THE GREAT BOOK OF MODERN WARPLANES

Featuring 200 full-color illustrations and over
1000 photographs in color and black-and-white

Portland House
New York

THE GREAT BOOK OF MODERN WARPLANES

Featuring 200 full-color illustrations and over 1000 photographs in color and black-and-white

This 1987 edition published by
Portland House, distributed by
Crown Publishers, Inc.,
225, Park Avenue South,
New York, New York 10003.

Printed and bound in Belgium

Library of Congress Cataloging-in-Publication Data

The Great book of modern warplanes.

1. Airplanes, Military. I. Sweetman, Bill.
II. Bonds, Ray.
UG1240.G675 1987 623.74'6 87-2226

ISBN 0-517-63367-1

All correspondence concerning the
content of this volume should be addressed to Bedford Editions Ltd.,
52 Bedford Row, London WC1R 4LR.

h g f e d c b a

Credits

Project Manager: Ray Bonds

Editors: Bernard Fitzsimons, Philip de Ste. Croix, Ray Bonds, Tony Hall

Designers: Grub Street Design, Tony Dominy, Rod Teasdale, David Allen, Barry Savage, Nick Buzzard, Lim & Lim, Mark Holt, Philip Gorton

Diagrams: TIGA, Arka Graphics (©Salamander Books Ltd.), Pete Coote, Danny Lim, Phil Adams and Mike Badrocke

Cutaway drawings: Mike Badrocke ©Pilot Press Ltd. Salamander Books Ltd.

Line three-view and side-view drawings, and color profiles: ©Pilot Press Ltd., Mike Badrocke (©Salamander Books Ltd.), Mike Trim (©Salamander Books Ltd.), Salamander Books Ltd., Keith Fretwell, Terry Hadler, Stephen Seymour, TIGA, Mike Trim and Tudor Art (©Salamander Books Ltd.)

Scrap view drawings: Mike Badrocke (©Salamander Books Ltd.)

Filmset by SX Composing Ltd., Tradespools Ltd., The Old Mill.

Color reproduction by Rodney Howe Ltd., Bantam Litho Ltd., Melbourne Graphics, Tempus Litho Ltd.

Printed in Belgium by Proost International Book Production, Turnhout

Contents

Picture Credits

The publishers would like to thank the following organizations and individuals who have supplied photographs for this book:
Aviation Photographs International; Belgian Air Force; British Aerospace; Boeing; Canadian Armed Forces; Robert F. Dorr; Fairchild; Ferranti; Fokker; Ford Aerospace; General Dynamics; General Electric; Goodyear; Grumman; Hughes Aircraft Corp; Israel Aircraft Industries; Israel Defense Force, Air Force; Kaiser Electronics; Marconi Avionics; McDonnell Douglas Corp; Ministry of Defence, London; NASA; Netherlands Ministry of Defense; Northrop; Lindsay D. Peacock; Pratt & Whitney; Royal Air Force; Royal Australian Air Force; Royal Danish Air Force; Royal Navy; RNAS, Yeovilton; Royal Netherlands Air Force; Rockwell International; Rolls Royce; Jim Rotramel; Spanish Air Force; Sperry Corp; Swedish Air Force; TASS; Texas Instruments; USAF; US Department of Defense; US Navy; Vehicle Systems Development Corp; Westinghouse.
Austin J. Brown: top: **304-305**. Copic (via Rotramel): top right: **573**. E & TV Films: sequence: **424-425**. Eaton-AIL: **507**; bottom: **508**. Flight International: bottom: **406-407**; top left; **436**; center: **439**. Bill Gunston: center: **450-451**. Hindustan Aeronautics Ltd: bottom left: **404**; **416**. IAI: bottom left: **580**. Interinfo: top: **423**; bottom: **426-427**; bottom: **436**. Marty J. Isham Collection: center left: **598**. Kongsberg Vapenfabrikk: bottom: **181**. Robert L. Lawson: center right **567**. LTV Aerospace: top and center right: **52-53**. Logan (via Roth/Rotramel): bottom right: **575**. MARS/K.Niska: **395**. Matra: top: **134**; center left: **558-559**. PPI/Mi Seitelman: bottom right: **32-33**. PPI/K. Tokunaga: **9**. Photo Research International: top right: **293**. Republic of Vietnam: top: **419**. Roth (via Rotramel): bottom left: **566**: top right: **575**; top left: **576-577**. SABCA: **149**. Salamander: top left: **565**. SEO/PPI: center right: **321**; top: **323**. Lear Siegler: center left: **174**. Seven Stridsberg (via Robert F. Dorr): bottom right: **433**. Yugoslav Federal Directorate of Supply and Procurement: top: **408**.

Introduction

This book tells the story of many of the most important combat aircraft flying today. Each story is told in considerable depth, and was written in close collaboration with the manufacturer of the aircraft concerned. The quality of the results is obvious from the fact that some of the chapters of this book are used by the relevant manufacturer as the official all-embracing description, purchased from the publisher in order to be given to anyone from a five-star general to a potential foreign customer.

This volume therefore contains a unique record of advanced Western technology. Certainly the Western Allies can be grateful for the brilliant engineering carried out, with perfect accuracy while at high pressure, by the prime contractors of these aircraft and by the design and development teams in the hundreds of suppliers involved in each program.

Most of these teams have been American, some British, and a few have worked in other countries. No nation has a corner in advanced technology — though in the most far-out fields of activity, often called the "leading edge" technologies, some countries have massive expertise of a kind that others find difficult to rival. Nothing promotes this kind of world leadership quite so well as major programs to build new combat aircraft. Looked at from another angle, no program to develop a new combat aircraft can succeed without vast armies of engineers, highly qualified and experienced in the extremely challenging and specialized fields of advanced technology, which determine the design of every part of the aircraft, both hardware and software.

At least 98 per cent of the world's countries could not even contemplate creating a modern combat aircraft. On the basis of the recent "track record", the United States appears to be way out in front, because it consistently creates new combat aircraft in a total elapsed time of under five years, measured from start of design to combat service. Typically, the first aircraft have reached squadrons two years from first flight. In Western Europe, France has occasionally attempted to emulate this performance, while Sweden and Israel are also attempting to create new fighters, though with massive help from offshore, and to timescales which by United States' standards are protracted. Other European nations have worked in collaboration on such programs, the biggest example being the Tornado, but if anything this method of development has probably made the project take longer.

The one country every defense analyst in the West watches most keenly is, of course, the Soviet Union. Nobody has ever doubted the ability of the Soviets to create tough and serviceable hardware that can be relied upon in the harshest environments, but in comparison with United States' equipment in the same class, the Soviet warplanes have often appeared — on paper at least — to be rather unimpressive. In recent years the Soviet designers have clearly striven hard to close what is often, and perhaps slightly optimistically, referred to in the West as the "technology gap". Some of the latest Soviet warplanes appear to be excellent designs, with formidable capability, but they appear to share certain traits which really do give the Western analyst some cause for guarded relief.

One of these traits is that almost every one of the latest Soviet combat aircraft appears to have been very strongly influenced by a much earlier United States' design. Another is that, by comparison with United States' aircraft, the Soviet warplanes have taken much longer to develop. Six years from issue of the official requirement to the first

Below: A view of an F-111A showing the maximum sweep allowed by its variable wing profile. This wingspan is known for giving crews a rough ride.

Below right: A Hornet of VMFA-314 Marine Corps fighter attack squadron during a live firing exercise. The missile is the AIM-9 Sidewinder.

flight appears to be common, followed by a further six years to operational service. In 12 years the whole situation is likely to have changed, so that the new warplane may be admirably designed to win types of combat that will never take place.

Thus, though the Russians are certainly not to be regarded as technological simpletons, they are not geniuses either. We must never forget, however, that the Soviet Union's history of aircraft design is a long and proud one, renowned for its innovation and willingness to thrust ahead into the unknown. It is very interesting that the apparent very strong influence of United States' combat aircraft designs on the latest Soviet types is almost unprecedented. One wonders if the Soviet planners have for the first time tried to cut down on both elapsed time and on risk, by using American aircraft as a starting point? Or can it be merely that attempts to solve similar design problems inevitably lead to similar conclusions?

There is unquestionably a strong element of pure fashion in aircraft design. Ever since World War II, the writer has campaigned for fighters (and indeed, other types of aircraft as well), with canard foreplanes instead of tailplanes (horizontal stabilizers). It seems no more than common sense to balance an aircraft longitudinally by pushing up at the front, adding to the lift, rather than by pushing down at the back, adding to the effective weight. Nobody appeared to want to know. Then, in the early 1960s, SAAB of Sweden published the STOL (short takeoff and landing) configuration of the Viggen. The worth of this "double delta" layout very gradually permeated the almost closed minds of other design teams, and gradually canards came into fashion; or perhaps one should say "came back", because that is how the Wright brothers designed their first flyer of 1903!

Today there is no longer any mental barrier blocking acceptance of the canard, and readers may expect to see plenty grouped together in a future book such as this. But today vectored-thrust STOVL (short takeoff, vertical landing) aircraft are restricted to just two long-established families; one having its roots in the old Hawker works at Kingston in Britain, and the other created by the Yakovlev bureau in the Soviet Union. To the writer it is simply common sense to make a jet engine do more than merely push out a plain jet through holes at the back, especially when the aggregate thrust exceeds the loaded weight of the aircraft! Today, with obvious reluctance (because some feel it is almost tantamount to copying the British), American engine builders are beginning to test engines with 2-D (two dimensional, or rectangular) nozzles which can vector the jet through limited angles upwards and downwards; but not in order to escape from the desperate vulnerability of airfields. Even the future ATF (Advanced Tactical Fighter) of the United States Air Force will be parked on the most heavily missile-targeted spots on this planet!

Another victim of fashion is the VG (variable-geometry) swing wing. In the 1960s it seemed so obviously superior that media copywriters vied with one another to find better ways to explain how marvelous it was to fly in an aircraft which the pilot could "redesign" in flight. The wings could be spread out to wide span, with powerful slats and flaps, for short takeoff and landing with heavy loads, and then tucked away for a supersonic dash through dense sea-level air. The F-14 even has a Mach-sweep programmer which in combat keeps pivoting the wings to and fro without the pilot having to worry about which angle is best at any particular time. But today the swing wing is out of fashion. It will come back of course, because it makes sense; but at the moment all the blinkered establishment can see is its so-called "penalties". They have the same lunatic approach to STOVL design as well.

Bill Gunston

Chapter 1

A-10

THUNDERBOLT II

Bill Sweetman

A-10 Thunderbolt II

Contents

Acknowledgements

The author and editor would like to thank all those who have contributed information and pictures to this chapter. Photograph sources are credited individually at the beginning of the book, but particular thanks are due to George Thune, Bill Lowenstein and Dave Wright of Fairchild Republic Company.

The following works were consulted in the course of preparing this chapter:
Flight International, particularly the 24 January 1976 issue
Air Force Magazine, particularly the July 1983 issue
Aviation Week and Space Technology
Defense Week, May 31, 1983
International Defense Review, 2/79
Freidrich Wiener, *The Armies of the Warsaw Pact Nations*, Carl Ueberreuter 1981

Author

Bill Sweetman is Interavia's Western USA correspondent. Between 1973 and 1979 he was on the staff of *Flight International*, where as well as covering the air transport industry he launched the 'Flight Intelligence' series of detailed technical analyses of modern Soviet military aircraft, including the first accurate descriptions published of Backfire, Foxbat and Flogger. From 1979 to 1981 he was Air Correspondent of the national Sunday newspaper, *The Observer*, and since moving to California he has contributed to the Washington-based *Defense Week*, in addition to *Interavia, International Defense Review* and *Interavia AirLetter*. His books include *A Concise Guide to Soviet Military Aircraft* (Hamlyn/Presidio, 1982) and *Aircraft 2000* (Hamlyn, 1984), as well as contributions to the Salamander titles *Soviet Air Power* (1978), *Air Forces of the World* (1979) and *The Chinese War Machine* (1979).

Introduction

The A-10 is most unusual among modern American combat aircraft. Built in a single model, in strictly limited numbers, for one specialized role, and without a single export order to its name, it is the antithesis of such predecessors as the Phantom or the nearly contemporary F-15 and F-16, which are notable for their popularity and versatility.

Critics would explain the A-10's lack of sales by pointing to its apparently outdated performance figures, its lack of sophisticated avionics and its airliner engines, all of which add up to no more than an absence of spurious glamour. In fact, for its uniquely demanding role of visual-range tank-busting, the A-10 Thunderbolt II– 'Warthog' to its intimates – is uniquely well-suited.

Down on the deck, under the cloud and in visibility that would ground almost any of its contemporaries, it can hide from missile and AA radars for all but the few seconds needed for a devastating gun or Maverick attack; it can out-turn high-speed interceptors; and its gun is as deadly against aircraft as against main battle tanks.

Paradoxically, the Warthog's strengths are a principal reason for the limit on numbers built. Hard to break, easy to mend, with a unique capability to fight, take punishment, regenerate their strength and fight again, A-10s simply do not suffer the kind of attrition associated with other modern fighters.

And other aspects of the design are equally original and impressive. The engines, unique among modern combat aircraft, are ideally suited to the role; the GAU-8/A Avenger cannon gives it a positively awesome punch; and in an era of supersophisticated fighters with appallingly accident-prone systems, an aircraft that has to be flown from the cockpit, rather than by means of a battery of black boxes, is one of the most sought-after assignments the Air Force has to offer.

Development

The requirements of the close air support mission could not be met by the big, complex supersonic jets developed for Tactical Air Command during the 1950s: in Vietnam, they were met instead by slow, propeller-driven aircraft whose virtues were long endurance, good weapon-carrying ability, low-speed manoeuvrability and good visibility. All the latter qualities are embodied in the A-10, which originated in the Attack Experimental programme initiated, at least partly as a result of pressure from the US Army, in 1966, and which has found its main role as a tank-killer on NATO's Central Front.

Close support is one of the least standardized missions in military aviation. It can, perhaps, be best defined as the use of airpower to attack hostile ground forces which are already in contact with friendly troops, or are on the point of engaging them. Some air forces do not even use the term 'close air support' (CAS), preferring phrases that emphasise offensive strike slightly to the rear of the battlefield. The Soviet Union's tacticians believe that the most intimate forms of close support should be the province of the ground forces' own helicopters. The infantry commander cares little for such fine distinctions. He wants some friendly firepower to deal with an imminent unpredicted attack by a superior force, and he wants it without delay.

The Fairchild Republic A-10A, officially named Thunderbolt II and universally known as the Warthog, is the only fixed-wing aircraft in the world which has been designed without compromise for the CAS mission. All of its many unique characteristics stem from CAS requirements, including its low speed, its long endurance, its unparalleled protection and its awesome built-in armament. However, its dedication to the CAS mission has also been the reason why it has been overshadowed by its sinuous supersonic contemporaries.

The basic controversy over CAS is nearly half a century old and still kicking. Is it best handled by a specialized aircraft, or by a fighter with bomb racks? Advocates of the CAS type argue that the 'fast-mover' fighter can hardly perform the mission at all. Its relative delicacy and poor low-speed handling tend to confine it to a single run against a previously identified or designated target. Their opponents argue that it is foolish to design any aircraft to the requirements of land warfare, to the detriment of its ability to fight and survive in the air.

The Western Allies' experience in the 1939-45 war was decisive. The Luftwaffe's favoured CAS weapon, the Ju 87 dive-bomber, won high renown in the early stages of the war, but the Royal Air Force found its measure and defeated it. The RAF and the US Army Air Force had already ordered quite large numbers of dive-bombers, but hardly any of them were used in action. Instead, the most successful CAS weapons in Northern Europe were Typhoons, Tempests, P-51 Mustangs and P-47 Thunderbolts, second-generation fighters armed with newly developed rocket projectiles and heavy gun armament.

The 1944-45 campaign was to influence planning into the 1960s. Its lessons were fresh in mind when Tactical Air Command was formed in 1947, and when the independent US Air Force followed later that year. One of the first things that the USAF did was to eliminate the 'Attack' category from its designation system, along with the obsolete 'Pursuit'. The fighter-bomber became the backbone of TAC. At the same time, though, the concept of close support began to melt into the 'strike' mission. TAC's main new project for the 1950s was an aircraft designed to fly at supersonic speed at low level, to navigate to a known ground target in bad weather and hit it with a nuclear bomb: the Republic F-105 Thunderchief.

Fighter design trends

The F-105 typified a great many trends in fighter design. It was bigger and more complex than its predecessors and cost a great deal more to buy and maintain, so there would be fewer of the new aircraft built. Because of its great complexity, it would demand more maintenance, so each aircraft would fly fewer missions and each mission would be preceded by many hours of preparation and equipment checks. The F-105 would operate only from well-equipped bases, safely in the rear of the war zone. Its range was excellent, at a high cruising speed; its endurance, in hours, was poor. In brief, there was no way in which an F-105 unit could respond to a call for immediate support.

By 1960, TAC's less sophisticated fighter-bomber types were getting older. Far from planning a replacement, TAC was busily working on SOR-183, a requirement which defined an aircraft much bigger and more sophisticated than the F-105. Nobody appreciated the implications of this trend more clearly than the customers for close air support in the US Army. For a time, the Army seriously considered acquiring its own CAS aircraft, and the Northrop N-156F (which had not yet received its first Air Force order) and the Fiat G.91 were both evaluated in 1961. The Army also received presentations on a quaint British machine called the Hawker P.1127. The sight of jet fighters in Army insignia touched off an inter-service dispute over the roles and missions split between the USAF and Army. Finally, the Army had to accept tight restrictions on the types of fixed-wing aircraft which it could operate, but the US Air Force was told by the Defense Secretary, Robert McNamara, to rebuild its ability to provide battlefield air support to the Army.

To begin with, CAS was closely linked to the 'limited war' theories of the time, and to the perceived US need to contain Soviet-inspired 'insurgencies' directed at allied states. The revival of CAS within TAC was originally directed at defeating guerrilla-type forces, using limited effort in an unsophisticated air environment. The first practical application of new 'counter-insurgency' (COIN) air power was to be Vietnam, where the first of the USAF's COIN detachments arrived in late 1961.

COIN operations against concealed ground troops called for the accurate delivery of small weapon loads, and with the weapon-aiming technology of 1961 this meant using an aircraft with good manoeuvrability at low speed. Such a light combat aircraft had been conceived in the late 1950s by North American: a strengthened, re-engined

Left: The A-X specification that gave rise to the A-10 was the product of a long process of analysis of close air support requirements: the resulting prototype is seen here with instrument boom attached to its nose.

Right: Slow, but tough and manoeuvrable at low speeds, and able to loiter for long periods with a heavy weight of ordnance, the A-1E Skyraider proved to be the most useful CAS aircraft available in Vietnam.

adaptation of a surplus T-28A trainer. The French had produced the conversion in quantity, as the Fennec, for use in Algeria, and TAC's Special Air Warfare Center at Eglin AFB, Florida, created the similar T-28D for use by Vietnamese forces and the rapidly growing force of US 'advisors'. A three-service requirement was issued for a successor aircraft: a highly versatile, carrier-capable machine of about the same size, power, warload and speed as the T-28D. This was the Light Armed Reconnaissance Aircraft (LARA), and was to be built in huge numbers for the USAF, Navy and Marines and for US allies.

But plans for LARA were upset by the Viet Cong, who began to demonstrate disturbing proficiency with their Soviet-supplied light anti-aircraft artillery (AAA), mostly of 12.7mm calibre. T-28D losses mounted steadily in 1963-64, and TAC's COIN experts attributed many losses to the type's modest speed. Even before the LARA contest winner – Rockwell's OV-10 Bronco – made its first flight, TAC had decided that it was to be confined to the forward air control mission. By late 1964, there were references to a Super-COIN aircraft with a minimum speed – at low level, with a full weapons load – around 315kt (580km/h).

But the need to replace the increasingly vulnerable T-28D was urgent, and the situation became worse in early 1964 when the heavy-lift contingent of the Vietnam-based attack force – Douglas B-26s – was grounded en masse by structural problems. Fortunately, a replacement was at hand in the burly shape of the A-1 Skyraider, which had been under evaluation at Eglin AFB since the previous year. The A-1 was not fast, but it was reasonably tough, it was manoeuvrable at low speeds – its massive dive-brakes were an asset – and it had a long endurance with a heavy weapon load, thanks to the efficiency of its piston engine.

The A-1 proved to be by far the most successful CAS improvisation in Vietnam, and one even shot down a MiG-17 which strayed in front of its four 20mm cannon. It was a decisive participant in many rescue operations, because it could remain on station and continue to fire long after any jet would have turned for home, out of fuel and ammunition. In the CAS mission, its endurance allowed it to loiter just behind the battle area and respond to a call for support faster than any jet. The A-1's low-speed manoeuvrability, and the all-round visibility from its high-perched bubble canopy (infinitely better than that of any contemporary fighter) meant that its pilot saw targets that a jet pilot would miss, and could keep them in sight as he swung the A-1 around to attack. A small turning radius allowed the A-1 to manoeuvre and turn among hills and low cloud, in conditions where jets were confined to a single pass at the target.

Endurance at a premium

The USAF did use other aircraft for CAS in Vietnam – such as the F-100 and the A-37, a version of the T-37 jet trainer – but none had the A-1's endurance, so they had to be kept on the ground until needed. Too often, they arrived too late, or found the tactical situation had changed, and their pilots could not see targets quickly enough to attack on a single pass. Experience in Vietnam convinced the USAF that a manoeuvrable, long-endurance aircraft, primarily relying on the 'Mark One Eyeball' for target acquisition, was the only way to provide effective CAS. The payload and endurance of the A-1 became the baseline for the Super-COIN studies.

Another piece of the jigsaw dropped into place in 1966, when the USAF ordered the A-7D development of the Navy's Corsair II. This was an aircraft about the same size as the Skyraider, but had a longer range, higher operating speeds and much more sophisticated equipment. Its presence in the TAC inventory would help fight the temptation to upgrade a COIN aircraft into another fast, expensive long-range strike type.

Meanwhile, the increasing strength of the Viet Cong was making the early-

Below left: The A-10's World War II namesake, the P-47 Thunderbolt. Shown here with 2,000lb (907kg) bombs, the P-47 was also a useful tank-buster with guns and rockets.

Below: Another Republic product, the F-105 Thunderchief was designed as a supersonic strike aircraft, but spent much of its career delivering iron bombs over Vietnam.

Bottom: The T-28D attack version of the T-28A trainer, seen here in 1962 at Bien Hoa AB, South Vietnam, with gun pods, rockets and bombs, proved too vulnerable to ground fire.

Below: The USAF's acquisition of the A-7D Corsair II in the late 1960s provided a capable long-range attack bomber and cleared the way for a dedicated COIN aircraft.

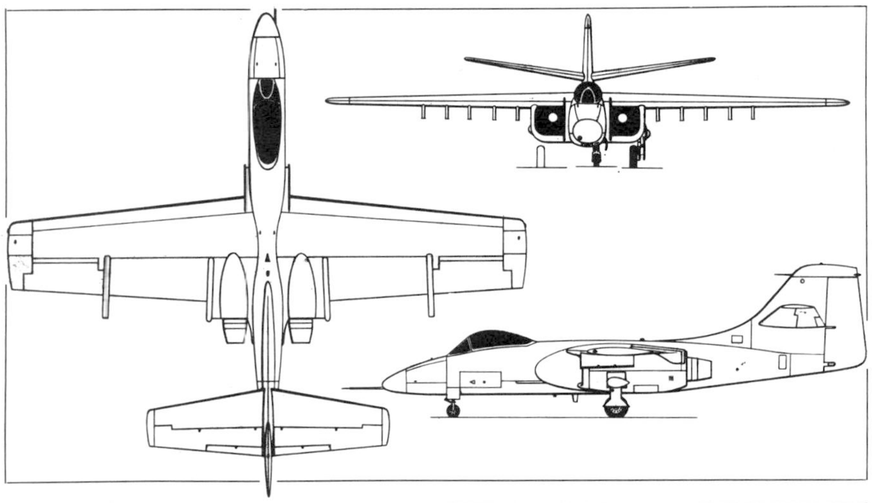

Top: Northrop's A-X contender, the YA-9A, was of conventional layout, with shoulder-mounted wing, single fin, and engines faired neatly into the fuselage sides.

Above: The first YA-9A on an early flight in June 1972. Although the fly-off results were close, the Northrop design lost out in terms of maintainability and survivability.

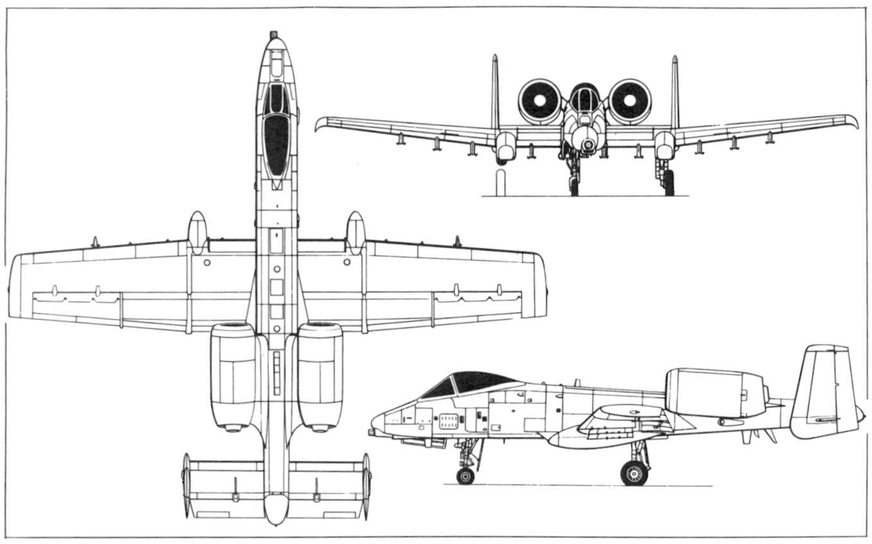

1960s image of a limited war look positively peaceful. Radar-directed AAA was encountered over Laos in 1964, and was expected to spread elsewhere. On the ground, North Vietnamese Army regular forces were encountered in late 1965, in the Ia Drang Valley. The possibility of encountering hostile armour could no longer be ruled out. Any future CAS aircraft, it was clear, would have to be able to destroy heavier targets and survive against more sophisticated defences than had been envisaged a few years earlier.

In the course of 1964, the US Army began to talk about an Advanced Aerial Fire Support System (AAFSS). The non-specific programme title masked the fact that AAFSS was to be a 220kt (410km/h) all-weather strike aircraft, which the Army could pursue and develop because it would be a compound helicopter. While the USAF would have produced a CAS aircraft in any case, the timing and details were certainly influenced by the constant pressure from the Army aviators.

The A-X programme

In mid-1966, these factors came together with the launching of the Attack, Experimental (A-X) programme by USAF Chief of Staff Gen. John P. McConnell. A request for proposals (RFP) was issued to 21 companies in March 1967, outlining the current state of USAF thinking on the new aircraft and seeking the views of the industry. The RFP was couched in broad terms, and it was not expected to lead directly to full-scale development. However, it laid out the most significant features which had been deemed necessary by the USAF experts.

The A-X was to combine A-1-type endurance and weapon load with a minimum speed of 350kt (650km/h) – the old A-1 was limited to 240kt (444km/h) with a heavy load. Despite its increased speed, it was to be able to manoeuvre hard at low airspeeds; the USAF wanted an aircraft which could turn in a limited amount of space, in order to attack an objective without overflying its defences, or make a complete turn in poor visibility without losing sight of the target.

The speed of A-X would not be enough to avoid ground fire completely, so it would be designed to survive when hit. In Vietnam, too many US fighters were being lost to small-calibre or fragment strikes in vulnerable areas, revealing design flaws in most of the service types. Although systems were duplicated, they were seldom protected, and the two channels often ran close together where a single hit would destroy both. In parallel with the A-X programme, several companies were placed under contract to study the specific question of combat aircraft vulnerability.

Above left: In complete contrast to the YA-9A, Fairchild's A-10 design was thoroughly unconventional in layout, with low wings, twin fins and podded engines high on the rear fuselage.

Left: The first YA-10A after roll-out from Fairchild's Farmingdale, Long Island, plant. Concern over the company's future, with no major order on its books, was an important factor in the USAF's choice.

Below: Airborne on a test flight, the first YA-10A demonstrates its ordnance-carrying capability.

In addition to its external armament, A-X was to carry a heavy internal gun. Vietnam experience had led the USAF back to the gun as a fighter weapon, and it was the only class of weapon with which a low-cost CAS aircraft could hit a small moving target. A scaled-up version of the very successful General Electric M61 was the obvious starting point. A-X would also have to be cheap, compared with supersonic fighters, and as simple as possible to maintain and operate. It would be designed to use short, unprepared strips, and to function with the limited maintenance facilities available at such bases. The type's low-speed manoeuvrability, and the heavy gun, were intended to eliminate the need for costly automated weapon-aiming systems.

All in all, the A-X requirement was a great deal more difficult than the updated Skyraider which many people thought it was at the time. With the jet engines available at that time, it would not be possible to match the Skyraider's endurance. A low-bypass-ratio engine (such as a Pratt & Whitney TF30 or Rolls-Royce/Allison TF41) has poor propulsive efficiency at low speeds. The A-7, which uses those engines, has excellent range at Mach 0.75-0.8, but will burn fuel almost as fast at half the airspeed. Its loiter capability is therefore limited. Improving propulsive efficiency at lower

Above: Tanker's eye view of a bomb-laden YA-10A during in-flight refuelling trials. The dummy slipway was not connected to the fuel system.

Left: The two YA-10As in formation. Comparative evaluation was carried out at Edwards AFB, California, during the last three months of 1972.

speeds means imparting a lesser acceleration to a larger mass of air, and in 1967 the only established way of doing so was the propeller.

Propellers, however, bring their own problems. Because of the survivability requirements, A-X would have to have two engines, and the speed and short-takeoff-and-landing (Stol) capability desired by the USAF meant that the A-X would have to be quite powerful for its size. The Stol and low-speed manoeuvrability requirements would demand large propellers, so the engines would be well out from the centreline of the aircraft. It became difficult to design the A-X so that it would be controllable if one engine failed at low speed, just after takeoff. Northrop looked at the possibility of coupling two turboprops in the tail, as on the Learfan business aircraft, but this would have made the entire aircraft vulnerable to a hit on the single propeller and gearbox. An alternative proposal was to install a cross-shaft between the two engines, but this added weight and complexity. The overall effect was that the turboprop-powered A-X became steadily bigger, approaching 60,000lb (27,200kg) maximum takeoff weight, and accordingly more expensive.

While the industry worked on responses to the RFP, the USAF worked on refining the A-X requirement, to minimize the size and cost of the aircraft while ensuring that all the service's essential needs were met, and on setting up the programme structure to avoid the risk of delays and cost escalation. The USAF was in deep political trouble over two major programmes, the F-111 and the C-5, and had no desire to add A-X to the list. Moreover, while cost increases could be tolerated for an advanced-technology aircraft, they would be the end of the road for A-X, which was billed as a low-cost, low-risk concept.

A-X was beginning to gain even greater importance in Air Force planning. Shocked by the lack-lustre performance of its F-4s against obsolescent MiG-17s and boy-racer MiG-21s over Vietnam, and by the sudden advent of the (apparently) awesome Mach 3 Mikoyan Foxbat, the USAF had directed its FX advanced fighter programme towards maximum performance in air-to-air combat. To suggest compromise for CAS or strike was heresy. From 1968-69 onwards, the entire Air Force CAS mission was riding on the A-X; if the A-X did not materialise, the plans for the new fighter would have to be changed, to add some strike capability, and the Army would demand and get all the money it wanted for the AAFSS, which had now materialised as the amibitious, sophisticated and expensive Lockheed AH-56A Cheyenne.

Four years elapsed between the first A-X discussions and the issue of a final RFP: a long interval, certainly, but understandable in the light of the fact that A-X was a completely new type of aircraft. The most important change during this initial development period came about as a result of improved engine technology. High-bypass-ratio turbofan engines were being run by all the major engine manufacturers, and were proving capable of everything claimed for them. While they had initially been designed for huge freighters and airliners, the technology turned out to be readily 'scaleable'. Small high-BPR engines for a variety of aircraft – airliners as well as military types – were soon under development and seemed to offer modest risks. On the A-X, the high-BPR engines were efficient enough to meet the endurance requirement. They could be mounted close to the centreline, easing the one-engine-out design case, and the adverse stability and trim effects associated with large propellers were absent. The turbofan, with a single fan stage driven directly by a turbine, is also inherently much simpler than the turboprop, with its gearbox and variable-pitch propeller.

Two other changes were related to the adoption of turbofans by nearly all the companies participating in the A-X programme. The speed of the A-X increased toward 400kt (740km/h), closer to the optimum for the turbofan, and the USAF set its final runway-length objective at a somewhat greater value than had been expected earlier: A-X was to operate from a 4,000ft (1,200m) strip at maximum weight. This was a fairly modest aim. With the thrust/weight ratio and the wing loading already dictated by the low-speed manoeuvre requirements, the field-length target could be met without complex high-lift devices or thrust reversal. Again, this helped reduce the weight and cost of the aircraft.

Another significant change of emphasis began to enter the programme in 1967-68. The North Vietnamese Army had, by that time, made their first use of tanks against US forces, and conventional warfare in Europe was once more being considered now that the 'nuclear trip-wire' philosophy had been abandoned. The anti-armour capability of A-X began to be considerably more important. Meanwhile, in June 1967, the Israeli Air Force had succeeded in knocking out a large number of tanks with the 30mm cannon fitted to their Dassault Mystères. What had happened was that while tank guns and frontal armour had made considerable advances since 1945, tanks remained, inevitably, more vulnerable at the rear, on the sides and, particularly, on the top. The 20mm M61 would not suffice though, so the USAF began to draw up requirements for a new gun for A-X, of larger calibre and with a higher muzzle velocity. This would be a destructive and very accurate weapon, but it would also be a great deal larger than the M61, and it would only fit in a specially designed aircraft. Quietly, and with very little public attention, the A-X turned from a general-purpose bomb truck into a cannon-armed 'tankbuster', a breed which had been considered extinct since 1945.

Specific requirements

The final RFP was issued in May 1970. Performance requirements included a speed of 350-400kt (650-740km/h). The maximum external load was to be 16,000lb (7,250kg), but this could be traded for internal fuel or for 1,350 cannon rounds. The A-X was to be able to carry 9,500lb (4,300kg) of external ordnance and internal ammunition over a 250nm (460km) radius, and loiter for two hours in the target area. Low-speed manoeuvrability was identified as the route to adverse-weather operations. The A-X, according to the USAF, would be so manoeuvrable that it could operate safely and effectively under a ceiling of 1,000ft (305m) with one nm (1.85km) visibility. "Weather conditions worse than this exist only 15 per cent of the time," noted an official USAF statement, without specifying to what part of the world this figure applied.

Contestants would be assessed on three other requirements. Survivability, or the ability to avoid or survive hits from a range of current and projected Soviet AAA weapons, was the most novel. Fuel system protection, duplicated and dispersed system runs and armour were basic requirements, but the USAF was keen to have an aircraft which could lose large segments of itself and stay airborne.

Simplicity, another prime requirement, was related to survivability in one respect; a survivable aircraft is of little use if it cannot be quickly repaired. But it was also important from the point of view of reducing the unit and operating cost – and saving money for the sophisticated FX. A-X was to use no new or untried technology, both to reduce costs and to eliminate, as far as possible, the danger of problems in the programme. 'Design to cost' was the watchword: if necessary, weight increases would be accepted and performance sacrificed to meet cost targets. Simplicity was also part of the last main requirement, for rapid response. The A-X might be based at forward operating bases, close to the battle line, for quicker response to any calls for support, and maintenance facilities would be limited.

The programme was novel in another respect; it would be the first in 15 years to involve a head-on, competitive evaluation between two prototypes. This reversion in policy stemmed from the problems with the F-111 programme, which had been launched simultaneously into production and development. Technical problems were encountered, and by the time they were fixed a great many aircraft had been built. It had also been necessary to modify many aircraft on the production line, and costs had escalated enormously.

The revived 'fly-before-buy' philosophy would avoid such problems, because the new aircraft would be flown and thoroughly tested before a production decision was taken. In the case of A-X, which was to be a low-risk design, this aspect of fly-before-buy was perhaps less important than the psychological factor. The manufacturers would be kept under strong competitive pressure until a much later stage in the programme, and by the time they had built and flown prototypes they would have a much greater stake in success.

Six companies responded to the 1970 RFP by the August 10 deadline: Cessna, Fairchild, Boeing-Vertol, Lockheed, General Dynamics and Northrop. The programme was significant, in that the USAF and US Navy had already selected contractors for their other important new aircraft. The A-X was – at that time – the last major combat aircraft programme in sight for many years. The field of contenders was strong. Lockheed and GD were among the most capable of aerospace companies, even if both were in the Pentagon's doghouse over the C-5 and F-111. Cessna had experience with the A-37 Dragonfly. Northrop had shown great expertise in building effective combat aircraft with comparatively low purchase and operating costs. Boeing-Vertol, a helicopter manufacturer, was an unexpected participant, with the only remaining propeller-driven design.

Fairchild – to be more precise, the Republic Aviation Division of Fairchild-Hiller – had learned a great deal from the performance of its F-105 in combat, but had produced no new aircraft since then. Thunderchief production had been terminated prematurely in favour of the F-4C Phantom; Republic had been involved in two separate efforts to develop highly advanced, supersonic, variable-sweep V/Stol fighters, in collaboration with European countries, but neither had borne fruit; and the company had been a finalist in the F-X competition, losing to McDonnell Douglas. Of all the A-X contenders, the Republic organisation was the only one which risked disappearing from the scene as a prime contractor if its bid did not succeed, and its best people were assigned to the preparation of the A-X proposal.

Weapon for the A-X

Also in 1970, the USAF issued an RFP couched in similar terms for what would now be the primary weapon, the internal gun. Designated GAU-8, it was to be a 30mm weapon with a 4,000 rounds/min rate of fire; the latter requirement effectively dictated that it would be a Gatling-type weapon, with multiple barrels. While the calibre was not as large as that of earlier airborne anti-tank guns, the weapon would make up the lost impact energy in muzzle velocity: 3,500ft/sec (1,067m/sec), equal to the best 20mm weapons in service and considerably better than most heavy cannon. It should be remembered, too, that the size of a

Right: This mock-up of the A-10 forward fuselage was mounted on a rocket-powered sled and used to test the McDonnell Douglas Escapac IE-9 ejection seat at Holloman AFB, New Mexico, in August 1974. Later A-10s were fitted with the Escapac II.

Below: The ejection seat saved the life of this pilot, who banged out after experiencing control problems. One of a batch of six Development, Test and Evaluation machines, the A-10 is carrying Air Force Systems Command markings; the incident occurred during filming of gun firing as part of the successful programme to eradicate the dangerous build-up of explosive gases from the gun barrel experienced with early GAU-8/As.

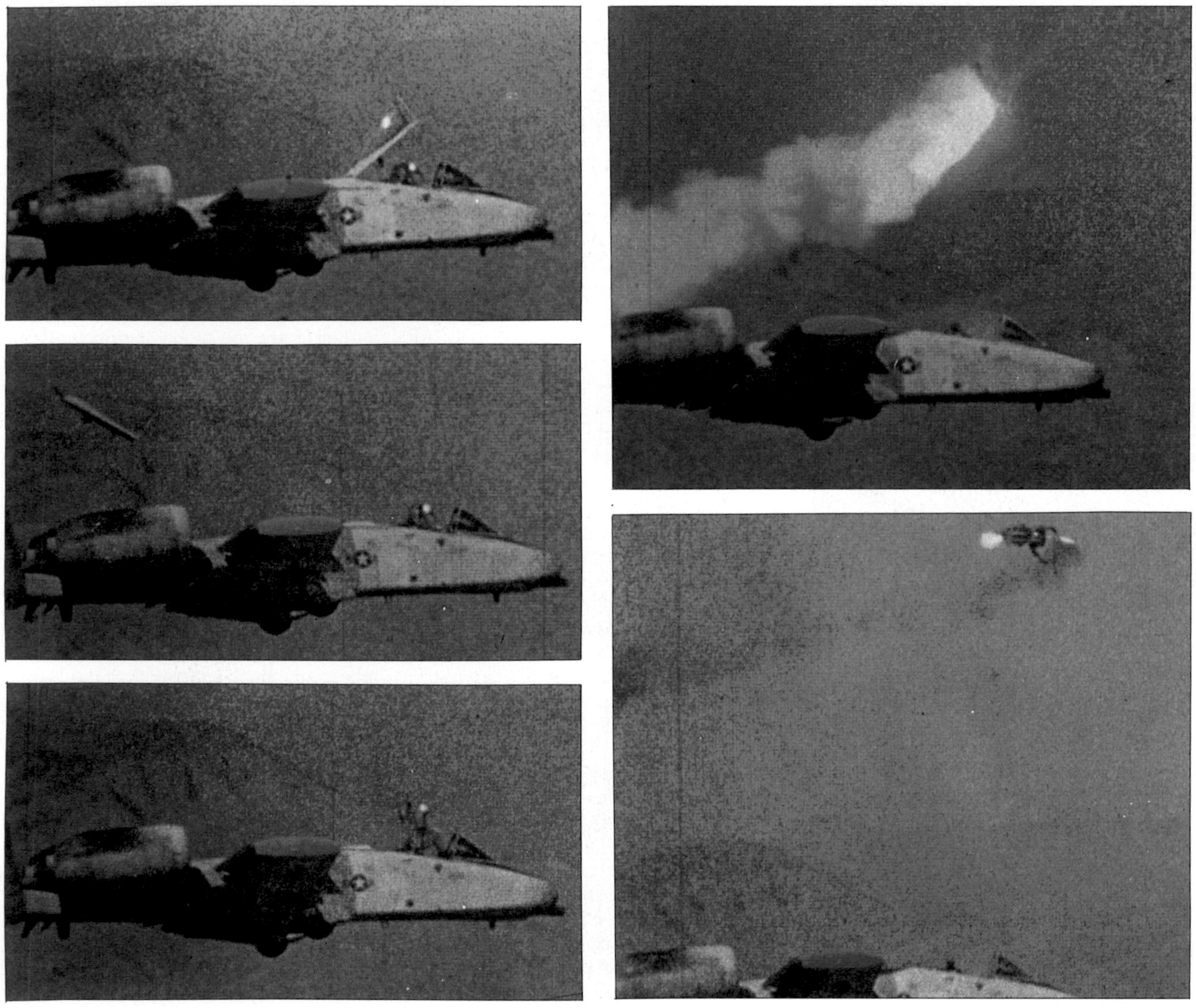

Below: The second YA-10A with its port outer wing and tailfin painted white for spin and recovery testing at Edwards in November 1974. This aircraft was retired in June 1975 after logging 548.5hr in 354 flights.

Above: Early firing trials with a prototype of the GAU-8/A 30mm cannon were carried out by the first YA-10A at Edwards AFB from September 1974. The fireballs formed by unburnt gun gas are apparent.

Above: The spin chute container installed on the tail of the second YA-10A, serial 71-1370, to help recovery during spin trials.

Left: Heavy-duty nose installation used to dispel the gun gases during early GAU-8/A firing trials.

gun increases rapidly with greater calibre. The mass of each round rises with the cube of the calibre, and the loads on the breech, the barrel and the feed systems follow suit. Barrel length increases with the calibre and the velocity. By the time the RFPs were issued, it was clear that the GAU-8 would be among the largest guns ever mounted on an aircraft, eclipsing even the 75mm weapons which had been tried in the 1940s. As in the case of A-X itself, the gun was to be selected after a competitive prototype evaluation. Four companies responded to the GAU-8 RFP – General Electric, which had built the original M61, Philco-Ford, Hughes and General American Transportation.

After so many studies of the A-X requirement, the USAF's needs were quite clear, and the final evaluation was quick. Four months after the closing date for proposals, the USAF announced that Northrop and Fairchild would each build two A-X prototypes. Northrop's contract for the YA-9A was worth $28.9 million, and Fairchild would receive $41.2 million for the YA-10A. The main reason for the difference was that Fairchild planned to build an aircraft close to production standards, while Northrop preferred to build something closer to a classic prototype, which would show what the production aircraft could do, but would not necessarily resemble it internally. The decision on the gun was announced later: General Electric and Philco-Ford were to build competing prototypes under $12.1 million contracts. The gun prototypes would thus cost one-third as much as the four A-X contenders themselves. The prototypes would be armed with the trusty M61 while GAU-8 development continued.

A common characteristic of all the USAF competitive flight evaluations or 'fly-offs' in the early 1970s was that the finalists were very different from each

Above: The first DT & E A-10, serial 73-1664, with three fuel tanks and instrumented nose boom during testing at Edwards in mid-1975.

Right: Underside view of the same aircraft carrying 18 1,000lb (907kg) bombs and reflecting the golden rays of the setting sun.

other. This was contrived quite deliberately, because one advantage of the fly-off approach was that a promising, but unconventional configuration or solution could be tested without risking the entire programme if it turned out to have some inherent and unacceptable flaw. The A-X finalists were different in many ways, and gave the USAF a very real choice of design philosophies; the contest was, however, the closest of all the fly-off evaluations.

The differences between the two aircraft started with their external shape. Where the Northrop design followed conventional fighter practice, with a shoulder wing, single fin and engines mounted close to the fuselage, the YA-10A resembled no previous combat aircraft apart from a few last-days-in-the-bunker German projects from 1945. The engines were mounted on the rear fuselage, airliner-style, there were twin fins and rudders and the main landing gear retracted into pods under the wing. The low-slung YA-9A was a design of elegant solidity, with its engines faired smoothly into the fuselage and the fin sweeping upwards from the aft body; its rival was a gangly beast, its long, skinny fuselage and broad wing improbably mated atop a stalky undercarriage.

Another material difference between the two aircraft was the choice of engine. Two high-bypass turbofans in the right thrust bracket were available in the USA. Fairchild selected the General Electric TF34, already under development for the US Navy's Lockheed S-3A anti-submarine warfare aircraft. Northrop chose a smaller engine, the Avco Lycoming ALF 502, which had been launched as a private venture in 1969. It received the military designation YF102-LD-100. It delivered 15 per cent less thrust than the TF34, but was 23 per cent lighter and only just over half as long. It was based on the world's first high-bypass turbofan, the PLF1, which had run in late 1963. The main selling point of the F102 was that it was derived from the T55 turboshaft, which had a long and distinguished record of peacetime and combat service in military helicopters. The YA-9A's cleaner shape largely made up for its lower installed thrust; the mission performance of the two aircraft was very similar, both meeting the specification, but the YA-10A would do so at slightly higher weights. Both contestants, though, were required to provide performance data with either engine.

Control surfaces

Both A-X contenders featured combined aileron/speedbrake surfaces on their outer wings; these resembled conventional ailerons, but were split into upper and lower panels. When opened, they produced a powerful deceleration effect with virtually no trim change, unlike a fighter-type dorsal or ventral brake. The YA-9A went somewhat further than its rival, featuring a unique side-force control (SFC) system. This linked the speedbrakes and the very large rudder, and could be engaged or disengaged from the cockpit. If the pilot commanded a move to the left, the SFC system would deflect the rudder to the right, opposite to the usual direction. At the same time, the left speedbrake would open, preventing the aircraft from turning to the right. Instead, the thrust of the rudder would move the aircraft bodily to the left, without turning or banking. With SFC, the pilot could track a ground target without constantly worrying about the bank angle and fuselage direction changes that accompany a conventional turn; Northrop estimated that SFC could double the tracking accuracy of a typical attack.

Before either design left the ground, the entire A-X programme had to survive the first of many critical reviews by Congress. By the end of 1970, there were no fewer than three very active CAS programmes under way in the USA: A-X, the Army's Cheyenne, and the US Marine Corps' acquisition of the Hawker Siddeley Harrier. Congressional critics demanded to know why all three types were needed. The Department of Defense – which, of course, oversaw all three services – launched its own extensive study of CAS doctrine, tactics and requirements in February 1971. At about the same time, the USAF was working on its own study, TAC 85, which covered the entire spectrum of tactical missions. One of the most significant aspects of these studies was that they marked a break from Vietnam-oriented attitudes, and concentrated instead on the situation in Europe.

Emphasis on Europe

The DoD told Congress that the US military simply did not have anything in service which could perform CAS effectively. Delivery accuracy, acquisition of small tactical targets and response times were all inadequate to a greater or lesser extent. For the first time, the report referred to the imbalance of ground armoured forces in Europe, and to the potency of new and forthcoming Soviet air defence systems (such as the SA-6 missile and the ZSU-23 mobile anti-aircraft gun system, although these were not specifically mentioned in the unclassified version of the report). The DoD argued that the extent of the threat made CAS a critically important mission, and also a very complex one. Each of the three CAS types, in the DoD's view, was best suited to some part of the requirement: "Cheyenne in discrete, responsible, highly mobile units, operating as part of the ground manoeuvre force;

Left: Line-up of early A-10s at Edwards in mid-1975. The two prototypes (furthest from camera) were retired in May and June as soon as three of the six DT & E aircraft (foreground) were available.

Above: **Seen from the cockpit of an A-37, a DT & E A-10 without ordnance but with eight pylons installed, rolls to port over a gun range where M48 and T-62 tanks will be attacked.**

Harrier in rapid response to urgent firepower requirements during amphibious operations; and A-X in concentrating heavy firepower, matching selected munitions to different targets, at threatened sectors from dispersed bases". The DoD conceded that the capabilities of the three types might overlap "in less demanding situations", but concluded that all three would be needed for the full spectrum of operations.

The A-X programme survived this first brush with politics, but with some conditions. The A-X would not be launched into full production as soon as a winner emerged from the fly-off. Further testing would have to prove the type's prowess in the CAS role, including its ability to survive against defensive systems and the lethality of its internal gun against armoured vehicles. As the initial development of the GAU-8 was not due to be completed until mid-1973, there would clearly be some delay to the programme, but the DoD regarded lethality and survivability as essential to the A-X and would not release the type for production until it had proved itself.

The fly-off competition called for both A-X candidates to be delivered by road to Edwards AFB, where they would make their first flights in the hands of company test pilots before being handed over to a specially formed USAF joint test force (JTF). The Air Force evaluation was to start in late October 1972. The YA-10A was the first to fly, taking to the air in the hands of Howard 'Sam' Nelson on May 10, 1972. Its Northrop rival followed 20 days later. The second YA-10A flew on July 21, and the second YA-9A joined the programme on August 23. The manufacturers had five months to unearth and fix any operationally significant problems in the design, because the rules of the contest prohibited any design changes during the JTF evaluation unless safety was in jeopardy. The only externally visible change concerned the YA-10A. Not surprisingly, stalling the aircraft sent turbulent airflow into the TF34s, which responded by stalling themselves. A fixed slot was fitted to the inboard wing to smooth out the airflow. The second YA-10A, too, was involved in the only incident of the test programme, blowing both main tyres in a heavy landing and sustaining minor damage to its nosewheel.

JTF evaluation

These and other problems had all been taken care of by the time the JTF took the four aircraft over, on October 24. The JTF was a new type of organisation, designed specifically to handle the competitive evaluation. It comprised test pilots from USAF Systems Command, which is responsible for the engineering and procurement of all USAF aircraft, and from TAC, which would use the A-X. Other experts were assigned to the JTF from the USAF Logistics Command and the Air Training Command, and their task would be to assess the maintenance requirements of the competing aircraft. All JTF team members worked and reported on both contestants. The evaluation was planned to include 123hr flying for each type, but eventually the YA-9As flew 146hr in 92 sorties, while the Fairchild aircraft logged 138.5hr in 87 sorties. Just under half the time was spent firing 20,000 rounds from the M61 cannon and releasing 700 'iron' bombs – no guided weapons were used at this stage – while about a third of the flying hours were devoted to performance and handling tests. Flight tests were followed by a week of maintenance demonstrations.

Left: The second DT &E A-10, 73-1665, armed with Hobo and Paveway guided bombs, fires a burst from its cannon during the weapons test programme which it shared with the third pre-production aircraft.

While the fly-off was unquestionably important, it was certainly not the only factor in the evaluation. Systems Command carried out its own theoretical assessment of the competing aircraft in parallel with the fly-off, covering areas which flight-testing could not be expected to explore. These included operational aspects, such as the degree of protection provided against gun and missile attack in the two aircraft; industrial considerations, such as the amount of work needed to set up production, and future concerns, including the potential of each type for development. The two engines were the subject of a parallel evaluation. An unprecedented series of tests was carried out at Systems Command's headquarters at Wright-Patterson AFB, Ohio, where representative components of both A-X designs were set up on stands, blasted with a simulated slipstream from a jet engine, and bombarded with 23mm shells from a Soviet-built anti-aircraft gun, to determine whether their foam-filled fuel tanks would withstand such hits without ignition.

Political pressure

Politically, there was pressure on the Air Force to select Fairchild. The aircraft industry in New York State had historically been dominated by Republic and Grumman. The latter, in 1972, was in serious trouble with the F-14 programme, and there were doubts about its future. Fairchild's Republic division had also been the largest single subcontractor on the Boeing SST programme, scrapped the previous year. Unless Fairchild was awarded the A-X, Long Island's aerospace industry might suffer permanent damage. It was not exactly possible to say the same about Northrop and Los Angeles.

Congressional pressure alone would not be enough to swing an Air Force decision against the service's own assessment, but neither was it in the USAF's interest to let a major contractor lose its capability to design and build a complete military aircraft. Competition was – and remains – a key element in the USAF procurement system, and the service had come to expect at least half-a-dozen responses from qualified suppliers to any of its RFPs. Other things being equal, this factor would tend to favour Fairchild.

Results from the fly-off competition were close. The Northrop type displayed better handling qualities in some respects; the YA-10A proved slightly superior from the maintenance viewpoint; but both aircraft improved on the specification. Systems Command's analysis showed a significant advantage for the Fairchild aircraft in the important area of survivability. The YA-10A, due partly to its unconventional configuration, appeared to be better protected against attack. The most important difference, though, was that the YA-10A was much more representative of a production-type A-X than the YA-9A, something which had been reflected in the higher price quoted and paid for the Fairchild prototypes. This would mean an easier transition to production with lower risks and smaller learning costs.

Above: For trials with Paveway laser-guided bombs and the Pave Penny laser seeker pod, 73-1665 – showing the effects of a strenuous test programme – is equipped with cameras under the nose and tail.

Left: The ability to fly from forward bases close to the battle area was a prime A-X requirement: one of the first production batch of 52 A-10As kicks up the dust as it comes in to land on the dry lake bed at Edwards.

Barely two weeks after the close of the fly-off and maintenance comparison, on January 18, 1973, the USAF announced the selection of the Fairchild aircraft. In the following weeks, the USAF and Fairchild negotiated a $159 million contract, covering ten development, test and evaluation (DT & E) aircraft for further testing. (This batch was later cut to six aircraft by Congress, and the remaining four pre-production aircraft were completed under the first production contract.) The contract included an option for initial production of 48 aircraft, but the A-10 would not be ordered in quantity until further tests of the aircraft had been completed, and the effectiveness of the GAU-8 had been demonstrated.

At the same time, the General Electric TF34 was selected to power the new aircraft. This was not a foregone conclusion, because an Avco-powered A-10 and a GE-powered A-9 had both been studied, and Avco Lycoming was offering a developed version of the F102 with greater power and growth potential. While the F102 was being offered at a considerably lower price than the TF34, the GE engine had one tremendous advantage: it was three years into a full-scale development programme for a military aircraft. The USAF also planned to use eight TF34s to power the Boeing AWACS (the idea was dropped a few weeks later) and large-scale orders held the prospect of lower unit costs in the future. Moreover, Fairchild and GE had worked together on a package of low-risk modifications to the TF34 which would reduce its cost without degrading its performance in the A-X.

Three days before the decision on the airframe and engine was announced, the two GAU-8A prototypes began side-by-side ground firing trials at the Armament Development and Test Center at Eglin AFB, Florida. Initial trials concerned the accuracy and general functioning of the guns; the advanced family of ammunition types was tested from a single-barrel stand in March, and tests proceeded with both guns until a firing rate of 4,000 rounds/min was attained. GE's experience with Gatlings, and the company-funded research on advanced 30mm weapons which it had started in 1968, told heavily in its favour, and it was selected for Phase 2 GAU-8 development in June 1973. GE was awarded a $23.7 million contract for 11 pre-production models, three for quality testing, and eight for installation in the pre-production A-10s.

Unofficial name

A less official event in the history of the programme can also be traced to Eglin AFB and the summer of 1973. Discussing the A-10 in the Tactical Air Warfare Center's *TAWC Review*, Major Michael G. Major closed his article by proposing a name for the new aircraft. Republic's first jet fighter, the F-84, had a less-than-sparkling take-off performance which earned it the nickname 'Groundhog' or just 'Hog'. Its swept-wing development, the F-84F, became the 'Super-Hog', and the concrete-hungry F-105 was christened 'Ultra-Hog'. "What do you suppose the A-10 will be called?" wondered Major. "The 'warthog'?" The name was too appropriate not to stick to an ugly beast with a thick hide and dangerous tusks.

The two YA-10As flew from Edwards throughout the rest of 1973 and 1974, although at a slightly lower rate than in 1972. The main thrust of the programme was the definition and completion of the pre-production aircraft, the first of which was due to be delivered at the end of 1974. The No 2 aircraft tested refinements to the design, including a package of aerodynamic changes which reduced drag both in cruising and manoeuvring flight: the wingspan was increased by 30in (76cm), cutting induced drag, the canopy and windscreen shapes were refined, the engine pylons were shortened and streamlined and the landing gear pods were reduced in cross-section. The temporary fixed slats were replaced by automatic retractable slats. All of these were to be incorporated on the pre-production aircraft. The second YA-10A explored the spinning and recovery envelope in late 1974.

Another series of trials took place as a result of Congressional pressure to replace the A-10 with the A-7D. After scaling down the pre-production programme in mid-1973, as mentioned above, the Senate Armed Services Committee threatened to make further cuts and divert the money into additional A-7D orders. In September 1973, it was agreed that the A-10 programme could continue, provided that a second fly-off contest was arranged between a YA-10A and an A-7D. This took place in April-May 1974 at Fort Riley, Kansas. The A-10 was found to offer significant advantages, particularly in less-than-perfect visibility where targets might merge into a dull background. Air Force testimony to Congress after the trials was unanimous: the A-10 was the only aircraft for the short-range CAS mission.

Operationally related testing included the installation of a standard 'slipway' for the USAF flying-boom refuelling system in the nose of the No 1 YA-10. This was a departure from normal fighter practice – most US fighters have receptacles behind the cockpit – but was found to be an improvement. The slipway was not plumbed into the fuel system on the prototypes, which instead took off at high gross weights to simulate the behaviour of the aircraft towards the end of the fuel transfer operation. The refuelling tests were concluded in August; in the same month, a mock-up forward fuselage, attached to a rocket-powered sled, was used for successful tests of the Escapac IE9 ejection seat at Holloman AFB, New Mexico. August 1974 also saw the start of

Right: Carrying its Paris Air Show number on the engine pod, a 355th TTW A-10 en route back to its base at Davis-Monthan in June 1977.

Above: A formation flight of four early production A-10s assigned to the 355th TTW. The wing's 333rd Tactical Fighter Training Squadron received its first A-10s in March 1976, and was the first operational unit to be equipped with the type, training pilots for service with combat wings.

Left: While two of its aircraft visited the Paris Air Show before going on to tour USAFE bases, three of the 355th TTW's A-10s carried out a series of demonstrations of their capabilities at PACAF bases, including this one in Korea, during June and July, 1977.

Below: A 355th TTW A-10 in the asymmetric colour scheme used for only 17 of the early production aircraft.

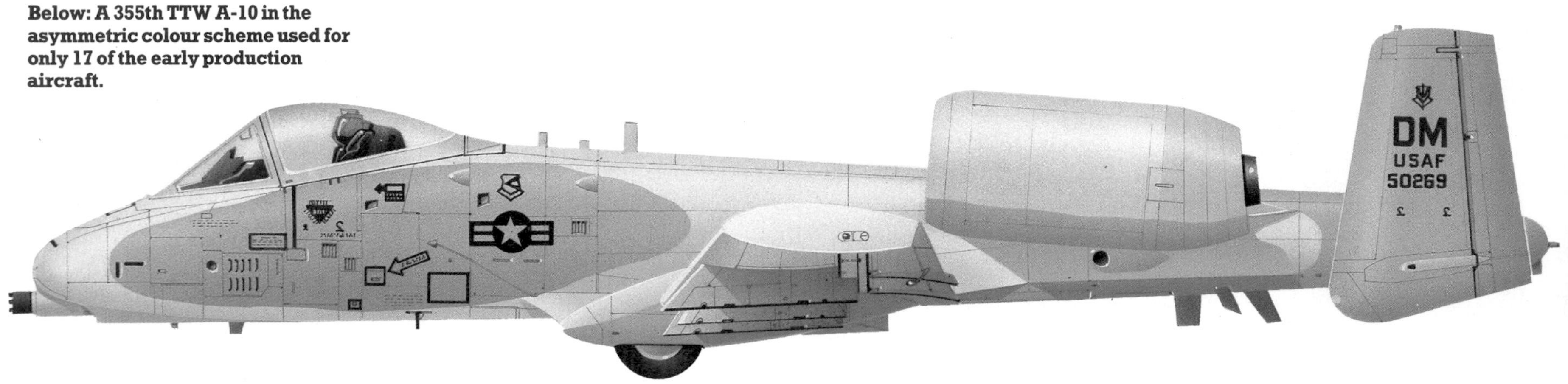

a series of unguided launches of the Hughes AGM-65A Maverick television-guided 'fire-and-forget' missile. Along with the GAU-8/A, Maverick was to be a standard weapon for the A-10. Eleven missiles were launched during the first evaluation flights.

Development of the gun and its three types of ammunition – armour-piercing incendiary (API), high-explosive incendiary (HEI) and target practice (TP) – continued in parallel with that of the aircraft. By September 1974, a prototype GAU-8/A was installed in the first YA-10A for preliminary trials. These disclosed a potentially serious problem. The explosive gases generated by the propellant were not being fully burned in the barrel, and the remnants were being expelled and ignited in front of the aircraft, forming a large and dangerous fireball. This was the most serious technical problem facing the A-10 programme towards the end of 1974, but was solved by adding a potassium nitrate additive to the propellant: a technique borrowed from the US Navy's battleship guns. This change also increased the projectile velocity to some degree. The gun itself passed its Critical Design Review in September 1974.

Production problems

Completion of the Critical Design Review on the production-standard airframe, with its aerodynamic changes, provision for the GE gun and other operational equipment, had been announced in May 1974. USAF people at Fairchild's Farmingdale plant, however, were growing concerned about the progress of production. The company had not run a major programme since the F-105 line had closed ten years before; many of its management people lacked experience in production, and the plant's machinery was outdated. (Some of it, one USAF officer asserted, had been used to build P-47s.) Both the cost and schedule targets of the programme were in danger. An Air Force inquiry led to a series of changes in Fairchild production management and organisation, and the USAF increased its staff at Farmingdale. Fairchild acquired new numerically-controlled machine tools to replace equipment from the F-105 era, and, on the recommendation of the Air Force, placed more of the A-10's critical machined components – the first parts to be assembled in any aircraft, which have the greatest potential to delay or disrupt production – with subcontractors.

Generally, progress with the A-10 was considered to be encouraging by mid-1974, and the GAU-8/A was also going well, although it had yet to be fired from the A-10. The Department of Defense accordingly gave the production programme an amber light at the end of July, releasing $39 million to start production of 52 production A-10As: the 48 aircraft which the USAF had taken on option at the start of the programme, plus the four aircraft which Congress had cut from the original DT & E contract. However, options to buy a smaller quantity were to be kept open. Five months later, with more aircraft and weapon trials completed and the DT & E fleet in final assembly, production of the A-10 was unconditionally authorized by the DoD.

The first DT & E aircraft was completed at Farmingdale in late 1974, and after preliminary ground tests it was stripped of its wing and empennage and flown to Edwards AFB in a C-5A transport, where it made its first flight on February 15, 1975. (On the previous day, the 1,000th YA-10 flight hour had been recorded.) The first DT & E aircraft was 'heavily instrumented' – that is to say, packed with sensors to measure temperature, vibration and strain in every component, and warrened with wiring runs linking all the gauges to a central digital recording system. It was not fitted with a gun, and its task was to measure and evaluate performance, handling, aerodynamic efficiency, loads and flutter.

The second of the pre-production batch was the first A-10 to make its first

Below: With the wing's old A-7Ds parked in the background, A-10s of the 355th TTW form up on the runway at Davis-Monthan AFB, Arizona.

Left: During 1977 the 354th TFW at Myrtle Beach began to convert to the A-10: here one of the wing's new aircraft refuels from a KC-135.

Below: A pair of 354th TFW A-10s in the new European camouflage scheme in flight with Mk bombs (foreground) and Maverick missiles.

Below: The new standard colour scheme of 30 percent and 50 percent grey was introduced with the 23rd production aircraft.

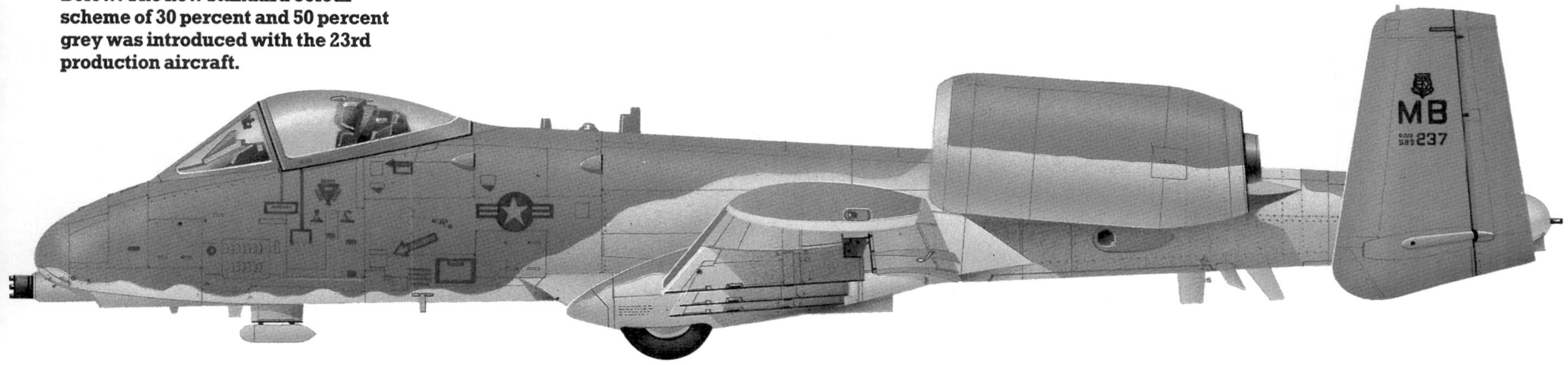

flight from Farmingdale, on April 26; it was also the first new aircraft to fly from Farmingdale since the last F-105 was completed. Fairchild, however, had sold the company airfield for general-aviation use some years before, and it was too crowded to be used for acceptance-test flying once the production programme got into its stride. By April, it had been decided to move A-10 final assembly and testing to another Fairchild facility at Hagerstown, Maryland, after the completion of the 10th aircraft.

The second DT & E aircraft was to share weapons and systems testing with the third of the batch, which flew on June 10. Both had GAU-8/A cannon installed. From June onwards, one A-10 joined the test programme every month. The fourth DT & E aircraft backed up the first for performance tests, and like the first, it did not have a gun. The fifth would lead the initial operational test and evaluation programme, and the sixth would be used for climate testing.

As the second DT & E aircraft joined the test programme in April 1975, the first YA-10A was retired and placed in 'flyable storage' after 467 flights and 590hr. Likewise, the second YA-10A was withdrawn from the programme in June, once the third pre-production aircraft was available. It had flown a total of 548.5hr in 354 flights.

Testing progressed with few problems. By the end of the year, it was revealed that the original weight estimates for the DT & E aircraft – including a 2,000lb (907kg) weight saving compared with the YA-10s – had been optimistic, and that the type was somewhat overweight. The USAF, however decided that the resulting degradation of overall performance was not critical. One failure occurred during static testing of the fatigue-test airframe at Farmingdale; a minor redesign of a forged fuselage/wing fitting was carried out to solve the problem.

Snags were overshadowed, though, by the performance of the second DT & E aircraft in the first live gun-firing tests, conducted against surplus US M-48 tanks and Soviet T-62s obtained via Israel. The A-10/GAU-8 combination confounded the sceptics, and clearly demonstrated that design aims had been achieved. Accuracy, range and destructive firepower were incomparably superior to anything achieved before. Strikes against the side and top armour of the T-62s, not only with the API ammunition but also with the HEI shells – which had been designed originally for use against softer-skinned vehicles – penetrated the heavy tanks' protection and set off secondary explosions of internal fuel and ammunition. The targets were totally destroyed, by what was effectively point-blank shooting: even at long ranges, the GAU-8/A's velocity was such that ballistic drop and windage could be ignored.

The first production A-10 flew in October 1975, and was delivered to the USAF on November 5. Along with the next three aircraft off the line – numbers 7 to 10 of the originally planned DT & E batch – it joined the test programme at Edwards AFB, but subsequent aircraft, starting in March 1976, were delivered to the first operational unit. This was the 333rd Tactical Fighter Training Squadron (333 TFTS), which had been designated as the first A-10 squadron in November 1974; part of the 354th Tactical Fighter Trianing Wing, it was based at Davis-Monthan AFB, Arizona.

Production build-up at Hagerstown was steady, rather than spectacular, and it was April 3, 1978, before the USAF accepted the 100th production A-10A. Present at the handover ceremony were two retired USAF officers: Brig. Gen. Francis S. Gabreski and Col. Robert S. Johnson. Both had distinguished themselves by destroying more than two dozen enemy aircraft in an earlier Republic product, so it was only fitting that the USAF should choose the occasion to give the A-10 a name, one that had ben proposed unofficially four years earlier: Thunderbolt II.

Below: The switch to European camouflage and the Maverick armament carried by this 354th TFW A-10 reflect the type's new role.

Structure

Those who describe the A-10 as the world's ugliest combat aircraft are unjust. The Soviet Mil Mi-24 Hind-D helicopter gunship is the clear winner in this category, by two warts and a proboscis, but the A-10 runs a respectable second. Standing high on its landing gear, its fins and engines reaching out toward the clouds, it is an imposing machine. Its weights and dimensions set it well above most Western support and attack types: it is similar in overall length to the formidable Tornado interdiction-strike aircraft, and its wing span is almost equal to that of the F-111A.

Above: The size and weight of the A-10 were largely dictated by the requirement for the massive cannon installation, and the need for sufficient protection to enable it to survive close-quarter tank-busting.

Basic dimensions, though, are misleading; the A-10 may be large, and its maximum take-off weight is considerable, but its normal in-service operating weights are considerably lower. Its configuration springs from the fact that it is designed to excel in a unique flight regime: constant manoeuvre at low speed and low altitudes. Its size is a product of its flight regime and its intended warload.

A heavy weapon load was one of the best features of the A-1, and it was carried over into the A-X requirement. A lesson of Vietnam was that effective intervention in the ground battle called for heavy firepower; dug-in troops or armour were generally unimpressed by the loads delivered by adapted fighters. Endurance requirements also drove the weight upward. The use of external fuel for the normal mission was ruled out from the survivability standpoint, and this meant all the fuel had to be accommodated internally. Morover, the need to protect the internal fuel compromised the conventional fighter-design approach, which is to use every available cubic inch in the air-frame for fuel.

The need for long endurance, and the low operating speeds, ruled out that great weight-saver, the afterburner. The result was higher engine weight for a given thrust level. The advent of the high-BPR turbofan was a major breakthrough, because its low fuel consumption helped make up for that weight penalty.

A-X also set standards for protection around vital areas – the pilot, the fuel system, and the internal ammunition – so that part of the empty weight was virtually independent of the overall size of the aircraft. Given a certain 'defeat level' – the maximum strike which the aircraft must survive – the amount of armour around the cockpit, for example, was the same however large or small the aircraft might be.

These requirements in themselves would have driven A-X beyond the size and weight of the Skyraider. As the requirement evolved toward tank-busting, however, the weight of a phenomenally large cannon installation, several times as heavy as an M61, had to be figured into the equation. So did the added airframe size, weight and drag incurred by carrying such a weapon internally, together with the large quantity of ammunition needed for even tens of seconds of firing time. While the A-10 may look large and beefy, its armour, its gun and its ammunition amount to some 25 per cent of its empty weight. It is no larger than an effective platform for the GAU-8/A, armoured to the levels specified by A-X, needs to be.

Wing design

Given the size and weight of an aeroplane, the next feature to be defined is the wing. In the case of the A-10, as with most combat aircraft, the main factors behind the wing design are speed and manoeuvre; other factors, such as range and field performance, tend to fall into place.

The high end of the speed envelope in the A-X requirement was not demanding. The maximum operating speed was to be only 400kt (740km/h), and the Fairchild designers selected a maximum design speed (VD) of 450kt (833km/h), allowing a normal safety margin in case a pilot allowed his aircraft to overspeed in combat. Wing designers care more about Mach number, or the relation of speed to the speed of sound, than pure airspeed; in the case of the A-10, the maximum speeds are to be attained at sea level, where the local speed of sound is higher than at medium altitude, so the wing does not have to be designed for more than Mach 0.68. It is possible to encounter high-Mach buffet at such speeds, particularly if the aircraft has to manoeuvre, but the A-10 is not required to manoeuvre tightly at its top speeds.

Below: Although of unconventional layout, the A-10 prototype, seen here during final assembly, was built using conventional materials and straightforward techniques.

Right: The large Fowler flaps and split-aileron airbrakes, displayed here by the second DT & E A-10, form the key to the A-10's low-speed manoeuvrability, and are readily accommodated on the large wings.

USAF tactics of the late 1960s were another important factor in the wing design. Attack aircraft, including the A-X, were not generally required to fly for long periods at high speed and low level. 'Ingress' profiles were invariably flown more than 1,000ft (305m) above ground level, in level flight above the roughest air. This, combined with the modest speed, meant that there was no need for the A-10 to have the short, swept, highly loaded wing that were required by contemporary Royal Air Force tactics, for example.

The peak performance of the A-X specification, instead, called for the ability to turn in a small radius and short elapsed time, at modest airspeeds; the A-10, pulling a 3.25g turn at 275kt (510km/h), can manoeuvre in a smaller radius than a fast-jet fighter, and can actually change heading more quickly. The implications of low speed and high g are important. The total drag generated by any aircraft is made up of a number of components, most of which increase with the square of the airspeed. A major exception is induced drag, or the drag due to lift, which increases with the lifting force generated by the wing. In a 3g turn at 275kt, the lift and the induced drag are at three times their normal value, but the other components of airframe drag are still modest. The main thrust of the A-X aerodynamic design, therefore, was to cut down the induced drag in a medium-speed manoeuvre, and the best way to do this was to increase the wingspan.

The A-10 design benefited from the steady advance in the basic design of wing sections. Classic wing sections of

Above: Tufts attached to a YA-10's wings to monitor the airflow, and the stall slats fitted to smooth turbulence at high angles of attack.

Right: Assembly of the A-10 port, starboard and centre wing sections prior to mating with the fuselage.

the 1950s produced most of their lift close to the leading edge; this was to say that the airflow over the wing underwent a single rapid acceleration at this point. This made the wing prone to buffet at even modest Mach numbers, and the only way to delay the buffeting was through the use of sweepback or a thinner section. Thin-section wings are heavier for a given strength, because the spars are not as deep (think of the way beams are placed in a building) and are less efficient at low speeds. In the 1960s, though, the use of computers enabled aerodynamicists to improve their mathematical 'models' of the airflow over the wing. This allowed them to design new sections in which the lift was more evenly distributed along the chord; they were called 'rooftop' sections, because a chart showing chordwise lift distribution was more symmetrical, like a house roof. Rooftop-section wings could be deeper, and hence lighter, for an equivalent Mach number.

The A-10 accordingly has a long-span, lightly loaded wing, which allows excellent low- to medium-speed turning performance with low drag and a low power requirement. The wing has a rooftop section and a 16 per cent thickness/chord ratio. The deep section makes it possible to build a wing which is reasonably light, has a long span and a high aspect ratio, and can withstand high g loadings. The depth of the wing, and its bluff leading edge, make for high lift and efficiency at low speeds. Another drag reduction is provided by the down-turned Hoerner wingtips, which act as small, lightweight endplates, reduce vortex flow at the tips and improve aileron effectiveness near the stall.

The big, thick wing also provides ample lift for take-off and landing, meeting all the A-X field-length requirements without the use of complex high-lift devices. The A-10 has classic area-increasing Fowler flaps, driven out along curved tracks to increase the area and camber of the wing. Fairchild did study alternative wing designs, with less area and double- or triple-slotted flaps, but the increased complexity and cost more than cancelled out the reduction in weight, while straight-line drag and manoeuvrability would have been somewhat worse. The simple Fowler flaps create little additional drag when extended, and can be partially lowered for manoeuvre at very low speeds.

Another advantage of the generously sized wing is that the flaps need extend over only part of the span, leaving room on the trailing edge for large ailerons for effective low-speed roll control; the A-10 has no wing spoilers. The ailerons also incorporate the only unconventional feature of the mainly straightforward aerodynamic control system. Each aileron is split on the horizontal plane, aft of its leading edge. An actuator and linkage in the aileron leading edge drive the two sections apart to form a powerful airbrake. This arrangement gives effective deceleration with virtually no trim change, unlike a dorsal or ventral brake, and does not interfere aerodynamically with the empennage as fuselage-side brakes can do. Similar airbrakes were used on the Northrop YA-9A; in fact, the devices were originally invented by Northrop in the 1940s for its flying-wing designs.

Low-wing advantages

While most contemporary attack aircraft, including the Northrop YA-9A, had shoulder-mounted wings, Fairchild chose a low-wing configuration for the A-10, for a number of reasons. The most important was that the A-X requirement called for at least ten separate weapons pylons under the aircraft. With a low wing it is possible to put the most highly loaded pylons under the fuselage itself, and, generally, to concentrate the heaviest stores near the centreline. This substantially reduces the rolling inertia of the aircraft with a maximum weapon load, and improves its handling. The low wing also provides for a wide-track landing gear with a simple retraction sequence. Some aspects of ground handling are simplified; it is easier to work around the aircraft with the engines running, for instance. On the debit side, all the maintenance has to be done with ladders and platforms.

The wing design is the key to the A-10's performance in the most important flight regime, sustained low- to medium-speed manoeuvre. This regime dictates the installed thrust, so there is plenty of excess thrust available to meet the comparatively relaxed straight-line speed requirement. Reducing drag by the classic means – streamlining, blending and fairing, and reducing surface area - was not necessary to meet the specification and was therefore not considered worthwhile. It can also be argued that achieving, say, a five per cent reduction in clean airframe drag is a futile exercise

Above: A-10 fuselage assembly line. Long and deep, the fuselage accommodates the pilot and gun forward, fuel tanks above the wings, and engine aft.

Above: The fuselage shell, showing the massive gun compartment and smaller nosewheel well, with the pilot's armoured 'bathtub' above, is hoisted along the line.

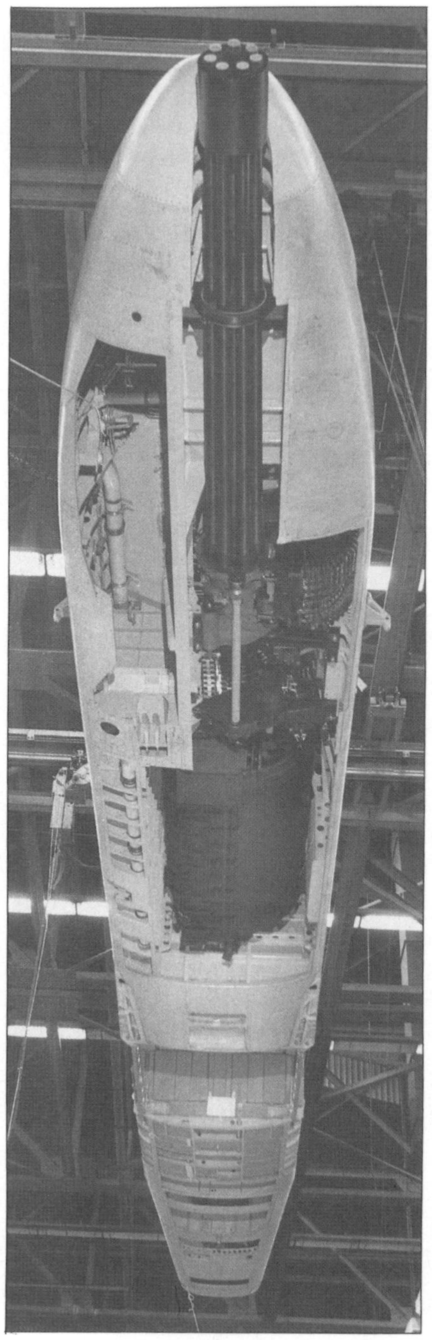

Above: One stage further along, the fuselage, with nose cone in place, gun installed and nose gear hydraulics fitted, is moved into position for mating with the wing assembly.

Above: The imposing, long-legged aspect of the A-10 on the ground is a result of the low-mounted wing and wide-track landing gear.

Right: The second DT & E A-10 with avionics and armament bay doors open for final installation of equipment prior to roll-out.

on an aircraft which will spend most of its life carrying a very large, drag-evoking external payload. Recognizing these factors, Fairchild designed the A-10 fuselage, engine location and empennage according to the demands of utility as well as those of aerodynamics.

The first requirement in the fuselage design is capacity. In most aircraft, a big, thick wing provides the natural home for the fuel, but it was clear from the start of the A-X programme that large wing tanks presented an unacceptably large vulnerable area to the enemy. Instead, the A-10 carries most of its fuel in fuselage tanks, which have a much higher ratio of volume to surface area. To minimize changes in trim as the fuel was used, the tanks were located in the centre fuselage, above the wing.

The forward fuselage is designed around the GAU-8/A cannon and its ammunition drum. The weight of the latter can drop by more than 1,000lb (454kg) as propellant and projectiles are expended (the cartridge cases are recycled back into the drum) so it is located to the rear of the gun, just ahead of the fuel tanks and close to the centre of gravity. The sheer power of the gun itself defines its position. The mass of its shells, its muzzle velocity and its rate of fire generate a constant recoil thrust of 9,000lb (40kN). Unless the recoil thrust vector was aligned precisely on the aircraft's centreline, this would make accurate shooting impossible.

Blast from the gun means that the muzzle must be well clear of any structure, so the only possible location is the nose of the aircraft, right on the centreline. The gun is set below the centre of gravity, so the firing angle is very slightly depressed (by about 2deg) to eliminate any pitch change. The YA-10As featured an automatic elevator compensator, to counter any pitch effects from firing the gun, but this was found to be unnecessary. The seven-barrel rotary gun is offset slightly to the left, and its mechanism is arranged so that the firing barrel is in the nine o'clock position, placing it exactly on the centreline. This makes room for the nose landing gear, which retracts into the right side of the fuselage.

The A-10's long forward fuselage provides room for the 21ft (6.4m) weapon, and the pilot occupies a lofty perch above the feed and breech mechanism. The narrow, flat-sided fuselage, the short nose and the bubble canopy, set well above the wing plane, give the A-10 pilot an all-round view matched by few other aircraft. The forward fuselage design also provides ample room for a second cockpit, which can be accommodated by rearranging some of the internal avionics. (Otherwise, the only change in the design of the two-seater is a slight increase in the size of the tailfins, to compensate for the added side area.)

The rear fuselage is the controversial part of the A-10 design, aesthetically and functionally. The skinny tail section carries the two engines, mounted high on the rear fuselage in airliner style, and the twin-fin tail assembly. It looked strange in the extreme to anyone used to fighter design, but Fairchild had sound reasons in its favour.

The only basic requirement affecting the location of the A-X's engines was that they should be far enough apart that a single hit would not disable both. To Fairchild's designers, it seemed that a conventional installation, with the engines under the wings, eliminated too much of the stores-carrying space on the

Left: The finished product, its bluff lines betraying few concessions to aesthetic considerations, but with an air of purpose and aggression in its strictly functional design.

aircraft. This was particularly true with the fat high-bypass engines, which were being used for the first time on a combat type. Neither were these engines very suited to being built into the fuselage, because of their large airflow requirements and their bulk. It seemed less risky, aerodynamically speaking, to house the engines in straightforward pods with short inlets. Fairchild studied overwing pods, as used on the unsuccessful German VFW 614 jet feederliner, but it would have proved difficult to change the engines without using special lifting equipment, particularly in the confines of a standard concrete hangarette.

The high-mounted rear-fuselage location which was finally chosen has a number of advantages. The engines are well out of the way of any dirt or foreign objects thrown up from the nosewheel when operating from unimproved strips; this is important, because high-bypass engines make superb vacuum-cleaners when placed too close to the ground and their high-pressure cores are very sensitive to erosion caused by dirt and grit. The inlets are also well to the rear, allowing gun gases more time to disperse. Also, as noted earlier, the engines can be kept running while the aircraft is being served and re-armed. One drawback of this arrangement, the fact that changes in thrust could change the trim of the aircraft in pitch, has been avoided by canting the engine nozzles 9deg upwards relative to the rest of the engine.

Tail layout

Rear-engined airliners have mid-set or high tail units, but the risk of a 'deep stall' – a condition in which the wing is stalled, the aircraft is sinking, and the tailplane, trapped in the turbulent wake of the wing and engine pods, has no power to recover the aircraft – immediately ruled out such a layout for the A-10, so the tail is low. Twin fins are partly a result of the engine location. It was felt that the engines could create some odd airflows around the rear fuselage, and might cause spin-recovery problems by shedding turbulent wakes on to a conventional single fin. The complexity of a twin-fin layout is justified, because it is almost impossible for both fins to be rendered ineffective at the same time.

Where the resulting layout scored very high points was in survivability. Control power in pitch and yaw can be retained even if one side of the entire empennage is shot away. More important, though, is the protection afforded to the engines. The fuselage and wing tend to conceal one or both of the engines from groundfire, from many different angles. The vertical and horizontal tail surfaces form what is almost a shroud around the engine exhausts, helping protect the aircraft against early-technology infra-red homing missiles: these weapons, such as the SA-7 Strela, need to 'see' the hot metal of the jetpipe before they will lock on to a target.

Testing of the YA-10s revealed some not unexpected problems with the engine installation. When the wing stalled, turbulent airflow from the wing-fuselage junction entered the inlets and stalled the compressors. The solution was to fit a flow-smoothing slat to the wing, inboard of the landing gear pods, which extended automatically under hydraulic power when the angle of attack exceeded the stall angle. A stall strip – a small spanwise fence, a few inches long

Right: The capacious forward fuselage proved readily capable of accommodating a second cockpit, and the second DT & E A-10 was converted to two-seat configuration for evaluation purposes.

Fairchild A-10A Thunderbolt II cutaway

1 Cannon muzzles
2 Forward radar warning antenna (one each side)
3 ILS antenna
4 Air refuelling ramp door
5 Air refuelling receptacle
6 AAS-38 Pave Penny laser seeker pod
7 Rudder pedals
8 Hinged windscreen panel (for instrument access)
9 Head-up display
10 Control column
11 Pilot's intrument display
12 Engine throttle levers
13 McDonnell Douglas ACES II ejection seat
14 Canopy jettison strut
15 Canopy actuator
16 Leading edge stall strip
17 Starboard wing stores pylons
18 Cockpit canopy cover
19 Pitot tube
20 Starboard navigation and strobe lights
21 Starboard aileron
22 Split aileron/airbrake
23 Airbrake operating jack
24 Aileron hydraulic actuator
25 Aileron tab
26 Cockpit air valves
27 IFF antenna
28 Tab balance weight
29 Anti-collision light
30 UHF/Tacan antenna
31 Starboard single slotted Fowler flaps
32 Flap guide rail
33 Flap hydraulic actuator
34 Fuselage fuel cells
35 Conditioned air delivery duct
36 General Electric TF34-GE-100 turbofan engine
37 Engine oil tank
38 Engine accessory equipment gearbox
39 Bleed air ducting
40 Air conditioning system intake and exhaust duct
41 Heat exchanger
42 Fire extinguisher bottle
43 Starboard tailfin
44 X-band antenna
45 Rudder mass balance
46 Rudder
47 Fan air exhaust duct
48 Core engine exhaust duct
49 Trim tab actuator
50 Elevator tab
51 Starboard elevator
52 Elevator hydraulic activators
53 Rear radar warning receiver
54 Tail navigation light
55 Port elevator
56 Port tailfin
57 Rudder hydraulic actuator
58 Formation light
59 IFF antenna
60 Elevator mechanical linkage
61 UHF/Tacan antenna
62 VHF/AM antenna
63 Fuel jettison
64 Air system ground connection
65 Hydraulic reservoir
66 VHF antenna
67 Hydraulic system ground connectors
68 APU exhaust
69 Auxiliary power unit (APU)
70 Air conditioning unit
71 Port Fowler flaps
72 Flap self-aligning torque shaft
73 Trim tab control rod
74 Aileron trim tab
75 Split aileron/airbrake
76 Strobe light
77 Port navigation light
78 Port aileron
79 Cambered wing tip fairing
80 Airbrake operating jack
81 Aileron hydraulic actuator
82 ECM pod
83 Aileron mechanical linkage
84 Flap hydraulic actuators
85 Hydraulic retraction jack
86 Main undercarriage pivot bearing
87 Chaff/flare dispenser
88 Forward-retracting mainwheel
89 Leading edge stall strip
90 Port wing stores pylons
91 Maverick air-to-ground missile
92 Wing centre section integral fuel tank
93 Main undercarriage wheel housing
94 Inboard wing stores pylon
95 Pressure refuelling connection
96 Slat hydraulic actuators
97 Inboard leading edge slat
98 Fuselage stores pylons (3)
99 Multiple ejector rack
100 Rockeye cluster bomb
101 Airflow smoothing strakes

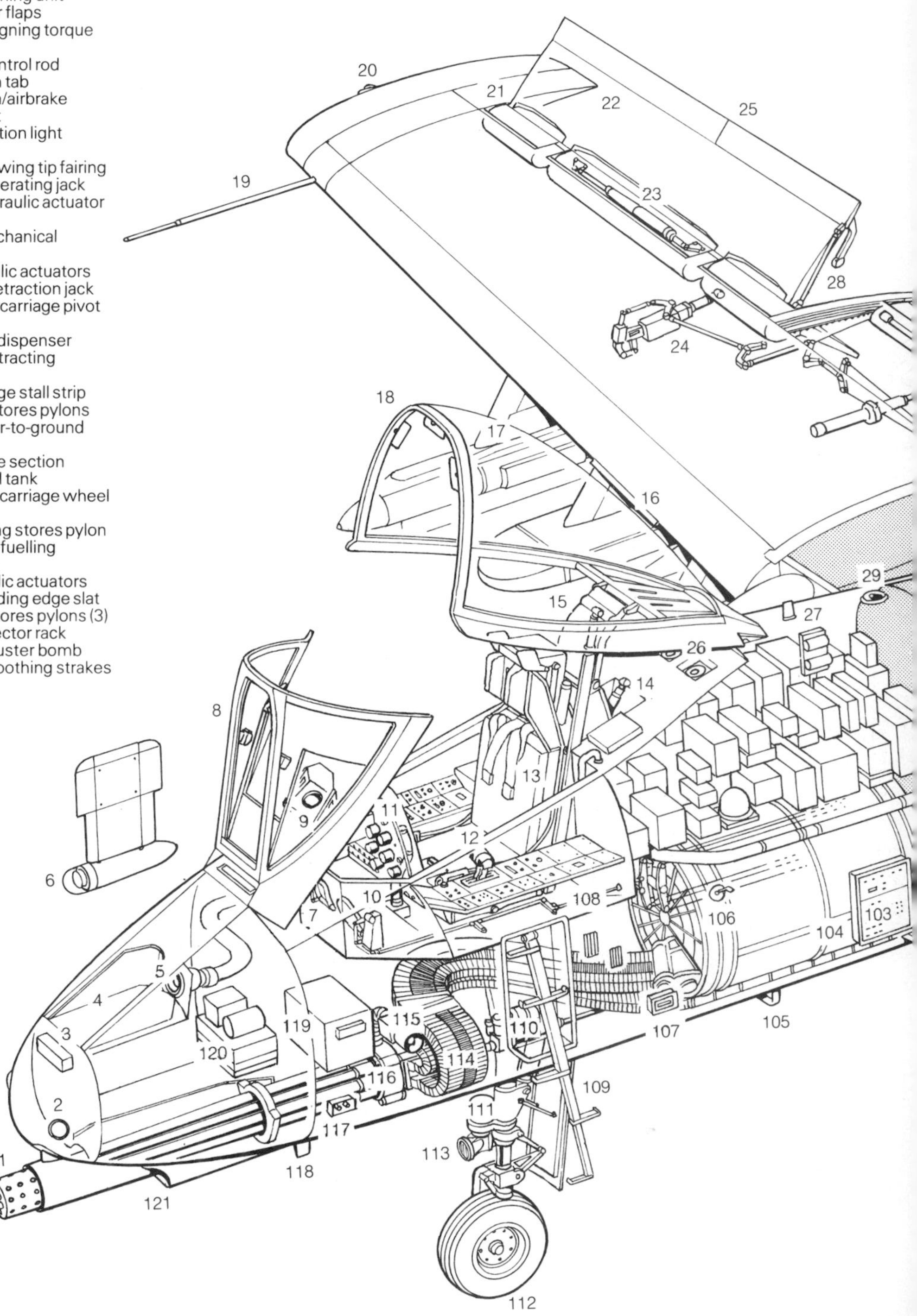

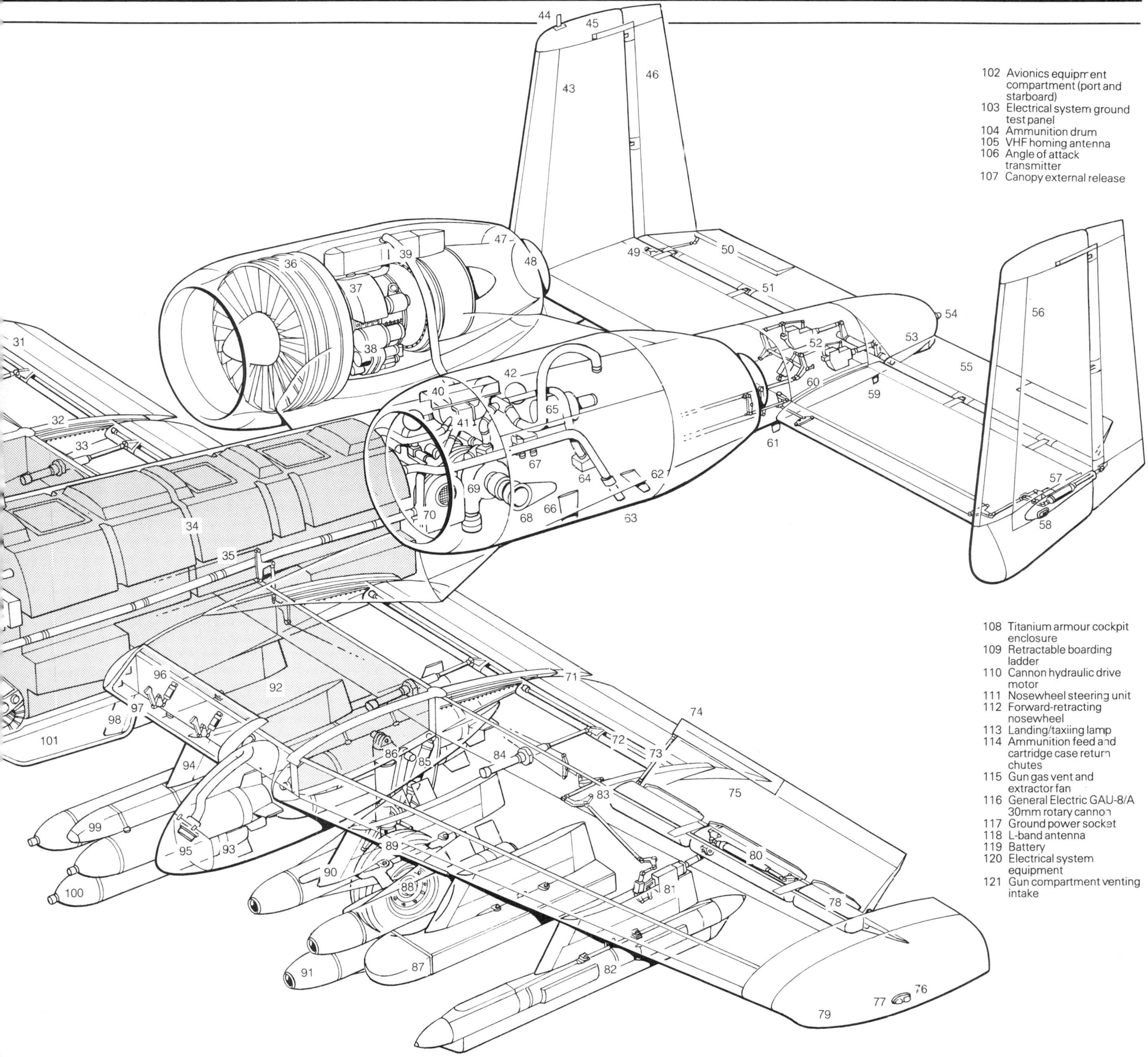

102 Avionics equipment compartment (port and starboard)
103 Electrical system ground test panel
104 Ammunition drum
105 VHF homing antenna
106 Angle of attack transmitter
107 Canopy external release
108 Titanium armour cockpit enclosure
109 Retractable boarding ladder
110 Cannon hydraulic drive motor
111 Nosewheel steering unit
112 Forward-retracting nosewheel
113 Landing/taxiing lamp
114 Ammunition feed and cartridge case return chutes
115 Gun gas vent and extractor fan
116 General Electric GAU-8/A 30mm rotary cannon
117 Ground power socket
118 L-band antenna
119 Battery
120 Electrical system equipment
121 Gun compartment venting intake

Above: The short nose and high-mounted cockpit with bubble canopy give the A-10 pilot a superb view, readily apparent in this phothograph of an 18th TFS pilot preparing for a mission from Eielson AFB, Alaska.

– was attached to the outboard leading edge to restore the natural stall warning. Two other devices were also added to cure the wing-engine interaction: prominent vertical strakes, fitted to the fuselage beneath the leading-edge wing root, and a trailing-edge fillet. Otherwise, the A-10 is aerodynamically straightforward, devoid of ventral fins, strakes, vortex generators and other fixes.

The final element in the A-10's unusual shape is provided by the main landing gear, which retracts forward into prominent underwing pods. This arrangement has a number of advantages, and the extra drag which it creates is not critical to the A-10. Unlike a sideways-retracting gear, it takes up little stores-carrying space beneath the wing. (The A-1 had a rearwards-retracting gear, for the same reason.) The entire landing-gear mechanism is attached beneath the wing itself, and the wheel is stowed ahead of the front spar, so there are no cut-outs in the structure.

The retraction mechanism is simple, and all three of the undercarriage legs retract forward; this is the ideal arrangement if the hydraulics are gone and the

Above: The A-10's forward-retracting landing gear legs, simple and rigid, with single wheels and low-pressure tyres, were designed to lower under gravity and wind resistance in the event of hydraulics failure, and the main gear and wheels are stowed in pods to maximize stores loading.

Right: Even in the event of landing gear collapse, the configuration should ensure that the main airframe structure sustains minimum damage.

gear must free-fall into the locked position, because gravity and the airstream both help to extend the gear. If even this next-to-last resort fails, the A-10 gear is designed, like those of the DC-3 or B-17, so that the mainwheels protrude from the gear pods and are free to rotate in a belly-landing. The A-10, in theory, will come to rest on its mainwheels and the lower tips of the fins with barely a bent antenna.

The landing gear itself is simple. The A-10 is designed to use short strips of prepared concrete, of the type that would be left on an airfield where the main runway had been cut in two by bombs, but is not really a rough-field aircraft. The landing gear, therefore, has simple rigid legs rather than more complex levered-suspension units, and there is only one wheel to each leg, carrying a single low-pressure tyre.

Odd as the A-10 may appear, its design has avoided any trace of unusual or unexpected handling qualities. This was a fundamental A-X requirement, and was one of the most important factors in the original fly-off competition; the USAF's view as that the A-X pilot, flying, navigating and acquiring targets at low level with a minimum of artificial help, would have no time to deal with any idiosyncratic handling behaviour.

A-10 pilots report that the aircraft feels much smaller than it looks, to the point where it is necessary to bear in mind that the wingtip may be nearly 30ft (9.15m) closer to the ground than the pilot in a steep turn over rolling terrain. The aircraft will tolerate a great deal of abuse, and gives plenty of notice when the limits of its tolerance are approached. The A-10 will remain controllable after the stall, and will only spin if pro-spin controls – full nose-up pitch and full rudder – are applied and held for several seconds; it will recover as soon as the controls are released.

Overall, the aircraft has been summed up as "an easy aircraft to fly safely, but difficult to fly precisely". Perhaps the

Left: Preparing for takeoff during Operation Gunsmoke '81 at Nellis AFB, A-10 pilots enjoy an unmatched all-round view from their cockpits, while only minimal ground support equipment clutters the flight line.

A-10 production manufacturing plan

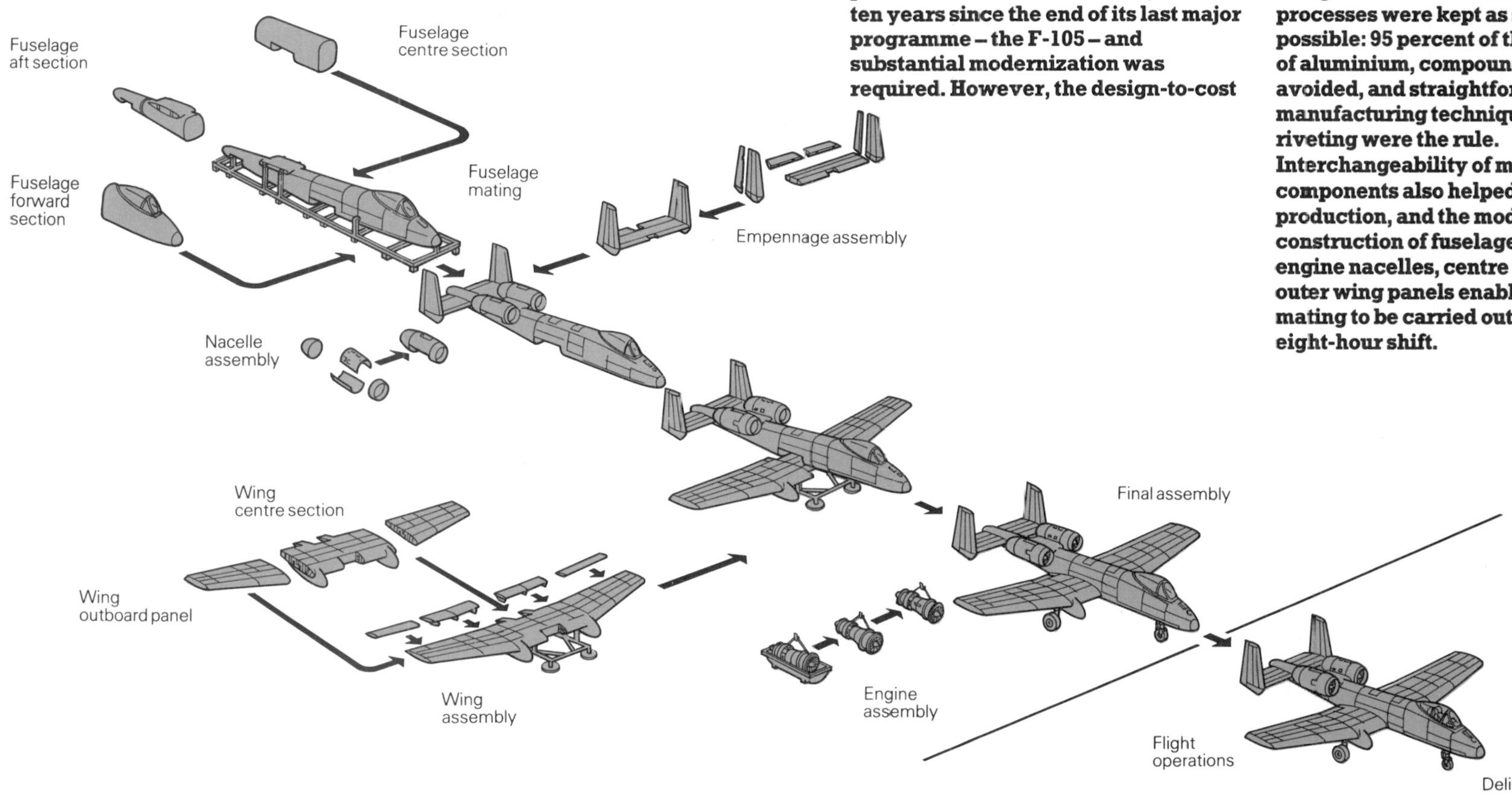

Below: By the time Fairchild secured a production order for the A-10, it was ten years since the end of its last major programme – the F-105 – and substantial modernization was required. However, the design-to-cost philosophy which had governed detail design meant that manufacturing processes were kept as simple as possible: 95 percent of the airframe is of aluminium, compound curves were avoided, and straightforward manufacturing techniques such as riveting were the rule. Interchangeability of many components also helped simplify production, and the modular construction of fuselage, empennage, engine nacelles, centre wing box and outer wing panels enabled final mating to be carried out in a single eight-hour shift.

Left: From the 11th aircraft onward, final assembly of A-10s was transferred to Fairchild's facility at Hagerstown, Maryland, where the company was able to conduct flight testing, its old airfield at Farmingdale having become too cluttered to permit such activity. Here one of the first production batches reaches the end of the assembly line, where the engines are installed and final checks are carried out on the structure and systems, though the line has been cleared for the photographer.

strongest testimony to the A-10's basic flying qualities is that Fairchild selected a very similar configuration when it competed for the USAF's Next Generation Trainer (NGT), and won the contest with what became the T-46A.

Internal arrangement

Beneath the skin, the design of the A-10 reflects two main considerations: survivability and design-to-cost. The ability to take hits from a variety of weapons, and survive, pervades both the structure and the systems of the A-10; design-to-cost mainly affects the construction and manufacture of the aircraft.

Design-to-cost was a new philosophy for military aircraft, but has always been a way of life for the designers of light aircraft and, to a limited extent, the airliner industry. While military aircraft, even the most exotic types, were never designed and built with total disregard for cost, the importance of price decreased rapidly with the move from basic to detailed design. The manufacturing cost would be estimated before any of the detail drawings were prepared, on the basis of the manufacturer's experience with earlier aircraft and the relative complexity of the new aircraft's structure and systems. The customer would base his procurement plan on that estimate.

Once detail design started, however, performance took priority over cost. If a part proved more highly loaded than had been expected, the normal practice was to make it from a higher-grade material and to accept the resulting cost increase. The same would be true if an assembly procedure was more complex than expected. On the other hand, there was no strong incentive to look for ways in which components could be made more simply, or manufactured from cheaper material than had been envisaged. It was therefore inevitable that costs would increase during the design and development stage.

Under the design-to-cost approach, the manufacturing cost was to be estimated, as usual, as part of the basic design: the A-X requirement set a $1.5 million cost target for the entire aircraft. What was new was that the cost was to be held down to the design level, even if it meant increasing weight and degrading performance. This policy was easier to implement on the A-10 than on a high-performance fighter, because a given mass of excess weight at 3g saps only one-third as much performance as the same mass at 9g. Nevertheless, the cost target was not easy to reach, and fundamentally affected the design.

Cost considerations

Design-to-cost, to begin with, ruled out the use of promising advanced composite materials. Closely contemporary designs such as the F-15 and F-16 used such materials to save weight, but, at the time, the costs of mass-producing composite components could not be safely predicted. A-X would be a conventional light-alloy aircraft, with the exception of some specialized components. The well-proven 7075 and 2024 alloys were chosen, due to their known resistance to stress and chemical corrosion.

During development, any proposed weight-saving was examined for its effect on manufacturing costs. A yardstick of $75/lb ($165/kg) empty weight was used, and if a proposed change cost more per unit saved, it was automatically discarded. Conversely, if a design change would add weight, but save more than $75/lb of extra weight, it would stand a chance of being implemented. This was the first time in a military aircraft programme that an actual dollar value had been put on empty weight.

Another basic principle, followed throughout the design and apparent in the external shape of the A-10, was the avoidance of 'double curvature': as far as possible, the A-10's shape is composed of flat planes or cylindrical or conical sections, reducing the need for slow and costly stretch-forming processes in the manufacturing stage. The fuselage sides are flat; the engine nacelles are cylindrical, rather than teardrop-shaped. Fuselage panels are overlapped and riveted, avoiding the smoother but more complex butt-jointing.

The A-10 is also unique in the degree to which components are interchangeable between the left and right sides of the aircraft: the fins and rudders, main landing gear, wing-root slats, inboard flaps, many fuselage skin panels and all pylons are examples. It was the first twin-jet USAF aircraft on which the engines were not 'handed', and this has now become a requirement for other new USAF types.

The advantages of this philosophy are two-fold: it cuts production cost, by doubling the output of a single part, and it simplifies spares support. In wartime, it may be critical, because the only spares that are any use at all are those that can be found on the base, whether in the normal supply system or aboard a damaged or otherwise inactive aircraft.

A related thrust in the production engineering of the A-10 was to ensure that components would be interchangeable between individual aircraft. This is not always the case: some aircraft have major components which are individually fitted at the factory, and a piece from another aircraft or an 'out of the crate' spare may fit only after precise, time-consuming adjustments, if at all.

Ultimately, the A-10 taught the USAF a lesson in manufacturing economics. After all the effort put into reducing the designed-in cost of the airframe, the Department of Defense revised its budget plans and authorised initial production of only 15 A-10s a month, rather than the 20 aircraft originally planned. This raised the price of the aircraft from the target of $1.5 million to $1.8 million. The USAF itself requested some changes in the avionics fitted to the aircraft, further increasing the price to $2 million. (These figures are compared to the target price and expressed in the same 1970 values; the dollar cost of A-10s as finally delivered was, of course, much higher due to general economic inflation.) Against this 33 per cent increase in the basic cost of the aircraft, the cost savings made through detail design seemed rather insignificant.

Survivability

The other major influence on the internal design, survivability, was equally new as a philosophy. It is strange but true that, before 1968, the ability of an aircraft to absorb battle damage and survive – specifically, to regain its base, with its pilot unharmed, and be repaired to fight again – had never been systematically studied. It was known that some aircraft were good in this respect (such as the B-17) and some were bad (the B-24), but there was no telling, or even guessing, which was the better aircraft until they were committed to combat.

Part of the reason for this state of affairs was a lack of basic data. Vietnam changed the situation. A great many modern aircraft, of a great many types, were used. The defensive fire was more intense, and more dangerous, than anything encountered since 1944-45, and came from a wide range of contemporary weapons. Modern ejection seats were more reliable under a wider range of circumstances; pilots were more easily tempted to stay with a damaged aircraft, if only to increase their chances of rescue by friendly units, and came back to report how they had been shot down.

F-105 experience

Survivability data began to arrive in quantity: the picture was mixed and confusing. One F-105 survived a direct hit on the wing from a 85mm AAA shell, and another was perforated in 87 places by an SA-2 missile and regained its base. But other F-105s were felled in seconds by small-calibre or fragment strikes. The same paradoxical situation applied to other types; Fairchild, however, had an early start in the field, because its F-105 bore the brunt of the Rolling Thunder operations in 1965-68, and F-105 experience was the first large single body of data. Before the A-X programme was initiated, too, Fairchild was upgrading and hardening the surviving F-105s.

It was soon found that the inconsistency of the hit-survival record stemmed directly from the fact that the question had never been seriously investigated. Structural design was driven by strength requirements, and systems design by reliability. While the F-105, designed for supersonic low-level flight, was structurally tough, and would stay together at reduced airspeeds after suffering quite serious damage, the designers had seen no reason not to run the two independent hydraulic systems close together in the belly of the aircraft. A minor strike in this area could knock out the F-105's hydraulics and, in consequence, its flying controls.

The positive lesson drawn from this experience was that survivability could be dramatically increased by attention to a few key areas, and by improvements which added only a modest amount to the empty weight; there was no need to encase the entire aircraft in an armoured carapace.

Guns were the main cause of losses in Vietnam, particularly in the close support mission. Often, the main function of the SA-2 missile was to force the attackers to use low altitude, within the range of AAA. Cannon projectiles were taken as the measure of the A-10's survivability. Among the most dangerous of these was the 23mm armour-piercing incendiary shell, lethal against fuel tanks; direct hits from 57mm guns were also encountered, but these, like SAMs, were more dangerous as fragments. Since then, the defensive armoury has been modernized; however, studies of vulnerability have shown that the effectiveness of protection does not decline abruptly as the calibre of the threat increases.

Another batch of combat data concerned the vulnerability of the aircraft to damage in different areas. No fewer than 62 per cent of losses of single-engined aircraft, in Vietnam and the Middle East, were caused by damage to the fuel system; 18 per cent to pilot incapacitation; 10 per cent to flying-control damage; 7 per cent to loss of engine power; and 3 per cent to structural damage. These losses reflected heavy missile kills as well as gunfire; however, the A-X operational envelope would be biased towards heights and speeds where AAA would be more effective. The A-X also embodied a new vulnerable zone, in the shape of a very large drum of ammunition. The loss statistics were an indication of what to do on A-X, but not a complete guide.

Survivability has been taken into account in every area of the A-10 design. Important features of the basic configuration include the widely separated engines, the duplicated tail surfaces, and large and powerful controls in all three axes. The combination of these features is intended to allow the A-10 to stay airborne even after sustaining gross airframe damage such as the loss of half the tail assembly, a complete engine or part of the wing.

Internally, the A-10 structure is designed so that any member can be severed by impact without causing a total failure. The wing and the tail surfaces are all designed around three spars of approximately equal size and strength, any two of which can absorb all anticipated air loads. Both the tailplane and the wing are continuous one-piece structures from tip to tip and, as noted above, the landing gear configuration was chosen partly because it eliminated structural breaks in the wing. The fusel-

The A-10 can survive massive battle damage, including the loss of any one of four surface attachments, any of the airframe subassemblies indicated or any two opposing longerons.

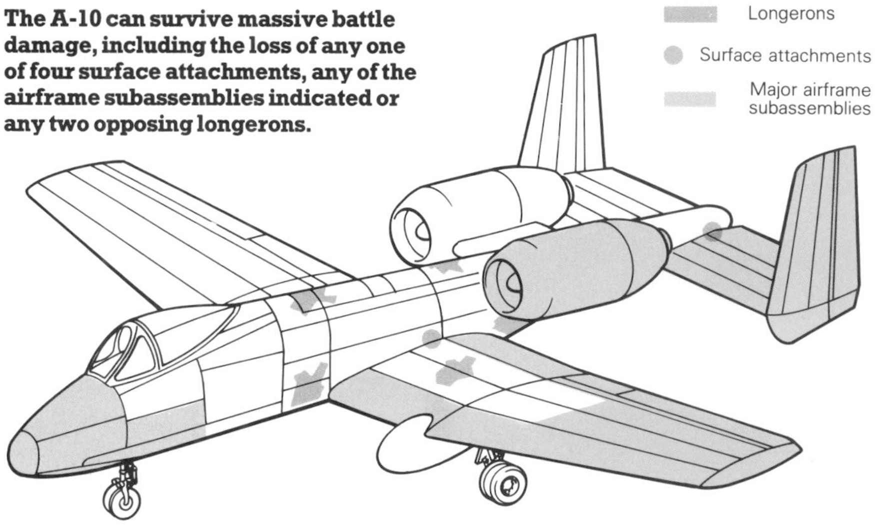

A-10 structural survivability

Above: The effects of 7.62mm armour-piercing projectiles on the bullet-proof/bird-proof front windshield fitted to the A-10.

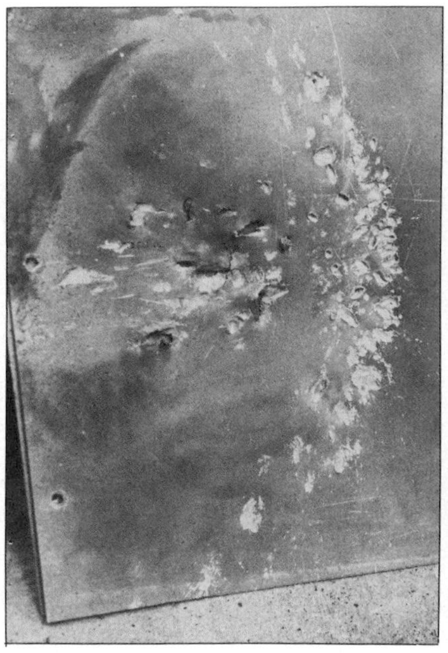

Above: A panel of the armour used for the GAU-8/A ammunition drum after being hit by a 23mm high-explosive projectile during tests.

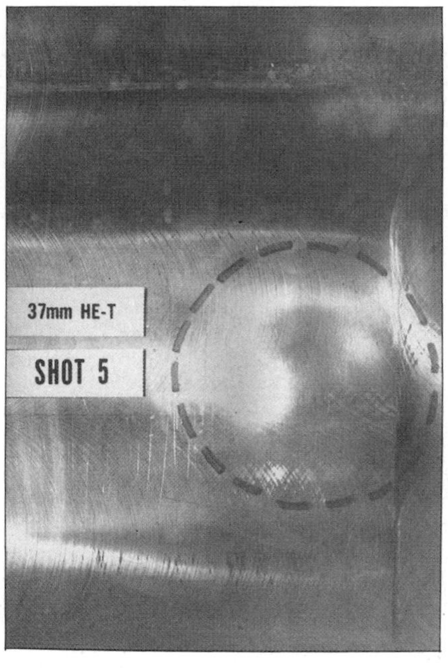

Above: Further tests were carried out on the titanium armour panels used for the pilot's 'bathtub': the back of one is shown after a 37mm HE hit.

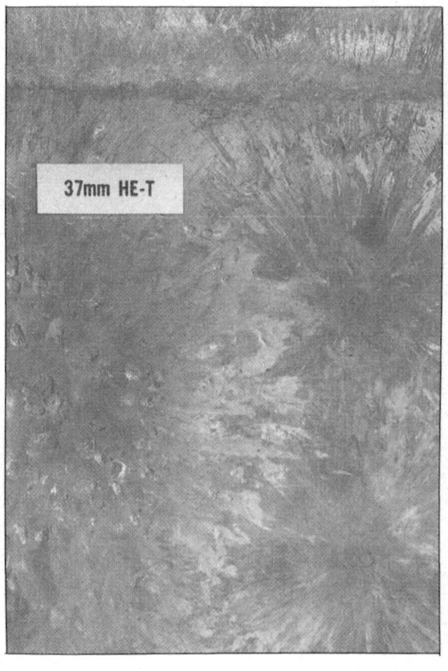

Above: The front of the same panel – used for the bathtub side – showing the effects of one 37mm and two 23mm rounds hitting at 90 deg.

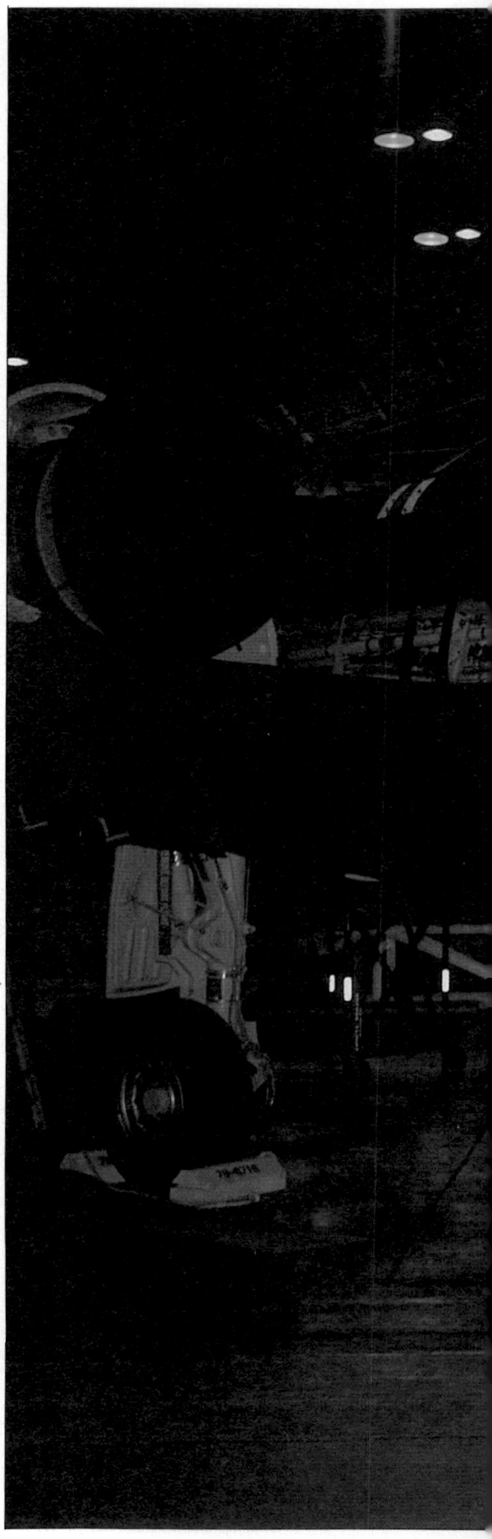

age incorporates four main longerons, any three of which can take the full structural loads. Most of the skin area is unstressed, greatly simplifying the repair task.

The structure would have presented no problems had the A-10 been used as it was intended, spending most of its time above the worst turbulence. In Europe, however, the A-10 was routinely flown at high speed and low level for most of its training missions. After cracks began to appear around fastener holes in the lower wing skin (which carries the peak tension loads in high-g flight) the USAF fitted accelerometers to some operational aircraft and found that they were experiencing high g loadings more than three times as often as had been expected. The simplicity of the aircraft, too, means that it spends a great deal of time in the air. A-10s are being fitted with thicker lower wing skins, during routine maintenance, to extend their useful lives to 8,000 hours.

Unique protection

Dealing with the cause of the majority of losses called for action to make the internal components less vulnerable to damage, and to protect them when this was not possible. It is this sort of protection which is unique to the A-10. It exceeds in degree anything applied to any helicopter, with the possible exception of the Mi-24, and is different in nature from the protection accorded to any fighter aircraft.

The fuel system had proved the weakest spot on the aircraft used in Vietnam. This was, perhaps, not surprising. Self-sealing fuel tanks had been developed before the 1939-45 war; they had an intermediate lining made from a rubber compound, which expanded when a puncture in the inner wall allowed it to be soaked with fuel. They had proved to be a vital feature in combat, but were abandoned in the early 1950s in favour of integral tanks, which were much more efficient and were almost essential to the design of a supersonic fighter with a useful range. It was argued that future air combats would involve missile strikes, which would be lethal regardless of fuel system design, and that jet fuel was less inflammable than the high-octane gasolines used in 1939-45.

Above: Warthog pilots – this one is wearing the badge of the 354th TFW – have expressed great confidence in their aircraft, and they are certainly as well protected as any.

Below: The wide separation of critical systems and control runs, as well as the ready access for maintenance, is apparent in this view of an 81st TFW A-10 in the hangar at RAF Bentwaters/Woodbridge.

In the Vietnam environment, unprotected fuel tanks were as dangerous as ever. Operating altitudes were low, speeds were high, and oxygen-rich air would swirl into any perforation in the airframe, scouring up any fuel leakages in the structural cavities and creating an instantly explosive atmosphere. The high fuel flows of jet engines meant that the fuel would spill more quickly from broken lines.

The A-10 fuel system is fundamentally different from the usual fighter system. For every USAF mission, apart from ferry flights, all the fuel is carried internally. (For ferry purposes, the centreline station and two wing pylons are plumbed, and can each carry a 600US gal (2,271lit) tank.) The 10,700lb (4,853kg) internal tankage is concentrated around the centre-section, so that the vulnerable area presented to hostile weapons is as small as possible, and the fuel lines are short. (This also effectively eliminates trim change with fuel use, making the aircraft simpler and easier to fly.) Most of the fuel is housed in true tanks, rather than integral cells formed by the aircraft skin and structure, although the inner wings include integral tanks.

The tanks are protected in several ways. The fuselage tanks, supplied by the Goodyear Tire & Rubber Company, are tear-resistant, and self-sealing in the event that they are perforated. All the tanks are filled with 'reticulated' rubber foam – that is to say, foam panels folded to fill the tanks. The foam serves several purposes: it slows the spillage of fuel, keeps airflows out of a punctured tank and inhibits the movement of flame fronts through the cavity. Protective firewalls and panels of rigid foam are installed between the individual tanks, and between the tank compartments and the remainder of the airframe, and more foam is fitted between the tanks and the fuselage sides; the object is to prevent any fuel which escapes from the tanks from flooding other airframe cavities.

Fuel provision

Fuel lines and valves are protected, as far as possible, by running them through the tanks. The final stages of the fuel lines are located in the upper section of the fuselage and on top of the engine pylons, where they are protected from damage by the rest of the airframe. The pipes are self-sealing, and the system is fitted with check valves which prevent fuel from flowing into a damaged tank. The single long fuel line leading to the flight-refuelling point in the nose is provided with its own purging system to clean out any remnants of fuel after use. If all else fails, the entire main tank system can be cut off, and two small, self-sealing sump tanks between the engines will provide a 200nm (370km) reserve for a safe return to base.

Equal attention is given to the flight control system, which has some unusual features for a modern combat aircraft. Control signals are transmitted to the hydraulic actuators by cables, rather than rods, because cables are less likely to be jammed by airframe damage. The cable system is duplicated, and either channel can be cut off from the cockpit if it jams. To provide greater protection for the critical pitch and roll axes, the control channels are completely separate from the control surface to the point where they enter the protected cockpit enclosure.

Dual hydraulic systems power the controls in normal operations, but if all power fails, the elevators and rudders can be moved directly by the pilot, through the control cables. Electrically powered trim tabs are fitted to the elevators, and help reduce the considerable control forces needed to fly the A-10 without hydraulic boost. The ailerons are too heavy for direct manual control; instead, if hydraulic power is lost, the control cables move small 'servo-tabs' attached to each aileron, which deflect in the opposite direction to the control input. Aerodynamic forces move the ailerons the other way, creating the desired rolling force. The A-10 is the only Western combat aircraft since the 1950s to be designed with this 'manual reversion' feature.

Each complete control channel runs through one of a pair of accessory tunnels built into opposite sides of the fuselage. These tunnels also carry duplicate hydraulic, electric and pneumatic runs, so that no single hit on one side can deprive the aircraft of any of its services. However, the manual back-up in the control system, and the fact that the landing gear is designed to free-fall into the locked position, means that the A-10 can, in theory, regain its base and land without further damage as long as at least one engine and one flight control channel remain operational.

Conventional systems

Other systems are largely conventional. Each engine powers one of the two 3,000lb/sq in (211kg/m^2) hydraulic circuits, which provide power to the controls, airbrakes, flaps, landing gear, brakes and gun mechanism. Engine bleed air is used for pressurization, airconditioning and windshield anti-icing and rain clearance (the rest of the airframe is not de-iced) and is also used to clear gases from the gun compartment after firing. A Garrett auxiliary power unit (APU) is installed in a titanium firewall box in the rear fuselage, between the engines, and provides power for engine starting and 'ground loitering'.

The other major areas for specialized protection are in the forward fuselage. One of these is the ammunition drum, which presents a unique potential for catastrophic damage; a single hostile round exploding in the ammunition drum could set off the A-10's magazine and destroy the aircraft instantly. The solution is to provide a layered protection system, designed to protect the drum from the direct impact of an armour-piercing explosive shell. The drum is placed at mid-height in the fuselage, as far from the skin as possible, and is armoured against fragments. The fuselage around it is not armoured in the normal sense, but is provided with trigger plates of various thicknesses to detonate any incoming round, whether armour-piercing, explosive or incendiary, before it reaches the drum.

The pilot himself is protected by a unique structural assembly called 'the bathtub'. This is a bolted-together box, made of heavy titanium sheets – ranging from 0.5in (12.7mm) to 1.5in (38.1mm) in thickness – and built into the forward fuselage, the sides of the box forming the upper sides of the airframe. It extends up to the canopy and windscreen frame, and provides side, front, rear and ventral protection. It accommodates the pilot, on his ejection seat, the flying controls and the instruments.

The sides of the bathtub are intended to defeat a direct hit from a 23mm API shell; the impact is likely to cause 'spalling' or the shedding of titanium fragments at high velocity from the inner surface of the armour, so the tub is lined internally with layers of ballistic nylon. Weighing some 1,200lb (544kg), the tub is the heaviest single piece of protection in the aircraft. Overall, it is estimated that 2,887lb (1,310kg), or 14 per cent of the A-10's empty weight, goes strictly to protection, without counting the survivability features of the structure and the configuration.

The final layer of protection is provided by the pilot's ejection seat. Initial production A-10s used the then-standard McDonnell Douglas IE-9 Escapac seat, one of the first to feature zero-height, zero-speed capability. However, the same company's ACES II (Advanced Concept Ejection Seat) has since been substituted; it provides better performance, considerably improved pilot comfort (an important factor, given the A-10's long endurance), and is common to the F-15 and F-16.

Above: A ground crewman checks the pressure refuelling panel of a 355th TFS, 354th TFW, A-10 prior to takeoff on a training mission.

While it was clearly not practical to verify the effectiveness of the protection system by shooting an A-10 to pieces, the USAF carried out a unique programme of static tests in the course of development. Representative wing and fuselage sections, complete with their fuel loads, were placed on ground rigs and subjected to a 400kt (740km/h) airstream generated by a turbofan engine. Tests with a Soviet 23mm AAA gun, firing API and HEI ammunition – the most dangerous types against fuel cells – demonstrated the fire-suppressing qualities of the foam system around the tanks, and advantages of the foamed tanks. The same weapon was used to evaluate the effectiveness of the titanium armour, in comparison with ceramics and aluminium.

All in all, 707 rounds of 23mm API and HEI were fired at A-10 structural specimens: 430 at the cockpit, 250+ into the fuel tanks, and nearly 60 into the ammunition drum. Among 108 rounds of other calibres were a burst of 7.62mm API fired into the windscreen. It was concluded that the area within which a single 23mm HEI/API strike would be lethal

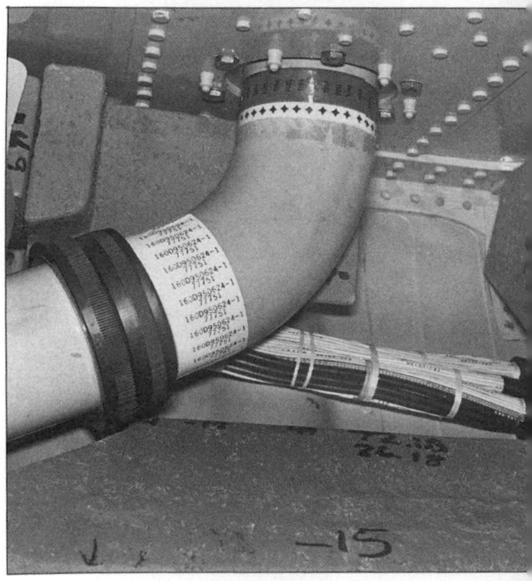

Above: Studies of aircraft losses over Vietnam showed that a principal cause was the concentration of fuel, hydraulic and electrical systems in small volumes, increasing their vulnerability to a single round: in the A-10 all systems are well protected and widely separated.

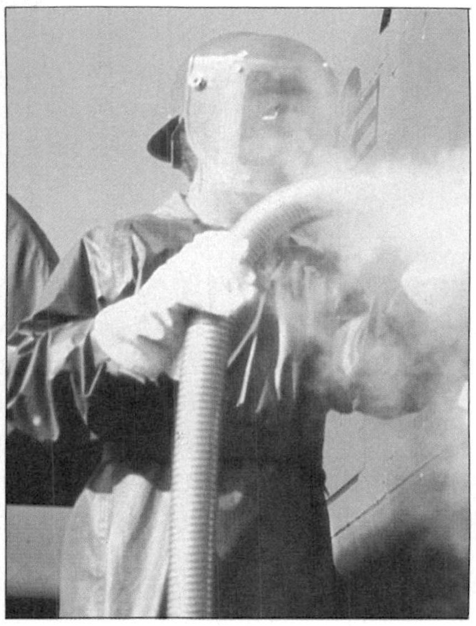

Left: Quick turnaround between sorties is vital to the effectiveness of close air support: here an A-10 of the 174th TFW, New York Air National Guard, is supplied with liquid oxygen during Exercise Sentry Castle '81.

Below: Realistic training is an essential part of TAC and reserve force readiness: chemical warfare clothing is worn by an ANG Technical Sergeant of the 104th TFG during an A-10 rescue exercise at Phelps-Collins ANG Base, Michigan.

Bottom: Refuelling an A-10 during Exercise Coronet Sail at Lechfeld AB, Germany. The fuel in the inner wing tanks should be used up by the time an A-10 reaches the battle area, further reducing its vulnerability.

Flight control separation

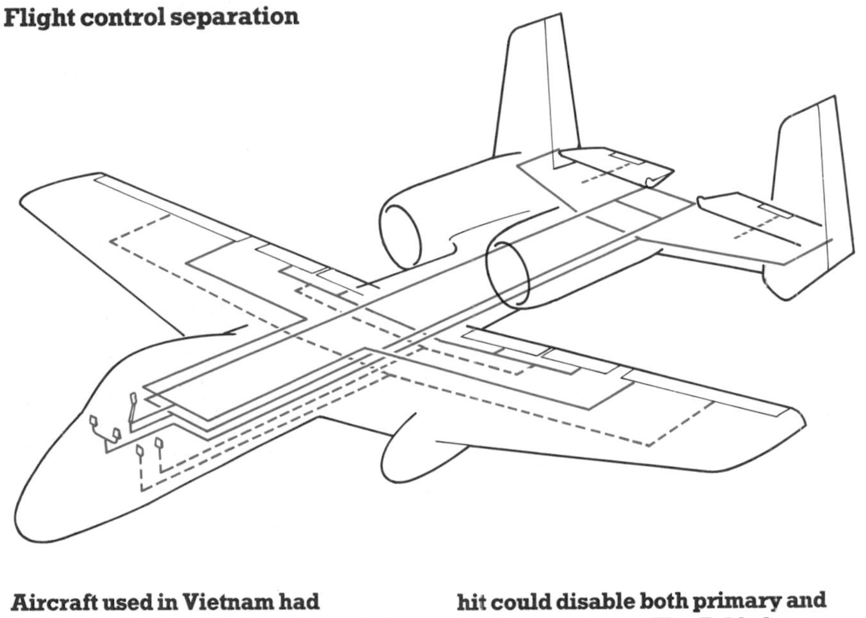

Aircraft used in Vietnam had duplicate flight control systems, but these were provided to guard against system failure: they were not physically separated, so that a single hit could disable both primary and back-up systems. The A-10s has duplicate, spatially separated control channels, and a manual back-up, indicated by the broken lines.

was one-tenth the equivalent area on a smaller, but unhardened, aircraft.

The idea that the A-10 can survive the physical loss of half a wing, half the tail, one engine or all its hydraulics, and even survive several such losses, may appear far-fetched. Consider, though, the case of a certain F-15. The Eagle is a close contemporary of the A-10, and its design drew upon very similar combat experience; while survivability was not a prime requirement in the F-15 design, McDonnell Douglas certainly incorporated many hard lessons from F-4 experience.

In the summer of 1983, an Israeli F-15 was engaged in mock combat with an A-4 when the two aircraft collided. The impact tore off 90 per cent of the Eagle's starboard wing, leaving an 8in (20cm) stump. The A-4 crashed; the Eagle survived thanks to lift from the wide body, survivable hydraulics, jam-resistant control circuits and its powerful tail surfaces. The F-15 was repaired and back in service within weeks.

The tactical value of such toughness is considerable, particularly when it is combined with the structural and systems simplicity of the A-10. Because of the A-10's design, strikes which might require major repair on another aircraft may simply call for a non-structural patch on the A-10. A heavier hit might destroy a conventional aircraft, but leave the A-10 able to regain its base. An A-10 in such a condition might well be beyond repair, and would almost certainly be too badly damaged to be returned to combat status at a front-line base, but, in wartime, that is not the whole story. The aircraft has recovered its irreplaceable pilot, and now represents a large stockpile of spares; the basic simplicity of the aircraft makes it easier to use the undamaged parts to restore other aircraft to fighting condition.

The A-10's aerodynamic and structural design has proved successful. Like the rest of the weapon system, it accomplishes what it set out to do at the estimated cost. Its design, incomprehensible in terms of pure fighter engineering or aesthetics, represents an uncompromised approach to a clearly defined requirement, and every feature of its gnarled and complex configuration responds to some part of the A-X specification.

Above: Twin engine pods, mounted high on the rear fuselage, form one of the principal elements in the A-10's startlingly original appearance.

Powerplant

In the definition of the A-X programme, the specific requirement which caused most problems was for endurance, or the ability to remain airborne behind the battlefield, ready to deliver a rapid response to any call for support. The reason that it was a problem was that the classic fighter engine is a poor way of providing endurance. The solution was to use a type of engine which had evolved to meet the payload and range requirements of passenger aircraft: the high-bypass-ratio turbofan. The A-10 was and remains unique among combat aircraft in using these inherently efficient and quiet engines.

Jet engines, turbofan engines and propellers all drive in the same way: they seize the air through which the aircraft flies and accelerate it rearwards, and Newton's 'equal and opposite reaction' forces the engine to accelerate forwards. This acceleration is transmitted to the airframe through steel-tube or forged engine mountings, and pulls it through the air.

The difference between the jet and the propeller is that the jet takes a smaller quantity of air, and accelerates it to a much greater degree. The effect on performance and efficiency is fundamental. A good analogy is an oarsman, who is also developing thrust by accelerating a fluid. He rows efficiently when the tips of the oars are almost static in the water with each sweep; he is imparting the smallest possible amount of acceleration to a large mass of water. If he moves his oars twice as fast with the same amount of energy, he will simply move a smaller mass with each stroke. His style will be inelegant and much of his energy will be dissipated in splashes and vortices. The same principle of propulsive efficiency – that the ideal is to apply the minimum acceleration to the maximum mass, disturbing the working fluid as little as possible – applies to aircraft engines.

There is one other basic point to consider. It is impossible for the rower to go faster than he can move the ends of his sculls. When the speed of the boat equals that of the fastest stroke, thrust equals zero. Likewise, each aircraft engine has a theoretical maximum speed at which it will no longer produce thrust – although most have practical speed limits which are lower, for other reasons. At lower speeds, though, the engine will no longer produce thrust equal to its own drag.

Selecting the right type of engine for an aircraft is a matter of defining the desired performance profile, and choosing the type of engine which is best suited to the most critical performance regime. The problem, in the early stages of the A-X programme, was that no engine had yet flown which possessed the desired characteristics.

Jet engine characteristics

The most important attribute of early jet engines was that they could operate at speeds well above the normal limits for propellers. Their main disadvantage was their poor fuel consumption, due to their low pressure ratio – a measure of how much air had to be moved to generate a given amount of power – compared to highly refined piston engines. During the 1950s this disadvantage was reduced by increasing jet pressure ratios through improved high-temperature materials and better compressor design. Higher exhaust velocities went hand-in-hand with increased pressure ratios – the engine drew in less air, squeezed it harder and expelled it faster. At subsonic speeds, the oars were skating over the water, and the gains in efficiency within the engine were wiped out by propulsive losses.

By the mid-1960s, there were two alternatives to the pure-jet engine. One was the turboprop, in which a high-pressure turbine engine was coupled to a conventional propeller through a power turbine and reduction gearbox. The other was the turbofan engine; this had been created by modifying a pure-jet engine with oversized forward compressor stages. Roughly half the air taken in by the engine 'bypassed' the compressor and turbine. The high-velocity exhaust from the compressor and high-pressure turbine was fed to a second turbine, and drove the fan. The turbofan produced a higher-mass, lower-speed exhaust than the pure jet, and was much more efficient at high subsonic speed: it powered the first jet airliners which could match the range capability of propeller-driven aircraft.

In 1963 the US Navy ordered the LTV A-7, a long-range light attack aircraft designed around a single TF30 turbofan. But this 'low-bypass' engine, although it represented a great advance over the pure-jet, was well out of its element at speeds under 350-400kt (650-740km/h). At higher speeds, fuel flows were too high to provide the endurance needed for the A-X mission.

The turboprop was much better adapted to low-speed cruising, and its maximum speed was acceptable to the USAF. Its disadvantages, outlined in the first chapter, were mainly concerned with the difficulty of integrating two powerful turboprops and their large propellers into a combat aircraft with a wide speed range, and making the resulting aircraft survivable.

Interestingly, a turboprop aircraft in the A-X class had been extensively tested more than a decade before the USAF formulated its requirement. This was the US Navy's Douglas A2D-1 Skyshark, which had started its development life as a turbine-powered version of the A-X's forebear, the Skyraider, and evolved into a different aircraft with a thinner wing and almost exactly the same top speed as the ultimate A-10.

The Skyshark was aimed at achieving twin-engine performance without the engine-out handling problems of a conventional twin. Like some of the early A-X studies, it had two engines deliver-

Below: The General Electric TF34 engine selected for the A-10 was only developed after the original A-X specification had been written.

Right: Originally developed for the US Navy's S-3A, the TF34 was operated for 400 hours under the wing of this B-47 test aircraft.

ing their power along the centreline – the coupled powerplant was the Allison T40, consisting of two T38s with a common gearbox. It was the powerplant that proved the Skyshark's undoing; the Skyshark's designer, Ed Heinemann, likened it to a chronic toothache. One prototype crashed when one turbine unit failed; the dead engine, still coupled to the live powerplant, acted as a huge air pump and drained all the power from the system. Other problems – with the separate engine and propeller control systems, with the reduction gear and overheating of the entire installation – prevented the engine from reaching its projected 5,500shp output.

In 1954 the Skyshark programme was cut back to purely experimental status, and replaced by Heinemann's far simpler Skyhawk. Its significance to the A-X programme lay not only in the similarity of its design goals to those established for the later aircraft, but in the fact that the Skyshark represented the last serious attempt, before A-X, to design a high-performance combat aircraft around turboprop power. The fundamental problem, as before, would be to steer a path between the conventional twin-turboprop installation, with its drag, weight and engine-out-condition penalties, and the risks and complexity of some type of coupled layout. The latter offered better performance, but it would be hard to ensure or demonstrate that it would not be vulnerable to a single hit.

High-bypass turbofans

The arrival of the classic compromise, the high-bypass turbofan, was entirely unexpected; neither of the engines eventually tested under the A-X programme had been designed with it in mind. The concept originated independently with several manufacturers in the early 1960s. Rolls-Royce and Pratt & Whitney approached it through extrapolation from their existing large commercial engines. Lycoming saw it as a means to break into the fixed-wing turbine power market, making the maximum use of its existing T55 turbine engine; the company was the first to run a true high-bypass engine, in late 1963.

General Electric's route into the market was different again. In the late 1950s GE had started work on a design for a vertical takeoff fighter using lift fans. These resembled enlarged jet engine rotors, and were designed to be buried within the wing of a small aircraft; they were driven by exhaust from small jet engines, impinging on small turbine blades fixed to the outside of the lift fan.

Very early in the 1960s the lift-fan research spawned a demonstration programme for a cruise fan – essentially, a lift fan turned through 90deg to give propulsive thrust. The biggest test rig comprised an 80in (205cm) fan driven by the exhaust of a J79. Results showed that the big fan could operate at high subsonic speeds with much greater efficiency than previous turbofans. Data from these tests was passed to the USAF in 1962, while the service was in the early stages of formulating its requirement for a huge strategic freighter.

In 1962-63, GE moved from the cruise fan, in which the fan and the gas generator were separate, to a more integrated concept in which the fan was driven by a conventional turbine, via a shaft running through the engine. Up to eight times as much air passed through the fan as went through the compressor, combustor and turbines (the 'core engine'); that was to say, the engine had an 8:1 bypass ratio.

Above: The TF34 test installation on the Navy's B-47, with the associated wiring runs carried along the leading edge of the wing.

This was the basis for the GE1/6 demonstrator engine, the foundation for GE's August 1965 victory in the contest to provide power for the USAF's new C-5.

This early experience and background set the pattern for GE high-bypass engines. GE's fortunes in jet propulsion had been founded on the J79, a single-shaft engine with a large number of stages and a great deal of internal variable geometry, and its later turbojet engines featured similar configurations. Its new high-bypass fan engines sustained the family tradition. They had long, many-staged 'cores', resembling GE's single-shaft turbojets, with the fan added to the front and the fan turbine at the rear. Unlike its rivals' engines, GE's big-fan engines did not have low-pressure compressors, although one or two 'booster' stages might be attached to the fan shaft behind the fan.

While GE's heavy brigade worked on the TF39 for the C-5, the company's small-engine group at Lynn, Massachusetts, was looking at smaller high-bypass engines. As Lycoming had done, GE started with a proven turbine core; the first high-bypass test engine built at Lynn was based on a T64 turboshaft engine, fitted with a scaled-down version of the TF39 fans and a new multi-stage power turbine. Otherwise, the geometry was unchanged. There was no booster stage, although the overall pressure ratio was slightly increased by the presence of the fan stage.

The existence of engines such as the Lycoming and GE demonstrators was to bring about a decisive change in the A-X programme. The new engines were not as efficient as turboprops in the A-X speed range, but they had many other advantages. They were easier to install; with no propellers, they could be located close to the centreline where engine-out

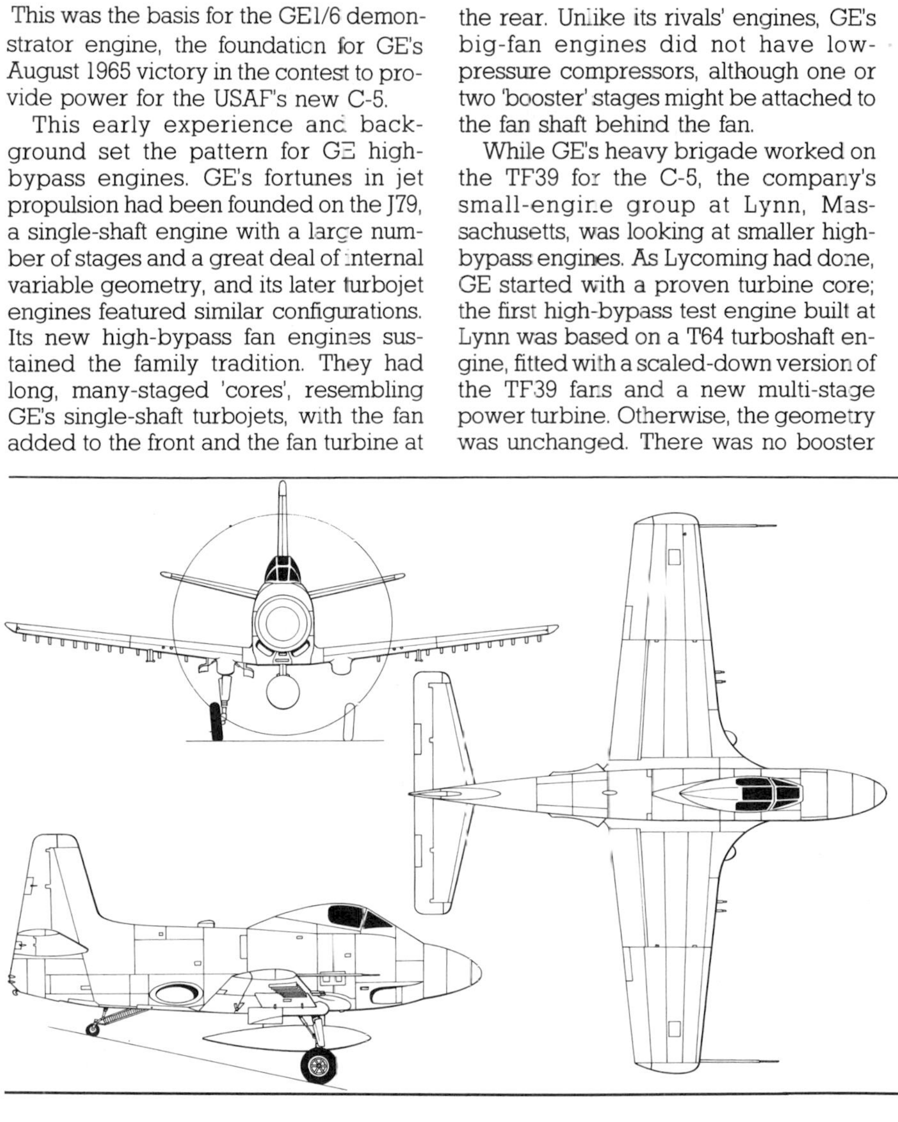

Douglas A2D-1 Skyshark

Designed in the early 1950s, the twin-turboprop Skyshark illustrated the difficulties of using such engines in an aircraft with performance similar to that proposed for the A-X.

Dimensions	
Wing span	50ft 2in (15.23m)
Length overall	41ft 2in (12.54m)
Height	17ft (5.18m)
Wing area	400sq ft (37.2m²)
Powerplant	Allison XT40-A-2
Power	5,500shp (4,105kW)
Weights	
Operating empty	12,994lb (5,894kg)
Max takeoff	21,764lb (9,872kg)
Performance	
Max speed	435kt (806km/h)
Max speed at SL	406kt (752km/h)
Cruising speed	249kt (461km/h)
Combat range	553nm (1,024km) at 320kt (593km/h)

Above: The first DT & E A-10 was the first to have the USAF-standard T34-100, the prototypes having flown with US Navy development engines.

Right: A-10s with external tanks form up before a ferry mission. Despite doubts in some quarters about the advisability of using a high-bypass turbofan on a combat aircraft, the high mounting keeps the intakes well clear of runway debris, and upward-pointing exhausts reduce the risk of FOD in a stream takeoff.

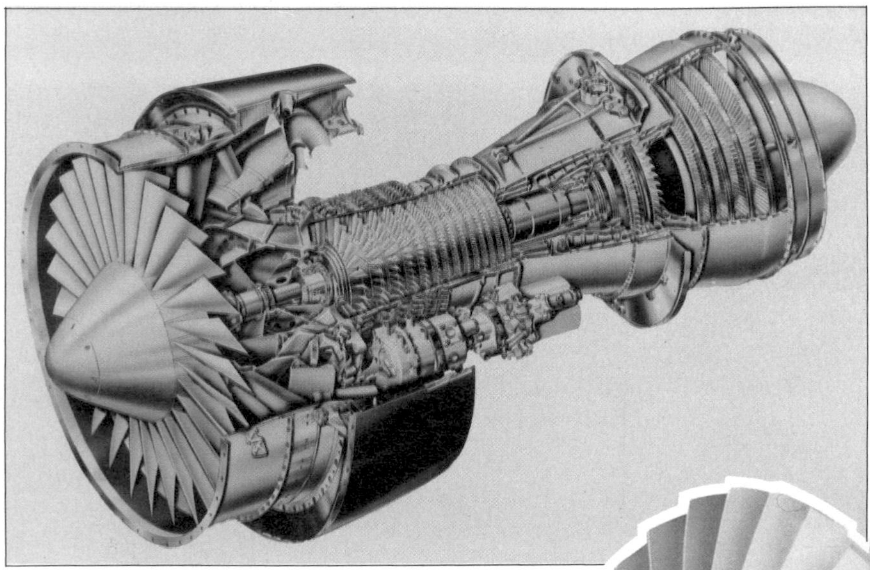

Below: TF34 cutaway, showing the single-stage fan, 14-stage compressor derived from GE's T64, and high- and low-pressure turbines.

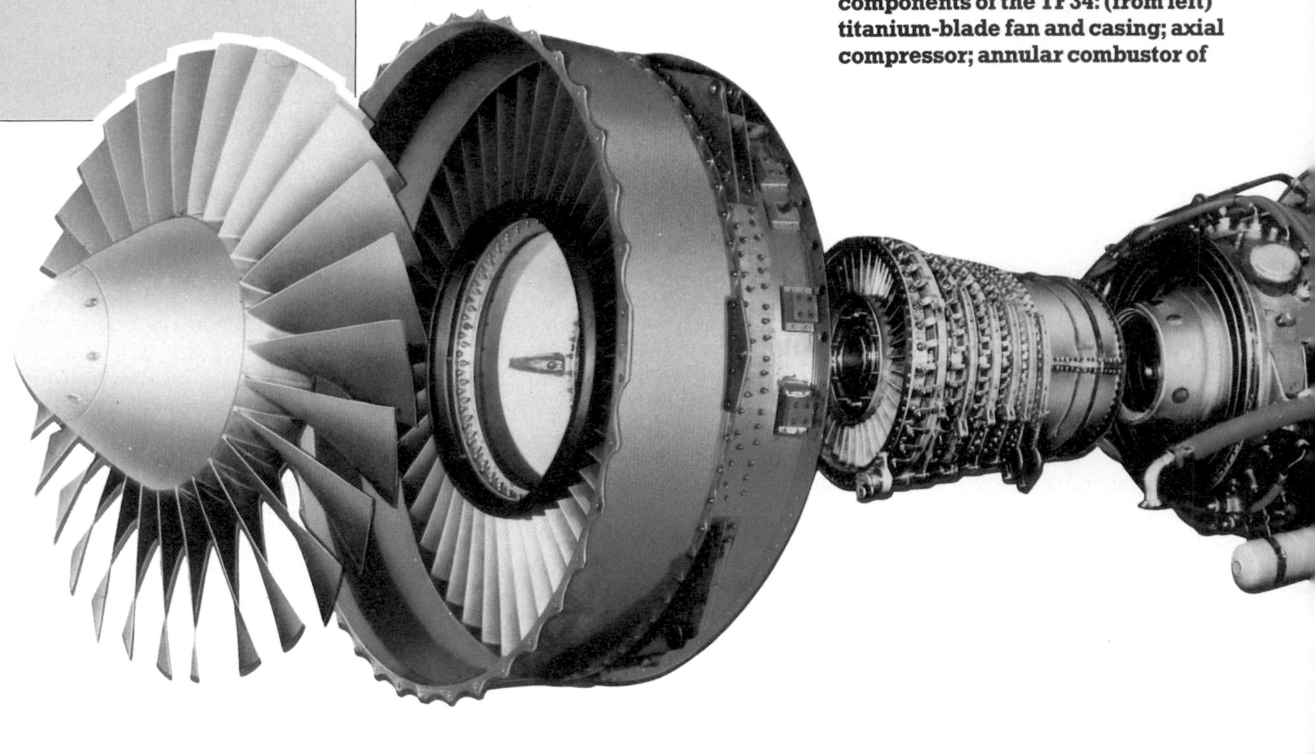

Below: The five basic modular components of the TF34: (from left) titanium-blade fan and casing; axial compressor; annular combustor of

effects would be minimal. They were simpler, dispensing with complex and critical components such as the propeller and reduction gear. (While the Lycoming engine did have a reduction gear, it had a much smaller ratio than a turboprop's gear and was much less complicated.) All in all, their advantages were overwhelming.

While the A-X requirement was still being refined, the US Navy followed a similar line of reasoning, and specified high-bypass turbofans for its new VSX – the replacement for the S-2 Tracker carrier-based antisubmarine warfare aircraft. GE based its proposed VSX engine on data from the test engine run at Lynn, although it would be a basically different engine from the T64. In late 1966 the Navy awarded design contracts for the GE engine, now designated TF34, and the Allison TF32, and definitive proposals were submitted in January 1968. In April GE was announced the winner, and Lockheed was awarded the contract to build the S-3A airframe. According to a GE official history, the victory came as a complete surprise to many of those associated with the programme.

Development of the TF34 moved ahead smoothly, and the engine made its first run in May 1969. In January 1971 it started a 200-hour test programme beneath the port wing of an obsolete Boeing B-47 bomber, leased by GE as a test-bed and operated from the company's flight test centre at Edwards AFB. Meanwhile, development of the S-3A Viking proceeded smoothly, and the compact ASW aircraft made its first flight in January 1972; the engine was qualified for US Navy use in August of that year.

There were several factors favouring the TF34 over any other engine proposed in the A-X competition. The most important was that the development of the engine, and initial production, were already fully funded under the S-3A programme, and USAF development expenditures would be confined to any changes needed for the A-X mission; none of these would be fundamental, whereas the production version of the Lycoming F102 would combine a higher-powered core, based on the T55-L-11B, with a redesigned fan. The TF34 was also at the beginning of its development life, and GE had identified a series of changes which could make extra thrust available if it were needed. The USAF already planned to use eight TF34s to power the new airborne warning and control system (Awacs) under development by Boeing, so there was some potential for commonality. Lastly, GE was an established supplier of combat engines to the USAF (unlike Lycoming, for instance) and already had the facilities and resources to develop the A-X engine.

GE's main disadvantage was cost. The TF34 was not a particularly simple engine, and had been developed for a quite demanding Navy mission; it would cost almost $140,000 more than the proposed production version of the Lycoming F102. (Both Fairchild and Northrop were required to provide data for both engines in their final proposals to the USAF, so in that sense the two engines were in direct competition.) However, it proved possible to reduce the cost of the TF34 by eliminating some features which were unnecessary for the A-X mission, and the GE engine emerged victorious.

Since that time, the TF34 has done steady rather than spectacular business for GE. Just after the A-10 decision was announced, Boeing and the USAF decided to use the older TF33-P-7 for the Awacs, to save the cost of developing a new version of the TF34 and its twin nacelle. Production of 187 S-3A Vikings ended in 1978, and A-10 production has also ceased. The basic engine is now in low-rate production in a commercially

Above: Large access doors allow the TF34 to be maintained 'on condition', removal of modules only being necessary when a problem arises.

Below: Ladders are needed to reach the engines, but the pod mounting makes them readily accessible when the access doors are opened.

nickel alloy with low-pressure fuel injection system; two-stage high-pressure tubine; and four-stage low-pressure turbine.

certified version, the CF34, for the Canadair Challenger 601 business jet, and a marine turboshaft version, the LM500, has been demonstrated.

An engine *aficionado* would immediately recognise the TF34 as a GE engine. There is no low-pressure compressor, although incoming air is slightly compressed by the fan before being split into bypass and core flows. The mechanical layout of the compressor is similar to that of the T64, with 14 axial stages, and the stators, or static blades, in the first five stages can be varied in pitch. Variable stators were developed by GE for the J73 and J79, and their use in large numbers is a GE trademark. Their function is to vary the airflow through the engine, making it easier to start a single high-pressure-ratio spool and improving handling; other manufacturers generally split such a long compressor into two spools. The compressor is driven by a conventional two-stage turbine.

Titanium fan blades

Aerodynamically, the fan is based on TF39 technology, although the design is modified to cater for the lower bypass ratio of the TF34 – 6:1, versus 8:1 for the C-5 engine – and does not feature the complex and unique one-and-a-half-stage configuration of the TF39. The fan has a single stage, with no booster stage. Each blade is forged and machined to shape from a solid piece of titanium alloy, the only material available at that time with sufficient lightness, tensile strength and rigidity to meet the requirements of a high-bypass engine.

Mechanically, the fan was different from that of the TF39. Because of its smaller size, it was not necessary to brace the blades by linking them together, so the annular mid-span shroud could be eliminated. The TF34 is also designed so that each blade can be removed individually by pulling out a securing pin, rotating the fan and withdrawing the blade through a slot in the fan case. The fan is driven by a conventional four-stage turbine.

Perhaps the most technically important feature of the TF34, at the time of its appearance, was the combustor section. Previous combustors had comprised sheet metal assemblies, called 'liners', built into the engine case. These promoted good combustion, and were cheap; the snag was that they had limited lives and needed frequent maintenance, and any work on the combustor called for dismantling the entire engine. The TF34, however, was the first engine to feature a more durable combustor, which was machined from a nickel alloy originally developed for turbine blades.

The TF34's fuel-injection system was also novel, relying on a two-stage swirler to generate powerful aerodynamic shearing forces which would vaporize the fuel before ignition. While these caused development problems in late 1971, they were fixed before they could delay the entire programme, and the Navy engine was qualified on schedule.

Later in the decade, GE's advanced combustor technology was to be a major factor in the success of its F404 and F110 fighter engines. Not only did the combustor prove efficient and durable, but the injector/burner system proved to be virtually free of visible smoke emission. GE, of course, had good reasons for working in this area: not for nothing was the twin-J79-powered F-4 nicknamed 'Ol' Smokey'. Smokeless exhaust is a tactically important feature of the A-10.

Modular maintennce

The TF34 is one of the first service engines to be designed with easy maintenance as a major consideration. It is a 'modular' engine, designed so that the main mechanical components can be separated from each other without disconnecting and stripping all the accessories. All the compressor blades can be individually removed and replaced by opening the engine carcass – which is split along the centreline – without dismantling the entire engine. The TF34 is also supplied with strategically located borescope ports, which allow the mechanic to insert a fibre-optic probe and survey the engine's interior for damage while it is still 'on the wing' (although that expression does not apply to the A-10).

Generally, the TF34 is designed to be maintained 'on condition': that is to say, the engine is only removed or serviced when regular performance checks, metal chip detectors in the oil system, or external and borescope inspections indicate that there is a problem. If the difficulty can be traced to a given module, it can be replaced without removing the engine from service, and, in some cases, without pulling the engine off the aircraft. (In the case of the A-10, though, it is probably easier to bring the engine down to ground level.) This is a great advance on earlier engines, which had to be removed, disassembled and inspected every few hundred hours, the intervals being determined on the basis of service experience.

Approaching the A-X competition, the GE engineers determined that they could easily match the opposition on performance, but were vulnerable to price comparisons. There was little point, therefore, in making changes to the basic aerodynamic and thermodynamic characteristics of the engine, which

Above: A 355th TFW A-10 makes a low pass over the Gila Bend range, Arizona. The turbofan's high thrust at low speeds formed the key to the A-10's low-level manoeuvrability.

Left: A Warthog touches down on the runway. Landing distance, even at maximum weight, is an economical 2,500ft (762m), while a fully-loaded A-10 can take off in 4,500ft (1,372m).

Right: A-10s of the 917th TFG refuelling from a 78th Air Refuelling Squadron KC-10 during an AFRES Aerials exercise held at Carswell AFB, Texas, in September 1983.

would accomplish little in terms of useful performance and add to the overall cost of the engine to the USAF. Instead, GE concentrated on cutting the manufacturing cost of the engine, without making extensive changes that would add to its development cost.

The only mission-related changes to the TF34 for the A-X concerned its installation. Even these were quite small. The main thrust and support bearings for the engine remained on top, as they had been designed for the S-3A's underwing engine installation; in the A-10, the engines were to be hung from dual forged outriggers projecting from the top of the fuselage. Some accessories were moved, to facilitate maintenance and satisfy the USAF requirement for left-to-right interchangeability.

The engine installation itself was conventional, except for the near-full length fan cowlings, the first on a high-bypass engine. They were chosen so that the exhaust nozzles could be angled slightly upwards, reducing changes of trim with changes of engine power. The engines were set higher than was ideal for maintenance purposes; by way of compensation, the cowlings, including the inner wall of the fan duct, were split and top-hinged, providing easy access to most of the engine without removing a single component. Provisions for hoisting the engines were built into the engine mounts, eliminating the need for external lifting devices.

Most of the differences between the Navy and USAF engines were the result of GE's effort to identify and implement savings in production costs. These were possible because the USAF requirement was, in some ways, less severe than that of the USN. The S-3, for example, was required to loiter for long periods at low speed in icing conditions. Because of the low speed the engines would not be at maximum power, and the icing bleed air would be cooler than normal. The Navy TF34 needed a complex, large-volume de-icing system to cope with these conditions; the USAF, however, had no icing requirement for the A-X, and the entire system could be eliminated.

Another specific Navy requirement was to operate at low thrust, but with high power being drawn from the engine to feed the S-3A's complex systems; draining power from the compressor caused aft-end temperatures to rise higher than they would on the A-X, at least in sustained operation. In some cases, it proved possible to use cheaper materials for the A-X engine. Other changes simply involved eliminating machining operations such as the removal of excess material and the drilling of lightening holes, trading a slight weight increase for lower cost. The USAF engine also required, and received, a simpler and cheaper control system.

The first YA-10s flew with Navy-standard development engines. The modified USAF engine, designated TF34-GE-100, made its first run in July 1973. Production-configured engines were put through 2,181 hours of testing on GE and USAF ground-testing facilities, including two 150-hour endurance cycles. The engine was declared qualified for military use in November 1974, and flew on the first pre-production A-10 early in the following year.

Reliability in service

The TF34 has posed few problems in development and service, and had logged two million flight hours by the end of 1982. The service environment has been more strenuous than was envisaged at the start of the programme, mainly because the lower-flying, higher-energy tactics now used keep the engines close to their full-power ratings much of the time. Largely for this reason, hot-section wear and tear has caused some 10 per cent of TF34s to need main-base overhaul and repair only 500 hours after being rebuilt in the field. To correct this situation A-10 powerplants are being upgraded to the new TF34-GE-100A model by the introduction of a modified combustor and high-pressure turbine module.

The most important change is the introduction of 'directionally solidified' DSR80 material in the first-stage turbine blades. DS blades are cast in a special furnace and are allowed to cool from the root to the tip. The metal forms long, uniform crystals instead of a random crystal structure: this means that some of the elements in a conventional casting alloy, which are added to bond the crystal boundaries and which are otherwise undesirable, can be removed. The DSR blades are more costly to produce than conventional blades, but the longer life more than makes up for the cost difference.

The -100A update includes a number of other changes: combustor modifications, to reduce 'hot spots' in the gas flow striking the turbine, changes to shrouds and seals and other new materials. The hot-section life of the -100A should be 2,000 hours, including 360 hours at maximum power, both figures being twice those attained by the -100 engine. The TF34-GE-100A was qualified for service in August 1983.

The TF34 has proved resistant to foreign-object damage (FOD) in service, despite those who doubted the wisdom of using a high-bypass engine on a combat-type aircraft. The high engine mounting keeps the inlets well clear of runway FOD, while the high exhaust position and upward-pointing exhaust reduce the problems of FOD in a stream takeoff. In 1982, A-10s involved in exercises in Egypt flew through heavy sandstorms with no problems, and the engines did not even need to be washed. Neither has the A-10 suffered unduly from birdstrikes, even in Northern Europe.

Above: Post-flight inspection of an A-10's TF34. The titanium fan blades have proved highly resistant to bird strikes over Europe, and have shrugged off heavy sandstorms during exercises in Egypt.

Non-problems are rarely investigated, but the most likely reason for the toughness of the TF34 lies in its basic front-end layout. The fan itself, with solid titanium blades and a modest 7,800rpm speed, is unlikely to suffer much damage from a birdstrike. The inlet to the core, where FOD can do far more damage, is not very prominent, being flush with the inner wall of the duct, and is well behind the fan. If a bird hits the fan, the heavier fragments will be thrown outwards, well clear of the core inlet. The same applies for any objects denser than the inlet air, including sand and water. Some other high-bypass engines, which have encountered more serious problems with ingestion and erosion, feature core inlets immediately behind the fan.

Operating their engines at constant full power in combat, A-10 pilots have

Below: A fuel tank is fitted under the wing of an A-10 in JAWS (Joint Attack Weapon System) colour scheme ready for deployment to Europe in 1978.

Above: Even without air refuelling, the A-10 has a ferry range of 2,240nm (4,148km) with a 20min reserve against 50kt (93km/h) headwinds.

Above: the unusual nose position for the refuelling receptable proved to be an improvement on the more normal location to the rear of the cockpit.

encountered no serious handling problems. In 1980 some engine stalls were being reported during prolonged gunfiring; this is understandable, since the GAU-8/A spits out 24lb (10.9kg) of used propellant every second when firing at its maximum rate. Usually this is not too much of a problem: there are few targets which can absorb more than a short burst from the A-10.

Another feature of the TF34 is that it is inherently much quieter than any other fighter engine. The advantage of this attribute in the tactical arena may be in dispute, but it has certainly been welcome to the people in the neighbourhood of the A-10's operating bases in Europe.

A higher-powered version of the TF34 was to have been developed for the Awacs programme, and would have improved A-10 performance in some respects, but GE's plans for uprated engines have not yet been implemented. Using the same fan as the existing version, the TF34 could be taken up to 10 000lb (4,540kg) thrust by increasing the turbine entry temperature; the standard core, mated to a larger fan and operating at the same temperatures, would yield around 11,500lb (5,100kg) thrust. There is no current requirement for an engine in this class, however: the only active development programme for a TF34-powered aircraft is the US Navy's S-3B, and modifications to this improved version of the Viking are likely to centre on the aircraft's avionics rather than the powerplant.

Engine change proposal

Briefly, in 1976, alternative engines were studied for the A-10, in an effort to generate more interest in the A-10 among Western European customers. Although the European F-16 programme was under way by that time, the Tornado was still several years away from service and its future was by no means assured. The prevailing view among Western European air forces was that the A-10 was too slow, and that airborne loiter was, in European conditions, a costly and unnecessary tactic. Fairchild therefore investigated a version of the A-10 in which some endurance would be traded for higher speed by installing different engines.

At the 1976 Farnborough Air Show Fairchild showed a model of an A-10 with longer, slimmer cowlings, and suggested that the aircraft could be powered by unreheated versions of two current fighter engines: General Electric's own J101, a very-low-bypass engine developing more than 10,000lb (4,540kg), and Europe's Turbo-Union RB.199. Either engine would generate more net thrust than the TF34 at higher airspeeds, and the modified aircraft would have been some 30-50kt (55-93km/h) faster than the standard A-10 in level flight, with weapons carried. The A-10's airframe limit of 450kt (830km/h) was however, too slow for the taste of European commanders, who continued to regard the A-10 as something of a curiosity, and no serious discussions took place as a result.

The engines of the A-10 are unique among the world's fighter and attack aircraft, and the key to its unusual performance. Their basic configuration is more akin to the typical modern airliner engine than to the normal fighter powerplant: for the mission which the A-10 was designed to perform, though, they are ideal.

Left: An A-10 of the 174th TFW, New York Air National Guard, its refuelling panel open, is de-iced with warm air during a deployment to Lechfeld AB, Germany, in 1981.

Weapons and Avionics

No other aircraft approaches the A-10 in its ability to carry a heavy load of hard-target ordnance; a single Warthog can carry enough weaponry to disable 16 main battle tanks. The primary weapon, unique to the A-10, is the massive GAU-8/A Avenger Gatling cannon, and this powerful gun is backed up by the highly accurate fire-and-forget Maverick missile, which offers a choice of television, scene-magnification TV or – soon – infra-red guidance. With these weapons the A-10 accomplishes its mission without the need for sophisticated – and costly and unreliable – weapon-aiming avionics. Meanwhile, the navigation and ECM systems have been upgraded as a result of operational experience.

Above: The 9,000lb (40kN) recoil thrust of the GAU-8/A cannon demanded a centreline location, and the forward fuselage was designed around the gun and its ammunition.

If the infantry commander has one recurrent nightmare, it is the unexpected rumble of armour. It signifies that he is about to be engaged by a force which his defensive weapons may blunt, but which they will probably not neutralize, and that it is too late to call for friendly armour to support his unit. In a ground-only battle, the options are immediate retreat, or destruction.

The nightmare came true more than once in Vietnam, and it can happen to a front-line unit at almost any time, even with the best reconnaissance and intelligence. Its importance for the A-10 is that it represents the most critical test for close air support (CAS). Only air power can rescue the unit under attack, and it can do so only if it arrives quickly, can distinguish friend and enemy, and can engage and defeat the attackers. This leads to a few basic requirements for effective CAS.

It can be taken for granted that the CAS aircraft will be outnumbered by main battle tanks (MBTs) and their escorts and support vehicles. Almost by definition, the CAS aircraft is responding to an emergency, and there will be no time to muster a superior force. The first essential for an effective CAS system is the ability to kill several targets in a single sortie.

The primary target is the MBT, a notoriously difficult machine to kill. Its resistance to blast weapons is sufficient to make their use uneconomical, and light cluster weapons, dispensing a shower of submunitions over a wide area, are also ineffective. Another basic requirement for CAS, therefore, is an airborne weapon that can guarantee a direct, lethal hit on a tank under operational conditions. Modern armoured formations, particularly in Soviet practice, carry their own defensive systems, so the weapon must have sufficient range to be fired from a position of relative security. Finally, even the fastest-responding CAS may not reach the fight before the attacking armour has engaged the friendly force. Telling friend from foe, when the position of the target is no help, is a great deal more difficult than simply acquiring, tracking and shooting a target which is known to be hostile.

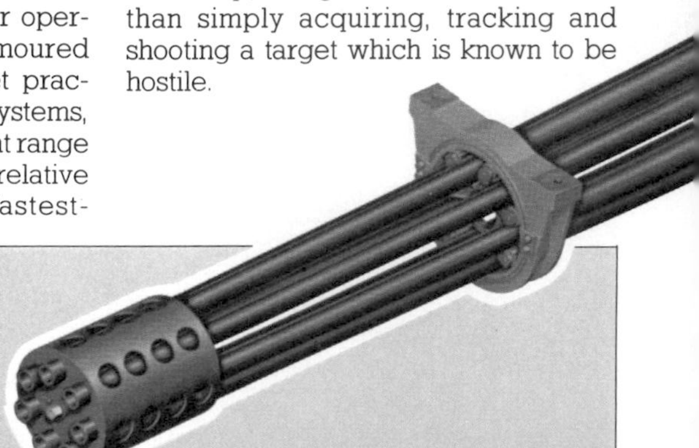

Below: 354th TFW ground crew prepare to reload a GAU-8/A's ammunition drum, using the Ammunition Loading System.

General Electric GAU-8/A Avenger 30mm armament system

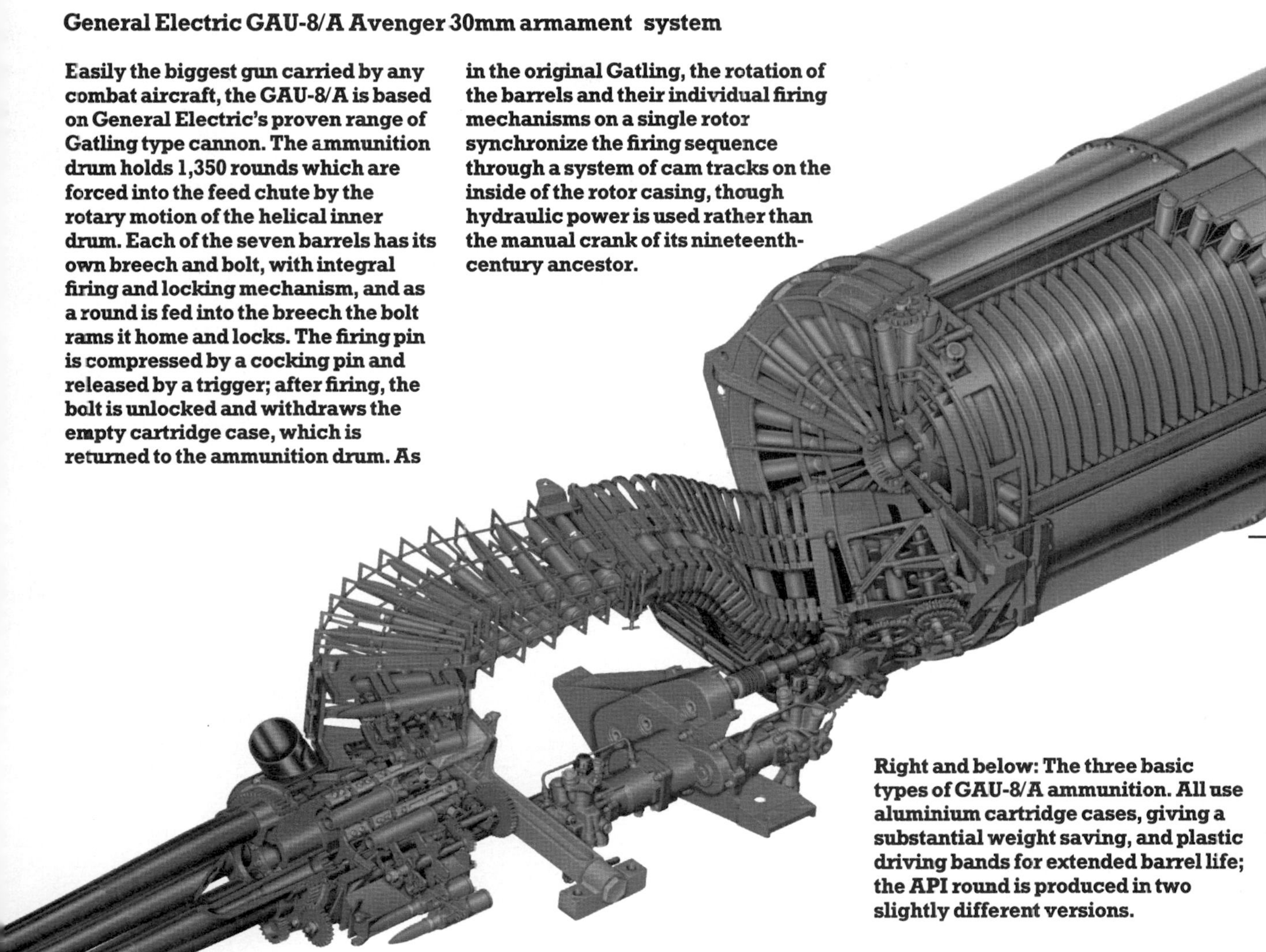

Easily the biggest gun carried by any combat aircraft, the GAU-8/A is based on General Electric's proven range of Gatling type cannon. The ammunition drum holds 1,350 rounds which are forced into the feed chute by the rotary motion of the helical inner drum. Each of the seven barrels has its own breech and bolt, with integral firing and locking mechanism, and as a round is fed into the breech the bolt rams it home and locks. The firing pin is compressed by a cocking pin and released by a trigger; after firing, the bolt is unlocked and withdraws the empty cartridge case, which is returned to the ammunition drum. As in the original Gatling, the rotation of the barrels and their individual firing mechanisms on a single rotor synchronize the firing sequence through a system of cam tracks on the inside of the rotor casing, though hydraulic power is used rather than the manual crank of its nineteenth-century ancestor.

Looking at these basic requirements in the mid-1960s, the USAF planners realised that there was no combination of weapons and sensors in the inventory, or even envisaged, which could meet the requirement. Unguided weapons and iron bombs were not accurate at safe ranges. Autonomous air-to-surface missiles guided by TV cameras were under study, but even if they worked as advertised, they would not kill a tank with every shot (the air-to-air battles over Vietnam had been a cold shower for those who believed in theoretical kill probabilities, as defined in the early 1960s). The cost-per-kill numbers, placed against the relatively low cost of the cheap, unrefined Soviet MBT, were not encouraging.

Reviewing the history of aircraft-versus-tank battles in the 1939-45 war, the USAF came across a few successes for the aircraft. Most of these involved the use of a heavy-calibre gun: the British Hurricane IID in the North African desert, with its two 40mm cannon; the German Ju 87G, with two 37mm weapons; and the Soviet Il-2, with 23mm or 37mm cannon. There was also the German Hs 129, with its massive 75mm gun, designed to tackle the huge Josef Stalin MBT.

The gun became the standard weapon of the A-X by a process of elimination: there was simply no other weapon in sight that could kill a tank from a fast-moving aircraft at a reasonable cost. The encouraging lesson from history, and from experience and tests with the more modern 30mm calibre weapons used by Britain and France, was that a tank could be destroyed by an airborne gun of moderate calibre, because the aircraft could attack the more lightly armoured sides and top of the tank. The tanks of the 1960s were a great deal better protected than those of the 1940s, but the design of guns, and, to a greater extent, the design of ammunition, had made advances as well.

Gun design

The design of an airborne anti-tank cannon had barely been considered since the mid-1940s. The principles of gun design, though, are constant regardless of the intended use of the weapon. Since the modern gun was conceived in the mid-1880s, these principles have become fairly well established.

The gun has been likened to a piston engine, with the barrel as the cylinder and the shell as the piston. Its power is proportional to the pressure generated by the expansion of the burning gases inside the barrel, and there are physical and practical limits, such as gun strength and durability, to that pressure. The power of the gun, and the speed of the shell, can be increased by adding more propellant without increasing calibre. But if the peak pressure is to be held constant, the propellant gases must have more time, and more room, to expand. This means a longer barrel, and is the reason why the ratio of barrel length to calibre is a basic parameter in gun design.

The speed of the shell – muzzle velocity – is a contributor to absolute range, but it is a vital quality in two specific types of gunnery. These, conveniently, are airborne gunnery and shooting tanks.

In airborne gunnery accuracy is the main requirement. No system, including a gun, is absolutely consistent in operation. Rounds may vary – to a tiny degree – in the burning rate of their propellant. Firing from a warm barrel is not quite the same as firing from a cold barrel. Outside the barrel, the weight of the shell and the wind take effect, and cause the shell to deviate from the straight and narrow path. An added factor in an aircraft is the varying speed and g loading when the gun is fired. All these add up to 'dis-

GAU-8/A ammunition

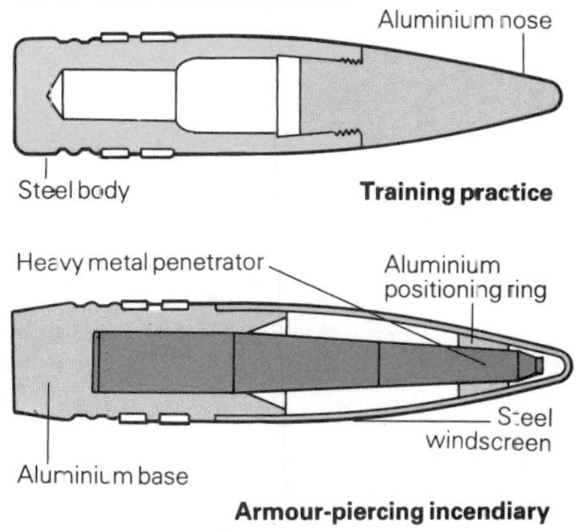

Right and below: The three basic types of GAU-8/A ammunition. All use aluminium cartridge cases, giving a substantial weight saving, and plastic driving bands for extended barrel life; the API round is produced in two slightly different versions.

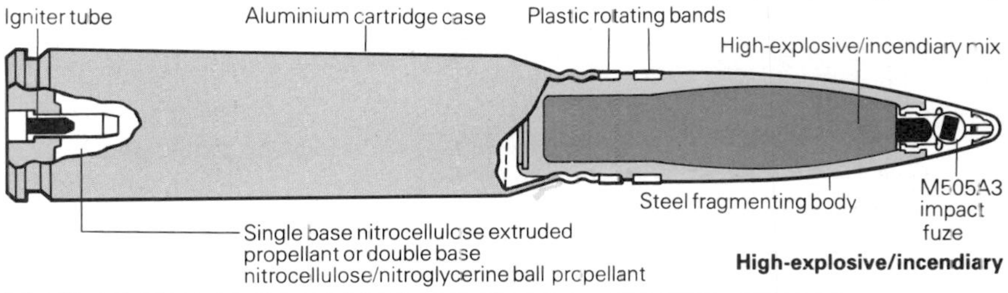

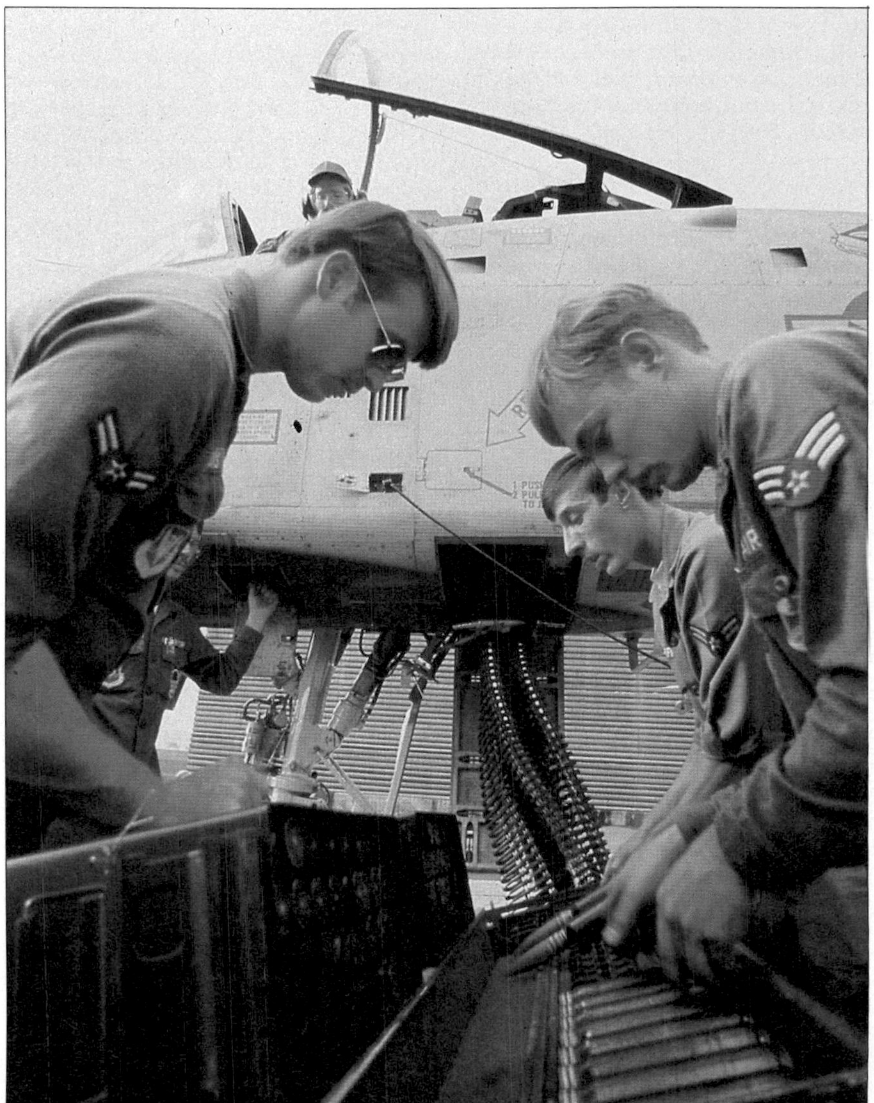

Right: Hand-loading 30mm rounds for early firing trials with the GAU-8/A. Each round is 11.4in (290mm) long, and the complete API round weighs an impressive 2.05lb (930g).

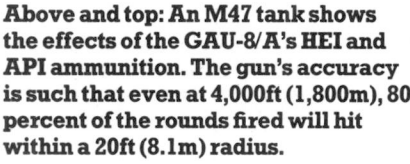

Above and top: An M47 tank shows the effects of the GAU-8/A's HEI and API ammunition. The gun's accuracy is such that even at 4,000ft (1,800m), 80 percent of the rounds fired will hit within a 20ft (8.1m) radius.

persion', the fact that shells diverge slightly in flight. Dispersion cannot be eliminated, but most of the factors that cause it are reduced by higher muzzle velocity.

The importance of velocity to antitank gunnery is in the nature of the target. Tanks are invulnerable to blast explosives, except in extremely large quantities. The common feature of all antitank munitions is that they concentrate their force on a single point, either in the form of a solid piece of hard metal or, in the case of a hollow-charge warhead, as a high-velocity jet of vaporized metal. The hollow charge is too bulky to be fired from a gun; the effectiveness of the solid penetrator is proportional to its impact velocity, and thus to its muzzle velocity.

Finally, antitank and airborne gunnery share a common feature. The fighter or attack pilot has neither the means nor the time to consider the ballistic drop of the shell with distance, and it is certainly impractical to fire and observe a ranging shot before firing for effect. While it may be possible for a ground-based antitank gun to fire a ranging shot before engaging a tank, it is definitely inadvisable. The effective range, in both cases, is the maximum range at which ballistic drop can be ignored: 'point-blank' shooting, in the original and accurate sense of the term. This range is almost directly proportional to muzzle velocity.

Given the basic principles of gun design and gunnery, and the state of the art in projectile design and propellant composition, the shape of the A-X gun became a factor of the operational requirements. These could be summarized as the need to assure the destruction of a T-62 tank at 4,000ft (1,200m) range. However, the phrase 'assure the destruction' introduced a new parameter into the requirement: rate of fire.

High muzzle velocity could reduce dispersion, but not eliminate it, particularly in airborne firing. It was reasonable to expect the new gun to put half its shots within an approximately tank-sized area from a given point at maximum effective range. The problem was that no two shells would be fired from the same point, because the aircraft would be moving. Again, this was a factor which could never be eliminated. It could, however, be reduced. The key was a very high rate of fire, so that the movement of the firing point between each round would be as small as possible.

The requirement for the A-X gun took shape in 1968-69. It soon became clear that the weapon would be of awesome size, and would utterly dwarf any aircraft gun since the 75mm freaks of 1939-45. Its shells would be more than twice as heavy as those of any gun with a comparable muzzle velocity or rate of fire, and the rest of the weapon would naturally grow in proportion. The multiple-target-kill capability required by the USAF, together with the high rate of fire, also meant that the A-X would carry more rounds of its heavy ammunition than other aircraft.

The rate of fire demanded by the USAF determined the basic configuration of the gun. It would be a design which dated back two decades or a century, depending on your historical perspective. It was in 1861 that Richard Jordan Gatling patented the first operable machine gun, a weapon which could load, cock and fire itself at a far faster rate than any human operator could attain. The Gatling gun consisted of six independent barrels and breeches, arranged in a circle and revolving around a common axis under the power of a hand crank, and it was used in the American Civil War, and later by the British Army. Its limitation was its need for external power, and by the turn of the century it had been replaced by weapons such as the Maxim, which used

Range estimation

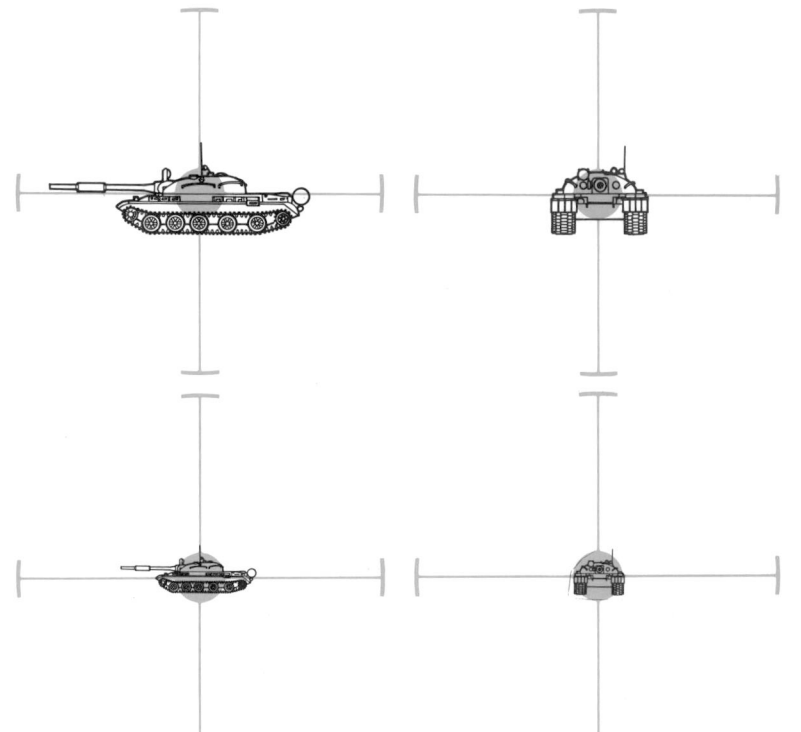

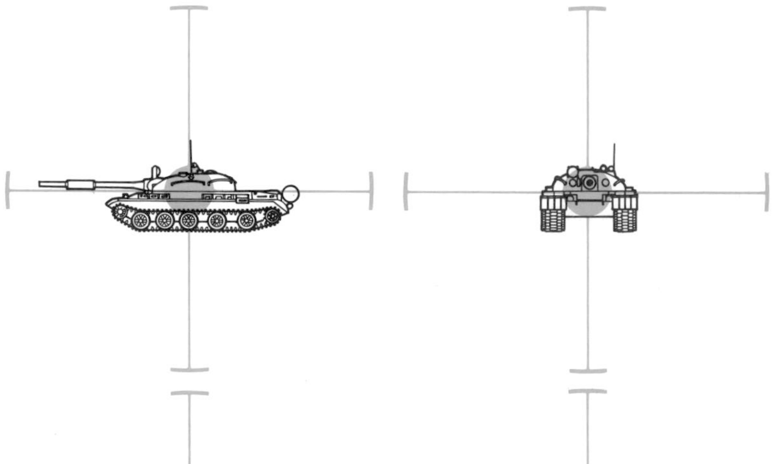

Right: During trials, pilots found a quick method of estimating target ranges based on the HUD gun cross: the upper and lower views show a T62 as it appears at 2,000ft (610m) and 4,000ft (1,220m).

Above: The GAU-8/A expels 24lb (10.9kg) of used propellant a second, causing occasional engine stalls, but few targets can withstand more than a very short burst.

Below: An M48 on the receiving end of a burst of fire from the GAU-8/A: as the rounds penetrate the tank armour, ammunition and fuel inside ignite to cause secondary explosions.

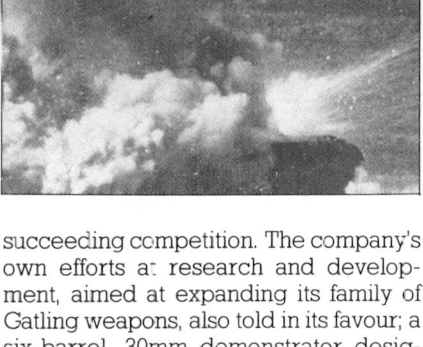

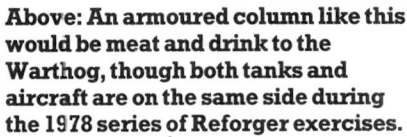

Above: An armoured column like this would be meat and drink to the Warthog, though both tanks and aircraft are on the same side during the 1978 series of Reforger exercises.

recoil energy to operate the mechanism.

The Gatling remained a museum piece until 1946, when the US Army Air Force began serious investigations of a new type of aircraft gun. In 1939-45 German aircraft cannon had proved superior in most respects to the Anglo-French Hispano, and vastly more effective than the USAAF's standard .5in (12.7mm) machine gun. The invading Allies also discovered prototypes of the Mauser MG 213 revolver cannon, which could fire twice as fast as any previous weapon for a modest increase in weight.

Post-war development of aircraft guns followed two parallel tracks. The development of the MG 213 was completed independently in Britain, France and the USA. The other route was started by the USAAF which intended to create an ultimate aircraft gun, combining high velocity with an unheard-of rate of fire: the aim was to arm a fighter or defend a bomber with a single gun.

This was Project Vulcan, and a development contract was awarded to General Electric's Armament Systems Department in 1946. GE's response to the USAAF requirement was to resurrect the Gatling. There were a number of reasons for this apparent throwback to the past. The most important was that the Gatling, coupled with a modern-technology feed system, could reach and sustain otherwise unthinkable rates of fire. The MG 213, firing at 1,400rds/min, was close to the limits on barrel life and barrel heating. A six-barrel Gatling, by contrast, could fire at 6,000rds/min, but each barrel would be firing at little more than two-thirds the rate of the MG 213 barrel.

The Gatling's need for external power was no longer a problem, now that fighter aircraft carried their own reliable electrical power supplies; in fact, it could be seen as a positive advantage. While a recoil-powered gun might run out of power if a round failed to fire, the Gatling's external power provided a number of options for clearing a misfired round from the cycle. A final mechanical advantage of the Gatling was that many of its functions were driven by the rotary movement of the barrel assembly; rotary movements are inherently more reliable, and impose fewer loads on the rest of the system, than the reciprocating motions of a conventional gun.

GE ground-tested its first T-171 20mm Gatling in 1949, successfully firing up to 6,000rds/min. The cannon's only real drawback was its unusual, bulky shape, which made it very difficult to install in an aircraft not specifically designed to carry it; it did not enter service until early 1958 first on the Lockheed F-104 and later on the Republic F-105, under the military designation M61A1. It proved its worth on the F-105 over North Vietnam, was squeezed into the nose of the F-4, packed into the USAF A-7 and fired in broadsides from AC-119 and AC-130 gunships. GE had developed a 7.62mm baby Gatling, the Minigun, which was fitted to helicopters, AC-47 'Puff-Ships' and the A-37B. By the time the A-X requirement emerged, the USAF was thoroughly convinced of the merits of the Gatling.

The fact that GE had designed every operational Gatling gun in the world gave it something of a head start in the succeeding competition. The company's own efforts at research and development, aimed at expanding its family of Gatling weapons, also told in its favour; a six-barrel, 30mm demonstrator designated T-212 was tested in 1967-68, before the formal USAF requirement was issued. As outlined in the first chapter, the contest to produce the GAU-8/A weapon for the A-10 led to a 'shoot-off' between rival prototypes from GE and Philco-Ford, which had developed the MG 213-based M39 for the F-100 and F-5. GE was announced the winner in mid-1973, and the production cannon was first fired from the A-10 in 1975.

GAU-8/A Avenger

The GAU-8/A Avenger is more than a scaled-up M61. Such a weapon could have been designed and built, but would have been unacceptably heavy. The first of many design differences is that the heavier weapon has seven barrels, instead of six. The maximum firing rate is lower (4,200rds/min versus 6,000), and the firing rate per barrel is lower again; each GAU-8/A barrel fires a maximum of 10rds/sec, while the M61 barrel fires nearly 17. Essentially, maximum firing rate has been traded for a heavier, more accurate and more lethal round; each shell is far heavier than the M50 round fired by the older weapon, and the more modest firing rate per barrel is necessary to ensure a long barrel life. The USAF specified a minimum 21,000-round life for each set of barrels. The GAU-8/A also has an improved and more compact bolt design which reduces the overall length and weight of the gun. The GAU-8/A is relatively compact, being only fractionally larger in diameter than the much less powerful M61.

The basic GAU-8/A gun closely follows the philosophy of Richard Gatling's original. Each of the seven 30mm barrels is a simple non-repeating rifle, with its own breech and bolt; the cocking and firing mechanism is built into the bolt. The bolt rams the shell into the breech and locks into position; a cocking pin compresses the firing spring, and a trigger releases it. The bolt is unlocked, and slides back to withdraw the empty cartridge case.

None of the barrels, though, can fire without some force to move and lock the bolt, and cock and release the trigger. The genius of the original Gatling concept is that all these operations are carried out and synchronized through the movement of a single component: the multiple barrels, built into one rotating assembly (which GE calls the 'rotor') and revolving on a common axis inside the gun casing. The firing mechanisms for each individual barrel are located on the outside of the rotor, and engage fixed cam tracks on the inside of the casing. As the rotor spins, the curving cam tracks engage and move the bolt, the locking mechanism and the firing pin, and take the barrel through a complete, perfectly synchronized firing sequence for each revolution of the rotor. This, essentially, is what happens in all the GE weapons.

Each GAU-8/A barrel is some 80 calibres in length. The muzzle velocity of the GAU-8/A is about the same as that of the M61, but the heavier, more advanced ammunition is not only more destructive but has better ballistic properties. It decelerates much less rapidly after leaving the barrel, so that its time of flight to 4,000ft (1,200m) is 30 per cent less than that of an M61 round, and the projectile drops a negligible distance – barely 10ft

AGM-65 Maverick

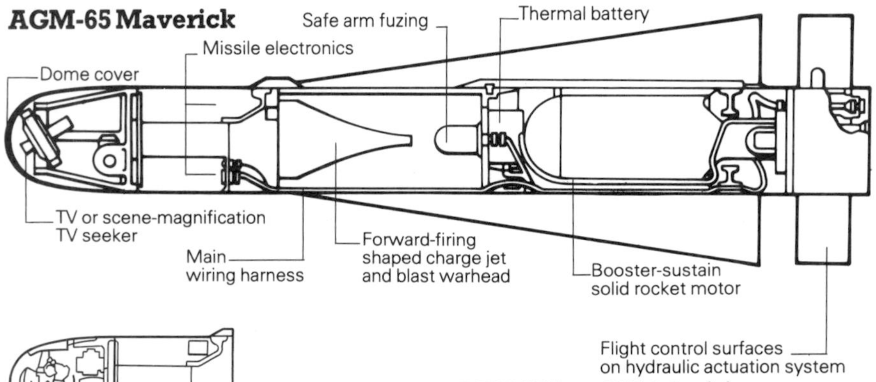

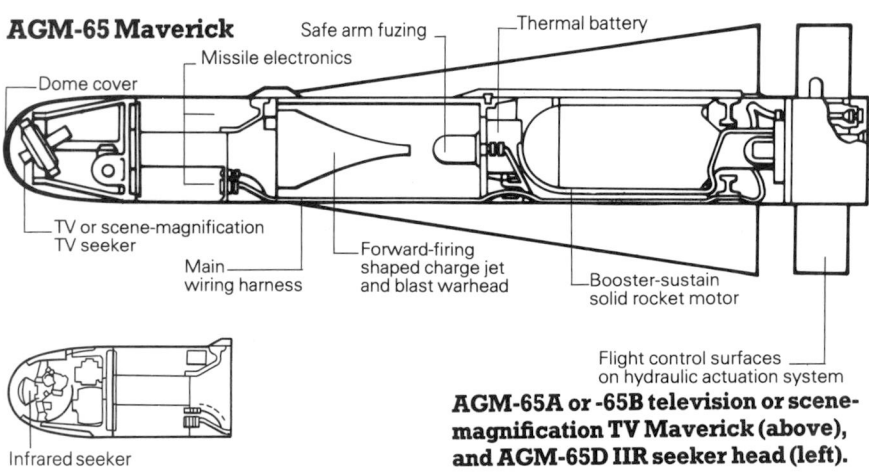

AGM-65A or -65B television or scene-magnification TV Maverick (above), and AGM-65D IIR seeker head (left).

Maverick launch zones

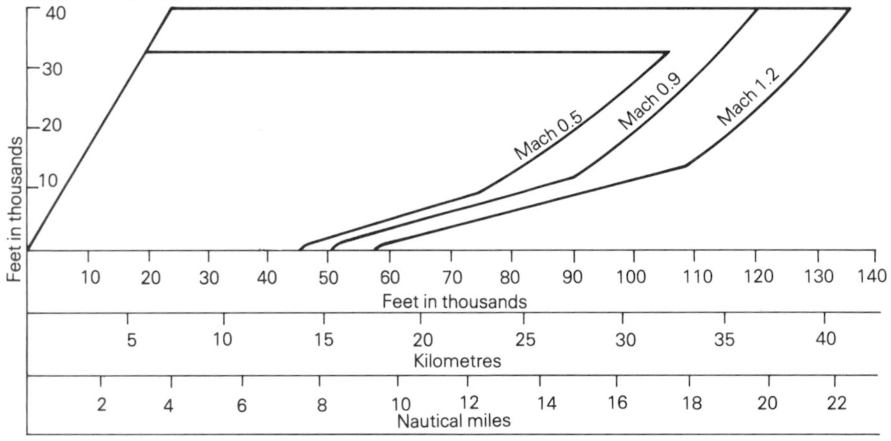

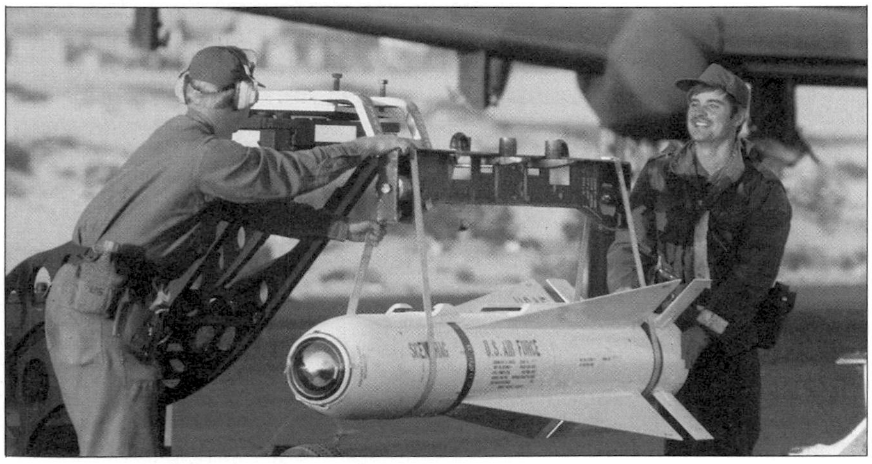

(3m) – in the process. The accuracy of the GAU-8/A, installed in the A-10, is rated at '5mil, 80 per cent', meaning that 80 per cent of rounds fired at 4,000ft (1,800m) will hit within a circle of 20ft (6.1m) radius; the M61 is rated at 8mil.

A very important innovation in the design of the GAU-8/A shells is the use of aluminium alloy cases in place of the traditional steel or brass. This alone adds 30 per cent to ammunition capacity for a given weight. The shells also have plastic driving bands to improve barrel life. They are imposing to examine and handle, measuring 11.4in (290mm) in length and weighing 1.53lb (694g) or more. There are four types in service. Two are common to most aircraft cannon: a practice round, and a general-purpose shell loaded with high-explosive/incendiary (HEI) compound. Specially developed for the A-10, however, are two armour-piercing incendiary (API) rounds. The USAF chose two companies, Aerojet and Honeywell, to develop and produce API shells for the A-10 under its 'second-source' philosophy: when items are acquired in large quantities, the USAF buys them from two organizations, and lets them bid competitively for each year's order.

The two API rounds are slightly different in detail, but basically are similar. Neither contains any explosive. Instead, they consist of a lightweight aluminium body, cast around a small 'penetrator' of smaller calibre than the shell. (The calibre is about 15mm.) It projects from the blunt body section, and the shell has a thin aluminium 'windscreen' to keep the shape aerodynamic. The penetrator is made of depleted uranium, a by-product of the enrichment process used to make nuclear fuel. The material has an extremely high density, comprising roughly two-thirds of the projectile's weight.

The result is that two-thirds of the total impact energy is concentrated in the small-calibre penetrator: enough energy to lift a thirty-ton weight one foot, delivered instantly to a penny-sized area. Not only is this ammunition capable of penetrating the top and side armour of an MBT, but the depleted uranium ignites on impact, sending a jet of flame into the vehicle.

Above left: The Maverick's launch envelope varies with the speed and altitude of the launch aircraft, and with target range, though the Warthog pilot will be most concerned with the bottom left-hand corner.

Left: Preparing to load an AGM-65B scene-magnification Maverick onto an A-10 at Cairo West AB during a Bright Star exercise in 1981.

Below: After being loaded onto LAU-88 launchers, Mavericks are transferred to the special launcher rack, seen here at RAF Bentwaters, ready for mounting on the aircraft.

Ammunition and feed system

The GAU-8/A ammunition is linkless, reducing weight and avoiding a great deal of potential for jamming. The feed system is double-ended: the spent cases are not ejected from the aircraft (which takes a great deal of force if the possibility of severe airframe damage is to be eliminated) but are cycled back into the ammunition drum. The feed system is based on that developed for later M61 installations, but uses more advanced design techniques and materials throughout, to save weight.

Inside the cylindrical outer drum is a rotating inner drum, resembling a huge, deeply cut worm gear. The helical channel which winds around this rotor holds the 1,350 shells; they are stored radially, with their tips toward the axis of the drum, and their bases are held in channels running the length of the fixed, outer drum. As the rotor turns, the shells are forced forward along the drum and into the complex of turning mechanisms and chutes leading to the gun.

Power for the gun and its feed mechanism is drawn from the A-10's dual hydraulic systems. Two hydraulic motors provide the total 77hp (57.4kW) needed to drive the system at its maximum firing rate. If either hydraulic system fails, the remaining motor can sustain the alternative 2,100rds/min rate.

Loading the linkless ammunition is the function of the only specialized piece of ground equipment used by the A-10. The Ammunition Loading System (ALS) resembles a trailer-mounted version of the GAU-8/A ammunition drum and feed system, and operates on the same principle, loading rounds and extracting empty cases simultaneously. A full load can be changed in less than 13 minutes.

GAU-8/A derivatives

Some of the GAU-8/A technology has been transferred into the smaller 25mm GAU-12/U Equalizer developed for the AV-8B, which is about the same size as the M61 but is considerably more lethal. GE has also developed the GAU-13, a four-barrel weapon using GAU-8A components, which has been tested in podded form, and the Avenger forms the basis for the Dutch-developed Goalkeeper naval air-defence gun. No current or contemplated aircraft other than the A-10, however, carries the full-up Avenger system. The weapon is simply too large. It measures 19ft 10.5in (5.06m) from the muzzle to the rearmost point of the ammunition feed system, and the ammunition drum alone is 34.5in (87.6cm) in diameter and 71.5in (181.6cm) long. With full ammunition, the system weighs 4,029lb (1,830kg).

In short, the GAU-8/A system, fully armed and ready to fire, is just about as long and as heavy as a Rolls-Royce or a full-size Cadillac. At its maximum firing rate, its average recoil force of 9,000lb (40kN) thrust is equal to the power of one of the A-10's engines. Operationally, the

Above: Medium altitude test launch of a Maverick by a DT & E A-10. Maverick allows attacks at longer ranges than the gun, though at considerably greater expense.

Left: Unlike earlier command-guided air-to-surface missiles such as Bullpup, Maverick is a fire-and-forget weapon: the pilot designates the target as seen by the TV or infrared seeker head and displayed on his cockpit CRT, launches the missile and takes evasive action while it homes automatically on the selected target. This sequence shows the destruction of an M113 APC.

performance of the gun makes it as vital to the A-10's mission as the wings and engines. It has many unique attributes, and no other weapon, in service or under study, can take its place.

The gun gives the A-10 the ability to attack multiple targets in one mission. It is designed to fire its full ammunition load in ten two-second bursts, with one minute to cool down between bursts; in normal use, the bursts and the cool-down time would be much shorter. A one-second burst from 4,000ft (1,220m) will put 40 shells into a circle little bigger than the length of a tank, and half-a-dozen hits are considered to be a lethal strike. With the theoretical ability to deliver 15-20 such bursts, the A-10 is unlikely to have to abort an attack for want of firepower.

The gun also eliminates the need for many of the systems which have been considered standard on other attack aircraft since the late 1960s. Its shells travel at Mach 3; from 4,000ft (1,220m) they are on target in 1.2 seconds. This means that the movement of an MBT is irrelevant to the aiming problem; to the A-10, all ground targets are fixed. Because of the flat trajectory of the shells, too, the distance to the target does not have to be accurately estimated or measured. Within the normal maximum range, the trajectory is a straight line in front of the aircraft, represented by a fixed dot on the head-up display. The absence of inertial platforms, laser rangefinders and other systems from the weapon-aiming loop not only simplifies the aircraft, but makes the pilot's workload less as well. Without the point-and-fire simplicity of the GAU-8/A, the A-10 concept of manoeuvring, medium-speed CAS with visual navigation and target acquisition would probably collapse due to excessive pilot workload.

The gun is extremely reliable. Stoppages are predicted to occur once in 150,000 rounds, or once in more than 100 missions when every round is fired. Even then, the weapon can often be cleared in flight by reversing the gun and feed mechanism and trying again. There is no guidance system to fail and nothing to be jammed or deceived. All this adds up to the fact that the kill probability of a GAU-8 burst is high: tests have shown that as many as half the bursts may be effective in a diving attack on the rear of a tank, and one third in side attacks.

AGM-65 Maverick

The gun is not only the primary weapon of the A-10, but it is one of only two weapons generally used by the aircraft. The other, the Hughes AGM-65 Maverick air-to-surface missile, complements the gun; it is also designed for attacks against hard, mobile precision targets, but from rather greater standoff distances. On the other hand, the Maverick does not give the A-10 the same sustained firing capability as the gun, and is not as fast-acting, and its cost per kill is very much greater. The cost of an early-model Maverick was quoted at $60,000 in 1981, versus $1,800 in ammunition and maintenance costs for a two-second burst from the cannon. The two systems, however, had a very similar kill probability (Pk) per pass, so the gun was far more economical.

Maverick was developed after the miserable failure of the command-guided Bullpup to accomplish anything in Vietnam. It was a very advanced concept for its day: a compact missile, designed for multiple carriage, which could guide itself autonomously to a precision target and destroy it with a large shaped-charge warhead. Its guidance system was based on television technol-

Alternative mission loads

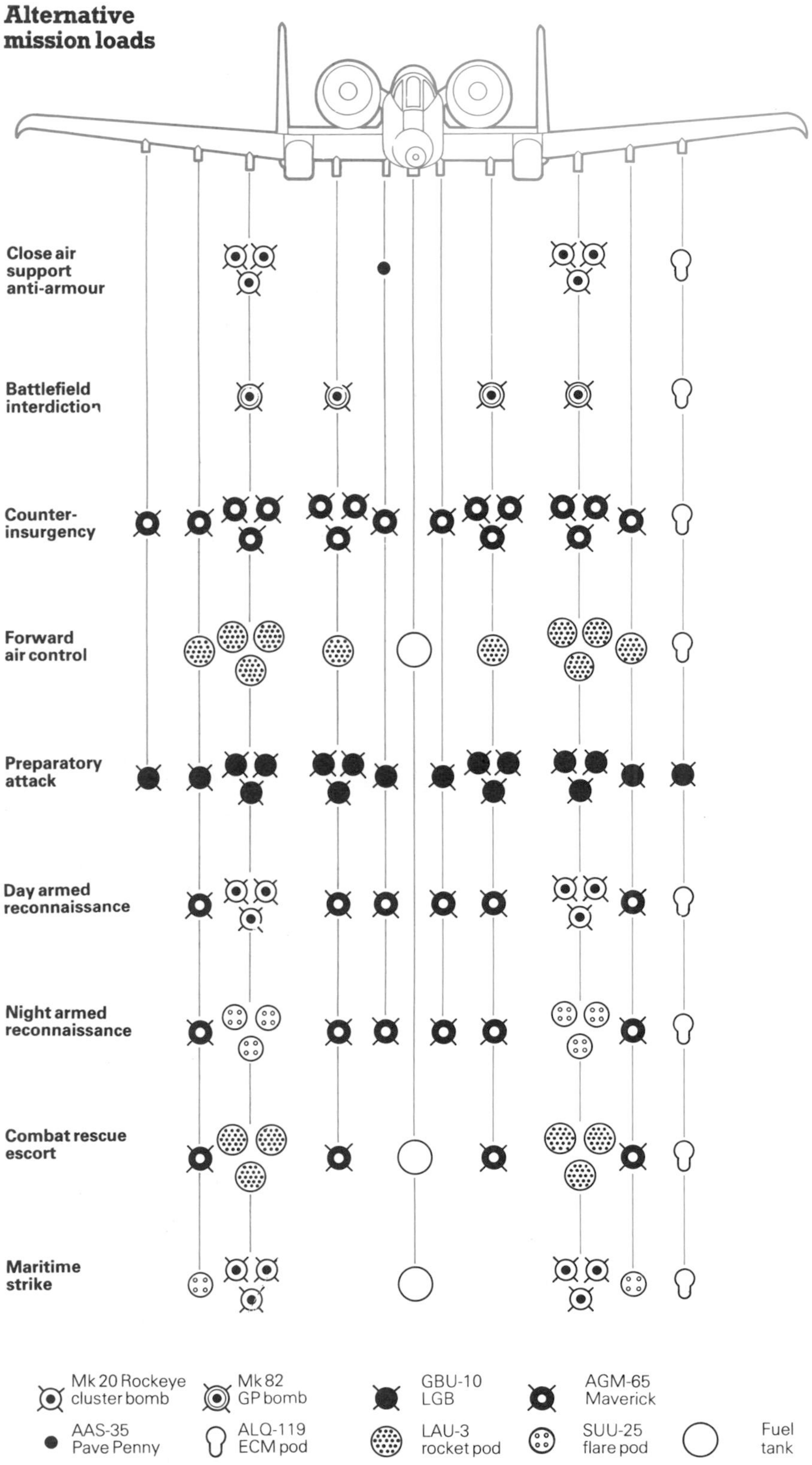

Left: During operational evaluation, the USAF found the A-10 well-suited to the preparatory role, and unmatched as an escort; FAC capability was judged satisfactory, while other roles have been suggested by the makers.

Below: 333rd TFTS, 355th TTW A-10 en route to the Gila Bend range, with 25lb (11kg) BDU-33 practice bombs on wing-mounted triple and fuselage multiple ejection racks.

ogy. A stabilized video sensor provided a picture to a cockpit display, and fed a simple image-processing system in the missile. The pilot pointed the camera at the target using cockpit controls, commanded the seeker to lock on and launched the missile. The guidance system sensed relative movement by analyzing the video signal, and generated correction signals to keep the missile on target.

Two production versions of Maverick were built in the 1970s. The first was the basic AGM-65A, with an optical system designed to cover a 5deg cone in front of the aircraft – equivalent to the field of view of a 200mm lens on a 35mm camera. It was replaced in production by the AGM-65B, originally known as the Scene Magnification Maverick, which has a 2.5deg field of view, and is carried as a standard weapon by the A-10. Underwing pylons 3 and 9, immediately outboard of the landing gear pods, are each fitted to carry the LAU-88/A triple launcher for the AGM-65. Maverick is controlled from its own panel in the cockpit, consisting of a video screen and controls for slewing the seeker, switching from low to high magnification and locking the missile on to the target.

Maverick has proven to be successful and reliable, and 85 per cent of all missiles fired – including some fired in anger, in South-East Asia and the Middle East – are claimed to have hit their targets. More than 30,000 Mavericks have been built for the USAF and export customers. The weapon has only one serious drawback: it has to be fired from a point uncomfortably close to the target. The missile itself has a theoretical range of 6-7nm (11-13km) even under the most unfavourable conditions – launch from a slow aircraft, such as an A-10, at low level. However, its TV tracker will not normally lock on to a target outside 2-3nm (3.7-5.5km). This is because air is not perfectly transparent, and the attenuation of optical wavelengths with distance prevents the guidance circuitry from getting the clear, high-contrast image that it needs. Maverick takes 4–8 seconds to lock on, which is a long time in air combat, and particularly so when the launch sequence takes place within the envelope of standard air-defence systems such as the SA-8 Gecko. Multiple launches in a single attack pass are not practicable.

Right: A powered hoist is used to load a Mk 83 1,000lb (454kg) GP bomb under the wing of a 354th TFW A-10.

A-10 stores options

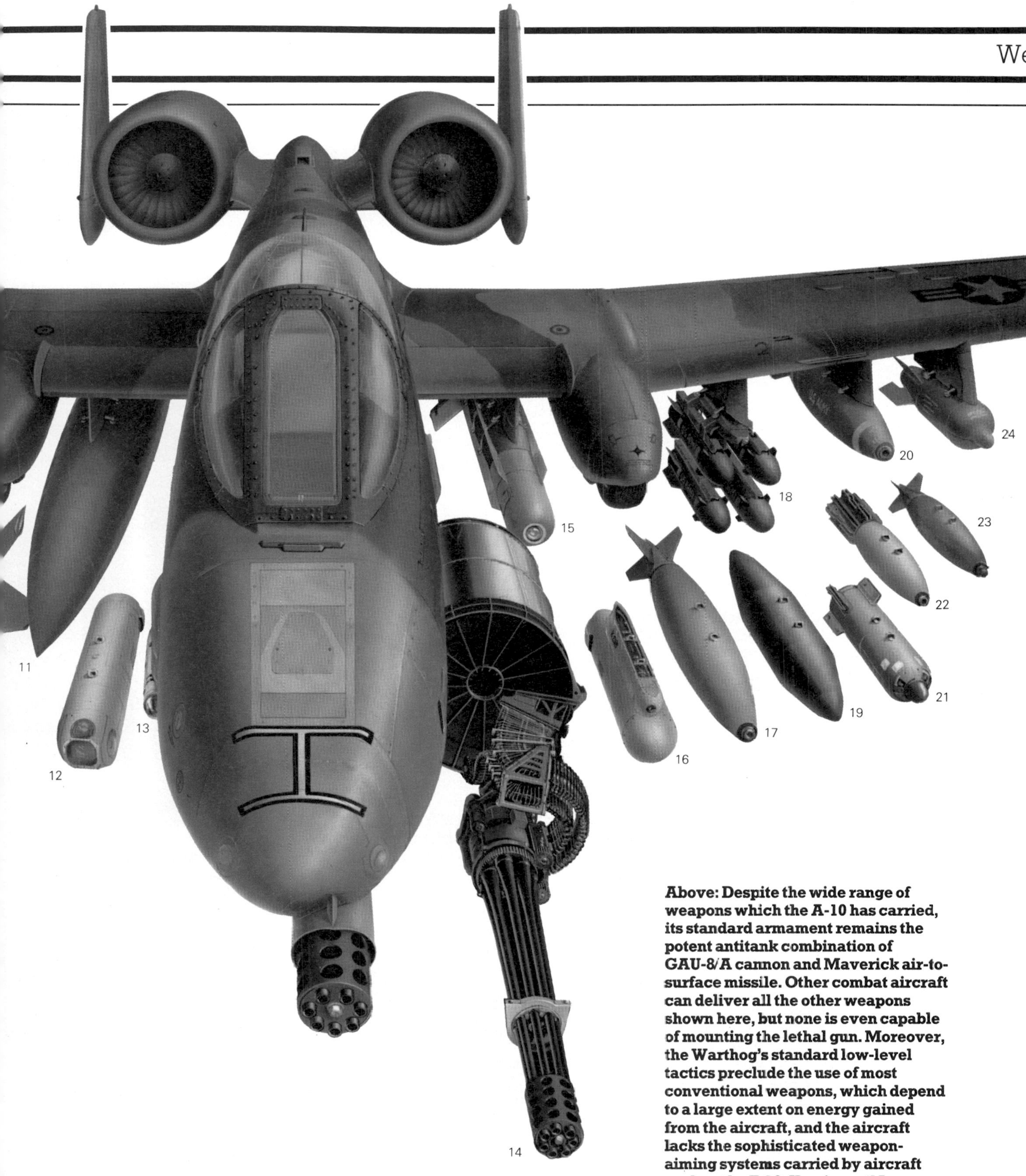

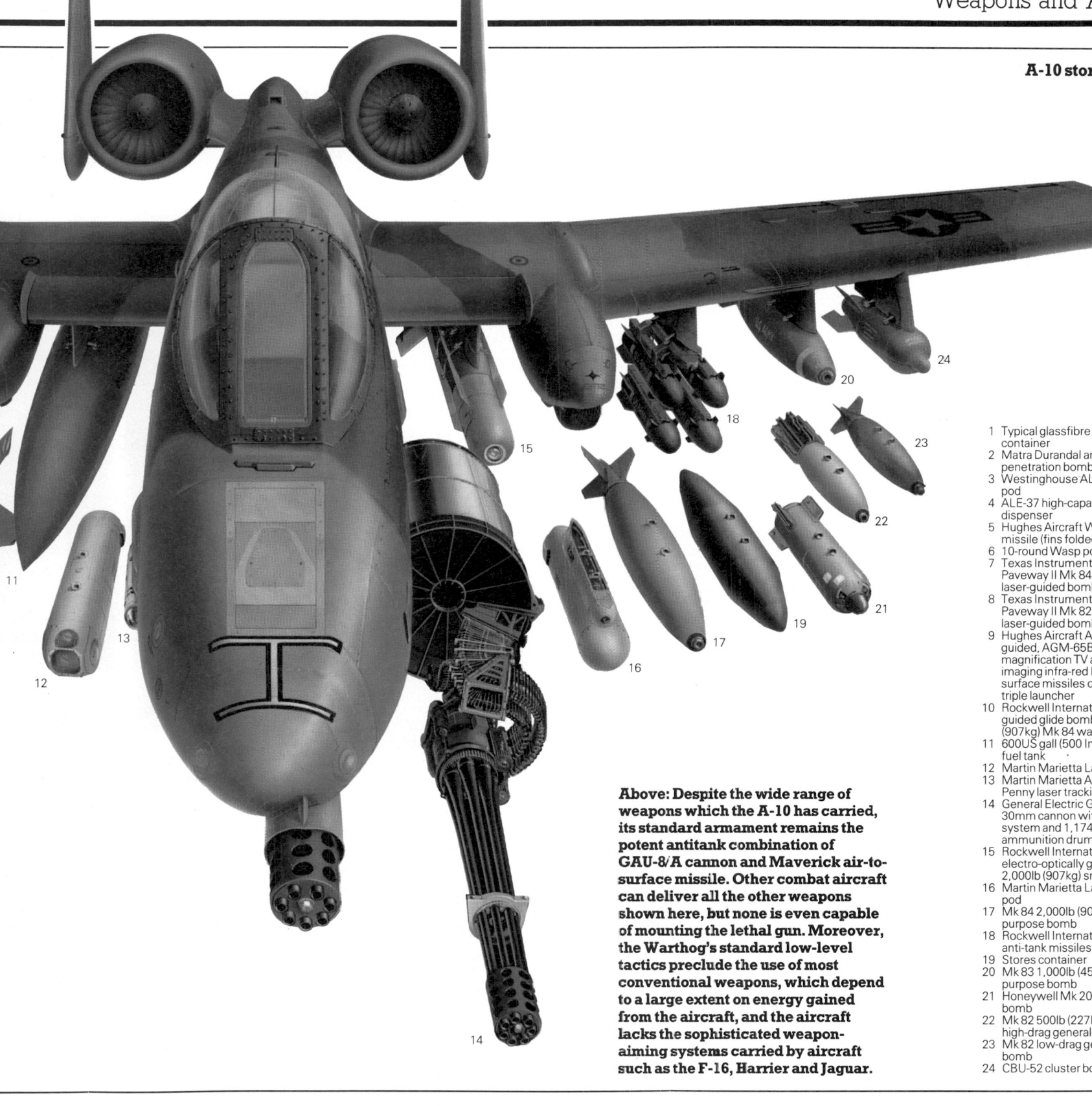

1 Typical glassfibre weapon storage container
2 Matra Durandal anti-runway penetration bomb
3 Westinghouse ALQ-119(V) ECM pod
4 ALE-37 high-capacity chaff dispenser
5 Hughes Aircraft Wasp anti-armour missile (fins folded)
6 10-round Wasp pod
7 Texas Instruments GBU-10E/B Paveway II Mk 84 2,000lb (907kg) laser-guided bomb
8 Texas Instruments GBU-12D/B Paveway II Mk 82 500lb (227kg) laser-guided bomb
9 Hughes Aircraft AGM-65A TV-guided, AGM-65B scene-magnification TV and AGM-65D imaging infra-red Maverick air-to-surface missiles on LAU-88/A triple launcher
10 Rockwell International GBU-15 guided glide bomb, 2,000lb (907kg) Mk 84 warhead
11 600US gall (500 Imp gall/2,273lit) fuel tank
12 Martin Marietta Lantirn navigation
13 Martin Marietta AAS-35 Pave Penny laser tracking pod
14 General Electric GAU-8/A Avenger 30mm cannon with hydraulic feed system and 1,174-round ammunition drum
15 Rockwell International Hobo electro-optically guided Mk 84 2,000lb (907kg) smart bomb
16 Martin Marietta Lantirn targeting pod
17 Mk 84 2,000lb (907kg) general-purpose bomb
18 Rockwell International Hellfire anti-tank missiles
19 Stores container
20 Mk 83 1,000lb (454kg) general-purpose bomb
21 Honeywell Mk 20 Rockeye cluster bomb
22 Mk 82 500lb (227kg) Snakeye high-drag general-purpose bomb
23 Mk 82 low-drag general-purpose bomb
24 CBU-52 cluster bomb

Above: Despite the wide range of weapons which the A-10 has carried, its standard armament remains the potent antitank combination of GAU-8/A cannon and Maverick air-to-surface missile. Other combat aircraft can deliver all the other weapons shown here, but none is even capable of mounting the lethal gun. Moreover, the Warthog's standard low-level tactics preclude the use of most conventional weapons, which depend to a large extent on energy gained from the aircraft, and the aircraft lacks the sophisticated weapon-aiming systems carried by aircraft such as the F-16, Harrier and Jaguar.

For this reason, the forthcoming introduction of the AGM-65D infra-red (IR) Maverick is very significant for the A-10 force. IR video technology has been available for many years, but it has taken new advances in electronics to create missile-sized and missile-priced image-processing systems which will cull guidance data from IR images. Because IR wavelengths are relatively little affected by attenuation in 'clear air', the AGM-65D can lock on at twice the stand-off range possible with the AGM-65B. This is close to the maximum range of the SA-8, and brings multiple launches within the realms of possibility. These are being facilitated by the development of a rapid-fire modification for the LAU-88/A, incorporating a circuit which slews the seeker of the second missile on to the target area as the seeker of the first is locked-on.

The IR weapon is also less affected by dust and smoke on the battlefield, and the better-quality image allows the pilot to discriminate between different types of vehicle according to their characteristic IR 'signatures'. The weapon requires no mandatory modifications to any aircraft already fitted to fire the AGM-65B. However, it is equipped to receive targeting data from the aircraft's weapon-aiming systems, and this capability can be used if the necessary control channel is installed.

The IR weapon's most important attribute is, for the time being, of limited use to the A-10: it operates identically by day and by night, the quality of the IR image being basically the same. As the A-10 gains night-operating capability, it will be able to use this characteristic.

Photographs of the A-10 loaded from wingtip to wingtip with weapons have helped to spread the impression that the aircraft was designed as an ordnance truck, primarily intended to carry a massive external load. This is not exactly true. The A-10 can lift a large warload because it was designed to use short fields, manoeuvre and fight while carrying a more moderate load. If the manoeuvring requirements are less severe, and a longer runway is available, the aircraft can lift a larger load. For an anti-tank mission from a forward operating base, however, six Mavericks and ammunition for the GAU-8/A constitute a full offensive load. Between them, the missiles and the gun are well suited to the A-10's primary mission, like most other aspects of the design.

In service with the USAF, the A-10 has been cleared to drop and fire a wide variety of weapons. These include the straightforward Mk 82 '500lb' bomb (which actually weighs 565lb/256kg); the A-10 can carry 28 such weapons. For use against troops or soft-skinned vehicles, the A-10 can carry cluster weapons such as Rockeye, CBU-52/58/71 and the British BL755. More sophisticated weapons include the GBU-12 laser-guided glide bomb, based on the 3,000lb Mk 84.

The A-10, however, is not particularly suited to deliver many of these weapons

Left: Bomb-carrying trials with the first DT & E A-10. Maximum load is 16,000lb, distributed between 11 pylons, though the extreme outboard wing pylons, limited to 1,000lb (454kg), are rarely used for anything but an ALQ-119 ECM pod.

Standard and INS HUD symbology and control units

The A-10 was designed for visual navigation and target acquisition, and the original avionics suite was as simple as possible, the head-up display using only the basic symbology shown below. The switch to low-level tactics, especially in poor visibility, made an inertial navigation system necessary, resulting in the expanded symbology shown right.

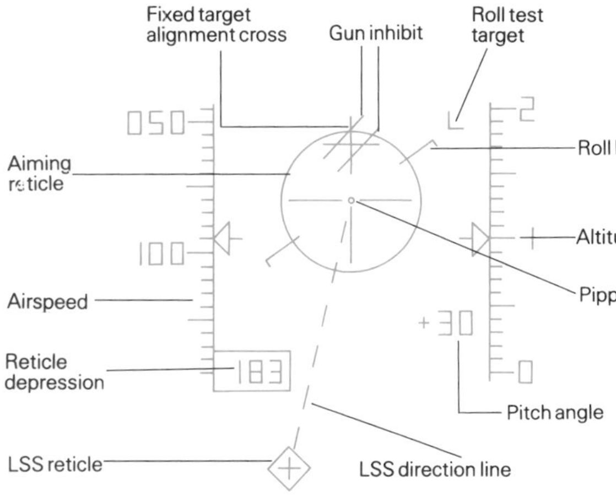

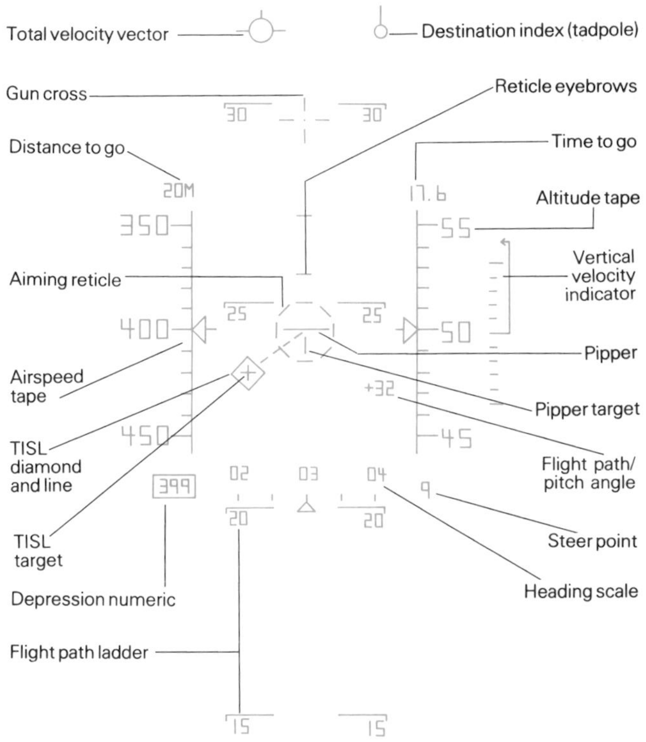

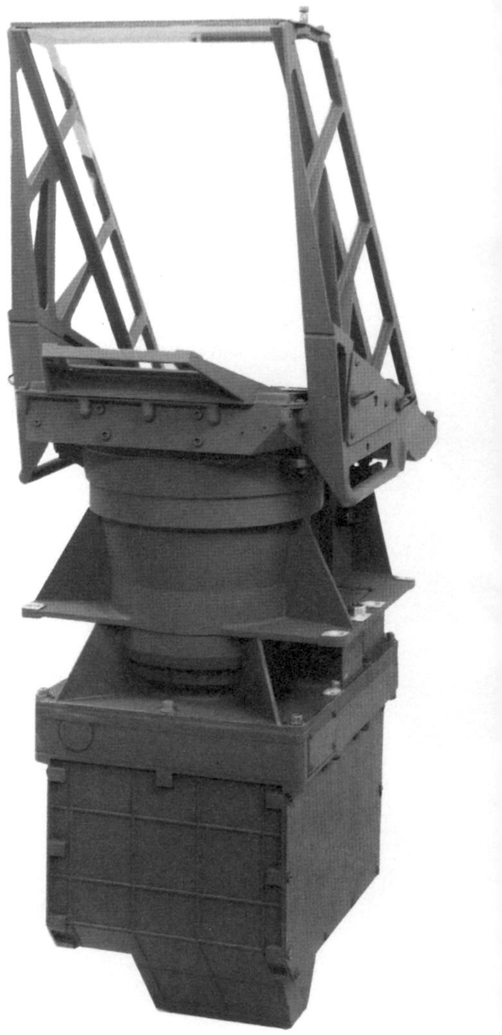

Above: The head-up display unit developed by Kaiser Electronics specially for the A-10 has been improved to incorporate inputs from the inertial navigation system.

Standard HUD control unit

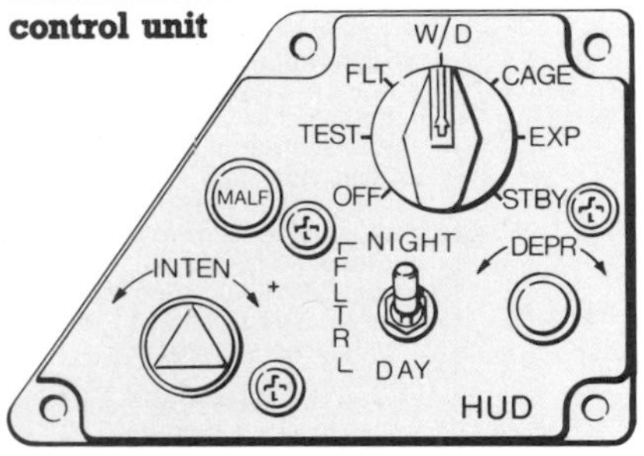

INS HUD control unit

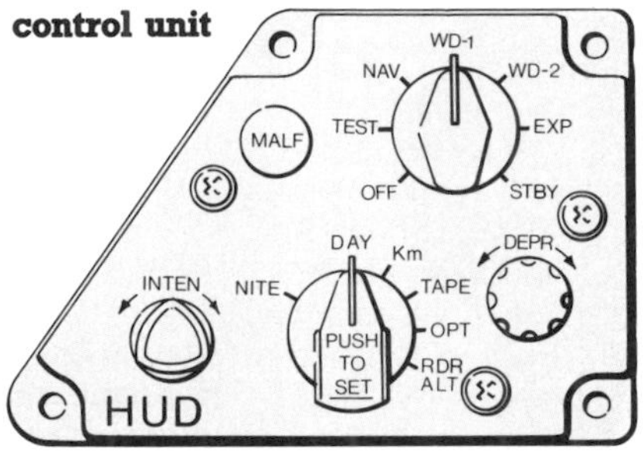

in the face of intense defences. As noted earlier, it does not possess many of the features which are standard on other light strike types, such as the F-16, Harrier and Jaguar. All these aircraft have some sort of weapon-aiming system which can measure the velocity of the aircraft relative to the ground and the distance to the target, compute the trajectory of whatever ordnance may be on board and indicate the precise moment to release the weapon. The A-10 has no means of measuring ground velocity, such as a high-accuracy inertial platform; it has no means of measuring range to the target and no weapons-release computer. Accurate attack with any weapon other than Maverick and the GAU-8/A is possible only in a steep, low-airspeed dive from medium altitude, a somewhat foolhardy tactic in the presence of SAMs or AAA.

It is not that the A-10 is deficient in its relative inability to use such weapons safely and effectively; just that it is a specialized aircraft, and is used as such. In the GAU-8/A and Maverick, it carries two proven and reliable precision-attack weapons which operate without complex aiming systems. The aircraft can dispense with them, and is thereby made more reliable and less costly.

Avionic systems

The original concept of the A-10 was for an aircraft that would be as devoid of avionics as the original Skyraider: no inertial navigation system, no complex displays, and no automatic flight control system or other pilot aids. It would be equipped with communications equipment, simple beacon-type navigation gear, and a straightforward head-up display with limited weapon-aiming symbology. While the A-10 is still closer to the Skyraider than any other aircraft in the USAF inventory, contact with reality has, as usual, changed plans to some extent.

The changing threat and the changing tactics needed to meet it have been the main motivations behind additions to the A-10's equipment list. More mobile missile systems, and the need to fly the entire mission at low altitude, are among them. The basic system has been little changed, though. The instrument panel facing the pilot is simple, with standard flight instruments and dual sets of gauges for the TF34 engines. To the pilot's right is the video display for the Maverick missile. The primary flight instrument is the Kaiser Electronics head-up display. This is a specially developed, uncomplicated unit which displays aircraft pitch and roll attitude, airspeed and altitude. Weapon-aiming systems on the initial production aircraft amounted to a fixed gunsight reticle on the HUD and the Maverick control panel.

The only addition to the weapon-aiming system to date is the Martin Marietta AAS-35 Pave Penny laser target-identification set, introduced to squadron use in early 1978. Pave Penny acts as a link between the attack aircraft and a forward air controller (FAC), who may be in a ground vehicle, a helicopter or an OV-10 reconnaissance aircraft. It is a low-cost, compact and lightweight device, 32in (81cm) long and weighing 32lb (14.5kg), which scans the area ahead of the aircraft for laser radiation. The FAC designates a target with his own laser equipment; Pave Penny picks up the reflection of the coded beam, and places a HUD symbol over the target. The A-10 pilot then takes over and attacks in the usual way. Pave Penny is carried on an unusual pylon mounting, attached to the starboard side of the forward fuselage; the usual nose installation is ruled out by the proximity of the gun muzzle with its associated shockwaves and vibration.

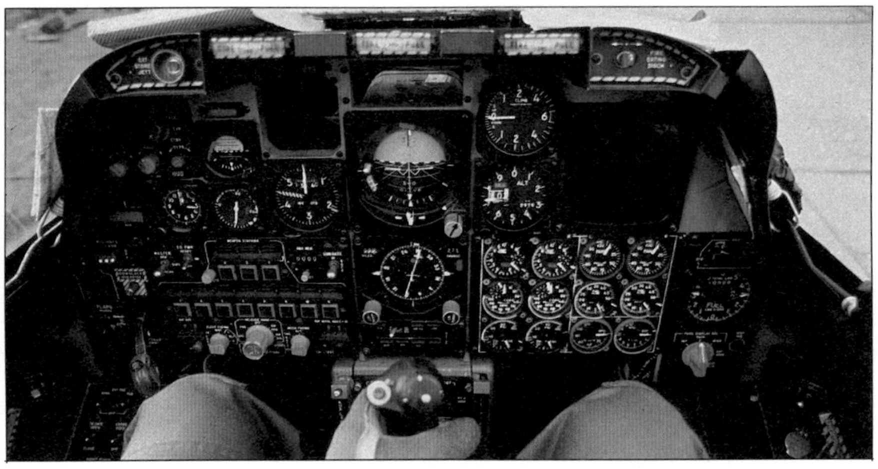

Above: The cockpit reflects the absence of sophisticated avionics, with standard flight instruments and the Maverick TV display to the right.

Defensive avionics on the first A-10s were confined to the Itek ALR-46 radar-warning receiver (RWR) system, a fairly simple piece of equipment with antennae built into the nose and tail of the aircraft. This has since been upgraded to the improved ALR-64 and ALR-69 models, to cope with the changing frequencies of Soviet air-defence radars. All the systems feed a simple plan-position indicator (PPI) scope in the cockpit, and show the bearing and approximate range of threatening radars. The system is most useful against the Shilka air-defence gun; the RWR shows the Shilka's position before the A-10 gets within range of its quad-barrelled 23mm cannon.

ECM protection

For active ECM protection in a high-threat environment, the A-10 normally carries a single Westinghouse ALQ-119 electronic countermeasures (ECM) pod on the outermost starboard pylon. The ALQ-119 has been superseded by the same company's ALQ-131 on later USAF aircraft such as the F-16. This is not to say that the older pod is ineffective or obsolete, but the newer system is effective against a wider range of threats, and can jam a greater number of frequencies.

The A-10 does, however, carry a very comprehensive internal decoy system, in the shape of the Tracor ALE-40. Built into formerly empty space in the landing gear pods and wingtips, the ALE-40 consists of 16 batteries of small tubes – 30 tubes to a battery – housing a total of 480 pyrotechnically-fired decoys. Some of these are flares, designed to lead an infra-red homing missile away from the A-10; the rest contain chaff, or thin strips of aluminium foil, and deploy into a loose cloud of metal after being ejected from the aircraft. Chaff is the oldest form of ECM, and under certain circumstances is still one of the most effective deception techniques and one of the hardest to counter. Decoys are a last-ditch defence

Typical head-up displays

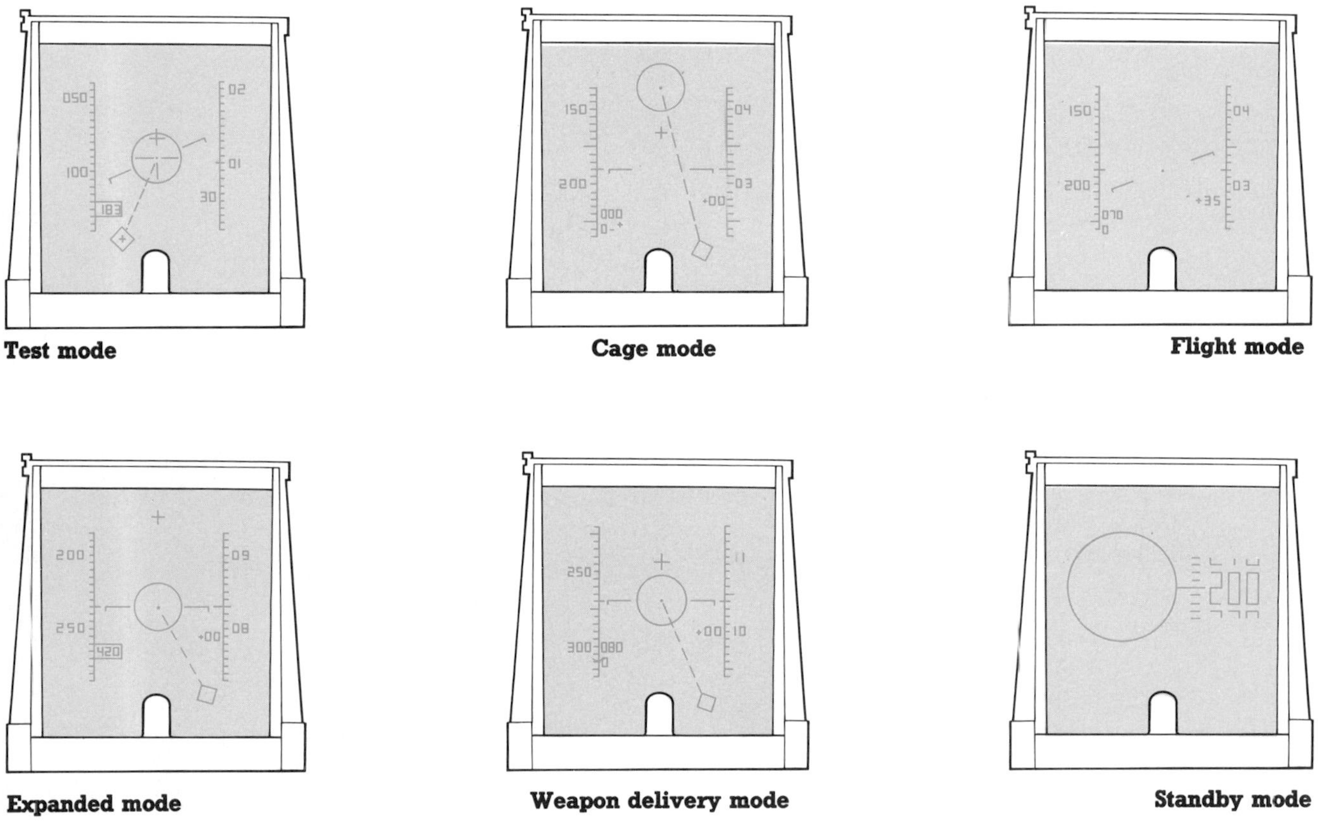

against missile attack; the pilot fires his decoys and simultaneously pulls a hard break, hoping that the missile's tendency to assume that the aircraft will continue in a straight path will lead it to follow the decoys rather than the real target.

Essentially, the USAF considers that tactics are more important than ECM to the close-support mission. This is why the A-10's equipment is relatively unsophisticated, and why the aircraft is not scheduled to receive the ALQ-165 advanced self-protection jammer (ASPJ), when it becomes available later in the 1980s. ECM is most necessary when an aircraft is exposed for long periods of time to the larger and more sophisticated missile systems: A-10 tactics are geared to avoiding such systems. Also, the A-10 is intended to carry the attack to close quarters, where large and complex systems are close to their minimum range and increasingly cumbersome. In brief, the A-10 is designed and used to need less help from sophisticated ECM than an F-16 or F-15.

Flight control and navigation

The A-10 has no automatic flight control system (AFCS), but is fitted with a stability augmentation system (SAS). The primary function of the SAS is to improve the stability of the aircraft as a weapons platform, and to make the aircraft respond more consistently to the controls; it is a simple, single-channel system and has been upgraded since the aircraft entered service. The SAS also provides warning of an excessive angle of attack, and impending stall, via a stick-shaker.

In one major respect, it was soon discovered, the philosophy of austerity had been taken too far: the A-10's lack of a built-in, autonomous navigation system. Like many features of the aircraft, this went back to the original A-X concept, and to US tactics of the late 1960s. The A-10 was expected to cruise to its loitering point at low-to-medium altitude, where the pilot would not have to follow terrain and Tacan beacons would provide necessary navigational data. But at low level Tacan is of limited use because its line-of-sight transmissions are usually blocked by terrain or the curvature of the earth. A-10 pilots in Europe found themselves navigating with 1/50,000-scale maps across their knees, while trying to avoid both the defences and the ground.

The solution was to add an inertial navigation system (INS) to the A-10. While some critics charged that installing INS ran counter to the basic philosophy of the A-10, there was nothing else to be done: in sustained low-level flight, the need to map-read pushed the pilot's workload to unacceptably high levels, while the need to pull up periodically to search for landmarks compromised the security of the formation.

A standard USAF INS, the ASN-141, was incorporated in the last 283 A-10s, starting in 1980, and the INS-equipped aircraft were first delivered to Europe, where the need was greatest. As production of new A-10s ran down, modification kits were produced for earlier aircraft; a contract covering the last batch of these was announced in April 1984, and the entire fleet is to be upgraded by mid-1987.

In the original A-10, the HUD gave the pilot basic flight information – speed, altitude and aircraft pitch and roll angle. The new system adds a wealth of data: vertical speed and flightpath (the angle at which the aircraft is climbing or diving), actual heading, the direction to steer to a pre-programmed waypoint or target location, and the distance and time to go to the next waypoint. Essentially, it relieves the pilot of the need to map-read and fly evasively at the same time. Navigation inputs can be made when convenient, and appear as clear directions on the HUD. The new equipment calls for little change to the cockpit; the HUD control unit is modified to control the new functions and an INS panel is added.

Because INS data would be projected on to the head-up display, Kaiser was made responsible for devising the INS installation. The chosen solution was to improve the HUD, and link it to the existing central air-data computer and the INS through a digital data-handling system or 'bus'. The existing HUD projection system is retained, but a completely new symbol generator of much greater power is installed. It is still fed with data from the conventional heading, attitude and reference system, but this pitch and roll information is used for back-up purposes only. The most important data is fed to the HUD through dual digital buses, designed to the USAF's MIL-STD-1553B standard.

Another improvement accompanies the introduction of INS. The A-10 was originally fitted with a conventional pressure altimeter, providing readings above sea level, but this was soon found to be inadequate on prolonged low-level flights over Europe's rolling hills. A standard APN-194 radar altimeter has re-

Pave Penny attack scenario

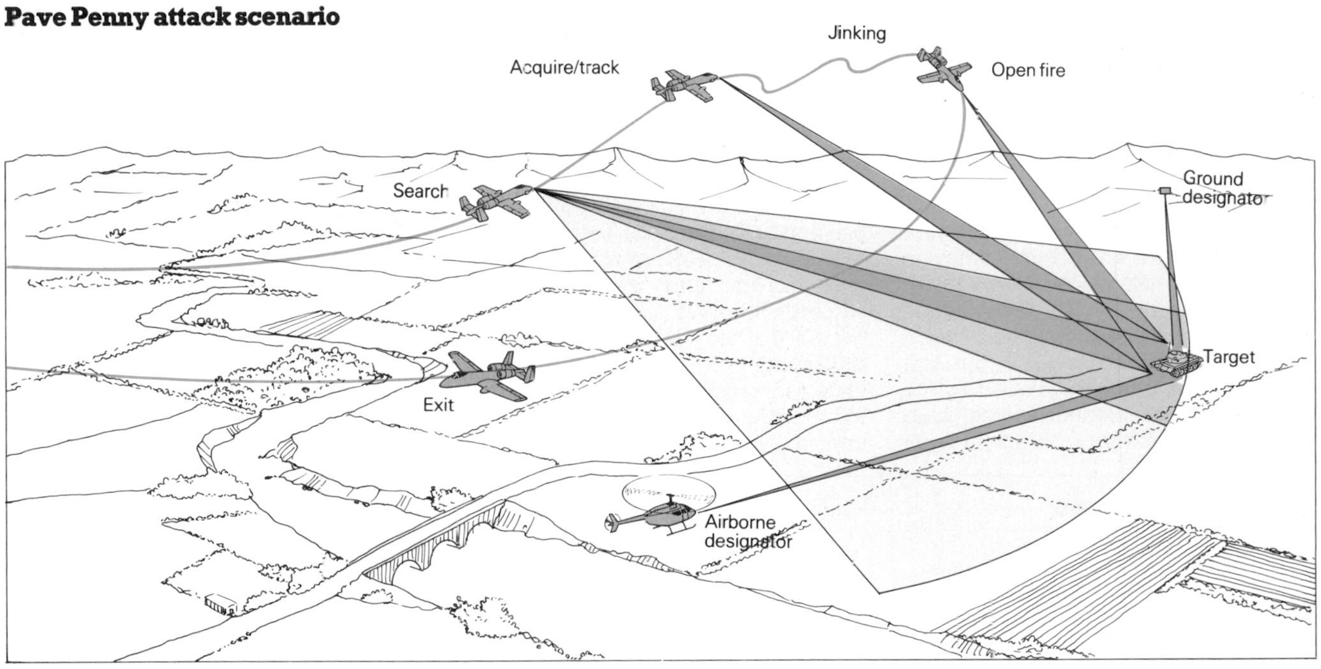

Above: the AAS-38 Pave Penny laser seeker pod allows the A-10 to acquire targets designated by forward air controllers, who may be airborne or with the troops on the ground. The pod detects the reflected radiation from the target and indicates it on the HUD, and the pilot then manoeuvres into position for a standard gun or Maverick attack.

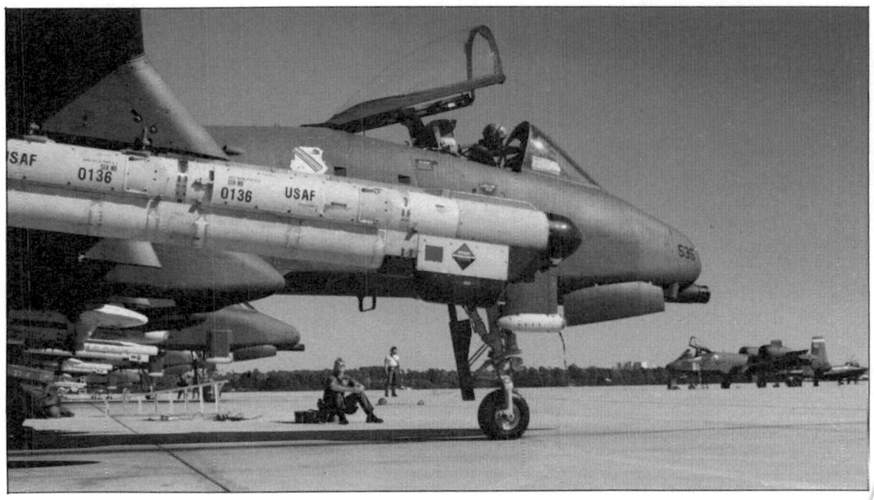

Right: External avionics pods on a 354th TFW A-10 at Myrtle Beach AFB. The Pave Penny is offset from the usual nose position to avoid the gun blast; the ALQ-119 jamming pod is normally carried on the outboard starboard wing pylon.

Above: A pair of 81st TFW A-10s, each carrying two Mavericks under each wing, and equipped with Pave Penny and ALQ-119 pods.

placed it on late-production and retrofitted A-10s.

Lantirn

The digital databus system may also provide the basis for a vast step forward in the A-10's operational capability: the introduction of the Lantirn (low-altitude navigation, and targeting by infra-red at night) night-attack system in the late 1980s. Lantirn, being developed by the USAF and Martin Marietta with the help of a team of major subcontractors, is an ambitious programme aimed at creating a single affordable, easily installed package which will give any of TAC's aircraft the ability to penetrate at low level, and find and strike precision targets, at night.

Lantirn has drawn some fire from critics, and its future is not completely assured. However, it is now an integral part of the very important F-15E dual-role fighter programme, and there is definitely increasing concern over the ability of Soviet armoured units to operate effectively at night. At present, only a few specialized TAC aircraft can operate outside daylight hours, and they are certainly too few in number to make much of an impact against a large-scale armoured assault. Lantirn is planned to make 700 more TAC aircraft capable of flying in terrain and weather cover at night, and carrying out precision attacks in clear air at night.

The Lantirn system consists of a set of highly miniaturized sensors and image-processing equipment, mounted in two external pods and feeding data via 1553B databuses to an advanced HUD. One pod handles navigation, and the other handles targeting. The navigation pod houses an advanced terrain-following radar (TFR) developed by Texas Instruments, together with a wide-angle forward-looking infra-red (Flir) system.

On a clear night, the pilot will fly at low level using a Flir image, superimposed on the real world by means of the HUD. The latter is planned to be a Marconi Avionics design, using holographic techniques; these are based on the diffraction of light, rather than reflection. A holographic HUD screen can be almost perfectly transparent to most light wavelengths, and be an almost perfect reflector of the wavelength chosen for HUD imagery. It is therefore possible to superimpose a detailed Flir image without obliterating the real world. It also differs from the normal HUD in that it can include the wide-angle picture needed for low-level navigation.

The Flir is useless, however, in cloud or rain. The TFR is needed to penetrate low cloud en route to the target and to let down through the weather when the cloudbase is low or unknown. It takes advantage of new processing techniques to allow higher rates of turn under

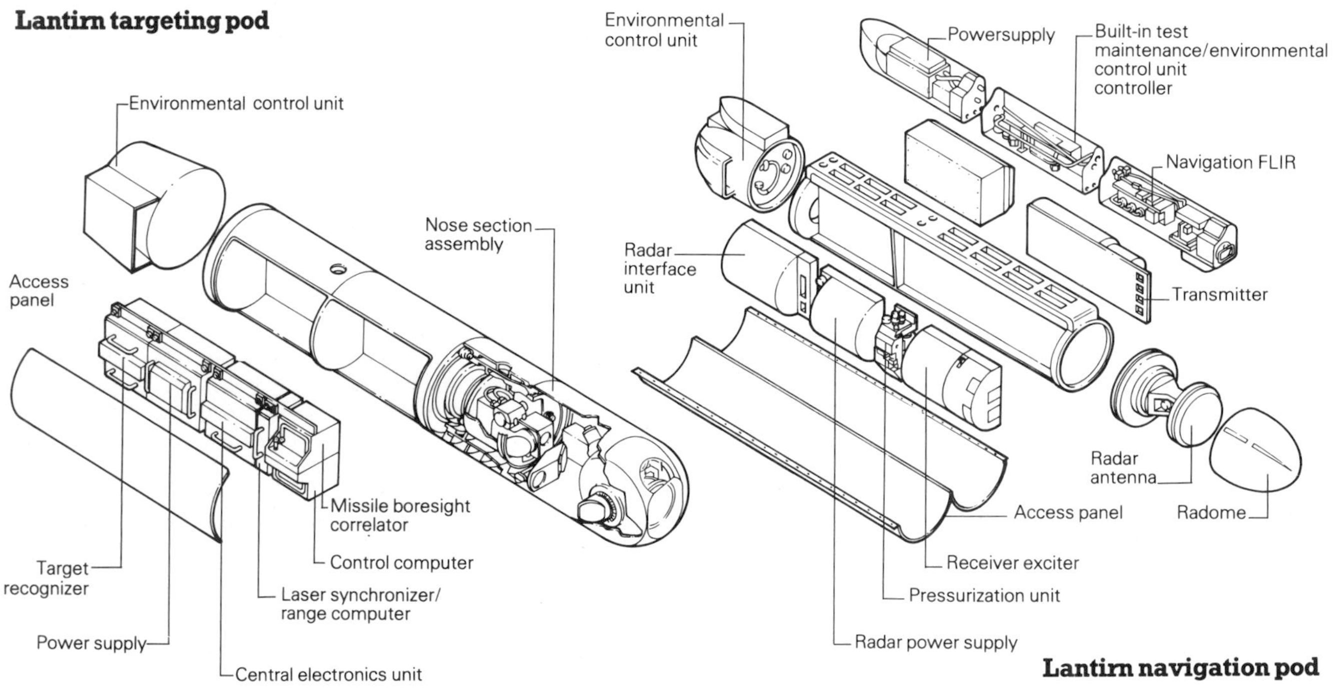

Left: The most important addition to the A-10's capabilities will come with the Lantirn night and all-weather navigation and targeting pods.

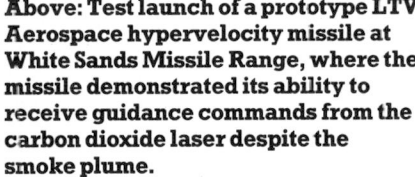

Above: Test launch of a prototype LTV Aerospace hypervelocity missile at White Sands Missile Range, where the missile demonstrated its ability to receive guidance commands from the carbon dioxide laser despite the smoke plume.

Right: Model of an A-10 with two hypervelocity missile (HVM) pods.

Hypervelocity missile pod installation

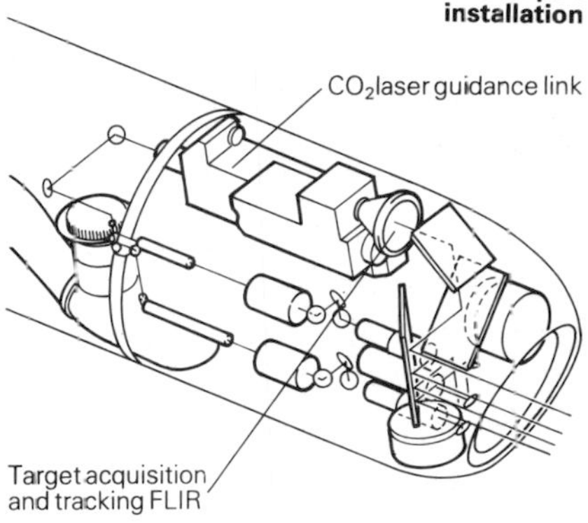

Fire control installation

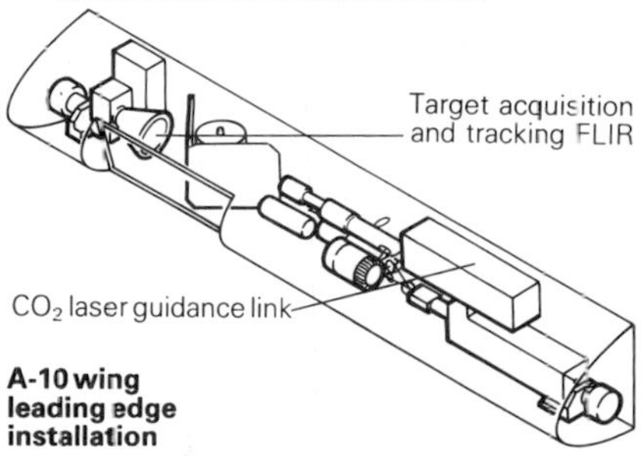

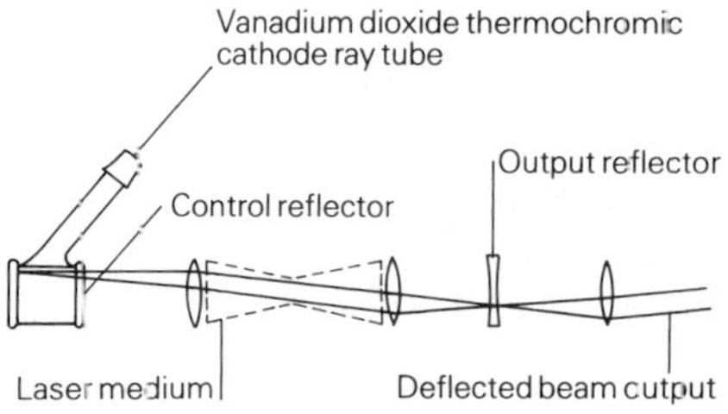

Electronically scanned laser radar sensor

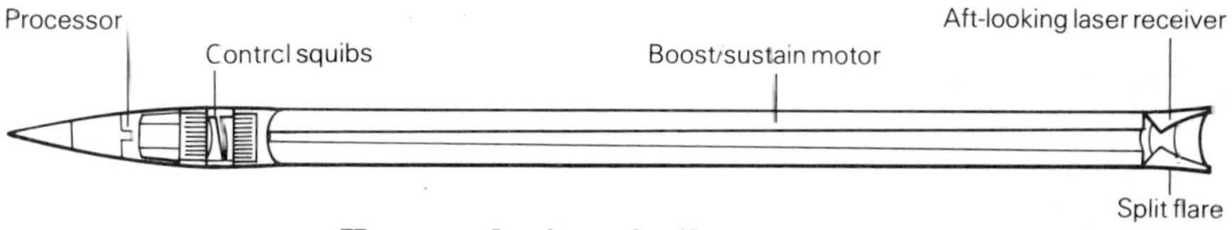

Hypervelocity missile

Right and above right: The components of the HVM system, which could provide a logical extension of the A-10's standard armoury: the high speed of the rocket will minimize exposure to defensive systems, and the single laser scanner can direct several missiles at once.

TFR control than was possible with earlier systems, and, in straight flight, to provide the maximum possible cover with the least possible transmission power and time, reducing the possibility of detection by hostile EW systems. The advanced HUD can display Flir imagery and TFR data simultaneously.

The targeting pod contains a narrow-angle Flir, feeding a 'telephoto' image to a head-down display in the cockpit, and a laser system which can act either as a rangefinder or a designator for laser-guided weapons. Spotting a target in the Flir image on the HUD, the pilot can bring the targeting pod's Flir to bear, and identify the target. He then has a number of options. Probably the most potent weapon for use with Lantirn is the IR Maverick. As noted earlier, the missile's seeker can be 'cued' on to the target by the aircraft systems, so the lock-on would be automatic and immediate. The pilot need only check that the missile has locked on, fire it and slew the targeting Flir to the next objective. Alternatively, he can use the laser system, either designating a target for a laser-guided bomb, or obtaining accurate range information for the release of a free-fall iron or cluster bomb.

Lantirn was launched into accelerated development in the late 1970s, but in September 1981 the pace of the programme was slowed down sharply, so as not to start production before the system had been thoroughly developed and tested. One of its more advanced features, an automatic target recogniser (ATR) intended to discriminate between MBTs, mobile SAMs and other armoured vehicles, was judged in 1983 to be too ambitious for near-term development, and has been 'uncoupled' from the rest of the programme; development of the elements outlined above was reported at that time to be proceeding according to plan. In mid-1984, prototype testing of the complete Lantirn system was under way aboard an F-16B at Edwards AFB, and this was due to continue until the end of the year. The current schedule calls for delivery of the first production Lantirn system in July 1987.

Of 720 Lantirn sets to be acquired by the USAF, 100 will be allotted to the A-10 force, according to plans in early 1984. The larger navigation pod will be carried on the starboard fuselage pylon, and the targeting pod will be slung beneath the port inboard wing. However, it is probably fair to say that the F-15E will enjoy top priority for Lantirn, followed by the F-16, with the A-10 bringing up the rear. In any event, the balance of the A-10 force will remain daytime-only aircraft in the foreseeable future.

Another improvement under consideration for the A-10 force is a ground proximity warning system (GPWS), similar in principle to the computerized alert system now fitted to most Western airliners and developed by Sundstrand, a world leader in GPWS. TAC issued the requirement after reviewing the A-10 accident record and discovering that a number of mishaps were due to high pilot workload or 'task saturation' – the latter being defined as concentrating on one task for more than five seconds. Scanning for targets, seeking firing opportunities and evading defences at low level, some pilots had simply flown into trees or the terrain.

A prototype GPWS was under test on an A-10 in early 1984. Like a civil GPWS, the system integrates airspeed, attitude and radar altimeter data and provides an electronically synthesized voice warning; however, the warning 'modes', or the envelopes within which the system will command or advise the pilot, are different. In low-level flight, the system will warn if the aircraft is below a preset altitude, and will also issue a 'roll out' command if the aircraft is low and the bank angle exceeds 45deg. The GPWS will also warn the pilot if the aircraft is too close to rising terrain – taking into account speed, the slope of the ground and the performance of the aircraft – and will order the pilot to abort an attack if he is in danger of hitting the ground.

Hypervelocity missile

Another proposed change for the A-10, not yet part of official planning, is its use as the first carrier for a new type of weapon, the hypervelocity missile (HVM) under development by Vought. As its name suggests, the HVM flies at extremely high speeds: almost 3,000kt (5,500km/h) or Mach 4.5. Because of this high speed, and the missile's accordingly short flight time, the launch aircraft can track the missile to impact without becoming vulnerable to defensive systems; costly, bulky fire-and-forget guidance systems are therefore unnecessary. The missile hits the target so fast – 50 per cent faster than the muzzle velocity of the GAU-8 – that the warhead can be eliminated as well, because a bundle of depleted-uranium or tungsten rods will destroy any conceivable armour.

The guidance system tested by Vought in 1983 consisted of a laser beam scanning a raster pattern (like the electron gun in the TV tube). The missile's electronics sense its position in the raster, and steer it towards the centre; control of the projectile is carried out by firing small explosive squibs through ports in its side. However, the missile itself is spin-stabilised and automatically guided to maintain its trajectory. Its speed renders target movement relatively insignificant, so it needs no more than the occasional mid-course update on the way to its target. Because of this feature, the single laser scanner can direct several missiles simultaneously on to different targets.

Vought estimates that a tank-killing HVM weighing less than 80lb (36.3kg) would have a range of 3 miles (4.8km), several times that of the GAU-8/A. On the A-10, an HVM system would use Lantirn or a similar device for targeting, and the HVM guidance system could be built into the wing leading edge. Two underwing pods would each accommodate 19 HVMs. With its explosive control system the HVM has no moving parts, and the cost of each round was estimated at $5,000 in 1981. The missile and guidance system were demonstrated in 1983, and Vought has proposed a two-year prototype programme leading to live firings from an A-10. By April 1984, however, funding for such an effort had not been obtained. But it would be a suitable first for the A-10, sustaining its position as the most lethally armed of all tactical aircraft.

Deployment

Almost every tactical command in the US Air Force has an A-10 unit on strength, and the biggest of all is the 108-aircraft 'superwing' assigned to the critical European theatre. Reserve and Air National Guard units also use the A-10. However, the USAF bought no more A-10s than it had originally planned, and acquired only the basic single-seat A-10A version. Fairchild's efforts to sell a two-seat night-capable version to the USAF went unrewarded, and neither did the type find export customers, who preferred the more glamorous supersonic fighters. The last A-10 was delivered to the USAF early in 1984.

Above: Checking the gun on a Warthog of the 23rd TFW at England AFB, Louisiana. The original 23rd Tactical Fighter Group was formed in China in 1942, and the present unit perpetuates the nose markings of the American Volunteer Group.

As a rule, unless things go badly wrong, the USAF buys more of every type of aircraft than it originally planned. As the end of planned production approaches a number of factors conspire to keep the line open. The aircraft is cheap to buy, compared with new types: newer aircraft are seldom ready as soon as had been envisaged, and there may be gaps in the front line to fill. New versions of the type may have been developed to carry out different missions, expanding the service's requirement.

At the same time, US combat aircraft nearly always find export markets. While US aircraft manufacturers often bewail the advantageous terms offered by foreign competitors in the commercial aircraft market, they are less vocal about the excellent credit facilities provided to their military customers through the Pentagon's FMS (foreign military sales) organization.

The A-10 has been an exception. Production ceased in 1984 after the exact quantity planned had been delivered. The last aircraft off the line was the same subtype as the first – in this respect, the A-10 was unique among US combat aircraft. Nor have any A-10s been sold for export. A disappointing outcome for Fairchild, this has been no fault of the aircraft or those who developed it; the programme has been trouble-free, and what cost overruns did occur were due to outside circumstances such as production-rate cutbacks and inflation. The aircraft does exactly what it was designed to do, and does it well.

The A-10's real problem came from outside the programme; it was fast, it was manoeuvrable, it was everything that a fighter should be, and it was called the F-16. It did not even exist, except as General Dynamics' Model 401 design study, when the USAF ordered the YA-10A prototypes, and it was a year away from its first flight when the A-10 was selected for production. At that time, in early 1973, the YF-16/YF-17 fly-off was not expected to lead to a production programme. Within just over a year, the two types were competing for a massive USAF order. The change had come about under pressure from Secretary of Defense James Schlesinger, and was motivated by two factors: concern over the cost of replacing all the USAF's fighters with the costly and sophisticated F-15, and the prospect of securing a massive order from Europe. The latter could, and did, assure US dominance of the international fighter scene for a decade or more.

The F-16 emerged victorious in the fly-off, and won the European order. It was not intended as a substitute for the A-10, but as a running-mate for the F-15; however, the simple laws of manufacturing economics put the GD and Fairchild aircraft in a kind of competition. Like any manufactured object, aircraft are cheaper if built in the largest possible quantities. Moreover, the graph of unit cost versus production rate is not a straight line, but a curve, and the price for each aircraft increases very rapidly at low rates. In the second half of the 1970s the USAF was in the middle of a post-Vietnam budgetary squeeze. There was simply not enough money available to buy three types of fighter – F-15s, F-16s and A-10s – at economical production rates. If the USAF continued indefinitely to buy all three types at the low rates it could afford, it would get far fewer aircraft at much higher prices.

Losing to the F-16

The F-15 was sacrosanct. The Air Force wanted, and still wants, as many F-15s as possible from every year's budget. Between the A-10 and the F-16 there was very little room for choice. Four NATO allies were committed to the F-16, and if the USAF was to stop after buying, say, 650 aircraft, they would be faced with a massive price increase for any future batches of F-16s. The Europeans were relying on USAF partnership in upgrading and improving the aircraft. Neither should it be forgotten that TAC, more than any other air command in the world, is a fighter pilot's service, and as a result has a built-in aversion to an aircraft that cannot chase MiGs.

The F-16 was also a dual-role fighter/strike aircraft, a concept which had been poison when the A-10/F-15 requirements were drafted, but which was now returning to favour thanks to economic pressure and new technology. Improved radar, better HUDs and accurate INS were making it possible for a relatively simple fighter to deliver ordnance with acceptable accuracy. There was no clear point at which the USAF decided to stop the A-10 programme; all purchases are negotiated independently, year by year. By the late 1970s, however, it was

Above: An 81st TFW A-10 ready for collection alongside a Virginia ANG F-105. The pilots of the 91st collected new Warthogs as their old ones fell due for maintenance.

Below: An 81st TFW pilot prepares for a mission during a Reforger '82 exercise. Despite the addition of an inertial system, maps are still important for visual navigation.

becoming increasingly clear that the USAF would stop production of the A-10 after buying the 700+ aircraft which had been set as the necessary force level to handle a strictly defined CAS mission. All other air-to-ground tasks would be handled by the dual-purpose F-16.

The A-10's technical and operational success helped to bring production to a close. This sounds paradoxical, but consider the cumulative impact of the following facts. At any time, the USAF's frontline A-10s have a mission-capable rate around 75 per cent – that is to say, three-quarters of the aircraft in the squadrons are fit to fly under wartime conditions. Despite being used almost exclusively in low-altitude, visual close-support missions, the A-10 has one of the lowest accident rates of any USAF fighter in history. It can be turned round between missions faster than any other USAF aircraft, and it can sustain operations from dispersed locations close to the front; for these reasons, it can sustain the kind of sortie rates which other aircraft only reach in an all-out surge. Lastly, its toughness, simplicity and ease of repair give the operating units a unique capability to 're-generate' after taking hits in action. Unfortunately for Fairchild, the foregoing adds up to one conclusion: a few A-10s go a long way.

Deliveries of the A-10 to operational units began in March 1977, a few months after the first aircraft had reached the designated training wing. As is normal practice, a unit based in the continental USA (CONUS) was assigned the first aircraft: the 354th Tactical Fighter Wing (TFW) at Myrtle Beach AFB, South Carolina. One reason for the choice of base was its proximity to a large gunnery test and training range. The first of its squadrons to be declared fully operational was the 356th Tactical Fighter Squadron (TFS), in October 1977.

Deployment proceeded steadily rather than rapidly, because the production decision had been delayed until flight tests were well advanced, and Congress had repeatedly reduced the number of A-10s to be bought each year. By mid-1977 the USAF still had only 55 A-10s, divided among the 354th TFW at Myrtle Beach, the designated training organisation – the 355th Tactical Fighter Training Wing (TFTW) at Davis-Monthan AFB, Arizona – and the 57th Tactical Training Wing at Nellis AFB, which was tasked with developing A-10 tactics.

From 1977, however, USAF priority was to field the A-10 in Europe. In August six A-10s of the 355th TFTW flew to Sembach, West Germany, to participate in the Autumn Forge series of exercises. Together with the JAWS tests carried out in late 1977, this experimental deployment provided a great deal of information on the best way to use the A-10 against typical Warsaw pact targets in European weather.

Left: Although based in England, the 81st regularly deploys to Germany for training: one of the wing's aircraft waits for takeoff clearance at a dispersal point during Reforger '82.

81st TFW

In February 1978 the USAF announced that the 81st TFW, based at RAF Bentwaters/Woodbridge (the two bases are so close together that, administratively, they are a single unit) and equipped with F-4C and F-4D Phantoms, would use the A-10 in Europe. Instead of deploying two wings, as had been planned, the 81st would be expanded into a 'superwing' with six 18-aircraft operating squadrons instead of the usual four. From early 1978, the main thrust of USAF A-10 activity was to get the 81st operational as soon as possible. The 355th TFTW took a leading role in the programme, using experience gained in the European tests and JAWS trials, and processing pilots and new aircraft – the 81st was to receive only factory-fresh A-10s to the latest build standard – at Davis-Monthan.

Pilots for the 81st TFW were drawn from four groups, in roughly equal numbers: new graduates from T-38 training; T-38 instructor pilots, ready for their first operational wing; the 81st's own F-4D pilots, with European experience; and pilots returning to flight status from other assignments. The balance worked well: the F-4 pilots and the last-mentioned group included a great deal of combat support and FAC experience, but the unit was not so loaded with experience that the younger pilots would be denied any chance of leadership.

The first squadron to complete training was the 92nd TFS, which ferried its 18 aircraft to Bentwaters on January 25, 1979. Thanks to specialized training by the 355th TFTW, with the help of senior 81st TFW personnel, the 92nd was considered mission-ready as soon as it arrived. By late 1979 four squadrons were operational and two forward operating locations (FOLs) had been activated, at Sembach and Ahlhorn. The remaining two squadrons arrived at Bentwaters by mid-1980, and the two remaining FOLs became operational.

The 81st continued to be the priority A-10 unit. As its aircraft became due for major maintenance, the pilots would ferry them back to the Air Logistics Center at McClellan AFB, Sacramento, the centre of all A-10 overhaul and modification, and then travel to Hagerstown and pick up a factory-fresh replacement for the squadron. In this way the 81st became the first unit to have INS and other important features on all its aircraft.

Right: The shark's mouth nose markings made famous by the American Volunteer Group in China were adopted by the 23rd TFG that replaced it, and are still used by the 23rd TFW, one of only two A-10 combat wings based in the continental United States. The 23rd and 354th TFWs, along with the rest of TAC's combat wings, constitute the USAF's ready reserve element.

Tactical Air Command has added only one CONUS-based A-10 unit since 1978 – the 23rd TFW at England AFB, Louisiana. Together with the 354th TFW, still at Myrtle Beach, the 23rd is assigned to TAC's primary role of rapid reinforcement worldwide. The 355th TTW is still at Davis-Monthan, and conducts all basic A-10 training for the USAF. Completing the regular USAF A-10 force are three independent squadrons: one at Nellis AFB, one in Korea and one in Alaska.

AFRES and ANG

The balance of the A-10 force in CONUS is assigned to the US Air Force Reserve (AFRES), with four squadrons, and the Air National Guard (ANG) with five. With its moderate maintenance requirements, the A-10 is a logical choice for these forces. Both are manned by part-time volunteers and operate in a similar way, training on a regular schedule and participating in frequent exercises and other operations with regular USAF units. ANG and AFRES A-10 units are assigned to reinforce the 81st TFW in Europe in time of need, and deploy to Europe as often as budgets permit. Additionally, the 81st regularly exchanges pilots with the part-time units; the AFRES/ANG pilots directly involved gain experience in Europe, the pilots at the home bases gain by contact with the European-trained 81st TFW pilots, and the programme also gives the 81st TFW pilots the chance to take part in major exercises such as Red Flag.

The USAF had planned to acquire some 750 A-10As, and production reached a peak rate of 13 aircraft a month in 1980. However, Congressional budget cuts in 1982 reduced the service's production orders to 707 aircraft, excluding the two non-standard YA-10A prototypes and the six development aircraft. Fairchild completed its last contract for A-10As in February 1984.

The end of production came about despite efforts to expand the A-10 market. Fairchild leased an A-10 from the USAF in September 1976, to make the type's first appearance outside the USA at the Farnborough Air Show. An appearance at the Paris show in the following year ended disastrously on the opening day, when the A-10 failed to complete a loop under a low cloudbase and crashed, killing its pilot. But the USAF itself had not yet devised satisfactory tactics for the A-10, and although professional observers were impressed by the power of the GAU-8/A, little serious interest was forthcoming.

Above: The 118th TFS, 103rd TFG, Connecticut ANG, based at Bradley Field, is one of five Air National Guard squadrons equipped with the A-10.

Right: The USAF's other part-time volunteer element, the Air Force Reserve, has one training and four regular A-10 squadrons: the distinctive Warthog nose marking is the trademark of the 917th TFG.

Two-seat A-10s

The longest and most costly campaign was aimed at developing the A-10 into a specialized night/adverse weather (N/AW) attack aircraft. While the USAF had no stated requirement for such an aircraft, there was enough interest to persuade Fairchild that a full-scale demonstration programme would be worthwhile. In late 1977 the company began to discuss such a programme with the USAF and avionics suppliers, and work started in April 1978, supported by USAF research and development money, Fairchild company funds and contributions of time and materiel from interested avionics suppliers.

The demonstrator was based on the first of the A-10 development aircraft, and the modification took only 13 months, the N/AW aircraft making its first flight on May 4, 1979. Provision for a second seat had been made in the original design: the second cockpit occupied the space above the ammunition drum, displacing a few avionics boxes, which were relocated in the fairing behind the canopy. The fins were increased in height by 20in (51cm) to compensate for the extra side area, but the airframe was otherwise unchanged. The two-seater could be flown from either cockpit, with the elevated rear seat and back-up flight controls.

The most important feature of the aircraft, though, was a pair of pods housing a suite of avionic subsystems. Assembled from proven and available components, these were designed to allow precision attacks at night, en route navigation in weather at low level and, to some extent, precision attacks in adverse weather.

Equipment on the N/AW demonstrator included a modified Westinghouse WX-50 radar in an underwing pod. Based on a standard weather radar, it was modified to act as a short-range, multi-mode navigation and attack radar. It had three functions: simple mapping, terrain-avoidance and attack, and as an attack radar it was capable of picking out small moving targets on the ground. The second pod, on the centreline pylon, contained a Texas Instruments AAR-42 Flir and a Ferranti 105 laser designator, on a single mounting which could be steered to search for targets. A forward-looking low-light TV system was mounted in place of the Pave Penny sensor, and a Litton LN-39 inertial navigation system completed the suite. The avionics fed a modified Kaiser A-10 HUD and a pair of cathode-ray-tube (CRT) displays in the rear cockpit.

The system was much simpler than that on a fast-mover night strike aircraft such as the F-111, because it was not automatic; with only half the speed, it did not need to be. And because it was not directly controlling the aircraft, the navigation/attack system did not have to be designed to be fully operational after a major failure, the single biggest complicating factor in the F-111 systems. The pilot flew the aircraft at all times, with the help of terrain-following radar (TFR) and Flir data, superimposed on the HUD to give a single picture with limited depth cues. The back-seat weapons system operator (WSO) would use the INS for en route navigation, and could use the Flir to search for targets to either side of the track; in that case, the pilot would use LLTV in place of Flir.

The WSO would operate guided weapons, and the pilot would carry out gun attacks. The concept of the two-seat aircraft was that the WSO would search for a second target as the pilot attacked

the first. The WSO would enter its exact coordinates on the INS, and the pilot would follow INS instructions for an accurate, first-pass attack. The laser would be used for accurate ranging and to designate targets for laser-guided bomb attacks.

The demonstrator was extensively evaluated during 1979-82, and just under 300 hours of testing proved that precision night attack was possible with the simple sensor fit. Fairchild proposed a production version, with the Flir and radar built into the landing gear pods, and the laser and LLTV installations buried in the wing leading edge. Avionics integration would have been more refined than on the 'breadboard' prototype. The N/AW aircraft would also have had a cleaner one-piece windshield and a single clamshell canopy, and the rear cockpit would have been protected by alloy/titanium/nylon side panels.

Night attack options

The N/AW A-10 would have cost $1.5 million more than the standard A-10A, and in 1979 Fairchild was offering new-built aircraft for delivery in early 1983. In retrospect, it is clear that this would have provided the USAF with a versatile nocturnal interdiction type much more quickly than any other programme. Fairchild also offered a number of cheaper options based on the demonstrator programme. One of these was a single-seat night attack (SSNA) configuration, with underwing Flir/laser and radar pods, as on the demonstrator, modified HUD and two head-down multifunction CRTs. There was also an 'austere' SSNA version with no radar, but with Flir/laser pod and INS for night attack on targets of known location and an austere two-seater.

Unfortunately, all these A-10 variants were designed to do the same job as Lantirn, which was still scheduled to be available before 1985. Lantirn promised a great many advantages. Its high-technology features, such as its automatic target recognition system and advanced HUD, would provide all the performance of the fully-equipped two-seater, through a simple modification of the single-seat aircraft; one of the USAF's biggest reservations about the N/AW programme was that the WSO represented superfluous weight and cost on daytime missions and in some night operations in clear air. Lantirn, too, could be applied to the F-16 and F-15 as well as to the A-10.

Most of the USAF's testing of the de-

Left: Four A-10s of the 917th TFG, based at Barksdale AFB, Louisiana, participating in AFRES Aerials exercises over Texas.

N/AW mission profile

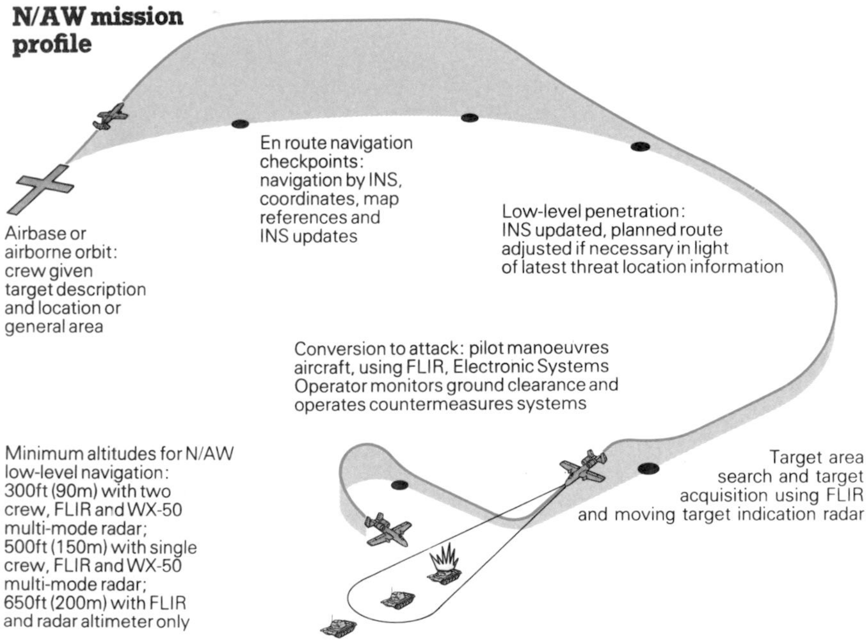
En route navigation checkpoints: navigation by INS, coordinates, map references and INS updates
Airbase or airborne orbit: crew given target description and location or general area
Low-level penetration: INS updated, planned route adjusted if necessary in light of latest threat location information
Conversion to attack: pilot manoeuvres aircraft, using FLIR, Electronic Systems Operator monitors ground clearance and operates countermeasures systems
Minimum altitudes for N/AW low-level navigation: 300ft (90m) with two crew, FLIR and WX-50 multi-mode radar; 500ft (150m) with single crew, FLIR and WX-50 multi-mode radar; 650ft (200m) with FLIR and radar altimeter only
Target area search and target acquisition using FLIR and moving target indication radar

Single-seat N/AW cockpit

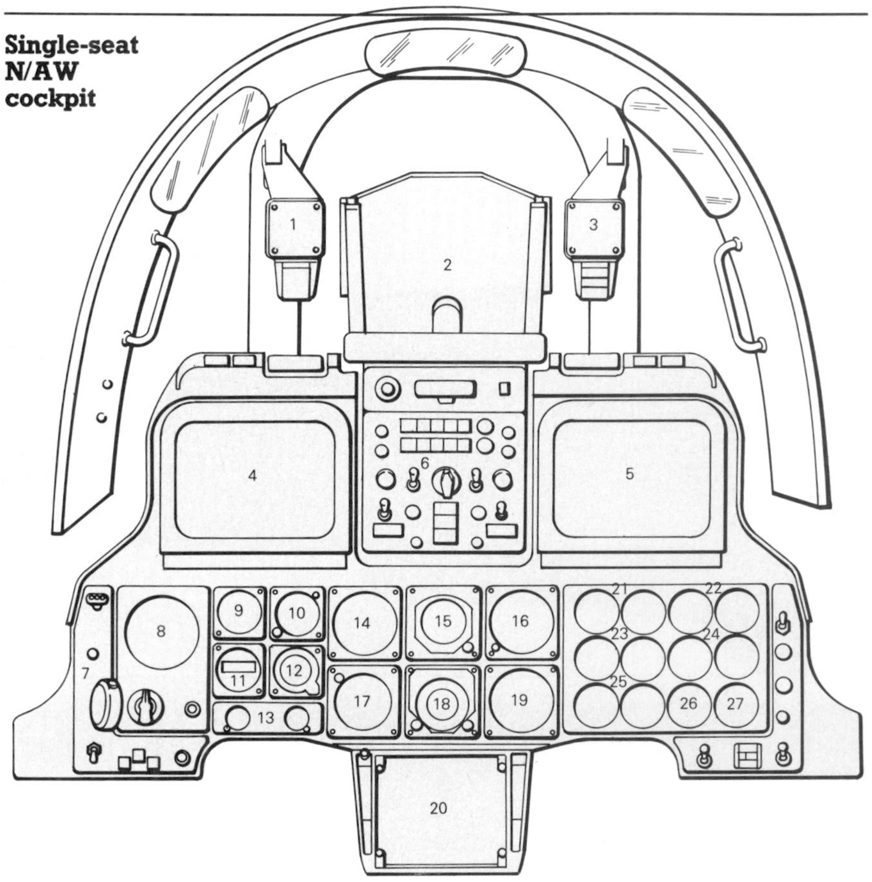

The cockpit proposed by Fairchild for the radar-equipped single-seat night attack A-10 would have allowed both fixed and moving targets to be attacked at night in low to moderate threat areas; an austere version without radar was also offered, as well as the two-seater.

1 Acceleration indicator
2 Head-up display
3 Standby compass
4 Left multifunction display
5 Right multifunction display
6 Display controls
7 Landing controls
8 Fuel quantity indicator
9 Angle of attack indicator
10 Clock
11 Channel frequency indicator
12 Standby attitude indicator
13 Hydraulics systems indicators
14 Airspeed indicator
15 Attitude director indicator
16 Barometric altitude indicator
17 Radar warning receiver azimuth indicator
18 Horizontal situation indicator
19 Vertical velocity indicator
20 Armament control panel
21 Engine temperature indicators
22 Engine fan RPM indicators
23 Engine core RPM indicators
24 Engine fuel flow indicators
25 Engine oil pressure indicators
26 Auxiliary power unit RPM indicator
27 Auxiliary power unit temperature indicator

Top: The two-seat night/adverse weather A-10 conversion prepares for a night takeoff with FLIR/laser pod under the fuselage and WX-50 radar pod under the port wing.

Above: Typical mission profile for a night/adverse weather attack in the A-10, with the avionics pods facilitating penetration, target acquisition and attack.

monstrator was dedicated to proving the service's contention that such a type could be operated successfully by a single pilot, as would be the case with Lantirn. It was not until late 1981 that the DoD decided to delay production of Lantirn until the basic principles had been proven, and by that time the opportunity for the all-weather two-seat A-10 had passed. The USAF did order 30 two-seat A-10Bs in 1981, but these were to have been combat trainers with standard cockpits. They would have been used by AFRES and ANG units, but Congress cancelled funding for these aircraft and no A-10Bs were built. Fairchild did try to find export markets for the A-10 – such as Morocco, the target of extensive presentations – but the type was hampered by specialization; with fighter unit costs climbing towards $20 million, few potential customers could afford economically sized fleets unless they standardized on a single type. The A-10's inability to take on the air-to-air role was apparent, while its sleek supersonic competitors could, at least, make an impressive show of putting bombs or A-model Mavericks on to simulated targets.

Soviet counterpart

The development of an equivalent type in the Soviet Union should have spurred some interest, but the East seems to have reflected Western ambivalence towards a specialized, subsonic close-support aircraft. The existence of such a type was reported in mid-1977; it had been observed on test at Ramenskoye, near Moscow, and was assigned the provisional codename of RAM-J. Little more was heard of the aircraft until mid-1982, when a small trials unit of Sukhoi Su-25s, allotted the NATO reporting name of Frogfoot, was deployed to Shindand, Afghanistan.

The Su-25 was originally hailed as a copy of the A-10, but analysis has suggested that it is a faster aircraft, powered by pure turbojet engines such as the Tumansky R-11. The aerodynamic configuration is more like that of the YA-9A, with fuselage-mounted engines; in detail, the aircraft looks not unlike a Sepecat Jaguar modified with a straight wing. The Su-25 is somewhat smaller than the A-10, and has equal or slightly greater installed power, and its engines are more efficient at higher speeds. It may be considered as a replacement for fast-

Right: The first of the development batch of A-10s was converted to the two-seat configuration, making its first flight in May 1979. Although the extended capabilities of the N/AW version were impressive, the Air Force expected Lantirn to enable one man to do the job, and the A-10B made no further progress. The production version would have had the avionics incorporated in the landing gear pods and wing leading edge.

Above and below: The N/AW A-10 was tested for nearly 300 hours between 1979 and 1982, successfully demonstrating its ability to carry out precision attacks at night.

Right: The Su-25 Frogfoot was originally thought to be a copy of the A-10, but is now believed to be a pure-turbojet fast-mover strike aircraft in the Su-20 class.

Sukhoi Su-25 Frogfoot

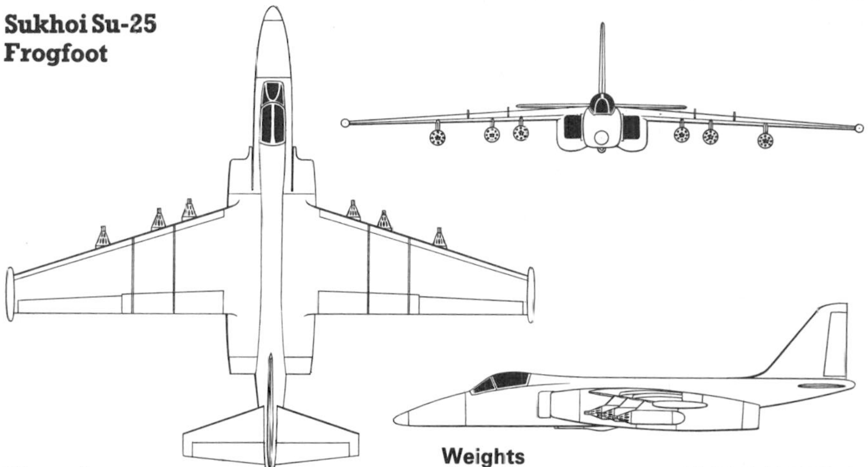

Dimensions	
Wing span	49ft 3in (15m)
Length overall	45ft 10in (14m)
Wing area	505sq ft ($37.6m^2$)

Powerplants	
	Two Tumansky R-13
Thrust (each)	11,240lb (50kN)

Weights	
Operating empty	21,000lb (9,500kg)
Maximum takeoff	42,000lb (19,000kg)
External load	9,000lb (4,000kg)

Performance	
Max speed at sea level	500kt (915km/h)
Max speed with stores	475kt (880km/h)
Combat radius	300nm (555km)

mover strike aircraft such as the Su-20 series. Despite its much lower absolute maximum speed, Frogfoot would have a comparable maximum speed with an external weapons load, because it would need less external fuel. Its cruising speed might even be faster under some circumstances, thanks to its high unreheated thrust.

Frogfoot undoubtedly carries some form of internal gun, but the overall size of the aircraft suggests that it is unlikely to be a weapon in the class of the GAU-8/A. New tactical ASMs developed by the Soviet Union could form the main armament of the type, but in Afghanistan it has been armed with conventional free-fall cluster weapons. Interestingly, the Afghan-based Frogfoots have been observed practising joint tactics with Mi-24 Hind attack helicopters, just as A-10s practise with US Army gunships.

By late 1983, however, there was no positive indication that the Su-25 was to be adopted as a standard service type, even though it had been flying for six years, and it was not reported in Eastern Europe until mid-1984. It may be that the type has been delayed while its design bureau worked on completing development of the Su-24 Fencer; alternatively, the unexpected success of the Mi-24 Hind may have overtaken it. The Mi-24, according to most accounts, is used in much the same way as a conventional attack aircraft.

Export attempt

The last battle to save the A-10 was mounted in 1982-83, when the type was proposed to several nations as a multi-role 'flying artillery' system, useful against many targets other than tanks. Following the Falklands war, Fairchild pushed the use of the A-10 as a maritime strike aircraft, particularly in areas such as South-East Asia. Equipped with the WX-50 radar, already tested on the N/AW demonstrator, and exploiting its long endurance, the A-10 could have proved a useful maritime strike weapon, carrying missiles such as Harpoon or Exocet. Air battles in the Falklands and Middle East, too, had shown the effectiveness of the new 'point-and-shoot' AIM-9L missile, and Fairchild's simulations demonstrated that the A-10 would defeat most opponents if armed with a weapon in that class.

At the 1983 Paris Air Show, Fairchild salesmen did their best to sound optimistic. Three customers, two in the Middle East and one in South-East Asia, were leading candidates for A-10 sales. The type was seen as a useful complement to an interceptor such as the F-5E, and Fairchild expected to sell 70-80 aircraft in 1983-85. At the same time, in Washington, the company and its Congressional friends were making a final and unsuccessful attempt to reverse the 1982 production cutback and keep the line open until export orders could be secured.

One Fairchild man at Paris gave a penetrating analysis of the factors favouring and hampering his company's sales efforts. "Essentially, our competitors are fighters which could cost twice as much as an A-10," he told Dave Griffiths of the US publication *Defense Week*, but went on to define what was probably the A-10's biggest negative in the export market: "Of course, a Mach 2 plane is sexier, and some pilots may think hitting ground targets is a grunt's job." Even more accurately, the executive added: "If there were any armies in the world that had their own tactical aviation, they'd love the A-10." Unhappily for Fairchild, and, perhaps, unhappily for the 'grunt' in the field, soldiers seldom if ever have any say in buying fighters.

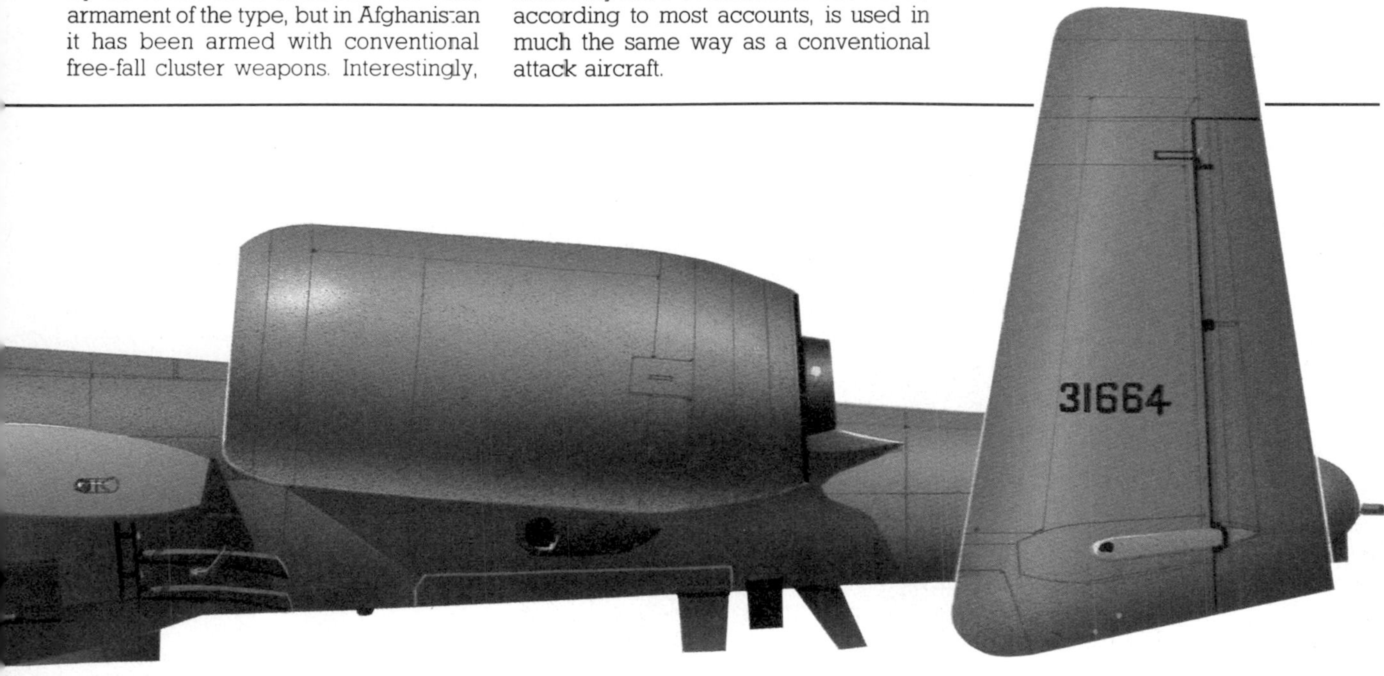

Performance and Tactics

Above: **Although ostensibly lacking in glamour, the A-10 mission is one of the most demanding in the USAF – and one of the most sought-after by pilots.**

A-10 tactics have been constantly revised and improved to meet a changing threat, and are tailored to the unique slow-flying, quick-turning performance of the aircraft. Originally intended to loiter at medium altitudes until required, A-10s now operate at extremely low altitude to counter defensive weapons, and can fly and fight effectively under low cloud and in poor visibility. The A-10 can sustain operations from austerely equipped forward bases, and can even 'ground loiter' on a good stretch of road. The A-10 complements the US Army's attack helicopter force in action against advancing armour, and unique coordinated tactics have been developed to make the best use of all resources.

January 25, 1979, was an English winter day like most others. There was a penetratingly damp chill in the air, and the overcast hung over RAF Bentwaters like an inverted bowl of frozen porridge. It was on this uncompromisingly European day that the A-10A arrived in Europe as an operational fighting aircraft.

It is not considered gentlemanly to cast aspersions upon an ally's newest weapon system, but concern over the effectiveness of the A-10 in Europe had reached very high levels in the NATO command structure. The USAF A-10s would replace McDonnell Douglas F-4C/D Phantoms. These were not the newest types in service, and were certainly not designed for blind precision attacks, but they had two seats, inertial navigation systems and secondary air-defence capability, and the back-seater was available to operate the whole range of first-generation targeting pods and guided weapons.

All NATO's senior air officers had seen films of A-10s delivering deadly, accurate anti-tank attacks from the gin-clear skies of Nevada, and most of them were not convinced that the same effect could be achieved in Europe, which is dark for 19 hours of the day in winter and overcast more often than not. The same officers had been briefed on the A-10's ability to withstand multiple hits from 23mm shells; they were also well aware of the existence of the Soviet SA-8 Gecko missile system, which had made its public debut in 1975. Generally, the feeling was that the European air forces had managed to prevent the USAF from fielding the F-16 in a form ideally suited to a central front in Vietnam or, preferably, Nevada, but that they might have failed to do so in the case of the A-10.

The controversy over the A-10 has remained active, and has kept the pressure on TAC to devise effective tactics against the changing threat, and demonstrate how they would be used in action. Certainly, the way in which the A-10 is used in training and exercises today is very different from the projections of the A-X planners. But it is also true that current A-10 tactics exploit virtually all the unique features of the aircraft; and even if some things might have been done differently had the present mission been envisaged from the outset, the A-10 is available, works well and is no sense inadequate for its mission.

The threats

The concept and design of the A-10 were based on an accurate perception of Soviet military equipment and tactics in the late 1960s. (In this, at least, the Warthog is one up on the aristocratic F-15 Eagle, which was strongly influenced by an immensely flattering assessment of the MiG-25 Foxbat). The primary attack weapon was the tank, used in large concentrations and dedicated to the advance. Unlike contemporary Western tank units, Soviet armoured

Below: An 81st TFW pilot demonstrates the Warthog's surprising agility: the same degree of manoeuvrability, translated to low levels, is the key to the A-10's ability to survive combat in high-threat areas.

Flight envelope

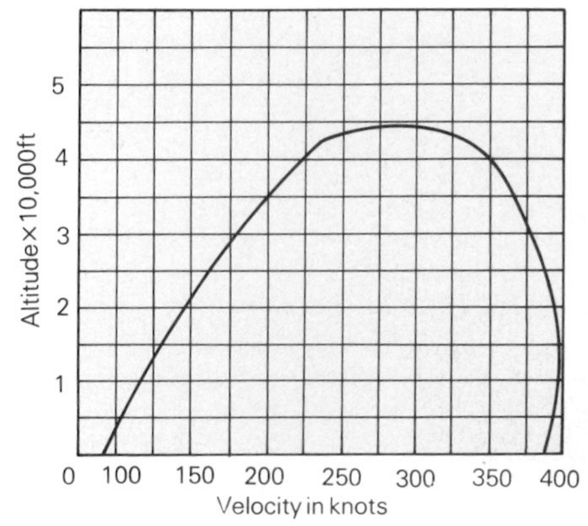

Performance graph for the A-10 in standard day conditions, at a design weight of 31,170lb (14,138kg), with six pylons fitted and at maximum thrust.

Turn performance

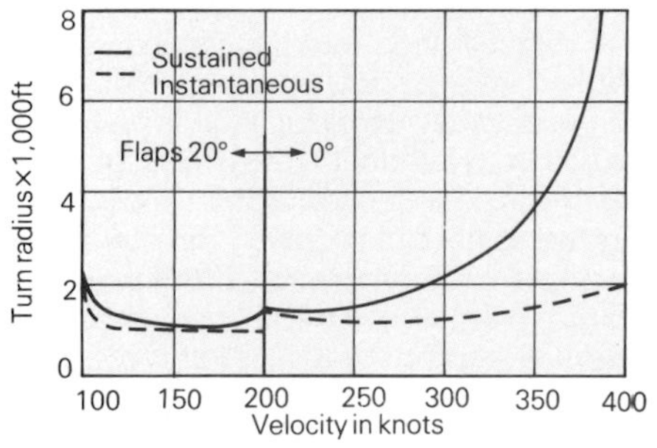

Standard day sustained and instantaneous turn rates for an A-10 with six Mk 82 bombs for a weight of 31,000lb (14,061kg) at 5,000ft (1,524m).

Load factors

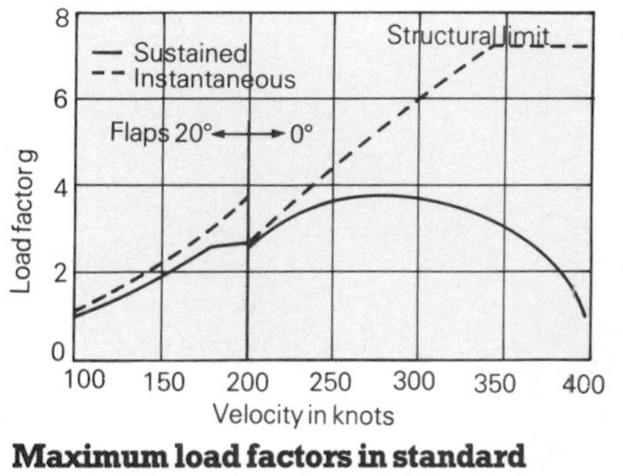

Maximum load factors in standard day conditions at an altitude of 5,000ft with six Mk 82 bombs for a gross weight of 31,000lb (14,061kg).

Above: Medium-altitude Maverick launch from the lead ship of a standard two-aircraft formation. The threat level in Europe forced a revision of the tactical concepts.

formations carried their own air defence systems. The most formidable of these was the ZSU-23-4 Shilka, a close-range defence weapon with no direct equivalent in the West.

The Shilka is designed to run with the tanks, on a PT-76 tracked amphibious chassis. It is armed with four 23mm cannon, with a total firing rate of 4,000 rounds/min, carries a great deal of ammunition and features liquid-cooled gun barrels, so it can sustain high rates of fire over a relatively long period. Considering the effectiveness of much less sophisticated light AAA over Vietnam, it was understandable that TAC perceived the Shilka system as a prime threat in the CAS arena long before its combat debut in 1973.

The threat from Soviet aircraft was not considered to be much of a problem for A-X in the late 1960s. Soviet air-to-air fighters were used defensively, to protect airbases and rear-area assets. TAC's fighter squadrons were equipped to keep the skies cleared over friendly ground all the time, and over hostile ground where necessary. A-X was not intended to penetrate far beyond the FLOT (forward line of own troops), and any encounters with MiGs would be accidental. However, the threat of aircraft or missile attack on airbases, particularly those closest to the battle line, was certainly present.

Tactical concepts

The A-10 was designed and equipped with European weather in mind, contrary to some opinion. But it was designed to cope with weather in a completely different way from an F-111 or Tornado. The theory was that zero-zero weather – no ceiling and no horizontal visibility – was not only rare but would halt all military operations, so there was no need for such extreme in-weather capability in a CAS type. Instead, the A-X was planned to operate under, rather than in, the weather and in reduced visibility.

Low ceilings and poor visibility are a cage for the fighter pilot. Unknown terrain lurks beyond the limits of visibility, and, as pilots say, the ground has a kill probability of 1.0. The ceiling is not dangerous in itself, but is a one-way exit from the air-to-ground fight. The pilot loses his target, and has to find a hole in the cloud if he is to descend and rejoin battle. The A-10 was designed to manoeuvre and fight visually within this confined space.

The A-10 is not a high-g, high-powered aircraft, but the one thing that it can do better than any supersonic fighter is turn at low speeds. A fighter like the F-16 is designed to catch a victim or lose an attacker in a turn, and does it with brute power installed in the lightest possible airframe. Low speeds represent loss of energy, and are avoided at all costs. The A-10 is different in concept. Low turning airspeeds are accepted, because air combat capability is not required. Because the airspeed is low, the

Below: Medium-altitude loiter, World War II style, was out of the question in the context of NATO's Central Front, but could still have applications in low-threat environments.

Designed close air support mission

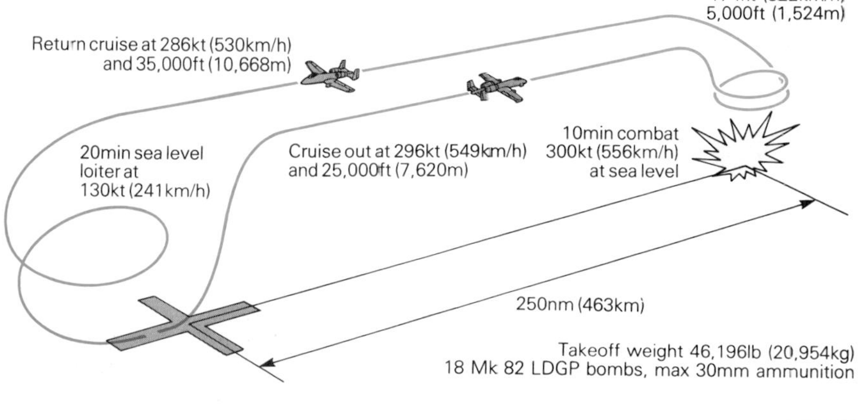

Below: From target recognition to Maverick launch takes the same time, during which the fast-mover gets much closer to the target and its associated defensive systems.

A-10/F-16 Maverick attack ranges

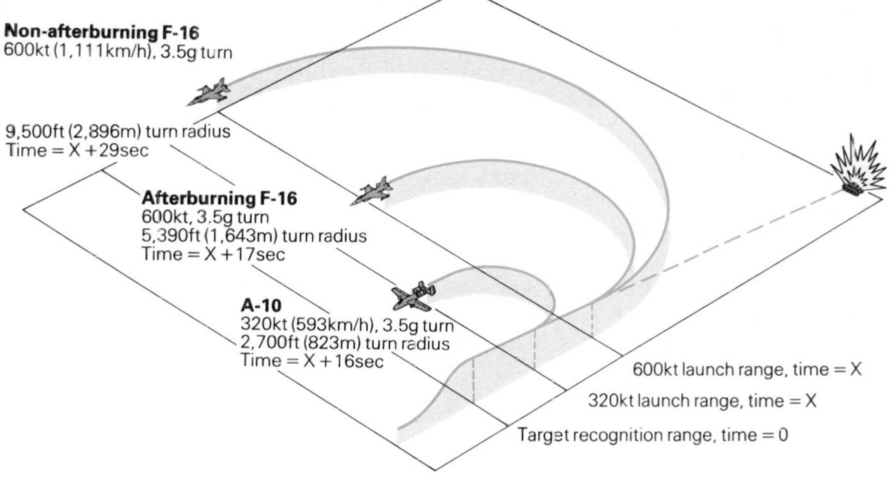

A-10 can attain a high rate of turn, in degrees/sec, without the high g forces that would be associated with the same rate at higher speeds. Low airspeed and high turn rate combine to give a small turning radius; the first lesson in geometry states that the circumference of the turn, the distance which the aircraft actually travels, is smaller too. The aircraft will therefore take less time to complete its turn.

Translating theory into fact, it is paradoxical but true that the A-10 will out-turn even an F-16 in full afterburner when the two aircraft are carrying similar loads. At 320kt (590km/h) and 3.5g, the A-10 can complete a half-turn, radius 2,700ft (824m), in 16 seconds. The F-16, at 600kt (1,110km/h) and 6g, makes a 3,620ft (1,043m) turn, and takes 17 seconds.

It is because of this emphasis on a quick turn rather than a fast turn that the A-10 can fight in the cage – the limited volume defined by ceiling and visibility. Early operational tests with the A-10 showed that this concept worked, and that the A-10 pilot could run into the target area, identify a pinpoint target, turn and attack it under a 1,000ft (305m) ceiling, with 1.5-2 miles (2.4-3.2km) visibility. Even in a European midwinter, TAC's records showed, similar or better conditions could be expected, on average, for eight hours a day.

By contrast, the apparently better equipped F-4D could not venture below the clouds unless the ceiling was at least 3,000ft (915m) and visibility 3 miles (4.8km). Conditions that good are encountered, on average, only four hours a day in midwinter, and only six hours a day from the beginning of November to the end of February. And as any European knows, the daily weather pattern does not conform to some arbitrary seasonal average. The difference between the A-10 and the fast mover could amount to weeks on end in which the A-10 would be the only aircraft that could attack ground targets at all.

Another objective set down by the original A-X philosophy was quick reaction, to be attained by a number of means. Airborne loiter was among the most important. The A-10 was designed to be launched from a relatively safe base, 250nm (460km) behind the battle line, and loiter for two hours before carrying out an attack. This meant that the A-10 could, in theory, be used on the 'cab-rank' principle developed by the 2nd Tactical Air Force in Western Europe in 1944-45. A-10s would be launched at regular intervals and join a loose traffic pat-

tern, the 'cab-rank', behind the battle line. They could respond immediately to any call for support, while other A-10s would be launched to relieve aircraft on the rank after their two hours on station expired.

In combat, the A-10 was designed to be relatively invulnerable to light AAA or shoulder-fired SAMs. Heavier SAMs presented a different type of threat. In the late 1960s these did not travel with the main armoured force, and if they were encountered in the CAS zone, would have been emplaced in a hurry. Moreover, the A-10's manoeuvrability would enable it to stay below the minimum altitudes of such weapons, and inside their minimum range, as it roamed around the battlefield shooting tanks.

The foregoing represents a brief summary of A-10 tactics as they were envis-

Terrain following at high and low speeds

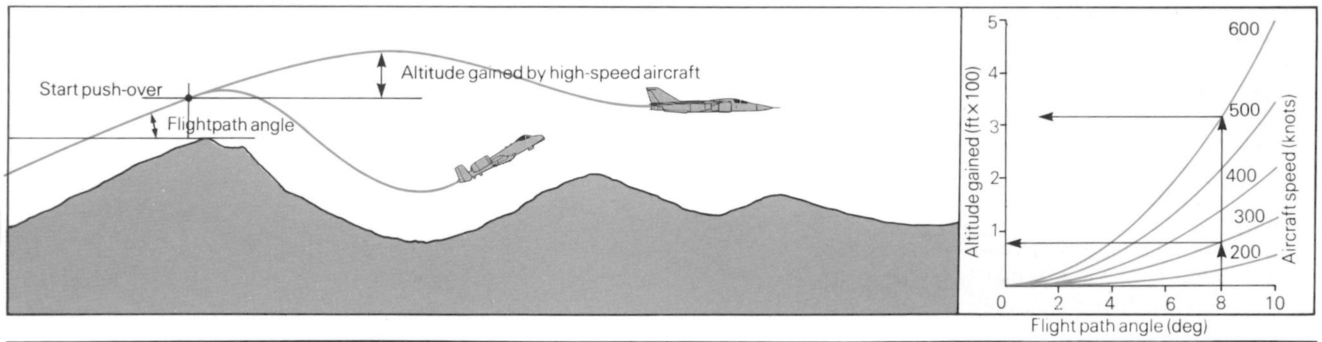

Above: While the A-10 at 300kt (555km/h) gains a modest 80ft (24m) in the push-over, an F-111 in hard-ride terrain-following mode climbs a dangerous 330ft (100m).

Left: The deployment of the Soviet SA-8 surface-to-air-missile with armoured columns contributed to a major rethink of CAS tactics.

SA-8 avoidance tactics

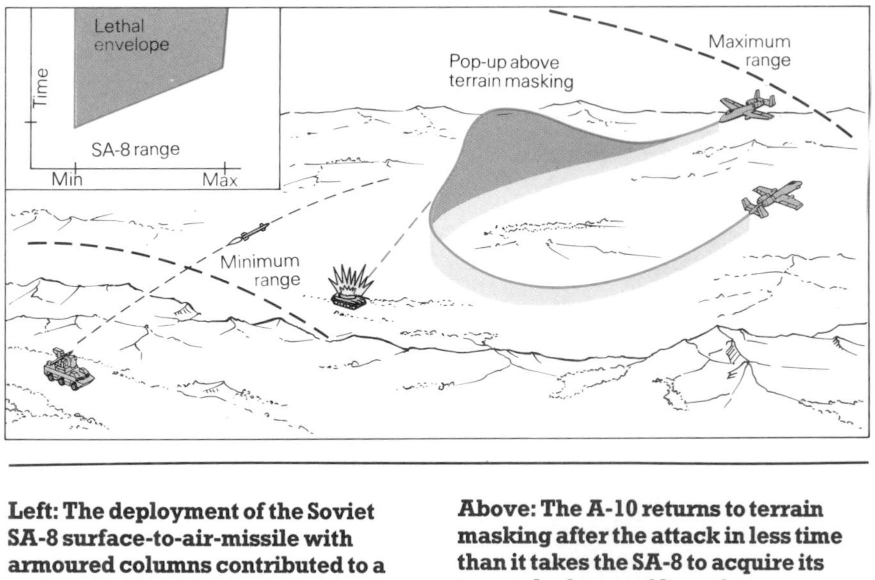

Above: The A-10 returns to terrain masking after the attack in less time than it takes the SA-8 to acquire its target, lock on and launch.

Above: Manoeuvrability at low altitudes allows the A-10 to exploit natural cover to the full, allowing air defences only the briefest glimpse of its armoured form.

ZSU-23-4 avoidance tactics

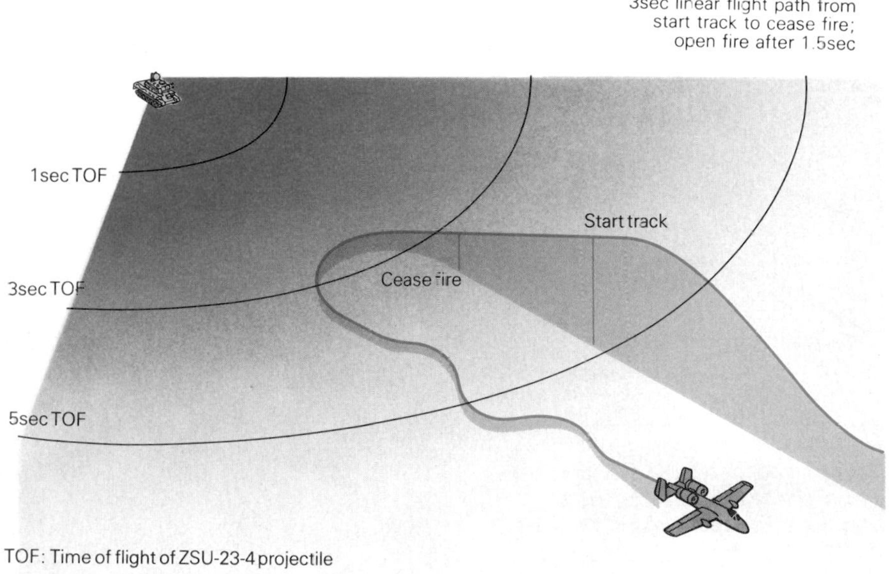

Left: At GAU-8/A range, the Warthog can carry out its attack and be back under the Shilka's minimum elevation before the deadly stream of 23mm projectile can reach it.

Below left: The ZSU-23-4, seen here in Polish army service, was always considered a major threat, but its lethality was not fully appreciated until the 1973 Arab-Israeli war.

aged in the early days of the programme. It is probably fair to say that most of them were completely invalidated by the time the A-10 came to Europe at the beginning of 1979. There were at least three critical factors which were not anticipated in the formulation of the A-X requirement, and between them they have made life a great deal more difficult for the A-10.

New threats

One factor was the performance of the ZSU-23-4. It was known to be a dangerous system, but its lethality was not fully appreciated until the Arab-Israeli war of 1973. The projectile is nearly twice as heavy as that of the M61A-1 Vulcan, at 0.41lb (0.19kg), and muzzle velocity is a respectable 3,200ft/sec (970m/sec). More importantly, however, the barrel cooling and other features give the four-barrel mount a very low dispersion. Combined with the sustained 4,000rds/min rate of fire, this makes the ability to withstand one or two 23mm strikes more or less academic. Like the GAU-8/A, the Shilka tends to hit its targets more than once or twice, and the effects have been compared to those of a rotary saw. The Shilka's effectiveness drops off very sharply beyond about 3,000-3,300ft (920-1,000m), but this certainly does not mean that the threat which it poses can be ignored.

The West got another unpleasant surprise in 1975, with the unveiling of the Soviet SA-8 Gecko mobile SAM system. Western experts had expected the Soviet Union to field a new short-range SAM. It would be much more effective than a pursuit-course heat-seeking weapon, but it would be more mobile than the bigger SA-6 system, which is carried on two vehicles, and it would have a shorter minimum range and lower minimum altitude. Everyone assumed, though, that the Soviets would design a small, simple system like the Roland or Rapier. Instead, they adapted the design of a sophisticated naval missile, the SA-N-4.

The SA-8 is a heavy, complex system, indicating its importance in Soviet planning and tactics. Mounted on a specially developed 25-30 ton (27.5-33 tonne) wheeled vehicle, the SA-8 system is complete with surveillance and tracking radar, and two independent high-power, narrow-beam radio command links. If radar is jammed or ineffective for other reasons, SA-8 has an electro-optical tracking and guidance system and according to some sources the missile may have infra-red terminal homing. The round is considerably larger than those used by Western fully mobile systems and carries a 110lb (50kg) blast-fragmentation warhead. The initial SA-8 configuration carried four missiles, but the improved SA-8B carries six, in sealed box launchers.

A third unexpected development was the extremely rapid introduction into service of the MiG-23 Flogger B/G fighter. The MiG-23 itself had been seen in 1967, but Western intelligence – hypnotised by the MiG-25 – failed to appreciate its importance to Soviet tactical airpower. Production accelerated at breakneck speed in 1972-75, in parallel with development of its new radar and missile armament. Not a dogfighter, but fast, heavily armed and comprehensively equipped, Flogger B/G is the first Soviet fighter designed to carry the air war into NATO's territory, beyond the reach of ground control.

The effect of these three developments on planned A-10 tactics was profound. The A-10 pilot was supposed to identify and select his target on the first pass, keep it in sight in a tight turn and attack on a second pass. Against Shilkas and SA-8s, this would be suicide. The aggressive MiG-23, meanwhile, put an end to the absolute security of airspace over friendly ground: so much for loiter and transit at medium altitudes. Between 1975 and 1979 the ground rules of A-10 operation were completely rewritten to cope with the changing threats while still exploiting the unique attributes of the aircraft. The changes affected survival and defensive tactics, attack profiles and targeting, and operational deployment.

Tactics for survival

Survivability has been at the centre of the A-10 controversy. The aircraft has most often been criticized on account of its speed. Most NATO strike aircraft are designed to attack at speeds of 600kt (1,110km/h); the A-10 attacks at barely more than half that speed, being capable of 325kt (602km/h) with a typical weapons load. TAC and Fairchild contend, however, that when the A-10 is properly used it can survive against Soviet defensive systems, and fare better than other aircraft. Tactics have presumably been evaluated not only against simulated Soviet systems on the USAF's Nevada ranges, but also against the real thing: captured SA-8s and Shilkas, and clandestinely obtained MiG-23s, are all believed to be in use.

The first point made by the A-10's advocates is that in the battle area, where the A-10s operate, the air defence system is not operating at peak efficiency. Firing positions will have been selected under pressure, on unfamiliar ground, and fields of fire of the different systems will not overlap in the optimum pattern. Communications, command and control will all be degraded to some extent. Even the advancing second echelon is subject to similar pressures.

Another important observation is that a Mach 0.9 speed is not a primary defence against a Mach 2.3 missile, let alone a Mach 3 shell. The only benefit of speed itself is to reduce the time in which an aircraft is exposed to defensive systems on a given flightpath. It is also a factor in generating high crossing rates relative to the defensive weapon's sight-line.

Under some circumstances, higher speed may actually militate against the best defensive tactic, which is to interpose a hill between the gun or SAM system and the target. TAC has been a late but enthusiastic convert to the doctrine of very-low-level flight, and A-10 units are the command's leading exponents of the tactic. Once again, it is the A-10's ability to manoeuvre hard at low airspeeds that is important. Cruising at its normal and most efficient speed, the A-10 can make sharp flightpath changes without incurring as much g as a faster aircraft following the same trajectory. Clearing the top of a hill, the A-10 will have less upward momentum than the faster aircraft, and can descend more rapidly on the other side without en-

Below: Warthog pilots do not consider MiGs a major threat: they can turn more quickly, and their guns are very effective against aircraft.

Survival against interceptors

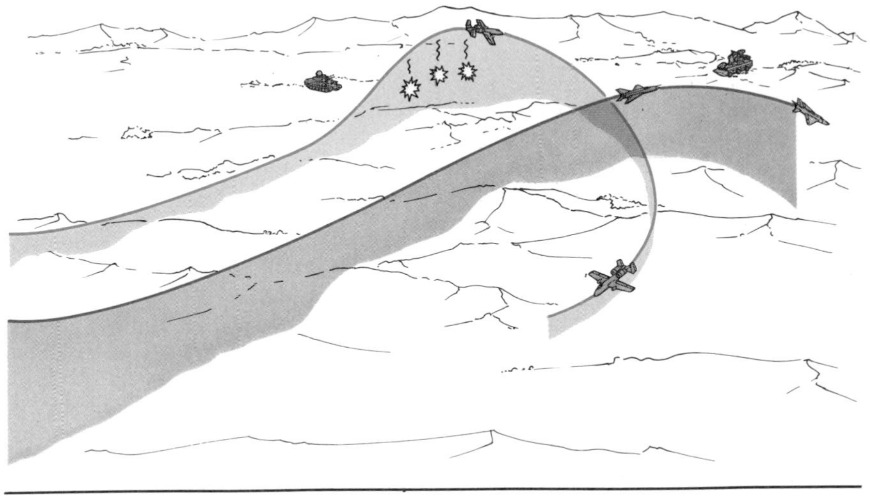

Battlefield air support mission

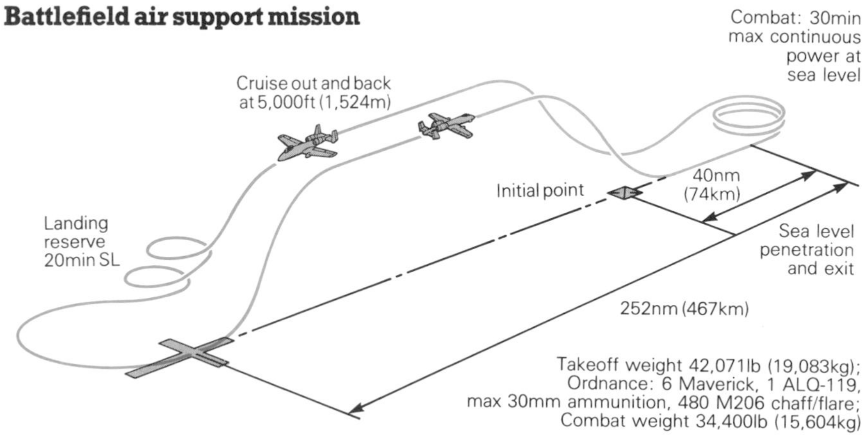

Above: Revised A-10 tactics emphasise sea-level penetration and combat in the face of the intense air defenses likely to be encountered.

Right: In battle, this would almost certainly be an opposing tank commander's last view of an A-10 – or anything else.

countering excessive levels of negative g. (Faster aircraft can, of course, roll inverted and pull their way around the top of the hill under positive g, but this tactic is only recommended if you are absolutely certain that the terrain does fall away on the opposite side of the crest.)

The A-10's small turning radius gives it a wider choice of tracks across uneven terrain which may not give a faster aircraft room to change course, and its low speed gives the pilot more time to plan the next manoeuvre. Light and natural handling takes a further weight off the pilot's mind.

At these low speeds, the A-10 can actually pull higher g than an F-16 in similar trim. When both aircraft are loaded for anti-armour operations, the A-10 can sustain a 3.25g turn at 250-300kt (460-555km/h). The F-16 can only match this performance with the use of reheat, and on dry thrust can manage only 2-2.5g in the same speed range. On dry thrust it can match the A-10's performance only by speeding up above 400kt (740km/h) and accepting a larger turning radius.

It is true that a fast-mover attack aircraft can follow terrain at reduced speeds and emulate some of the A-10's tactics. The snag is that only the A-10 and its engines are designed for such speeds. Fast-movers do not usually reduce their speed, because by doing so they drop out of their efficient cruising regime and suffer unacceptable warload/radius penalties. It is this consideration that makes the A-10's performance unique.

A-10s have been operated successfully by service pilots at average altitudes of 100ft (30m) above ground level, although most training is carried out at higher altitudes, mainly because of peacetime restrictions. Slightly higher altitudes are acceptable where the threat comes from Floggers rather than SAMs, but on the final run to the target the A-10s fly substantially lower than any other fixed-wing aircraft.

Low-level operation protects the A-10 in a number of ways. Simply concealing the aircraft for as long as possible from the sightline of the defensive system is one of them. Fairchild studies show that in hilly terrain, such as the Fulda Gap in West Germany, a ZSU-23-4 can engage targets in just 22 per cent of the area covered by its effective range if the target stays below 200ft (61m).

Again, one of the defender's advantages is the ability to see and identify the attcking aircraft before its pilot can pick out a SAM or gun system among ground clutter and other targets, but this 'first-look' advantage can be wiped out if the aircraft breaks cover at close quarters. With radar-guided or command-guided systems such as the SA-8, low flying also reduces the SAM's advantage due to greater maximum range. Also, such weapons are not 'fire and forget' – they need a certain amount of time to lock on, fire a missile and guide it to the target. Breaking ground cover at the last moment, and returning to it as soon as possible, gives the operator the shortest possible time to engage the target.

Even with a target in sight, extremely low altitudes present problems for SAMs. Simple IR-homing SAMs have to be launched at a minimum elevation angle, because of their short range and their tendency to fly into the ground. Their effective envelope is shaped like an inverted cone with its apex at the launch point, and the lower an aircraft flies, the shorter its flightpath through the cone. An aircraft flying at 300kt (555km/h), 100ft (30m) over a SAM with a 20deg minimum launch elevation – typical of unsophisticated weapons – will be in and out of the operator's launch window in less than one second.

Radar-guided SAMs have other limitations, and can be confused by a very-low-altitude target. Radar signals bounce off a target in all directions, and will be reflected again when they strike the ground. Usually, such echoes will be well outside the narrow cone of a missile tracking beam, and will not be detected by the radar's receiver. But if the aircraft's altitude is less than twice the width of the beam, the ground echoes will be close enough to create false targets on the radar screen. Multiple echoes are another problem which increases with low altitude.

Operation at very low altitudes also protects the A-10, to some extent, from 'snapdown' attacks by MiG-23s or similar aircraft firing IR or semi-active radar-guided missiles from higher altitudes. The latest Flogger G variant is considered to have "some look-down/shoot-down capability" according to the US Department of Defense, and this implies that its High Lark radar and AA-7 Apex missile would be of limited use against a small target 100ft (30m) off the ground.

IR missiles such as the AA-8 Aphid, also carried by the MiG-23, are probably of little use against an A-10 at a lower altitude than the launch aircraft. Such all-aspect IR missiles home on the heat energy generated by friction between an airframe and the air. The A-10 is slow and relatively small, and is therefore a weak target, and the sensitivity of an IR missile is limited; if the seeker is too sensitive, it will lock on to false targets on the ground. While low-level operation does not provide a complete defence against fighters, it does mean that if the MiG-23s want to shoot down the A-10s they probably have to come down to the A-10's level to do it.

The main disadvantage of low-level operation is probably the great stress

Low-level gunnery

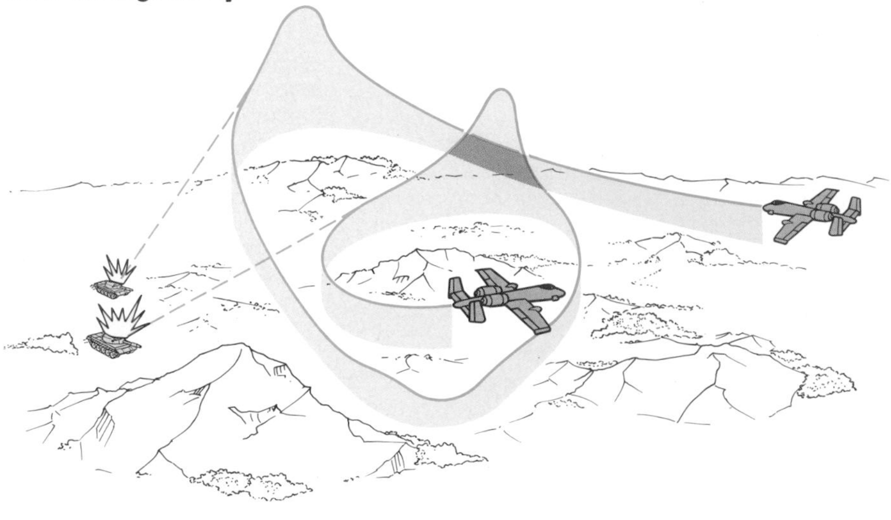

Above: Spending most of its time less than 100ft (30m) above the ground, the A-10 pops up to between 200ft (60m) and 500ft (150m) to destroy tanks with brief bursts of gunfire.

Below: The same terrain-masking and three-dimensional jinking are employed in the run-up to a Maverick delivery from 500ft (150m); a cloud base of 1,000ft (300m) is no problem.

Low-level Maverick delivery

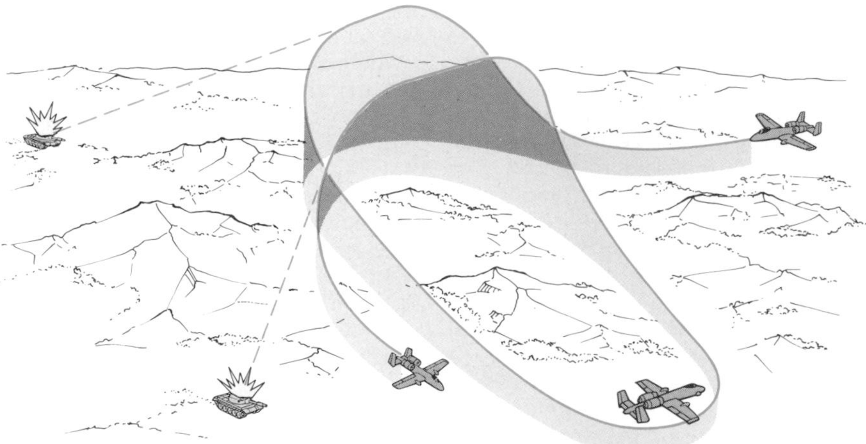

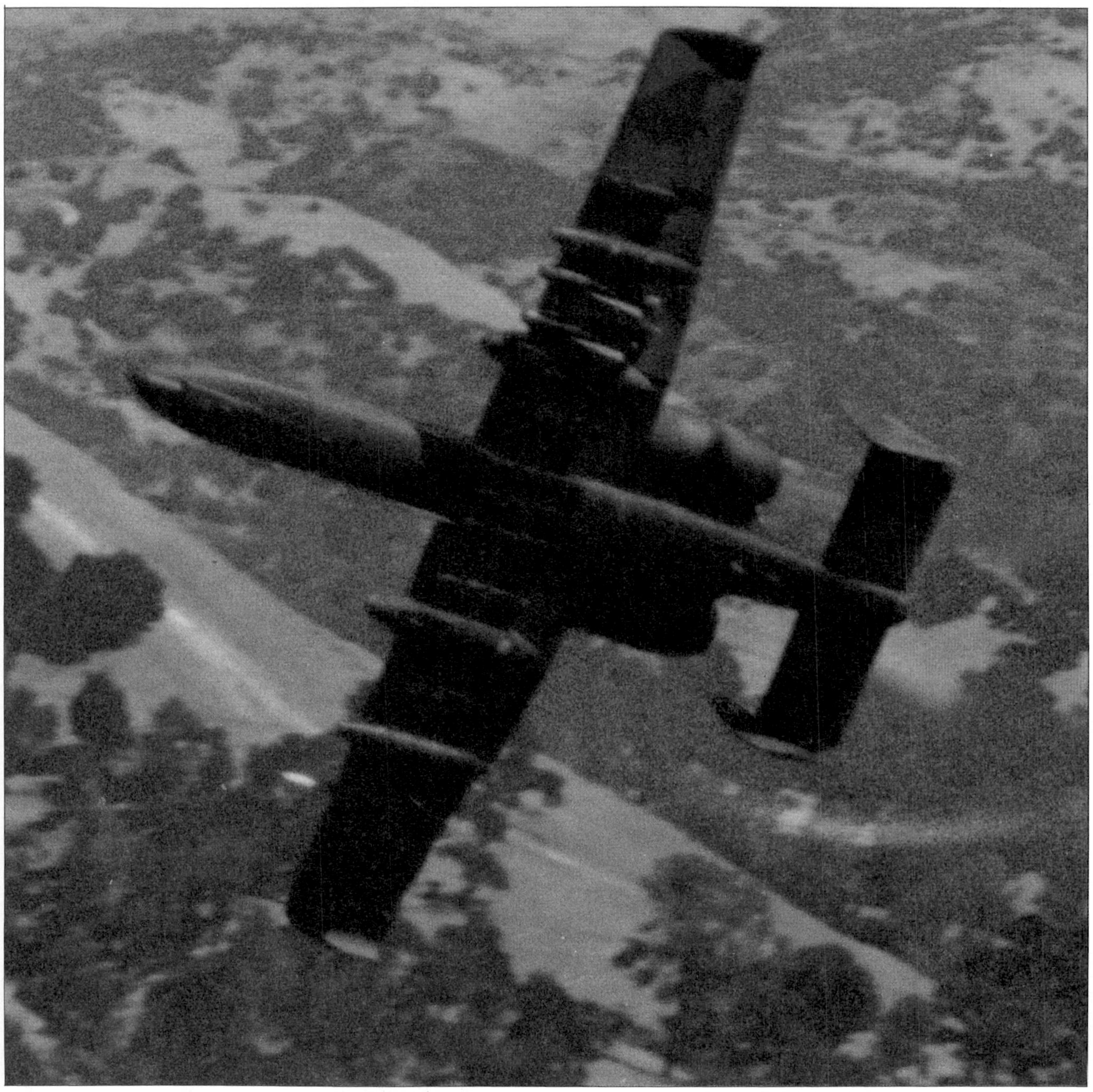

which it places on the pilot. This has been a major factor in the abandonment of the cab-rank loiter concept. Loitering at medium altitudes is unsafe, but the physical and mental demands of flight among the treetops at 300kt (555km/h) make it inadvisable to add two hours to the mission. At that point, pilot fatigue could become a limiting factor on a squadron's ability to sustain its readiness to fight.

In combat, the A-10 is to survive partly by means of its manoeuvrability, and partly by its ability to counter-attack, with the help of its built-in and podded EW and decoys. The basic attack manoeuvre in the SA-8 era is the pop-up, or, in TAC argot, the 'bunt-up', in which the aircraft emerges from the protection of terrain, engages its target, attacks and dives back into cover.

Once again, the most important characteristic is not high speed, but low exposure time; if it is shorter than the time that the SA-8 takes to engage and hit the target, the missile operator can do nothing. The A-10's ability to manoeuvre in small radii and short time is its main asset here. Its lower speed means that it can drop back into cover at a higher descent rate than a fast jet: in a bunt, or negative-g pushover, the limiting factor is pilot tolerance rather than aircraft power, so the g force will be the same, and the slower aircraft will follow a steeper and shorter downward trajectory.

Speed is also of secondary importance in avoiding hits after a weapon has been fired at the aircraft, because any sophisticated defensive system can measure speed accurately and compensate for it. (In deference to the fast mover, it should be noted that sheer speed does reduce the time in which the target is within the lethal envelope, all other things being equal.) In the case of guns and radar-guided SAMs, however, it is possible to 'generate miss distance'. Translated, this means that when the projectile arrives where the fire-control system says the target ought to be, it is safest for the target to be somewhere else.

A common weakness of both guns and command-guided SAMs is that they work on a projection of where the target will be in one or two seconds' time, rather than shooting at its present position. This is commonsense in the case of the gun, with its dumb, unguided projectile, and less obvious in the case of the missile; but even the missile system takes a finite amount of time to detect the movement of the target, process the movement into a command signal and transmit it to the missile. Then, the missile control surfaces move, and – not quite immediately – the missile's flightpath will begin to change according to the target's motion. Unless some degree of prediction is built into the system, the combined delay will be enough to guide the missile behind the target.

The Shilka's fire-control system assumes that the aircraft will continue on a straight path at constant speed, and the SA-8 system probably does the same. The rate at which the target can diverge from that straight path is largely a matter of the g force which it can generate: in this case, the important parameter is instantaneous, short-period g rather than sustained g, because evading instant destruction is a great deal more important than preserving energy or avoiding a stall. Loaded for air-to-ground operations, the A-10 can pull as much instantaneous g as most other aircraft.

In the case of the gun, the miss distance will be a function of g and the firing

Left: Even during the brief periods when the A-10 might be exposed to fire, its structure makes it uniquely able to survive major damage.

range. At 300kt (460km/h), and with a five-second flight time for the shell, the gun will miss by 1,310ft (400m). In a missile attack, the important factors are g and the distance between the aircraft and the missile when the manoeuvre starts. According to Fairchild figures, apparently based on SA-8 characteristics, a 4g manoeuvre, initiated when the missile is 12,000ft (3,660m) away, will cause the weapon to miss by 500ft (150m); not much, but better than nothing.

Tactics such as these would be used in conjunction with the A-10's countermeasure systems. Chaff would be dropped during a bunt-up manoeuvre, to keep multiple false returns coming into the hostile radar as the A-10 itself leaves the safety of the low-level confusion zone. The ALQ-119 pod and the chaff clouds can degrade the SA-8 command link, even if the system reverts to electro-optical tracking. Flares would be used during the bunt-up, to create similar multiple-target problems for IR missiles.

The A-10 carries no specifically defensive armament, although trials have shown that an advanced IR missile such as the AIM-9L Sidewinder would be a formidable addition to its armoury. The AIM-9L is a particularly good match for the A-10. Its critical advantage over earlier weapons is that it can lock on to a target from almost any direction. This eliminates the need for the classic tail-chase, in which the attacker tries to manoeuvre into the enemy's rear quarter. Instead, the advantage goes to the aircraft which can swing its nose on to the target most rapidly, and at low altitude this will usually be the A-10. Even without the AIM-9L, though, the instant firepower of the GAU-8/A, coupled with the A-10's rapid turn ability, make the Warthog a dangerous beast to tackle.

In particular, the effective range of the GAU-8/A has been shown to be greater than that of the Shilka, and the USAF's A-10 weapons school at Nellis AFB teaches the use of the GAU-8/A to suppress the Soviet gun in a classic High Noon shoot-out. The attack starts with a bunt-up, which takes the A-10 to the Shilka's maximum range. The Shilka starts tracking and fires, while the A-10 simultaneously enters a three-second diving attack, including a two-second burst from the cannon. At the point which the Shilka's projectiles will reach three seconds after firing, and just before the first rounds arrive, the A-10 breaks and heads for cover, and the shells miss. By that time, the first of the 130-plus shells fired by the A-10 will be hitting the vehicle. This tactic was first demonstrated at Nellis AFB in February 1979 against a simulated Soviet tank battalion array, including four Shilkas. Two pairs of A-10s from 422 TFW attacked the formation, killed the Shilkas and, in four minutes, killed 23 tanks.

In the air-to-air regime the A-10 is, technically speaking, unarmed, because it has no way of aiming the cannon against a rapidly crossing target. But the first A-10 pilots to engage in dissimilar air combat training simply disregarded this factor and followed their instincts, pulling the quickest possible turn and spraying the adversary with simulated GAU-8/A fire. The 'Warthog stomp' has since proved extremely effective. In 57 sorties flown by the USAF's Aggressor unit at Nellis against A-10s, the A-10s survived as long as they saw their attackers. Only once, when an A-10 was attacked by two F-5Es, did an A-10 pilot even have to jettison external weapons.

In more recent Red Flag exercises, even the most manoeuvrable fighters have found it advisable to avoid close-quarters engagements with the A-10s, preferring a less effective but safer shoot-down pass from above. A-10s enjoy a special exception from the Red Flag safety rule which prohibits close-quarters head-on attacks, and are permitted to close to 1,000ft (305m) before breaking off.

In action, the A-10s would usually have the advantage of sighting the enemy first. The MiG-23's High Lark radar would give advance warning of an attack and its direction, via the A-10's radar-warning system, while the A-10 itself has no emitting devices to give its location away to a Sirena 3 or similar Soviet radar-warning

Right: Conus-based A-10 units train for worldwide deployment and a variety of threat levels: the 354th TFW uses a 300 acre (120 hectare) wooded area of its South Carolina base for realistic training for Europe.

device. The aircraft are difficult to spot against the ground in their subfusc green finish – one operational problem is that A-10 pilots have been known to lose sight of their wingmen – while any attacker will be outlined against the sky. The problems presented by snap-down attacks against the A-10 have already been mentioned, so any combat will take place at low level. In all, according to Brig.Gen. Rudolph Wacker, the commander of the Europe-based A-10 force in August 1979, "At the altitudes we expect to fly, enemy interceptors pose almost a negligible threat. Interestingly,' he continued, "a careless interceptor pilot quickly changes from the hunter to hunted, and generally will find himself outmanoeuvred by the A-10, and always outgunned."

Trained in low-level tactics, schooled to take advantage of every chink in the defences, and equipped with their jamming and decoy suites, the A-10 units have become confident that their ability to survive is as great as that of any other system in clear air above a European battlefield. The controversy over the A-10 has receded, and its unique place within the NATO Central Region line-up is beginning to be appreciated.

In current thinking, the most important of the A-10's attributes is its ability to sustain combat. Against armour, its firepower is more than twice that of any other aircraft in the TAC inventory. With 1,174 GAU-8/A rounds and six Mavericks, the A-10 can deliver 16 lethal anti-armour attacks in a single mission, or even more given efficient use of the GAU-8/A. No other type can deliver more than six Mavericks, or is armed with an effective anti-armour gun.

The A-10 can also stay in combat longer than other types, even though they may appear to have a superior range on paper. As noted earlier, an A-10 can sustain a higher turn rate than an F-16 with a comparable ordnance load, unless the

Above: During annual Thunderhog exercises, the 354th TFW uses its 'European' environment to simulate deployment, complete with all supporting elements, to austere forward operating locations.

Right and below: A-10s are also based in Alaska with the 18th TFS, 343rd Composite Wing, at Eielson AFB. During Exercise Cool Snow Hog 82-1, held at Kotzebue Air Station, this Warthog was given an unusual black and white paint scheme for evaluation purposes. The A-10s of Alaskan Air Command, along with a squadron of 0-2A forward air control aircraft, provide the primary air support for the US Army's ground forces stationed in the Alaska defence region.

F-16 uses reheat; but the use of reheat is highly demanding of fuel. Again, with a comparable ordnance load and the same mission profile, the F-16 comes close to the A-10's radius of action, but only if it uses dry thrust exclusively in the combat area. Two minutes of combat afterburner are enough to cut the F-16's operational radius to 60 per cent of the A-10's. Four minutes of afterburner, and the F-16 can go only 40 per cent as far. With its typical anti-armour ordnance load, an ALQ-119 pod, a full load of 480 decoys and full internal fuel, the A-10 can fly 252nm (466km) to the target, including 40nm (74km) at low level, and remain in the fight, on full power, for 30 minutes.

While that mission is an indicator of the A-10's performance, it is not typical of the way the A-10 would be used in service, because one of the type's other attributes – an unusual one, but not quite unique – gives the commander a better option. The quality in queston is the A-10's ability to operate from short strips and rudimentary bases. Supersonic fighters, in general, still need 8,000-10,000ft (2,440-3,050m) of concrete for normal operations. The A-10, with full fuel and weapons, can take off in 3,600ft (1,097m) and land in 1,140ft (347m).

The landing distance is particularly significant. Combined with the A-10's slow approach speed and docile handling, it means that the aircraft can be recovered safely on a short strip with a large safety margin. Even with reduced hydraulic power, no flaps or a fatigued pilot, the A-10 can recover to a 4,000ft (1,200m) strip with no trouble at all, and without using an emergency arrester hook.

Forward operating locations

At the same time, the A-10's simplicity, and the absence of any critical non-mechanical systems, means that the aircraft can not only operate from dispersed bases, which most aircraft can do, but can also sustain operations from such bases, which is a rare ability indeed. In Europe, the A-10s are based at RAF Bentwaters, well behind the battle line, in an efficient, consolidated organisation. They would operate in wartime, however, from a group of six bases 100nm (185km) from the West German border: from north to south, Ahlhorn, Noervenich, Sembach and Leipheim, plus two more bases which are not revealed. These forward operating locations (FOLs) have stocks of fuel, ammunition and Mavericks, together with a few of the most important spares.

With most aircraft, an attempt to sustain operations from an austere base would rapidly result in an airfield full of damaged and defective airframes 250nm (463km) nearer the battle line than the spares and people needed to

81st TFW forward operating locations

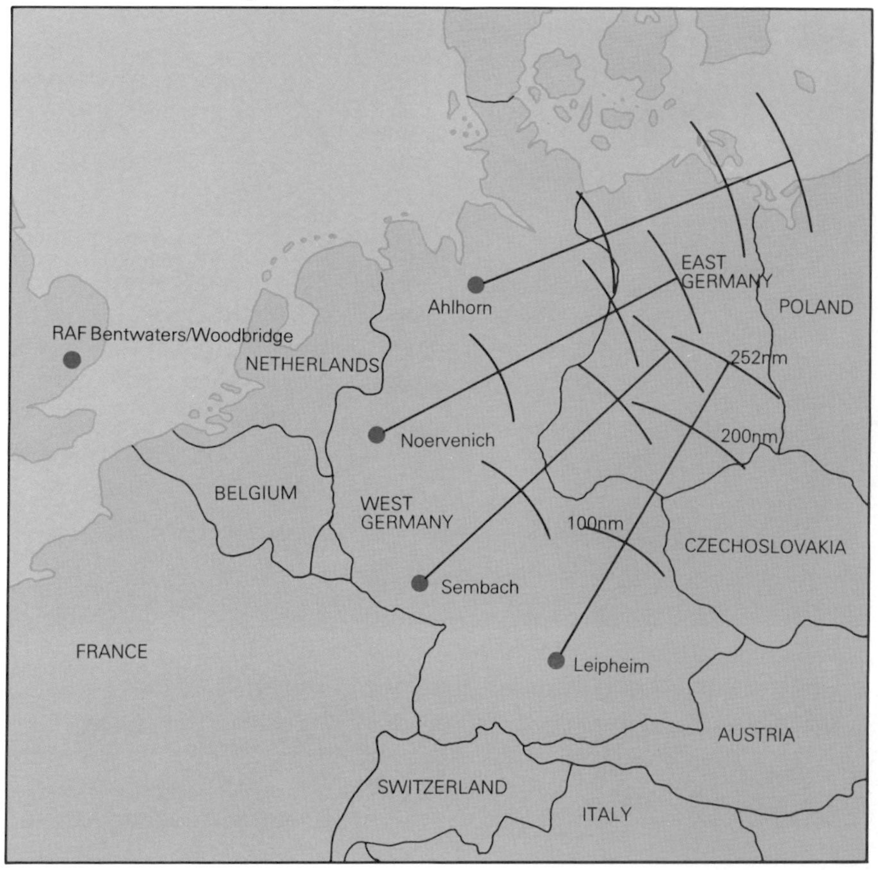

Top: Pilots of the 511st TFS, one of the six squadrons that make up the 81st TFW, are briefed before a mission during the Cold Fire 83 exercise at Wiesbaden Air Base, Germany, in September 1983.

Above: Off-loading a Maverick from a 511st TFS A-10 after a Cold Fire 83 training mission. A total of 18 aircraft were deployed to Wiesbaden in support of the German army's Brave Lion exercise.

Left: A 511st TFS pilot at the end of a Cold Fire mission. Cold Fire and Brave Lion both formed part of the annual Autumn Forge series of combined NATO manoeuvres in Germany.

repair them. The A-10's simplicity and survivability features change the picture. A hit, or close miss, which would send a more complex and less resilient aircraft down for extensive repairs may well simply pepper the A-10's secondary structure, calling for nothing more than a few temporary patches. Again, a less survivable aircraft might regain a friendly base after being hit, but might not be airworthy enough to be flown back to its home base. A maintenance team must be dispatched, to fix it for the flight home, before the main work of repair can even start. Experience has shown that the A-10 can, under the same circumstances, often ferry itself back from the FOL to the main base.

The FOL has several major advantages. It is an effective and more efficient substitute for airborne loiter in decreasing reaction time; not only are the FOLs close to the front line, but the force is spread out so that no part of the line is very far from A-10 support. Because the FOL is closer to the front line than any main base, it takes less time for the A-10s to return to base, rearm and rejoin the fight, so more sorties can be flown in a day. A related benefit is a reduction of pilot flying time and fatigue for each mission.

FOL basing also makes the force less vulnerable to counter-airfield attack, for a number of reasons. Splitting the fleet among a number of FOLs forces the enemy to carry out several raids against less valuable targets. Not only that, but it is more difficult to deny an airfield to A-10s than it is to close it to fast-mover operations. The A-10s can operate from half a runway, or from a long taxiway, while their lower landing and take-off speeds mean that runway repairs need not be completed to the same standard.

Also, the FOLs can, if necessary, be covertly changed and concealed. The A-10 is an easy aircraft to fly, and operations from an unfamiliar field would present no prblems. It uses only one piece of specialized ground equipment, the ammunition loader, and supplies held at the FOL are, in general, compact and limited. Changing the position of a FOL does not, for example, call for the movement of dozens of spare engines.

Using FOLs close to the battle line, A-10 units have demonstrated their ability to fly more sorties per aircraft per day than any other type in the inventory. In early tests of the FOL concept, in April 1978, A-10s averaged nearly 15 missions per day over a three-day period and surge rates above 10 sorties have been attained in later exercises. The average sortie surge rate, though, is above six missions per day, greater than that of any other USAF aircraft.

Firepower, endurance, short reaction time, resistance to counter-air attacks and high sortie rates make the A-10 force a unique asset. Live exercises and studies have repeatedly shown that the A-10 not only performs better than other systems in its own specialized arena, but does many things which no other weapon can do at all. For example, a secondary mission assigned to the 81st TFW is to escort the USAF's combat rescue helicopters, should they have to penetrate hostile territory in the daytime. Armed with cluster weapons and the cannon to suppress groundfire, the A-10's endurance and speed make it a much more suitable escort than any other fighter.

To the ground commander or forward air controller (FAC) the A-10's 'combat persistence' is, perhaps, its salient advantage. The fast-mover strike aircraft, with its limited endurance, may be able to respond quickly to a call for help, but the support which it can offer is not only limited in duration, but also tied to a certain time. The FAC knows that the F-16 strike requested some time ago will arrive at 1543 hours precisely, and the activities of other systems on the battlefield must be geared to that time. The A-10, by contrast, can be held in reserve until another weapon has had time to attack, or can be vectored to another part of the engagement zone after completing one effective attack.

One way of using the A-10, which has been practised to the limited extent possible in peacetime, is 'ground loiter', a technique otherwise confined to the Harrier. If the A-10s are required to wait near the battle for any extended period, they can alight easily on a good stretch of road – and Germany's autobahns are the best in the world – and wait for a call to action. The APU keeps all the systems running while using a minimal amount of fuel, so the aircraft can start engines and take off at shorter notice than any other type.

The A-10 is the only weapon which offers this sort of performance without sacrificing the full mobility of airpower; this is one of the factors which distinguishes the A-10 from the tank-killing helicopter. The helicopter is slow and short-legged, and the commander at the scene is, for practical purposes, limited to the helicopter force in his immediate vicinity. The available helicopter resources

Left: From these four forward operating locations, the A-10s of the 81st TFW have the range to cover the whole of the frontier between East and West Germany.

Below: The rolling plains of northern Germany are ideal tank country: they are also ideal Warthog territory, especially when winter weather grounds other types for days on end.

Below: An A-10 of the 57th TTW, now the 57th Fighter Weapons Wing, in one of the camouflage schemes evaluated during the JAWS (Joint Attack Weapons Systems) trials held at Fort Hunter Liggett, California, in November 1977. New tactics were tested against a variety of threats.

have to be spread out along the entire battle line, so the numbers available at any one spot will not be large enough to mount a strong counterattack. The A-10, however, is available for rapid reinforcement at any point.

Another attribute of the A-10 versus the helicopter is the ability of the faster fixed-wing aircraft to survive at close quarters with enemy SAM and AAA units. The helicopter is, essentially, an ambush weapon, unparalleled in its ability to find and exploit cover and attack from concealment. Its limitation is that it is most effective against the front and forward flanks of an advancing unit, and that it is unable to strike targets deep within the formation. Apart from the new AH-64, too, no helicopter has more than half the A-10's firepower, measured in effective anti-armour weaponry.

The tasks assigned to the A-10 in each phase of the battle reflect the type's strengths. In the early stages, as the advancing enemy spreads out through the van of the defences, the A-10s are available to respond quickly as advance ground forces engage the first enemy units. The ground forces delay the advance, and provide targeting information for effective attacks by A-10s.

Once the main force is engaged, the A-10 force can be used to provide 'fire-hose' CAS, a constant flow of sorties to the battle area which the commander can direct as necessary. The aircraft may support a unit in danger of being broken through, or exploit the brief opportunity offered by a new unit joining battle, and not yet fully deployed. In the case of a breakthrough, the A-10 force can be rapidly concentrated to slow the advancing force, attack the flanks of forces moving through the breach, and disrupt the movement of forces to the front. The last-named mission is not regarded as CAS, but is termed 'battlefield air interdiction', or BAI.

JAWS and JAAT

The way in which these operations are commanded and controlled is unique. The A-10 was the first TAC aircraft designed to work in such close proximity to hostile armoured forces, and the first which would be so closely integrated with the battle on the ground. It was in early 1977 that USAF and US Army officers began to discuss a common problem: that it was clearly wasteful and dangerous to confront an armoured attack in increments, each service sending in its own systems independently. The discussions led to the development of a concept called JAWS (joint attack weapons systems), in which the strong and weak points of the helicopter, artillery and the A-10 would be blended into a single system. Early trials took place at Fort Benning, Georgia, in September 1977, followed two months later by a full-scale JAWS exercise at Fort Hunter Liggett, California.

Above left: The mottled paint schemes used for the JAWS tests were applied to every part of the aircraft, and were varied from day to day to match weather and terrain conditions.

Above: Following the JAWS trials, a 57th FWW A-10 in mottled camouflage was deployed to Ramstein AB, Germany, to participate in evaluation of infrared Maverick performance.

The JAWS trials were highly successful. The A-10's main task was to shoot tanks. Freed from that major burden, the Cobra helicopters concentrated on attacking the air defence systems, using the highest possible degree of concealment and the longest possible stand-off ranges. The presence of two airborne threats, with completely different speed and manoeuvrability characteristics, confused the air defence operators. A helicopter popping out of cover might be about to attack; the Shilka operator would traverse his turret and lock on, and the helicopter would promptly drop back behind the treeline, having simply intended to decoy the gunner away from an attacking A-10. Safe separation was assured by a simple rule of thumb: the attack helicopters held the airspace from the ground to the treetops, and the space above belonged to the A-10.

To the A-10 pilot, racing at low level with no overview of the battlefield, the presence and alignment of helicopters were always a clue to the presence of tanks over the hill. The helicopters would launch their first attack on the air-defence units as the A-10s passed them on their way in; then, as the A-10s left the scene, the gun and missile systems engaged the aircraft, betraying their positions for a second attack.

Once the scores were added up, it was found that the Cobras and A-10s working together had killed three to four times as many targets as had been hit in previous exercises by similar forces working separately. The vulnerability of both types was also greatly reduced. A Joint Air Attack Team (JAAT) manual was prepared, and the techniques developed in the JAWS exercises were written into regular A-10 operations.

Below: An A-10 in JAWS markings outside its aircraft shelter at Ramstein AB. Testing of IIR missiles concentrated on performance in bad weather and battlefield smoke.

Above: During the JAWS trials, no live ammunition or missiles were fired, but data links to the range instrumentation system facilitated precise analysis of the results.

Good forward air control (FAC) – observation of battlefield targets, and the assignment of targets to different air assets – is crucial to successful JAAT operations. The A-10s and helicopters work within a common FAC structure, but tactics are not rigid. One important reason for flexibility, besides the fact that it leaves room for individual initiative, is that easy and reliable communications are not to be expected in the face of intense hostile jamming. Moreover, the A-10 pilots, in manual terrain-following flight en route to the battle area, have no time to take down attack instructions in exhaustive detail.

Instead, the JAAT philosophy stresses the importance of frequent joint practice and training sessions involving A-10s and helicopters, so that the A-10 pilots learn to fill their role in the JAAT with a minimum of briefing and only a few moments of communication with the FAC. The USAF's OV-10 FAC aircraft, with their long endurance, are important in maintaining an overview of the action, and act as the 'traffic police', directing the A-10s to the starting points for their attack runs. Immediately before entering the target area, the A-10 pilots receive a last update from a front-line FAC in a helicopter, jeep or armoured personnel carrier.

The A-10 mission in Central Europe is highly demanding, and commanders say that even an experienced A-10 pilot transferred from the US will take at least a year to understand the mission completely. The need to comprehend the command and control system along an extended stretch of the front, possibly involving British, Dutch, Belgian and German forces, is added to the demands of the mission itself. In Europe, the A-10 pilots fly and train for a high-threat environment. In an engagement, they will jink constantly to throw off the defensive systems, and will pull more than 7g positive and 2.5-3g negative in the process. With its combination of long endurance and heavy armament, together with high sortie rates, the A-10 can spend far more time in combat than any other aircraft. The European A-10 force has a higher ratio of pilots to aircraft (28 pilots per 18-aircraft squadron) than the TAC average, because the ability of the aircraft would otherwise be limited by sheer pilot fatigue.

Training is intensive. The new arrival is introduced to two-ship formation flying at progressively lower altitudes, and, when operating from the FOLs, the pilots simulate wartime sortie rates, flying two or three missions a day. A-10s in Europe practice regularly with the Aggressor unit at RAF Alconbury. In the 1982 fiscal year, the European A-10s alone accounted for 24 per cent of all the flying hours in US Air Forces Europe, and more hours than that of the next two wings combined.

Ugly and aggressive, the Warthog has a talent for arousing strong feelings. It certainly lacks the Lamborghini glamour of the F-16, or the puissant grace of the Eagle. Ground troops like the Warthog, possibly because it is the only TAC aircraft that will never be chasing MiG-23s five miles above their heads while the T-72s are running over their toes. An 81st TFW pilot summed up the A-10 pilots' attitudes: "Fighter pilots used to be short guys with big wristwatches and little airplanes who stayed far above the conflict. Warthog jockeys have little wristwatches and big airplanes, and go looking for a fight."

Glossary and abbreviations

AAA Anti-aircraft artillery, or all tube AA weapons. Usually spoken as "triple-A"
AB Air Base (USAF base outside USA)
AD Air Division (TAC formation)
AF Air Force (USAF formation)
AFB Air Force Base
AFRES (US) Air Force Reserves
AGM- US designation prefix for any air-to-ground missile
AIM- US designation prefix for any air-to-air missile
ALQ- US designation prefix for any active countermeasures equipment
ALR- US designation prefix for any radar-warning receiver
ANG Air National Guard
API Armour-piercing incendiary (ammunition)
APU Auxiliary power unit
A-X Attack, Experimental: programme designation used before selection of A-10
BAI Battlefield air interdiction
BPR Bypass ratio
Bunt Wings-level, negative-g entry into a dive
Bypass ratio Ratio of the total airflow through a turbofan engine to that passing through the core section
CAS Close air support
CBU- US designation prefix for a cluster-bomb unit
Cobra US Army Bell AH-1 attack helicopter
COIN Counter-insurgency
CONUS Continental US
CRT Cathode-ray tube (computer/TV-type display screen)
DT & E Development, test and evaluation
Egress USAF term for flight out of combat area
ECM Electronic countermeasures
EW Electronic warfare
FAC Forward air control, or forward air controller
Flir Forward-looking infra-red
FOD Foreign-object damage
FOL Forward operating location
FWW Fighter Weapons Wing (Nellis-based TAC unit)
g Unit of acceleration
GBU- US designation prefix for an unpowered guided bomb system
GE General Electric (the US company, no connection with the British company of the same name)
GPWS Ground-proximity warning system
Grunt Infantryman (US slang)
HEI High-explosive incendiary (ammunition)
HUD Head-up display
HVM Hypervelocity missile
Induced drag Drag due to lift, and proportional to lift
Ingress USAF term for flight into combat area
INS Inertial navigation system
In-weather Conditions of zero effective visibility due to cloud or rain. Term mainly used in connection with low-level flight or attack
IR Infra-red
JAAT Joint Air Attack Team
JAWS Joint Attack Weapons Systems
JTF Joint Test Force
Lantirn Low-Altitude Navigation, and Targeting by Infra-Red at Night
LLTV Lowlight television
Lock-on The action of a missile or other system maintaining contact with a target using its own sensors
Manual reversion Provision for a control surface to be moved by human force alone in the event of power failure
Maple Flag Regular USAF/Nato combat exercises, held in Canada to combine large range with European-type weather
N/AW Night/adverse-weather
Pk Kill probability of a weapon, expressed as a decimal of 1. Single-shot pK of 0.5 means that one round in two will kill the target
Red Flag Regular USAF exercises held at Nellis AFB, Nevada
RFP Request for proposals
RWR Radar-warning receiver
SA- Nato-assigned designation prefix for Soviet surface-to-air missile system, including all ground equipment
Suite A group of avionics systems dedicated to the same task
TAC Tactical Air Command
TFG Tactical Fighter Group (ANG or AFRES formation only)
TFR Terrain-following radar
TFS Tactical Fighter Squadron (nominal strength 18 aircraft)
TFTS Tactical Fighter Training Squadron
TFTW Tactical Fighter Training Wing
TFW Tactical Fighter Wing (normally, four TFS)
TFWC Tactical Fighter Weapons Center, Nellis AFB
TP Target Practice (ammunition)
USAF United States Air Force
USAFE United States Air Forces in Europe
ZSU- Zenitny Samochodnaya Ustenovka (self-propelled anti-aircraft gun): Soviet designation prefix for mobile AAA systems

Specifications

		Fairchild A-10A	Definition	Northrop YA-9A
Dimensions	Wing span	57ft 6in/17.53m		58ft/17.67m
	Length overall	53ft 4in/16.26m		56ft 6in/17.22m
	Height overall	14ft 8in/4.47m		16ft 11in/5.16m
	Wing area	506sq ft/47.01m²		580sq ft/53.9m²
Powerplant		Two GE TF34-GE-100A		Two Avco-Lycoming YF102-LD-100
	Thrust (each)	9,065lb/40.3kN		7,500lb/33.3kN
	Bypass ratio	6.2:1		
Weights	Operating empty	24,959lb/11,321kg	Pilot, oxygen, unusable fuel and oil, gun and six pylons	
	Basic design weight	30,384lb/13,782kg	Maximum weight at 7.33 g	
	Internal fuel	10,700lb/4,853kg		
	Max external load	16,000lb/7,250kg		
Take-off weights	Clean			26,000lb/11,800kg
	Maximum	50,000lb/22,680kg		42,000lb/1,905kg
	CAS mission	47,094lb/21,362kg	18 565lb (256kg) Mk 82 bombs, 750 rounds of ammunition and full internal fuel	
	Anti-armour mission	42,071lb/19,083kg	Six Mavericks on triple launchers, 1,174 rounds of ammunition, ALQ-119, 480 flare/chaff cartridges and full internal fuel	
	Ferry	49,774lb/22,577kg	Full internal fuel and three 600 US gal (2,271lit) external tanks	
Performance	Never-exceed speed	450kt/834km/h		390kt/723km/h
	Max level speed at sea level, clean	381kt/706km/h		
	Combat speed at 5,000ft (1525m) with six Mk 82 bombs	380kt/704km/h		
	Cruising speed at sea level	300kt/555km/h		270kt/500km/h
	Sea-level rate of climb at design weight	6,000ft/min/1,828m/min		
	Service ceiling	45,000ft/1,3715m		
Combat radii	Anti-armour configuration, 30min combat, 40nm (74km) sea-level penetration and exit	252nm/467km		250nm (463km) with 2hr loiter
	CAS configuration, 1.88hr single-engine loiter at 5,000ft (1525m), 10min combat	250nm/463km		
	Ferry range, 50kt (93km) headwinds, 20min reserve	2,240nm/4,148km		

Deployment

USAF A-10 units

Command	Formation	Operating unit	Base
Air National Guard		128th TFW	Truax Field, Wisconsin
		174th TFW	Syracuse, New York
		103rd TFG	Windsor Locks, Connecticut
		104th TFG	Westfield, Massachusetts
		175th TFG	Baltimore, Maryland
Alaskan Air Command	343rd Composite Wing	18th TFS	Eielson AFB, Alaska
Pacific Air Forces	5th Air Force	25th TFS	Suwon AB, South Korea
Tactical Air Command	9th Air Force	23rd TFW	England AFB, Louisiana
	9th Air Force	354th TFW	Myrtle Beach AFB, South Carolina
	12th AF, 836th AD	355th TTW	Davis-Monthan AFB, Arizona
	TFWC	57th FWW	Nellis AFB, Nevada
USAFE	3rd Air Force	81st TFW	RAF Bentwaters/Woodbridge, England
US Air Force Reserves	434th TFW	45th TFS	Grissom AFB, Indiana
	442nd TFG	303rd TFS	Richards-Gebaur AFB, Missouri
	917th TFG	47th TFS	Barksdale AFB, Louisiana
	917th TFG	46th TFTS	
	926th TFG	706th TFS	New Orleans NAS, Louisiana

Chapter 2

F-15

EAGLE

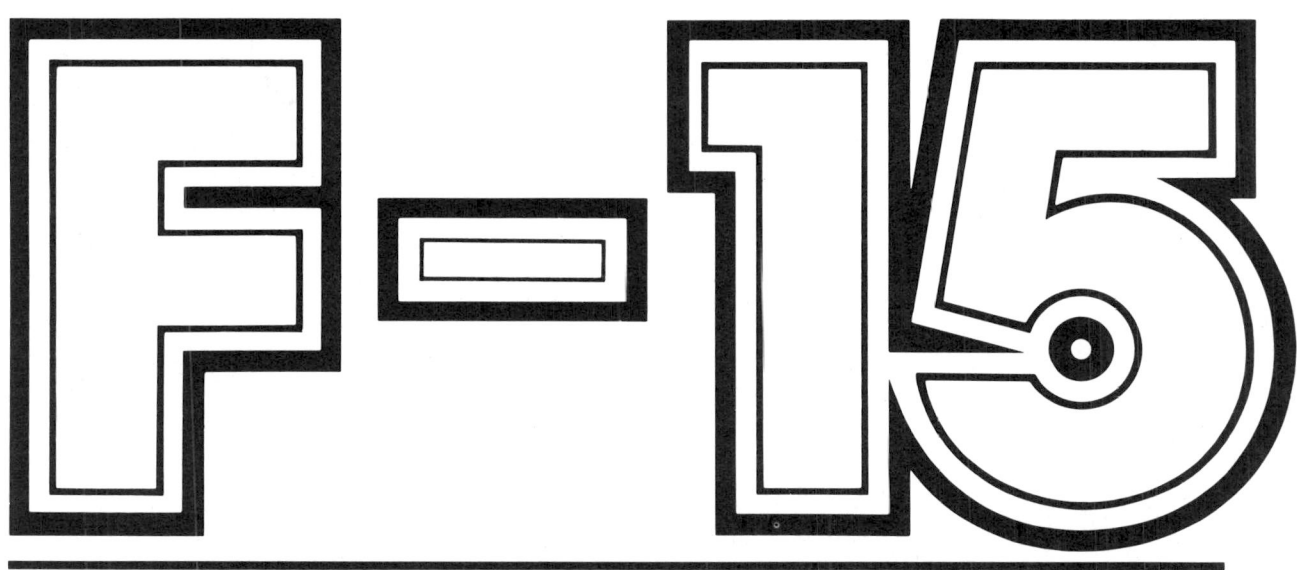

Michael J. Gething

F-15 Eagle

Contents

Acknowledgements

The author and editor are grateful to the following individuals who have helped in the preparation of this chapter: Geoffrey Norris, Karen Stubberfield and Jeffrey Fister of the McDonnell Douglas Corporation; Major Dito Ladd, formerly of the 36th TFW, USAF; and Colonel Wendell H. Shawler, formerly Director of the F-15 Joint Test Force.

The Powerplant section is based on the equivalent section in the companion chapter *F-16 Fighting Falcon* by Doug Richardson. The author is further grateful to Don Parry, Lindsay Peacock and Bernard Fitzsimons who contributed the sections on Avionics, Deployment and Combat, and Structure and Performance and Handling respectively.

Author

Michael J. Gething is Managing Editor of the Whitton Press *Defence* series of publications and Editor of *Defence*. Before joining the staff of the magazine in 1976 he had worked for the Defence Operational Analysis Establishment at West Byfleet, and had been Assistant Editor of the Royal Aeronautical Society magazine, *Aerospace*.

Fascinated by aviation history since his youth, he began his career as an aviation journalist by writing on scale modelling subjects. Although he has less time to build models, he keeps in touch with the scene through the International Plastic Modellers Society.

In his spare time he is a squadron officer with the Bracknell Squadron of the Air Training Corps, having been commissioned in the Royal Air Force Volunteer Reserve (Training Branch) in 1972. Among his other books are *NATO Air Power in the 1980s*, *Warsaw Pact Air Power in the 1980s* and *Military Helicopters*.

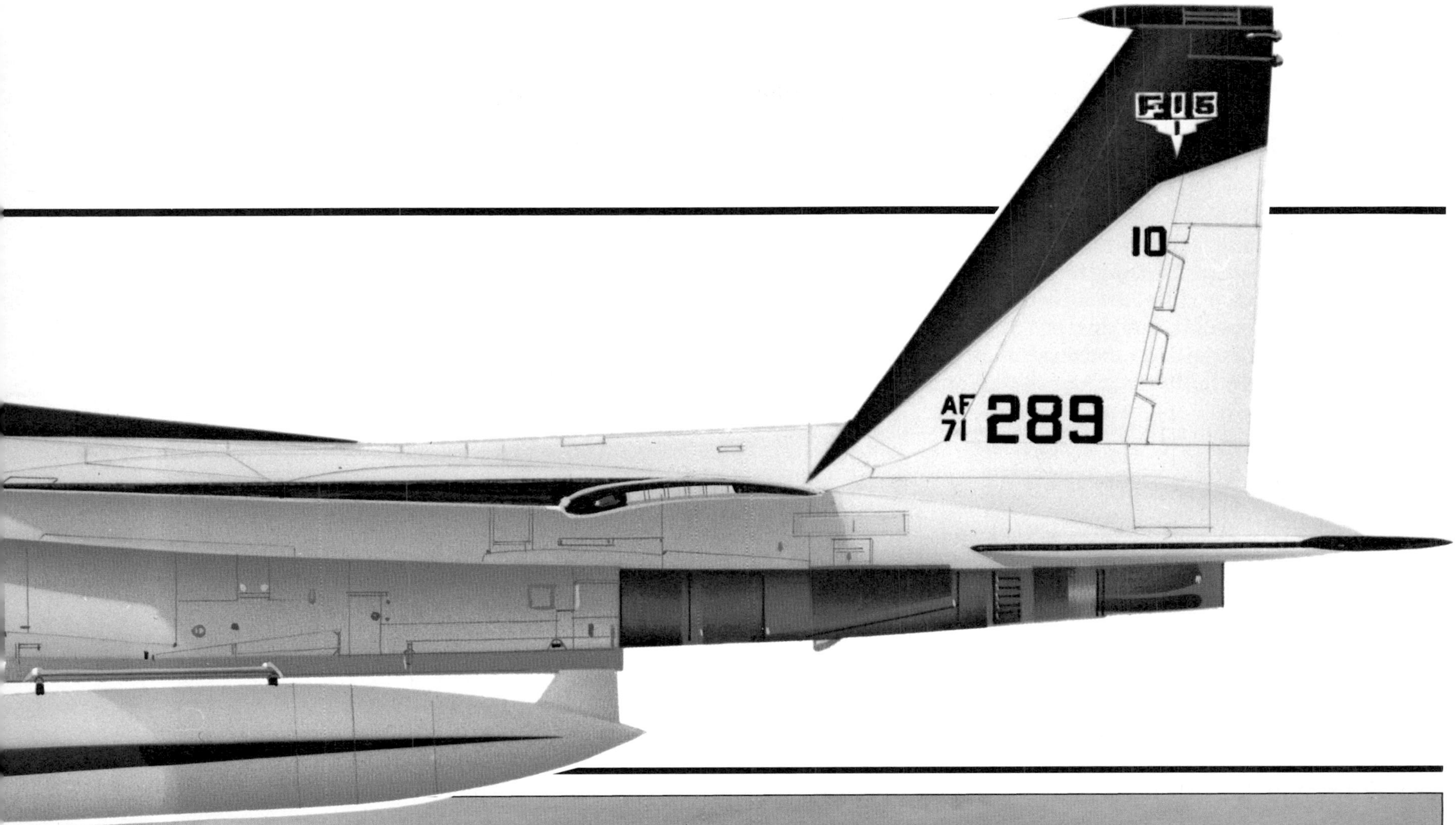

Introduction

Fighter aircraft have always held a special fascination, from the apparently flimsy scout biplanes of the First World War, through the legendary Spitfire, Mustang and Zero of the Second World War and the F-86 Sabre that fought over Korea to the F-4 Phantom of the 1960s. Even compared with such predecessors the F-15 Eagle sets a completely new standard, and one that only today is even beginning to be matched by the Soviet Union.

The Eagle's exceptional capabilities are the product of a combination of features. Two powerful F100 engines provide the 50,000lb (22,700kg) of thrust for record-breaking climb and acceleration; an airframe refined through thousands of hours of computer studies and wind-tunnel tests translates raw power into outstanding manoeuvrability; digital avionics and a powerful long-range radar enable targets to be detected at ranges of up to 100 miles (160km); and new versions of the medium-range radar-guided Sparrow and short-range heat-seeking Sidewinder, along with a high-speed Gatling gun, form the Eagle's deadly claws. All these aspects are dealt with in authoritative detail in the following pages, along with accounts of the type's performance and handling qualities, its deployment and combat record with the Israel Defence Force Air Force and the future versions currently under development for the specialized ground-attack and anti-satellite roles.

The one major drawback with this exceptional aircraft is its price: only Israel, Japan and Saudi Arabia have so far found the wherewithal – and the official approval – to acquire their own F-15s, and not even the US Air Force can afford all the Eagles it would like. However, it was inevitable that the best fighter in the world, would also be one of the most expensive, and in terms both of current capability and of potential for development, it would seem that the size of the bill is equalled by the stature of the product.

Development

Confronted with a new generation of Soviet combat aircraft in 1967, while it was fighting in Vietnam with the 'second-hand' F-4 Phantom, the US Air Force began serious work on a new fighter of its own. Designated FX, and intended to provide air superiority in friendly and hostile airspace alike, the new design was to be optimized for combat, with the power and agility to overcome any current or projected Soviet opponent. In the resulting F-15 Eagle, with its unequalled combination of performance, firepower and sophisticated avionics, the USAF believes it has such a machine.

Above: Air superiority blue and dayglo orange paint scheme on one of the pre-production F-15s during the flight test programme.

There are two adages which apply to the McDonnell Douglas F-15 Eagle: 'if it looks good, it is good' and 'if you design a good fighter, it can be adapted to other roles successfully'. The basic objective of the F-15 programme was, according to Major General Benjamin N. Bellis, F-15 System Program Director, "to efficiently acquire a fighter capable of gaining and maintaining air superiority through air-to-air combat". Although the Eagle has yet to be flown in action by the US Air Force it has fulfilled its purpose, again according to Maj Gen Bellis of being "a high performance, extremely agile aircraft to meet the projected threat of the late 1970s and early 1980s" at the hands of Israeli pilots over the Lebanon. The air-to-ground capability built into the original design is now being enhanced to produce the F-15E 'Strike Eagle', and the type is also being procured as an air defence interceptor to replace the F-106 Delta Dart.

The F-15 Eagle is the first air superiority fighter to stem from USAF requirements since the F-86 Sabre of 1948. The previous TAC (Tactical Air Command) fighter was the F-4 Phantom II, designed for the US Navy and, together with the A-7D Corsair II, forced on the USAF by the circumstances of the Vietnam War. Having to procure Navy aircraft was anathema to the Air Force, and despite the success of both Phantom and Corsair, when the time came for a new tactical fighter the Air Force was determined that it should be of their own choosing.

New Soviet fighters

The genesis of the Eagle can, perhaps, be traced back to a Russian airfield at Domodedovo, near Moscow in July 1967. At an airshow there, in front of the world's press, the Soviet Union unveiled a new generation of combat aircraft. Of particular note were a swing-wing fighter, condenamed Flogger by NATO, and a high-speed, twin-fin fighter codenamed Foxbat, both from the famous Mikoyan-Gurevich (MiG) design bureau. Later information was to identify the Flogger as the MiG-23 and the Foxbat as the MiG-25, while a later ground-attack version of the MiG-23 was designated MiG-27 Flogger D.

The MiG-23 Flogger was a single-seat air-combat fighter powered by a single Tumansky R-29 afterburning turbojet with a Mach 2.2 capability. Armed with a twin-barrel 23mm GSh-23 cannon and four air-to-air missiles – later known to comprise a pair each of AA-7 Apex and AA-8 Aphid AAMs – its range of 1,200 miles (1,930km) and service ceiling of 61,000ft (18,600m) made it a potent fighter. It was to supplement the MiG-21 Fishbed series of fighters, then in their second and now in the third stage of their development.

The MiG-25 Foxbat was also a single-seater, but powered by a pair of Tumansky R-31 afterburning turbojets. Initially a missiles-only interceptor, with a pair of AA-6 Acrid (one infra-red homing and one radar homing) plus a single AA-7 Apex and a single AA-8 Aphid, it carried a high-power radar codenamed Fire Fox. It has a Mach 2.8 capability, could fly 1,610 miles (2,580km) and had a service ceiling of 80,000ft (24,400m). Initially the design was thought to have been a counter to the American B-70 Valkyrie bomber cancelled in 1961, but the Foxbat was continued as an air superiority and reconnaissance fighter. The implication was obvious to the Pentagon: here was a fighter that could prove immune to the standard USAF fighter of the day, the F-4 Phantom.

The FX study

Work on a new air superiority fighter had begun within the USAF as a general feeling of need for an aircraft in the best traditions of the P-51 Mustang and F-86 Sabre. This was in the early 1960s, and by April 1965 the USAF fighter lobby were looking at a Fighter Experimental (FX) type. In October 1965 the USAF asked for funding of full scale studies, and two months later issued a Request for Proposals (RFP) for a Tactical Support Aircraft. The Concept Formulation Study (CFS) which came out of the RFP went to Boeing, Lockhead and North American Rockwell in March 1966, the McDonnell Aircraft Company (MCAIR) being one of the losers at this stage. However, none of the submitted designs was considered further, mainly due to the aerodynamic configurations and bypass ratio of the powerplants.

From mid-1966 to autumn 1967 activity on the FX was minimal, although the USAF maintained its own CFS team in being until autumn 1968. The impact of the Domodedovo revelations was felt,

Below: Silhouetted against the setting sun, a pair of F-15As in the skies they were designed to dominate.

Top left: The 60,000lb (27,000kg) variable-geometry proposal produced by MCAIR in early 1968.

Above left: slightly later design study with fixed delta wing.

Top: Variable-camber leading edges were envisaged for this wing form developed in early 1969.

Above: Wooden mock-up of the F-15 used for NASA wind-tunnel tests.

and in August 1967 a second RFP for a CFS was issued. This time the words Tactical Support Aircraft were changed to one – Fighter – and this time MCAIR, along with General Dynamics (formerly Convair) were awarded the six-month study.

Among the objectives set by the USAF was a speed range of Mach 1.5 to 3.0. General Dynamics offered both a variable geometry and a fixed-wing FX: MCAIR recommended a fixed wing, twin engines and a single crewman. This second CFS was completed in May 1968, and in September of that year the FX Concept Development was authorized. In the same month the RFP for Contract Definition stage was offered to the aerospace industry, and MCAIR, along with Boeing, Fairchild Hiller, General Dynamics, Grumman, Lockhead, Ling Temco Vought and North American, bid for the contract. By December 1968 only MCAIR, Fairchild Hiller and North American were in the running.

By now the FX was designated F-15 and the three contenders were hard at work. A Development Concept Paper issued by the USAF defined the overall parameters of the design, and justified it against pressure from the US Navy to take a modified version of their VFAX/F-14 on four counts: it would be a single-seat, fixed-wing, twin-engined fighter of approximately 40,000lb (18,000kg); there would be no competitive fly-off, as this was not thought desirable; the VFAX was not considered a suitable replacement for the F-4E Phantom, nor could the F-4E be modified to meet the threat; and an air-to-ground capability would be included, but only as an offshoot of the primary air-to-air role.

Initiated under the Total Procurement Package, the programme thus left a large volume of work for the contractors bidding. No hardware competition

Right: The first F-15A prototype airborne for the first time from Edwards AFB on July 27, 1972.

Below: A month earlier, the same aircraft was photographed before the roll-out ceremony at St Louis.

Above: The third development F-15A, used to test the avionics, is seen here in the markings of the USAF Flight Dynamics Laboratory Advanced Environmental Control System.

Above: The second development TF-15, later redesignated F-15B, was flown for the first time on October 18, 1973, and has subsequently been seen in a variety of configurations.

F-15 Project demonstration milestones

Preliminary design review	Sep 70
Radar contractor selection	Sep 70
Critical design review	Apr 71
Avionics review	June 71
Major sub-assembly tests	Jun 72
Engine inlet compatibility	Mar 72
First flight	Jul 72
Bench avionics complete	Sep 72
First aircraft performance demonstration	Sep 72
First airborne avionics performance	Dec 72
Fatigue test to reach one lifetime	Jan 73
Static test 2 critical concluded	Jan 73
Armament ground test	Jun 73
1g flight envelope	Aug 73
Fatigue test to reach 3 lifetimes	Dec 73
USAF evaluation summary	Dec 73
Equipment qualified	Mar 74
Category II aircraft and equipment in place	Mar 74
Training equipment in place	Oct 74
Fatigue test to reach 4 lifetimes	Oct 74
External stores flutter and release	Aug 74
AGE equipment in place	Oct 74
Category I flight tests complete	Nov 74
First aircraft delivered to TAC	Nov 74

meant an enormous amount of paper studies and documentation, while the contract itself had to include tooling, development, testing and production. Later, in response to criticism from Congress and the public over cost overruns on the C-5A Galaxy and F-111 programmes, the USAF worked in demonstration milestones which the contractor had to meet before receiving the next stage of funding. These are listed in the accompanying table.

The bids were made by June 1969, and from July to December the USAF's Aeronautical Systems Division made their evaluation. Selection of the McDonnell Douglas bid was announced on December 23, 1969. Major General Bellis announced in Washington the next day that in the technical, operational, management and logistic areas McDonnell Douglas had been placed first. In addition he went on to say that the MCAIR price had been lowest of the three. Selection of the winning contractor was the responsibility of Secretary of the Air Force Robert G. Seamans Jr, after hearing presentations from the F-15 source selection evaluation board and the source selection advisory council, neither of which made specific recommendations. Secretary Seamans' choice was favourably received throughout the USAF.

The initial contract called for 20 development aircraft: a preliminary batch of 10 single-seat F-15A (71-0280–71-0289) and a pair of two-seat trainer TF-15A (71-0290 and 71-0291, later redesignated F-15B) Category I versions; and eight Category II full scale development (FSD) aircraft in single seat F-15A form (72-0113–72-0120). The FSD batch were closely matched to the production configuration.

The first F-15 was rolled out officially at MCAIR's plant at St Louis on June 26, 1972 with due ceremony. In July it was taken apart, loaded into a USAF C-5A Galaxy transport and airlifted to Edwards AFB, California. There it was reassembled, checked out and prepared for its maiden flight. On a typical Californian clear day, with blazing sunshine, MCAIR's Chief Test Pilot Irving Burrows took the first Eagle (USAF serial 71-0280) into the air on July 27, 1972.

The Eagle's missions

In the terms of the FX Development Concept Paper (DCP), the F-15 is "optimized for counter-air missions" operating as part of TAC. These missions, which come under the general heading of air superiority, include escorting friendly strike forces over enemy airspace, making fighter sweeps ahead of such a strike force, combat air patrol between friendly strike aircraft and enemy bases, and tactical air defence of friendly territory.

According to the DCP, the most difficult of these roles is combat over enemy airspace, where "the counter-air fighter must protect the strike force from enemy fighters while under the disadvantage of being in the enemy's GCI network and exposed to potential attack from his fighters, SAMs and AAA". It is no surprise, therefore, to learn that the DCP calls for the F-15 to be "superior in air combat to any present or postulated Soviet fighters both in close-in, visual encounters and in stand-off or all-weather encounters".

According to the DCP assessment, neither an improved F-4E, with new wings and engines, or a version of the VFX (F-14 Tomcat) for which a contract was placed in February 1969, were considered able to meet the FX requirement. USAF politics aside, the configuration as a carrier aircraft for the basic role of fleet air defence and its consequent cost ruled out the VFX. However, an 'escape clause' was written into the DCP, which considered a

Left: An August 1975 view of the second F-15B, seen here carrying out trials with the Fuel and Sensor Tactical (FAST) pack conformal fuel tanks on the intake sides.

F-15 pre-production aircraft flight test roles

Serial	First flight	Function
71-0280	Jul 27, 1972	Open flight envelope; explore handling qualities; external stores carriage
71-0281	Sep 26, 1972	F100 engine tests
71-0282	Nov 4, 1972	Avionics development; calibrated air speed tests
71-0283	Jan 13, 1973	Structural test airframe
71-0284	Mar 7, 1973	Internal gun, external fuel jettison and armament tests
71-0285	May 23, 1973	Avionics tests; flight control evaluation; missile fire control
71-0286	Jun 14, 1973	Armament and fuel stores tests
71-0287	Aug 25, 1973	Spin recovery, high AOA and fuel system tests
71-0288	Oct 20, 1973	Integrated aircraft/engine performance tests
71-0289	Jan 16, 1974	Tactical EW system, radar and avionics evaluation

Below: F-15B 71-0291 in the Bicentennial paint scheme worn by this much repainted Eagle during 1976 as part of the celebrations of 200 years of American independence.

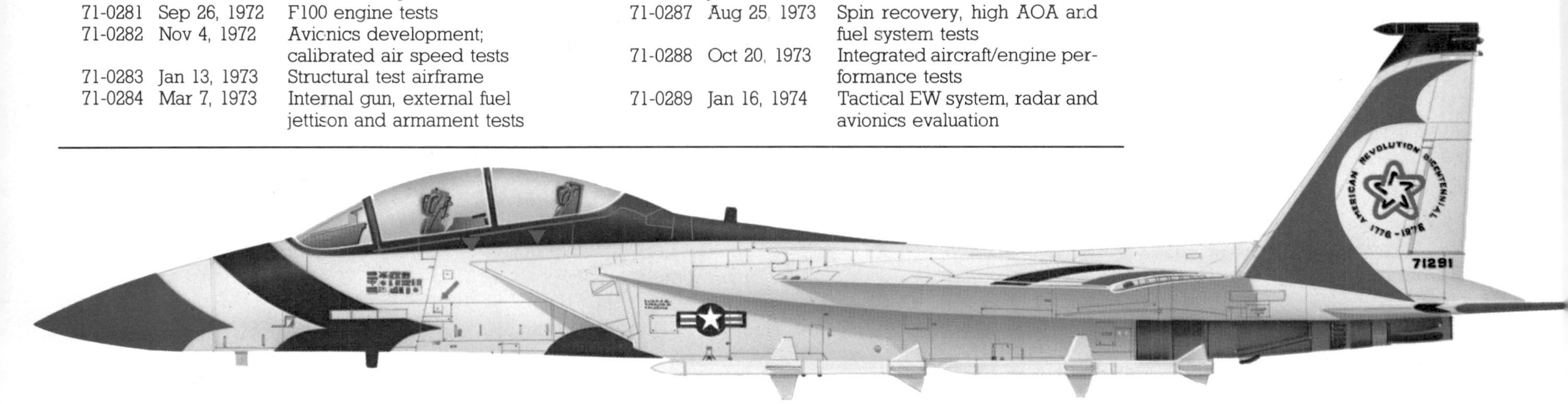

further examination when "revised, detailed information on the tradeoffs between VFX-2 (with new engines and lighter avionics) and FX will be available to enable a decision as to whether to pursue one or both of these aircraft".

It is further interesting to note that the Eagle itself was later considered for adoption by the US Navy. This occurred in July 1971, when the Secretary of Defense asked the Navy to investigate the possibility of an F-15N, via the Systems Program Office. A minimum modification study by MCAIR to equip the Eagle for carrier operations increased the weight of the aircraft by some 2,300lb (1,043kg). The Navy Fighter Study Group III then did their own appreciation, disregarding the MCAIR data, which resulted in further weight increases and the addition of AIM-54 Phoenix AAM. In this configuration the weight and drag sent the performance down and the costs up to a level where the F-15N was deemed unacceptable.

The navalized Eagle made one more appearance before being finally rejected. Investigative testimony before the Senate Armed Services Committee's ad hoc Tactical Air Power subcommittee started new discussions on a modified Eagle for the Navy. This was in March 1973, at a time when the F-14 Tomcat programme was under pressure. Deputy Secretary of Defense Packard wanted to look at a lower-cost F-14, the F-15N and improved F-4s as alternatives for the Navy mission. The result was the formation of Navy Fighter Study IV, where these alternatives were discussed, and out of it came the concept of the Naval Air Combat Fighter to partner the F-14 in a maritime equivalent of the Air Force F-15/F-16 hi-lo mix. Ironically, MCAIR was selected as prime contractor on this programme, which involved navalizing the Northrop YF-17 as the F-18 Hornet.

Each of the ten pre-production Eagles was allocated a specific task in the flight test programme. Their roles were as outlined in the table. The first two-seater, 71-0290, was first flown on July 7, 1973, and was used for the two-seater evaluation. The second two-seater was flown on October 18, 1973. The first two-seater was slotted between the seventh and eighth aircraft, and since then every seventh aircraft built has been in two-seat configuration.

Right: The Bicentennial Eagle in flight, sporting the flags of the many countries where it had been demonstrated below the canopy.

Below: Back to a more familiar colour scheme, but still sporting an array of flags below the canopy, 71-0291 touches down with speed brake deployed.

Right: 72-0118, the sixth of eight full-scale development aircraft produced for the USAF's own Category II flight test and evaluation programme.

The first 12 Eagles were allocated to Category I of the test programme (now known as Contractor Development, Test and Evaluation) under the manufacturer's test pilots. The eight FSD aircraft allocated to Category II testing (now the Air Force Development, Test and Evaluation) were flown by a USAF Joint Test Force of Air Systems Command test pilots and Tactical Air Command fighter pilots. Category III of the test programme (now the Follow-on Operational Test and Evaluation) was conducted by the USAF. Later some of the Category I aircraft were passed on to the USAF.

By October 29, 1973, when the 1,000th test flight was flown by an F-15, 11 of the 12 Category I airframes were flying. Those aircraft had expanded the flight envelope of the Eagle to a speed of Mach 2.3 and a height of 60,000ft (18,300m). While development proceeded reasonably smoothly, it was not without its problems, and MCAIR Chief Test Pilot Irving Burrows and Colonel Wendell Shawler, the USAF's Director of the Joint Test Force 'went public' on a number of these in a joint lecture to the Society of Experimental Test Pilots in 1973.

The first problem discussed related to the stick force per g value. As a result of simulator experience prior to the first flight, it was thought that the aircraft might not be as nimble as expected, simply because of the stick forces. As designed, it was thought that these stick forces would be comfortable for manoeuvring, while not being so low as to suggest the chance of a pilot-induced oscillation or aggravate high g sensitivity. There are two sets of controls: a conventional hydromechanical system, and a Control Augmentation System (CAS). Both are capable of flying the aircraft, though the former was considered a back-up system in the event of the CAS failing.

The hydromechanical system determines the basic control deflections,

Above: Underside view of the 43rd production F-15A, the 61st of all single-seat Eagles.

Below: An early production F-15A in the markings of the 58th Tactical Fighter Training Wing, based at Luke AFB, Arizona, and wearing the standard Compass Gray two-tone paint scheme.

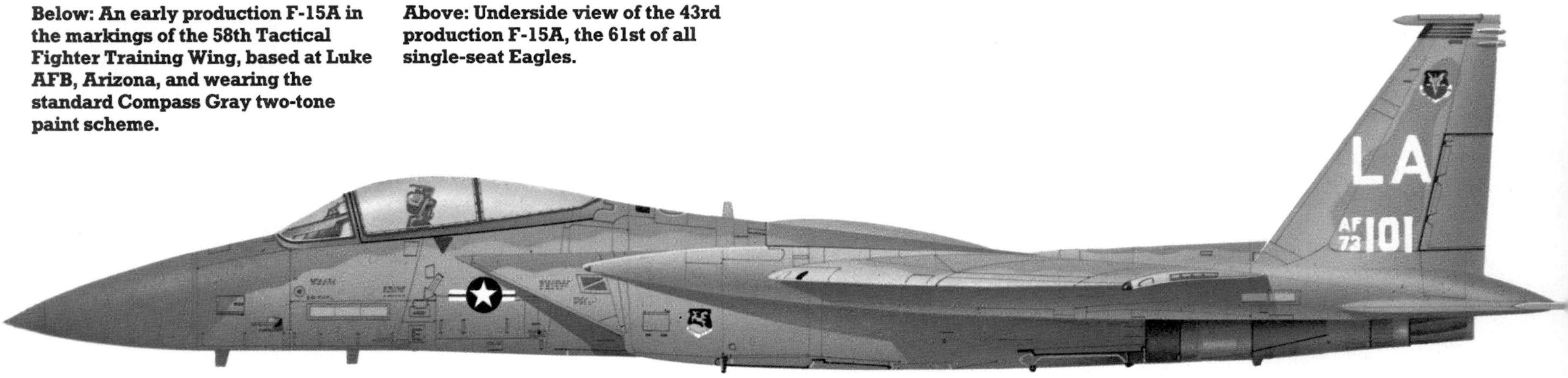

Below: One of two F-15Bs which, along a pair of F-15As, all from the 58th TFTW, were painted in a special attitude-deception three-tone grey camouflage scheme devised by aviation artist Keith Ferris.

Right: F-15Cs on the McDonnell Douglas production line in June 1981, when over 600 Eagles had been delivered to the USAF.

while the CAS operates over the hydromechanical system and modifies the control surface deflections which provided aircraft response in line with the stick position. In the mechanical longitudinal system a spring cartridge provided the linear force gradient. There was much debate as to what was the optimum setting for the cartridge, but as the evidence was based on simulator experience only there was some reluctance to make changes. Besides, it was thought unwise to lighten the stick forces too much in case the aircraft was accidentally overstressed. Thus with a stick force (ie the pressure required to be applied to the control column in order to move the control surfaces) of 3.75lb (1.7kg) per g, manoeuvres in excess of 6.5g required some 25lb (11.3kg) of stick force to initiate a response to control demand. In such high-g situations this meant some considerable strain on the pilot.

Modified stick forces

Early flight testing confirmed the initial simulation findings. With the CAS off the manoeuvring forces were too heavy for a fighter with the inherent capability of the F-15. With the CAS on these forces were more comfortable, but there was room for improvement. A dual-gradient longitudinal spring cartridge was evaluated, and found to be an improvement, while modifications were also made to the CAS pitch computer, enabling a satisfactory match between the CAS and the hydromechanical system. Flight testing of these fixes confirmed their suitability, and were incorporated in production aircraft. Forces around the neutral position are considered 'comfortable' at all speeds within the flight envelope, and there was no excessive longitudinal sensitivity or trend towards oscillation with the CAS either on or off. Pilots can now fly 6g manoeuvres one-handed with no trouble.

The lateral sensitivity of the Eagle also came in for some criticism. Although, again, it was recognized on the simulator, it was partially masked by the lack of physiological cues. The original specifications called for rolling capabilities in excess of previous accelerations. These could only be achieved by using a large amount of lateral control – quickly. This meant that lateral control surface deflections were 'sudden and big'. While the ailerons, with plus or minus 20deg of travel, are mechanically served, the differential stabilator (all-moving tailplane) is connected to both the mechanical and CAS circuits.

Normal smooth manoeuvring was highly responsive, but comfortable. However, any sudden small lateral movements of the stick, such as might be expected during formation flying, gun-tracking or air-to-air refuelling, caused an undesirable jerkiness resulting in a possible pilot-induced oscillation. While not as simple to correct as was the longtitudinal system, a two-point solution was arrived at. A dual-gradient force system coupled with a higher setting on the CAS transducer prevented the CAS from augmenting roll commands at small stick deflections was the first fix; the second involved a modification to the CAS in order to

Right: Tanker's eye view of a two-seat Eagle, with the refuelling boom positioned in the F-15's receptacle. In-flight refuelling has enabled Eagles to fly non-stop the 7,000 miles (9,620km) between Okinawa and Florida.

Above: Three brand new F-15As in flight early in 1976 before delivery to the 1st TFW at Langley AFB.

Below right: Streak Eagle easily beat the F-4's climb records, and was faster than an Apollo moonshot to 15,000m.

negate some of the roll rate demanded by small sharp deflection of the stick.

The need to retract the undercarriage into the fuselage led to a rather narrow track of 9ft 0¼in (2.75m) and a wheelbase of 17ft 9½in (5.42m). To have considered another configuration would have incurred an unacceptable weight penalty. The narrow track promised to produce a few problems, and these duly appeared during the flight testing. During crosswind landings the upwind wing would come up, causing the aircraft to tend to weathervane into the wind, and again drift downwind. Holding the nose up on landing only accentuated the problems, and so pilots always tried to get the nosewheel on the ground as quickly as possible.

The causes of the problems were soon identified. The first involved the aileron-rudder interconnect (ARI) system: as the stick was moved laterally (assuming a neutral or aft longitudinal position) rudder movement was initiated in sympathy. So, if the right wing came up and the stick was moved to the right to counteract it, the rudder motion would make the aircraft yaw to the right, and thus aggravate the tendency to weathervane. The second problem occurred with the stick aft, as if to hold the nose up, when the aircraft systems washed out some lateral control. This had been designed into the controls so as to mimimize lateral deflections of the stick at high angles of attack. As the pilots said, "Rolling out on the runway was not the place to reduce lateral control, particularly in a very lightly wing-loaded fighter with a narrow gear".

In these circumstances, the wind would blow the wing up, and the aircraft would start weathervaning. The normal response by the pilot would be to move the stick into wind, but this did nothing to level the wings, and succeeded only in worsening the yaw into wind, giving the pilot the impression that the aircraft wanted to tip up and over onto the downwind forward quarter. Once the nosewheel was down, the situation improved slightly, but all the characteristics remained to a lesser degree, and the resultant roll-out was described as 'uncomfortable'. The whole problem was exacerbated by the oleo struts on the mainwheels tending to stroke at different times in the roll-out and on a calm day, there could be a 2 or 3deg difference until the up-wing oleo would stroke. A further weak point was the low-gain steering on the nosewheel.

Streak Eagle world time-to-height records

Altitude	Time	Date	Previous time	Margin
3,000m (9,843ft)	27.57sec	Jan 16, 75	34.52sec (F-4B)	20 per cent
6,000m (19,685ft)	39.33sec	Jan 16, 75	48.79sec (F-4B)	19 per cent
9,000m (29,528ft)	48.86sec	Jan 16, 75	61.68sec (F-4B)	21 per cent
12,000m (39,370ft)	59.38sec	Jan 16, 75	77.14sec (F-4B)	23 per cent
15,000m (49,212ft)	77.02sec	Jan 16, 75	114.50sec (F4-B)	33 per cent
20,000m (65,617ft)	122.94sec	Jan 19, 75	169.80sec (MiG-25)	28 per cent
25,000m (82,021ft)	161.02sec	Jan 26, 75	192.60sec (MiG-25)	16 per cent
30,000m (98,425ft)	207.80sec	Feb 1, 75	243.86sec (MiG-25)	15 per cent

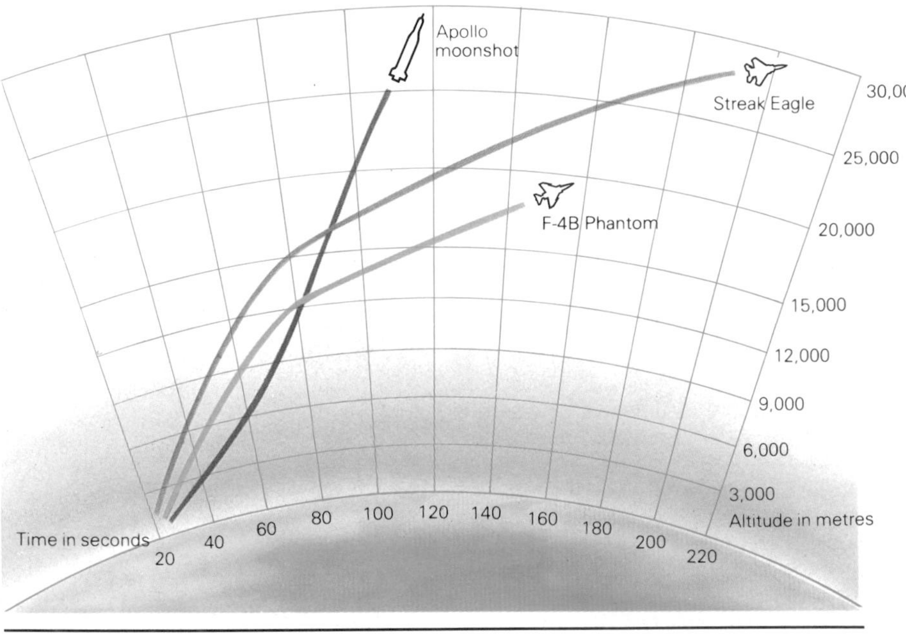

Above: The record-breaking Streak Eagle, 72-0119, over the familiar St Louis skyline.

The full plus or minus 15deg steering should have assisted three-point directional control, but because of the pedal-to-wheel deflection, long, strong legs were required to get positive response.

Considerable effort went into fixing the whole dilemma of cross-wind landing, and the Eagle can now accept such landings in 25–30kt crosswinds. To begin with, the ARI was all but eliminated on touch-down, as it had no essential function on the ground. The mechanical ARI was made to deactivate on sensing wheel-spin on the ground, which was almost instantaneous after touch-down. This effectively eliminated the effects of the ARI, but did retain it in a static condition until the ground checks were made. The CAS ARI was also largely eliminated during the roll-out in a similar fashion.

The mechanical lateral control wash-out with the stick aft was eliminated with the undercarriage down, while the gain was increased on the nosewheel steering so that the response was swifter.

Right: Major D.W. Peterson, who piloted the Streak Eagle to the 15,000m and 25,000m records on January 16 and 26, 1975, by the nose of the specially prepared F-15A.

Above: An early production F-15C refuels from a KC-135A tanker with an example of MCAIR's previous USAF fighter, the F-4, in attendance.

This fix was primarily to improve the taxying qualities of the Eagle, but the benefits to directional control on the runway were welcomed. The mainwheel oleo struts were significantly modified, so as to achieve a greater load stroke quicker on touchdown, while the remainder was taken up at lower speeds: Overall the Eagle had a more solid feel following touch-down.

The time and effort expended on this series of fixes have paid dividends for Eagle operations. The 25–30kt crosswind component allows crab angles of up to 12deg to be used on landing. With the nose held at 12deg pitch, for maximum braking effect, the Eagle's velocity vector is simply held straight down the runway with the rudder until the nose is lowered at about 80kt, where the nosewheel steering takes over. All the pilot needs do is to fly down the runway using normal aerodynamic control until the nosewheel is lowered to contact with the ground.

The handling qualities of the F-15 Eagle in flight are described as 'excellent' using either the conventional hydromechanical system or the CAS to fly the aircraft. However, several modifications known as Engineering Change Proposals (ECPs) were made, though by autumn 1974 only 36 had been recommended, of which 13 did not involve the Eagle itself. Of the 23 ECPs made to the aircraft, only three are externally visible: the raked wing tips, the dogtooth stabilator, and the enlarged speed brake.

Early in the test programme MCAIR discovered a buffet and wing-loading problem at certain altitudes. After attempting to solve the problem with wing fences, the solution adopted was to remove 4sq ft (0.37sq m) diagonally from the wing tip to create a raked appearance. The cutting of the dogtooth into the leading edge of the stabilator was the solution to a flutter problem discovered in wind tunnel testing. This produced a minor shift in the coefficient of pressure and a change in the moment of inertia sufficient to remove the flutter. The enlargement of the speedbrake from 20 to 31.5sq ft (1.86 to 2.93sq m) allowed the required drag to be produced from lower extension angles, and removed a buffet caused by the original brake at the desired drag configurations (and higher extension angles).

Below: One of the virtues of the F-15 is the minimal amount of ground support equipment needed, as illustrated in this view of pre-flight checks at a snow-covered base.

Radio-controlled models

One of the more interesting aspects of the F-15's flight test programme was the use of large glider models of the Eagle, which were dropped from a Boeing B-52 of the NASA Flight Research Center flying at 45,000ft (13,700m) at 175kt. Termed 'remotely piloted research vehicles', these models were built of aluminium and glass fibre to three-eights scale, having a wing span of 16ft 1¼in (4.91m) and a length of 23ft 10¾in (7.28m) and weighing some 2,000lb (907kg). Radio-controlled from the ground, they performed their manoeuvres, deployed a parachute and were recovered in mid-air by a helicopter. Among their tasks were to conduct high angles of attack, stalling and spinning manoeuvres ahead of the live flight tests performed by the eighth development Eagle.

All these ECPs, many of a minor nature, have contributed to making a good flying aircraft into a fighter with excellent handling qualities. Following its first flight, the F-15 Eagle met all its milestones on time with one exception: because of technical problems concerned with F100 engine durability tests, this part was some months late. The test programme's deliberately slow pace was, according to Major General Bellis, able to provide "a significant capability to profit from information derived from the initial and intensive ground-test programme and the current joint Air Force and contractor F-15 flight test activities". Such a pace is totally in keeping with the 'test before fly' and 'fly before buy' attitude adopted by the USAF in their procurement procedure.

Final proof of the new fighter's capabilities was provided by Operational Streak Eagle, a joint USAF/MCAIR operation to break a number of time-to-height world records, previously held

Above: St Louis again forms the background for this February 1979 view of the first F-15C before its delivery to TAC.

by the F-4 Phantom and Soviet MiG-25 Foxbat. The 19th pre-production aircraft (the 17th single-seater) was totally stripped down: radar, cannon, missiles, tail hook, utility hydraulic system, one of the generators, and several actuators were removed, along with the paint finish, leaving a bare metal aircraft. Between January 16 and February 1, 1975, Majors W. R. Macfarlane, D. W. Peterson and R. Smith established a total of eight new time-to-climb records flying from Grand Forks AFB. The Eagle was some 2,800lb (1,270kg) lighter than a standard production aircraft and only sufficient fuel was carried for the specific flight and return to the airfield.

The Category I and II flight test programme was completed by the delivery of the first production Eagle, a TF-15A (F-15B) to the USAF's Tactical Air Command at Luke AFB on November 14, 1974. On July 1, 1975, the first operational F-15 Eagle squadron within Tactical Air Command – the 1st Tactical Fighter Wing (TFW) – was formed at Langley AFB, and six months later, on January 9, 1976, this wing received its first aircraft.

As with most aircraft in production, improvements and refinements are constantly emerging. The current production models of the Eagle are the F-15C and F-15D, which replaced the single-seat F-15A and twin-seat F-15B respectively from mid-1979, when a total of 443 had been produced.

Externally there is no major difference between the two sets of Eagles. Internally, the APG-63 radar has been improved by the addition of a programmable signal processor (PSP), details of which are given in Chapter 4; the fuel capacity has been increased by some 312.5USgal (260Imp gal/1,188 litre); and the aircraft has been modified to accept two conformal Fuel and Sensor Tactical (FAST) packs on either side of the fuselage, enabling the internal fuel capacity to be increased by a further 1,523US gal (1,268Imp gal/5,738 litre) altogether.

The first F-15C Eagle flew on February 27, 1979, with the first F-15D following on June 19, 1979. These versions entered service with the USAF in September 1979, when the 18th TFW at Kadena AB, Okinawa, Japan, received their first squadron. The F-15C/D model represents the baseline from which the F-15 Multi-stage Improvement Programme (MSIP) begins. In addition to the enhancements already noted, the MSIP will take in a new programmable weapon control set, with provision for the AIM-120 AMRAAM, AIM-7M Sparrow and AIM-9M Sidewinder missiles; expanded electronic warfare (EW) equipment, including an enhanced radar warning receiver (RWR), an internal ECM system and the addition of chaff/flare launchers; and expanded communications facilities, Seek Talk, HF radio and provision for JTIDS. Although further versions with enhanced roles are under development, the F-15C/D model of the Eagle remains the current production standard, and is likely to continue as such in the near term.

Below: Three-view drawing of the production F-15C; the upper side profile shows the two-seat F-15D. Without the FAST packs, the F-15C is externally identical to the A.

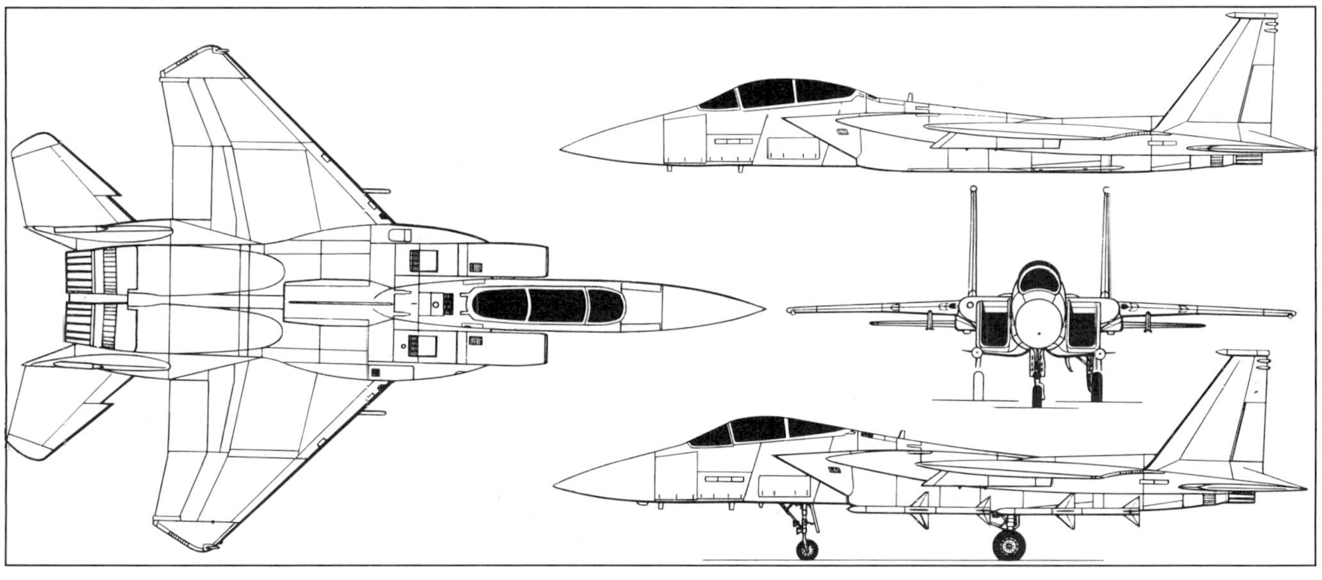

Structure

Thousands of hours of computer studies and wind-tunnel tests went into the F-15's design; billions of dollars have been spent on building the aircraft and its essential systems. Much of this effort and expense was devoted to keeping the basic structure as simple as possible, for maximum survivability in combat and ease of maintenance on the ground. In service, the Eagle may not have quite matched its designers' expectations, but an outstanding safety record and an improving rate of availability demonstrated by Tactical Air Command Squadrons are testimony to its basic soundness.

By mid-1967 the early conception of the FX as a 60,000lb (27,000kg) variable-sweep multirole aircraft had been rejected in favour of a 40,000lb (18,000kg) fixed-wing fighter, and by September 1968, when the Contract Definition RFP was issued, a number of design criteria had been established. Several of these were directly concerned with structural features, while others involving specific operational requirements imposed their own indirect constraints on the physical details of the resulting aircraft.

Since the Eagle was to be used for air combat, a combination of high thrust-to-weight ratio and low wing loading were stipulated, within the overall gross weight limit of 40,000lb. A high degree of survivability was called for in structure and subsystems, involving comprehensive testing of components used, along with extended component life and reduced maintenance requirements. And the single crew member, who would be provided with a comprehensive suite of automated avionics to enable him to carry out his mission unaided, was to be given all-round visibility.

Computer evaluations

During the preliminary FX design studies – which ultimately involved some 2,500,000 man-hours and resulted in 37,500 pages of documentation – MCAIR engineers carried out extensive computer evaluations comparing the weights of hypothetical aircraft of given cost resulting from a variety of basic design features. For example, if a two-man, all weather avionic suite were installed, the gross weight of the aircraft was calculated as 46,000lb (20,865kg), while single-seat, clear-air avionics required a gross weight of only 31,500lb (14,290kg). Similar comparisons were made between theoretical aircraft with varying degrees of energy manoeuvrability and maximum speeds ranging from Mach 0.8 sea-level dash to a sustained Mach 2.7.

The parameters for the structural component of the computer evaluation were represented by an upper limit of 8g with 100 per cent fuel and a lower capacity for 6.5g with only 60 per cent fuel, giving respective gross weight figures of 41,500lb (18,825kg) and 38,000lb (17,235kg). The actual design limitation of 7.33g was achieved within the specified 40,000lb weight limit.

Considering that the external dimensions of the F-15 are marginally greater than those of the F-4 Phantom, it is remarkable that the maximum takeoff weight of the newer fighter should be nearly 6,000lb (2,700kg) less than that of its predecessor. Part of this reduction is a result of the lighter internal fuel load, which with the Eagle's more efficient

Above: Viewed from above, the contours of the Eagle fuselage clearly show the central pod and twin boom structural configuration.

Below: June 1981, and among the F-15Cs and Ds on the MCAIR assembly line is the distinctive tail of an F/A-18 Hornet.

engines still gives a longer range, and the rest is accounted for by the higher percentage of titanium and advanced composite materials used in its construction. As originally designed the F-4 was built with more titanium than any previous fighter, but even in its later versions this only amounted to some 9 per cent by weight of the total structure, whereas the Eagle airframe includes 25.8 per cent titanium, only 5.5 per cent steel and 37.3 per cent aluminium.

The titanium is largely concentrated around the engines and the inboard sections of the wings. The fuselage itself is of conventional semi-monocoque construction, and its pod and twin boom configuration is apparent in the contours of the upper surfaces. The frames of the central pod and of the air intakes on either side and their skin are of machined aluminium, as is the front wing spar, but the three main wing spars and the bulkheads connecting them and the frames of the engine pods are of titanium, also machined. Aft of the forward main wing spar the fuselage skin is also of titanium, and the same metal forms the cantilever booms outboard of each engine which carry the twin fins and horizontal stabilators, the stabilator attachments and the spars of the fins.

Titanium strength

There are several advantages to the use of titanium in these areas. The resulting structure is strong enough to transmit the control forces from the tail surfaces, and the strength of the twin engine bays, with titanium firewalls between them, reduces the risk of a fire or explosion in one engine damaging or incapacitating the other. Similarly, the titanium skin of the inboard underwing skin covers the integral fuel tanks, which are filled with sealant foam injected through channels in the joints between the spars and the aluminium upper skin. Moreover, the titanium wing spars and supporting bulkheads are strong enough to allow the aircraft to keep flying with any one spar in each wing completely severed.

Further weight savings are achieved by the use of composite materials over honeycomb cores for the wing flaps and ailerons and the tailfins and stabilators. The central sections of the tail surfaces, where the titanium structural members form torque boxes, as well as the rudders, are covered with boron composite skins with aluminium and Nomex honeycomb between, while aluminium skins cover the honeycomb flaps and ailerons and the raked outboard sections of the wings. The speedbrake, similarly, has a graphite composite skin

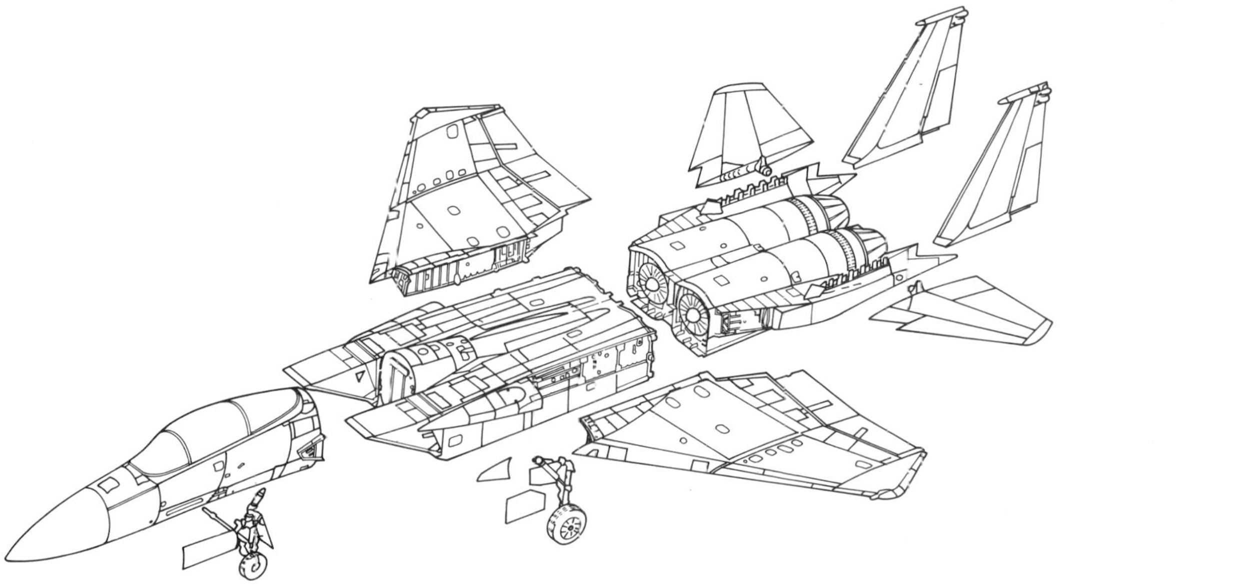

Below: The bubble canopy is the only external feature of the Eagle to interrupt the aerodynamically clean contours of the airframe.

Above: Major structural assemblies of the F-15 airframe. Tail surfaces and wings are interchangeable between aircraft.

Top: Automatic drilling machines in action, forming the attachment holes around the edges of the acrylic windshield destined for an F-15.

over a core of aluminium honeycomb.

The wing torque box assembly is based on the three titanium spars, extended by aft and outer spars of aluminium, and the wings are attached to the titanium bulkheads by pin joints which allow interchangeability between aircraft. The flaps and ailerons are similarly interchangeable, as are the windshield, canopy, speedbrake and fibreglass nose radome, while the vertical stabilizers, rudders and stabilators are interchangeable between right and left sides of the aircraft.

The aircraft is constructed in stages, with individual assemblies built up separately and progressively integrated. The main assemblies are the rear, centre and forward fuselage sections, the vertical and horizontal stabilizers and the wings, and various techniques are used in forming the multitude of sub-assemblies involved.

Sheet aluminium parts are drilled and routed automatically, with more substantial aluminium sections formed in a two-storey press exerting a pressure of 7,000 tons. Titanium forgings are also finished by computer-controlled milling machinery, and titanium sheets are formed in a furnace at temperatures of 1,650deg F (900deg C) and pressures of 250psi (45kg/sq cm). Graphite skins for the speedbrake are shaped by a high-speed laser cutter, while the honeycomb core is mechanically carved to match. Other automated processes include computerized pipe bending and robot drilling of the attachment holes for the acrylic windshield.

Meanwhile, sheets of the boron epoxy composites used for the tail surfaces are assembled by hand before being bonded by high-pressure steam in an autoclave. Metallic parts are spray-painted individually to protect them from corrosion, and critical sub-assemblies such as the engine intake ducts and wing leading edges are drilled and riveted by hand. Another job for

Above: Ground crew work under floodlights to prepare a 49th TFW F-15A for a sortie during Red Flag exercises at Nellis AFB in 1980.

Below: A ground crewman sporting an 'Eagle Keeper' badge takes advantage of the ready accessibility of the F-15's internal systems.

Left: An F-15B from Nellis AFB's 57th TTW in its hangar for routine servicing during a Red Flag desert warfare simulation.

skilled technicians is the assembly of the 290 bundles of electric wiring: these are installed during the build-up of the fuselage sections, as are fuel and hydraulic systems.

The final assembly stage brings together the three fuselage sections and the wings, and the final connections of all the power, control and environmental systems. These are checked before the final stage, which involves the installation of engines and avionics, and after a final checkout the aircraft is flown by a company test pilot to ensure that all systems are functioning.

As well as the parts fabricated in MCAIR's own plant, the F-15 involves the use of parts supplied by some 1,200 sub-contractors whose value is approximately half that of the total aircraft cost. By 1980 total cost of the F-15 programme had amounted to $16.58 billion, giving an average unit cost for the 749 aircraft involved of rather more than $22 million (in FY 1980 dollars). The 60 F-15s sold to Saudi Arabia cost a total of $1.92 billion, while Israel's first 40 Eagles were worth $907 million.

Design rationale

The wing configuration is relatively straightforward, though it was only selected after several hundred had been analysed and more than 100 were tested in almost a year of solid wind-tunnel trials. Ultimately, variable camber, with movable surfaces on both leading and trailing edges as used on the F-16, was rejected, since an alternative design with a fixed leading edge employing conical camber was found to offer only slightly higher supersonic drag and marginally reduced subsonic performance, both of which were more than offset by advantages in terms of weight, simplicity of manufacture and ease of maintenance. The chosen design has a straight leading edge swept at an angle of 45deg, an aspect ratio of 3, zero incidence and 1deg of anhedral.

As outlined in the previous chapter the wingtips were modified from their original shape, a total of 3sq ft (0.28sq m) being removed from each tip to reduce excessive lift at the wingtips and consequent severe buffeting at high g loads and high subsonic speed at altitudes of 30,000ft (9,000m) or so. Another change made as a result of flight testing was the increase in chord of the outer portions of the horizontal stabilators, creating the characteristic notched leading edges of these surfaces, to eliminate flutter. At the same time, the original speedbrake was increased in size by more than 50 per cent, again to eliminate a buffet problem.

Overall, the F-15 profile is designed to minimize wave drag at high speeds, with the single exception of the bubble canopy, which is a feature of both the Eagle and the USAF's other new fighter, the F-16 Fighting Falcon. The aerodynamic penalties imposed by such a canopy are regarded as unavoidable if the pilot is to be enabled to perform his air superiority mission effectively.

The canopy itself is a single transparency with only one transverse frame, hinged at the rear and counterbalanced by a single strut, with a second strut immediately behind the pilot's seat for emergency jettison of the canopy. The size of the canopy is the only external difference between single-seat and two-seat Eagles: the latter have a longer canopy to accommodate the rear crew member, while the single-seater has an avionics bay behind the pilot's seat. This

Right: For maximum maintainability the F-15 airframe features a total of 570sq ft (53sq m) of access doors and panels, as demonstrated here.

houses several avionics 'black boxes' associated with the Tactical Electronic Warfare System in current models but is largely empty and offers ample room for additional avionic equipment; it is unpressurized, and when the canopy is lowered it is isolated by an integral seal.

Directly behind the avionics bay are the fuselage fuel tanks, and between the forward and aft tanks, below the speed-brake, are the ammunition drum and feed system for the M61 cannon. The gun itself is housed in the starboard wing root fairing, while the equivalent fairing at the port wing root contains the flight refuelling receptacle.

The only examples of variable geometry in the F-15's structure are the engine air inlets on either side of the forward fuselage. Because the aircraft was designed to be flown at high angles of attack in combat, the intakes are able to 'nod' up or down to keep the aperture facing directly into the airflow in order to maintain an adequate supply of air to the engines. The intakes are pivoted at their lower edge and adjusted to angles of 4deg above or 11deg below the horizontal by hydraulic actuators controlled by the air data computer. The intake angle can also be adjusted to prevent more air than necessary being

Right: Extending steps built into the fuselage side of the F-15 can be used instead of the normal ladder for cockpit access.

Below: An 8th TFW Eagle is given an automatic wash at Kwang Ju air base in Korea, during Exercise Cope North in June 1982.

Left: The remarkable slenderness of the F-15's twin vertical tails is achieved by the use of boron composite skins on honeycomb cores.

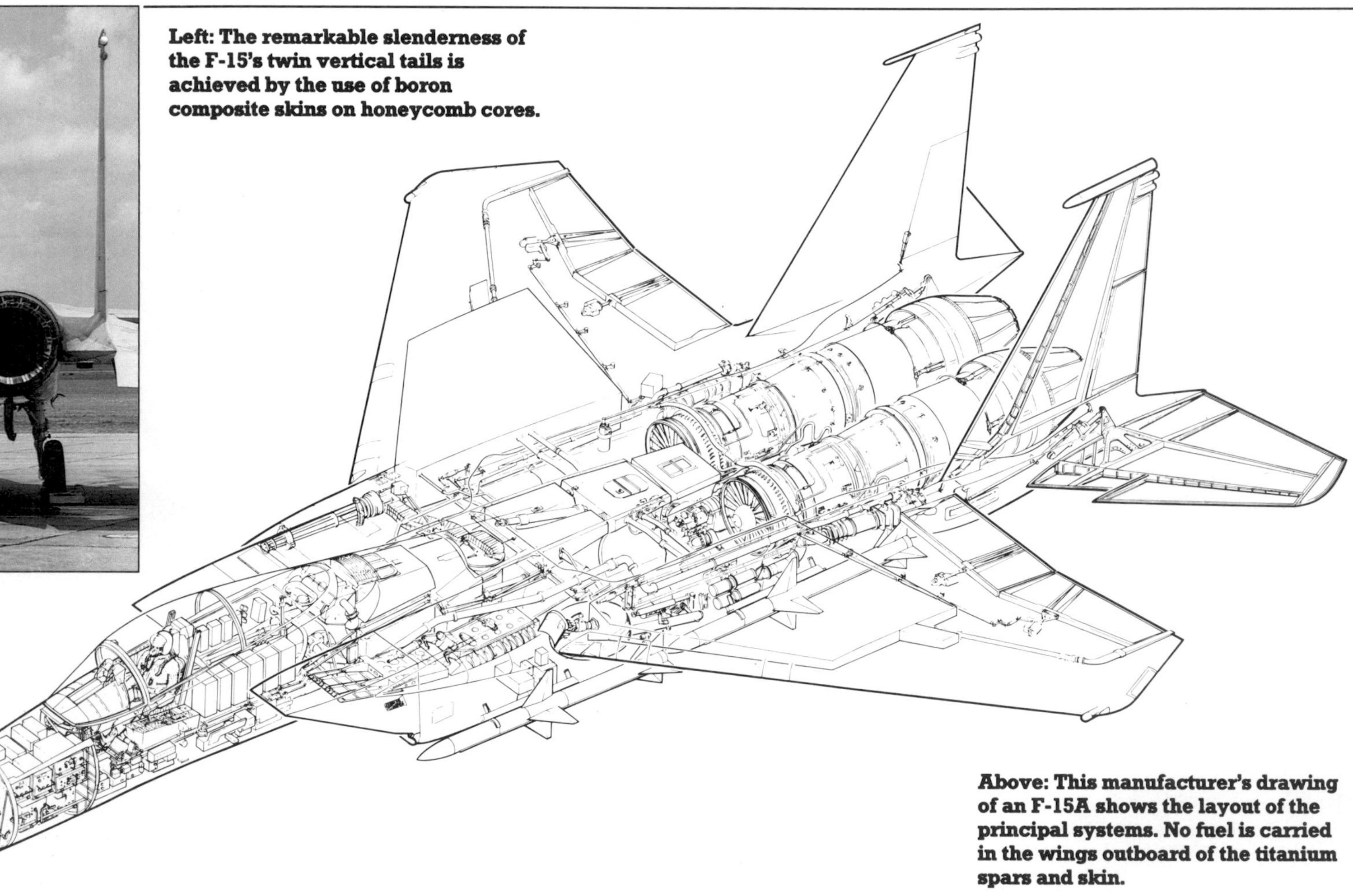

Above: This manufacturer's drawing of an F-15A shows the layout of the principal systems. No fuel is carried in the wings outboard of the titanium spars and skin.

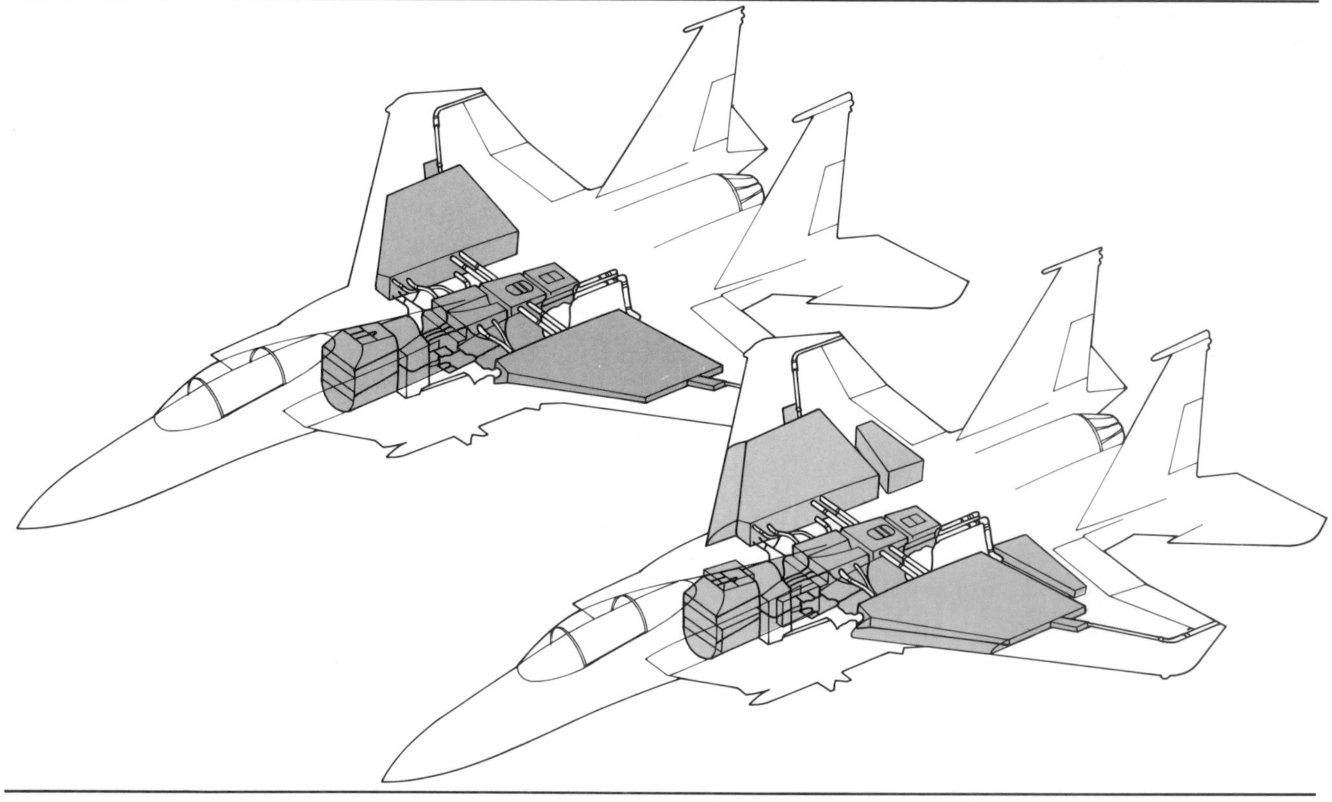

Right: Wing leading and trailing edge tanks, and additional tanks in the centre fuselage, allow the F-15C to carry an extra 1,855lb (880kg) of fuel internally.

taken in, and the intake surfaces have a further function in providing additional manoeuvring control in a similar manner to canard foreplanes. At supersonic speeds their effectiveness is almost a third as great as that of the stabilators, whose size and weight were enabled to be reduced in consequence. Immediately aft of the intakes themselves are twin mechanically linked ramps to control the shockwaves created in the incoming air.

Of course, structural and aerodynamic efficiency are prerequisites in any aircraft, but a combat aircraft must also be designed to survive the inevitable wear and tear of battle. In this respect the Eagle's main assets are reckoned to be its overall superiority in such areas as pilot visibility, radar detection ability, weapons systems and performance, but a number of less obvious safety features were included, largely as a result of experience with the F-4 in Vietnam, in addition to the basic structural elements described above.

Hydraulics and fuel

As well as twin engines, the F-15 has three separate hydraulic systems which can detect and isolate leaks in their associated subsystems and each of which is capable of sustaining the flight control system on its own. Similarly, twin electrical systems, powered by 40/50kVA AC generators operating through DC conversion units, are capable independently of fulfilling the aircraft's power requirements, while a standby hydraulic generator is fitted to supply critical systems in an emergency. Either the electronic control augmentation system or the hydromechanical system can provide independent flight control should one or the other be put out of action.

Fuel supply is another vital system, and this too is designed to cope with various emergencies. The fuel tanks themselves are filled with foam, and the fuel lines are also self-sealing. In the event of electrical failure, the fuel system will continue to operate on standby power, providing fuel flow adequate for engine operation up to the mid-afterburner range.

Additional protection against fire is provided in the form of a fire-suppression system. A pressurized bottle containing a non-corrosive agent is located between the engine bay firewalls, with three nozzles able to release the agent into either engine or in the space between them. The provision of this fire suppression system is one of the direct results of the F-4's experiences in Vietnam, and the Eagle is one of the few fighter aircraft to be fitted with such equipment. The physical separation of the fuel tanks from the engine bays is another precaution against fire.

Another aspect of the F-15 design intended to maximize its efficiency in combat is the emphasis placed on ease of maintenance and relative independence of ground support equipment. The airframe features a total of 570sq ft (53sq m) of access panels, allowing most routine maintenance to be carried out without the use of work stands. The overall simplicity of the airframe is a major factor in reducing maintenance requirements: by comparison with the F-4E, the F-15 has only 202 lubrication points against the earlier fighter's 510; seven hydraulic filters, all of which are interchangeable and which incorporate visual indications of the need for replacement, are used in place of the Phantom's 21; plumbing connections in the fuel system are reduced from 281 to only 97, and the interchangeable fuel pumps are of a plug-in design that allows them to be changed in only 30 minutes; and whereas the F-4E had 905 potted electrical connectors, whose waterproof compounds were subject to deterioration, the F-15 has a total of 809 silicone grommet connectors to avoid this problem.

The digital avionic systems used also help to reduce the maintenance workload. No routine servicing is needed for these: they are line replaceable units (LRUs), readily removable in the event of failure for testing and repair, and faulty units can be located by means of a built-in test panel located in the nosewheel well. The cockpit is also equipped with a caution light panel to indicate system failures and a built-in test (BIT) panel for the avionic systems. To reduce dependence on support equipment the secondary power system which provides power for the jet fuel starters can also power the electrical and hydraulic systems for up to 30 minutes while maintenance work is carried out or for munitions loading.

Power for the electrical generators

Left: The separation of the engine bays, with titanium firewalls between, has contributed to the F-15's excellent safety record.

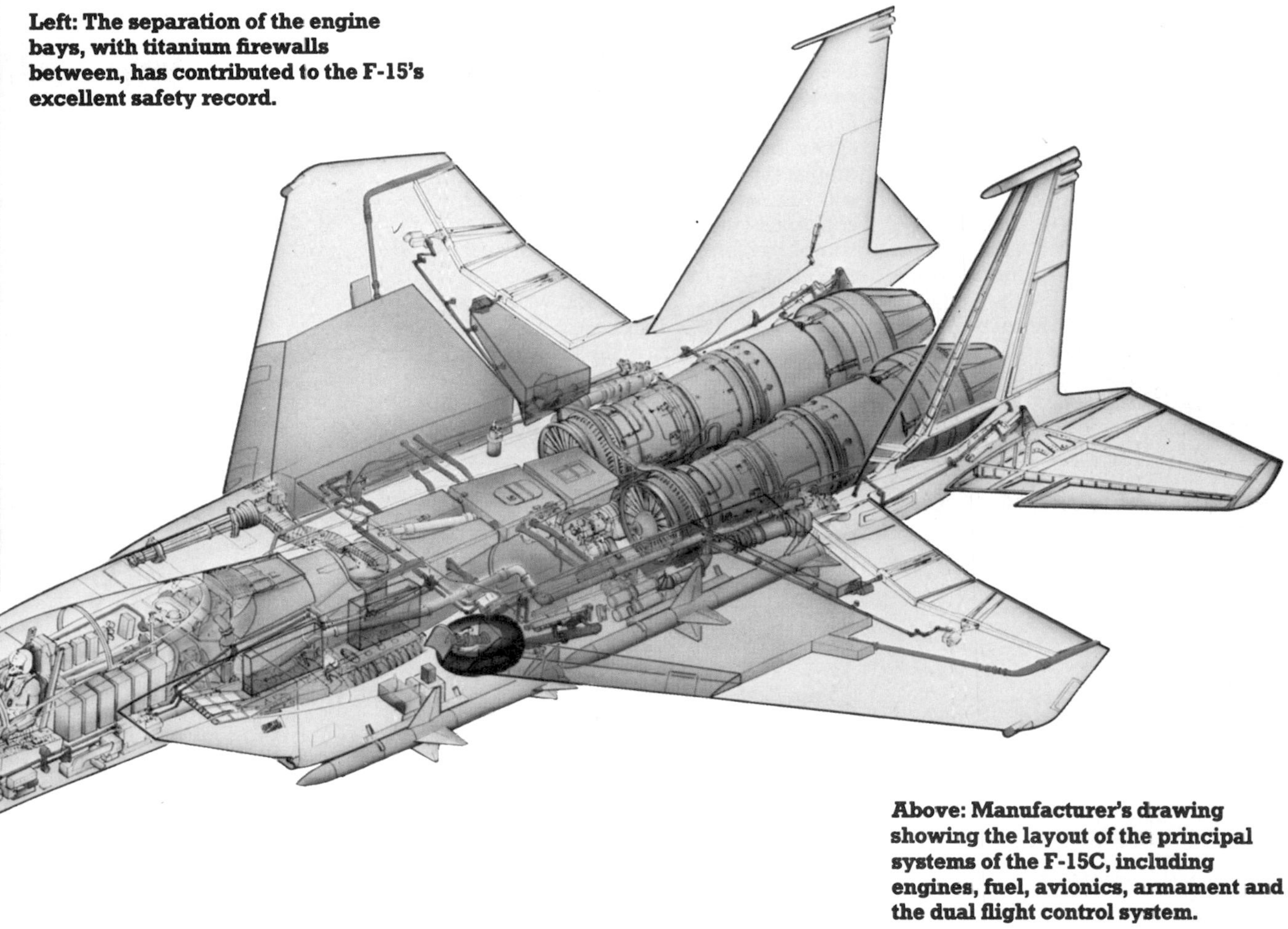

Above: Manufacturer's drawing showing the layout of the principal systems of the F-15C, including engines, fuel, avionics, armament and the dual flight control system.

Left: The increased maximum takeoff weight of the F-15C necessitated strengthening of the undercarriage, tyres and brakes. A 36th TFW F-15C shows its landing gear.

and hydraulic pumps is derived from the main powerplant via an aircraft-mounted accessory drive shaft. Being mounted on the aircraft rather than in the engines themselves, this allows the engines to be interchangeable between right and left. To simplify engine maintenance, each F100 turbofan can be broken down into five main modules, consisting of the inlet and fan, the gearbox, the fan drive, the engine core and the augmentor (afterburner) duct and nozzle. Any of these can be removed for maintenance while another module is substituted, so that a malfunction in one part of the engine does not put the whole powerplant out of action while it is repaired. The engines themselves are removed quickly and easily, sliding out of the rear of the bays on integral rails onto a cart with matching rails, and with only ten disconnections necessary before removal. Complete engine change can be accomplished well inside the 30 minutes minimum specified by the Air Force. And with the engines installed internal inspections can be carried out by means of 12 borescope ports on each engine.

The overall intention behind this careful planning of maintenance features was to meet a USAF requirement for a maximum of 11.3 maintenance man-hours per flight hour (MMH/FH), just under half the requirement of the F-4E, which would allow a 15 per cent reduction in the number of maintenance personnel. In practice, however, this figure has not been achieved: reduced to 19 by the time type testing was complete, the MMH/FH figure had risen to around 35 by 1980. One reason for this was the continuing difficulties with the engine, as described in the following chapter, with the powerplant absorbing nearly half the total maintenance effort. Another was the continuing shortage of skilled maintenance personnel, partly as a result of the comparatively low rates of pay which such personnel received compared with those available elsewhere.

An equally serious problem was the difficulties encountered with the Avionics Intermediate Shops (AIS), the second of three stages in the F-15 planned maintenance programme. The first level of maintenance takes place on the flight line, where routine servicing is carried out and line-replaceable units are removed as necessary. The second stage, of which the AIS forms part, is the repair on base of faulty units, and the third is depot repair at Air Logistic Centres.

Among the problems encountered with this system was the difficulty of repairing LRUs on base with nearly half of the avionics LRUs being returned to the depots. This in turn meant that stocks of replacement LRUs were quickly exhausted. The principal reason for this state of affairs was the repeated failures of the automated testing stations which comprise the AIS, to the extent that only half the AISs were operational at any time. And the problem was compounded by the failure of the AIS to agree in its diagnosis of the fault with the indications of the on-board BIT equipment in a large percentage of cases.

The natural consequence of all these problems was a high rate of cannibalization, with parts being removed from one aircraft to keep another flying. Consequently, by 1979 availability of the F-15 within TAC had fallen to an alarmingly low 56 per cent. On the other hand, a high degree of readiness has been achieved on numerous exercises, and the Eagle has compiled an impressive safety record. Overall availability by 1983 had risen to more than 65 per cent, and an official inspection of the 1st TFW at Langley in August 1982 found a record 98.6 per cent of aircraft operational: this compares with an availability of only 35 per cent of the same wing's aircraft three years earlier.

New model

Meanwhile, the original F-15A and B production models were replaced by the improved C and D from June 1979. Again, external differences between the single and two-seat version are limited to the slightly longer canopy fitted to the F-15D, and the principal external distinguishing feature of the later models is the provision of the FAST Pack conformal fuel tanks.

The FAST Packs are attached to the outside of each air intake, and can carry an additional 4,875lb (2,211kg) of fuel. Alternatively, sensors such as reconnaissance cameras or infra-red equipment, radar warning receivers and jammers, laser designators and low-light TV cameras, or a combination of such sensors with reduced quantities of fuel, can be carried. When the FAST Packs are fitted, the four Sparrow missiles are mounted on their corners, and bombs or air-to-surface missiles weighing up to 4,400lb (1,995kg) can be carried as an alternative.

Internal fuel capacity of the F-15C/D is also increased by 1,855lb (880kg), with additional tanks located in the centre fuselage and in the wing leading and trailing edges. The effect of this increased fuel capacity is to raise the potential gross weight of the F-15C to 68,000lb (30,845kg) with full internal fuel, FAST Packs and three external tanks. As a result, tyres, wheels and brakes have been strengthened to cope with the increased weight.

The FAST Packs alone carry slightly less fuel than the normal three external tanks, but allow the aircraft to be flown at considerably higher speeds. Compared with the clean configuration, an F-15 equipped with FAST Packs experiences only slightly increased profile drag at subsonic speeds, and compared with the standard external tanks the conformal tanks contribute only a fraction of the former's drag at supersonic speeds. Ferry range with the increased internal fuel, FAST Packs and wing and fuselage tanks is increased to 3,450 miles (5,560km). According to the manufacturers, unused space in the outboard sections of the wings could accommodate a further 900lb (400kg) of fuel.

The manufacturers have also proposed to exploit currently unused internal space, particularly in the rear of the cockpit and in the tail booms, to equip the Eagle for other roles. As much as 56cu ft (1.6cu m) of growth space is claimed to be available for additional avionics, and in the Strike Eagle/Advanced Fighter Capability Demonstrator version of what was originally the second development F-15B the company has already installed a weapon system operator's station in the rear cockpit. Other roles envisaged for developed versions of the Eagle include specialized reconnaissance and Wild Weasel defence suppression models.

The latter would be intended to replace, respectively, the RF-4C and F-4G versions of the aging Phantom, though USAF evaluations during 1983 were concentrated on the dual-role fighter/ground attack role, for which the Eagle was subjected to comparative trials with the F-16XL.

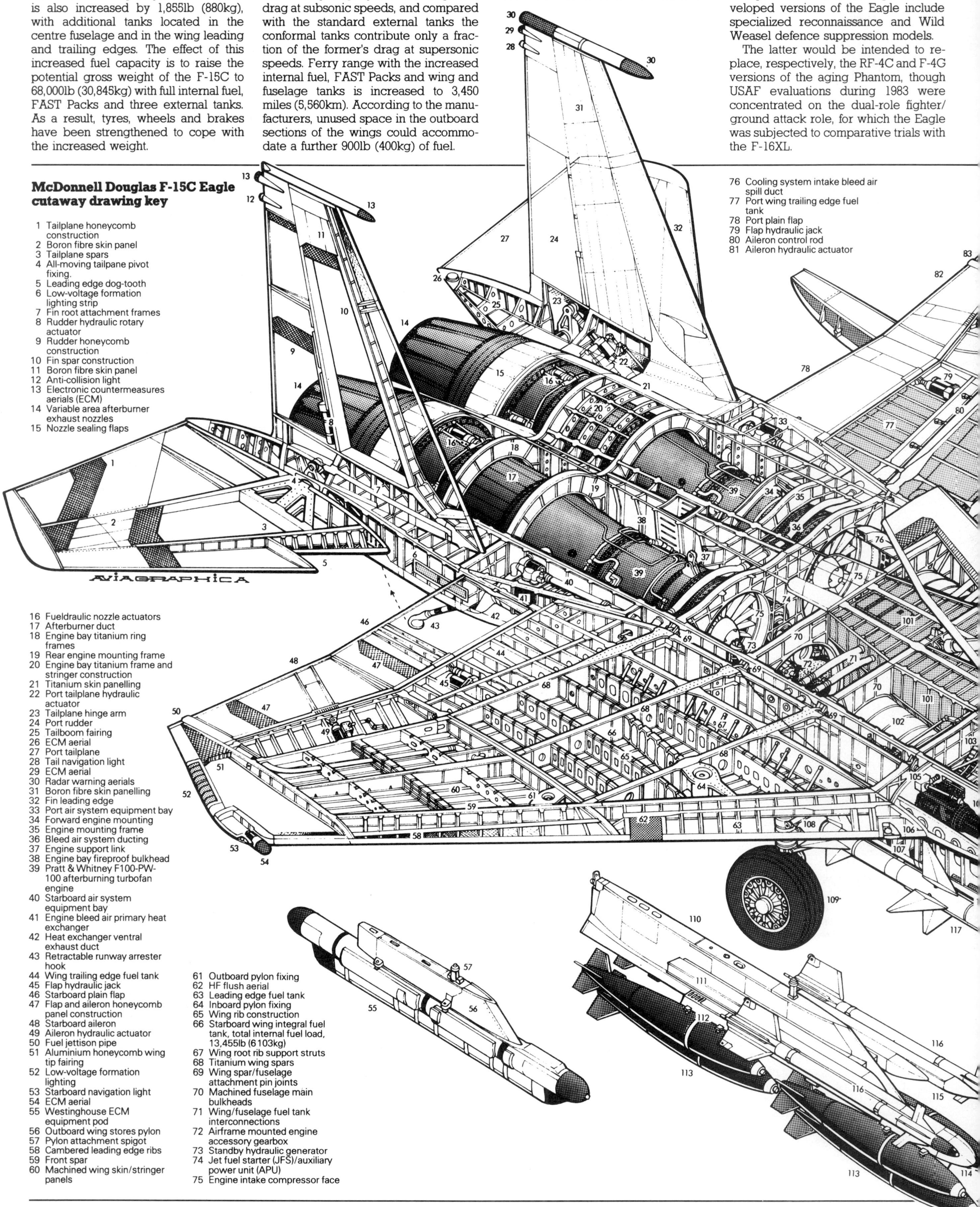

McDonnell Douglas F-15C Eagle cutaway drawing key

1 Tailplane honeycomb construction
2 Boron fibre skin panel
3 Tailplane spars
4 All-moving tailpane pivot fixing.
5 Leading edge dog-tooth
6 Low-voltage formation lighting strip
7 Fin root attachment frames
8 Rudder hydraulic rotary actuator
9 Rudder honeycomb construction
10 Fin spar construction
11 Boron fibre skin panel
12 Anti-collision light
13 Electronic countermeasures aerials (ECM)
14 Variable area afterburner exhaust nozzles
15 Nozzle sealing flaps
16 Fueldraulic nozzle actuators
17 Afterburner duct
18 Engine bay titanium ring frames
19 Rear engine mounting frame
20 Engine bay titanium frame and stringer construction
21 Titanium skin panelling
22 Port tailplane hydraulic actuator
23 Tailplane hinge arm
24 Port rudder
25 Tailboom fairing
26 ECM aerial
27 Port tailplane
28 Tail navigation light
29 ECM aerial
30 Radar warning aerials
31 Boron fibre skin panelling
32 Fin leading edge
33 Port air system equipment bay
34 Forward engine mounting
35 Engine mounting frame
36 Bleed air system ducting
37 Engine support link
38 Engine bay fireproof bulkhead
39 Pratt & Whitney F100-PW-100 afterburning turbofan engine
40 Starboard air system equipment bay
41 Engine bleed air primary heat exchanger
42 Heat exchanger ventral exhaust duct
43 Retractable runway arrester hook
44 Wing trailing edge fuel tank
45 Flap hydraulic jack
46 Starboard plain flap
47 Flap and aileron honeycomb panel construction
48 Starboard aileron
49 Aileron hydraulic actuator
50 Fuel jettison pipe
51 Aluminium honeycomb wing tip fairing
52 Low-voltage formation lighting
53 Starboard navigation light
54 ECM aerial
55 Westinghouse ECM equipment pod
56 Outboard wing stores pylon
57 Pylon attachment spigot
58 Cambered leading edge ribs
59 Front spar
60 Machined wing skin/stringer panels
61 Outboard pylon fixing
62 HF flush aerial
63 Leading edge fuel tank
64 Inboard pylon fixing
65 Wing rib construction
66 Starboard wing integral fuel tank, total internal fuel load, 13,455lb (6103kg)
67 Wing root rib support struts
68 Titanium wing spars
69 Wing spar/fuselage attachment pin joints
70 Machined fuselage main bulkheads
71 Wing/fuselage fuel tank interconnections
72 Airframe mounted engine accessory gearbox
73 Standby hydraulic generator
74 Jet fuel starter (JFS)/auxiliary power unit (APU)
75 Engine intake compressor face
76 Cooling system intake bleed air spill duct
77 Port wing trailing edge fuel tank
78 Port plain flap
79 Flap hydraulic jack
80 Aileron control rod
81 Aileron hydraulic actuator

Above left: With its paint removed the Streak Eagle clearly shows the boron composite skins of its rudder and vertical stabilizer.

Above: Control surfaces of the F-15 are limited to wing flaps and ailerons, twin rudders and all-moving horizontal stabilators.

82 Port aileron
83 Fuel jettison pipe
84 Wing tip fairing
85 Low-voltage formation lighting
86 Port navigation light
87 ECM aerial
88 Cambered leading edge
89 Outboard pylon fixing
90 Port wing internal fuel tank
91 Fuel system piping
92 Inboard pylon fixing
93 Leading edge fuel tank
94 Anti-collision light
95 Boom-type air refuelling receptacle
96 Bleed air duct to air conditioning plant
97 Control rod runs
98 Dorsal airbrake, open
99 Airbrake glass-fibre honeycomb construction
100 Airbrake hydraulic jack
101 Centre fuselage fuel tanks
102 Intake ducting
103 Ammunition feed chute
104 M61A-1 Vulcan 20mm cannon
105 Hydraulic rotary cannon drive unit
106 Starboard anti-collision light
107 Ventral main undercarriage wheel bay
108 Main undercarriage leg strut
109 Starboard mainwheel
110 Inboard stores pylon
111 Air-to-air missile adaptor
112 Bomb rack
113 Mk 82 low drag 500lb (227kg) HE bombs
114 Bomb triple ejector rack
115 Missile launch rail
116 AIM-9L Sidewinder air-to-air missile
117 AIM-7F Sparrow air-to-air missile
118 Sparrow missile launcher unit
119 Cannon muzzle aperture
120 Cannon barrels
121 Central ammunition drum, 940 rounds
122 Airbrake hinges
123 Forward fuselage fuel tanks
124 UHF aerial
125 Intake duct bleed air louvres
126 Intake bypass air spill duct
127 Variable area intake ramp hydraulic actuator
128 Air conditioning system cooling air exhaust duct
129 Canopy hinge point
130 Air conditioning plant
131 Intake incidence control jack
132 Intake duct variable area ramp doors
133 Intake pivot fixing
134 Starboard engine air intake
135 Nosewheel leg door
136 Nose undercarriage leg strut
137 Nosewheel
138 Landing/taxying lamps
139 Nosewheel retraction strut
140 Rear underfloor equipment bay
141 Tactical electronic warfare system (TEWS) racks
142 Cockpit coaming
143 Rear pressure bulkhead
144 Canopy jack
145 Cockpit pressurization valves
146 Structural space provision for second crew member (F-15D)
147 Cockpit aft decking
148 Canopy arch
149 Port intake external compression lip
150 Fuel and sensor tactical (FAST) pack, conformal fuel pallet, capacity 5,000lb (2268kg)
151 600US gal (2270 litre) external fuel tank
152 Cockpit canopy cover
153 Ejection seat headrest
154 Seat safety handle/arming lever
155 Canopy emergency jettison linkage
156 Ejection seat launch rails
157 Safety harness
158 McDonnell Douglas ACES II "zero-zero" ejection seat
159 Cockpit sloping bulkhead
160 Pilots side console panel
161 Air conditioning ducting
162 Forward underfloor equipment bay, built-in test equipment (BITE) and liquid oxygen converter
163 Low-voltage formation lighting strip
164 Port side retractable boarding ladder
165 TACAN aerial
166 Angle of attack probe
167 Rudder pedals
168 Control column
169 Pilot's head-up display (HUD)
170 Instrument panel shroud
171 Frameless windscreen panel
172 ADF sense aerial
173 Radio and electronics equipment bay, port and starboard
174 Cockpit front pressure bulkhead
175 Pitot tube
176 UHF aerial
177 Radar mounting bulkhead
178 Radome hinge mounting
179 ILS aerial
180 Radar scanner mounting and tracking mechanism
181 Hughes APG-63 pulse doppler radar scanner
182 Scanner mounted IFF aerial array
183 Glass-fibre radome

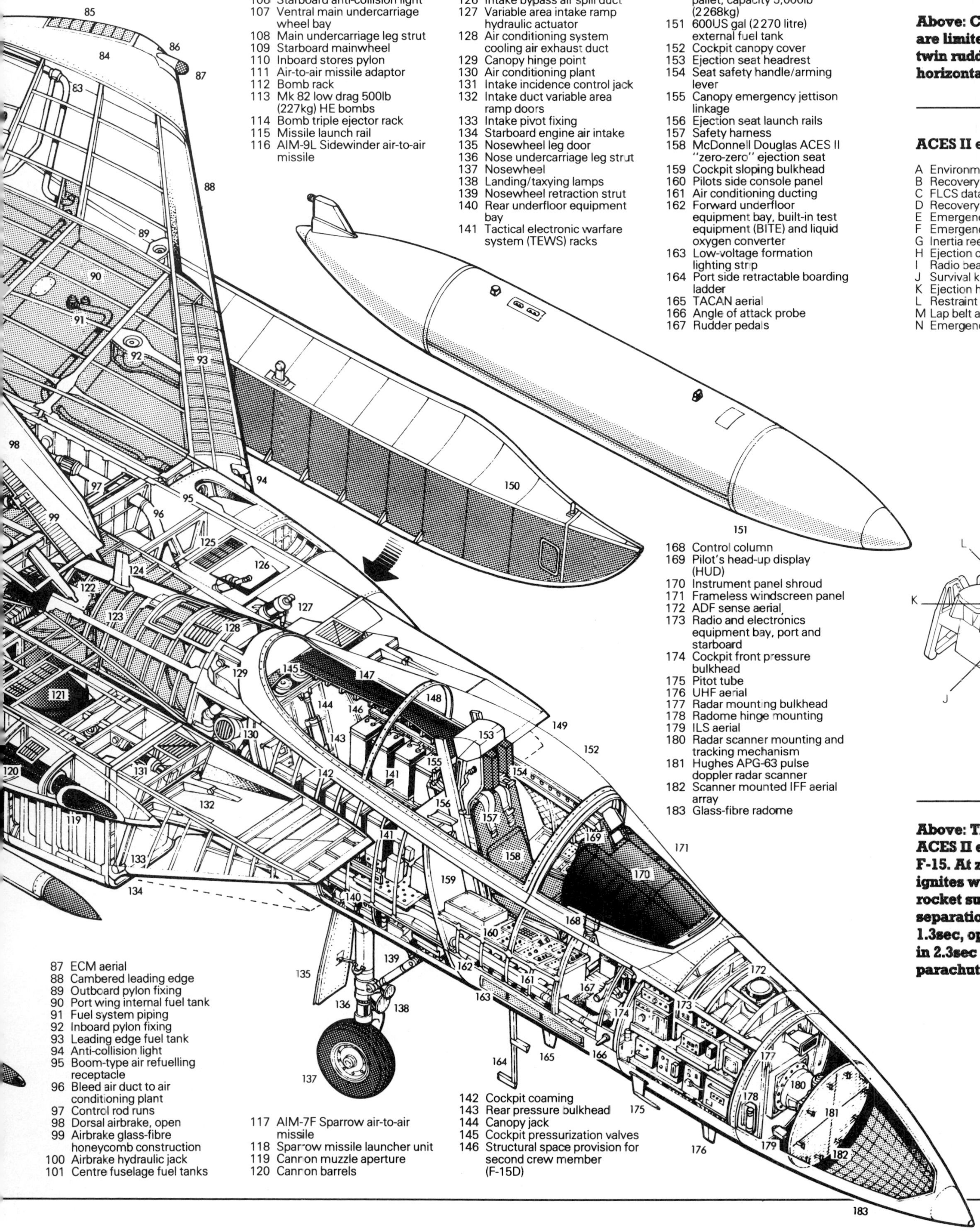

ACES II ejection seat

A Environmental sensor pitots
B Recovery parachute container
C FLCS data recorder
D Recovery parachute risers
E Emergency oxygen bottle
F Emergency oxygen pressure gauge
G Inertia reel knob
H Ejection control safety lever
I Radio beacon switch
J Survival kit (under seat pan)
K Ejection handle
L Restraint emergency release handle
M Lap belt and survival kit attachment
N Emergency oxygen fitting

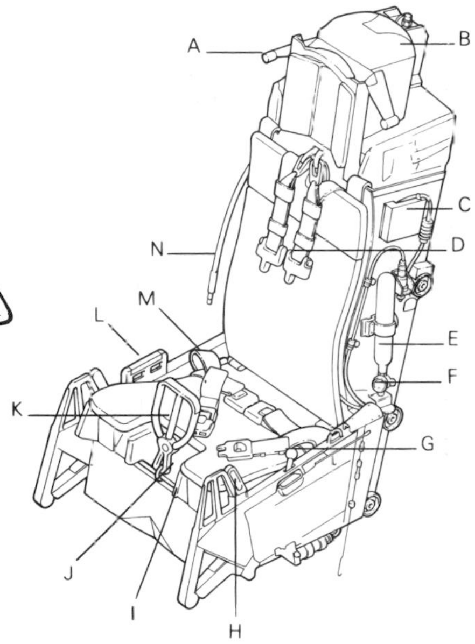

Above: The McDonnell Douglas ACES II ejection seat as fitted to the F-15. At zero airspeed the catapult ignites within 0.3sec, followed by the rocket sustainer in 0.45sec, separation of pilot from the seat after 1.3sec, opening of the parachute pack in 2.3sec and full inflation of the parachute in about 5sec.

Powerplant

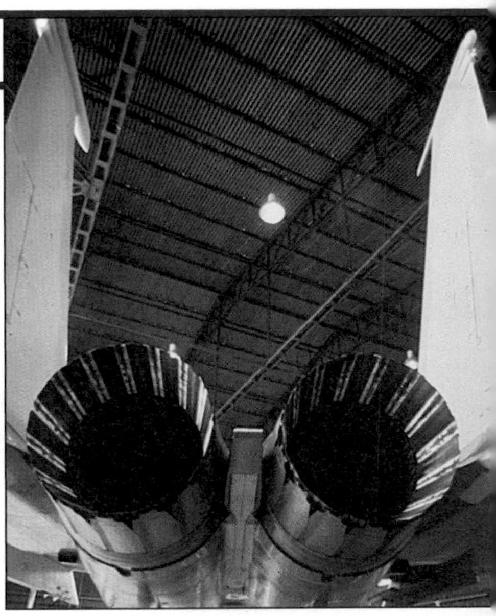

A fighter pilot needs as much power as he can get, so a fighter designed to be the best in the world needs most power of all. The thrust demanded for the F-15 pushed US engine technology to its limits, and the F100 turbofan has had its share of problems. But when a principal source of engine wear turns out to be pilots flying aircraft in ways that were never possible before the manufacturers have reason to congratulate themselves. Meanwhile, the F100 has formed the basis for newer powerplants, and there are new engines under development as possible replacements in a new generation of Eagles.

Above: The convergent/divergent nozzles of an F-15's twin Pratt & Whitney F100s fully open in the afterburning position.

Development of the Pratt & Whitney F100 turbofan started in August 1968, when the USAF awarded development contracts to P&W and General Electric for engines suitable for use in the planned FX fighter. In view of the high thrust-to-weight ratio planned for the new fighter, the resulting engines would have to push the technology of the time to its limits. P&W faced the daunting task of developing a powerplant producing 25 per cent more thrust per unit of weight than the then-current TF30 turbofan used in the F-111, and twice that of the J75 turbojet used in the F-105 Thunderchief and F-106 Delta Dart.

Both companies built and ran demonstration engines whose light weight, high thrust and low fuel consumption were well in advance of previous designs. The P&W engine was selected by the USAF for further development, contracts being awarded in 1970. Two versions were originally planned – the F100 for the USAF and the F401, intended to power later models of the US Navy's F-14 Tomcat, but the latter was cancelled when the USN was ordered by the Department of Defense to cut back the size of the planned F-14 fleet.

The F100 is an axial-flow turbofan with a bypass ratio of 0.7:1. It has two shafts – one carrying a three-stage fan driven by a two-stage turbine, the other carrying the ten-stage main compressor and its two-stage turbine. The completed engine is 191in (4.85m) long and 34.8in (0.88m) in diameter at the inlet, and weighs 3,068lb (1,391kg).

Powder metallurgy

New technologies used in the F100 included powder metallurgy. Instead of forming some metal components in the traditional manner, P&W reduced the raw material to a powder. This could be heated and formed under high pressure to create engine components better able to tolerate the high temperatures planned for the F100 core.

Operating temperature of the F100 turbine was far above that of earlier engines. Successful turbojets of earlier vintage, such as the GE F85 which powers the F-5E, or the GE J79 used in the F-4 and F-104, had turbine inlet temperatures of around 1,800deg F (982deg C). P&W had achieved figures of just over 2,000deg F (1,093 deg C) in the TF30 turbofan, but to meet the demanding requirements of the F100 specification involved temperatures of 2,565deg F (1,407deg C).

Use of such advanced technology resulted in an engine capable of providing the high levels of thrust required. Maximum thrust is normally described as being 'in the 15,000lb (6,800kg) thrust class' when running without afterburner, and 'in the 25,000lb (11,340kg) class' when full augmentation is selected.

Normal dry (non-afterburning) rating is 12,420lb (5,634kg), rising to a maximum of 14,670lb (6,654kg) at full Military Intermediate rating – the maximum attainable without afterburning. Specific fuel consumption (sfc) – the amount of thrust produced for each pound of fuel burned per hour – is 0.69 at normal rating and 0.71 at Military Intermediate. At full afterburning power, the F100 develops 23,830lb (10,809kg) of thrust at an sfc of 2.17. At this rating, the engine swallows an impressive 860lb (390kg) of fuel per minute.

By the time the F-15 was ready for its first flight in July 1972, the F100 had completed most of its test programme, meeting 23 out of 24 critical 'project milestones'. Between February and October of the following year, a series of turbine failures dogged attempts to complete the 150-hour running trial which formed part of the formal Qualification test. The latter was the most punishing series of tests to which any US military jet engine had ever been subjected, according to P&W. It included 30 hours of running at a simulated speed of Mach 2.3, and 38 hours of running at a simulated Mach 1.6.

Following completion of this test, the F100 was subjected to a further series of intensive trials, including 150 hours of running at over-temperature conditions, and a long series of accelerated Mission Tests. Conducted on the ground, but designed to simulate the stresses of operational service, these were intended to build up running time and detect potential problems. The latter were not serious enough to delay the start of production. The powerplant is

Below: An F-15A of the 32nd TFS, its engines in full afterburner, accelerates down the runway at Camp New Amsterdam.

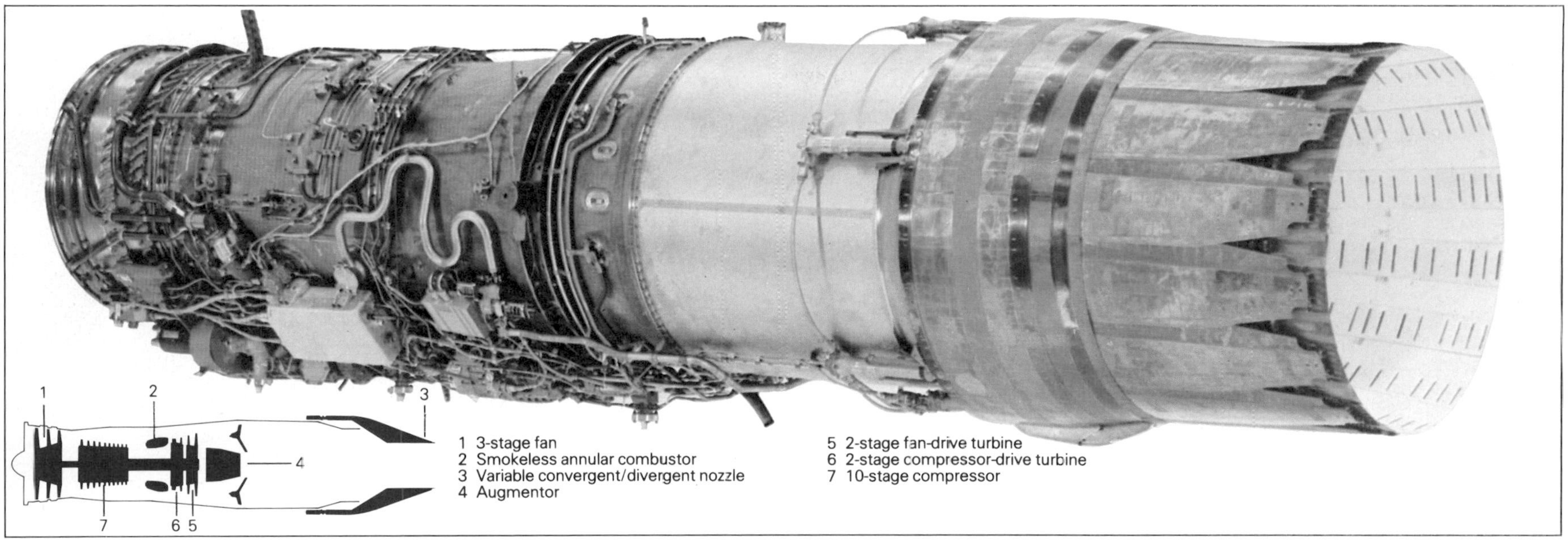

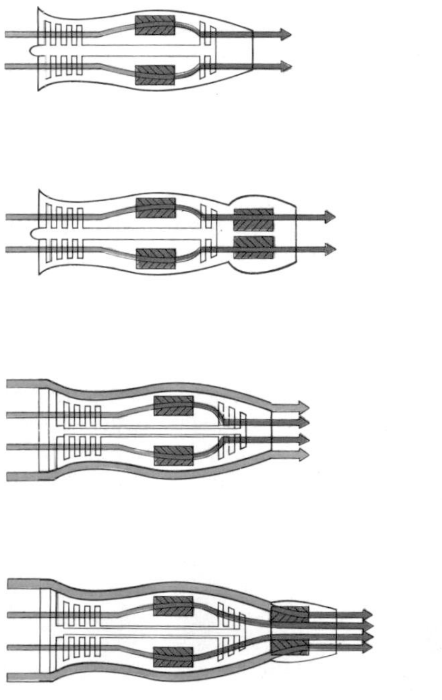

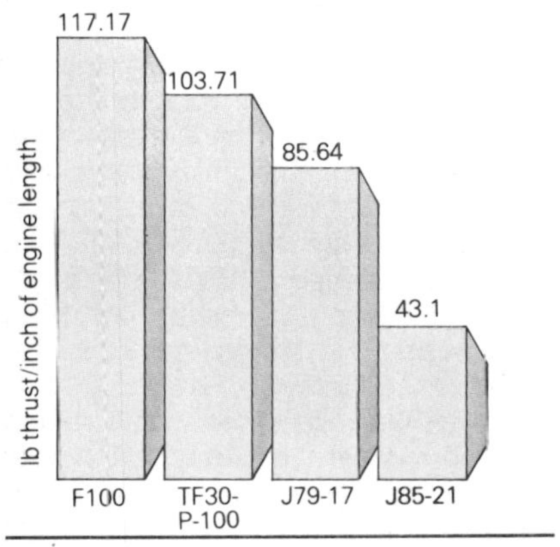

Above: Comparison of the thrust available per inch of engine length from powerplants of (left to right) the F-15, F-111F, F-4E and F-5E.

Top: Exterior of the F100, with diagram of its principal components. Nearly half its length is occupied by the augmentor chamber and nozzle.

Above: Evolution of the afterburning turbofan (bottom) via the turbojet (top), afterburning turbojet and straight turbofan.

Above: Factory inspection of an F100. The engine weighs 3,068lb (1,391kg) and has a thrust-to-weight ratio of nearly 8:1 at full augmentation.

designated F100-PW-100 by the company and JTF22A-25A by the USAF.

USAF hopes that the F100 would be a fully-reliable powerplant by the time the F-15 entered service were confounded by a series of technical and operational problems. Strikes at two major subcontractors delayed the delivery of engines, while service experience showed that the F100 was wearing out twice as fast as had been predicted. By the end of 1979 the USAF was being forced to accept engineless F-15 airframes, and by the spring of the following year around 30 were in storage. A massive effort by P&W brought the delivery situation under control, but for a long time the F-15 fleet remained short of engines.

A modification introduced into the fuel pump of the F100 created problems for the F-15 early in its career. In cruising flight, cavitation could begin in the pump, badly damaging the pump vanes. The solution adopted was simple – revert to the original design. In the case of the single-engined F-16 Fighting Falcon, which also uses the F100, a pump failure would be more serious, so Sunstrand developed an alternative dual-element pump for this aircraft. This runs at a lower speed, and should one section fail, the other can continue to deliver fuel at a lower rate.

The electronic engine control unit uses the fuel as a coolant. This technique for obtaining 'free' cooling led to problems when the F-15 first entered service. During training missions at Luke AFB, aircraft sometimes had to wait for 45 minutes or more before takeoff, with engines running at idle settings. This gradually heated the mass of fuel in the Eagle's tanks to the point where it was no longer cold enough to cool the engine control unit.

Modified fuel flow

Given the high temperature of the desert environment at Luke, the unit could not radiate the excess heat away, so tended to overheat. This resulted in engine overspeed problems and turbine failures. The fix in this case, according to the Burrows/Shawler paper presented to the Society of Experimental Test Pilots in 1975, was to cut back the fuel flow rate of the electronic engine control, based on the rate of temperature increase, just prior to full military power. Acceleration time was reduced by this modification to less than 50 per cent of the original time.

Another early problem was that the afterburner light-up envelope was considered too restrictive. Among the more important changes was one involving the five-segment afterburner range (practically mandatory for all fan engines) designed to make a smooth transition between segments, where the main problems were either too rich a mixture causing a light and then a blow-out, or too lean a mixture preventing a relight at all.

The spray-ring of each segment of the afterburner has a quick-fill capability which controls the light-up of each segment. The amount of fuel in each segment was the same for all altitudes and speeds, resulting in insufficient fuel at sea level and too much at high altitudes. The solution was the provision of a barometric sensor to reduce the amount of fuel fed into the quick-fill area as altitude was increased. The improvement is described as 'the biggest increment' on this problem.

The other major afterburner change was to reduce fuel flow in full reheat mode, which countered the effects of excess fuel for airflow and afterburner size. By reducing the total fuel flow by a nominal 4,000lb/hr (1,814kg/hr), the blow-out difficulty at full reheat was eliminated. An additional benefit was equal or greater thrust for less fuel flow.

The limited throttle movement came in for some criticism at this stage of the flight testing. Originally, the rpm was to be kept to a minimum at all altitudes, thus allowing 65 per cent rpm at 40,000ft (12,000m). This caused problems in getting the engine out of idle, due to low fuel flow, while requiring a slow throttle movement for acceptable acceleration. The fix was simple enough, involving

Right: Test equipment is positioned on an F100 at Pratt & Whitney's Government Products Division, West Palm Beach, Florida.

increasing the idling rpm in line with increasing altitude.

On the air intakes, which incorporate a variable-geometry ramp to adjust the airflow at varying speeds and heights to the optimum required by the engine, months of wind-tunnel research paid off. The amount of travel provided for the ramp was found to be more than necessary, and the engine inlet compatibility testing was completed in four months. Similar testing with the F-4 Phantom took 22 months, and with the F-101 Voodoo some 30 months.

Early operational and durability problems with the F100 during the late 1970s were largely overcome by modifications plus improvements in materials, maintenance and operating procedures. Production of spare parts was accelerated, and field maintenance teams were increased in size.

Part of the problem lay in the fact that the USAF had underestimated the number of cycles which engines aboard such high-performance types as the F-15 and F-16 would actually undergo. (A cycle is defined as the temperature variation experienced in a mission from engine start to maximum power and afterburner, then back to the lower settings used for landing). In 1977 the service estimated that each engine would undergo 1.15 cycles per flight hour. In practice the rate was 2.2 for the F-15 and 3.1 for the F-16.

At one time, designers had assumed that the most arduous duty which a jet engine had to face was running for long periods at high power levels. By the late 1960s, research had shown that this was simply not the case. Many failures were due to this type of running, but others were created by the heating and cooling resulting from an engine being run up to high power then throttled back.

Technicians dubbed this 'low-cycle fatigue', but had to admit that it was difficult to measure. To aid the design of future engines such as the F100, estimates were made of the average number of thermal cycles to which an engine would be exposed per flying hour. Unfortunately for the F100 programme, these estimates were wrong. In practice, engines were being subjected to far more thermal cycles than the designers had allowed for.

Overworked engines

Paradoxically, the additional stress which the engines were receiving was largely due to the F-15 and F-16 being such good aircraft. Given the high manoeuvrability of their new mounts, pilots were flying in a manner not possible on earlier types, pushing the aircraft to high angles of attack and making full use of the extended performance envelope. In the heat of a dogfight, the throttle setting would be changed much more often than on earlier fighters. All this spelled hard work for the engine.

Critical components such as first-stage turbine blades showed signs of distress, condemnation rate during repair being 60 per cent instead of the predicted 20 per cent. Maximum gas temperature was reduced to conserve component life, while R&D funding was concentrated on improvements to reliability rather than increasing thrust. Despite these problems, the F-15 had a better engine related safety record by the end of the 1970s than any other USAF fighter at a comparable point in its service career.

Another problem which was to dog the F100 during the first years of its service career was stagnation stalling. The compressor blades in a jet engine are of aerofoil section, and, like the wing of an aircraft, can be stalled if the angle at which the airflow strikes them exceeds a critical value. Powerplant stalls are occasional occurrences in most jet engines, particularly in the early stages of development, and the F100 was to prove excessively vulnerable to stagnation stalling during its first few years of operational service.

Turbofans are prone to a particularly severe type of stall from which recovery is not possible. As the flow of air through

Above: The split tail of the F-15 allows the stabilators and vertical stabilizers to be kept well clear of the efflux from the engines.

Below: The titanium frames of an F-15 engine bay, with the powerplant about to be installed, as seen by the wide-angle lens.

the compressor is disturbed, the engine core looses speed, while the combustor section of the engine continues to pass hot gas to the turbine, causing the latter to overheat. If this condition is not noticed, the turbine may be damaged.

Experience with the F-15 showed that in the event of a mild hard start, the pilot might not notice that a stall had occurred, as the loss of acceleration on the twin-engined aircraft was often not sharp enough to indicate to the pilot that one engine had failed. Unless he checked the temperature gauge, low-pressure turbine entry temperature could reach the point were damage might occur. To avoid this problem, an audible-warning system was devised.

Some stagnation stalls were found to be due to component failures, but most were linked with afterburner problems. The latter usually took the form of 'hard starts' – virtually mini-explosions within the afterburner. In some cases the afterburner failed to light on schedule; in other instances the burner extinguished. In either event, large amounts of unburned fuel were sprayed into the jetpipe, creating a momentary build-up of fuel. When this was ignited by the hot efflux from the engine core, a pressure pulse was created – the aerospace equivalent of a car backfiring.

Deliberate hard start

A reporter from the journal *Aviation Week* gave this account of a deliberately-induced hard start on a test stand: "The force of the auto-ignition was sufficient to rock the heavily sound-insulated concrete test building. A large gout of flame at the afterburner exhaust was seen on the closed-circuit color-television system."

The pressure in the afterburner resulting from a hard start sent a shock wave back up through the fan duct. When this reached the front section of the engine, it could cause the fan to stall, the high-pressure compressor to stall, or, in the worst case, both. It was sometimes possible for a series of stagnation stalls to occur, with each resulting in the afterburner hard start needed to trigger off another.

Stagnation stalls usually took place at altitude and at high Mach numbers, but rarely below 20,000ft (6,100m). Normal recovery method was for the pilot to shut down the engine, and allow it to spool down. Once the tachometer showed that engine rpm had fallen below the 50 per cent mark, the throttle could safely be reopened to the idle position, and the F100 would carry out its automatic relight sequence. Critical factor in restarting the engine after a stagnation stall is the low-pressure turbine-inlet temperature. This must fall to 450deg F (232deg C) before the engine can be restarted.

Several modifications were devised to reduce the frequency of stagnation stalls. The first approach taken was to try to prevent pressure build-ups in the afterburner. A quartz window in the side of the afterburner assembly allowed a flame sensor to monitor the pilot flame of the augmentor. If this went out, the flow of fuel to the outer sections of the burner was stopped.

When the F100 engine-control system was originally designed, P&W engineers allowed for the possibility that ingestion of efflux from missiles might stall the engine. A 'rocket fire' facility was designed into the controls in order to cope with such an eventuality. When missiles were fired, an electronic signal could be sent to the unified fuel control system which supplies fuel to the engine core and to the afterburner. The angle of the variable stator blades in the engine could be altered to avoid a stall, while the fuel flow to the engine was momentarily reduced, and the afterburner exhaust was increased in area to reduce the magnitude of any pressure pulse in the afterburner.

Tests had shown that the 'rocket fire' facility was not needed, but P&W engineers were able to use it as a means of preventing stagnation stalls. Engine shaft speed, turbine temperature and the angle of the compressor stator blades are monitored on the F100 by a digital electronic engine control unit. This normally serves to 'fine-tune' the engine throughout flight to ensure optimum performance.

By monitoring and comparing HP spool speed and fan exhaust temperature, the engine control unit is able to sense that a stagnation stall is about to take place, and send a dummy 'Rocket Fire' signal to the unified fuel control system to initiate the anti-stall measures described above. At the same time, a second modification to the fuel control system reduces the afterburner setting to zone 1 – little more than a pilot light – in order to help reduce pressure within the jetpipe.

In an attempt to prevent any pulses coming forward through the fan duct from affecting the core, P&W engineers devised a modification known as the 'proximate splitter'. This is a forward extension to the internal casing which splits the incoming airflow coming from the engine compressor fan, passing some to the core of the engine and diverting the remainder down the fan duct, past the core and into the afterburner. By closing the gap between the front end of this casing and the rear of the fan to just under half an inch (1.3cm), the engine designers reduced the size of the path by which the high-pressure pulses from the burner had been reaching the core.

Engines fitted with the proximate splitter were test-flown in the F-15, but this modification was not embodied in the engines of production Eagles, whose twin engines made the loss of a single engine less hazardous. It was, however, fitted to engines destined for the single-engined F-16.

The improvement in reliability as a result of the modifications to the fuel control system and nozzle was dramatic. Back in 1976, the F-15 fleet experienced a stagnation stall rate of 11–12 per 1,000 flying hours: by the end of 1981 this had dropped to 1.5 per 1,000 hours.

Above: The 'nodding' air intakes on either side of the F-15's forward fuselage are necessary to maintain the optimum rate of airflow to the engines, and for operation at high angles of attack.

Below: Eagles rendezvous with a KC-10A tanker. Specific fuel consumption of the F100 is 2.17 with full augmentation.

Above: A two-seat F-15 approaches a tanker boom for refuelling. Economical at normal ratings, the F100 consumes 860lb (390kg) of fuel per minute in full afterburner.

Efforts are under way to further reduce the smoke output of the F100 as part of a planned component-improvement programme. For example, the combustor has been modified to increase the velocity of the airflow in its front end, resulting in improved mixing of air and fuel and leading to more complete combustion and less residual smoke.

Traditional engine-servicing techniques involve replacing critical components at the end of a statistically-calculated lifetime. This often results in components being removed and scrapped while still perfectly servicable, giving good safety margins, but at a high cost to the operator. The USAF now wants engine designers to develop parts with greater tolerance to crack damage so that these may be left in the engine until inspection by non-destructive test (NDT) methods shows that cracks are starting to develop and a replacement is needed. Life-cycle costs may be cut by up to 60 per cent.

The service's Damage Tolerant Design (DTD) programme involved both Pratt & Whitney and General Electric, and focussed much of its attention on the F100. One of the programme's first achievements was a new pattern of F100 fan disc having five times the life of the original component. Key design elements under DTD are high quality control of the raw material, and the avoidance of shapes and configurations such as sharp radii which cause stress concentrations.

The Air Force plans to begin testing engine discs currently under development as part of the DTD programme in 1984, and hopes to fit these into operational engines before the end of that

Below left: The General Electric F110 has been test-flown in an F-15, and is one candidate to power future variants of the Eagle.

Top: The P&W PW1120 is based on the core of the F100: smaller and lighter, it is to be used in the Israel Aircraft Industries Lavi fighter.

Above: The other potential replacement for the F100 is P&W's own PW1128, which began test-flying in March 1983.

year. By 1985 or 1986 the F100 may be fitted with second and third-stage turbine blades and vanes manufactured using a single-crystal technique. Although more expensive than components made from traditional materials, these will probably have a lifetime at least twice that of current vanes and blades.

The USAF was the first F100 user to take advantage of a warranty scheme offered by P&W in 1980. The company undertook to repair or replace certain high-pressure turbines unserviceable as a result of wear or mechanical failure at no extra cost to the USAF. Engines covered by the deal were from production lot IX and were due for delivery between February 1981 and January 1982.

To qualify for free treatment, faulty engines would have to have carried out less than 900 equivalents of the TAC engine operating cycle (about two years of normal use) or develop the fault within three and a half years of delivery. If the HP failure had caused secondary damage to the engine, P&W undertook to cover costs up to 75 per cent of that of a new engine.

Pratt & Whitney are continuing research into new engines based on the F100 and its technology. During a series of tests carried out in late summer of 1982, the company ground-tested an F100 fitted with a two-dimensional nozzle. Rectangular in cross-section, this is a convergent/divergent design featuring moveable upper and lower surfaces which could be used to vector the thrust. This design was developed under a USAF contract, and while no production applications is planned, the new nozzle could be used in a modified F-16 or F-15.

Angles of up to 20deg were demonstrated, but P&W is confident that the design would be good for up to 30deg. Coupled with the use of thrust reversing, this technique could greatly increase the agility of current aircraft, and could cut the take-off run to 1,200ft (366m) or less. Earlier attempts to design axisymmetric nozzles with vectoring and thrust-reversing have resulted in complex and heavy units which paid a high penalty in thrust loss. The latest P&W design could be offered as an add-on modification, weighing only a few hundred pounds, to the standard F100 gas generator section.

Using experience gained from the F100 programme, P&W was able to begin development of the cropped-fan PW1120 afterburning turbofan. Based on the core of the earlier engine, this is a low-risk development with 60 per cent commonality, but incorporating a new low-pressure compressor and turbine and a simplified afterburner. Operating temperatures have been slightly reduced, and the PW1120 has a slightly lower thrust-to-weight ratio of 7.25:1 instead of 7.9:1. The PW1120 is some 20in (51cm) shorter than the F100 and 7in (18cm) narrower in diameter. It is rated at 20,620lb (9,342kg) and is due to fly early in 1984. The first application of the PW1120 to be announced was the planned Israel Aircraft Industries Lavi air combat fighter.

Two other engines are currently under development, aimed at re-engining the F-15, F-16 and, possibly, the F-14. An up-market version of the F100, variously known as the F100EMD, PW1130 and now the PW1128, has its mass flow increased to 248lb/sec (112.5kg/sec), a turbine entry temperature of 2,700degF (1,482degC) single crystal blades and digital electronic controls. The PW1128 began test-flying in March 1983, with a rating of 26,900lb (12,200kg). Its production rating will be 27,410lb (12,430kg).

Competing with the PW1128 is the General Electric F110 (formerly the F101 DFE – derivative fighter engine) rated at 27,500lb (12,470kg), which has flown in both the F-14 and the F-16XL. Both engines may well be bought, but the split has yet to be determined: one possibility is the installation of the PW1128 in the F-15, and the F110 in the F-14 and F-16.

Avionics

The key to the Eagle's combat capability is its sophisticated suite of avionics: long-range, look-down radar that can detect even low-flying targets at ranges of up to 100 miles (160km); a tactical electronic warfare system to warn of any threat; and displays and controls that present the pilot with almost all the information he needs and allow him to control weapon systems and radar without looking inside the cockpit. The addition of programmable signal processing has further increased the radar capability, and for the ground-attack role still more improvements are planned.

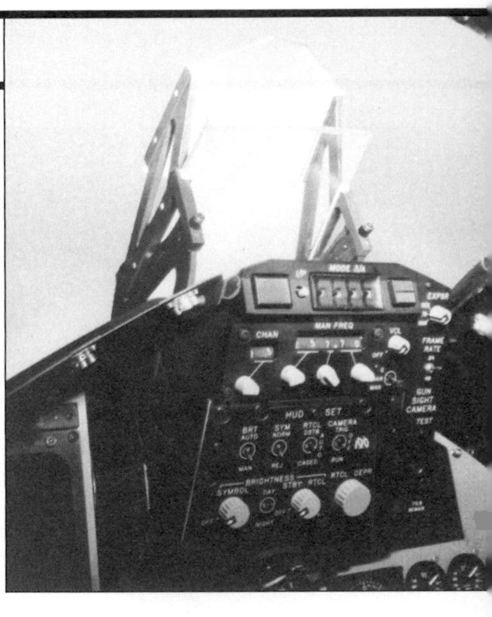

Above: The McDonnell Douglas head-up display present all essential navigation and attack information to the Eagle pilot.

When considering the anatomy of a modern aeroplane the airframe can be likened to the skeleton and flesh, the engines provide muscle and the onboard computers and avionics can be considered as the brain and nervous system. For many years the avionic systems were relatively simple and were purely add-on items to assist in communication and navigation: failure of any one item did not create any great problem, and the aeroplane could fly quite happily under human control and judgement. Then came the great electronic revolution and the emergence of the silicon chip.

The evolution of the integrated circuit – an entire microelectronic system embodied in a chip of semiconductive material, normally crystalline silicon – brought immediate gains to the designers of avionic equipment. The size and weight of 'black boxes' could be drastically reduced; power consumption fell, the associated need for complicated cooling systems; reliability increased; and, perhaps most significantly, the new devices allowed for a considerable expansion of functions.

Computers that had once required large storage space shrank to shoe-box size, offered great reliability and could be programmed for a variety of complex tasks. With programming came the new word 'software', denoting an arcane, subjective art that can achieve the apparently impossible.

Generally, software can be considered as the process of telling a computer what to do and how to do it, while making the process understandable to the computer itself. This last consideration is crucial to efficient operation, since a computer totally lacks judgement and intuition and cannot relate in any useful manner to past experience. Consequently, the software must be able to dictate behaviour under all operating conditions including abnormal situations.

High-speed operation

A major advantage of electronic systems is that they operate at the speed of light, allowing a considerable number of operations to take place in a very short space of time. If a pilot operates a switch which affects a circuit under computer control and at that point the computer is working hard it may introduce a delay of perhaps one tenth of a second. This is a valuable breathing space for the computer, yet so short as to be entirely unnoticeable to the pilot.

As well as operational functions, software programs can be used to carry out automatic test and system monitoring, constantly evaluating the health of the associated hardware and providing an indication of malfunction to the pilot. This is an extremely important part of a modern avionic system, usually referred to as built-in test equipment (BITE). It enables failures to be identified and isolated, allowing the pilot to carry on with the operation by selecting alternate systems. One manufacturer of such equipment is on record as saying that a typical system with 100,000 computer instructions may use almost three quarters of this capacity for diagnostic purposes.

As the electronic revolution gained pace so avionic equipment became more complex. By the early 1970s systems were evolving with considerable computational powers, and with digital computers forming an integral part. Reliability had improved and maintenance had been simplified by the use of self-checking systems. More and more critical functions came under the control of electronic systems and the avionic suite now ranked alongside airframe and engine as an essential and fundamental element. Integration of these three areas has reached the point where it is now inconceivable that any part of a modern military aircraft should not be under some form of electronic control of influence.

A modern aeroplane such as the F-15 depends upon electronic systems for communication, navigation, flight management, weapons management, automatic flight control (auto-pilot), systems control and management (eg hydraulics and pressurization), control and management of electronic warfare (EW) systems and the continual monitoring of all aspects of engine and airframe operation and maintenance. Indeed, the pace of change in modern technology and military tactics to meet evolving threats is such that any simple list of electronic devices is necessarily incomplete. Although the aeroplane appears externally unchanged, its black boxes can undergo constant evolution and refinement, and the practised eye can sometimes note the addition of certain lumps, bulges and antennas on the external surface of the airframe.

Below: Nose radars, HUDs and bubble canopies give these F-15s unmatched target detection ability.

Air-to-air gun mode

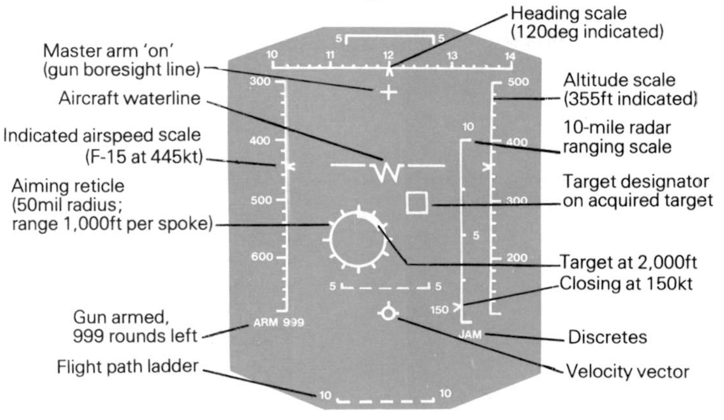

Air-to-air medium range missile mode

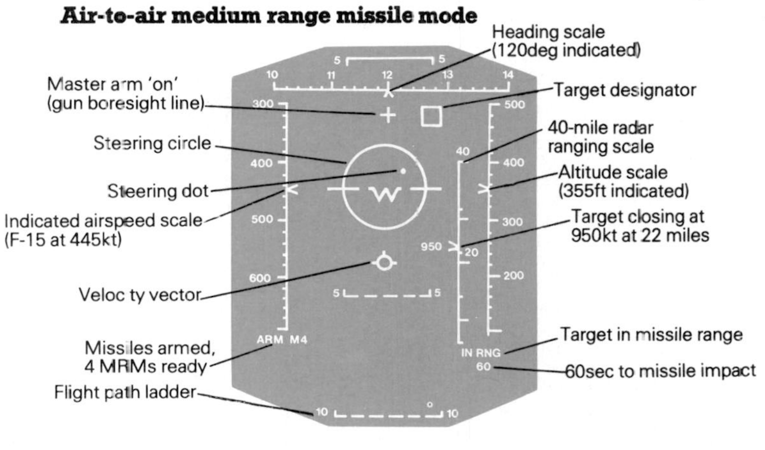

Air-to-ground automatic mode

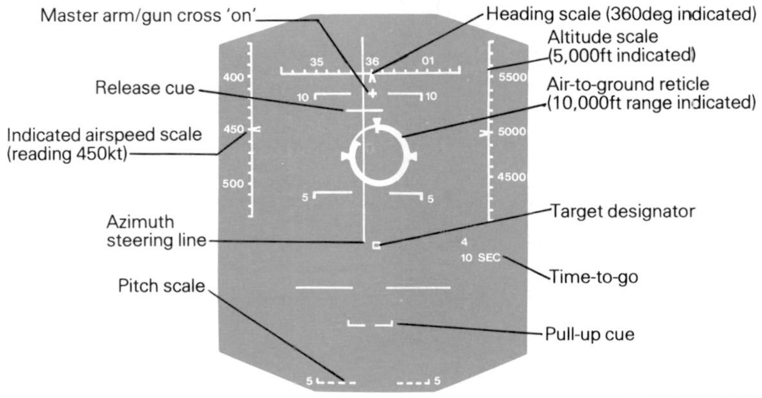

Air-to-ground CDIP mode

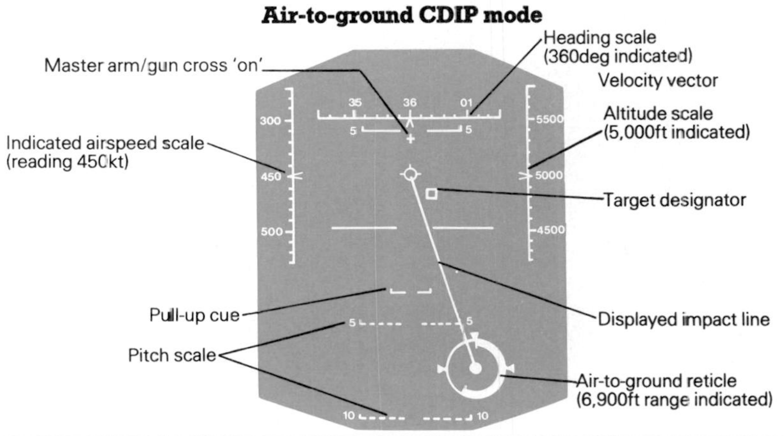

Above: Typical displays presented by the F-15 HUD showing the symbology used in various air-to-air and air-to-ground attack modes.

This is an important aspect of avionic innovation as it can enhance abilities and performance even though the aircraft is still restricted by its own basic dynamic performance. In other words, the power/weight ratio tends to remain constant, but its electronic eyes and brain can become more far-seeing and powerful so that it can be a more effective fighting machine.

The basic electrical power of the F-15 is provided by engine driven generators manufactured by the Lear Siegler Power Equipment Division. These feature a 40/50kVA generator constant speed drive unit, produced by the Sundstrand Corporation, which ensures that the generator itself is always driven at a constant speed regardless of engine speed or revolutions. This in turn ensures a constant, steady output of closely controlled electrical power in terms of voltage, frequency and phase and does away with the need for additional on-board devices to ensure such basic integrity of power supplies. Power is then distributed throughout the aircraft via other control systems, circuit breakers, distribution boards and transformer-rectifiers to ensure adequate power, of the correct type, for each sequence of operation. For instance, certain switched selection circuits can accept fairly brutal power sources while other types of instrumentation require highly accurate and sensitive power inputs.

Much of the flight information can be presented to the pilot on a cathode ray tube (CRT) display, which can accept inputs from radar or electro-optical sensors. This is in line with the current trend for information to be presented in visual terms, often supported by colour. The pilot can assimilate more information more efficiently and ambiguity is reduced. An IBM on-board digital air data computer is used to process information from other sensors such as al-

Below: View through the head-up display following the launch of a medium-range AIM-7 Sparrow. The missile itself is visible in the target designator box.

Left: The front panel of the F-15C cockpit has all the most frequently used controls conveniently mounted and a minimum of instruments.

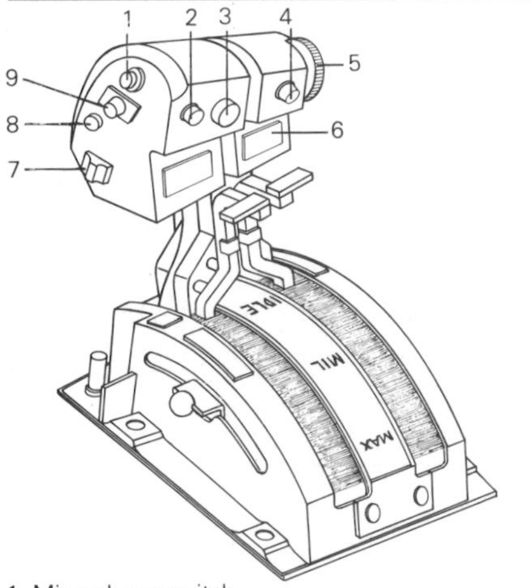

1 Microphone switch
2 IFF interrogate button
3 Target designate control
4 Gunsight reticle stiffen/reject short-range missile
5 Radar antenna elevation control
6 ECM dispenser switch
7 Weapon selection switch (gun, short-range missile or medium-range missile)
8 Spare
9 Speed brake switch

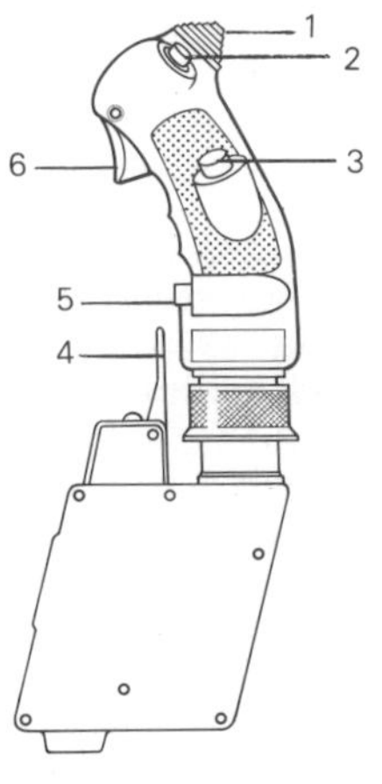

1 Trim button
2 Weapon release button
3 Radar auto acquisition switch
4 Autopilot/nose gear steering release switch
5 SRM/EO weapon seeker head cage/uncage control
6 HUD camera and gun trigger

Above: The throttles (top) and control stick carry all the weapons and radar controls needed in combat, enabling the pilot to keep his eyes attention on the target or HUD.

timeters, and this too is presented on the CRT display.

Communication is usually through VHF/UHF links, which essentially form a line-of-sight system. In other words, the range of the equipment is directly proportional to the aircraft's height above the ground. For long-distance flights, therefore, the communications system is supplemented by HF to provide the necessary range. Interference by the enemy is always a problem in communications and several programmes have been undertaken to overcome the problem. Typically, the signal can be spread over a wide spectrum to reduce the chances of detection and require a widely spread jamming signal with consequent dissipation of power and loss of effectiveness.

The aircraft's Litton ASN-109 navigation system is based upon inertial navigation techniques. This is a completely passive, on-board system which does not have to rely on ground-based aids and is largely automatic in operation. It depends upon highly sensitive gyroscopes which are used to accurately align a platform in relation to true North. The pilot tells the computer the start point and can add several desired destinations or waypoints, and as the aircraft moves off, accelerometers on the platform detect rates of movement. All the information is then processed by a digital computer, which comes up with a variety of answers which are displayed to the pilot. This information includes position, time to go to next waypoint and wind conditions.

The high degree of accuracy of platform stabilization can give attitude information for the aircraft's flight instruments providing pitch, roll and heading data at all times. This navigation system is backed up by ground-based navaids such as TACAN, ADF and ILS allowing the F-15 to integrate with any type of traffic pattern. In a cross-country mode these aids can be used to update the inertial system.

Among the most classified equipment is that concerned with aspects of electronic warfare (EW). This is also likely to be the system most often modified, changed and reprogrammed. EW systems can be used to detect radars, notify the pilot of various types of hostile EW and allow a degree of offensive reaction such as jamming enemy signals. Such is the state of modern electronics that many of these devices act completely automatically and can recognize the difference between friendly and hostile emissions. They are capable of reacting to rapid changes in the enemy scenario and can fire off decoys such as chaff or infra-red (IR) flares to confuse the seeker of enemy missiles. The F-15 carries such a system in the Northrop ALQ-135, which is part of the aircraft's tactical electronic warfare system (TEWS) and is associated with the active jamming role.

More readily apparent is the Loral ALR-56 radar warning receiver, four external antennas mounted at each wing tip and on top of each fin give them a distinctive, easily recognizable shape. A fifth blade-shaped antenna is mounted under the forward fuselage. Associated equipment includes receivers, power supply, receiver controls and a display of an alpha-numeric type which indicates the degree of lethality and range of the emerging threat. The all-solid-state ALR-56 is based on a digitally controlled dual channel receiver which scans from H-band through to J-band (6-20GHz), while changes in the perceived threat can be accommodated by changes in software.

The APG-63 radar

While it is invidious to suggest that any one part of the avionic system is more important than any other in these days of integrated and interrelated systems, it is hard not to admit that the awesome capability of the Hughes APG-63 radar is really the heart of the F-15 and the

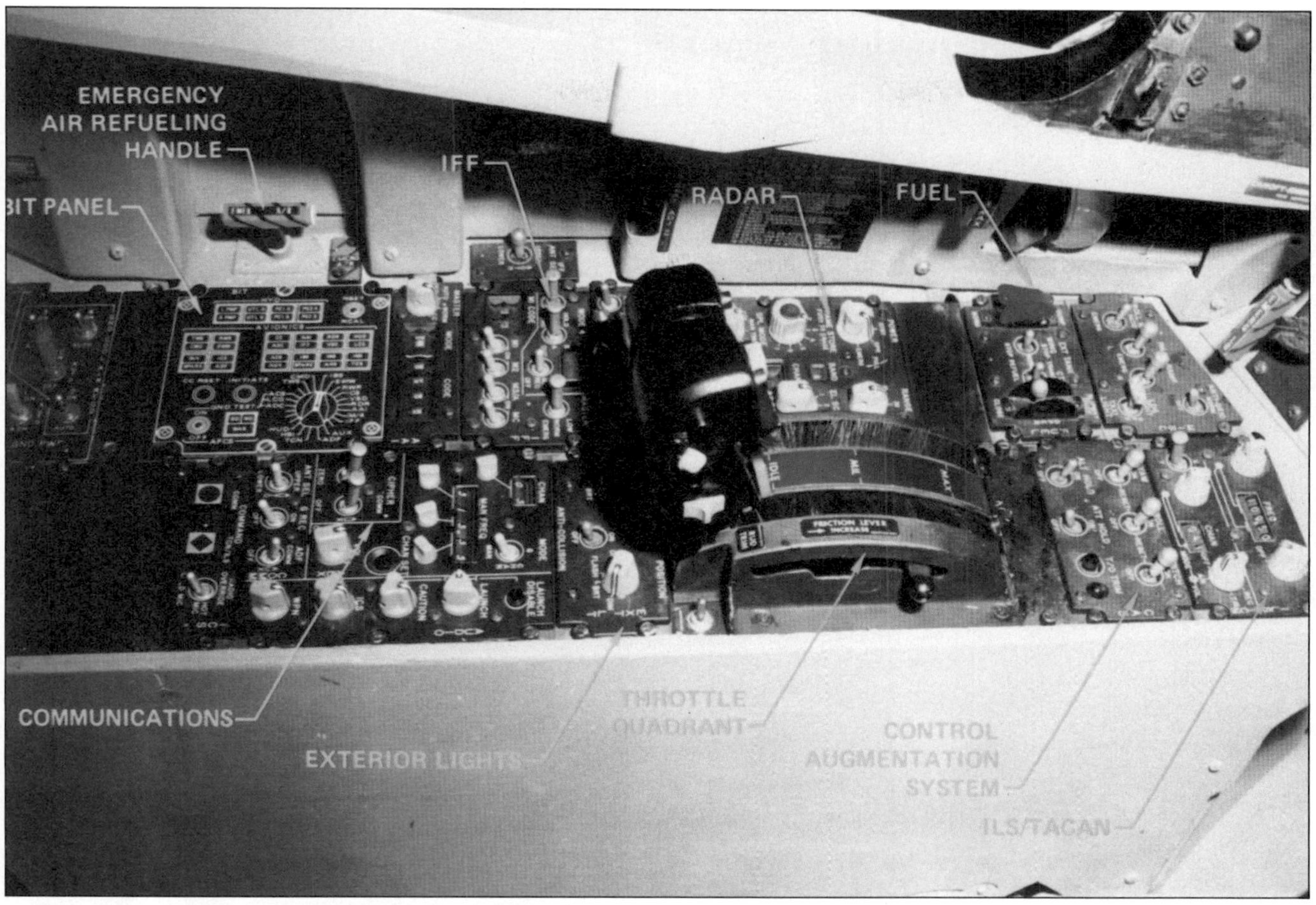

Left: A feature of the left console is the BIT (built-in-test) equipment panel, allowing the pilot to locate faults in the avionics.

Below left: Adjusting the head-up display controls of an F-15D during pre-flight checks at Kadena Air Base, Okinawa.

foundation of its air combat efficiency.

When the F-15 was designed its primary mission of air superiority depended on an advanced fire control radar. The daunting specification numbered among its requirements: use in a single-seat aircraft to track targets at extremely long ranges; close-in and look-down operation that would blind other radars; a clutter-free radar display which would show all target information; the ability to provide tracking and steering data on a head up display (HUD) allowing the pilot to keep his eyes on the target; ease of operation; weapons control and coordination; and selected air-to-ground capabilities. In addition it was expected to reach high standards of reliability and maintainability.

Such a requirement would have been unthinkable a few years earlier and showed just how much influence the new electronics could have on the capabilities of a new aircraft. Even so, to meet the specification certain compromises had to be reached and innovative techniques employed to the full.

Most airborne radars work in the X-band (8–12.5GHz) and choice of frequency is the first area of compromise. The critical factor in an aircraft is the size of the antenna: in a fighter the most convenient position is in the nose, where space is restricted by aerodynamic considerations. It so happens that X band produces a good compromise antenna size. Dropping to S band demands a larger antenna, while going further up, say to K band, offers a small and neater antenna but a signal which is adversely affected by meteorological conditions such as rain – hardly a good choice for a modern fighter aircraft.

Pulse repition frequency

Another fundamental choice is that of the pulse repetition frequency (PRF) which refers to the number of transmitted pulses per second. This is often classed as high or low, with high considered to be energy transmitted at 100,000 or more pulses per second while low is only some 1,000 pulses per second. In general terms, the use of a high PRF in the pulse-Doppler radars common in fighters gives good long-range detection of head-on targets, but a restricted detection of tail-on targets and a tendency to lose track of manoeuvring targets.

In comparison, the low-PRF radars then commonly employed for air combat proved to be good for ground mapping but could not detect targets in a look-down mode. It seemed that the compromise choice of a medium PRF would offer improved performance against manoeuvring targets, but at the expense of long range detection.

Hughes overcame the difficulty by developing a radar that had all three PRF modes. High and medium operate together, while low is used for ground mapping. So emerged the APG-63 multi-mode pulse-Doppler radar with an all-altitude, all-aspect attack capability and a maximum detection range in excess of 100 miles (160km). It can also guide radar-controlled missiles against all

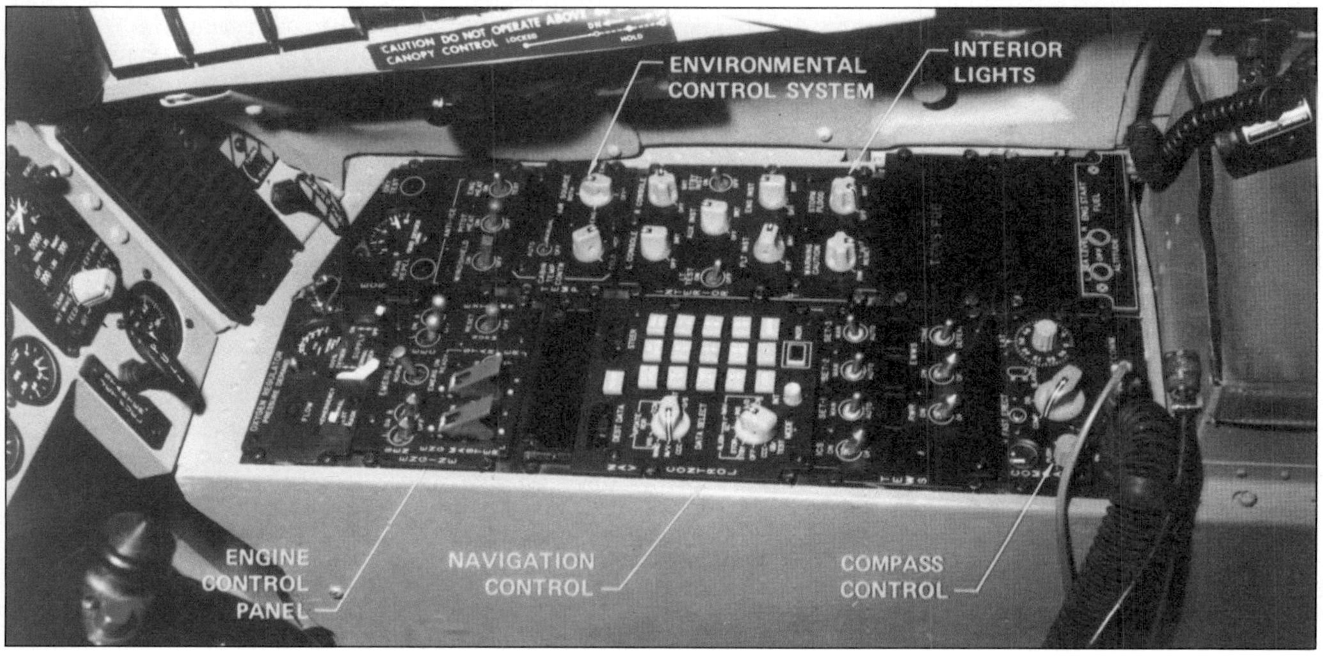

Left: Layout of the navigation, engine and environmental system controls on the F-15 cockpit's right console.

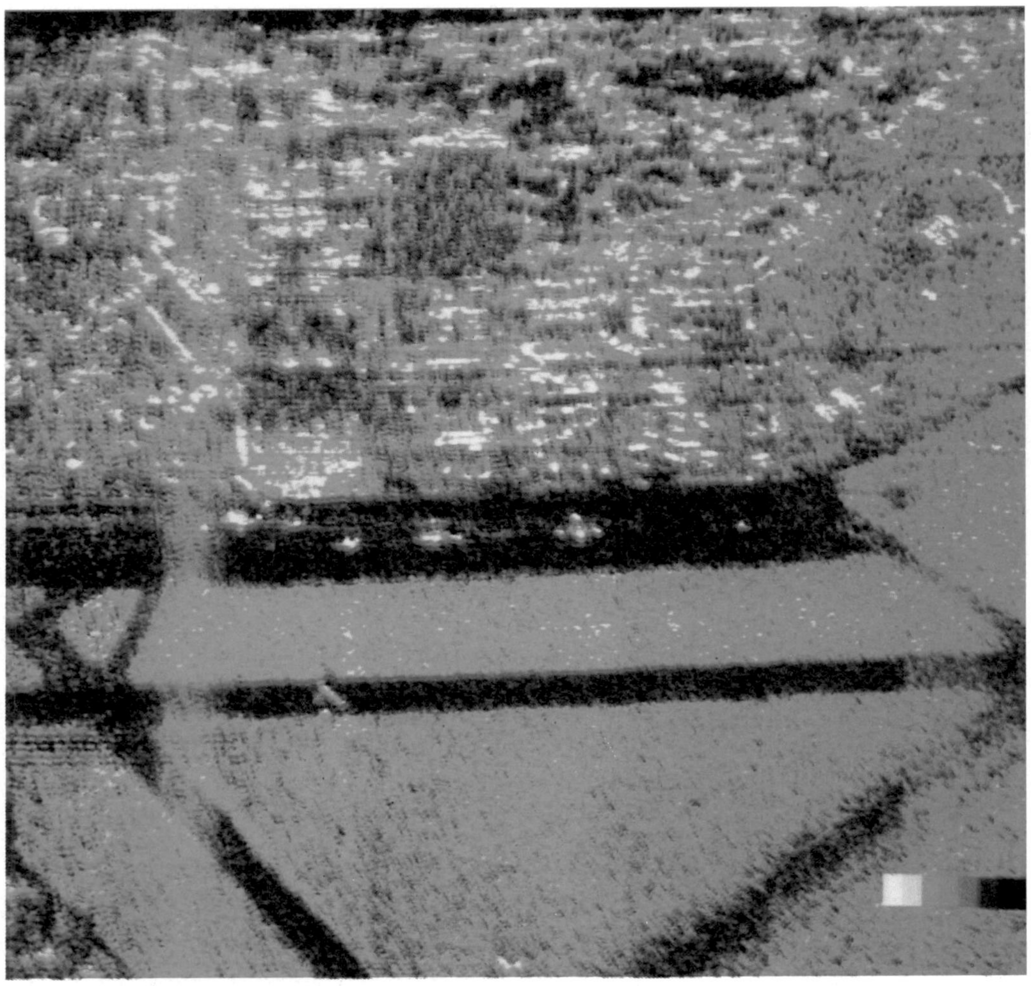

Above: Scott AFB, Illinois, as seen by the camera (right) and as an 8.5ft (2.6m) resolution ground map produced by the F-15 AFCD radar.

Below: The radar display format used in the Strike Eagle includes a window which can be moved to select enlarged patch maps.

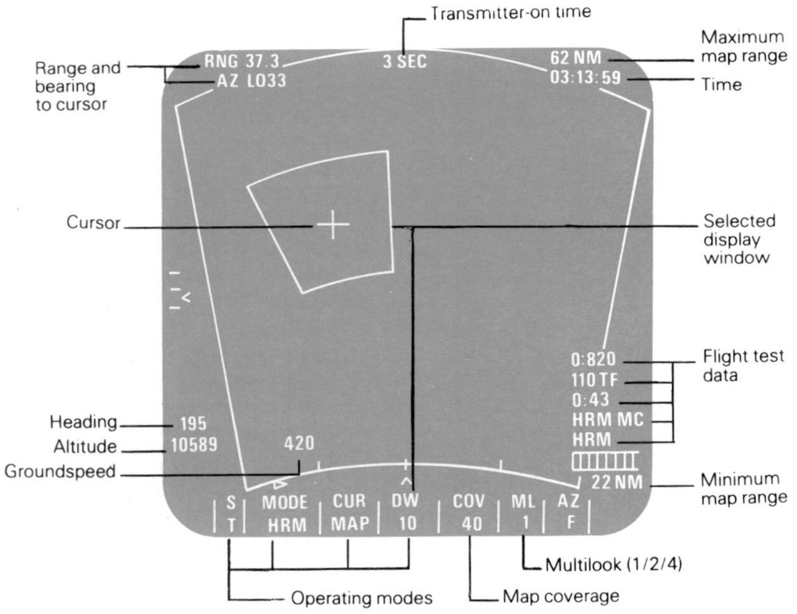

Bottom: Comparative effective ranges of the F-15's APG-63 and the MiG-25's Fox Fire radars, showing the former's clear advantage.

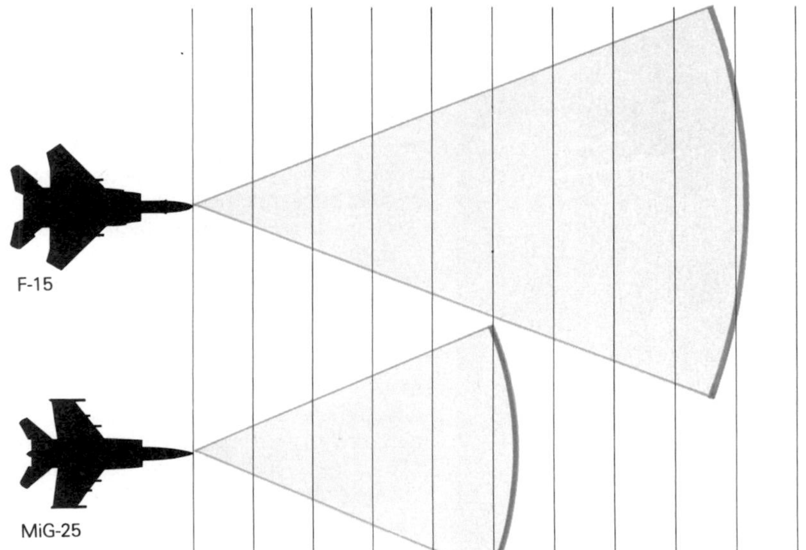

types of target. The primary radar controls are mounted on the aircraft's throttle so allowing the pilot to keep his head up during combat. The HUD shows target positioning, steering, range data and weapons release data.

The radar display provides a clear, clutter-free presentation and look-down view of any target aircraft even in the presence of heavy ground clutter. This ability is the result of a combination of both high and low PRF; digital processing of data, and the use of Kalman filtering in the tracking loops. The last process is a computer technique which continually compares the relative errors of the on-board equipment and data from the external sensors – in other words, a form of averaging of available data. In addition, the radar uses a gridded travelling wave tube that permits variation of the radar waveform to suit the prevailing situation.

Another problem with radar is that of false alarms. These are eliminated by the use of a low-sidelobe antenna – which is a good preventative against enemy EW – a guard receiver and frequency rejection of ground clutter and ground moving targets. Air-to-ground modes include target ranging for automated weapon release, a mapping mode for navigation and, thanks to the Doppler element, a velocity update for the INS. The nose-mounted antenna is a planar array that is hydraulically driven and gimballed in three axes.

Combat evaluation

When the radar first came into operation in the F-15 a series of air combat evaluations were carried out by USAF pilots flying the aircraft against seven different types of aircraft modified to simulate leading threats, and the F-15 won by a handsome margin. More significantly, perhaps, it took part in a series of exercises in which an E-3A Sentry AWACS faces attack by a large force. The F-15 proved to be successful in 38 out of 39 intercepts and its radar overcame the effects of jamming techniques.

Further improvement came with the development of a programmable signal processor (PSP). This is a feature of all new APG-63s and is available as a retrofit item to earlier models. When it appeared, in 1979, this was the only known deployed PSP and was considered to be a key element in expanding the F-15's tactical air interdiction role while enhancing its tactical air superiority capability. The PSP is a high-speed, special-purpose computer which controls the radar modes through its software rather than through a hard wired circuit design; this allows rapid switching of modes for maximum operational flexibility. PSP-modified radar is fitted to the 420th and subsequent Eagles, which are designated F-15C (single-seat) and F-16D (two-seat).

The use of the PSP paved the way for the modification of an ANAPG-63 to provide synthetic aperture radar (SAR). The modification followed on from earlier SAR work in the USAF Forward-looking Advanced Multimode Radar (FLAMR) programme. The PSP in this instance is a fourth-generation model which performs over seven million operations per second.

SAR imagery sharpens mapping details and provides the pilot with an overhead view, as if he were flying directly over the target, when in fact he can be 100 miles (160km) away. Previously, such imagery had to be processed on the ground because suitable equipment was too large to be easily fitted into an aircraft and processing speed was too slow for real time display.

The first flight of the new radar in an F-15 took place in November 1980, and initially a radar mapping resolution of 127ft (39m) was obtained. Within a month it was down to 60ft (18m) – still not good enough for the recognition of small tactical targets. By the 40th test flight, however, resolution was down to the stipulated level of just 10ft (3m).

Above: Routine maintenance on an F-15A's APG-63 radar. All the equipment is readily accessible, and individual components are easily removable for repair.

This degree of resolution means that at a distance of 20–30 miles (30–50km) from the target street patterns, power lines and field boundaries are visible. At 10 miles (16km) from an airfield a ⅔-mile (1km) square radar map can be displayed and aircraft as little as 8ft 6in (2.6m) apart can be clearly recognized. Other targets may be seen equally clearly, making target selection easy and unambiguous. The radar maps are updated every few seconds and linked to the navigation systems and weapons modes for ground attack preparations.

By this time, too, MCAIR had developed low-drag fuel pallets to increase the F-15's ferry range. These are two close fitting packs known as fuel and sensor tactical (FAST) packs. In addition to increased fuel tankage, the FAST packs allow a greater range of electronic sensors to be carried, including optical cameras, low light level TV cameras and a laser designator.

Enhanced Eagles

Coincident with this development, the manufacturers suggested that the USAF needed an all-weather fighter capable of performing long-range, air-to-ground interdiction missions while maintaining its air-to-air capabilities, and suggested than an enhanced Eagle would fulfil these requirements.

Two-seater F-15 Eagles had been built and were externally identifiable only by their larger cockpit canopy. This allowed them to function as trainers as well as being combat capable. The manufacturer used one of these two-seaters in a company-funded project known as Strike Eagle to create an all-weather, day/night ground attack aircraft using the new SAR radar integrated with forward looking infra-red (FLIR) system of the Pave Tack pod. The rear cockpit was modified to allow a specialist crew member to handle the radar and FLIR inputs.

The rear cockpit was fitted with four electronic displays and two hand controllers which allow the crew member to focus his attention on the displays while operating systems and controlling display content. Two of the displays are used for navigational purposes, one for weapon selection and one to monitor enemy tracking systems.

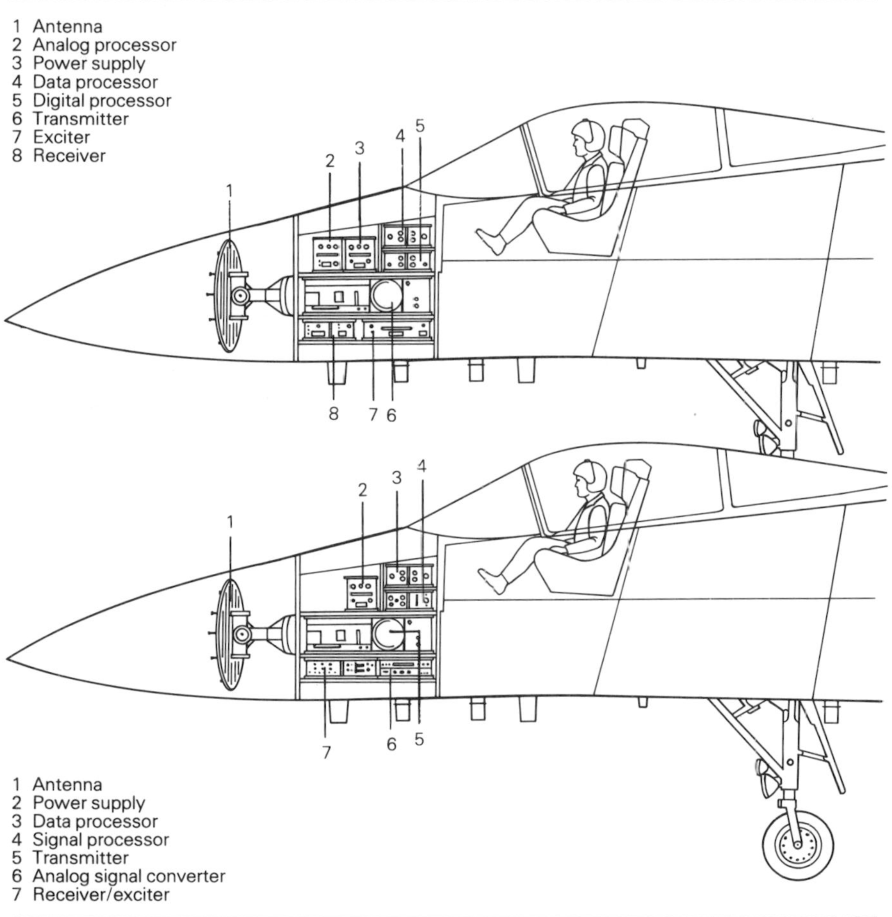

Above: Comparison of the standard APG-63 (top) and the PSP-modified equipment carried by the F-15C.

At the same time, improving electronic systems had created more sensitive electronic countermeasures sensors and the manufacturers proposed an Advanced Wild Weasel F-15. The outcome of these projects is described elsewhere in this book though they deserve mention in the evolution of the aircraft's avionic systems.

In 1981, another advanced avionic feature became linked with the F-15, when the Integrated Flight/Fire Control (IFFC) and Firefly III programmes were initiated. The IFFC 1 programme, being undertaken by MCAIR under a $14 million contract from the Air Force Flight Dynamics Laboratory, is for the design, development, integration and flight testing of a system which couples the Eagle's fire control and flight control systems to accept dual control inputs and tailor flight control response to the various weapons delivery modes. The Firefly III programme, being conducted by the General Electric Aircraft Equipment Division under a $7 million Air Force Avionics Laboratory contract for the further development of the fire control system.

The IFFC/Firefly III coupling will allow automatic positioning of the aircraft to attack targets detected by an electro-optical target designation pod. This is expected to shorten engagement times and enable the aircraft to drop its bombs or stores without having to overfly the target. The F-15 in the Firefly programme carries a Martin Marietta-built Atlis II designator pod in the port forward missile well and this is linked to the aircraft's fly-by-wire system via an intermediate additional digital computer.

As had been predicted by the manufacturers at the start of the Strike Eagle project, the USAF is becoming acutely aware of its need to have a long-range all-weather aircraft with a good air-to-ground capability. The current F-4 is nearing retirement and the possibility of an all-new multi-role fighter is unlikely to be translated into reality much before the mid-1990s.

A more practical solution would seem to be the upgrading and modification of an existing aircraft, principally through the use of improved avionics. This is now the subject of a USAF programme which is comparing the relative performances of the F-15 and F-16. Three F-15 advanced fighter demonstrators will be used to evaluate both single pilot and pilot/specialist officer crew complements. The single-seater is an F-15C; one two-seat F-15D is fitted with a Ford Aerospace FLIR and laser tracker/marker pod while the other two-seater is the original Strike Eagle with Pave Tack FLIR and laser pod and synthetic aperture radar. The rear cockpit of the last is still configured with an array of special displays and controls for operation of the sensors, and the aircraft is now known as the Advanced Fighter Capability Demonstrator. Although the Pave Tack pod is expected to be the standard fit, it was considered prudent to gain additional operational experi-

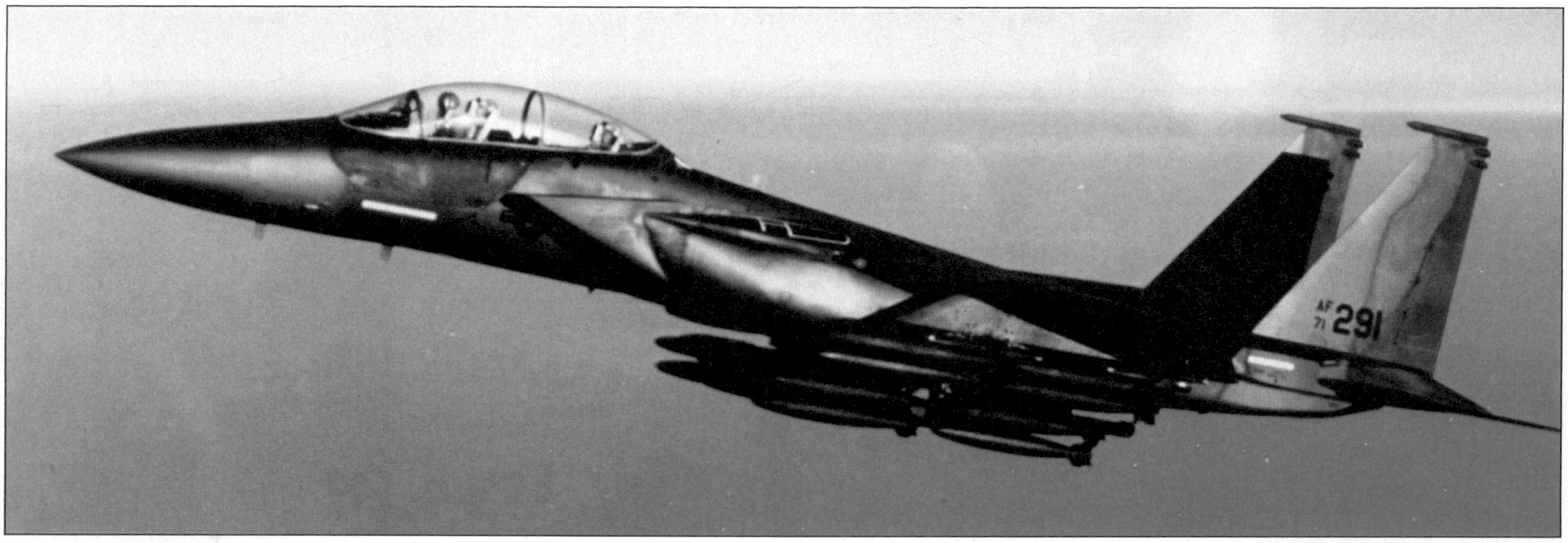

Above: The Strike Eagle's APG-63 was modified to use synthetic aperture radar techniques for high resolution ground mapping.

ence by using the Ford Aerospace system, which has been derived from a similar pod developed for the F/A-18 Hornet.

Another alternative option for the enhanced Eagle is the Martin Marietta LANTIRN (Low Altitude Navigation and Targeting Infra-Red for Night) system currently under development for the USAF's F-16 and A-10 aircraft. The system consists of two pods and cockpit displays: the navigation pod contains a wide-field-of-view FLIR sensor, terrain-following radar and associated electronics, while the targeting pod contains a stabilized wide- and narrow-field-of-view targeting FLIR sensor, automatic trackers, laser designator and ranger, automatic target recognizer, missile boresight correlator and supporting electronics. Interface with the pilot is through a wide-field-of-view, diffractive optics HUD, built by Marconi Avionics in the UK. The system is still under development, and its inclusion on an enhanced Eagle is subject to its successful service entry on the F-16 and A-10.

Possibly the greatest operational problem that has to be overcome in the advanced role is that of survivability. This can be achieved only by the use of advanced sensors and more capable avionics, probably with a two-man crew, while Visionics will be needed for all-weather, low-altitude flight using terrain-following radar and a new radar altimeter. Some of this innovation will evolve as part of the constant product improvement programme that companies tend to pursue during the lifetime of their products. In the USAF this is epitomized by the Multi-Stage Improvement Programme (MSIP) which is currently monitoring enhanced radar, improved software and the introduction of Seek Talk and JTIDS.

Seek Talk is the codename for a long term programme to reduce the vulnerability of UHF radios to enemy jamming by modifying existing radios with the addition of spread spectrum techniques and the use of a null steering antenna.

JTIDS stands for Joint Tactical Information Distribution System, an ambitious programme intended to provide a high-capacity, reliable, jam-resistant, secure, digital information distribution system which will allow for a very high degree of interoperability between various elements of deployed forces and command and control centres. An interesting feature of the JTIDS system is a relevant navigation characteristic: Implicit in the signalling structure is a highly accurate measurement of message time of arrival which is readily convertible to transmitter/receiver range. This could prove to be a most useful device in future tactical roles and in a supplementary role to INS, whose principal virtue is its independence of ground installations.

Although a great deal of current development is obscured by the needs of security it is possible to visualise an advanced version of the F-15 in the required role. Current systems of the Strike Eagle standard could be integrated with the results of the Firefly III programme and with new HUDs such as the Marconi Avionics wide field-of-view diffractive-optics system. These systems would operate in conjunction with advanced versions of missiles, guns and laser-guided bombs. Trials were due to start in 1983 of the AGM-65D IIR Maverick air-to-ground missile and the General Electric 30mm gun pod.

The next event in the evolving avionic scene will be the introduction of the Global Positioning System (GPS), which

Left: The IFFC/Firefly III F-15B, with Martin Marietta ATLIS II optical sensor and tracker pod on the port wing missile pylon.

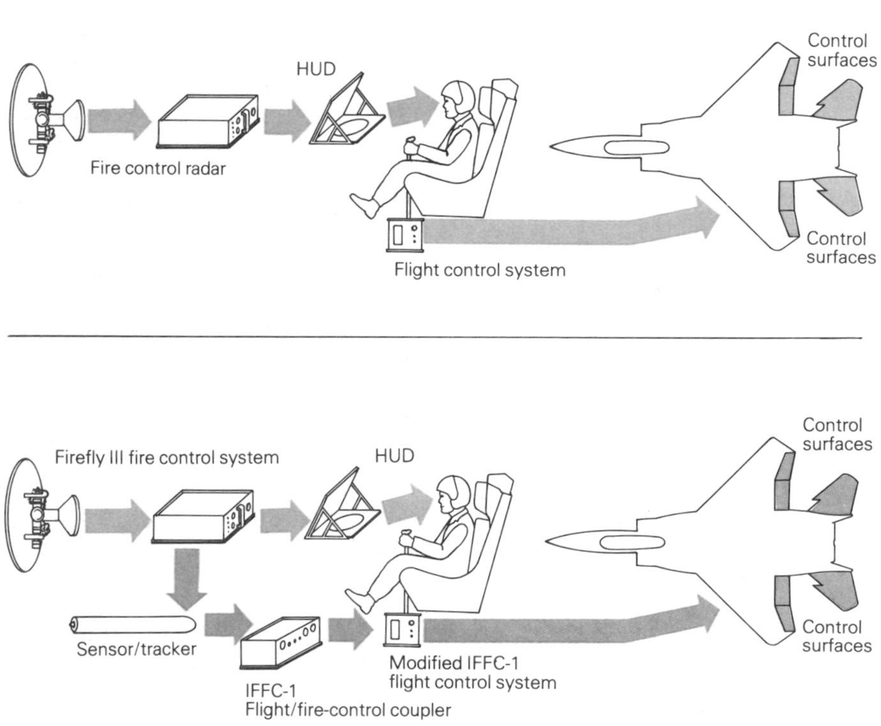

Below: Modifications introduced on the IFFC/Firefly III flight and fire control system, compared with the standard F-15 system.

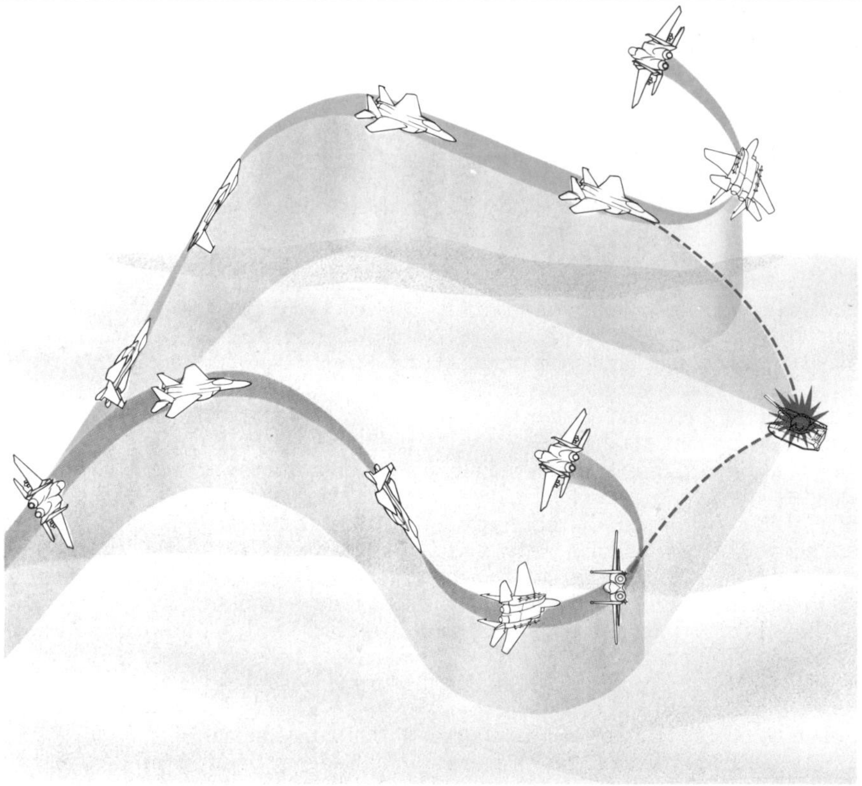

Below: Typical manoeuvring attack made possible by the IFFC system (bottom) compared with the conventional pop-up attack profile.

is expected to revolutionize navigation, though it requires satellites which could be vulnerable in war. Currently two F-15s are conducting GPS trials and it is expected that the complete system will be operational by 1987. It will eventually consist of a network of Navstar satellites circling the earth. Thousands of ground receivers mounted in all types of military vehicles and even carried by foot soldiers will translate satellite signals into navigation information that will be accurate to within 10–20m anywhere in the world, day or night and regardless of weather. The information will include altitude, longitude, latitude, velocity to 0.1m/sec and a precise time in nanoseconds.

The Navstar satellites will orbit the earth at an altitude of 12,500 miles (20,000km), each one continuously broadcasting time and position messages. This information will greatly enhance tactical air operations and should prove to be a potent all-weather navigation system. Advanced anti-jamming techniques are built into the system to permit continuing operation under the most stringent of enemy EW operations.

The GPS tactical air configuration will provide continuous signal tracking under all flight conditions and the system will be integrated with other on-board avionics so that the GPS-derived data can be used to refine other flight systems.

Below: Illuminated indicators on the front panel include fire warning (top left), canopy unlocked (top right), air-to-ground mode button and beacon light (centre) landing gear (bottom left) and caution panel (bottom right).

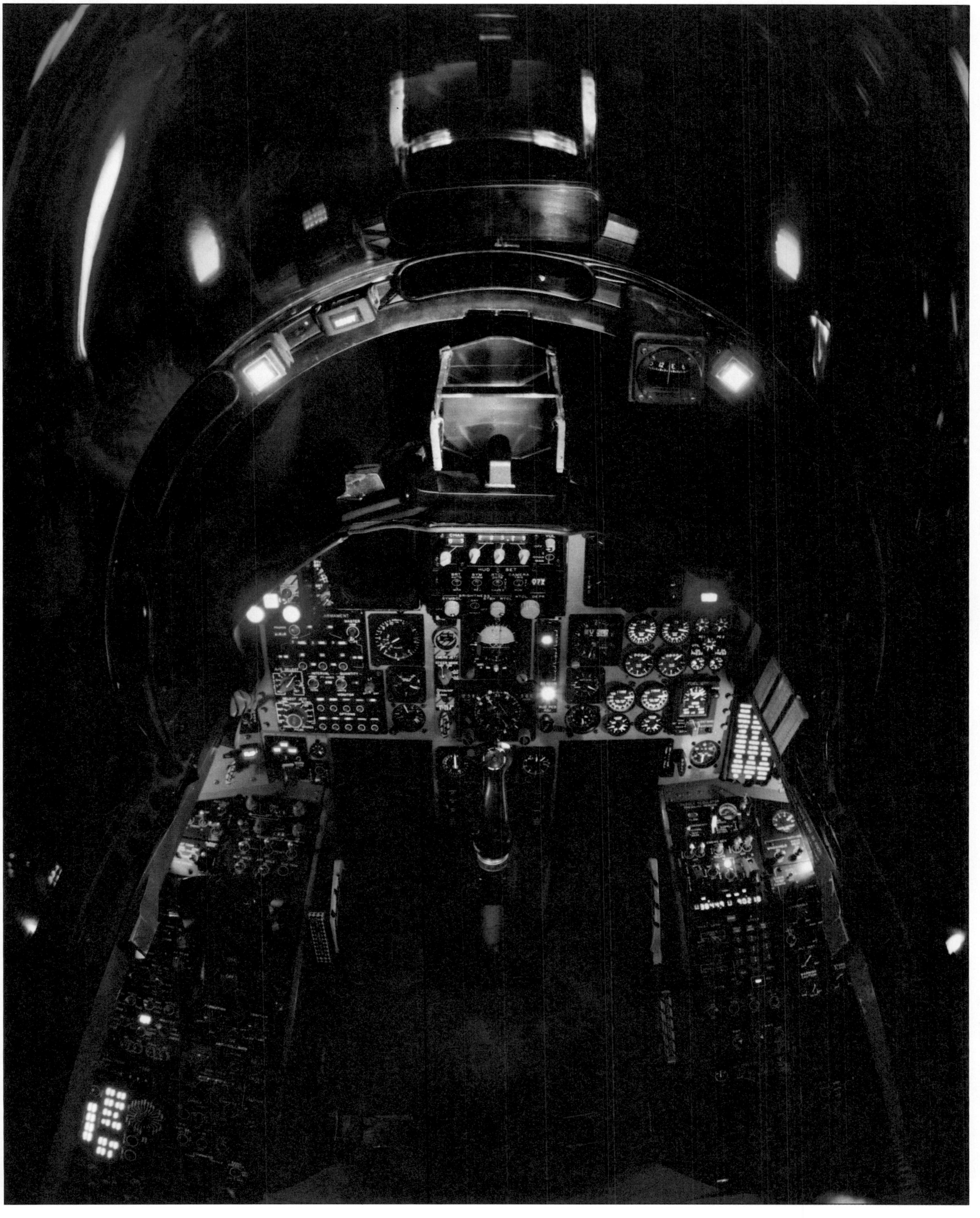

Armament

The missiles-only fighters produced for the USAF in the late 1950s and early 1960s were found to be at a severe disadvantage over Vietnam, and the Eagle weapon system was planned from the outset to include a gun. At the same time, improved versions of the medium-range, radar-guided Sparrow and short-range, heat-seeking Sidewinder were provided. New weapons planned for the Eagle include the AIM-120 AMRAAM, while the type has also proved able to deliver air-to-ground weapons with a high degree of accuracy, leading to the possibility of orders for a dual-role fighter development.

Above: F-15 in standard air superiority configuration, with four AIM-7s and four AIM-9s.

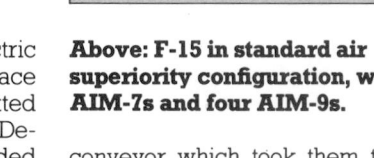

The basic requirements of the Eagle weapons system, as outlined in the Development Concept fall into three distinct categories: guns, air-to-air missiles and air-to-ground weaponry. In addition, we must also consider the use of external fuel and EW pods to enhance the basic capability of the Eagle.

During the late 1950s and early 1960s air combat with guns was thought by many to have had its day, and the latest American fighters had no guns, relying solely on air-to-air missiles. Air combat during the Vietnam War, however, revealed such an urgent need for gun armament that a new version of the F-4 Phantom, TAC's principal fighter, had to be developed with an internal 20mm gun.

From the beginning, therefore, the FX was planned with an internal gun as an integral part of its weapons system. Initial production models were to rely on the tried and true M61A1 20mm Vulcan cannon, produced by the Aircraft Equipment Division of the General Electric Company. Later models of the Eagle were to have a new 25mm cannon, using a new type of caseless ammunition, which would have the advantage of eliminating cartridge extraction and ejection systems, resulting in a simpler mechanism. General Electric and Philco-Ford (now Ford Aerospace and Communications) both submitted designs, and after evaluation in December 1971 Philco-Ford was awarded the contract for the new gun, designated the GAU-7.

Left: Armourers use a conveyor belt to load 20mm ammunition into an F-15 ammunition drum. The links are stripped during the loading process.

Although potentially a simpler weapon, the advantages mentioned above were offset by other problems, basically involving the ammunition. With caseless ammunition there is no spent cartridge to be wasted (or collected) after the round is fired, promising potentially enormous savings. However, the US Army had been trying to get caseless ammunition right for the previous 15 years with a continuing lack of success. (The world's first weapon designed with a successful caseless ammunition is the Heckler & Koch G-11 rifle, with ammunition from H&K in collaboration with Dynamit Nobel.)

The GAU-7 ammunition was being developed by the Brunswick Corporation. The propellent half of the 25mm round was covered with a flame retardant covering, which was stripped off mechanically as the rounds entered a conveyor which took them to the five barrels of the weapon. This stripping mechanism was causing the ammunition conveyor to jam. Another problem involved the development of a moisture-protective material for use with the ammunition, whose final drawback was inconsistent ballistic action. In theory the higher muzzle velocity of 4,000ft/sec (1,200m/sec), compared with the 3,200ft/sec (975m/sec) of the M61, meant that not only did the projectile reach the target sooner than an M61 round, but also that it had a flatter trajectory, producing a more concentrated hit pattern on the target and giving a higher probability of kill. Unfortunately, the whole system proved too unreliable.

By September 1973, with over $100 million spent on development, the problems with the GAU-7 had still to be overcome, and with other new-technology items on the Eagle running reasonably smoothly, the Air Force decided to

Right: Missile launch as seen from the back of a two-seat F-15. At one stage the USAF switched to an all-missile armament, but during the Vietnam war the F-4 had to be revised to accommodate a gun, since many engagements took place at ranges too short for a missile to be launched effectively.

Below: Radar-guided Sparrow for BVR engagements and short-range Sidewinders form a potent combination.

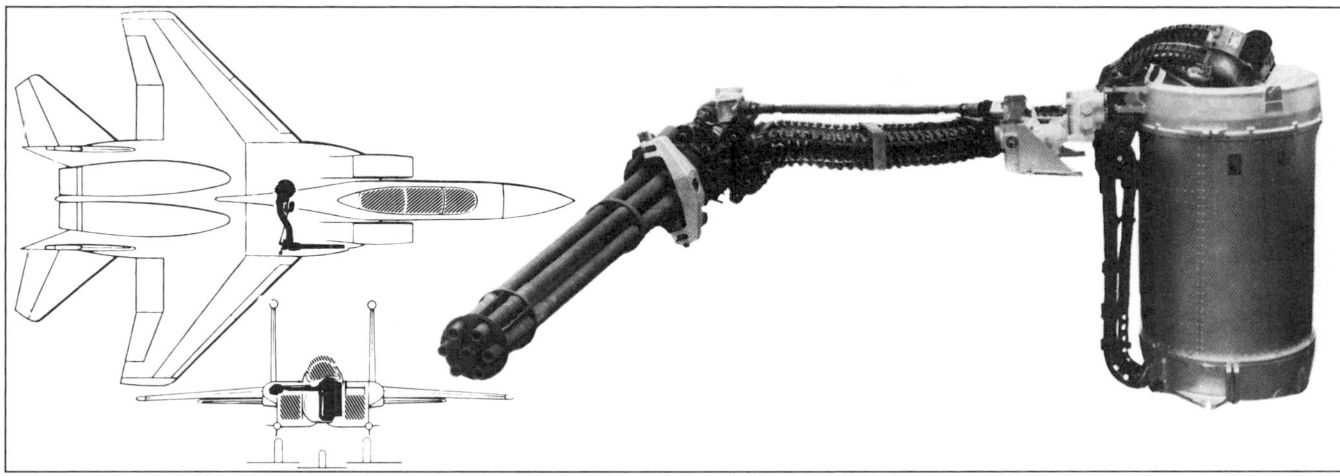

Left: The General Electric M61 Vulcan 20mm gun system, and details of its location in the F-15 airframe. The gun could not be mounted in the nose, since this would interfere with the radar, and the wing root alternative was found to be eminently satisfactory. The ammunition drum, housing 940 rounds, is mounted in the centre fuselage; a linkless feed system transports the rounds to the gun and carries the spent cartridge cases back again. This system has proved extremely reliable in operation.

cut its losses. Although Philco-Ford proposed a year's delay on the programme, it was cancelled and replaced by the M61, of 1954 vintage.

The M61A1 is an exceptionally reliable system. Its rotary action allows a rate of fire of some 6,000 rounds per minute (although only 940 rounds are carried on the Eagle). The use of six barrels minimizes erosion, thus ensuring long life for the weapon. The high rates of fire dictate a special linkless feed for the M61, and while some aircraft systems expel the used cases, others collect them. The ammunition used is in the M50 series, and includes armour piercing (with or without tracer elements) and incendiary types. The rotary action of the weapon as installed in the F-15 is provided by hydraulic/electrical power.

Locating the gun

The choice of location for the internal gun was not easy. Ideally it should have been placed as close to the fighter's cg as possible in order to reduce aiming errors when the weapon was fired, but a nose mounting was ruled out because the vibration of the weapon firing would upset the microcircuitry of the APG-63 radar. A second location, further aft on the fuselage centreline, was rejected because of possible gun-gas ingestion problems. The final solution, approached with some trepidation was to mount the gun in the starboard wing root, where there was plenty of room for the weapon and its ammunition drum and feed system. Tests later showed that the comparitively large separation of the gun from the fore-and-aft axis of the aircraft produced no aiming or recoil problems. In addition, the gun alignment could more easily be varied to give maximum tracking time on target, a facility initially demonstrated in simulation, and later proved in practice.

For the future, there is a new General Electric 25mm cannon, the GAU-12/U, under development for the AV-8B Harrier II/Harrier GR.5. Present plans do not call for its use beyond the AV-8B, but the possibility exists that it might be adapted for installation in the F-15E. Another gun option for the F-15E is the carriage of three General Electric GE 430 GEPOD-30 30mm gun pods on fuselage and underwing pylons. The GEPOD-30 is a lightweight four-barrel version of the GAU-8/A gun used in the A-10A Thunderbolt II, and fires the standard GAU-8/A ammunition. The main role of the GEPOD-30 would be

Right: The rocket motor fires as an AIM-7 Sparrow is launched from the first F-15C Eagle. The aircraft has an instrumented nose probe.

air-to-ground, but there is nothing to preclude its use in the air-to-air mode if the tactical situation allows.

Although the gun has been restored, the missile remains the Eagle's primary air-to-air weapon. The new fighter's missile armament was originally to consist of the AIM-7F Sparrow for beyond visual range (BVR) engagements, and a new short-range IR-homing missile, designated AIM-82. The latter missile was cancelled well before it reached the hardware stage, and the AIM-9L Sidewinder took over. For the future, the AIM-120 AMRAAM will replace Sparrow, with the projected European ASRAAM a possible successor to Sidewinder.

AIM-7 Sparrow

The AIM-7 Sparrow originated as Sperry Gyroscope's Project Hot Shot in 1946, and by 1955 it was in service as the beam-riding AAM-N-2 Sparrow I with the US Navy. The active-radar Sparrow II was cancelled in 1957 and the AIM-7F comes from the third generation of Sparrow, the Raytheon AAM-N-6 Sparrow III, which became the AIM-7C when the US services changed nomenclature in 1962. The AIM-7C introduced semi-active radar homing with continuous wave (CW) guidance and was in service by 1958. The AIM-7E, later versions of which armed early Eagles, featured a continuous-rod warhead, consisting of a 66lb (30kg) explosive charge enclosed in a tight drum made from a continuous rod of stainless steel. On detonation, this rod shatters into some 2,500 lethal fragments. The more manoeuvrable AIM-7E2 was developed to reduce the missile's minimum range as a result of experience in Vietnam, when the demand for visual identification of targets inhibited its use, and this version armed the initial batches of F-15 Eagles.

The AIM-7F, designated missile for the Eagle, brought the Sparrow into the solid-state electronic age. Reducing the size and weight of the guidance package, still CW, allowed a more powerful motor, the Hercules Mk 58, to be used, resulting in an increased range of 62 miles (100km), and enabling a larger 88lb (40kg) warhead to be carried. Introduced in 1977, the AIM-7F is claimed to be able to lock-on to a target against clutter up to 10dB.

The most recent version of the Sparrow is the AIM-7M, which has an inverse monopulse seeker, a digital signal processor, a new autopilot and a new fuze. It is expected to offer greatly

Above: The Sparrow accelerates towards its maximum speed of approximately Mach 4. Range of the AIM-7F is 62 miles (100km).

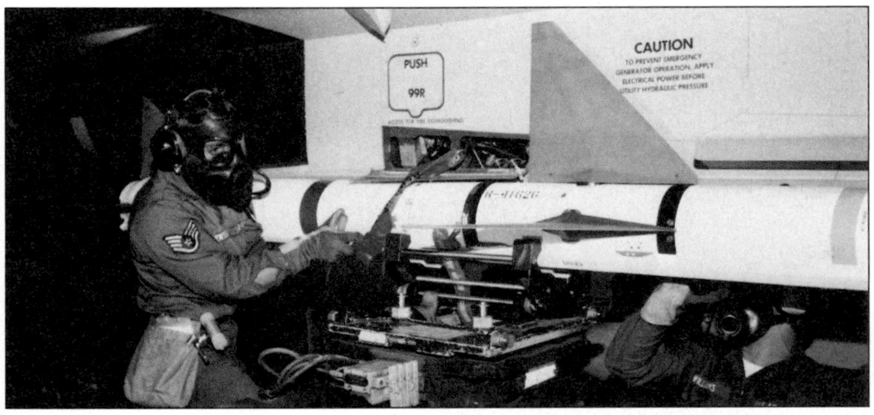

Left: Armourers in protective clothing and respirators install a Sparrow on its fuselage mounting.

Below: In its air superiority configuration, the F-15 can have its fuel, oil and liquid oxygen replenished, and Sparrows and ammunition reloaded, in a turnaround time of only 12 minutes.

improved results in adverse weather conditions, as well as in an ECCM environment, and starting with the FY 1981 budget funding, Sparrow production has been concentrated on this variant.

AIM-9 Sidewinder

The Sidewinder is the original simple, low-cost air-to-air missile, capable of being carried by practicaly any combat aircraft. Since its development in 1949 by a team of scientists at the Naval Ordnance Test Station (now the Naval Weapons Centre) at China Lake, it has been produced in seven major variants, with at least one further derivative under consideration. US production of the initial AIM-9B variant reached a total of 80,900 missiles, while a European consortium produced about 15,000. The usefulness of the missile is exemplified by the fact that during the Falklands conflict of 1982 the RAF modified their Nimrod maritime patrol and ASW aircraft to carry four Sidewinders in a matter of weeks in order to give them a measure of self-defence capability.

Sidwinder has an infra-red seeker which homes onto heat emissions from the jet efflux of the target. A variety of guidance heads, and six major forward fin configurations have been used, and many of the later versions combined older airframes with new seekers and fins. The AIM-9L, which represents the third generation of the missile, features a new double-delta forward fin configuration of larger span than previous missiles and a new seeker head. Part of the DSQ-29 guidance and control system, the new head uses AM-FM conical scan, with a fixed-reticle, tilted-mirror system, and is cooled by Argon gas. The new seeker offers greater sensitivity and improved tracking stability, while lethality is increased by the use of the DSU-15B active optical laser fuze, allied to the WDU-17B annular blast fragmentation warhead.

Once the pilot has energized the missile homing head, he listens for the 'growl' in his headset that signifies it has acquired a target. Should he be set up for a perfect shot straight up the tailpipe of a target, the growl intensifies to a strident tone, and the pilot launches the missile. In this respect Sidewinders (of whatever mark) are simple to use in air-to-air combat.

AIM-120 AMRAAM

Despite all the advances made over the years with the Sparrow AAM, it retains one basic drawback – its semi-active radar guidance system requires the target to be continuously illuminated throughout an engagement, so that the pilot can only deal with one target at a time. Consequently, the prime requirement during development of the Advanced Medium Range Air-to-Air Missile (AMRAAM) was that it should be a launch-and-leave missile, allowing several targets to be engaged simultaneously beyond visual range without monopolizing the fire-control radar and leaving the pilot blind to other threats. AMRAAM was also required to be usable in all weathers, fired from or at all aspects and with a look-down/shoot-down capability. With the proliferation of Sparrow throughout the US Air Force, Navy and Marine Corps, it had to be able to integrate with existing fighters and fire control radar, and physically fit where a Sparrow was previously located. The final requirement was considerably higher reliability than that of Sparrow.

This was a demanding specification, and in 1976 a joint USAF/US Navy project office was set up at Elgin AFB to organize the development of the new missile. By February 1979 the conceptual studies had been narrowed down to submissions from Hughes Aircraft and Raytheon, who were awarded contracts for ten prototype missiles each to be fired from F-14, F-15 and F-16 aircraft in a competitive evaluation.

After only three firings of each contender the trials were halted, with the Hughes entry a clear winner, and in December 1981 the company received a 50-month full scale development contract valued at some $421 million. The resulting missile, designated AIM-120 but still known as AMRAAM at the time of writing, is some two-thirds of the weight of the Sparrow, and similar in configuration, though the main fins are somewhat smaller. It has an estimated speed of Mach 4, and an active X-band radar terminal seeker using a high-power solid-state transmitter with a low-sidelobe, wide-gimbal antenna, and a built-in radio-frequency processor. Navigation, autopilot, radar, datalink, fuzing, sequencing and self-test functions are all handled by a single 30MKz microprocessor.

The last two of the Hughes test firings were from an F-15, following one from an F-16, and the second launch, on November 23, 1981, scored a direct hit on a QF-102 target drone The F-15 was flying at 6,000ft (1,830m) at Mach 0.75, and the missile was launched in a look-down/shoot-down mode at the QF-102 flying at 1,000ft (300m) at Mach 0.7. The missile was cued by the APG-63 radar and launched by the aircraft's stores

Top left: A fully armed F-15 stands ready for takeoff, with safety tags on missiles and airframe and cockpit canopy open.

Centre left: An armourer removes the cover from the seeker head of a Sidewinder as the aircraft is prepared for a sortie.

Left: Mock-up of the Hughes AIM-120 AMRAAM is assembled on the fuselage station of an F-15.

Below left: First captive flight test of a Hughes AMRAAM Instrumented Measurement Vehicle, used to test the new missile's aerodynamic compatibility with the F-15.

Below: During the firing trials that resulted in its selection, a prototype of the Hughes AMRAAM is launched from an F-15B.

control system. It demonstrated inertial midcourse guidance and then acquired its target against ground clutter.

The final prototype firing came late in 1982 and demonstrated the missile's ability to intercept a low-flying aircraft using self-screening ECM. It was launched from an F-15 flying at 16,000ft (4,900m) some 10.8nm from a QF-102 drone flying towards the launch aircraft at 400ft (120m). It was launched with command-inertial guidance and then switched to active radar in order to acquire and intercept the target, which passed within lethal range of the AMRAAM's warhead.

Further development firings are scheduled to take place in 1984 from the F-16 (on which the AIM-120 will enter service in 1986) followed by the F-18, F-15 and F-14. The USAF requirement for AIM-120 is upwards of 20,000 missiles, and already further improvements are planned for the missile's 25-year projected life. The AIM-120B will feature passive terminal homing, and will be introduced from 1990, while the AIM-120C will have overall improvements in range, speed and manoeuvreability, and will be available from the mid-1990s. All variants of the AIM-120 will be able to be launched from either rails or ejection units.

AMRAAM is the subject of an agreement signed between the United States and France, Germany and the UK, which will see the missile become the NATO-standard BVR weapon. In turn, the European partners will develop the Advanced Short Range Air-to-Air Missile (ASRAAM) to replace Sidewinder in both US and European service. Although agreements over ASRAAM are in existence, the missile is unlikely to be available before the late 1980s.

Air-to-ground Weapons

While primarily an air superiority fighter, the Eagle possesses a substantial air-to-ground secondary capability, as the accompanying table illustrates. Work is also under way on a dedicated air-to-ground variant, designated F-15E, which will be a two-seat strike fighter. The basic stores capability of the F-15A/C has five weapons pylons, in addition to the four Sparrow missiles, capable of carrying up to 16,000lb (7,257kg) of bombs, rockets, ECM equipment or external fuel tanks.

The Strike Eagle demonstrator, on which the F-15E will be based, can carry up to 24,000lb (10,886kg) of stores. Among the stores compatible with the Eagle in this role are the AGM-88A High-speed Anti-Radiation Missile (HARM), AGM-65 Maverick TV-guided missile, AGM-84A Harpoon anti-ship missile, Mk 20 Rockeye bombs on MER-200 multiple ejection racks, Matra Durandal runway denial weapons, 500lb (227kg) Mk 82 bombs in Slick (low-drag) and Snakeye (retarded) configuration, 2,000lb (907kg) Mk 84 bombs in Slick, Laser, Electro-optical and Infrared homing versions, ALQ-131 ECM pods and 600US gal (500Imp gal/2,280 litre) drop tanks.

1 ECM antenna
2 ALQ-119(V) jammer pod
3 600US gal (500Imp gal/2,273 litre) fuel tank
4 MER (multiple ejector rack) carrying three Mk 82 500lb (227kg) slick (low-drag) general-purpose bombs (one with a stand-off contact fuze) plus one AIM-9J and one AIM-9L Sidewinder AAMs
5 FAST (Fuel and sensor tactical) pack conformal fuel tank
6 MK 20 Rockeye cluster bomb
7 Tactical nuclear bomb
8 MK 82 Snakeye high-drag bomb
9 M61 cannon with 940 rounds of 20mm ammunition
10 GBU-10E/B (Mk 84 2,000lb) Paveway II laser-guided bomb
11 AVQ-26 Pave Tack sensor pod
12 GBU-12D/B (Mk 82 500lb) Paveway II laser-guided bomb
13 CBU-52B/B cluster bomb dispenser
14 AIM-7F/M Sparrow AAM
15 AGM-84A Harpoon anti-ship missile
16 SUU-20 practice bomb dispenser
17 MK 84 2,000lb (907kg) general-purpose bomb
18 GBU-15(V)-4-B modular guided glide bomb
19 AGM-88A Harm anti-radar missile
20 AGM-65D IIR (imaging infra-red) Maverick air-to-surface missile
21 Two AGM-65A (TV) or AGM-65C (laser) Mavericks
22 General Electric GPU-5/A gun pod housing 30mm GAU-13/A gun, ammunition and drive system
23 AIM-120 AMRAAM (advanced medium-range air-to-air missile)

The MER-200 multiple ejection bomb rack is designated BRU-26A/A, and allows the Eagle a high degree of flexibility in its weapons carriage. It is in production to equip all Eagles assigned to the US Rapid Deployment Joint Task Force, as well as for the Japanese Air Self Defense Force F-15Js. Its main advantage is that it allows supersonic carriage and release of up to six weapons, and can jettison them in any loading configuration. It is strong enough to allow the pilot to pull 7.3g during combat manoeuvres, and has been flight tested to Mach 1.4, although MCAIR, the manufacturers, claim carriage, jettison and release of stores up to Mach 2. Production of this low drag multiple ejection rack was running at 40 units per month by mid-1983.

In addition, the Eagle can enhance its range by the use of the FAST (Fuel And Sensor Tactical) packs mounted on the fuselage side, and these retain the ability to mount Sparrow or AMRAAM missiles on the lower corners, or carry some 4,400lb (1,996kg) of air-to-ground stores. Each of the FAST packs can carry 849US gal (707Imp gal/3,228 litres) of fuel. Alternatively, or in combination with fuel, they can house cameras and IR sensors for reconnaissance; low-light television (LLTV), forward looking IR (FLIR) and laser designators for the strike role; or Wild Weasel equipment for defence suppression.

FAST packs were first flown on an F-15B on July 27, 1974. MCAIR claim that carriage of the conformal tanks only slightly reduces the subsonic profile drag relative to the clean aircraft and represent only a fraction of the supersonic drag of the three standard drop tanks, which between them carry 20 per cent more fuel than the FAST packs. Installation or removal is possible in 15 minutes, despite their complex shape Pand size. With FAST packs and the three drop tanks, the F-15C has demonstrated an unrefuelled ferry range of 2,660nm (4,903km). In this configuration, the F-15C has a maximum gross weight of 68,000lb (30,840kg), while the F-15D model is only some 800lb (363kg) heavier with the same internal fuel.

Weapons configurations

In the basic air-to-air role, the F-15A/C Eagle carries four AIM-7F Sparrows, four AIM-9L Sidewinders and the internal 20mm gun. In addition, it usually carries a 600US gal drop tank on the centre-line pylon and the inner wing pylon can also carry a similar drop tank without sacrificing the Sidewinder capability.

The basic attack configuration of the non-dedicated Eagle retains the basic air-to-air configuration, possibily including the centre-line tank, and adds extra stores. Any range enhancements required can be provided by air-to-air refuelling. The prime requirement was for the attack mission not to detract from the basic air-to-air combat mission which is certainly the case.

Below: The second F-15B in early 1976, before its development into the Strike Eagle. Even at this stage MCAIR were keen to demonstrate the F-15's ground-attack capability, and 71-0291 is seen here armed with 18 500lb (227kg) Mk 82 slicks.

Left: The impressive array of stores that have been launched by the Eagle or are designed to be compatible with the aircraft's delivery system.

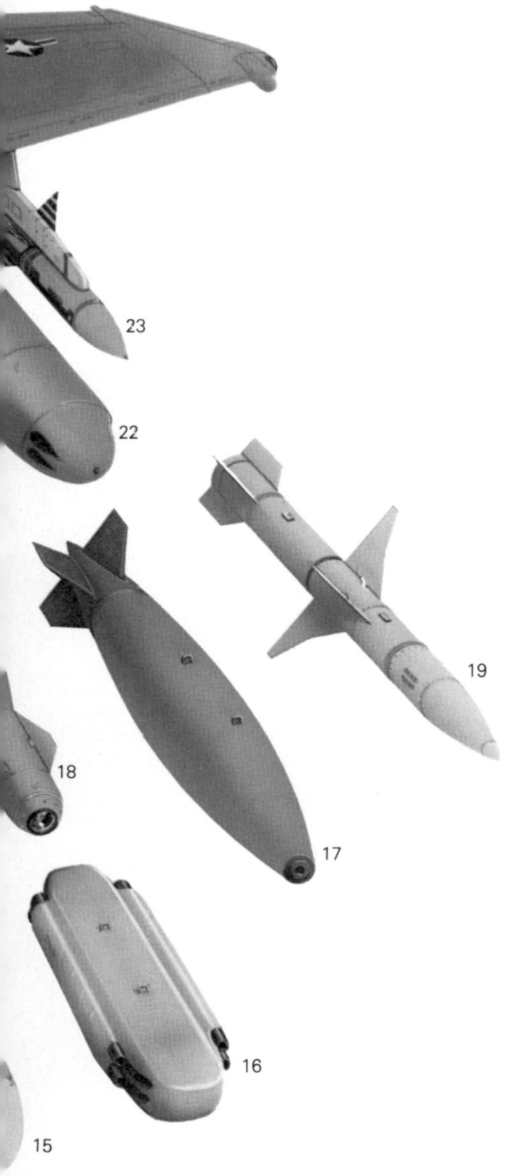

Right: Multiple stores can be carried by a standard F-15 without disrupting the normal armament of Sparrows and Sidewinders.

Deployment and Combat

Following its service introduction with the 'Triple Nickel' 555th TFTS, the Eagle achieved operational status in 1976 with the 1st Tactical Fighter Wing. Subsequently the type has been deployed with USAF units in Europe, the Far East and Alaska, as well as equipping selected units of TAC's Air Defense Command, while export customers have included Israel, Japan and Saudi Arabia. Only Israeli pilots have seen combat in the type, achieving predictably impressive results: elsewhere, the F-15 continues to be the USAF's principal front-line fighter.

The operational career of the F-15 effectively began on November 14, 1974, at Luke AFB, Arizona, when President Gerald Ford accepted TF-15A 73-0108 on behalf of Tactical Air Command (TAC). The Eagle had been flying in full USAF insignia for some time by then, but the handful of Air Force units which had used the type prior to November 1974 were essentially test organizations, unlike the 58th Tactical Fighter Training Wing (TFTW), the unit which was to operate the first TF-15A. This aircraft, incidentally, was christened 'TAC 1' during the ceremonies that marked the type's introduction to service.

The first F-15 squadron was the 555th Tactical Fighter Training Squadron (TFTS). This unit, the famed 'Triple Nickel', had racked up an impressive air combat record in Vietnam when, equipped with another MCAIR product, the F-4 Phantom. It accounted for no less than 40 MiGs. The 555th quickly set about the task of qualifying instructor pilots and formulating a training syllabus, a process which was largely completed by about the middle of 1975 when personnel earmarked to serve with the first fully operational wing were present in some considerable numbers at Luke.

Below: Ready to get airborne on an interception in less than five minutes, a fully-armed F-15A waits in its hardened shelter.

Mission-ready status

The responsibility of bringing TAC's newest piece of hardware to mission-ready status was entrusted to the 1st Tactical Fighter Wing (TFW), which shared Langley AFB, Virginia, with TAC headquarters, and the next 18 months or so proved to be a period of intense activity at this base as more and more personnel were posted in to join the team.

As with most modern combat aircraft, introduction of the Eagle did not go entirely according to plan. One of the most significant difficulties concerned delays in the output of qualified pilots by the 58th TFTW, this arising directly from the rather lower than anticipated sortie production rate (SPR). In fact, low SPR levels affected the entire project for quite some time, and although the decision in November 1975 to eliminate the air-to-ground portion of the training syllabus went some way towards alleviating the pilot shortage, the situation was compounded by the AIMVAL/ACEVAL (Air Intercept Missile Evaluation/Air Combat Evaluation) test programme of 1976-77 which called for the 58th TFTW to surrender six aircraft to the 57th Fighter Weapons Wing (FWW) at Nellis. An example of the effect that these difficulties had on the overall pace of the project is provided by the fact that the 1st TFW was still some 18 pilots short of its authorized level in May 1976, about five months after it had been fully equipped with 72 Eagles.

Above: An unarmed 36th TFW F-15A on deployment over Norway. The 36th was the first USAFE unit to be equipped with the Eagle.

A key factor in the SPR shortfall was the low rate of aircraft serviceability during the early stages of the Eagle's career mainly because of difficulties involving the F100 engine and the fire control system and its associated APG-63 radar. Engine-related problems such as compressor stalls, slow acceleration and stagnation with a corresponding loss of thrust have continued to cause concern and were certainly not helped

by the production difficulties experienced by Pratt & Whitney in the late 1970s.

As far as the avionics are concerned, the picture is somewhat brighter. Most early problems resulted from poor performance of on-base Avionics Intermediate Shop (AIS) test equipment and the consequent need to send many defective LRUs (Line Replaceable Units) back to the contractor for repair and rectification work. This, in turn, brought about a 'domino' effect as cannibalization became necessary to maintain aircraft in an 'up' condition, the situation eventually reaching a point where, when engine difficulties were taken into account, the expected degree of reliability was being missed by in excess of 50 per cent. Hardware and software fixes incorporated in the latter half of the 1970s have gone some way toward improving avionics performance but AIS test equipment is still causing more than a few headaches for maintenance personnel.

Despite these trials and tribulations, training of 1st TFW personnel forged ahead steadily, being highlighted by delivery of the first F-15A (74-0083 'Peninsula Patriot') to the 27th TFS at Langley on January 9, 1976. By the end of that year two further squadrons, the 71st and 94th TFSs, had also received their allotted number of aircraft and the 1st TFW was fully equipped if not yet fully operational.

Not surprisingly, the pilots spent most of 1976 familiarizing themselves with their new mounts and exploring the capabilities of the F-15 in the air combat role. This involved extensive training exercises against each other and against dissimilar types such as the T-38 Talon, A-4 Skyhawk, F-4 Phantom, F-5E Tiger II and F-106 Delta Dart. The opportunity to participate in Red Flag exercises at Nellis was also taken: during September and October no less than 24 aircraft deployed to Nevada for Red Flag VIII. They performed creditably, the SPR rising significantly along with pilot confidence in the aircraft and its systems.

By the end of 1976 both the 27th TFS and the 71st TFS were adjudged to be mission-ready but the emphasis was already shifting toward Europe, home of the next wing to convert. This was the 36th TFW, then operating the F-4E Phantom from Bitburg AB, West Germany. However, rather than accomplish transition at Bitburg it was decided that a new concept would be used in an attempt to curtail the 'down-time' which is usually associated with major re-equipment programmes. Accordingly, the 1st TFW was tasked with assisting the 36th TFW to attain operational readiness on the F-15 under the code name Ready Eagle.

36th TFW build-up

Maintenance personnel for the 36th TFW duly began training at Langley in September 1976 while aircrew for the first squadron – a mix of experienced F-15 pilots from Luke and Langley plus some former F-4E pilots from Bitburg – gradually accumulated at Langley. Responsibility for overseeing the Langley-based phase of flying training rested with the 94th TFS and was highlighted by the first pilot achieving mission-ready status in mid-January of 1977. On January 5, the first two Eagles had reached Bitburg for maintenance familiarization training, where they were joined by two more during March.

In the meantime, delivery of those Eagles earmarked for service with the 36th TFW was being effected to Langley and it was from here that some 20 F-15As and a trio of TF-15As left for the first mass transatlantic migration to Bitburg on April 27, these all reaching Germany safely during the afternoon of the same day. Within 12 hours of arrival the 525th TFS was in business, some of the new arrivals already standing 'Zulu'

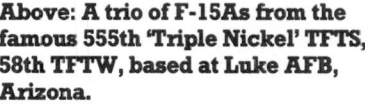

Above: A trio of F-15As from the famous 555th 'Triple Nickel' TFTS, 58th TFTW, based at Luke AFB, Arizona.

Below: A pair of F-15As from the 1st Tactical Fighter Wing, the first operational Eagle unit, based at TAC's Langley HQ.

Below: A 1st TFW F-15A banks over one of the world's most expensive flight lines at Langley AFB, Virginia, also home of the 48th FIS.

Bottom: Three F-15As and a two-seat F-15B of the 57th Fighter Weapons Wing, based at Nellis AFB, Arizona, in formation.

Above: A trio of 36th TFW F-15As during the Arctic Express exercise held in 1978 to test combat readiness in Arctic conditions.

alert duty and providing a fitting testimonial to the success of the initial phase of Ready Eagle.

Back in the USA, training of the second 36th TFW squadron, the 53rd TFS, followed similar lines. Deployment of the 53rd to Bitburg followed in July, while the third squadron – the 22nd TFS – brought the re-equipment process to a successful conclusion when it took up residence at Bitburg in October. It should be noted that transatlantic ferry flights of aircraft for these two squadrons were made over a fairly lengthy period, groups of half-a-dozen or so being deployed at a time during the summer and autumn of 1977 until the planned level of about 80, including several spares, was achieved.

Holloman AFB in New Mexico was the next base to welcome the Eagle, re-equipment of the resident 49th TFW's three squadrons being accomplished during 1977-78. Another new procedure, code-named Ready Team, was employed on this occasion, the intention being to permit some existing fighters – in this case F-4D Phantoms – to remain combat-ready during the initial phases of conversion. The process of transition got under way in June 1977 when the first pilots for the 7th TFS reported to Luke for training with the 58th Tactical Training Wing (TTW) as it had become known during 1977. The 58th TTW had itself been expanded in June 1976 when the 461st TFTS was organized as the second F-15 training squadron, and it grew still further while the 49th TFW was undergoing conversion, gaining the 550th TFTS in September 1977. Initial qualification of the 7th TFS was managed by the 461st and 555th TFTSs, and was followed by a brief assignment to the 550th TFTS for mission-ready checkout, culminating in reassignment to Holloman where F-15s began to arrive in October 1977. Re-equipment of the 8th TFS was accomplished with effect from January 1978 while the 9th

Right: One of the 36th TFW's Bitburg-based F-15As parked outside its hardened aircraft shelter for routine maintenance.

USAF F-15 operating units

Formation	Base	Squadrons	Remarks
1st TFW, TAC	Langley AFB, Virginia	27th TFS 71st TFS 94th TFS	F-15A/B from Jan 76 Re-equipped with F-15C/D from Dec 81
18th TFW, PACAF	Kadena AB, Okinawa	12th TFS 44th TFS 67th TFS	Equipped with F-15C/D 1979–80
1st TFW	Elmendorf AFB, Alaska	43rd TFS	First F-15As received Mar 82
33rd TFW, TAC	Eglin AFB, Florida	58th TFS 59th TFS 60th TFS	To receive F-15C/D during 1984
36th TFW, USAFE	Bitburg AB, W Germany	22nd TFS 53rd TFS 525th TFS	F-15A/B from Dec 76; re-quipped with F-15C/D from Aug 80
49th TFW, TAC	Holloman AFB, New Mexico	7th TFS 8th TFS 9th TFS	Received first F-15A/Bs Oct 77; completely equipped by Apr 78
405th TFW, TAC	Luke AFB, Arizona	426th TFTS 461st TFTS 550th TFTS 555th TFTS	555th was first USAF F-15 squadron, Nov 74
FWW	Nellis AFB, Nevada	422nd TES F-15 FWS	Former 57th FWW/433rd FWS; equipped 76/77
USAFE 17th AF	Soesterberg AB, Netherlands	32nd TFS	F-15A/B late 78; F-15C/D summer 80
ADTAC	Langley AFB, Virginia	48th FIS	Equipped from Aug 81; Det 1 at Tyndall AFB, Florida
ADTAC	McChord AFB, Washington	318th FIS	First F-15 received Jun 83

TFS took delivery of its first F-15s during April, the conversion process being successfully concluded during July, by which time Ready Eagle 2 was well under way.

This code name referred to the re-equipment of just one squadron, namely the 32nd TFS at Soesterberg in the Netherlands, and training of air and ground crews began during May 1978. However, since the number of aircraft involved was small, it became necessary for the 1st TFW to cover alert commitments once the F-4E Phantoms previously assigned to the 32nd TFS had departed. Accordingly, exercise Coronet Sandpiper brought the deployment of 18 F-15As on September 13, 1978. These remained in the Netherlands for approximately three months, being manned by 71st TFS pilots for the first 45 days and by members of the 94th TFS for the rest of the deployment. The 1st TFW aircraft were accompanied by the first two F-15As for the 32nd TFS for maintenance training, while the bulk of the F-15s destined for service at Soesterberg followed during November and December 1978, enabling those aircraft involved in Coronet Sandpiper to return home to Langley. By mid-January of 1979 the 32nd TFS was fully equipped and operational with 18 F-15As and a brace of F-15B two-seaters.

Tactical Air Command's fourth F-15 wing was the 33rd TFW which again followed the Ready Team procedure. Stationed at Eglin AFB, Florida, the 33rd was equipped during the first six months of 1979 with sufficient aircraft for just two squadrons, the 58th and 59th TFSs. Shortly afterwards, however, a third squadron, the 60th TFS, was organized to provide training support for the 18th TFW. This was active at Eglin between July 1979 and April 1980 when, with transition of the PACAF (Pacific Air Forces) unit successfully concluded, it deactivated, only to reappear during 1981 with F-15As and F-15Bs made available by the re-equipment of other units.

Flown for the first time in late February 1979, the F-15C was quickly introduced to operational service, with most of the initial production batch joining the 18th TFW at Kadena AB, Okinawa.

Right: An F-15A of the 49th TFW, from Holloman AFB, New Mexico, demonstrates its ability to climb vertically.

Below: Another of Holloman's F-15As. The 49th TFW's three squadrons – the 7th, 8th and 9th TFS – were equipped with Eagles during 1977–78.

Above: 49th TFW F-15As rendezvous with the first KC-10A Extender tanker/transport to be delivered.

PACAF's first, and so far only, F-15 wing entered the transition phase during 1979 and, as already noted, the 60th TFS at Eglin was closely involved in Ready Eagle 3. Highlighted by the successful transpacific deployment of 16 F-15Cs and F-15Ds of the 67th TFS in late September 1979, re-equipment of the 18th TFW was completed in April 1980, other squadrons attached to this wing being the 12th and 44th TFSs.

The conversion of the 18th TFW can essentially be considered as marking the conclusion of the initial phase of Eagle deployment, all subsequent new-production F-15C and D models being used to modernize some of those units which had earlier received F-15As and Bs. Inevitably, this resulted in the appearance of yet another generic codename – Ready Switch – and began with the 32nd TFS at Soesterberg which disposed of its F-15As and Bs during May and June 1980, replacing them with an identical number of new-build Cs and Ds between May and August of the same year. Attention then shifted to Bitburg's three squadrons which were progressively re-equipped between August 1980 and December 1981, TAC's 1st TFW at Langley was the most recent wing to convert, in a transition programme which began in December 1981 and which was scheduled for completion in mid-1983.

Left: An F-15A of the 33rd TFW, based at Eglin AFB, Florida, sports the unit's distinctive Eagle crest on the inside of its vertical stabilizer.

Below: A 59th TFS, 33rd TFW, F-15A with non-standard serial number marking in formation with Canadian Armed Forces CF-104.

In addition, some F-15Cs and F-15Ds have also been delivered to the 405th Tactical Training Wing, a unit which appeared in August 1979 when it was decided to reorganize training elements at Luke into two separate wings. Consequently, the three F-15 squadrons previously assigned to the 58th TTW split away to form the 405th TTW, leaving the former wing to concentrate mainly on F-4 Phantom crew training. Looking to the future, Eglin's 33rd TFW is due to receive the newer models of the Eagle during 1984.

The substantial numbers of older F-15As and F-15Bs being released by this re-equipment programme have in turn permitted conversion or activation of several other units, one such being the 60th TFS which was organized at Eglin during 1981 and which brought the 33rd TFW up to full strength with three squadrons. Additional training capacity was also made available following the transfer of the 426th TFTS from the 58th TTW to the 405th TTW at Luke and its re-equipment with the F-15.

Perhaps more significant, however, was the opportunity to update those units dedicated solely to the air defence of the continental United States. This process got under way on August 10, 1981, when the 48th Fighter Interceptor Squadron (FIS) at Langley AFB received its first F-15A for maintenance familiarization training. Previously equipped with the F-106 Delta Dart – a fine interceptor but now fast approaching veteran status – the 48th FIS had taken delivery of half of its planned complement of 20 aircraft by January 1982 and duly attained operational status later in that year. The 48th subse-

Above left: A pair of 18th TFW F-15Cs over the Pacific. The 18th is PACAF's only Eagle unit.

Above: An F-15C of the Soesterberg-based 32nd TFS, which transferred to the newer model in mid-1980.

quently joined four other F-15 units taking part in the William Tell air defence weapons meet at Tyndall AFB, Florida, in October. Despite this being the Eagle's first participation in the event, the type generally performed well, with Kadena's 18th TFW fighting off the challenge posed by F-4, F-101 and F-106 interceptor squadrons to win the overall competition.

ADTAC's (Air Defense Tactical Air Command) four remaining F-106 squadrons – the 5th, 49th, 87th and 318th FISs at Minot, Griffiss, Sawyer and McChord AFBs respectively – were all expected to convert to the F-15 in the next two or three years, and the 318th received its first Eagle on June 10, 1983. The type was also scheduled to equip ADTAC's Air Defense Weapons Center at Tyndall.

One other unit also benefited from the availability of early model Eagles this being the Elmendorf-based 43rd TFS which took delivery of its first examples on March 1, 1982 and which is now fully equipped with 27 F-15As and F-15Bs. Tasked with the air defence of Alaska and the approaches to the northern United States, the 43rd TFS forms part of the 21st TFW. As well as conducting operations from Elmendorf also maintains alert detachments at Eielson AFB, Galena Air Force Station and King Salmon Airport.

No survey of USAF Eagle operations would be complete without some mention of the 57th Fighter Weapons Wing at Nellis, which played a major part in bringing the F-15 to full operational status. More recently known as the 57th TTW, this unit is principally concerned with test and evaluation of weapons systems and the formulation of the best tactics for their use. Accordingly, it features examples of most of the major tactical aircraft types in the USAF inventory. The 57th took delivery of its first F-15s during 1976, these joining the 433rd Fighter Weapons Squadron (FWS), initially for the AIMVAL/ACEVAL project and in later years for the refinement of tactics. A further influx of F-15s in 1977 permitted some to be assigned to the 422nd FWS for follow-on operational test and evaluation work but the Nellis-based unit has recently undergone a major reorganization which has seen the disappearance of these two squadrons and their replacement by the F-15 Division of the Fighter Weapons School and the 422nd Tactical Evaluation Squadron (TES) respectively. Despite these changes in nomenclature the work performed at Nellis remains essentially the same.

Following the Eagle's introduction to operational service in November 1974, the next three years or so were essentially a period of consolidation. It was not until early in 1978 that the F-15 really began to flex its wings, when, in Operation Condor, eight aircraft from the 1st TFW flew to Osan AB, Korea. This was the first overseas deployment by a US-based F-15 wing and one which involved local exercises with PACAF and RoKAF (Republic of Korea Air Force) elements.

Right: The three squadrons of the 36th TFW traded in their F-15As and Bs for C (shown) and D models starting in August 1980.

Below: Two F-15As of ADTAC's Langley-based 48th FIS retract their landing gear following a formation takeoff in October 1982.

As already noted, Coronet Sandpiper brought 18 of the 1st TFW's F-15s to Soesterberg in the last three months of 1978 to cover the 32nd TFS's 'Zulu' alert commitment while that unit converted to the Eagle, and the new year celebrations were barely over before the 1st TFW took to the road again. A detachment of 12 aircraft headed for Saudi Arabia on January 13 and spent ten days overseas during which time operations were conducted from several Saudi air bases including Khamis Mushayt, now one of three RSAF (Royal Saudi Air Force) F-15 operating locations. In addition to overseas visits, the 1st TFW was a regular participant in Red Flag manoeuvres at Nellis and also headed north to Canada to participate in Maple Flag during April and May 1980. The latter is a similar exercise although it is predicated more upon a European environment, a scenario which is greatly helped by the striking resemblance of the local terrain to that of Europe.

Further deployments in 1980 saw 12 aircraft from Kadena's 18th TFW visit Kwang-Ju AB in Korea during March for Team Spirit '80, a simulated combat exercise against RoKAF and other USAF elements. Team Spirit now appears to be an annual endeavour for the 18th TFW, as many as 24 aircraft taking part in 1981 and 1982. Also in 1980, the 33rd TFW took some of its Eagles overseas for the first time when 18 flew to Bremgarten in West Germany. Codenamed Coronet Barrel and running from October 3 to November 5, this exercise, like others of the Coronet series, was intended to provide aircrew with experience of the area in which they may at some future date be required to fly and fight.

Multiple deployments

For the 49th TFW, 1981 was a particularly memorable year. The months of August and September were dominated by no less than three Coronet deployments – to Jever and Lahr in West Germany and to Aalborg in Denmark – each of which involved 12 F-15s. Meanwhile, the 1st TFW returned to Europe in May 1982 after an absence of more than three years when, in a split exercise, they conducted two back-to-back visits to the Netherlands. The first of these, Coronet Sidewinder I, brought F-15s to Gilze-Rijen between May 17 and June 4, and was followed on June 7 by Coronet Sidewinder II, in which 12 more aircraft visited Soesterberg for a stay lasting 16 days.

Later in the same year, as part of the regular autumn NATO exercises, virtually half of the 33rd TFW flew to West Germany under the Crested Cap dual-based commitment; they stayed for almost a month, with 24 Eagles going to Bremgarten and a further 12 to Sollingen. However, perhaps the most remarkable demonstration of mobility during 1982 was the deployment of six F-15Cs of the 18th TFW from Kadena to Florida at the beginning of October. The record-breaking 7,000 mile (9,620km) ferry flight accomplished non-stop in 15

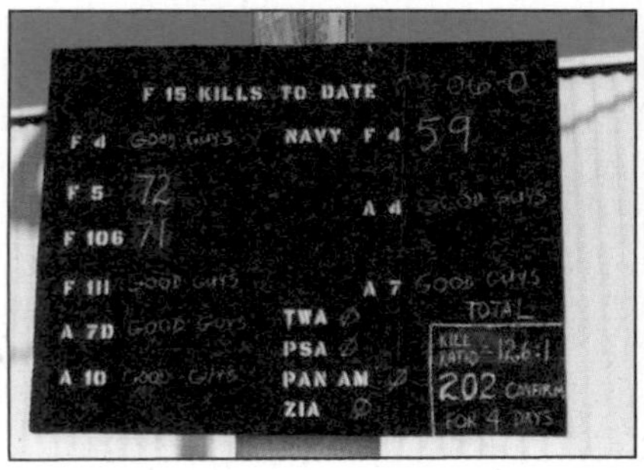

Above: The scoreboard for a Red Flag exercise held at Nellis AFB, Nevada, in May and June, 1980.

Opposite, top: AIM-7 Sparrow missiles are brought out to arm a 36th TFW F-15C during the William Tell 82 weapons meet.

Left: Demonstration of rescue methods for Japanese ground crew during a deployment to Nyutabaru AB as part of Exercise Cope North 81-3.

Below: An F-15C of the 18th TFW is the centre of attention after flying from Okinawa to Florida for the William Tell 82 meet.

Right, top to bottom: The 38th TFW's F-15Cs followed their non-stop 7,000-mile (9,620km) flight by taking first place in the William Tell meet at Tyndall AFB. This sequence shows one of the unit's six Eagles, armed with Sidewinders but no Sparrows, scrambling to an interception.

hours, with aerial refuelling and other support was furnished largely by just one KC-10A Extender from the Douglas side of the McDonnell Douglas Corporation. Each of the six Eagles was refuelled no less than ten times during this epic flight, the accompanying KC-10A itself receiving fuel three times from another Extender and some KC-135A Stratotankers. Arriving at Eglin in good shape, five of the six F-15Cs subsequently made the short hop to Tyndall where they participated in the William Tell 82 weapons meet, providing further proof of the type's capability by emerging as the overall winners of this air defence competition.

Eagle exports

By mid-1983 the only export customers for the Eagle were Israel, Japan and Saudi Arabia. Israel was the first to receive Eagles when it accepted a batch of three aircraft on December 10, 1976, these plus one other of the initial order for 25 aircraft (23 F-15As and two F-15Bs), being reconditioned USAF evaluation machines. More recently, a further 15 Eagles, almost certainly F-15Cs were delivered to the Israeli Defence Force – Air Force (IDFAF) and another 11 are known to be on order although these are currently embargoed as a result of Israel's adventures in Lebanon.

As far as operating units and bases are concerned, Israel has maintained its usual near-impenetrable degree of secrecy although numerous reports indicate that No 133 Squadron was the first IDFAF squadron to equip with the F-15.

Almost inevitably, Israel became the first to utilize the Eagle in combat. Although, again, relatively little first-hand information has been forthcoming, it is known that the F-15 has performed most satisfactorily. It was first committed to action in late June 1979 against a sizeable force of Syrian MiG-21s, six of which were apparently destroyed by six F-15s and two Kfirs. All types of primary ordnance – AIM-7 Sparrow, AIM-9 Sidewinder and M61 Vulcan 20mm gun – were used in achieving these successes. Further kills followed in September, when four MiG-21s were destroyed in an abortive Syrian attempt to down an IDFAF RF-4E Phantom engaged on reconnaissance duties. More recently, at least one Syrian MiG-23 has fallen to Israeli Eagles over Lebanon, and it is interesting to note that IDFAF pilots do not seem unduly concerned about degraded-system operation. Combat is usualy conducted at close quarters with infra-red homing missiles and, of course, the 20mm cannon, underlining the continuing requirement for the classic dogfighting type of aircraft.

Japan selected the Eagle to be its fourth-generation interceptor during December 1976, after a lengthy evaluation which initially considered no less than 13 potential candidates. The seven still in contention by 1975 comprised the Viggen, Tornado, Mirage F1, F-14 Tomcat, F-15 Eagle, F-16 Fighting Falcon and F/A-18 Hornet. These were reduced to just three – the F-14, F-15 and F-16 – in January 1976, and further detailed studies during the summer of that year finally resulted in the decision that a derivative of the Eagle known as the F-15J was best suited to Japan's peculiar defence requirements.

Initial plans anticipated the acquisition of 123 Eagles for service with five squadrons, but this figure was later cut to exactly 100, comprising 88 F-15J single-seaters and 12 F-15DJ two-seaters. Two of the F-15Js and all of the F-15DJs were to be manufactured by the parent company in St. Louis, Missouri. The remaining 86 F-15Js will be built by Mitsubishi Heavy Industries at Komaki, the first eight from knocked-down assemblies provided by MCAIR.

Japanese service

With the type still in the early stages of its operational career with the JASDF (Japan Air Self-Defense Force), plans current in June 1983 anticipated an ultimate total of four squadrons operating Eagles by 1986. Flying for the first time on June 4, 1980, the first F-15J was formally handed over to JASDF representatives at St Louis on July 15. It then went to Luke AFB where, in company with F-15J number two, it spent several months on weapons firing trials and other tasks, and it was not until March 1981 that these two aircraft became the first JASDF Eagles to fly in Japan. Both joined the Air Proving Wing at Gifu AB for further evaluation and test work, and they were later joined at Gifu by some Mitsubishi-built examples and a few of the two-seat F-15DJs.

Above: Israel was the first export customer for the Eagle, receiving its first three in December 1976. Here four IDF-AF F-15s fly over the historic Masada fortress.

The first Komaki-assembled F-15J made its maiden flight on August 19, 1981 and was eventually delivered to the JASDF during December, in time for the formation of the F-15 Temporal Squadron at Nyutabaru AB on January 1, 1982. This unit was equipped with a handful of F-15Js and F-15DJs and tasked with initial conversion training duties. Formal training of JASDF pilots actually began several months earlier at Luke AFB, Arizona, under the aegis of the 555th TFTS, which temporarily operated at least four of the F-15DJs in full USAF insignia. The F-15 Temporal Squadron lasted only three months before metamorphosing into No 202 Squadron at the same base on April 1, 1982 and operating subsequently as part of No 5 Air Wing.

By the end of 1982 production at Mitsubishi's Komaki Factory was beginning to pick up, some 13 F-15Js having been completed and flown with most of these going to No 202 Squadron. The next phase of service introduction was scheduled to begin in 1983. No 203 Squadron at Chitose AB near Sapporo was the second JASDF unit to receive Eagles, followed in 1984 by No 204 Squadron at Nyutabaru. Chitose is also expected to be the home of a fourth squadron in Fiscal Year 1985 (April 1985–March 1986), and it seems likely that procurement of up to 50 additional aircraft will eventually permit the formation of at least two more squadrons in the late 1980s.

Above: A Royal Saudi Air Force F-15C armed with Sidewinders flies in formation with one of the Lightning interceptors it has now replaced with No 13 Fighter Squadron.

The third customer for the Eagle is Saudi Arabia which has contracted for a total of 62 aircraft comprising 47 F-15Cs and 15 F-15Ds. Because one of the stipulations of the 'Camp David' agreement lays down that no more than 60 Eagles may be present in Saudi Arabia at any give time, two of the single-seat F-15Cs are to be held in the United States as attrition replacements.

Deliveries to the Royal Saudi Air Force (RSAF) actually began during January 1981 although, again, a small number of aircraft initially went to Luke AFB for pilot training under the 555th TFTS and like the Japanese examples these were operated in full USAF insignia while at Luke. RSAF Eagles began to reach Saudi Arabia during 1982, and by the end of that year a total of 47 had been delivered, with the balance due to be handed over by the summer of 1983. Details of actual service use are scarce but it is thought that No 13 Squadron, previously equipped with the Lightning, is the first F-15 unit, and that three air bases – at Dhahran, Khamis Mushayt and Taif – will support F-15 operations. It therefore seems reasonable to assume that each will host one squadron of about 20 aircraft. Their primary task is air defence.

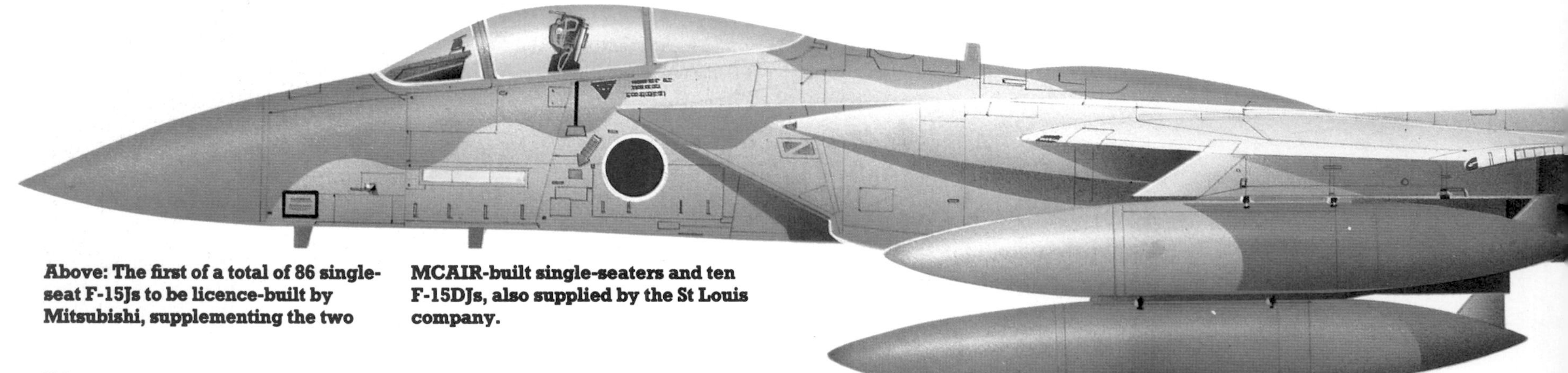

Above: The first of a total of 86 single-seat F-15Js to be licence-built by Mitsubishi, supplementing the two MCAIR-built single-seaters and ten F-15DJs, also supplied by the St Louis company.

Above: One of the 15 F-15Ds which Saudi Arabia has bought along with 47 single-seaters.

Above: Israeli deployment is shrouded in secrecy, but it is known that the country's initial order for 25 F-15A and B Eagles went to equip No 133 Squadron of the IDF-AF.

Below: One of the two MCAIR-built F-15J Eagles arrives at Gifu air base in Japan after a ferry flight from St Louis.

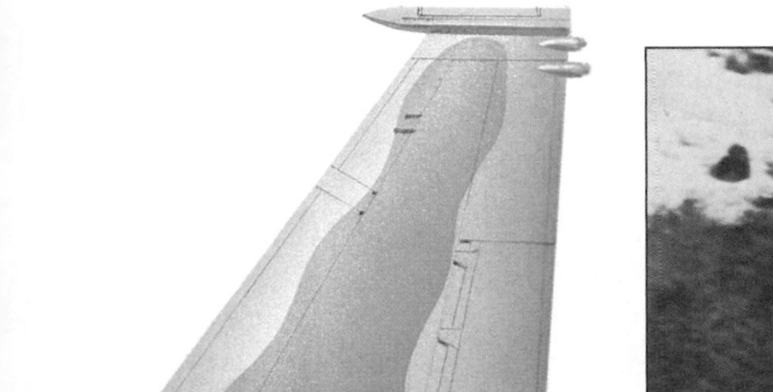

Performance and Handling

One of the fundamental aims of the FX programme was to produce a fighter capable of out-performing any actual or potential Warsaw Pact opponent, though there was considerable debate over the precise details of how this was to be defined. With its unprecedentedly high thrust-to-weight ratio and low wing loading for maximum manoeuvrability, the Eagle has demonstrated the required level of performance, and its handling qualities at speeds ranging from 100 knots to Mach 2.5 have won unqualified praise from pilots as well as providing a thrilling spectacle for air show audiences.

The performance requirements embodied in the FX Request for Proposals were intended to equip the resulting fighter to better all existing and projected Warsaw Pact opponents. As of the late 1960s these were represented by the small, agile MiG-21 and the rather bigger but highly manoeuvrable MiG-23, expected to be encountered at all altitudes; the fast, high-altitude MiG-25; and the Su-15 interceptor, for which the look-down radar capability was likely to be needed.

At the same time, some compromises had to be accepted, so that the USAF's original requirement for a maximum speed of Mach 2.7 at high altitudes, for example, was reduced to Mach 2.3, with a Mach 2.5 minimum burst capability. The higher speed would not only have prevented the use of a bubble canopy, added up to 3,000lb (1,360kg) to gross weight and reduced dash radius, it would also use up fuel at a rate of 65,000lb/hr (29,480kg/hr), equivalent to consuming the entire internal fuel load of an F-15A in about 11 minutes. The fuel flow at Mach 2.3 was estimated at a significantly lower 45,000lb/hr (20,400kg/hr). It was also argued that higher speeds were in any case irrelevant to most missions.

Other performance figures specified included a top speed of Mach 1.2 at sea level, which it was felt would provide a useful margin of superiority over potential opponents. The wing was to be optimized for buffet-free performance at Mach 0.9 and 30,000ft (9,100m). More generally, performance was to be a consequence of high thrust-to-weight ratio and low wing loading, which had been recognized as the fundamental elements in providing the desired degree of superiority in performance and agility.

Wing loading

In its production form, at a takeoff weight of 41,500lb (18,820kg) with full internal fuel, the F-15A's 608sq ft (56.5sq m) of wing area gives a loading figure of just over 68lb/sq ft (333kg/sq m), and with half internal fuel this figure falls to 57lb/sq ft (279kg/sq m). Similarly, thrust-to-weight ratio at takeoff, with the F100s in full afterburner and full internal fuel, is 1.15:1, and by the time half the fuel has been used the ratio increases to nearly 1.4:1. By comparison, wing loading of the F-4E at combat weight is 80lb/sq ft (390kg/sq m), with a thrust-to-weight ratio of approximately 0.85:1.

When translated into actual flying qualities these figures have important consequences. The four forces acting on an aircraft in flight are thrust, drag, weight and lift, and all are inter-related. Lift and drag increase as airspeed rises; both lift and drag are increased by increasing the angle of attack, and increasing the angle of bank in a turn also increases drag. Lift is considered as acting perpendicularly to the surface of a wing, and in a steep turn it has to counteract both the weight of the aircraft and the centrifugal force acting on it. Lift can be increased by increasing the angle of attack, but this also results in more drag, which in turn demands more power if the turn is to be sustained.

It is in this context that the theories of former fighter instructor Major John Boyd assume such importance. By the time Boyd was assigned to the FX programme in October 1966 he had already developed his theory of energy manoeuvrability in conjunction with Tom Christie, a mathematician working at Eglin AFB. By subtracting drag from thrust and multiplying the residue by velocity, Boyd realized, it was possible to express the 'energy rate': when drag exceeds thrust the energy rate becomes negative, so that either more thrust must be made available or the aircraft will lose altitude, airspeed or both. This in turn gives rise to the concept of specific excess power (Ps), or the amount of 'spare' thrust available in a turn, and explains the importance of the F-15's unprecedentedly high thrust-to-weight ratio.

Wing loading also has an important effect on turning performance. As an aircraft banks, the amount of life needed to counteract the combination of gravity and centrifugal force increases as the bank angle increases; and since the

Above: The F-15's thrust-to-weight ratio is such that it can accelerate in a vertical climb to supersonic speeds – the first fighter to do so.

Below: A 32nd TFS F-15A leaves the Camp New Amsterdam runway at a speed of 135kt after a takeoff run of only 900ft (274m).

radius of turn at a given airspeed depends on the bank angle, it follows that the turn radius of which an aircraft is capable is dependent on the extent to which it can continue to develop lift with increasing bank angles. The high available thrust enables the Eagle to maintain or increase speeds in high banked turns, thus enabling it to fly turns at high rates. Thus the F-15's low wing loading and high thrust-to-weight ratio combine to make it exceptionally manoeuvrable. Compared with the F-4, the F-15 can take off in a shorter distance, accelerate faster to a higher maximum speed, turn with a reduced radius and at a higher rate and fly higher; alternatively, it can climb at a lower airspeed.

To allow pilots to make maximum use of the Eagle's power and agility a dual flight control system was developed. The conventional hydromechanical system operates through push rod linkages acting on the valves of hydraulic actuators which deflect the control surfaces. The pitch-roll control assembly is a mechanical system which modifies the response of the system and the aileron-rudder interconnect couples the rudders and stabilators so that the former are operated automatically in conjunction with the stabilators, allowing manoeuvres to be carried out using the stick alone.

Meanwhile, the automatic control augmentation system (CAS) forms a separate fly-by-wire system using electrical signal signals and servo motors to operate the hydraulic actuators. The CAS system includes pitch and yaw rate, angle of attack and dynamic pressure sensors, as well as accelerometers to monitor vertical and lateral acceleration. It is thus able to compute the correct settings for the control surfaces at any combination of speed and g forces.

The CAS also senses the stick forces applied by the pilot, translating them into electrical signals to the control surface actuators: should the mechanical system fail the CAS would continue to operate the control surfaces. For

Above: A 36th TFW F-15A in formation with an F-5E in the blue-grey camouflage of an Aggressor squadron. The Aggressors simulate MiG-21s for combat training.

Below: Even with a full load of three external tanks, the F-15 is capable of impressive takeoff performance and rapid climb.

Above: Three 405th TTW F-15As in a steep climb over the Arizona desert with engines in full afterburner delivering 11 tons of thrust each.

Right: Performance envelope of the Strike Eagle ground-attack version of the F-15 remains impressive even with external stores.

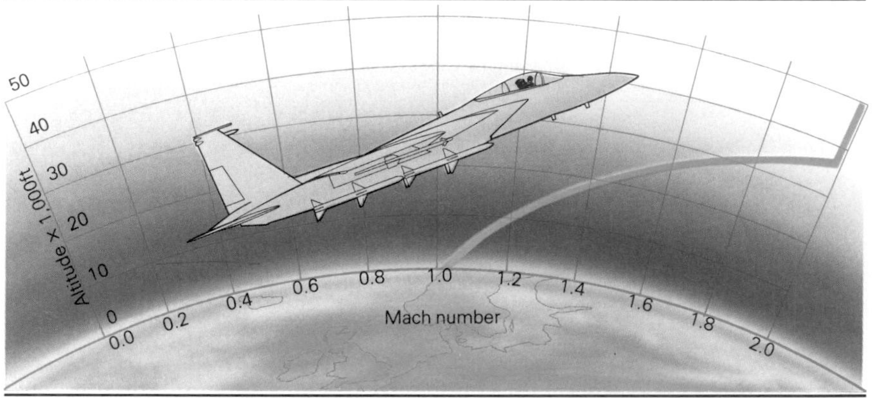

safety, the CAS is a dual-channel system in which the signals carried by each channel are continuously compared with each other, and if an error greater than a predetermined maximum is detected both are automatically disengaged. The Eagle can be manoeuvred with the CAS off using the mechanical system alone: in this mode, control is reportedly equal to that of earlier fighters, with the CAS providing a marked improvement in handling and effectively intervening to point the aircraft in whatever direction the stick is moved.

The control surfaces themselves are straightforward. The all-moving stabilators act in unison for pitch control and differentially for roll control in conjunction with the ailerons. Being mounted outside the engines, the stabilators could be positioned out of the wing wake without interference from the jet efflux, and at high angles of attack, when the ailerons become progressively less effective, the tail surfaces generate all required roll moments. The twin vertical stabilizers are tall enough to maintain stability at high angles of attack, and the twin booms on which the tail surfaces are mounted are braced to each other via the titanium engine bay assembly to provide a rigid structure for transferring the torsional loads from the tail to the aircraft.

Modifications to the aerodynamic configuration and control system as a result of flight testing are described in detail in the first chapter. Structural alterations included the clipping of the wingtips to reduce buffeting at high subsonic speeds and high g at around 30,000ft (9,100m); the increased chord on the outer sections of the stabilators to eliminate flutter, producing the notched leading edges of these surfaces; and the doubling in size of the speedbrake.

At the same time, several changes were made to the flight control system, such as the reduction in stick control forces during high-g manoeuvring to make CAS-off control easier. The CAS itself was modified to be less responsive to small, sharp stick deflections, since its original bias towards rapid rolling made the aircraft's response alarmingly jerky during more precise manoeuvres such as formation flying, air-to-air refuelling and target tracking with the gun. Similarly, the aileron-rudder interconnect system was made to disconnect on touch-down to eliminate the accentu-

Right: The F-15 has demonstrated an ability to turn well inside an F-4E, or climb 7,100ft (2,164m) while matching the Phantom's tightest level turn.

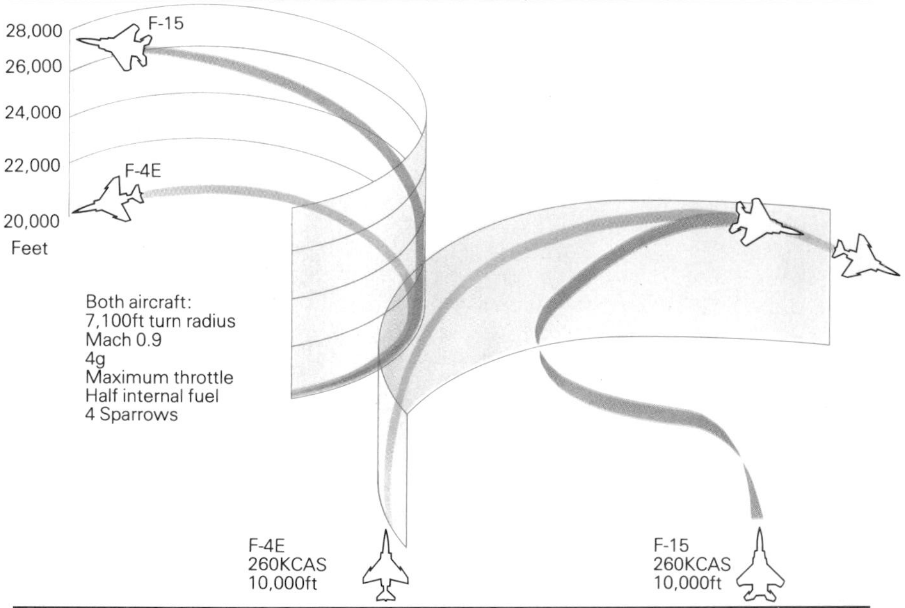

Above: Superb performance is matched by a magnificent view from the cockpit: a 49th TFW F-15A is in the background.

ation of weathervaning during cross-wind landings.

While all these problems were being identified and corrected during the flight test programme, the new fighter was demonstrated to a number of journalists during 1974. Clark Martin, of the US journal *Aviation Week and Space Technology*, flew in an F-15B when the aircraft was still subject to a limit of +5.9g: the left afterburner failed to ignite until after liftoff, but the takeoff was still impressive, a 3,300ft (1,000m) ground roll taking 18 seconds to a liftoff speed of 175kt. This compares with a ground roll of only 900ft (274m) for a production single-seater in standard interceptor configuration, when the nose-wheel is rotated at around 100kt and liftoff takes place at 135kt.

Following liftoff the F-15B went into a 50deg climb at 300kt, reaching a height of 14,000ft (4,267m) by the time it was over the end of the 15,000ft (4,572m) runway. During subsequent manoeuvres Clark reported that CAS-off flight was equal to that of earlier fighters, enabling tracking manoeuvres at up to 4g to be carried out at 10,000ft (3,000m) and 350kt. Climb and acceleration were also demonstrated, with a climb at better than 6,000ft/min (1,800m/min) in Military (non-afterburning) power to 32,000ft (9,750m) followed by acceleration in full afterburner from Mach 0.9 to Mach 1.1 in 10 seconds and Mach 1.2 in 20 seconds.

Left: A pair of 57th FWW Eagles demonstrate the type's excellent low-level handling qualities over Nellis AFB, Arizona.

Another close observer of an early demonstration flight was Captain Robert J. Hoag, Editor of the USAF *Fighter Weapons Review*. Following in an F-4 chase plane, Captain Hoag watched the Eagle lift off after a ground roll of 1,200ft (366m) and reach 10,000ft (3,000m) over a ground track of less than 5,000ft (1,500m). To compare the turning performance of the two aircraft, the F-4 initiated a 5½g turn in full afterburner, starting from a speed of 350-400kt and at an altitude of 12,000ft (3,650m). The Eagle, starting at the same speed and altitude and at a slant range of 6,000ft (1,830m) was able to close to a minimum range on the Phantom's tail within 540deg of turn, using only military power and with no trace of the severe buffeting experienced by the F-4.

Another manoeuvre which particularly impressed Captain Hoag, who was moved to describe the F-15 as a "Superfighter", was a transition from 110kt flight, with landing gear and flaps down, to an Immelmann in full afterburner with gear and flaps up. The transition was immediate, and the Eagle was able to accelerate throughout the manoeuvre.

The implications for combat of the

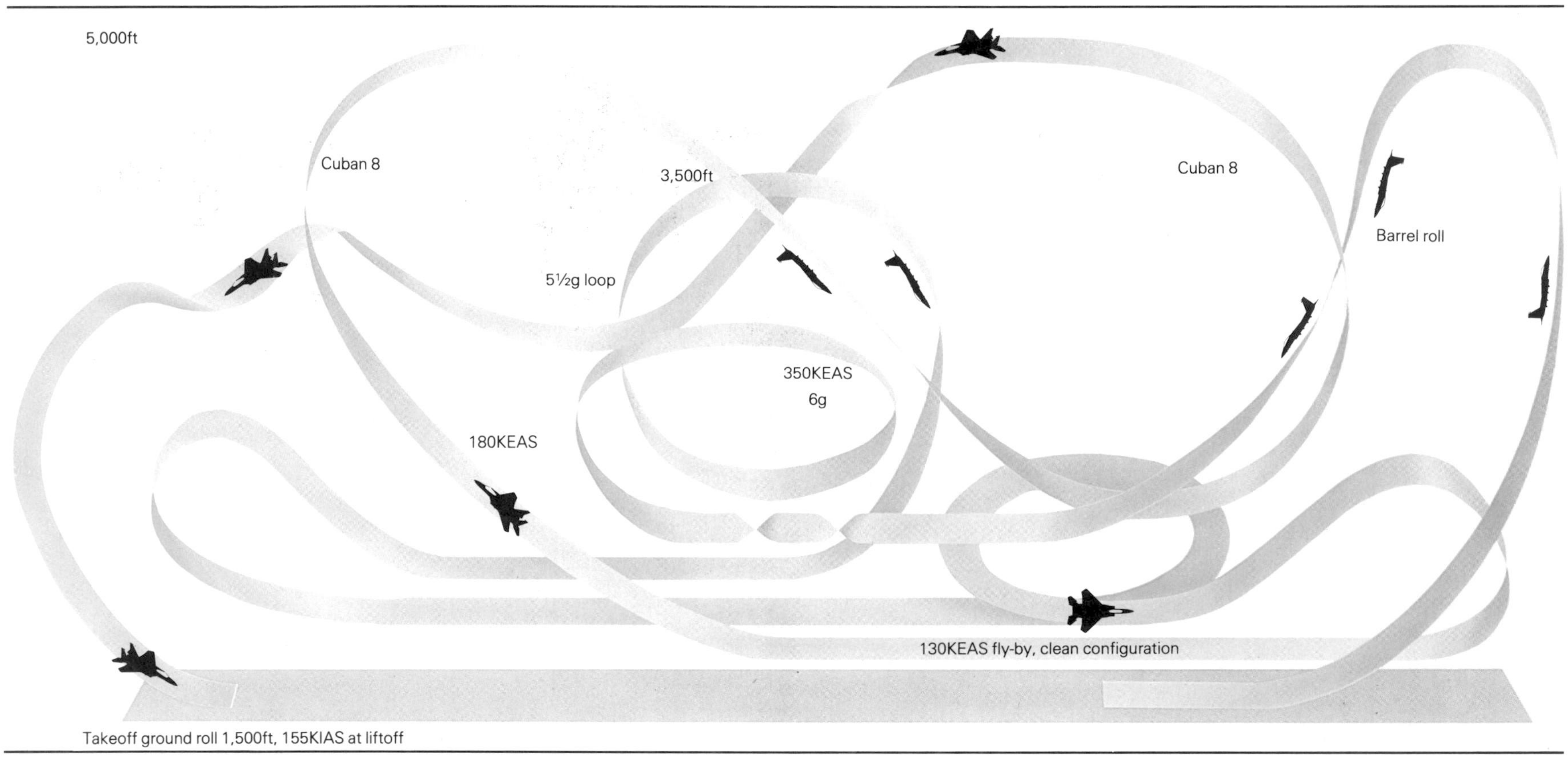

Above: Fair-weather flying display given by the Strike Eagle during its public premiere at the 1982 Farnborough Air Show.

power implicit in such demonstrations are obvious. While the Eagle should be able to accelerate out of trouble fairly easily, an opponent would find it extremely hard to get away. The F-15's ability to maintain controllable flight over a wide range of speeds and at angles of attack up to 26deg can enhance the effectiveness of both missiles and guns. And the ability to maintain acceleration at steep angles is a significant advantage against the high-speed, high-altitude MiG-25, allowing the target to be tracked by the radar against a clutter-free background in a snap-up intercept.

Overall, the Eagle's air combat superiority is directly attributable to the high lift and excess power specified in the original requirement. Whereas the pilot of an F-4 must be aware of the need to conserve energy, and will often have to build up energy in combat by diving away into a zoom climb, the F-15 has so much power available that it can accelerate straight into high-g manoeuvres, and sustain them for long periods without losing altitude or airspeed.

Of course, there are other requirements in combat than pure power and manoeuvrability: above all, the pilot must be able to use them effectively. In this respect the bubble canopy and the exceptional visibility it provides is of fundamental importance – according to Captain Hoag, "The pilot feels as if he is riding astride the bird, rather than in it". There is also room for him to twist around in his seat without banging his head against the canopy.

Below: 36th TFW F-15A touches down with airbrake at full 45deg extension. Early control problems on the rollout were corrected by modifications to the control system.

Cockpit layout

The cockpit layout itself was given an enthusiastic welcome. The most frequently used controls are positioned at the top of the centre instrument panel (HUD, UHF radio, Mode 3 IFF and position identification) or on the left console near the throttle (radar controls, fuel jettison, ILS TACAN, landing lights, BIT control panel auxiliary radio and master IFF). Other instruments on the front panel include the air-to-air and air-to-ground weapons monitoring systems, the radar display, standard flight instruments and engine instruments. The right console contains the engine controls, INS control panel and environmental controls. Altogether there are 30 per cent fewer gauges than in an F-4 cockpit, and with the HUD acting as the primary source of flight information and the communications controls located just below it the time spent looking inside the cockpit is reduced to a minimum.

The pilot is further helped to keep his head up by the location of the main weapon and radar controls on the stick and throttle. With the CAS translating the pilot's inputs into electrical signals, finger and thumb pressure on the stick is enough to maintain control, while the controls for a number of other functions are also carried on the stick. A trim button allows the aircraft's attitude to be adjusted in pitch or yaw axes; the trigger engages the HUD camera and fires the gun; the weapon release button, depending on the mode selected, will engage the HUD camera, launch a selected missile, release bombs, designate a target or illuminate a target for a Sparrow; another button uncages or cages the seeker heads of heat-seeking Sidewinders or laser-guided bombs; and the air refuelling receptacle re-

Below: Touchdown by a 555th TFS Eagle. Even without a brake parachute the F-15 needs a shorter landing run than the F-4.

lease switch, when the radar is engaged, enables the pilot to engage the radar's boresight or super-search modes. The former commands the radar to scan directly ahead and lock on the first target it detects within ten miles (16km), while in super-search the radar scans the 20deg HUD field of view up to ten miles ahead and locks on any target detected, displaying a box in the HUD to indicate its position to the pilot.

The throttles also carry a variety of controls. Apart from the microphone and IFF transmitter, there is an ECM dispenser switch for releasing chaff or flares, a weapon mode selector for the air-to-air radar mode appropriate to gun, Sparrow or Sidewinder, and the speedbrake control, plus more radar controls. The antenna elevation control allows the radar scan pattern to be adjusted up or down, while the target designator control adjusts the position of the radar scope target acquisition gate, used to designate a target detected in normal search modes.

HOTAS philosophy

The thinking behind the head-up HOTAS (hands on throttle and stick) system of combat is summed up succinctly by Colonel Wendell H. Shawler, Director of the F-15 Joint Test Force, 1973–76: "Everything you need is on the throttle and stick". However, he adds that these functions need to be simplified to avoid confusion during the heat of battle. According to Jack Cranes of MCAIR, addressing the Society of Experimental Test Pilots on the F/A-18 HOTAS system, the average pilot can only use three functions intelligently, wisely and properly. Air-to-air weapon selection on the F-15 is split into three functions: gun, Sidewinder or Sparrow.

Again according to Colonel Shawler, on selecting guns, "you automatically got everything up there (in the HUD) you needed for guns, including short-range radar on your radar selection". The same applies to the two types of AAM. "The fact that you were selecting one of three functions – you got everything you needed. You couldn't do much else – you don't want to. When you start getting all these complexities where you put 50 functions on the stick and throttle, if you select one thing over here, you get three choices there, it gets very difficult." During Colonel Shawler's time HOTAS did not strain the pilot's workload; but later, when all the ECM and EW aspects were added to the one-man cockpit, it did, in his opinion, "put the workload over a lot of people's capabilities".

This view has been echoed by at least one experienced F-15 pilot, Major Dito Ladd, who until transferring to the 527th Aggressors was Chief of Weapons and Tactics with the 525th TFS, 36th TFW. In May 1983 Major Ladd recalled: "There are times when you feel like 'Yeah, I've got this thing whipped, I can take advantage of every opportunity the weapon provides.' That was generally after a period of intense flying. Flying once a day or twice a day over a period of two to three weeks there are times when the airplane can be fun, with one man it can be extremely effective, but it take the time and practice to do it. It's just like anything, you've got to practice."

Right: 36th TFW F-15Cs practise a formation takeoff from a West German autobahn. Nose-up normally takes place when the Eagle reaches a speed of 100kt.

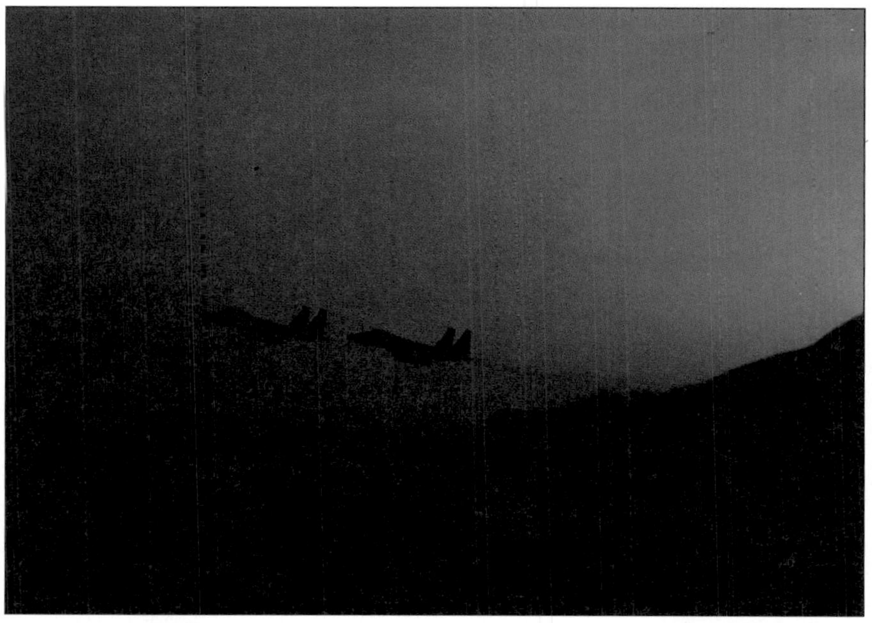

Right: Two F-15Cs of the 18th TFW take off at sunset from Kwang-Ju air base, Republic of Korea, in April 1982 during one of PACAF's annual Team Spirit exercises.

Future Variants

Although intended purely as an air-superiority fighter, the Eagle has proved a ready convert to the ground-attack role, and the manufacturer's Strike Eagle demonstrator has paved the way for a potential dual-role derivative. In addition, the type's rapid acceleration to high altitudes made it the obvious candidate as launch vehicle for the USAF's new anti-satellite missile, and other proposed variants include tactical reconnaissance and defence-suppression replacements for the RF-4C and F-4G Wild Weasel versions of the venerable Phantom.

Above: Dive-bombing demonstration by the second development F-15B, 71-0291, in its Strike Eagle configuration in 1980.

By 1983 the F-15 Eagle had progressed through three distinct phases. The first was its development to the F-15A production fighter, designed primarily for air superiority, but with a secondary ground attack capability. Phase two was to increase the internal fuel capacity (and thus the maximum takeoff weight)m offer provisions for conformal tanks, and add a programmable signal processor to the radar system, to produce the F-15C and two-seat F-15D. The current Multi-stage Improvement Plan (MSIP) for the F-15C/D will offer provision for the AIM-120 AMRAAM, improved ECM and C³ (command, control and communications) systems, a programmable armament control system, enhanced radar and an improved internal computer.

The next version to appear, the F-15E, was originally known by the manufacturers as Strike Eagle and was, in effect, a dual-role fighter offering improved weapons system flexibility and avionics/radar performance in the ground attack role without sacrificing its proven air-to-air capability. The first public demonstration of the new model was its appearance at the Farnborough Air Show in September 1980. The Strike Eagle, a converted F-15B flown for the first time in its new configuration on July 8, 1980, was a private venture by MCAIR and their subcontractors. It featured the extra underwing pylons, provision for the FAST pack conformal tanks and the developed APG-63 radar with SAR techniques, and its projected role was that of an all-weather interdiction aircraft to supplement, and later replace, the remaining F-111s in the TAC inventory.

The key to the Strike Eagle's expanded capabilities lay in the improvements to the radar and avionics. In essence, these advances make it possible to use the radar more intelligently with the aid of PSP (programmable signal processing). Taking advantage of the aircraft's forward speed to give real-time ground mapping, it is possible to achieve much better resolution, allowing the radar to be operated on a time-share basis between the three separate

Left: Among the weapons carried by the Strike Eagle company-funded demonstrator were the Matra Durandal anti-runway weapon.

Below: Strike Eagle demonstrates its ability to carry a heavy load of Mk 20 Rockeye cluster bomb dispensers – plus four Sidewinders – in 1981.

Above: Command and status, tactical situation, radar, and duplicate of the pilot's HUD displays dominate the aft cockpit of the F-15 AFCD.

Left: Strike Eagle carries out a simulated ground attack with the General Electric 30mm gun pod over Wisconsin in 1980.

modes of terrain-following and avoidance, ground-mapping and air search. Based on a two-seat F-15B, the Strike Eagle carries a second crew member to manage the increased number of avionics systems, which could also include FLIR and LANTIRN.

The USAF were impressed with the Strike Eagle and its potential, especially as the air-to-air capabilities are not impaired by the air-to-ground enhancements. Although a new Advanced Tactical Fighter was planned for the 1990s, there was a requirement for 398 dual-role fighters to enter service in the mid-1980s. To this end, a comparable evaluation in 1982–83 examined the enhanced capabilities of both the F-15 and the delta-winged F-16XL. The projected F-15E would have terrain avoidance built in to its radar and linked to a radar altimeter, but despite being little more than a software change, automatic terrain-following using the LANTIRN system is only considered as a growth option. Some of the USAF's mission requirements would require an F-15E to

Above: In its new guise of dual-role fighter demonstrator, 71-0291 carries 22 Mk 20 Rockeyes over St Louis in May 1983.

penetrate to the target by night and in bad weather at around 500ft (150m), using FLIR for target identification and delivering its weapons with the possible assistance of a laser designator, which MCAIR consider calls for a two-man crew.

During the six-month trial at Edwards AFB, California, more than 200 test flights were conducted. During the evaluation, the four aircraft demonstrated their capabilities in a number of areas: long-range, all-environment radar; extended flying range and increased payload; high-speed, low-altitude missions; improved survivability; accurate weapons release; and a two-man crew configuration. As an indication of the increase in payload and range performance, MCAIR quote a 7,000lb (3,175kg) increase in take-off weight to 75,000lb (34,020kg). Another F-15, equipped with conformal tanks, three drop tanks and eight 500lb (227kg) Mk 82 bombs, demonstrated long range combined with a dual air-to-air and air-to-ground role, while 16 differing stores configurations were flight tested on the Eagle's five pylons and four semi-recessed missile stations.

The Eagle evaluation, which began on November 1, 1982, and was concluded on April 30, 1983, used four aircraft. The F-15B Advanced Fighter Capability Demonstrator (formerly Strike Eagle), with the specially-equipped rear cockpit, APG-63 radar with SAR capability and the Ford Aerospace Pave Tack FLIR laser pod, flew 66 sorties and notched up 121·1 hours; an F-15C with conformal tanks and weapons adapters to increase number of the air-to-ground weapons pylons from three to five flew 104 hours in 50 sorties; and two F-15Ds, one of which was equipped with the Ford Aerospace/Texas Instruments FLIR and laser tracker/marker pod, made a combined total of 88 flights, involving nearly 130 hours in the air. Advanced rear cockpits equipped with four multi-pur-

Below: Formation takeoff from Lambert-St Louis, home of MCAIR, with the F-15 dual-role demonstrator in the foreground.

Left: The Advanced Fighter Capability Demonstrator equipped with bombs, Sidewinders, forward-looking infra-red pod and long-range ground-mapping radar takes off from Eglin AFB, Florida.

Above: The MCAIR Strike Eagle in its original form, before conversion to AFCD and dual-role demonstrator for USAF trials.

pose video screens allowed the occupant to control the various radar, navigation and communications displays simultaneously, and the Eagle successfully completed USAF flight requirements for carrying the 500lb (227kg) Mk 82 and 2000lb (907kg) Mk 84 bombs, BDU-38 and CBU-58 weapons. MCAIR officials are quoted as saying the F-15s "achieved accurate visual and radar weapons delivery" during the trials.

Relating some of these claims to sample mission profiles, an F-15C with conformal tanks plus one centreline tank could take off from a base in the south of the Sinai peninsula and conduct a hi-lo-lo-hi mission, including a 50nm dash at Mach 0·9, to attack a target in the extreme north of Greece with 12 Mk 20 Rockeye bombs. Alternatively, an aircraft with conformal tanks and three external drop tanks could undertake a ferry mission, with reserves, from Bitburg AB in Germany to the southern part of the Persian Gulf, a distance of some 2600nm.

An accuracy of between 4 and 8 mils, better than the A-7D Corsair II, F-4E Phantom or F-111E/F, has been claimed by MCAIR, and CEP (cumulative error probabilities) have ranged between 36ft (11m) and 85ft (26m) using Continuously Displayed Impact Point (CDIP) deliveries in various conditions. These include airspeeds ranging from 420kt to 480kt, dive angles of less than 20deg to more than 40deg, and slant ranges of less than 5,000ft (1,500m) to more than 10,000ft (3,000m). MCAIR also claim to have demonstrated a CEP of 77ft (23·5m) in *blind* bombing, using the F-15B AFCD.

A decision on which of the competing types should be the subject of requests for further funding was due by the end of 1983 and, capabilities apart, the cost factor was certain to influence the selection process. The contract to evaluate

Below: Despite insistence that the FX programme included "not a pound for air-to-ground", high performance, automated systems and a second crew member have made the F-15 a leading candidate for the USAF's dual-role fighter requirement.

Above: The Vought seeker head for the USAF's ASAT missile combines laser gyros, infra-red seekers and rocket motors for satellite tracking.

Left: HARM, anti-radar missile, Snakeye bombs, Sparrows and Sidewinders arm the proposed defence suppression Eagle.

Below left: A full-size model of the USAF's ASAT missile ready for loading on an F-15A at Boeing's Seattle facility in August 1982.

the capabilities already described was valued at $13 million, and USAF sources indicate that development of an F-15E Eagle to production status would cost in the region of US $350 million, with procurement of the 398 models adding a further $16,000 million.

The basis for the F-15E would be the MSIP-standard F-15D two-seater. To this would be added a fail-operative flight control augmentation system; provision for carrying and launching a variety of weapons, including tactical nuclear bombs; VHF and HF communications; provision for the LANTIRN system, including a modified intertial navigation system, radar altimeter and the Marconi Avionics diffractive-optics, wide-field-of-view HUD; and the new cockpit displays and controls associated with the extra avionics for both pilot and weapons system operator. Additionally, an internal countermeasures set would be installed in the ammunition bay of the F-15E, as two-seat models currently do not carry ECM. Should problems occur with LANTIRN, the Ford Aerospace FLIR pod, derived from that used on the F/A-18 Hornet is available as an alternative, as is the Pave Tack system from the same manufacturer.

Another option for the F-15E, which could come as an MSIP, is the Manoeuvring Attack System, derived from the Integrated Flight and Fire Control/Firefly III developments described in Chapter 4. This would allow weapons to be delivered accurately, or guns fired, during tactical manoeuvring. The first live air-to-air trial of the IFFC took place on August 19, 1982, when an F-15 shot down a PQM-102 target drone over the White Sands Missile Range, New Mexico. The drone was closing at 400kt from a near-frontal position, and both aircraft were in sharp right turns. The IFFC on the F-15 was activated at a target range of 10,000ft (3,000m) and a closure rate of 760kt, so that in the space of a single two-second burst, comprising 171 rounds of target practice ammunition, target distance shrank from 5,800ft (1,770m) to 3,800ft (1,160m). Under normal circumstances, a fighter has to manoeuvre behind his opponent and open fire from an angle of 30deg or less off the tail. In this case the F-15 attacked from 130deg approaching from the front and right, but the drone was hit and caught fire.

Another planned role for the Eagle is that of satellite killer. While the Soviet Union has been developing its own 'killer' satellites, the United States has adopted a different approach to the problem. In 1979, the Vought Corporation was awarded a US $78·2 million contract to develop an ASAT (anti-satellite) system to be operational in 1985. This takes the form of an advanced interceptor missile to be launched from the centreline pylon of an F-15 Eagle, with guidance so accurate that destruction of its target will be by collision, making a warhead unnecessary. Funding of $82·3 million in the FY '80 budget and $268 million in FY '81 was enough for flight testing to continue through 1984.

ASAT system

The ASAT missile is intended to be carried by the F-15 on a pre-directed flight trajectory to the launch point. The missile itself consists of a first stage based on the Boeing AGM-69 Short-Range Attack Missile (SRAM), and a second stage powered by a 6,000lb (2,722kg) thrust Altair III Thikol rocket motor, which for many years has formed the fourth stage of Vought's Scout launch vehicle. A simple seeker combining laser gyros and infra-red sensors operates small rocket motors for course correction during the tracking stage until impact is achieved. Information available by mid-1983 indicated that the ASAT weighs some 2,700lb (1,225kg) and is 17ft 9¾in (5·43m) long and 1ft 7¾in (0·5m) in diameter. Attitude control is provided by two fixed and three movable fins. The F-15 launch pylon incorporates a back-up battery, electrical connections, a communications link, a microprocessor and a gas-generated cartridge ejection unit, and the first two test firings are scheduled by October 1983.

The ASAT programme, also known as

Above: The Boeing-developed ASAT launch pylon incorporates a microprocessor and communications link between missile and aircraft.

the Prototype Miniature Air-launched Segment (PMALS) of the Space Defense Program, is managed by the USAF's Space Command. Boeing Aerospace is responsible for the SRAM first stage, integration services and the missile control centre, while Vought have overall responsibility for the programme as prime contractor and McDonnell Douglas carry out the necessary modifications to the aircraft. A total of 36 F-15s, equipping two squadrons, are expected to be committed to the ASAT role.

A number of other roles have been considered for the F-15C, including tactical reconnaissance and defence suppression to replace the ageing RF-4C and F-4G Wild Weasel variants of the Phantom. However, such developments would be subject to budgeting considerations. The US House Armed Services Committee in its report on the FY 84 budget request, published in May 1983 quotes the flyaway cost of an F-15C as $25·2 million, compared with $12·78 million for an F-16. The budget request for 48 Eagles in FY 84 was reduced to 30 by Congress, who in addition, "would disapprove multi-year procurement". They feel "there is merit in maintaining two fighter aircraft production lines" for the USAF, and they recommend that F-15 production is maintained at "a minimum sustaining rate". Planned procurement of 696 more F-15s at a total cost of $26 billion, they consider "unaffordable". It is not surprising, therefore, that the same report, when considering tactical fighter derivatives of both the F-15 and F-16, recommends deletion of the $21·4 million requested for long lead items for whichever type is selected.

Below: Vought ASAT is carried by a Space Command Eagle for vibroacoustic trials as part of the captive flight test programme.

Right: The USAF's antisatellite programme involves using the F-15's rapid climb to launch the missile at an altitude of around 80,000ft (24,400m). SRAM first stage and Altair III second stage carry the warhead/seeker to intercept altitude.

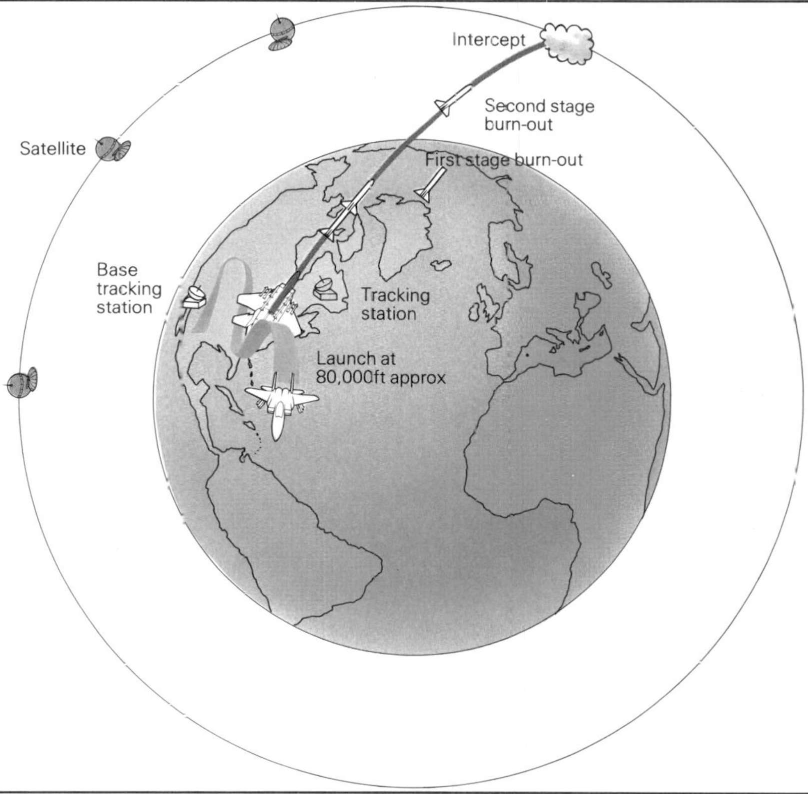

Glossary and abbreviations

AAA Anti-aircraft artillery
AAM Air-to-air missile
AAR Air-to-air refuelling
AB US air base (on allied territory)
ADF Automatic direction finding (system)
ADTAC Air Defense Tactical Air Command
AFB US Air Force Base (on sovereign territory)
AFCD Advanced Fighter Capability Demonstrator (ex-Strike Eagle)
AGM- US designation for air-to-ground missile
AIM- US designation for air intercept missile
AIS Avionics intermediate shop
AMRAAM Advanced medium-range air-to-air missile
analogue Electronic system in which quantities are represented by electrical signals of variable characteristics, i.e. by electrical analogues
anhedral Angle of wing, canard or tailplane below horizontal
ARI Aileron-rudder interconnect
ASAT Anti-satellite (missile system)
aspect ratio Wing slenderness in plan form, numerically span^2/area
ASRAAM Advanced short range air-to-air missile
ASW Anti-submarine warfare
augmentation afterburning (reheat)
AWACS Airborne warning and control system (Boeing E-3A Sentry)

BIT(E) Built-in test (equipment)
BVR Beyond visual range
bypass ratio Ratio of total airflow through a turbofan engine to that passing through the core section

camber Curvature of the centreline of a wing aerofoil
CAS Control augmentation system
CDIP Continuously displayed impact point
CEP Circular error probability
CFS Concept formulation study
chord Imaginary line joining the leading and trailing edges of a wing or aerofoil section
clutter Spurious returns on a radar scope
CRT Cathode ray tube
CW Continuous-wave radiation

DCP Development concept paper
DFE Derivative fighter engine (now the GE F110)
digital Electronic system in which quantities are as on/off signals coded to represent numbers
dihedral Angle of wing, canard or tailplane above the horizontal
Doppler Radar which measures changes in frequency between reflections in the ground ahead of and behind the aircraft, thus giving accurate measure of speed over the ground; Doppler effect is also used to pick out moving targets.
DTD Damage tolerant design

ECCM Electronic counter-countermeasures
ECM Electronic countermeasures
ECP Engineering change proposals
EO Electro-optical
EW Electronic warfare

FAST packs Fuel and sensor tactical packs (also known as conformal tanks)
FIS Fighter interception squadron
FLAMR Forward looking multi-mode radar
FLIR Forward looking infra-red
FSD Full scale development
FWW Fighter weapons wing
FY Fiscal year (as in US budgets)

g Acceleration due to standard gravity, unit of linear acceleration
GE General Electric Company (USA)
GHz GigaHertz (Hertz × 1,000,000,000)
GPS Global positioning system

HF High frequency
HUD Head-up display
Hz Hertz, cycles per second

IDFAF Israeli Defence Force – Air Force
ILS Instrument landing system
INS Inertial navigation system
IR Infra-red, heat radiation

JASDF Japanese Air Self-Defense Force
JTIDS Joint tactical information distribution system

KHz Kilo Hertz (Hertz × 1000)

LANTIRN Low-altitude navigation and targeting infra-red for night
LLTV Low-light television
LRU Line replaceable unit

Mach Unit equal to the speed of sound
Maple Flag Series of tactical air exercises carried out over Canada in as realistic manner as possible, including EW
MCAIR McDonnell Aircraft Company (part of the McDonnell Douglas Corporation)
MMH/FH Maintenance man hours per flight hour
MSIP Multi-staged improvement programme
MTBF Mean time between failure
MW Megawatt

NDT Non-destructive testing

PACAF US Pacific Air Force
Pave Tack FLIR sensor/laser designator system carried on F-111F and F-4 Phantom, and tested on F-15; produced by Ford Aerospace
PRF Pulse repetition frequency
PSP Programmable signal processor
P&W Pratt & Whitney

Red Flag Series of tactical air exercises carried out in Nevada in as realistic manner as possible, including EW
RFP Requests for proposals
RoKAF Republic of Korea Air Force
RSAF Royal Saudi Air Force
RWR Radar warning receiver
R&D Research and development

SAM Surface-to-air missile
SAR Synthetic aperture radar
Seek Talk Codename for a secure communications system under development
semi-active Homing on radiation reflected from a target illuminated by radar carried in fighter or other vehicle (but not the missile itself)
slick Streamlined (Aero-1A shape) bomb
SPR Sortie production rate
SRAM Short range attack missile

TAC USAF Tactical Air Command
TACAN Tactical air navigation
TEWS Tactical electronic warfare system
TFS Tactical fighter squadron
TFTS Tactical fighter training squadron
TFTW Tactical fighter training wing
TFW Tactical fighter wing

UHF Ultra-high frequency
USAF United States Air Force

VFAX Project designation for a carrier-based fighter/attack aircraft
VFX Project designation for a carrier-based fighter aircraft
VHF Very-high frequency

Wild Weasel Codename for defence-suppression aircraft (as in F-4G Wild Weasel)
wing loading Aircraft weight divided by wing area

'Zulu' alert Aircraft maintained on constant readiness to scramble against unidentified air targets 365 days a year

Specifications

	F-15A	**F-15C**
Length	63ft 9in/10.43m	63ft 9in/10.43m
Wingspan	42ft 9¾in/13.05m	42ft 9¾in/13.05m
Height	18ft 5½in/5.63m	18ft 5½in/5.63m
Weights		
Empty	28,000lb/12,700kg	28,000lb/12,700kg
Takeoff (air-to-air)	41,500lb/18,824kg	44,500lb/20,185kg
Maximum takeoff	56,000lb/25,401kg	68,000lb/30,844kg
Wing area	608sq ft/56.5sq m	608sq ft/56.5sq m
Load factor	+9g/−3g	+9g/−3g
Combat thrust: weight ratio	1.4:1	1.3:1
Maximum speed	>Mach2.5	>Mach2.5
Service ceiling	65,000ft/19,813m	65,000ft/19,813m
Range		
Ferry (with external tanks)	>2,500nm/4,630km	>2,500nm/4,630km
Ferry (with FAST Packs)	—	>3,000nm/5,556km
Internal fuel	11,635lb/5,278kg	13,455lb/6,103kg
Number of hardpoints	5	5
Maximum ordnance load	16,000lb/7,257kg	16,000lb/7,257kg

Chapter 3

F-16

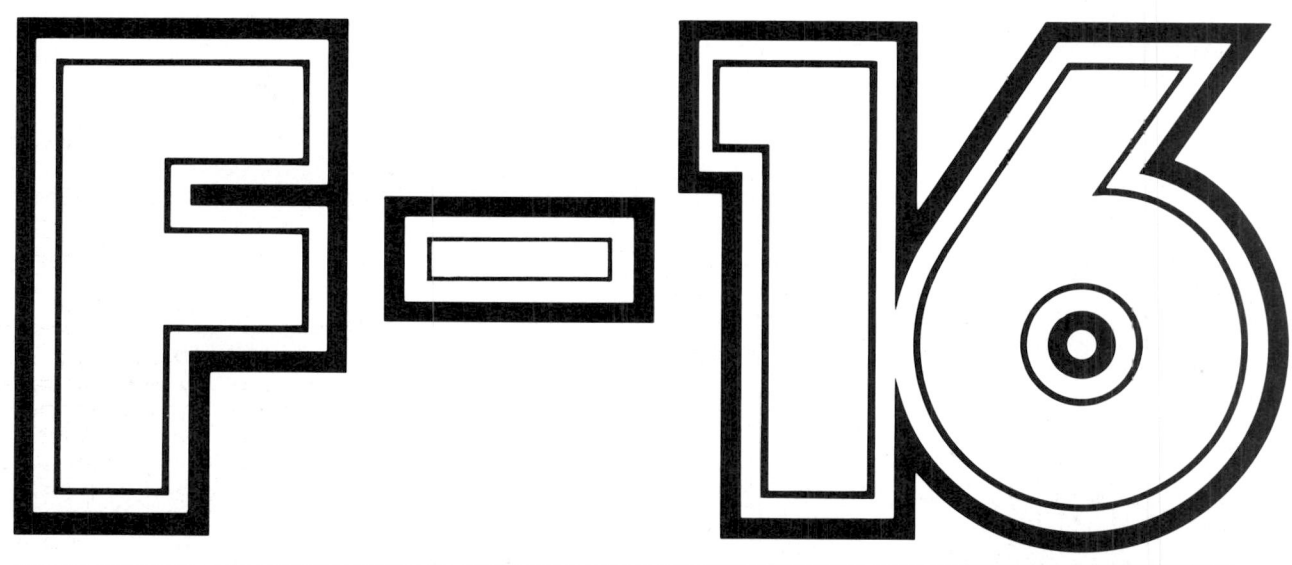

FIGHTING FALCON

Doug Richardson

F-16 Fighting Falcon

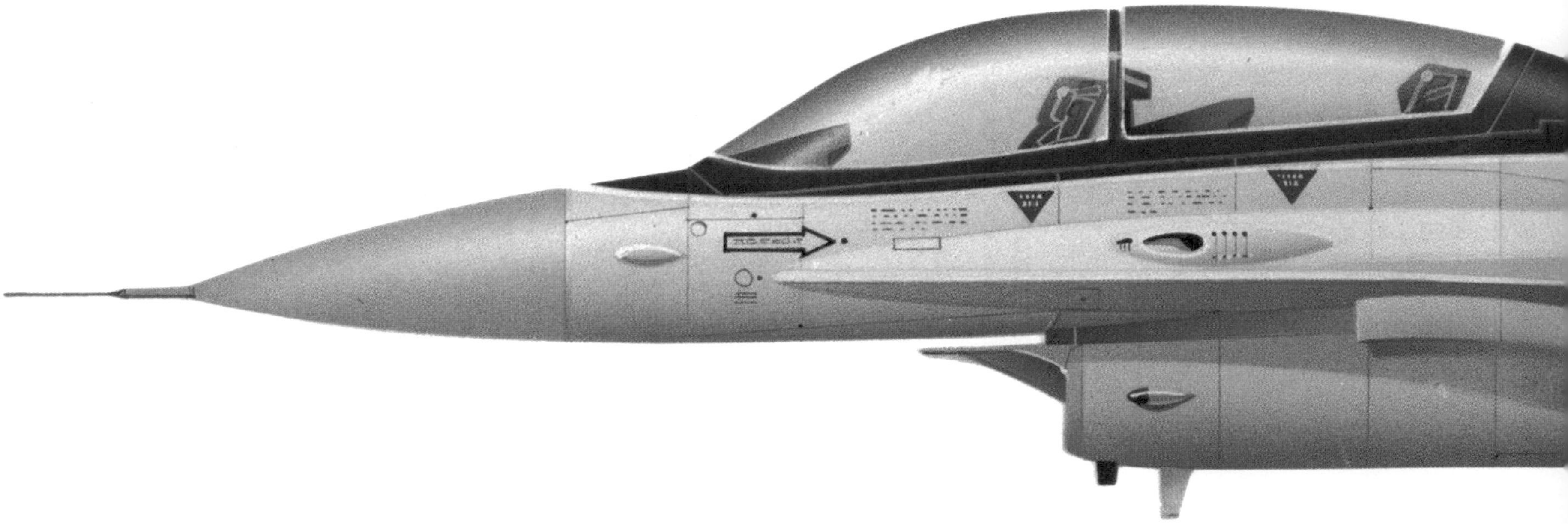

Contents

Acknowledgements

This chapter would not have been possible without the unstinting help over the years of current and former members of the public relations department at the Fort Worth Division of General Dynamics, and of technicians on the assembly and flight lines. Many other companies have provided material: apart from those credited for supplying photographs, these include Itek, Martin Marietta, McDonnell Douglas, and Oldelft. Thanks are also due to many departments and units of the USAF, to the air arms of Belgium, Denmark, the Netherlands and Norway, and to their military attaches in London, and to the Editor and Defence Editor of *Flight International* for research facilities.

Author

Doug Richardson is a defence journalist specializing in the fields of aviation, guided missiles and electronics. Editor of *Defence Materiel*, the journal devoted to the British defence industry, he trained initially as an electronics engineer, starting his career as a technician with an R&D team working on avionics for the Buccaneer and the cancelled TSR-2 project.

After an electronics R&D career encompassing such diverse areas as radar, electronic warfare, rocket engine control systems, computers, automatic test equipment and missile trials, he switched to technical journalism as a member of the staff of the internationally respected aerospace journal *Flight International*, serving as Defence Editor before moving on to become Editor of the international technical defence journal *Military Technology and Economics*.

His previous work for Salamander includes *The Illustrated Encyclopedia of Modern Warplanes* and contributions to *The Balance of Military Power*, and he has also written for such technical and defence journals as *International Defense Review, NATO's 15 Nations, Defence, Technologia Militar* and *Wehrtechnik*. In 1981 he edited *Defense Review*, a Chinese-language report on the British defence industry prepared for controlled circulation in the Chinese government, industry and armed forces.

Introduction

General Dynamics' Fighting Falcon was one of the stars of the 1977 Paris Air Show. In those not-so-distant days it was simply designated F-16 and only a handful of aircraft were flying, but the type was regarded by many observers as the hottest and probably the most controversial fighter in the Western world.

As the aircraft stood on display in the flight line, many individuals stopped to photograph it, but one in particular caught the writer's eye. Dressed in a suit of distinctly out-of-date style and equipped with a Russian camera fitted with a large telephoto lens, he was photographing the aircraft not from close up but from a range of several hundred yards.

The resulting clandestine photographs were no doubt eagerly examined in an East European Defence Ministry a few days later, but the whole exercise might have been made easier had the anonymous photographer simply marched boldly up to the F-16 and accepted one of the colour photos of the aircraft which the two GD men on duty beside it were handing out to anyone who asked!

At a time when most of the Western European media saw the F-16 as a potential political scandal, and news reports knocking the aircraft were commonplace, the Warsaw Pact was clearly taking the new GD warplane very seriously – even if one of their intelligence-gathering methods was a trifle crude.

Subsequent events can have done little to allay their concern. Far from being the 'can of worms' which its opponents had suggested, Fighting Falcon is a highly capable aircraft likely to enter service with many more friends and allies of the West and to remain in production into the 1990s.

Moreover, the undoubted success of the initial production models seems certain to lead to future variants beyond the F-16C/D. As it enters service in ever-growing numbers, many MiG and Mirage pilots must be wondering how long they will have to wait before receiving aircraft in this performance class.

Development

No other combat aircraft has packed as much multirole military capability into a single airframe as does the F-16 Fighting Falcon. Agile enough to outfly opponents such as third-generation MiG-21s, yet able to carry heavy ordnance loads over long ranges during strike missions, the F-16 will form a major component of Western air strength during the 1980s and 1990s. For the first time in modern fighter design 'lightweight' is not a euphemism for 'limited performance', and Fighting Falcon is a triumph for the advocates of smaller, lighter and less expensive fighters.

In following up the F-86 Sabre of the late 1940s, US fighter designers developed an expensive fascination with the sophistication made possible by improvements in technology. The larger the aircraft, the more capable it became, but while succeeding designs saw massive increases in combat capability, the price was paid in terms of both money and ever-diminishing fleet numbers. From the P-51 Mustang to the F-15 Eagle, each new US land-based fighter was on average 2·4 times more expensive than its predecessor, and Eagle production over 15 years may never reach a tenth of the 15,000 Mustangs built in a third of that time.

This philosophy was challenged briefly in the light of Korean War experience. The F-104 should have ended up a US equivalent of the MiG-21 Fishbed, but like the earlier F-100 evolved into a strike fighter instead of an air-combat fighter. Early models were used in Vietnam for a short time, but the USAF found itself having to combat the agile and lightweight MiGs of the North Vietnamese air force with the heavy and expensive F-4 Phantom – a type originally developed as an all-weather naval interceptor. The subsequent addition of wing slats and a built-in 20mm cannon enhanced the aircraft's usefulness as an air combat fighter, and the F-4E was to have a long and successful combat career, but the original design had never been intended for dogfighting.

The Vietnam experience

Over North Vietnam, the US pilots found themselves unable to match the kill rates of the Korean War. Instead of a 10:1 or better kill ratio of the earlier conflict, they achieved at best just over 3:1, a figure which steadily fell to still lower values. For a long time, the US services claimed to have maintained permanent superiority over the MiGs, quoting rates of just over unity at worst. In practice, the ratio at times came out slightly in favour of the Vietnamese.

Part of the problem was training programmes which had placed little emphasis on air-to-air combat. The accepted dogma was that the traditional dogfight had a hallowed place in the history of air fighting, but none at all in modern warfare. Even in the early 1940s, the Spitfires and Hurricanes used to defend British skies from the attentions of the Luftwaffe were committed to combat using elaborate pre-planned tactics which virtually denied the possibility of individual 'free-style' air-to-air engagements. The Luftwaffe pilots had no such illusions, and took a heavy toll of the defenders in early encounters.

With the arrival of the high-speed jet fighter, and the subsequent development of supersonic fighters, the 'no-dogfighting' dogma re-emerged virtually unchanged from its early 1940s RAF form. In view of the speed of the latest warplanes, the firing time available to an attacker was thought to be so small that pilots attempting to dogfight would have little chance of hitting their targets. Long-range combat using air-to-air missiles was thought to be the likely pattern of future combat. In the skies above Korea, Suez, and the Indo-Pakistan border the falsehood of this theory has been demonstrated time and again. In the light of the Vietnam experience it was rejected by the USAF.

As early as 1965 the USAF began concept-formulation studies of new high-performance fighters. These included a heavy 60,000lb (27,000kg) interceptor/air-superiority fighter designated Fighter Experimental (FX), and a lightweight Advanced Day Fighter (ADF). FX would have been heavier than the F-4 Phantom, with twin engines and a variable-geometry wing, while the 25,000lb (11,000kg) ADF design specified a thrust-to-weight ratio and wing loading intended to better the performance of the MiG-21 by a margin of 25 per cent.

The appearance of the Soviet MiG-25 Foxbat fighter in the mid-1960s created a hiatus in USAF future fighter plans. Foxbat posed the threat of the Soviet air force and its Warsaw Pact allies being equipped with Mach 3 fighters at a time when the USAF had only a handful of experimental Mach 3 YF-12 fighter prototypes and no plans for production of aircraft in this performance class. Development of the massive North American F-108 Rapier interceptor had begun in the late 1950s, but this Mach 3 design

Above: Contrasting styles in fighter design – 15 years separated the first flights of the F-4 Phantom (left) and the YF-16 (right).

Below: Dogfighters old and new in formation provide graphic evidence that Fighting Falcon is hardly bigger than the 1940s P-51 Mustang. Note the 'bubble' canopies.

was cancelled in September 1959, 18 months before the first of two prototypes was due to fly.

Foxbat's Mach 3 capability provoked a redirection of USAF fighter planning. The urgent goal now was to develop a design capable of matching both the existing MiG-21 and the new MiG-25, shifting the emphasis to an FX design – the F-15 – offering a high top speed and long-range missile armament.

Although on 'back-burner', the concept of a lightweight fighter similar to ADF was not dead. Two individuals who did much to keep the concept of a lightweight fighter alive were former fighter instructor Major John Boyd, and Pierre Sprey, a civilian working for the assistant Secretary of Defense for Systems Analysis.

Boyd had already had a strong influence on the FX project and was the inventor of the concept of energy manoeuvrability – a vital element in assessing fighter performance. "Let's pretend that manoeuvrability is an energy problem", he once suggested to a group of thermodynamics students. "When you manoeuvre an airplane you need energy ... you lose energy either in gaining altitude, airspeed or both.

"Normally you lose energy in turning. What happens is that your drag exceeds your thrust, and at that point you have a negative energy rate. That negative rate has to come out of altitude, airspeed or out of a combination of the two. You reach a point, even with your military afterburner, at which drag is greater than thrust. That means you have a negative vector ... you multiply net drag by velocity and that tells you how much energy you're going to have to pump up."

Measuring performance

At first Boyd could hardly believe that this simple idea was a new method of looking at fighter performance. Once he had accepted the fact, he considered how combinations of aerodynamics and engines could be devised to create better aircraft. "You just turn the problem of manoeuvrability around and look at it from a different viewpoint. And the result of that was obvious.... The right thrust-to-weight ratio could give you an important edge over your adversary." Fighter performance could be measured at different combinations of altitude, airspeed and manoeuvring situations in terms of what is now designated Specific Excess Power – Ps in engineering jargon.

Boyd's theory showed that the FX would require an engine with a thrust-to-weight ratio significantly better than that of current designs. The resulting F100 turbofan was not only used to power the F-15, but also created the possibility of a lightweight single-engined design of high performance.

Traditional USAF thinking prior to the early 1970s equated light weight with short range. To some degree, this was justified in view of the technology of the time. The MiG-21 was a lightweight developed using mid-1950s technology, and the original Fishbed C day fighter gave rise to the quip among export users that it was a 'supersonic sports plane' – an aircraft with very limited range and even more limited payload.

In the late 1960s, Boyd and Sprey devised a 25,000lb (11,340kg) design designated F-XX – a dedicated air superiority fighter of high endurance. Later studies took this weight down even lower to around 17,000lb (7,700kg). The concept met much opposition, since some saw it as a threat both to traditional thinking on the subject of fighters and to the existing F-15 project.

By 1971, Boyd was working for the Air Force Prototype Study Group. Consequently, he was able to push the concept at a time when the idea of competitive flight-testing of prototype designs was returning to vogue after the massive and highly controversial Total Procurement Package contracts of the 1960s which had resulted in the F-111 and C-5 Galaxy.

Main driving force in getting the LWF project off the drawing board and into the experimental shop was Deputy Defense Secretary David A. Packard, who saw the concept of competitive prototyping as a method of reversing the ever-growing cost of new weapon systems. A series of ground rules for such prototyping exercises drawn up by Air Force Secretary Robert C. Seamans specified that funding would be limited, with initial performance goals and military specifications kept to a minimum. Contestants should not be constrained by the existing force structure of the USAF, but should not assume that any long-term production commitment existed.

Two USAF requirements were chosen for prototyping: a medium STOL transport intended to replace the C-130 Hercules, and the lightweight fighter. These resulted in the Boeing YC-14 and McDonnell Douglas YC-15 jet transports and the YF-16 and YF-17 fighter prototypes. Instead of the 'XC-' and 'XF-' designations which would have been traditional for such programmes, the 'Y' (development) prefix was used in order to stress that a mixture of off-the-shelf and experimental technologies were being used.

Above: The Convair F-106 was built only in small numbers, but the YF-16 from the same Fort Worth plant was the first of at least 2,000.

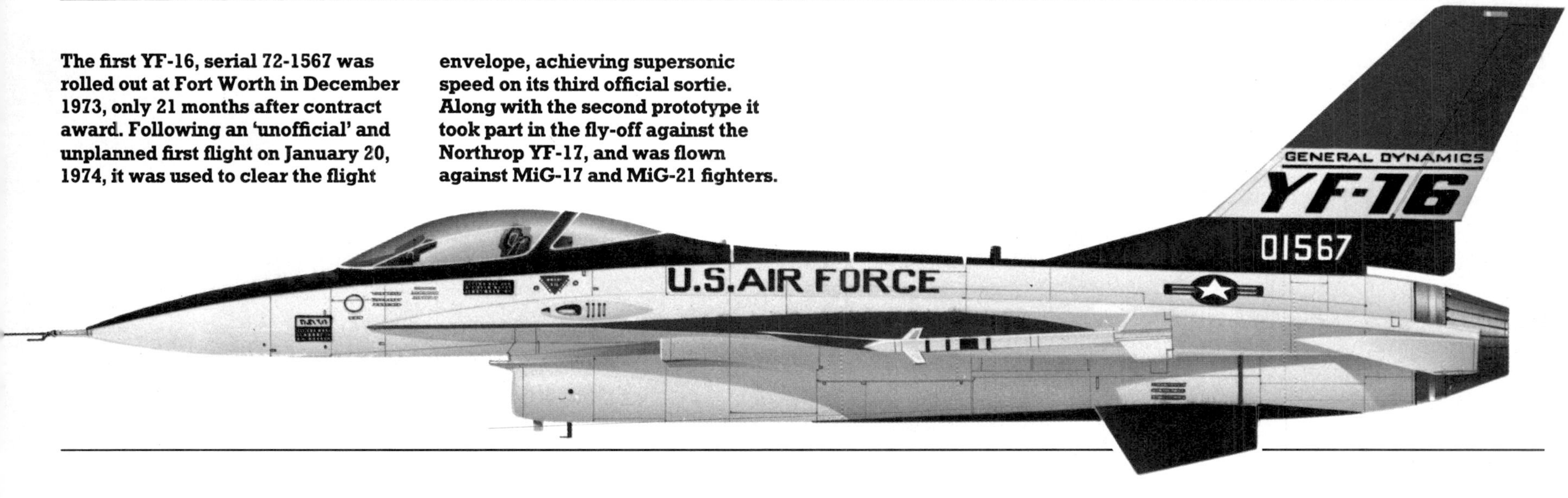

The first YF-16, serial 72-1567 was rolled out at Fort Worth in December 1973, only 21 months after contract award. Following an 'unofficial' and unplanned first flight on January 20, 1974, it was used to clear the flight envelope, achieving supersonic speed on its third official sortie. Along with the second prototype it took part in the fly-off against the Northrop YF-17, and was flown against MiG-17 and MiG-21 fighters.

Above: The YF-16s did much experimental work with ordnance and missiles. Here the second aircraft carries Paveway laser-guided bombs on underwing pylons and an Atlis laser designator under the intake.

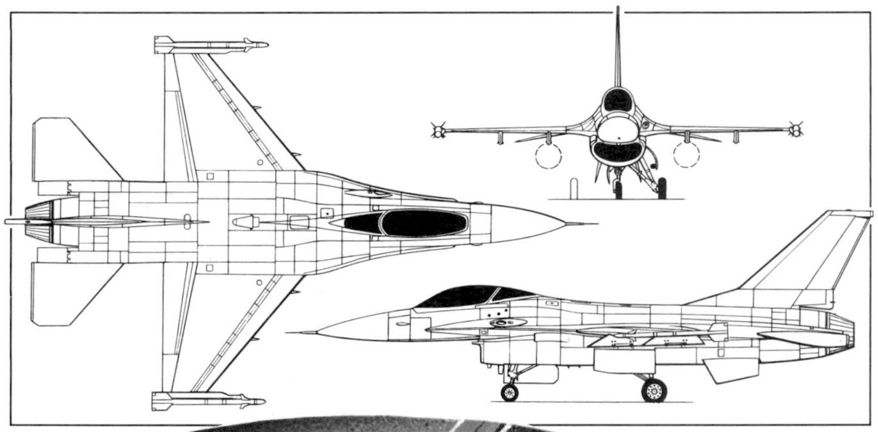

Above right: Definitive F-16 configuration with the enlarged tail.

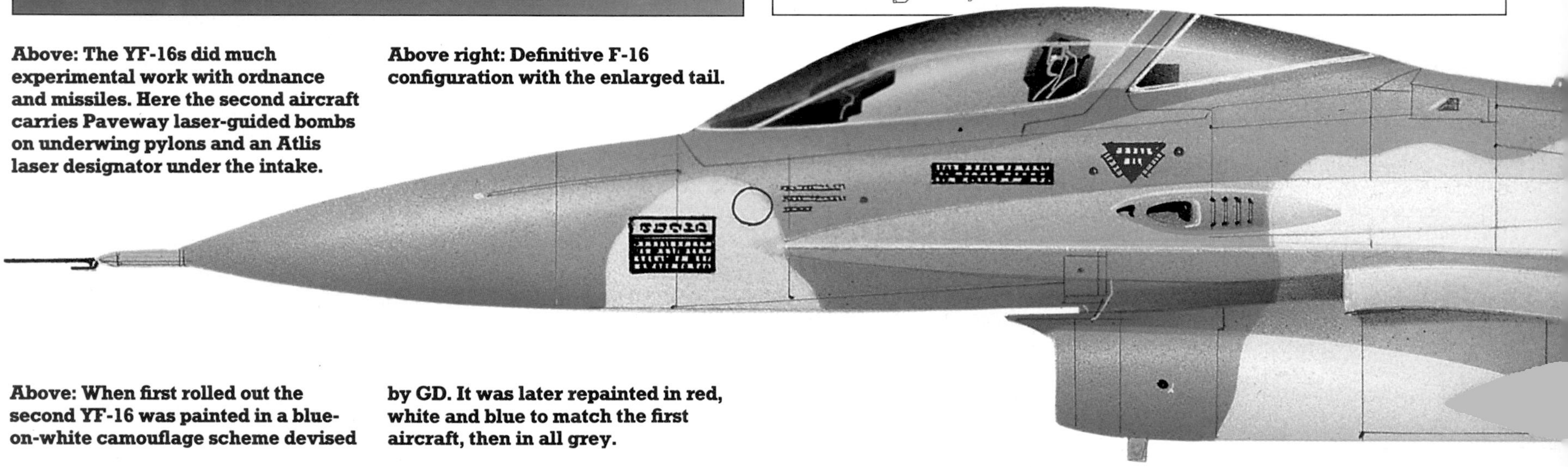

Above: When first rolled out the second YF-16 was painted in a blue-on-white camouflage scheme devised by GD. It was later repainted in red, white and blue to match the first aircraft, then in all grey.

Four contracts worth a total of around $100 million were placed early in 1972 under the LWF programme. General Dynamics was given $38 million to develop and fly two YF-16s, while Northrop was awarded $39 million for two prototypes of the rival YF-17. Contracts were also given to Pratt & Whitney for development of a version of the F100 turbofan specifically for single-engined installations, and to General Electric for the new and smaller YF101 engine.

In submitting a Request for Proposals (RFP) for what was now designated the Lightweight Fighter (LWF) to industry in early 1972, the USAF specified three main objectives. The resulting design should fully explore the advantages of emerging technologies, reduce the risk and uncertainties involved in full-scale development and production of a new fighter, and provide the Department of Defense with a variety of technological options available to meet military hardware needs.

Instead of trying to match the 'brochure' capability of Soviet fighters, the USAF decided to optimize the LWF for the likely conditions of future air combat – altitudes of 30,000 to 40,000ft (9,000 to 12,000m) and speeds of Mach 0.6 to 1.6 – with no attempt to equal the performance of the MiG-25 Foxbat. It was designed not for the top right-hand corner of the performance envelope, but for a wide range of flight conditions, and with the emphasis on turn rate, acceleration and range. This combination of parameters would allow the resulting aircraft to intercept and engage not only existing Warsaw Pact types such as the MiG-21, MiG-23 and Su-7, but also more advanced aircraft such as developed MiG-23 versions and the Su-24 Fencer.

The choice of likely operating height would raise a few eyebrows today, when most combat aircraft must fly at treetop height in order to survive, but reflects a time before the surface-to-air missile threat had literally brought the USAF down to earth. Even in the mid-1970s, the concept of flying into hostile airspace at medium altitude under the cover of advanced ECM had still not been abandoned.

Prototype technology

Following industrial submissions by five companies, General Dynamics and Northrop were chosen to develop flight-test hardware, and a contract was awarded to General Dynamics on April 13, 1972. This was a 'cost plus fixed fee' contract worth $37·9 million, and covered the design, construction and test of two prototypes under the USAF designation YF-16, plus one year of flight testing.

Although development and testing of these light fighters was a technology-demonstration programme, the USAF retained the option of carrying on to develop the design into a service aircraft. The contract with GD specified an average flyaway unit cost target of $3.0 million in 1972 dollars, (rather more in 1983 prices), assuming a production run of 300 examples at a rate of 100 per year. Complete design responsibility for the aircraft lay with the contractors, in order to reduce paperwork and maintain the pace of the programme, under the direction of the Aeronautical Systems Division at Wright-Patterson AFB, which monitored both projects throughout subsequent development.

No attempt was made in designing the YF-16 to push individual technological advances: the intention was to produce and test an aircraft capable of being developed into an operational type. New technology was used in instances where it would have the greatest effect in meeting performance targets, but proven systems and components were retained in areas where such new technology was not required. Components and detail assemblies were designed for ease of manufacture, using low-cost materials wherever possible. Hardware was standardized wherever possible, the design of the air-

Above: According to some critics, the F-16 should have retained the YF-16 configuration shown here – a simple day fighter armed with two AIM-9, a cannon and minimal avionics.

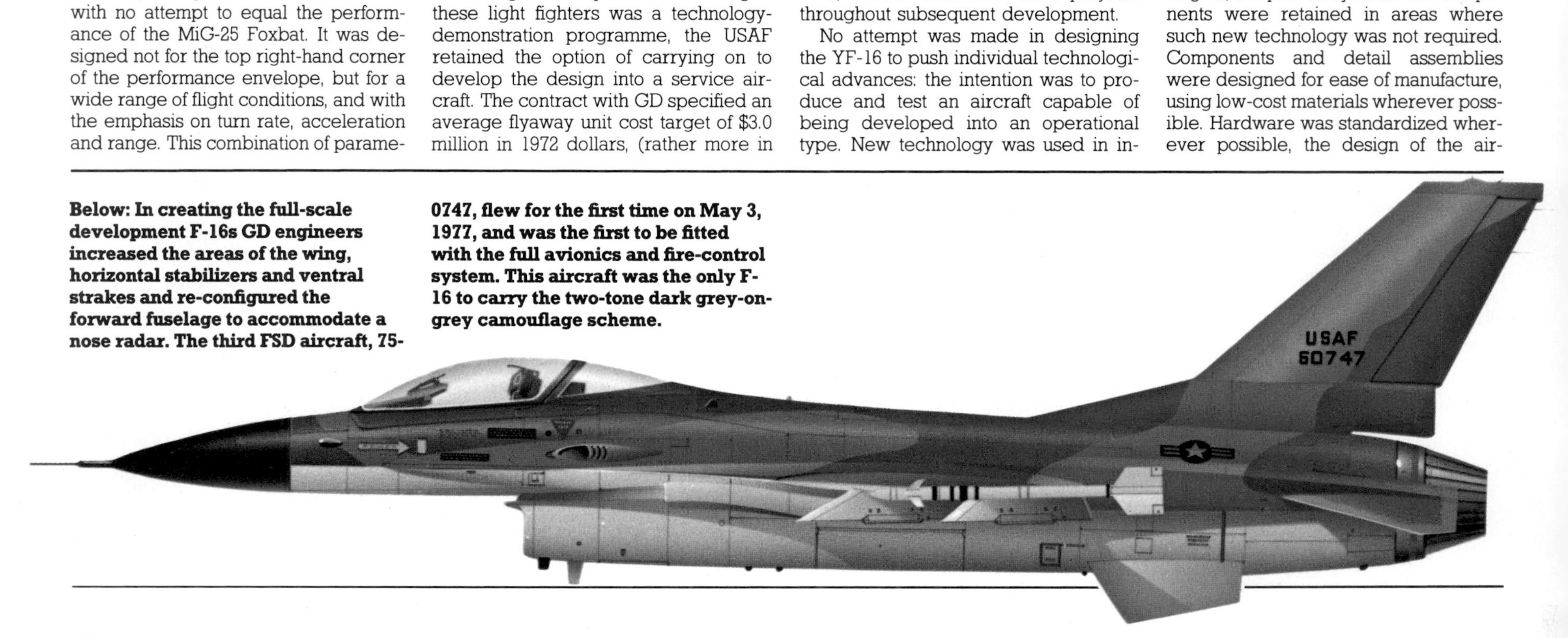

Below: In creating the full-scale development F-16s GD engineers increased the areas of the wing, horizontal stabilizers and ventral strakes and re-configured the forward fuselage to accommodate a nose radar. The third FSD aircraft, 75-0747, flew for the first time on May 3, 1977, and was the first to be fitted with the full avionics and fire-control system. This aircraft was the only F-16 to carry the two-tone dark grey-on-grey camouflage scheme.

Left: After completion at Fort Worth the first prototype was flown to Edwards Air Force Base aboard a Lockheed C-5A Galaxy transport. It was then reassembled to allow flight trials to begin. First tests were high-speed taxi runs.

Above: This head-on view of a YF-16 shows the wing leading-edge strakes and the way the wing is blended smoothly into the fuselage.

frame often incorporating multi-use parts and assemblies.

Flying advanced technology features on the YF-16 gave the USAF confidence to adopt them in a service aircraft. "If we hadn't put them in the prototype, we'd still be arguing about putting them into a production airplane", F-16 director of engineering Willian C. Dietz told the US magazine *Aviation Week & Space Technology* in 1977. Although high-technology features such as relaxed stability, fly-by-wire control, wing/body blending and strakes, variable camber and the reclining seat were used to improve F-16 performance, these were not seen as high risks in terms of production or maintenance.

Specific cost goals were set at an early stage, and careful studies were carried out to establish areas where a trade-off between cost and performance or operational capability would be acceptable.

Prototype design

Design objective of the YF-16 was to create the maximum agility and manoeuvrability in a small aircraft with minimum avionics capable of conducting air combat operations some 500nm (575 miles/926km) from its own base.

Small size not only dictated design simplicity, but brought a series of other advantages. Factors such as material, detail design and construction being equal, airframe cost is largely dependent on airframe weight, so the move towards a smaller aircraft promised lower costs. At the same time, drag was minimized, allowing a lower thrust setting to be used during aircraft cruise, and increasing the thrust-to-weight ratio possible with any given powerplant. And as experience in Vietnam had shown, the small size of the MiG-17 and MiG-21 made them difficult to detect visually, adding to the problems of aircrew engaging these types in air combat.

One factor which helped focus USAF attention on the virtues of the YF-16 and YF-17 was the Middle East War of 1973. The USAF has always fought its wars under conditions of numerical superiority, but October of that year saw a close ally struggling to win air and battlefield superiority against forces abundantly equipped along Soviet lines. The need of quantity as well as quality was brought home in a conflict in which one observer estimates that some 40 per cent of the Israeli fighter force was lost, or damaged to the point where it was not available for combat, within the first two days.

One influence on the size of the design was the likely avionics payload. While the LWF requirement specified minimal avionics, the design team recognized that an operational aircraft would probably require a heavier and bulkier payload of electronics. Accordingly, the decision was made not to size the basic aircraft to handle radar-guided missiles such as the AIM-7 Sparrow, but to assume an air-to-air armament of heat-seeking AIM-9 Sidewinder missiles plus a General Electric M61 cannon, while making provisions within the design to allow Sparrow-class missiles to be incorporated at a later date, should this be desired.

Military requirements specified a load factor of 7·33g while carrying 80 per cent internal fuel. GD decided to increase this figure to 9·0g at full internal fuel, and to increase the service life of the airframe from the normal 4,000 hours to 8,000 hours.

Accepting the fact that fighters invariably end up carrying external fuel tanks, the GD team decided to capitalize on this trend. Assuming that a YF-16 pilot would use externally-carried fuel on the outbound trip to the combat zone, then fight and return on internal fuel, the design team allocated internal fuel volume accordingly, reducing the airframe size. This move shaved 1,470lb (667kg) off the airframe empty weight, and reduced all-up weight by 3,300lb (1497kg). More importantly, turn rate could as a result be increased by five per cent, and acceleration by 30 per cent.

Before deciding on a configuration for the new aircraft, GD engineers considered the effect of 78 variables, running theoretical analyses and wind-tunnel tests. The latter testing totalled 1,272 hours, and was carried out at speeds from Mach 0·2 up to Mach 2·2, at angles of attack of up to 28deg and at yaw angles of up to 12deg. Parameters identified as having a significant influence on performance included wing sweep, camber and aerofoil section, inlet position and shape, the incorpora-

Above: Rival of the YF-16 during the USAF competitive fly-off was the Northrop YF-17. Developed from the California team's P-530 Cobra, this design featured twin vertical tail fins and was powered by two General Electric YF101 'leaky turbojet' engines.

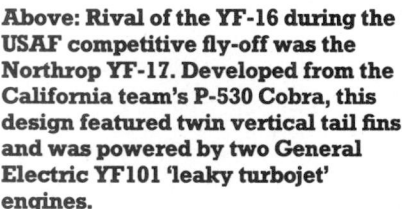

Above: Formation take-off by the first and second full-scale development aircraft. The latter sports its third paint scheme – the all-grey finish which replaced the earlier blue-on-white and red/white/blue markings. Both aircraft are fitted with instrumented nose probes.

tion of wing/fuselage blending, fore-body strakes and canards, plus the number, planform and location of the tail surfaces.

Combat priorities laid down by the LWF requirements were turning performance at Mach 1·2 (demanding low wave drag), turning performance at Mach 0·9 (demanding optimum drag-at-lift), acceleration (requiring minimal wave drag) and maximum lift at Mach 0·8/40,000ft (12,000m) (again requiring optimum drag-at-lift). These conflicting demands made the selection of a wing planform difficult. In many ways, a straight wing fitted with leading edge flaps offered the best compromise, but wave drag was high. Wave drag of a swept wing would have been better, but penalties would have been paid in terms of handling qualities and drag-at-lift.

Previous fighters from the same design stable were the delta-winged F-102 Delta Dagger and F-106 Delta Dart, and the variable-geometry F-111, but neither of these proven technologies seemed right for the new fighter. Delta wings offer high volumetric efficiency, along with low structural weight and wave drag, but suffer penalties in trim drag and drag-at-lift. Variable geometry can give optimum aerodynamic performance in all flight conditions, but imposes problems at weight and balance.

The design finally adopted traded wing loading against aspect ratio to achieve the optimum balance between the conflicting demands imposed by the turn rate and acceleration requirements. Leading-edge sweep angles of 35deg, 40deg and 45deg were tested, along with six aerofoil sections. The latter included constant thickness and camber, and designs in which these parameters were varied from root to tip. The selected design has a leading edge sweep of 40deg, an aspect ratio of 3·0 and a wing loading of 60lb/sq ft (2·53kg/sq m).

A wing of fixed camber could not have satisfied the conflicting demands of takeoff and landing, subsonic cruise, combat manoeuvring at high G levels and supersonic flight, but the use of variable camber played a major part in maintaining aircraft handling qualities and performance, particularly throughout the likely range of air combat speeds (Mach 0·8 to 1·6). It also allowed the use of a low aspect ratio and a thickness of only four per cent, factors which helped to optimize drag-at-lift and thus transonic manoeuvring.

To achieve this, the YF-16 wing was fitted with leading and trailing-edge flaps: if used throughout the flight envelope, these would help match the wing to changing Mach number and angle of attack. And instead of the slotted pattern of leading-edge flaps often used in other aircraft during takeoff and landing, the YF-16 wing incorporated a plain single-in-chord flap. Flap positions are automatically adjusted by the flight-control system.

Design similarities

At first sight, the competing GD and Northrop designs looked very different, but both made use of moderately swept wings and long root extensions. This was no coincidence, both teams having concluded that the vortexes cast by such extensions at high angles of attack would maintain a good airflow across the wing, even beyond stalling point, thus promising good handling at high angles of attack.

Another area of advanced technology in the YF-16 design was the adoption of wing-body blending. Near the root, the wing's depth is increased to the point where it blends smoothly into the fuselage. Company engineers had originally devised this technique in the late 1940s during studies of jet-powered seaplane fighters, though the definitive Convair YF2Y fighter which flew in 1953 did not in practice use wing-body blending. The technique was also used on the Douglas Skyray and Saab 35 Draken, in both cases providing sufficient internal volume for a substantial payload of fuel.

The YF-16 centre of gravity was located far enough aft to reduce longitudinal stability and increase manoeuvrability. Since lift acted ahead of the c.g., the tailplane was required to push the tail of the aircraft up rather than down in order to maintain level flight. It thus added to the lift rather than subtracting from it as on normal designs. At supersonic speeds, the centre of pressure moved aft, reducing the amount of downward force which the horizontal tail surfaces had to apply.

To 'tame' the resulting flying characteristics, the GD design team had to provide a full-time fly-by-wire stability augmentation and flight-control system to translate the pilot's control demands into movements of the aircraft control surfaces. Without the confidence gained with the YF-16, the Air Force probably would not have adopted a fly-by-wire control system in the production aircraft, a service project director stated in 1977.

In selecting an engine for the new fighter, the GD designers had to consider not only the virtues of single and twin-engined installations, but also the effects of different engine cycles (bypass ratio and pressure ratio). The most obvious candidates were a single Pratt & Whitney F100 or a pair of General Electric YF101s. The former was already under development for use in the F-15 Eagle, and its medium bypass-ratio turbofan design offered high thrust and good fuel economy.

The Fort Worth team did look into the possibility of creating a much lighter aircraft powered by a single YF101, but studies suggested that this would be unable to meet the performance requirements. This approach was in fact to

Below: In creating the production configuration (right), GD engineers slightly increased the dimensions of the original YF-16 (left), and reprofiled the nose section to accommodate the APG-66 radar. This photograph shows the second YF-16 and the first FSD aircraft.

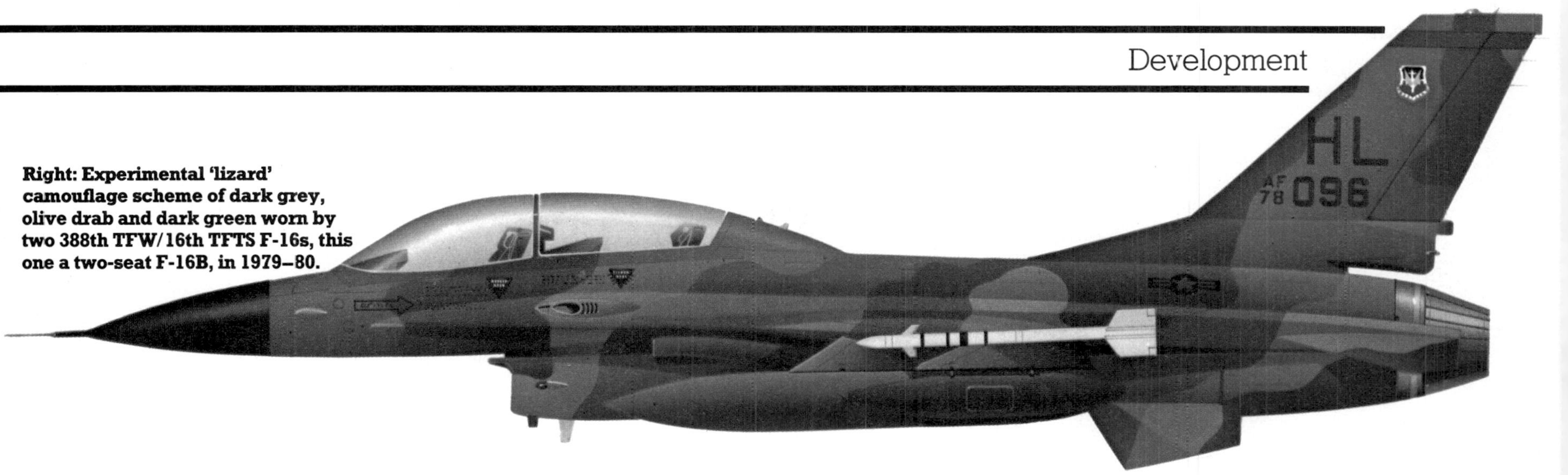

Right: Experimental 'lizard' camouflage scheme of dark grey, olive drab and dark green worn by two 388th TFW/16th TFTS F-16s, this one a two-seat F-16B, in 1979–80.

Above: The moment of liftoff as the third FSD aircraft leaves the Forth Worth runway to begin an avionics test mission. The nose radome carries the normal pattern of probe, while the small black 'teardrop' fairing immediately behind the radome is for a radar-warning receiver.

Above: Near-plan view of the third FSD aircraft during a sortie from Edwards Air Force Base. The muzzle port for the 20mm M61 cannon is a prominent feature on the port-side strake. The black-and-white film used has increased the contrast of non-standard markings.

be adopted in the late 1970s by Northrop, when the latter company set out to create what eventually became the F-20 Tigershark, but this is a 'shorter-legged' design less able to carry out long-range bombing missions.

The safety factors involved in single and twin-engine designs are more difficult to quantify. Discussing this problem in a technical paper on YF-16 development, Deputy Program Director Harry Hillaker stated "Many evaluations of accumulated accident-rate data have been made with varying conclusions. The number of variables involved in these evaluations make it impossible to arrive at a specific conclusion. I will debate, however, the argument that safety is the primary consideration in determining the desired number of engines." The merits of single versus twin-engined designs are still a subject of debate, and one which was later to play a significant rôle in persuading some nations to adopt the twin-engined F-18 Hornet rather than the GD fighter.

First flights

The first YF-16 prototype was rolled out at Forth Worth on December 13, 1973, a mere 21 months after GD received the $37·9 million contract. First flight of the YF-16 took place on January 20, 1974 at Edwards AFB – ahead of schedule and much to the surprise of GD pilot Phil Oestricher and all the technicians watching what should have been a high-speed taxi trial to check pitch and roll response.

As the aircraft gained speed and was rotated into a nose-up attitude, a diverging rolling oscillation built up. Distracted by this, and still relatively unfamiliar with the YF-16's high thrust-to-weight ratio, Oestricher allowed the speed to build up to around 150kt. Realizing that the horizontal tailplane had hit the runway, Oestricher decided that the best way of handling the problem was to get airborne. A brief six-minute circuit followed, and the YF-16 was successfully brought in to a smooth landing.

The subsequent investigation showed that the oscillation experienced during the roll down the runway had been pilot-induced, largely as a result of the gain of the flight-control system. The 'fix' was simple – the gain was reduced by 50 per cent while the aircraft was on the ground, then automatically raised to its full value once airborne.

The official first flight followed on February 2, with Oestricher once again at the controls. The prototype was taken up to 15,000ft (4,500m) with the undercarriage extended. The gear was then retracted, the speed increased to 300–350kt and 2–3g turns carried out. The sortie lasted for 90 minutes. Three days later, Oestricher took the aircraft supersonic for the first time, reaching a top speed of Mach 1·2 and remaining supersonic for five minutes. Manoeuvres at up to 5g were also carried out during this third flight of the YF-16.

By the time that the second prototype joined the programme in May of that year, temporary flying restrictions had been placed on the type following two incidents in which the F100 turbofan had lost power. Both were traced to contamination of the fuel-control valve which had caused this component to jam at the idle position, but until the problem was cleared up the YF-16 had to remain within 'dead-stick' landing distance of the runway.

To allow spinning and spin-recovery characteristics to be safely explored, along with handling at high angles of attack, a 0·3-scale flying model was flown at Edwards AFB in 1975. Built from glass fibre with an aluminium sub-structure, this was 14ft (4·27m) long, had an 8ft 9in (2·67m) wingspan and was stressed to handle loads of up to 5·5g.

Below: Delivered in November 1977, FSD aircraft No 5 was initially used to explore aircraft handling qualities. It was later assigned to Eglin Air Force Base in Florida to take part in Seek Eagle – a USAF programme to determine the limits of the F-16's weapons carrying capability.

An operational fighter

Even before the second prototype had flown, the LWF programme was no longer just a technology demonstration. In April 1974 US Defense Secretary James R. Schlesinger decided that the successful LWF contender was to be developed into an operational type designated ACF (Air Combat Fighter). As flight testing of the YF-16 and the rival YF-17 continued throughout 1974, pilots from the USAF, US Navy and US government were able to evaluate both types. Trials included air-to-air combat against the A-37B Dragonfly, F-106 Delta Dart, F-4 Phantom and MiG-21. These tests were completed by the end of 1974.

Selection of the YF-16 was announced on January 13, 1975. Secretary of the Air Force John McLucas stated that performance of the GD aircraft had been 'significantly better' during the fly-off, particularly at supersonic and near-supersonic speeds. The YF-16 had also exhibited better acceleration, endurance and turning capability.

An initial development contract awarded by the USAF covered 15 development aircraft – 11 single-seat fighters and four two-seat trainers – and was worth $417·9 million. A separate $55·5 million contract to Pratt & Whitney covered engine development.

The production aircraft was effectively a slightly scaled-up version of the prototype design. The latter had not been fitted with nose radars, and original USAF planning had assumed that the ACF design would carry a small search radar similar in peformance to the Emerson APQ-159 fitted to the Northrop F-5E. The subsequent decision to adopt a more powerful multi-mode set required an increase in nose volume, nose length being extended by 7in (17·8cm), while nose diameter was increased by 4in (10·2cm). The number of access doors on the airframe was increased in the revised design, while the number of weapon stations was increased from seven to nine.

Selection of the YF-16 ended any chance that four NATO countries – Belgium, Denmark, the Netherlands and Norway, all of which were looking to replace their F-104 Starfighters – might adopt the YF-17, although Northrop pointed out that their design had been flown with prototype engines which had clocked up less than 1,000 hours of test running. Production engines would have provided eight per cent more thrust, raising aircraft performance.

The USAF concluded that the GD aircraft outperformed the Northrop design in several areas, although the latter was superior in some respects. Around Mach 0·7, the YF-17 could outturn the YF-16, but from Mach 0·8 upwards the YF-16 was better. The GD aircraft had greater range, and was considered to be closer in standard to a production design in terms of weight, fuel capacity, and thrust-to-weight ratio.

USAF studies suggested that flyaway costs of the F-16 would be some six to seven per cent lower than those of the F-17, and that savings could also be anticipated in development and operation. Engine choice was not a factor in the selection, but the twin-engined design would have consumed 20 per cent more fuel, an important factor as the price of oil continued to rise following the 1973 Middle East War.

US Navy interest

In the meantime, the GD aircraft remained a contender for the US Navy's contemporary NACF (Navy Air Combat Fighter) programme to replace the F-4 Phantom and A-7 Corsair. One configuration proposed by the Fort Worth team was a single-seat design using the fuselage of the two-seat trainer in order to obtain more internal volume for avionics or fuel. The YF-16 had 18cu ft (0·51cu m) of volume for internal avionics, a figure which was reduced in practice to 12·8cu ft (0·36cu m) by the installation of flight test avionics. The new proposal would have provided up to 25cu ft (0·71cu m) of space.

Above: An international quartet poses on a snow-cleared taxiway – production F-16s in the markings of Norway (bottom left), Netherlands (upper left), Belgium (upper right) and Denmark (bottom right). All are two-seat F-16B versions.

The four NATO nations sent a delegation to the US in May 1974 to discuss possible LWF procurement. At that time the USAF were thinking of ordering 650 fighters, with the US Navy taking a further 800 examples. Selection of the USAF's new fighter was not scheduled until May 1975, but the European air arms wanted a decision by the end of September 1974.

This date was impossible to attain, but the deadline for USAF source selection was brought forward to January 1975 by speeding up the flight test programme. Flight refuelling was used to extend the duration of individual flight-test sorties, while the programme was revamped to avoid unnecessary duplication of flight test conditions. Instead of the two and half years normally required to complete Category 3 flight testing on a new aircraft, the YF-16 and -17 tests were completed in sufficient detail to allow source selection in January 1975, barely a year after first flight. At this point the US Navy, considering that it did not have sufficient data to make a choice, quit the LWF programme to continue its own studies of both aircraft.

Meanwhile the deadline for submission of proposals to the NATO Governments had been extended to January 1975 at the request of the US. The formal F-16 proposal was submitted on January 14, a day after the Swedish proposal (for the SAAB-Scania 37E Viggen) and a day ahead of the French (for the M53 turbofan-powered Dassault-Breguet Mirage F.1E).

The formal decision to adopt the F-16 came as no surprise when announced on June 7, 1975, although many observers noted that Belgium planned to deploy 102 aircraft rather than the anticipated 116. The resulting cost savings were intended to be invested in research and development work directed towards a new West European combat aircraft.

F-16 production

In developing the F-16 from the YF-16, changes were kept to a minimum. Fuselage length was extended by 10in (25·4cm), while the wing area was increased by 20sq ft (1·85sq m), and fitted with two additional hard points. The horizontal tailplane was increased in size, and a jet starter was added to the F100 turbofan.

Assembly of the first full-scale production F-16 began in December 1975, and involved GD in a major modernization of its Fort Worth plant. Since the F-111 programme, the latter (officially USAF Plant 4) had been under-utilized, and had seen no major investment or updating since the 1960s. GD initially hoped to get Department of Defense funding for the modernization needed for the F-16 programme, but the US Government had already decided that it was no longer prepared to finance capital facilities needed for military projects. The Pentagon agreed that the plant would require updating, but expected GD to finance this themselves. By the summer of 1982 the company had invested $70 million, and was planning to spend $25 million more.

In laying out the production line, GD allowed for production of up to 45 aircraft per month. By the end of 1980, production was running at 16 per month and the manufacturer estimated that the current tooling could be used to build another 23–25 per month if required.

Under the 1975 agreement, a total of 348 F-16s for the European partners were to be assembled in Europe, 184 at the Fokker plant at Schiphol in the Netherlands, and 164 by SABCA at Gosselies in Belgium. The four nations are also entitled to offsets of 10 per cent of the dollar value of each aircraft sold to the USAF, and 15 per cent on aircraft sold to other export customers.

The Memorandum of Understanding covering European purchase and co-production of the F-16 ensured that the European companies involved in the project would receive work not only on USAF aircraft but also on Fighting Falcons built for Third World operators. It also stipulated the payment to the US government of a $471,000 research and development levy on the price of each aircraft delivered to the four air arms. The latter figure includes a recoupment charge for F100 R & D.

Preliminary contracts for the F-16 were placed in 1975 with European industry. It is impractical to detail all the suppliers in a programme of this mag-

Left: Demonstration flight by two brand new F-16As of the USAF. In the clean configuration shown here the aircraft could easily outfly the MiG-21 and could probably cope with the new MiG-29 Fulcrum. These particular Fighting Falcons were delivered in April 1980.

Above: F-16s on the final assembly line at Fokker's Schipol plant in the Netherlands. Co-ordination and control of the multi-national assembly programme was a formidable management task comparable to that of the Apollo space programme.

nitude, but the main contracts were awarded as follows.

Two aircraft assembly lines were set up, one at the SABCA plant at Gosselies in Belgium, where Belgian and Danish airframes are assembled, the other at the Fokker plant at Schiphol-Oost in the Netherlands. At the same time, the Belgian company SONACA – formerly Fairey SA – was reconstituted with new management and was contracted to build the aft fuselage.

Assembly of aircraft for the Netherlands and Norway is handled by Fokker, who also build the centre fuselage, the leading edge flaps, the trailing edge panel and flaperon. SABCA facilities at Gosselies and Haren in Belgium tackle the wing structure box and assembly of the complete wing. Other components such as the vertical fin box and the wing and centreline pylons are built in Denmark by Per Udsen, while the undercarriage is tackled by DAF in the Netherlands, and the wheels by Raufoss in Norway.

European assembly of the F100 engine is handled by the Belgian company Fabrique Nationale, which invested around $35 million in new test cells, machine tools and other equipment. Kongsberg builds the engine fan-drive turbine module in Norway, while Phillips in Holland is responsible for the augmentor nozzle module.

Contracts for avionics are widely scattered throughout the four nations. MBLE (Belgium) has overall responsibility for the APG-66 radar, while Signaal and Oldelft (Netherlands) are responsible for the radar antennae and HUDs respectively. Also involved in HUD work are Marconi Avionics in Britain (the original designer of the unit) and Kongsberg. Danish Industrial Group One (Neselco and LK-NES) supply the fire-control computer, the radar displays are built by Danish company Nea Linberg, and Kongsberg handles the inertial navigation system as well as its other contributions.

The creation of European F-16 production facilities was not an easy task. European industry had earlier built the Lockheed F-104G Starfighter, but the latter aircraft was not in USAF service. Since the F-16 is a front-line US warplane, and would be assembled on both sides of the Atlantic, many procedures had to be agreed, standardized and in some cases made the subject of compromise. In the early days of the YF-16 project, paperwork had been kept to a minimum in order to maintain the pace of the programme, but with the adoption of the F-16 by four NATO nations, Fighting Falcon became what is probably the most complex management task that the US Department of Defense has ever undertaken. In 1977 programme director Brigadier General James Abrahamson described the task he faced as "a management nightmare". More than 3,000 suppliers and subcontractors were involved in the international programme, and even under the 998-aircraft production run originally planned, some 20,000,000lb (9,000,000kg) of raw material and three million individual manufactured items were due to cross the Atlantic.

In an ideal world, the F-16 would not have been committed to large-scale overseas production until the design had been frozen and proven, and until the Fort Worth line had ironed out the inevitable production 'bugs'. In practice, however, the aircraft entered production on a similar timescale in both the US and Western Europe, with production facilities being planned before the design was fully refined or production techniques checked out. Not since the days of the original US ICBM programmes had such pressures been placed on project management.

Project management

Since the programme involved contractors in five nations, it was essential to set up procedures under which proposed changes to the design could be jointly discussed and agreed, so that a common standard of hardware would be produced by all of the nations involved. Before components and aircraft could be built, technical standards, acceptance procedures, working practices and even accounting methods had to be jointly agreed. In some cases fundamental differences in procedure and outlook were uncovered.

The US aerospace worker is mobile in outlook, and will tend to 'follow the contracts', working for whatever company needs his services. Two-shift production working is common on large programmes, maintaining production speed and helping to amortize the cost of expensive tooling. In Western Europe, staff are less mobile, with companies placing greater emphasis on long-term workload, and providing greater job security for their employees. Single-shift working is normal, and expensive overtime often frowned upon. It is not uncommon for aerospace plants to shut down completely for anything up to a month during the holiday period.

Such practices may be thought desirable in Europe, but they penalized the performance of the many non-US F-16 contractors. In 1977 it was estimated that European co-production would add over a million dollars to the cost of each F-16 purchased by the NATO air arms. A penalty was also paid in terms of time. As production began, GD estimated the lead time on its Fort Worth line as 24 months, while in the case of the European assembly lines, this rose to 36 months.

In both cases, the end result was increased cost. Unit flyaway price of a USAF F-16 was originally set at $4·55 million in 1975 dollars. The price tag agreed for the NATO aircraft was $6·09 million. Part of this increase was due to R&D levy of $470,000 per aircraft, but the remainder was a reflection of the increased tooling costs and longer lead times.

Methods by which US aerospace suppliers added fixed charges to production costs in order to recover administration and other overhead costs had all been devised to cope with production carried out mostly in the US by US companies. In instances where raw parts might be fabricated in the US, shipped to Europe for finishing, then returned to the US for incorporation within USAF aircraft, normal procedures became distinctly cumbersome.

Above: F-16 centre-fuselage sections on the production line at Fokker's Ypenburg plant in the Netherlands. These sections show how wing/body blending was used by GD engineers in creating the F-16. The central tunnel houses the F100 turbofan.

European co-production

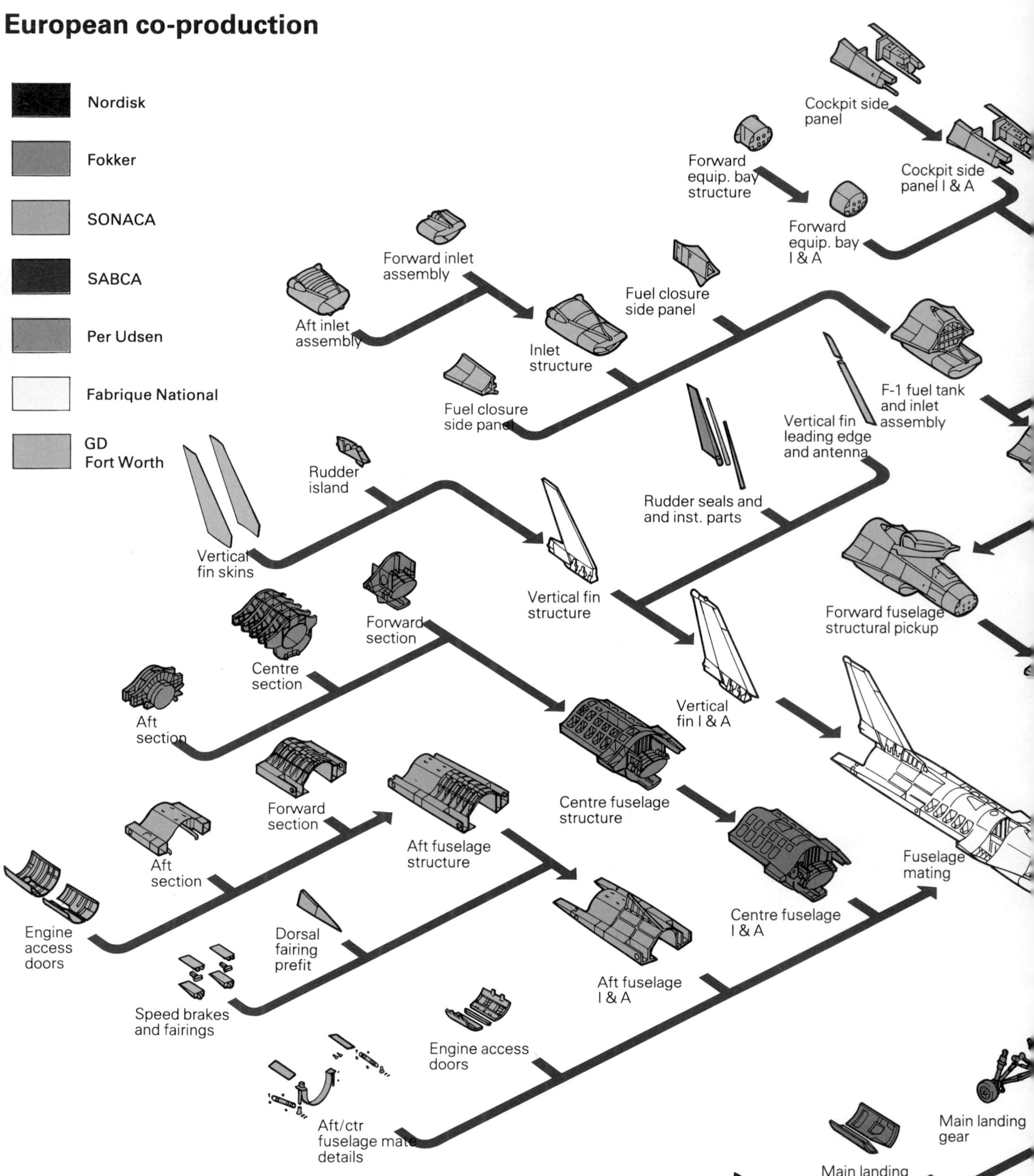

Bookkeeping was further complicated by the fact that US procurement procedures dictate that the financial records of companies supplying defence hardware be officially audited, but the European companies involved in F-16 assembly were, not unnaturally, reluctant to allow the US government access to detailed financial data. A compromise was devised under which the individual companies were checked by auditors from their own national governments.

Late in 1976, the smooth running of the programme was disrupted when the USAF decided to standardize on the McDonnell Douglas ACES 11 ejection seat without fully consulting the West Europeans.

The NATO air arms requested a total of 18 changes to the F-16. Seven were subsequently cancelled, six were adopted by all five operators and decisions on five more were deferred. These NATO requests added useful facilities to the aircraft, including:

* improvements to the radar to suppress the effects of sea clutter, and to allow a radar image to be 'frozen' on the display
* navigation update capability
* an altitude-hold facility in the aircraft autopilot
* installation of a radar electro-optical video recorder
* improved anti-corrosion treatment

Despite such problems, and the inevitable political haggling over the distribution of offset work, the programme flowed smoothly during the second half of the 1970s. First European co-production contracts were formally signed in July 1976, and the following October saw the first full-scale development aircraft rolled out at Forth Worth, with the first flight following in December.

Full-scale production

The third full-scale development aircraft was used for avionics testing. The radar was delivered two months later, but came with an unexpected bonus – it incorporated a more advanced standard of hardware and software than had been planned – and did not affect the timescale of avionics flight testing.

At the start of 1977 the USAF announced plans to purchase an additional 738 aircraft. Formal authority for full-scale production was given the following October, two months after the first two-seat F-16B flew.

By February 1978 the Belgian production line had opened, followed by the Dutch line in April. The first F-16 to be delivered to Europe arrived at Gosselies on June 9, 1978, having crossed the Atlantic aboard a USAF C-5 Galaxy. It was used for assembly tests at the SABCA plant. The following month, the first European-built F-16 components – a set of wings – were fitted to a USAF aircraft on the Fort Worth line. The two-way flow of components across the Atlantic had become a reality.

Meanwhile, in the spring of 1978, the US General Accounting Office published a report on the F-16 which drew attention to a number of development problems, including engine malfunctions, structural cracks, minor problems with the radar, and instability at high angles of attack. The report called for the review of the programme and the likely threats which the aircraft would face in service, but pointed out that the problems met to date '. . . do not seem to be any more severe than those previously experienced in other major systems. And experience with the systems shows that these problems are resolved over time'.

This report attracted some unfavourable publicity for the type, with several knocking reports appearing in print and on TV, but these overlooked the fact that the GAO was to some degree reporting past history. Fixes to many problems were already at hand.

First flight of a production aircraft from the Fort Worth line took place in August 1978, with the maiden flight of a European F-16 following on December 11, 1978, from Gosselies. This was a two-seat F-16B, and was flown by Neil Anderson and Serge Martin, the latter having spent two weeks on familiarization training at Forth Worth prior to the historic sortie.

Deliveries to the user air arms started in January 1979 when aircraft were delivered from US and European production lines to the 388th TFW at Hill AFB, Utah, and to the FAéB (Force Aérienne Belge, or Belgian Air Force) respectively. In May the first Fokker-built aircraft flew, and four US aircraft completed a four-month series of tests in Europe. A month later the KLu (Koninklijke Luchtmacht, or Royal Netherlands Air Force) accepted its first F-16s, and in January 1980 deliveries began to the air arms of Denmark, Norway and Israel.

By the end of 1979, the unit flyaway cost of the F-16A was $10·2 million. In numerical terms this may have been far above the $3·0 million originally envisaged back in 1972, but in 1975 dollars was around $4·7 million – well below the USAF 1975 target price of $5·0 million.

Until 1980, the F-16 lacked a name. The unofficial use of 'Falcon' resulted in objections by Dassault-Breguet who already used the name for their range of business jets. At a time when the USAF was re-using Second World War nomenclature, the F-16's high performance, long range, bubble canopy and ventral air inlet suggested 'Mustang II' to may observers, but this had been pre-empted by an automobile manufac-

Right: The second European F-16 assembly line is at the SABCA plant at Gosselies, Belgium. Deliveries to the air arms of Belgium and Denmark started in January 1979.

Below: This flow chart shows the principal structural assemblies of European-built F-16s and identifies the major suppliers. The use of European and American components in aircraft built on both sides of the Atlantic involved an immense administrative effort, and European industrial practices were largely responsible for each locally-built NATO aircraft costing a million dollars more than the USAF equivalent. I & A indicates Integration and Assembly.

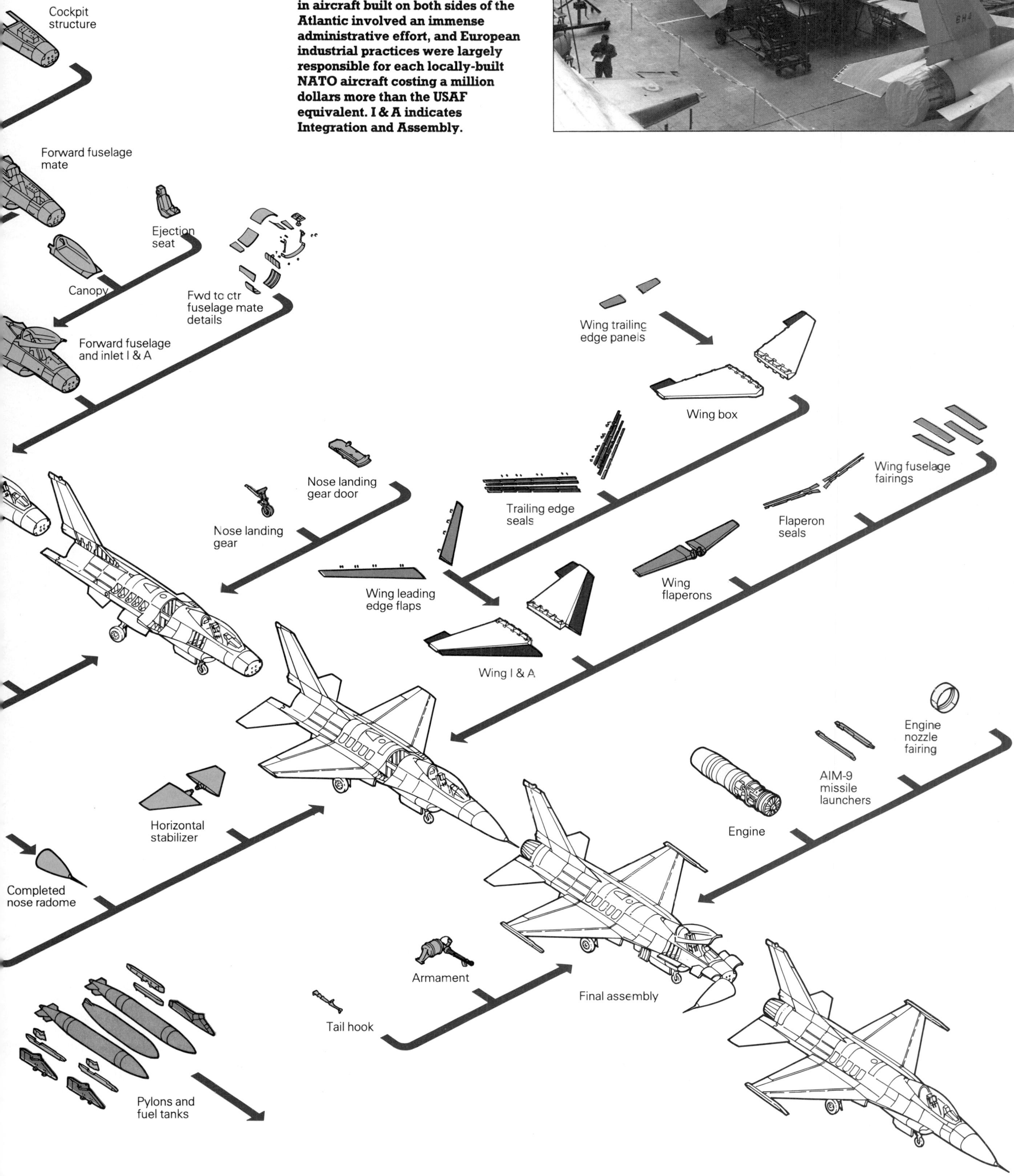

turer. Final choice, made in 1980, was the unimaginative 'Fighting Falcon'.

First phase of the F-16 Operational Test and Evaluation programme was carried out at Hill AFB, Utah, but this was followed by international trials. Nine aircraft took part in the MOTE (Multinational Operational Test & Evaluation) programme, including two from the Belgian and Netherland Air Forces. Six aircraft, plus one of the two reserves and more than 120 personnel, spent six weeks in each of the participating nations during the second half of 1980, so that operating experience could be built up.

The F-16/79 export fighter
In the first weeks of 1980 a new shape was given to future US fighter exports when President Carter reversed his 1977 decision that the development of military aircraft specifically for the export market would not be allowed. The guidelines laid down for the proposed FX export fighter called for performance and cost to be between those of the F-5E and the F-16A.

Designs were to be multirole, but optimized for air-to-air combat and with deliberately restricted strike capability. Payload/range performance had to be clearly inferior to that of current front-line types, but deployment and maintenance had to be easier, and the new fighters must not be easily upgradable without US permission. Finally, development of FX fighters was to be a commercial undertaking by the companies concerned, who had to accept all marketing and financial risks. The two obvious candidates were GD with a downrated derivative of the F-16, and Northrop with its new F-5G single-engined member of the Freedom Fighter/Tiger II family.

In order to create the resulting F-16/79 prototype, GD acquired a two-seat F-16B from the USAF in June 1980. The aircraft supplied was 75-0752, one of the original pair of full-scale development F-16Bs. General Electric created a new J79-GE-17X version of this, well-proven single-shaft engine specifically for the project, modifying it to match the F-16 airframe and to give a useful amount of extra thrust.

To keep airframe modifications to a minimum, the J79 installation locates the front face of the engine compressor in a similar location to that of the compressor face in the F100-powered aircraft. Since the GE engine is 18in (46cm) longer than the F100, the rear fuselage has had to be extended aft of the taileron pivot point by an equivalent amount.

The GE turbojet requires a lower airflow than the F100, so GD devised a new pattern of intake. The standard intake had been designed as a single removable component, which made substitution of the new version an easy job. The new unit looks externally similar to the original, but the upper surface extends much further forward, making an easy recognition feature. This new intake incorporates a fixed compression ramp in its roof, and a bypass valve designed to supply a flow of cooling air to the engine bay.

A steel heat shield weighing almost 2,000lb (900kg) surrounds most of the length of the new engine, and accounts for most of the increased structural weight of the new version. This protects the structure of the aft fuselage from the high level of heat generated by the turbojet. Being a turbofan, the F100 passes relatively cool air from the fan along a duct just below the outer casing, consequently radiating less heat.

Private venture
Like the rival Northrop F-20, the F-16/79 was developed as a private venture. Total cost of construction and flight test – some $18 million according to a GD estimate – was shared by the airframe and engine manufacturers. Unit flyaway cost was $8·0 million in 1980 prices.

Being only a minimal change from the standard aircraft, the F-16/79 required no new fatigue or other structural testing, and its assembly could be fitted easily into the normal Fort Worth line. Single and two-seat F-16/79 models were planned, and GD intended to begin deliveries to a customer two years after signing the letter of authorization.

The conversion task was quickly accomplished, and the single F-16/79 prototype flew for the first time on October 29, 1980. By early June of the following year it had clocked up a total of 122 flying hours in 131 sorties, demonstrating a top speed of Mach 2·0 and and altitude of 50,000ft (15,000m) along with 9g manoeuvres. The first flights were naturally for trials purposes, but evaluation flights followed, and by July 1981 28 pilots had flown the aircraft. These included GD personnel and pilots from the USAF, USN and three foreign air forces.

The formal US Department of Defense policy on FX was spelled out in the autumn of 1982, days before Northrop rolled out the F-20 prototype, in a letter from Deputy Defense Secretary Frank Carlucci to Air Force Secretary Verne Orr and Navy Secretary John Lehman. "There are several friends and

allies that are now, or soon will be, engaged in the process of modernizing their respective tactical air forces. Only a few can afford first-line fighters, and because of fiscal and other restraints it is important that the United States has alternatives to front-line aircraft available for export.

"The alternative is the FX either as a stand-alone capability or as an element of lo/hi mix. It is clearly in the US national security interest to have our friends and allies equipped with systems that will still be militarily capable in the late 1980s and into the 1990s.

"For this reason, we must selectively but actively encourage the foreign procurement of the FX, not leave this marketing effort just to the manufacturers. Wherever possible and appropriate, your departments will encourage representatives of foreign governments and defence establishments to include the FX in their aircraft modernization plans."

Countries identified as potential FX customers are Bahrain, Egypt, Indonesia, Jordan, Malaysia, Oman, Philippines, Saudi Arabia, Thailand, Turkey and United Arab Emirates. Sales of FX will also be promoted in South America. GD salesmen predicted that up to 20 air arms were potential customers for the F-16/79 and that as many as 1,000 aircraft might be built. Nations briefed on the F-16/79 included Austria, Jordan, Malaysia, Nigeria, Singapore, Taiwan and Thailand.

Austria seemed the most likely launch customer when that nation tested the GD aircraft and the rival Dassault-Breguet Mirage 50 in December 1980. Since the single prototype was unlikely to be available for an overseas sales tour so soon after first flight, GD drew up plans to lease an F-16A from the USAF.

Above: Even if the tail markings had been omitted, the extended jet pipe and modified inlets on this two-seater would identify it as an F-16/79.

Right: The F-16/79 was developed as an FX-class export fighter, but it remains to be seen whether potential customers will be prepared to accept this deliberately-downgraded design when others are being offered the standard F100-powered aircraft.

Above: First Fighting Falcon to use the General Electric F110 turbofan (formerly the F101 Derivative Fighter Engine) was the F-16/101. The F110 was developed from the F101 powerplant of the B-1 bomber.

The F-16/101

While the F-16/79 was taking part in a highly-publicized test programme, GD was also testing a second re-engined version of the Fighting Falcon. On December 19, 1980, GD flew the first F-16 to be powered by the General Electric F110 turbofan. Originally known as the F101 DFE (Derivative Fighter Engine), this was an experimental engine intended to maintain GE design expertise in the field of high-thrust afterburning turbofans and to be a possible new engine for the F-14 Tomcat and F-16.

F-16/101 flight testing went smoothly, all trials objectives being accomplished by May 29 of the following year in 58 sorties and 75 flying hours – 25 hours less than planned. Twelve pilots flew the aircraft during a programme of development trials which included close-support, strike and air-to-air missions. The only major incident which marred this fast-moving and successful test programme was a single dead-stick landing in January 1981 due to a fuel leak.

Staged improvements

While development of the F-16/79 was being carried out, work on other versions continued. The Fighting Falcon finally achieved Initial Operating Capability (IOC) with the USAF in November 1980, while in January 1981 349 squadron of the Belgian air force became the first F-16 unit to qualify for NATO service in Europe.

A project as large as the F-16 is certain to attract critics. The most common complaint levelled by its detractors, particularly in the earliest stages of the full-scale development programme, was that what started out as a cheap and simple lightweight fighter had grown into a complex and considerably heavier multirole design. To confuse the issue further, a second school of thought claimed that the aircraft and its systems were too simple, and that the Fighting Falcon would have difficulty in operating effectively in Western Europe's often-foul weather.

Simple day fighters of the type originally conceived by the 1972 Lightweight Fighter programme do have a useful operational role, but almost certainly not on NATO's Central Front. The general trend of USAF thinking has been that future version of the F-16 would need more sophisticated systems in order to fight and survive in any 1980s conflict. To create and phase in such new equipment with a minimum of disruption to the Fighting Falcon production programme, the USAF and its NATO allies have devised the Multinational Staged Improvement Programme (MSIP). This will add improvements in a gradual manner.

The first MSIP Phase 1 aircraft was USAF aircraft no 330, which entered final assembly in the summer of 1981. The NATO consortium introduced the same build standard early in 1982.

Also known as F-16+, the MSIP Phase 1 standard incorporates Engineering Change Proposal 0350, which adds the structural changes and new wiring required by beyond-visual range (BVR) AMRAAM missiles, electro-optical nav/attack systems, internal ECM and other new avionics. A further modification, ECP 0425, involves increasing the size of the horizontal tail, in order to increase the surface's ability to cope with changes of c.g caused by heavy weapon loads. Tail surface area is increased by 30 per cent over the 49sq ft (4·55sq m) of earlier aircraft, empty weight being increased by around 200lb (90kg) as a result. The original component used a titanium pivot shaft and sub-spar, but the opportunity was taken to eliminate this expensive material for the stabilizer. This decision reflected a dramatic increase in the cost of titanium in the late 1970s following the Soviet cutback in exports of the metal.

Under the Pacer Loft programme the European F-16 fleet is being modified to match the USAF standard.

External differences

The most obvious external sign of Pacer Loft is a grey camouflage finish on the nose radome in place of the earlier black. A new pattern of canopy is physically interchangeable with those on other F-16s, but the remaining improvements are all internal. These include changes intended to cure potential minor problems detected during early service experience. Rain water had been observed accumulating at some locations within the structure, so drainage holes have been drilled in the forward fuselage area and vertical fin. Maximum takeoff weight is increased from 35,500lb (16,103kg) to 37,000lb (16,783kg), while the all-up weight for 9g manoeuvres has risen from 22,500lb (10,206kg) to 25,300lb (11.476kg).

MSIP Phase 1 prepares the aircraft for Phase 2 – the incorporation of the improved radar, LANTIRN compatible HUD, multifunction head-down CRT displays, uprated environmental control equipment and expanded 'core' avionics including a revised fire-control computer.

Aircraft to be built to this standard are designated F-16C (single seat) and F-16D (two-seat). Target-acquisition and lock-on performance of the APG-66 is improved, and a new movable control stick replaces the earlier unit. If the pilot attempts to fly the aircraft close to the allowable aerodynamic limits, an audible warning is given in his headset.

Two new items of avionics are a data recorder incorporated in the ejection seat in an attempt to ensure that flight-system data survive an accident, and a ground-test panel which checks that secondary power for the flight-control system is available.

Test-flying of some items of the new avionics due to be introduced under MSIP Phase 2 started in 1982. The first Phase 2 aircraft should be assembled on the Fort Worth line in the summer of 1984 and is due to be delivered in July of that year. Production deliveries could start in the following December or early in 1985.

Total cost of F-16C/D all-weather development has reached $5,800 million – two and a half times the previously projected $2,300 million. In order to save money, the first 350 F-16s are not to be updated with MSIP modifications.

MSIP Phase 3 may follow shortly behind Phase 2, depending on the timescale of the new systems. These will include the LANTIRN pods, 30mm gun pod and the Seek Talk secure voice system. Final modifications such as the ASPJ jammer and AMRAAM missile will not enter service until 1985 or later.

While plans for such future versions were being drawn up, the US and European lines continued to deliver the F-16A/B models in ever-growing numbers. In June 1982 the 200th European aircraft was delivered, and the 750th Fighting Falcon to be built was handed over in the following month. Another month brought delivery of the 800th example, and by the end of the year total flying hours of the F-16 had passed the 275,000 mark. By the spring of 1982, the USAF was predicting a total F-16 buy of 2,333 F-16s, having announced

USAF F-16 improvement plan

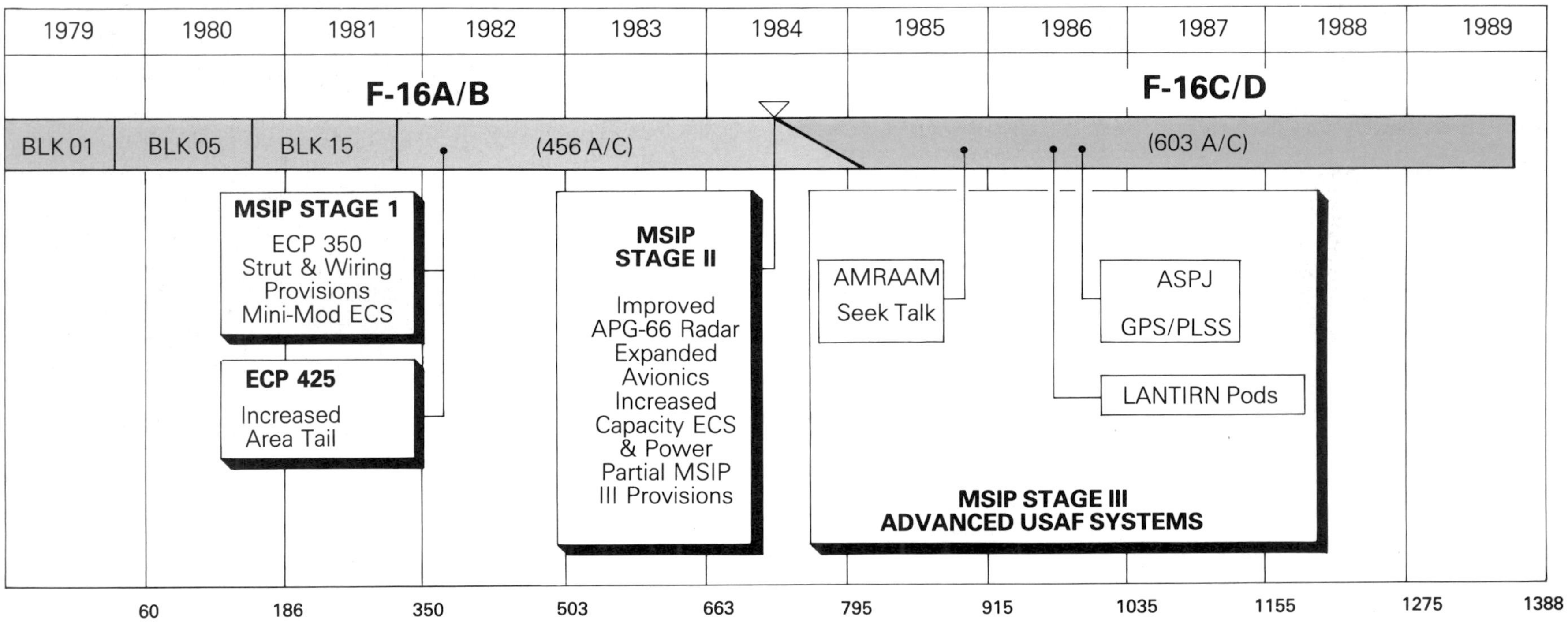

plans to buy an additional 945, including 597 enhanced derivative versions.

US military procurement is traditionally handled year-by-year, but the F-16 is one of the few aircraft being purchased under multi-year production plans. This results in real savings to the customer since the manufacturer has the confidence to negotiate with suppliers and subcontractors for larger quantities of components and materials, and to procure long lead-time items for aircraft to be built in the later stages of the contract. When this scheme was mooted in 1982, GD pointed out that 120 aircraft could be delivered per year under a multi-year contract for the level of funding which would pay for only 96 under annual procurement methods.

The 1984 US defence budget allocates a total of $2,300 million to F-16 procurement in 1984, and $3,200 million in 1985, which will allow production to run at 120 aircraft per year. This may seem a long way from the original concept of a 'cheap' fighter, but if spent on F-15 Eagles the same money would buy only half that number.

Right: Jet pipes of the F110-powered (left) and standard F100-powered (right) versions of the F-16.

Below: Fighting Falcon has now flown with the GE J79 turbojet, GE F110 (formerly F101 DFE) turbofan and the standard P&W F100 turbofan.

Current F-16 production delivery schedule

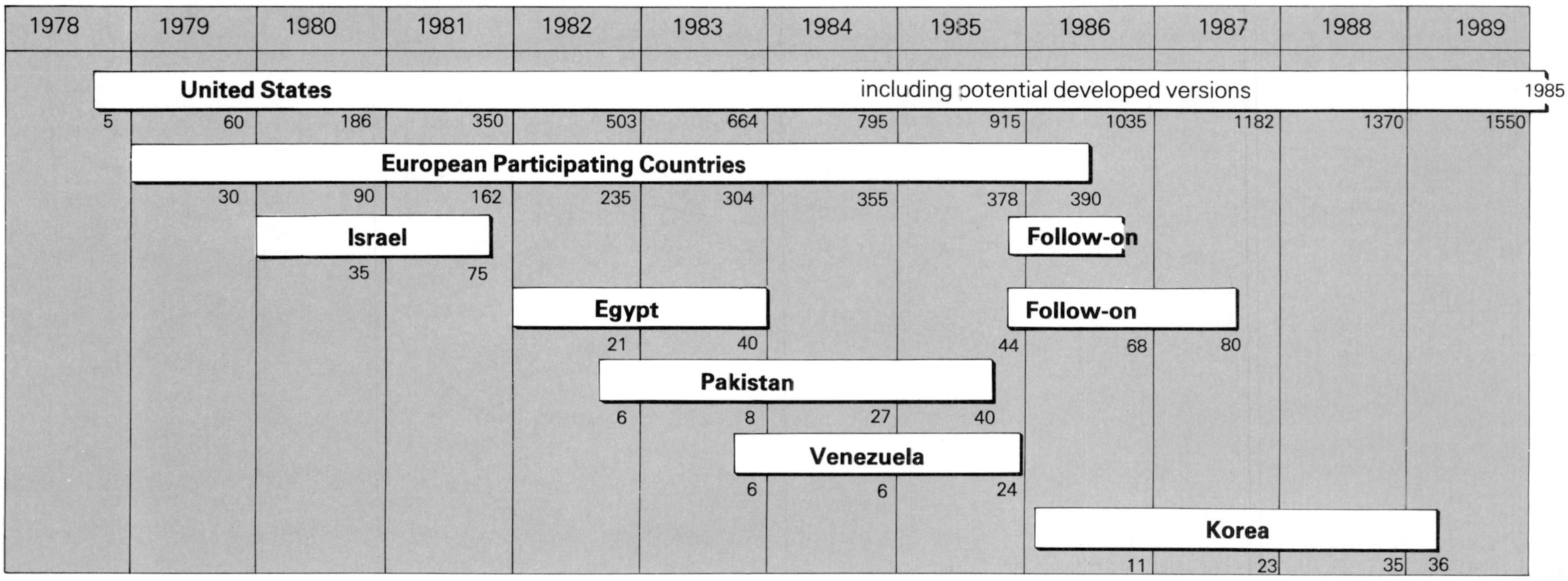

Structure

In designing the structure of the F-16, General Dynamics engineers never lost sight of the fact that the end product must be easy to produce. Wherever possible, the attractions of advanced constructional methods such as chemical milling and exotic materials such as titanium and carbon-fibre composites were rejected. Without compromising the performance of the aircraft, the GD team created hardware which would eventually be assembled on three production lines by Belgian, Dutch and US workers, using components built to a common standard by sub-contractors on both sides of the Atlantic.

Above: Production aircraft on the Fort Worth assembly line. At this stage the canopy and radome still have protective coverings.

Fighting Falcon may be a high-performance aircraft of advanced aerodynamic form, but in designing its structure the GD engineers eschewed wherever possible sophisticated constructional techniques and materials. The USAF wanted an inexpensive fighter, so a modularized and simplified structural design was adopted.

Despite the aircraft's high performance, some 80 per cent of the structure is manufactured from aluminium alloy. A little less than 8 per cent is made from steel, composites account for less than 3 per cent, and titanium for a mere 1.5 per cent. Around 60 per cent of the structural parts are made from sheet metal, while less than 2 per cent require chemical milling.

The weight savings resulting from the use of advanced technology such as relaxed stability and wing/body blending are very significant, resulting in an empty weight some 1,300lb (590kg) less than would have been the case with a more conventional design. During full-scale development, GD estimated the cost of the F-16 airframe structure as $60 per lb, so this reduction in theory reduced airframe costs by around $80,000.

The development of a military aircraft is often a long saga of ever-increasing takeoff weight. This problem had dogged the F-111, the previous Fort Worth design, but in engineering the production F-16 the GD team maintained rigorous control over weight growth. Between April 1975 and January 1978 the takeoff weight increased by just over 5 per cent from 22,197lb (10,068kg) to 23,357lb (10,595kg), but more than half of this 'fat' reflected increased operational capability, producibility or maintainability.

Fatigue tests

In parallel with the flight-test programme a series of ground fatigue trials were carried out on the fifth development airframe. A test rig set up in a hangar at Fort Worth used more than 100 hydraulic rams to apply stress to an instrumented airframe, simulating the loads imposed by takeoff, landing and combat manoeuvring at up to 10g. By the summer of 1978, this airframe had clocked up more than 16,000 hours of simulated flight in the rig. These tests were carried out at a careful and deliberate pace which sometimes lagged behind schedule.

As the tests progressed, cracks developed in several structural bulkheads. News of this problem resulted in hostile comments in the media, but GD pointed out in its own defence that the cracks had occurred not in flying aircraft but on ground test specimens. If the risk of such cracks during development testing was not a real one, a company spokesman remarked to the author at the time, no-one would be willing to pay for ground structural test rigs. GD redesigned the affected components, thickening the metal, and installed metal plates to reinforce existing units.

Built up from three major sub-sections – nose/cockpit, centre and aft – the fuselage is based upon conventional frames and longerons. The forward manufacturing break point is just aft of the cockpit, while the second is located forward of the vertical fin.

Combined with advanced aerodynamics and the low sfc of the F100 turbofan, the increase in fuselage internal volume created by wing/body blending accounts for the GD fighter's impressive range performance. Some 28 per cent of the weight of a loaded F-14 is fuel, while the equivalent figure for an F-16 is 31 per cent.

Anyone who has seen an F-16 undergoing an engine change cannot help noticing the effect of wing/body blending on the aircraft's internal fuel capacity. Visiting the Fort Worth flight line in 1977, the author was shown an engineless F-16 – one of the development aircraft on the flight line was undergoing an engine change. Looking up through the tail and out through the air inlet, his first reaction was "Where do you keep the fuel?". At first sight it seemed impossible for so much kerosine to be stowed in the limited space which remained.

Wing/body blending was carried out in three dimensions. Seen from the front or rear of the aircraft, the wing gradually blends in cross section with the fuselage, making it impossible to define where the wing ends and the fuselage begins. This blending is varied lon-

Below: Belgian ground crew prepare an F-16 for flight. The avionics technician needs no steps or ladder in order to work on the radar.

gitudinally in order to 'tailor' the cross-sectional area distribution.

In planform, the wing leading edge also blends with the fuselage thanks to the leading-edge strakes. At high angles of attack, these create vortexes which maintain the energy of the boundary air layer flowing over the inner section of the wing. Wing root stalling is thus delayed, and directional stability maintained. Vortex energy also provides a measure of forebody lift, reducing the need for drag-inducing tail trim. Graphic proof of the existence of these vortexes may be seen during tight turns if local condensation results in a 'con-trail' from the strakes. At air shows, the aircraft has been flown with smoke generators whose plumes have clearly shown the trailing vortexes. And by keeping the inner-wing boundary layer energized, the strakes allowed a reduction in wing size, aspect ratio and weight – a saving of around 500lb (227kg) in structural weight.

The combination of wing/fuselage blending and variable camber resulted in several advantages, including the additional space provided in a location close to the centre of gravity for internal fuel, avionics and other systems. Without this feature, the F-16 would have been about 5ft (1.5m) longer and the structure some 570lb (259kg) heavier.

Gradually increasing thickness of the wing in the region of the wing root resulted in a stiffer wing than would have been possible with a conventional design. Stiffness was increased by the fact that the lift-increasing manoeuvring flaps allowed a smaller wing of reduced span to be used. The wing structure itself incorporates five spars and 11 ribs. Upper and lower wing skins are one-piece machined components.

Above: By early 1979 the production line in GD's mile-long assembly building was picking up speed. The aircraft nearest the camera was delivered to the USAF in May.

Aerodynamic performance

Fineness ratio of the F-16 configuration is lower than the ideal for supersonic flight, but transonic drag is minimized. In conventional designs, wing lift normally falls off at high angles of attack, but the F-16 obtains a useful amount of body lift.

The leading-edge manoeuvring flap and trailing-edge flaperon can be moved at up to 35deg/sec to match Mach number and angle of attack. Maximum speed of movement is matched to the aircraft's ability to respond to changes in pitch, so that flaps and aircraft attitude are always matched.

By shaping the wing aerofoil to match aerodynamic conditions, the moving flaps reduce drag, maintain lift at high angles of attack, improve directional stability, and minimize buffeting. The latter qualities are useful during tight turns in air combat, or while 'jinking' at low level to confuse hostile air defences. The wing is only around 1.5in (3.8cm) deep at the point where the leading-edge rotary actuator is installed, so the design of this component was a significant challenge.

In the spring of 1982 actuator failures caused the USAF temporarily to ground all F-16s which had exceeded 200 hours of operational flying – 240 of the 400 F-16s in service at that time – for inspection of the wing leading-edge flap. A routine inspection had revealed signs of excessive wear in the actuation mechanism which controls the position of the leading-edge manoeuvring flap. More than 40 aircraft required repair, the remainder being returned to service once this component had been inspected – a process which took around five man-hours per aircraft. As an interim solution pending a definitive 'fix', aircraft were re-inspected every 100 hours.

The vertical stabilizer has a multi-spar and multi-rib structure made from aluminium alloy as is the unit's top cap, but the skins are fabricated from graphite epoxy. The two ventral fins beneath the rear fuselage section are made from glass fibre. Also located under the rear fuselage is a runway arrester hook.

The original pattern of horizontal stabilizer is being replaced by a larger component under the MSIP Phase I programme, details of which are given later in this chapter. Inboard of each are the air brakes. Stowed in the horizontal position when not in use, these are of the split type, the upper and lower sections of which open through an angle of 60deg.

The main undercarriage units retract forwards into the lower fuselage, and the large doors were found to offer a good – although unconventional – mounting location for Sparrow or Sky Flash radar-guided missiles. The nose gear is located aft of the intake, so that debris or other foreign objects thrown up by the wheel will not be ingested into the engine air intake.

The location of the intake is certainly unconventional, but wind tunnel tests showed that the ventral location is subject to minimal airflow disturbance over a wide range of flight conditions and aircraft manoeuvres, since the forward fuselage tends to shelter it from the effects of aircraft manoeuvres. At an angle of attack of 25deg, for example, the air flows into the intake at an angle of only 10deg.

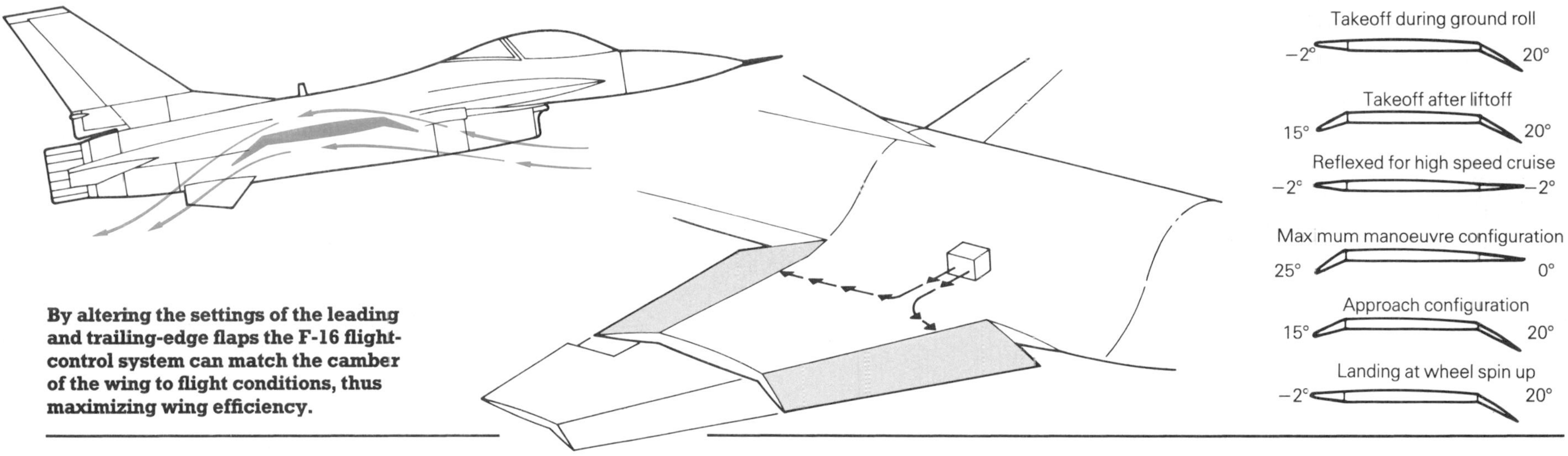

By altering the settings of the leading and trailing-edge flaps the F-16 flight-control system can match the camber of the wing to flight conditions, thus maximizing wing efficiency.

Critics who predicted in the mid-1970s that the F-16 would suffer a high incidence of engine damage due to FOD (foreign object damage) have been proved wrong. The lower edge of the intake lip is 38in (97.5cm) above the ground, high enough to minimize the chances of small objects or fragments of debris being sucked in. A study of the limited clearance between intake and runway surface on types such as the Boeing 707 (inboard engines) and 737 airliners might have suggested that all would be well, but such obvious comparisons were often overlooked during the wave of F-16 knocking carried out by some 'experts' as Europe was tooling up to build the type.

Conventional wisdom suggests that the complexities of variable geometry are mandatory in an intake for use at Mach 2. Like the creators of the earlier Saab-Scania J37 Viggen, however, the GD engineers ignored the rule book and devised a simple fixed-geometry unit incorporating a boundary-layer splitter plate. This was designed as a single assembly to make future updating easy (a feature later found useful during the development of the turbojet-powered F-16/79 variant). A more traditional variable-geometry intake assembly had been designed, but at present it seems unlikely see service.

In order to reduce the number of spare parts which F-16 units must hold, some components are designed to be interchangeable between port and starboard. These include the horizontal tail surfaces, wing flaperons, 80 per cent of the main landing gear components, and many of the actuator units.

Like any aircraft, the Fighting Falcon is only as good as its pilot. Aircrew assigned to the F-16 are housed in the most sophisticated cockpit that the technology of the early 1970s could devise. Later fighters such as the F/A-18 Hornet may have more advanced electronics, but no other aircraft in the Western world – and probably in the entire world – has the combination of reclining seat and sidestick controller used in the F-16.

Research suggested that a pilot's tolerance could be increased by the use of a reclining seat whose back was tilted at angles of up to 65deg. GD engineers compromised by adopting a tilt of 30deg and by raising the pilot's knees and legs. In terms of providing extra pilot tolerance to high-g manoeuvres the cockpit layout was probably a success, but the disadvantages of such a configuration seem to have prevented its being used in later designs. Studies carried out by other manufacturers suggest that the raised leg position markedly reduces the panel area which may be used to house displays and instruments.

Good all-round visibility is provided by a canopy whose forward and centre sections are made from a single piece of polycarbonate. An impressive item of plastics engineering, this suffered from 'teething troubles' early in its development. The transparency was required to withstand the impact of a 4lb (1.8kg) bird at 350kt, and passed initial tests with flying colours. Following some minor problems with the canopy protective coating on the YF-16, the USAF modified the latter, but the revised

General Dynamics F-16 Fighting Falcon cutaway

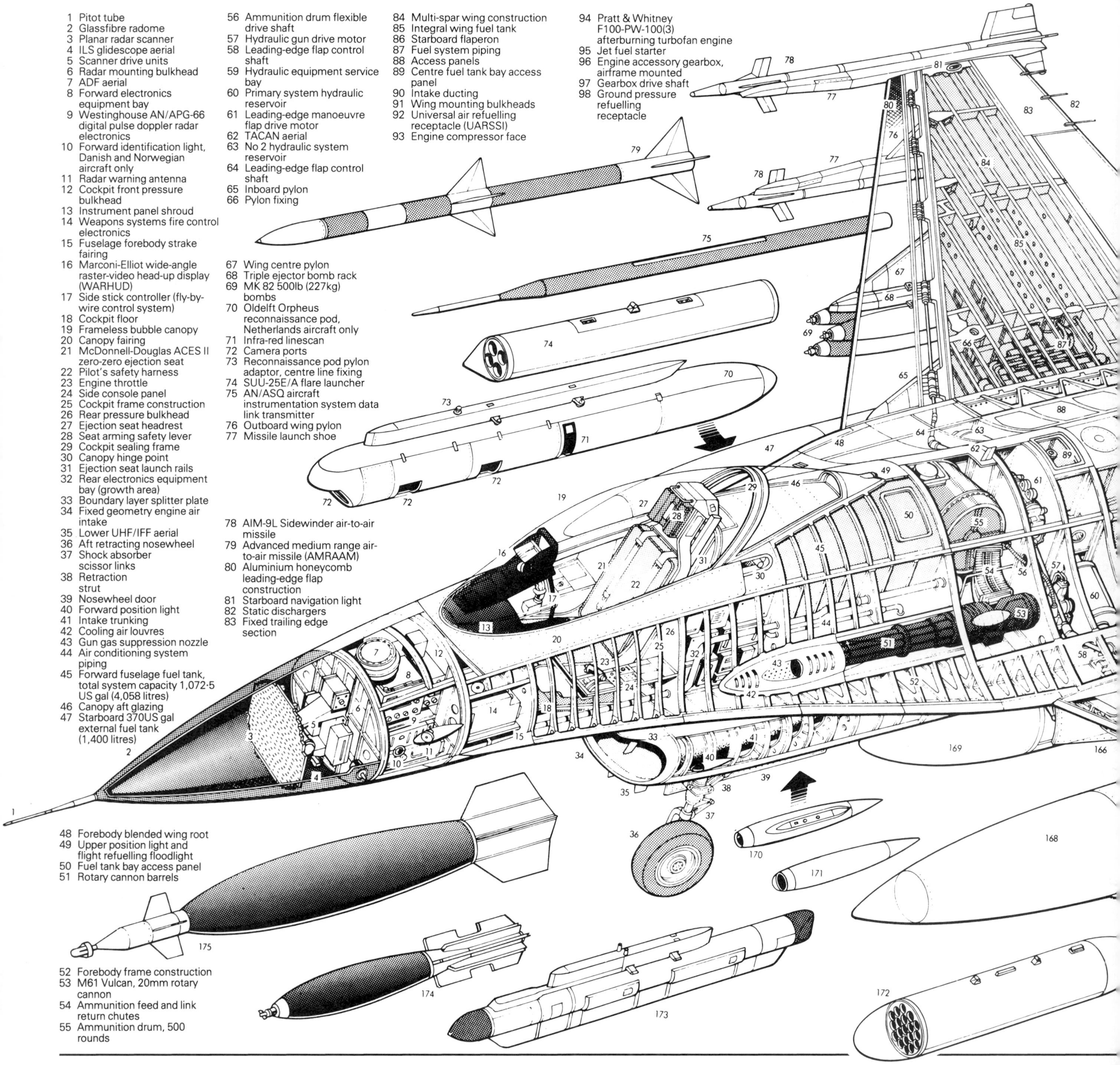

1 Pitot tube
2 Glassfibre radome
3 Planar radar scanner
4 ILS glidescope aerial
5 Scanner drive units
6 Radar mounting bulkhead
7 ADF aerial
8 Forward electronics equipment bay
9 Westinghouse AN/APG-66 digital pulse doppler radar electronics
10 Forward identification light, Danish and Norwegian aircraft only
11 Radar warning antenna
12 Cockpit front pressure bulkhead
13 Instrument panel shroud
14 Weapons systems fire control electronics
15 Fuselage forebody strake fairing
16 Marconi-Elliot wide-angle raster-video head-up display (WARHUD)
17 Side stick controller (fly-by-wire control system)
18 Cockpit floor
19 Frameless bubble canopy
20 Canopy fairing
21 McDonnell-Douglas ACES II zero-zero ejection seat
22 Pilot's safety harness
23 Engine throttle
24 Side console panel
25 Cockpit frame construction
26 Rear pressure bulkhead
27 Ejection seat headrest
28 Seat arming safety lever
29 Cockpit sealing frame
30 Canopy hinge point
31 Ejection seat launch rails
32 Rear electronics equipment bay (growth area)
33 Boundary layer splitter plate
34 Fixed geometry engine air intake
35 Lower UHF/IFF aerial
36 Aft retracting nosewheel
37 Shock absorber scissor links
38 Retraction strut
39 Nosewheel door
40 Forward position light
41 Intake trunking
42 Cooling air louvres
43 Gun gas suppression nozzle
44 Air conditioning system piping
45 Forward fuselage fuel tank, total system capacity 1,072·5 US gal (4,058 litres)
46 Canopy aft glazing
47 Starboard 370US gal external fuel tank (1,400 litres)
48 Forebody blended wing root
49 Upper position light and flight refuelling floodlight
50 Fuel tank bay access panel
51 Rotary cannon barrels
52 Forebody frame construction
53 M61 Vulcan, 20mm rotary cannon
54 Ammunition feed and link return chutes
55 Ammunition drum, 500 rounds
56 Ammunition drum flexible drive shaft
57 Hydraulic gun drive motor
58 Leading-edge flap control shaft
59 Hydraulic equipment service bay
60 Primary system hydraulic reservoir
61 Leading-edge manoeuvre flap drive motor
62 TACAN aerial
63 No 2 hydraulic system reservoir
64 Leading-edge flap control shaft
65 Inboard pylon
66 Pylon fixing
67 Wing centre pylon
68 Triple ejector bomb rack
69 MK 82 500lb (227kg) bombs
70 Oldelft Orpheus reconnaissance pod, Netherlands aircraft only
71 Infra-red linescan
72 Camera ports
73 Reconnaissance pod pylon adaptor, centre line fixing
74 SUU-25E/A flare launcher
75 AN/ASQ aircraft instrumentation system data link transmitter
76 Outboard wing pylon
77 Missile launch shoe
78 AIM-9L Sidewinder air-to-air missile
79 Advanced medium range air-to-air missile (AMRAAM)
80 Aluminium honeycomb leading-edge flap construction
81 Starboard navigation light
82 Static dischargers
83 Fixed trailing edge section
84 Multi-spar wing construction
85 Integral wing fuel tank
86 Starboard flaperon
87 Fuel system piping
88 Access panels
89 Centre fuel tank bay access panel
90 Intake ducting
91 Wing mounting bulkheads
92 Universal air refuelling receptacle (UARSSI)
93 Engine compressor face
94 Pratt & Whitney F100-PW-100(3) afterburning turbofan engine
95 Jet fuel starter
96 Engine accessory gearbox, airframe mounted
97 Gearbox drive shaft
98 Ground pressure refuelling receptacle

design promptly failed its final qualification tests.

This failure triggered off a re-examination of the canopy design and test procedures, and studies of alternative canopy designs. A newer and heavier pattern of canopy was developed in order to ensure adequate resistance to bird strikes. The final design meets all USAF requirements, and offers a level of visibility which must leave MiG-21 and Mirage III pilots drooling with envy. Its high 'bubble' profile may result in some penalty in terms of supersonic drag, but the F100 engine has more than enough thrust to cope. Visibility from the cockpit covers a full 360deg in the horizontal plane, and from 15deg down over the nose through the zenith and back to directly behind – a total of 195 deg. Sideways visibility extends down to a depression angle of 40deg. The polycarbonate is 0.5in (1.3cm) thick, but its optical quality is high, and the curved surfaces offer minimal distortion of the outside view.

Above: A technician examines the forward undercarriage leg of a Belgian Air Force F-16. Note the inlet strut for increased rigidity

The ejection seat selected for production F-16s was the McDonnell Douglas ACES II (Advanced Concept Ejection Seat) used on the F-15 Eagle. This is a rocket-powered unit with a vectored-thrust STAPAC pitch-control system. Mounted beneath the seat, STAPAC consists of a small vernier rocket motor with a thrust of 235lb (107kg) and a 0.3sec burn time. As the seat leaves the cockpit, a gas generator spins up a pitch-rate gyro. This is uncaged and the vernier motor lit. The latter normally has its thrust axis aligned with the nominal centre of gravity of the seat and its occupant: should the seat pitch forwards or backwards due to aerodynamic forces or a low or high centre of gravity, the STAPAC vernier will be vectored to apply a corrective force.

ACES II offers zero-zero performance. From a stationary aircraft parked on the ground, it will lift to a height of more than 100ft (30m) and carry rearwards by at least 50ft (15m). Built-in survival equipment includes emergency oxygen, a URT-33C radio beacon, a liferaft and a rucksack.

The Multinational Staged Improvement Plan (MSIP) approved in February 1981 brought in a series of improvements developed under Engineering Change Proposal ECP350. This included modifications to the structure and wiring of the wings to allow the carriage of AMRAAM, the provision of hardpoints on the intake sides to carry

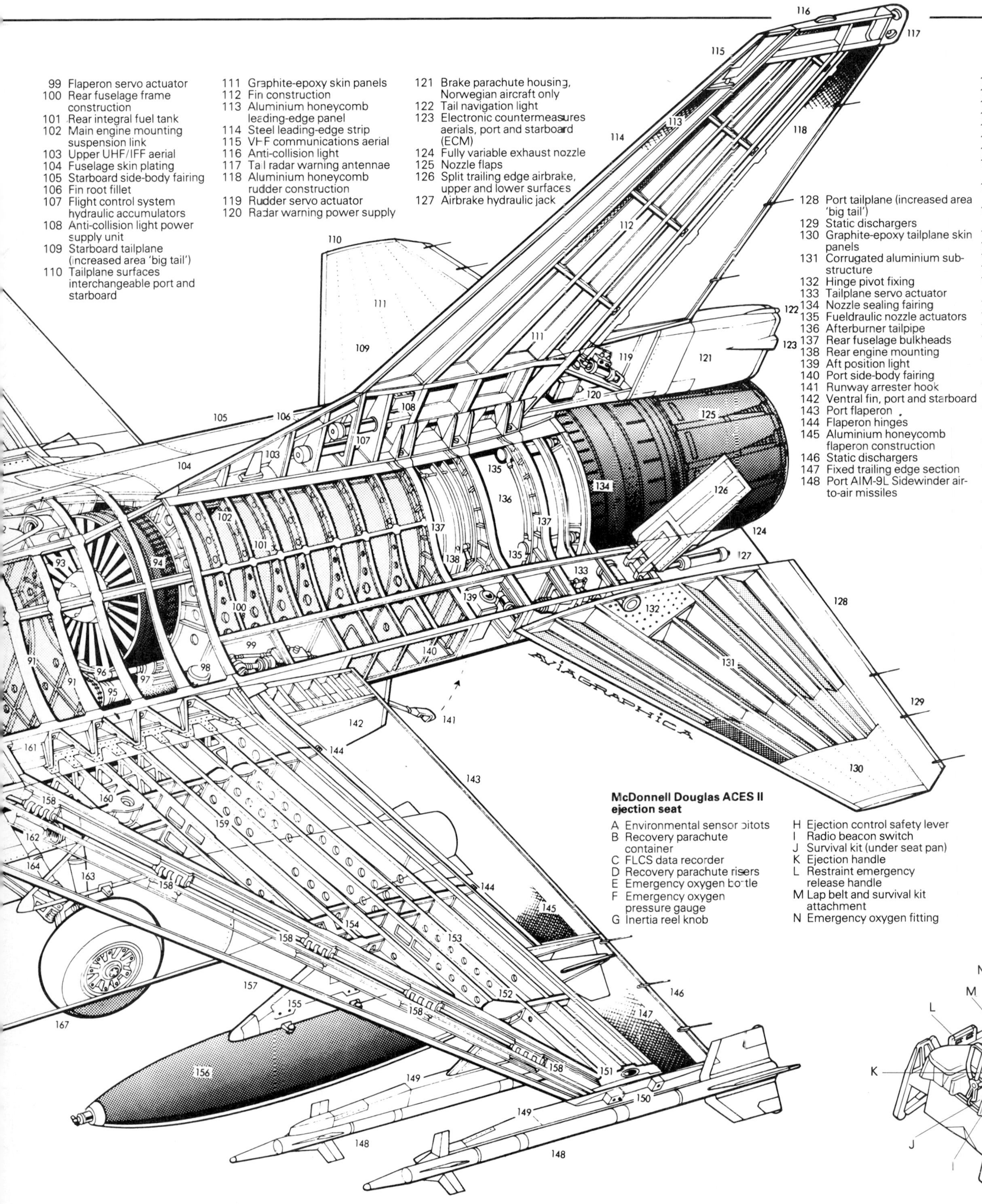

99 Flaperon servo actuator
100 Rear fuselage frame construction
101 Rear integral fuel tank
102 Main engine mounting suspension link
103 Upper UHF/IFF aerial
104 Fuselage skin plating
105 Starboard side-body fairing
106 Fin root fillet
107 Flight control system hydraulic accumulators
108 Anti-collision light power supply unit
109 Starboard tailplane (increased area 'big tail')
110 Tailplane surfaces interchangeable port and starboard
111 Graphite-epoxy skin panels
112 Fin construction
113 Aluminium honeycomb leading-edge panel
114 Steel leading-edge strip
115 VHF communications aerial
116 Anti-collision light
117 Tail radar warning antennae
118 Aluminium honeycomb rudder construction
119 Rudder servo actuator
120 Radar warning power supply
121 Brake parachute housing, Norwegian aircraft only
122 Tail navigation light
123 Electronic countermeasures aerials, port and starboard (ECM)
124 Fully variable exhaust nozzle
125 Nozzle flaps
126 Split trailing edge airbrake, upper and lower surfaces
127 Airbrake hydraulic jack
128 Port tailplane (increased area 'big tail')
129 Static dischargers
130 Graphite-epoxy tailplane skin panels
131 Corrugated aluminium sub-structure
132 Hinge pivot fixing
133 Tailplane servo actuator
134 Nozzle sealing fairing
135 Fueldraulic nozzle actuators
136 Afterburner tailpipe
137 Rear fuselage bulkheads
138 Rear engine mounting
139 Aft position light
140 Port side-body fairing
141 Runway arrester hook
142 Ventral fin, port and starboard
143 Port flaperon
144 Flaperon hinges
145 Aluminium honeycomb flaperon construction
146 Static dischargers
147 Fixed trailing edge section
148 Port AIM-9L Sidewinder air-to-air missiles
149 Missile launcher shoe
150 Wing tip launcher fixing
151 Port navigation light
152 Outboard pylon fixing rib
153 Multi-spar wing construction
154 Centre pylon attachment rib
155 Wing centre pylon
156 MK 84 2,000lb (908kg) low-drag bomb
157 Leading-edge manoeuvre flap
158 Leading-edge flap rotary actuators
159 Integral wing fuel tank
160 Inboard pylon fixing
161 Wing attachment fishplates
162 Landing/taxying lamp
163 Main undercarriage shock absorber strut
164 Mainwheel leg strut
165 Retraction strut
166 Mainwheel door
167 Forward retracting mainwheel
168 Port underwing fuel tank, 370US gal (1,700 litres)
169 Centre line external fuel tank, 300US gal (1,378 litres)
170 Electro-optical forward looking infra-red pod (EO-FLIR)
171 Laser target designator pod (LAST)
172 LAU-3/A rocket launcher, 19 × 2·75in (6,98cm) ground attack rockets
173 Westinghouse AN/ALQ119-1 electronic suppression system radar jamming pod (ESM)
174 Snakeye, 500lb (227kg) retarded bomb
175 GBU-10C/B 2,000lb (908kg) laser guided bomb

McDonnell Douglas ACES II ejection seat

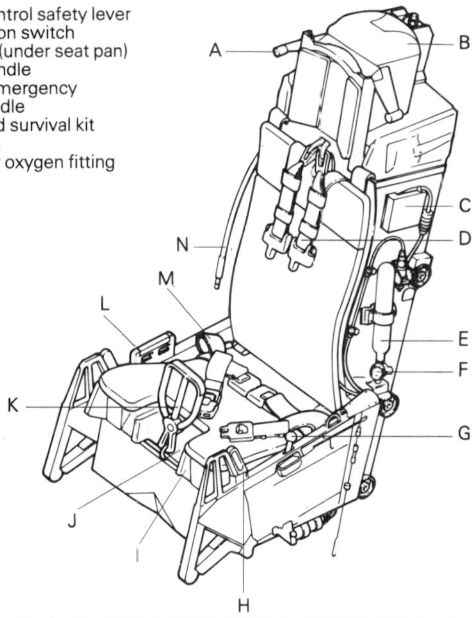

A Environmental sensor pitots
B Recovery parachute container
C FLCS data recorder
D Recovery parachute risers
E Emergency oxygen bottle
F Emergency oxygen pressure gauge
G Inertia reel knob
H Ejection control safety lever
I Radio beacon switch
J Survival kit (under seat pan)
K Ejection handle
L Restraint emergency release handle
M Lap belt and survival kit attachment
N Emergency oxygen fitting

the LANTIRN electro-optical system, and wiring and structural provisions in the cockpit for the LANTIRN HUD, head-down multi-function displays and other improved avionics.

Load capacity of the centre wing pylons rises from 2,500lb (1,135kg) to 3,500lb (1,590kg). Other modifications prepare the aircraft for the ASPJ ECM system and make provision for a radar altimeter. Control logic of the aircraft environmental control system was also modified to increase system efficiency.

MSIP I modifications

Although the USAF does not expect to take delivery of the new avionics items until the end of 1984, it programmed the associated structural and wiring modifications into the production line in 1981 under the MSIP I programme. These changes added approximately 200lb (90kg) to aircraft weight.

A new horizontal tailplane of increased area is the most obvious external evidence of the MSIP I modifications. Introduced by Engineering Change Proposal 425, this provides the greater control force required to cope with heavy munition loads. When large ordnance loads are carried, aircraft centre of gravity is moved further forward, increasing stability and making the F-16 more difficult to manoeuvre.

The revised tail is easier and less expensive to produce, since its structure does not incorporate titanium. The rising cost and poor availability of this metal led GD to redesign the tailplane spar and pivot in aluminium as part of ECP 425, resulting in a cost saving of 20 per cent. Corrugated aluminium alloy, mechanically fastened to the carbon-fibre skins, replaced the earlier filling of aluminium honeycomb, which was bonded into place. The finished stabilizer is thicker than the original component, but thanks to the increased span the thickness-to-chord ratio remains unchanged. At the same time, the need for a braking parachute led GD to modify the vertical fin to allow the fitting of this item should customers so desire.

Wherever possible, the design makes maintenance easy. Ground crew working on the F-4 Phantom had to cope with 510 individual lubrication points, 281 fuel line connections, more than 900 individual electrical connectors and 294 avionics units. In the case of Fighting Falcon, lubrication points have been cut to 84, and fuel line connections to 90, while the avionics technicians have only 52 units to deal with. The number of connectors remains high at 841, but these now incorporate silicone grommets, so are easier to service than earlier patterns of connector which were potted (sealed) with rubberized compound after assembly. As a further aid to maintenance, around 60 per cent of the surface of the aircraft is removable, the Fighting Falcon design incorporating 228 access doors. Only four tools are required to open these, and 80 per cent of the aircraft systems are accessible without stands.

Old technology

Some technology from earlier General Dynamics fighters – the Convair F-102 Delta Dagger and F-106 Delta Dart – was used in the F-16 programme. Tests have shown that a fuel tank sealant designated AF-10 Scotchweld which was used on these 1950s designs had a better performance and required less maintenance than the more modern polysulphide rubber-like compounds now in use, and offered cost savings of 25 per cent or more. During tests on F-16 centre-fuselage and aft-fuselage tanks, the older type of sealant successfully withstood the standard 5psi (0.35kg/sq cm) air-pressure test.

The most drastic structural modification which the Fighting Falcon has undergone was that imposed by the 'cranked-wing' F-16XL project, whose new delta wing uses a planform originally proposed for use on supersonic airliners. Developed in conjunction with NASA's Langley Research Centre, it is intended to offer low drag at high subsonic and supersonic speeds without losing low-speed manoeuvrability. It is of multispar delta design with a leading edge sweep angle varying from 50deg to 70deg. Area is 120 per cent greater than that of the basic wing, while wing weight rises by 2,600lb (1,179kg). Weight is reduced by the use of carbon composite materials for the upper and lower skins. Had these been made of aluminium alloy, the wing would have been some 600lb (272kg) heavier.

During the conversion work, the length of the aircraft fuselage was extended by 56in (142cm) This was accomplished by adding two new fuselage sections at the junctions between the three main fuselage sub-assemblies. One 30in (76cm) section is located at the front split point, and a 26in (66cm) section at the rear. This increase in fuselage and wing size allowed internal fuel capacity to be increased by 82 per cent. The latter factor dramatically increases the payload/range performance of the modified aircraft. The F-16XL is intended to carry twice the payload of the F-16 40 per cent further.

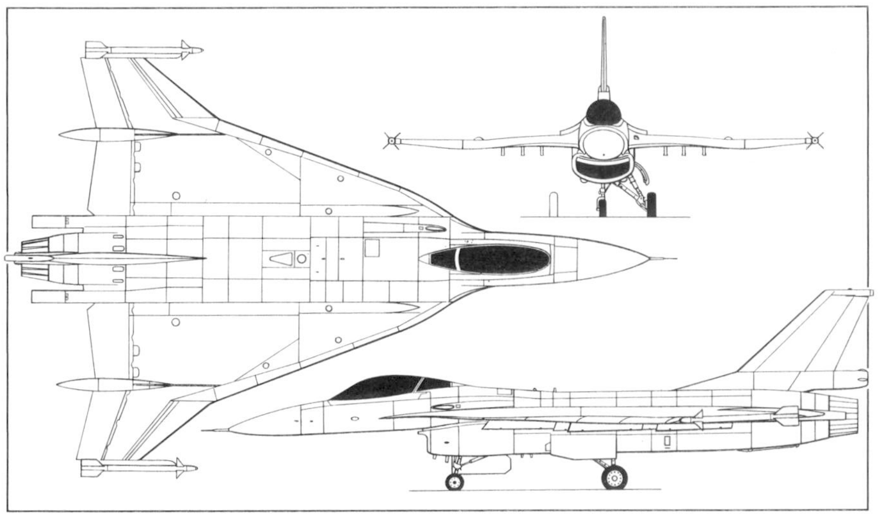

Above: Single-seat version of the F-16XL

Below: The modular design of the basic F-16 fuselage allowed new sections to be spliced in to create the longer fuselage of the F-16XL.

Below right: The first F-16XL was a single-seat aircraft powered by a P&W F100 turbofan and with a wing area increased by 120 per cent.

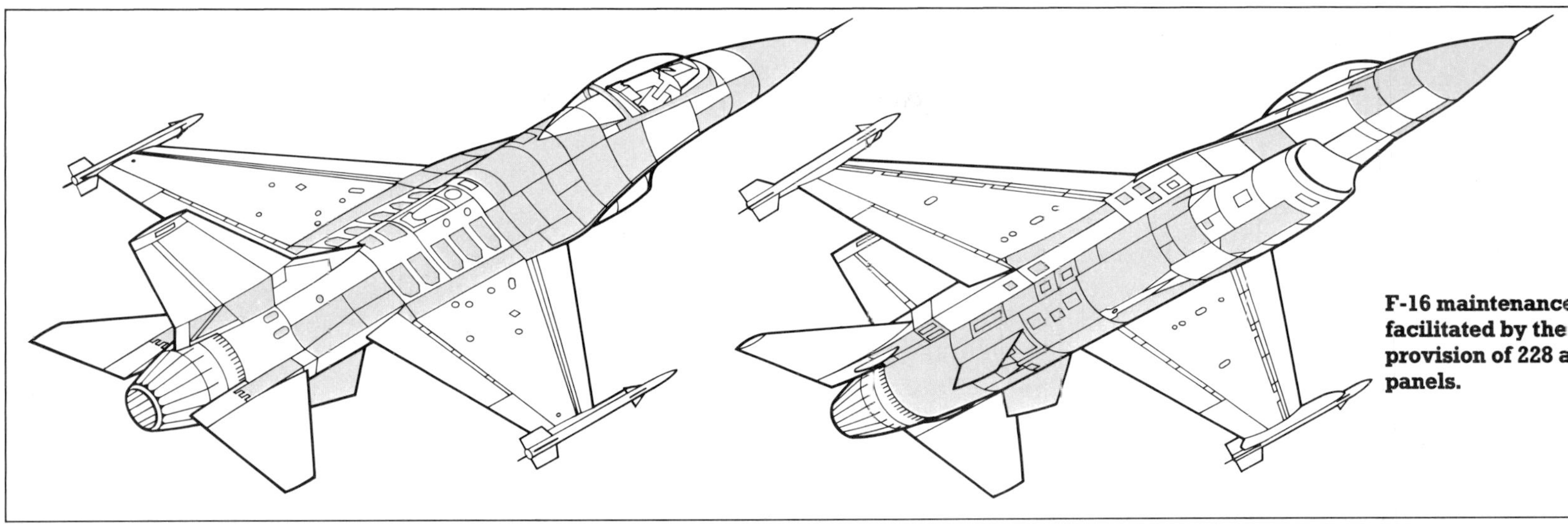

F-16 maintenance is facilitated by the provision of 228 access panels.

Above: A USAF technician removes an access panel from the wing of a 428th Tactical Fighter Squadron F-16 during Exercise Cope Elite 1981.

Right: Although the wing planforms of the F-16/79 (lower) and F-16XL are very different, the fuselage displays a high degree of commonality.

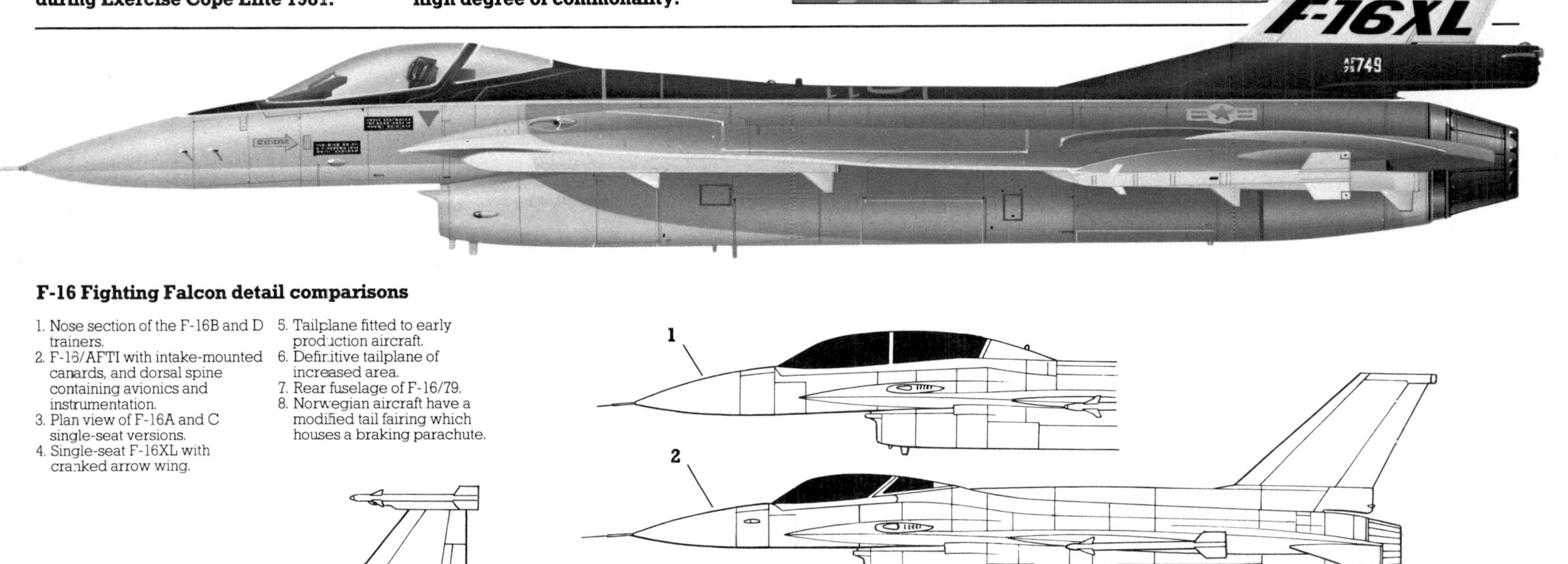

F-16 Fighting Falcon detail comparisons

1. Nose section of the F-16B and D trainers.
2. F-16/AFTI with intake-mounted canards, and dorsal spine containing avionics and instrumentation.
3. Plan view of F-16A and C single-seat versions.
4. Single-seat F-16XL with cranked arrow wing.
5. Tailplane fitted to early production aircraft.
6. Definitive tailplane of increased area.
7. Rear fuselage of F-16/79.
8. Norwegian aircraft have a modified tail fairing which houses a braking parachute.

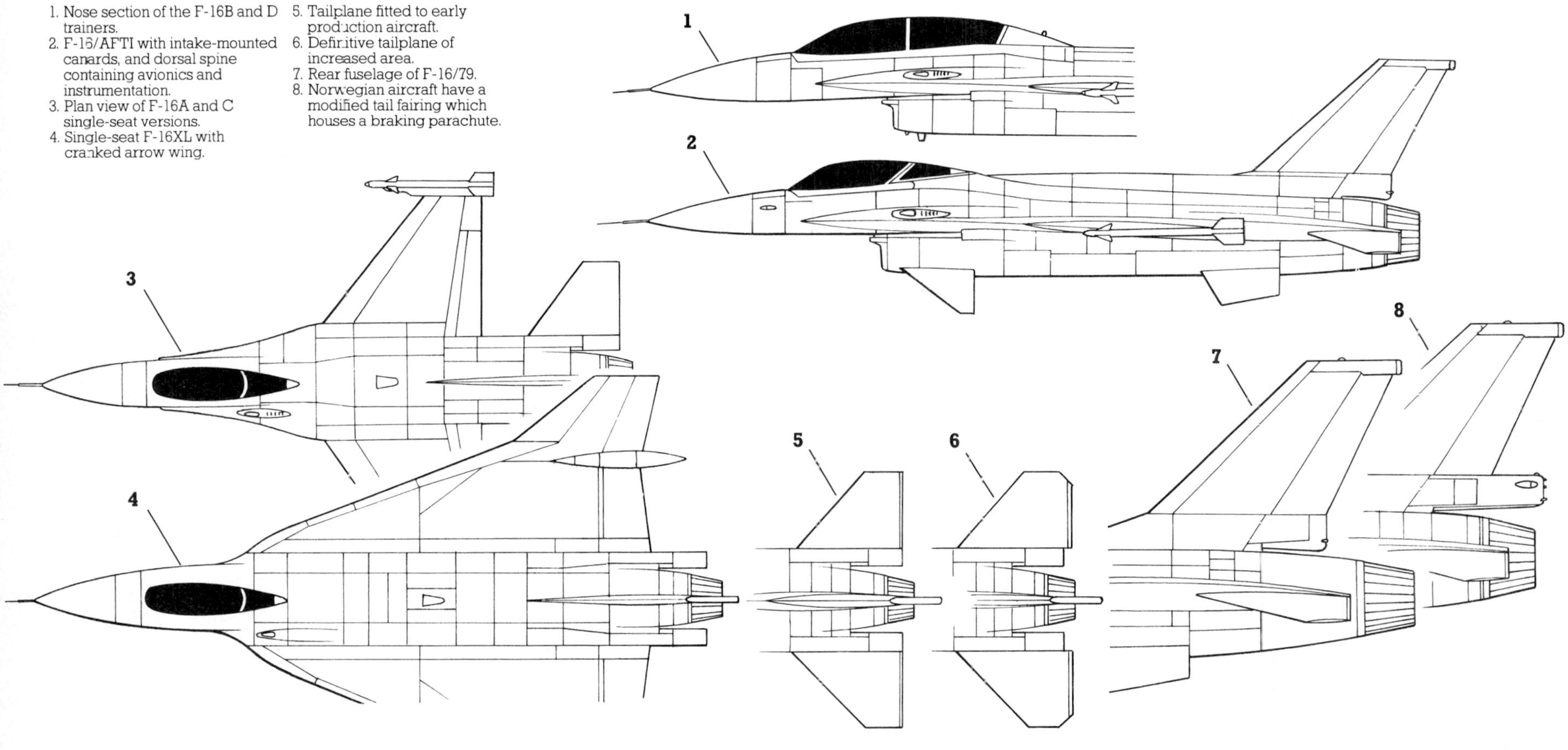

Powerplant

John Boyd's concept of Specific Excess Power called for the F-16 to have a high thrust-to-weight ratio, which in turn required an engine of superlative performance. Such a powerplant was already available in the form of the F100 turbofan devised by Pratt & Whitney for the earlier F-15 Eagle programme. The F100 could deliver the thrust, but its development and deployment stretched US engine technology to the limits. Despite a series of teething troubles, however, the USAF and P&W persisted with development work until all problems were solved.

Development of the Pratt & Whitney F100 turbofan started in August 1968, when the USAF awarded development contracts to P & W and General Electric for engines suitable for use in the planned FX fighter – later to become the F-15 Eagle. In view of the high thrust-to-weight ratio planned for the new fighter, the resulting engines would have to push the technology of the time to its limits. P&W faced the daunting task of developing a powerplant producing 25 per cent more thrust per pound of weight than the contemporary TF30 turbofan used in the F-111, and twice that of the J75 turbojet used in the F-105 Thunderchief and F-106 Delta Dart.

Both companies built and ran demonstration engines whose light weight, high thrust and low fuel consumption put them well ahead of previous designs. The P&W engine was selected by the USAF for further development, contracts being awarded in 1970. Two versions were originally planned – the F100 for the USAF and the F401 intended to power later models of the US Navy's F-14 Tomcat, though the latter was cancelled when the USN was ordered by the Department of Defense to cut back the size of the planned F-14 fleet.

The F100 is an axial-flow turbofan with a bypass ratio of 0.7:1. It has two shafts, one carrying a three-stage fan driven by a two-stage turbine, the other carrying the ten-stage main compressor and its two-stage turbine. The completed engine is 191in (4.85m) long and, 34.8in (0.88m) in diameter at the inlet, and weighs 3,068lb (1,392kg).

New technologies used in the F100 included powder metallurgy. Instead of forming some metal components in the traditional manner, P&W reduced the raw material to a powder. This could be heated and formed under high pressure to create engine components better able to tolerate the high temperatures planned for the F100 core.

Operating temperature of the F100 turbine was far above that of earlier engines. Successful turbojets of earlier vintage, such as the GE F85 which powers the F-5E, or the GE J79 used in the F-4 and F-104, had turbine inlet temperatures of around 1,800deg F (982 deg C). P&W had achieved figures of just over 2,000deg F (1,093deg C) in the TF30 turbofan, but to meet the demanding requirements of the F100 specification involved temperatures of 2,565deg F (1,407deg C).

Use of such advanced technology resulted in an engine capable of providing the high levels of thrust required by the F-15 and F-16. Maximum thrust is normally described as being 'in the 15,000lb (6,800kg) thrust class' when running without afterburner, and 'in the 25,000lb (11,340kg) class' at full augmentation.

Normal dry (non-afterburning) rating is 12,420lb (5,634kg), rising to a maximum of 14,670lb (6,654kg) at full Military Intermediate rating – the maximum attainable without afterburning. Specific fuel consumption (sfc) – the amount of thrust produced for each pound of fuel burned per hour – is 0.69 at normal rating, 0.71 at Military Intermediate. At full afterburning power, the F100 develops 23,830lb (10,809kg) of thrust at an sfc of 2.17. At this rating, the engine swallows an impressive 860lb (390kg) of fuel per minute.

By the time the F-15 Eagle was ready for its first flight in July 1972, the F100 had completed most of its test programme, meeting 23 out of 24 critical 'project milestones'. Between February and October of the following year, a series of turbine failures dogged attempts to complete the 150-hour running trial which formed part of the formal Qualification Test. The latter was the most punishing series of tests to which any US military jet engine had ever been subjected, according to P&W. It included 30 hours of running at a simulated speed of mach 2.3, and 38 hours of running at a simulated Mach 1.6.

Following completion of this test, the F100 was subjected to a further series of intensive trials, including 150 hours of running at over-temperature conditions, and a long series of Accelerated Mission Tests. Conducted on the ground, but designed to simulate the stresses of operational service, these were intended to build up running time and detect potential problems. None of these was serious enough to delay the start of F-15 production, and the first

Above: A USAF crewman at Kunsan Air Base in South Korea fuels an F-16. Engines in the F100 thrust class require large amounts of fuel.

Below: At full afterburning thrust, the F100 consumes more than 800lb of fuel per minute. This aircraft is from the 8th TFW, based at Kunsan.

aircraft were delivered to the USAF in November 1974. The F-15 powerplant is designated F100-PW-100 by the company and JTF22A-25A by the USAF.

Despite the obvious merits of the P&W F100 turbofan, including the fact that this engine had already been selected for use on the F-15, GD carried out many studies of the smaller General Electric YF101 engine. The P&W engine was very much a product of late 1960s thinking – a high bypass ratio turbofan offering good and economical performance at its military (dry) rating – while the GE powerplant was a more modern engine with a much lower bypass ratio. Only a small amount of air was ducted past the core in this design, which GE had dubbed a 'leaky turbojet'.

In many ways, the GE engine was more conservatively designed, emphasis having been placed on reliability rather than ultimate performance. GE personnel made no secret of their view that the P&W engine was pushing the technology of the time close to the limits.

Factors considered by GD during the engine evaluation were the weight of the rival powerplants plus the fuel needed for cruise, combat and reserve. The YF-16 design mission included a 500nm cruise to the target area at high subsonic speed, acceleration to combat speed using maximum afterburner, a period of combat in full afterburner involving sustained turns and supersonic and subsonic speeds, then a return to base with a 20-minute sea-level reserve.

Above: To clear the F100 for service, the engine was subjected to the most demanding series of ground tests ever devised for a USAF powerplant.

Weight calculations

Combined fuel and engine weight for this mission was calculated to be 7,882lb (3,575kg) using a single F100, or 10,234lb (4,642kg) for twin YF101 engines. Two YF101 engines plus installation would weigh 1,024lb (464kg) more than would be the case with a single F100, while an extra 1,328lb (602kg) of fuel would have to be carried. Using the twin GE installation, the F-16 design team would have come up with an aircraft with a mission weight of 21,470lb (9,739kg) instead of the 17,050lb (7,734kg) promised by the P&W engine.

If aircraft weight were kept constant, an F100-engined YF-16 would have a 70 per cent greater mission radius than a twin-YF101 design, GD estimated. Some 90 per cent of this increase was due in roughly equal proportions to the lower engine weight and fuel load required by an F100-powered design, the remainder to reduced drag and airframe weight.

The lower bypass ratio and lighter weight of the F100 installation produced dividends in many areas, GD estimated. Under static conditions at sea level, a pair of YF101 'leaky turbojets' would produce an extra 5,200lb (2,359kg) of thrust, but at Mach 1.2 the turbofan offered an additional 7,500lb (3,402kg). The difference at 30,000ft (9,000m) and Mach 2 was less marked, but the P&W engine still offered a useful 2,850lb (1,293kg) of extra thrust.

In cruising flight, the big turbofan offered a thrust-to-weight ratio seven per cent better than that of the two YF101 engines, and with a 25 per cent lower fuel flow. At 30,000ft and Mach 2, fuel flow was more evenly matched, but thrust-to-weight ratio was dramatically improved. The P&W engine would consume 6.5 per cent less fuel, but produce a 41 per cent higher thrust-to-weight ratio.

In one instance the F100 turned out to have too much thrust. The residual thrust from an idling F100 was 670lb (304kg) – too high for F-16 operations on icy runways. In theory, this residual thrust could have sent a lightly-loaded F-16 moving at speeds of up to 50kt, rather too much for taxying. A test programme using the second YF-16 showed that the engine could be adjusted to give a lower idling speed, reducing the taxying speed to a more acceptable figure.

USAF hopes that the F100 would be a mature powerplant by the time the F-16 entered service were dimmed by a series of technical and operational problems. Strikes at two major subcontractors delayed the delivery of engines, while service experience showed that the F100 was wearing out twice as fast as had been predicted. By the end of 1979 the USAF was being forced to accept engineless F-15 airframes, and by the spring of the following year some 30 were in storage. A massive effort by P&W brought the delivery situation under control, but for a long time the F-15 and F-16 fleets remained short of engines.

A modification introduced into the fuel pump of the F100 created problems for the F-15 early in that aircraft's career. In cruising flight, cavitation could begin in the pump, badly damaging the pump vanes. The solution adopted on the F-15 was simple – revert to the original design. In the case of the F-16, a pump failure would be more serious, so Sundstrand developed an

Below: Specifically developed for use in the F-16, the F100-PW-200 has additional anti-stagnation-stall features for single-engine safety.

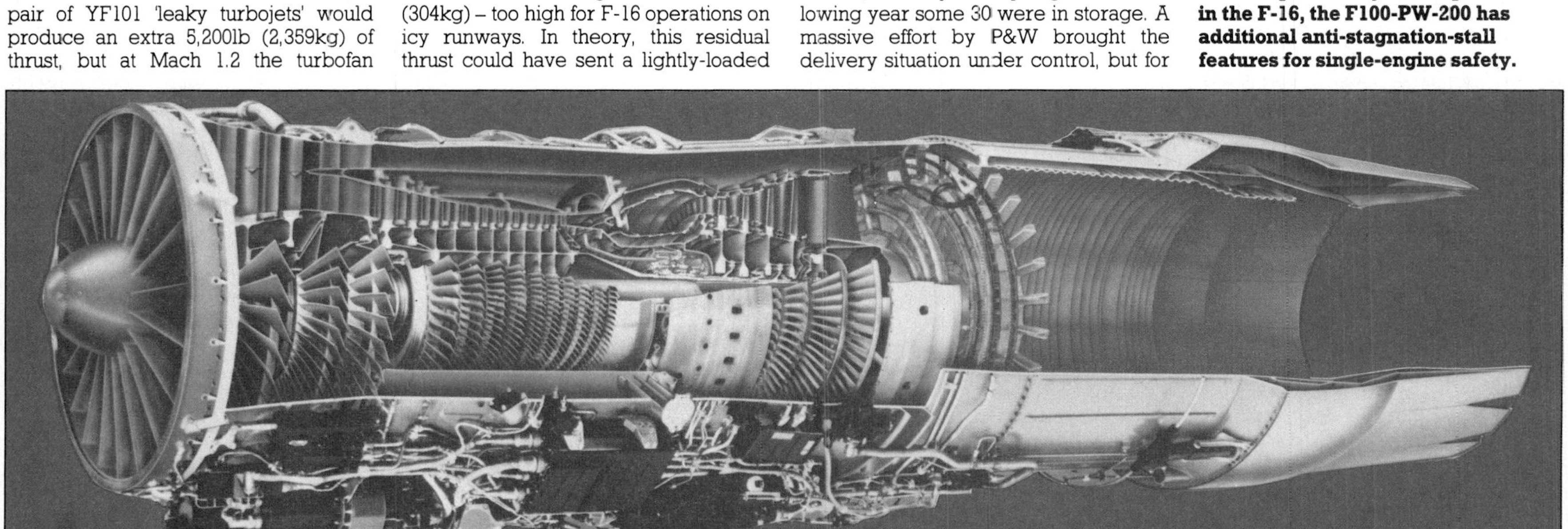

Above: Dwarfed by the bulk of the McDonnell Douglas KC-10A Extender, an F-16 connects the 'flying boom' to its receptacle during tests of the new tanker/cargo aircraft.

alternative dual-element pump for this aircraft. This runs at a lower speed, and should one section fail, the other can continue to deliver fuel at a lower rate.

The electronic engine control unit uses the fuel as a coolant. This technique for obtaining 'free' cooling led to problems when the F-15 first entered service. During training missions at Luke AFB, aircraft sometimes had to wait for 45 minutes or more before takeoff, with engines running at idle settings. This gradually heated the mass of fuel in the Eagle's tank to the point where it was no longer cold enough to cool the engine control unit. Given the high temperature of the desert environment at Luke, the unit could not radiate the excess heat away, so tended to overheat, resulting in engine overspeed problems and turbine failures.

Early operational and durability problems with the F100 during the late 1970s were largely overcome by modifications, plus improvements in materials, maintenance and operating procedures. Production of spare parts was accelerated, and field maintenance teams were increased in size.

Part of the problem lay in the fact that the USAF had underestimated the number of cycles which engines aboard such high-performance types as the F-15 and F-16 would actually undergo. (A cycle is defined as the temperature variation experienced in a mission from engine start to maximum power and afterburner, then back to the lower settings used for landing.) In 1977 the service estimated that each engine would undergo 1.15 cycles per flight hour, but in practice the rate was 2.2 for the F-15 and 3.1 for the F-16.

At one time, designers had assumed that the most arduous duty which a jet engine had to face was running for long periods at high power levels. By the late 1960s, research had shown that this was simply not the case. Many failures were due to this type of running, but others were created by the heating and cooling resulting from an engine being run up to high power then throttled back.

Technicians dubbed this 'low-cycle fatigue', but had to admit that it was difficult to measure. To aid the design of future engines such as the F100, estimates were made of the average number of thermal cycles to which an engine would be exposed per flying hour. Unfortunately for the F100 programme, these estimates were wrong. In practice, engines were being subjected to far more thermal cycles than the designers had allowed for.

Paradoxically, the additional stress which the engines were receiving was largely due to the F-15 and F-16 being such good aircraft. Given the high manoeuvrability of their new mounts, pilots were flying in a manner not possible on earlier types, pushing the aircraft to high angles of attack and making full use of the extended performance envelope. In the heat of a dogfight, the throttle setting would be changed much more often than on earlier fighters. All this spelled hard work for the engine.

Air combat demands

The F-16 places more strain on the engine than does the F-15, since the Fighting Falcon is used in the demanding air-combat role. P&W studies showed that throttle excursions placed a greater strain on the engine than long runs at a constant setting. Studies involving instrumented test aircraft gathered data on the number of throttle movements and the amount of afterburner use which test F-16s were clocking up, and the company carried out a series of accelerated mission tests to clear the F100 for use in the GD aircraft.

Critical components such as first-stage turbine blades showed signs of distress, condemnation rate during repair being 60 per cent instead of the predicted 20 per cent. Maximum gas temperature was reduced to conserve component life, while R&D funding was concentrated on improvements to reliability rather than increasing thrust. Despite these problems, the F-15 had a better engine-related safety record by the end of the 1970s than any other USAF fighter at a comparable point in its service career.

Another problem which was to dog the F100 during the first years of its service career was stagnation stalling. The compressor blades in a jet engine are of aerofoil section, and, like the wing of an aircraft, can be stalled if the angle at which the airflow strikes them exceeds a critical value. Powerplant stalls are occasional occurrences in most jet engines, particularly in the early stages of development, but the F100 was to prove excessively vulnerable to stagnation stalling during its first few years of operational service.

Turbofans are prone to a particularly severe type of stall from which recovery is not possible. As the flow of air through the compressor is disturbed, the engine core looses speed, while the combustor section of the engine continues to pass hot gas to the turbine, causing the latter to overheat. If this condition is not noticed, the turbine may be damaged.

Experience with the F-15 showed that in the event of a mild hard start, the pilot might not notice that a stall had occurred, as the loss of acceleration on the twin-engined aircraft was often not sharp enough to indicate to the pilot that one engine had failed. Without a check on the temperature gauge, low-pressure turbine entry temperature could reach the point where damage might occur. To avoid this problem, an audible-warning system was devised for the Eagle. This is not needed on the Fighting Falcon, since a stall of the single engine produces an immediate loss of acceleration.

Some stagnation stalls were found to be due to component failures, but most were linked with afterburner problems. The latter usually took the form of 'hard starts' – virtually mini-explosions within the afterburner. In some cases the afterburner failed to light on schedule; in other instances the burner extinguished. In either event, large amounts of unburned fuel were sprayed into the jetpipe, creating a momentary build-up of fuel. When this was ignited by the hot efflux from the engine core, a pressure pulse was created – the aerospace equivalent of a car backfiring.

Deliberate hard start

A reporter from *Aviation Week* gave this account of a deliberately induced hard start on a test stand: "The force of the auto-ignition was sufficient to rock the heavily sound-insulated concrete test building. A large gout of flame at the afterburner exhaust was seen on the closed-circuit colour-television system." The pressure in the afterburner resulting from a hard start sent a shock wave back up through the fan duct. When this reached the front section of the engine, it could cause the fan to stall, the high-pressure compressor to stall, or, in the worst case, both. It was sometimes possible for a series of stagnation stalls to occur, with each resulting in the afterburner hard start needed to trigger off another.

Stagnation stalls usually took place at altitude and at high Mach numbers, but rarely below 20,000ft (6,100m). Normal recovery method was for the pilot to shut down the engine and allow it to spool down. Once the tachometer showed that engine rpm had fallen below the 50 per cent mark, the throttle could safely be reopened to the idle position, and the F100 would carry out its automatic relight sequence. The F-16 is fitted with a jet-fuel starter, but from a height of 35,000ft (10,700m) a pilot would probably have enough time to attempt at least three unassisted starts using ram air. Critical factor in restarting the engine after a stagnation stall is the low-pressure turbine-inlet temperature. This must fall to 450deg F (232deg C) before the engine can be restarted.

Several modifications were devised to reduce the frequency of stagnation stalls. The first approach taken was to try to prevent pressure build-ups in the afterburner. A quartz window in the side of the afterburner assembly allowed a flame sensor to monitor the pilot flame of the augmentor. If this went out, the flow of fuel to the outer sections of the burner was prevented.

When the F100 engine-control system was originally designed, P&W engineers allowed for the possibility that ingestion of efflux from missiles might stall the engine and a 'rocket fire' facility was designed into the controls. When missiles were fired, an electronic signal could be sent to the unified fuel control system which supplies fuel to the engine core and to the afterburner. The angle of the variable stator blades in the engine could be altered to avoid a stall, while the fuel flow to the engine was momentarily reduced, and the afterburner exhaust was increased in area to reduce the magnitude of any pressure pulse in the afterburner.

Tests had shown that the 'rocket fire' facility was not needed, but P&W engineers were able to use it as a means of preventing stagnation stalls. Engine

Above: A night-time engine test at the Pratt & Whitney plant. The F100 is in full afterburner, and the nozzle has been fully opened to allow the hot exhaust gases to expand.

shaft speed, turbine temperature and the angle of the compressor stator blades are monitored on the F100 by a digital electronic engine control unit, which normally serves to 'fine-tune' the engine throughout flight to ensure optimum performance.

By monitoring and comparing HP spool speed and fan exhaust temperature, the engine control unit is able to sense that a stagnation stall is about to take place, and send a dummy 'Rocket Fire' signal to the unified fuel control system to initiate the anti-stall measures described above. At the same time, a second modification to the fuel control system reduces the afterburner setting to zone 1 – little more than a pilot light – in order to help reduce pressure within the jetpipe.

In an attempt to prevent any pulses coming forward through the fan duct from affecting the core, P&W engineers devised a modification known as the 'proximate splitter'. This is a forward extension to the internal casing which splits the incoming airflow from the engine compressor fan, passing some to the core of the engine and diverting the remainder down the fan duct, past the core and into the afterburner. By closing the gap between the front end of this casing and the rear of the fan to just under half an inch, the engine designers reduced the size of the path by which the high-pressure pulses from the burner had been reaching the core. Engines fitted with the proximate splitter were test-flown in the F-15, but this modification was not embodied in the engines of production Eagles, whose twin engines made the loss of a single engine less hazardous.

When it first flew, the F-16 seemed almost free of stagnation stall problems, but while flying with an early-model F100 engine, one of the YF-16 prototypes did experience a stagnation stall,

Right: Ready for refuelling during a 4,350 mile (7,000km) flight across the United States intended to simulate a transatlantic deployment, an F-16 approaches the boom of a KC-135.

though this occurred outside the normal performance envelope. Three incidents were noted later during flight tests at high angles of attack. All took place at Edwards AFB during low-speed flight tests at high altitude. The first production aircraft to experience a stagnation stall was an FAéB aircraft operating near the limits of the performance envelope. The pilot was able to restart the engine and landed safely.

Given the amount of development work, the stagnation stall problem was soon mastered, although never completely eliminated. To suit the F100 for the single-engined F-16, the USAF decided to adopt the modifications already fitted to the engines of the F-15, plus the proximate splitter.

The F-16 powerplant is designated F100-PW-200 by the manufacturer, JTF22A-33 by the USAF. It weighs 54lb (24.5kg) more than the original version fitted to the F-15, and incorporates a back-up fuel-control system and a modified cooling system for the control system, which has a hydromechanical back-up.

The improvement in reliability was dramatic. Back in 1976, the F-15 fleet experienced a stagnation stall rate of 11–12 per 1,000 flying hours. By the end of 1981 this had dropped to 1.5 per 1,000 hours thanks to the modifications to the fuel control system and nozzle. Engines fitted to the F-16 fleet (and incorporating the proximate splitter) had an even lower rate – 0.15 per 1,000 hours.

The need for greater engine reliability in the single-seat F-16 has forced the USAF to be cautious when problems emerge. In the summer of 1980, for example, engines in USAF, European and Israeli service were inspected following the discovery of a broken control cable in the wreckage of an aircraft which crashed at Hill AFB during a low-level training flight. This was seen as a precautionary measure for the single-seat aircraft: for the twin-engined F-15 spot checks were deemed sufficient.

Efforts are under way to reduce further the smoke output of the F100 as part of a planned component-improvement programme. For example, the combustor has been modified to increase the velocity of the airflow in its front end. This results in improved mixing of air and fuel and leads to more complete combustion and less residual smoke.

Traditional engine-servicing techniques involve replacing critical components at the end of a statistically calculated lifetime. This often results in components being removed and scrapped while still perfectly serviceable, giving good safety margins, but at a high cost to the operator. The USAF now wants engine designers to develop parts with greater tolerance to crack damage so that these may be left in the engine until inspection by non-destructive test (NDT) methods shows that cracks are starting to develop and a replacement is needed. Life-cycle costs may be cut by up to 60 per cent.

The service's Damage Tolerant Design (DTD) programme involved both Pratt & Whitney and General Electric, and focussed much of its attention on the F100. One of the programme's first achievements was a new pattern of F100 fan disc having five times the life of the original component. Key design elements under DTD are high quality control of the raw material, and the avoidance of shapes and configurations which cause stress concentrations – sharp radii, for example.

F100/J79 comparative data	**F100**	**J79**
Manufacturer	Pratt & Whitney	General Electric
Type	turbofan	turbojet
Bypass ratio	0.71	–
Dry thrust (lb/kg)	14,670/6,654	11,810/5,357
Afterburning thrust (lb/kg)	23,830/10,810	18,730/8,496
Weight (lb/kg)	3,835/1,740	3,847/1,745
Thrust:weight ratio (with afterburning)	6.2:1	4.87:1
Turbine inlet temperature (deg F/deg C)	2,565/1,149	1,810/821
Number of components	31,100	22,000
Maintenance man hours/flight hour (1978)	4.2	1.7

New components

The USAF plans to begin testing engine discs currently under development as part of the DTD programme in 1984, and hopes to fit these into operational engines before the end of that year. By 1985 or 1986 the F100 may be fitted with second and third-stage turbine blades and vanes manufactured using a single-crystal technique. Although more expensive than components made from traditional materials, these will probably have a lifetime at least twice that of current vanes and blades.

The USAF was the first F100 user to take advantage of a warranty scheme offered by P&W in 1980, whereby the company undertook to repair or replace certain high-pressure turbines unserviceable as a result of wear or mechanical failure at no extra cost to the USAF. Engines covered by the deal were from production lot IX and were due for delivery between February 1981 and January 1982.

To qualify for free treatment, faulty engines would have to have carried out less than 900 equivalents of the TAC engine operating cycle (about two years of normal use) or have developed the fault within three and a half years of delivery. If the HP failure had caused secondary damage to the engine, P&W undertook to cover costs up to 75 per cent of that of a new engine.

The F-16/79

The General Electric J79 turbojet seemed an obvious choice as powerplant for the planned FX export version of the F-16 in view of that engine's widespread use. Production of the J79 in the US ended in 1979 after a total of 13,686 had been built for use in the B-58 Hustler, F-104 Starfighter and F-4 Phantom. Licence production in Japan ended early in 1980, but the powerplant remained in production in Israel for the Kfir fighter.

The J79 is a single-shaft axial-flow turbojet with a 16-stage compressor and three-stage turbine. The former incorporates variable inlet vanes and six stages of variable stators. The combustor is of cannular type with ten burners. For the F-16/79 project, GE engineers devised a new version designated J79-GE-17X, and incorporating a new feature which the company called Combat Plus. When this is demanded by the pilot, fuel flow to the engine is slightly increased, while the exhaust nozzle closes slightly. The net result is to increase exhaust gas temperature by around 100deg F (56deg C), producing several hundred pounds of extra thrust.

Combat Plus cannot be used at all times. The engine must be running in full afterburner, compressor inlet temperature must not exceed 15deg F (–9 deg C), and certain combinations of low altitude and high speed would place excessive strain on the engine casing due to excessive internal pressure resulting from the high airflow involved.

The exact level of thrust increase created by Combat Plus varies depending on engine operating conditions. On a ground test bed, maximum thrust in full afterburner rises from 17,900lb (8,119kg) to more than 18,700lb (8,482kg). In a high altitude test chamber, maximum thrust with Combat Plus rises to 20,840lb (9,453kg) at Mach 2/35,000ft (10,700m) operating conditions.

Ratings when installed in an airframe will be further modified by the inlet configuration, but for many flight conditions GE claims that the uprated J79 will result in minimal performance loss. The superiority of the F100 is very marked in terms of fuel consumption, however. At military (non-afterburning) ratings the turbojet burns more fuel than the turbofan, although this is not a problem in the range-constrained FX mission. When the afterburner is lit, the difference in fuel consumption is minimal, according to GE.

Another modification required to match the J79 to the F-16 airframe was the addition of a transfer gearbox designed to mate with the airframe-mounted gearbox on the F-16 which drives electrical generators and hydraulic pumps. The engine also incorporates safety features originally devised for use on single-engine installations such as the F-104 Starfighter and Kfir.

Three development engines were built. The first was used to carry out 60 hours of formal Preliminary Flight Rating Tests, running for five hours under simulated Mach 2 conditions. The second was supplied to GD for use in the F-16/79 prototype, while the third acted as a back-up.

Although the F-16/79 has not yet entered service, and by mid–1983 had yet to attract an order, the future of the Combat Plus feature of the J79 may be assured. Development of Combat Plus was originally begun as a means of improving the performance of the F-4, but some development work was carried out in the mid–1970s for Israel. The latter work led to further developments by Israeli engineers, and the IDFAF is reported to be considering its use in the J79-IAI-J1I powerplant of Kfir.

The F-16/101

In the search for an alternative engine for the F-14 Tomcat and the F-16, the US Department of Defense awarded General Electric a $100 million contract to build five F101 Derivative Fighter Engines (DFE) for flight test. The first engine reached full power on December 30, 1979, the first day of ground testing. During the following month it clocked up 60 hours of running at all power levels. It was designed to be a direct replacement for the F100 in the F-16 airframe, and to be installed in the Tomcat by means of extended fore and aft mountings.

As well as serving as an alternative powerplant, the F101 maintained General Electric design expertise in high-thrust engines, ensuring that two com-

Below: A pilot of the 429th Tactical Fighter Wing carries out a pre-flight inspection of his Fighting Falcon's ventral intake.

Above: Final adjustments are made to an F100 turbofan at the Pratt & Whitney works.

Left: Technicians manoeuvre an F100 into the second FSD aircraft. The multi-flap articulated nozzle is seen here in the open position used when the afterburner is lit. When dry thrust is selected, the nozzle closes to a narrower diameter.

panies would be able to offer designs for future engines of this performance level.

By the autumn of 1980 the F101 had completed 430 hours of accelerated mission testing – the equivalent of 1,000 hours of F-16 flying. Since testing had begun, maximum thrust had fallen by less than two per cent, while specific fuel consumption in afterburning mode had increased by just over one per cent. The engine was stripped down for examination, found to be in good condition, then rebuilt to undergo testing intended to simulate 1,000 hours of flying in the F-14.

F100 developments

Pratt & Whitney are continuing research into new engines based on the F100 and its technology. During a series of tests carried out in late summer of 1982, the company ground-tested an F100 fitted with a two-dimensional nozzle. Rectangular in cross-section, this is a convergent/divergent design featuring movable upper and lower surfaces which could be used to vector the thrust. This design was developed under a USAF contract, and while no production application is planned, the new nozzle could be used in a modified F-16 or F-15.

Angles of up to 20deg were demonstrated, but P&W is confident that the design would be good for up to 30deg. Coupled with the use of thrust reversing, this technique could greatly increase the agility of current aircraft, and could cut the take-off run to 1,200ft (366m) or less. Earlier attempts to design axisymmetric nozzles with vectoring and thrust-reversing have resulted in complex and heavy units which paid a high penalty in thrust loss. The latest P&W design could be offered as an add-on modification weighing only a few hundred pounds to the standard F100 gas generator section.

Using experience gained from the F100 programme, P&W was able to begin development of the PW1120 afterburning turbofan. Based on the core of the earlier engine, this is a low-risk development with 60 per cent commonality, but it incorporates a new low-pressure compressor and turbine, and a simplified afterburner. Operating temperature has been slightly reduced, and the PW1120 has a slightly lower thrust-to-weight ratio – 7.25:1 instead of 7.9:1. The PW1120 is 20in (50.8cm) shorter than the F100 and 7in (17.8cm) narrower in diameter. First application to be announced was the planned Israel Aircraft Industries Lavi fighter.

Avionics

Advanced aerodynamics and a high thrust-to-weight ratio are not enough to make an advanced fighter. Without its complex payload of avionics 'black boxes', Fighting Falcon would not be able to search for and locate its targets under typically poor European weather conditions, or confuse hostile ground-based or airborne radars. And without the assistance of the complex fly-by-wire flight-control system, the F-16 pilot would probably be unable to cope with the inherent instability of his aircraft. With these systems installed, however, a basic lightweight fighter becomes a formidable multirole combat aircraft.

Above: Westinghouse engineers install line-replaceable units in a development APG-66 radar to be test-flown in an F-4 Phantom.

Like most US military aircraft, the F-16 carries a comprehensive suite of avionics. The basic installation in the F-16A/B is already greater than many proponents of the original Lightweight Fighter scheme may have envisaged, but this reflects the combat environment of the 1980s rather than any desire by GD or the USAF to 'gold plate' the aircraft. Under the MSIP and F-16C/D programmes even more systems will be added to improve all-weather capability. Some critics attack the Fighting Falcon as being over-complex, but the original concept of a simple day fighter is no longer suited to Western European operations.

Integration of the F-16 avionics makes extensive use of the MIL-STD-1553 multiplexed databus – a significant step forward in avionics design. The significance of computer languages and interfaces may seem obscure, but the complexity of modern warplanes makes standardization of these as important as the standardization of more tangible objects such as fixings, fastenings, connectors and weapon attachment points.

Traditional methods of avionics integration involved the use of bulky and expensive bundles of electric wiring for the distribution of signals and data. Multiplexing is a technique under which various equipments share a common electrical connection on a time-sampled basis – the electronic equivalent of time-sharing an apartment. If the number of times per second during which a signal has access to the electrical connection – databus – is sufficiently high compared with the rate at which that signal may change, the end result will be as acceptable as a fixed piece of wire. Lightweight digital switching electronics may therefore be substituted for heavy and bulky cabling.

Avionics standardization

By specifying an agreed 'code of conduct' for using the databus, MIL-STD-1553 greatly reduces the electronic interfacing problems experienced in earlier digital avionics systems, in which each manufacturer selected his own independent software (computer programs and instructions) as he saw fit.

GD was an enthusiastic supporter of avionics standardization, and all avionics for the F-16 were developed using a common interface and computer language. For the avionics improvements planned as part of the MSIP programme, the company standardized on the latest version of MIL-STD-1553, the Jovial computer language and a new standard interface for stores and stores-management systems.

The APG-66 radar

Primary target-detection sensor of the F-16 is the Westinghouse APG-66 radar. As originally conceived, the F-16 would have carried only a simple search set, probably similar in performance to that in the Northrop F-5E. Some individuals in the Department of Defense even suggested the use of a basic range-only unit with a fixed antenna.

Experience during the Vietnam War had shown how enemy aircraft could avoid detection by flying close to the ground, where the clutter experienced on normal pulse radars could hide them from observation. The need to have 'look-down' radar capability forced the adoption of a pulse-Doppler radar, but the traditional high complexity and cost of such equipment made the design of the much smaller APG-66 a difficult task.

In order to carry out a radar-controlled interception, an aircraft requires data on the bearing of the target and its range. Bearing can be measured by means of a highly-directional antenna giving good angular discrimination, but range data can most easily be obtained by pulsing the radar transmitter on and off again at a rate known as the pulse-repetition frequency (PRF). In the simpler types of radar equipment, sufficient time is allowed for one pulse to travel out to the target, be reflected, and return to the radar before the next pulse is transmitted. Engineers describe such radars as low-PRF sets.

Until the 1960s, airborne radars were almost blind when attempting to look downwards to detect low-flying aircraft. The latter were able to hide in the clutter produced by the strong radar echo from the terrain background against which they were being viewed.

Below: Marconi Avionics' holographic HUD begins flight trials in the front cockpit of an F-16B. The large combiner glass gives the unit the wide field-of-view needed for use with LANTIRN.

By the 1960s a new source of microwave power known as a travelling-wave tube (TWT), along with the use of digital signal processors, allowed the creation of pulse-Doppler radars with a good look-down performance.

The use of stable and coherent (phrase-related) pulses from a TWT allows the radar to measure the Doppler shift in the radar returns from the target – the tiny change in frequency caused by target motion relative to the signal source. Using this technique, the relative velocity of the target against the terrain background allowed the wanted target signal to be extracted from the massive background returns. This technique is known as pulse-Doppler radar.

TWT transmitters cannot match the high levels of power available from the magnetron transmitters used in low-PRF radars, so the designers were forced to use high PRFs in order to illuminate the target with sufficient power. Since each pulse would be transmitted before the previous pulse had completed the round trip out to a distant target and back, each pulse had to be electronically 'labelled' by a low-frequency modulation at the time of transmission.

Medium PRFs

The range data obtained by processing the labelled pulses is of low accuracy, and high PRFs are also poor at detecting targets whose closure rate is low. In the 1970s, therefore, designers of airborne radar turned to medium PRFs. These allow traditional methods of ranging to be used at most combat ranges, while still allowing pulse-Doppler techniques to be used for look-down operation.

Since the PRFs best suited to range measurement are different to those effective against low closing-rate targets, a practical design of medium-PRF set has to switch rapidly from one PRF value to another. This made the design of hardware able to carry out pulse-Doppler signal processing virtually impossible. The solution lay in the use of software-controlled digital signal processing. By making the characteristics of the filter dependent on a computer program (software) rather than physical components (hardware), the designers could contrive near-instantaneous reconfiguration of the filter to match each PRF waveform used by the radar. The first radars to use medium PRFs and digital signal processors were the Hughes APG-65 in the F-15 Eagle and the L.M. Ericsson PS-46/A in the Viggen JA37 intercepter.

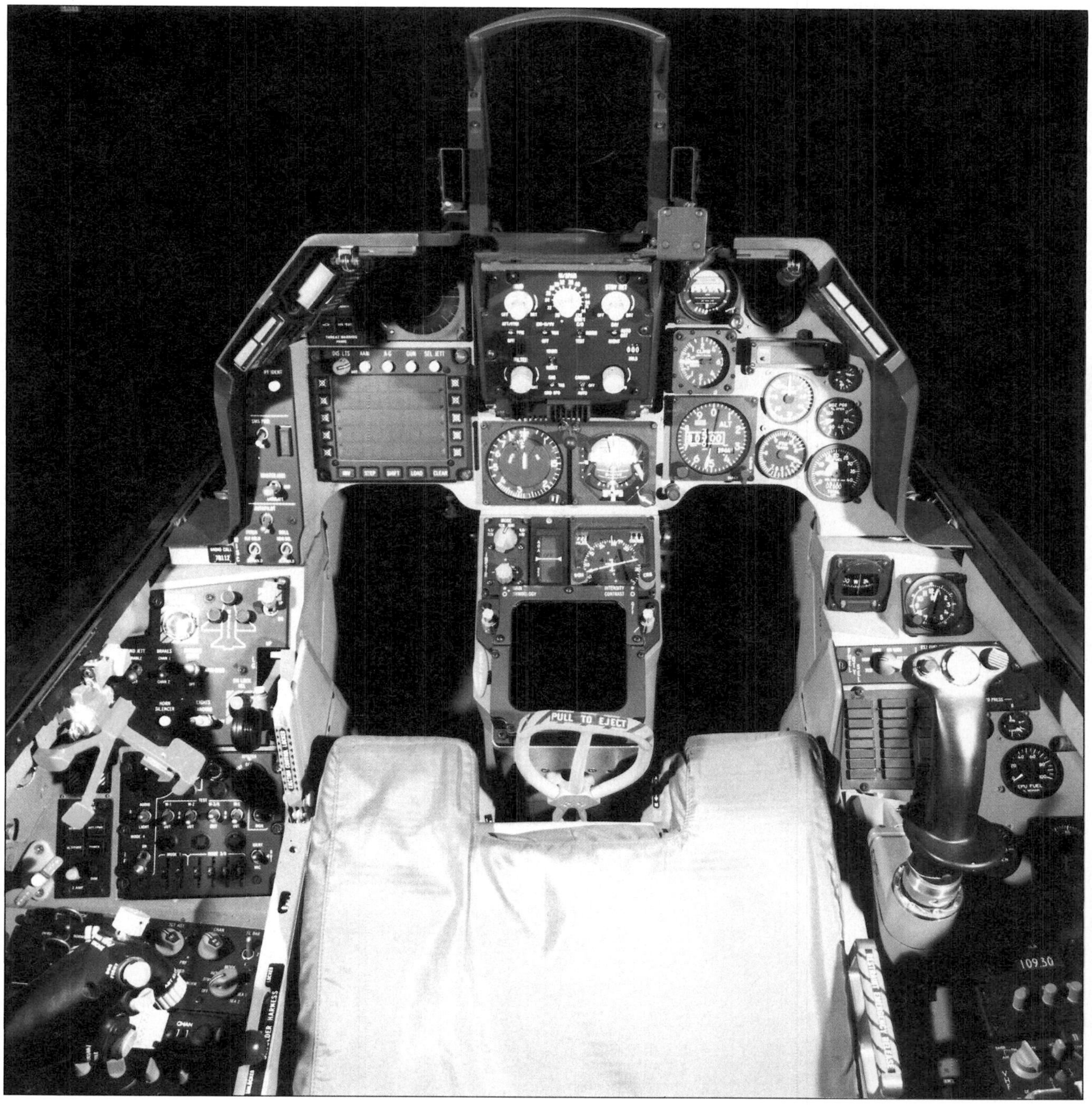

Above: Primary sources of nav/attack data for the F-16A pilot are the HUD (top) and square CRT display (between the pilot's knees).

Development contracts for the F-16 radar were awarded to Hughes and Westinghouse, and both companies test-flew prototypes in a competitive evaluation before Westinghouse was awarded the contract for what became the APG-66. The specification was very demanding, calling for a medium-PRF pulse-Doppler set capable of being installed in the modestly-sized nose section of the Fighting Falcon.

The set was initially optimized for the air-to-air role, but air-to-surface modes were also requested soon after the fly-off. To minimize possible delays and cost increases, some compromises in air-to-ground performance were accepted. At high altitudes, for example, radar ground-mapping performance is lower than would have been possible with an antenna optimized for this role.

The APG-66 used in the F-16A/B is a medium-PRF radar (typically 10 to 15kHz). It operates in I/J band and incorporates a 'flat-plate' planar array antenna. Sixteen operating frequencies are available within the band, and the pilot may select between any four. Total weight is 296lb (134kg), and the set occupies a volume of 3.6cu ft (0.1cu m). A mean time between failures of 97 hours has been demonstrated.

Radar operating modes may be selected by the pilot using the throttle, sidestick controller or radar control panel. Like most modern sets, the APG-66 is designed so that all the controls needed during air combat are located on the control stick and throttle. When the set is tracking a target, the range scale is switched automatically to reduce pilot workload.

Primary air-combat mode is Downlook, which provides clutter-free indication of low-flying targets. Fighter-sized aircraft may be detected head- or tail-on at ranges of more than 30nm (34.5 miles/55.6km). If the target is flying at a higher altitude than the Fighting Falcon, the pilot may select Uplook mode, gaining a useful 33 per cent increase in detection range.

Below: The final FSD aircraft was temporarily fitted with a mock-up of an enlarged nose able to house the APG-65 radar used in the F/A-18.

Below: Performance of the APG-66 radar against typical aircraft targets: the figures for the Soviet aircraft are estimates based on results with US types. Ranges obtained in look-up mode are better than those in look-down mode – in the latter case the set must carry out sophisticated signal processing to distinguish between the target and unwanted radar reflections from the ground.

Opposite: All controls needed during combat are mounted on the sidestick controller (top) and throttle (below). The Dogfight/MSL override switch on the latter can be set to the 'Dogfight' position to select radar Air Combat mode.

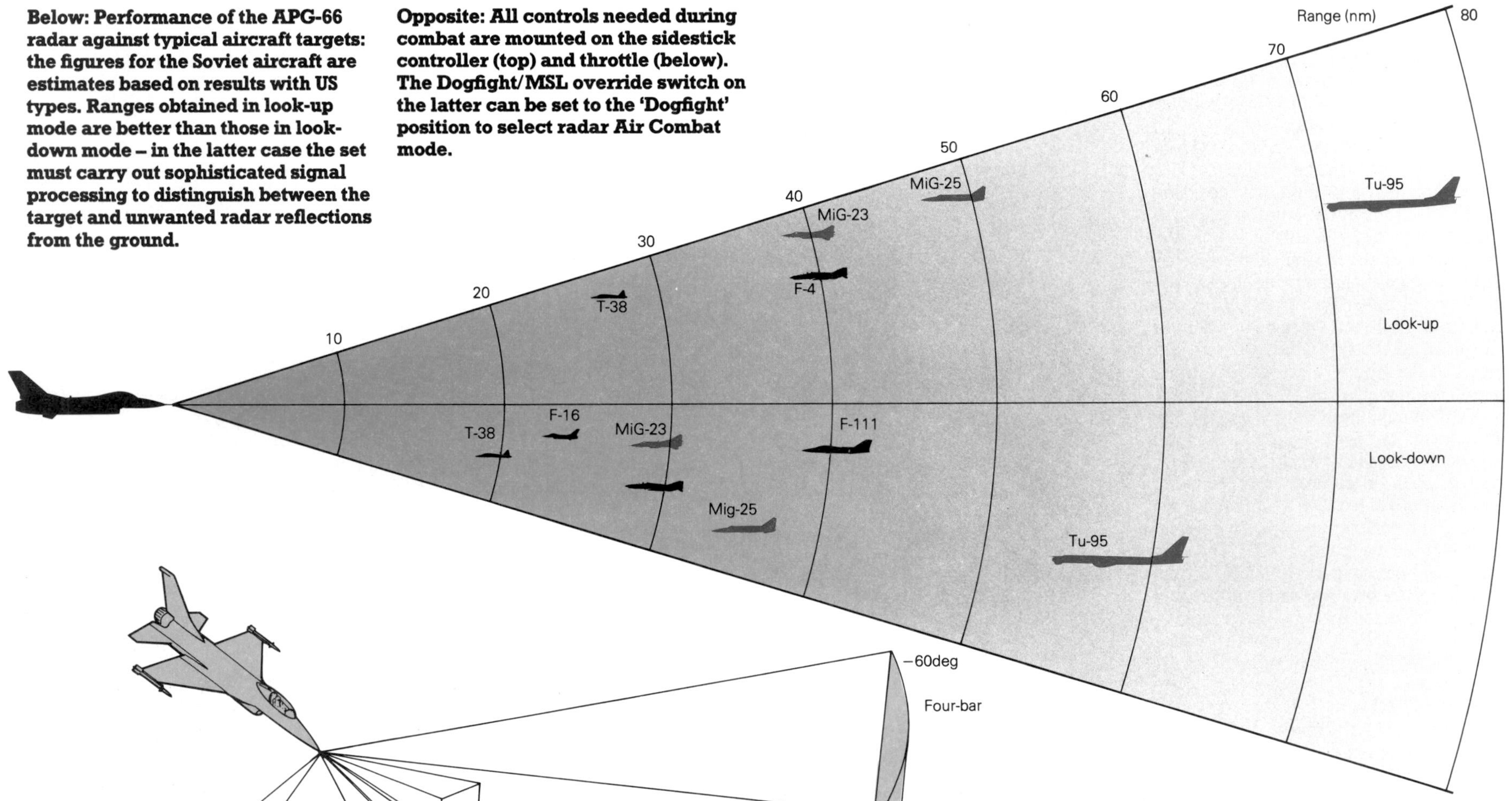

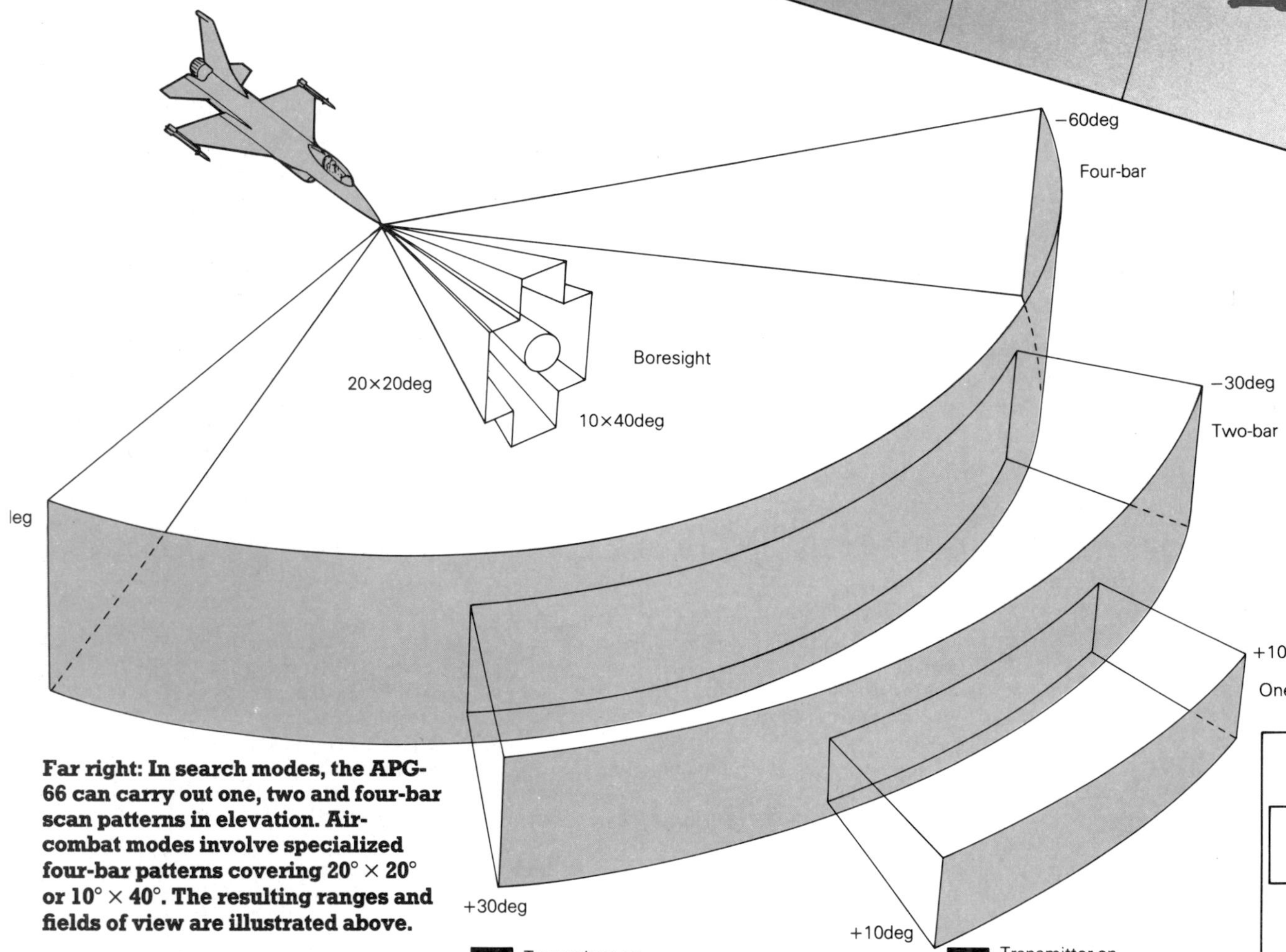

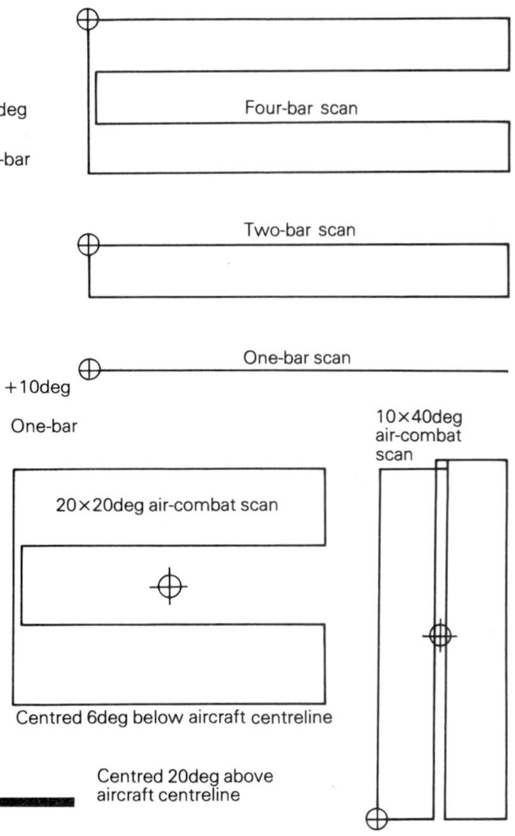

Far right: In search modes, the APG-66 can carry out one, two and four-bar scan patterns in elevation. Air-combat modes involve specialized four-bar patterns covering 20° × 20° or 10° × 40°. The resulting ranges and fields of view are illustrated above.

Right: A pulse radar transmits for short periods of time only, spending the intervals listening for echoes from the target.

Four modes are available for air-to-air combat. In the Dogfight mode, selected by means of a throttle-mounted switch, the radar automatically scans a 20deg × 20deg field. If the pilot can see the target in his HUD, and the range is less than 10nm, the radar will automatically lock on. If high-g manoeuvres are to be carried out, the area to be searched can be altered to a 40deg × 10deg pattern.

If faced with several closely-spaced targets, the pilot can press the Designate button on his sidestick controller. The radar will then operate in a slim narrow-beam mode, and by manoeuvring his aircraft the pilot can place the beam on to the required target. When he releases the Designate switch, the radar will acquire and track the chosen victim.

Slewable air-combat mode can give the Fighting Falcon pilot the edge during combat manoeuvres. A cursor-control button on the throttle grip allows e scan pattern to be moved to antici- target manoeuvres. This is particularly useful when both aircraft are manoeuvring in the vertical plane.

Seven modes are provided for air-to-surface use. Air-to-ground ranging is automatically selected during continuously-computed impact point (CCIP) and dive-toss attacks, measuring the slant range to a designated point on the ground.

CCRP attacks

Continuously-computed release point (CCRP) attacks use the set's ground mapping modes. Real-beam ground mapping gives a plan position indicator (PPI) display at 10, 20, 40 or 80nm range, and scan widths of plus or minus 10deg, 30deg or 60deg. This image may be used for navigational updates, the location and detection of ground targets and for direct or offset weapon delivery.

Dedicated sea-surface search modes may be used in the maritime role. Sea 1 is a frequency-agile mode for use against stationary or moving vessels in up to sea state 4, while Sea 2 uses a narrow Doppler notch to detect moving targets in higher sea states, and may also be used to indicate moving targets on land.

Beacon mode also uses a PPI display format. It may be used in conjunction with ground-located radar beacons to take navigation fixes or to carry out offset weapons delivery. In the air-to-air role, this mode is used to locate flight refuelling tankers by interrogating their beacons.

Several auxiliary methods of presenting imagery may be used in these PPI modes. If Freeze mode is selected, the radar carries out a final scan, the image of which is 'held' on the display, following which the radar transmitter is turned off so that the aircraft cannot be detected by passive means. A moving symbol on the display continues to indicate aircraft motion. Expanded-beam real map mode provides an optional ×4 magnification on all PPI modes. The pilot selects the 'patch' to be expanded from anywhere within the radar's scan and range limits.

Highest definition of ground features is given by a special Doppler beam sharpened mode. Usable when the set is ground mapping at ranges of 10 or 20nm, this provides a further ×8 magnification over that in expanded-beam real map mode. Since this mode relies on the processing of Doppler shift, it is only available at angles between 15deg and 60deg off the aircraft's velocity vector. Should the aircraft's subsequent flight path bring the area being viewed to within 15deg of the aircraft centreline, the radar automatically switches to the normal ground-mapping mode. Doppler beam sharpening is likely to be much used when projected specialized off-boresight guided weapons finally enter service.

Development of an effective pulse-Doppler radar of such small size was a formidable technical undertaking, so it was hardly surprising that several problems were experienced during early tests, particularly in look-down mode. Pulse-Doppler radars measure the Doppler shift created by target velocity in order to discriminate between genuine

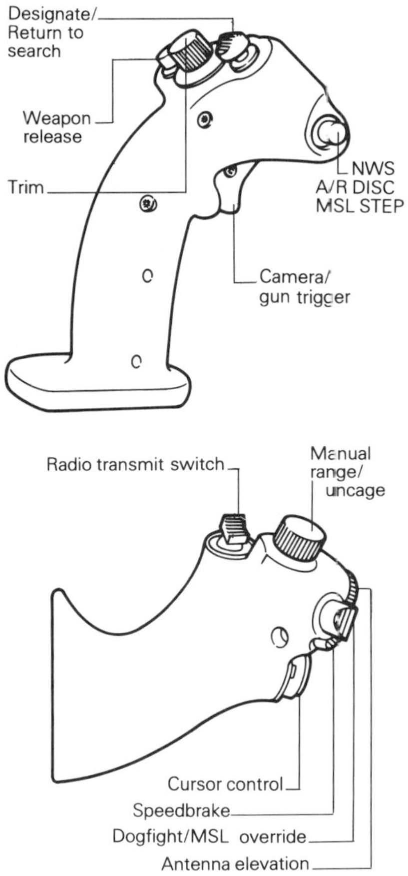

targets and ground clutter. This involves defining a threshold velocity – a speed at which targets must be moving in order to be accepted as valid. Vehicles on West German autobahns often move at speeds of 100mph (160km/h) or more, and were sometimes registered as low-level targets.

During tests over water in Norway, false targets registered on the radar were found to be due to stray radiation from the radar antenna. In designing an antenna, the engineer would like to see all of the signal being directed into the main beam, but in practice some always escapes in the form of sidelobes – unwanted weak beams at an angle to the main beam. A good design will reduce these sidelobes as much as possible, but it is virtually impossible to eliminate them. Radar energy escaping from these sidelobes was being reflected off the water in fjords, creating false targets.

Synthetic imagery

Earlier radars presented a direct radar picture to the operator, who could to some degree use his own skill and experience in deciding which targets were real. Sets such as the APG-66 reduce all radar data to digital form, and present the pilot with a synthetically generated image made up of pre-defined symbols. The screen is free from clutter and is much easier to read than that of earlier types of radar which showed 'raw' data, but the discrimination between real and false targets must be achieved automatically by signal-processing equipment. In the case of the early APG-66 sets, this feature required modification.

During other early trials, the radar showed poor detection range and low performance in the Doppler beam-sharpened air-to-ground modes. Clearing up these and other 'bugs' took much time and effort, but the situation was under control by the summer of 1979. Modifications were made to the low-power RF circuitry, digital signal processor and system software, and the revised equipment was under flight test and evaluation by the end of 1979.

Improvements to the APG-66 form part of the MSIP update programme. In 1980 Westinghouse was awarded a $25 million contract to begin development of a programmable signal processor (PSP) and dual-mode transmitter for the APG-66. The latter would use low PRFs for air-to-ground work, and medium to high PRFs in air-to-air combat. These modifications were intended to match the performance of the AMRAAM missile, and to improve air-to-ground capability and ECCM performance. The set would also receive track-while-scan and raid-assessment modes. Both new sub-units were designed to occupy the same space as the equipment they replaced.

The design of TWTs able to operate efficiently over a wide range of PRFs is difficult. Given low or even medium PRFs, the transmitting tube of a radar spends more time silent than transmitting. In engineering jargon, the 'duty cycle' of time 'off' to time 'on' is low. The tube thus has plenty of time to cool between individual pulses, so the designer can work the device hard while it is actually radiating, obtaining high levels of peak power.

Above: If the one-piece canopy were to fail, the combiner glass of the HUD would act as a windshield.

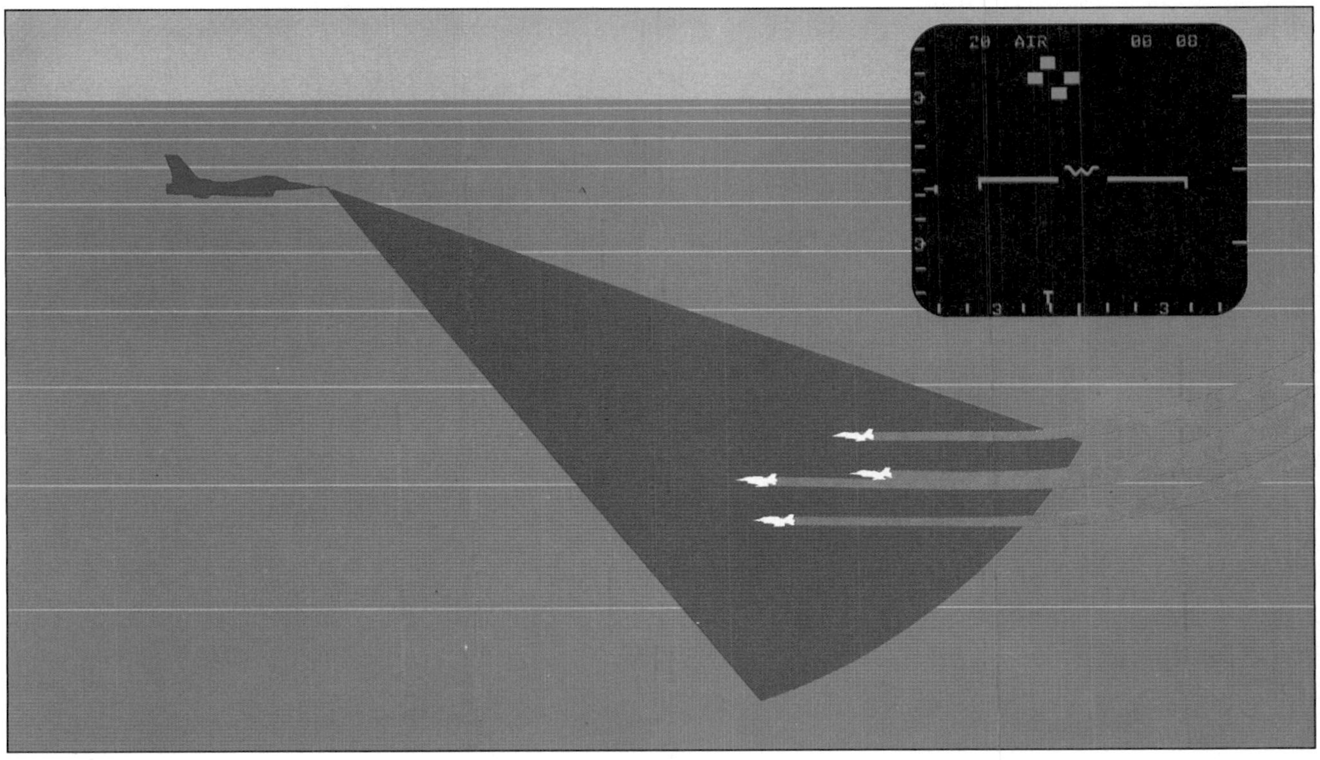

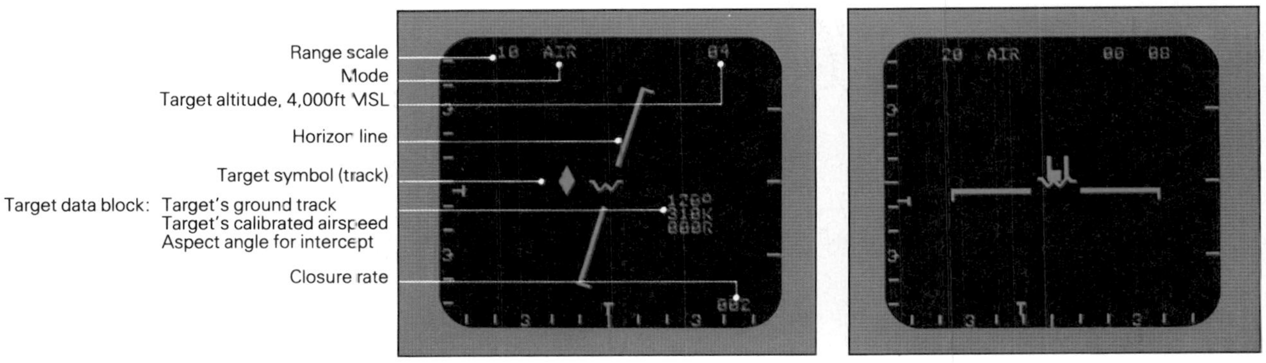

Above right: Primary air-to-air radar mode is Downlook, a medium-PRF search and track mode able to detect low-flying intruders. According to Westinghouse, the set has a low false-alarm rate of less than two per minute. The radar displays use computer-generated alphanumeric and other symbology, to present the pilot with clean imagery, while the effects of clutter and system noise are filtered out by signal processing. Earlier-generation radars presented 'raw' analogue radar imagery to the user, requiring skilled interpretation.

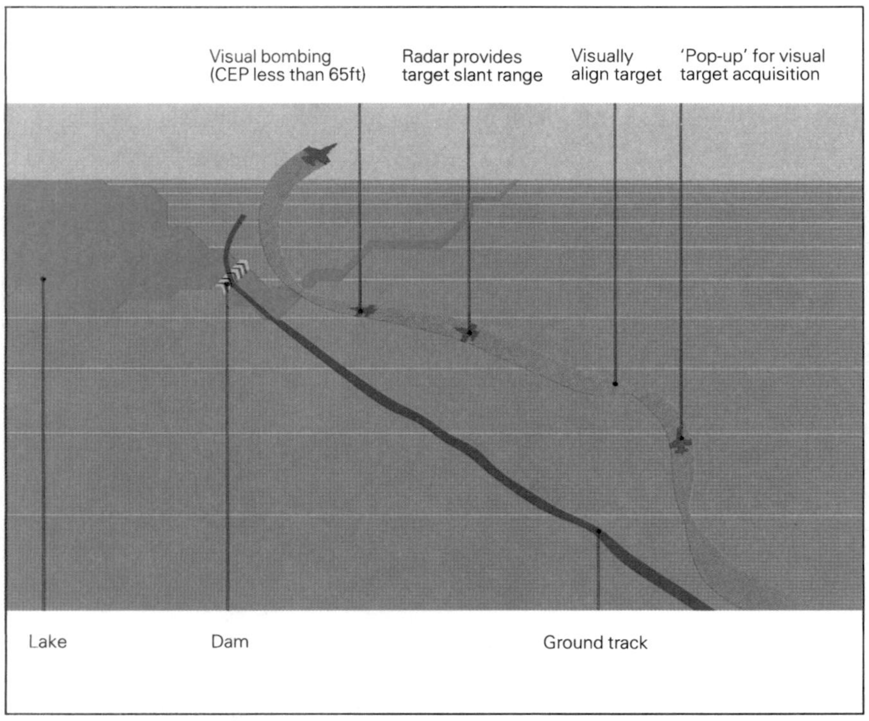

Above: During CCIP (continuously-computed impact point) attacks, the APG-66 radar is used to measure slant range to the target during the final run.

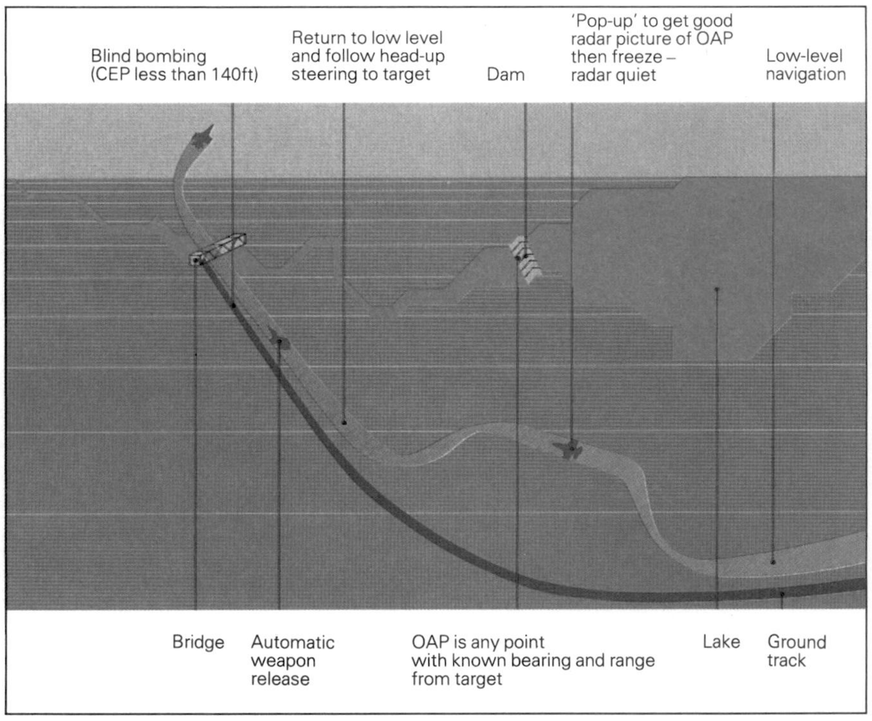

Above right: CCRP (continuously-computed release point) attacks use the the ground mapping radar modes. A radar map may be created and 'frozen' during a pop-up manoeuvre.

At high PRFs, the tube spends much more of its time transmitting, and has less time to cool down between pulses, involving a duty cycle of 50 per cent or more. As a result, the amount of power which can be extracted in each individual pulse is reduced.

By the time that Westinghouse faced the problem of updating the APG-66, its great rival in the airborne radar business had developed a new type of TWT which made dual-mode operation much more efficient. Working in conjunction with Litton, Hughes had created a TWT able to cope with the high peak-power demands of low- and medium-PRF operation, while still operating efficiently at the high duty cycles required by high PRFs. Long-range detection performance at medium PRFs could now match that at high PRFs.

All-round improvements

The revised MSIP radar's high-PRF modes are expected to raise radar range by at least 30 per cent, and perhaps as much as 60 per cent. Track-while-scan facilities will match the set to the fire-and-forget multiple-target attacks made possible by the AMRAAM missile, while the extended range performance should allow maximum advantage to be taken of the weapon's long range. The higher resolution of the modified set also allows the provision of a Raid-Assessment mode in which individual aircraft within a tight formation may be detected and tracked.

Improved air-to-ground facilities include new operating modes for ground target detection and tracking, plus Doppler beam-sharpening facilities for high-resolution ground mapping. These modes will complement the performance of the LANTIRN sensors.

Under the initial contract, seven radars were built for software development, ground trials and flight testing. Flight testing of the updated radar began in 1982. Earlier trials had involved the use of an F-4 testbed, but the new version was mounted in a modified Rockwell International Sabreliner business jet. The nose section of the aircraft was modified to carry the distinctive drooping profile F-16 radome. Delivery of revised radars should begin in 1984.

A second application for the APG-66 is the F-4EJ version of the Phantom. As part of a retrofit programme intended to extend the service life of the Japan Air Self-Defense Force fleet of Mitsubishi-built Phantoms, the existing APQ-120 radar is to be replaced by the APG-66J derivative of the Fighting Falcon set. A total of 100 aircraft are to be reworked.

Hardware from the APG-66 is also being used in the new Offensive Radar System due to be fitted in the nose of the Rockwell International B-1B bomber. This equipment will be used for tasks including low-altitude terrain-following and avoidance, high-resolution ground mapping and target detection/tracking.

Development potential of the APG-66 is by no means exhausted. Westinghouse engineers are already predicting that future versions might be able to establish the identity of a target by analyzing the radar return, and that new air-to-ground modes might include terrain-following and high-resolution surveillance using synthetic-aperture techniques.

The LANTIRN programme

In the late 1980s, the APG-66 will be backed up by the Martin Marietta LANTIRN (low-Altitude Navigation and Targeting Infra-Red for Night) system. This equipment will allow the pilot of a single-seat aircraft to fly sorties by day or night and in adverse weather. It can provide terrain-following radar and FLIR (forward-looking infra-red) imagery for navigation; automatically acquire, identify and categorize tank targets, passing target information to the aircraft's fire-control system so that Maverick missiles may be launched against several targets in a single pass; and can acquire and track fixed ground targets using FLIR or visual techniques, then designate them for attack using a built-in laser.

The basic installation comprises two avionics pods containing the sensors for navigation and target acquisition/tracking respectively. Martin Marietta is prime contractor for both. On the F-16, the pods will be carried on hardpoints under the inlet. They can operate autonomously, so an aircraft could fly into action with only one should this meet the requirements of the mission. Although the programme was formally launched in 1980, it was suspended just over a year later, and reshaped to reduced the technical risks involved.

The navigation pod is 12in (30.5cm) in diameter, 78in (198cm) long and weighs about 430lb (195kg). Main subsystems are a Ku-band terrain-following radar, wide field-of-view FLIR, pod computer and the associated power supply. Sophisticated signal processing is used to give the radar a wide azimuth coverage, allowing high-rate turns at low level in order to avoid or confuse the defences. This should give greater survivability than earlier-generation equipments which simply issued pitch commands to the pilot. The latter may have allowed him to avoid the terrain ahead, but exposed the aircraft to ground fire during the 'pull up' manoeuvre.

FLIR field of view is 28deg in azimuth and 21deg in elevation. The resulting wide-angle imagery may be superimposed on the outside scene by means of the HUD. In darkness or bad weather the HUD provides an image of TV-like quality and sufficient width to allow the pilot to look in the direction of his turn in order to 'preview' the terrain.

Targeting pod

The larger targeting pod has a movable nose section containing a FLIR sensor, laser transmitter/receiver and a stabilization system able to compensate for aircraft movements and vibration. A fixed centre section houses the tracker electronics and signal-processing systems and the boresight correlator used to pass target data to the aircraft's air-to-ground weapons. Environmental control of these systems and the nose-section sensors is handled by equipment in the aft section of the pod.

Flight testing using dummy fairings began in September 1982. The simulated pods have the same weight and mass distribution as the actual equipment and were instrumented to allow measurements of flutter, vibration and loads to be carried out. Test flying with functional equipment was scheduled to

LANTIRN navigation pod (right) and targeting pod (below)

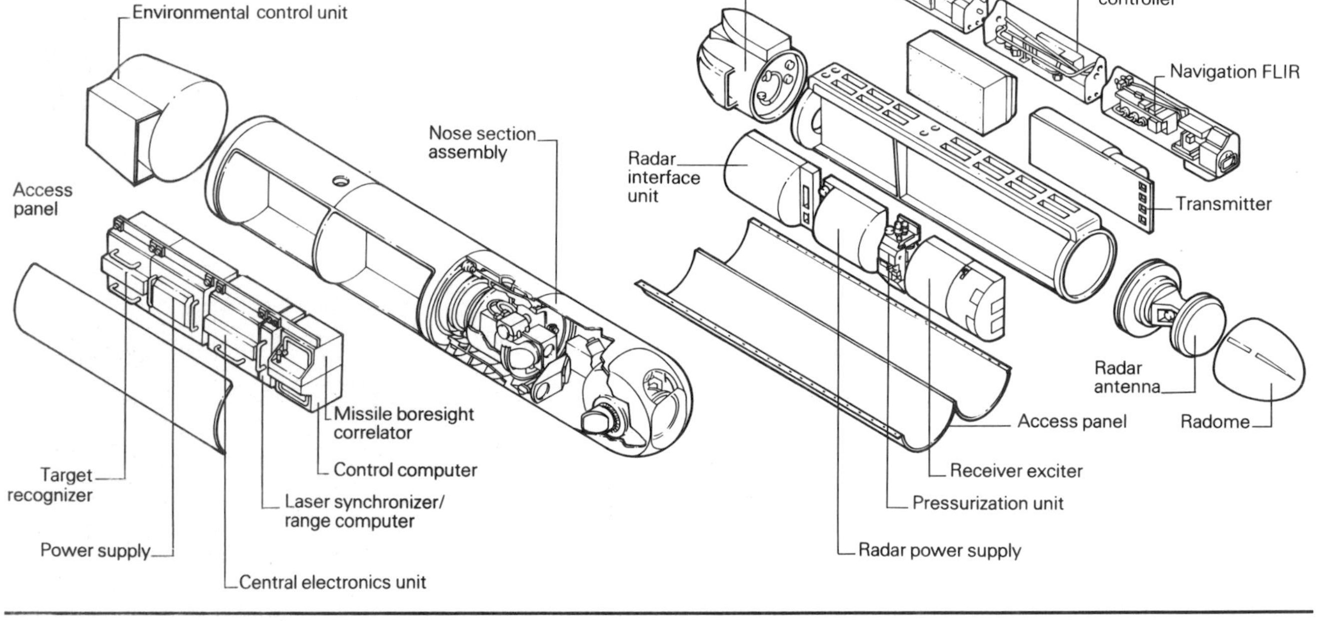

begin in the summer of 1983 using two F-16B and two A-10A trials aircraft. By the winter of 1984, LANTIRN equipment is scheduled to have completed tests under adverse operating conditions during combined development test and evaluation/initial operational test and evaluation trials in Europe.

In a typical LANTIRN attack, the aircraft will perform a 'pop-up' manoeuvre at the initial point. Scanning to either side of the flight path, the sensors pass IR imagery to the target-recognition systems. Once targets have been assessed, they will be shown to the pilot on his head-down display, while the HUD marks the first to be engaged. Using a second cockpit CRT display to show IR imagery from the Maverick missiles, the pilot will assign the first round to its target. As one round is launched, the system will automatically set up for the next, allowing up to six targets to be engaged during a single pass. LANTIRN can also handle laser-guided munitions. In this case, the system would illuminate the pre-selected target as the aircraft pulled up and released its weapon.

The most technologically risky part of LANTIRN is the Automatic Target Recognizer (ATR) sub-system. The USAF no longer plans to incorporate this equipment into LANTIRN from the start, but to add it under a later retrofit programme. Competitive designs are being developed by Hughes and Martin Marietta for evaluation in mid-1984, and the result of this trial will determine whether either is to be committed to full-scale development.

Central components of the LANTIRN cockpit display are the Marconi Avionics HUD, and two head-down multifunction CRT screens. The latter are able to display data from the radar and infra-red imagery from the LANTIRN sensors or the Maverick missile seeker head, plus the system-status displays required by the pilot.

LANTIRN funding

LANTIRN costs have been criticized by the US GAO, which ordered the USAF to re-evaluate its need for the equipment. In practice, says the USAF, the cost over-run has been less than 10 per cent – much of the alleged cost increase was due not to cost growth but to a change in accounting methods. The latter came about when LANTIRN was reclassified from being a retrofit programme of an existing weapon and upgraded to the status of being a programme in its own right. When this was done, the costs of development, testing and support became chargeable to the project and not to the F-16 programme. Further funding was added to allow for extra testing, and the programme has been stretched in timescale by about two years. To ease development, the USAF has dropped its requirement for LANTIRN to embody automatic laser correlation.

Flight trials of the LANTIRN HUD began in the summer of 1982, a year or so ahead of flight tests of the complete navigation and targeting pods. Congressional support for the project was waning, largely due to the high cost of the system, and the House Armed Services Committee reported that it had seriously considered 'recommending denial of all 1983 authorization of funding'.

Ford Aerospace has developed a FLIR pod for the US Navy, which will use it on the F/A-18 Hornet, and Congress has directed that this be tested in competition with LANTIRN before a production decision on the latter is taken in 1985. The USAF has in the meantime been prohibited from ordering LANTIRN into production until competitive flight tests have been carried out.

Cockpit displays

Data from the radar and Nav/attack systems of the Fighting Falcon are presented to the pilot on head-up and head-down displays. In the F-16A and B the head-down CRT display is manufactured by Kaiser, but for the HUD the USAF turned to the British company Marconi Avionics. A specialist in HUD technology, this Rochester-based company created the first HUD to enter service on a production aircraft – the Hawker Siddeley Buccaneer – back in 1960, and subsequently became an established supplier of HUDs to the USAF, building units for the A-7 Corsair II.

The original Buccaneer unit was primitive by modern standards, using analogue electronics and simple symbology. The A-7 HUD used digital electronics for computing and the positioning of the symbology, establishing the style of HUD now produced by many companies around the world. More than 2,000 units have been delivered for the Corsair II, and one of the company's HUDs was removed from the wreckage of an A-7 shot down in Vietnam, returned to the UK and found to be still in working order.

In addition to supplying the USAF, Marconi Avionics also provides equipment for other advanced military aircraft such as the Panavia Tornado, and had even developed the HUD for the Mirage F1.E contender for the NATO fighter order. For the Fighting Falcon programme, the UK company was involved from the beginning, having been awarded a contract to develop HUDs for the original two YF-16 prototypes. All subsequent patterns of HUD flown on or planned for the F-16 were designed by the same team.

In developing the F-16 HUD, the company placed great emphasis on the air-to-air gunnery role, aiming to create a system capable of giving a good first-burst hit probability. Radar ranging would normally be used, but a rotary switch on the HUD front panel provides for the more traditional stadiametric ranging, using the known wing span of the target as a reference from which to compute range.

Since the entire canopy of the F-16 is a one-piece polycarbonate component, its loss in an accident or in preparation for ejection would expose the pilot to the full force of the slipstream. Design of the optical components of the HUD was contracted to the UK company Pilkington PPE, whose designers ensured that the combiner glass of the unit was strong enough to withstand the slipstream. With the canopy gone, the HUD can thus act as a temporary windshield.

Field of view of the F-16A/B HUD is 13·5deg in azimuth by 9deg in elevation. For the AFTI project a wider field of view was required, so the Rochester design team pushed conventional optical technology to its limits to produce an impressive 20 × 15deg field. For use with the LANTIRN pod, the USAF asked for a HUD with an even larger field – 30 × 20deg. This forced the design team to return to the first principles of optics and devise an entirely new type of display.

The constraints on the HUD designer include the need to interfere as little as possible with the pilot's field of view, to take up as little of the instrument panel as possible, and not to intrude beyond the confines set by the windscreen and the ejection line. The last boundary is set by the space needed by the pilot's legs and feet during ejection.

To maximize the field of view the designer could mount the combiner glass as close to the ejection line as

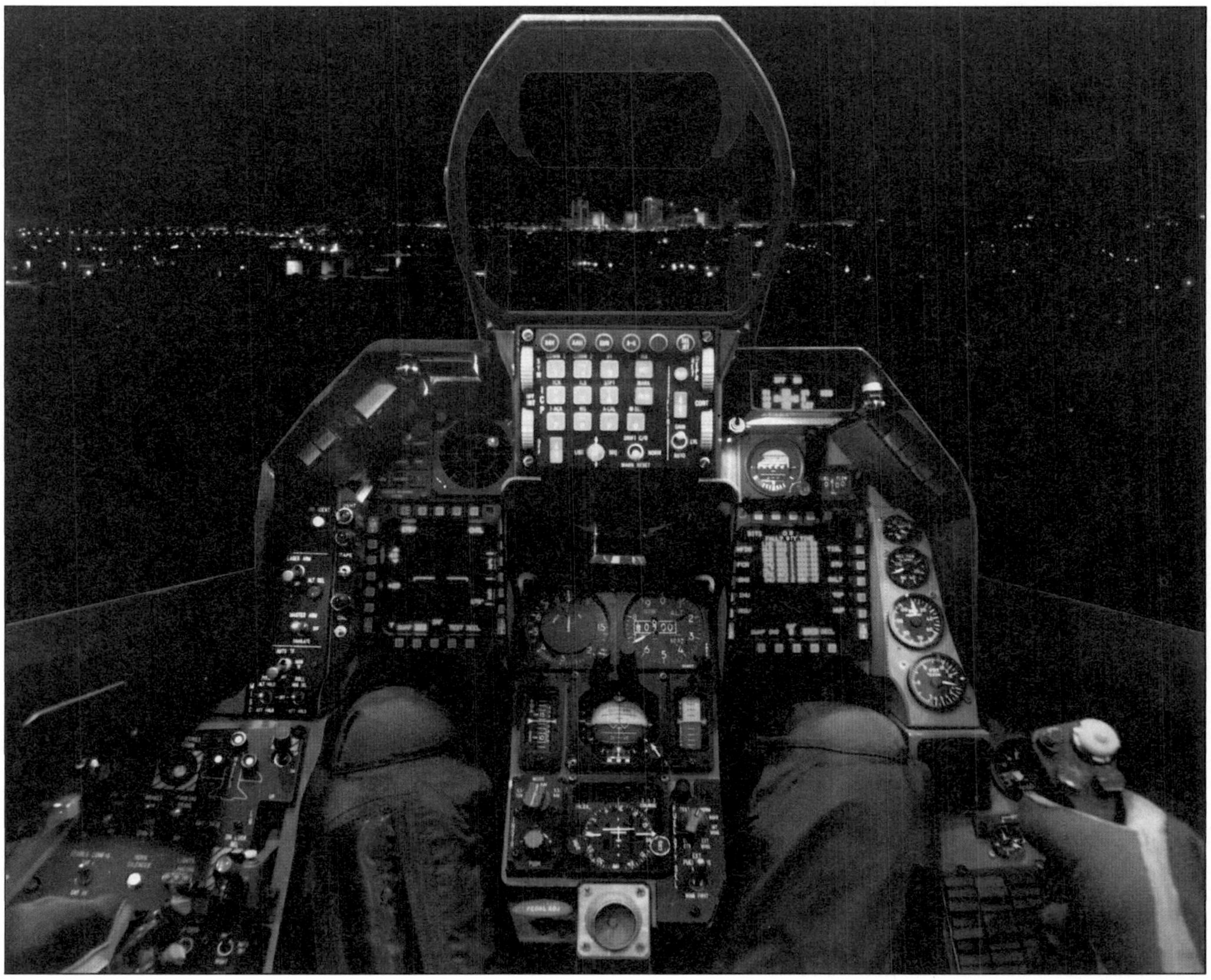

Above: A wide-angle HUD and two multipurpose CRT head-down displays are the main new features of the F-16C/D cockpit. The HUD was originally intended to be a holographic unit.

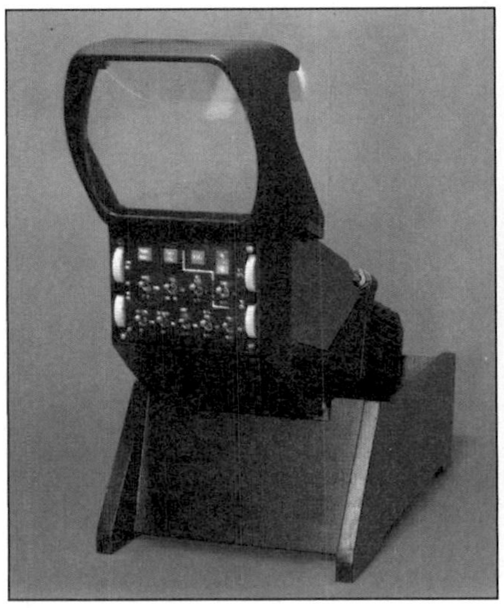

Above: Like the LANTIRN system itself, the Marconi Avionics holographic HUD is not certain to find a place in future F-16s. The USAF may modify the more conventional F-16C HUD to accept imagery from LANTIRN or other EO systems.

Above: Standard Marconi Avionics head-up display in an F-16A. The rectangular display seen below and to the left of the HUD control panel is not a radar display but forms part of the Fighting Falcon's sophisticated stores-management system.

possible. This leaves no room for the traditional pattern of CRT image-injection system, since the latter is mounted on the pilot's side of the combiner glass and would thus project over the ejection line. A complex optical path involving 'folding' the light rays was devised, but this had a low efficiency, resulting in a dim view of both the CRT-generated imagery and the outside world.

The final solution entailed the use of a combiner consisting of a reflective hologram or diffraction grating to create the effect of a mirror surface. Holograms reflect light of only a certain colour, allowing light of all other colours to pass freely. In the LANTIRN HUD design, the colour chosen for reflection is the green associated with the CRT used to generate symbology. The combiner can thus act simultaneously as an efficient mirror and as a transparency. To quote Robin Sleight, Technical Manager of the Marconi Airborne Displays division, "We have found one of the rare conditions in life where we are getting something for nothing: a surface which transmits 90 per cent of the light hitting it, yet apparently also reflects to a similar value!"

The first unit was handed over to the USAF in March 1982, and flight tests aboard an F-16 started the same summer. Like the LANTIRN system itself, the holographic HUD faces an uncertain future. Early in 1983 Marconi Avionics announced that it had been awarded a contract to build a new pattern of HUD for the F-16C and D, but this is largely based on the AFTI unit rather than on the holographic design. It seems likely that the new unit will be modified for use with LANTIRN.

Under the MSIP programme, the F-16 will also receive new patterns of head-down cockpit displays. General Dynamics will install a moving-map display

Above: The wide-angle HUD devised for the AFTI/F-16 forms the basis of the F-16C HUD. This design offers the widest field of view possible using conventional optics.

on an instrument panel between the pilot's knees, displacing conventional mechanical standby flight instruments. This system was chosen in preference to the synthetic raster-scan display favoured by GD, which would have allowed moving-map data to be displayed on any of three multi-function cockpit CRT displays being developed by Sperry.

ECM systems

In addition to its offensive avionics, the Fighting Falcon is equipped with defensive electronic countermeasures (ECM) systems intended to help it survive in the face of modern air defences. Secrecy is essential if ECM techniques and tactics are to remain effective, so very little detailed information has been published concerning the performance of the equipment mentioned below.

The most basic item of ECM equipment is the radar-warning receiver (RWR). This is designed to detect the signals from hostile radars, and to alert the pilot that he is under observation. Most patterns of RWR give an approximate indication of the threat bearing, frequency and signal characteristics, while some identify the threat using a built-in catalogue of threat parameters.

When a threat radar is first detected by the RWR, the threat may not yet have detected the incoming aircraft. The RWR has the relatively simple task of detecting the powerful signal transmitted by the hostile radar, but the receiving system of the latter must attempt to detect the small amount of energy reflected by the target.

The threat radar will almost certainly be fitted with a relatively large and highly-directional antenna, while the RWR has only a low-gain omni-directional antenna array, but despite this inequality the RWR will usually detect the radar before the latter has detected the aircraft. Given this warning, the pilot may change course to avoid the radar, reduce cruise height in order to fly beneath the radar's horizon, or turn on some form of ECM. The warning provided by the RWR gives him a clear advantage.

The same techniques may be used if a tracking radar manages to lock on to the aircraft. The RWR display will probably give the first indication to the pilot that his tactics have been successful in 'breaking the lock' of the hostile system.

Basic RWR carried by the F-16 is the Itek ALR-69. Based on the earlier ALR-46, this was developed for the USAF and US Navy and consists of five general-purpose surveillance receivers plus a sixth frequency-selective receiver. The latter is probably used to detect signals associated with semi-active homing missile systems such as the Soviet SA-6 Gainful, and gives an indication of the direction of attack.

The US desire to limit exports of this sensitive equipment led to Pakistan rejecting its first batch of F-16s in 1982. These were to have been fitted with the Itek ALR-46. Widely exported to nations such as Egypt, Iran, Portugal, Saudi Arabia, South Korea, Switzerland, Taiwan, Thailand and West Germany, the ALR-46 covers the radar spectrum from 2.0 to 18GHz. Alarm indications are given on CRT cockpit displays and in the pilot's headset. Pakistan was eventually cleared to receive the ALR-69, but the older equipment may still be supplied to F-16 operators who do not face the most sophisticated threat systems.

At a later date, USAF aircraft could receive the latest RWR currently under development, the Itek ALR-74. This uses some of the technology developed for the US Navy's ALR-69, and is intended to counter Soviet threats anticipated for the late 1980s. Both programmes have attracted criticism from the US GAO, which wants to see a common RWR developed for both services.

Many F-16 operators have already opted to fit their aircraft with further ECM protection in the form of active jamming systems or chaff dispensers. The equipment selected is often specific to the individual air arm, although a degree of standardization is being attempted.

Modern jamming systems operate in noise and deception modes. Noise jamming aims to swamp the hostile radar signal or communications link with unwanted radio-frequency noise, so that the genuine and wanted signal cannot be distinguished from the background.

F-16 antenna locations

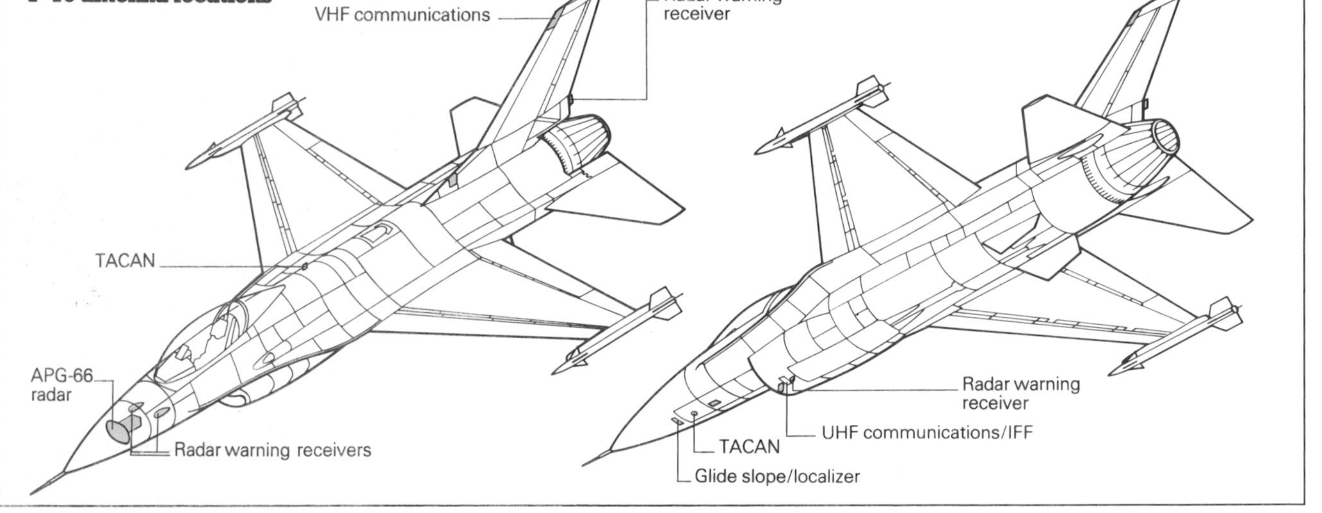

The technique is simple to implement, since very little needs to be known about the characteristics of the threats. If the exact operating frequency of the latter is known, the jammer may be pre-tuned to concentrate its output power on these frequencies. This is known as spot jamming.

If the threat frequency is not known exactly, or if the threat is frequency-agile, the simplest technique is to radiate the noise output of the jammer over a range of frequencies likely to contain the threat. This is known as barrage jamming, and is a simple technique, but the need to spread the power of the jammer reduces its effectiveness. Since the aircraft-mounted system can only generate a relatively modest level of jamming power, the signal-to-noise ratio received by the threat radar or system will be much lower than with spot jamming, easing the task of filtering out the wanted signal from the unwanted.

Rather than attempt such brute-force solutions, the modern jamming system uses a built-in search (or 'set-on') receiver to monitor the frequency of all detected threat signals. The output from this receiver may be used to control the frequency of the jammer transmitters, so that the spot jamming may be used against a threat of unknown or variable frequency.

Deceptive jamming

More complex patterns of monitoring receiver may be used to allow subtler forms of jamming – a family of techniques known as deceptive jamming. These involve receiving the threat signal, processing it in some way, then re-transmitting it in the hope of persuading the threat system to accept the doctored signal as genuine. By choosing the manner in which the signal is processed before transmission, the ECM designer can feed false range or bearing information to an enemy radar, or even cause multiple false targets to be detected.

Demonstrating such false target jamming to the author several years ago, Westinghouse technicians effectively blanked out the circular PPI (plan-position indicator) display of a surveillance radar by generating thousands of false targets simultaneously. So closely were these spaced on the display that the CRT face literally turned an even shade of white.

In a modern jamming system the search receiver monitors all radar signals received, comparing their parameters with a built-in threat library. Once those representing the greatest threat to the aircraft have been identified, the jammer assigns the power available from its various jamming transmitters accordingly. This technique is known as power-management.

The type of jamming to be used will be chosen to match the threat, and the receiver will often monitor the hostile transmission at regular intervals in order to assess the effect of its jamming. If the latter is not proving effective, a different jamming method may be automatically selected.

In the early stages of the full-scale development programme, Tactical Air Command contemplated an internal ECM system. Studies of possible aircraft installations were carried out, and the likely balance between cost and aircraft survivability assessed. It was appreciated that an internal system would require the use of new technology and would take some time to develop and deploy.

All external stores had to be flutter tested, and some problem was initially experienced with the ALQ-119 ECM pod. When the aircraft was loaded with one specific configuration of stores, a speed limit had to be imposed. Tests with the ALQ-131 showed that carriage of the more modern pod required no such restraint.

Both the USAF and the Royal Netherlands Air Force adopted the ALQ-131 pod for the protection of their F-16 force. Selection of an ECM system for the F-16 became a major political issue in the Netherlands, with the Christian Democrat/Liberal coalition Government supporting the ALQ-131 and the Labour party being opposed to its adoption. The controversy was marked by Parliamentary hearings and debates. The US offer in August 1980 of a batch of 75 ALQ-131 ECM pods at a total cost of $63.5 million was the final factor which persuaded the RNethAF to adopt the standard USAF pod. This was seen as being cheaper than an internal ECM fit, and offered the advantages of standardization within NATO. Denmark and Norway were due to select an ECM fit in 1981, but lack of defense funds made it likely that no ECM would be fitted.

Development of the ALQ-131 started in the early 1970s to meet a USAF requirement. Following successful development and flight tests, the unit was ordered into production in 1976. ALQ-131 is a 573lb (260kg) modular pod-mounted system able to cope with a wide range of threats, particularly the radars and guidance systems of air-defence systems.

By selecting internal modules, the user may configure the pod to handle threats spread over one to five frequency bands. Modules are available to cope with all frequencies used by current anti-aircraft missile systems, and both noise and deception-jamming modes are available. The pod is power-managed, and the software can easily be modified to cope with the tactical situation which the user faces, or to take into account changes in threat tactics or parameters. Such modifications may be easily carried out, and may even be implemented on the flight line.

The struggle between the ECM designer and the latest tactics and systems is a continuous one. If the prospective enemy introduces new radar bands or techniques, hardware modifications may be needed. The USAF initiated the classified Have Exit update programme in 1980, four years after the equipment entered service. In this case, the system was probably being updated to cope with new Soviet threat systems featuring monopulse radars.

The USAF carries the ALQ-131 pod on the fuselage centreline hardpoint, thus losing the ability to carry an additional 300US gal (360Imp gal/1637l) of external fuel. It also left internal space available for follow-on systems such as AMRAAM-related equipment and the JTIDS (Joint Tactical Information Distribution System) data terminal.

The Rapport III system

After a study of the merits of pod-mounted and internal ECM systems, the Belgian Air Force decided in 1979 to adopt the Loral Rapport III (Rapid Alert Programmed Power Management of Radar Target) internal ECM suite. The original version of Rapport was developed for the FAéB following a study of the Mirage 5B carried out in the light of Israeli experience during the 1973 Middle East War.

Requests for proposals for an internal ECM installation were circulated to US and European electronics companies early in 1974. Three companies were contracted to carry out feasibility studies, a team consisting of Loral and MBLE being chosen to develop the prototype Rapport II. This was flight

Above: If pod-mounted electronic countermeasures are carried on the F-16, the ventral hardpoint is normally used. This 388th TFW aircraft is equipped with a Westinghouse ALQ-119, almost certainly the (V)-12 version.

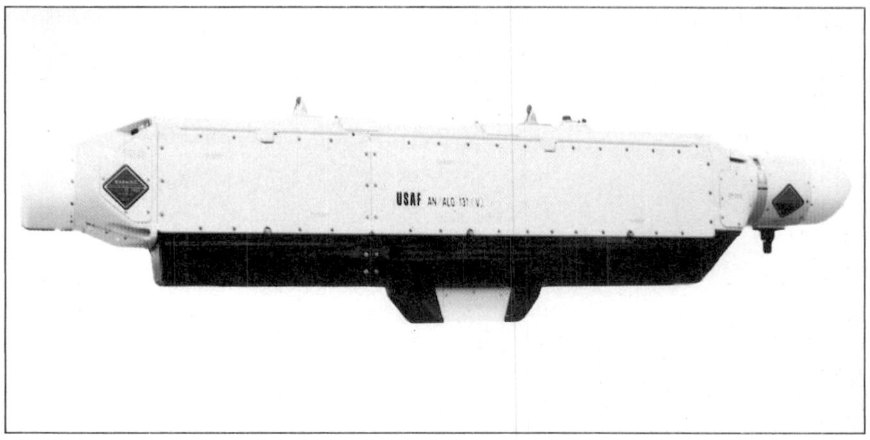

Right: Main recognition features of the Westinghouse ALQ-131 ECM pod are the full-length ventral gondola and two ventrally-mounted antennae. The red and black markings near the fore and aft-mounted radomes warn personnel to keep at least 15ft (4.6m) away when the pod is transmitting.

tested in 1977 and entered production a year later.

Belgium demonstrated Rapport II to its NATO F-16 partners, but failed to arouse much interest. It then funded GD to carry out a study of a Rapport installation for the F-16. The GD response was favourable, so contracts for two prototypes of the Rapport III system for the F-16 were awarded to Loral and GD in 1979. Part of the system is carried in an extended fairing at the base of the tail fin. Rapport III is designed to be compatible with the Rapport II equipment still carried by Belgian Mirage 5R and 5BA fighters.

Before adopting Rapport the Belgian Air Force studied rival equipments, but concluded that the former system was likely to be cheaper than alternative US equipments. Being internally mounted, Rapport also has the advantage of not taking up a hardpoint and does not add to aircraft drag. One penalty which Belgium was forced to pay was the loss of internal avionics growth space, and the fact that the packaging of future avionics adopted by the NATO F-16 users would be non-standard on Belgian aircraft.

Flight trials of Rapport III were carried out during the summer of 1981 at Eglin AFB, Florida, using two Belgian Air Force F-16s. Units were flown against simulated threat systems and other equipment at the Eglin EW range.

The USAF did not carry out a full test of the equipment itself, but concluded from limited studies that the effectiveness of the ALQ-131 and Rapport III were broadly comparable. Minor technical problems delayed completion of the test programme, and while the equipment was shown to meet all requirements, the delays resulted in an overrun in the trials budget.

This increased cost posed additional strains on what was already a tightly-funded programme, so Belgium was faced with the option of either voting additional funds or reducing the number of aircraft to be equipped from the planned 72. Not all Belgian F-16s will have Rapport, as the system will not be carried by aircraft assigned to the training role. Deliveries of hardware are due to end in 1985. The only other F-16 operator to adopt Rapport was the Israeli Air Force. The first Israeli order was for units to equip at least some of the 75 F-16s on order at that time.

According to Loral, Rapport is the first ECM system to integrate the tasks of detecting signals, identifying the threats and transmitting the required type of jamming signal. The system is reprogrammable on the ground in order to cope with new threat systems. Rapport systems for the Belgian Air Force are supplied by the Belgian company MBLE.

The wide-band RWR used in Rapport monitors all incoming radar signals, identifying the type of radar involved and displaying the resulting data to the pilot on a CRT. Power-management algorithms are used by the system's microprocessor-based jammer-control system in order to determine the best ECM tactics to cope with a constantly changing situation. Rapport employs forward and backward-facing jammers, whose output power and frequencies are set to match the characteristics of high-threat enemy equipments.

In 1979 the US Congress ordered the USAF and US Navy to evaluate Rapport III, but both declined to adopt the system. The USAF rejected Rapport III, pointing out that it was incompatible with the ALR-69 RWR, while the USN described the system as 'entirely unacceptable'. Both services were already collaborating on the inter-service Advanced Self-Protection Jammer (ASPJ) project.

Development of the ASPJ started as a competition between two industrial groups, with Westinghouse and ITT eventually defeating the Northrop/Sanders team. Space for ASPJ was always available within the F-16, but ECP350 introduced the necessary internal holes and ducts for the system's waveguides and wiring.

Right: Aircraft cruising at medium altitude should be sitting ducks for hostile defences, but the ALQ-131 pod's noise and deception jammers can counter all known SAM systems.

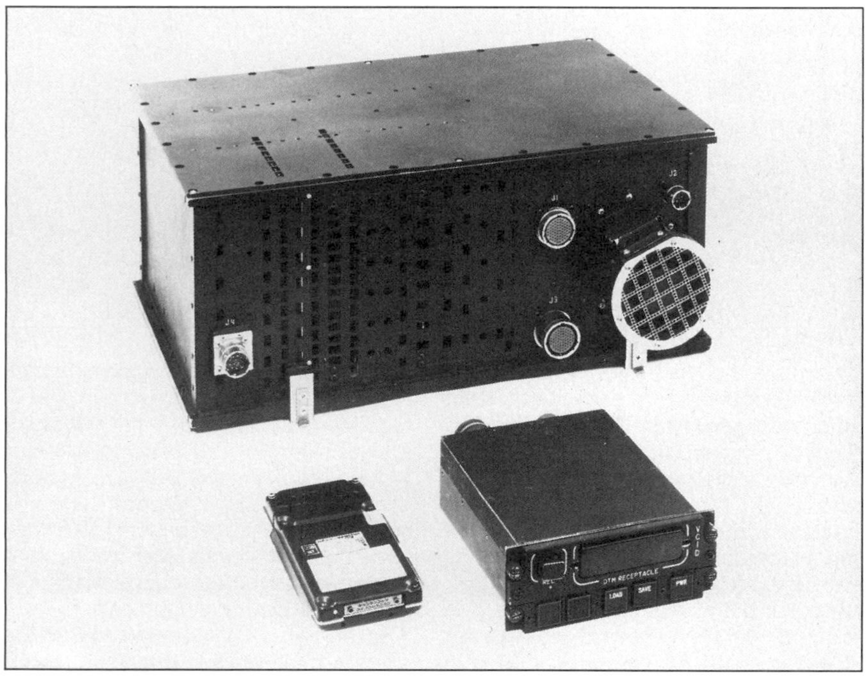

Left: Lear-Siegler voice-control system from F-16/AFTI.
Below: Infra-red image obtained from the Oldelft Orpheus recce pod, to be used by RNethAF F-16s.

Above: The USAF has no current plans to deploy a dedicated reconnaissance version of the F-16, but the 6th full-scale development aircraft was flown with a dummy camera pod.

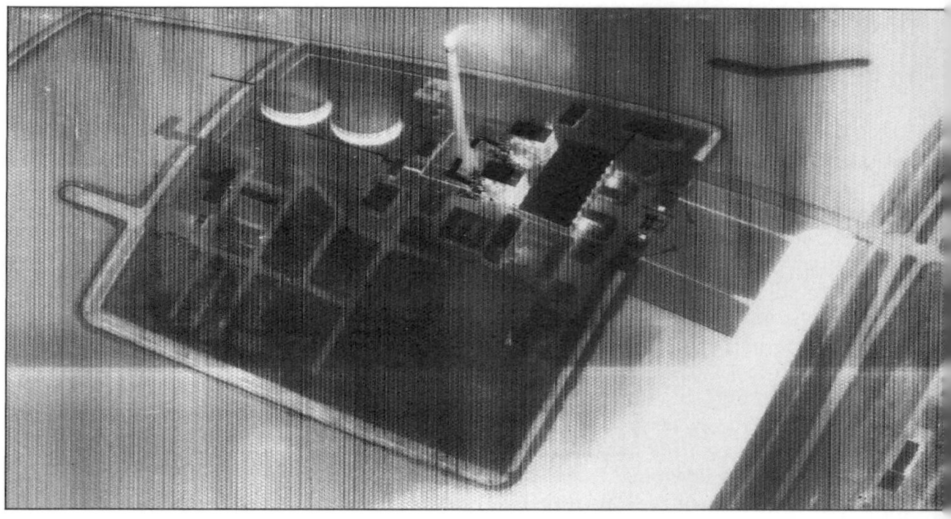

So advanced is the design of the ALQ-165 ASPJ that the job was thought impossible by many people, according to Westinghouse. The Services were determined to obtain a system which would not suffer from early obsolescence as the threat systems it faced were updated. The designers decided to sever the pre-set relationship between threat and countermeasure which has been a feature of earlier ECM systems, and to rely on the ASPJ computer to select the appropriate countermeasure techniques in accordance with a combination of established threat data and real-time information obtained from the system's built-in receiver/signal processor.

The operational requirement called for ASPJ to cover several octaves of frequency, handling multiple threat signals against a dense background of other signals. The system can simultaneously jam many threats using its power-managed dual-mode transmitters. These have parallel TWT tubes which can be used to cope with pulse or CW signals in response to demands from the system software.

Design of the system is modular; the five basic sub-units plus the optional augmentation receiver and high-band transmitter may be installed aboard a range of aircraft. In the case of Fighting Falcon, the equipment is being mounted internally as part of MSIP Phase III. For the US Navy's F-14 Tomcat and F/A-18 Hornet, it will take up the internal space currently occupied by the ALQ-100/126 ECM equipment, while the US Marine Corps AV-8B will carry the system in an external pod.

Communications equipment

Basic communications installation in the F-16A and B consists of Collins ARC-186 VHF AM/FM and Magnavox ARC-164 UHF transceivers, a Magnavox KY-58 secure voice system and an interference blanker by Novatronics. Between 1984 and 1986 the USAF F-16 force will be equipped with the new JTIDS jam-resistant command, control and communications system, plus the Seek Talk ECM-resistant voice-communications equipment should this survive budget cut-backs.

Part of the MSIP Phase III programme, these units will be introduced at the same time as the LANTIRN electro-optical system, AMRAAM missile and the ASPJ electronic countermeasures system. Also introduced around this time will be new navigation equipment which will utilise the GPS satellite system. This will supplement the current Singer-Kearfott-developed SKN-2000 inertial navigation system.

One unusual item of communications equipment being pioneered in the AFTI/F-16 is a Lear-Siegler voice-control system. Designated Voice-Controlled Interactive Device (VCID), this is used to control the AFTI avionic systems. In its initial form the VCID system has a vocabulary of 32 words, but this will eventually expand to a maximum of 256. Early tests used words such as 'menu', 'data', 'entry', 'plus', 'minus', and 'recall', plus numbers, phonetic letters, and the points of the compass.

In the early stages of AFTI flight tests only single-word commands were used. These control nav/attack and flight-control modes, and later tests will evaluate the use of connected phrases. There are no plans at present to use voice command to handle critical safety-related functions such as primary flight control or weapon release.

In theory, electronic systems should be able to deal with complete sentences, searching for and extracting the relevant nouns and verbs. This type of parsing operation – a development of artificial intelligence research – can already be done via the keyboard of all but the smallest computers, and has been incorporated into computerized 'adventure' games such as Zork.

One problem with voice-recognition systems is that not only are they voice dependent – that is, they tend to respond accurately only to the voice for which they were set up – but that the accuracy also depends on voice characteristics remaining, if not constant, at least predictable. To explore this area GD conducted tests to see how voice quality changes owing to factors such as time of day, stress, fatigue, and G-loading. Other tests explored the effect on voice-operated systems of extraneous noise in the aircraft cockpit or in the pilot's oxygen mask, for example.

Noise level in the cockpit of a high-performance aircraft is very high; in the F-16 it can exceed 120dB during 9g manoeuvres. High g forces also make speech difficult or even impossible. During GD centrifuge tests, few pilots could talk at levels of more than 5g, although one individual managed to keep grunting commands at up to 9g. Under these rigorous circumstances, experimental voice-recognition equipment managed an impressive 90 per cent success rate in identifying his spoken commands. The USAF sees the major application of voice-operated cockpits as future night/all-weather single-seat fighters.

Another technique being tested in the AFTI/F-16 is a helmet-mounted sight for target designation. Instead of positioning target-identification cross-hairs by means of a throttle-mounted cursor control, the AFTI pilot need only look at a target in order to acquire it. The pilot aligns the target with a set of 0·5in (12·7mm) long cross-hairs incorporated in the visor of his helmet. He then depresses the 'target designate' button on his sidestick controller. Orientation of the helmet within the cockpit is measured by a magnetic system incorporating a transmitter mounted on the canopy immediately behind the pilot's head, and a 4oz (113gm) receiver system on the helmet; the radar or FLIR is automatically slewed to achieve lock-on. Final adjustment is carried out using

This diagram illustrates an automated manoeuvring attack by the AFTI/F-16. During the initial run-in (1) the pilot engages the attack system, then carries out a pop-up manoeuvre (2) to acquire the target and command lock-on. After a period of jinking flight (3) he updates the lock-on (4), then gives the system permission for weapon release (5).

the cursor controller or by voice command via the VCID system.

If the aircraft systems have detected a target, the location of the latter may be passed to the pilot via the helmet-mounted sight. In this case, miniature lamps at the tips of the visor cross-hairs indicate to the pilot the direction in which he must move his head to acquire the target. When all four are illuminated, the target is in the centre of the cross-hairs.

Flight control system

Probably the boldest step in the original YF-16 design was the decision to adopt an all-electronic fly-by-wire (FBW) flight-control system, instead of the traditional pattern of hydromechanical system with linkages and cables. This was a high-authority command and stability-augmentation system of quadruplexed (four-channel) analogue type, and this configuration was retained for the production aircraft. The weight reductions resulting from the elimination of a mechanical system could be used to allow the large-scale use of fail-safe and fail-operative design techniques, ensuring the high reliability of the electronic equipment.

When details of the F-16 system were first published, they caused some misgivings at Saab-Scania in Sweden, where design of the JA-37 Viggen flight-control system was in hand, since the Swedes had opted for a quadruplexed digital system. Despite momentary misgivings, the Swedish decision was a correct one – Fighting Falcon was born too soon to embody a quadruplexed digital system. The latter first entered service in 1977 on the Space Shuttle and a year later on the F/A-18 Hornet.

Without the FBW system, the GD designers could not have positioned the aircraft centre of gravity behind the centre of pressure to give a reduced or negative static margin. The resulting inherent instability is controlled by the FBW system, making the aircraft easy to fly, but gives the controls a high response rate and allows the use of relatively modest amounts of tail deflection during high-g manoeuvres or supersonic flight. During the design of the YF-16, GD engineers estimated that the consequent reduction of trim drag allowed 400lb (181kg) to be shaved off the mission weight of the aircraft.

Lifting tail

The use of relaxed stability also allowed the size of the tail to be reduced, as less force was needed to alter aircraft attitude. Since the tail effectively pushes the rear of the aircraft upwards in order to maintain level flight (the tail on a conventional aircraft pushes downwards), tail trimming forces increase the overall lift.

Adoption of FBW was a bold step, but one that paid off. The system has generally proved trouble-free in service, except for a brief period in August 1981 when most F-16 operators placed restrictions on flying following the discovery of a problem in the flight-control emergency power system.

Ground test runs carried out following the loss of an F-16 in an earlier flying accident had focussed attention on an air-bleed valve. Following the crash of a 388th TFW aircraft on August 6, Time Compliance Technical Order 30 specified that this valve be inspected between flights until a modification was carried out. The check took 1–2 man-hours to perform, so most operators virtually grounded the aircraft until the valve had been modified to prevent 'chattering'.

Tests had shown that faulty valves could cause voltage fluctuations able to affect the flight control system's emergency backup systems, causing spurious and unpredictable pitch, yaw and roll inputs. Modifications to eliminate the problem took around 12 manhours per aircraft.

FBW systems have been test-flown since the late 1960s, and a rudimentary single-channel analogue system even flew as long ago as 1952 aboard a Tay-engined Viscount airliner testbed. The Panavia Tornado was the first production design to adopt FBW, but this aircraft retained a mechanical backup. The GD team was the first to take the step of eliminating mechanical backups, trusting the safety of the aircraft completely to electronics. Mechanical backups were also eliminated on the later F/A-18 Hornet, Mirage 2000 and JA-37 Viggen designs, but Fighting Falcon showed the way. For this reason alone, the GD warplane is assured of a place in aviation history.

For the AFTI/F-16, a full-authority triplex digital flight-control system is used. This is designed to be fault tolerant, so that no single fault should affect correct operation. In the event of a second fault developing, the system is able to revert to a standby condition which will permit safe flight to continue, allowing the aircraft to return to base in such an emergency.

Failures resulting in complete loss of control will be rare, the AFTI specification calling for not more than one per 10 million flight hours. To guard against unforeseen failure modes the system incorporates a simple analogue backup flight-control system. Designated the Independent Backup (IBU), this will allow control to be maintained should some drastic failure result in the digital flight-control system being unable to maintain control.

Armament

Ordnance carried by the Fighting Falcon ranges from simple weaponry such as unguided rockets and 20mm cannon shells to nuclear weapons. Air-to-air, air-to-ground and specialized anti-ship missiles, along with laser-guided 'smart' bombs, have all been cleared for service, and the F-16 is already slated to receive the most advanced types of weaponry currently under development, including the 'fire and forget' AMRAAM missile needed to cope with next-generation Soviet fighters. Even using straightforward 'iron' bombs, Fighting Falcon can hit its target with greater accuracy than the F-111.

Above: 20mm cannon shells are loaded into the magazine of an F-16 at Kunsan Air Base, South Korea. A full load consists of 500 rounds.

Despite its age, the General Electric 20mm M61A remains the standard USAF fighter cannon. The Service did attempt to develop a caseless 25mm weapon for the F-15 Eagle, but this project bogged down in technical difficulties, so the 20mm seems destined to soldier on through the 1980s.

The M61A1 may be a proven weapon, but its adoption in the F-16 resulted in some initial problems. Gun firing from the type was temporarily forbidden in September 1979 following two incidents in which this resulted in uncommanded yawing movements. Gun vibration was found to be affecting an accelerometer in the flight-control system, causing it to feed false data to the control computer, which in turn demanded the yaw.

A simple modification insulated the accelerometer from vibration. Ten aircraft were modified, assigned to Hill AFB, and successfully participated in a Red Flag exercise. The modification was then introduced into production aircraft, and all 106 operational F-16s delivered with the original pattern of accelerometer installation were modified during 1980.

In its F-16A/B form, the Fighting Falcon was armed with AIM-9 Sidewinder missiles for air-to-air combat. Today's Sidewinders are greatly improved versions of the primitive weapon which first entered production in the mid-1950s. Early Sidewinders may not have required the full co-operation of the target during air-to-air combat, but were restricted to use in classical tail-chase attacks in good weather.

With the arrival of second- and third-generation seeker heads, Sidewinder matured into an agile 'dogfight' missile. European F-16s were originally scheduled to carry the AIM-9J – a rebuilt and modernized version of the early AIM-9B or -9C – but the US Government eventually agreed to make the AIM-9L available. This is a highly agile weapon with all-new guidance seeker and proximity fuze. A total of at least 16,000 are likely to be built in the US, and a further 9,000 or more by a European manufacturing consortium.

BVR missiles

In Vietnam, the MiG-17 and MiG-21 interceptors which challenged US warplanes were equipped only with cannon or short-range guided missiles. US pilots could opt to engage targets under beyond-visual-range (BVR) conditions using the Raytheon AIM-7 Sparrow, or close in to engage in a dogfight with guns and AIM-9 Sidewinders. By the time the F-16 was entering service in significant numbers, it faced the threat of aircraft such as the MiG-23 armed with AA-7 Apex long-range missiles. To engage these in a Sidewinder-armed F-16 would put the Soviet pilot in the same position as US aircrew had been in over Vietnam.

Without improvements, the Fighting Falcon stood the risk of becoming the late-1980s equivalent of the Japanese Zero – lightweight and agile but seriously under-armed. Romantics might argue otherwise, but the day of the simple fighter was coming to an end. Testifying before Congress in 1980, Undersecretary of Defense for Research and Engineering William J. Perry described the F-16A as "an incomplete airplane". Detailing the need for BVR combat capability, he said that "we kidded ourselves a little bit on the F-16, thinking we were buying an inexpensive airplane".

As originally planned, the APG-66 radar was not intended to have the capability of handling BVR missiles. What the customer asked for – and Westinghouse delivered – was a multimode set sized for the air-to-air mission but offering the many modes necessary for effective ground attack in the 1980s and beyond.

The definitive solution to the problem was the planned AMRAAM (Advanced Medium-Range Air-to-Air Missile), which was due to enter service in the mid-1980s, but USAF planners considered a number of interim solutions for service in the first half of the 1980s. French missile company Matra could offer a radar-guided version of the R.550 Magic. The US, meanwhile, had already fielded and withdrawn a radar-guided AIM-9C version of Sidewinder and had the technology available to develop an updated version of this as a result of the

Below: The smoke pouring from the F-16 on the target range comes not from the engine but from the 6,000rds/min M61A1 cannon.

Above: As a private venture, GD has test-fired radar-guided AIM-7 Sparrow missiles from the YF-16, though no customer has requested Sparrow armament.

Below: This unconventional door-mounted pylon was used for test firings of the Sky Flash shown here, as well as for Sparrow. No F-16 user has ordered the BAe weapon.

Below: the AIM-9 Sidewinder may be a lightweight missile, but lifting its 172lb (78kg) weight into place on the wingtip launch pylon requires significant muscle power.

Semi-Active Medium Pulse-Repetition-Frequency Seeker Demonstration project carried out at China Lake. Either weapon would have given the F-16 a radar capability, but would have done little to improve the engagement range.

Obvious solutions were the longer-range AIM-7 Sparrow or British Aerospace Sky Flash radar-guided missiles. Although larger than AMRAAM, both missiles could provide the required range but would require modifications to the APG-66 in order to provide target-illumination facilities.

Evaluation of a Sparrow-armed YF-16 was carried out by GD, using company funding, with inert rounds carried on wingtip, underwing and fuselage-mounted pylons. The last location involved the pylon being fitted directly on the undercarriage door, and was used for test firings in November 1977. A test firing of the British Sky Flash missile followed a year later, using pylons in the same location.

The need for interim BVR missiles was questioned by some analysts, who claimed that the problems of target-identification would often inhibit BVR attacks, while the higher cost of the missiles would reduce the amount of live-firing training which would be possible. Adoption of either weapon would have been expensive, and AMRAAM development showed no signs of significant slippage in time-scale, so plans for the older missiles were shelved.

AMRAAM and ASRAAM

Fighting Falcon will be the first aircraft to carry the new Hughes AIM-120 AMRAAM. This missile is intended to combine the performance of the AIM-7 Sparrow in an airframe not much larger than that of the AIM-9 Sidewinder. The weapon weighs only 326lb (148kg) at launch, compared with 115–195lb (70–88.5kg) for Sidewinder and 503lb (228kg) for the latest versions of Sparrow. Maximum range is more than 30 miles (48km), and the missile is likely to fly at around Mach 4.

AMRAAM flies the initial portion of its trajectory under the control of a mid-course inertial guidance unit which can be updated if neccessary by the launch aircraft. In the later stages of flight, the missile switches on its high-PRF radar seeker and homes onto the target. Since this seeker uses active radar, it does not require the launch aircraft to carry a target illuminator antenna or to continue to track the target after launch. If the target attempts to protect itself with jamming, AMRAAM's seeker can be set to operate in a medium-PRF home-on-jam mode during the midcourse or terminal stages of flight.

Hughes and Raytheon developed rival AMRAAM designs in the late 1970s. Each contractor was due to fire ten prototype rounds from F-14, F-15 and F-16 test aircraft. Firings started in 1981, but after only six shots Hughes was declared the winner in December of that year.

The company launched its first test round in February, with the first guided shot (from an F-16) following on August 26. The round scored an almost central hit on a QF-102 target, which burst into flames and crashed. The missile did not carry a warhead. In a series of six design-validation flight tests, AMRAAM scored two direct hits, one near-miss well within the lethal radius of the warhead, and three failures. The design has now been modified to take account of the experience gained. Test firings will resume in 1984.

Under a $420-million 50-month contract awarded after the 'shoot-off', Hughes is to build some 100 development missiles, 87 of which will be launched from F-14, F-15, F-16 and F/A-18 aircraft during a two-year series of development and operational test/evaluation firings. Delivery of production rounds will begin in the second half of 1985.

AMRAAM was nowhere near ready for service when the Multinational Staged Improvement Plan (MSIP) was approved in February 1981, but the associated Engineering Change Proposal ECP350 included changes to the aircraft structure and wiring of the wings to allow the weapon to be retrofitted easily at a later date.

The aircraft may eventually carry the shorter-range ASRAAM (Advanced Short-Range Air-to-Air Missile) being developed by a European consortium consisting of British Aerospace Dynamics and Bodenseewerk Geratetechnik. This missile is intended for US and NATO use and would be built under licence in the USA. Development has been painfully slow, and any resulting weapon is unlikely to see service until the late 1980s.

In studying possible guidance systems for ASRAAM, the two companies looked at infra-red, active-laser and active-radar systems. One possibility would have involved using a combination of methods, some rounds with radar seekers supplementing others with IR heads in order to lessen the chances of enemy countermeasures proving successful. Marconi Space and Defence Systems proposed an active-radar seeker with a three-axis gimballed antenna able to provide the acute look-angles needed to acquire off-boresight targets.

Vectored thrust seems the most likely control system, since it would allow the

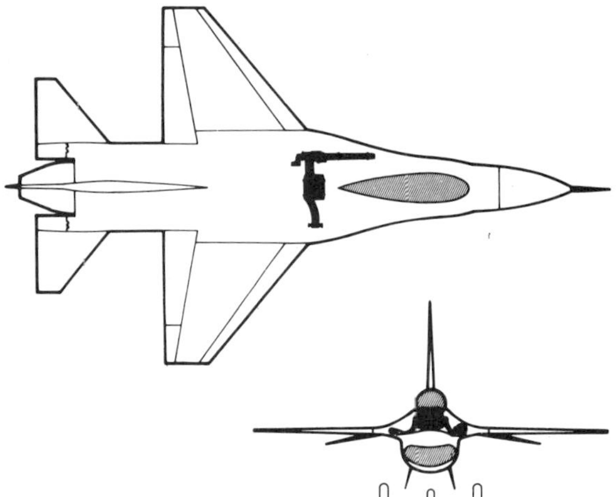

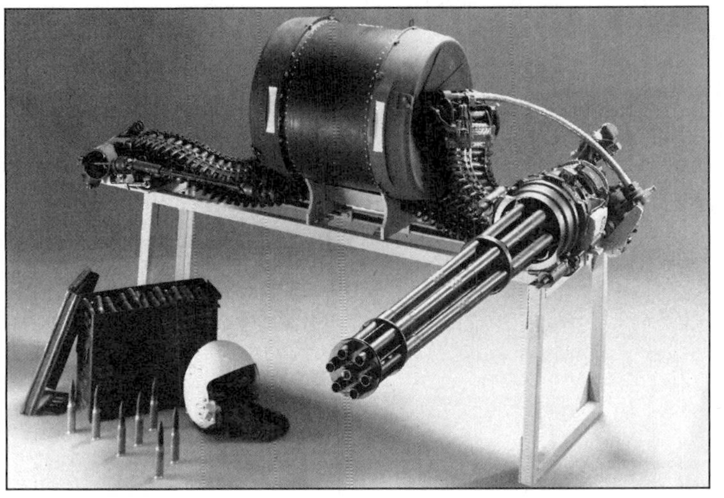

Far left: Location of the M61A1 cannon, ammunition drum and feed in the F-16. GD studies have shown that 30mm DEFA, 27mm Mauser or 30mm Oerlikon KCA could be accommodated should a heavier and more destructive projectile be desired. Left: In creating the M61 series of aircraft cannon, the Armament division of General Electric revived the rotary principle first devised by the legendary Dr Gatling. This involves rotating the entire barrel assembly: while one barrel is firing, the remaining five are at different stages of the loading/unloading cycle. The result is a very high rate of fire and high reliability.

high initial manoeuvrability needed to engage off-boresight targets. By eliminating wings, the design would allow three missiles to be carried on a single pylon.

AGM-65 Maverick

The six underwing pylons and single under-fuselage hardpoint of the F-16 allow a heavy ordnance load to be carried, including air-to-surface missiles, 'smart' bombs, tactical nuclear weapons and conventional iron bombs. One of the most important warloads of US F-16s will be the Hughes AGM-65 Maverick used for precision attacks against point targets. This is available in AGM-65A, AGM-65B and AGM-65D forms, which use TV guidance, scene-magnification TV guidance and imaging infra-red (IIR) guidance respectively. The last can be used in day, night or adverse-weather conditions. Currently under development are the AGM-65E laser-guided version and AGM-65F IR-guided variants, but these are intended for use by the US Marine Corps and Navy respectively. All versions use common aft and centre sections and have the same aerodynamic configuration.

More than 26,000 TV-guided rounds were built, demonstrating an 86 per cent hit rate in 1,221 firings. Average miss distance during a series of tests against tank-sized targets was only 3ft (0.91m). A vidicon (TV) seeker in the nose of the missile may be slewed upon its two-axis mounting and used to view the target area. Using a TV image on the cockpit display, the pilot can align the target on the aiming mark, then command lock-on.

AGM-65A has a 5deg field of view, while the AGM-65B Scene Magnification variant has a 2.5deg field of view but can detect targets at longer range thanks to the increased image scale. These early-model Mavericks are not ideally suited to use from single-seat fighters due to the time needed to acquire the target and lock-on the missile seeker. Moreover, visibility conditions in many parts of the world can reduce target detection range to the point where the pilot of a high-speed aircraft no longer has time to operate the weapon. This problem has been appreciated for some time, spurring development of the IR-guided AGM-65D.

Imaging infra-red

The operating principle of the IR version is similar to that of the -65A and -65B, but in this case a thermal image is displayed in the cockpit instead of TV. Two magnifications are provided – wide angle for target acquisition, and narrow angle for final identification and lock-on. One difference is that Maverick operations normally involve using the missile seeker to locate the target: with the IIR version, the seeker may be slaved to or cued by target-acquisition systems such as Pave Penny or LANTIRN.

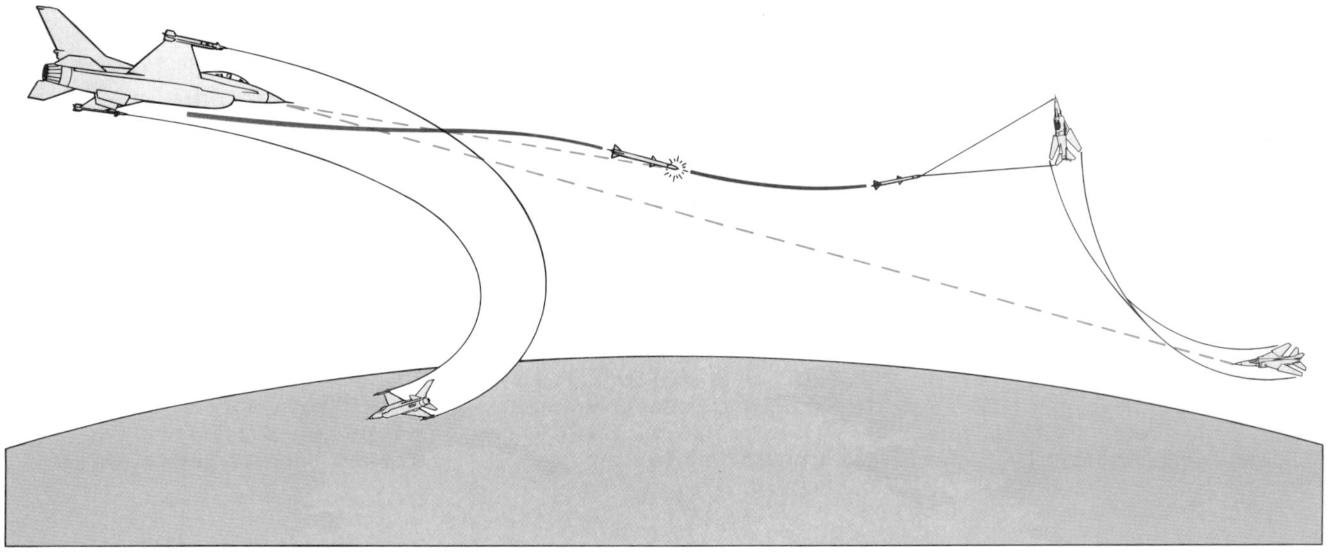

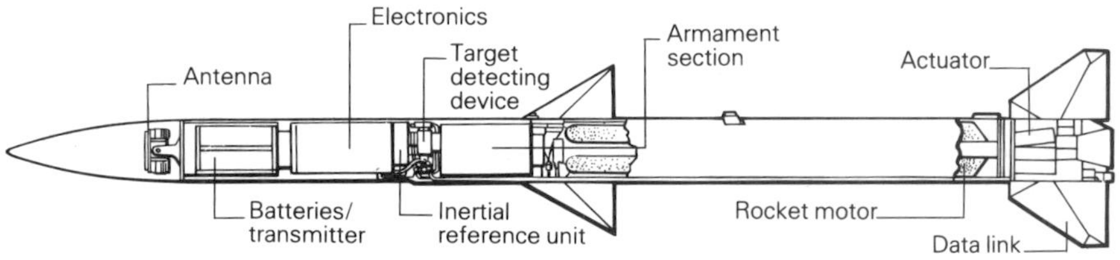

Above: After launching the fire-and-forget AMRAAM missile, the F-16 pilot will be able to turn away. The round will home onto the target during the final stages of flight using an active-radar seeker. Right: Internal arrangement of AMRAAM.

After launch, the round flies a proportional-navigation course, cruising under the impulse given by a solid-propellant rocket motor. All versions of Maverick have roughly the same launch zone. The missile can be launched at dive angles of up to 60deg, while maximum launch altitude varies according to aircraft speed, and generally lies between 33,000 and 40,000ft (10,000–12,000m). Above this height the round would become aerodynamically unstable.

Maximum range varies according to aircraft speed and height – from more than 22nm (25 miles/41km) at Mach 1.2/40,000ft down to around 7nm (8 miles/13km) at Mach 0.5 at low level. At lower altitudes, maximum range is dictated by the loss of kinetic energy during the coasting stage of flight. Above 10,000ft (3,000m) or so, endurance of the thermal batteries used to provide on-board electrical power is the limiting factor. There is no minimum launch altitude, but the minimum launch range is constrained by the limitations of the guidance and the need for the launch aircraft to avoid the exploding warhead.

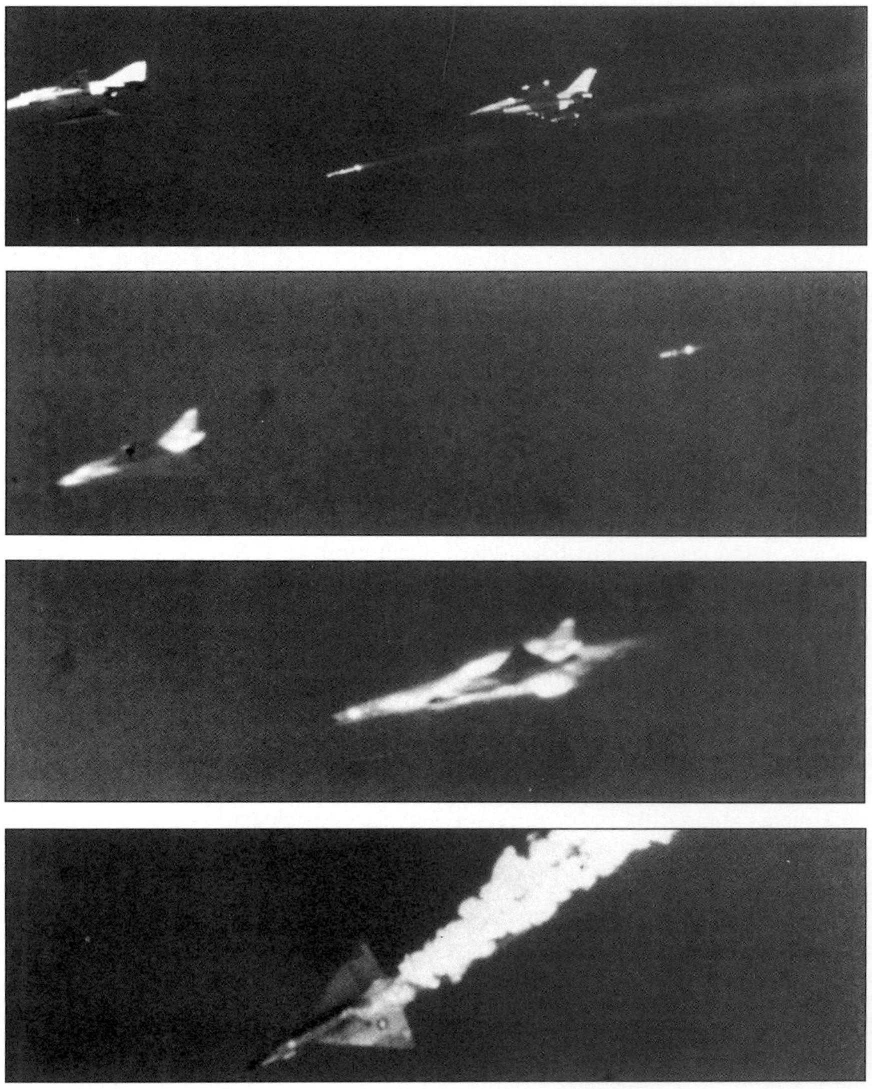

Right: Destruction of a QF-102 drone by the first guided AMRAAM launch.

Below right: Internal arrangement of the TV-guided Maverick.

Below: Maximum range and height of Maverick launching have been declassified following the export.

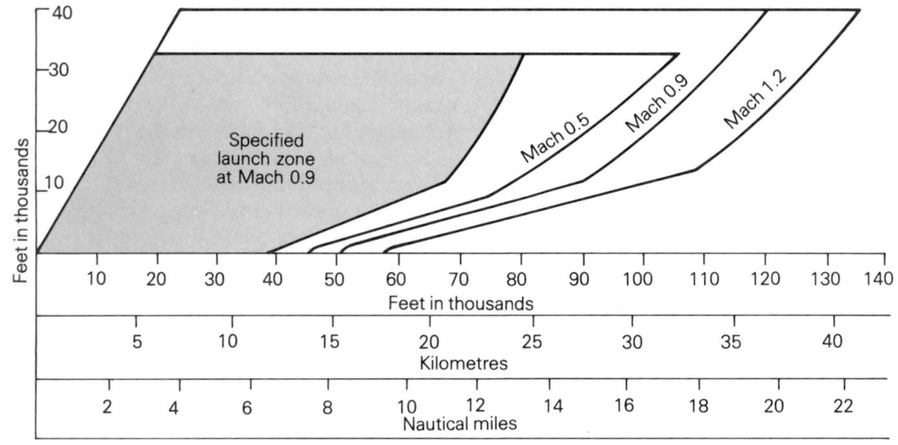

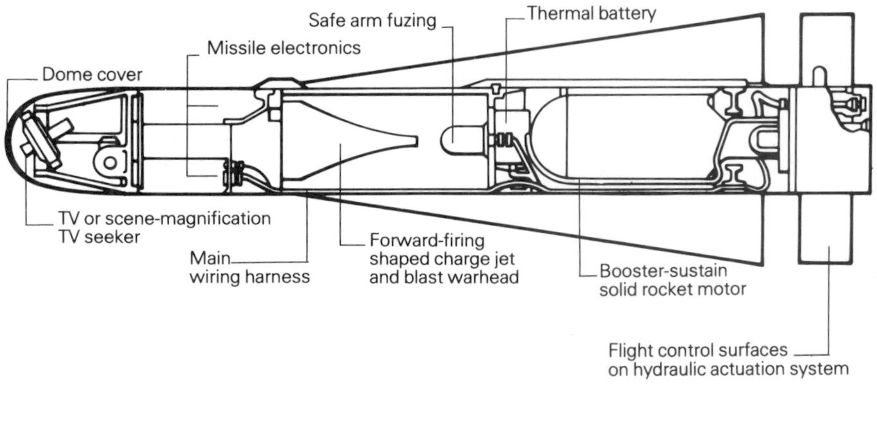

The first full-scale development F-16B releases a Maverick in a diving attack. An operational launch at such altitudes would require massive ECM protection for the aircraft.

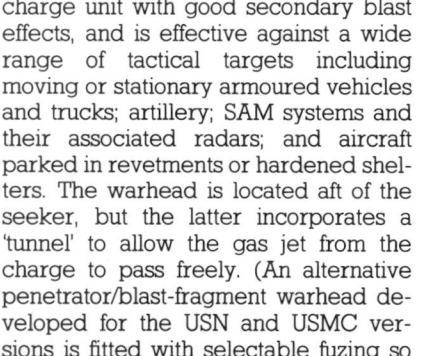

The warhead is a 125lb (57kg) shaped charge unit with good secondary blast effects, and is effective against a wide range of tactical targets including moving or stationary armoured vehicles and trucks; artillery; SAM systems and their associated radars; and aircraft parked in revetments or hardened shelters. The warhead is located aft of the seeker, but the latter incorporates a 'tunnel' to allow the gas jet from the charge to pass freely. (An alternative penetrator/blast-fragment warhead developed for the USN and USMC versions is fitted with selectable fuzing so that it can be set to detonate either on initial impact with the target, or after penetration.)

Maverick requires little modification of the parent aircraft, and can be carried on the three-round LAU-88/A and LAU-88A/A launchers or the single-rail LAU-117/A. A modified version of the LAU-88/A with drag-reducing fairings, including a 'boat-tail' aft section, is intended for use on high-performance aircraft such as the F-16. Drag is reduced by some 45–60 per cent depending on flight profile. Mavericks can be loaded on to the launcher and go/no-go tested as a complete assembly.

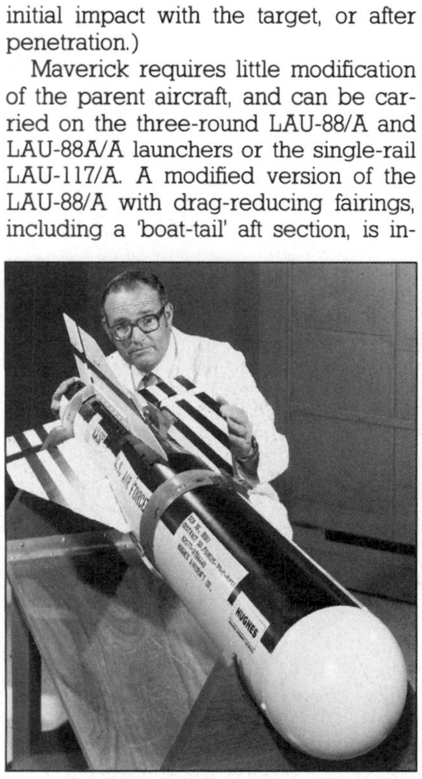

Above: The weapon which Fighting Falcon may never see – funding for the Hughes Wasp mini-missile was effectively cancelled in 1983.

Above: 1,000lb (454kg) iron bombs are released from the first F-16XL.

Top right: Two-seat F-16/79 launches a Paveway laser-guided bomb.

Above: The F-16/79 releases iron bombs over a US range. European air arms have long since abandoned medium altitude dive attacks, but the USAF has great faith in ECM.

Right: 388th TFW Fighting Falcons set course on a training mission.

Below right: Penguin anti-ship missile under the wing of an RNoAF F-16.

Modifications to the LAU-88/A have been devised to allow rapid fire against multiple targets. The modified launcher contains facilities for: ground boresighting all missiles to the 'pipper' of the aircraft sighting system; operating two missiles at the same time, with the seeker head of the second slaved to that of the first; holding the aim of the second round after the launch of the first; and providing a safe time interval between dome cover ejection and missile launch.

One Maverick tactic tested during AGM-65D trials during 1982 involved the use of an F-16 and an F-111 working as a 'hunter-killer' team. Using a belly-mounted AVQ-26 Pave Tack FLIR pod, an F-111F was able to locate and designate a ground target, then use a voice link to call in the Maverick-armed F-16.

An important future weapon for the F-16 might be the Hughes Wasp mini-missile. Intended to be a relatively inexpensive and lightweight (approximately 105lb [48kg]) weapon, Wasp will be launched in multi-shot 'fire-and-forget' attacks. Most tactical guided missiles must be locked on to their target before launch, but the advanced-technology millimetre-wave (94GHz) active radar seeker fitted to Wasp will be able to search for, locate and identify tactical targets after being launched, and without assistance from the launch aircraft. Wasps will be fired from 12-round launch pods, two of which would be carried by an F-16. Flight tests began in November 1982.

In August 1978 one of the YF-16s became the first single-seat aircraft to deliver smart bombs without assistance from a second target-designating aircraft during a series of 46 industry-sponsored test flights carried out in 1978. For these tests, the aircraft carried a Martin Marietta/Thomson-CSF Atlis pod under the intake.

Developed by Martin Marietta and the French company Thomson-CSF, Atlis (Automatic-Tracking Laser Illumination System) is a pod-mounted system consisting of a stabilized TV system able to lock on to targets selected by the pilot, and a target-designation laser able to 'mark' targets during missile or smart bomb attacks. It allows the aircraft to break away immediately after missile launch in order to avoid being engaged by enemy point-defence systems. During the first trial, the aircraft delivered a GBU-10 bomb from an altitude of 5,000ft (1,524m), entering a 4g turn immediately after weapon release.

Simulated Sabre trials

As part of the same series of tests, the YF-16 carried out a series of simulated attacks to prove the concept of the planned British Aerospace Sabre air-to-ground missile. Based on the well-proven Rapier anti-aircraft missile, Sabre was intended to allow Royal Air Force pilots to engage several off-boresight ground targets during a single pass.

There was no significance in the use of the YF-16 for these tests – BAe engineers needed a trials aircraft fitted with modern avionics and HUD, and took advantage of the US programme. The test flights at Edwards AFB followed a series of tests in the Martin Marietta combat simulator, and thousands of mathematically modelled 'firings'.

The results of these tests showed that the number of targets engageable in a single pass would be roughly equal to the range in kilometres of the distance at which the first was detected: some four seconds were needed to align the laser system on to the first target, and re-aiming on to a fresh target following the kill would take several seconds. A typical squadron pilot would manage a kill rate of around 70 per cent.

Development of Sabre cost £1.5 million of company funding, but the weapon was not adopted by the RAF. That service opted instead to fund development of the Hunting Engineering VJ291 guided cluster bomb, but the latter project was itself abandoned in the summer of 1981 owing to technical problems and escalating costs. Atlis was not adopted by the US services, but is due to equip some French Air Force Jaguars and Mirage 2000s.

Some F-16 operators will carry their own specialized weapons on the F-16. To guard against the possible effects of a future arms embargo, Israeli aircraft might be modified to carry the indigenously-developed Raphael Shafrir 2 heat-seeking missile or the follow-on Python 3. The former entered service in 1969 and is reported to have scored more than 200 'kills', with a single-shot kill probability of 60 per cent. Python was scheduled to enter service in 1983 or 1984, but pre-production rounds were given a baptism of fire during the 1982 air combats over Lebanon.

Norwegian Air Force F-16s will carry the Kongsberg Vapenfabrikk Penguin 3 anti-ship missile. Derived from the sur-

HL
HL
HL
HL

293

face-launched Penguin missile, this lacks the solid-fuel booster rocket of the standard missile and has smaller wings. It can carry a 250lb (113kg) high-explosive warhead over ranges of up to 25 miles (40km), depending on the speed and height of the aircraft at the moment of weapon release.

Warload of the arrow-winged F-16XL is much improved over that of the standard aircraft. A total of 29 hardpoints beneath the wings and fuselage can carry 15,000lb (6800kg) of stores, allowing a payload of 16 Mk82 bombs to be carried under the wings and on the centreline.

The F-16XL was the first aircraft to be designed for semi-conformal carriage of weaponry. If an aircraft carries a heavy load of external ordnance and stores on the conventional patterns of external pylon, the drag of such equipment may exceed that of the airframe, dramatically reducing range and speed while increasing radar cross-section. If conformal carriage is adopted, stores and weapons are designed to 'blend' into the airframe.

Such a technique offers dramatic reductions in drag, but taken to its extreme would involve stores being redesigned to match the shape of the parent aircraft. In practice, however, much of the promised advantage may be obtained by less drastic redesign efforts.

In 1970, the USAF and US Navy jointly funded a programme of conformal-stores trials, during which Boeing installed a large, shallow ventral pallet under the fuselage of an F-4B test aircraft. This could carry several configurations of stores, such as a load of 12 Mk82 500lb (227kg) bombs mounted in four rows across the width of the fuselage. Each row contained three bombs stowed nose-to-tail.

Flight trials showed that the modified aircraft had less drag than a clean F-4, the pallet having improved the area distribution of the Phantom design. Loaded with weaponry, it could fly in clean condition a mission which would normally demand the carriage of two 370US gal (308Imp gal/1,402 litre) external fuel tanks, while the maximum speed at around 30,000ft (9,000m) with a payload of up to 12 500lb (227kg) bombs rose from Mach 1.1 to Mach 1.8.

Despite such obvious success, the services did not retrofit their F-4 fleets. The modification would have cost no more than $75,000 per aircraft in 1971 prices, but the planning of the time was based on the erroneous assumption that the Phantom would be phased out by 1982.

Range improvements

In the case of the F-16XL, stores are semi-buried in the airframe. Wind-tunnel tests carried out prior to the aircraft's first flight suggested that gains of up to 50 per cent in mission radius might be possible.

Positioning of the bombs on the XL follows the contours of the aircraft underside. On the inboard stations, the bomb nearest the front is carried slightly nose-up, those further back are virtually level, while the aft bomb is mounted nose down. Individual stores are distributed around the aircraft centre of gravity in order to eliminate destabilizing effects. According to GD, the positioning of bombs is staggered to create a drag-reducing effect similar to that produced by area ruling of the airframe cross-section.

Instead of using the traditional pattern of stores pylon and ejector units, the GD designers substituted a lightweight 30lb (13.6kg) ejector, shaving a total of 1,500lb (680kg) from the weight of the complete aircraft.

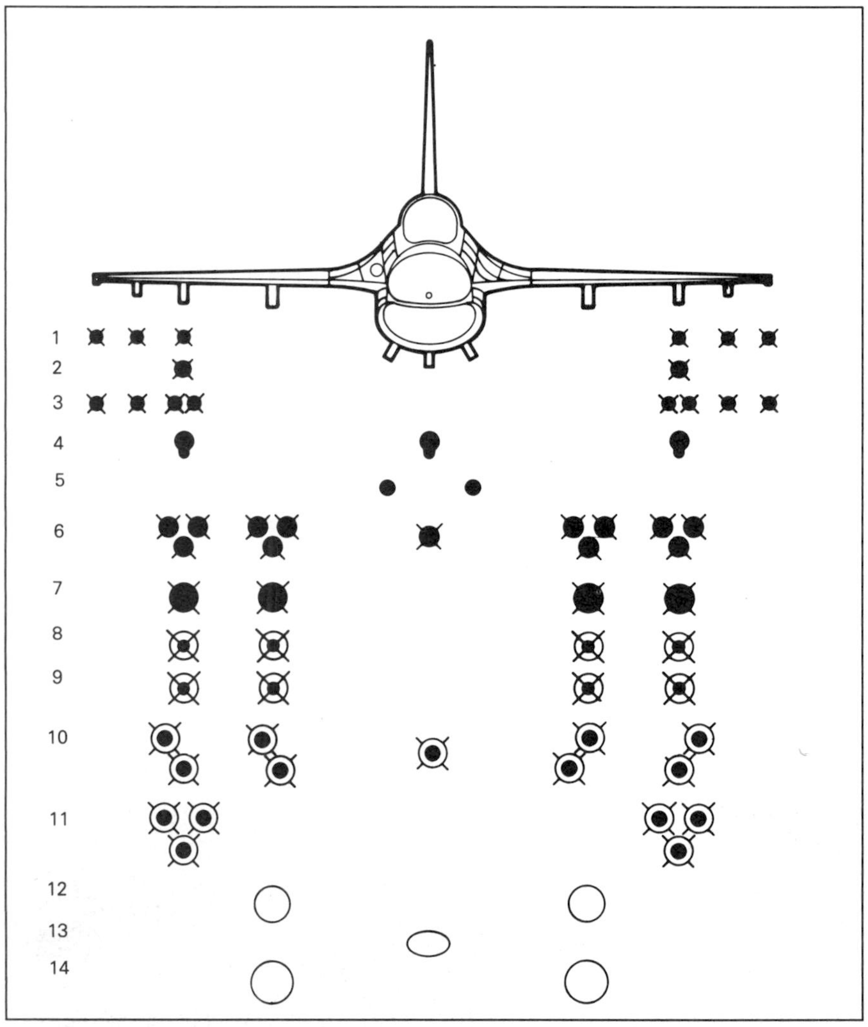

USAF F-16 stores loadings: 1: AIM-9 Sidewinder. 2: AIM-7 Sparrow (proposed). 3: AIM-120 AMRAAM. 4: ALQ-131 ECM pods. 5: Electro-optical/infra-red/terrain-following radar pods. 6: Up to 25 Mk82 1,000lb (454kg) bombs. 7: Mk84 2,000lb (907kg) bombs. 8: and 9: Paveway or GBU-15 laser-guided bombs. 10: Up to 17 cluster bombs. 11: AGM-45 Maverick. 12:370gal fuel tanks. 13:300gal fuel tank. 14:600gal fuel tanks.

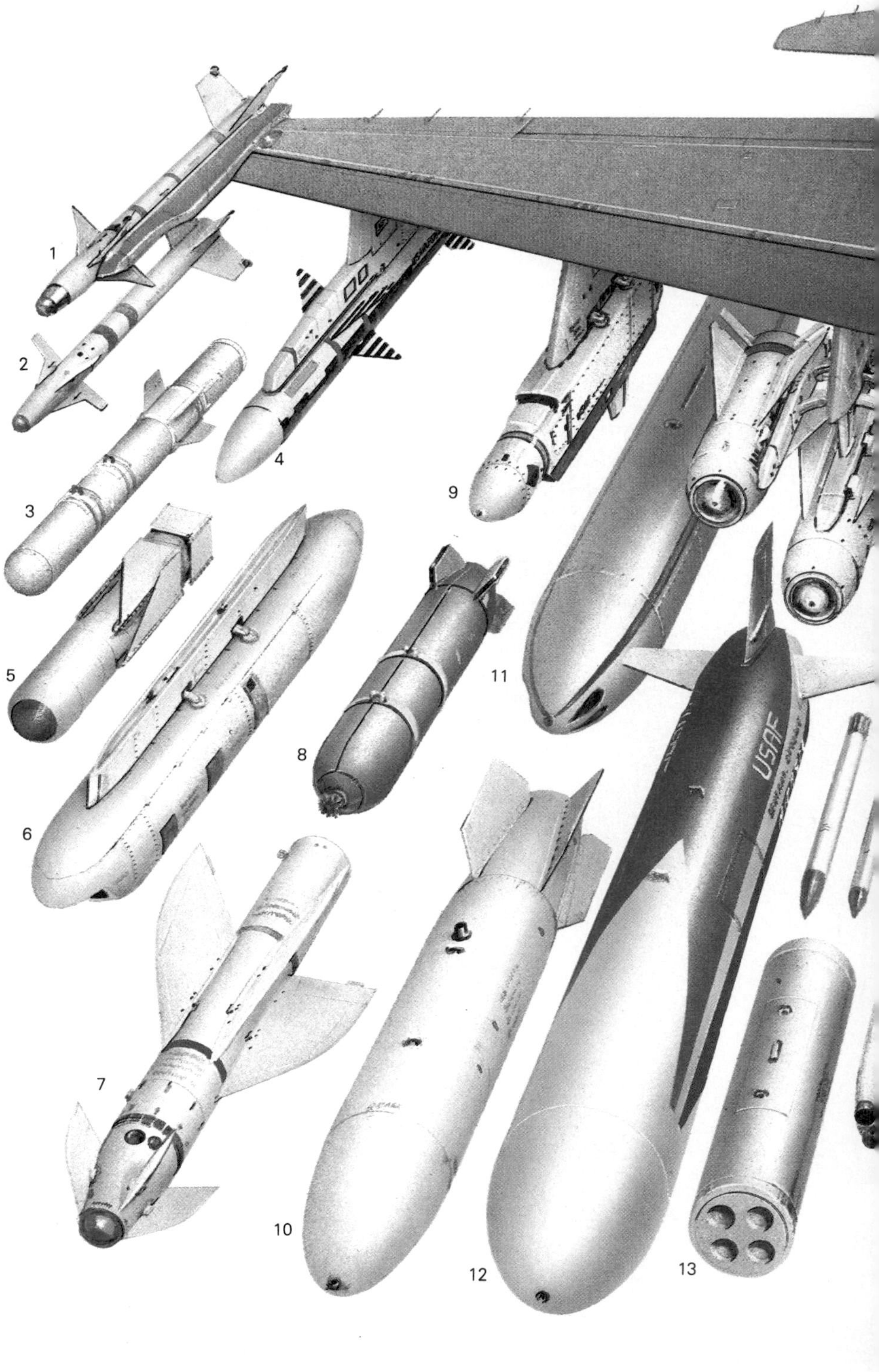

1 AIM-9L Sidewinder
2 AIM-9J Sidewinder
3 Durandal anti-runway weapon
4 AIM-120 AMRAAM
5 Wasp air-to-surface mini-missile (proposed)
6 Orpheus recce pod (RNethAF only)
7 Penguin Mk 3 anti-ship missile
8 Cluster munition
9 ALQ-131 ECM pod
10 Nuclear bomb
11 GEPOD 30mm gun pod
12 AGM-109 MRASM cruise missile (proposed)
13 SUU-25 flare
14 TV or IIR-guided AGM-45 Maverick
15 SUU-20 practice carrier
16 LAU rocket launcher
17/18 proposed electro-optical, FLIR and radar pods
19 ATLIS II designator pod (trials only)
20 Paveway laser-guided bomb
21 Mk 82 500lb (227kg) general-purpose bombs
22 HOBO 'smart' bomb
23 Mk 84 2,000lb (907kg) general-purpose bomb
24 Mk 82 Snakeye retarded bomb
25 External fuel tank
26 AGM-78 Standard ARM anti-radar missile
27 Mk 83 1,000lb (454kg) bomb
28 Mk 117 750lb (340kg) bomb
29 AGM-45A Shrike anti-radar missile
30 AGM-88 HARM anti-radar missile
31 Radar-detection pod (for proposed Wild Weasel two-seater)

Left: Even with simple iron bombs, the F-16 offers exceptionally accurate delivery. During some trials, diameter of the weapon impact area was only one third of the specified figure.

Right: During low-altitude attacks, the tail fins of the Snakeye 500lb (227kg) bomb open to retard the weapon. The impact point is thus well to the rear of the aircraft, protecting it from blast and debris.

Above: The impressive array of stores carried by, tested on or designed to be compatible with the Fighting Falcon belies the type's original conception as a cheap and simple lightweight fighter.

Right: USAF technicians check 500lb (227kg) bombs on a munition cart, prior to loading them aboard an F-16 during exercise Cope Elite 81. As a result of MSIP modifications, all hardpoints are likely to be cleared to a 9g load factor.

Combat and Deployment

Ordered by the USAF, adopted by four NATO air arms and high on the shopping list of the Imperial Iranian Air Force, the F-16 was never far from the headlines in the late 1970s. With three production lines tooled up, aircraft were delivered in ever-increasing numbers, and other air forces joined the queue to take delivery of General Dynamics' latest creation: by mid-1983 Fighting Falcon had already been ordered by ten nations in five continents. And if Israel's 1967 air strikes were the best advertisement for the Mirage III, the Osirak raid may yet boost sales prospects for the F-16.

The USAF accepted its first production F-16 on August 17, 1978, and the first delivery to an operational unit followed on January 6, 1979. First unit to be equipped was the 388th Tactical Fighter Wing at Hill AFB, Utah, which built up to its full strength of 102 Fighting Falcons by the end of 1980, and trained aircrew for TAC and export customers.

In the hands of 388th TFW pilots, the Fighting Falcon began to show its mettle. Three days of war games held at Hill AFB in March 1980 showed how the aircraft could be used to reinforce the NATO Central Front or any other trouble spot. Refuelling from KC-135 tankers, 12 aircraft carried out a 7,000km (4,350-mile) transit flight lasting 10 hours to simulate overseas deployment, followed by two days of intensive flying.

Despite the sophistication of the new warplane and its avionic systems, the care taken during design and development to ensure reliability and easy maintenance paid off from the beginning, and unit after unit converting to the type found itself clocking up flying hours at a higher-than-predicted rate. In 1979 the average number of hardware failures per flight hour for USAF aircraft was around 1·2, against an eventual goal of only 0·34. During the second half of 1979 the actual failure rate of the F-16s at Hill AFB varied from just under 1·2 down to around 0·75, and this showed signs of falling to the target figure by the early 1980s.

By 1980 the F-16 was displaying impressive reliability in the field. Tactical Air Command standard for mission capability is 70 per cent, but by 1980 the Fighting Falcon was averaging 74 to 76 per cent, making it the most reliable fighter in the US inventory. Both figures quoted refer to the number of aircraft completely or partly mission capable.

A study carried out in 1976 identified many areas of F-16 operations which would be cheaper than those associated with the earlier F-4. This assumed a typical TAC squadron of 24 aircraft and identified the cost changes (in 1976 prices) detailed in the accompanying table. All other cost such as support equipment and base matériel support were assumed to be unchanged. On this basis the annual operating cost of an F-16 squadron would be 30 per cent less than an equivalent F-4 unit.

Above: Infantrymen watch an F-16 take off during Exercise Team Spirit 82. Fighting Falcons have taken part in many recent exercises.

Fighting Falcon officially started its operational career with the USAF on November 12, 1980, when the 4th Tactical Fighter Squadron – part of the 388th TFW – achieved Initial Operational Capability. In March of the following year this unit took 12 Fighting Falcons overseas for the first time during a month-long deployment to Flesland in Norway. If further proof were needed that the Fighting Falcon was a success, this was provided in June 1981 when seven 388th TFW aircraft won the Royal Air Force-sponsored tactical bombing competition held at Lossiemouth in Scotland, defeating RAF Jaguars and Buccaneers and USAF F-111Es.

Below: The long range of the Fighting Falcon allows staging flights from the US to Western Europe without assistance from European-based tankers. On trials, aircraft have flown 2,000nm without refuelling.

Delivery of the 400th aircraft took place in May 1981, the 500th production example following in August of the same year. First USAF pilot to clock up 1,000 hours was Lt Col Dean Stickell of the 16th Tactical Fighter Training Squadron at Hill AFB. He reached four figures of Fighting Falcon flying time in the autumn of 1981, his involvement with the aircraft having begun at Edwards AFB during the type's development and evaluation programme.

Increasing orders

By this time the USAF had 1,388 Fighting Falcons on order, and was talking of ordering a total of almost 1,750 examples for regular Air Force units, plus enough to re-equip the Thunderbirds display team. A possible order to re-equip Air National Guard units was seen as likely to add 600 to 800 further aircraft to the production run. Consideration was also given to storing 150 aircraft in Israel in kit form.

By the summer of 1981 overseas deployment of the Fighting Falcon had begun with the first deliveries to the 8th TFW. Part of the Pacific Air Forces and based at Kunsan in the Republic of Korea, the wing began converting from the F-4D in September 1981. Although a long way from the continental USA, the wing has maintained good operational readiness despite a shortage of spares – a common F-16 problem as more and more squadrons converted to the type. The majority of newly-built components were immediately embodied in new-production aircraft, rather than being shipped to the user as spares. Availability rates of 70–75 per cent were reported early in 1983, partly as a result of earlier Block 10 aircraft being swapped for the then up-to-date Block 15 standard. Basic mission of 8th TFW is strike and interdiction, but air-to-air combat training is also carried out. F-4s released from service at Kunsan were returned to the USA and re-assigned to Air Force Reserve units.

F-16s from USAF Korean bases act as 'friendly enemies' for F-15 units in Japan, allowing USAF aircrew assigned to the latter location to practise dissimilar air combat. During other exercises, techniques have been developed for operating the two types in a co-operative manner. Fighting Falcons can join an F-15 formation to take advantage of the latter's longer-ranged Hughes APG-63 radar and the attrition inflicted by the Eagle's AIM-7 Sparrow missiles in the opening stages of an air combat.

By the spring of 1982, the USAF fleet had exceeded 100,000 flying hours. A total of 345 was in service at that time, 270 with TAC operational units. Deployment of the aircraft to USAFE in West Germany started in December 1982, and the 50th TFW became operational on the type at Hahn Air Base in July 1982.

The first unit to become operational at Hahn was the 313th TFS. Following initial training at Zaragoza in Spain, the unit took its 24 F-16s to Hahn in the spring of 1982. Later that year the 50th TFW and 496th TFS also began re-equipping to bring the Hahn wing up to strength. Aircraft assigned to Hahn were to Block 15 production standard. This includes the larger horizontal tail surfaces, and inlet hardpoints for AMRAAM missiles and LANTIRN sensors.

One highly-publicized conversion to the Fighting Falcon was that of the USAF's Thunderbirds display team. The team made no public appearances in 1982 following a four-aircraft crash which killed four members of the group. At that time, the team was using T-38 Talon trainers, but eight F-16s were assigned to the unit in the autumn. Several paint schemes were evaluated before the definitive black/red/white finish was approved. The Thunderbirds completed the transition to the F-16 in November 1982, and were thus able to fly the new type during the 1983 display season.

Starting in October 1982, the US Air National Guard began to deploy the F-16. First ANG unit to re-equip was the 169th Tactical Fighter Group at McEntire AFB, which received 24 Fighting Falcons in 1983 as replacements for its A-7 Corsairs. First AF Reserve unit to get the F-16 will be the 466th TFS at Hill AFB, Utah. Currently equipped with F-105 Thunderchiefs, this unit will re-equip with Fighting Falcons in 1984.

As aircraft continue to roll off the production lines, the USAF Fighting Falcon strength will continue to build up. In 1983, another F-16 wing, the 401st TFW, became operational at Torrejon in Spain. Next to become operational will be the 86th TFW at Ramstein AFB, West Germany.

Above: Fighting Falcons often carry a ventral tank, but runway clearance when this store is fitted is clearly minimal.

Comparative annual operating costs
(one TAC squadron of 24 aircraft, 1976$ × 1,000,000)

Element	F-4	F-16
Fuel	4·3	2·1
Training	1·1	0·3
Munitions & missile training	1·1	0·9
Spares	1·8	1·2
Base operating support	1·7	1·3
Depot Maintenance	2·9	2·3
Safety/logistic modifications	0·4	0·6
Military pay & salaries	7·5	5·4
Medical facilities	0·3	0·5

Above: First USAFE Fighting Falcon unit was the 50th TFW at Hahn. Deployment started in December 1982 and was completed in 1983.

Below: The 'bubble' canopy of Fighting Falcon gives good visibility. Even at high angles of attack, the pilot has a clear view over the nose of his aircraft.

Below right: The 388th TFW was the first operational F-16 unit. During Exercise Yellow Alpha in 1980, 18 of its aircraft flew an impressive total of 72 'combat' sorties.

Above: It is rare to see Fighting Falcons in the clean condition of these KLu examples – even the wingtip rails are empty on the two nearest aircraft.

Left: Two decades of aerospace technology lie between the lumbering Tu-95 Bear and its KLu 'escort'. The Soviet aircraft may have been on a mission aimed at measuring the 'scramble' response time of the F-16.

An additional F-16 wing made up of two squadrons – 50 aircraft in all – is scheduled for deployment at Misawa air base in northern Japan from 1985 onwards. This is intended to help offset the build-up of Soviet arms in the region. The deployment plans were attacked as 'provocative and hostile' by the Soviet Union when they were announced in the autumn of 1982.

The 1984 US defence budget allocates a total of $2,300 million to F-16 procurement in 1984, and $3,200 million in 1985. This will allow production to run at 120 aircraft per year. This may seem a long way from the original concept of a 'cheap' fighter, but if used to buy F-15 Eagles, the same money would enable only half that number to be procured.

F-16 exports

In 1977 the US estimated the likely market for Western-built fighters over the next two decades as 6,000. Main candidates at that time were seen as the US Grumman F-14 Tomcat, McDonnell Douglas F-15 Eagle, General Dynamics F-16 Fighting Falcon and McDonnell Douglas F-18 Hornet, the Anglo-German-Italian Panavia Tornado, and the Dassault-Breguet Mirage 2000 from France. This impressive line-up was joined within a few years by the General Dynamics F-16/79 and Northrop F-20 Tigershark from the US, and the Dassault-Breguet Mirage IIING, and the future may see further candidates in the shape of the Saab-Scania JAS 39 Gripen from Sweden, Israel Aircraft Industries' Lavi, the Dassault-Breguet ACX, and the planned tri-national Advanced Combat Aircraft (ACA).

The Fighting Falcon was to be a candidate for many export orders. The type's adoption in 1975 by the air forces of Belgium, Denmark, the Netherlands and Norway was a major boost, but the F-16 was soon to be locked in competition with its rivals in the search for overseas orders.

In the early stages of the programme, the USAF opposed early delivery commitments being made to nations outside the multi-national manufacturing consortium, except Iran. In order to avoid a shortage of aircraft and spares, the service did not want to see further export commitments until 1981. In practice, however, the Department of Defense and General Dynamics continued to promote the aircraft, but no early sales agreements were reached.

The Force Aérienne Belge/Belgische Luchtmarcht (Belgian Air Force) was the first European operator to take delivery of locally-built Fighting Falcons. The original Belgian order was for 116 aircraft – 96 single-seaters and 20 two-seat trainers – and the first example was accepted on January 29, 1979.

On January 16, 1981, 349 Sqn of the FAéB was officially assigned to NATO, and on May 6 it was declared fully operational. Belgium will deploy three F-16 wings. No 1 Wing at Beauvechain consists of two squadrons – 349 and 350 – each with 32 aircraft. The latter squadron was the second FAéB unit to convert to the type. 10 Wing at Kleine-Brogel consists of 23 and 31 Squadrons. As F-16 conversion continued, the MTU was transferred from Beauvechain to Klein Brogel. Once conversion is completed it will disband, and key staff will move to the FAéB Technical School at Saffraanberg.

Within two years of taking delivery of its first F-16As the Belgian Air Force reported an availability rate of 88 per cent. Mean time between failures was 2·9 hours, while the 12 man-hours of maintenance required per flying hour was well below that of many earlier types. Turnaround time was between 15 and 45 minutes, depending on the type of mission being flown.

The Belgian Air Force was the first to use the Fighting Falcon in the somewhat unwarlike role of target tug. Tests carried out at Solenzara in Corsica using a No 1 Wing aircraft tested various underwing and fuselage locations for the pods associated with Tetraplàn and Secapem B90 targets, as well as the newer Taxan design which incorporates an acoustic scoring system. These tests included jettison trials in which an Alpha Jet was used as photographic chase plane.

Belgium's F-16 force will be boosted by a further wing in the late 1980s when the Dassault-Breguet Mirage 5B is phased out of FAéB service. The Mirages currently serve with Nos 2 and 3 Wings, attrition having reduced the number operational to around 60. Starting in 1988, therefore, the service will replace the Mirage force with a follow-on batch of 44 F-16s due to be delivered in 1988/9. The deal is worth $625 million. Industrial offset arrangements offered by GD would be 58 per cent – the figure used in the original F-16 deal – plus a further 22 per cent going to Flemish companies in northern Belgium. When the new aircraft are operational, Belgium will field eight Fighting Falcon squadrons, or a total of 160 aircraft.

Continuing production

Production of the F-16 in Belgium would have ended in 1984 once the 116 aircraft ordered under the original 1975 deal had been completed, but GD has offered to place enough offset work on USAF and export aircraft to keep the line moving until work starts on the next Belgian batch in 1987.

Beginning in September 1981, a total of 35 early-production Belgian Air Force F-16s were rotated back through the SABCA factory at Gosselies in Belgium for cockpit modifications and updating of the avionics, including the APG-66 radar. This work followed the completion of intensive operational evaluation of the aircraft.

At the same time, the Rapport III ECM system was installed internally. This involves rewiring the aircraft, and since only a few technicians can work within the confined space of the cockpit and nose section at any one time, the work is slow. Each aircraft spends about six months at the factory, and the modified Falcons are delivered back to the user at a rate of around one a month. At this build standard they are known as Block 10 aircraft. The same factory continues with new production work, Belgian aircraft from the 54th onwards being built to the revised standard.

Deliveries of F-16 aircraft to the Kongelige Danske Flyvevåbnet (Royal Danish Air Force) started on January 28, 1980. The current order is for 46 single-seat F-16A fighters plus 12 two-seat F-16B trainers, and the first squadrons to convert were Esk 727 and 730 at Skrystrup. The former unit was declared

Left: Belgian Fighting Falcon prepares for an operational task not foreseen in the original US Light Fighter specification – target towing!

Below: From 1988 onwards, these Belgian Air Force F-16s will be joined by a follow-on batch of 44 aircraft destined to replace the present Mirage 5 fleet. Despite an attractive offset package devised by Dassault, the FAéB ordered the GD aircraft.

Above: Norwegian airfields are snow-covered for much of the year, a factor which caused the RNoAF to request braking parachutes in its F-16s.

operational to NATO on August 26, 1981. Four Danish instructors were trained at Hill AFB, and were assigned to Esk 727 to begin the task of training further instructors.

The next stage of the operation involved the conversion of the most experienced pilots of Esk 727 to the Fighting Falcon. Both squadrons had formerly flown F-100 Super Sabres, and the transition involved the units being split into sub-units designated by the suffixes -100 and -16. While the -100 unit maintained Danish AF combat strength using the F-100, -16 tackled the task of conversion to the GD fighter. As the Fighting Falcon units approached full strength, the Super Sabres were withdrawn from service late in 1982.

Denmark plans to withdraw the Lockheed F-104G Starfighter from operational service in 1984. Esk 723 – one of the two squadrons which currently flies the type – will probably convert to the F-16.

The 1975 agreement between the United States and the four European F-16 operators covered work on 998 aircraft – 348 for the European air arms and 650 for the USAF. This workload is tailing off, but the US has offered further work in return for F-16 follow-on orders being placed in 1983. Denmark looks likely to follow the Belgian lead in placing a follow-on order, but nothing had been announced by mid-1983.

Rather than operate 'twinned' squadrons, the Koninklijke Luchtmacht (Royal Netherlands Air Force) opted to shut down each of the units converting to the Fighting Falcon for the year or so that the transition required. The first F-16 was accepted on June 6, 1979, an operational conversion unit having been set up at Leeuwarden, home base of 322 Sqn, the first to convert from the F-104G. The first instructors were trained at Hill AFB in the USA. Local pilot and crew training started at Leeuwarden in October 1979, and the first newly-converted pilot joined 322 Sqn in December of the same year.

322 Sqn completed conversion by the end of April 1981. 323 Sqn (also based at Leeuwarden) was the next to be stood down to begin conversion to the Fighting Falcon. A second OCU was set up at Volkel, home base of 306, 311 and 312 Sqns to tackle the conversion of these units, a task which started in 1982.

Fighting Falcon in the KLu

Like all European F-16 operators, the KLu plans to use the Fighting Falcon primarily in the close support role. In addition to carrying out air-to-ground attacks, Dutch F-16s will also be used as air-superiority fighters both in the battle area and in the air-defence region allocated to the KLu by NATO.

The last squadron to convert, Nr 306, formerly flew the RF-104G reconnaissance aircraft. When re-equipped with Fighting Falcon, it will continue to specialise in reconnaissance, carrying the Oldelft Orpheus recce pod. This role requires only minor adaption of the F-16. Originally deployed on the Starfighter, the Orpheus pod carries five cameras and an infra-red line scanner.

In March 1980 the Netherlands announced plans to increase its F-16 fleet from 102 aircraft (80 F-16A and 22 F-16B) to 213, but the only follow-on announced by the summer of 1983 was for 22 aircraft intended to act as attrition replacements.

Delivery of 60 F-16A and 12 F-16B aircraft to the Kongelige Norske Luftforsvaret (Royal Norwegian Air Force) started on January 25, 1980, and four squadrons will operate the type by 1984. Like its NATO partners, the RNoAF sent an initial batch of personnel to Hill AFB for training. On their return to Norway, these instructors were assigned to Skv 332, Norway's first Fighting Falcon unit, for conversion training. By the autumn of 1981, Skv 332 was fully equipped with F-16s and Skv 331 – the first operational unit – had already received many of its aircraft.

Skv 331 and 332 are based at Bodo, and formerly flew F-104G Starfighters. They were followed through the conversion process by Skv 338 from Norland (a former F-5 unit) and Skv 334 from Bodo (formerly an anti-shipping unit whose CF-104D/G fighters were armed with Bullpup missiles). For attacks against surface vessels, RNoAF F-16s will be equipped with the indigenously developed Penguin Mk 3 missile.

Norway's small F-16 force was intended to fulfil a national requirement for a weapon system capable of area defence and anti-invasion strikes, but the numbers ordered were not sufficient to protect all airfields. Funding was allocated under the 1983 defence

Right: The immaculate condition of this Danish Air Force F-16A, its hangar, mobile tool kit and work platforms would satisfy the most fastidious inspecting officer.

Left: Deployment of the F-16 no doubt strained the logistic facilities of the Egyptian Air Force, but will dramatically improve Egypt's technological capability.

budget for low-level air defence missiles, but this might be used to purchase more F-16s.

Non-NATO customers

Given the capability of the F-16, further orders for the aircraft were inevitable. On May 7, 1975, both YF-16s were flown to Cecil Field, Jacksonville, Florida to carry out flight demonstrations for the Shah of Iran and King Hussein of Jordan. The programme watched by the monarchs included a mock dogfight between the GD aircraft and an F-4 Phantom.

Iran became the first third-party nation to adopt the F-16. A letter of intent signed by the Imperial Iranian Government on October 27, 1976, covered the procurement of 160 aircraft, and a follow-on buy of a further 140 was also discussed.

Following the Iranian revolution early in 1979, the new Iranian Government cancelled all the massive arms contracts signed by the former Shah, including the F-16 deal. Work on these aircraft had already started, but only minor components had been built. Discussing the cancellation with the author at the time of the announcement, a GD spokesman pointed out that hardware already built could be switched to other customers, and that the likely beneficiary was Israel.

In terms of cost, the loss of the Iranian order had a more marked effect. The likely cost increase for the USAF was estimated at $175,000 per aircraft, while the price rise of European-built examples was predicted to be $129,000 or more per aircraft.

Israel was virtually a captive market for the F-16. After the 1967 arms embargo on the Mirage 5 fleet, Israel was unlikely to place a major order for warplanes with France, and given the importance of the Arab world as a market, it is unlikely that Dassault-Breguet would want the undesirable publicity of another Israeli aircraft deal.

Price information was originally sought on a package of 250 aircraft, and the Tsvah Haganah le Israel – Heyl ha'Avir (Israel Defence Force – Air Force) was reported to have a long-term requirement for a further 150 to 200 examples. In August 1978 Israel announced plans to procure 75 aircraft under a contract valued at around $1·2 billion. This purchase was split between 67 F-16As and eight F-16Bs, and was expected to lead in the longer term to a total purchase of 225 aircraft by the end of the 1980s.

A total of 17 modifications to the Fighting Falcon were requested by the IDFAF: Israeli aircraft would carry weapons not used by other F-16 operators, while IDFAF training and mission-management techniques differed from USAF/NATO practice. Hardware and software had to be modified to meet these specific national requirements.

Deliveries to Israel started on July 2, 1980, at a rate of four per month under a schedule which should have seen the last handed over in November 1981. Flown by US personnel drawn from the 16th Tactical Training Squadron, the first four made the journey from Florida to Israel in 11 hours. An excellent demonstration of the type's long range, this delivery sortie required the use of full external tanks and three in-flight refuellings.

The near-paranoid Israeli rules concerning military security prevent individual IDFAF squadrons or pilots being identified. The identity of the squadron chosen to operate the first Fighting Falcons has never been released officially, but it is known to have a history of pioneering new types. The first Israeli squadron to fly jets, the unit in question equipped with Gloster Meteor F.8 fighters in August 1953, and in 1956 it was the first to receive the Mirage III.

The Osirak raid

Less than 14 months after entering IDFAF service, the Fighting Falcon went to war. On June 7, 1981, eight were used in a precision air strike against the Osirak nuclear reactor being built at Twartha near Baghdad. Due to become operational in the late summer or early autumn of 1981, this facility was seen as a threat to Israeli security. According to Israeli intelligence, if allowed to 'go critical', the 70MW Osirak reactor would have turned out sufficient plutonium to allow Iraq to construct up to five 20kT nuclear weapons by the mid-1980s.

Timing of the raid was critical. The longer it was delayed, the more complete Osirak would be at the moment of its destruction, and thus the greater the losses in equipment suffered by Iraq. At the same time, it was essential that the raid be conducted before the reactor began operating, lest its destruction released a cloud of intensely radioactive material into the atmosphere.

Selection of the F-16 for the Osirak mission resulted from several factors, including the type's long range, the ground-mapping modes available on the APG-66 radar, and the accuracy of the navigation and attack systems. Eight aircraft formed the strike component of the mission, while six F-15 Eagles flew top cover in order to protect the Fighting Falcons using the longer-range APG-63 radar and AIM-7 Sparrow missiles.

Exact details of the raid have never been published: Israeli accounts contain minimal information, often verging on hagiography rather than combat reporting. The eight aircraft, plus their escort of six F-15s, probably took off from Etzion air base, near Eilat in southern Israel. External tanks were carried and the formation may have begun by topping up from tanker aircraft.

First leg of the flight probably took the formation across southern Jordan and then into Saudi Arabian airspace.

Below: One result of the Soviet invasion of Afghanistan was clearance for Pakistan to receive US warplanes – F-16s rather than the A-7 Corsair IIs originally requested.

Right: As US/Israeli relations grew more strained following the Osirak raid and 1982 invasion of Lebanon, the supply of further F-16s to the IDFAF was repeatedly embargoed.

Reports published shortly after the raid suggested that during this phase of the mission the Israeli aircrew deliberately set their radios on frequencies normally used by the Jordanian Air Force. Speaking in Arabic and using Jordanian calls signs, they pretended to be Jordanian crews on a training mission.

One report claims that the formation was detected by Saudi radars, but that the aircrew were able to allay suspicions. Probably flying at low level to minimize the risk of interception, the raiders were able to cross the desolate northern part of the country, then turn north into Iraq.

On crossing the Iraqi border, the attackers were fired on by anti-aircraft units, but no hits were scored. Time over the target was 0630, the combination of the early hour and the fact that the day was Sunday being thought to minimize the chance of French technicians being on duty.

Complete surprise

Tactical surprise was complete, the raiders approaching from the west and reporting some anti-aircraft fire, but no interceptors or SAM launches. The Fighting Falcons attacked in two waves, each consisting of two pairs of aircraft. Prime target was the 105ft (32m) diameter concrete cupola covering the reactor. Individual bomb runs took less than two minutes, the first wave scoring at least two hits with 2,000lb (907kg) Mk 84 bombs.

Early reports suggested that 'smart' bombs were used – perhaps Texas Instruments Paveway LGBs guided by Pave Spike designator pod – but Israeli spokesmen claimed that 'iron' bombs were used in conjunction with what IDFAF commander General David Ivri described as 'a new technique ... based on the excellence of our pilots'.

The reactor was badly damaged, the protective dome collapsing and burying the complex in rubble, while laboratories and other facilities were also damaged and one French technician was killed. The second wave is reported not to have bombed. The attackers were not engaged during the return flight, which took them westwards, back across Jordan and into Israeli airspace. The Reagan administration told Congress that the raid may have been a 'substantial violation' of US/Israeli mutual defense agreements, and placed a temporary embargo on F-16 deliveries to the IDFAF.

Delivery of further F-16s was temporarily embargoed once again on July 17, 1981, following a week-long series of attacks on Palestinian bases in the Lebanon. At this point 53 aircraft had been delivered, and ten more were due to begin their flight to Israel that day. Delivery of all 75 aircraft to Israel was eventually completed by the end of 1981. In May 1982 the US Congress was told that the Reagan Administration intended to supply a further 75 F-16s to the IDFAF, with deliveries starting in 1985.

The spring and summer of 1982 saw IDFAF Fighting Falcons in action once again. In the course of air combat over the Bekaa valley in Lebanon the Israeli Air Force claimed the destruction of 92 Syrian fighters, more than half of which were MiG-23 Floggers. In this air-to-air fighting the F-16 emerged as the top-scoring 'MiG-killer', downing 44 Syrian warplanes, while the F-15 accounted for a further 40. Most of the kills were scored using the AIM-9L 'all-aspect' version of Sidewinder.

Aircraft most commonly met in combat by the Israeli pilots were the MiG-21, MiG-23 and Su-22. Syrian tactics were poor, according to the Israeli pilots, with little evidence of careful pre-flight planning. There was no shortage of bravery, however – wave upon wave of Syrian aircraft rushed into combat despite their heavy losses.

In an interview with the magazine *Flight International*, an unidentified senior Israeli officer ascribed the Syrian loss rate to a combination of shortcomings in the command structure and in the individual aircrew. "In the 1973 war the Syrian pilots fought aggressively, this time it was different ... they could have flown the best fighter in the world, but if they flew the way they were flying, we would have shot them down. It wasn't the equipment at fault, but their tactics ... They fired missiles, they fought, but in a peculiar way ... in our opinion, they acted without tactical sense." One immediate result of this Israeli success was yet another temporary embargo on Fighting Falcon deliveries, with President Reagan banning the supply of the follow-on batch of aircraft. This was duly lifted in May 1983.

On June 25, 1980, Egypt signed a letter of agreement covering the supply of 40 F-16s. The deal was worth more than $960 million and included the 40 aircraft, ten spare F100 engines, and ordnance including 600 Maverick rounds, 500lb (227kg) and 1,000lb (454kg) bombs and 20mm cannon ammunition. Also included were a simulator plus other support equipment and manuals.

Egypt originally wanted the F-15, and despite having the F-16 on order still wanted the Eagle, presumably as part of a 'Hi-Lo' mix. By 1980 it was obvious that the McDonnell Douglas warplane was too expensive for Egypt's limited budget and the likely level of US military credit available, so this plan was abandoned, at least for the time being.

Diversions to Egypt

Growing unserviceability of Soviet-supplied warplanes made early delivery of the Fighting Falcon essential, and in order to meet Egyptian requests that deliveries be speeded up 30 examples were diverted from the USAF. Between December 1981 and May 1983 monthly deliveries to the USAF were cut from 15 aircraft to around 13. The remaining ten EAF F-16s were built from scratch as export aircraft.

Aircraft for the Egyptian Air Force started down the production line in 1981, and all 40 were due to be delivered by early 1984. Egyptian aircraft are F-16A & B standard and not equipped with the MSIP avionics or provision for AMRAAM missiles. The EAF would like to have the Hughes missile, but any agreement covering its supply would have to form part of a future and separate agreement.

The current mixture of US, French, Soviet and Chinese equipment deployed by Egypt clearly places great strain on that nation's IFF systems. All EAF fighters, including the F-16 and Soviet types, are equipped with IFF units developed and supplied by Teledyne.

Egypt has a total requirement for 120 F-16s to replace part of the aging fleet of Soviet-supplied MiGs and Sukhois. Given the high cost of Western defence equipment compared to Soviet products, the EAF will be unable to replace Fishbeds and Fitters on a one-for-one basis, so the nominal size of the service will decline during the 1980s.

Being short of modern aircraft, Egypt uses the Fighting Falcon for both air defence and ground attack. The Egyptian Air Force sees an eventual need for up to 150 examples, and has already requested a second batch of 40. Even before the first examples of the F-16 were operational in Egypt, the US Defense Department was planning to allow Egypt to place a follow-on order. As part of a $1,300 million package of military sales credits for Egypt requested from Congress in 1982, the Pentagon wanted to supply a further 40 aircraft, with deliveries beginning in 1985. An agreement covering the supply of these follow-on aircraft was signed in May 1982. The 40 aircraft in this second batch will be delivered between late 1985 and the autumn of 1987.

Having built up experience in the construction of modern aircraft by assembling Alpha Jets for the Egyptian Air Force, Egyptian industry is keen to co-produce more advanced types. Both the F-16/79 and the F-20 have been proposed as possible successors, but the problem of funding such a programme seems immense: a price tag of $2,000 million has been estimated.

F-16s for Korea

President Carter's idealistic plan, announced in 1977, to withdraw 39,000 US troops from South Korea was soon to be suspended as the 1970s drew to a close, but triggered off that nation's equipment upgrading plans. A requirement for 100 new fighters was identified, and US approval for the purchase of 72 aircraft was requested in 1979.

Below: Painted with temporary US markings and loaded with external tanks, a Fighting Falcon begins the long trip which will end some 11 hours later in delivery to the Israeli Defence Force – Air Force.

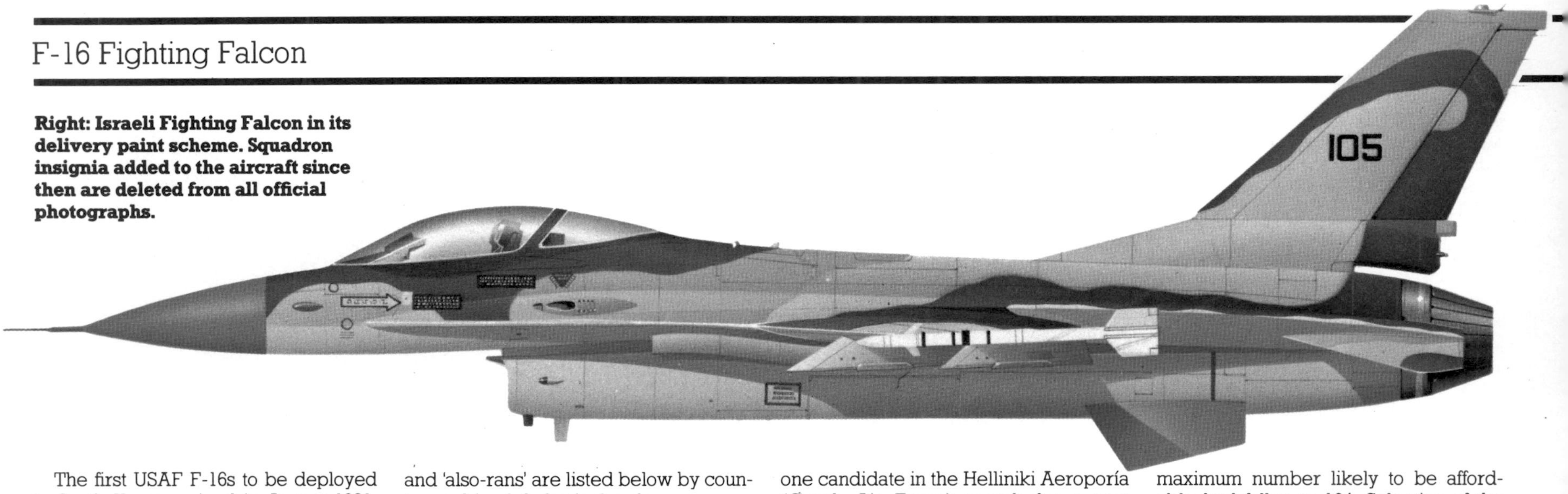

Right: Israeli Fighting Falcon in its delivery paint scheme. Squadron insignia added to the aircraft since then are deleted from all official photographs.

The first USAF F-16s to be deployed to South Korea arrived in August 1981, but the South Korean government signed a letter of offer for 36 aircraft of its own at the end of that year. Worth $930 million, the deal covered 30 single-seat and six two-seat aircraft, with deliveries beginning in February 1986 at a rate of one per month. It also covered spares, training and technical assistance.

The supply of advanced warplanes to Pakistan was clearly a politically sensitive issue, plans to supply the Vought A-7 Corsair II having been abandoned in the mid-1970s when Pakistan insisted on proceeding with plans to purchase a nuclear fuel re-processing plant from France – a possible key step along the route to developing indigenous nuclear weapons. Following the Soviet intervention in Afghanistan, however, the US State Department finally sanctioned the supply of 40 F-16s, Pakistan becoming the ninth nation to adopt the type when contracts were signed in December 1981.

Pakistan is to get 40 aircraft, the first six of which were delivered at the end of 1982, while the remainder are covered by a separate contract. The Fighting Falcon will probably replace part of the current fleet of Shenyang F-6 Farmers (Chinese-built MiG-19s).

Next customer for the Fighting Falcon was the Fuerzas Aéreas Venezolanas (Venezuelan Air Forces), which needed to replace the elderly Mirage IIIE fighters operated by Esc 34 at Palo Negro. Venezuela's proposed order for 16 single-seat and eight two-seat aircraft was sent to the US Congress for formal approval at the end of 1981, and the contract was signed in May 1982. Deliveries are due to begin in the autumn of 1983, with six aircraft being delivered in that year and six in 1984. The remaining 24 should be delivered in 1985.

Other evaluations

To date, the Fighting Falcon has attracted no other export orders, but this has not been due to any lack of marketing effort. The aircraft was a candidate in several fighter evaluations of the late 1970s and early 1980s, and is under consideration by several nations. For convenience, these current evaluations and 'also-rans' are listed below by country and in alphabetical order.

Australia's requirement for a Mirage IIIO replacement called for the procurement of up to 160 aircraft, and GD attempted to create an attractive package of F-16 work for Australian industry, despite the inexperience of the latter. Final assembly of the aircraft in-country was proposed, although the modest size (75) of the planned order made the economies of such a move questionable. Company estimates suggested that at least 150 aircraft would have to be assembled to justify the initial capital costs.

In both the Canadian and Australian fighter-selection competitions, the F-16 has lost out to the larger, twin-engined McDonnell Douglas F/A-18A Hornet. The reasons cited were generally those of genuine all-weather avionics in the standard aircraft, plus the extra safety of the twin-engine propulsion system. The Australian evaluation did highlight the lower overall programme cost of the GD fighter, although it suggested that the support and attrition costs over the lifetime of the planned fleet might substantially reduce the difference.

A four-man Österreichische Luftstreitkräfte (Austrian Air Force) team evaluated the F-16A in 1980. During one test the aircraft took off just under two minutes after engine start, reaching Mach 2 at 40,000ft (14,000m) within six minutes of brake release. Theoretical winner of this evaluation was the Dassault-Breguet Mirage 50, but plans to place an order have been suspended. Air defence is not highly placed in the Austrian government's list of priorities.

Initial goal of the Canadian Armed Forces was to select its next fighter in December 1977, and to begin deployment of the chosen aircraft in 1980. At least 120 were wanted, with perhaps a further 200 being ordered in the longer term. At the end of a three-year study, Canada finally selected the F/A-18 in April 1980. Factors influencing the choice included the greater safety offered by a twin-engined design, the higher performance of the F/A-18 systems and the avionics growth space.

Greece, which attempts to maintain a close military balance with Turkey, requested data on a possible procurement of 150–200 F-16s. The F-16 was one candidate in the Helliniki Aeroporía (Greek Air Force) search for a new fighter, being evaluated in competition with the F/A-18, F-18L, Mirage 2000 and Tornado. A total of 100 aircraft are needed, with a possible follow-on order for 30 more, but selection of the winner has been long delayed and no decision had been announced by mid-1983. Reports in the local press favoured the F-18L and Tornado, but the US government is thought to favour an F-16 deal, since the last-named aircraft could also be supplied to Turkey, maintaining the local military balance.

Japan chooses F-15

Japan's defence budget is not over-lavish. When 'shopping' for a new fighter in the late 1970s, the Nihon Koku Jieitai (Japan Air Self-Defense Force) appreciated the need to obtain the most effective force which the limited funding would permit. What was required was not only a new fighter, but also an early-warning and control system.

Japan evaluated the F-14, F-15 and F-16: the last could have allowed a larger fleet, but an order was finally placed for 123 F-15 Eagle fighters to be built under licence by Mitsubishi.

In the autumn of 1982 it seemed the Fuerza Aérea del Peru (Peruvian Air Force) might become the first South American FX customer. Data on price and availability of the F-16/79 were requested, and the FAP was thought likely to acquire 26 examples. After considering a subsequent US offer, Peru opted later the same year to order 24 Mirage 2000 fighters for delivery beginning in late 1984.

During negotiations held in the late 1970s over the future of US bases on Spanish territory, the Spanish government asked for 72 F-16s or aircraft of similar performance to be supplied.

The F-16 was clearly a front runner in the Spanish FACA (Futuro Avion de Combate y Ataque, or future fighter and attack aircraft) competition, being evaluated against the Mirage 2000, F/A-18 and Northrop F-18L. The Ejército del Aire Español (Spanish Air Force) wanted 144 aircraft, but by mid-1981 the maximum number likely to be affordable had fallen to 104. Selection of the F/A-18 was announced in July 1982, but only 82 examples could be afforded. The planned procurement was reviewed in 1983, a limited re-evaluation of the competing types being carried out before a final decision to acquire 72 F/A-18 Hornets was announced.

A Saudi Arabian requirement for 150 lightweight fighters for interception duties was reported in 1977. Despite the subsequent purchase of 60 McDonnell Douglas F-15 Eagles by the Al Quwwat al Jawwiya as Sa'udiya (Royal Saudi Air Force) under the Peace Sun programme, the US government still considers Saudi Arabia a potential customer for FX-class fighters.

With the growing diplomatic ties between the US and China in the 1970s, Taiwan found itself increasingly isolated in diplomatic terms. The Air Force wanted the F-16, but the range of the GD aircraft would have given the Fighting Falcon a significant strike capability against the Chinese mainland. Supply of the F-16, F-16/79 or Northrop F-20 was vetoed by the US government – largely as a result of political pressure from the People's Republic of China – so Chung-kuo Kung Chuan (Chinese Nationalist Air Force) re-equipment plans are now based on the F-5E Tiger.

During the late 1970s and early 1980s, a number of ambitious plans were conceived by the Turkish government in its attempts to set up a viable national aerospace industry. A requirement for 150 to 200 F-16s was discussed with the US, but serious study of this was hampered by the arms embargo enforced by the US following the invasion of Cyprus in 1974, and by Turkey's acute shortage of funds for new equipment. The equipment finally adopted by the Türk Hava Kuvvetleri (Turkish Air Force) is likely to be supplied as US military aid, and will probably be influenced by the final choice of fighter made by Greece. The US Government will almost certainly ensure that a military balance in terms of quality and quantity of equipment is maintained between these rival air arms.

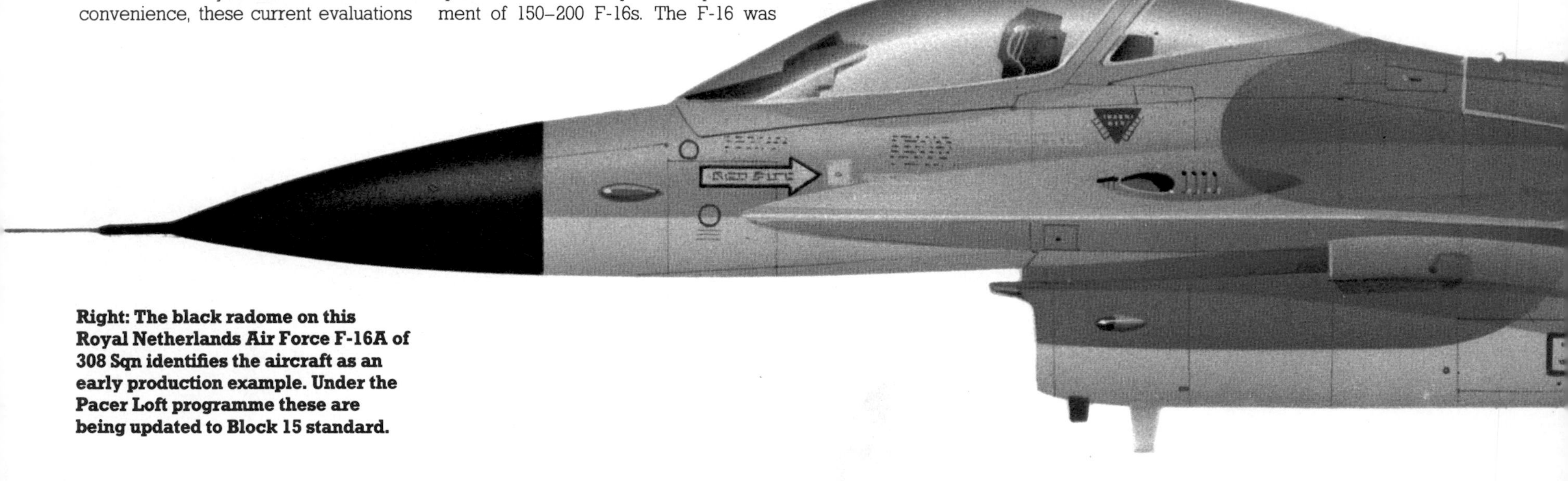

Right: The black radome on this Royal Netherlands Air Force F-16A of 308 Sqn identifies the aircraft as an early production example. Under the Pacer Loft programme these are being updated to Block 15 standard.

Right: F-16A of the 35th TFS, 8th TFW – the 'Wolf Pack' – from Kunsan Air Base, South Korea. Note the wolf's head insignia, which appears on both sides of the fuselage.

Right: Royal Norwegian Air Force F-16s are finished in an overall grey paint scheme, and carry the fuselage national markings below the aft section of the canopy.

Right and below: The emblem on the intake of this USAF Fighting Falcon identifies it as an aircraft of the 4th Tactical Fighter Squadron, 388th TFW, based at Hill AFB, Utah.

Performance and Handling

Ready for takeoff on an air-combat mission with no external tanks, Fighting Falcon tips the scales at around half the weight of an F-4 or F-15 tasked with a similar mission. Even by the standards of classic lightweight designs such as the MiG-21 Fishbed and Dassault-Breguet Mirage III, the F-16 is still a light fighter, weighing about one third more than the Soviet fighter and twelve per cent more than the Dassault delta. The GD aircraft matches its light weight with combat performance which the Mirage or MiG pilot can only dream about and a weapon delivery accuracy better than that of the F-111.

A lightly loaded F-16 with full internal fuel has a thrust-to-weight ratio of just over 1:1 in full afterburner. Working with the lightweight YF-16 prototypes, GD test pilots carried out pre-takeoff engine and system checks at 80 per cent power. Application of full afterburning power would have caused the wheels to slide.

Fighting Falcon begins its take-off roll with the wing leading and trailing-edge flaps positioned 2deg up and 20deg down respectively. After brake release, the aircraft quickly picks up speed. Rotation is usually at around 125kt, liftoff at around 140kt.

When Robert Ropelewski of *Aviation Week* flew the F-16B for the first time in 1979, GD Chief test pilot Neil Anderson was able to demonstrate the takeoff performance: "Anderson ... rotated the nose upwards, stopping at 60deg pitch as the aircraft began climbing out". Given the 30deg reclining tilt of the Fighting Falcon ejection seat, this climb angle meant that the torsos of the two pilots were literally horizontal. The F-16 can climb vertically, but this would result in the pilot hanging head-down in his seat.

"Acceleration continued, even in that attitude", reported Ropelewski, "the aircraft passing through 170kt about 30 seconds after brake release. A wing-over manoeuvre was used to level the aircraft at around 8,000ft (2,450m) altitude, still within the length of the Carswell (AFB) runway. A USAF Northrop T-38 chase aircraft which had started its takeoff roll on the same runway five seconds after the F-16 was just lifting off the runway below."

When the undercarriage is retracted the leading edge changes to 20deg down, while the gain of the flight-control system is doubled to reach its normal flight value. (The 50 per cent reduction while on the ground was incorporated as a result of the inadvertent first flight of the original YF-16 prototype). Throughout the mission the flight-control system remains at full gain, except when the door which covers the refuelling receptacle is opened. The latter operation reduce the control response in pitch and roll by an amount designed to make the aircraft 'less nervous', during the approach to the tanker, refuelling and subsequent separation.

One of the most novel features of the F-16 cockpit is the sidestick controller used in place of the traditional control column. This is located on the starboard side of the cockpit, and incorporates an adjustable armrest mounted on the cockpit wall. This is essential in high-g flight conditions, and includes an optional wrist rest which may be folded back against the wall if not required.

The original pattern of sidestick controller did not move, but was force sensitive only. Although effective, this scheme provided no indication to the pilot of when maximum input was being demanded. To avoid sprained wrists in the excitement of high-g manoeuvres, the USAF decided to allow the definitive design of stick a few millimetres of movement to provide the required degree of 'feedback' to the pilot. The rudder pedals have around 0.5in (1cm) of movement.

The flight-control system ensures that the pilot cannot over-stress the airframe. No matter how hard he operates the controls, the angle of attack and load factor are limited, ensuring that he cannot demand more than 25deg angle of attack or 9g load factor.

In practice, the 9g figure is probably close to the limit that the human body can take while performing a useful military mission. In conventional cockpits, pilots often experience tunnel vision – commonly known as grey-out – at levels of around 6 or 7g, but the semi-reclining seat of the F-16 seems to extend this limit by up to 2g. *Aviation Week*'s Robert Ropelewski noted no vision problems at manoeuvres of 8g or more, despite having had grey-out at around 7g in other aircraft.

Above: Even in dry thrust the F-16 is capable of impressive aerobatics. In combat, the added impetus of the afterburner offers the pilot 'brute force' solutions to any desired manoeuvre, while his opponent might have to conserve energy.

Right: The superb visibility of the F-16's canopy is illustrated by this view of aircraft from the 8th TFW. If the pilot looked round he would be able to see his own vertical stabilizer.

The brisk acceleration of the F-16 is a feature which has attracted much comment from pilots. Neil Anderson quotes one of the USAF pilots who tested the YF-16 as saying that flying the F-16 was '... like riding on top of a telegraph pole. Every time you light the afterburner, you are a little nervous that it is going to run out from under you'.

Any feeling that the pilot rides on top of the Fighting Falcon rather than within it is heightened by a bulbous canopy large enough to allow the pilot to look over his shoulder and observe his vertical stabilizer and see whether or not he is leaving a con-trial. Pilots used to the more traditional pattern of low-drag canopy used on such aircraft as the F-4 or A-7 are likely to feel somewhat exposed. At relatively modest bank

Above: Neil Anderson (left), Chief Test Pilot at General Dynamics, played a major role in the F-16 programme. Colleague James McKinney (right) flew the aircraft during the 1979 and 1981 Paris Air Shows.

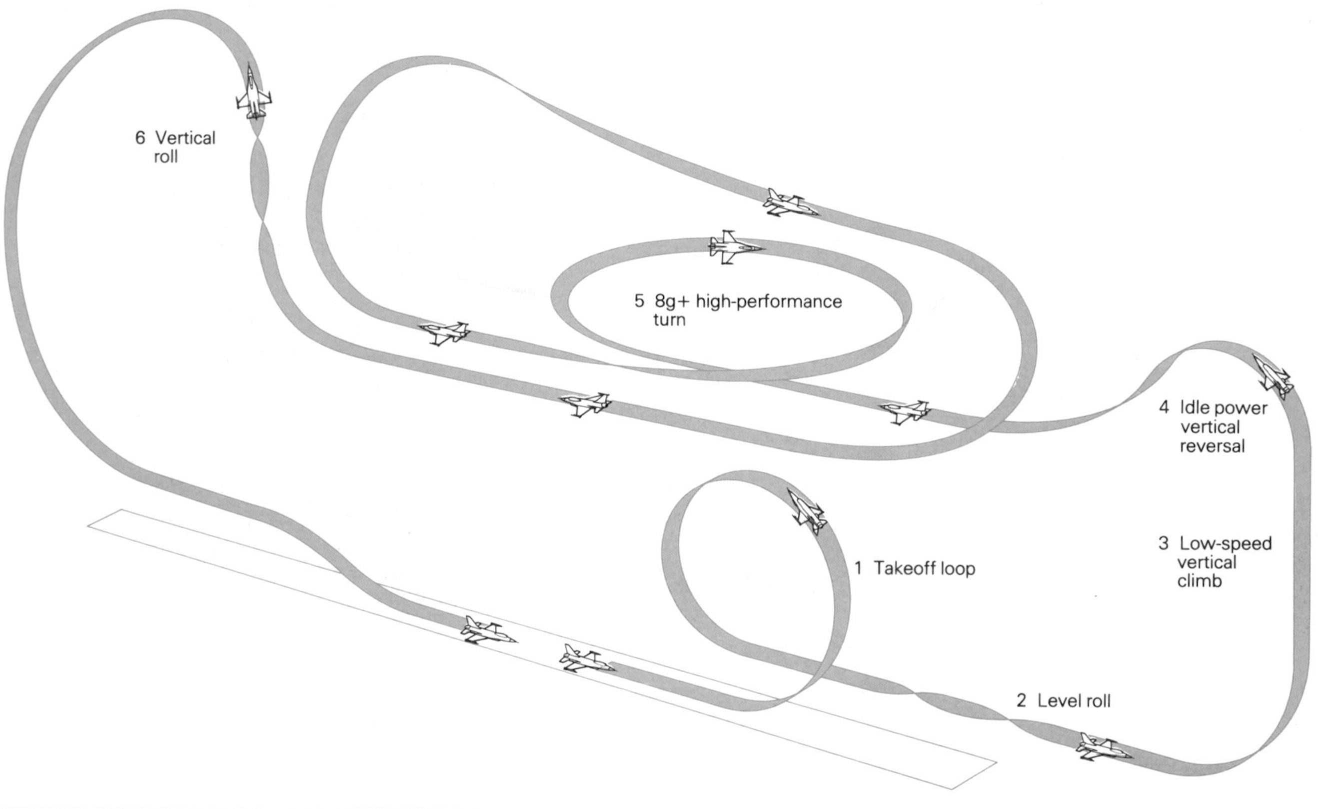

Left: This composite diagram illustrates some of the manoeuvres flown by the F-16 at Farnborough and Paris Air Shows during the late 1970s.

angles the pilot is able to look vertically downward at the terrain below, while the absence of canopy frames in the forward field of view removes the reference points by which pilots instinctively position the horizon during normal flight. During initial Fighting Falcon sorties, new pilots are recommended to fly by instruments until they become accustomed to the external view.

In high-speed cruise the wing leading and trailing-edge flaps are positioned 2deg above centre. Should the pilot attempt maximum-rate manoeuvres, the leading edge will move to 25deg down and the trailing edge will move to neutral. Vortexes generated by the leading-edge strakes play a significant part in improving the handling of the Fighting Falcon, producing improved

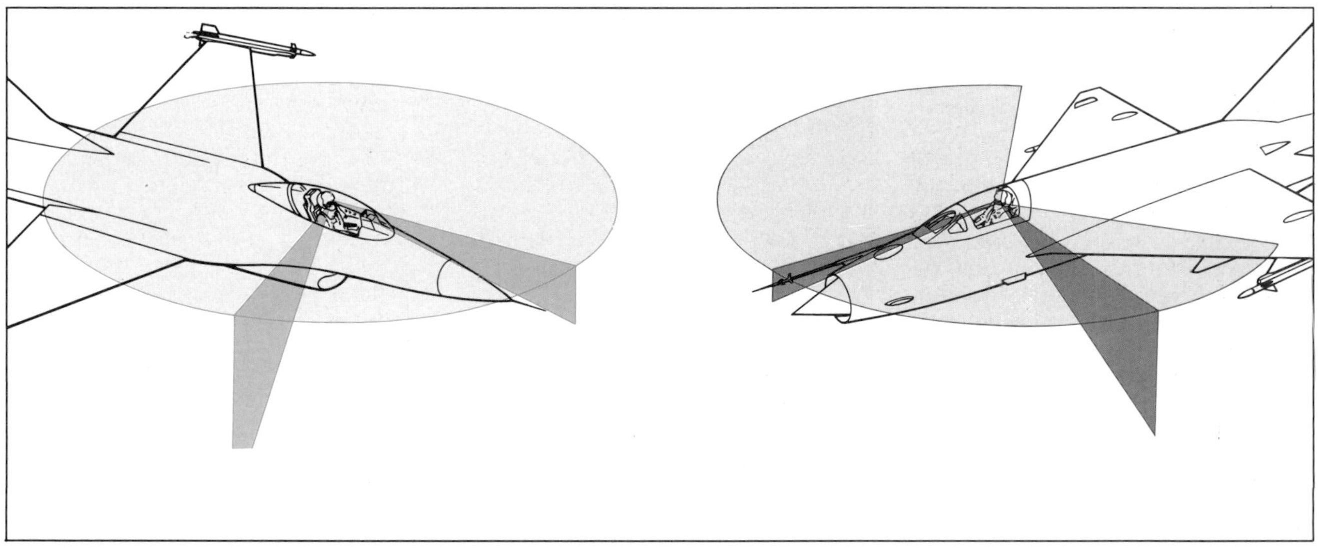

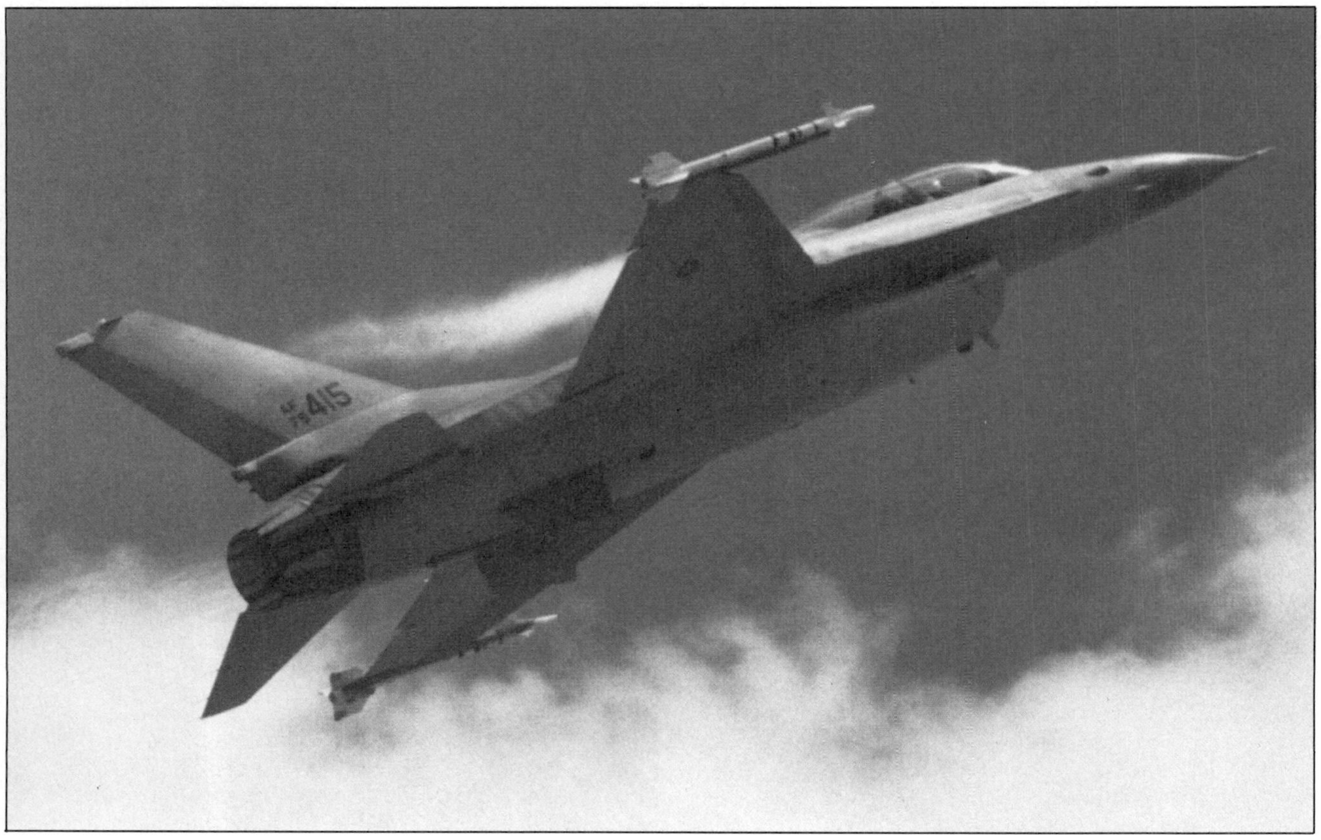

Above: Visibility from the cockpit of the F-16 is greatly superior to that from the MiG-21bis.

Left: F-16B two-seater flies an impressive-looking 9g climbing turn.

airflow over the wings and vertical tail. Lift, pitch and directional stability are all improved, while buffet intensity is reduced. Hard manoeuvring at high supersonic speeds can result in some buffeting, according to GD, but for most of the performance envelope Fighting Falcon is buffet-free. Transition through the transonic region is smooth, with only a slight buffeting as speed is increased through Mach 0.95.

Full details of the performance of the F-16A and C had not been released by June 1983. Unclassified brochures on the J79-powered version include the manoeuvre-capability charts reproduced here, but the equivalent charts for the F-16 bear no numerical data. During test flights, however, the F-16 has been flown at speeds in excess of Mach 2, and at altitudes greater than 60,000ft (18,300m). Thanks to the massive thrust of the F100, Fighting Falcon can climb at virtually any airspeed.

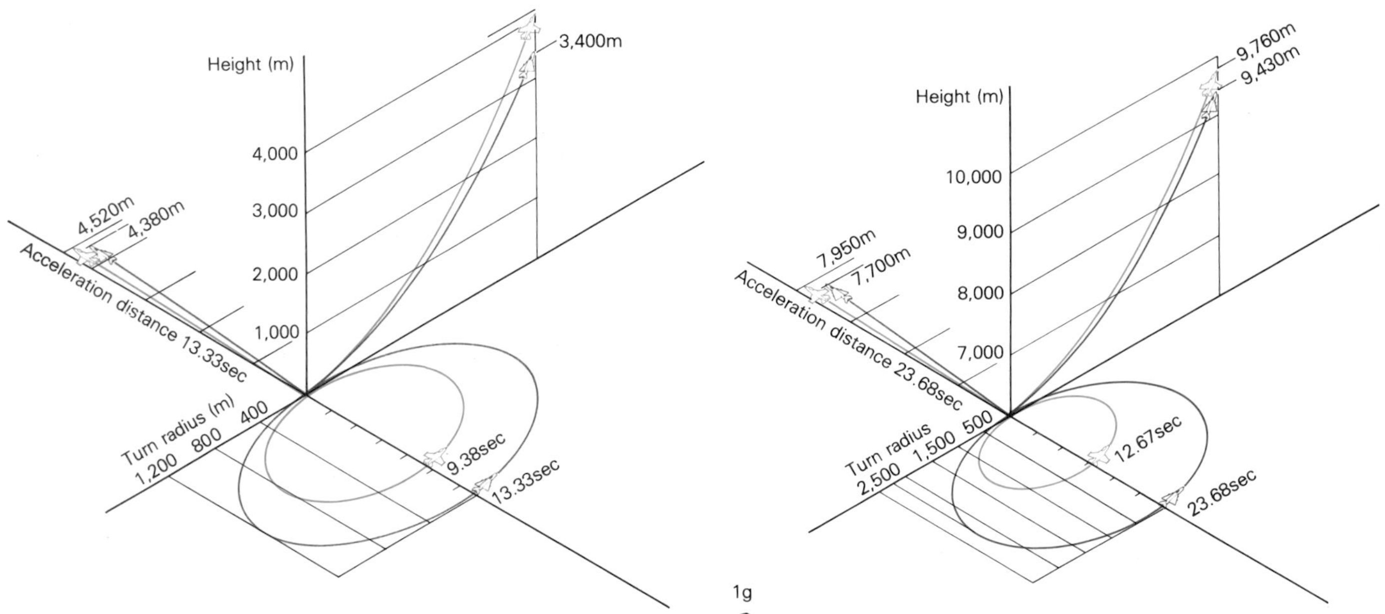

Performance of the F-16A compared with that of the MiG-21bis third-generation version of the Fishbed fighter. The diagrams assume a speed of Mach 0.85 at sea level (above) and 20,000ft (6,000m) (right). In all cases turning performance, acceleration and rate of climb are superior to those of the MiG.

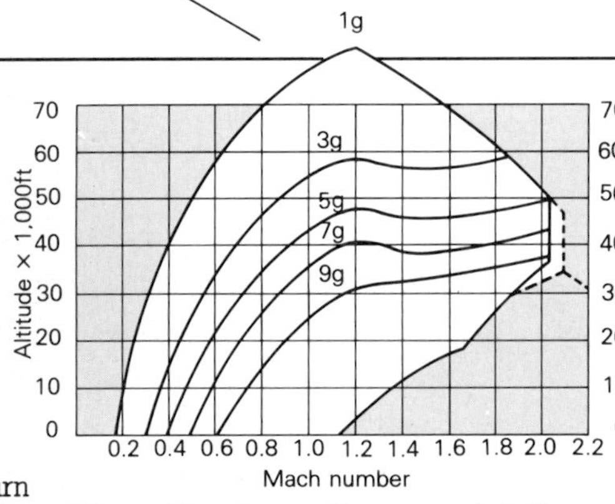

Above: Precise performance details of the F-16A are classified, but this chart shows the F-16/79's instantaneous manoeuvre capability.

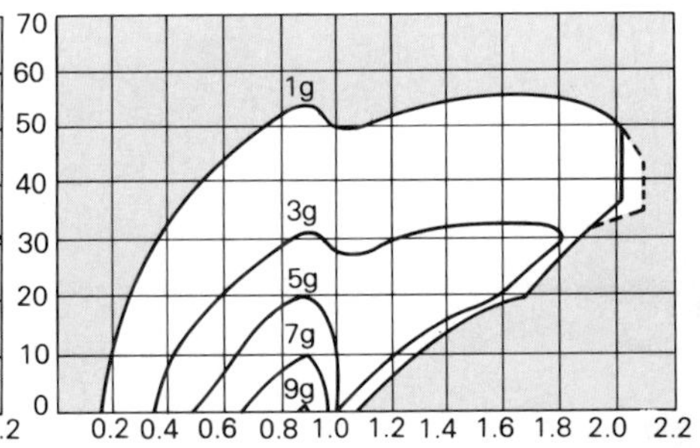

Above: Sustained manoeuvre capability of the F-16/79 is lower than the instantaneous capability, but the ability to sustain 7g is available in the most likely combat conditions.

Few fighters will be able to out-turn the Fighting Falcon. Flown in a 325–350kt turn against an F-4, a YF-16 prototype was able to carry out a full 360deg turn by the time the older fighter had managed some 240–250deg. Even at sea level the F-16 is able to out-turn the Mikoyan MiG-21bis. In terms of rate of climb, acceleration and turning performance, Fighting Falcon easily exceeds the performance of the Soviet fighter at altitudes of up to 30,000ft (9,000m). Comparative date for greater altitudes is not available.

According to one unclassified chart (produced by a rival US company) detailing comparative aircraft performance, maximum instantaneous turn rate of Fighting Falcon is just over 20deg/sec – virtually the same as that of the F-14 Tomcat and F-20 Tigershark. This figure is marginally bettered only by the Mirage 2000 and F/A-18 Hornet, and is a 50 per cent improvement over that associated with older types such as the Mirage III, F-4 Phantom and F-5E.

According to the RNethAF, the F-16 is "unbeatable" in simulated air combat. By early 1981 the aircraft had been flown against USAFE F-15 Eagles from Bitburg and Soesterberg in West Germany, and against RNethAF Mirage 5B fighters. The radar gave the service a level of look-down performance totally lacking in earlier types such as the F-104G.

Fighting Falcon is also an effective strike aircraft. Even at high speed and low altitude, air turbulence does create significant aircraft instability. Ropelewski has reported flying at 600kts at 100ft (30m) altitude with impressive results. "The aircraft was flyable hands-off, with no indication of gust upsets or even the slightest vertical or lateral accelerations."

During bombing practice, F-16 crews have displayed accuracies well above those obtained with earlier tactical fighters. According to the USAF, 2,000lb (907kg) iron bombs can be dropped within 30ft (9m) of a target, compared

Right: Con-trails forming from the strakes of this F-16 trace the path of the vortexes passing over the wing. These streams of energized air greatly enhance flying qualities.

Above: Despite its relatively large wing area, the Fighting Falcon offers pilots a smooth ride at low altitudes and high air speeds, essential qualities for the strike role.

with the 150ft (45m) typical using the F-4. The best crews of the Korean-based 8th TFW were scoring CEPs (circular error probable) of 9ft (2.74m) during 10deg diving attacks, while the average figure for the unit was 35ft (11m). Given this sort of accuracy, some pilots argue, there is no need to carry guided missiles or 'smart' bombs unless small hard targets such as bridges are to be attacked.

In substituting the GE J79 turbojet in place of the F100 to create the F-16/79 FX export fighter, GD has paid some performance penalty. Two years after his F-16B sortie, Ropelewski was able to fly the F-16/79 and noted a lower takeoff performance. "Acceleration is slower than with the F100 engine and the initial climb attitude is less impressive – in the neighbourhood of 30deg pitch compared with around 60deg for the standard aircraft – in a typical air-to-air configuration."

As the undercarriage is lowered prior to landing, the wing leading and trailing-edge flaps return to the 15 & 20deg down high-lift configuration used for the initial climb, while control sensitivity is reduced by 50 per cent to eliminate any possibility of over-correction.

Typical approach speed is around 125kt, with the aircraft touching down at or just below 120kt. After landing the nose is held up at an angle of 13deg to obtain aerodynamic braking, the nose-wheel not being lowered until speed has dropped to around 100kt. Typical landing runs at an aircraft weight of 20,000lb (9,000kg) are around 3,000ft (900m) on dry asphalt or concrete.

The problem of dead-stick landing is of concern to the pilot of any 'hot' single-engined aircraft. The earlier F-104G Starfighter had been particularly unforgiving in this respect, since the wing flaps were blown with engine air to improve lift. To make sure that the Fighting Falcon driver would have confidence in his aircraft should the engine fail, a series of dead-stick landing trials were carried out using the YF-16 prototypes. Initial tests showed that the aircraft could glide at around 150kt with undercarriage and flaps down, but a figure of 170kt was later chosen.

Below: Without its electronic fly-by-wire system the F-16 would not be controllable.

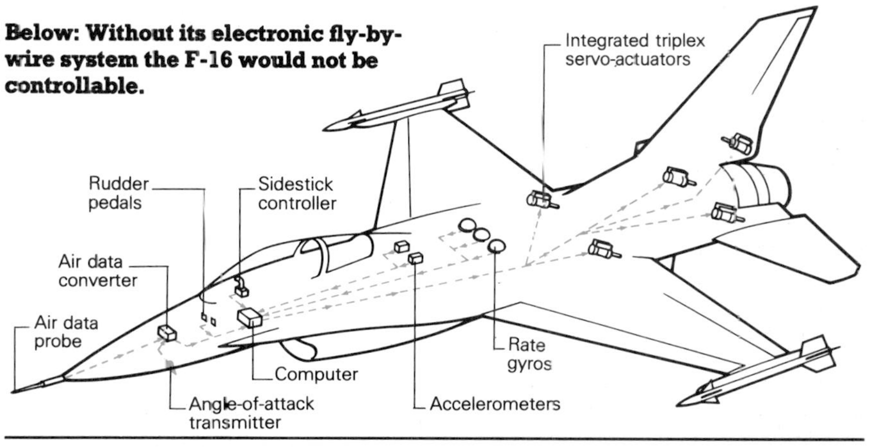

Right: In seeking a replacement for the ageing Northrop T-38 Talon, the USAF's Thunderbirds display team finally adopted the Fighting Falcon. It was first used during the 1983 season.

Experimental Variants

Like most successful designs, the F-16 has the potential for development into more advanced versions. Few aircraft can have been subjected to quite so many re-engining and rebuild programmes at such an early stage of their career: within ten years of the first flight by a prototype experimental versions have included an aircraft able to taxi on rain-drenched soil, experimental delta-winged variants, CCV configurations pioneering new ways to fly, forward-swept wings and even a proposed vectored-thrust STOVL model. One thing is certain – the story is unlikely to stop with the aircraft described here.

Above: The FloTrak wrap-around may look clumsy if not downright agricultural, but trials have shown that with its aid an F-16 could be towed across waterlogged ground, or taxied over a rough field.

Fighting Falcon has been used as a testbed for several experimental programmes. In some cases the aircraft was simply a convenient guinea-pig, but other projects involved drastic rebuilds and could lead to more advanced future versions of the F-16.

One of the YF-16 prototypes was used in 1982 to test a novel method of operating high-performance aircraft from damaged airfields. The USAF asked Vehicle System Development Corporation of California to devise a method of allowing jet fighters to be taxied over rough or soft ground. This would allow aircraft trapped in hardened shelters at bases attacked by anti-airfield weapons such as JP233 to be taken from their shelters and taxied to a takeoff site without using the damaged or mined taxiways.

Below: Fighting Falcon of the future? Equipped with intake-mounted canards and a MiG-21 style dorsal spine, the AFTI/F-16 is engaged in research which could lead to entirely new types of combat manoeuvre.

Wrap-around tracks

The solution devised was to fit wrap-around tracks to the nose and main wheels. These effectively widened and lengthened the 'footprint' of each wheel, reducing ground pressure and, consequently, the chance of the aircraft bogging down in soft terrain. Normal ground pressure of an F-16 is around 275lb/sq in (19kg/sq cm), but the use of the FloTrak wrap-arounds reduces this to just under 80lb/sq in (5·5kg/sq cm). During trials held at Wright-Patterson AFB, Ohio, a YF-16 fitted with FloTraks was able to taxi over rough ground at speeds of up to 35kt, and was towed across rain-soaked soft ground. At one point during the latter test the wheels of the towing tractor began to sink into the waterlogged soil, but the YF-16 was still free to move.

One of the YF-16 prototypes was rebuilt in the mid-1970s as part of the USAF Flight Dynamics Laboratory Control-Configured Vehicle (CCV) programme. Canard surfaces were added beneath the air intake, one on each side of the nose wheel, the fuel system was modified to allow greater control over the position of the aircraft centre of gravity, and the flight-control system was modified to allow the aircraft to be manoeuvred in ways not possible with conventional controls.

In a normal aircraft, movements in one plane are often related to movements in another. For example, in order to turn, a conventional aircraft must bank. On the YF-16/CCV, movements are fully independent or 'decoupled'. The aircraft can rise or fall using direct lift, move laterally by direct side force, or yaw, pitch or roll independently of direction of flight.

GD test pilot David J. Thigpen flew the modified aircraft in its new configuration for the first time on March 16, 1976, starting what was scheduled to be a programme of 85 flights. While coming in to land at the end of the 29th CCV test mission on June 24, 1976, the aircraft suffered a loss of engine power

while still some half a mile from touchdown. Thigpen brought the aircraft down in a rough landing, but the undercarriage collapsed under the strain. Subsequent repairs took more than six months, flights resuming in the spring of 1977.

The flight-test programme was completed by the end of July of that year. After 125 hours of experimental flying (87 flights), the YF-16/CCV proved that the new degrees of freedom such as fuselage pointing measurably improved mission effectiveness, and that future aircraft incorporating CCV technology could be designed to be smaller, lighter, less expensive and more manoeuvrable than conventional types.

The AFTI/F-16

Advances in electronic technology resulting from digital systems and large-scale integrated circuits suggest that future fighters will be able to incorporate new types of flight-control and nav/attack systems. To evaluate these, the USAF has devised the Advanced Fighter Technology Integration (AFTI) programme. This uses a heavily modified F-16 as a testbed, GD having been awarded a contract on December 26, 1978, to rebuild one of the full-scale development F-16s. The aircraft was handed over to the company in March 1980.

The AFTI/F-16 is immediately recognizable by the presence of intake-mounted canard surfaces and a dorsal spine similar to that fitted to third-generation MiG-21s. The latter modification provides the internal volume needed to house flight-test equipment. The AFTI/F-16 has a triplex digital flight-control system which will give the pilot CCV-type freedom of manoeuvre. All movements are fully decoupled.

First flight of the modified aircraft was delayed by software problems, but finally took place at Fort Worth on July 10, 1982. The first three test flights were carried out at Fort Worth by GD pilots, and the aircraft was then flown to Edwards AFB, California, to begin a two-year programme of 275 test flights.

The first year of flying explored the unorthodox flight modes such as fuselage pointing and direct-force translation. Early sorties checked aircraft behaviour over a large portion of the performance envelope, before work began on proving the digital flight control system and the new degrees of freedom which it permits.

Pilots will explore the effects of adding decoupled degrees of freedom to normal flight, determining how the new freedom of manoeuvre can best be used, and how unconventional motions and attitudes affect the pilot. If some manoeuvres cause vertigo or nausea in pilots, they will be of little use in combat, so this type of man-machine interaction must be explored. The USAF anticipates that trials will confirm that normal coupled flight modes are best for most of a sortie, handling the major changes to the flight path. Decoupled modes will probably be reserved for 'fine-trimming' aircraft position in simulated combat.

At the end of this phase, the aircraft will be returned to Fort Worth for further updating, so that integrated flight and fire-control tests can begin. This will involve the installation of the Automatic Manoeuvring Attack System (AMAS), whose main components are a Westinghouse sensor pod containing a FLIR sensor and laser rangefinder, a helmet-mounted sight, digital fire-control computer, radar altimeter and a Standard Avionics-Integrated Fuzing (SAIF) unit.

The sensor pod will be mounted in the port wing root, and will share the digital programmable signal processor of the APG-66 radar. In operational use, the pod may be slaved to the radar, helmet sight, or inertial navigation system so that targets detected by the latter can be tracked by passive infrared means. This will reduce the amount of time during which the aircraft must transmit. The pod may also be used to acquire targets independently. Data from the FLIR will be passed in turn to the integrated flight/fire-control system, which will generate the commands needed to steer the aircraft automatically towards the target.

The two years of test flying will be intensive, making use of flight-test facilities originally devised for the Space Shuttle programme. These will allow data from the aircraft to be processed in real time, so that the results of a sortie will be available before the aircraft has landed. Testing is due to culminate in a tactical evaluation during a Red Flag exercise at Nellis AFB, Nevada.

In 1980, news of a new and drastically modified F-16 variant was leaked to the US technical press. Designated SCAMP (Supersonic Cruise and Manoeuvring Prototype), this was based on studies carried out by GD between 1976 and

Above: Seen from this angle the F-16/XL bears a distinct resemblance to Fort Worth's biggest delta – the Convair B-58 Hustler. Note how the stores are mounted close to the underside of the wing.

Below: First F-16 to explore the strange world of decoupled flight movements was the YF-16/CCV. A series of 87 flights by the rebuilt prototype the mid-1970s paved the way for the more recent AFTI/F-16.

New ways to fly

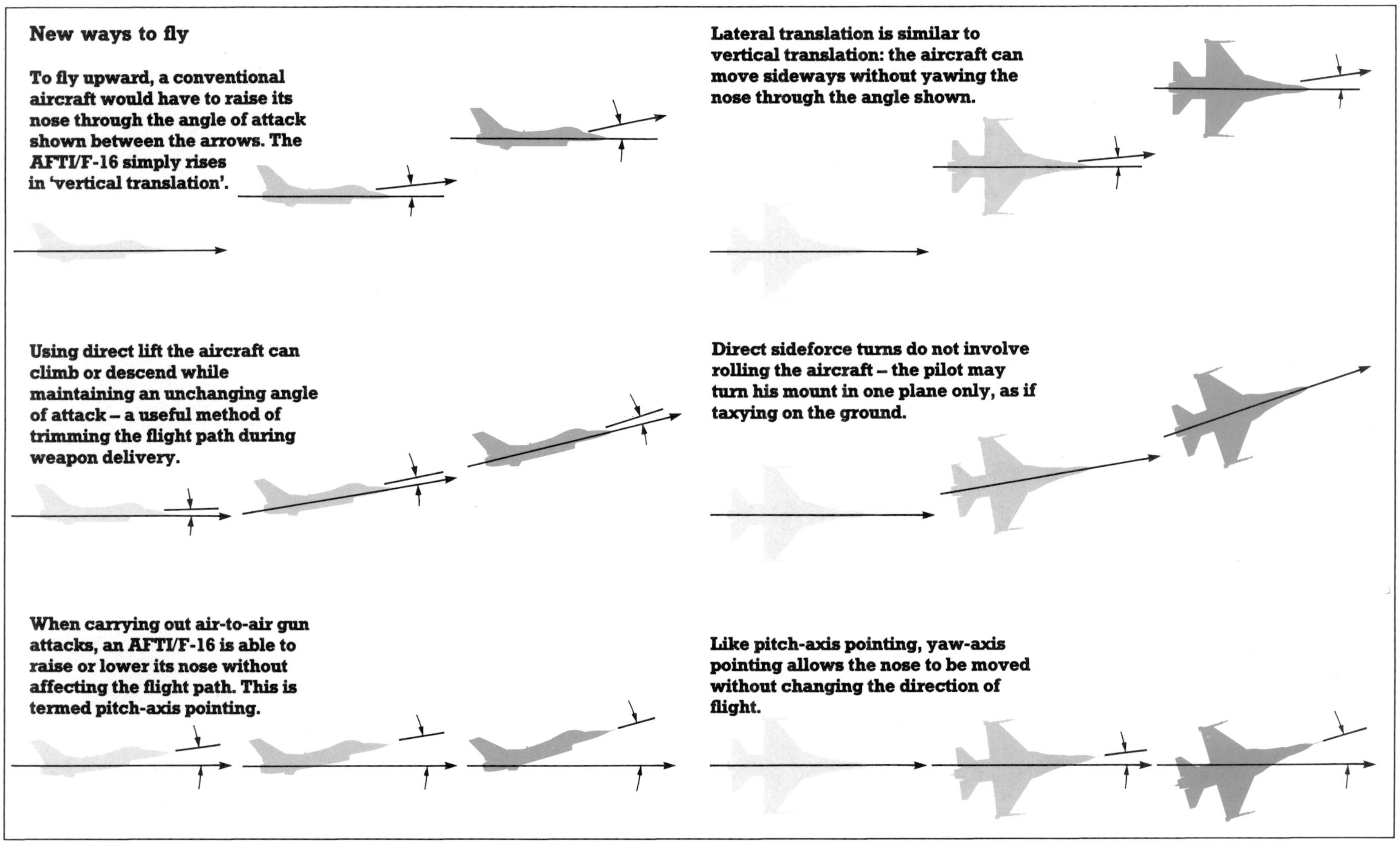
To fly upward, a conventional aircraft would have to raise its nose through the angle of attack shown between the arrows. The AFTI/F-16 simply rises in 'vertical translation'.
Lateral translation is similar to vertical translation: the aircraft can move sideways without yawing the nose through the angle shown.
Using direct lift the aircraft can climb or descend while maintaining an unchanging angle of attack – a useful method of trimming the flight path during weapon delivery.
Direct sideforce turns do not involve rolling the aircraft – the pilot may turn his mount in one plane only, as if taxying on the ground.
When carrying out air-to-air gun attacks, an AFTI/F-16 is able to raise or lower its nose without affecting the flight path. This is termed pitch-axis pointing.
Like pitch-axis pointing, yaw-axis pointing allows the nose to be moved without changing the direction of flight.

1980, and featured a 'cranked' delta wing, a configuration proposed to the USAF by GD in February 1980. Although the programme was at this stage a private venture by the manufacturer, the USAF did provide support, and the third and sixth full-scale development F-16s were returned to GD in the summer of 1981 for conversion to the new configuration.

Given the large production base of the F-16, GD designers tried to capitalize on existing components and experience in order to reduce the potential cost of the new variant. Wings and horizontal tail account for about 11 per cent of the total cost of the F-16, and these are the main all-new components in what was now designated the F-16XL. Although the rebuild did involve a modest fuselage stretch, the new designation did not, as some humorists suggested, stand for 'Xtra Length'!

Despite the significant external differences between the F-16A and the F-16XL, the airframe of the latter has more than 70 per cent commonality with the standard fighter. If a production version were to be ordered by the USAF, this would probably have MSIP-standard avionics, including the modified radar and LANTIRN.

F-16XL flight tests

First flight of the F-16XL took place at Fort Worth on July 15, 1982. This first sortie was all-subsonic, the aircraft reaching a top speed of Mach 0·9, a height of 30,000ft (9,000m), a maximum load factor of 3g and 20deg of angle of attack. At takeoff the angle of attack was 8deg, rising to 10deg at landing. Both values are well below those associated with traditional delta designs. Test pilot Jim McKinney reported that handling was 'very different' from that of the basic F-16, offering a 'solid ride'.

Following a small number of flights, the aircraft was transferred to Edwards AFB to begin a joint USAF/GD trials programme. Due to run for 240 flights over a period of nine months, this exercise involved both prototypes – the single-seat F100-powered version and the later GE F110-powered two-seater. Tests assessed the 'ride' which the aircraft offers at low level, and the use of high-speed tactics for defense penetration without the use of afterburner.

The second F-16XL is a two-seat rebuild of a full-scale development F-16A which was damaged in a landing accident. Ground proof-load tests of this aircraft suggested that the aft wing spar would fail at around 85 per cent of the planned limit, so the centre 22in (56cm) section of aluminium spar was replaced by a steel component.

First flight of the second F-16XL took place on October 29, 1982, again from Fort Worth. This aircraft, powered by the GE F110 turbofan, reached Mach 1.4 on its first sortie, with test pilot Alex Wolf in the front cockpit and Jim McKinney in the rear.

During the first 53 hours of F-16XL flight tests a total of seven GD and USAF pilots flew the aircraft. Highlights of this first period of testing included speeds approaching Mach 2·0 and altitudes of up to 50,000ft (15,240m). The aircraft refuelled from a KC-135 tanker, reached a speed of Mach 1·2 while carrying 12 Mk 82 bombs, and ripple-released the same ordnance load during dropping tests. After a brief grounding while further vibration trials were carried out and a braking parachute was installed, the aircraft began a series of stability and control tests, including an exploration of high angles of attack.

An evaluation of the two cranked-wing F-16XL prototypes by the USAF began in the summer of 1982. The FY 1983 budget included $21 million to cover the cost of the two F-16XL prototypes, as well as $57 million for the rebuilding of an F-15 Eagle fighter to the proposed F-15E strike configuration.

At one time the existence of the F-16 seemed to threaten USAF plans to develop a heavy strike fighter based on the F-15. The GAO asked the service in the summer of 1981 to justify its announced need for dedicated strike versions of the McDonnell-Douglas fighter and the F-16. Throughout the tests, the USAF was careful to avoid suggestions that the aircraft were in competitive evaluation, but the US Congress will not allow the USAF to buy both types.

One exotic F-16 variant which never left the Fort Worth drawing boards was the SFW/F-16 developed for the Defense Advanced Research Projects Agency (DARPA) forward-swept wing programme. Forward-swept wings offer good low-speed handling characteristics and low drag, but are very difficult to manufacture using conventional technology. The use of advanced composite materials allows the wing to be made strong enough to prevent the unwanted flexure which aerodynamic stresses

Left: The F-16 that never was – the forward-swept wing demonstrator proposed to DARPA in the mid-1970s.

tend to set up, but without an unacceptable weight penalty.

DARPA awarded study funds to GD, Grumman and Rockwell International under a project which started in 1976. Several configurations were studied by GD, including one with canards and an aft-mounted wing, but the final SFW/F-16 design was rejected by DARPA in January 1981 in favour of the Grumman 712 – now designated X-29A.

Both the USAF and US Navy are already considering next-generation fighters, and plan to test-fly technology demonstrators based on current aircraft. Fighting Falcon is a natural candidate for these programmes. In 1986 or 1987 the USAF intends to test-fly a flight-technology demonstrator as part of its study effort into next-generation fighters. This could involve a heavily modified F-16 airframe, perhaps mated with a more modern engine such as the P&W PW1130 derivative of the F100.

STOVL proposal

The most exotic F-16 derivative currently under study is the STOVL (short takeoff/vertical landing) E7 design offered by GD as a solution to the US Navy's specification TS169. This demanding requirement calls for a technology demonstrator capable of hovering for up to four minutes while using only 5 per cent of its fuel load; accelerating from Mach 0·8 to 1·6 at 35,000ft (10,700m) in only 80 seconds; and carrying out a sustained turn rate of 5·5g at 10,000ft (3,000m).

The service wants the aircraft to be built around existing hardware, so GD plans to mate a delta wing with an F-16-derived fuselage, installing a 28,000lb (12,700kg) thrust General Electric F110 (formerly F101 DFE) turbofan engine. To give hovering ability, an ejector system based on a de Havilland Canada design would be used. Air from the engine fan would be collected in a plenum chamber then used either to help provide vertical lift or to boost forward speed during transition and horizontal flight.

In the case of the Rolls-Royce Pegasus engine used in the British Aerospace Harrier, air from the fan is ducted to the forward pair of swivelling nozzles, while core exhaust is ducted to the rear nozzles – the 'four-poster' configuration. In the hover, the E7 would rely on a 'three-poster' scheme having two forward-located thrust sources and a single aft-mounted vectoring nozzle. The forward thrust component would be provided not by vectored nozzles but by the ejector system.

Fan air would be ejected from a series of nozzles arranged in a fore-and-aft line at the root of each wing. Fuselage and wing-mounted doors would direct the fan air downwards. This flow of fan air would draw a further supply of air through a series of louvres in the upper surface of the wing, augmenting the thrust.

In theory, such a scheme could augment fan-air thrust by a factor of up to 1·7, but in practice the gain will be less. The designers of the ill-fated Rockwell XV-12A of the mid-1970s used an augmentation scheme based on ejectors arranged laterally along the wing, but because of unpredicted losses in augmentor efficiency their creation stubbornly refused to hover. As a result of subsequent research into augmentors, GD considers that the technique is now usable. Its great advantage over afterburning 'four-poster' configurations is that it minimizes ground erosion and heating. The hot 'footprint' left by an afterburning Harrier derivative would allow the take-off point to be detected by infra-red sensors long after the aircraft had departed.

During transition the E7 would duct part of the plenum air to an aft-facing tailpipe, while still supplying some thrust via the ejector system. The core exhaust would be vectored and afterburned in the rear nozzle to balance and accelerate the aircraft. The tailpipe incorporates an afterburner, but this would not be used during transition. In horizontal flight the ejector system would be shut down, and all fan air ducted to the tail-pipe. The rear nozzle and tailpipe afterburners would be used as required.

There are still formidable technical problems to be solved, particularly with the ejector system, but GD plans to spend $2 million during 1984 on refining its design. Tactical radius and air-to-air performance of the E7 would be lower than that of the Fighting Falcon, but GD expects better manoeuvrability in the air-to-ground role.

Above: This head-on view of the F-16/XL illustrates the excellent shape of the basic F-16 canopy. The pilot has good downward visibility on both sides of the fuselage.

Below: Offered as a STOVL technology demonstrator to meet a US Navy requirement, the E7 is the most drastically modified F-16 proposed to date. Powerplant would be a single GE F110 turbofan.

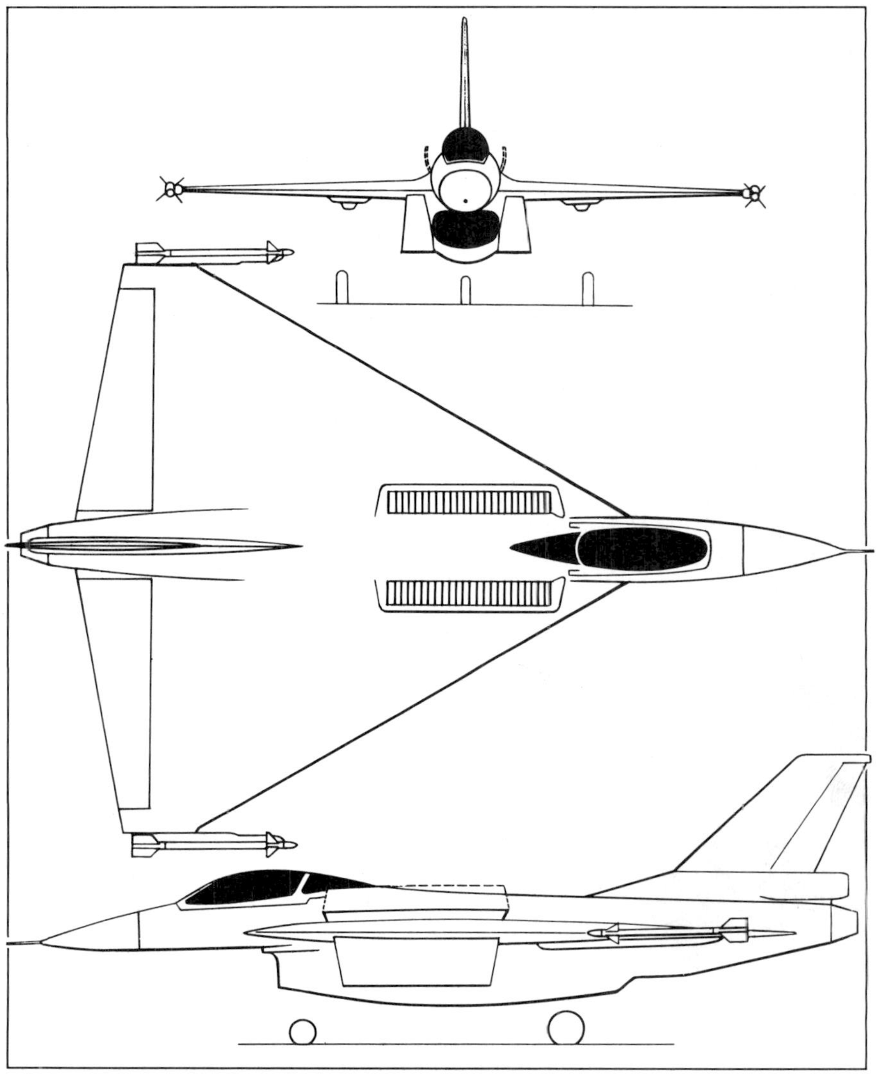

Glossary and abbreviations

AIM-	US designation for air-to-air missiles
AFB	Air Force Base
AGM-	US designation for air-to-surface missiles
AFTI	Advanced Fighter Technology Integration
Algorithm	Mathematical process for achieving a desired result
AMRAAM	Advanced Medium-Range Air-to-Air Missile
Analogue	Electronic system in which quantities are represented by electrical signals of variable characteristics, i.e. by electrical analogues
ANG	Air National Guard
ALR-	US designation for a radar-warning receiver
APG-	US designation for a nose-mounted fighter radar.
APQ-	US designation for jamming system
Aspect ratio	Ratio of the span of a wing to its chord
ASPJ	Advanced Self-Protection Jammer
ASRAAM	Advanced Short-Range Air-to-Air Missile
Bypass ratio	Ratio of the total airflow through a turbofan engine to that passing through the core section
Camber	Curvature of the centreline of a wing aerofoil
Category 3 flight test	Operational stage of US certification process – now called Air Force Development, Test and Evaluation
CCV	Control-configured vehicle
Centre of pressure	Point at which all the lift on the chord of a wing would act if the distributed pressure were to be replaced by a single resultant force
c.g.	Centre of gravity
Chord	Imaginary line connecting the leading and trailing edge of a wing
CRT	Cathode-ray tube (computer/TV-style display screen)
DARPA	Defense Advanced Research Projects Agency
dB	Decibel (unit of gain or attenuation)
Dead-stick	Flight operation carried out with engine(s) shut down or otherwise inoperative
Digital	Electronic system in which quantities are as on/off signals coded to represent numbers
Drag-at-lift	Drag created under high-lift flight conditions
ECM	Electronic countermeasures
ECP	Engineering Change Proposal
ECP 350	MSIP modification scheme
Envelope	Engineering term for the area defined by a series of limits
Esc	see Escadrille and Escuadron
Escadrille	Squadron (Belgium)
Escuadron	Squadron (Venezuela)
Esk, Eskadrille	Squadron (Danish)
EW	Electronic warfare
FAéB	Force Aérienne Belge, or Belgian Air Force
Fail-operative	System element which will allow a system to continue to operate in its active state in the event of a failure
Fail-safe	System element which will revert to a safe condition should it fail
FBW	Fly-by-wire (term for electrically signalled flight-control systems)
FLIR	Forward-looking infra-red
g	Unit of acceleration
GAO	General Accounting Office (an investigative branch of the US Congress)
GD	General Dynamics
GE	General Electric
GHz	GigaHertz (Hertz × 1,000,000,000)
HUD	Head-up display
Hz	Hertz (unit of frequency)
I&A	Integration and assembly
IDFAF	Israel Defence Force – Air Force
IIR	Imaging infra-red
I/J-band	Radar frequencies from 8 to 12GHz
IOC	Initial operating capability
IR	infra-red
iron bomb	conventional free-falling high-explosive bomb
JTIDS	Joint Tactical Information Distribution System
KHz	kiloHertz (Hertz × 1,000)
KLu	Koninklijke Luchtmacht, or Royal Netherlands Air Force
kT	Kiloton
Ku-band	Radar frequencies from 12 to 20GHz
LANTIRN	Low-Altitude Navigation and Targeting by Infra-Red at Night
Mach	Unit equal to the speed of sound
MSIP	Multinational Staged Improvement Programme
MTU	Maintenance Training Unit
MW	Megawatt
nav/attack	Navigation and attack (e.g. 'nav/attack system')
Nr	Number (Dutch)
OCU	Operational Conversion Unit
Pacer Loft	Modification programme for European F-16s
P&W	Pratt & Whitney
Raster scan	Method of building up a TV-style image on a CRT by scanning the image in a series of lines
R&D	Research and development
RNethAF	Royal Netherlands Air Force
RNoAF	Royal Norwegian Air Force
RWR	Radar-warning receiver
PRF	Pulse repetition frequency
Program	Instructions for a computer
Programme	Spelling used to designate a programme of research or work
Ps	Engineering abbreviation for specific excess power
PSP	Programmable signal processor
SCAMP	Supersonic Cruise Aircraft Modification Programme
sfc	Specific fuel consumption (unit of fuel consumed per unit of thrust per hour)
SFW	Swept-forward wing
smart bomb	Free-falling bomb with built-in guidance system
Software	One or more programs for a computer
Synthetic-aperture radar	Technique by which a small radar antenna on a moving vehicle may simulate a larger unit in terms of resolution
TAC	Tactical Air Command
Taileron	All-moving tailplane able to move differentially as a substitute for traditional aileron control
TFG	Tactical Fighter Group
TFS	Tactical Fighter Squadron
TFTS	Tactical Fighter Training Squadron
TFW	Tactical Fighter Wing
Trim drag	Component of drag due to the deflection of an elevator or elevon in order to maintain lateral balance of an aircraft
TWT	Travelling-wave tube (power source used in many modern radar)
USAF	United States Air Force
USN	United States Navy
Wave drag	Component of drag resulting from the formation of shock waves
Wing loading	Weight of an aircraft divided by the wing area

Specification

	YF-16	F-16A	F-16/79A	F-16XL
Length	48ft 5in/14.75m	49ft 6in/15.09m	49ft 6in/15.09m	54ft 2in/16.51m
Wingspan	31ft 0in/9.45m	31ft 0in/9.45m	31ft 0in/9.45m	34ft 3in/40.92m
Height	16ft 3in/4.95m	16ft 8in/5.08m	16ft 8in/5.08m	17ft 7in/5.36m
Weights				
Empty	13,595lb/6,167kg	15,586lb/7,070kg	17,041lb/7,730kg	
take-off (air-to-air)	21,600lb/9,798kg	23,810lb/10,800kg		
Maximum take-off	27,000lb/12,247kg	35,400lb/16,057kg	35,400lb/16,057kg	
Wing area	300sq ft/27.87sq m	300sq ft/27.87sq m	300sq ft/27.87sq m	646sq ft/60.02sq m
Wing loading (air-to-air)		73lb/sq ft/30.81kg/sq m		
Thrust:weight ratio (air-to-air)		1.1:1		
Maximum speed	Mach 1.95	>Mach 2	>Mach 2	
Service ceiling	>50,000ft/15,200m	>50,000ft/15,200m		
Range				
Ferry (with ext. tanks)		>2,100nm/3,890km		
Tactical radius		>500nm/925km		c.730nm/1,340km
Internal fuel		6,972lb/3,162kg		c.12,700lb/5,760kg
No. of hardpoints		nine	nine	17
Maximum ordnance load		20,450lb/9,280kg	15,200lb/6,890kg	

USAF F-16 units

Wing	Base	Tail code
Tactical Air Command		
9th Air Force		
56th TTW	Macdill AFB, Florida	MC
363rd TFW	Shaw AFB, South Carolina	SW
12th Air Force		
388th TFW	Hill AFB, Utah	HL
474th TFW	Nellis AFB, Nevada	NA, WA
832nd Air Division		
58th TTW	Luke AFB, Arizona	LA
US Air Forces in Europe		
16th Air Force		
401st TFW	Torrejon, Spain	TJ
17th Air Force		
50th TFW	Hahn AB, West Germany	HR
Pacific Air Forces		
5th Air Force		
314th Air Division		
8th TFW	Kunsan AB, South Korea	WP
Air National Guard		
169th TFG	McEntire ANGB, South Carolina	

Chapter 4

F/A-18

HORNET

Mike Spick

F/A-18 Hornet

Contents

Acknowledgements

The author and editor would like to thank all those who have contributed information and pictures to this chapter. Photograph sources are credited at the beginning of the book, but particular thanks are due to Timothy J. Beecher and Al Gingerich of McDonnell Aircraft Company, Saint Louis; Geoffrey Norris and Karen Stubberfield of McDonnell Douglas Corporation (UK); Robert F. Dorr, who compiled the table on page 259; Robert L. Lawson of *The Hook*; Kearney Bothwell and V. Leon Levitt of Hughes Aircraft Company, Radar Systems Group; B. McCoy and John E. James of Kaiser Electronics; Anna C. Urband of the US Naval Office of Information; and J. K. Corfield of the Northrop Corporation.

Author

Mike Spick was born in London less than three weeks before the Spitfire made its maiden flight. Educated at Churchers College, Petersfield, he later entered the construction industry and carried out considerable work on RAF airfields. An interest in wargaming led him to a close study of air warfare and a highly successful first book, *Air Battles in Miniature* (Patrick Stephens, 1978). His subsequent work includes a historical study of the evolution of air combat tactics, *Fighter Pilot Tactics* (Patrick Stephens, 1983), and he is co-author of a previous Salamander book, *Modern Air Combat* (with Bill Gunston, 1983), as well as later chapters in this book, *B-1B*, *F-4 Phantom II* (with Doug Richardson) and *F-14 Tomcat*.

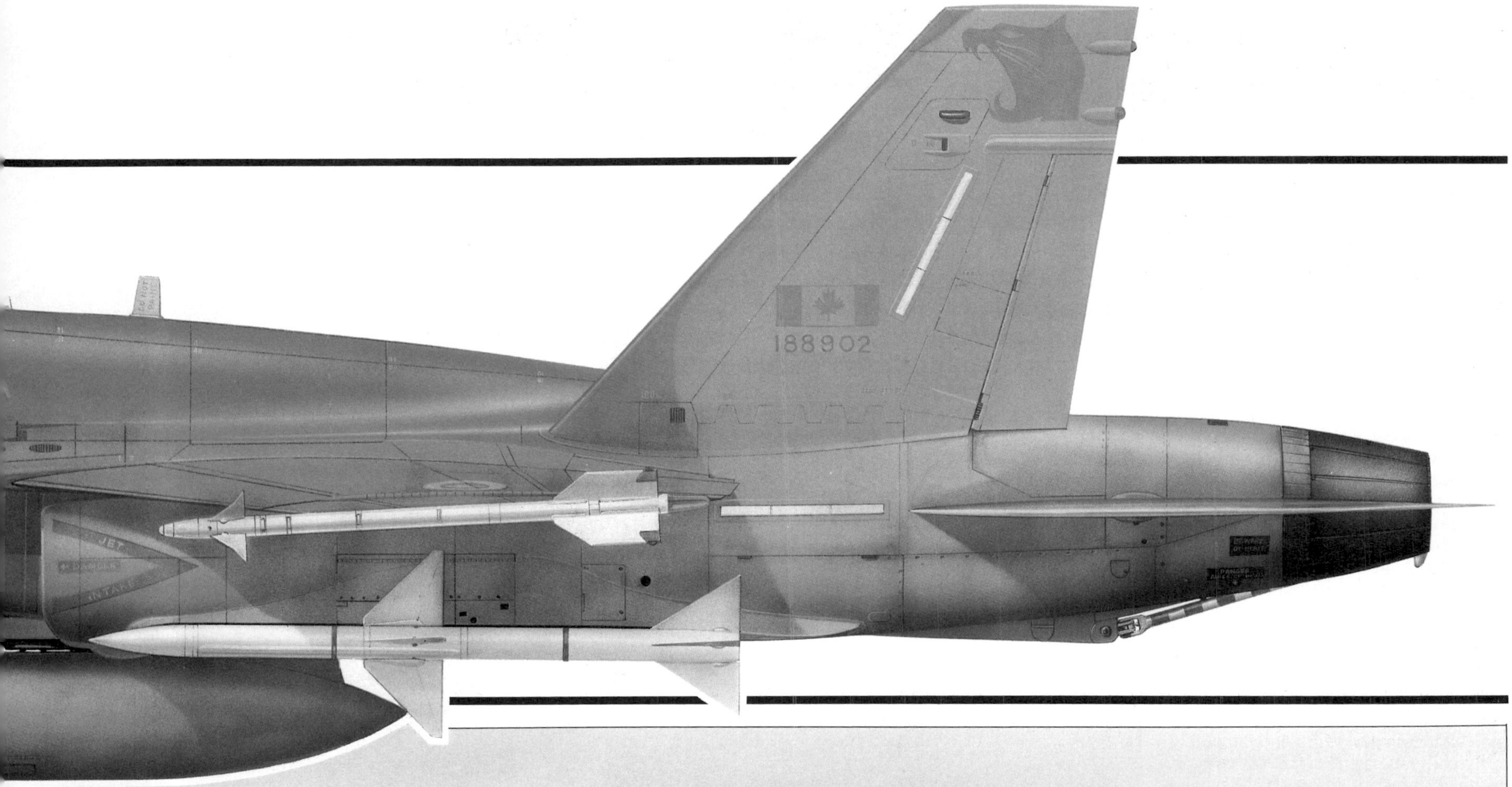

Introduction

Criticism of Western fighter designs has been a growth industry for more years than I care to remember, largely because of the inability of the experts to predict accurately the form that future war in the air will take. Thus the first homing missiles were expected to put an end to manoeuvring close combat and make guns redundant: in fact, whereas it had often been possible to evade a gun attack by accelerating out of range, the reach of the new weapons made such a course distinctly unwise; the ability to turn hard became more rather than less necessary, in order to make the missile work hard to catch the target and increase the chances of failure. Manoeuvre may start at longer ranges, but is more vital than ever before.

The F-18 has received more than its fair share of criticism. It is not as capable as the F-14 in the fleet defence role; it is inferior to the F-16 in close combat; it lacks the range of the A-7; and so on. Yet the Hornet has the task of replacing not one but two types in the US Navy inventory, the A-7 Corsair and the F-4 Phantom – and the latter, the most versatile and capable fighter of its generation, is a particularly hard act to follow.

It should not be forgotten that almost every fighter ever built has sooner or later been festooned with ordnance and asked to do something for which it was not originally designed. The fact that the Hornet has rather more provision than usual for weapons delivery built in from the outset must be a major point in its favour. It must also be remembered that all modern fighters are the result of a series of compromises.

The other main grounds for criticism is the fact that the F-18 is derived from the YF-17, the loser to the YF-16 in the USAF's lightweight fighter competition in the 1970s. But it is too easy to say that the Navy bought the loser: the YF-17 performed extremely creditably in the competition and in some areas was actually superior to the YF-16. The F-18 in turn is a much improved machine, and the Navy is satisfied that it is getting the best aircraft for its purposes.

Development

Speaking on June 30, 1981, Vice Admiral Wesley L. McDonald, US Navy, addressed the critics of the F/A-18 programme: "After seven years of design, development, open testing and intensive study, the capability of this aircraft is well understood. While some factions have been criticizing legitimate problems that typically are not known until much later in service, others have been fixing those problems. Today, no significant discrepancies remain . . ." While these comments certainly seem justified, the Hornet's origins can be traced back beyond those seven years to Northrop design studies of the 1960s.

The first half-century of air warfare saw fighters grow larger, faster, heavier, less manoeuvrable, much more versatile, and vastly more expensive. No nation has an unlimited defence budget, and with the increase in costs came a diminution in fleet size. The trend firmly established itself: fewer aeroplanes, but of greater capability. As combat aircraft grew more expensive, attempts were made to break out of the vicious circle of rising costs with such aircraft as the lightweight Folland Midge and its Gnat derivative. But a main argument against the concept was that the number of young men with both the desire and the ability to fly complex fast jets was not large; it made little sense to equip them with anything less than the very best. This attitude was fine for the wealthier industrial nations, but not so good for the others.

An early, and very successful example of an austere lightweight fighter was the F-5 Freedom Fighter, manufactured by the Northrop Corporation. As early as 1954, a Northrop team toured both Europe and Asia, sounding out the defence needs of many nations. Their findings led to the development of the N-156, later to become the F-5, as a private venture.

Basically, the fighter force that a nation thinks it needs and the fighter force that it can afford are two different things. Force size and quality are limited by capital outlay, maintenance costs and skilled manpower resources, while the number of fighters available for action at any one time is governed by force size and maintainability. The F-5 was designed to offer supersonic performance as a fighter and a secondary strike capability, coupled with the simplicity, reliability and maintainability to provide a high sortie rate. Its sole concession to complexity was in the use of two engines, an early example of systems redundancy, although its fuel costs were assessed as less than half those of the single-engined F-104. It first flew on July 30, 1959.

The United States Defense Department ran a Military Assistance Program (MAP) to help the smaller aligned nations acquire suitable defence equipment. On April 25, 1962, the DoD designated the F-5 as the MAP all-purpose fighter, which effectively meant that it could be supplied to friendly nations on very advantageous, heavily subsidized terms. As a result the F-5 was to see service with the air arms of more than two dozen countries.

With the F-5 an on-going project, it was time to look to the future. Northrop had no way of knowing how long the F-5 would stay in production, and that 20 years later it would still be in the process of up-grading (their F-5G has recently been redesignated F-20). Every aspect of aviation tends to be evolutionary rather than revolutionary: Northrop had identified a market need and filled it; the obvious next step was to consider a successor.

This meant staying in the export market rather than trying to produce a fighter for US service, and involved special considerations, the main one being technical and manufacturing participation by the main customer countries. By allowing the customer to have a hand in producing the aeroplane, the deal could be made much more attractive, as much of the money spent would benefit indigenous industry. The overall cost had to be attractive, both in capital outlay and in terms of operational life expenditure. The aeroplane would have to be mission-capable; while it could hardly approach the standards of the superfighters then under development, it would have to do a convincing job for the money. Cost-effectiveness was not a term current at the time, but this was the aim. In the event, the success of the cheap but potent F-5 has probably proved a hindrance to early sales of the new fighter. Finally, any

Right: This unusual planform view of the prototype Northrop YF-17 high over the Mojave desert shows many of the unique features of this fighter. The cut-outs in the LEX, through which the ground can be seen, the sharply swept, high aspect ratio horizontal tailplanes and the forward set of the vertical tail surfaces are all clearly apparent.

deals with foreign countries had to be politically acceptable to the DoD; the United States was hardly likely to countenance sales to a friendly country which was likely to use the equipment in a conflict with another friendly country.

Left: An early picture of the YF-17. The small strakes on the nose cone have not yet been added.

In the mid-1960s, Northrop initiated discussions with F-5 users and other interested parties to determine their requirements. They also postulated the most likely threat, and as many of the early F-5 operators were members of NATO, the discussions took on a distinctly European aspect. The fighter threat at that time was of course the Soviet-designed MiG-21, which was in service in large numbers with the Warsaw Pact countries: the projected threat was its successor, expected to be a simple, cheap, lightweight air superiority fighter, likely to enter service in the mid-1970s.

From the requirement studies emerged five basic missions: interception, air superiority, reconnaissance, close support and interdiction. These roles have conflicting requirements and an aircraft optimized for any one of them would be compromised in the others to a greater or lesser degree.

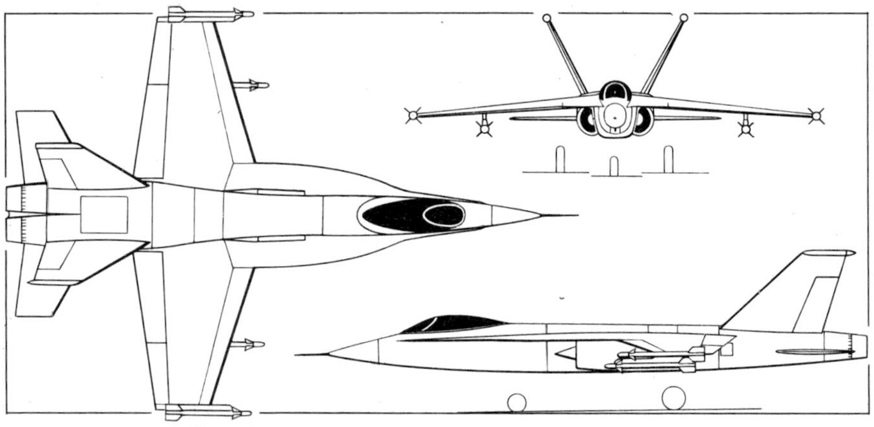

Above left: The Northrop F-20 Tigershark is, like the Hornet, descended from the F-5A, which the F-20 closely resembles.

Left: Development stage – the P-530 Cobra. The early requirement for Mach 2 capability is reflected in the Starfighter-like fuselage shape and the half cones to the inlets.

Below: F-5E of the 425th TFTS. The success of Northrop's earlier lightweight fighter has probably inhibited sales of the company's F-18L.

Lee Begin takes charge

Back in 1956, Northrop's Lee Begin, Jr., had made the first drawing of the N-156, later to become the F-5. Now, ten years later, he took charge of the Northrop project office team whose function it would be to translate ideas and requirements for the new fighter into hardware. Early studies showed that optimization for air superiority would result in the minimum compromise for the other roles. This was hardly surprising, as the aerodynamic requirements of an air superiority fighter themselves demand a great deal of compromise.

The role requirements are: (1) high rate of climb; (2) fast acceleration; (3) high turn rate combined with small turn radius; and (4) good transient performance (i.e., the ability to change the direction of flight rapidly). Items (1) and (2) require a high thrust/weight ratio, plenty of specific excess power (P_s) and the lowest possible drag, all of which are achieved by wrapping the smallest possible body around the largest possible engine. Item (3) demands a low wing loading which in turn calls for a relatively large wing (with its attendant weight and drag), plenty of P_s, and a high aspect ratio. Item (4) is conferred by good performance in pitch, and particularly in the rolling plane, with a fast rate of roll and rapid roll rate acceleration. This calls for a relatively small wing with a low aspect ratio. The art is to produce the best compromise between these conflicting requirements.

By 1967 the decision had been taken to design a Mach 2 air superiority fighter with secondary capability in other roles. The potential market was assessed at about 3,000 aircraft, of which the Northrop share could be about one-third, and the main types the new fighter could be expected to replace were the F-5, the Lockheed F-104 Starfighter and the Dassault Mirage III.

Gradually the outlines of what was to become the P-530 Cobra emerged. The original 'paper aeroplane' formulated in 1966 clearly showed its F-5 ancestry. The wing was of similar shape although greater in area, and featured a small leading edge extension (LEX) at the root, although it was high mounted. The engine inlets were set forward, just behind the cockpit, while the vertical and horizontal tail surfaces were almost identical. By the following year, larger LEX had been added, and the inlets were now positioned beneath the wings, which had developed a taper on the trailing edge from a point at about one-third of the span to the fuselage.

YF-17 configuration: seven stages of development

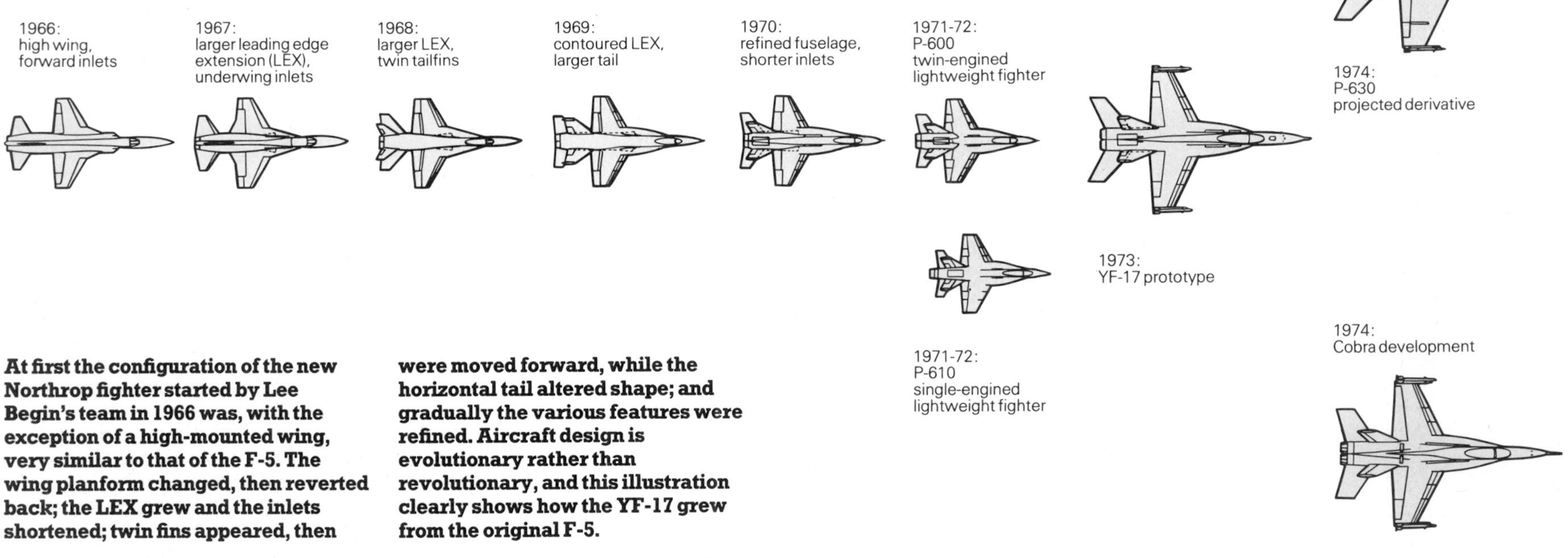

At first the configuration of the new Northrop fighter started by Lee Begin's team in 1966 was, with the exception of a high-mounted wing, very similar to that of the F-5. The wing planform changed, then reverted back; the LEX grew and the inlets shortened; twin fins appeared, then were moved forward, while the horizontal tail altered shape; and gradually the various features were refined. Aircraft design is evolutionary rather than revolutionary, and this illustration clearly shows how the YF-17 grew from the original F-5.

The most radical departures in layout came in 1968. The wing had reverted almost to its original shape, while the LEX had been extended much farther forward. They were now definite strakes rather than mere extensions, and their function was to generate large vortices across the upper surface of the wing which would inhibit the spanwise movement of the boundary layer air across the wing surface to give better handling qualities at high angles of attack (AOA). They also provided a destabilizing effect at transonic and supersonic speeds as the wing centre of lift moved aft, thus reducing trim drag. Finally the LEX served as compression wedges, reducing the intake Mach number by lowering the local AOA at the intakes. Running along the inside edge of the LEX were cut-outs, or slots. The purpose of these was to draw off the stagnant fuselage boundary layer air before it could be ingested by the engines, and expel it into the low pressure area above the wing roots.

Tail redesign

The tail had undergone the most radical changes. The horizontal surfaces were more sharply swept than before, and were of increased area, but the single fin and rudder had vanished, to be replaced by small twin vertical surfaces canted outwards, set above the engines at the extreme rear of the fuselage. Wind tunnel tests proved this layout unsatisfactory, and in 1969 the design showed that the LEX had been contoured, and the vertical tail surfaces were much larger, and had been moved forwards on the fuselage to a position where they overlapped both the trailing edge of the wing and the leading edge of the horizontal tail. This position produced some area rule effect, and good lateral stability was provided by the vortices from the LEX impinging on the fins, which were canted outwards at the startling angle of 30deg to obtain maximum benefit.

To achieve a thrust/weight ratio close to or exceeding unity, the two engines were required to have a static thrust in afterburner of about 12,000lb (5,445kg) each. The two main contenders for the supply of the engines were Rolls-Royce, with the RB.199, and General Electric with their new GE 15. General Electric agreed to develop their engine specifically for the Cobra, and the GE 15, later to become the YJ101-GE-100 was chosen. The twin-engined configuration selected was a follow-on from the F-5, giving extra safety and reducing operating costs due to attrition. Much controversy surrounds the twin versus single engine debate; it is believed, although figures differ widely, that a twin-engined design gives an engine-related attrition rate about 60 per cent of that suffered by single-engined designs.

By 1970 the P-530 Cobra looked much as the F-18 does today. The engine inlets had been shortened and the vertical tail surfaces were not canted at quite such an extreme angle. Meanwhile Northrop had set up other design teams. One team produced a layout for a single engined variant, the P-610, while another team, for reasons best known to the manufacturers, came up with a design called the P-600, almost identical to the P-530.

Unlike many fighters designed earlier, the Cobra always featured guns as part of its armament. At one stage two 20mm M39 revolver cannon were featured, but the final choice was the six-barrel General Electric M61, mounted under the nose. Wingtip launch rails were provided for Sidewinders, although theoretically the choice of missile was left to the customer, and seven hardpoints were provided for the carriage of up to 16,000lb (7,260kg) of stores. A one-piece bubble canopy gave the pilot excellent all-round vision.

By 1972 Northrop had invested a great deal of money in the Cobra project. More than 4,000 hours of wind tunnel testing had been completed and nearly 750,000 engineering man hours expended. Now they needed partners to further the programme who would be prepared to invest $100 million in the construction and testing of two pre-production machines, and whose requirements would total between 300 and 400 Cobras. The pre-production machines would allow the customer to evaluate the aeroplane before placing a firm order, and the initial payment would be offset against the total cost of the order. Provision had been made to allow the Cobra to be split up into production packages to share manufacture between customer nations, and both Holland and Norway were showing interest, but the vast capital expenditure involved in replacing a major portion of a nation's air force makes it a political and financial as well as a military issue. In practice, politicians become both military and financial experts and the resulting hot air delays the proceedings.

Hard lessons

Meanwhile wars had been fought and lessons learned. Vietnam 1965-1972, the Middle East wars of 1967 and 1969-70 and the Indo-Pakistan conflict of 1971 had all involved much air fighting, and one thing had become evident: close combat, the old-fashioned dogfight, was still very much a part of air warfare. The F-4 Phantom, arguably the most capable aircraft of its era, had found itself hard pressed by the comparatively cheap, lightweight Soviet designs. One of the truisms of air combat is "Don't fight the way your opponent fights best", but the Phantom often had no choice.

The historical record had until that time shown that the fastest fighter possessed a clear advantage in combat, both in attack and in defence. Until the Korean War, the difference between combat cruising speed and maximum speed rarely exceeded 15 to 20 per cent, but with the advent of Mach 2 capable fighters the difference became a factor of between two and three. Consequently, the advantage passed from the fastest aircraft in terms of capability to the fastest moving aircraft at the time of engagement. Over Vietnam, this was often the defending MiGs. The attempt to find an answer took two forms: better weapon systems with reliable beyond-visual-range (BVR) kill capability, and fighters which could beat the MiGs at their own game.

Two men who played a large part in developing the latter concept were defence systems analyst Pierre M. Sprey, and USAF Major John Boyd. Major Boyd is well known for formulating

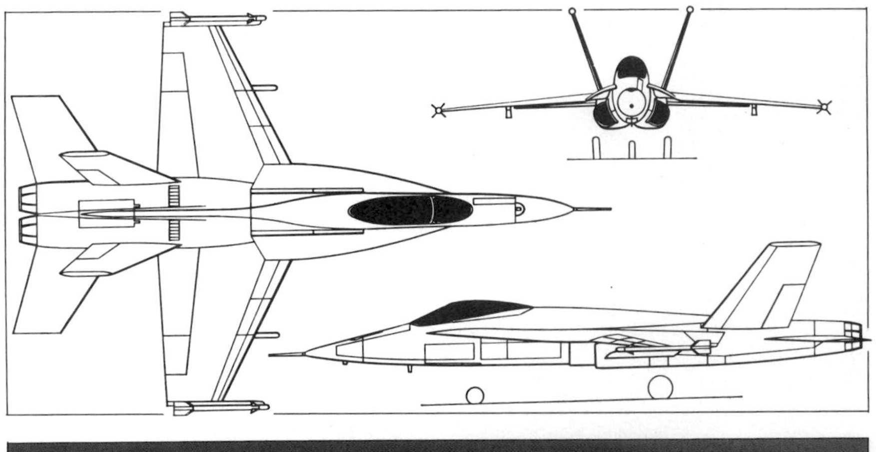

Right: The use of ultra-violet light allows the photography of airflow patterns formed in the wind tunnel. This picture of a YF-17 model on test, taken nearly a year before the first flight, shows the vortices formed by the LEX leading edge extensions.

the concept of energy manoeuvrability, and perhaps less so for his development of a flying technique to counter roll reversal by using rudder instead of aileron, 'setting the hook' as he called it. Their early studies centred around a design for a dedicated air superiority fighter, and priorities were established from the lessons of the past. The most obvious lesson was that the majority of air victories were the result of a surprise attack, so the problem became a question of how best to achieve surprise. Part of the answer lay in keeping the fighter small and therefore difficult to see. This was at the time almost heresy. The latest US fighters were the Grumman F-14 Tomcat and the McDonnell Douglas F-15 Eagle, both very capable, colossally expensive and extremely large.

Doubts were beginning to surface as to whether the established trend was the correct one. There could be little doubt that however capable a fighter was, it would stand little chance in close combat if heavily outnumbered by simple, austere (and cheap) fighters. This was in fact borne out by later Red Flag exercises, where the big superfighters performed wonderfully well in numerically small engagements but achieved a kill ratio in multi-bogey combats barely in excess of 1:1 against F-5Es of the Aggressor Squadrons.

Above: Having lost the USAF ACF competition to the YF-16, the YF-17 was then evaluated by the US Navy for the strike fighter role, resulting in the semi-naval markings.

Below: Trailing smoke, a YF-17 lifts off the runway. Compare the flimsy landing gear and single nose wheel with the beefy-looking undercarriage subsequently added to the F-18.

Below left: Three-view drawing of the YF-17, showing the basic configuration finalized in 1973.

Below: The P-600 differed from the YF-17 in wing and tailplane planform, and in the cant angle of the fins.

Below right: The two YF-17s were later redesignated F-18L by Northrop for evaluation purposes.

Bottom right: The hooded aspect of the YF-17, which inspired the name Cobra, is seen at takeoff.

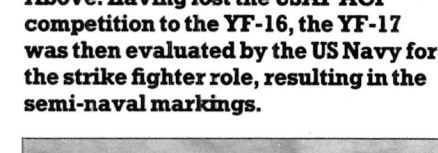

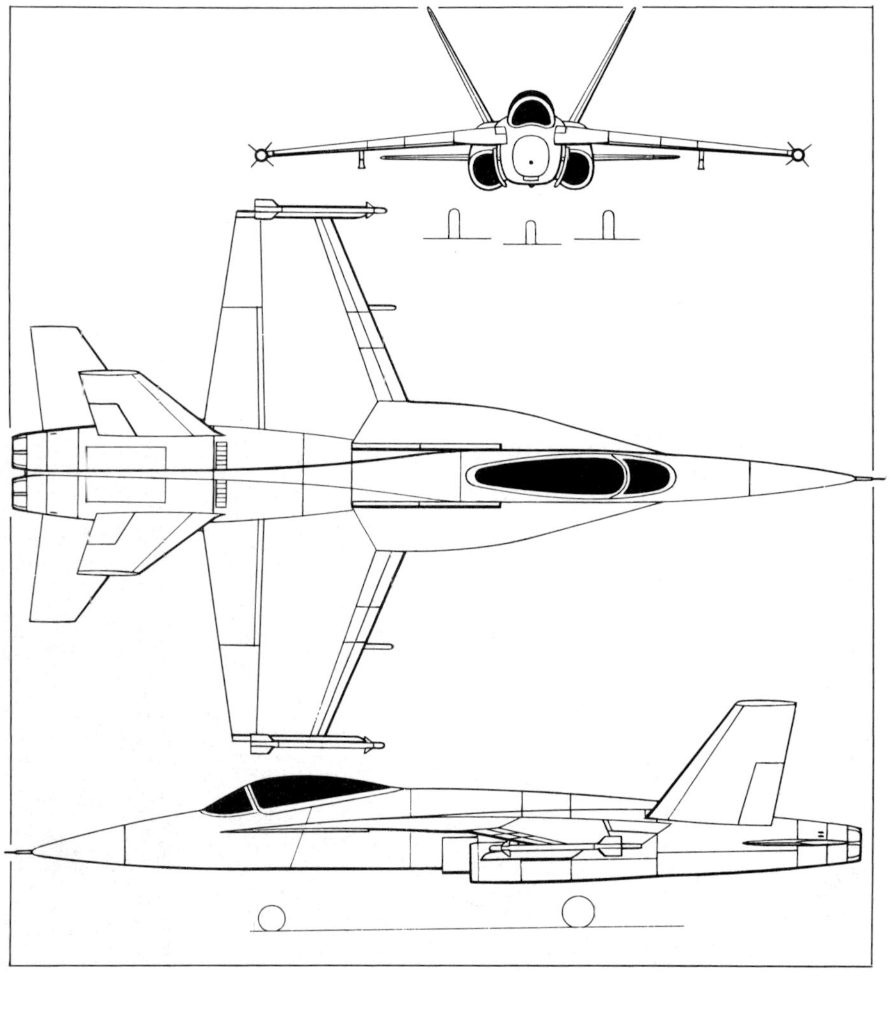

By 1971, Major Boyd was working for the Air Force Prototype Study Group, and was in a position to push the light fighter concept. At the same time, the Department of Defense resorted to the time-honoured custom of ordering prototypes which could be evaluated by flying against each other. Prototyping was regarded as a systems management technique to be pursued as a possible method of achieving continuing technical superiority cheaply, or as the jargon has it, 'in an austere funding environment'. It can be summarized as "let's see the goods before we buy".

LWF requirement

On January 6, 1972, the USAF issued a request for proposals for a lightweight fighter (LWF). Little in the way of performance minima was specified, thus freeing the designer to concentrate on the main requirements, which were to demonstrate exceptional manoeuvre and handling capability in the transonic regime. In short, the LWF was to be designed for greatest effectiveness in the middle of the flight performance envelope.

A minimum load factor of 6.5g was specified, along with limited avionics for navigation, communications and fire control for guns and missiles. The new design had to demonstrate advanced technology while keeping both weight and cost down.

LWF proposals were submitted by Boeing, Ling-Temco-Vought, General Dynamics and Northrop. The Northrop proposal was based not on the P-530 but on the virtually identical P-600. On April 13, 1972, the field was narrowed to two, contracts being placed with General Dynamics and Northrop, worth \$38 million and \$39 million respectively. Each was to build two prototype fighters for evaluation. They were to be technology demonstrators, and no Air Force requirement was to be presumed. A cost limit of \$3 million was set based on a procurement of 300 aircraft in Fiscal Year 1970 terms. This allowed the competing design teams to make cost/performance tradeoffs, rather than be forced to keep tweaking the performance up a little to meet firm specification requirements, usually at disproportionate cost.

Bearing the Air Force designation YF-17, the first Northrop prototype was rolled out on April 4, 1974, its maiden flight took place on June 9, and it was followed into the air by the second prototype on August 21 of the same year. It had taken nearly eight long years, but the concept had finally made the transition from paper aeroplane to flyable hardware. The YF-17 was a single-seat fighter powered by two afterburning General Electric YJ-101 low bypass ratio turbojets, each rated at about 15,000lb (6,800kg) static thrust. The wings were set in the mid-fuselage position with 5deg of anhedral, and were of trapezoidal planform reminiscent of the F-5, with an area of 350sq ft (32.52m^2), a 20deg sweep at quarter-chord, with LEX and slots as drawn for on the P-530. Variable camber was featured, in the form of leading edge manoeuvring flaps and plain trailing edge flaps which deflected automatically as a function of AOA and Mach number.

The fuselage had grown to about 4ft (1.22m) longer than the P-530, and narrow strakes had appeared on both sides of the nosecone. The pilot sat on a Stencel Aero 3C ejection seat, which was raked back at an angle of 18deg. The bubble canopy gave excellent rearward visibility although this was somewhat negated by the airbrake when extended, this being located on top of the fuselage between the twin fins, which were canted outwards at about 20deg, rather less than those of the P-530. The all-moving tailplane showed most changes, being mounted low on the rear

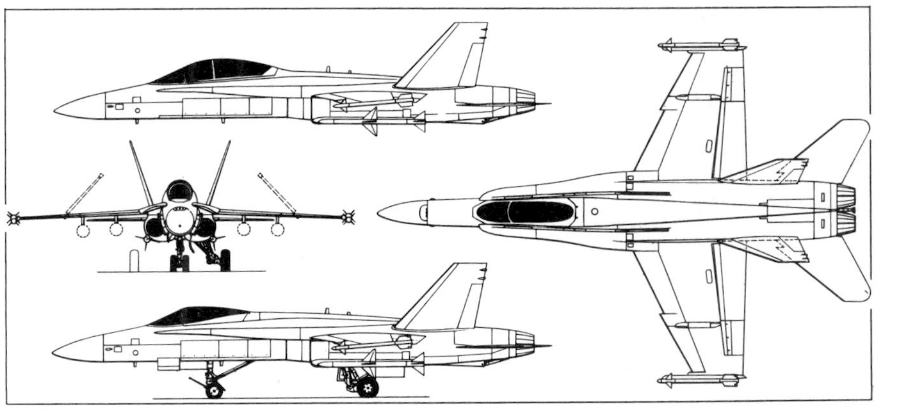

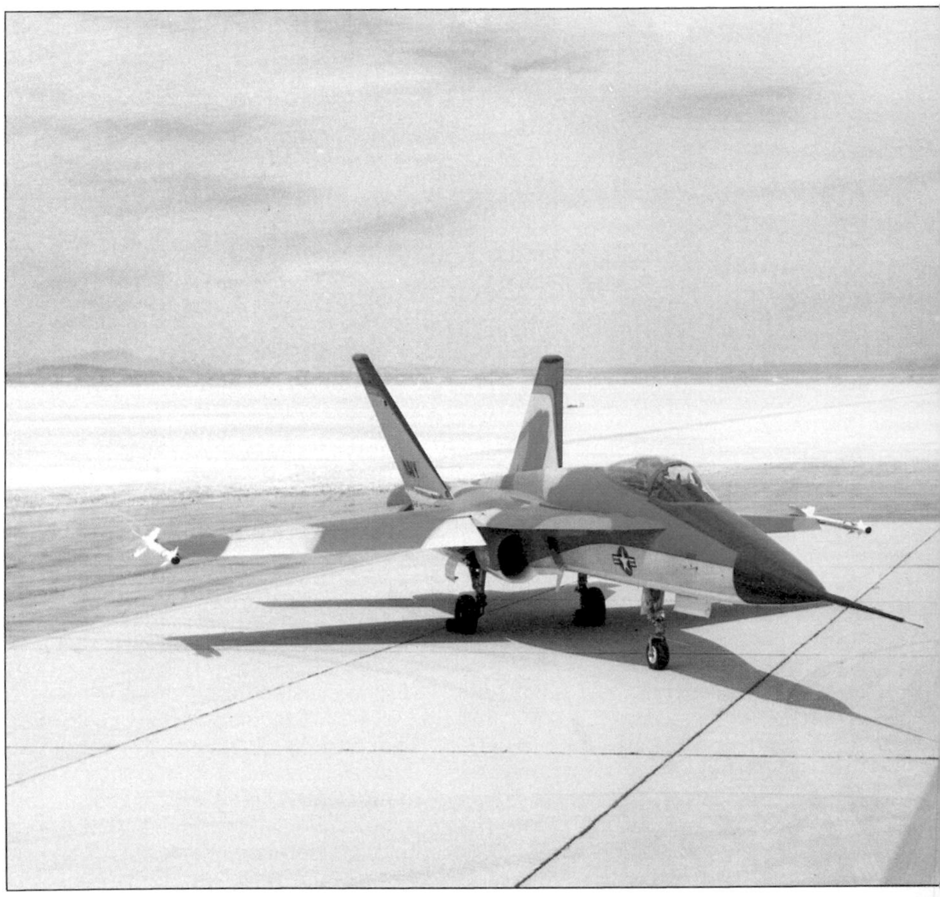

Above: The first prototype F-18 on an early flight demonstrates its variable camber wing.

Top: Hornet 1 looks rather weary after nearly four years of test flying. Navy and Marine Corps markings are on opposite sides.

Right: Hornet 3, the carrier suitability trials aircraft, flies over USS *America* on October 30, 1979, prior to making the first deck landing. During the next four days Hornet 3 carried out what the US Navy called, "the most successful sea trials in naval history", including 32 catapult launches.

Left: The original configuration of the F-18, plus a profile of the two-seat TF-18. The notched wing and tailplane leading edges are McDonnell Douglas innovations, along with the arrester hook and folding wings needed for carrier operations, and the altered tailplane planform.

Below: A contrast in prototypes. The YF-17 (left) is noticeably smaller and less chunky than the Hornet 3, and while both aircraft carry Sidewinders on wingtip rails, the F-18 also carries two Sparrows under the fuselage.

fuselage and swept more sharply than on the Cobra, while its span had increased to 22.21ft (6.77m) and its aspect ratio had risen considerably. Fly-by-wire (FBW) systems operated ailerons, rudder and tailplanes, with mechanical pitch and roll backup for the tailplane.

The YF-17 retained the nine external store stations of its predecessor and its air-to-air armament consisted of a Sidewinder mounted on a rail on each wingtip, and the M61 cannon mounted high in the nose instead of underneath as formerly. Avionics were basic: an air-to-air ranging radar by Rockwell International with a small phased array antenna; the Litton Industries LN-33 Inertial Navigation System (INS); a Teledyne transponder; and a gunsight head-up display (HUD) by JLM International. The clean takeoff weight had been held down to 23,000lb (10,430kg), which gave a very favourable thrust/weight ratio. Considerable weight savings had been achieved by redesigning the undercarriage, which on the Cobra had been intended for rough field operations and was consequently more rugged and heavier than necessary for runway operations.

In the air, the YF-17 performed well. During flight tests it demonstrated a top speed of Mach 1.95 (there was no requirement for Mach 2 and considerable weight and complexity savings had been achieved by using fixed inlets), a peak load factor of 9.4g, a maximum altitude of 50,000ft (15,250m), and a sea level rate of climb exceeding 50,000ft/min (254m/sec). Handling was excellent: the YF-17 could achieve AOA of up to 34deg in level flight, and 63deg AOA was reached in a 60deg zoom climb, while the aircraft remained controllable at indicated speeds right down to 20kt (37km/h). Northrop were consequently able to claim that their contender had no AOA limitations, no control limitations, and no departure tendencies. It was certainly an impressive performance.

A decision was taken in April 1974 that the LWF was no longer to be just a technology demonstrator, but that the successful contender would be developed into a USAF Air Combat Fighter (ACF). The general reasoning was that basic commitments demanded more fighters than the number of F-15s or F-14s that could be purchased with the funds available, so a nucleus of expensive high-technology fighters was to be supported by austere and much cheaper ones. This became known as the hi/lo mix, in which the fighter force was to have adequate numerical strength containing a significant level of high technology.

The flight test programme for the ACF contenders was rushed through in a few months instead of the normal two years. Formal evaluation took place towards the end of 1974, and the result was announced on January 13, 1975: the new air combat fighter for the USAF would be developed from the General Dynamics YF-16. The contest had been far from a walkover and the YF-17 had proved superior in some regimes, but the award had gone to its single-engined rival.

Navy fighter requirement

Meanwhile another potential market had emerged. Back in 1971 the US Navy had become concerned at the cost of the F-14 Tomcat, which had caused both rate of procurement and total number to be restricted to the extent that the Navy could not afford the number of Tomcats that it deemed necessary. Furthermore, the ageing Phantoms and Corsairs would need to be replaced in the not too distant future, and various alternative solutions were examined, including a cheaper F-14, a navalized F-15 and improved F-4s. A group called Fighter Study IV discussed and rejected these alternatives, formulating instead the requirements of a new Naval Air Combat Fighter with a secondary attack capability, known as VFAX (fighter/attack experimental aeroplane) and to be armed with both the short range Sidewinder and the medium range Sparrow. It was anticipated that this would be a totally new design, but Congress decreed that the USN should study derivatives of the ACF contenders.

Below: Maiden flight. Carrying dummy Sparrows and Sidewinders, Hornet 1 lifts off the runway at Saint Louis on November 18, 1978, with McDonnell Douglas Chief Test Pilot Jack Krings at the controls.

Northrop, inexperienced in the particularly demanding requirements of carrier-based fighter design, teamed up with McDonnell Douglas, makers of the very successful Phantom, and the result of this collaboration was a navalized version of the YF-17, known initially as the Northrop P-630 and later as the McDonnell Douglas Model 267. In retrospect, it seems probable that Congress had in mind the use of a common type by both Air Force and Navy, with cost savings resulting from a large order. The precedent had been set years earlier by the F-4 Phantom, which was designed for carrier operations and went on to form a major part of the USAF inventory.

Navy assessment

The US Navy took a long, hard look at both the ACF contenders. Quite apart from the constraints imposed by carrier operations, their requirements differed considerably from those of the Air Force. The F-16 was a close combat dog-fighter *par excellence*, whereas the Navy needed a machine that could be used to modernize both fighter and attack squadrons. In particular, fitting out a fighter to carry the medium-range Sparrow was a major task. The procurement limit set for the Tomcat was sufficient to equip only 18 of the 24 squadrons in the Carrier Air Wings, leaving a further six to be modernized, plus 12 US Marine Corps fighter squadrons, as well as six Navy and Marine reserve squadrons to be re-equipped. In addition, there were 24 front-line and six reserve attack squadrons then flying the A-7 Corsair, which would need new aircraft from the early 1980s. Allowing an annual attrition rate of 4.5 per cent, the result was a total requirement of 800 aircraft.

To fulfil the dual roles, the Navy needed a fighter which could easily be adapted to carry the Sparrow, and which could equally easily be converted for the attack role. The original P-530 had been designed as a strike fighter, so there were few problems in that direction. But the Navy, unlike the Air Force, carried out most of their missions over the sea. Engine malfunction leading to the loss of the aeroplane was bad enough, but over the sea it was also likely to cause the loss of a hard-to-replace piece of software – the pilot. General Dynamics had teamed with LTV (Vought) to produce a navalized variant of the YF-16, but the two engines of the Northrop/McDonnell Douglas fighter offered better safety, and this was a major factor in influencing the Navy's decision, although the YF-17 was also able to demonstrate better carrier recovery performance than its rival. A further consideration was that the design had more multi-mission potential.

The choice of the future F/A-18 as the Navy's new fighter/attack aeroplane was announced on May 2, 1975. A frequent accusation against the Navy during the following years was to be that they had bought the loser in the ACF competition. Of course, they had, but they had also bought the aeroplane that they considered was better suited to their needs. A comparison of USN requirements with the projected figures for the new fighter, now redesignated F-18, shows how closely they matched (see table). The only serious shortfall in the figures was on minimum approach speed, but it was felt that this could be improved.

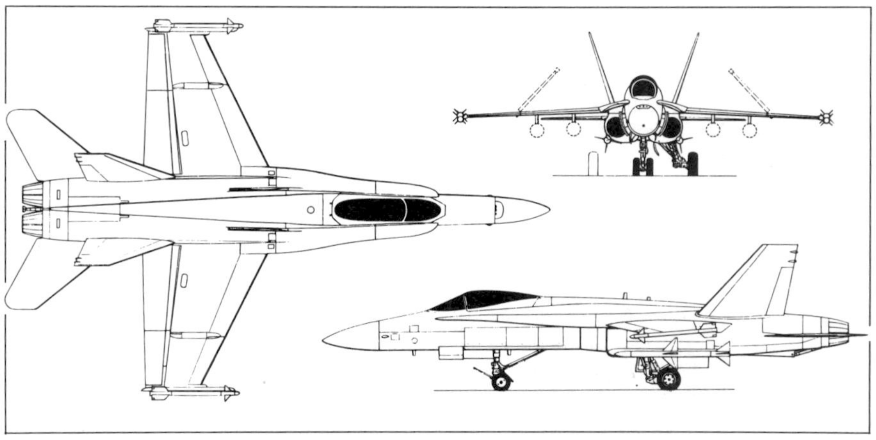

US Navy VFAX requirement/projected F-18 comparative data

	VFAX	**F-18**
Vmax dry power	Mach 0.98-1.0	Mach 0.99
Acceleration Mach 0.8-1.6	80-110 seconds	88.3 seconds
Combat ceiling (000ft/000m)	45-50/13.72-15.25	49.3/15.03
P_s, Mach 0.9/10,000ft (3,050m)	750-850ft/sec 229-259m/sec	756ft/sec 230.5m/sec
Buffet-free sustained load factor	5.0-5.5g	6.6g
tructural load factor	7.5g	7.5g
Single-engine climb rate	500ft (152m)/min	565ft (172m)/min
Minimum approach speed (kt/km/h)	115-125/212-230	131/241
Escort fighter radius (nm/km)	400-450/737-829	415/765
Strike radius (nm/km)	550/1,013	655/1,027

McDonnell Douglas, with the McDonnell Aircraft Corporation's extensive background of designing carrier fighters, became the main contractor for the F-18, with Northrop as a major subcontractor, the construction work being split approximately 60/40. At the same time, Northrop were to develop a land-based version of the fighter for the export market under the designation F-18L and, in the event of orders being placed, the work share was to be reversed. One thing was certain: the naval F-18 would be a much heavier beast than the YF-17, and more powerful engines would be required. This was resolved on November 21, 1975, when General Electric received a letter contract to proceed with the new F404, a developed and uprated version of the YJ-101. McDonnell Douglas received their letter contract on January 22, 1976, for the Full Scale Development (FSD) batch of 11 aircraft, nine single- and two twin-seaters: the first flight was scheduled for July 1978.

Adapting a land-based fighter to become carrier-capable is a very complicated process, and the aircraft also had to be fitted out to meet the Navy's dual-role mission requirements. Provision had to be made for the carriage of Sparrow missiles together with a compatible fire-control system, and all-weather avionics. A Hughes multi-mode radar was selected, and the nose had to be fattened by 4in (10cm) to accommodate the antenna, but no lengthening was needed.

Above: Dust billows up behind Hornet 3 as it carries out one of a series of cross-wind landing trials at Edwards AFB, California, during the summer of 1980. The flaps and ailerons are right down, and the stabilators are deflected to their maximum extent. A total of 119 landings were made in crosswinds of up to 30mph (48km/h).

Left: The Hornet after several fixes. The notches in the wing and tailplane leading edges have disappeared, as has almost all the slotted area in the wing root leading edge extensions.

Above: Hornet 3 aboard the aircraft carrier USS *Dwight D. Eisenhower* in February 1982. The complexity of the main landing gear, which retracts rearward while rotating through 90deg in order to avoid the Sparrow positions, is clearly apparent.

To meet the long-range patrol requirements, provision for an extra 4,460lb (2,023kg) of fuel had to be made, bringing the total internal fuel capacity to 10,680lb (4,844kg) – compared with the 6,400lb (2,903kg) of the YF-17 – in four fuselage tanks plus an extra tank in the inboard section of each wing. A further 2,000lb (907kg) of fuel could be carried in drop tanks, and provision was made for in-flight refuelling.

For carrier operations a nosegear towbar and an arrester hook were added, and the undercarriage was redesigned to cope with the extra weight and the high stresses of catapult takeoffs and arrested landings, while to save space below or on deck, the outboard wing panels were made to fold. Alll these changes involved additional weight, bringing the projected gross weight of the F-18 to 33,580lb (15,232kg) at this stage, compared with the 23,000lb (10,433kg) of the YF-17. Considerable structural strengthening was required to cope with both the stress of catapult launching and arrested deck landings, or 'traps', and the weight increases. These modifications took the wing loading past acceptable limits. In consequence the wing area was increased from the 350sq ft (32.52m^2) of the YF-17 to 400sq ft (37.16m^2). This was done by increasing the span by 2.5ft (0.76m), and extending the chord by adding to the leading and trailing edges.

Much attention was paid to improving the carrier approach characteristics. The aerodynamic shape of the LEX was refined, and they were extended further forward on the fuselage, with a consequent increase in area. The deployment angles of the leading and trailing edge flaps were increased from 30deg to 45deg, and the ailerons were programmed to droop at a maximum angle of 45deg in low-speed flight. The horizontal tail surfaces, or stabilators, changed shape yet again, to give a lower aspect ratio than before, and a snag was added to the leading edges of both the wing and the stabilator to generate high energy air and reduce spanwise drift during carrier approaches.

Left: Stropped up on the catapult ready for launch. The rudders are toed in at a 25deg angle to provide a nose-up moment at takeoff.

It was predicted that these improvements would reduce the approach speed to 125kt (230km/h), at an AOA of 6-7deg, giving the pilot an excellent view over the nose. This compared very favourably with the Phantom, which approached nose-high at an AOA of 13-14deg. It was also anticipated that operation with very heavy payloads in zero wind over deck (WOD) conditions would be possible, and that the WOD requirements at maximum loads would be very low.

Cost and complexity

Another important factor that influenced final design, and one by no means unique to the Hornet, was the sheer complexity of modern fighters. This had a knock-on effect, as complexity caused costs to soar and greatly increased the lead time from design inception to service entry. Soaring costs also reduced procurement levels, increasing the temptation to soldier on with the existing equipment for a few more years, and this in turn increased the operational life of fighters already in service to unprecedented levels – the life span of the Phantom, for example, looks likely to exceed 30 years. As a result, the production Hornet was designed to have a very long service life of 6,000 flying hours, including 2,000 catapult launches and 2,000 traps. Low procurement levels also meant that fighters had to be designed to fulfil more than one role, which put survivability and maintainability at a premium. In time of war, a prime requirement is a high sortie rate. The Hornet was therefore designed for high survivability and extreme ease of maintenance, while its dual role was stressed by the unofficial but widely used F/A-18 designation.

Below: The third FSD Hornet steps delicately (or so it seems) from the edge of the flight deck. As the weight comes off the wheels, the main gear takes on a totally different appearance (compare this view with the picture above).

At the same time, a single-seat aircraft was being asked to supplement the two-seat Tomcat, and replace both the single-seat Corsair and the two-seat Phantom. This was a hard act to follow, and the question is still frequently posed whether one man can handle the workload. McDonnell Douglas rose to the challenge and, in a *tour de force* of cockpit design, took the experience and technology gained on the F-15 and improved on it by a considerable margin. The hands on throttle and stick (HOTAS) concept was adopted, with all the controls necessary for the combat mission placed on either the throttle or the control column. This appears to have been remarkably successful, although it does seem to demand from the pilot some of the qualities of a concert pianist. Information is presented on three cathode ray tube (CRT) displays, thereby eliminating at a stroke most of the hordes of dials that cover the dash and side consoles of most modern fighters. The desired information is to be called up as needed by a little simple switchology.

First flight

The F-18 made its maiden flight on November 18, 1978, only four months late. Flown by McDonnell Douglas chief test pilot Jack Krings, the first Hornet, Bu. No. 160775, resplendent in a white, blue and gold paint scheme, lifted off the runway at Lambert Saint Louis International Airport at shortly after 1100 hours local time. The flight, during which no problems were encountered, lasted 50 minutes, and a speed of 300kt (550km/h) and an altitude of 24,000ft (7,300m) were recorded.

After the initial flight test phase at Saint Louis the first Hornet moved to the Naval Air Test Center (NATC), NAS Patuxent River, Maryland, for the FSD test programme, which was to last from January 1979 to October 1982. This was not to be without its tribulations but, after all, that is what test programmes are for. The eleven FSD aircraft and their functions are shown in the accompanying table.

Above: Hornet 6 in orange and white high-visibility livery. This aircraft was used for high AOA and spinning trials, for which the gaudy paint job was an asset.

Right: Different-coloured AIM-9s – port red, starboard white – assist aspect identification on film of the high AOA and spin tests.

Below right: Hornet 7 takes on fuel from a KA-3 tanker. The US Navy uses the probe and drogue system for in-flight refuelling rather than the USAF's boom and receptacle.

Full Scale Development roles

Aircraft	Bu. No.	Test function
Hornet 1	160775	Flight test and flutter
Hornet 2	160776	Propulsion and performance
Hornet 3	160777	Carrier suitability and ECS
Hornet 4	160778	Structural flight test
Hornet 5	160779	Avionics and weapon systems
Hornet 6	160780	High AOA and spinning
Hornet T1	160781	Armament and systems
Hornet 7	160782	Armament and systems
Hornet 8	160783	Performance and systems
Hornet T2	160784	Accelerated engine service test
Hornet 9	160785	Maintenance engineering

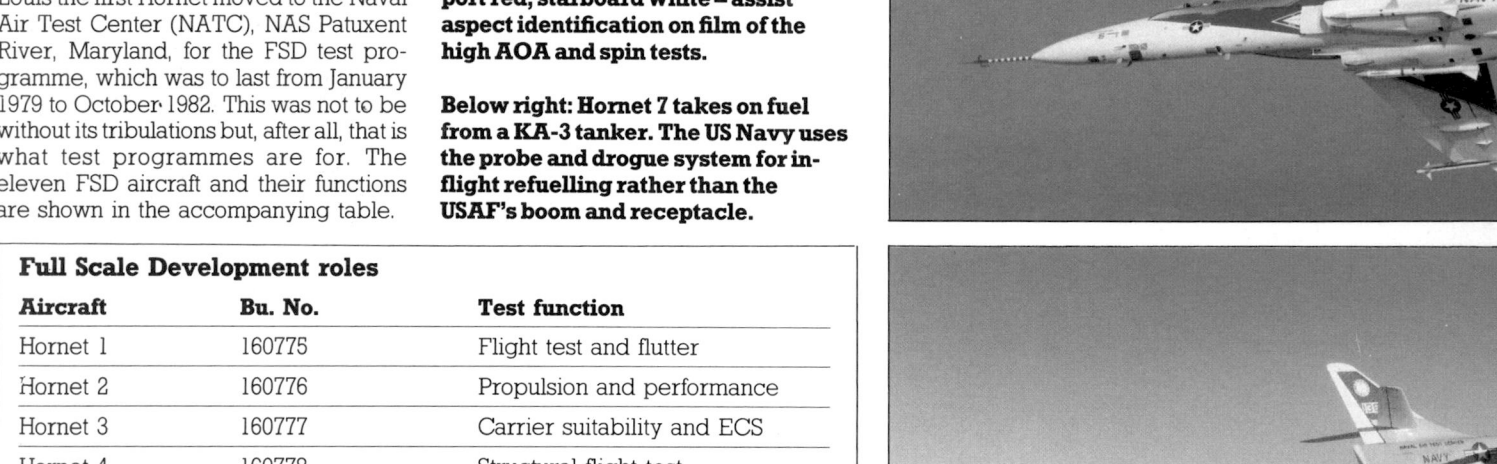

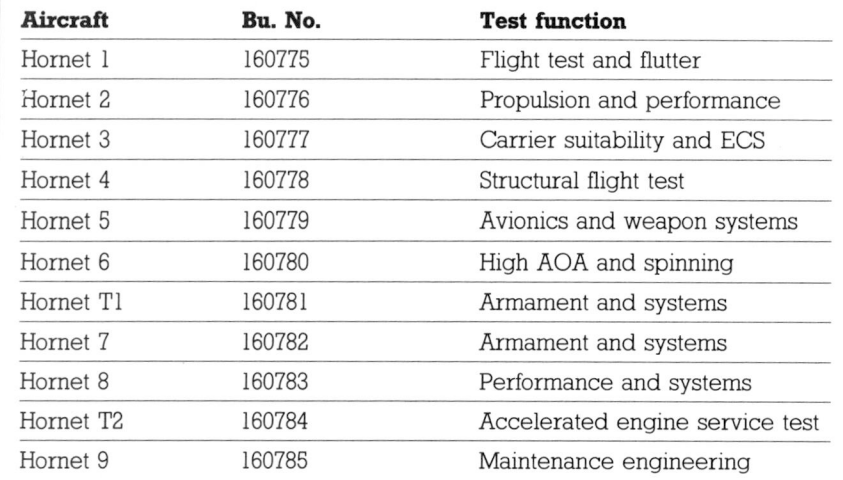

Previous test programmes had been carried out at a variety of locations, depending on which function was under test, but in the case of the F-18 the new Principal Site Concept was applied, with almost all flight testing taking place at Patuxent River. Apart from logistical advantages, this provided the opportunity for Navy and McDonnell Douglas personnel to work closely together, both in the air and on the ground, thus ensuring full naval participation in design improvements. The test programme called for no fewer than 3,257 test flights and involved two shifts, six days a week for both the Navy and the main contractor and the principal subcontractors. By mid-1981 over 3,500 flight hours had been logged in more than 2,600 flights.

The gestation period of the Hornet was surrounded by controversy. Some of this, mainly political in nature, was caused by the cost increases attendant upon the development of a lightweight fighter (a term thought to be synonymous with cheap) into a capable middle-weight. Unfortunately the Hornet's development period coincided with a period of high inflation and this had the effect of making things look much worse than they were. The vast sums being spent had the effect of making the programme highly visible, and a considerable amount of speculation took place as to whether it would be cancelled.

With hindsight it appears unlikely that cancellation was ever a possibility, although alternative programmes were kept constantly under review. Potentially more damaging were the questions raised by the test programme itself. Certain technical problems and performance shortfalls emerged, some of which led to vociferous criticism, not only from the press and the politicians, but also from sections of the military whose personal prejudices ran counter to the F-18 concept.

An underlying cause was the proposed dual role of the new fighter. The F-4 Phantom, originally developed as a fleet defence fighter, had been turned into the greatest multi-role aircraft of its time. It had, however, been found wanting in the close combat arena, and there was a subsequent stress on the air superiority fighter role. Now here was McDonnell Douglas taking the *losing* fighter in the ACF competition and fitting it out to become not only a fighter but an attack aircraft as well. This gave some people the impression of a retrograde step, especially in view of the doubts that had been raised about the ability of one man to cope with the workload. Finally, there were those in the Navy who felt that the aircraft had been foisted on them by the DoD decision that the choice had to be made between the contenders in the Air Force competition, rather than commissioning a purpose built design. With this background, the Hornet had many detractors from the outset.

Early test flights confirmed that the nosewheel lift-off speed was unacceptably high, at 140kt (258km/h), and Hornet 3 (Bu. No. 160777) was modified to overcome this problem. The snag in the leading edges of the stabilators (a modification made by McDonnell Douglas) was

filled in, and a software programme change was made which automatically 'toed-in' the rudders 25deg at takeoff, while the weight was still on the wheels, providing a downward moment aft of the rotation axis. These modifications reduced the nosewheel lift-off speed to an acceptable 115kt (160km/h).

Hornet 2 (Bu. No. 160776) showed performance deficiencies which caused considerable acrimony. Navy Preliminary Evaluation (NPE) 1 revealed a shortfall of 12 per cent in specific range in cruise conditions, and a lesser but still significant shortfall in combat conditions, while acceleration from Mach 0.8 to Mach 1.6 at 35,000ft (10,670m) took longer than the 110 seconds predicted. A number of contributory causes were found. The engines were early standard, with performance levels below those subsequently achieved. The leading and trailing edge flaps were automatically actuated, and a programming fault had set the angle between two and three degrees too low to achieve optimum cruise performance. A software change cured this particular problem. There were also a number of faults in the environmental control system.

When all the changes had been made the shortfall on range reduced to 8 per cent, this being due to unanticipated drag. As a result, a Hornet was tufted to assess the airflow patterns on its surface. The slots in the LEX were found to cause a considerable proportion of the excess drag, and on Hornet 8 they were filled in for further tests. This did not cause the anticipated adverse effect on the airflow into the intakes and became a standard fix, along with two further drag reducing modifications: the wing leading edge radius was increased, and a fairing was installed over the environmental control system efflux under the fuselage to direct exhaust air rearward instead of straight out across the airstream. These fixes increased the range, but had little effect on the acceleration problem.

On the credit side, the engine response was excellent, the transition from flight idle to full afterburner taking less than four seconds, and afterburner lightup was satisfactory, being demonstrated at 45,000ft (13,700m), and 150kt (276km/h). Slight deficiencies in specific fuel consumption (sfc) were shown, but these were partially corrected by a change to the main fuel control.

Above: The dropping of objects from an aircraft in flight is a process fraught with peril: here an empty fuel tank is successfully discarded. For this series of trials in December 1980, Hornet 7 is equipped with a camera on the tailhook assembly and three more on each wingtip. In the event, the elliptical-section drop tank was replaced by a conventional tank.

Top: The seventh FSD Hornet built was the first two-seater, T1. Initially wearing white, blue and gold livery, it is seen here on October 26, 1982, in orange and white at NATC Patuxent River. Behind it are Hornet 6, also in high-visibility finish, and Hornet 3 with wings folded and Sidewinders still in position on the wingtips.

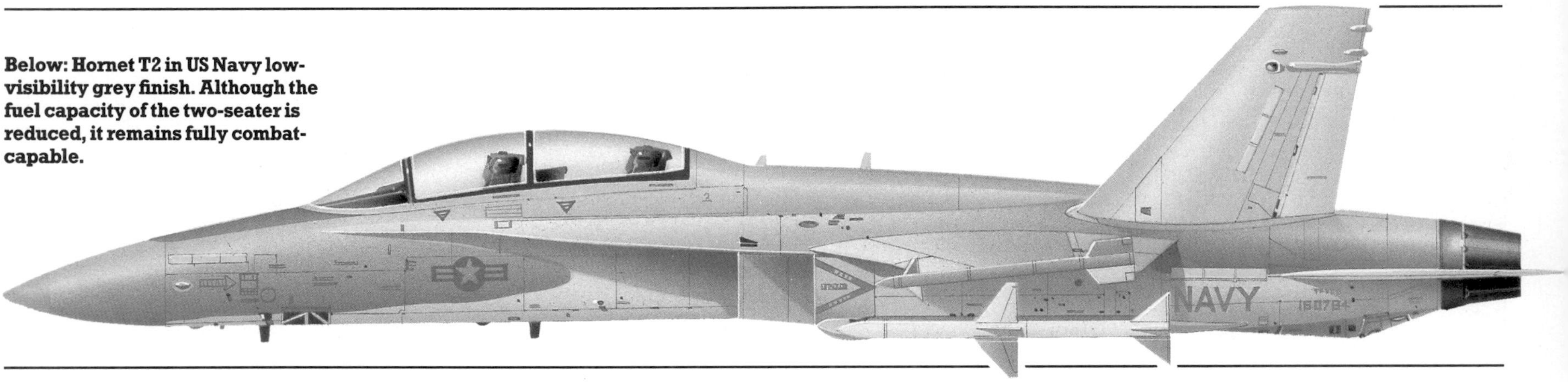

Below: Hornet T2 in US Navy low-visibility grey finish. Although the fuel capacity of the two-seater is reduced, it remains fully combat-capable.

The range shortfall was to have serious repercussions. The Navy specification called for a range of 444nm (818km) in the fighter role and 635nm (1,170km) for attack missions. As at November 1979, the range limits had been set at 404nm (745km) in the fighter and 580nm (1,068km) in the attack configurations. Additional fuel tanks were not an acceptable solution, since the initial specified weight of 20,146lb (9,138kg) had already been exceeded by 1,962lb (890kg). An excess of 1,600lb (762kg) was considered acceptable, and a weight reduction programme was instituted to save 341lb (155kg), although this was not to take effect until the 123rd aircraft.

The most serious problem of all concerned rate of roll, which was well below the specified rate of 180deg/sec. Figures released early in 1980 gave the achieved roll rates as 185deg/sec at Mach 0.7, 160deg/sec at Mach 0.8, and 100deg/sec at Mach 0.9, all at 10,000ft (3,050m). At 20,000ft (6,100m) the roll rate was on specification at Mach 0.9, but as velocity increased so roll rate diminished. Analysis and observation showed the problem to have two main causes, namely flexing of the outer wing panels, and roll damping with the wingtip Sidewinders in place: when the outboard aileron was deflected in the transonic speed range, the wing bent in the opposite direction to counter the aileron action. The leading edge could actually be seen curling up from the cockpit!

The solution was a compound one. The snag in the leading edge, which incidentally did not feature in the YF-17, was eliminated, and the trailing edge box was strengthened to increase torsional stiffness, at the same time strengthening the trailing edge box into the wing root. This involved using monolithic graphite material instead of the sandwich in the inner wing and aluminium in the outer section. The trailing edge spar was also thickened, together with its webs and caps, while the ailerons were extended outboard to the wingtips, increasing their area by 36 per cent, and differential movement of the leading and trailing edge flaps was introduced. The differential horizontal authority of the stabilator was also increased. A spin-off effect of the increased aileron size was a 7kt (13km/h) reduction in the undesirably high carrier approach speed.

The Hornet encountered certain other problems during the test programme. The No. 4 fuel cell in the fuselage was very prone to leakage, and only a redesigned and strengthened cell cured the problem. Structural testing also revealed some flaws, details of which are given in the following chapter.

Carrier suitability trials

Hornet 3 (Bu. No. 160777) was slated for carrier suitability trials. After extensive testing at Patuxent River, during which over 70 catapult launches and 120 arrested landings were made, Navy test pilots Lt. Cdr. Richards and Lt. Grubb flew out to the USS *America* for initial sea trials during the late afternoon of October 30, 1979. During the next four days the Hornet carried out what were later described as "the most successful sea trials in Naval Aviation history". Between them, the two pilots carried out 32 catapult launches and traps, plus 17 touch-and-go landings, or 'bolters', and demonstrated vertical descent rates of 19.5ft/sec (5.9m/sec). Serviceability was 100 per cent throughout the trials, with no hold-ups recorded, and general characteristics, including deck handling, were recorded as excellent. Most catapult launches were made using intermediate power although full afterburner was used during two. The on-board auxiliary power unit (APU) was used for starting the engines, thereby keeping the 'yellow stuff' on deck to a minimum.

However, on its return from the trials Hornet 3 blotted its copybook when, arriving at NAS Oceana, it suffered, of all things, a landing gear failure. The fault lay in the centering mechanism to the main gear axle, which was experiencing a higher than predicted stress level. A new dual-chamber shock strut had to be developed, and this cured the fault.

This same aircraft was detached to Edwards AFB in California during the summer of 1980 for crosswind landing tests, and a total of 119 landings were made in crosswinds up to 30mph (48km/h). On March 17, 1981, Hornet 3 was again in trouble when, after a high sink rate approach at Patuxent River, the end of the fuselage-mounted rod on one of the main gears pulled out of the side

Below: In the attack role, FLIR and LST/SCAM pods replace the Sparrows on the fuselage mountings.

Above: Hornet 8, assigned to performance and systems tests, poses for the camera during IFR trials in May 1981. The refuelling probe can be seen extended, and the tanker is, slightly unusually, a USAF KC-10 with drogue gear.

Left: The ninth single-seat Hornet to be built was the first to receive the low-visibility grey finish. Seen here in fighter configuration, it is unusual in having no FSD number on the tailfin.

Below: With a payload of four Mk 84 1,000lb (454kg) slicks, this aircraft – also shown opposite – demonstrated the Hornet's attack range with the simulated attack on the Pinecastle range, 620nm (1,150km) from NATC Patuxent River, in September 1981.

brace actuator. After touchdown, the gear moved outboard and collapsed, causing damage to the flaps, wingtip, and engine intake.

The first fully automatic hands-off landing was made at Patuxent River on January 22, 1982, with McDonnell Douglas test pilot Peter Pilcher at the controls. This was the Hornet's first flight carrying the automatic landing system, and it is believed that this was the first time a fully automatic landing had been made on an initial flight. On January 26 Navy pilots started using the system, and by August of that year sufficient experience had been gained for the second batch of sea trials to be made, this time aboard the USS *Carl Vinson*. Two Navy pilots shared 63 catapult launches and traps, and numerous bolters, with various load combinations both by day and by night

Weapons trials

Other tests were going well, and the air-to-air and air-to-ground weapons trials were particularly successful. The first live missile firing was carried out by Hornet 5 (Bu. No. 160779) during December 1979, with McDonnell Douglas test pilot Bill Lowe at the controls, and the Sidewinder passed within 2.5ft (0.76m) of the BMQ-34 radio controlled target, well within lethal range. By October 1980 eight missile firings with both Sidewinder and Sparrow had been carried out against radio-controlled drone targets, with a 100 per cent success rate. No fewer than five of the eight missiles scored direct hits.

The ground and air firing tests of the M61 cannon also proved satisfactory. The ground tests involved firing the complete 570-round magazine in one long burst, while in the air tests six short bursts were used to empty the magazine. Both the 4,000 and 6,000 rds/min modes were used, and firing the gun was found to have no detrimental effect on either radar tracking or engine operation. The gun position above the nose was suspect, since it was thought that it might interfere with air to ground visual tracking at night, and that the accumulation of gas particles on the windscreen might degrade night visibility, so another test involved firing at a flare on a one-man liferaft on a cloudy night. No tracking difficulty was encountered, and no problems were caused by the gas particles.

Nor was the attack capability of the Hornet neglected. After early release trials of various stores, following which it was found necessary to move the store racks 5in (12.5cm) forward due to a flutter problem, one of the batch of nine pilot production Hornets (Bu. No. 161248) took off from Patuxent River bound for the Pinecastle Range Complex near Orlando, Florida, some 620nm (1,150km) away. It carried four Mk 83 1,000lb (450kg) bombs, two AIM-9 Sidewinders and three 315US gall (1,192lit) external tanks, with a Martin-Marietta laser spot tracker and Perkin-Elmer strike camera (LST/SCAM) pod on the right inlet position, a Ford Aerospace forward looking infra-red (FLIR) pod on the left inlet and a full load of 570 20mm cannon shells in its magazine. The Hornet's gross takeoff weight was 48,253lb (21,900kg), and after depositing its ordnance on target it returned in just over three hours with 1,600lb (726kg) of fuel remaining.

One change that was found necessary involved the drop tank designed specifically for the Hornet. Manufactured from spun fibre impregnated with aluminium, it was elliptical in cross-section to give better ground clearance, but the stresses imposed by catapult launches and traps proved too much and it was replaced by a cylindrical tank holding an extra 15US gall (57lit) of fuel.

The General Electric F404 engine, despite being a relatively new design, was one of the success stories of the programme. As a previously untried engine it was subjected to an accelerated test programme – referred to as the 'Hornet Hustle' – involving Hornets T2 (Bu. No. 160784) and 9 (Bu. No. 160785). In just 55 flight days the two Hornets flew 116 missions, totalling just short of 150 flying hours, and on three occasions Hornet T2 achieved six flights a day, a remarkable performance. The F404 was found to have excellent throttle response, to be virtually stall-free, and to have little trouble relighting in flight.

Serious incidents

Only three serious incidents occurred. Trouble with a No. 4 bearing caused an engine shut-down in flight, but an improved bearing in production engines overcame the problem. An engine fire shortly after takeoff caused a mission to be aborted, and on examination three non-adjacent turbine blades were found to be fractured, although none had pierced the engine casing.

The most serious incident occurred on September 8, 1980, the day after the Farnborough Air Show, when Hornet T2 took off en route for Spain; the pilot was Jack Krings, by now the Director of Flight Operations for McDonnell Douglas, with Lt. Col. Gary Post of the USMC in the rear seat. At about 18,000ft (5,500m) on the climb-out there was a loud explosion, followed by a rapid temperature rise in the right turbine. The engine was immediately shut down and an attempt was made to reach the A&AEE airfield at Boscombe Down, but the throttle for the left engine appeared to be jammed, and control problems were experienced. Finally Krings and Post were forced to eject, at a speed of about 400kt (740km/h) and an altitude of 4,000ft (1,200m). The stricken Hornet crashed at Middle Wallop, Hampshire.

The affected engine was a pre-production model which contained a different type of material in the low-pressure turbine from that used in production standard engines. It had done about 300 flight hours at the time of the failure, which was due to the low-pressure turbine fracturing in flight. After extensive testing it was recommended that some redesign work be undertaken on certain rotor parts, although the fact that flight testing was resumed shortly afterward indicates that the failure was of a type unlikely to recur frequently.

The final FSD Hornet successfully completed its portion of the trials in October 1981. As well as the maintenance engineering inspection, it had participated in the Hornet Hustle and undergone electro-magnetic compatibility tests. The design case for the Hornet, based on the calculated radiation levels for the deck of an aircraft carrier, was 200V/m, compared with the 20V/m specified for the land-based F-16, and an average of 2V/m for the previous generation of aircraft. A couple of channels were found to have insufficient protection and new filter connectors were provided in the flight control system.

Climatic testing was carried out at the McKinley Climatic Laboratory, operated by the USAF's 3246th Test Wing at Eglin AFB, Florida. The Hornet was exposed to rigorous weather tests in a gigantic hangar, with temperatures fluctuating between −65deg F and +125deg F (−54/+52deg C). Winds of up to 100mph (160km/h) were simulated, and the Hornet was subjected to precipitation ranging from monsoon rains falling at 20in (50cm) per hour to blizzards.

Pilot reports on the Hornet had been unanimous in their praise of its handling qualities – it had reached higher AOA without control loss than even its F-16 rival, and it appeared virtually spin-proof. It was therefore extremely puzzling when a pilot production aircraft (Bu. No. 161215) crashed in Chesapeake Bay on November 14, 1980. Lt. C. T. Brannon, a naval test pilot attached to test and evaluation squadron VX-4, was on a routine handling flight when he lost control at about 20,000ft (6,100m). Failing to recover the aircraft, he ejected, and was fished out of the sea unharmed.

Accident investigation

Hornet 6 (Bu. No. 160780), painted orange and white for high visibility and with an anti-spin chute carried in a small box mounted above and between the engine nozzles, had carried out the high AOA and spin tests successfully. The Hornet had been found to be reluctant to spin at all, and when the control settings for inducing the spin were released it tended to fly out of it with no further ado. Points well outside the USN specifications had been reached without difficulty, including 78deg AOA coupled with 12deg of yaw; 74deg AOA coupled with 25deg of yaw; and, amazingly, 65deg AOA with a sideslip of −15deg to +30deg.

Tests were immediately instituted to duplicate the flight conditions leading to the accident, at first with no success. No fewer than 110 spin trial flights were

Above: A swarm of Hornets over the Mojave desert, as Naval Air Test and Evaluation Squadrons VX-4 from Point Mugu and VX-5 from China Lake join forces. All are single-seaters and all carry centreline tanks, while the rearmost aircraft also has wing tanks. Some carry Sidewinders while others have bombs on the wing pylons.

Left: Bu. No. 161248, first of the pilot production batch, and the Hornet that flew the Pinecastle strike demonstration, turns low over the water as if to line up for a deck landing, though as the hook is not down this is hardly likely.

Above: An atmospheric scene aboard USS *Constellation* as an aircraft launches at night, while three others of VX-5 stand by.

Right: A crowded deck on 'Connie' by day, with two Hornets on the catapults and a further four from VX-5 spotted, with wing tanks but no weapons.

made by both McDonnell Douglas and Navy pilots, and it took four weeks to duplicate Brannon's flight departure, which appears to indicate that it was an extremely unusual occurrence. On the first occasion, the pilot was able to regain control by cutting the engine on the outside of the spin to flight idle, while using full 'burner on the inside engine.

Once the problem had been identified, a solution was found. A spin recovery switch was added to the flight computer control which defeated the computer's logic and gave full control-surface authority to the pilot. In the test aircraft the cockpit displays were programmed to go blank when a yaw rate exceeding 15deg/sec was sensed, and the words 'spin recovery' appeared on the displays with an arrow indicating the direction the control column should be moved for recovery: once yaw reduced to less than 15deg/sec the pilot centred the controls and the aircraft flew out of the spin. With the switch added, Brannon's flight was duplicated for the second time, and the switch performed as advertised. The switch was incorporated on production Hornets, while improvements to the computer logic were put in hand to render it unnecessary on later models.

The training squadron VFA-125 was commissioned at NAS Lemoore, California, on November 18, 1980, and on February 19, 1981, it took delivery of its first Hornet. The way had been long, beset with difficulties, frustrations, and talk of cancellation. The Hornet had been roundly condemned as a can of worms, not as good as the types it was to replace, far too expensive and inferior to the contemporary F-14, F-15, and F-16. It is, however, worth noting that the criticisms came from those who had not flown it. It is a compromise aeroplane certainly, but a first class compromise.

Right: The sign outside MCAS El Toro, California, where the first operational Hornet unit, VMFA-314 Black Knights, converted from F-4Ns in January 1983. The loads shown – LGBs and targeting pods, Sparrows and Sidewinders – symbolize the dual role.

Structure

A modern fighter is a series of compromises, and trade-offs have to be made between many conflicting requirements. The transition from lightweight air combat fighter to middleweight multi-role carrier fighter and attack aircraft was not an easy one, with additional weight and the demands of carrier operations having to be accommodated without degrading performance. Nevertheless, with reliability, maintainability and survivability as fundamental design criteria, the F/A-18 has demonstrated an impressively high rate of availability, and the Hornet should be airborne to meet any threat as it arises.

Above: An unusual close-up belly view of FSD Hornet 7 taken during armament and systems trials in February 1980. The ECM fairings under the intakes and the chaff and flare dispensers show up well.

The Hornet is unusual in that there are two aircraft designs which externally appear almost identical, one known as the McDonnell Douglas F-18A Hornet, and the other as the Northrop F-18L Hornet. This unprecedented situation arose through the navalization of the Northrop YF-17 by the Saint Louis-based McDonnell Aircraft Company. MCAIR, as the company is known, is a division of the McDonnell Douglas Corporation, and was nominated as the main contractor for the F-18 due to its wide experience in the design and development of carrier fighters, with the Northrop Corporation as the major subcontractor, the work being split approximately 60/40.

Joint manufacture

McDonnell Douglas builds the forward fuselage and cockpit, wings, stabilators and landing and arresting gear, while Northrop manufactures the centre and aft fuselage sections, the splice between them, and the vertical fins. The joined fuselage sections, complete with all their associated plumbing and systems, are then shipped to Saint Louis for final assembly by McDonnell Douglas, who, with their carrier fighter background, retain overall responsibility for stress analysis. Major systems such as hydraulics, fuel, engines, environmental control, and secondary power are the responsibility of Northrop, while the crew station, avionics and flight control systems are down to McDonnell Douglas.

Both companies used full scale and very accurate engineering development jigs to work out the precise routings and positions of the plumbing and subsystems within the airframe. In the event of orders being placed for the F-18L, a lighter and simpler (and, some think, more potent) version of the F/A-18, the main contractor/subcontractor relationship would be reversed and Northrop would take the project leadership with a 60 per cent share of production.

The original Hornet contract was for eleven FSD aircraft, comprising nine single-seaters and two twin-seaters, plus one fatigue test and one static test airframes. Based on a purchase of 800 aircraft, the cost was predicted at $5.9 million each in Fiscal Year 1975 terms, including the cost of engines and avionics which were to be supplied through separate government contracts. Unfortunately, the cost was to escalate out of all proportion during the next few years, a period of very high inflation, and both politicians and the popular press were heard calling for cancellation.

In all fairness, the same vociferous protests had greeted just about every new American fighter project during the previous ten years, the F-111 being the outstanding example. A type of perverse logic seemed to prevail: if it was cheap it must automatically lack capability, whereas if it was capable it must be either too expensive or too complicated to work properly, and the slightest setback was blown up to assume the proportions of a major disaster. Fortunately, more sober counsels prevailed and a total of 1,377 Hornets, including the 11 FSD aircraft, were ordered for the US Navy and Marine Corps, although the USN stated that their actual requirement was for 1,845 aircraft, despite unit costs having risen to over $20 million in the interim. The rate of production had reached seven Hornets a month in December 1983 and is planned to peak at 18 per month in 1987, and to continue, albeit at a lower rate, until 1994.

Technically, the Hornet structure represents a transitional stage in fighter design. By weight, 49.6 per cent of the airframe is made up of aluminium, while steel accounts for 16.7 per cent, titanium 12.9 per cent and advanced composites 9.9 per cent. These proportions compare interestingly with the Air Force F-15 and F-16, which are at extremes of the scale. The F-15 contains by weight only 37.3 per cent aluminium and 5.5 per cent

Right: The structural flight test Hornet pictured in June 1979. Without paint the various materials are visible: the black areas are graphite/epoxy composites while the dark grey patch on the fin is titanium.

Below: A different view of the same aircraft. The composite areas under the LEX are access panels for the avionics LRUs.

steel, but 25.8 per cent of titanium, whereas the F-16, which deliberately avoided high technology materials, contains about 80 per cent of aluminium, just under 8 per cent steel, and only 1.5 per cent titanium and less than 3 per cent of advanced composites.

The use of advanced composites in the Hornet was, until the advent of the AV-8B Harrier II, more extensive than in any other operational fighter. Although contributing just under 10 per cent of the total weight, graphite epoxy composite material covers approximately 40 per cent of the surface area of the Hornet. Light in weight, of high strength, fatigue resistant and, most important in a carrier environment, corrosion resistant, it is used in the wing skins, trailing edge flaps, ailerons, stabilator, fin and rudder surfaces, most maintenance access doors, and the airbrake.

The fuselage is a semi-monocoque basic structure incorporating differential area ruling, with reduced area above the wings and increased cross-sectional area below them, both of which help to generate positive lift and reduce lift-induced drag. The forward position of the fins was also selected partially for its area-rule effect. The fuselage structure is mainly of light alloy, with machined aluminium fuselage frames. The engines are located in the extreme rear of the fuselage, with titanium firewalls between them. The engine bay face is formed by the production break between the rear and centre fuselage sections. The pressurized cockpit in the forward fuselage section is of fail-safe construction and is mounted above the nosewheel bay, which is probably longer in proportion to fuselage length than in any other aircraft. The 'barn door' type hydraulically actuated airbrake is mounted between the twin fins, and is of graphite epoxy material.

Two-dimensional inlets

Mach 2 was not a specified requirement, so the engine inlets are two-dimensional external compression types, allowing savings in weight and complexity. They also have a small radar cross-sectional area, thus reducing the risk of head-on detection. The inlets are preceded by 5deg fixed ramps, solid at the front and perforated just in front of the inlet proper in order to dispose of the sluggish boundary layer air from the ramp face. The only moving parts on the intakes are the bleed air doors, which exhaust upwards into the LEX flow field.

The wings are of cantilever construction, set in the mid-fuselage position with slight anhedral. Typically Northrop in their trapezoidal shape, they feature variable camber and, at first sight rather outlandish-looking, leading edge extensions (LEX). This combination, known as a hybrid wing, confers excellent manoeuvrability in the subsonic/transonic flight regime, and really outstanding high-AOA capability, rather better even than the vaunted F-16. The main wing construction is a six-spar machined aluminium alloy torsion box, with graphite-epoxy wing panels. The box is attached to the fuselage by six dual-fork attachment lugs.

Control surfaces

The variable camber is achieved with full-span leading edge flaps which have a maximum extension angle of 30deg, and single-slotted trailing edge flaps, actuated by Bertea hydraulic cylinders, with a maximum angle of 45deg. Computerized automatic actuation sets the optimum angle for the prevailing flight conditions, whether manoeuvre or cruise. The ailerons, with Hydraulic Research actuators, can also be drooped to an angle of 45deg, thus acting as full-span flaps to give low landing approach speeds, and the ailerons and flaps also provide differential movement for roll. The wing loading is modest and the variable camber gives the good gust response characteristics necessary for the attack role. The leading edge flaps and the ailerons have aluminium skinning, while the trailing edge flaps are of graphite epoxy. The wing fold essential for carrier stowage comes at the inboard end of each aileron, with a titanium hinge and an AiResearch mechanical drive, and a Sidewinder launch rail is carried on each wingtip.

Above: Small is beautiful in the close combat arena, and this head-on shot demonstrates the Hornet's small presented area.

Below: The work split between McDonnell Aircraft Company, Saint Louis, and the Northrop Corporation in California is approximately 60/40. As shown in the diagram, Northrop's contribution (shown in red) comprises the rear fuselage and fins, which are shipped to Saint Louis for final assembly with the MCAIR-built forward fuselage, wings, stabilators and landing gear.

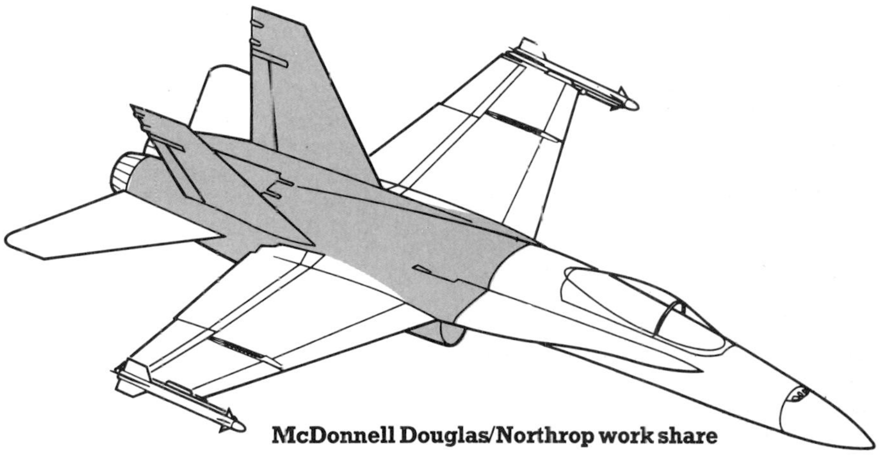

McDonnell Douglas/Northrop work share

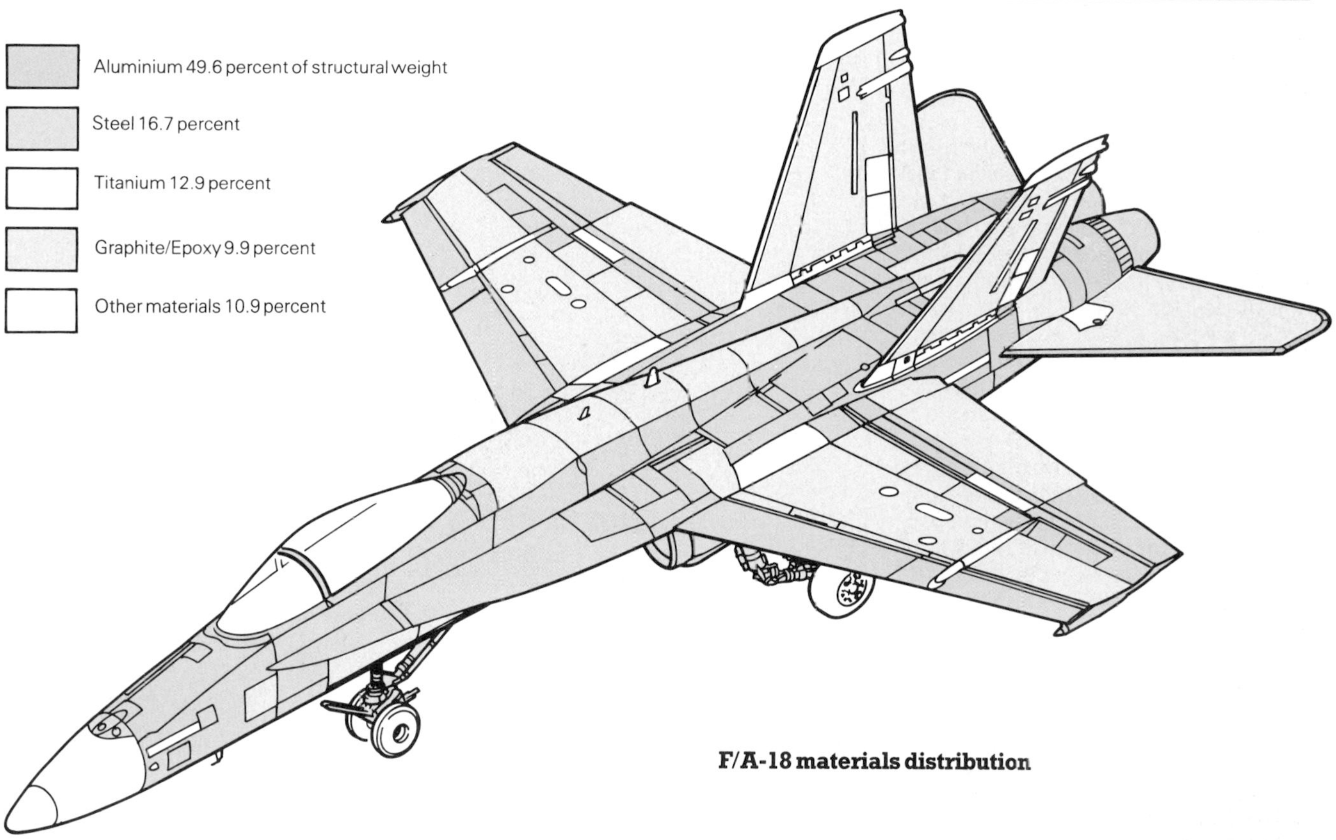

F/A-18 materials distribution

Right: Conventional materials and composites are combined in the Hornet's airframe for optimum strength and lightness. Graphite/epoxy composites cover 40 per cent of the surface area while accounting for under 10 per cent of structural weight. Titanium is used far more widely than in the F-16 but less than in the F-15.

Above: A VFA-125 Rough Raiders Hornet is prepared for a mission. The elliptical section drop tank being fitted gave greater deck clearance, but was unable to take the stresses of ship-based flight.

The most remarkable feature of the wing is the LEX, which extends forward past the cockpit. It acts as a giant vortex generator which scrubs the wing clean of slow-moving boundary layer air and permits controlled flight at AOA exceeding 90deg, although it should be noted that engine thrust is needed to maintain control of the aircraft in these regimes. The LEX also increases maximum lift by up to 50 per cent, and reduces lift-induced drag, supersonic trim drag and buffet intensity. Furthermore, it acts as a compression wedge to reduce the Mach number at the engine inlet face, and reduces the angle of the air entering the inlet by 50 per cent of the AOA.

Each LEX contains empty space that nothing other than fluid would fit into, but if the space were used for fuel it would be too far ahead of the centre of gravity, and damage would cause fuel spillage into the engine intake, which is undesirable to say the least. The LEX cannot house cannon without bulges spoiling the airflow, but one use has been found: the Hornet boarding ladder is integral, and retracts neatly into the underside of the left-hand LEX.

The Hornet's all-moving tailplanes, or stabilators, are unusual in that their span exceeds 50 per cent of the wing span, apparently to give adequate roll control as tailerons, where the effectiveness of the ailerons is insufficient. They are actuated by National Water Lift servo-cylinder hydraulic units, acting collectively for pitch and differentially for roll control. Like many modern fighters with engines mounted at the rear, the Hornet is close-coupled, and the pitch rates achieved have been described by Navy pilots as 'unbelievable'. The stabilators are constructed from aluminium honeycomb clad with graphite epoxy, but with aluminium leading and trailing edges, reinforced with titanium near the pivots.

Tail configuration

The twin fin and rudder arrangement has two outstanding advantages, in that it reduces or eliminates the effect of body vortices at high AOA, and also presents a smaller radar cross-sectional area than a single fin of the same total area seen from side-on.

The fins are of cantilever structure, with a six-spar torsion box connected to six fuselage/fin attachment frames with integral lugs. They are skinned with graphite epoxy, with titanium leading edges and detachable glass fibre tips. The mid-fuselage location and outward cant was selected to avoid blanketing by the fuselage at high AOA and also to avoid the possibility of biplane interference at low forward speeds. Titanium panels cover the rudder hydraulic actuator positions, and the rudders themselves are of one piece aluminium with graphite-epoxy skinning.

The retractable tricycle undercarriage is manufactured by Cleveland Pneumatic, and accounts for a great deal of the steel used in the Hornet, while the wheels and brakes, which are of the multi-disc type, are by Bendix. The nosegear consists of a forward retracting

Wing flap positions

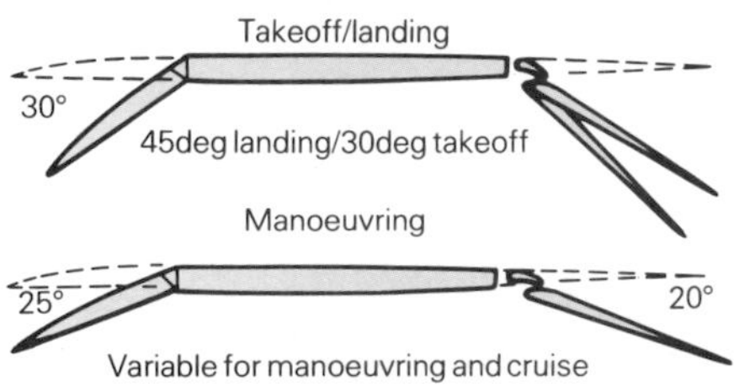

Above: The Hornet's wings feature variable camber, and computerized actuation which alters the section automatically to give optimum performance in all flight conditions. Variable camber also reduces gust response and improves the ride quality at low level and high speed.

Right: January 1982, and VFA-125 deploy to Yuma for ACM. A couple of adversary aircraft can be seen in the background, as can an AV-8A Harrier in hovering flight.

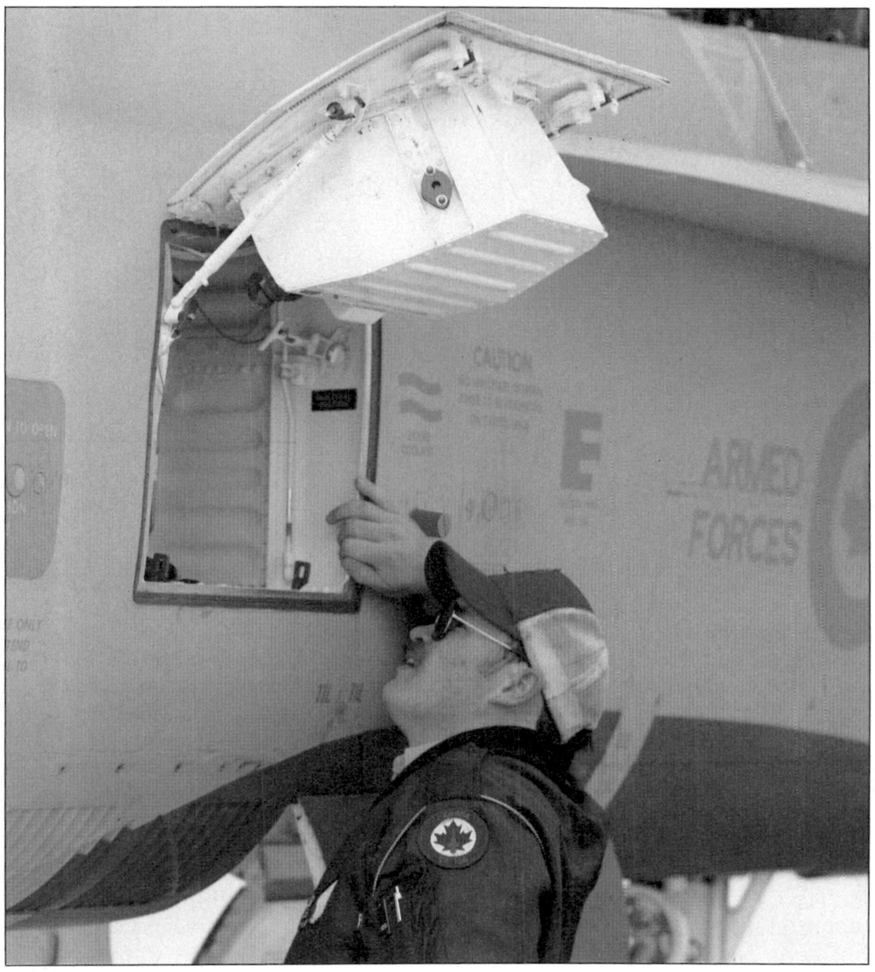

Above: The Canadian Armed Forces were the first foreign purchasers of the Hornet, with an order for 148 aircraft. A Canadian ground crewman peers intently into the gun mechanism access panel.

(approximating to 4,000 hours of aircraft life), a crack was discovered in the bulkhead which holds the main landing gear uplock system. This was caused by an error during the manufacturing process resulting from a tooling problem. A quarter-inch (6mm) diameter hole had been drilled slightly out of position. To correct this a half-inch (13mm) diameter hole had been drilled and plugged, and the new hole had then been drilled in the correct position, through the plug, creating a weakness. Only the first eight Hornets had been affected by this error before the tooling was corrected, and fatigue testing was suspended for nearly two weeks while McDonnell Douglas evaluated the use of bonding material on both sides of the affected part of the bulkhead.

At the same time, further minor cracks were found in the No. 453 bulkhead. These emanated from a group of four

Left: A two-seat Hornet is given a thorough wash, with intakes and AOA vanes protected by covers. Note the boarding ladder extended from its stowage in the LEX.

Below: A Canadian Armed Forces two-seat CF-18 in the hangar with the avionics bay access panels open. The avionics are LRUs and designed for rapid substitution.

$^3/_{16}$in (5mm) diameter holes which had been drilled in the bulkhead to hold a hydraulic line swivel link fitting. In this case, the fix was to discontinue drilling these holes and attach the fitting to the bulkhead by a different method. Other minor defects included fatigue cracks found after 2,702 hours of fatigue testing in the leading edge flap drive lugs, which were redesigned to incorporate shorter pins, while a failure in the leading edge flap transmission was fixed by increasing the thickness of the wing gear, which had the effect of reducing the concentration of stress at that point. It should be pointed out that this is by no means a catalogue of disasters, but the sort of minor events that occur in any test programme.

One of the greatest assets of a military aeroplane is a high sortie rate: it must be able to 'get up and go' as often as possible, and not be grounded by footling defects. Reliability is a key factor in achieving this state of affairs, but equally important is maintainability, which was a fundamental consideration in the design of the Hornet. No fewer than 307 access doors are incorporated in the surface, with the selection of the type of door fasteners being based on the anticipated frequency of access. Quick release latches are used on over 53 per cent of the door areas. The approach was to obtain positive locking with no special tools needed, and no locking wire, thus reducing the ever-present danger of foreign object damage, or FOD. Almost all the access doors are accessible from deck level; only 30 require the use of work stands to reach them.

Avionics black boxes are situated at chest height and only one deep, so that extracting a failed unit will not involve the removal and subsequent replacement of a serviceable unit. The black boxes are Line Replaceable Units (LRUs) and are designed for on-the-spot substitution, so that while the old unit is pulled out and taken back to the workshop for repair a new one is slotted into its place with a minimum of fuss. The radar is track-mounted and can be rolled out for ease of access and maintenance; the windscreen hinges forwards to allow access behind the instrument panel; and the ejection seat can be removed for servicing and replaced without affecting the canopy rigging.

Both avionics and consumables are covered by Built-In Test Equipment (BITE). The engine APU can provide power for check-out of all systems without the engines running and without the need for an external power source, and a fault causes a caution light to come on in the cockpit. The pilot then calls up information on the failure on his cockpit multimode display. In the nosewheel well, a position pioneered on the F-15, where it is easily accessible to the deck crew but sheltered from the elements, is the Maintenance Monitor Panel (MMP), which pinpoints systems failures visually. Equipment is fitted with 'fail' flags which provide confirmation that repair or replacement is needed when the relevant access door is opened.

For speedy pre-flight checking, deck crews have access to a separate consumables panel which indicates critical fluid levels on a 'go/no go' basis. Without this there would have to be a time-consuming series of checks on such things as engine oil, APU oil, drive system oil, hydraulic fluid, radar coolant, liquid oxygen, fire extinguishing fluid, and liquid nitrogen for cooling the seeker heads of the Sidewinders. Servicing points are so distributed as to minimize the risk of deck crew getting in each other's way. Significant maintenance data is recorded in flight by the Maintenance Signal Data Recorder, which measures data on the engines, avionics, and structural strain gauge and makes it available at the end of the mission in the form of a print-out.

Reliability demonstration

A formal reliability demonstration was completed in November 1980, comprising 100 flight hours in 50 flights. Only 12 failures were recorded, three of which were avionics related, and only two of which affected the satisfactory performance of the mission. This compared very favourably with the Navy's requirements, which were a Mean Time Between Failures (MTBF) of 3.7 hours against a demonstrated performance of 8.33 hours, and an ultimate target of 90 per cent probability of mission success against a demonstrated 96 per cent. The mean time for repair was 1.8 hours and the direct Maintenance Man Hours per Flight Hour (MMH/FH) figure was 3.4.

Maintainability checks were held at various points in the development programme. After 1,200 flying hours the planned level of unscheduled MMH/FH was 8; the Hornet demonstrated 7.47, and at 2,500 flying hours the target of 5 MMH/FH was easily bettered, the Hornet recording 3.62. The guarantee for Fleet Supportability evaluation is 3.35 MMH/FH; this was eventually bettered by a wide margin.

The Hornet compares very favourably with other USN aircraft. In the year between July 1982 and June 1983, the MMH/FH figure for production Hornets was 2.62, while comparable figures for other machines were 4.54 for the A-7E Corsair, 5.17 for the A-6E Intruder, 5.6 for the F-4S Phantom, and 5.86 for the F-14 Tomcat. During the same period, the Hornet's Mean Flight Hours Between Failures (MFHBF) was also remarkable, production aircraft turning in a figure of 2.1 against 0.7 for the Corsair, 0.6 for the Intruder, 0.8 for the Phantom and 0.6 for the Tomcat.

A further maintenance bonus results from the fact that the Hornet is to replace both the Phantom and the Corsair. Regardless of whether the Hornet is the F-18 fighter or the A-18 attack variant, it remains essentially the same aircraft, and only 4,000 different support items need to be stocked to maintain it. An all-Hornet air wing will dramatically reduce the spares inventory, not so much in terms of total quantity of items stocked, although the demonstrated reliability and maintainability of the McDonnell Douglas fighter will do much to reduce this, but in the number of types of spares. A current mixed air wing of Phantoms (12,500 support items) and Corsairs (8,000 support items) is something of a logistical nightmare. The all-Hornet air wing will show a reduction in the number of components to be stocked of the order of 80 per cent.

The Hornet is constructed in stages, with individual sections being fabricated separately before being brought together in a predetermined order for final assembly. The rear and centre fuselage sections are constructed in Northrop's Hawthorne plant, then put together before being shipped to the McDonnell Douglas factory in Saint Louis for final assembly. The vertical fins are also manufactured in Hawthorne. The other major sections are the wings, stabilators, forward fuselage and cockpit and the landing gear.

Aluminium sheet structures are automatically drilled and routed, while heavier aluminium structural sections are formed in a gigantic two-storey machine manufactured by the Hydraulic Press Manufacturing Co, which can exert a pressure of up to 7,000 tons (711,000kg). Components which will undergo high stress, fatigue, or high temperatures, such as the stabilator pivots or engine firewall linings, are made of titanium. A process known as super-plastic forming/diffusion bonding shapes titanium sheet, which is made plastic by a combination of temperatures of 1,650deg F (900deg C) and pressures of 250psi (16.8 bars), while the world's largest profile milling shop cuts the finished components from forgings using computer controlled machines.

Pipe bending is also computerized, and coloured plastic caps on the open ends of the tubes prevent contamination prior to assembly. The electrical wiring is installed in pre-made bundles during

Above: A contrast in styles. The enlarged LEX, canted fins and small fixed intakes are the major points of difference displayed by a two-seat F-18 alongside the same manufacturer's fourth pre-production F-15 Eagle.

McDonnell Douglas F/A-18 Hornet cutaway

1 Radome
2 Planar array radar scanner
3 Flight refuelling probe, retractable
4 Gun gas purging air intakes
5 Radar module withdrawal rails
6 M61A1 Vulcan 20mm rotary cannon
7 Ammunition magazine
8 Angle of attack transmitter
9 Hinged windscreen (access to instruments)
10 Instrument panel and cathode ray tube displays
11 Head-up display
12 Engine throttle levers
13 Martin-Baker Mk 10L 'zero-zero' ejection seat
14 Canopy
15 Cockpit pressurization valve
16 Canopy actuator
17 Structural space provision for second seat (TF-18 trainer variant)
18 ASQ-137 Laser Spot Tracker
19 Wing root leading edge extension (LEX)
20 Position light
21 Tacan antenna
22 Intake ramp bleed air spill duct
23 Starboard wing stores pylons
24 Leading edge flap
25 Starboard wing integral fuel tank
26 Wing fold hinge joint
27 AIM-9P Sidewinder air-to-air missile
28 Missile launch rail
29 Starboard navigation light
30 Wing tip folded position
31 Flap vane
32 Leading edge flap drive shaft interconnection
33 Starboard drooping aileron
34 UHF/IFF antenna
35 Boundary layer bleed air spill duct
36 Leading edge flap drive motor and gearbox
37 Engine bleed air ducting
38 Aft fuselage fuel tanks
39 Hydraulic reservoirs
40 Fuel system vent pipe
41 Fuel venting air grilles
42 Strobe light
43 Tail navigation light
44 Aft radar warning antenna
45 Fuel jettison
46 Starboard rudder
47 Radar warning power amplifier
48 Rudder hydraulic actuator
49 Starboard all-moving tailplane
50 Airbrake
51 ECM antenna
52 Radar warning antenna
53 Formation lighting strip
54 Variable area afterburner nozzles
55 Afterburner duct
56 Engine fire suppression bottles
57 Arrester hook jack and damper
58 Port all-moving tailplane
59 Afterburner nozzle actuator
60 Tailplane pivot bearing
61 Arrester hook
62 Tailplane hydraulic actuator
63 General Electric F404 afterburning turbofan engine
64 Engine digital control unit
65 Formation lighting strip
66 Engine fuel system equipment
67 Port drooping aileron
68 Single slotted Fowler-type flap
69 Aileron hydraulic actuator
70 Wing fold rotary actuator and gearbox
71 Port navigation light
72 AIM-9P Sidewinder air-to-air missile
73 Leading edge flap rotary actuator
74 Port leading edge flap
75 Airframe mounted engine accessory gearbox, shaft driven
76 Leading edge slat drive shaft
77 Auxiliary power turbine
78 Flap hydraulic jack
79 Twin stores carrier
80 Outboard stores pylon
81 Aft retracting mainwheel
82 Mk 83 general purpose bombs
83 AIM-7 Sparrow air-to-air missile
84 Mainwheel shock absorber strut
85 Inboard stores pylon
86 Main undercarriage pivot bearing
87 Hydraulic retraction jack
88 Radar equipment cooling air spill valves
89 External fuel tank
90 Air conditioning system heat exchanger
91 Radar equipment liquid cooling units
92 AAS-38 forward looking infra-red (FLIR) pod
93 Boundary layer splitter plate
94 Air conditioning system water separator
95 Centreline fuel tank
96 Forward fuselage fuel tanks
97 Avionics equipment bay
98 Liquid oxygen converter
99 Nose undercarriage hydraulic retraction jack
100 UHF antenna
101 Retractable boarding ladder
102 Forward retracting nosewheels
103 Nosewheel steering unit
104 Landing/taxiing lamp
105 Carrier approach lights
106 Catapult strop link
107 Control column
108 Rudder pedals
109 Gun gas vents
110 Ammunition feed mechanism
111 Pitot head
112 UHF/IFF antenna
113 Radar equipment module
114 Formation lighting strip
115 Forward radar warning antenna
116 Radar scanner tracking mechanism

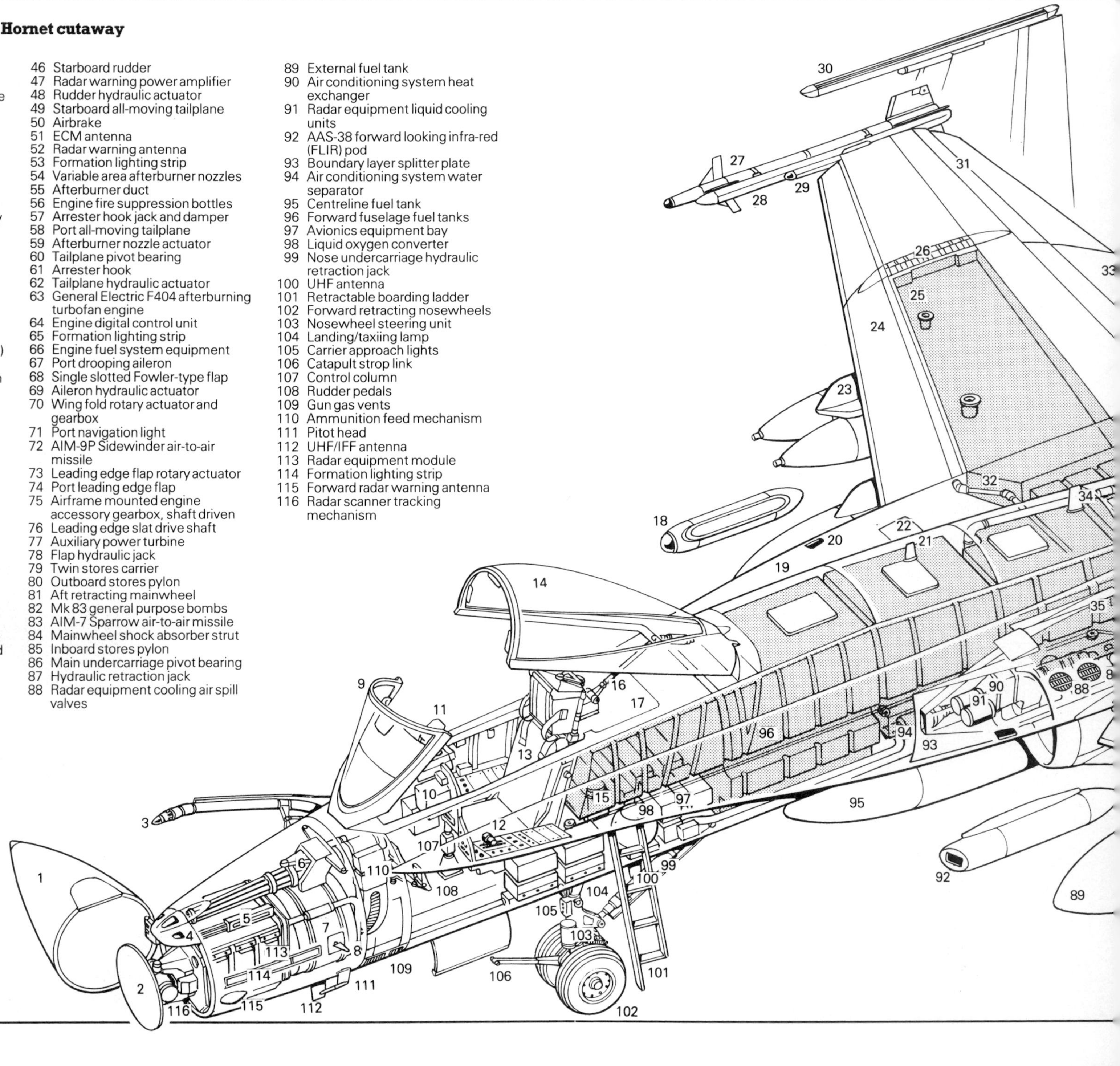

Left: Worker participation is encouraged as the 100th Hornet shipset manufactured by Northrop is officially handed over. The placards remind the workforce of their importance to the project.

Right: A TF-18A is loaded for action with two low-drag bombs on each outboard wing pylon and three cylindrical fuel tanks. AAS-38 FLIR and LST/SCAM pods occupy the Sparrow positions.

the build-up of each section, as are fuel and hydraulic lines. The fuselage, wings and empennage come together at final assembly and the systems are connected and checked. The final stages are the installation of the avionics and engines. After a comprehensive ground check, the aircraft is rolled out ready for its first flight in the hands of a company test pilot.

One production process not touched upon so far, and one which the Hornet utilized more than any other production aircraft before the advent of the Advanced Harrier, is carbon fibre composite material, in this case graphite epoxy. Composites possess high strength to weight and stiffness to weight ratios, have unique flexibility qualities and low thermal conductivity, and are extremely resistant to corrosion and fatigue. In certain applications they can be stronger than steel, stiffer than titanium, and, very significantly, lighter than aluminium. They consist of carbon/graphite or other high-performance fibres bound in epoxy resin or other matrix. In their fibre form they show near-perfect crystalline structure, and it is the parallel alignment of the crystals along the filament axis which provides the great strength and stiffness. The Hornet uses a total of 1,326lb (597kg) of graphite epoxy, giving a weight saving of 25 per cent which, coupled with strength in certain applications plus corrosion resistance, makes the extra cost involved worthwhile.

Although McDonnell Douglas has the world's largest facilities for making aircraft parts from advanced composites – more than 500,000sq ft (46,500m^2) of floor area – only 55 of the Hornet's 220 graphite epoxy panels are made there. This is partly due to the highest concentration of composites occurring on the sections made by Northrop.

Composite fabrication

The process is complex. The wing skins are the most highly stressed panels, and these have titanium inserts, with the metal bonded and tapered into the panel at the root. The sheets of composites are carefully oriented on top of one another to get the plies correct, then bonded in an autoclave with heat and pressure. To cut single ply thicknesses, McDonnell Douglas use a 1,000-watt CO_2 laser manufactured by Photon Sources Inc. which can achieve cutting speeds of between 5 and 7in (12.7 to 17.7cm) per second.

For multiple-ply cuts a reciprocating knife cutter produced by Gerber Garment Technology is used. With a 2in (50mm) carbide blade operating at 4,000 strokes a minutes, cutting rates of 7½in/sec (19cm/sec) can be achieved. Machining the panels produces fine graphite dust, which with the epoxy, can be toxic. Consequently, many operations have to be carried out under watersprays, which wash the resultant slurry into a collection point ready for disposal. Drilling composites is also an operation which needs careful judgement, and McDonnell Douglas has had to improve its drilling techniques, especially for holes through composite material/titanium/aluminium in the structure.

With all these problems, it might be thought that the difficulties of repairing battle damage in composite panels would be enormous. While admittedly it is not that easy, the following methods are believed to have been developed by the Israeli Defence Force-Air Force. Providing the damage is not so severe as to warrant a complete replacement component, the technique is to drill a hole just large enough to insert a reciprocating jigsaw, cut neatly around the damaged area to remove it, then simply insert a rubber bung! Alternatively, where this method is impracticable, composites can be patched with titanium.

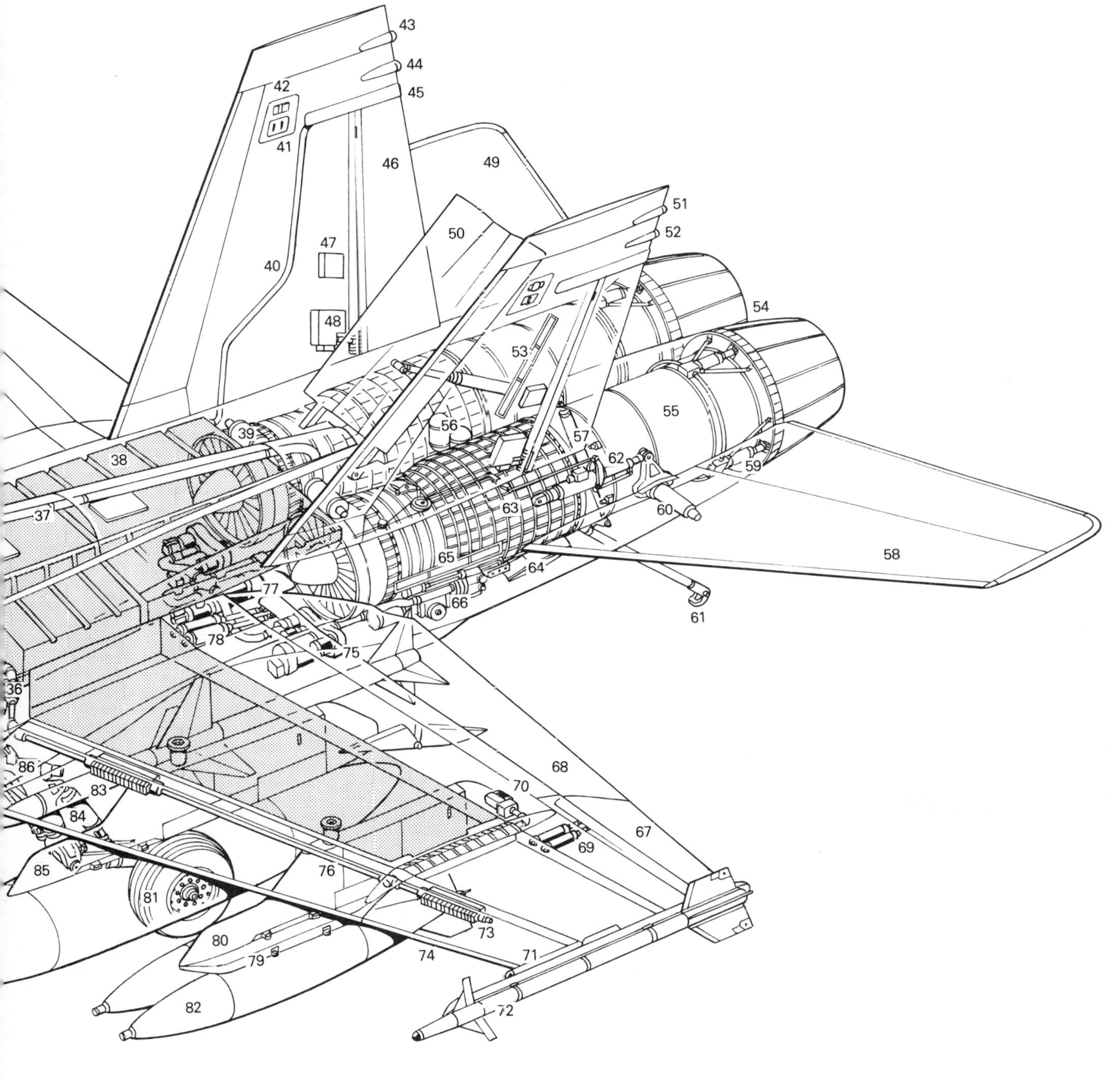

Powerplant

Above: This head-on view of the F404-GE-400 augmented turbofan strikes the essential keynote of simplicity. From the outset, the accent has been on reliability rather than ultimate performance.

The evolution of the Hornet's General Electric F404 low-bypass turbofan was closely linked with that of the aircraft itself. Starting out as the YJ101, developed specifically to power the Northrop P-530 Cobra and designed for economy and reliability rather than ultimate performance, it first took to the air along with the prototype YF-17 in June 1974. When the Northrop lightweight fighter was upgraded into the McDonnell Douglas F/A-18 strike fighter for the US Navy, the engine grew with the project, gaining in size, weight and thrust to become the F404-GE-400.

The Northrop design concept for a lightweight fighter was twin-engined from the outset. Two engines conferred a lower attrition rate and greater safety, but carried built-in penalties of their own. The structure to contain them was perforce more complex than that of a single-engined fighter, and therefore heavier, and more weight would be added by the duplication of fuel and other engine-related systems. Another penalty which is often overlooked is that two engines have twice the potential to go wrong, and double the amount of servicing and maintenance needed. Ideally then, the engine needed to be simple and easily maintainable, and to have exceptional reliability. At the same time, it had to give the high thrust to weight ratio and rapid throttle response essential for fighter operations.

The choice of engines originally lay between the Rolls-Royce RB.199 and the General Electric GE 15. General Electric agreed to develop their engine specifically for the new Northrop fighter, and the choice was made, not that it ever seemed very likely that an American aircraft manufacturer would design a new product around a British engine. Redesignated J101, the new powerplant was first seen in public at the Paris Air Show in May 1971. The GE 15 had incorporated technology from the F101 turbofan, then under development to power the Rockwell B-1 supersonic bomber, and many of the ideas were carried over into the J101.

Emphasis in design of the J101 was placed on reliability rather than ultimate performance. Cost was naturally an important consideration, and the 'design to cost' concept was treated as part of the technology of the engine. Although bearing the J prefix used to denote a turbojet, it was in fact a turbofan engine, albeit with a very low (0.2) bypass ratio. General Electric described it at this stage as a continuous-bleed turbojet, with the excess delivery from the low-pressure (LP) compressor being discharged around the core. For this reason it was semi-facetiously referred to as a 'leaky turbo-jet'.

Turbofan advantages

In pure turbojets, the afterburner and efflux nozzle is exposed to the superheated exhaust gases from the turbine. In a bypass engine, or turbofan, while some of the bypass air mixes with the core exhaust and is burned in the afterburner, the remainder is used to cool the engine external skin and nozzle, and no secondary flow for cooling the engine or exhaust nozzle is required, thereby considerably reducing complexity, drag, weight and cost. A further advantage is gained during afterburning in that the bypass air is still relatively rich in oxygen, whereas the core exhaust has already passed through the engine where much of its oxygen has been consumed.

The J101 was a physically small engine, 12ft 1in (3.68m) long and with a maximum diameter of 2ft 8½in (0.83m). With three low-pressure and seven high-pressure compressor stages, it achieved a compressor pressure ratio exceeding 20:1, and an annular combustor eliminated the smoky exhaust trails that war has shown lead to MiG pollution. It featured just two turbine stages, one high- and one low-pressure, and a variable converging-diverging nozzle. Its static thrust rating was 9,000lb (4,082kg) at full military power, and 15,000lb (6,800kg) with full afterburner, which gave it a thrust/weight ratio in the region of 8:1.

The J101 was made up of seven major modules, a feature which greatly facilitated ease of repair and maintenance. At the front was the LP compressor, a three-stage axial flow design. Variable inlet guide vanes regulated the engine air flow. Behind it came the HP compressor, of seven stages, which had been developed from the F101 turbofan. Some of the stages featured variable geometry to ensure efficient operation. Under the HP compressor was positioned the electrical-hydro-mechanical engine control module, designed to provide stall-free operation regardless of any rate of throttle movement anywhere in the flight envelope and thrust range. Between the HP compressor and the HP turbine came the combustor.

The next module in line was the single-stage HP turbine driving the HP compressor. Both the blade design and cooling in this stage were derived from the F101. Then came the LP turbine which drove the LP compressor at the front of the engine. This featured convection cooled blades, and convection cooled vane segments brazed into pairs on the nozzle. Finally there was the afterburner module, the design of which was based on that of the tried and proven J85, as used in the F-5E. This had an annular pilot flame holder, and a single-stage main fuel distributor provided smoothly modulated thrust variation.

Having the advantage of using proven technology from the F101, development of the J101 was comparatively rapid, so that initial component testing occupied just 14 months. Testing of the first core engine began in March 1972, and the first complete engine test took place during the following July. In the meantime, the USAF had issued its request for proposals for the LWF, an Air Force contract following at the end of April 1972, and the Y prefix, denoting preproduction was added. The engine thus became the YJ101-GE-100.

Simulated flight testing, carried out at the Arnold Engineering Development Center at Tullahoma, Tennessee, covered the performance envelope from high altitude to sea level supersonic speed, and various speed/AOA combi-

Above: The J101 low bypass ratio turbofan was developed to power the Northrop YF-17. It is often forgotten that for the fly-off against the YF-16 the YF-17 was using early development engines. The J101 was designed for ease of maintenance, with seven modules.

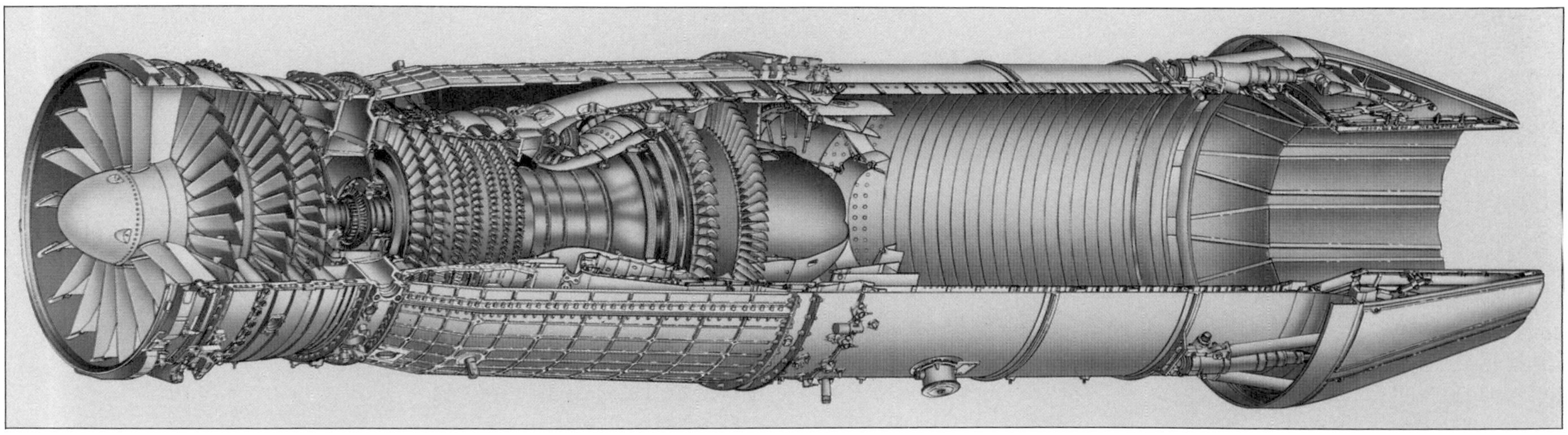

Above: Cutaway view of the F404, showing the simplicity of the layout by comparison with earlier turbojets. Accessories are mounted on the airframe rather than the engine, so it is not 'handed'.

nations. The Prototype Preliminary Flight Rating Test (PPFRT) was completed in December 1973, using a single engine, in just 101 test hours, and the USAF cleared the engine for unrestricted operation throughout the entire flight envelope. The YJ101 first flew in the YF-17 prototype on June 9, 1974.

Altogether, seven engines were used in the short YF-17 flight test programme. A total of 302 flights, amounting to 719 flight hours, were clocked up, during which the YJ101 proved to be remarkably fault-free, not one engine-related delay being recorded. Peacetime operations are considerably more arduous for an engine than those flown in war. Not only do training sorties tend to last longer, but at least one, and possibly several combats may be simulated, whereas on a war mission none at all may occur. Reliability in peace and survivability in war are the keynotes.

It should be remembered in this context that for the ACF competition the YF-17 was using what was to all intents and purposes an experimental engine, while the rival General Dynamics YF-16 was powered by the Pratt & Whitney F100 engine already developed for the F-15. In fact, the Fort Worth company did consider using two YJ101s in their machine, but the YF-16 was a rather smaller aeroplane than the YF-17, and the weight and drag penalties of accommodating two engines were shown by design studies to be unacceptable. As we have seen earlier, the single-engined design was declared the winner of the competition.

The YF-17's two engines and larger airframe were to prove a blessing in disguise. Although the ACF competition had been lost the YF-17 was considered by the Navy to be the most suitable aeroplane for development to meet their multi-role requirement. But to turn a lightweight fighter into a carrier-suitable, multi-mission machine was obviously going to promote it into the midleweight class, and more thrust would be needed if a dramatic and unacceptable reduction in the new fighter's performance was to be avoided.

Upgrading the J101

The obvious answer was to upgrade the YJ101, which so far had proved outstandingly successful. The result was the F404-GE-400, the F designation acknowledging that it was a turbofan rather than a turbojet, although it was at first referred to as an augmented turbojet, while the number in the 400 range denoted that the project was funded by the US Navy. The new engine was very similar to the YJ101, but scaled up by about 10 per cent and with the bypass ratio increased to 0.34, still less than half the ratio of the F100. Corrosion-resistant materials, essential to counter the salt-laden environment of carrier operations, were used throughout.

The F404, at 13ft 2in (4.01m), was 13in (34cm) longer than the YJ101, and the fan diameter was increased by one inch (2.5cm). The mass airflow was raised about 10 per cent to 140lb/sec (63.5kg/sec) and combined with a 50deg F (28deg C) increase in turbine inlet temperature, and the pressure ratio was increased to 25:1. The thrust ratio remained at 8:1. These improvements resulted in a dry thrust of 10,600lb (4,800kg) and a maximum afterburning thrust of 16,000lb (7,250kg). This put it in the same thrust class as the General Electric J79, used to power the ubiquitous Phantom among other aircraft, which could reasonably be described as the F404's predecessor.

To see how far engine technology had progressed in 20 years, a brief comparison is in order. In achieving comparable thrust, the F404 was, at 2,121lb (962kg), barely half the weight and two-thirds the length of the J79. A 25:1 pressure ratio achieved with just ten stages compared very favourably with the 13.5:1 ratio of the J79's 17 stages, while the total number of components per engine was just 14,400 against 22,000.

Below: An F404 engine on the test rig. Accelerated mission oriented testing condensed the operational mission cycles, concentrating on areas of maximum stress. Each AMT hour represents five flight hours.

The small size of the F404 contributed directly to the weight saving: fewer parts, only three structural frames and sumps, with their attendant lubrication systems, and just five main bearings. Yet weight reduction, although important, was not the only consideration, because the F404 could have been made lighter still. As with the YJ101, design to cost was an integral part of the programme and in several areas weight was the trade-off to keep cost down. Typically, these were the use of solid rather than hollow compressor blades, cast rather than fabricated structures, and solid metal rather than honeycomb material in casings and ducts. Steel was also used instead of titanium where the substitution was found cost-effective.

Powering a carrier fighter is the most demanding role for an engine in the entire aviation spectrum. It must be both reliable and durable, able to withstand not only the thrust and environmental changes encountered in the fighter mission, but also the repeated stresses of catapult launches and arrested landings, for which a design factor of 11g was built in. Furthermore, the deck idle thrust must be very low, so as not to cause embarrassment to either the pilot or deck-handling crew in a crowded area.

The development programme for the F404 was the most comprehensive for an engine ever. While components were originally scheduled to undergo some 5,000 test hours, in the event about 8,000 hours were clocked up, and 14 development engines underwent more than 13,000 factory test hours over a period just short of five years. The first F404 engine test took place in January 1977, a month ahead of schedule, and quickly demonstrated the required sea-level performance, and the first of six engines arrived at the Naval Air Propulsion Test Center (NAPTC) at Trenton, New Jersey, shortly afterward. Nine engines were delivered in 1978 and a further 24 in 1979. PPRFT took place in May 1978, and the first flight, in Hornet 1, in November of the same year; the Model Qualification Test (MQT) was completed in July 1979; and the first production engine was handed over in January 1980.

Above: The nozzles of the F404 are variable, with a 12-petal external cover. Here they are shown in the fully closed flight idle position.

Engine test modes

Testing took place in three basic modes. The Simulated Mission Endurance Test (SMET) duplicated the throttle movements and power settings used in the fighter and attack missions. Three tests were held, each of 750 hours, approximating to three years of operational service. The Accelerated Mission Test (AMT) used the SMET missions as a basis, condensing the operational cycles and concentrating on the areas where damage was most likely to be caused. Each AMT hour represented five hours of operational usage, so that the 2,000 plus hours of AMT logged in the development programme represented more than 10,000 flight hours. Finally, Accelerated Service Testing (AST), the so-called Hornet Hustle, was flown by Hornets 9 and T2. The AST was a 1,000-hour programme, the first half of which was flown by McDonnell Douglas test pilots and the remainder by Navy pilots. The flight programme was very intensive: on three separate occasions, Hornet 9 flew six sorties per day.

F404/J79 comparison

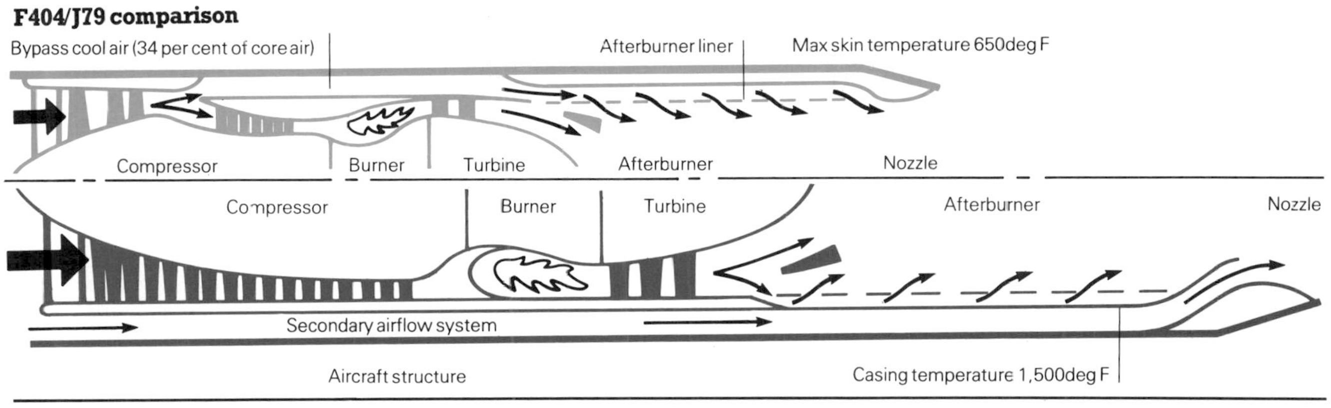

Left: Comparison of the F404 (top) with the J79, used to power the F-4 and F-104. Comparable thrust is achieved for half the weight and two-thirds the length of the earlier engine.

Below left: The auxiliary power unit (APU) gives the Hornet a self-starting capability and also provides power for systems checks from internal sources.

Below: Engine fires are extinguished by selective discharge into any of three areas: starboard engine and AMAD, port engine and AMAD, or the auxiliary power unit.

F/A-18 secondary power system

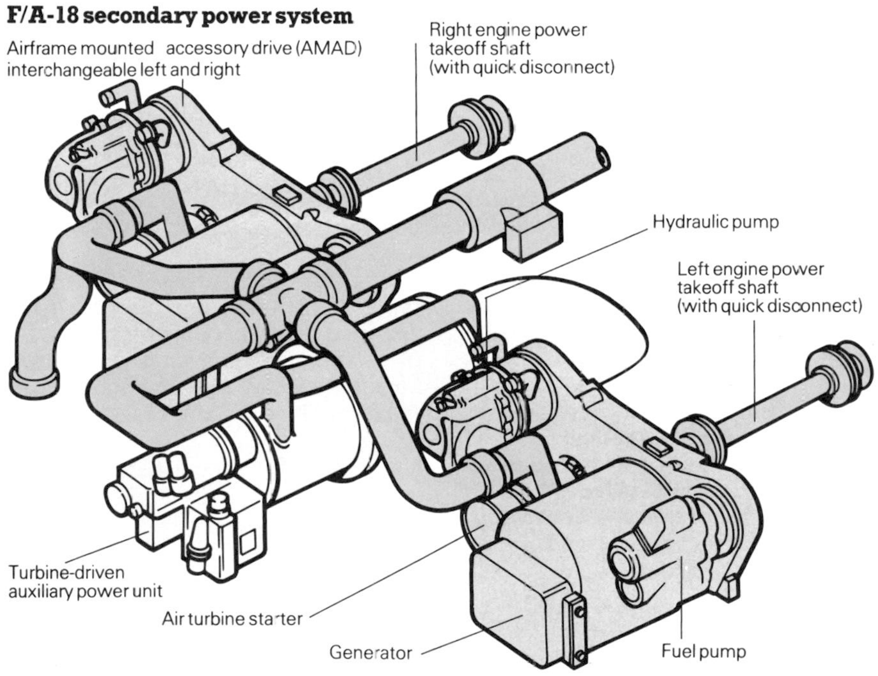

Engine fire extinguishing system

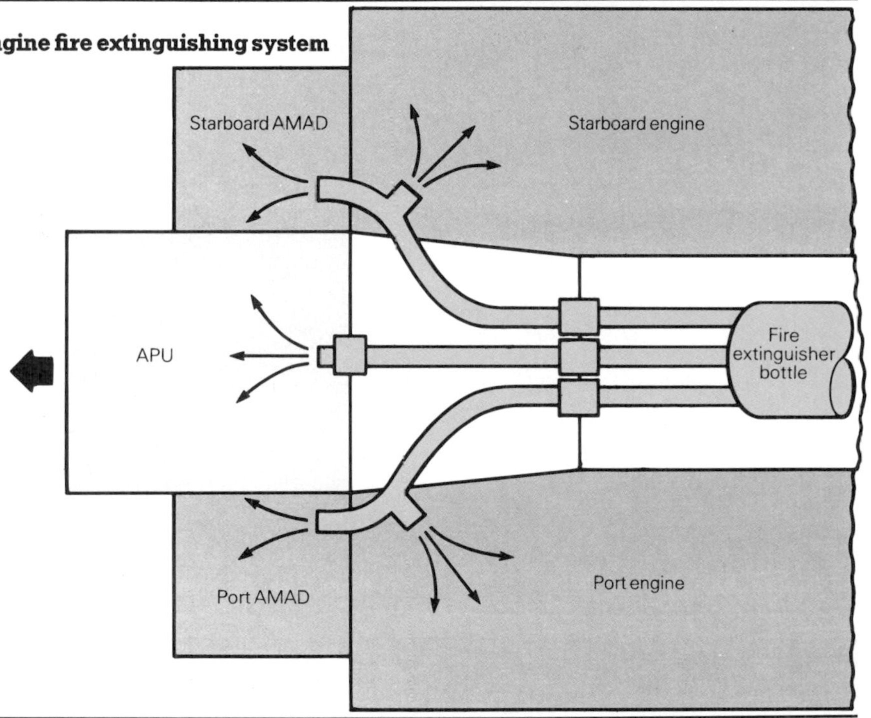

The F404 flight test programme proved remarkably trouble-free. The engine was shown to be extremely stall-resistant at high AOA and various combinations of yaw and sideslip, and no compressor stall was experienced in the first 300 flights from Patuxent River. This was in part due to the careful integration of the airframe and inlet design, particularly the LEX, with the engine. The LEX reduced the angle of the airflow into the inlets to approximately half the angle of attack. Some stalls, afterburner blowouts, and engine flameouts were later experienced at AOA of between 50deg and 90deg, but the stalls quickly corrected themselves and both engine and afterburner were found to relight automatically. The engine was also found to be wonderfully responsive, accelerating from idle to full afterburner in less than four seconds, and throttle slams from flight idle to maximum power and back were tested and found to cause no problems.

Below: The lack of requirement for Mach 2 performance allowed simple fixed inlets to be used, with a saving in both weight and cost.

All this is not to suggest that the F404 was entirely fault-free. The specified acceleration time from Mach 0.8 to Mach 1.6 was not achieved, although the Hornet showed that it could match even F-15s in drag races up to Mach 1.2. Certain shortfalls were revealed in specific fuel consumption – the amount of fuel burned per unit of thrust per hour – but although these could only partially be compensated, this was not felt to be particularly serious. The sfc of the F404 at military power is 0.85lb per pound of thrust per hour. Other engine-related problems were a single case of a No. 4 bearing failure, and turbine blade fractures, which are described in the previous chapter.

One fault was discovered as a result of a small power loss to both engines in the same aircraft, following relight tests. With the engines stripped down, the blades of the HP turbine were found to be worn approximately 20 mil (0.5mm). Checks made on other engines revealed a wear range of between 4 and 8 mil (0.1-0.2mm). It was concluded that a temperature difference between the blades and the casing had caused rubbing and resultant wear. As the performance of both the affected engines was still above specification, no action was taken and they were re-installed.

Much more serious was the engine failure that led to the loss of Hornet T2 on September 8, 1980. The LP turbine disc suffered a catastrophic fracture and flew to pieces, causing irremediable damage. The casing of the F404 is designed to retain fractured turbine blades, which are, after all, a fairly common failure with any engine, but great lumps of a 90lb (41kg) metal disc revolving at very high speeds contained far too much kinetic energy to be stopped. Parts of the disc were not recovered, which hampered the investigation into the cause of the crash.

At that time, 33 flight test engines had been delivered. The discs in 12 of these had been formed with conventional castings, while the remainder had been manufactured by a 'fine mesh' powder metallurgy process known as hot isostatic forming developed by General Electric. In this process the raw material, called Rene 95, was reduced to a powder before being poured into a mould where it was subjected to extreme heat and pressure, the end result being known as '60 mesh'. The failed LP turbine disc was of 60 mesh, and turbine discs of this material were replaced immediately pending the results of the enquiry.

The findings were inconclusive, due to the fracture having occurred in a part of the disc that was never found, but it was thought that either a flaw in the material or a defect in the manufacturing process was responsible, and that the incident could be described as a 'worst case' event. General recommendations included redesigning all F404 rotor parts for maximum life. The turbine disc was to be strengthened, and holes formed between the existing holes to reduce stress concentration. The isostatic forming and forging process was not fully understood; in an on-going technology programme the process had been refined still further to produce '150 mesh' which tests showed to have four times the reliability of 60 mesh, which was used in all further engines.

Maintainability

Ease of maintenance is another facet of reliability. In line with the entire Hornet concept, the F404 engines were designed for maximum maintainability. One feature carried over from the YJ101 was the modular construction, which allowed entire sections to be replaced rapidly with a minimum expenditure of manhours. It will be readily appreciated that in the cramped confines of an aircraft carrier at sea, both manpower and space is at a premium.

Special consideration was given to rapid engine changes. Unlike most twin-engined designs, there are no left and right engines on the Hornet; any engine can be fitted on either side. This was achieved by mounting engine accessories on the airframe instead of on the engine. The engine has only ten connections, or interfaces, with the aircraft and can be changed without special equipment being used, 'within the shadow of the aircraft'. Large engine bay doors under the rear fuselage open inward toward the centreline, exposing everything that needs servicing, all of which are mounted on the underside quadrant of the engine. The engine is changed by lowering it vertically out of the bay. With practice, a four-man team can complete an engine change in 20 minutes, although demonstration teams have often beaten this figure.

Servicing has been made particularly easy. There are no scheduled overhauls; just what is called 'on-condition' maintenance, which means putting right what needs attention. The necessity for this is established by an In-Flight Engine Condition Monitoring System, or IECMS, in which trained electrons whiz about the engine to check that all is well. Faults are displayed in the form of flags in the cockpit to warn the pilot, and read-outs for maintenance personnel. Engine removal therefore only takes place when a fault is recorded that requires remedial action, or one of the modules has reached the end of its scheduled life.

Left: The F404 was designed in seven modules for ease of repair and maintenance. The engine is suspended vertically to allow the modules to be disconnected.

Below: Engine removal only takes place when remedial action is necessary, or when a module reaches the end of its scheduled life. With practice, a four-man crew can change an engine in less than half an hour, and any engine can fit either side.

Borescope inspection

Apart from the IECMS, each engine contains 13 ports to allow internal inspection by borescope, although only nine of these are accessible with the engine installed. The F404 should require workshop maintenance less than twice for every 1,000 flight hours, and the target mean time between maintenance actions is 175 flight hours. This compares well with the corresponding figures for the J79, which are 3.1 per 1,000 hours and 90 hours respectively. The mission abort rate for the F404 is once every 2,000 hours.

Engine accessories, called line-replaceable units, are placed on the underside of the engine and are replaceable through the engine bay door. Each engine has an Airframe Mounted Auxiliary Drive (AMAD) System, which drives a fuel pump, a hydraulic pump, and a 40kVA General Electric VSCF generator.

An unusual feature of the Hornet is that the pilot can climb aboard and start the engines just as though he were in a car

(well, almost), which saves a lot of ground support equipment, or 'yellow stuff', from cluttering up the carrier deck. The secret lies in the Garrett AiResearch Auxiliary Power Unit, or APU, which is mounted on the aircraft centreline just ahead of the twin engine bays, and is accessible through a quick-release door on the underside of the fuselage. It is a compact unit, weighing 112lb (51kg), and it develops 200hp (150kW).

The APU is started from the cockpit by battery power. It then supplies high-pressure air to the turbine starter to start the engine. Once one engine has been started, a power shaft drives the AMAD and thereby the pumps and generator, so that cross-bleed air can be used to start the second engine. Of course, the engines can always be started from an external power source if necessary.

The APU has another valuable function. By disengaging the accessory drive from the engines, all the aircraft systems can be run independently of either the engines or an external power source. This enables a full ground checkout to be made of all systems that require electrical power, hydraulic power, fuel pressure, or cooling, entirely from the Hornet's own resources. The APU can also be used to supplement air conditioning on a very hot day when engine bleed air proves insufficient for both the environmental control and avionics bay cooling systems.

Fuel system

Internal fuel is contained in four fuselage and two wing tanks, which are self-sealing and protected by foam in the wing and fuselage voids. Shaft-driven motive flow boost pumps in each AMAD unit pump fuel from the main wing and fuselage tanks to the engine feed tanks. The fuel, either JP-4 or JP-5, is supplied to the engines from separate feed tanks which interconnect for cross-feeding and are self-contained and self-sealing to provide a 'get you home' facility if the main tanks are damaged. The only fuel lines to enter the engine compartments are a main feed to each engine fuel control. This minimizes the chance of a broken or damaged fuel line spilling fuel into the hot engine compartment.

The total internal fuel capacity is 11,000lb (4,990kg) which can be augmented by three external tanks each containing 350US gall (1,324lit), bringing the maximum fuel load to approximately 17,800lb (8,075kg). A single refuelling point on the left side of the front fuselage is used for both ground refuelling and purging the fuel system, while the fuel vents and dumps are located on the top of the fins. In-flight refuelling can be used to increase the range; a retractable probe is located in a compartment at the top of the starboard side of the nose, just ahead of the cockpit.

A slight problem encountered with the Hornet's fuel system during the FSD programme was that the specification requirement of 10 seconds of normal engine operation at negative g was not being consistently achieved. The Parker jet pumps, mounted in a small reservoir designed to trap sufficient fuel for 10 seconds of negative g operation, tended to pump air pockets trapped in the fuel as readily as the fuel itself. The remedy was to replace the jet pumps with Sundstrand turbine-driven fuel boost pumps, which would not suck air.

The F404-GE-400 is the engine developed specifically for the Hornet, but other F404 variants are in the pipeline. The F404-GE-100 has been developed to give 17,000lb (7,700kg) of thrust for the Northrop F-20 Tigershark, while the F404J, with 18,000lb (8,150kg) of thrust will power the Swedish Gripen. General Electric predict that the F404 will be uprated to 19/20,000lb (8,600/9,100kg) during the next four years.

Left: Care and concentration as the engine dolly is positioned ready for the start of an engine change. Such changes are done 'within the shadow of the aircraft' as a matter of routine – an important consideration at sea.

Below: Engine accessories are placed on the bottom quadrant and are accessible through the engine bay door, as seen here. Accessories are all LRUs (line replaceable units).

Right: Flaps down for the photo call, an F-18A Hornet lights the afterburner for the benefit of the camera. The nozzles are small by present-day standards and are a direct aid to reducing the risk of detection.

Avionics

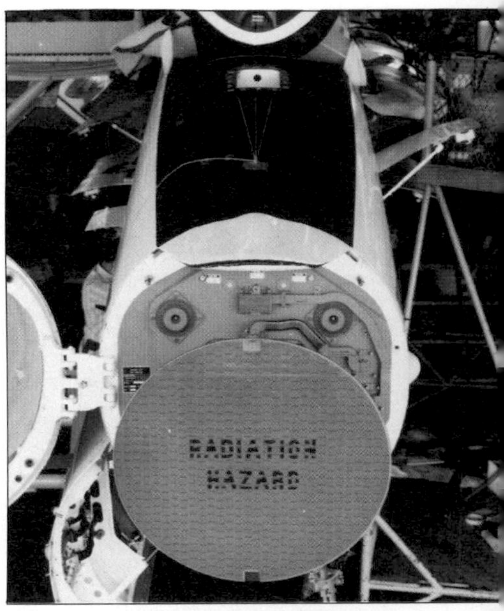

It is not enough for a modern fighter to have outstanding performance and handling qualities. It also needs clever systems for target location, weapons delivery, threat detection, navigation and communications if it is both to survive and to carry out its mission successfully. Current technology allows very sophisticated systems to be designed small enough to fit a single-seat aeroplane, and the Hornet's cockpit is a *tour de force*, presenting the information in such a manner that one man can fly the demanding spectrum of missions required of an aircraft designed for both fleet defence and long-range attack.

At the heart of the Hornet's complex avionics system is the cockpit, where all the information comes together for use by the pilot. Much of the controversy surrounding the aircraft has been based on quite justifiable doubts as to whether one man could handle all the information to be thrown at him and still fly the mission successfully. Previous Navy fighters, the F-4 Phantom and the F-14 Tomcat both had two-man crews, and they could be pretty hard-pressed at times.

The challenge to McDonnell Douglas was formidable: to take the Northrop YF-17 lightweight fighter and dress it out as a carrier-borne multi-role combat aircraft involved a tremendous increase both in the complexity of the systems and in the amount of information that would need to be presented. The Hornet had to be able to replace both the Phantom and the Corsair, and also to supplement the Tomcat in the fleet defence role; the systems and instrumentation requirement for all these tasks was enormous. Moreover, the ejection seat, raked back at an angle of 18deg as compared with the 15deg of the F-15's seat, brought the pilot's knees higher, reducing the instrument panel and console area available to only about 60 per cent of the usable area in the F-15 cockpit, but with more systems to control and display.

Starting from scratch

To design an effective cockpit, McDonnell Douglas started with the proverbial clean sheet of paper. Mission analysis was the first step. Whether flying an air-to-air or air-to-ground mission, the pilot would have up to three different air-to-air weapons, a combination chosen from more than two dozen air-to-ground weapons, all the aircraft systems and about 250 switchology functions to handle. Originally, the A-18 version was to have a moving colour map display that was not required in the F-18, while the Marine Corps wanted one UHF and one VHF radio in their aircraft rather than the two UHF sets that were to be the standard Navy fit. These differences were resolved by fitting moving map displays in all Hornets and adopting the Navy radio fit as standard.

Mission analysis identified three main workload areas: (a) weapon and sensor management during combat, in which time was critical; (b) communications, navigation, and identification (CNI) systems management throughout the entire flight spectrum, with special emphasis on carrier operations in conditions of poor visibility; and (c) systems mode management and miscellaneous requirements, which were usually not time-critical, but still occupied valuable console space as well as units of the pilot's mental capacity.

Cockpits of other aircraft were studied, in particular the company's own F-15, and work done as part of the US Navy Advanced Integrated Modular Instrumentation Systems programme was examined, as was the cockpit proposed by McDonnell Douglas for the Model 263 VFX contender. McDonnell Douglas had also been building a large simulator complex which had been extensively used during the design stage of the F-15. The simulator was heavily involved during the design and development of the Hornet, not least for the cockpit layout, in which both test and service pilots could try out proposed systems and suggest improvements.

The final solution lay in more intensive use of computer-aided controls and displays than on any previous aeroplane. The time-critical combat weapon and sensor management was achieved via the hands on throttle and stick (HOTAS) concept pioneered on the F-15. A pilot in

Above: Hornet pilots have been known to describe the cockpit as being "out of Star Wars". The displays reflected in this pilot's visor heighten the impression.

Top: The planar array antenna of the Hughes APG-63 radar is quite small, a fact made apparent by this assembly line photograph.

Right: One-man operability is the keynote of the Hornet cockpit layout. Information is called up as required on the CRT displays at the touch of a few of the surrounding buttons.

combat usually flies with his left hand on the throttle(s) and his right hand on the control column: using HOTAS, all necessary switches for weaponry or essential data displays are mounted on one or the other of these controls. The pilot is therefore able to control the necessary weapons, sensors or displays without moving his hands away from either control, and without taking his eyes off either the target or the head-up display (HUD). Management of the CNI functions was incorporated in the up-front control (UFC) panel located in the centre of the dash, while systems mode management is accomplished by switches surrounding three head-down cathode ray tube (CRT) displays.

Cockpit displays

The most striking aspect of the Hornet cockpit is the almost total lack of dials and conventional instrumentation. Prominent are the three 5in (12.7cm) square CRTs on the instrument panel. These are linked to the two mission computers and also the HUD. The HUD is of the twin-combiner type, with a comparatively wide 20deg×20deg field of view; its optics are located behind the CNI panel, and it is the main flight instrument for both weapon delivery and navigation, including both manual and automatic carrier landing modes. Data such as speed, heading, attitude, AOA, altitude, g loading, steering commands and cues for attack are projected either as symbols or in alpha-numeric format on the combiner glass and focussed at infinity, so that the pilot is enabled to assimilate the information without losing sight of the target or the carrier deck.

CRTs were chosen for the three head-down displays (HDDs) for their sheer versatility in showing different kinds of information in a small space. It is easier and quicker for the pilot to assimilate the information that he requires than from a conventional presentation because flight, sensor and weapon information are all grouped conveniently together on the CRT display. This has had the effect of allowing the conventional armament panel and more than a dozen electro-mechanical servoed instruments of dubious reliability to be deleted from the aircraft cockpit. CRTs also offer the best combination of contrast and resolution, two conflicting requirements, in bright sunlight.

Two CRTs are set high on the instrument panel; the multi-function display (MFD) on the right, and the master monitor display (MMD) on the left. Manufactured by Kaiser Aerospace, they are identical and interchangeable units: in the event of a failure of one, their functions also are interchangeable in flight and the mission would not have to be aborted. Each contains symbol generators, capable at need, depending on the complexity of the modes, of driving two or three displays, while the HUD can be driven by either. Each CRT has 20 push-button controls around its perimeter, which allow different operating modes or stored programs to be called up, and the software-programmed display processors can operate all the computerized displays. Between them, they have the added advantage of allowing the pilot to select the information he wants and present it where he wants it.

The MFD is the primary sensor display for radar attack and radar mapping information, and the digital computer gives a processed and clutter-free presentation. Also presented in an alpha-numeric format is flight information such as speed, attitude, weapon status, altitude etc. The symbology can be either cursive or TV raster (525 or 875 lines). The MMD is the primary warning, electro-optical and infra-red sensor and armament display, as well as projecting cautionary and advisory information on the aircraft systems.

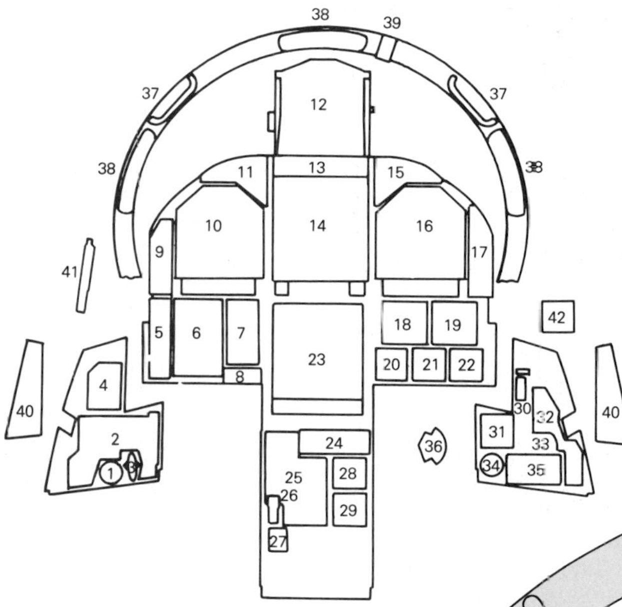

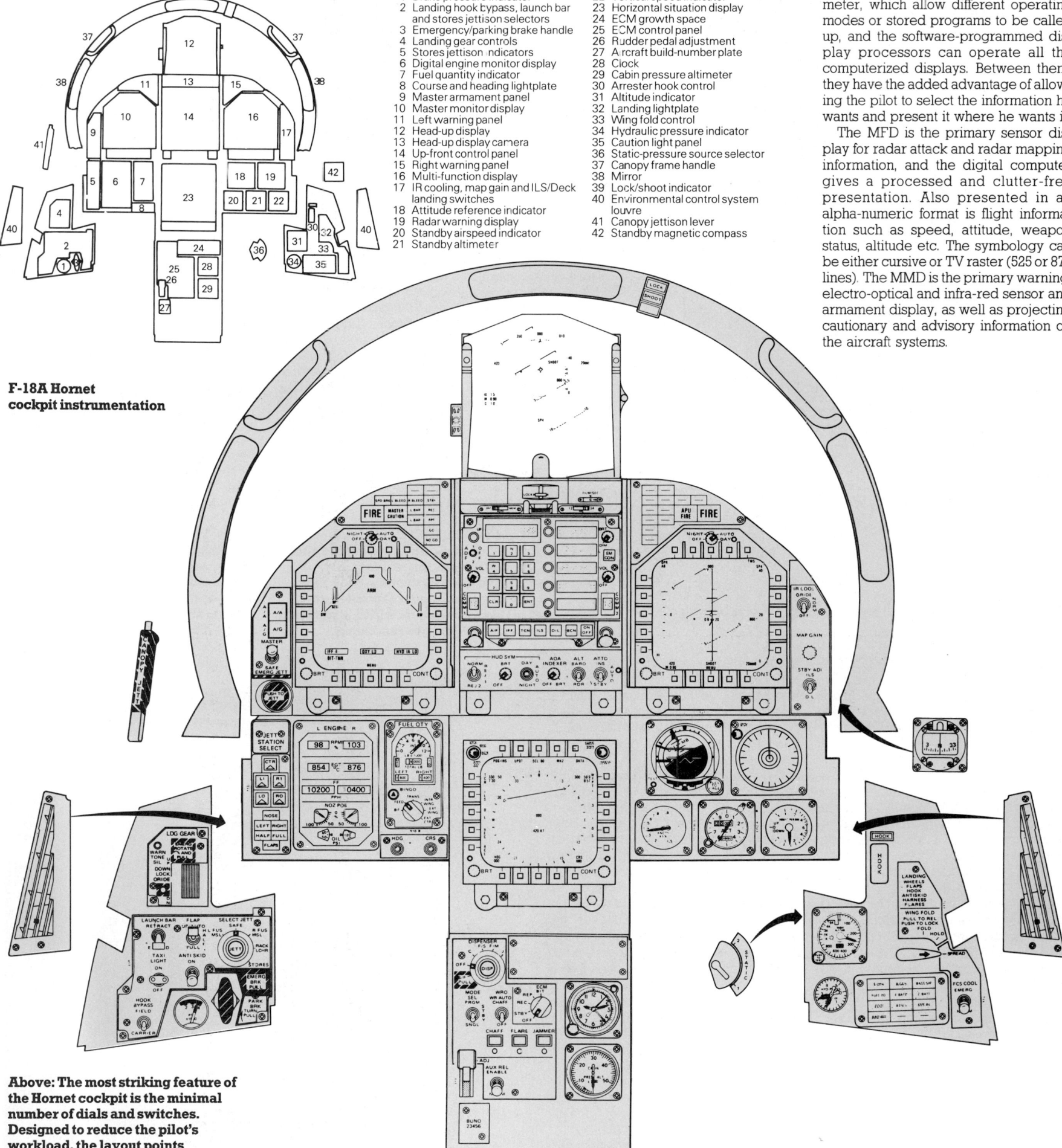

1 Brake pressure indicator
2 Landing hook bypass, launch bar and stores jettison selectors
3 Emergency/parking brake handle
4 Landing gear controls
5 Stores jettison indicators
6 Digital engine monitor display
7 Fuel quantity indicator
8 Course and heading lightplate
9 Master armament panel
10 Master monitor display
11 Left warning panel
12 Head-up display
13 Head-up display camera
14 Up-front control panel
15 Right warning panel
16 Multi-function display
17 IR cooling, map gain and ILS/Deck landing switches
18 Attitude reference indicator
19 Radar warning display
20 Standby airspeed indicator
21 Standby altimeter
22 Vertical speed indicator
23 Horizontal situation display
24 ECM growth space
25 ECM control panel
26 Rudder pedal adjustment
27 Aircraft build-number plate
28 Clock
29 Cabin pressure altimeter
30 Arrester hook control
31 Altitude indicator
32 Landing lightplate
33 Wing fold control
34 Hydraulic pressure indicator
35 Caution light panel
36 Static-pressure source selector
37 Canopy frame handle
38 Mirror
39 Lock/shoot indicator
40 Environmental control system louvre
41 Canopy jettison lever
42 Standby magnetic compass

F-18A Hornet cockpit instrumentation

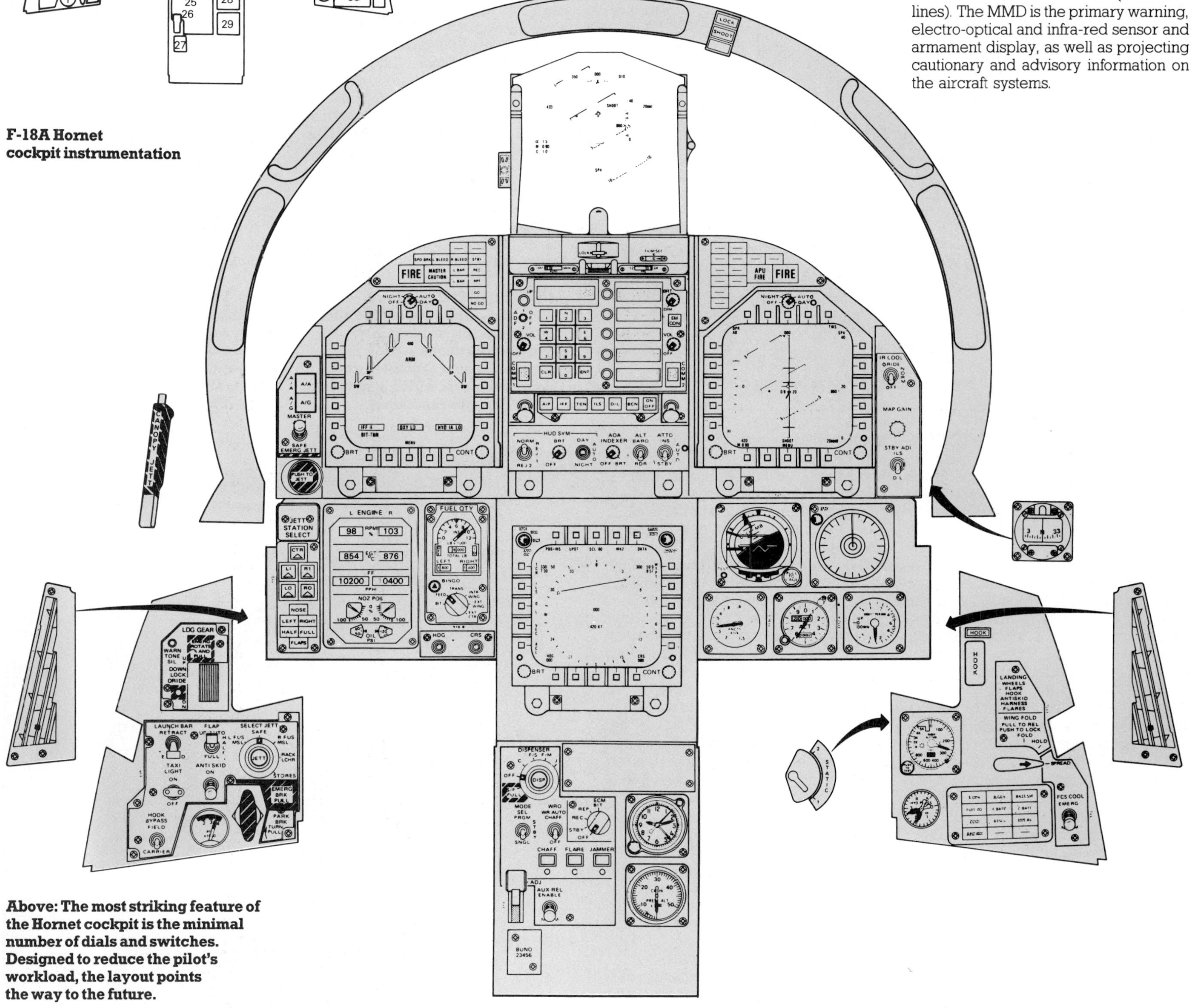

Above: The most striking feature of the Hornet cockpit is the minimal number of dials and switches. Designed to reduce the pilot's workload, the layout points the way to the future.

Left (from left): The Hornet's primary cockpit displays are the master monitor display (MMD), horizontal situation display (HSD), head-up display (HUD) and multi-function display (MFD). Functions of the MMD and MFD are interchangeable, and either can drive the HUD.

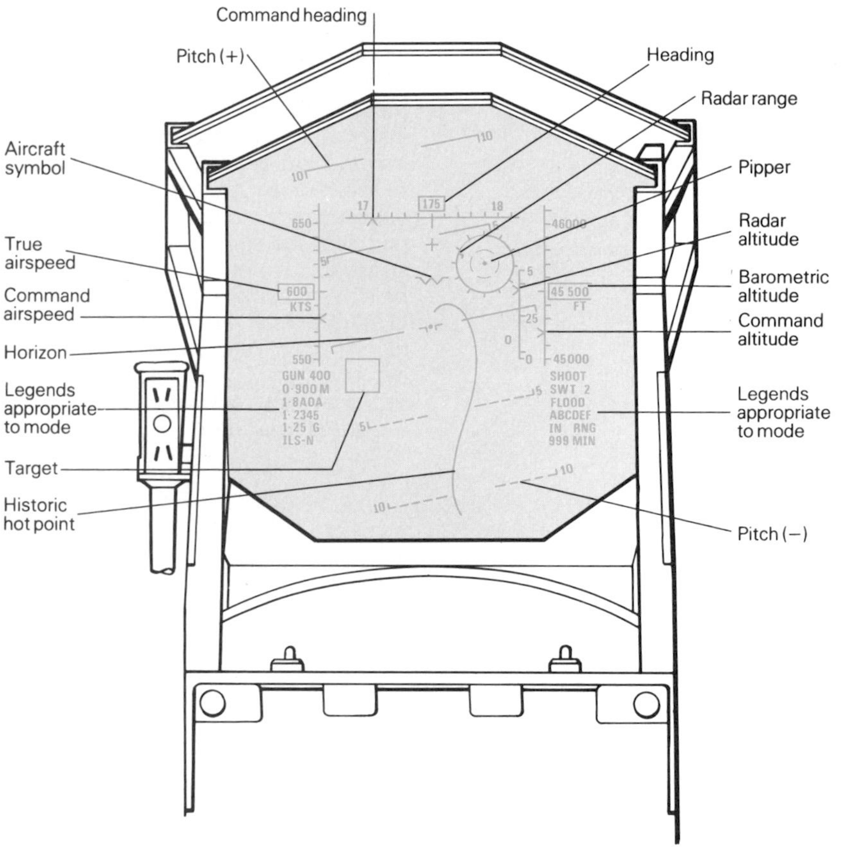

F/A-18 head-up display symbology

Left: Typical HUD symbology, showing all the information the pilot needs as he closes on his target. Among the data displayed are range, height, speed and weapon selected – in this case the gun, which is shown as having 400 rounds remaining.

At a lower level, below the UFC panel, is a third CRT. This is the horizontal situation display (HSD), based on the British Ferranti system but repackaged and licence-built in America by Bendix. It consists of a coloured, film-projected moving map acting both as a horizontal position indicator and as a display for attack information such as time/range to target, Tacan steering and INS waypoint steering commands, and it updates position as required. It also presents electronic warfare and threat indications. The HSD has push-button controls in the same manner as the MFD and MMD, which call up the information requested. An ingenious feature of the HSD is that it has a lens system that effectively forms an aperture 10in×7in (25.4cm×17.8cm) for the pilot to see the display in bright lighting conditions as though it were hooded. At night, the pilot can lean slightly forward, which effectively removes the aperture to a point outside his line of vision and prevents him being dazzled by the display. Almost every avionic system is linked to the three CRTs, as described below in connection with the specific functions.

Situated between the MMD and MFD, and below the HUD, is the up-front display, which deals with CNI functions. Supplied by McDonnell Douglas Electronics, it is so positioned that only a slight glance down from the HUD is necessary. The bottom row of buttons, reading from left to right, select autopilot, Identification/Friend or Foe (IFF), Tactical Air Navigation (TACAN), Instrument Landing System (ILS), Data Link, and Beacon, with an on/off switch on the extreme right. Just above, at extreme left and extreme right, are the switches controlling the two UHF radios. Other switches control the Automatic Direction Finding (ADF) system and essentials such as brightness, volume, etc.

The main area of the panel is taken up with a keyboard and electronic readout panels. The pilot selects a function and the readout panels display the options on that particular function; the desired option(s) are selected and the data is entered via the keyboard. The UFC panel then automatically clears, ready for further use. All controls are within easy reach of either hand, and with practice numerous CNI functions can be performed under instrument conditions.

The remaining instruments are nearly, but not quite, standard. Master warning lights are used to indicate that all is not well, but the detailed information on the malfunction appears immediately in a corner of either the MMD or the MFD. Engine and fuel state data is presented in digital form using mechanical drum counters. A departure for the Navy is the use of white cockpit lighting at night. In the unlikely event of complete power failure or loss of displays, standby instruments are located at the bottom right of the dash. They consist of pneumatic airspeed, altitude, and vertical speed indicators, and a gyroscopic Attitude Director Indicator.

HOTAS control

Not quite as way out as the displays, but still very advanced, is the HOTAS concept, which gives the pilot control of the major sensors, weapons, and displays without removing his hands from the throttle and stick, which of course is where he wants them in the heat and confusion of combat. No longer is he reduced to groping in the cockpit to find the correct switch while trying to maintain visual contact with a distant opponent.

The HOTAS system looks at first sight as though the pilot will need the manual dexterity of a concert pianist to operate the ten switches mounted on the throttles and a further seven on the stick, but experience gained on the F-15, which also uses HOTAS, plus extensive simulator tests, and, of course, the rapidly mounting flight time of the Hornet itself, has shown that the use of HOTAS lies well within the abilities of the average pilot. In this connection, it should be noted that not all the functions will be needed at once, but just a few at a time to meet the needs of the moment. Incorrect mode selection is always a potential problem, but the error becomes instantly apparent on the feedback on the visual displays, and corrections can be made almost instantaneously.

Only three of the HOTAS switches are primary to air combat; others are secondary, or are related to carrier landing functions. The primary switches are the Air-to-Air Weapons selector and the Automatic Lock-on selector on the stick, and the Target Designator control on the left-hand throttle. It should be remembered that the Hornet has two engines and therefore two throttles; while the throttles are so shaped as to be operated as a single control, there can be no guarantee that this will always be the case.

The Air-to-Air Weapons selector has three positions for selection of Sparrows, Sidewinders or guns as appropriate. The selection cues the radar automatically to the nominal parameters for the weapon chosen for range and azimuth, elevation and pulse repetition frequency. This has the added advantage of allowing the pilot to vary his search pattern by altering the weapon selected. For long-range work, Sparrow is selected and the radar automatically enters range-while-search

Below: The original Ferranti combined map and electronic display unit on which the Hornet horizontal situation display is based. A coloured film map is projected on the screen, and additional navigation information can be displayed as required.

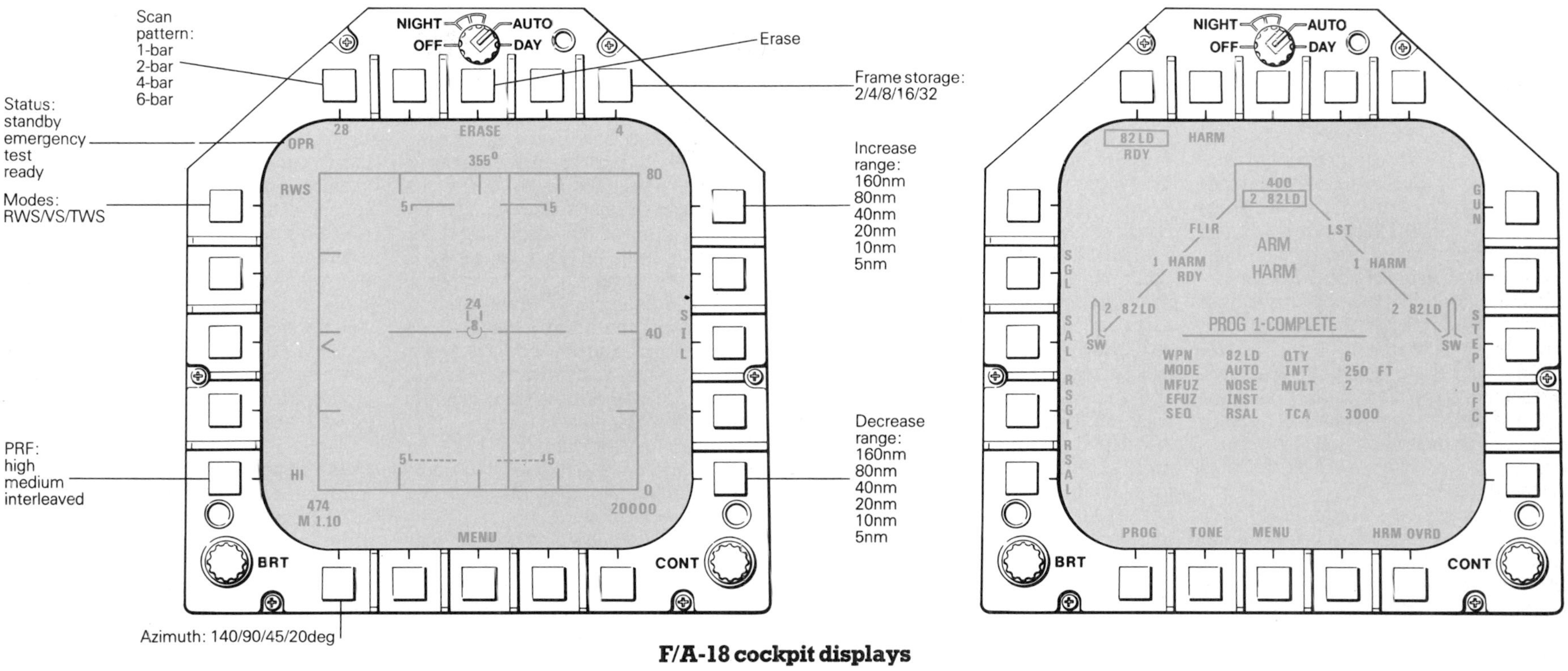

F/A-18 cockpit displays

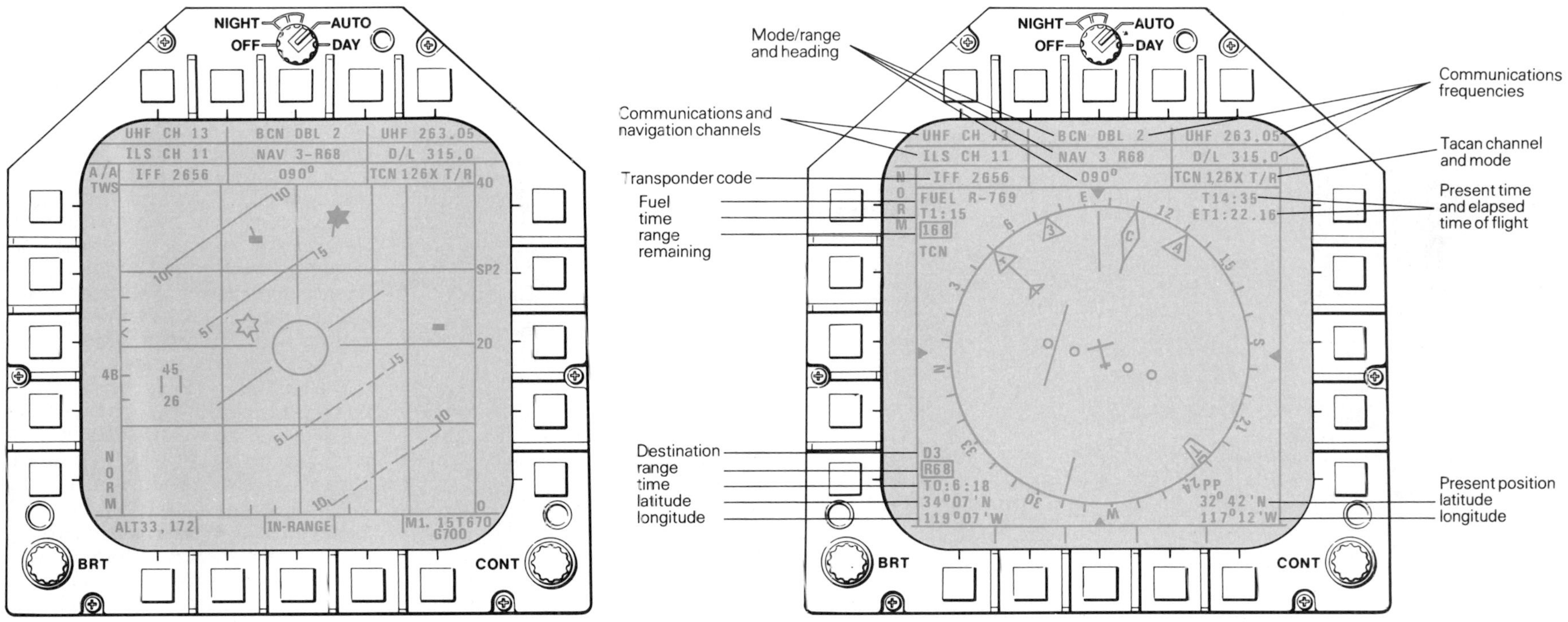

mode, out to a maximum of 80nm (147km). For Sidewinder, the search range automatically switches to 20nm (37km), with four-bar elevation scans and plus or minus 70deg in azimuth; while for guns, the search range reduces to 5nm (9km), with six-bar scans and plus or minus 45deg in azimuth. A check on the weapon selected is given on the HDDs.

The Automatic Lock-on selector is also three position and offers three modes for visual lock. These take the forms of: (1) a 3deg boresight circle on the HUD for pinpoint fly to lock-on; (2) a 20deg circle on the HUD, which gives rapid search and target acquisition within the HUD field of view; and (3) a vertical scan racetrack which opens off the top of the HUD. This is used for off-boresight lock-on, and the acquisition method used for a visual target is for the pilot to roll his aircraft until the target appears to be positioned directly above the centre of the front canopy arch. Tightening the turn then pulls the target (relatively speaking) down into the radar acquisition area, or even better, into the HUD field of view.

In all these modes target lock-on is automatic and is displayed on both the HUD and the MFD, and a 'shoot' symbol comes up on both displays when the electrons are satisfied that a satisfactory firing solution has been achieved for the weapon selected. Back-up is supplied by flashing light indicators for both lock and shoot on the top right-hand quadrant of the canopy arch. This is particularly useful when the off-boresight mode is being used, as the pilot will be visually tracking the target at a high angle-off well outside the HUD field of view in many cases.

The Target Designator Control (TDC) mounted on the left throttle is an isometric/force transducer switch which moves the designator symbol on the displays in any direction. To describe its function as simply as possible, if the pilot wishes to alter a radar mode or function, whether it be range, elevation, scan, mode, azimuth or whatever, he uses the switch to move the TDC brackets on the displays to cover whichever parameter he wishes to change, then operates the switch until the desired parameter appears. Alternatively, he can slew the brackets to cover a target symbol then, by pressing the button, designate and lock on to it. The TDC can also be used to alter the line of sight of the infra-red and laser sensors if they are carried.

Other combat-related components of the HOTAS system are the gun/missile trigger and air-to-ground weapon

Above: Typical cockpit displays. Top left is the radar display for the range-while-search mode, using high PRFs out to a distance of 80nm (147km). Top right is a stores management display, showing a bomb release programme for the six Mk 82 LD bombs; Harm and Sidewinder are also indicated. Bottom left is air-to-air track-while-scan radar mode, while bottom right is a sample horizontal situation and mission data display.

Below: Fighter pilots have always needed to fly with one hand on the throttles and the other on the control column, but as weapons and sensors grew more complex this became more difficult to achieve. The solution, pioneered on the F-15 and subsequently adopted for the F-18, is for all time-critical functions to be mounted on these controls, using the HOTAS (hands on throttle and stick) approach pioneered by the F-15.

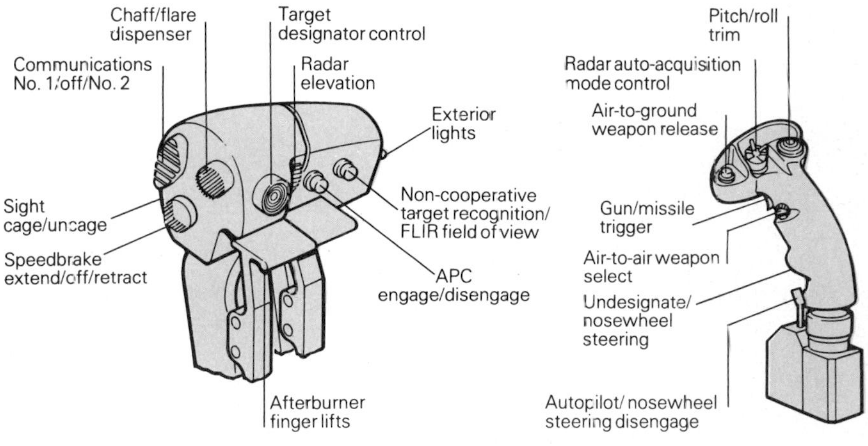

F/A-18 throttle and control stick

release switch which are mounted on the control column; the airbrake control; the infra-red seeker head cage/uncage button for the Sidewinders, which automatically slaves the IR sensor to the line of sight of the radar; a three-position communications selector switch; the three-position chaff/flare dispenser switch; and the radar elevation control, which are all on the left-hand throttle; and the non-co-operative target recognition/FLIR field of view control on the right throttle. Non-combat related functions are the autopilot/nosewheel steering disengage switch; the nosewheel steering cancel switch; and the pitch and roll trim, which are all on the control column; and the automatic power compensator engage/disengage switch (part of the automatic carrier landing system); exterior lighting switch; and finger lifts to engage ground idle power, all mounted on the throttles.

The pilot sits on a Martin Baker SJU-5/A ejection seat which is based on the tried and proven Mk 10. It provides a zero speed, zero altitude escape capability, and is effective up to 600kt (1,110km/h). Excellent all-round visibility is provided by a tear-drop shaped canopy made of laminated acrylic plastics. Visibility is possibly not quite as good as from the F-16, but there is little in it, and it is certainly good enough to make Fishbed and Flogger drivers suck their teeth. Oddly enough, two different manufacturers are involved, PPG Industries making the windshield while the canopy itself is from Swedlow.

The Hornet is more than just an aeroplane; it is a fine example of an integrated weapons system, and it is difficult to single out any one item as being particularly outstanding, especially as the degree of integration is such that almost everything seems interlocked with everything else. Having said that, the AN/APG-65 radar, manufactured by the Hughes Aircraft Company Radar Systems Group, is a fine piece of kit containing many advanced features never before incorporated in a tactical aircraft. The requirements were stringent: to produce a radar which lacked nothing in the air-to-air modes, and was equally good for navigation and air-to-ground functions; to be one-man operable and small enough to fit a medium-sized fighter; to be easily maintainable; and to have an unprecedented level of reliability, with a target MTBF of no less than 106 hours. Proposals were originally submitted by both Hughes and Westinghouse, with the Hughes design being selected at the end of 1977.

APG-65 radar

The APG-65 is a coherent pulse-Doppler radar operating in the X-band (8-12.5GHz), which is fairly standard for airborne radars as it requires a fairly small antenna – an important consideration when space is restricted, as it always is in fighters. Coherent pulse-Doppler radar dates back to the late 1950s, when the travelling wave tube (TWT) was developed.

The function of the TWT is to increase the level of power of a signal that is fed into it. Essentially, a radar sends out massive signals and gets minute ones back in return, and the more powerful the signal transmitted, the better the return. Using a signal from a continuously running coherent oscillator, the TWT produced pulses suitable for radar in which every pulse is exactly in phase with the preceding and following pulses. This enabled the Doppler shift – the observable frequency change when the range between the transmitter and the receiver is altering – to be used in radar for the first time.

One immediate advantage was that for the first time a low-flying aircraft could be detected against the ground returns, or radar echoes from the surface, since a moving target gives a shift in frequency returns which makes its echo different from the echoes bouncing back from the ground. Digital computers then sort out the echoes that are different. Most returns are likely to be shown to be moving in conformity with the flight path of the radar-carrying aircraft, and as these are in most cases the echoes from the ground, a threshold can be established, the unwanted returns filtered out, and only those which are not showing a Doppler shift which is in conformity with the flight path are presented on the radar display. These are likely to be targets.

In the air-to-air mode, the system contains two weaknesses. There is little point in detecting a horse and cart simply because it is moving, so a bottom limit must be set to the velocity of non-flight-path-conformal echoes. This is usually about 90mph (144km/h). Consequently, slow-flying machines such as helicopters can be filtered out, while very fast moving surface vehicles can be acquired. Furthermore, an aircraft flying at a right angle to the flight path is also likely to be filtered out, as its relative velocity will not exceed the threshold limit. Of course, this only applies to a radar searching downwards against the ground clutter; against a clear sky background it will not apply.

Pulse repetition frequency

A fundamental choice to be made with pulse-Doppler radar is the pulse repetition frequency (PRF). The range is wide: 100,000 transmitted pulses per second and upwards is classed as high PRF, while 1,000 pulses per second is low PRF. In between these extremes comes medium PRF, which, as we shall see, is very useful. High PRF has one great advantage: the greater the number of transmitted pulses per second, the higher the average power radiated, and the higher the average power, the greater the detection range. A high PRF waveform is also excellent at detecting a target coming in head-on with a high closing speed, but it is not so good at detecting targets with a low closure rate, such as would be encountered from the tail-on aspect with a low overtaking rate. Neither is it much good at measuring range; although a low degree of frequency modulation (FM) can be impressed on the pulse as a sort of identity tag, ranging information gained in this manner is not very accurate.

The inaccuracy inherent in measuring range in the high PRF mode stems from the short time lapse between each pulse. It is difficult to tell which pulse has engendered which echo, and ambi-

Left: The APG-65 radar runs out on rails for ease of access. The antenna uses electric drive, and the WRA modules are apparent.

Below: Much of the flight testing with the APG-65 radar was carried out by this specially modified T-39D Sabreliner. The picture at left is also of this aircraft.

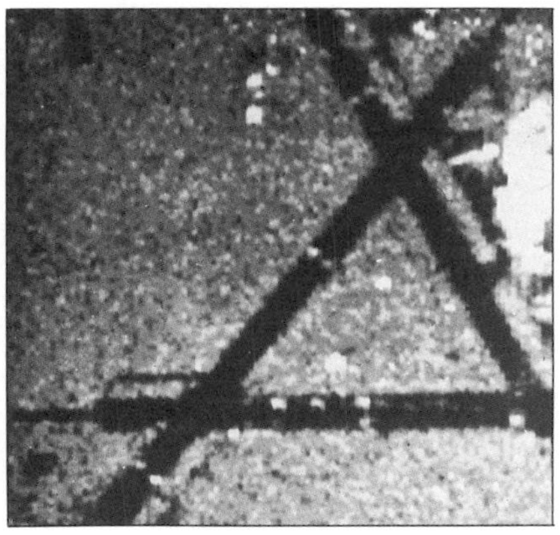

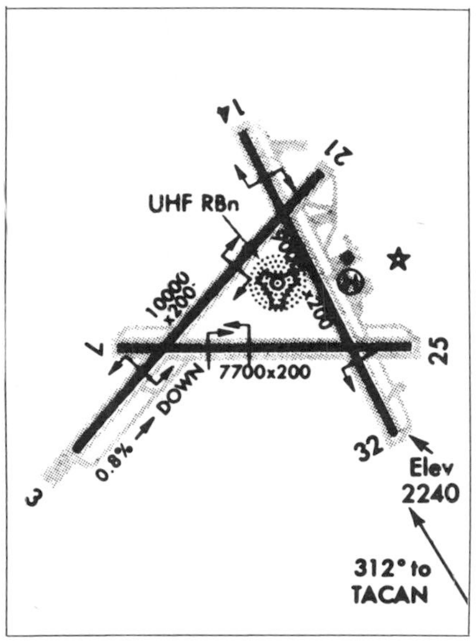

Above: Doppler beam sharpening techniques give excellent ground mapping resolution. Compare the upper picture of a DBS patch mode map with the airfield layout below it. Computer techniques are used to give a vertical picture.

guities arise in consequence. Low frequency PRF has much better ranging capability, the time lapse between pulses enabling a return to be received from a considerable distance before the next pulse is transmitted, which removes the ambiguity of high PRF.

A compromise solution of medium PRF was first used operationally in the F-15 radar, the APG-63. Medium PRF confers many advantages in the medium-range detection and accurate tracking of small, high-speed targets, the accuracy being sufficient to enable data for weapons delivery to be processed. In the APG-65, a medium PRF waveform is interleaved with high PRF. The medium PRF used is not a constant waveform, but a series of PRFs in the medium band. This in practice gives good average solutions to the problems posed by the varying velocities of different targets. The PRF variation is accomplished by the programmable gridded TWT.

The use of rapidly varying PRFs was made possible by the use, for the first time on a production fighter, of a programmable signal processor, which has the staggering ability to perform up to 7.2 million operations per second; what are called real time calculations. This allows incoming echoes to be sampled and analyzed to adjust and set the processing boundaries. Range gate and filter configurations are pre-programmed on software, unlike those of the APG-63, which give a fixed choice of selections. On the

Right: The USM-469 Radar Test System for the APG-65 radar installed at NAS Lemoore, California.

Below: The WRA modules in the APG-65 are designed for speed and ease of replacement in the field.

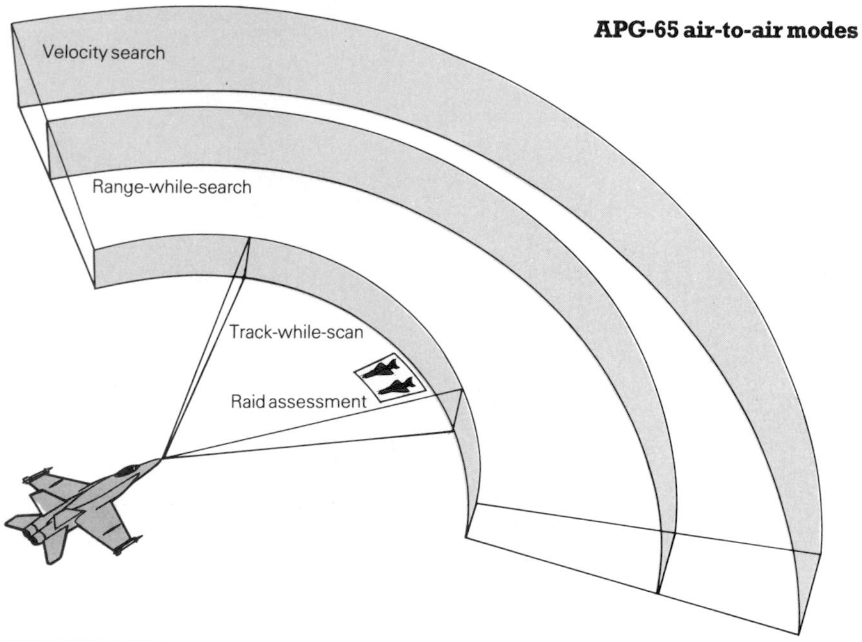

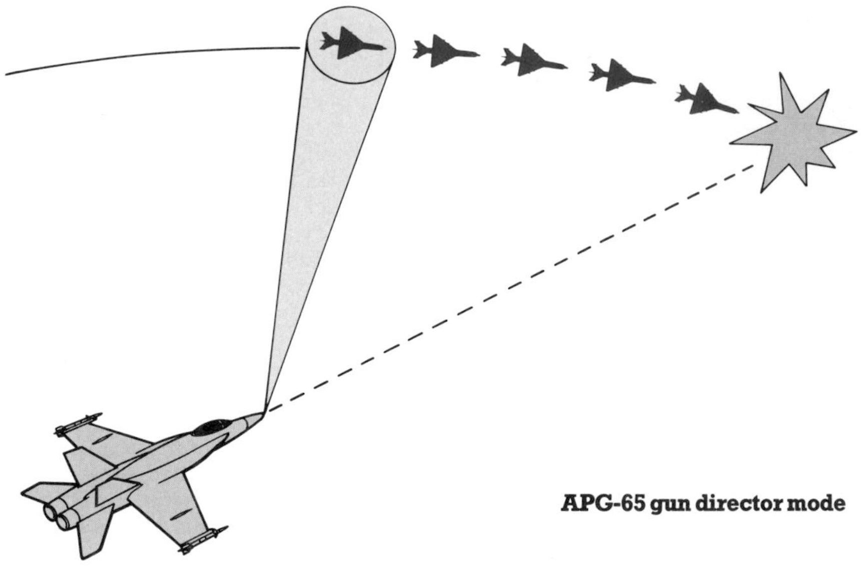

Hornet, if new modes are needed due to the requirements of new weapons or changes in the nature of a threat, or existing modes need modification, a software change will suffice.

The APG-65 is, considering its capability, remarkably small. It weighs just 340lb (154kg) excluding the rack, and its volume, excluding the antenna, is only 4.49cu ft (0.127m^3). It contains approximately 14,000 parts, compared with the 27,000 parts of the AWG-9 on the Tomcat, and on test it has exceeded its MTBF guarantee of 106 hours, which compares remarkably well with the in-service figure of 8.2 hours for the AWG-9. Modular for easy maintenance, like so much of the Hornet, it consists of five primary subsystems which are all known as weapon replaceable assemblies (WRAs).

Radar servicing

As in all the other systems, BITE is incorporated, and can detect 98 per cent of potential or actual failures and indicate in which WRA the malfunction exists. Any WRA can be substituted in 12 minutes. One great advantage of the WRAs is that they are all digital, and need no special alignment or adjustment when being fitted. For servicing, the dielectric radome (by Brunswick) swings open to the right, and the APG-65 can be run out on an extending track; the radar is fully operable even with the track extended.

The antenna is a fully balanced, low side-lobe slotted waveguide planar array, using direct electric drive, thus saving the weight and complexity of a hydraulic system. The transmitter contains the X-band gridded TWT, which alone among the WRAs is liquid-cooled to reduce both the necessary voltage and the thermal stresses, both of which reductions contribute to reliability. All other WRAs are air-cooled. The radar data processor stores instructions for the different operating modes on a floppy disc unit with a 256K 16-bit word capacity; on demand, the instructions are transmitted to a 16K capacity solid-state memory, which controls the operation of the radar.

The digital signal processor is the key element in the radar: without its real-time handling of the masses of incoming information, the entire sequence would fail. The receiver/exciter unit converts the incoming signals from analog to digital form; it consists of low-noise field effect transistor (FET) amplifiers, which give great reliability for low cost, a low-noise exciter with multiple channels, and the analog/digital converter.

The APG-65 carries out a great deal of work on its own programs, but the net

Above: Velocity search detects long-range closing targets; range-while-search detects all-aspect targets; and track-while-scan follows ten targets, displaying eight.

Above right: Gun director mode uses pulse-to-pulse frequency agility to track targets and set the correct lead for a gun attack.

Right: Three air combat manoeuvre modes are available, all of which provide automatic lock-on to the first target acquired. Top is boresight acquisition, centre is vertical acquisition, used against either a higher or a turning target, while bottom is head-up display acquisition, which covers the area directly ahead of the HUD and locks on to the first target detected. A 'step-through' facility is provided to allow the pilot to reject targets successively until he acquires the one he wants.

results still have to be presented to the pilot on the cockpit displays, partly with symbology and partly in alpha-numeric form. Gone are the days when the raw data was presented on the CRT in analog form, and the pilot or a second crew member had to exercise a great deal of expertise in deciphering what it all meant.

We have seen that the APG-65 is a very sophisticated piece of kit: precisely what can it do? Its mission modes fall into three basic categories, air-to-air, air-to-ground, and navigational functions, which also contain some capabilities that we have not so far examined. Air-to-air modes are:

Velocity search. This mode utilizes high PRF for long-range detection. As we have seen, high PRF works best at long range on rapidly closing targets. The priority for this mode is early detection of targets that are likely to pose a threat within a timespan measured in minutes, rather than those that are heading in an entirely different direction and will not become a threat unless a radical change of course is made. The information is presented to the pilot as azimuth and velocity only, in other words the direction the target is coming from, and how fast it is approaching.

Range while search mode uses both high and medium PRF waveforms to detect targets at all aspects and relative velocities out to about 80nm (150km) range. The high PRF pulses are FM coded for ranging while the medium PRF utilizes the range gate filtering incorporated in the PSP. The purpose of range while search is to detect anything out there, regardless of aspect, heading, velocity, or threat potential.

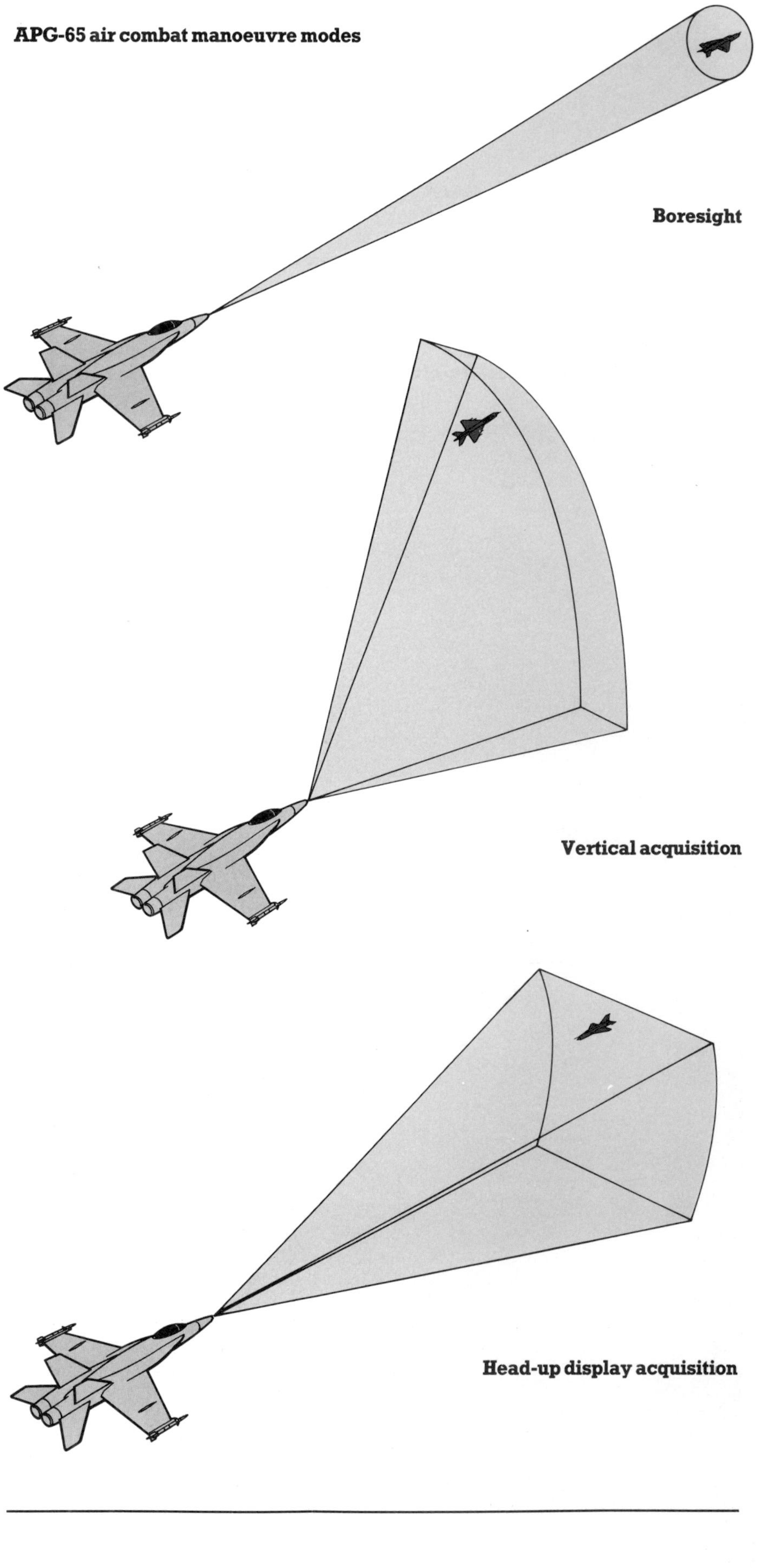

Right: The terrain avoidance mode coupled with precision velocity update confers a first-pass blind strike capability in the attack mode.

Far right: Doppler beam sharpening improves ground mapping; sector mode uses a 19:1 sharpening ratio, while patch mode uses a 67:1 ratio.

Below: High-resolution radar mapping modes greatly simplify navigation as well as target location and identification.

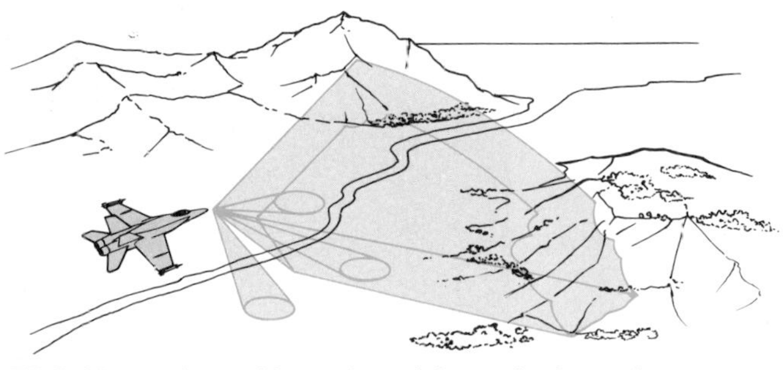
APG-65 terrain avoidance/precision velocity update

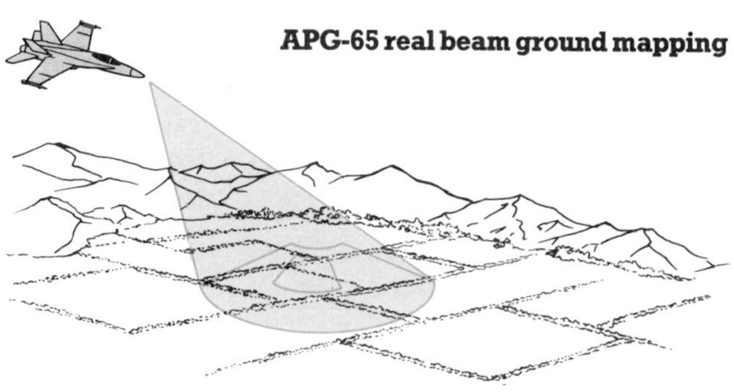
APG-65 real beam ground mapping

F/A-18 radar navigation and attack

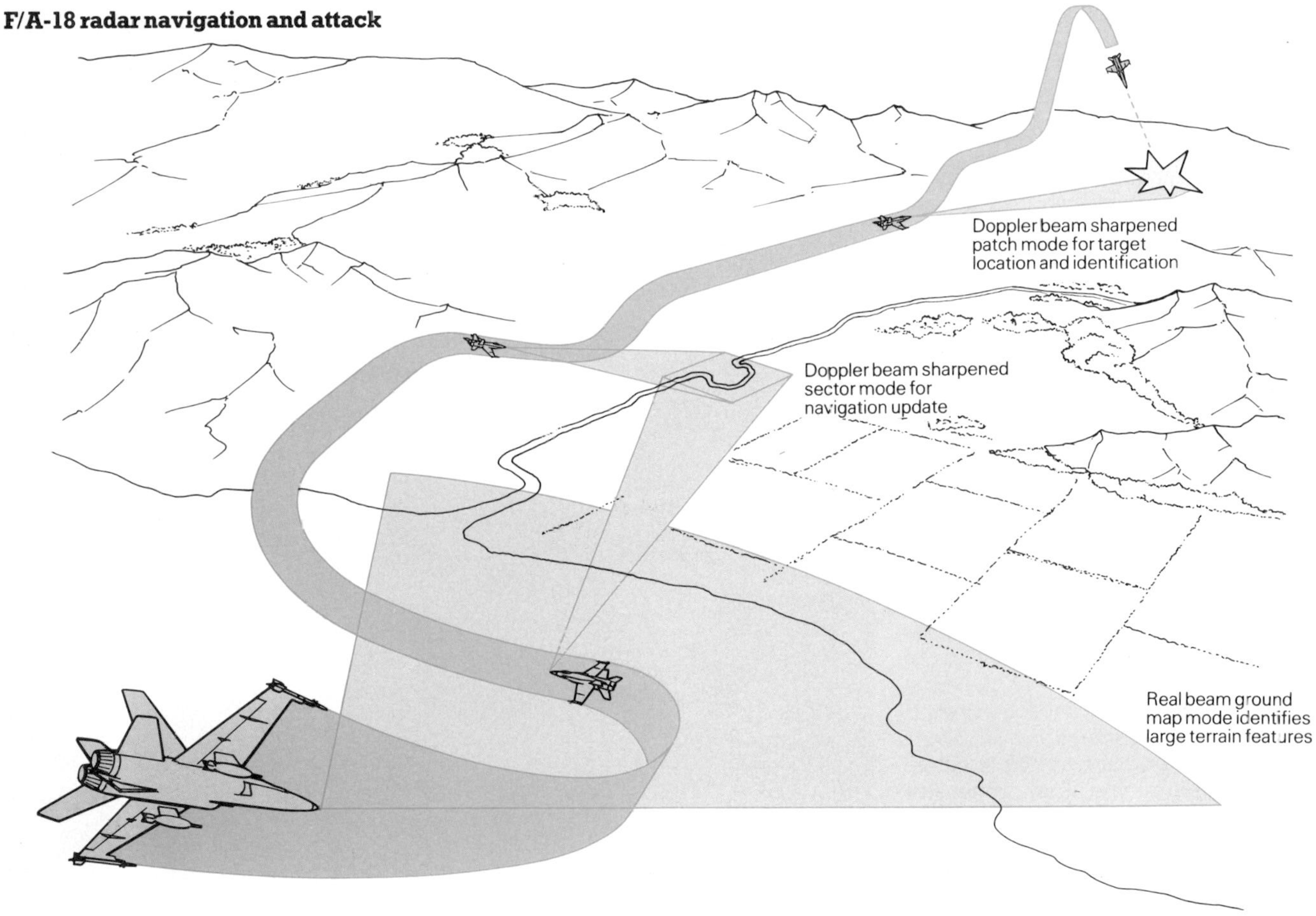

Track while scan is a medium PRF mode used during the closing phase at ranges below 40nm (75km). While not in the same league as the Tomcat's big AWG-9, the APG-65 has the more than useful ability of maintaining files on the tracks of ten separate targets, while displaying the eight most likely ones to the pilot, eight being considered the maximum number, in terms of workload, that the pilot can cope with. The aspect, altitude, and speed of the highest priority target, i.e., the greatest threat, is also displayed.

At some future date, the Hornet is to be equipped with the launch and leave AIM-120 AMRAAM (Advanced Medium Range Air-to-Air Missile). When this happens, it will provide the Hornet with the capability of engaging separate targets simultaneously.

Single target track mode is automatically cued on the HUD when the target comes within range while the radar is in the range while search mode. The pilot then switches to STT mode, which uses two-channel monopulse angle tracking able to follow the target through most manoeuvres, although computer logic is needed to extrapolate 180deg turns and Split-S and Immelmann type manoeuvres by the target. Provided only that the antenna gimbal limits are not exceeded, the radar should not break lock in the STT mode. Attack steering commands and data for weapon launch are shown on the HUD, while the velocity, aspect and altitude of the target are displayed on the MMD.

In addition to target tracking, the system continually computes launch parameters, and 'shoot' cues are displayed when a firing solution has been achieved. A special high pulse rate provides illumination for the semi-active radar homing (SARH) AIM-7 Sparrow missiles. As the range reduces to below 20nm (37km) the pilot has the option of using the heat-seeking Sidewinder, and uncaging the seeker head with the throttle-mounted switch slaves the IR sensor to the line of sight of the radar. A visual check of which target has been acquired, essential in a confused tactical situation, is provided on the HUD.

Raid assessment mode has been developed to solve the perennial problem of hostile aircraft flying in such close formation that radar discrimination is insufficiently sensitive to be able to separate them. In consequence, they appear on the display as one target. This is a matter of particular concern in the NATO defence area, and also the Middle East, where such 'bunching' tactics were brought to a fine art in 1973. In essence, the raid cannot be hidden, but the single blip gives no clues as to the composition of the force, and therefore allows no intelligent guesses to be made as to its intentions until the moment it splits up, which is generally far too late for effective counteraction to be taken.

The raid assessment mode, effective at ranges of up to 30nm (55km), provided that the enemy formation has a minimum separation between aircraft of about 500ft (150m), uses Doppler beam sharpening techniques based on expanding the area around a single target return to give increased resolution, which in turn should allow the radar to separate the individual components of a formation.

Air combat manoeuvre modes

These break down into three forms.

Boresight utilizes a narrow 3.3deg beam placed on a target which is within the boresight axis, or centreline, of the radar-carrying aircraft, the time-honoured method of pointing one's nose at the enemy, although in a manoeuvring engagement this is really of most use in the traditional pursuit attack from astern.

Vertical acquisition scans an arc 5.3deg wide by 60deg above boresight and 14deg below, once every two seconds, and is most useful for tracking a target when either the tracking aircraft or both it and the target are in a hard turn. The pilot rolls the Hornet into the same plane of motion as the target, positioning the target above the centre of the canopy arch. Vertical acquisition is most useful when both aircraft are turning hard with the target less than 60deg angle-off.

Head-up display acquisition is the third air combat mode. This scans the 20deg by 20deg field of view of the HUD, which is plus or minus 10deg in azimuth, and 14deg above boresight to 6deg below in elevation, once every two seconds.

In all these modes, which can be used over ranges varying between 500ft (150m) and 5nm (9km), the radar locks on to the first target acquired automatically, with visual cues indicating lock and shoot appearing on the CRT displays, the HUD, and via flashing lights on the canopy bow. Despite the automatic acquisition of targets, the pilot can always reject them in turn until he reaches the one he really wants; alternatively he can designate the target with the moveable cursor.

Gun director mode can be used for ranges of less than 5nm (9km) and the radar provides position, range and velocity data on the target, which drive the gun aiming point, or pipper, on the HUD. Glint, or erratic changes in the apparent radar centre of the target, which can under some circumstances move off the target altogether, is overcome to a large degree by the use of pulse-to-pulse frequency agility. This method also provides very accurate data for lead-angle prediction, simplifying high angle-off shooting; the pilot places the pipper on the target and presses the trigger. A conventional sight is used as back-up in the event of a malfunction.

The air-to-ground modes are no less impressive. In particular, the long-range surface mapping, using high resolution modes never previously incorporated in a tactical aircraft, is outstanding. To identify large geographical features from long distance, necessary, for example, when approaching a hostile coastline, the **real beam ground mapping** mode is used. This combines low PRF with pulse compression to confer long range, and non-coherent pulse to pulse frequency agility to avoid glint. The mode provides a rather crude small-scale radar map of the terrain ahead, from which large features such as river

Right: Pilot's eye view of the vertical acquisition mode. A target is seen (left) off to the right and turning. The pilot rolls his aircraft (centre) into the plane of motion of the target by positioning his aircraft in such a way as to make the target appear to be above the centre of his canopy bow. Acquisition should be automatic, but if a firing solution can not be achieved he tightens the turn, causing the target to appear to move down into the HUD. In this mode, the 5.3×74deg arc is scanned every two seconds.

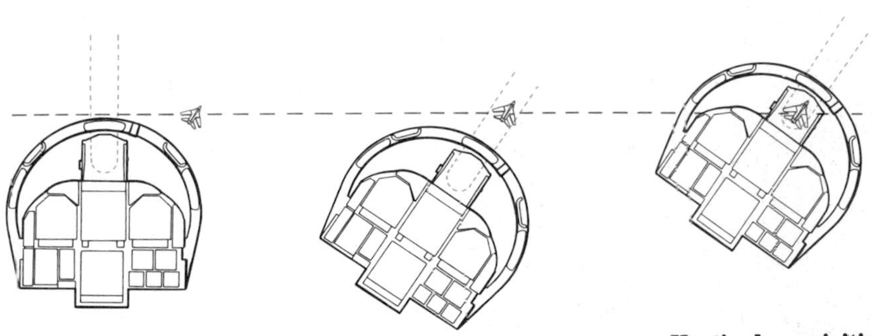
Vertical acquisition

estuaries can be readily identified. In all the ground-mapping modes, the display presentation is computer-adjusted to present the map from a vertical viewpoint rather than from the shallow angle obtained from the aircraft, which would give a distorted view and make recognition of features much more difficult. Other ground mapping modes give better resolution over smaller areas by using doppler beam sharpening (DBS). In the **DBS sector** mode, a beam sharpening ratio of 19:1 is used, while the **DBS patch** mode utilizes a 67:1 ratio.

Terrain avoidance mode is used for low-level strikes in poor visibility. An automatic terrain-following system would of course be far better but this is not a built-in capability; instead, terrain avoidance shows the pilot where the ground is, and it is then up to him to avoid it. Two sets of data are presented; one is the ground profile along the velocity vector of the aircraft (the direction in which it is travelling, which is not necessarily the same as the direction in which it is pointing), while the other shows the ground profile at a preset level below the direction of travel. Obstacles projecting through this preset level of clearance are clearly shown on the displays, which allows avoiding action to be taken. In a dive the terrain along the direction of travel is displayed, but in a climb the display shows the terrain parallel to the ground. This prevents the pilot from levelling out too soon in the event of there being a peak ahead of him.

Precision velocity update is another radar capability. It can be used to provide the Doppler input to the computer for weapon delivery, and also to improve navigation by updating the inertial platform of the INS for velocity errors. It also provides for in-flight alignment, although the demonstrated accuracy of the Litton ASN-130 INS, at 0.5nm per hour (far better than the specification requirement), is such that little correction is likely to be needed.

A carrier fighter perforce spends much of its time flying over water, and anti-shipping strikes are part of its function. To detect ships, **sea surface search** mode can be selected, although tracking is not a feature of this function. Radar clutter from the surface of the sea varies considerably according to the sea state (how rough it is). When the sea surface search mode is selected, the radar first samples the sea state. This is then analyzed by computer and a filter threshold is established to filter out the background clutter and present only those returns that do not conform, which are likely to be ships.

Other air-to-ground modes are concerned with ranging and attack. Either fixed or moving targets may be attacked, using two-channel monopulse angle tracking combined with coherent frequency agility, and ranging on designated targets is accomplished by one of two methods, depending on whether the depression angles are large or small. For large depression angles, split-gate range tracking is used, and monopulse tracking is used if the depression angles are small. A designated target is automatically acquired in this mode, which can also be used to provide ranging information when the target is designated by laser or infra-red means.

The outstanding reliability of the radar is no accident: from the outset it was a primary requirement, since it is obviously of little use to have the most capable radar in the world if it spends half its time in the repair shop. Simplicity of design was primary, as was an intensive test programme. Comprehensive testing during production is also used to detect potential or actual faults (infant mortality is the manufacturer's term) with both high and low temperature and exacting vibration conditions an integral part of the highly automated tests.

The specified requirement of 106

Right: View from the seat of the Sperry Operational Flight Trainer. Simulation is playing an increasingly important part in training pilots on new types. The realism here is excellent, apart from the fact that the pilot is not wearing gloves.

hours MTBF was met in June 1983, a whole year ahead of schedule. At this time, the requirement for the development stage achieved was only 85 hours MTBF, but as Hughes Program Reliability Manager Terry Rostker explained: "After we met that requirement, we decided to continue the test at our own risk to show that the radar can meet the mature system requirement of 106 hours MTBF (equivalent to 148 hours of failure-free running in the test chamber). At 149 hours, we stopped the tests to analyze the results and to review them with McDonnell Douglas and the Navy. Then an additional 54 hours of test were run to validate the highly successful demonstration."

The tests were stringent, to say the least. Each radar was sealed in an environmental chamber and subjected to a series of nine-hour operational cycles. Each nine-hour segment consisted of 90 minutes of cold soaking at −65deg F-(−54 deg C), followed by a further 90 minutes at −40deg F (−40deg C). The set was then switched on and allowed to warm up for just six minutes, before being continuously operated for six hours at temperatures of up to 160deg F (71deg C).

In line with the overall maintenance-free concept of the Hornet, the APG-65 requires no regular maintenance inspections, calibration, or adjustment. Only when a malfunction manifests itself does it receive any attention.

Radar Test System

An essential back-up to the APG-65 is the USM-469 Radar Test System (RTS), also designed by Hughes. When a fault is located through the Hornet's BITE, the affected WRA is removed from the aircraft and a fresh one installed. The faulty unit is connected to the RTS, whose operator keys in a test programme which is then run automatically. The problem is identified and presented on a visual display unit (VDU) which is part of the RTS, and if necessary a print-out is given. The faulty component is replaced by the operator, and the test programme is re-run as a check. The RTS also has a complete self-diagnostic facility which enables it to check itself to ensure that it is functioning correctly.

The APG-65 has automatic electronic counter-countermeasures (ECCM) built into all the operating modes, and the set is designed to resist hostile jamming. Frequency agility plays a large part in this capability but some of it is managed through the software. An advertised advantage is that the software can be rapidly reprogrammed to meet changing threats. From a practical point of view, this can be done quite easily, but it does contain a problem from the com-

Above: Air combat is simulated in the Hughes Weapons Tactics Trainer, in which the fledgling Hornet pilot spends about 50 hours. Consisting of two domes, each containing a Hornet cockpit, the WTT enables trainees to fly against each other or the computer.

Left: The first night landing is one of the less dull moments in a Navy pilot's life. Simulated carrier landings and takeoffs, coupled with emergency procedures, ensure that the pilot is as well prepared as possible.

Right: Like all USN and USMC combat aircraft, the Hornet is equipped with the ALE-39 countermeasures dispenser system. A total of 30 rapid-bloom chaff, flare and jamming cartridges are carried in each of the two dispensers mounted just behind the inlets on the underside of the Hornet's fuselage.

mand point of view. The question must arise: who decides the priorities? Is it the higher echelons of command who, with masses of data at their disposal for analysis, make a considered, global judgement, then alter all modes in a standard way for all units; or should it be the commander on the spot, who has just become aware of a major threat change and wishes to counter it before tomorrow morning's strike is launched? The question is complicated by the fact that not only would the aircraft program need alteration, but the RTSs would also need adjustments in order to be able to continue their checking functions.

Central computers

The total computer memory requirement of the Hornet was 741K 16-bit words at the outset, with room for growth. This is almost half as large again as the capacity of the F-15, which has some 500K words at its disposal. In total, the Hornet contains more than two dozen computers, which fall into two basic regimes, sensor-related and mission-related. The sensor-related computers are concerned with detection and navigation, while the mission-related computers concentrate on weapon delivery and display management.

At the heart of the Hornet's avionics are two Control Data Corporation AYK-14 mission computers, each with a 64K core memory capacity, one of which handles navigation and support while the other concentrates on weapon delivery. Should one fail, and battle damage is always a possibility to be reckoned with, the other can provide sufficient backup to give a 'fight your way home' service. They also control the multiplex bus system which consists of three channels, each containing two multiplex buses, one of which is active while the other is redundant. Two of the channels connect with other avionic systems, while the third connects the two mission computers.

Clever avionics are essential to the operational capability of the Hornet, and the software, with its own development programme running parallel to that of the aircraft, is a subject on its own. It is, for example, used to auto-release air-to-ground weapons in situations where the pilot of a Corsair would be busy hitting rows of switches on a console. The same software principle applies to the navigation and communication systems, the Automatic Carrier Landing System (ACLS), the Litton Industries ASN-130 Inertial Navigation System (INS), etc.

Threat warning is provided by the Itek ALR-67 Radar Warning Receiver (RWR), which is able not only to locate but also to identify the threat by checking its emission characteristics against a memory bank, then presenting it on a cockpit display. Electronic countermeasures are also built in. Full ECM details are naturally not available, but it is to be expected that the standard forms such as barrage jamming, range-gate stealing, and other deception jamming measures are incorporated. Once the receiver detects the presence of a hostile radar which appears to present a threat (which is half the battle), its emissions are then compared with those of known threats and identified. Further processing reveals which emission appears to pose the greatest threat, and countermeasures are automatically instituted. Passive countermeasures are also fitted, in the form of the Tracor ALE-40 flare and chaff dispenser.

The pilot must be kept warm (or cocl) in his cockpit, which must also be

Above: In the attack role the Hornet carries the AAS-38 FLIR pod on the port Sparrow station. Using thermal imagery, this produces a picture on the cockpit MMD of terrain or targets at night. Definition is remarkably sharp, as evidenced by this series of pictures of a US Navy amphibious assault ship.

Above: The FLIR pod in position on FSD Hornet 7. The optical head rotates and swivels automatically to follow a designated target.

pressurized: failure to keep within the set limits would lead very quickly to pilot failure. Much the same principle applies to the avionics, and many failures are caused by high operating temperatures. Avionics cooling lies within the field of the environmental control system, and the original specification for cooling air to the avionics required it to be delivered at a temperature of 62deg F (17.7deg C) at altitudes up to 30,000ft (9,150m), with a proportionate decrease at 42,500ft (12,950m) to zero degrees F (−17.8deg C).

In practice, these limits were improved considerably, and the temperatures of avionics microcircuit junctions ran at up to 95deg F (35deg C) cooler than their specified operating temperatures, making a direct contribution to systems reliability. Another factor which directly improved reliability and helped to keep operating temperatures down was the fact that many components were derated, some operating on as little as 15 per cent of their design power level. For example, the radar has a range performance comparable to that of the much larger APG-63, yet it operates at less than half of the peak transmitter power level.

FLIR and laser pods

In the attack role, two avionics pods can be carried in the positions otherwise occupied by the two Sparrows. These are the Ford Aerospace AAS-38 forward-looking infra-red (FLIR) pod, and the Martin-Marietta Laser Spot Tracker/Strike Camera (LST/SCAM). The FLIR pod flight testing on the Hornet was completed by December 1981. It provides a round-the-clock bad weather attack capability by providing the pilot with a picture of the terrain over which he is flying in conditions too bad for visual target acquisition.

To locate the target, the pilot initially selects a field of view 12deg×12deg, along a line of sight which can be varied between 30deg up and 150deg down. The pilot also has the freedom to roll up to 540deg either way before the system gives up and sulks. The area thus surveyed is presented at apparent actual size on the MMD by thermal imagery, the equipment receiving infra-red impulses (it should be noted that infra-red is just another electromagnetic wavelength, slightly above the level of visual light) and converting the energy into a televisual format electrical impulse. In this form it is displayed on the MMD as a picture of the object being observed, with remarkably clear definition. A function is also included to ensure that the image displayed in the cockpit appears the right way up, i.e., as the pilot would normally see it.

When a target is identified, the field of view can be closed down to 3deg×3deg, which gives an image magnification of about four times, although ×10 magnification has been experimented with. The auto-tracker can then be engaged, and the AAS-38, which is integrated with both the avionics and the mission computer, presents accurate data for the calculation of weapon release solutions. The optical head can also see the target after the aircraft has passed over it, giving it the capacity for assessing the weapon's effectiveness, and in the event of the target being a bridge or other fixed, known location the FLIR pod can be used to update the navigation system.

The AAS-38 is small, 13in (33cm) in diameter, 6ft (1.83m) long and just 340lb (154kg) in weight. Like much else on the Hornet it is modular (with 10 components), easily maintainable and has a very high MTBF. It is planned to expand the AAS-38 to incorporate a laser designator/ranger in the pod, and provision has been made to accommodate the transceiver, pulse-forming network, and necessary power supply.

The LST/SCAM pod has a dual function. It searches for, acquires and then tracks laser pulse-coded energy from a pre-designated target, thus giving a bad weather/visibility first pass strike capability. It allows the target to be acquired from beyond visual range, and provides for speedy acquisition during a manoeuvring, defence-evading approach. Once the target is acquired, the LST passes data to the mission computer, which in turn presents a visual indication of the target's position, on the HUD. At the same time, aiming and weapon release information is presented.

The SCAM part of the pod uses a 35mm Perkin-Elmer panoramic camera. Directed by the mission computer, this covers the target area before, during and after the attack. The LST/SCAM pod is longer but narrower and lighter than the FLIR pod, being 8in (20cm) in diameter, 7ft 6in (2.29m) long and only 162lb (73kg) in weight.

Below and below right: The LST/SCAM pod occupies the starboard fuselage station. The crewman is fitting the pod's WRA-203 centre section.

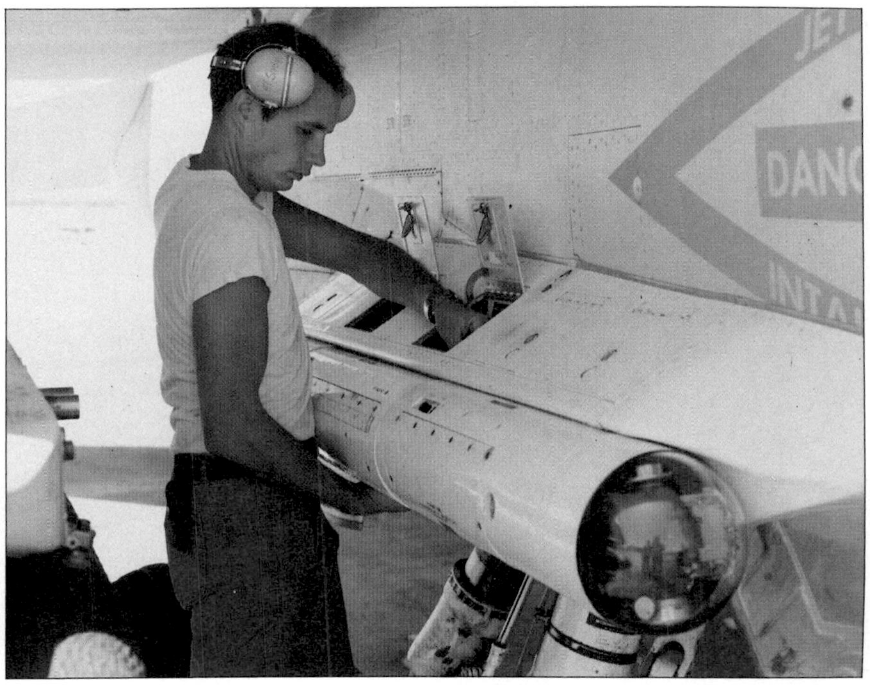

Armament

Like its insect namesake, the Hornet carries a vicious sting. For the air-to-air role it has Sparrow and Sidewinder missiles and a 20mm Vulcan cannon, and it will eventually be equipped with the launch-and-leave AMRAAM. For the air-to-ground mission it can carry a wide variety of ordnance to match the task in hand, from laser-guided weapons to old-fashioned iron bombs, while for anti-shipping strikes specialized weapons such as Harpoon are available. While none of these is unusual, the Hornet really scores as a true multi-role fighter, rather than a fighter dressed out for alternative tasks.

Despite the return to fashion of the aircraft gun, missiles are the primary weapons of the modern fighter in air-to-air combat. Missiles have a chequered history, and have been the source of many misconceptions and misunderstandings. Before examining the weapons relevant to the Hornet, perhaps we should take a brief overview of the entire subject.

For a start, the term 'guided missiles' has found wide currency in the argot of aviation. This is a misnomer. Very few missiles are in fact guided, which term implies positive control by the firer, and the air-to-air missiles carried by the Hornet certainly do not come into this category. Homing missiles, or target-following missiles would be a more accurate description.

To digress briefly, missiles that can manoeuvre to follow their targets seem to have caused a certain amount of confusion in the United States in their early days, as the first manoeuvring air-to-air missile in the world to enter service, the AIM-4 Falcon, was originally allotted an experimental fighter designation as the XF-98. There was, of course, some justification for this; Hughes Aircraft had for all practical purposes created a small pilotless kamikaze aeroplane!

A myth widely disseminated in the early days of homing missiles was that they would obviate the need for manoeuvring combat between fighters. Future air encounters were to be fought at long range, with the victory going to the side which detected the enemy earliest, got into position first, deployed the longest-ranged weapons and had the best countermeasures. War in the air was to become a war of technology: the new missiles would manoeuvre unerringly in tracking down their targets, and they could not be out-run except at the very limit of their range, and then only in the unlikely event of their being detected in time. But as Admiral of the Fleet Lord Fisher commented at the start of the century, "The best scale for an experiment is 12 inches to the foot!" And so it was to prove: experience was to show that the elaborate theorizing had been almost entirely wrong.

Let us take a brief look at the characteristics common to almost all homing missiles. They are rocket-propelled, and are accelerated to a very high speed within a few seconds, after which they coast along, gradually losing speed until finally control is lost, when they either explode at the end of their run or fall harmlessly (from the opposing pilot's viewpoint) to the earth. For most of their travel they are too fast to be outrun, so, leaving aside countermeasures for the moment, evasive action is the only recourse.

In the long-gone days when guns were the only effective air-to-air weapon, a standard method of evasion was to dip the nose of the aircraft and accelerate away out of range. Against

Above: Close-up of the large and drag-inducing twin store rack and pylon as armourers practice bombing up a Hornet at sea. The bombs do not yet have fuzes attached.

Below: A Canadian Armed Forces CF-18 carries eight BL-755 cluster bombs on its four underwing pylons.

missiles, with effective ranges measured in miles, this was futile. The new homing missiles had not ended manoeuvring combat; rather, they had made manoeuvre much more important. Yet the missiles were supposed to be able to out-manoeuvre the fighters. This idea appears to have arisen from the fact that some missiles were advertised as being able to perform 30g turns, whereas fighters were designed to a limit of 7g or a little over.

There are three ways of measuring turning ability. One is in multiples of acceleration, or g; a second is in terms of radius of turn, measured in linear distance; while the third is in rate of turn, expressed in degrees per second. As turning performance is a function of speed, the number of gs that can be pulled is largely irrelevant. The quoted 30g is for a very high velocity only, and as the velocity of the missile decays, so does its ability to manoeuvre. In this it is like an aircraft, but a much more extreme case.

Missile versus aircraft

Major John Boyd's concept of energy manoeuvrability applies to missiles exactly as it does to fighters. A missile travelling at Mach 4 at the tropopause and describing a 30g turn would have a radius of turn of about 14,600ft (4,450m) and a rate of turn slightly exceeding 14deg/sec. By comparison, a fighter flying at its 'corner velocity' – the point where its turning ability is best, or about 400kt (737km/h) – can turn on a radius of only 8,180ft (2,494m) with a mere 2g acceleration, and achieve a turn rate of 16deg/sec at 6g. Naturally, the missile does not necessarily have to match either the turn radius or turn rate of its target, as it can cut the corner, but having to manoeuvre bleeds off energy and reduces its further capability, while at the same time the difficulties of tracking are greatly multiplied. This, of course, applies to a missile coming in from the stern quadrant of the target; from any other direction an energetic manoeuvre may easily take the target outside the missile's flight envelope.

Missiles perform simple tasks best, so the role of the pilot of the target aircraft is to make himself as difficult to hit as possible. Discounting countermeasures for the moment, he does this by generating as much angle-off as he can and hopefully puts himself outside the missile's reach. If he either knows or suspects that the missile tracking him is a heat-seeker, he will attempt to shield his hot exhaust behind the cooler body of his machine.

To summarize, missiles are not yet ten feet tall. Like aeroplanes, they have clearly defined flight performance envelopes, and a pilot under attack will often survive if he can draw it either beyond the limits of the envelope or out toward the boundaries where it will perform less well. The really clever part is knowing when he is under attack, particularly from BVR (beyond visual range) missiles.

While missiles have flight performance envelopes, these are conditioned to a large extent by the relative speeds and aspects of the launching aircraft and its target, so that performance data that is generally available must be qualified. For example, speed is generally stated in terms of Mach number, but many factors affect this, including the velocity of the launching fighter and the altitude at launch. Ideally, the launching fighter should be flying as fast as possible at launch to impart as much of its own velocity, and thus energy, to the missile, in this way maximizing the total energy of the missile at motor burn-out. This in turn will increase range and also kill probability (P_k), especially with BVR weapons.

Launch at low altitude will not only reduce the speed of the launching aircraft, and thus the amount of extra energy that it can impart, but also the maximum velocity of the missile. The air at low level is denser, creating more drag, and the higher pressure on the backchamber of the missile will decrease thrust. Maximum speed data for missiles should therefore be viewed with caution, as, for the same reasons, should flight-time and range.

Still other factors affect speed and range. An obvious example arises in the case of a missile being launched at a target high above, when the missile has to use a considerable portion of its energy in lifting itself to a great height, instead of propelling it as far and as fast as possible, although this is to a small extent offset by the benefits of falling air pressure on the backchamber and reducing drag as the altitude increases and the air gets thinner.

Above: FSD Hornet 7 launches a Sparrow during early armament trials at NAS Patuxent River. Sparrow confers a BVR kill capability.

Right: AMRAAM is a launch-and-leave missile using inertial guidance for the midflight phase and active radar terminal homing.

Right: Target speed and relative heading vary an air-to-air missile's launch envelope considerably – by 10nm in this example.

Below: Three types of missile homing: AMRAAM (top), Sparrow (centre) and Sidewinder.

AIM-120 AMRAAM

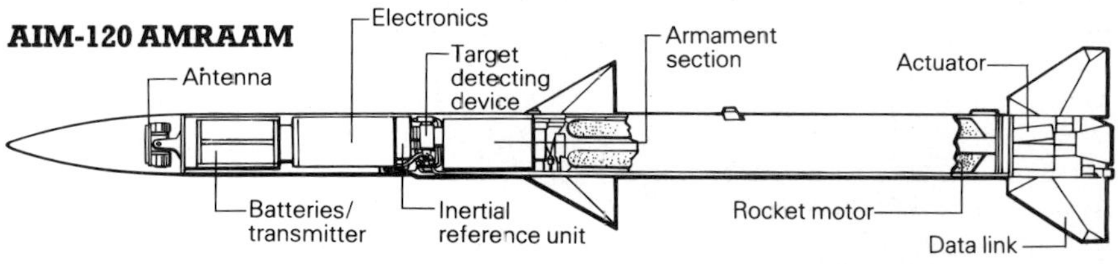

Semi-active radar homing missile attack ranges

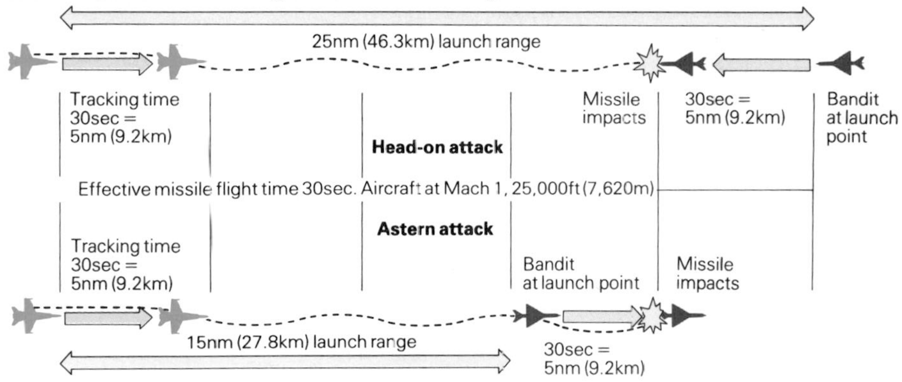

Missile homing methods

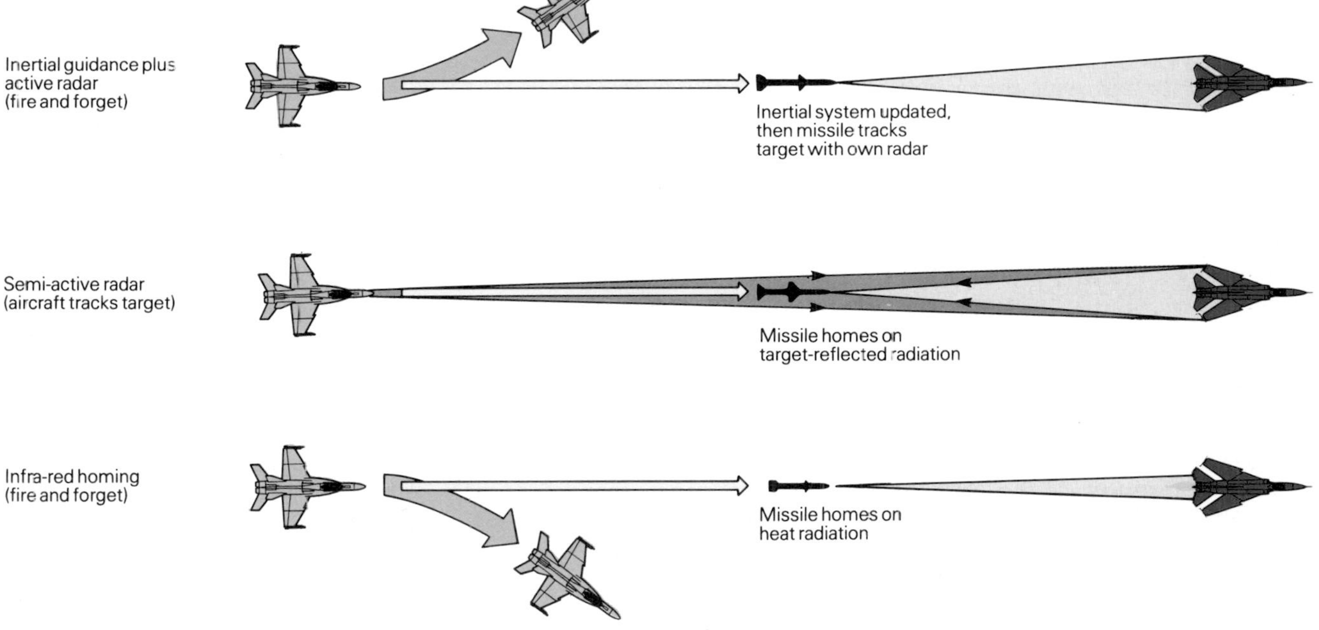

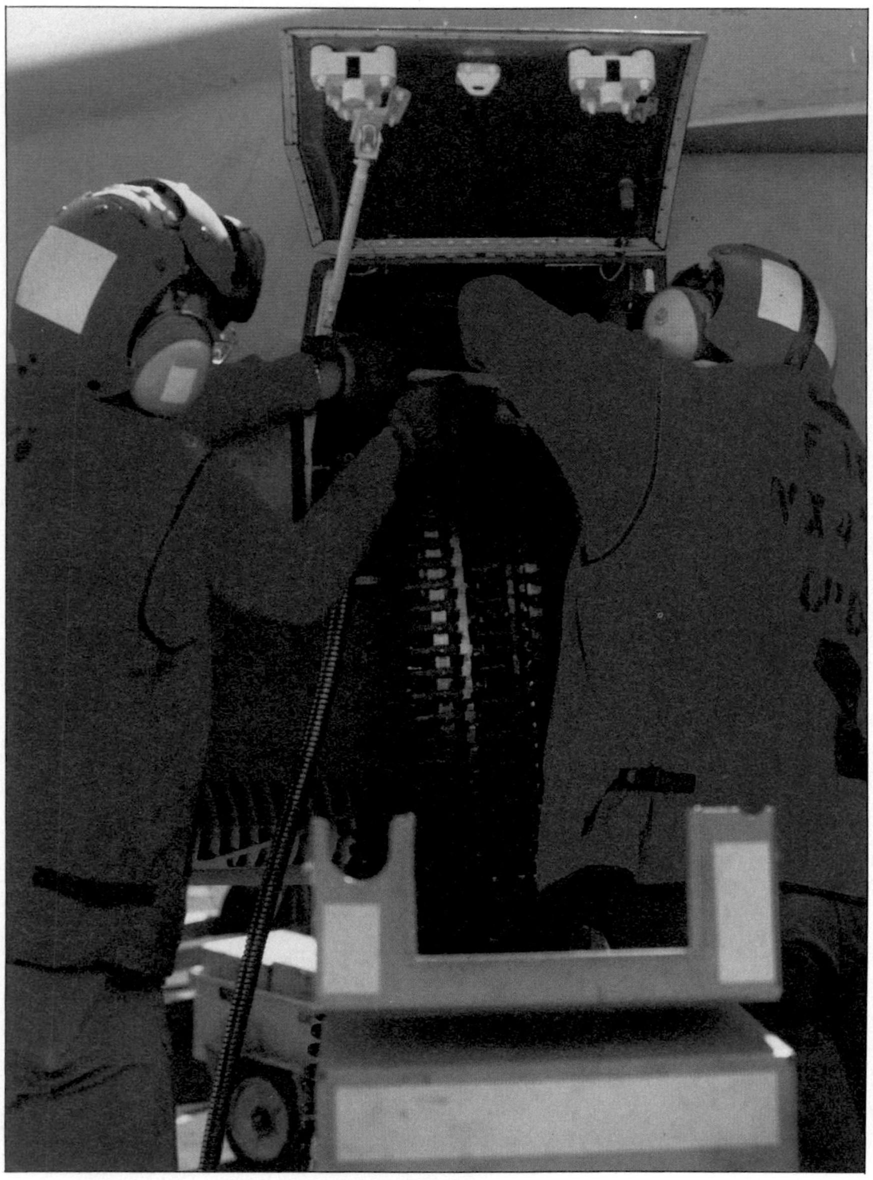

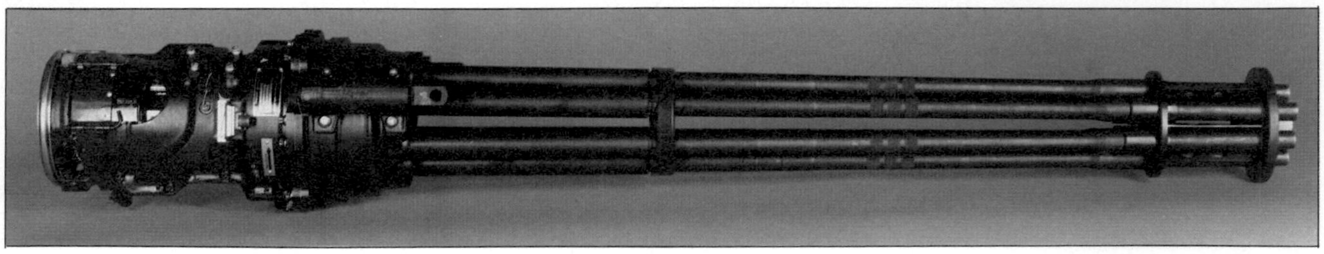

Above: Ears protected against noise and heads helmeted against hard edges, armourers reload a Hornet's M61 Vulcan cannon.

Right: The six barrels of the M61 give a maximum rate of fire of 100 rounds per second and help achieve a high degree of reliability.

Range is generally stated in terms of distance, which is a fixed measurement, but since a missile is launched from a dynamic object at a dynamic target this can be very misleading. If we compare hypothetical cases of head-on and stern-on attacks using a missile with a flight time of 30 seconds and a static range of 20nm (37km), given a target velocity of Mach 1 in both cases, and provided the homing system is up to the task, the missile can be launched against the head-on target while it is still 25nm (46km) away, whereas from astern the missile must be launched at a maximum range of 15nm (28km) to allow it to overhaul the target. The difference is the distance that the target moves during the time of flight. Launch range parameters are thus almost infinitely variable, depending on comparative aircraft velocities, aspects, headings and, of course, relative altitudes.

M61 hit probability

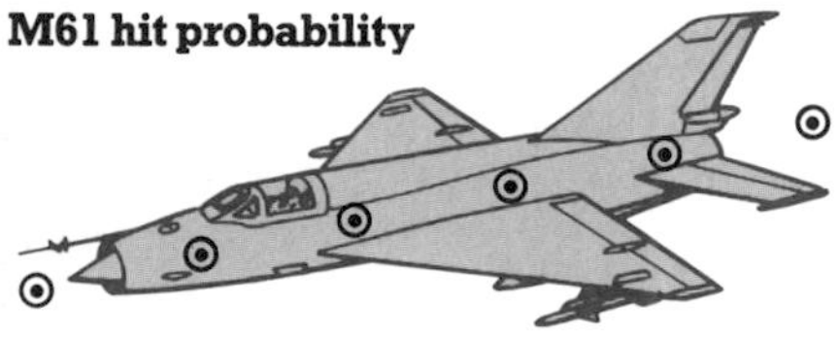

Above: A MiG-21 at 500kt (921km/h) and 90deg angle-off should be hit at least four times by an accurately aimed burst from a Vulcan.

F-18 nose gun and radar installation

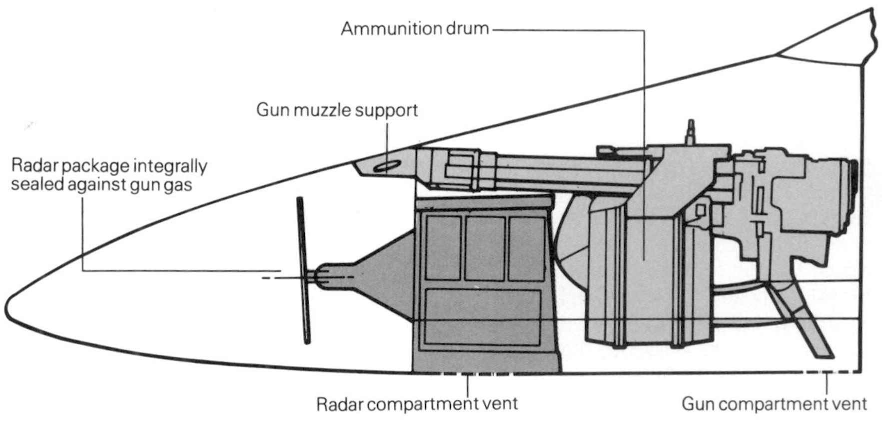

Right: The close proximity of the M61 cannon and the radar equipment in the nose of the Hornet required some very clever design work to damp antenna vibration down to an acceptable 30 g during gun firing.

AIM-7 Sparrow

The primary air-to-air weapon of the Hornet is the AIM-7F Sparrow, and probably in the future the AIM-7M. A semi-active radar homer, conferring the ability to engage targets from beyond visual range, Sparrow originated nearly 40 years ago as Project Hot Shot for the US Navy. Since that time it has been continually up-graded and improved to the extent that it represents one of the biggest missile programmes in history, with a projected grand total approaching 55,000 of all variants built by the time production ends.

Sparrow saw extensive service in Vietnam, although its BVR capability was severely curtailed following a couple of unfortunate 'own goals' in the early days. This was not a reflection on the capabilities of Sparrow, merely an indication of the inadequacy of the electronic identification methods of those days. At first, a strict insistence on visual target identification prevailed, although subsequently Sparrow BVR attacks were allowed under strictly controlled conditions. Modern identification systems have improved considerably, although it remains possible that operational restrictions will have to be imposed on BVR attacks in certain situations.

Sparrow offers many operational advantages. While it is hardly sporting, the ability to kill from medium to long range, and certainly from beyond visual distance, has obvious attractions. It also finally nails the old myth about the chivalry of the air, which in truth has never really existed. Air combat is and has always been a matter of creeping up unseen and shooting one's adversary in the back. Victory goes not to the bravest or the strongest, as the old legends would have us believe, but generally to the sneakiest, and few weapons are more sneaky than Sparrow, which comes hurtling in out of nowhere, fired by an unseen assailant.

Used in conjunction with the parent fighter's pulse-Doppler radar, which illuminates the target with the radar impulses whose echoes the Sparrow homes on, the missile is at its best against a head-on target with a high closing rate. As was sometimes the case in Vietnam, opposing fighters are forced to run the Sparrow gauntlet before they can close the range to a point where they can fight back. A classic instance of this took place near Yen Bai on the morning of May 10, 1972, when the four Phantoms of Oyster Flight took out two of four intercepting MiG-21s before closing to visual distance.

Sparrow has come in for heavy criticism in recent years because its SARH system demands that the parent fighter

illuminate the target with its radar during the entire homing phase. A second, and far more valid criticism is that it forces the pilot to concentrate on one target to the exclusion of all others. But to return to the first point, the launch aircraft, having fired a Sparrow, has to fly a more or less head-on course towards the target to illuminate it. The supposedly inevitable consequence is that the target makes a visual sighting just before the Sparrow blows it from the sky, and fires a launch-and-leave missile of its own, the destruction of the target being followed in short order by the destruction of its attacker.

Even with the advantage of numerical superiority, swapping one for one is not a good way to fight a war; it certainly does nothing for a pilot's morale. But while the argument has a great deal of merit, it seems unreasonable to assume that a one-for-one swap will be the outcome in a majority of cases, even though it must be admitted that the risk does exist. There must be many cases when the target will be splashed without seeing its assailant, particularly when there is a great height disparity between the two, and especially when the Sparrow has been launched from a lower level. A beam or front quarter attack would also reduce the possibility considerably.

In this connection, the Hornet is a fairly small aeroplane with smokeless engines and, very importantly, small engine intakes tucked away beneath the wings. It is a very difficult aeroplane to spot from head-on. And in mediocre weather visual acquisition will be even more difficult. Much of the case against Sparrow arose from the AIMVAL/ACEVAL series of exercises, which were held in Nevada, where the climate and visibility are near perfect for much of the time.

Nevertheless, there can be no doubt that having to illuminate the target with radar for relatively long periods is tactically undesirable, the illuminating fighter being visible and predictable for far too long. Using the radar for protracted periods is like lighting a huge electronic beacon in the sky saying, "This is where I am, this is who I am, and this is what I am doing". There can be no doubt that a BVR launch-and-leave weapon would be preferable to Sparrow, but to look at the positive side, Sparrow does confer genuine BVR capability.

Psychological impact

Another positive aspect, which unfortunately cannot be quantified, arises from the emissions that accompany a Sparrow launch. The chances are that the RWR of the target has warned the pilot that a Sparrow-type radar is locked on to him, as it can detect when a hostile radar changes from search to attack mode, but he has no way of knowing whether a missile has been launched or not.

There is an element of psychological warfare here: the pilot of the target (or group of pilots in close formation) will feel threatened by the radar emissions, which may tend to lower their mission effectiveness. While the launch-and-leave weapon is tactically preferable as a weapon, it can have no such effect, although one psychological effect common to all BVR weapons is the bolt from the blue, when one of the formation is suddenly blown away without any prior warning. Even the sight of a big Sparrow steaming past in the event of a near miss will hardly be reassuring.

The Sparrow is a big missile. It is 8in (20cm) in diameter and 12ft (3.66m) long, with a 3ft 4in (1.02m) span. Maximum speed is about Mach 4, and the stated range of the AIM-7F is 62 miles (100km). One telling comment on the missile's size was provided by a paper study done a few years ago to assess the effect of equipping the F-5E to carry it, when the general effect was described as "like putting an anchor on the airplane". The Hornet, however, is large enough and powerful enough to carry it with no problems.

Above: FSD Hornet 8 during gun firing trials in April 1980. Unusually for a modern fighter, the cannon is located just above the aircraft centreline. This is as close to the ideal position as the radar allows.

Below: A Hornet of VMFA-314 Black Knights lets fly with a Sidewinder from the starboard wingtip rail. Previously equipped with F-4Ns, the Black Knights converted to the Hornet in March 1984 and are assigned to CVW-13 on USS *Coral Sea*.

Left: FSD Hornet 7 configured for the attack mission, with three Paveway laser-guided bombs and an AGM-84 Harpoon on pylons, Sidewinders on the wingtips and fuselage FLIR and LST/SCAM pods.

First introduced in 1977, the AIM-7F Sparrow has Raytheon solid-state guidance with a conical scan seeker head. Propulsion is by the Hercules Mk 58 solid fuel motor, and the warhead consists of 88lb (40kg) of high explosive, contained in a drum made from a continuous stainless steel rod which shatters into about 2,600 fragments on detonation. With these tiny, high-velocity fragments flying about, the probability of lethal damage being caused to the target is very high. Detonation is triggered either by impact or by proximity fuze.

The latest Sparrow variant is the AIM-7M, which is fitted with an inverse monopulse seeker and a digital signal processor, which should give improved look-down and ECCM capability. Also featured are a new autopilot and a new fuze. Hornet will carry the AIM-7F at first, but is expected to convert to the AIM-7M at some future date.

To counteract the shortcomings of Sparrow, the AIM-120 AMRAAM was developed by Hughes. A launch-and-leave missile, it initially flies towards its target using inertial mid-course guidance, then activates its own X-band radar seeker in the nose for the terminal phase of flight. As there is no necessity for the parent fighter to illuminate the target, this missile will give the Hornet a multi-shot capability, engaging more than one target simultaneously rather than having the radar concentrate on one target to the exclusion of all else. AMRAAM has successfully demonstrated a look-down capability in test firings, but little firm information is available. Its overall dimensions are similar to those of Sparrow, but at 326lb (148kg), it is much lighter. Maximum speed is estimated to be about Mach 4, and its range is believed to exceed 30nm (55km).

AIM-9 Sidewinder

The AIM-9L Sidewinder carried by the Hornet is almost certainly one of the last variants of a very long line dating back to 1949. It started life as a simple and very cheap (about $2,500 at the time) missile using an infra-red (heat) homing system. From dead astern, aimed at the hot jet efflux of a non-manoeuvring target, it was very reliable, but targets are rarely cooperative. As the years passed, it was developed into a much more capable weapon with greatly increased range and tracking ability, but at the penalty of vastly increased cost.

Above: FSD Hornet 4, the structural test prototype, photographed in August 1981 carrying four Mk 84 2,000lb (907kg) on wing pylons. Blue and white Sidewinders are carried for attitude identification.

Right: Close-up of the underwing pylons, the nearer mounting a pair of Mk 82 slicks on a twin store carrier. Underwing stores carriage is a cumbersome business.

All versions before the L were stern attack weapons, although the J can under some circumstances acquire targets from other angles, and it is generally considered that if the pilot of the target aircraft knows that his opponent is behind him, and if he has sufficient energy manoeuvrability, he can deny a valid Sidewinder shot. Sidewinder has been manufactured in greater numbers than any other Western missile, with production currently approaching the 130,000 mark.

Sidewinder is essentially a visual distance weapon. The seeker head developed for the L variant uses Argon-cooled Indium Antimonide, which is extremely sensitive to IR emissions, and has an all-aspect capability. An aircraft in flight is warmed by friction heating due to the air passing over its skin. This is more pronounced where the local airflow is accelerated, such as the nose, or the leading edges of the flying surfaces, and the seeker head is sufficiently sensitive to detect this heating against the cold ambient background of the sky.

Clever filters are incorporated to ensure that the missile does not home on the sun or other IR source, although in the Gulf of Sidra incident in August 1981, when Libyan Air Force Su-22s clashed with US Navy F-14s, one of the Tomcat pilots reported that he waited until the target cleared the sun before launching a Sidewinder, which seems to imply a certain lack of faith on his part – or, of course, total professionalism! Sidewinder has many advantages over Sparrow, not the least of which being that it is a launch-and-leave weapon. It is small, with a diameter of only 5in (12.5cm) and a length of 112.2in (2.85m), and it weighs only 188lb (85kg). It can be fitted to almost any aircraft with ease, needing little more than a launch rack or rail, a few wires, and earphones. The wingtip mounting rail on the Hornet has the advantage of increasing the effective aspect ratio of the wing, which reduces its lift-dependent drag. This confers better cruise performance and sustained manoeuvrability compared with underwing racks.

The Hornet's wings fold to reduce storage and deck space required. When it is being armed before a mission, it is obviously an advantage to be able to load the Sidewinders onto the wingtip rails with the wings in the folded position. This is possible, although the safety aspects are reported to give ordnance officers pink fits! The main disadvantage of Sidewinder is that its detection range drops dramatically in cloud or heavy rain; in extreme conditions it becomes unusable.

Sidewinders in combat

Sidewinder has an operational history dating back to September 1958, when Sabres of the Chinese Nationalist Air Force, operating from Taiwan, clashed with communist Chinese MiGs. Four MiGs were claimed to have fallen to Sidewinders in what was the very first operational use of any air-to-air homing missile. In the Vietnam war early-model Sidewinders were widely used, achieving a kill ratio of about 15 per cent. This was considerably better than the kill ratio achieved by the Sparrow, which varied between 8 and 10 per cent. Sidewinder is an inherently more accurate weapon than Sparrow, due to its ability to 'see' a heat source more clearly than Sparrow can sense the fuzzy, wandering epicentre of a target provided by reflected radar emissions. This is one reason for the Sidewinder's better kill ratio, but it should be remembered that it was a better and more reliable short-range weapon than Sparrow and was consequently used on the easier targets.

The AIM-9L received limited use by Sea Harriers in the South Atlantic in 1982. There were 23 missile engagements in which a total of 26 missiles were fired, causing the destruction of 19 Argentinian aircraft. On three occasions two missiles were fired at the same target. This gives a kill ratio of 73 per cent. While this record is very impressive it should be noted that the all-aspect capability of the AIM-9L was not really tested. Most missile firings were from astern and from fairly low angles-off and rarely were the targets manoeuvring energetically. An Argentinian pilot later commented that missiles could be out-manoeuvred if they were seen coming in time; he was referring to surface to air missiles during low level attacks but his remark has a certain validity. On one occasion, two Sidewinders were launched without success at an Argentinian Canberra manoeuvring hard at low level over the sea, while on others the missile succeeded in tracking and hitting evading fast jets.

Right: A Hornet of VFA-113 Stingers en route to the Leach Lake range in California (top). After releasing two Mk 82 slicks in a shallow dive (centre), the aircraft banks away (bottom), showing the empty racks.

Above: The BL-755 cluster bomb unit is not a new weapon, but it still had to be cleared for use by the Hornet. This Canadian CF-18 carries eight, with cameras attached in five positions to record the drop.

Sidewinder is very easy for the pilot to use. With the seeker head uncaged, i.e. live, the missile announces that it is looking at something warm with a noise variously described as a 'growl' or a 'rattle' in the pilot's earphones, which increases in intensity as the target indications improve. The missile is then locked on to the target it is looking at and a squeeze of the trigger sends it on its way. AIM-9L has a stated range of 11 miles (18km) and a speed of about Mach 2.5, with a flight time of one minute. Its warhead is of the annular blast fragmentation type, with 22lb (10kg) of high explosive, and it carries fuzes for detonation of both impact and proximity types.

Gun armament

In common with all modern fighters, the Hornet carries a gun. Once upon a time, when the new wonder missiles were emerging, guns were thought to be superfluous except for ground strafing. But that is another story, and not everybody believed the theory anyway. Soviet fighters were almost without exception armed with guns; notable exceptions to the missiles-only trend in the West were Dassault with the Mirage III and, of course, Northrop with their F-5.

One further factor, which has a certain relevance to the Hornet, was that Western fighters of the period were being made far more capable than hitherto, able to fly their missions at night and in adverse weather conditions. This, plus the illumination requirements of the SARH missiles, resulted in the nose of the fighter being almost entirely occupied by a large radar set, while wing mountings, so widely used in World War II, apart from being poor places to mount guns, were hardly practicable, as the demands of Vmax had made them too thin. It was consequently difficult to find a suitable location which would also avoid gun exhaust gases being ingested by the engine with undesirable results.

Combat experience in the skies over North Vietnam soon had the American fighter pilots screaming for guns. With visual identification requirements reducing Sparrow effectiveness considerably, and a cruising speed of about 480kt (884km/h), the missile-only Phantoms often found themselves embroiled in 'knife-range' combats with the North Vietnamese MiGs. On May 4, 1967, Major Bill Lafever, then a young Lieutenant, was flying as backseater to the famous commander of the 8th TFW, Colonel Robin Olds. After a hectic fight in which four Sparrows and three Sidewinders (the other suffered a malfunction) were fired and a MiG-21 shot down, Olds led his flight straight over Hoa Loc airfield. There were about five MiG-17s in the circuit and Olds made several dummy passes on them at extremely close range. Without a gun, he could do little else.

MiG kill statistics

More than ten years afterward, Bill Lafever's comments on gunless fighters were still vividly descriptive, although hardly fitting for these pages. The two months immediately prior to the encounter just described had thrown up a relevant statistic. During this period 10 MiG-17s were downed, all by gunfire from the huge and unwieldy F-105 Thunderchief fighter-bombers, while their missile-only Phantom escorts could claim but two MiG-21s.

The M61A1 Vulcan cannon was the gun chosen to arm the Hornet, with 570 rounds of 20mm ammunition allowing about six seconds of firing at its maximum rate of 100rds/sec. The Vulcan utilizes six rotating barrels on the Gatling principle and is a fairly large weapon, so that locating it in a smallish aeroplane presented problems. The best place for any aircraft gun is on the centreline of the aircraft, where the recoil causes no asymmetric loading, but an immediate problem arises from the fact that this position is invariably occupied by the radar. The priority then becomes finding the best possible compromise position.

The same problem had been encountered on both the F-15 and F-16. On the F-15, the gun has been mounted in the starboard wing root, while on the F-16 it is accommodated in the port side of the fuselage, and both aircraft have the magazine in the centre fuselage behind the cockpit. In both cases it was considered preferable to accept the disadvantages of asymmetric mounting – even to the extent of automatically calling up rudder to counteract the yawing moment generated when the gun was fired – in order to keep the tremendous vibration caused when firing the gun away from the sensitive radar. In the Hornet, the designers took the bull by the horns and placed the gun in the nose, just above the centreline, in close proximity to the radar. The gun and its magazine were pallet-mounted to give quick and easy access for changing.

The vibration problem was then

Above: One of the principal anti-ship weapons carried by the Hornet, the AGM-65F variant of Maverick uses imaging infra-red homing.

tackled. Ground firing trials showed that the vibration level at the top of the planar antenna could reach a totally unacceptable 400g. Hughes overcame this problem by putting four anti-vibration mounts on to each bulkhead at the back and front of the radar. This allowed the radar assemblies to 'float' between the bulkheads and damped the vibration down to about 30g, which, although it sounds a lot, was reckoned acceptable.

Only the position of the muzzle, on top of the nose and immediately ahead of the pilot, appears suspect. When the gun is fired at night, the muzzle flash would seem to be in the perfect position to interfere with the pilot's night vision. As recounted earlier, a night-firing trial was held, after which it was reported that no difficulties were encountered in tracking a flame float at night, but a flame float is an entirely different proposition to an unlit air or ground target.

The General Electric M61A1 Vulcan cannon has been the standard USAF aircraft gun for many years, and is a most reliable weapon, with an average stoppage rate of just one round in 10,000. One reason for its reliability is the fact that it is externally powered, and the feed does not depend on the gun's own action, unlike the previous generation of gas-operated revolver cannon such as the M39. The six rifled barrels rotate anti-clockwise (looking in the direction of fire), and the fact that there are six barrels reduces wear and heat dissipation, giving longer weapon life.

The tremendous rate of fire requires a linkless feed; it also gives a very high hit probability against a fast-moving, high-angle-off target. M50 series ammunition is used, with a muzzle velocity of 3,400ft/sec (1.036m/sec). With a firing rate of 6,000 rounds per minute, the shells are spaced 34ft (10.36m) apart on leaving the muzzle, and this distance reduces during the time of flight. A 44ft (13.46m) long MiG-21 Fishbed at 90deg angle-off and with a velocity of 500kt (921km/h) travels its own length in 0.052 seconds. If the aim of the Vulcan is accurate and the target motion is in plane, the Fishbed is going to be hit at least four times.

A criticism of the Vulcan heard from some quarters is that it takes time to wind up to the full rate of fire. In fact, it takes all of 0.3 seconds, and a further half-second to wind down again. The argument goes that the first placement of the gun aiming dot, or pipper, on the target, is generally the best; after that it tends to wander off. Because of this – the criticism stems from a paper written a few years ago by defence analyst Pierre Sprey entitled *First Rounds Count* – the time taken for the Vulcan to wind up to full speed is considered a disadvantage, as it is still gathering speed at a time when the aim is at its truest.

Below: Infra-red images produced by the AGM-65F's IIR seeker and displayed on the cockpit CRT: the destroyer USS *Bagley* at the limit of the pilot's visual range (upper) and at the terminal homing stage.

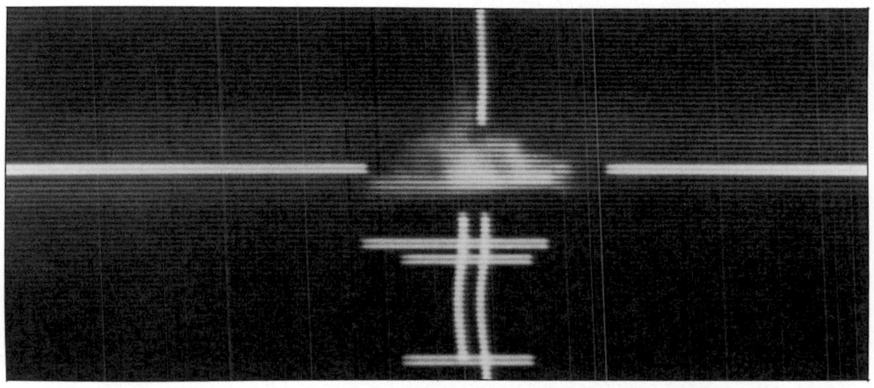

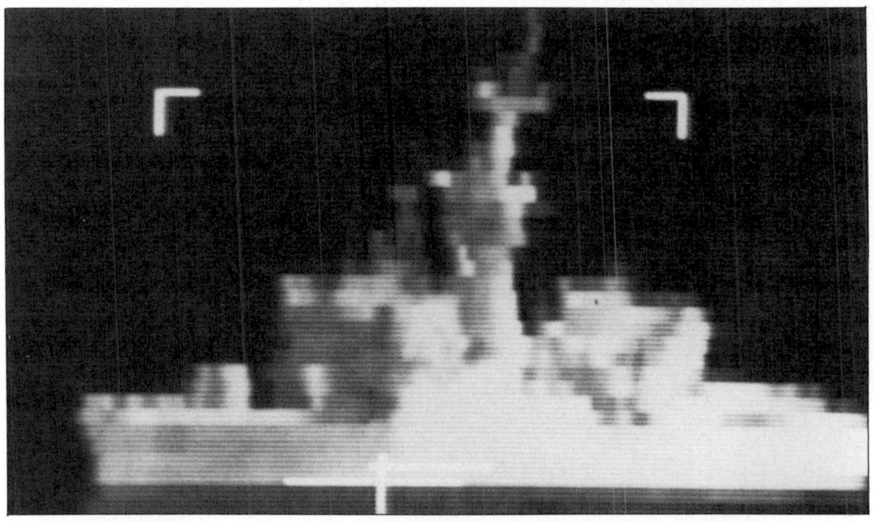

Below: Another weapon test carried out by the CAF Aerospace Engineering Test Establishment, this time involving unguided rockets.

The answer to this is fairly simple. Gas-operated revolver cannon such as the M39 do hit their full rate of fire instantly. The trouble is that the full rate of fire for an M39 is only 1,500rds/min, so it would take four of them to exceed the output of the M61 in the first half-second of firing. Fitting one gun, albeit a bulky one, into a Hornet was a difficult task. Where would four M39s go?

The aircraft gun can be summarized as an essential close-range weapon of great reliability, with a snap-shot capability unequalled by any missile yet built. It also increases the number of potential on-board kills considerably: each missile can be used but once, whereas the gun is a repeating weapon. Short on range and of limited application it may be, but an adversary ignores it at his peril. Finally, the only effective countermeasure against it is manoeuvre. The radar may be solid with jamming and decoys may render heat missiles useless, but the gun-armed fighter will always possess the means to shoot an opponent from the sky.

Ground-attack weapons

The load-carrying capacity of the Hornet is stated to be a maximum of 17,000lb (7,700kg), though it seems that this weight is unlikely to be carried operationally. The two wingtip Sidewinders will be carried on the attack mission to give a self-defence capability, but the Sparrows will be supplanted by the FLIR and LST/SCAM pods.

If long range or endurance is required, the centreline and the two inner wing hardpoints are wet and can be used to carry jettisonable tanks which add 6,435lb (2,920kg) of fuel. While multiple ejection racks (MERs) on the four wing hardpoints and a triple ejection rack (TER) on the centreline allow a total of 19 Mk 82 bombs of 500lb (227kg) nominal weight each to be carried, this is not a typical load. The drag penalty of loaded MERs and TERs is very high, and against strongly defended targets it is possible that only twin store vertical ejection racks (VER-2s) will be carried. A typical load would therefore be four Mk 83s and six Mk 82 low drag bombs (slicks), carried in pairs.

The drag penalty of MERs and TERs arises not only from the racks and weapons considered individually, but also from the interference drag they cause in combination. In flight, the airflow accelerates past the bombs and their racks, reaching a maximum just ahead of their maximum width. Consequently, clusters of bombs grouped close together on an MER impinge upon each other's and the rack's accelerated airflow, and interference drag results. This affects not only aircraft performance but also bombing accuracy, as drag-induced forces tend to impart pitching and yawing moments to the weapons at the moment of release, especially with current attack speeds approaching 600kt (1,110km/h).

Operational handling of the bombs is simple. The ground crew load the weapons and make the fuze code settings. The pilot then checks the loading on the MMD, and sets up to three delivery programs on the attack computer. Even these are not immutable, as both the programs and the weapons' status can be changed during flight.

The range of weapons that can be carried by the Hornet is fairly comprehensive. Apart from the Mk 82, 83, and 84 slicks, laser-guided versions of all these weapons can be carried. The principle of laser-guided bombs (LGBs) is fairly simple: the target is marked by a laser designator, either from the ground or from another aircraft, which produces a funnel of reflected laser light over the target, rather like the basket in basketball. The trick is for the attacking aircraft to deliver the bomb into the top of the funnel, whereupon it will glide down on to the target.

The LGB can be delivered into the top of the funnel in a variety of ways. In a heavily defended area, the dive-toss method is preferred: the attacking aircraft approaches low and fast, then at a pre-calculated point and speed, pulls up and launches the bomb in a high trajectory towards the top of the funnel.

Also in the inventory are Mk 82 retarded bombs, which allow the attacker to get clear of the explosion of a bomb dropped from very low level. Various

US Navy F-18 ordnance loads

Weapon	Armament Station								
	1	2	3	4	5	6	7	8	9
Air-to-air missiles									
AIM-9G/H/L Sidewinder	1	2						2	1
AIM-7F Sparrow		1		1		1		1	
Air-to-surface missiles									
AGM-65E/F Maverick		1	1				1	1	
AGM-88A Harm		1	1				1	1	
Conventional weapons									
Mk 82 LD/HD		2	2		2		2	2	
Mk 82 LGB		1	1				1	1	
Mk 83 LD		2	2		1		2	2	
Mk 83 LGB		1	1				1	1	
Mk 84 LD		1	1				1	1	
Mk 84 LGB		1						1	
Mk 20 or CBU-59/B Rockeye		2	2		2		2	2	
BLU-95 FAE-II (fuel-air explosive)		2	2		2		2	2	
AGM-62 Walleye		1						1	
Walleye data link pod					1				
Practice bombs									
Mk 76/Mk 106 dispensers		1	1		1		1	1	
BDU-12/20		1	1				1	1	
BDU-36		1						1	
Rocket launchers									
LAU-10D/A, -61A/A or -68B/A		2	2				2	2	
Special weapons									
B57 or B61		1						1	

Above left: Defence suppression is a task that an air arm ignores at its peril. Here, the first firing of an AGM-88A Harm by an F-18 is carried out by FSD Hornet TF1 over Wallops Island test range in October 1983.

Left: The cameras carried during separation trials show up clearly on wingtips, in Sparrow positions and under the rear fuselage as an inert B61 'special weapon', designated BDU-12/20, falls clear of FSD Hornet 7.

rocket launchers can be fitted – LAU-10/D, -61A, and 68B/A – while among the more exotic weapons are the fuel/air explosive BLU-95/B and the CBU-59B Rockeye cluster bomb, which covers the target area with a pattern of bomblets, effective against soft vehicles, personnel, and parked aircraft.

Among the 'smart' weapons carried is the AGM-62 Walleye glide bomb, an electro-optically guided weapon with a data link for extended range. Walleye is released in the general direction of the target then, via the television camera in the nose of the weapon, the pilot acquires the target on his monitor screen. He then focusses the camera on the target and locks it on. A powered weapon of similar concept is the AGM-65A/B Maverick, which has a range of 14 miles (22km), although other versions of this weapon use imaging infra-red (IIR) to provide the target picture, or laser seekers; respective designations are AGM-65D and AGM-65C/E.

Against shipping targets, AGM-84 Harpoon is used. Harpoon is a long-range – 68 miles (109km) – missile: steering commands are programmed into the strapdown inertial system before launch and height above the sea is controlled by a radar altimeter, while propulsion is by a small turbojet which gives it a high subsonic speed at very low altitude. Skimming in low over the water, at a predetermined point it switches on an active radar seeker which searches, then automatically locks on to a target. During the final phase of the approach it pulls itself up, then dives on to the target from above. As it is a launch-and-leave missile, the Hornet will at no time have to make a close approach to a hostile fleet in order to carry out a Harpoon attack. Supersonic and IIR versions of Harpoon are under consideration.

AGM-88A Harm

A totally different type of weapon is AGM-88A Harm (High Speed Anti-Radiation Missile). Harm is a radiation-seeking missile with a range exceeding 11 miles (18km), and superior detection capabilities and higher speed than either of its predecessors, Shrike and Standard. Its function is to seek and destroy hostile ground radars, and it operates in three modes: self-protect, target of opportunity and prebriefed.

In the self-protect mode, the Hornet's RWR will detect threat emissions and the mission computer will assess threat priorities, prepare a program and feed the necessary data to the missile, all in a matter of milliseconds, whereupon Harm can be launched and will home on the emissions selected. In the target of opportunity mode, the missile seeker operates automatically using methods which are carefully concealed under a blanket of woolly terminology. In the prebriefed mode, Harm is used in a rather speculative fashion. It is launched from within range and in the direction of known emitters (radars): if one comes on the air and starts to radiate, then Harm will immediately home on to it, whereas if nothing happens, Harm explodes in mid-air at the end of its run.

With this arsenal of weapons at its disposal, Hornet is a very potent fighting machine indeed. Whether it operates as a fighter or as an attack aircraft, it has the systems and the weaponry to successfully tackle a broad spectrum of threats, tasks and targets.

Above: Some idea of the wide variety of stores that the Hornet can carry is given here, though the list is by no means comprehensive. The operational use of TERs is restricted because of the high degree of drag they induce in flight.

F/A-18 Hornet stores options

1 AIM-9L Sidewinder AAM
2 AIM-9J Sidewinder AAM
3 AGM-65 Maverick ASM
4 AGM-62 Walleye ASM
5 AGM-109 Harpoon anti-ship missile
6 Drop tank, 315US gall (262 Imp gall, 1,192lit)
7 B57 tactical thermonuclear bomb
8 Durandal anti-runway weapon
9 SUU-20 practice dispenser
10 ASQ-173 laser spot tracker/strike camera (LST/SCAM) pod
11 AIM-7 Sparrow AAM
12 AGM-88A Harm anti-radar missile
13 Gun port
14 M61A1 Vulcan 20mm cannon with 570-round ammunition drum
15 GBU-10E/B Paveway II Mk 84 2,000lb (907kg) laser-guided bomb (LGB)
16 AAS-38 forward-looking infra-red (FLIR) pod
17 Mk 84 2,000lb (907kg) low-drag (LD) general-purpose bomb
18 Three Mk 82 500lb (227kg) low-drag (LD) 'slick' general-purpose bombs on TER (triple ejection rack)
19 Mk 82 high-drag (HD) 'Snakeye' retarded general-purpose bomb
20 M117 750lb (340kg) general-purpose bomb
21 Stores carrier
22 Data link container for Walleye guidance or flight test monitoring
23 CBU-59/B or Mk 20 Rockeye antitank cluster bomb
24 Two Mk 83 1,000lb (454kg) low-drag (LD) general-purpose bombs
25 LAU-61A/A rocket pod
26 LAU-68B/A rocket pod

Hornets in service

On June 30, 1981, Vice Admiral Wesley L. McDonald, US Navy, gave his verdict on the Hornet's value to the service: "The versatility of the F/A-18 to effectively perform both the fighter and the attack missions provides the battle group commander with options never before available. When in a defensive posture, the Hornet will counter either air or surface threat. Offensively, it will provide both fighter escort and a survivable ordnance delivery vehicle with finite accuracy. This force multiplication effect is not available with any other aircraft in the world . . . All indications are that the Navy/Marine team has a superb machine in which to move forward into the future."

Experimental squadrons VX-4 and VX-5 were the first USN units to fly the Hornet, but the first true Hornet squadron was VFA-125 – the Rough Raiders – which was commissioned at NAS Lemoore, California, on November 13, 1980. VFA-125 is a fleet readiness squadron, charged with training both ground and air crew for the operational units. As such, it will have at its peak a far greater complement than a normal squadron, with a total strength of 60 Hornets, a high proportion of them two-seaters, 75 officers, including 30 pilots, and about 600 enlisted men. It will convert operational squadrons to the Hornet at a rate of four per year. A second fleet readiness squadron, VFA-106 Gladiators, was commissioned at NAS Cecil Field, Florida, in April 1984, while a third is planned to be activated at MCAS Yuma, Arizona, probably in late 1986.

The Rough Raiders are a unique mixed Navy and Marine Corps outfit. Their first commanding officer was Capt. James W. Partington, USN, and the executive officer was Lt. Col. Gary R. VanGysel, USMC. Their backgrounds were, as one might expect with a dual-role aircraft like the Hornet, dissimilar. Captain Partington has extensive attack experience flying Skyhawks and Corsairs, while Lt. Col. VanGysel is a very experienced Phantom driver. At first, the squadron build-up was slow. The first Hornet arrived on February 19, 1981, and was followed by two more aircraft from the pilot production batch. The first full-scale production Hornet did not arrive until September, and by the end of the year, the Rough Raiders had eight Hornets.

Approximately 150 of the Hornets on order will be two-seat TF/A-18As, about one in every nine of the total order, and following the precedent of the F-15 and F-16, they will probably be redesignated F/A-18B at some future date. The two-holers are fully combat-capable, although carrying less fuel, they are slightly short on range compared to the single seater. They feature an extended canopy, with the rear seat set 6in (15cm) higher than the front seat to give the guy in the back good visibility, and the rear cockpit is identical to the front except that it does not have a HUD. The second seat displaces a fuel tank, and the TF/A-18A carries 600lb (272kg) less fuel internally. Any performance differences between the two are marginal.

By August 1981 the VFA-125 pilots had reached the stage in their training where they were ready for Air Combat Manoeuvring (ACM) experience, despite the fact that at this point only three Hornets had been assigned to the squadron, and these had to be shared between 16 pilots. ACM is an unproductive exercise when carried out between fighters of the same type as the only difference is that of pilot quality, so adversary aircraft were provided in the form of an A-4 Skyhawk of VA-127 (the Cylons), from NAS Lemoore, and an F-5E Tiger II from the US Navy Fighter Weapons School (usually known as 'Top Gun') at NAS Miramar, near San Diego.

An adversary aircraft is a type selected for its performance similarities to known or likely 'threat' aircraft. The Skyhawk represents the MiG-17 while

Above: Two F-18As and two TF-18As of the Rough Raiders in a neat formation during the deployment to MCAS Yuma in January 1982.

Below: A Hornet of VFA-125 takes the wire aboard USS *Constellation* during the Rough Raiders' first carrier qualifications in October 1982.

the F-5E doubles for the MiG-21. In most cases, adversary aircraft wear Warsaw Pact camouflage, with Soviet-style 'buzz numbers' on the nose. Adversary pilots are trained in Soviet techniques and tactics, and with their specially chosen aircraft simulate the most realistic threat possible for training purposes.

The four-day exercise consisted entirely of one versus one encounters. The adversary pilots, both very experienced men, were as keen as anyone to see what the Hornet could really do, especially after all the controversy that had surrounded it. They were most impressed, Major George Stuart of the USMC describing the Hornet as being as capable as any aircraft in the inventory, while Lt. John C. Forrester, USN, felt afterwards that there was no comparison between the Hornet and the two adversary types. He was also impressed by the fact that the Rough Raiders, although inexperienced on the type, had reached such a high level of competence, the sign of an easy aeroplane to fly.

The next stage was a ten-day deployment to MCAS Yuma with five Hornets in November 1981, followed by an extended deployment, also to Yuma, by nine Hornets, lasting from January 5-27, 1982, to complete ACM training for the initial batch of 16 pilots assigned to VFA-125, and to finalize the ACM syllabus for the squadrons to be trained on the Hornet. The advantage of Yuma is that it has an electronically instrumented range able to track up to eight aircraft at a time, while simulating and assessing missile firings and recording the proceedings on video tape. The entire mission is then replayed to the pilots on their return. Skilled debriefers beware! This elaborate system, produced by Cubic Corporation's Defense Systems Division in San Diego, rejoices in the acronym of TACTS/ACMI (Tactical Aircrew Combat Training System/Air Combat Manoeuvre Instrumentation). Electronic pods are attached to the participating fighters: these emit signals which are received by a network of solar-powered antennas on the ground for transmission back through a series of micro-wave relay stations to a mobile recording centre. The combats can then be reconstructed and evaluated.

The bulk of the opposition for the second deployment was provided by Skyhawks of the Cylons, although Top Gun Skyhawks, Canadian F-5s from No. 433 Squadron, and Tomcats from VF-51 and VX-4 also participated. The anti-Tomcat sorties were flown one versus one, while the others were generally multi-bogey encounters at odds of up to three to one against the Hornet. The multi-bogey engagements pressurized the Rough Raiders into using their systems capability to the full, whereas in one versus one encounters there is always a tendency to close quickly to visual range, then stay visual.

Naturally, the Hornet did not win every encounter – there is no aircraft/pilot combination in the world capable of pulling that off – but the results achieved left the Rough Raiders full of enthusiasm for their mount. Navy Lt. Phil Scher of the Cylons hitched a ride in the back seat of a Hornet during one exercise. An experienced adversary pilot who had previously flown against the Tomcat, Eagle, and Fighting Falcon, he commented afterwards: "From close up, I can honestly say that the F/A-18 is magic. I don't think that there are many airplanes, if any, that are capable of physically beating the Hornet in the air."

Shoot-out at Yuma

Questions that are frequently posed are, how good is the Hornet in the air-to-air arena, and how would it shape up against the F-16? The following account of an engagement that took place during the second Yuma deployment in part answers the first question.

Through Telegraph Pass at 420kt (774km/h), two F/A-18 Hornet jet fighters enter the range, level at 'Angels one-five', and scan the early morning sky for the enemy. Hornet One's radar locks on to a target. He transmits:

"Contact . . . a single . . . on the nose at 15,000ft (4,570m)."

Hornet Two climbs to 25,000ft (7,620m) to gain an offensive position. Suddenly the radar blip separates.

"We've got two . . . the wingman is splitting high and left," replies Hornet Two. "I'm showing 1,000kt (1,840km/h) overtake."

Above: A Hornet of VFA-125 photographed at high altitude. The strangely foreshortened effect is a result of distortion caused by the canopy of the A-7 camera ship.

Below: Hornets of VMFA-314 Black Knights prepare to launch during their first sea deployment in July 1983. The Black Knights are assigned to CVW-13 aboard USS *Coral Sea*.

Above: In military power only, a clean Hornet of VMFA-323 Death Rattlers leaves the flight deck. The Hornet can be flown off the catapult 'hands-off'. VMFA-323 partners VMFA-314, VFA-131 and VFA-132 as part of the air wing embarked on *Coral Sea*.

Left: As a direct result of combat experience, pilots of modern fighters have an unobstructed view to the rear. The Hornet is comparable to any in this respect, as this view of a TF-18A back-seater shows.

Below: Pilot's eye view astern as a Hornet climbs gently away from the carrier it has just left in December 1982. It can be seen that blind spots, potentially so dangerous in air combat, have been reduced to a minimum.

"Six miles . . . in the box . . . four miles, tally-ho," replies Hornet One. "It's an A-4, shoot, shoot!"

"Fox One," calls Hornet Two, and the computer sends the simulated missile on its way to a lethal kill. As Hornet Two pitches back to assist, he hears Hornet One call a shot on the remaining bogey. The computer scores the shot as a miss as the bogey pilot hauls his aircraft into a vision-dimming 6g turn. Hornet Two manoeuvres into a cover position while Hornet One strives to regain the offensive advantage.

"Fox Two," calls Hornet One. "Good kill" is the call over the radio from the computer monitor station. Both aircraft turn west and 'bug out' in full afterburner, streaking towards 'good guy' country at the pass. The entire fight is over less than 30 seconds after the pilots initially sighted each other.

Pilots and aircraft

It may, of course, be argued that this exercise involved adversary aircraft which were far inferior to the Hornet and was therefore an unfair match. On the other hand, adversary pilots are men of high experience and ability levels, who do not do the job to be beaten and thus bolster their opponent's confidence; they play to win. Despite the discrepancy in the hardware, pilot ability historically always has been, and for the foreseeable future will continue to be the dominant factor in air fighting. Better technology helps a lot, but it is not the be-all and end-all.

In a contest between the Hornet and the Fighting Falcon, with pilots of equal ability, the result appears to be wide open. At the time of writing, the Hornet's weapon system is superior, and the Fighting Falcon has no effective answer to the 'shoot-in-the-face' capability conferred by the AIM-7 Sparrow. It then becomes a question of tactics. Initially, the Hornet pilot should try to keep his energy levels high and maintain his distance, taking Sparrow shots from any angle as opportunity offers, thus forcing the F-16 to manoeuvre hard to evade and deplete his energy. If this succeeded, the Hornet could then close for a heat missile or gun shot. In one versus one close combat, the contest would be fairly even.

It is the author's opinion that transient performance is more important than sustained turning ability. While no fighter in the world can match the sustained turn ability of the F-16, the pitch rate and the high AOA capability of the Hornet are believed to be better than those of the F-16, so that pilot ability would be the dominant factor in any contest between the two, and especially the ability of each pilot to use the strong points of his machine, which, rather surprisingly, is not always the case. For example, an Aggressor Squadron F-5E versus F-16 combat in 1982 saw the austere Northrop fighter achieve a good attacking position, whereupon the F-16 pilot evaded by a series of 9g loops which the F-5E was unable to match. The Aggressor pilot later commented: "I just flew around a while and waited for him to get tired!" This was not a good example of the use of sustained turn.

Multi-bogey combats

It must be remembered that one versus one combats are just peacetime training; they are not war. In war, multi-bogey combats are the norm, and they are, regardless of technical superiority, a great leveller. Leaving aside the BVR attack capability of the Hornet, one would expect the results of a multi-bogey contest between the F-16 and the Hornet to come out about equal, given equal numerical quantities. Given equal cost quantities, the cheaper F-16 would have a slight edge, but there are limits to the cost quantity equation. Given equal cost quantities, the austere F-5E is probably the greatest of them all, but procurement levels would be so high that pilot standards would have to drop to fill the empty cockpits. Moreover, the equal cost quantity argument, if carried to extremes, also involves the acceptance of an adverse kill ratio, which would be counterproductive due to the effect on morale. But to return to the Hornet, it may be fairly assumed that in the fighter role, it will perform extremely creditably.

The built-in reliability and maintainability of the Hornet paid handsome dividends during the second Yuma detachment. Originally, 288 sorties were planned, an average of 1.5 per aircraft per day. In the event, a total of 326 sorties exceeding 400 hours flight time were carried out, and every sortie had full systems operable. Only one sortie had to be cancelled, when a minor fault caused a 20-minute delay, which was enough to prevent the pilot from arriving at the range at his allotted time. Each Hornet averaged 44.7 hours of flight time during the deployment, and the remarkably low average of 11 MMH/FH was recorded. Not one fuel leak or hydraulic failure occurred during the deployment, a stark contrast to the Hornet's predecessor, the F-4 Phantom, of which it is often said, with some justification, that if it doesn't leak, it must be empty. The air combat training syllabus was satisfactorily finalized, and two months later a three-week deployment to NAS Fallon, in Nevada, served a similar function for the attack training syllabus.

Performance analysis

The original specification deficiencies either have been cured or do not seem to worry the pilots. The slow roll rate is now up to about 220deg/sec, about as much as a pilot can reasonably handle. The Hornet still does not accelerate from Mach 0.8 to Mach 1.6 in the required time, which was to give maximum energy at missile launch, but it is faster up to Mach 1.2 than virtually anything else, having beaten even the F-15 in 'drag races' up to this speed, and as hardly any air combat is likely to take place at speeds exceeding Mach 1.2, the pilots consider this deficiency to be unimportant.

The Hornet has attracted a lot of flak over its range capability, but many of the comparisons drawn seem suspect, especially those involving the Corsair. Fuel flow management and close attention to flight profiles for the attack mission have produced improvements, and although a Hornet in the attack configuration does not have the radius of action of the Corsair that it replaces, the difference is reportedly less than 10 per cent. The Hornet's far greater survivability due to its vastly superior performance is considered by the pilots to be more than an adequate trade-off for a reduction in maximum range.

From the staff point of view, an operational evaluation in 1982 stated that the unrefuelled capabilities of the Hornet cause a reduction in the stand-off range of a battle group, an important consideration in the event of an action against a Soviet fleet equipped with SS-N-12 or SS-N-19 surface-launched anti-shipping missiles with a range of 300nm (550km). Nevertheless, it appears that the criteria for the Hornet should not be performance comparisons against other types, but how well it performs its allotted role.

In the final analysis, theoretical ranges attainable at certain speeds under precise conditions with defined weapon loads are irrelevant. With the attack role specifically in mind, the only question worth asking is, can the Hornet deliver a worthwhile load at a sufficient distance (not necessarily greater in either case) with greater accuracy and a greater margin of survivability than the aircraft that it is to replace? In the air combat role, the question becomes, can the Hornet perform both as an interceptor and close combat fighter in an effective manner without being outclassed by the opposition? In both cases, the answer must be an unqualified yes. The pilots genuinely praise the Hornet's handling qualities, although with neutral speed stability the control column does not have a lot of 'feel', and a certain amount of care must be taken to avoid overstressing the airframe. Maximum lift, achieved at about 35deg AOA, can be reached with a one-handed pull on the stick, while to reach higher AOA two hands are needed. The aircraft is almost spinproof, while if it does depart controlled flight, recovery is simple. It is stable in both roll and yaw, and is a good gun platform up to 30deg AOA.

Carrier qualification

A further milestone in finalizing the Hornet training syllabus was reached between September 27 and October 4, 1982, when the Rough Riders completed their first carrier qualification operations aboard the USS *Constellation*. Six pilots using two single-seat Hornets logged ten bolters as well as 57 day and 24 night traps during this period, and no problems were encountered.

Catapult launches are regarded as easy. The Hornet taxis to the cat, and the launch bar, which is attached to the nose gear, is positioned in the shuttle on the catapult track. The pilot makes his final checks, then waves to the catapult officer that he is ready to go. The Hornet is trimmed to fly 'hands off', though it is normal for the pilot to put his left hand on the throttle to prevent it slipping back under the 4g acceleration as the catapult fires.

Landing is carried out either manually or automatically. For a manual landing the pilot sets up the speed, line-up and glideslope. 'On-speed' is taken from the aircraft's instruments, while line-up is judged from the centreline on the carrier

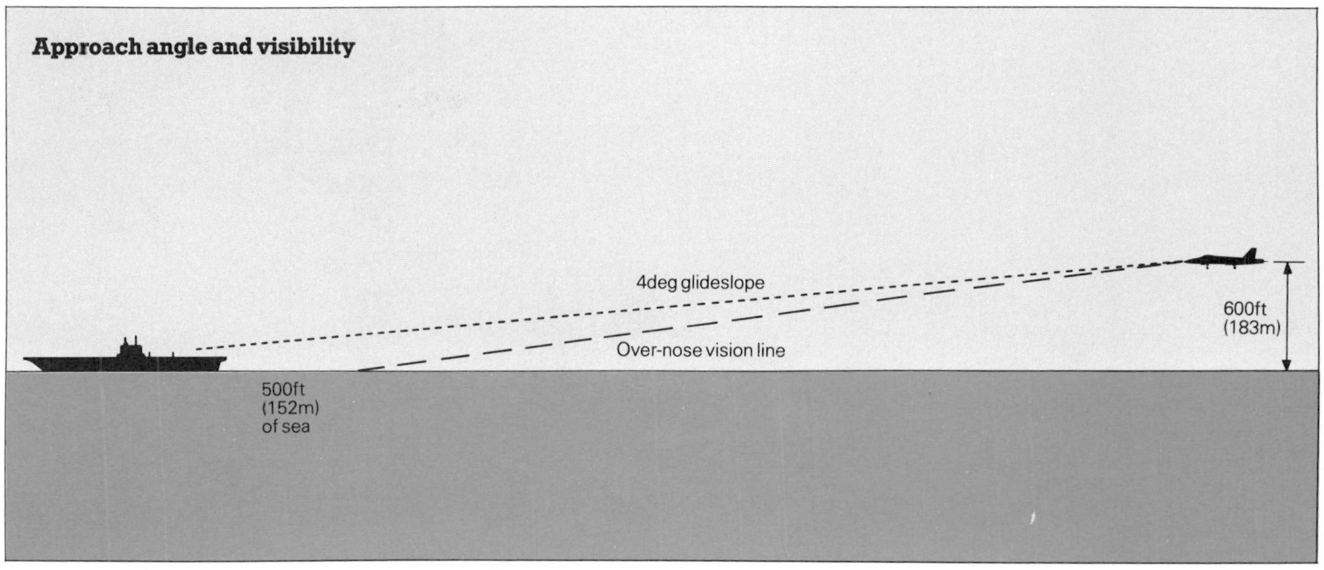

Above: The Hornet has a low AOA on the final approach, and the excellent visibility over the nose simplifies landing on a carrier deck to a considerable degree.

Below: The carrier suitability trials Hornet launches from a 6deg ski-jump ramp at NATC Patuxent River. The attitude of the main gear suggests that a fair proportion of the aircraft's weight, though not yet all of it, has been transferred to the wings.

deck. The glideslope, an angle of about 4deg, is taken from the Fresnel Lens, which is a series of directional lights on the carrier: the pilot watches the mirror of the Fresnel Lens and the correctness of his approach is shown by the colour of the light reflected in the mirror, an orange light indicating that the glideslope is correct. At touch-down the throttles are advanced to full military power; if the hook misses the wires the Hornet flies right on past the carrier and tries again.

The automatic system is different again. At a set distance out on the approach the pilot couples his ACLS to the ACLS SPN-42 system on the carrier. This transmits signals to the Hornet's auto-pilot which guide the aircraft straight on to the carrier deck, making due allowance for deck motion. The throttles are controlled automatically in this mode by the Hornet's approach power compensator (APC).

Training syllabus

The pilot training syllabus evolved by VFA-125 lasts five months, a little longer than the course for maintenance personnel, and consists of four phases: transition, air-to-air, air-to-ground, and carrier qualification. Instruction begins in the brand new Hornet Learning Center at Lemoore, where computer-assisted

Left: Final checks are carried out as one of the VMFA-314 Hornets prepares to launch from the catapult aboard USS *Constellation* during carrier operations in July 1983.

Below: Deck crew cluster round Hornets of VMFA-314 as they get ready to launch. The coloured vests indicate the various functions to which the individual crewmen are assigned – purple and a white 'F' identify the fuelling team.

audio-visual techniques cover procedures, switchology and systems operation, and the fledgling Hornet pilot then progresses to the simulators. The first of these is the Part-Task Trainer (PTT), consisting of simplified Hornet cockpits, in which familiarization with HOTAS is begun and the manipulative skills needed to operate the controls is acquired. Then comes the Operational Flight Trainer (OFT), which simulates actual flight from takeoff to landing by means of three visual displays and uses a g-suit/g-seat buffet system for extra realism. OFT training covers both airfield and carrier takeoffs and landings, the complete instrument syllabus, and emergency procedures.

Then comes the Weapons Tactics Trainer (WTT), consisting of two 40ft (12.2m) domes with a cockpit in each and seven televisual projectors. The WTT, in which each student will spend an estimated 50 hours, provides advanced air-to-air radar training and ACM practice. Each dome can be operated solo, or combined into a 'twin-tub' to allow the pilots in each dome to 'fly' against each other. The projectors generate a realistic earth/sky backdrop on the inside of the domes on which target, missile and gunfire images are also generated. After sufficient time has been spent in the simulators, flight training begins. This consists of around 70 sorties, supplemented by the simulators as necessary, followed by a further 20 sorties for carrier qualification.

Operational squadrons

The first operational Hornet squadron was VMFA-314, the Black Knights, commanded by Lt. Col. Peter Field, who had played a major part in the Hornet FSD programme at Patuxent River. The Black Knights were part of the Phantom-equipped 3rd Marine Air Wing based at MCAS El Toro, California, and the inaugural ceremony took place on January 7, 1983, at El Toro. At a press conference immediately afterwards, Lt. Col. Field had a number of points to make about the Hornet in reply to questions from reporters.

The first concerned the accuracy of weapons delivery, which was described as better than ever before, with a weapon system "literally out of Star Wars". The second point concerned the sheer pleasure of flying the Hornet. This contrasts with the Phantom, which has never been regarded as an easy aeroplane to fly and requires a lot of concentration. The third point concerned the maintainability of the Hornet, with MMH/FH reduced to one-third of the figure for the Phantom. He commented that the squadron had achieved more flight hours over a given period with their first four Hornets than they had been used to getting from their full complement of 12 Phantoms. Later in the year, the Black Knights participated in Red Flag 83/5 at Nellis AFB, where they flew as aggressors, clashing with Air Force F-15s and F-16s. Unfortunately, the details are still classified at the time of writing.

The Black Knights were followed on to the Hornet by their fellow squadrons of the 3rd MAW, VMFA-323 and VMFA-531, and the Navy was not far behind, VA-113 Stingers commencing training for the Hornet on March 26, 1983. They became operational in August of the same year, a full two months ahead of schedule. The Stingers were previously equipped with Corsairs, and their commanding officer, Cdr. William Pickavance, was quick to comment that for years the squadron had needed fighter escort, whereas they now had an aircraft with an excellent self-defence capability.

Two of the biggest controversies about the Hornet appear to have been largely silenced since its operational debut. The first concerned the multi-role capability insofar as it affected the pilot. Some pilots are natural air fighters, while others really enjoy moving mud. The opinion has been widely held that never the twain should meet, and while units had specialist roles, pilots tended to be assigned to squadrons where their natural bent could best be utilized. Reports from the squadrons appear to indicate that interchangeability appears to be working, although doubts will continue to exist for some time yet. Of course, a squadron contains more pilots than aircraft, so it seems logical that if the split between natural fighter and natural attack pilots is about even, then the nature of the mission can be allowed to affect the allocation of the pilots within certain limits.

Solo mission capability

The other doubtful area has been whether one man can fly the type of mission that has come to be regarded as the prerogative of the two-seater. The general opinion of those who fly the Hornet appears to be that the advanced avionics, and especially the cockpit, enable one man to perform satisfactorily, although this verdict is not unanimous. Some former Skyhawk and Corsair pilots would prefer a back-seater to help with the workload, despite, or perhaps because of their previous experience. It is, however, accepted in the Hornet squadrons that this is a minority opinion. As the old saying goes, "Combat is the ultimate, and the unkindest, judge."

At least 40 USN and USMC squadrons are planned, although this number, as well as the total planned procurement of the Hornet, may change if Navy and Marine Corps mission requirements are revised. On the large carriers, the Hornet will supplement the Tomcat in the fleet defence role, but it is planned that the two smaller carriers, USS *Midway* and *Coral Sea*, which will both remain in service into the 1990s, will deploy four squadrons of Hornets each.

Hornet squadrons

US Navy and Marine Corps F/A-18 Hornet squadrons as of May 31, 1984

Unit	Tailcode	Name and base	Carrier assignment	Remarks
Operational Test and Evaluation				
NATC	7T	(none) NAS Patuxent River, Md	(none)	From 1978, operational tests.
NWC	(none)	(none) NWC China Lake, Ca	(none)	From 1984, weapons tests.
VX-4	XF	Evaluators NAS Point Mugu, Ca	(none)	From 1981, operational test and evaluation; carrier trials with CVW-15/USS *Vinson* Fall 1982; carrier trials with VFA-125 on USS *Constellation* Fall 1982; CO Capt J. Michael Welch.
VX-5	XE	Vampires NAS Point Mugu, Ca	(none)	From 1981, operational test and evaluation; carrier trials with CVW-15/USS *Vinson* Fall 1982; CO Cdr Michael P. Curphey.
Pacific Fleet Replacement Air Group (RAG)				
VFA-125	NJ	Rough Raiders NAS Lemoore, Ca	(none)	Commissioned Nov 13, 1980, first F-18 squadron; received first aircraft Feb 19, 1981; ACM deployment to MCAS Yuma, Az, Jan 5-27, 1982; bombing deployment to NAS Fallon, Nev, Mar-Apr 1982; carrier trials with VX-4 on USS *Constellation* Sep-Oct 1982; CO Capt James W. Partington.
Pacific Fleet				
VFA-25	NK	Fist of the Fleet NAS Lemoore, Ca	CVW-14 USS *Constellation*	Commissioned Jul 1, 1983; received first aircraft Nov 11, 1983; to deploy with VFA-113.
VFA-113	NK	Stingers NAS Lemoore, Ca	CVW-14 USS *Constellation*	Commissioned Mar 25, 1983; received first aircraft Aug 16, 1983; to deploy with VFA-25; CO Cdr Craig A. Langbehm.
Atlantic Fleet Replacement Air Group (RAG)				
VFA-106	AD	Gladiators NAS Cecil Field, Fla	(none)	Commissioned Apr 27, 1984; CO Cdr David J. L'Herault.
Atlantic Fleet				
VFA-131	AK	Wildcats NAS Cecil Field, Fla	CVW-13 USS *Coral Sea*	Commissioned Mar 29, 1984.
VFA-132	AK	Privateers NAS Cecil Field, Fla	CVW-13 USS *Coral Sea*	Commissioned Feb 10, 1984; CO Cdr Robert E. Lakakri.
VMFA-314	VW	Black Knights MCAS El Toro, Ca	CVW-13 USS *Coral Sea*	Converted from F-4N Jan 7, 1984; assigned to CVW-13 Mar 29, 1984; CO Lt Col Pete Field.
VMFA-323	WS	Death Rattlers MCAS El Toro, Ca	CVW-13 USS *Coral Sea*	Converted from F-4N 1983; assigned to CVW-13 Mar 29, 1984; CO Lt Col Gary Vangysel.
Other units				
VMFA-531	EC	Gray Ghosts MCAS El Toro, Ca	MAG-11, 3rd MAW	Converted from F-4N 1983; CO Lt Col Jim Lucas.
VFA-136	AK	(unassigned) NAS Cecil Field, Fla	CVW-13 USS *Coral Sea*	To be commissioned 1985; with VFA-137 to replace VMFA-314 and VMFA-323 aboard *Coral Sea*.
VFA-137	AK	(unassigned) NAS Cecil Field, Fla	CVW-13 USS *Coral Sea*	To be commissioned 1985; with VFA-136 to replace VMFA-314 and VMFA-323 aboard *Coral Sea*.
VFA-146	(unassigned)	(unassigned) NAS Lemoore, Ca	(unassigned)	To convert from A-7E about 1986.
VFA-147	(unassigned)	(unassigned) NAS Lemoore, Ca	(unassigned)	To convert from A-7E about 1986.
VFA-303	ND	Golden Hawks NAS Miramar, Ca	CVW-30 Naval Air Reserve	To convert from A-7E about 1986 as first Reserve F-18 squadron.

NOTE: *Coral Sea* is currently being refurbished and will be the first carrier with four F/A-18 squadrons (replacing two A-7E and two F-4S squadrons); the assignment of Marine Corps squadrons is temporary pending the formation of VFA-136 and VFA-137.

CO: Commanding Officer **CVW:** Carrier Air Wing **MAG:** Marine Aircraft Group **MAW:** Marine Aircraft Wing **NATC:** Naval Air Test Center **NWC:** Naval Weapons Center **VFA:** (US Navy) Strike Fighter Squadron (formerly Fighter Attack Squadron) **VMFA:** Marine Fighter Attack Squadron **VX:** Operational Test and Evaluation Squadron

LOCATIONS: Az Arizona **Ca** California **Fla** Florida **Md** Maryland **Nev** Nevada

The excellent high AOA handling of the Hornet, coupled with its high thrust to weight ratio, have led McDonnell Douglas to suggest that it might be capable of a ski-jump takeoff in the manner of the Harrier. Tests are currently underway at Patuxent River using 6deg and 9deg ramps, and it has been suggested that a 25deg ramp may eventually be tried. As the Hornet does not have vectored thrust, the full operational implications are at present unclear, although two-dimensional thrust vectoring has been suggested for the F404 engine. The great advantage of a ramp takeoff for shipboard operations is that no matter how heavy the swell, the aircraft is launched upwards away from the sea. But whether a combined ramp and catapult is intended, or even feasible, remains to be seen.

Many air forces have evaluated the Hornet with a view to re-equipping with the type, and to date Canada, Australia, and Spain have placed firm orders. One of its main competitors has been the Hornet's original rival, the General Dynamics F-16, which has been very successful in securing overseas orders. The two main criteria appear to be cost and mission effectiveness: where the F-16 can perform the required missions it is definitely an attractive proposition due to its lower cost, whereas the more capable Hornet is able to meet more stringent operational specifications but at greater cost.

Export advantages

Nevertheless, the F-16 drew considerable flak in Europe when it first entered service for its lack of adverse weather BVR capability, and its limited armament. The original two Sidewinders would not last long in a major air battle, and the consequent lack of on-board kills was likely to seriously limit its combat persistence. The F-16 is also stuffed full of fuel in a manner that arguably increases its vulnerability to battle damage. By contrast, the Hornet has a genuine adverse weather capability and was equipped with BVR weaponry from the outset. In the fighter configuration, it has never had less than four missiles, and can easily carry more. Its two engines give greater flight safety, and it has exceptional built-in survivability.

Canada is a country of vast size with a sparse population over most of its area. It also has air defence commitments in Europe, and the McDonnell Douglas CF-101 Voodoos, Lockheed CF-104 Starfighters, and Northrop CF-5 Freedom Fighters operated by the Canadian Armed Forces were looking distinctly long in the tooth by the end of the 1970s. After an intensive evaluation of many contending fighters, the Canadian government became the first export customer for the Hornet, signing a contract for 137 aircraft, including 24 two-seaters, in the summer of 1980 later adding another 11 single seaters.

Above: Two CF-18B two-seaters of the CF take on fuel from a CC-137 tanker. Flight refuelling is essential for the Canadian Forces, given the vast size of the country. Dummy canopies are painted on the undersides of all Canadian CF-18s for aspect deception of opponents in combat.

The trials had ended in a straight contest between the F-16 and the Hornet, and two key factors were cited in the decision to adopt the Hornet rather than the F-16. The first was twin-engined safety. Flying over Canada has certain similarities to flying over the sea; airfields are few and far between, and a pilot forced to eject could be lost almost as easily in the inhospitable wilderness as over water. The second reason was that the Canadian authorities felt that the larger F/A-18 had more growth potential than its single-engined rival.

The Canadian Hornet features three changes from its US Navy counterpart.

Right: the Royal Australian Air Force has ordered a total of 75 Hornets to replace three squadrons of Mirage IIIs. Among the distinctive features of the RAAF Hornets are the IFF antennae under the nose.

On the left side of the forward fuselage is mounted a 600,000-candlepower spotlight, a standard Canadian item used to make visual identification of bogeys at night. A different ILS is fitted, and in lieu of the USN sea survival gear, a cold-weather land survival kit is carried.

Canadian camouflage

A further difference, though hardly a modification, is the painting of a false canopy on the underside of the nose. The brainchild (and also patent) of American aviation artist Keith Ferris, it is intended to deceive opponents as to which way the aircraft is turning. Extensive experiments have been carried out in the United States with this and other forms of deception camouflage, but with inconclusive results. It obviously works some of the time, as complaints have been received about it being a potential collision hazard in peacetime training exercises, although it cannot work at very close ranges nor yet at extreme visual distances. In wartime it could have a certain value, as it interferes with what former US fighter instructor Major John Boyd calls the opposing pilot's OODA loop (Observation, Orientation, Decision, Action). The deception interferes, even if only briefly, with the orientation phase, thus delaying the decision and action phases, which in a time-critical situation could be valuable indeed. The false canopy is generally painted matt black with irregular gloss black splodges to represent the glint of sunshine on a canopy.

The first two CF-18s – the name Hornet has not been adopted by the Canadian Armed Forces – CF 901 and 902, were delivered to the Aerospace Engineering Test Establishment at Cold Lake, Alberta, on October 25, 1982, and the first CF-18 unit to be formed was No. 410 Operational Training Squadron, whose pilots had been through the VFA-125 training syllabus. The three operational squadrons to be formed will be Nos. 421 and 441 Squadrons, while in June 1985, the Hornet will be introduced to European service by No. 439 Squadron, presently flying Starfighters out of Soellingen in West Germany.

Above: The first Canadian Forces unit to be formed was No. 410 Operational Training Squadron at CFB Bagotville, Quebec, to which this gleaming new two-seater is assigned. Unit badge is a cougar head.

Below: The first two CF-18s to be delivered fly in formation. The 600,000-candlepower spotlights carried by Canadian aircraft can be seen ahead of and below the LEX.

Australian Hornets

In many ways, the problems of the Royal Australian Air Force duplicate those of the US Navy and Canadian Armed Forces. Much of the RAAF's flying will be done over water; sea surveillance is high on its list of priorities; and like Canada, Australia is a large, sparsely populated and inhospitable country. In a hard-fought contest against the F-16, the Hornet was selected for three main reasons, principally for its twin-engined safety and better growth potential; thirdly, it was decided that the proposed up-grading of the F-16's avionics, in particular the radar, all-weather targeting system and navigation equipment, presented a risk, whereas the Hornet systems were adequate without alteration. A total of 75 aircraft, of which 18 will be two-seaters, were ordered to replace the three squadrons of ageing Dassault Mirages.

The Australian Hornet will differ from the standard in minor details. They include the elimination of catapult launch equipment, the replacement of carrier ILS by a conventional ILS, and the provision of HF radio for long distance communications, indigenous fatigue monitoring, Tacan and IFF systems, a landing light, and an aural 'gear down' warning system. The first Australian Hornet components reached the Saint Louis assembly line in August 1983, and handover of the first two aircraft is expected to take place in October 1984. These will then be used to train OCU pilots before being flown to Australia in April 1985. The third Hornet will be supplied in knock-down kit form for re-

Above: A considerable effort was made to sell the Hornet overseas. This 1980 photograph shows an early prototype, with unfilled LEX slots and notched wing leading edge, in Swedish Air Force markings.

assembly by the Government Aircraft Factory at Avalon, which will be responsible for the assembly of the remaining 72 aircraft. The F404 engines for the Hornet will also be assembled in Australia, by Commonwealth Aircraft at Melbourne. The Australian-assembled Hornets are scheduled to commence delivery from April 1985.

A major construction programme is currently underway at Williamtown in New South Wales involving hangarage, a maintenance complex, a simulator building, and other facilities for Hornet operations. In addition, major works are taking place at Tyndal in the Northern Territory, some 300 miles (480km) south of Darwin, which will be another Hornet's Nest. The first operational unit to receive Hornets will probably be No. 75 Squadron, currently based at Darwin, followed by Nos. 3 and 77 Squadrons. It has also been proposed to establish another base at Weipa, in northern Queensland, which would bring Papua, New Guinea, within range of the Hornet. One additional and not inconsiderable advantage of the Hornet in RAAF service may accrue from the fact that US Navy carrier groups operating in the Pacific and Indian oceans would be using the same type, thus facilitating mutual assistance.

Spanish Hornets

The third nation to order the Hornet was Spain, with the F-16 being the final alternative once more. The aircraft to be replaced were F-4C Phantoms (with which the Ejercito del Aire had never been very happy), Mirages and Freedom Fighters. Originally 144 aircraft were required, but budgetary considerations saw this reduced to 72 Hornets, plus an option on a further 12, and the contract was signed on May 31, 1983, with first delivery due in 1986.

The Spanish operational requirement was for an adverse-weather, day or night aircraft able to operate in either the fighter or attack roles, although attack was given the greater emphasis. Recent head-to-head sales contests against the F-16, notably those involving Greece and Turkey, as in many previous cases, have been lost to the cheaper single-engined fighter. Yet it has been noticeable that whenever operational requirements were more demanding, the Hornet has been the aircraft selected.

The Luftwaffe is currently evaluating the Hornet, together with the McDonnell Douglas F-15, the General Dynamics F-16, the Northrop F-20 Tigershark, and the Dassault Mirage 2000. Air superiority is the prime requirement, with a procurement of 200 to 300 aircraft at stake. If capability regardless of cost is the aim, the F-15 Eagle has to be the favourite, whereas if cost is the main consideration, the Tigershark should win hands down. If maximum performance in the top right-hand corner of the performance envelope is required, the Mirage 2000 cannot be ruled out. But for a good all-rounder at an in-between price, the contest is likely to devolve upon those old adversaries, the Fighting Falcon and the Hornet.

In fact, it is widely believed that the West German evaluation is being performed in order to establish a datum for the proposed TKF fighter specification. But this being so, the development period of a totally new fighter is such that the existing F-4F Phantom fleet will reach the end of its effective life before the new fighter is ready, in which case the Hornet, with its all-round capability, would make a more than useful stopgap. It appears to be the aircraft to beat.

The Hornet, like most combat aircraft, will doubtless see service in many specialized roles during its lifetime, and one of these is already emerging in the shape of the reconnaissance RF/A-18. It was originally planned to produce a dedicated two-seat variant for this role, but studies showed that extensive structural changes would be needed, as well as a new environmental control system to cool the additional avionics.

Reconnaissance conversion

Consequently, it was decided to produce a reconnaissance pallet which would be interchangeable with the Vulcan cannon. The gun cavity door on the underside of the nose was also to be replaced by a bulged fairing with viewing ports and provision for extra sensor mountings, and the entire package was designed to be installed or replaced at squadron level in about eight hours. Testing began in October 1982 and was scheduled to continue until September 1984, but the package concept, like many another lash-up before it, proved unsatisfactory, and early in 1984 the US Navy reverted to its original scheme and awarded a development contract to McDonnell Douglas to produce a dedicated reconnaissance Hornet. The gun is to be removed and cameras installed in its place, while heating and cooling lines are to be modified, and the software is to be reprogrammed to suit the sensors. Flight testing is scheduled to commence in the summer of 1984 and be completed sometime during the following year. It is possible that extra fuel will be accommodated by raising the 'spine' of the aircraft behind the cockpit.

Another possible variant that has been under discussion for some time is the two-seat heavy attack aircraft to replace the A-6E Intruder. No designation has

Below: A reconnaissance Hornet is the next step, and MCAIR received a development contract in early 1984. Sensors will replace the gun, the 1982 proposal for pallet-mounted equipment having been rejected.

Reconnaissance conversion proposal

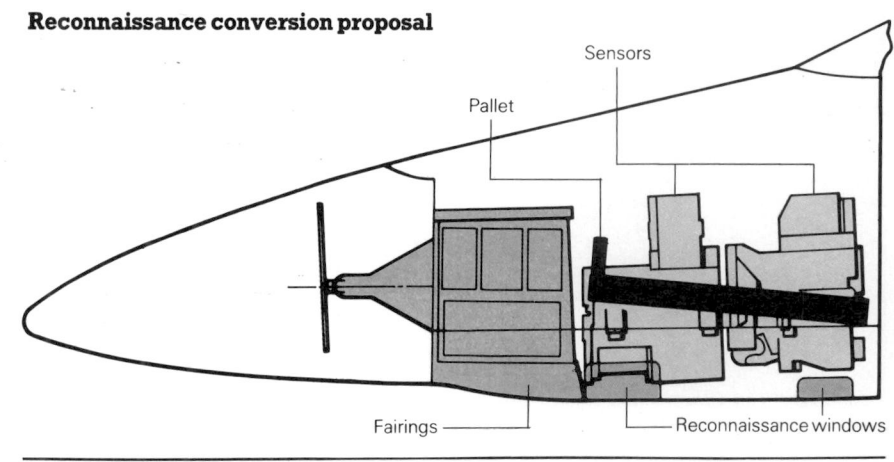

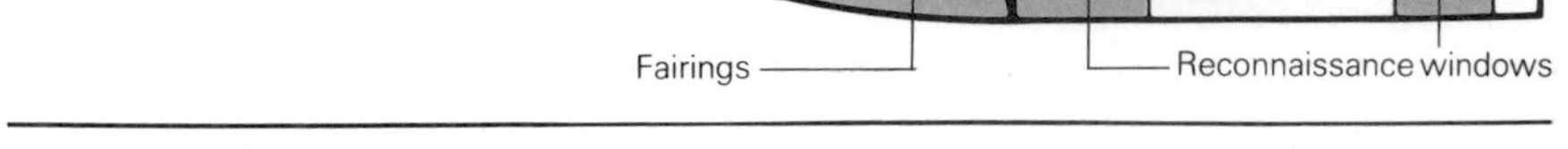

Right: Spain was the third export customer for the Hornet, the 72 ordered being due for delivery from 1986. By mid-1984 no decision had been made on colour schemes for the Ejercito del Aire, but this illustration shows how an F-18 might appear in similar camouflage to that worn by Spanish Air Force Phantoms.

Left: Mock-up of the two-seat Northrop F/A-18L. Sparrows occupy the wingtip launch rails, while Sidewinders are carried on extra underwing pylons. The Northrop proposal has lost out to the F-16 and F-18A in terms of sales.

been assigned as yet, but it is unofficially referred to as the Advanced A-18. A McDonnell Douglas proposal incorporates modifications to the trailing edges and flaps, uprated F404 engines in the 18,000lb (8,165kg) thrust class and expanded air-to-surface radar modes based on experience with the Strike Eagle programme. Additional internal fuel capacity, a mission-adapted rear cockpit and larger external fuel tanks are also proposed.

Northrop F-18L

As related in the development chapter, McDonnell Douglas took the Northrop YF-17 lightweight fighter and upgraded the design into a carrier-compatible multi-role fighter, the F/A-18A. At the same time, Northrop produced a design for a land-based multi-role variant with about 90 per cent commonality in terms of high-value, high-usage parts, which was originally intended to be about 20 per cent cheaper than the F/A-18A carrier fighter, but with the same versatility. It was designated F/A-18L.

Not being intended for carrier operations, the Northrop Hornet has a simpler and much lighter undercarriage, stressed for descent rates of up to 14fps (4.27m/sec). This allows greater external stores carriage on the fuselage, and also leaves an extra 18cu ft ($0.51m^3$) available for extra avionics and fuel. A smaller and lighter hook is fitted for runway arrestment, and the fuselage missile housings of the F/A-18A are not featured, thus saving weight and drag; Sparrow or Skyflash missiles are carried on underwing pylons, or even on the wingtips in lieu of Sidewinders.

There is no necessity for the wings to fold and the hinges and hydraulic folding gear have been eliminated. This has allowed the wings to be strengthened to carry the much heavier SARH missiles on the tips, and an extra hardpoint has been included on each wing. Instead of the ailerons and flaps on the F/A-18A, flaperons are used which incorporate ride control by varying the lift and apparent AOA to reduce the gust response, thus giving a smoother ride in high-speed low-altitude flight. On touchdown the flaperons deflect vertically and increase the download on the undercarriage, which makes the brakes more effective, and reduces the landing run. The flap deflection on the F/A-18L varies from its naval counterpart. The maximum flap deflection is 20deg for the leading edge flaps and 30deg for the trailing edge, compared with 30deg and 40deg respectively for the F/A-18A. Integral wing tanks are an optional extra, while USAF type 600US gall (1,756lit) drop tanks can be carried on the inner underwing hardpoints.

The overall effect of these changes is to reduce the aircraft weight by nearly a tonne. Thus wing loading is reduced, which improves manoeuvrability, and thrust loading is increased, which benefits acceleration, takeoff, climb and sustained turn. Alternatively, a heavier payload can be carried: the stated maximum is 20,000lb (9,072kg), which is rather more than the carrier fighter. With these advantages, it would seem that if the F/A-18A is a handful in the dogfight, the F/A-18L would be even more so. Yet no orders have been placed, and the F/A-18L bids fair to become the fighter that never was. The two YF-17s were judged sufficiently similar to be redesignated F/A-18L prototypes by Northrop for evaluation purposes, but not one F/A-18L has been built, and it is beginning to look as though none ever will be. This is the more surprising as the market potential was originally assessed as being around the 2,000 mark.

Part of the problem has been that the F-16 has been in competition, and the F-16 is a very fine fighter indeed. The other part arises from the fact that McDonnell Douglas have been energetically marketing their Hornet abroad, often in competition with the Northrop Hornet. Evaluation teams can go to Fort Worth or Saint Louis and see a finished product, whereas at Hawthorne this is not possible. One feels that Northrop and the F/A-18L Hornet deserved better. In early 1984 lawsuits pending between the rival companies were alleging what is in essence to be described as poaching. The legal situation is complex, involves Department of Defense rulings and is beyond the scope of this work. Although part of the Hornet story, with a decision anticipated late in 1984, it is of little interest from a strictly aviation viewpoint. What does matter is that the Hornet is a very fine warplane and a worthy successor to the ubiquitous Phantom.

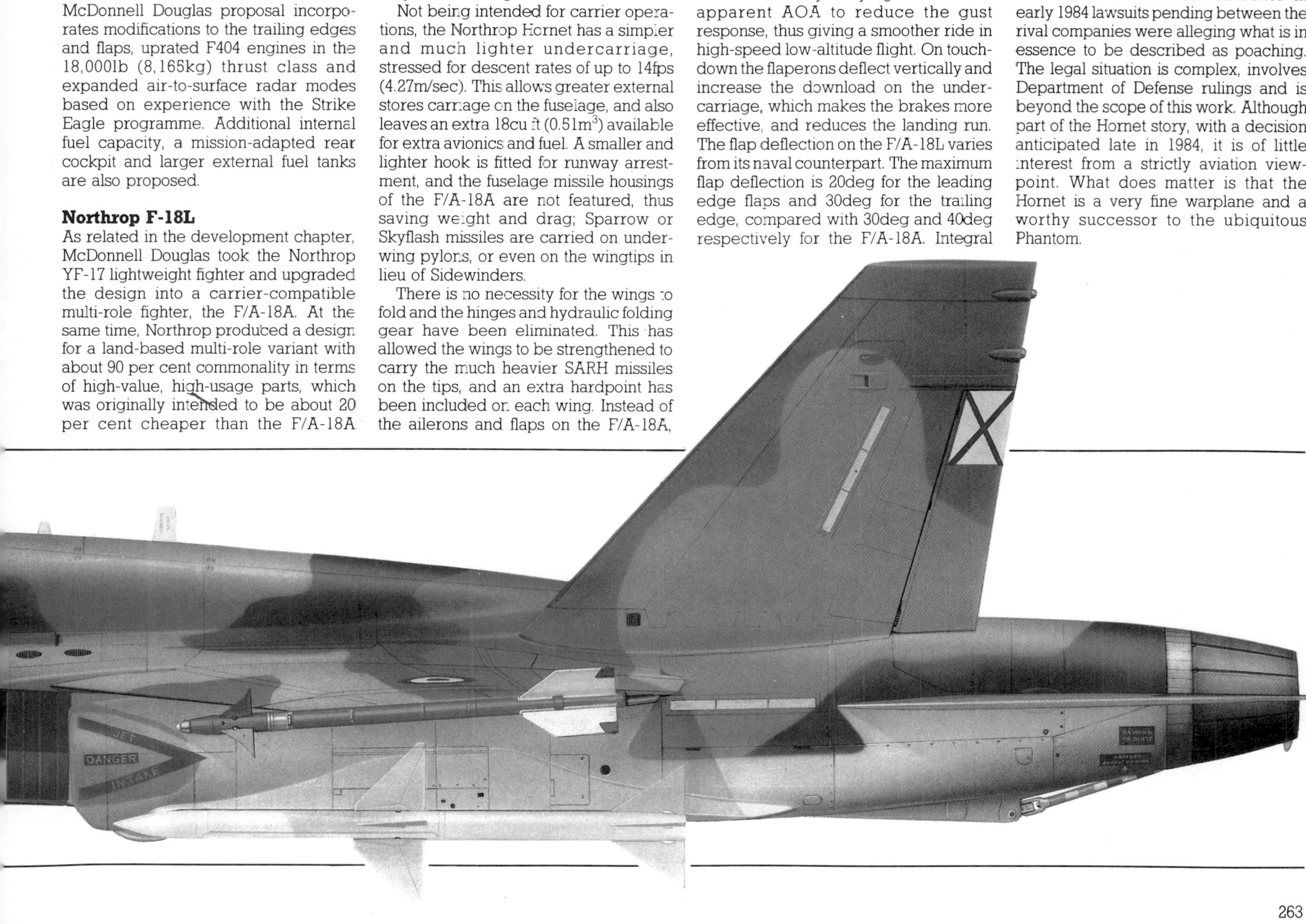

Glossary and abbreviations

A&AEE Aircraft and Armament Experimental Establishment (UK)
ACF Air Combat Fighter (USAF)
ACLS Automatic carrier landing system
ACM Air combat manoeuvring
ADF Automatic direction finding
AFB Air Force Base (USAF)
AGM Air-to-ground missile
AIM Air interception missile
AIMVAL/ACEVAL Missile and air combat evaluation programme carried out in Nevada in 1977
Alpha-numeric Information presented in the form of letters and/or numbers
AMAD Airframe mounted accessory drive
AMRAAM Advanced Medium-range Air-to-air Missile
AMT Accelerated mission test
Analogue Electronic system in which quantities are represented by electrical signals of variable characteristics, i.e., by electrical analogues
Anhedral Downward angle of wing or tailplane
AOA Angle of attack (the angle at which the wing meets the airflow)
APC Approach power compensator
APU Auxiliary power unit
Aspect ratio Ratio of the wingspan to the wing area, expressed as span squared divided by wing area
AST Accelerated service testing
Azimuth Bearing or direction in the horizontal plane
BIT(E) Built-in test (equipment)
Bolter Touch-and-go deck landing (usually unintentional)
Boundary layer Thin layer of slow-moving air that tends to cling to the skin of an aircraft
Bug out Depart the area
Bu. No. Bureau of Aeronautics number
BVR Beyond visual range
Bypass ratio Ratio of total volume of air passing through the engine to that passing through the core section.
CNI Communications, navigation, identification
CO_2 Carbon dioxide
CRT Cathode ray tube
CW Continuous wave (radar emission)
DBS Doppler beam sharpening
Departure The point at which an aircraft goes out of control
Dielectric Radar non-reflecting material
Digital Electronic system in which quantities are represented as on/off signals coded to represent numbers
DoD Department of Defense (US)
Doppler Radar making use of shift in frequency of signals reflected from the earth's surface ahead of or behind an aircraft to give measurement of true groundspeed, or of signals reflected from earth and moving targets to indicate the latter
ECCM Electronic counter-countermeasures
ECM Electronic countermeasures
FBW Fly-by-wire (electronic flight control system)
FET Field effect transistor
Flaperon Control surface doubling as flap and aileron
FLIR Forward-looking infra-red
FM Frequency modulated
FOD Foreign object damage
Fox One Pilot call on launching a Sparrow
Fox Two Pilot call on launching a Sidewinder
FSD Full scale development
g Unit of acceleration
GHz Giga Hertz; 1,000,000,000 Hertz (cycles per second)
Glint Apparent movement of the radar centre of a target
HDD Head-down display
HF High frequency
HOTAS Hands on throttle and stick
HP High pressure
HSD Horizontal situation display
HUD Head-up display
IFECMS In-flight engine condition monitoring system
IFF Identification friend or foe
IFR In-flight refuelling
IIR Imaging infra-red
INS Inertial navigation system
IR Infra-red
Knot Nautical mile per hour
kVA kiloVolt Amperes
LEX Leading edge extension (at the wing root)
LGB Laser-guided bomb
Lock-on Radar concentrating on targets in the attack mode
LP Low pressure
LRU Line replaceable unit
LWF Lightweight Fighter (USAF)
MAP Military Assistance Programme
Mach number Speed stated as a function of the local speed of sound
MCAS Marine Corps Air Station
MER Multiple ejection rack
MFD Multi-function display
MFHBF Mean flight hours between failures
MMD Master monitor display
MMH/FH Mean maintenance hours per flight hour
MMP Maintenance monitor panel
MTBF Mean time between failures
NAS Naval Air Station
NATC Naval Air Test Center
Nm Nautical mile (= 1.15 statute miles, 1.85km)
NPE Naval Preliminary Evaluation
OFT Operational Flight Trainer
OODA loop Sequence of pilot's mental processes: observation, orientation, decision, action
Overtake Closing speed irrespective of relative aspect or heading
Passive Non-emitting
Pitch Vertical movement or angle of aircraft longitudinal axis
PPFRT Prototype Preliminary Flight Rating Test
PRF Pulse repitition frequency
Ps Specific excess power
PSP Programmable signal processor
PTT Part Task Trainer
Raster Television picture built up line by line
Red Flag Tactical exercises held at Nellis AFB
RTS Radar Test System
RWR Radar warning receiver
SARH Semi-active radar homing
Sfc Specific fuel consumption (unit of fuel consumed per unit of thrust per hour)
SMET Simulated mission endurance test
Stabilators All-moving one-piece tailplane
STT Single target track
Tacan Tactical air navigation
TACTS/ACMI Tactical Air Combat Training System/Air Combat Manoeuvre Instrumentation
Taileron All-moving tailplanes with differential movement to provide control in the rolling plane
TDC Target designator control
TER Triple ejection rack
TFTS Tactical Fighter Training Squadron
TFW Tactical Fighter Wing
Trap Arrested deck landing
TWT Travelling wave tube
UFC Up-front control
UHF Ultra-high frequency
US gall US gallon (= 0.83Imp gall; 3.785lit; 6.5lb [2.95kg] JP-4 fuel)
VDU Visual display unit
VER Vertical ejection rack
VHF Very high frequency
Vmax Maximum velocity
WRA Weapon replaceable assembly

Specification

	YF-17	F-18A	F-18L
Dimensions			
Span (without missiles)	35ft 0in (10.67m)	37ft 6in (11.43m)	37ft 6in (11.43m)
Length	56ft 0in (17.07m)	56ft 0in (17.07m)	56ft 0in (17.07m)
Height	14ft 6in (4.42m)	15ft 3½in (4.66m)	14ft 7in (4.44m)
Tail span	22ft 2½in (6.77m)	21ft 7¼in (6.58m)	21ft 7¼in (6.58m)
Wheel track	6ft 10in (2.08m)	10ft 2½in (3.11m)	8ft 5in (2.57m)
Wing area	350sq ft (32.52m²)	400sq ft (37.16m²)	400sq ft (37.16m²)
Weights			
Empty	17,000lb (7,700kg) approx	21,830lb (9,900kg)	19,600lb (8,900kg) approx
Fighter configuration	23,000lb (10,430kg)	34,700lb (15,740kg)	32,000lb (14,500kg) approx
Maximum		51,900lb (23,540kg)	
Performance			
Vmax	Mach 1.95	Mach 1.8	Mach 2+
Combat ceiling	50,000ft (15,240m)	50,000ft (15,240m)	55,000ft (16,765m)
Combat radius – fighter	>500nm (927km)	>400nm (740km)	
Combat radius – attack		575nm (1,065km)	
Ferry range (unrefuelled)	2,600nm (4,816km)	>2,000nm (3,706km)	2,500nm (4,630km)
Initial climb rate	>50,000ft/min (254m/sec)	50,000ft/sec (254m/sec)	56,000ft/sec (285m/sec)
Maximum payload	9,800lb(4,445kg) approx	17,000lb (7,710kg)	20,000lb (9,070kg)

Chapter 5

F-111

Bill Gunston

F-111

Contents

Acknowledgements

The author and editor would like to thank the public relations staff of General Dynamics and Grumman Aerospace for their help in providing material for this chapter. In addition to the other individuals and organizations whose contributions of photographs are credited elsewhere, we are particularly grateful to Thomas B. Street, EF-111A Deputy Program Director, and M.J. Lancaster, of the Royal Australian Air Force Public Relations Office. Captain Jim Rotramel, USAF, author of the section beginning on page 306, has also provided many of the outstanding photographs included.

Author

A former World War II RAF pilot and flying instructor, Bill Gunston has spent most of his working life accumulating a wealth of information on the history of aviation and military technology. Since leaving the service in 1948 he has acted as an advisor to several major aviation companies and become one of the most respected authors on scientific and aviation subjects as well as a frequent broadcaster. His numerous books include the Salamander titles *The Illustrated Encyclopedia of Modern Military Aircraft* and *The Encyclopedia of the World's Combat Aircraft*.

A regular contributor to many leading international aviation and defence journals, he is a former technical editor of *Flight International* and technology editor of *Science Journal*. Among the many other authoritative journals for which he has carried out assignments are *Battle*, *Aeroplane Monthly*, *Aircraft* (Australia), *Aviation Magazine* (France), *Aerospace International*, *Aircraft Production*, *Flying*, *World Airnews*, and the *Journal of the Royal United Services Institute for Defence Studies*. He is an assistant compiler of *Jane's All the World's Aircraft* and has contributed to Brassey's *Annual and Defence Yearbook*, *Aircraft Annual* and Salamander's *The Soviet War Machine*, *The Encyclopedia of Air Warfare* and *The US War Machine*.

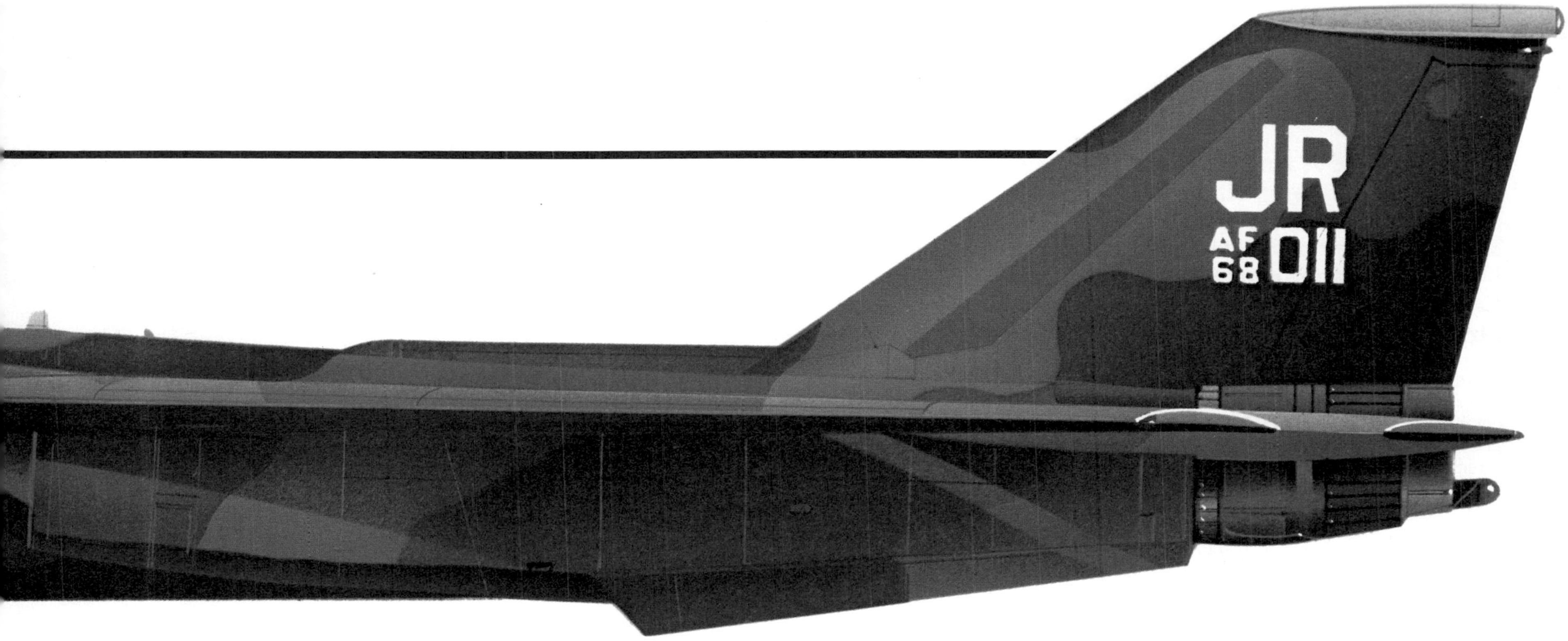

Introduction

Nobody even remotely connected with aviation needs to be told that the early years of the F-111, the planned all-can-do tactical fighter for the USAF in the 1960s, were marked by the biggest row in aviation. The row was triggered by the belief that the USAF had bought "the second-best airplane at the higher price" (than its immediate rival design), but the situation was exacerbated by the prolonged efforts of the Defense Secretary to make the same basic design suit the very different needs of the US Navy. Once the F-111 was actually flying everyone wanted to look ahead to quick development and high-rate production, but this was thwarted by technical problems whose extent and scale were almost unbelievable – so that the Australians did not get the F-111s they had bought in 1963 until ten years later. Even the attempts to demonstrate the F-111's capability in action were thwarted by extraordinary combat losses which had nothing to do with the enemy.

Having painfully recapitulated all this it may sound naive or even wishful thinking to suggest that in fact the F-111 was an aircraft of very great stature and unprecedented capability, which for many years has not only more than met most of its numerical design requirements but has served as the exact model for the Sukhoi Su-24, its counterpart in the Soviet Union. Does the F-111 do a good job? Of course. Need it have had all the problems and arguments? Of course not. But wisdom after the event is not particularly valuable.

What is rather odd is, first, that the more unusual features of the F-111, notably the pivoted swing-wings which so captivated the popular media, played no part in the years of technical difficulty and political in-fighting. It was certainly wrong to ask for a long-range bomber and call it a fighter. Had this aircraft been given an 'A' (for Attack) designation, instead of 'F' (for Fighter), it is very doubtful that anyone would have tried to bulldoze through a plan for one aircraft for both the USAF and Navy.

Development

During the 1950s American design teams worked on fighters to fly at over Mach 3, with weights in the 40-ton class. Such monsters, fortunately never built, helped create a mental climate for the TFX, planned in 1960 as the US Air Force's new all-can-do multirole fighter. The Secretary for Defense said it had "the speed of a fighter, the bombload of a heavy bomber and the range of a transport". Despite the protestations of the customer – the Commanding General of TAC said "I am not going to accept any goddamned 70,000lb airplane" – the end product was a 100,000lb fighter. This caused a few headaches.

When a major air force such as the USAF organizes for the next-generation combat aircraft, it is subject to inputs and pressures which pull in different directions. It wishes the new equipment to be the best, and in particular to beat anything likely in the same timeframe by the real or potential enemy. It wants it to replace particular aircraft that are nearing the end of their first-line career. It is highly desirable to make maximum use of the latest technology, yet it wishes to use only well-tried hardware and techniques that will not cause expensive delays and price escalation. And there is a fair amount of fashion influencing the sort of aircraft the generals have in mind.

At the time of Korea they were shocked at being outflown by pilots in MiG-15s and were receptive to any manufacturer who could promise more speed and height, even if it meant carrying less fuel or weapons. But by the end of the fast-moving 1950s they had overcome this fixation on performance, and in doing so had tended to move in what now appear to have been wrong directions.

New technology was abundant. In the context of the aircraft described in this book the most important was probably the pivoted swing wing (like other technical details, this is described in the next chapter). Another was the high-compression two-spool gas turbine, with its superior fuel economy, and the turbofan engine with its much better propulsive efficiency (and, by virtue of its reduced jet velocity, dramatically diminished noise). Combining these engine advances with full augmentation promised a highly superior fighter powerplant. Other new developments included titanium alloys used in primary structure; thrust reversers able to be used in flight; thrust vectoring for jet lift and STOL or even VTOL capability; complete crew capsules able to be ejected from a doomed aircraft with the crew inside; and a positive wealth of new avionics for blind navigation, terrain-following, weapon delivery and many other duties including protection against hostile defence systems.

In 1960 it would have been possible to combine all these in such a way as to produce a fabulous multirole fighter, essentially equal to an F-15 except in one or two relatively trivial areas where the technology had not then sufficiently matured (the cockpit displays and pilot interfaces are an example). But USAF thinking in 1960 was quite different from the thinking of seven years later that produced the F-15. In 1960 the USAF was trying to steer a course between experts, not only in Britain, who proclaimed the manned fighter obsolete, and other experts who said it was vitally needed but only as a long-distance 'stand-off kill' interceptor armed with large missiles. Yet other experts pointed out the vulnerability of airfields, and urged that all future combat aircraft should be VTOLs, or at the very least V/STOLs, able to rise thunderously off the ground from a thousand isolated sites where they would be safe from the dreaded nuclear missiles.

Ground-attack requirements

Still others insisted that the main role in practice was likely to be attacks on surface targets; and here again there was sharp division of opinion between the diehards who believed in the 'nuclear tripwire' policy and the newer adherents to the 'flexible response' doctrine. The former said the new fighter only needed to carry one or two bombs and deliver them somewhere in the general area of the target, while the conventional-warfare believers demanded the ability to carry about 48 bombs and achieve a delivery accuracy of about 50 metres.

It was clear that a new USAF fighter would have to be procured, but it could have been an agile replacement for the disappointing F-104 or a stand-off killer for Air Defense Command in place of the lately terminated Mach 3 F-108 Rapier. The man who got the ball rolling was the new Commander of Tactical Air Command, General Frank F. Everest. TAC had always been very interested in the air-to-ground business, and under Everest's supervision plans were drawn up for a new fighter-bomber to replace the F-105 Thunderchief.

In fact, the F-105 had never been a true fighter at all, but rather an all-weather attack bomber with an internal bay for a nuclear weapon. In many ways it was a great aircraft, but it needed the best runways available. TAC had made a study of F-105 operations, especially in Europe, which showed that, as the available runway length was reduced below 10,000ft (3,000m), so did the incidence of overruns and barrier crashes increase. Everest's predecessor, Otto P. Weyland, had written a detailed analysis of future TAC missions and equipment needs, and Everest was determined to get new hardware into the inventory as soon as possible.

Above: Not a 'bit more poke' but the container for the anti-spin chute on the 4th RDT&E prototype. Note the streamlined fairings outboard of the engine nozzles.

Below: From the top of a hangar at Fort Worth a photographer records the pre-rollout preparations, with technicians preparing the prototype under the scrutiny of a camera crew.

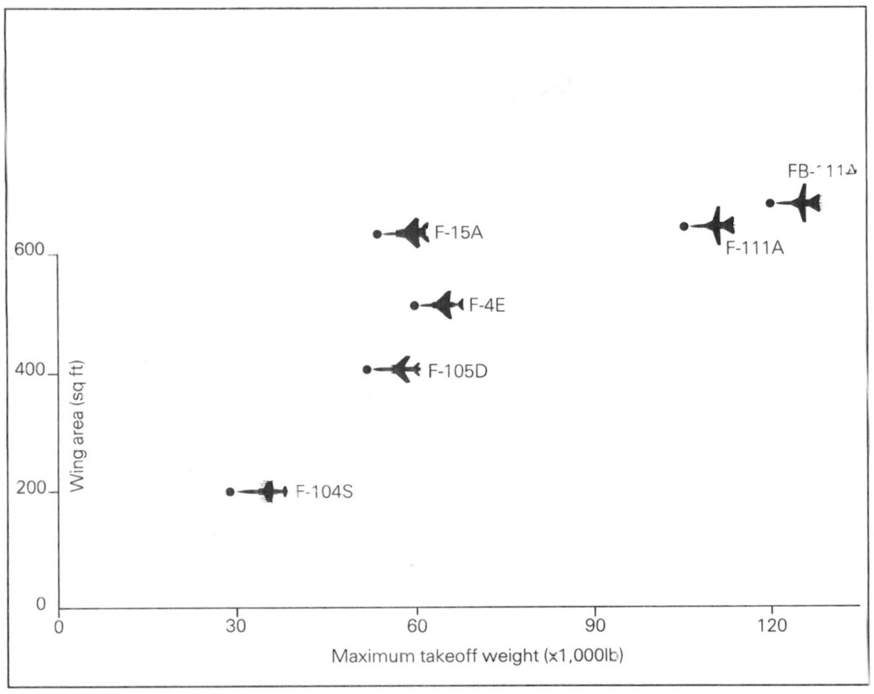

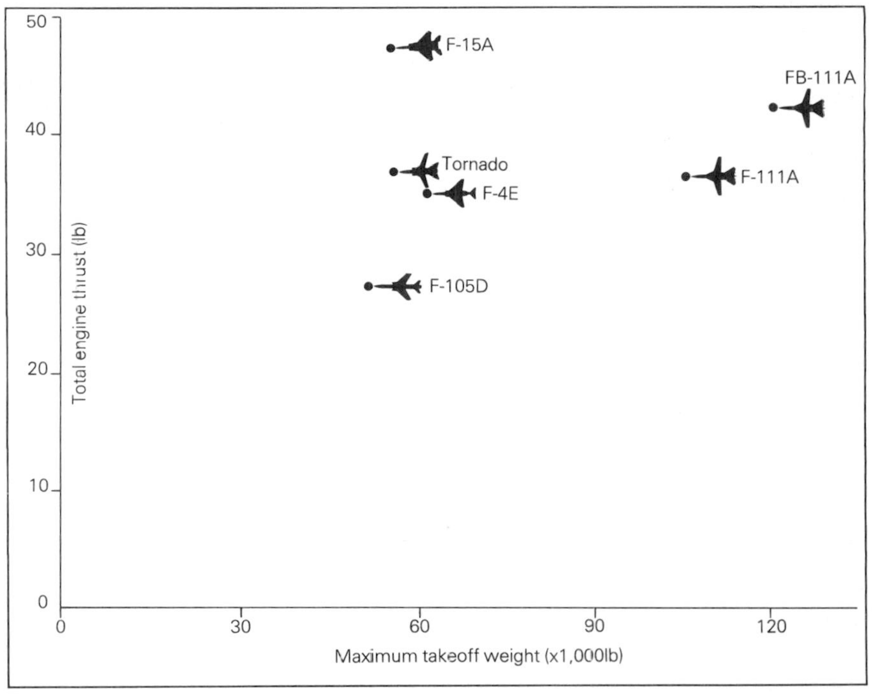

Above: The third and sixth RDT&E aircraft formating with wings at maximum sweep. Even at this stage they were quite different from 63-9766 seen opposite – and from each other.

Top left: Wing loading of all One-Elevens is high by any standard. This is fine for low-level attack but it makes the aircraft a bit of a non-starter where air combat is called for.

Top right: Power loading is gross weight divided by total engine thrust. Again, the One-Eleven's great weight makes it a 'non-fighter'.

In retrospect it is unfortunate that the studies revolved around long-range attack missions, overseas deployment and, instead of true STOL capability, merely a runway requirement less demanding than that of the F-105. TAC had already studied the Zell (zero-length launch) technique in which combat aircraft are blasted like missiles off a launcher using a giant rocket; this was unattractive on such counts as flexibility, safety, convenience and cost. VTOL was all the rage in Europe, where some of the basic techniques had been sewn up in patents by Rolls-Royce and Bristol Aero-Engines Ltd, and this provoked a large measure of prejudice against it in TAC. It was commonly felt, and not without justification at that time, that a VTOL was too limited in range and weapon load to be much use. This was before the era of efficient STOVLs like Harrier II with its ski-jump technique.

So, instead of concentrating on what would happen when the Soviets fired the hundreds of their nuclear missiles which are targeted on NATO airfields, the USAF planners considered only attack by conventional bomb-dropping aircraft. They came up with the answer that any substantial improvement – such as 50 per cent – on the F-105 runway requirement would be most welcome. It became fashionable to talk of "taking off between the craters".

Leaping into the mid-1980s we now have the situation in which protesters campaign against the so-called 'cruise' as likely to invite nuclear retaliation, despite the fact that no enemy can know its whereabouts in advance, while the alternative long-range delivery system in the European NATO context is the F-111 whose whereabouts are in general known to within a few metres. It seems common sense to equip an air force only with combat aircraft capable of dispersal away from nuclear rocket attack, but the evidence of discussion on this point in the TAC thinking of 1960 is hard to discover.

In contrast, there is abundant evidence that any real attempt to move towards V/STOLs was thought undesirable. Not only was it thought to result in rather useless aircraft, but the problems of logistics and what later became known as C^3 (Command, Control and Communications) were considered to negate the advantages. No less an expert than the USAF Director of Operational Requirements, Major-General Bruce K. Holloway, said: "In order to disperse one or two flights at appreciable distances from each other we would require major changes in the supporting base structure. A fleet of VTOL supply aircraft would be required. A vastly increased communica-

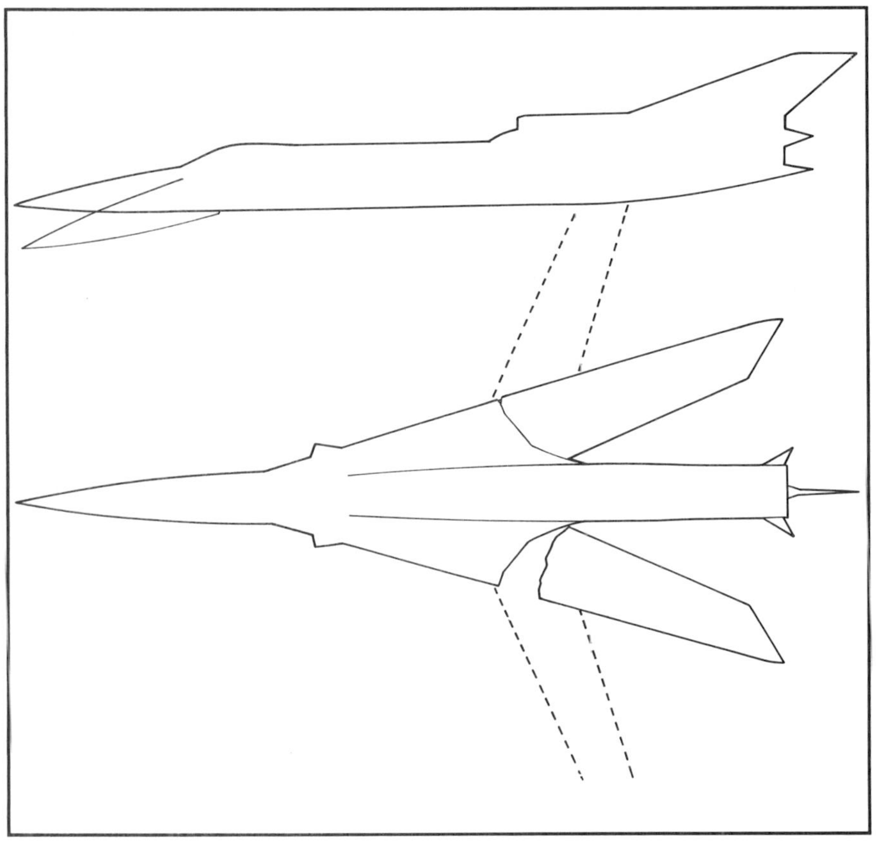

Left: The original spur to NASA's swept-wing work was the swing-wing (and droop nose) work of Vickers-Armstrongs at Weybridge in 1958–9.

Left: The unpainted fourth prototype with anti-spin chute, full flap/slat deployment and four dummy Phoenix long-range air-to-air missiles.

Below left: Boeing-Wichita destroyed almost all their records on their excellent TFX submission. This three-view at least survives.

Above: The seventh RDT&E aircraft with wings at the minimum sweep angle of 16deg and carrying four dummy nuclear bombs.

Below: The first air-to-air picture at maximum sweep. It was secured on the same January 1965 sortie as the adjacent illustration.

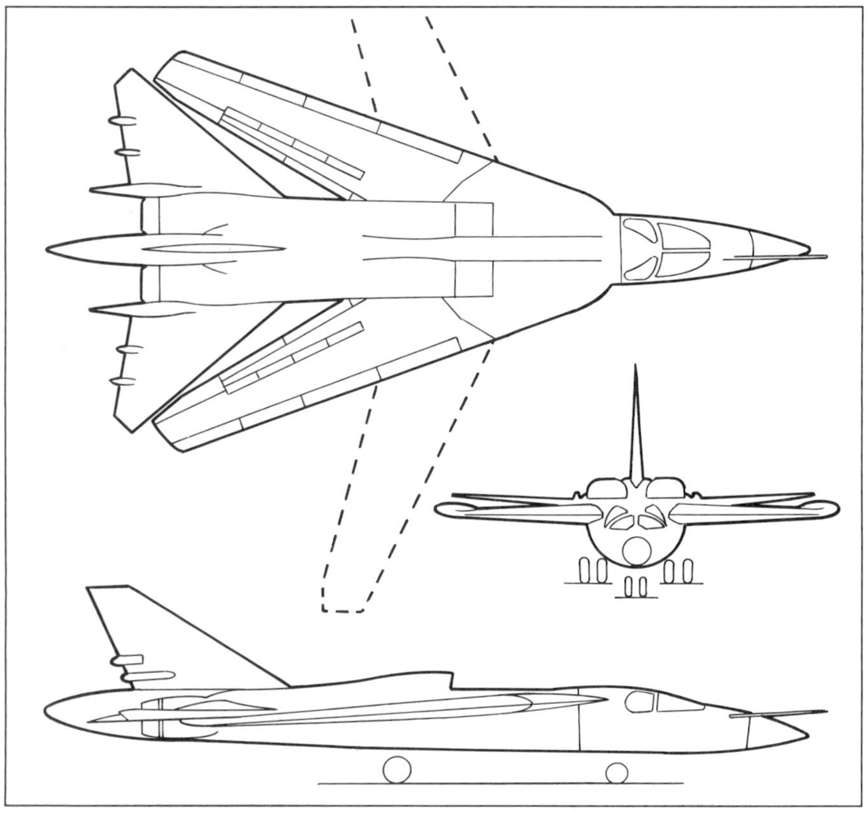

Above: Another view of the seventh prototype on test with B61 'nukes'. The outer pylons, on the swinging wings, sometimes failed to pivot.

Below: For comparison with the picture opposite, this shows the dramatic way the F-111 can change its shape on command of the pilot.

tions net would also be necessary ...".

We cannot pursue the argument, because in almost a quarter century since that time little more has been done to make air power survivable on the ground. But 1959–60 was a crucial era in which the USAF had the power to steer the thinking of the world's air forces in this direction.

As it was, it was only after considerable argument that SOR-183 (Specific Operational Requirement) was drawn up in the first half of 1960. Nobody argued about the central demand, which was the ability to carry two nuclear weapons internally and fly at Mach 1·2 (912mph/1,468km/h) at treetop height over very long distances to a major ground target. It was also agreed there had to be a considerable capability with conventional 'iron bombs', but here the bombload could vary from 5,000lb to 30,000lb (2,268kg to 13,608kg), and in 1960 the general view was that 10,000lb (4,536kg) was an acceptable minimum. Very curiously, as the aircraft was called a fighter, there appear to have been no numerical demands for SEP (specific excess power, a measure of surplus propulsive thrust available for the extra energy needed for climb or manoeuvring), or for turn radius or any other manoeuvre demands, and very limited and uncertain specification of air-to-air weapons.

Ultimately SOR-183 was issued on June 14, 1960, calling for a Future Tactical Strike Fighter. Somebody subsequently omitted the vital word 'strike' and it became Tactical Fighter Experimental or TFX. With hindsight it is self-evident that, as the entire emphasis of SOR-183 was on long-range attack, the aircraft ought really to have been called an attack aircraft, with a DoD number such as A-7 (pushing the 1964 Vought Corsair II down the list to become the A-8). This would have saved a fantastic amount of time, money and aggravation, because the new US Administration of John F. Kennedy which assumed office on January 20, 1961, brought with it a man determined to be a new broom to sweep the Pentagon clean: Robert S. McNamara.

A former Vice-President of the Ford Motor Co, McNamara was an incisive businessman who, probably rightly, believed the Pentagon to be a vast house peopled by costly bureaucrats who needed a good shakeup in order to deliver better value for money. Sadly, he also got involved in technical matters. He is quoted as watching a Navy flypast and asking "What good are all

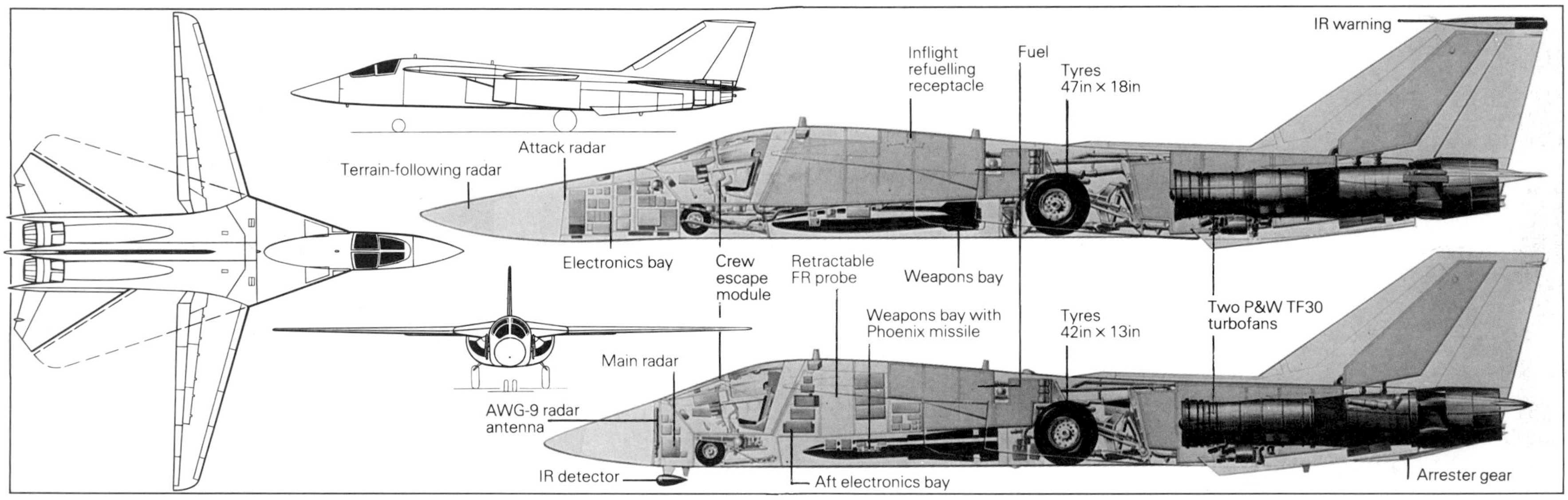

Above: Simple three-view of the F-111B. The main distinguishing feature was the non-Aardvark nose.

Above: Comparative inboard profiles of the F-111A (upper) and F-111B, published by GD on June 15, 1965.

those different kinds of airplanes?" – the implied belief being that one, or possibly two, types could have flown all the Navy's missions. One of the first things he did on taking office was to be told all the biggest new DoD procurement programmes. He believed many could be combined, to the taxpayer's benefit.

It so happened that running in parallel with the USAF SOR-183 was a Navy programme called the Fleet Air Defense Fighter. This called for the longest possible time on CAP (Combat Air Patrol), armed with a heavy load of long-range AAMs and powerful radar to spot hostile aircraft at distances of at least 100 miles (160km). After many studies the Navy had discovered that, provided the AAM had sufficient flight performance, the carrier aircraft could almost be a modified S-2 with a speed of about 180mph (290km/h)! By 1959 the FADF had centred on the Douglas F6D Missileer, a subsonic aircraft with long mission endurance, the powerful Hughes AWG-9 radar and six or even eight of the giant Bendix Eagle AAMs. But many people could not understand the concept of a subsonic fighter, and in one of his last acts the outgoing Navy Secretary, Thomas S. Gates Jr, cancelled the F6D.

Consequently, when McNamara was briefed on the TFX he was also briefed on the FADF, which was in a very fluid state. Many companies in the US industry were preparing proposals for either or both, and it seemed obvious that both TFX and FADF were going to be programmes of the first magnitude, together replacing such important types as the F-105, F-101, F-104, F-100, F-6, F-8, F-3, the new F-4 Phantom in all versions for all services, and also all derived reconnaissance models of each type. When Allied purchases were added, the total production was likely to run into several thousand, and as a former Ford man McNamara believed in getting the price down by building lots of identical items.

Thus was born the drive for commonality between the TFX and FADF. Like many aspects of the F-111 story it has been aired in countless Congressional reports, hardback books and articles in the media throughout the world. Most readers will already know that, against almost all the professional advice of people in the Air Force and Navy, the new SecDef actually did bulldoze through a common programme for a new fighter for both services. He insisted on the maximum commonality

Below: This beautiful 'profile' depicts the second production F-111B, the final example completed of the Navy version. We ought to shed no tears at its demise.

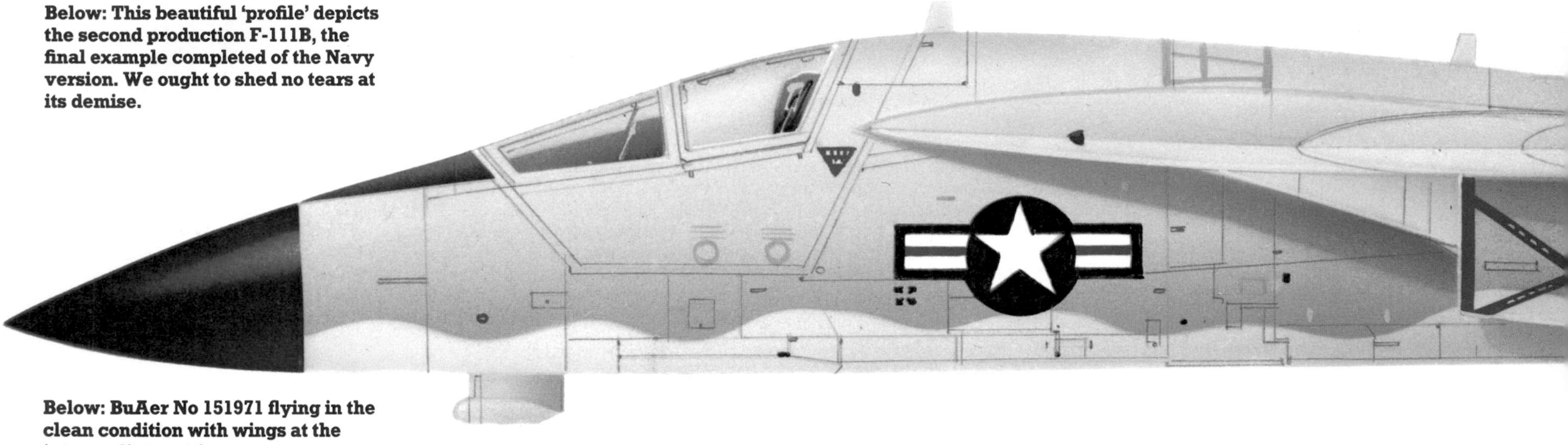

Below: BuAer No 151971 flying in the clean condition with wings at the intermediate setting.

even to the extent of personally telling the rival bidders how to design the aircraft.

The eventual winner, the Fort Worth Division of General Dynamics (GD), was selected – again in the face of almost all the expert opinion in the Air Force – largely because, even though its price was higher, it offered to build with a higher degree of commonality than the second-placed bidder. The latter was Boeing-Wichita, whose excellent engineering team lost out largely because it recognized that to meet what actually were two entirely different sets of requirements you have to build two different aircraft.

At all times the basic design was dictated primarily by the USAF requirement, the unfortunate Navy being instructed to demand the fewest possible essential changes. Thus the aircraft finally built was not significantly compromised by the Navy FAD mission except in the single matter of the cockpit arrangement. The Air Force had originally specified tandem seating for a pilot and WSO (weapon-system officer), which offered lower drag and better all-round view for both men. The Navy favoured side-by-side seating because this made it slightly less impossible for the 'common' design to meet the severe limitation on overall length for compatibility with aircraft carriers. The increased drag did not matter to a stand-off interceptor carrying AAMs with a range in the order of 100 miles (161km), and for most naval missions the side-by-side arrangement was actually an advantage.

Thus the F-111A for the Air Force and F-111B for the Navy were built with side-by-side seating. After agonizing problems the F-111B ground to a halt in 1968 and was replaced by the F-14, and it does not appear again in this book. But the legacy it left of arguments and problems – quite apart from being one of the very few 'fighters' ever built with side-by-side seats – certainly never saved the US taxpayer the anticipated billion dollars.

Also omitted from this book are details of the scandals which rocked not only Washington but the entire United States after the F-111 contract was awarded to GD on November 24, 1962. These began with the widespread belief that Mr McNamara had picked the wrong aircraft; as an official Report to the US Senate later stated, "The preliminary enquiry soon revealed that there was substantial reason to believe that the decision had been made to buy the second-best airplane at the higher price". This particular row raged for years, and has still not entirely subsided, though it was eventually surpassed in popular appeal by Watergate.

What was much more serious was that the F-111 itself ran into an extraordinary succession of serious technical difficulties. Not one of these stemmed from any of the radically new features in the design, but they combined to have a major effect on the overall programme. One effect was still further to reduce the capability of the F-111 as an air-combat fighter, to the extent that – though for purely emotional reasons today's F-111 jocks insist they are *fighter* crews, and regard the word 'bomber' as a studied insult – the aircraft has never been used in any kind of fighter role whatsoever. Another effect was that, in the sharpest contrast to the sausage-machine production envisaged by McNamara, the total programme comprised a mere 562 aircraft split up into batches of nine types.

Today the Royal Australian Air Force has 20 F-111C aircraft and four modified F-111As, while the USAF has one wing each of the F-111A, F-111D, F-111E and F-111F, and two squadron-size wings of the FB-111A. To make life harder, shortages of both aircraft and crucial spares have resulted in some squadrons having to operate a mix of different sub-types, greatly increasing the cost and complicating training and maintenance.

Almost the only part of the programme that has worked more or less as planned has been the newest version, the unarmed EF-111A electronic-warfare aircraft. Here 42 F-111As are being completely rebuilt by Grumman, as described in the penultimate chapter. Earlier versions were procured in reduced numbers either in order to switch to an improved model or because of the effect of inflation on the purchase price.

Above: The first colour air-to-air of the first F-111B. Interesting that Grumman went for tandem seats in the F-14 Tomcat!

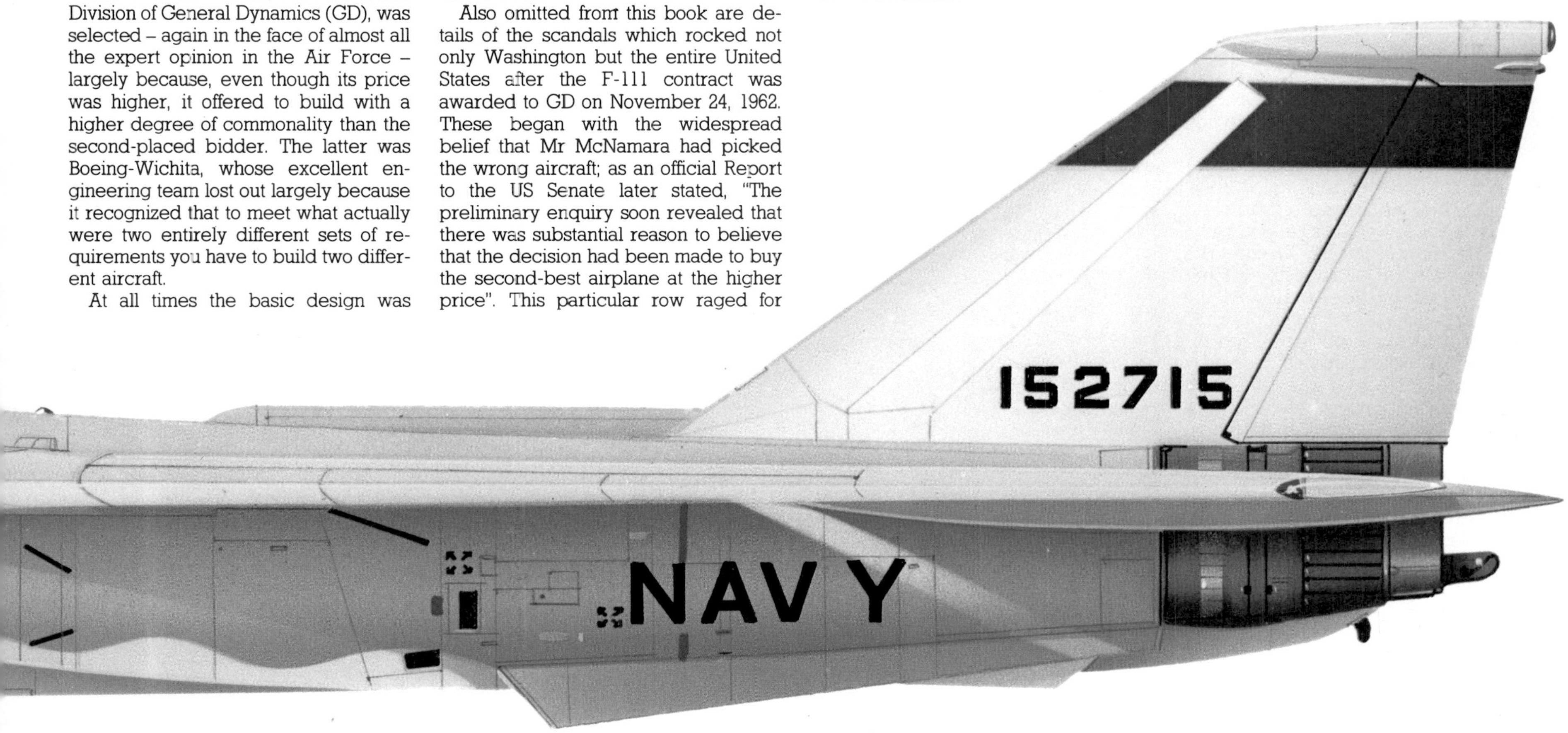

Triumph in adversity

Thus, instead of being the global smash-hit that Mr McNamara and many other people expected in 1961, the F-111 programme has suffered many disappointments, amplified by the close attentions of a generally hostile press. Yet if only it were possible to forget the difficulties – and the unfortunate word 'fighter' which caused half the problems – no objective observer can but conclude that the F-111 will go down in history as an aircraft of immense stature and capability which ushered in a new age in military aviation. Though the popular media often cannot see beyond its swing wings, that design feature is purely incidental. Its true importance lies in the fact that it was the first aircraft to make blind first-pass attacks on point targets, and to penetrate hostile airspace in the TF (terrain following) mode.

The first accomplishment means it can fly as straight as an arrow to a known fixed point on the ground, day or night and in any weather, and drop a bomb within a circle of maybe 50 metres radius. Both the TAC and SAC versions have such a string of success behind them in pinpoint navigation and bombing competitions that this capability is not in doubt. As a bonus, which in some theatres is vital, the range of the F-111 even without air refuelling handsomely exceeds that of any other military jet except large subsonic aircraft (the Soviet Su-24 is probably comparable). One has only to study the Su-24 to see that the Sukhoi designers have paid the engineers who created the F-111 the greatest of all compliments. They have probably been able to set up a better programme, however, building many hundreds of the same model.

Design

The fact that today's One-Elevens can do their job is testimony to the basic rightness of the design: however, nobody today would build the aircraft in this way. Even eliminating any suggestion that the aircraft has any air-combat capability, it would be preferable to use tandem seating, and with gross weights of 100,000lb and over the propulsive thrust could well be increased by at least 50 per cent. Alternatively the basic demands for mission radius and ferry range should have been pitched much lower. But the sincerest form of flattery is imitation, and the Soviet counterpart, the Su-24, is almost a copy!

Above: The reason for the swing-wing is that, ideally, a transonic low-level attacker can almost lift itself on the fuselage!

SOR-183, the USAF document which launched the TFX programme which led to the F-111, merely spelled out a list of requirements. It did not specify how many engines, or even how many wings, the successful proposal aircraft might have; but at the same time the document itself was drawn up in a curious manner which virtually dictated that the successful design would have a swing wing.

Back in the early 1950s the US National Advisory Committee for Aeronautics, largely in the ebullient person of John Stack, chief of supersonic tunnels at the Langley Laboratory, had cast an attentive eye over the concept of the pivoted swing wing, or VG (variable-geometry) aircraft. No elegant way of using the idea seemed possible until October 1957, when a proposal came out of the blue from Vickers-Armstrongs (Aircraft) in Britain.

NACA had just begun a further study of swing wings when the US Mutual Weapons Development Program office in Paris advised Langley that a disgruntled Barnes Wallis at Vickers was looking for someone to replace the UK Ministry of Supply which had just abandoned the swing wing (because it had been decreed that manned combat aircraft were no longer going to be needed). To cut a very long story short the end result was not funds going to Weybridge but the very considerable Vickers research information going to Stack.

In October 1958 NACA was renamed NASA (National Aeronautics and Space Administration), and by this time not only had Stack completed tunnel testing of a basic swing-wing shape but the Langley model-makers were being given drawings of possible future fighter shapes. Stack spent much of his time in heated discussion with planemakers, and almost as much in the company of generals. By this time he was Langley's Deputy Director, and probably the most important man in the Western world when it came to getting new aerodynamics into practical designs of aircraft. He played a central role from the very start in helping Gen Everest draft the SOR-183 requirements, and the numbers stipulated stemmed directly from Langley's results in tunnel testing swing-wing models.

The key features in the Vickers-derived NASA configuration were: the left and right wings were each pivoted far outboard from the aircraft centreline, the pivots being fixed (many earlier ideas featured sliding wing roots) even well beyond the sides of the broad fuselage; inboard of the pivoted swing-wings was to be a large, acutely swept fixed portion called a glove; and the wing was mounted high so that the two gloves and the upper surface of the broad fuselage formed a large lifting surface, which with the pivoted wings folded fully back would provide more than half the total lift. The range of sweep angles adopted by GD, which was typical of all the NASA studies and rival bidders, was 16deg to 72·5deg.

It is one of the larger examples of the dictates of fashion in aircraft design that the swing wing was so universally regarded as a panacea in 1960, eagerly adopted by all the six bidders on the TFX programme, yet so widely discounted in the Western world today. Naturally, the F-111 was such a major advance in the design of military aircraft that it was virtually copied by the Soviet Union; moreover TsAGI, the Moscow-centred aerodynamics institute, also perfected a configuration for turning swept-wing aircraft into swing-wing ones and this has been used in the Sukhoi single-engined attack family (derived from the Su-7) and the Tupolev supersonic bomber family (derived initially from the Tu-22). For the past several years there have been conferences at TsAGI and even at the Kremlin to reaffirm that the swing wing is frequently the best answer despite its non-

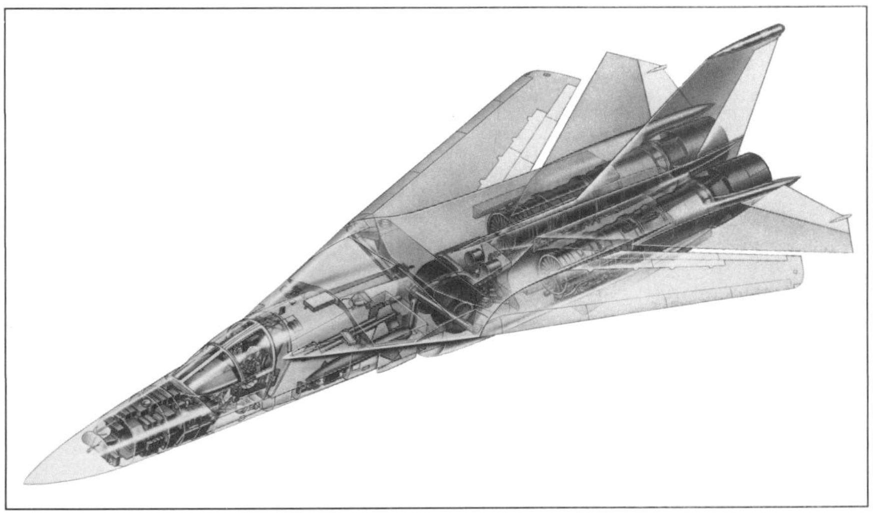

Left: Long before first flight GD put out this cutaway F-111A showing a Bullpup ASM and two Sidewinder AAMs in the internal weapon bay!

Below: British Aerospace tear 'em apart and rebuild 'em: UH = Es from Upper Heyford's 20th TFW, and LN = Fs from Lakenheath's 48th TFW.

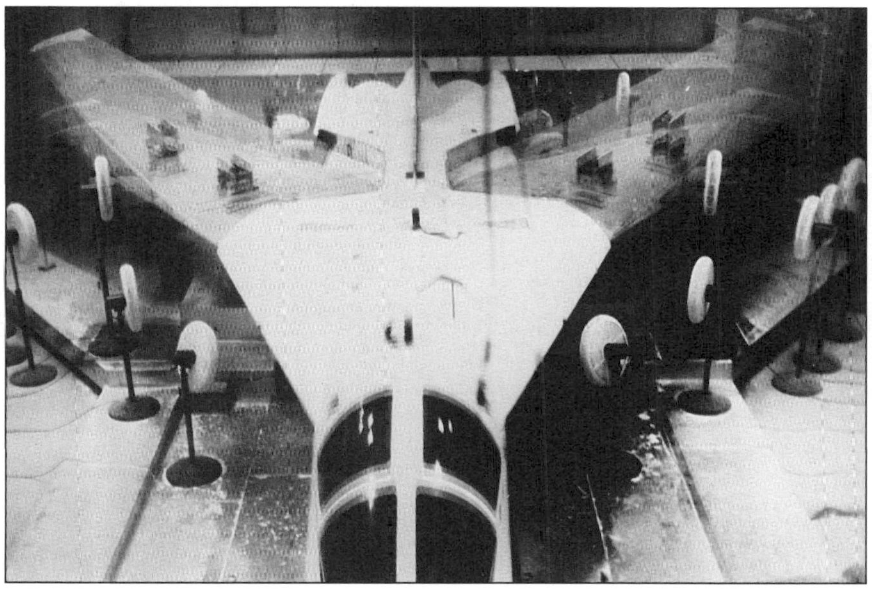

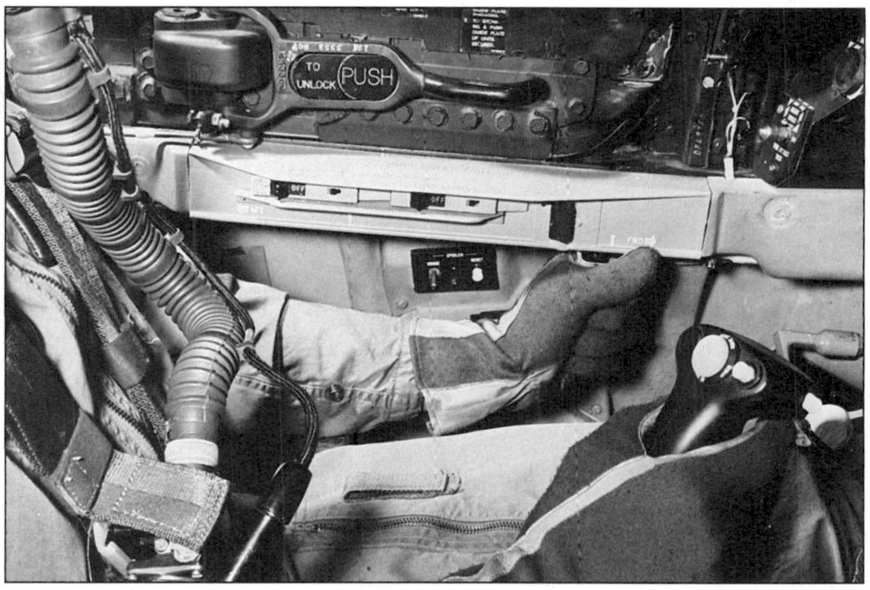

Top: A triple exposure in one of the Fort Worth refrigerated 'torture chambers' showing the way the wings were bent in proof testing.

Above: Close-up of the swing-wing pivot junction, showing how the glove vane rotates nose-down while its bottom half opens like a book.

Top: A GD engineering pilot grasps the 'trombone handle' which commands wing sweep angle. There is nothing to show which way is right!

Above: An F-111D of the 27th TFW shows the complex geometry of the slat, glove vane and pivot junction in the minimum-sweep position.

appearance in all the latest Western military aircraft except the B-1B, whose roots go back to the late 1960s when the swing wing was fashionable.

Variable geometry

It may not always be apparent that an aircraft of fixed shape has to be designed to perform at its best at one particular combination of flight speed, atmospheric density/temperature, aircraft weight and engine power setting. If any of these things (and a few others) is altered, the aircraft becomes less efficient. Half a century ago the first major elements of variable geometry were adopted in the form of leading-edge slats (which open to keep the air flowing back across the upper surface of the wing at high angles, for example at low speeds) and trailing-edge flaps (which when lowered slightly give a considerable increase in wing lift, and when lowered fully also cause a large increase in drag). Such forms of variable geometry are universally accepted; indeed in modern fighters the ability continuously to vary the wing cross-section profile to suit different speeds, manoeuvres or other flight conditions is put forward by their designers as a good alternative to the swing wing.

In fact, while variable wing profile is a powerful method of adapting the aircraft to changing conditions, it cannot possibly be regarded as a replacement for the swing wing. The latter offers an even more powerful means of, in effect, redesigning the aircraft in flight to fit it to different parts of a mission. At takeoff the wings are spread out to the maximum span, and the high-lift devices comprising full-span leading-edge slats and full-span trailing-edge double-slotted flaps are all extended; in addition, the outer portion of fixed glove is opened into upper and lower portions, the lower forming a near-vertical guide vane around the inboard end of the slats and the upper (called the glove vane) being rotated nose-down to guide airflow over the wing above the inboard end of the slats, rather in the way a Kruger flap guides airflow at the wing root of a modern jetliner.

Cleaned up after takeoff the ugly duckling turns into a graceful swan, long-necked and with long slender wings considerably more efficient in subsonic cruise than the stubby wings of fixed-wing fighters – and, in fact, even more efficient than the wings of many jetliners! A typical cruise setting is 26deg, or 10deg of added sweep. This lines up the fixed outermost pylons with the airflow and is the only setting at which it is possible to carry the maximum external load. To sweep the wings further it is necessary to jettison the outermost pylons, if these are fitted (they seldom are). It would be possible to incorporate a Mach/sweep programmer to adjust wing sweep automatically to flight Mach number or some other parameter, but as in practice the F-111 is not intended to indulge in air combat there is no incentive to do so. Maximum sweep is needed only for supersonic dash, and though Mach numbers exceeding 2 are attainable at over 35,000ft (10,700m) the more familiar regime is at low level, invariably below 1,000ft (300m) AGL (above ground level) and in heavily defended areas below 300ft (90m), where hostile radars may be expected to have blinkered and unreliable vision.

Penetration of hostile territory was recognised as early as 1944 to call for flight at the lowest possible altitude, to escape detection by radar until the last possible moment and give the defenders minimum warning and many other problems, but it was not until the 1950s that a few design teams were given the chance to come up with designs for dedicated low-level bombers. Such aircraft are a class apart, and in many respects their design has to be the exact opposite of that of an air-combat fighter. Thus, it is sheer nonsense to claim that machines such as the F-15, F/A-18A or Mirage 2000 can be 'designed' to fly both the fighter and the attack missions.

Immutable laws

Publicity managers can get very hot under the collar, but unfortunately they do not have the power with their press releases to alter the fact that the fighter needs the biggest wing it can get, while the attack aircraft needs the smallest. Not only does the attack aircraft need the highest possible wing loading (aircraft weight divided by wing area, in other words the average weight supported by each bit of wing) but it also needs the smallest possible span. Ideally it would like a mere sliver of a wing, with maximum chord (front to rear distance) but hardly any span. Imagine an F/A-18A with just its long wing-root extension, and with the main wing removed: that is the kind of shape that does well in penetrating hostile airspace at supersonic speed at treetop height.

The F/A-18 driver does not have the ability to remove his main wings, except with dire consequences, but this is just what the swing-wing jock can do by the mere touch of a lever. Sweeping the F-111 outer wings back to 72·5deg has only a modest effect on the total area but a dramatic effect on the span, which is reduced to around half its maximum value. Why is it important to change the shape of the wing in this way? There are five main reasons, but the chief one is that not only is drag greatly reduced, so the aircraft can fly faster than sound, but also the variation of lift with AOA (angle of attack) is greatly reduced.

AOA is the angle at which the wing meets the air. A normal unswept wing held at near-zero AOA will give no lift at all. As AOA is increased, while holding airspeed constant, so does the lift increase in a fairly uniform way until, at an AOA of around 16deg, the wing runs out of steam. It then cannot lift any more (not without increase in airspeed, which at high AOA means tremendous increase in engine thrust), and any attempt to increase AOA further will result in a stall, the aircraft dropping like a stone. The slender wing, such as an F-111 at 72·5deg, shows very much less variation in lift with AOA; it is said to have a 'flat lift-curve' when the results are plotted on a graph. It so happens that AOA can be increased to seemingly crazy angles without the aircraft dropping out of the sky, but these are not part of an F-111 driver's normal repertoire.

The crucial advantage of a flat lift-curve is that, since the air at low levels is both very dense and very turbulent, because of the effect of wind on hills, buildings and other terrain features, a high-speed attacker inevitably finds his wings flying through an endless succession of upcurrents and downcurrents of an unpredictable nature. This means that AOA is constantly changing in a

Above: Crew modules from McDonnell Douglas lined up at Fort Worth for installation. Each cost as much as a complete F-86.

Below: Three landing and taxi lights adorn the nose gear, which has twin steerable wheels. It folds forward, pulling the doors after it.

Bottom: This crew module was seen on inspection in the Fort Worth plant prior to being built into 63-9783, the eighteenth Research, Development, Test and Evaluation aircraft, which was subsequently rebuilt as the first prototype FB-111A for Strategic Air Command.

random and often violent manner. With a normal (long-span) wing the ride is so rough that, to use aircrew parlance, "you get your eyeballs shaken out". In contrast the F-111 or Tornado or Soviet aircrew have a smooth ride, and can fly their mission with professional precision. (The only other kind of aircraft that can do this is the TSR.2 type with extremely high wing-loading in a short-span wing, rather like a swing wing at maximum sweep, and with very powerful flap blowing to get enough lift for takeoff and landing.)

We in the West must be careful not to forget that such recent aircraft as the F-16, F/A-18 and Mirage 2000 have fixed wings not as a matter of fundamental choice. These aircraft were originally designed for the air-combat mission; and, having been thus designed, their wings could not readily be given pivots. Their manufacturers thus have a vested interest in trying to avoid discussion of their limitations in the attack mission.

To be frank, if a fixed-wing aircraft slows down to about 450 knots and maintains a good height AGL – say, 1,000ft (300m) – it can fly a respectable attack mission, such as that achieved by F-16s against a nuclear reactor in Iraq. In missions over the sea, which is flat and has relatively unturbulent air above it, the F/A-18A can fly a fair attack mission at the same speed at considerably lower heights. But put any fixed-wing aircraft on the Central European NATO front, and it becomes a totally different ball game. Indeed, put it on a mission against Hanoi in the early 1970s and it would find low-level flight on a cloudy night through the mountains with rings of SAM batteries ahead to be an unacceptable situation. No amount of hard-sell shouting can alter the laws of nature. Certainly, we must guard against thinking the swing wing outmoded.

At the same time, though the F-111 will forever be remembered as the first production swing-wing aircraft, it is certainly not above criticism. GD cannot be blamed for the side-by-side seating, which in 1962 became inevitable, but in many other respects the design left much to be desired. US interest in the BAC (which absorbed Vickers-Armstrongs) swing-wing and TSR.2 research, all of which was passed to the USAF, triggered corresponding BAC interest in TFX, and when B.O. Heath at

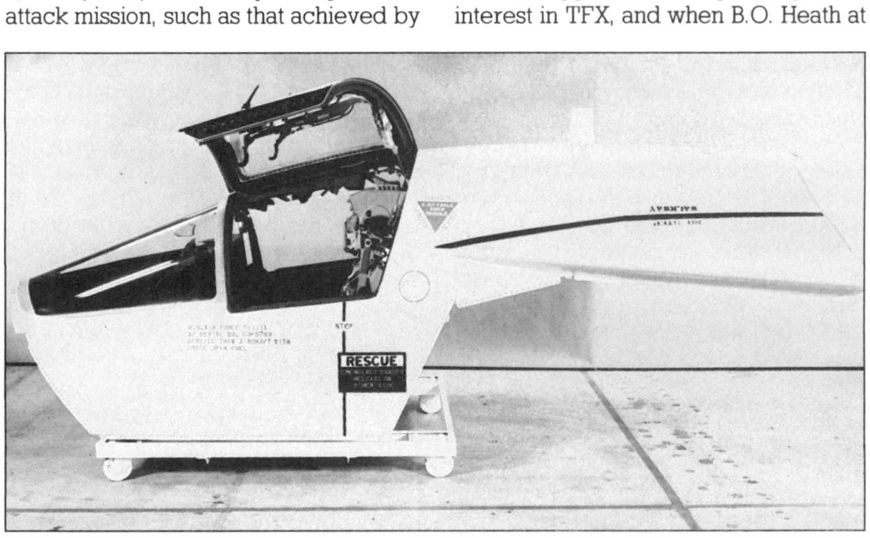

Far left: The left taileron (stabilator) of an F-111F, parked at full positive incidence. Note the ECM aerial and static dischargers located on the trailing edge.

Left: The high-lift devices of an F-111F are clarified by the distinctive red paint of the internals. The flaps in this photograph are not at maximum deflection.

Below left: White number 5 is for RAF Strike Command's Tactical Bomb Competition, held at Lossiemouth: this 48th TFW F-111F was taking part in 1981.

Above: Flightline of the 48th TFW at the 1981 Tac Bombing Contest. The F-111 (even the F) has to try hard today to beat the F-16!

BAC Warton saw a three-view of the F-111 he thought it worth writing a brief critique. He pointed out that it was undesirable to have the tailplane at the same level as the wing, so that the wing and tailplane almost became one surface at 72·5deg sweep; that the wing pivots were not in "quite the right place"; that there was too much length of body upstream of the inlets, so that a thick boundary-layer of sluggish air would have to be disposed of inboard of the inlets; that the inlets were too close to the engines, so that distorted airflow would be likely to cause serious engine compressor stalls; and that base drag at the tail would be excessive.

It so happened that the British government later threw away Heath's own aircraft (TSR.2) and regarded the F-111 as the perfect replacement, completely ignoring this critical appraisal. But everything Heath predicted was proved to be true, and in addition he might have added that it is undesirable and unnecessary to design main landing gears which make it impossible to carry a heavy weapon, tank or ECM load under the fuselage. Heath later played a central role in the design of the much smaller Tornado which regularly carries an 8,000lb (3629kg) bombload without having to use a single wing pylon.

Ejectable capsule

One of the most unusual features of the F-111 is that instead of having ejection seats the crew ride in an ejectable capsule. The only company with previous experience of ejectable capsules on a production aircraft was GD Fort Worth itself, with the B-58, which had three in a row. The F-111 has just the one capsule, inside which is the complete side-by-side cockpit. McDonnell Douglas played the prime role in developing this so-called 'crew module'. In emergency either occupant can grab a lever beside his knee and, with a press-squeeze-pull movement, initiate the jettison sequence. Explosive cutting cord severs the module from the aircraft, and a 40,000lb (18,000kg) thrust rocket zooms it up and back at any flight Mach number down to zero and at any height. A large portion of wing goes with the module to give inflight stability, the internal pressurization is discontinued but oxygen supply is maintained, and the controlled descent is retarded by a parachute with impact cushioned by ventral airbags. There are cases of crews surviving with nothing more than a shaking after a capsule has rolled down a craggy mountainside. On land the capsule forms a survival shelter; on sea it behaves like a self-righting boat, the pilot's stick serving as the handle of the bilge-pump!

The troubled development history of the F-111 is well known, and it is unprecedented for a single modern combat aircraft to have suffered so severely on the counts of excessive aerodynamic drag, engine/inlet mismatch (to the point that the TF30 engine installation was officially described as "a hazard to safe flight"), excessive weight, shortfalls in range, speed and height, and, later, catastrophic structural failures. Coming on top of the thundering row over the contract award, with its overtones of incompetence and individual self-interest among the highest members of the Defense Department, all this had a most damaging effect on what was actually a very fine aircraft.

In retrospect the author still believes that the SOR-183 figures were ill-conceived from the start. The ferry range without air refuelling was stipulated at 3,000nm (3,455 miles/5,560km); this was responsible for GD having to show in-

Below: Basic features of the unique jettisonable crew module. The bilge pump is driven by the joysticks should the module land in water.

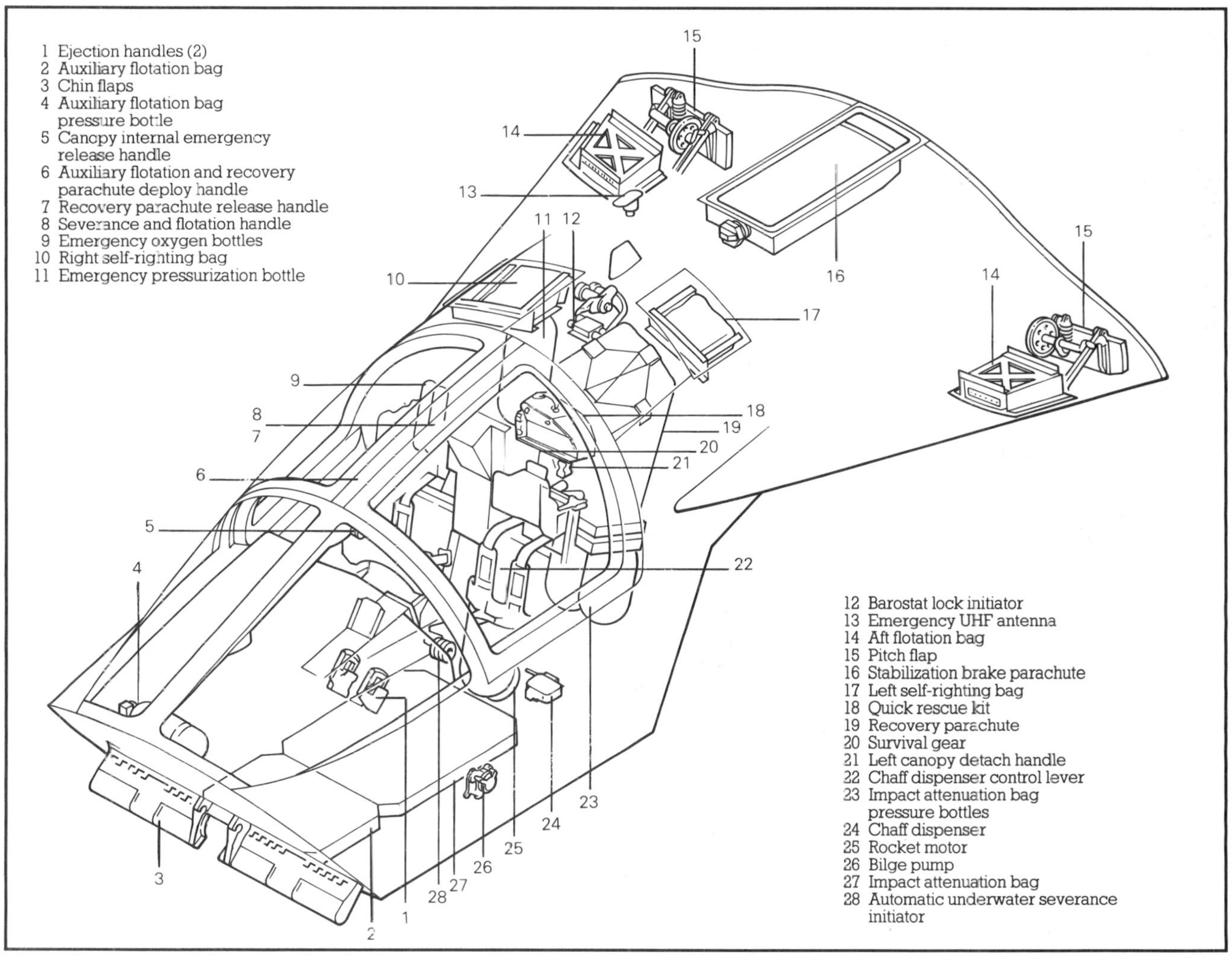

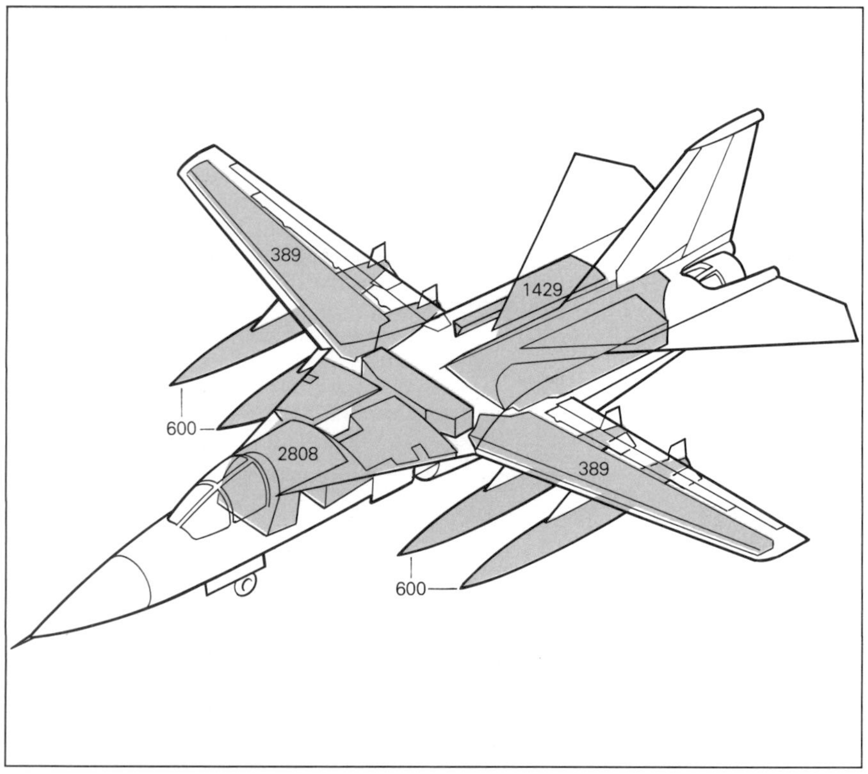

Above: Based on a USAF illustration, this diagram shows the fuel tanks of an F-111A or E (most tactical versions are similar). The figures are capacities in US gallons: the main cutaway drawing below gives corresponding capacities in Imperial gallons and litres.

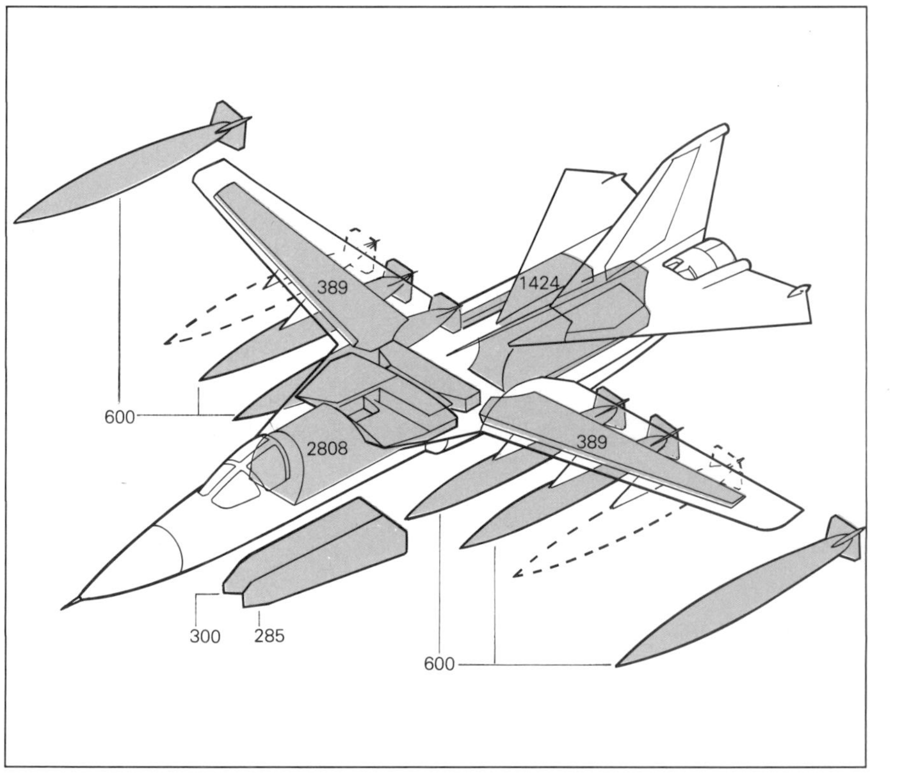

Above: An equivalent diagram showing the tankage of the FB-111A bomber, with optional weapon-bay tanks (and 5US gal less internal).

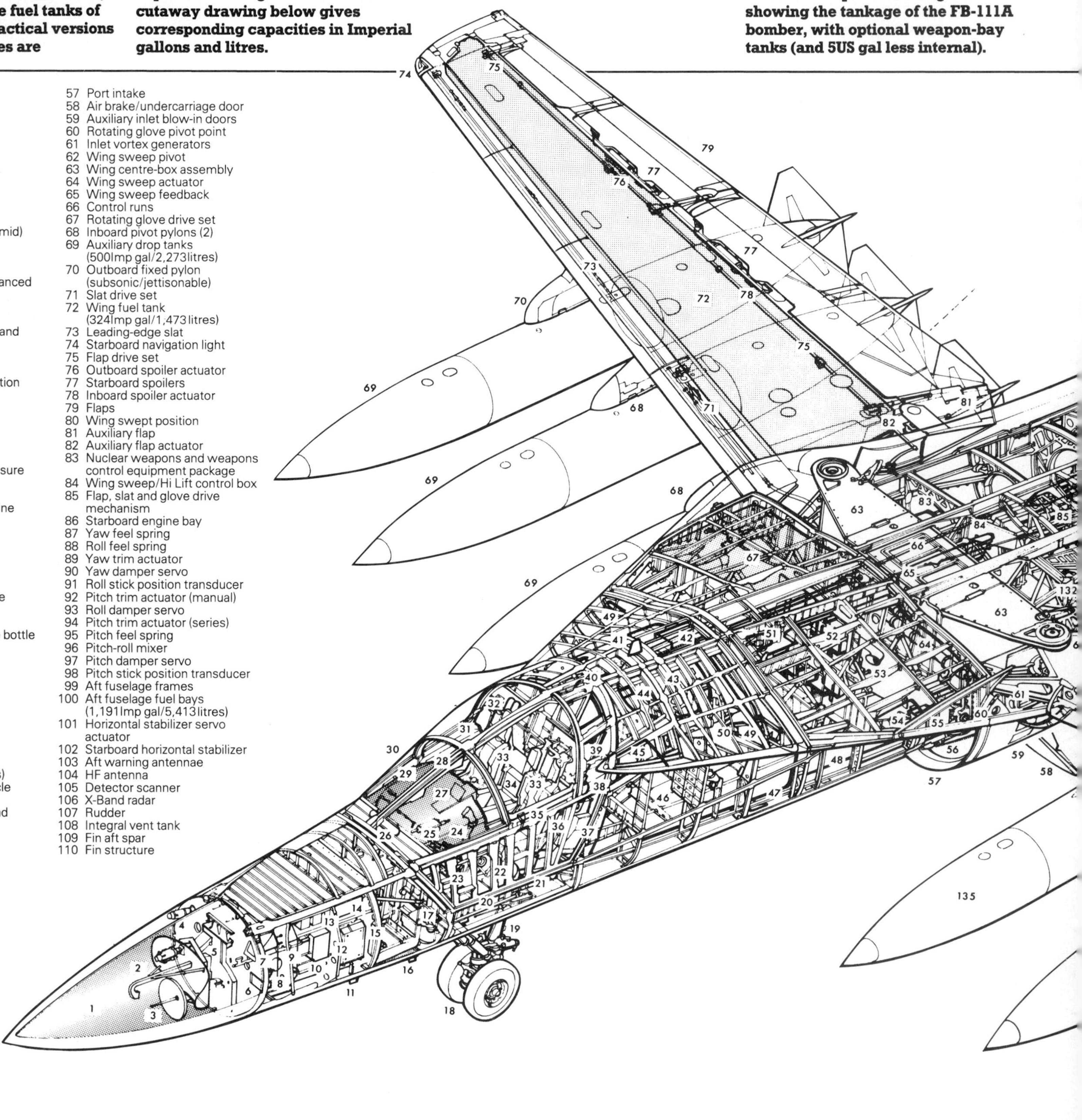

F-111D cutaway

1 Hinged nose cone
2 Attack radar
3 Terrain-following radar
4 Nose hinges (2)
5 Radar mounting
6 Nose lock
7 Angle-of-sideslip probe
8 Homing antenna (high)
9 Forward warning antenna
10 Homing antenna (low and mid)
11 ALR-41 antenna
12 Flight control computers
13 Feel and trim assembly
14 Forward avionics bay (Advanced Mk II digital computer)
15 Angle-of-attack probe
16 UHF Comm/Tacan No 2
17 Module forward bulkhead and stabilization flaps (2)
18 Twin nosewheels
19 Shock strut
20 Underfloor impact attenuation bag stowage (4)
21 Nosewheel well
22 LOX converter
23 Rudder pedals
24 Control column
25 LOX heat exchanger
26 Auxiliary flotation bag pressure bottle
27 Weapons sight
28 Forward parachute bridle line
29 De-fog nozzle
30 Windscreen
31 Starboard console
32 Emergency oxygen bottle
33 Crew seats
34 Bulkhead console
35 Wing sweep control handle
36 Recovery chute catapult
37 Provision/survival pack
38 Attenuation bags pressure bottle
39 Recovery chute
40 Aft parachute bridle line
41 UHF data link/AGIFF No 1 (see 123)
42 Stabilization-brake chute
43 Self-righting bag
44 UHF recovery
45 ECM antennae (port and starboard)
46 Forward fuselage fuel bay (2,340Imp gal/10,638litres)
47 Ground refuelling receptacle
48 Weapons bay
49 Module pitch flaps (port and starboard.
50 Aft flotation bag stowage
51 Air refuelling receptacle
52 Primary heat-exchanger (air-to-water)
53 Ram air inlet
54 Rate gyros
55 Rotating glove
56 Inlet variable spike
57 Port intake
58 Air brake/undercarriage door
59 Auxiliary inlet blow-in doors
60 Rotating glove pivot point
61 Inlet vortex generators
62 Wing sweep pivot
63 Wing centre-box assembly
64 Wing sweep actuator
65 Wing sweep feedback
66 Control runs
67 Rotating glove drive set
68 Inboard pivot pylons (2)
69 Auxiliary drop tanks (500Imp gal/2,273litres)
70 Outboard fixed pylon (subsonic/jettisonable)
71 Slat drive set
72 Wing fuel tank (324Imp gal/1,473litres)
73 Leading-edge slat
74 Starboard navigation light
75 Flap drive set
76 Outboard spoiler actuator
77 Starboard spoilers
78 Inboard spoiler actuator
79 Flaps
80 Wing swept position
81 Auxiliary flap
82 Auxiliary flap actuator
83 Nuclear weapons and weapons control equipment package
84 Wing sweep/Hi Lift control box
85 Flap, slat and glove drive mechanism
86 Starboard engine bay
87 Yaw feel spring
88 Roll feel spring
89 Yaw trim actuator
90 Yaw damper servo
91 Roll stick position transducer
92 Pitch trim actuator (manual)
93 Roll damper servo
94 Pitch trim actuator (series)
95 Pitch feel spring
96 Pitch-roll mixer
97 Pitch damper servo
98 Pitch stick position transducer
99 Aft fuselage frames
100 Aft fuselage fuel bays (1,191Imp gal/5,413litres)
101 Horizontal stabilizer servo actuator
102 Starboard horizontal stabilizer
103 Aft warning antennae
104 HF antenna
105 Detector scanner
106 X-Band radar
107 Rudder
108 Integral vent tank
109 Fin aft spar
110 Fin structure

Above: An F-111D of the 27th TFW undergoing hangar maintenance at Cannon AFB, near Clovis, New Mexico, in August 1981.

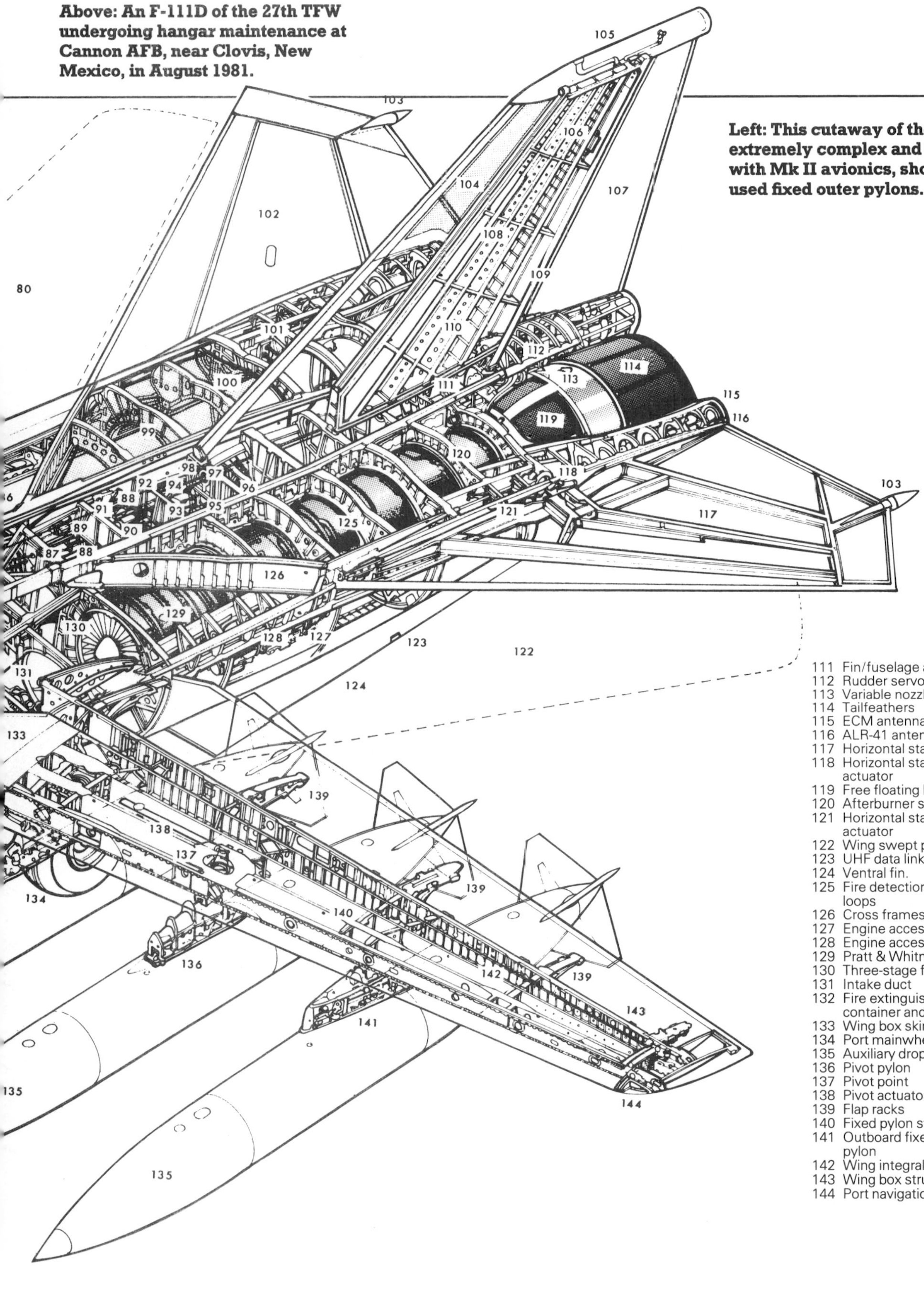

Left: This cutaway of the F-111D, the extremely complex and costly version with Mk II avionics, shows the never-used fixed outer pylons.

111 Fin/fuselage attachment
112 Rudder servo actuator
113 Variable nozzle
114 Tailfeathers
115 ECM antenna
116 ALR-41 antenna
117 Horizontal stabilizer structure
118 Horizontal stabilizer servo actuator
119 Free floating blow-in doors
120 Afterburner section
121 Horizontal stabilizer servo actuator
122 Wing swept position
123 UHF data link/AG IFF No 2
124 Ventral fin.
125 Fire detection sensing element loops
126 Cross frames
127 Engine access hatches
128 Engine accessories
129 Pratt & Whitney TF30 turbofan
130 Three-stage fan
131 Intake duct
132 Fire extinguishing agent container and nozzles
133 Wing box skinning
134 Port mainwheel
135 Auxiliary drop tanks
136 Pivot pylon
137 Pivot point
138 Pivot actuator
139 Flap racks
140 Fixed pylon strong point
141 Outboard fixed jettisonable pylon
142 Wing integral fuel
143 Wing box structure
144 Port navigation light

genuity in packing fuel into every last nook and cranny apart from the fin, with a consequent rise in takeoff weight on the conventional (HE) mission to over 100,000lb (45·36 tonnes). The demand for Mach 2·5 at high altitude resulted in prolonged tinkering with inlets, and in fact was never met even with the much more powerful F-111F because it reduces airframe life and appears to have been quite unnecessary (it was written in largely because of the belief that the F-111 would be used for high-altitude fighter and reconnaissance missions). Not least, the TAC baseline mission of an attack on a surface target at a distance of 800nm (921 miles/1,482km) stipulated that the final 200nm to the target should be flown at Mach 1·2; though the fuel for the required ferry mission could marginally also meet this demand it caused numerous problems and, of course, was impossible with a conventional bombload.

It is easy to be wise after the event, but it is difficult to avoid the conclusion that it has always been folly to write a specification for a strategic bomber (according to McNamara "with the range of a transport") and expect it also to be a superior aircraft in any kind of fighter mission. The extremely severe problems encountered in development, including massive deficiency in aircraft range, ceiling, speed and manoeuvrability, could not have been predicted – because, despite a background research programme exceeding that for any previous aircraft of its size in history, none of these things *was* discovered in advance. There appears to be some justification for the oft-repeated American belief that it is better to design a world-beating fighter and then hang bombs on it, though the European experience with Tornado and Viggen shows that the reverse is possible if the basic design is a success.

Another of the bits of mythology that has grown up around the One-Eleven is that, while the Navy was crippled by weight restrictions, the Air Force was unconcerned. In a standard hardback reference, *McNamara: His Ordeal in the Pentagon* (Harper & Row, 1971) the author, Henry L. Trewhitt, writes "the Air Force wanted a plane that weighed no less than 75,000 pounds (34,000kg) . . ." In fact during the crucial years of SOR-183 the thinking in TAC was that a way had to be found to keep the weight down to levels with which the command was familiar. The actual target gross weight in June 1959 was 45,000lb (20,412kg), and Gen Everest is on record as saying "I am not going to accept any goddamned 70,000-lb (31,750kg) airplane". As late as December 1961, well into the unprecedented four rounds of competitive bidding by the rival contractors, Everest with extreme reluctance agreed to raise the absolute upper limit on gross weight to 60,000lb (27,216kg), and only as a last-ditch tradeoff in order to achieve the desired lo-lo-hi penetration radius of 800nm.

There is no doubt whatsoever that it is the difference between weights of this order and those actually reached by the production versions of F-111 that effectively killed the aircraft as a fighter. Indeed, one feels there must have been some optimism on the part of the contractors or a gross breakdown in communications for the customer to fix an absolute upper limit at 60,000lb for an aircraft that fully laden turns the scales at various levels (depending on subtype) between 98,850 and 119,243lb (44,838 and 54,088kg). But, conversely, it is these awesome weights that give the F-111 its still-unrivalled range/bombload combination for a tactical aircraft.

Powerplant

One of the key technological advances which made possible the concept of the TFX was the high-compression augmented turbofan, which can combine very high maximum thrust with fuel economy far better than for the older generation of turbojets. Pratt & Whitney won the potentially enormous job of powering the F-111 with the promising TF30. The dour and conservative engine supplier suffered beyond belief in this programme (and in others using this engine), not least because of the design of the aircraft inlet system. The result was a succession of new TF30 models, combined with crippling price inflation.

Above: The whole engine slides out to the rear, the variable nozzle always being outside the aircraft. Here an 18,500lb thrust TF30-P-3 is checked over for an F-111E of the 20th TFW at RAF Upper Heyford.

Among the many curious facets of the F-111 design is that although the USAF never stipulated two engines, no contractor ever submitted any other number. The aircraft TFX was intended to replace, above all others, was the single-engined F-105. The engine of the F-105 was a large and extremely robust two-spool turbojet augmented by a large afterburner with a fully variable multi-flap nozzle. In its day it was a fine engine, and in fact the same engine minus the afterburner has today been refurbished and used in the TR-1. But by the end of the 1950s the advent of the turbofan, pioneered by Rolls-Royce under the name 'bypass turbojet', opened the way to superior fuel economy.

To a first approximation the fuel consumption of a jet engine of given power depends upon the mean jet velocity. At subsonic speeds it pays to use an engine that handles a larger airflow and discharges it at lower velocity, though compared with a high-velocity simple turbojet such an engine is likely to be larger, heavier and more complicated. In fighters it is often not just fuel consumption that matters but the total weight of the powerplant plus the fuel burned in each mission that determines how the aircraft is designed. For a lightweight air-combat fighter the need for agility in combat may well outweigh the need for range, and it pays to use a simple engine even though it burns more fuel. In the case of the F-111 quite the opposite considerations applied.

Never before had such range been demanded of any fighter-type aircraft. It was clear from the outset that the propulsion equations more nearly resembled those of a supersonic bomber, where the increased size and complexity of a high-compression turbofan handling a large airflow are amply rewarded in reduced weight of fuel consumed.

Turbofan advantages

Compared with a turbojet, a turbofan extracts more power from the jet with additional stages of turbine blading and uses this power either to drive a separate fan at the rear or a greatly enlarged low-pressure compressor at the front. In either case, the added fan blades pump fresh air which does not pass through the rest of the engine but is discharged as a relatively slow-moving cooler jet surrounding the hot 'core jet' from the rest of the engine.

Not only does this reduce the mean velocity of the combined hot central jet and surrounding fan jet, thus reducing fuel consumption, but it has the bonus of dramatically reduced noise. Moreover, as the air in the surrounding fan jet still has all its oxygen (because no fuel has been burned in it) it is possible to burn a great deal of extra fuel in it to give very large thrust boost for supersonic flight. In ordinary turbojets the afterburner is fed not with fresh air but with already very hot gas whose oxygen has partly been consumed. Thus an ordinary afterburner cannot burn much additional fuel before either the oxygen is all used up or the temperature becomes excessive. One of the chief technical advances in the engines of the F-111 was that, for the first time, an efficient turbofan was combined with a thrust-boosting augmentation system which injected fuel into both the hot core jet (as in previous afterburners) and also into the fresh air compressed by the fan.

Turbofans had been built previously, but only for subsonic bombers and transports. For the F-111 the engine had to be cleared to Mach 2·5 in the stratosphere and – an even more severe demand – to operate at sea level for long periods at a sustained supersonic Mach number of 1·2. It went without saying that the overall propulsion system would have fully variable inlets, as well as the variable nozzle forming part of the engine itself.

One reason for the choice of two engines was to provide a degree of twin-engine safety. Modern engines are reliable, but the F-111 was clearly going to spend much of its life at low level where birdstrikes are a major hazard, causing expensive shedding of blades and either loss of an engine or at least a precautionary shutdown. Another reason was that total thrust for takeoff or Mach 1·2 dash was going to be approximately 40,000lb (18,000kg), and nobody

Below: What Americans call afterburner (usually abbreviated to 'burner) is often called reheat in Britain, though the strict term for a turbofan is augmentation. RAAF F-111C.

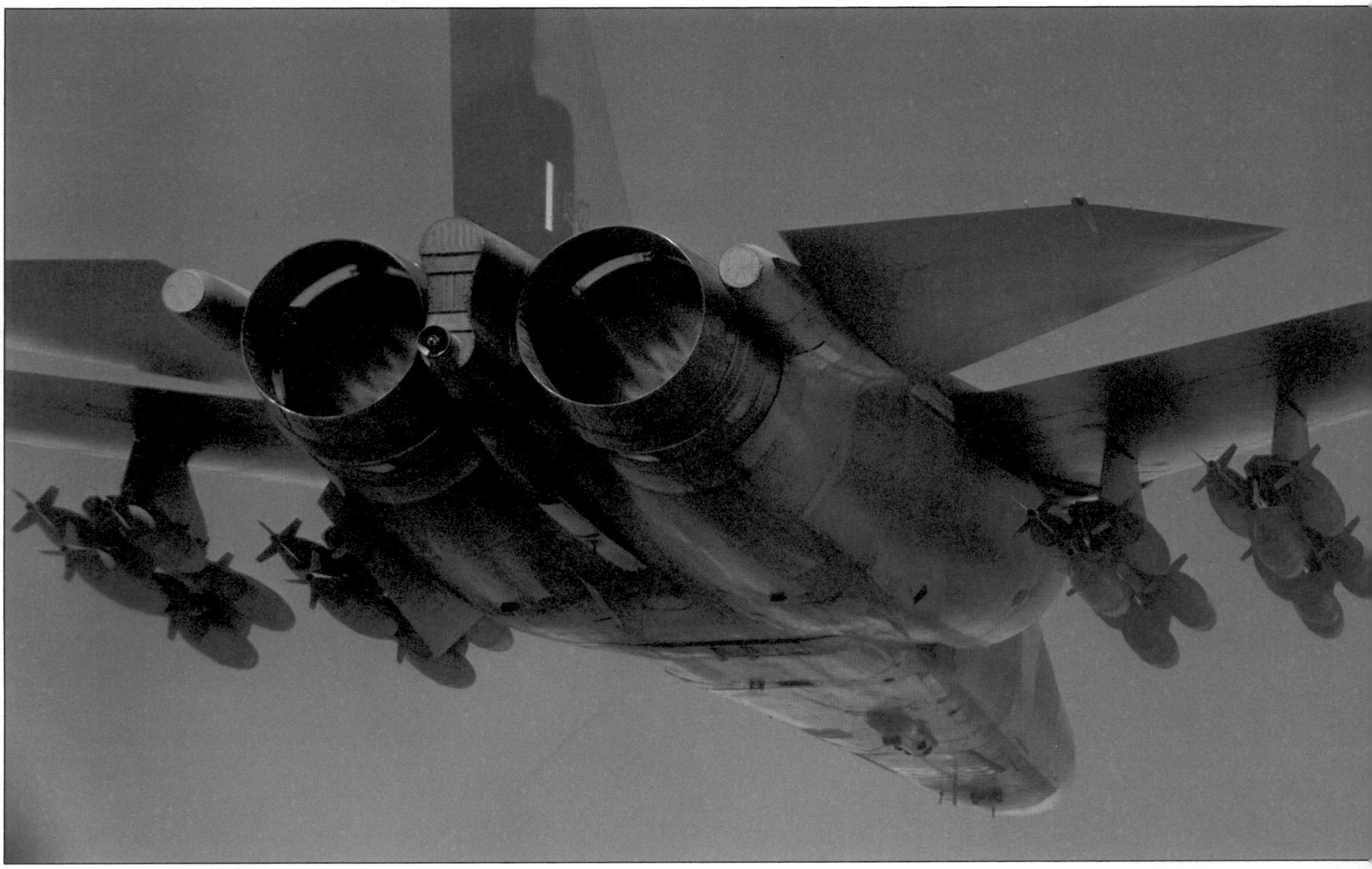

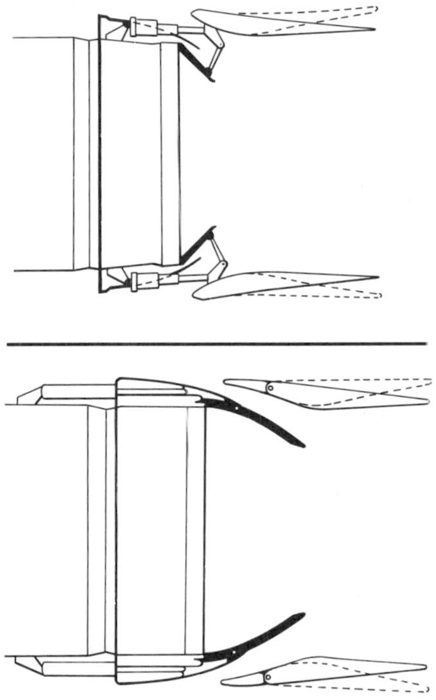

had built a production military engine of this size. In contrast, 20,000lb (9,000kg) was a handy and familiar size, well suited to field engine-change operations without outsize handling gear.

It was logical for bidders to place the engines side-by-side, with sufficient space between them for considerable fuselage fuel (though the largest tanks tended to be further forward, aft of the cockpit). How the inlets should be arranged was up to the aircraft designer. One of the best inlets on a USAF supersonic fighter had been the striking dorsal installation of the F-107A, and most bidders, including GD, studied inlets in the top of the fuselage.

The losing finalist, Boeing-Wichita, proposed to use dorsal inlets, and these would have had many advantages including reduced sensitivity to FOD (foreign-object damage) and possibly to birdstrikes. Another would certainly have been reduced RCS (radar cross-section), because engine inlets are among the most reflective parts of any aircraft and those on the F-111 today enable the hostile radars to 'see' right inside to the fronts of the engines. Another of the unexplained puzzles of the F-111 is that, in his explanation to Congress of why he picked the GD design, SecDef McNamara specifically mentioned the low RCS of that bidder's proposal, yet it must surely have been higher than for the Boeing aircraft with 'invisible' inlets?

In practice there were three candidate engines: the Allison AR.168, General Electric MF-295 and Pratt & Whitney JTF10. The Allison was based squarely on the Rolls-Royce Spey. Had it been chosen it would probably have filled the bill beautifully, with no significant trouble, but its 'foreign' origin prevented it from being judged on its merits. The MF-295 was possibly the most advanced of the three engines, but it existed only on paper and was finally deemed 'unacceptable' by the SSSB (Systems Source Selection Board). Boeing had preferred the GE engine but was given a paid study contract to switch to P&W, whose engine had originally been designed for the stillborn DC-9 four-engined passenger liner of 1958. For the F-111 the proposal was designated JTF10A-20, with a completely new afterburner and multi-flap nozzle. Accessories were grouped underneath, one of them being a large 60-kVA alternator (on both engines). Cartridge starting is possible, but the usual method is pneumatic, by air turbine, with cross-bleed to start the second engine.

Top: A beautiful Pratt & Whitney artwork showing the fundamentally improved TF30-P-100, which powers the final new-build One-Eleven, the F. Hardly any part is unchanged from the earlier models.

Above left: One of the areas of total redesign in the P-100 is the variable nozzle (bottom), with a translating primary iris replacing the original flaps (top) and giving a consequent reduction in drag.

Above: A production TF30-P-3 is checked before delivery in 1967.

Right: Tank boom operator's view of an FB-111A during inflight refuelling.

Above: Takeoff, in this case by an FB-111A, momentarily has the engines at full power fighting the vast barn-door airbrake which encloses the gear.

Above: The original Triple Plow 1 inlet (F-111A, E and EF) has a large splitter plate close to the fuselage.

The Connecticut company's slogan had always been "Dependable engines", and in the F-111 engine it stuck to its principles of accepting greater engine weight than its rivals in order to secure solid reliability. This belief that the JTF10 would give less trouble than the alternative candidate engines was the chief factor in its choice. Designated TF30-P-1 it was on test by mid-1964, and two flight-cleared engines were installed in the first YF-111A at the ceremonial rollout on October 16, 1964, 16 days ahead of schedule. All went well on the first flight, but on Flight No 2, on January 6, 1965, Dick Johnson attempted to exceed Mach 1 with the wings fully swept and found severe compressor stall as soon as he tried accelerating in full afterburner.

Engine aerodynamics

The hundreds of blades in the fans and compressors of modern jet engines are each like a small wing, and subject to the same rules, though with the added complication that the flow past any one blade is determined by the blades upstream and downstream. Suppose the air downstream cannot get through the narrow, constricted high-pressure blades fast enough: this will slow up the flow in the early stages, and the angle of attack of each blade can become excessive, causing it to stall. Any sudden turbulence can trigger a stall, and a stall in one part of a compressor can quickly cause general breakdown of flow.

Compressor stalls can be violent; they can sound like major explosions to the pilot, and in extreme cases they result in the engine spewing broken blades out of the jetpipe. Designers therefore leave a clear 'stall margin' so that, in normal operation, a compressor stall just cannot happen. But the bigger the stall margin, the higher the fuel consumption. In trying to make their engine more efficient the P&W engineers had cut it too fine, and hewed too close to the stall line for the short F-111 inlet system.

P&W jet engines have almost as much flight time as those of all other Western makers combined, but experience and conservative design do not always result in a troublefree product. It is fair to assess the basically excellent TF30 as the most troublesome engine of the past 20 years, and the Navy is still seeking a replacement in the F-14. In the F-111 it retained its position as the sole engine, but only by being developed through eight main models (including one for the Navy F-111B) and with price-escalation of more than 300 per cent.

The first main variant to overcome the more critical shortcomings of the P-1 was the P-3 (Air Force engines have odd-numbered suffixes). This has a redesigned stator inlet, compressor spools spinning at different speeds from the P-1 and with changed blade angles, a sixth-stage bleed to improve stall tolerance in combat manoeuvres or at supersonic speeds, a new afterburner fuel system, and modified nozzle. Still the engines coughed, banged and spluttered, and several losses of aircraft were attributed to engine behaviour.

GD discovered that much of the trouble lay in their inlet system, which – as predicted by 'Ollie' Heath in far-away Lancashire – was failing to get rid of the large boundary-layer flow and deliver smooth non-turbulent air to the very touchy engine. Engineers at Fort Worth spent four years improving the F-111 inlet system, despite the fact that an unprecedented effort had been applied to get it right at the outset.

The first major redesign was called Triple Plow I. Most unusually, the inlet that had been adopted for the F-111 took the form of a quarter-circle, with quarter of a conical centrebody, the location being well back under the wing root. The whole inlet was positioned outboard of the fuselage, from which it was separated by a large vertical wall. In Triple Plow I it was again moved a small further distance outboard, standing away from this wall, with a third plow (plough) to extract boundary layer between the top panel and the underside of the wing.

This remained the inlet for the F-111A, which was the most numerous variant, but by late 1967 GD had perfected a better Triple Plow II inlet with 14sq in (90sq cm) more area, positioned 4in (10cm) further out from the fuselage, with a longer and reprofiled corner cone to improve behaviour at high AOA

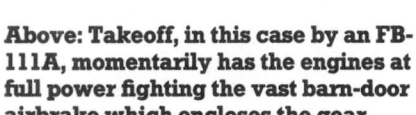

Right: Tail-on aspect of a torn-down aircraft (being rebuilt into an EF). Ahead of the main inlet frame the inlet ducts curve outwards, with the inner walls covered in vortex vanes to re-energize boundary-layer airflow.

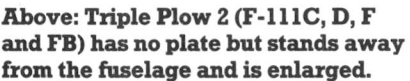

Above: Triple Plow 2 (F-111C, D, F and FB) has no plate but stands away from the fuselage and is enlarged.

and enabling the full Mach 2·5 performance to be realized at high altitude. This inlet also introduced three suck-in auxiliary doors in the wall about 12in (30cm) downstream, and it went into production for the F-111E. Unfortunately, as this retained the original engine it has insufficient power to reach this Mach number, and the vehemently expressed belief of the Senate TFX Investigation that there should have been "a constructive decision to stop F-111 production" pending the arrival of the Triple Plow II inlet appears unwarranted.

This inlet did, however, make possible the introduction of new versions of the TF30 which gradually made up some of the gross deficiency in power/weight ratio resulting from the massive escalation in F-111 weight. Discounting the stillborn Navy version, the next major advance in propulsion came in 1969 with the P-7 engine for the SAC bomber version, the FB-111A. This incorporates small changes, and has turbine entry temperature limit raised from 2,050deg F (1,121deg C) to 2,100deg F (1,149deg C) and rotational speeds appreciably increased (*see main data section, p000*). In the same year the P-9 succeeded the P-3 as powerplant of the basic TAC models, but this was fitted only to the F-111D. Turbine temperature is the same as for the P-7, but further increase in rotational speed results in increased thrust.

All this time P&W had been busy with major redesign to produce a greatly improved TF30 engine, and this finally matured as the JTF10A-32C, with military designation TF30-P-100. This was new from inlet to nozzle. The new fan and LP (low-pressure) compressor have a bulged inner profile, with backwards-canted blades at the front of the LP spool, removing flow-separation at the roots and dramatically improving tolerance of the engine to distorted flow in the inlet duct. The eight combustor cans are of a new Finwall pattern which are lighter, need only half as much cooling air, and give smokeless combustion with gas temperature raised to no less than 2,300deg F (1,260deg C), which is high even today.

To handle this increased temperature a completely new HP (high-pressure) turbine is fitted, with blades made from P&W's patented directionally cast process in which the metal crystals are aligned along the length of the blade, and with film-cooled stator vanes. Engine speeds are again increased, to a peak of 14,870rpm. And the afterburner is completely new, with five zones of combustion and a new electronic ignition system giving gentle 'soft-light' which reduces pressure excursions during light-up by almost 40 per cent compared with the previous fuel-squirt ignition. The nozzle is also quite new, with translating (rotary sliding) iris segments in the primary variable nozzle and a ring of 'tailfeathers' downstream which instead of being power-actuated are allowed to float to any position they assume.

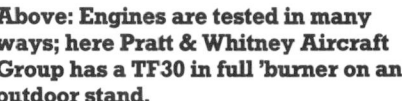

Above: Engines are tested in many ways; here Pratt & Whitney Aircraft Group has a TF30 in full 'burner on an outdoor stand.

The P-100 was such a tremendous improvement over all previous F-111 engines it really is a pity that "a constructive decision to stop production" could not have been taken until it was ready. It improved the takeoff thrust/weight ratio from 0·39 in the F-111A (hardly a 'fighter' type ratio!) to a more respectable 0·53 though even this is unimpressive compared with the figures of better than 1·0 for the F-15 and F-16. Sadly, the Air Force could not afford more than 106 of the final F-111 tactical model, the F-111F, nor could it retrofit the P-100 in any of the earlier aircraft.

P&W pressed on with TF30 improvement, and by 1970 had designed, and completed the underlying programme or research for, the next-generation engine designated JTF10A-39. Installationally interchangeable with the P-100, and actually lighter than any previous F-111 engine, this featured a modest increase in airflow and a further major jump in turbine temperature to 2,400deg F (1,316deg C), putting the engine in the 30,000lb (13,000kg) thrust class. The F-111 with this engine was calculated to have 5 per cent better rate of turn, 8 per cent faster climb after takeoff and 18 per cent faster supersonic acceleration, but the Air Force could not afford to buy the engine and instead terminated the F-111 programme.

Left: Not sixteen-inch guns but the overhauled P-3 engines being dollied back in to a newly converted EF in the Grumman Aerospace plant. The fuselage is tilted nose-down to bring the engine axes horizontal.

Avionics and Armament

Above: The USAF Rome Air Development Center (Systems Command) put the 15th RDT&E F-111A on a pedestal to measure avionics radiation patterns.

To the media the One-Eleven is important because of its swing wing. In fact this is to a large degree incidental. What is central to its mission capability is a somewhat bulky and heavy array of electronic 'black boxes' which are described in this chapter. To be brutally frank, building these into any modern tactical aircraft would result in a much more effective interdiction attack system than one of today's One-Elevens with the avionics removed. Unfortunately the USAF ended up with a succession of One-Elevens with progressively better nav/attack systems but remarkably little commonality.

So far this book has discussed the F-111 purely as a flying machine. It is not to be forgotten that its purpose is to carry air-to-ground weapons and deliver them accurately to a target, or a heavy payload of EW (electronic-warfare) systems and operate them in precisely the correct place. And, to a degree surpassing that attained by any previous fighter-type aircraft, the F-111 has to fly these missions regardless of the time of day or the weather.

This chapter, therefore, deals with the basic on-board systems for navigation, flight control and weapon delivery, and with the added external devices for improved delivery accuracy or EW self-protection. The task is slightly complicated by the fact that the F-111 matured as a family of aircraft with several totally dissimilar avionic installations, which in turn results in each model having its own distinctive cockpit.

Indeed, whereas the need to introduce so many improved versions of the TF30 engine had never been considered, it had been half expected from early SOR-183 days that there might be a case for progressive updating of the avionics. This is because, as a deliberate USAF policy, the basic F-111 had been planned around what might be called 'state of the art' black boxes, instead of the very latest solid-state digital technology. Thus, the avionics originally fitted were (and many still are) relatively bulky and heavy; and they consume a lot of electrical power, turning it into heat which has to be dissipated. Such penalties were willingly accepted in order to reap the expected large benefits of having hundreds, if not thousands, of F-111s all equipped with the same mature and reliable on-board systems fully meeting the tough numerical demands imposed by the customer in the matters of reliability and maintainability.

These demands, which were in many respects novel when written in 1960–61, were the most stringent that had been imposed at that time on any new aircraft. A few of them are the ability to: fly 30 hours per aircraft per month; move off within five minutes of an unpremeditated alert; take off within 30 minutes of returning from the previous mission; demand not more than 35 man-hours per flight hour for all maintenance purposes; require no more than 15 minutes for identifying any fault in any system; require no more than 15 minutes for operational preflight checks; remain on continuous alert for five days; and be operationally ready 75 per cent of the time.

Thus, it was the original intention that the avionics should be in standardized modules, if possible one layer deep and with Bite (built-in test equipment) for rapid self-test and isolation of faults. Every area is covered by an easily opened door, almost all of which can be reached from ground level. Fundamentally the One-Eleven is a very superior aircraft in its design for maintainability, and the Air Force has only itself to blame for the increasingly troublesome situation in which no two wings fly the same version, and some wings have non-standard 'foreign' variants parked on the flightline.

In all versions the avionic fit is subdivided into three main groupings: fire-power control, penetration aids and MTC (mission and traffic control). The actual equipments installed are listed in the main data section. Apart from the progressive improvements in engine sub-type the avionics are the principal areas of difference between the five attack versions and one strategic version of the F-111. Avionics also include the flight-control system and instrumentation.

Flight control relies on the dual part-redundant and totally separated hydraulic systems and triplex (fully redundant) electronic autopilot. The system is self-adaptive, in that pilot input to the stick gives the same response at all aircraft speeds and altitudes and irres-

Below: A practice combat mission by the 474th TFW in the early days, with tandem triplets of Mk 83 bombs.

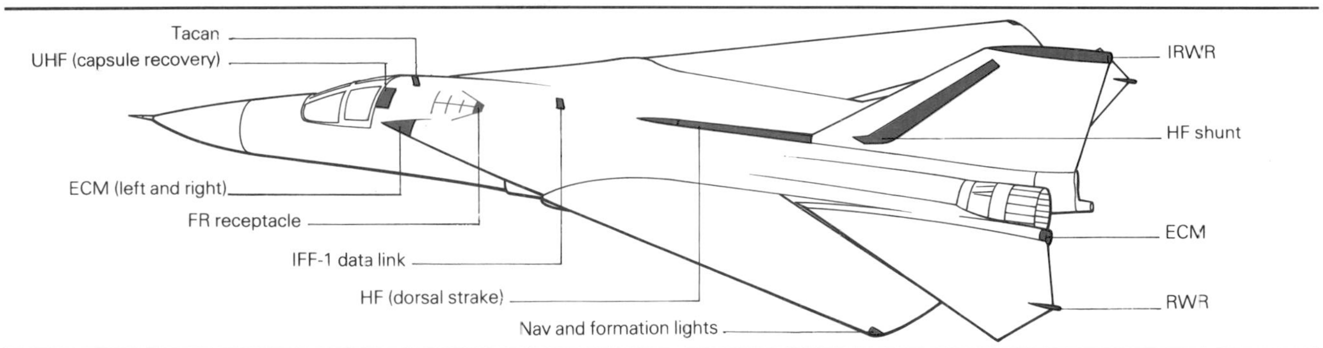

Top: Newest of the ECM pods carried by tactical One-Elevens, the ALQ-131(V) is the latest mass-production type of the Westinghouse company.

Above: Simplified key to some of the external avionics aerials (antennae) of an F-111A.

Left: Tail of an F-111F of the 48th TFW (the wing commander's aircraft) showing the tip pod, low-voltage formation light (pale cream strip) and blunt-ended ECM emitter.

Left below: Close-up of an F-111F showing the left ECM transmitter.

from the very start, and it was also probably the first to have an internal integrated warning system for all radar and IR (infra-red) wavelengths.

The initial RHAWS (radar homing and warning system) was the Dalmo-Victor APS-109 and 109A, with the main miniature spiral receiver aerials in pointed pods facing astern from the rearmost points of the tailplanes and the side-looking aerials beneath glassfibre panels which made a prominent and distinctive pattern on each side of the nose until, from about 1978, they began to be painted over. The cockpit display, surrounded by no fewer than nine control knobs, is at the top right of the panel immediately to the right of the TFR scope.

The original IRWR (IR warning receiver) was the Cincinnati Electronics AAR-34 backed up by the same supplier's ALR-23, of which some 700 pairs were supplied for the F-111 programme. These are tuned to warn of the approach of any burning hydrocarbon gas such as would trail behind a SAM, AAM or hostile fighter. Avco supplied the original ECM receiver subsystem, though the Transco ALR-4 was one early fit.

Like the Elint (electronic intelligence) passive receivers just described, the offensive ECM have varied greatly from one F-111 version to another, and also because of progressive updating. The F-111 could have been modified to house internal jammers and dispensing systems, but the objections were time, cost, supposed inflexibility of a built-in system, difficulty of getting good all-round coverage and the penalty of always having an item installed that usually (in peacetime) would not be needed. Even today there is much argument, and external pods remain the favoured answer. The chief contractor for dispensed payloads was originally Lundy, with the ALE-28, and the same company has later supplied the ALE-44. Both are mounted upstream of the rear ECM aerials, inboard of the tailerons, and dispense chaff or flares. The WSO controls the operation from a panel at upper right which shows the number of payloads of each type remaining, and provides for selection of burst rates, burst intervals and payload units per burst.

The F-111 pioneered internal ECM systems in slender fighter-type aircraft, in the Western world at least, though details of where the boxes are installed have not been made public. The original system designed for the F-111 was the ALQ-94, by Sanders Associates, a company previously a supplier of EW equipment for Navy aircraft. A reported 500-plus sets were delivered, each providing both noise and deception jamming along dual channels and with a CW (continuous-wave) capability which certainly antedated the 'shock discovery' in the Yom Kippur war in 1973 that no Israeli or US ECM was effective against the SA-6 SAM. Today the -94 is being replaced by the -137, as noted later.

External ECM pods

A major objection to external jammer pods is that they not only add drag but they occupy pylons, but in the F-111 this is much less important because the pod pylons are under the fuselage and cannot be used for dropped stores such as bombs. In the early years of the F-111 the standard ECM pod was the General Electric ALQ-87, a modest pod yet considerably better than those available in the mid-1960s. On entering service in partnership with the F-111A in 1967 the ALQ-87, previously called the ORC-160-8 from its ancestry in the prolonged ORC-160 research programme, was intended to be an effective barrage jammer against both surface threats and interceptor radars. Using a backward-wave oscillator it was extended to cover G/H (previously C) band followed by I/J (previously X and Ku) bands by the time it went to Vietnam in 1968. A year later it was further extended into the shorter wavelengths in the upper J band. Its electric power is generated by a self-contained ram-air windmill, and a distinctive recognition feature is the pair of ventral blade aerials.

Usually two ALQ-87s were carried in tandem on the widely separated racks under the internal bomb bay and between the rear ventral strakes. Subsequently the widely used Westinghouse ALQ-101 pod was also used. Stemming from the QRC-335 programme, these pods are available in several versions, some (notably the ALQ-101(V)8, deployed in large numbers) having a ventral gondola to give an approximately doubled spread of frequencies covered. Unlike the GE pod this family

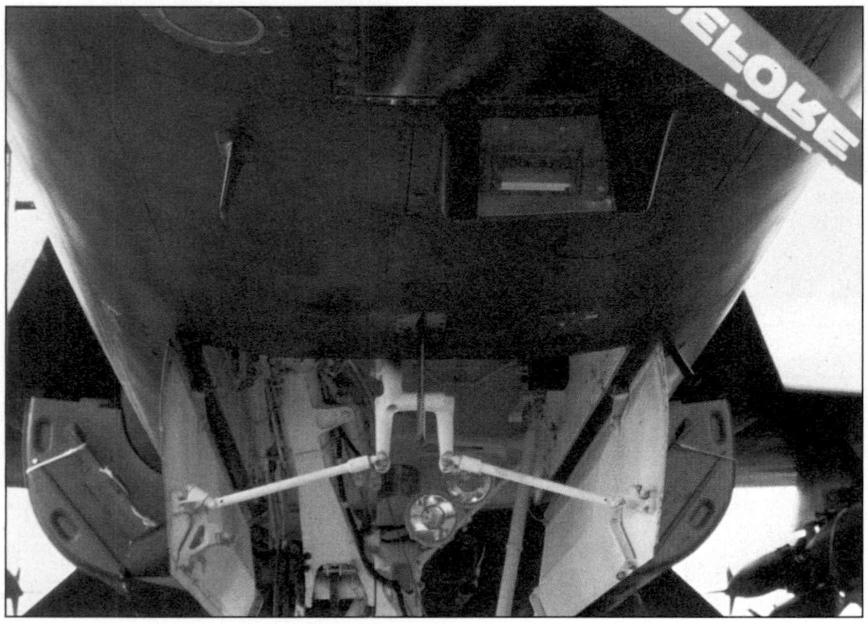

Top: A gun-equipped F-111D of the 27th TFW at Cannon AFB. Proposals still exist to rebuild this model into SAC bombers.

Above: The strike camera installation of an F-111D, typical of most tactical models. It looks obliquely forward but the outer window is skin-flush.

have no windmill, but have hemispherical radomes emitting to front and rear.

This overall avionic fit was retained with only very minor changes in the second production version, the F-111E. The RAAF virtually accepted the entire Mk I avionics for the F-111C, though this has a modified airframe, as explained in a later chapter. But as early as 1963 the USAF Systems Command had begun detailed investigation of a Mk II avionics fit, and though this may be fractured English it eventually came to describe a totally new aircraft, but packaged inside virtually the same airframe as the A and E models. The reason was simply that by the mid-1960s the Mk I black boxes had begun to look distinctly dated, with analog technology, large printed-circuit boards often bearing discrete components, and a general level of technology hardly different from an F-4. Clearly, it was possible to do much better with more modern technology, and it looked as if the F-111 could be transformed into a virtually new-generation aircraft.

By 1964 the Mk II avionics specification and equipment list had been agreed, and the prime contract for systems integration was placed with North American Aviation's Autonetics Division, today called Rockwell International Electronics. Some parts of mission/traffic control and penaids were left alone, but the central firepower control and associated cockpit displays were virtually designed from a clean sheet of paper.

It was planned to switch to the Mk II at the 100th production F-111 in 1968, the new model being designated F-111D. What actually happened was that the exciting new Mk II system – which at one time the British government thought it could have in the RAF in 1968 also – took so long to develop that costs multiplied frighteningly, delays became severe and eventually it went into a mere 96 aircraft, compared with a planned 315. Even so, major elements of the Mk II system were omitted, one being CW illumination for AIM-7 Sparrow AAMs to restore some capability in the air-to-air mission.

Largest item in the firepower control is the attack radar, and in the Mk II system this is the Autonetics APQ-130. Essentially the next generation after the same company's ASB-12 (REINS) radar bombing system for the A-5 Vigilante, APQ-130 is a digital solid-state device with more operating modes than the APQ-113. It can offer considerably improved picture sharpness in ground map modes, especially at the very shallow grazing angles of tree-top TF flight, offers MTI (moving-target indication) in being able to pick out a moving target against a stationary surface background, and in particular has vastly improved performance in conditions of heavy precipitation (rain or snow) or enemy countermeasures.

In the early days of the F-111 WSOs who came from older aircraft would not allow that there could ever be a better radar than the APQ-113 but the 130 is a new-generation set with many capabilities not dissimilar to the F-15's APG-63 and Tornado's TI attack radar. In theory such a radar needs less cooling and is far more reliable than older sets, but in practice the abort rate of the F-111D has generally been worse than that of all other variants, largely because of problems with the temperamental avionics.

Other items making up the Mk II suite are listed in the detailed data section.

Supplier of the APQ-128 TFR is Sperry, the APN-189 doppler comes from Canadian Marconi, GD and IBM produced the totally new general-purpose digital computer, and in the cockpit the D has a very advanced HSD (Astronautics Corp AYN-3) which superimposes aircraft position, track and target data over projected maps or reconnaissance photographs, while directly ahead of

Below: The Pave Tack pod is normally housed inside the weapon bay. As the target approaches it is quickly extended (Mach limit is 1.4) and pointed within the limits shown.

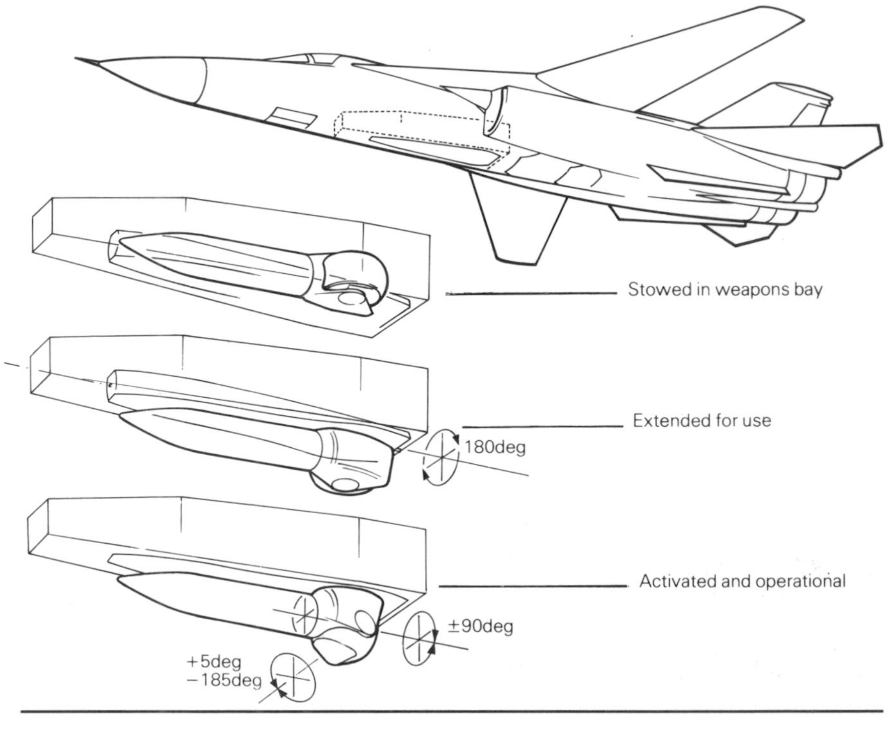

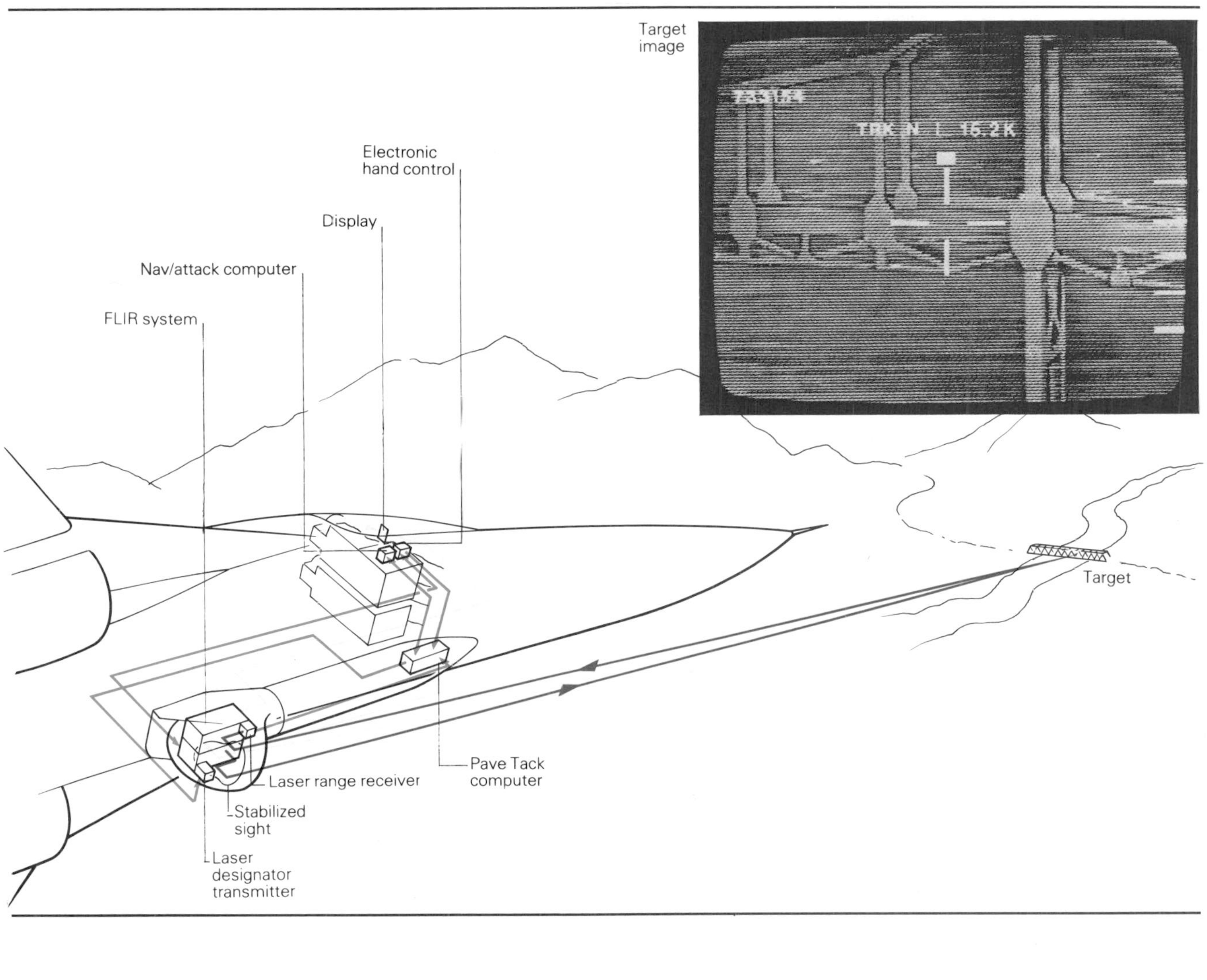

Above: Pave Tack became operational on 15 September 1981 with F-111Fs of the 48th TFW at RAF Lakenheath. This F-111F is carrying a 2,450lb (1,111kg) GBU-15.

Left: Simplified Pave Tack functional diagram, with an inset video image (in this case of a bridge target).

both crew members is an AVA-9 HUD, by Norden Division of what is today called United Technologies, one of the first head-up displays in the USAF and a major cause of Mk II delays and problems. In the centre of the pilot's panel is a VSD (vertical situation display) almost as impressive as the giant HSD on the right, and more than half the other cockpit items look different from those in the A and E versions.

As noted earlier the D introduced a more powerful TF30 engine, and a more important advance was the introduction of a 'bootstrap-cycle' ECS (environmental control system), though this was yet another cause of severe technical problems. One of the few changes in the D that showed externally was the replacement of the often-criticized manually operated scope camera, used for photographing targets, by a KB-18A automatic strike camera. This looks obliquely ahead from a small blister under the forward fuselage, and has been retrofitted on most F-111As and Es, in some cases after relocation of an ALE-23 or ALR-41 blade aerial.

Left: Trials with the Hughes version of Pave Mover have been flown with this F-111E, mainly at White Sands Missile Range, New Mexico. The radar components and data link ride in the large underbelly pod.

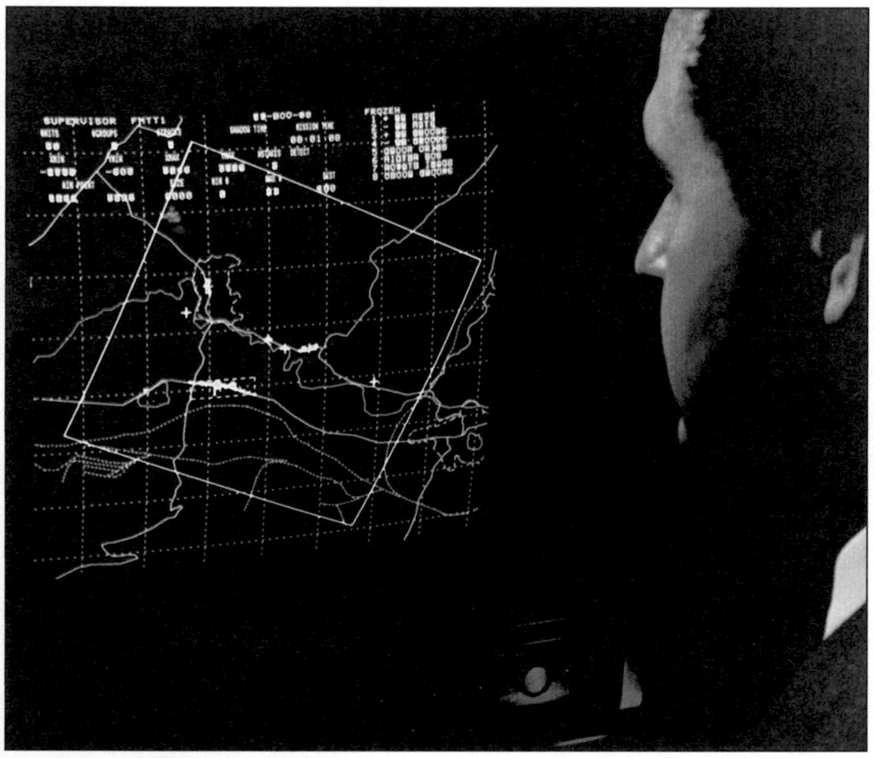

Left below: The Pave Mover data link sends the radar target information to a mobile ground station to create this full-colour battlefield display. Computers display the alphanumeric data on all significant targets.

Left bottom: An F-111D lets go 12 Mk 82 bombs over Nevada in July 1972.

Altogether the F-111D is unquestionably a superior aircraft, and one with a bit more accent on air combat, a facet also shown by the invariable installation of the gun, as described in the next chapter. But the CW illumination of air targets for Sparrow AAMs has never been used, and there is no plan to fit either these weapons or the later Amraam. On balance, therefore, the D remains a questionable programme, which has absorbed very large sums of money, given relatively poor mission availability and required the training of flight and ground crews who cannot operate or maintain other F-111s.

The situation would have been better had the D become the standard model; indeed, there was even discussion in the 1964–5 period of retrofitting the Mk II avionics to the F-111A. Cost proved to be prohibitive, and the Mk II research bill alone escalated from a projected $60 million to more than $280 million by 1969. At quite a late stage the decision was taken to go ahead with the planned fitment of larger mainwheel tyres and a stronger landing gear, but the increase in gross weight thus permitted was minimal, and in fact seldom used. The D had also been planned as the standard photo and multisensor reconnaissance model, designated RF-111D.

The original idea was that TAC would buy large pallets carrying optical cameras, a SLAR (side-looking airborne radar) and IR linescan, and clip them into the weapon bays of regular F-111As. It was found difficult to do this, and in December 1967 the 11th development aircraft (63-9776) began a flight programme as the RF-111A, with a multisensor installation which was not readily removable. Over $118 million was spent on the RF system, and as late as 1968 it was hoped to buy 60 RF-111Ds with a similar installation, managed by a separate digital computer, but the RF programme was cancelled. This left the RAAF later to spend a lot more money on a quite different RF-111C programme of its own.

Final tactical version

Chronologically the next variant was the FB-111A, discussed in a later chapter. The tactical models were completed with the F-111F, and had it not been for Pratt & Whitney it is doubtful that this model would ever have been purchased. Though the earlier One-Elevens can do their job, and in *Airman Magazine* for August 1969, the most experienced of all F-111 pilots, Maj Tom Wheeler (USAF Chief of Flight Test and Acceptance at GD), wrote "The power plant on this bird is so good that you can do a lot of flying on one engine", the fact remains the thrust/weight ratio of the fully loaded aircraft was unimpressive even for a bomber, and about one-third as high as modern fighters. There was certainly an urge to counter the unplanned and awesome increase in gross weight with additional engine thrust, but it took a long time to do this, in part because P&W were busy getting the engine to an acceptable standard of reliability when installed in the F-111A. As noted earlier they finally came up with the P-100 engine offering a welcome 35 per cent more power than the F-111A and E engines, and with other big advantages, and this tipped the scales in favour of a planned buy of 219 of the F version.

Ideally these should otherwise have had the standard Mk II avionics to maximise both capability and commonality, but the mixture of technical problems and astronomic costs spurred a search for a more affordable alternative. This was realised in the Mk IIB system (a designation originally applied to the FB-111A avionics), which were considered the best compromise between capability and price. Officially said to cost just half as much as the Mk II system, the IIB has the AYK-6 digital computer from the Mk II but used to tie together generally simplified black boxes and with a cockpit much more familiar to a driver of an A or E.

New Mk IIB avionics

The attack radar is the APG-144, based on the GE radar of the FB-111A but with the addition of 0·2-microsecond pulsewidth (half the previous minimum) and a 2½nm (4·63km) display scale, again half the previous minimum and giving double the 'magnification'. GE wished to add DMTI (digital moving-target indication) and a reduced wavelength in the K-band, but though these were flown they were never incorporated in production sets. (Later the same radar formed the basis of those used in prototype B-1 bombers.) Another new item was the Loral ALR-41 CMRS (countermeasures receiver set), but by 1980 this was being replaced by the new-generation Dalmo-Victor ALR-62 as part of the USAF's across-the-board efforts to update the EW suites of all F-111s. The ALR-62 RWR is now the chief sensor in the updated F-111 kit for the remainder of the 1980s, which also includes the AAR-44 and ALQ-137.

Though still partly classified, the AAR-44 is the latest in a series of IRWRs (infra-red warning receivers) by Cincinnati Electronics, and it retains the fin-top location of the receiver cells – which, of course, are refrigerated by a cryogenic system. This installation can continue its non-stop search of the entire hemisphere below the aircraft whilst locking-on and tracking any oncoming SAM or AAM and processing the resulting data for display to the crew. IRCM (countermeasure) action can be automatic, in other words the AAR-44 can itself trigger the release of flare cartridges from the ALE-28 installation at the optimum times and with the best frequency and burst characteristics to protect the aircraft without the crew having to work out the answers under extreme stress. The system can handle attacks by several missiles simultaneously, and is claimed to have near-perfect ability to discriminate true targets against solar radiation or the

Sun's reflection on glass or water, and known kinds of IRCM background.

ALQ-137 is an internal EW system developed specially for the F-111 family as a replacement for the same company's ALQ-94. The 137 may be expected to have higher ERP (effective radiated power) and will certainly have more advanced digital processing to manage the electric power for the maximum result, with either or both noise and deception signals being sent out not to all points of the compass but towards the threat being countered. Trials began in 1974 and the first production contract was placed in 1977, the installation being integrally linked with the ALR-62 to form the first really modern

Above: An F-111A with 24 Mk 82 bombs operating with the 366th TFW.

Right: Standard MER (multiple ejector rack) of the kind carried by F-111s for conventional bombing.

Below: An F-111A of the 474th TFW on Constant Guard Five deployment to Southeast Asia in December 1972. It is shown on a combat mission from Takhli RTAFB loaded with CBU-42 cluster bombs.

Foot of page: An unidentified F-111A photographed in 1971 with a display showing the number carried of each store (white bombs are nuclear).

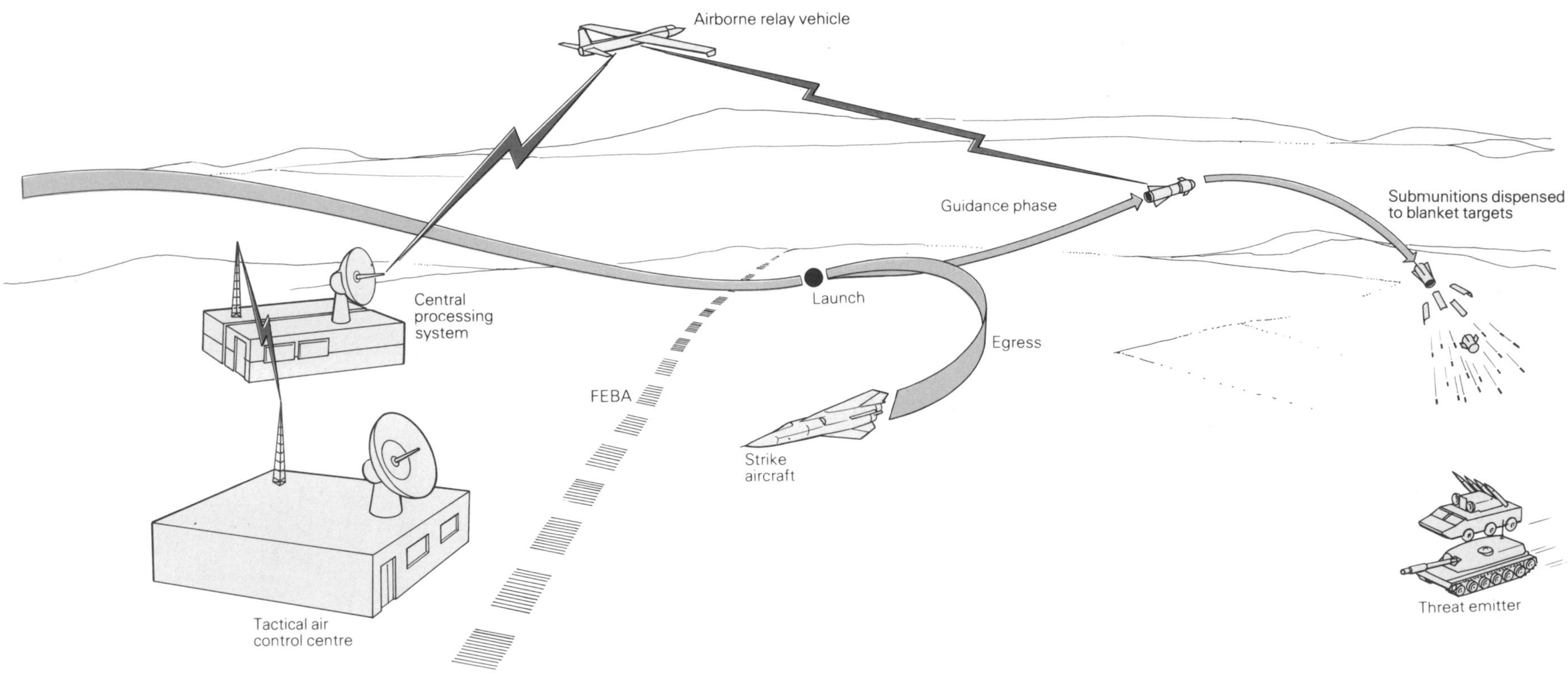

Above: The Advanced Location/Strike System uses TOA (time of arrival of radar pulses) and DME (distance measuring equipment) to hit enemy radars with GBU-15s.

EW package in any tactical aircraft. Of course, it is likely that by the mid-1980s the ITT/Westinghouse ALQ-165 ASPJ (advanced self-protective jammer) will be installed in the surviving F-111s, as well as in all front-line combat aircraft of the USAF, Navy and Marines. This extremely advanced installation is intended to be internal in all aircraft, and to counter threats at frequencies up to 20 GHz from the start, 35 GHz by about 1989 and perhaps 140 GHz by the end of the century, given the expected improvements in capabilities.

New Avionics

Remarkably, in view of the extremely comprehensive internal fit of sensors and weapon-delivery systems, the F-111 has in recent years been a favoured vehicle for extra avionics in these categories. As far as combat effectiveness is concerned, by far the most important of the add-ons is AVQ-26 Pave Tack, one of the many 'Pave' projects initiated by USAF Aeronautical Systems Division. It is briefly described as a versatile target designator for use at all times of day and in all kinds of weather. Prime contractor is Ford Aerospace but key elements include a FLIR by TI, a laser by International Laser Systems and a virtual image display by GE. Flying in an F-111F began in August 1978, the sensor pod being mounted on a cradle which extends it upon command from its normal retracted position in the weapon bay. When extended the sensor head can view the entire hemisphere beneath the aircraft.

The pod comprises a streamlined tubular Base Unit packed with electronics, digital computer and refrigeration, and a spherical Head Unit able to be rotated at high speed and with great precision to look in any direction. The

Below: A fine January 1983 portrait of one of the 48th TFW's F-111Fs with Pave Tack and four Paveway IIs.

Above: Though the F-111 has always been nominally a 'fighter', and early prototypes were cleared with the AIM-9 Sidewinder, it is only very recently that such self-defence AAMs have appeared in use. This bombed-up F-111F shows the neat way that AIM-9 is carried on the side of the pylon.

Right: The fourth F-111B Navy fighter flying with four dummy AIM-54 Phoenix long-range AAMs. The same powerful air-to-air interception weapons were also flown on the fourth USAF F-111A RDT&E aircraft, but no attempt was subsequently made to give USAF F-111s stand-off interception capability.

Head contains the AAQ-9 FLIR and AVQ-25 YAG (yttrium/aluminium garnet) laser, both boresighted exactly parallel to a precision-stabilized optical sight. All sensors are isolated from vibration, and look through a large window of ZnS (zinc sulphide). The FLIR provides a ×1 or ×2 video picture of a narrow 3deg or wide 12deg field of view on 525 or 875 lines, on which can be superimposed the bright reticle of the laser designator and a great variety of alphanumeric information. The line of sight may be aimed by a hand controller or controlled automatically by various systems.

Once the target is being tracked it remains in the display no matter what evasive manoeuvres are performed, and while the sightline gives exact angle information the laser gives range information, within much less than 10ft (3m), for precision weapon delivery. The laser emits at 1·06 microns and is thus compatible with Paveway-series and other smart weapons. The head swivels aft to give damage information on leaving the target, everything if necessary being taped for subsequent playback.

The display was accommodated by taking the space previously occupied by the APQ-144 (main radar) indicator/recorder system. Funding limitations have restricted Pave Tack buy for F-111Fs to a mere 49 pods, though all active aircraft are being converted to take them. Operational clearance with the 48th TFW was reached in 1981, since when the training burden has been considerable. Pave Tack has also been purchased for RAAF F-111Cs.

Another Pave system not yet cleared for use on any aircraft is Pave Mover. This ambitious TAWDS (target acquisition/weapon delivery system) is based on an SAR (synthetic-aperture radar) which, as described earlier in this book, emits sequenced signals as if from a giant antenna to give very high resolution. Two Pave Mover SARs are flying in F-111s, a Hughes in an F-111E and a joint Norden/Grumman in an F-111A. Norden/Grumman was the team on the A-6 Intruder for the US Navy, and their Pave Mover was based on work done in

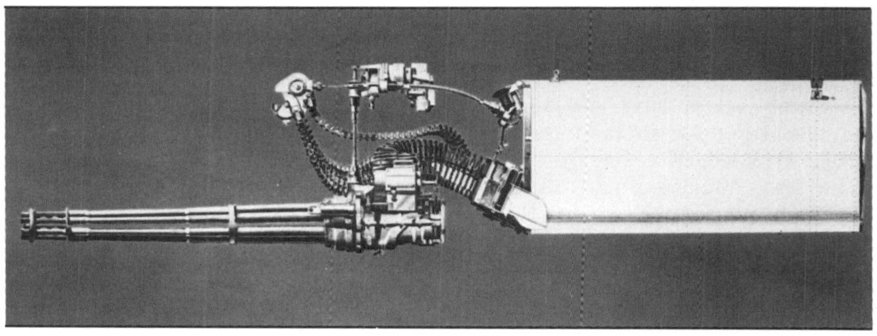

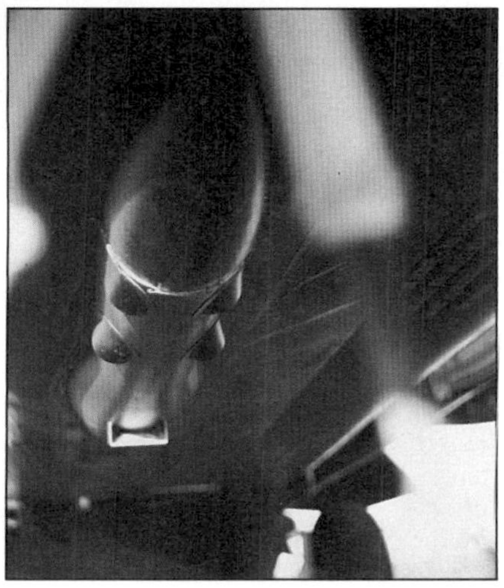

Top: The M61A-1 gun installation includes the biggest ammunition tank ever fitted to any fighter, with a capacity of up to 2,084 20mm rounds.

Above: The box containing the M61 gun seen installed but with the weapon bay doors open. The gun is on the right side, with muzzles to the left.

Right: The gun in an F-111F of the 366th TFW, showing the muzzle fairing carried to reduce drag.

Left: A full load of 24 Mk 82 bombs rain down from an F-111F serving with the 366th TFW operating from Mountain Home AFB in 1973.

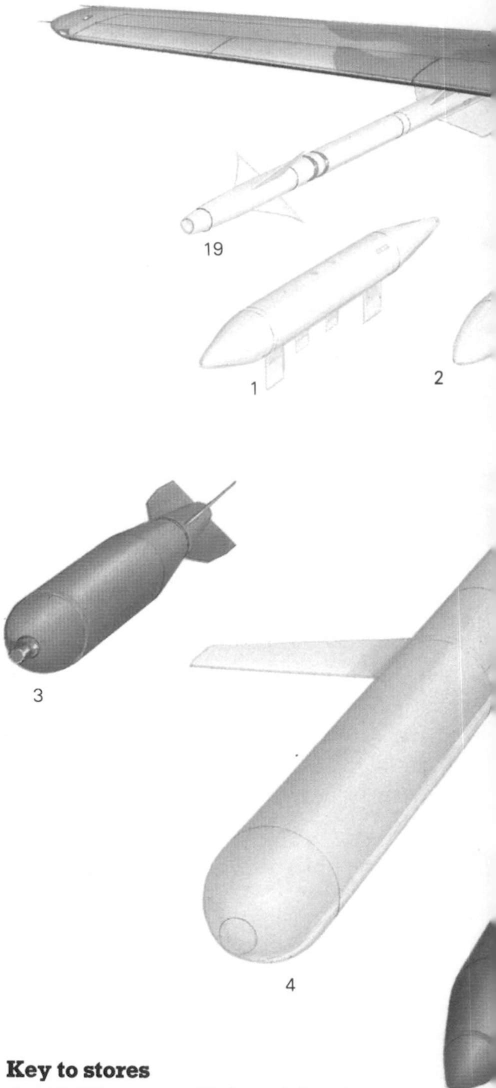

Key to stores
1 ALQ-87 jammer pod (being withdrawn)
2 ALQ-131 jammer pod (entering service)
3 Mk 117 750lb (340kg) GP bomb
4 AGM-109 MRASM cruise missile
5 Twin bomb dispensers
6 Stores container
7 Mk 82 Snakeye retarded bomb
8 AGM-69A SRAM (FB-111A only)
9 M61 20mm cannon
10 B61 nuclear weapon
11 Nuclear weapon (type undisclosed, possibly B28 carried by FB-111A)
12 Mk 83 1,000lb (454kg) GP bomb
13 600US gal drop tank
14 GBU-15 laser-guided bomb
15 B43 nuclear weapon
16 Mk 84 2,000lb (907kg) GP bomb
17 ALQ-119(V) ECM jammer pod
18 Durandal anti-runway weapon
19 AIM-9L Sidewinder AAM

updating that programme. The Norden/Grumman set is long and slim and required extensive aircraft modification but is mounted on a quickly removed pallet and gives little drag. The Hughes radar is fatter and mounted largely external below the weapon bay, needing modest aircraft modification but imposing higher drag. Both are SLARs (side-looking aircraft radars) working in I/J band with aerial arrays 11·5ft (3·5m) long, and both use the latest combinations of frequency hopping, spread spectrum PRN (pseudo-random noise) techniques to make it very difficult for enemy ECM to get a good lock or determine their direction or range. This is vital, because the carrier aircraft would be the first thing to be destroyed and extremely vulnerable, orbiting at about 49,000ft (15km) for long periods and playing a crucial role in directing air attack on the enemy.

Pave Mover has been used mainly in connection with the USAF Assault Breaker concept for stopping a thrust by vast forces of armoured vehicles. Attacks could be made by manned aircraft, such as normal F-111s, or by missiles with single warheads or missiles with dispensed submunitions with or without individual guidance. All these, including even the unguided submunitions, could benefit from Pave Mover surveillance, which gives a pin-sharp picture of stationary objects on the battlefield and also can detect and track moving objects.

The radars flying in the two F-111s can each detect and track six separate "target arrays" each comprising up to 12 objects such as tanks, whilst simultaneously transmitting target guidance updates to two missiles or aircraft. Trials from Holloman AFB began in June 1981 and in 1983 decisions on the next stage were expected. There are problems with C^3 – command, control, communications – and with discriminating between high-value tanks and SP guns and low-value targets or even decoys. Moreover, there is never enough money to progress in the way needed to stay even abreast of the threat on the European Central Front.

Yet another F-111 add-on is the AXQ-14 data-link which rather surprisingly is needed to allow GBU-15 missiles to be guided effectively. Though GBU-15 is a Rockwell weapon, also known as CWW (cruciform-wing weapon), the data-link is a Hughes Aircraft product, and it is hung on the rear fuselage, displacing the ECM jammer pod to a new location under the weapon bay. In the photograph a full-size F-111 mock-up is mounted upside-down to avoid ground interference while the data-link is tested at full power (with an ALQ-119 jammer further forward). The AXQ-14 emits from a phased-array aerial system to guide the missile into its target, whilst at the same time relaying the image seen by the missile's EO nose seeker to the F-111 cockpit display. The pod also includes the usual mission recorder.

Weapons for the One-eleven

As the original concept of SOR-183 was an aircraft to replace the F-105 it is not surprising that the F-111 ended up with plenty of pylon capacity, an internal weapon bay and a 20-mm M61 'Gatling gun'. At the same time, in view of the extremely high price of so large and complex an aircraft, and the desire to fly fighter missions, and perhaps enjoy commonality with the Navy air-dfence fighter, it is a little surprising that weapons for the air-combat and interception roles appear to have been almost overlooked.

Dealing with this mission first, several early development aircraft were used in flight test programmes with AAMs. The No 7 aircraft (63-9772) was fitted with a remarkably complex system of twin staggered pairs of rails for launching Sidewinder close-range AAMs. Each pair of rails was hung on parallel links from the top of the weapon bay and with the bay doors open could pivot down to place the missiles out in the airstream well below the fuselage. This fit was not adopted, though on all tactical versions Pylons 3,4,5 and 6 can have shoes for launching any model of AIM-9 Sidewinder (though they are almost never carried).

The No 4 aircraft (63-9769) was flown with dummy AIM-54 Phoenix AAMS on the four inboard wing pylons (Nos 3, 4, 5 and 6). This large and extremely long-ranged AAM was to have been the primary armament of the F-111B, and its great performance was naturally of interest to the USAF, though the associated AWG-9 radar could not handle parts of the Air Force attack mission. Predictably, the more the F-111 became a bomber, the less the USAF thought about Phoenix. Unlike Sidewinder, Phoenix was never actually fired from any Air Force version of F-111.

The wish to add the AIM-7 Sparrow medium-range AAM to the weapon kit of the F-111 has already been related. The MK II avionics suite was specially designed so that the main attack radar would have an AAM mode in which it could provide a CW pencil beam to illuminate a hostile aircraft. This mode is not used, and no Sparrow ever flew on an F-111, though should this capability be thought important it could fairly readily be provided.

As it is, the gun is today the only part of the regular weapon fit regarded as an air-to-air weapon, and it is not normally carried except by the F-111D and occasionally by other models. Except for the 27th TFW, most One-Eleven crews have never even seen it, far less fired it. The installation is not unusual, the gun being mounted on the right centre of the forward part of the bomb bay, faired inside a blister built into the right-hand bay door which is provided with a removable front fairing. The door and fairing can be swung open for access to the gun. A round-trip flexible guideway feeds ammunition from the enormous 2,084-round drum in the rear of the bay, to which empty cases are returned. The gun is aimed with the pilot's LCOS (or HUD in the F-111D) and is considered useful against certain ground targets.

When the gun is not installed, the bomb bay can be used for various purposes including carriage of ECM dispensers (for bulk chaff in particular), fuel and/or water tanks, special instrumentation, and, in the RF-111C, a reconnaissance installation. The brochures say that two 750lb (340kg) bombs can be carried in the bay, but in fact the standard USAF stores loadings

Below: a selection of stores carried by the F-111 (the aircraft is typical of all tactical attack versions).

do not include any internal items except nuclear bombs, practice bombs and the gun.

Standard nuclear bombs which can be carried by the F-111 include the B43, B57 and B61, all in tactical versions and the former with at least five different yields. In each case one bomb can be carried in both the left and right bays. When the gun is carried only the right bay is fully occupied but none of these weapons can be carried on the left side. As noted later, the FB-111A can carry two SRAMS, internally; AGM-86B ALCM cannot be accommodated.

The only fuselage pylons are for ECM pods, and for practical purposes in conventional warfare the only armament is what can be carried on the wing pylons. The outer wings have four hardpoints on each side, and weapon loads have been published which require eight pylons, but though these were flown during early test programmes they are not used in practice, and the outermost pylons, Nos 1 and 8, positioned at BL (buttock-line) 309 (ie, 309 in or 25ft 9in [7·85m] from the aircraft centreline) are not fitted.

This leaves a maximum capacity of six pylons. The outers, Nos 2 and 7, each at BL 250, are fixed to the wing at such an angle that they are aligned with the fore/aft axis only when the wings are at the 26deg sweep position. In theory it would be possible to take off with the wings fully forward with these pylons installed, though it is certainly not normal practice. At any sweep angle greater than 26deg these pylons must be jettisoned. The only load normally carried on these pylons is the 600US gal (500gal, 2,273-litre) drop tank.

Thus in practice there are just four pylons available for conventional weapons: Nos 3,4,5 and 6, located at BL 189 and 118 on each side of the aircraft. These pylons are the only ones normally installed, and they were the first in the world to be mounted on pivots with internal linkage to keep them aligned with the airstream at all wing sweep angles. All are stressed to 5,000lb (2,268kg) to 4·6g, the heaviest load being the 600US gal tank which weighs almost this amount when filled. Other possible loads are listed in the data. Normal maximum bombload is thus 19,800lb (8,981kg), comprising 24 M117A1 GP bombs each of 750lb nominal weight but an actual weight nearer to 825lb (374kg).

Nuclear bombs, such as B43, B57 and B61, the Mk 84 family of 2,000lb (907kg) bombs and the M118 bomb of 3,000lb (1,361kg) nominal mass are all carried singly. Other stores are carried in multiple, either four or six to each of the four pylons. This requires the addition of an MER (multiple ejector rack) to each pylon. The F-111 has its own unique design of MER which, while preserving the usual basically triangular section, has a waisted centre and a bulged front and rear, with ventral strakes, giving it an area-ruled appearance. It carries all stores in tandem triplets, the heaviest load of six CBU-58s (cluster bomb units, each housing 800 bomblets of 1lb) having roughly the same aggregate mass as the 600US gal tank.

There is no reason to doubt that Maverick could be carried in tandem triplets, but this is not a certified F-111 weapon (one is reminded of the story of the F-111 pilot who, newly arrived in southeast Asia, was asked "Do you have smart missiles?" and replied, "No, we have smart airplanes"). The one recent exception is the GBU-15, Rockwell's modular guided weapon system, which fits precision guidance to either a 2,000lb bomb or to the CBU-75 clustered munition dispenser. This has been certified for use from all TAC F-111 models, which can carry one on each of the four pylons. This TV/data-link system is normally part of the major F-111 force update which also includes the installation of the Pave Tack system in the weapons bay.

Deployment and Combat

In March 1968, only eight months after TAC had received its first One-Eleven, six of the new bombers were deployed to Thailand for operations over North Vietnam. Within weeks half the force had been lost, but the lessons learned were put to good use when the type returned in 1972. Escalating costs and media criticism had taken their toll, however, and the current force is thinly spread, with most units having a mixture of variants, and maintenance problems further compounded by shortages of spares. Nevertheless, the F-111 remains one of NATO's most capable long-range penetration bombers.

Above: A Combat Lancer aircraft with ALQ-87 pods and Snakeye bombs on the outer pylons leaves Takhli in March 1968.

By 1967 GD had flown all 18 RDT&E (research, development, test and evaluation) aircraft of the Air Force F-111A, as well as over 50 production aircraft. On the other hand Cat I (Category I, testing by the prime contractor, in this case GD) was nowhere near completed, and Cat II (by USAF Systems Command) had not even started. There was pressure on the Air Force not only to get the big new bird into the squadrons but to fly some effective missions to try to counter the torrent of highly adverse publicity in the media.

The first chance to gain favourable headlines came on May 22, 1967, when two production aircraft, still in contractor's hands, were flown across the North Atlantic. One landed at RAF Wethersfield to give USAFE (USAF Europe) their first sight of what was slated to be one of their most potent weapons in the years to come. The other went on to Le Bourget for the Paris Air Show. Like its companion it had taken off from Loring AFB, Maine, and flown non-stop without air refuelling, completing the mission in 5 hours 54 minutes with 2½ hours fuel remaining. The pilot was Maj Tom Wheeler, and the unprecedented flight for a fighter-type aircraft at last drew grudging admission from the media that the F-111 might in fact be quite an airplane.

The urgent task of clearing the aircraft for service delivery was complicated by the fact that up to No 42 no two F-111As were exactly alike, though often the differences were small. Flying rates increased markedly in 1967, and by mid-year it was clear that the stipulated 35 maintenance man-hours per flight hour would be likely to be met. At last, on July 17, Col Ivan H. Dethman, cigar-smoking CO of Detachment I, 448th TFS, collected the first of TAC's One-Elevens and flew it to Nellis AFB, north of Las Vegas.

Below: F-111As of the 474th TFW over the Pacific heading for Thailand on Combat Lancer deployment. A KC-135 provided tanker support.

Operational testing

Cat III (user unit) testing could thus begin, and though everyone had much to learn Dethman's style was to work men and aircraft around the clock, in a gruelling programme called Harvest Reaper. Officially the F-111A became operational with the 448th in October, in which month each aircraft on strength flew an average of 59·7 hours, which was actually fractionally lower than the figure for September but double the 30 hours demanded by the Air Force.

Few people liked the side-by-side cockpit, but on the whole initial impressions were highly favourable. Gradually the P-3 engine, attack and TF radars, ECM gear and other items became universal on all aircraft, and as crew skills increased so did confidence in flying lone missions deep into hostile territory. It took a while to trust one's life to the TFR, and it was found that heavy rain was interpreted as solid ground and, as it might start at a great height, some crews found themselves at plus-3g and at 10,000ft (3,000m) AGL before they could take over manually and dive back to what were supposed to be safer levels "in the weeds".

Another item that took some getting used to was the crew module. Everyone appreciated the comfort of not having to wear a parachute, but traditional ejection seats and parachutes were known quantities. A former GD flight test engineer, 'Ted' Tate, recalls: "For months Col Henry Brown, a 17-victory P-51 ace, had been giving me pure hell about the 'Chinese New Year, Mickey Mouse' escape system, which he was sure would fail to work at the vital moment. He was airborne with Maj Joe Jordan (F-104 altitude record-holder) on gun tests, when gun gas in the weapon bay exploded, causing mortal damage. These gentlemen had a very smooth ride back to Earth. Col Brown's Command magazine wanted him to write about it, and his article was filled with superlatives of praise for the system he had condemned the previous day".

Everyone wanted to prove the One-Eleven a winner, and air shows were attended whenever possible. On

Armed Forces Day Fred Voorhies, GD test pilot, put on a sparkling show at Holloman AFB, and then came in at minimum speed in dirty configuration with everything hanging out and down. He planned to clean up, hit afterburner, sweep the wings and go into a steep climb. To his horror he found he had got into the 'back of the drag curve' in which, as speed falls further, drag actually increases. He slammed the throttles wide open but could not avoid hitting the ground violently just short of the runway. When the dust cleared Fred could be seen climbing out. He took off his helmet and drop-kicked it (football style) far into the desert; then he pounded the One-Eleven with his fists, yelling "Dumbhead... Dumbhead..." All this in front of major network TV cameras. Later the extremely capable Voorhies flew the One-Eleven spin programme.

Deployment to Vietnam

By the start of 1968 TAC had demonstrated takeoffs and landings at light weights with ground rolls less than 2,000ft (600m), carried bombloads up to 29,000lb (13 tonnes), made 40 refuelling hook-ups in a single flight, and achieved navigational accuracies described as "eight times better than TAC's next-best fighter/bomber" and bombing accuracies that were "consistently amazing". The Joint Chiefs of Staff took a political decision to take a calculated risk and send six aircraft from the Nellis 428th TFS to Vietnam in the expectancy that they would prove the concept of deep interdiction by individual unescorted aircraft, with no backup from tankers, ECM or any other aircraft, and show what the One-Eleven could do. The project was called Combat Lancer, and the Detachment was put in Col Dethman's charge, as CO of the squadron.

They crossed the Pacific in a group, accompanied by a single KC-135 simply to take care of any fuel emergency, without even carrying drop tanks and navigating on the F-111 inertial systems. Litton could take pride in hitting the tiny island of Guam right on the nose after an uncorrected flight of 3,000 miles (4,800km) from Hickam AFB, Hawaii. The force arrived at Takhli Royal Thai AFB, 85 miles north of Bangkok on March 17, 1968. They flew a few training sorties in the unfamiliar environment and then began the arduous task of flying long missions by night, completely alone, no matter what the weather. Typically they carried 24 Mk 82 bombs and two ALQ-87 pods.

The result was quite unexpected. On March 28 a One-Eleven went out on a mission and never came back. The same thing happened two days later, and again on April 27. As each crew planned its own mission and thereafter maintained radio silence, nobody had the slightest idea what had happened. Altogether 55 missions were flown in Combat Lancer, most by night and more than half in bad weather. Yet the 52 missions that came back reported complete success: they achieved what appeared to be total surprise, and the RHAWS and ECM receivers did not once indicate any illumination by a hostile radar, nor was there the slightest evidence of combat damage. Yet half the force had simply vanished. This was not at all what the Air Force had wanted, or expected; predictably, the media took it for granted the missing aircraft had been shot down.

Fortunately one of the crews had managed to eject. Their testimony, and examination of the crashed aircraft, made it clear there had been a sudden catastrophic failure in the tailplane system, and this was traced to fatigue failure of a welded joint in the power unit of the left tailplane. Its effect would be to put the aircraft into a violent left roll and pitch-up, whilst slamming the sticks back into the crew's stomachs. On May 8, before the cause had been pinpointed, a Nellis aircraft was lost in precisely these circumstances. This accident was positively attributed to failure of the weld. Loss of six aircraft (three in Vietnam) in just over 5,000

Left: A Combat Lancer aircraft landing after an air test at Takhli, without MERs on the pylons. Note the Combat Lancer badge on the rudder.

Above: A classic photograph of TFR operations over Vietnam in 1968, showing an F-111A with wings at intermediate setting 'skiing' up a peak.

Below: F-111As were used in the Igloo White programme to drop sensors which picked up sounds or vibrations from Viet Cong trucks.

Top: A fine picture taken during the early years of training missions from Nellis AFB, Nevada. The aircraft is the 105th F-111A (including RDT&E).

Above: Similar externally, apart from the Triple Plow 2 inlets, this F-111F (then with the 389th TFS, 366th TFW) is a totally different weapon system.

hours flying with the Air Force was a record that compared very well with other supersonic types, but it is galling to think that, had the weld failures been avoided by different design or stricter quality-control the total would probably have been just one aircraft.

This was only the start of a prolonged period of major structural problems which were totally unexpected and which should have been avoided by the extremely comprehensive test programme carried out by GD and its suppliers. The structural heart of the aircraft is the WCTB (wing carry-through box) which carries the 8½in (21·6cm) pins on which the wings pivot. Ruling material of this massive component is Ladish D6AC, a high-strength steel known for its good ductility and freedom from brittle fracture which earned particularly good marks during the TFX bid evaluations. The precision-fit bolts holding the WCTB together were carefully mated with holes reamed and ground to avoid the slightest scratch or sharp edge, yet in static fatigue testing potentially catastrophic cracks were discovered in late 1968 around several bolt-holes. An order went out restricting all F-111s to +3·5g manoeuvres until GD had taken each aircraft back and added 500lb (227kg) of thick reinforcing gussets. This cost several million dollars. Then on December 22, 1969, the left wing came clean off a Nellis aircraft being flown quite properly and with a fully reinforced WCTB. The crew did not have time to trigger the capsule.

All aircraft grounded

This was perhaps the all-time low point in the entire F-111 programme. The 223 aircraft then flying were grounded while the holiday period was spent in a frantic investigation to discover if any further flaws lurked in the WCTB or wing pivots. One F-111A was found to have a major flaw resembling a miniature bomb crater, about an inch across and extending almost the full depth of the D6AC steel, in the lower plate of the wing pivot fitting, which is the very strong area of the swinging outer wing surrounding the pivot pin. How this escaped three successive tests by ultrasonic and magnetic-particle means was a mystery, but the Scientific Advisory Board undertook the unprecedented step of ordering the inspection and proof testing of every single F-111 in existence. Four complete new test facilities had to be built, two at Fort Worth, one at Waco and one at Sacramento, in which the One-Elevens – some from as far afield as Upper Heyford, England – were bent and twisted to +7·33g and −2·4g with the wings at 56deg sweep after prior refrigeration to −40deg F (−40deg C). No flaw was found in a wing pivot, but two potential crashes may have happened on the ground when a tailplane pivot shaft broke at Forth Worth and a WCTB lower plate parted in tension at Sacramento. This test programme eventually embraced more than 330 aircraft of the USAF, including 70 of the new SAC bomber version, but not the 24 for the RAAF which were delayed for almost ten years.

The technical troubles which afflicted the One-Eleven in its early years were far outside anything normally encountered, and strongly suggested the malignant hand of fate. They certainly did not reflect any failure on the part of any contractor's design process or quality control, and in no way could be construed as evidence of what the notorious Senator William A. Proxmire called "an unsafe and defective plane". Today F-111s have flown more than a million hours, almost all in the most demanding conditions of high speed at low level and in every kind of weather. The fact that none of this ever gets into the newspapers is the best evidence of what kind of aircraft the F-111 really is.

The F-111 was never named, but by 1968 its universal 'pronunciation' of One-Eleven had been supplemented by an unofficial name as curious as it was inappropriate: Aardvark. Assuming that the reason had nothing to do with coming first in alphabetical listings, it stemmed purely from the aircraft's long nose, also a feature of the South African animal whose name literally means earth-pig. The name was *not* chosen because of the One-Eleven's ability to hug the ground!

The slightly modified F-111E, whose only real difference lies in improved inlets but not the improved engines, entered service at Cannon AFB in October 1969. Congress criticized GD for making so many of the A-model, with supposedly inadequate inlets, but the only real criticism is that there was inadequate money to buy uprated en-

Above: An unusual near-vertical view of two F-111As of the 430th TFS, 474th TFW, operating out of Nellis over the dry watercourses of Nevada.

Left: Another view of one of the same aircraft. Note the unpainted HF shunt aerial (diagonal stripe along the fin) and the white colour of the flexible strips which admit the rear of the swing-wing root.

Below: An F-111F flying in TF mode over Idaho mountains in 1972.

Top: Two of the first F-111As to join the Air Force flying with a full load of 'slicks' with the 428th TFS, 474th TFW, from Nellis AFB in 1967.

Above: Another aircraft of the 474th, in this case with the wings at the intermediate position. Unusually, no badges are carried by this F-111A.

gines to make the F-111E's inlets have some value. To the men in the cockpit it is virtually impossible to tell from the aircraft's performance or handling whether they are in an A or an E, though the E was the first to introduce improved ECM, a slightly different TFR, automatic ballistics computing and the strike camera under the nose.

Though large numbers of One-Elevens had been delivered by 1972, the only combat-ready ones were still those of the 474th TFW at Nellis, and when it was decided to take the bull by the horns and send the F-111 back to Vietnam the choice fell not on the 428th, the Combat Lancer veterans, but on the wing's other two squadrons, the 429th and 430th. The Viet Cong forces from the North had broken through into the South in April 1972 and not only was help wanted but it looked like being an opportunity really to put the One-Eleven to work in a way that might never return. This time the F-111A was a mature weapon system and the involvement was on a major scale, with two squadrons each of 24 aircraft, and they stayed for five months. It was called Constant Guard Five.

The two squadrons were determined to do it right, and if possible not only demonstrate what a fine interdiction platform can do but also set new records of many kinds. They planned to start by arriving at Takhli and straight-away flying a combat mission. To make this a sensible objective the 429th sent six crews on ahead to get some rest and plan their mission, while other crews ferried the aircraft, departing Nellis on September 27. They went 13½ hours non-stop to Andersen (Guam) with four tanker hook-ups. The last 6½ hours needed a single tanker hook-up over the Philippines, and a final run at high speed and low level across South Vietnam to check out all the systems. Everything was fine, the aircraft arrived fully serviceable and the combat crews were waiting.

About four hours were available for servicing, then after nightfall the mission – to RP-5 (Route Package 5) in north-west Vietnam – was on. Three of the six aircraft aborted with equipment failure prior to takeoff, the fourth had ECM failure in the air and aborted, another could not hit the primary target and had to choose the alternate, and the last never came back. Such was the unimpressive start to what was to become the opening of a new chapter in air warfare. The One-Eleven had been planned as the first of the new generation of sophisticated attack aircraft able to make deep interdiction penetrations of heavily defended regions and bomb with great precision and with no external assistance whatsoever.

In fact, so lone a game did the One-Elevens play that when aircraft did go missing nobody had the slightest idea whereabouts they might have gone in. The crews were more than happy to accept the serious consequences of not being found by their friends in return for guaranteed security of the mission. Security in South Vietnam had the reputation of being the leakiest of sieves, and if a crew did its own planning, worked out its own routes, profiles, turn points, radar offsets and target run-up, there was a fair chance that this information would not be passed to the enemy. But it was not long before four aircraft had been lost – all with a callsign ending in 3 and all on a Monday night – and political pressure came even from Washington itself for all crews to file detailed flight plans, and to call the airborne command post by radio at each turn point. This was most unpopular. Flight plans as filed were fragmentary, and at 450 knots at 300ft in foul weather on a pitch-black night the pilot and WSO had plenty to do without chatting with people interested in one's precise whereabouts and timing for the next turn point.

By late 1972 the defences were tremendous. In the Hanoi/Haiphong area flak was denser than over wartime targets in the Ruhr, and SAM sites were numbered in scores. The One-Elevens were facing this very much 'for real', and their crews were often frankly at the very limit of what their nerves could stand in demonstrating to the world that they could hack the new kind of air warfare. The idea of getting 'under the radar' was a joke: early warning, AAA and SAM radars were on every mountain, hill and small eminence, and it was not uncommon for the RHAWS lights to be on for minutes at a time, with occasional bursts of warning from the IRWS as well, watching from the top of the fin.

Never before had lone crews each of two men personally planned their mission and pitted their skill and courage against perhaps 20,000 people determined to stop them. How random could the route be? What about double-bluff, and repeating the previous route exactly (something ordinarily never done)? Dare one go through the middle of this narrow defile, or through that narrow gorge? What height AGL would be best at each point? Would a Hard Ride be possible? The vicious faces of the outcrops of karst, a kind of blackish limestone, meant that selecting Hard would almost pull the wings off, first going up to breast the crest and then bending the wings down to seek the bottom of the terrain on the far side. This was worse than any terrain in Nevada, and crews found it "absolutely incapacitating". Medium Ride was preferred except in fairly open country.

Pilots' impressions

Several crews talked about their low-level 'skiing' missions to *Air Force Magazine*. Former F-105 jock Capt Jackie Crouch said: "Think about flying around in daylight and good weather only 200ft above the ground, and going up and down over hills and into valleys, keeping this height. Now do this at night, in mountains and in heavy cloud when you can't see anything outside the cockpit. This is really, really exciting, even without the enemy threat.

"It takes real discipline to come up over these mountains, as we did at night, out on top of the cloud layer in the moonlight. We'd see those jagged peaks all round us poking through the cloud tops, and we'd have to put the nose down back into that mist. And as we went down the moonlight would fade, and the cloud get darker, and we'd know we were descending far below those peaks and were depending on our radars and our autopilots – and with Hanoi coming up. I won't say that I wasn't worried.

"One night, when the weather was *very* bad, I was in cloud for the last 11 minutes before bombs away. That means at the lowest level of the whole flight, at 250 or 200ft going up and down the hills. We didn't see a thing outside the cockpit, not even after the bombs left us. For me, this thing was really remarkable. Even now I can't explain how fantastic it was ... the confidence I gained in the airplane, it made a believer out of me. Given a choice on a

Right: An F-111D of the 27th TFW, Cannon AFB, New Mexico, USAF 68-151. It is fitted with the internal gun and two practice bomb dispensers.

Below: Today F-111s have low-visibility markings, with tail code, insignia (except for unit badges) and stencils in black.

night strike of going in Hi or going in Lo, I'll take Lo, every time. And I'll go anywhere in the F-111."

To give the WSO's viewpoint Lt Steve Glass recalled the mission he flew on December 18, 1972 at the start of a critical Linebacker II period that took on the massed SAMs that were knocking down the B-52s, and effectively silenced them. "The delta weather was way down, ceiling 200ft or thereabouts and cloud piled up to 28,000ft.... We came skiing down the mountains and plunged out into the open under the lower edge of the overcast, and it seemed to us the entire Hanoi Valley was lit up like Las Vegas. Hanoi was bright with neon and street lights and the port of Haiphong was aglow in the distance. On the roads leading out of town and on the mountain switchbacks to the south the truck headlights were blazing like strings of pearls.

"We happened to arrive about ten minutes to eight in the evening, Hanoi time. We were coming so fast we were almost on release point before any of those lights started going out. Sections of the town blacked out one at a time, and we knew sirens were screaming and somebody down there was pulling master switches, even as the bombs left us."

The 429th and 430th flew over 4,000 missions, more than 3,980 of them in the TF mode at low level, and took just six losses, the lowest of any attack aircraft in actual warfare. This is despite the intense defences, the very limited number of targets and the extreme alertness, skill and long practice of the enemy gunners, radar operators and SAM crews. So far as is known, every one of the 74,000 bombs dropped by the F-111s was on target; in the case of one vital target, surrounded by Hanoi city, which was 'off limits', no other type of aircraft was permitted to bomb it, but the F-111s made repeated attacks, all at very high speed at low level and in all weathers, and destroyed it without one bomb falling outside the small target area. The two squadrons rotated back to Nellis from January 1973, the last mission being the 4,030th on February 22.

Deployment to England

No other version of F-111 except the A has actually gone to war. The next model in service, the E, was transferred from Cannon AFB to re-equip the 20th TFW which was re-formed at RAF Upper Heyford, Oxfordshire. The first pair of Es swept in from a leaden sky on September 12, 1970 and found that the old RAF base was being torn apart for new facilities including simulators, full-size training rigs (for example, for the fuel and wing-sweep systems) and an awesome amount of maintenance capability.

The three squadrons, the 55th, 77th and 79th, at first each had their own tail codes, and altogether the base built up to an active establishment, excluding dependents, of about 4,000, many of whom are at two satellite fields, Barford St John and Croughton. Though aircraft of the 20th have to keep in practice at tanker hook-ups they need no such support in Europe, nor any forward operating base. From the heart of England they can fly every mission with which they are tasked by the NATO commanders, and their low-level training missions frequently pass within a few feet of shepherds high in the Alps as they thunder in TF flight to drop practice bombs on the range at Aviano in the foothills above Venice. Early in the F-111 era no aircrew were posted to fly the type unless they had at least 1,000 hours, including 750 hours jet time. Conversion has always taken place at Nellis, typically with 13 missions in 45 hours' flying, followed by a further 13 trips upon joining the user squadron.

The totally different F-111D began at last to come off the production line at aircraft No 216 in autumn 1970. Service entry took place from October 1971 with the only unit ever to operate this model, the 27th TFW at Cannon AFB, New Mexico, replacing the wing's F-111As. Deliveries were completed in February 1973, and the 27th have ever since maintained an image which bravely accentuates the fact that F stands for Fighter. The gun is normally carried, together with the occasional AIM-9 Sidewinder, and though the 27th do not reckon to be second-best to anyone in air/ground delivery, they have been successful in projecting their belief that they fly the best One-Elevens ever built. It is significant that in 1979, when the USAF was urgently trying to get Congress to agree on a stretching programme to turn TAC and SAC F-111s into long-range FB-111B/Cs, as described in a later chapter, they picked the F-111Ds of the 27th as those best suited to conversion. A cynic would say it is because they are already so non-standard, and hard and expensive to maintain.

Last of the tactical attack versions, and last new-built One-Eleven of any sort, the F-111F seeks to get the best avionics features of the D but at less cost, plus the increased flight performance from the excellent P-100 engine. In fact this engine was not ready when the F-111F replaced the D at the 456th aircraft, and the first 30 were delivered with the same P-9 engine as the D. The Mk IIB avionics likewise were not fully available, and it took about a further year for the USAF to receive a fully developed F-111F. This is certainly the best all-round F-111, not so much because of the engine but because it offers considerably greater mission/avionic capabilities than the A and E (virtually identical to those of the D) with considerably fewer and less-costly problems and with a higher availability and reliability. The engine certainly confers improved performance, which every F-111 crew would appreciate, but this is very seldom of any significance because it is possible to fly the missions on

Left: An early picture of the eighth F-111E before application of unit insignia. Note the clearly visible ECM flush aerials on the nose.

Above: View from a KC-135 boomer's station of two F-111E aircraft of the 20th TFW, Upper Heyford, refuelling over solid cloud in 1980.

Below: When the 20th TFW was first re-equipped with the F-111E the tail codes differed for each squadron. JT was the 77th TFS.

the old low-powered P-3 engine. Indeed, though the P-100 is in every way a much better engine than any previous TF30, its extremely high price was the chief reason for the small number of F-models built. Buying them in a small trickle, 12 a year in the final four years, also helped to make the price soar, and it is small wonder that the 12 for 1975 were cancelled.

Idaho to Thailand

The F joined the 347th TFW at Mountain Home AFB, Idaho, in February 1972, where there is plenty of rugged country and extremes of weather. The aircraft were only with the 347th little over a year; in 1973 the wing was ordered to Thailand, flying F-111As, and the very last combat mission in the SEA (south-east Asia) theatre was flown by one of the 347th's swing-wingers over Cambodia on August 15, 1973, closing out nine years of non-stop warfare.

The F-111Fs were reassigned to the 366th TFW, still at Mountain Home and with unchanged MO tail codes, even when in August 1976 one squadron, called 366 Detachment 1, was temporarily sent to the Republic of Korea to show that sudden belligerence by North Korea had not gone unnoticed. The Fs did particularly well to make the totally overwater transit to Taegu AB in just 11½ hours elapsed time from Idaho. On return from Korea the 366th had only another few months before, like the 347th, they had to switch to the Brand-X

Above: The first mission from RAF Lakenheath by the 48th TFW, on April 9, 1977. Note the white tail codes and the blister for the gun.

Left: The 48th Wing Commander's F-111F photographed in June 1981 during the RAF Strike Command Tac Bombing Competition. By this time the tail codes were in black.

Right: An F-111E, 68-062, being delivered by the 20th TFW to British Aerospace at Filton for major rework and refurbishing in April 1982.

Below: Air-to-air of F-111F 70-2369 of the 48th TFW, still with white tail codes in late 1978.

Above: A 1983 portrait of one of the 48th TFW's F-111Fs showing the large bulge of the Pave Tack (also visible in the photograph at centre left). Under the wings are four Paveway II (GBU-16B/B of 1,000lb size) laser-guided 'smart bombs'.

version, the F-111A. Their aircraft were taken from them and ferried non-stop on internal fuel to RAF Lakenheath, Suffolk, where they replaced the F-4D Phantoms of the 48th TFW in March 1977.

After conversion the 48th worked up quickly to combat-ready status, unquestionably becoming the most formidable long-range interdiction outfit in the entire European theatre (on the NATO side, at least). Despite weather markedly more depressing than Idaho, the Fs settled down to hard work of many kinds, some of it classified, and put up an enviable safety record which in 1982–83 was suddenly shattered by the loss of six aircraft in as many months, two of the crews failing to eject and one aircraft, in May 1983, simply going straight into the North Sea on return from a mission, with no radio call. The importance of the 48th is shown by its selection as one of the first USAF units to be completely equipped with Pave Tack, as described earlier. The next chapter tells more.

Servicing in England

Location of what are for geographical reasons the two most important F-111 wings in the United Kingdom clearly means that, over a long period, aircraft have to be maintained more than 5,000 miles (8000km) away from the true parent organization, the Air Force Logistics Command's Sacramento Air Logistics Center at McClellan AFB. For almost a decade the USAF either ferried or shipped One-Elevens all the way to California for major overhaul. Then in 1978 it put out an exploratory contract with British Aerospace. The Weybridge-Bristol Division was given a small package of maintenance work on UK-based F-111s including renewal of the pyrotechnics of the cockpit ejection capsule. This is a particularly tricky and crucial task, which has to be repeated every four years; moreover, though the crews' lives depend on it, it can hardly be functionally tested after renewal!

Bristol did so well on this first contract that by 1983 work had built up to a complete major overhaul of 20 F-111 aircraft a year, from both Upper Heyford (Es) and Lakenheath (in mid-1983 temporarily detached to Sculthorpe while Lakenheath runways are resurfaced) which has the F model. Aircraft are completely torn apart, and continued excellent performance was rewarded in 1983 by the offer of a four-year contract instead of an annual one, with throughput raised to between 36 and 40 aircraft per year. The work is done in the former 'Brabazon Hangar' where Concordes were later assembled. Since 1982 aircraft have been given low-voltage formation light strips and a complete repainting to the new strict specification before being returned to their units.

Flying the Mission

Above: About to start engines of an F-111F of the 390th TFS (Detachment 1 of the 366th TFW) prior to the first mission from Taegu in August 1976.

The author was once privileged to fly a training mission in a One-Eleven, but that single flight, memorable though it was, hardly qualifies him to write about flying it, or even in it. We asked a member of the 493rd Tactical Fighter Squadron, 48th Tactical Fighter Wing, United States Air Force, to tell us in simple terms what it is like. Captain Jim Rotramel is widely known to aviation readers, and especially to plastic modellers, but in between the demands of a heavy and very varied workload he finds time to climb into the right seat of an F-111F.

What's it like to fly the F-111?

That's a question that Aardvark drivers – like all fighter pilots – get asked a lot. It would seem to be an easy question to answer, but it's not. I've read many "pilot reports", but quoting a mountain of statistics has never imparted what it FEELS like to fly a fast jet – and the F-111 is one of the fastest. So this pilot's report, written by a weapon systems operator, is going to be different.

Perhaps we should start with who flies F-111s. There are two of us, sitting side-by-side: the pilot – we call him the AC, for aircraft commander – on the left and the navigator/weapons systems operator – known professionally as WSO, pronounced "wizzo" – on the right, both officers.

Pilots have gone through a year of undergraduate pilot training, and WSOs through at least six months of undergraduate navigator training. After completing these schools they go to lead-in fighter training for a couple of months, to learn the basics of flying fighters in aircraft that are familiar to the pilots, allowing them to concentrate on the flying instead of the airplane.

Only then do they begin flying the Aardvark – the F-111's unofficial, but universally accepted, nickname. It takes about a year for a newcomer to the airplane to become MR, mission ready. It takes almost another year to become comfortable with operating all of the systems in this very complex war machine.

Our missions begin with flight planning. They're planned to help us accomplish a set of tasks we're required to perform every six months. An individual mission takes anywhere from a couple of hours to a couple of days to plan. The actual day of the flight, the crew shows up to take care of the final details about 3½ hours before takeoff, and conduct a briefing an hour later.

About an hour before takeoff time we "step" to whichever aircraft the maintenance section has assigned us that day. Although AC and WSO names are stencilled on the nosegear doors, it's only by chance if we actually fly "our own" jet.

The jet is BIG. Our internal fuel load weighs more than a fully loaded F-16! Technically a fighter by designation, it's really a tactical bomber, roughly combining the range and payload of a B-66 with the speed and manoeuvrability of an F-105.

The AC does the detailed walk-around inspection, while the WSO checks any external stores and does a quick look at the jet before climbing on board and strapping in. The cockpit, by fighter standards, is quite roomy – similar to the front of a compact-sized (ie, European) car. The seats are very hard – especially after we have been strapped into one for more than three hours! But that hardness helps protect us from serious injuries if we have to eject. Unlike all other fighters, the F-111 doesn't have ejection seats, but an escape capsule. In an ejection, the entire cockpit area separates from the airplane. This virtually eliminates the wind-blast injuries which can be encountered when ejecting at high air-speeds in other aircraft. More than one F-111 crew owe their lives to this feature.

Ready for takeoff

Engine start comes 45 minutes prior to takeoff, and for the next 25 minutes we're busy powering up and checking out all the different systems. Twenty minutes before takeoff, we taxi to the runway where we're checked over one last time. Once on the runway and cleared for takeoff, the engines are run up – first to military (MIL) power and then into the afterburner range, one at a time, while we check them out.

At brake release, power to both engines is increased to maximum afterburner, and we accelerate quickly but smoothly to 145 knots, when the AC rotates the nose up, followed shortly by liftoff. The takeoff roll takes 15 seconds and 2,500 feet for an F model, which, with engines even more powerful than the F-15's, is noticeably quicker than other F-111s.

A typical training sortie will include an hour of high-level cruise, a half-hour of low-level practice, with 15 minutes or more dropping practice bombs. If we've enough fuel left, we will practise various types of landing approaches when we get home.

After a 2½ to 3-hour flight, it will take another hour to park the jet, debrief any maintenance problems, and get back to the squadron for a flight debriefing and paperwork session (even this job isn't done until the paperwork is finished!) taking about another hour. As you can see, flying just once is an all-day affair.

A lasting impression is the amount of

Right: A departure sequence from the Forth Worth runway of 74-0188, the 106th F-111F and 562nd and last One-Eleven. It was accompanied by an even more sprightly performer, the first YF-16A – which, unlike the One-Eleven, is in MIL (dry) power.

Above: A pilot of the 48th TFW runs through his checks prior to entering the cockpit of his F-111F inside its HAS (hardened aircraft shelter) at RAF Lakenheath in 1983.

Right: A different photographer took this picture a few minutes later as the aircraft exited the HAS.

USAF

Above: A March 1983 photograph of an aircraft of the 48th TFW, 70-2399, carrying practice-bomb dispensers and an ALQ-131 jammer pod.

flame which comes out the engines in full afterburner. The only thing I've seen that belches more fire is the SR-71. One young observer of an F-111 takeoff at night said it appeared they were "riding on a star". I can't think of a more apt description.

With all the flame comes a lot of noise. Which is probably why F-111 bases are usually situated far from large population centres. All that is more noticeable when watching an F-111 than when flying one. In the Aardvark it's impossible to see your own engine, tail, or inner portions of the wings. The ear-splitting blast of the engines is virtually unnoticeable in the cockpit, where the noise level is comparable to a commercial airliner.

Despite its ungainly appearance on the ground, when the gear comes up and the wings go back, the true purpose of the airplane's design becomes clear – SPEED. Ask any air-to-air fighter pilot how much fun it is to convert on an F-111 flying at 200 feet doing 570 knots or more. The little folded wing, that makes us one of the slowest-turning airplanes around, also lets us go as fast and low as we can stand – and with a ride that's normally as smooth as glass.

The wings are swept with a small handle on the left wall, mounted above the pilot's throttles. There's a gauge we can both see to tell us what angle they're at, and they're manually swept to provide the best flying qualities for any given aircraft weight and speed. From the right seat, you notice a faint jerk when the wings begin moving, but

Below: Pulling negative g down the slope to TFR height over Loch Ness, Scotland, on a practice mission by the 48th in June 1982.

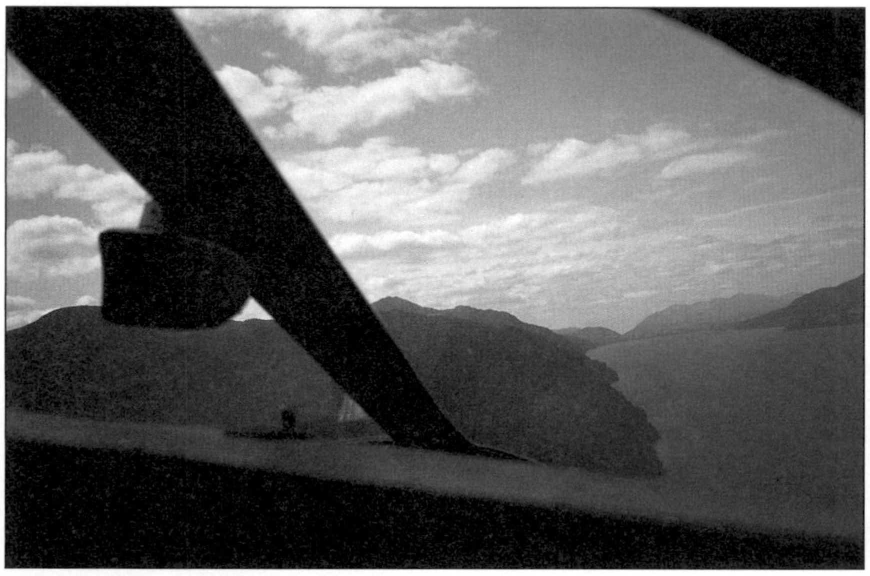

Below: Another view from the right-hand seat of an F-111F, in this case of mountainous terrain passing the wingtip at 450 knots.

Foot of page: The low-voltage strip lights stand out on this F-111F of 494 TFS, 48 TFW (70-2384) snapped from its companion in May 1983.

Above: Taken in December 1982, a fine air-to-air of 70-2366 over rugged terrain. Terrain-following flight would be much lower.

aside from that it doesn't feel any different than any other airplane.

We earn our keep by carrying substantial payloads at high-subsonic cruise speeds, at low altitudes, and in any weather, deeper into enemy territory than other non-strategic aircraft could even imagine. Cruising at eight miles a minute, 500 feet off the ground, is exciting and beautiful. You're low enough to get a really good look at the countryside, and in the United Kingdom that's rugged coastlines, lakes, mountains and castles. After a while, 500 feet seems quite high – you can get comfortable there, at least in daylight.

On the other hand, 200 feet never seems high – it's an incredible thrill, but one you never take for granted, especially when approaching the speed of sound. The sensation of speed is amazing, and if the pilot decides to convert all that airspeed into altitude, your altimeter can read 15,000 feet in about 20 seconds! There's not a ride in a carnival anywhere that comes close to it.

Terrain Following, or "TFing", is what set the F-111 in a class by itself for more than a decade. The ability to fly as low as 200 feet AGL (above ground level) at as fast as 1·2 times the speed of sound in almost any weather is of great tactical significance – not to mention scary! Flying at 1,000 feet AGL in mountainous terrain at night, while seeing nothing but the hazy grey/black of the inside of a cloud, punctuated only by the occasional red flash of the rotating beacon, is guaranteed to focus your attention on the task at hand, which is ensuring that the automatic TF system is working properly.

Terrain-following flight

Basically, what happens is that the TF antenna nods up and down, scanning a narrow sector in the aircraft's flight path to determine terrain elevation. This information is processed and transmitted to the flight control system which adjusts the aircraft's pitch attitude to avoid the ground. It's up to the pilot to make any necessary power adjustments. The actual path across the ground is determined by the points set into the navigational computers. Even though the aircraft has the ability to avoid the terrain in its path, it's up to the crew to plan a flight path which best uses the terrain to mask the airplane from enemy defences.

During TF flight, the atmosphere on board becomes very businesslike, the small talk ceases, and we each monitor our instruments to make sure everything is working as intended. The commentary is terse; we each tell the other only what we see in front of us. The AC monitors the aircraft response to the terrain depicted on his TF radar presentation. This, combined with the larger picture of the terrain that the WSO is describing to him from his attack-radar presentation, indicates a properly functioning system. Safe TFing requires excellent crew coordination, which means practice and trust. Complacency towards TFing is unwise and could be fatal. We may argue about the percentage lethality of Triple-A or SAMs, but we all know the ground rates 100 per cent.

Questions about performance are difficult to answer. For instance, "How fast do you go?" Normally, we roar by at about 480 knots, but if someone is trying to shoot us down, we go as fast as we can stand it. It also depends on the speed limits of the bombs we're carrying or their fuzes, as well as a lot of other things. The airplane itself certainly isn't speed-limited!

Maximum speeds

There's no quoted top speed for the F-111. When the skin temperature gets hot a timer begins counting the number of seconds it can keep up the speed before parts start to weaken from the heat. In reality, that type of speed performance is of little practical value, since, while it's possible to outrun an attacker, it would also quickly exhaust our fuel. A kill is a kill, be it by gun, missile or a case of the terminal stupids!

The same answer applies to "How far can you go?" and "How much can you carry?" All those classic yardsticks of performance really don't work well in the real world. There are too many shades of grey for a simple black-and-white answer.

What you can count on is that our mission in a real war would be tailored to get us to our target and back with as many of the right type of bombs as we could carry. The further away the target, the fewer the number of bombs. At any rate, we wouldn't expect to come home with loads of gas sloshing around our fuel tanks!

This small piece of the F-111 story wouldn't be complete without a few words about the people on the ground. They're legion, from the mail clerks and cooks, to the security police and families. Their work, support and tolerance makes our job possible. But most of all, the maintenance people: for even though the Aardvark is a magnificent and capable airplane, it's not as maintainable as the new airplanes which have benefited from its experience. So that we can do our job, a lot of young people have to work long hours, sometimes in miserable weather. Although the fliers get the glory, we never forget whose shoulders we stand on.

The Bombers

Nobody can turn a fighter into a strategic bomber, but when the fighter is the One-Eleven there is enough internal fuel to make the idea worth careful study. For more than 20 years General Dynamics and the US Air Force have been only too keenly aware of the highly effective bombers that could be produced from today's F-111 by drastic modification, but Congress has never voted the money. Instead SAC has a small and elite force which flies a bomber only slightly different from the tactical models. Their consistently high scores in competition have been a source of embarrassment to the long-established SAC wings.

Above: A 48th TFW One-Eleven is loaded with Snakeyes under pressure during the Quick Turnround section of the 1981 RAF Strike Command Bombing Competition.

Since the earliest days of the TFX programme, SAC (USAF Strategic Air Command) had eyed the aircraft as a possible basis for a small supersonic bomber. The command never thought of just buying the resulting F-111, but the impressive range figures appeared to indicate the possibility of future stretching into a larger bomber to fly SAC missions. GD began work on possible SAC versions in 1962, and several were three-engined, with the centre engine fed by an S-duct. Other models had larger and more powerful engines, most of which existed only on paper, and at all times the SAC One-Eleven was regarded as suitable for the nuclear role only, the payload being used for fuel rather than for massive loads of conventional bombs.

In any case, it was clear that not even a stretched F-111 could fly the global missions of SAC, even with flight refuelling. Like the B-47 and GD's own B-58 before it, the F-111 could at best be a limited aircraft relying heavily on in-flight refuelling and on some missions either departing from a forward operating location in a friendly country or recovering to a friendly base outside the United States, and in general being assigned to targets on the periphery of possible enemies.

Having pointed out its deficiencies it is fair to claim that the F-111 offered many advantages. Compared with the B-52, the command's only global carrier vehicle, it had a very much smaller radar cross-section, and could carry at least as good a suite of EW/ECM systems for its own protection. It could be made hard against nuclear explosion effects, where the B-52 was soft. It could fly much faster, at much lower heights above the ground. Its 'penetrability' was assessed as several times better, especially against the most heavily defended targets. Not least, it could be built from the start with more modern avionics, and in particular with a more precise navigation system.

In the course of 1964, while SAC hardened in its belief that the F-111 should form the basis for an interim low-level penetrator, ideas of gross stretching began to fade, on grounds of timing, cost and the demonstrable fact that most of the stretched models were still range-limited. What was called the FB-111 (later FB-111A) was first drawn in that year, combining a wing almost identical to the long-span wing of the Navy F-111B with a regular F-111A fuselage and tail but with main landing gears having larger tyres and increased-capacity brakes, to which were soon added strengthened legs to handle increased gross weights. The heaviest loading envisaged was two of the new SRAMs (short-range attack missiles) in the weapon bay and eight 600US-gal drop tanks under the wings, a configuration never realized in practice. Flight crew were to number three, comprising pilot, copilot/navigator and defence-systems operator.

Thrust and weight

It was an important part of the concept of the FB that it need not have a thrust/weight ratio as high as a fighter version. Thus a third TF30 engine was not needed, even though from the start the gross weights were planned to be in the region of 100,000lb (45,000kg), at a time when it was hoped the 'fighter' model would gross about 55,000lb (25,000kg). What was completely unpredicted was that the so-called fighter models would themselves escalate in weight to the 100,000lb level, resulting in essentially the same thrust/weight ratio as for the SAC aircraft. Moreover, the TAC versions do not have the long-span wing.

Development of the FB was interwoven with models for two export customers, who were confidently expected to be the first of many. Back in 1963 Britain had hoped to sell its TSR.2 aircraft to Australia, but internal British troubles based on inter-service rivalry and narrow party politics had already begun to unite to torpedo this programme, and the Australians naturally began to doubt that TSR.2 could be relied upon. The obvious alternative was the F-111, and despite frantic pleas from the British, Aussie Prime Minister Menzies and Defence Minister Athol Townley signed on October 24, 1963 for 24 F-111s at a total 'ceiling price' of A$112 million, or US$90,749,040. It

Below: Inflight refuelling compatibility test with the eighteenth RDT&E F-111A, which served as the original FB prototype – complete with SAC badge.

seemed the obvious choice. Menzies said "No government could spend money on anything else", and to the charge that the price might escalate Townley replied "There is far more chance it will be reduced, because our figure is based on the present production run". This run was for 1,726 aircraft, more than three times the number actually built.

By 1965, when the FB was at the stage of detailed planning, the newly elected Labour government in Britain was determined to do away with TSR.2, and it cancelled the programme on April 6 of that year. In its election campaign that government had announced not only its intention to kill the homegrown aircraft but also its wish to replace it with the American TFX, which was presented to the British people as a far superior and much cheaper alternative. In the announcement of cancellation of TSR.2 the Ministry of Defence stated: "An order for 150 TSR.2 aircraft would have meant each one would have cost £5 million ... a full programme based on the F-111 would be £300 million less. ..." In other words, the RAF F-111s would cost £450 million in all, or £3 million each, "allowing for all future charges and payments". This was just double the price of the Australian aircraft, but still seemed much better than £5 million.

Britain and Australia engaged in detailed talks during 1965 both to sew up the contracts, which were not with GD but with the US Government, through the Department of Defense, and also to establish the precise standard of build of their respective aircraft. Both countries agreed to have the long-span wing, strengthened landing gear with larger tyres and brakes, and other features of the SAC bomber version, which by the end of 1965 was designated FB-111A. The Australian (RAAF) aircraft became the F-111C and, though it was officially described as the F-111A by British spokesmen, the British (RAF) variant received the odd designation of F-111K. In February 1966 Defence Minister Healey announced that Britain was buying ten for a start, with a further 40 to follow in April 1967, at a 'ceiling price' of US$5·95 million each. This compared with a unit price of $7·8 million on the original 1965 calculation (which saved £300 million) and $3·8 million for the Australians. There were to be 46 F-111Ks (XV902/947) and four TF trainers (XV884/887). The British involvement was convoluted in the extreme, and involved offset deals with the USA and third-party nations and much more besides, but fortunately the whole house of cards collapsed in January 1968 when Prime Minister Wilson announced that the F-111K had, like TSR.2, been cancelled.

Above: The seventh F-111A was used for stores separation tests with all eight pylons fitted. Such loads have never been carried, even by today's FB-111A.

By this time most of the parts had been made for all 50 aircraft, 19 were visible on the Fort Worth assembly line and the two YF-111K flight-test aircraft were almost complete and painted. Because of their close similarity to the FB-111A the decision was taken to convert

Right: An FB-111A over Lake Worth on contractor flight test. The configuration is that which would be used on most SAC missions in a nuclear war, with four tanks but no external weapons. The widely publicized bomb-toting capability of the FB is probably only of academic interest, though six tanks might be an important configuration giving intercontinental range.

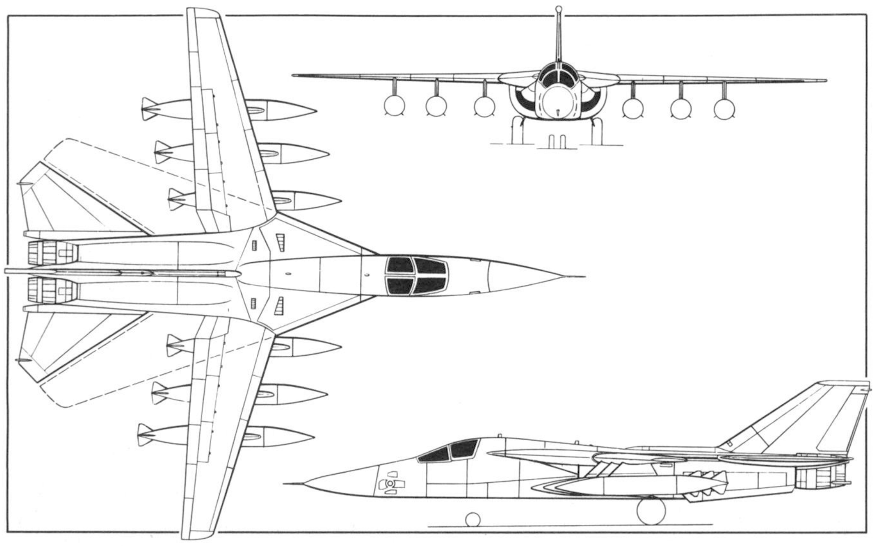

Above: Three-view of the FB-111A with six underwing tanks

Below: Three-view of the proposed FB-111H strategic bomber

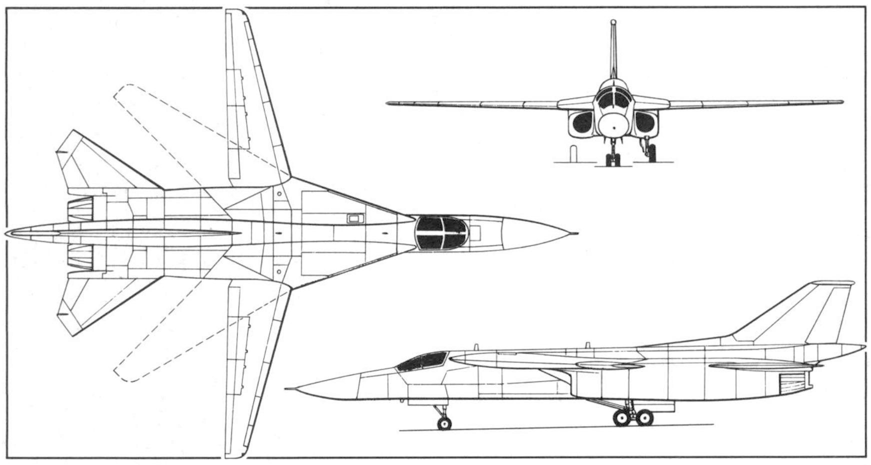

as many F-111Ks as possible into this version, but the first two machines, both of them TFs, were too different for ready conversion. Eventually they were completed as YF-111A aircraft of the USAF (67-149/150) with provision for very complete instrumentation in R&D programmes, as explained in the last chapter. The other 48 were completed as FB-111As for SAC.

The force structure and detail design of the FB-111A were all settled during 1965, the only differences compared with the F-111E, with Triple-Plow II inlet, being the long-span wing, new main gears, Mk IIB avionics with an added astrocompass and other small variations, SRAM missile provisions, and the more powerful P-7 engine. This engine was the first uprated model to enter service, running well ahead of the less-powerful engine of the F-111D, and it stemmed from the Navy-sponsored P-12 engine of the defunct F-111B. In fact, the first two production FBs were delivered with P-12 engines, but were re-engined later with the standard P-7.

To speed development the 18th of the original development batch of F-111As, 63-9783, was completed as the FB-111A prototype. It flew in gull grey and white on July 30, 1967, and played the chief role in early proving of FB capabilities other than SRAM firing. The first production machine, 67-159, with temporary P-12 engines, flew on July 13, 1968 and handled the SRAM compatibility and launch programme during Cat II testing.

More than any other part of the F-111 programme the FB suffered from escalation in price. The stated intention had been to assign this new swing-wing bomber as a replacement for 345 B-52C, D and F heavy bombers and 80 B-58As and TB-58s. The planned force to do this numbered 210, plus 53 extra aircraft for use as spares and to make good attrition losses, and Defense Secretary McNamara said the total cost would be "in the order of a billion and three-quarters". Subsequently the specification for the FB-111A hardly altered beyond refinement of the avionic systems into the Mk IIB which also went into the F-111F with minor differences, but the general rise in price brought a reduction in the numbers bought to a mere 76, costing $1·2 billion, not far short of the total for 263.

First SAC unit

The first FB-111A unit was the 340th Bomb Group of SAC, which was specially formed to introduce the type to SAC service, while Systems Command was engaged in Cat II testing, and before Cat III tests of the complete FB-111A/SRAM system had started. The 340th received its first aircraft on September 25, 1969. Based at Carswell AFB, adjacent to the manufacturer's plant at Fort Worth, the 340th's principal role was to train FB-111A crews. Like all SAC units it set a very high standard in all things, the qualifications for pilots including more than 2,000 hours in command and at least two years in a combat-ready squadron, with at least 1,500 hours demanded of navigators.

The FB has dual flight controls, but the right-seater has an exceptional amount to do because EW/ECM is even more important in this model than in the tactical versions, and was at one time thought to merit the inclusion of a third crew-member. Initial crew training was handled by a unit of the 340th BG, the 4007th Combat Crew Training Squadron. Using selected material and with an outstanding navigation/bombing system in the FB-111A these small two-seaters quickly established a great reputation in SAC and fairly consistently have carried off top honours in the annual Bombing Competition. One of the crews from the 4007th took the chief awards at the 1970 competition, when the type was still weeks away from becoming operational.

The first delivery to a user unit took place on December 16, 1970, when an FB was ferried by a crew of the 509th BW to their operating base at Pease AFB, New Hampshire. Ultimately SAC built up an active inventory of 70 aircraft, which has since been reduced to 58, assigned equally to the 509th, which handles crew training, and the rival 380th BW at Plattsburgh AFB, in upper New York, to which the 4007th was also relocated. Crews fly about four practice missions a month, each of 3½–4½ hours duration and involving hookups with a KC-135 (either of the USAF or, often, of a New England ANG unit) and plenty of low-level penetration including electronically scored free-fall bombing. Very occasionally a SRAM is fired, at White Sands Missile Range, New Mexico, but real SRAMs are seldom flown. SRAM accuracy has been consistently better than for the same missile fired from the B-52.

In general the emphasis in training is the maintenance of a very high degree of professional skill without burning

Right: In most respects the Royal Australian Air Force F-111C is similar to the FB-111A, though the avionics and engines are no more advanced than those of the original F-111A. Professional aircrew in 6 Sqn have become wholly attuned to a heavy but low-thrust aircraft which often has to fly in a tropical atmosphere.

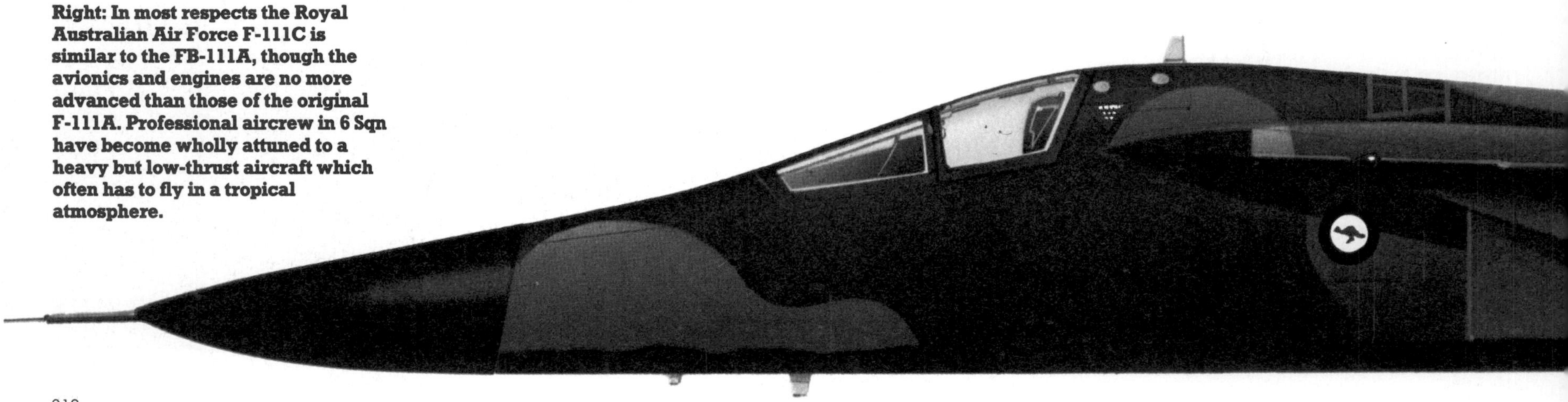

Above: FB No 68–0264 just after takeoff from Pease AFB, New Hampshire, during Global Shield 79, SAC's biggest exercise for years.

much fuel and without aircraft attrition (because FBs cannot be replaced). The much-publicized capability of flying with 50 Mk 117 bombs, each weighing a nominal 750lb (340kg) but in fact nearer to 825lb (374kg) and thus representing a total load of 41,250lb (18,711kg), is never even approached, and it is relatively unusual to fly with any significant load of conventional bombs. With the theoretical maximum load the ceiling is so poor that the aircraft could not clear the summit of Pike's Peak, Colorado, which is at 14,110ft (4,301m). The FB was castigated back in the 1960s on this account, but it is of no importance to an aircraft whose operational life is centred on altitudes below 1,000ft (300m) and often below 300ft (90m).

Today the normal maximum payload of the FB can be regarded as six free-fall nuclear bombs, such as the Mk 43 or Mk 57 or TX61, or six SRAMs, two internal and four on the four swivelling inner wing pylons. Quite often two bombs or SRAMS are carried internally and two or four tanks externally, but it is extremely rare for six pylons to be fitted, and there is no present plan ever to fit the theoretical eight. Low-level bomb runs normally work up to Mach 0·75 or 495 knots (570mph/917km/h), and though it is common to practise stall recoveries there is no incentive to do anything that would eat into airframe fatigue life, because already the average fleet age of the FB is just over 13 years (October 1983) and they may well have to go on for a further 13.

Service experience has in general been exemplary. At the 100,000 hour mark, achieved in January 1976, there had been just two fatal accidents and a total of four write-offs. Performance in the SAC bombing and navigation competition has been consistently superior, largely because the FB has no other modern aircraft against which to compete – despite costly updating of the B-52G and H and the best efforts of their very experienced crews.

At the time of writing the most recent (November 1982) contest again proved a runaway win for the swing-wingers. The 509th BW took the Fairchild Trophy as the SAC wing with the highest bomber and tanker scores (the FB sharing the honours with the KC-135s of the 509th ARS). FB-111As have won this trophy in seven of the past eight years. The 509th also took the Mathis Trophy, awarded for maximum total points in both high and low-level bombing; FBs have taken this trophy in five of the previous six years. The 509th also took the John C. Meyer Trophy, awarded to the unit achieving the highest expectancy of damage on the basis of bombs delivered on target. The award for the best single FB-111A crew, however, was won by the rival 380th BW.

At the same meet the award for the Best F-111 Crew went to crew A-1 from the RAAF, who flew their F-111C all the way from Amberley, at Ipswich in south-east Queensland, 50 miles from Brisbane. The RAAF went into the One-Eleven programme with sky-high hopes in 1963, and had not the slightest inkling that they would end up almost cancelling, and not receive a single aircraft Down Under for another ten years! Yet, despite the problems, the F-111C has given Australia interdiction muscle it has never had before, and will certainly never have again.

It will be recalled that the Australian government had signed for 24 aircraft in 1963 at a unit price of A$3·8 million, the build standard being essentially a mix of the F-111A airframe and engines with

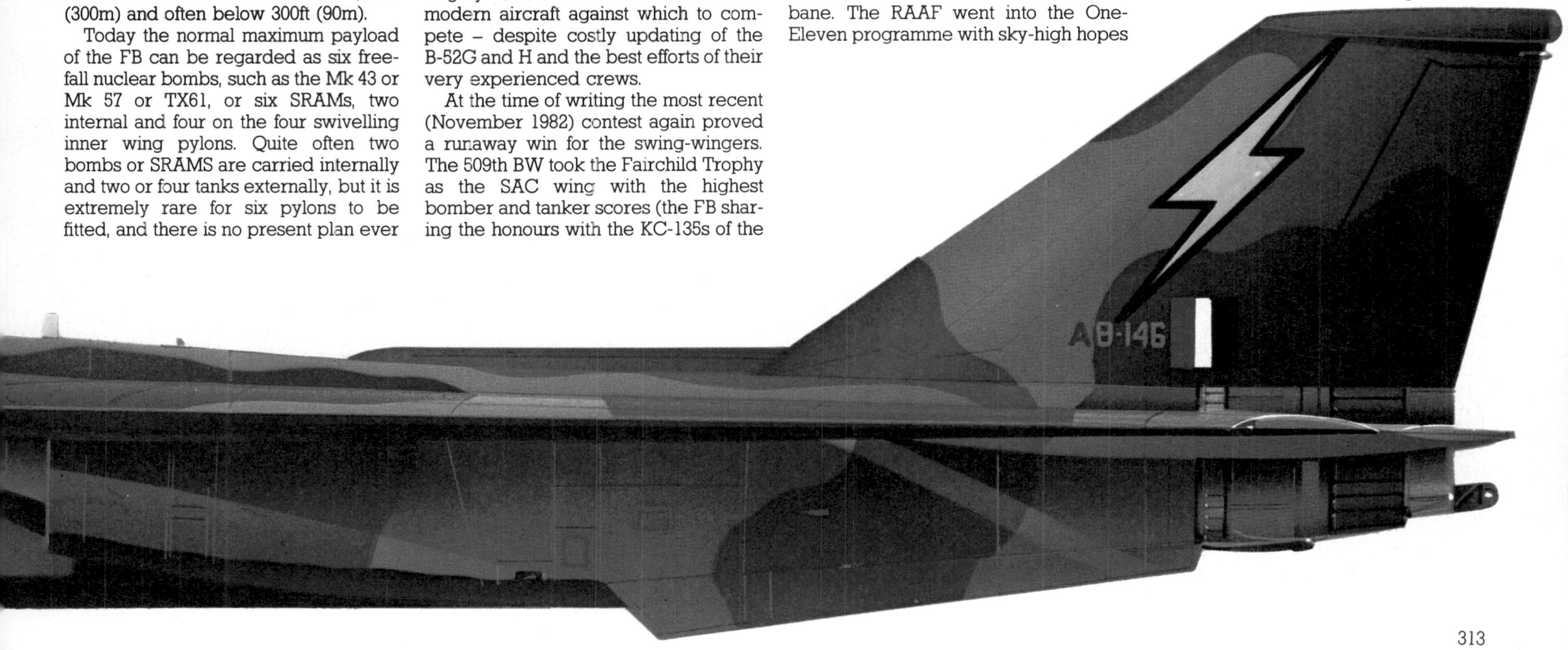

long-span wings and strengthened landing gear, and a removable stick on the right side, but retaining F-111A avionics. It was claimed the new wing and landing gear would 'significantly increase the range and payload', though as the fuel capacity is the same as for the F-111A the difference cannot be significant. In fact, the combination of a heavier aircraft with the least-powerful of all F-111 engines with early Triple Plow I inlets makes the F-111C theoretically the most sluggish model, with rate of roll reduced by the increased span, but the differences are unimportant because the aircraft can do all that has been asked of it. In theory it replaced the Canberra, but as the US supplied F-4E Phantoms as an interim stop-gap RAAF Nos 1 and 6 Sqns got a taste for air-combat capability which they were reluctant to part with.

Another complication was that in July 1966, by which time the manufacture of the RAAF aircraft had started, new Air Minister Peter Howson announced that six aircraft would be flown back to the USA for conversion into RF-111Cs, with the USAF/GD removable multi-sensor pack in the weapon bay. Howson stressed "The striking power of the RAAF will not be affected, because the six modified aircraft can be reconverted to the strike role within hours". The Australian government made regular progress payments on its bill totalling A$7·98 million for RF-111C costs, but this project temporarily collapsed with termination of the RF-111A.

Delayed delivery

Training of F-111C maintenance crews began in 1967, with the start of flight-crew training following in 1968. It was admitted that delivery of the 24 aircraft would slip by about two months, being completed between September and December 1968, but structural problems caused further delays and a team led by Air Vice-Marshal E. Hey spent three weeks at Washington, Fort Worth and Nellis. Howson's successor, Gordon Freeth, pointed out that, while the USAF could accept F-111s that might need extensive rework, Australia was a long way off and "would face tremendous difficulties".

The first F-111C was flown by GD in July 1968 and was formally accepted two months later. It was then completely dismantled by the USAF and, with the

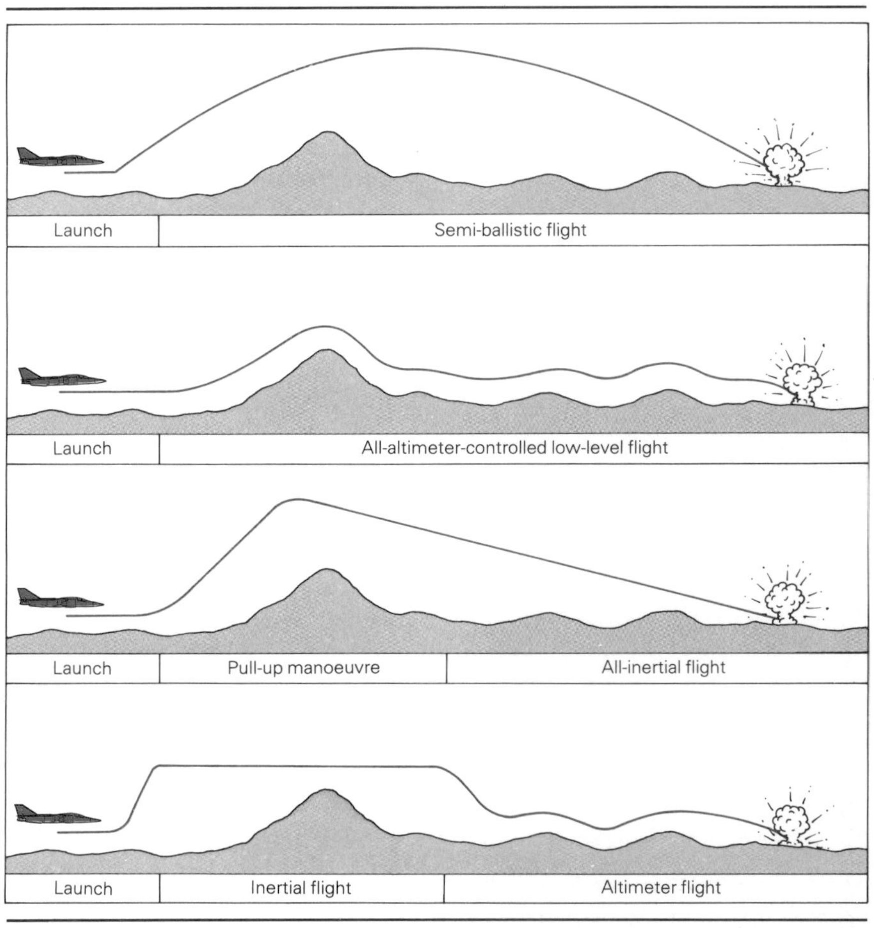

Below: The FB-111A aerodynamic prototype, originally the 18th RDT&E F-111A 63–9783, did a lot of flying with possible SAC loads, one of which was this combination of four tanks and two B61 nukes. In practice the external stores have invariably been tanks and SRAMs.

Above: Release of SRAM at low level over White Sands Missile Range.

Left: Simplified outlines of SRAM trajectories, showing the inherent versatility of this neat weapon. Moreover, these ignore the complete flexibility available in the horizontal direction followed.

Right: Another SRAM shot, this time from an FB at medium altitude.

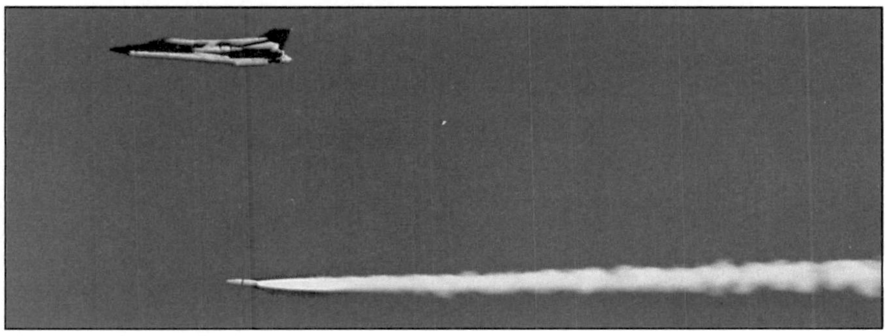

other 23, put into long-term storage. Avionics were carefully packed into a thermostatically controlled hangar at Fort Worth. Wings were stacked inside the GD plant, while the fuselages, largely gutted of engines and equipment, rested on their wheels at Carswell AFB.

The usually decisive Aussies found the F-111 hard to handle. The Defence Minister, Malcolm Fraser, announced on December 5, 1969, he had formally asked the USAF to reactivate the 24 F-111C aircraft "so that they can be taken over by the RAAF as soon as possible". In the same month the wing parted from an F-111A and the situation was worse than before. The F-111Cs were actually the only F-111s in existence in 1969 that were never subjected to a static proof test, despite the intense concern of the Australians with structural integrity. It was not until March 14, 1973 that another Defence Minister, Lance H. Barnard, announced that the Australian government was going ahead with the F-111, and that the first F-111C would be accepted by its RAAF crew at Nellis on the following day.

In fact, the flow of aircrew to Nellis, broken off five years previously, had resumed in January 1973, and eventually the whole force of 24 aircraft were ferried via McClellan AFB (California), Hickham AFB (Hawaii), and either Pago Pago (American Samoa) or Nadi (Fiji),

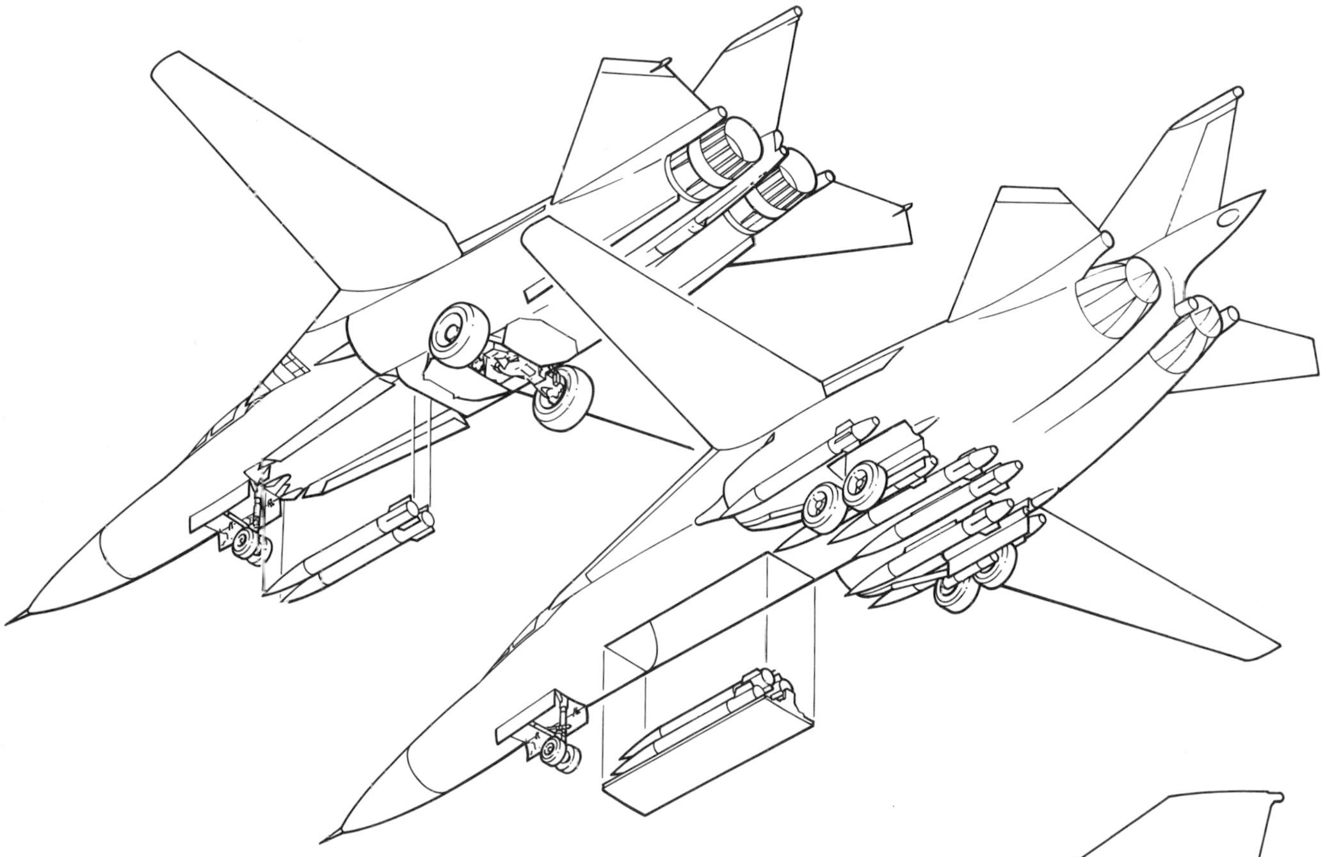

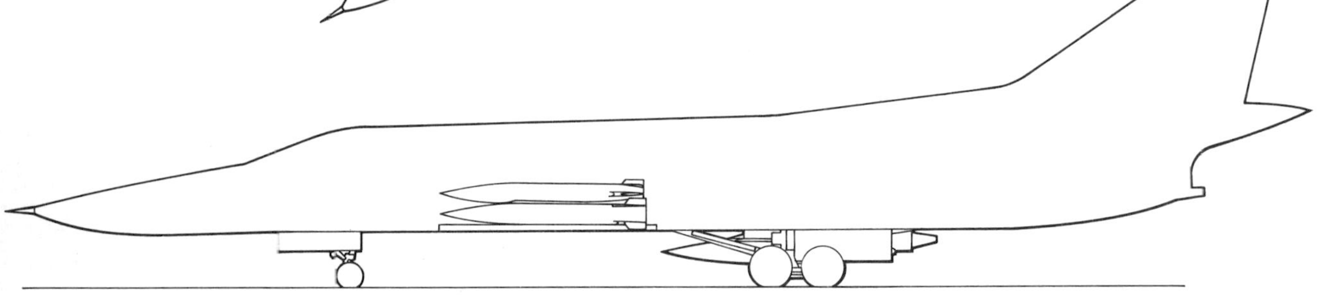

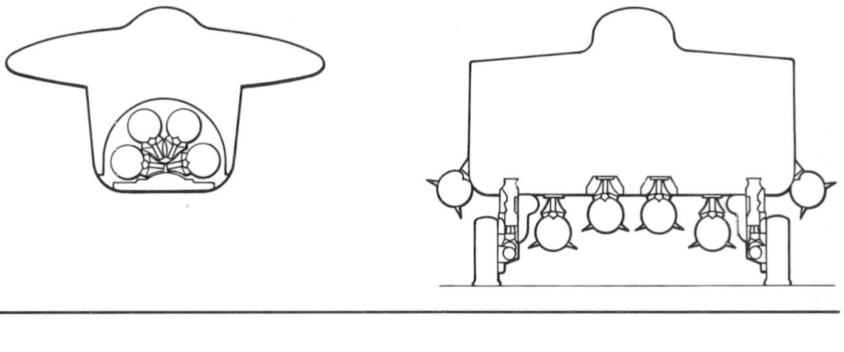

Above: The proposed stretched bomber version would have been powered by two GE F101 engines and carried eight SRAMs without using the wing pylons, and would have been able to fly missions over a radius extended to more than 2,600 miles (4,185 km).

Left: Partly for reasons of money the RAAF has been unable to think in strategic terms. Armourers of 482 Maintenance Sqn get 24 Snakeye bombs aboard each F-111C.

Above: Three aircraft of 6 Sqn curve in over the Gold Coast – as they call this bit of Queensland – homeward bound to Amberley, about 50 miles inland.

in four groups of six in the course of 1973. The first six arrived at Amberley on June 1, 1973. The much-loved Phantoms were returned, batches of six and five (one was lost in Australia) going back in 1972 and two final batches of six on June 6 and 20, 1973, to allow 1 and 6 Sqns to re-equip. The second group of six F-111Cs arrived at Amberley on July 27, and the third and fourth groups in September and November. Once Nos 1 and 6 Sqns were at last in business, forming No 82 (Strike) Wing, most of the political acrimony faded into history. The One-Elevens settled into a training routine which takes them as far as Butterworth (Malaysia), Hawaii and even the USA, with various trips to Indonesia and other south-east Asian countries. The official figure for final capital cost was A$324 million, roughly four times the original 'ceiling' price quoted.

Australian service

In service the C has proved adequate in almost all respects, and 21,000 hours were flown before the first was lost on April 28, 1977. The pilot was a USAF officer on exchange posting, and it was said he only settled an old score as an RAAF pilot ejected from a USAF One-Eleven in 1973. Subsequently three further RAAF aircraft were lost; each was replaced by an ex-USAF F-111A purchased at what was said to be a price of A$5·95 million agreed in 1969 and not subsequently altered.

Like the USAF the RAAF now inevitably has a mix, in this case 16 Cs and four As. Further lack of standardization has followed the introduction after exactly 20 years of study of the reconnaissance pallet. The final decision to continue with the removable multi-sensor package was taken by Defence Minister Barnard in December 1974, when a US$280,000 contract was placed with GD for a study to determine the work required to modify four aircraft. After some discussion, particularly over

Below: Liftoff of the first RAAF F-111C in GD hands at Fort Worth in April 1979. Inset: customer inspection of first RF installation.

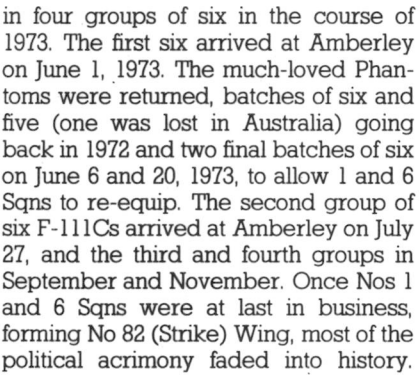

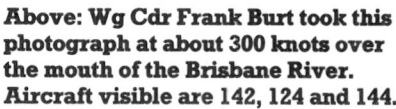

prices and offsets, GD went ahead with a complete pallet mounting cameras, optical sights, IR linescan and a TV system, with sensor controls and displays in the right-hand cockpit. An F-111C flew to Fort Worth in late 1978 and was rolled out on 18 April 1979 for flight testing by GD and RAAF crews. By 1980 three further kits had been shipped to Amberley for installation by personnel of 452 Sqn, who look after the aircraft assigned to 1 and 6 Sqns (No 6 has the four convertible F/RF aircraft).

The RAAF's aircraft have increasingly been tasked with maritime and anti-ship missions. If funds can be made available it seems likely that an anti-ship missile will be purchased, and it is known that evaluations have been made of Harpoon, Exocet and Sea Eagle, and probably of other weapons in this category.

To return to the FB-111A force of SAC, it is only natural that, as with the B-58 before it, GD should have been active in canvassing advanced or stretched versions. By far the most important was a substantially enlarged model for SAC, which was discussed from the mid-1970s and finally began to firm up as the FB-111H in 1977. Powered by two GE F101 engines, the same as then planned for the B-1, the H would have had a largely new fuselage, tandem-wheel main gears freeing the belly for weapons, and many other major and minor changes. It had the full support of everyone in the USAF from David C. Jones, Chief of Staff, down. Cost of rebuilding 65 FB-111As was put at $2·3 billion. Congressional approval was not forthcoming, so what happened next was a scaled-down plan of September 1979 to rebuild 66 FB-111As and 89 F-111Ds (essentially the surviving force of each type) to a rather lower standard called FB-111B/C, the B being the rebuilt FB and the C the rebuilt D. These would have had greater commonality with the existing aircraft, but F101 engines, more fuel and completely revised avionics and weapons would have turned them into very effective penetrators. Inflation, however, made the price of this reduced programme soar to $6·5 billion, or more than $40 million per aircraft and far more than the original estimated cost of a whole programme for 1,704 F-111s in 1963!

Above: Wg Cdr Frank Burt took this photograph at about 300 knots over the mouth of the Brisbane River. Aircraft visible are 142, 124 and 144.

The FB-111B/C likewise never got the go ahead, and all that the USAF has so far been able to do is find $300 million for a programme to upgrade 65 FB-111As to improve their equipment. The Air Force Air Logistics Center at Sacramento began work in 1980 to add the Afsatcom (Air Force satellite communication system) terminal for sending and receiving teletype messages whilst airborne in any part of the world to effect a great improvement in operational readiness. A stall-warning system had been deemed urgent enough to be added, as well as the ALR-62/ALQ-137 mix described in an earlier chapter. At almost $5 million per aircraft, this modest avionics fit, which could just about fit into a Jeep, compares in price with that of a new F-111A. There is no plan at present to fit the AGM-86B ALCM, which in principle could be carried on the four wing pylons.

Left: Fortunately the Australian procurement of the F-111C is at present unique in human experience! For just under five years the whole force was dismantled and stored: here the fuselages are packed like sardines in a hangar at Carswell AFB.

The EF-111 Electric Fox

The air defence system encountered over North Vietnam, with its combination of SAMs, ground-controlled interceptors and radar-directed AAA based on a comprehensive network of surveillance radars, and consideration of the even more sophisticated system deployed by the Warsaw Pact, belatedly led the USAF to consider the need for a specialized tactical electronic warfare aircraft. Luckily, a suitable combination was found in the form of the ALQ-99 tactical jamming system used in the US Navy's EA-6B Prowler and the F-111A airframe: even so, it was to take another 15 years before the first EF-111A 'Electric Fox' was in service.

Above: A salvaged F-111A is mounted on its side and subjected to giant electromagnetic pulses for the EF-111A programme.

This final chapter dealing with a One-Eleven for the inventory describes a version far removed from anything contemplated in SOR-183, one whose purpose is not to carry traditional weapons but weapons of a purely electronic kind. As far back as 1942 the RAF was flying aircraft in the face of the enemy purely in order to find out about his emitters (ground and airborne radars, navaids and communications) and to interfere with them. Today the EF-111A is the newest and most advanced aircraft in the West carrying on this vital work.

Of course, any air force that takes its job seriously fits all its combat aircraft with EW (electronic warfare) systems. RWRs (radar warning receivers) are carried to indicate when the aircraft is being illuminated by a hostile radar, and advanced equipments give details about the illumination and perhaps even identify the type of radar and indicate its exact location. ECM (electronic countermeasures) may then be brought into play if the threat seems serious.

Powerful jammers can blanket the enemy wavelength(s), either by a 'brute force and ignorance' method in which the jammer simply has greater power (which is difficult, because small emitters in fighters can hardly overpower giant radars on the ground), or by deceptive techniques, involving sending out just the right signals in the right directions at the right times to stop the enemy radar from getting a good lock on. At the same time, small jammers can be ejected in dispensed cartridges, along with hot flares to defeat IR (heat) homing missiles. By far the commonest ECM of all is chaff, small slivers of reflective foil or aluminized film, which when dispensed in large clouds form a barrier that ordinary radars cannot penetrate.

Despite all this, modern airspace is becoming so perilous that even the latest tactical aircraft may not have a very good chance of penetrating it deeply and surviving. This is particularly true of the airspace over the countries of the Warsaw Pact in eastern Europe, where the overall anti-air defence system is by far the strongest in the world. In several areas a NATO aircraft penetrating at a height of 10,000ft (3,000m) could be caught in the beams of 1,000 surface-based radars simultaneously. Behind this dense electronic barrier are the world's greatest concentration of rapid-fire guns, SAMs of many kinds and high-performance manned interceptors. Consequently, an attacking aircraft needs all the extra

Left: The first prototype, 66-049, which was aerodynamically but, at this time, not electronically representative of the definitive EF.

Below: This photograph of the rather gaudy first EF, 66-049, was taken at Grumman's Calverton, NY, facility in June 1978.

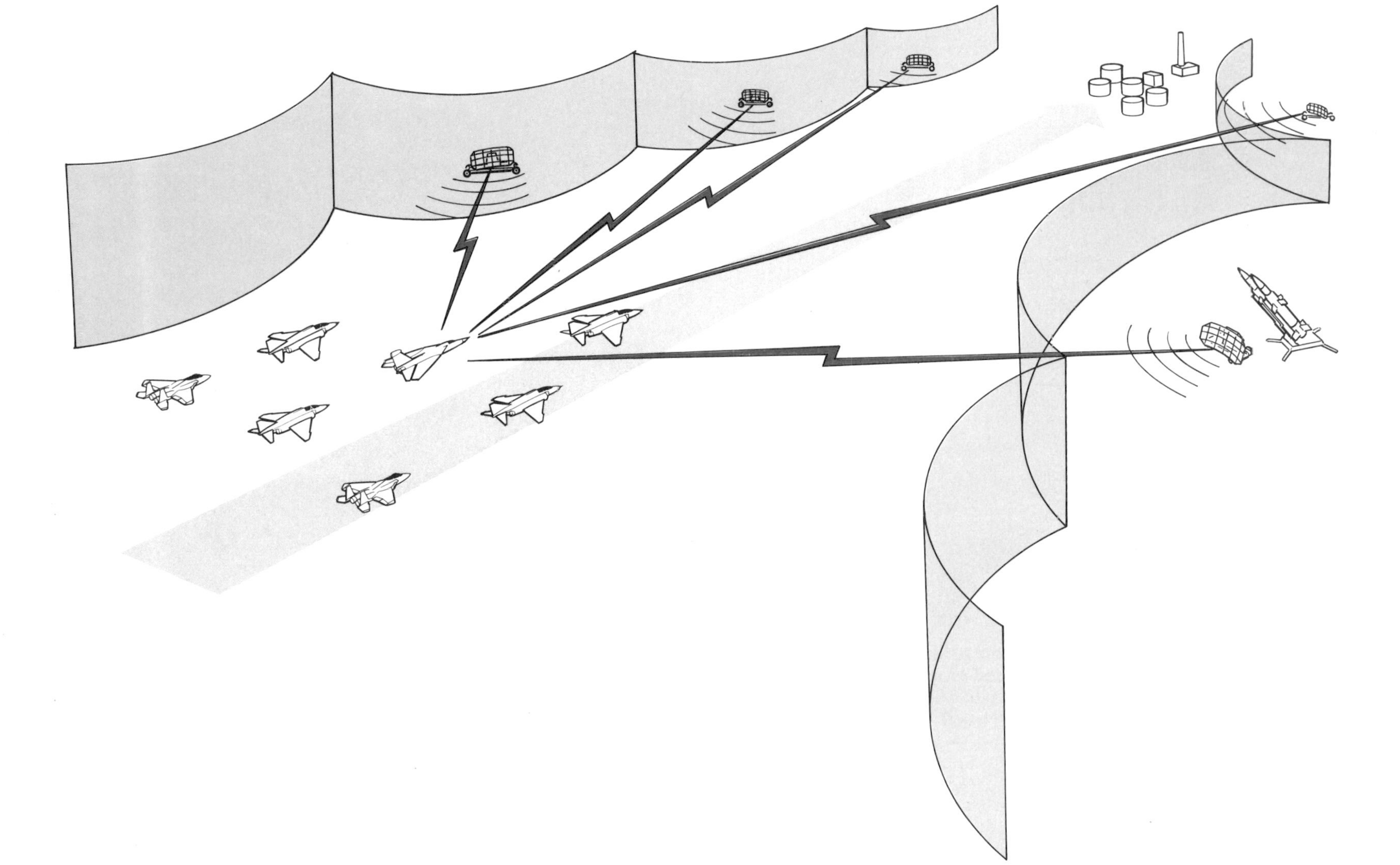

help it can get in order to have at least a reasonable chance of surviving.

Some two decades earlier the recognition that North Vietnam was beginning to construct electronic anti-air defence led to the urgent re-introduction of dedicated EW aircraft. The USAF completely rebuilt B-66 bombers and turned them into various species of EB-66, while the Navy did the same thing with F3D Skyknight interceptors and turned them into EF-10Bs. The Navy went on to buy much better purpose-designed EW aircraft, first the EA-6A Intruder and then the EA-6B Prowler, but the Air Force dragged its feet.

Urgent updating

Throughout the first half of the 1960s specialist agencies in the Air Force, and many experienced officers, grew increasingly alarmed as nothing appeared to be happening to counter the swiftly growing anti-air network facing the NATO air forces. Lieutenant-General Robert C. Mathis, Vice-Commander of the giant AFSC (Air Force Systems Command), said "In southeast Asia long-range Soviet radars detected our aircraft from gear-up to their attack run". He said a total updating of the USAF airborne EW capability was urgently needed "to support the tactical strike forces worldwide with high-power steerable, directional ECM jamming against early-warning, heightfinder, GCI (ground-control intercept) and acquisition radars".

It was one of the many times that, by default, the mighty USAF had let itself get into a situation that can fairly be called a crisis, and it was saved only by the sheer chance that it did not have to do any actual fighting. When it is realized that 15 years elapsed from the first move to update its pathetically inadequate EW capability in 1967 to the time that the first new EW aircraft became fully operational in 1982 the magnitude of the problem is thrown into focus. Politicians still like to imagine that peacetime deficiencies can somehow be put right in time of crisis by working around the clock for a few days. To get the Electric Fox took 15 years, and that was only possible because it was based on an existing tactical jamming system (ALQ-99) and an existing airframe (the F-111A).

Back in 1967 there were no EW tactical support aircraft in the Air Force except the EB-66s and a few EB-57s. All were ineffective electronically and overaged as aircraft, and it was planned to phase out the last in 1970. A new system was needed, as several lone voices had been explaining since 1963, but one always has to go through the motions of 'saving money' by studying lash-ups and interim stop-gaps, and by 1968 a lot of money had been spent on the ITEWS (interim tactical EW system) which was a proposal to re-equip, re-engine and re-wing the EB-66s.

As anyone could have predicted without charging the taxpayer a cent, this proved to be costly and impracticable, besides leaving the Air Force with an aircraft totally inadequate to meet the growing threat. So the next study, in 1968-70, focussed on a straightforward buy of Navy EA-6B Prowlers. This aircraft, the standard EW platform aboard Navy carriers until at least the year 2000, packages the powerful and properly designed ALQ-99 system into an A-6 Intruder airframe stretched to accommodate two extra crew, with the jamming emitters carried externally in up to five underwing and centreline pods, each with its own ram-air windmill to generate electric power.

Above: A grossly simplified portrayal of the way an EF-111A is intended to roll back the coverage of hostile air-defence radars and communications.

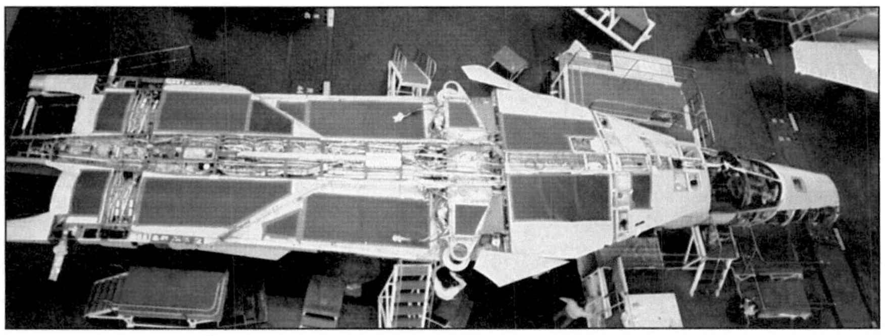

Left: This is the state to which the incoming F-111As are reduced in the Grumman teardown section (Station A) prior to rebuilding as an EF-111A.

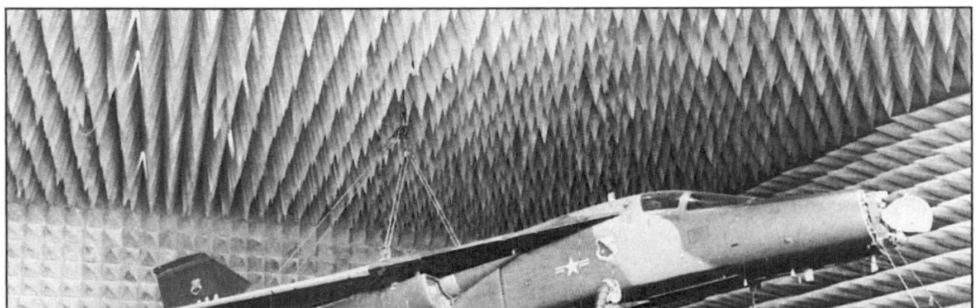

Centre above: An unserviceable F-111A mounted in the Grumman anechoic chamber for testing its electromagnetic compatibility.

Above: Fully instrumented 66-041 airborne in late 1978 after a year of generally very successful testing of the on-board systems and ALQ-99E.

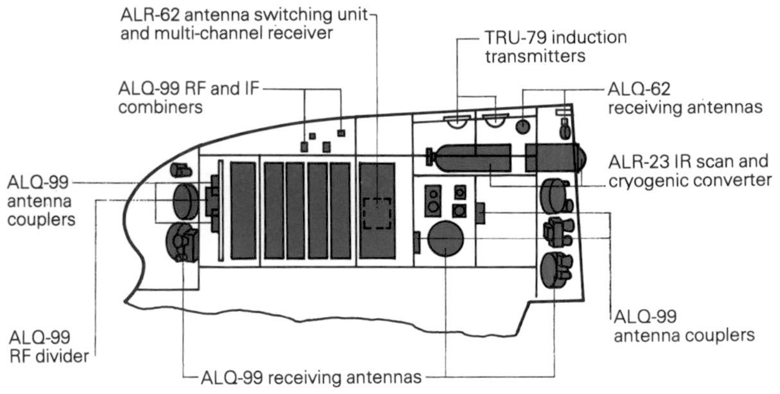

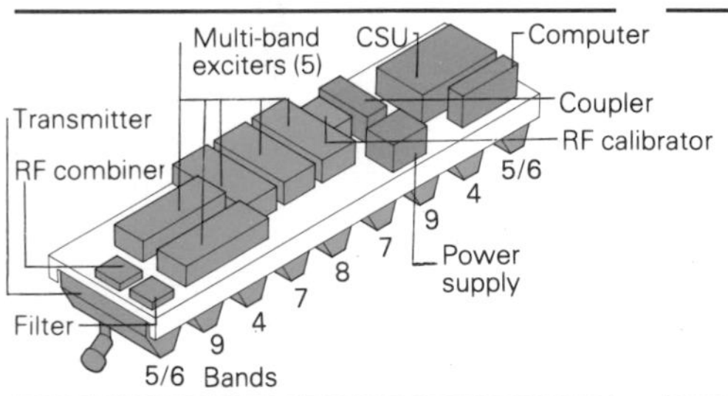

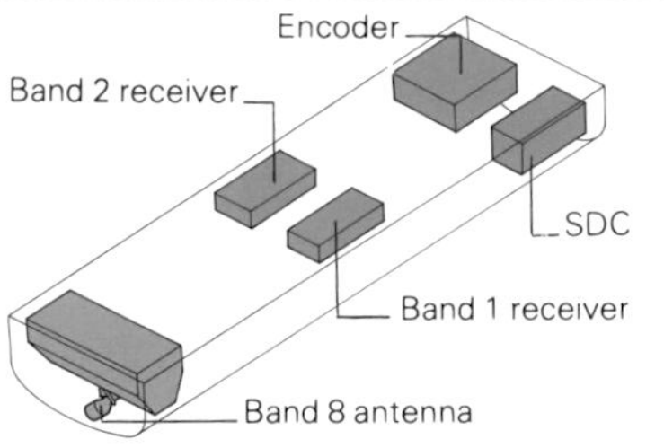

Top: Major elements housed in the fin-tip pod, which weighs 370lb (168kg) and contains 583lb (264kg) of electronic receivers.

Above left: Simplified outline of items mounted on the equipment pallet in the weapon bay. Transmitter aerials emit through the 'canoe' radome.

Above left centre: The main pallet in the weapon bay door weighs 4,738lb (2,149kg) of which 4,274lb (1,939kg) comprises ALQ-99E avionic boxes.

Above: The pilot's side of the EF cockpit is not very different from an updated F-111A, which is hardly surprising; differences are at right.

Below: A comprehensive diagram of locations of external receiver and emitter aerials (antennas in the US) of the standard EF-111A.

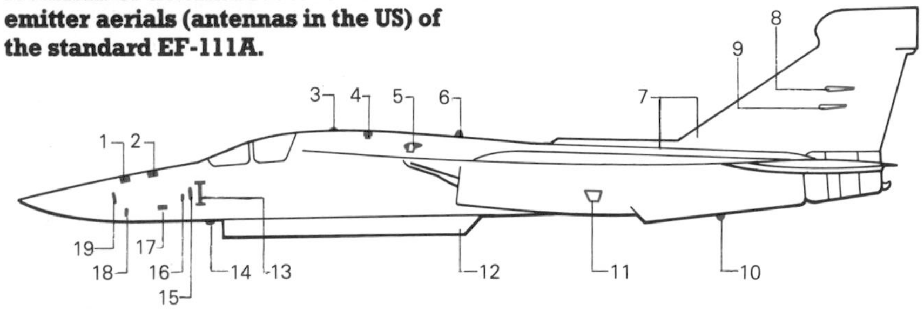

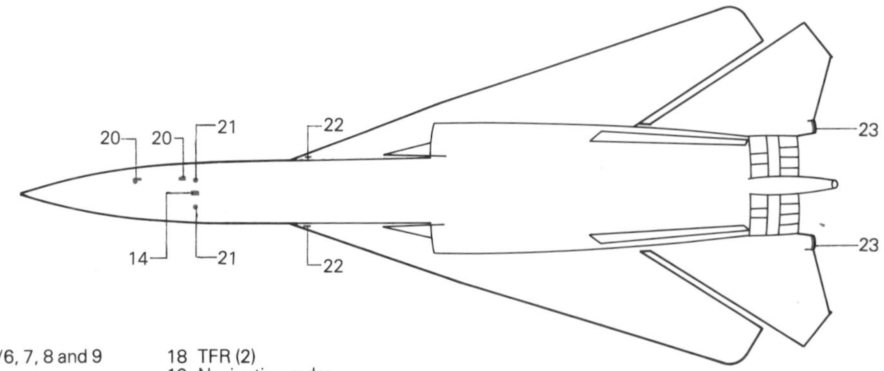

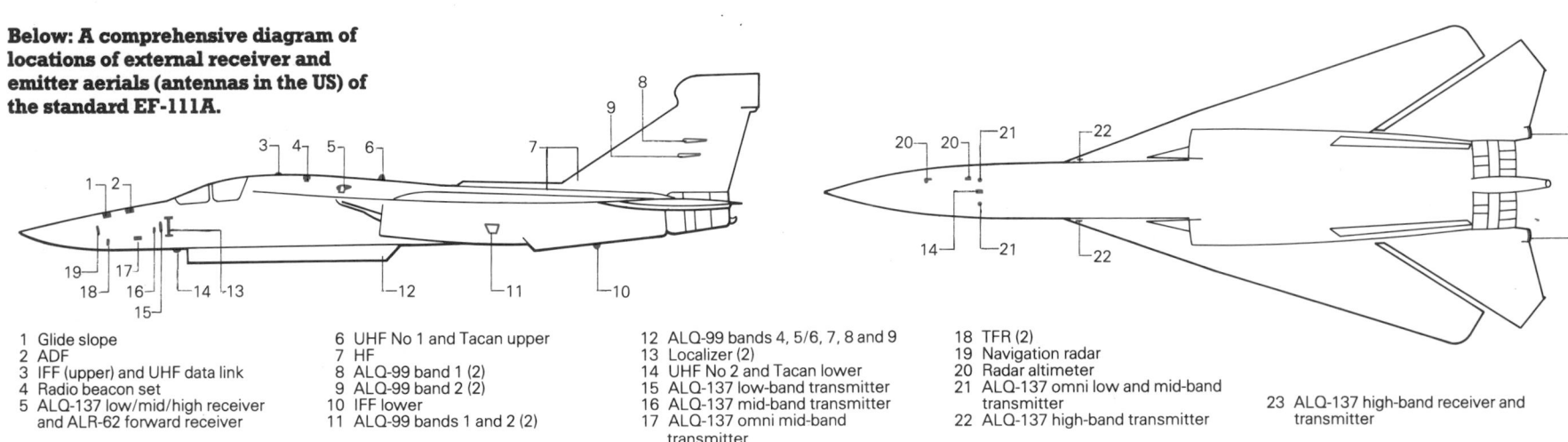

1 Glide slope
2 ADF
3 IFF (upper) and UHF data link
4 Radio beacon set
5 ALQ-137 low/mid/high receiver and ALR-62 forward receiver
6 UHF No 1 and Tacan upper
7 HF
8 ALQ-99 band 1 (2)
9 ALQ-99 band 2 (2)
10 IFF lower
11 ALQ-99 bands 1 and 2 (2)
12 ALQ-99 bands 4, 5/6, 7, 8 and 9
13 Localizer (2)
14 UHF No 2 and Tacan lower
15 ALQ-137 low-band transmitter
16 ALQ-137 mid-band transmitter
17 ALQ-137 omni mid-band transmitter
18 TFR (2)
19 Navigation radar
20 Radar altimeter
21 ALQ-137 omni low and mid-band transmitter
22 ALQ-137 high-band transmitter
23 ALQ-137 high-band receiver and transmitter

The EA-6B does a good job, but it is open to criticism. The Air Force faulted it because it lacks supersonic performance, though it is arguable how often such performance would be needed in practice. Certainly, on some missions the EW aircraft has to fly in company with the attacking force, but with an external bombload no attack aircraft can fly much faster than an EA-6B, and the Navy has not often wished for greater speed.

A second criticism of the USAF was lack of range. This again is arguable. Like other A-6s the EA-6B has 15,940lb (7,230kg) of internal fuel, and depending on how many jammer pods are carried it can add to this up to four large drop tanks, so it could not be too heavily criticized on this score and certainly could fly useful tactical overland missions. On the other hand, it cannot equal the exceptional fuel capacity of the One-Eleven, nor the latter's high speed in the clean condition. The final black mark against the EA-6B was high price, but again this is relative and in fact is probably lower than for the EF-111A, though as it is impossible to compare a new-build aircraft with a rebuild such an assertion is of little value. One suspects there was also a bit of reluctance to accept a Navy aircraft, and a far from new one at that.

What seemed a better alternative was to try to package the TJS (tactical jamming system) of the EA-6B into the F-111. There was little chance of getting the F-111 production run extended, though this possibility was examined at length. The only alternative was to convert existing F-111s, and though the USAF later described these as 'surplus', all One-Elevens are actually pretty useful and converting a substantial number inevitably meant withdrawing the oldest and least effective examples from the inventory of Tactical Air Command. In fact almost exactly half of TAC's F-111A force were earmarked for conversion.

Fortunate coincidence

It is partly a matter of chance that it was found possible to convert the F-111A into an outstanding EW platform. Though said at the time to be not only cost-effective but also the lowest-risk solution, Grumman Aerospace, prime contractor for the EA-6B to the Navy and brought into the USAF programme at the very outset, was initially by no means certain the conversion could be done. Fitting two extra seats would have cut into the internal fuel because there were reasons why it was not desirable to extend the F-111 forward fuselage. Grumman received a Phase 1A contract in 1974, by which time it had already carried out deep study of an EW F-111, and in January 1975 an $85.9 million contract was received for the conversion of two F-111As into prototype EF-111As.

In addition to the hostile radars listed earlier a modern TJS aircraft has to counter the AI (airborne interception) radars of interceptors and IFF (identification friend or foe) systems. It can do this in various ways, and in most scenarios the USAF will also use Wild Weasel F-4Gs with Harm and other anti-radar missiles, as well as EW equipment such as ALQ-131 or ASPJ pods on each of the fighter or attack aircraft in the theatre. The powerful EW platforms can orbit well back from the battlefront, along with the TR-1 recon platforms, Awacs platforms and tankers. Here they would normally operate at high altitude, screening all air activity on the friendly side from hostile radars in what is called the Barrier Standoff role, with jamming tuned to the enemy's early warning, GCI, height-finding and target-acquisition radars and his IFF systems. In roughly similar locations they can also operate in the AI-jam role, with emissions tuned to obliterate the AI radars of enemy interceptors and thus further protect the aircraft on the friendly side.

Alternatively, the EF-111A can orbit closer to the enemy, either in the CAS (close air support) role, flying at low altitude to jam mobile battlefield radars for SAMs and AAA, or in the BAI (battlefield air interdiction) role, flying at medium level to jam all SAM/AAA radars as well as communications and data links. Finally, the EF can fly penetration escort missions accompanying

Left: A general view of the cockpit used by Grumman for development purposes, without ejection seats, with all wiring and panels installed.

1 Auxiliary brake handle
2 Landing gear control panel
3 Arresting hook handle
4 External stores jettison button
5 Agent discharge/Fire detect test switch
6 Fuselage fire pushbutton warning lamp
7 Engine fire pushbutton warning lamps
8 Angle-of-attack indexer
9 Wing sweep flap/slat position indicator
10 Engine tachometers
11 Engine turbine inlet temperature indicators
12 Engine fuel flow indicators
13 Engine nozzle position indicators
14 Engine pressure ratio indicators
15 Hydraulic pressure indicators
16 Engine oil pressure indicators
17 Control surface position indicator
18 True airspeed indicator
19 Horizontal situation indicator
20 Airspeed Mach indicator
21 Attitude director indicator
22 Altitude vertical velocity indicator
23 Threat indicator
24 Standby airspeed indicator
25 Left status indicator
26 Self-contained attitude indicator
27 Standby vertical velocity indicator
28 Radar altimeter indicator
29 Right status indicator
30 Fuselage fuel quantity indicator
31 Fuel quantity indicator test button
32 Landing gear position indicator lamps
33 Instrument system coupler control
34 Total/select fuel quantity indicator
35 Takeoff trim indicator lamp
36 Takeoff trim button
37 Fuel quantity indicator select knob
38 Main caution lamp panel
39 Lower caution lamp panel
40 ILS control panel
41 Ram doors/oil quantity panel
42 Annunciator indicator
43 Standby altimeter
44 Master caution lamp
45 Magnetic compass
46 TFR scope panel
47 Nav radar scope panel
48 UHF radio control panel
49 TTWS control indicator panel
50 Inertial nav control panel
51 Stores jettison select panel
52 Landing gear emergency release handle
53 JSS/SPS warning and caution panel
54 Angle-of-attack indexer
55 Clock
56 Digital display indicator
57 Jammer status panel
58 JSS modes select panel
59 Disposables control panel
60 Digital display indicator control panel
61 Stowage bag

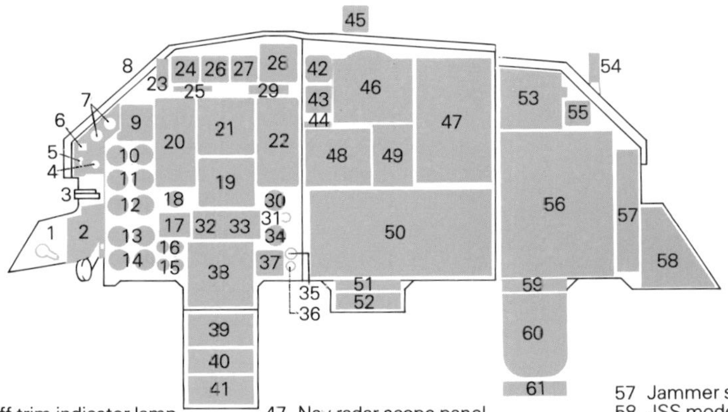

Left below: Schematic diagram of the main front panel of the EF-111A with major items identified.

attacking aircraft on deep penetration strikes into hostile territory. It was clearly essential to select an aircraft able to accompany not only existing USAF attack aircraft but also those likely to enter the inventory during the remainder of this century, and at maximum weight an EF-111A can maintain 507 knots (584mph/940km/h) at low level over enemy territory. This is considerably slower than a clean One-Eleven in the nuclear role, but is considered adequate by the USAF.

As in the EA-6B the EF-111A carries its sensitive receiver subsystem in a large fairing on top of the fin. Six spiral antennae (aerials) are arranged looking to all points of the compass 60deg azimuth apart. They give full coverage of all threat frequencies, and indicate LOS (line of sight) to each emitter. The information they collect is used to manage the high-power jamming subsystem, prime contractor for which (under overall Grumman management) is Eaton's AIL Division at Deer Park, NY. In the EA-6B an IBM 4-pi computer manages a distributed external jamming system hung on pylons, as noted previously, but in the EF-111A ten powerful jammers are mounted on a large pallet housed in the weapon bay and radiating through a 16ft (4.9m) 'canoe' radome along the underside of the fuselage.

Smart jammer

ALQ-99 was thus a 'smart' (computer controlled) jammer from its inception in 1965. Its features included individual CW transmitters with higher than 1kW continuous power; high-gain aerials giving ERP (effective radiated power) in the megawatt range; closed-loop jammer control (for example, if a threat ceases emitting, the ALQ-99 instantly ceases to jam it); millisec (thousandth of a second) look-through to study the hostile emissions while jamming is in progress; real-time signal processing by the computer, which also handles BIT (built-in test) and fault isolation; and EMC (electromagnetic compatibility) testing of the complete radiating aircraft in a giant anechoic chamber to confirm that the massive jamming emissions would not interfere with or damage the aircraft's own delicate avionics.

In 1970–73 the XCAP (expanded capability) ALQ-99A came into use on the EA-6B. This offered doubled frequency coverage, greater computer capacity, new wide-band transmitters, a recording capability for future threat analysis, a new Raytheon multimode exciter giving many new features including track-breaking and CFAR (constant false-alarm rate) jamming, and a lot of new computer software. Next, in 1974, came ICAP (increased capability) ALQ-99D, with digital tuning to exact frequencies; a multi-format cockpit display and keyboard; peripheral processor; a faster encoder and 8-MHz clock; broad-beam jamming aerials and further improved software to speed up response in the auto mode; and an expanded frequency sector mode, jamming individual threats.

These considerable improvements

Above: Main cooling-air outlets at the rear of the pallet from which hot air blasts while ALQ-99E is operating. The rear of the radome can be seen.

Left: Close-up of the fin-tip pod on 66-041 after delivery to Mountain Home AFB. There is little hint of the complex array of internal receivers.

Left: A fin and pod for an EF-111A in the Canadair plant at Montreal. This section posed structural as well as aerodynamic and avionic problems.

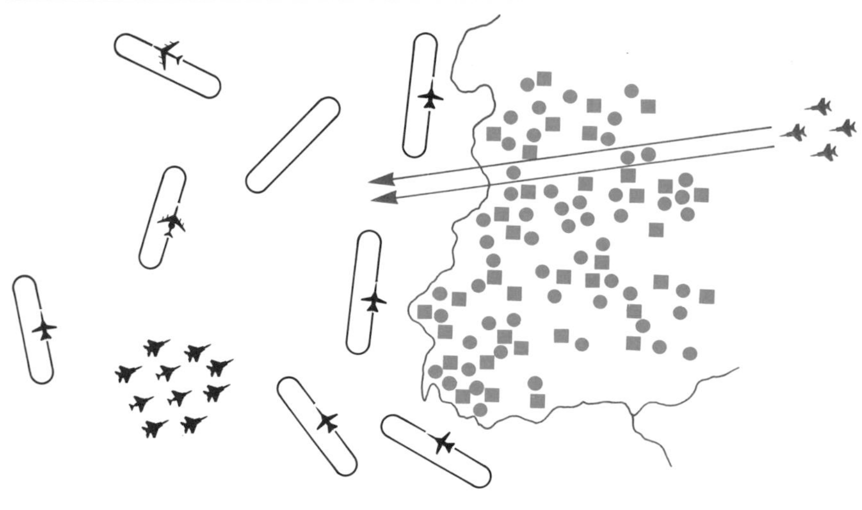

Above: Simplified representation of the barrier standoff and AI jammer roles which will be flown by the EF-111A to protect friendly aircraft.

Right: In the penetration escort role the EFs would accompany the friendly attacking aircraft (here depicted as F-4s) throughout hostile airspace.

Below: The close-in role demands that the EF-111A should fly racetrack patterns at different heights close to the edge of hostile airspace. At the same time, other EF-111As orbiting at higher altitudes would guard supporting aircraft against attacks by enemy interceptors.

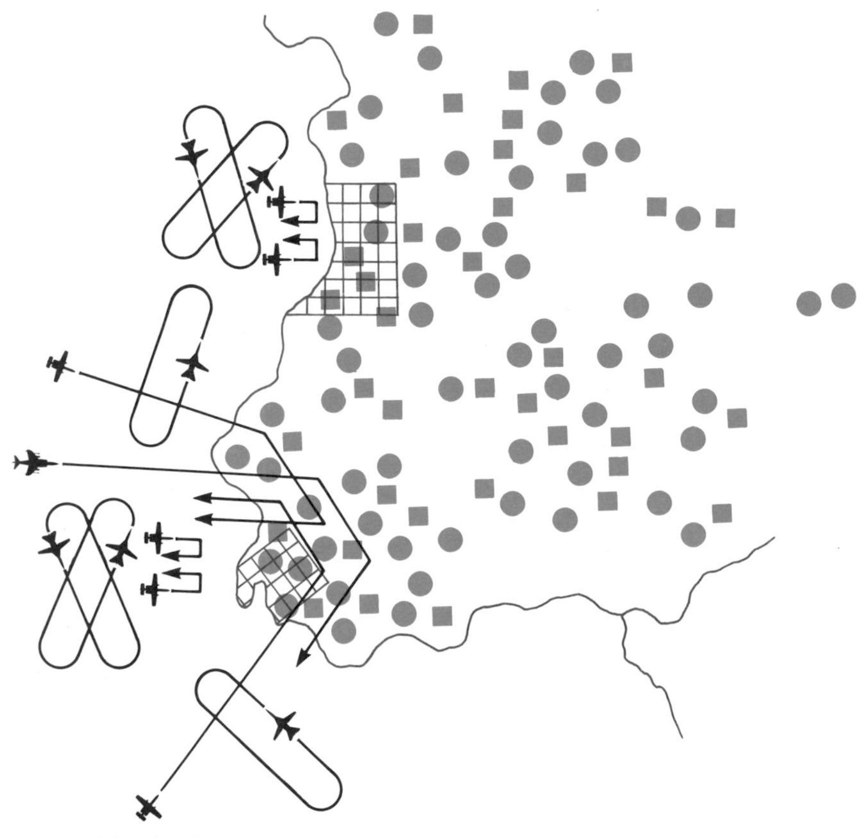

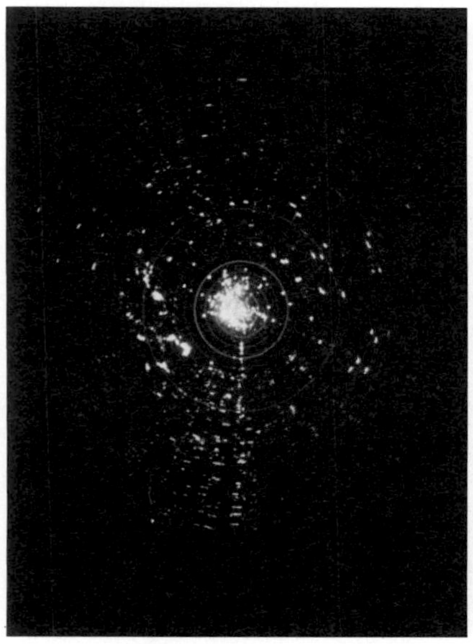

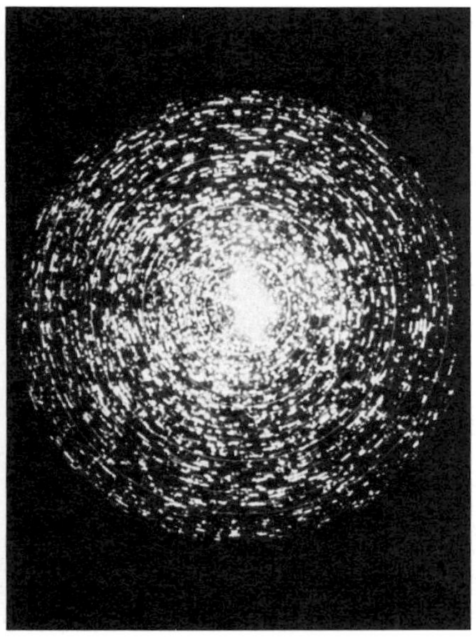

Left: Actual photographs showing the screen of a ground air-defence surveillance radar (far left) with the normal unjammed picture; when the receiver is jammed by transmissions from the airborne ALQ-99E it becomes impossible to decipher the radar returns (near left).

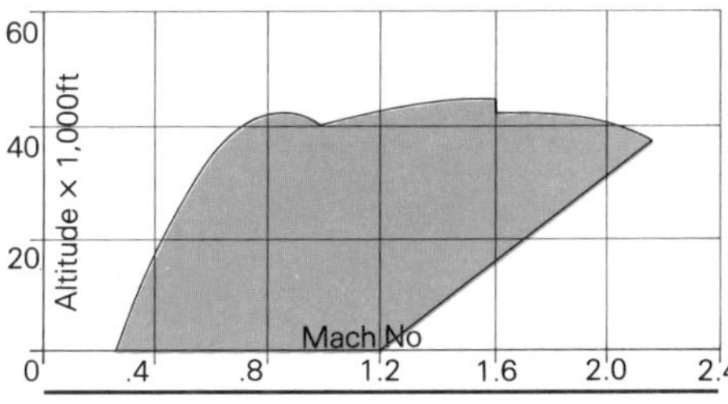

Above: The EF-111A performance envelope is essentially the same as that of other F-111 versions, though Mach 1.2 at sea level would be rare.

Above: The first EF delivered to TAC was the twice-rebuilt 66-041, seen here with MO tail code after arrival at Mountain Home in January 1982.

not only enabled the ALQ-99 installation to handle more hostile threats faster, but also opened the way to the desired system for the EF-111A which, by virtue of increased automation and further improved software, enables one man to do what in the EA-6B takes three. The system is the ALQ-99E, developed in 1974–78. Apart from the single-operator computer control it features inflight-adaptable aerials; a new multiband, multispot exciter with its own modulation microprocessor; digital CFAR jamming; and complete isolation of active and passive systems, the latter comprising the ALR-62 (V)-4 TTWS (terminal threat warning subsystem), as well as the active ALQ-137 (V)-4 SPS (self-protection subsystem). Thus, to recapitulate, the main JSS (jamming subsystem), the ALQ-99E detects, identifies, locates, records and jams every kind of hostile emitter using computer control to give high-power jamming with highly effective signal modulations in just the right directions and at precisely the right times. It is universally considered the best EW system in the world at present.

Turning an F-111A into an EF is a major rebuild operation, but as far as possible it preserves the F-111's basic flight qualities and manoeuvre envelope. Thanks to the prior exhaustive test programme the basic airframe has a 10,000-hour life, and this is also the life put on all new structure added in producing an EF. The F-111A airframes typically had about 2,000 hours when they were grounded for conversion, and it is calculated that at normal peacetime utilization the remaining 8,000 hours will take them up to about the year 2010, possibly with occasional local rework.

New equipment

The main changes are the fin receivers and installation of the jamming equipment pallet. Canadair supplies the fin, which is reinforced to carry 370lb (168kg) of pod structure loaded with 583lb (264kg) of internal electronics (see diagram). Grumman assembles the main jammer installation, which mounted on its pallet weighs 4,274lb (1,939kg), while the canoe radome and door adds a further 464lb (210kg). Thus it is generally agreed that, not surprisingly, the EF flies like an F-111A with a 6,000lb (2,700kg) bombload, though as most of the extra weight is internal the rate of roll is perhaps a bit better. On Red Flag and other exercises EFs have repeatedly demonstrated their ability to fly formation with other F-111s making high-speed attacks.

The rebuilding of the fin and weapons bay are by no means all the airframe changes involved. As the jamming system is internal it cannot use ram-air windmill generators, and a new EPS (electric power system) is needed. The original 60-kVA IDGs (integrated-drive generators) on the engines are replaced by large machines rated at 90 kVA, supplying the jamming pallet via a completely new rewired electrical subsystem. Rewiring is partly responsible for reducing weight by 1,600lb (726kg). At least as important is the installation of two new ECS (environmental control system) installations, the air-cycle system used in the F-111F, with a ram inlet under the front of the right-hand main engine inlet duct, and a liquid (Coolanol) refrigeration system to provide cold air at 40deg F (4.4deg C) to cool the high-power avionics which, being internal, have no slipstream cooling. The liquid system rejects heat overboard via two RAHEs (ram-air heat exchangers) located at the roots of both tailplanes. Another local modification is the addition of a blade aerial on the right side of the fuselage under the wing trailing edge, and flush skin aerials in both glove leading edges.

Prototype testing

In 1974–76 Grumman Aerospace at Calverton, the USAF Rome Air Development Center and Kirtland AFB used five prototype or early production F-111A aircraft in exploring radiative patterns, EMC and nuclear hardness with giant electronic pulses. On December 15, 1975, Grumman began a 29-flight programme at Calverton with an F-111A fitted with a dummy canoe aerial to check basic flight performance and handling. It was followed on March 10, 1977, by the first of the two EF-111A prototypes funded in 1975. This aircraft, gaily painted 66-049, was aerodynamically representative of the definitive aircraft, with the fin pod and other modifications, but did not have a fully operative jamming system. An almost complete operative system was flown on the second prototype, 66-041, painted in the low-visibility pale grey of the production aircraft and flown from Calverton on May 17, 1977.

Subsequent testing confirmed predicted aircraft performance and handling, and generally excellent jamming effect (on one occasion a New England ANG unit called up to request that jamming be switched off so that it could find out where its own aircraft were). A minor redesign of the fin was called for and there were just over 200 other snags, mainly in the area of reliability and maintainability, all speedily corrected to the point where in 1979 direct maintenance was averaging an impressive 20 man-hours per flight hour, less than that required for regular F-111s. Totally Blue Suit (ie, by Air Force personnel) follow-on testing began in April 1979 and was completed in October after 261 hours in 86 flights. Reliability and maintenance easily bettered all targets, despite severe surge demands and sustained high sortie rates, all in the hands of the 366th TFW at Mountain Home AFB assisted by

Above: A superb study of 66-019, the third production EF, after delivery to Mountain Home.

personnel from Eglin AFB's Tactical Air Warfare Center.

Particularly bearing in mind the patchy record of the basic One-Eleven for reliability – described by a USAF spokesman at Mountain Home during EF testing as "not enviable" – it is especially gratifying to record that the complex and challenging EF is not only much better than the unmodified aircraft but considerably better than the USAF's requirements. As a result, in November 1979 the DSARC (Defense Systems Acquisition Review Council) breathed a sigh of relief and lifted all production constraints. Grumman has since been in production with conversion kits, with an average of six airframes at Calverton at any one time.

Production Lot I consisted of one aircraft – the completely refurbished 66-049 – which was rolled out at Calverton on June 19, 1981. This was the first time anyone had seen the definitive production cockpit, which has only one set of flight controls and a very neat set of displays for the EWO in the right seat. This aircraft vanished into Grumman's anechoic chamber for additional EMC testing, and the first example actually delivered to TAC was 66-041, likewise completely brought up to production standard and delivered to the 366th TFW 17 months behind schedule in November 1981. This was the first of the two aircraft in Lot II, while Lot III comprised four aircraft, all delivered in 1982. Lot IV included eight aircraft delivered by the late summer of 1983, and IOC (initial operational capability) was to be achieved in November 1983. Lot V, comprising 12 aircraft, was in the Grumman plant in 1983 and were then all due for delivery by September 1984. The final batch, Lot VI, comprises 15 aircraft due for delivery at monthly intervals between September 1984 and November 1985. Originally all were to have been in use before 1983.

In service six Electric Foxes – which seems a better name than the pretentious Electronic Warrior favoured by the Air Force – are being held for training and attrition, while 24 are assigned to the 388th Electronic Combat Squadron at Mountain Home and 12 to a second ECS at RAF Upper Heyford. The aircraft based in Britain will clearly be those 'at the sharp end' in the immediate future. One of the most severe problems has been trying to find a friendly block of airspace with any kind of air defence system rivalling that in Warsaw Pact countries. Nothing like this exists anywhere in NATO, and virtually all the really tough evaluation of how the EF will perform against dense emitter concentrations has been done on simulators, notably those at Calspan's REDCAP facility in Buffalo.

There is every reason to believe that this potentially outstanding aircraft would in practice perform as advertised, though it is extremely hard to demonstrate this in advance. Eventually it will have JTIDS (Joint Tactical Information Distribution System) terminals with which it will be able to plug in in real time to ground bases or to an Awacs aircraft, both to protect the latter more effectively and to feed Elint (electronic intelligence) information as fast as it is collected. Certainly the only big problem with the EFs is their rather limited numbers, which will mean that combat losses will at least temporarily leave significant gaps in a particularly vital part of the inventory.

Below: Another Electric Fox, 66-013, showing the overall remarkably clean appearance of this extremely capable jamming platform.

Experimental Variants

As well as enabling it to penetrate hostile airspace at low levels and high speeds, the One-Eleven's swing wings offer unique opportunities for aeronautical research, allowing wings of various configurations to be tested at any required sweep angle. Since 1970 NASA has exploited these opportunities in a series of programmes investigating the technology of supercritical wings, which offer greater efficiency at high subsonic speeds. Most recently the F-111 has become the recipient of the uniquely flexible Mission Adaptive Wing, whose profile can be adjusted for any flight condition without the use of flaps or other drag-inducing devices.

Above: Another picture of 63-9778 in original TACT form, showing the fully instrumented wing with considerable wash-out of incidence from root to tip.

From early in the TFX programme it was evident to such people as NASA's John Stack that the F-111 would be a uniquely valuable aircraft for R&D (research and development) purposes. Unlike previous aircraft it can test wings at any desired angle of sweepback, and in some programmes this is a considerable asset. But in the early 1960s NASA was more concerned with lunar exploration than with lift-drag ratios, and little was done for a further ten years, though NASA's aerodynamicists were hard at work.

Probably the single most important advance in subsonic and transonic wing technology in the past 25 years is the so-called supercritical wing, which compared with a classic wing is much thicker (around 17 per cent thickness/chord ratio), having a bluff leading edge and almost an upside-down profile, with a flatter top and more bulging camber on the underside. It sounds like an absurd idea, and the only reason it might appear to give lift upward instead of downward is that the trailing edge is curved gently downward, so at least the air comes off the wing with some downward momentum. In fact it is a brilliant idea, because the air over the upper surface is less violently accelerated and thus the wing can be driven to a higher airspeed before it encounters sonic speed at the line of peak suction on the upper surface, with its attendant shock-waves and high drag.

Supercritical wings in practice are not so much used to make aeroplanes go faster as to enable them to fly at the same speed with greater efficiency. The supercritical wing can be made so much deeper that the skins can be thinner and the weight much less. Compared with a normal thin wing the aspect ratio (the slenderness in plan form) can be greatly enhanced, giving greater efficiency in subsonic cruising flight. There is room for more fuel inside the wing, and the bluff leading edge improves takeoff and low-speed handling without the need for adding false bluffness with a Kruger flap. Altogether the supercritical wing has transformed the latest generation of large passenger jets and executive aircraft, though Rockwell's Columbus Division, which received NASA's original contract, has been unable to reap much business benefit.

Early applications

A rather imperfect supercritical wing flew under NASA contract on a T-2C Buckeye in November 1970, and on a NASA F-8 Crusader on March 9, 1971. By this time the USAF interest in the B-1 was beginning to trickle more money into the idea, and in early 1973 the 13th F-111A was assigned to test a supercritical wing at different sweep angles. Ostensibly part of NASA's TACT (Transonic Aircraft Technology) programme, aircraft 63-9778 was painted in the badges and initials of a remarkable lot of sponsors. For the USAF there was the AFFTC (Air Force Flight Test Center) and AFFDL (Flight Dynamics Lab). For NASA there was the ARC (Ames Research Center), FRC (Dryden Flight Research Center) and LRC (Langley Research Center, where the F-111 had it earliest origins).

Curiously, instead of fitting a long slender wing, of the kind used on modern transports, the TACT wing fitted was blunt and of short span, with much reduced aspect ratio and broad-chord tips. Sweep angles were reduced to 10deg (min) and 58deg (max), and there was very marked washout (wing twist reducing AOA progressively from root to tip). Droop leading-edge flaps and area-increasing trailing-edge flaps were fitted, with roll spoilers well outboard. Prolonged test flying took place to give results evaluated against those measured previously in 24 NASA flights in the unmodified configuration. This programme, in 1965–68, provided a considerable amount of data, and for good measure one TF30 engine was also fitted with a new IPCS (integrated propulsion control system) which instead of the usual hydromechanical control used digital electronics to control the engine, its inlet and variable nozzle.

NASA and the USAF said little about the results of the supercritical wing programme, but continued tinkering with the wings and by summer 1979 had moved on to flying large wing gloves intended to provide what was called "natural laminar flow". Since 1949 many organizations have sought to fly an aircraft whose boundary layer, instead of being turbulent, was maintained in a smooth laminar condition. This would significantly reduce drag, so that in 1953 Handley Page in England was rash enough to publish ideas for subsonic jetliners able to fly from Britain to Australia non-stop. Neither that company nor anyone else ever succeeded in building an aircraft in which laminar flow was truly practical. A fly on the leading edge will instantly result in a turbulent boundary layer, as will dirt, manufacturing imperfections and even an already turbulent atmosphere, but by 1979 NASA wished to see how far it would be possible to use the new technology of deep supercritical wings to maintain a favourable (accelerating) pressure gradient over most of the chord and thus preserve laminar flow by natural means, without any of the sucking or blowing of the previous active schemes. (Even this was not new, the deep Griffith aerofoil having been produced in 1945.)

First, the One-Eleven had to be flown without the use of any wing movables, and it was soon confirmed that at 10deg

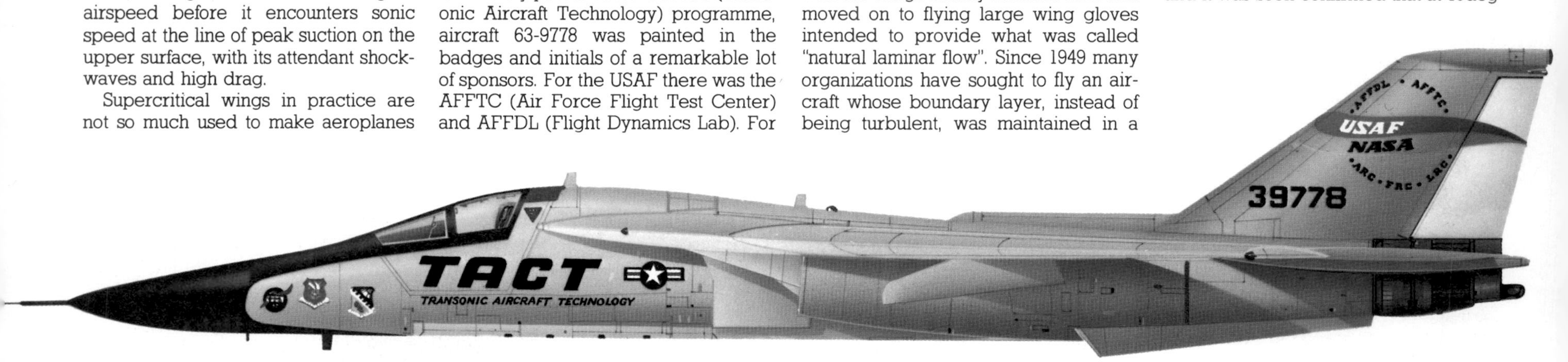

Above: Specially drawn for this book, this side elevation (profile) shows 63-9778 in its first rebuilt form with the original supercritical wing.

Right: The TACT aircraft with the wings in the intermediate sweep position. In fact, the wings are no more advanced than those of the A310 Airbus.

Opposite: In contast the attempt to achieve a large degree of 'natural' laminar flow was a major challenge. Note the added glove on each wing.

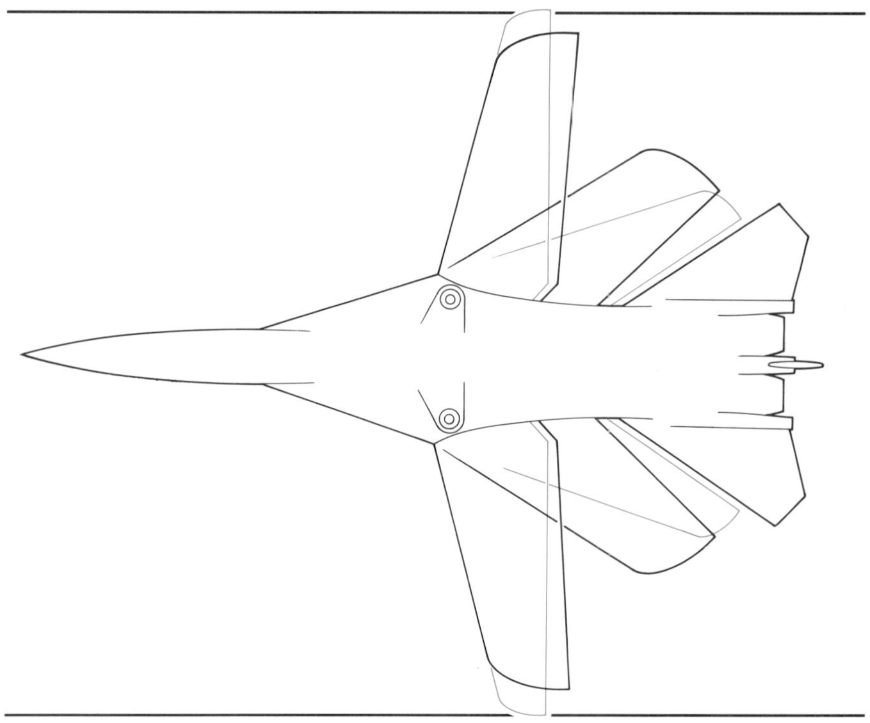

Above right: This version of a simple NASA drawing shows the low aspect-ratio plan shape of the supercritical wing superimposed on the original F-111 outline in blue.

sweep it was possible to take off and land without using droops or flaps. Large gloves were then built around the wings near mid-span, made with extremely accurate profile which then had to be slightly marred by adding instrumentation to measure surface pressures, pitot-rake ram pressures and other unknowns, such as where transition to a turbulent boundary layer actually took place. In all, 19 flights were made at heights up to 30,000ft (9,000m), at Mach numbers to 0.85 and with sweep restricted to 10–26deg. Again, no results have been published, though this does not necessarily mean that laminar flow has yet again proved an elusive pipe-dream.

Mission-Adaptive Wing

This was not to be the end of the road for the NASA/USAF One-Eleven. As part of the far-reaching AFTI (Advanced Fighter Technology Integration) programme the USAF wishes to investigate what is called the MAW, for Mission-Adaptive Wing. It is the logical next stage beyond today's crude rigid wings to which crude rigid slats, droops or flaps are hinged. Birds do it better: their wings can change shape in smooth curves exactly adapted to each flight condition. For many years aerodynamicists have wished to do the same, the only objection being that it is very difficult. Fortunately the AFFDL found $20 million, and a contract for a pair of almost totally new wings was awarded to, of all people, the losing TFX finalist, Boeing-Wichita.

Boeing had already devoted a lot of thought to how, and how far, it would be possible to replace crude wings by flexible ones. Indeed, as far back as 1969 the first 747 had flown with giant leading-edge flaps with skins largely made of glassfibre composite able to take up a strongly arched shape as they extend from the main surface. With the One-Eleven it was planned to go the whole hog and make the entire pivoted wing flexible apart from the original torsion box. The two boxes, stripped of their previous overlays and gloves, were removed from ship 778 and sent to Wichita in late 1981. Meanwhile, Boeing had already built a full-scale wing section to determine loads and stresses, structurally proved each component for the MAW, and also shown in tunnel

Right: The Mission-adaptive wing in model form set up for high-speed tunnel test at the USAF Arnold Engineering Development Center, Tennessee.
Right below: The Boeing-Wichita artist faced a challenge in trying to produce a popular picture of the MAW in action.
Foot of page: Far more informative is this photograph of the left-hand MAW at Boeing Military Airplane Co in Seattle. Protractors are measuring deflections prior to AFTI/F-111 flight.

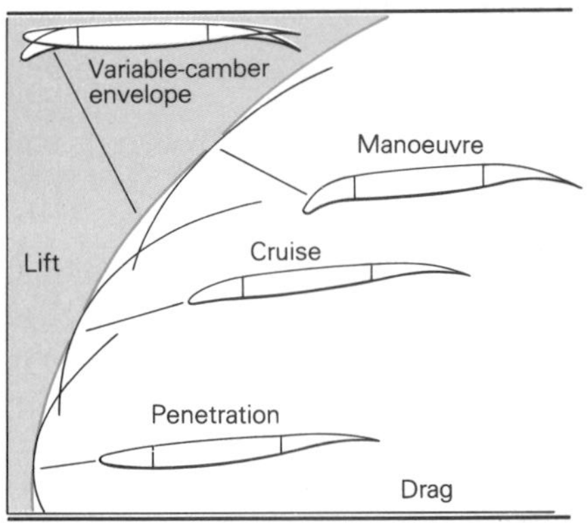

Above: The thing that matters about the MAW is not plan shape but the variable section profile. Other aircraft, such as the F-16, can pivot leading and trailing edges, but only in a crude way with hinged rigid surfaces. The MAW is flexible.

testing that the MAW might be expected to improve buffet-free lift by 69 per cent, sustained lift by 25 per cent and reduce cruise drag by 6 per cent at subsonic speeds and 7 per cent in supersonic flight. A company spokesman said it could be "the single most innovative development in years".

Design details changed slightly in 1980–82, but it has always been the intention to maintain an unbroken flexible upper skin from leading edge to trailing edge, using basically a GRP (glass-reinforced plastics) structure. Prolonged studies appeared to show that the compression of the underside in the low-speed or manoeuvre regime would cause buckling unless some form of spanwise discontinuity was accepted, allowing one part to slide over its neighbour. The leading edge behaves as a fully variable droop flap, driven by a powered system from root to tip. The trailing edge likewise is fully powered, behaving as both ailerons (with asymmetric flexure) and flaps (with symmetric flexure). Features include high actuation power and rapid movement when demanded, the objective being trailing-edge rotation at 30deg/sec.

Test programme

Flight control modes to be tested include cruise camber control for peak efficiency, manoeuvre load control for quicker dogfight manoeuvres without overstressing the wing root, and DLC (direct lift control) to permit the pilot either to change the aircraft longitudinal pitch angle nose-up or nose-down without diving or climbing, or alternatively to cause the aircraft to make sudden movements in the vertical plane without altering the pitch attitude at all. It should also be possible to effect automatic alleviation of gust loads to give passengers (and structures) a smoother ride.

Naturally, the flight control system with the MAW will be of the fully redundant digital FBW (fly-by-wire) type, coupled to a dual electro-hydraulic wing actuation system. In mid-1983 it was expected that limiting leading-edge angle would be 15deg down, while the trailing edge is expected to move 4deg up and 19deg (the original objective was 30deg) down. The programme has slipped by about a year from the original objective of autumn 1982, but as this was written it was clear that flight with the MAW wings under manual control should be possible well before the end of 1983. In 1984 it is expected that fully automatic flight will be possible, the pilot merely inserting flight Mach number, altitude and manoeuvre condition and leaving it to the FCS (flight control system) digital computer continuously to select the best wing profile.

The F-111 wing has a reasonable amount of internal room for the power actuation system and linkages. Future transports might have even more, but from the viewpoint of the USAF prime candidates for the MAW are the F-16 and other advanced fighters, and it remains to be seen whether their small wings will prove mission-adaptable.

Glossary and abbreviations

AAA Anti-aircraft artillery
AAM Air-to-air missile
Active Emitting radiation
ADF Automatic direction finding system
Aerial British word for antenna
AFB US Air Force Base
AGL Above ground level
AI Airborne interception
Antenna American word for aerial
AOA Angle of attack
Aspect ratio Wing slenderness in plan-form, numerically span^2/area
ASPJ Advanced self-protection jammer
Awacs Airborne warning and control system
Azimuth Bearing, direction or angular rotation in horizontal plane

BG Bomb Group
Bite Built-in test equipment
BW Bomb Wing

CAP Combat air patrol
CAS Close air support
CFAR Constant false-alarm rate
CG Centre of gravity
Chord Distance across wing from leading to trailing edge measured parallel to longitudinal axis of fuselage
CNI Communications, navigation, identification
CRT Cathode-ray tube
CW Continuous-wave radiation

DF Direction finding
Digital Operating with discrete on/off pulses or bits which instead of being measured are counted
DLI Deck-launched intercept
DME Distance measuring equipment
DoD Department of Defense
Doppler Radar which measures changes in frequency between reflections from ground ahead of and behind the aircraft, thus giving accurate measure of speed over the ground (doppler effect is also used to pick out moving targets)

ECCM Electronic counter-countermeasures
ECM Electronic countermeasures
EM Electromagnetic
EO Electro-optical
EW Electronic warfare

FADF Fleet Air Defense Fighter
FBW Fly by wire, electrically signalled
FLIR Forward-looking IR
FOD Foreign-object damage
FOV Field of view

G Acceleration due to Standard Gravity, unit of linear acceleration
GCI Ground-controlled interception
GD General Dynamics Corporation
GE General Electric Company (USA)
GHz Gigahertz, thousands of millions of cycles per second

HAS Hardened aircraft shelter
HE High explosive
HF High frequency
HUD Head-up display
Hz Hertz, cycles per second

I-band EM radiation 8 to 10GHz
IFF Identification friend or foe
ILS Instrument landing system
INS Inertial navigation system
IR Infra-red, heat radiation
Iron bomb Ordinary HE bomb
IRCM IR countermeasures
IRWR IR warning receiver

J-band EM radiation 10 to 20GHz
Jammer ECM emitter designed to smother hostile radars or radios
JTIDS Joint tactical information distribution system

kHz Kilohertz, thousands of cycles per second
kT Kilotonnes yield
kVA Kilovolt-amperes, unit of electrical power
kW Kilowatt, unit of DC electrical power

Lantirn Low-altitude navigation and targeting IR at night
LGB Laser-guided bomb
Lo As close to the Earth's surface as possible typically 200 to 1,000ft (90–300m)

Mach Unit of airspeed equal to the local speed of sound
MHz Megahertz, millions of cycles per second
MTI Moving-target indication

NACA US National Advisory Committee for Aeronautics
NASA US National Aeronautics and Space Administration
NIS NATO identification system
nm Nautical mile

OKB Soviet experimental construction (ie, design) bureau

Passive Not emitting
PD Pulse doppler type of radar
Pod Streamlined container carried externally
PPI Plan position indication
PRF Pulse-recurrence frequency (or repetition)

RAAF Royal Australian Air Force
RAF Royal Air Force
Raster TV picture built up line-by-line
RCS Radar cross-section
RDT&E Research, development, test and evaluation
RHAWS Radar homing and warning system
RMTS Ranger and marked-target seeker
RTAFB Royal Thai Air Force Base
RWR Radar warning receiver

SAC USAF Strategic Air Command
SAM Surface-to-air missile
SAR Synthetic-aperture radar
Semi-active Homing on radiation reflected from a target illuminated by radar carried in fighter or some other vehicle (not the missile)
SecDef US Secretary for Defense
SIF Selective identification facility
Signature Characteristic form of each emitter's radiation, forming a kind of fingerprint
Smart Self-guided to home on an illuminated target, especially using laser radiation
Slick Streamlined (Aero-1A shape) bomb
SOJ Stand-off jammer
Solid-state Based on semiconductor materials instead of vacuum tubes
SOR Specific operational requirement
Span Distance measured across tips of wings
STOL Short takeoff and landing

TAC USAF Tactical Air Command
Tacan Tactical air navigation
Taileron Tailplanes able to move together as primary control in pitch and opposite sense as control in roll (tailplane/aileron)
TF, TFR TFR Terrain following, terrain-following radar
TFS USAF Tactical Fighter Squadron
TFW USAF Tactical Fighter Wing
TFX Tactical fighter experimental
TI Texas Instruments Inc
TJS Tactical jamming system
TsAGI Soviet central aero and hydrodynamics institute
Turbofan Turbojet with oversize low-pressure compressor delivering excess airflow bypassing core of engine to add to jet downstream

UHF Ultra-high frequency
USAF US Air Force
USN US Navy

VG Variable geometry, especially variable sweepback
VHF Very high frequency
V/STOL Vertical or short takeoff and landing

Wing loading Aircraft weight divided by wing area
WSO Weapon-system officer (wizzo)

Specifications

	F-111A/E	F-111C	F-111D
Engine	TF30-P-3	TF30-P-3	TF30-P-9
Inlet	Triple Plow 1*	Triple Plow 1	Triple Plow 2
TO thrust	18,500lb/8,390kg	18,500lb/8,390kg	20, 840lb/9,453kg
Wingspan 16°	63ft 0in/19.2m	70ft 0in/21.34m	63ft 0in/19.2m
Wingspan 72½°	31ft 11½in/9.74m	33ft 11½in/10.35m	31ft 11½in/9.740m
Wing area 16°	525sq ft/48.78sq m	550sq ft/51.1sq m	525sq ft/48.78sq m
Length	75ft 6½in/23.03m	75ft 6½in/23.03m	75ft 6½in/23.03m
Height	17ft 0½in/5.19m	17ft 0½in/5.19m	17ft 0½in/5.19m
Fuel (internal)	4,191gal/19,052lt	4,191gal/19,052lt	4,191gal/19,052lt
Fuel (external)	2,000gal/9,092lt	3,000gal/13,638lt	2,000gal/9,092lt
Weight empty	46,172lb/20,943kg	47,303lb/21,456kg	46,631lb/21,151kg
Weight max TO	91,300lb/41,400kg	110,000lb/49,900kg	100,000lb/45,360kg
Avionics			
Radar	APQ-113	APQ-113	APQ-130
TFR	APQ-110	APQ-110	APQ-128
Radar altimeter	APN-167	APN-167	APN-167
RHAWS	APS-109A	APS-109A	APS-109C
CMDS	ALE-28	ALE-28	ALE-28
CMRS	ALR-23	ALR-23	ALR-41
INS	AJQ-20A	AJQ-20A	AJN-16
Tacan	ARN-52	ARN-52	ARN-52(V)
ILS	ARN-58	ARN-58	ARN-58A
IFF (AIMS)	APX-64	APX-64	APX-64(V)
IFF	—	—	APX-76
Optical sight	ASG-23	ASG-23	AVA-9 (HUD)
Doppler	—	—	APN-189
Astrocompass	—	ASQ-119	—
ECM jammer	pods	pods	pods
SPS	—	—	—
TTWS	—	—	—

	F-111F	FB-111A	EF-111A
Engine	TF30-P-100	TF30-P-7	TF30-P-3
Inlet	Triple Plow 2	Triple Plow 2	Triple Plow 1
TO thrust	25,100lb/11,385kg	20,350lb/9,230kg	18,500lb/8,390kg
Wingspan 16°	63ft 0in/19.2m	70ft 0in/21.34m	63ft 0in/19.2m
Wingspan 72½°	31ft 11½in/9.74m	33ft 11½in/10.35m	31ft 11½in/9.74m
Wing area 16°	525sq ft/48.78sq m	550sq ft/51.1sq m	525sq ft/48.78sq m
Length	75ft 6½in/23.03m	75ft 7in/23.04m	76ft 0in/23.17m
Height	17ft 0½in/5.19m	17ft 0½in/5.19m	20ft 0in/6.1m
Fuel (internal)	4,184gal/19,020lt	4,673gal†/21,243lt	4,173gal/18,970lt
Fuel (external)	2,000gal/9,092lt	3,000gal/13,638lt	none
Weight empty	47,481lb/21,537kg	47,980lb/21,763kg	55,275lb/25,072kg
Weight max TO	100,000lb/45,360kg	119,243lb/54,088kg	89,000lb/40,370kg
Avionics			
Radar	APQ-144	APQ-114	APQ-160
TFR	APQ-146	APQ-134	APQ-110
Radar altimeter	APN-167	APN-167	APN-167
RHAWS	APS-109	APS-109B	—
CMDS	ALE-28	ALE-28	ALE-28
CMRS	ALR-41	ALR-41	ALR-23
INS	AJN-16	AJN-16	AJQ-20A
Tacan	ARN-52(V)	ARN-52(V)	ARN-52
ILS	ARN-58A	ARN-58A	ARN-58
IFF (AIMS)	APX-64(V)	APX-64(V)	APX-64
IFF	—	APX-78	—
Optical sight	ASG-27	ASG-25	—
Doppler	—	APN-185	—
Astrocompass	—	ASQ-119	—
ECM jammer	pods	pods	ALQ-99E
SPS	—	—	ALQ-137(V)4
TTWS	—	—	ALR-62(V)4

* F-111E, T Plow 2; † with bomb bay tanks (2)

Performance

All versions can briefly exceed Mach 2 (1,320mph, 2124 km/h) above 30,000ft (9144m) in clean condition and at MAX power (afterburner). At low levels the clean maximum is typically Mach 1.2 (912mph, 1468km/h), but the EF-111A is limited to about 500kt.

Deployment

F-111A 4520th Combat Crew Training Sqn, Nellis AFB, Las Vegas, Nevada; 4480th TFW, Nellis; 474th TFW, Nellis; 347th TFW, detached to Takhli RTAFB; today serving only with the 366th TFW, Mountain Home AFB, Boise, Idaho, and the 57th Fighter Weapons Wing, formerly McClellan AFB, now at Nellis. Support for all USAF One-Elevens by Sacramento Air Logistics Center, McClellan AFB, Sacramento, California.

F-111B Test programmes from NAS Patuxent River, Miramar, Point Mugu and Lakehurst, but never operational.

F-111C No 6 Sqn, RAAF, Amberley, Ipswich, Queensland.

F-111D 27 TFW, Cannon AFB, Clovis, New Mexico.

F-111E Briefly at Cannon, then 20th TFW, RAF Upper Heyford, Oxon.

F-111F 347th TFW, Mountain Home (and Takhli RTAFB and Taegu AB); 366th TFW, Mountain Home; now only with 48th TFW, RAF Lakenheath, Suffolk (temporarily detached to RAF Sculthorpe, Norfolk).

FB-111A 340th Bomb Group, Carswell AFB, Fort Worth, Texas; 4007th Combat Crew Training Sqn, Carswell; 4201st Test Sqn, Eglin AFB, Fort Walton Beach, Florida (SRAM test); today serving with 380th BW, Plattsburgh AFB, Plattsburgh, NY, and 509th BW, Pease AFB, Portsmouth, New Hampshire.

EF-111A 366th TFW, Mountain Home; today serving with 388th ECS (Electronic Combat Sqn), Mountain Home, which is training crews for other ECSs including one to be formed at RAF Upper Heyford.

Inventory

Numbers built, and in USAF/RAAF inventory, December 1982:

Model	Built	12/82
F-111A	159	105
F-111B	7	0
F-111C	24	20
F-111D	96	84
F-111E	94	81
F-111F	106	92
FB-111A	76	63
Total	562	445

Chapter 6

HARRIER

Bill Gunston

Harrier

Acknowledgements

The author and editor would like to thank everyone who has contributed information and photographs for this chapter. Particular thanks are due to John W. Fozard, OBE, British Aerospace Divisional Marketing Director, who studied the text in meticulous detail. We are also grateful to John Godden, British Aerospace Aircraft Group, Kingston; Timothy J. Beecher, Lon O. Nordeen and Doree L. Martin of McDonnell Aircraft Co, St Louis; Geoffrey Norris and Karen Stubberfield of McDonnell Douglas Corporation (UK); David W. Hall, Rolls-Royce Marketing Manager for Pegasus and V/STOL and John Hutchinson, Rolls-Royce Ltd., Bristol; J. R. Ford of Ferranti plc; L. F. E. Coombs of Smiths Industries; and to the many people in MoD (RAF), MoD (RN) and the USMC who have assisted with the project.

Author

A former World War II RAF pilot and flying instructor, Bill Gunston has spent most of his working life accumulating a wealth of information on the history of aviation and military technology. Since leaving the service in 1948 he has acted as an advisor to several major aviation companies and become one of the most respected authors on scientific and aviation subjects as well as a frequent broadcaster. His numerous books include the Salamander title *The Illustrated Encyclopedia of Modern Military Aircraft* as well as an earlier chapter in this book: *F-111*.

A regular contributor to many leading international aviation and defence journals, he is a former technical editor of *Flight International* and technology editor of *Science Journal*. Among the many other authoritative journals for which he has carried out assignments are *Battle, Aeroplane Monthly, Aircraft* (Australia), *Aviation Magazine* (France), *Aerospace International, Aircraft Production, Flying, World Airways,* and the *Journal of the Royal United Services Institute for Defence Studies*. He is an assistant compiler of *Jane's All the World's Aircraft* and has contributed to Brassey's *Annual and Defence Yearbook, Aircraft Annual* and Salamander's *The Soviet War Machine* and *The US War Machine*.

Contents

Introduction

The story of the Harrier is without parallel. It began with a rather unwieldy scheme conceived by a Frenchman for vectoring jet thrust not only backwards, to achieve high forward speed, but also downwards, to make the aircraft rise vertically off the ground. Engine designers at Bristol translated the concept into a more elegant solution: a new type of aircraft engine able in one neat package to provide lift, thrust and even inflight braking. But the British, into whose lap the concept fell in 1957, had just been shortsighted enough to predict that the RAF was never going to need any more fighters or bombers. Future wars were going to be fought exclusively with missiles, which seemed a more attractive option because they were cheaper.

Despite these extraordinary circumstances, the completely new idea of a single-engined "jump jet" managed to survive. This was because American money paid for three-quarters of the engine, and one man – Sir Reginald Verdon Smith – said his company would pay for the remainder. A little later Sir Sydney Camm at Hawker Aircraft managed to persuade his board to pay for two prototypes of the novel P.1127 aircraft his team had designed. And in June 1960, four years from the start, British officials actually thawed enough to sponsor the P.1127 itself, provided that it was understood it was purely for research, and had nothing to do with such a taboo subject as a future combat aircraft!

With the passage of a complete decade, reason returned. The P.1127 was permitted to be turned into the Harrier, which gave the RAF the only kind of airpower that can survive in a future war, by being dispersed away from known airfields. It was also obvious that similar aircraft could completely transform airpower at sea, but, true to form, Britain put its foot in it a second time. Having, without actually announcing the fact, come round to recognizing that fighters and bombers were going to continue to exist, the government then pronounced that fixed-wing airpower in the Royal Navy was henceforth terminated, and that no more carriers would be built.

So we went through the charade a second time, permitting the development of the Sea Harrier provided that the ship to carry it was known by the strange title of "through-deck cruiser" (because to call it by the forbidden name "carrier" would have caused frightful ructions). Thus, by a second lot of back-door methods the Sea Harrier entered service, and so by the merest chance Britain was able to recover the Falkland Islands. Without the little jump jets the only response in April 1982 would have been to fume and bluster, and for the first time in modern history naked aggression would have paid off.

Where do we go from the Harrier and Sea Harrier? Why, on to the next generation, the AV-8B. This time the British government excelled itself. By announcing in 1975 that there was "not enough common ground" for a joint programme with the USA, Britain handed its birthright over to McDonnell Douglas. Now, freed from Whitehall at last, it will really go places.

The Jump Jet

In the mid-1950s the aeronautical world was becoming increasingly occupied with ideas for lifting fixed-wing aircraft vertically off the ground with the thrust of jet engines. For the next ten years every possible arrangement was studied, and more than 30 different schemes were actually flown. It is ironic that one of the least favoured of them should, after many years of fighting against not only the predictable ignorance, entrenched positions and totally closed minds, but also self-imposed political problems peculiar to Great Britain, eventually have won through to show the world that you can have airpower without either airfields or giant carriers.

Above: The pioneer free-flying jet VTOL device was the first Rolls-Royce TMR (thrust-measuring rig), popularly called The Flying Bedstead. The two Nene engines supplied air for four reaction control nozzles.

The self-imposed political problems stemmed from the now notorious *White Paper on Defence* of April 1957, which stated in the clearest terms that Britain's Royal Air Force was "unlikely to require" any more fighters or bombers – ever! Indeed, the phrase was interpreted in even stronger terms, to the extent that all combat aircraft programmes for the RAF were cancelled, excepting only the Lightning interceptor, which, said the Minister "has unfortunately gone too far to cancel". The very mention of future combat aircraft was enough to damage the career of officers or civil servants, and there was absolutely no point in anyone in the aircraft industry coming up with a new design.

It so happened that, just over a year earlier, Michel Wibault had put the finishing touches to a proposal for a combat aircraft unlike anything seen previously. One of the most famed French designers between the wars, Wibault had the vision to see that the numerous new NATO airfields being built in the 1950s might eventually become vulnerable to attack by nuclear missiles. Immovable, and littered with costly warplanes, they would present the ideal target. After much thought he came to the obvious conclusion: the only way to make airpower survivable is to divorce it from airfields.

Various VTOL (vertical takeoff and landing) aircraft already existed. Some were tail-sitters, pointing skywards, while others were flat-risers with swivelling engines or some other arrangement for obtaining both lift and thrust. Wibault devised a strange solution in which a gas turbine drove four large centrifugal compressors through gearboxes and shafts. Around each blower was a delivery casing – variously called a snail, a scroll, a diffuser or a volute – which could be rotated through 90°. With the four nozzles pointing downwards, the result was lift; with the nozzles facing rearwards, the result was thrust.

Wibault named his aircraft a Gyropter. He was not bothered about whether it should be a fighter or an attack aircraft; in the mid-1950s NATO was becoming interested in VTOL for both purposes. He was concerned with the basic principles, such as the need for the resultant VTOL lift force to pass through the aircraft CG (centre of gravity). He also knew that aircraft able to hover, a condition in which ordinary control surfaces are useless, have to have an extra control system using RCVs (reaction control valves) at the extremities, fed by compressed air. To drive his blowers he picked the Bristol Orion, with a sea-level potential of 8,000hp, as the most powerful turboshaft engine available, though the portly shape of his aircraft, and its relatively low-energy jets, precluded it from being supersonic.

Wibault failed to get much reaction from the Armée de l'Air or US Air Force, so he next took his proposal to the MWDP (Mutual Weapons Development Program) office in Paris. This was the agency through which a bountiful USA funded promising European military projects unsupported by their own nations. The MWDP director, Col Johnny Driscoll, USAF, was intrigued. Two years earlier he had supported the Bristol Orpheus, which was unwanted in Britain, and this had been the engine choice for all the contenders in the NATO light strike fighter competition, which was won by the Fiat G91. He asked the man behind the Orpheus, Bristol Aero-

Right: Typical of many free-flying rigs of the 1960s, this German VTOL helped in developing the VAK 191B strike fighter. Note the four RB162 lift jets, fed from two fuel drums amidships, and the wind anemometer!

Right: A Harrier GR.3 of RAF No 1(F) squadron recovers to its ship during Operation Corporate in spring 1982. It was the inherent simplicity of the single-engine vectored-thrust concept that enabled it to produce invaluable no-airfields airpower.

Engines technical director Stanley (later Sir Stanley) Hooker, to review Wibault's proposal. Hooker criticised the clumsy shafts, gearboxes, compressors and rotatable scrolls, but strongly favoured the use of a single engine for both lift and thrust, in a flat-rising jet. He showed the idea to his friend, the great Theodore von Kármán, who instantly said "Ah, vectored thrust" – today a common term.

Hooker took the scheme back to Bristol and handed it to his team: Charles Marchant, Gordon Lewis, Pierre Young and Neville Quinn. It did not take these brilliant young engineers long to come up with a scheme that retained the benefits while eliminating the drawbacks. Instead of bevel gears and transverse shafts to four blowers they proposed a single 1·5:1 reduction gear to drive two stages from the LP (low-pressure) compressor of the new Olympus BOl.21 turbojet, discharging through left and right vectoring nozzles. From this projected engine, the BE.48, further work gave the BE.52, in which the Orion was replaced by the lighter, simpler and cheaper Orpheus. Next, the BE.53 was produced by making the big front compressor an integral part of the engine, with a single front inlet, the inner part of its airflow going to supercharge the core engine and the outer part being discharged through the vectoring nozzles.

Fortunately Wibault was delighted at the transformation of his idea, and in December 1956 he and Lewis jointly applied for a patent for the first aircraft to look vaguely like a Harrier. This historic patent drawing not only showed two cold fan nozzles and two hot rear jet nozzles but it also featured contra-rotating spools and PCB (plenum-chamber burning). Making the HP (high-pressure) and LP spools rotate in opposite directions almost cancelled out the previously very large gyroscopic forces caused by the spinning masses in the engine, which in hovering flight would otherwise have caused severe problems. PCB is the vectored-thrust equivalent of afterburning or reheat, in that by burning extra fuel upstream of the cold and/or hot nozzles the thrust can be greatly increased for short periods. PCB was for the moment put on one side, to avoid its potentially thorny development problems. Without it the BE.53 would only give about 8,000lb (3630kg) thrust, but the immediate objective was to get something built and tested.

By great good fortune Driscoll's successor at MWDP, Col Willis (Bill) Chapman, was an enthusiast for VTOL. In the subsequent period of nearly 30 years the USAF has consistently stuck its head in the sand whenever it is asked what would happen if the many hundreds of Soviet missiles currently targeted on NATO airfields (including all those in the USA) were ever to be fired. In 1956, however, it was still possible to keep an open mind, and Chapman positively raced to find money to pay 75 per cent of the development bill of the BE.53. Equally quickly, Sir Reginald Verdon Smith, chairman of the Bristol Aeroplane Co (parent of the engine firm), agreed to finance the remainder, as he had done previously with the Orpheus. This was the crucial decision that got the whole project started.

Above: **Seemingly perhaps the most attractive way to build a jet VTOL, the tilting-engine aircraft still poses many problems. Germany's VJ101C had six RB145 engines, two in the fuselage and two twin tip pods, and reached supersonic speed.**

Below: When the Hawker P.1127 was being designed the only VTOL with official sponsorship in Britain was the Short SC.1, a slow five-RB108 aircraft (four for lift, one for thrust) which carried out a vast amount of fundamental research.

Hawker gets involved

Sadly, Wibault died at this juncture, and never saw his idea bear fruit. Another casualty was Maj Gerry Morel, brave French member of the British SOE who succumbed to his wartime treatment by the Gestapo and Vichy police. Director of the Société Franco-Britannique, he played a leading role in launching both the Orpheus and Pegasus, and as agent for Hawker he hosted Sir Sydney Camm at the 1957 Paris airshow just before he died. Camm said he had been watching the Rolls/ Ministry VTOL schemes, with numerous special lift jets, with increasing disbelief. Morel asked him if he had seen the BE.53. On return to Kingston Camm sent a famous letter: "Dear Hooker, what are you doing about vertical takeoff engines?"

At the time Camm was immersed in trying to turn the Mach 2 P.1121 into the twin-engine, two-seat P.1129 to meet the TSR.2 requirement. Jet lift was a second-

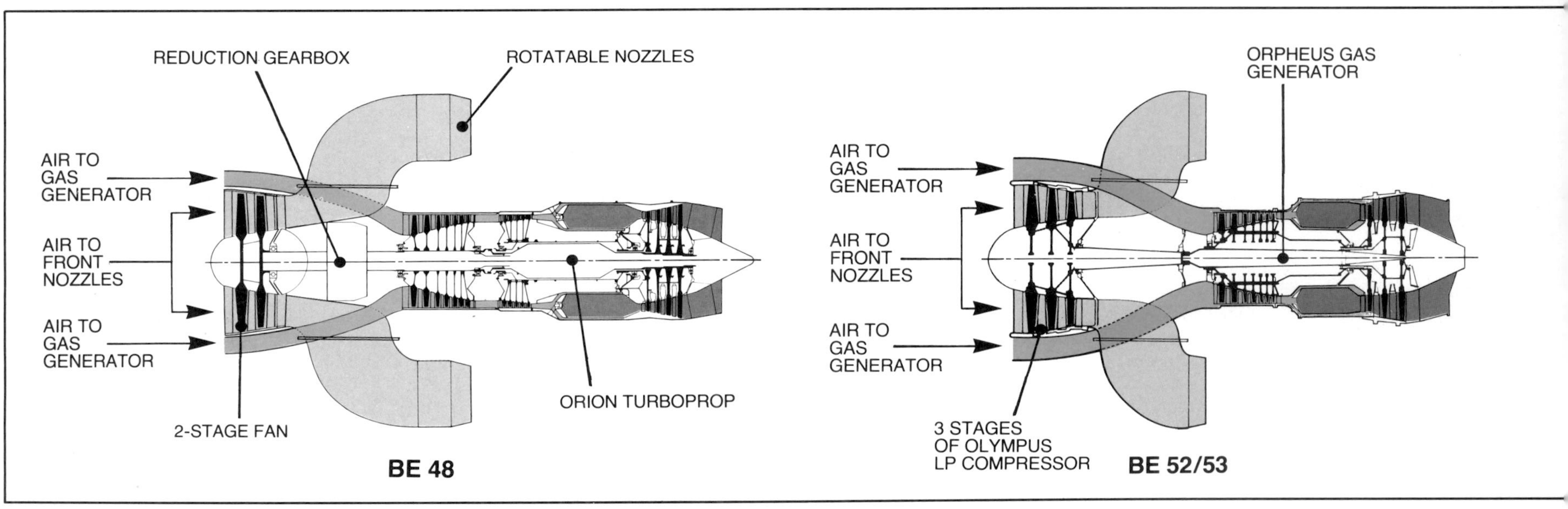

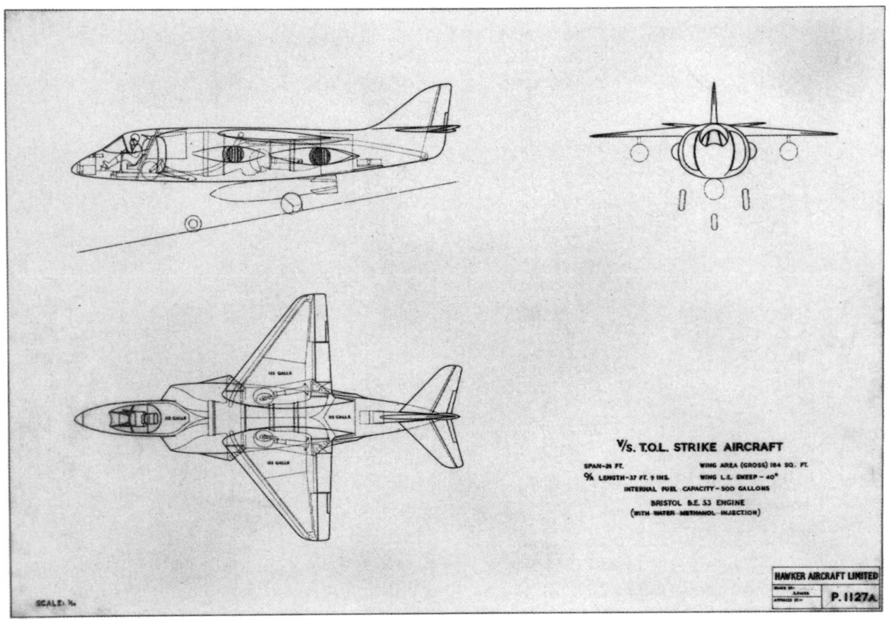

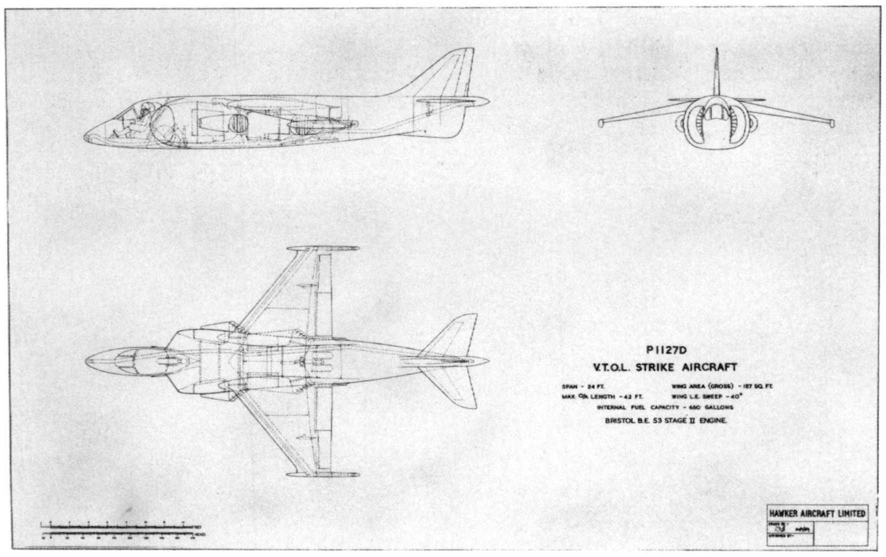

Top: An original company drawing from Kingston of the first of the P.1127 project studies. The words WITH WATER METHANOL INJECTION have been deleted by the designer. Note the conventional landing gear.

Above: The P.1127D was the aircraft actually built, and at company risk. This drawing, dated 20 September 1959, conforms closely to the first prototype, XP831, which began its hovering trials at Dunsfold in 1960.

ary matter, and in any case 8,000lb of lift from an engine based on the Orpheus seemed, in Camm's book, a typical engine-maker's overstatement. Hooker sent along the first BE.53 brochure, and Camm passed it to two of his best young engineers, Ralph Hooper and John Fozard. On 28 June 1957, in the same month as the Paris airshow, Hooper signed the first Hawker vectored-thrust drawing. As the jetpipe was not deflected, only the cold front jets were aligned with the CG, and the aircraft had to be STOL (short takeoff and landing), not VTOL. It was a rather slow three-seat battlefield surveillance aircraft. A little later it was refined into a two-seat support aircraft with lateral inlets. Meanwhile, down at Bristol the engine was developed into the BE.53/2, the first Pegasus, with mirror-image fan blading, to give contra-rotating spools to cancel out gyroscopic torques, and with the hot jetpipe bifurcated to a second pair of vectored nozzles.

Now the hare-brained scheme was suddenly looking plausible. As the P.1129 project became bleaker (because the RAF kept increasing the TSR.2 demands), so did the jet-lift work become more important. In August 1957 the first P.1127 brochure described a new aircraft designed around the Pegasus, with the four nozzles disposed around the CG under a high wing. This time it was a single-seater for attack and reconnaissance, and as it was a true VTOL it had air-bleed RCVs for control in hovering flight. Col Chapman was pleased with the proposal, but thought the range too short to be of real value to NATO air forces. Bristol raised the thrust to over 11,000lb (4990kg) by substituting the high-airflow HP compressor of the Orpheus 6, the result being the Pegasus 2. In early 1958 MWDP put up 75 per cent of the money for six of these engines, Bristol agreeing to pay the other 25 per cent, while Hawker Aircraft agreed to fund continued aircraft design and testing.

In the Pegasus 2 the engine had become a neat turbofan with the original bent pipe nozzles replaced by short nozzles with multiple cascade vanes to guide the flow. Bypass ratio was set at about 1·35, to match the thrusts from the cold and hot nozzles, and one major change was that the bleed power for the RCV nozzles was taken through stainless-steel pipes from the HP spool, Hooper having found that bleeding cooler fan air through aluminium pipes needed such enormous airflow that the pipes would not fit inside the wings! As there were only small gyroscopic effects, Camm was hopeful that complex triply-redundant three-axis autostabilization would not be needed. Hugh Conway, former managing director of Shorts and well up in the SC.1 autostab problems, later became managing director of Bristol Siddeley Engines. He gave a long briefing to Camm on what had to be done. After he had gone, the Hawker boss said "We are only ignorant buggers here at Kingston, and don't understand all that science. We'll leave the P.1127 simple, and let its pilots fly it".

The company-funded P.1127

The last major changes to the P.1127 were to adopt bicycle landing gear, with the wingtip outriggers made shorter by sharply sloping the wings down to 12° anhedral, the wing being placed above the fuselage so that it could be removed in order to change the engine. By mid-1958 Hawker Aircraft were busy testing models to investigate the novel airflows with sucking at the inlets and blowing at the four nozzles angled in various directions. In June 1958 the Ministry of Supply permitted tests to be done in government tunnels, and later extensive research was done at NASA in the United States, largely because the P.1127 was such an interesting aircraft. In March 1959 the Hawker Siddeley board boldly decided to fund two P.1127 prototypes, and work on these went ahead at high speed. By this time both the RAF and RN were daring once again to consider manned aircraft, including VTOL. Unfortunately, at the same time, Rolls-Royce, pushing its multiple lift-jet concept, announced collaboration with Dassault of France on a VTOL Mirage.

This seriously damaged the prospects of the P.1127. Having no home market, it was dependent on NATO, whose offices were already funding three-quarters of the vital engine. But the French made it clear they would have nothing to do with a British project, especially in view of Dassault's programme. To cut an extremely long and involved story short, while by April 1959 the RAF was at last openly thinking about a Hunter-replacement in the class of the P.1127, NATO had begun to plan a more ambitious scheme for a VTOL supersonic aircraft to meet NBMR-3 (NATO Basic Military Requirement 3). The latter resulted in a plethora of submissions from companies throughout the NATO aircraft industries, most of them as international collaborative projects. Hawker proposed a grossly stretched supersonic P.1127, the P.1150, powered by an uprated Pegasus with PCB.

NATO upgraded the NBMR-3 specification in its final form in March 1961, and the resulting Hawker submission was the P.1154 powered by the completely new Bristol Siddeley BS.100 engine of 33,000lb (14970kg) thrust. In April 1962 the P.1154 was declared the "technical winner" of the competition, but to appease France the rival Mirage IIIV was said to be "of equal merit". Moreover France predictably said it would never

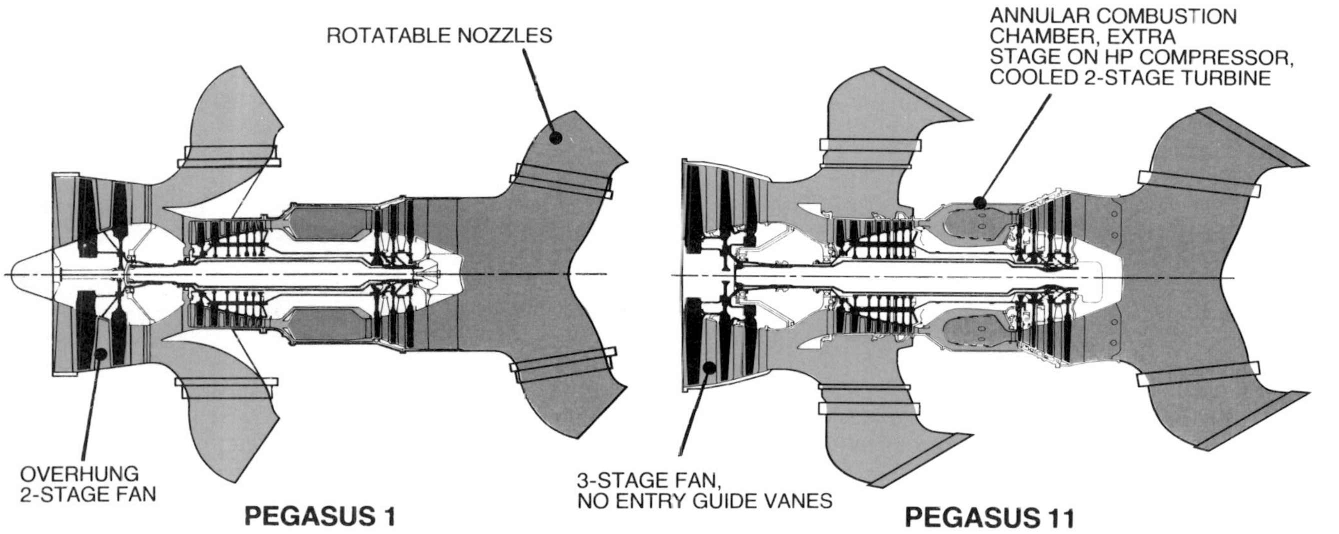

Evolution of the Pegasus

Simplified drawings showing how the first Wibault-derived scheme devised at Bristol, the BE.48, evolved over a decade into today's Harrier engine. The first two drawings, the BE.48 and 52/53, are slightly falsified in that the two inlets to the gas generator were actually at the top and bottom of the engine, while the front nozzles were on the sides. The significance of the colours is that magenta shows the hot portions of each engine, and blue the cooler elements. In today's Pegasus 11 the front nozzles discharge 110°C jets at 1,200ft/s (366m/s) and the rear 670°C jets at 1,800ft/s (549m/s).

accept any candidate but the Mirage IIIV, which it would continue to develop. This caused the whole NATO house of cards to collapse, and eventually the IIIV along with it, but it left both the RAF and RN looking for aircraft in the class of the P.1154. Eventually versions of the big supersonic Hawker aircraft were developed for both customers, but the RN did all it could to damage the programme by insisting on the maximum number of differences. Eventually the RN pulled out in February 1964, buying long-takeoff Phantoms (which it soon lost as the result of the 1965 decision to phase out British carriers). The RAF P.1154 was simply cancelled by the government in February 1965. The reasons were purely political, but, to explain the decision to the public, Prime Minister Wilson said that the P.1154 "will not be in service in time to serve as a Hunter replacement".

Below: The only serious rival to Hawker's V/STOL programme in the early 1960s was Dassault of France, which followed the Rolls-Royce formula (also supported by the British official establishment) in having a battery of separate lift engines. This was the first nine-engined Balzac.

More Phantoms were bought, which in fact cost more than the predicted P.1154 price and were available no sooner (and of course Hunters are still serving today in many air forces).

At the time, the cancellation of the P.1154 appeared a mistake of great magnitude, and certainly the decisions by the RN and the British government were taken for erroneous and very short-sighted reasons. Looking on the bright side, the British services were left with a nucleus of officers who understood a little about V/STOL, and industry was left with a wealth of experience. In any case, while the big supersonic V/STOLs were all the rage, the original Pegasus-powered subsonic programme had made great progress, though without any obvious eventual production application.

Bristol Siddeley Engines ran the first Pegasus 1 at Patchway in September 1959. Rated at 9,000lb (4082kg), this used LP bleed air for aircraft control and was for ground running only. The Pegasus 2 ran in February 1960, and at first all that Bristol could promise Kingston was 10,000 lb (4536kg). Hawker experimental pilot Hugh Merewether had been invited by NASA to fly the Bell X-14

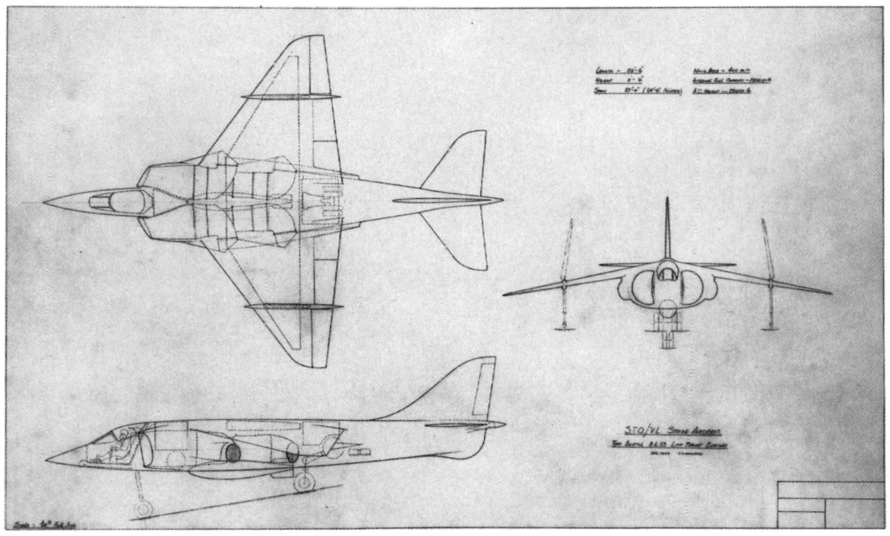

Above: Not previously illustrated, the Hawker P.1132 was an amazingly advanced aircraft for August 1958. It would have had two BE.53 engines, handed left and right to discharge on the outboard side of the engine only. Even at 1958 thrust ratings these would have allowed a gross weight of 29,000lb, the same as today's Harrier II, as well as transonic speed. This "STO/VL" was not built.

Below: Dated 30 September 1961, this drawing shows the P.1150/3 which was planned to meet the NATO NBMR-3 competition.

Bottom: The initial form of P.1154, which succeeded the P.1150/3 in the NBMR-3 contest. Later this impressive machine was further developed for the RAF, only to be cancelled in 1965.

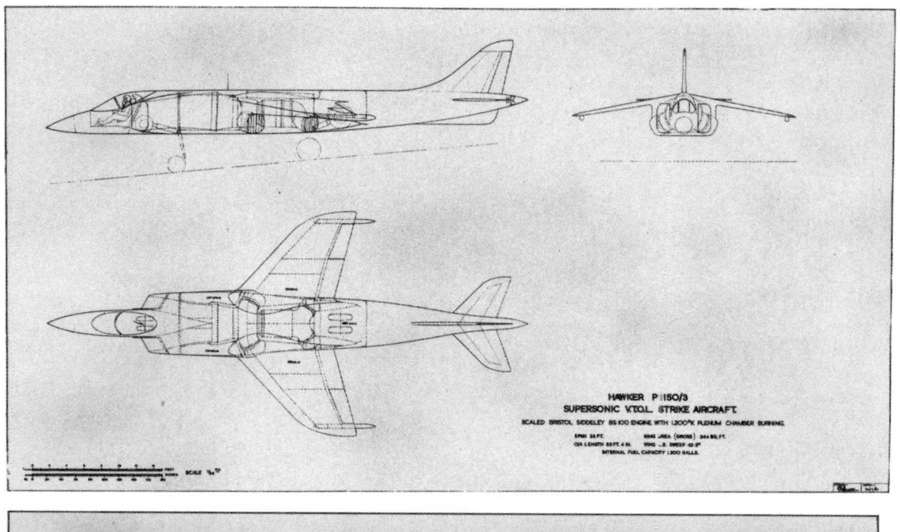

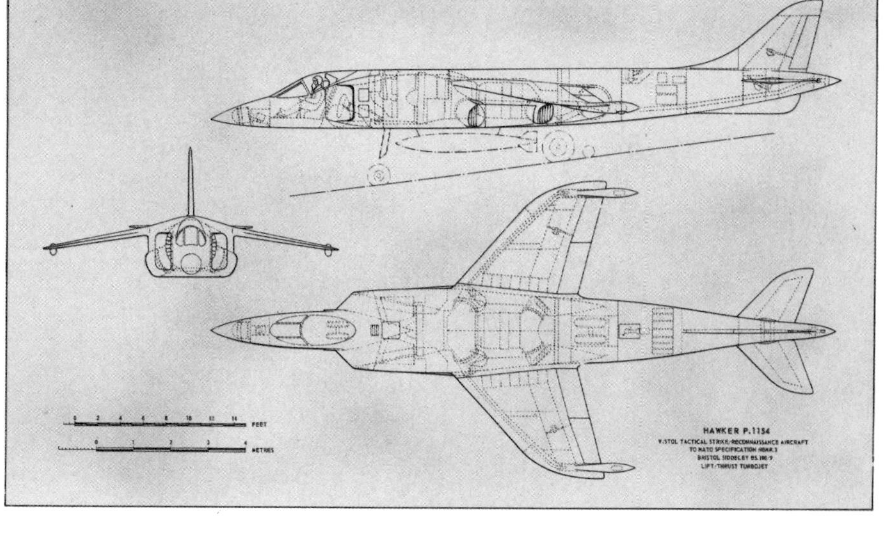

with vectored jets, and in making a vertical landing (VL) he ran out of roll power, even though both jets were at high power, and damaged the aircraft. Extra RCV power seemed a good idea for the P.1127, but it would mean even less thrust for lift, and Hawker's estimate of the first P.1127's empty weight was about the same as the promised engine thrust. Fortunately another 1,000lb (454kg) was then forthcoming from the installed engine, and in August 1960 it was cleared at 11,000lb (4990kg) for 30 min of VTOL or 20 hours of conventional flight.

By this time the two P.1127s were visible at Kingston, and to avoid embarrassment at having them emerge with no serial number the Ministry had at last coughed up some money in June 1960 and drafted a contract, both aircraft meeting experimental requirement ER.204D which was written around them. Serial numbers XP831 and 836 were allocated. Meanwhile, because the excess thrust for lift was so small, it was recognised that recirculation of hot efflux gas back into the engine inlets had to be avoided, so Hawker's airfield at Dunsfold was fitted with a special grid designed to channel gas well away from the aircraft. Hooker suggested to Camm that perhaps the first flight should be in the conventional (runway) mode, to check handling qualities. Camm snapped back "All Hawker aircraft have perfect handling qualities, the first flight will be a VTO"!

Testing begins

Ground running of XP831 began on 31 August 1960. Large bell-mouth inlets were fitted for these initial trials, and the aircraft carried the minimum of removable equipment. For hovering, in October, it was positioned over the grid with loose tethers to heavy weights. Even the wheel doors were removed, and the radio replaced by an intercom link. Chief test pilot A. W. "Bill" Bedford may even have wondered if the weight of plaster on his broken leg (gained as a car passenger in Switzerland) would prove the last straw, but on 21 October 1960 he got daylight under the wheels of the small prototype that was to lead to a new era in aviation.

There were problems, but also solutions. At rest the aircraft naturally tipped over on to one outrigger; always, on the next liftoff, there was inadequate RCV power with the Pegasus 2 to bring the wings level, so the aircraft would skid sideways across the grid and slew around in yaw. Again, inadequate RCV power made it impossible, even with full rudder, to stop the aircraft pirouetting tail-on to any wind, because of the powerful momentum drag in the inlets. And the tethers themselves caused great difficulty, so that Merewether said his task was "like trying to learn to ride a bike by riding down a narrow corridor".

On 19 November 1960 the hated tethers came off, and Bedford said it was "like freeing a bird from a cage". Free hovering proved most successful, and with progressive increases in engine thrust the missing removable items were replaced. A further improvement in RCV control came when, instead of having a swivelling rear pitch jet, the tail installation comprised separate pitch and yaw RCVs. But when high-speed taxi tests began it was found that the main gear hung lower than the outriggers, giving undue freedom in roll; poor nosewheel steering was combined with severe shimmy of the freely castoring outriggers, and the latter began leaving wavy lines of black molten rubber across the Dunsfold runway.

These problems were fixed by locking the outriggers and increasing their extension so that both touched the ground together. XP831 was sent to the RAE at Bedford, and after further high-speed runs Bill Bedford made the first conventional flight on 13 March 1961, far out-accelerating the chase Hunter. On 7 July 1961 the second aircraft opened its flight programme in the conventional mode from Dunsfold, and soon demonstrated speeds of well over 500 knots (576mph, 927km/h) at low level. By December 1961 this machine had gone on to pull 6g in sustained turns, reach over 40,000ft (12·2km) and achieve Mach 1·2 in a shallow dive. Then, because of a

Left: The first photograph of the first prototype P.1127, taken outside the Dunsfold hangar in August 1960 before the serial XP831 had been painted on. Later doors and other items were taken off to save weight

Below: Hawker Siddeley paid for this fully equipped ground-running pen long before there was any suggestion of Ministry funding. The picture was taken as the 2,000lb/sq in air bottles were starting the engine.

fault in the construction of the moulding, the glassfibre left front engine nozzle came off in the air. Bedford tried to land at RNAS Yeovilton, but when he lowered the flaps he entered a roll which could not be arrested, and he had to eject. A few days later a farmer arrived at Yeovilton with the missing nozzle, and though this facilitated diagnosis it took years before really satisfactory front nozzles were achieved. Eventually, though they do not really "need" such material, they were made of steel like the hot rear nozzles.

On the whole, flight development of the first two examples of this radical aircraft had been remarkably smooth, and there had been no need for any significant alteration to the aircraft or engine. This early phase was completed on 12 September 1961 by the achievement of complete transitions. Aircraft XP381 was either lifted off in VTO, accelerated forwards to high speed and then brought back to a VL, or taken off in the conventional mode, slowed in the air to the hover and then accelerated again for a rolling landing. In October 1961 operations were made from grass and other rough surfaces, and an especially important development was the start of STO trials, the nozzles being vectored down to 50° or 55° after a quick acceleration to about 60 knots.

In November 1960 the Ministry had funded four further P.1127s, actually calling these "development aircraft" as if they might be for something more than pure research. Soon there were plenty of detail differences as these came into use and, along with XP831, were progressively modified. Among the new features were a kinked wing leading edge giving increased chord at the tips, a row of upper-surface vortex generators to prevent wing drop at high Mach numbers, improved outrigger gears without pointed-nose fairings, Küchemann streamwise wingtips, modified tailplanes with greater area and 18° anhedral, improved RCV fairings and, for a time, inflatable rubber inlet lips that could be puffed up to a large radius for hovering and deflated to give a sharp lip for high-speed flight. Variable-radius inlets are needed for all jet V/STOLs, but a good scheme has never been devised. Rubber simply failed to stand up to high-speed flight.

Design improvements

Back in 1959 attitudes in the RAF and the Ministry had been changing. The TSR.2 project was well under way, and the Air Staff felt they could test the situation by writing a requirement for General Operational Requirement 345 for the simple Hunter replacement, which might well be a V/STOL. Though many officers scorned the P.1127 for its puny capability and lack of Mach 2 speed, some saw the possibility of future development. This obviously hinged upon what Hooker's team could do at Bristol, and they were already busy fitting the HP turbine with aircooled blades. This enabled gas temperature to jump from 977°C to 1,177°C, giving higher thrust. When combined with a new three-stage fan without inlet guide vanes, an annular combustor and other improvements, the result was the Pegasus 5, which soon gave 15,500lb (7030kg).

This at last enabled Hawker to design an improved P.1127 able to carry a little warload as well as fuel, but it is very doubtful that anything more would have happened – apart from the NATO fixation on much heavier supersonic V/STOLs – had not the United States come to the rescue a second time. Larry Levy, a wealthy American, had joined MWDP in Paris and had the vision to see that what was wanted was for NATO actually to get some service experience in, to see how jet V/STOLs could be operated in the field. He had the political clout to persuade the American, British and Federal German governments to fund a Tripartite Evaluation Squadron. Originally each nation was to put up the money and pilots for six aircraft, but – against German advice – this was cut to three on British pressure for economy. By early 1962 the RAF had given up GOR.345, and with it any hope of using a simple Pegasus-engined aircraft, deciding instead to go all out for Mach 2 with the P.1154. Despite this, the TES survived, because other nations were involved, and the aircraft were ordered by the newly created British Ministry of Aviation (formerly Ministry of Supply) on 21 May 1962.

The improved aircraft were called Kestrels. Powered by the Pegasus 5, they featured a new swept wing, with a thicker centre section causing a hump in the fuselage, which had first flown on XP984, the final P.1127. In its ultimate form this wing had small dogtooth discontinuities and extended-chord outer sections. A better relationship between the nozzles, wing and aircraft CG was obtained by splicing in extra fuselage sections above the front nozzles and below the rear nozzles (in effect moving the wing aft, as well as lengthening the

Right: Taken in 1964, this photograph shows the fifth P.1127 after it had received streamwise wingtips, inflatable inlet lips, eleven vortex generators on each wing, and the odd kinked-anhedral tailplane.

Flying controls

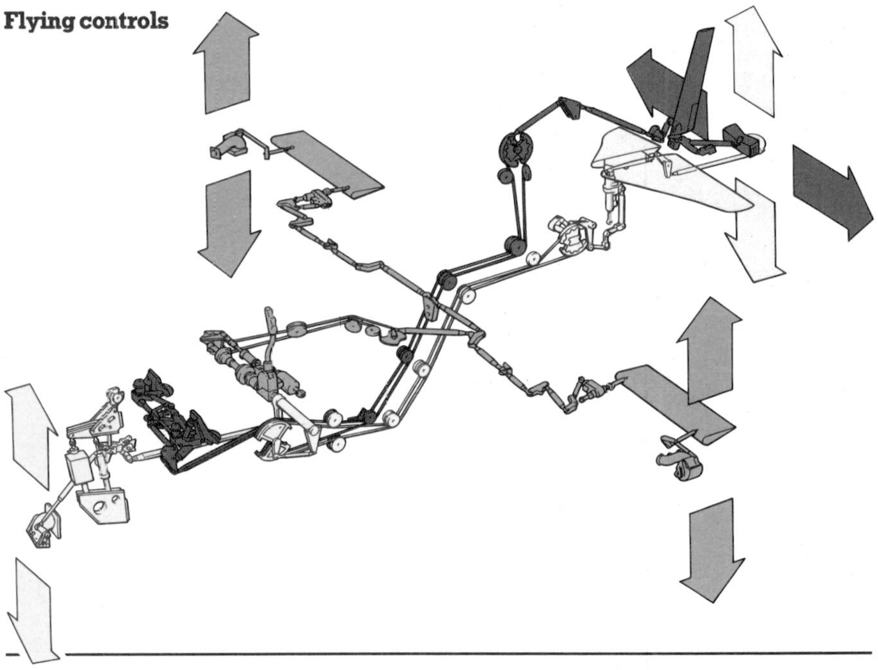

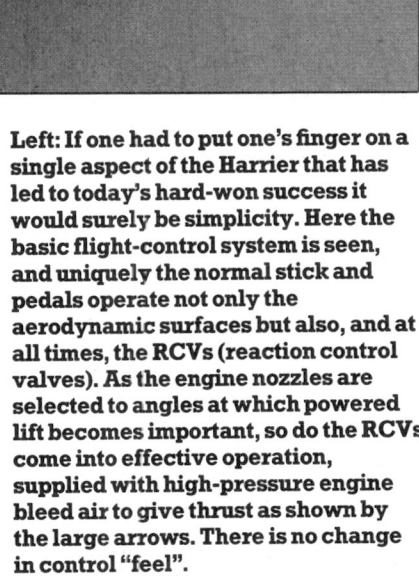

Left: If one had to put one's finger on a single aspect of the Harrier that has led to today's hard-won success it would surely be simplicity. Here the basic flight-control system is seen, and uniquely the normal stick and pedals operate not only the aerodynamic surfaces but also, and at all times, the RCVs (reaction control valves). As the engine nozzles are selected to angles at which powered lift becomes important, so do the RCVs come into effective operation, supplied with high-pressure engine bleed air to give thrust as shown by the large arrows. There is no change in control "feel".

Below: Not many photographs were taken of XP836, the second P.1127. This was chiefly because the glassfibre left front engine nozzle, clearly seen here, was made with an inherent structural weakness which led to nozzle separation in late 1961.

fuselage) and giving a sharper bifurcation to the jetpipe to move the hot nozzles forwards. By this time the hot nozzle fairings were all of the rectangular "spade" type instead of the "pen nib" type originally used, the flaps were extended in to the wing root, and toe-operated wheel brakes were standard. The Kestrels also had main-gear doors stressed for use as airbrakes, ventral strakes, taller fins, and eventually all had a substantially larger tailplane with a 16° anhedral and a kinked leading edge.

XS688, the first Kestrel but not quite up to full standard, flew on 7 March 1964. The TES was formed at Dunsfold under Wg Cdr D. McL. Scrimgeour, RAF, on 15 October 1964, and from April 1965 operated at RAF West Raynham and various unprepared dispersed sites in the neighbourhood. Its pilots were drawn from the RAF, Luftwaffe, USAF, USN and US Army. Two came from the latter service, though it had no hope of operating high-speed jets, whereas the Marines were not included despite their intense interest. The Kestrels had the pitot head on the fin, as in late P.1127s, and instead of a long nose probe a forward oblique camera was fitted. Under each wing was a pylon intended to carry a wide variety of stores, but these hardly ever carried anything during TES flying except 100gal (455lit) drop tanks, though on other occasions Kestrels dropped practice bombs.

Altogether 938 sorties were flown by the TES prior to disbandment in November 1965, roughly 24 missions per aircraft per month, with a total of some 600 hours. Takeoffs were made from concrete, tarmac, grass, compacted soil, various plastics and rubber sheets, aluminium sheet, glassfibre sheet, a portable pad constructed from interlocking aluminium planks, and plenty of surfaces covered with wartime PSP (pierced steel planking). Except for a US pilot who tried a rolling takeoff with the parking brake on, there was no serious incident, and the general opinion was extremely favourable. One of the most important benefits was that the TES got used to operating without a fixed airfield with centrally heated brick-built accommodation, which air forces had taken for granted since 1945.

Above: One of the first air-to-air pictures of the first Kestrel, taken in March 1964 with Dunsfold's Hunter T.7 two-seat chase aircraft in attendance. Rubber lips were fitted.

Below: Another view of the first Kestrel. This was still an immature combat aircraft, but apart from the engine designers, few knew what might later be derived from it.

Following TES use, six Kestrels went to the USA. By this time the USAF had decided it preferred airfields to V/STOL and chose to regard them as quaint foreign devices, despite their new US joint-service designation of XV-6A; according to *Aviation Week* it was "trying to think what to do with them". NASA, on the other hand, used XV-6As both at Dryden and at Langley for serious research, and found them valuable tools limited only by the 50-hour overhaul life on each engine.

This limited life was constantly being improved at Bristol, where, even if no funding had been forthcoming, Hooker's team would have kept on cranking in improvements. By early 1964, when no Kestrel had flown and all attention was focussed on the BS.100 engine for the P.1154, Bristol Siddeley was well advanced with a greatly improved Pegasus, the Mk 6, which first ran a year later. Its titanium fan handled substantially greater airflow, the combustion system was further improved with vaporizing burners and water-injection for short periods at enhanced power, both HP turbine stages were aircooled, two-vane hot nozzles were fitted, the fuel system was again revised and a life recorder was added. Despite its greatly increased thrust of 19,000 lb (8618kg), the Pegasus 6 was lifed at 300 hours.

The P.1127 (RAF)

This outstanding performance by the engine company, which had already more than doubled the thrust of the Pegasus with more yet to come, at last made it obvious that a Kestrel successor could fly useful combat missions. Though there continued to be factions within the

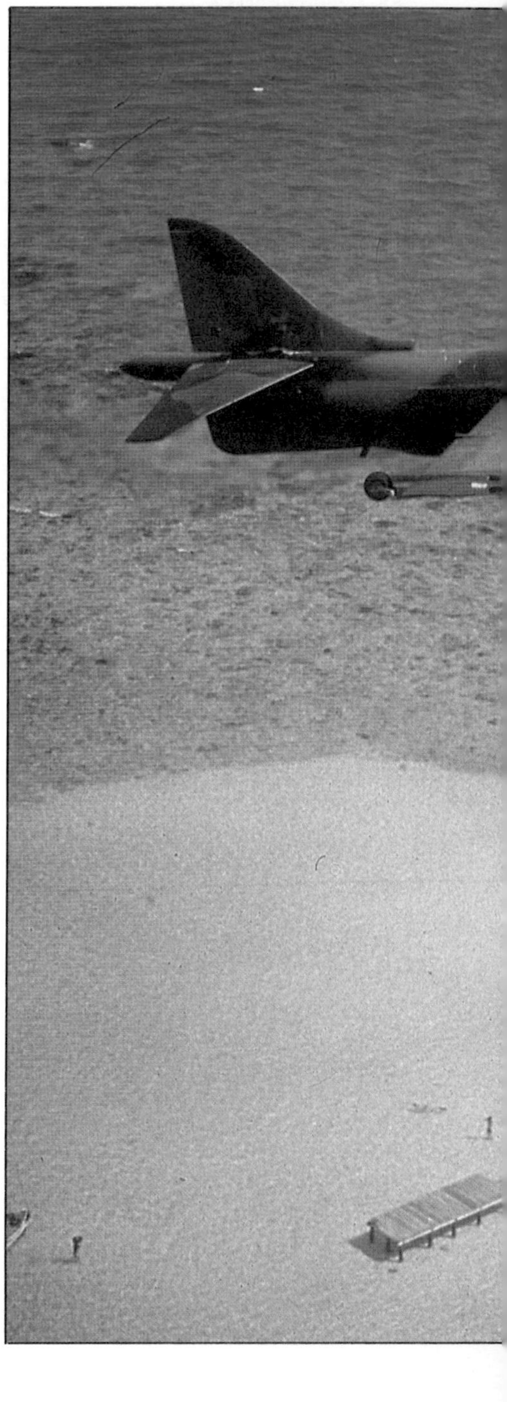

Left: Large grab-holds near the front nozzles identify this as an XV-6A, a Kestrel in the USA (actually aboard CV-62 USS *Independence*), seen in May 1966 during carefully measured carrier suitability evaluations.

RAF that scorned any Pegasus-powered subsonic aircraft, those who took the trouble to examine the possibilities came up with surprising results. Thanks to its economical engine even the Kestrel had demonstrated mission radius and endurance as good as the best Hunter, and with the Pegasus 6 it was possible to combine this with a warload considerably greater than the Hunter could carry. In any case, V/STOL capability means that aircraft could be dispersed into front-line bases not only untargetable by missiles but also close to the enemy, thus enabling weapons to be carried in place of external fuel. It is fortunate that the CAS (Chief of the Air Staff), Sir Thomas Pike, took pains in 1962-3 to keep the Pegasus aircraft alive in parallel with the big BS.100-powered machines, and in 1963-5 his successor, Sir Charles Elworthy, did likewise.

When the Labour government took office in October 1964 it had campaigned partly on the fact that it would do away with British military aircraft. It informed the Air Staff that two of the three main programmes would be cancelled (later the third went, also). One of the first casualties was the P.1154. The Air Staff had seen this coming and began writing a new requirement, ASR.384, for a simple replacement for the Hunter in the tactical attack and reconnaissance roles, derived from the P.1127. The aircraft itself became known as the P.1127(RAF), but eventully was named Harrier, a name previously picked for the P.1154 and, back in 1927, for a Hawker bomber powered by an earlier Bristol engine, the Jupiter.

In a nutshell the proposal was that Hawker should produce an improved Kestrel powered by the Pegasus 6, and pack into it whatever avionic items from the P.1154 might fit. Even this fall-back proposition was only won with difficulty. Prime Minister Wilson, still professing to hate British planemakers, refused to sanction any suggestion of a possible production programme. The best deal the RAF could get was that the Ministry, which had just been renamed the Ministry of Technology (Mintech), would fund a small development batch. Then a decision would be taken on whether the P.1127(RAF) was worth putting into service.

Mintech came through with an order for six development aircraft, XV276-281, only two weeks later, on 19 February 1965. By this time Sir Sydney Camm had been Chief Designer for 40 years, and he had handed over the reins to John Fozard as Chief Designer P.1127(RAF). In 1966 Camm passed peacefully away on his local golf course, so like Mitchell with the Spitfire he never saw his last creation get into production But for "Foz" and his design team it was a time of hectic action. Compared with the P.1154 the P.1127(RAF) was supposed to be easy, but it was not possible just to put the new engine and combat equipment into a Kestrel. Many parts of the airframe had to be redesigned, and it all had to be done in a very short time indeed, because first flight date had been fixed for 31 August 1966.

Left: The first military unit to fly the Harrier was No 1(F) squadron, RAF, which converted during 1969. This photograph shows a 1 Sqn GR.1 over the disputed territory of Belize, which this handful of aircraft have protected for over ten years.

The Harrier

When the "P.1127(RAF)" was at last allowed to be produced, after cancellation of the much more powerful P.1154(RAF), it bore the stigma of appearing superficially to be a second-best alternative. Because it was small and subsonic, many of the Air Staff still doubted that it would be of much real value, a belief heartily echoed by the USAF which by this time (1965) had ceased to show much interest in V/STOL because it could not see beyond supposed percentage penalties. It needed real dedication for the Hawker engineers to produce the Harrier right first time, and to a very challenging timescale.

Above: Completion of a NATO exercise in Norway, in temporary winter camouflage, highlights the way RAF Harriers have operated around the clock for 15 years.

While the P.1154 lived, nobody in the RAF was particularly interested in the smaller V/STOLs powered by the Pegasus. After the issue of ASR.384 and the contract for a development batch (DB) of six aircraft, the simplistic belief of many in high places was that the P.1127(RAF) already existed in the Kestrel; all that was needed was to install the Pegasus 6 engine and the extra equipment items that its power made possible. The team at Kingston knew better, but even they did not immediately realize that they would have virtually to start again with a different airframe. In fact, the redesign changed well over 90 per cent of the drawings.

Airframe

For reasons already emphasized, the P.1127s and Kestrels had been made as light and simple as possible, but the P.1127(RAF) had to meet full service requirements. The structure had to be stressed to higher factors, the symmetric limit being 7·8g at maximum weight. The weights were all going to be considerably increased, yet the landing gear had to be stressed for more severe landings, with rates of descent to 12ft/s (about 3·66m/s). The entire airframe had to be designed for a safe life of 3,000 flight hours, to a most severe mission load spectrum, virtually all at very high speed at the lowest possible level, which meant demonstrating 15,000 hours on a specimen. Low-level jets suffer severely from the birdstrike problem, and though this mainly affected the inlet and engine it also meant the windscreen had to withstand the nominal 1lb (0·45kg) bird at 600 knots (1111km/h).

The wing managed to retain the original main structural box, which comprises two triangular boxes joined on the aircraft centreline. Upper and lower skins are machined from heavy plate to provide integral stiffening, and the inboard portion of the box on each side forms a sealed integral fuel tank, each of 172·5gal (784lit) capacity. The wing is tiny, because it was originally designed for high-speed flight, and low-level attack aircraft need the smallest possible wing in order to have minimum gust response, and thus give the pilot an acceptably smooth ride in rough air even at full throttle. Despite this small size, the extra lift of the wing on short rolling takeoffs is important in enabling more fuel or weapons to be carried, and later still the RAF took a leaf from the book of the US Marine Corps and studied the Harrier as an air-combat fighter, where a larger wing would show to advantage.

In any case, the wing differs greatly from that of the Kestrel. The section profile did not alter, remaining an NPL (National Physical Laboratory) "peaky" section with a generous nose radius, with thickness/chord ratio varying from 10 per cent at the root to 5 per cent at the tip. The leading edge was again redesigned, with extended chord outboard

Below: G-VSTO was a production Harrier GR.1, XV742, which in 1971 was painted in glossy epoxy camouflage and civil registration, with HSA logo on the fin. It was used as a demonstration aircraft pending completion of the company's own G-VTOL.

Below: A Harrier GR.1 of RAF No 20 Sqn, shown with gun pods attached but otherwise in the clean configuration. Subsequently the appearance was markedly altered by the addition of the LRMTS on the nose and the RWR installation at the tail. No 20 Sqn later re-equipped with Jaguars.

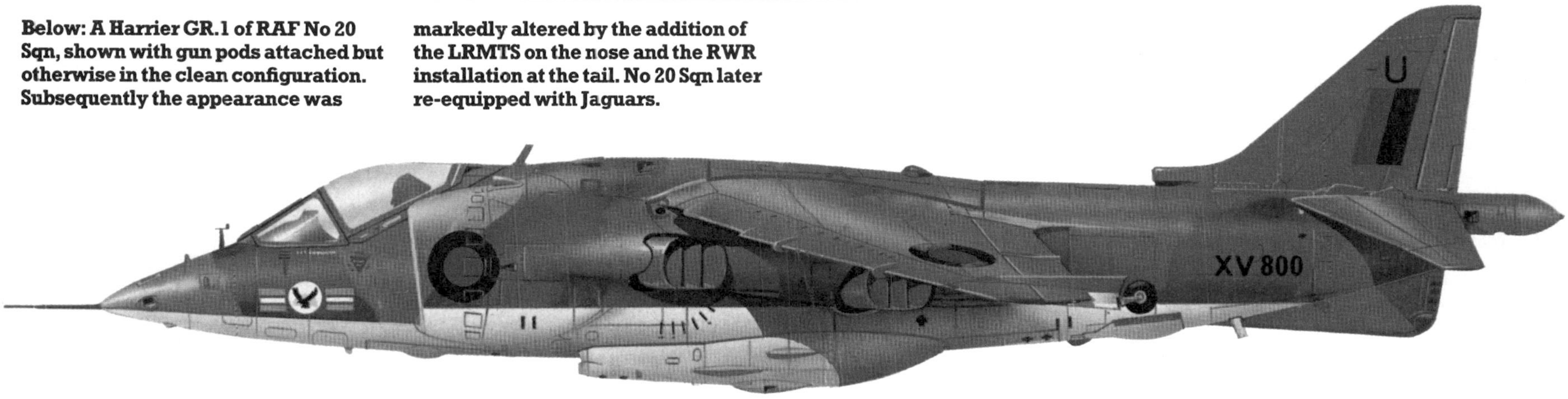

Left: Taken in 1963, this picture shows the first Kestrel being built (the same aircraft is shown airborne on p.10). The integral-tank wing sits on the fuselage above the engine.

Below: Slinging test at Dunsfold to demonstrate compliance with the requirement to hoist the aircraft with maximum fuel, weapon load, and pilot in the cockpit. If dropped from this height, the landing gear would absorb the energy.

and initially a double kink leading to the inboard section; later this was replaced by a single dogtooth some way inboard of the inner small fence. Vortex generators were also needed. The Kestrel had finally had ten on each wing, but the Harrier began with four and ended with a row of 12.

More significant was the need to preserve longitudinal stability with full external stores, because this was before the CCV (control-configured vehicle) technology had matured sufficiently for an unstable fighter to be attempted. The specified stores loading was two pylons under each wing, rated at 1,200lb (544kg) inboard and 630lb (286kg) outboard. To retain adequate CG margins it was necessary to move the aerodynamic centre of the wing to the rear, and the obvious way to do this was to add area outboard. In fact, two tips were designed, both added immediately outboard of the outrigger gears. The normal tip can be unbolted and replaced by a larger tip giving extra span for improved cruising efficiency, and thus greater range for ferrying.

As before, the ailerons and plain flaps are of bonded aluminium honeycomb construction, both being hydraulically driven and the ailerons being positioned by Fairey powered flight-control units. Previously Fairey and Dowty had alternated for the contracts for the P.1127, Kestrel and P.1154. Despite Camm's dislike of clever devices, autostabilization was provided, but in a simple form with limited authority on pitch and roll only, without duplication. A light bobweight was added, and later the yaw axis was also brought in, but flight with autostab switched off is no problem. Hovering in gusty conditions is easier than with a helicopter, because the mean density of the Harrier exceeds 25lb/cu ft (400kg/m^3) and it needs little pilot input.

In solving the thorny problems of longitudinal control it was found that, aerodynamically, the final Kestrel tailplane shape could do the job, though with increased trim range. Structurally, it was back to the drawing board, because even with the Pegasus 5 the Kestrel tailplane had vibrated frighteningly during ground running, with jets aft, becoming a blur with 6in amplitude at a frequency of about 13Hz! To permit running with engine nozzles aft, the TES had had to anchor the tailplanes to the ground to meet the stipulated life of 1,000h. With the Harrier the required life was trebled, and engine power greatly increased, yet the final tailplane came out weighing 211lb (95·7kg), only 32lb (14·5kg) more than before. One of the many remarkable successes of Harrier flight development was to clear the aircraft with all combinations of external stores with impeccable handling up to AOA (angle of attack) exceeding 20°, despite the destabilizing effect of some 30,000 jet horsepower blasting a few inches beneath the tailplane.

Though closely related to that of the Kestrel, the fuselage was completely redesigned, with room for many extra items and stressed to much greater loads. A few items, such as Tacan and the nav/attack computer (avionics are described later), were fitted into the small nose, along with an F.95 oblique camera looking diagonally ahead on the left side. The seat became a Martin-Baker rocket-assisted H.9 or 9D, mounted on the sloping rear pressure bulkhead of the cockpit, which has the modest dP (pressure differential) of 3·5lb/sq in (24kPa). Though a flat front windscreen was required, for good view directly ahead, rear and aft vision were compromised by retaining a low-mounted seat and a canopy level with the top of the fuselage. There is a small rear-view mirror, but the view is limited both by the fuselage itself and the large inlets on each side. The canopy, opened manually along sloping tracks, contains MDC (miniature detonating cord) to shatter the acrylic moulding a split second prior to ejection.

The centre fuselage was restressed to carry two gun pods, as alternatives to belly strakes which, first used on the Kestrel, help to increase pressure on the undersurface in low-altitude hovering. In addition there is a centreline hardpoint for stores of up to 1,000lb (454kg). Two fuselage bulkheads, Nos 9 and 11, are stressed above the left inlet for a large oblique inflight-refuelling probe, which is attached on the rare occasions when it will be needed. Fuel is carried in five modest tanks, all integral with the structure: 51·5gal (234lit) each side aft of the inlets, 39gal (177lit) each side between the nozzles and 104gal (473lit) above the main-gear bay immediately behind the wing. Under the wing, immediately behind the engine, is the titanium drum containing 50gal (227lit) of demineralised water for injection into the engine combustor to restore thrust during VTOL operations on a hot day.

The rear fuselage was redesigned to house the main avionics bay and lox (liquid oxygen) container, with the associated air-conditioning bay immediately to the rear, served by a ram inlet in the base of the fin. The cockpit air-conditioning was located immediately behind the seat, in the space between the inlet ducts, with two projecting ram inlets in the dorsal surface and the system exhaust ejecting into the inner faces of the two inlet ducts.

Like other areas the inlets were again redesigned. Not only did the Pegasus 6 need a greater airflow, but this time there had to be a definitive inlet able to give acceptable efficiency at all speeds from flying tail-first up to over Mach 1, while at the same time withstanding severe birdstrikes on the inlet lip and on the curving wall which forms the inner skin of the forward tanks. By this time it was evident that the problems of any flexible variable-radius lip were not going to be solved quickly, if ever, so as well as reshaping the duct itself the problem of variable geometry focussed attention on metal mechanical systems. The final answer was a very short, sharply curved duct with a strong lip having the same peaky aerodynamic profile as the front of the wing, and provided with six suck-in auxiliary doors around the outside of each duct, mating with six more doors on the inner wall. The boundary-layer bleed slit on the inner wall, first used on the Kestrel, was enlarged and reprofiled to reduce drag and airflow distortion.

Unfortunately, no way could immediately be found to avoid distortion of the inlet airflow caused by the six auxiliary doors, which while admitting a large extra airflow caused cross-stream flow and turbulence and reduced pressure recovery. Further distortion was inevitably caused by the stream of hot air on the inner wall from the cockpit air-conditioning heat exchanger. While five of the six DB (development batch) aircraft had the inlet as described, a better configuration was eventually finalized after the DB drawings had been committed to manufacture. Thus, the production Harrier has a superior inlet system, outwardly distinguished by having eight large doors forming an almost continuous auxiliary-inlet ring. After flight development this system was made to behave almost perfectly over a range of inlet airflow angles and engine throttle rates equalled by very few other jet aircraft.

The last major development effort concerned the landing gear, which even in the Kestrel had been only passable rather than good. The primary objective of much greater energy absorption was met chiefly by increasing oleo stroke, without significantly increasing the loads to be absorbed at the attachments. Weak and spongy nosewheel steering was curable, but problems with excessive freedom in roll remained. In fact in early DB aircraft the heelover angle in turns worsened from 1·5° to 3·5°. The first of the six aircraft just made the due date, 31 August 1966, with a brief hover by Bill Bedford. Later, in fast runway operations, the unsatisfactory lateral stiffness on the ground became obvious, and in 1967 the decision was taken to redesign the main oleo into what was called the self-shortening form. On alighting, the new leg collapsed almost without resistance for the first 7·0in (178mm), by which time the outriggers were firmly on the ground. From that time on the landing gear, and all ground behaviour, has been better than that of most normal aircraft. Bay doors were arranged to close after extension of the gear to keep out foreign matter disturbed by the jets. Tyre pressures are typically 90lb/sq in (620kPa), or slightly higher for two-seat versions; this is fine for off-runway operations, and not much more than a quarter of the figure for the main gears of an F-15.

British Aerospace Harrier GR Mk 3 cutaway

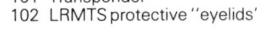

1 Pitot head
2 Laser Ranger and Marked Target Seeker (LRMTS)
3 Windscreen washer reservoir
4 IFF aerial
5 Yaw vane
6 Windscreen wiper
7 Pilot's head-up-display (HUD)
8 Martin-Baker Mk 9D, zero-zero ejection seat
9 Boundary-layer air exhaust ducts
10 Cockpit air-conditioning system
11 Engine oil tank
12 Twin alternators
13 Engine accessory gearbox
14 Auxiliary power unit (APU)
15 Starboard wing pylons
16 Starboard wing integral fuel tank
17 Aileron power unit
18 Starboard navigation light
19 Roll control RCV (reaction control valve)
20 Outrigger wheel fairing
21 Starboard aileron
22 Hydraulic reservoir
23 Plain flap
24 Anti-collision light
25 Water tank
26 Water filler cap
27 Flap jack
28 Rear-fuselage fuel tank
29 Emergency ram-air turbine
30 Turbine release control
31 Equipment bay air-conditioning system
32 HF aerial tuner
33 HF notch aerial
34 Starboard all-moving tailplane
35 Rudder control linkage
36 Total-temperature probe
37 Forward radar warning receiver
38 VHF aerial
39 Rudder
40 Rudder trim tab
41 Yaw control RCV
42 Rear radar warning receiver
43 Pitch control RCV
44 Port all-moving tailplane
45 Tail bumper
46 Tailplane power unit
47 UHF aerial
48 Control system linkages
49 Twin batteries
50 Chaff and flare dispensers
51 Avionics equipment racks
52 Airbrake hydraulic jack
53 Liquid-oxygen converter
54 Hydraulic-system nitrogen pressurising bottle
55 Airbrake
56 Fuel jettison
57 Aileron hydraulic actuator
58 Port aileron
59 Aileron/roll RCV mechanical linkage
60 Hydraulic retraction jack
61 Outrigger wheel leg fairings
62 Port outrigger wheel
63 Roll RCV
64 Port navigation light
65 Bleed air ducting
66 Rocket pack
67 Outboard wing pylon
68 Aileron control linkage
69 Port wing integral fuel tank
70 1,000lb (454kg) GP bomb
71 Rear (hot stream) swivelling exhaust nozzle
72 Inboard wing pylons
73 Mainwheels
74 Pressure refuelling connection
75 Ammunition tank
76 Main undercarriage hydraulic jack
77 Fuselage flank fuel tank
78 30mm Aden cannon
79 Forward (fan air) swivelling exhaust nozzle
80 Engine monitoring and recording equipment
81 Ventral gun pod, port and starboard
82 Hydraulic-system ground connectors
83 Forward fuselage fuel tank
84 Rolls-Royce Pegasus Mk 103 vectoring-thrust turbofan
85 Supplementary air intake doors (free-floating)
86 Nosewheel
87 Landing/taxiing lamp
88 Nosewheel hydraulic jack
89 Hydraulic accumulator
90 Boundary-layer bleed air duct
91 Ejection-seat rocket pack
92 Engine throttle and nozzle control levers
93 Instrument panel
94 Control column
95 Rudder pedals
96 Pitch feel and trim actuators
97 Inertial platform
98 Pitch RCV
99 Camera port
100 Camera
101 Transponder
102 LRMTS protective "eyelids"

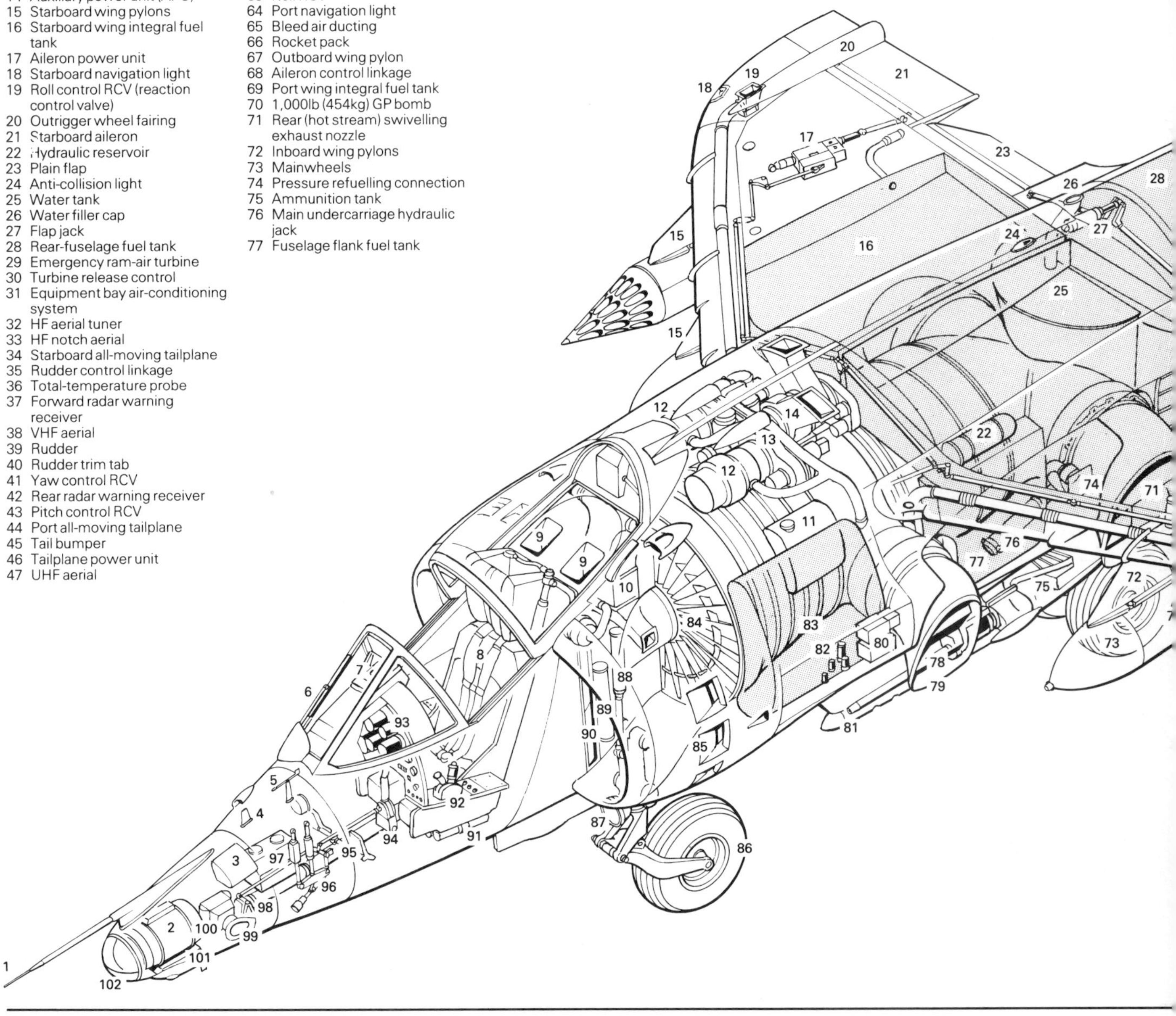

Above: AV-8A Harriers for the US Marine Corps on the line at Kingston in 1971. Because the wing is removed on each engine-change the fuselage and wing were virtually completed before the two came together at the flight-test airfield at Dunsfold, near Cranleigh, Surrey.

Powerplant

In many respects the Pegasus is unique. Conceived by Bristol Aero-Engines, developed by Bristol Siddeley and finally put into production after the takeover by Rolls-Royce, it is not only totally new in conception but it even broke much new ground in its basic design. The first time it was seen by the public it was doctored to resemble a conventional civil turbofan, the BS.58 (though bulges at the sides confirmed the rumours of vectored thrust with lateral nozzles), and even this looked novel with its inlet face completely devoid of any struts or inlet guide vanes (IGVs). Instead the front face of the engine comprised the first stage of the

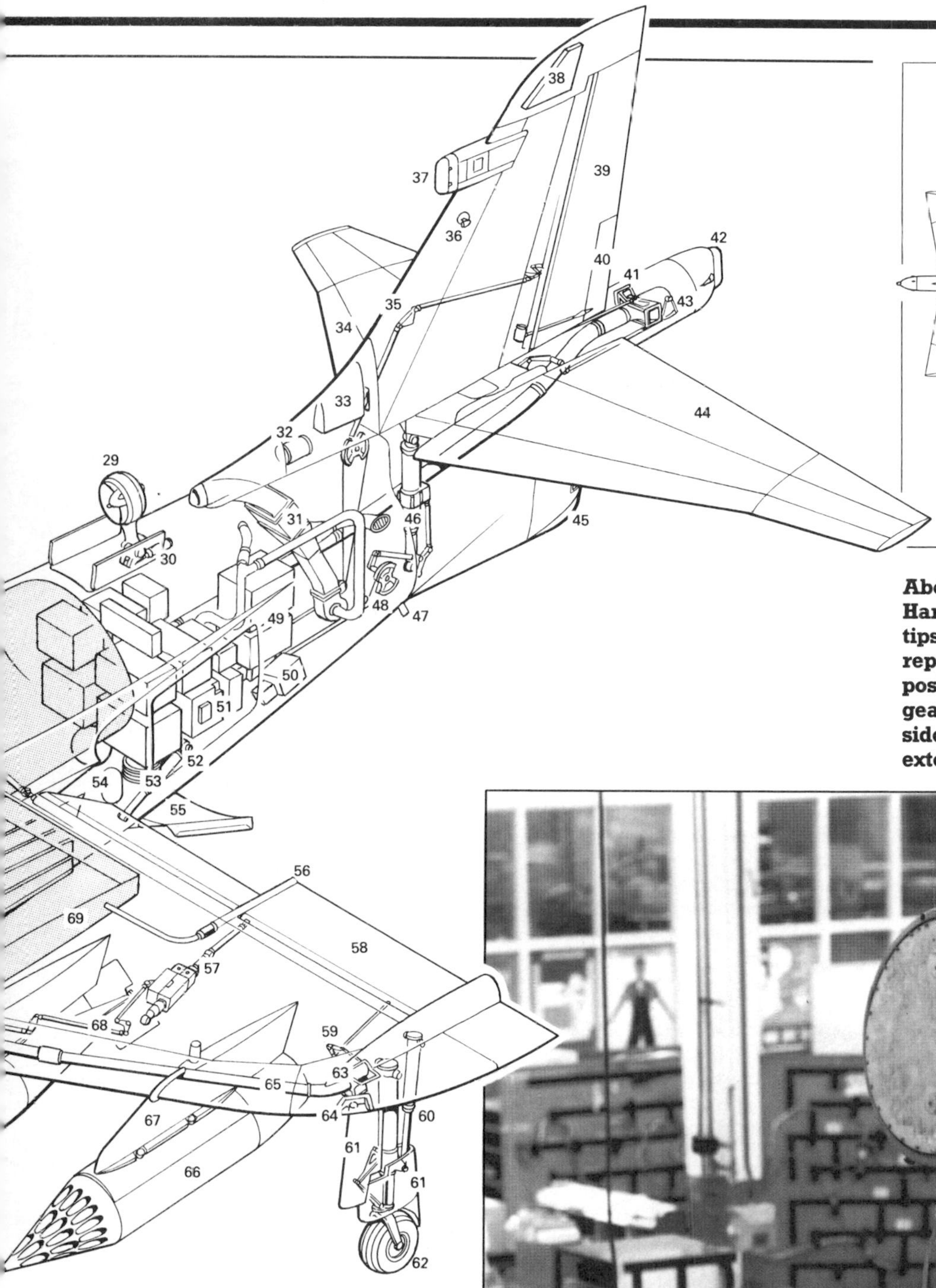

Above: Disposition of operational equipment in the Harrier GR.3, with shading showing the location of internal fuel. It is not yet possible to publish a similar illustration showing the Zeus active ECM system which is due in the late 1980s.

fan itself, though today most turbofans are built this way.

Dr Hooker's team were able to do away with IGVs because of the onward march of gas-turbine aerodynamics. IGVs had been needed in earlier engines to swirl the incoming air in the direction of rotation of the moving blades downstream, in order that the Mach number of the flow past the outer parts of the blades should always be well below 1. The development of thin, sharp-edged blades of so-called lenticular form enabled Mach number at the tips to go well into the supersonic region, up to about 1·5. Once the flow was supersonic, there was no point in having IGVs. Their omission saved engine length, weight and cost, improved resistance to bird-strikes and made it possible to eliminate all inlet anti-icing systems.

A further innovation, bold at the time but today commonplace, was to make the entire fan overhung, in other words to cantilever it ahead of the front bearing. The fan's light weight, large diameter and enormous airflow made vibration a problem, and there was bound to be severe vibration because of the extremely short inlet ducts, which in turn stemmed from the fact the engine had to be centred around the aircraft CG. The

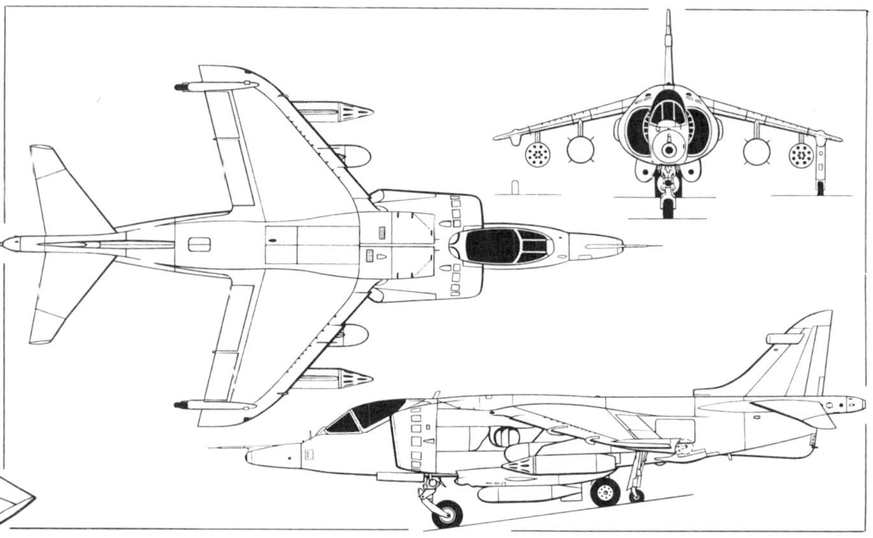

Above: Three-view of the standard Harrier GR.3, showing normal wing-tips, nozzles aft, gun pods and a representative ordnance load. The position of the retracted outrigger gear is shown by a broken line in the side elevation. LERX wing-root extensions flew on one GR.3.

Below: The bare (undressed) Pegasus looks very stark, compared with the finished engine. Here fitters at Rolls-Royce Bristol are installing the GTS (gas-turbine starter) on top of the intermediate casing of a Pegasus 11 Mk 103 for a Harrier GR.3 of the RAF. Engine weight is 3,113lb (1412kg).

main resonant blade frequencies thus had to be kept outside the running speed range, and this was achieved by fitting snubbers (mid-span shrouds) to the blades, so that they all touched each other. This also solved the problem of distortion of static pressure distribution downstream of the fan, where it discharges into a plenum chamber which feeds the two front nozzles. The production engine has three stages of fan blades, all made in Hylite 45 titanium alloy in place of the Pegasus 3's aluminium, and all with snubbers.

In the same way, the need to split the hot gas downstream of the turbines and discharge it through left and right nozzles demanded a sharply bent exhaust duct, and this induced vibration in the LP turbine blades. The method of attack was rather similar, in that all blades in the second HP and both LP stages were drilled near mid-span and heat-resistant wire laced through to give an anti-vibration link joining all blades in each stage. (Today, in the AV-8B, new shrouded LP blades are used instead, avoiding the loss in efficiency of the gas flowing past the wires.)

There are many other technically interesting parts of the Pegasus, including the combustion system which, in sharp contrast to the original Orion and Orpheus, has a fully annular chamber with vaporizing burners. The latter were among the technologies inherited when Armstrong Siddeley joined Bristol to form Bristol Siddeley, and after careful tests the Bristol team were not too proud to admit that the Coventry firm's idea was superior. As a result the Harrier's combustion has generally been perfection, and its absence of visible smoke adds to its elusiveness which is a great bonus in warfare.

All other aspects of the Pegasus, however, pale into insignificance compared with the underlying need to vector the entire engine thrust through 98·5°. No other engine of such power has ever been thus vectored, nor fitted with four nozzles. It was clear from the start that the four nozzles simply *had* to move in unison, in the same way that the wings have to stay fixed to the fuselage. Moreover, with thrust often much greater than the total weight of the aircraft, the angles of the nozzles had to be controlled accurately. Thus, all four nozzles had to move together and, in any setting, all four had to be positively locked.

The final scheme adopted is to bleed HP air, the same 400°C supply as that fed to the RCVs, and use it to power two motors driving a differential gearbox in such a way that, if either motor jams, the other continues to drive but at half-speed. From this gearbox the scheme echoes the Wibault concept, in that a drive shaft along the underside of the engine is geared to two cross shafts. Instead of then using further gears, Hooker wisely elected to use chains. The chain drives have proved to be totally reliable, light and free from backlash or other problems. Credit for the air servo-motor goes to the Plessey company, though the entire system was produced by Hawker. It is controlled by a single lever in the cockpit, which is the only control in the Harrier cockpit not found on normal aircraft. It can drive the nozzles at rates up to 100°/s. As explained later, the system eventually matured as an extra flight trajectory control for use in air combat.

Systems

The flight control system in a V/STOL aircraft really has to comprise two systems, one for use in V/STOL flight and the other, the conventional system, for use only at speeds sufficiently high for

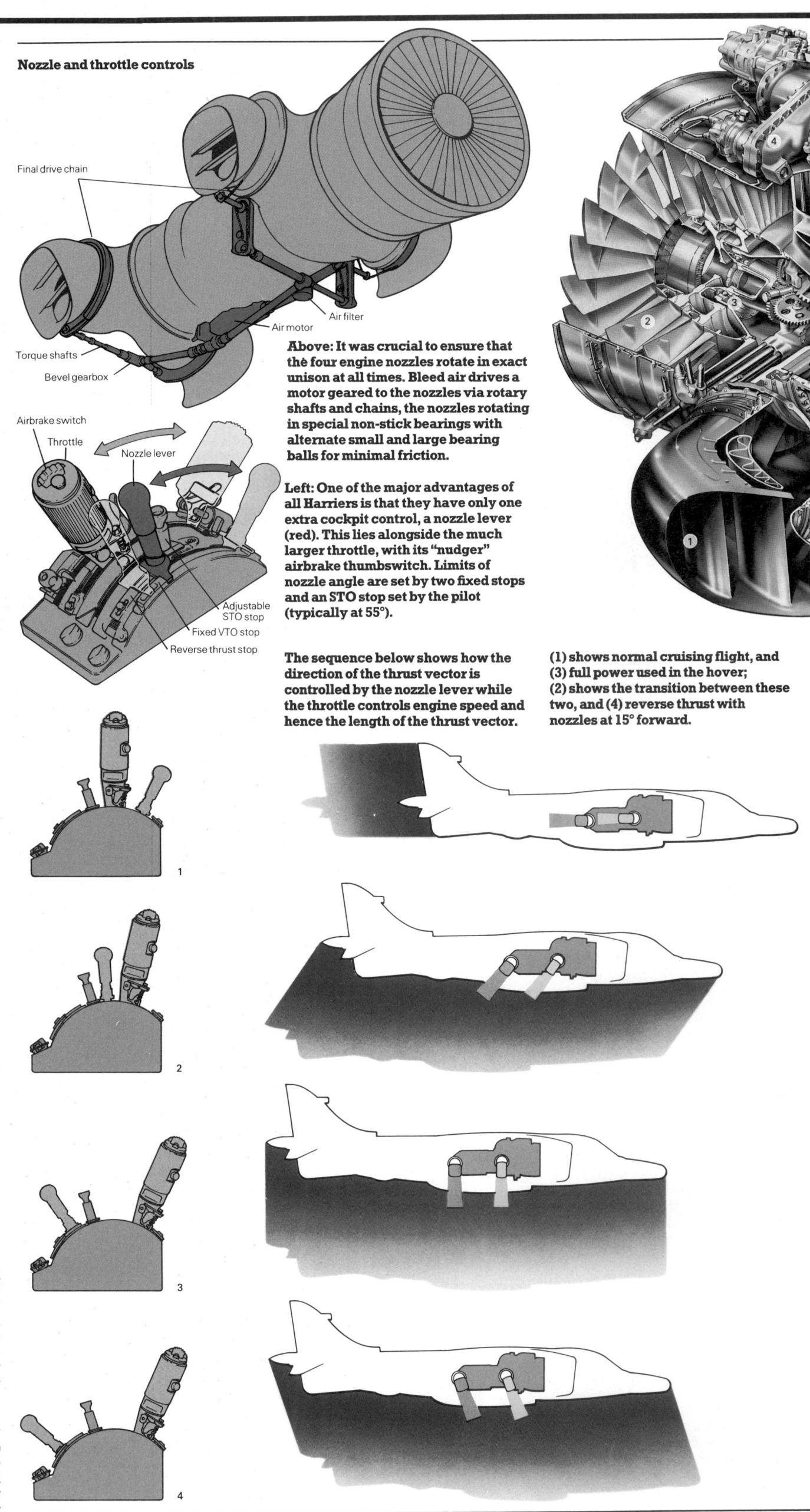

Nozzle and throttle controls

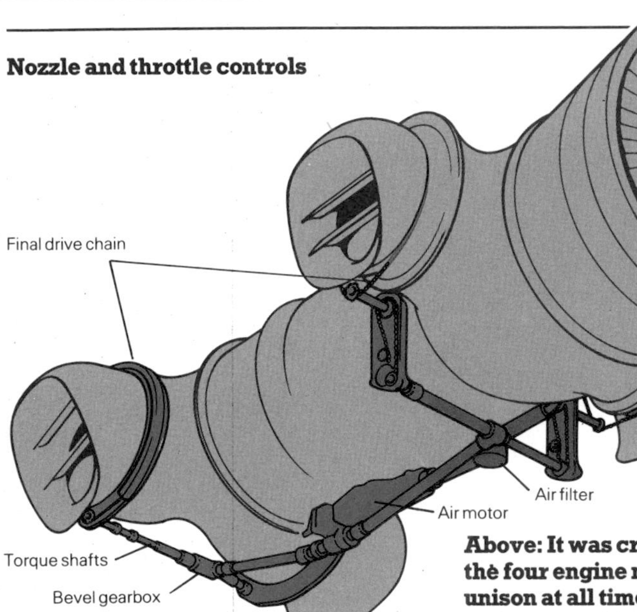

Above: It was crucial to ensure that the four engine nozzles rotate in exact unison at all times. Bleed air drives a motor geared to the nozzles via rotary shafts and chains, the nozzles rotating in special non-stick bearings with alternate small and large bearing balls for minimal friction.

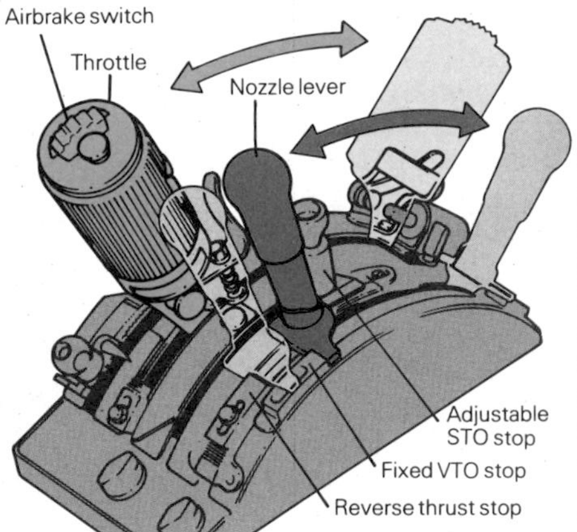

Left: One of the major advantages of all Harriers is that they have only one extra cockpit control, a nozzle lever (red). This lies alongside the much larger throttle, with its "nudger" airbrake thumbswitch. Limits of nozzle angle are set by two fixed stops and an STO stop set by the pilot (typically at 55°).

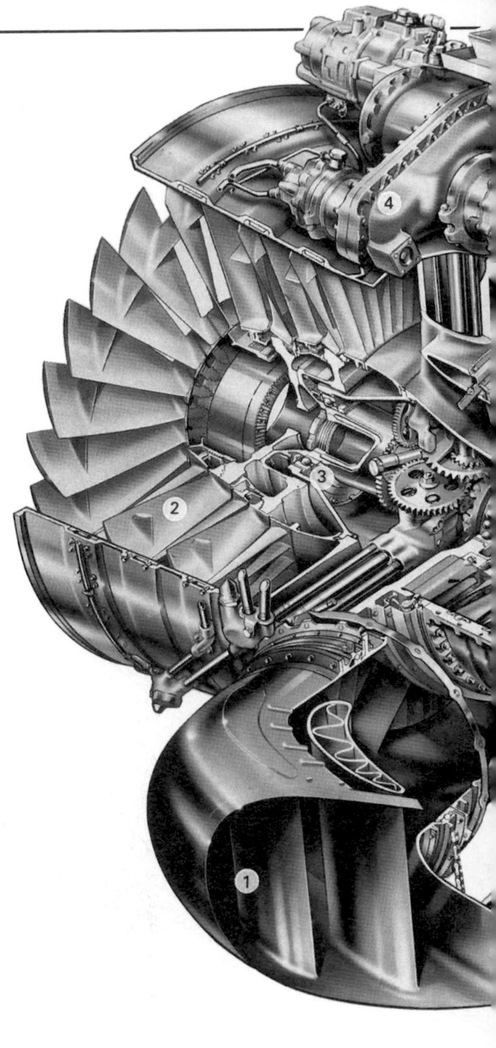

The sequence below shows how the direction of the thrust vector is controlled by the nozzle lever while the throttle controls engine speed and hence the length of the thrust vector.

(1) shows normal cruising flight, and (3) full power used in the hover; (2) shows the transition between these two, and (4) reverse thrust with nozzles at 15° forward.

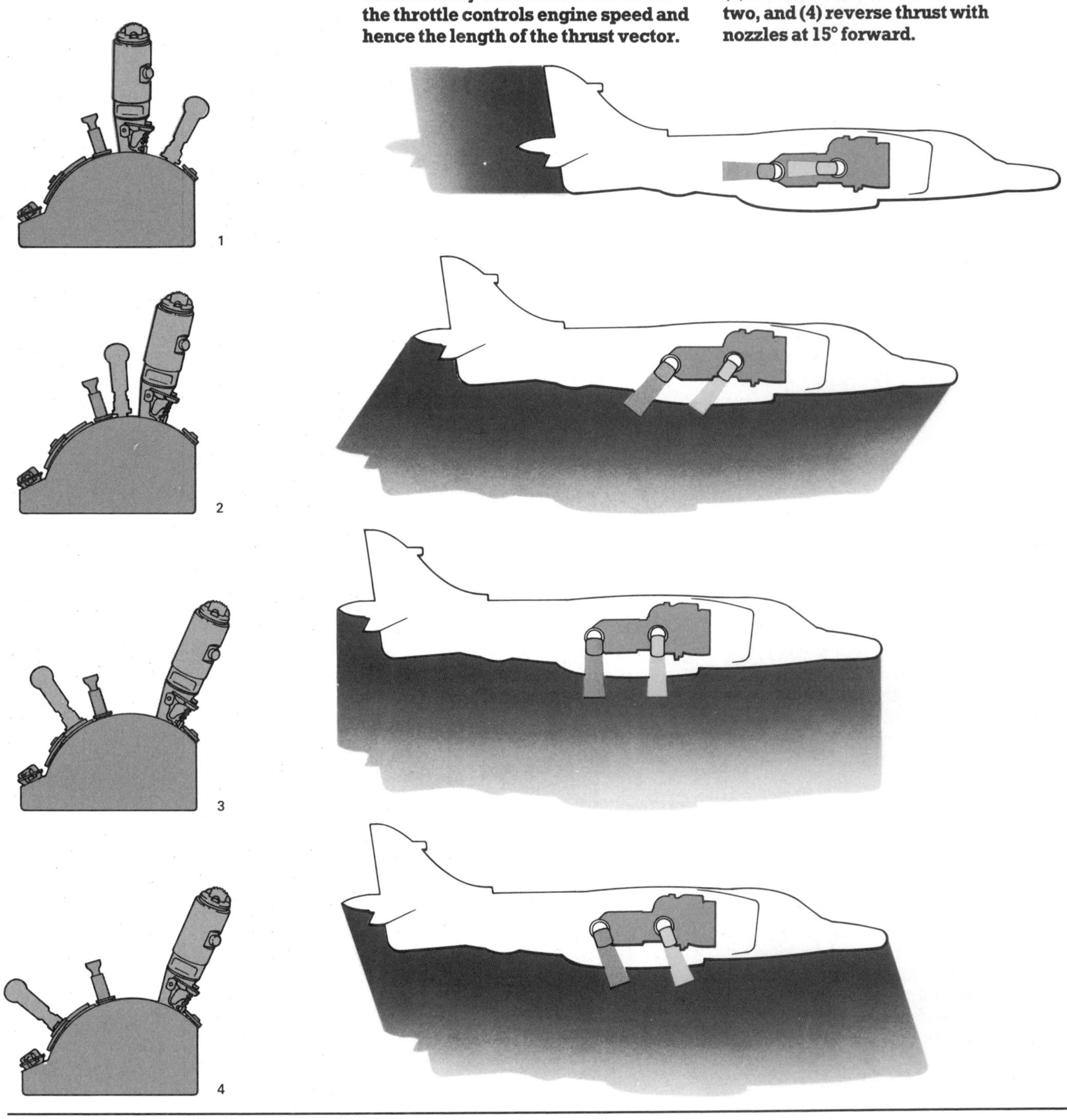

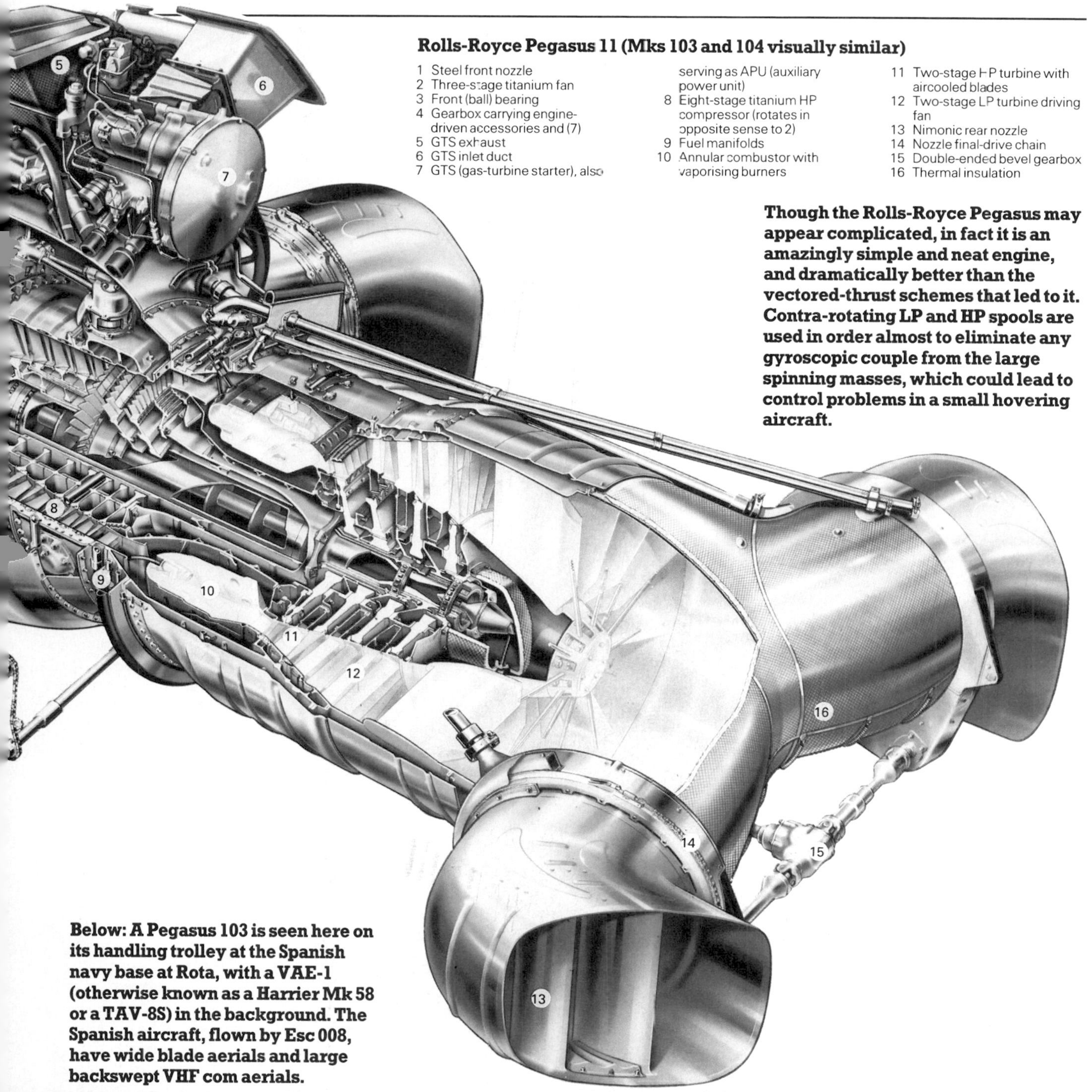

Rolls-Royce Pegasus 11 (Mks 103 and 104 visually similar)

1 Steel front nozzle
2 Three-stage titanium fan
3 Front (ball) bearing
4 Gearbox carrying engine-driven accessories and (7)
5 GTS exhaust
6 GTS inlet duct
7 GTS (gas-turbine starter), also serving as APU (auxiliary power unit)
8 Eight-stage titanium HP compressor (rotates in opposite sense to 2)
9 Fuel manifolds
10 Annular combustor with vaporising burners
11 Two-stage HP turbine with aircooled blades
12 Two-stage LP turbine driving fan
13 Nimonic rear nozzle
14 Nozzle final-drive chain
15 Double-ended bevel gearbox
16 Thermal insulation

Though the Rolls-Royce Pegasus may appear complicated, in fact it is an amazingly simple and neat engine, and dramatically better than the vectored-thrust schemes that led to it. Contra-rotating LP and HP spools are used in order almost to eliminate any gyroscopic couple from the large spinning masses, which could lead to control problems in a small hovering aircraft.

Below: A Pegasus 103 is seen here on its handling trolley at the Spanish navy base at Rota, with a VAE-1 (otherwise known as a Harrier Mk 58 or a TAV-8S) in the background. The Spanish aircraft, flown by Esc 008, have wide blade aerials and large backswept VHF com aerials.

ordinary control surfaces to be effective. As already noted, the conventional system is fully powered and irreversible, apart from the rudder which has a trim tab and manual drive. The horizontal tail is made up of left and right "slabs" without elevators, and it resembles that of the F-4 Phantom in having a large angular movement and marked anhedral. Roll is controlled solely by the small ailerons, though partly because of the short span the rates of roll are good.

At low speeds and in hovering flight the RCV system is progressively energized. There is no sudden transfer from one system to the other; the aerodynamic surfaces continue to be deflected, but as speed is reduced down to the hover, so does the RCV system progressively and smoothly take over. The linkages to the RCV system are, in fact, driven from the local conventional flight-control circuits. The ailerons drive roll RCVs at the front of the outrigger gear fairings. The rudder drives the yaw RCV in the projecting tail end of the fuselage. The tailplane drives the nose-down pitch RCV at the tail, while the nose-up RCV under the nose is driven directly from the stick.

The RCV system is not brought in by q-feel (dynamic pitot pressure) or an airspeed sensor, but simply according to the position of the main engine nozzles. When the nozzles are fully aft, the master shut-off valve under the engine HP compressor delivery is closed; thus, though pilot flight-control demands move both the aerodynamic surfaces and the RCVs, the latter's shutters open and close without any compressed air emerging. As soon as the engine nozzles move away from the fully aft position, the master shut-off valve begins to open. Rapidly the supply pressure in the stainless-steel pipes builds up until, when the engine nozzles are at about 20°, the master valve is fully open. Pilot control demands now result in the aerodynamic surfaces being accompanied by extremely powerful blasts from the associated RCVs.

It might not be appreciated just how powerful the RCV system has to be. The air supply is at 400°C (750°F), almost a dull-red temperature, and at a nozzle exit pressure of 150lb/sq in (1034kPa). The RCVs are heat-resistant steel, with convergent nozzles opened or closed by shutters sealed by sliding carbon bearings. In action, each RCV emits a supersonic jet moving at about 1,700mph (2740km/h). At full control demand the Harrier RCV system is transmitting energy at a rate of several thousand horsepower.

The early P.1127s had a constant-bleed system for the RCVs, and pilot demands merely shut down some valves and opened others wider. Such a system would be unacceptable in the Harrier, for the loss in available engine thrust would be serious, quite apart from denuding the engine turbines of air pumped by the compressor, thus increasing gas temperature. The Harrier instead has a demand system. When the pilot's cockpit controls are centred, no air is consumed. Stick and rudder movements open the appropriate RCVs progressively, to give a smooth and natural aircraft response. Particular effort was needed to perfect the roll RCVs, and achieve exactly the right "gearing", in terms of matching roll response to pilot stick deflection. The roll RCVs are especially interesting in that each is cunningly made to blast air either upwards or downwards, depending on the pilot demand, thus doubling the roll control power in comparison with that from a unidirectional RCV installation.

Most secondary power functions in the Harrier are served by the hydraulic system. This is duplicated, energized by two engine-driven pumps to a pressure of 3,000lb/sq in (20.69MPa). It serves the flying control system, flaps, landing gear and doors (the latter closing with gear down), airbrake, adaptive anti-skid wheel brakes, windscreen wiper and the jack which extends the RAT (ram-air turbine). The latter, normally retracted in a box in the top of the rear fuselage, can be extended to provide emergency system pressure. It provides ample power for flight control, but in view of the special nature of the Harrier, and the demanding nature of a dead-stick (engine off) landing, the RAT is being removed from RAF Harriers. In emergency, hydraulic items can be moved by stored nitrogen pressure.

Electrical power is generated as AC (alternating current) by two 12kVA alternators projecting ahead of the accessory gearbox above the engine fan case. TRUs (transformer/rectifier units) convert some power to DC, part of which charges the two batteries. The latter, in the rear fuselage, provide power to start a Lucas gas-turbine APU (auxiliary power unit), which is mounted on the rear of the accessory gearbox where it fits above the Pegasus plenum chamber. It can be started from the cockpit in the most extreme climatic conditions, and makes the Harrier completely independent of any ground power. Among other things it drives a 6kVA alternator for ground servicing and stand-by, and also serves as the starter for the Pegasus. The APU draws in air from a rectangular inlet in the top of the fuselage and discharges exhaust from a second flush aperture nearby.

Pilot oxygen is supplied from a Normalair-Garrett lox converter of 1gal (4·5lit) capacity. Like other system components, this is located in the rear fuselage, in this case immediately above the airbrake.

Fuel tankage in the airframe has been described, and it can be supplemented by two drop tanks carried on the "wet" (plumbed) inboard wing pylons. Originally the Harrier was cleared with combat tanks of 100gal (455lit) or ferry tanks of 330gal (1500lit), the latter seldom being needed in European service. During Operation Corporate (see later chapter) new tanks of 190gal (864lit) size were also flown, though these are not used by the RAF. The ground pressure-fuelling connection is immediately ahead of the left rear engine nozzle. The flight-refuelling probe, roughly 10ft (3m) in length, is attached above the left inlet and coupled to the inflight-refuelling valve in the aircraft fuel system. The probe is inclined upwards and outwards so that its tip is easily visible to the pilot. Finally, the large airflow and power of the Pegasus tend to give a false idea of the Harrier's fuel consumption. In the worst condition, hovering at full weight at sea level, fuel burn is 220lb (100kg)/min. This is one-sixth that of an F-4 Phantom on take-off.

Avionics

When the P.1127(RAF) was rather suddenly invented, upon cancellation of the P.1154(RAF), there was no background of an RAF OR (operational requirement) or official specification. As time was pressing, the Air Staff merely issued ASR.384 as a re-issue of the most recent

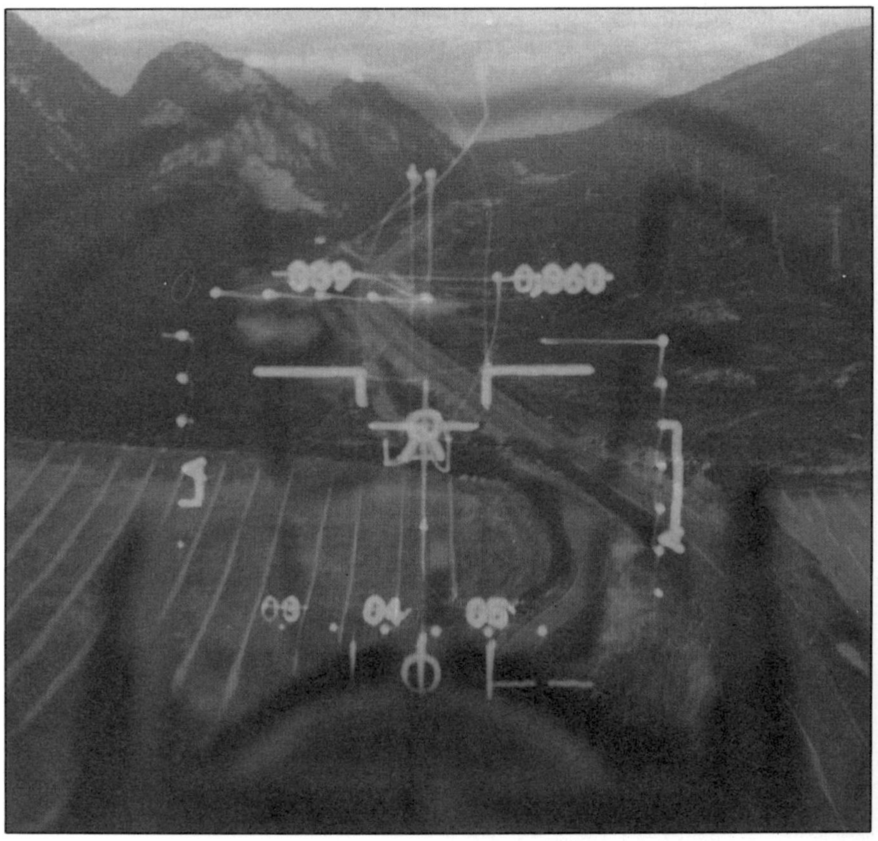

Right: Taken during an actual RAF low-level training sortie, this photograph shows how the pilot can look simultaneously both at the HUD display and at the scene ahead. The Harrier is diving into the valley.

Above: The cockpit of an RAF GR.3, showing the traditional dial instruments. The HUD and head-down moving-map display are on the centre-line; left are flight instruments with the weapon panel below.

Harrier GR.3 Cockpit Layout

1 Pilot display unit
2 Flying instruments
3 PDU controls
4 Weapon control panel
5 V/UHF controls
6 Throttle and nozzle box
7 Hand controller
8 F.E. 541 NDC (navigation display computer) unit
9 Engine instruments
10 Fuel instruments
11 F.E. 541 NDC control
12 Centralised warning system panel
13 Tacan controls
14 Voice recorder
15 IFF (identification friend or foe) controls

Left: Though well-known, this is still the best photograph yet taken of SNEB rockets being fired from an RAF Harrier. This Ministry of Defence (RAF) picture dates from GR.1 days. The photographer was looking almost straight up at the diving aircraft, firing on a ground target.

draft of OR.356, which was the document covering the P.1154(RAF), but with the radar omitted and the mission numbers down-graded to suit the anticipated mission capability of the smaller, subsonic Pegasus-powered aircraft.

The radar was omitted because it would have been extremely difficult to include it, there was no mention in ASR.384 of air combat missions, and the equipment itself did not yet exist (the supplier, Ferranti, had not even been awarded the full development contract). Apart from this item, much of the P.1154(RAF) avionics suite was written in without change, notably including the INAS, HUD and NDC.

The INAS (inertial navigation attack system) is the Ferranti FE.541, which because of its NBMR-3 application was actually designed for the P.1154(RAF). Its basis is the inertial platform in the nose, bolted to the cockpit front pressure bulkhead, which feeds positional information to the IMS (inertial measurement system) and present-position computer, which in turn feeds position information to the NDC (navigation display computer) and trajectory information to the WAC (weapon-aiming computer). The NDC is also called a projected map display, because its main display is a circular screen on which is projected optically a 35mm cassette containing a selected topographic map covering typically 800nm (921 miles, 1483km) north/south and 900nm (1,036 miles, 1668km) east/west.

There are two other inputs to the NDC. One is traditional Tacan, the long-established radio navaid which gives R-theta (radius and bearing) information from an interrogated ground station. The other is the Sperry C2G gyrocompass, providing an additional source of heading information. Present position is at the centre of the NDC, and the pilot himself has inputs in the form of buttons on the NDC, and a separate pistol-grip hand controller with a rolling-ball input and white "fix" button, which is depressed as the aircraft overflies a point whose position must be recalled or which must later be regained.

The third major avionic item specified at the start was the HUD (head-up display). This was designed by a small firm called Specto, which was taken over by Smiths Industries. It receives height and speed information from the ADC (air-data computer) and cockpit HUD control panel (and, after this item had been fitted, the LRMTS, as described in the next chapter). The HUD provides basic flight guidance information for all modes of flight, including a vital cue showing any tendency to sideslip at speeds too low for natural weathercocking by the fin, as well as the primary steering information for all air-to-ground or air-to-air attacks.

A HUD camera was specified to record the display as a training aid, and other basic avionics included HF, VHF and UHF radio, and IFF (identification friend or foe). Tactical VHF was also called for, but in fact this was never fitted until it appeared on AV-8 series aircraft of the US Marines and Spanish Navy.

After delivery, two very important extra items changed the appearance of Harriers of the RAF. These, the LRMTS and RWR, are described in the next chapter. EW (electronic-warfare) installations are also discussed there, and in the account of Operation Corporate.

Weapons

No internal weapons were called for. Like the P.1154(RAF) the Harrier was to rely solely on externally carried stores, though the supersonic predecessor's emphasis on guided missiles (such as Red Top and AS.30) was replaced by simpler weapons thought more appropriate to a tactical battlefield situation: bombs, rocket pods, and external gun pods. Hawker designed the pods to accommodate a single Aden Mk 4 gun of 30mm calibre together with its ammunition. The ammunition box accommodates 100 rounds, and 130 can be accommodated without causing feed problems if the capacity of the feed chutes is utilized. For minimum aircraft drag the firing aperture at the front of the pod is covered by a frangible cap, blown off by the first round. These pods have a useful effect as LIDs (lift-improvement devices), and when removed are replaced by thin strakes serving the same purpose.

Details of weapon loads are given in a diagram. The maximum weight of external loads can reach 9,000lb (4082kg), but the limit for normal operations is 5,300lb (2400kg). For the reconnaissance mission, the centreline fuselage pylon can carry a Hawker pod housing five optical cameras, two left and two right oblique F.95 Mk 7s and a forward F.135. Since the Falklands campaign RAF Harriers have carried AIM-9 Sidewinder self-defence AAMs.

Below: Selected weapons carried by the RAF and US Marine Corps, the American stores being in brackets.

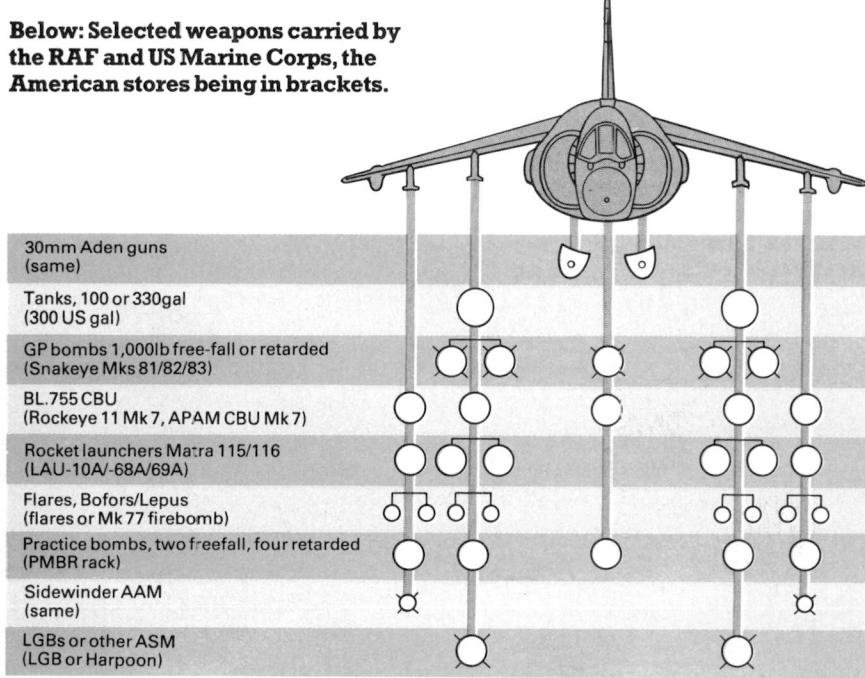

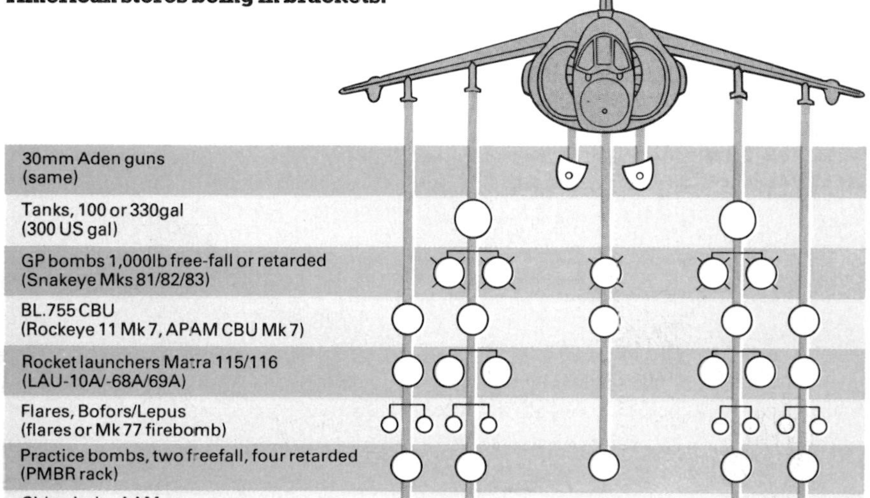

Harrier in Service

Since April 1969 Harriers have flown half a million operational hours, almost all under conditions of peculiar severity. Unlike other aircraft, a proportion of this time has been high-power hovering balanced on four thunderous jets which often kick up debris from the ground. Yet FOD (foreign-object damage) has been less than for many conventional aircraft, and even the birdstrike problem has been no worse than for other low-level attack aircraft. Unexpectedly, the Harrier has also turned out to have unique advantages in air combat; surely all fighters will one day have vectored thrust?

XV276, the first of the six DB prototypes, made its first hover on 31 August 1966. Subsequent development was most successful, and progressed from a simple unpainted aircraft with a long nose probe, no guns or pylons, six blow-in inlet doors and four vortex generators on each wing, to aircraft indistinguishable except to a real expert from the first production Harrier GR.1 (GR, ground attack and reconnaissance). The latter aircraft, XV738, was the first of 60 ordered in early 1967, sufficient to equip an OCU (Operational Conversion Unit), a front-line squadron in Britain and another in RAF Germany.

In the course of 1967 numerous carry-trials flights at Dunsfold proved various external stores, and the process gained momentum in 1968 with five aircraft at the Aeroplane & Armament Experimental Establishment, Boscombe Down. Indeed, it has never stopped, and even today new weapons and EW fits are being cleared both in Britain and in the USA. Among the early clearances was the AIM-9B Sidewinder AAM, envisaged as a light self-defence weapon. Photographs of the installation, on the outboard pylons, were taken in January 1968; but no provision was made for it in RAF Harriers, so in Operation Corporate 14 years later the trials had to be flown as a crash programme!

In early 1968 Hawker Siddeley Aviation hosted the media at Dunsfold. Though it was a new experience to witness a pirouetting display by seven jump jets, many of the pressmen failed fully to appreciate that they were witnessing the start of a new era in warfare

Above: A brace of RAF Harrier GR.3s on a training mission in 1980 from 233 OCU, Wittering. Individual aircraft letters are in pale blue above the fin flash. Aircraft L, on the right, is probably XV807. Each aircraft is carrying two tanks and two practice-bomb carriers.

Right: When new this Harrier was designated as a Hawker Siddeley AV-8A, or Harrier Mk 50, and it is shown in its original markings in service with VMA-231. Note the big tactical VHF mast above the fuselage, the bolted-on probe and the light practice bombs carried in tandem.

Above: This US Marine Corps Harrier was the fourth to be built and the third to be delivered (on 12 March 1971), but it was photographed in July 1982 after updating to AV-8C standard. For most of its career it has served with VMA-513.

Above left: Four AV-8As of the US Marine Corps – probably from VMA-513, though this is not certain – en route to air/ground rocket firing during a practice deployment to MCAS Yuma, Arizona. Attacks would be made in 20° dives.

in which airpower can be provided with neither airfields nor aircraft carriers. Bob Lickley, assistant managing director, reported good results with dropped stores, dry contacts with Victor K.1A tankers, ceiling climbs to beyond 50,000ft (15·24km) and the company's offer to sell Harriers at "£750,000 to £1 million, depending on quantity and equipment". He also announced further growth in thrust of the Pegasus, all of which could be translated into greater fuel or weapon loads.

During 1968 a massive effort was made to perfect the nav/attack system, which in some respects was new to British experience and at the time was fully competitive with anything flying elsewhere. Even in 1967, when it worked properly, accuracy of the basic inertial system degraded at less than 1nm (1·15 miles, 1·85km) per hour, and weapon delivery accuracies were the best ever achieved with RAF attack aircraft, and similar to results with the contemporary F-111. By autumn 1968 the main advance had been reliability and consistent performance. Several important trials were also flown from ships, following earlier experiments with P.1127s, as related in the next chapter.

Enter a customer

Overseas interest in the Harrier was in some places intense, though in most cases without the slightest thought of purchase. The only serious acquisition interests were shown by a few navies, and in any case Hawker Siddeley's main marketing effort was a low-key one aimed at educating military aviators whose usual understanding of vectored-thrust V/STOL was based on deeply rooted misconceptions. It was certainly a great surprise when, at the 1968 Farnborough air show, a commissionaire at the Hawker Siddeley chalet announced that at the door were three officers of the US Marine Corps who would like to fly a Harrier!

In fact, the Marines had been looking at the Harrier for eight months. One of the Corps' basic needs is effective airpower over a beach-head where its tough "Leathernecks" might be making an assault on a foreign shore. It had the choice between helicopters and total reliance on the giant carriers of the US Navy. The best helicopter seemed to be the Lockheed AH-56A Cheyenne, incredibly complex and costly and yet seemingly vulnerable because of its modest speed. For eight years a further alternative had been sought in SATS (short airfield for tactical support), but this meant the beach assault had to arrive complete with shiploads of aluminium planking, gas-turbine catapults, arrester installations and much more, as well as a complete Seabee construction battalion to fasten it all together. There had to be a better answer.

From the 1950s, largely because of the unswerving belief of Col, later Gen, Keith B. McCutcheon, the Corps had decided that the future lay with a V/STOL, when the technology matured. Though the Marines had played no part in the TES, they had carefully studied the six XV-6A (Kestrel) aircraft which from 1966 flew from Edwards, NASA-Dryden, NASA-Langley and the Naval Air Test Center at Patuxent (Pax) River, where Marine pilots at last flew them. In April 1966 an XV-6A flew from the LPD (assault ship) USS *Raleigh*, and for the first time the Marines began to wonder if the little Hawker jet might not represent the germ of something they could use. There was no doubt it had all the performance they wanted, and it had the most flexible basing possibilities anyone could wish. But not until 1968 was it clear that the more powerful version, the Harrier, might be able to do a useful job in the close-support mission.

Thus, despite the outpourings of the uninformed media, whose universal view in the United States was "the Harrier couldn't carry a box of matches across a football field", Gen Leonard C. Chapman, Commandant of the Corps, ordered that the British aircraft should be thoroughly evaluated. Brig-Gen Johnson came to England with two outstanding pilots, Col (later Gen) Tom Miller and Lt-Col Bud Baker. The Minister of Technology granted each Marine pilot ten flights, and their searching evaluation confirmed that the Harrier could do rather more than the popular American – and, in fact, world – opinion, and was close to being the ideal air weapon that the Corps had long dreamed of. It quickly drew up plans for a buy of 114 aircraft, sufficient to support four 20-aircraft squadrons plus training and attrition.

At Christmas 1968 the Marines announced their interest, and that they had received Department of Defense (DoD) approval for an initial buy of 12 aircraft to get the programme started. Funds for these were slashed from the DoD budget in the final rounds of Congressional cuts in January 1969, but this was only a temporary setback. A line

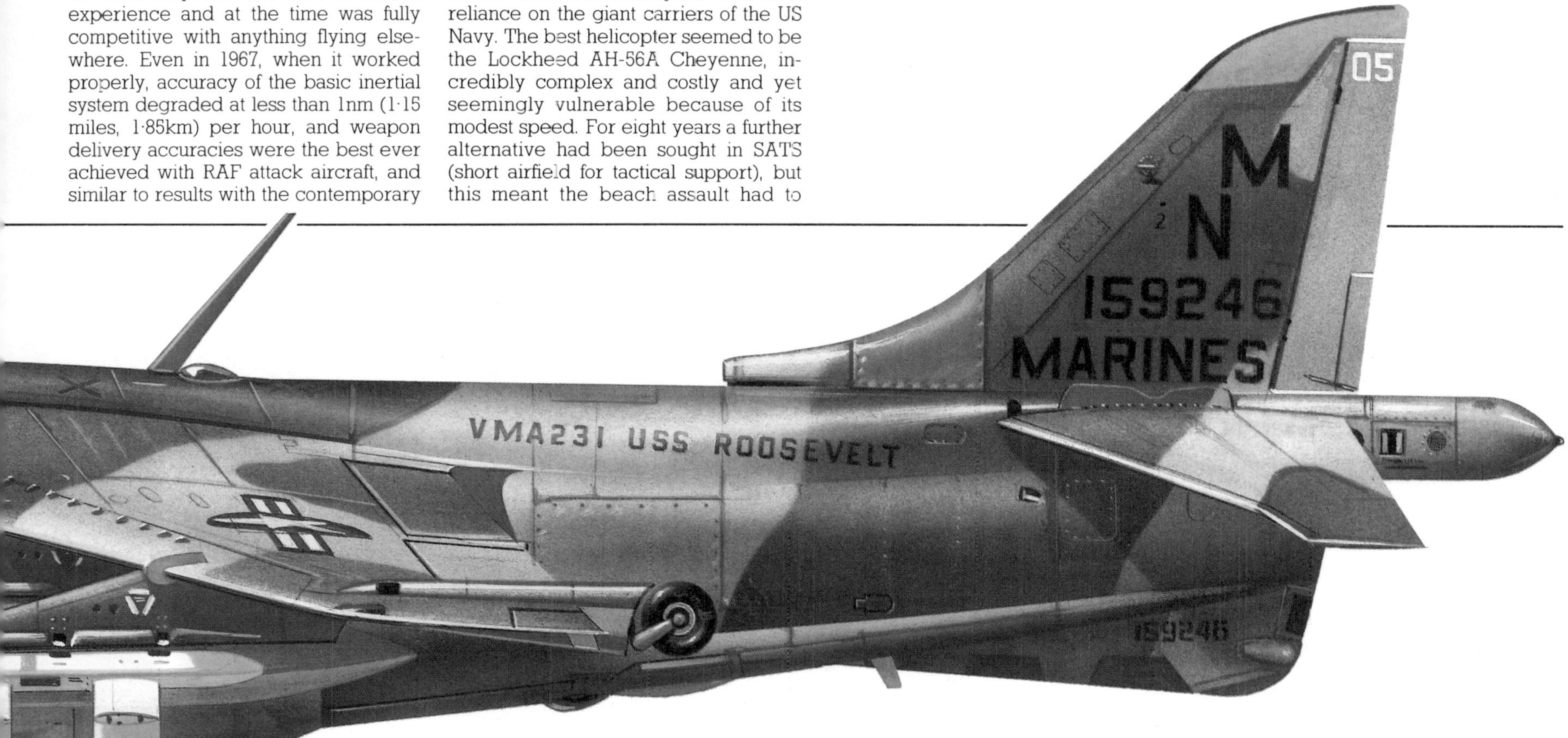

item in the FY70 (Fiscal Year ending 30 June 1970) budget was $58 million for 17 new F-4J Phantoms. The Marines willingly gave up these aircraft and used the money to pay for the initial 12 Harriers, which received the US designation AV-8A. They were to be made in Britain, and as nearly as possible copies of the RAF Harrier. Subsequent AV-8As were to be licence-built in the USA, and Baker and Miller visited all the chief American aircraft companies. Instant interest came from Douglas, which saw the AV-8A as the replacement for its own A-4 Skyhawk. But the California company had just come under the control of MCAIR (McDonnell Aircraft of St Louis). To everyone's surprise, not only did Sandy McDonnell express support, but he even got the British V/STOL project transferred to MCAIR! A 15-year agreement was signed with Hawker, not only for making the AV-8A but also for mutual exchange of all subsequent vectored-thrust V/STOL data and drawings. Pratt & Whitney signed with Rolls-Royce in October 1971 for joint future development of the Pegasus, under the US designation F402, with an option on a manufacturing licence.

In October 1969 the US Navy (on behalf of the Marines) and in January 1970 the USAF carried out evaluations of Harriers at Dunsfold. Both reports were highly positive, despite the tragic death on 27 January 1970 of Major Charles R. Rosberg, USAF, who got into uncontrollable roll during the tricky narrow band of airspeeds accelerating away from a VTO, when a flat turn or yaw is dangerous. This was the first fatal accident to any Hawker jump jet.

One of the changes specified in the AV-8A was the new Pegasus 11, with increased mass flow, improved water injection and turbine cooling and further revisions to the fuel control. This went into production as the Mk 103 for the RAF and Mk 803 for the AV-8A, but in fact these engines were too late for the first ten AV-8As which were delivered with Mk 802 (Pegasus 10) engines. Another obvious change was clearance with American ordnance, and the USMC interest in air combat prompted the obvious carriage of AIM-9 Sidewinder missiles. Though these had been fitted to a P.1127(RAF) at the A&AEE, the wiring was never installed. Amazingly, after the wiring to fire Sidewinders had been designed and fitted for the AV-8A, the RAF insisted that it should be specially *omitted* from its own Harriers, thereby causing a "crash" modification programme in April 1982! The Marines planned to replace the Aden guns at an early date, but these soon built up such a fine reputation they have remained in use to this day, even though they do not fire standard US ammunition. American communications radio, IFF and certain other avionic items replaced British equipment, an armament safety switch isolating the weapon circuits whenever the main landing gear oleo was compressed was fitted, and a direct manual throttle for use in emergency was also specified.

While the AV-8A programme got under way, deliveries began of Harrier GR.1s to the RAF. The first aircraft, XV738, had flown on 28 December 1967. Carriage and weapon-release trials and nav/attack refinements occupied 1968, and in January 1969 the first RAF unit, the Harrier Conversion Unit, was formed at Dunsfold. The first delivery to an operational squadron, appropriately No 1 Sqn, based at Wittering, took place on 18 April 1969. On paper No 1 had actually received XV741 and 744 on 9 April, but both were diverted to take part in the transatlantic air race held in May. They were fitted with ferry tips, 100gal (455lit) tanks and refuelling probes and flew from the centre of London to the centre of New York and back. The first takeoff, from a disused coal-yard at St Pancras station, was notable for the amount of coal-dust blown over assembled dignitaries. The NY pad was a site at the Bristol Basin, in mid-Manhattan, so named because it had been filled with rubble from bombed buildings in Bristol, home of the Pegasus! Times for the 3,490 miles (5616km) were 5h 57min westbound, the best of any competitor, and 5h 31min eastbound.

Below: Rising above the solid century-old ironwork of St Pancras station, London, XV744 was a very new GR.1 when it took part in the transatlantic race to New York City in May 1969. It had 100gal tanks, probe and bolt-on ferry wingtips.

Entry into service

QFIs (qualified flying instructors) who had completed Harrier conversion at Dunsfold then trained pilots of No 1 Sqn, followed in due course by Nos 4, 20 and 3 (in that order) forming a wing in RAF Germany at Wildenrath, the total RAF buy having been increased as listed in the Appendix. In early 1970 the HCU was restyled 233 OCU (Operational Conversion Unit) and moved to Wittering. It was true to RAF form that all the early Harrier conversion was done without the benefit of a dual two-seater, though this had been studied at Kingston since 1960. Some of the early two-seat P.1127 studies were novel, but reflected the unusual problems of putting a second cockpit in such a tight-knit V/STOL with four nozzles disposed around the CG. It was

Below: XZ146, an RAF two-seater, seen at Dunsfold in 1978 after it had been updated to T.4A standard with RWR and LRMTS. Curiously, it still has the original short fin. The same machine is seen above in its final paint scheme.

Below: Here XZ146 (see below) is shown resplendent in the markings of RAF No 4 Sqn, based at Gutersloh and carrying guns and bomb pods.

Below: In contrast, USMC 159380 is seen serving with VMA(T)-203 with the definitive tall fin, but of course no RWR, LRMTS or gun pods.

eventually clear that the only solution was a direct stretch of the fuselage with tandem seating.

When the RAF got round to drafting a requirement (ASR.386) for a two-seat Harrier, it made life harder by demanding that the aircraft should be able to take its place in the operational inventory, flown from the front seat with normal fuel and weapons. It was by no means certain that this was achievable, but once a contract for two two-seat development aircraft (XW174-5) had been received in 1967, work began in earnest. It was only rendered possible by the continued dramatic increases in thrust of the engine, because a two-seater was clearly going to be appreciably heavier.

Right: G-VTOL, the British Aerospace civil demonstrator, churning up the desert during a rolling vertical landing on an overseas trip in 1973. This aircraft has full "airways" avionics, and can go at short notice anywhere in the world.

It is simple to list the design changes in producing the two-seat Harrier T.2 (T = trainer), but in fact it was no simple task. The nose, with pupil cockpit, was cut off and moved 47in (1·19m) forward. The instructor cockpit was inserted in the gap, at a level some 18in (457mm) higher than the pupil. To provide room for the rear seat and pressure bulkhead, the cabin air-conditioning system was removed from its previous location immediately behind the seat. It was replaced by a new system, of greater capacity matched to the volume of the dual cockpits, packaged in the large new fairing behind the canopy. The latter was redesigned as a single large framed structure hinged open along the right side. To reduce the pitch moment the F.95 camera and inertial platform were moved from the nose to a location under the rear seat, immediately in front of the nose gear. To maintain control power, the forward RCV was brought even further into the nose, being moved forward by 56in (1·42m). To balance the destabilizing effect of the larger nose the entire tail was moved 33·3in (846mm) to the rear, and the vertical fin enlarged by mounting it on an extra root section 11in (279mm) high. The ventral fin was changed in shape and enlarged. The fuselage tailcone was lengthened, partly to increase the moment arm of the pitch/yaw RCVs and partly to house ballast to counter the extra mass ahead of the CG. This ballast, and the instructor seat, are removed when the aircraft is flown as a single-seat combat aircraft. The horizontal tail was not altered, apart from adding shot-filled tubes near the tips to damp resonance caused by the fact that the long fuselage has a natural frequency that is a sub-harmonic of that of the tailplane. Thus, ground crew must be careful never to bolt a single-seat tailplane on a two-seater.

The first two-seater flew on 24 April 1969, but this crashed from fuel-control contamination and the real development was done with XW175. There were few problems apart from inadequate yaw (weathercock) stability at high AOA (angle of attack). This proved a most intractable problem, taking until the late summer of 1971 to cure. By this time pro-

1 Classical dispersed operation

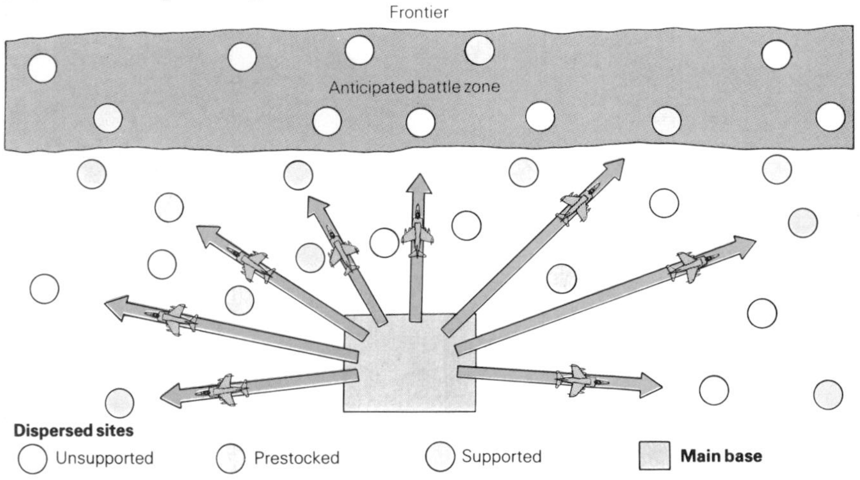

2 Operations from unsupported sites

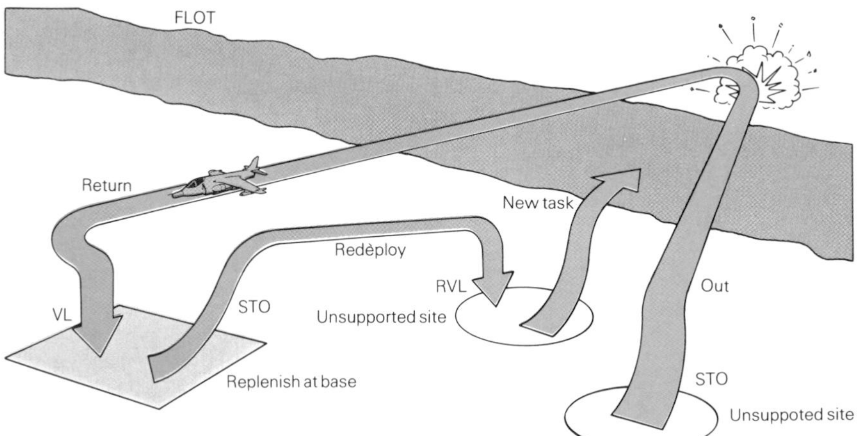

3 Rapid-reaction operations

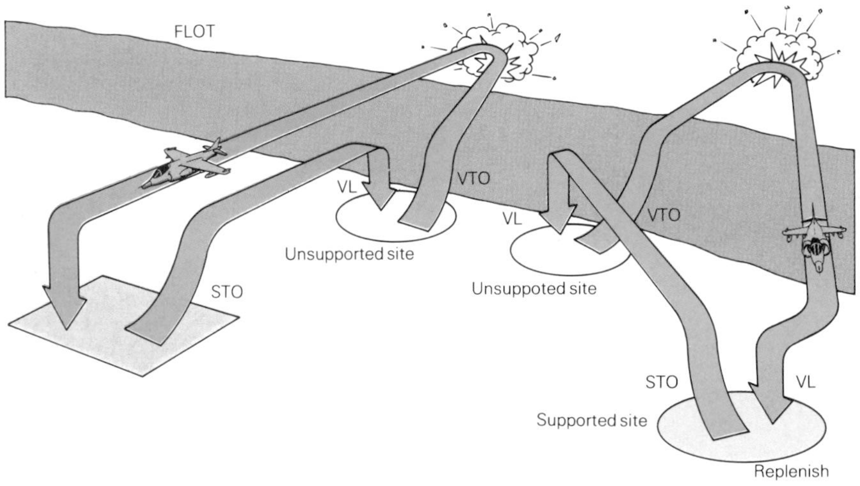

4 Operations from prestocked sites

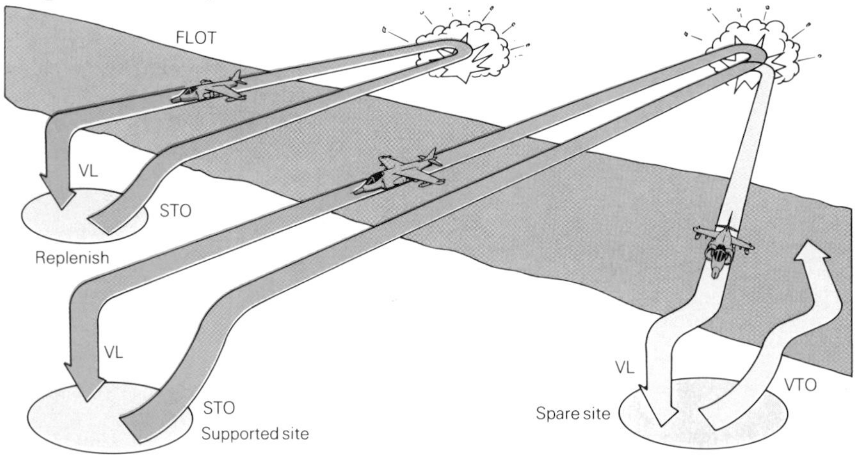

1 In the classical pattern Harriers work from a main base near the land battle but disperse away from it in emergency or whenever the need arises. This stylized plan view shows a front-line area dotted with the three kinds of dispersed site.

2 Here the main base has been heavily attacked and is being used only as a logistics centre. The unsupported sites are bare plots used as "ground loiter" positions close to the FLOT (forward line of own troops). Pilots are summoned by radio communications.

3 This is the "cab rank on the ground" concept, which among other things saves fuel compared with the cab rank method of 1944. Note that one dispersed site here is big enough for an STO, which gives more payload or mission endurance.

4 Here there is no main base, and all operations are from prestocked sites (with fuel, weapons and a few support personnel) or supported sites (which also have full frontline servicing and briefing facilities, and radio communications).

Above: Harrier GR.3s of RAF No 1(F) Sqn temporarily in removable Arctic camouflage while on detachment to RNorAF base Bardufoss in 1979. The occasion was a NATO exercise called, appropriately, Cold Winter.

duction T.2s were in service, and many were modified with the final cure, which, after several adjustments, is a broader vertical tail with 18in (457mm) extra height, together with automatic opening of the airbrake to 26° whenever the horizontal tail is commanded to large negative angles.

Prolonged further trials, including carriage of stores, were flown with the first production T.2, XW264, which first flew on 3 October 1969. Subsequent details of production mark numbers, serials and numbers built are given in the Appendix at the back of the book. The RAF uses the two-seaters for pilot conversion at 233 OCU and on each Harrier squadron for weapon-delivery instruction, instrument ratings and various other checks. From 1971 the two-seaters greatly eased conversion problems, improved general proficiency standards and enabled inexperienced first-tour pilots to join Harrier squadrons.

Units in operation

Operational flying was approached in easy stages. An early overseas deployment was No 1 Sqn's armament practice camp at RAF Akrotiri, Cyprus, in March 1970, when a great deal of live firing at ground targets was combined with a long transit flight, but without using air refuelling. Then followed a busy round of off-base operations in various climates, Tacevals (tactical evaluations) in which the operational performance of a unit is numerically assessed in simulated front-line conditions, introduction of a succession of aircraft improvements, and solution of some of the major operating problems, other than the intractable one of birdstrikes. At first "everything but the kitchen sink", and sometimes that too, was taken to each dispersed site in order to make things as much like a well-equipped airfield as possible. Though NATO has never attempted to emulate the Warsaw Pact air forces in spartan dispersed-site exercises, at least the RAF Harrier squadrons have acquired great experience in how to sustain high-intensity operations for a week or more without going near an airfield and with the minimum of special equipment. Even so, such an exercise still needs eight C-130 loads, not counting fuel.

No 20 Sqn converted from Harriers to Jaguars in 1977, and Nos 3 and 4 were brought up to 18 aircraft each and relocated at Gutersloh, nearer East Germany than any other NATO airfield. Both units have scored maximum possible marks in many exercises, including NBC (nuclear, biological, chemical) simulations. On most exercises each Harrier has flown an average of from four to 12 combat missions a day, with full briefings and complete changes of weapons and other "consumables", but without inertial realignment. In Exercise Oak Stroll in 1974 a total of 24 serviceable aircraft flew 1,121 missions in nine days, while in Big Tee (Tee = Tac eval exercise) in the same year No 1 Sqn flew 364 missions in three days with 12 aircraft, one machine flying 41 sorties. The CO said "Try *that* with an F-teen jet!"

The STO technique

Very soon it was obvious that the optimum type of mission is STVOL (short takeoff, vertical landing), the STO greatly increasing possible weapon loads for a given mission radius. The technique could hardly be simpler: the aircraft is lined up with the park brake on, the ASI bug (marker on the rim of the airspeed indicator) is set to a pre-computed takeoff speed, such as 140

knots, and the nozzle angle stop locked at 50°. The throttle is then moved to 55 per cent, brakes released and the throttle slammed to 100 per cent. A quick glance to check that full power has been obtained, and then, as the needle rotates past the bug, the nozzle lever is quickly whipped back to the stop. The Harrier leaps off the ground, gear is retracted and, as the aircraft climbs away on a mixture of engine thrust and wing lift, the nozzle lever is inched forwards, at the same time raising the flaps, until at about 180 ASI the aircraft is fully wingborne. At speeds up to 400 ASI, with nozzles aft, a Harrier out-accelerates everything else in the sky.

Above: Taken in 1971, this picture shows the lavishly equipped kind of hide with which RAF Harrier units played early in the aircraft's career. In a real war hides might be more spartan, and less visible.

Curiously, in view of its major extra capability of vectored-thrust V/STOL, the Harrier is in almost all respects simpler to fly than other tactical combat aircraft. As explained in a later chapter, it can operate when all other jets are grounded. It can also be operated from small pads, platforms and heaving ship decks by pilots who have never even seen a ship previously. (The very important ski-jump technique appears in the next chapter.) The one standard departure from the STOVL operating routine comes when operating from unprepared surfaces, in which case an RVL (rolling vertical landing) is made, touching down with as much forward speed as the available run allows – typically 40 ASI – to minimise FOD (foreign-object damage) and recirculation of jet gas.

Below: An early GR.1 on Ministry trials in 1971, hovering near a simulated blasted runway while laden with guns, tanks, rocket launchers and recon pod.

From the earliest days of the P.1127 great attention has been paid to the increased importance of reingestion and FOD in V/STOL aircraft. Flow patterns round a hovering Harrier in ground effect are complex, and strongly modified by the extremely high energy supersonic blasts from the RCVs, but the underlying pattern is that there are four slightly divergent pillars from the main engine nozzles which spread out on impact across the ground. Jet temperatures are roughly 100°C for the front nozzles and 600°C for the rear (the RCV jets are at around 300°C), but absence of smoke means that the only way to see the jets is by "heat haze" light refraction. Air

Comparative mission radii that can be flown by a conventional attack aircraft (red) and a Harrier GR.3 (blue), in all but the last case with 5,000lb (2268kg) bombload. When available runway shortens, Harriers win out.

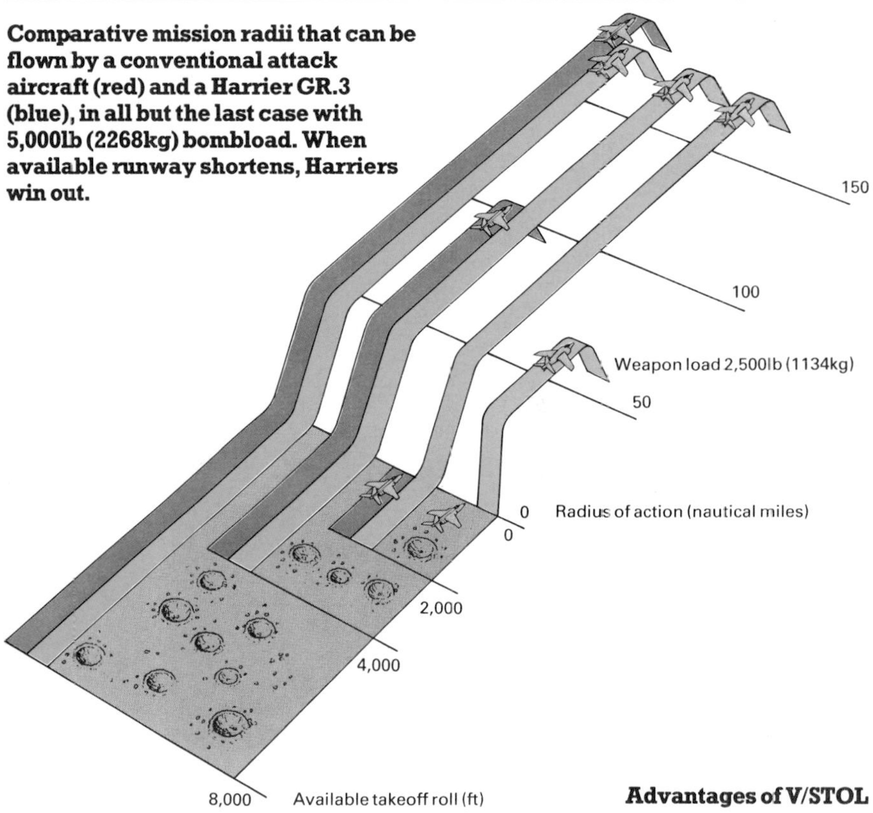

Advantages of V/STOL

and gas spreads outwards along the ground, rapidly losing energy, but the flows spreading inwards, for example from the two left-hand nozzles, almost immediately meet the mirror-image flow from the other side of the aircraft. The only place to go is up, resulting in a fountain jet rising vertically and striking the belly of the aircraft. This might seem advantageous, like the fountain that supports the ball at a shooting gallery, but in fact the high-velocity flow round the fuselage tends to act like the air flowing over the curved surface of a wing and suck the Harrier downwards. It is the designer's task to arrange strakes and dams to contain this flow, rather like the design of an air-cushion vehicle, to create a high-pressure area that will more than overcome the suck-down and instead add to the lift.

RAF Harriers and related aircraft have a simple LID (lift-improvement device) in the form of the two gun pods. These break up the impacting flow and, even though it can freely escape past the landing gears to front and rear, create a region between the pods where pressure is significantly above atmospheric. When the pods are removed, their effect is achieved by fitting strakes along the belly in the same locations.

FOD is an enormous subject. One aspect is birdstrikes, which cause significant attrition of low-flying aircraft everywhere that there are birds. Peculiar to the Harrier is FOD caused by poor operating procedures, which at the least can leave the aircraft covered in dirt blasted from the ground, and at worst can write off the engine fan, or the complete engine, or the complete aircraft. Despite its large fan and sea-level airflow of 432lb (196kg)/s, the Pegasus is a tough engine, and the Hylite fan blades stand up particularly well to most FOD, but at the same time it is essential for all Harrier personnel, especially pilots, to bear the problem in mind.

This is especially important when operating from unprepared sites. The Harrier obviously needs to be as self-sufficient as possible, and though (surprisingly) ladders are still deemed essential for cockpit access, various changes have made the RAF aircraft normally independent of ground services. Electrical power has been considerably uprated, both by fitting the Mk 2 version of the Lucas APU, with electrical output raised from 1·5kVA to 6kVA, while the original pair of engine-driven 4kVA alternators have given way to the 12kVA machine which was fitted to the AV-8A from the start.

One reason for wanting more electrical power has been the introduction of additional equipment. Of course, the recon pod consumes a little power, and this is often carried by No 4 Sqn. All RAF Harriers in front-line service have since the late 1970s also carried two items that alter the appearance of the aircraft. One is the RWR and the other the LRMTS.

Above: Not many photographs are available showing Harriers making rocket attacks. One of them is this portrait of the very first production Harrier, after conversion to GR.3 standard, on a range in Sardinia.

New equipment

The LRMTS (laser ranger and marked-target seeker) occupies the thimble extension on the nose. The Ferranti 106 laser, similar to that fitted to the Jaguar, is a Nd-YAG type which can be fired actively as a super-accurate measuring device which can be aimed by either the nav/attack system or the pilot within a 20° cone ahead. It provides target range, range-rate and angles, presented on the HUD. In the passive (MTS) mode it detects and locks on to any target illuminated with Nd-YAG (IR "black light") by friendly troops, providing the same weapon-guidance information as before. The ground illuminator and airborne receiver can be coded together to avoid spoofing IRCM (IR countermesures) or false lock-ons.

The RWR (radar warning receiver) is the MSDS ARI.18223, a typical 1960s-style installation which warns the pilot if his aircraft is being illuminated by a hostile radar. It covers the E to J frequency bands, of wavelengths from 15 down to 1·5cm, and receives at two aerials (antennae) mounted at the tail, that near the top of the fin leading edge covering the 180° facing ahead and that at the tip of the tailcone covering the 180° to the rear. The installation is rudimentary, the warning in the cockpit being merely a four-sector display which illuminates any 90° sector in which a hostile emitter is operating, and indicates its frequency band. Audible warning can also be given. In later aircraft the RWR is linked with an EW installation, but until May 1982 nothing had been provided to protect RAF Harriers. This subject is dealt with in the chapter on Operation Corporate, where EW protection was suddenly needed.

While these items were being retrofitted, more powerful engines became

Right: LRMTS with the lid off, a Ferranti picture showing the nose laser of a GR.3 and particularly laying bare the gimballed optical system of Cassegrain-telescope type.

British Aerospace Harrier GR.3

Below: The RAF Harrier GR.3 is here illustrated with a selection of its ordnance. The very advanced Wasp missile (shown with a tube launcher) will not now be selected for use by the RAF. In the Falklands, GR.3s were fitted with the Royal Navy rocket launcher, with 36 tubes of 2in calibre (see pages 38-9).

1 AIM-9B Sidewinder AAM (for the Falklands campaign the improved AIM-9L, now in production in Europe, was quickly made available, and a twin carrier was also cleared for use)
2 Hunting JP.233 dispenser (short type)
3 Lepus flare
4 Drop tank, 100gal (455lit); for the Falklands conflict a 190gal (864lit) pattern was quickly cleared for use
5 Wasp ASM launching pod (12 round)
6 Wasp ASM (unloaded); development of this weapon has recently been suspended
7 Practice-bomb dispenser with bombs installed
8 BAe reconnaissance pod with horizon-to-horizon optical cameras, forward oblique and various low-level cameras, plus BAe D type 401 IR linescan
9 Gun pod (one of two) containing 30mm Aden and ammunition
10 Ammunition, typically 120-130 rounds per gun, maximum being 150
11 Two Matra retarded bombs, 882lb (400kg)
12 ML twin carrier with two GP bombs, 1,000lb (454kg)
13 Rocket launch pod and rockets; one common type is Matra 155 with 18 tubes of 2·68in (68mm) for SNEB rockets
14 GBU-13/18 Paveway II smart (laser-guided) bomb which was based on the British 1,000lb (454kg) free-fall bomb
15 Hunting BL.755 cluster bomb, 611lb (277kg), (contains 147 bomblets in seven bays)

Right: Almost all RAF Harrier flying in Europe has been from airfields. Here XV738, the very first RAF Harrier (also illustrated opposite) is making a rolling takeoff with 3 Sqn.

Below: A standard RAF Harrier GR.3, XZ134 was one of the final batch of 12 aircraft ordered in 1974 (later buys were for attrition). It flies with 3 Sqn at RAF Gutersloh.

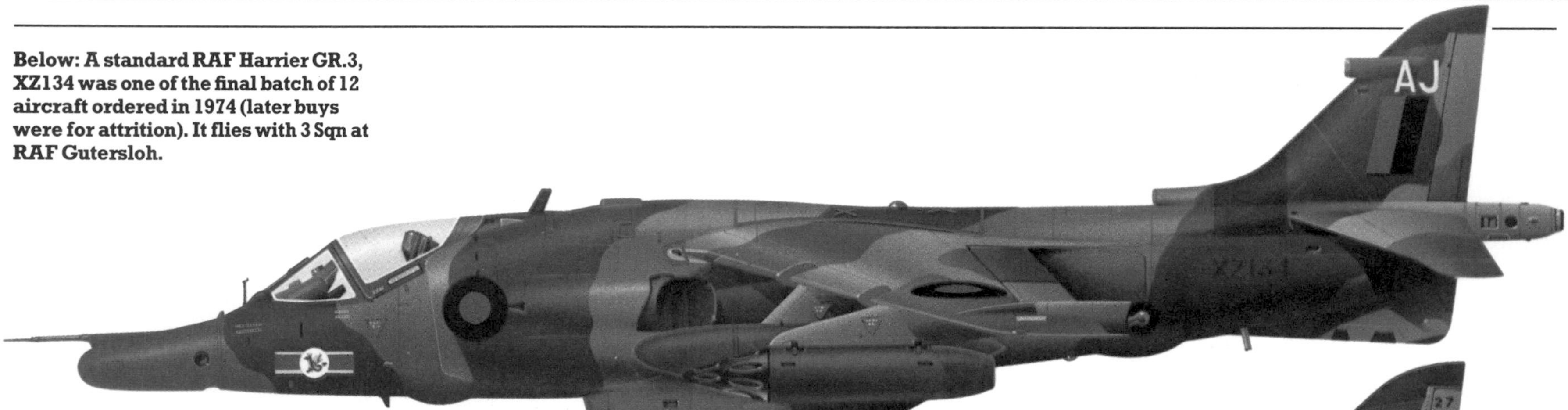

Below: AV-8A No 159241 was delivered in 1974 to Marine Corps squadron VMA-231, and is shown here in today's toned-down national markings. Home base is MCAS Cherry Point, NC.

available. The Pegasus 102, production mark of the Pegasus 10 which had run in 1969 at 20,500lb (9299kg), introduced a higher turbine entry temperature and was a field modification. The uprated aircraft became the GR.1A and T.2A. The Pegasus 103 (Pegasus 11), rated at 21,500lb (9752kg), became available in 1972, and by 1976 had replaced all earlier engines. The mark numbers were changed to GR.3 and T.4, while new two-seaters fitted with the Mk 103 from the start were styled T.4A.

Clearly one of the shortcomings of first-generation Harriers, especially those of the RAF, has been a lack of any EW (electronic warfare) capability. The addition of a rudimentary RWR gives 360° coverage of hostile emitters, but what does the pilot do about it, except perhaps perform a smart change of course or start jinking? In the Falklands war we saw the embarrassing spectacle of chaff bundles being jammed in under the airbrake and between bombs and their ejector-release units! Now at last even the existing GR.3s are to get a proper EW kit, and as MSDS (Marconi Space & Defence Systems) estimates the potential order (with RDT&E and all spares) as worth "£100 million plus", each installation must be costed at more than the original price of the Harrier GR.1! MSDS is providing a new RWR which will be linked with an internal multimode RF jammer produced by Northrop. Known as Zeus, the system will be installed by BAe in RAF Harriers, perhaps from 1985, and MSDS/Northrop will market it elsewhere. It has not been announced whether Zeus will be specified from the start for the GR.5 described later, which will carry the outstanding BAe Dynamics Alarm anti-emitter missile.

As noted earlier, the USMC specified the Pegasus Mk 803 (export 103, also called F402-RR-401) but had to accept temporary installation of the Mk 802 (export 102, or F402-RR-400) in the first ten AV-8As. Deliveries began on 26 January 1971, and in late 1972 all AV-8As were cycled through NAS Cherry Point to bring them up to definitive standard. This included not only the Dash-401 engine but also the back-up manual fuel control, which was later added to RAF engines, for control following a bird-strike and consequent surge and flame-out. The planned American licence production never materialized because of the funding in small annual batches, in the teeth of opposition by Congress, which made transfer of production prohibitively costly. Thus, to the 12 FY70-funded aircraft were added 18 funded in FY71, 30 in FY72 and 30 in FY73. This left 24 for FY74, but in fact plans changed.

At the start the Marines suffered encouragingly low attrition, but after three years the rate increased sharply. Almost all incidents appeared to reflect on the pilot rather than the aircraft, and after prolonged enquiries it was decided that the AV-8A was a mount for ex-fighter pilots, who in the initial stages had been selected exclusively, rather than ex-helicopter pilots, who were finding it very hard to stay mentally abreast of what was happening. While the pilot selection procedures were tightened and training patterns revised, the decision was taken to buy some two-seaters in the final batch. Fearful of Congress withholding funds, the Marines

Below: RAF No 4 Sqn is the only unit which routinely carries out reconnaissance missions, using the multisensor pod on the centreline. These GR.3s were on a mission from Wildenrath in May 1983. Aircraft letters come yellow, orange or red.

Left: Marine Corps No 158385, the second AV-8A to be built, was delivered to VMA-513 on 5 February 1971 and is seen here on the deck-edge elevator of USS *Guam* during the AV-8A's first sea deployment.

stuck 100 per cent to single-seaters in the first four increments, and only felt safe in buying trainers in the final year. Extra costs of the two-seaters and various weapon clearances ate into the budget so that in the final year, instead of 24, only 20 aircraft could be afforded. These comprised 12 AV-8As and eight two-seaters, which were expected to be called AV-8Bs but instead received the designation TAV-8A.

Marine modifications

Modifications kept being made to the Marine aircraft, as a result of operating experience. Though the value of the INS was not in doubt, the Marines wanted a rough-and-ready nav/attack system needing no warm-up/alignment time and less skilled maintenance, and in 1973 the FE.541 system was replaced by a Baseline nav/attack system comprising the HUD fed with data from a Smiths IWAC (interface/weapon-aiming computer) which usually provides CCIP (continuously computed impact point) steering markers for air/ground visual delivery. Another change was to replace the Mk 9D seat by the American Stencel SIII-S3, on national policy grounds, and another was to fit a non-toppling attitude/heading reference system. Hawker had also fitted tactical VHF radio to many AV-8As, and to all two-seaters, with a large inclined aerial mast above the fuselage. The two-seaters are specially equipped with both tactical VHF and UHF, for use in the Airborne Tac Air Commander role in control of ground forces.

The first combat unit, formed in April 1971, was VMA-513 at Beaufort (pronounced Bewf't) MCAS in South Carolina, under Bud Baker. This squadron did many of the weapon trials at China Lake and Point Mugu, both in California. Next came the remaining units of Marine Air Group 32, all at MCAS Cherry Point, North Carolina: VMA-542, VMA-231 and training squadron VMA(T)-203. All have operated intensively from every kind of site or ship, including carriers (CV-42 *Franklin D. Roosevelt*), assault ships or Landing Platform, Helicopter (LPH-3 *Guam* in particular) and LHAs (Landing Helicopter Assault). It is largely because of Marines experience that Harriers made more than 13,000 missions from ships at sea before there was an accident of any kind, as noted in the next chapter.

In early 1970 Col Baker asked a fellow Marine, Capt Harry Blot, to be project officer for developing ACM (air-combat manoeuvring) with the AV-8A. Blot quickly decided the basic aircraft had excellent handling, a good engine that kept going in all combat situations, and an excellent thrust/weight ratio, but was penalized by its high wing-loading and poor rear view. Blot was under the impression that Viffing (VIFF, vectoring in forward flight) was common practice in RAF squadrons. In fact, Hugh Merewether had briefly toyed with "cracking the nozzles" at various speeds in the first 1127(RAF), and so had at least two RAF test pilots, but it was strictly absent from RAF Pilots Notes. Oddly, there had never been a deliberate attempt to see how well the Harrier

Left: Activity aboard USS *Guam* in 1974 as AV-8As of VMA-542 fly training missions. Each AV-8A is clean, without even guns, but inflight-refuelling probes are installed, for A-4 "buddy" contacts.

Defensive Break by Harrier

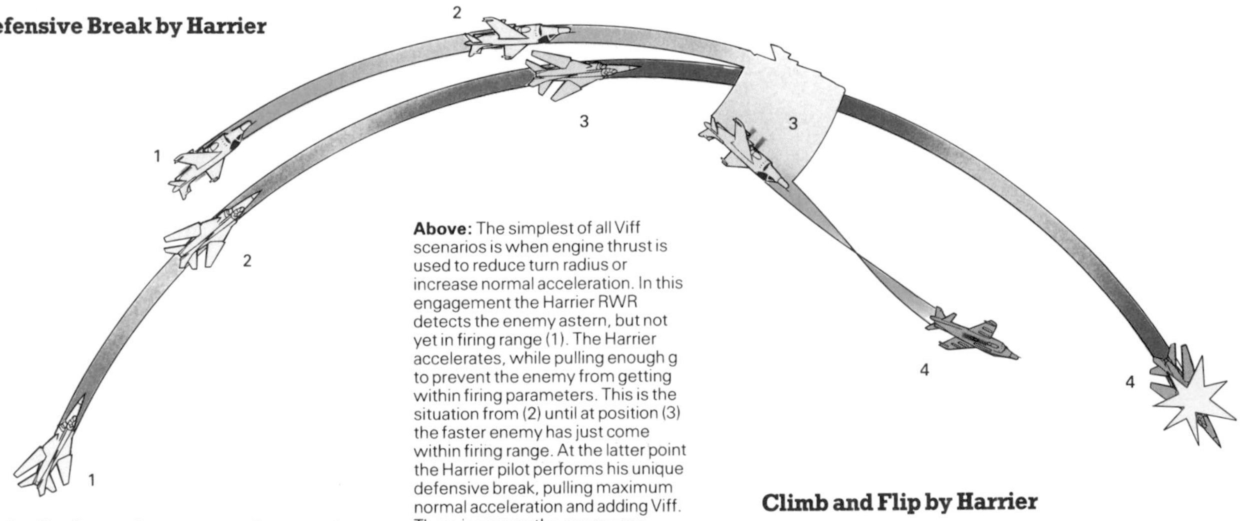

Above: The simplest of all Viff scenarios is when engine thrust is used to reduce turn radius or increase normal acceleration. In this engagement the Harrier RWR detects the enemy astern, but not yet in firing range (1). The Harrier accelerates, while pulling enough g to prevent the enemy from getting within firing parameters. This is the situation from (2) until at position (3) the faster enemy has just come within firing range. At the latter point the Harrier pilot performs his unique defensive break, pulling maximum normal acceleration and adding Viff. There is no way the enemy can avoid overshooting, and he then becomes an easy close-range target (4). Variables are numerous, one being that at (3) the Harrier pilot could even set the nozzles to 98·5° for more violent deceleration; another is that at (4) the half-roll may not be necessary, especially if AAMs are used.

Right: In these three sets of artwork the Harrier appears as an RAF GR.3, but in fact the drawings are based on originals stemming from the US Marine Corps, who pioneered the use of Viffing as an extra advantage in combat.

could look after itself if intercepted, but this is just what Blot was asked to do with the AV-8A.

Test sorties at the US NATC (Naval Air Test Center) were at a premium, so he decided to go straight to the limit: achieve 500-kt speed and then slam the nozzles to 98°! In his own words: "The airplane started decelerating at an alarming rate, the magnitude of which I could not determine because my nose was pressed up against the gunsight . . . the violence of the maneuver had dislodged me from the seat, and I was now straddling the stick, with my right hand extended backwards between my legs trying to hold on for dear life . . ." This was the start of the discovery that the Harrier can be a most difficult opponent in close combat.

The point has already been made that the Harrier is very small, smokeless and an odd shape, so that it is peculiarly difficult for an enemy to see at a glance what it is doing. Its IR signature is low and diffuse. On top of these factors, its ability to Viff was obviously worth exploring. NASA ran fresh trials with an XV-6A, while Blot organized computer simulations which showed, discouragingly, that Viffing would entail such loss in energy as to nullify any gains in manoeuvre. The computer program was then loaded into the twin-dome ACM simulator at MCAIR in St Louis, and this showed a very different picture. Most of it was impressive, but at low speeds there were results that conflicted with Blot's findings. He was, in particular, told that no aircraft could turn in the way he reported, while harsh demands at low speeds resulted in end-over-end tumbling resulting in a crash. Blot went back to NATC and spent many sorties carefully approaching these computer situations. He found that the uncontrolled tumbling was an error in the simulation, while the turn-rate discrepancy resulted from the actual aircraft being able to achieve a form of blown-wing effect, due to the pumping action of the jets, which with skill could result in turns that no other aircraft can equal.

Tests were also run in Britain, notably at the RAE, but the RAF has shown only marginal interest in ACM and its Harriers try to avoid combat, which is not part of their mission. The US Marine Corps, however, not only found exciting possibilities but even succeeded in getting British Aerospace (as Hawker Siddeley became on 1 January 1978) and Rolls-Royce to remove two limitations on Viff potential. The nozzles were modified with greater strength and a higher-

Climb and Flip by Harrier

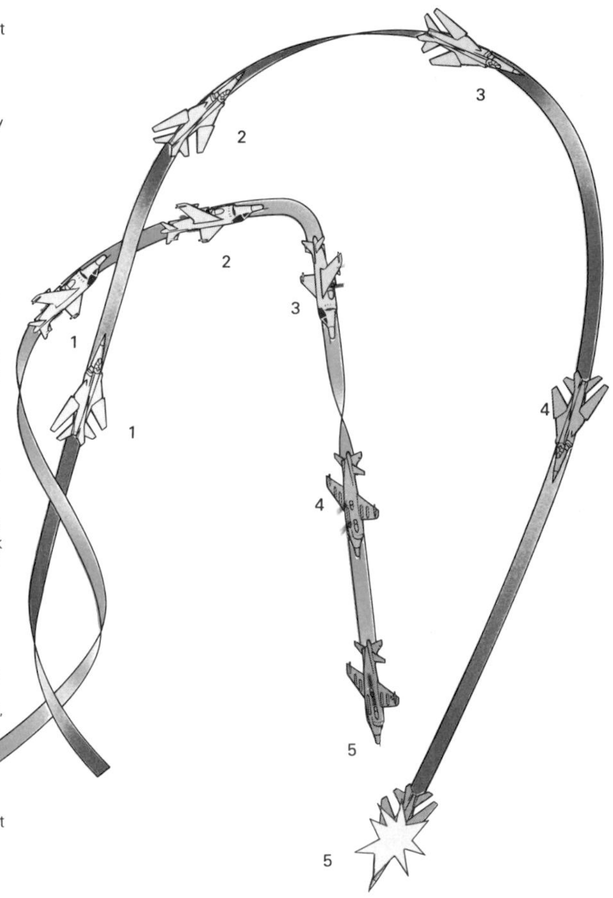

Right: In this so-called "climb and flip" the Harrier performs one of its numerous "impossible" manoeuvres, which are now part of the routine air-combat repertoire of all experienced US Marine Corps Harrier pilots. The sequence begins with the Harrier (whose trajectory is indicated by a blue line in all these illustrations) and its adversary (red line) climbing in a steep spiral and losing speed, the enemy close behind and eager to get within firing parameters before the Harrier can pull one of its tricks. From this position (1), with the enemy in close trail, the Harrier pilot using light stick forces pulls well past the vertical (2) and, as the speed bleeds away through the 200-knot level, he adds a small nozzle angle (3). The Harrier very quickly flips to a 90° nose-low attitude. The enemy has no option but to follow a semi-ballistic arching curve to end up going steeply downhill. Still travelling quite slowly, the Harrier goes into full reverse (4). There is no way the enemy can avoid going on down past what seems to be a Harrier stopped in mid-air. When the enemy gets to position (5) he presents the simplest possible target, for guns or AAMs.

Harrier as the Attacker

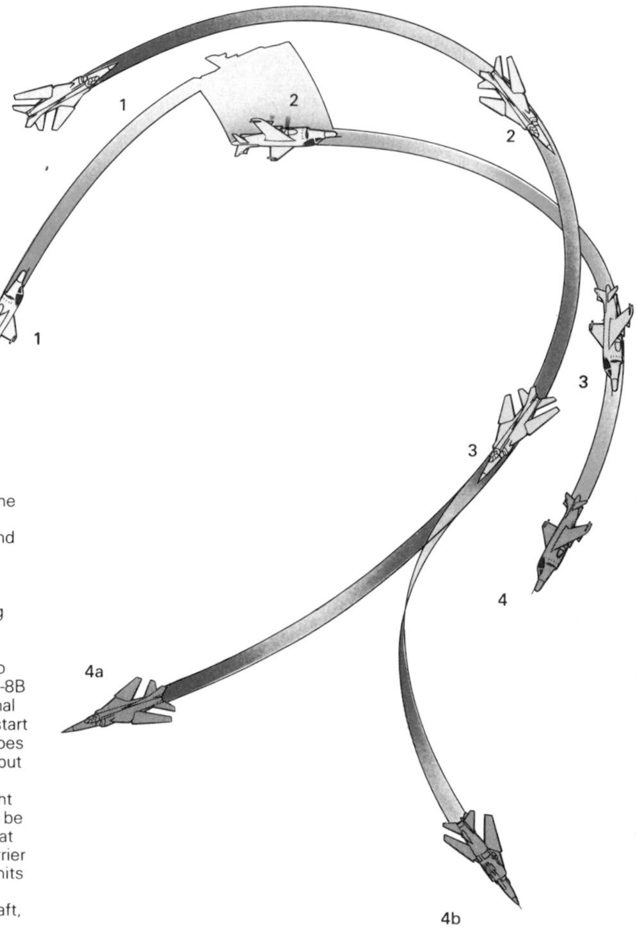

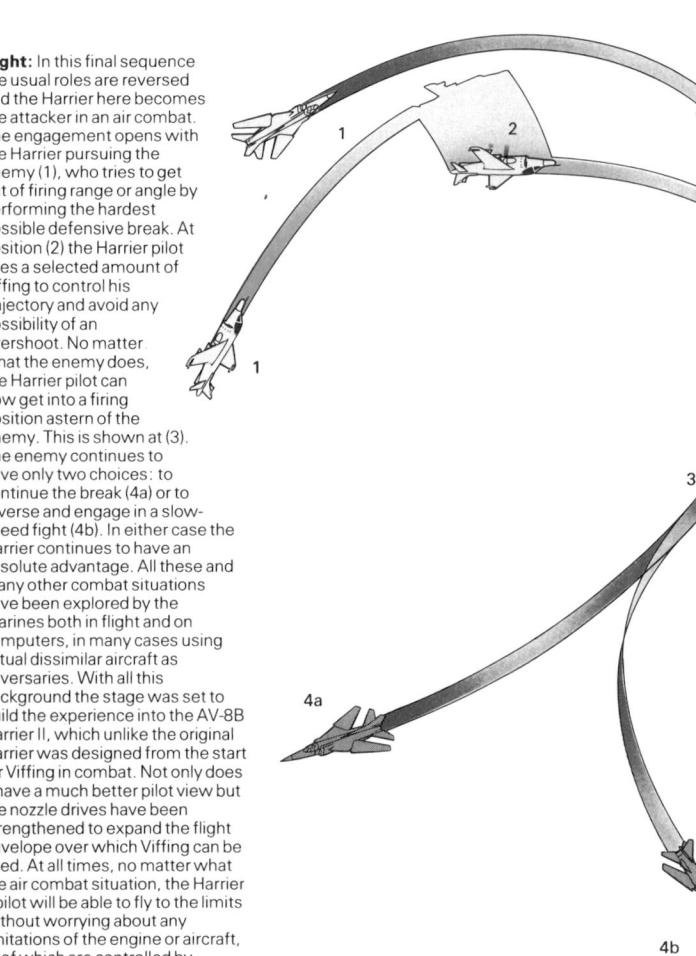

Right: In this final sequence the usual roles are reversed and the Harrier here becomes the attacker in an air combat. The engagement opens with the Harrier pursuing the enemy (1), who tries to get out of firing range or angle by performing the hardest possible defensive break. At position (2) the Harrier pilot uses a selected amount of Viffing to control his trajectory and avoid any possibility of an overshoot. No matter what the enemy does, the Harrier pilot can now get into a firing position astern of the enemy. This is shown at (3). The enemy continues to have only two choices: to continue the break (4a) or to reverse and engage in a slow-speed fight (4b). In either case the Harrier continues to have an absolute advantage. All these and many other combat situations have been explored by the Marines both in flight and on computers, in many cases using actual dissimilar aircraft as adversaries. With all this background the stage was set to build the experience into the AV-8B Harrier II, which unlike the original Harrier was designed from the start for Viffing in combat. Not only does it have a much better pilot view but the nozzle drives have been strengthened to expand the flight envelope over which Viffing can be used. At all times, no matter what the air combat situation, the Harrier II pilot will be able to fly to the limits without worrying about any limitations of the engine or aircraft, all of which are controlled by computers.

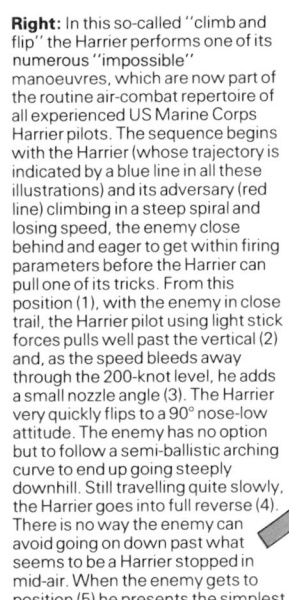

Left: Another photograph of Marine Corps rocket training on the Yuma ranges, in this case with monster Zuni rockets, which are the largest of their kind used by any Western air forces. The AV-8A, 158957 of VMA-542, was lost in 1976.

power drive, while the engine was provided with a combat plug, a screw-in turbine temperature control fuse, that for 2½ minutes allows the engine to give full power in wingborne flight, instead of a maximum of 75 per cent. This removed all restrictions on Viffing, at all speeds, attitudes and altitudes, without ever having to keep an eye on instruments. The potential discovered is described by Blot, now a colonel, as "absolutely eye-watering". It has been utilized to the full in the AV-8B.

In the mid-1970s the US Marine Corps began working on a major CILOP (conversion in lieu of procurement) programme to update surviving AV-8As for continued use through the 1980s. The scheme was put into operation at Naval Air Rework Facility, Cherry Point in 1979. It was planned to rework 60 aircraft, but the figure was cut by budget pressures to only 47, and these have been upgraded to AV-8C standard. The chief task is an airframe audit and rework under a SLEP (service life extension programme) for a further 4,000 hours flying. The LIDs of the AV-8B Harrier II (described later) are installed to enhance payload/range. Surprisingly, no laser or other weapon delivery system is installed, but EW gear is vastly augmented. The ALR-45 radar warning receiver is installed, with aft-facing aerials in the tailcone and forward-facing on the wingtips. A Goodyear ALE-39 dispenser for chaff, flares or jammers is installed in the rear equipment bay. An Obogs (on-board oxygen generation system) similar to that described in the AV-8B chapter is installed, and new radios include a new UHF and the KY-58 secure voice transmission system. AV-8C conversions are supported by kits from BAe Kingston-Brough division and MCAIR St Louis.

The plane in Spain

There is another operator of regular Harriers: the Spanish naval aviation, or Arma Aérea de la Armada. The Franco government began discussions in 1972, and, following a demonstration by chief test pilot John Farley which showed that the wooden deck of the old carrier *Dédalo* would barely get warm, far less burst into flames, a requirement was announced for 24 V/STOLs and an initial order was placed for six single-seat Harrier Mk 55s and two two-seat Mk 58s. Because it was feared a possible British Labour administration would tear up the deal, the order was placed via Washington and MCAIR, the aircraft being shipped to St Louis for final assembly and delivery as AV-8S and TAV-8S machines with BuAer numbers. They were assigned to Escuadrilla 008, with Spanish designation VA-1 Matador and, for the trainer, VAE-1. In 1977 a repeat order was placed for five more single-seaters. They are broadly to AV-8A standard, but with a broad VHF blade aerial for communicating with helicopters at sea. Operations from *Dédalo* and shore base Rota, near Cadiz, have been most successful and the new carrier, *Principe de Asturias* will operate 12 Harrier IIs.

Left: A pair of VA-1 Matadors of the second batch, alias Harrier Mk 55 or AV-8S, seen at BAe Dunsfold in company with G-VTOL. Because of the change in the Spanish government, there was no objection to placing this order direct with BAe.

Sea Harrier

Harriers of all kinds have operated from more ships, of more diverse types, than any other aircraft in history. Certainly no other aircraft comes close to the Harrier in logging over 13,000 missions from ship decks before there was a single incident involving damage to an aircraft. This chapter describes the special multirole Harrier developed for operations at sea. It can be based on large carriers, small carriers with ski jumps, small carriers without ski jumps, surface warships with a flat pad 80ft by 50ft (24m×15m), and also on container ships which 48 hours previously had no military equipment on board, and ships fitted with a novel Skyhook.

Above: Royal Navy No 809 Sqn was assembled at short notice by Lt-Cdr (now Cdr) Tim Gedge, and here most of its beautifully painted aircraft are seen immediately before departure from Yeovilton.

It is curious that, while some air staffs still ignore the destruction of their airfields during – if not immediately prior to – any future war, naval staffs the world over have recognized that the Harrier opens up totally new possibilities for deploying air power anywhere that a ship, not necessarily a carrier, can go. Back in February 1963 the P.1127 ran a programme of demonstrations from the carrier HMS *Ark Royal*, test pilots Bedford and Merewether discovering that operations from a deck were, they said, "simpler than from an airfield."

It may be that, in pursuing an elusive commonality with the RAF in 1963-64, and seeking the Mach 2 V/STOL P.1154RN, the Royal Navy was biting off more than it could chew. There would probably have been major problems in operating these heavy and expensive machines, though it is doubtful if they would have cost more than their replacement, the Spey-Phantom, which needs a large ship with full catapult and arrester gear. But the abrupt decision of the 1966 Labour government to terminate British fixed-wing airpower at sea, and to cancel the new carrier (CVA-01) then in design, brought a totally new situation. It is difficult for a service to argue against Government cuts in defence. If Their Lordships had said "What would we do if Argentina invaded the Falklands?" the Defence Minister in 1966 would have replied, in effect, "We really cannot concern ourselves with such unlikely eventualities!" So the fixed-wing Fleet Air Arm wound down to a full stop, and, after a while, saddened and perturbed people all over Britain stuck labels in their cars saying FLY NAVY.

Below: Taken in the post-Falkland period in late 1982, this photograph shows a Sea Harrier FRS.1 streaming fuel from the jettison pipes. It has Training Sidewinder missiles installed.

By the late 1960s P.1127s, Kestrels, XV-6As and Harriers had demonstrated the complete absence of hassle in operating from many warships, some with nothing but a small helicopter pad, in various sea states with winds gusting to 40kt and with the ship doing anything from full speed to being at anchor. Several major shipbuilding companies were studying "Harrier carriers", with displacements down to a mere 6,000 tons, and without the need for catapults and arrester gear. The British Admiralty, having been informed that there would be no more fixed-wing seagoing airpower, and that there would be no replacements for the ageing fleet carriers *Ark Royal* and *Eagle*, was clearly faced with a lunatic situation. The government view was that future maritime airpower would be provided by the land-based RAF, a service already over-extended and unable to operate except around the shores of Britain! The US Navy could not be relied upon to provide airpower for purely British actions around the world, and the only possible, and obvious, alternative was to deploy a specially developed maritime version of the Harrier from a new class of V/STOL ship. Special ships were clearly indicated, though the V/STOL aircraft could also operate from simple helicopter pads on existing warships. The Admiralty was kept continuously updated on Hawker Siddeley's Maritime Harrier studies, yet, if the official story is to be believed, the decision was taken in 1968 to deploy a new class of V/STOL carrier – known as a "through-deck cruiser"

Below: One of the third batch of production Sea Harriers, this FRS.1 is depicted with a single victory symbol. It later destroyed a second Mirage in the South Atlantic war while serving with 809 Sqn.

Left: France has always eyed the Harrier, and especially the Sea Harrier, with extreme interest. Here an RAF GR.1 is seen aboard the *Jeanne d'Arc*, a most useful ship of over 12,000 tons displacement, in October 1973. Sea Harriers would fit this ship ideally, though there might be political obstacles to such a mating.

Above: In 1971 RAF No 1(F) Sqn took their Harrier GR.1s aboard HMS *Ark Royal*, trying to assist a stupid political scheme whereby, in the absence of such ships, the RAF would provide air cover for the Royal Navy! No 1 has enough to do in connection with warfare on land, but the trials on this ship were impressively simple.

Below: When delivered the Sea Harriers were factory-finished in Royal Navy dark grey and white, with squadron tail badge, in this case 800 Sqn.

Below: In the South Atlantic aircraft were repainted for reduced visibility, as noted in the next chapter. This former 899 Sqn machine served with 800 Sqn.

(TDC) to avoid any hint that it might be used for the forbidden fixed-wing aircraft – which was to be designed *for helicopters only.* This is so beyond belief that it could be discounted, were it not for the fact that the initial form of TDC ship was indeed not optimised for fixed-wing V/STOL operation!

Part of the trouble was that, like many air staff at that time (1968-72), the RN Air Warfare department totally overlooked the air defence capability of the Harrier because it had (an official quote) "too short an endurance" and did not fly at Mach 2. Indeed, when RAF No 1 Sqn received an unprecedented clearance to go aboard RN carriers and fly combat missions (which the squadron did in March 1970, without the slightest trouble), the author was advised by an RN spokesman that "Of course, this idea that the fleet might be defended by Harriers is laughable!" Despite this, Hawker was asked by MoD to modify No 1 Sqn Harriers for shipboard operation by adding tie-down shackles to the outrigger gears and add a relay to the nosewheel steering so that, whenever the anti-skid brakes were switched off, the nosewheel steering would be engaged, preventing the aircraft from pirouetting round on a rolling deck. The RAF had plenty of other tasks for 1 Sqn – which could well have been wiped out on the first day of a war, anyway – and in any case looked askance at the whole idea of a Maritime Harrier. The "light blues" doubted the ability of such an aircraft to intercept supersonic "Backfires", judged its ship to be costly and vulnerable, and feared that resurrection of naval air-power would result in cutbacks in the RAF's own budget. Meanwhile, the "dark blues" were not only mentally locked-in to the concept of Big Ship air-power but still wanted highly supersonic speed and a backseat crew-member.

Thus in true British fashion, the environment was confused and unfavourable. Despite this a few farsighted and dogged individuals, mostly at Kingston, kept on studying the possibilities for what in 1971 was called the Maritime Support Harrier. Though the RN Ship Department at Bath was well into the design of the TDC ship, its form was still somewhat fluid and there was no official requirement for it to carry any aircraft except helicopters. As for the MS Harrier, this too was fluid, because Hawker and MCAIR were busy with a next-generation aircraft, the AV-16 family, powered by the more powerful Pegasus 15 and in some forms capable of supersonic speed on the level. It was partly because of this vision of increased performance that, in early 1971, the RN Air Warfare staff began to consider an MS Harrier seriously; but the whole situation was made academic by the fact that there was no money.

The "Through-Deck Cruiser"

From the start of the TDC ship design it had been policy that these ships would serve in an ASW (anti-submarine warfare) role, act in a command/control role for both naval and air forces, and "make a contribution to area air defence". When the author asked what the latter meant he was told that it was interpreted as meaning a requirement for the Sea Dart SAM, and as finally designed a twin launcher for this missile represented virtually the only armament of these large and costly vessels! But at some time in late 1971 the Admiralty not only made a case for a Maritime Harrier but got Treasury permission for it, and this not only resulted in a rethink of the TDC ship but also enabled Hawker to authorize a firm design programme. Rather than being an AV-16, the Maritime Harrier was to be a minimum-change Harrier, and when the Naval Staff Target for its previously forbidden new jet was issued in August 1972 it was seen to be written round the Harrier GR.3 with the minimum of alterations.

At last there was a programme for a V/STOL and a ship to carry it. Vickers received the contract for the first ship in April 1973, with a planned commissioning date of 1980. The TDC designation was gradually replaced by others:

Left: An unusual formation off the Devon coast in 1981 made up of Sea Harriers of 899 Sqn (lead aircraft, tail code VL for Yeovilton), 801 (nearest, code N for HMS *Invincible*) and 800 (tail code H for HMS *Hermes*).

Left: Today HMS ***Invincible*** **has close-in Phalanx guns (small white thimbles at bow and stern) as well as her Sea Dart launcher. On deck in late 1983 were two Sea Harriers and a Sea King HAS.5.**

official documents since 1980 have called these ships Command Cruisers, ASW Cruisers, AS Cruisers and CAHs (for Carrier, Assault Helicopter). At Kingston, Hawker received the development study contract for what was called the Naval Harrier. As studies had been going on in depth for several years previously, and money (equated with time) was tight, the job should have been completed quickly. Sadly, funding was administered in trickles, and often dried up entirely, and the planned go-ahead was delayed until January 1973, when an order for 24 aircraft was arranged. This was then delayed until June, when a complete review of the UK's defence commitments put the whole programme back into the melting pot. At last Hawker were advised in December 1973 that the go-ahead had been agreed, and would be announced the following week. What actually happened was a "fuel crisis", soaring inflation and industrial unrest. In 1974 there were two General Elections, a series of Defence Cuts and a near-total loss of hope. Then on 15 May 1975, as chief test pilot Farley and chief designer (Harrier) Fozard were on short finals at Dunsfold in the company Dove, the tower advised them "The BBC has just announced they're ordering 24 Sea Harriers!"

Designation of the aircraft is Sea Harrier FRS.1, for fighter/reconnaissance/strike. This versatility has rarely been attempted in any one aircraft, and it was not so much making the best of a bad job as the result of prolonged tests to establish the missions that can be flown from a small deck. The three roles actually spelt out in the Naval Staff Target were: (F) a 400nm (741km) radius of action at altitude carrying guns and Sidewinders against any ship-based or long-range shore-based aircraft; (R) sea search of at least 27 000sq miles (70 000sq km) in one hour at low level; and (S) at least 250nm (463km) radius (depending on mission profile) carrying a wide range of anti-ship or ground-attack stores, with accurate delivery.

In fact, mission radius and load were already known to depend on the takeoff run available, as with any other fixed-wing machine, and in the early 1970s a further major variable came into the picture: the ski jump. Before describing this, it is worth noting that by 1972 the Hawker test pilots had deeply explored Harrier operations from ships and come up with basic operating rules. If mission load is not important, the fastest reaction time, typically 90s from initiation of engine start to wingborne flight, is achieved with a VTO, and this also burns the least fuel (a matter of a mere 100lb, 45kg, to wingborne flight, compared with over 1,000lb (454kg), for an F-14). VTO enables aircraft to be spotted only 30ft (10m) apart, gives least sensitivity to ship motion and hardly ever requires the captain to alter course or speed. STO, on the other hand, enables heavier loads to be carried for any given radius, and a 500ft (152m) run with 30kt (55km/h) WOD (wind over the deck) gives exactly double the mission load that can be lifted from VTO. It was found that the ideal deck markings were white "tram lines" just 7ft (2·13m) apart, and that the takeoff clearway need be no more than 38ft (11·6m) wide. Harriers can line-up nose to tail and takeoff at full power with nozzles pointing aft. As for landings, these were always VL, and not only simpler but safer than using conventional carrier aircraft which hit the wires at 120kt (222km/h) relative speed.

Below: The island of HMS *Hermes* shelters XZ450, the first Sea Harrier to fly, on board for operational trials in the Irish Sea in October and early November 1979.

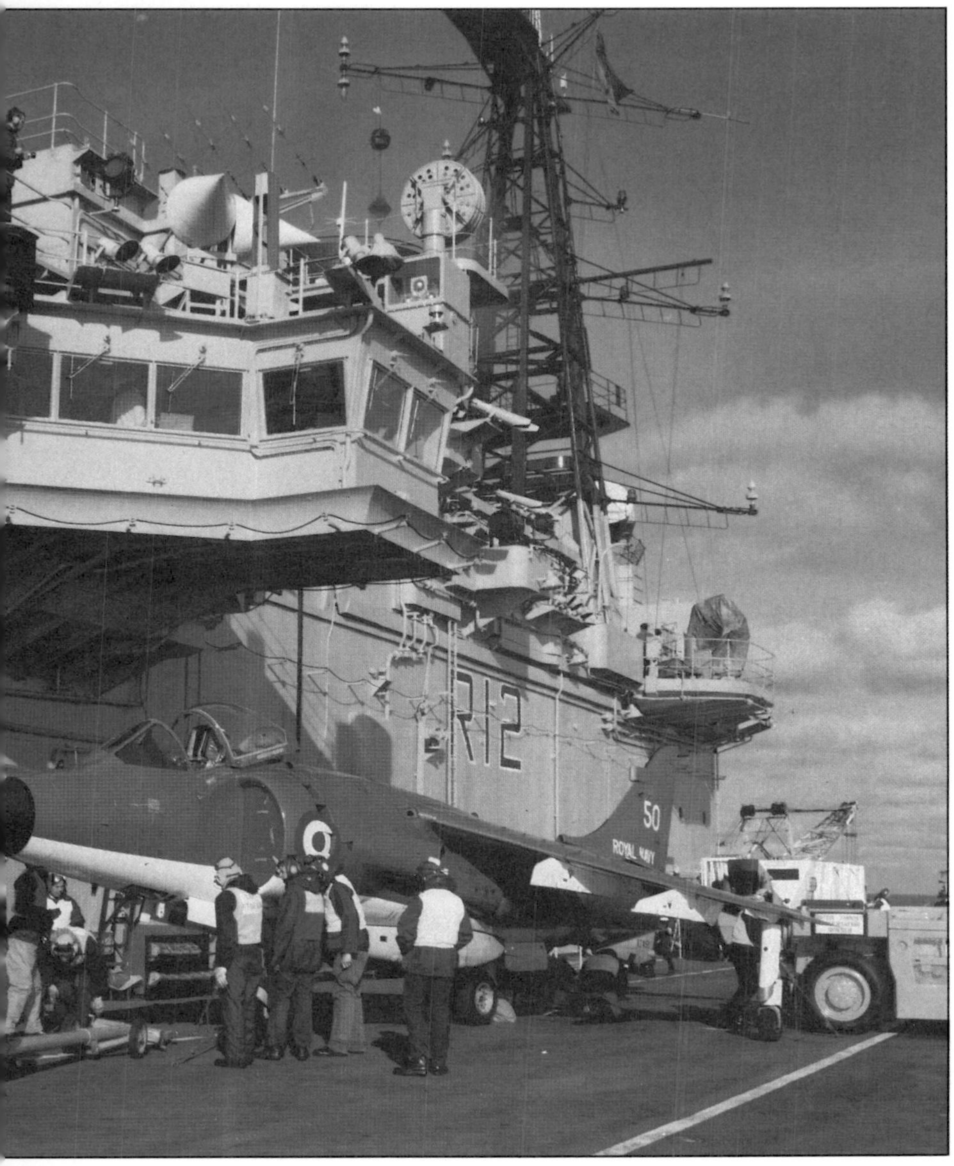

Sortie performance

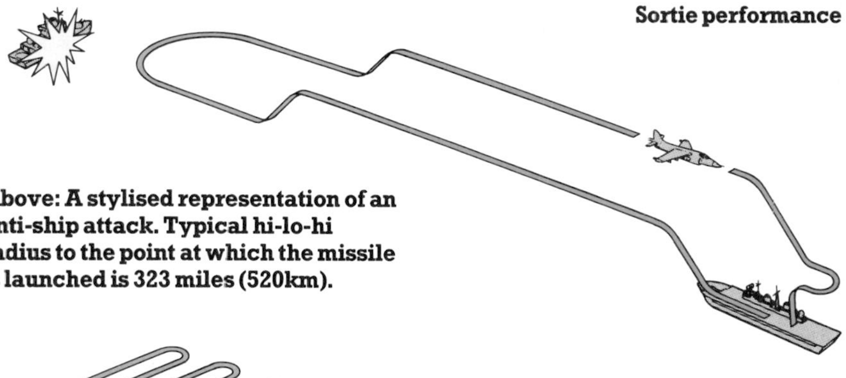

Above: A stylised representation of an anti-ship attack. Typical hi-lo-hi radius to the point at which the missile is launched is 323 miles (520km).

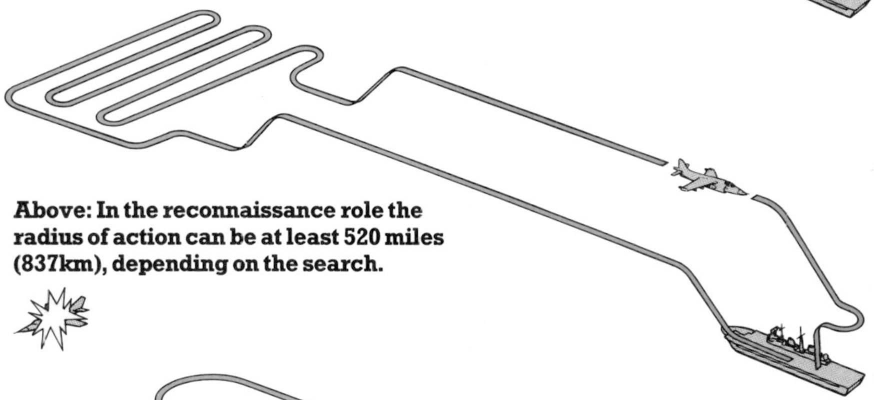

Above: In the reconnaissance role the radius of action can be at least 520 miles (837km), depending on the search.

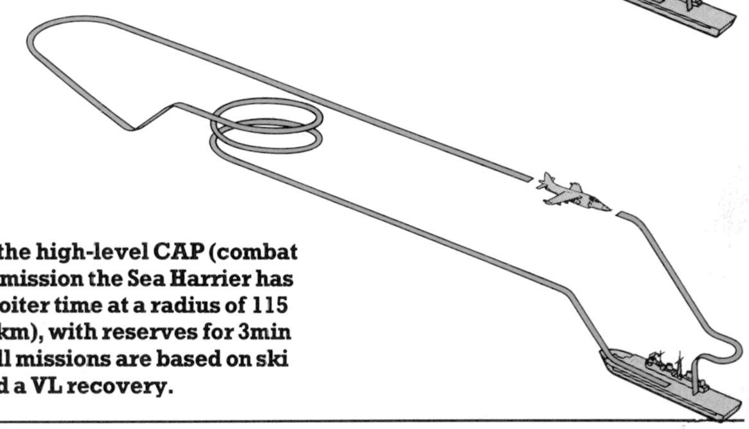

Above: In the high-level CAP (combat air patrol) mission the Sea Harrier has 1½ hours loiter time at a radius of 115 miles (185km), with reserves for 3min combat. All missions are based on ski takeoff and a VL recovery.

Left: The DB (development batch) GR.1 Harrier XV281 made the first ski jump trials at the RAE Bedford, beginning with the ramp set at 6° on 5 August 1977. Here 281 goes off the end in the spring of 1978 with the ramp set at 15°, which is close to the best angle for operational use.

All this had been worked out in detail, and remains valid, and one particular series of trials was to take off at lower and lower airspeeds to investigate the limiting value of ASI and AOA, so that in any situation the maximum safe weapon load or minimum safe deck run could be assessed. Unlike a runway takeoff, the aircraft is instantly out of ground effect as it runs off the edge of the deck. On the other hand, it can be allowed to sink, because the deck is something like 50ft (15m) above the sea. But there is not a lot of time or space, and if total engine failure were to occur as the aircraft left the deck, it would go into the sea in 2½s, barely time for the pilot to eject. The dynamics of carrier flying have been studied by many people, some of whom in the mid-1940s were convinced landing gears could be replaced by flexible decks, while others believed it would help if the deck moved relative to the ship! Vectored thrust introduced a new situation, and an officer studying for an MPhil thesis at the University of Southampton came up with an answer whose importance is matched by its elegant simplicity.

Lt-Cdr Doug Taylor RN wrote his thesis on the subject of V/STOL operations from confined spaces – not necessarily ships – and showed that if the takeoff surface ends in an upward curve, great benefits ensue. As in any STO departure, there is a choice between length of run (for any given wind) and mission load. Taylor calculated that leaving with a trajectory inclined upwards at about 10° would add an upwards velocity component that would counter the "fall" resulting from insufficient airspeed, and thus compensate for an initially inadequate combination of jet thrust plus wing lift to balance the weight. In other words, the Harrier could start its flight with deficient lift (resulting from either too much mission load or insufficient STO run). Over the next ten seconds or so the thrust component from the nozzles set at 50° accelerates the aircraft to about 35kt (65km/h) higher airspeed, by which time there is no lift deficiency, and from this point on the aircraft can climb away normally. The big advantages are that it is possible either to take the air with a much heavier load or at greatly reduced airspeed, the entire initial trajectory is much higher above the sea or ground, and in the event of engine failure there is much more time in which to assess the situation and eject. In the case of a ship launch in severe weather, a ski ramp ensures a positive upwards trajectory even in the worst case of the ship pitching bows-down into the sea.

It is a yet further grave reflection on the British Official Establishment that from 1972 until mid-1975 there was very little support for the ski-jump idea, even though – at considerable expense – Hawker had done extensive studies and model tests which fully confirmed the most sanguine predictions. Indeed, the ruling view in the Admiralty was that such a disturbing idea was unwelcome, to the extent that Fozard called the ship experts "The Flat Deck Preservation Society". Doggedly, the first ship was built with a flat deck and a Sea Dart launcher bang in the bows on the centreline, so that a ski ramp would obstruct its arc of fire!

Ski-jump – at last!

In 1976 Hawker at last managed to get the MoD to fund the construction of a ski ramp for research on land, and this was built by Redpath Dorman Long at RAE Bedford. The first ski launch was made by P.1127(RAF) XV281 on 5 August 1977 at an exit angle of 6°. Subsequently this aircraft and others, including two-seaters, made 367 launches at angles up to 20°, at which angle the landing-gear oleos were just bottoming with the 4g vertical acceleration. Over 100 pilots had a go – they queued up – and Harriers took the air at 100kt (185km/h) below the normal STO speed of 142kt (263km/h)!

Not least of the many good features of this brilliant idea was that no aircraft modifications whatsoever were called for. This was doubly welcome, because the Sea Harriers had really become quite new aircraft, and in any case were,

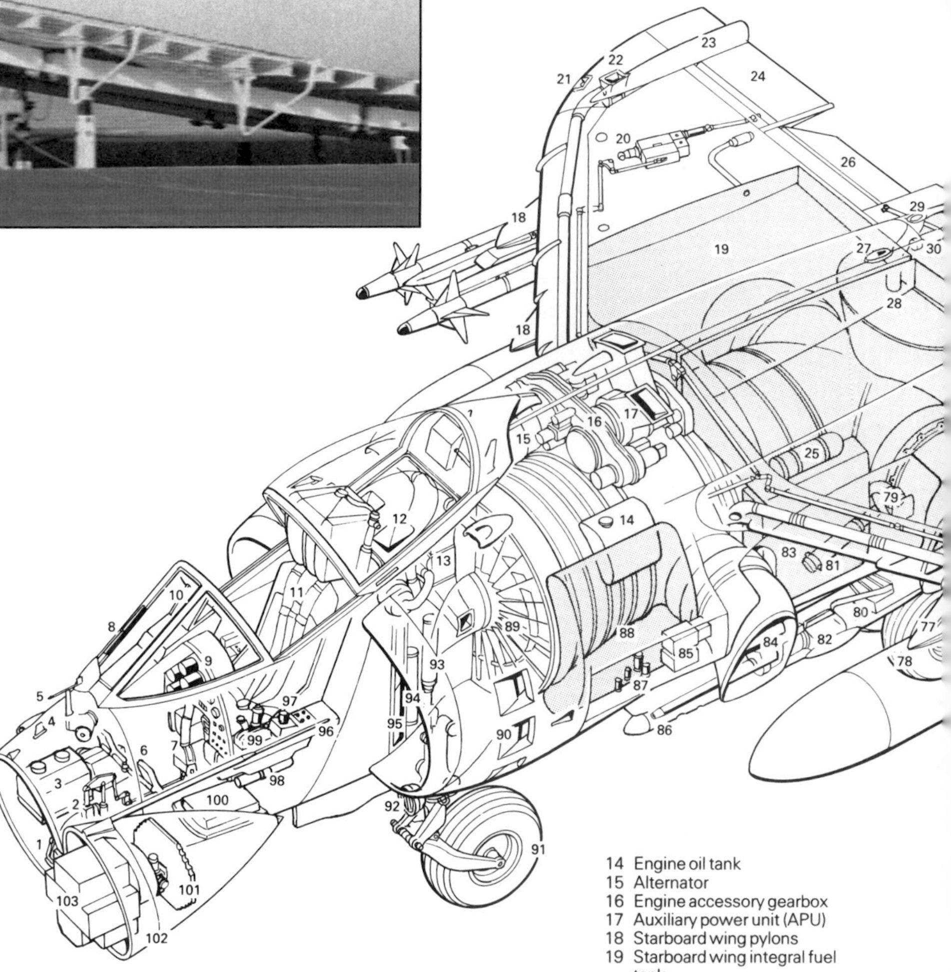

British Aerospace Sea Harrier FRS.1 cutaway

1 Pitch RCV (reaction control valve)
2 Pitch feel and trim actuators
3 Inertial platform
4 IFF aerial
5 Yaw vane
6 Rudder pedals
7 Control column
8 Windscreen wiper
9 Instrument panel
10 Pilot's head-up-display (HUD)
11 Martin-Baker Mk 10H zero-zero ejection seat
12 Boundary-layer air exhaust ducts
13 Cockpit air-conditioning system
14 Engine oil tank
15 Alternator
16 Engine accessory gearbox
17 Auxiliary power unit (APU)
18 Starboard wing pylons
19 Starboard wing integral fuel tank
20 Aileron power unit
21 Starboard navigation light
22 Roll control RCV
23 Outrigger wheel fairing
24 Starboard aileron
25 Hydraulic reservoir
26 Plain flap
27 Anti-collision light
28 Water tank
29 Water filler cap
30 Flap hydraulic jack

Ski jumps save lives

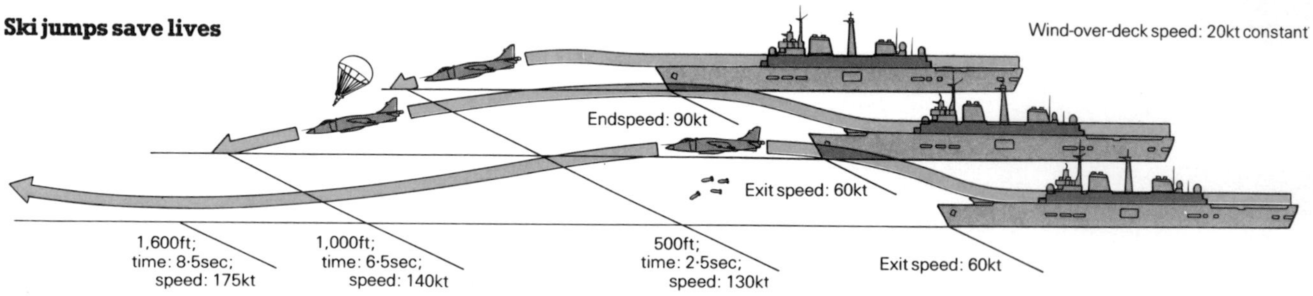

Above: Even though failure of the nozzle drive happens much less often than once in 10,000 launches, it is a factor to be reckoned with. In takeoff – jets aft – from a flat deck (top) the pilot has to eject, but has barely enough time to realize it before he hits the sea. With a ski jump at maximum weight he has almost three times as long (centre drawing). Alternatively, by smartly jettisoning external stores, he can even climb away despite the failure.

Below: Another, quite unrelated, benefit of the ski jump is that it enables a Sea Harrier either to carry a bigger load or to use a much smaller deck. In the traditional flat deck (upper ship drawing) the aircraft goes off the end after a run of 600ft (180m) at a speed of 120kt (222km/h), carrying 10,000lb (4536kg) of fuel and weapons. With a ski jump it can become airborne at only 70kt (130km/h) (middle), or else can carry 13,000lb (5900kg) of fuel/weapons.

Ski jumps add weapons

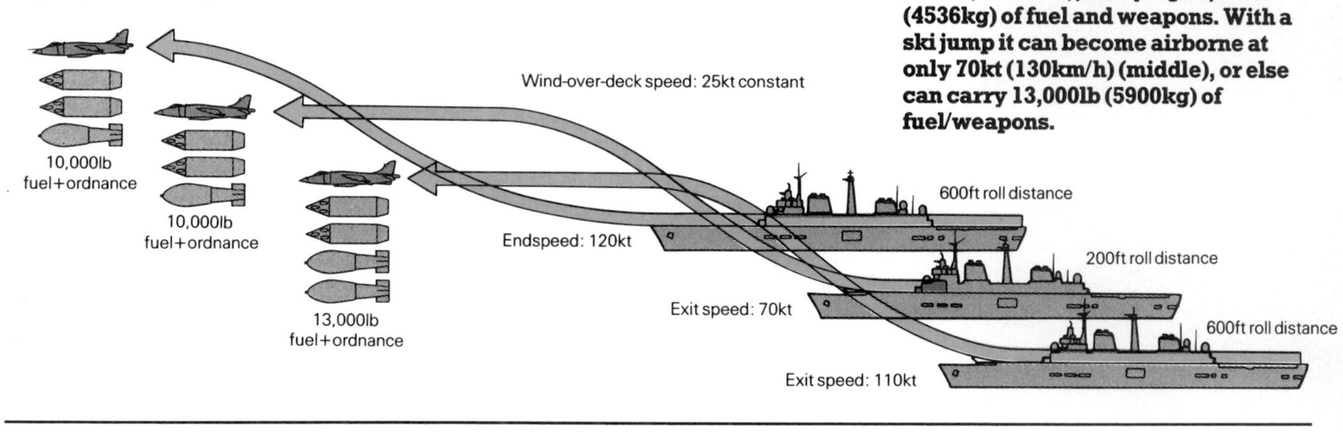

Below: A simple cutaway showing the main items of fuel, on-board equipment and weapons of the Sea Harrier FRS.1.

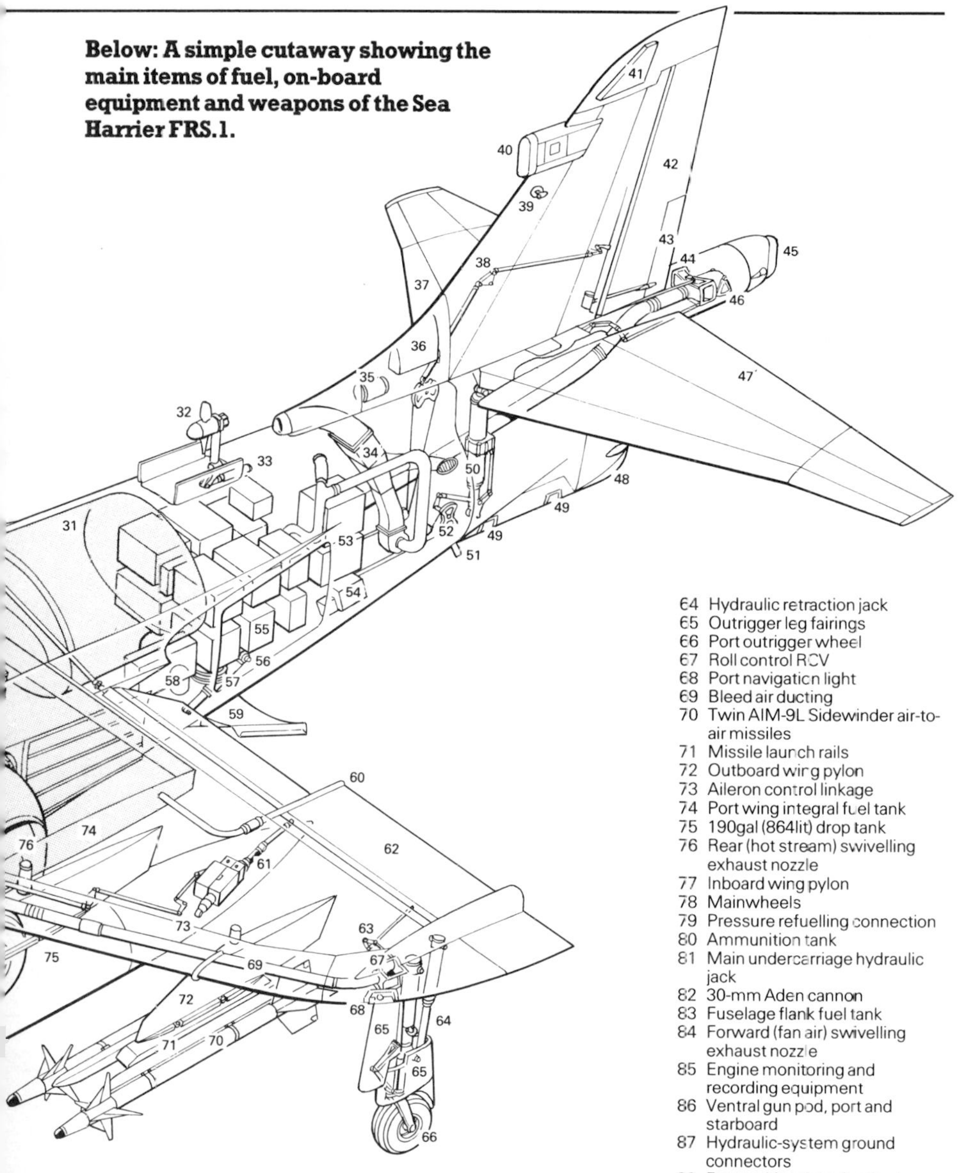

31 Rear fuselage fuel tank
32 Emergency ram-air turbine
33 Turbine release control
34 Equipment bay air-conditioning system
35 HF aerial tuner
36 HF notch aerial
37 Starboard all-moving tailplane
38 Rudder control linkage
39 Total-temperature probe
40 Forward radar warning receiver
41 VHF aerial
42 Rudder
43 Rudder trim tab
44 Yaw control RCV
45 Rear radar warning receiver
46 Pitch control RCV
47 Port all-moving tailplane
48 Tail bumper
49 Radar altimeter aerials
50 Tailplane power unit
51 UHF aerial
52 Control system linkages
53 Twin batteries
54 Chaff and flare dispensers
55 Avionics equipment racks
56 Airbrake hydraulic jack
57 Liquid-oxygen converter
58 Hydraulic-system nitrogen pressurising bottle
59 Airbrake
60 Fuel jettison
61 Aileron power unit
62 Port aileron
63 Aileron RCV mechanical linkage
64 Hydraulic retraction jack
65 Outrigger leg fairings
66 Port outrigger wheel
67 Roll control RCV
68 Port navigation light
69 Bleed air ducting
70 Twin AIM-9L Sidewinder air-to-air missiles
71 Missile launch rails
72 Outboard wing pylon
73 Aileron control linkage
74 Port wing integral fuel tank
75 190gal (864lit) drop tank
76 Rear (hot stream) swivelling exhaust nozzle
77 Inboard wing pylon
78 Mainwheels
79 Pressure refuelling connection
80 Ammunition tank
81 Main undercarriage hydraulic jack
82 30-mm Aden cannon
83 Fuselage flank fuel tank
84 Forward (fan air) swivelling exhaust nozzle
85 Engine monitoring and recording equipment
86 Ventral gun pod, port and starboard
87 Hydraulic-system ground connectors
88 Forward fuselage fuel tank
89 Rolls-Royce Pegasus Mk 104 vectoring-thrust turbofan
90 Supplementary air-intake doors, free floating
91 Nosewheel
92 Landing/taxiing lamp
93 Nosewheel hydraulic jack
94 Hydraulic accumulator
95 Boundary-layer bleed air duct
96 Pitot head
97 Radar hand controller
98 Ejection-seat rocket pack
99 Engine throttle and nozzle control levers
100 Doppler radar
101 Radar scanner
102 Radome, folded to port
103 Ferranti Blue Fox radar

Above: The family relationship imparted by Sir Sydney Camm is obvious as one of Yeovilton's Hunter T.8M Blue Fox radar trainers formates with a Sea Harrier of 899 Sqn. Every Sea Harrier pilot trains on the Yeovilton T.8Ms.

like the new ships, delayed by industrial unrest and other factors quite unconnected with the aircraft itself. The original build standard had been discussed in 1972, but it was not finalized until after the go-ahead in 1975.

Almost all the changes were confined to the front end, which was completely redesigned. Apart from this the main differences were: substitution of aluminium alloy for magnesium or Mg-Zr alloy to avoid sea-water corrosion (the only items not changed were the nose and outrigger wheels and the engine gearbox); a 4in (100mm) increase in fin height, mainly from building in the RWR as an extra section; addition of an emergency wheel-brake system; various system changes, including a liquid oxygen converter of a different make; addition of lashing lugs to the nose gear; increase in tailplane nose-up travel by 2°; increase in wingtip RCV roll power for use in turbulent ship wakes; and a switch to the Mk 104 engine, still a Pegasus 11 but with complete anti-corrosion protection and an uprated gearbox drive for a 15kVA alternator to supply the greater electrical loads. To facilitate checking engine thrust prior to launch it was planned to add a hold-back link to the main gear, secured to a hydraulic snubber below deck and severed by the pilot via a release button on the nozzle lever, but this was never fitted.

The aircraft nose, however, is totally new, and aesthetically vastly improved. The chief alterations are addition of a multimode radar, installation of a totally different nav/attack system, and accommodation of the extra avionics and cockpit panels by raising the entire cockpit 11in (279mm), which automatically improves pilot view. Cockpit displays were completely redesigned.

Never before had so much mission capability been built into so small an aircraft, and this is combined with the ability to operate from almost any warship, in any weather, with only one man on board and with no external assistance or ground power supplies. The avionics were therefore a major challenge, and the result has proved to be an excellent compromise that has scarcely needed any alteration.

Blue Fox radar

As it is by far the largest sensor, the radar can be dealt with first. Ferranti was the logical supplier, because of its major involvement with the RAF Harrier and its work on the P.1154 radar. In fact the Blue Fox radar was derived more nearly from the Seaspray fitted to Navy Lynx helicopters, but considerably augmented. Operating in I-band, it is a neat modular 186lb (84kg) package, aircooled and installed in a nose which hinges 180° to the left to reduce aircraft length. There are four main mission operating modes: search, with a B-type (sector) scan, PPI, multi-bar (raster) or single scan; attack, with intercept and lead/pursuit or chase in the air-combat mission, and weapon-aiming via the HUD in anti-ship or surface attack; boresight, for quick ranging on targets of opportunity; and xpdr (transponder) for immediate identification of friendly targets. Two two-seat Hunters were rebuilt as T.8M radar trials aircraft, later serving with a third conversion as Sea Harrier radar trainers at Yeovilton. A P.1127(RAF), XV277, was flown in 1974 with a metal mock-up nose. While this was satisfactory aerodynamically, it would not have been adequate to house the desired radar dish. This was the factor that drove the Kingston designers to adopt the raised cockpit configuration.

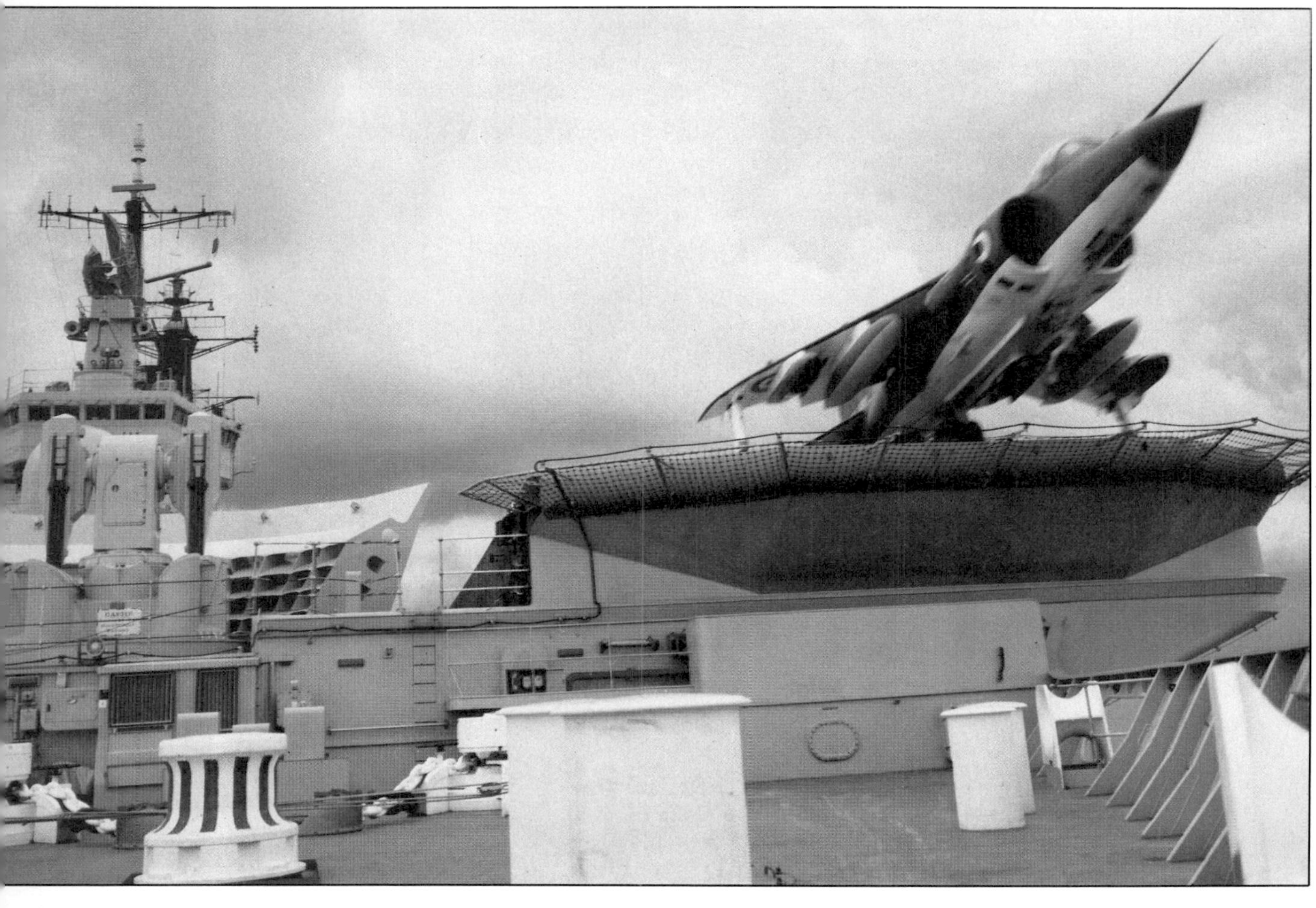

Left: One of the first ski-jump takeoffs by a Sea Harrier FRS.1 in early 1980 from the newly commissioned HMS *Invincible*, whose ramp is limited to 7° by the location of the Sea Dart SAM launcher (seen, unloaded, on the left). The aircraft has two tanks and three practice bomb carriers.

The nav/attack system installed in the Sea Harrier bears little resemblance to that of the Harrier. It reflects the ship-based environment, which, for example, imposes inertial alignment problems, and the unusual spread of missions. Two digital computers are used, one 20k (20,000 words) WAC (weapon-aiming computer) associated with the HUD and used to provide symbology and weapon-aiming graphics, and an 8k navigation computer which ties together that series of equipments and feeds a nav control/display panel on the right console. Navigation inputs come from: a Ferranti all-attitude TGP (twin-gyro platform) which, while avoiding most INS problems, provides a continuous measure of aircraft attitude and acceleration; a Decca 72 doppler radar and Sperry flux valve, which provide independent ground speed and heading inputs and monitor the TGP; and Tacan, UHF homing, an I-band transponder and an ADC (air-data computer). Even at sea the system takes only 2min to align, and provides: present position as a lat/long or tactical grid reference; range, bearing, course-to-steer and time to any of ten waypoints (any of which can be assigned a velocity, because it might be a ship); estimates of time remaining on task, derived from fuel contents and flow-meter readings; range/bearing to a Tacan station or an offset position; groundspeed/track and wind-speed and direction; and immediate update by pilot input by overflying a known waypoint, radar fix or Tacan.

An improved cockpit

Designing the cockpit to accommodate an exceptional amount of display information in a small space was a real challenge, but it has proved popular with pilots and very easy to learn. Thanks to the raised position, the side consoles are wider than in the Harrier, yet more panel space has also been provided ahead. The latest miniaturized displays are used, examples being the row of CWS (centralized warning system) lights around the coaming. The HUD is newer than that of the GR.3, with a larger display linked to the programmable computer interfacing with numerous weapon-aiming and navaid equipments. On return to the ship the approach and landing are assisted by MEL Madge (microwave aircraft digital guidance equipment) which can feed through the WAC to the HUD. The main radar display is to the right, and the pilot has a hand controller at the rear on the left console.

Not only does the seat's elevated position give a better all-round view, but the canopy is bulged at the sides. View to the rear compares favourably with that in any other fighter, and with gear extended the pilot can look across the inlet ducts and check the outrigger gears, which cannot be seen in a GR.3. The seat itself is the latest Martin-Baker type, the Mk 10H, one of the rocket-assisted zero/zero variety (usable at zero height and zero airspeed), and its main parachute is deployed in 1·5s, compared with 2.25s for the Mk 9D of the GR.3. Ahead of the flat bulletproof windscreen is a yaw vane, centred instead of offset as in the GR.3, and the reconnaissance and strike camera is relocated to look out of the right side of the nose. Another addition is a radar

Above: British Aerospace Dynamics is now in production with the Sea Eagle long-range anti-ship missile, two early examples of which were flown on the first Sea Harrier, XZ438, during carry trials in 1981.

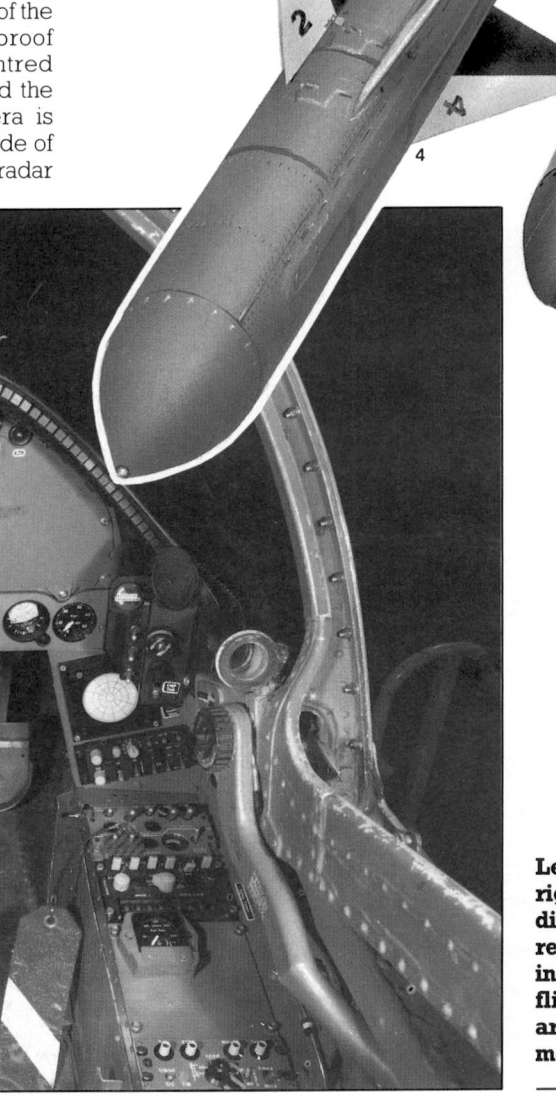

Left: A Sea Harrier cockpit. On the right side of the main panel the radar display (here blanked off for security reasons) replaces the engine/fuel instruments of the GR.3, and basic flight instruments occupy the central area which in the GR.3 is filled by the moving-map display.

British Aerospace Sea Harrier FRS.1

Below: Artwork showing stores normally carried by the Sea Harrier. Item No 8, the reconnaissance pod, could easily be carried, as it is by RAF Harriers, but is not currently required by the Royal Navy. Several other stores could readily be cleared for use.

1 Matra 550 Magic AAM (used by Indian Navy)
2 AIM-9L Sidewinder AAM
3 AIM-9B Sidewinder AAM
4 Sea Eagle ASM
5 Harpoon ASM
6 100gal tank (190gal, 864lit, is now used)
7 Lepus flare
8 Reconnaissance pod
9 30mm Aden gun pod
10 30mm ammunition
11 1,000lb (454kg) GP bomb
12 Matra retarded bomb
13 ML twin carrier with Matra 155 launchers
14 RN 2in (50·8mm) rocket launcher
15 BL.755 cluster bomb

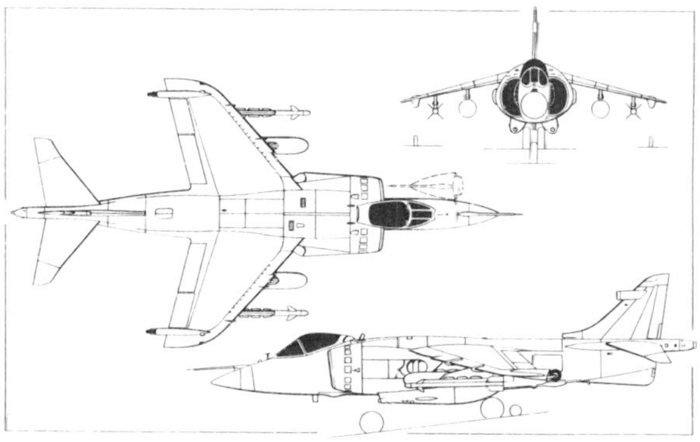

Above: Three-view drawing of a BAe Sea Harrier FRS.1. The position of the nosecone containing the Blue Fox radar main unit when folded back is shown in dotted outline.

Right: Elements of the Ferranti Blue Fox multimode radar, with the mechanically steered aerial (antenna) mounted in its yellow transport cradle. In front are the cockpit push-button and pistol-grip hand controllers.

Below: A selection of stores carried by Sea Harriers. Inboard wing stations have a maximum capacity of 2,000lb (907kg), twice that of the outboard stations.

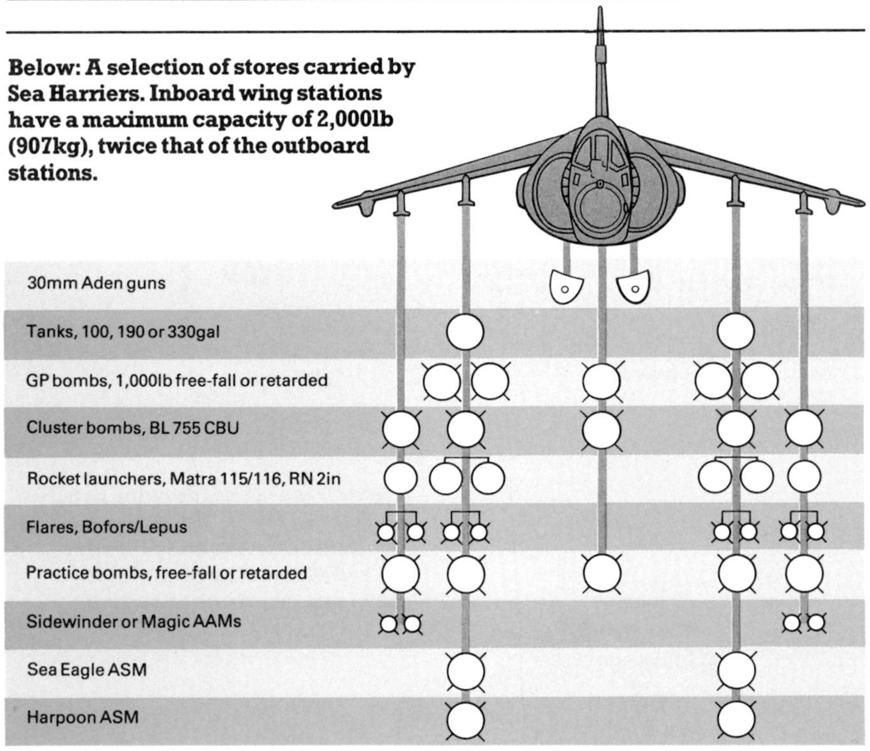

altimeter, with display prominent on the main primary panel fed by aerials recessed in the ventral fin similar to those of the AV-8C.

RWR and armament generally is the same as for the GR.3, though the pylons were strengthened. Weapons, however, have always been different and more diverse, including Sidewinder AAMs, RN 2in (50·8mm) rocket pods and anti-ship missiles. No wiring is provided for a reconnaissance pod.

The original plan was to go ahead with the 24 production aircraft, but in May 1978 the plan was changed, ten additional Sea Harriers being ordered and the first three being earmarked as special trials aircraft (XZ438-440). Because of the complexity of their instrumentation, these aircraft were overtaken by XZ450, the first of what had become 31 production aircraft, and despite delays due to industrial unrest this flew in its primer paint on 20 August 1978. Two weeks later, in Fleet Air Arm livery, it did ski jumps from a new 15° sagging-catenary ramp built by Royal Engineers at the Farnborough airshow using standard Fairey MGB (medium girder bridge) components. The first instrumented aircraft, XZ438, flew on 30 December 1978, and subsequent progress was rapid. XZ451, with Modex number 100, was delivered to RNAS Yeovilton on 18 June 1979, the IFTU (Intensive Flying Trials Unit), No 700A Sqn, commissioned there on 19 September, and a month later an extremely successful sea trials programme was flown from HMS *Hermes* in the Irish Sea.

Subsequently 700A became 899 Harrier HQ Sqn, with Nos 800 and 801 Sqns as the combat units, the plan being to assign one to each Command Cruiser: *Invincible, Illustrious* and *Ark Royal.* By sheer chance it was decided to retain the old carrier *Hermes* for Sea Harrier training, despite a decision to send her to the breakers' yard in 1982 on the commissioning of *Illustrious.* After much argument it was decided to carry out a refit in late 1979 and fit her with a 12° ski ramp. How momentous this narrow decision would be, could not be dreamed of.

Overseas sales

Subsequent RN work-up of the Sea Harriers is discussed in the next chapter. Meanwhile, navies around the world continued to watch the progress of these unique aircraft with growing interest. India remained at the top of the list of serious potential customers, and Australia planned to buy HMS *Invincible* in 1983 (though remaining undecided about fast V/STOL jets). The first customer to follow the RN's lead did, in fact, turn out to be India, which had long used Hawker (Armstrong Whitworth) Sea Hawks from INS *Vikrant.* In July 1972 John Farley flew the company demo two-seater, G-VTOL, to give requested demonstrations from the ageing carrier despite the 30°C steamy monsoon atmosphere. Farley flew 22 times in two days, and, when he left, the Indian Navy was totally sold on this amazing aircraft. It placed an order for six Sea Harrier Mk 51 single-seaters, and two two-seat Mk 60s, for delivery in 1983.

During the Falklands war the Indian

Left: XZ492 of No 800 Sqn flying over HMS *Hermes* in 1981, with AIM-9B Sidewinders, tanks and guns. At that time *Hermes* was earmarked for immediate scrapping; nobody could foresee how vital she would later be.

Above: XZ457, aircraft "713" of 899 Sqn at Yeovilton, destroyed two Mirages and a Skyhawk but is seen here over Somerset in company with a newly-acquired Harrier T.4(RN), the Royal Navy's two-seat trainer version.

Navy team at British Aerospace watched for a sudden speed-up on their aircraft, indicating that they were being rushed through for delivery to the Royal Navy instead. This never happened, and the first Mk 51, bearing the white tiger badge of No 300 Squadron, was handed over at Dunsfold on 27 January 1983. Pilots and ground staff were trained at Yeovilton before the first FRS.51s flew out to *Vikrant* in late-1983. Differences between the Mk 51 and the RN FRS.1 are minor; for example a gaseous oxygen system is fitted, and the AAM is the Matra Magic.

Today the Sea Harrier is not only a formidable and exceptionally versatile warplane but it has been proved so in unusually tough circumstances. In the longer term it will require updating, and though there is every indication that the airframe will need little attention, BAe has given the question of an MLU (mid-life update) prolonged consideration and come up with a comprehensive package which it is expected will be funded for incorporation in the late 1980s. The basic aircraft might receive several AV-8B-type changes including zero-scarf front nozzles, LERX for combat agility, detail changes to improve aerodynamics and STO lift, and increased internal fuel. In the nose will be a new and more advanced radar, funded by the MoD from Ferranti's private-venture Blue Falcon, with all the expected features of a high-power pulse doppler set, including: look-up/look-down; improved combat performance at high altitude; TWS (track while scanning); segregation of multiple targets; and allocation of threat priorities. New wing-tip launchers will be added for AIM-9L, later replaced by the European Asraam (advanced short-range AAM), while the wing pylons may be tailored to single or paired AIM-120A (Amraam, advanced medium-range AAM), which will give a stand-off "fire and forget" kill capability. Other changes may include an Obogs (on-board oxygen generating system) and an internal EW installation as in the updated RAF GR.3.

Left: Now intensively used by the Indian Navy's No 300 Sqn, IN601, the first Sea Harrier FRS.51, is seen here in primer paint and temporary SBAC registration G-9-478 on its first flight on 6 August 1982. A month later it was at the Farnborough Air Show (see above).

Above: Externally there are few differences between the Indian Navy FRS.51 and the regular FRS.1, apart from the white tiger badge of 300 Sqn. Internally a gaseous oxygen system is fitted, and the Indian Navy's AAM is the Matra 550 Magic.

Operation Corporate

The recovery of the Falkland Islands from the occupying forces of Argentina was quite unlike any other campaign in the history of human conflict. Operation Corporate was mounted at very short notice, and involved all the armed forces of the Crown in a land/sea/air war utterly unlike anything for which those forces had been trained, and in a remote and inhospitable part of the globe some 4,000 miles from the nearest friendly base! The success of the entire operation depended upon the Sea Harrier, later joined by the RAF Harrier, both of which at the start were unproven weapon systems.

Above: Unusually approaching from dead astern, a Sea Harrier recovers aboard *Hermes* at twilight. One Sidewinder has been fired, but tanks are retained. All touchdowns are vertical.

The refusal of a group of Argentine scrap-metal dealers to leave British territory on South Georgia gave a clue that a direct confrontation was possible, and on 31 March 1982 Admiral Sir John Fieldhouse RN, who had just returned to Britain from Exercise Springtrain in the Mediterranean, was ordered to begin preparing Task Force 317, of which he was to be overall Commander. Indeed, he had ordered Rear-Admiral "Sandy" Woodward to prepare a detachment before he left Gibraltar. Immediately plans were put into action involving all the fighting services.

Crucial to the possible retaking of the islands was airpower, because Argentina possessed powerful fighter and attack brigades within both its air force and naval aviation. Thanks to the decision of the British government in 1966 there was no seagoing British airpower whatsoever, except for the small force of Sea Harriers, which had barely settled down and whose pilots were mostly inexperienced. Even this force had only come into existence in the teeth of opposition from defence officials and the Treasury.

At RNAS Yeovilton, Somerset, were the three Sea Harrier squadrons: 800 (Lt-Cdr Andy Auld), 801 (Lt-Cdr Nigel Ward) and the HQ unit 899 (Lt-Cdr Tony Ogilvy). To make things more difficult, 801 were on leave on the day of mobilization (2 April) and 800 were due to go on leave at mid-day! Each had an establishment of five aircraft, but 899 was split up to augment the two first-line squadrons, so that on 5 April, with spare aircraft added to the establishment, HMS *Hermes*, the Task Force flagship, sailed from Portsmouth with 11 Sea Harriers of 800 Sqn which had landed on an already overcrowded deck, and a few miles out a 12th landed on. The brand-new HMS *Invincible* was almost as crowded, and among her air units was 801 Sqn with eight aircraft. Among the mountains of stores, all loaded in less than three days but which were to sustain a campaign lasting three months, were the newest and best Sidewinder AAMs, the AIM-9L. Not previously used by the RN, though in production by a European industrial group, AIM-9L has a completely new guidance system, more powerful control fins and a high-power warhead.

Above: An aircraft of No 800 Sqn on the slippery deck of *Hermes* in a force 10 gale. In the background are the flagship's "goalkeeper" (*Broadsword*) and, on the skyline, *Invincible*.

The unknown quantity

Thus, from the start, the Task Force had a small air component equipped with a unique aircraft which, though it was relatively new and untested in battle, promised to be outstandingly versatile. In particular, it was expected to be able to intercept and destroy attacking Argentine aircraft, including the Mach 2 Mirage and Dagger – all are called Mirages here, for simplicity – which in low-level attack are extremely subsonic. By an accident of geography the Falklands are at such a distance from the several large mainland airbases that, while low-level attacks by the Argentine aircraft were perfectly capable of being mounted, there would not be a lot of fuel to spare, especially if afterburner was used. At the same time, the Task Force was going to stand off at a considerable distance, and the Sea Harriers likewise were not going to have much time on station either. Not least, the Argentine aircraft were several times more numerous. Put another way, the total embarked force of 20 British fixed-wing aircraft was so small that even a single combat loss was going to be significant.

At an early stage it was clear that more aircraft would be needed. There were other Sea Harriers and pilots, and there were also the Harriers of the RAF, and preparations were made to bring as many into the South Atlantic as the two flat-top ships could accommodate. Lt-Cdr Gedge was ordered to form a third Sea Harrier squadron, and he immediately located Sea Harriers at Boscombe, Dunsfold and other locations, though none was in front-line condition and almost all were in various stages of refit, rebuild, special trials or still being completed by the maker. All were urgently hurried through to the latest combat-ready state – without, incidentally, commandeering a single one of the FRS.51 aircraft building for the Indian Navy. Lt-Cdr Gedge just managed to scrape together an adequate number of Sea Harrier pilots, including some on exchange posting in Australia and the USA. By April 30 Gedge had formed 809 Sqn, though he had to import two RAF

Below: This profile shows XV787, first flown on 9 September 1970 and heavily engaged on combat missions with 1(F) Sqn in the Falklands in 1982. Note the chin transponder and Paveway LGB.

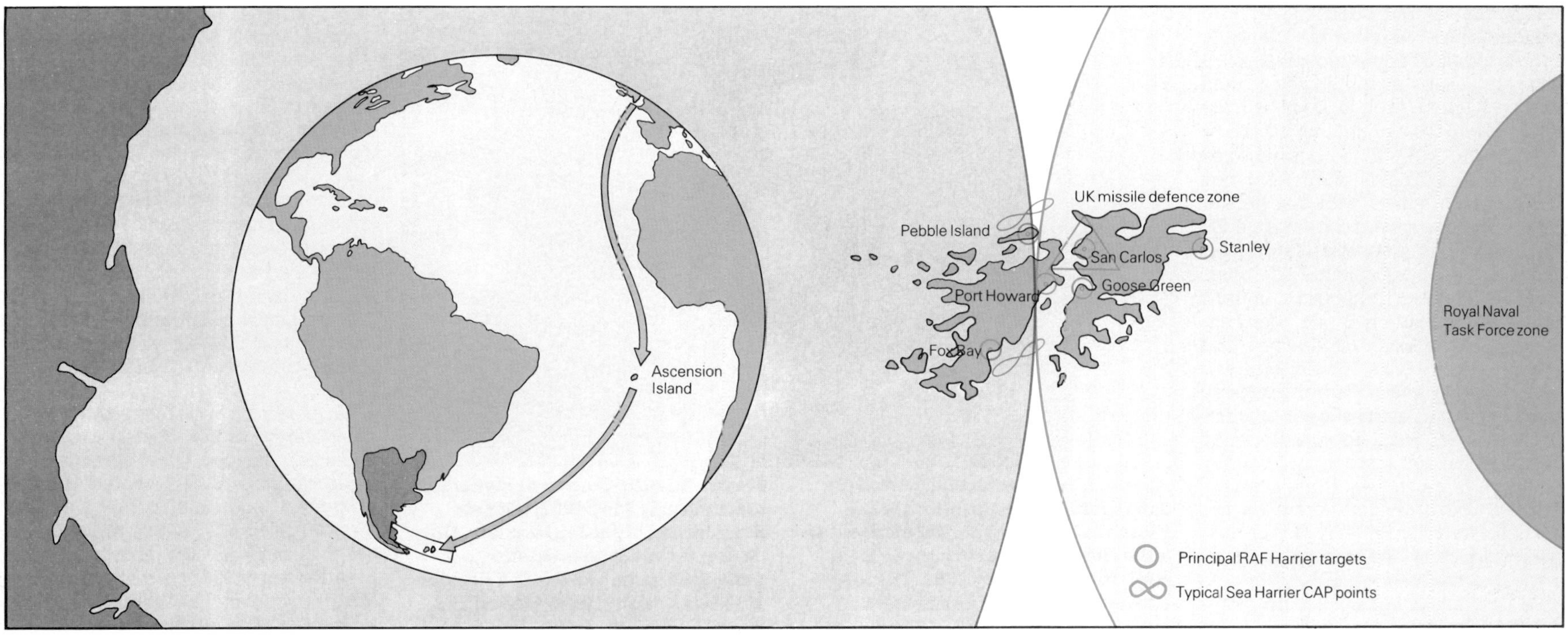

Above: An overall idea of the geography is provided by these two maps, one of the globe superimposed on a larger-scale map of the Falklands. The former emphasizes the colossal distance from Britain, as far as New York to New Zealand. The local map shows a 400 nautical mile radius from Argentina in red and a 200 nm radius from the Task Force in blue.

Right: Sea Harrier XZ498 of No 800 Sqn makes a VL aboard *Illustrious* in Falklands waters in 1983. During the war she served with 801 on *Invincible*.

Harrier pilots who had Lightning interceptor experience, and he also had to leave two aircraft behind to carry on essential development and training.

The eight aircraft of the new squadron were to a slightly later standard than other Sea Harriers, and they later had twin Sidewinder launchers and 190gal (864lit) tanks. They were factory-painted in a shade of light "barley" grey which RAE experts calculated would blend in best with winter South Atlantic environments. The other squadrons had left Britain painted in standard dark sea grey with white undersides, with bold unit insignia on the tails. Clearly they had to be toned down for warfare, and the decision was taken to paint the undersides the same colour as the top, to apply Type B (red/blue) roundels and low-contrast black serial number and Modex numbers, and no other markings. The repainting was done on the journey south. *Invincible*'s modern air-conditioning enabled spray-painting to be used, but in *Hermes* 800 Sqn had to be laboriously painted by hand.

Back at Yeovilton No 809 readied itself for combat, the two hijacked RAF pilots quickly learning how to use the Blue Fox radar and launch over a ski jump. The flight-refuelling probes were fitted, and on 31 April/1 May the whole squadron flew out to Ascension Island. All aircraft refuelled a total of 14 times from Victors, though few pilots had ever made an AAR (air/air refuelling) contact before. As in all such deployments the objective was to keep all tanks nearly filled, so that, if the next refuelling were to fail for any

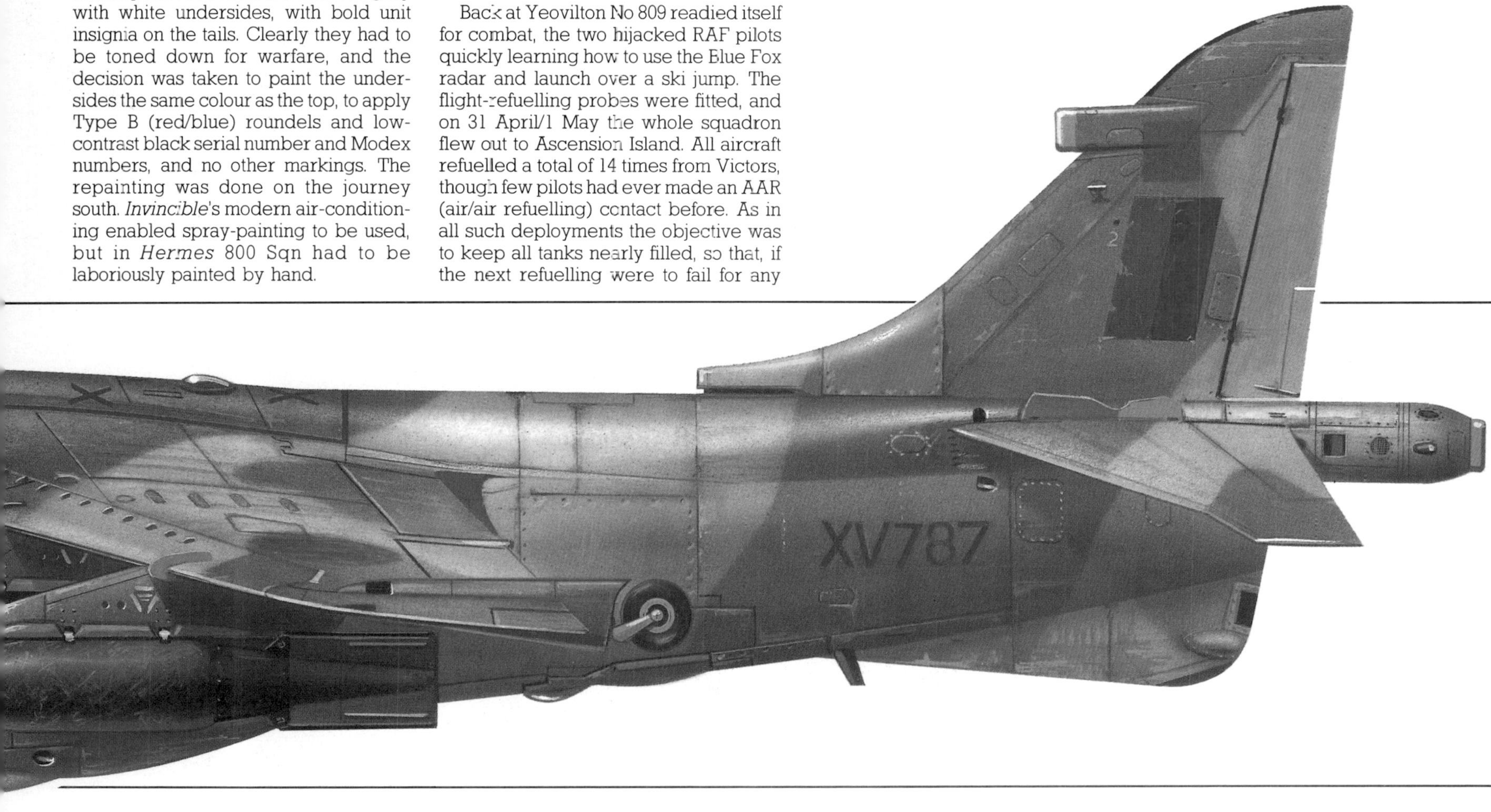

reason, the aircraft could still fly to a friendly airbase. At Ascension the newly formed squadron parked awaiting a ship, and every possible crevice and hole was taped over to keep out the wind-blown volcanic grit and sand.

By Easter, 3 April, the decision had been taken to commit RAF No 1 Sqn (W/C Peter Squire), with the Harrier GR.3, but in this case much remained to be done. The prime mission was expected to be air defence, for which the RAF Harrier units were initially neither trained nor equipped. Many aircraft modifications were required, and as with the RN units the situation was compounded by the squadron's planned imminent departure for a major exercise in Canada. S/L Bob Iveson, a No 1 Sqn flight commander, was sent to Liverpool to study a large and fast container ship, *Atlantic Conveyor*, and report on her suitability as a Harrier ferry. It was clear she could carry the aircraft as deck cargo, but no flying would appear possible, and there were major problems with personnel accommodation.

She had been laid-up at Liverpool, but was quickly readied, and while still at Liverpool a Sea Harrier carried out deck trials; but she had to sail, jammed with stores, on 23 April without any fixed-wing aircraft aboard. By this time the Harriers, 14 in number, had already been substantially modified. The largest task was to insert along the wings the wiring for Sidewinders on the outer pylons. Launch rails for these missiles were added, and the complete installation was tested with live firings from Llanbedr on the Aberporth range. In the interest of ordnance commonality the aircraft was cleared to use the RN rocket launcher, housing 36 rockets of 2in (50·4mm) calibre instead of the usual RAF Matra 115 which takes 18 (or 19 if the centre tube is used) of 68mm. Another new weapon cleared in a hurry was the Mk 13/18 Paveway II LGB (laser-guided bomb), which was thought to be particularly appropriate to the GR.3 since this aircraft has a compatible 10·6 micron laser. Under the nose a blister appeared covering a transponder added to enhance the GR.3's response to the ship aircraft direction radars. Also to be cleared for use were the big 330gal (1500lit) drop tanks, which were to be needed on the long flight south.

A "marinised" GR.3

Apart from these modifications, all the GR.3s were put through an environmental protection programme, as many holes and joints as possible being sealed to prevent salt-water ingress even if waves were to break over the aircraft. Where ingestion could not be prevented, new drain holes were provided. Lashing-down lugs were added to the outrigger gears, and other changes were made to facilitate shipboard operation. Meanwhile, Ferranti Ltd had worked around the clock updating Finrae (Ferranti inertial rapid-alignment equipment) to ready the GR.3's INS immediately prior to each mission. The trolley-mounted package was based on the FIN 1064 (updated Jaguar) INS, and continuously provided north and horizontal references over long periods. Three Finraes were flown to Ascension and taken aboard *Atlantic Conveyor*, and the final software program was sent via communications satellite direct to the South Atlantic.

It had been planned for each pilot of No 1 Sqn to qualify by making three takeoffs over the ski ramp at Yeovilton, but it was evident after a few attempts that there was "nothing to it", and a single launch apiece was sufficient. Close air combat was another matter, and every pilot put in intensive DACT (dissimilar air-combat training), including air combat against Mirages of l'Armée de l'Air and Super Etendards of l'Aéronavale. Then the first group of nine Harriers flew from Wittering to St Mawgan, Cornwall, and from there went on to Ascension on 3-5 May. Each was met five times by Victors, the procedures again providing for diversion to a friendly base should the next AAR fail to top up because of malfunction. Typical flight time was 9h 15min, easily a record for any Harrier in RAF service. Not for the first time the RAF resolved to rethink the traditional "relief tube" and rubber bottle, with a Velcro slit in the immersion suit.

At Ascension three of the aircraft were temporarily commandeered to provide local air defence. The other six air-taxied across to the moored *Atlantic Conveyor*, each making a VL on the newly added VTOL spot in the bows, then turning aft and taxiing down a narrow canyon left between walls of two-high containers – which provided the only protection against the sea – to a

Above: A tradesman of RAF No 1(F) Sqn together with the pilot use the Finrae to align the inertial platform of a Harrier GR.3 prior to a sortie from HMS *Hermes* in May 1982. The Sea Harrier in the rear had different navaids and did not need Finrae.

Below: *Atlantic Conveyor* steaming south in early May 1982, with six Harriers and eight Sea Harriers. Only the former really needed the protective bags, and one Sea Harrier of 809 was parked fully fuelled and armed on the bow spot.

marshalled spot, where the aircraft were parked and wrapped in Driclad envelopes. Few of the pilots had been aboard a ship before. The ship also took aboard the eight Sea Harriers of 809 Sqn, and various helicopters. The final Sea Harrier was parked at readiness on the VTOL spot, for local defence. On 18 May *Atlantic Conveyor* passed lat 52°S and closed with the Task Force, whereupon the GR.3s, freed from their garments, air-taxied across to *Hermes*. This time their pilots experienced a deck pitching and rolling in what were soon to be recognized as normal South Atlantic conditions. Meanwhile 809 put six aircraft on *Hermes* and two on *Invincible*, though later this squadron had four on each ship as planned.

In late May five more GR.3s, completing No 1's total of 14, were flown out to Ascension. Four were taken aboard the *Contender Bezant*, a Ro-Ro ship whose conversion had caused major problems. The remaining aircraft, plus the three now released from defending Ascension, flew all the way south to the Task Force, one pair on 1 June and the other pair on 8 June. This time the landlubber pilots viewed 4,000 miles (6440km) of cold ocean with anxiety. There was no question of there being any possibility of diversion to any land base whatsoever, and for the last 800 nautical miles (1500km) they were entirely alone, and though they could use Tacan they had to preserve radio silence. To cap it all, one pair arrived on the deck of *Hermes* in the middle of an Argentine air attack.

On its way south the original Task Force had launched CAPs (combat air patrols) with increasing frequency. These ranged out as far as 120 miles (193km), usually to the south-west, and as the TEZ (the 200-mile, 322km Total Exclusion Zone) was approached a lot of flying was done at night. In any case, with the onset of winter, daylight gradually shortened to a narrow band between about 1100 and 1730 local time, and weather progressively worsened. Much of the hardest action, in late May and June, took place with gale-force winds, mountainous seas, and everything on deck being covered in condensation which froze at night. Towards the middle of June it snowed heavily. For much of the time cloud base was at 200ft (90m) and occasionally it was half this, with visibility typically being half a mile (800m) with high winds. Under these conditions the Harriers and Sea Harriers experienced no special difficulty, whereas conventional carrier-based aircraft in a similar situation would not have been able to fly at all.

Meeting the "Argies"

Contact with what had become the enemy was made on 25 April when a Sea Harrier of 801 intercepted an FAA (Fuerza Aérea Argentina) 707 on long-range reconnaissance looking for the Task Force. It was outside the TEZ and, the rules of engagement at that time being restrictive, it was not attacked.

The first combat missions were flown by 12 aircraft from *Hermes* at dawn on 1 May. With top cover provided by 801 from *Invincible*, nine Sea Harriers made a carefully planned low-level attack on Port Stanley airfield, which had been bombed on the previous night by a Vulcan. The first four came in at 520kt (963km/h) at 100ft (30m) with variously fuzed 1,000lb (454kg) bombs to hit the SAM and gun defences, attacking in a forwards toss. This went well, the air-burst weapons being seen to explode directly over their targets. Four of the other five aircraft each had three BL.755 cluster bombs, for use against aircraft and support areas, while the fifth had three 1,000lb (454kg) with contact fuzes. All aircraft also had two tanks and the gun pods. Despite intense ground fire, only one aircraft was hit, taking a 20mm shell through the fin. The holes were quickly repaired with Speedtape (adhesive-backed aluminium tape). The three other Sea Harriers from *Hermes* hit Goose Green, again encountering intense hostile fire.

During the daylight hours of 1 May several pairs of 801's Sea Harriers encountered Mirages, at least three of which very inexpertly fired semi-active Matra R.530 AAMs at long range, all of which were evaded by the RN aircraft. The CO of 801, Lt-Cdr Ward, frustratingly chased three T-34C Turbo Mentors on FAC duty through low cloud without managing to nail one. But later on that day 801 launched two aircraft to intercept a high-altitude raid and met at least two Mirages head-on. Lt Steve Thomas used his radar to control the two aircraft into firing positions, while two enemy missiles zipped harmlessly over his cockpit. F/Lt Paul Barton, RAF, then let go a locked-on AIM-9L and saw his target disappear in a fireball, which was the invariable result of a -9L strike. A few seconds later Thomas also got into firing parameters and probably bagged the other Mirage, but it entered dense cloud with the -9L chasing it. At dusk Lt Alan Curtis and Lt-Cdr Mike Broadwater carried out a textbook autonomous radar interception of two Canberras, scoring one confirmed and one probable. The day was rounded off by *Hermes*, which launched two aircraft against another high raid. Again the enemy opened fire at long range, the Sea Harrier evading the missile, and the second Sea Harrier,

Left: On 8 June 1982 Marshall of Cambridge flew the first C.1(K) tanker version of the RAF Hercules, which can operate from Stanley. Here a "Herc tanker" refuels an RAF Harrier GR.3 over the South Atlantic in 1983.

Below: Hosing down the flight deck of the Task Force flagship shortly after the Argentine surrender, when the worst of the blizzards were over. In the theatre all Sea Harriers on *Hermes* were administered by 800 Sqn.

Above: Flying practice continued on the journey south in April 1982. Ready for the first real mission aboard *Hermes* are 1,000lb retarded bombs, AIM-9Ls and Mk 46 AS torpedoes for the ship's Sea King HAS.5 helicopters.

Harrier Force Deployed

Sea Harrier	Harrier GR.3	Method of Transit
12	0	Embarked in UK, HMS *Hermes*
8	0	Embarked in UK, HMS *Invincible*
8	6	Flown UK to Ascension Island, embarked *Atlantic Conveyor*
0	4	Flown UK to Ascension Island, flown to 52°S, vertical landing on HMS *Hermes*
28	**10**	**Total**
0	4	Flown UK to Ascension Island, embarked *Contender Bezant*, flown off to Port Stanley having arrived after ceasefire

Harrier Force Missions

Sorties	2,000+ South of Ascension Island
	1,650 within Total Exclusion Zone
Combat Missions	**Sea Harrier:**
	1,100+ CAP sorties
	90 offensive support
	GR.3:
	125 ground attack and tactical reconnaissance
Flying Rate	approx 55 hours/aircraft/month
	up to 10 sorties/aircraft/day
	3-4 sorties/pilot/day
	up to 10 hours/day in cockpit
Pilot/aircraft ratio	1.2 initially
	1.4 later
Aircraft availability at beginning of each day	95%
Operational loss rate/sortie	0.38%
Overall loss rate/sortie	0.61%
Known successful ejection attempts	100%

Confirmed Sea Harrier Kills

Aircraft	AIM-9L Sidewinder	30mm guns	Total
Mirage	11	0	11
A-4 Skyhawk	6	2	8
Canberra	1	0	1
Pucará	0	1	1
C-130 Hercules	½	½	1
Puma helicopter	0	0	1*
Total	**18½**	**3½**	**23**

* Hit ground during evasive action

Confirmed Kills on Ground

	Aircraft	30mm guns	Cluster bomb	Total
Sea Harrier	A-109	1	0	1
	Islander	0	1	1
	Pucará	0	1	1
	Puma	2	0	2
Harrier GR.3	Chinook	1	0	1
	Puma	2	1	3
Total		**6**	**3**	**9**

Harrier Force Losses

Reason	Sea Harrier	Harrier GR.3
Air-to-Air combat	0	0
Ground Defences	2	3
Slid off deck	1	0
Hit sea after take-off	1	0
Collided or flew into sea	2	0
Total	**6**	**3**

again flown by an RAF officer on exchange, F/Lt Bertie Penfold, bagged a Mirage with a -9L.

Few days were to be as busy as this, and losses began with Lt Nick Taylor, who was killed by AAA at Goose Green on 4 May. By mid-May the Sea Harriers had completely covered the islands with photo reconnaissance, and on 20 May the first RAF Harriers also got into action. The pilots of No 1 Sqn were, on the whole, far more experienced in low-level attack missions, and though they had looked forward to flying air defence sorties, the Royal Navy took the view that this was best left to the Sea Harriers. It was therefore decided that the GR.3s should be rewired to carry offensive stores outboard and they subsequently took over most of the low-level attack and reconnaissance, leaving the Sea Harriers to fly CAP and other air-defence duties.

GR.3s join in

Prior to the arrival of the GR.3s the Sea Harrier pilots had decided to fly attack missions by day and night using a mix of medium level bombing and low-level tosses. The RAF Harriers worked almost exclusively at the lowest possible level, and, because even with the help of the surviving Finrae (two went down with the sunk *Atlantic Conveyor*) navigational accuracies could not quite equal those achieved with stationary alignment on an airfield, it was decided to navigate and attack visually wherever possible.

The first mission by No 1 Sqn, tasked on 20 May, was a strike against fuel and oil dumps at Fox Bay. Led by the CO, with both his flight commanders, S/Ls Bob Iveson and Jerry Pook, the tight formation made a single pass at low level straight over the target and used BL.755 CBUs (cluster bomb units). There were many secondary explosions, culminating in a giant fireball. Subsequently the GR.3s flew 125 sorties on attack and reconnaissance, the latter using the centreline pod. Three aircraft were lost, all due to ground defensive fire, which was usually intense and caused so much aircraft damage as to depress serviceability below the amazing figure of "above 99.9 per cent" set by the Sea Harriers.

The three losses were: XZ963, 21 May, hit by Blowpipe missile at Goose Green, F/Lt Jeffrey Glover ejected and captured (the only British PoW); XZ998, 27 May, hit by two large-calibre shells when at high speed at below 100ft supporting 2 Para near Goose Green, S/L Iveson losing flight control and hydraulic pressure, the aircraft then catching fire, arresting dive by vectoring nozzles but finally having to eject, evading capture and being picked up by Royal Marine flying Army Gazelle over two days later; XZ972, 30 May, after flying through heavy fire on 19 previous missions took several hits at low level when attacking a helicopter landing site west of Stanley and began losing fuel rapidly, and though S/L Pook thought his chance of survival poor because of loss of radio he was in fact accompanied by his wingman who had alerted *Hermes*, and when Pook ejected 45 miles (72km) short of the ship he actually heard the Sea King that was waiting to collect him.

Pook was only off operations for one day, because of a stiff neck, and in the closing stages he was one of the GR.3 pilots to use smart LGBs against difficult point targets. The hills around Port Stanley enabled all such attacks to be made behind cover, the Harrier approaching on the far side of Mounts Harriet, Tumbledown, or Two Sisters and lobbing the weapon in a toss over the summit. On two occasions the FAC (forward air controller) fired the Ferranti designator too soon and the LGB failed to achieve lock, but on all other FAC-designated smart attacks there was a direct hit. This weapon would have been valuable on many earlier attacks, almost all of which were against small targets that were exceedingly difficult to locate, but it might have been difficult to set up a friendly designator and a good launch trajectory. On at least one occasion, over Stanley airfield, an LGB failed to lock-on when designated by a GR.3's own laser. On some occasions attacks on heavily defended point targets were made at just above ground level by groups of GR.3s directed by a Sea Harrier overhead at much higher altitude who could see the target and send minor course changes.

In the whole of Operation Corporate the RN Sea Harriers flew 2,376 missions for a total of 2,675·4 hours. Seldom, if ever, has so much depended on so few aircraft. Despite the appalling weather, aircraft averaged 55 hours per month, flying 6 to 10 sorties per day. It was common for pilots to fly two combat missions without leaving the cockpit, and the serviceability never fell below 95 per cent. HMS *Invincible*'s aircraft flew 99.97 per cent of the tasked sorties, losing only

Right: Sea Harrier development aircraft XZ440 was used for the urgent clearance of the 190gal (864lit) drop tank and the twin Sidewinder AAM launcher, here loaded with the newly available AIM-9L.

Above: The Task Force flagship returned to Portmouth on 21 July, to a welcome that was deeply moving. Sea Harriers urgently needed at Yeovilton were flown off from the Bay of Biscay, but six were ranged on deck, together with the entire ship's company.

part of one sortie through unserviceability. Operations continued at a high intensity in conditions far below peacetime limits, and were assisted by local extensions given to various component lives, including the complete engine, and by allowing interchange between Harrier and Sea Harrier engines and fuel system components.

After the shock of meeting the Sea Harrier on 1 May, the Argentine FAA and CANA (naval air arm) avoided any clash with "the Black Death" for three weeks. Despite this, there was no let-up in round-the-clock CAPs, and sadly two aircraft, XZ452 and 453, flown by Lt-Cdr John Eyton-Jones and Lt Alan Curtis, disappeared on 6 May while on CAP in very bad weather; almost certainly they collided in cloud. On 24 May ZA192 hit the sea shortly after takeoff on a stormy night, Lt-Cdr G. W. J. Batt being killed. On 29 May ZA174 slid off the rolling icy deck of HMS *Invincible* while moving forward for the next takeoff; Lt-Cdr Mike Broadwater ejected and was picked up by a Sea King. The sixth and last loss was on 1 June when 801's air-warfare instructor, F/Lt Ian Mortimer, RAF, was shot down by a SAM while at 15,000ft (4572m) in XZ456. Mortimer was snatched from under the noses of the enemy in an amazing night search/rescue mission lasting nine hours.

During the lull in enemy air activity, 800 Sqn knocked out the reconnaissance trawler *Narwhal* on 9 May, and just a week later crippled the supply ship *Bahia Buen Suceso* and damaged the *Ric Carcarana*. On 22 May a patrol boat was strafed and forced to beach. By this time the RAF Harriers were flying the bulk of the attack missions – to the RAF's disgust because, though it had shown antipathy towards air combat when specifying the Harrier in the 1960s, it now naturally wanted a share of the air combat glory.

"Black Death" dominant

This continued to be cornered by the Navy, which had many brief but intense combats. All hell was let loose on 21 May (which happened to be Argentine Navy Day) at the start of the British assault landings. No. 800 downed four A-4s with Sidewinders and one with guns on that day, bagged a Mirage on 24 May, and had a particularly good day on 8 June when two of its aircraft splashed a formation of four Mirages: F/Lt Dave Morgan, RAF, getting two, Lt Dave Smith downing one, and the fourth Mirage hitting the sea during evasive action. The detailed analysis of Operation Corporate at first credited Sea Harriers with 20 confirmed and three probable kills, but this was later revised to 23 plus three probable, one of the additions being the C-130.

In late May Nos 11 and 59 Sqns Royal Engineers constructed an FOB (Forward Operating Base) at Port San Carlos. It comprised an 850ft (259m) strip made of MEXE aluminium planking, with taxi and parking loops at one end where fuel was stored in large flexible pillow tanks. The FOB was not used for reloading ordnance, but it enabled Harriers and Sea Harriers to put in almost twice as much time on CAP or cab-rank attack patrol by eliminating the round trip of some 400 miles back to the ship to refuel. One GR.3 sank through a joint in the metal matting, the nose gear going in up to the landing light. Using RE heavy lift gear the aircraft was bodily wrenched free; then it went straight back into action. On another occasion W/C Squire was making the authorized slow approach, with gear down and landing light on to avoid being engaged by British Rapiers, when his jet blast lifted a section of matting which struck his aircraft, XZ989. The impact drove the nozzles to the aft position, and the Harrier hit the ground hard careered through the strip, severing it, and continued up a nearby hill and over the brow before coming to rest in a Rapier crew's slit trench. The runway was quickly repaired.

Throughout the campaign nobody was more impressed by the performance of the Harrier and Sea Harrier than the men who flew and maintained them. Over 2,000 sorties had been flown, in the harshest conditions imaginable, and each day aircraft availability for both types together averaged better than 95 per cent. Unserviceability lost less than 1·0 per cent of the planned missions, despite the fact that virtually every aircraft took damage from ground fire. Many aircraft, mainly RAF Harriers because of their low attack tasking, took numerous hits from calibres up to 20mm yet were operational on the next day. one GR.3 was hit in the RCV hot-air duct near the tail. On its approach to *Hermes* with nozzles down, the rear end quickly cooked up until it was almost red hot, but XW919 was back in action 36h later; a performance that seems to typify the achievement of these aircraft during this arduous campaign.

Left: Removing the protective nosecap from one of the newly added AIM-9Ls on a GR.3 of No 1(F) Sqn at the forward base at San Carlos. Note the badge of HarDet (Harrier Detachment). Even in operations from this land site the INS was seldom used, aircraft using dead-reckoning and the pilots' eyeballs.

Harrier II

Above: Still obviously a Harrier, the AV-8B Harrier II is at the same time a totally new aeroplane. Sadly for Britain, government policy in 1975 has transferred control to the United States.

McDonnell Aircraft (MCAIR) of St Louis became associated with the original Hawker V/STOL programme in 1969, with an AV-8A licence agreement which also included the right for the US company to develop derived aircraft using the vectored-thrust principle. With staggering shortsightedness the British government opted out of a collaborative programme in 1975, leaving the next generation to St Louis. The next generation is Harrier II, and most of the production will take place in the United States.

By 1971 the Harrier was in production for the RAF and the almost identical AV-8A for the US Marine Corps. Though a few dissenting voices were still heard, which for reasons of ignorance or vested interest claimed that jet V/STOL was not cost/effective, or immature, or merely "foreign", it was obvious to any thinking person that it represented the dawn of a new era in aviation. So Hawker and MCAIR, and Rolls-Royce and Pratt & Whitney, did the obvious and began studying advanced developments of both the Harrier and its Pegasus engine.

Unlike previous aircraft, the Harrier and its Pegasus engine are intimately integrated. Quite apart from the patent situation, no other engine could provide both thrust and lift, and as the future of the Harrier appeared to depend crucially upon the provision of more of both of these factors, the foundation for the Advanced Harrier appeared to be a more powerful Pegasus.

Rolls-Royce Bristol decided to build a demonstrator engine to show the kind of performance possible with a few modifications. The new engine proposed was given the designation Pegasus 15, but the demonstrator was an intermediate engine using the existing Pegasus 11 core and adding only the proposed Pegasus 15 fan, with a diameter increased by 2¼in (57mm) to handle a significantly increased airflow. The Pegasus 15 was aimed at 24,500lb (11 113kg) thrust, so the Bristol team were pleased when the lash-up demo engine gave a figure of 24,900lb (11 295kg) on its first testbed run in May 1972. Hawker and MCAIR felt safe in assuming 25,000lb (11 340kg) in their aircraft studies.

Not least of the encouraging aspects of the Advanced Harrier was that this time there appeared likely to be four major launch customers: the RAF, Royal Navy, US Marine Corps, and US Navy. The latter had decided to deploy a major force of advanced V/STOL fighters aboard its Sea Control Ships, which in many ways were to be like the Royal Navy's *Invincible*. A Joint Management Committee was set up at government level with representatives of the civilian defence ministries (Mintech for Britain), the four customer services and the four main industrial partners. Hawker at Kingston produced the P.1184 and P.1185 project studies. MCAIR produced the AV-8C (not today's AV-8C), a minimum-change Harrier development with a long-span swept wing based on Douglas work with NASA's Richard T. Whitcomb with a supercritical profile matched to Mach 0·92 cruise (and originally studied for a developed DC-9). Such a wing could house more fuel and greatly increase STO lift, besides having enough span for numerous stores pylons. All the studies featured a raised cockpit with all-round view, and of course the inlets had to be enlarged, though it was just posssible to squeeze the Pegasus 15 into the existing size of fuselage.

The AV-16 design

Though Hawker and MCAIR collaborated closely, and had growing technical teams at each other's plants, they pursued their studies independently. By 1973, after agonizing evaluations, it had been decided to let the Pegasus fan grow a further half-inch, to get 25,000lb (11 340kg) with lower turbine temperature and thus achieve long low-cost life, even though this meant a redesign of the fuselage. The AV-8-Plus also introduced a further improved high-airflow elliptical-lip inlet provided with a second row of suck-in auxiliary doors. Both teams also began to discover ways in which local modifications could increase VTO or STO lift without any appreciable penalty. Wisely, both judged that the right course was to modify the proven Harrier as little as possible, and to do so only when a major gain appeared possible with small technical risk. Both adopted the designation AV-16, meaning twice the capability of an AV-8.

Unfortunately, some customers, including both navies, kept harping on the supposed primitive simplicity of the basic Harrier – which in fact is why it has survived and succeeded – and on the apparent advantages for naval missions of a highly supersonic V/STOL. The US Naval Air Systems Command asked both airframe companies how they would design such a machine, and Hawker dusted off its latest series of S (for supersonic) family of studies. These featured a PCB-boosted four-poster engine, of the kind described in the final chapter, which in turn pushed the main gears out into the wing as in the P.1154RN. The wing itself was naturally not only unlike that of a Harrier but utterly unlike that of the AV-8-Plus, which far from yielding

Left: Shown with an assortment of tanks and weapons in the plan and head-on views, the S-6 was one of the "might have been" supersonic designs studied at HSA Kingston in 1973-4.

Below: A direct plan view emphasizes the more obvious new features of the AV-8B, especially the new wing. Low-visibility markings highlight the APU (GTS) inlet and exhaust apertures.

supersonic speed would actually make the aircraft slower. Thus, the AV-16 S-6 had a well-swept wing of low aspect ratio and very low thickness/chord ratio, with broad streamwise tips and long root extensions. High-altitude Mach number was 1.95.

With a PCB thrust of 34,500lb (15650kg) the attractions of such a machine were obvious, and it would probably have met with the approval of the US Navy, which did not wish to bother with a mere "warmed over" version of the existing Harrier. But the likely costs were already daunting, inflation was beginning to bite, and the only really definite and urgently concerned customer, the Marine Corps, was horrified at the idea of such a complete redesign and merely wanted a more capable subsonic bomb truck. At the time it seemed tragic that, because of narrow-minded conflict of interest and perhaps also the sheer diversity of possible aircraft, the idea of a really big two-nation, four-customer programme was by 1973 falling apart.

It was especially disheartening to lose the US Navy, because in terms of numbers this was potentially the No 1 customer. On 13 October 1972 Navair, the Naval Air Systems Command, awarded a major V/STOL development contract to North American Rockwell for the extremely advanced and complex XFV-12A. This was expected to hover in August 1974 and make transitions a month later. We are still waiting for the XFV-12 to fly, and in fact the whole project fell so short of prediction it was abandoned in 1980. But its very existence could easily have caused MCAIR to look for easier lines of business, and it is to the credit of Sandy McDonnell – who inherited from his uncle a very tough and canny business sense – that instead of dropping the rejected AV-16 the St Louis company continued to believe that it was the right way to go.

To offer encouragement, in 1973 the US Marine Corps issued a formal requirement for such an Advanced Harrier, and MCAIR and Hawker began doing joint studies, which culminated in a submission to the US and British governments of an "AV-16A" on 13 December 1973. It had the MCAIR long-span supercritical wing, the Pegasus 15 engine, and numerous lift-improving detail refinements throughout the airframe. But

Above: This unusual 1981 formation of AV-8B 161396 and an AV-8A 159255 shows the much greater volume available in the new nose and cockpit areas. Another contrast is the lateral area of the twin under-fuselage strakes.

Left: Never has an aircraft programme of recent years started out so good on paper yet proved so great a disappointment as the US Navy Rockwell XFV-12A. Planned as a supersonic successor to the AV-8A, it never flew.

factors outside the programme were casting a deepening shadow. One was the continuing uncertainty of what the customers wanted. Only the Marines simply wanted an AV-16A. The RAF wanted an Advanced Harrier whose major improvements could be retrofitted to its existing Harriers, and on this count the MCAIR wing and Pegasus 15 engine were both non-starters. The Royal Navy had by this time become committed to the design that became the Sea Harrier. Worst of all, inflation was beginning to bite, and not only was the development cost of the AV-16A and its engine put at $1 billion but this was expected to double because of inflation by the time the aircraft entered service.

Increasingly the meetings dwelt on problems rather than progress, and what seemed to be the *coup de grâce* was the announcement of the British government on 19 March 1975 that: "There is not enough common ground on the Advanced Harrier for us to join in the programme with the US". In fact, this was not true, because one aeroplane will now serve both countries, but that particular government simply wanted to cut defence spending and was delighted to latch on to any project that seemed to be in difficulties. In the United States Navair cancelled its sponsorship of the AV-16A due to lack of funds. The Navy itself had already picked the XFV-12A, and terminating the "foreign program" pleased a lot of partisan Congressmen.

Pegasus 15 abandoned

Though this was the low point in a protracted story, the crunch in 1975 did allow each airframe partner, if it chose to, to press ahead with its own unfettered studies for its own customers. Both quickly came to the same conclusion regarding the Pegasus 15. It is possible that, had PCB development never been shelved by Rolls-Royce following cancellation of the P.1154, a 34,500lb (15650kg) PCB Pegasus 15 would have been funded in 1975, with dramatic long-term results. But the Mk 15 engine alone was costed at $600 million to US qualification, and, when it was found that this equated to $200,000 per pound of extra thrust, the whole project seemed not worth while. The crucial decision was taken to abandon any immediate major Pegasus development, and concentrate on the airframe instead. Navair funded a study of Pegasus alternatives, carried out jointly by Pratt & Whitney and Rolls-Royce, which suggested: 1, the Pegasus 104, as later adopted for the Sea Harrier; 2, the Mk 104 with internal changes to improve maintainability and give a TBO (time between overhauls) of 1,000h; 3, the Pegasus 11D with small internal changes giving 800lb (363kg) more thrust; and 4, an 11D with 1,000h TBO. Not submitted, Rolls also studied the 11D+ with increased temperature and 22,500lb (10206kg) thrust.

For a possible Advanced Harrier for the Marines, Navair picked the second choice above, the improved Mk 104 with 1,000h TBO, and with virtually all the detail improvements aimed at improving ease of maintenance and reducing total costs over perhaps a 20-year period rather than at increasing performance. Despite this, MCAIR had already shown in 1975 that by airframe modifications alone, the payload/range capability of the AV-8A could be at least *doubled*! MCAIR were in any case determined to continue Advanced Harrier development for the Marines, and in 1975 had put a growing technical team on the job. It could have elected to go it alone, but wisely chose to continue collaboration with Hawker, who retained liaison engineers at St Louis and played a significant part in the design of what by 1975 had become the AV-8B. Before the end of 1975 MCAIR had completed the basic project design, and had already carried out extensive test programmes. One of the latter was to rebuild a crashed AV-8A to look broadly like the AV-8B, and this impressive non-flying demonstration aircraft was rolled out as early as 7 August 1975.

The obvious new feature of the AV-8B was the wing. This was a refined version of the Whitcomb supercritical wing, designed by an MCAIR team under T. R. Lacey. Its chief new feature is that, in one of the boldest structural decisions for many years, its entire primary structure is carbon-fibre composite (called graphite composite in the USA), and it is the largest carbon item in any aircraft, excepting the Rockwell B-1 horizontal tail. On any count it is larger than the Harrier wing, with span over 30ft (9·1m) and a much deeper cross-section, the average t/c (thickness to chord) ratio being 10·5 per cent compared with 8·5. Thus it can accommodate almost twice as much fuel as the original wing, 4,950lb (2245kg) compared with 2,834lb (1285kg), besides giving far greater STO lift and providing for three pylons on each side. It has eight spars, each with an undulat-

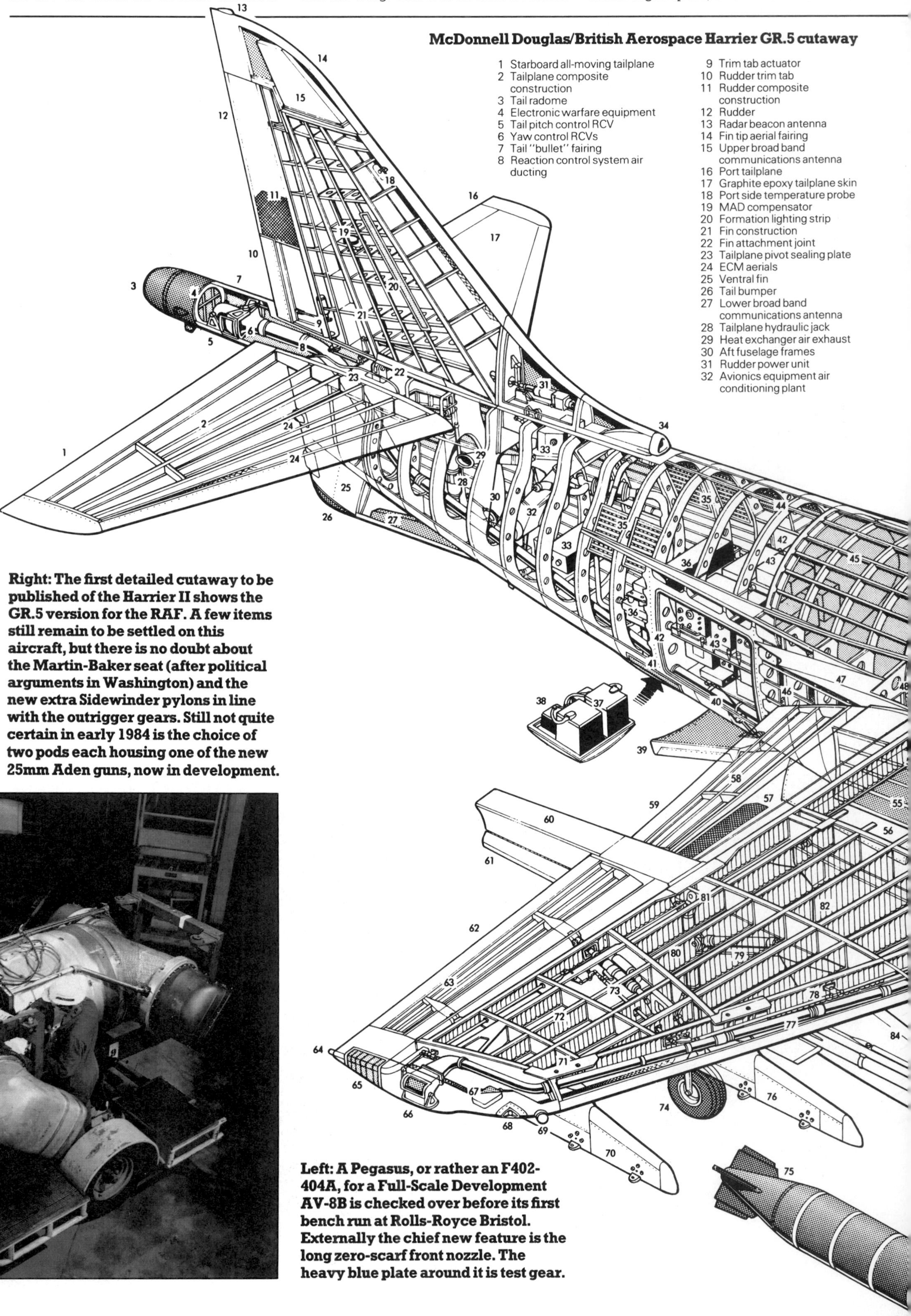

Right: The first detailed cutaway to be published of the Harrier II shows the GR.5 version for the RAF. A few items still remain to be settled on this aircraft, but there is no doubt about the Martin-Baker seat (after political arguments in Washington) and the new extra Sidewinder pylons in line with the outrigger gears. Still not quite certain in early 1984 is the choice of two pods each housing one of the new 25mm Aden guns, now in development.

Left: A Pegasus, or rather an F402-404A, for a Full-Scale Development AV-8B is checked over before its first bench run at Rolls-Royce Bristol. Externally the chief new feature is the long zero-scarf front nozzle. The heavy blue plate around it is test gear.

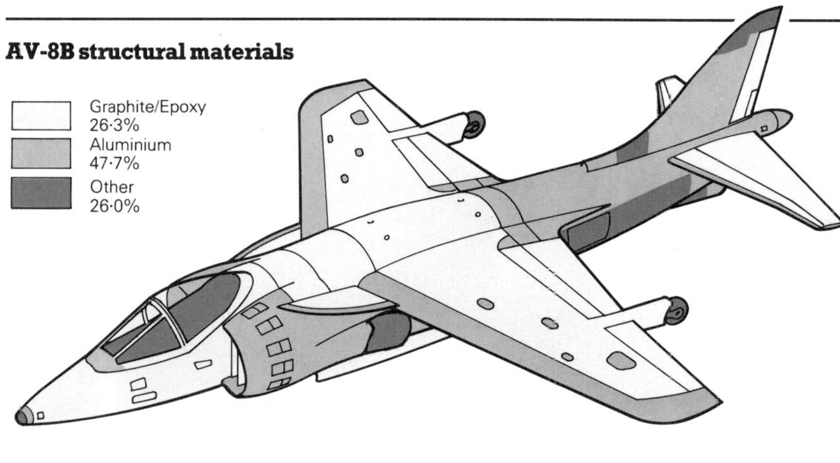

Above: Another far from obvious new feature of all Harrier II aircraft is the widespread use of graphite composite. **The 26·3 per cent by weight equates to about 40 per cent by volume, because of the low density of this material.**

ing (sine-wave) web, yet the switch to carbon and deeper profile enables the new wing to weigh 330lb (150kg) less than an equivlent all-metal wing.

The leading edge is now swept at 36° instead of 40°, and is a simple aluminium alloy structure which after flight development has only a single outboard fence. The trailing edge is totally new. While the RCVs are right at the tip, for maximum roll power, the outrigger landing gears have been moved inboard between the ailerons and flaps, reducing track to 17ft (5·18m) for easier manoeuvring and with the leg fairings replaced by doors. Inboard are the enormous double-slotted flaps which in the STO mode are extended to 62° and react powerfully with the wing circulation induced by the angled nozzles. MCAIR and NASA conducted prolonged tests to rearrange the nozzles, wing and flaps to obtain the most favourable circulation around the inboard wing in STO. This work also led to new longer zero-scarf front engine nozzles which give 200lb (91kg) more thrust. It is planned to switch to titanium, saving 50lb (22·7kg). This wing/flap/nozzle improvement provides the largest of the many increments in STO lift, no less than 6,700lb (3039kg) on a 1,000ft (300m) run.

The new engine inlets were further refined to increase airflow and reduce drag, and the geometry of the double row of auxiliary inlet doors improved. Eventually, at the seventeenth production AV-8B, it was found possible to use large single doors. These increase VTO lift by 600lb (272kg), but instead of this

33 Avionics equipment racks
34 Heat exchanger ram air intake
35 Electrical system circuit breaker panels, port and starboard
36 Electronic warfare equipment
37 Chaff and flare dispensers
38 Dispenser electronic control units
39 Ventral airbrake
40 Airbrake hydraulic jack
41 Formation lighting strip
42 Avionics bay access door, port and starboard
43 Avionics equipment racks
44 Fuselage frame and stringer construction
45 Rear fuselage fuel tank
46 Main undercarriage wheel bay
47 Wing root fillet
48 Wing spar/fuselage attachment joint
49 Water filler cap
50 Engine fire extinguisher bottle
51 Anti-collision light
52 Water tank
53 Flap power unit
54 Flap hinge fitting
55 Titanium fuselage heat shield
56 Main undercarriage bay doors (closed after cycling of mainwheels)
57 Flap vane composite construction
58 Flap composite construction
59 Starboard slotted flap, lowered
60 Outrigger wheel fairing
61 Outrigger leg doors
62 Starboard aileron
63 Aileron composite construction
64 Fuel jettison
65 Formation lighting panel
66 Roll control RCV
67 Radar warning signal processor
68 Starboard navigation light
69 Radar warning aerial
70 Outboard pylon
71 Pylon attachment joint
72 Graphite epoxy composite wing construction
73 Aileron power unit
74 Starboard outrigger wheel
75 BL755 600lb (272kg) cluster bomb (CBU)
76 Intermediate pylon
77 Reaction control air ducting
78 Aileron control rod
79 Outrigger hydraulic retraction jack
80 Outrigger leg strut
81 Leg pivot fixing
82 Multi-spar graphite wing construction
83 Leading-edge wing fence
84 Outrigger pylon
85 Missile launch rail
86 AIM-9L Sidewinder air-to-air missile
87 External fuel tank, 300US Gal (1135lit)
88 Inboard pylon
89 Aft retracting twin mainwheels
90 Inboard pylon attachment joint
91 Rear (hot stream) swivelling exhaust nozzle
92 Position of pressure refuelling connection on port side
93 Rear nozzle bearing
94 Centre fuselage flank tank
95 Hydraulic reservoir
96 Nozzle bearing cooling air duct
97 Engine exhaust divider duct
98 Wing panel centre rib
99 Centre section integral fuel tank
100 Port wing integral fuel tank
101 Flap vane
102 Port slotted flap, lowered
103 Outrigger wheel fairing
104 Port outrigger wheel
105 Torque scissor links
106 Port aileron
107 Aileron power unit
108 Aileron/air valve interconnection
109 Fuel jettison
110 Formation lighting panel
111 Port roll control RCV
112 Port navigation light
113 Radar warning aerial
114 Port wing reaction control air duct
115 Fuel pumps
116 Fuel system piping
117 Port wing leading-edge fence
118 Outboard pylon
119 BL755 cluster bombs (maximum load, seven)
120 Intermediate pylon
121 Port outrigger pylon
122 Missile launch rail
123 AIM-9L Sidewinder air-to-air missile
124 Port leading-edge root extension (LERX)
125 Inboard pylon
126 Hydraulic pumps
127 APU intake
128 Gas turbine starter/auxiliary power unit (APU)
129 Alternator cooling air exhaust
130 APU exhaust
131 Engine fuel control unit
132 Engine bay venting ram air intake
133 Rotary nozzle bearing
134 Nozzle fairing construction
135 Ammunition tank, 110 rounds
136 Cartridge case collector box
137 Ammunition feed chute
138 Fuel vent
139 Gun pack strake
140 Fuselage centreline pylon
141 Zero scarf forward (fan air) nozzle
142 Ventral gun pack (two)
143 Aden 25mm cannon
144 Engine drain mast
145 Hydraulic system ground connectors
146 Forward fuselage flank fuel tank
147 Engine electronic control units
148 Engine accessory equipment gearbox
149 Gearbox driven alternator
150 Rolls-Royce Pegasus 11 Mk 105 vectored thrust turbofan
151 Formation lighting strips
152 Engine oil tank
153 Bleed air spill duct
154 Air conditioning intake scoops
155 Cockpit air conditioning system heat exchanger
156 Engine compressor/fan face
157 Heat exchanger discharge to intake duct
158 Nose undercarriage hydraulic retraction jack
159 Intake blow-in doors
160 Engine bay venting air scoop
161 Cannon muzzle fairing
162 Lift augmentation retractable cross-dam
163 Cross-dam hydraulic jack
164 Nosewheel
165 Nosewheel forks
166 Landing/taxiing lamp
167 Retractable boarding step
168 Nosewheel doors (closed after cycling of undercarriage)
169 Nosewheel door jack
170 Boundary layer bleed air duct
171 Nose undercarriage wheel bay
172 Kick-in boarding steps
173 Cockpit rear pressure bulkhead
174 Starboard side console panel
175 Martin-Baker Mk 10 ejection seat
176 Safety harness
177 Ejection seat headrest
178 Port engine air intake
179 Probe hydraulic jack
180 Retractable inflight-refuelling probe (bolt-on pack)
181 Cockpit canopy cover
182 Miniature detonating cord (MDC) canopy breaker
183 Canopy frame
184 Engine throttle and nozzle control levers
185 Pilot's head-up-display (HUD)
186 Instrument panel
187 Moving map display
188 Control column
189 Central warning system panel
190 Cockpit pressure floor
191 Underfloor control runs
192 Formation lighting strips
193 Aileron trim actuator
194 Rudder pedals
195 Cockpit section composite construction
196 Instrument panel shroud
197 One-piece wrap-around windscreen panel
198 Ram air intake (cockpit fresh air)
199 Front pressure bulkhead
200 Incidence vane
201 Air data computer
202 Pitot tube
203 Lower IFF aerial
204 Nose pitch control air valve
205 Pitch trim control actuator
206 Electrical system equipment
207 Yaw vane
208 Upper IFF aerial
209 Electronic warfare equipment
210 ARBS heat exchanger
211 MIRLS sensors
212 Hughes Angle Rate Bombing System (ARBS)
213 Composite construction nose cone
214 ARBS glazed aperture

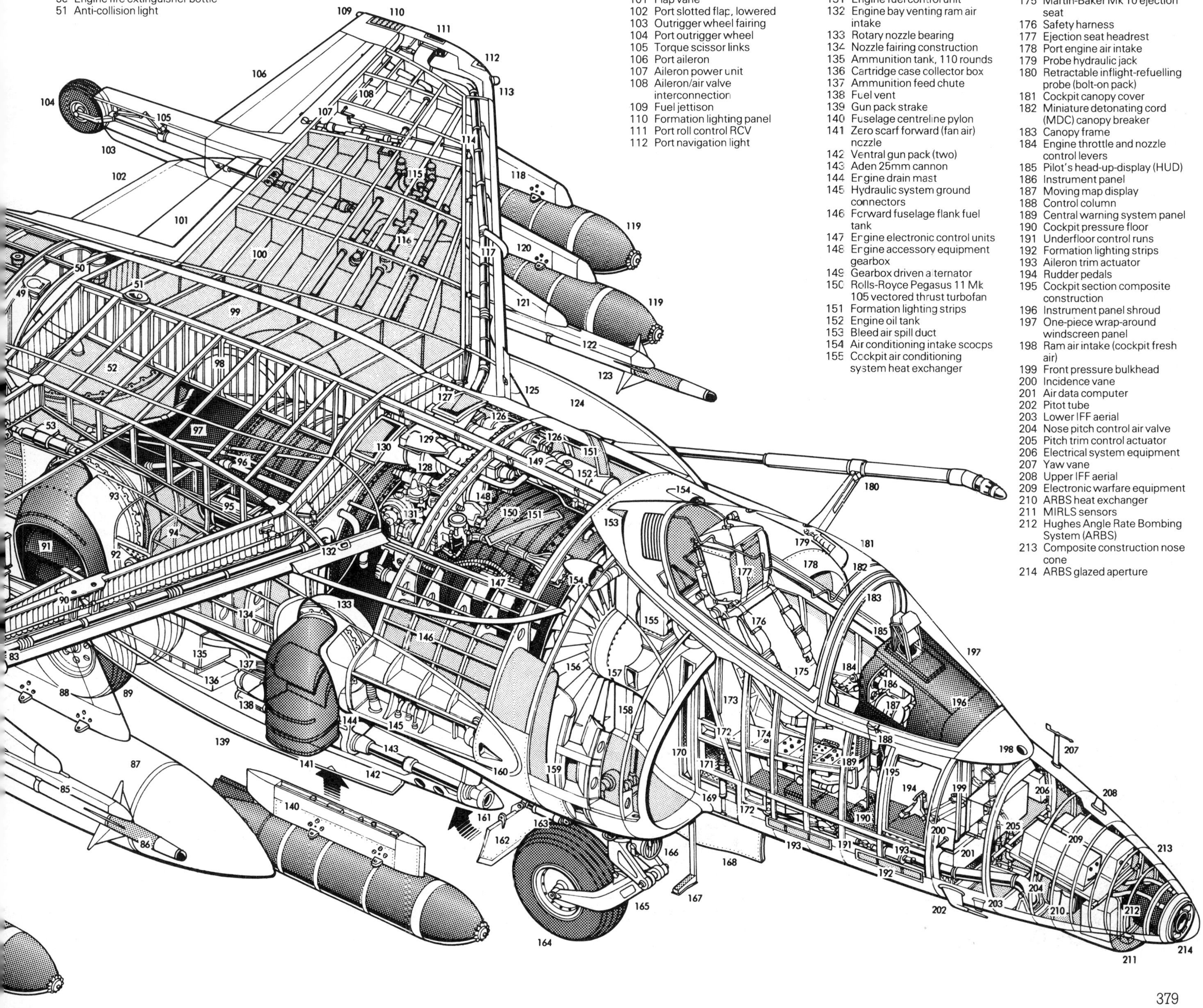

being at the cost of poorer high-speed behaviour the drag in cruising flight is actually reduced. Another very large contribution (1,200lb, 544kg) to VTO lift is furnished by the greatly improved LIDs (lift-improvement devices), which were devised jointly by BAe and MCAIR. Even the mid-1975 AV-8B mock-up had strakes added to the gun pods, with the inter-pod space boxed in by a hinged surface upstream – called a dam, but looking like an airbrake – which when tested on an AV-8A not only increased low-altitude lift by 1,220lb (533kg) but also reduced hot-gas reingestion and lowered inlet temperature by 20°C.

As well as being modified in shape, the complete forward fuselage, horizontal tail, rudder and the removable panels covering the top of the fuselage were all redesigned in carbon fibre. An incidental advantage is the elimination of tailplane resonance problems, and this is hoped to extend also to the proposed TAV-8B two-seater. As for the cockpit, this has been raised 10·5in (267mm) and provided with a giant circular-profile canopy giving an outstanding all-round view. The cockpit is descibed later. The whole nose was greatly enlarged, to provide additional space for avionics and other equipment, and the front windshield was increased in size and made a single curved piece of very thick multilayer stretched acrylic, with deicing but no wiper.

These were the chief improvements proposed by MCAIR for the AV-8B, which continued at full pressure at St Louis, assisted by NASA, though not yet funded by the Navy. By early 1976 another damaged AV-8A had been rebuilt with many AV-8B features, including the wing, flaps, LIDs and engine inlets, and initially put through engine-running and lift interaction tests resting on tall supports out of doors. By September 1976 it was in the giant 40×80ft tunnel at NASA's Ames Research Center. This full-scale model, whose wing was made of aluminium and wood, completed 319h of testing, and smaller models completed over 4,000h in perfecting the new high-lift features of the AV-8B.

Above: The third FSD aircraft, seen here near St Louis in April 1982, was the first to be fitted with LERX at the wing roots. This photograph illustrates the excellent visibility from the cockpit; the pilot is head up during air-to-air and air-to-ground combat.

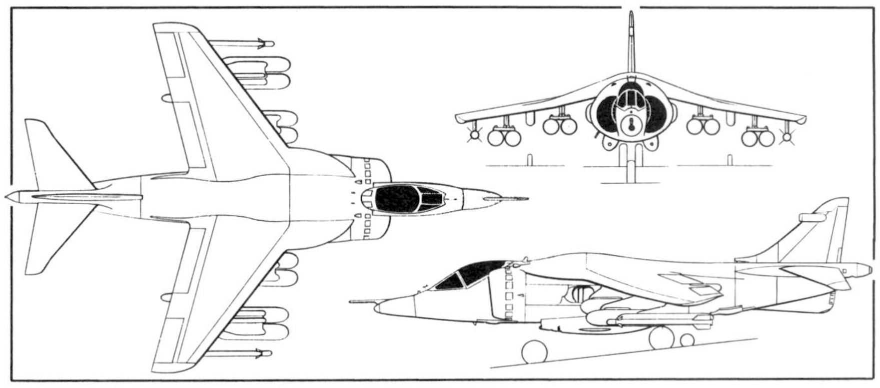

Above: In some respects the Kingston alternative, the Big Wing Harrier, would have been superior to the GR.5 which the RAF will now receive. It was particularly designed for higher speed and better manoeuvrability.

Funding is authorized

In March 1976 William P. Clements Jr, the US Deputy Secretary for Defense, announced agreement in principle to a programme for 342 AV-8B aircraft for the Marine Corps, comprising two YAV-8B prototypes, four FSD (full-scale development) prototypes and 336 production machines. Later the 336 were to be divided into 12 pilot production, 18 limited production and 306 full production. Limited funding was authorized, including cover for the two prototypes, and a complete test example of the new wing. To save time and cost the two YAV-8Bs were rebuilt AV-8As, Nos 158394 and 158395. These incorporated the complete new wing, with carbon (graphite) structure, but not yet incorporating production-style manufacturing methods, as well as the new inlets, and LIDs, but retaining the original tailplane, forward fuselage, cockpit and internal systems. The first YAV was completed 53 days ahead of schedule and at 188lb (85·3kg) under the calculated empty weight, so that it weighed almost exactly the same as a regular Harrier. AV-8B Project Test Pilot Charley Plummer lifted off from the concrete apron at Lambert St Louis airport for the first time on 9 November 1978.

In March 1979 ski takeoffs began from the Fairey-built MGB 12° ramp which had been purchased by the US Navy and airlifted from Farnborough to Pax River. A month later, in April 1979, MCAIR was awarded the long-awaited contract for the four FSD aircraft, and a long-lead contract for $35 million to begin preparation for production. At the same time it was by this time all too evident that the AV-8B was still tainted with the hated label "foreign" in influential sections of Congress. Though it had no historical precedent, the Carter administration decided to put the screws on the RAF to buy the AV-8B rather than the home-grown Big-Wing Harrier by making a full go-ahead on the AV-8B contingent upon export sales. Many partisan things were said, and certainly there existed a powerful lobby who wanted all the Navy vote to be poured into the colossal and escalating funding-trough of the F/A-18A Hornet (from the same contractor) and major ship programmes. SecDef Harold S. Brown called the F/A-18A-only choice a "more efficient" solution, overlooking the fact that a distant Marines beachhead might offer no conventional airbase. Another DoD spokesman called the AV-8B "an inefficient project that consumes funds needed for overall force modernization".

Probably the most serious result of the three years of delaying tactics for political ends was an increase in the estimated US price for the programme of no less than £920 million, due solely to infla-

Below: Aerodynamicists festoon prototype aircraft with tufts to explore airflow and look for flow breakaway. Here a YAV-8B, 158394, has tufting covering the entire top and bottom of both wings. Inboard stores are Snakeye bombs.

Above: BuAer No 158394, the first YAV-8B, caught by the camera in a tight turn over the Patuxent River runways in early 1982. Note the two cine cameras under the rear fuselage, aft of the old Aden-shape gun pods.

tion. Had the RAF simply bought the AV-8B at the start there might have been no delay at all, but the British situation was not easy to resolve. The RAF's needs continued to be for an improved Harrier able not only to fly far and fast at the lowest possible level, in the face of bad weather and intense hostile electronics and ordnance, but also to dogfight when necessary against agile opponents. Air Staff Requirement 409 stipulated various numerical parameters, including a maximum speed not less than that of the GR.3 and a sustained turn-rate of 20°/s. Hawker (BAe from 1978) strove to meet all the RAF's needs, and also to do so with changes which could be retroactively applied to existing RAF Harriers. It succeeded on all counts, with its proposed Big-Wing Harrier, produced to MoD study contract in 1978-80 and noteworthy for a fully swept long-span (over 34ft) wing made in metal and not only retrofittable but also with a high-speed profile for low drag and high manoeuvrability. Prominent at the roots of the leading edge were LERX (leading-edge root extensions) to add area at high AOA and create strong vortices, and thus delay the onset of flow separation from above the wing. They have a deliberate destabilizing effect and, seen in various forms on most modern air-combat aircraft, they enhance manoeuvrability. Tested on a GR.3 (XV277) they enabled pilots to pull 1g extra at any given engine thrust.

The Big Wing Harrier proposed many other new features, and would have had no fewer than ten stores attachments on the wings alone. BAe thought it at least as saleable as the AV-8B, which was slower than the GR.3 and missed meeting the RAF turn rate by miles with a limit of under 14°/s. It therefore produced brochures to try to convince governments, notably the British, that it had the better product and that it would be better for Britain to have the whole of an initially modest RAF programme, with a big export potential, than a minor share of the AV-8B. The decision was agonizing but the carpet was rather pulled from under BAe when the Minister of Defence announced in 1980 that "the Big Wing is unlikely to be any part of an improvement programme for the GR.3". Though deadlock appeared to continue, in fact BAe very reluctantly came round to the view that half a cake is better than the whole of a non-starter, and in January 1981, as the new Reagan administration took office in Washington, BAe recommended acceptance of the AV-8B as the most commercially viable solution.

At last the Minister of Defence announced in July 1981 that the AV-8B would be bought for the RAF, with an expected total of 60 aircraft. Much fewer than the original Harrier buy, this will equip new squadrons to serve alongside GR.3 units, the latter aircraft being given a major mid-life update. At once there was what previous SecDef Brown had

Below: AV-8B No 5, the first true production Harrier II, in the St Louis plant with F-15s in the rear in April 1983. Note the double row of inlet doors, which have now been replaced by single doors of improved form.

Above: The "pretty" FSD aircraft, 161397, on test from St Louis in April 1982 with gear extended and a touch of airbrake. LERX and LIDs are installed.

called "a new situation", and an MOU (Memorandum of Understanding) was signed on 24 August 1981 authorizing full-scale development. MCAIR and BAe decided on the family name Harrier II. The deal at the industrial level finally thrashed out is: for all US and 75 per cent of third-country sales, MCAIR is prime contractor with BAe a subcontractor; for all UK and 25 per cent of third-country sales, BAe is prime, with MCAIR a subcontractor; actual split of airframe work is about 60 MCAIR to 40 BAe; and systems and equipment are split about 80 US to 20 UK. The engine is a far better deal for Rolls-Royce, which merely has to relinquish up to 25 per cent of the production content to Pratt & Whitney, and for the Marine Corps buy only.

One advantage of the delay in launching full-scale development was that it was possible to crank in numerous further updates to both the aircraft and engine. The latter progressed from the YF402-RR-404, used in the YAV-8B aircraft, to the F402-404 with an improved 1st fan stage with wide-root blades to permit higher rpm, a higher-output gearbox and a new bulkhead matched to the production AV-8B. This was cleared at 21,700lb (9843kg) in 1980, and in the same year running began on a further improved sub-variant, the Dash-404A, with a revised swan-neck (intermediate casing) with a more efficient air path, and an increased-capacity No 2 bearing. In the same year, 1980, testing began of the full production engine, the F402-RR-406, with the shrouded LP turbine, triple interstage labyrinth seals, improved HP turbine cooling and a forged combustion-chamber outlet. Rated at 22,000lb (9979kg), this promises to be cleared to 1,000h TBO, with a hot-end inspection at 500h. In RAF service it will be designated Pegasus 105. The Dash-406 will enter service with the Marines in 1985, replacing the Dash-404A now being used in AV-8Bs.

The advantage of composites

The first of the four FSD aircraft flew in Plummer's hands at St Louis on 5 November 1981. All four were flying by June 1982, and two further airframes were built for structural testing, a novel feature of the AV-8B being that as no fatigue is yet known in carbon composite structures the wing and tailplane should have unlimited life. By July 1982 the fatigue specimen had completed 24,000h, equal to two planned lifetimes each of 12,000 flying hours. Further work led to the introduction of improved structural manufacturing and test methods, such as accurately cutting out large numbers of stacked carbon composite plies (laminates) simultaneously, and automatically traversing an ultrasonic scanner over the entire wing skins to check on perfect inter-laminate bonding.

More fundamental have been the improvements to the on-board systems. Nobody was ever totally satisfied with the original Harrier stability and control which in one band of airspeeds during a transition could lead via a yaw and involuntary roll to complete loss of control The Harrier II has a new high-authority SAAHS (stability and attitude-hold system) with a pitch/roll autostabilization computer and an electronic interface to the front RCV. Longitudinal and lateral margins are greatly improved, and with SAAHS operative throughout the flight envelope the pilot workload is greatly reduced, and anxiety virtually eliminated. Writing in *Rolls-Royce Magazine* the AV-8B Program Manager at Pax River, Maj Richard H. Priest, commented "It sounds good, but how does that translate when I'm trying to land on a 72ft by 72ft pad in the trees, or on a pitching deck on a dark night? I lower the nozzles and begin deceleration. I quickly realise that almost no lateral stick inputs are required, and the classic AV-8A nose wander is just not there any more. Continuing the decel to hover I am again impressed by the rock-steady feel of the aircraft, and how cool the engine is running under these demanding conditions.

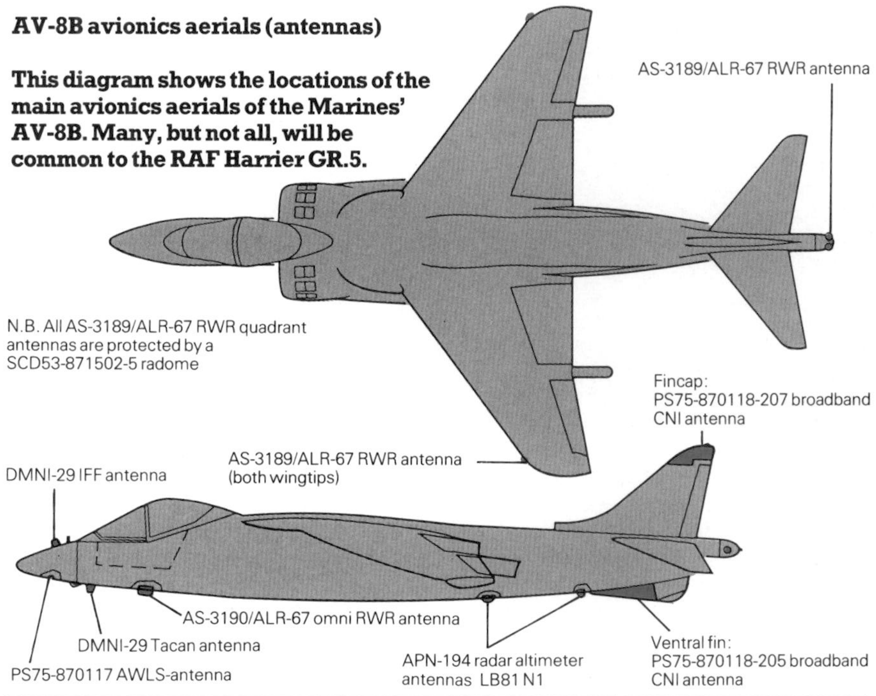

AV-8B avionics aerials (antennas)

This diagram shows the locations of the main avionics aerials of the Marines' AV-8B. Many, but not all, will be common to the RAF Harrier GR.5.

Reducing the power to descend to about 15ft I wait for the cobblestoning [random attitude disturbances] to begin, but it never occurs." In fact, so effective are the LIDs that AV-8B pilots just let the aircraft mush down on to the air cushion, where it refuses to sink any further until the power is brought back.

In production AV-8Bs propulsion management is handled by a Fadec (full-authority digital electronic control) produced by the new group DSIC (Dowty and Smiths Industries Controls). The AV-8B is the first production application for a Fadec, which again reduces pilot workload and any peaks in turbine gas temperature. As part of a far-ranging five-year NASA research programme into AV-8B stability and vectored-thrust aircraft behaviour generally, which will spin-off into future fighter designs, it is planned in late 1984 to integrate the throttle and nozzle controls into a single cockpit control, so that the pilot can fly in true Hotas (hands on throttle and stick) style, without ever having to move his left hand from one control to another. This will give perfect Viffing control for air combat, in which the AV-8B is already proving formidable, and will also ease the pilot's task in bad weather landings and other challenging phases of flight.

The NASA study has further tasks, including the refinement of simulator models to develop new navigation and guidance concepts for use in bad weather, including essentially blind landings impossible with other combat aircraft.

System improvements

Typical of system improvements throughout the aircraft, the Harrier II flap control system is digital FBW (fly by wire). It is self-monitoring, and controls the two electrohydraulic power units, each of which can push with 30,000lb (13·6 tonnes) to move the flaps at 7°/s down to 25° and at 64°/s from 25° to 62°. In earlier Harriers breakage of the torque tubes linking the flaps could cause flap asymmetry and force the pilot to eject. With the Harrier II the flap system can suffer any kind of failure and even shut down, yet the pilot can still fly the aircraft. The system also controls droop of the two ailerons, which improves lift in STO or at high AOA, and eliminates the need for the pilot to adjust flap setting in flight. Other major system improvements include constant-frequency AC electrics, an updated inertial navigation system (ASN-130 in the AV-8B, possibly a different system for the GR.5) and an Obogs (on-board oxygen generating system) which passes engine bleed air through filter beds which remove everything but the oxygen, as it is needed.

Left: The original planning cockpit used in defining the standard for the Harrier GR.5. The head-down moving-map display is on the right, and the MFD on the left is shown in the stores readout mode.

Below left: An early AV-8B simulator (July 1979), though with a cockpit not very different from those in today's production aircraft. Here the RAF moving-map display is replaced by the panels for fuel and ALE-39 ECM.

It goes without saying that the Harrier II cockpit is totally new. A great deal was fed in from the F/A-18A programme, including a large MFD (multifunction display) on the left and a prominent and easily used UFC (up-front control) for CNI (com/nav/ident) which incorporates a fibre-optic data converter. Above the UFC is the large Smiths Industries HUD, with dual combiner glasses, and on the right is a fuel panel and another controlling the Goodyear ALE-39 chaff/flare dispenser in the rear fuselage (in the GR.5 the RAF plan to have a moving-map display here instead). The armament control panel is low on the left, below the MFD.

At present all Harrier IIs have an approximately similar Hotas system, the stick and throttle grips including the following control functions: SAAHS control, air start, manoeuvre flaps (for combat), com selection, sensor selection, sensor cage/uncage, slew control/designation, weapon selection, weapon release, gun firing and aircraft trim. Viffing for combat will later be added to this impressive list. Pilot view is superb, and unlike the original low-canopied Harrier the pilot can sit well upright yet still find that the HUD is dead centre in his forward FOV (field of view). Previously, pilots sat as high as possible to try to see out, and then could not get down to use the HUD; "Harrier hunch" became famous throughout the Marine Corps. With the second-generation aircraft there is no need to hunch, and all controls also are comfortably situated without need to move the body.

Above: This drawing depicts an RAF Harrier GR.5. Stores shown include GP bombs, BL.755 CBUs and Lepus flares. LIDs strakes are fitted, though the expected gun pod is the new 25mm Aden. The RWR installation is the same ALR-67 as used by the US Marine Corps, with forward-facing aerials on the wingtips, though a different RWR may be selected.

There would be little problem in accommodating a modern multimode radar, but in all Harrier IIs at present planned the primary weapon delivery sensor is the Hughes ARBS (angle rate bombing system). This is mounted in the extreme nose and comprises a laser spot tracker and TV contrast tracker working together. They can be locked on to any surface target and thereafter continuously feed the appropriate angle rate information to the HUD and, if it is set in the attack mode, the MFD. The laser receiver also detects and locks on to any target illuminated by a correctly coded friendly laser from elsewhere. The pilot need make only one pass, and can lay down iron bombs manually, or by computer-controlled AWR (auto weapons release) mode, or by the CCIP (continuously computed impact point) line or depressed-sightline modes. Alternatively he can select missiles, such as any variant of Maverick or LGBs (laser-guided bombs).

Harrier GR.5s will probably stick to the Aden (though presumably in a 25mm developed version), but the AV-8B is the first aircraft to use the American General Electric GAU-12/U. This is the newest of the GE "Gatling" family, and has five barrels of 25mm (0.984in) calibre. MCAIR and GE developed a unique armament system in which the gun is mounted in the left-hand pod and 300 rounds of ammunition are housed in the right pod, which is aerodynamically identical. Behind the gun is the 35hp pneumatic drive motor running on engine bleed air. Rate of fire is 3,600spm (thrice the 30mm Aden rate) and muzzle velocity is 1,065m/s compared with 790. The magazine is very easy to reload, and with a linkless feed nothing is left behind on board. As previously noted, the pods have been configured to enhance the air-cushion effect as part of the LIDs programme. Other ordnance and external loads are listed in a diagram. The maximum weapon carriage of 9,200lb (4173kg) has been demonstrated.

In-flight refuelling

MCAIR test pilot Jack Jackson flew the first of the 12 pilot-production AV-8Bs in a 1h shakedown from Lambert St Louis on 29 August 1983. The general feeling at St Louis is that each Harrier II is coming out better than its predecessors, but with the pilot-production machines the definitive standard is very closely approached. A few weeks previously Jackson had made the first wet hookup with a Marine KC-130 tanker operating from Edwards. The neat refuelling probe, which is removable, retracts into the top of the left inlet duct fairing and when extended is easily visible to the pilot. Despite what Jackson knew from experience was severe turbulence behind the tanker, which often causes other aircraft to make an inadvertent disconnect, the AV-8B was rock-steady. Jackson said his workload was "about half that needed with an AV-8A".

Later, in late November 1983, the Navy reached final agreement on several important procurements in FY83 and FY84. The total obligational funding (paying for everything) for the AV-8B for these two fiscal years was planned to be 18 in FY83 costed at $942·9 million and 30 in FY84 at $979·8 million. The actual contractual figure for the basic aircraft (minus engine) for FY83 had been set at $423·6 million, for an increased buy of 21 aircraft, but this has been further pruned to $401·3 million. Delivery of pilot-production aircraft to the Marine Corps began in October 1983, and, as this book went to press, production was gradually building up to the planned 4·5 aircraft per month. The pilot-production aircraft are followed by the 18 so-called limited-production AV-8Bs, beyond which come the 306 full-production aircraft.

It is planned that by late 1988 the Marines should have 260 of these aircraft, with IOC (initial operational capa-

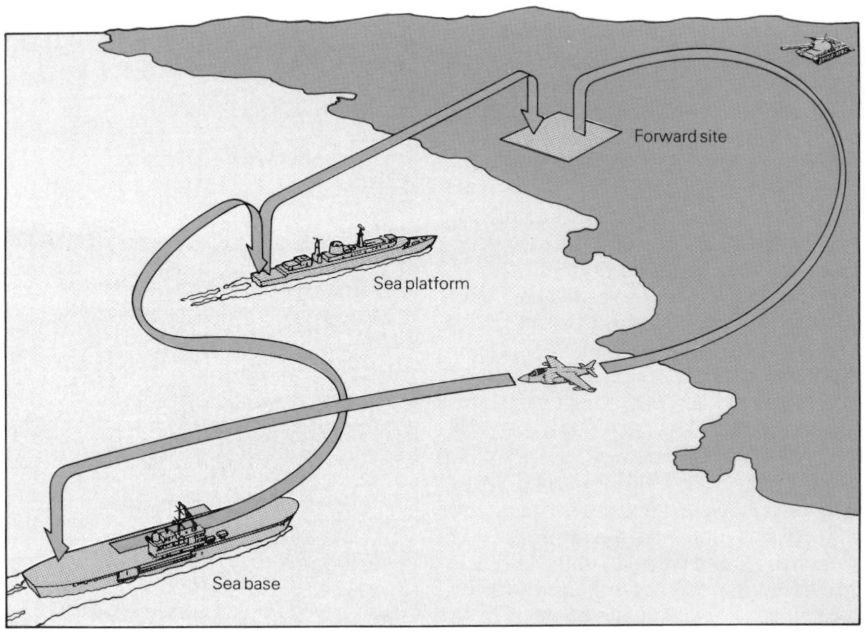

Below: Stores carried by the AV-8B are disposed on six wing and three fuselage store stations; maximum load: 9,200lb (4,173kg).

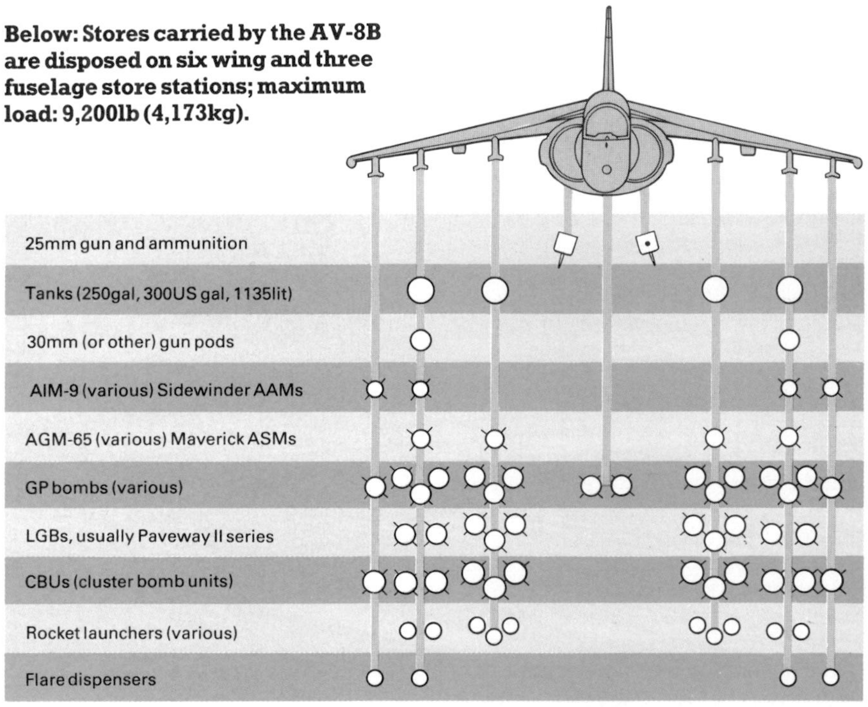

Below: An assortment of wing-mounted or centreline stores (not the gun pods) carried during Navy Board of Inspection and Survey trials. In front are a Sidewinder training store, an AIM-9L and a pair of AIM-9Ns.

Harrier II mission profiles

Left: Simplified mission diagram showing AV-8B operation from sea bases against land targets. The very flexible Harrier family could do a VTO or, as shown on a *Tarawa* class ship, an STO. A brief visit is made to the helicopter pad of a surface warship, followed by a VL at a forward site on land, before returning to the original ship.

Right: Here a selection of possible AV-8B shore-based missions is shown. A rolling takeoff would usually be made wherever possible, and certainly at the main base (unless rendered totally unusable). The forward sites would if possible be camouflaged, and most would probably offer only a very restricted run. Tanks imply hostile ground forces.

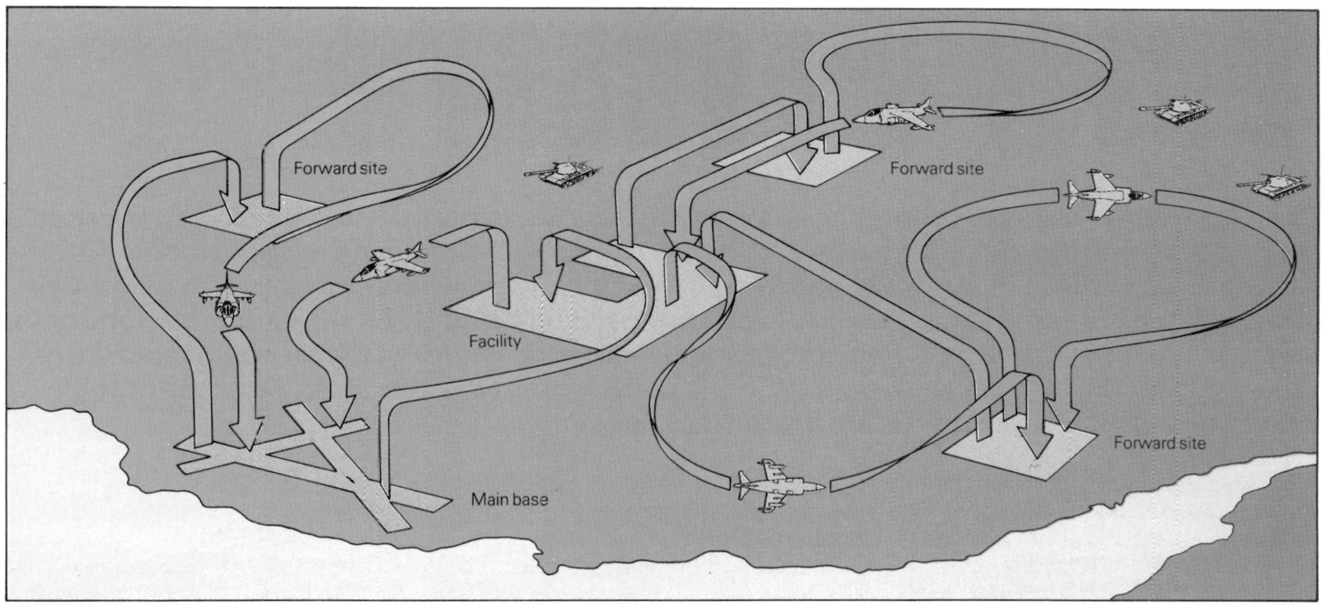

Above: A September 1983 photograph of a production AV-8B showing the ARBS in the nose and the GE 25mm gun and ammunition pod installation. The only change since then has been a further improvement in the inlets.

bility) achieved from mid-1985. Initially the Harrier IIs will replace the AV-8C in VMAT-203, VMA-231 and VMA-542, the surviving older Harriers going to reserve units. Further Harrier IIs will then replace the A-4 Skyhawk in the five Marine squadrons still flying this aircraft. To support the pilot training requirement, especially in conversion of the A-4 pilots, it is planned to purchase 18 two-seat TAV-8Bs. These are likely to differ substantially from the British two-seater even in the changes compared with the single-seat version. Length would be increased by 4ft (1·22m) and tail height by 17in (432mm), both close to the British figures, but the AV-8B starting point has a totally new forward fuselage and the trainer will have a shorter tailcone. The front (pupil) cockpit would omit the ECM systems and, initially, weapon-delivery controls, though the TAV-8B would be designed to be used if necessary as a combat aircraft.

With the Harrier II now firmly established as a production aircraft it must be expected that it will become the standard international version. British Aerospace are only too aware of the possibilities, and may be expected, in partnership with MCAIR, to offer a naval shipboard variant in due course. Meanwhile the first export order, for 12, was announced by the Spanish Navy in April 1983. These aircraft will be very close to the Marine Corps AV-8B, though they may be delivered with the 11-21 engine. The contract is priced at $378 million, with spares and training included. From early 1987 these aircraft will equip the new squadron to be based aboard the *Príncipe de Asturias*, the new Spanish V/STOL carrier. The VA-1 Matadors will continue in service with Esc 008, unlike the early Harriers of the US Marine Corps. The Spanish AV-8B squadron has not yet been announced.

Below: Dry and later wet contacts were made with FSD aircraft 161397 in March and April 1983, the KC-130R coming from VMGR-352. Unlike all previous Harriers the AV-8B has a retractable inflight-refuelling probe.

Below: Weapon release trials from Patuxent River in October 1982, using the third aircraft, included this set of two triplets of inert Snakeye retarded bombs. Delivery accuracy has been consistently excellent.

The Future

The regrettably limited acceptance so far of the Harrier, especially in its air force versions, is a damning indictment of air staffs who believe in the sanctity of airfields. British Aerospace and MCAIR know the penny will eventually drop, and are busy with new ways of using Harriers and with higher-performance derived designs. As the conflict in the South Atlantic revealed, the very newness of going to war with vectored thrust means that we are as yet only on the brink of the possibilities. SCADS, Skyhook, PCB: these are some of the concepts that may come to fruition during this decade.

Above: Some people might get the idea McDonnell Douglas was trying to corner the market in advanced combat aircraft. The chief point that emerges from this June 1982 formation picture is the relatively small size of the Harrier II, compared with the F-15 (nearest) and F/A-18 (furthest).

In October 1981, just before roll-out of the first AV-8B, the MCAIR AV-8B engineering director, Larry Smith, was interviewed in the following terms:

Q. In the grand scheme of things, how important is the AV-8B?

A. It's extremely important, even historic. The move to V/STOL tactical aircraft is of comparable importance to the move from propeller to jet aircraft, and I believe history will record it that way.

Q. What makes this evolution historic?

A. It's a combination not possible earlier in the history of flight, a marriage of the advantages of the fixed-wing aircraft with the advantages of the rotary-wing aircraft. If the development of those two types was historic, and it was, then the advent of fixed-wing jet V/STOL is of equal significance.

These facts are all so basic and familiar that they are easily overlooked. This is especially the case in peacetime, when the superb airbases still exist. It is only after the airbases have been blasted – even if only conventional weapons are used – that vectored thrust takes over as the only survivable form of airpower. But in many parts of the world the costly and immovable airfields have never even existed, or perhaps the only ones available belong to the enemy. Harriers can still thunder into action, in every kind of tactical role, operating from jungle clearings, highways, warship pads, merchant vessels, or anything else offering about 75ft (23m) of clear space.

Of course, it helps greatly if a ski jump is available. Nobody appreciates this better than the current users of the Harrier, and it would be strange if they had not years ago have completed detailed surveys of all the many thousands of sites around the world where their V/STOLs might suddenly have to go into action from a natural ski ramp formed by the terrain. Even in desert regions it is possible to find dispersed sites offering natural ski ramps, though sandy deserts pose ingestion problems and generally make concealment difficult. Alternatively, it is possible to drive around with one's own airfield, but the early ideas for mobile ramps are now regarded as too costly.

However, there is no reason to doubt that a much simpler so-called skeletal ramp could make the task of erecting, folding, transporting and re-erecting much easier. British Aerospace proposed such a ramp in 1979. The key feature is a central rail with a deep channel section tailored to the twin-wheel main landing gear. All the pilot need do is set up the nozzle stop and bang the throttle open. The aircraft will be steered precisely and automatically, so that all the outrigger gears need are two narrow rails, possibly only 1ft (0·3m) wide. The 1979 display model showed only two support trusses, each fitted with

Below: Today's GR.3? Sure, but what other aeroplane – anywhere in the world – can deploy real airpower without needing any kind of airfield or carrier? This aircraft from 233 OCU demonstrates the aerodynamics – using rainwater – of a rolling VL.

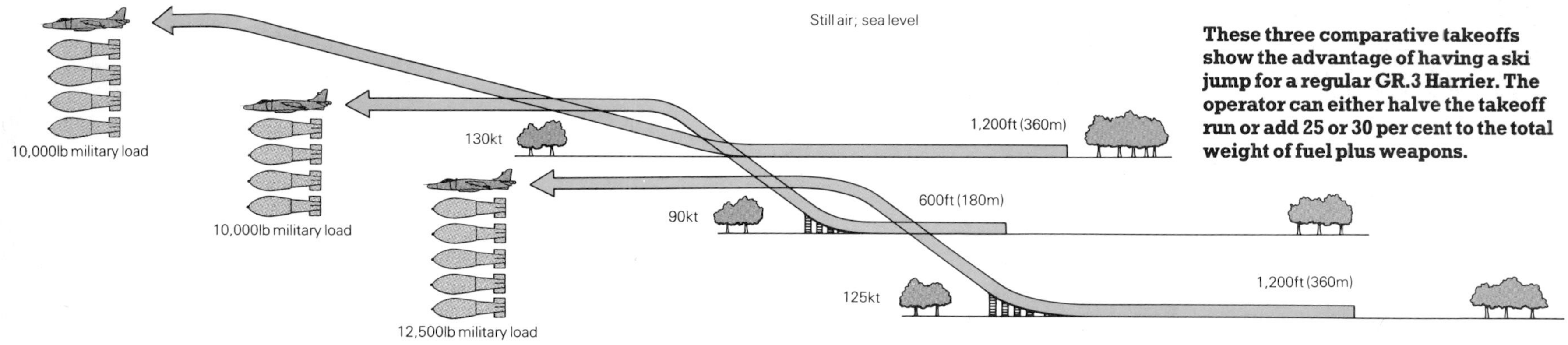

Ski jumps on land: performance gains

These three comparative takeoffs show the advantage of having a ski jump for a regular GR.3 Harrier. The operator can either halve the takeoff run or add 25 or 30 per cent to the total weight of fuel plus weapons.

Right: G-VTOL, the company demonstrator, has been used for hundreds of ski-jump takeoffs to show potential customers there really is nothing to it. Here it is using the RAE Bedford ramp which is set at 20°. The development of mobile, land-based ramps must be a priority for the future.

transport wheels but anchored to the ground prior to aircraft operations. Such a ramp would weigh approximately one-tenth as much as the MGB plate type of ski ramp, and several could be airlifted in a single C-130.

Incidentally, as more and more nations realize that a mobile ski ramp is less vulnerable than an airfield, the supply of ramps for both combat operations and training will become important. It started when in 1979 the US Marines bought the Farnborough ramp and set it up at NAS Pax River, moving it to MCAS Cherry Point as a routine training facility in 1981. They bought a second MGB ramp for the US West Coast, and are buying the kit for a ramp for their Mobile Reserve. The first permanent training ramp was designed by BAe for the Royal Navy at Yeovilton, and is unique in several respects. Its first 100ft (30m) is concrete, but the final portion can easily be adjusted in 1° intervals to any setting between 7° and 15°, which enables the ramp to duplicate those of *Invincible/Illustrious* at 7° and *Hermes/Ark Royal* at 12°.

In the maritime context the possibilities for Harrier deployment are open-ended. Consider the case of Sub-Lt Ian Watson, who ran out of fuel over the Atlantic, far from land, in June 1983. He merely alighted on a small (2,300ton) Spanish merchant ship, an operation which Watson had neither trained for nor even considered, saving a £7 million aircraft which, without vectored thrust, would have sunk. But when operations from merchant ships are premeditated, the results can be impressive. Two fascinating proposals, with possibilities which grow each time they are studied, are Skyhook and SCADS.

SCADS: a force multiplier

SCADS (shipborne containerized air-defence system) is unique in warfare. Thanks to the capabilities of the Harrier, or in this case Sea Harrier, it enables equipment to be prepared and stored which, in a matter of a few hours, could multiply the number of oceangoing V/STOL bases. In the distant past similar schemes were studied for the conversion of merchant vessels into helicopter or even fixed-wing carriers, but the job always took weeks to months. Today, with such machines as the F-14, F/A-18 and E-2, such conversion is out of the question; indeed, the number of nations with seagoing fixed-wing airpower of the conventional kind has fallen to three (USA, France and Argentina) and will decline further during the current decade. In contrast, jet V/STOL technology has already put this kind of airpower aboard front-line ships of five nations (USA, Soviet Union, Spain, Britain and India), and others, probably led by Italy, will be added in the current decade. SCADS gives further impetus, in that for a relatively modest outlay a dozen other nations could almost overnight join the growing club of those with multirole seagoing airpower.

The advantages of a bolt-on system are obvious. In sudden emergencies there are never enough flight decks, and except for the US Navy the loss of a single one would be serious (in the case of two navies it would halve the number available, and in three others it would eliminate seagoing airpower entirely). With prestocked SCADS two, three or four more multirole V/STOL warships could be produced in a matter of hours.

The ideal starting point is a container ship, of 30,000 deadweight tonnage and capable of 25 knots (46km/h) in order to reach a trouble-spot quickly. In the form studied by British Aerospace the SCADS ship would become the operating base for six Sea Harriers and two Sea King helicopters, the latter being tasked primarily with AEW (airborne early warning). The ship is far more than a mere transporter of the aircraft; it provides every facility needed for their sustained operation for 30 days, as well as the ship's own defence system against air attack. In effect, it becomes a powerful warship, able to supplement the air defence and long-range attack capability of a task force or to serve as a convoy's outer defence perimeter.

To do the whole job takes about 230 ISO (International Standards Organization) containers, each 8ft × 8ft × 40ft (2·4m × 2·4m × 12m). Accompanying artwork shows how most of these would house aircraft fuel for the 30 day period,

SCADS ship layout

Below: SCADS (shipborne containerized air-defence system) is something that in the early 1980s is highly exciting, but it is almost certainly by no means the only bright idea to be triggered off by vectored thrust. This diagram shows how any modern container ship could be adapted so that, at less than 48h notice, it could be converted into an operating base for the world's most versatile combat aircraft. There are an unlimited number of ways in which Harriers and ships can be wedded, but SCADS appears in 1984 to be very hard to beat – whatever the budget!

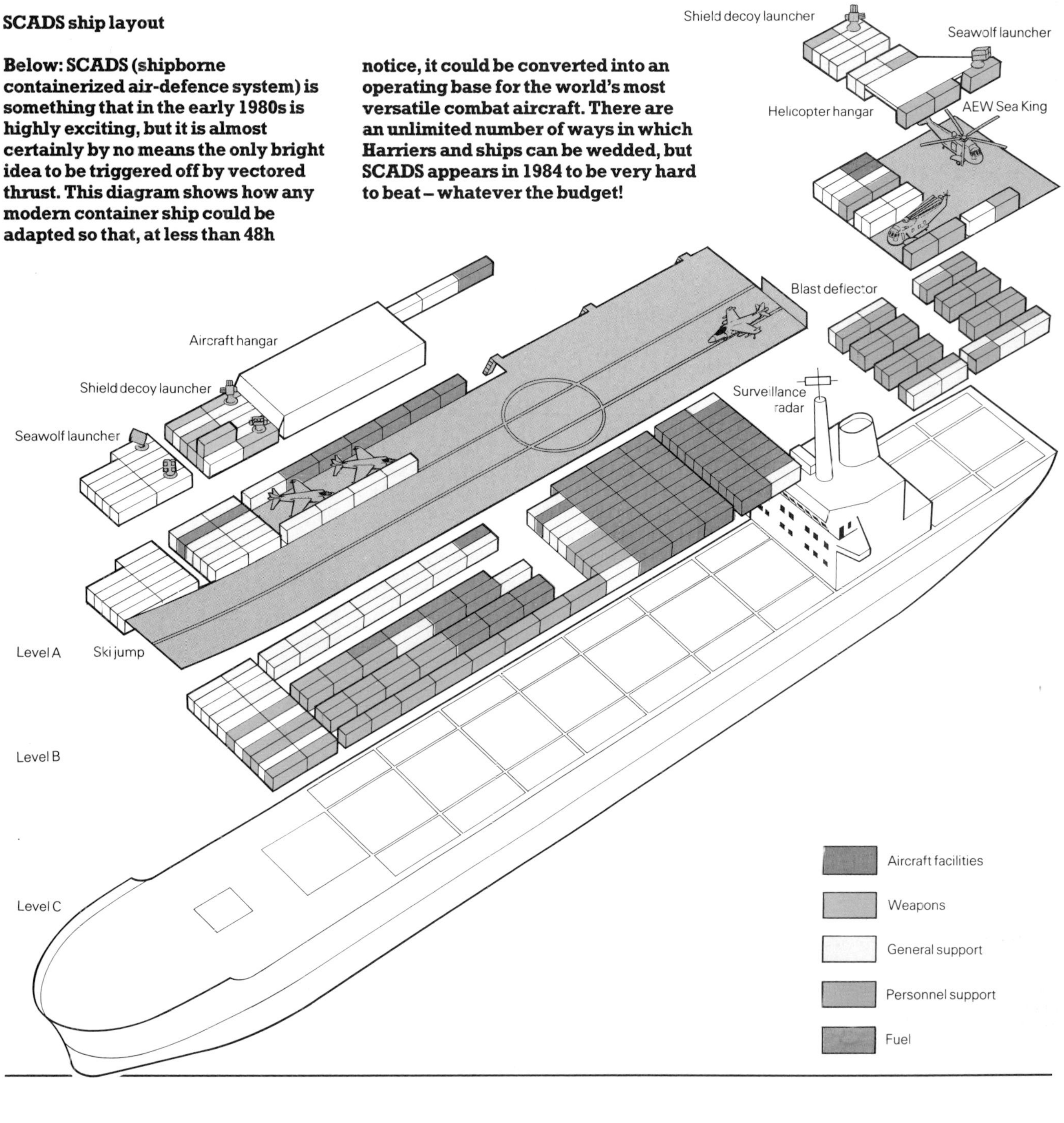

Right: Airpower en route to war: aboard the ill-fated *Atlantic Conveyor* in May 1982, showing the GR.3s (left) and 809 Sea Harriers. The SCADS system would turn such vessels into effective fighting ships in their own right.

assuming 50h flying per aircraft (a figure greatly exceeded during Operation Corporate). Others would be accommodation units and offices for the extra crew of some 190 men, while others would house drinking water, food, domestic/utility power supplies and other essential services. The operational side would have containers loaded with aircraft spares, workshops and test gear, aircraft ordnance, and a complete range of air defence systems including Seawolf missiles, their handling gear and (possibly vertical) launchers, surveillance and Seawolf direction radars, active countermeasures and passive/decoy systems (Shield is favoured). There would also be a flying control station, Plessey aircraft direction radar, homing and blind-landing aids and extra communications. Prefab sections would add the helicopter pad and MGB runway/ski jump.

All the evidence shows that with such a system established in service, and once fitted to a ship to find and eliminate snags, a containership could be at sea again as a multirole warship two days after entering the conversion port. Proof of several elements of SCADS was furnished by the *Atlantic Conveyor*, but of course that vessel was hastily converted as a mere V/STOL transporter and had no previously designed installations, no runway and no defences. At the time of writing, the Royal Navy is testing the RFA (Royal Fleet Auxiliary) *Reliant* in the South Atlantic, having converted her from the containership *Astronomer*, but with helicopters only. Clearly, the next step is to test a full V/STOL conversion.

Incidentally, the point must be made in this book that several almost off-the-cuff tests have shown that the AV-8A, and certainly the Sea Harrier, has a large potential in the ASW (anti-submarine warfare) role because of its high speed, versatile weapon capability (such as Stingray), agility and ability to hover. This is unlikely ever to be a primary role, but the Sea Harrier in particular could certainly add ASW to the missions it could perform in the SCADS method of deployment.

The startling Skyhook

If SCADS will revolutionize a nation's rapidly available airpower at sea, Skyhook seems to border on science fiction, until one recalls that BAe have tried out its essential elements. In a nutshell it is a shipboard crane which reaches out and grabs a Harrier in the hover. Thereafter the aircraft can be refuelled and released; or it can be swung inboard and tucked into a parking slot below decks, all under precise control as if done by an extremely capable giant. At first glance it looks as if the ship merely swings out the jib of a crane fitted with a hook mechanism, but in fact the system is quite sophisticated.

British Aerospace has studied the design and operation of a Skyhook installation on a frigate, but of course it could be applied to any warship, or merchant vessel, of above about 5,000 tons displacement. In a typical frigate installation the Skyhook could form part of a standard package measuring 55ft×170ft ×18ft (16·8m×51·8m×5·5m) providing the total installation needed for the operation of four Sea Harriers and two Sea Kings, complete with below-decks hangar space and two Skyhook cranes.

To recover aboard a Skyhook ship the pilot uses only standard piloting techniques to make a decelerating transition and then to formate alongside at the speed of the ship. The Skyhook, extended from its normal stowed position on deck, is automatically controlled by ship motion sensors and hydraulic rams so that its pick-up head is space-stabilized; in other words, it moves ahead at the speed of the ship in a perfectly straight line no matter how the ship may heave and roll. Attached to the pick-up system is a day/night hover sight which, using two vertical lines and one horizontal line in one plane and two horizontal index markers nearer to the pilot, gives clear guidance information so that the pilot can move inboard to the correct distance from the ship, at the right height and correctly located fore-and-aft. The precision demanded is not onerous: the pilot merely has to maintain position within a box with 10ft (3m) sides, so an

Skyhook in action

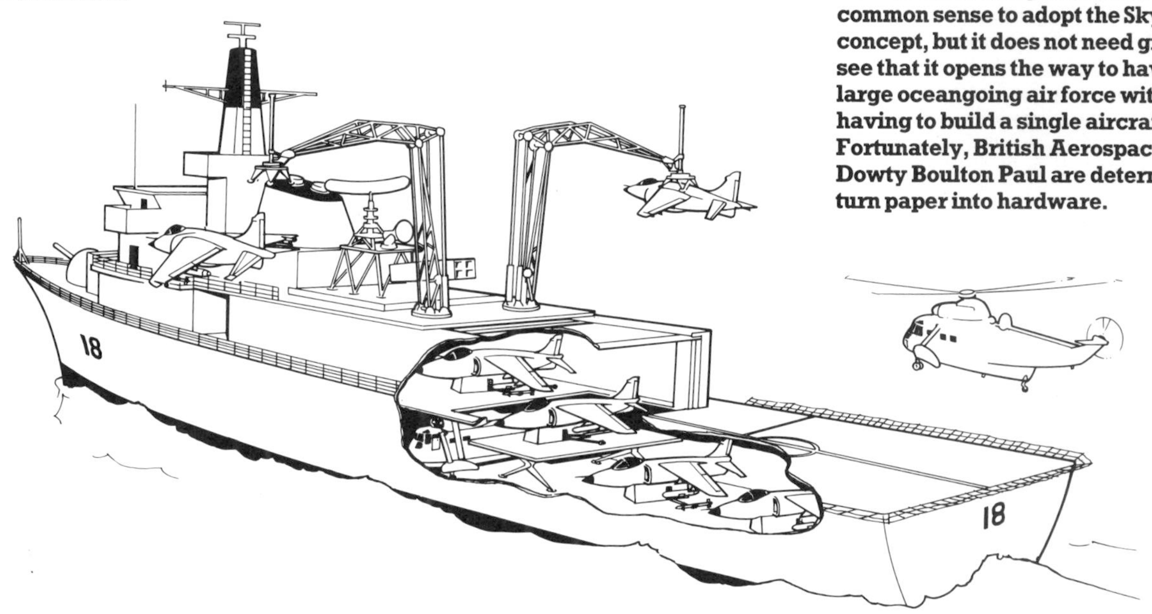

Left: So far no navy has had the common sense to adopt the Skyhook concept, but it does not need great IQ to see that it opens the way to having a large oceangoing air force without having to build a single aircraft carrier. Fortunately, British Aerospace and Dowty Boulton Paul are determined to turn paper into hardware.

Right: Sea Harrier FRS.1s recovering aboard *Hermes* in May 1982, with an RFA oiler and plane-guard Sea King in the background. At the time of writing no Sea Harrier has even been damaged in recovering aboard its ship.

The hover sight

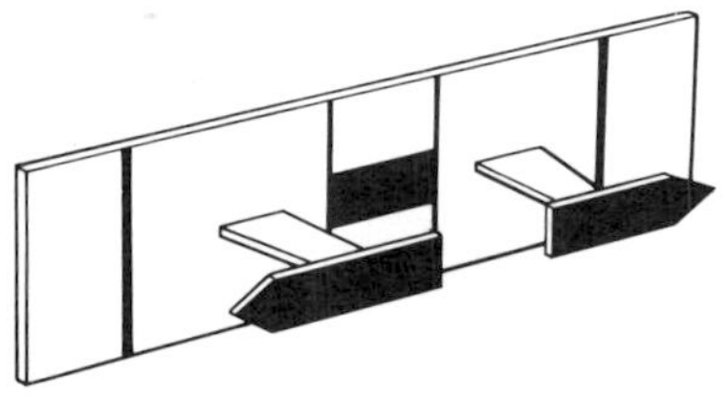

Below: A sequence showing how aircraft capture by the BAe-promoted Skyhook is envisaged. The guidance display – simplicity itself – is carried on the end of the Skyhook. It uses parallax to allow the pilot to formate his aircraft correctly in the contact window.

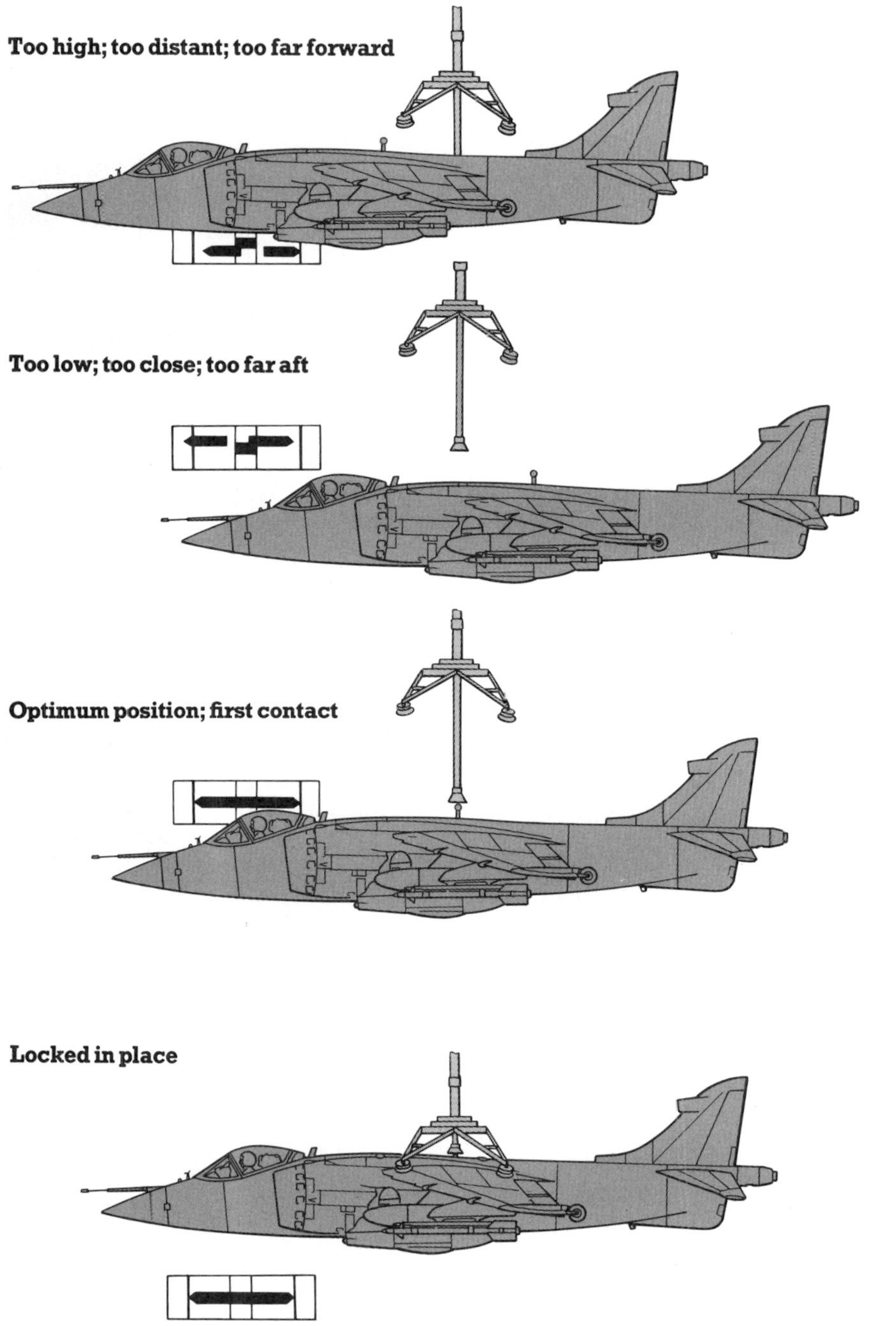

Skyhook is space-stabilised

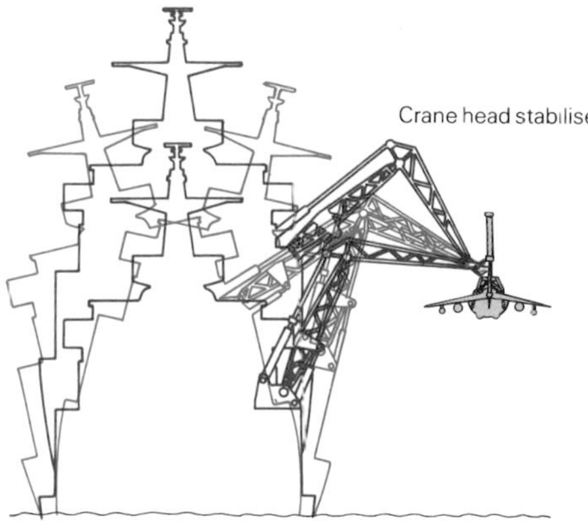

Skyhook details

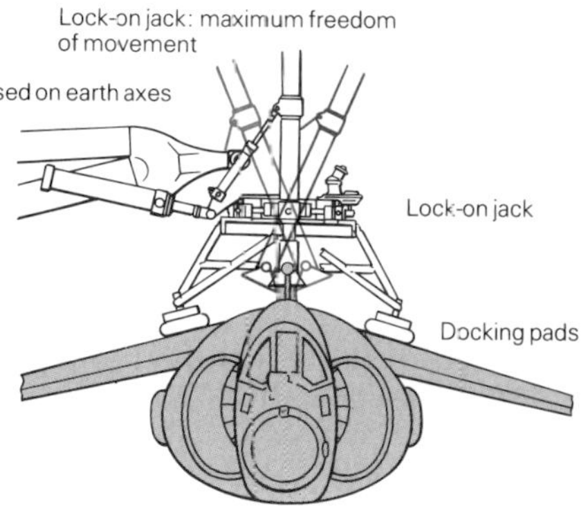

exhausted pilot with only basic training ought to have no great difficulty.

Once it is moving at the speed of the ship within the contact window (the 10ft cube) the Sea Harrier is acquired by an on-board optical system which looks down from the Skyhook and measures the exact angle and distance to a small pick-up probe extended above the aircraft. Tests have shown that there is no problem in automatically guiding the lock-on jack over the pick-up probe in an elapsed time of about one second, with the aircraft anywhere in the capture window. Lock-on is indicated to the pilot by a series of lights and/or by R/T. He at once slightly reduces power, putting load on the pick-up, and the jack simultaneously pulls the aircraft upwards firmly against the resilient docking pads. The capture is then complete, after a total time of only a few seconds.

For fluid replenishment the pilot stays aboard, with the engine at ground idle, while the fuel and water tanks are topped up. At 1,100lb (500kg)/min, this task takes 5 minutes or less. The existing sockets for these fluid systems could be used, with large articulated hose-arms, or, without much difficulty, the Sea Harrier could be provided with new fuel/water sockets close to the pick-up probe. Alternatively, for change of pilot or for rearming, the engine is shut down as soon as capture is complete and the Skyhook officer swings the aircraft inboard, the action automatically and progressively phasing out the space-stabilization. By the time the aircraft arrives inboard it is fully ship-stabilized, pitching and rolling with the ship. If the aircraft is needed for another sortie it is lowered through the deck access on to a trestle already pre-loaded with all the external stores needed. The latter are automatically elevated by powered crutches on to their ejector/release units, and the entire rearming can be automatic. Within the trestle the gun pods can be replaced by new pods with full magazines. Complete rearming takes just under ten minutes.

If the aircraft is not tasked with an immediate sortie it can be released from the Skyhook and then moved to its allotted parking space below deck. The trestle carrying the Sea Harrier is moved completely mechanically, under remote control, to the selected location. This calls for no sweating manpower, eliminates damage, is unaffected by the roughest of seas, and enables aircraft to be parked almost touching each other, and with great saving in time. Skyhook design has been based on a 4,000 ton ship and Sea State 6, which means conditions would be unacceptable for only about 1 per cent of the time on an averaged worldwide basis.

When an aircraft below decks is needed for a sortie, the hangar access is opened and the Skyhook programmed to lock-on to the aircraft. As soon as this is confirmed, the trestle releases the aircraft and the Skyhook swings the Sea Harrier outboard, at the same time changing to the space-stabilized mode. Meanwhile the pilot has been starting the engine and doing his cockpit checks, in telebrief contact with the ship. When his checks are complete, the pilot signals he is ready for takeoff. The jack slowly pushes the Sea Harrier down away from the pads, the pilot at once beginning to feel the need for small hovering flight control movements, while checking that the nozzles are at about 90°. He opens up to high power over a period of 10 seconds, taking load off the Skyhook jack until green lights flash on the lock-on board. The pilot then adds a trifle more power; as soon as the jack senses an up-load it disconnects and withdraws rapidly upwards. The pilot then rolls slightly away from the ship and begins an accelerating transition.

Obviously such a system could turn frigates and even destroyers into potent aircraft carriers. Something like it seems bound to come into increasingly wide use, despite its drawback in making all takeoffs VTO instead of STO. The latest Vosper escort carrier gets the best of both worlds by using a ski jump for takeoff and Skyhook for recovery. BAe has teamed up with Skyhook subcontractor Dowty Boulton Paul to search for a customer. Its importance is so inescapably great that in the course of time it is bound to happen. The Soviet Union has no inhibitions, and simply adopts good ideas when it sees them. It could well be that in that country the Skyhook will first go into mass production, though they have some catching-up to do.

Left: If any of the local farmers around Dunsfold had been watching these early experiments in 1982 they might indeed have thought Kingston-Brough Division were mad. G-VTOL proved that, from the pilot's point of view, the Skyhook concept is "a piece of cake".

The Super Harrier?

Even Skyhook does not exhaust the list of possible future methods of operating Harriers, but the remainder of this chapter must turn to future developments of the aircraft itself. Though it is unwise in aviation to suggest that an ultimate has ever been reached, the AV-8B looks close to the limit of what can be flown with today's Pegasus engine. The writer has long believed that a case could be made for a tandem-wing aircraft, which could probably have favourable jet-induced circulation round the wings (better than AV-8B) and would show advantages in compactness, agility and the ability to change the engine upwards without removing the wing. This is just one of several configurational possibilities, but – though there has never been a time in aviation when so many diverse configurations and propulsion arrangements presented themselves – this book is not about V/STOL but about the Harrier. Future possibilities are therefore confined to aircraft that can be regarded as Super Harriers.

Though there is still an unfortunate element in many countries, most notably in the United States, that continues to regard the Harrier concept as too limited or outdated to be worthy of consideration, in fact its simplicity has always been its greatest strength. Almost all the alternative V/STOL fighter schemes being proposed in the USA today would have made Sir Sydney Camm's hair stand on end. They would be not only astronomically expensive and trouble-ridden, but in a real war would undoubtedly impose a severe burden on supporting personnel and highly vulnerable to battle damage. Moreover, not one could join a combat unit within ten years, and if the XFV-12A is any guide, most will fall by the wayside.

It seems infinitely more sensible to start with a Harrier and see how it can be developed. Unlike the situation at the start of the AV-8B project, this time it is essential to seek further progress with the engine. For several years, 1969-82, virtually all Pegasus development was directed towards longer life, improved reliability and reduced costs. Now the emphasis is returning to climbing further up the thrust ladder, and there are two immediate paths to take. One is PCB (plenum-chamber burning), described later. The other is going on with the normal progression made with almost all gas turbines in increasing the mass flow, raising the gas temperature, improving component efficiencies, and tightening up clearances and improving seals throughout the engine to reduce air or gas leakage.

The immediate Pegasus prospect is the 11-21D, already bench tested, in which significantly improved HP turbine cooling can lead to either extended life or increased thrust, a typical compromise being 1,000h TBO at a rating of 22,001lb (9980kg). Planned as the engine of the AV-8B+, which could replace today's AV-8B on the line in about 1986, the Pegasus 11-35 introduces a rebladed fan which increases mass flow from 432lb (196kg)/s to 451lb (205kg)/s, with a 7 per cent increase in rpm. There are small modifications throughout the engine to cater for the increased pressures. This engine has been running since August 1981 and is rated at 23,200lb (10524kg), though it is installationally interchangeable with engines in current Harriers.

The importance of PCB

For the more distant future, later in the 1980s, the most important development is PCB (plenum-chamber burning). This is the burning of additional fuel in the plenum chamber between the fan and the front nozzles, and is precisely similar in principle to conventional afterburning in a jet pipe. The main difference is that in an afterburner the extra fuel is sprayed into very hot gas, much of whose oxygen has already been consumed. In the Pegasus plenum chamber the added fuel encounters relatively cool air with all its oxygen present, so the potential thrust gain is very large. Gains in thrust at the front nozzles of 100 per cent can readily be obtained, and as the front nozzles provide roughly half the thrust of the engine the overall boost in power is about 50 per cent.

PCB is an essential for any supersonic V/STOL. It was a feature of the BS. 100 engine for the P.1154, and this was preceded by PCB-boosted Pegasus research for the P.1150 in 1961. It is a pity that so many years have been wasted, though at company expense Rolls-Royce continued with small PCB investigations in the early 1970s, for the AV-16 and other Advanced Harrier projects, and eventually PCB tests began to pick up again in 1980, latterly with MoD funding. So far all the full-scale engine running has been done with one of the oldest and least-representative Pegasus engines, a Mk 2.

Basically there is nothing very clever about PCB. All that has to be added are fuel manifolds, an internal burner to hold the flame while imposing minimum pressure drop on the airflow, and variable-area nozzles. Almost the only significant factor complicating the design of a PCB system is that the flow turns corners while combustion is taking place, but prolonged testing has established a successful system. In 1962-64 this was tested in sea-level static conditions with the Pegasus 2 mounted upside-down on an open-air bed, so that with PCB in operation the hot luminous jets from the front nozzles pointed skywards, causing noise but not erosion or reingestion problems. As the programme is based at the MoD Proof and Experimental Establishment at Shoeburyness the PCB tests cause no noise nuisance.

Following basic calibration and performance measurement, the tests moved on to study behaviour with distorted inlet airflow and with varying water ingestion, simulating torrential rain or snow. Water flow was increased until it was a veritable Niagara, extinguishing combustion on one side and then, with water reduced, checking that the PCB was

Above: This Pegasus 2 was used for the first phase of sea-level tests at the MoD Proof and Experimental Establishment, Shoeburyness in 1981. The giant front nozzles do not represent a definitive design.

Below: The PCB rig at Shoeburyness during test operation. The water spray visible is to cool ground-based instrumentation during the initial running-up test phase. Note PCB flames visible in front nozzles.

immediately relit by the burner on the other side of the engine. Simulated high-altitude testing followed at the National Gas Turbine Establishment. The results enabled the temperature rise, and thus the thrust boost, to be increased for further testing which by 1983 had the engine mounted in a refurbished Harrier airframe slung from a large gantry at Shoeburyness. The main purpose of the 1984 testing is to study the interaction of the aircraft and ground when suspended at all heights up to over 50ft (15m), and with the aircraft and nozzles at various angles. Subjects studied included surface erosion and temperature and, especially, engine performance deterioration due to hot-gas reingestion and the effectiveness of various methods of minimising reingestion.

Problems of erosion, reingestion and FOD are much intensified by PCB, which multiplies gas velocity and temperature of the forward pair of jets. The difficulties looked intractable, but today Rolls-Royce say the entire technology is well advanced and solutions to all the problems are in sight. The high-altitude testing had to explore handling and relighting up to altitudes well over 60,000ft (18·3km) and over an extreme range of AOA, because PCB engines are likely to power extremely agile air-combat aircraft whose lives will by no means be restricted to treetop height. Like modern afterburners, PCB needs to be fully modulated, rather than an on/off system.

There is every indication that the preferred operating method for a PCB-boosted supersonic Harrier derivative will be STOVL. The high thrust will enhance acceleration in an STO, and there are ways of solving the increased problems of jet scrubbing, intense noise impingement on the fuselge skin and, especially, fuselage heating with the jets aft. The nozzle control system, at present rigidly linking all four nozzles in unison, may have to cater for the fact that the front nozzles may or may not have PCB in operation, with a consequent possible doubling of front-nozzle thrust. Again, there are ways of keeping the resultant thrust vector at the optimum angle and passing through the aircraft CG.

A supersonic Harrier

As accompanying curves show, PCB is a "must" for a supersonic V/STOL. Even with an inlet system more or less like a Harrier, Mach 1·6 can be seen at the tropopause at around 36,000ft (11km). With more complex sharp-lipped fully variable inlets Mach 2 could be achieved, but there seems little advantage in doing so. The one big change that will almost certainly be called for in a supersonic Harrier is that the engine must be a three-poster, the two rear nozzles being replaced by a single central reheat jetpipe. Vectoring jetpipes are not new, Rolls-Royce itself having done prolonged testing with the RB.153 in the 1960s which had a rear afterburner and 90° vectoring nozzle. The method of vectoring such a pipe is usually to insert a doubly tapered portion which can be rotated by an external power source. Such a pipe is called a "lobsterback".

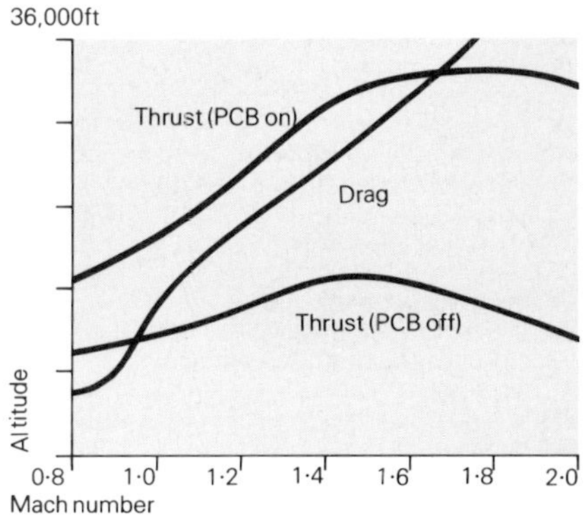

Above: Even the most generalized curves show that PCB makes an enormous difference to V/STOL aircraft performance at 36,000ft (11 800m). Though fuel burn is increased, as in normal afterburning, Mach number is doubled.

There are several advantages of the three-poster for a supersonic V/STOL. One is that it is possible to use an afterburner in the central rear nozzle. Another is that in cruising flight the flow through the engine is more direct than with four nozzles at the sides, and this is important at Mach numbers as high as 1·6. Most important of all, the installed drag is reduced and there are no projecting rear nozzles downstream; with PCB in action life would be hard for the rear nozzles of a four-poster engine. On the other hand, moving the front nozzles towards the underside of the fuselage and keeping the rear nozzles at the side has been shown to be practical. Front nozzles located diagonally downwards would send down PCB jets in the hovering mode which would strike each other above ground level and eliminate the hot fountain that results from two vertical front jets. This arrangement, with canted front nozzles and two rear side nozzles has been favoured by MCAIR in both the proposed AV-8SX and Model 279-3.

AV-8SX was a proposal dated 1981 by MCAIR and Rolls-Royce to gain experience with a rebuilt AV-8A. The PCB four-poster engine would be a Pegasus 11-03B initially, rated at 27,000lb, and later an 11-33B derived from today's 11-35 but with PCB to give a dry thrust of 24,500lb (12 247kg) and a maximum PCB rating of 34,000lb (15 422kg), in all cases in the static condition at sea level. The fuselage would be stretched, the inlets would be configured for Mach 1·6, and the wing would be of greater area but thinner, and fitted with larger flaps. The Model 279-3 is a study for a definitive supersonic V/STOL with the same four-poster PCB engine. Though clearly a Harrier descendant, it would hardly have one part in common, and the variable inlets and nozzles would have to be accepted as an inevitable surrender of the Harrier's present simplicity. With a 400ft (122m) STO the 279-3 could carry a weapon load of 18,000lb (8165kg), and a very large proportion of the airframe would be of lightweight composite construction.

Much depends on whether the customer accepts that the obvious way to recover to a land or seaborne base is by a VL. Almost all takeoffs would be an STO, but a landing at substantial forward speed poses all the difficulties of conventional fighter operation, which in wartime, with blasted bases and a lack of large decks, may just prove insuperable. Time and again it has been shown that it is safer to stop and then land than to land and then hope to stop. But even at light weight a VL could demand PCB, and it is to clear PCB engines in a landing at zero forward speed that much of the current research is directed.

Of course, both MCAIR and British Aerospace have countless proposls for other forms of future V/STOL. Some bear no relation to the Harrier at all, but most recognise the vital pioneering of the Harrier in establishing vectored thrust as the way that future land and sea fixed-wing airpower will surely go.

Tomorrow's V/STOL engine

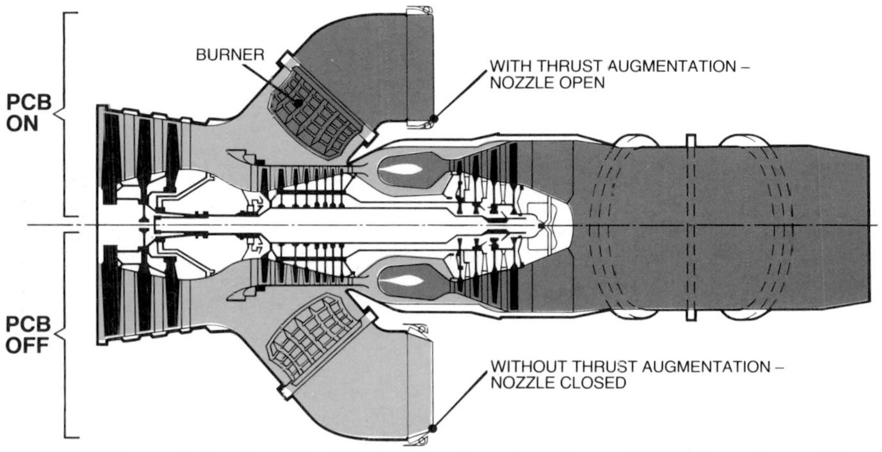

Above: This again is simplified, but the diagram shows the chief features of a three-nozzle STOVL vectored-thrust engine with PCB, such as will be needed for the highly supersonic combat aircraft of the 1990s.

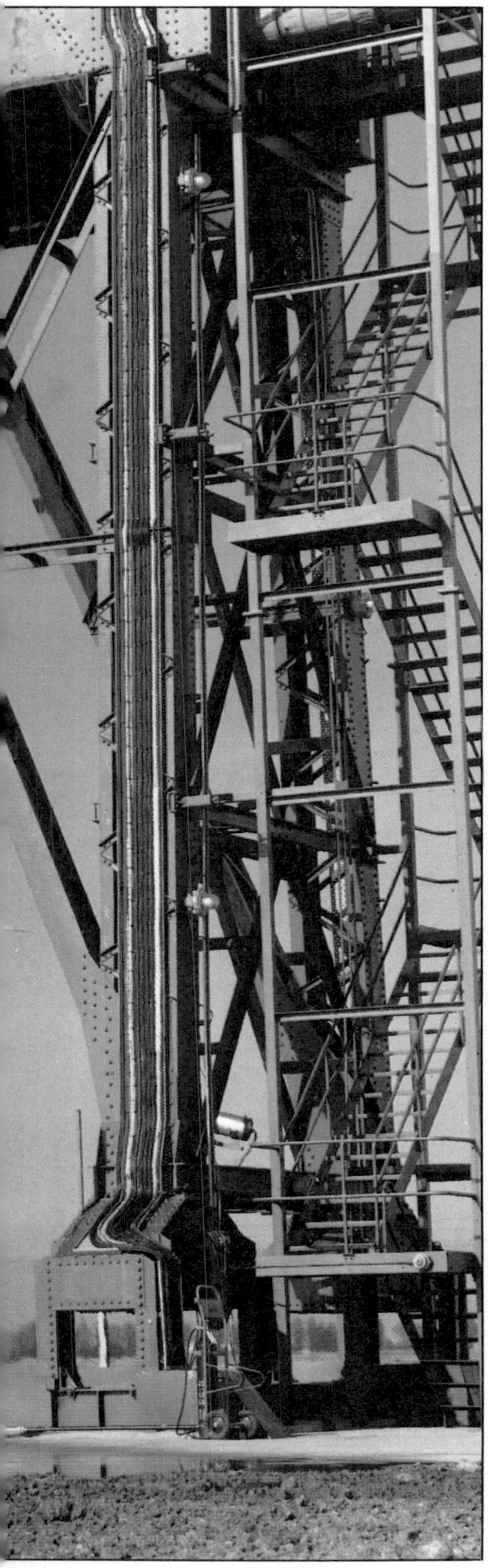

Above left: Published by British Aerospace in 1983, this shows a possible appearance of a Royal Navy Sea Harrier after a mid-life update.

Left: Much less certain is the Model 279-3, envisaged by McDonnell Douglas as the preferred next generation after Harrier II. Powered by a PCB Pegasus, it could fly by 1990 if customers make up their minds this is sensible.

Abbreviations

AAA Anti-aircraft artillery
AAM Air-to-air missile
AAR Air-to-air refuelling
A&AEE Aeroplane and Armament Experimental Establishment, Boscombe Down
ACM Air-combat manoeuvring
ADC Air-data computer
AOA Angle of attack
APU Auxiliary power unit
ASI Airspeed indicator
ASM Air-to-surface missile
ASW Anti-submarine warfare
BAe British Aerospace plc
CAH Code for helicopter or V/STOL ship
CANA Argentine naval aviation
CAP Combat air patrol
CAS Chief of the Air Staff (UK)
CBU Cluster bomb unit
CCIP Continuously computed impact point
CCV Control-configured vehicle
CG Centre of gravity
CILOP Conversion in lieu of procurement
CNI Communications/navigation/identification
CWS Central warning system
DB Development batch
ECM Electronic countermeasures
EW Electronic warfare
FAA Argentine air force
FAC Forward air control
Finrae Ferranti inertial-navigation rapid alignment equipment
FOB Forward operating base
FOD Foreign-object damage
FRS Fighter/reconnaissance/strike
GR Ground-attack/reconnaissance
GTS Gas-turbine starter
hi High altitude, around 30,000ft (9·1km) or over
HP High pressure
HSA Hawker Siddeley Aviation Ltd
HUD Head-up display
IFF Identification friend or foe
IGV Inlet guide vane
INAS Inertial nav/attack system
INS Inertial nav system; Indian Navy Ship
IR Infra-red
IRCM IR countermeasures
LERX Leading-edge root extension
LGB Laser-guided bomb
LIDs Lift-improvement devices
lo At minimum safe level above ground
LP Low pressure
LRMTS Laser ranger and marked-target seeker
MAD Magnetic anomaly detection
MCAIR McDonnell Aircraft Co (also written McAir)
MCAS Marine Corps Air Station
MDC Miniature detonating cord
MEXE Military Engineering Experimental Establishment (now MVEE)
MFD Multifunction display
MIRLS Miniature infra-red line scanner
MOU Memorandum of understanding
MWDP Mutual Weapons Development Program
NAS Naval Air Station
NASA National Aeronautics and Space Administration
NATC Naval Air Test Center
NBC Nuclear/biological/chemical
Obogs On-board oxygen generating system
OCU Operational Conversion Unit
PCB Plenum-chamber burning
PoW Prisoner of war
PPI Plan-position indication
RAE Royal Aircraft Establishment
RAF Royal Air Force
RAT Ram-air turbine
RCV Reaction control valve
RDT&E Research, development, test and engineering
RN Royal Navy
RNAS RN Air Station
RVL Rolling vertical landing
RWR Radar warning receiver
SAAHS Stability-augmentation and attitude-hold system
SAM Surface-to-air missile
SL Sea level
SLEP Service life extension program
STO Short takeoff
STOVL STO/vertical landing
Tacan Tactical air navigation
TBO Time between overhauls
TDC Through-deck cruiser
TES Tripartite Evaluation Squadron
TEZ Total Exclusion Zone
TGP Twin-gyro platform
TO Takeoff
TRU Transformer/rectifier unit
TWS Track while scanning
UFC Up-front control
UHF Ultra-high frequency
USMC United States Marine Corps
Viff Vectoring in forward flight
VL Vertical landing
VMA Marine fixed-wing attack squadron
V/STOL Vertical or short takeoff and landing
VTO Vertical takeoff
WAC Weapon-aiming computer
WOD Wind over the deck

Specifications

	Harrier GR.3	Harrier T.4	Sea Harrier FRS.1	AV-8C	AV-8B/Harrier GR.5
Engine type	Pegasus 103	Pegasus 103	Pegasus 104	F402-RR-402	F402-RR-406/Pegasus 105
TO thrust (wet)	21,500lb (9752kg)	21,500lb (9752kg)	21,500lb (9752kg)	21,500lb (9752kg)	21,700lb (9843kg)
Span	25ft 3in (7·7m)	25ft 3in (7·7m)	25ft 3in (7·7m)	25ft 3in (7·7m)	30ft 4in (9·25m)
	29ft 8in (9·04m) with ferry tips				
Length	46ft 10in (14·27m)	55ft 9·5in (17·0m)	47ft 7in (14·5m)	45ft 7in (13·89m)	46ft 4in (14·12m)
Height	11ft 4in (3·5m)	13ft 8in (4·17m)	12ft 2in (3·71m)	11ft 4in (3·45m)	11ft 7·75in (3·53m)
Wing area	201·1sq ft (18·68m²)	201·1sq ft (18·68m²)	201·1sq ft (18·68m²)	201·1sq ft (18·68m²)	230sq ft (21·37m²)
	216·0sq ft (20.1m²) with ferry tips				
Fuel capacity	630gal (2865lit)	630gal (2865lit)	630gal (2865lit)	610gal (2775lit)	915gal (4163lit)
Basic op'g weight	12,640lb (5734kg)	13,440lb (6096kg)	12,990lb (5892kg)	12,565lb (5699kg)	12,922lb (5861kg)
Max TO weight	26,000lb (11794kg)	26,000lb (11794kg)	25,600lb (11612kg)	25,000lb (11340kg)	29,750lb (13494kg)
Max speed (SL)	735mph (1183km/h)	720mph (1159km/h)	740mph (1191km/h)	740mph (1191km/h)	668mph (1075km/h)
Dive limit	Mach 1·3	Mach 1·3	Mach 1·25	Mach 1+	Mach 0·93
Service ceiling	51,200ft (15·6km)	50,000ft (15·24km)	51,200ft (15·6km)	51,200ft (15·6km)	(Not disclosed)
Strike radius	230 miles (370km)	—	345 miles (555km) max	As GR.3	692 miles (1113km)
Ferry range	2,340 miles (3766km)	—	2,300 miles (3700km)	As GR.3	2,830 miles (4555km)

Notes: length for GR.3 with laser, for T.4 without; strike radius is 1,000ft (305m) STO without ski ramp, hi-lo-hi and with max bombload possible plus two tanks; ferry range is without inflight refuelling.

Harrier variants

RAF

P.1127 Original prototypes, XP831, XP836, XP972, XP976, XP980 and XP984, Pegasus 2 engine rated at 11,000lb, later 12,000lb.
Kestrel FGA.1 Development and evaluation aircraft, XS688-696, Pegasus 5 engine rated at 15,500lb. Equipped TES, six later shipped to USA as XV-6A, 64/18262-18267. Total 9.
P.1127(RAF) Also designated Harrier GR.1 DB (Development Batch), XV276-281, used for trials and other work by BAe, Rolls-Royce, A&AEE, RAE and other operators, Pegasus 6 rated at 19,000lb. Total 6.
Harrier GR.1 First production aircraft, XV738-762, XV776-810, XW630, XW763-770 and XW916-924 (last batch preceded 763-770). Pegasus 6 Mk 101 rated at 19,000lb. Equipped RAF No 233 OCU and Nos 1, 3, 4 and 20 Sqns. Total 78.
Harrier GR.1A Designation of GR.1 aircraft after conversion to Pegasus 10 Mk 102 engine rated at 20,500lb. Total 61.
Harrier T.2 Tandem-seat dual trainer with combat capability, two development aircraft XW174-175, and 12 production XW264-272 and XW925-927 (last two completed as T.2A). Pegasus 6 Mk 101.
Harrier Mk 52 Company demonstrator built approximately to T.2 standard but with strakes in lieu of gun pods, later re-engined with Mk 103 Pegasus, one aircraft variously G-VTOL or ZA250.
Harrier T.2A Designation of T.2 after conversion to Pegasus 10 Mk 102, total 9, plus XW926-927 completed to this standard.
Harrier GR.3 Designation of updated Harrier GR.1/1A re-engined with Pegasus 11 Mk 103 rated at 21,500lb, plus RWR and laser nose. Total 56 conversions, plus XZ128-139, XZ963-973, XZ987-999, an additional 36 built as GR.3 (RAF single-seat total 114).
Harrier T.4 Designation of T.2/2A aircraft after conversion to Pegasus 11 Mk 103, and most with RWR and laser nose. Total 10.
Harrier T.4A Two-seaters built with Mk 103 engine, XW933-934, XZ145-147, XZ445 and ZB600-603. Total 9.
Harrier GR.5 RAF version of Harrier II with Pegasus 11-21E Mk 105 engine rated at 21,700lb. Serials begin with ZD318-320. Total to be 60.

Royal Navy

Sea Harrier DB Development batch aircraft of new multirole RN single-seater with Pegasus 11 Mk 104 engine rated at 21,500lb, XZ438-440. Total 3.
Sea Harrier FRS.1 Production aircraft for Royal Navy, XZ450-460, XZ491-500, ZA174-177, ZA190-195, ZD578-582 and ZD607-615. Equip 800, 801, and 899 Sqns and previously 700A and 809 Sqns. Total 45.
Harrier T.4RN Two-seaters to T.4 standard for Royal Navy, ZB604-606. Total 3.

USA

Harrier Mk 50, AV-8A Original aircraft for US Marine Corps, first 10 delivered with F402-RR-401 (Mk 802) engine and retrofitted, all others with F402-RR-402 (Mk 803) engine. BuAer Nos 158384-158395, 158694-158711, 158948-158977, 159230-159259 and 159366-159377. Equip VMA(T)-203 and VMA-231, 513 and 542. Total of 102.
Harrier Mk 54, TAV-8A US Marine Corps two-seater, F402-402 engine, BuAer 159378-159385. Equip VMA(T)-203. Total 8.
AV-8C US designation of AV-8As rebuilt with numerous airframe, avionic and equipment improvements. Total 47.
YAV-8B Two AV-8B development aircraft rebuilt from last two of first batch of AV-8As, BuAer 158394-158395. Total 2.
AV-8B FSD Four full-scale development AV-8Bs to second-generation design, with F402-RR-404A engine rated at 21,700lb, BuAer 161396-161399. Total 4 plus 2 static test airframes.
AV-8B Pilot-production aircraft, F402-RR-406 (Pegasus 11-21E) engine rated at 22,000lb. BuAer 161573-161584. Total 12.
AV-8B Limited production, F402-RR-406 engine. BuAer 162068-162085. Total 18.
AV-8B Full production, F402-RR-406 initially, possibly a version of Pegasus 11F-35 later. Planned procurement 306.
TAV-8B Two-seater of new design for US Marine Corps, derived from AV-8B. Planned procurement 27.

Spain

Harrier Mks 50 and **55, VA-1 Matador** Single-seaters for Spanish Navy to AV-8A Mod standard, US designation AV-8S with BuAer Nos 159557-159562 (Mk 50) and 161174-161177 (Mk 55), equip Esc 008. Total 10.
Harrier Mks 54 and **58, VAE-1 Matador** Two-seaters for Spanish Navy to TAV-8A Mod standard, US designation TAV-8S with BuAer Nos 159563-159564 (Mk 54) and 161178 (Mk 58). Total 3.
Harrier II (Spain) Single-seaters to same standard of build as AV-8B for Spanish Navy, designation not yet allocated. Total 12.

India

Sea Harrier FRS Mk 51 Single-seaters completed close to FRS.1 standard for Indian Navy, 601-606, equip 300 Sqn. Total 6.
Harrier T. Mk 60 Two-seaters for Indian Navy to approximate T.4RN standard, Nos 621-622. Total 2.

Chapter 7

MiGs

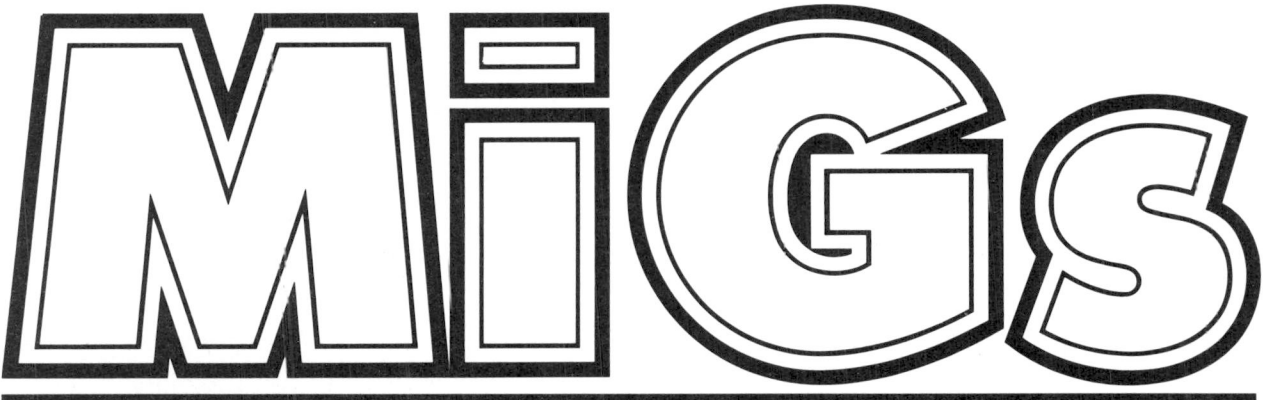

Bill Sweetman

MiGs

Contents

Acknowledgements

Anyone seeking to write about Soviet aircraft must trawl every source with a fine net. A full set of references for a chapter such as this would probably be half as long as this book itself, and it would be invidious to select specific examples. However, *Air International, Flight International,* the *Interavia* publications and *Aviation Week & Space Technology* were extensively farmed for the information in these pages.

The author would like to extend a particular word of thanks to Richard Ward of General Dynamics for advice, encouragement and help.

The publishers are also grateful to all those who contributed photographs, particularly Bill Green, Malcolm Passingham and the US Department of Defense.

Author

Bill Sweetman is Western USA correspondent for the Interavia Group, contributing extensively to *Interavia, International Defense Review* and *Interavia AirLetter*. Between 1973 and 1979 he was on the staff of *Flight International*, where as well as covering the air transport industry he launched the 'Flight Intelligence' series of detailed technical analyses of modern Soviet military aircraft, including the first accurate descriptions published of 'Backfire', 'Foxbat' and 'Flogger'. From 1979 to 1981 he was Air Correspondent of the national Sunday newspaper, *The Observer*, before moving to California. His books include *A Concise Guide to Soviet Military Aircraft* (Hamlyn/Presidio, 1982), and an earlier chapter in this book, *A-10 Thunderbolt II*.

Introduction

For most people, the word "MiG" is purely and simply synonomous with a Soviet fighter. Not literally true, this reflects the fact that the vast majority of Soviet fighters in the jet age have stemmed from the design bureau named after Artem Mikoyan and Mikhail Guryevich.

Soviet warplanes are seldom described with any accuracy in the West. They are portrayed as highly capable threats, comparable to the best of the West's fighters, when it is time to make defence plans and draft budgets; but when the astronomical unit costs of Western systems have to be explained to the public, the Soviet fighter is depicted as a crudely designed and rudely constructed agricultural implement.

If there is one central theme in this book, it is that MiGs are neither Porsches nor wheelbarrows. Rather, they are fighting machines designed to rigidly utilitarian standards, many of them set by factors which do not apply or are not considered important in the West. Another difference is that many of the criteria by which the Soviet Union's planners assess the merits of an aircraft design can be applied equally to a tank, ship or missile system.

It is from the world of armour that the author's favourite parable about the differences between Soviet and Western design practices is drawn. In the course of the Eastern campaign of World War II, the Wehrmacht captured one of the Red Army's deadly T-34 tanks and shipped it back to one of the German manufacturers for assessment. The engineers' response, in essence, was that they could never build a T-34 because it would not pass their quality control inspection. The rest is history.

The Bureau and the System

Soviet designers work in a completely different environment from the familiar Western system, and some understanding of the differences is essential if Soviet design philosophy is to be understood. The Soviet designer's job is to respond to a specification drafted by the unified Soviet armed forces, using a comprehensive set of standards and guidelines developed by the Soviet industry over the years. The Mikoyan-Guryevich bureau rose to prominence through the design of the MiG-15, MiG-17 and MiG-19, rugged, uncomplicated fighters that exactly met the armed forces' demands.

No Westerner can be unaware that the affairs of the Soviet Union are managed differently from those of the United States, Britain or France, but it is sometimes difficult to appreciate just how deep those differences run. In historical perspective, the Russian Empire had barely emerged from feudalism before 1917, when the rule of the Tsars collapsed. Attempts at Western constitutional democracy had been made, but their effects were superficial. Politically, the vast domain of the Romanovs was an unpolluted culture, a laboratory-clean environment for the first experiment in Marxism.

Post-revolutionary Russia, and the Union of Soviet Socialist Republics established in 1922, was not the first society to be governed according to a set of writings and precepts, or in which decisions and laws were made by the interpretation of such principles. A great many theocracies – countries ruled by a religion and its priests – have existed throughout history, and some still do. Marxism, however, is not a religion. Marxists regard it as a scientific theory applying to all the workings of society.

Most aviation books do not start with a discussion of political doctrine. In Western terms, it is out of place. But in dealing with the development of Soviet military aircraft, some reference to the importance of Marxism is not merely relevant; it is essential.

Very often, new Soviet weapons have been over-rated or under-estimated in the West, and to a startling degree. Examples of this have included the MiG-21, which was regarded as virtually useless until it started taking a heavy toll of 'superior' US Air Force fighters over Vietnam. In the case of the MiG-25 the reverse was true: US analysts greatly overestimated its performance. The latter error cost the American taxpayer dearly, because the exaggerated threat was fed into the design of the F-15 fighter and substantially increased its size and cost.

In both cases, Western observers could not resist the temptation to draw direct parallels between Soviet and Western aircraft. Given that East and West are equally subject to the laws of mechanics and aerodynamics, this can be valuable. When it is a matter of requirements, goals and design priorities, it can be grossly misleading; it has sometimes been called 'mirror-imaging'. Its root cause is the failure to put the weapon in the right context.

Constant references to the teachings of the Communist party, and the presence of political officers and functionaries at all levels, are not just the outward trappings of a one-party state. They are real fundamental guidelines in all aspects of endeavour. The relationship between the industrial managers, the military, the technologists and the Party is not a one-way affair; successful people in all walks of life tend also to be influential in the Party.

There are no exceptions to the rule of Party and doctrine. The process by which Soviet aircraft are brought from the requirement stage to the front line, and the way in which they would be used in action, are fundamentally affected by such considerations. At every phase, decisions are made in accordance with larger principles of 'military art' or 'technical art' which apply to all military operations, or to the design of all military vehicles. These principles, in turn, are founded not only on experience and experimentation, but also on doctrine.

According to Western observers and Soviet defectors, the core of power in the Soviet Union is the Defence Council, a group within the Politburo that encompasses the Party, the armed forces and, probably, the KGB. The position of the aircraft industry reflects that structure. It is entirely geared to meeting the needs of a single 'customer' – the Ministry of Defence (MoD), from which all aircraft requirements and specifications emanate. Commercial aircraft, too, are built to military standards, and would be used for airlift tasks in wartime; the effect of military requirements can be seen in many features of their design, some of which are inexplicable in commercial terms.

The MoD is the administrative head of the Soviet armed forces. These are unified to an extent which is almost incomprehensible in the West, where, for instance, the US Army, Navy and Air Force will debate roles, missions and funding among themselves at the highest level. In the Soviet Union, resources and responsibility are divided along functional lines.

A warning should be entered at this

Above: First design from the MiG bureau was the MiG-1, a high-altitude fighter whose stubby lines indicated a concern with weight reduction and high performance.

Below: This simplified chart of Soviet procurement procedures shows the central place of the experimental design bureau (OKB) within the much larger overall system.

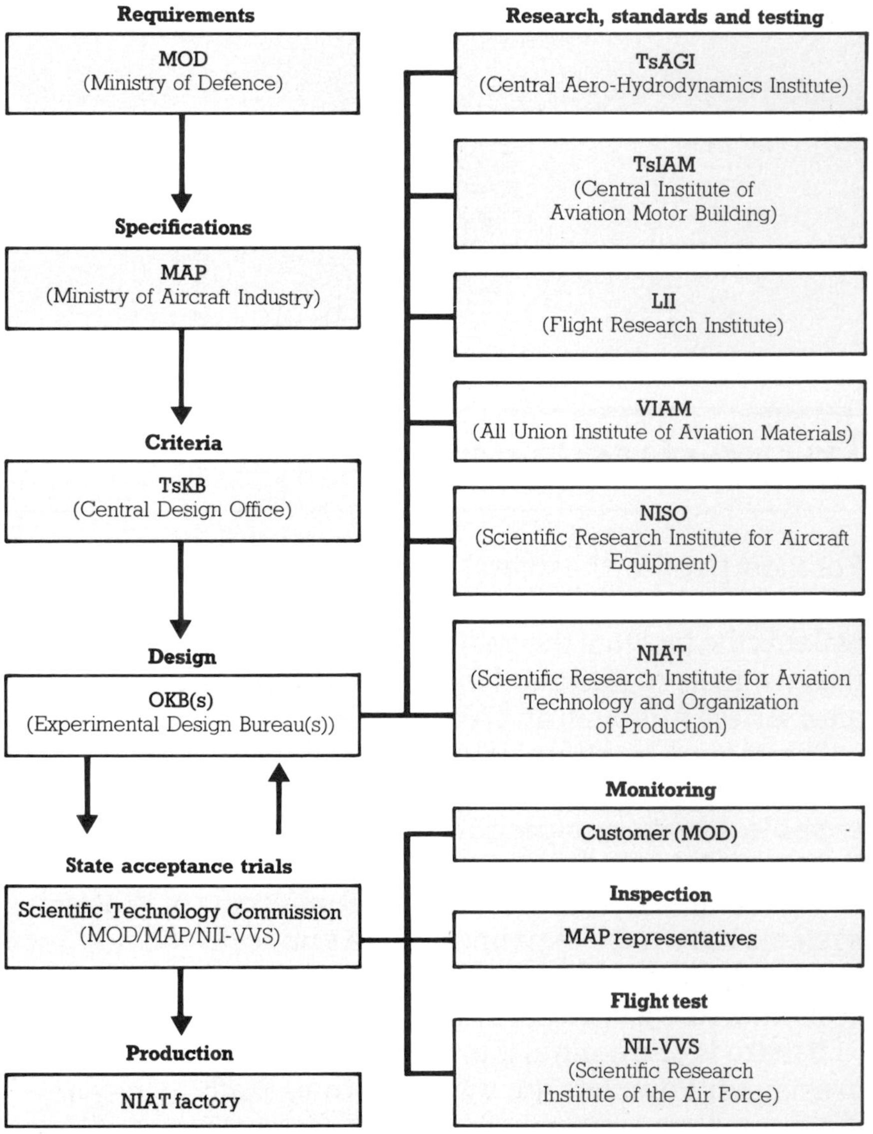

Left: Artem I. Mikoyan, photographed in March 1966. Aged 34 when the MiG bureau was founded, he headed it until he literally died at his drawing board in 1970. The status and influence of leading Soviet engineers such as Mikoyan is almost unbelievable in Western terms.

Right: "For Stalin!" reads the legend on this MIG-3 interceptor, assigned to the defence of Moscow. Even in 1942, MiG fighters were distinguished by cowling bumps and bulges.

Below: MiGs were not the most distinguished of Soviet wartime fighters. This MiG-3 has fallen into German hands, and its base has been taken over by Bf 109s.

Right: These MiG-3s seem to be split into elements of three, with lead aircraft and wingmen distinctively marked. Rigid tactics compensated for expertise lost in pre-war purges.

point: in the early 1980s, it became apparent in the West that many components and relationships within the Soviet military organization had been changed, but by late 1984, the precise details of the changes had not been identified. What follows is based on the 1984 assessment by the International Institute of Strategic Studies.

The casual observer of the Soviet military may get an impression of a Western-type structure, because an organization named the 'Soviet Air Forces' (VVS) does exist under the MoD. However, the VVS lacks one vital element of an independent force: it does not command its assets in combat. In the case of tactical fighters and strike aircraft, the VVS is responsible for supplying, training and supporting some 25 large combat units, some described as Regional Commands and some designated as Air Armies. The majority of the aircraft produced by the Mikoyan bureau serve with these formations. Up to 1983, these forces were generally referred to as Frontal Aviation (FA), and were all designated as Air Armies; however, the FA designation appears to have been abandoned.

For military operations, these units are commanded by an entirely separate hierarchy, reporting to the MoD. As far as is known, the vast Soviet tactical forces are divided into three main theatres, each aligned in a direction of critical interest: the Western theatre faces NATO, the Southern deals with the Middle East and Afghanistan, and the Far Eastern theatre stands opposite China and the Far East. The Western theatre, which is the largest, is believed to be subdivided into three smaller 'theatres of military operations,' or TVDs. The Regional Commands and Air Armies are assigned to the theatres or, in the Western theatre, the TVDs.

The structure reflects the Soviet view that fighting units are for combat, and should be burdened as little as possible with support tasks such as logistics, maintenance and training. It is also significant that the operating VVS units are not necessarily under the command of ex-pilots – as it happens, most TVD commanders have risen through the land forces, while tactical air officers find promotion in the VVS; even so, a TVD commander is expected to think like one, not like an armour or motor-rifle type.

Below: The OKB is a compact organization, with its own design, prototype manufacture and flight test facilities. A 'skunkworks' operation is an approximate Western parallel.

Experimental Design Bureau (OKB) organization

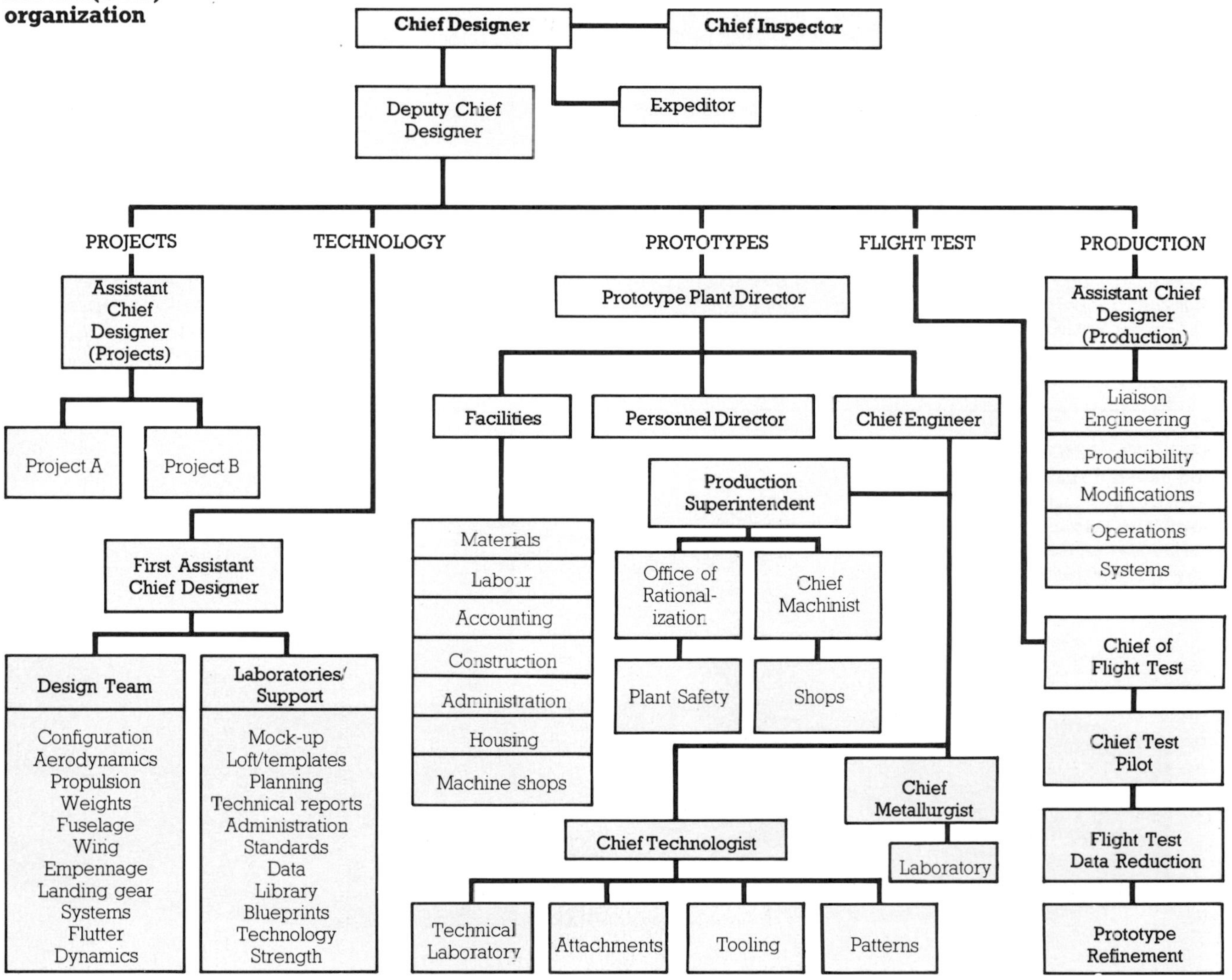

Above: One can only wonder what happened to the German-derived engines of the pre-production MiG-9 when the pilot discharged the mighty 37mm Nudelman-Suranov NS-37 fowling-piece on the intake splitter.

Above: Most MiG-9s had a more conventional armament installation. Not the prettiest of fighters, the type made the most of low-thrust engines.

Above: The MiG-15UTI – known under the NATO reporting system as 'Midget' – was the standard trainer for Soviet fighter pilots for decades until the introduction of the Aero L-39. This example was photographed after being overhauled in Prague for the Iraqi Air Force, which used the type into the late 1970s.

Right: This Czech-built CS-102 (MiG-15UTI) featured an Izumrud search radar, and probably had a reserve role as an interceptor. In the 1950s, Warsaw Pact allies were permitted to build such aircraft.

Another difference between the VVS and a Western air force is that its tactical fighters are assigned only to the defence of military targets in the theatre of operations. The defence of the Soviet Union itself is the task of a different organization, Voyska-PVO (National Air Defence Troops), which encompasses interceptors, surface-to-air and anti-ballistic missiles, and the command, communications, warning and control systems without which they would be useless. PVO formations are assigned to specific targets and regions and vary in size according to the importance of the target and its vulnerability to attack; the largest single PVO command is the Moscow Air Defence District. The PVO is the other user of MiG designs.

PVO reorganization

In the major reforms observed in the early 1980s, the main effect on the PVO was the removal of virtually half its fighter aircraft. The loss was not as great as one might think, though, because the aircraft eliminated were older types which could hardly expect to catch a B-52, and would have no chance at all against a B-1. The older aircraft were transferred to the VVS, and are assigned to the theatre commands, as auxiliary interceptors and reserves.

In their respective fields, the VVS and PVO are responsible for training, including the development of tactics. They are responsible for ensuring that their systems are able to defend against the threat where needed, and to carry out their missions in the face of defensive systems. They are responsible for maintenance and reliability, and must ensure that their weapons will be available to execute their missions.

One important feature of Soviet procurement in the past has been the fact that the PVO and VVS have presented fundamentally different requirements, not only in terms of weaponry, avionics and flight performance, but also in terms of maintenance levels and base specifications: the difference is as great as that between the USAF and US Navy. There is currently a trend towards common equipment, but it may yet reverse.

A third organization may now be issuing requirements for combat aircraft: the construction of a true aircraft carrier on the Black Sea indicates that a new generation of naval fighters must be under development, with requirements being developed by the AVMF (Soviet Naval Aviation). Apart from this specialized and secret endeavour, all requirements for new fighters start at the headquarters of the PVO or VVS.

In the case of a major development programme, one that is expected to lead into production, the MoD's decision is likely to be made – or at least approved – at Politburo level. Both MoD and Politburo decisions will take very similar factors into account. In the Soviet system, money is not central to the economy; since virtually the entire legal economy is governed by the state, the flow of money from the public to the private sector and back again, the factor which determines most Western budgets, is negligible. Instead, decisions are taken in terms of resources. The MoD considers whether to expand missile production, or whether to increase its capacity for building combat aircraft. Again, it may advise doing both, but this could mean using labour, factory space and materials that could have been used to build airliners (earning relatively hard cash from the Warsaw Pact) or even consumer goods.

Strategic decisions of this sort must be considered by the Politburo. There are limiting factors involved in the allocation of resources to the MoD, as opposed to other users. The most important concern such things as agriculture, energy, raw materials and communications – the infrastructure without which the MoD cannot function. There is also a minimum standard of living to be considered, below which the people will be neither healthy nor trustworthy. The Defence Minister, as the head of the MoD and a member of the Defence Council, sees such decisions from both sides. Once the decision is made, the Politburo will hand it down to the Council of Ministers – in theory the Soviet Cabinet, but in fact the Politburo's administrative staff – for execution by the Ministry of Aircraft Industry (MAP).

This process has a fundamental impact on the design of Soviet aircraft. A

Below: This MiG-15bis, in bright red and pale blue colour scheme, was used by the Moskovsky Okrug PVO aerobatic display team – the Red Falcons – and flown at early Aviation Day demonstrations in the mid-1950s.

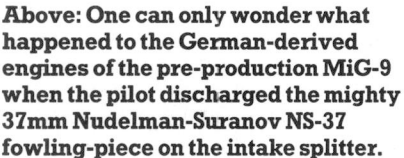

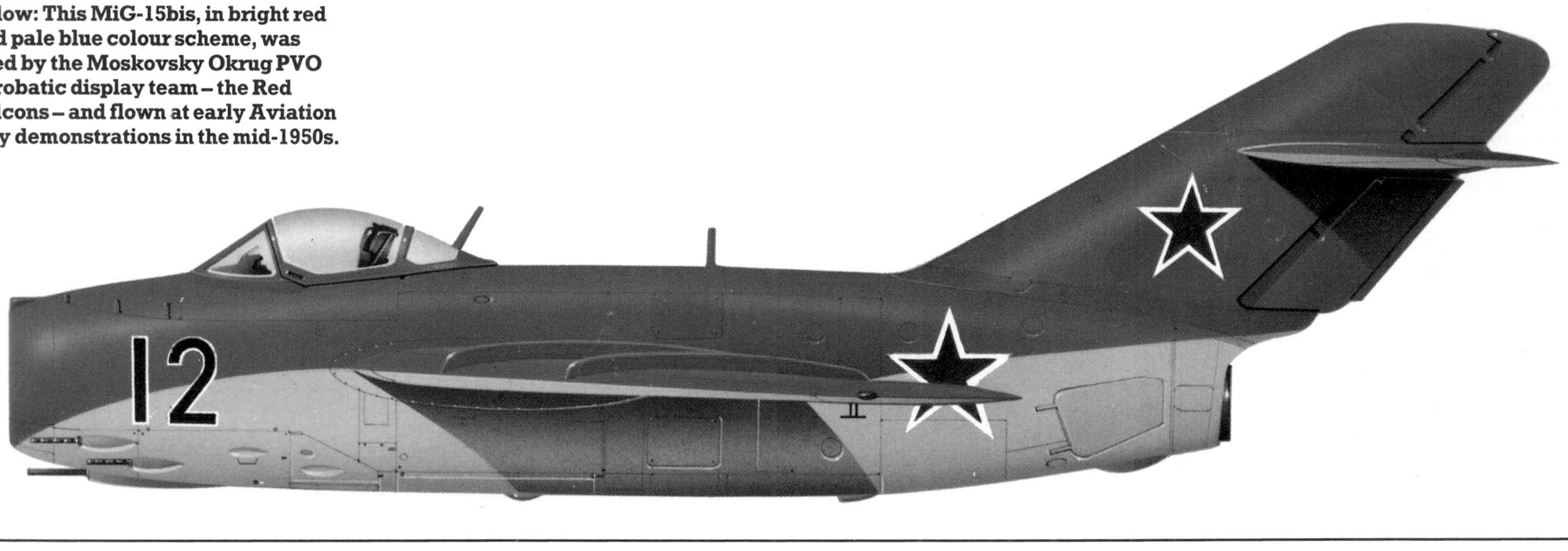

Above: Under Project Moolah, the USA offered asylum and money to any pilot defecting with a MiG-15. The project was successful, and analysis and testing of the MiG-15 helped to define tactically important modifications to the F-86 Sabre, such as the importance of the all-moving "flying tail" for high-speed pitch control. (See below for original markings.)

requirement for a new tactical fighter, for instance, will be framed by the VVS in terms of the threat it will face, the targets which it will be expected to attack, and the development of tactics at the theatre and tactical level. Its costs (in terms of resources) and merits will be assessed by the MoD, and weighed quite objectively against the needs of other branches of service. If it is considered a priority, and the Politburo has made sufficient resources available to the MoD, the industry will be asked to fill the requirement – but that is the industry's first official involvement in the process.

Requirement pull

The result is that Soviet aircraft developments are the result of what is called 'requirement pull': the service has a requirement, and once it is approved the industry directs its technical and industrial rescurces to meet it. Western military aircraft, on the other hand, are more often defined by 'technology push'. The industry carries out research and predicts the performance and characteristics of future weapons using new technology; the military reviews the potential of the technology, and selects for development those weapons which offer the greatest military advantage.

This distinction can illuminate many of the differences between Soviet systems and Western systems, and the way in which they are developed and introduced to the fleet. For instance, a requirement-pulled procurement system tends to be driven by the threat, as well as by offensive military objectives. There is an inevitable lag between the time that Western plans become clear, or the time that a Soviet strategy change is made final, and the fielding of a system that responds to such a development. In some cases, this explains why the Soviet Union appears slow to introduce one new technology, while it is very quick to field another.

Technology that does not respond directly to the needs of the user will usually be bypassed, or left to a later generation. The importance of this lies in the fact that the user is the TVD or theatre commander. His first priority is numerical strength; Soviet military doctrine stresses the fact that the stronger force starts with an advantage. In the case of aircraft, producibility times reliability equals availability, or the number of aircraft ready to be flown against the target at any time.

Defining objectives

When the TVD commander needs a major improvement – the ability to extend conventional bombardment behind the battlefield, to implement a change in strategy or to counter improvements in the threat – what Soviet texts call 'military-technical art' will be employed to provide it. But from the commander's perspective, an improvement in any given performance number – an increase in range, turn rate, radar detection range or transonic acceleration – is not significant unless it meets a specific objective at a higher level. It does not of itself justify a replacement of an existing type, and will be cheerfully traded for easy production.

An excellent example of this mechanism in action is the development of look-down, shoot-down (LDSD) radar/missile systems. The first of these was tested in the USA in the late 1950s, long before the Soviets had low-altitude, all-weather offensive aircraft in service. Such aircraft were still not in the Soviet inventory when the AWG-9/Phoenix LDSD system was first ordered into production, in the early 1960s. That is a case of 'technology push'. The Soviet Union did little about LDSD capability until the number and importance of low-altitude, adverse-weather penetrators in the Western arsenal began to climb, in the early 1970s. In the later years of that decade, an interim LDSD system entered Soviet service, and testing of full-capability systems surged ahead, in a classic example of 'requirement pull'.

The task of the MAP – the Ministry of Aircraft Industry – is to respond to the requirement. Essentially, MAP is the Soviet aircraft and engine industry. It embraces production, design, development and basic research, together with the control of standards and specifications. Its organization, however, makes it less of a monolith than its size might imply.

Most of MAP's facilities and personnel are spread among its large subdivisions.

Below: The MiG-15 made its combat debut in the markings of North Korea, but usually flown by Chinese or Soviet pilots. This MiG-15bis was flown to Kimpo, near Seoul, South Korea, by Snr Lt Kum Suk No of the Korean People's Army Air Force, on September 21, 1953, and evaluated by the US Air Force.

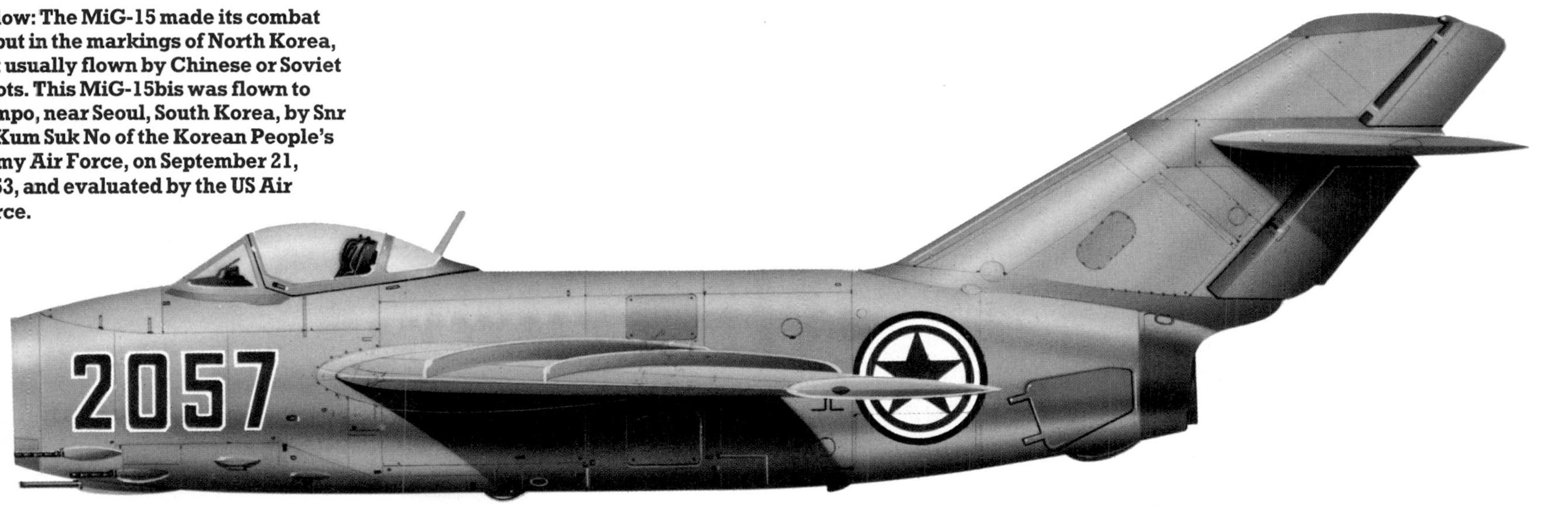

Four of them are each associated with one discipline of aircraft design: aerodynamics, engines, avionics and systems, and materials. Another is responsible for advanced flight research. To that extent, these divisions of MAP constitute a Soviet equivalent of the National Aeronautics and Space Administration, but they are much more than that. The propulsion and the avionics/systems organizations include the design offices, for one thing. For another, they do not merely provide data for the aircraft designers, or conduct research in support of aircraft programmes, but directly influence the way aircraft are designed. The results of their research are summarized in manuals and technical memoranda, and issued as guidelines to the engine and airframe designers. They cover many basic aspects of design; most of the combat aircraft in Soviet service have planforms and air inlet designs which were centrally defined and selected in this way.

One complete division of MAP is responsible for manufacturing technology, and the maintenance and equipment of State Aviation Factories (GAZ). This organization carries out its own research into ways of making aircraft easier to build – reducing the number of parts, using new processes to eliminate scarce or costly materials, making assembly sequences easier – and, no doubt, issues its own guidelines to the designers.

Also under MAP is an organization with no Western equivalent: the Central Design Bureau (TsKB). The role of the TsKB is highly influential in the evolution of Soviet aircraft, because it is the means by which the advantages of competition, and the incentive to build a better product, are introduced into the planned, quota-dominated world of industry.

The TsKB carries out many of the functions of a Western company's advanced-design department. When a requirement is submitted to MAP, it is the TsKB which carries out the feasibility study and determines what sort of aircraft will be needed to meet it; what sort of new technology will have to be incorporated in the structure, engines and avionics; and, ultimately, whether the requirement can be met and with what resources. In the process, it collaborates with the other MAP divisions and draws on their specific expertise. Once the initial studies are complete, and approved by the military customer, the TsKB passes its work on to another set of organizations: the design bureaus.

What makes the TsKB most unusual in the Soviet structure is that it heads a group of organizations which, often, compete with one another. These are the Experimental-Design Bureaus, or OKBs. Despite its title, an OKB is more than a design office; it is a substantial organization, capable of designing an advanced combat aircraft, building a number of prototypes, and – with the assistance of the MAP's flight-test department – carrying out the complete development programme. It also oversees preparations for production. The largest OKBs can handle multiple programmes.

OKB constraints

The OKBs are not autonomous. Their task is to interpret a fairly tight specification laid down by the TsKB, and produce a prototype which responds to it. They interpret that specification in accordance with the standards set by the other MAP organizations, and design to incorporate components – engines, avionics, ejection seats and so on – available from those organizations. The design task is probably simpler and quicker than starting from scratch.

In the past, the TsKB has often instructed two OKBs to build prototypes, with the better one being selected for production. Alternatively, on occasion, a single OKB has built two prototypes sharing common components, but with a different basic layout. More recently, there has been less evidence of such 'fly-off' contests, probably because they take up a great deal of time and materiel. (One factor which facilitates fly-offs in the West – the fact that manufacturers will usually provide competing prototypes below cost, in hopes of future profits after they win - does not apply in the Soviet Union.) However, paper designs and computer simulations are undoubtedly still compared.

To talk about 'competition' is, perhaps, not quite accurate, and 'comparison' may be a better word. The OKBs, unlike Western design teams, do not depend on winning contests for their survival; some of them have remained active for many years without designing a production aircraft, and have even won awards for the usefulness of their work. (Take Kamov as an example. Only two production designs, and one derivative, have emerged from Kamov in the past 30 years, but the bureau has pioneered many useful helicopter technologies.) Under whatever name, the process gives the TsKB a choice of approaches to its requirement.

To the Western eye, the MAP may look like a vast bureaucracy, within which progress would be impossible. However, there are a number of features which make the system work more smoothly than one might expect. The staffs of the different organizations are very stable, and lines of promotion are

Above: A radar-equipped MiG-17PF 'Fresco-D' interceptor on final approach. The intake bullet houses the conical scan search element of the Izumrud radar, and the bulged lip contains the ranging set. The large area of the wing is apparent.

Below: This Shenyang FT-5 (Chinese two-seat trainer version of the MiG-17PF), photographed at its Pakistan AF base in March 1981, illustrates the generally high quality of workmanship apparent on most of the south-of-the-border 'bootleg' MiG designs.

Above: A North Vietnamese MiG-17F under attack by US Navy F-8 Crusaders on December 14, 1967. In such low-level engagements subsonic speed was no handicap.

Below: This high-altitude reconnaissance photo – quite possibly taken from a U-2 or a drone – shows two MiG-17Fs at Phuc Yen, 20 miles northwest of Hanoi, in October 1966.

clear and mostly vertical. The result is that, firstly, the individuals within the system have a great deal of experience in their specific jobs; and, secondly, that working relationships between individuals are of very long standing. The Soviet system contrasts sharply with most Western organizations. Consider Britain, where virtually none of the Civil Service policy-drafters with access to the Cabinet level has any background in engineering, or take the case of the USA, where programmes are managed by serving officers who are promoted and transferred every couple of years.

Stable cross-departmental relationships can be accommodated within the Soviet system, because there is no contractor/customer relationship involved, so issues of 'conflict of interest' do not arise. People within the MAP aerodynamics, engine, systems and production organizations are even assigned to, and work alongside, the designers of a specific OKB for years at a time. The designer faced with a problem may not have to submit a memorandum in triplicate to the MAP production branch. Instead, he walks three doors down and discusses the problem with the production-branch representative in the bureau, with whom he has worked for five years. It may not always work that way, but it works better than Western foes of socialism might care to admit.

OKBs are not lightly formed or disbanded in these days, but that was not always the case. Many OKBs, now unknown, were formed and fell under Stalin; some major bureaus of their day simply vanished before the mid-1950s. Most of today's leaders, however, were operating in the years before the 1939-45 war – or the 1941-45 war, as it should properly be termed in discussions of the Soviet Union – and rose to prominence during the war years. They included Yakovlev, Ilyushin and the only design bureau to carry two names: the OKB headed by Artem Mikoyan and Mikhail Guryevich.

Mikoyan and Guryevich had both been involved in major programmes before they joined forces on a new VVS fighter requirement in 1938. Mikoyan had worked on the Polikarpov I-153 biplane fighter; his partner had just returned from the highly un-Stalinist atmosphere of Santa Monica, California, where he had been helping Boris Lisunov turn the DC-3 licence into hardware.

The bureau is established

Mikoyan was 34, and Guryevich 46, when the new bureau was formally established in October 1939. Among early recruits to the OKB was a young man named Rostislav Belyakov, who at the time of writing heads the MiG team. The bureau's first fighter prototype flew in April 1940.

The team's first objective was the design of high-performance, high-altitude fighters. Initial results were not impressive. The badly flawed I-200 prototype was rushed into service as the MiG-1, and suffered a catastrophic accident rate. The MiG-3 was an improved version, but entered service just in time for the German invasion. The VVS found itself fighting a low-level, tactical air war, and production of the MiG-3's highly supercharged, high-altitude AM-39 engine was terminated in 1942, bringing to an end wartime production of MiG designs.

The bureau's work on high-altitude fighters continued; the sporadic but potentially dangerous threat from very-high-altitude bombers and reconnaissance aircraft was enough to sustain support for such programmes. A series of successively improved prototypes appeared, incorporating such advanced features as turbosupercharging, cockpit pressurization and laminar-flow aerofoil sections. The last of the series was the excellent I-225, designed for medium-to-high altitude and offering better all-

Above: Two MiG-17Fs maintain an unnervingly close formation on an Il-18 transport. Not the fastest fighter in service at that time, the late 1950s, the MiG-17 was still the standard Soviet fighter-bomber.

Below: Possibly taken at the Mikoyan OKB's home near Moscow, this photo shows two service MiG-17Fs climbing away, and a gaggle of variously marked MiG-19PMs, along with one MiG-17F, in the background.

round performance than any contemporary Soviet type. It flew in March 1945; Germany was defeated before it could enter production, and it was superseded by more advanced jet aircraft.

A contemporary of the I-225 deserves mention: the MiG I-250, which may have been the fastest propeller-equipped fighter to enter service. Together with the very similar Su-5, it was developed in great haste to meet the potential threat from German jet aircraft such as the Arado Ar 234 bomber. The Soviet Union's own work on jet engines was lagging far behind Germany's and Britain's; to produce a high-speed interceptor, the MAP developed a unique powerplant coupling a piston engine with a Campini-type jet. Also called an 'accelerator', this resembled a conventional jet without the turbine; instead, the compressor was driven by a shaft from the back of the engine. The auxiliary jet exhausted through a variable rear nozzle.

The I-250 was a notably small aircraft for its power, and used an advanced wing section with slotted flaps. It was claimed to be capable of 513mph (825km/h) in level flight – slightly faster than some early jets. A few I-250s were built, and, designated MiG-13, served with shore-based navy air defence units until 1950.

With fighting in Europe at an end, the wartime East-West alliance died almost as quickly as the pre-war German-Soviet non-aggression pact had done. The effect of the sudden shift in policy on the fortunes of the MiG bureau was immense; in fact, it was to catapult the OKB to the leading position among Soviet fighter design teams, in less than three years. The possibility of an invasion from ruined Europe could be ignored; instead, the threat came from the United States, with its nuclear weapons, a vast fleet of B-29s in being and the intercontinental B-36 under development. The Soviet Union needed jet interceptors, and the MiG OKB, for all its lack of production designs during the war, was pre-eminent in all the necessary technologies: pressure cabins, high-speed aerodynamics, and advanced structures. In April 1946, the MiG bureau flew the first Soviet jet aircraft.

This aircraft, the I-300, was a bulky but basically clean design with two engines in the belly, fed by a nose intake. It entered production as the MiG-9. Its aerodynamics were based to some extent on those of the smaller I-250; it carried a heavy armament and had a respectable internal fuel capacity. Its main drawback was an uninspiring thrust/weight ratio, but this was hardly the designers' fault. The Soviet Union's own jet engines were not ready to fly; however, most of the German aero-engine industry had been overrun by Soviet forces, and the entire operation was evacuated to the Soviet Union. (This included many leading designers, who remained there, well treated, until they were permitted to leave in the late 1950s.) Unfortunately, German industry had never produced a

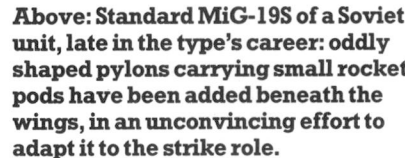

Above: Standard MiG-19S of a Soviet unit, late in the type's career: oddly shaped pylons carrying small rocket pods have been added beneath the wings, in an unconvincing effort to adapt it to the strike role.

Left: A MiG-19PF with Izumrud radar and the inevitable external tanks. Not a large aircraft, the MiG-19 weighs about as much as an A-4 Skyhawk, but with its twin engines it is significantly more powerful.

Below: A Bulgarian MiG-19PF undergoing line maintenance. Note the hinged access panels over avionics and systems bays in front of the cockpit, beneath the forward fuselage and over the wing.

Below: Tyres smoke gently as a Pakistan AF Shenyang F-6 – a Chinese reproduction of the MiG-19 – touches down. The relatively large external tanks are common to all of the small, powerful MiG designs.

good turbojet over 2,500lb (1,100kg) thrust, despite its early start, and this limited what early Soviet jets could do.

The breakthrough came in September 1946, when the British Government agreed to provide samples of the 5,000lb (2,720kg) Rolls-Royce Nene engine to the Soviet Union. The Nenes arrived in October, and were promptly and efficiently 'reverse-engineered' by Vladimir Klimov's design team: they were disassembled, all components and tolerances were measured, the materials were analyzed, and the results were translated into new engineering drawings. The first Soviet-built RD-45s were completed early in 1947.

The availability of an engine galvanized an already existing effort to develop a high-performance interceptor, which had been proceeding under Guryevich's leadership while Mikoyan led the urgent effort to get the MiG-9 into service. The MiG team had studied many documents from Germany, and the design which emerged – initially known as Aircraft S – to some extent resembled Dr Kurt Tank's Ta 183, including such features as a swept wing with slight anhedral, a short rear fuselage and a large, highly swept fin carrying the tailplane. As the I-310, it flew at the end of 1947. Tests revealed no problems that could not be tolerated or quickly overcome, and the design was ordered into production in March 1948 as the MiG-15.

Reputation for fighters

The MiG-15 was not merely the best Soviet fighter of its generation; it was the only one to be built in significant numbers, and it established the OKB as the Soviet Union's leading fighter design team. The MiG-15bis, with a more powerful VK-1 engine (the Soviet equivalent of the Rolls-Royce Tay/J48), quickly followed the initial version into production. In Korea, the type proved superior in some respects to the F-86 Sabre, which owed its overall superiority to important features such as its radar gunsight, and benefited from better pilot training and tactics. The MiG-15UTI became the standard Soviet-bloc advanced trainer for decades, while the basic fighter version was built in vast numbers, both in the Soviet Union and in Poland, Czechoslovakia and China.

One of the MiG-15's deficiencies was its inability to exceed Mach 0.92 safely; in fact, the Mach sensor and airbrakes were connected to prevent such a thing from happening. Development of a version without this limitation began in early 1949; the first prototype was flown in January 1950, but was destroyed soon afterwards. The improved SI-2 flew some months later, and production of the new aircraft – the MiG-17 – was authorized in mid-1951.

The MiG-17 was distinguished by a new, more sharply swept wing and tailplane, and a longer and less sharply tapered rear fuselage. Many components, such as the entire forward fuselage, the engine, the armament installation and the landing gear, were similar or identical to those of the MiG-15. The modifications raised the limiting Mach number of the aircraft, but also increased its weight while the thrust remained the same.

The new aircraft did not replace the MiG-15 in production until it was fitted with an augmented VK-1F engine; the result was the MiG-17F, the first reheat-equipped (afterburning) fighter in the Soviet inventory. A radar-equipped version, the MiG-17PF, was developed for the PVO, and was followed by the MiG-17PFU, with four underwing K-5M missiles. MiG-17 production ran to over 6,000 aircraft in the Soviet Union, and the type was also built in Poland, Czechoslovakia and, in very large numbers, in China. Although technically obsolete by the mid-1960s, the type proved a dangerous opponent for US fighters in Vietnam.

Supersonic speed in level flight was the logical next step. It was approached by evolution from the MiG-15 and MiG-17, the first supersonic prototype using the same forward and centre fuselage geometry, mated to a yet longer rear fuselage, a more powerful engine and a new wing and tail of increased sweepback. As was the case with similar developments in the West, it proved more difficult than expected. The mid-set tail of the early prototype aircraft, the I-350, caused flutter problems. The single-engined version was dropped in favour of a parallel development, using two small, very light but respectably powerful AM-5 engines, designed at the Mikulin OKB by Sergei Tumansky. The third prototype in the series, the I-350M, flew

Above: The potential handling problems of the MiG-19's highly swept wing were countered by the use of very large wing fences. One wag suggested that their function was to prevent the airflow from defecting to the tips.

Left: All-round vision hood, two heavy cannon and effective airbrakes made the MiG-19 a fairly effective dogfighter, by the standard of the day.

in September 1953, featuring two engines and a fuselage-mounted tailplane.

The first production aircraft in the series was the MiG-19F, with afterburning AM-5F engines, but the type was barely acceptable for service because of poor handling characteristics. The first effective version was the MiG-19S, with an all-moving slab tail, roll spoilers and other critical changes, which entered service in 1955. Like its immediate predecessor, the MiG-17, the MiG-19 was also delivered with a limited-performance radar (MiG-19PF) and K-5M missiles (MiG-19PM). Some 2,500 MiG-19s were built in the Soviet Union; an even greater number may have been built in China, which reverse-engineered the type after the Sino-Soviet rift of 1960. The MiG-19 copy, the Shenyang J-6, led to the locally developed JT-6 trainer, and to the considerably modified Q-5 attack fighter; all the Chinese developments have been extensively exported in recent years under the export designations F-6, FT-6 and A-5.

By the mid-1950s, the MiG OKB had achieved every significant 'first' in the development of Soviet jet fighters: first jet to fly, and first in service; first swept-wing fighter in service, and first in combat; first jet fighter with reheat, and first with missile armament. Finally, with the MiG-19, the team had produced not only the first and only workable supersonic fighter in the Soviet Union, but the first in the world. The MiG bureau had come a long way in ten short and eventful years.

MiG-21 'Fishbed'

Small, fast, and austere to a fault, the MiG-21 epitomises the Soviet approach to warplane design and development. The MiG-21 has been in production longer than any other fighter in history, has been built in greater numbers than any other supersonic fighter and has taken part in every air war, bar the South Atlantic, since 1965. Even now, serious studies of re-engined MiG-21s with new sensors and other improvements are being undertaken, because the MiG-21 is such a good answer to the needs of the smaller air force. For an aircraft which Western analysts once dismissed as useless, this is not bad going.

Above: The small size of the MiG-21F is apparent in this view. The design of the canopy was influenced by that of the Folland Gnat; it formed a blast shield to protect the pilot in the event of ejection.

Once the physical and psychological barrier of Mach 1 had been breached, aerospace technology advanced at a gallop. The 1950s saw all previous records for speed and altitude shattered. They were a time of serious work on near-hypersonic aircraft, airborne nuclear power, radical chemical fuels and previously undreamt-of weapons and sensors. It was also the decade in which the Cold War between East and West froze solid.

The Soviet Union's development of nuclear and thermonuclear weapons, and the Korean War of 1950-53, set the international tone for the decade, and there was very little change in the atmosphere from 1950 to 1960. The mood was one of sullen confrontation, and East and West both armed themselves – almost exclusively – for total war.

The 1950s concept of total war was not the same as today's. Nuclear weapons still had to be delivered by subsonic bombers, far more susceptible to interception than today's missiles. The total number of warheads on either side was smaller, because nuclear weapons were difficult and expensive to produce, and so large that only a handful could be carried on one aircraft. Moreover, the public at large was kept blissfully unaware of the hazards of radioactive fallout. For these reasons, it was felt that non-nuclear combat could still be important, even in the case of an all-out thermonuclear exchange. Another difference between the 1950s and the two subsequent decades was that defence against nuclear attack was considered to be feasible and essential.

Neither the Soviet Union nor the United States, however, could afford to maintain vast land forces while racing to develop new systems for strategic attack and defence. The US had moved to consolidate its alliances in Europe, leading to the establishment of the North Atlantic Treaty Organization in 1949. In 1955 a 'Treaty of Friendship, Mutual Assistance and Cooperation' was signed in Warsaw by the USSR and six other East European states, ostensibly as a defensive response to NATO; in fact, the Warsaw Pact formalized relationships which had existed since the establishment of Communist governments in Eastern Europe in the aftermath of the war. In both cases, there was a need for conventional weapons to equip these forces, as well as the Soviet and US units that would be based alongside them.

In the USA, the advance of technology had driven the air-defence interceptors and tactical fighters apart by the early 1950s, to the point where the aircraft designed for one mission were incapable of performing the other, even with adaptation. The Soviet Union, however, continued to require all-purpose fighters in the mould of the MiG-15, MiG-17 and MiG-19.

The strategic bomber threat

Several factors influenced Soviet planning for advanced fighters in the early 1950s. One was the rapid expansion of the USAF force of jet bombers. In just four years of production, starting in 1952, the USAF built the staggering total of 2,000 Boeing B-47s, whose Mach 0.9 cruising speed rendered the MiG-15 and MiG-17 impotent, and the MiG-19 of marginal usefulness. The low-time B-50 bombers which the B-47s replaced were converted into tankers; together with the availability of bases in Britain and else-

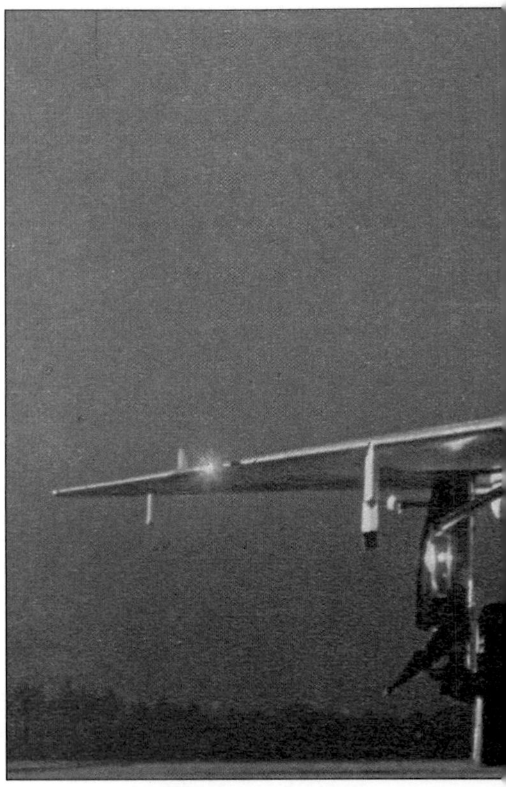

Below: Czech-built MiG-21Fs, produced at the Aero factory near Prague and designated S-107, can be distinguished from otherwise similar Soviet-built machines by the lack of a glazed rear section to the canopy.

Bottom: The Tumansky R-11 was a remarkable engine. The two-spool powerplant has a high thrust/weight ratio, and contains only 3,500 parts, fewer than the much smaller J85, thanks to good basic design.

Below: A pristine S-107 (MiG-21F). Note that the port gun has been removed, making way for additional electronics. The combined pitot boom and yaw/pitch sensors is a standard piece of equipment.

Mikoyan Ye-2A prototype

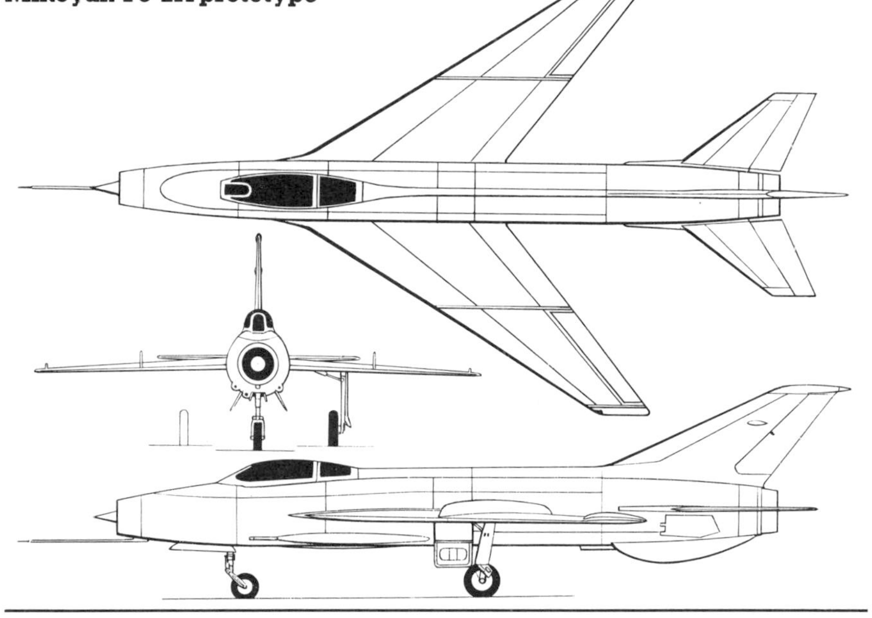

Above: The aerodynamic configuration of the Ye-2A was based on a thin-winged MiG-19. The less conventional delta-winged Ye-5, with a lower empty weight, proved to have better performance in all respects.

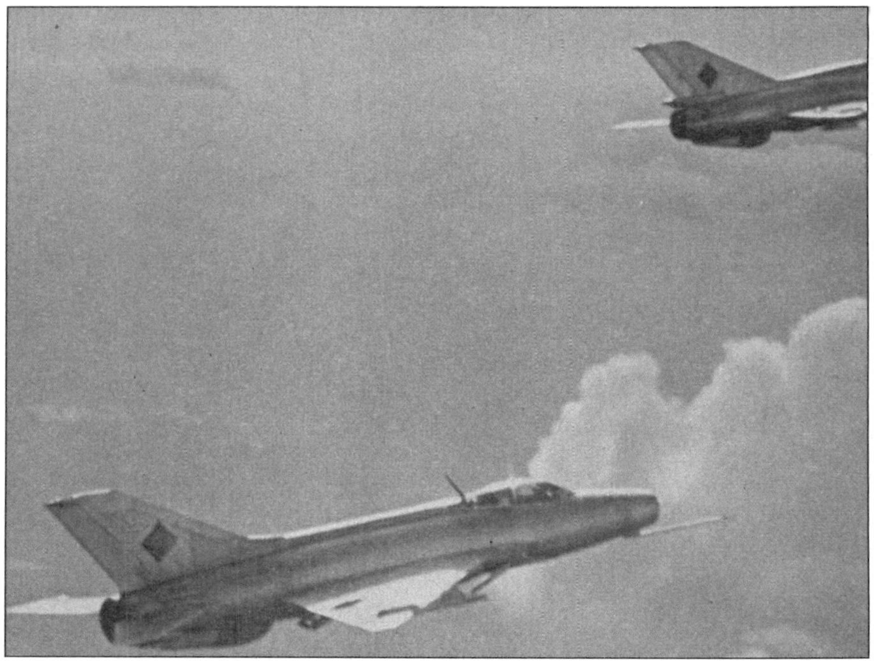

Above: a MiG-21F of the DDR Luftstreitkrafte slows down for the camera, displaying its three small ventral airbrakes. The aircraft in the background is a later model, with a broader fin and relocated brake chute.

Below: Through ingenious design, it proved possible to fit a radar in the already tightly packed airframe, creating the MiG-21PF. Note the oversize, low-pressure tyres common to all MiG-21s.

where, this made the B-47's relatively short range very much less important. B-47 attacks could be expected from almost any direction. Meanwhile, the intercontinental B-52 was well advanced in development. As well as adding a truly global dimension to the jet bomber threat, it would carry more extensive countermeasures than the B-47 and would cruise at higher altitudes.

Combat experience in Korea was also important. While the kill/loss ratio had been heavily in favour of the USAF (probably about 4:1, rather than the 10:1 claimed at the time) there was little dispute that the basic design of the MiG-15 had proved sound. A few small but significant items of equipment, and much better training and experience, had decided many engagements. In terms of performance and firepower, the MiG-15 had held its own against the much larger F-86. Korea also demonstrated that tactical air warfare could still come down to a close-range, turning engagement, and that absolute performance, including speed, acceleration and rate-of-climb, was important; an aircraft with the advantage in performance gave its pilot the initiative in starting or ending an engagement.

Basic Soviet military doctrine, however, introduced a complication into the conception of any new Soviet fighter: numerical superiority was vital. Western Mach 2 fighters were, without exception, more complex and more expensive than their subsonic and transonic predecessors. There were fewer of them, and they needed more maintenance. Such a development would have been unacceptable to the Soviet front commander, who then as now considered numbers first and technical quality second. Resolving the dilemma by increasing the resources devoted to fighter production was out of the question; bomber production took absolute priority, and it would be years before the Soviet strategic strike force attained parity with Strategic Air Command.

The requirement

The solution was to issue a requirement in late 1953, calling for a fighter with Mach 2 speed, and a service ceiling close to 66,000ft (20,000m) – both figures based on what was necessary to engage a B-52 – but demanding that the aircraft be little bigger than a MiG-17, and actually smaller than a MiG-19. Moreover, the aircraft had to carry a range-only radar, air-to-air missiles and a pair of heavy cannon, and it had to possess conventional flying characteristics, good manoeuvrability and reasonable field performance.

By the standards of the time this was a very stiff requirement indeed. The small size was the root of most of the problems it posed. Many of the components of the aircraft were basically fixed in size and weight; the pilot, seat and cockpit enclosure, the radar and radio equipment, the guns and the missiles were examples. They tended to make a fixed contribution to the weight and drag of the aircraft, and some of them imposed other constraints, such as the cockpit, which required a minimum cross-section forward of the wing. The main reason why Western designs had grown in weight and size was to reduce the weight and drag of these fixed items as a proportion of the total-aircraft figures.

The call for high supersonic speed compounded the difficulties. The aircraft was to be small, its internal fuel capacity would not be great, and it accordingly

Left: Details apparent on this S-107 include the ogival centrebody and the large vertical wheel wells. Note the large Fowler flaps, fully extended for take-off. The aircraft may be taking off on dry thrust in order to conserve its limited supply of fuel.

Mikoyan SM-12PM

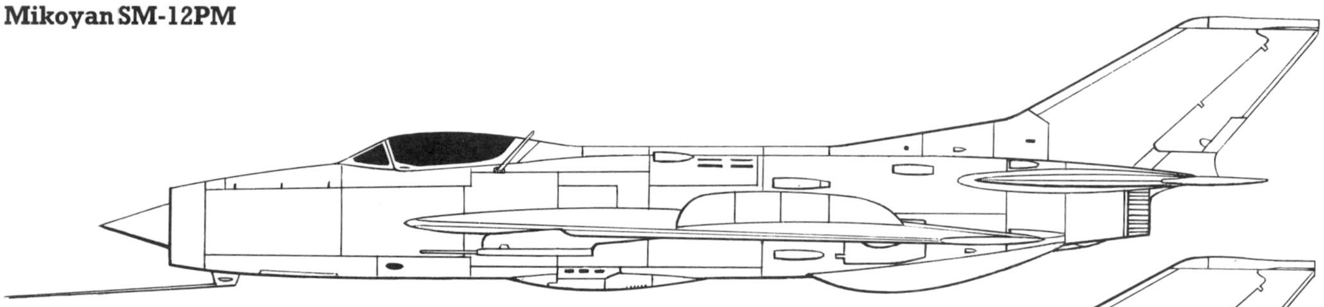

Mikoyan SM-12PMU

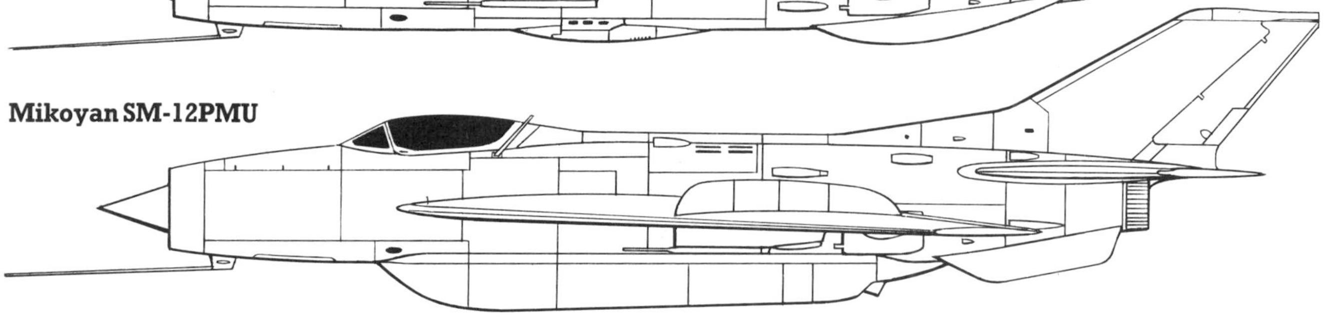

Above: The more advanced inlet and radar nose configuration of the MiG-21PF was tested on two highly modified MiG-19s with broad-chord vertical fins. The SM-12PMU added a large ventral rocket pack.

Right: The MiG-21PFM featured plain, blown flaps. These were less efficient on take-off than the original Fowler flaps, so provision was made for the execution of flapless, rocket-assisted short take-offs.

could not afford an oversized engine. An efficient supersonic configuration was vital. The Area Rule called for a smooth, and not excessive, variation in cross-sectional area from nose to tail, and the need to reduce wave drag meant that the fuselage must be as slender as possible. Neither was readily compatible with a light, efficiently packed airframe of small overall dimensions.

The new fighter would be single-engined – there is no evidence that any other layout was considered. The development of the Tumansky RD-9 had built up experience in small, light, powerful turbojets to the point where the design of a slightly larger engine would not present too many problems, and a single-engined aircraft would have a more slender, lighter rear fuselage than a twin of the same size.

The overall layout of the aircraft was strongly influenced by the aerodynamicists at the MAP's Central Aero-Hydrodynamics Institute (TsAGI). At that time TsAGI's influence was at its zenith, and its technical authority was such that its recommendations were almost read as law. However, TsAGI itself was strongly influenced by the success of the earlier MiG fighters, whose mid-set wings and circular-section fuselages may have been less than ideal from the systems-packaging standpoint, but were aerodynamically straightforward and contributed to low drag and uncomplicated handling. Under TsAGI control, the MiG trademarks appeared on everything from cruise missiles to the Mya-4 heavy bomber.

Another feature which was probably assumed from the start was the inlet design. All previous Soviet fighters and prototypes had featured nose intakes, so the adoption of any other configuration would have meant a simultaneous move into a new internal geometry and a new speed range. The design has advantages of its own: it mandates long, gradually curved ducts, which tend to generate few surprises; the inlet itself is free from problems caused by wakes and vortices from the airframe or gun gas ingestion; and the air enters the inlet as it has to enter the engine, equally distributed in a circular pattern. The two main drawbacks are that such a layout takes up a large volume in the forward fuselage, and makes it almost impossible to install an engine with greater mass flow at a later date.

Planforms for supersonic flight were many and various in the early 1950s. Thin, moderately swept wings, tailless deltas, ultra-thin straight wings and other layouts were all being tried, with varying degrees of success, but most of them were ruled out for the new Soviet fighter by the terms of the requirement. Medium sweep angles were limited to about Mach 1.5 with contemporary powerplant technology; tailless deltas and F-104-type thin wings would not have achieved the necessary runway performance with existing technology.

Alternative solutions

TsAGI proposed two solutions. One was to modify the MiG-19 wing for a higher Mach number; the other was a new layout, combining a sharply swept delta wing with a tailplane. The basic delta had been flown in 1949, on the Convair XF-92A prototype, and despite its outlandish appearance it had shown itself to be free of vices or surprises. Its drag was little higher than that of a swept wing, but it offered much more volume, had more area for the same weight, and was inherently stiff. Its main disadvantage was that it replaced the normal tailplane; at low speed, instead of flaps lifting the aircraft, the delta wing had up-elevon weighing it down. The delta also generated its maximum lift at very high angles of attack, which were impractical for conventional aircraft. Finally, the fact that the relatively short trailing edge had to provide all the pitch and roll forces for the aircraft, with a short moment arm, made the delta less manoeuvrable than a conventional aircraft.

Adding a conventional tail relieved many of the problems and produced a layopt with inherently good stability and handling. In particular, the delta's ability to maintain stable airflow up to high angles of attack – as a result of vortices shed by its sharply swept leading edge – was retained. This was important for a fighter, because it meant that the ailerons remained effective at virtually all times, and the pilot could pull very hard manoeuvres without worrying about losing lateral control.

The only serious limitation of the layout was that its short span, thin section and high sweep militated against high wing loadings. Even with large and effective flaps, the TsAGI-type tailed delta would not be a champion weight-lifter, and growth potential would be limited. (The West's only tailed delta, the A-4 Skyhawk, carries heavy external loads, but has a thicker, slatted wing.) However, future growth beyond the scope of the requirement was not something which the Soviet system considered important.

In early 1954, the MAP directed the MiG bureau to build prototypes of the small supersonic fighter with both swept and delta wings. A near-parallel programme, also started in 1954, called for swept-wing and delta-wing prototypes of very similar configuration, but larger. Clearly, MAP was concerned that the MiG-17 sized aircraft might not meet all the requirements, particularly the evolving needs of the PVO.

The challenge facing the MiG bureau was to fit all the components of an advanced fighter aircraft into the close confines of the TsAGI configuration. This was done with considerable ingenuity, and work on the new prototypes – all designated with the Soviet letter written as E, but pronounced Ye - forged ahead. To a Western eye, the internal layout of the new aircraft would have seemed ran-

Above: The introduction of the Mach 2, radar-equipped MiG-21PF was a major step forward for the non-Soviet Warsaw Pact forces. This example is a member of a single regiment of MiG-21PFs supplied to Romania.

Below: Each Soviet fighter regiment contains two or three two-seaters for conversion training. In this scene at a SovAF base, a MiG-21U 'Mongol-A' taxies out for a training mission, with an Su-7 following it.

Below: MiG-21FL was the designation of this subtype, built by HAL at Nasik. It was basically similar to a late-production MiG-21PF, but had an export-model radar and a more powerful version of the R-11 engine.

Below: The second-generation MiG-21s were the first to have radar, a major omission from the original. Note that the HAL aircraft, built later than the Soviet types, has a GP-9 gun pack housing a twin-barrel GSh-23.

Second-generation MiG-21s

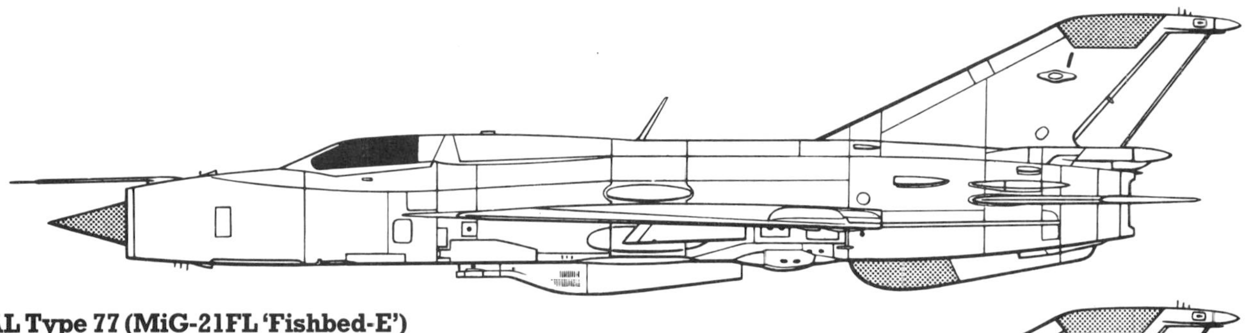

HAL Type 77 (MiG-21FL 'Fishbed-E')

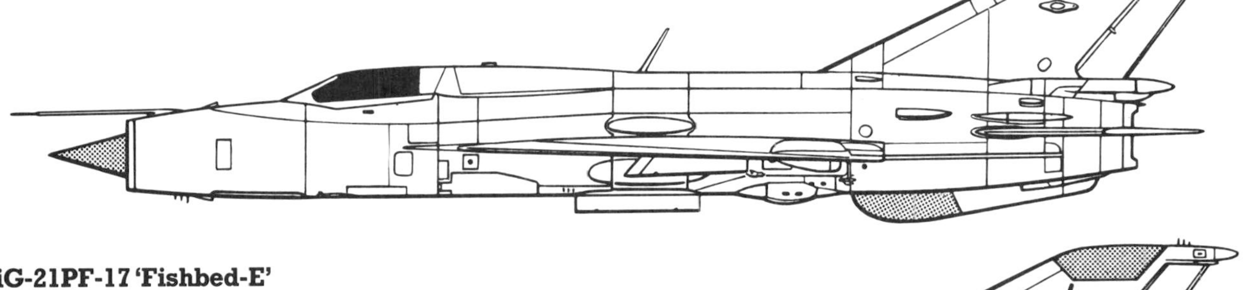

MiG-21PF-17 'Fishbed-E'

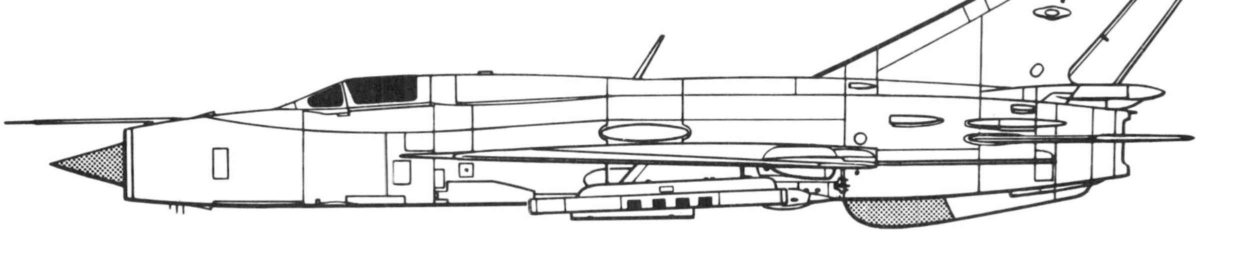

MiG-21PFM 'Fishbed-F'

dom and disorganized, and the exterior appearance untidy. However, the nature of the design becomes much clearer when the packaging problem is considered.

The core of the design was a new engine from the Tumansky bureau, the R-11. There has been some controversy over whether this engine was a two-shaft design. Its thrust and diameter, however, suggest a pressure ratio in the region of 10:1-12:1. In the West, such pressures have been combined with acceptable handling by two means: the use of a two-spool layout, the extensive use of variable stators or the use of a large number of compressor stages. The R-11 emerged as a two-spool engine, the first Soviet engine to feature such a layout. For its day (it was probably first run in prototype form in 1953), the R-11's design thrust/weight ratio of 5:1 was quite ambitious; it was achieved partly by straightforward, economical design – the engine was astoundingly simple, with a total of only 3,500 different parts – and partly by deliberately sacrificing durability.

The latter aspect is important. In Soviet terms, reliability is distinct from durability. Reliability directly affects the performance of the weapon in combat, and there is nothing to be done if a critical failure occurs in action. Absolute reliability is the goal. Durability, on the other hand, is something which is only vital to a certain degree. In Western terms, an engine which must be returned to a large maintenance depot, stripped, disassembled and checked and repaired where necessary every 250 hours is an abomination. In the Soviet Union, a time between overhauls (TBO) of 250-300hr is not uncommon, and the reasoning behind this fact is interesting.

Maintenance logistics

As noted in the previous chapter, the combat units are not expected to worry about fixing their aircraft and engines, beyond the most elementary maintenance (which is made as easy as possible, with plenty of small, quick-opening panels for routine inspections). Instead, they run them for their allotted lifetimes and exchange them for newly overhauled equipment, fresh from the maintenance depot. The conservative TBOs mean that unscheduled removals are rare, and the engines need little inspection in service. The logistics system is geared to handle all the overhaul work and the traffic in repaired components, and generally works smoothly because nearly all the work is scheduled.

In fact, the TBO requirement is set by the needs of the Front commander. He knows that his logistic system will not work smoothly in wartime; essentially, he needs enough time on the weapons he has available to fight the war. Assuming that, at any given time, his fighter engines will have an average of half their TBO left, the target TBO is twice as many hours as the fighter is expected to fly in the course of the main offensive.

In the case of engines, the short TBOs make it possible to achieve higher thrust/weight ratio and better fuel consumption. Both these figures improve with increasing engine pressure ratio, but this also means higher temperatures in the engine. Much of the advanced and expensive technology in Western engines is devoted to achieving long life with high temperatures; Soviet metallurgy is not quite as advanced as that of the West, but engine performance is closely comparable because long TBOs are not required.

Given the size of the R-11, the fuselage design of the MiG prototypes was built up around the engine and its inlet trunk, which was split vertically just behind the inlet lip and merged just ahead of the engine. Structurally, it was basically similar to the earlier MiGs. The wings were separate – being removable for transport and repair, as MAP requires – and attached by lugs and bolts to high-strength forged steel ring-bulkheads with stainless-steel fittings. These bulkheads were the heart of the aircraft. The inlet ducts, and the main fuel tanks between them, fitted inside the ring. The rear fuselage bolted to the rearmost bulkhead, and the forward fuselage – designed around the pilot's seat, the electronics bay and the inlets – was attached to the front. The nosewheel bay served a dual purpose, providing access to the lower electronics bay; a single bonnet-like panel ahead of the windscreen hinged forward to give access to the upper part of the bay.

Internally, the design reflected the need for minimum cross-section, with a number of notable features. In the nose, a single aluminium panel on each side extended from just behind the inlet to the leading-edge wing root, and from the cockpit sill to the lower part of the fuselage; it formed both the side of the fuselage and the outer wall of the inlet duct. Neither of the small, thin-section wings

Above: A Yugoslav Air Force MiG-21PFM, fresh from its regular overhaul. Soviet support practice relies on frequent major overhauls, conducted at factory-type rates.

Below: Two Soviet MiG-21PFMs, ready to roll on a night intercept training mission. With reheat used for take-off, the operational radius will not be substantial.

Right: The number of early-production MiG-21PFs, codenamed 'Fishbed-D', with the same narrow-chord fin as the MiG-21F, was not large. This example was assigned to a display team, possibly formed by the Moscow Air Defence District.

Right: The third-generation MiG-21, represented by this Yugoslav MF, was a major advance. The mix of air-to-air and air-to-surface weaponry shown on this aircraft was theoretically possible, if unusual. The outboard pylons were plumbed for fuel tanks.

Left: A well-used early-model MiG-21PF of the Polish Air Force. The prominence of the rivets is due to the use of steel rivets, which are prone to surface corrosion.

would accommodate the landing gear without the use of small high-pressure tyres, but these would have been operationally unacceptable because of the requirement to operate from quickly prepared strips or cleared tundra. A fuselage-mounted gear, however, would have had too narrow a track. The answer was an ingenious inward-retracting gear, in which the wheels were attached to the legs by a complex but sturdy mechanical linkage. As the legs folded into the wing, the wheels remained in a near-vertical position and retracted into the fuselage sides between the main bulkheads.

Above: A mixed Polish Air Force formation containing three MiG-21PFMs and (furthest from camera) an early MiG-21PF. Operationally, the aircraft were interchangeable.

New design trademark

Because the wheels were a little too large for the space available, the designers added small bulges in the fuselage and gear doors above and below the wheel wells. This proved to be the start of a design trademark. Soviet designers, unlike their Western counterparts, never seem too afraid of adding small bulges in the skin to ease a problem of internal design, to add strength or simplify construction, or to avoid having to enlarge the overall cross-section. They do nothing for the looks of the aircraft, but cause very little extra drag, especially toward the rear, where the airflow over the skin is already broken up.

The design of the stabilizer also deserves special note. The aim was the slimmest possible rear fuselage, but the aerodynamic configuration called for an all-moving stabilizer at mid-height, in line with the wings. On the MiG-19 the stabilizer was set at the top of the fuselage, and the two halves were deeply rooted in the structure; that would not be possible with the new aircraft, because the jetpipe was in the way. Both stabilizers would have to transmit their loads separately into the side of the fuselage.

The solution was to adopt the same geometry as used for the MiG-19. The trunnions on which the tail pivoted were angled in line with the sweepback at half-chord. In Western designs, the trunnions are usually at 90° to the fuselage; the MiG method carries the loads into the fuselage further forward so that the main load-bearing structure can be shortened. The tailplanes were linked by bellcranks and rods (one bellcrank accounts for another pimple on each

Below: An unusual interim (or, possibly, updated) MiG-21PF with the early narrow-chord fin, later braking-chute arrangement and provision for rocket-assisted take-off.

side) to the single actuator and the artificial-feel system, in the leading edge of the fin. This layout also placed the stabilizer and rudder actuators close to the engine ancillaries, reducing the length of the hydraulic system.

That much was common to the two different versions. The swept wing was based on the MiG-19 structural design, with two spars and ribs at right angles to the leading edge. The delta featured a full-span swept main spar, supported by two unswept booms forming another structural box. Large, area-increasing Fowler flaps were fitted to the trailing edge of the delta wing.

The first in the series to fly was the swept-wing Ye-50, in late 1955. The R-11 was not ready, so the Ye-50 was fitted with a single RD-9 (the MiG-19 engine) and a rocket engine in the tail. It attained Mach 2.3, and while the mixed-power fighter was never adopted for service use, the Ye-50 demonstrated that the swept wing was structurally and aerodynamically sound. The definitive R-11-powered prototypes – the swept-wing Ye-2A and the delta Ye-5 - flew in May and June 1956 respectively, and made the short flight from GAZ 155 to Tushino for the Aviation Day flypast.

This brief appearance had an interesting sequel. Firstly, Western intelligence failed to appreciate the small size of the MiG fighters, believing them to be about the same size as the Sukhoi types which made their debut at the same time. Secondly, the Western analysts became convinced that the Ye-2A, codenamed 'Faceplate', had entered production, while the delta-winged Ye-5 'Fishbed' had been abandoned. In mitigation, it should be pointed out that the simultaneous fielding of two Sukhoi fighters with very similar layouts confused the situation. However, the misconceptions concerning the MiG fighters were to endure for half a decade.

Above: Another unusual variant: an early-model MiG-21PFMA, first of the third generation, delivered to Czechoslovakia before the GSh-23 internal gun was available. The anti-ingestion strakes are also absent.

Below: A Soviet pilot poses for the camera with his MiG-21MF. The boom-mounted pitch and yaw sensors, absent from the second-generation types and the PFMA, made a comeback on this and later versions.

In fact, it was the Ye-5 that was selected as the basis for the production aircraft, mainly because its thicker wing gave it more internal fuel capacity, at the end of 1956. Neither type had shown any serious aerodynamic vices; the problems that were encountered affected the Ye-2A and Ye-5 equally. The two most serious of these concerned engine/inlet matching and the flight control system.

Problems with the first true supersonic inlet in the Soviet Union were not surprising. The design was classically simple, a derivative of the conventional blunt-lipped circular inlet used on earlier MiGs; that design worked well up to Mach 1.4, but shock-waves formed from the lip generated an increasing amount of drag at higher speeds. The Ye-2A/Ye-50 inlet had a sharp lip, and a pointed central cone. The aerodynamic function of the inlet cone was to form a shock wave – the primary shock – ahead of the inlet aperture, decelerating the air (relative to the aircraft) before it entered the inlet. This type of inlet is simple, and works well under test conditions; the problem with the original Ye-2A/Ye-50 inlet was that it had no variable geometry whatsoever, and could not accommodate the full range of speeds and altitudes of which the aircraft was capable.

Adjustable inlet

The solution was an adjustable three-position centre-body, automatically controlled according to airspeed, which allowed the airflow to be matched to the flight conditions and the needs of the engine. Also, the area of the basic inlet was reduced to avoid compressor stalls, while to aid in starting, relighting and low-speed flight, small auxiliary suck-in doors were added just below the wing leading edge. A final addition was a spill door on each side of the nose, to relieve

Mikoyan MiG-21MF 'Fishbed-J' cutaway

1 Pitot-static boom
2 Pitch vanes
3 Yaw vanes
4 Conical three-position intake centrebody
5 'Spin Scan' search-and-track radar antenna
6 Boundary layer slot
7 Engine air intake
8 Radar ('Spin Scan')
9 Lower boundary layer exit
10 Antennas
11 Nosewheel doors
12 Nosewheel leg and shock absorbers
13 Castoring nosewheel
14 Anti-shimmy damper
15 Avionics bay access
16 Attitude sensor
17 Nosewheel well
18 Spill door
19 Nosewheel retraction pivot
20 Bifurcated intake trunking
21 Avionics bay
22 Electronics equipment
23 Intake trunking
24 Upper boundary layer exit
25 Dynamic pressure probe for q-feel
26 Semi-elliptical armour-glass windscreen
27 Gunsight mounting
28 Fixed quarterlight
29 Radar scope
30 Control column (with tailplane trim switch and two firing buttons)
31 Rudder pedals
32 Underfloor control runs
33 KM-1 two-position zero-level ejection seat
34 Port instrument console
35 Undercarriage handle
36 Seat harness
37 Canopy release/lock
38 Starboard wall switch panel
39 Rear-view mirror fairing
40 Starboard-hinged canopy
41 Ejection seat headrest
42 Avionics bay
43 Control rods
44 Air conditioning plant
45 Suction relief door
46 Intake trunking
47 Wingroot attachment fairing
48 Wing/fuselage spar-lug attachment points (four)
49 Fuselage ring frames
50 Intermediary frames
51 Main fuselage fuel tank
52 RSIU radio bay
53 Auxiliary intake
54 Leading edge integral fuel tank
55 Starboard outer weapons pylon
56 Outboard wing construction
57 Starboard navigation light
58 Leading edge suppressed antenna
59 Wing fence
60 Aileron control jack
61 Starboard aileron
62 Flap actuator fairing
63 Starboard blown flap
64 Multi-spar wing structure
65 Main integral wing fuel tank
66 Undercarriage mounting/pivot point
67 Starboard main wheel leg
68 Auxiliaries compartment
69 Fuselage fuel tanks Nos 2 and 3
70 Mainwheel well external fairing
71 Mainwheel (retracted)
72 Trunking contours
73 Control rods in dorsal spine
74 Compressor face
75 Oil tank
76 Avionics pack
77 Engine accessories
78 Tumansky R-13 turbojet (rated at 14,550lb/6,600kg with full reheat)
79 Fuselage break/transport joint
80 Intake
81 Tail surface control linkage
82 Artificial feel unit
83 Tailplane jack
84 Hydraulic accumulator
85 Tailplane trim motor
86 Tailfin spar attachment plate
87 Rudder jack
88 Rudder control linkage
89 Tailfin structure
90 Leading edge panel
91 Radio cable access
92 Magnetic detector
93 Tailfin mainspar

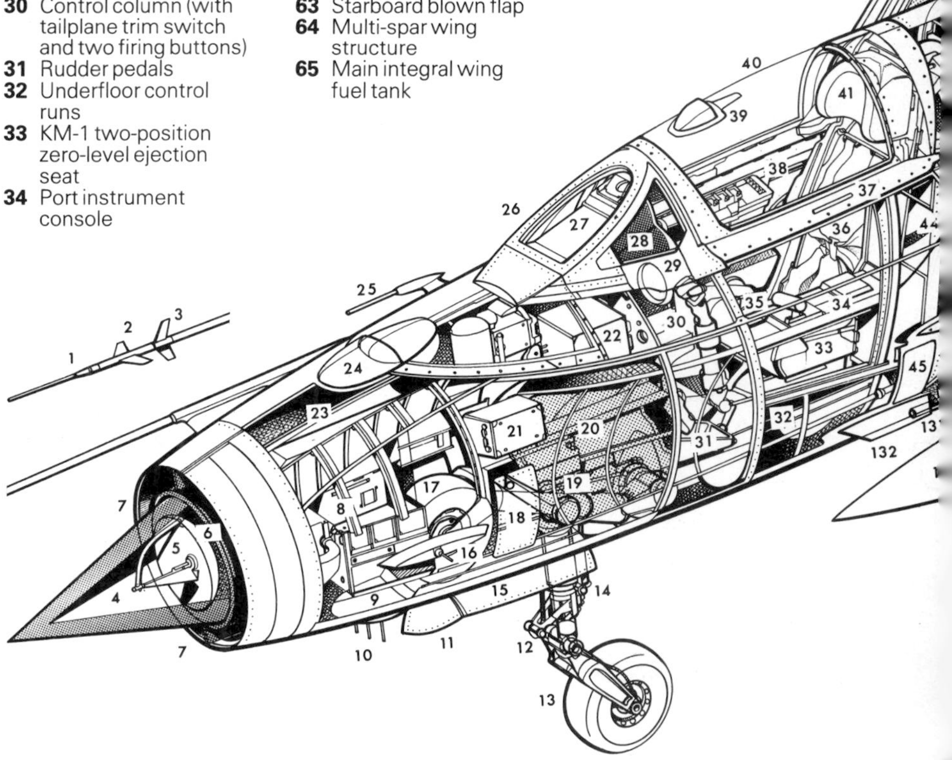

excessive pressure in the inlet. Meanwhile, a programme of research into more efficient Mach 2 inlet configurations got under way, using modified MiG-19s.

The control problem was essentially one of systems design. In pursuit of light weight and efficiency, the MiG OKB had provided only a single hydraulic system, with manual back-up for the rudder and ailerons and a standby electrical system for the stabilizer. The first pre-production prototype, the Ye-6, was lost after the engine stalled, and the standby stabilizer control proved inadequate; after that, the system was redesigned around dual hydraulics. The modified aircraft was cleared for production in 1957, as the MiG-21, and deliveries started in the following year.

The initial version, known to NATO as 'Fishbed-A', was not built in large numbers. The flight control system still needed development, handling characteristics still had to be refined, and the engine was not only short of thrust but its TBO of 100 hours was unacceptable even by Soviet standards. However, the initial MiG-21 incorporated most of the features of the production aircraft, including armament and operational systems.

The main weapon was the K-13A air-to-air missile, known to NATO as AA-2 'Atoll' and very similar to the US Sidewinder. It has often been suggested that the K-13A was copied from one of the US weapons which had been fired from a Chinese Nationalist Air Force F-86 over Quemoy, had struck its target – a Chinese MiG-15 – but had failed to explode, due to simultaneous failures of its proximity fuze, impact fuze and self-destruct system. But this story has never been confirmed, and the resemblance may be one of flattery rather than imitation; most of the world's other missiles in this class bear a strong resemblance to the Sidewinder. Like the early Sidewinder, the original K-13A was a pursuit-course weapon – its IR homing head needed an intense source of radiation, such as the hot metal at the rear of the

Right: Simple, proven construction methods are used in the MiG-21. Note also how components that do not fit the fuselage shape are accommodated in fairings and conduits.

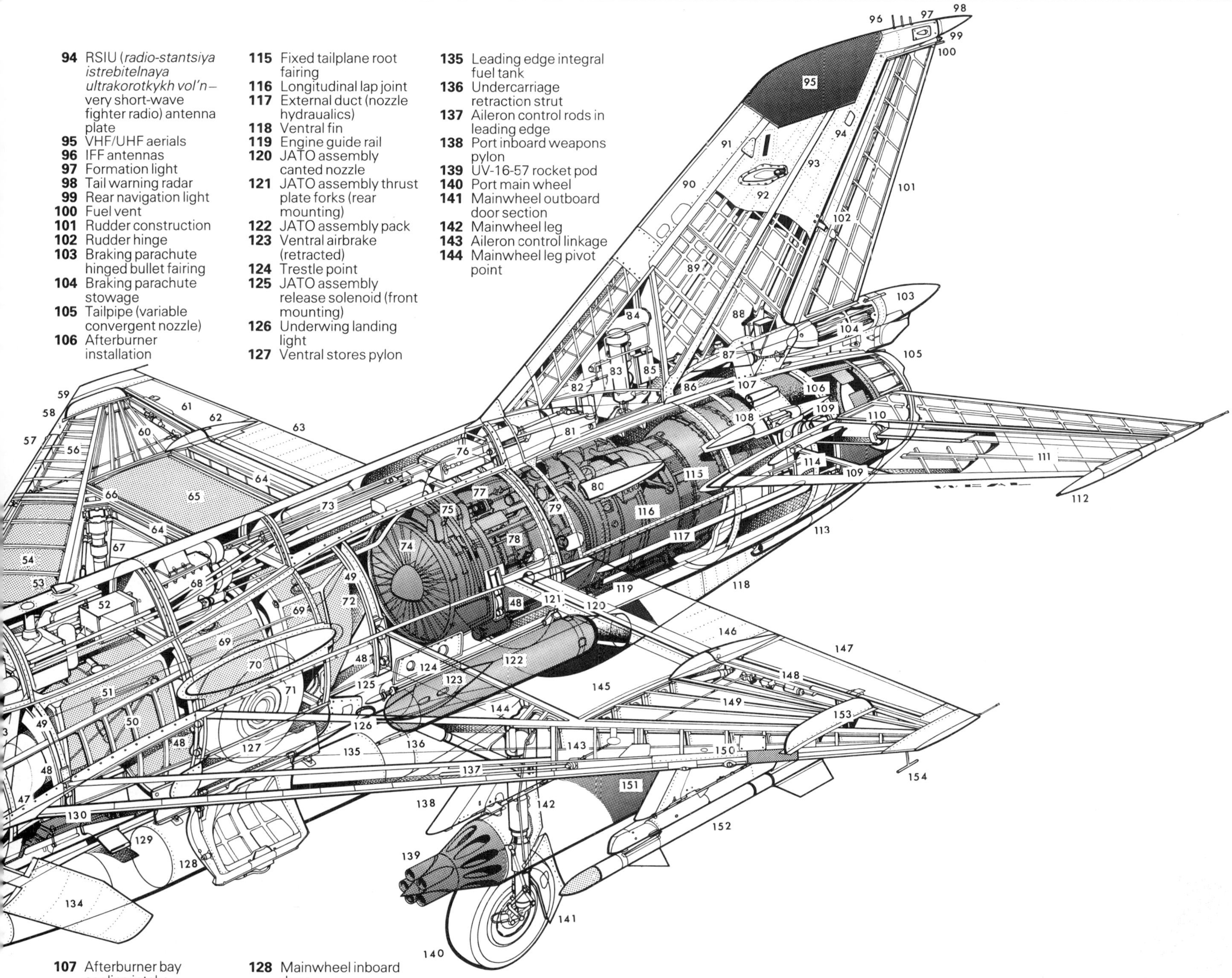

94 RSIU (*radio-stantsiya istrebitelnaya ultrakorotkykh vol'n* – very short-wave fighter radio) antenna plate
95 VHF/UHF aerials
96 IFF antennas
97 Formation light
98 Tail warning radar
99 Rear navigation light
100 Fuel vent
101 Rudder construction
102 Rudder hinge
103 Braking parachute hinged bullet fairing
104 Braking parachute stowage
105 Tailpipe (variable convergent nozzle)
106 Afterburner installation
107 Afterburner bay cooling intake
108 Tailplane linkage fairing
109 Nozzle actuating cylinders
110 Tailplane torque tube
111 All-moving tailplane
112 Anti-flutter weight
113 Intake
114 Afterburner mounting
115 Fixed tailplane root fairing
116 Longitudinal lap joint
117 External duct (nozzle hydrauallics)
118 Ventral fin
119 Engine guide rail
120 JATO assembly canted nozzle
121 JATO assembly thrust plate forks (rear mounting)
122 JATO assembly pack
123 Ventral airbrake (retracted)
124 Trestle point
125 JATO assembly release solenoid (front mounting)
126 Underwing landing light
127 Ventral stores pylon
128 Mainwheel inboard door
129 Splayed link chute
130 Twin 23mm GSh-23 cannon installation
131 Cannon muzzle fairing
132 Debris deflector plate
133 Auxiliary ventral drop tank
134 Port forward air brake (extended)
135 Leading edge integral fuel tank
136 Undercarriage retraction strut
137 Aileron control rods in leading edge
138 Port inboard weapons pylon
139 UV-16-57 rocket pod
140 Port main wheel
141 Mainwheel outboard door section
142 Mainwheel leg
143 Aileron control linkage
144 Mainwheel leg pivot point
145 Main integral wing fuel tank
146 Flap actuator fairing
147 Port aileron
148 Aileron control jack
149 Outboard wing construction
150 Port navigation light
151 Port outboard weapons pylon
152 AA-2-2 'Advanced Atoll' infra-red-guided AAM
153 Wing fence
154 Radio altimeter antenna

Not an inch of space in the MiG-21MF is wasted. Note the ring frames that carry wing loads around the inlet ducts and fuel tanks, the tailplane actuator in the fin, and the ancillary equipment moved into the dorsal spine to make room elsewhere.

Above: Head locked firmly into the radar hood, and ears cocked for GCI instructions, were standard procedure for a successful interception in this Polish MiG-21PFM. The small optical sight was for back-up use only.

target's engine, in order to guide correctly.

Faired into the lower fuselage of the MiG-21 were two Nudelman-Rikhter NR-30 cannon, of the type originally used on later production MiG-19s. A revolver cannon of the same general type as the British Aden, French Defa and US M-39, the NR-30 was a powerful weapon with a 14.4oz (410g) projectile, a 2,550ft/sec (780m/sec) muzzle velocity and a rate of fire between 850 and 1,000 rounds per minute. The projectile size, larger even than that of the A-10's fearsome GAU-8/A, is particularly notable.

The weapons were aimed with a simple gyroscopic gunsight, with range information provided by the small radar in the nose cone. The rest of the cockpit was equally simple. Beacon receivers were provided for navigation, but the main emphasis was on ground-to-air links through which the fighter could be vectored to its target. The ejection seat was a specially developed lightweight design, and was linked to the unusual one-piece, forward-hinged canopy; the hood separated from the aircraft with the seat, forming a screen against wind blast.

The first full-scale production version appeared in late 1959. The main change to the MiG-21F was the switch to an uprated engine, the R-11F, with about 10 per cent more power. A number of other significant changes, however, were incorporated in the early stages of production, including a broader-chord fin for improved stability at high Mach numbers. Most MiG-21Fs possessed only one gun, the port NR-30 being removed. It is quite possible that the space was needed for datalink equipment, or for another system displaced by the introduction of the new VHF device.

Airbrake location

Another change during MiG-21F production was the incorporation of two extra airbrakes beneath the fuselage, level with the leading edge, augmenting the original small airbrake ahead of the ventral fin. Three separate airbrakes for a small fighter may seem a lot, but, it seems that one of the requirements common to all Soviet combat aircraft is that extending the airbrakes must not disturb the aircraft in pitch. Neither are brakes allowed to displace the central pylon. The result is that there are few good locations for a single large airbrake, and Soviet fighters tend to have two or more oddly positioned airbrake panels.

The MiG-21F was found to have solved most of the problems of the original MiG-21, and went into large-scale production at Gorkii. The type was also built in Czechoslovakia, at the Aero plant near Prague; the Czech-built aircraft were distinguished by the absence of rear-vision panels behind their canopies. In April 1963, the first batch of ten MiG-21Fs arrived in Finland, and the Western myth of the 30,000lb (13,600kg) MiG-21 was finally exploded.

In addition, a number of MiG-21Fs were supplied to China in early 1960, before the rapid deterioration of Sino-Soviet relations which started later in that year. All technical assistance had been cut off by the end of 1960, but the MiG-21s, their engines and their missiles were rapidly dissected and reverse-engineered at the Xian State Aircraft Factory. The first Chinese-built aircraft, designated Xian J-7, was flown in December 1964; the R-11F engine was copied at Shenyang as the WP-7B. In the late 1960s, production was suspended, but output resumed following the political changes of the late 1970s.

Recent J-7s, such as the 80 aircraft delivered to Egypt from 1982 onward, incorporate a number of changes, including a conventional rearward-hinged canopy with a separate three-piece windshield, and a small radar warning receiver in a bullet at the base of the rudder. Other J-7s have reportedly been assembled in Egypt and passed on to Iraq.

The MiG-21F corresponded very closely to the 1953 specification; the problem was that the specification itself did not realistically reflect operational needs. By the time the aircraft entered service, it was realised that the limitations of the unaided human eye made a search-and-track radar not merely a desirable option for a high-altitude supersonic interceptor, but a complete necessity unless ground control was extremely tight and accurate. By the time the MiG-21F entered service, design and testing of the radar-equipped second-generation MiG-21 was well under way.

The chosen radar was the R1L, known to NATO as 'Spin Scan' and providing some 100kW of power in I-band, and taking its name from its spiral scanning pattern. Originally designed for the much larger Su-9 'Fishpot-A' interceptor, the R1L represented a substantial item of equipment for a fighter as small as the MiG-21, and incorporating it without loss of performance was a challenge.

The response to the challenge was to develop a new forward fuselage, probably incorporating many of the lessons learned in the difficult development of the original MiG-21 inlet. A very similar inlet was tested on a modified MiG-19, the SM-12PM, in 1957-58. The new nose was almost untapered, and the inlet was greatly increased in diameter. The capture area was unchanged, being dictated by the engine mass flow; the central cone could therefore be large enough to house the radar antenna. The fact that the cone was larger in relation to the inlet also improved its aerodynamic efficiency, particularly at high speed. The cone slid forward between Mach 1 and Mach 1.2, so as to spill the primary shock past the inlet.

Radar cooling

Another new feature was a narrow annular slot girdling the cone, directly behind the radome. This bled the turbulent boundary layer off the surface of the cone, further improving efficiency. The airflow through the slot was used to cool the radar electronics, mounted in a single pack behind the antenna, before being exhausted through vents above and below the nose. However, cooling airflow was cut off at speeds above Mach 1.2, as the cone slid forward.

Installation of the radar displaced the systems which had previously been fitted ahead of the cockpit, and in order to add internal volume, the designers exploited their understanding of the Area Rule. In place of the minimal dorsal spine, which on the MiG-21F covered the control runs, the OKB extended the top and sill lines of the canopy further aft, providing space for extra equipment. The result was to smooth out the variation of cross-section over the length of the aircraft, reducing drag at Mach 1.2 by 20 per cent and causing no increase in drag at higher speeds, though it did diminish rearward visibility from the cockpit.

The recontoured fuselage was tested on a prototype aircraft, designated Ye-66A, which was also fitted with a belly pack containing a 6,500lb (3,000kg) thrust U-2 liquid-fuel rocket engine and

Below: The spartan cockpit of a MiG-21MF. Note the robust ejection handles and the reliable, low-maintenance toggle switches, protected by metal rings from inadvertent operation.

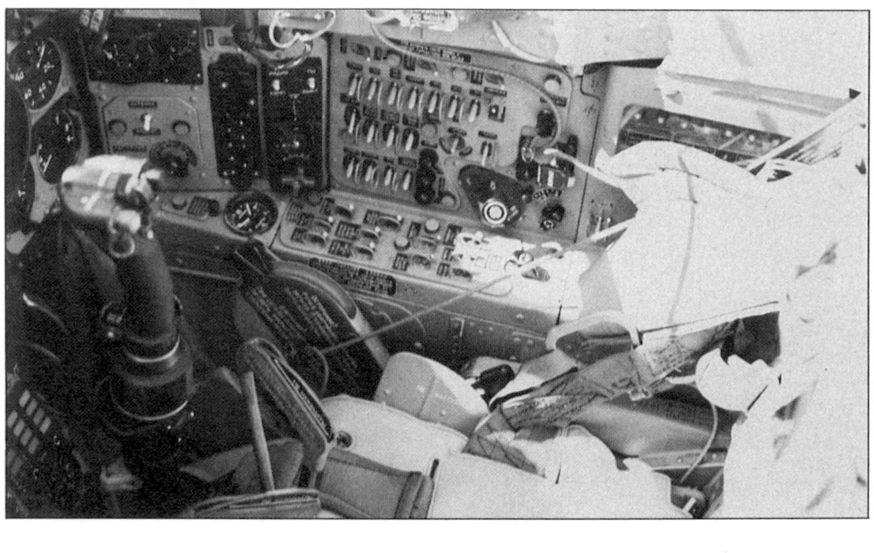

Right: The multi-role MiG-21MF had a less obtrusive radar display than the pure interceptor versions. The prominent master caution panel, above and to the right of the radar scope, is also noteworthy.

MiG-21 stores options

1 AA-2-2 'Advanced Atoll' radar-guided air-to-air missile (compatible with 'Jay Bird' radar)
2 UB-16-57 rocket pod
3 57mm rockets
4 500kg general-purpose bomb (a total of 48 types of free-fall bomb, including nuclear, napalm, chemical and fuel-air explosive types, are qualified for use on the MiG-21)
5 108Imp gal (490lit) drop tank; 176Imp gal (800lit) and 286Imp gal (1,300lit) tanks also available
6 GP-9 pack (GSh-23 gun and ammunition)
7 23mm ammunition (normal load 200rds)
8 Reconnaissance pod with forward plus three lateral oblique cameras, IR linescan printer and ECM chaff dispenser
9 AA-8 'Aphid' IR-homing air-to-air missile
10 AA-2 'Atoll' IR-homing air-to-air missile
11 ECM jammer pod

MiG-21 weapons provision and avionics

1 GSh-23 cannon with 200rds ammunition
2 Centreline pylon, capacity 500kg (1,100lb)
3 Inboard wing pylon, capacity 250kg (550lb)
4 Outboard wing pylon
5 'Spin Scan' radar
6 'Odd Rods' IFF antennas
7 Main avionics bay
8 HF notch antenna, ILS
9 Radar altimeter
10 VHF/UHF antenna
11 Radar warning receiver
12 VHF communications and data link antenna

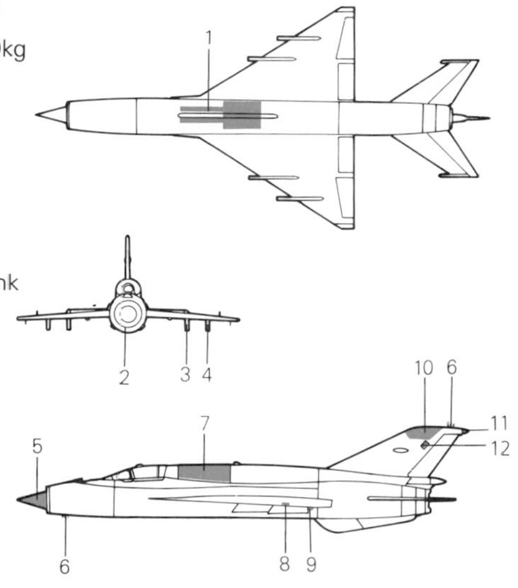

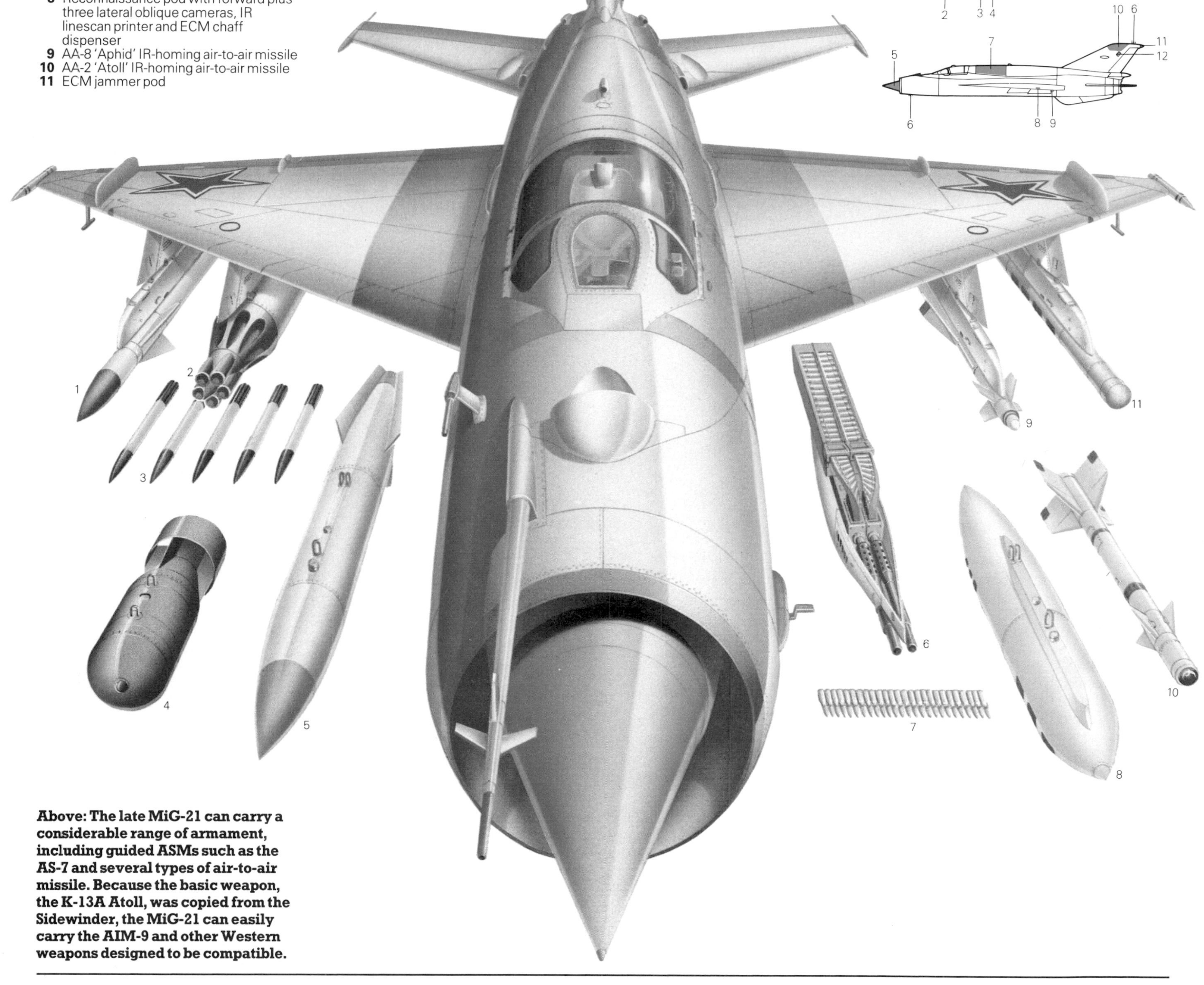

Above: The late MiG-21 can carry a considerable range of armament, including guided ASMs such as the AS-7 and several types of air-to-air missile. Because the basic weapon, the K-13A Atoll, was copied from the Sidewinder, the MiG-21 can easily carry the AIM-9 and other Western weapons designed to be compatible.

Left: The unguided rocket has been a favourite Soviet weapon since the 1940s, providing great firepower and reasonable accuracy without sophisticated aiming systems. This is a UB-16 pod (16 S-5 57mm rockets).

its propellant tank. There is no sign that this layout was being considered for production, but it was used to probe the speed and height limits of the design and set an official world altitude record of 113,891ft (34,714m) on April 28, 1961.

The new version – which flew around 1959, as the Ye-7 – also dispensed with the remaining gun and the corresponding bulges, simplifying the design of the forward airbrakes. Despite the removal of the guns, it was heavier than the MiG-21F, and required larger mainwheels and brakes, evidenced by slightly larger bulges in the fuselage; powerplant was the R-11-F2S, with a slightly higher augmented rating to retain high-speed performance at higher weights. The new aircraft entered production in 1961, as the MiG-21PF, and was codenamed 'Fishbed-D' by NATO.

Another new version, appearing at about the same time, was the MiG-21UTI conversion trainer. The airframe was a mixture of features, with the MiG-21F inlet – the trainer had no need for radar – the larger mainwheels of the MiG-21PF, and the pitot boom above the inlet as on the later all-weather fighter. The instructor's cockpit replaced a large part of the MiG-21's internal fuel capacity, so the

Above: The spine profile identifies this aircraft as a MiG-21bis, known to NATO as 'Fishbed-L'. This aircraft has a similar gunsight to the MiG-21MF; later versions have a true head-up display.

MiG-21UTI – 'Mongol-A' to NATO – had only a short endurance.

The MiG-21PF launched a rapid-fire process of development, in which the production configuration seemed to change almost every year. The history of the type, from this point, resembles a Russian novel: there are dozens of characters, each with a number of different names. In this case, the nomenclature is complicated by the NATO designation system, which reflects external changes rather than internal differences.

A PF development incorporating a further increase in fin chord, probably compensating for the larger nose, made its appearance in 1964. Just before that, it appears, the braking parachute was moved from the rear of the ventral fin to an acorn fairing at the base of the dorsal fin. In most aircraft, the tip of the fin incorporated a large plastic tip insert. The significance of this was that it covered the antenna for a high-capacity VHF communications and data link, known in various versions as ARL-S, RSIU and, in the West, Markham.

MiG-21PF 'Fishbed-E'

The importance of this data link was that it allowed the MiG-21 to be steered by ground controllers towards its target, whch in a high-speed intercept would be out of sight until the final seconds of an engagement. This version was regarded by the Soviet Union simply as a MiG-21PF, but was designated 'Fishbed-E' by NATO. The MiG-21US 'Mongol-B' was a trainer version with a similar fin.

The late-production MiG-21PF was quickly followed by two new versions, each of which introduced a single important change. The MiG-21PFS featured plain flaps, blown by air bled from the engine, in place of the original Fowler flaps. Takeoff performance may have suffered slightly, but the new arrangement reduced the approach and landing speed, and shortened the landing run. About the same time, a short-takeoff capability was added, by making provision for booster rockets on the sides of

Above: Standard MiG-21MF of the Soviet Air Force. One of the most widely produced single variants, the MiG-21MF was regarded as a true multi-purpose aircraft capable of air combat and strike missions.

Below: Another MiG-21MF, photographed on the same occasion as the example illustrated above. An unusual feature of these individuals is that the inboard wing pylons have been removed.

Right: Two MiG-21MFs in long-range trim with three external tanks. The 'wet' outer pylons of the third-generation MiG-21s added some 30 per cent to the maximum usable fuel capacity of the type.

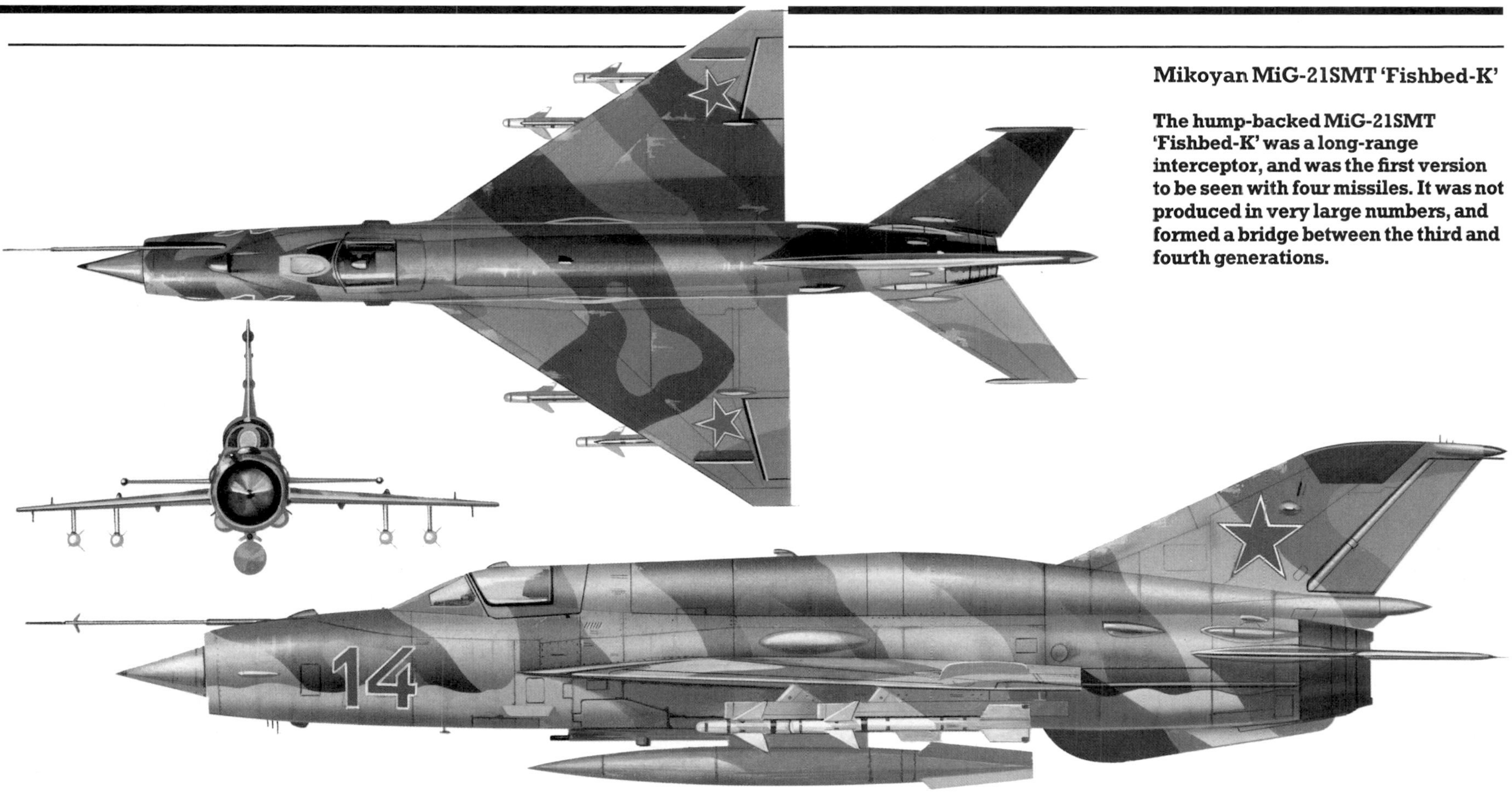

Mikoyan MiG-21SMT 'Fishbed-K'

The hump-backed MiG-21SMT 'Fishbed-K' was a long-range interceptor, and was the first version to be seen with four missiles. It was not produced in very large numbers, and formed a bridge between the third and fourth generations.

the fuselage. As this version was virtually indistinguishable from its predecessor, it was also known as 'Fishbed-E' in the NATO system.

The late-production MiG-21PF formed the basis of the first MiG-21 variant to be built in India. Designated MiG-21FL, it was a combination of old and new features, with the MiG-21PF airframe and the uprated R-11-F2S-300 engine (see below). Like other export versions of the aircraft, it carried the R2L 'Spin Scan-B' radar, a cheaper and less capable modification of the R1L designed for exports and wartime production. It entered production at Hindustan Aeronautics Limited's specially built Nasik plant, near Bombay, around 1967-68, while the R-11 was built at Koraput. The HAL-built aircraft were also equipped to take a locally manufactured ventral pack housing a GSh-23 cannon (see below) and 150 rounds of ammunition; the pack was attached to the centreline pylon.

Observed at almost the same time as the PFS was the MiG-21PFM, distinguished by its conventional, separate windshield and sideways-hinged canopy and known to NATO as 'Fishbed-F'. It is probable that the main reason for the change was to improve the effectiveness of the ejection system; the time required to hinge the canopy forwards, as opposed to blowing it off, and the delay while the seat and canopy separated, must have increased the minimum safe altitude for ejection. The PFM is also thought to have introduced the R-11-F2S-300, with a further 5 per cent thrust increase.

The next phase in development almost certainly reflected combat experience in Vietnam. The MiG-21PF had proved useful, but the MiG-17 had been, if anything, more successful; the more modern fighter had a poor endurance, its radar was not good enough to be a major improvement, and – crucially – it had no guns. The solution to many of these problems was found in a quite extensive redesign of the MiG-21, which began to enter service in 1968.

The basic airframe of the new MiG-21PFMA was similar to that of the PFM. The dorsal spine, however, was enlarged once again with a straight top line and a wider base; this change was not hard to implement, since the dorsal spine is a secondary fairing structure, added to the fuselage in the last stages of construction. The spine is not believed to contain any fuel, with the possible exception of a small header tank to provide the engine with a back-up gravity feed. Instead, the spine is used to contain avionics and ancillary equipment, possibly including a gas- or battery-powered emergency power unit.

The other main external change on the PFMA was the addition of an extra pylon under each wing. These could be used for weapons, but were also plumbed to accept the same 108gal (490lit) tanks as the centreline pylon. The PFMA could therefore carry twice as much ordnance as earlier versions, or could be configured with a much greater operational radius.

Most PFMAs featured another significant change: the return of the internal gun. This was the GSh-23, successfully developed within extremely tight restrictions on space and weight. Its design was based on the Gast principle, devised in Germany during the 1939-45 war; it incorporated two side-by-side barrels, with their firing mechanisms coupled by a horizontal rocker arm so that the recoil energy of one barrel was used to cock and fire the other one.

The system was extremely light, weighing only 130lb (60kg) without ammunition, required no external power and imposed low recoil forces on the airframe. Together with 200 rounds of 23mm high-explosive/incendiary ammunition, it fitted neatly into a small space in the belly of the MiG-21. The equipment previously housed in that position – possibly a battery, or the oxygen system – was presumably relocated in the enlarged spine. Because of the weapon's small size, the ventral drop tank could still be carried; the splayed-out ammunition chutes protruding from the gun-pack kept the spent cases away from the tank. Another external feature associated with the gun was the small strake beneath each blow-in auxiliary inlet, designed to prevent the ingestion of gun gas.

GSh-23 performance

The GSh-23 was also notable for the shortness of its twin barrels. In gun design, a key parameter is the barrel length expressed as a multiple of the calibre. The Gsh-23 barrels are only 40 calibres long, while most aircraft cannon measure 70 calibres or more. The statistics for the GSh-23, as reported in the West, appear to be impressive: the weapon fires a 6.35oz (180g) projectile and is said to have an 'effective range' of 2,950-3,300ft (950-1,000m) and a 3,000rds/min rate of fire. But its true effectiveness is hard to assess without knowing its muzzle velocity, which must be limited by its barrel length, and dispersion, both of which are crucial in determining the amount of energy that the gun can put on to its target. In any event, the combat record of the later MiG-21s does not appear to show the substantial proportion of gun kills that show up in Western claims of the same period.

Codenamed 'Fishbed-J' by NATO, this third-generation development of the MiG-21 was also produced in India, as the MiG-21M; production at Nasik started in 1970. In the Soviet Union, however, it was quite rapidly superseded by the MiG-21MF, powered by the new Tumansky R-13-300. An increase of nearly 20 per cent in unreheated thrust, coupled with a slight reduction in engine weight – probably achieved through the greater use of titanium alloys – significantly improved the fighter's all-round performance, and probably made the full five-pylon capacity more useful in practical operations. To NATO, the MiG-21M and MiG-21MF were also 'Fishbed-J', being externally similar to the MiG-21PFMA. The MiG-21UM 'Mongol-C' was the trainer equivalent.

Avionics changes on the MiG-21MF included a modified R1L radar operating in J-band, and accordingly named 'Jay Bird' by NATO. It probably included a ranging function for use with the GSh-23. The MiG-21MF also featured an improved air-data system – evidenced by a yaw-rate sensor on the nose boom and a pitch sensor on the port side of the nose – which may have been associated with newly introduced autostabilization equipment or a simple bomb-aiming computer.

The third-generation MiG-21 was also adapted for the tactical reconnaissance role, in a number of slightly different versions; like snowflakes, no two seem to be quite alike, and NATO sidesteps the issue by referring to them all generically as 'Fishbed-H'. One version, designated MiG-21R and operated by Egypt, features a camera pack built into the belly, replacing the GSh-23 installation and other avionics behind the nosewheel bay. The pack contains oblique and vertical cameras.

Another type is operated by Soviet and Warsaw Pact forces, and is believed

Below: Points of interest on the very powerful R-25 engine – this is a HAL-built example – include the neatly packaged accessories and the engine's simplicity: there is no variable geometry whatsoever.

Below: The rear fuselage of the MiG-21bis, looking aft from the transport break joint. Auxiliary air ducts are visible. Note the deeper, stronger frames around the final jetpipe, which carry the tailplane loads.

Bottom: The MiG-21bis line at Nasik. Note that the spine is one of the last elements added to the basic fuselage structure, which is common to all MiG-21s. An in-service MiG-21M is being overhauled on the left.

to be designated MiG-21RF; it carries an external reconnaissance pod on the centreline pylon and different pods configured for optical and electronic reconnaissance have been observed. It has no gun and no anti-ingestion strakes, and a conduit connects the gun-bay area with the sensor pod. Small antennas, probably connected with an electronic support measures (ESM) listening system, are fitted to the wingtips. A large antenna is built into the dorsal spine, and is probably a downlink through which real-time information can be transmitted to a ground station or relay aircraft; this capability has been attributed to the MiG-21RF by USAF sources.

The last of the third-generation MiG-21s was something of an oddity. Observed in 1971, it was readily distinguished by a still fatter dorsal spine, which now sported a slightly convex top line peaking level with the wing trailing edge. The hunchbacked aircraft was the MiG-21SMT, known to NATO as 'Fishbed-K', and there is no reasonable doubt that the MiG-21SMT's spine contains extra fuel, to extend the range of the aircraft. Despite this attempt at curing one of the type's main shortcomings, the MiG-21SMT was not exported outside the Soviet Union, and was replaced in production by models which approximated to the earlier aerodynamic shape.

The explanation probably lay in changing requirements. The MiG-21PFMA was equipped to carry a four-missile armament, but in fact it very seldom did so in service, and neither did the MiG-21MF. The likely reason was that the weight and drag of the extra missiles reduced the fighter's endurance, which was short enough in any case, to an unacceptable level, and the SMT was designed to rectify the situation. The internal layout of the spine is not known, but it is likely that avionics and ancillary equipment were installed in the forward part, with some 60-100gal (270-450lit) of extra fuel to the rear. Given the normal rule of thumb that half the fuel in an external tank is used to propel the tank through the air, the SMT's extra internal fuel was roughly equivalent to the two extra tanks that could be carried by the MiG-21PFMA and subsequent aircraft.

In any case, the MiG-21SMT was the first version of the type to be depicted carrying four missiles; the outboard pair were usually of a new type, known as the AA-2-2 'Advanced Atoll' and combining the standard AA-2 airframe and motor with a semi-active radar-homing guidance system. In theory, the AA-2-2 could function outside visual range, but in practice is more likely to have been designed for use outside the IR missile's effective envelope, in beam or collision-course attacks. A similar variant of the Sidewinder, the AIM-9C, was developed in the USA, but enjoyed little success, being withdrawn from service before it was used in combat. Whether the AA-2-2 is more useful is not known.

The modifications to the MiG-21SMT may have adversely affected the speed or manoeuvrability of the aircraft. However, it was outside factors that would shape the development of the MiG-21 family in the early 1970s. The USAF had digested its own Vietnam lessons, and was developing the new F-15. The McDonnell Douglas fighter promised great advances in flight perform-

Right: A Soviet MiG-21bis 'Fishbed-L', seen here with its optional armament of two IR-homing AA-2 'Atoll' and two radar-homing AA-2-2 'Advanced Atoll' air-to-air missiles.

Mikoyan MiG-21Mbis 'Fishbed-N'

The most heavily armed MiG-21bis variant carries AA-2-2s outboard and AA-8s inboard. This aircraft carries no centreline tank, suggesting a very short mission radius.

Above: The arrival of MiG-21Fs in Cuba in November 1962, revealed in this USAF reconnaissance photo, pushed US-Soviet relations closer to the crisis point, despite the limited capacity of those aircraft.

Above: Nearly a quarter-century later, MiG-21s in Cuba were still regarded as a threat. This reconnaissance photo of San Julian airfield was released by the US State Department in early 1985.

Below: Despite its poor quality, this photograph, released by the US DoD and State Department in March 1985, shows that Cuba has received the updated MiG-21bis, with its generally improved combat capability.

Below: A once-unthinkable formation: an F-16 and an A-10 of Tactical Air Command with a MiG-21 and a MiG-15UTI. The Soviet aircraft are in Egyptian service; the occasion was the Bright Star 82 joint exercise.

ance, and would pose a significant threat to Soviet airpower. Meanwhile, the MiG-23 was being prepared for service, and would be available in large quantities from 1971-72. The MiG-23 had excellent range, even with four missiles, but was not as agile as the MiG-21.

Apparently, the Soviet armed forces decided to field a mixed force of MiG-23s assigned to the long-range fighter and escort missions, and MiG-21s dedicated to the tactical air defence role. Extended range was no longer a priority for the MiG-21, but higher performance and improved equipment were desirable. The result was the fourth and final generation of MiG-21s.

The final generation

The first of these was the MiG-21bis, which entered production in the early 1970s, but which was not publicly reported until 1978, when it was offered to Finland. The MiG-21bis resembles the MiG-21MF very closely, and it requires careful scrutiny to see that the dorsal spine has been modified once again, reducing drag and accommodating a larger header tank. Internally, too, the airframe is reported to be revised and strengthened, increasing internal fuel capacity, and the avionics are improved. It is known to NATO as 'Fishbed-L'.

The new model was closely followed by the very similar MiG-21Mbis 'Fishbed-N' (the '-M' suffix is not used; because of possible confusion), distinguished by two small antennas, each resembling a miniature bow and arrow, on the nose and tail; these are usually stated to be associated with a new instrument landing system, standard on all Soviet

types in the 1970s and known as 'Swift Rod.'

The most important change, however, was introduced after the MiG-21bis had entered production: the use of a completely new engine, the Tumansky R-25. Originally believed to be rated at 16,500lb (7,500kg) thrust, it is now known to produce over 19,800lb (9,000kg) with full afterburner, 36 per cent more than the R-13; the lightweight MiG-21bis, therefore, has only 20 per cent less thrust than the much larger F-16. The R-25 has the highest thrust/weight ratio of any pure-jet engine in service, being no heavier than the R-13.

The thrust increase has been made possible by a number of changes. The R-25 appears to have one more compressor stage than the R-11 and R-13; the mechanical and aerodynamic design of the compressor has been improved, and more advanced materials have presumably been used. Unreheated thrust is probably some 20 per cent higher than that of the R-13-300. The augmentor, however, is completely new, and gives the new engine an augmentation ratio (the ratio of augmented thrust to dry thrust) of 1.5:1, compared with 1.3:1 for the R-13. The new augmentor is also claimed to provide better handling at high altitude.

Left: MiG-21PFs were the main subtype used in North Vietnam; had a cannon-equipped version been available earlier, the Vietnamese pilots might have been even more successful in air-to-air combat against their USAF and US Navy adversaries.

The late-model MiG-21bis has a revised cockpit, with a head-up display (HUD) replacing the prominent head-down scope of earlier versions. It also carries the R-60 (known to NATO as the AA-8 'Aphid') missile originally developed for the MiG-23. The R-60 is an unusual weapon, optimized for high-g manoeuvrability rather than range; it is much smaller than the AA-2 or Sidewinder. It is not believed to have an all-aspect capability, but its high agility gives it an expanded firing envelope against manoeuvring targets at short range. Paired with the radar-guided AA-2-2, it makes up an effective armament combination.

In 1979 the MiG-21bis and R-25 entered production in India, and about 120 had been built by 1984. Indian sources officially describe the aircraft as 'the last of the MiG-21 series'; there has been no sign of any further development of the MiG-21 in the Soviet Union, and production of the type is declining in favour of newer fighters. Quite possibly, the Xian J-7 will be the last member of the family in production by 1986-87.

Exactly how many MiG-21s were built is hard to assess, but there is little doubt that the total has easily topped the record of just over 5,000 set by the F-4 Phantom. A study of the size of the world-wide MiG-21 fleet – which probably peaked at about 5,000 aircraft in the mid-1970s – combined with some allowance for combat losses, attrition and the replacement of obsolete variants, suggests that about 6,500-7,000 MiG-21s of all types have been built in the Soviet Union. HAL has built about 400, and a similar quantity of 'bootlegged' J-7s have come out of the Xian facility. Czech production was probably on a smaller scale, with perhaps 200 aircraft being delivered in the early 1960s. The grand total of 7,500-8,000 deliveries makes the MiG-21 the most widely built of all supersonic combat aircraft.

'MiG diplomacy'

It was the MiG-21 that brought the phrase 'MiG diplomacy' into the international lexicon. Many newly independent or post-revolutionary countries received a small unit of MiG-21s at a subsidized price, on excellent terms and with payment in their own currency. Many saw little, if any, use: Indonesia's MiG-21Fs lay idle for many years after a political rift interrupted the spares supply. The type was, however, standard equipment for Middle Eastern and North African allies of the Soviet Union, and in most cases still made up the bulk of their fleets in 1985. Neither was 'MiG diplomacy' quite dead: the mere rumour that MiG-21s were on their way to Nicaragua in late 1983 caused a US reaction which, in the opinion of some observers, would have been more appropriate for the arrival of a regiment of Backfires.

The MiG-21 has been delivered to more nations than any other supersonic fighter, and has fought in virtually every major conflict since it entered service. Western assessments of its qualities have varied widely: at times, it has been condemned as being useless for any mission more demanding than the Liberation Day flypast; at other times, it has been used as a reference point for an

Egyptian Air Force Mig-21PF 'Fishbed-D'

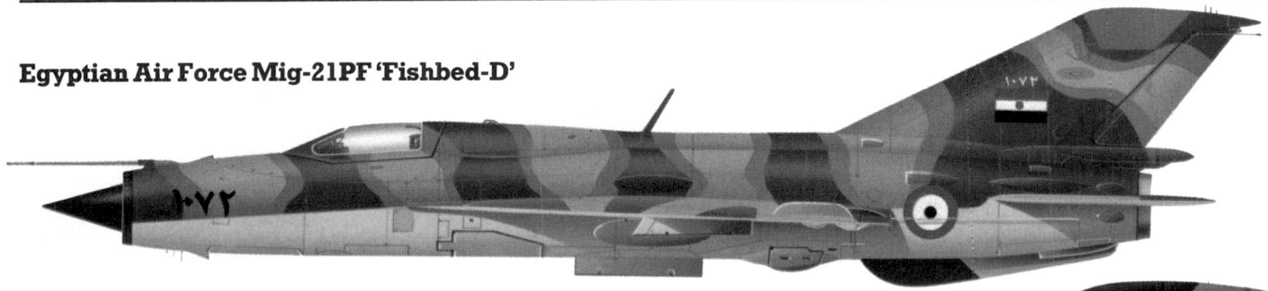

Egyptian Air Force MiG-21PF 'Fishbed-E'

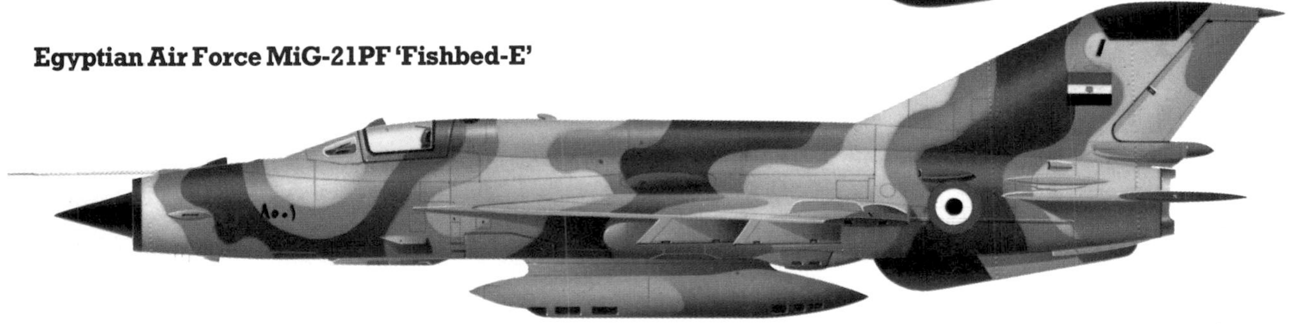

Egyptian Air Force MiG-21RF 'Fishbed-H'

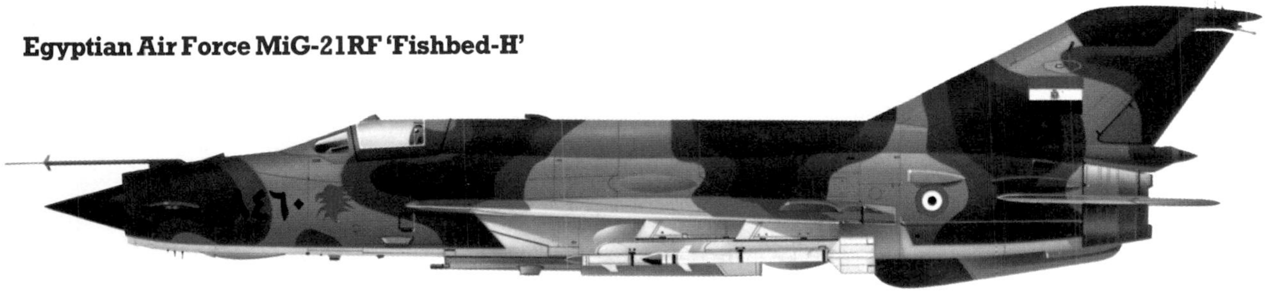

Egyptian Air Force MiG-21MF 'Fishbed-J'

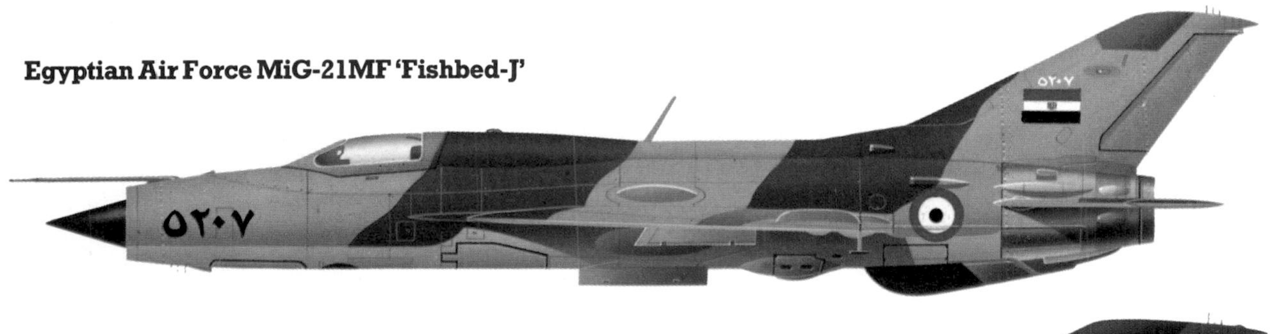

North Vietnamese Air Force MiG-21PFMA 'Fishbed-J'

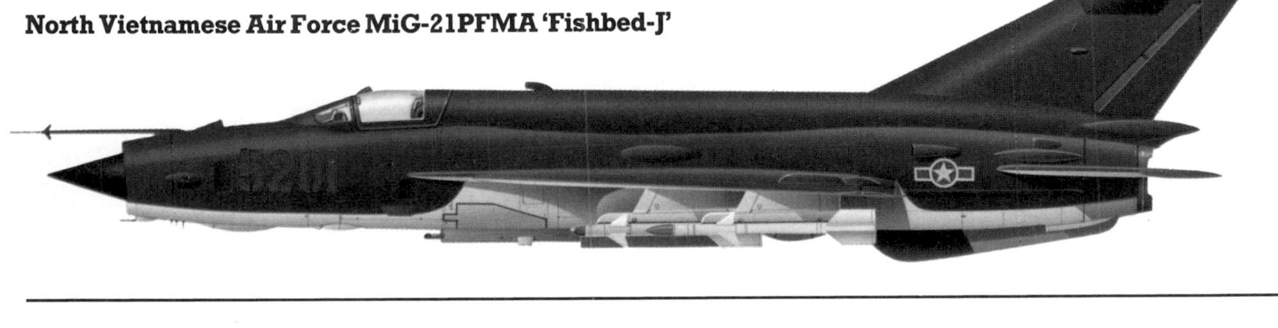

Left: The MiG-21 is the world's most widely built and widely used supersonic fighter. Egypt, in particular, has used nine different subtypes, while those supplied to North Vietnam saw extensive action.

Right: Non-Soviet pilots have praised the MiG-21 for its straightforward handling and ruggedness. In this ground-to-air photograph an Indian pilot shows off a specially marked display aircraft.

Above: Soviet Air Force MiG-21PFs participating in the 1967 Aviation Day display at Domodedovo.

Above right: The MiG-21 configuration was adapted for a series of larger aircraft, culminating in the Ye-166 testbed for high-Mach propulsion technology.

entire generation of fighter development. The truth does not lie between these two viewpoints, because both of them are accurate.

If flight performance and handling make a fighter, the MiG-21 has stayed near the top of the heap for more than two decades. The design has no basic handling vices, and can be pushed to its aerodynamic limits without courting a violent departure from controlled flight. This is mainly due to the delta wing, which is highly resistant to stalling; instead of suffering an abrupt break-up of the airflow, leading to the loss of aileron control, a sudden wing drop and a spin, the delta can exploit this attribute to a greater extent than a conventional tailless configuration. Because of its long tail arm, it is more stable in yaw and has more control power in pitch. Another reason for the MiG-21's tractability and tolerance of abuse is the nose inlet, which is free from all airframe effects and feeds the engine efficiently even at high angles of attack.

Handling limitations

The main limitation on handling is that the drag of the delta builds up much more quickly than the lift, so the MiG-21 must lose either speed or height when it pulls a sharp manoeuvre. At Mach 0.9 and 15,000ft (4,570m), even the F-4E can sustain a turn rate 20 per cent faster than the MiG-21MF, and the F-16 and F-15 are in a completely different class. However, the MiG-21's instantaneous turn rate – the highest rate it can generate, irrespective of whether it loses speed or height – is virtually equal to that of the F-4E at Mach 0.9, and much better at Mach 0.5, at which speed the MiG-21 can use its flaps to improve its manoeuvre performance. Clearly, the answer for the MiG pilot is to avoid long tailchases, and concentrate on manoeuvres that combine abrupt turns with the opportunity to accelerate rapidly up to fighting speed. With the MiG-21bis – which has a thrust/weight ratio in the same class as the F-15 and F-16, combined with a low-drag airframe – this would be a particularly attractive tactic.

It should be noted, moreover, that the slatted F-4E, the F-15 and F-16 are by no means true contemporaries of the MiG-21. Direct contemporaries included the F-104 and Mirage, which were very much less manoeuvrable than the MiG, and the early F-4, which was subject to a highly dangerous stall-spin departure if flown beyond its limits.

Pilots have described the MiG-21 as a straightforward aircraft to fly. It seldom earns the description 'pleasant', probably because it has a rather basic artificial-feel system which leads to uncomfortably high stick forces. While there is autostabilization in pitch and roll, the pilot is mainly kept within the operating envelope by the artificial feel system, which provides very high stick forces at high airspeeds. One point in favour of the aircraft is the simplicity of its systems, which make the piloting task less complicated. Of all supersonic fighters, the MiG-21 is probably best suited to the inexperienced pilot.

Low-speed handling is particularly good. The ailerons remain effective down to 130kt (240km/h), and the usual touchdown speed is about 140-145kt (260-270km/h). With the brake parachute used immediately on landing, the MiG-21 stops after a 1,320ft (400m) roll, providing a comfortable margin even on a short runway.

But flight performance and handling are not everything. The MiG-21's best known drawback is basic to the design and resistant to easy fixes. Because of several design features – the minimal cross-section, the small volume of the wing and the location of the engine – virtually all the fuel is well ahead of the centre of gravity. As the fuel is burned, the aircraft becomes progressively

Right: One modified MiG-21PFM airframe became the 'Fishbed-G', a low-speed, fixed-gear testbed for the jet-lift Stol concept and a predecessor of the 'Faithless' Stol fighter. Note down elevator on the approach.

Below: In the early 1970s, the MiG-21MF was considered mature enough to let Western observers close to it, and it was used on goodwill exchange visits to France and Sweden. This gave the West its first close look at a Soviet combat aircraft – albeit a type which was no longer at the technological forefront.

more tail-heavy, until the centre of gravity passes outside limits and the aircraft becomes susceptible to a sudden, out-of-control pitch-up.

The severity of the problem varies from subtype to subtype; the R-13-powered aircraft, with a lighter engine may be better off than the R-11-powered variants. Another factor may be piloting skill and qualifications – Soviet instructors probably teach foreign students to stay well away from the danger zone. However, the CG problem makes between 110 and 175gal (500-800lit) of the less than generous 570gal (2,540 lit) capacity unusable, and severely restricts the aircraft's endurance.

The other main problem is the spartan simplicity of the fighter's systems. As delivered, even the MiG-21MF lacked any navigation system other than a compass and basic beacon receivers, its gunsight toppled at 2.75g and it had no system for aiming bombs with any degree of accuracy. The 'Jay Bird' radar has a range of only 20 miles (32lm), and is masked by ground clutter below 3,000ft (915m) altitude. The MiG-21bis has a better cockpit, but still uses the antiquated 'Jay Bird' radar.

Western weapons and systems

A solution adopted by a number of operators has been to retrofit MiG-21s with improved systems, and Egypt, estranged from the Soviet Union, has gone farthest in this direction. The first step, in 1982, was to replace the K-13. This missile – at least in its export-standard model – is not the best of IR-homing weapons, and the Egyptian Air Force reckons to have doubled the effectiveness of its fleet by fitting the AIM-9P3 Sidewinder. (The AIM-9P3, too, is an export-standard weapon, and is not as capable as the legend-in-its-time AIM-9L.) Iraq has followed suit, clearing its MiG-21s to fire the Matra 550 Magic. Meanwhile, Egypt's MiG-21MFs are being further upgraded with the Emerson APQ-159 radar, similar to that of the F-5E, British GEC Avionics head-up displays, and provision for the medium-range AIM-7F Sparrow missile. Emerson is prime contractor, and the first modified aircraft was due to start ground tests in mid-1985, and to fly in early 1986.

Ferranti and Smiths Industries have also developed combined head-up display and weapon-aiming computer systems (Hudwacs) for retrofit to small combat aircraft, including the MiG-21. Most such contracts are regarded as highly confidential; however, India is definitely a target, and China is offering the J-7M, a J-7 with British avionics. Ferranti has announced a new radar named Red Fox, designed to replace 'Jay Bird'. A repack-

aged version of the Sea Harrier FRS.1 radar, Red Fox would provide much better air-to-air performance, and could also be used for air-to-sea search. There is even a possibility of an entire engine change, both the GE F404 and the PW1120 having been studied. However, this would be very expensive, as either engine probably costs more than a new J-7.

One final attribute of the MiG-21 is its sheer ease of operation. It embodies the Soviet philosophy of simplicity and ruggedness; nothing on the aircraft is not absolutely essential, and considerable attention has been given to ensuring that routine flight-line activities such as re-arming and inspection are easy, and require a minimum of equipment. The fighter is regarded as highly reliable, and can be turned round between missions in ten minutes.

The best way of summing up the MiG-21 is probably to say that it has a mix of good and bad qualities, but that it carries them to greater extremes than most other fighters. In combat, it has been demonstrated that the MiG-21 is very effective when the situation permits tactics which exploit its good attributes, but suffers severely when the tables are turned and the adversary's tactics are aimed at its weak spots.

India and Vietnam

The first potential use of the MiG-21 in combat was a non-event. India had received six MiG-21Fs in February 1963, followed by another 24 aircraft in 1964-65, but when war broke out between India and Pakistan in September 1965, only 10 aircraft were believed to be operational. The use of the MiG-21 was sporadic, and the only reported encounter involved a Pakistan Air Force F-104 which encountered four MiG-21s when at the limit of its endurance. The PAF pilot used the F-104's speed to outrun the MiG-21s on the deck. The Indian Air Force also tried to intercept the PAF's single RB-57F reconnaissance-bomber, but its high altitude frustrated their efforts.

The Vietnam theatre, where the MiG-21PF arrived at the end of 1965, was near-ideal for the Soviet fighter. The mission was air defence over a relatively small area, and the fighters were working within a Soviet-supplied system that also included acquisition radars, surface-to-air missiles and the control systems to tie them all together. The MiG pilots were scrambled as needed, and vectored accurately towards their targets by ground control. The US Air Force and Navy strike aircraft and escorts were operating at long range, and their endurance over the target was limited.

Other factors favoured the North Vietnamese pilots. The US pilots were not permitted to launch missiles without positive visual identification, a restriction which not only rendered the radar and medium-range missiles of the Phantom of little use, but if anything left the MiG-21 at an advantage; because the MiG-21 was smaller than the F-4, and had a less smoky engine, the MiG-21 pilot could visually identify an F-4 long before an F-4 pilot could identify the MiG. The MiG pilots also had quite limited objectives. If they could jump the incoming strike aircraft and force them to dump their weapons, they had succeeded. Finally, as noted above, the MiG-21 was clearly superior in a close fight to the early F-4, having the edge in visibility and manoeuvrability, and the MiG-21 remained a dangerous adversary throughout the war.

Above: Yugoslav Air Force MiG-21PFMAs – the examples shown here are early models without an internal gun – in a tunnel-type underground hangar. More often, MiG-21s are protected by dispersal and their ability to use sod runways.

The inability to sustain air superiority over the theatre to the extent which had been possible in Korea came as a shock to the USAF, and had a number of consequences. The slatted wing of the F-4E was a short-term counter to the MiG-21; for smaller allied nations, the USAF launched development of the F-5E, designed to emulate the MiG-21's performance. Finally, air-to-air dogfight performance became the key parameter in the new US fighters of the 1970s.

Debut in the Middle East

The MiG-21's debut in the Middle East theatre was unexpectedly cancelled on June 6, 1967. Egypt's apparently formidable fleet of MiG-21s was a priority target for Israel's meticulously devastating air-strike that morning, and not one made it into the air. The aircraft were replaced by the end of 1968, and air battles resumed in March 1969. Seven Egyptian MiG-21s were claimed in a single battle in September 1969, and the Israeli Air Force began to make increasingly bold incursions into Egyptian airspace.

In late January the Soviet Union moved a complete Soviet-manned air defence organization into Egypt, including the new MiG-21MF 'Fishbed-J' fighters. The Soviet force, according to Israeli sources, included 72 MiG-21MFs drawn from Frontal Aviation assets in Hungary. Confrontation was inevitable, and the IAF launched attacks on Soviet radar and missile sites in early July. On July 30, two F-4s and two Mirages on an armed reconnaissance mission engaged a group of a dozen MiG-21MFs, claiming five kills without loss. The victory was ascribed to the lack of experience shown by the Soviet pilots, and to the Israelis' use of the new and secret Rafael Shafrir missile, then among the best weapons in its class. Compared to the contemporary export-model Sidewinder, or the K-13, the Shafrir was more reliable and could be fired over a wider manoeuvring envelope.

Right: India has both built and operated a variety of MiG-21s, including these HAL-built MiG-21Ms.

In the 1973 Middle East war, the EAF used its MiG-21s for close support, (armed with rockets and 550lb (250kg) bombs) as well as for battlefield air superiority. Because of the extensive use of SAMs, air combat was largely confined to very low altitudes and, very often, to low airspeeds. The MiG-21's low-speed performance was extensively used, and the gun was regarded as the main air-combat weapon – some early MiG-21PFMAs were retrofitted with the GSh-23 during the war. The EAF claimed to have held its own in the conflict, particularly in air-to-air actions, but – once again – the Shafrir was a powerful factor on the Israeli side.

Since 1973, the MiG-21 has been used in combat by Iraq, in the largely hidden war against Iran, and by Syria. The Syrian-Israeli conflicts will be discussed in the chapter on the MiG-23; to avoid repetition, it will suffice to say that the technical quality of the MiG-21 was not a major issue.

Overall, the MiG-21 has qualified itself as a classic design. Despite its age, it remains a very credible dogfighter. Even now, a late-model MiG-21, with updated electronics and effective weapons, could be one of the most cost-effective combat aircraft on the market.

Right: A mixed formation of two MiG-21R reconnaissance fighters (second and third from camera) and two escorting MiG-21MFs, all of the Egyptian Air Force.

Left: In October 1973, a MiG-21 is destroyed by cannon fire from an Israeli F-4E Phantom. Despite good performance on paper, the Soviet fighter's own gun has not proved as lethal as the M61 carried by later models of the F-4.

Below: A mortally hit Egyptian MiG-21 falls in view of Israeli tank crews in 1973. The Israeli forces have a firm respect for MiG fighters, and – perhaps because of this – have consistently maintained high kill-to-loss ratios in combat.

MiG-23/27 'Flogger'

Few fighters of the 1960s have been built in such large numbers as the very fast and predatory-looking MiG family of swing-wing fighters that carry the NATO codename 'Flogger'. With no direct equivalent in the West, the MiG-23 and MiG-27 represent a uniquely Soviet approach to the tactical fighter problem: powerful, quite large and remarkably simple to build in quantity. It was the last of these qualities that shocked the West, making the types far more readily affordable than any Western fighter of comparable capability, and allowing them to be deployed with unprecedented speed.

Above: A MiG-23M and flight-suited aircrew photographed at a base in the cis-Carpathian Military District. The aircraft carries a centreline fuel tank, with very little ground clearance on this version.

In the early 1960s, it seemed that almost every air arm in the world was taking delivery of new and advanced equipment. Genuine Mach 2 performance, the province of a very few aircraft in the late 1950s, was beginning to reach the squadrons. In the Frontal Aviation inventory, the MiG-21 was well established in production, the radar-equipped versions were entering service, and the merits and deficiencies of the type were clearly appreciated in the Soviet Union if not in the West.

Western fighters of the 1960s thoroughly outclassed their Soviet counterparts, not only in payload and range but also in operational equipment: more effective air-to-air missiles, carried in larger numbers; air-to-air radars large enough to detect and track targets beyond visual range, and guide missiles on to them; improved navigation equipment permitting routine operations beyond the range of ground control. The pinnacle of fighter design at that time was the US Navy's new F-4 Phantom: compared with the contemporary MiG-21PF, the Phantom carried four times as many missiles and eight times as many bombs, could pick up targets three or four times as far away and, in theory, could shoot them down before coming within range of their weapons.

While the supremacy of numbers is paramount in Soviet military doctrine, the related discipline of 'military-technical art' concerns the technical quality of military equipment. It involves the identification of the most important factors in weapon performance, and the standards which must be met to ensure that an opponent does not enjoy some overwhelming advantage due to technology. At the same time, military-technical studies single out performance standards which are less important, and can be sacrificed in the interests of easy production.

It was clear in the early 1960s that some of the deficiencies of the existing MiG-21 could become critical by the end of the decade. An aircraft in the class of the F-4 would have some vital advantages: the 'first look', because of its radar, the 'first shot', because of its long-range missiles, and, importantly, the ability to accept or decline an engagement, because of its higher performance. Against the MiG-21, the F-4 would be able to fight when the circumstances were favourable and show discretion at other times. It should be noted that in Vietnam, the MiG-21 showed up well when circumstances were in its favour; on the few occasions when F-4 units mounted an aggressive fighter sweep, the kill-to-loss ratio was heavily in favour of the F-4.

As the new fighter requirement made its way through the system, this type of comparison helped define the most important qualities of a new type. A basic building block was the ability to detect and engage targets beyond visual range (BVR), calling for a long-range search and tracking radar and reliable radar-guided missiles. Like the F-4, the new fighter would carry shorter-range IR-homing missiles for close combat.

Performance requirements

The new type was to be faster in level flight, climb and acceleration than the MiG-21, while greater range would also be desirable; although no dramatic increase in the internal fuel capacity, as a fraction of clean gross weight, was demanded, it could be assumed that the MiG-21's CG problem would be avoided and general advances in design would provide a further improvement. The MiG-21 was judged correctly to be more manoeuvrable than most of its contemporaries, so no increase in sustained or instantaneous turn rates was required.

Right: An excellent sequence showing the first swing-wing MiG, the Ye-231 (or Ye-23-1). The original and much cleaner configuration of the prototype is clearly visible.

Below: The MiG-21DPD was strictly a low-speed test aircraft, with a fixed landing gear. The lightweight, compact lift engines were probably developed by the Kolesov bureau.

Below: The MiG-21DPD was part of a complete V/Stol technology programme. Together with the Yak-36, it led to the operational Yak-38, as well as the Ye-230 prototype.

Soviet V/Stol fighter development

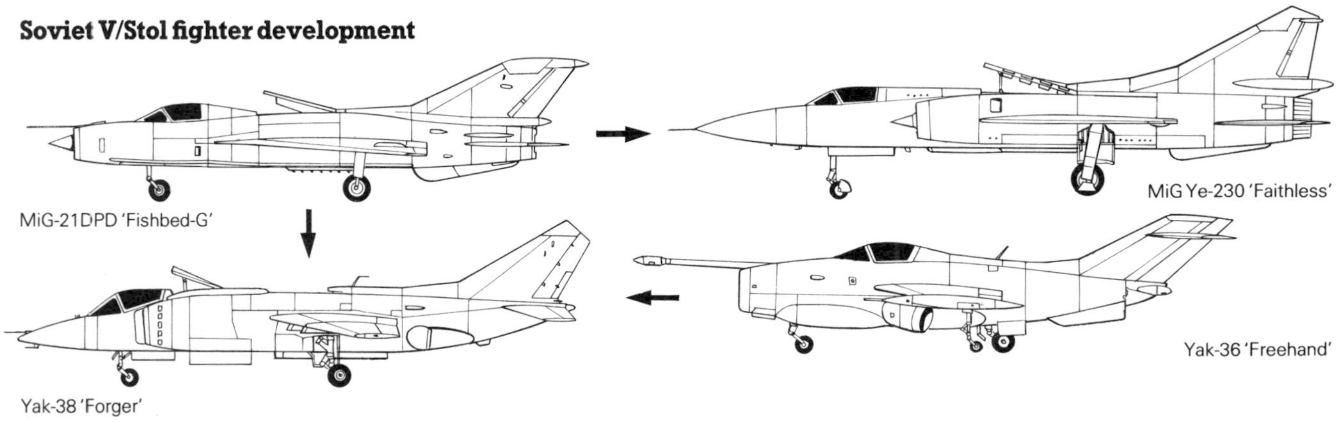

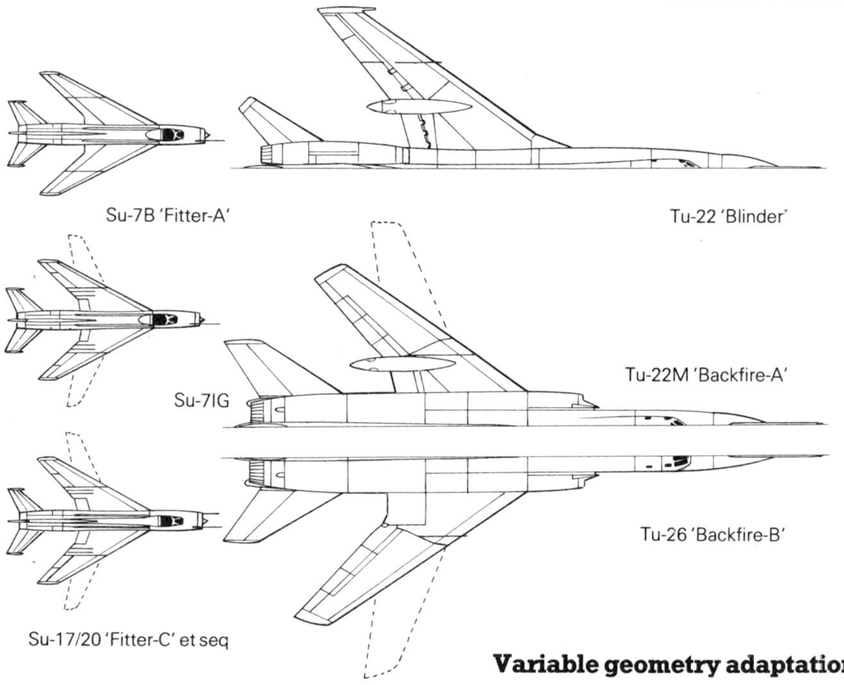

Variable geometry adaptations

Above: One TsAGI VG configuration was intended for adaptations of existing aircraft, such as the Su-7 and Tu-22. The Su-7IG and Tu-22M test/evaluation types led to the definitive Su-17/20 series and the Tu-26.

Below: The wing of the Ye-231 prototype was cleaner and smaller than that of the subsequent production aircraft; the main part of the vertical fin was the same size, but the dorsal fin was noticeably smaller.

Field performance was also pegged at MiG-21 levels. The final requirement was – as usual – that the size and cost of the aircraft be kept to a minimum. The requirement was probably issued by the TsKB in late 1963 or early 1964.

It must have been clear that the requirement would probably have to be met by a new aircraft. The most advanced Soviet fighters under development were the PVO's new interceptors, the Mikoyan Ye-26 (MiG-25) and the Sukhoi Su-15. The Mach 3, short-range MiG-25 was far too specialized for the FA, and while the Su-15 might have seemed superficially close to the requirement in terms of flight performance, capacity for avionics and weapons and size, it was a specialized PVO weapon. Its radar was optimized for counter-countermeasures performance rather than range, it was heavily dependent on maintenance facilities and it needed too long a runway. The same objections applied to the series of tailed-delta MiG prototypes developed between 1959 and 1962.

The requirement was tougher than it might appear at first sight. The speed and payload targets, coupled with a limitation on field lengths, eliminated the straightforward tailed delta. The classic Western compromise would have been a thin-section, moderately swept wing, as on the F-4, Mirage F.1 and Crusader. The MiG OKB was already developing an aircraft, the Ye-26, with such a wing, but it does not seem to have been considered for very long in the case of the new FA aircraft. The reason for this probably lies in the basic design trades: the speed requirement would have driven the wing loading upward to the point where the field-length target was out of reach.

The solution was to evaluate what were, at the time, two radically new technologies which promised to relieve the aerodynamic problems involved in attaining high speeds without long runways. One was variable sweep, the other was propulsive lift.

The latter, as applied to a basically conventional supersonic fighter, was not

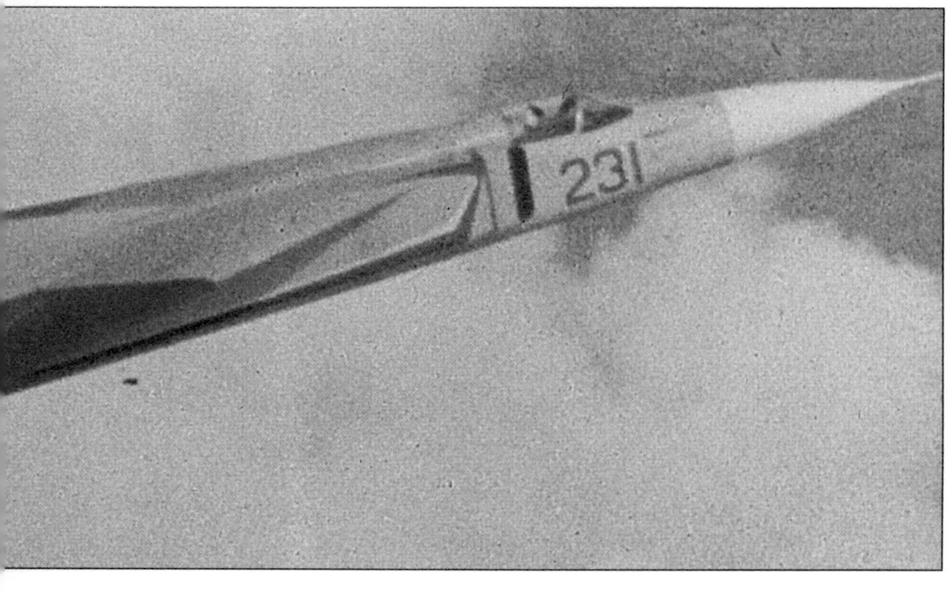

Left: This view shows clearly how the prototype's stabilizer, further forward than that of the production aircraft, fits neatly into the overall planform so that the wing and stabilizer tips align when the wing is in the fully swept position with the leading edge at an angle of 72°.

New variable geometry fighters

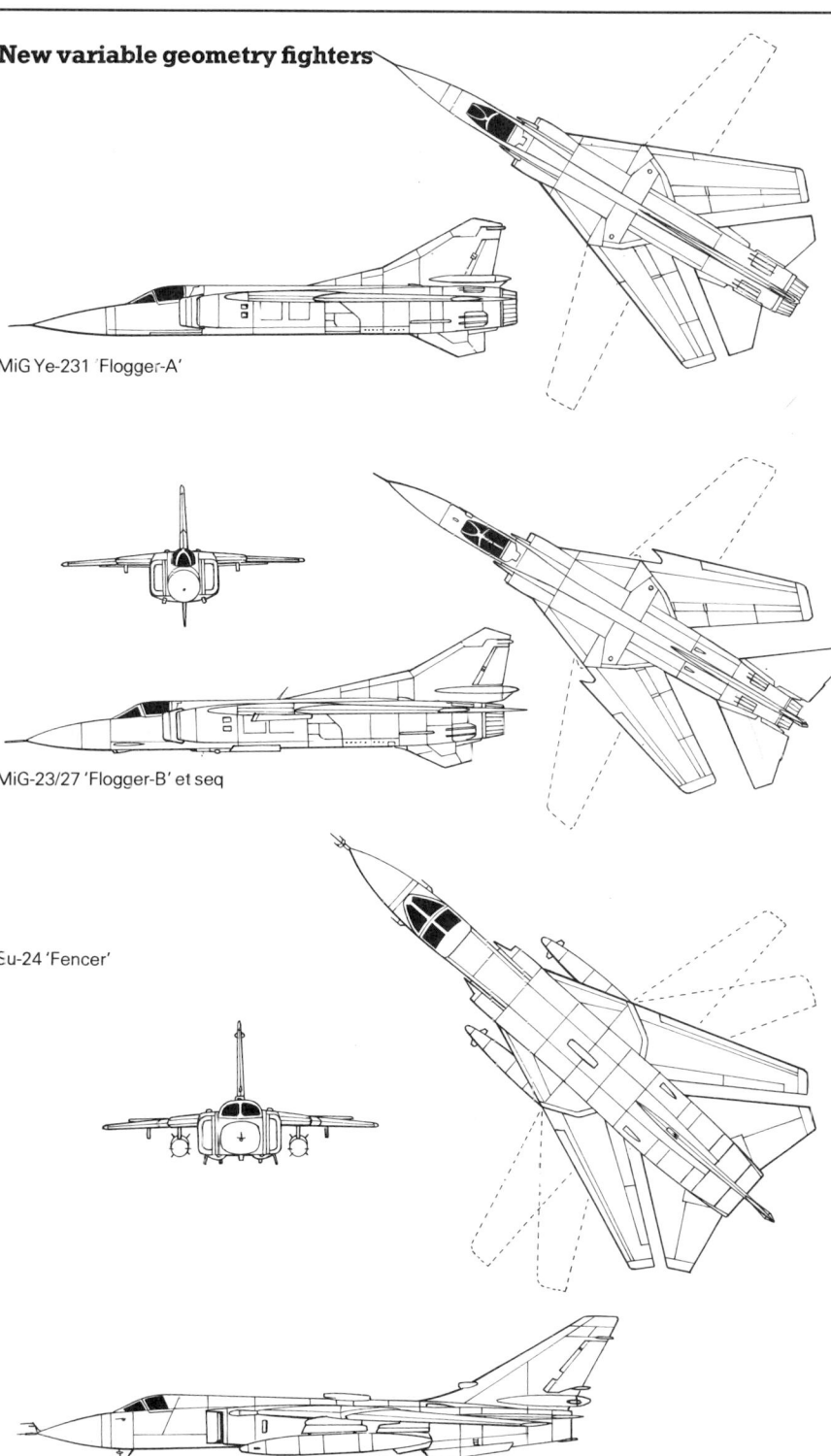

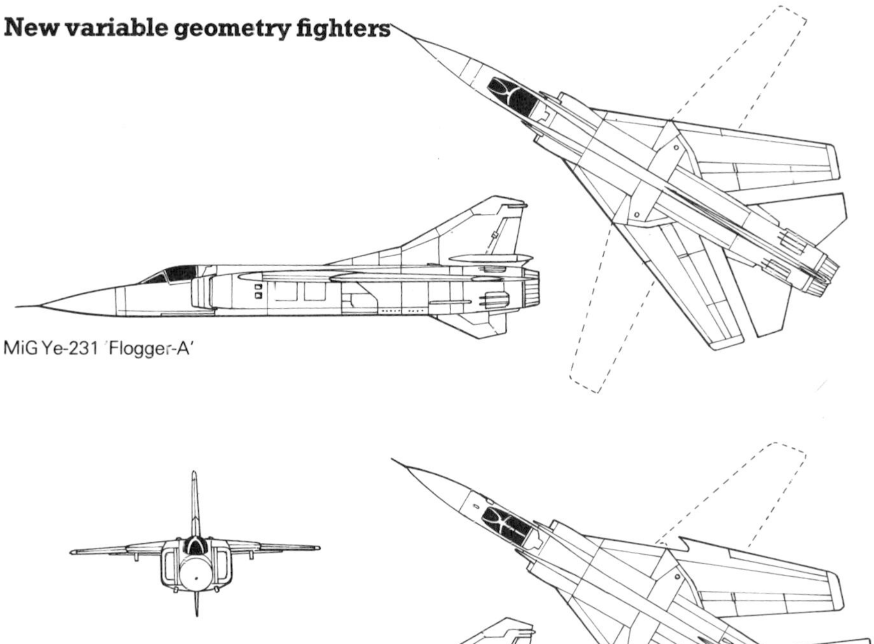

Above: TsAGI developed a neat planform for new VG aircraft such as the Ye-231, which featured a simple wing/fuselage junction and, unlike most Western layouts, had room for a high-capacity stores pylon under the glove. Modified for the production MiG-23, it was retained for the Su-24.

Left: A MiG-23M 'Flogger-B' in the initial production configuration. The heavy glove pylons are associated with the big AA-7 'Apex' missile, and shoes for the older AA-2 'Atoll' are carried on the belly pylons.

quite unique to the Soviet Union, being evaluated almost in parallel by Saab in the early days of the Viggen programme. The fighter would be equipped with two or three small lift jets mounted vertically in the fuselage, slightly forward of the CG and exhausting through variable louvres in the belly. On takeoff and landing, these engines would provide a vertical thrust equal to between a third and a half of the total weight of the aircraft, reducing the need for lift. All things being equal, the aircraft would take off and land more slowly.

There was a further benefit. As the speed of an aircraft is reduced from its maximum, it is given more 'up elevator' to raise the nose, increase the wing's angle of attack and maintain lift for level flight. The elevator (or stabilizer) is generating an increasing amount of downward thrust, and the wings have to provide more lift to compensate for this force. Supersonic combat aircraft tend to have short tails, for reasons of weight and drag. The stabilizer is working with a short lever, and the downforce must be higher; look at any supersonic combat aircraft on take-off or on the approach, and you can see the stabilizer angled sharply nose-down, and thrusting the whole aircraft towards the ground.

In the jet-lift-assisted fighter, the lift-jets would provide a powerful and drag-free force to raise the nose, being ahead of the CG. At low speeds, the stabilizer could actually be used to lift the tail, and yet the aircraft would remain stable. In effect, the lift-jets allowed the area of the stabilizer to be added to that of the wing, rather than subtracted from it. The potential reduction in landing and takeoff speed was very large indeed, and – apart from the extra internal volume occupied by the lift engines – the fighter could retain an uncompromised supersonic configuration with a small-area, low-drag wing and no complex high-lift devices.

The other formula considered for the new FA fighter, variable sweep, was more familiar in the West. TsAGI was entirely familiar with the history of variable sweep, although it had never been tested in the Soviet Union. The concept was little younger than the swept wing itself, having been first studied as soon as the unfavourable low-speed characteristics of the swept wing were detected. It had been tried on two manned aircraft in the USA, with indifferent results, mainly because it was thought necessary to slide the entire wing root fore and aft to keep the wing's aerodynamic centre in the same position.

British research work into Sir Barnes Wallis' Swallow concept pointed the way to eliminating this complication, by moving the pivot points away from the centreline and tapering the moving panels. Finally, in the late 1950s, John Stack's work at NASA's Langley Research Center showed that a fixed-root, outboard-pivot variable-sweep wing was within the state of the art and could be provided with effective aerodynamic controls.

Right: MiG-23U trainers are attached to each operational regiment. They have a back-up combat mission, but are compromised operationally by having a much less effective radar than the single-seat variants.

Below right: Photographed around 1975, this MiG-23M has a full complement of operational equipment including the IRST (infra-red search and track) set under the nose. The black panel ahead of the IRST forestalls reflection problems.

Below: The basically clean and straightforward lines of the MiG-23 – a direct result of the Soviet emphasis on ease of production – are very apparent on what appears to be a factory-fresh MiG-23M.

Right: Even with the aid of top and side periscopes, the instructor's view from the MiG-23U rear cockpit is less than panoramic. Most performance monitoring is presumably carried out via instruments.

This work was thoroughly documented and discussed, and formed the starting point for TsAGI's investigations. Another source of inspiration was the General Dynamics F-111, revealed in mid-1964 but doubtless known to the Soviet Union before that time.

VG benefits

Although 'variable sweep' is an accurate description of the mechanical functioning of such a wing, some of its benefits and implications are connected with the fact that the aerodynamic shape of the wing changes in other ways as it swings back. The term coined by NASA – 'variable geometry' or VG – is not mere verbosity, but is more complete and accurate. The wing not only has variable sweep, but also variable span and variable thickness, all being significant.

Varying the sweep angle itself has certain benefits. Some high-lift devices work best on a virtually unswept wing. Highly swept wings, on the other hand, have some advantages: they have low drag at very high speeds, because the wing lies behind the main shock wave from the nose, and are relatively little affected by gusts in high-speed, low-level flight. Wings with more than 60° sweep have very poor low-speed behaviour, and such sweep angles are practical only with VG.

VG also means variable span. A long-span wing generates more lift for takeoff, and less induced drag – drag due to lift – in medium-speed cruising flight. At higher speeds, the drag due to the size of the wing, and Mach effects, become more important, and a shorter-span wing is more efficient. To some extent, too, a VG wing has variable area, because part of the trailing edge retracts into the fuselage or glove as it sweeps back. This increases the wing loading, reduces high-speed drag and improves the aircraft's low-level, high-speed ride.

As the wing sweeps back, its chord – measured parallel with the centreline – increases. Its physical thickness stays the same, so its aerodynamic thickness, defined as the ratio of thickness to chord, is reduced. Thick wings generate more lift at low speeds, thin wings produce less drag at high speeds, and the VG aircraft gets the best of both worlds again.

VG complications

It was these qualities that made VG attractive in the early 1960s, and made it the basis for so many design studies. Its implementation presented some challenges, however. Stability and control were complicated by the gross changes in aerodynamic shape: in particular, the aerodynamic centre (AC) of the aircraft tended to move aft with the sweeping of the wing, and moved further aft at supersonic speed, threatening to cause high trim drag. The rearward AC shift affected pitch stability as well, making the size and the position of the stabilizer more critical than ever. Lateral (roll) and directional (yaw) stability were also

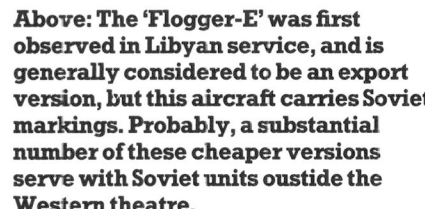

Above: The 'Flogger-E' was first observed in Libyan service, and is generally considered to be an export version, but this aircraft carries Soviet markings. Probably, a substantial number of these cheaper versions serve with Soviet units oustide the Western theatre.

Below: Seen here undergoing pre-flight checks is another unusual specimen – a MiG-23M 'Flogger-B' with the large weapon shoes, and the dielectric head above the pylon, which are normally associated with strike versions of the type. It may be a development aircraft.

affected to some degree. Structurally, the chief problem was the design of small pivot mechanisms that would be completely reliable and yet would carry some of the highest loads in the airframe.

All the problems connected with AC shift could be reduced by moving the pivot points further outboard, and this also reduced the loads on the pivots because more of the flight loads were carried on the fixed part of the wing. But there were costs involved with this approach. Chiefly, the benefits of VG were reduced along with the risks.

TsAGI studies of these problems produced two different VG planforms. One was similar to that of the F-111, with a few variations which, without greatly affecting performance, made it easier to integrate into an aircraft design. The pivots were slightly farther apart, the distance between them being 22 per cent of the total span, rather than 17 per cent, and the maximum sweep angle, measured from the pivots, was slightly smaller.

As a result of these two differences, much less of the TsAGI wing actually retracted into the fuselage when it was swept back, and the fixed root or 'glove' was shorter than that on the F-111. This made the design of the fuselage less difficult, by reducing the size of the cut-out and cavity needed to accommodate the wing, made the glove shape compatible with conventional inlets, and increased the span of the glove just enough to provide room for a high-capacity stores pylon. Another difference was a larger gap in plan view between the wings and the stabilizer, but like the F-111, and unlike later VG designs, the wings and stabilizer were at the same level.

Above: Ordnance fit on this MiG-23M appears to include dual AA-8 shoes, with provision for another store, under the gloves, an AA-2 shoe under the starboard belly pylon and a bomb rack to port.

The other layout produced by TsAGI was originally intended for use on modified versions of swept-wing aircraft, and was based on an Su-7 planform, the pivots being set at 30 per cent span. This layout formed the basis for the Su-20/22 and the Tu-22M 'Backfire' bomber, both originally derived from fixed-geometry designs, but worked well enough to be adapted for the completely new Tupolev 'Blackjack' strategic bomber.

It was the more ambitious, F-111-style planform that was evaluated for the new tactical fighter, alongside the propulsive-lift concept. The decision to do so was almost certainly taken during 1964, and represented a significant break with Western practice. In the West, VG was regarded as a feature of complex, expensive aircraft, and was used only where its perceived cost and complications were needed to meet specific mission requirements. TsAGI and the TsKB, however, intended to implement VG as cheaply as possible, using it to increase the mission efficiency of a basic tactical combat aircraft and thereby contain its size and cost.

Rival prototypes

Apparently, both MiG and Sukhoi OKEs were asked to build prototypes in response to the requirement. Sukhoi's aircraft was to be a short takeoff and landing (Stol) variant of the Su-15 interceptor, using jet lift, while Mikoyan was to build two tactical fighter prototypes, to test the jet-Stol concept and variable sweep in parallel. Mikoyan also adapted a MiG-21 airframe into the purely experimental MiG-21DPD 'Fishbed-G', for early tests of the concept.

At the same time, the Tumansky bureau started development of a new engine for the MiG types. Whether this engine is a turbojet or a turbofan has been disputed by different sources for

Mikoyan MiG-23MF 'Flogger-B' cutaway

1 Pitot tube
2 Radome
3 'High Lark' J-band radar scanner dish
4 Radar dish tracking mechanism
5 'Swift Rod' ILS antenna
6 Avionics cooling air scoop
7 Radar and avionics equipment bay
8 Ventral doppler antenna
9 Yaw vane
10 Dynamaic pressure probe (q-feel)
11 SRO-22 'Odd-Rods' IFF antenna
12 Armoured windscreen panel
13 Head-up display
14 Instrument panel shroud
15 Radar head-down display
16 Instrument panel
17 Rudder pedals
18 Angle of attack transmitter
19 IR sensor housing
20 Nosewheel steering unit
21 Torque scissor links
22 Pivoted axle beam
23 Twin aft-retracting nosewheels
24 Nosewheel spray/debris guard
25 Shock absorber strut
26 Nosewheel doors
27 Hydraulic retraction jack
28 Control column
29 Ejection seat firing handles
30 Wing sweep control lever
31 Engine throttle control lever
32 Pilot's ejection seat
33 Electrically-heated rearview mirror
34 Ejection seat headrest
35 Upward hingeing cockpit canopy cover
36 Canopy jack
37 Starboard air intake
38 Canopy hinge point
39 Screw-jack-actuated adjustable boundary layer splitter plate
40 Boundary layer bleed air holes
41 Port engine air intake
42 Intake internal flow fences
43 Retractable landing/taxying lamp (port and starboard)
44 Temperature probe
45 Variable-area intake ramp doors
46 Boundary layer bleed air ejector
47 Avionics equipment bay
48 ADF sense aerial
49 Boundary layer air duct
50 Forward fuselage fuel tank
51 Ventral cannon ammunition magazines
52 Ground power connections
53 Intake suction relief doors
54 Weapons system electronic control units
55 SO-69 Sirena 3 radar warning antennas
56 Fuselage flank fuel tanks
57 Wing glove fairing
58 Starboard Sirena 3 radar warning antennas
59 Jettisonable fuel tank (176Imp gal/800lit capacity)
60 Nose section of MiG-23U Flogger-C tandem-seat trainer
61 Student pilot's cockpit
62 Folding blind flying hood
63 Rear seat periscope (extended)
64 Instructor's cockpit
65 MiG-23BN Flogger-F dedicated ground attack variant
66 Radar ranging antenna
67 Laser ranger nose fairing
68 Raised cockpit canopy
69 Armoured fuselage side panels
70 Wing leading edge flap (lowered)
71 Starboard navigation light
72 Wing fully forward (16° sweep) position
73 Port wing integral fuel tank (total internal fuel capacity 1,265Imp gal/5,750lit)
74 Full span plain flap (lowered)
75 Starboard wing intermediate (45° sweep) position
76 Starboard wing full (72° sweep) position
77 Two-segment spoilers/lift dumpers
78 Non-swivelling jettisonable wing pylon (wing restricted to forward swept position)
79 Wing glove sealing plate
80 Wing pivot bearing
81 Wing pivot box carry-through unit (welded construction)
82 VHF antenna
83 Wing sweep control screw jacks
84 Fin root fillet
85 Rear fuselage fuel tank
86 Tumansky R-29B afterburning turbojet
87 Afterburner duct cooling air scoop
88 Cut-back fin root fillet (Flogger-G)
89 Tailplane control and hydraulic equipment bay
90 Starboard all-moving tailplane
91 Tailfin
92 Short wave ground control communications antenna
93 UHF antenna
94 ILS antenna
95 Sirena 3 tail warning radar
96 ECM antennas
97 Tail navigation light
98 Static discharger
99 Rudder
100 Rudder hydraulic actuators
101 Brake parachute housing
102 Split conic fairing parachute door
103 Variable area afterburner nozzle
104 Fixed tailplane tab
105 Static discharger
106 Port all-moving tailplane
107 Afterburner nozzle control jacks (6)
108 Tailplane pivot bearing
109 Tailplane hydraulic jack
110 Airbrakes (4), upper and lower surfaces
111 Airbrake hydraulic jack
112 Afterburner duct
113 Ventral fin, folded (undercarriage down) position
114 Ventral fin control jack
115 Lower UHF antenna
116 Ventral fin down position
117 Engine accessory equipment bay
118 Wing root seal
119 Port spoilers/lift dumpers
120 Flap guide rails
121 Port plain flap
122 Fixed spoiler strips
123 Static discharger
124 Port navigation light
125 Leading edge flap (lowered)
126 Port wing integral fuel tank
127 Wing pylon mounting rib
128 Extended-chord sawtooth leading edge
129 Port mainwheel
130 Mainwheel door/debris guard
131 Shock absorber strut
132 Hinged axle beam
133 Articulated mainwheel leg strut
134 Hydraulic retraction jack
135 Fuselage stores pylon
136 Twin missile launcher
137 AA-8 'Aphid' short range air-to-air missile
138 GSh-23L twin-barrel 23mm ventral cannon pack
139 Gun gas venting air scoop
140 AA-2 'Atoll' air-to-air missile
141 Fuselage centreline pylon
142 Ventral fuel tank (176Imp gal/800lit capacity)
143 Wing glove pylon
144 Missile launch rail
145 AA-7 'Apex' long range air-to-air missile

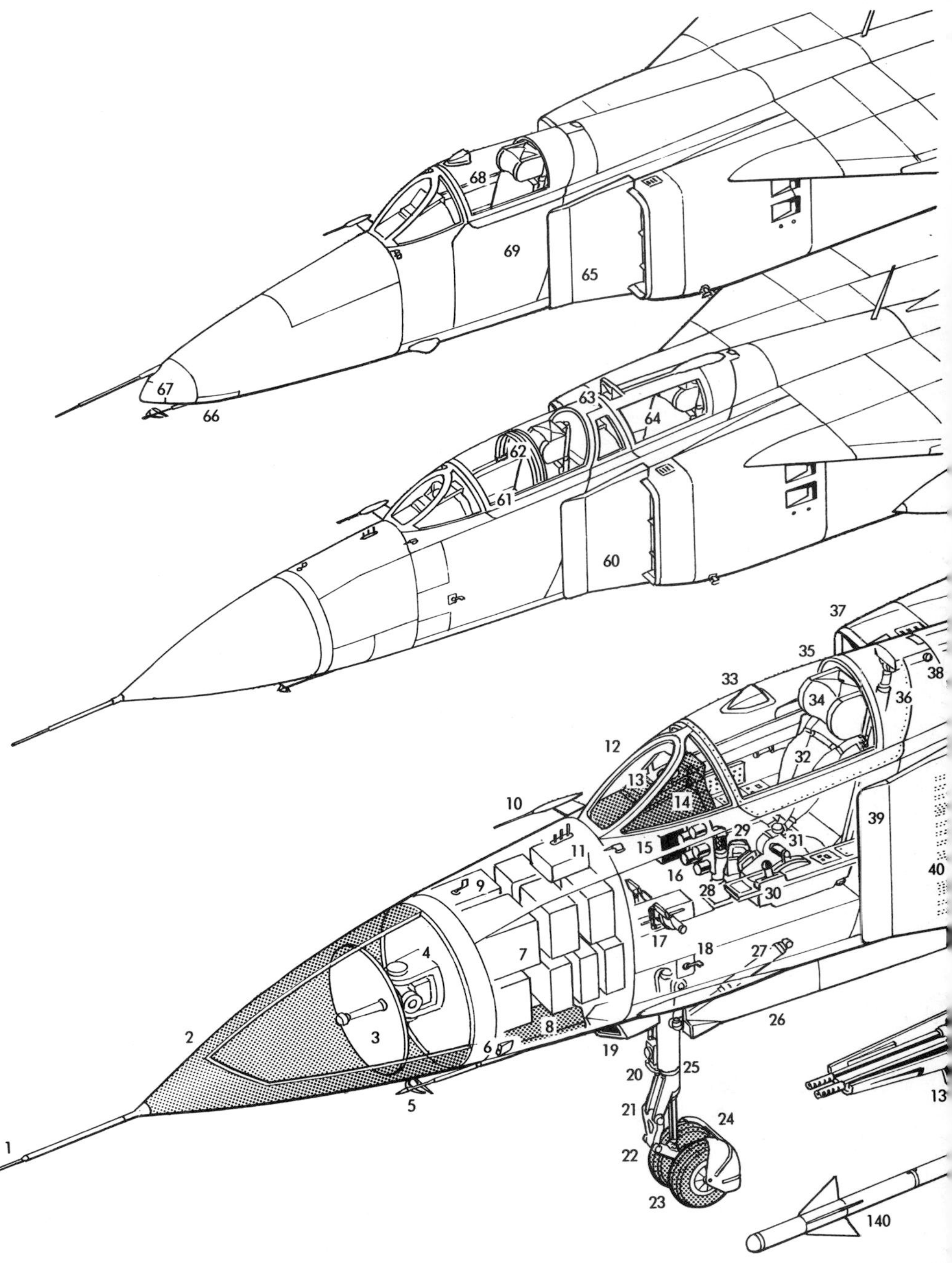

some years; both were probably considered in the development stages. The turbofan is an attractive partner for the VG layout. Without reheat, its specific fuel consumption (SFC) is much better than that of the pure jet, leading to a substantial improvement in range. Because of its large-volume, oxygen-rich exhaust, it can also provide a tremendous thrust boost in reheat, so that its augmented thrust/weight ratio – a key factor in combat performance – is superior to that of the turbojet.

All Western VG aircraft have augmented turbofan powerplants. However, they are all designed for missions that include either long low-level sectors or long loiter times. The engine is in dry thrust nearly all the time, and the lower SFC of the turbofan is critical. That was not the case for a tactical fighter such as the new MiG.

A common factor in nearly all Western augmented turbofans is that their development has been extremely difficult. The most commonly encountered problem is that the augmentor fails to run smoothly in the mixture of hot and cool air fed to it by the engine, and that fluctuations in the augmentor pressure send pulses up the bypass duct and into the fan, which is also the low-pressure compressor. The disturbance thus affects the airflow into the high-pressure compressor, causing the engine to suffer from chronic stalls.

Turbofans also run hotter than turbojets. Much of the airflow bypasses the 'core', which comprises the high-pressure compressor, combustor and turbine, but these components provide all the engine's power: the fan merely converts it into thrust. They are smaller than the same components in a turbojet of the same thrust, and in order to generate as much power from half as much air, they must have a higher pressure ratio. This is one of the reasons why turbofans are more efficient than turbojets. However, increasing temperatures go hand in hand with higher pressures, and temperatures in the hottest part of the engine – just downstream of the combustor, and ahead of the turbine – are much higher in a turbofan.

Supersonic complications

In a supersonic aircraft, the problem is compounded. At high speeds, the inlet compresses and heats the incoming air, and the temperature at the compressor face rises rapidly with increasing speed. This temperature increase is then multiplied by the pressure ratio of the engine. The result is that supersonic turbofans must run at turbine entry temperatures (TET) some 600°F (330°C) higher than a

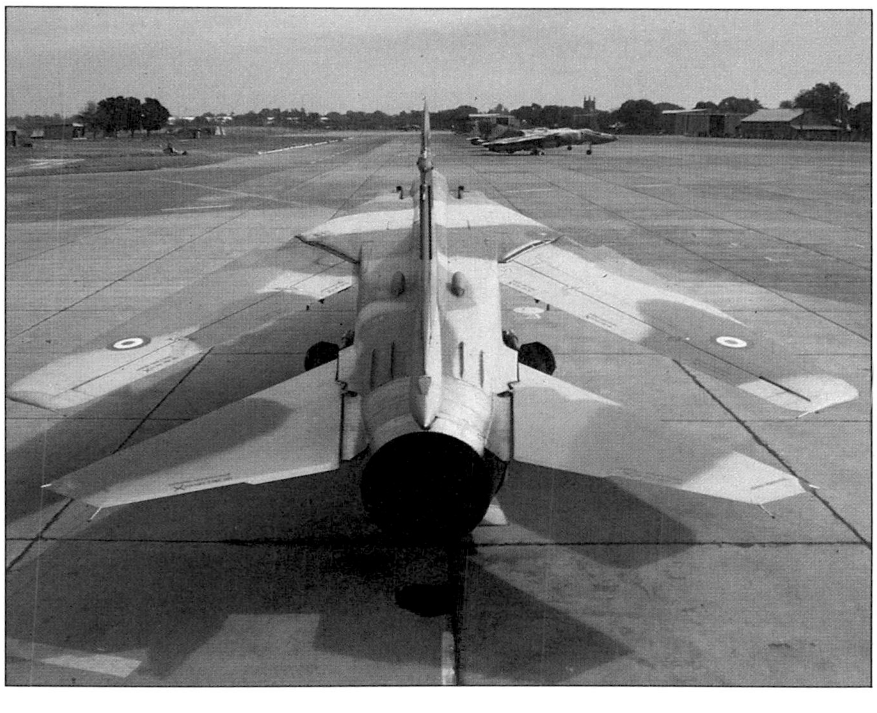

Above: India is a major operator of the 'Flogger' family, with three variants in service: the MiG-23BN strike fighter, MiG-23M fighter and the MiG-27M, the last-named being built at Nasik by HAL and bridging the gap between the MiG-21 and MiG-29.

Below: Rugged simplicity of construction is a hallmark of the MiG-23 design. Note in particular the robust forgings which form the heart of the design. Also, large access panels are almost absent; these are not required by Soviet maintenance philosophy.

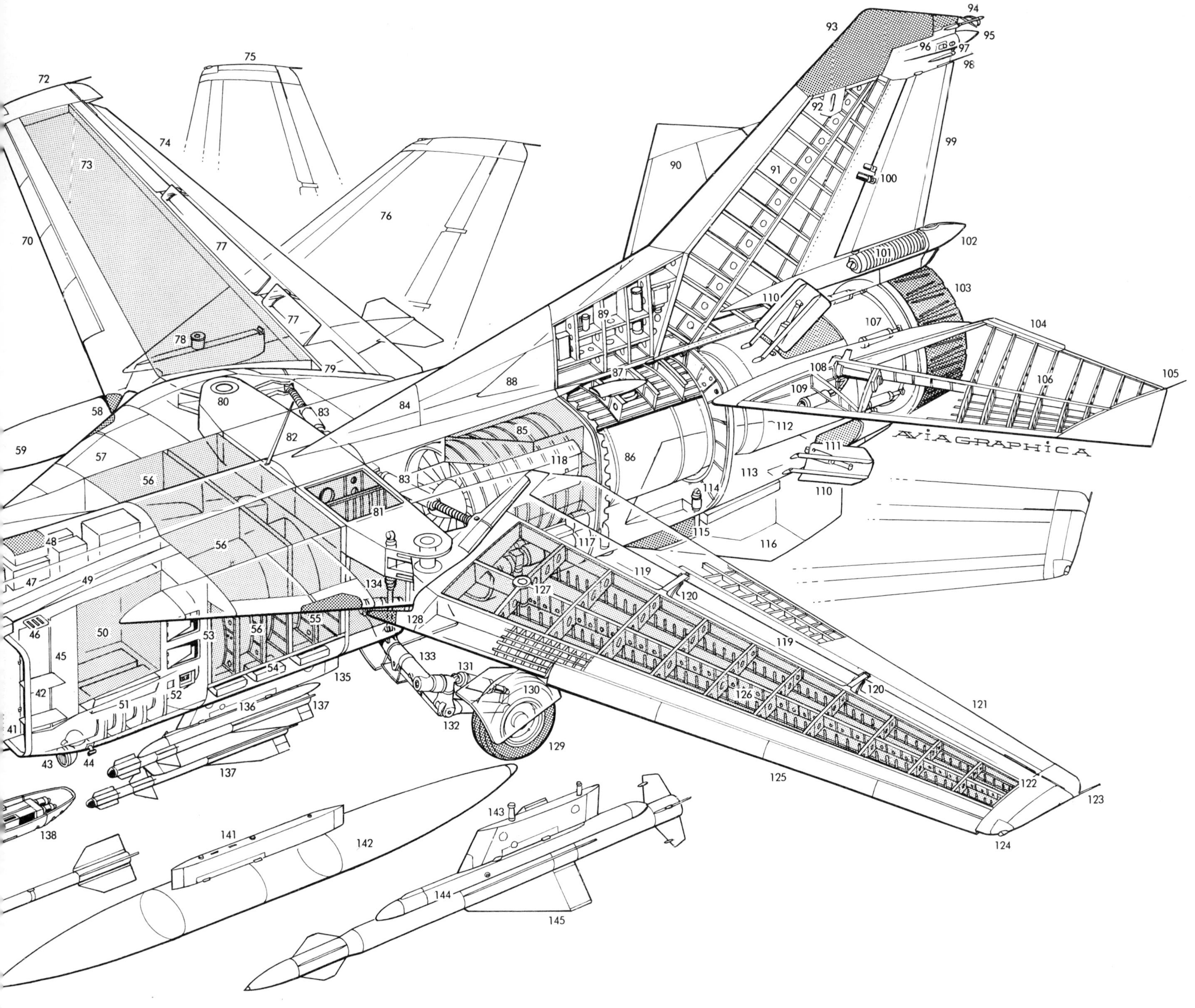

turbojet at the same speed. Turbine life has been the other main problem in the development of supersonic augmented turbofans.

High temperatures and pressures have another effect on the engine. Increasing heat calls for different, more exotic materials and more sophisticated cooling techniques, while higher pressures demand closer tolerances in manufacture and maintenance. The result is that a turbofan is inevitably more expensive than a turbojet, by a considerable margin.

Considering the potential difficulties and costs of the turbofan against its performance advantage, the Soviets decided to stay with the turbojet. (Such a decision would probably be taken by MAP, with inputs from the engine and airframe OKBs and the production organization, and would be approved by the MoD.) Published and apparently reliable data for the Tumansky powerplant, which was designated R-27, overwhelmingly fall into line with values for a turbojet.

Like the Tumansky engines developed for the MiG-21, the R-27 was a two-shaft powerplant with little if any variable geometry. Its pressure ratio was similar to that of Western turbojets such as the J75 and J79, but, being a decade later in design, it used more advanced aerodynamics to achieve a greater pressure rise in each stage, so the number of stages was smaller (eleven in all, compared with 15 for the J75 and 17 for the J79). The engine was accordingly shorter and lighter, developing 25 per cent more thrust than the later models of the J79 but weighing about the same as the older engine.

The Tumansky engine had a similar mass flow and diameter to the older Lyulka AL-7 turbojet. Later, the R-27

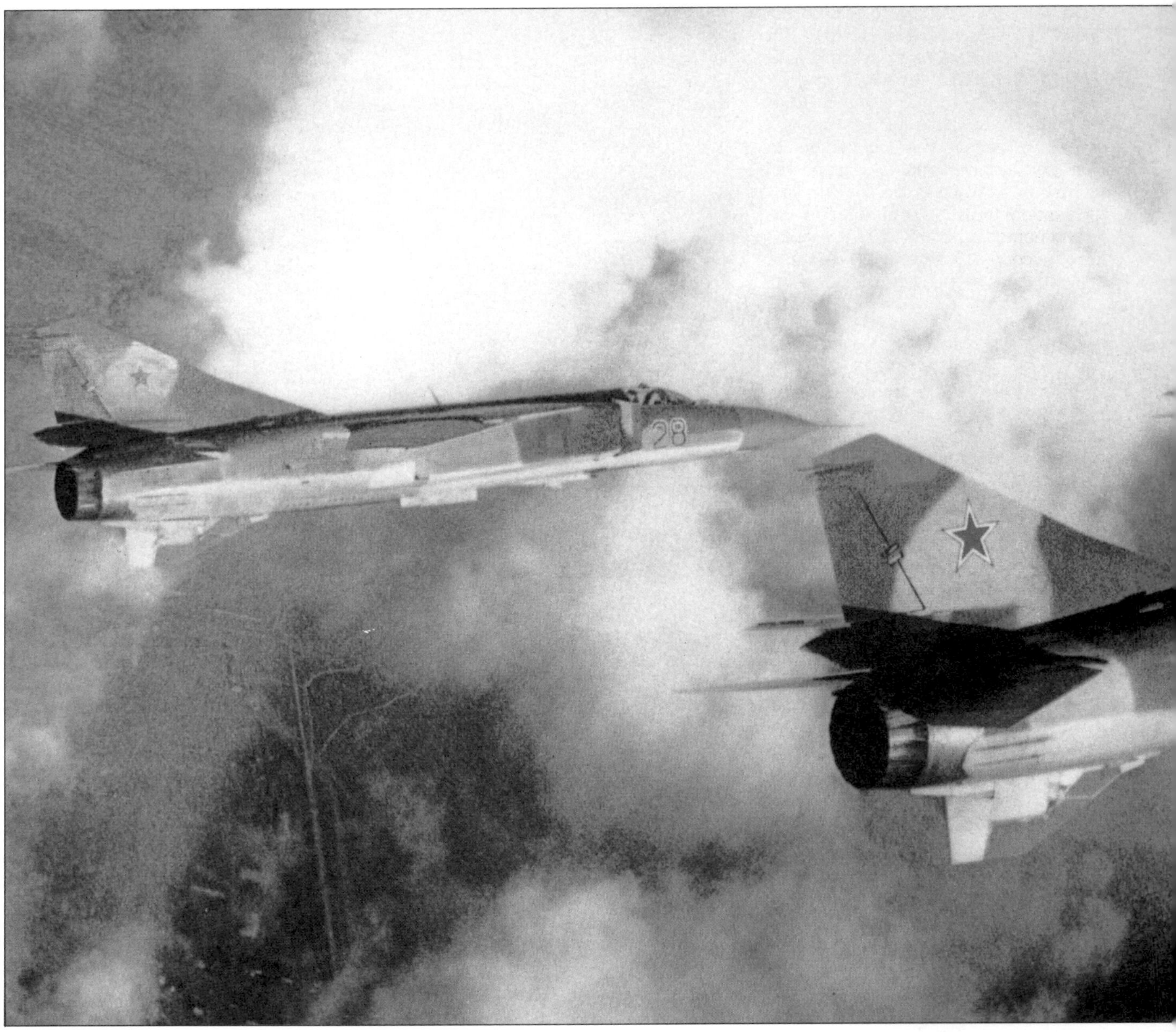

Top: Czech Air Force MiG-23BNs are similar to those supplied to India. Clearly visible on the nearer aircraft is the armour plate – almost certainly titanium – applied to the sides of the cockpit.

Above: Apparent in this view of an Indian Air Force MiG-23BN is the improved downward view provided by the attack fighter's shorter, wedge-shaped nose. The head-up display combiner is also visible.

Left: Medium sweep probably gives the best compromise between speed and agility. This sequence shows that the overwing spoilers are used to aid roll control up to fairly high speeds.

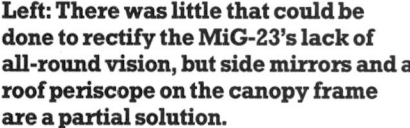

Left: There was little that could be done to rectify the MiG-23's lack of all-round vision, but side mirrors and a roof periscope on the canopy frame are a partial solution.

Above: The later MiG-23bis 'Flogger-G', first seen in late 1978, is distinguished by its cut-back dorsal fin. These aircraft have no IRST set, a subsystem that reappeared later.

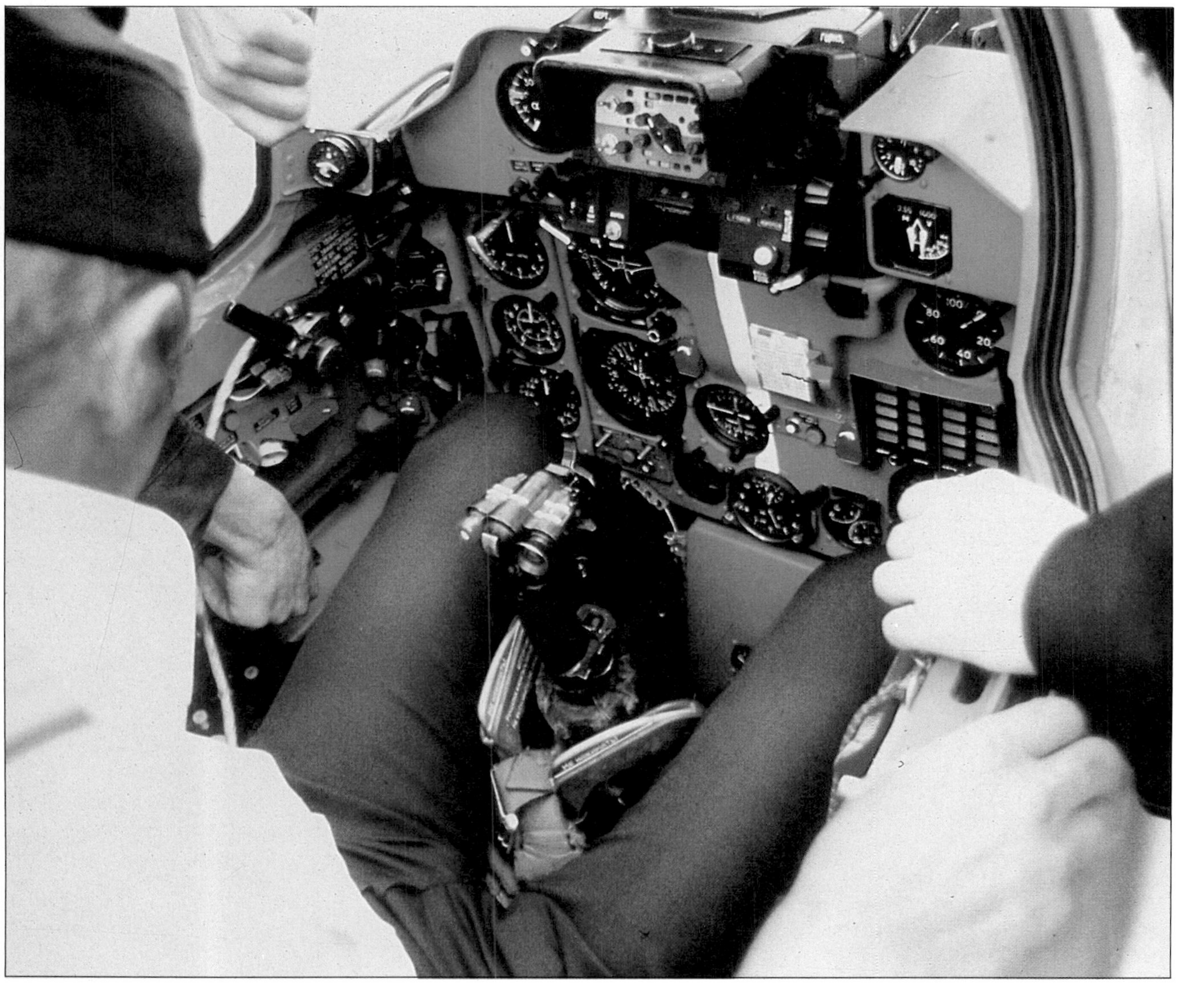

Below: The MiG-23 cockpit is basically simple and features a large number of single-message caution and warning captions. Critical radar and weapon data is displayed on the HUD.

would replace the AL-7 in developed versions of the Sukhoi 'Fitter', but this commonality may well have allowed the Mikoyan OKB to use the AL-7 as a reliable and proven substitute for the R-27 during early flight tests of its new fighter prototypes.

Despite its unusual powerplant, the Ye-230 Stol prototype appears to have been completed earlier than the VG aircraft, making its first flight in 1966. The Ye-230 was a handsome design. Aft of the front wing attachments, it was basically a MiG-21, scaled up by about 1.25:1. The wing planform, circular-section fuselage and landing gear geometry were all similar to those of the smaller type. The forward fuselage was entirely new. Ahead of the wing, it widened to accommodate half cone, axisymmetrical side inlets, flanking a compactly designed, oval-section nose containing the cockpit, above the nosewheel well, with avionics racks behind the cockpit and the radar bay and radome in front. A bay in the centre fuselage, between the inlet ducts, accommodated two lift-jets in the 5,500lb (2,500kg) thrust class, probably developed by the Kolesov bureau.

The Ye-231 VG prototype – the entire programme bore the Ye-23 designation, different configurations being identified by three-digit designators – flew in early 1967. Apart from the forward fuselage and nosewheel, which were identical to those of the Ye-230, it was a completely different aircraft, and owed no specific features to any other MiG design. Typically, though, it was logically laid out and full of interesting detail.

The wing itself was slender and quite thin in section, and carried plain, full-span trailing-edge flaps split into three segments, and overwing spoilers for low-speed roll control and lift dumping. The movable outer wings could be moved into three positions – 16°, 45° and 72° – under manual control. There was no provision for movable wing pylons. Sealing around the junctions with the glove and fuselage presented no great problems, because the wing was thin and the apertures were short, and was carried out with small spring-loaded metal panels. The wing incorporated a certain amount of taper and twist, tending to offload the tips and reduce the shift of the aerodynamic centre. The tailerons had cropped tips in the new standard style, to avoid flutter problems, and were independently actuated to provide high-speed roll control.

Structural features

Structurally, the new type followed MiG-21 practice, with a mix of conventional light alloy and high-strength steel. MAP's production organization continued to display a fondness for massive forging presses, and these were used to make the key bulkheads, the wing carry-through structure and the spars.

The inlets were of the vertical-ramp type, but were based on the design developed by the central propulsion bureau, TsIAM, for the new Sukhoi Su-15. A primary splitter wedge performed the dual function of clearing off the turbulent air close to the fuselage and forming the primary shock wave ahead of the inlet aperture. Hinged to the rear of this plate was a movable ramp, back-to-back with another ramp inside the inlet. The two ramps moved outward to narrow the inlet at high speed, while boundary-layer flow adhering to the inlet ramp was drawn through tiny perforations in the ramp and vented overboard. Simple in function, these inlets had been shown to work well at speeds up to Mach 2.4 At low speeds, two suck-in auxiliary doors in each inlet wall provided additional airflow.

The main landing gear was unique. Each levered-suspension unit was attached to a massive beam, pivoted close to the aircraft centreline and shaped to fit in the space between the inlet duct and the fuselage side. As the gear retracted, the beam swung upward into the fuselage side, and the wheel folded downward to lie behind and parallel to the beam. While heavy and complex in itself, the gear design took up very little volume in the fuselage and incredibly little of the valuable area on the surface, while clearing both wing and centreline stores and providing a wide track for ground stability. Its only drawback was that it was rather short, giving the aircraft a tail-down, waddling gait and failing to provide more than minimal ground clearance for under-fuselage stores.

Directional stability was clearly an issue, because of the high design speeds and the rearward movement of the aerodynamic centre. The fin was large, and carried a massive dorsal extension which stretched almost half-way along the fuselage. For a further increase in vertical area, with its effect enhanced by the dynamic pressure under the fuselage, the designers incorporated a single very large ventral fin, which folded upward and to the right as the landing gear was extended. Also prominent in the design of the rear fuselage were the four separate airbrake segments, above and below the tailplanes, which provided powerful deceleration without any trim changes.

VG and jet-lift offered different advantages, but it does appear that they were pursued as alternative approaches to the design of a tactical fighter. However, VG proved convincingly superior overall. Even the mid-span-pivot demonstrator, the Sukhoi S-22I, was unexpectedly adopted as a production aircraft. The Ye-231 was selected as the basis for the next tactical fighter, but it also served as an aerodynamic technology demonstrator for a new all-weather strike aircraft developed by the Sukhoi bureau. The resulting Su-24 is virtually a 1.2:1 linear scale-up of the Ye-231 planform.

Jet-lift Stol disadvantages

Precisely why jet-lift Stol was abandoned is not known. Obviously, combat radius would be compromised by the loss of internal volume to the vertical propulsion system, but this would be offset to some degree by the ability to take off without using reheat, and the Stol fighter could also operate from shorter strips close to the front. Other disadvantages might be harder to accept. The combination of low flight speeds and a large mass of air passing vertically through the fuselage must have had effects on stability that were interesting, to say the least. Also, any severe pitch-up would have caused simultaneous reduction in lift and a reverse thrust component. Experience from the programme, however, helped development of the Yak-38 shipboard Vtol fighter.

Strategic changes may also have contributed to the ending of the Stol programme. In 1967, NATO had shifted from a strategy of nuclear retaliation to a doctrine of 'flexible response', emphasizing a gradual increase in the commitment of military force and a delayed use of nuclear weapons. Among Soviet doctrinal changes in response was a new emphasis on mobility, and the ability to make rapid and deep advances into enemy territory. The role of tactical air power, too, became more offensive, with the stress on destroying enemy air assets rather than defending and supporting the ground troops. The changes in doctrine were important for the MiG-23. In particular, the FA now needed a 'counter-air' fighter of much greater range than the MiG-21, and it was in this area that the VG aircraft excelled.

Above: Taken during the same display as the photograph below, this shows the same aircraft turning with medium sweep. At any sweep angle, however, the MiG-23 does not match the manoeuvrability of later fighters.

The Ye-231 made a brief appearance at the Domodedovo air show in June 1967, and received the NATO codename 'Flogger'. Thereafter, it disappeared from Western eyes for almost four years. Even its true service designation, MiG-23, was thought to apply to the 'Foxbat'.

Development was not fast, and its course is not entirely clear. Prototype testing is believed to have continued through the rest of the 1960s, until by 1969-70 the future of the programme had been settled: it had been decided to defer large-scale production, pending substantial modifications to the design. Meanwhile, a small batch of service-test aircraft, based on the prototype but carrying some operational equipment,

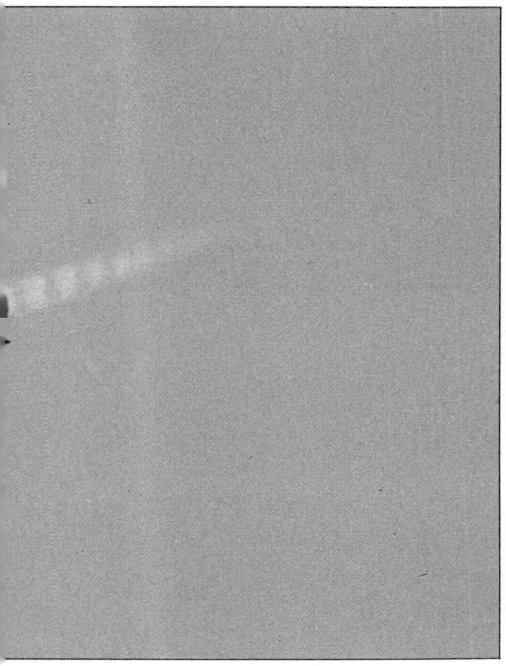

Above: Indian Air Force MiG-23BN climbs out with full afterburner. The variable inlets and fully variable nozzle of this version are of little use in its normal operating regime – high subsonic speed at low level.

would be issued to FA units for further evaluation. Designated MiG-23S, and known to NATO, like the prototype, as 'Flogger-A', these aircraft were in service by 1971.

By that time the first true production model was flying. The MiG-23M, later named 'Flogger-B' by NATO, incorporated some major changes. These have been consistently misrepresented by so many authoritative sources that the correct version is seldom heard.

The new version retained virtually all the structure of the prototype. The centre-section wing structure was retained, including the gloves and the pivots, and most of the fuselage was externally similar to the original. The overall fuselage length was unchanged. It is important to note that the fuselage was not shortened, nor were the wing pivots moved forward on the gloves; it is obvious that the latter step would have been geometrically impossible without closing the gap between the pivots, redesigning the carry-through structure and revising the fuselage.

The main external changes were confined to the outer wing panels and the tail surfaces. The outer wing panels were new. While the span and tip chord were unchanged, a very large leading-edge extension was added to the planform, increasing chord at the root of the moving panel by more than 20 per cent. This extension terminated abruptly in a huge 'claw' outboard of the glove, so that the pivot geometry remained unaltered. The design of the claw was such that it formed a narrow slot at minimum sweep, a streamwise dog-tooth at intermediate sweep, and a streamlined discontinuity with the wings swept aft. The trailing-edge flaps were unchanged, roll-control spoilers were added, and the outer two-thirds of the outer-panel leading edge were made into a simple nose flap.

The tailerons and most of the fin and rudder were structurally unchanged, but were moved aft by about 24in (61cm). The dorsal fin extension, already large, was further stretched to retain its original starting point on the fuselage. The ventral fin was not moved.

The reason for the changes is not known. The original Ye-231 layout was retained with great success in the Su-24, so it presumably had no fundamental shortcomings. However, the aerodynamic effects of the modifications can be broken down as follows:

☆ Increased wing area and lift coefficient (through the new leading-edge flaps), permitting higher weights at take-off;
☆ Increased taper, reducing the shift of aerodynamic centre with wing-sweep changes;

Left: Wings fully aft and throttle fully forward, a MiG-23bis pulls up during a display in Sweden. The stable pattern of precipitation along the leading edge shows that the notch is doing its job and preventing tip stall.

Right: An Indian Air Force MiG-23BN rolls out after landing. The brake parachute is used routinely, but it is interesting to note that neither spoilers nor airbrakes are deployed.

Below: Landing after its demonstration in Sweden, a MiG-23bis deploys its brake chute. The more level ground attitude of the later version, with its revised landing gear, is notable.

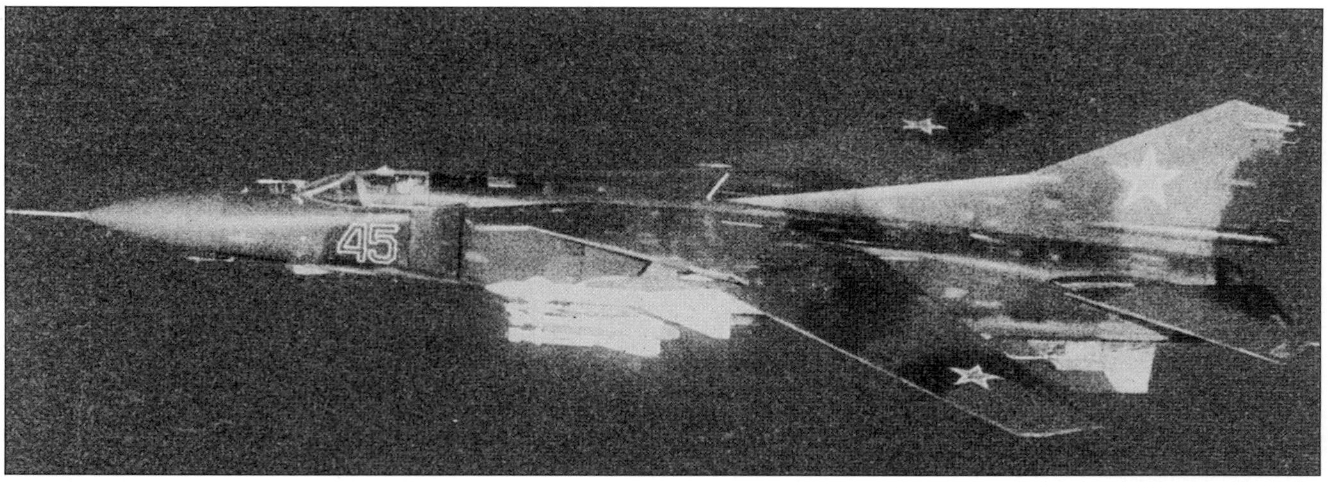

Right: In the early 1980s, MiG-23s were first observed carrying AA-8 'Aphid' short-range AAMs in pairs on the belly pylons. The double row of forward fins can be seen clearly in the missiles carried by this MiG-23M.

☆ Moving the aerodynamic centre forward, and the tail surfaces aft, lengthening the tail 'moment arm' and increasing the effectiveness of the control surfaces;
☆ Moving the aerodynamic centre forward while, if anything, moving the centre of gravity rearward, reducing static stability margins;
☆ Moving the tailerons clear of the wing wake;
☆ Providing a leading-edge break to shed a strong vortex over the wing, inhibiting outward airflow and delaying tip-stall and pitch-up.

It is almost certain that the main aim of the modifications was to make the aircraft more manoeuvrable. The F-111, which has a very similar wing and tail geometry, becomes excessively stable in pitch – that is to say, nose-heavy – as the wings sweep back. The result is a reduction in manoeuvrability and, because a greater amount of control power is required to trim and manoeuvre the aircraft, an increase in drag in both level and manoeuvring flight. By making the configuration less naturally stable and increasing the control authority, the modifications applied to the MiG-23 increased the instantaneous turn rate; lengthening the moment arm also reduced the trim drag, while the vortices shed by the claws would inhibit a complete departure from controlled flight, which might be made more likely by the reduced stability margin. The Su-24, which does not need improved manouevrability, retains the original TsAGI shape.

Apart from these major changes, there were relatively few modifications other than those connected with operational equipment. One was the introduction of horizontal vanes into the inlet, behind the variable ramp, a simple but effective way of curbing unruly airflows at high angles of attack. The clean shape was disrupted by some semi-external conduits, but the fuselage remained basically unaltered.

Above: Illustrating the Soviet Union's confidence in its allies is this export-model 'Flogger-E' of the Libyan AF, with the radar/missile system of the MiG-21MF. One Libyan MiG-23 pilot crashed in Italy, probably while trying to defect.

Right: A SovAF MiG-23bis. In sharp contrast to the aircraft above, it has an incomparably better radar, IRST set (not the same as that of the MiG-23M), missiles of a later generation, more power and provision for much more fuel. Released in 1985, this is the first shot of a MiG-23bis with three tanks.

MiG-23M operational equipment

The new MiG-23M was a fully operational aircraft, with a full range of equipment. The nose was occupied by the fire-control radar; its Soviet designation is unknown, but it is codenamed 'High Lark' by NATO. It is a J-band radar working on the pulse-Doppler principle, with circuitry that analyzes the Doppler shift in return echoes. Emissions from the original 'High Lark', recorded by Western electronic intelligence assets, were considered to be suspiciously similar to those of the Westinghouse AWG-10 fitted to the F-4J Phantom; some F-4Js had been lost over Vietnam in 1967-68, and it has been suggested that the original 'High Lark' owes a great deal to recovered AWG-10 specimens. In any event, the 'High Lark' was a respectable performer for its time, with some ability to detect low-flying targets against ground clutter. (This 'look-down' capability must be distinguished from 'look-down, shoot-down'; 'High Lark' cannot guide a missile on to a low-flying target.)

In consideration of the changes in the fighter mission, and the possibility that the new fighter might operate beyond the range of ground control, the MiG-23 became the first Soviet fighter to feature a long-range navigation system, in the form of Doppler. Beneath the nose of the MiG-23M was a prominent housing with an optically flat glass front. This is generally considered to house an infra-red search and tracking device, for passive target tracking and positive identification.

Other antennas, built into the nose, the tailfin tip, the gloves and the tips of the claws, betrayed the presence of defensive and communications systems. The large dielectric panel at the tip of the fin housed the datalink antenna; a rear-facing bullet on the fin, and forward-facing antennas on the wings, probably housed the Sirena radar-warning receiver (RWR) system. The three differently shaped vertical aerials of the 'Odd Rods' IFF system spout ahead of the windshield, and bow-and-arrow antennas, reported to be part of the 'Swift Rod' instrument landing system, are carried on the nose and fin. In the lower rear fuselage is an array of 20 small holes; their purpose is not known for certain, but they may well be dispensers for flares and chaff cartridges, used as last-ditch missile decoys.

From the outset, the MiG-23 was designed to carry an internal GSh-23 cannon. (Interestingly, the Ye-230 had appeared at Domodedovo in 1967 with an accurate mock-up of the gun pack, before the weapon itself was known in the West.) The installation was similar to that of the MiG-21PFMA and subsequent variants, as discussed in the previous chapter.

The primary armament of the new fighter was to comprise the new R-23 and R-60 missiles, respectively designed for long-range interception and dogfighting. The R-23 was a new departure for the Soviet Union, being the first Soviet weapon intended for BVR attacks on small targets; known to NATO as AA-7 'Apex', its most striking characteristic is its size. It is about 20 per cent longer than its closest Western equivalent, the Sparrow, and its body diameter is 30 per cent larger. Taken together, these figures suggest that the R-23 weighs some 950lb (430kg), or about twice as much as the Sparrow. However, its effective range is no greater than the Sparrow's.

R-23 design rationale

These characteristics, unimpressive on paper, probably reflect a conservatism that was justified at the time. In Vietnam, the only theatre where BVR missiles had been used, the results had not been good, with kill probability (PK) figures in the 0.1-0.2 range: one shot in five or ten would be successful. The answer was either to improve the technology – which the Soviet Union could not count on doing, because this was a first-generation fighter-versus-fighter weapon – or to be more conservative in what was expected of each part of the system. The key was probably to trade greater weight for an acceptable PK. Whether this was accomplished successfully is hard to assess, since the R-23 has never been used in action.

The layout of the R-23, with foreplanes, delta wings and tailfins, suggests a concern with providing enough aerodynamic manoeuvrability to pursue a target through an evasive manoeuvre: Vietnam had shown the difficulty of achieving surprise with a missile shot, because of radar signals and the missile's thick exhaust plume. In addition, the R-23 may have a larger fraction of its weight devoted to the warhead, and to multiple fuzing systems to ensure that it detonates.

In common with Soviet interceptor-borne missiles, the R-23 is carried in two versions, one with infra-red homing and one with semi-active radar homing. The missiles can be released separately or in sequence, complicating the opponent's countermeasures problem and increasing the chances of a hit. One advantage of the TsAGI VG configuration is that it provides space below the gloves for the substantial pylon which this weapon requires.

MiG-23 stores options

1 Tactical air-to-surface missiles
2 AA-8 'Aphid' (R60) air-to-air missiles
3 GP-9 pack (23mm GSh-23 and ammunition)
4 176Imp gal (800lit) centreline fuel tank
5 AA-2 'Atoll' R-homing air-to-air missile

High speed and a heavy armament are the MiG-23's strong points. While AAMs are the primary armament, anti-radiation missiles and other air-to-surface weapons not requiring specific guidance systems can also be carried.

MiG-23 combat avionics

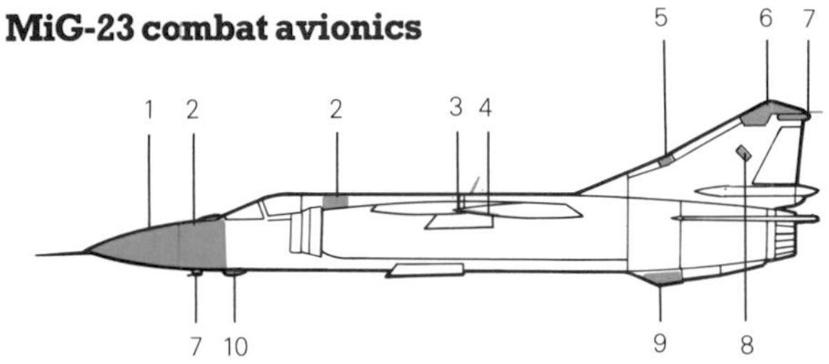

1 'High Lark' radar
2 Main avionics compartments
3 Sirena 3 radar warning receiver
4 VHF antenna
5 HF notch
6 VHF/UHF antenna
7 'Swift Rod' ILS antenna
8 VHF omnidirectional range antenna
9 Not known
10 Laser ranger and marked target seeker

MiG-23 stores provision

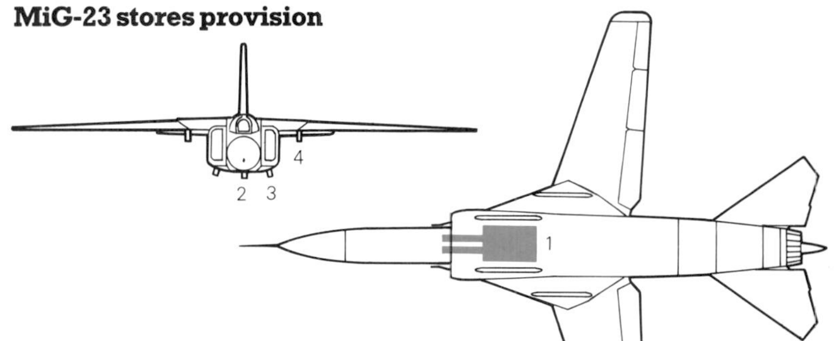

1 GSh-23 with 200rds ammunition
2 Centreline pylon for 176 Imp gal (800lit) fuel tank
3 Fuselage pylon, capacity 1,650/2,200lb (750/1,000kg)
4 Wing glove pylon, capacity 2,200lb (1,000kg)

The other missile developed for the MiG-23 was the R-60. This, by contrast, is the smallest of all fighter-launched guided weapons. With its relatively large delta wings and its double nose fins, it is clearly designed for high agility, so that it can turn rapidly from its launch path on to the target and confound any evasive manoeuvre. This should give it a small minimum range, and the ability to engage any target of sufficient brightness within the range of its seeker head. The forward nose fins are fixed, and may act as 'slats' for the aft set of fins, turning the airflow towards them and delaying a stall at very high g. The R-60, known to NATO as AA-8 'Aphid', is also used in semi-active radar and IR versions, the former being used for front-aspect attacks.

Missile deployment

Production of the MiG-23 seems to have run ahead of the development of the new missiles. When the type was first observed in East Germany, in the course of 1973, it was seen to be carrying launch rails for K-13-type missiles. The new weapons probably entered service in the Soviet Union in the mid-1970s, and were kept away from the less secure areas of Eastern Europe and the Baltic until the early 1980s. Initially, the glove pylons each carried a single R-23, and the belly pylons each mounted one R-60; dual launchers for the R-60 or K-13-class weapons have been seen on the glove pylons, replacing the R-23 rail; also, twin R-60 rails can be fitted to the belly pylons. While the MiG-23 can in theory carry eight short-range missiles, two R-23s and four R-60s seem to constitute the normal armament.

A routine and parallel development was the production of a two-seat conversion trainer variant, the MiG-23U. The second cockpit, with poor natural visibility ameliorated by a retractable periscope, displaced some of the fuel and avionics. Part of the latter was relocated to the nose, and the smaller 'Jay Bird' radar replaced the 'High Lark' system to make room for it.

The MiG-23 was fast, heavily armed, and had a respectable range, but NATO observers were not, to begin with, very disturbed by its arrival. It was clearly not in the class of the new US fighters then under development, and was generally more comparable with the F-4. As 1973 gave way to 1974, however, Western economies recoiled under the impact of the oil embargo and subsequent price rise, and defence plans everywhere came under budgetary pressure. Meanwhile, the number of MiG-23s in the field continued to increase at an ever faster rate, and the West started to take notice.

It soon became clear that the MiG-23 was an outstanding achievement in producibility, even by Soviet standards. This did not result from any single breakthrough, but from the fact that ease of production was a priority at all stages of design. The TsAGI VG planform, for example, was designed to be compatible with a simple fuselage and simple inlet design. The strength of the structure primarily relied on a few components of high-tensile steel, reinforcing the straightforward riveted-alloy airframe. The inlet was a proven design that had been demonstrated to perform properly without a complex control system. Tumansky's engine used advanced design in the aerodynamics to reduce the number and cost of the individual stages. This philosophy was carried right through the airframe.

Above: One of a batch of photos taken at Tripoli in 1975, which revealed the existence of the 'export' MiG-23.

Right: Points of interest in this nose-to-nose confrontation between MiG-23BN and Jaguar at an Indian Air Force base include the similarity of the forward fuselage design, the much larger inlets (and greater power) of the MiG, and the Soviet type's short, stout landing gear.

Right: Egypt took delivery of a number of MiG-23 export models – fighters and MiG-23BNs – before its rift with the Soviet Union. Some of the aircraft seen here may still be in service, at a well concealed airfield on Nellis AFB, Nevada.

Above: Indian Air Force MiG-23BNs of the first production batch delivered from the Soviet Union. HAL is now building the more capable MiG-27M, and MiG-23M fighters have been delivered direct from the Soviet Union.

By the end of 1973, MiG-23 production was probably running at 150 aircraft a year. While the MiG-21 still offered superior manoeuvrability, and would be retained for the tactical air defence mission, the newer fighter was far superior to the MiG-21 and Su-7 in any role that involved long range or an appreciable warload. With sizable fleets of such obsolescent types in being, the opportunity to carry out a rapid replacement programme, and to reply firmly to NATO's flexible response strategy, could not be missed. It was decided to accelerate production of the MiG-23 to unprecedented levels.

The factors behind individual Soviet planning decisions are kept secret. It is no secret, however, that Soviet industry's forte is the production of mechanical devices: airframes, engines, tanks and the like. In the case of almost any weapon system, it is found that the production of electronics and electronics-based subsystems lags behind that of the platform itself. In the case of the MiG-23M, the most likely components to present such a problem would be the 'High Lark' radar and the new missiles.

In the case of a Western aircraft in the same position, production would probably not be started until the radar production rate could match that of the airframe. The Soviet front commander, though, would rather have the faster, more powerful aircraft as soon as possible. It is possible that considerations of this sort underlay the development of new versions of the MiG-23, the first of which appeared quite suddenly on the scene in mid-1975.

Left: MiG-23BNs of the IAF's No 10 'Winged Dagger' Squadron. All these aircraft feature a small dielectric cap on a fairing above the starboard glove pylon; however, this is not always present on IAF aircraft of the type.

The simplest adaptation, and possibly the first to be developed, was basically a MiG-23M with the 'High Lark' radar, IR system and missile-control electronics removed, and replaced by a version of the MiG-21's 'Jay Bird' radar. Armament comprised four K-13-class missiles. It was this version that was supplied to Syria, Iraq and Libya in 1974-75. However, it has also been seen in Soviet markings.

A more extensively modified aircraft was developed to supersede some of the many Su-7s, MiG-21s and older MiGs in the tactical strike role. The first step in this line of development was a basic MiG-23 up to the rear cockpit bulkhead, but with a completely new forward fuselage which was shorter, lighter, cheaper to manufacture and offered a better downward view. It also carried armour on the cockpit sides. The new nose had no provision for a large attack radar, but contained a laser rangefinder. This version was designated MiG-23BN.

Strike variant

At the same time, a more extensive revision of the design was carried out, to produce an optimized strike aircraft. To reduce empty weight, at the cost of operationally useless Mach 2+ capability, the new type was fitted with simple fixed inlets and a shorter, lighter nozzle, while its payload was increased through a number of modifications. To increase the under-fuselage capacity, the fuselage weapon pylons were moved from the underside of the fuselage proper to the inlet ducts, making it possible to carry larger stores; new landing gear support beams increased ground clearance so that a large store or a drop tank could be carried on the centreline; and a small rack was added on each side of the rear fuselage These racks are usually described as mountings for auxiliary take-off rockets, but in fact carry additional stores, or flare or chaff dispensers.

For long-range missions, non-swivelling hardpoints were provided for two more 175gal (800lit) fuel tanks under the wings; the tanks would be used at the start of the flight, and jettisoned before the wings were swept. The wheels and

Mikoyan MiG-27 'Flogger-D'

The MiG-27 is a fully developed, extended-range strike version of the family. Excess weight – including the variable inlets and nozzle – is removed and replaced by extra fuel, more weapons and additional avionics. Virtually all the aircraft of this type have been delivered to Soviet units.

Above: Apparent in this view of a MiG-27 are the repositioned pylons, bulged wheel bays and taller main landing gear.

Right: An excellent view of a MiG-27. Note the electro-optical and electronic installations above the glove pylons, nose laser rangefinder, ventral six-barrel Gatling gun, 'scabbed-on' cockpit armour and rear-fuselage stores pylons.

brakes were enlarged to handle the higher gross weight of the new type, and were covered by bulged doors. Almost certainly, the new type introduced the Tumansky R-29 engine, uprated by 15 per cent over the R-27.

Another important change was the provision of a new gun, a six-barrel Gatling-type weapon of 23mm calibre. Not only did this offer a higher firing rate than the GSh-23 – probably in the region of 4,000-5,000 rds/min – but it also had a more sensible 70-calibre barrel length. An unusual – in fact, unique – feature of the installation was that the gun was uncovered, its workings completely exposed to the elements. This suggests that the gun is free to move in elevation, a technology that the Soviet Union is known to have exploited in later systems.

Gun performance

The rationale behind such a weapon is simple. A shell drops after it is fired, and the distance it drops below the barrel datum line varies with the firing range. When a fast-moving aircraft is shooting at a much slower ground target, both the range and the ballistic drop change rapidly during the burst. The later shells cover less distance and drop less, so the strikes tend to form an elliptical pattern with its long axis on the flightpath. Now, if the gun is trainable, and controlled by an automatic system with access to accurate range data (from a laser rangefinder) and accurate groundspeed data (from Doppler), the barrel can be steadily depressed during the burst, compensating for the shorter range and closing up the hit pattern. Even a simpler system, based on airspeed or a pre-set depression rate, could reduce the shell dispersion and increase the number of hits.

The improved ground-attack aircraft also featured a further outbreak of avionics: upgraded Doppler beneath the forward fuselage, an unidentified dielectric panel, possibly for a terrain-avoidance radar, under the nose, and two small dielectric bulges on the sides of the nose. The most significant additions, though, were installed on the gloves, directly above the pylons: an electronic antenna to starboard and an electro-optical head to port.

These were directly connected with the new air-to-surface guided weapons under development in the Soviet Union. Even in 1985, very little is known about these weapons. The only one to have been carried outside Soviet airspace is the AS-7 'Kerry', a radio-command guided weapon in the same class as the obsolete US Bullpup. More advanced weapons include the AS-10, a semi-active, laser-guided weapon, the heavier laser-guided AS-14 and the anti-radar AS-12. There is also a 1,100lb (500kg) laser-guided bomb. Seven new ASMs have been deployed since the mid-1970s, according to the DoD.

Increased payload, structural changes and, above all, provision for stand-off ASMs made the new variant a very different machine from the fighter versions, or the original strike aircraft. Accordingly, it received the designation MiG-27. Its arrival in East Germany, in mid-1975, came as a total and unpleasant surprise to NATO; even worse, the 16th Air Army had four regiments of this highly effective strike aircraft by the end of the year. It was a quantum jump in capability over the Su-7, and its appearance threatened to end NATO's large margin of qualitative superiority over the Warsaw Pact.

Some, but by no means all, of the improvements incorporated in the MiG-27

Left: This was the first photo of a 'duck-billed' MiG-23 to be seen in the West. It is a hybrid, with MiG-23 inlets and the MiG-27's duct-mounted pylons, and is almost certainly a development aircraft.

Left: The MiG-27 HUD is similar to that of the MiG-23. The canopy has no central frame; this may mean that the ejection seat is designed to break through the transparency.

were applied to the MiG-23BN, which became the export-model ground-attack variant of the family. Something of a mongrel, it had the Mach 2.3 propulsion system of the original MiG-23, but with no search radar it was virtually useless in the high-altitude air-to-air regime. Most of the advanced avionics appear to be missing, including those connected with advanced ASMs, the structure is similar to that of the MiG-23 and the less effective GSh-23 gun is retained. MiG-23BNs delivered to Warsaw Pact air forces have the same small nose antenna fairings as the MiG-27; these may be command antennas for the AS-7, or part of another earlier-technology ASM system. Some Soviet units also operate this type.

The MiG-23BN served a multiple purpose. Despite its simplified systems, it is an effective 'bomb truck', and is easier and cheaper to produce than the more complex MiG-27. The retention of variable inlets seems paradoxical, but it does mean that the same basic airframe can be changed to a fighter configuration at the final assembly stage if national needs require it.

The new variants were identified by NATO in order of observation; the MiG-23U trainer was 'Flogger-C'; the MiG-27, 'Flogger-D'; the 'export model' MiG-23, 'Flogger-E'; and the MiG-23BN became 'Flogger-F' for Middle East and other export customers, and 'Flogger-H' in its WarPac version.

With the introduction of the MiG-27, a second State Aircraft Factory was brought into the programme, and production surged ahead. By the late 1970s, the Soviet Union was estimated to be building more than 500 MiG-23s and MiG-27s per year. The type was exported throughout the Middle East, to Cuba and to Vietnam, and production of the MiG-27M was licenced to HAL in India, deliveries starting in 1979. The MiG-23S was supplied not only to Frontal Aviation, but also to the PVO, providing some measure of capability against low-flying aircraft and replacing many obsolescent types.

It should be remembered, though, that not all of the aircraft delivered were of the top-grade types. Neither the MiG-23M nor the MiG-27 was confirmed to be in use outside Soviet units – with the exception of the East German Luftstreitkraefte (LSK), which is under full-time

Left: The MiG-23BN is another 'export model' which in fact is extensively used by the Soviet Union's own forces; recently, it has been more widely illustrated than the MiG-27, but the latter is probably more important.

Soviet command – until the early 1980s, when India and Syria acquired the MiG-23M. Soviet units operate some 2,100 fighter versions of the series, and over 700 strike types. Some of these are of the subtypes usually described as 'export models'. In recent statements of fighter doctrine, for example, it has been made clear that only one aircraft in each fighting pair need be equipped for BVR.

Analysis of the destruction of a Korean Air Lines 747 in September 1983 has suggested that it was intercepted by a pair of aircraft: a BVR-equipped Su-15 and a MiG-23, probably a 'Flogger-E'. The 'Flogger-E' and MiG-23BN are probably in the minority overall, but may predominate in the Southern and Far Eastern theatres. Even if 75 per cent of the Soviet fleet consists of the full-capability variants, it is quite possible that downgraded versions have accounted for half the production run.

'Flogger-G' and 'Flogger-J'

Development continued through the later 1970s. An improved fighter version was first seen in late 1978 when a squadron of the type paid a visit to Finland. Believed to be designated MiG-23bis, the type incorporated a number of changes. The most obvious was a shorter, smaller dorsal fin extension, the precise reason for which is not clear. The type also featured a redesigned landing gear. The new nosewheel leg carried larger tyres, like those of the MiG-27, and the doors were bulged to accommodate it; the mainwheel legs were like those of the MiG-27, providing ground clearance for a 175gal (800lit) tank on the centreline. Like the MiG-27, too, the MiG-23bis can carry underwing tanks of the same capacity on fixed-sweep, jettisonable pylons. Compared with the original fighter version, its fuel capacity is increased by 525gal (2,400lit), or the equivalent of a MiG-21's internal fuel load.

The 'High Lark' radar has been improved, with more 'look-down' capability against low-flying targets (although it cannot guide AA-7 missiles on to them), and the cockpit instrumentation appears to have been modified; the Soviet fighter's usual head-down radar scope has been eliminated, and data is presented instead on the head-up display. This version is known to NATO as 'Flogger-G'.

The most recent version of the family to be identified is a MiG-27 variant known as 'Flogger-J' and featuring a slightly different nose profile. The EO and RF heads above the glove pylons have been deleted, and the pylons often carry gun pods with depressable barrels. Some 'Flogger-J' aircraft have been seen with narrow leading-edge root extensions; these seem too small to have much of an effect on the turn rate, and may house antennas.

MiG-23 exports started just after the Arab-Israeli war of 1973. It was an unlikely harbinger of peace, but it was to be eight years before the type was used in action. In June 1982, the MiG-23 made its combat debut, and emerged on the wrong side in the greatest military disaster in the history of air warfare.

Following Israel's invasion of Lebanon, Syria moved to install SAMs in the Beka'a Valley. The Israel Defence Force-Air Force (IDF-AF) moved to destroy the missiles and the advancing Syrian troops, and MiG-21s and MiG-23s were deployed to protect them. The combat zone was only two minutes from Syrian bases, while the IDF-AF aircraft had to fly between 10 and 40 minutes to reach the combat zone. The IDF-AF was also under a self-imposed prohibition against entering Syrian airspace.

Within one week, the IDF-AF had destroyed more than 80 Syrian aircraft, including 36 MiG-23s; its own losses did not exceed two aircraft. The general verdict, however, was not that the aircraft itself was totally inferior, since there were many factors in the Israeli success. The IDF-AF certainly displayed better tactics, and the Syrian tactics were judged less effective than they had been in 1973. The IDF-AF also had the advantage of better missile armament, with the developed Shafrir and the all-aspect AIM-9L. (According to the IDF-AF, Syria's MiG-23s were armed with R-23s and R-60s.)

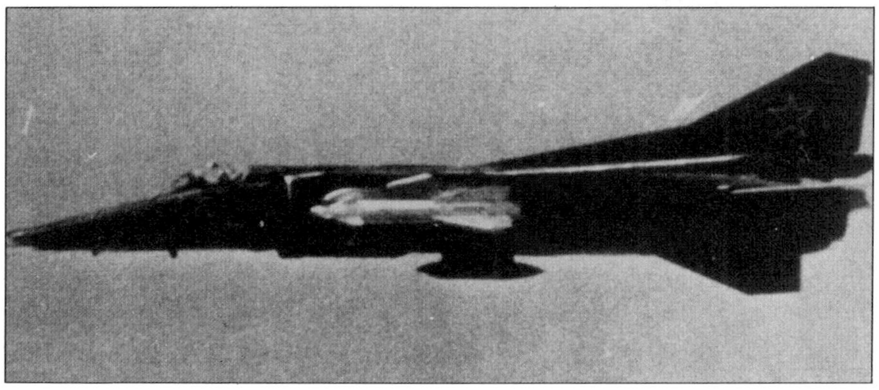

Above: Published here for the first time, this shows a MiG-27 carrying a very large (length 13.5ft/4m) ASM. Bigger than the AS-7 'Kerry', it may be the semi-active laser-guided AS-14, or the anti-radiation AS-9. The pod under the fuselage resembles the underwing gunpods of the 'Flogger-J'.

Possibly the most important single factor, though, was the highly developed Israeli battle management system, including E-2C Hawkeyes and a fleet of electronic intelligence (elint) platforms ranging from balloons, through OV-1 Mohawks and modified RF-4Es to specially equipped RC-707s. The Syrian fighters were tracked as soon as they left their runways, and the IDF-AF usually had the advantage of surprise. The IDF-AF fighters all had datalinks, and could receive information as it was gathered: the Syrians' own Soviet-supplied datalinks had been effectively jammed by the IDF.

Details of individual actions are hard to come by. However, published figures have suggested that the MiG-23 is outturned by both the MiG-21 and the F-4E, and is in a different class of manoeuvring performance from new generation fighters such as the F-16. In fact, its performance has been compared to that of the F-104: very fast in a straight line, but very slow in a turn. Its assets, however, include a long range, thanks to low overall drag, respectable internal fuel capacity and VG: the operational combat radius of the three-tank 'Flogger-G' has been stated at 600nm (1,100km) by USAF intelligence sources.

'High Lark' performance

The MiG-23 also has a greater radar detection range, and a greater missile range, than some Western types. According to figures supplied by the US Air Force to *Aviation Week* in early 1981, 'High Lark' can detect a fighter-sized target at 42-45nm (78-83km) at 20,000ft (6,100m) and Mach 0.9. At the same altitude, the maximum range for a radar-guided AA-7 launch is 14nm (26km). This is slightly better than the engagement range for the F-4E/AIM-7E combination, but not by a significant amount; worse than the performance of the F-15/AIM-7F; and considerably better than the performance of the F-16/AIM-9 combination. The 'first-look, first-shot' advantage which the MiG-23 enjoys over the F-16 is a major problem for NATO, and will remain so until the long-delayed introduction of the Hughes AIM-120 Amraam.

MiG-23/27 production was scaled down in the early 1980s; probably, one of the plants involved was converted to production of a new design such as the MiG-29. However, the effect of its contribution to the rapid modernization of Soviet and allied units in the 1970s will be felt for a long time. Apart from the F-16, no comparable Western type has proved to be anything like as affordable, and no similarly affordable type can be considered comparable. The MiG-23 and MiG-27 may not be the newest technology, but they will not become obsolete in this decade, and they provide the Warsaw Pact with a firm numerical foundation for its latest modernization efforts.

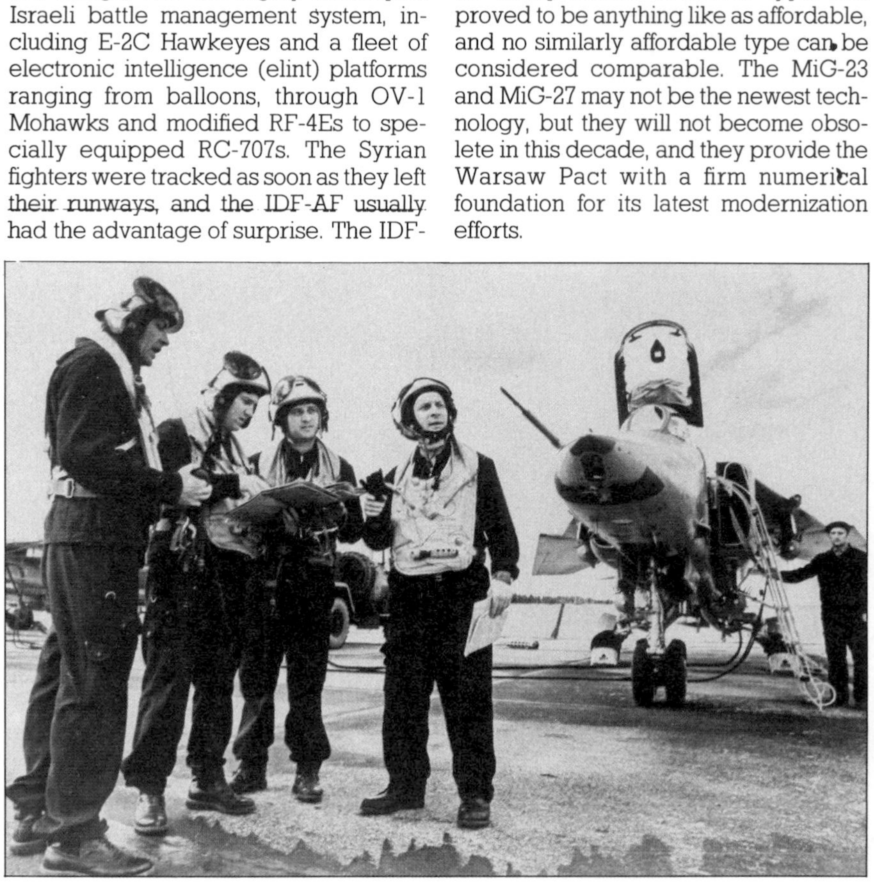

Right: Another photo showing the extensive range of sensors carried by the MiG-27. The four-bomb armament carried here is probably little more than a practice load.

MiG-27 stores options

1 FAB-250 550lb (250kg) general-purpose bomb
2 FAB-500 1,100lb (500kg) general-purpose bomb
3 Tactical air-to-surface missile
4 AA-2-2 'Advanced Atoll' air-to-air missile
5 23mm Gatling gun and ammunition
6 1,100lb (500kg) low-drag bomb
7 176Imp gal (800lit) centreline fuel tank

The most heavily armed member of the series, the MiG-27 can carry and launch most of the new tactical ASMs and smart weapons introduced by Soviet forces over the past ten years.

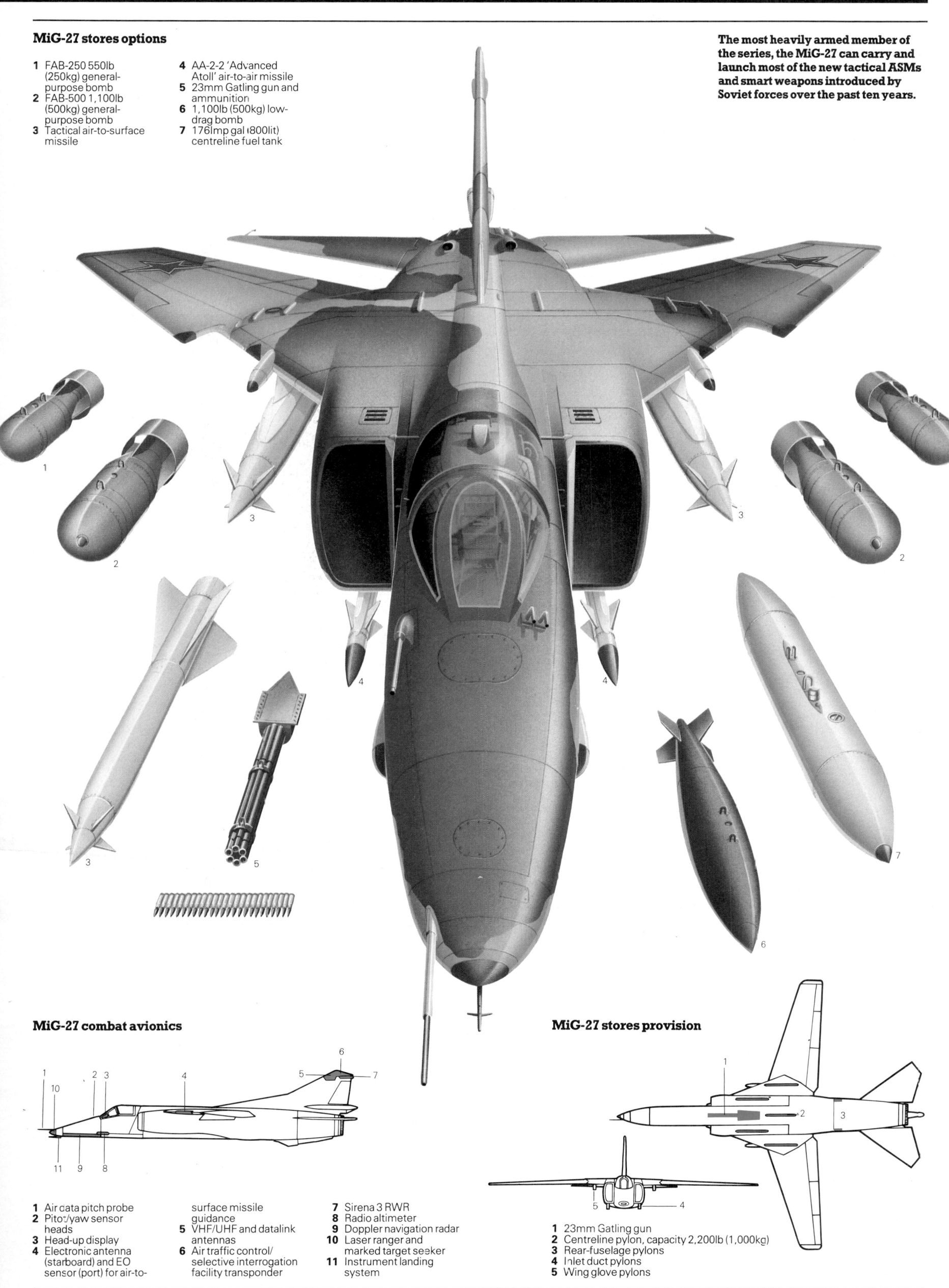

MiG-27 combat avionics

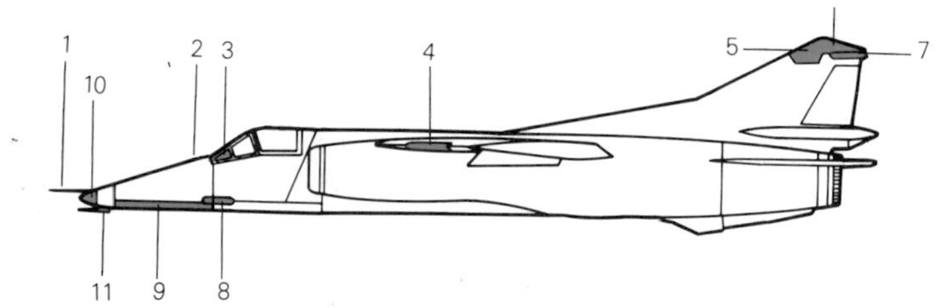

1 Air data pitch probe
2 Pitot/yaw sensor heads
3 Head-up display
4 Electronic antenna (starboard) and EO sensor (port) for air-to-surface missile guidance
5 VHF/UHF and datalink antennas
6 Air traffic control/ selective interrogation facility transponder
7 Sirena 3 RWR
8 Radio altimeter
9 Doppler navigation radar
10 Laser ranger and marked target seeker
11 Instrument landing system

MiG-27 stores provision

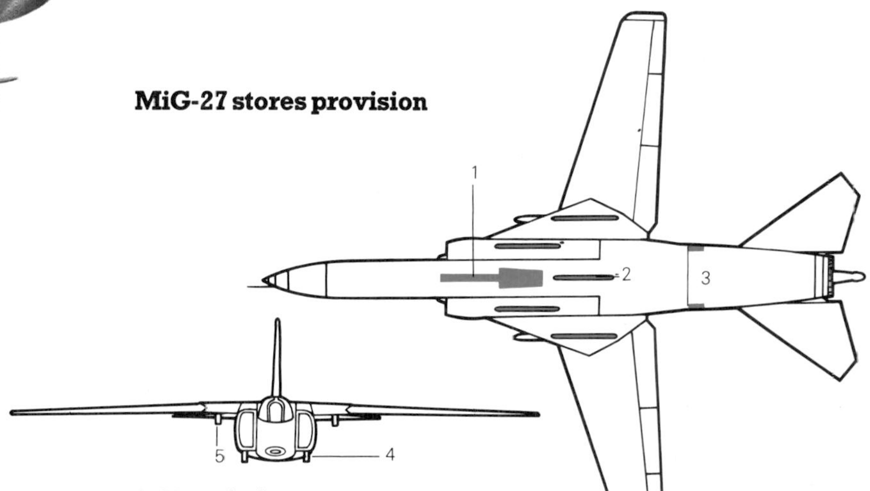

1 23mm Gatling gun
2 Centreline pylon, capacity 2,200lb (1,000kg)
3 Rear-fuselage pylons
4 Inlet duct pylons
5 Wing glove pylons

MiG-25 'Foxbat'

Solid and aggressive in appearance, and uniquely fast in level flight and climb, the MiG-25 has inspired respect since its first appearance. Initially developed as a counter to the cancelled B-70 Valkyrie, the new interceptor was consistently mis-assessed by Western intelligence, with results that permanently affected Western planning. The US Air Force, in particular, incurred enormous expense in developing the F-15 as a counter to what proved to be a mythical aircraft. And the West's errors would probably still stand uncorrected had it not been for a once-in-a-lifetime intelligence windfall in the mid-1970s.

Aviation history is full of surprises. One of the biggest was probably inflicted on the personnel of Hakodate Airport, in northern Japan, one overcast September afternoon in 1976. At 13.50, just as the daily All Nippon Airways 727 lifted off the 6,000ft (1,830m) runway, a jagged steel-grey shape dropped from the clouds, dead in its path. A collision was averted at the last second as the intruder's pilot turned sharply around the 727 and dived for the runway. The aircraft was still moving at 220kt (405km/h) as it touched down, and following a tyre-scorching, parachute-streaming gallop down the length of the remaining concrete it came safely to rest 800ft (243m) into the overrun zone. The airport people stared with slowly diminishing disbelief at the new arrival, the unmistakable red stars of the Soviet Air Forces vivid against its dull skin. Lt Viktor Belenko had defected to the West with his own aircraft, a Mikoyan MiG-25 'Foxbat-A'.

It was as though the paleontological community had discovered a live Tyrannosaurus rex in some South American jungle. Many aerospace professionals heard the news over breakfast in their hotels in London or the English countryside, because the Farnborough Air Show was on. The news had reached Washington in the middle of the night, but the best men of the USAF's Foreign Technology Division were leaving Wright-Patterson AFB before dawn aboard a pair of VC-135s.

The MiG-25 was the most feared and least known of all Soviet aircraft. It was considered to be almost as fast as the Lockheed SR-71, but it had already been built in far greater numbers and was still in production. According to some assessments, its unrefuelled range was comparable to the SR-71's, allowing it to escort Backfire bombers over the North Atlantic or reconnoitre the whole of Western Europe; even the less flattering estimates credited it with range at least equal to that of the new McDonnell Douglas F-15. The MiG-25 had thumbed its nose at Israel's formidable air force. What nobody could understand was how the Soviet designers had packed so much performance into an aircraft that could be built in such numbers.

A myth exposed

The Foreign Technology Division, and the intelligence community in general, were next in line for a surprise. Examination of the aircraft – before it was returned, in pieces, to the Soviet Union – and Belenko's own extensive debriefing, showed that the West had grossly mis-assessed the MiG-25 from the day of its first public appearance nine years earlier. For almost a decade, a great deal of Western defence planning had been influenced by a mythical aircraft.

The story had started just about two decades earlier, when the US National Advisory Committee on Aeronautics (NACA) published the results of some theoretical work in high-Mach aerodynamics. The theory put forward by Alfred Eggers and Clarence Syvertson was that a supersonic aircraft could be designed to trap its own shock wave beneath its wings, turning otherwise wasted energy into useful lift.

The 'compression lift' theory went unnoticed until January 1957. At that time, Strategic Air Command was looking for a supersonic replacement for the B-52, but the target performance was proving hard to attain, except with an enormous aircraft which, in effect, was 'staged' like a rocket; much of its structure would contain only fuel, and would be jettisoned as the fuel was used. The last few hundred miles to the target would be flown at Mach 2, but cruising speed would be subsonic. Boeing and North American proposed such aircraft to meet the Weapon System 110A (WS-110A) requirement, and both designs were rejected.

In pursuit of an alternative approach, North American turned to the compression-lift theory, and by mid-1957 was proposing a design which was not only more practical, but would fly at Mach 3 throughout its mission, 1,720kt (3185km/h) at an altitude of 70,000ft (21,330m). In December 1957 North America was chosen to build the new bomber, and in the following month SAC cancelled full-scale development of an alternative nuclear-powered bomber in favour of an accelerated schedule for the WS-110A programme. The new bomber would fly in December 1962, and the first operating wing of 12 aircraft would be operational by August 1964. First details of the programme were released in February 1958, and the designation B-70 was adopted.

To the PVO-Strany, responsible for defending the entire Soviet Union and all its military and industrial centres from bomber attack, the B-70 was a real problem. There were many analysts at the time who would not have agreed with this view. Only months earlier, British officials and Defence Minister Duncan Sandys had rebuilt the country's entire military production programme around the omnipotent guided missile. In the Soviet Union, where amateurs are not encouraged to make policy decisions, a more reasonable view prevailed.

A 200-ton Mach 3 bomber may be an easy target to detect, but it is certainly not easy to kill. Problems start with the mechanics of destroying a large aircraft. Blast is relatively weak in the thin air of high altitude, so a kill requires either a direct hit, by chemical explosives or some heavy kinetic projectile (such as the metal hoop formed by a continuous-rod warhead), or a nuclear blast. Nuclear warheads make the guidance problem less severe, but at the expense of a bigger delivery system.

At the time, the fastest Soviet interceptor was the new Sukoi Su-11. It would not even touch the B-70. Its maximum sus-

Left: A MiG-25R 'Foxbat-B' undergoing flight-line inspection. The sharp waisting of the fuselage between the inlets is very clear in this view, as is the gradual widening of the upper ramps from front to rear.

Above: One of the Ye-26 prototypes takes a bow over Domodedovo on July 9, 1967. Note the vertical fins, much smaller than those adopted for the production MiG-25. The nose is black, but there is probably no radar inside.

tained altitude was far lower than that of the B-70, its speed was 30 per cent lower, and its AA-3 'Anab' missiles were designed for use against subsonic bombers.

The Soviet weapon with the greatest capability against high-altitude targets was the new V750VK surface-to-air missile (SAM) system, a large solid-rocket-powered missile with an effective altitude around 75,000ft (22,900m). Despite this, it was a long way short of an effective defence against a B-70, and even a much larger SAM would also suffer certain limitations.

One of these is that a solid-rocket SAM is a 'boost/coast' vehicle: its engines burn out after a few seconds of flight, leaving it with only its momentum. Its ability to turn and manoeuvre is limited by its remaining energy, and beyond a certain point it 'goes ballistic' and will no longer respond to guidance signals. The problem is compounded at high altitudes, where a design conflict arises: the missile's wing size is limited by the need to accelerate rapidly at low altitude, and to keep weight down, but its small wings are inefficient in thin air at higher levels.

On the other hand, the target can manoeuvre: not rapidly, but to an unlimited degree. It also has plenty of warning of an attack, because of the powerful radar signals needed to guide a missile from a ground station. Providing enough of an energy margin to follow an evasive manoeuvre on the part of the target eats further still into the missile's lethal radius.

Speed is a related problem. All missile systems work, to some extent, on prediction, because there is always a time lag between the target's movement and the missile's response: a missile which was guided to the target's actual position would always pass just behind it. With a large command-guided weapon like the V750VK, over a long enough range, the time lag can be quite considerable, and if the target is manoeuvring, and the missile is in its last, sluggish flight phase, the predicted and actual positions of the target may be well apart. Speed also reduces the time available for an engagement, and makes the tracking problem more difficult.

A final point is that the missile is relatively small and expendable, while the aircraft is large, has plenty of onboard power, and is protected by powerful jamming systems. It is probably an accurate generalization to say that jamming gets more effective as the missile approaches the target and flies further from its launch and control system. Because of these and other factors, even a very large SAM would only have a limited effective radius against an aircraft such as a B-70.

Alternative approaches to a similar problem were being tried in the USA. Because of the 'technology push' mechanism, however, US air defence planning had always been aimed at a projected threat well in advance of anything fielded by the Soviet Union, and by mid-1958 work on an interceptor capable of countering supersonic-cruise bombers was quite well advanced. This was the North American F-108, a large, long-range, two-seat Mach 3 aircraft, equipped with a radar/missile system that could initiate an engagement at 85nm (160km) range. Rather further along in development was the formidable Boeing IM-99 Bomarc, a massive strategic SAM with ramjet propulsion and its own active radar system.

Neither would have worked in the Soviet system. The F-108-type aircraft, with its highly sophisticated electronics, would not have been achievable in time to meet the B-70 threat. In any event, the long-range interceptor was less attractive to the Soviet Union; the land-mass is so large that an adequate multi-layered defensive system can be operated over Soviet territory, where range is not critical, and still protect major targets. As for the Bomarc, the cost of such a large missile, and the chances of actually hitting the target so far from the launch point, were always in doubt.

Instead, the PVO-Strany opted for an extrapolation of the current Soviet interception system. As it stood in 1957-58, the Soviet air defence environment reflected the country's lack of a good radar-equipped interceptor. The IA-PVO – the interceptor component of the force – was divided into a great many small units, usually no larger than a division (three or four regiments of 36 aircraft), each tasked with the defence of a given area or target. The backbone of the force was made up of single-seat interceptors, with limited radar capability.

The fighters were held at readiness on the ground until a target was detected; they were then scrambled and directed to the interception point by ground controllers. Training and tactics stressed tight control and instant obedience on the part of the pilots, because it was only through close adherence to procedures that a fighter with a low-powered radar could be brought within detection range of its target.

This force structure had some important implications for fighter design. Because the system was originally built around the MiG-15 and MiG-17, each unit's area of operations was restricted to the 160nm (300km) operational radius of those types, and the command and control facilities at unit level were designed to handle the air battle in that area. Now, if a longer-range interceptor were to be introduced, the command and control facilities would have to be expanded to cope with a larger area of operations, and the units' air defence zones would overlap. Without restructuring and re-equipping the ground units, the PVO-Strany simply did not require greater range from its interceptors.

Interceptor performance

Quick reaction, on the other hand, was important, and became more so as the speed of the threat increased. Fighter requirements accordingly stressed speed, rate of climb and reliability. The ability to ensure destruction of the target was also important, and air-to-air missiles received a great deal of attention in the 1950s.

During 1958 the PVO-Strany worked on defining the system needed to intercept the B-70, and what emerged was a requirement for a new single-seat fighter of extremely high performance. It would be designed for a ground-controlled interception (GCI) mission, but the concept would be taken a step further: the fighter would be under automatic control from the ground, and a datalink would connect the fighter's radar to the ground station. The radar would be powerful enough to burn through jamming at close range, providing the ground station with the exact target data needed for the final intercep-

Right: The MiG-25 'Foxbat-E' has been produced by fitting older airframes with the more effective and less compromised radar of the MiG-23bis, together with a similar IRST system.

Left: Lt Viktor Belenko's MiG-25 rests in the overrun area at Hakodate airport, in northern Japan, following its pilot's defection. It was the largest single windfall of technical intelligence in the superpowers' history.

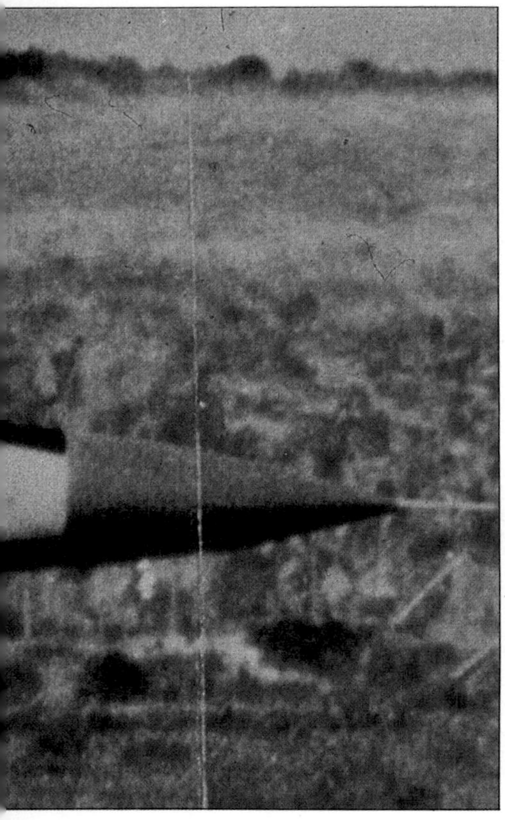

Below: Although it has a new radar, the 'Foxbat-E' has the same AA-6 missiles as the older aircraft. The appearance of the nose is slightly changed, because the new radome is closer to an ogive than a cone, and is shorter than that of the original.

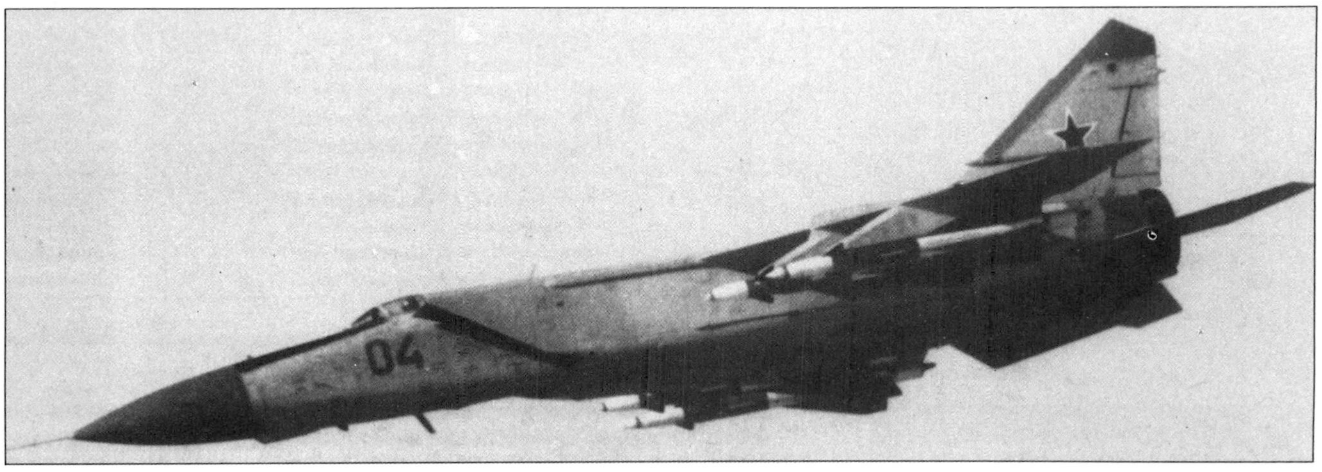

tion. The armament would be a battery of four missiles, each capable of felling a heavy bomber, but with only a modest range; the final attack would be made by the aircraft, not the missiles alone. Maximum speed, with missiles aboard, was to be in excess of 1,620kt (3,000km/h), and the type was to be suitable for mass production.

In speed and range, the new system was not unlike the Bomarc. The main differences were that instead of being expendable, it was recoverable; that it had the ability to make multiple firing passes at the target, increasing its PK; and that it had the added flexibility of a pilot in the loop.

The beauty of this requirement was that, although it stretched the state of the art and was by no means easy, it did not demand any immense advance in any one technology. It avoided the need to develop a long-range radar/missile system, while the modest specified range brought the airframe-design problem within reason. Also, while the datalink would involve new technology, the philosophy of automated GCI meant that many of the complex problems, such as discriminating against jamming and working out the best interception track, could be handled on the ground. Another advantage was that the target would be detected and tracked by ground-based radars; until the final seconds of the interception, when the interceptor turned on its radar, the target's crew need not be aware that they were under attack.

Go-ahead for Mikoyan

The requirement was probably issued in 1959; both Mikoyan and Sukhoi are likely to have been consulted, since both were engaged in developing technology for Mach 2.8 aircraft, but no details of Sukhoi's design, if it existed, are known. In any case, the Mikoyan design was given the go-ahead, probably in early 1960.

In terms of sheer performance, the Mikoyan bureau did not need to aim as high as the Lockheed Skunk Works, which started design of the A-12 reconnaissance aircraft at about the same time,. but were working within far tighter constraints of producibility and reliability. Also, the Soviet system had not encouraged the development of technology for its own sake during the 1950s, and the result was that some of the basic knowledge available to Lockheed was not available to the Mikoyan team.

Even so, building a practical aircraft to carry four heavy missiles and a powerful radar to Mach 2.8 posed problems in many areas. The best known, at the time, was kinetic heating: friction and compression between the air and the airframe generate heat, and above Mach 2 the temperatures begin to reach levels that degrade the structural properties of aluminium, and bring down its fatigue life. The only answer is to substitute a more heat-resistant material.

Above: This was the first photograph released in the West to show the MiG-25 carrying the two-stage AA-6 'Acrid' missile. Semi-active radar-homing weapons are carried on the outer pylons, and IR-homers inboard.

Aerodynamics also present challenges. As Mach numbers increase, the shock waves shed by the nose and leading-edge surfaces slant back more sharply, and may interact with the rest of the airframe: for instance, the wing leading edge may cut into the nose shock wave, possibly causing excessive drag. Putting the wing completely inside the shock wave either means a very sharply swept wing (with poor low-speed characteristics) or a long and heavy nose; the alternative is a thin-section wing, which is structurally difficult to build. Overall, the design becomes dominated by wave drag.

Stability and controllability

Stability is also an issue. The aerodynamic centre moves rearward at high speeds, so that the aircraft becomes more stable, but it may become excessively stable and more difficult to control. Meanwhile, as Mach number increases, all the aerodynamic surfaces become less affected by changes in angle of attack, and since the tail surfaces stabilize the aircraft by responding to such changes, the dynamic stability of the aircraft decreases. The problem is worse at high altitude, where aerodynamic damping of aircraft movements decreases due to the thinner air. The changes in static and dynamic stability with Mach number make the design and sizing of vertical and horizontal tail surfaces peculiarly critical. The task was particularly difficult in the case of the new interceptor, since it would have to possess some degree of manoeuvrability at its maximum operating speed.

Propulsion for a Mach 3 aircraft is an area for careful trade-off studies. The design of the propulsion system becomes dominated by the ram effect – the high pressure and temperature created when the air entering the inlets at a relative speed of 2,720ft/sec (830m/sec) is slowed down to zero relative speed before entering the engine. This is not quite enough for a ramjet to offer high efficiency, but it creates problems for a conventional turbojet. If the pressure at the compressor face is further multiplied by the engine's own pressure ratio, temperatures within the engine rise to levels where even exotic materials will not be adequate. Also, the design of the inlet system becomes critical, because even a small drop in the amount of ram pressure recovered can have a very large effect on efficiency.

Above: The fuselage shape of the MiG-25, with the augmentors, forward fuselage and inlet blended into a solid central box, is well depicted in this view of a 'Foxbat-E'. Note also the anti-glare panel ahead of the IRST set.

Mach 3 flight takes a great deal of power, so the overall efficiency of the propulsion system is important. Even a slight increase in specific fuel consumption translates into a lot of extra fuel. It was this problem that hit the Bristol 188 research aircraft; because the powerplants were not efficient enough, the 188 simply could not carry enough fuel to complete a mission at its design speed.

The fuel system is yet another problem area, for several reasons. High temperatures can detonate empty tanks; heat also causes thermal expansion, making it difficult to seal the tanks properly. On the other hand, as much of the airframe as possible must contain fuel, because of the high thrust requirements.

With these problems in mind, the Mikoyan team threw out all previous designs, along with the normal evolutionary design approach, and started with a clean sheet of paper. The first clear point to emerge, in all probability, was the fact that the new aircraft would be big. The missiles would be large, because of the need for high speed, effectiveness at high altitude and a heavy warhead. The radar system would be heavy, have a large antenna and require a startling amount of power. The resulting rough figures for the size of the aircraft pointed clearly to a twin-engined type, because no single engine would be big enough.

The Mikoyan OKB's trade-off studies on the configuration would make fascinating reading. It is possible to guess that the tailless delta or canard were considered, but probably rejected on the grounds of poor manoeuvrability at high altitude. The familiar tailed delta was probably ruled out, indirectly, by weight: with fuel for Mach 3 and the required operational equipment, its wing loading would be too high for any high-altitude manoeuvring, and its short span would probably have raised the spectre of inertia coupling.

This left a thin, moderately swept wing as the best practical option. As it happened, the same conclusion had been reached some years earlier by another design team, one which was also aiming for high speed and high altitude, and which also faced requirements that ruled out the otherwise attractive delta wing. Their final design was the highly elegant North American Vigilante, and there can be no question that this very advanced Mach 2 carrier-based bomber, unveiled in 1958, was the starting point for the Mikoyan OKB's design.

Design genealogy

To allocate credit correctly, it must be noted that some key features of the Vigilante configuration stemmed from the Vought F-8 Crusader, flown in 1954, and the first supersonic aircraft to feature a thin swept wing in the structurally convenient shoulder position. The slab tail was set at mid-height on the fuselage, out of the wing wake, another first and a great help to high-speed stability, avoiding the pitch-up problems of a T-tail. At a time when exaggerated 'wasp-waisted' fuselages were the rage, the F-8's clean, straight-lined fuselage demonstrated a clearer understanding of the Area Rule.

The Vigilante inherited these characteristics, adding an advanced propulsion system with variable-geometry, wedge-shaped inlets. The inlet design was more sophisticated than that of the contemporary F-4, and could achieve more efficient ram pressure recovery. The sharp, thrust-forward upper lip split the primary shock past the inlet, but the variable ramps inside the inlet were designed to capture and stabilize the subsequent shock waves. With careful control of bleed valves in the inlet system, this layout was capable of high efficiency across a wide range of flight conditions.

The width of the fuselage and the inlet lips could be a problem at high angles of attack, possibly shedding vortices over the fin. To reduce this effect, the Vigilante designers provided the original design with twin outward-canted vertical fins. These were replaced by a single all-moving slab fin before the prototype was completed.

The twin fins were retained on the new Mikoyan fighter, as were many other aspects of the Vigilante configuration: the thin, shoulder-mounted wing, the inlets, the slab-sided fuselage and the tail position. The detail execution of the design was different, reflecting the different missions, but the two aircraft turned out to be remarkably similar in shape, size and weight.

The characteristics of the engine, and in particular its thrust and fuel consumption, would determine the size of aircraft needed to meet the mission requirement, while the choice of engine was driven by the timescale and the technical problems. A new turbojet with a normal pressure ratio would have to survive unprecedented operating temperatures, for the reasons discussed above, and development would simply have taken too long. However, there was an alternative available and in production.

During the 1950s, a number of design teams had advocated the development of a specialized, simplified 'supersonic turbojet', in which efficiency and low-speed thrust/weight ratio were deliberately sacrificed in the interests of high-speed performance. By 1960, two such engines had been built: the British de Havilland Gyron, and a cruise-missile engine built by the Mikoyan bureau's close associates at the Tumansky OKB. It was this engine that formed the basis for the new interceptor.

The engine's poor low-speed characteristics were of secondary importance, because there was no requirement for subsonic cruise, high-subsonic combat or loiter. However, its appetite for kerosene at Mach 3 would be phenomenal. Studies soon confirmed that the fighter would, indeed, be large, with a loaded takeoff weight of 35-40 tons.

Given the size and the general configuration, the design – now known as the Ye-266 – began to take shape. The size of the wing was set by manoeuvre, climb and sustained altitude requirements, which dictated a maximum wing loading at the top of the climb. (With well over half the fuel gone, this would be much lower than the take-off wing loading.) Sweep angle and thickness/chord ratio were traded off, based on the minimum depth that was structurally practical: a 4 per cent thick wing, swept 40° on the leading edge, was selected, providing low drag but making some room for fuel in the wing. The wing's moderate sweep and low aspect ratio made it stiff enough to accept four pylons for large AAMs, and to allow conventional ailerons to be used for all lateral control. Take-off and landing speed were of secondary importance, and high-lift devices were confined to plain flaps.

The wing was not quite as much of a plank as it appeared. A certain degree of washout – reduction in incidence towards the tips – was introduced by gradually reducing the leading-edge camber from the outer pylon to the tip. At some angles this feature could give a strong impression of compound sweep, and it has confused many observers over the years.

Below: The truck by the left-hand MiG-25U carries all the diagnostic equipment for the type, tools for routine maintenance and a ground power unit, and also acts as a tug.

Fuselage design

The shape and size of the engine dictated the build-up of the fuselage. The rear fuselage was wrapped around the huge afterburners, each measuring 49in (1.5m) in diameter. The centre fuselage was a deep, wide box containing the engine tunnels, much smaller in diameter than the augmentors, the simple, forward-retracting main landing gear and much of the fuel. Just ahead of the leading edge, the structure broke into three elements: the two big variable inlets and their ramps, flanking a long nose containing the cockpit and the radar system.

The detailed aerodynamic design of the fuselage was one of its best features. The cross-sectional area was allowed to expand steadily, from the nose back to the wing. In plan view, the nose section tapered from its maximum width, immediately aft of the radome, to a deep but slender 'neck' between the inlets, reducing total cross-section and avoiding what would otherwise have been a drag-evoking kink in the area-versus-length chart. In fact, the wave drag coefficient of the new design was better than that of the more slender MiG-21 at any speed above Mach 1.5.

The horizontal tail trunnions were angled, as on the MiG-19 and MiG-21, so

Mikoyan MiG-25 'Foxbat-A'

Features of the MiG-25's shape which are frequently overlooked – the straight wing leading edge, the slender 'neck' of the forward fuselage between the inlets, and the tapering inlet lips – are apparent in this old but generally accurate drawing.

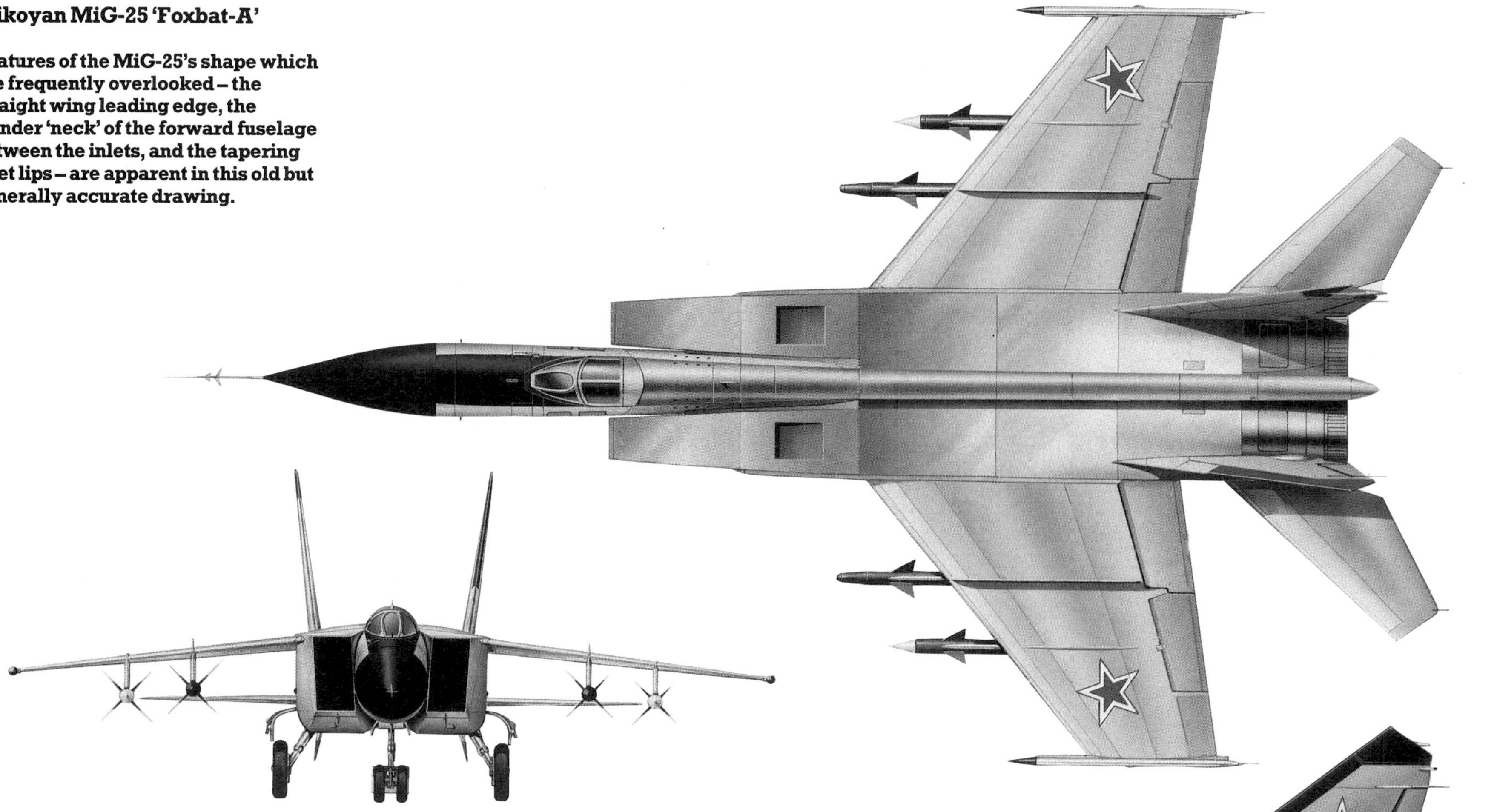

that the stabilizers seemed by Western standards to be mounted on little more than thin air. The tips of both the vertical and horizontal surfaces were sawn off at right angles to the quarter-chord line, in what was later recognized as a simple and effective precaution against flutter.

The most original feature of the airframe, though, was its construction. As explained above, aluminium alloys were unsuitable for the main parts of the airframe. In the USA, steel honeycomb and titanium were regarded as alternative substitutes in high-Mach aircraft; by 1960, quite large amounts of titanium had been used in a number of US aircraft (including the Vigilante), production facilities were in place, and it was possible to conceive of a small production run of all-titanium aircraft. The Soviet Union had less experience and fewer facilities. Moreover, the idea of mass-producing an all-titanium fighter by the mid-1960s was out of the question, as it would have been in the USA. Like Lockheed, the Mikoyan OKB had more sense than to try their luck with steel honeycomb.

What the Soviet Union did have was a great deal of experience with ordinary steel. Steel has never been part of the Western aircraft designer's culture, although steel alloys are cheap, have competitive strength-to-weight ratios – even at high temperatures – and are easy to work with. Aluminium is superior for most aircraft structures, because it is more ductile and more easily fabricated into large, light, load-bearing assemblies. It is also more tolerant of holes; thin aluminium sheet can be riveted, but steel of the same weight is too thin to stand such treatment, and demands welded joints which are mistrusted by the Western designer. Steel is more suited to concentrated loads, and, in 1960, had been used for the frames and load-bearing bulkheads in all the Mikoyan jet fighters.

Structural materials

The Ye-26, therefore, was mainly built out of high-strength steel alloys. Most of the structure was arc-welded: the skins were stiffened with welded-on steel stringers, and welding was used to build up complex structural components that, in a Western type, would be forged. Forged steel was used for spars and main structural members; titanium was used for the leading edges and around the tailpipes where the temperatures were highest; and some cooler parts, such as the trailing edges, flaps and ailerons, were of aluminium.

The structure weight, in total, came to 17 per cent more than that of the Vigilante, a similarly sized aircraft. This figure was respectable, but was achieved by carefully trading strength for weight. The Ye-26 was designed to pull a maximum of 5 g during the interception, when the fuel tanks would be much more than half empty; with full tanks, the maximum g was much lower. Most current fighters are designed to pull 9 g with half fuel, so their airframes must be more than twice as strong as that of the Mikoyan fighter. Neither was the airframe stressed for high speeds at low level.

The fuel system represented a unique answer to the problems of heating and sealing associated with high-speed operations: the designers simply abandoned integral tanks in favour of discrete fuel tanks built from continuously welded steel sheet. The system added some weight, but it was virtually leakproof, was easily fitted with a nitrogen inerting system, and furthermore insulated the fuel from the worst of the skin heating. In theory, the tanks reduced internal fuel volume; in practice, the 31,000lb (14,000kg) fuel load was 41 per cent of clean gross weight, an excellent figure.

Above: Groundcrew give scale to the heavyweight MiG-25, its tall verticals and mighty afterburners. One man is standing on the stabilizer, a testimony to the type's rugged construction.

The propulsion system, as noted above, was based on a modified Tumansky missile engine. It was a single-shaft, fixed-geometry engine with five compressor stages and a single turbine stage without air cooling: its basic layout resembled a small jet engine such as a Rolls-Royce Viper. Static pressure ratio – the usual measure of an engine's efficiency – was only 7:1, considerably less than that of the MiG-21 powerplant. Despite its simplicity, the engine was large: its mass flow of 275-300lb/sec (125-135kg/sec) put it in the same class as the biggest contemporary pure jets. It was mostly made of steel, with some titanium.

The engine, however, was merely the core of the powerplant. It breathed through a long convergent duct fed by a cavernous two-dimensional inlet; a spill door for excess air was located on top of the inlet, and a small flap on the lower lip could be drooped to admit more air at low speeds. Two ramps on the top surface of the inlet were deflected downward under hydraulic power and electronic control at high speed, to constrict the throat and control the pattern of shock waves in the duct. Further back along the duct were a group of vanes to smooth out irregularities in the airflow, and a system for injecting methanol and water into the airstream. (Some 1,100lb (500kg) of the mixture was carried in tanks in the fins, and fed to the inlets through external conduits.) The methanol mixture cooled the air as it evaporated, and allowed thrust to be increased within the engine's temperature limitations.

Behind the engine was a monstrous augmentor, 50 per cent larger in diameter than the engine itself, fed with fuel from four injection manifolds and with three concentric flameholders. Ignition was by a pilot burner on the rear of the engine, which was lit at all times. The convergent-divergent nozzle was driven by 12 hydraulic jacks.

Powerplant performance

A propulsion system of this type was a sluggard at low speed. The low pressure ratio translated into poor specific fuel consumption. It also meant that the 'core' had a poor thrust/weight ratio, because it produced little power in relation to its size and airflow. The gargantuan inlet and augmentor, too, represented little more than dead weight and parasite drag at subsonic speeds, where the inlet could not compress the air enough to run the augmentor efficiently.

High speeds were a different story. Compression in the inlet duct increased with the square of the speed, probably attaining ratios in excess of 30:1. Because of the engine's low pressure ratio, it could swallow the high-pressure air from the inlet without encountering astronomical thermal loads, and without having to be throttled back like a more complex, high-pressure engine. The air expanded through the turbine, but only enough to drive the compressor, so the air leaving the back of the engine was still highly compressed. Also, because of the vast mass of air swallowed by the inlet, and the relatively small amount of fuel burnt in the engine, the efflux was still rich in oxygen. Further oxygen was provided by engine cooling air, drawn from the inlet.

Augmentor thrust

The entire system was geared to providing near-ideal conditions of temperature, pressure and oxygenation at the augmentor. In fact, the main function of the core was to further compress and heat the air, making the augmentor more efficient; at high speed, its contribution to thrust was small. Virtually all the thrust at high speed was generated by expansion through the convergent-divergent nozzle, driven by the combustion of massive quantities of fuel in the augmentor.

This type of powerplant has been called a 'turboramjet', or a 'supercharged ramjet', and the term is accurate to a degree. While the components of the propulsion system are the same as those of any supersonic turbojet, most of the compression is done in the inlet and most of the thrust is generated at the final nozzle, just as happens in a pure ramjet. Perhaps 'turboramjet' is appropriate, since the other type of powerplant to carry the name – in which the jet is switched out of the cycle at high speed – has never been flown.

Just how much sheer thrust this sort of engine can produce at high speed is best illustrated by example. The F-15, judged a high-speed fighter, weighs just over half as much as the MiG design, when both are carrying missiles and half internal fuel, but the MiG has only 12 per cent more static thrust, and moreover its missiles are far larger and less efficiently carried. Yet the Soviet type is 60 per cent faster, mainly because it has a completely different type of powerplant. This is no discredit to the F-15, which was designed with entirely different missions in mind, but points out the unique thrust-producing characteristics of the turboramjet engine.

The engine and augmentor were installed for early flight tests in a test-bed aircraft derived from the MiG tailed-delta series. Designated Ye-166, it flew in 1961 and set a series of speed and altitude records in the following year. It tested the engine up to the design Mach 2.8 maximum speed.

Meanwhile, work on the Ye-26 continued. The aircraft systems were mostly conventional: thanks to the limited supersonic endurance, the aerodynamic heat from the skin would not soak through every part of the aircraft, as it did on the contemporary A-12. Apart from a new high-temperature synthetic hydraulic fluid, and a special cooling system for engine accessories – a single-pass methanol/water system was used to cool the generators, the hydraulic pumps, and the avionics, the hot liquid being dumped into the inlets – the systems could have been taken off any contemporary Soviet aircraft, with two hydraulic circuits for the flight controls and pneumatics for the brakes.

Development of the fire-control system and the missiles proceeded in parallel. Unquestionably the most advanced feature of the fire-control system was the datalink, which was one of the first airborne systems anywhere to use a digital computer. The task of the computer was to translate high-speed digital pulses, which were easy to send by radio, into analogue signals that the aircraft systems would understand, and vice versa. The 'downlink' carried the radar imagery from the aircraft to the ground controller; the 'uplink' transmitted steering com-

MiG-25 'Foxbat-A' cutaway

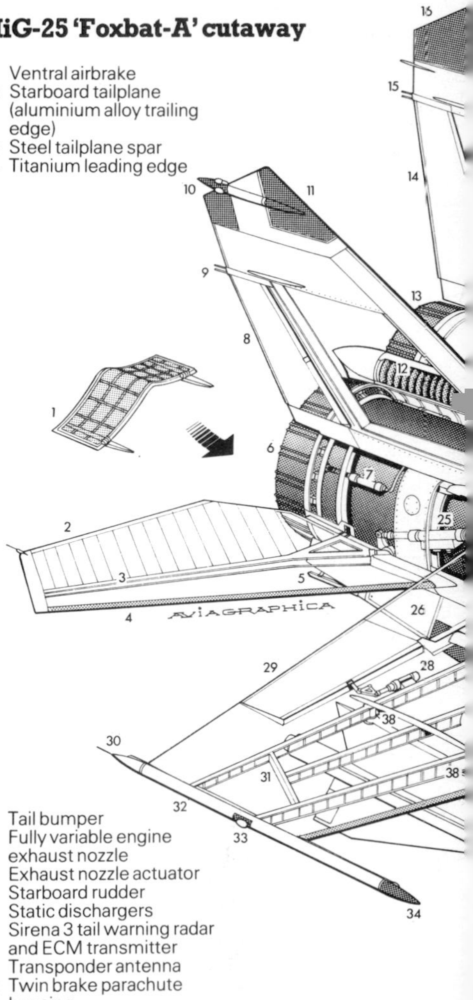

1 Ventral airbrake
2 Starboard tailplane (aluminium alloy trailing edge)
3 Steel tailplane spar
4 Titanium leading edge
5 Tail bumper
6 Fully variable engine exhaust nozzle
7 Exhaust nozzle actuator
8 Starboard rudder
9 Static dischargers
10 Sirena 3 tail warning radar and ECM transmitter
11 Transponder antenna
12 Twin brake parachute housing
13 Port engine exhaust nozzle
14 Port rudder
15 Static dischargers
16 VHF antenna

mands from the ground control system to the autopilot. The pilot's task was to ensure that the aircraft and its systems were functioning properly, and he would not assume control until the aircraft's own radar had unambiguously locked on to the target.

Specialized radar

The radar itself was unusual. Unlike most airborne radars, it was not designed to detect or track the target: ground-based radar would have done so before the aircraft left the ground. Instead, its role was to provide a final, accurate fix on the target, in the face of extremely heavy jamming, to enable the pilot and ground controller to fly the aircraft into a position to launch missiles. The emphasis was on power: the radar was to be so powerful that even the reflection of the beam from the target would be stronger than any jamming signal. (The fighter radar was at an advantage, because its beam is concentrated, while jamming is seldom accurate in direction.)

'Burn-through' range varies with the radar cross-section of the target, and the power and efficiency of its jamming systems, but the Ye-26 radar was probably designed to acquire a B-70 at about 50nm (90km), in order to give accurate guidance over at least the last 60sec of an interception, despite the speed of the interceptor and the target. Beam or collision attack was the normal tactic.

Given the size of a B-70 and an estimate of its jamming system, this implied a radar power of 600kW, at least three times more than any previous fighter radar. Transistor technology was then in its early stages, so – rather like some hi-fi buffs of the same era – the Soviet designers elected to stay with vacuum tubes. These, however, had to meet new requirements: the sheer power of the new radar, combined with the heat in the nose of a Mach 3 aircraft; and the stresses incurred in going from arctic cold on a Siberian runway to maximum operating temperature in under ten minutes. The result was the biggest fighter radar ever built, weighing over 1,100lb (500kg). Another, theoretical drawback of the radar – a direct result of its high power – was that powerful ground clutter rendered it ineffective against targets below 1,650ft (500m) altitude.

Other systems aboard the MiG-25 were designed to resist or offset jamming. Communications were assured by large flush antennas in the fin, and emissions from hostile radars were detected by an electronic surveillance measures (ESM) system housed in slim wingtip pods. A final touch was a small optical sight in the cockpit: if all else failed and the B-70's mighty Westinghouse ECM system did its duty, the pilot had one last chance to get parameters with his IR missiles.

The missiles were of similarly heroic proportions, though range was not the reason for their size: the need for lethality and assured performance was more important, and each missile carried a 220lb (100kg) high-explosive/fragmentation warhead. The requirement to destroy a Mach 3 target pushed the weapon's speed upward, to Mach 4 or more, while the high operating altitude dictated large wings for the sake of manoeuvrability. All of these requirements drove the size and drag of the missile up. The resulting missile was twice as large as any Western AAM, and in fact was slightly bigger than a Hawk SAM.

Uniquely, the missile has three exhaust nozzles, two smaller nozzles being located on the body sides level with the wing trailing edges. Almost certainly, this indicates the use of a two-stage propulsion system, with a booster in the tail and a sustainer exhausting through side nozzles (see photo overleaf).

The missile was built in two versions: semi-active-radar (SAR) or infra-red (IR), and according to most accounts the normal operating technique is to fire one of each type in close succession. While IR is normally considered to have a limited range, this particular weapon was designed for use against a large Mach 3 aircraft – its entire airframe radiating at 220-330°C – at high altitudes, where the normal attentuation of IR radiation with distance would be sharply reduced due to the thin air. The maximum range for effective missile launch was probably in the 25nm (50km) range, giving just enough time for a second salvo in a single pass should the first miss its mark.

While the entire system was still in the earliest stages of development, what could have been a fatal blow descended: the US Government cancelled the B-70 production programme. The first cancellation came in December 1959; a reprieve came in mid-1960, but the new Kennedy Administration wasted no time in putting a final halt to SAC's plans for deploying a Mach 3 bomber. Nevertheless, development of a system to shoot it down continued, although at a slightly more relaxed pace.

There were several reasons for this decision. The B-70 was still in being as a prototype programme, so the cancellation could still conceivably be reversed. The performance of the new fighter would also be useful against the B-58 and any successor aircraft; in 1960, the possibility of further B-58 production and development still existed. In all probability, too, the Soviet intelligence community knew that another long-range Mach 3 aircraft was under development in the USA, in the shape of the Lockheed A-12. A mock-up of a version of this aircraft with internal bays for nuclear weapons or reconnaissance sensors was completed in mid-1962, and following the Cuban missile crisis in October of that year it was ordered into production. The RS-71 would have full global range, with refuelling, and an equivalent bombload to the B-58. From the Soviet viewpoint, therefore, the threat of a high-altitude, high-Mach strategic attack force did not vanish with the cancellation of the B-70.

The first Ye-26 was flown in 1964. One early prototype, the Ye-266 set a 1,000km (540nm) closed-circuit speed record in April 1965, sustaining 1,252kt (2,320km/h) with a 4,410lb (2,000kg) payload. In those days, high-resolution satellite imagery of Soviet test centres was not available, so no inkling of the new type's shape appeared until July 9, 1967, when two of the aircraft appeared at the Aviation Day display at Domodedovo, near Moscow. They were officially described as being in the Mach 3 class, and confirmation of that performance came in October, when the Soviet Union claimed 500km (270nm) and 1,000km (540nm) closed-circuit records at speeds around Mach 2.8.

Record performance

The records beat the closed-circuit speeds set by the YF-12A (a member of the A-12 family) in May 1965, but there were two significant points which most observers missed. The YF-12A's 500km speed was slower than its 1,000km record, indicating that turning capability, rather than high-speed endurance, was the limiting factor. In the case of the Ye-26, the reverse was true: the 500km record was faster, showing that the aircraft was near its speed and endurance limits. The other observation that nobody made was that the Soviet team had not beaten the YF-12's 80,257ft (24,462m) altitude mark, or its Mach 3.12 straight-line speed record.

Instead, Western analysts tended to assume that, like the YF-12, the Ye-26 was much faster in the straight line than in the circuit, and was probably capable of Mach 3.2 or more. They also mirror-imaged the construction of the YF-12, and assumed that the Ye-26 had an ad-

Below: An uncomplicated cutaway reflects basic simplicity of design, with forged steel structural members and titanium used mainly for high-temperature secondary structure.

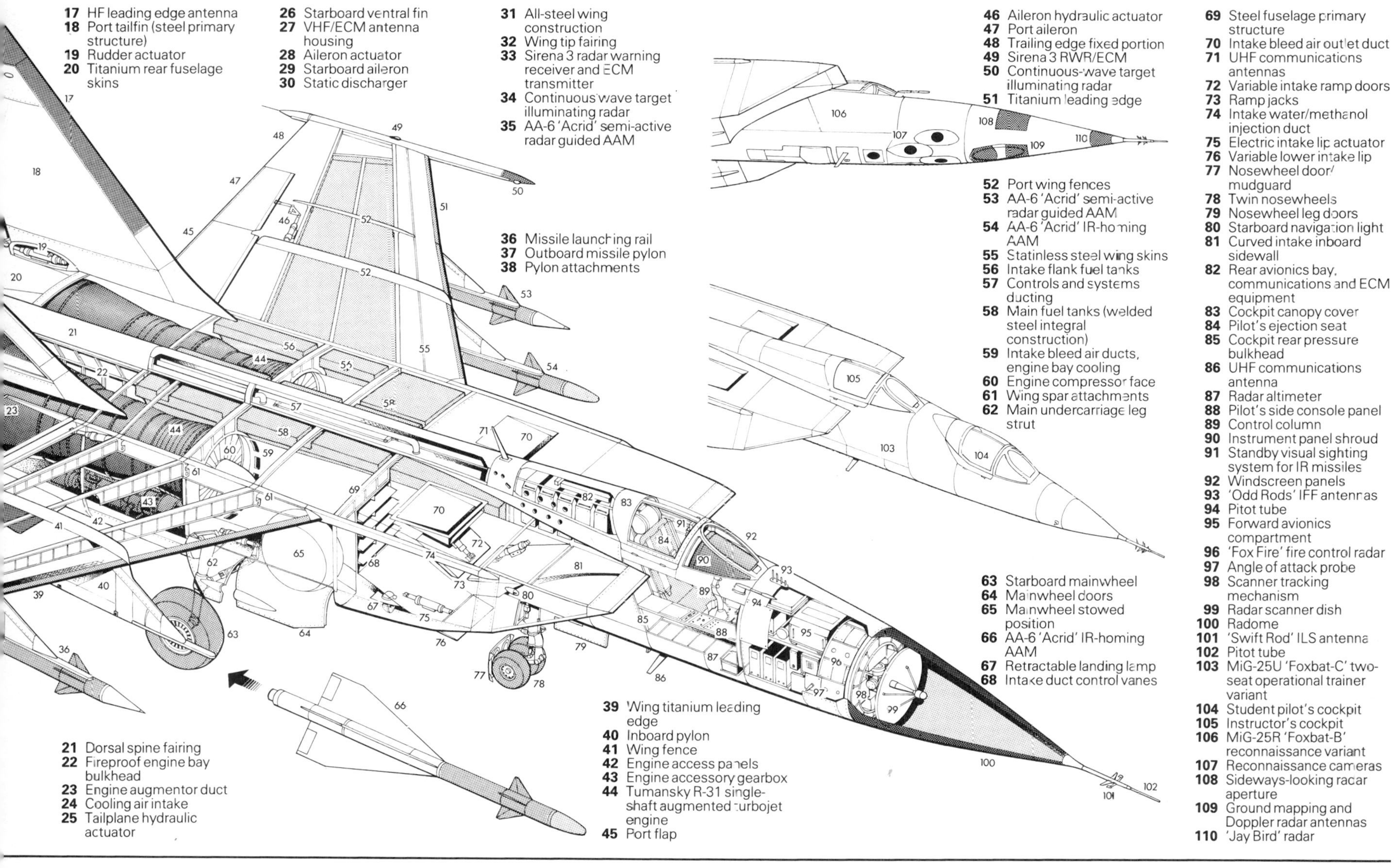

vanced, lightweight all-titanium airframe. The result was that Western estimates of empty weight were almost 25 per cent too low, and estimates of normal gross weight were almost 35 per cent low.

Another snare for Western analysts lay in the engine installation. The mass flow of the R-266 was, coincidentally, about the same as that of an advanced augmented turbofan engine of the same thrust rating. It was all too easy to believe that a high-pressure-ratio turbofan provided the Ye-26's motive power.

The impact of this assumption on estimates of range and transonic thrust/weight ratio was profound: as noted above, the R-266 is very inefficient outside the maximum speed regime, but a turbojet or turbofan would have been far better. Western estimates generally credited the Ye-26 with a normal combat radius of 600nm (1,120km), equal to that of an F-4 with maximum external fuel. The analysts then combined their thrust/weight ratio with their wing loading (which, along with the weight, was much too low) and deduced that the Ye-266 would be well able to hold its own in close-in combat. It was also naturally assumed that only an advanced pulse-Doppler radar would account for the large size of the Ye-26 radome.

Threat inflation

The final element in the 'Foxbat' myth was that from 1968 to 1972 the West thought that the Ye-26 was the MiG-23. Reports of preparations for large-scale MiG-23 production may well have reached the West, and further confused the picture. The Soviet Union made no attempt to dispel the confusion.

The result was that the Ye-26 – now codenamed 'Foxbat' by NATO – became the classic case of threat inflation. Combined with the accurately estimated dimensions, the known record-breaking flights and the quoted engine thrust, the picture that emerged was of a combat aircraft which sacrificed little efficiency or versatility in return for unmatched speed and altitude performance.

The USAF – then in the process of writing its requirements for a new tactical fighter – proved particularly susceptible to 'Foxbat' hysteria. The original F-X specification, which would have produced something like an F-18, was hastily revised to demand a top speed of Mach 2.5 and more radar detection range. The higher speed meant that complex variable-geometry inlets were needed, while the demand for improved radar implied a larger antenna, a wider forward fuselage and, ultimately, a heavier aircraft. The resulting aircraft, the F-15, is generally considered the Porsche 928 of fighters: supreme in performance and handling, full of sophisticated equipment, and so expensive that hardly anybody can afford it. It could be argued that the Ye-26 made its most significant contribution to the East-West military balance before flight tests were completed.

Meanwhile, development of the real Ye-26 proceeded rather more slowly than previous Soviet fighter programmes, partly because of its high performance and partly because of its complexity. There seems to have been no problem in attaining the required flight performance, as the 1967 records showed, but stability and control were clearly a problem area. Large-area ventral fins, operating in the high-pressure zone beneath the fuselage, were apparent on the aircraft shown at Domodedovo, and proved partially effective. One prototype tested endplate fins on the wingtips, which further improved directional stability at high speeds. The final solution was more conventional: the vertical fins were substantially enlarged, being increased in area by some 50 per cent, so that the leading edge overlapped the trailing edge of the wing, and the ventral fins were retained but considerably reduced in size.

Other detail differences apparent on at least one of the Ye-26 prototypes included a low-drag conformal fuel tank of about 175gal (800lit) recessed into the belly of the aircraft, and two small struts connecting the fuselage nose to the lower lips of the inlets, perhaps intended to solve a vibration problem.

Production of the new type apparently started in 1968, but was suspended after a senior PVO officer was killed in the crash of a Ye-26 prototype; it was resumed about a year later, and the type entered service in 1970-71 with the service designation MiG-25. It is possible that the armament initially comprised AA-5 'Ash' missiles, as used on the Tu-28P 'Fiddler' interceptor, but the missile specially developed for the aircraft, known to NATO as AA-6 'Acrid', was in service by 1975. The basic interceptor version was known to NATO as 'Foxbat-A'; its radar was identified as 'Fox Fire'.

Above: Apparent in this view of a Libyan MiG-25 are the three propulsion nozzles of the AA-6 missile, which have passed unnoticed in all previous publications. The two small nozzles on the sides of the missile, between the wings, are probably the exhausts of the cruise motor, the booster being in the tail.

As is normal Soviet practice, a conversion/proficiency trainer version entered service in parallel, the MiG-25U adding a second cockpit in the nose, ahead of the normal cockpit – the fuselage aft was too narrow – and this replaced the fire-control system and radar.

The MiG-25, with its supporting ground environment, was certainly the best high-altitude interception system of its day. In service, it turned out to meet the requirements laid down for it, and it would probably have been effective against the B-70. Lockheed's Skunk Works, however, had gone one better than the Soviet planners had anticipated: cruising at altitudes up to 95,000ft (29,000m), the SR-71 was safely outside the MiG-25/AA-6 envelope. But the USAF had no way of knowing this, and the presumed capability of the MiG-25 was a major factor in the US Government's decision not to use SR-71s or D-21 drones for penetrations of Soviet airspace, denying itself – in the words of USAF intelligence chief Gen George Keegan – 'vast amounts of intelligence.'

Given the success of the basic design, the lack of high-altitude targets and the Soviet Union's lack of a high-flying reconnaissance aircraft, it was logical to adapt the MiG-25 for such a mission. The MiG-25R entered service in parallel with the basic interceptor; it was identical up to the front cockpit wall, and in aerodynamic shape, but the nosecone contained a much smaller forward-looking radar, probably related to the MiG-21's 'Jay Bird'. This made space and payload available for a useful sensor package.

Two versions of the type have been observed: 'Foxbat-B', with conventional and video cameras and side-looking radar, and the electronic intelligence (elint) 'Foxbat-D', without cameras, but with a more extensive array of flush-mounted antennas. Both versions use the advanced datalink to relay real-time information to ground stations, and may be guided from ground stations.

A small group of MiG-25Rs were deployed to Cairo West, Egypt, in 1971 as part of the Soviet expeditionary force, remaining there until 1974. Without missiles, and possibly using drop tanks, the MiG-25R had better range and altitude performance than the fully loaded fighter. Between October 1971 and March 1972, MiG-25Rs based at Cairo covered the Israeli-held coastline from Haifa to Port Said, and flew the length of the Sinai Peninsula, both missions calling for 270nm (500km) penetrations of Israeli airspace and a total range in the region of 500nm (900km). Longer missions were flown at slightly reduced speeds, around Mach 2.5, but combined with the 80,000ft (24,000m) cruising altitude they were enough to confound Israel's air defences.

Flights and interception attempts continued into 1973. One MiG-25R was tracked at Mach 3.2 over Sinai, and the word soon went around the souks that the aircraft barely made it back to base, its engines having suffered severe damage. It was not appreciated at the time that this was the normal and inevitable consequence of flight outside normal speed limits.

In the same year, in June and July, the Ye-266 captured a series of time-to-height records, reaching 98,430ft (30,000m) in 4min 4sec and attaining a peak altitude of 118,900ft (36,240m), far higher than any aircraft had ever gone without rocket boost. The McDonnell Douglas F-15 Streak Eagle took the time-to-height records in January-February 1975, but in May the Ye-266 struck back and regained the title. The aircraft used for the 1975 records was designated Ye-266M, and apparently used RD-F engines rated at 31,000lb (14,000kg) thrust. (Not too much reliance should be placed on such numbers, because the thrust of the original engines was never accurately stated in record claims.) McDonnell Douglas analyzed the Soviet figures, and has claimed that they could not have been achieved without rocket boost.

The time-to-height records gave the 'Foxbat' myth another boost, but worse was to come. In mid-1975, 'Foxbat-Bs' were deployed to Poland, making some sorties to East Germany. Immediately afterward, NATO surveillance radars started tracking Mach 2.8 targets emanating from Poland at 90,000ft (27,430m) altitude, flying as far as the North Atlantic ports and returning at the same speed. In the light of such observations, even the original estimates of the MiG-25's range seemed low; the tracking data suggested an operational radius of 650nm (1,200km) at sustained high-supersonic speed. From this, one analyst deduced that the MiG-25 should be capable of a 1,080nm (2,000km) radius fighter mission, cruising at Mach 2.2 and including 2min combat. This was awesome performance indeed, suggesting that Polish-based MiG-25s could present a threat to NATO aircraft as far away as the Greenland-Iceland-UK gap.

The scare had been caused by a simple confusion. Western intelligence was entirely unaware that the Soviet Union's reconnaissance formations had deployed a new surveillance drone with a Mach 2.8 cruise speed and a range of about 1,600nm (3,000km). Derived from Soviet cruise-missile technology, it was launched from a mobile ramp and recovered by parachute. The MiG-25s based in Poland, as well as being tasked with high-altitude probes into Western airspace, formed the perfect cover for this new system.

'Foxbats' for export

Then came Hakodate, and the legend was punctured. With the MiG-25's cover blown, it became available to trusted export customers such as Algeria, Libya and Syria, which took delivery of the 'Foxbat-A' complete with AA-6 missiles in 1979-80. In 1982, India replaced its ageing Canberra PR.9s with eight MiG-25Rs. The reconnaissance aircraft are certainly useful, but it is hard to see what purpose the fighter variants serve apart from prestige. The 'Flogger-B/G', with its greater endurance, is unquestionably a better all-round fighter against the targets such nations are likely to face. And even the MiG-25 is not invulnerable, as the Israeli Defence Force-Air Force demonstrated in June 1982. Two Syrian MiG-25s were destroyed over Lebanon, probably by well-planned 'snap-up' F-15/Sparrow attacks.

Most of the Soviet MiG-25 fighter fleet – some 300 aircraft strong – has been retrofitted to 'Foxbat-E' configuration, with the same radar/missile system as the MiG-23. The 'High Lark' radar and IR search-and-track set give improved capability against manoeuvring and low-altitude targets, of the type which the MiG-25 is now more likely to face. The 'Foxbat-E' also features an extended tail bullet, probably indicating the presence of upgraded electronic countermeasures equipment. 'Foxbat-E' fighters based in Eastern Europe have been scrambled in response to SR-71 flights along the East-West border, and pose a significant threat to NATO air assets such as E-3 Awacs aircraft.

The 'Foxbat-E' represents an interim step to the ultimate development of the line, which responds to the B-1 as the original responded to the B-70: the MiG-31 'Foxhound', discussed later in the book. Its significance now, 25 years after the design of the original MiG-25 got under way, is material testimony to the outstanding qualities of the original design.

MiG-29 'Fulcrum'

Still largely a mystery to the West, partly because of a lengthy and perhaps difficult development process, but mainly because of the effectiveness of Soviet security precautions, the MiG-29 'Fulcrum' represents the state of the art in Soviet fighter design. There is little doubt that few, if any, key aviation technologies developed in the West have gone unmatched in the Soviet Union, and the MiG-29 will, like the MiG-21, MiG-23 and MiG-25 before it, represent a massive advance over earlier Soviet fighters. What remains to be seen is whether such a complex aircraft can match their outstanding producibility.

Above: Satellite reconnaissance is able to produce early and good planform data, but other details can remain uncertain. This sketch of a MiG-29, released in April 1984 by the US Department of Defense, suggests an F-18-like fuselage geometry with lateral inlets built into the fuselage sides.

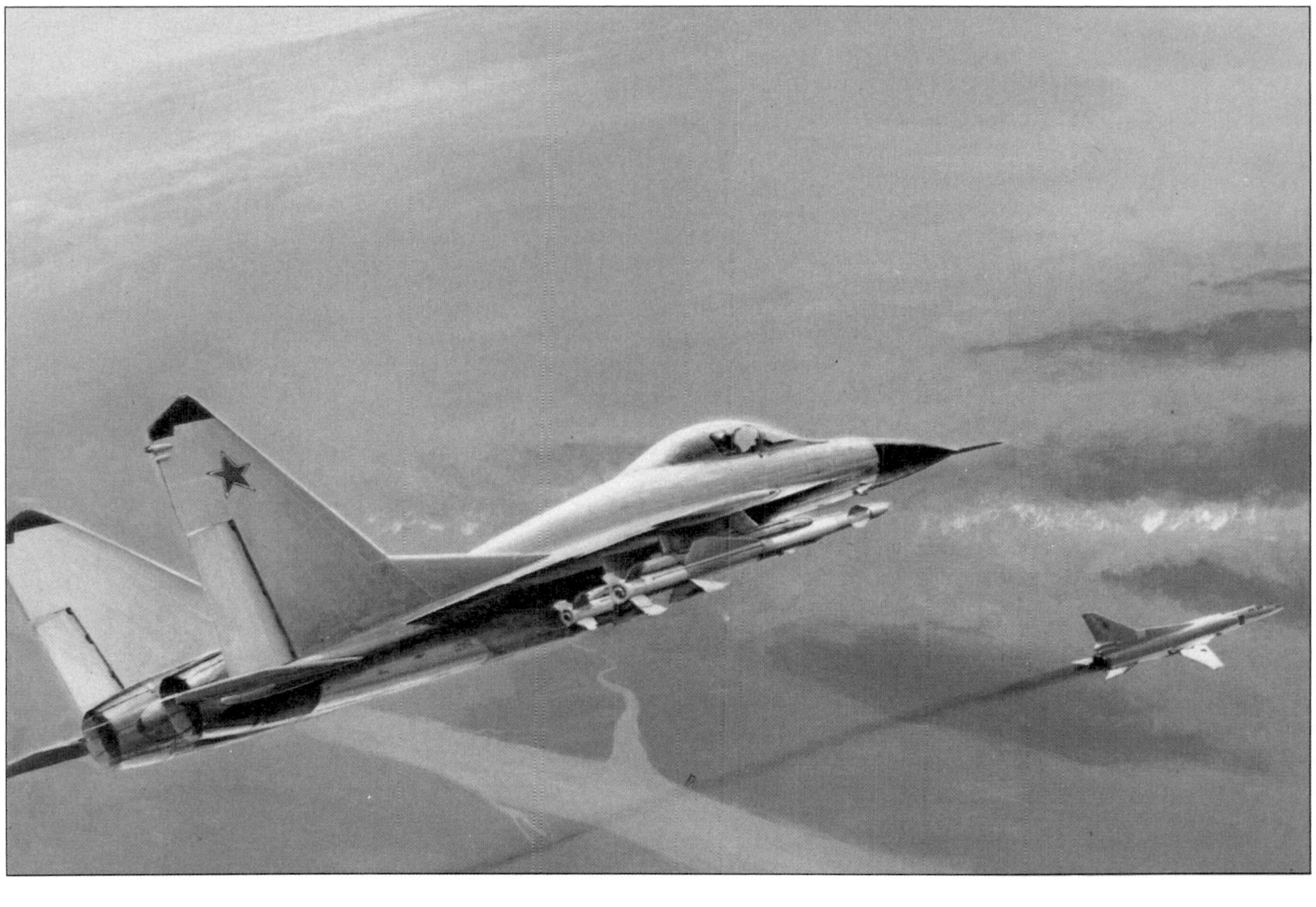

Above: The latest DoD impression of the MiG-29 suggests a cross between an F-16 and an F-14, with ventral inlets and separate engine nacelles. Details, either sensitive or unknown, are coyly hidden behind a quartet of R-23R missiles. It also shows tailbooms carrying the fins and tailerons.

Of all the new combat aircraft to appear in the 1960s, the MiG-23 was by far the most successful. While the Mikoyan swing-wing fighter was built in thousands, new Western types in that decade were overshadowed by the continued dominance of the F-4 and Mirage, designs which dated back to the 1950s. In the 1970s, as a consequence, Western and Soviet fighter developments were out of phase. Mass production of the MiG-23/27 series dominated the Soviet scene: in the West, a generation of new fighters appeared to replace the F-4, Mirage and F-104 as the primary tactical combat aircraft.

The new Western types were characterized by an emphasis on long-neglected qualities, particularly manoeuvrability in the high-subsonic regime and pilot visibility. This was not a fad: it reflected a careful analysis of combat experience in Vietnam, the Middle East and other theatres. Two fundamental lessons had emerged from this analysis.

One lesson was that beyond-visual-range (BVR) combat was much more difficult than the analysts of the 1950s had believed. Speed, confusion, fog of battle, unreliable IFF, low altitudes, better ECM, radar warning systems and the sheer complexity of the BVR radar/missile guidance loop all tended to diminish the probability that the first long-range salvo of BVR missiles would hit their targets. IR-homing missiles were more reliable, and guns were better still, but both had to be used in close combat.

Energy for combat

The second lesson was that success in air combat was highly dependent on energy. The typical fighter of the 1950s entered the ring fast and high, with a great deal of momentum, but as it turned to close on an enemy's tail its weight and its small wing told against it, and its momentum began to bleed away faster than its engines could put it back. The fighter quickly began to lose speed, height and the initiative.

The Western fighters of the 1970s had efficient, relatively long-span wings for good turning performance, and – equally important – light and extremely powerful new engines. While their predecessors could generate an instantaneous 7g break *in extremis*, these new machines could turn at 9g until they ran out of fuel.

It is not in the nature of the Soviet system to emulate the West as a matter of habit. But facts are facts, and as the details of the new F-15 and F-14 emerged in the early 1970s it must have become increasingly clear that, even in small numbers, they posed a problem for the MiG-23. The Soviet type would be at a disadvantage in the BVR phase, but even if this proved indecisive – the best one could hope for – the US fighters would almost literally fly rings around their adversary in close combat. Despite major modifications applied in advance of production, the MiG-23 was an inherently poor dogfighter, becoming steadily more stable (harder to manoeuvre) at increasing speeds.

Against the smaller F-16, the MiG-23 has an undisputed first-shot advantage. But this is significant only in the uncertain world of BVR, and in close combat the MiG-23 is, once again, outclassed. If the F-16 pilot can evade or spoof the first BVR salvo, he immediately more than reverses the MiG-23's advantage.

Another steadily increasing threat (as viewed from the Soviet side) has been the ability of NATO to operate at very low level. When the MiG-23 was conceived, it was generally considered that ultra-low-altitude operations, 250ft (75m) or less above the treetops, would be the province of a few specialized and expensive aircraft. The Royal Air Force, however, showed that single-seat attack fighters could operate 'down in the weeds', given an inertial navigation system and a head-up display. This tactic put most of NATO's attack aircraft out of the MiG-23's BVR envelope; during the 1980s, new systems will extend ultra-low-level flight to night operations.

All these developments in the threat emerged in the late 1960s. In a way, the timing was awkward for the Soviet Union. Although the trend in technology and operations was clearly apparent, there was no practical alternative to the MiG-23: any new fighter reflecting combat lessons would take years to develop, and would not be available in quantity until the late 1970s, while to rely on the MiG-21 and Su-7 for so long was unthinkable. The MiG-23 was made the subject of a major production programme, alongside new versions of the MiG-21 and Su-7.

The next generation

New fighters in the post-Vietnam mould were accordingly deferred to the next generation. Serious planning probably started in 1971-72, giving rise to an operational requirement in 1973-74. While there is no way of knowing exactly what planning steps were taken, subsequent events make it possible to reconstruct the planners' logic.

Agile fighters and low-level attack aircraft were, in all probability, two of the most important factors taken into account. A look-down shoot-down (LDSD) radar/missile system, capable of engaging fighter-size targets in ground clutter, was a basic requirement. This meant a sophisticated radar, with a larger antenna than that of the F-16; in fact, there was probably little chance of making the system smaller than the MiG-23 radar. The missiles would also be larger than simple IR-homing weapons. All of this tended to drive the weight of the aircraft upwards. Comparable agility to the F-16 and F-15 was also required.

Up to this point, the requirement was not too demanding for an aircraft which would appear some years after the US fighters. However, the new aircraft was also planned to match the range and speed of the MiG-23. The high installed thrust dictated by manoeuvrability objectives made it more difficult to achieve a long range, while a Mach 2.3 speed requirement added weight – in the form of variable inlets, for example – and complicated the aerodynamic design. The requirement could be met, but only by an aircraft as big as an F-15, something which would put the basic Soviet requirement for numerical superiority far out of reach.

US Department of Defense analysts currently believe that the Soviet Union solved the dilemma by developing two aircraft: a large, F-15-sized aircraft for the long-range fighter mission, and a smaller, less costly type, differing mainly in having a shorter range, and intended for both air-to-air and strike missions. The larger aircraft is the Sukhoi Su-27 'Flanker', while the latter is the newest Mikoyan type, the MiG-29 'Fulcrum'.

It should be noted that this explanation of the two types' design missions is not universally accepted. It has been suggested that the Su-27 may be intended for use on the Soviet Union's new aircraft carrier, as well as on land; and there may be other workable hypotheses. The DoD view certainly smacks of 'mirror imaging', reflecting the way that the USAF uses the F-15 and F-16, while the MiG-29 and the F-16 are two very different aircraft.

RAM-L in production

A prototype or technology demonstrator for the MiG-29 started flight tests at Ramenskoye, near Moscow, in 1977, and was initially known in the West as RAM-L. (If early Western figures were reasonably accurate, this aircraft may have been smaller than the production aircraft, with a maximum take-off weight in the F-16A class, and with R-13 or R-25 engines.) By early 1979 the RAM-L was considered to be a strong candidate for production, and by mid-1982 it was known that production was under way. An operational test unit formed in late 1983, and full production started in 1984 at a plant near Moscow.

Early Western impressions of RAM-L showed a basic configuration similar to that of the Northrop P530/YF-17/F-18, with very large leading-edge root extensions (Lerxes) reaching to the nose. In 1981-82, however, nearly all sources, including USAF and DoD publications, showed a modified MiG-25 shape, with smaller Lerxes and vertical-ramp inlets, and it was not until the trials unit formed that the public consensus settled on the original Northrop-type configuration.

The starting point for the MiG-29 design was clearly the MiG-25, from which it derived its wing sweep and aspect ratio and the relative size and location of its tail surfaces. This may seem odd, because the MiG-25 is no dogfighter: but it was designed to manoeuvre in the very difficult high-Mach, high-altitude environment, where some of the problems, such as high angles of attack and low control power, are surprisingly similar to those encountered in medium-altitude air combat. It is also a compact, low-drag configuration in which most of the main aerodynamic loads are conveniently concentrated in the close-coupled rear and centre fuselage.

Plan-view drawings of the MiG-29 suggest that the only trailing-edge control surfaces are set well inboard. This implies that the horizontal tail provides the primary roll control, perhaps with the aid of spoilers at low speed, and that the wing surfaces are plain flaps. There is no sign of the full-span leading-edge and trailing-edge flaps, operable over the entire flight envelope, that are found on the F-16 and F-18.

The main aerodynamic difference between the MiG-25 and the MiG-29 is the addition of Lerxes. These sharply swept surfaces do several things to help the aircraft manoeuvre. Their main characteristics are their high sweep and low aspect ratio: taken together, these mean that they have little effect in level flight, and develop progressively more lift as the aircraft pitches upward. Like a delta wing, the Lerx provides a smooth increase in lift with increasing pitch, and does not stall in the conventional way. At high angles of attack, it also sheds a strong vortex over the upper surface of the wing.

As the aircraft turns, the Lerx provides a gradual increase in lift, destabilizing the aircraft and reducing the amount of stabilizer downforce needed to sustain the turn. The effective wing loading and the induced drag are also reduced, and the spanwise lift distribution becomes more biased towards the centreline, reducing bending moments on the wing. At the same time, the vortex shed by the Lerx inhibits spanwise flow, and helps to prevent tip stall. The vortex generates its own low-pressure region over the wing, and provides a powerful lift boost of its own.

There are as many different patterns of Lerx as there are design teams working the problem. The MiG-29 Lerx (also used on the Su-27) is one of the simplest, forming a highly swept, straight-edged extension of the wing. Lerx design is not easy, introducing problems such as interaction of the vortices and the vertical tails, and involving what one distinguished Western designer has called the 'black art' of vortex lift. Lerxes similar to those on the MiG-29 appear on Northrop P530 studies dated 1968; the much more complex curved shape used on later designs and, eventually, on the F-18, was substituted in the following year, because it was considered to provide more lift and a better vortex.

Above: The relationship of the MiG-29 planform to that of the MiG-25 is apparent in the plan view: the size, shape and relative positions of the wings, tailerons and ventral fins are all similar.

The size of the Lerxes suggests strongly that the MiG-29, like the F-16 and F-18, is unstable in pitch – that is to say, the aerodynamic centre may be ahead of the centre of gravity some or all of the time. This brings considerable advantages: in level flight, the tail is providing an upward force, contributing to lift rather than subtracting from it, so that the drag usually caused by tail downforce is absent. In a sustained turn, where the normal lift and downforce are multiplied by the g load, relaxed stability provides even greater benefits.

If the MiG-29 is pitch-unstable, as seems likely, it must have full-time, redundant artificial stability, probably provided by an electronically signalled – 'fly-by-wire' (FBW) – flight control system. This could have been the first system of its type on a Soviet aircraft, but the technology was mature enough to be used on the An-124 transport, flown at the end of 1982.

The uncertainties involved in Lerx design and the technical risks of FBW may account for the West's confusion over the MiG-29's basic layout in 1981-82. It is the author's view that at least one prototype was completed in a lower-risk, naturally stable back-up configuration with smaller Lerxes, MiG-25-type inlets and a conventional mechanically signalled control system. Another reason for testing such a type could lie in inlet design. The MiG-25 inlet is one of the most efficient designs for high Mach numbers and high angles of attack, but is difficult to combine with a full-length Lerx because of its length and width. A fly-off between two similar aircraft would have clearly brought out the strengths and weaknesses of the two.

The size of the MiG-29 is set by the need to carry an LDSD radar/missile system, with the result that it is much bigger than the F-16, and slightly larger and more powerful than the F/A-18. It is also large enough to have two engines as a matter of necessity rather than choice. The fuselage layout is reminiscent of the F-15, in that the engines are set widely apart, on either side of the main keel. One difference in favour of the Soviet

Mikoyan MiG-29 'Fulcrum'

This provisional drawing of the MiG-29 was prepared in the first half of 1985, based on information from a variety of sources. It should be noted that many of these contradict each other, and that no clear and unambiguous description of the aircraft had been released to any unclassified source at the time of writing. Similarly, details of the AA-X-10 missile, said to make up the primary armament of the new fighter, are not yet available.

Above: It is likely that the MiG-29 will carry a large and powerful radar/ missile suite, and an IRST set. At the same time, all-round vision may not attain the same levels as on the fighter's US contemporaries.

design, though, is that the swept, canted fins and the canted stabilizer trunnions make it possible to attach all the tail surfaces directly to the rear fuselage, eliminating the tailbooms seen on the F-15. The spacing of the engines allows straight ducts from the underwing inlets – possibly of the MiG-23-style vertical-ramp type – to the engines, and provides a wide track for a simple landing gear. The width of the forward fuselage is set by the radar, and it may taper in plan view towards the rear, like that of the MiG-25. The canopy design does not seem to offer quite as much unobstructed visibility as that of the new US fighters.

Structural details are uncertain. The Soviet Union has worked extensively on composite materials, particularly carbon (graphite) fibres. However, titanium is abundant in the Soviet Union, and the country has a great deal of processing capacity, so it may make a more attractive alternative to carbon-fibre materials than it does in the West. One Soviet brochure, interestingly, shows a carbon-fibre-skinned honeycomb taileron similar to that of the MiG-29. Given the nature of the Soviet system – in particular, the fact that technology usually responds to a clear and definite need – it might be surprising to find a great deal of composite structure on the MiG-29. The required performance can be achieved with aluminium, steel and titanium.

The MiG-29 is, not surprisingly, powered by a pair of Tumansky engines. These are of a new type, designated R-33D, and are reported to be the first augmented turbofans to be used on a Soviet fighter. A very low bypass ratio, minimizing cost and handling problems, is to be expected.

Details of the avionics carried by the MiG-29 are sketchy. The radome diameter, one external indication of the potential of the forward-looking radar, is in the same class as the F-15 and MiG-23. US sources have ascribed a 60nm (110km) search range and a 45nm (83km) tracking range to the MiG-29 radar, but this figure is hard to evaluate in the absence of a radar cross-section for the target. The MiG-29 is also likely to carry an improved version of the infra-red tracker fitted to the MiG-23, and a high-capacity, ECM-resistant datalink.

According to US sources, the MiG-29 is to be armed with the AA-10, a new missile with a 25nm (46km) range and an active terminal seeker. The total armament is quoted as six missiles but, as in the case of the MiG-31, the maximum load probably reflects a mix of BVR weapons and small dogfight missiles in the R-60 (AA-8 'Aphid') class.

The MiG-29 certainly carries at least one internal gun. Some plan views show two heavy-calibre single-barrel weapons above the Lerxes, in positions similar to that of the F-16's single M61A1. These would be more effective than the GSh-23 and lighter than the MiG-27's Gatling. The installation leaves the underside of the aircraft clean for external stores, and keeps the burnt gases well clear of the inlets.

Full-scale production of the MiG-29 is reported to have been delayed for about a year by technical problems, before starting in 1984. Remarkably, the Indian Air Force is scheduled to receive the type in 1985; the delivery of 45 complete aircraft will be followed by a licence-production programme at HAL's Nasik facility, where some 150 MiG-29s will be assembled or built, starting in 1987-88. The agreement to supply MiG-29s followed an urgent request from India for an aircraft capable of meeting Pakistan's F-16s on equal terms. The IAF aircraft, however, will carry two R-23 (AA-7 'Apex') and four R-60 missiles, and it would not be surprising to find an updated version of the 'High Lark' radar.

The DoD suspects that the MiG-29 may be used in the strike mission in the future. This is certainly possible: like current US fighters, the MiG-29 has a strong structure, a generously sized wing and plenty of power, and this means that it has the potential for carrying a large external load. The common-sense application of such ideas as conformal fuel tanks and tandem stores carriage, as used on the F-15E, would turn the MiG-29 into a capable attack aircraft. One question, however, is whether the full-up MiG-29, with its advanced radar and missiles, would be used for such a mission, or whether a strike version, analogous to the MiG-27, would be developed.

From what little we have seen of the MiG-29, it appears to be another crisp and economical response to a sensible requirement. Apparently comparable to the F-18, but slightly faster, it will certainly not be at a disadvantage in close-in combat against any modern aircraft. In a dogfight, the numbers for the F-18, F-16 and MiG-29 are so similar that differences in tactics, pilot skill level and – very important – missile capability will prove decisive.

As it stands in 1985, the MiG-29's long-range armament and systems outclass those of the F-16, and are in the same category as those of the F-18. To some extent, too, its high altitude and speed may give it the ability to accept or refuse combat according to whether the tactical situation is favourable. Developments in Soviet fighter training and doctrine – de-emphasizing the textbook, and placing more stress on instant response, initiative and flexibility – will allow the Soviet Air Force to take full advantage of the type.

Production slow-down

One remaining question, though, will be answered only in the course of time. So far, fighter production rates in the Soviet Union have not returned to the levels reached in the late 1970s, having dipped in the early 1980s as four largely or completely new types – the MiG-29, MiG-31, Su-25 'Frogfoot' and Su-27 – entered production. The MiG-29 is undoubtedly a capable aircraft. It is also, by Soviet standards, a fairly complicated one, with its advanced radar and missile system and its twin engines. The same applies to the Su-27, only more so, and even the Su-25 is a twin-engined aircraft. The result is that if fighter output is to be maintained, engine output will have to be virtually doubled.

Again, three of the new types have advanced radars. As noted in the chapter of the MiG-23/27, production of the fully equipped fighter with the 'High Lark' look-down radar has only been a fraction of the whole, probably running at under 200 aircraft a year. The output of even more sophisticated radars will have to reach four times that level if fully equipped MiG-29s, MiG-31s and Su-27s form the bulk of production at 1970s rates. The delays in Su-27 and MiG-29 production reported by US sources in 1985 are therefore far from surprising, and output will almost certainly climb more slowly than US sources have implied.

Meanwhile, the total of comparable new-generation fighters in service with NATO and other Western allies is well over the 2,000 mark: in the light of this figure, the importance of the MiG-29's success to the Soviet Union is difficult to overstate.

MiG-31 'Foxhound'

Faced with a requirement for a new long-range interceptor able to detect, track and destroy low-visibility B-1 bombers carrying out their attacks at low levels, the Soviet Union appears to have selected a development of the fast, heavily armed but short-legged MiG-25. Looking at the likely shape of the requirement, and at the potential of the original design, however, it seems that a much altered MiG-25, with more efficient engines, new missiles and an improved radar and fire-control system, and with large external tanks for increased range, could form the basis for the world's most powerful interceptor.

Politicians and public were quick to react when the MiG-25 'Foxbat-A' interceptor, as delivered to Japan by Lt Viktor Belenko, turned out tc be spectacularly different from the aircraft that Western intelligence had described. It was, to say the least, a bad time for the credibility of such Western assessments. Perhaps in order to save face, it was leaked that Belenko had described an improved version of the MiG-25, which was undergoing flight tests at the time of his departure from the Soviet Union, and which might possess some of the threatening attributes that the real MiG-25 lacked.

This new aircraft is not known as well as the MiG-23 was known at a similar stage in its career. At the time of writing, no photograph of the type has been published. However, the US Department of Defense has released a general-arrangement drawing of the type, presumably derived from satellite observation (and, probably, from ground observation as well) which forms the basis for the following preliminary assessment.

'Foxbat' derivation

The new aircraft is now identified as the MiG-31 (although it appears to have preceded the MiG-29 into service) and carries the NATO reporting name 'Foxhound'. The most important single observation to be made from available evidence, however, is that the MiG-31 is very closely related to the MiG-25. It has been reported that its designation before service entry was MiG-25M, and this would not be surprising given the high commonality between the original version and its new development.

There is very little uncertainty about the MiG-31's primary role: it has clearly been developed to counter the USAF/Rockwell B-1 bomber, just as the MiG-25 was developed to intercept the B-70. Development of the B-1 was launched in the summer of 1970 – after several years of debate over what sort of performance would be required of a future bomber, if one was needed at all – and the type was due to become operational in the early 1980s.

To put it baldly, the B-1 threatened the entire Soviet air defence system with obsolescence, despite the billions of roubles which had been poured into it during the 1960s, and despite the fact that it was better equipped and vastly larger than any other air defence organization in the world. Unfortunately, none of its fighters or missiles had any ability to acquire a low-flying target against the ground, let alone track it or guide a missile on to it, while the B-1, with its fighter-type configuration and highly efficient turbofan engines, could fly at very low altitudes throughout the Soviet Union.

Moreover, the B-1's design was not only efficient, but took account of investigations into reducing the radar cross-section (RCS) of an aircraft. This would make it even more difficult to find. The Soviet air defence system was particularly vulnerable to low-level penetration, because of the reliance placed on ground-controlled interception (GCI): if both the target and the pursuing aircraft dropped below the controller's radar horizon, the game was up.

At the end of 1972, the Soviet-supplied and Soviet-maintained air defence system of North Vietnam was put to its biggest test, as the Linebacker II raids sent dozens of B-52s directly over Hanoi. The loss of 14 B-52s, with others damaged, was regarded at the time as a defeat for the USAF; but for the Soviet interceptor community, Linebacker II was an unmitigated disaster. Faced with huge waves of heavily laden bombers, flying at high altitude in broad daylight over a complete air defence system, the MiG-21PF interceptors missed the lot: all the damage to the B-52 force was caused by SAMs. To add insult to injury, B-52 tail-gunners shot down at least two MiG-21s as they manoeuvred to fire their missiles.

The advent of the B-1 and the catastrophe of Linebacker II made a complete reform of the manned fighter component of the Soviet air defence system inevitable. (Missiles retained their target-defence role, within the existing organization.) The basic philosophy of using thousands of limited-range fighters, operating in many small cells under strict GCI rules, as the primary means of air defence had to be abandoned. This was to have a profound effect on the shape of the next interceptor.

The basic requirement for a new interceptor was presumably issued as the B-1 programme started, in 1970-71. Capability against low-visibility, low-level targets called for greater operating autonomy, a considerable search range and a look-down/shoot-down radar/missile system, and a two-man crew to operate the system. The result would automatically be a large, heavy and expensive aircraft. Most Western analysts would have bet on a derivative of the Su-24 being adapted fill that role, but it did not work out that way, for sound and fundamental reasons.

There is only one way to offset the advantage of surprise enjoyed by a low-altitude attacker, and that is to place the acquisition radar on an aircraft. In fact, the definition of an advanced airborne early warning and control (AEW&C) aircraft probably preceded that of an interceptor. The first-generation Tu-126

Soviet territorial air defence

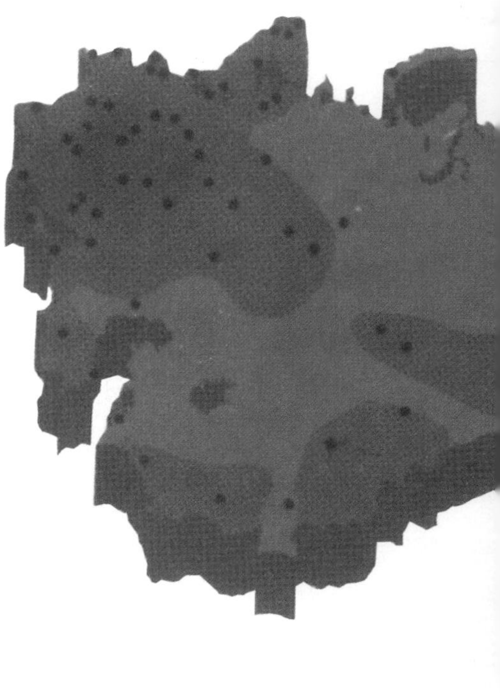

Above: US DoD map showing the Soviet Union's territorial air defence system. The MiG-31 will provide the

Below: The MiG-31 is heavier than the MiG-25, but its overall dimensions are about the same. The plan view shows that the length of the main fuselage has been considerably increased – the tailpipes have been extended aft, and the inlets forward – while room has been made for a second cockpit by widening the fuselage.

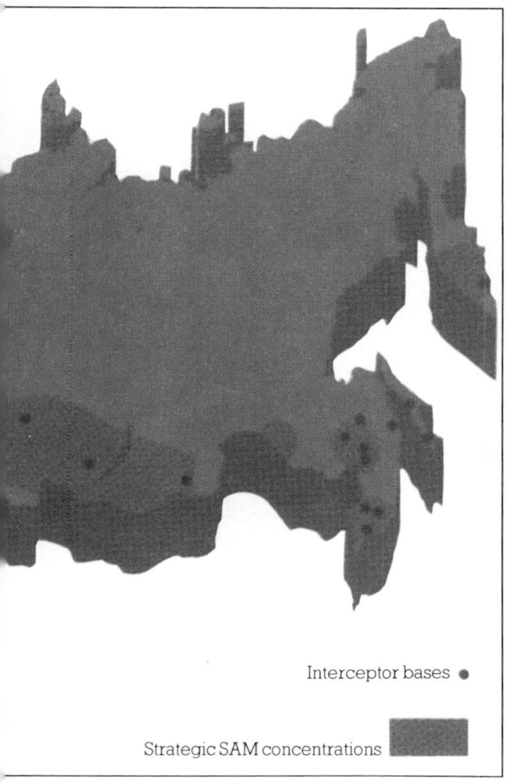

look-down/shoot-down capability essential to deal with the threat posed by the USAF's new B-1B bomber.

Above: Fast, stealthy and manoeuvrable, the USAF/Rockwell B-1B presents a difficult target at low altitude to even the most sophisticated air defence system. The ability of a well designed and properly equipped manned bomber to avoid detection and interception was confirmed during tests with the B-1 prototypes.

Mikoyan MiG-31 'Foxhound'

The DoD illustrations upon which this drawing is based show an aircraft directly derived from the MiG-25. In detail, the aircraft may differ more substantially from its predecessor, reflecting its lower design speed and greater range. However, it does appear to be a true derivative of the earlier design.

Above: The MiG-31 has been depicted with very large drop tanks on its outer pylons, but its primary weapon – the AA-9 missile – has not yet been seen in any unclassified presentation. However, it is generally described as bearing a close resemblance in size and performance to a late-model AIM-7 Sparrow. The eight-missile armament suggests that belly weapon stations are also available.

'Moss' – probably intended to provide AEW cover for the Soviet Navy, as much as anything else – had no look-down capability, and a much more sophisticated system would be required for strategic air defence. It would need an advanced radar and powerful digital computers to cope with the many real and false targets within its detection range. It would need sophisticated displays to help its human operators manage the air battle, and multiple data links to guide the fighters to the interception point. The entire system would have to be effective against a fast and wily adversary with a highly advanced jamming system and, quite possibly, the means to shoot back.

The result is that AEW&C types are the most expensive of all military aircraft, and are inevitably limited in numbers. The new Soviet AEW&C platform, the Ilyushin 'Mainstay-A' derived from the Il-76 freighter, is no exception. It is expected that no more than four will be built each year, and that a maximum of 50 may eventually enter service.

Even the best AEW&C aircraft can handle only a limited number of fighters and targets at any moment. Now, the rate at which these scarce systems can handle targets is directly related to the interval between the first detection of an intruder and the point at which the airborne controller 'hands off' the target to the fighter crew. In the Soviet environment the nearest fighter may easily be hundreds of miles away, so the fighter's speed becomes critical – and the MiG-

25's shape is remarkably efficient at supersonic speeds.

Endurance is less important. Most Soviet targets are deep inside Soviet territory, so it is possible to mount an effective air defence from usable bases on the perimeter. The fighters can either scramble and dash to the target area, or remain on patrol without ever straying far from a refuelling base.

Even with a relaxed range requirement, the MiG-25 might look like a non-starter. But its normal 160nm (300km) operational radius is mainly a result of the very high speeds which it attains, and the extremely poor efficiency of its engines outside their normal high-speed envelope. The short span and high wing loading are the only inherent disadvantages of the airframe; on the other hand, its internal fuel capacity is remarkably high. A reduction in dash speed makes it possible to use more conventional powerplants, which would be more advanced and efficient than the 1950s engines of the MiG-25, and for a mixed subsonic/supersonic mission the type could easily be modified to carry large external fuel tanks. Such changes would increase combat radius to a remarkable degree.

The new aircraft, flown in 1974-75, appears to retain most of the MiG-25's structure. The wing, the tail surfaces and the entire centre-section seem basically unchanged, although the wing-tip avionics pods are gone, and small leading-edge root extensions (Lerxes) are added to the wings and vertical tails. The forward fuselage has been redesigned; both the fuselage and the inlet ducts have been extended by about 40in (100cm), and the fuselage between the inlets is wider, accommodating a second cockpit. The nose ahead of the cockpit is shorter than that of the MiG-25, and at the rear, the tailpipes extend about 60in (150cm) further aft.

According to the DoD, the MiG-31 has a maximum speed of Mach 2.4 This is an important figure. The MiG-25 powerplant was defined by the need for high thrust at high speed; a Mach 2.4 aircraft, however, could easily be powered by a conventional afterburning turbojet, corresponding to a scaled-up Tumansky R-29. Such an engine, with about 25 per cent more mass flow and thrust than the R-29, would be far more efficient in the cruise regime. It would also, in all probability, be slightly longer than the R-31 – accounting for the extended jetpipes – but its airflow and weight would be compatible with the airframe of the MiG-25.

In theory, the Mach 2.4 top speed would make it feasible to build a lighter, more efficient aluminium-alloy structure, but the close likeness between the MiG-25 and MiG-31 makes it improbable that such a thing has been done. However, the MiG-31 is reported to have a stronger airframe than the MiG-25, lifting the older type's tight speed and manoeuvre limits at low altitude, and this may have been achieved at little cost in weight by substituting titanium alloys for steel. (Since the MiG-25 was designed, Soviet work in titanium has made great advances, and the Soviet Union is now the world's largest titanium producer.)

MiG-31 armament

The MiG-31's armament includes at least four air-to-air missiles of a new type, known to NATO as AA-9, mated to a new pulse-Doppler radar and fire-control system. Tests with the AA-9 were first observed in August 1977. According to US sources, the MiG-31 with the AA-9 has a true look-down/shoot-down capability, including the ability to intercept targets with an RCS of under $1m^2$, at altitudes as low as 200ft (60m) above ground level, from a launch at 20,000ft (6,100m). In other tests, the system is reported to have engaged four larger targets – UR-1 supersonic drones, with a $5m^2$ RCS – within 40sec, all at different altitudes; it has also intercepted a UR-1 at 70,000ft (21,300m), after a launch at 54,000ft (16,500m), demonstrating a 16,000ft (4,900m) 'snap-up' capability. In that test, the missile coasted to 125,000ft (38,000m) after passing close to the target. The missile has a range of 25-40nm (46-74km), and has its own active radar for guidance in the final stages of its flight, like the US Navy's AIM-54 Phoenix.

The significance of this information – which US intelligence apparently acquired by intercepting telemetered data during test firings – is that the MiG-31/AA-9 system can probably intercept any known aircraft, from an F-111 or B-1 in terrain-following flight to an SR-71 at its maximum altitude. Its capability against cruise missiles – which have a very small RCS, well below $1m^2$ – is probably limited. The problem, in that case, is that the range and resolution of the missile's active terminal homing radar is limited by its antenna size. For the same reason, the system will have to be modified to cope with the forthcoming 'stealth' Advanced Technology Bomber.

Given its performance, the AA-9 is probably a large missile by Western standards; it may be in the same size class as the AA-7. The DoD credits the MiG-31 with the ability to carry eight missiles, but it is likely that this would be a mixed load, with four AA-9s on the wing pylons and four smaller missiles, on twin launchers, on the under-fuselage pylons. The DoD-released impression also shows a pair of 440gal (2,000lit) fuel tanks on the outer pylons, which presumably displace a pair of missiles. The MiG-31 is reported to carry an internal gun, probably in the lower fuselge.

Adding up the stretched fuselage, the corresponding increase in internal fuel capacity, the second crew station and the increased external load, it quickly becomes apparent that the MiG-31 is a big aeroplane, much heavier than any Western fighter (its empty weight is equivalent to the all-up weight of an F-15 with missiles and some external fuel).

The cancellation of the original B-1A production contract in June 1977 did not materially affect the MiG-31 programme. Development of the new bomber continued, and the production programme could have been reinstated at any time. This happened in October 1981, by which time the design had been significantly improved.

The MiG-31 is believed to have become operational in late 1982, and, even though its shape dates back a quarter of a century, it is a very potent combat aircraft and poses some serious problems for NATO. Unlike recent Western air-defence types, the MiG-31 is not compromised in the least for close-in combat: its wing loading and thrust/weight ratio clearly rule it out of the air-superiority envelope.

From its MiG-25 ancestor, the MiG-31 inherits an airframe that runs into no real limits at high speed and high altitude. The aerodynamic design is optimized for low supersonic drag, with few compromises. Its turbojet engines are sized for straight-and-level flight, rather than manoeuvre, and are more efficient at high Mach than turbofans.

The result is that the MiG-31 is a very honest Mach 2.4 aircraft. It should be able to attain Mach 2.4 even with four large missiles under its wings, and, because of its better-matched engines and large internal fuel capacity, it will have a greater supersonic endurance than in-service Western types. It operates routinely above 70,000ft (21,300m), well above the normal operating ceiling of any Western fighter.

With plenty of fuel and a reasonably efficient powerplant, the 800nm (1,500km) interception radius quoted by the DoD is probably realistic. This represents a mixed subsonic/supersonic mission with external fuel, and only a short burst of supersonic combat; however, it translates into the ability to cover a large area of the Soviet Union against a subsonic target such as a B-1, given accurate guidance by 'Mainstay' AEW&C aircraft to the target area. Alternatively, and unlike any other Soviet or Western fighter, the big MiG-31 can dash 400nm (750km) to the target area at Mach 2.4.

In the tactical theatre, the MiG-31/'Mainstay' combination poses a definite threat to Western deep-interdiction aircraft, which have up to now been fairly safe at low altitude; the smaller MiG-29 and Su-27 fighters do the same. The unique threat from the MiG-31, though, is directed at NATO assets such as the vital E-3 Awacs, and the increasing number of stand-off reconnaissance and control platforms. Operating at high speed and high altitude, the MiG-31 can make snap-down missile attacks against these vulnerable targets with very little warning. While the type is certainly not immune to interception, it operates close to the limits of most Western systems, and interception becomes considerably more difficult under such circumstances.

Interceptor deployment

With the advent of the MiG-31 and 'Mainstay', the re-equipment and re-organization of the Soviet interceptor force is nearing completion. Re-equipment of the air defence force has, so far, proceeded in two phases. A first, interim stage was represented by the arrival of MiG-23M 'Flogger-B/G' fighters, originally developed for tactical use but possessing at least some capability against low-flying targets, and the retrofit of the 'High Lark'/AA-7 missile system to the MiG-25 fleet. The MiG-31 and the 'Mainstay' constitute the second stage of improvement.

Meanwhile, the former IA-PVO (Interceptors of National Air Defence) force has been separated into two parts. More than half the pre-1980 force has been transferred to the VVS (Soviet Air Forces), and re-assigned to a generic point defence role under the local joint-services command. The entire fleet of Su-15s – the most modern interceptors in the world in 1972 – has been transferred to this force, along with other older types. A numerically smaller, better equipped core, dedicated to strategic air defence, still functions as part of the National Air Defence Troops (Voyska-PVO), and it is this force that will, increasingly, standardize on the MiG-31 and, possibly, more advanced aircraft.

The MiG-31 is, unquestionably, one of the world's best interceptors, and is one of the few aircraft that represent a problem for the B-1. Its development represents an economical use of an old airframe in a new role: a lesson which the West might do well to study.

Above: The 'Mainstay' AEW&C aircraft, based on the Il-76 freighter, goes hand in hand with the MiG-31. The interceptor, in fact, was designed as the best possible operational complement to the AEW&C aircraft.

Below: The importance of the new MiG-31 'Foxhound' in the modernization of Soviet air defences is grapahically illustrated in this DoD projection of Soviet interceptor radar capability.

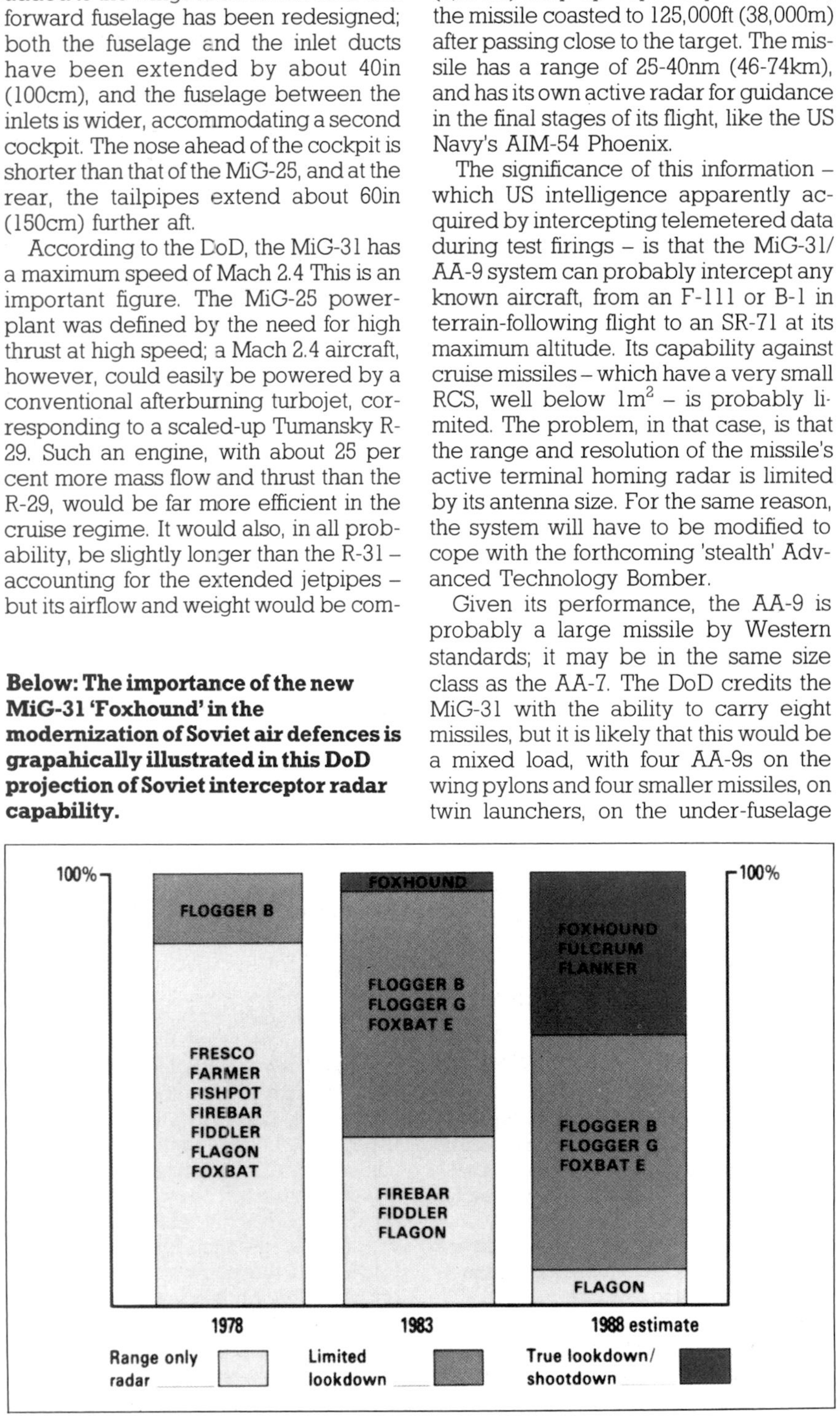

Specifications

Mikoyan MiG-21F 'Fishbed-C'

Dimensions	Span	23ft 6in/7.16m	
	Length overall	51ft 4in/15.65m	
	Length exc probe	44ft 2in/13.46m	
	Height	14ft 9in/4.5m	
	Wing area	247sq ft/22.9m²	
Powerplant		One Tumansky R-11F turbojet	
	Thrust (dry)	9,500lb/42.2kN	
	Thrust (augmented)	12,650lb/56.2kN	
	Internal fuel	540Imp gal/2,470lit	
			Definition
Weights	Empty	11,000lb/4,980kg	
	Normal take-off	16,250lb/7,370kg	Clean
	Max take-off	19,025lb/8,630kg	2 AAM, 1×108Imp gal/490lit tank
	Wing loading	77lb/sq ft/375kg/m²	
Performance	Max speed	1,150kt/2,125km/h (Mach 2)	
	Max sea level speed	590kt/1,100km/h	
	Initial climb rate	25,900ft/min/132m/sec	
	Combat radius	120nm/220km	4 AAM, 1 tank
Armament	One or two internal 30mm NR-30 cannon; two wing hardpoints for AA-2 'Atoll' AAMs; centreline pylon for drop tank.		

Above: Combining a radar nose with the fin of the original 'Fishbed-A', this is probably the Ye-7 prototype for the entire MiG-21PF series.

Mikoyan MiG-21Mbis 'Fishbed-N'

Dimensions	Span	23ft 6in/7.16m	
	Length overall	51ft 4in/15.65m	
	Length exc probe	47ft 11in/14.16m	
	Height	14ft 9in/4.5m	
	Wing area	247sq ft/22.9m²	
Powerplant		One Tumansky R-25 turbojet	
	Thrust (dry)	13,000lb/57.8kN	
	Thrust (augmented)	19,850lb/88.2kN	
	Internal fuel	640Imp gal/2,900lit	
Weights	Empty	13,500lb/6,200kg	**Definition**
	Normal take-off	19,300lb/8,750kg	2 AAM, 1×108Imp gal/490lit tank
	Max take-off	22,000lb/10,000kg	2 AAM, 3 tanks
	Wing loading	89lb/sq ft/435kg/m²	
Performance	Max speed	1,200kt/2,230km/h (Mach 2.1)	
	Max sea level speed	Just over Mach 1	
	Initial climb rate	58,000ft/min/284m/sec	
	Combat radius	175nm/320km	4 AAM, 1 tank
Armament	One internal 23mm GSh-23 cannon; four wing hardpoints for up to 3,300lb (1,500kg) ordnance, inc. AA-2, AA-8, AS-7, rockets or bombs; centreline and outboard wing pylons for drop tanks.		

Above: This sequence shows the sometimes confusing changes of spine shape in the later MiG-21s. The narrow, straight-topped spine on the MiG-21MF 'Fishbed-J' (top) was introduced in the MiG-21PFMA. The MiG-21SMT 'Fishbed-K' (centre) has a very fat spine with a curved top line, ending in a mould line running across the entire chord of the fin. Finally, the MiG-21bis 'Fishbed-L' has a spine shape much closer to that of the MiG-21MF, but still fatter than that of the older aircraft; note downward curve of spine/fuselage junction, and the longer 'crease' where spine merges into fin.

Above: Close-up of a MiG-21Mbis 'Fishbed-N', showing the panels which give access to control runs and fuzes. The large ground service connectors visible on the fuselage beneath the wing root are clearly designed with gloved hands and the rigours of Siberian weather in mind.

Mikoyan MiG-23MF 'Flogger-G'

Dimensions	Span (wings spread)	46ft 9in/14.25m	
	Span (wings swept)	27ft 2in/8.3m	
	Length overall	59ft 10in/18.25m	
	Length exc probe	55ft 6in/16.9m	
	Height	14ft 4in/4.35m	
	Wing area	325sq ft/30.2m²	
Powerplant		One Tumansky R-29B turbojet	
	Thrust (dry)	17,500lb/78kN	
	Thrust (augmented)	25,350lb/113kN	
	Internal fuel	1,270Imp gal/5,750lit	
			Definition
Weights	Empty	25,000lb/11,500kg	
	Normal take-off	38,000lb/17,250kg	
	Max take-off	42,500lb/19,250kg	6 AAM, 3×175Imp gal/800lit tanks
	Wing loading	130lb/sq ft/635kg/m²	
Performance	Max speed	1,350kt/2,500km/h (Mach 2.35)	
	Max sea level speed	730kt/1,350km/h (Mach 1.1)	
	Combat radius	500nm/930km	4 AAM, 3 tanks
Armament	One twin-barrel 23mm GSh-23 cannon in lower fuselage; two medium-range R-23 (AA-7 'Apex') or four short-range R-60 (AA-8 'Aphid') on glove pylons, plus two or four R-60s under intake ducts		

Above: A MiG-23MF 'Flogger-G' in dirty condition on the approach. Inevitably a more complex aircraft than the MiG-21, the MiG-23 is nevertheless markedly less so than its Western contemporaries.

Mikoyan MiG-27 'Flogger-J'

			Definition
Dimensions	Span (spread)	46ft 9in/14.25m	
	Span (swept)	27ft 2in/8.3m	
	Length overall	58ft 1in/17.7m	
	Length exc probe	54ft 10in/16.72m	
	Height	14ft 4in/4.35m	
	Wing area	325sq ft/30.2m^2	
Powerplant		One Tumansky R-29-300 turbojet	
	Thrust (dry)	17,500lb/78kN	
	Thrust (augmented)	25,350lb/113kN	
	Internal fuel	1,270Imp gal/5,750lit	
Weights	Empty	25,000lb/11,500kg	
	Normal take-off	41,000lb/18,500kg	6,000lb stores
	Overload take-off	44,500lb/20,200kg	6,000lb/2,700kg stores, 2× 175Imp gal/800lit tanks
	Wing loading	137lb/sq ft/670kg/m^2	
Performance	Max speed	980kt/1,820km/h (Mach 1.7)	
	Max sea level speed	730kt/1,350km/h (Mach 1.1)	
	Combat radius	500nm/930km	6,000lb, 3 tanks
Armament	One six-barrel 23mm cannon, movable in elevation, in lower fuselage; up to 10,000lb (4,500kg) of stores under inlet ducts, wing gloves and rear fuselage. Options include: free-fall bombs on multiple racks, expendable decoy pods on rear fuselage; up to four AS-7 (radio command), AS-10 (laser-homing) or AS-12 ASMs; two AS-9 anti-radiation missiles; TV/laser-guided bombs; gun pods.		

Above: A murky but interesting shot of a MiG-27 'Flogger-J', showing its small leading edge root extensions. This aircraft is believed to be carrying a laser-guided bomb beneath the nearer inlet duct, and what may be an associated tracker/designator pod beneath the fuselage.

Mikoyan MiG-25 'Foxbat-A'

			Definition
Dimensions	Span	46ft/14m	
	Length overall	74ft 10in/22.8m	
	Length exc probe	71ft 4in/21.75m	
	Height	18ft 5in/5.60m	
	Wing area	730sq ft/68m^2	
Powerplant		Two Tumansky R-31 turbojets	
	Thrust (dry)	20,500lb/91kN	
	Thrust (augmented)	27,120lb/120.5kN	
	Internal fuel	3,900Imp gal/17,800lit	
Weights	Empty	44,000lb/20,000kg	
	Max take-off	82,500lb/37,500kg	4 AA-6
	Wing loading	113lb/sq ft/550kg/m^2	
Performance	Max speed	1,6250kt/3,010km/h (Mach 2.82)	
	Service ceiling	78,000ft/24,000m	2 AA-6 or 4 AA-7
	Initial climb rate	41,000ft/min/208m/sec	
	Interception radius	160nm/300km at Mach 2.8	
Armament	Four AA-6 'Acrid' or, on 'Foxbat-E', R-23 (AA-7 'Apex') AAMs.		

Left: MiG-25Rs. The 'Foxbat-B' (right) has some unusual features, such as modified upper and lower inlet lips and a small fairing alongside the inlet. In the rear is a 'Foxbat-D' fitted with side-looking airborne radar.

Above: This view of a MiG-25R 'Foxbat-B' shows the transparencies for long-focus oblique and vertical cameras, and the dielectric panels covering Doppler navigation equipment and electronic sensors.

Mikoyan MiG-29 'Fulcrum-A'

			Definition
Dimensions	Span	39ft 6in/12m	
	Length overall	59ft/18m	
	Length exc probe	57ft/17.4m	
	Height	16ft 6in/5m	
	Wing area	450sq ft/42m^2	
Powerplant		Two Tumansky R-33D turbofans	
	Thrust (dry)	11,250lb/50kN	
	Thrust (augmented)	18,300lb/81.3kN	
	Internal fuel	1,500Imp gal/6,750lit	
Weights	Empty	22,500lb/10,200kg	
	Normal take-off	37,000lb/16,750kg	6 AAM, int fuel
	Max take-off	41,500lb/18,800kg	6 AAM, 3×175Imp gal/800lit tanks
	Wing loading	92lb/sq ft/450kg/m^2	
Performance	Max speed	1,320kt/2,450km/h (Mach 2.3)	
	Max sea level speed	730kt/1,350km/h (Mach 1.1)	
	Combat radius	350nm/650km	6 AAM, 3 tanks
Armament	Internal cannon armament, possibly comprising two 30mm single-barrel weapons in Lerxes; wing and belly pylons for two R-23 plus four R-60 or four to six AA-10 air-to-air missiles.		

Mikoyan MiG-31 'Foxhound-A'

			Definition
Dimensions	Span	46ft/14m	
	Length overall	75ft 8in/23m	
	Length exc probe	72ft 6in/22.14m	
	Height	18ft 5in/5.6m	
	Wing area	730sq ft/68m^2	
Powerplant		Two Tumansky RD-F turbojets	
	Thrust (dry)	22,000lb/98kN	
	Thrust (augmented)	32,000lb/142.5kN	
	Internal fuel	4,100Imp gal/18,800lit	
Weights	Empty	47,500lb/21,500kg	
	Max take-off	90,500lb/41,000kg	4 AA-9, 2×440Imp gal/2,000lit tanks
	Wing loading	125lb/sq ft/600kg/m^2	
Performance	Max speed	1,385kt/2,560km/h (Mach 2.4)	
	Service ceiling	75,000ft/23,000m	
	Initial climb rate	41,000ft/min/208m/sec	
	Interception radius	800nm/1,500km	Subsonic cruise, 100nm/185km supersonic dash
		400nm/740km	Mach 2.4 dash
Armament	Four AA-9 air-to-air misisles, plus four smaller weapons.		

Chapter 8

B-1B

Mike Spick

B-1B

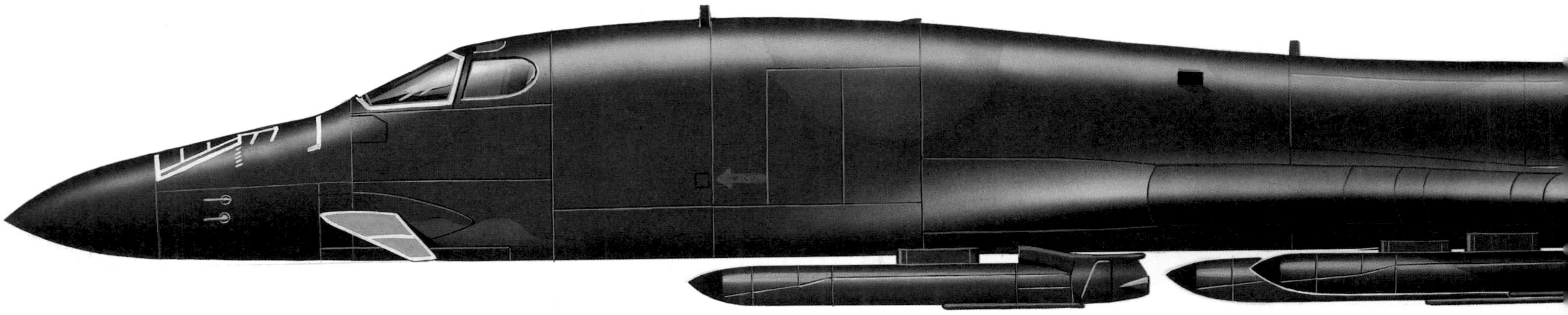

Contents

Acknowledgements

The author and publisher are grateful to all those who have contributed information and illustrations to this chapter. Photograph sources are credited at the beginning of the book, but particular thanks are due to Earl Blount, Lyn Castorina, Jack L. Hefley, Mike Matthews and Scott L. White of Rockwell International; Major Ron Hinkle and Major George H. Peck, HQ Aeronautical Systems Division, Wright-Patterson AFB; Dr Richard Hallion, Edwards AFB; DoD Public Affairs, the Pentagon; Major William H. Austin, USAF Office of Public Affairs; Dwight E. Weber of the General Electric Company; Peter B. Dakan of Boeing Military Airplane Company; Richard L. Palmay of Eaton Corporation AIL Division; Robert F. Dorr; and Air Force Magazine.

Author

Mike Spick was born in London less than three weeks before the Spitfire made its maiden flight. Educated at Churchers College, Petersfield, he later entered the construction industry and carried out considerable work on RAF airfields. An interest in wargaming led him to a close study of air warfare and a highly successful first book, *Air Battles in Miniature* (Patrick Stephens, 1978). His subsequent work includes a historical study of the evolution of air combat tactics, *Fighter Pilot Tactics* (Patrick Stephens, 1983), co-authorship of the Salamander book *Modern Air Combat* (with Bill Gunston, 1983), and three other chapters in this book, *F/A-18 Hornet, F-4 Phantom II* (with Doug Richardson) and *F-14 Tomcat*.

Introduction

The gestation period of the B-1 has been long and difficult even by modern standards. The aircraft was conceived in 1965 after five years of study programmes, the contract was placed on June 5, 1970, and the first aircraft flew on December 23, 1974. The production programme was subsequently cancelled by the Carter Administration, only to be reinstated, albeit in a different though externally similar form during President Reagan's first term in office, and initial operating capability was finally achieved in 1986.

During its chequered career it has been called many things, not all of them flattering: the last of the dinosaurs, an essential leg of the nuclear deterrent triad, a threat to world peace, too expensive, tremendously capable, too vulnerable and – perhaps most insulting of all – an interim solution. Perhaps the most misleading label to have been applied is that of bomber, a word that evokes a big, vulnerable aircraft plodding through the skies at the mercy of both fighters and surface-to-air missiles as it seeks to drop old-fashioned gravity bombs onto a fixed target.

Both the tax-paying public and the politicians knew what a bomber was, though the military did not seem so sure, and for many years controversy abounded as to the exact role of the B-1 and the qualities it should possess. This uncertainty was reflected in the record number of acronyms that the project collected during the early years, a phenomenon that served only to muddy the waters still further.

Two main issues arise. First, can a carrier of strategic weapons penetrate a modern air defence system without incurring an unacceptable level of attrition? Second, has it any significant advantage over the ICBM, the SLBM and the cruise missile? The answer to the first question is that no-one really knows: we can only guess. The answer to the second is an unqualified affirmative, at least in the political sense, since it allows a much greater degree of flexibility.

The final answer will only be known in 40 or 50 years: if the world is still unravaged by nuclear war, the B-1B will have played the part for which it was intended – not by going to war, but by its presence.

The Manned Bomber

It is easy to regard the manned strategic bomber as an anachronism. Intercontinental ballistic missiles allow a fast strike to be made against almost any part of the globe: by comparison, the response of the strategic bomber is almost tortoise-like. Moreover, no effective defence is yet possible against the big missiles with their multiple warheads, whereas the bomber is faced with a combination of fighter and missile defences that, over the last quarter of a century, have made it seem increasingly vulnerable. The question is therefore one of credibility: how viable a proposition is the B-1B?

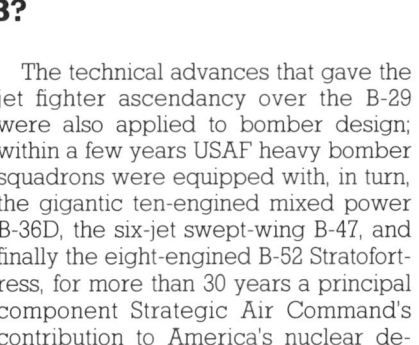

Above: The world's first strategic air-to-surface missile was the Bell GAM-63A Rascal, which saw service between 1957 and 1959. Supersonic, with a range of 75 miles (121km), it is seen here being test launched from a DB-47E Stratojet.

World War II in Europe ended with Germany in ruins and, on the far side of the world, Japan well on the way to the same fate. Then, in August 1945, a single nuclear weapon dropped from a single bomber over Hiroshima was followed by a second bomb over Nagasaki. These devastating attacks effectively finished the war, and with them the strategic bomber came of age. The destructive power of the new weapons had made it totally convincing. There could be no further argument.

The early carriers of nuclear weapons were the USAF Boeing B-29, which also saw service with the RAF as the Washington, and its Soviet copy, the Tupolev Tu-4. Normal attack altitudes and speeds were something in excess of 30,000ft (9,000m) and 200kts (370km/h) – far short of their maximum stated performance figures, but necessary to achieve a worthwhile operational radius. At these heights and speeds they were fairly safe from interception by piston-engined fighters, which took up to 30 minutes to reach attack altitudes, but vulnerable to the new generation of jet fighters. In the strategic role their range was such as to rule out the possibility of fighter escort, and while they could fly in close formation for mutual protection during much of the mission, when the time came to attack they were forced to split up and go their separate ways.

The next operational use of B-29s was for conventional bombing during the Korean War. They proved vulnerable to jet fighters in daylight, even with fighter escorts, and were forced to seek the cover of darkness. In turn, this caused a resumption of the electronic war waged over Germany a decade earlier but which had lapsed after 1945.

The factor which had traditionally made the bomber vulnerable to the fighter was the disparity in performance that allowed the fighter to reach the bomber's altitude and overtake it. The arithmetic was simple: detection of a bomber at a mere 50nm (93km) range gave defending fighters some 15 minutes to scramble, reach the bomber's altitude and intercept it before it could reach their airfield. And as detection distance increased so did the time available for interception. It should be noted that intercepting a B-29 was no pushover, and actually shooting it down was something else again. But as the probability of the bomber completing its mission was eroded, so too was its credibility.

The technical advances that gave the jet fighter ascendancy over the B-29 were also applied to bomber design; within a few years USAF heavy bomber squadrons were equipped with, in turn, the gigantic ten-engined mixed power B-36D, the six-jet swept-wing B-47, and finally the eight-engined B-52 Stratofortress, for more than 30 years a principal component Strategic Air Command's contribution to America's nuclear deterrent force.

New performance levels

For interceptors, the B-52 was a totally different proposition from the B-29. The new bomber's operational altitude was one-third higher and its cruising speed about double that of the latter. As a consequence, while reaction times for the defending fighters were halved, they had to climb far higher to intercept. Furthermore, if ground control failed to position the fighters correctly it would take them far longer to catch up, even assuming they had sufficient fuel, and in many cases they would not.

Military aircraft design is a dynamic process, and by the time a prototype leaves the ground for the first time new shapes appearing on drawing boards are intended to render it obsolete. The B-52 was not expected to be any exception to a clear trend: bombers needed to survive to carry out their mission, survival was enhanced by evading interception by fighters, and interception was evaded by flying higher and faster. There was nothing new about this. The higher and faster progression had been established during World War I, and the technology of the 1950s simply allowed it to proceed faster than ever before.

The USAF's next stratagic bomber, the Convair B-58 Hustler, was designed to fly its mission at over 50,000ft (15,200m) and to maintain supersonic speeds for more than 1,000nm (1,850km): the initial penetration would be made at high subsonic speed, culminating in a Mach 2 dash over the target, and a supersonic dash could also be used to penetrate heavily defended areas. The Hustler entered service with Strategic Air Command in 1960, and for reasons which will be touched upon later was phased out 10 years later.

The last American strategic bomber in the ever higher, ever faster tradition was North American Rockwell's XB-70 Valkyrie, intended to fly its entire mission at 80,000ft (24,400m) and Mach 3. At that speed and altitude it was detectable and its course was fairly predictable, but travelling at just under 29nm (53km) per minute and an altitude of 13nm (24km) it would have posed a formidable task for the manned interceptor. However, just as engines, airframes, avionics and weaponry had made giant strides, so had costs, and Valkyrie was cancelled in 1960 despite very encouraging trials.

The fly in the ointment was the missile, or more properly the rocket. Both projectiles and guidance systems had made tremendous progress, and many people

Left: The gigantic Convair B-36D was the link between earlier piston-engined bombers and later fast jet types, being powered by six piston engines with four jets for takeoff and over-the-target dash speed.

Right: The long-range stand-off missile reduced the time that the bomber was at risk to the defences. A B-52G launches a GAM-77 Hound Dog, which could carry a 1MT warhead for up to 710 miles (1,143km).

Above: The B-58 Hustler was designed to penetrate at high altitudes and high subsonic speeds, culminating in an extended Mach 2 dash over the target. It entered service in 1960 but was unsuitable for low-level missions and was phased out in 1970.

Above: The ultimate high-speed, high-altitude bomber was the North American XB-70 Valkyrie, designed to fly the entire mission at Mach 3 and at 80,000ft (24,383m), where it would have been beyond the reach of defending interceptors.

forecast that the missile would replace both the manned bomber and the manned interceptor. To be fair, the prospects of this happening looked bright. Giant ballistic rockets could carry nuclear and thermonuclear warheads over vast distances with a fair degree of accuracy in a matter of minutes, and were unstoppable by any known means. Clever guidance systems enabled other rockets to follow unerringly and destroy manned aeroplanes. At least, that was the theory. In practice it didn't quite work out, but at the time it looked perfectly possible.

One immediate result was that the new wonder weapons inherited the funding that might otherwise have been used to build more and better aeroplanes. It cast doubt on the viability of manned fighters and bombers, and made some people wonder whether air warfare as it had developed during the previous half-century was an evolutionary aberration. In future, missiles were to deliver the strategic attacks, while the old fashioned flying machine would be ruthlessly hacked from the sky with robot-like precision by defensive missiles. The aeroplane still had a tactical role to play over the battlefield, but as a strategic weapon it was finished. Or so it was thought in some circles.

Certainly the high flying strategic bomber was beginning to look distinctly vulnerable, a view that was reinforced when Gary Powers' U-2 was shot down by an SA-2 missile over the Soviet Union in May 1960. While the destruction of a single U-2 did not automatically mean that a massed bomber force flying at a lower altitude and using the latest electronic countermeasures would be decimated, it was a clear pointer to the future. The time was sure to come when the defences would have a distinct advantage over the high-altitude bomber.

Contemporary estimates of the effectiveness of the SA-2 'Guideline' varied between 80 and 95 per cent. Later experience was to show that the estimates were an order of magnitude too high; they derived partially from theory and partially from test results, both of which

Below: The Valkyrie is seen here in Mach 3 cruise configuration, with the wingtips folded down to give high-speed stability. This state-of-the-art bomber was cancelled, mainly because of the predicted lethality of new missile air defence systems.

tend to be misleading: theory tends not to work in practice, while test firings are conducted in a sterile environment by people with a vested interest in making them work. But at the time the future of the manned bomber looked bleak.

In the event, the Nuclear Triad concept of ICBMs, SLBMs and manned bombers was adopted. ICBMs were tied to fixed bases whose locations were known, and they were vulnerable to a preemptive strike by enemy ICBMs. SLBMs launched from under the sea were safer, although shorter in range, but they had the inherent disadvantage that only a small fraction of the force could be on station at any given moment, and it was impossible to be absolutely certain that they had not been detected. The bomber is also vulnerable – Pearl Harbor is never very far below the surface of the American military mind – but keeping a handful of bombers in the air, armed and ready to go, meant the bomber force could never be totally wiped out by a surprise attack.

The Triad concept had some basic advantages. Any surprise attack would need to hit all three elements simultaneously and targeting all three elements in all locations would be very complicated and tremendously difficult, while defence against the Triad involves protection against three different forms of attack, so that the defence against any single one is diluted.

Manned bomber advantages

There were further arguments in favour of the manned bomber. Firstly, there could be no guarantee that a conventional war might not have to be fought at some stage, perhaps against a less technically advanced nation, in which the strategic bomber could be used to advantage in a conventional (non-nuclear) role. Secondly, in times of tension, strategic bomber forces could rapidly be deployed to sensitive areas, thus expressing the determination of the nation to resist, and as a last resort a full scale strike could be launched yet still recalled at the last minute. An ICBM, by contrast, was irrecoverable and unstoppable, leaving the politicians no time for second thoughts. More immediately, there were a lot of bombers in existence or under construction. To scrap them, along with their supporting infrastructure, could have been disastrous not only in terms of national morale and the economy, but because a potential aggressor might interpret such a move as indicative of a lessening of the collective will to resist.

The performance of the B-58 was sufficient to make it a formidable opponent for some years to come, but only 116 were built, including training variants. Valkyrie could hardly have entered service before 1970 and – electronic countermeasures notwithstanding – could not be expected to constitute a credible threat for long in the face of improving defensive systems. Its colossal expense meant that procurement would be low, and the whole concept of a trisonic bomber was dubious.

Following the Valkyrie's cancellation, efforts were concentrated on giving added survivability, and therefore credibility, to SAC's principal bomber, the B-52. Nearly 750 had been built, of which the first had been delivered in June 1955; it was a relatively new type, and had a lot of operational life left in it if only it could be made capable of penetrating the defences. ECM kit went without saying; other means of enhancing survivability included stand-off missiles, which would allow it to attack the target from a distance rather than overfly it, and defence suppression missiles to blast a hole in enemy defensive systems through which it could penetrate.

Another interesting idea was the Quail decoy missile, whose radar signature was enhanced to simulate that of the parent bomber and which followed a pre-programmed course to distract the defenders from the real bomber. Of course, gadgets like Quail are nice to have, and each one launched could have diverted an attack, but only a limited number of decoys could be carried and each one reduced the effective warload.

The nub of the matter lay in detection, and in defence reaction times. Bombers generally have large radar reflective surfaces, so they can be detected from great distances, and the quest for ever greater heights and speeds had some drawbacks. High altitude was effective against interceptors, whose time to height had become critical, but less so against SAMs, which took off vertically after little preparation.

At the same time, height made bombers visible from further away. For all practical purposes, radar emissions travel in straight lines, so the horizon blocks the line of travel; a bomber flying at a constant altitude follows the curvature of the earth, and the higher it flies the sooner it will appear over the radar horizon, increasing the warning time given to the defences. ECM could help the bomber to remain undetected, but it was far from being the whole answer. Very high speeds reduced the defenders' reaction time, but curtailed the bomber's powers of manoeuvre and made its course more predictable. Something new was needed.

Low-level penetration

The response, designed to reduce detection ranges and defence reaction times, as well as the effectiveness of surface-to-air missiles and fighters, was really very simple: penetration would be undertaken at low level, below the radar horizon.

Effective defence against the bomber was entirely dependent on effective detection: any reduction increased the bomber's chance of completing the mission in proportion. The SAMs of that era were not designed to engage low-flying targets, and at low levels the interceptor fighters lost much of their ostensibly overwhelming performance advantage. Naturally there was a price to be paid – fuel burn is much greater at low altitudes, reducing radius of action, though long-range attack weapons helped make good the deficiency – but there was a degree of compensation in the fact that the defending fighters would be in

Above left: To confuse the defences, B-52s could each carry two GAM-72 Quail decoys, fitted with reflectors in their noses to augment their radar signatures to that of a B-52 and equipped with jamming devices. Flying a pre-programmed course, Quail's function was to distract the defences from the real bomber; it was phased out in the late 1970s.

Left: The first aircraft in SAC service to be fully capable of low-level all-weather penetration, achieved using terrain-following radar, was the FB-111, seen here carrying four SRAMs. The FB-111 also proved the operational validity of variable geometry, and much of the technology of the B-1 was based on experience gained with this aircraft.

even worse straights. With full afterburner they would consume fuel at a colossal rate while barely reaching Mach 1. By contrast, the speed of the bomber at low level would be little affected.

The shooting down of Powers' U-2 had little or no effect on the decision to switch to low level penetration; SAC had initiated it some months earlier, and the process was complete after about three years. Both the British and the French nuclear deterrent forces also switched to low-level penetration at the same time.

The RAF's adoption of night bombing early in World War II had represented an attempt to make the raiders invisible to the defenders, and the switch to low-level penetration in the early 1960s was aimed at the same target, although low level in a B-52 was not at all the same thing as low level in a modern aircraft such as Tornado GR.1.

Another approach to invisibility was represented by the use of ECM to blind defenders, an interesting illustration of which came in the later stages of the Vietnam War. Before April 1972 strategic targets in the North were attacked by tactical fighter-bombers, while B-52s were engaged in bombing targets further south. The obvious inference was that the B-52s were considered too vulnerable to attack the heavily defended targets in North Vietnam. However, during the Linebacker II campaign at the end of 1972, B-52 raids on the North were mounted under cover of darkness, assisted by jamming and defence suppression aircraft. The B-52s flew at the optimum engagement height of the SA-2 missiles, which were launched at them in large numbers, but instead of the slaughter predicted some years earlier, only about two per cent of the B-52 sorties were lost, while the SA-2s' kill ratio was also only about two per cent. MiG-21 fighters also attempted to intervene, losing two of their number for no result.

It should be remembered that these were conventional (iron) bomb attacks, and that the bombers flew in cells of three to maximize their ECM effect, whereas had they been carrying out a nuclear strike they would have flown singly and at low altitude. What difference that would have made is difficult to predict, although it seems likely that casualties would not have been too severe.

To summarize, the quest for ever-increasing altitude and speed had been abandoned in favour of trying to sneak past the defences at low level using intensive ECM and on-board defence suppression weapons. The aircraft used were already in the inventory rather than being of a purpose-built type. Valkyrie, at that time the most advanced bomber in the world, had been abandoned, and a new bomber was needed: the road to the B-1B had started.

Above: The B-52 in its different forms has been the mainstay of SAC since 1955. Its internal bomb bays can hold a formidable load, while even more weapons can be carried externally, as this B-52G, preparing to take off with a dozen SRAMs on underwing pylons, demonstrates.

Below: As the B-1B enters service, the elderly B-52 will be relegated to the role of stand-off cruise missile carrier. Its main weapon will be the AGM-86 ALCM, seen here being test launched, whose range is sufficient to allow the bomber to keep well clear of the defences.

Development

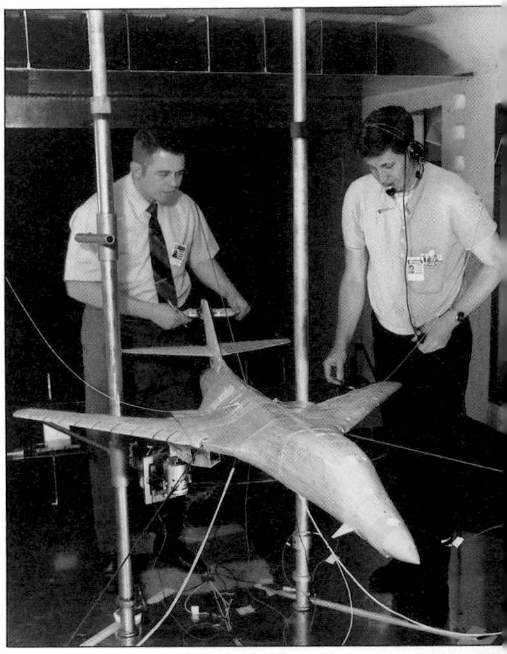

Above: Wind tunnel tests vary from the simple examination of airflow patterns to the very exotic. The amount of wiring attached to this B-1 model indicates the latter.

The plethora of names and acronyms applied to the B-1 during its protracted gestation could give the impression that the US defence procurement staff did not really know what they were about. An insight into the problems was given by Lt Gen Kelly H. Burke in an address to the NAC in March 1982: "I've always thought that if military history teaches us anything, it ought to teach us humility, because we never have been very good at predicting the next war . . . we've not always done a good job in acquiring the right sort of weapons to fight those wars." The years of chopping and changing that preceded the B-1B's service entry represented a determined effort to get it right.

AMSA 1967

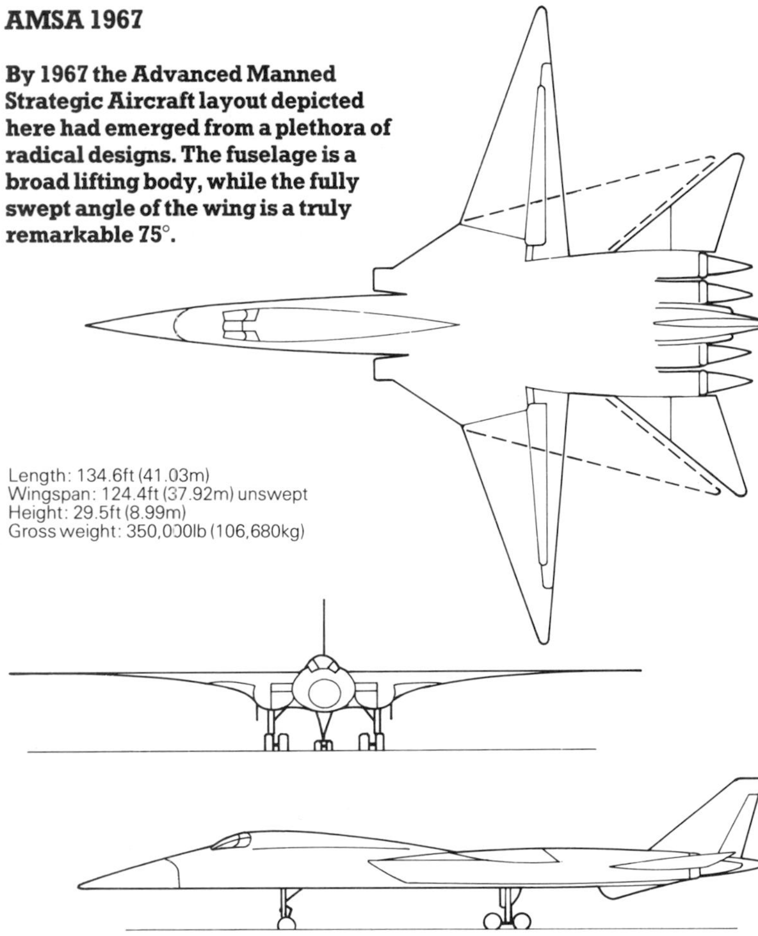

By 1967 the Advanced Manned Strategic Aircraft layout depicted here had emerged from a plethora of radical designs. The fuselage is a broad lifting body, while the fully swept angle of the wing is a truly remarkable 75°.

Length: 134.6ft (41.03m)
Wingspan: 124.4ft (37.92m) unswept
Height: 29.5ft (8.99m)
Gross weight: 350,000lb (106,680kg)

The shooting down of Gary Powers' U-2 over the Soviet Union in May 1960 did not immediately invalidate the high-altitude bomber, but it was an indication that the route to survival lay in avoiding radar detection by flying below the radar horizon, and in 1961 the United States Air Force initiated exploratory studies of a new concept, the Subsonic Low Altitude Bomber, or SLAB. The SLAB studies were followed in 1962 by Project Forecast, a USAF examination of the force structure requirements for the strategic triad for the period through to the 1980s: concluded in 1969, it made a strong case for the retention of the manned bomber as an essential part of both deterrent and conventional forces.

In 1963, while the USAF pursued new research on the Extended Range Strategic Aircraft (ERSA) and Low Altitude Manned Penetrator (LAMP), other studies were carried out by industry on government contract under the titles Advanced Manned Penetrator (AMP) and Advanced Manned Penetrating Strategic System (AMPSS). AMP consisted of preliminary design and evaluation of the technical and economic feasibility of four basic mission concepts: low altitude subsonic; subsonic low altitude and medium supersonic high altitude; subsonic low altitude and high supersonic high altitude; and V/STOL. The two main questions to be answered were essentially what the Air Force could reasonably expect in a given time scale, and what it could afford. At an early stage the second solution seems to have been favoured, as the AMPSS study concerned the optimization of this concept.

During 1965 the AMP and AMPSS studies were concluded and a new one started on the Advanced Manned Strategic Aircraft, or AMSA, later lampooned as "America's Most Studied Aircraft". The AMSA programme lasted for the next four years, and in essence consisted of the development of a point design in a flexible manner. The AMSA study was carried out by three airframe companies, Boeing, General Dynamics, and North American Rockwell, and funded by the Air Force.

The primary mission of AMSA was officially stated as being to deter nuclear war through the ability to survive an enemy first strike, successfully penetrate enemy defences (both actual and projected) and accurately deliver either stand-off or laydown weapons on both military and industrial targets, and the basic point design required that initial survivability, penetration capability and payload/range be better than those of the B-52, at that time the mainstay of Strategic Air Command.

AMSA 1968

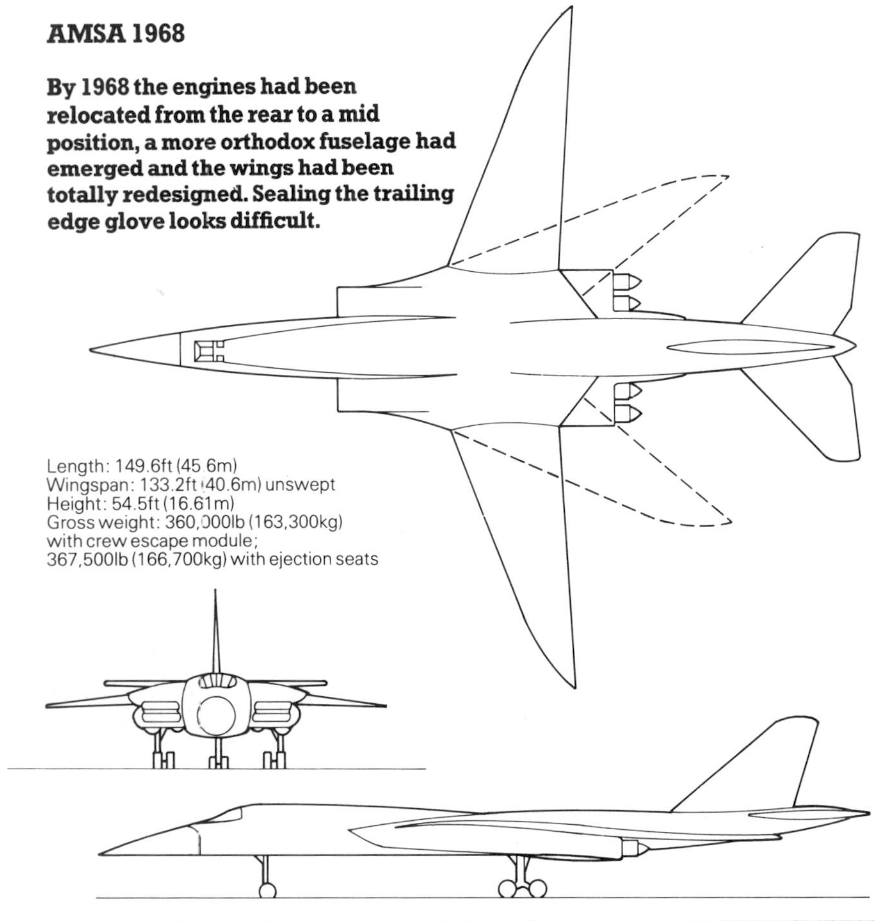

By 1968 the engines had been relocated from the rear to a mid position, a more orthodox fuselage had emerged and the wings had been totally redesigned. Sealing the trailing edge glove looks difficult.

Length: 149.6ft (45.6m)
Wingspan: 133.2ft (40.6m) unswept
Height: 54.5ft (16.61m)
Gross weight: 360,000lb (163,300kg) with crew escape module;
367,500lb (166,700kg) with ejection seats

B-1 proposal 1969

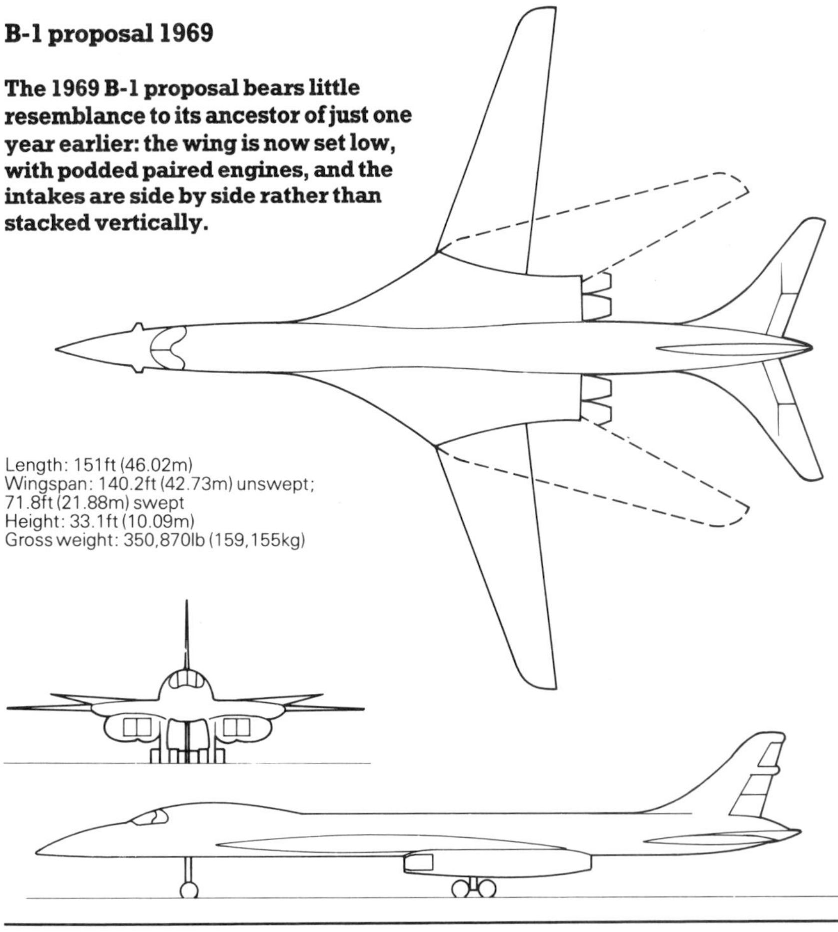

The 1969 B-1 proposal bears little resemblance to its ancestor of just one year earlier: the wing is now set low, with podded paired engines, and the intakes are side by side rather than stacked vertically.

Length: 151ft (46.02m)
Wingspan: 140.2ft (42.73m) unswept;
71.8ft (21.88m) swept
Height: 33.1ft (10.09m)
Gross weight: 350,870lb (159,155kg)

Above: The B-1 mockup is seen here at an early stage. Access to the interior is through a door on the side of the nose, but this was not a feature of the finished product.

Above right: Two fixed wing models are shown, along with three AMSA proposals whose wing sweep angles exceed 90° to form rhomboidal lifting bodies. AMSA 1968 is at far right.

The earlier studies had shown that the best chance of successful penetration of a heavily defended area lay in high subsonic speed at low altitude, while supersonic performance at high altitude gave greater flexibility, as well as reducing the transit time through lightly defended areas. This was the point design around which AMSA was developed, and in November 1969 the USAF was able to issue Requests for Proposals. The three companies that had participated in the AMSA studies made their submissions, and in June of the following year Rockwell International, as North American Rockwell had become, were selected as B-1 system contractors.

Winning design

An interesting development process had led to the winning design. The most modern weapons available at the time were the Short Range Attack Missile (SRAM), for which Boeing Aerospace were awarded a contract in October 1966, and another Boeing product, the Subsonic Cruise Armed Decoy (SCAD), which was designed to be interchangeable with SRAM. The B-52 was intended to carry eight of these missiles internally on a rotary launcher, and consideration of cost-effectiveness dictated that the B-1 be able to do better, the obvious way ahead being multiple launchers. Accordingly it was decided to mount three rotary launchers internally, giving three times the striking power of the B-52, but since the relationship between weight and cost dictated that AMSA was to be a rather smaller aircraft than the B-52 tripling the internal weapons load was going to be difficult. Some idea of the problem is presented in the following table.

Weight as percentage of the gross	B-52	AMSA
Structure	22	22
Systems	20	22
Weapons load	5	15
Fuel	53	41
	100	100

The structural percentage had to be held down to the same level as the B-52, even though the aeroplane was smaller. Again, the systems could not be allowed to increase by more than two per cent of the gross weight: even though such extras as terrain-following radar, addi-

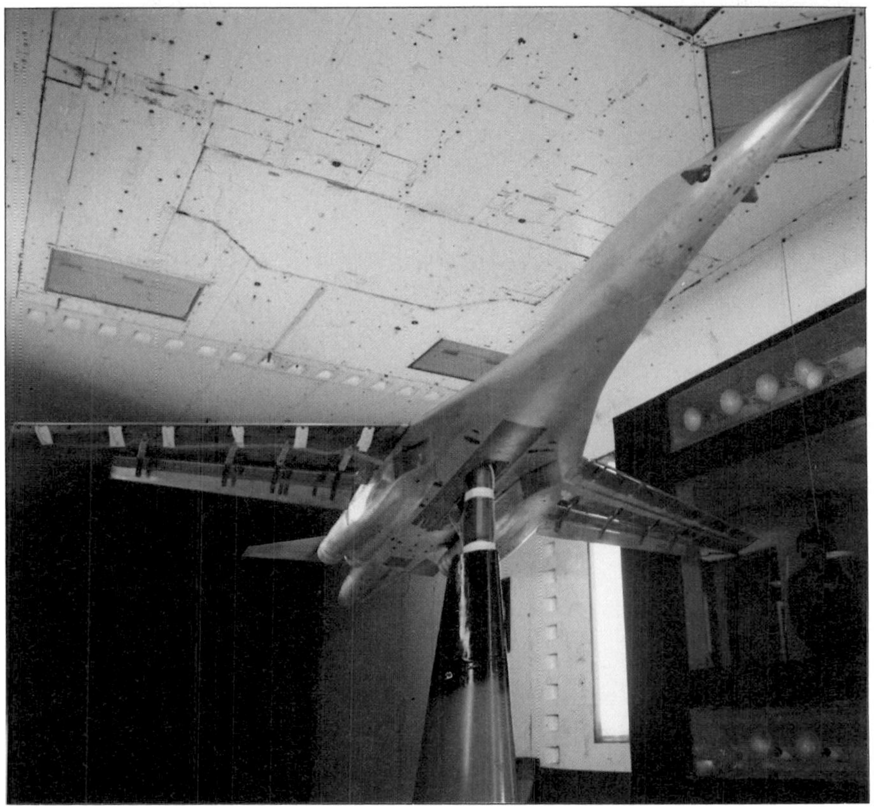

Above: Wind tunnel model of the B-1 showing the leading edge slats and the complicated double translating flaps originally proposed. Also shown are the original horizontally raked supersonic inlets.

Below: The mockup, complete with Strategic Air Command insignia on the nose, against a scenic backdrop with star filter effects. The date is December 1971, some three years before the B-1's maiden flight.

Above: The underside of the rear fuselage of the B-1 contains some interesting compound curves. Here the left fuselage and the inside of the inner left engine nacelle are tufted to examine the airflow.

Top: The first B-1A, the flying qualities test vehicle, shown with the SAC nose stripe at medium altitude over the Mojave desert. The barber pole pitot was carried for flight instrumentation reasons only.

Above: Final approach to one of the 79 landings made by the first prototype during a career that included 405.3 hours of test flying during the four years that followed its first flight on December 23, 1974.

tional penetration aids and extra sensors had to be fitted, the reduction in gross weight meant they actually had to weigh less than those of the B-52. This only left one area in which savings could be made – fuel – so a range comparable to that of the B-52 had to be achieved with a reduction in fuel fraction amounting to 29 per cent.

Matters were further complicated by the decision to use a variable-geometry (VG) wing. This had many operational advantages, allowing short takeoffs and landings, which aided dispersal, while full sweep gave a good configuration for supersonic flight and low gust response, an invaluable quality in the low-level penetration role. On the other hand, it meant that valuable space would be taken up by the wings and their pivots, actuators and hydraulic systems. In terms of weight fraction, VG added to the section called systems. If payload and range were not to suffer, some very interesting tradeoffs would have to be made.

In fact, the first tradeoff had already been made, when vertical takeoff and landing was considered and rejected. If not totally beyond the state of the art at that time, it was certainly considered to carry too high a development risk, while the added weight and cost could only have been balanced by a reduction in payload, range or both. In-flight refuelling was always available, but the demands would have been excessive and the increase in the size of the tanker fleet very costly, and while survivability in the event of a surprise attack would have been greatly enhanced, a VTOL bomber ideally needs a VTOL tanker.

Efforts to hold down the structural weight percentage involved the examination of new materials and design concepts. Boron and carbon composites were investigated, along with high-strength steel and aluminium alloys, but the main effort was directed towards the use of titanium. From the design angle, concepts such as blended wing bodies, which permitted maximum structural depth and minimized wetted area, were carefully considered.

Power for AMSA was the subject of a separate programme aimed at a minimum length lightweight afterburning turbofan incorporating a short annular combustor, a short mixer and augmentor, a high temperature turbine and cooled blades. Contracts were let for the development of two technology demonstrator engines, the final choice falling on a General Electric design.

The avionic systems, both offensive and defensive, were to be the most comprehensive yet seen, and keeping the weight percentage down posed a challenge. The main emphasis was on the use of digital systems and multi-function phased array antennas. A development programme on the radar system was established, and a breadboard apparatus was constructed and test flown in a C-135. The avionic systems were obviously going to be very complex and demand a lot of power; a 230-volt electrical system was proposed, combined with a lot of electrical multiplexing, but new technology offered better reliability and general simplification.

Survivability requirements

The need to survive a surprise attack had a considerable impact on systems requirements. The key to survival lay in wide dispersion, and while this would normally be to SAC bases in the United States, the use of quite small and spartan civil airfields was not discounted in times of political tension. The variable-geometry wing was an advantage in getting in and out of small fields, but there were many other considerations. AMSA had to be stand-alone capable, able to operate with little or no flight line equipment. In the event of an alert, it had to be capable of self-starting, and airborne within a very few minutes. Good communications at the airfield were not essential, as the on-board systems could be used, but what was essential was the ability to check that the bomber was ready to go with all systems available. This was accomplished by means of an on-board Central Integrated Test System (CITS), which provided data on serviceability status.

The final requirement, which bit into the strutural and systems weight percentages, was the need to incorporate nuclear hardening against both blast (for the airframe) and electro-magnetic pulse (EMP) for the avionic systems.

B-1A first prototype (74-0158)

All B-1As were finished originally with white anti-flash paint, but this made them far too visible at low level.

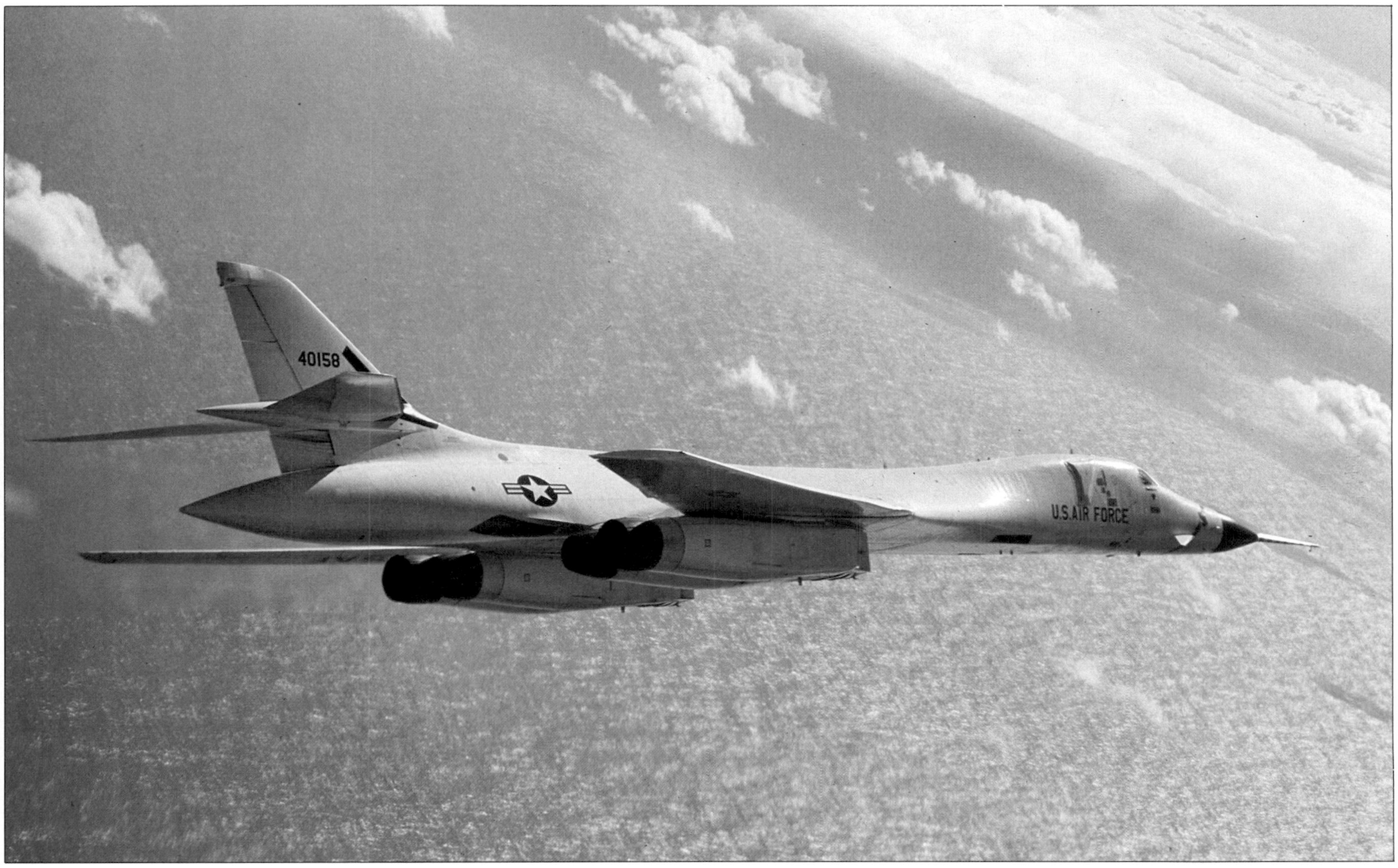

Above: The first B-1A with wings fully swept in a climbing turn at high altitude. What appears to be slight skin wrinkling can be seen aft of the crew area, and there is no transparency in the rear cockpit.

With all these factors taken into consideration, the required mission range had still to be achieved while using a smaller fuel fraction. The high-technology turbofans promised between 10 and 15 per cent better specific fuel consumption than the Pratt & Whitney J57s of the B-52, which contributed greatly to the solution of the problem; the rest had to be down to the aerodynamicists. Once again the variable-sweep wing was the largest single contributing factor, and this was developed from the same NASA data base as that of the F-111.

By 1967 the thousands of configurations had been whittled down and a point design had emerged, though this paper aeroplane bore little resemblance to the B-1 ultimately built. AMSA 1967 was 134.6ft (41.02m) long, 29.5ft (8.99m) high at the single fin, and spanned 124.4ft (37.92m) with the wings at minimum sweep. The four turbofans, located at the rear of the fuselage, were fed from sharply raked two-dimensional intakes set out from the forward fuselage. The single fin was mounted on the end of the fuselage which projected slightly back behind the engines, and the abiding impression was that it was rather undersized, though it was supplemented by two small ventral fins set on the outside of the twin engine nacelles. The cockpit formed a bulge on the top of the forward fuselage, and was faired gently back almost to the halfway point.

Most remarkable of all in appearance were the wings. The wing gloves commenced just behind the intakes, and were set high, sweeping back at approximately 55°, and the wings themselves were almost perfectly triangular in shape, with lightly rounded tips. At minimum sweep of around 20° the trailing edge actually swept forward, while maximum sweep angle was a spectacular 75°, the wings folding back to form an almost continuous surface with the horizontal stabilizers, which were set in a marginally lower plane than the wings. The wings had a very slight dihedral; the stabilizer a slightly larger one. Despite all efforts, the structural weight percentage had crept up to 24, though the systems were down at 18, as was the weapons load, now 14 per cent, leaving the fuel fraction to make up the difference at 44 per cent. The design gross weight was 350,000lb (158,760kg).

Both the design and the requirements continued to develop. The weapons load

Above: 'Burners cooking, the first B-1A departs Edwards. The rather clumsy wing glove fairing can be seen to advantage from this angle. It was revised on the B-1B.

was increased from 24 to 32 SRAMs carried internally, and the point design had to change considerably to accommodate an effective 33 per cent increase. Obvicusly, on a combat mission, the weapons load is expended, either gradually or fairly rapidly, and this greatly effects the aerodynamic balance of the carrier aircraft. It was therefore necessary to place the engines near the aerodynamic centre of the aircraft rather than at the tail, but this in turn caused other problems, such as heating of the rear fuselage from the engine exhausts, while the location of the horizontal stabilizers had also to be amended.

As a result of these changes, AMSA 1968 bore little likeness to its predecessor of the year before, but had begun to bear a passing resemblance to the future B-1. The length had increased to 149.6ft (45.60m), height to the top of the fin had jumped 46 per cent to 54.5ft (16.61m) while the span at minimum sweep had increased slightly to 133.2ft (40.60m).

The engines were located in pairs in twin nacelles on each side of the fuselage; the intakes showed little change, but were now clearly paired, one on top of the other. The single fin was greatly increased both in height and in area, and moved forward a few feet, while the ventral fins had gone, since there was nowhere to locate them. The cockpit bulge was much more smoothly faired into the fuselage, and the wing gloves, starting high on the intakes and much reduced in size, no longer blended into the fuselage but ended in a fillet above the twin engine nacelles, with the wing sweeping back into the fillet. The wings also had a new shape, a straight leading edge curving gently toward the tip to give a sharp point where it met the trailing edge, which now had a slight sweepback when fully extended.

At this stage the design was beginning to harden, and a great many tradeoff studies were initiated. Cost effectiveness had always been important, and now it became paramount, the basic parameter being relative effectiveness in destroying a specific target complex or system set against the overall system cost. Previous cost comparisons had been based on weight, but the point design, in the form of AMSA 1968, was now used as the basis of a more comprehensive cost analysis against which tradeoff costs could be compared. Many studies were undertaken, the most important of which were:

(a) Landing gear flotation requirements against dispersal capability (involving a worst-case assessment of small dispersal airfields.

(b) Crew escape module compared with ejection seats. The normal operational crew consisted of four men, but on training missions two instructors would bring the number up to six. Rather surprisingly, the study showed savings using a six-man module based on that of the two-man F-111, which was some 6,750lb (3,062kg) lighter overall, taking into account the individual life support systems. The USAF also felt that crew effectiveness would be greater in the shirt-sleeve environment than in all the normal paraphernalia of flying gear, as efficiency is improved when the crew can communicate with each other direct rather than using communications equipment. A further consideration was that in the event of an ejection at high altitude and high supersonic speeds, the crew module was much more survivable.

(c) CITS capability as compared with AGE (automated ground environment). This was an easy one to resolve, as although the CITS added weight, cost, and complexity to the aircraft, its omission greatly increased the bomber's vulnerability to surprise attack while reducing its credibility as a combat system.

(d) Ride quality against crew effectiveness. As a rule of thumb, the lower the altitude, the rougher the ride. The planned ultra low level penetration at high subsonic speeds gave the best chance of mission success, but subjected the crew to a bone-jarring series of jolts at intervals of two or three seconds. This is uncomfortable in the short term, and for the extended periods that would be necessary for deep penetration, would be so fatiguing as to considerably affect crew efficiency. The answer partly lies in the gust response of the aircraft, the conditioning factors of which are a low aspect ratio and a high wing loading. The AMSA project, with wings fully swept, fulfilled both these conditions admirably in terms of design, but the size of the aircraft caused problems, its sheer length tending to induce a whipping motion, with the aircraft flexing as it rode the gusts. There were two possible ways to reduce this motion to acceptable levels: either to make the fuselage much more rigid, though the weight penalty of doing this was prohibitive; or to use low altitude ride control, in which small sensor actuated vanes were mounted on the sides of the nose, reacting automatically to gusts and smoothing out the ride.

(e) Nuclear hardness versus initial survival. This is a sensitive area, and no firm information was released on this study, but it seems reasonable to speculate that nuclear hardening beyond a certain point demands extra weight and a longer takeoff run, reducing dispersal capability, which in turn reduces the probability of surviving a surprise attack.

By 1969 the years of study were ready to bear fruit. Concept definition was complete, and the Department of Defense authorized the USAF to proceed

Above: The first B-1A lets it all hang out on finals, giving a good view of the stalky narrow track gear and the movable ramps of the horizontally raked supersonic engine inlet configuration.

Right: The B-1A was intended to have a Mach 2 capability at high altitude. Wings fully swept, the second prototype sets off on a high-speed run, the flared position of the nozzles indicating full throttle.

Left: Three B-1A's on the flight line was a rare sight. The second B-1A, restored to flying order after eight months of load testing during 1975, is in the foreground, with the first and third aircraft to left and right respectively.

further Until this point, most of the studies had been concerned with relative cost effectiveness, and two things were certain: this would be the most studied and easily the most expensive combat aircraft in the world. As related earlier, Requests for Proposals were issued, the submissions were studied, and the weapon system contract was awarded to Rockwell. No longer just a project, the design had ceased to be AMSA, and had become the B-1.

The Rockwell proposal bore a close resemblance to the B-1 as it finally flew. Compared to AMSA 1968, overall length was slightly up at 151ft (46.02m), height to the top of the fin was considerably reduced, to 33.1ft (10.09m), while span at minimum sweep had grown to 140.2ft (42.73m).

In plan view the Low Altitude Ride Control (LARC) vanes were clearly visible on either side of the nose just ahead of the cockpit, area ruling was readily apparent for the first time, and the leading edges of the wing glove boxes, freed now from proximity to the engine intakes, described a gentle concave curve outward from the fuselage. The wings, more blunted at the tips, ranged from a minimum sweep angle of 15° to a maximum of 75°, producing a rather odd shoulder effect reminiscent of an F-14 using oversweep for deck parking. The horizontal tail surfaces also featured the same graceful curve on the leading edge as the glove box, the overall effect being rather similar to the Handley Page Victor.

Fuselage refinement

From the front the departures from AMSA 1968 were equally marked. Instead of a rather square-section fuselage flanked by squat double intakes, a more rounded fuselage flanked by thickish wing gloves with little sign of wing/body blending presented a more pleasing aspect, while the paired engines mounted in nacelles beneath the gloves showed side-by-side intakes instead of the previous horizontal split. With the wing moved to the low position the engine nacelles formed a tunnel from which the main gear depended, unlike AMSA 1968, in which the main gear was retracted into the nacelles. This considerably reduced undercarriage track from 17.8ft (5.43m) to 12.1ft (3.69m), narrower than the ideal, but unavoidably so. The wings showed a slight anhedral, while the horizontal tail, mounted level with the wings, showed several degrees of dihedral.

The side elevation was much like that of the B-1 as we know it, except for the position of the horizontal tail, while the engine nacelles were considerably shorter than those on AMSA 1968, and featured a horizontal rather than a vertical rake to the inlets.

The Defense System Acquisition Review Council authorized full scale development on June 4, 1970, and the contract awarded to Rockwell International was for five flight test and one static test aircraft. There was, however, a fly in the ointment: there simply was not enough money available, and Air Force approval to proceed with development was conditional on the project being tailored to suit the purse, so radical changes were inevitable. All the studies had assumed that the advanced avionics, defensive and offensive, would be made available, but in the event this was not the case. The requirements had been aimed far into the future, beyond immediate needs, and avionics development was halted, entirely through lack of funds. Instead, existing avionics were to be used, though provision was to be made for advanced equipment to be fitted at a later date.

Left: Defense Secretary Donald Rumsfeld prepares to board a B-1A at Edwards AFB on April 19, 1976. On landing after an hour-long flight during which he took a turn at the controls, former US Navy pilot and firm B-1 supporter Rumsfeld commented that the aircraft had handled "exceedingly well".

Right: In-flight refuelling was essential to the B-1A mission as originally envisaged and the first prototype is shown here conducting refuelling trials with a KC-135 tanker. The lines of the B-1 often belie its size, which can be judged here in comparison with the tanker.

After nearly nine years of the most careful studies and design work, it was ironic that the first major task after the contract had been awarded was to redefine the performance parameters and redesign the aircraft to fit the budget, a programme called Project Focus. The driving force was no longer cost effectiveness but cost limitation, a change of emphasis that was to have serious repercussions for the future, as it undermined the credibility of the B-1 in the eyes of the American public and, worse, the politicians.

It is a truism that in any field of endeavour the best is the enemy of the good; while there can be no doubt that the revised B-1 concept was very good indeed, it is equally certain that it was not as good as the original. Public and politicians naturally assumed that if the original aircraft was what was needed to fly the mission successfully, the new and degraded version could not possibly have the necessary capability. Predictably, in view of the enormous cost, the project became a political football, though it still retained many supporters.

After avionics, the next area to come under close scrutiny was that of the structural materials used. The original design contained a high proportion of titanium (approximately 40 per cent of structural weight), and while titanium is a great weight saver compared to steel, it is also much more expensive. Rockwell were very experienced in the use of this material after building the XB-70 Valkyrie, and had developed a fabrication process known as diffusion bonding (described in detail in the following chapter) which gave great strength and was used in conjunction with welding and bolted joints. As well as saving weight – basically, the more titanium that can be substituted for steel, the greater the weight saved – titanium can also be used instead of aluminium in areas subject to aerodynamic heating, since it retains its strength in conditions where aluminium gradually weakens, such as flight at speeds exceeding Mach 2.2.

Both weight and cost in aircraft structures are very sensitive to the proportion of titanium used. Below about 12 per cent, in the specific case of the B-1, both cost and weight fall dramatically as the replacement of heavy steel sections with lighter titanium ones causes a knock-on effect through the design. Above this point, the weight continues to reduce while the cost levels out, until the proportion reaches 20 per cent, after which weight continues to diminish, albeit at a reduced rate, but costs start to spiral upward as many cheaper members are being replaced by the more expensive material. In the end, the proportion of titanium was reduced to about 21 per cent.

Materials specifications

Problems had arisen from the use of high strength steel alloys in the F-111, and the very long service life envisaged for the B-1 meant that this had to be avoided, so a requirement was added for the use of materials with superior fracture mechanics. In essence, this involved very strict manufacturing controls coupled with advances in non-destructive testing methods. It also involved the flaw size for a component being specified at an undetectable level; the component had then to be manufactured in such a way that the flaw could not become critical during the aircraft lifetime, which in the case of the B-1 was some 13,500 flying hours.

Project Focus had reduced the weapon load to 24 SRAMs instead of the 32 projected earlier, but design gross weight still increased from 350,870lb (159,155kg) to 360,000lb (163,296kg), and the operational requirements were relaxed slightly. On paper these appear fairly marginal. The fully laden takeoff distance was extended by 500ft (152m); the supersonic dash distance was decreased by 100 statute miles (161km); the altitude for refuelling was reduced by 500ft (152m); and the thrust/drag ratio was reduced by about 10 per cent.

From Project Focus emerged the repackaged B-1, heavier but smaller, with length reduced to 143.5ft (43.74m), height to the top of the fin slightly increased at 32.4ft (9.88m), and span at minimum sweep reduced to 136.7ft (41.66m), while the wing gloves were smaller in span and no longer showed the graceful concave leading edge.

At the same time, two really major changes were apparent, the most obvious being the blending of the wing glove and the fuselage. This was adopted primarily to provide extra structural strength and extra volume while reducing the overall dimensions; it also helped to reduce the radar cross section (RCS) by smoothing out angles which would othewise have made excellent radar corners, though Rockwell staff remember this as more of a spinoff than a deliberate design feature.

The second major external change was the horizontal tail. That on the original proposal had been set low on the fuselage, roughly 5ft (1.52m) above the thrust line, where benefits in terms of both weight and stability were greatest, but in close proximity to the engine effluxes. The change from titanium to aluminium meant that the tailplane could not be exposed to such a demanding acoustic and temperature environment, and it was relocated halfway up the vertical fin. Altered flutter characteristics made a complete redesign necessary, and the revised horizontal tail was of much more orthodox appearance than its predecessor. Although this increased the weight, it provided additional usable area in the tailcone for avionics.

A third, less obvious change concerned the engine intakes, The B-1 had two important flight regimes; Mach 2 at high altitude and low-level subsonic, and to provide the best solution to these

Above: The third B-1A transits the Mojave desert at about 500ft (150m). The fully swept wings notwithstanding, the power setting is only moderate. From this angle, the aircraft seems to be peering ahead.

Below: The third prototype during terrain following trials in September 1977 on its forty-eighth flight. The rear fuselage and the base of the fin are tufted.

Right: The third B-1A at medium altitude over one of the California dry lakes. The contrast with the T-38 chase aircraft gives an impression of size; the bomber's AoA is higher than that of the trainer.

Above: Condensation ripples from the trailing edge as the third B-1, seen here in polished natural metal, nears the contrail belt. Distinct vortices can be seen arising from the wing glove seal area.

Below: A slow pass with wings at minimum sweep by the third aircraft at Edwards. This could have been a minimum speed test but is probably a speed calibration check.

conflicting requirements a rather complex mixed compression intake had been adopted. Further studies showed that the use of a simple external compression intake would slightly enhance subsonic performance at the price of a corresponding restriction in the top right-hand corner of the performance envelope, but more than that, a weight saving of roughly 1,400lb (635kg) could be achieved.

By the middle of 1971 the basic configuration had stabilized, and in July of that year the Preliminary Design Review was held. This signalled the start of a new phase in which any changes would at the very least involve the preparation of new drawings, and in a worst case tooling and materials would have to be scrapped an inevitably expensive process. Unfortunately further changes were unavoidable, as the emphasis on cost control had become even stronger than the previous stress on cost effectiveness. In some cases it was found that the cost of a particular feature would be more than anticipated so that an alternative would have to be sought, the wing high-lift systems being a case in point. Originally these were conceived as double-slotted translating flaps, but the detail design soon showed that such a system would be both heavy and complicated, so an alternative was sought. A single slotted flap was designed and subjected to wind tunnel tests, which confirmed that it could meet the requirements. The leading edge slat was then extended inboard slightly, with the result that the high lift capability exceeded requirements.

Escape module revision

Another area subject to revision was the crew escape module. As first proposed it featured two rocket motors, one for primary propulsion and the other for manoeuvring, the latter being gimbal-mounted to allow manoeuvre in two axes. It was found that for a slight reduction in low-altitude adverse-attitude capability, one rocket motor, designed to give control in both roll and pitch, could do the job. The cost saving was considerable.

The contract placed with Rockwell on June 5, 1970, had been based on cost plus incentive fee and was planned on a series of milestones, at each of which approval had to be given before proceeding to the next phase. These were: (a) Preliminary design review of engines and avionics; (b) Mockup review; (c) Engine run to 90 per cent power; (d) Contract award for avionics integration; (e) Design review of engine; (f) Avionics mockup; (g) Engine preliminary flight rating test; (h) Rollout; (i) First flight; and (j) Production decision.

Unfortunately, inflation was beginning to bite, and cost overruns on other programmes, notably the C-5 Galaxy, were raising fundamental questions

Above: The setting sun highlights the fourth B-1A at Edwards in March 1981, shortly before the termination of the initial flight test programme. This unusual view emphasizes the great bulk of the bomber.

about procurement methods. Standard service practice before this time had been for the contractor to comply with the specification regardless of cost, but the first few months of the B-1 programme saw the USAF studying alternative methods. The result became known as the Innovative approach, with the head of the System Program Office, at that time Major-General Douglas Nelson, given a clear mandate to pull the basics of the programme together in such a way that costs would be reduced. In other contexts this would be known as horse trading.

The impact on the development programme was considerable. Two of the original five aircraft ordered for the flight test programme were eliminated, and the number of development engines was reduced from 40 to 27, while the target date for the first flight slipped by five months from December 1, 1973, to May 1, 1974. Worse still, the production decision, scheduled to be made six months after first flight, was deferred for a further six months, giving a total delay of 17 months. A high element of risk was attached to this programme, as it involved the lion's share of the flight test programme being borne by the first prototype, so a serious mishap could have incalculable consequences.

Before the design finally settled down, a few minor changes took place. A radome replaced the tail cone, while a further, bullet-shaped sensor position appeared behind the junction of the vertical and horizontal tail surfaces. The overwing fairing was modified, as was the trailing edge fairing between the engine nozzles; the main landing gear strut was beefed up a bit; and the horizontal tail sweep angle was also modified. Span remained the same, but length showed a slight increase to 152.2ft (46.39m), as did overall height, to 33.58ft (10.23m). These were the final dimensions of the prototype B-1A.

The halting of the advanced avionics development caused a major headache, but with previous requirements as a guide, a package of existing sub-systems was put together. The big question mark against advanced systems is always whether they are going to work as advertised, whereas with existing equipment the reverse is the case: the question then is, in a long-term programme, are the items still going to be manufactured and available when they are wanted? The uncertainty was aggravated by the long service life envisaged for the B-1. Naturally, mid-life updates were anticipated, but it could just turn out that a particular item would perform well enough to be retained, and might well be wanted 30 years in the future. If it was ten years old to start with. . .?

Avionics selection

The package selected consisted of such systems as a stellar-inertial navigation platform, forward-looking and terrain-following radar, radar altimeter and other items combined with a central computer complex. Examination deemed the computer complex risky and expensive; consequently, a modified off-the-shelf computer was substituted. At this point the avionics were split into two packages, offensive and defensive, and defensive systems were recategorized to allow open competition in order to reduce the risks, both technical and fiscal. In April 1972 Boeing was selected to integrate the offensive avionic systems, and after a period of intensive evaluation the AIL Division of Cutler-Hammer secured the order to do the same job on the defensive avionic systems. This award was made in January 1974, barely four months before the first flight was scheduled to take place, but by this time the programme had slipped a few months.

In 1973, construction started of the first B-1 prototype, and even as this happened further ventures to improve later variants or to upgrade standard models were under review. Many of these were in the field of avionics, and one improvement that did get through in the end was a new, cheap, but highly accurate inertial navigation platform, but there were some other very interesting ideas which seem to have been all but forgotten in the years since 1973. One was a new wing carry-through box by Advanced Metallic Structures. Two concepts were evaluated and one was to be constructed and tested, the design conforming to the

B-1A fourth prototype (76-0174)

The first B-1 to wear camouflage, 76-0174 also carried a dorsal spine housing a waveguide for a monopulse jamming system called Cross-Eye.

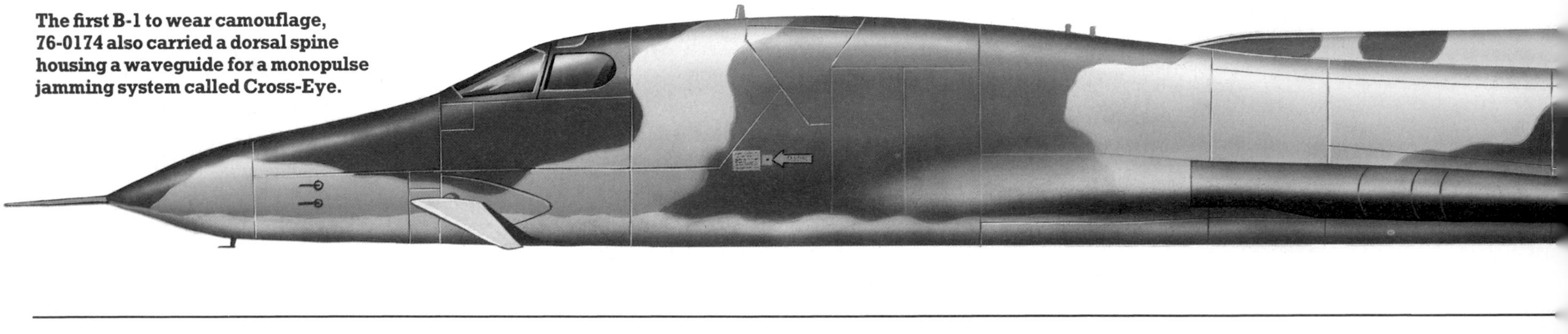

Above: The dorsal spine on B-1A No 4 is clearly shown. This was not featured on any other aircraft and does not appear on every picture of this one. Also highlighted is the original wing seal fairing.

dimensions and structural needs of the B-1. Little has ever been released, except that the use of advanced materials and concepts was expected to produce large savings in both weight and cost, and it might be incorporated into later B-1s on the production line.

The other possibility was the supercritical wing, at that time about to be flown on the F-111, which was designed to offer higher cruising speeds, simpler construction and, almost certainly, reduced costs. To retrofit the supercritical wing is a fairly easy job with a variable-sweep aircraft, and might have been done as a mid-life update, but little has since been heard of the programme, and its use for the B-1 has long since been shelved.

As if the impact of the so-called Innovative approach had not been bad enough, the programme schedule was disrupted yet again in July 1973 by the USAF's new fly-before-buy policy. This slowed progress up still further, with the projected date for first flight being delayed several months; even worse, from a production point of view, was that the time between first flight and the decision to commence production was doubled from 12 to 24 months. This was difficult for Rockwell. The third prototype would be completed early in 1976, after which manufacturing would grind to a halt; then, if the decision proved favourable, it would have to restart at the end of the year. At this stage some 3,000 suppliers and subcontractors were involved in the project, and the task of rescheduling that lot, as well as finding interim work for many thousands of direct employees, was no joke. Once skilled workers are laid off, getting them back in times of full employment is not easy.

By this time the US Senate Armed Services Research and Development Subcommittee was growing worried about the situation. In the late summer of 1973 Air Force Secretary John L. McLucas ordered an independent review, headed by Raymond Bisplinghoff, at that time the Deputy Director of the National Science Foundation. The report

Above: No 4 before the application of camouflage and without the dorsal spine. The black dielectric panels on the wing glove roots accentuate the waisted effect of the central fuselage.

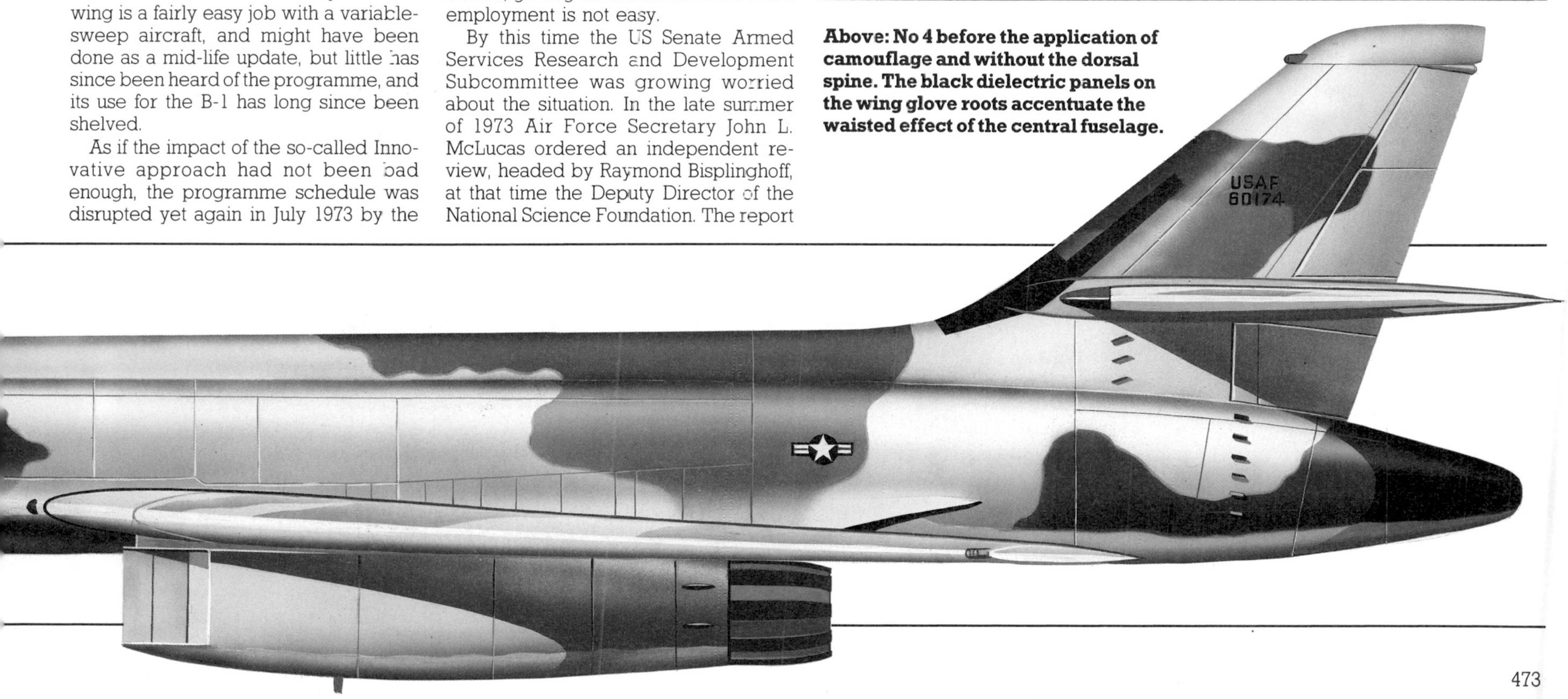

produced by Bisplinghoff's team of technical and management experts was critical of the development programme in a number of areas, but particularly the cheeseparing environment.

While the report's conclusions were largely ignored, it is worth examining the salient points in order to appreciate the difficulties under which the project operated. Firstly, the programme was so totally success-oriented yet so austerely funded that it would be difficult to switch over from development to full scale production. Secondly, three prototypes were inadequate for the development of such a complex design. Thirdly, the rephased development programme would cause both delays and extra costs, estimated as not less than $300 million. Fourthly, insufficient funding was available to ensure programme flexibility. Fifthly, the flight test programme envisaged would be "minimal", and heavily dependent upon the first prototype for at least the first year. And finally, several technical and design aspects were criticized, among them the overwing fairing and the electrical multiplex system.

The USAF agreed with almost all these points, but stated that they arose largely from budgetary constraints, so contractor management procedures were tightened up after the preliminary report, and it was agreed to try and fund a fourth prototype. The only reason that the project had not been terminated was the absolute belief that the B-1 would be vital to the security of the United States.

Development and design refinement remained a dynamic process throughout this period. One of the suggested changes was to eliminate the variable-sweep wing, thereby saving weight and complexity, and to fix the wing at an angle of 50°. This would have been self-defeating in terms of the mission requirements, and the B-1½, as it was mockingly called, was returned to the closet.

Above: A busy scene at Edwards, with all four B-1As under one roof. Seen clockwise from the left are No 2, with the aft radome open; No 4; No 1; and No 3, seen here with starboard wing spoilers extended.

One major change stemming from test results, which found the crew capsule to be unstable at speeds above 300kt (556km/hr), came in October 1974, when the decision was taken to revert to ejection seats for the four crew members. If the two instructors were carried, they would be forced to leave the aircraft through the belly hatch. The first three

B-1 cruise missile carrier proposal

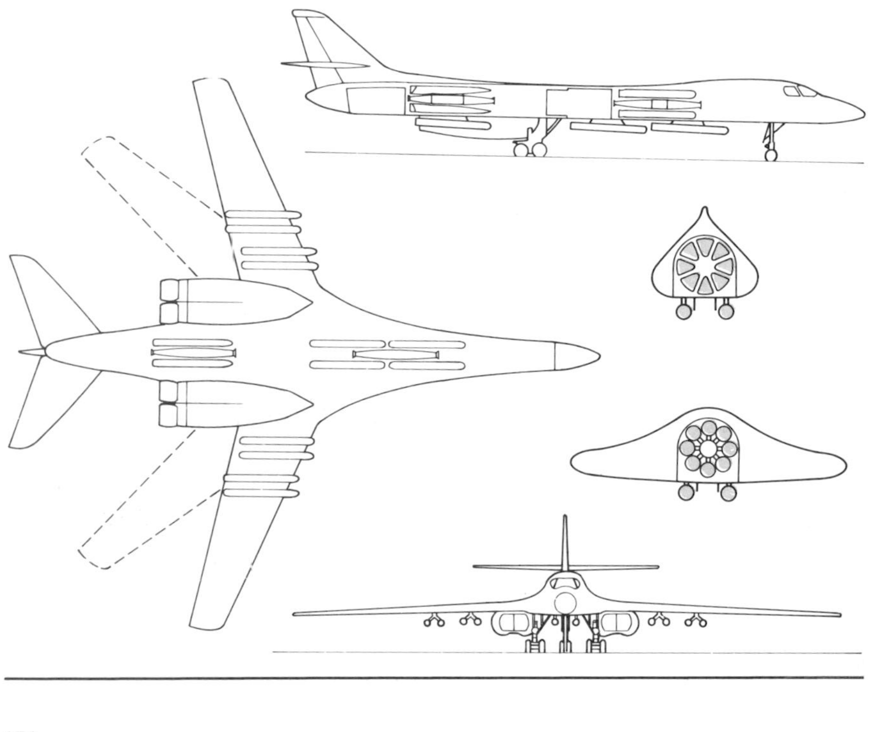

Left: In the wake of the programme's cancellation in 1977, Rockwell proposed this fixed-wing version of the B-1 optimized for internal and external carriage of 30 Tomahawk or ALCM cruise missiles.

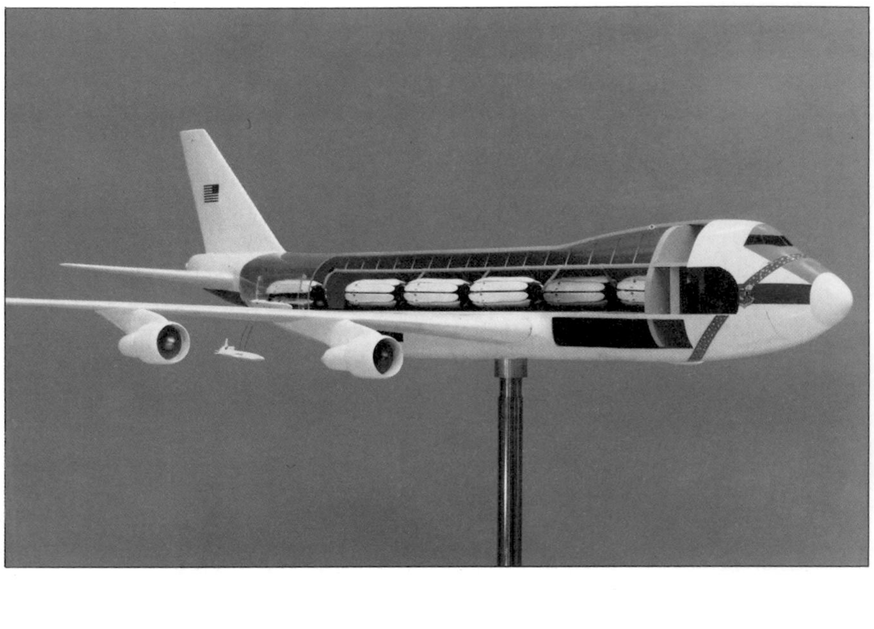

Below: Boeing proposed a 747-200F for the stand-off missile launcher role, with a payload of between 70 and 90 weapons. ALCMs were to be carried internally and launched through a side door at the rear.

B-1 core aircraft proposal

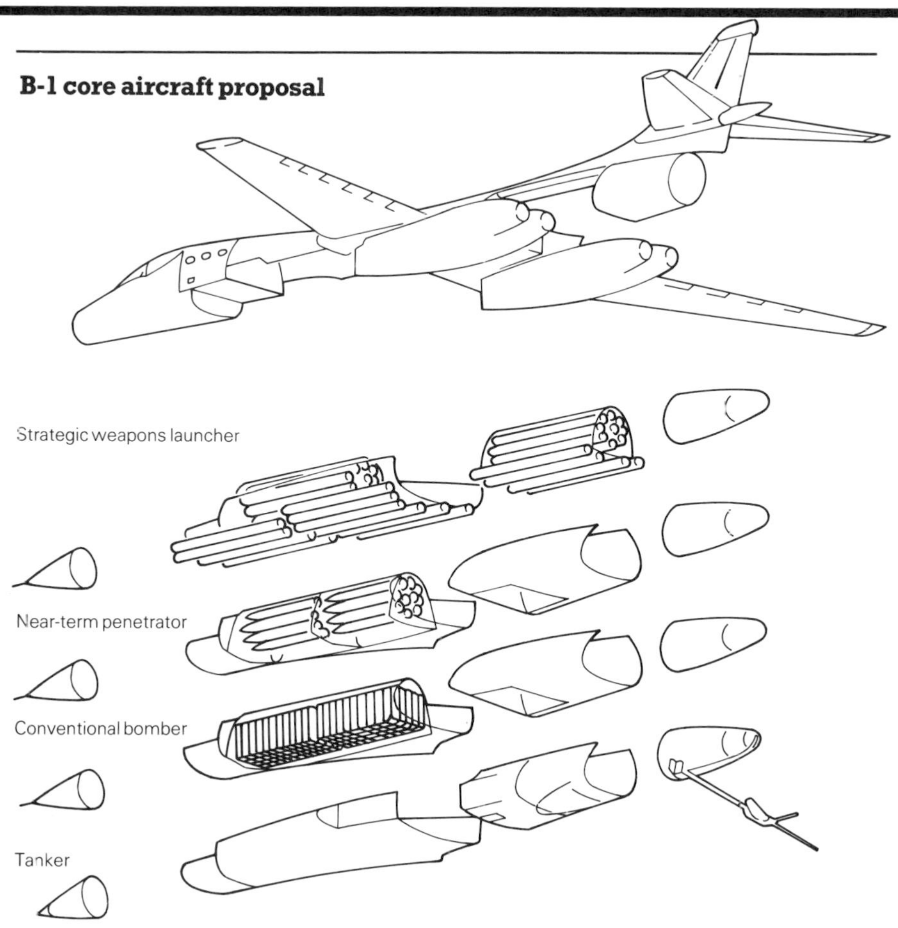

By 1979 Rockwell had produced this scheme for a family of aircraft based on the B-1 and adaptable to various roles. The wings were to be fixed at a 25° sweep angle and limiting the aircraft to subsonic speeds would enable the percentage of titanium to be reduced to 8 per cent: along with other changes, these would allow the cost per aircraft to be reduced by more than one third. The strategic weapons launcher would carry up to 30 cruise missiles; the near-term penetrator would accommodate two eight-round SRAM launchers and a fuel tank, bridging the gap between the B-52 and the next generation of bombers; the conventional bomber would replace the penetrator's SRAMs with bombs, mines or Harpoon missiles; and the tanker would have a fuel tank module forward with more fuel and a boom operator's compartment aft; in each case a nose radome and tail equipment bay appropriate to the mission would be carried.

prototypes were too far along the manufacturing process to be altered, but aircraft No. 4 and all subsequent models would have ejection seats. The maximum weight had also crept up to 395,000lb (179,172kg).

The first B-1 was rolled out at Palmdale, California, on October 26, 1974, at a ceremony presided over by Defense Secretary Dr. James R. Schlesinger. In his speech, he commented: "Deterrence, it is said, lies in the eye of the beholder. It works by acting on the psychology, on attitudes, and the perceptions of difficulties recognized by the potential attacker. In this respect, the bomber is unique: there is no satisfactory substitute for its contribution to that overall panoply of forces which achieve deterrence." He also sounded a warning note. "A prerequisite for any affirmative decision [on production] is that the B-1 continues to perform throughout the entire Research and Development sequence in a manner that is highly acceptable."

After extensive ground checks the first B-1, 74-0158, left the ground at Palmdale on December 23, 1974, and after a flight lasting 78 minutes, it landed at Edwards Air Force Base. There were no untoward incidents, and the aircraft, the flying qualities test vehicle, immediately began its allotted test programme.

At this point more than 20,000 hours of wind tunnel testing had gone into the project, the final effort being full scale tests to verify that the engines were compatible with the intakes. Predicted lift/drag ratios, stability and control over the entire gamut of flight conditions had all been checked out. Now the proving time had come, with the start of what would later be described as "probably the most successful flight test programme of all time." (This was an Air Force comment, not manufacturer's hype.)

As originally planned, the flight test programme was to start with clearance for low-level flight at speeds up to Mach 0.85, with a minimum of 18 flights to be made in the first six months. In spite of using telemetry for in-flight data transmission, the factor determining progress would be the rate at which the data from each flight could be analyzed and processed. In-flight refuelling was to be used to extend mission time where practicable, and this was particularly valuable for flutter testing at maximum weight, as the aircraft did not need to land to top up with fuel to bring the weight back up to the required level.

As it proceeded, the test programme deviated somewhat from that originally planned. There is obviously some risk in low flying, and with only one flight test aircraft available for some time, a more cautious course was adopted, with the flight envelope only gradually explored. Both in the air and on the ground, further milestones in the development programme were passed, and April 10, 1975, was notable for two: the first supersonic flight was made, a speed of Mach 1.05 being reached; and on the same mission in-flight refuelling was used for the first time. Meanwhile, the second development aircraft, No. 74-0159, was undergoing the full-scale static/strength and proof loading tests. These were conducted at Palmdale by the Lockheed Aircraft Corporation and were completed during July of that year.

Right: Flight testing continued after 1977, with the fourth prototype concentrating on evaluation of its ability to use its defensive systems to penetrate hostile airspace.

The next event was particularly momentous: Rockwell were awarded a contract for a fourth B-1. In line with previous decisions, this would have ejection seats, a redesigned forward fuselage with the crew capsule deleted, revised engine nacelles and a bay aft to accommodate defensive avionics.

Low-level flight testing began in earnest on September 19, 1975, when the first, and still the only flying B-1 reached Mach 0.75 at 500ft (152m), over the Pacific test range. The limits were gradually pushed faster and lower until, on November 11, speeds ranging from 165kt (306km/h) to a maximum of Mach 0.83 – roughly 550kt (1,020km/h) – were demonstrated over the main runway at Edwards at an altitude of 200ft (61m).

Second to fly

The burden of the entire flight test programme was carried by the first B-1 for a total of 15 months before it was joined by the third development aircraft. No 74-0160 was rolled out on January 16, 1976, and made its first flight on April 1, and the arrival of this aircraft, scheduled for offensive avionics, terrain-following, and weapons delivery trials, must have occasioned a huge sigh of relief among those closely concerned with the programme. It was quickly joined by the second B-1, No. 74-0159, which, its loading test function completed, had been put back into flying order. It was rolled out on May 11, and made its first flight on June 14.

With three B-1s flying, the test programme proceeded apace, and the Initial Operational Test and Evaluation (IOTE) flights, which were simulated Strategic Air Command missions, were successfully completed in September of that year. These were followed on December 1 by the completion of DSARC III, the production decision: including those already existing, a total of 244 B-1 bombers would be procured.

After all the trials, tribulations and general abuse, including the appellation B-1 Bummer that the project had suffered during its long and penurious life, it now seemed to be riding the crest of a wave. This feeling was reinforced in April 1977, when the entire B-1 team, both civil and military, was awarded the prestigious Collier Trophy, presented annually for "The greatest achievement in aeronautics or astronautics in America, in respect of improving the performance, efficiency, or safety, of air or space vehicles." At this point, the 100th test mission had just been flown. Taken by the third B-1 on March 29, it had covered over-water navigation and terrain-following tests and simulated SRAM missile release. The 34th flight by this aircraft, it brought total flight hours to 542.

But already the storm clouds were gathering, and in March a Pentagon study had proposed that the total number of B-1s be cut to 150. Arms reduction negotiations with the Soviet Union were in progress at the time, and President Carter had retained the option to delete the B-1 entirely if satisfactory progress was made towards disarmament. Then, in May, it was revealed that the unit cost of the aircraft would top $100 million. This caused a furore among the opponents of the B-1, to put it mildly, and even gave many moderates pause for thought. Once again, the project begun all those years and all those dollars ago was teetering on the brink of disaster.

The axe fell on June 30, when President Carter announced the he would not approve production of the B-1. His decision was made on the recommendation of Defense Secretary Harold Brown, who later defended the Pentagon's reasoning in the following terms: "My recommendation to the President . . . [was] based on the conclusion that aircraft carrying modern cruise missiles will better assure the effectiveness of the bomber component of US strategic forces in the 1980s . . . I concluded that on the basis of new design features resulting from progress in cruise missile technology, and in the light of proven test results, the assurance of successful operation of the cruise missile against future Soviet defences is now very high. I further concluded that . . . the cruise missile options offer more certainty of high effectiveness. Moreover, the cruise missile option is less expensive." The carrier for the new weapon was to be the already elderly B-52, and another acronym nearly joined the already long list in the B-1 story: MROOBA (Must Refurbish Our Old Bombers Again).

Immediately following the President's announcement, the Air Force imposed a 90-day stop order on B-1 production, pending the termination, which came on July 6, of all B-1 production contracts by the Defense Secretary. The only gleam of light remained in the fact that the existing aircraft were to be retained for a research and development programme, and that the fourth B-1, at the time about 45 per cent complete and slated to develop the full avionic system capability, was not affected by the stop order. The first production aircraft, Nos 5, 6 and 7, which had already been started, were halted.

Termination of the programme was a heavy blow to Rockwell International. Over 8,000 workers had to be laid off, and many others redeployed, though the nucleus of the team was kept together by seeking subcontract work wherever it could be obtained – from Boeing on 747 and 757 airliners, from Airbus Industrie, from British Aerospace and so on. The engineering team was subcontracted out to whoever needed it for periods varying between six months and three years while remaining on Rockwell's payroll; in this way it generated turn-

over, as it was hired out on a cost plus basis, while being kept together; without it, Rockwell could have been out of the big league for good. A spin-off benefit was that the engineers were kept current on technology.

Less than two weeks after cancellation of the B-1A, Rockwell began submitting proposals for R&D programmes to the Air Force, which in turn submitted a restructured programme for B-1 development to the Defense Secretary on October 7. The outcome was the Bomber Penetration Evaluation (BPE), which was to last until January 1981, and during which the B-1 gained five new acronyms: NTP (Near Term Penetrator), SWL (Strategic Weapons Launcher), CMCA (Cruise Missile Carrier Aircraft), MRB (Multi Role Bomber), and finally LRCA (Long Range Combat Aircraft). The NTP was intended as an interim bomber to bridge the gap between the B-52 and something better than the B-1; otherwise the descriptions are self-explanatory.

Relegated to research

Once again the B-1 took to the skies, although now relegated to the role of a research vehicle, in an exhaustive programme that was, although nobody realised it at the time, to involve more than 1,350 flying hours and last some three and a half years.

On October 5, 1978, the second prototype attained its highest ever speed of Mach 2.22 at an altitude of 50,000ft (15,240m). The programme was further augmented on February 14, 1979, when the fourth B-1, No. 76-0174, made its maiden flight from Palmdale to Edwards. This was the full capability aircraft, so avionic systems testing could now begin in earnest. This aircraft was slightly different in appearance from its predecessors in that it featured a dorsal spine housing some temporary test equipment for the avionic suites. Much of its flight time was taken up in comprehensive test sorties in a Red Flag environment, to evaluate how well it performed against both American and simulated Soviet

Above: The mission profile of the B-1 includes a subsonic cruise at high altitude to conserve fuel while in friendly or neutral airspace. This is its natural habitat on the outbound and homeward legs.

Below: The second B-1A, seen here on March 23, 1983, the day it initiated the B-1B flight test programme. The modifications carried out during the previous nine months resulted in few external changes.

B-1A second prototype

74-0159 resplendent in the livery of the B-1B test programme. Widely hailed as the first B-1B, it was really only a modified B-1A.

Above: The underside of 74-0159 showing the modified weapons bay doors. Some extra dielectric panels have appeared, but most of the other modifications carried out are not readily apparent.

Below: In-flight refuelling is not necessarily a straight and level process, but must occasionally be carried out in a turn, as this picture shows. Despite its size, the B-1 is easy to fly accurately.

defensive systems, a task in which it was aided by the third prototype.

The BPE dragged along on a hand-to-mouth basis, never quite knowing when it might be terminated. The first reprieve came in October 1979, when Congress appropriated funds to continue the evaluation of operational penetration techniques and the defensive avionics, and was followed on January 29, 1980, by an official extension of the BPE to June 30, 1981, although the flight test programme would be completed long before then. It was also planned to convert the third B-1 to carry Air-Launched Cruise Missiles (ALCMs) both in the internal weapons bays and on pylons externally, while the fourth aircraft continued to fly against various radars and missile defences until October 27, when the decision was taken to concentrate on Airborne Controlled Intercepts.

Meanwhile, behind the scenes the pot was once again coming to the boil. Yet another study group had been set up on August 22 to evaluate bomber alternatives, headed by Dr. Zeiberg of the Office of the Secretary of Defense and divided into five panels covering mission and requirements, the threat, aircraft system design, planning and programme, and systems evaluation. The consideration of low observables is conspicuous by its absence, since it was becoming clear that stealth technology was of primary importance in the penetration missions: indeed, the existence of such a programme was sprung on the unsuspecting nation just three days later by Defense Secretary Harold Brown, when he announced a research programme into the subject as the basis of an advanced technology project for the future.

In the early days of the B-1A its radar cross section had been quoted as anything between 1/35 and 1/25 that of the B-52. The BPE had shown just how important low observability was in aiding penetration; countermeasures were valuable, but were emissions that might prove counter-productive by giving away the position, or at least the presence, of the aircraft.

On December 2 General Mathis, Vice Chief of Staff of the Air Force, issued a letter formally designating the new strategic bomber proposal the LRCA; six days later it was decided to extend BPE flight testing through April 1981. By the beginning of 1980 new-generations of offensive and defensive avionics were being used in the tests, which still concentrated on airborne controlled interception. (Although never officially stated, it was obvious that the interceptor fighter was regarded as the main threat.)

BPE completion

The final flight test in the BPE, flown by the fourth B-1A on April 29, 1981, concluded all B-1 test flying; since the first flight in December 1974 a total of 1,895.2 flight hours had been accumulated, shared among the four prototypes as follows:

No 1: 79 missions, 405.3 hours
No 2: 60 missions, 282.5 hours
No 3: 138 missions, 829.4 hours
No 4: 70 missions, 378 hours

In addition more than 25,000 hours of wind tunnel testing had taken place, the engines had accumulated nearly 7,600 flight hours, and the structural article had been subjected to fatigue testing designed to simulate three aircraft lifetimes, while weapons tests had included the dropping of some 45 B-61 inert nuclear weapons and the air launching of two SRAMs.

On April 7 the Bomber Alternatives Study Interim Report had been submitted to Congress, and June 4 saw the completion of the Manned Bomber Penetrativity Evaluation Flight Test Results and Report by the Air Force Test and Evaluation Center at Edwards AFB. The contenders were: the refurbished B-52, equipped with updated electronics; an extensively modified FB-111 – the FB-111H – a cheap but definitely interim solution with longer range than the standard version but no ALCM carrying capability; a jumbo jet type modified to carry a heavy load of ALCMs; and the B-1 modified for greater range, a heavier and much more diverse payload, and lower observability, traded

Above: The first production B-1B taxies out at Edwards AFB in October 1984. The small transparency added to the avionics operator's station is just visible, while the shadow of the wing betrays the slat detail.

Below: August 1984, and 74-0159 demonstrates its short takeoff roll at Edwards. Compare the tailcone and fin fairing with those of the aircraft pictured above: the B-1A's are pointed whereas on the B-1B they are blunt.

Bottom: 74-0159 leaves the Edwards runway, with the new dark paint scheme giving it a menacing aspect. It is noteworthy that even the engine intakes are dark rather than the more usual white.

against the Mach 2 capability, which was by this time looking a handicap rather than an asset.

The B-52 was not immortal, but at this time it was judged still capable of carrying out the penetration mission at least until the late 1980s. The Advanced Technology Bomber (ATB), still a dream of the future, could not be certain within the required timescale, and should the B-52 be selected for further service life extension there would still be a gap in penetration ability from about 1987 to 1995. The modified FB-111 was attractive from a cost standpoint, but while its penetration capability was undoubted, its inability to carry a heavy enough payload told against it; a buy of about 150 was contemplated, but they would have been inadequate for the task. The large cruise missile carrier was always an outsider in the contest: it would have been limited in every respect apart from weapon load, since it lacked dispersal capability and mission flexibility.

Against these options, the B-1B, beefed up to carry an extra 82,000lb (37,195kg) of payload, with a longer range and lower radar signature than the B-1A, plus a flight proven airframe and engines, looked a very good bet indeed. The report had concluded that the next strategic bomber should be capable of fulfilling requirements additional to the nuclear strike role – basically the iron bomb mission, maritime patrol, and minelaying – and that the B-1 derivative was the best option within the projected need for an Initial Operational Capability (IOC) by 1986.

It was becoming obvious that the United States needed a new long range multirole aircraft and that the B-1B was the only real contender, a fact confirmed on October 2, 1981, when President Reagan announced the decision to build 100 B-1Bs to have an IOC some time in 1986. This would coincide with the predicted inability of the B-52 to carry out the low-level penetration mission, leaving the surviving B-52s to carry out the less demanding role of stand-off cruise missile carriers. In the meantime, the ATB, or stealth bomber, could be developed in a less urgent atmosphere.

President Reagan's announcement was followed in November by a joint letter to Congress from Defense Secret-

Above: Flaps and slats extended and a touch of right rudder as 74-0159 lines up on the runway. This shot was taken just 12 days before the aircraft's fatal accident, which occurred during a test flight on August 29, 1984.

Below: Farnborough 82, and 76-0174 joins the static display after flying non-stop from California. The dorsal spine, blunt tailcone and camouflage scheme are the distinguishing features of this aircraft.

ary Caspar Weinberger and the Director of the CIA, confirming that the B-1B would be able to penetrate the projected Soviet defences until well into the 1990s, and in December the Senate approved full funding. The total cost of the B-1B procurment programme had been fixed at $20.5 billion calculated at Fiscal Year 1981 rates.

Contracts awarded

1982 might well be described as the year of the contract. Full scale development and Lot 1 production was awarded to Rockwell on January 20; the first batch of engines was ordered from General Electric on April 1; the AIL Division of Eaton Corporation (formerly Cutler Hammer) received the order for Lot 1 of the defensive avionics on June 8; and just three days later the offensive avionic suite Lot 1 was awarded to the Boeing Military Airplane Company. Also in June the initial review for the B-1B was completed.

At this point, of course, the B-1B did not exist, though tremendous effort had gone into making the B-1A – the only available hardware – a multirole aircraft. The vast increase in payload had to be achieved at little or no cost in structural weight, despite the obvious necessity to beef up the undercarriage to carry the increased gross weight at takeoff, and was to be achieved by a weight trimming programme. Some weight could be saved by trading off the Mach 2 capability, and more by revising the wing seals, while improved aerodynamic efficiency would also help. At the same time, to increase penetration capability, and with it mission survivability, the avionics suites were to be upgraded using off-the-shelf products as far as possible.

One suggestion which was not adopted was to limit the wing sweep angle to a maximum angle of 60°. As the wings transitioned, they caused changes in the aircraft centre of gravity, which was compensated for automatically by the transfer of fuel between various internal tanks. A simplified system could have saved weight, but would have reduced the excellent low-level ride qualities as it increased aspect ratio.

A new 1,100-hour flight test programme was planned: the first and third aircraft, which had the highest time, were to be stored and subsequently cannibalized for spares, and the new programme was built around the two low-time B-1As, the second and fourth prototypes. Production B-1Bs were also scheduled to join the programme as various later stages were reached. Meanwhile, the flying ceased as the Air Force and Rockwell sorted out exactly what they were going to do. The fourth B-1A made a brief excursion across the Atlantic in September 1982 to the Farnborough Air Show, during which it clocked up a further 28 flying hours; it was then grounded for avionics modifications, and was not to fly again before the summer of 1984.

During the summer of 1982 work started on the second prototype to modify it for the B-1B programme. Changes included new weapons bay doors and modifications to some bulkheads and the flight control systems. It was originally anticipated that this work would take about 21 months, but in the event the aircraft was flying again on

March 23, 1983, just nine months later. Its test functions were to cover stability and control, flutter, and weapons release, and although it was widely hailed by the Press as the first B-1B, it was actually just a modified B-1A. Once again the flight test programme depended on a single aircraft for a protracted period, but at least this time it was a flight-proven aircraft.

The fourth B-1A rejoined the test programme with a flight on July 30, 1984. Equipped with new avionic systems, both defensive and offensive, it was scheduled to fly some 380 hours in the next phase, and some idea of the rate of progress is given by the fact that during the next nine months it flew 24 missions, totalling 120 hours. The accent was on testing the defensive avionic systems first before switching to full system clearance. Meanwhile, the second prototype has been making good progress, and was only four flights away from concluding its allotted programme when, on August 29, 1984, it crashed, killing the chief test pilot of Rockwell International, Doug Benefield, and seriously injuring the other crew members.

This fateful flight was, until the unfortunate accident, quite routine. The original flight plan called for takeoff at 06.30 hours and a duration of 4 hours 20 minutes; takeoff was to be at a 9° pitch attitude, followed by airspeed calibration tests in the Edwards tower flyby pattern, then static and dynamic minimum speed control tests in the Cords Road area. After refuelling in flight, the aircraft would head for the Edwards Precision Impact Range Area (PIRA), where it was to make to weapons release passes, the first simulated, and the second releasing five Mk 82 high-drag bombs whose warheads were filled with concrete.

The mission would end with touch-and-go landings back at Edwards with Doug Benefield acting as instructor pilot to the command pilot, Major Richard V. Reynolds; 69 days had elapsed since Major Reynolds had made a landing in the B-1, whereas to remain current on type a landing is required every 60 days (in all other aspects of flying the B-1 Major Reynolds was current). The final point was a landing touchdown load test followed by a full stopping test on maximum braking effectiveness.

The engines were started at 05.43, and the big bomber began to taxi out at 06.18. During the taxiing phase ground load survey turning tests were carried out on the ramp, after which the aircraft proceeded to Runway 22, where a final preflight check revealed that scuffing during the turning tests had caused excessive wear to both nose gear tyres, and tyres 3 and 8 on the main gear. The aircraft then returned to the ramp for remedial work, completed by approximately 08.30.

Edwards AFB is one of the busiest in the world, and the delay, caused by a trifling matter, meant that the order of the mission had to be rescheduled so as to avoid disruption of other activities planned for that day. The revised test sequence was now: takeoff; weapons release; airspeed calibration; minimum speed control; and landing. The first two phases were uneventful, though the airspeed calibration tests were curtailed after two passes due to thermal turbulence threatening to make the data obtained invalid.

At 10.12, some 43 minutes after takeoff, the B-1, accompanied by its F-111 chase aircraft, climbed to 6,000ft (1,830m) in the Cords Road area, and was configured for the static minimum control speed points, with wing sweep at 55°, flaps, slats and gear retracted, and the centre of gravity at 45 per cent of Mean Aerodynamic Chord (MAC). This test was successfully carried out at a speed of about 250kt (463km/h). Normally the centre of gravity changes would be carried out auto-

Below: The first production B-1B, 82-0001, inaugurates a new chapter in the long and tortuous story of Strategic Air Command's new bomber. Having just taken off from Palmdale on its maiden flight, it passes overhead en route to Edwards AFB.

Below: The first production B-1B in Rockwell's vast checkout facility at Palmdale, which can accommodate four aircraft at a time. Behind the aircraft is one of the control rooms for the test engineers; around three-quarters of the tests have been automated.

matically, but the nature of this test series called for manual operation.

The next test was dynamic minimum control speed, with the wings fully extended at 15°, flaps, slats, and landing gear all down, the centre of gravity at the aft limit for that configuration of 21 per cent MAC, and a speed of 138kt (256km/h). The B-1A accelerated to 300kt (556km/h), whereupon sweeping the wings commenced, a process that took 46 seconds. The flaps, slats and landing gear were all extended, but the centre of gravity was left unchanged, far outside the limit for that particular configuration, and as the airspeed decayed through 145kt (269km/h), with the angle of incidence rising to 8.5°, the aircraft suffered an uncontrollable pitch-up to an angle of 70°. Despite the application of full forward stick and left rudder, the aircraft was in an irrecoverable position, and Major Reynolds intitiated the ejection procedure.

Even now all should have been well for the crew. This aircraft was one of the original three with the crew escape module which had been designed to separate at low altitudes and adverse attitudes, correct its attitude and regain sufficient height for the parachutes to deploy, then make a soft landing on the impact bladders. However, one of the explosive repositioning bolts failed to function, and the module made a hard nose-down landing, with tragic results.

The main finding of the accident investigation board was as follows. "There was deviation from flight manual procedures in that the wings were brought forward without either resetting the CG control panel from 45 to 21 per cent (21 per cent was the minimum for that particular configuration) MAC or checking that the CG was within limits before sweeping the wings. This resulted in the aircraft exceeding the aft CG limits as defined in the flight manual."

Meanwhile, back at Palmdale, an exciting event was about to take place: the rollout of the first production aircraft, a genuine B-1B, on September 4, 1984. On October 18 it made its maiden flight to Edwards, to join the test programme as a full capability aircraft. Much more development lay ahead – even when this book appears it will not be complete – but 23 years after the initiation of the first exploratory studies by the USAF, a production bomber had appeared, to enter service within a year, and to achieve IOC within two years,

This was indeed a milestone. An earlier loss of the second prototype might have proved much more serious, but as it was, although tragic, it did nothing to further hurt or delay the programme. The first B-1B, No. 82-0001, was to join the fourth prototype, and the work slated for the lost prototype was taken over by the ninth production aircraft.

Below: 82-0001 at the moment of lift off from Palmdale, on its way to join the fourth B-1A in the flight test programme at Edwards. Camouflage details are more clearly shown in this picture than most – note the tiny star and bar marking.

Below: July 27, 1985, and Air Force Secretary Verne Orr formally hands over the first operational B-1B to General Bennie L. Davis, Commander in Chief of Strategic Air Command, at Offutt AFB, Nebraska, the command's HQ. This is the second production aircraft, serial number 83-0065.

Structure

Conflicting requirements for rapid start-up and getaway, the use of short runways and austere airfields, Mach 2 at high altitudes and extended penetration at high subsonic speeds at low levels, and very heavy payloads and intercontinental range, made the use of a variable-sweep wing for the B-1 almost inevitable. At the same time, the decision to carry the payload and fuel internally, although later amended, placed a premium on available volume, leading to wing/body blending and in turn reducing radar signature. The reduction in radar signature, in fact, was so marked that much further effort was concentrated on this aspect, especially for the B-1B, even to the extent of dropping the Mach 2 requirement.

The B-1's main fuselage is a traditional monocoque, with frames, skins and longerons forming a cohesive whole, although to make maintenance easier as many as possible of the load carrying paths are internal, thus reducing the number of external structural panels. The internal structure is very concentrated, with frames spaced at roughly 10in (250mm) intervals for the entire length of the fuselage.

The fuselage is manufactured in sections, and these are assembled first, before the wings, undercarriage, engine nacelles and empennage are attached. The forward fuselage section contains the radome, the radar avionics bay, the nose gear bay which is beneath the crew compartment, the environmental equipment bay, a section of the forward fuel tank, and most of the avionics bays, which fill almost the entire cross-section of the fuselage just astern of the crew compartment. Next comes the forward intermediate section, which contains the front and intermediate weapons bays, with integral fuel tanks to each side.

The wing/body blending begins here. As previously related, this was adopted for many reasons, among which were the need to increase strength and volume. It reduced structural weight by more than 5 per cent and slightly reduced transonic drag without increasing subsonic and supersonic drag. Yet another advantage lay in the amount of body lift generated – about 50 per cent in the high-speed low-altitude regime – while the additional fuel housed would otherwise have occupied some weapons bay volume. More avionics are also sited in this area. Behind the front intermediate fuselage section comes the massive titanium wing carry-through (WCT) box, which also serves as an integral fuel tank.

Astern of the WCT box, the aft intermediate fuselage section houses the main gear well, with a fuel tank above it, and a flight controls mixer compartment. Further avionics are accommodated in a 14in (35m) wide compartment between

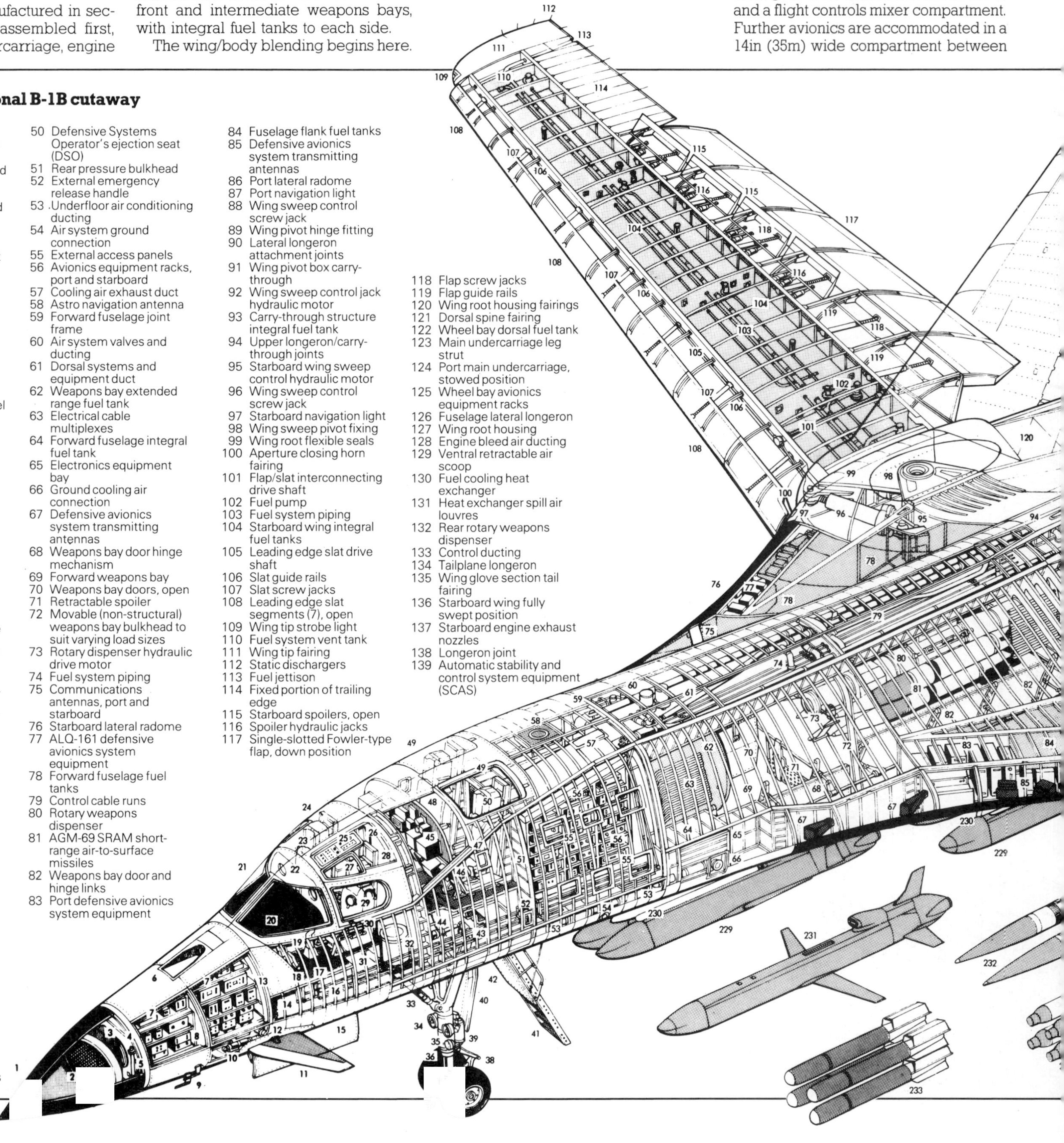

Rockwell International B-1B cutaway

1 Radome
2 Multi-mode phased array radar scanner
3 Low-observable shrouded scanner tracking mechanism
4 Radar mounting bulkhead
5 Radome hinge joint
6 In-flight refuelling receptacle, open
7 Nose avionics equipment bays
8 APQ-164 offensive radar system
9 Dual pitot heads
10 Foreplane hydraulic actuator
11 Structural mode control system (SMCS) ride control foreplane
12 Foreplane pivot fixing
13 Front pressure bulkhead
14 Nose undercarriage wheel bay
15 Nosewheel doors
16 Control cable runs
17 Cockpit floor level
18 Rudder pedals
19 Control column, quadruplex automatic flight control system
20 Instrument panel shroud
21 Windscreen panels
22 Detachable nuclear flash screens, all window positions
23 Co-pilot's ejection seat
24 Co-pilot's emergency escape hatch
25 Overhead switch panel
26 Pilot's emergency escape hatch
27 Cockpit eyebrow window
28 Ejection seat launch/mounting rails
29 Pilot's Weber ACES 'zero-zero' ejection seat
30 Wing sweep control lever
31 Cockpit section framing
32 Toilet
33 Nose undercarriage drag brace
34 Twin landing lamps
35 Taxiing lamp
36 Shock absorber strut
37 Twin nosewheels, forward retracting
38 Torque scissor links
39 Hydraulic steering control unit
40 Nosewheel leg door
41 Retractable boarding ladder
42 Ventral crew entry hatch, open
43 Nose undercarriage pivot fixing
44 Hydraulic retraction jack
45 Systems Operators' instrument console
46 Radar hand controller
47 Crew cabin side window panel
48 Offensive Systems Operators' ejection seat (OSO)
49 Cabin roof escape hatches
50 Defensive Systems Operator's ejection seat (DSO)
51 Rear pressure bulkhead
52 External emergency release handle
53 Underfloor air conditioning ducting
54 Air system ground connection
55 External access panels
56 Avionics equipment racks, port and starboard
57 Cooling air exhaust duct
58 Astro navigation antenna
59 Forward fuselage joint frame
60 Air system valves and ducting
61 Dorsal systems and equipment duct
62 Weapons bay extended range fuel tank
63 Electrical cable multiplexes
64 Forward fuselage integral fuel tank
65 Electronics equipment bay
66 Ground cooling air connection
67 Defensive avionics system transmitting antennas
68 Weapons bay door hinge mechanism
69 Forward weapons bay
70 Weapons bay doors, open
71 Retractable spoiler
72 Movable (non-structural) weapons bay bulkhead to suit varying load sizes
73 Rotary dispenser hydraulic drive motor
74 Fuel system piping
75 Communications antennas, port and starboard
76 Starboard lateral radome
77 ALQ-161 defensive avionics system equipment
78 Forward fuselage fuel tanks
79 Control cable runs
80 Rotary weapons dispenser
81 AGM-69 SRAM short-range air-to-surface missiles
82 Weapons bay door and hinge links
83 Port defensive avionics system equipment
84 Fuselage flank fuel tanks
85 Defensive avionics system transmitting antennas
86 Port lateral radome
87 Port navigation light
88 Wing sweep control screw jack
89 Wing pivot hinge fitting
90 Lateral longeron attachment joints
91 Wing pivot box carry-through
92 Wing sweep control jack hydraulic motor
93 Carry-through structure integral fuel tank
94 Upper longeron/carry-through joints
95 Starboard wing sweep control hydraulic motor
96 Wing sweep control screw jack
97 Starboard navigation light
98 Wing sweep pivot fixing
99 Wing root flexible seals
100 Aperture closing horn fairing
101 Flap/slat interconnecting drive shaft
102 Fuel pump
103 Fuel system piping
104 Starboard wing integral fuel tanks
105 Leading edge slat drive shaft
106 Slat guide rails
107 Slat screw jacks
108 Leading edge slat segments (7), open
109 Wing tip strobe light
110 Fuel system vent tank
111 Wing tip fairing
112 Static dischargers
113 Fuel jettison
114 Fixed portion of trailing edge
115 Starboard spoilers, open
116 Spoiler hydraulic jacks
117 Single-slotted Fowler-type flap, down position
118 Flap screw jacks
119 Flap guide rails
120 Wing root housing fairings
121 Dorsal spine fairing
122 Wheel bay dorsal fuel tank
123 Main undercarriage leg strut
124 Port main undercarriage, stowed position
125 Wheel bay avionics equipment racks
126 Fuselage lateral longeron
127 Wing root housing
128 Engine bleed air ducting
129 Ventral retractable air scoop
130 Fuel cooling heat exchanger
131 Heat exchanger spill air louvres
132 Rear rotary weapons dispenser
133 Control ducting
134 Tailplane longeron
135 Wing glove section tail fairing
136 Starboard wing fully swept position
137 Starboard engine exhaust nozzles
138 Longeron joint
139 Automatic stability and control system equipment (SCAS)

Left: The first B-1A seen from below in company with an F-111 chase aircraft, providing a clear comparison of SAC's two swing-wing bombers.

Right: This view gives an indication of the extra volume gained by the wing/body blending and the absence of radar trapping angles.

the wheel wells and in the structural compartments outboard of the gear. Behind the gear well is the aft weapons bay, again with integral fuel tanks, and from about halfway down the weapons bay double frames extend outboard to carry the engine nacelles. They reach as far as the nacelle centre beams. Finally, the aft fuselage section contains another fuel tank, another avionics bay and the dielectric tailcone.

Design of the aft fuselage section posed problems. Frames extending into the dorsal area give support and torsional stiffening to the tail assembly. The design of the horizontal tailplane was tailored around the stiffness originally specified, but it was later discovered that for the high-Q environment at low altitudes greater static strength would be needed. The obvious solution was to incorporate a dorsal spine made from steel alloy, which would be heavy but relatively cheap, but instead a five-section boron epoxy spine running from

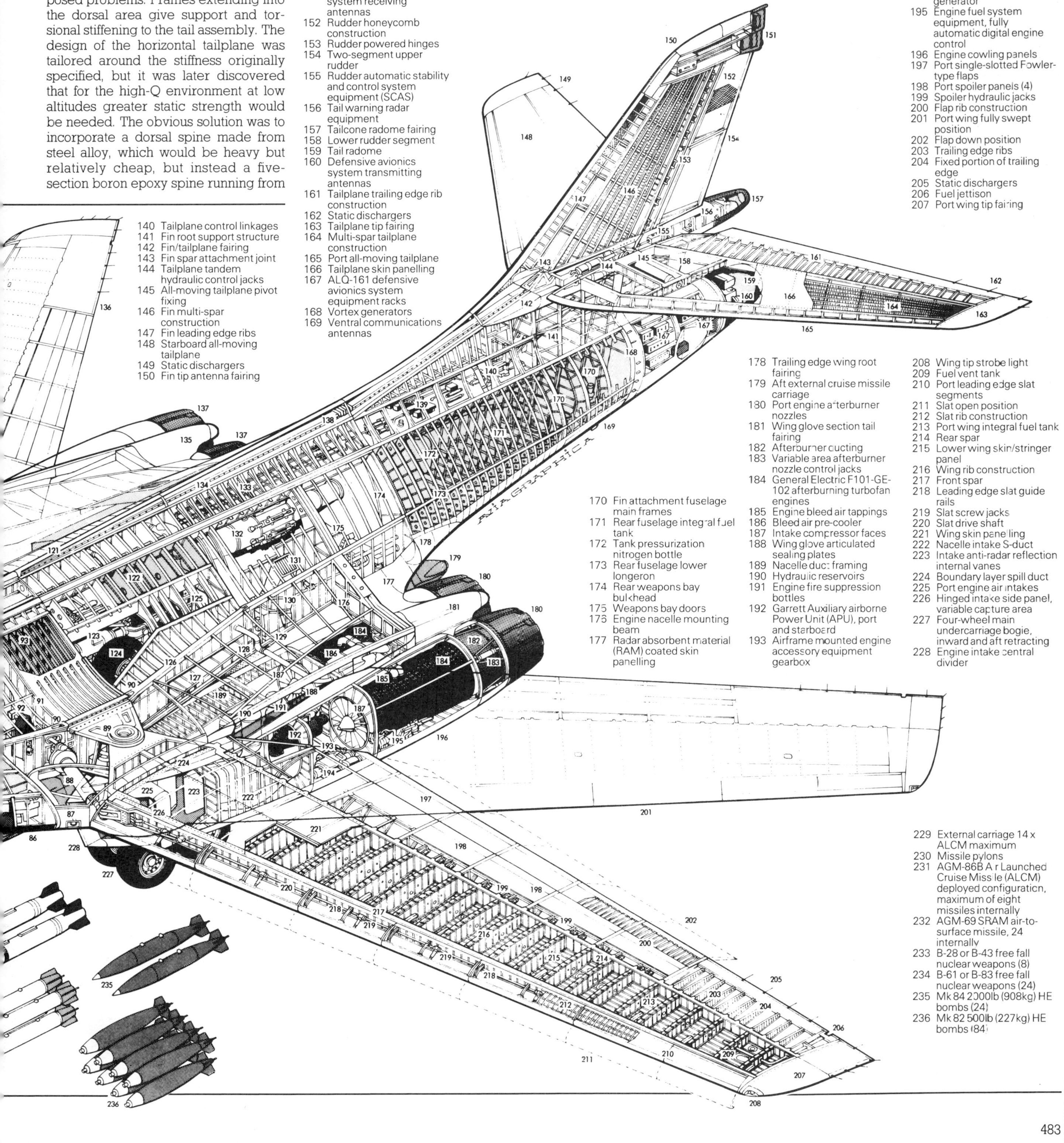

140 Tailplane control linkages
141 Fin root support structure
142 Fin/tailplane fairing
143 Fin spar attachment joint
144 Tailplane tandem hydraulic control jacks
145 All-moving tailplane pivot fixing
146 Fin multi-spar construction
147 Fin leading edge ribs
148 Starboard all-moving tailplane
149 Static dischargers
150 Fin tip antenna fairing
151 Defensive avionics system receiving antennas
152 Rudder honeycomb construction
153 Rudder powered hinges
154 Two-segment upper rudder
155 Rudder automatic stability and control system equipment (SCAS)
156 Tail warning radar equipment
157 Tailcone radome fairing
158 Lower rudder segment
159 Tail radome
160 Defensive avionics system transmitting antennas
161 Tailplane trailing edge rib construction
162 Static dischargers
163 Tailplane tip fairing
164 Multi-spar tailplane construction
165 Port all-moving tailplane
166 Tailplane skin panelling
167 ALQ-161 defensive avionics system equipment racks
168 Vortex generators
169 Ventral communications antennas
170 Fin attachment fuselage main frames
171 Rear fuselage integral fuel tank
172 Tank pressurization nitrogen bottle
173 Rear fuselage lower longeron
174 Rear weapons bay bulkhead
175 Weapons bay doors
176 Engine nacelle mounting beam
177 Radar absorbent material (RAM) coated skin panelling
178 Trailing edge wing root fairing
179 Aft external cruise missile carriage
180 Port engine afterburner nozzles
181 Wing glove section tail fairing
182 Afterburner ducting
183 Variable area afterburner nozzle control jacks
184 General Electric F101-GE-102 afterburning turbofan engines
185 Engine bleed air tappings
186 Bleed air pre-cooler
187 Intake compressor faces
188 Wing glove articulated sealing plates
189 Nacelle duct framing
190 Hydraulic reservoirs
191 Engine fire suppression bottles
192 Garrett Auxiliary airborne Power Unit (APU), port and starboard
193 Airframe mounted engine accessory equipment gearbox
194 Electrical system generator
195 Engine fuel system equipment, fully automatic digital engine control
196 Engine cowling panels
197 Port single-slotted Fowler-type flaps
198 Port spoiler panels (4)
199 Spoiler hydraulic jacks
200 Flap rib construction
201 Port wing fully swept position
202 Flap down position
203 Trailing edge ribs
204 Fixed portion of trailing edge
205 Static dischargers
206 Fuel jettison
207 Port wing tip fairing
208 Wing tip strobe light
209 Fuel vent tank
210 Port leading edge slat segments
211 Slat open position
212 Slat rib construction
213 Port wing integral fuel tank
214 Rear spar
215 Lower wing skin/stringer panel
216 Wing rib construction
217 Front spar
218 Leading edge slat guide rails
219 Slat screw jacks
220 Slat drive shaft
221 Wing skin panelling
222 Nacelle intake S-duct
223 Intake anti-radar reflection internal vanes
224 Boundary layer spill duct
225 Port engine air intakes
226 Hinged intake side panel, variable capture area
227 Four-wheel main undercarriage bogie, inward and aft retracting
228 Engine intake central divider
229 External carriage 14 x ALCM maximum
230 Missile pylons
231 AGM-86B Air Launched Cruise Missile (ALCM) deployed configuration, maximum of eight missiles internally
232 AGM-69 SRAM air-to-surface missile, 24 internally
233 B-28 or B-43 free fall nuclear weapons (8)
234 B-61 or B-83 free fall nuclear weapons (24)
235 Mk 84 2000lb (908kg) HE bombs (24)
236 Mk 82 500lb (227kg) HE bombs (84)

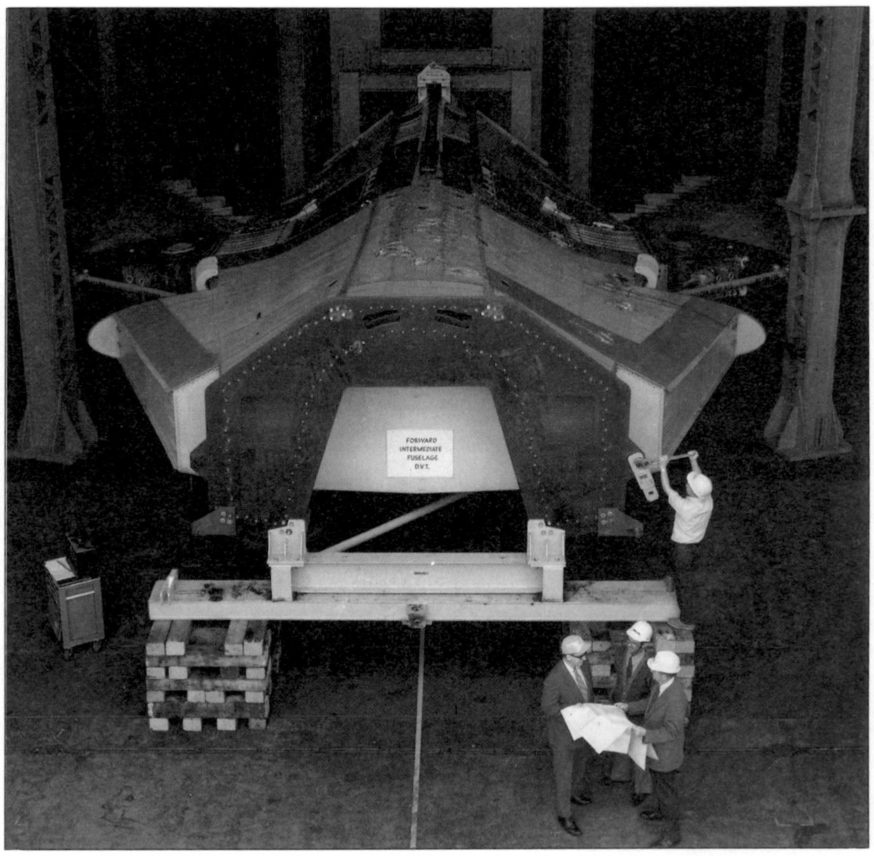

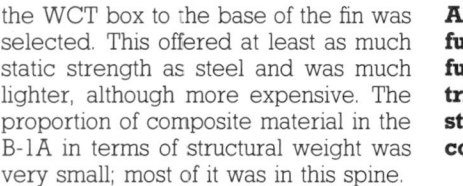

the WCT box to the base of the fin was selected. This offered at least as much static strength as steel and was much lighter, although more expensive. The proportion of composite material in the B-1A in terms of structural weight was very small; most of it was in this spine.

Fuselage changes between the B-1A and the B-1B were fairly major, although mainly beneath the surface. The fuel load carried by the B-1A at takeoff was restricted by the takeoff gross weight (TOGW) limit of 395,000lb (179,172kg), which meant it was dependent on IFR to carry out its mission, taking off with half-empty tanks and rendezvousing with a tanker before proceeding.

The TOGW of the B-1B was increased by a colossal 82,000lb (37,195kg) to 477,000lb (216,367kg) – which, as Rockwell's Scott L. White stressed at the 1985 Paris Air Show, was all additional fuel and weapons carriage capability: "The gross weight increase involved basically no empty weight increase to the aircraft. We didn't have 50,000lb (22,680kg) of structural weight to carry 32,000lb (14,515kg) extra weight of weapons and fuel. We were able to go through and reduce weight in several areas, and beef it up in others to carry this higher gross weight. We added a few thou here in wing skin thickness, and a few thou there in longerons, and did other things, like reworking the rear wing spar."

One main cause of the increase in TOGW was the carriage of external weapons; the other was the requirement that the aircraft be able to take off with a full fuel load. A stronger undercarriage and more powerful engines were the main factor in making this possible, and while Rockwell International's efforts to hold the empty weight constant represented an engineering *tour de force*, it is equally a testimony to the soundness of the original design.

Another major change between the B-1A and the B-1B resulted from alterations to the proposed weaponry. The basic B-1 has three weapons bays, each 15ft (4.57m) long, designed to accommodate the SRAM, and although the ALCM was originally intended to be similar in size later development work increased its length by nearly a third, so that it would no longer fit the B-1's weapons bay. The remedy was to make the front and intermediate weapons bays flexible by making the intervening bulkhead removable, providing a bay long enough to take the new ALCM, allowing growth space for new weapons and giving the option of carrying a small fuel tank at the front of the enlarged bay along with the ALCMs. This meant that structural loads in this area had to be carried through without the integral stiffening provided by the bulkhead.

Above: The fin is fitted to the rear fuselage section of the first B-1B. The fuselage section at the join is nearly triangular, and has already been stuffed with the control and electrical connections.

The B-1A's weapons bay doors were metal, but the B-1B's are made of composites, which has both reduced radar reflectivity and improved acoustic characteristics, and on the B-1B an aerodynamic spoiler has been fitted to prevent the slipstream from entering the bays when the doors are open.

At the heart of the structure is the WCT box, a massive titanium structure likened by Rockwell to "the Brooklyn Bridge built like a Swiss watch". Its basic function is to carry the variable-geometry wings, but it also has to carry and support the main gear, in which function it must be able to cope with some 90 per cent of the maximum TOGW, and it also houses about 20,000lb (9,072kg) of fuel. Its overall length is something over 26ft (7.92m), it is 5ft (1.52m) from front to rear, and it is built in three large sections, mainly of diffusion bonded titanium.

Diffusion bonding

Diffusion bonding is a process developed by North American Rockwell for the XB-70 Valkyrie; in Scott L. White's words: "We get a large titanium plate, plus maybe about 40 smaller, individually machined pieces, and put them in a two-way box. The two-way box is a tool, and it accurately positions all those pieces. The tool is then evacuated, and subjected to high temperatures and pressures for between ten and twelve hours, it forms into one piece of material which needs little or no machining. It is just as though it has been cut from a single piece of metal. Then we weld two

Right: "The Brooklyn Bridge built like a Swiss watch", is how Rockwell describe the WCT box. Constructed mainly of diffusion bonded titanium, it supports the main undercarriage as well as the variable-sweep wings.

or three sections together to get a major section; the crossplates in the structure perform like an eggcrate."

The upper and lower cover then have to be fitted; the lower cover is duplicated, and the entire structure is designed to have a redundancy factor high enough that if one plate cracks the other can carry the entire load. Both upper and lower covers are bolted, using tapered bolts. These naturally need tapered holes. The taper is fairly marginal towards a point, and contributes considerably to structural strength. Tolerances on the whole unit are very tight – hence the Swiss watch analogy. As it is also a fuel tank, the WCT box is then sealed before undergoing a special heat process.

The pin on which the wing pivots is about 17in (430mm) in diameter and of the order of 600lb (272kg) in weight. Made of titanium, it is hollow, and is carried on a two-race spherical bearing.

The wing, a conventional two-spar aluminium box structure, with machined spars and ribs, also serves as a fuel tank and has machined aluminium single piece covers to both top and bottom. Segmented slats along the entire leading edge open only for takeoff, while a six-section single-slotted flap extends along most of the trailing edge, the two inner sections of which are locked closed when the wing sweep exceeds 20°. Roll control is by means of differentially moving tailplanes, assisted by spoilers on the upper wing surfaces, the outer sections of which also lock automatically at speeds exceeding Mach 1. The trail-

Above left: The front intermediate fuselage section is seen here mated to the WCT box and aft intermediate section, with wings already pinned in place. The cross section has changed appreciably at this point.

Above: The front fuselage section of the first B-1B is built in two halves, then stuffed with all the wiring and plumbing before the two halves are mated and the nose section, with its avionics bays, added in front.

Below: With only the aft fuselage section remaining to be mated, the varying concave sections to the area behind the cockpit are shown clearly by the differentially curving shapes of the open panels.

Left: Fully assembled, the first B-1B is seen undergoing a thorough systems checkout at Palmdale prior to rollout. The black areas on and around the SMCS vanes are probably radar absorbent material (RAM).

Above centre: The massive forged steel box support and spindle acts as a rear frame for the fuselage stub while joining both the fin and the stabilizers to the fuselage.

Above: The bottom section of the three-piece rudder, located below the horizontal tail, provides the SMCS control in the lateral plane, damping out unwanted yaw effects.

ing edge of the wing is notched where it joins the fuselage to preserve as much volume in the fuselage as possible when the wings are fully swept.

Wing fairing seals are always a problem on variable-geometry aircraft; even after wind-tunnel tests it is difficult to predict exactly how the full-scale article will behave, particularly in terms of drag. On the B-1A a hinged panel mounted behind the wing pivot line was fitted over the movable section of the wing as a fairing, backed by two fixed fairings blending the fuselage to the wing. The seal itself was a bulky and expensive system of mechanical fingers designed to contour-articulate over the wing as it swept back, but this was draggy, heavy, complicated and costly, and when the B-1B was mooted, Rockwell examined all other alternatives. To the surprise of those who considered that the American aerospace industry led the world in every field, the best system was found to be that adopted for Europe's Panavia Tornado of sliding 'feathers' supported by an inflatable bag, and this was duly incorporated into the design of the B-1B. The inflatable bags, made by the Chesterfield, England, firm of Woodville Polymers, are 20ft (6.10m) long, and each has 21 pressure relief valves, also British-produced by Normalair-Garrett of Yeovil.

It was originally planned to have an empennage of composite construction, but that on the B-1A was primarily of aluminium. The fin consisted of a single box component, attached to the aft fuselage with a double shear attachment and bolted to the horizontal stabilizer spindle. The rudder was in three sections, two above the line of the horizontal stabilizer and one below, the last being linked to the low-altitude ride control, and the design and sizing of the horizontal tail surfaces was largely determined by flutter characteristics.

The horizontal stabilizers were also of aluminium box construction, with GRP leading and trailing edges and tips. The structure was fitted directly onto the steel spindle and the two surfaces rotated independently of each other to give both pitch and roll control, with deflections of 10° up and 25° down for pitch control and plus or minus 20° for roll. Flight testing showed that under extreme aerodynamic loads the stabilizers had insufficient authority in both pitch and roll; this was overcome by altering the hinge point to limit the moment on successive aircraft.

Composite construction, scheduled to be used for the stabilizers on the fifth and succeeding B-1As, is a feature of the B-1B, for which advanced composite technology has been used to build both horizontal and vertical tail surfaces; the structures of both are now of high strength titanium sine wave beams – hailed as a breakthrough in advanced welding processes and unique in the aerospace industry.

Developed by Rockwell in conjunction with Martin Marietta, the subcontractor for the tail surfaces, the process achieves maximum strength and integrity with minimum weight penalty; the beams are very similar to standard structural I-beams, but the central section is very precisely corrugated to match sine wave dimensions, and narrow caps of titanium sheet are welded to the edge of the corrugation; the sine wave is tracked from the outside of the cap by the welding torch, using heat sensors.

At the heart of the tailplane assembly is a massive box support and spindle, forged from HP9-4-20 steel alloy and weighing about 4,950lb (2,245kg). This huge spindle is a major structural component which not only serves as a rear frame for the fuselage stub beneath the fin, but also joins both the fin and the stabilizers to the fuselage while supporting the bottom of the three rudders.

One of the most innovative, if not the most obvious features of the B-1 is the Structural Mode Control System (SMCS), which in its early days was known as the Low Altitude Ride Control (LARC). Penetration of defended areas at high subsonic speeds and very low altitudes is a good way to evade detection and interception, but the turbulence encountered near ground level gives rise to bumps. These can be very severe; for example, a B-52 travelling at a fairly sedate 325kt (602km/h) and 1,000ft (305m) can experience gust loads of +4g and −2g in the cockpit, even in moderately turbulent conditions, as a result of aeroelastic fuselage whipping.

A large aircraft is more prone to this flexing effect than a small one, and the faster it flies the worse it gets. Under these conditions the aircraft is difficult to control, the instruments are difficult to read and making the correct switch selections becomes a matter of great care, and a prolonged period of low-level flight lowers crew efficiency significantly. The solution to the problem was the SMCS.

After the Valkyrie bomber programme had been cancelled the two flying examples had undertaken a research programme, mainly into high-altitude very high-speed flight, but also into the effects of turbulence on large high-speed aircraft. Exciter vanes had been installed on an XB-70 as part of the latter programme, providing the basis for SMCS. The basic idea is that small canard surfaces on the nose of a long aircraft can damp out the bumps by providing forces that will oppose flexing, and in the early days of the B-1 project it was calculated that the system could reduce the vertical acceleration loadings to barely one-third of their undamped level. Lateral loading would need to be taken care of by means of yaw dampers. The only alternative would be to increase the rigidity of the aircraft and thus reduce the bouncing effect at the extremities, but Rockwell calculations showed that this approach would have incurred a penalty of 5-10,000lb (2,268-4,536kg) in weight. By contrast, the SMCS weighed in at just under 500lb (227kg)

SMCS operation

SMCS is an automatically controlled system which uses two small vanes, mounted either side of the nose at a pronounced anhedral angle, and the bottom section of the three piece rudder. When switched on the system responds to accelerometer signals which detect turbulence and react very rapidly, damping out lateral motion through the rudder section, while the vertical motion is corrected primarily by the nose vanes, which can travel through an arc of plus or minus 20° at speeds of up to 200°/sec. The system is reported to be working better than anticipated; there was originally some mistrust on the part of certain pilots, but experience quickly converted them. On the B-1A, the nose vanes were of aluminium, but on the B-1B they are primarily of graphite epoxy bonded to an aluminium honeycomb, with titanium leading and trailing edges and mounted on a steel trunnion superstructure.

The engines are mounted in pods under the wing gloves. The intakes were the subject of a complete redesign for the B-1B, as described in the following chapter.

Another area of major redesign was the cockpit, although as we have seen, this was part of the B-1A development programme. The original scheme had been for a crew escape module with close to zero/zero adverse attitude capability, the design of which had been based on that of the General Dynamics F-111. This had been chosen because it offered the best survival prospects for the crew in the event of a stratospheric bale-out at Mach 2, while performing well at high subsonic speeds and low altitudes, and improving crew efficiency by permitting a shirt-sleeve operating environment. It was also water-tight, and would remain afloat in the sea, and in the event of an ejection over inhospitable terrain it would provide shelter for the crew while they awaited rescue. Finally, initial studies predicted a weight saving with its use.

The crew escape module was fitted to the first three aircraft only. Separation is initiated by pulling either the pilot's or the co-pilot's ejection handles, or both rear seat ejecting handles, whereupon

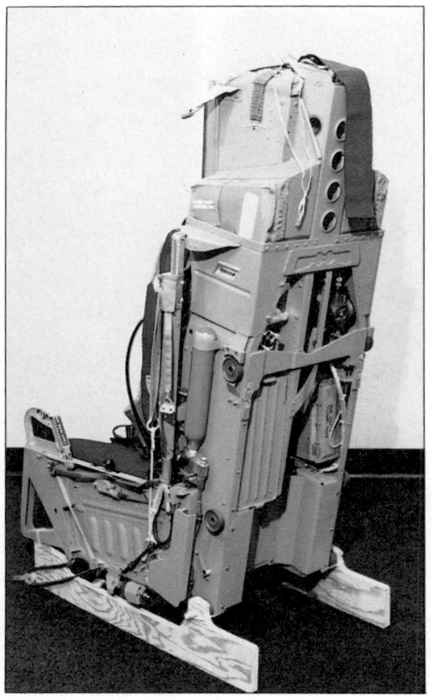

Above: Three-quarter rear view of the ACES ejection seat fitted to all production aircraft. It has zero/zero capability for low-level emergency ejections.

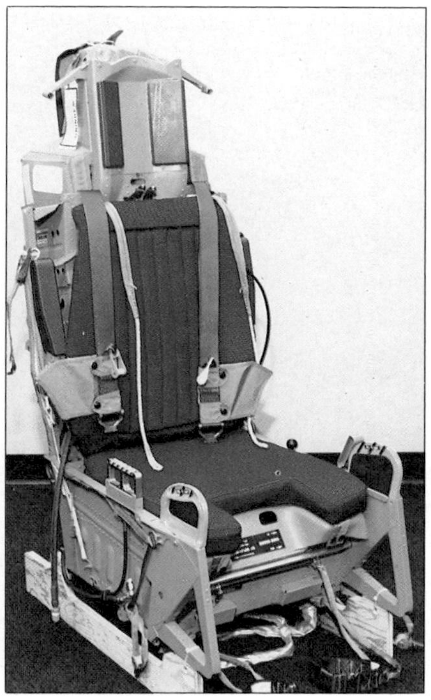

Above: The ACES ejection seat from the front, showing the harness and the leg restraints and the padded headrest designed to prevent whiplash injuries to the occupant's neck.

Above: The crew escape module used on the first three B-1As is seen here carried inverted beneath the wing of a B-52 as part of intensive proof of concept trials.

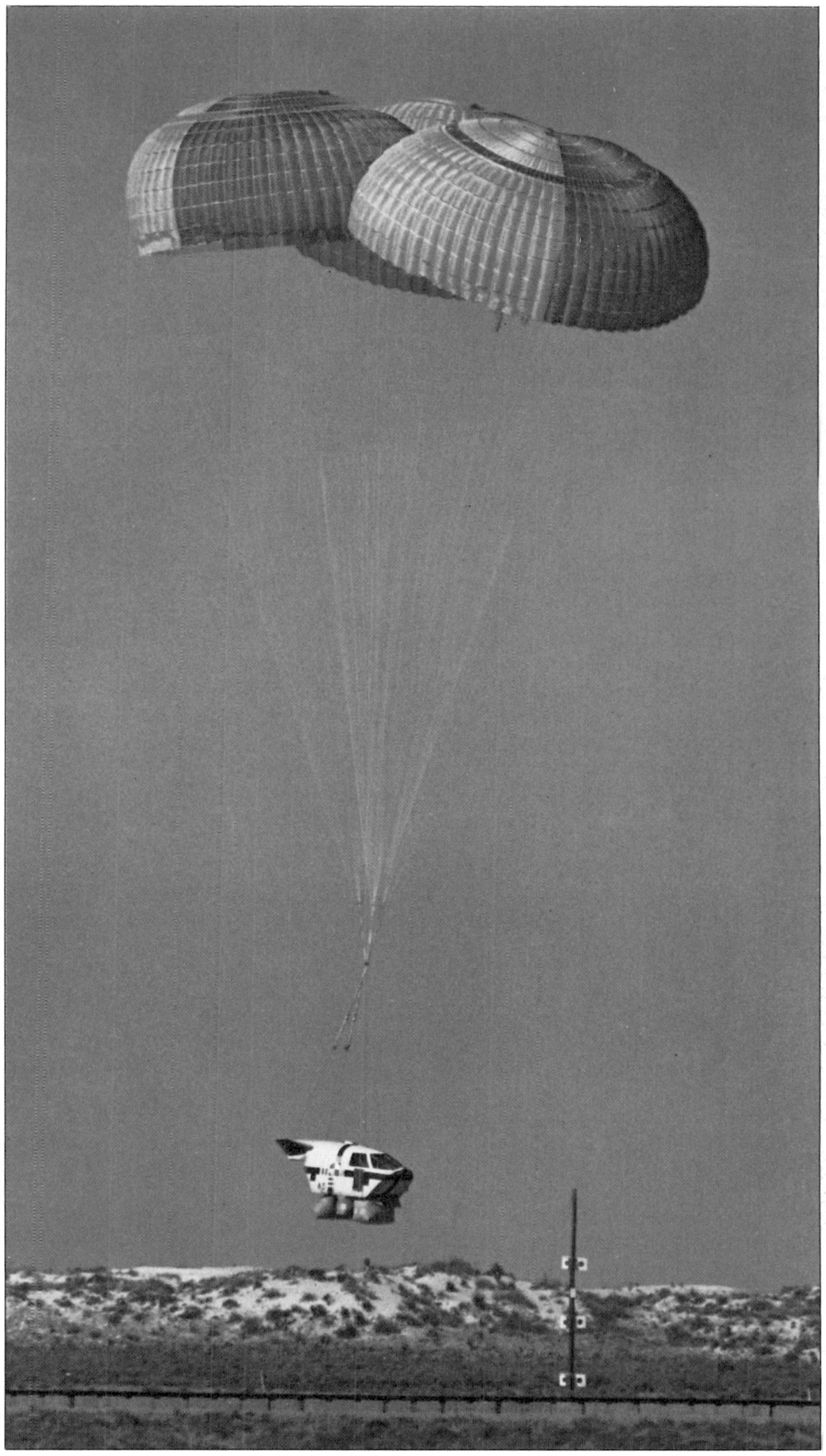

Above: The crew escape module about to impact during trials. The fins can be seen deployed at the rear, and the impact attenuation bags are fully inflated for landing.

Below: The crew board what appears to be the fourth B-1A. The first man to arrive hits a switch on the nose gear which starts the APUs, providing power to the systems.

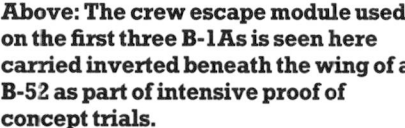

an explosive system shears the module from the aircraft, a drogue parachute is deployed, and a pair of fins situated on top of the fuselage extend to stabilize it during the deceleration period. During this time a rocket motor flies the module automatically to a safe altitude and attitude, and when sufficient speed has been lost three recovery parachutes are released; a five-bladder landing impact attenuator system inflates before ground contact.

Entry to the module was through a belly hatch by means of an extending ladder, and an emergency exit hatch was also incorporated. The crew section could be pressurized for an equivalent altitude of 8,000ft (2,438m), while an unpressurized section housed the escape chutes and rocket motor system. The module was exhaustively tested, with 48 major parachute tests, ten aerial drops of the module, 17 stabilization component sled tests, and five crew escape module sled tests, but it was eventually rejected due to instability in certain flight regimes, although it was also found to be very expensive to maintain, and removal for checking was a complex and time-consuming operation. A temporary bulkhead had to be inserted in the junction frames to maintain the structural integrity of the aircraft while it was removed, and an incredible number of systems had to be discon-

Above: The construction of the heavy and complicated nose gear is clearly depicted, with the figure alongside giving scale. The good downward visibility over the nose is apparent from this angle.

Right: In-flight view over the nose while traversing the Grand Canyon at low level. The photograph appears to have been taken from the co-pilot's seat, with the result that the forward view is slightly degraded.

nected, then reconnected on completion. From the fourth prototype onward the module was deleted and ACES II ejection seats substituted.

The crew of the B-1 normally consists of the pilot, co-pilot, and two avionics systems operators, one for the defensive and one for the offensive systems. Provision also has to be made for two instructors, and in the early days of the project the possibility of carrying two extra crewmen was considered, in order to fly missions of up to 36 hours. The cockpit of the B-1B is fairly roomy, allows the crew to get up and stretch, and incorporates a hot cup and a chemical convenience, while the avionics operators also have a window in the B-1B, presumably for psychological reasons. The instructors position leaves a little to be desired – the four regular crew positions all have ejection seats, but the instructors are left to depart manually through the belly hatch – but overall the B-1 is a remarkably comfortable aeroplane; the longest flight to date, from Edwards to Farnborough in 1982, lasted 11 hours 25 minutes, and the crew reported no undue fatigue at the end of the trip.

Forward visibility is excellent: the nose slopes steeply away to give good vision for landing, and the windshields are large, with overhead transparencies for a vertical view which is necessary during in-flight refuelling. The windshields themselves consist of an outer glass layer, which provides an abrasion and heat resistant surface, combined with an electrical demisting and deicing system, and an inner 12mm ply lightweight, high impact-resistant polycarbonate plastic layer which incorporates a 4mm thick spall shield on the inside face; the entire structure is bonded with a silicone interlayer material resistant to temperature changes. The windshield is designed to withstand a birdstrike of 4lb (1.81kg) at a speed of 600kt (1,112km/h).

The cockpit is also the nerve centre of the flight control system. In the early design stage, fly-by-wire was in its infancy and its use was considered to be a technical risk, so it was decided to go for a complete electro-hydraulic control system, using rods, cables, pulleys and bell-crank levers, with linear gearing to the flight controls. It was quadruplex, and consisted of four simultaneously operating but independent hydraulic systems functioning at 4,000psi, systems 1 and 2 running off the two left-hand engines while 3 and 4 were powered by the right-hand engines. The mission can be completed with a single system failure, while a double failure permits a safe landing.

A 4,000psi system represented the state of the art at that time; most other aircraft used 3,000psi systems, though a notable exception was Tornado, which made its maiden flight some three months earlier. This entirely mechanical system involved penalties in space and weight, but was felt to be justified by the reliability of a tried and trusted system,

Right: The main gear is designed to be able to cope with 90 per cent of the B-1B's takeoff gross weight of more than 220 tonnes on landing, though seen from this angle, it looks decidedly flimsy for the task.

Above: The cockpit transparencies are designed to give good front quarter vision, while those overhead are used mainly in air refuelling. It can be seen that a marginal view behind the beam is possible.

while the higher pressure produced weight savings.

The Automatic Flight Control System (AFCS) provided roll attitude, flight path, airspeed, auto-throttle and Mach holds. A systems routing tunnel is provided in the upper fuselage structure between the longerons, while the wing sweep actuators and flap and slot drive mechanisms are located in the forward intermediate fuselage, in the wing blended section. The Sundstrand wing sweep actuation system was (and probably still is) the largest aircraft actuation system in the world. Another first is the hinge-line geared rotary actuation system for the rudder, also by Sundstrand, which had never before been used in a production aircraft.

The B-1B contained certain changes to the flight control system. Non-linear gearing was introduced to improve handling, particularly for the precision flying involved in in-flight refuelling, and fly-by-wire was introuduced alongside the mechanical controls, the pilot's control system being FBW while the co-pilot's system is mechanical. This produces a considerable saving in weight, although it is safeguarded by a reversionary link in which if one system fails, the two sets of controls can be tied together. This provides systems redundancy. The wing spoilers were modified to eradicate a tendency to float up.

The undercarriage consists of a rather long main gear with two four-wheel bogies which retracts into the centre fuselage section, with a twin-wheel nose gear retracting forward into a well beneath the crew compartment. The fuselage ground clearance is about 9ft (2.74m), while the engine nacelle clearance is about half this distance, and retraction or extension is completed in 12 seconds by means of electronically controlled actuators.

The gear is designed to cope with nearly 90 per cent of the TOGW when landing and is accordingly substantial, the main landing gear cylinders being forged from 300M steel and weighing roughly 3,000lb (1,361kg) each while the nose gear, which is not subject to the same stresses, has a main cylinder forged from 7175 aluminium alloy and weighs in at 1,000lb (454kg). No reverse thrust or braking parachute is fitted, but five-rotor carbon type brakes are supplied by Goodyear, who also make the tyres. Ground steering is provided by the nose wheel, which can turn through 76° right or left or, for manoeuvring by support vehicles in confined spaces, can be released to give full 360° rotation.

The B-1 was designed to be survivable, not only in the accepted sense of surviving battle damage and successfully penetrating hostile defence zones, but also in the event of a surprise nuclear attack. While nothing can ensure survival of an aircraft in the event of a near miss, there is much that can be done to maximize the chances of survival and serviceability to carry out the mission.

The hazards from a nuclear explosion are blast, heat, overpressure and radiation. A certain amount can be done to minimize the effects of the first three by strengthening the structure, although too much strength is counter-productive as the weight increase rapidly becomes prohibitive, but this is a sensitive area,

Left: Nose gear retraction tests at Rockwell's Palmdale facility. The plethora of hydraulic lines and wires within the gear bay are seen as the gear retracts forwards.

and no specific details of blast and overpressure hardening have been released. The original B-1As were painted white as a protection against flash, but with the increasing accent on low level penetration this ceased to be acceptable; white would make the defending interceptors' task easier by day or in moonlight by highlighting the aircraft against the terrain below.

The compromise mooted for the B-1B was to use light and dark grey camouflage, which would break up the outline of the aircraft in low level flight, with the light grey used to cover the heat-sensitive zones such as the avionics compartments and the flight deck. This scheme was dropped, and production B-1Bs are sprayed in the European One scheme of Dark Olive Green, Dark Green and Dark Grey, although the constantly changing angle of the light on the sweeping curves, and the deliberate use of paints of varying reflective qualities, makes this difficult to discern clearly. The approach has been to concentrate on a feature that will actively assist the completion of the mission rather than one that will aid survival in what must be marginal circumstances at the outset.

The main enemy in the event of a surprise nuclear attack is radiation in the form of Electromagnetic Pulse (EMP), which is capable of disrupting or completely destroying electronic circuits. Even such large and coarse things as street lights can be affected, and an aircraft like the B-1, packed with electronic gadgetry, is very vulnerable, and there would be little point in surviving the blast, heat, and overpressure of a nuclear explosion only to find that the vital avionic systems had all been taken out. A lot of research has gone into solving this problem, much of it by the avionic system contractors, but certain items have been incorporated into the structure and can be described here, although others cannot be commented on as yet.

Basically, guarding against EMP involves shielding wiring with overbraided cable, or, in areas such as the avionics compartments, where the density of wiring would make this impractical, by shielding the entire compartment with a contrivance similar to a Faraday cage. Avionics bays and doors are also

Below: The first step in inserting a wing pivot pin is to shrink the pin by immersion in liquid nitrogen. This is done at the assembly point by engineers specially suited and visored against spillage.

Bottom: Positioning the pivot pin takes about five minutes, but the assembly is expected to remain in place for 30 years, making precision of manufacture and positioning of components to exact clearances vital.

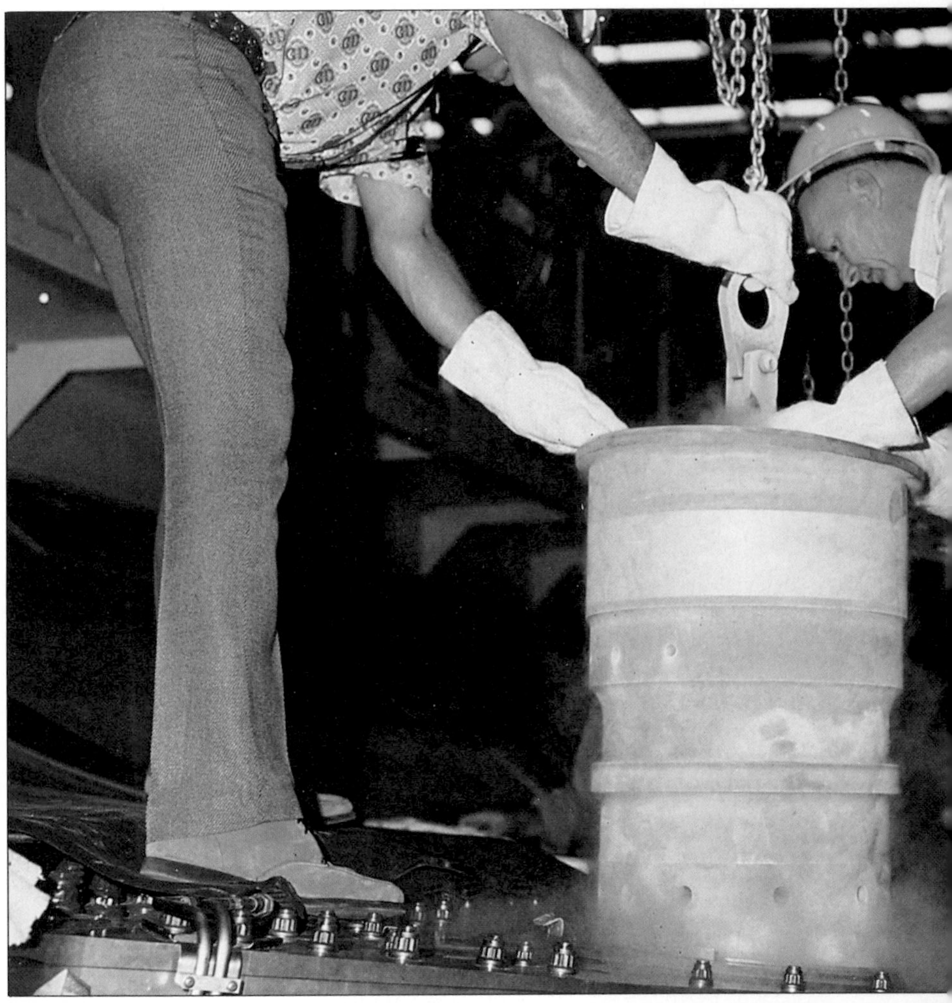

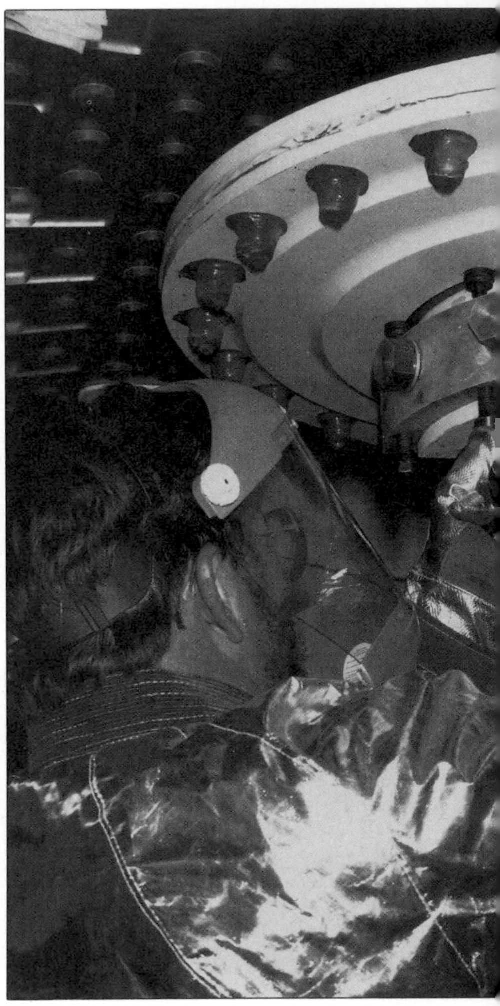

shielded by creating paths of low electrical resistance around them, again using braided cables. By these means, it is hoped, the EMP will be diverted from sensitive systems.

Central to the mission of the B-1 is its ability to penetrate hostile defences unseen and undetected, and since air defence systems are heavily reliant on radar, a lot of effort has gone into reducing the bomber's RCS. As we saw earlier, the small RCS of the B-1A was largely a spin-off from the evolving design: in the beginning, ECM was expected to be the principal form of protection. Quite early in the programme it was discovered that the B-1 would have a very small RCS compared with that of the B-52 – authoritatively quoted by certain European magazines as either 1/35 or 1/25 the latter's.

Of course, the study of radar signatures was at that time in its infancy; there was probably no deliberate intent to mislead anyone. So what is the truth? The RCS of the B-1A is widely stated to have been 1/10 of that of the B-52, while the RCS of the B-1B is equally widely stated to be 1/10 that of the B-1A. The B-52 is reckoned to have an RCS of $100m^2$, which would make that of the B-1B just $1m^2$. For comparison, a normal fighter sized target is reckoned to be about $5m^2$, while the small MiG-21 is supposed to have an RCS of $2m^2$ from the head-on (ie, smallest) aspect. In fact, the RCS of the B-1B is highly classified information, despite the fact that the above figures are widely reported even in official USAF releases; but we can be certain that the B-1A was a vast improvement over the B-52, and that the B-1B shows a further reduction in RCS.

The improvement shown by the B-1A was primarily a result of its less reflective shape, while the B-1B was the subject of an extensive programme to reduce radar reflectivity in three areas: avionics, structure and radar absorbent material (RAM). As far as avionics were concerned, the main change was to the radar antenna, as described in the Avionics chapter. Structurally, the engine inlets were completely redesigned to reduce radar signature, a change dealt with in the Propulsion chapter; more significantly, the front and rear bulkheads were canted downward so that radar pulses meet them at an oblique angle and are more likely to be scattered than reflected straight back. Both these changes, very worthwhile in themselves, were made even more effective by the extensive use of RAM.

The search for a radar absorbent material was started by the German Navy during World War II. The Kriegsmarine wanted to make its U-boats invisible to British airborne radar, something beyond the state of the art for a number of years, but in fairly recent times a radar absorbent coating has been developed which can capture the tiny electronic impulses emitted by radar and convert them into heat instead of reflecting them back. It was not perfect, but it reduced the radar echo considerably.

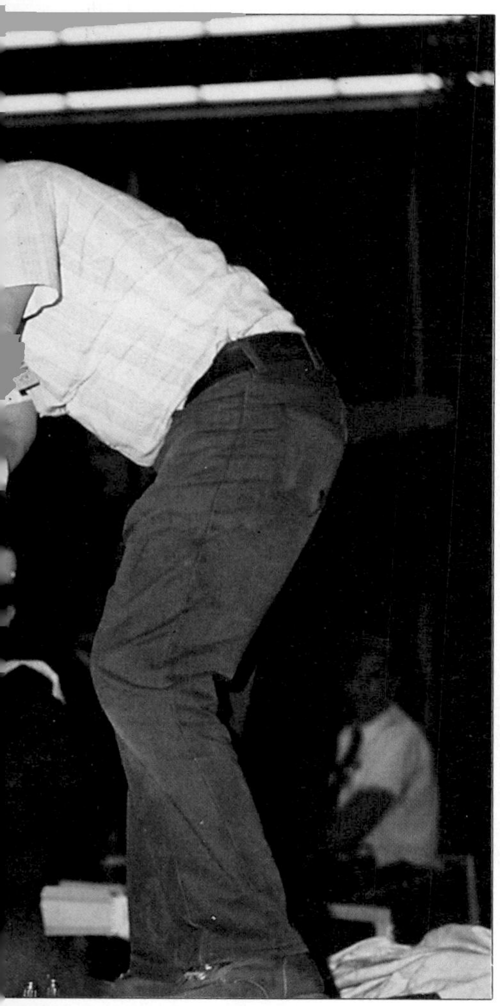

Left: The cooled pin is lowered into position in an area prewarmed by heating blankets to increase the tolerance; the fitters have to wear special gloves. The minute precision of the WCT box can be seen.

Below left: The engineers in their special suits make final adjustments from underneath, fitting what seems to be a ring collar. The double titanium wing connector plate is clearly visible from this angle.

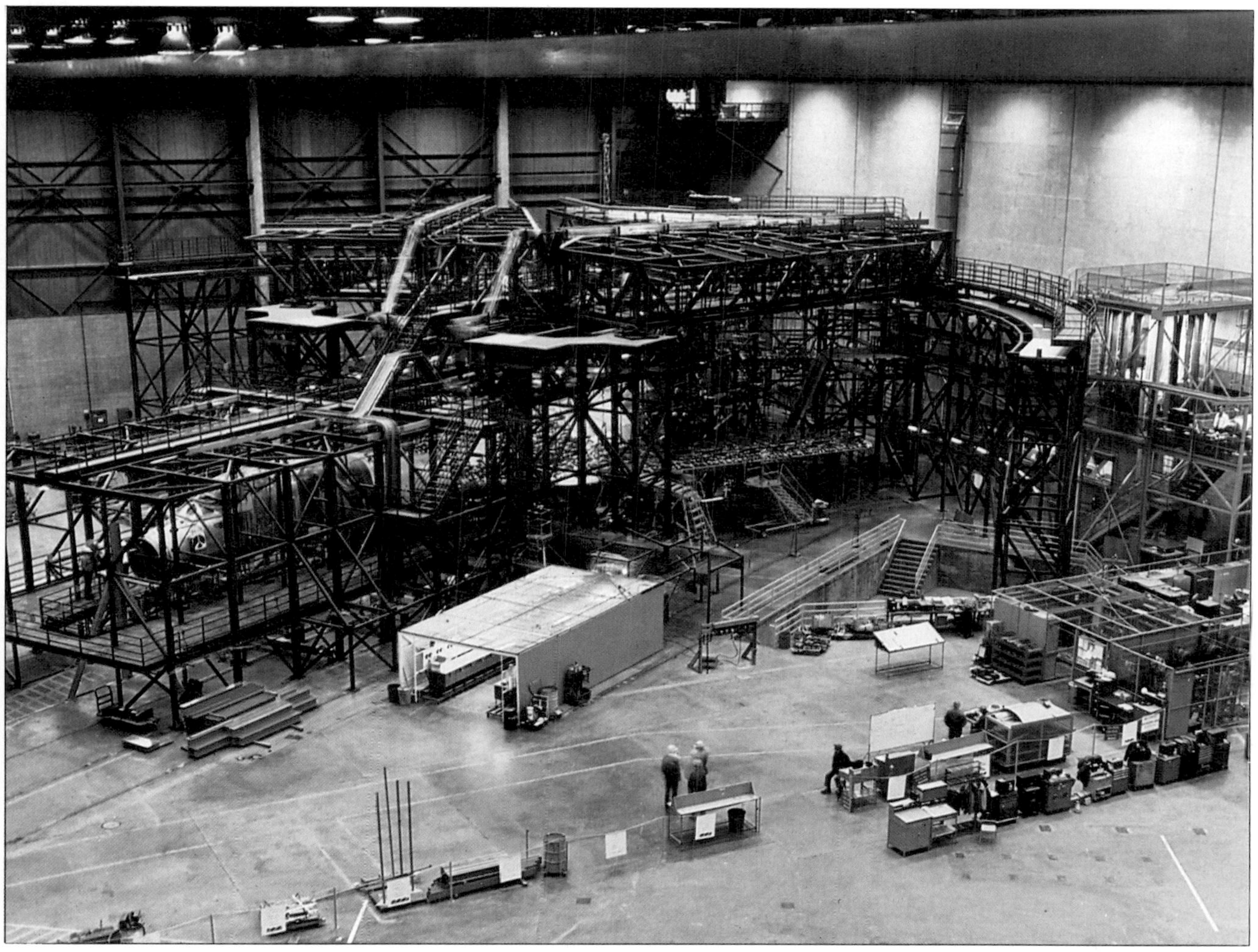

Below: The second B-1A prototype, the structural test vehicle, is seen here undergoing airframe proof and calibration evaluation in Lockheed-California Company's structural test rig at Palmdale.

RAM applications

The RAM used on the B-1A and B-1B is, once again, a sensitive subject, and no specific details are forthcoming, but it is widely known that RAM materials are sensitive to wavelength, and that what works on one wavelength will not work on another. The probem with the B-1 was simplified by its flying at low level, where the only wavelengths likely to be used against it were those in the 3cm I/J band. Although it can only be speculation, it seems likely that the RAM used on the B-1B is optimized for this wavelength, where it will be most effective.

Having developed the material, the designers had to decide where to locate it for the best effect. The engine intakes were one obvious choice, and RAM was used extensively in this area even on the B-1A. For the rest, the fore and aft canted bulkheads were shrouded with the substance, because they were behind cones made of dielectric material transparent to radar signals, and it is also applied around the glove vanes, on the front of the wing fairing and wing root fairings, around the spoilers and flaps and on the horizontal stabilizers – anywhere, in fact, that there is an angle that could trap and reflect back radar energy.

In fact, with an aeroplane so packed with avionics, it has been an exercise of considerable ingenuity to allow the sensors, both active and passive, to look out, detect and positively identify threat radars, while actively deflecting or absorbing their emissions in other areas. Another problem has been the flight deck transparencies: a threat radar could look right through these, and receive an echo from the interior, so an electrically conducting coating was developed to channel the impulses away. All in all, defeating enemy radars by passive means such as clever design and special materials has been a major task, brilliantly executed.

The construction of the B-1B has been a major operation, and a list of the companies involved reads like a directory of the American aerospace industry. Apart from the four associate contractors, there are 50 major subcontractors and over 3,000 suppliers. At the peak of the programme, Rockwell International estimate that no fewer than 50,000 people will be working on the project, including 22,000 directly employed by Rockwell in plants at Palmdale, El Segundo, Colombus and Tulsa. Early in 1986 production was ahead of schedule (the first B-1B was delivered some months ahead of time), and exactly on budget.

Some of the statistics are mind-boggling. The B-1B has required some 18,000 engineering drawings, 61,000 manufacturing orders have been placed, and 25 five-axis milling machines, which can cut and grind metals to an almost infinite variety of shapes, have been acquired. No fewer than 460,500 individual items are required as spares for each aircraft, and 4,800 items of support equipment, of which nearly three-quarters are peculiar to the B-1B.

Structural testing, which began in 1970, was designed to develop processing and fabrication methods and to check strength limitations of structural elements and assembled components. An exhaustive series of tests included more than 2,000 on materials, 2,600 on fracture mechanics and 2,400 on fastener

Above: A busy scene at Palmdale, with assembly work on the first B-1B finally approaching completion. An interesting detail evident here is the nacelle fairing between the starboard engine effluxes.

Left: The size and shape of the B-1 mean that a large number of work stands have to be employed. The wing/body blending necessitates a special stand on the aft fuselage.

systems; altogether, 682 specimens were used to establish the basic design concepts, check out the exact configurations and verify the predicted results.

The next stage comprised Design Verification Tests (DVTs), in which nine full-scale sections, all structurally critical, were put through extensive fatigue and static tests.The WCT box was the most important of these: static tests were carried out for 12 simulated flight conditions, four of them with the gear down, with the wing sweep varied from 15° to 67½°. The WCT box was also tested to 100 per cent of its design limit loading on a dozen occasions, and once taken to 150 per cent of the design loading without failure.

Materials selection also came under close scrutiny. The B-1 was the first major programme to have a fracture mechanics requirement, and much emphasis was placed on developing techniques to measure and control the fracture resistance of aluminium, steel, and titanium. One of the main findings was that much closer quality control had to be exercised.

Located at Rockwell's El Segundo plant, the System Development Tool (SDT) is virtually a mockup of the full size aircraft. Originally built in sections for the B-1A programme, it was later modified to represent the B-1B and assembled into a complete structure. Its function is to allow planning and manufacture of the wires, cables, and tubing that make up the intestines of the aircraft.

For example, the route of a particular system is planned to fit in with the other systems that must also pass through the same area, and where a change in direction or a junction occurs a mockup of the fitting needed is made and check-fitted into the SDT. Once its correctness is established, the mockup piece is fed into a numerically controlled machine which records the exact specifications, and these are in turn fed into a bending machine, which produces the actual hardware to very tight tolerances.

Close tolerances, complexity and planning are the three main factors in the production process. Planning includes organizing the material flow, so that everything is in its appointed place at the proper time, and getting the optimum major sections broken down to give maximum production rates.

Questioned on the production process, Scott L. White explained: "It's all very similar to the B-1A except for the forward fuselage and the nacelles. These are the two critical paths, the forward fuselage because the preponderance of wiring is in it, and the nacelles because they had to be completely redesigned, and we had to start from scratch. What we were originally going to do on the forward fuselage was to build it in what we call the 'cigar', but

B-1B structural components

First stage in the mating of primary structural assemblies is the attachment of forward intermediate and aft intermediate fuselage sections to the wing carry-through box. The vertical stabilizer is attached to the aft fuselage section before it and the forward fuselage are joined to the intermediate fuselage structures; then comes installation of the nacelles, undercarriage, wings and horizontal stabilizers. Engines and landing gear and weapons bay doors are added during final installation.

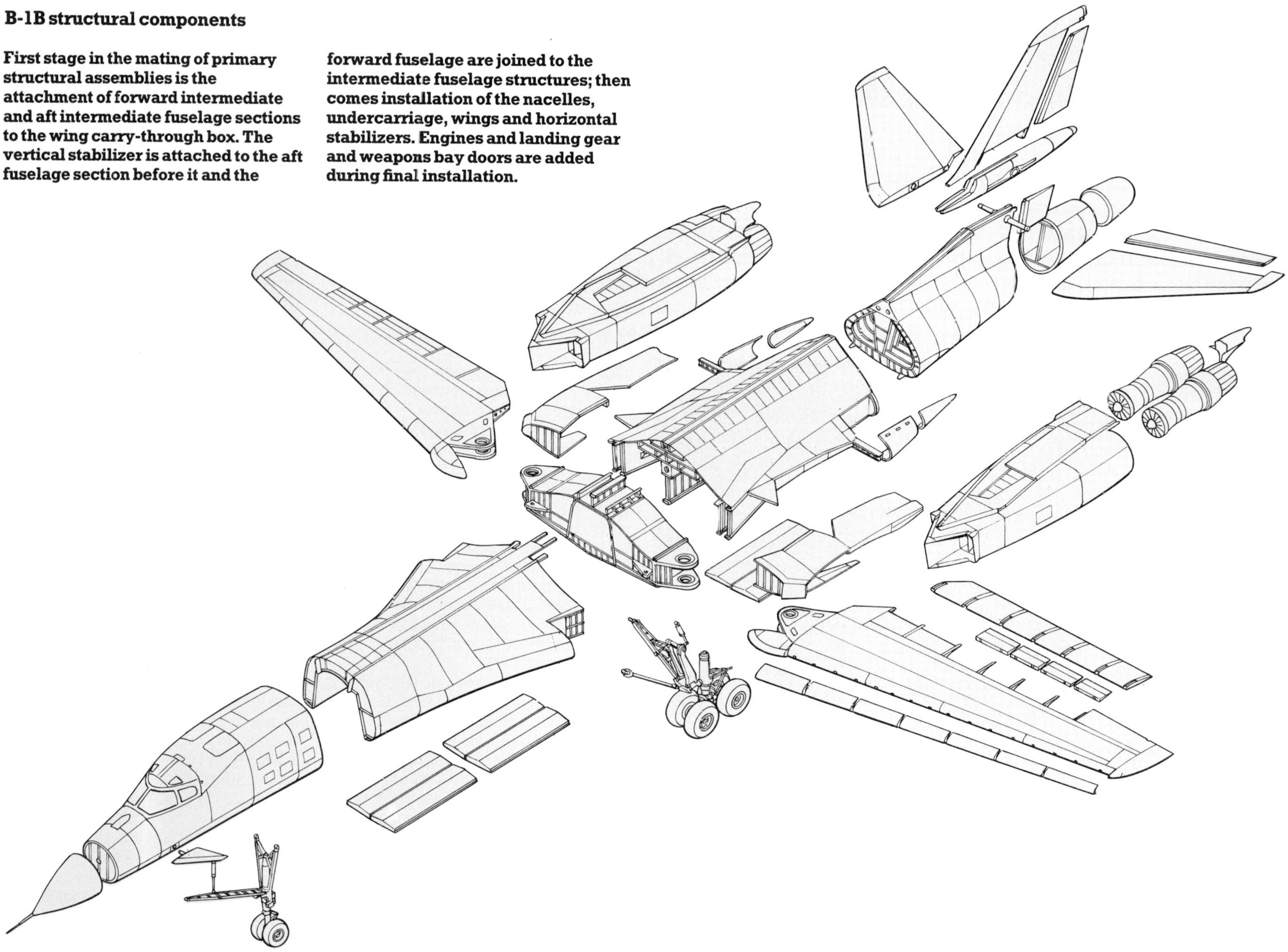

then we had all the people in the world doing the wiring inside it and getting in each other's way.

"What we have done now is to split this section in half, and the majority of the wiring, amounting to about 35,000 wire segments, is done in a separate building. It really cuts down on time and big problems. On the assembly line there is a tram, and each half section runs down to the final assembly position. The assembly line has five mate stations where the entire fuselage is put together. We have generated a lot of capability and quality in this process, and we also utilize a lot of automatic fastenings. The system is that the automatic fastening machine drills the hole and serves the fastener. If it happens to be in a fuel containing area, it also automatically puts the sealer in. All this improves the quality and repeatability from aircraft to aircraft.

Wing mating procedure

"When the fuselage is assembled, the landing gear is attached, then it is rolled forward on the gear to the wing mating stations. No levelling equipment is needed to assemble the wings because only at one point do they attach. The wings are on tools [jigs] and the tools are on airglides. The fuselage is pulled in between the wings, and then the wing is pushed into position by three men. To fix the wing pivot pin, heating blankets are placed on the wing carriage fittings to warm and expand them, while the pin is put into liquid nitrogen to shrink it. The pin, which is hollow, is then lifted out by crane and dropped into position; it takes about five minutes. As long as we do it within fifteen minutes there is no problem. The men have to wear special gloves. Then the final touches are applied, and the job is done."

Right: The B-1B project embraces more than 5,000 subcontractors and suppliers: here the first aft intermediate fuselage arrives by Super Guppy at Palmdale from Vought Aero products in Dallas.

However meticulous the planning, things still go wrong. Murphy's First Law provides that if a thing can be put on upside down, sooner or later it will be, and it duly happened with the first production B-1B, although it should be pointed out that Rockwell were not at fault. On the upper fitting that joins the WCT box to the wing there is a bearing which is not quite concentric, and the supplier is supposed to stamp it "this side up". Unfortunately, the supplier stamped the wrong side; the bearings were put in upside down and the wing pins were inserted, then Rockwell performed the final measurements to check that the clearances were correct, whereupon the error was discovered. The wing would function as it was, but would be subject to fatigue and wear, and would not meet the 30-year life requirement.

Now, this particular aircraft was scheduled to join the test programme: it was not going to be subject to the stresses of operational aircraft, and the temptation must have existed to let it pass, then take remedial action at a later date. Against this, the B-1B programme was a fishbowl, subject to intense public scrutiny, not only for performance and cost, but also quality. Had the press got hold of the story, they would have had a field day, and faith in the programme would have been seriously undermined.

The discovery was made at about midday on a Thursday. Within hours, the decision had been made to pull both pins. Somewhere along the line this would have to be done anyway; the Air Force would need to know the correct procedures and the method would have to be physically verified when the manual was prepared. So the procedures were scheduled, with video cameras installed to record events, and the engineers went to work.

The method was the reverse of the installation procedure: the hollow pins were filled with liquid nitrogen to shrink them, the crane was positioned, and one pin came straight out; the other stuck slightly but virtually no difficulty was encountered. By the morning of the following Monday, the pins had been pulled and the bearings checked and replaced correctly. In Scott White's words: "We went back to the supplier and made sure that it could never happen again."

Powerplant

The AMSA specification, with its emphasis on low-level penetration, called for an engine that was both economical and flexible: the answer was the General Electric F101 turbofan. During the long gestation of the B-1B, however, the priorities changed, so that supersonic speed lost much of its initial importance and the high-speed, low-level flight regime became paramount, allied to durability and reliability. In producing the F101-102 derivative of the original F101-100, General Electric also had to meet a requirement for neutral installation, enabling any engine to be installed in either side of either nacelle.

Above: Underside view of the right engine nacelle of the third B-1A, showing the excellent access to the engines afforded by removing a two-part cowl. The inner engine nozzle is contracted, the outer dilated.

Left: An F101-GE-100 undergoing a full throttle run in a test rig at night. Comparison with pictures of fighter engines in similar tests reveals a bigger and more visible exhaust plume.

The choice of qualities for the engine to power the B-1 naturally involved trade-offs between certain desirable features. The demands of the mission were: unrefuelled intercontinental range; sustained high subsonic speeds in the turbulent air found at low levels; and high initial thrust to get it out of a short airfield. The first three put a premium on fuel economy, which in turn dictated the use of a turbofan with a relatively high bypass ratio for a military aircraft, and the new engine was derived from a General Electric test programme designated GE9 Phase II, a demonstrator of which had been produced in 1965.

Development started in that year at the same time as the AMSA studies, and culminated in the award on June 5, 1970, of a USAF contract for the development of 40 YF101-GE-100 engines, a quantity reduced to 27 when the number of prototype B-1s was cut back. The design goals can be summarized by a simple comparison with two J79s: a single YF101 was intended to do the same amount of work while occupying less than 30 per cent of the volume, with an improvement on the specific fuel consumption (sfc) at cruising speed of about 25 per cent and with no visible smoke emission.

The turbofan engine is basically a standard jet engine with an oversized fan in the front acting as a low pressure compressor. The throughput of air from the intake is therefore much larger than that in a pure jet engine, and this produces a high-mass exhaust of lower velocity. Much of the air from the intakes is led around the engine core and does not pass through the engine proper. This is termed the bypass, and the bypass ratio refers to the amount of air which passes the engine in relation to the amount that actually goes through it.

Below: Cutaway of the original B-1 engine, the F101-GE-100. The length of the power-producing core, from the compressor to the augmentor rings, can be seen to be barely half of the total engine length.

General Electric F101-GE-100 turbofan

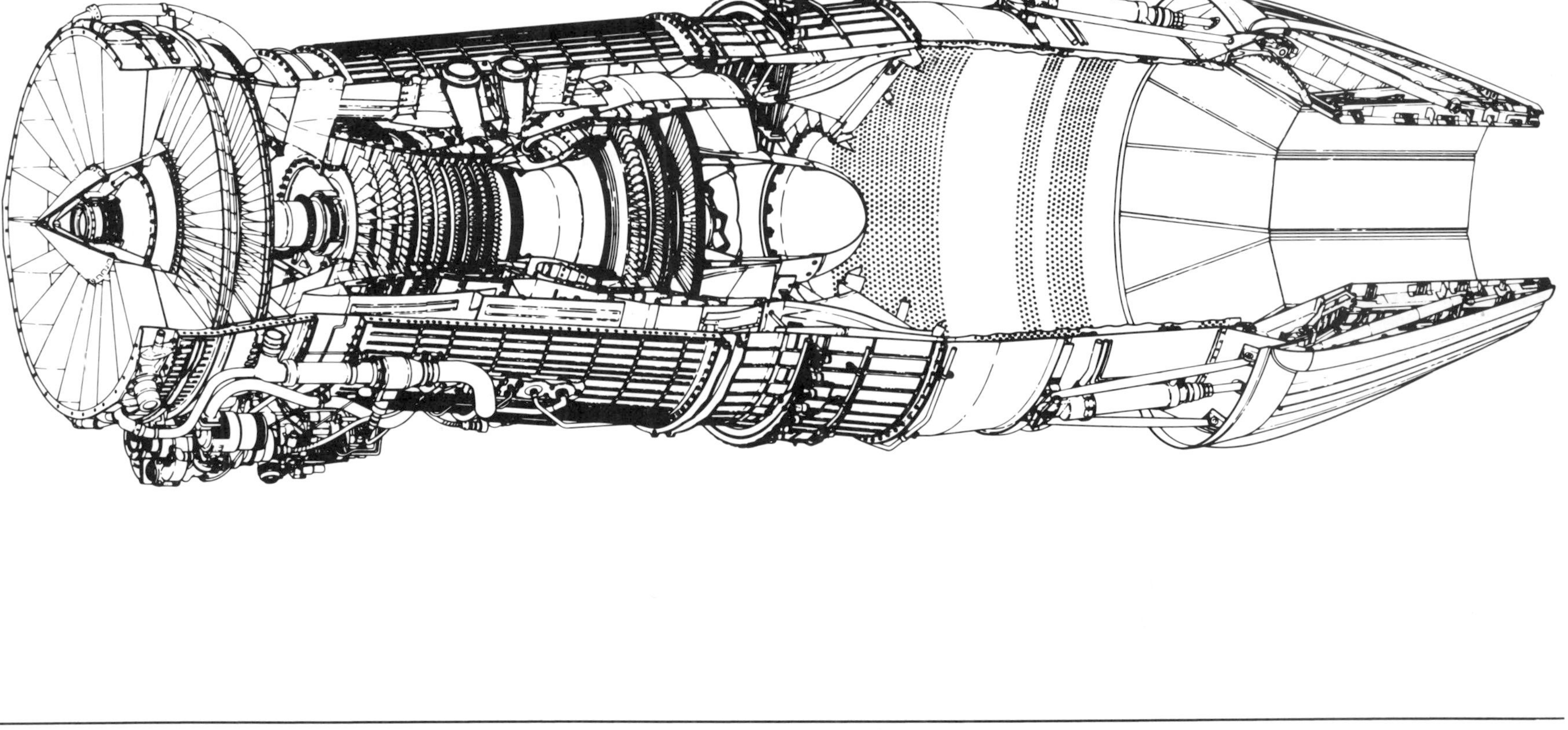

The fan is driven by a spool from the turbine, which is in turn driven by the compressed and heated air from the combustion chambers. Modern airliners typically use a high bypass ratio engine which is very efficient at subsonic speeds, producing a lot of thrust for a relatively small amount of fuel. The bypass air also serves a cooling function, enabling higher turbine temperatures to be used than would otherwise be the case, which further increases efficiency. Much of the inherent efficiency of the turbofan is lost at supersonic speeds and high altitudes, and for a high-performance aircraft the bypass ratio must be carefully sized to give the best possible combination of performance throughout the flight envelope.

The F101 is a twin spool turbofan engine with an original bypass ratio of 2.2:1, later reduced to 2:1, which means that twice as much air goes through the bypass as through the core. This figure is relatively high for a fast jet engine, as we can see by comparing it with the slightly earlier TF30 that powers the F-14 and the F100 powerplant of the F-15 and F-16, whose bypass ratios are 0.9 and 0.7 respectively.

The F101 features two fan compressor stages and nine high-pressure (HP) compressor stages driven by two low-pressure (LP) and one HP turbine stages. The average pressure rise per compressor stage is 1.35:1, far exceeding the 1.20 and 1.25:1 of the TF30 and F100, for a total pressure ratio of 27:1, some 50 per cent higher than that of the fighter engines. Thrust in both military power and full augmentation of 17,000lb (75.6kN) and 30,000lb (133.4kN) respectively also far exceeded the power of the TF30 and the F100. But they were designed to meet an altogether different mission requirement; the driving factor for the B-1 engines was power with economy to meet the demanding operational radius tempered with speed requirements.

In fact, the F101 was later optimized to meet fighter needs, first as the F101DFE (Derivative Fighter Engine) and subse-

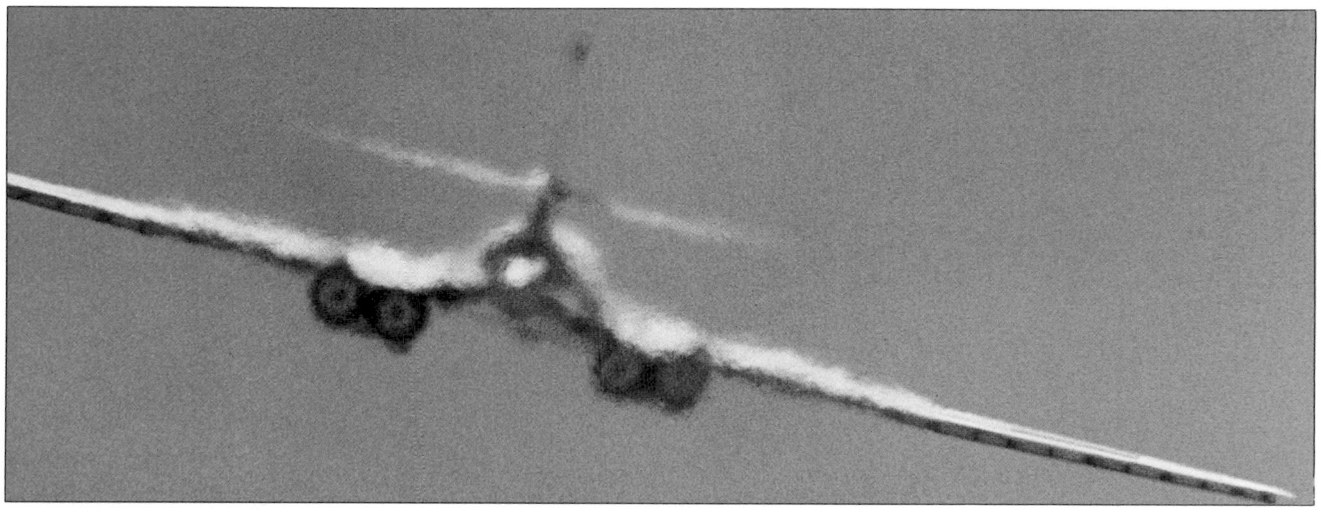

Top: This rear view of the second B-1A using full augmentation shows the low visibility of the engines when seen from astern in daylight, while the exhaust plume is for all practical purposes smoke-free.

Above: Same aircraft, same day, slightly different angle showing the nozzles dilated. The spacing between engines in each nacelle is an insurance against damage to one affecting the other.

Below: Four YF101 flight test engines at Rockwell's Palmdale facility, ready to be installed in a B-1A. A total of 46 YF101s were built, of which half had been delivered to Rockwell by 1977, when B-1A production was cancelled.

Top left: The mission profile of the B-1 calls for quick reaction and good short field capability, demonstrated here by the second B-1A prototype.

Left upper centre: The same aircraft demonstrates a two-engined takeoff. No significant asymmetric handling problems have been found.

Left lower centre: The B-1A demonstrates single-engined flight, the pilot using a large bootful of left rudder to stay straight.

Left: Finally, an unaugmented (non-afterburning) takeoff is demonstrated. Although this requires a reduction in takeoff gross weight and a long runway, it is quite within the B-1's capabilities.

quently the F110, which has been selected to power later versions of all three fighters. The core of the DFE is virtually identical to that of the F101, but the bypass ratio has been lowered to 0.85, an extra fan stage has been added and the overall pressure ratio has been increased to 30:1, to produce slightly more thrust at military power, and about 10 per cent less at full augmentation. On the other hand, the weight and frontal area have been reduced, the specific thrust shows a considerable improvement and throttle response is more rapid. This is not to imply that either engine is better than the other; each is best for the task for which it was designed.

June 1971 saw the Initial Design Review (IDR), which was carried out by the USAF, and a full-scale engine mock-

up was despatched to Rockwell International during the following October. GE began testing the core engine on October 29, some 17 days ahead of schedule, and the first complete engine to be fitted with the afterburner was tested during the following April, achieving 90 per cent of its rated speed.

The YF101 development engine passed its Critical Design Review in July 1972, and the first engine was delivered to Rockwell International for installation trials 11 months later. The first flight test YF101 was delivered on March 22, 1974, immediately after the successful completion of the Preliminary Flight Rating Test (PFRT), and a further three engines for the first B-1 prototype had arrived by mid-May. Also tested was the ability of the secondary power system to start all four engines simultaneously while providing enough power for all the aircraft systems.

The F101 has been claimed to be America's most tested engine. The original F101 development programme had contained many new concepts, such as multiple milestones and non-concurrent development and production etc, and the first flight of the B-1A, on December 23, 1974, was to be followed by two very important milestones: the completion of the Product Verification Programme (PVP) by mid-1976; and the key item for the entire B-1 project, DSARC III, the production decision, which was scheduled for November 1976. Meanwhile, the USAF had been considering alternative test programmes, and between 1970 and 1974, analysis had been conducted in parallel with the development of the F101, though without impinging on it.

Most of the problems in previous engine programmes had stemmed from the lack of a good aeromechanical data base over the entire flight envelope, and from differences between operational usage and endurance testing during the development phase. In other words, the theoretical data on which previous test programmes had been based bore little relationship to what actually happened when the operational units got their hands on the hardware, and as aircraft became more capable, they were being used much harder than had been foreseen, whereas during the development programme, test pilots flew strictly regulated flight profiles which were related to ground test data. Consequently, there was a tendency for weaknesses to show up only when the aircraft reached the squadrons, a little late in the day for remedial action to be taken. Also, there had been an emphasis on either meeting performance and/or weight limits in full; this had often led to a tradeoff with reliability, through squeezing the last ounce out of the new engine.

After extensive reviews of past programmes, the Air Force Aeronautical Systems Division devised a method of improving the development process. The emphasis was on achieving the initial operational Time Between Overhauls (TBO), and the development engines (YF) were to be used to attain a balance between performance, weight, cost, reliability and durability rather than attaining one absolute figure at the expense of any other. Furthermore, it was suggested that development should be aimed more at the production engines at the expense of the pre-production examples, while the post-Product Verification (PV) phase prior to the production phase should be used to examine logistics and maintenance aspects. This was called the New Development Concept.

In 1974 the Air Force System Program Office decided to adapt the New Development concept to the F101 programme, which was already well advanced, and a comprehensive review of the entire programme followed. At that time, the programme for the F101 was the most detailed ever, containing all the elements of the past engine programmes with extra design and testing requirements in the areas of airframe compatibility, low cycle fatigue, and structural integrity. Certain military specifications had been identified as unnecessary, where past results had proved irrelevant, or the items were covered by component testing, items eliminated including the ingestion of sand, and salt water.

Examination of the endurance testing schedule for the F101 revealed some anomalies. The requirement was based on a modified milspec, but in many areas it failed to cover the B-1A's operational profile, with the maximum thrust limits for takeoff and climb too low by a substantial margin, while supersonic cruising had been overestimated by almost a factor of three. Worst of all, there was no provision at all for the demanding terrain following regime, and while engine starts were on target – they could hardly be otherwise – the number of shutdowns was too low by a factor of 4. A number of revisions to the programme were obviously needed.

Realistic test schedule

The first step was to provide a test schedule which truly reflected the B-1's operational cycle. A start was made by isolating those areas of the flight regime which make the greatest demands on the engines. These were found to be hot running, which in operational usage tends to gradually increase until red line limits are reached; throttle transients, which are experienced in rapid accelerations and decelerations and in the case of the B-1 occurred during overshoots on landing and touch-and-go training; the throttle juggling involved in terrain-following flight and in-flight refuelling; high cycle fatigue resonance; and start-up and shutdown. Rather surprisingly, shutdown was found to be almost as bad as start-up, especially if maximum operating conditions had been reached during the test, due to the wide variation in temperatures experienced. At the other end of the scale, the less demanding areas were taxiing, cruising, landing approach, and time spent on station throttled back for maximum endurance.

Once these criteria were established, the next step was to revise the test schedule on a more realistic basis. The first decision was to double the initial operational TBO specification needs to provide an endurance test equivalent to

Left: In-flight refuelling is an integral part of the B-1 mission, and either the Air Force flying boom shown in operation here or the US Navy drogue system can be used.

Below: An intimate rear view of the F101-GE-102 reveals details of the 12-segment variable nozzle and the 28-chute mixed flow augmentor. The flameholders are in the centre.

General Electric F101-GE-102 turbofan

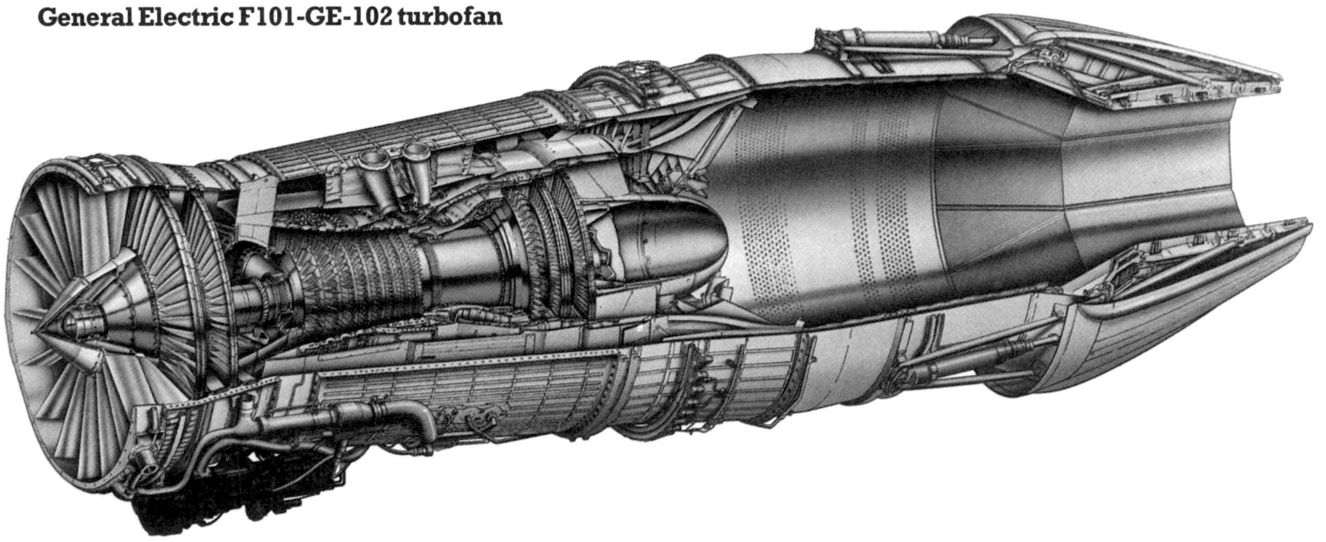

Left: Cutaway of the definitive B-1B engine, General Electric's F101-GE-102. Almost identical to the earlier -100 in appearance, it features greater durability and is slightly heavier.

1,000 hours. Secondly, with the exception of the high cycle fatigue resonance conditions, all the more demanding areas would be reproduced on a one-for-one basis, while terrain-following transients were to be included.

These recommendations were adopted, with the result that the 300-hour Product Verification test included some 200 starts and shutdowns and 440 throttle transients, while 225 hours of the 300 were devoted to climb and terrain-following flight regimes, representing the demanding parts of 200 five-hour missions.

A further recommendation was for the adoption of a Continued Engineering Development (CED) programme. Previously the QT had been accepted as qualifying an engine for mass production, but CED was intended to use early production engines to uncover problems early, rather than to wait for them to occur during operational service, and included logistics and maintenance in addition to actual operational experience. The crtical design review was approved by the USAF in July 1975, PV was completed, and CED commenced in August 1976. The production decision was made in November of that year, and a production contract issued to GE, who at this point had built a total of 46 YF101 engines, of which 23 had been delivered to Rockwell International.

The cancellation of the B-1A by the Carter Administration in June 1977 put the F101 programme on the backburner, and CED continued through to March 1981, shortly before the B-1 flight test programme ground to a halt, when roughly 7,600 flying hours had been recorded on the four B-1As. The intention was threefold: engine maturity had to be established, component life extended and engine procurement and running costs reduced. It should be remembered in this context that the F101DFE, with an identical core engine to the -100, was under development, and at the same time there was a groundswell of optimism that the B-1 would one day be resurrected.

This optimism was not misplaced; in September 1981 a Presidential go-ahead was received for the B-1B, to be powered by the F101-102. The -102 was almost identical to the -100, but with the accent on durability and operability, and the proposed weight increase for the B-1B required rather higher turbine temperatures to maximize performance and improve operating efficiency. Other changes were neutral installation, so that any engine could be installed in any position, and a simplified nozzle, while the intakes could also be greatly modified with the relaxation of the Mach 2 speed requirement.

The F101-102 was the first engine to utilize Accelerated Mission Testing (AMT) as a tool for product verification, the latter being completed in February 1982. Two 381-cycle AMT blocks run on

Centre left: The F101-GE-102 is somewhat larger than a typical fighter engine, partly because its greater bypass ratio calls for a fan of greater diameter. It is giving more thrust than expected.

Left: This view shows clearly the rear nacelle details of the first production B-1B during preparations for a test flight. Details of the main gear are also visible, as is the unusual cross-section of the main gear well doors.

a -102 during its PV programme involved some 790 hours of running time, more than half of which was at full thrust, including 4,713 afterburner lightups, 830 low fatigue cycles and 9,427 full thermal cycles – a rough equivalent of ten years of service usage. PV was complete by February 1982, and the production contract, worth $182 million, was received by GE on April 1 of the same year.

Full scale development was completed during September 1983, and the first production -102 engine was delivered that same month, taking to the air aboard the first B-1B in October 1984. At a casual glance the -102 is identical to the -100, and its dimensions are the same, but it is about 400lb (180kg) heavier. Extremely reliable in service, it is reportedly very stall-proof, and early shortcomings found in sfc were fairly marginal – between 3 and 5 per cent – and were deemed to be acceptable.

The F101 in detail

The F101 is a two-spool turbofan with a bypass ratio of roughly 2 and a mass flow of approximately 350lb (160kg) of air per second. Overall dimensions are identical for both the -100 and the -102, length being 15.08ft (4.60m) and maximum diameter 4.58ft (1.40m), but while the dry weight of the -100 is approximately 4,000lb (1,814kg), the -102 shows an increase, mainly due to improved durability, to 4,400lb (1,996kg). Each produces the same static thrust at military and augmented settings of 17,000lb (75.6kN) and 30,000lb (133.4kN), although the actual flight performance of the -102 is rather the better of the two, as one would expect, being the latest development of a design nearly 20 years old. The F101 is modular, which assists maintenance and repair, and has many borescope ports to allow visual inspection of such areas as the compressor, the combustors, and the turbine, particularly the compressor and turbine blade clearances.

The low-pressure (LP) compressor is the two-stage fan, which also has inlet guide vanes with variable trailing edge flaps. Originally both fan stages had solid titanium blades with tip shrouds for improved clearance control, but in the -102, the first stage LP fan blades are made of a directionally solidified DSR80H nickel based alloy, and the front frame and fan section have been amended due to the adoption of fixed inlets on the B-1B. This, combined with other improvements, led GE to anticipate a 17°C temperature improvement and 2½ per cent more thrust: in fact, they got a 33°C improvement in temperature and 5 per cent extra thrust. The effect on takeoff performance was dramatic, the B-1B lifting off five seconds earlier than with the -101. The fan casing is designed to split horizontally for ease of maintenance, allowing the individual vanes and blades to be replaced as required, and the shroud was designed with a short chord as a weight reduction measure.

The outer fan duct is a separate module, and it directs the bypass air around the core engine. The first module in the core engine is the high pressure (HP) compressor, which incorporates high stage loading from the earlier X370 engine, and a cooled aft casing provides blade clearance control. Like the fan casing, the HP compressor casing splits horizontally for access, the front section being made of titanium and the rear section of steel. The compressor itself has nine stages, the first three of which have variable stators, and the rotor is fabricated by inertia-welding the separate rotor discs together to form a rigid steel drum.

Behind the HP compressor comes the heart of the engine, the combustor, in which the fuel is mixed with air and burnt to produce power. The first machined ring type combustor used in a high performance engine, it is a short annular type with fuel injected through dual cone nozzles into the dome area scroll cups for ignition. This gives a uniform temperature distribution at the HP turbine nozzle, through its ability to mix fuel and air over a very short distance.

Next in line comes the HP turbine, which drives the HP compressor by way of a concentric outer shaft, and has but a single stage with 85 blades. The turbine disc forging was originally to be Rene 120, a development by GE in the powder metallurgy field, but this gave trouble and its replacement, Rene 95, was also unsatisfactory in the early stages, so the -102 uses DA718 nickel alloy in both the turbine and compressor discs. The problem was finally solved by adding an extrusion step prior to forging, and using an improved Rene 95 alloy. The HP turbine blades and vanes are hollow aerofoils with compressor air cooling through film holes on the rear edge of the blades, and the inclusion of more film holes on the back edge of the blades is stated to reduce temperatures at the trailing edges by as much as 110°C. In the -102, the blades are made of directionally solidified DSR80H nickel based alloy. Since 1982 lasers have been used to drill these holes. This is a cleaner and faster process than either electro-discharge machining or electro-steam drilling, the methods that were used previously. This cooling system makes the expansion characteristics compatible with those of the rotor, which aids control of tip clearances.

Just behind the HP turbine is the LP turbine, which drives the fan through a central shaft or spool. A two-stage design, it is uncooled and has shrouded tips to the blades. The LP turbine blades are individually replaceable, but the second stage vanes are only replaceable in segmented groups. The LP turbine is immediately ahead of the afterburner, or strictly speaking for a turbofan engine, the augmentor.

The augmentor is of the mixed flow type, with 28 chutes handling the core exhaust gases and a further 28 to carry bypass air. A convoluted flow mixer provides for the efficient mingling of the two air sources in the plane of the

Above right: Ground testing for high altitude, high speed operation is carried out in a test cell which can simulate the conditions required at Air Force Systems Command's Arnold Engineering Development Center.

Right: The shrouds surrounding the afterburner section can be seen in this study of the starboard engines being fitted to the seventh B-1B. The exhaust nozzles of the F101-102 were simplified to save weight.

Above: To achieve speeds in excess of Mach 2 an external shock inlet was adopted for the B-1A. The three-piece vertically aligned ramp is in the centre and the variable inlet lips can be seen in the open position which is adopted for takeoff.

flameholders, which are radial, and are sited in the hot core exhaust, which is the best place for both lighting up and stable high-altitude operation.

Augmentor operation is electronically controlled, and a self-balancing cycle for the airflow mix is incorporated. One of the considerations in determining this cycle was the reduction of infra-red signature, although no specific details have been released. Augmentation operation is reported to be very smooth, and completely variable over the entire range. Light-up begins on the inner flameholder and works progressively outward; GE have stated that about nine-tenths of the core exhaust is burned before the oxygen-rich bypass air is used. This helps to even out the rise in temperature as increasing amounts of fuel are fed into the augmentor. The augmentor liner is cooled by bypass air.

At the extreme end of the engine comes the nozzle, which is naturally a convergent-divergent type made up of primary and divergent leaves with outer flaps and seals. Optimum area for each flight condition is achieved by means of a translating actuator ring which adjusts the flaps and seals by way of cams and links; the actuator ring is moved by hydraulic rams. Trouble was experienced with the nozzle during the early flight test phase when several leaves were shed at high speeds and altitudes, and a certain amount of redesign was necessary to cure the problem.

Nacelle installation

The engines are housed in pairs in nacelles under the wing root, and although the nacelles are widely spaced flight testing has established that the failure of both engines in one nacelle, although causing asymmetric thrust, will not cause undue control problems. The Automatic Flight Control System (AFCS) will compensate aerodynamically for any potential yaw arising from this condition. The B-1B can even be flown on one engine, although fuel must be jettisoned to lighten the aircraft to acceptable levels.

Rapid starting is essential to survive a surprise attack, and the externally powered electric starter originally con-

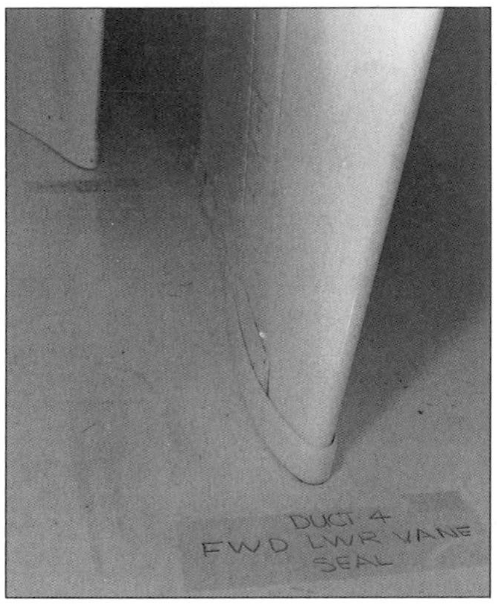

Above: In order to help shield the engine face from the emissions of hostile radars, the vertical inlet guide vanes have been repositioned at various angles to deflect the impulses, as seen here.

sidered was rejected because of its vulnerability to EMP. Orthodox start carts would have reduced stand-alone capability, and in any case were not really conducive to a rapid escape from a threatened airfield. Instead, a gas turbine Auxiliary Power Unit (APU) in each nacelle has a power shaft to each engine, coupled through a gear box.

The APU not only provides power to start the engines: each engine in a nacelle can be started simultaneously with the other using low pressure air; alternatively either APU can start the engines in the opposite nacelle; but power and bleed air are provided for static ground operation. The engines themselves provide power for all hydraulic and electrical systems, plus bleed air for the environmental control system. The B-1B is rather quicker to start than the B-1A; in the event of an alert, the first crew member to reach the foot of the access ladder hits a switch mounted on the nosegear, and by the time the crew reach their stations, both APUs are running and power is reaching all systems. All four engines can then be started simultaneously.

The front of the nacelle contains the intakes, and these have changed considerably during the development period, as the original requirement for Mach 2 performance at altitude with the B-1A was dropped in favour of greater stealth on the B-1B. Early in the B-1A's development a highly efficient but rather complicated mixed external and internal shock system was considered, but this was abandoned after cost-effectiveness studies, and a slightly less efficient external shock system was adopted.

B-1B intake layout

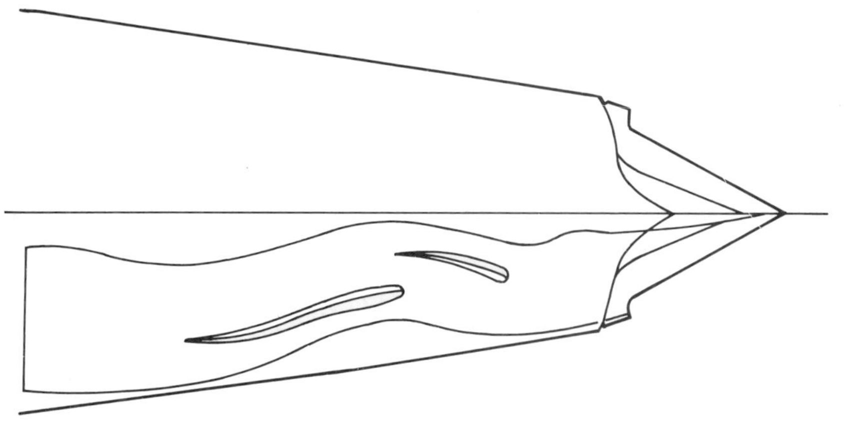

Above: Low observables technology has been applied to the intakes, resulting in a serpentine duct with angled guide vanes and baffles to deflect or trap radar energy. Heated vanes are shown in red.

Below: The B-1B intake is quite different from that of the B-1A, (top left). A plain intake with no variable ramp, it retains the movable lips which are needed to increase air ingestion at takeoff.

Regardless of the speed of the aircraft, air entering the engines must be slowed to subsonic speed before it reaches the face of the LP compressor, and setting up a shock wave or a series of shock waves is the best way of doing this. The inlets are raked back sharply as on many modern fighters, but they are aligned horizontally instead of vertically. The main ramp on the B-1A was therefore vertically aligned, and consisted of three hinged panels, hydraulically actuated and controlled by computer, and the first and third panels, the ramp and the throat, move independently as a function

Left: A closeup of the front of a B-1B engine nacelle, showing how well the engine compressor face is shielded from hostile radar emissions. In this pre-installation picture, the variable lips are constricted into a normal in-flight position.

Right: The B-1B achieves its intercontinental range by carrying an enormous load of fuel, which is distributed around the aircraft as shown here. The centre of gravity is maintained by automatically transferring fuel from tank to tank.

of the Mach number. Basically they remain collapsed, or fixed, at Mach numbers up to about 1.4. At takeoff, the inlet lip moves outward to increase the mass air flow. Boundary layer control in supersonic flight is achieved by the use of two-position louvres on the underside of the nacelle, while the Mach number in the duct diffuser is controlled automatically using a bypass door just ahead of the engine face.

Given the present state of the art, bisonic speed and stealth are mutually exclusive. Mach 2 is only achieved at high altitudes in full view of enemy radar; afterburning greatly increases the aircraft's IR signature; and the inlet design allows radar to look straight down the intake to the face of the engine. The rapidly rotating compressor blades are excellent radar reflectors; since there is always at least one blade at the exact angle to bat the electromagnetic pulse straight back on a reciprocal course, which is exactly what is not wanted if the aircraft is to escape detection. The engine face can only be shielded from the emissions by an inlet that precludes Mach 2 speeds.

With the accent on stealth, the B-1B mission profile altered somewhat. Range could be given by high altitude economical cruise in friendly or neutral environments, but the growing difficulty of successfully carrying out a mission involving a deep penetration of hostile airspace placed the highest premium on remaining undetected. Mach 2 at altitude thus became of little importance, while stealthy low-level penetration for protracted periods became an absolute essential.

To reduce the radar signature of the B-1B the intake ducts were made serpentine to prevent hostile radars looking straight down the throat of the engine, vertical inlet guide vanes were repositioned at an angle, and baffles were inserted to deflect electromagnetic impulses on a winding course both on their way down the intake duct and on their return journey. Extensive use was also made of radar-absorbent materials, so that while radar pulses can still enter the intake, they are either absorbed or deflected downwards, amounting to a tremendous reduction in the B-1B's radar cross section.

Intake simplification

The complicated system of moving ramps and electronic controls on the original B-1A intake would have been self-defeating, and these have been deleted from the B-1B along with the Mach 2 capability, and maximum speed at altitude is now somewhere in the region of Mach 1.3-1.4, but since the supersonic flight regime is considered of little consequence, it is difficult to see exactly where it will fit into the revised mission profile. Invisibility is always better than high performance, though it has been noted that should the USAF ever have a requirement for an ultra long-range interceptor, the original intakes could be fitted to restore the Mach 2 capability.

The B-1B is packed full of fuel. While exact figures have not been released, simple arithmetic gives an approximate figure of 32,000 US gallons, or around 93 tons, carried in eight tanks in the fuselage, in the blended wing body and in the wings, while the forward weapons bays are plumbed for auxiliary tanks. Needless to say, simply leaving all this fuel to slosh around under the influence of gravity would upset the balance of the aircraft, and it will be remembered that an out-of-balance condition led to the loss of the third prototype. Matters are further complicated by the variable-sweep wing, which also alters the centre of gravity.

The answer lies in the Fuel and Center of Gravity Management Subsystem (FCGMS), which automatically maintains balance by pumping fuel around the tanks. It measures the fuel weight in each tank, then combines this information with weapon load data from the stores management system, and the undercarriage, flaps and wing sweep position, Mach number, pressure altitude and aircraft attitude, and from this calculates the actual centre of gravity. The FCGMS then compares this data with stored moment arm data, and if an out-of-balance condition exists it gives control signals which open and close valves and start and stop fuel pumps to transfer fuel around the system to achieve a balanced flight condition. Pressure in the tanks is maintained by pumping nitrogen in through the vent subsystem, which also prevents the buildup of an explosive fuel vapour/air mixture.

There are two separate main tanks, and each has two booster pumps and one cooling fuel pump. These supply fuel to the engines and to two cooling fuel loops, while cross-feed valves permit the supply of fuel to all four engines from either tank. The cooling loops are used to regulate the temperatures of the accessory drive gearbox, the avionics bays, the oil for the hydraulic systems and the integrated drive generator by way of environmental control heat exchangers. Fuel is also supplied to the APU in each nacelle, enabling the APU and cooling systems to operate during ground alert status. Fuel transfer can also be operated manually from the cockpit, where a fuel management panel is fitted. In the main, fuel transfer is a fore-and-aft operation, with a separate line and isolation valve providing unobstructed flow between the front and rear fuselage tanks.

B-1B fuel stowage

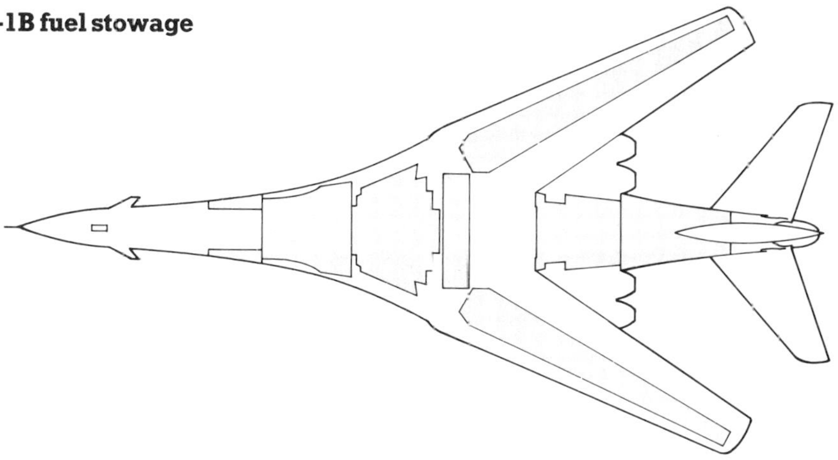

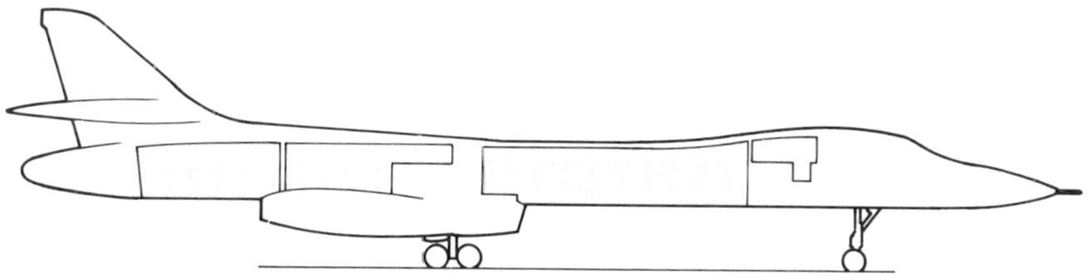

Below: The operational pre-flight scene will be much more spartan, as the B-1B will deploy to small fields for periods of 30 days, depending entirely on its own resources once it has topped up with fuel.

Avionics and Armament

To enable it to carry out its design role of penetrating the most intense defences to deliver nuclear weapons, day or night and in any weather, the B-1B carries two comprehensive suites of avionics, one offensive and the other defensive in character and each with its own specialist operator. Many details of these systems are highly classified, and it is impossible to give a comprehensive account of their operation; moreover, the hiatus between the cancellation of the B-1A in 1977 and its reinstatement as the B-1B in late 1981 allowed many technological improvements to be incorporated into the later aircraft's systems, and in some areas there is little similarity between the two.

From the outset, defining the avionics needs of the B-1 was seen to be a major task. It was originally proposed to keep costs down by assembling asuite of off-the-shelf avionic subsystems tied together with a central complex of computers, but it was soon realized that development and integration would be both expensive and technically risky, so it was decided to assemble the highly specialized defensive avionics suite as a separate package.

Rockwell International and General Electric were selected as weapon system and engine contractors respectively in June 1970, but selection of the avionic system contractors was delayed while proposals were evaluated. Boeing Military Airplane Company (BMAC) were eventually nominated for the offensive avionics system (OAS) in April 1972, while the AIL Division of Cutler-Hammer, now the Eaton Corporation, was not appointed to develop the defensive avionics system (DAS) until January 1974 – less than a year before the maiden flight of the first B-1A.

Although two separate contractors were concerned with the main B-1 avionic systems, and there were certain flight control and other systems that lay outside the scope of either of them, the avionics suite has to be interdependent and operate as part of a cohesive whole and there are parts of the system which are either integrated with both the OAS and the DAS, or which have multiple functions within the electronic innards of the aircraft.

At the heart of the B-1 avionic systems are four redundant MIL-STD-1553 data buses, which have replaced the avionics multiplex (AMUX) system used in the B-1A. A data bus can be considered as a single-track loop railway with many

Above: Not the B-1B impersonating the Space Shuttle, but an avionics test rig for the antenna systems. Some idea of the importance of the avionics can be gained by the extreme lengths and cost to which the USAF and contractors have obviously gone.

Below left: The pilot's console is dominated by the central CRT, which in this instance apparently shows the aircraft to be in a gentle left turn at low level. There is no HUD, but the CRT is set only just below the pilot's normal line of vision.

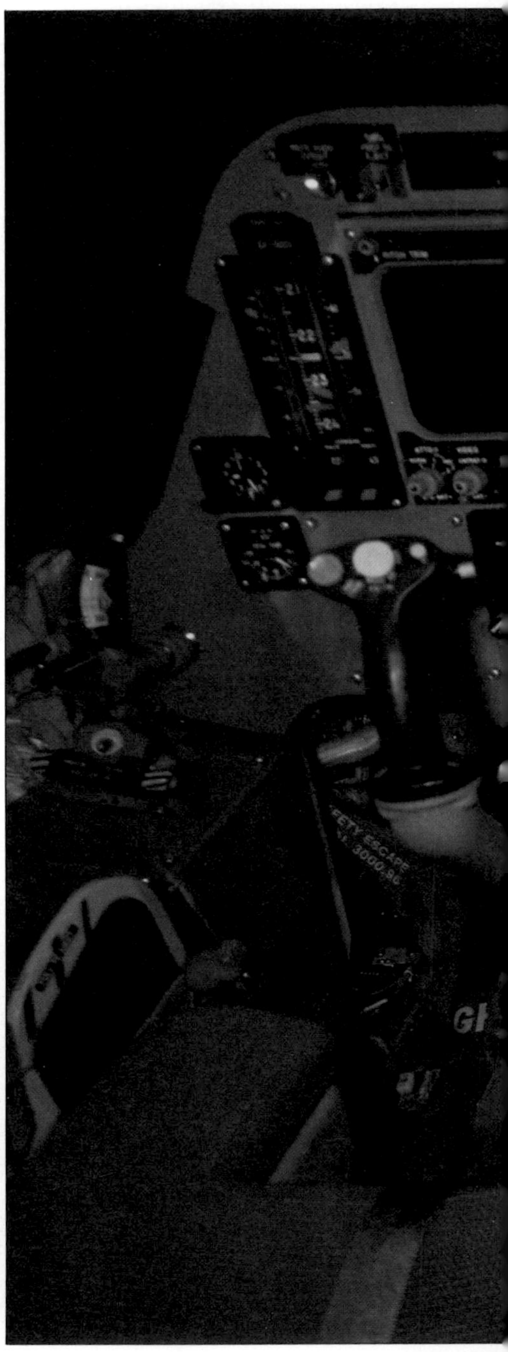

other lines leading off it: information is fed into the loop from one of the lines, and coded so that it is automatically taken off at the appropriate intersection. The data buses sort information from the radars, navigation, flight monitoring systems and so on and feed it to the relevant compartments.

If the data buses are at the heart of the system, then electronic multiplexing (EMUX) forms the arteries, using only two two-wire cables to transfer more than 9,000 inputs and outputs selectively, from any point in the aircraft to any other point via a common data bus. Routing is done via a controller/processor which can also solve combined sequence or interlocking equations and from them produce output commands. EMUX saves a colossal amount of wiring – some 32,000 wire segments with a total length of 80 miles (129km) – a great deal of complexity, and some 3,000lb (1,360kg) in weight.

Onboard test system

Vital to the efficient operation of the B-1 is the Central Integrated Test System (CITS). This is an onboard digital data processing system which continually monitors and verifies the performance of various parts of the system, both in flight and on the ground, including offensive and defensive avionic systems, the AFCS and the powerplant, recording in-flight failures and battle damage, and, although almost all systems have a measure of redundancy built in, projecting the systems status onto a display in the centre of the avionics panel. CITS uses an IBM AP101F computer for monitoring and programming, and a program is presently under development to augment its capabilities still further by adding an Expert Parameter

Above left: There are remarkably few instruments in front of the pilot, and only one old-fashioned dial type to be seen from here.

Above: The co-pilot's station is almost identical to that of the pilot. Only the side console and the wing sweep control are handed.

Below: The flight controls are more like those of a fighter, with the stick-type control column and the quadruple throttles set under the left hand in both positions.

Avionic systems control console

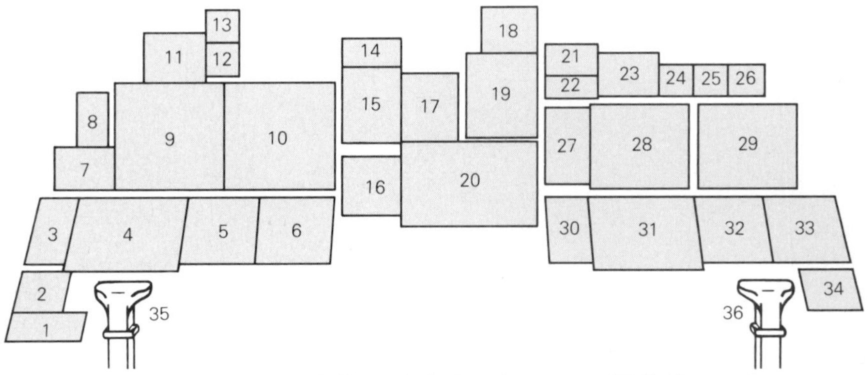

1 CITS (Central Integrated Test System)
2 Lights
3 DSO (Defensive Systems Operator) power
4 Multi-function display
5 Integrated keyboard
6 ALQ-161 RFS/ECM (Radio Frequency Surveillance/ Electronic Countermeasures)
7 ICS (Integrated Communications System)
8 Environmental controls
9 Electronic display unit (EDU)
10 Electronic display unit (EDU)
11 Caution panel
12 Attitude/director indicator
13 Flight performance
14 High frequency radio
15 AFSATCOM (Air Force Satellite Communications) printer
16 AFSATCOM keyboard
17 AFSATCOM control panel
18 Lights
19 Naviation auxiliary panel
20 CITS
21 Coded switch panel
22 Transponder
23 Caution panel
24 Flight performance
25 Attitude/director indicator
26 Horizontal situation indicator
27 Bomb/navigation panel
28 Radar display unit
29 Multi-function display
30 Radar control panel
31 Multi-function display
32 Integrated keyboard
33 Stores management system
34 ICS
35 DSO tracking handle
36 OSO tracking handle

System called CITEPS, which will more accurately diagnose faults using artificial intelligence software. The self-testing facilities can also detect EMUX failures and bypass the affected areas using redundant circuitry or boxes.

Power for the avionic systems is supplied by three integrated drive generators rated at 105/110kVA, while one single essential bus for the Central Air Data Computer (CADC) can be driven by an emergency 15kVA generator. This is needed particularly for the AFCS which, being tied into virtually everything to do with controlling the aircraft in the air, makes an invaluable contribution to relieving stress on the airframe, particularly in the terrain-following mode, and extending its operational life. As well as terrain following the AFCS provides flight path, airspeed, altitude, automatic throttle operation, roll attitude and Mach holds.

The flight director panel can also be used to establish heading hold, navigation and automatic approach modes, but as we saw in the Structure chapter its most valuable contribution is in damping out gust response. The AFCS has 11 Systron Donner servo/accelerometer packages distributed around the aircraft, containing a total of 27 individual inertial sensors. These monitor the linear acceleration in both vertical and horizontal planes, while providing angular rate inputs about all three axes of motion to the stability and control augmentation system. Extra packs also give lateral and vertical axes plus linear acceleration inputs to the automatic flight controls, and further contributions come from flight director computers and the military avionics systems.

The B-1B OAS differs considerably from that of the B-1A and nowhere more than in the radar fit. The B-1A carried two radars in the nose: the General Electric APQ-144 scanning radar, used for ground mapping and to obtain positional fixes for navigation, target location and weapons targeting; and the Texas Instruments APQ-146 terrain-following radar, both of which were derived from similar items used on the F-111. Both were replaced on the B-1B by the Westinghouse APQ-164 multimode radar which could be used for all these tasks and more besides.

The change stemmed partly from improved technology and partly from the need to reduce observables, and the APQ-164 was derived from the APG-66 fighter radar as used in the F-16, and the USAF Electronically Agile Radar re-

Above: At the heart of the OAS is the APQ-164 radar, the antenna of which is shown here during system integration. The black assembly on the mounting frame is a dummy load for testing without radiation.

Above right: The avionic systems operators' consoles are dominated by three CRT displays each side on which information is presented. While the systems are highly automated, the operators retain overall control through the integrated keyboards.

Right: The phased array antenna of the APQ-164 radar is canted down to reduce its radar reflectivity. Although in this picture it looks movable, it is fixed, and the radar beam is steered and pointed as required by electronic means.

Below: The baseline configuration for B-1B avionics is divided into five interacting parts. Many existing units are incorporated along with several entirely new ones, all linked by a quadruple MIL-STD-1553B EMUX (electronic multiplex) bus.

Avionic system baseline configuration

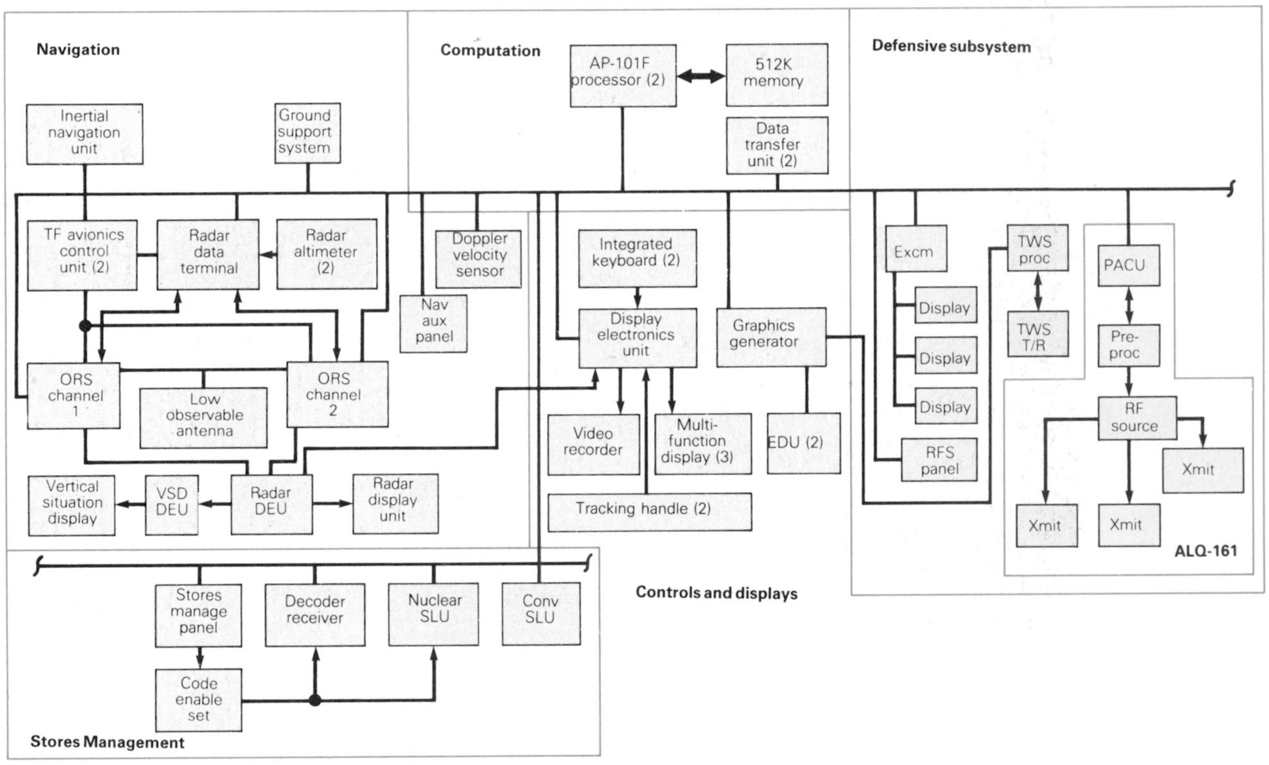

Left: The offensive avionic system operator's station and, below the CITS console on the central panel, the entrance to the tunnel giving access forward to the flight deck.

search programme, initiated in 1974. APG-66 technology included the dual mode transmitter, the Programmable Signal Processor (PSP), and certain other components, the resulting commonality saving an estimated $350 million, while the EAR programme contributed low-observable phased-array technology. The APQ-164 was selected in competition with a hybrid Hughes radar which combined features of the APG-63 and APG-65 as used in the F-15 Eagle and F-18 Hornet respectively.

APQ-164 is a dual-channel multimode coherent pulse-Doppler radar with a low observable antenna. The dual channel is used to provide systems redundancy and only one channel is actively used, the other being purely a backup. Unlike previous radars it has a fixed instead of a moving antenna and scanning is carried out electronically by the phased array, a feasible procedure because the scanning angles needed by a fighter radar are not required, and the angular variation can be more restricted. The antenna is pointed down, which helps reduce its radar return, as emissions from hostile radars will tend to be deflected downward rather than straight back on a reciprocal bearing. It is reported that its reflectivity to hostile radars is about two orders of magnitude less from the critical elevation and direction than were the two antenna carried by the B-1A.

APQ-164 operating modes

Recent information credits APQ-164 with 13 modes – real beam and high resolution ground mapping, terrain following, terrain avoidance, Doppler velocity up-date, rendezvous for in-flight refuelling, ground moving target indication and ground moving target track, weather detection and avoidance, ground or air beacon, monopulse measurement, and high altitude calibration. The two most important for the B-1B mission are likely to be ground mapping, which will be used for route navigation, updating waypoints, target location and attack, and terrain following.

Real beam mapping uses low pulse repetition frequency (prf) combined with non-coherent pulse-to-pulse frequency hopping (which avoids glint) to produce a small-scale radar map of the terrain ahead. This is good enough to identify large natural features such as lakes, although it does not have the definition to cope with small natural or man-made features. It is computer adjusted to give a vertical map presentation on the radar screen thus avoiding the possibility of misidentification of features due to slant distortion. Doppler beam sharpening can be used to give better definition over smaller areas, but the degree and ratios have not been released.

For really high resolution ground mapping, synthetic aperture radar (SAR) mode is used, and the definition provided is reported to be as good as low grade photography. The antenna can scan through any quadrant between 20° and 60° to either side of the aircraft's velocity vector – its mean course, taking into account drift and course corrections – and SAR works by receiving and processing the returning radar emissions over "a significant distance", which is the distance travelled by the B-1B during a

Left: OAS simulator in operation. A ground map is visible on the radar display unit, while alpha-numeric information is presented on the two multi-function displays.

set time. During this time the velocity of the radar returns from each particular point being illuminated alters in direct relationship to the changing angle; in other words, as the aircraft moves, so the angle to each individual point, and with it the characteristics of the radar reflection, alters. The general effect is that of having a radar antenna many hundreds of feet wide – wide enough, in fact, to present angular variation information. Further processing is then carried out to give a precise fixing for navigation updating, or an attacking solution for a target.

SAR is not new technology; it was first developed in the 1960s for reconnaissance purposes, but only in fairly recent times did the means become available for the extraction and presentation of radar data to permit targeting. The definition of SAR imagery on the B-1B is said to be so good that it will allow a landing on a damaged airfield at night or in bad weather without recourse to ground based landing aids, always suppossing that enough concrete remains. The full capabilities of SAR have not yet been released, but it seems reasonable to suppose that many functions will be enhanced by its use, apart from navigation and target acquisition.

When using either SAR or real beam mapping modes, the radar presents the picture on the radar display, or alternatively on one of the multi-function displays (MFDs) in the offensive avionics systems operator's position (the right-hand seat). When it becomes necessary to update the navigation via a pre-programmed waypoint, the display will place cross-hairs over the calculated position, and any deviation will show up as a displacement against the real point which will be depicted on the screen. The operator, via a tracking handle, then moves the cross-hairs to the exact spot, which automatically updates the navigation system and puts the aircraft precisely on track.

Terrain following modes

Terrain following is accomplished in a combination of three modes – hard, medium and soft – and any one of 11 ground clearance altitudes, the lowest of which is believed to be 200ft (60m) or less, selected according to the demands of the mission, the nature of the terrain to be traversed and the degree of threat. Obviously, in a high threat area hard ride and a low altitude will be optimum, but despite the low gust response of the B-1B and the smoothing effect of the SMCS system, prolonged flight in these conditions would be tiring, and would lower crew efficiency, so where it is reasonable to do so, a compromise solution is likely to be adopted between the demands of security and crew comfort.

Terrain-following radar scanning is not a continuous process, since although the beam is narrow, and fairly difficult to acquire by hostile monitoring stations, it is still an emission and thus subject to possible detection. Instead, a guidance algorithm developed by Boeing is used to compute the required flight path from the scan signal returns, and this also calculates when another scan should be made. The radar emissions are therefore intermittent rather than constant, making them more difficult to detect, especially over flat terrain where the intervals between scans will be less frequent than over hilly country. The flight path is scanned in a range/altitude profile out to roughly 10nm (18.5km) and the data passed to the radar and navigational computers, which calculate the flight profile to be followed and transmit the data to the terrain following control unit, which feeds commands into the flight control system.

Terrain avoidance, on the other hand, simply warns the pilot of obstacles, and it is then up to him to avoid them. Any of the 11 clearance altitudes can be selected according to the nature of the terrain, and the radar scan works to this level. Only obstacles that reach higher than the selected altitude are shown on the pilot's and co-pilot's situation displays whereas in terrain following mode both the flight path and the terrain profile are presented for monitoring.

The OAS contains a total of 66 LRUs of 41 different types, and the complete shipset weighs 2,883lb (1,308kg). In all, 20kVA of power are needed to run it. So far we have considered only the radar, but there many other systems, mainly to do with navigational functions, plus the computer bloc.

Precise navigation over very long distances is essential to the success of the mission, and while the radar modes can help considerably by pinpointing waypoints and geographical features, they are no more than aids. The inertial navigation system (INS), however, is of fundamental importance. The entire route is carefully planned beforehand and the details preprogrammed onto a cassette tape which is fed into the navigation system.

Above: The first B-1B in system checkout at Palmdale. Unpainted, the aircraft shows the dielectric panels at the wing root and the base and tip of the fin behind which receivers and transmitters for the ALQ-161 system are located.

The INS is precisely aligned before takeoff, or possibly in the air in the event of an emergency scramble, and a complex system of sensors feeds information into the INS during flight, enabling it to keep track of the aircraft's position to a high degree of accuracy. The B-1A carried redundant twin Litton inertial systems, but upgraded requirements for the B-1B, stated as a factor of 2.5 better unaided inertial accuracy, doubled accuracy (or halved error) in weapons release, and a three times more accurate attitude reference for the radar in the terrain following or avoidance modes, called for something better.

The unit chosen was the Singer Kearfott SKN-2440, two of which are installed in the development B-1Bs, although only one is to be carried in operational aircraft; should it be found desirable to retrofit a second, the wiring is already in place. SKN-2440 is a development of the SKN-2416 and SKN-2430 as used on the F-16, and the associated sensors are the Teledyne APN-218 Doppler velocity sensor, which is a modified variant of that used in the B-52, and dual Honeywell APN-224 radar altimeters, also used on the B-52. These items replaced their

ALQ-161 defensive avionic system configuration

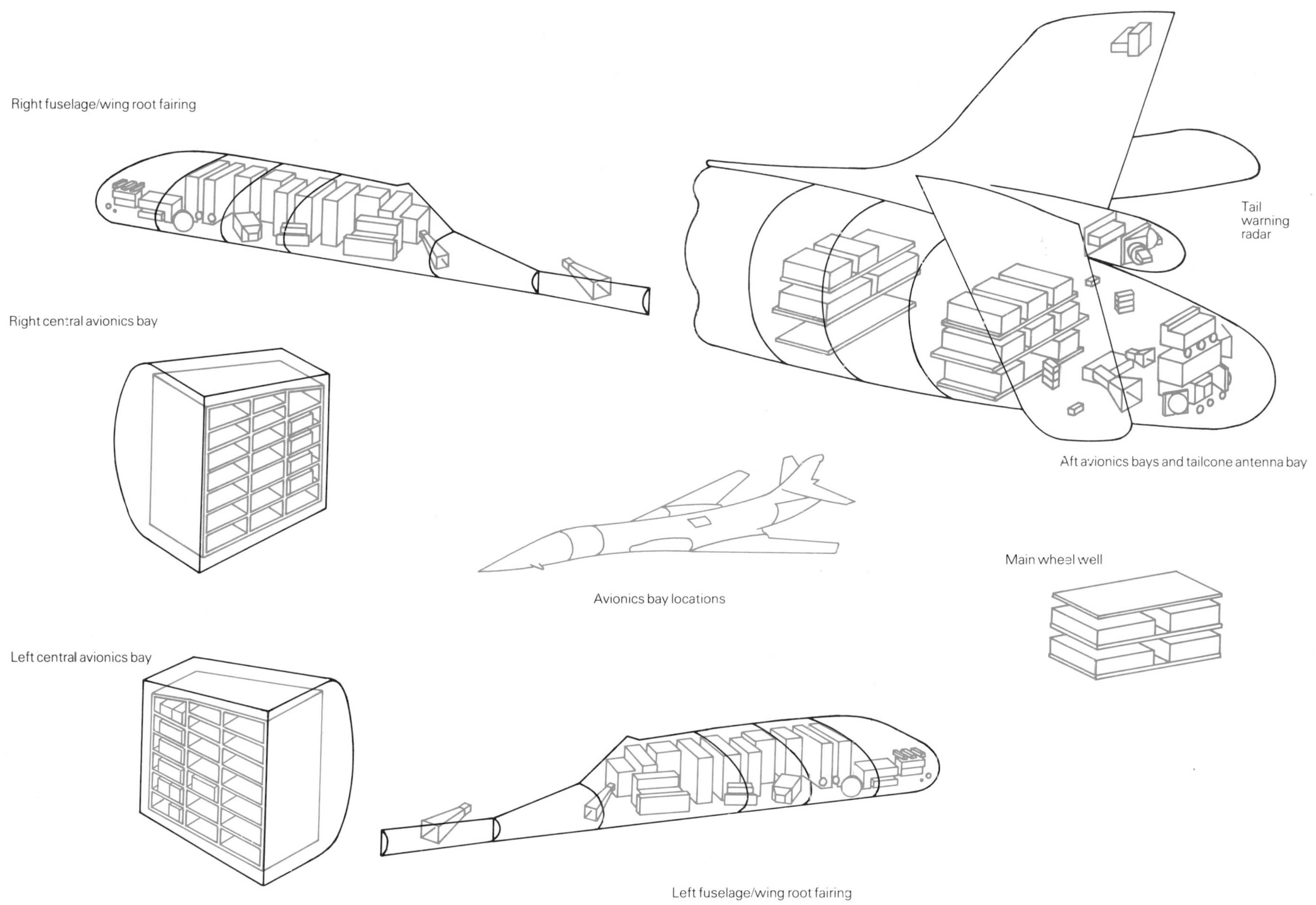

Above: The Eaton ALQ-161 defensive avionic system comprises no fewer than 107 separate units dispersed around the aircraft to give comprehensive coverage. It is designed to detect and defeat known and projected threats.

Right: Both the OAS and the DAS are heavily reliant on LRUs, one of which, a component of the ALQ-161, is seen here. Serviceability is greatly eased when a faulty unit can be replaced within minutes by a ground crewman wearing gloves.

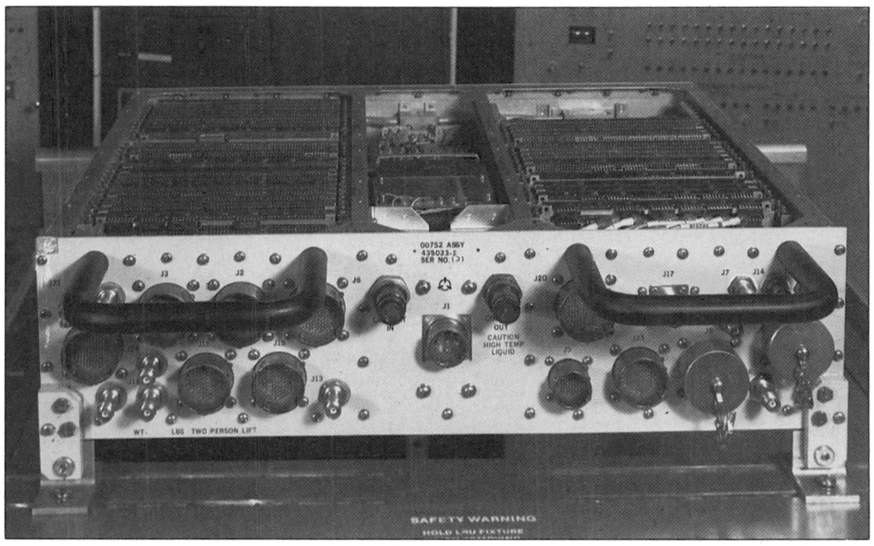

counterparts on the B-1A, whose gimballed Doppler motion sensor was found to be unsatisfactory and was replaced by the non-gimballed Teledyne APN-200 in 1976, and the Honeywell APN-194 radar altimeter.

It was proposed in 1982 to support APN-218 with the Honeywell AAN-131 precision navigation system, but this seems to have been dropped. Other aids proposed for the B-1A were a Hughes forward-looking infra red (FLIR) sensor and a Dalmo-Victor low light television (LLTV), which were to have made up the electro-optical viewing system. In 1976 it was reported that the FLIR was to be hardened against EMP and redesigned for a new location along the aircraft centreline, but this was never implemented, and no electro-optical sensors were scheduled for the B-1B by early 1986, although Low Altitude Navigation and Targeting Infra Red at Night (Lantirn) may well be incorporated if trials are successful.

Computers play a big part in tying the OAS and its associated systems together. The B-1A used the Singer Kearfott 2070 in the OAS, but in 1976 the USAF directed Boeing to look for a cheaper alternative as part of the design to cost directive. The B-1B uses the IBM AP-101F, a dual architecture computer compatible with both the MIL-STD-1553 and -1750 databuses, which was developed from the AP-101C as used in the OAS of the B-52, and it was originally anticipated that an updated variant of the B-52 model would be used, but the AP-101F turned out to be different enough to warrant a new designation. The radar incorporates two AP-101Fs dedicated to terrain following, one of which is on the backup system as described earlier. These compare the actual flight path with the calculated flight path and command corrections from the flight control system.

At the very centre of the OAS lie four AP-101Fs, navigation, control and display, and weapons control occupying one each while the fourth serves for backup while monitoring critical functions. All the computers connect with a mass memory unit with a capacity of 512K words, including the AP-101F in the CITS and another in the defensive avionic system. The taped mission instructions are fed into this via two Sundstrand data transfer units, while a mass of information, such as data on known hostile emitter characteristics, is also stored ready to be called up on demand. The memory unit is a development of that used in the B-52 OAS, and uses a core memory rather than the drum storage device used in the B-1A. It is believed that this unit is slightly more vulnerable to TREES (transient response of electronic equipment and systems), which is the effect of exposure to gamma rays and high energy particles, but that the advantages of the system more than outweigh the disadvantages.

More exotic items apart, the B-1B carries the usual sort of avionics kit one would expect – VHF and HF radios, TACAN, ILS and so on, plus secure voice communications. Most of these have been checked and in some cases modified to give the required degree of EMP and TREES hardening. The B-1A was fitted with the ASC-19 satellite communications set but, rather surprisingly, the Air Force is not planning to fit a satellite signal receiver for the Navstar Global Positioning System in the B-1B.

Rumour also has it that bistatic radar has been under consideration for the B-1B. This is a type of radar where the transmitter and receiver have separate antennas which in airborne use are mounted on separate illuminator and attacker aircraft. The transmitter, which is announcing its presence to the enemy by its emissions, remains in neutral or friendly airspace, while the receiver homes on the reflected emissions without betraying its presence. Presumably, if bistatic radar were adopted, the B-1B would carry the receiver while a B-52 operating in the stand-off role could carry the transmitter. A test programme was initiated by the USAF in 1980, at which time considerable technical problems remained to be overcome, not the

Above: Ergonomic checkout of the DAS console. The two EDUs show the EW environment in graphic form, while tabulated information is presented on the MFD.

Electronically steerable transmit antenna

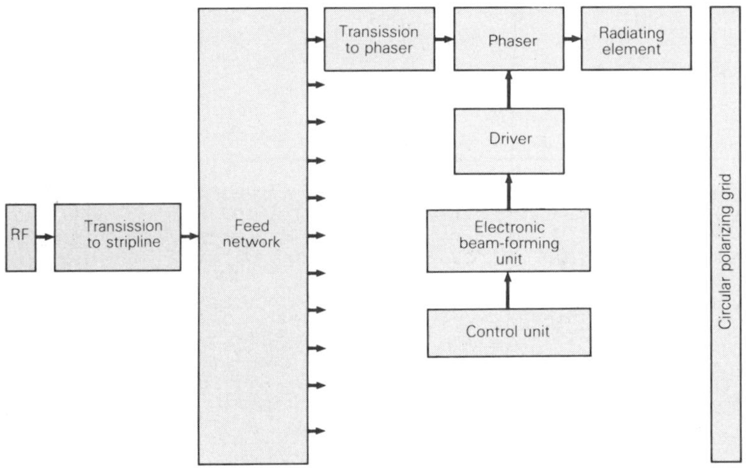

Left: The B-1B carries nine of these Sedco Systems antennas, three each for jamming on Bands 6, 7 and 8, with one for each band in each wing root and in the tailcone.

least of which were the ability to compensate for precise relative navigation and motion, and transmitter/receiver geometry. The operational use of bistatic radar by the B-1B appears to involve considerable difficulties, and no official announcements have been made.

Stores management is a separate subsystem within the OAS. Developed from a similar article on the B-52, it provides status information for the systems operator and control for both conventional and nuclear weapons. The weapon status data is provided by logic units mounted on the rotary launchers in the weapons bays and is shown on the OAS operator's MFD. At the same time, it can command signals to the weapons issued from the OAS switch panel via the computer system. As an obvious precaution against finger trouble or accidental release, the release of nuclear weapons demands two man operation, with controls too widely spaced for one man operability – standard procedure where nuclear weapon delivery systems are concerned. One set of switches is located in the front (pilot's) area of the cockpit while the other set is in the systems operators' section, and a quite complicated procedure is involved, a code enabler set being used to obtain two-station consent for release while a decoder/receiver provides the interface with the weapons.

The OAS consists of many different subsystems carrying out different functions, but linked together and monitored and controlled primarily by the OAS operator; the Defensive Avionic System (DAS), on the other hand, is a much more cohesive system, a fact reflected in its Air Force systems designation of AN/ALQ-161. ALQ-161 is an advanced system devoted mainly to electronic countermeasures, although some infra-red kit is included. In all, including antennas, black boxes, displays and controls, it totals 107 separate items, of which 52 are unique to the system. Most are LRUs weighing between 40lb and 80lb (18-36kg), easily accessible and very quickly replaceable. Total system weight, excluding cables, displays and control units, is about 5,200lb (2,360kg), and when its full jamming capability is utilized it consumes roughly 120kW of power, the equivalent of 120 microwave ovens working simultaneously.

Defensive avionics

Penetration is central to the primary B-1B mission: remaining undetected is the best aid to penetration, and the low-level terrain-following flight path and the low-observables technology built into the design are steps toward this goal. Even so, undetected penetration could only be assured by silence and invisibility – to radar and infra-red detection as well as to the human eyeball – and there is no way to conceal an aeroplane weighing more than 200 tons. This is where ALQ-161 comes in as a vital second line of defence.

Modern air defence systems are heavily reliant on radar. The human eye can be defeated by the cover of darkness, or by bad weather; the human ear was never much good against even high and slow targets, and the B-1B is certainly not that; and infra-red also has drawbacks as a means of primary detection. All of which leaves radar detection, which can sometimes, although by no means always, be circumvented by low flying and terrain masking. But sooner or later, in a comprehensive defensive radar system, even the low-observable B-1B will be located. The trick then is to conceal not its presence, but its exact location, course, and speed. ALQ-161 uses antennas, located around the airframe to give 360° cover, which can tell when it is being painted by a hostile radar. The system then deploys what amounts to protective electronic camouflage by jamming or deceiving the enemy radars. It cannot conceal its presence by these means – *something* must be there to cause the jamming – but it can conceal its location, identity and purpose from the detection system.

In hardware terms, the ALQ-161 has changed little between the B-1A and the B-1B. Although the computers and the data bus are of improved types with greater capacity, the main improvement comes from programmability. Far more advanced programs are now possible, and full use is being made of them.

ALQ-161 is for all practical purposes fully automatic, with the operator acting as a systems manager, monitoring operations but only actively intervening in circumstances where human judgement is felt to be superior to that of the computer programs. It is anticipated that programming advances will be able to keep pace with the abilities of threat radars for many years to come, with updated software obviating the need for new hardware.

The fourth B-1A featured a dorsal spine extending from just behind the cockpit to the fin. This was connected with an experimental monopulse radar

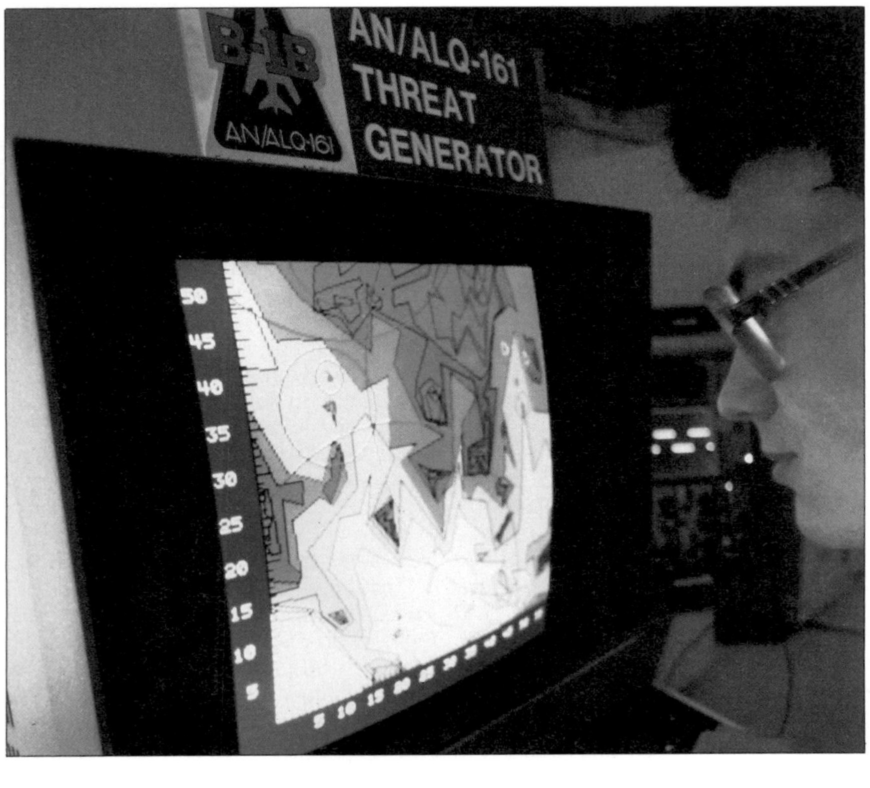

Left: Much of the development work for ALQ-161 was carried out on a simulator – the ALQ-161 Threat Generator, which depicts stylized terrain complete with threats.

ALQ-161 operation

This graphic representation of the ALQ-161's automatic response to detected threats shows threats of increasing frequency from bottom to top and the system's response as time progresses from left to right. The high-priority threat in the top row and the area surveillance radar in the row below are jammed (indicated by the box) until the system has ceased to receive transmissions, as is the high-priority radar in the third row. To deal with the two frequency-hopping radars in the fourth and sixth rows the jammer must transmit over a broader frequency band – using spot jamming against the former and a pulse repeat-back technique against the latter, which covers a wider range – and when a new high-priority threat of undetermined characteristics is detected (bottom row) the frequency-hopping area surveillance radar is left unjammed temporarily to allow power to be concentrated on continuous jamming of the new threat until its scan and pulse rate and other characteristics can be assessed and output can be matched to the individual pulses. Jamming of the continuous-wave radar is also interrupted when the system has to cope with the unclassified threat and the high-priority frequency-hopper, and again when pulses from the two remaining high-priority threats coincide. High-threat emitters would be those associated with AA systems.

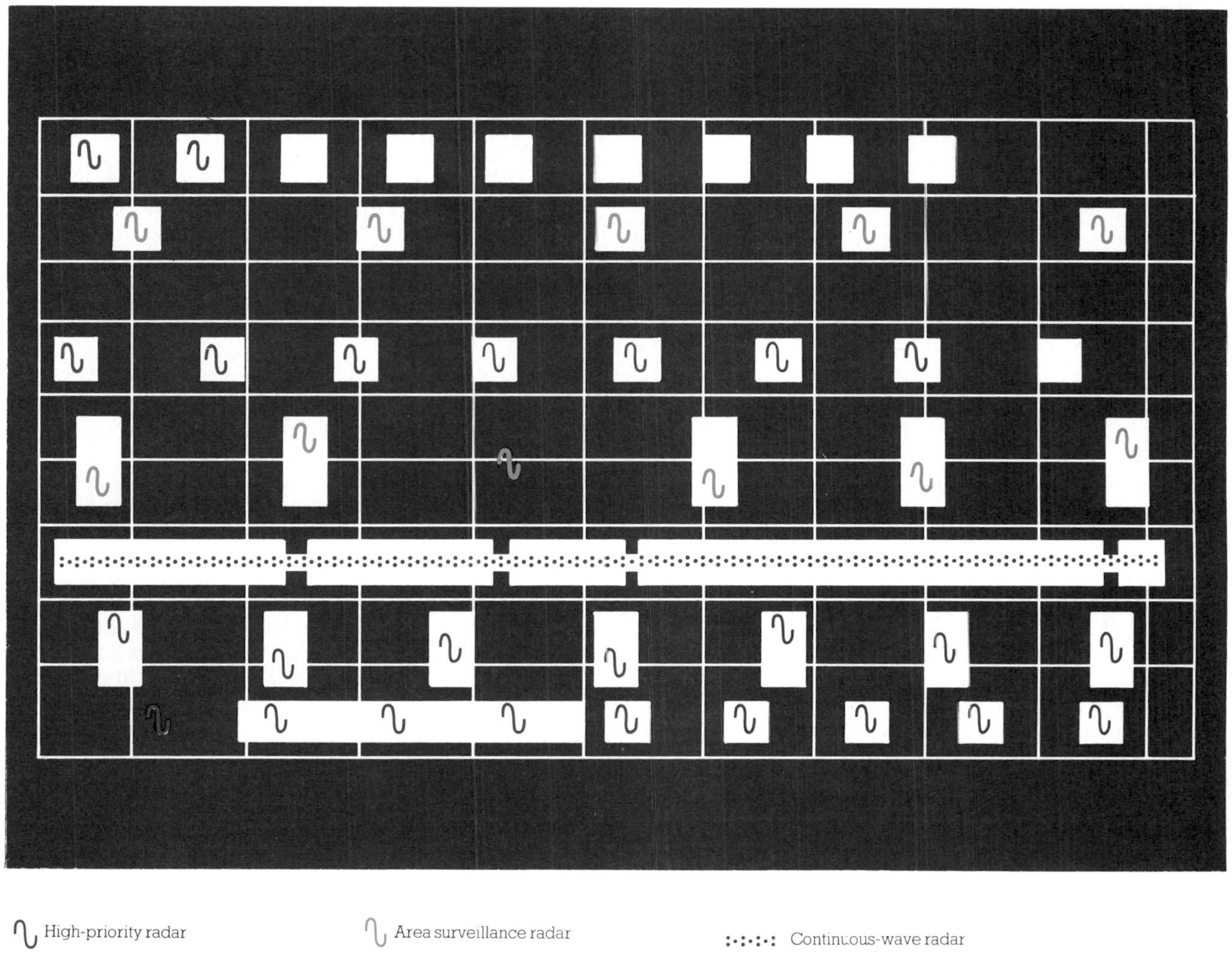

jamming system called Cross-Eye, developed by Kuras-Alterman, and housed a waveguide; little has been published on it, and it is not carried by the B-1B. The latter does, however, carry the Westinghouse ALQ-153 tail warning radar, the function of which is to detect both aircraft and missiles approaching from astern. As this is an emitter, it would appear to contradict the purpose of ALQ-161 by giving hostile defences something to track, but it is the only piece of equipment able to give warning of, say, a fighter making a visual, no-radar attack from this quarter, and will probably only be used in circumstances where a high risk of such an attack exists.

ALQ-161's operational sequence is listen, detect, classify, establish priority and activate countermeasures. Listening and detection is carried out by electronically steered phased array antennas mounted in the leading edges of the wing gloves and in the tail, each covering an arc of 120° in azimuth and 90° in elevation to provide all-round coverage. The band width is believed to range between VHF, which is used by some Soviet early warning and ground control interception radars, and I/J band, which is used by fighters and surface-to-air missiles. The system is designed to work in a very high threat environment, using jamming in near real time against multiple emitters, without becoming overloaded.

ALQ-161 is basically a passive listening system, only resorting to active countermeasures when absolutely necessary. This is a matter for fine judgement, either by the artificial intelligence of the computer program or by the Defensive Systems Officer, who can override the computer program and delay the onset of jamming if the circumstances warrant. For example, a few faint strobes from an early warning radar do not guarantee that the bomber has been detected, and if jamming is initiated too soon, it will simply confirm that something is out there and alert the system.

When the antennas on the B-1B start picking up hostile radar emissions they pass the basic data to the direction and frequency receivers. The directional receiver sorts out a location for the emitters while the computers analyse the frequency data, which includes tracking radar pulse trains and waveforms, enabling the types of emitter to be identified and assigned threat priorities. Near real-time processing is provided by six data buses which receive information from nine high speed computers called Jamming Logic Allocation Units housed in two black boxes referred to as Jam Logic A and Jam Logic B. The system is controlled by a single IBM AP-101F computer.

Speed and co-ordination are the keynotes of ALQ-161. It is impossible for the B-1B to carry enough jamming transmitters to deal with hostile radars on a one-for-one basis, and ECM is managed on a time-share basis, with jamming priority going to the greatest threat. Where possible, jamming emissions are broadcast on a narrow beamwidth to reduce the power necessary, hopping from threat to threat within milliseconds to give the greatest possible coverage. The number of emitters that the jamming transmitter can cope with simultaneously is quite amazing, and this over a wide frequency spectrum. The system is extremely flexible, and even when the jamming transmitters are heavily engaged the detection subsystem can continue to monitor old signals and detect new ones, even when the jammer is working in the same frequency band. ALQ-161 is configured in such a way that antenna pointing, frequency modulation, and activation are all optimized against the threat radars. If a threat radar ceases

Right: An articulated test assembly is used to check the pattern of emissions from ALQ-161 tailcone antennas. The hoist and platform have anechoic shrouds to eliminate unwanted echoes.

B-1B stores configurations

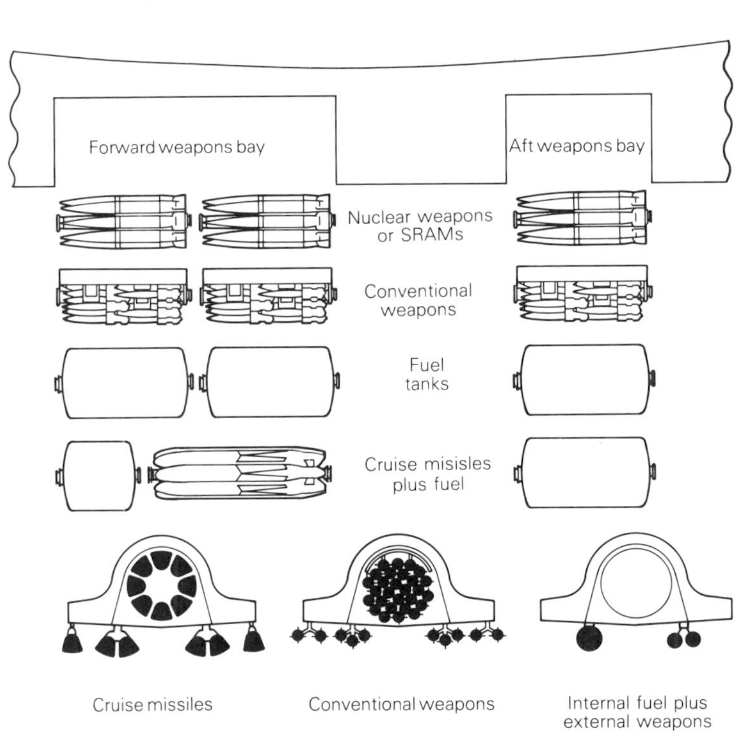

transmitting, the jamming directed against it is automatically stopped.

The Defensive Systems Officer is kept abreast of the situation via two Sanders CRT displays. One of these is a conventional Plan Position Indicator, which depicts the aircraft and its planned track against a background of threat emitters, which are presented in an alpha-numeric format. The other CRT gives a panoramic picture of the situation with details of the emitters. A cursor can be used to give a more detailed display of any desired area together with a list of both the emitter characteristics and up to five countermeasures modes that can be used aginst it. The DSO can hook in to the system by means of a keyboard if it becomes necessary to take any direct

Left: The movable bulkhead in the forward weapons bay allows ALCMs to be carried. It is unlikely to carry external weapons on missions involving low-level penetration.

Below: SRAMs are loaded onto one of the three rotary launchers that can be carried by the B-1B. Each launcher carries eight missiles for a total internal load of 24.

action to modify what ALQ-161 is doing automatically.

The B-1B also carries passive countermeasures in the form of chaff and IR flare decoys. The chaff and flare dispenser is in the top of the fuselage behind the crew compartment, in two rows, with forced ejection of both chaff and flares. Dispensing is automatic, controlled by ALQ-161, or manual, controlled by the DSO, who carefully monitors the supplies remaining at any given moment.

Another feature of ALQ-161 is the monitoring network, Status Evaluation and Test (SEAT), which is linked to the CITS. Any system degradation or failure is overcome by the CITS computer, an IBM AP-101F, which uses a data bus to bypass faulty units and thereby maintain full ECM capability.

Weapons

The weapons load carried by the B-1B is awesome in its destructive power, as the accompanying table shows. Of the nuclear gravity weapons, the B-83 is believed to be considered the primary weapon for the B-1B, with the B-61 a possible alternative, while the B-28 and B-43 are getting rather long in the tooth. The B-83 weighs 2,408lb (1,092kg) and

has a yield of one megaton. Fuzing takes place in flight and can be set for either air or ground burst. It is parachute retarded, and can be dropped from any altitude between 150ft and 50,000ft (46-15,240m), and a new parachute design allows air drops to be made at transonic speeds, and slows the bomb to 60mph (97km/hr). B-61 is a similar but lighter weapon, weighing about 800lb (363kg), and has a yield of between 10 and 500 kilotons.

	Internal	External
Nuclear gravity		
B-28	12	8
B-43	12	14
B-61	24	14
B-83	24	14
Nuclear guided		
AGM-69 SRAM	24	14
AGM-86B ALCM	8	14
Conventional		
Mk 82	84	14
Mk 84	24	14

The Boeing AGM-69 Short Range Attack Missile (SRAM) was developed during the 1960s as a supersonic rocket propelled defence suppression weapon. Both speed and range vary according to the speed and altitude of the launch aircraft, between Mach 2.8 and 3.2, and 35 to 105 miles (56-169km), and warhead yield is 200kT. Production ceased on 1975, but over 1,000 SRAMs remain in the inventory. Once launched it is a difficult weapon to stop, as it has an offset homing ability which enables it even to turn around and strike at a target astern of the launching aircraft.

In 1985 a competition was launched to develop a new short range attack missile, provisionally called SRAM II, to be carried by the B-1B. It is to be smaller than AGM-69 and rocket propelled, and the contending companies are Boeing Aerospace, Martin Marietta Aerospace, and McDonnell Douglas Astronautics. The decision was expected to be made in the first half of 1986, with production of some 1,900 missiles to begin in 1989.

The AGM-86B Air Launched Cruise Missile (ALCM), another Boeing product, played a part in the cancellation of the B-1A when it was thought that it could replace the manned bomber in the penetration role if launched from a stand-off carrier such as the B-52. A jet propelled subsonic missile with a speed of only about 435kt (805km/h), it has a range of some 1,300nm (2,500km) and carries a 200kT warhead. To reach its target it follows a terrain-hugging path using a sophisticated INS and Terrain Contour Matching (Tercom) guidance system, which compares the surface of the area that it is overflying with profiles stored in the computer memory.

The B-1B has also been considered for the maritime surveillance and patrol function. Both the MK-36 and MK-60 sea mine have been mentioned in this connection, while the AGM-84A Harpoon anti-shipping missile is said to be compatible with the B-1B wiring, although certain interface equipment would have to be installed and the correct pylons bolted on.

For self-defence against an air threat, Asraam is the most likely possibility. A short-range, all-aspect heat seeking missile, it would require certain modifications to be made to the OAS, and rails or pylons to be fitted.

While a considerable amount of ordnance can be hung on the outside of the B-1B, this cannot do other than prejudice its stealth qualities. For the deep penetration mission, it will probably rely on the content of its vast weapons bays. These contain quick-acting rotary launchers with eight weapons stations on each, and in theory all eight SRAMs on one launcher can be pre-targeted and released within 45 seconds. Undergoing trials at the moment is the Common Strategic Rotary Launcher (CSRL), which will also be used by the B-52. This consists of carbon fibre epoxy tubes 14ft (4.27m) long and 1.75ft (0.53m) in diameter. Aluminium collars at the ends attach the tubes to the aircraft, while six aluminium rings on each tube carry the weapons mounts. A weight saving of some 400lb (181kg) each is achieved by using aluminium instead of steel.

Right: The second prototype B-1 drops an inert B-61 nuclear weapon over the range. The parachute retards the weapon, allowing the fast-flying bomber to evade the explosions.

Below: The B-1 with all weapon bay doors open is an impressive sight, even though only a single bomb is falling. Release and separation appear to have been very clean.

Right: The T-38 chase bird keeps a close watch as iron bombs are discharged from the forward weapons bay at fairly low level over the PIRA, located not far from Edwards.

Deployment

The first B-1B was rolled out with due ceremony at Palmdale on September 4, 1985, five months ahead of schedule; the event was greeted by Air Force Secretary Verne Orr with the words, "We don't build bombers to go to war. We build them to keep from going to war. May it never fly in anger." While this laudable sentiment emphasized the deterrent nature of the B-1B, there has been no shortage of attempts to find alternative missions for what is, after all, the world's most expensive military aircraft. It is ironic that one of the alternative roles was described as "a show of force and an expression of national resolve" when the aircraft has been made as near invisible as possible.

Above: Originally, the B-1 mission was to involve refuelling after takeoff, but the revised requirement for the B-1B called for the ability to take off with full fuel and continue without support.

At the time of the first B-1B roll-out the first and third B-1A prototypes had been retired from the flight test programme while the second had been lost in a tragic accident. Meanwhile, the fourth B-1A was well along with flight testing the avionic systems in an intensive programme which had started during the previous July and was scheduled to continue for nearly two years, with a total of 380 flying hours, until mid-June 1986, when the official full scale development testing was due to terminate.

At first concentrating on the defensive avionics system, the fourth B-1A's flight programme, carried out from Edwards AFB, allowed flights every Thursday, with every third flight used as a backup to cover the scheduled test points that for one reason or another (and we saw examples of that in the account of the flight that ended in the loss of the second B-1A) had been missed or re-scheduled. High altitude calibration and initial air alignment for weapons release were also carried out by this aircraft.

To expedite the offensive avionics testing, a BAC-111 airliner was fitted out as a flying testbed for the radar systems. This had the advantage that the black boxes could be spread through the fuselage, giving ease of access during flight. The adapted BAC-111 first flew in this role on July 3, 1984, at the start of a year-long programme, concentrating at first on the detailed ground mapping modes.

The first production B-1B joined the flight test programme on October 18, 1984. Fully instrumented for testing such areas as structures, flight control systems and weapons separation, it also carried a fully working offensive avionics system on its first flight, and a considerable proportion of the flight test programme was devoted to working the (unspecified) bugs out of the OAS. The initial emphasis was placed on high resolution ground mapping and fix taking from both high and low altitudes, using synthetic aperture techniques with the radar trained up to 15° sideways. The INS also had to be checked out, and instrument approaches demonstrated in poor visibility with no ground landing aids, using the aircraft's on-board systems; and there were some simulated releases of gravity weapons.

For various reasons, which will become apparent, a certain amount of flight testing at very high all-up weights was not possible with this aircraft. Test flight day from Edwards AFB was Wednesday, so as not to clash with the B-1A, and a similar routine of two flights followed by a backup was adopted. In August 1985 the initial production configuration of the ALQ-161

Left: One effect of the European One camouflage scheme is the dramatic changes of colour that occur with changing light conditions: radar may be the main threat, but visual concealment still matters.

Above: KC-135 boom operator's view of the B-1B. The original black markings, seen here, caused the operators severe problems in judging depth while positioning the booms, especially in darkness.

Above: The solution was to add high-visibility white aim pattern markings around the receptacle and on the SMCS vanes, a move which the USAF is satisfied does not affect overall visual signature.

Below: To protect the crew against thermonuclear flash blindness aluminium shields with ceramic portholes are being installed to cover the cockpit transparencies within 150 microseconds.

defensive avionics system was fixed, and shortly afterward the first B-1B was withdrawn from the flight test programme to undergo structural proof loading tests until December of that year. The first SRAM launch had been scheduled for around August or September, but was deferred until after the next aircraft, the ninth production B-1B, joined the test programme.

No 9 is the first machine to incorporate the removable bulkhead between the front weapons bays, and is therefore the first B-1B capable of flying ALCM trials. It was scheduled for delivery on March 15, 1986, and in addition to ALCM and SRAM testing, it will also participate in the testing of flight control, flying qualities and flight at heavy all-up weights.

The 100,000lb (45,360kg) increase in the gross weight of the B-1B compared with the B-1A caused certain problems. The design does not stall in the classic manner where the wings lose lift at a certain combination of speed and angle of attack (AoA), accompanied by wing drop: instead, the aircraft tends to pitch up. The AoA limit is set by the neutral stability of the aircraft, and a Stall Inhibitor System (SIS) was developed to prevent the pilot going past the neutral AoA point by providing a limit in the flight control system with a small built-in safety margin. The SIS has been installed and successfully flown in the first B-1B and is being added to production aircraft on the line from No 10 onwards, and will at some point be retrofitted to the earlier aircraft.

However, at very heavy weights, flying at the AoA limit imposed by the SIS simply does not give sufficient lift in some flight regimes, and the only answer is to exceed the neutral stability limitations. In order to do this with safety, and in many cases to do so at all, some form of artificial stability must be provided, and a Stability Enhancement Function (SEF) has been added to the existing stability control augmentation system. The result is similar in effect to the fly-by-wire system used in the F-16, and by permitting safe controlled flight in what would otherwise be unstable regions of the flight envelope, will expand the envelope out to a full heavyweight condition. Manufactured by Sperry to a Rockwell design, SEF is first scheduled to fly in No 9, where it will be proved, and will be featured in production line aircraft from No 19 onward. SEF will also be retrofitted to the earlier aircraft at some unspecified date.

Below: Escorted by an F-111 and a T-38, the second B-1A prototype releases a SRAM over one of the Edwards weapons ranges during stores separation trials. This drop was made in July 1984.

Bottom: The fact that the rocket motor has not ignited indicates that this is a dummy round: the genuine article would already have started the process of accelerating to its top speed of around Mach 3.

The defensive avionic system is scheduled for a thorough workout in the first quarter of 1986, using the B-1A and the first production B-1B. It is to be subjected to a carefully programmed sequence of tests against simulated threat environments with both the variety and intensity of the emissions gradually increasing. Operational integration with AWACS will also take place at some stage, while the tail warning radar will be tested against simulated airborne interceptions. Finally, the DAS will be evaluated against a hostile multi-threat environment.

Weapons trials will continue, and the first carriage and launch trials with ALCM are scheduled to commence in August 1986, lasting for 13 months. These will of course use B-1B No 9, which will be joined by No 28, which should become available from October 31, 1986, and which has been designated to carry out extra ALCM trials and also weapons development work with new, stealthy cruise missiles.

The loss of the second B-1A had little or no effect on the test programme, which is on target for IOC by July 1986. The crash, did, however, cause modifications to the FCGMS to be considered. In the manual mode, mishandling of which led to the disaster, an out-of-cg condition causes an orange light to illuminate as a warning: this light is located low on the dash, and it is believed that it may have been obscured by the crewmen's knees. Following modifications the light is now red, and from aircraft No 19 on it is being relocated to the glareshield, directly in the pilot's line of vision, while an aural warning has also been added in the form of a horn, and neither light nor horn can be switched off until the out-of-cg condition has been corrected.

Automatic-to-manual

Another modification involves the procedure for changing from automatic to manual modes. In the original system a free-floating toggle switch was used, but this has been replaced, again from No 19 onward, by a double-action lever lock switch. Both modifications will be retrofitted to the earlier B-1Bs in due course.

A further modification, proposed but still not implemented by early 1986, is the adoption of a wing sweep detent, a mechanical stop similar to that used in the F-111. Pumping fuel around the bomber is all very well, but it takes a certain amount of time, and in the manual mode sufficient time may not be allowed. The detent is a reminder to the pilot to check the cg position before sweeping the wings further; it works by stiffening the wing sweep control so that the pilot needs steadily increasing force to move it, until it will physically go no further while an out-of-cg condition exists. It will of course adjust as the fuel transfers and the cg position shifts. Rockwell have also suggested that a voice warning system could be adopted in lieu of the horn. This would be rather similar to the system used in the F-15, but if it is adopted it can hardly be built in on the production line before No 32, which will leave a lot of retrofitting to do.

Several incidents have occurred involving foreign object damage (FOD) to the engines, mainly to the fan blades. A few of these have been mysterious, with material similar to that used in the aircraft being found in the engines although nothing has been missing, and improved

Right: The second production B-1B touches down at Offutt AFB on June 27, 1985. Scheduled to fly on to Dyess two days later it suffered FOD during the landing and the No 1 B-1B took its place.

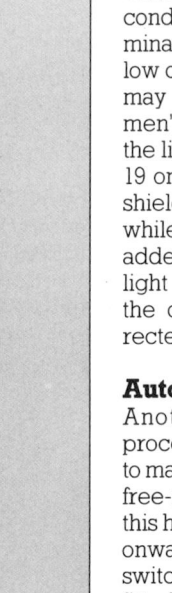

inspection procedures on the production line have been instituted as a preventative measure.

One incident involving B-1B No 1 was fairly straightforward. An avionics compartment forward of the intakes contains a special rack for test equipment, and a loose bolt from the rack came out from the compartment through a louvred cover. At least, so it appears: little FOD material was found in the engine, but what there was matched that of the missing bolt. A fix was easily found involving a new louvred cover with smaller slots.

At least two other FOD incidents have involved the air cooler flapper doors, which control the flow of air through ram air ducts for the environmental control system. At speeds exceeding Mach 0.45 the flapper doors, which at 5in by 7in (127mm by 178mm) are quite small, open to permit the entry of ram air; below this speed a sensor-controlled hydraulic powered blower fan forces the doors to close as the ram air flow diminishes. In both cases the doors appeared to have come apart in flight, and as they were located forward and between each pair of engines the debris had been ingested.

One incident came at a rather embarrassing moment. B-1B No 2 was the much heralded first operational aircraft to enter Strategic Air Command service, and was due to be handed over with great ceremony at Dyess AFB, Texas, on June 29, 1985, but as it came in to land at SAC Headquarters at Offutt AFB, Nebraska, on June 28 the flapper doors duly came unglued and FODed both engines on one side. Of course the aircraft was grounded as a result, and No 1 had to be flown post-haste from Edwards for the handover. The ceremony was duly performed; some 50,000 spectators had a great day out, and the only harm done was to the accuracy of some of the Press reports.

However minor the cause, engine FOD is a potentially dangerous problem, so measures were immediately put in hand to cure it and with typical American thoroughness, these were implemented in three phases. Phase I addressed the immediate problem of keeping the aircraft flying, and consisted of securing the existing assembly by using thicker bolts, extra washers, and locking wires. Phase II was instituted to find out whether the cheap and easy Phase I solution could be made permanent: the plan is to fix instruments to the left engine nacelle of the No 4 B-1A in order to find out exactly what aerodynamic forces are operating within the duct to cause the failures. Phase III is a Rockwell redesign of the flapper door assembly to reduce the number of parts, in case Phase II shows that Phase I can only be an interim solution.

One of the latest B-1B revisions concerns the life support systems. Oxygen for the crew is normally carried in cylinders in the form of liquid oxygen (lox), or as high pressure gas. An added hazard in a crash or battle situation, these are being replaced with a recently developed oxygen generating system by Normalair-Garrett, which draws sufficient oxygen from the engine bleed air by using a Zeolite nitrogen filtering system.

First operational base

Dyess AFB, near Abilene, Texas, was announced as the home of the first operational B-1B bomber unit by President Reagan on January 21, 1983. The resident 96th Bomb Wing consisted of two squadrons, the 337th Bomb Squadron, equipped with B-52H Stratofortresses, and the 917th Air Refuelling Squadron with KC-135A Stratotankers. The B-52s were phased out between August 1984 and January 1985 to make way for their replacement, while the tanker unit prepared to develop in-flight

Above: The bomb bay doors are highlighted during a test flight. Only the forward bay is long enough to accommodate the 20.8ft (6.3m) length of the ALCM.

Below: The rotary launcher used for SRAMs and B-61 nuclear bombs is capable of carrying eight weapons with a combined total weight of 25,000lb (11,340kg).

Left: The crew access ladder is located immediately behind the nosewheel: in an alert the crew would be expected to get aboard and have the aircraft off the ground in a matter of minutes.

Above: Maintenance personnel infiltrate the wing glove fairing to work on the central hydraulic reservoir, which is located above and between the engines.

refuelling techniques for the B-1B. The 337th will also be responsible for instructing other tanker units which are part of future B-1B equipped wings.

As the first B-1B unit, the 96th BMW will differ slightly in composition from the ordinary. The 337th BS will be the first standard operational squadron, but it will be preceded into service by the 4018th Combat Crew Training Squadron, a dedicated aircrew training unit which was activated at Dyess on March 15, 1985. Also based at Dyess is Detachment 1 of the 4201st Test and Evaluation Squadron from Edwards. This unit is responsible for follow-on testing and evaluation on the B-1B and also for training the cadre of B-1B instructors assigned to the 4018th CCTS. The 4201st detachment will have no aircraft specifically assigned to them, but will use those of the 4018th, some 15 aircraft initially, notwithstanding that other seemingly authoritative sources put the figure at 10.

The 96th BW will take 11 aircraft on strength at first, plus three spares, a total three less than the normal squadron establishment of 16,plus one spare, though it will have a full complement of 22 operational crews. Doubtless this situation will regularize itself when the training role of the 4018th CCTS diminishes, as it will when all units are up to strength and the requirement is reduced to the replacement of time-expired crews. Delivery of the 100th and last B-1B was originally scheduled for July or August 1988, but has now been brought forward to April 30 of that year.

The original mission envisaged for the B-1A was the deep penetration of the Soviet Union to make precision strikes on defended targets, and critics have often asked why this could not be left to the ICBM and SLBM forces – why, in fact, a manned bomber was needed at all. To summarize what was written in the opening chapter, the ICBMs were felt to be too vulnerable to a preemptive strike, which if successful would leave no retaliatory capacity, while the SLBMs suffered from lack of accuracy, and in any case only a relatively small proportion of missile submarines would be on station at any one time, vastly reducing the striking power of the force as a whole. A further, less immediate consideration was the possibility that a sudden major improvement in submarine detection methods could render the entire SLBM force vulnerable to destruction before it could be used.

With those factors in mind, the manned bomber represented a second chance. A combination of dispersal and rapid reaction time should ensure that enough of the manned bomber force survives a surprise attack to represent a credible threat, and the force also represents a second-strike capability, unlike the other two delivery systems, which by their very nature are one-shot. As a delivery system, the manned bomber was accurate and flexible, capable of being retargeted or even recalled in mid-mission.

It should also be remembered that the manned bomber is the only proven method of nuclear weapon delivery, and in these days of heavy reliance on technology it is as well to remember that no-one really knows what would happen if the superpowers engaged in an all-out nuclear exchange. Certain conventional weapons have achieved remarkable results in the sterile, laboratory-like conditions of the test range, then failed to deliver the goods in combat.

Moreover, discussion of a limited nuclear exchange is arrant rubbish. When dealing with weapons of such destructive capability, a good analogy is that of a farmer giving a pig a condition pill: the pill is placed in a tube, which is inserted into the pig's mouth, and the farmer then blows down the tube, whereupon the pig swallows the pill. The trick is to make sure that the pig doesn't blow first! To apply the analogy to the current strategic situation, the pills are in place and the tubes firmly inserted, with both sides waiting for the first sign that the other is taking a deep breath.

It has been estimated that there are between 1,800 and 2,300 major targets in the Soviet Union, and that for the manned bomber to be a credible deterrent in its own right it should be capable of delivering some 2,000 nuclear weapons accurately on targets, regardless of where they are situated. In the majority of cases, this calls for deep penetration.

The cruise missile, for which the B-1 was nearly discarded, does not have the range to be effective, while its penetration capability against the Soviet defences has always been in question. There is a great difference between penetrating a hundred miles of hostile territory and a thousand. The Tercom terrain matching system is also susceptible to the vagaries of the Russian winter, as in many areas deep snow and iced-up rivers and estuaries would alter the appearance of the terrain, making matching difficult if not impossible. The difference between human and computer intelligence lies in the fact that the

Unrefuelled mission (SRAM and gravity weapons)

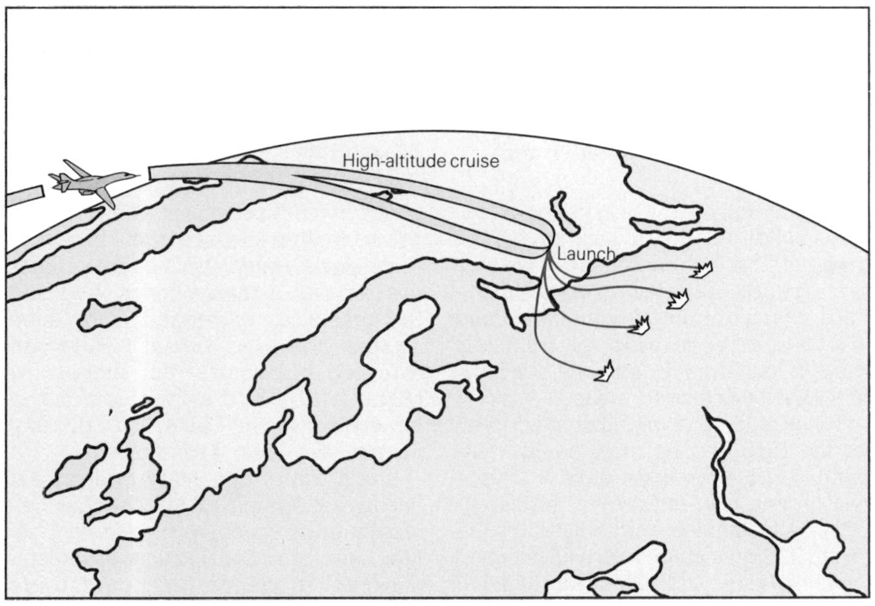

Unrefuelled mission (ALCMs)

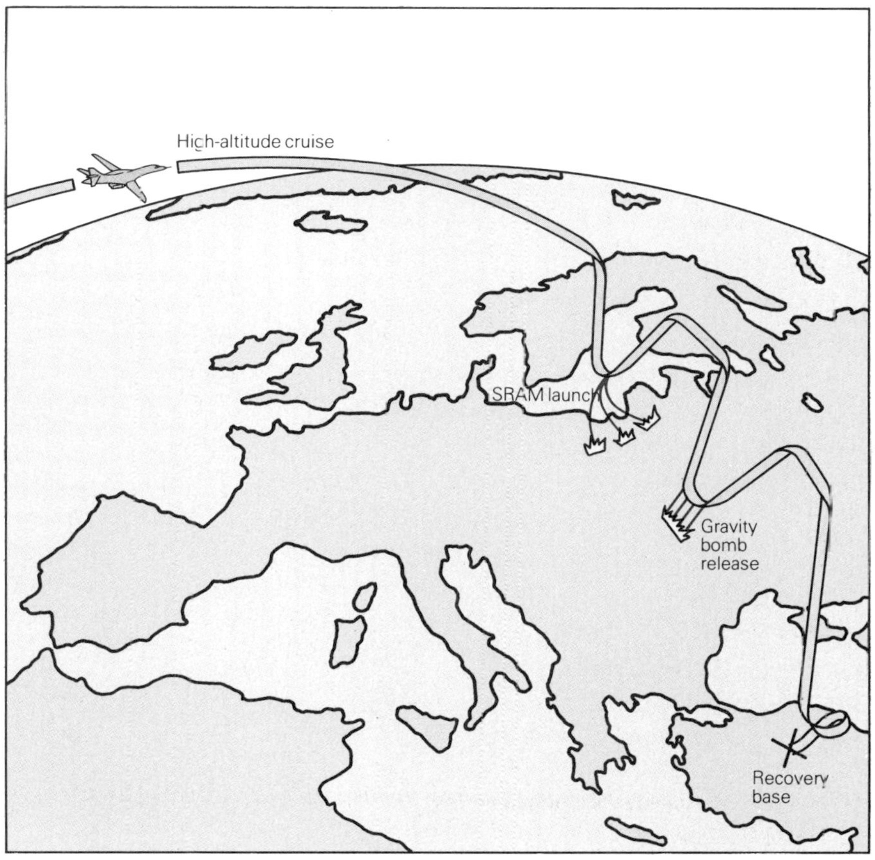

Above: One of the missions envisaged for the Long Range Combat Aircraft by the US Air Force bomber study group, set up to consider alternatives to the B-1A, involved the new high subsonic version of the B-1 carrying ALCMs in a high-altitude transatlantic return flight.

Right: Increased range, low observability and a more diverse payload were key features of the LRCA – subsequently the B-1B – so that the new bomber would be able to penetrate air defences at low level in support of theatre forces in Europe.

computer cannot have second thoughts, wonder whether it has just made a mistake and revise its judgement.

It has long been assumed that all strategic bomber bases in the United States are targeted by missiles, and in times of international tension the B-1 force is intended to be dispersed as widely as possible. There are at least 100 airfields capable of maintaining sustained B-1 operations, and another 250 FAA Grade III fields suitable for emergency dispersal – that is, sized for Boeing 727 type aircraft. The greatest threat comes from depressed trajectory SLBMs launched from just a few hundred miles offshore, which would allow very little reaction time. The B-1, with its stand-alone capability, is intended to be able to take off and be several miles away from the airfield, hopefully beyond the worst effects of the nuclear detonation, within just four minutes of the warning being given.

The B-1A was intended to take off with a full weapons load, but just enough fuel to take it to cruising altitude and a rendezvous with a tanker. This gave a reasonable certainty of the survival of a fair number of the bombers, but placed a premium on the survival of the tanker force, without which the bombers were impotent. It hardly needs saying that the tanker force could not be dispersed as widely or scrambled as quickly as the B-1s, and was therefore the weak link in the chain.

Crew/endurance limit

In the early days of the B-1 design period, when provision was to be made for two instructors as well as the four man crew, it was suggested that two extra crew could be carried, giving a maximum endurance of 36 hours with in-flight refuelling. This seems never to have been pursued, perhaps because the proposed number of B-1As, 244 in all, was too low to allow flying what amounted to standing patrols in times of crisis.

The B-1A was to continue its mission by taking on a full load of fuel from the tanker, climbing to altitude and cruising at Mach 0.85 to the edge of the threat area. Depending on the tactical circumstances, it would then penetrate at Mach 2 at high altitude or descend to very low level for a high subsonic penetration. Where possible it would try to bypass the defences; if this was impracticable SRAMs would be launched to suppress them. Nuclear gravity weapons would normally be carried as part of a weapons mix for use against major targets, as

Left: With wings fully swept for low-level penetration, the B-1B is literally faster than a speeding bullet. Full operation at the 200ft (60m) penetration altitude had not been demonstrated by the time the first operational aircraft was delivered.

Above: Wings fully forward is the normal position for landing, but the second B-1B landed successfully with the wings at 55° when a fault caused the wings to stick in that position during a training flight from Dyess in March 1986.

these generally had a greater yield than the smaller warheads carried by the missiles. The fuel consumed in Mach 2 penetration naturally reduced the operational radius substantially, and would have been used for relatively shallow penetration missions over the less heavily defended areas.

The approach to the mission adopted for the B-1B was far more realistic: its increased fuel tankage gave a 25 per cent increase in operational radius; its reliance on tankers was reduced by the fact that it can take off with a full fuel and weapons load, and has an unrefuelled range described as intercontinental; stealth and eluding the defences became much more important; and the Mach 2 requirement was dropped. The B-1B still retains a supersonic capability – Mach 1.4 to be precise – but this is largely residual, nice to have but rarely likely to be of any great value.

From a practical point of view, it is always easier to see the apparent shortcomings of one's own equipment than to assess objectively the problems it poses to the other side, and it is wise to slightly overrate the capabilities of an opponent until exact assessment is possible. While SAC has been concerned with such matters as reasonable attrition rates and mission success probabilities, the Soviet defence forces must have been very concerned about their chances of preventing both the B-1A and the B-1B from inflicting unacceptable damage.

Frankly, to talk about attrition rates in an all-out nuclear war can only be an academic exercise, but one useful consequence of the B-1 programme is that while the B-1B is an extremely costly machine, the cost of an even half-way effective defence against it for a country as vast in area and as lengthy in border as the Soviet Union would be many times greater, both in money and in effort, and the resources expended in defence against this one threat cannot be directed elsewhere. But success or failure for the B-1B will be determined by whether it ever has to fly its primary mission: if it does, it has failed.

It is a truism of military aviation that hardware optimized for one function usually ends up doing something else. Many aircraft of many nations have been designed as nuclear weapon delivery systems, but, fortunately, not one has ever been used for that purpose. Some have been engaged in reconnaissance; others have ended their lives as tankers; and just a few – the B-52 and the Vulcan spring to mind – have dropped some conventional iron bombs.

The B-1B seems to be heading the same way. It is now proposed to use it for a variety of missions, including maritime reconnaissance and mine laying, anti-shipping attacks using smart weapons such as Harpoon, and conventional interdiction. Official statements credit it with the ability to extend US Navy capability in both coastal and inland power projection, and with its range and payload it could bring force to bear until orthodox tactical reinforcements arrived.

It also seems probable that the B-1B may be used as part of the US Army Air/Land Battle doctrine, which requires rapid reaction to a superior enemy force on the battlefield, and would involve both hitting the attack spearhead and massive attacks against the support echelons which kept it supplied. It is also reported that plans are afoot for the B-1B force to interdict Warsaw Pact airfields to take the pressure off NATO fighter and strike aircraft and free them for the close air support mission. This mission could be flown from bases in the United States, presumably at fairly high altitude using stand-off weapons.

The last mission, however, would indeed be a desperate measure. Bearing in mind the colossal cost of a single B-1B and the severely limited numbers being acquired, it is very hard to envisage a situation outside total war where the loss of even one could be justified. It is also difficult to conceive of a conventional war situation even in central Europe where the B-1B could do a better job than equal-cost quantities of Tornados, or even F-111s, although the answer to this may emerge by the end of the decade: the SAC bombing competition is an annual event, and after Tornado teams from the RAF swept the board in the 1984 and 1985 competitions it is reasonable to assume that the B-1B will be entered as soon as the USAF thinks it has a fair chance of reclaiming some of its silverware.

Achieving Initial Operational Capability (IOC) in July 1986, the B-1B is scheduled to carry the burden of penetration for some ten years, at which point the Advanced Technology Bomber (ATB) is due to enter service. This new machine, using the very latest stealth techniques, will then take over the penetrator role, and the B-1B will revert to being a stand-off cruise missile carrier replacing the elderly B-52s. It should last in this mission from 1995 to approximately 2010. But will it?

The ATB, under development by Northrop, is variously rumoured to look like a cross between a wide-span Vulcan and the old Northrop flying wings; it is also rumoured to be small, with less carrying capacity than the B-1B. Certainly it will be more expensive; equally certainly it will have more than its fair share of detractors. Almost certainly history will repeat itself, and the ATB will be rubbished in favour of the more effective, low technical risk, and much cheaper B-1B – or, as it may well be, the B-1C or B-1D.

Handling properties

B-1B handling is reported to be very good, although little detail has been given, probably because unlike a fighter which has been designed to be hurled around the sky, the sedate manoeuvring required of the LRCA is not exciting by comparison. The cockpit features a stick rather than the wheel common to most large aircraft, and each pilot has a left-hand throttle quadrant. Major George W. Larson Jr gave an account of his impressions to *Air Force Magazine* in June 1976:

"Taxiing the aircraft is easy with nosewheel steering through the rudder pedals. Smooth, positive differential braking is effective in the event of a nosewheel steering malfunction. The old groaning and screeching and shuddering associated with other large aircraft braking systems is not evident. With the wings at full forward sweep, 15°, slats extended, and full flaps, the B-1 is configured for takeoff . . . in full augmentor there is a smooth, rapid acceleration to liftoff speed. Only minimum aft stick displacement is needed at rotation speed, and you find yourself airborne in approximately 3,000 to 4,000ft (914 to 1,219m). After takeoff retrimming is necessary as the flaps are retracted . . . Manoeuvring the aircraft in pitch or roll is a pleasant surprise. Only small control displacements (one or two inches depending on airspeed) are required. The response to a control stick input is rapid. There are no sluggish or delayed control responses . . . Refuelling the B-1 is much easier [than earlier large bombers]. Only very minimal control inputs are required, thrust response is rapid and effective, and visibility is excellent.

"[In low level flight] the already rapid control responses increase in this high dynamic pressure regime . . . In the traffic pattern, the B-1 is so responsive you can fly an ILS or an overhead pattern with equal ease and precision. Some pilot adaptation is required prior to touchdown on landing. I consistently feel that I'm higher than necessary when the main gear touches down. The reason is that the pilot sits considerably forward of the main landing gear and is flying the aircraft at an angle of attack of approximately seven degrees during the landing flare. While it makes a grease job more demanding, it does not detract from easily landing the aircraft."

Nor is the B-1B's handling in any way inferior. Air Force Chief Test Pilot Lt Col Leroy Schroeder has commented that handling is so good that "sometimes you've got to stop and think how big this aircraft is before you do some things because it handles so well."

Strategic bomber force modernization

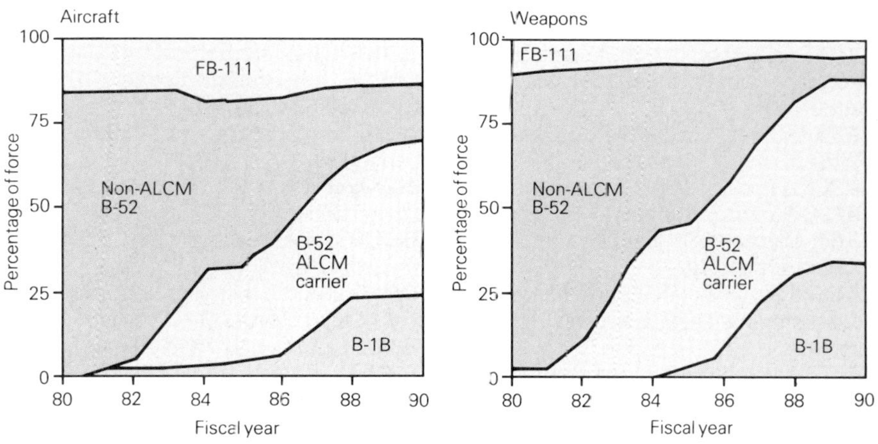

Above: By 1990 B-1Bs and ALCM-equipped B-52s will represent, respectively, 25 and 45 per cent of SAC's bomber force, and the combination will be responsible for over 85 per cent of its weapons.

Left: Badge and motto of the 96th Bomb Wing, whose 4018th Combat Crew Training Squadron and 337th Bomb Squadron are the first operational users of the B-1B. The 96th is at Dyess AFB, near Abilene, Texas.

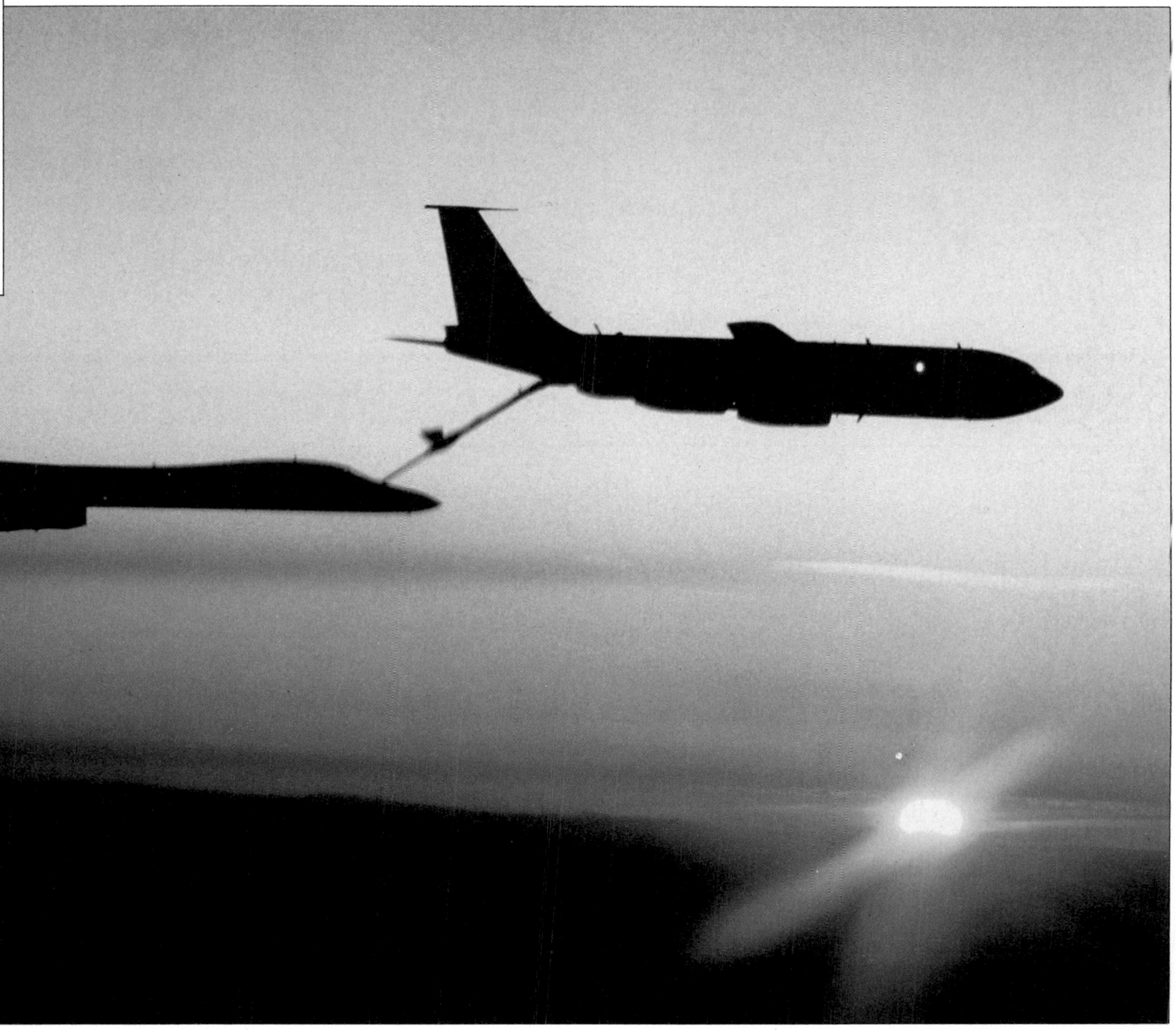

Below: Silhouetted against the rays of the setting sun, a B-1B refuels from a KC-135. Fuel and aircrew costs have made the idea of maintaining standing patrols with the B-1B a non-starter.

Glossary and abbreviations

ACES Advanced Concept Ejection Seat
acronym name composed of initial letters
AFB Air Force Base (USAF, continental USA only)
AFCS Automatic Flight Control System
AFSC Air Force Systems Command
AGE Automatic Ground Environment (defensive system)
ALCM Air Launched Cruise Missile
algorithm mathematical formula or process
AMP Advanced Manned Penetrator
AMPSS Advanced Manned Penetrating Strategic System
AMSA Advanced Manned Strategic Aircraft
AMT Accelerated Mission Testing
anhedral downward angle of horizontal flying surfaces
APU Auxiliary Power Unit
ARS Air Refuelling Squadron
aspect ratio ratio of span^2 to wing area
ATB Advanced Technology Bomber
beam sharpening radar technique giving better definition over a small area
BMAC Boeing Military Airplane Company
body lift lift gained from the fuselage area rather than from the wings
BPE Bomber Penetration Evaluation
breadboard experimental layout for electronic system
bypass ratio ratio of total air passing through the engine against that passing through the core section
BW Bomb Wing
CCTS Combat Crew Training Squadron
CED Continued Engineering Development
CITEPS Central Integrated Test Expert Parameter System
CITS Central Integrated Test System
CMCA Cruise Missile Carrier Aircraft
CRT Cathode Ray Tube
CSRL Common Strategic Rotary Launcher
dihedral upward angle of horizontal flying surfaces
DSARC Defense System Acquisition Review Council
DSO Defensive (avionics) System Officer
DVT Design Verification Testing
EAR Electronically Agile Radar
ECM Electronic Countermeasures
EMP Electromagnetic Pulse (from nuclear explosion)
empennage tail section
EMUX electronic multiplex
ERSA Extended Range Strategic Aircraft
Faraday Cage device for excluding unwanted electrical emissions
FBW Fly By Wire
FCGMS Fuel and Centre of Gravity Management System
FLIR Forward Looking Infra Red
FOD Foreign Object Damage (to engines)
fuel fraction proportion of fuel load to gross weight
GCI Ground Controlled Interception
gust response the reaction of the aircraft to rapid changes in wind direction and velocity
HF High Frequency
HP High Pressure
ICBM Intercontinental Ballistic Missile
IDR Initial Design Review
IFR In Flight Refuelling
ILS Instrument Landing System
incidence angle of attack
INS Inertial Navigation System
IOC Initial Operational Capability
IOTE Initial Operational Test and Evaluation
IR Infra-red
IRCM Infra-red Countermeasures
Lantirn Low altitude navigation and targetting infra-red at night
LAMP Low Altitude Manned Penetrator
LARC Low Altitude Ride Control
LLTV Low Light Television
LP Low Pressure
LRCA Long Range Combat Aircraft
LRU Line Replaceable Unit
MAC Mean Aerodynamic Chord
Mach Number Speed expressed in terms of the local speed of sound
MFD Multi-Function Display
MilSpec Military Specification
mockup full scale engineering model
MRB Multi-Role Bomber
NASA National Aeronautics and Space Agency
NATO North Atlantic Treaty Organization
NTP Near Term Penetrator
overpressure the difference between the aircraft internal pressure and the air pressure externally in the vicinity of a nuclear blast
PFRT Preliminary Flight Rating Test
PIRA Precision Impact Range Area
pitch movement about the vertical longitudinal axis
psi pounds per square inch
prf pulse repetition frequency (radar)
PVP Production Verification Program
q dynamic pressure
QT Qualification Test
R & D Research and Development
RAM Radar Absorbing Material
ramp hardstanding or apron
RCS Radar Cross-Section
red line 'never exceed' limits
SAC Strategic Air Command, USAF
SAM Surface to Air Missile
SAR Synthetic Aperture Radar
SCAD Subsonic Cruise Armed Decoy
SDT System Development Tool
SEAT Status Evaluation and Test
SEF Stability Enhancement Function
SIS Stall Inhibitor System
SLAB Subsonic Low Altitude Bomber
SLBM Submarine Launched Ballistic Missile
SMCS Structural Mode Control System
spoilers roll control surfaces which "dump" lift
SRAM Short Range Attack Missile
stabilizers tail flying surfaces
static thrust the thrust produced by the engines when stationary at ground level
SWL Strategic Weapons Launcher
Tacan Tactical air navigation
telemetry the relaying of information from instruments to ground receivers during a test flight
TES Test and Evaluation Squadron
Tercom Terrain contour matching
TOGW Take Off Gross Weight
TREES Transient Response of Electronic Equipment and systems (to a nuclear detonation)
Triad The three nuclear deterrent delivery systems
V-G variable geometry (actually variable sweep)
VHF Very High Frequency
VTOL Vertical Take Off and Landing
WCT box Wing Carry Through box

Deployment

PAA: Primary Aircraft Authorized
BAI: Back-up Aircraft Inventoried
FI: Flight Instructional
OP: Operational
IOC: Initial Operational Capability

Base	Activated	First delivery	Equipment complete	IOC	Unit	PAA	BAI	Crews
Dyess AFB, Texas	Mar 85	29 Jun 85	Nov 86	Sep 86	4018 CCTS	15	—	18 FI
					96 BW	11	3	22 OP
Ellsworth AFB, South Dakota	Oct 86	Dec 86	Jul 87	N/A	28 BW	32	3	44 OP
Grand Forks AFB, North Dakota	Feb 87	Aug 87	Jan 88	N/A	319 BW	16	1	22 OP
McConnell AFB, Kansas	Jul 87	Jan 88	30 Apr 88	N/A	384 BW	16	1	22 OP

Authorized strength: 90 aircraft plus 8 back-ups plus 2 at Edwards AFB (4200th TES) = 100 Total.

Specifications

Dimensions (ft/m)	B-1A	B-1B
Length (B-1A inc probe)	151.17/46.07	147/44.80
Height	33.58/10.23	34/10.36
Span at 15° sweep	136.67/41.65	137/41.76
Span at 67½° sweep	78.17/23.83	78/23.77
Main gear track	14.50/4.42	14.50/4.42
Wing area ft^2/m^2	1,950/181.2	1,950/181.2
Weights (lb/kg)		
Empty, approx	172,000/78,019	172,000/78,019
Gross takeoff	395,000/179,172	477,000/216,367
Max weapons load	115,000/52,164	125,000/56,700
Performance		
Speed lo	Mach 0.85	Mach 0.85
Speed hi	Mach 2.22	Mach 1.40
Ceiling (ft/m)	50,000/15,240 plus	49,000/14,934
Range unrefuelled (nm/km)	5,200/9,636	6,500/12,045
Power	Engines	4xF101-GE-100
4xF101-GE-102	Dry rating (lb/kN)	17,000/75.6
17,000/75.6	Wet rating (lb/kN)	30,000/133
30,000/133		

Production

Lot	Aircraft	Serials	Tail codes
I	1	82–0001	20001
II	2–8	83–0065—0071	30065—30071
III	9–19	84–0049—0059	40049—40059
IV	20–54	85–0062—0096	50062—50096
V	55–100	N/A	N/A

Chapter 9

F-4

PHANTOM II

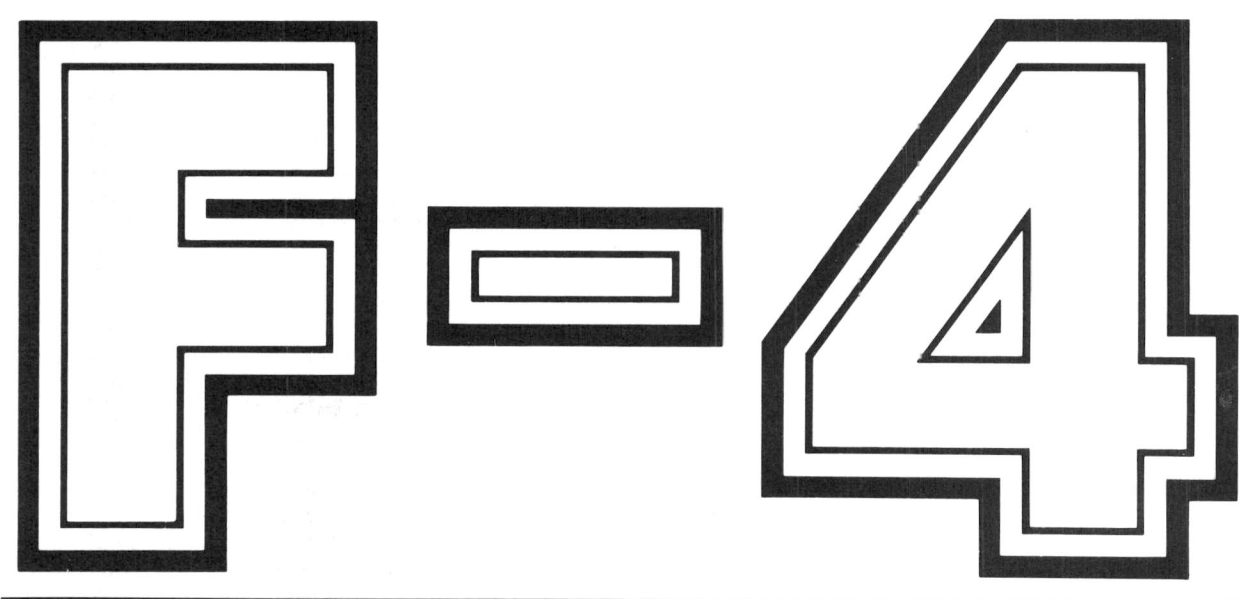

Doug Richardson, Mike Spick

F-4 Phantom II

Acknowledgements

The authors and editor would like to thank everyone who has contributed information and photographs for this chapter. Particular thanks are due to the personnel of McDonnell Aircraft Co., St. Louis – especially Timothy J. Beecher, Bob "Beaver" Blake, John S. Brooks and Frederick W. Ross – and Geoffrey Norris and Karen Stubberfield of McDonnell Douglas Corporation (UK); Captain Jim Rotramel; Robert F. Dorr, Captain Eric Coloney; US Department of Defense (US Navy, USAF); the Royal Air Force; Germany's *Luftwaffe*; Israel's Embassy in London; the Royal Australian Air Force; Westinghouse; General Electric; Boeing; and Pratt & Whitney.

Authors

Doug Richardson has been editor of *Defence Materiel*, defence editor of *Flight International* and editor of *Military Technology and Economics*. He has worked as an electronics engineer in radar, electronic warfare, rocket engine control systems, computers, automatic test equipment and missile trials. He is a frequent contributor to many technical defence journals, including *International Defense Review*, is the author/co-author of previous Salamander books (including *The Balance of Military Power, The Illustrated Encyclopedia of Modern Warplanes*, and the F-16 chapter in this book) and is a frequent broadcaster.

Mike Spick is the co-author of Salamander's *Modern Air Combat*, and two other books, *Air Battles in Miniature* and *Fighter Pilot Tactics* (both Patrick Stephens). He is a wargamer and broadcaster on aviation topics.

Contents

Introduction

"Phantom salesmen have been very successful, but it could be argued that they have had an easy task." Seldom can the merits of a modern warplane have been so neatly summed up as in this comment by the journal *Flight International* on the occasion of the roll-out of the 5,000th aircraft in 1978.

In terms of numbers of Mach 2 fighters delivered, only the MiG-21 can surpass the Phantom's 20-year production run. In the critical arena of air combat, the F-4 held its own against all-comers in the late 1960s and early 1970s. During the Vietnam War, more than 140 MiGs fell to the guns and missiles of USAF and US Navy Phantoms, around 70 per cent of the total number of North Vietnamese aircraft downed in air combat. As recent air-combat exercises have shown, a skilfully piloted F-4 can win in air-to-air trials against the latest generation of agile dogfighters.

Given the aircraft's long record, readers will know that the Phantom's career has already been documented. But with the enthusiastic help of the companies and air forces involved in the various F-4 programmes, this new Salamander book has been able to break new ground.

Readers will be able to follow the development of the aircraft from the relatively simple configurations originally proposed to the USN, through the long series of variants which were deployed and combat-proven—(including information on Israel's mysterious F-4P and RF-4E(S)—to the exotic but never-built single-seater, F-4T air-superiority variant, and swing-wing F-4(FVS).

The Phantom story is far from over. Even as this book was in preparation, a consortium of US companies was drawing up plans for the final version documented in these pages—the "Super Phantom" re-engined variant with modernised avionics and greatly-improved performance. The brutal shape of the F-4 seems destined to play a significant role in air power well into the 1990s at least.

Development

Above: James S. McDonnell, Founder and Chairman of the McDonnell Douglas Corporation poses with the 5,000th Phantom produced at the St Louis plant in Missouri. This F-4E was actually destined for Turkey.

When in 1953 the McDonnell Aircraft Corporation design for a carrier fighter lost out to the Chance Vought Crusader, their prospects looked bleak. Undaunted, they produced a design which could be adapted for many roles. Ordered by the USN as a fleet defence interceptor in 1955, it proved to be so outstanding that it became a true multi-role fighter. Thirty years later it remains a potent weapon, and looks like being so well into the 1990s.

Paradoxically, the origins of the F-4 Phantom lie in a failure. The McDonnell Aircraft Corporation was a relative latecomer to the aviation scene; during the late stages of World War II and in the years immediately after, it had established a reputation for designing and building jet carrier fighters. It all began on August 30, 1943, when the company received a letter of intent for a jet carrier fighter. Seventeen months later, on January 26, 1945, the prototype fighter, the XFD1 made its first flight, and later became the first United States jet aircraft to land aboard an aircraft carrier, the USS *Franklin Delano Roosevelt*, on July 21, 1946. Only 60 of the production aircraft were built, and it was quickly superseded. However, it did serve as a basis for more advanced fighters, notably the McDonnell F2H Banshee (895 built), which bore a distinct family resemblance to the FH1. McDonnell's next carrier fighter was the swept wing F3H Demon, of which 521 were built, and which remained in frontline service until 1965.

With this background of successful carrier-based fighters, the McDonnell Aircraft Corporation had every hope of winning the order to fill a US Navy requirement for a supersonic air superiority fighter in 1952. Eight designs were submitted by various companies, and in May 1953 the choice was made, the winning proposal being the Chance Vought design which became the F-8 Crusader. This left a vacuum, which both nature and McDonnell abhor. MAC set out to fill it, taking the bold decision to look to the future. The next step was to determine future requirements, simply by canvassing for opinions from any Naval personnel who were willing both to listen and to fill in questionnaires that MAC had thoughtfully provided. From the Chief of Naval Operations (CNO), the Head of the Fighter Branch, the Bureau of Aeronautics (BuAer), Naval Operating Commands, right through to the Overhaul and Repair people, information was amassed which, when analysed, yielded a consensus of opinion from which MAC was able to commence design studies.

Several studies gradually emerged from the mass of requirements, often conflicting, which had been gleaned from the Naval sources. Noteworthy among these were the F3H-C, a single-engined fighter bearing a family resemblance to the Demon; the F3H-E, also single-engined but of different and more advanced appearance than the -C; and, most important as it subsequently transpired, the F3H-G, a twin-engined design with more than a passing resemblance from side-on to the McDonnell fighter built for the Air Force, the F-101 Voodoo. The F3H-G was to be a single seater, powered by two Wright J65s (licence-built Sapphires) with afterburning. While technically a fighter, as shown by the "F" designation, the design was intended to cover a multitude of roles. To achieve this, several designs were produced for the nose and cockpit area, all of which could be spliced onto the basic design, and each of which optimised the aircraft for a different role.

The all-weather interceptor was equipped with the Mk 16 Mod 3 Fire Control System, as were all the other variants except the photo reconnaissance. The main armament was to be 56 2in (50mm) unguided Folding Fin Aircraft Rockets (FFARs) carried on retractable racks in the front fuselage. Nine hard points under the fuselage and wings could be used to carry any combination of external rocket packs. The APQ-50 radar was to be installed to give all-weather capability and to give information for the automatic firing of the rockets.

The all-weather attack fighter carried four 20mm Mk 12 cannon with 150 rounds per gun in place of the racks of FFARs. It also had provision for nine hard points to carry any combination of stores and "special" attack weapons. The radar carried was once again to be the APQ-50.

The day interceptor variant was to have six of the then-new Sparrow semi-active radar homing (SARH) missiles mounted externally on retractable racks. These were matched with the compatible APQ-51 radar.

Next came the jet attack version. This carried the Westinghouse lightweight radar which gave ranging for air to air combat. Its weapons fit was variable. It could be equipped with four 20mm cannon, or 56 FFARs carried internally, or two 20mm cannon with an in-flight refuelling probe (IFR), or 28 FFARs with an IFR probe. It also carried a Low Altitude Bombing System (LABS) for the accurate delivery of underwing stores.

In accordance with its policy of meeting any and all Navy requirements, MAC then proposed the Ferret Electronic Countermeasures Aircraft, thereby foreseeing the future need for the Wild Weasel. Its proposed armament was the internally carried 56 FFARs, with provision for a wide combination of external stores, which was matched with LABS. The main radar was to be the APQ-46; it was also to be equipped with the APR-9 ECM search radar receiver and the APA-70 ECM homing set which allowed detection, location, identification and destruction of enemy ground radar installations.

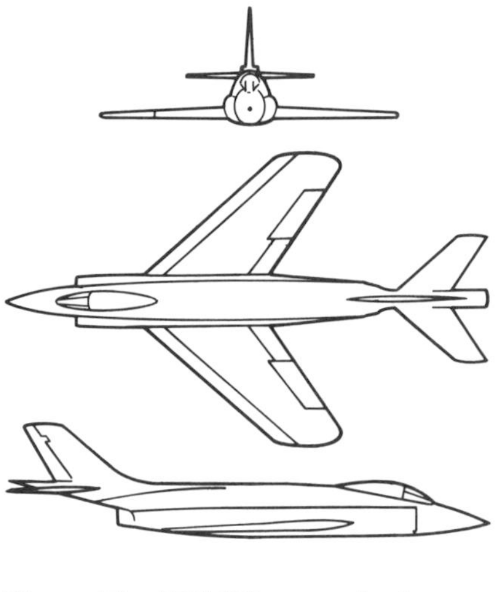

Above: The F3H-(C) was a single engined single seat fighter reminiscent of the Demon.

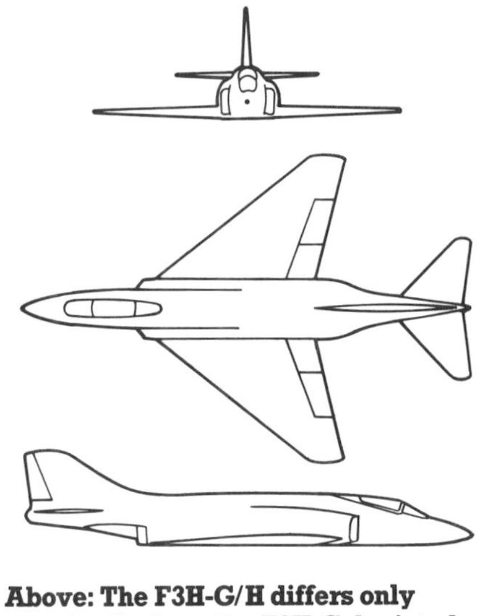

Above: The F3H-G/H differs only marginally from the F3H-G depicted at bottom left.

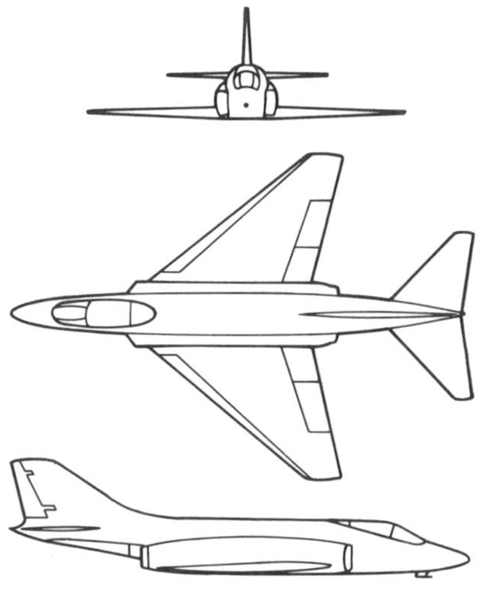

Above: The F3H-G, with two Wright J65 engines and one-man crew was to become the Phantom.

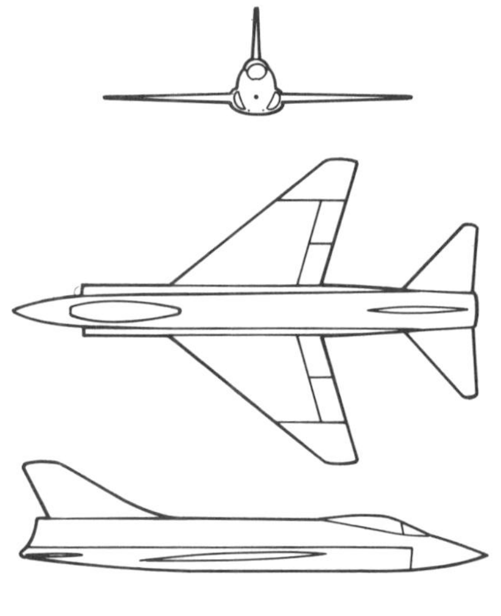

Above: The F3H-E was the most radical of the proposed designs, powered by a single J67 jet.

At this time, no-one was very sure whether a two-seat fighter would be better than a single-seater, given that air combat was becoming much more technical. Two seats obviously had their uses, such as in training, ECM missions, and the carriage of an Air Strike Coordinator. MAC hedged its bets on this one and produced a two-seat design armed with 56 FFARs and carrying an APQ-51 radar. The aircraft length had to be held down to 56ft (17.07m) to fit the central elevators on Midway class carriers, and the second crew position was accommodated by moving the pilot's position forward and down and squeezing the second crewman's position in behind him.

Finally, the most obvious need was for a photo-reconnaissance variant. This was also catered for, deleting all armament and installing one K-25 forward looking camera in the nose, three forward and aft rotatable CAX-12 cameras under the nose section, with a further two CAX-12s mounted just behind and below the pilot's seat to give detailed altitude coverage. Provision was also made for alternative use of night cameras and photo-flash cartridges. The cameras were aimed from a viewfinder in the cockpit showing a 60 degree forward view from under the nose.

In September 1953, MAC submitted an unsolicited proposal to NAVAIR (BuAer) for the F3H-G as an all-weather general purpose aircraft. Though all possibilities seemed to have been covered, the proposal was rejected in November of that year, partly due to the lack of a firm military requirement.

Undaunted, MAC went on to construct a full scale mock-up, which was completed early in the new year. Many senior Naval personnel were invited to the MAC works at St Louis, Missouri, to view it and pass comment. One of the main problems at this stage was that, as mentioned before, the F3H-G had not been designed for a specific role, but to carry out any task short of troop carrying. It was a series of solutions looking for the right problem.

Meanwhile, NAVAIR had also been looking to the future and in June 1954 evaluated four proposals for an all-weather fighter. The contenders were McDonnell's F3H-E single-engined fighter, the twin-engined F3H-G, and proposals by Grumman and North American. The BuAer team selected the F3H-G. This led to the Fiscal Year 1955 Procurement Programme including a recommendation that two proto-

Above: Mock-up of the F3H-G, in May 1954. The wings are not yet cranked, the stabilators are still horizontal and the inlets are plain. Two of the four gun ports can be seen.

Below: Mock-up of the F4H-1 in December 1955. The fin has become more angular, the stabilators are drooped, a second cockpit has appeared, as have ramps on the intakes.

type aircraft, to be designated AH-1, should be acquired, and on October 18 1954 a Letter of Intent was issued. Work began, but effective progress was almost impossible, as the Detail Specification had still to be agreed with BuAer, and there was still no firm military requirement for the aircraft.

Then in April 1955 the situation changed radically for the better. Two officers from BuAer and two more from CNO arrived at St Louis and, using blackboard and chalk, described exactly what they wanted in less than an hour. It was to be a fleet defence fighter that could take off from an aircraft carrier, cruise out to a distance of 250 nautical miles (463km), stay on patrol at that distance, intercept intruders, then return to the carrier three hours after takeoff. It was to be a missile-armed fighter and as such would not carry guns. The preferred weapon was to be the new Sparrow semi-active radar-homing missile.

At last MAC knew what was wanted, and within the next two weeks the concept was revised to suit. Four Sparrow missiles were to be the main armament, carried on extendable rails beneath the fuselage. The cannon, which had featured on the mock-up, were deleted, and the fire control system was changed. The AH-1 had an estimated maximum speed of Mach 1.5 on the power of the two Wright J65s. Now two of the more powerful General Electric J79-GE-2 engines, each giving 15,900lb (7,212kg) of static thrust with afterburning, were to provide the motive power, to give a maximum speed in excess of Mach 2. These were the most powerful engines in terms of thrust/weight yet developed, and their installation involved many changes.

One further major change occurred. No-one was entirely certain whether the new interceptor should be a single- or a two-seater (the argument continues with new designs to this day). In a single place version, the pilot workload would be very high, and this factor could possibly restrict further development, given the technology of the period. MAC therefore produced an alternative two-seat layout, differing from the original proposal, making space for the second crew position behind the pilot by removing a 150 gallons (US) (125 Imp gall/568 litres) from the forward fuselage and increasing the capacity of the jettisonable external fuel tank which was to be hung beneath the centreline, by the same amount. CNO and BuAer were offered the choice and within 36 hours had settled for the two-seater. The final main alteration was the deletion of all the hardpoints for carrying external stores with the exception of the one to carry the centreline tank.

Up to this moment, the F4H, as it had now been designated, had attracted little publicity. The 1950s was without doubt the most exciting decade ever in aviation development, and new experimental and fighter projects (and some also for supersonic bombers) hogged most of the limelight. At the time, "fighter" meant a single-engined, single-seater that clawed its way into the sky and flew the pants off anything that opposed it. Few could work up much enthusiasm at the idea of a twin-engined, two-place attack bomber (the AH designation) which was in the process of being converted into a fighter. And anyway, it had lost out in the

Below: The Phantom's first flight, on May 27, 1958. Problems with the undercarriage retraction were encountered, causing the flight to be terminated early. The "Sparrows" are in fact dummies.

Above: The first of the many: MAC's chief test pilot Robert C. Little at the controls of the first prototype, BuAer No. 142259. The sharply downswept tail and cranked wings are in evidence.

original competition to the F-8 Crusader, which was coming along very nicely. Nor was the revised design anything to attract comment; by the standards of the day, the F4H looked a very ordinary aeroplane. At the end of the two weeks, during which time the detail specification had been written, the mock-up had been rebuilt, but the only really noticeable differences from the original were that the horizontal stabilator had been drooped downwards at a shallow angle, and large fixed ramps had appeared in front of the intakes. The fact that a second crew position had been added was barely noticeable.

Just over three years were to elapse before the F4H made its first flight, and in that time many modifications were made. To give these in chronological order would be confusing and so we shall deal with them section by section. Wind tunnel tests and calculations showed probable stability and control problems. The stabilator, which had already been tilted down at a modest 15 degree angle, was now tilted down at a surprising 23 degree angle to remove it as far as possible from the turbulent wing downwash created at high angles of attack, although it was mounted just high enough to stay out of the direct path of the engine efflux.

The outer wing panels, which were made to fold for carrier operation, were given 12 degrees of dihedral. Wind tunnel data had indicated that 3 degrees of dihedral was desirable for the entire wing, but the same effect could be achieved by cranking the outboard panels upwards with far less effort and redesign. The outer panels were also increased in chord, which produced a snag or "dogtooth" in the leading edge. This acted as a vortex generator, fulfilling the same function as the wing fences seen on many contemporary, particularly Soviet, designs, in alleviating tip stall.

The wings featured flaps on both leading and trailing edges. The outboard leading edge flaps and the trailing edge flaps deflected to an angle of 60 degrees, with the inboard leading edge flaps deflected to 30 degrees. Both leading and trailing edge flaps incorporated boundary layer control blowing, a first for an operational fighter. This lowered the stall and approach speeds considerably, improved lateral control at low speeds, and reduced the angle of attack for a deck landing to about 10 degrees. For greater stability at supersonic speeds, more keel area was added by extending the chord of the vertical fin.

The combination of the upward cranked wings and the sharp anhedral on the stabilator was mainly responsible for the distinctive appearance of the F4H-1, and all subsequent models. Many disparaging remarks greeted the appearance of the F4H at first, such as "a triumph of thrust over aerodynamics". It certainly did not look right. Time, though, has gradually softened the adverse impact of its looks, and the record of the aeroplane has silenced critics.

Below: An unusual shot of an early F4H-1, BuAer No. 146817, carrying its full complement of six Sparrow air-to-air missiles.

The engine installation was very advanced for its time. The switch to the J79 required considerable enlargement of the inlets and ducts. Great pains were taken to ensure that they could be fabricated precisely the same on all aircraft. In order to achieve very high Mach numbers, the inlets were made variable, another first on a fighter. To keep the sluggish boundary layer air out of the inlets, a large sharp-edged ramp was set about 2 inches (50mm) out from the fuselage. Just behind this came a hydraulically actuated moveable ramp, thus creating a variable throat area, and an engine bypass. Boundary layer air on the ramps is removed through a vertical slot between them, and through thousands of tiny perforations in the moveable ramp, from where it is expelled through louvres above the ducts. The moveable ramp is programmed to operate automatically as a function of the free stream air flow, and the bypass operates as a function of duct Mach number. In this manner there is no drag-creating excess airflow, and the flow is at all times sufficient for the power. On early models, the fixed ramp was at 5 degrees, with a 10 degree variable ramp.

On the underside of each engine compartment is an auxiliary air door. This fulfils two functions: it admits more air during ground running when no ram pressure is available, and it is hydraulically loaded to blow open so that it acts as a valve to relieve excessive pressures caused by rapid throttling back, or compressor stall at high speeds.

Other changes involved the weapons system. On August 26, 1955, the fire control system became the AMCS-Aero-1A, and the APQ-50 Mod became the standard radar for early production models, with a 24in (610mm) scanner. Still later, this was supplanted by the APQ-72 radar with a 32in (813mm) scanner, which required a larger radome, and was to give the aircraft its characteristic droopy-nosed look.

The rails for the Sparrows were omitted and the missiles were to be carried "semi-submerged" in a shaped recess under the fuselage, which greatly reduced the drag. They were launched by a small explosive charge which blew the Sparrow away from the parent aircraft and the missile motor ignited as it fell clear. On May 23, 1956, came a requirement for the simultaneous carriage of Sparrows and Sidewinders. A folding fin version of the Sidewinder was undergoing development at the time, and this was to be carried, but in November 1957 the Naval Ordnance Test Station informed NAVAIR that its reliability was likely to be seriously impaired against the standard type. The

effect of this finding was for provision of a rack to carry either two Sidewinders or one Sparrow under each wing. Gradually the previously deleted hardpoints were being reinstated. Provisions were made for extra drop tanks under the wings, and a probe for in-flight refuelling was installed just behind the cockpit, capable of taking on over 260 US gallons (984 litres) per minute. An AAA-4 infra-red seeker was incorporated in a bulge under the nose. The total external load that could be carried was 16,000lb (7,258kg).

The first 18 aircraft built had the flush canopy as the mock-up, but later machines had the canopy raised to give a better forward view over the enlarged nose. The design generally was beefed up for carrier work, and stressed for a sink rate of 22ft/second (6.71m/sec) at a weight of 33,000lb (14,969kg) on landing, as well as catapult launching under zero wind conditions using military

Above: The fifth Phantom, BuAer No. 143390. After completing primary missile system tests, the aircraft was assigned to VX-5 at El Centro, California, for ground attack evaluation testing.

Right: The sixth Phantom, BuAer No. 143391, pictured during carrier suitability trials in April 1960. The nosewheel leg is extended as the aircraft is being prepared for catapult launch.

Above: The eleventh Phantom, BuAer No. 145310, demonstrating its ground attack capability with a load of no fewer than 22 500lb bombs. The photo was taken on 17 April, 1961.

power only. Other requirements were for a steerable dual nosewheel, and provision for dual control in the rear cockpit.

Ease of maintenance was also a consideration in a naval fighter, space being at a premium in the confined hangar deck of an aircraft carrier. Avionics were made generally more accessible, and no less than 199 external access doors were provided, including hinged doors which exposed both engines. Radars of the era were often temperamental, so provision was made for the set to run out on rails for all-round access, without the need to remove it from the aeroplane, a great advantage in those days.

Having established the military requirement for the F4H-1 type of fighter, BuAer invited Chance Vought to build a competing aircraft. MAC coyly suggested that this was to keep them honest, but the real reasons were far more valid than that. Having two aircraft competing for the same order allowed operational evaluation of contrasting solutions to the same problem, and at the same time prevented all the eggs being in one basket. The US Navy had earlier done this with the J40 engine, around which all future fast jet designs were to be based. Its failure caused some red faces and they were not going to be caught again.

The Chance Vought competitor was the XF8U-3 Crusader III. A single-place, single engined design, despite its name it bore little resemblance to the F8U-1 Crusader which had won the original competition. It was fast, but did not have the F4H-1's load-carrying capability.

At last the first prototype F4H-1 neared completion, and it was "rolled out" on May 8, 1958. The first flight had originally been scheduled to take place at Edwards AFB, but this had been changed, and on May 27, the new fighter (Bu No 142259) lifted off for a 20 minute maiden flight in the hands of company chief test pilot, Robert C. Little. Approximately 1,500 subcontractors and suppliers, based in 28 different states, were involved in the project, which up to that point had absorbed about 6,800 man/years. To make this figure more comprehensible, a comparable effort would be represented by the on-site work expended in building 9,000 houses.

The manufacturers' flight test programme went rather better than expected; then in September of that year, the F4H-1 was released to take part in Phase I of the Naval Preliminary Evaluation (NPE). This took place between September 15 and October 10, and involved the investigation of flying qualities and the performance of the basic configuration. This was coupled with the "fly-off" competition against the rival F8U-3 which, having made its first flight just six days after the F4H-1, was showing itself to be a quite remarkable aeroplane.

On December 17, the result was announced; the F4H-1 had been selected as the US Navy's first-line all-weather fighter. The choice of the McDonnell fighter in preference to the F8U-3 was mainly decided by two factors. The two-man crew was judged to be the more effective for the mission, given the complex nature of the weapons system, and two engines were also considered to be an advantage, conferring greater survivability in war and extra safety in peace, although this consideration was reported to be secondary. Two production contracts followed, for 24 aircraft in February 1959 and a further 16 in May, bringing the total number ordered at this point to 47. By the middle of the year, eight F4H-1s had been completed and flown. Their roles in the test programme were as shown in the accompanying table.

A/C No.	BuAer No.	Test Function.
1	142259	Aerodynamic and Propulsion System Development and Demonstration.
2	142260	Propulsion System Development.
3	143388	Equipment Evaluation.
4	143389	Armament Development—Primary Missile System.
5	143390	Primary Missile System Development.
6	143391	Carrier Suitability.
7	143392	Aerodynamic Development and Demonstration.
8	145307	Structural Demonstration.

The McDonnell Aircraft Corporation was, as previously noted, a relative newcomer to the aviation scene. On July 3, 1959, they celebrated their 20th anniversary; to mark the occasion a formal ceremony was held at which the F4H was officially named Phantom II by Mrs. Cecil Paton Milne; the wife of the Assistant Secretary of the Navy for Materiel. (While the correct name is Phantom II, to avoid confusion with the earlier MAC fighter, from now on it will simply be referred to as the Phantom. To avoid further confusion, we will also use the designation F-4 from this point, although this did not become official until 1962 when all aircraft were retrospectively designated and the first batch of 47 machines became F-4As. In March 1961 they were to be retrospectively designated F4H-1Fs!)

Of the initial batch of 47, the first 26 were used for research and development, and the remainder were issued to training units. As was to be expected, they varied considerably. The first 18 aircraft retained the flush canopy and small pointed nose housing the APQ-50 radar set, while the rest sported the raised canopy and bulged droopy nose necessary to house the larger scanner of the APQ-72 radar. The first prototype made its first 50 flights powered by J79-GE-3 engines before being retrofitted with -2s, then later -2As. The -2A was rather more powerful, rated at 16,150lb (7,326kg) static thrust at maximum power, and 10,350lb (4,695kg) at military power.

The next important phase in the development programme came with Phase II of the NPE which took place at the Naval Air Test Centre, Patuxent River, Maryland. Held between July 27 and August 13, 1959, this investigated carrier suitability and flying qualities at an expanded performance envelope. By this time the Phantom was turning in some exceptional performances, in many cases, better than expected, and exceeded its guarantees by an unprecedented 75 per cent. This sounds, and in fact *is*, spectacular, but it is a total, not an average. Some of the comparisons are given in the accompanying table, from which it can be seen that the bulk of the total percentage come from climb and acceleration, which were far better than predicted.

System Parameters	Required	Demonstrated
M_{max} at Max Power	Mach 2.04	Mach 2.03
M_{max} at Mil Power	Mach 0.99	Mach 1.01
Max Power Rate of Climb at 35,000ft (10,671m)	12,258ft/min (3,737m/min)	17,500ft/min (5,335m/min)
Acceleration Time from MRT V_{max} to M_{max} at 35,000ft	0.81 minutes	0.59 minutes
Time to Climb from Sea Level to 35,000ft (max power)	1.30 minutes	1.13 minutes
Supersonic Combat Ceiling Max Power	55,430ft (16,900m)	56,900ft (17,348m)
Max Specific Range (naut. miles per lb of fuel)	0.1107	0.1173
Combat Gross Weight	36,817lb (16,700kg)	36,817lb (16,700kg)

With the development programme going well, Phantom No. 6, BuAer No. 143391, commenced carrier suitability trials in October 1959, and on February 15, 1960 Lt. Cdr. Paul Spencer made the first carrier take-off from the 78,000-ton USS *Independence* and after a 15 minute flight made an arrested landing back on board. Lt. Cdr. Spencer, who as Commanding Officer of VF-74 "Bedevilers" was later to become the first Phantom "Centurion" by making 100 deck landings on type, commented shortly after this first carrier flight: "The F4H is a big airplane. It is twice the weight of the F-11F Tiger and nearly three times the weight of the A-4D Skyhawk, but with all its bulk, it handles better than any modern Navy fighter. Former single-engine fighter pilots will find the response of the F4H's twin J79 engines close to sensational."

Trials continued for several days. The *Independence* was at that time one of the largest carriers in the US Navy; further trials were held on the much smaller USS *Intrepid* (42,000 tons), with equal success. The way was now clear for the final phase of NPE in April, although the Carrier Suitability Demonstration was not completed until November. Then at 11am on December 30, 1960, the first Phantom to enter squadron service, No. 28, Bu No. 148256, was formally accepted by VF-121 at NAS Miramar.

The tremendous advances made in aviation technology during the 1950s had led to a spate of record-breaking as both nations and manufacturers sought to prove that their product flew higher, faster, or further than their rivals. It was a record-minded time and, given the exceptional performance of the Phantom, it was perhaps inevitable that the US Navy should be tempted to have a go at a few. In the event, this led to an unparalled series of record-breaking flights beginning in December 1959 and stretching over the next 28 months. It was an entirely convincing demonstration of what an outstanding aeroplane the Phantom was.

The records achieved were:

1. Project Top Flight, December 6, 1959. Cdr. Lawrence E. Flint, flying from Edwards AFB, set a new absolute altitude record of 98,557ft (30,048m), with the second prototype, Bu. No. 142260, the engine development aircraft.

2. 500km Closed Circuit, September 5, 1960. Marine Corps Lt. Col. Thomas H. Miller flying from Edwards AFB in Bu. No. 142260 set a new speed record of 1,216.76mph (1,958km/h). There were several points of interest about this flight. Drop tanks were carried under both wings and the fuselage centreline. The wing tanks were jettisoned prior to the acceleration phase, which was made with the centre line tank still on. The afterburners were lit 150 miles (241km) from the start line at a height of 36,000ft (10,976m) and a speed of Mach 0.92. After 120 miles (193km) the Phantom had reached an altitude of 48,000ft (14,634m) and accelerated to Mach 1.6. At this point the centreline tank was jettisoned. By the time the start line was reached the altitude had reduced to 42,200ft (12,866m) and the speed had increased to Mach 1.76. The Phantom

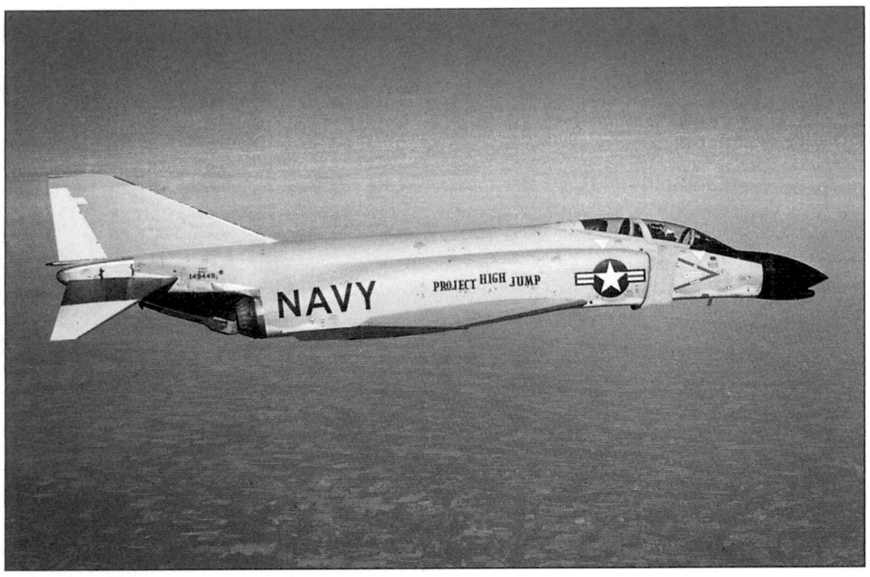

Left: Project High Jump Phantom, BuAer No. 149449, was a standard F-4B.

Right: Aircraft Commander Lt. Huntington Hardisty and his RIO, Lt. Earl "Duke" DeEsch, with the eighth Phantom, BuAer No. 145307, in which they set a low level speed record of 902.769mph (1452.82km/h).

Below: The fourth prototype sports different nose, canopy and intakes.

crossed the finish line 15min 19.2sec later at a height of 46,000ft (14,024m) and at a speed of Mach 2.10 having made a sustained afterburner run lasting 25½ minutes.

3. 100km Closed Circuit, September 25, 1960. Cdr. J. F. Davis, flying Bu. No. 142260 from Edwards AFB, set a new speed record of 1,390.24mph (2,237km/h). The Phantom entered the circular course at an altitude of 45,000ft (13,720m) at a speed of Mach 2.31 and held a 3g turn all the way round, finishing at 47,000ft (14,329m) and Mach 2.21.

4. Project Lana, May 24, 1961. This was a transcontinental speed record attempt designed to demonstrate the rapid deployment capability of the Phantom and at the same time celebrate the 50th anniversary of American Naval Aviation. LANA was in fact an acronym for 50th (roman numeral L) Anniversary Naval Aviation. The distance was 2,446 miles (3,936km), starting from Ontario Field, Los Angeles, and finishing at Floyd Bennett Field, New York. The run consisted of a subsonic military power climb-out to 50,000ft (15,244m), then a maximum speed dash, letting down to 35,000ft (10,671m) and subsonic speed for in-flight refuelling over New Mexico, Missouri, and Ohio. Three Phantoms took part; the fastest, flown by Lt. Gordon with Lt.(jg) Young as his Radar Intercept Officer (RIO), finishing with a time of 2 hours 48 minutes at an average speed of just over 873mph (1,405km/h).

5. Project Sageburner, August 28, 1961. Lt. Huntington Hardisty, pilot, and Lt. Earl DeEsch, flying Phantom No. 8, Bu. No. 145307 from Holloman AFB, set a world speed record at low level of 902.769mph (1,453km/h). The speed was the mean of four passes over a measured 3km (1.86 miles) course at an altitude not exceeding 328ft (100m). Without doubt, this was the most dangerous of all the record attempts.

6. Project Skyburner, November 22, 1961. Marine Lt. Col. Bob Robinson, flying the hard-working Bu. No. 142260 from Edwards AFB, set a new absolute speed record of 1,606.3mph (2,585km/h). At the end of the second run over the measured course, the Phantom was clocking Mach 2.62, something over 1,700mph (2,750km/h). This aircraft had earlier been retrofitted with the more powerful J79-GE-8 engines, and had been modified for the record attempt by installing a water/alcohol spray in the inlet ducts to cool the air ahead of the compressors.

7. Sustained Altitude, December 5, 1961. Cdr. George Ellis, flying from Edwards AFB, set a new sustained altitude record of 66,443.8ft (20,252m) over a measured course.

8. Project High Jump. This was a series of time-to-altitude records set by USN and USMC pilots between February 21 and April 12, 1962. The first five records were set by Phantoms from NAS Brunswick, Maine; the remainder from NAS Point Mugu in California. They are shown in the table.

Time-to-altitude records, 1962

Altitude	Time	Pilot	Date
9,842ft (3,000m)	34.52sec	Ltd. Cdr. John Young	February 21
19,685ft (6,000m)	48.78sec	Cdr. David Langton	February 21
29,527ft (9,000m)	1min 01.62sec	Lt. Col. W. McGraw	March 1
39,370ft (12,000m)	1min 17.15sec	Lt. Col. W. McGraw	March 1
49,212ft (15,000m)	1min 54.54sec	Lt. Cdr. Del Nordberg	March 1
65,616ft (20,000m)	2min 58.5sec	Lt. Cdr. Taylor Brown	March 31
82,020ft (25,000m)	3min 50.44sec	Lt. Cdr. John Young	April 3
98,424ft (30,000m)	6min 11.43sec	Lt. Cdr. Del Nordberg	April 12

On the final flight, Lt. Cdr. Nordberg's Phantom went over the top at more than 100,000ft (30,480m), thus bettering its Top Flight performance. On most of the record-breaking flights, the Phantoms were flown solo. Many of the flights were made carrying the four recessed Sparrows; the extra weight was more than compensated for by the reduction in drag.

The F-4A version of the Phantom II was the first of many variants. Perhaps the most remarkable testimony to the excellence of the design lies in the fact that its external appearance has changed so little over the years. Most of the subsequent improvements lie beneath the surface. The following text

Above and below: The most famous Phantom of all—the second prototype, BuAer No. 142260 which on December 6, 1959, set a new absolute altitude record of 98,557ft (30,040m), then on November 22, 1961, went on to set a world absolute speed record of 1,606.3mph (2,585km/h).

Phantom development

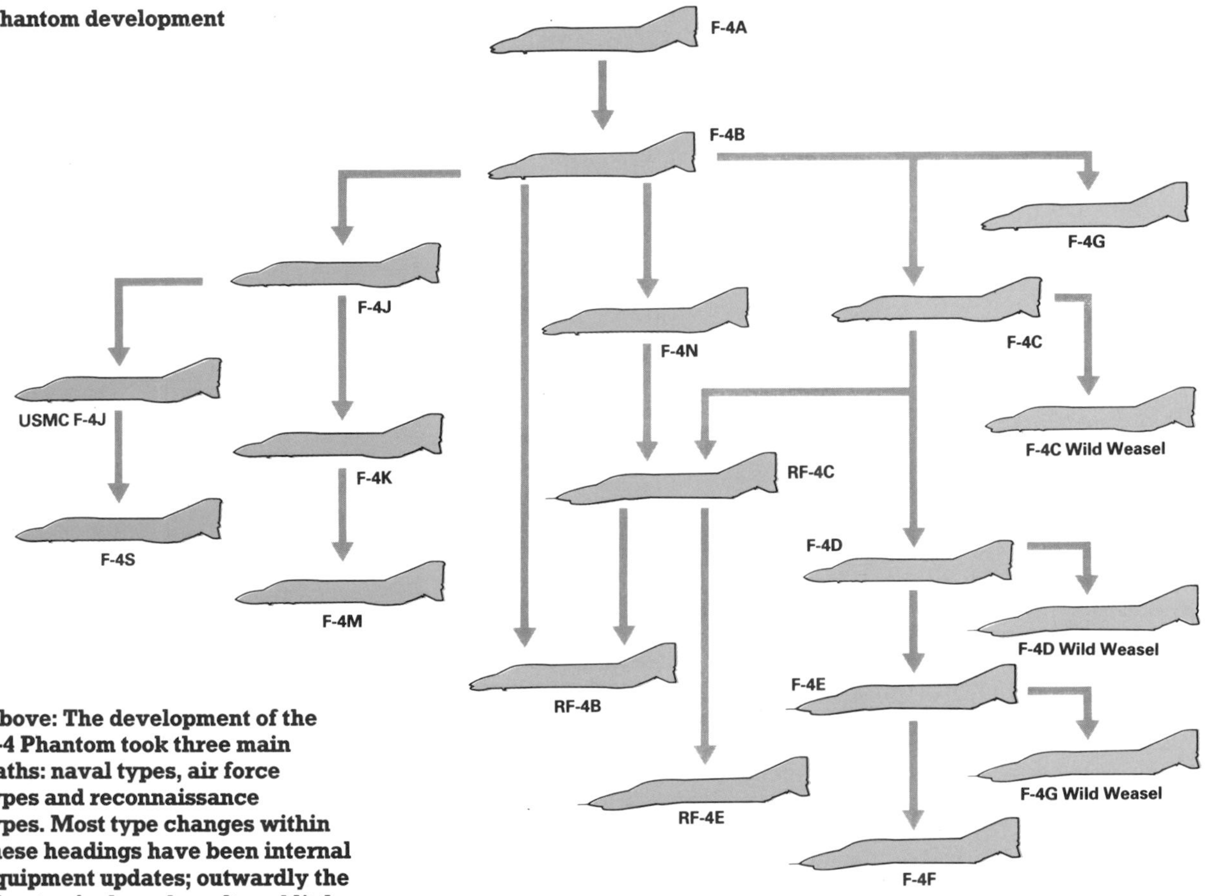

Above: The development of the F-4 Phantom took three main paths: naval types, air force types and reconnaissance types. Most type changes within these headings have been internal equipment updates; outwardly the Phantom's shape has altered little.

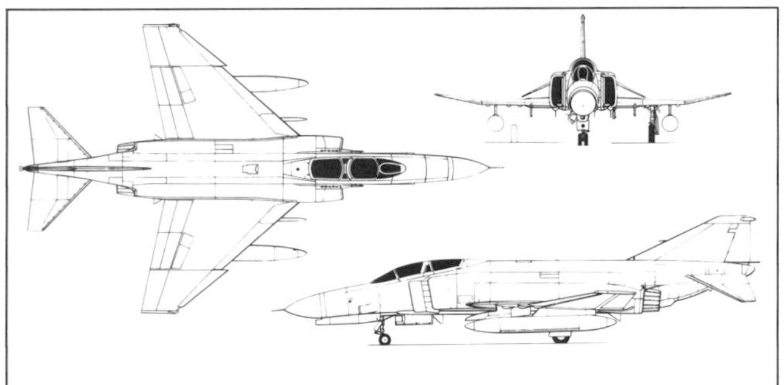

Above: The slatted winged F-4E.

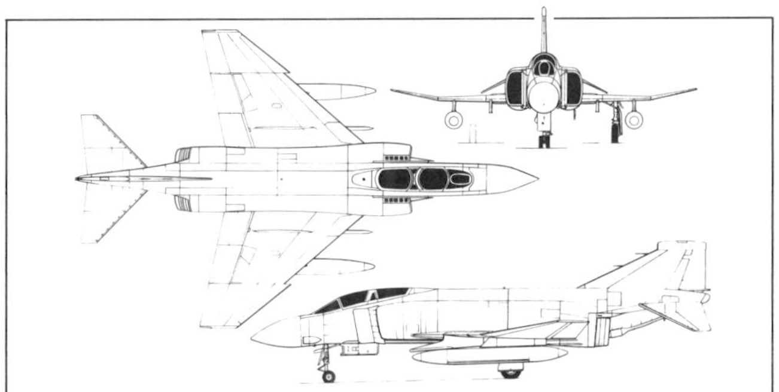

Above: The Spey-engined FG-1.

outlines the development of the sub-types, not in suffix order, but in chronological order based on the date of the first prototype of each sub-type. Given in this manner, the order of development comes out about right.

F-4B. March 25, 1961. USN and USMC.
This was the first major production version. The differences between the F-4A and the F-4B were basically as follows, although there was some overlap:
1. The enlarged radar antenna.
2. More powerful J79-GE-8 engines, rated at 16,000lb (7,484kg) static thrust on maximum power and 10,450lb (4,740kg) on military power. The airflow to the engines was increased marginally and the intake geometry altered from 5 degrees to 10 degrees for the fixed ramp, and from 10 degrees to 14 degrees for the variable ramp. The -8 employed a pre-compressor cooling system which sprayed a mixture of alcohol and water into the ducts ahead of the compressor sections to reduce temperatures at speeds exceeding Mach 1.9.
3. Early carrier trials had shown the need for three improvements. Structural and undercarriage changes allowed deck landings to be made at the increased weight of 34,000lb (15,422kg) with a sink rate of 24ft/second (7.32m/sec). A better view over the nose was achieved by the raised canopy coupled with provision to raise the pilot's seat for landing. The nose gear was made extendable by 20in (51cm) to increase the angle of attack during catapult takeoff.
4. The basic electronics fit was standardised as follows: the Aero 1A Fire Control System comprised the APQ-72 search and track radar; the APA-157 continuous wave radar for Sparrow semi-active homing missile guidance; and the AAA-4 Infra-red search and track scanner, which needed radar ranging information. The Communication-Navigation-Identification (CNI) package was made up of ARN-21 TACAN (Tactical Air Navigation), ARC-52 Communications, APR-40 Auxiliary UHF receiver, ARA-25 UHF-ADF (Airborne Direction Finding), APX-68 IFF (Identification Friend/Foe), APA-89 SIF (Selective Identification Feature), and AIC-14 intercomm. Also included was a miscellaneous selection of black boxes; the APA-138 fixed optical gunsight, the A-24 Central Air Data Computer, APN-22 Radar Altimeter, ASA-32 Autopilot, ASN-39 Dead Reckoning Navigational Computer, and the AJB-3A Loft/Toss Bombing Computer.

Above: This rare photograph, taken in January 1962, shows a US Navy F-4B (see small nose wheel) in US Air Force markings as the F-110A, with Tactical Air Command insignia on the fin.

F-4G (USN Version). March 20, 1963.
This designation was applied to a dozen F-4Bs which were fitted with a two-way Data Link incorporating an automatic carrier landing mode with automatic approach power compensation. To accommodate the extra equipment, a new compartment was formed by reducing the size of the No. 1 fuel cell, with access through a hatch on top of the fuselage. These F-4Gs were later reconverted back into F-4Bs, but the new compartment was to appear on many subsequent models.

F-4C. May 27, 1963. USAF.
Carrier fighters, hampered by folding wings, arrester hooks and such like naval impedimenta, had traditionally been out-performed by their land-based counterparts. As Navy Phantoms took almost every record in sight, and consistently turned in exceptional performances during operational exercises, it was perhaps inevitable that it should attract a wider audience. In 1961 the Department of Defense ordered a series of competitive evaluations to be held between the Phantom and current Air Force fighters. The results were startling for the light blue fraternity. The new Navy fighter was faster, climbed better, could detect at longer ranges, and carried heavier loads further than the best the Air Force could offer. This was combined with better serviceability rates and lower man-maintenance hours per flight hour.

In 1962 the Department of Defense approved the procurement of the Phantom for Tactical Air Command with the Air Force designation of F-110A. Changes were kept to a minimum, but some were inevitable. The F-4C, as it was later to be redesignated, differed from the Navy F-4B in the following respects:
1. J79-GE-15 engines were installed. These could be used for remote field

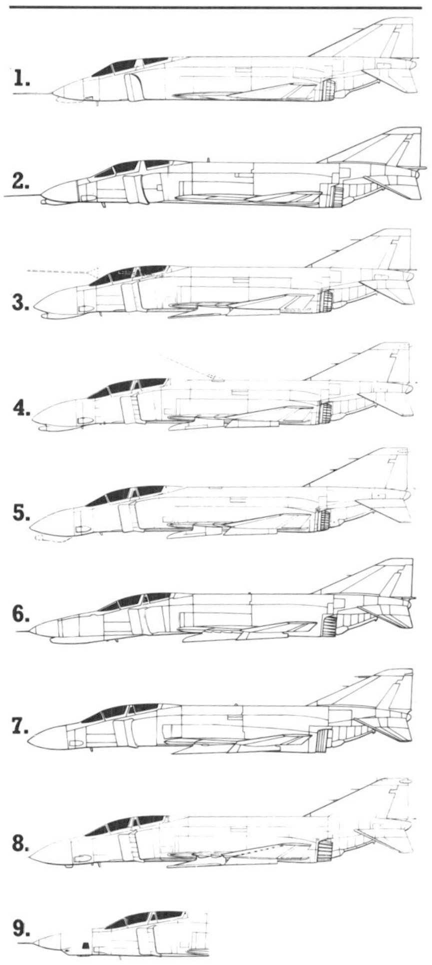

Above: Phantom variants (see also three-views).
1. XF4H-1 prototype.
2. F-4A carrier fighter.
3. F-4B carrier fighter, first major production version.
4. F-4C tactical fighter for the USAF.
5. F-4D strike fighter for USAF.
6. F-4F variant for Luftwaffe.
7. F-4K/M now in RAF service only.
8. F-4J USN replacement for F-4B.
9. RF-4 typical nose section.

Above: US Navy F-4G of VF-213 in experimental camouflage finish aboard USS *Kitty Hawk*, in July 1966. The white radome came from a repair facility. Black was the original colour.

operations as they incorporated a cartridge-pneumatic starting system instead of the compressed air turbine impingement used by the Navy. The 20kVA generators were moved from the waist gearbox to a fairing in the engine nose.
2. Tarmac-covered concrete runways are relatively soft when compared with the steel deck of a ship, and the wheels and tyres were increased in width from 7.7in to 11.5in (196mm to 292mm). The brakes were made more powerful and an anti-skid system was fitted, although this was regrettably not proof against a pilot with size 14 boots and a shot of adrenalin. The increased wheel and tyre width necessitated a shallow bulge in the wing to house them.
3. The Navy IFR probe was replaced by the Air Force boom receptacle.
4. Full dual controls were fitted; the early years in Air Force service saw the Phantom crewed by two rated pilots. Only later did the Weapon System Officer, commonly known as the "Whizzo", take over the back seat.
5. The APQ-100 radar, a modified APQ-72, was installed, complete with Plan Position Indicator (PPI). This gave better radar mapping.
6. The ASN-48 Inertial Navigation System (INS) replaced the Navy's navigation computer, giving better long-range independent navigation.
7. The AJB-7 bombing system and LADD timer were incorporated, as well as provision for the AGM-12 Bullpup command guidance air to ground missile.
8. Provision was made for the four Sidewinders to be replaced on the wing pylons by the cheaper AIM-4 Falcon.

RF-4C. (Prototype was converted F-4B.) August 8, 1963. USAF.

The obvious next step was to produce a reconnaissance version of the Phantom, and this was developed in parallel with the F-4C, featuring the same engine and undercarriage revisions, but with a redesigned nose which increased the overall length of the aircraft by 4ft 8in (144cm). The missile control systems were deleted, communications were made considerably more versatile, and a comprehensive package of reconnaissance equipment installed. Typically this consisted of:
1. APQ-99 forward-looking radar with terrain following and terrain avoidance modes; also a ground mapping mode which provided a general radar navigation facility.
2. A comprehensive array of cameras in the nose, with either a KS-72 or KS-77 forward framing camera for obliques, a KA-55A high altitude panoramic camera and a KA-56A low altitude panoramic camera, all combined with an LA 313 Optical Viewfinder in the front cockpit. In-flight data was recorded on all film frames by the Auxiliary Data Annotation Set (ADAS), and normally took the form of date, time, radar and barometric altitude, latitude, longitude, heading, pitch, roll, drift angle, and unit details. LA 307A and LA 308A photo flash ejectors were installed in the rear fuselage.
3. ASN-56 INS replaced the ASN-48 of the F-4C.
4. APQ-102 Side Looking Radar (SLR) with its reference computer and recorder. control gave a high-definition radar picture along both sides of the aircraft's track. Tied in with the cameras on most models was the ALR-17 ELRAC which automatically identified and classified hostile radars on photo-maps. Further electronic wizardry could be carried in pods.
5. AAS-18 Infra-red detection set used IR line scanning to produce a thermal map of the area flown over, by day or by night, even showing such details as the heated patch on a runway left by an aircraft that had earlier taken off.
6. The high frequency (HF) system extended communications far beyond the line of sight range limits normally associated with UHF. This seeming reversion to an earlier type of radio made voice communication with base possible over the entire range of the mission. The ARC-105 HF Communications Transceiver, with HF antenna coupler control and a shunt aerial occupying almost the entire leading edge of the fin made this possible.

RF-4B. March 12, 1965. USMC.

The United States Navy had no requirement for a reconnaissance Phantom, but a small number of carrier-suitable RF-4Bs were acquired for the Marine Corps. They differed from the RF-4C in the following respects:
1. J79-GE-8 engines.
2. Navy-type wheels and IFR.
3. Flight controls in front cockpit only.
4. The mounts for the KS-72 or KS-85 cameras were rotatable in flight, whereas those in the RF-4C could only be realigned on the ground.

F-4J. (Prototype was converted F-4B.) June 4, 1965. USN and USMC.

The F-4J was an updated and strengthened F-4B with the air defence role stressed. The differences between the F-4B and the F-4J were:
1. J79-GE-10 engines, rated at 17,900lb (8,119kg) s.t. and increased fuel capacity gained by adding No. 7 fuel cell in the rear fuselage above the engine nozzles.
2. DLGW increased to 38,000lb (17,237kg) at a sink rate of 23.3ft/sec (7.10m/sec). This involved considerable structural strengthening, and the Air Force type wide wheels and tyres were fitted. To maintain low carrier approach speeds at increased weights the inboard leading edge was fixed, the ailerons made to droop at a 16½ degree angle with the landing gear down, and a fixed inverted slot was incorporated along the leading edges of the stabilators. In addition, the ASW-25 One-Way Data Link with automatic carrier landing and approach power compensator was fitted.
3. AWG-10 fire control computer system, incorporating the APG-59 pulse doppler radar with a look-down capability.
4. AJB-7 Bombing System.
5. Miniaturised solid-state CNI.
6. Visual Target Acquisition System (VTAS) fitted as a helmet sight.
7. Electronic warfare equipment included APR-32 Radar Homing and Warning System (RHAWS) with a fin cap aerial.
8. Modified equipment cooling unit.
9. GVR-10 Vertical Reference Gyro

Above: An unusual view of a Royal Air Force Phantom FGR-2 fitted out for the long range interception role. The roundels in this low visibility scheme appear to serve little purpose.

10. 30kVA generators to produce the extra power required.
11. Martin-Baker rocket-assisted zero/zero ejection seats.

A special version of the F-4J was proposed for the USMC, with the primary task of attaining beachhead air superiority. It differed from the main version in two respects. The Weapon Control System became the digital AWG-10A, which gave more accurate data for missile launch, and computed air to ground conventional weapon delivery. It also incorporated manoeuvre slats on the wings as described for the F-4E.

F-4D. December 9, 1965. USAF.

The F-4D was basically the F-4C airframe and engines, with improved avionics and better strike capability. The differences between the C and D versions were:
1. APQ-109 partial solid state radar (modified APQ-100), which gave air to ground slant ranging, and for the first time, movable cursors on the display.
2. ASG-22 Lead Computing Optical Sight System (LCOSS) with lead computing amplifier and gyro.
3. ASQ-91 Weapons release computer.
4. ASN-63 INS.
5. 30kVA generators.

Much of the extra electronics kit was located in the compartment over the No. 1 fuel cell pioneered by the Navy F-4G. The accuracy of the air-to-ground conventional weapons delivery was greatly improved. Typical store capability of this model was: 18 750lb (340kg) bombs, or 15 680lb (308kg) mines, or 11 1,000lb (454kg) bombs, or 7 smoke bombs, 11 150 US gallon (125 Imp gall/568 litre) Napalm tanks, 4 Bullpup AGMs, or 3 20mm Vulcan gun pods.

F-4E. (Prototype was converted YRF-4C.) August 7, 1965. USAF.

The F-4E was developed in parallel with the Navy F-4J and was originally intended to be an F-4D but with much improved radar capability. The missile control system was to have been either the AWG-10, or the original Aero 1A with the addition of Coherent-On-Receive-Doppler System (CORDS). This component of the APQ-120 miniaturised radar promised excellent detection of low-flying aircraft, and even possible detection of moving targets on the ground. But CORDS was later found to be erratic, and in the event the APQ-120 pulse radar was fitted. Meanwhile the design was overtaken by events. Combat experience in Southeast Asia had shown the need for a gun in air-to-air combat. As an expedient, a pod containing the M 61 Vulcan cannon had been hung on the centreline of earlier models. This was far from satisfactory: it occupied a pylon and degraded the performance of the aircraft, and distortion of the pylon by flight and firing stresses led to innaccuracy.

Another problem arose from the fact that the Phantom had been designed as an interceptor rather than as a fighter. At that time, manoeuvre combat had been thought to be a thing of the past, as it had been previously and no doubt will be again. In fact, as weapons get cleverer, it is probably inevitable; the difficulty lies in knowing exactly when! The design of the Phantom had a built-in drawback, an unforgiving stall/spin characteristic. High AOA manoeuvring at low speeds or high weights easily led to the aircraft departing controlled flight. At altitudes above 10,000ft (3,050m) recovery was possible, but below this it was frequently fatal. In peacetime, pilots were educated to avoid the danger area, but dodging MiGs and missiles over North Vietnam did not permit this luxury. Literally dozens of Phantoms were lost to this cause.

This sparked off a programme called Agile Eagle. What was wanted was the best blend of high lift co-efficient for the least drag, improved handling at high AOA, with suitability for high lift configurations at take-off and landing. All had to be compatible with the existing F-4 wing planform and structural concept. Various solutions were tried. They included leading edge flaps and slats, leading edge camber, trailing edge flaps, and various combinations of these. Worthwhile improvements in energy/manoeuvrability were achieved in wind tunnel tests with leading edge flaps, and also leading edge slats. At high AOA the slats were found to have better lift/drag characteristics than flaps, and this modification became standard on aircraft delivered from June 1972 onwards. The remainder were retrofitted with slats at a later date.

The F-4E differed from the F-4D as follows:
1. M61-A1 cannon and 640 round ammunition tank were fitted. This involved a lengthened and redesigned nose with a fairing on the underside for the gun. The IR seeker was omitted.
2. Manoeuvre slats on leading edges of wings, with the inboard edge fixed and BLC deleted. In manoeuvring flight the slats extend automatically at about 6 degrees AOA and retract at about 4 degrees.
3. Slotted leading edges to the stabilator as on the F-4J.
4. APQ-120 pulse Doppler radar and intercept computer.
5. No. 7 fuel cell in rear fuselage as on the F-4J.
6. J79-GE-17 engines giving 17,900lb (8,119kg) s.t. max.
7. Hydraulic wing fold deleted.
8. Martin-Baker rocket assisted ejection seats with zero/zero capability.

F-4K. June 27, 1966. Royal Navy as FG-1.

The F-4K was developed from the F-4J for Britain's Royal Navy to supersede the sub-sonic Sea Vixen. The decision was taken at an early stage to use the Rolls-Royce Spey Mk.202 or 203 engines, rated at 20,515lb (9,305kg) s.t. maximum and 12,250lb (5,556kg) s.t. military power. The extra thrust was to give better acceleration, better climb, and more bleed air for BLC, thus improving low speed handling. The Spey also had a much better specific fuel consumption than the J79 which promised about a 30 per cent increase in range/endurance.

Considerable structural alterations were needed. The intakes and ducts were enlarged to accommodate a 20 per cent greater mass airflow and auxiliary air doors were installed in the

rear fuselage. Both fixed and moveable intake ramps were redesigned. The engine bays were enlarged, which involved the refairing of the lower aft fuselage and slight alteration of the location of the rear pair of Sparrows. One result of all these changes was that the fuselage had to be widened a few inches, although the wingspan remained unchanged. Alas, problems were encountered in matching the engine to the airframe, the result of which was that the anticipated performance improvements were never realised.

Other differences between the F-4K and the F-4J were:

1. DLGW 38,000lb (17,237kg) at a sink rate of 24ft/sec (7.32m/sec).
2. IR sensor deleted.
3. Arrester hook strengthened to withstand a deceleration of 4.8g.
4. To allow catapult launching at lower wind over deck speeds the nose gear was made extra-extendable from 20in to 40in (51 to 102cm) to give increased AOA at launch.
5. Many internal equipment changes.
6. Combustion starters for the engines.
7. Radome and antenna were made to swing through 180 degrees, thus reducing the overall length to 52ft (15.85m) to allow the F-4K to fit British aircraft carrier lifts.

F-4M. February 17, 1967. Royal Air Force as FGR 2.
The F-4M was based on the F-4K, with weapon delivery and tactical reconnaissance systems added to make it a true multi-role aeroplane. The main differences between the F-4M and F-4K are:

1. Drooped ailerons, slotted stabilator, catapult launch provisions and extra-extendable nose gear all deleted.
2. Anti-skid brakes.
3. Ferranti INAS.
4. HF long range voice communications.
5. LCOSS.
6. Strike camera.

RF-4E. September 15, 1970. Used by West Germany, Iran, Israel, Japan, Greece and Turkey.
The RF-4E is basically an F-4E airframe with armament provisions deleted and an RF-4C nose spliced on. The equipment fit varies with the customer.

F-4N. June 4, 1972. USN and USMC.
This is the designation given to selected F-4Bs which have been rebuilt to extend their service life and update their equipment. This project, codenamed Beeline, replaces certain structural sections which have reached the end of their safe fatigue life. It involves a complete rewire, new 30kVA generators, one-way Data Link, air-to-air IFF, VTAS, SEAM, Automatic Altitude Reporting, and a dogfight computer.

F-4F. May 18, 1973. West Germany.
In the late 1960s extensive studies were carried out on a possible single-seat Phantom (to be designated F-4EF) as a candidate in the US International Fighter Competition held to select a new export fighter for supply to friends and allies of the United States. The earlier Northrop F-5A/B had been able to match the performance of the MiG-19 Farmer and early-model MiG-21 Fishbed, but something "hotter" was needed to cope with the second-generation Fishbeds and the MiG-23 Flogger.

Above: Phantom FG-1 of No. 892 Squadron, Royal Navy, on board an American aircraft carrier, almost certainly USS *Saratoga*, from which the squadron first operated, in Autumn 1969.

Below: Phantom F-4D of USAF's 8th TFW "Wolfpack" over the Republic of Korea during Exercise "Team Spirit 78". It carries auxiliary fuel tanks and an AN/ALQ-119 ECM pod.

Above: Brightly coloured Phantoms of US Navy test squadron VX-4. The aircraft bringing up the rear is a QF-4B drone (here with pilot), painted red for maximum rather than minimum visibility. "Black Bunny" leads.

Right: Phantom No. 266, USAF serial No. 62-12200, flew 30 test flights from Edwards AFB with experimental canard foreplanes as shown here. It had also been a fly-by-wire (FBW) demonstrator.

The obvious choice was the then-new F-5E, but the competition saw various alternative designs being proposed. These included the single-seat Phantom, the Vought V1000 uprated version of the F-8 Crusader and Lockheed's high-wing/low tailplane CL-1200 derivative of the F-104.

In addition to having no rear cockpit, the F-4EF would have had a simplified and lightened structure with a slatted but non-folding wing, no refuelling receptacle and only six fuel cells. Other features included a light weapon load—normally a centreline tank and four AIM-9s plus the internal cannon.

However, the prospect of a relatively low-cost "stripped" version of the F-4 was seen by European aircraft companies as an alarming threat to their own products. Contemporary reports suggested a production price would have been less than $1 million, but this was probably unrealistic given the fact that at the time even an F-5A cost around $750,000, while the newly-developed F-5E had a price tag of around $1.3 million. Lowest recorded unit price for export Phantom was the $1.53 million which Spain paid for 36 refurbished F-4Cs delivered in 1971/2. The most expensive F-4 deal is reported to have been Iran's 16 RF-4Es, at a unit cost of $9.36 million.

The F-4EF was offered to the West German Luftwaffe to meet its requirement for a new air-superiority fighter. A Phantom order was finally placed, but (as mentioned earlier) the version selected was a less drastically modified F-4E variant retaining second cockpit and folding wing with F-4E-style leading-edge slats. Various weight-saving exercises give the type a higher combat thrust-to-weight ratio than the standard aircraft.

Other items differing from the F-4E are:

1. Simplified APQ-120 radar.

2. Sparrow missiles and their associated systems are deleted and the internal cannon and Sidewinders are the primary armament.

3. IFR, slotted stabilator, bombing avionics and No. 7 fuel cell are deleted.

F-4G (USAF version). December 6, 1975.

This variant must not be confused with the much earlier and numerically insignificant batch of USN Phantoms which also received the same designation. The USAF version of the F-4G is an F-4E airframe reconfigured for the Advanced Wild Weasel role. As electronic technology progressed, ground-to-air weapons became more deadly. Aircraft ECM was helpful, but defence suppression became necessary, and the Wild Weasel defence suppression aircraft was developed. The F-105F Thunderchief was one of the earliest and best known of these, but some earlier Phantoms, F-4Cs, Ds and Es, had been configured to carry out this mission by adding electronic detection gear and arming them with anti-radiation missiles and other weapons.

To meet the full requirements of the Wild Weasel role, the F-4G was developed. It differs from the F-4E as follows:

1. The internal gun was deleted and a chin pod housing radar detection antennae took its place. The only other readily discernible change in the external appearance is a further pod on top of the fin.

2. APR-38 RHAWS installed. This is a very comprehensive system with no less than 52 antennae. It provides threat information and also allows triangulation, giving distance to the target as well as the bearing provided by earlier systems. It can also supply data for weapon delivery, including automatic weapon release, and has a blind bombing capability. The rear cockpit is far more comprehensively instrumented than any previous Phantom. Primary weapons carried are the Shrike and Standard anti-radiation missiles, and the Maverick electro-optical guided bomb.

F-4S. July 22, 1977. USN.

This designation has been given to F-4Js which have undergone rebuilds to extend their service life and update their equipment, in a similar manner to the F-4N. The most radical modification is the addition of leading edge slats.

F-4CCV. MAC No. 266. AF Serial 62-12200.

This particular Phantom had an eventful history. Starting as an F-4B, it was converted to become the prototype YRF-4C. Still later it became the prototype YF-4E. It was then used for research into fly-by-wire (FBW) survivable flight control systems (SFCS), and was also known as the Precision Aircraft Control Technology (PACT) demonstrator. In this configuration it made its first flight on April 29, 1972, from Lambert St. Louis International. For this flight it retained back-up mechanical controls. As confidence was gained, the mechanical reversion was removed and on January 22, 1973, it made a 70 minute flight from Edwards AFB using FBW only. It was later fitted with experimental 40sqft (3.7sqm) canard foreplanes to evaluate Control Configured Vehicle (CCV) techniques for combat aircraft. In this form it retained FBW, and the outboard flap sections were modified to act as flaperons for manoeuvre loading and direct lift control. It flew 30 test flights in this configuration at Edwards AFB, and its working life ended on December 5, 1978, when it was donated to the USAF Museum.

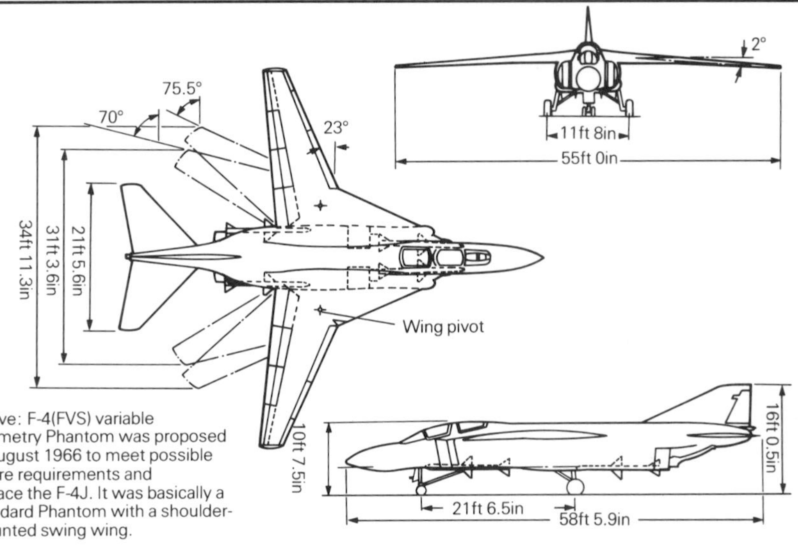

Above: F-4(FVS) variable geometry Phantom was proposed in August 1966 to meet possible future requirements and replace the F-4J. It was basically a standard Phantom with a shoulder-mounted swing wing.

QF-4B and DF-4B

A small number of F-4Bs were converted during the early 1970s to become Remotely Piloted Vehicles (RPVs) and "mother" aircraft (DF-4Bs). These are used for flight and weapon trials and research.

F-4 (FVS) variable geometry design

In the mid-1960s, McDonnell drew up plans for what would have been the most heavily-modified version of the Phantom family—the variable geometry F-4(FVS). This was intended as a follow-on to the US Navy's F-4J, and was designed to cope with the anticipated threats of the 1970s. The service could foresee a need for greater fleet-defence capability plus improved air-to-ground attack performance, but the demands of the steadily-escalating Vietnam War dictated that development time of any new fighter must be kept short.

Several missions were identified for the new design, including thwarting saturation attacks by subsonic and supersonic aircraft operating at heights ranging from sea level over to 40,000ft (12,192m), with some attackers releasing air-to-surface missiles at ranges of up to 100 miles (161km). This demanded the ability to carry out several simultaneous look-up, look-down and co-altitude attacks in the face of enemy ECM.

Long-range air-superiority and escort missions required improved range, as did the demand for an ability to deliver air-to-ground ordnance including nuclear weapons from over 600 miles (945km) distance.

The F-4(FVS) would have retained much of the existing Phantom structure, the main new component being the revised wing with pivots at 28 per cent span. Wing sweep would have been variable from 23deg to 70deg, while a revised horizontal stabiliser with zero dihedral was intended to improve supersonic manoeuvrability. To cope with the increased range, internal fuel capacity was to increase from the 1,998 gallons (7,563l) on the F-4J to 2,514 gallons (9,516l).

Attractive although the VG Phantom may have seemed on paper, it was hardly surprising that the project was abandoned. The ill-fated F-111B naval fighter was already in deep technical trouble, but the USN could see the possibility of repacking that aircraft's advanced weaponry into a new airframe while still attaining an early 1970s operational date.

The McDonnell design could not match the long radar range and multishot capability of the Phoenix missile and AWG-9 fire-control system, so the Navy was probably wise to insist on scrapping the F-111B in 1968 and beginning the VFX programme which was to result in the Grumman F-14 Tomcat. Had the F-4(FVS) been built as an interim fighter, its existence might even have resulted in the more capable F-14 being abandoned in the early 1970s as cost-escalation and inflation drove the price of the Grumman warplane to unprecedented levels.

F-4T air-superiority fighter

One further F-4 variant was to be stillborn in the late 1970s. In a final attempt to keep the Phantom line running, McDonnell Douglas proposed the F-4T air-superiority fighter. This would have been based on the F-4E, but would have been stripped of all equipment associated with air-to-ground missions. The chin-mounted M61 cannon would have been retained, along with an armament of four AIM-9 Sidewinders and four AIM-7 Sparrows, or an alternative warload of six Sparrows. A digital computer would have handled missile launching. It was never clear if the design had been slanted to meet the needs of a specific potential customer, but none came forward.

Super Phantom

Congressional funding (Fiscal Year 1984) has been approved for the US Air Force to carry out a flight demonstration programme of improved F-4Es (dubbed Super Phantoms), primarily for vast foreign military sales potential, but also with a view to extending service life of Phantoms in US service. Despite apparent USAF reluctance (because of the potential threat to funds for foreign sales of F-16s, development of F-16E or F-15E dual-role fighters, and advanced tactical fighter research and development), the Department of Defense is recommending upgrading of F-4s with new engines (Pratt & Whitney 1120, see chapter on Powerplant) and avionics.

Probably because they could envisage that a Super Phantom would compete for sales with the F-15 and F/A-18, McDonnell Douglas declined to participate in the project. In September 1983 Boeing and Pratt & Whitney proposed a flight test demonstration programme with the re-engined F-4 which would also be fitted with avionics already developed for other aircraft. The Department of Defense would like to have the test aircraft in the air by 1985's Paris Air Show, for obvious international marketing reasons. Main foreign users the sales pitch would be aimed at would be Israel, West Germany, South Korea and Japan, who are all looking at ways to improve their Phantoms. Of over 3,500 F-4s still in service worldwide, it is estimated that more than 2,000 will still be operating into the next century, based on the assumption that most air forces will not be able to afford replacements by existing or newly developed types, and the fact that there is scope for improving the F-4s in their inventories. The crux of USAF's reluctance appears to be concern at extending the life of aircraft whose airframes could aleady have up to 20 years of fatigue life.

Above: The "Super Phantom" proposal, which includes upgraded engines and avionics.

The Boeing/Pratt & Whitney proposal is claimed to offer marked performance improvements over the J79-engined Phantom, and modification costs per aircraft—including new engines, avionics refit and a conformal fuel tank under the belly—have been estimated at $7 to $9 millions. Avionics for the test aircraft would include the F-16's APG-66 radar, Marconi head-up display and Sperry cockpit display system, as well as the Teledyne avionics processors and Honeywell inertial navigation system which are fitted to Northrop's F-20 design.

Despite the opposition to the scheme, it looks very much as if many of the world's Phantoms are in for a new lease of life.

Below: The end of an era. The 5057th and last St. Louis-built Phantom, an F-4E, was flown away by the USAF on Friday October 26, 1979.

Structure

Pretty the Phantom may not be but, built to withstand the shocks and stresses of carrier-based operations, it has had the strength to carry out any task which its users might request. Although designed as a long-range interceptor, the Phantom has shown itself able to tote massive loads of ordnance. In RAF service, the big warplane has been used for low-level strike missions, flying so close to the ground that some aircraft have come home with tree branches caught in the flap mechanism.

Above: As this view of unpainted aircraft on the St. Louis production line shows, the F-4 structure is virtually all metal, apart from the radome and canopy. The diagram below indicates measures to minimise the weight problem.

Two qualities best sum up the structure of the Phantom—it was a good sound design, and it has proven able to take punishment. Despite the long process of evolution to which the aircraft was subjected, modifications to the structure were largely confined to changes dictated by revised roles and equipment. As wartime experience in the skies over Vietnam was to show, the structure of the Phantom could absorb damage by anti-aircraft fire and missile attack, and bring its crew home safely.

Construction of a mock-up was completed by the end of 1955, and the design was frozen the following August, allowing metal to be cut for the first XF4H-1 prototype. This lacked the bulbous nose fitted to all production aircraft, but was otherwise similar to the Phantom of today.

The F-4 defies the traditional rule of thumb which claims that "if it looks right—it is right". The F-4 may not look "wrong" but it cannot claim to be beautiful. Its shape is no triumph of brute force over aerodynamic ignorance—the distinctly odd lines are not engineers' crude attempts to "cure" aerodynamic deficiencies, but practical solutions to many of the problems faced during the design of any Mach 2 type, an example of how a bold design team can push back the accepted rules by using advanced technology.

The layout was no step in the dark, however. Most of its features—side intakes, low-set swept wing, and long tail section extending behind the jetpipes—may be seen in the earlier XF-88, F-101 and F-3 (F3H). Despite being a single-seat, single-engine design, the F-3 bears a strong family resemblance to the F-4.

Several landmarks in aircraft design were established by the F-4 team. Some 8 to 10 per cent of the airframe was made from titanium, the first time that this material had been used on a large scale for primary structural sections which would be exposed to high temperatures. Phantom was too early to take advantage of today's advanced materials, such as carbon-fibre composites. The main non-metallic structural material used was glass fibre, largely for parts such as the nose radome which needed to be transparent to radio or radar transmissions.

Large scale use was made for the first time in a fighter design of integral machining and chemical milling—good methods of making strong lightweight components. Coupled with the use of large pressings and forgings, these techniques allowed the design team to build the airframe from large sections, a move which reduced the number of fasteners and concentrations of stress. The use of honeycomb was restricted to non-critical parts such as fairings, wheel-well covers and trailing edges.

The Phantom is made up of seven major sub-assemblies: forward fuselage; centre fuselage; aft fuselage; wing centre section; wing outer sections; horizontal tailplane.

The soundness of the basic design was proven in the early 1970s when the US Navy rebuilt 228 F-4Bs to the F-4N standard. Airframes were selected according to the number of catapult shots, arrested landings and flying hours they had clocked up. In addition to installing new avionics, this modification program strengthened the structure, replacing some new sections so that these aircraft could serve into the 1980s.

Overall length of the aircraft was dictated by the size of the centre lifts aboard some patterns of US Navy carriers in service when the design was drawn up. This set a length of 56ft (17m), but this was later increased by around 2ft (61cm) to allow the installation of a larger radar antenna.

Lifts on UK carriers were only 54ft (16.4m) long, so a folding radome had to be developed for the F-4K. This allowed the entire radar in its radome to be swung backwards through 180 degrees in order to bring the aircraft length within this limit.

The forward fuselage was manufac-

Extensive use of titanium

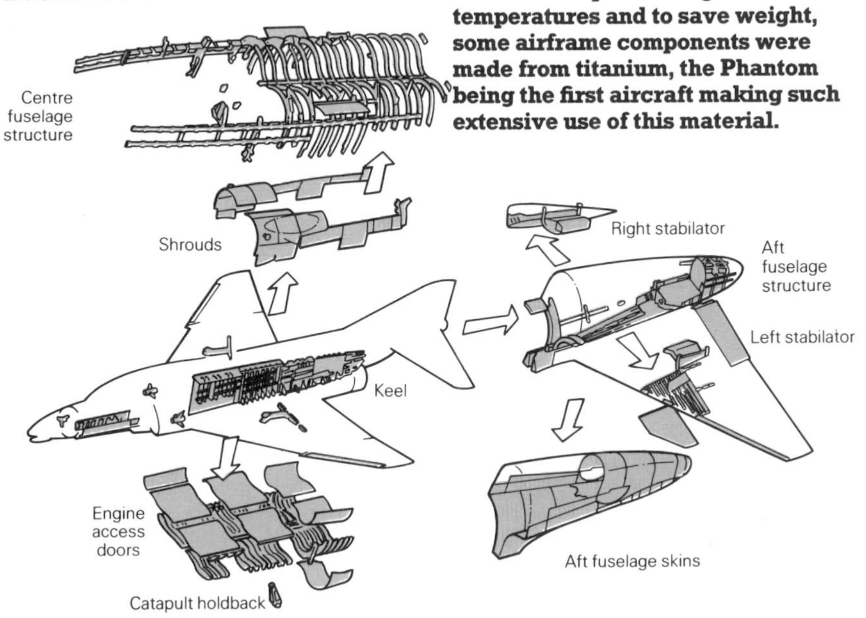

Below: To cope with high temperatures and to save weight, some airframe components were made from titanium, the Phantom being the first aircraft making such extensive use of this material.

Above: The variation in appearance of chin-mounted IR seeker is about the only discernible outward difference between an F-4C and F-4D. The standard pattern lacks the bulged rear section of the version fitted to the F-4D (upper).

Left: RAF technicians service the retractable refuelling probe on an F-4M. The engine inlets are shrouded to prevent the accidental entry of tools or debris.

tured in two halves (port and starboard), which were fitted with electrical cabling and pipework before being mated. It was largely manufactured from sheet aluminium, with forgings being used in areas of high stress such as the nose landing gear supports and the inlet leading edge.

Most of the major changes introduced to this section of the aircraft were in the nose profile. First major production change was on the F-4D. The chin-mounted fairing formerly used to house the AAA-4 IR sensor was no longer required, while the nose was increased in diameter to accommodate the new APQ-109 radar.

The extended nose of the recce version first appeared on the RF-4C, developed by the USAF as a replacement for the RF-101A Voodoo. It was first tested in 1963 on two F-4Bs converted as YRF-4C "recon" prototypes while still on the production line. Ultimate reshaping of the nose came with the F-4E, when a compact solid-state APQ-120 radar plus an internal gun replaced the earlier radar payload.

A new avionics compartment was introduced by the mid-1960s F-4G carrier-landing development aircraft. Located just behind the second cockpit, this made room for the ASW-21 data link, but reduced the size of the No. 1 fuel cell. Although these aircraft were later modified back to the standard F-4B configuration, the new avionics bay was to remain a feature of later variants such as the F-4D, E and J.

The centre fuselage section is just over 22ft (6.7m) long. Two bulkheads in this area transfer most of the fuselage loads into the wing spars via 16 close-tolerance bolts. Most of the titanium used in the F-4 is located in the aft fuselage, particularly in the main structural keel which runs between the engines, and in the engine bay inner liners.

Double-wall construction was adopted for the floors of the fuel tanks located above the engine bays. Cool air diverted from the engine bay is passed between these walls, then dumped overboard via louvres in the fuselage sides.

Since the lower surface of the aft fuselage is exposed to the effects of turbojet efflux, it is of double-wall section cooled by ram air, and incorporates insulating blankets. An outer layer of titanium "shingles" is held in position by oversized screws and washers in order to minimise buckling with changes of temperature.

Accessibility of internal equipment is good, the design team having fitted some 199 external access doors. These include hinged doors covering the engines, and removable top-fuselage covers which give access to the fuel system. Experience in Vietnam eventually led to the installation of armour plate over critical systems and on the rear fuselage.

The Phantom's fuel

Most of the internal fuel is housed in fuel cells mounted behind the cockpit and above the engine bays, while integral wing tanks raise the total capacity to around 12,400lb (5,624kg). The individual cells are of the bladder type, and are pressurised by engine bleed air. Each is mounted in its own sealed sheet-metal compartment. Fuel capacity was increased from the F-4E onwards by the addition of a seventh fuel cell in the rear fuselage. This carried an additional 618lb (280kg) of fuel.

The wing tanks were to give rise to some problems. Early-production Air Force F-4Cs had wing-tank leaks which had to be re-sealed after every flight, while similar problems were to be experienced by the USN, particularly as the F-4 fleet aged, At one point during 1982, three quarters of Naval Reserve squadron VF-201's aging F-4Ns (reworked F-4Bs) were grounded because of fuel leaks and wing cracks.

Refuelling on the ground is by means of a pressure-fuelling receptacle mounted beneath the aircraft. For flight refuelling, USN aircraft use a probe-and-drogue refuelling system. On the Phantom, a retractable probe was mounted on the starboard side of the cockpit area. USAF examples carry a spine-mounted receptacle able to mate with the flying boom carried by the KC-135 and other tankers.

The wing is of relatively low aspect ratio, and has a broad, flat centre section, plus outer panels which can be folded upwards to ease storage in the carrier's hangar. In the course of development, design engineers found that lateral stability could be greatly improved by the application of a constant 3 degree dihedral to the entire wing. Rather than redesign the wing and undercarriage, the designers applied 12 degrees of upward cant to the hinged outer wing panel, achieving the same effect in a simpler way. Seen in conjunction with the downward-canted tailplane, this gives the Phantom its characteristic 'bent" appearance. A dog-tooth in the wing leading edge helps control the flow of air across the wing.

Both the forward and main wing spars were machined from 14ft (4.2m) long forgings to create components of "C"-section. The centre section skin was manufactured from alloy billets just over 2in (5cm) thick. After being machined from the flat metal, they were bent to create the necessary slight curvature. The major skin components of the outer wing were made from roll-tapered sheets ranging in thickness from 0.1 to 0.3in (0.25 to 0.76cm) then chemically milled.

All control surfaces are hydraulically-actuated. The ailerons work in conjunction with spoilers on upper wing surface, two sections being mounted per side. To roll the aircraft, the spoilers on one side are raised, to disturb the airflow and reduce the lift, while the aileron on the other side is deflected downwards. The systems have generally performed well but several aircraft were lost in the mid-1960s due to failures of the aileron actuators—a problem whose final solution took more than a year.

Although the aircraft has seen extensive land-based service with the USAF and overseas air arms, the wing fold was never deleted, although the powered-mechanism was deleted on some USAF aircraft.

The wing is also fitted with leading and trailing-edge flaps, while airbrakes are located on the underside of each inboard wing section. The leading-edge flaps are in three sections, two on

Above: Moments from touchdown, an RF-4C gets extra lift from its trailing and leading-edge flaps and drooped ailerons.

Below: The overall dimensions of the Phantom had to be compact enough to fit the US carrier elevators, and even then the nose radome had to fold for the F-4Ks of the Royal Navy (not a unique feature of UK Phantoms).

Boundary-layer control on leading and trailing edge flaps

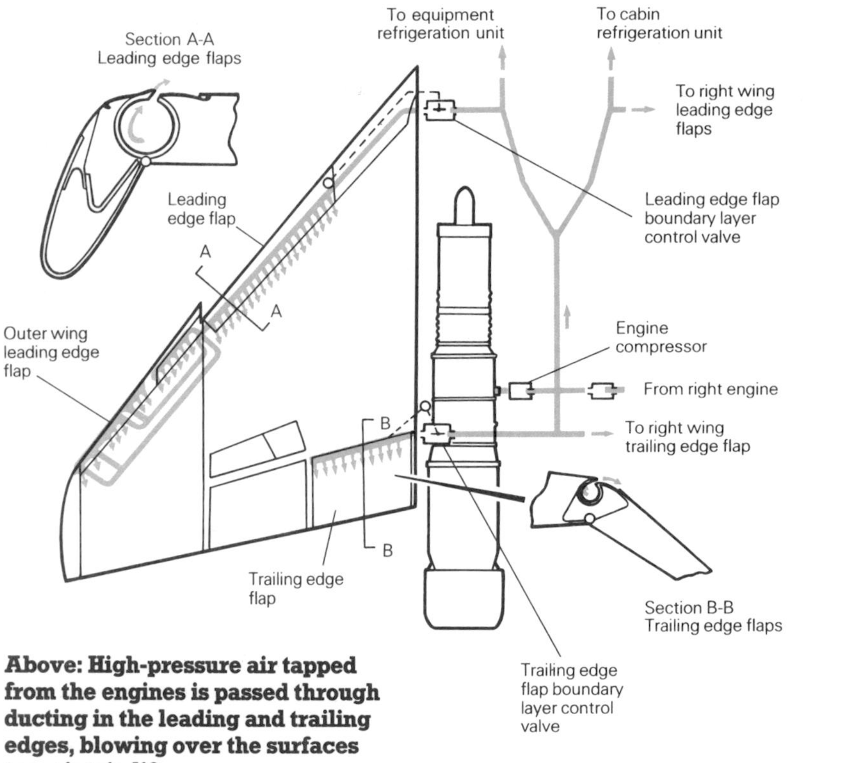

Above: High-pressure air tapped from the engines is passed through ducting in the leading and trailing edges, blowing over the surfaces to maintain lift.

Above: Missing panels on this production-line Phantom reveal much of the internal pipework inside the aircraft, including the wing leading-edge ducting for boundary-layer control described left.

the centre-section of each wing and the third on the outer wing panel. Although broadly similar in build to their USAF counterparts, Iranian F-4Ds were given a fixed leading edge on the inboard wing section.

To allow an aircraft in the weight and performance class of the Phantom to land on a carrier, the designers had to pay strict attention to boundary layer control. Hot air bled from the compressors of the engines is piped to the leading-edge droop flaps and across the trailing edge flaps.

The basic wing design has survived virtually unchanged aerodynamically throughout the life of the aircraft, although some mechanical strengthening was needed in order to overcome

McDonnell Douglas F-4E Phantom II cutaway

1. Radome
2. Radar disconnect unit
3. Pitot head
4. ADF sense aerial
5. Windscreen rain dispersal duct
6. Ammunition drum
7. Pilot's instrument display
8. Lead computing sight and indicator
9. Engine throttle levers
10. Pilot's Martin-Baker ejection seat
11. Forward cockpit canopy cover
12. Weapon's Systems Officer's instrument panel
13. Boundary layer spill ducts
14. Weapons Systems Officer's Martin-Baker ejection seat
15. Rear cockpit canopy cover
16. IFF aerial
17. Avionics equipment bay
18. Upper fuselage light
19. Leading edge wing fence
20. Starboard wing integral fuel tank
21. Leading edge manoeuvre slat
22. Radar warning antenna
23. Wing tip formation light
24. Retractable in-flight refuelling receptacle
25. Rearward identification light
26. Two-segment spoilers
27. Fuel jettison
28. TACAN aerial
29. Drooping aileron
30. Fuselage fuel cells
31. General Electric J79-GE-17 powerplant
32. Fuel system piping
33. Ventral airbrake
34. Airbrake hydraulic jack
35. Flap hydraulic jack
36. Tailcone cooling air intake
37. Arrester hook jack and damper
38. Tailplane artificial feel system unit
39. Tailplane control linkages
40. Anti-collision light
41. Artificial feel system pressure head
42. Formation lightning strip
43. VHF aerial
44. Tail navigation light
45. Radar warning antenna
46. Rudder mass balance
47. Rudder
48. Fuel jettison
49. Brake parachute housing
50. Parachute door
51. Rudder hydraulic actuator and damper
52. Tailplane hinge mounting
53. Tailplane hinge sealing plate
54. All-moving tailplane
55. Fixed leading edge slat
56. Tailplane hydraulic actuator
57. AIM-7 Sparrow air-to-air missile
58. Port plain flap
59. Afterburner nozzle control jack
60. Afterburner duct
61. Port drooping aileron
62. Variable area afterburner nozzle
63. Arrestor hook
64. Fuel jettison
65. Rearward identification light
66. Port wing tip formation light
67. Port navigation light
68. Radar warning antenna
69. Remote compass transmitter
70. Outboard leading edge manoeuvering slat
71. Outboard slat hydraulic jack
72. Aileron damper
73. Outboard spoiler hydraulic actuator

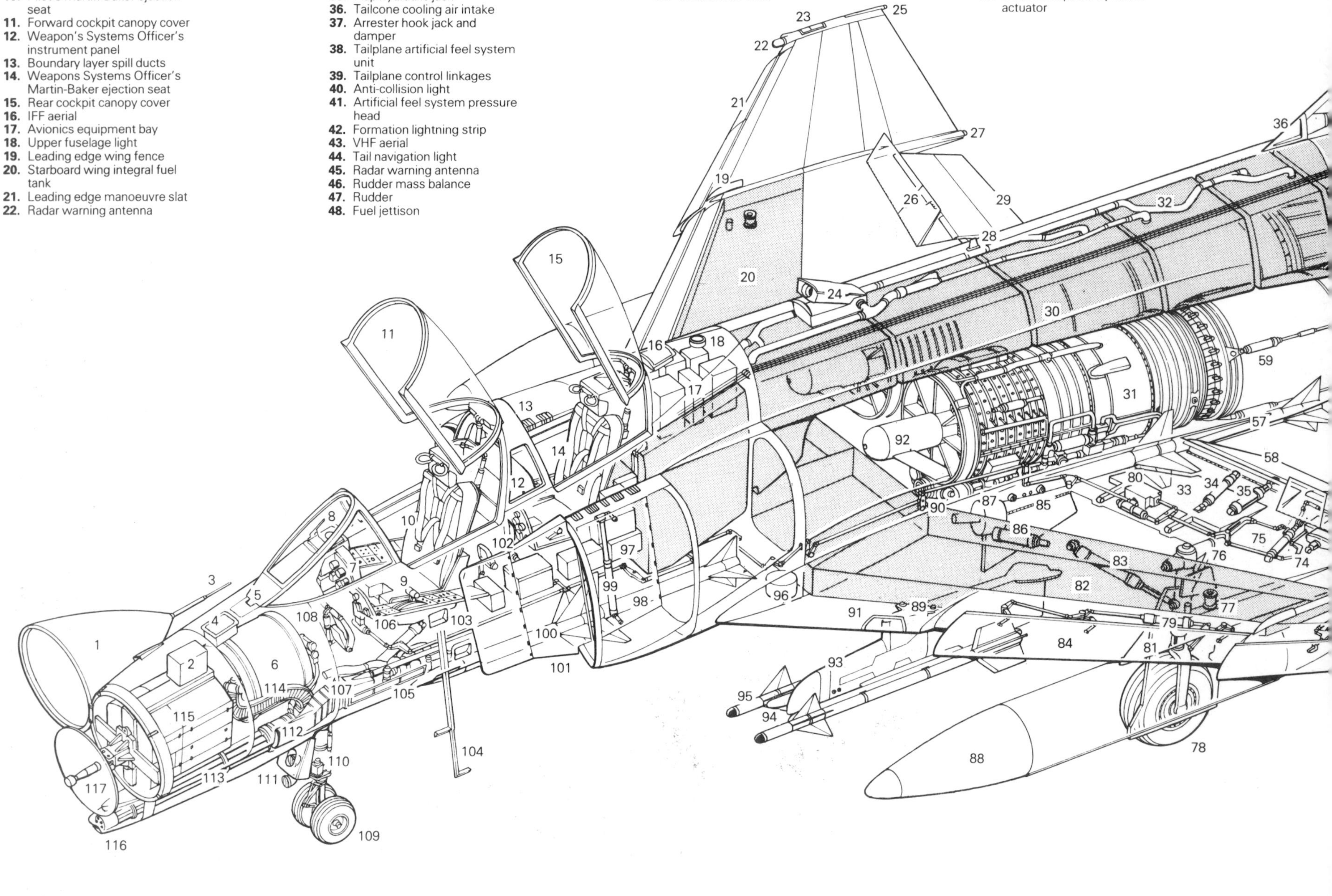

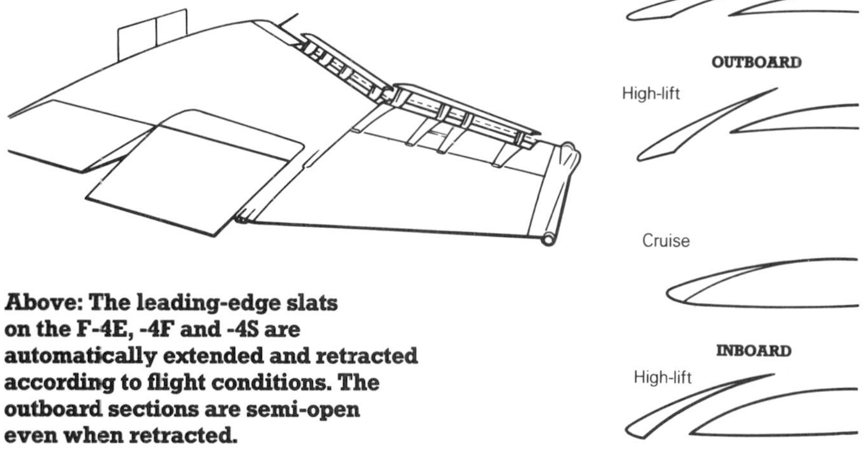

Above: The leading-edge slats on the F-4E, -4F and -4S are automatically extended and retracted according to flight conditions. The outboard sections are semi-open even when retracted.

Above: An F-4E displays the leading-edge slats devised to improve handling (see diagram, above right). The red-tipped pod in one Sparrow well is an EROS collision-avoidance system.

cracking problems. The USAF reported cracking ribs and stringers on the outer wing panels of early F-4Cs, but this was cured by the addition of a heavier stringer and extra rib. Embodied in new-production aircraft, these were retrofitted by the USAF to F-4Cs already in service.

The USN and USMC were not blind to the qualities of the F-4C and D, and started work on the F-4J in an attempt to field a broadly similar aircraft. The resulting F-4J has a landing weight of 38,000lb (17,237kg), so changes were needed in order to hold down the landing speed and preserve the low-speed handling characteristics—vital ingredients of good carrier-landing qualities. A drooped aileron configuration was adopted so that these components could be deflected 16.5 degrees downwards at take-off and landing in order to increase the available lift.

Most drastic change to the wing was the introduction of leading-edge slats on F-4Es built from 1972 onwards. Two are mounted on the leading edge of each wing in place of the earlier blown flap. The section mounted on the inner wing panel is fully retractable, but the other on the outboard section is semi-fixed, acting as a slat in both the cruise and high-lift configurations. At high angles of attack, these are automatically extended by hydraulic actuators, increasing the lift. At lower angles of attack, the drag of the wing with slats extended is greater than that with slats retracted. The actuation system is arranged to extend the slats only at angles where they will increase the lift. Once extended, they remain out until the angle of attack has fallen significantly below that for slat extension. Without such built-in inertia, there would be a risk of the slats being unstable under flight conditions, moving in and out repeatedly in response to tiny changes in angle of attack. With slats deployed, the aircraft can pull tighter turns, while approach speeds are reduced by around 12kts (22.2km/h) for the same all-up weight.

McDonnell Douglas built 350 slat kits in the early 1970s at a total cost of $93 million. These were used to modify pre-1972 F-4Es. The retrofit task involved removing the existing flaps and boundary-layer control system, adding an anti-fatigue reinforcing strap to the wing centre section, replacing the outer-wing panels, and fitting the new slats, actuators and support structure. Hydraulic and control systems were also modified. Deletion of the boundary-layer control system deprived the trailing edge flap of its supply of blowing air. This was no problem for the Air Force, but carrier-based aircraft needed the blown trailing-edge flap in order to reduce approach speeds.

When the USAF's Thunderbirds display team re-equipped with F-4Es in the summer of 1969, cracks were soon detected in the outer wing panels of the team's aircraft. These sections were duly reinforced. The loss of an F-4E in January 1973 led the USAF to embark on a programme of structural modifications, which would extend the service life of the aircraft from 3,000 to at least 4,500hrs.

Naval Phantoms were not to receive slats until the F-4J life-extension programme in the late 1970s. As part of the modification scheme which created the F-4S, some 248 naval F-4Js were rebuilt, receiving an F-4E-style slatted wing, new hydraulics and electrical wiring, plus some local strengthening of the airframe to permit higher landing weights.

The one-piece stabilisers are angled downwards at 23 degrees on each side—a simple method of keeping them clear of the wing wake at high angles of attack, and of compensating for the rolling effect of the upward-cranked outer wing sections at high speed. In this way, the designers avoided some of the handling problems which affected some other high-performance designs. The inner sections are made from titanium, in order to cope with the close proximity of engine exhaust gas.

The F-4J was the first model on which a fixed inverted slat was fitted to the horizontal stabiliser. This maintained the effectiveness of the control surface at high angles of attack without altering

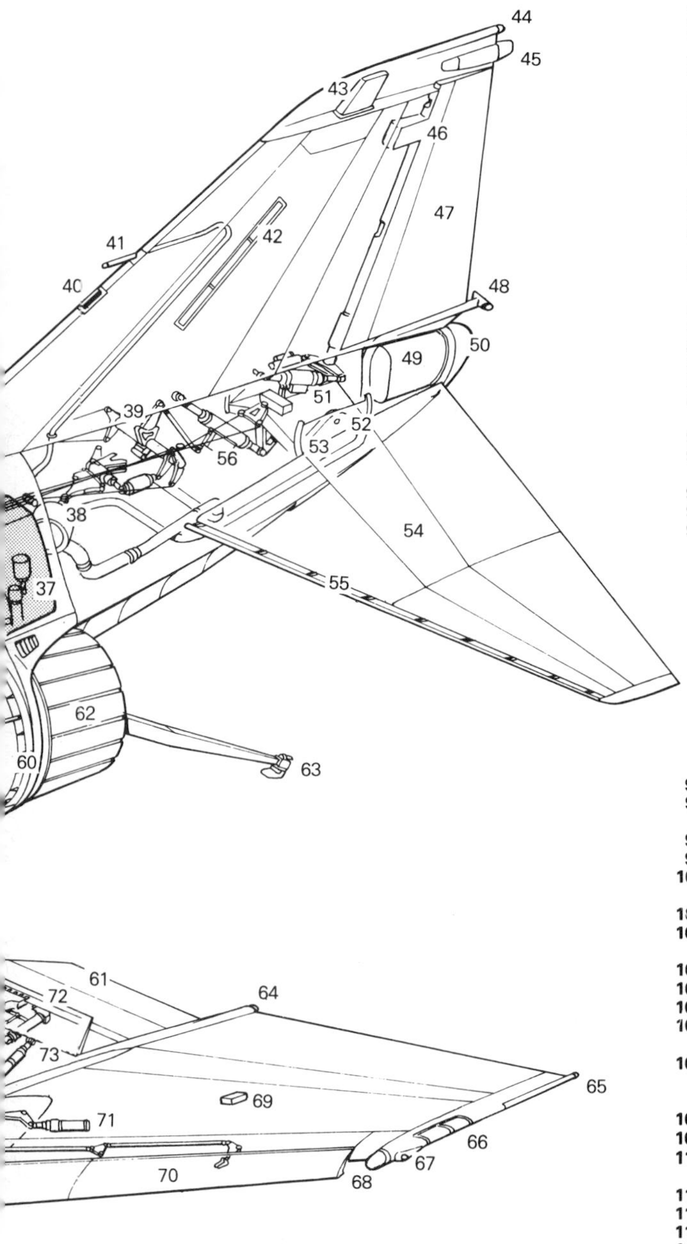

74. Aileron hydraulic actuator
75. Inboard spoiler hydraulic actuator
76. Main undercarriage hinge bearing
77. Pylon attachment point
78. Inward retracting mainwheel
79. Inboard slat hydraulic jack
80. Aileron and spoiler servo actuator
81. Outboard stores pylon
82. Port wing integral fuel tank
83. Main undercarriage hydraulic jack
84. Inboard leading edge manoeuvering slat
85. Systems ground connections
86. Hydraulic accumulator
87. Hydraulic reservoir
88. External fuel tank
89. Inboard pylon attachment
90. Engine accessory equipment gearbox
91. Radar ranging antenna
92. Engine driven generator housing
93. Inboard stores pylon
94. Missile launch rail
95. AIM-9 Sidewinder air-to-air missiles
96. Starter cartridge container
97. Lower avionics equipment bay
98. Variable area intake ramp
99. Intake area actuator
100. AIM-7 Sparrow air-to-air missile
101. Boundary layer splitter plate
102. Rear cockpit secondary flight controls
103. Boarding steps
104. Retractable boarding ladder
105. Formation lighting strip
106. Control column and mechanical linkage
107. Equipment air conditioning system, crew system on starboard side
108. Rudder pedals
109. Aft retracting nosewheels
110. Nosewheel steering control unit
111. Landing and taxying lamps
112. Heat exchanger ram air intake
113. M61 Vulcan 20mm cannon
114. Ammunition feed chute
115. Radar equipment unit
116. Cannon muzzle
117. Radar scanner dish

Below: US Marine Corps F-4J lands aboard USS *Nimitz*. Many F-4Js were rebuilt to the -4S standard, receiving leading-edge slats.

behaviour at the lower angles typical of high-speed flight. This feature was also adopted by the USAF on the F-4E.

The long tail section extending over the jetpipes reduces weight and minimises volume, while maintaining the required moment arm of the tail surfaces. In its simplest form, this technique was first seen on the MiG-15, but it has long been an accepted feature of McDonnell fighter designs.

Flight at up to Mach 2.4 requires a large vertical fin area to ensure directional stability. The most recent solution favoured by designers is twin surfaces (MiG-25, F-14, F-15, F/A-18 and most of the latest lightweight fighter designs). If a single fin is to be used this may be tall (as on Tornado), but the F-4 design team decided to choose a fin of normal height but of large chord. This incorporates a hydraulically-actuated slab-type rudder.

The variable engine inlets have a fixed forward ramp and a V-shaped adjustable ramp located further aft. The first variable-area inlets to be used on a production fighter, these are fully described in the chapter on propulsion. In the light of flight test experience with the F-4A, the inlets were slightly increased in area, and the ramp angles were increased. Twin ducts lead the air from the inlets back to the engine bay.

Introduction of the Rolls-Royce Spey turbofan on the F-4K and -4M required a fair degree of structural redesign. The rear fuselage was widened to accommodate the new engine, the area of the intakes was increased by 20 per cent and the duct increased in width by about 6in (15.2cm) in order to cope with the increased size and airflow demands of the new powerplant, and auxiliary doors were added near the tail. The aft lower fuselage also had to be modified, with some 300lb (136kg) of titanium being added to the engine bay in order to cope with the higher exhaust temperature of the British engine.

Triplicated 3,000psi hydraulic systems provide power for control surfaces, undercarriage retraction, and wing folding. This takes the form of twin systems each powered by a separate engine (via a hydraulic pump) and designated PC-1 and PC-2, plus a back-up utility system which drew power from both pumps. Phantom hydraulics proved vulnerable to ground fire, and could result in loss of control if an aircraft was hit. The utility system does not power the stabiliser, but combat experience in Vietnam showed how a damaged aircraft could still be flown.

If the main pressure lines started to fail, pilots were told to use the limited time available before stabiliser movement was lost to set that surface to a suitable cruise position. By maintaining a firm forward pressure on the control stick, a hydraulic lock could be induced in the system, "freezing" the now unpowered stabiliser in position. It was impossible to predict how long this situation would continue, since the lock could be broken by slow leakage through the system's one-way hydraulic check valves, or by minor leakage resulting from combat damage, but in many cases it gave sufficient flying time to get the aircraft out of hostile airspace so that the crew could easily be rescued.

Structural variations

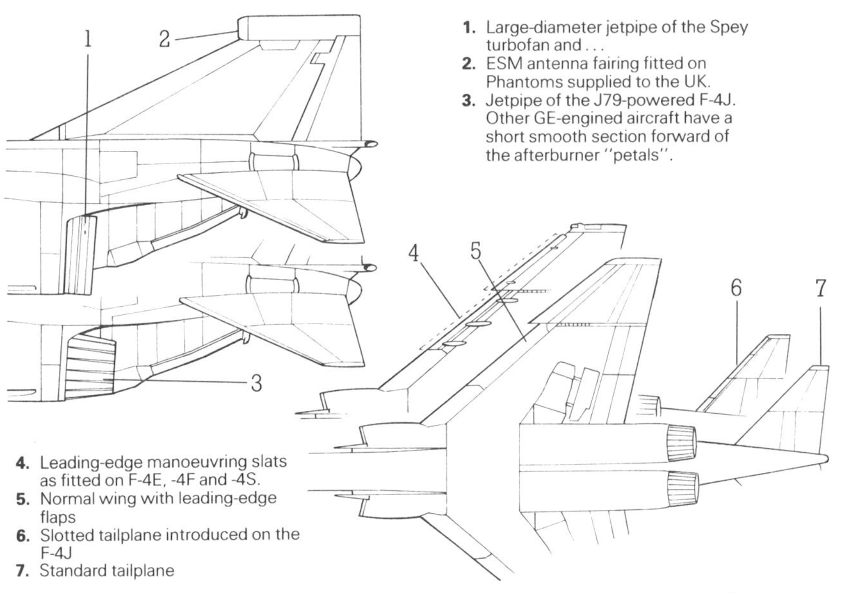

1. Large-diameter jetpipe of the Spey turbofan and . . .
2. ESM antenna fairing fitted on Phantoms supplied to the UK.
3. Jetpipe of the J79-powered F-4J. Other GE-engined aircraft have a short smooth section forward of the afterburner "petals".
4. Leading-edge manoeuvring slats as fitted on F-4E, -4F and -4S.
5. Normal wing with leading-edge flaps
6. Slotted tailplane introduced on the F-4J
7. Standard tailplane

Left: The high-lift wing is emphasised, and daylight can be glimpsed through the leading-edge slat as this USAF F-4E taxies down the runway in convoy. The stabilator is fully depressed.

Below: The massive structure of the forward undercarriage leg reflects the rugged qualities needed to cope with the stress of carrier-based operations. The various landing weights are given in the text.

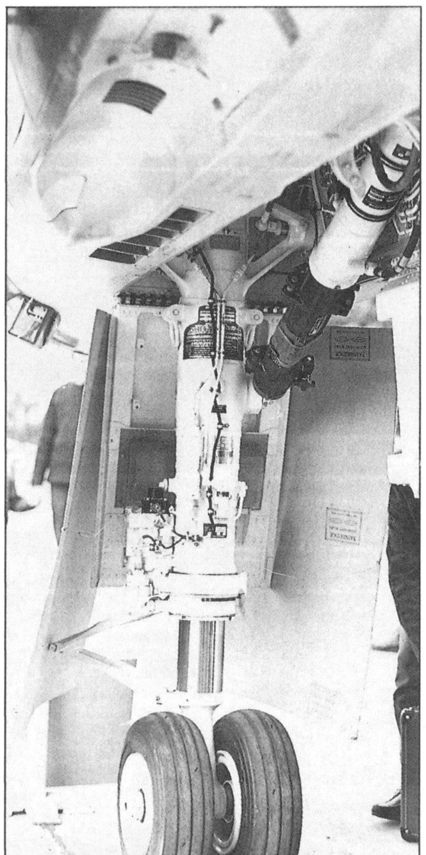

The USAF added an auxiliary power unit to the F-4E and RF-4C which was able to provide a limited range of stabiliser movement provided that the actuation system had not been damaged.

The tricycle undercarriage has a twin-wheel nose unit and single-wheel main units, stressed to accept a sink rate of 24ft/sec (7.3m/sec). The nosewheel was the first to apply full 360 degree steering to a fighter.

Undercarriages may not sound like high-technology items, but the stresses such components undergo are severe. On a typical sortie, a fighter will roll on its wheels for around 6 miles (9.6km). Taxiing out to the runway, then back to the hardstand at the end of the mission accounts for just over 3 miles (4.8km), while take-off and landing rolls are typically 1 mile and 1.5 miles (1.6 and 2.4km) respectively. In theory, an F-4 wheel has a design life of 1,000 miles (1,610km), but it is unlikely that many operators worry—those hard-working wheels keep on turning unless abused by unduly tight turns or excessive speed while taxiing.

Tyre pressures used by the USN (typically around 350psi) are suited to flight-deck operations rather than the demands of conventional operation from runways. In creating the F-4C, the USAF replaced the naval pattern of 7.7in (19.5cm) wide wheels with new 11.5in (29.2cm) wide units, reducing the tyre pressure to around 200psi. Exact pressures vary from model to model, but the figures given show the general trend.

To house the revised main gear, which also incorporated more powerful brakes (complete with an anti-skid system), a bulge had to be added to the upper and lower wing surfaces and to the undercarriage doors. The aft-mounted tail hook was retained on USAF aircraft.

British Phantom undercarriage

The undercarriage and tail hook of the British Spey-powered F-4s were strengthened to cope with landing weights of 36,000lb (16,330kg), almost a ton heavier than the F-4B. A modified pattern of nose landing gear was needed for the Royal Navy F-4K in order to give an increased angle of attack at launch in order to cope with the lower wind over deck speed associated with the RN carriers. The revised nose leg incorporated a 40in (101cm) extension, twice that of the equivalent USN component.

Structure of the F-4M for the Royal Air Force is broadly similar, but without the extending nose leg, catapult-related features and aileron droops. Like the USAF, the RAF specified anti-skid brakes.

Main undercarriage of the USN F-4J was restressed to cope with the higher landing weight—4,000lb (1,814kg) more than that of the F-4B—and given USAF-style wider wheels.

Cockpit visibility is limited in the rearward direction, a feature which the F-4 shares with contemporaries such as the Mirage III and Lightning and even later types such as the Mirage F1. On the first prototypes the situation was even worse. Until the 19th aircraft, the top of the canopy was kept flush with the fuselage top in order to minimise drag. When it came, the redesign was not in order to improve rearward vision—a quality not thought particularly important in a heavy missile-armed interceptor—but because it was considered necessary to give the crew a better forward view for landing.

When the USAF adopted the Phantom, it insisted on the rear cockpit being reconfigured to suit the Air Force doctrine that the "back-seater" be a pilot. A

Above: An RAF crew prepares to start engines. The movable ramps of the air inlet may be clearly seen, also the fine pattern of suction holes on the rear ramp. Note the restricted visibility from both cockpits, particularly to the rear.

more complete set of dual controls was fitted, and the height of the instrument panel was reduced to improve the forward view. They could have saved money by leaving well alone, since experience was to show that to obtain the best from the aircraft's avionics, the rear crew member should be a "black box" driver rather than a fully-qualified pilot.

Below: Spey-powered F-4K bearing the Omega tail insignia of 892 Sqn about to touch down aboard *Ark Royal* after firing 2inch rockets from underwing launchers.

Early aircraft had ejection seat problems, finally solved by the installation of a modified seat in 1969. This was more effective at low altitudes and low airspeeds, and featured a sequence control which prevented both crew members from ejecting simultaneously. The cockpit of later models such as the F-4E and J was fitted with Martin-Baker zero-zero ejection seats.

The F-4 has at times displayed a tendency to "lose its lid". Sources of inadvertent canopy loss range from accidental operation of the canopy selector or jettison control by the crew to failure to ensure that the canopy is locked before take-off, or a component failure in the locking system. Unlucky aircrew have discovered that "lidless" flight at speeds above 300kts (556km/h) is made difficult by wind blast pushing the pilot's head forward and down, but that conditions become more acceptable—albeit noisy—at lower speeds.

Phantom sub-contractors

Although all the Phantoms built for the US services and for all export customers apart from Japan were assembled on the St Louis production line, less than half of the airframe was actually built at St Louis. The list of companies which shared the mammoth task of assembling the Western world's most widely-built supersonic fighter reads like a "Who's Who" of the US aerospace industry, including names such as Beech, Cessna, Fairchild (Republic), Goodyear, and Northrop. European companies involved at a later stage included British Aircraft Corporation, Hawker Siddeley Aviation, MBB, and Short Brothers & Harland (Shorts).

When the F-4 programme began, the McDonnell team could have had no idea that the line would deliver more than 5,000 aircraft and that production would run for two decades, ending in 1979. The original production contract called for a total of 375 aircraft, with the line scheduled to close in 1965. The demands of the Vietnam war held the production rate at more than 50 aircraft per month between 1966 and 1968, peaking at 70 per month early in 1967.

Phantom major sub-contractors

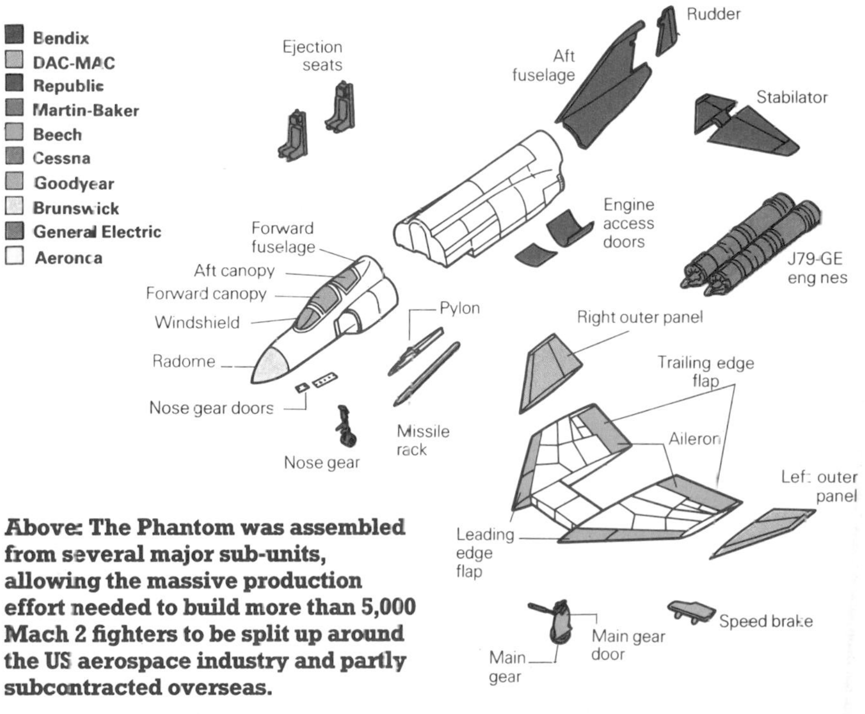

Above: The Phantom was assembled from several major sub-units, allowing the massive production effort needed to build more than 5,000 Mach 2 fighters to be split up around the US aerospace industry and partly subcontracted overseas.

Propulsion

In selecting a powerplant for the Phantom, the US Navy chose a winner. General Electric's single-shaft J79 may be longer and more complex than present-day engines in the same thrust class, but at the time was an advanced design. It proved powerful and dependable; aircrew sent to war could ask for little more. The only customer to specify an alternative powerplant was the UK, for its F-4K and -4M, but the anticipated increase in performance was not achieved .

Given the wisdom of hindsight, the choice of the General Electric J79 as powerplant for the Phantom hardly seems innovative. Widely used by types such as the F-104 Starfighter and IAI Kfir, and having powered the A-5 Vigilante and B-58 Hustler supersonic bombers, the J79 has clocked up more supersonic flying time than any other Western military engine.

However, when McDonnell engineers first drew up plans in 1954 for what was eventually to become the Phantom, selection of a suitable engine was difficult. For a start, the GE engine was still on the drawing board, while the US Navy still had painful memories of having chosen the wrong "advanced" engine for many of its 1950-vintage fighters and bombers. The US aero-engine industry was in the final stages of the transition from the piston-era to the jet age, with long-established companies and relative newcomers to the field struggling for survival at a time when the pace of the new technology was relentlessly driving the weaker organisations to the wall.

The US Navy had traditionally favoured Westinghouse as an engine supplier, using that company's J34 in a series of twin-engined aircraft such as the McDonnell F2H Banshee, the Douglas F3D Skynight carrier-based night fighter, and the experimental YF2Y Sea Dart water-ski seaplane fighter.

In addition to its use by the USN, it had also powered a long series of USAF experimental fighters such as the tiny McDonnell XF-85 Goblin "parasite" fighter, the ill-fated XF-87 Blackhawk all-weather fighter (the last aircraft to carry the Curtiss name), McDonnell's XF-88A Voodoo and Lockheed's XF-90 long-range escort fighters. (The name and general configuration of the XF-88 were later adopted for the F-101.)

This established relationship between the USN and Westinghouse broke up in the early 1950s with the failure of the J40 programme. Westinghouse was relatively new to the aero-engine business, having been asked during World War II to apply its steam and industrial turbine experience to the new field of jet propulsion, so that established manufacturers such as Pratt & Whitney and Wright could concentrate on conventional and much-needed piston engines.

The J34 had proven successful, but disguised the company's lack of expertise in the new field, giving it the confidence to embark on the ill-fated J40 and J46 programmes. Selected as the preferred high-power engine for future USN aircraft, the J40 was scheduled to develop 7,200lb (3,266kg) of dry thrust for subsonic applications and up to 11,600lb (5,262kg) with afterburner for use in transonic aircraft.

Douglas' aircraft the victims

Main "victim" of these powerplants was Douglas, which selected the 4,600lb (2,087kg) dry-thrust J46 for use in developed versions of the F3D Skynight, and the J40 in "dry" form for the A3D Skywarrior and with afterburning for the F4D (F-6A) Skyray. Both engines were failures, and it is little wonder that Bill Gunston—at the time a journalist with *Flight International*—recalls Douglas designer Ed Heinemann being "about ready to commit hara-kiri over Westinghouse". All the Douglas aircraft went into service with alternative powerplants.

The J40 was also installed in early-production examples of the McDonnell F3H Demon, a large number of which were eventually grounded for use as instructional airframes while the aircraft was redesigned to accept an alternative engine.

By the time an engine had to be selected for the F4H-G, the J40 debacle of a few years earlier forced McDonnell to look to other manufacturers—Allison, Pratt & Whitney, Wright and General Electric. All but the last were famous names of the piston era. Like Westinghouse, GE was a steam turbine company brought into the jet engine field during the war.

Allison's earlier J33 has been used in Navy fighters such as the F9F Cougar, and in afterburning form in the Air Force's F-94A Starfire all-weather fighter; but this was a bulky centrifugal engine not really suited to a supersonic design. Although the Allison J71-A-2, which developed 14,250lb (6,464kg) of thrust in full afterburner, had been used as the definitive powerplant of the F3H Demon it was not selected for the new fighter. Its only other application was as a replacement for the J57 when the USAF modified the Douglas Skywarrior to create the B-66 Destroyer.

Pratt & Whitney's J48 had already been used by the US Navy in early versions of the F9F Cougar, but this too was of centrifugal form. Maximum thrust offered was 8,500lb (3,856kg) when using afterburning and water-injection.

A more powerful and proven engine was available from P&W in the form of the J57-P-7, already selected for supersonic fighters such as the F-100 Super Sabre, F-102A Dagger, and F-8 Crusader, and used to "rescue" the A-3D Skywarrior and F4D Skynight.

The J57 was a landmark in engine history—the first to adopt the two-spool layout used by most current military jet engines. In "dry" form it powered most of the Boeing B-52s built, and its civil version was used on the Boeing 707 and Douglas DC-8. The afterburning version produced a reliable 14,000lb (6,350kg) of thrust, but was some 20ft (6.0m) long and weighed around 5,000lb (2,268kg)—slightly heavier than the J40, but offering substantial gains in efficiency, power and reliability.

General Electric's J79—at that time known as the X-24A—was being developed for the USAF as an advanced engine for future supersonic aircraft, and had already been selected to power the B-58 supersonic bomber and F-104 fighter. Thanks to the adoption by the GE designers of a novel type of single-shaft configuration, the X-24A seemed likely to match the thrust and fuel consumption figures of the P&W engine, but at a much lighter weight—around 3,500lb (1,588kg).

Instead of the P&W or GE engines, the F3H-G team turned to Wright, the company whose radial piston engines had powered bombers such as the B-17, B-29, and B-50, as well as the DC-4, -6, -7

Above: While running in full afterburner, the engines of this F-4J of VF-32 (thrusting off from the carrier USS *John F. Kennedy*) burn about 1,300lb (595kg) of fuel per minute.

Below: The McDonnell F3H Demon was delayed by the trouble-plagued J40 engine, produced by the relatively inexperienced Westinghouse, so when it came to choosing an engine for the F4H the US Navy and the company were understandably cautious, eventually getting it right with the J79.

and Lockheed Constellation airliners. For the new fighter, McDonnell opted to use a pair of afterburning Wright J65 engines. The choice was an unfortunate one—Wright was to become another victim of the turbojet era, and the single-spool J65 was to have a troubled life.

The Wright engine was a licence-built version of the British Armstrong-Siddeley Sapphire, and had been selected in 1950 as the powerplant of the F-84F Thunderstreak. According to an official USAF history, the Sapphire was "a hand-tooled production for which the Curtiss-Wright Corporation ... had acquired a manufacturing license". The engine was hastily Americanised, but the programme met unexpected difficulties. The US-built engine was overweight, gave less thrust than the UK original, and was to acquire a reputation for poor reliability.

To meet the demands of the Korean War, the engine was placed into production at Wright and the Buick Division of General Motors. The early YJ65-W-1 was speedily replaced by the improved -1A model (which was not interchangeable with the earlier version), while Wright struggled to create the definitive J65-W-3, which was eventually to power most of the F-84s built.

Despite a history of problems, the high thrust-to-weight ratio of the J65 still made it attractive, and the McDonnell team was not alone in adopting it. Uprated versions were used to power the North American F-1 Fury—a "navalised" F-86 Sabre—and the Martin B-57 version of the Canberra, while an afterburning version developing 10,200lb (4,627kg) of thrust was adopted for the Grumman F11F Tiger.

By August 1954, the F4H-G had been redesignated AH-1. The GE J79 had not yet flown, but confidence in the design was high enough to allow it to be chosen as the production powerplant. Use of the Wright J65 was now to be confined to the prototypes only. Faced with delays with the YJ79 hardware, Lockheed had followed the same course, adopting the afterburning J65 to power the prototype XF-104s, the first of which had flown in March of that year. At one time the Wright engine even seemed a likely powerplant for the first production batch of F-104As.

By the summer of 1955, the new McDonnell design had completed its metamorphosis into a two-seat Mach 2 fighter, while progress with the J79 allowed that engine to be specified for all prototypes and production aircraft. (Had the Wright engine been adopted for the Phantom, the company might have survived in the turbojet business for a longer period of time. Like Westinghouse, the company faded from the jet-engine business.)

The GE engine was flight-rated in its YJ79-GE-3 form before the end of 1954 for installation in the pre-production F-104A. On February 17, 1956, the first F-104A became the first J79-powered aircraft to fly. Engine troubles curtailed the first flight, but little more than a month later the aircraft had reached Mach 1.79, and the J79 was on its way to becoming a successful engine, finally entering operational service with the USAF early in 1958.

Progress with the J79

At this time the "bugs" had not been completely wrung out of the engine, and a number of incidents involving flame-outs caused the USAF to ground the F-104A for several months until the improved -3B version became available.

First flights of the XF4H-1 in the summer of 1958 were conducted using the J79-GE-3A. Rated at 9,600lb (4,355kg) of dry thrust, these engines developed 14,800lb (6,713kg) in full afterburner. After 50 flights had been carried out, the engines were swapped for the more powerful YJ79-GE-2. This was later followed by the -2A version which gave 10,350lb (4,695kg) dry, and 16,150lb (7,326kg) with afterburner. The latter engine was fitted to all 23 prototypes.

For the definitive F-4B, the USN selected the J79-GE-8, which offered still greater thrust, giving the aircraft Mach 2.4 capability. Dry thrust of this engine was 10,900lb (4,944kg), rising to 17,000lb (7,711kg) in full afterburner. This powerplant was also retained for the RF-4B and the F-4N.

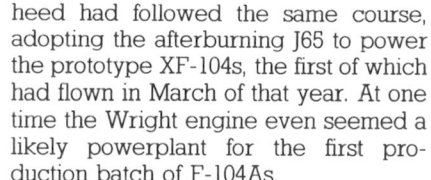

Airflow through J79-GE engine

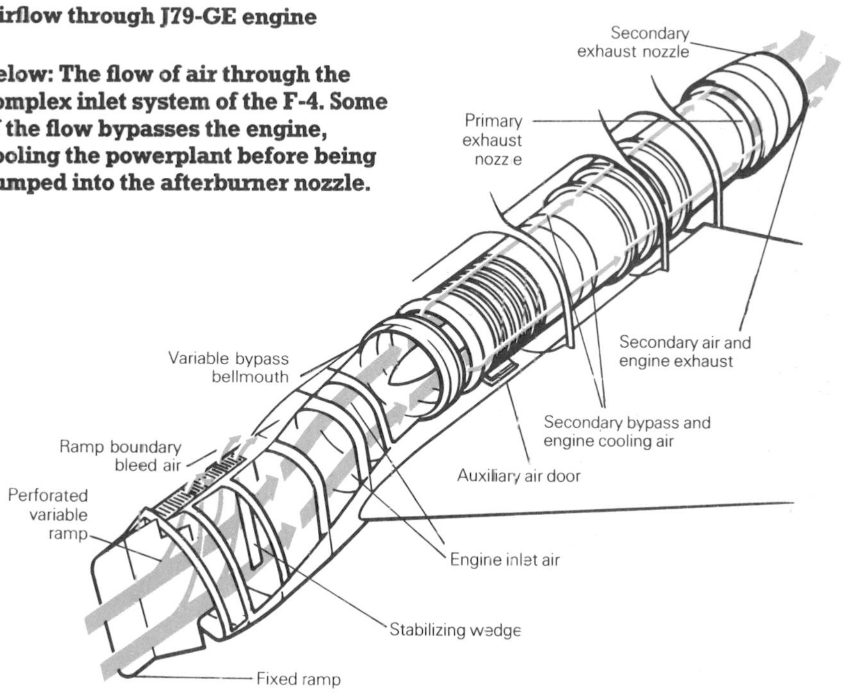

Below: The flow of air through the complex inlet system of the F-4. Some of the flow bypasses the engine, cooling the powerplant before being dumped into the afterburner nozzle.

The high performance and reliability of the J79 are the result of careful design. At the time when the original X-24A configuration was drawn up the GE engineers must have been tempted by the merits of the two-spool configuration as used on the J57. High engine efficiency demands a compressor able to deliver high pressures, and the two-spool solution devised by P&W is the most widely adopted method of creating a modern engine.

Virtually all the major engine manufacturers adopted the two-spool layout for the engines which power most of today's military aircraft and airliners. Only the French engine company SNECMA stuck doggedly with the well-proven single-shaft configuration used by all the early axial-flow jet engines, adopting this design solution in the 1970s for the M53 turbofan which powers the Mirage 2000.

In a single-spool engine, all the stages of the compressor and the turbine which powers it are mounted on a common shaft, and rotate at the same speed. On the early turbojet engines, such a simple scheme worked well, but the quest for increased efficiency demanded compressors with a higher compression ratio. Newer designs "grew" greater numbers of compressor stages, leading to increased problems with surges and stalls.

The two-spool layout uses two coaxial shafts. The compressor is divided into two sections—an initial low-pressure section followed by a high-pressure section. These are mounted on the inner and outer shafts respectively. The turbine stages are similarly divided between the two shafts, which are designed to rotate at the speeds best suited to their individual compressors. (This scheme was taken a stage further in the 1970s with the creation of the first three-spool engines such as the Turbo-Union RB.199 and the Lotarev D-36.)

Below: A Phantom centre-fuselage section seen on an early production line shows the massive engine bays, plus the extensive access panels which were devised to make servicing easy.

Below: A J79 turbojet fresh from the General Electric works and ready for installation in an F-4. This efficient, single-shaft engine did much to make the Phantom a great success.

Above: The internal shape of the F-4 inlet system required precision in design and manufacture. The probe signals inlet conditions to the automatic ramp control system.

Left: Demonstrating how huge the inlet of an F-4E is, maintenance work is being carried out on the variable ramp inlet system. Note the gap between the splitter plate (used to divert boundary air) and the fuselage side.

The two-shaft system works well, but is naturally more complex than a single-shaft design. For the J79, the GE design team devised a compromise configuration—a single-shaft engine whose later high-pressure compressor stages incorporated variable-incidence stator blades. These movable components were linked together mechanically so that their position could be controlled by an actuator driven by the fuel supply. The resulting engine was light but powerful, and was adopted for aircraft such as the B-58, F-104, A-5 and Kfir. Civil variants powered the Convair 880 and 990 airliners.

The J79 is just over 17ft (5.18m) long, slightly more than 3ft (0.9m) in diameter, and weighs around 3,600 to 3,800lb (1,633 to 1,724kg). (Exact dimensions and weights vary from model to model.) The compressor has 17 stages and is driven by a three-stage turbine. The combustion chamber is of the 10-section cannular type. A modulated (fully-variable) afterburner and a variable-area exhaust nozzle are fitted to all models.

Air is bled from the 17th compressor stage to operate the boundary-layer control system, the air conditioning of the cockpit and equipment bays, and the cockpit pressurisation. Air is also taken from the latter system to supply subsystems such as fuel tank pressurisation, engine anti-icing, and the pneumatic system air compressor.

The engine is easy to maintain. The casing of the compressor, combustor and turbine sections is split to give access to the internal parts, while compressor and turbine blades are individually replaceable. The entire turbine section may be lifted out as a single module, while the rotors and stators of

Left: This photo shows the smoke-emission problem which, with most models of J79, allowed MiG pilots and anti-aircraft gunners to spot the Phantom at long range. The problem was overcome with later versions.

both the compressor and turbine are interchangable (rather than matched units).

The J79 has proved a reliable powerplant, although problems occasionally emerged. Several Phantoms were lost in the late 1960s due to engine-bay fires. This resulted in a major reconfiguration of the engine and bay.

One persistent problem with the J79 was the high level of smoke emission. Despite much effort by GE and the US services, Phantoms continued to emit telltale trails of black smoke which allowed the enemy visually to detect, identify and track them from a range of up to 20 miles (32km). The latest models of J79 incorporate a low-smoke combustor, but this improvement came too late for most F-4 variants.

The J79-GE-8 was one of the variants plagued with this problem, and its retention in service into the 1980s on two squadrons of US Naval Reserve F-4Ns has attracted unfavourable comments as these older aircraft—dubbed "smokers" by the USN—fly alongside the more modern F-14s.

When the USAF adopted the Phantom in its F-4C form (initially designated F-110A Spectre, USAF having different designation systems from USN until September 18, 1962), a new J79 variant was devised to meet the service's specialised requirements. Main new feature of the J79-GE-15 was a self-contained cartridge starting system. In most other respects it was similar to the USN's -GE-8 version.

Next engine upgrade came with the US Navy's F-4J, which introduced the J79-GE-10. This introduced a further thrust increase, giving a total of 17,900lb (8,119kg) in full afterburner. The USAF was quick to introduce a powerplant of similar rating, adopting the J79-GE-17 for use in the F-4E. This variant was also built under licence in Japan by Ishikawajima-Harima Heavy Industries for installation in locally-built F-4E(J) Phantoms.

When run at this thrust level, the by now well-proven J79 began to display signs of stress. USAF's F-4s were particularly troubled by technical powerplant problems. In order to obtain the increased thrust, GE engineers had increased the exhaust gas temperatures. On the earlier -8 and -15 engines, maintaining the gas temperature and engine rpm had been easy, but the "hotter" engine was more temperamental in this respect. Greater effort and attention was needed on the part of the aircrew to maintain these parameters within limits.

Stall problems

A number of stalls and flame-outs were recorded early in the F-4E flight-test programme in the summer of 1968, but the evaluators concluded that the powerplant was basically a sound design. Aircraft being deployed overseas were hastily modified. During 1969, the failure rate rose, and engine life expectancy fell to 608 hours, while a labour strike in October of that year created a shortage of engines. Aircraft at MacDill AFB were "robbed" of engines so that an Eglin-based unit could be deployed to Southeast Asia on schedule.

With the arrival of aircraft equipped with leading-edge slats, F-4 pilots began flying at lower speeds and higher attack angles, and the engines were exposed to a flight regime even more likely to trigger stalls. Final clearance of this problem was now a matter of some urgency. Steady development eventually wrung these final "bugs" out of the design, and the -17 became as reliable and well liked as any other member of the J79 series.

Above: This view of an F-4 during refuelling operations also shows the channels behind the splitter plate and light-coloured grilles on the top of the inlet. Both are used to divert boundary air.

Another problem which was finally cured was the high level of smoke emission. The -19 version of the engine devised for the Italian Air Force's F-104S interceptor incorporated a smoke-free combustor. This was also fitted to the -10A version of the engine fitted to the F-4S.

Despite the "teething troubles" described above, the J79 must by any reckoning be considered a highly successful engine. More than 17,000 have been built, and some 11,000 are in active use. Around 30 million flying hours have been clocked up, and the engine has no lifetime or cyclic limits. USAF statistics on engine reliability show that for each flight hour, the J79 needs an average of 2.9 maintenance man-hours, while the bill for spare parts averages at $113 per flying hour. By private motoring standards these figures might seem high, but in the world of Mach 2 flight they make impressive reading (The turbine blades on the Tumanski turbojet which powers most MiG-21 Fishbed variants has a turbine-blade lifetime of only a few hundred hours.)

In the Phantom, air is fed to the J79 via a complex inlet system whose design features two ramps—one fixed and another moving. Most of the airflow passes through the engine, but some is bypassed around it and discharged through bellmouth nozzles surrounding the aft end of the jetpipes. Elaborate precautions were taken during the design to ensure that the boundary airflow (the air disturbed by having moved in close proximity to the fuselage or inlet ramps) is ducted away safely and not ingested by the engine.

The fixed ramp takes the form of a large metal plate mounted some 2 inches (5cm) away from the fuselage side. This allows most of the boundary air to be ducted away. Directly aft of this fixed ramp is the privoted variable ramp, which may be moved to vary the intake throat area and engine bypass as a function of free-stream total temperature (the temperature of the airflow) and duct mach number, matching the amount of incoming air to the demands of the engine. Penalties associated with insufficient flow to the engines or excess flow creating drag are avoided. Boundary air from the ramps is sucked away into a vertical slip between the two ramps and through more than 12,000 small holes in the variable ramp.

During engine startup, air is drawn into the engine ducts via an auxiliary air door in the lower surface of each engine compartment. Should duct pressure rise in flight due to rapid throttle retardation or a compressor stall, the door will open to dump the excess air overboard.

Royal Navy/RAF Speys

This basic design in inlet has now become a classic, and has been copied on other aircraft such as the MiG-23 Flogger. It has proved trouble-free in service, the only major redesign being that needed to cope with the UK decision to instal an afterburning version of the Rolls-Royce Spey turbofan in the Phantoms ordered for the Royal Navy and RAF. Originally developed as a civil engine, the Spey is a two-shaft turbofan designed in the early 1960s. The first engine ran in December 1960. First military version to enter service was the Mk 101 fitted to Mk2 versions of the Buccaneer, but this was a "dry" powerplant. In theory, an afterburning Spey should have greatly improved the performance of the F-4, but the UK industry's limited experience with afterburning systems should have sounded a note of caution. At the time when the design of the afterburning RB.168-25R was begun in 1964 the only afterburning British engines to have seen significant service were the Avon 210 series in the Lightning and the Bristol Siddeley Sapphire in the Gloster Javelin.

Until its amalgamation with Bristol Siddeley, Rolls-Royce design expertise in afterburning turbofans was limited to some experimental hardware tested on the RB.141 (the engine from which the Spey was derived, and which was offered in conjunction with Allison as a potential powerplant in the USAF's TFX programme) and on the RB.168.1 Spey (as part of the research and development on the West German VJ101 V/STOL fighter project).

The UK decision to adopt the Spey for its Phantoms was not simply a matter of national chauvinism or political expediency. The Royal Navy's carriers *Ark Royal* and *Eagle* had smaller flight decks than USN "flat-tops", and the service even planned to operate the Phantom from the even smaller *Hermes*. The Rolls-Royce engine offered 3,500lb (1,588kg) more afterburning thrust than the J79-GE-8 flying in the US Navy's F-4B, and a useful 2,600lb (1,179kg) more than the J79-GE-10 which was to power the later F-4J. Fuel consumption in normal flight was also improved, thanks to the turbofan's excellent specific fuel consumption in dry thrust.

In creating the new afterburning version, Rolls-Royce modified the materials used and restressed the engine, changes needed in order to suit the powerplant to conditions of supersonic flight. The design of the low-pressure compressor was changed to a more robust shaft-and-disc configuration, while the new afterburner section was developed complete with multi-bar fuel injection and self-contained ignition. A Plessey lightweight starter was fitted to cope with military start-up requirements.

Two versions of the engine were built—the Mk 202 and 203. This was necessary due to the faster afterburner light-up required by the Royal Navy in order to cope with overshoots from carrier landings. Complete with afterburner, the Spey weighs 4,093lb (1,856kg)—slightly more than the J79—but is 3 to 4 inches (7.6 to 10.1 cm) shorter.

What was not appreciated in the early stages of the UK Phantom programme was that the new engine and its airflow demands were not compatible with the existing fuselage and air intakes. In practice, considerable modifications were needed (see Structure chapter).

When the first Spey-powered F-4Ks began flying in the summer of 1966, and were joined the following February by the first F-4M for the Royal Air Force, it soon became apparent that all was not well. Afterburner instability at high altitude proved troublesome, and the compressor displayed a tendency to stall. Intake problems were also noted. "Fixes" were duly devised, but delivery of production aircraft to the Royal Navy and RAF was delayed from 1968 to 1969.

Even once these problems were ironed out, and early restrictions on the aircraft removed, the Spey engine was never able to match the performance of the J79 at high Mach numbers. Spey-powered Phantoms are restricted to a maximum speed limit of Mach 2.1 in order to keep the temperature of the compressor outlet within acceptable limits, a direct result of the decision to compromise on the high-temperature qualities of the materials used in the redesigned compressor section of the engine.

Faced with the saga recounted above, it is hardly surprising that the US services and all subsequent export customers stuck with the tried and tested J79, more powerful versions of which continued to become available to match new variants of the basic aircraft. The only other customer for the afterburning Spey was the People's Republic of China, which arranged for licence pro-

Far left: Although the afterburner outlets differed little between the various General Electric J79-powered models of the Phantom, compare this view of the rear fuselage of a Pave Tack-equipped F-4 with that of its British counterpart.

Left: The rear section of the British turbofan-powered Spey Phantom is much wider than that of the GE-engined aircraft, and has larger diameter jetpipes.

Left: Engineers prepare to install a Rolls-Royce Spey turbofan in the YF-4K prototype. Adoption of the British engine required significant redesign of the fuselage, and a reduction in maximum speed.

duction of the engine to power indigenously-designed military aircraft.

Alternative powerplants

The most exotic engine installation ever considered for a Phantom variant was the water-injection J79 proposed for the F-4X project. This owes its origin to a request by Israel (probably in the late 1960s) for General Dynamics RB-57F high-altitude reconnaissance aircraft complete with a HIAC camera system able to take high-resolution oblique photos without overflying the target area. The supply of RB-57Fs was ruled out by the US State Department, but in 1971 Israel was allowed to buy a pod-mounted version of the HIAC camera for use on the F-4.

The drag imposed by the massive G-139 camera pod cut the top speed and ceiling of the F-4 to less than Mach 1.5 and 50,000ft (15,240m) respectively, so the Israelis continued to press for a delivery platform able to climb to higher altitudes at which the HIAC would give its best performance.

In 1972, the special projects department of GD began an examination of the Israeli requirement, finally proposing an uprated F-4 able to reach Mach 2.4 and 78,000ft (23,774m) while carrying a built-in HIAC.

New variable-geometry intakes were devised to handle the high-speed flight conditions while still being compatible with the existing ducts and trunking. The new inlets were of larger area than the standard units, and used a complex mixed-compression design.

Like the Operation Skyburner aircraft, the F-4X would have used engines cooled by inlet water-injection. The system used for these early record-breaking flights had been somewhat crude, and the water did not always form a homogeneous spray. Trickles of water flowing back and into the engine are reported to have caused local cooling and contraction of hot engine parts, particularly the compressor shroud, resulting in minor damage to the engine.

For the F-4X, GD engineers devised a more elegant system of inlet spray bars, which was extensively wind-tunnel tested in 1972. Two long conformal tanks, each able to hold 2,500lb (1,134kg) of water, were designed to bolt on to the aircraft on either side of the fuselage above the inlet trunking and engines. Each was divided lengthwise into three independent sections, water being drawn in a carefully arranged sequence in order to maintain the stability of the aircraft. In parallel with this work, a revised nose was devised in order to carry an improved version of the HIAC camera.

In December 1974 a standard F-4E was delivered to GD for use as an F-4X mock-up. Using cardboard, the company engineers re-profiled one side of the aircraft to the new configuration, but time was running out for the project. Like the advanced F-4(FVS) swing-wing Phantom, the F-4 was seen as a possible threat to the newer and more expensive aircraft—in this case the F-15 Eagle. Factions within the USAF were only too happy to stonewall the project by insisting that yet further feasibility studies be carried out.

Faced with such delays, the customer lost patience, opting to have the same sensor payload installed in the less dramatically modified F-4E(S). Doubtless greatly relieved, the USAF quietly abandoned the F-4X programme.

New powerplant for the Super Phantom

The only other engine seriously mooted as an alternative powerplant for the F-4 is the Pratt & Whitney PW1120. A twin-shaft turbojet derivative of the F100 turbofan carried by the F-15 and F-16, the new engine is about 40 inches (102cm) shorter than the J79 and similar in diameter, and is compatible with the existing inlet system. It offers 25 per cent more dry thrust and 30 per cent greater output with full afterburner. The better specific fuel consumption of the turbofan would increase the Phantom's range by up to 18 per cent, while the smaller size could allow more internal fuel to be carried.

The PW 1120 will power Israel's Lavi light fighter. Five test engines were built, and had completed more than 1,000 hours of ground running by the end of 1983. The results of this intensive test programme cleared the way for the engine to begin flight tests in the summer of 1984.

Like the Spey, the new P&W engine offers just over 20,000lb (9,072kg) of thrust in full afterburner, but the US engine has the advantage of being based on more modern technology. It is some 25 per cent lighter than the J79-GE-19. Maximum diameter is 12 inches (30.4cm) less than that of the F100, the lower air flow being handled by a new pattern of three-stage LP compressor driven by a single-stage uncooled turbine. (The basic F100 uses a three-stage fan driven by a two-stage turbine. The hot "core" has a ten-stage compressor driven by a two-stage air-cooled HP turbine.) Part of the airflow from the LP compressor bypasses the hot section of the engine and is used to cool the engine casing and the liner and nozzle of the simplified augmentor. Despite these design changes, the PW 1120's commonality with the F100 is around 70 per cent.

Below: The white-painted augmentor spoolpiece, flange stiffening ring and side-mounting brackets on this Pratt & Whitney 1120 engine were required to ensure compatibility with the Phantom airframe. Re-engined aircraft will have a 55 per cent improvement in engine thrust:weight ratio, and the reduced fuel consumption plus extra fuel in conformal tanks will increase range.

Avionics

When the avionics of the Phantom were first designed, the transistor was in its infancy. Designers were forced to use fragile and power-hungry thermionic tubes (radio valves). Most F-4s operational today have transistorised avionics, while the proposed Super Phantom "rebuild" programme could see the introduction of avionic systems such as a pulse-Doppler radar and head-up display as used on latest-generation US fighters. Combat experience saw the aircraft improved in other ways, with the addition of a zoom-lens electro-optical viewing aid and pod-mounted ECM systems.

Above: USAF technicians service the APQ-120 radar of an F-4E. The good access given to the radar chassis and subsystems was a deliberate feature of the Phantom design, and was introduced to ease the maintenance of the older tube-based radars.

By the latest standards, the avionics of the Phantom are somewhat dated, but are nevertheless milestones in the development of airborne electronics. In updated and modernised form, they remain combat-effective even in the 1980s. In many earlier aircraft types, avionics consisted of temperamental "black boxes" which required endless nursing by trained technicians. The F-4 proved that complex avionics systems were not "hangar queens", but could go to war—and win.

Two rival "giants" of the electronics industry dominate the field of US-developed airborne radars—Hughes Aircraft and Westinghouse. The US Navy has always had a traditional preference for Westinghouse, a company that first became involved in airborne radar with the Douglas SBD Dauntless and Grumman Avenger torpedo bombers of World War II.

These early radars were made of a number of individual "black boxes" scattered about the interior of the aircraft, but when the Douglas F4D Skyray project came along, the Westinghouse engineers created the Aero-13, a radar set configured in a cylindrical shape which made it easy to instal and service in the nose of the aircraft. This configuration has been widely copied and remains the standard layout for fighter radars to the present day.

USN demands for high performance meant that the nose of the F-4A had to be enlarged to accept the larger antenna of the definitive Westinghouse APQ-72 radar which was to be standard set in the F-4B. This made extensive use of miniaturised tubes (valves) in its design, and the design of the receiver and integrating storage-tube indicator was optimised for maximum detection range–about twice that of earlier sets. The operator in the rear seat was provided with target-acquisition and tracking data, and had much electronic counter-countermeasures (ECCM) features (such as manual over-ride facilities) at his disposal. Separate pallets developed by Raytheon provided guidance and target-illumination functions for the AIM-7 Sparrow missiles.

During a 1961 test programme designated Operation Highspeed, the Phantom and its APQ-72 radar were shown to be superior to the F-106 Delta Dart and its MA-1 radar/fire-control system. This was a major factor in persuading the USAF to adopt the aircraft. For the F-4C, the USAF adopted a modified radar designated APQ-100. Closely modelled of the USN set, it featured a redesigned scope in the rear cockpit which offered a PPI mapping display option, and an adjustable range strobe for bombing. For air-to-ground missions, the radar interfaced with the aircraft's inertial platform.

When drawing up plans for the improved F-4D, the USAF wanted more emphasis to be placed on air-to-ground operations, and specified replacement of the APQ-100 radar with the more effective APQ-109. Significant additions in the new set included an air-to-ground ranging capability, a ground beacon identification and display capability, and an improved cockpit display able to handle TV imagery from weapons such as Walleye.

The USN set out to create its own improved Phantom in the form of the F-4J, and it selected another improved Westinghouse radar—the AWG-10 pulse-Doppler radar. To appreciate fully the importance of this new equipment, a brief digression into the esoteric world of radar theory is required.

Modern radars such as the APG-63 in the F-15 Eagle reduce all radar data to digital form, presenting the pilot with a clutter-free, synthetically-generated image made up of pre-defined symbols. Such luxuries were not available when the F-4 was designed. Its radars present a direct radar picture to the operator, who must use his own skill and experience in picking out targets from the clutter.

This task is particularly difficult when the radar is attempting to "look-down" and detect low-flying targets. Since the radar beam is very much larger in angular size than the target, much of the energy returned is reflected from the ground rather than the target. Combat experience in Vietnam showed such radar "clutter" could mask low-level attackers.

Until the 1960s, airborne radars were almost blind when attempting to look downwards to detect low flying aircraft, but then improved electronics allowed the creation of airborne radars with a good "look-down" performance. The key breakthrough was the use of pulse-Doppler radar technology. This requires the use of a highly-stable trans-

Front cockpit instruments (early)

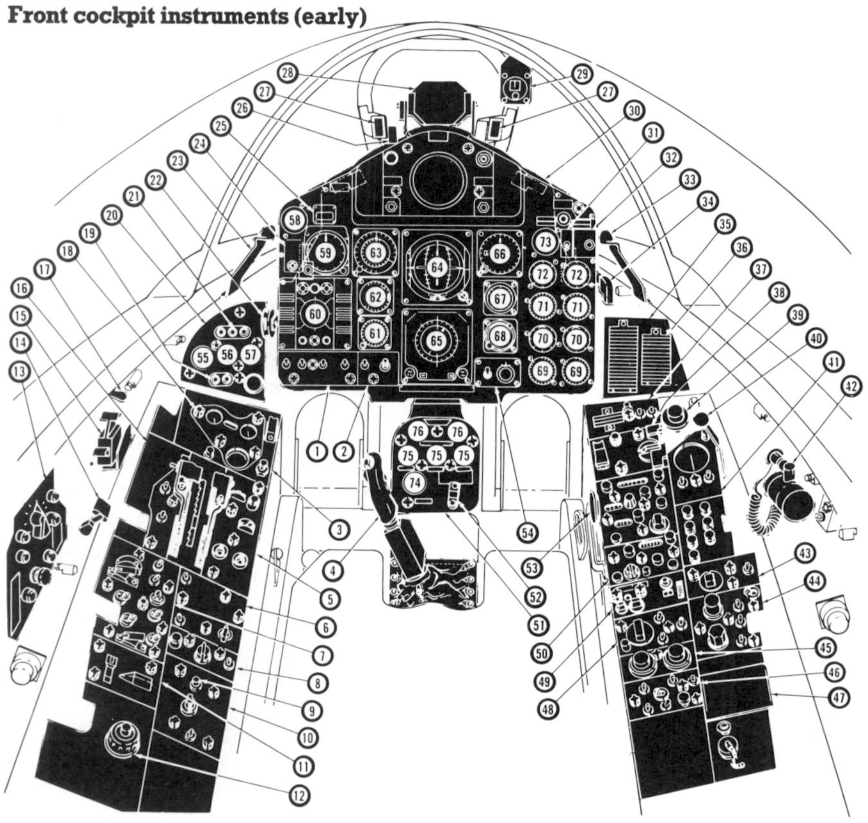

1. Missile control panel
2. Bomb control panel
3. Left utility panel
4. Control stick grip
5. Engine control panel (inboard)
6. Flight control panel
7. Fuel control panel
8. Intercom control panel
9. Steps position indicator
10. Auxiliary armament control panel
11. Pressure suit/oxygen control panel
12. Anti "g" suit control valve
13. Rack cartridge ground test panel
14. Emergency hydraulic pump handle
15. Flap controls
16. Engine control panel (outboard)
17. Canopy control handle
18. Engine control panel (centre)
19. Flap position indicators
20. Left vertical panel
21. Gear position indicators
22. Landing gear control handle
23. Emergency canopy release handle
24. Landing check list
25. UHF channel indicator
26. Labs light
27. Approach indexer light
28. Azimuth-elevation-range indicator
29. Standby compass
30. Main instrument panel
31. Feed tank check list
32. Take-off check list
33. Manual canopy unlock handle
34. Arresting gear control handle
35. Right vertical panel
36. Caution light panels
37. Electric control panel
38. T249A bomb control monitor panel
39. Emergency vent handle
40. Defog-foot heat handle
41. Right utility panel
42. Utility spot and flood light
43. Temperature control panel
44. Cockpit lights control panel
45. SIF control panel
46. Exterior lights control panel
47. Wingfold panel
48. IFF control panel
49. Compass system controller
50. Comm-nav. group control panel
51. Pedestal panel
52. Rudder pedal adjustment crank
53. Emergency brake handle
54. Mode-bearing/distance selector panel
55. Stabilator trim position indicator
56. Wing trim position indicator
57. Rudder position indicator
58. True airspeed indicator
59. Radio altimeter
60. Missile status panel
61. Accelerometer
62. Angle-of-attack indicator
63. Airspeed and mach number indicator
64. Attitude director indicator
65. Horizontal situation indicator
66. Altimeter
67. Vertical velocity indicator
68. Clock
69. Exhaust nozzle position indicators
70. Exhaust gas temperature indicators
71. Tachometers
72. Engine fuel flow indicators
73. Fuel quantity indicator
74. Pneumatic pressure indicators
75. Hydraulic pressure indicators
76. Oil pressure indicators

Below: Phantoms not fitted with an internal cannon could accommodate a larger radar antenna—this is probably an APQ-100 set in an F-4D. The handle-like fittings on the "dish" are dipole antennas for the IFF.

mitter in the radar set. This normally uses a travelling-wave tube (TWT) power source rather than the magnetron device used in more conventional radars. The output pulses from such a transmitter are what the electronics engineer terms "coherent"—they have an exact phase relationship with one another.

A very crude analogy which might illustrate the point would be to imagine a squad of infantry dressed in civilian clothing and heading into a busy railway station to travel home on leave. Although at first sight indistinguishable from other young male travellers of their age, their tendency to keep in step as they walked—acting as a "coherent" group—would allow them to be picked out in the crowd.

The AWG-10 was the first transistorised interceptor radar, and the first multi-mode set with pulse-Doppler look-down capability over land and sea. Considerably more complex than earlier Phantom radars, the new set offered a range of operating modes including: pulse air-to-air search and tracking; pulse-Doppler look-down; air-to-ground ranging; continuous wave (CW) illumination; high/low mapping. A comprehensive built-in test system able to check radar performance was also included.

Head-on detection in pulse-Doppler mode proved much better than that available from earlier radars. In look-down mode, the AWG-10 could detect air or surface targets of 53.8sq ft (5sq m) radar cross-section at range of 50nm (100km) or more. Range acceleration limiters and a guard channel improved ECCM capability.

When the UK ordered the Spey-powered Phantoms, the RN and RAF were determined to take advantage of pulse-Doppler technology. The AWG-11 and 12 chosen for the F-4K (Royal Navy) and F-4M (RAF) were slightly modified versions of the AWG-10. They were reworked in the late 1970s as part of a programme to extend the life of the RAF F-4 fleet.

Improved AWG-10 radar

Under a USN/USMC retrofit programme, the F-4J was equipped with the improved AWG-10A radar, an updated version of the original AWG-10. Reliability and maintainability were greatly increased by modifications such as the replacement of the original transmitter by a new solid-state unit whose only tube was a klystron power amplifier. Addition of a digital computer allowed the use of much more effective missile launch equations. At short range, for example, the radar can extract and utilise data on target manoeuvres. Weapon-aiming calculations for a full range of air-to-ground ordnance can also be handled. Another new feature was a servoed optical sight.

Several new operating modes were added by the rework. Air Combat Manoeuvring mode computes target manoeuvres. By making use of derived target data such as aspect, altitude, speed and acceleration, it optimises the choice of missile launch boundaries, ensuring that the steering error commands presented to the pilot are not unnecessarily confined. AWG-10A can cope with the AIM-7E, -7E2, -7F, -9D and -9G missiles.

In the AWG-10, the pilot's Command Indicator showed the same radar display as that available to the "back seater", but pilots rarely used it in combat. A typical reaction might have been that such head down gadgetry was OK for long range interception, but in close-in combat no pilot was "... going to look down at a ***** scope when it might mean that the ***** target would get onto his ***** tail!"

This perfectly understandable attitude often resulted in missiles being fired in combat by "rack of the eye" instead of by following the launch data on the command indicator. The servoed optical sight introduced on the AWG-10A displays all the data which the pilot will need, allowing him to fly with head up for all weapon launches.

A servoed reticle cross acts as the equivalent of the scope steering dot, while the circular "pipper" substitutes for the scope steering-error circle. To satisfy missile-launch requirements, the cross must be kept within the "pipper", while the end of an analogue "bar" indicating range must be at less than the 6 o'clock position. (The bar starts at the 12 o'clock position and extends round in a clockwise direction proportional to range.)

In gun attacks, the "pipper" must be aligned with the target. When the radar is locked on, the range bar is operative. If no lock-on has been obtained, the system assumes a range of 1,000ft (305m). In HEAT attacks, the seeker of an AIM-9G Sidewinder may be slaved to the pilot's line of sight independent of

Above: "Front office" of a USAF 414th TFS F-4E. The lower-profile instrument panel improves visibility.

Below: The "back-seater" of the same aircraft has very little forward view of the outside world—this cockpit is designed as a radar operator's workstation. Note the hooded radar display.

Direct mode weapons delivery

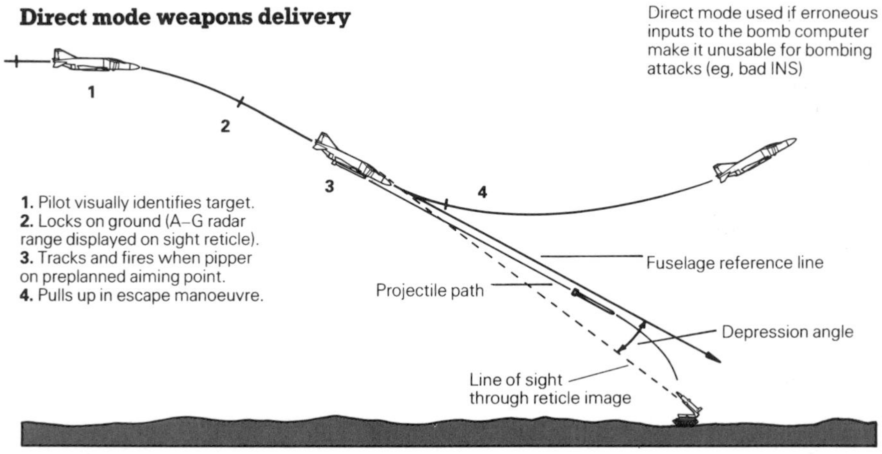

Direct mode used if erroneous inputs to the bomb computer make it unusable for bombing attacks (eg, bad INS)

2. Locks on ground (A–G radar range displayed on sight reticle).
3. Tracks and fires when pipper on preplanned aiming point.

Fuselage reference line
Projectile path

Line of sight through reticle image

Dive toss release

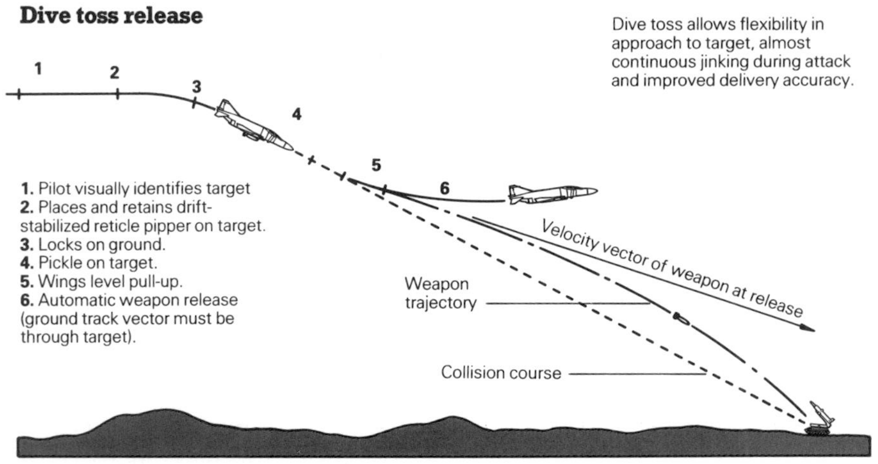

Dive toss allows flexibility in approach to target, almost continuous jinking during attack and improved delivery accuracy.

2. Places and retains drift-stabilized reticle pipper on target.
3. Locks on ground.
4. Pickle on target.
5. Wings level pull-up.

Velocity vector of weapon at release
Weapon trajectory

Dive glide release

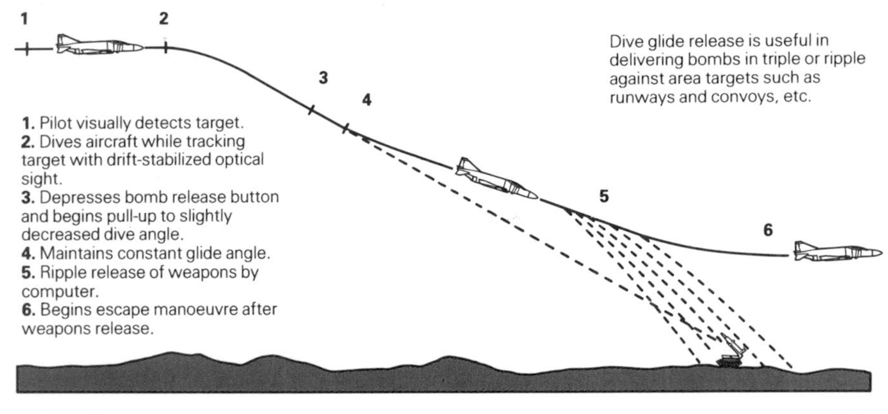

1
2
3
4
5
6
Dive glide release is useful in delivering bombs in triple or ripple against area targets such as runways and convoys, etc.
1. Pilot visually detects target.
2. Dives aircraft while tracking target with drift-stabilized optical sight.
3. Depresses bomb release button and begins pull-up to slightly decreased dive angle.
4. Maintains constant glide angle.
5. Ripple release of weapons by computer.
6. Begins escape manoeuvre after weapons release.

Offset bombing release

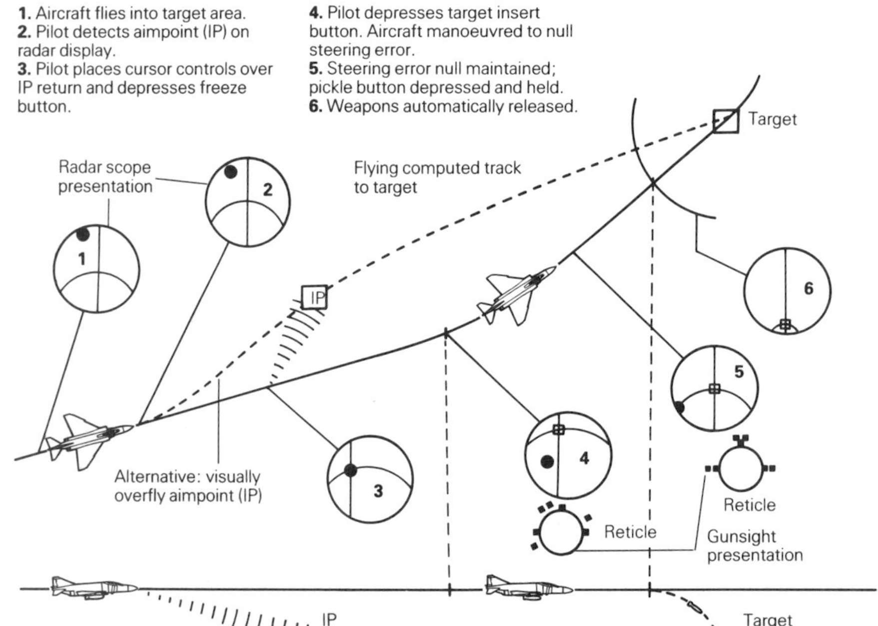

1. Aircraft flies into target area.
2. Pilot detects aimpoint (IP) on radar display.
3. Pilot places cursor controls over IP return and depresses freeze button.
4. Pilot depresses target insert button. Aircraft manoeuvred to null steering error.

Radar scope presentation
Flying computed track to target

Alternative: visually overfly aimpoint (IP)

Gunsight presentation

Above: Later models of the F-4 gave pilots a new freedom in planning bombing attacks. *Direct* mode (top) with pre-planned dive angles and target ranges is used only as a last resort. In *Dive Toss* and *Dive Glide* modes the pilot simply aligns his ground track vector with the target at the moment of weapon release. *Offset Bombing* allows attacks against targets not visible on radar—in this case the set is locked on to an offset aimpoint. Given details of the relative position of the aiming point and target, the nav/attack system could direct the ordnance.

Above: The rectangular fin-top fairing for the RWR and small antenna just above the tail insignia are features found only on UK F-4s, being associated with British-developed ESM and communications equipment.

the radar target track, or else to the radar antenna position.

Automation of the air-to-ground delivery of ordnance allows the pilot significant flexibility in planning his flight path to the target. Freed from the need to fly a rigidly pre-programmed flight path to the release point, the aircraft is much less vulnerable to ground fire.

In Continuously-Displayed Impact Point (CDI) mode, the back seater is able to set the system to cope with the calculation needed in order to handle the ordnance chosen by the pilot. All ballistic data are held in the computer, and the pilot simply flies to bring the "pipper" of his servoed optical sight onto the target.

For targets of opportunity, or targets whose elevation is not known, the pilot uses Freeze-Displayed Impact (FDI) mode, placing the optical sight "pipper" over the target, and depressing the "pickle" button to obtain radar range and elevation data which re-positions the "pipper". An attack pattern can then be flown, and the "pipper" re-aligned with the target.

Computer Released Visual (CRV) mode handles dive/toss delivery of ordnance. After obtaining target range and elevation data in FDI mode, the pilot keeps the "pickle" button depressed, and flies any suitable path in elevation, while maintaining the azimuth alignment with the target. The optical sight provides "time-to-release" data, and the pilot keeps the "pickle" button depressed until the system automatically releases the ordnance.

Effects of APQ-120

Introduction of the nose-mounted internal gun on the F-4E was made easier by the adoption of another new radar—the compact APQ-120. This has a 27.5in (70cm) antenna instead of the earlier 32in (81cm) unit, while its solid-state avionics were better able to resist the vibration resulting from gunfire than a thermionic-tube set would have been.

The APQ-120 was the first USAF F-4 radar to include a Westinghouse-developed missile guidance and illumination function as part of the design. Computation and semi-active radar guidance facilities were mechanically integrated with the complete package, with substantial savings in weight, volume and cost.

When the USAF modernised its F-4E fleet, some of the digital technology originally devised for the AWG-10A was added. Westinghouse shipped a total of 810 add-on computers intended to replace existing analogue missile-release computers. The radar now has Computer-Aided Acquisition of target (CAA) facilities, and can send launch information to the missiles in real time. As part of its Peace Rhine F-4F update programme, the West German Luftwaffe ordered 210 computers to give the aircraft better missile-launch capability, plus new head-up and head-down air-to-air gunnery capability.

In order to prolong the life of the Japan Air Self-Defense Force fleet of Mitsubishi-built F-4EJ Phantoms, the existing APQ-120 radar is to be replaced by the APG-66J derivative of the Fighting Falcon set. A total of 100 aircraft are to be reworked and will enter service as the F-4E (J) Kai. Following a first flight in 1985, the new version is expected to remain in service well into the 1990s.

Radar-warning receivers

In order to cope with the threat posed by enemy radars or radar-guided weapons, an aircraft must be able to detect when it is being sought, detected and tracked. This task is carried out by means of a radar-warning receiver (RWR).

The need for RWRs first became urgent during the Vietnam War. Following a study begun in August 1965, a contract was awarded in November for the APR-25, a simple crystal-video receiver covering the band of frequencies in which North Vietnamise defence systems operated. This equipment had been proposed by a small $5.5 million electronic company called Applied Technology, which later became a division of Itek. In the F-4C and RF-4C, this RWR was installed alongside the specialised APR-26 launch-warning receiver. USN F-4Bs were fitted with the APR-27, a Navy equivalent of the -26 built by Magnavox.

For the F-4D, the USAF turned to Bendix, fitting the APS-107 also carried by the F-105 and F-111. An update of the APR-25 and -26 to incorporate new techniques such as automatic time/video correlation circuits resulted in the improved Itek APR-36 and -37 fitted to USAF F-4Es. Equipment installed on export aircraft varied from customer to customer.

Magnavox RWRs were once again installed on the Phantom with the introduction of the APR-32 on the F-4J, but the rebuild to F-4S resulted in the Loral APR-43 Compass Sail Clockwise tactical warning receiver being substituted.

The ALR-46 was fitted to Luftwaffe F-4Fs under a retrofit programme. This is a development of the earlier ALR-36/37, and is a field-programmable broadband receiver covering frequencies from 2 to 18GHz.

Phantom combat avionics

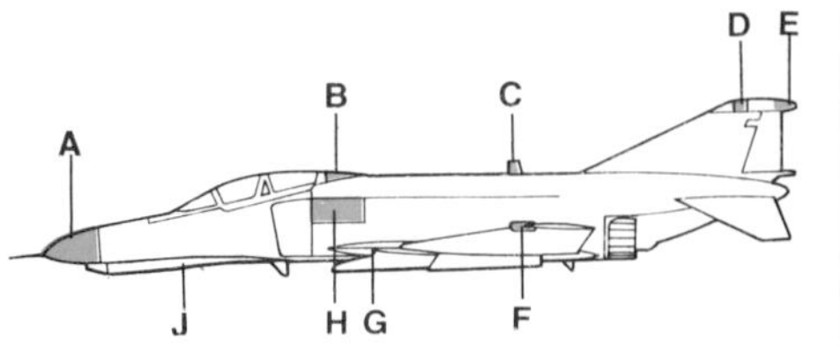

A. PQW-120 radar.
B. IFF.
C. Tacan.
D. VHF.
E. RWR.
F. Forward RWR.
G. Ranging aerial (right wing).
H. Avionics bays.
J. VHF/UHF.

Above: Avionics are not confined to the nose section of the F-4—location of individual units is often determined by their operational role. Here are shown some of the combat avionics carried by F-4 versions.

Above: Antennas in the fin-top and undernose fairing are just two items in the complex APR-38 radar detection and homing system carried by the F-4G Wild Weasel.

Wild Weasel avionics

The most complex receiving installation carried by any Phantom is the McDonnell Douglas APR-38 system in the F-4G Wild Weasel. The original F-4C Wild Weasels used the ALR-46 to detect and home on to hostile radar, but this was replaced in the definitive F-4G by a complex suite of EW avionics which would have required a massive platform in the EC-135 class had earlier technology been used.

The ALR-38 antennas are located in the chin fairing which originally contained the muzzle of the M61 cannon, and on the tip of the vertical fin. Incoming signals are detected, analysed and compared with the extensive on-board library of threat signatures contained in the aircraft's central computer. The resulting data is presented on specialised displays in the rear cockpit.

Perhaps the biggest problem associated with the system is the sheer volume of data which it can present to the system operator, whose operational duties while "stalking" a ground threat can make the speed of fast-moving arcade games such as Space Invaders or Galaxians seem sluggish. Typical time for aiming and firing a Maverick missile is around three seconds, while some tactical situations involve a SAM versus ARM shoot-out—both sides launching missiles, with the Weasel attempting to get his anti-radiation round on to the SAM guidance radar before the ground-launched missile has completed its trip from the launcher to the Weasel. The rule of thumb drummed into new operators is that if they have stared at the same display for more than five seconds in a combat situation, they have actually lost command of the fast-moving situation. The back-seater must be able to recognise that he has become "saturated" with data, and not attempt to struggle on.

Continuing an attack under overload conditions might result in the aircraft falling victim to anti-Weasel tactics. One such trick is dubbed "Here, Kitty Kitty" by Weasel crews—an enemy using one threat system to draw the Weasels into an attack which will bring them into the engagement zone of others. To cope with such tricks, Weasels often hunt in pairs in order to reverse the same trick. While one draws the attention of the bad guys loitering just out of engagement range, the second aircraft attempts to approach unobserved from the rear, landing a Maverick or Harm missile on the unsuspecting radar or SAM site.

Foreign warning receivers

Some nations equip their Phantoms with indigenously-developed RWR equipment. UK Phantoms are fitted with the Marconi Space and Defence Systems ARI 18228, which provides indications of threat bearing, transmission type and other data on a cockpit-mounted CRT display. It is believed Israeli F-4Es were supplied with US warning receivers, probably the APR-36/37, but it is likely that these have now been retrofitted by more advanced systems, perhaps of local manufacture. Israel's Elta company already offers RWR systems for export. Few details of the avionics fit of Japan's F-4E(J) have been released, but at least two RWRs (designated JAPR-1 and -2) are known to have been developed indigenously to match local threat conditions.

The Phantom's jammers

Jamming systems can attack the hostile radar using one of two techniques, or even both. Noise jamming aims to swamp the genuine target return by transmitting large amounts of radio-frequency noise. The human ear and brain are highly efficient at picking out the sounds of one conversation from admidst the babble of many others—psychologists even describe this ability as the "cocktail party effect"—but a radar is less versatile and cannot distinguish the genuine and wanted signal from the background noise created by the jammer.

Such "brute-force" methods of confusing a radar have been partly supplanted by deceptive jamming—a process which involves receiving the threat signal, modifying it in some way, then re-transmitting it in the hope that the threat system will accept the "doctored" signal as genuine. By choosing the manner in which the signal is processed before transmission, the ECM designer can feed false range or bearing information to an enemy radar, or even cause multiple false targets to be detected.

The F-4 has carried three main types of jamming pod, all developed by Westinghouse. The ALR-101 was developed in the late 1960s and is available in a range of variants. The original unit covered E/F and G/H bands. A more powerful V(3) version was briefly produced only to be replaced by the V(4) which added I/J band coverage. V(6) offered a further increase in coverage, while the extra electronics in the V(9) required installation of a "gondola" fairing on the lower surface of the pod to provide additional internal volume. V(8) is an updated version of the earlier pods, and has been widely exported. Further development led to the V(10) and V(12), which are similar in capability to the newer ALQ-119. The latter is a dual-mode self-protection pod which has seen extensive service on USAF F-4s. It entered service in Vietnam during 1972 and is believed to cover the radar spectrum form E to I band.

Development of the ALQ-131 started in the early 1970s to meet a USAF requirement. Following successful development and flight tests, the unit was ordered into production in 1976. ALQ-131 is a 573lb (260kg) modular pod-mounted system able to cope with a wide range of threats, particularly the radars and guidance systems of air-defence systems. By selecting internal modules, the user may configure the pod to handle threats spread over one to five frequency bands. Modules are available to cope with all frequencies used by current anti-aircraft missile systems. Noise and deception-jamming modes are available.

The pod is power-managed, and the software can easily be modified to cope with the tactical situation which the user faces, or to take into account changes in

Below: Test installation of the Pave Spike designator on an F-4. The pod has a gimballed and stabilised optical turret for the laser and TV system, used to identify and mark targets to be attacked with laser-guided weapons.

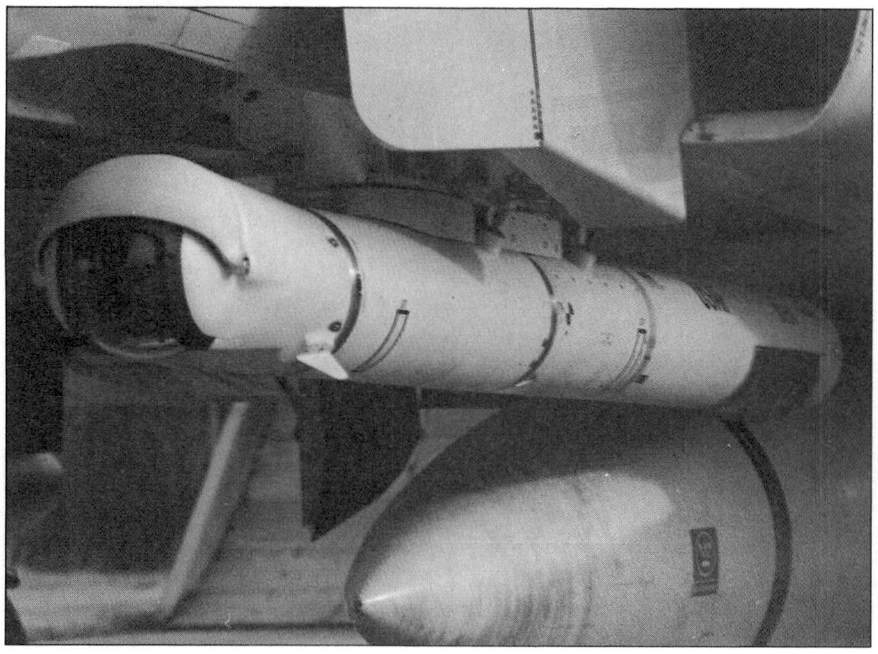

Below: F-4E with the larger Pave Tack adverse-weather designator pod. In this system a FLIR is used for target tracking and the gimballed optics are at the rear. Really bad weather can defeat the FLIR.

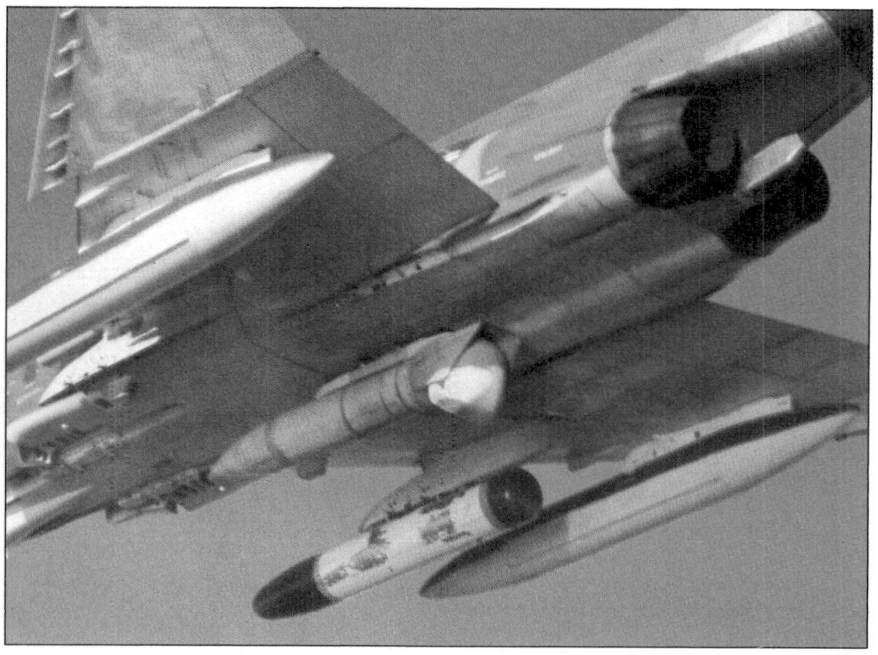

Above: USAF F-4D complete with chin-mounted infra-red seeker and ALQ-101 ECM pod. The fairing beneath the pod gives extra space for jamming equipment, and was to be a feature of the later ALQ-119 and -131.

Below: Two F-4Ds of the Wolfpack of USAF 8th TFW. Note the ventral hump on the chin-mounted IR sensor of the nearest aircraft, which also has the "towel-rack" antenna for AN/ARN-92 LORAN navigation gear.

Above: The nose section of the RF-4C has optical ports for the cameras and IR sensors. The two dark hemispheres are miniature radomes for radar-sensing antennas. Earlier RF- nose was similar but angular.

Below: Wing leading-edge fairing and optical sensor of the Northrop TISEO system fitted to some F-4Es to aid long-range target identification. The optics are stabilised and can be slaved to the APQ-120 radar.

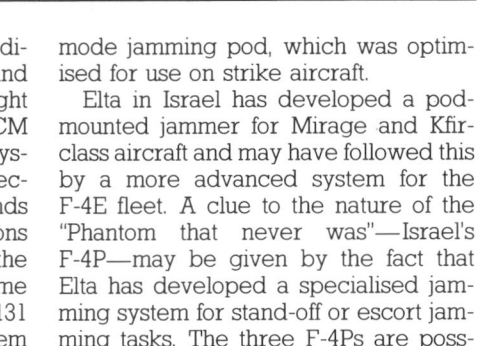

threat tactics or parameters. Such modifications may be easily carried out, and may even be implemented, on the flight line. The struggle between the ECM designer and the latest tactics and systems is a continuous one. If the prospective enemy introduces new radar bands or techniques, hardware modifications may be needed. The USAF began the classified Have Exit update programme in 1980, four years after the ALQ-131 entered service. In this case, the system was probably being updated to cope with new Soviet threat systems featuring monopulse radars.

Non-US Phantom operators may use pods or other EW systems of non-US origin, but details are rarely released. RAF aircraft are now assigned to interceptor rather than strike duties so are unlikely to receive the Marconi Space and Defence Systems Sky Shadow dual-mode jamming pod, which was optimised for use on strike aircraft.

Elta in Israel has developed a pod-mounted jammer for Mirage and Kfir-class aircraft and may have followed this by a more advanced system for the F-4E fleet. A clue to the nature of the "Phantom that never was"—Israel's F-4P—may be given by the fact that Elta has developed a specialised jamming system for stand-off or escort jamming tasks. The three F-4Ps are possibly the IDFAF equivalent of the USAF's EF-111A Electric Fox EW aircraft—a dedicated jamming aircraft able to protect formations attacking heavily defended targets.

Infra-red sensors

Radar is not the only means of detecting and identifying targets which the Phantom has utilised. The seventh F-4A prototype saw the introduction of the distinctive chin fairing used to house an infra-red sensor—the Texas Instruments AAA-4. The USN had already adopted a similar sensor for the F-8 Crusader, providing a passive back-up to the main radar, allowing targets to be tracked by the heat emissions from their engine exhaust and airframe. Much in vogue in the late 1960s and early 1970s, systems of this type were not particularly successful, so it was not surprising that the USAF decided not to retain the AAA-4 infra-red sensor as a standard feature on the F-4D. According to official documentation (and many books on the F-4), the F-4D carries no IR sensor, but in practice the system was retrofitted in a modified form. The revised housing features a ventral hump, distinguishing modified F-4D from the earlier F-4Cs which have IR sensors.

Located in a circular housing on the wing leading edge of late-production USAF F-4Es, the Northrop TISEO (Target Identification System Electro-Optical) displays a high-magnification stabilised image on a cockpit display, allowing long-range visual identification of targets. The optical telescope can be slaved to the radar antenna or operated independently, and offers two fields of view.

A total of 156 USAF D/E models have AVQ-23A Pave Spike television/laser designator pods. Suitable for daylight use, this 425lb (193kg) pod contains a TV tracker and a laser designator/ranger, plus stabilised and steerable optics. The back seater uses the equipment to acquire, track and designate targets for attack by laser-guided munitions. Export users include the UK and Turkey.

Israel's Peace Jack RF-4E(S)

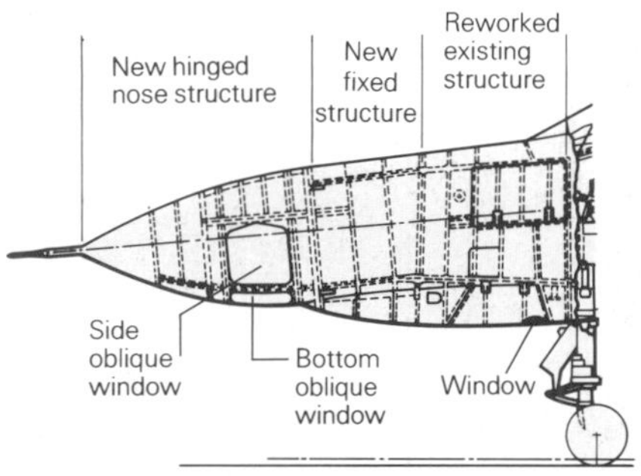

Above and right: The drawing and pre-delivery photograph show the modified nose (12in/30cm longer than F-4E) of Israel's General Dynamics-modified RF-4E(S) Peace Jack high-altitude recce aircraft. Note the optical port for the massive long-range camera used to take oblique images of heavily-defended targets.

The broadly similar AVQ-26 Pave Tack offers all-weather ordnance-delivery capability, thanks to the incorporation of a Texas Instruments FLIR system instead of TV. A built-in videotape recorder allows the imagery to be stored for post-strike assessment and the location of potential targets.

Reconnaissance Phantoms

The RF-4C featured many internal changes. Flight controls were fitted in the front cockpit only, allowing the back-seater to concentrate his attention on operating the payload of optical and electronic sensors, including in-flight film-processing equipment. Largest portion of the RF-4C payload was made up of optical cameras—usually one KS-72 or KS-87 forward oblique-framing camera plus one KA-56A low-altitude and one KA-55A high-altitude panoramic camera.

A Goodyear APQ-102A sideways-looking radar (originally installed) recorded a broad strip of terrain on each side of the flight path on a film which could be processed after landing, and was backed up by an AAS-118 infra-red detecting set. The ALR-17 allows hostile radars to be identified and classified on the photo imagery, while the ALQ-161 normally carried on the centreline handles the ELINT task. An HF communications transceiver allows voice communication between the aircraft and its base at all times.

Terrain-following radar

The days when reconnaissance aircraft could overfly target areas with impunity at high altitude are long since over. The viable methods of operating a recce Phantom against targets likely to shoot back is either to attempt oblique photography and sensing from a high-altitude location well out of range of the defences, or else to go in fast and low. For the latter type of mission, the recon version carries in the extreme nose a Texas Instruments APQ-99 radar, often referred to as the "forward looker" by aircrew. This allows the aircraft to fly in terrain-following mode. The antenna of the set covers a vertical angle from +10 to −15deg and scans from side to side over a narrow 5deg sector.

The radar display shows a profile of the terrain directly ahead of the aircraft, plus a solid line or template whose shape and location is defined by the height at which the aircraft is to fly. The pilot steers the aircraft in pitch according to instructions given by a climb/dive indicator needle. If the system is operating correctly, the terrain profile shown on the scope will always remain below the template. (Some slight overlap is allowed over hilly ground, but only at short range.) It is impossible for the aircraft to maintain an exact height above the ground at all times when flying across rough terrain. Flight over valleys will tend to be higher than the selected nominal, while clearance over high ground will be slightly reduced.

One of the biggest problems in tactical reconnaissance is that of getting imagery into the hands of ground commanders while it is still fresh. Front-line combat units need to receive the current tactical position, not a record of where the enemy was several hours ago or more. The RF-4C solved this by processing the film while the aircraft is in flight, and if neccessary ejecting the resulting photographs in a cartridge which could be picked up by front-line personnel.

The other photo-reconnaissance versions were broadly similar. The RF-4B of the Marine Corps combined the RF-4C systems and inertial navigation system with the airframe of the F-4B.

RF-4C's APQ-99 radar template

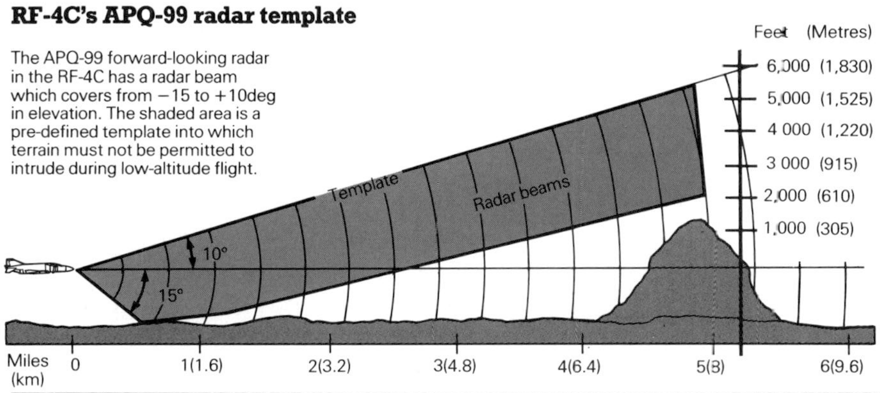

The APQ-99 forward-looking radar in the RF-4C has a radar beam which covers from −15 to +10deg in elevation. The shaded area is a pre-defined template into which terrain must not be permitted to intrude during low-altitude flight.

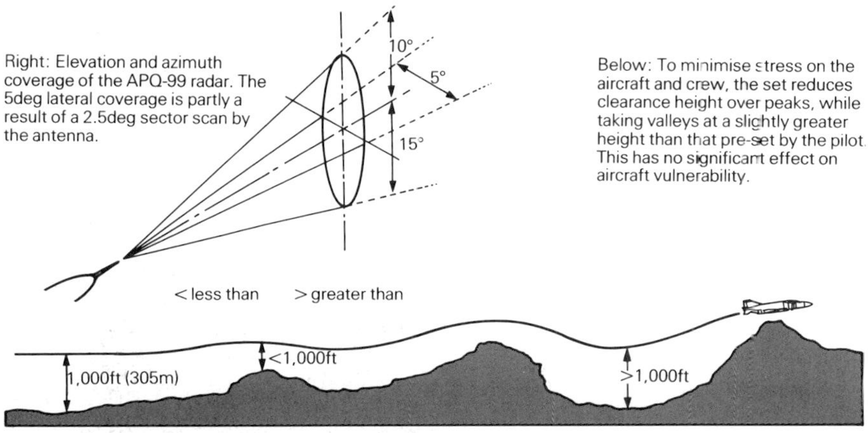

Right: Elevation and azimuth coverage of the APQ-99 radar. The 5deg lateral coverage is partly a result of a 2.5deg sector scan by the antenna.

Below: To minimise stress on the aircraft and crew, the set reduces clearance height over peaks, while taking valleys at a slightly greater height than that pre-set by the pilot. This has no significant effect on aircraft vulnerability.

Below: The antenna is stabilised in the horizontal plane, giving the RF-4C good warning of approaching high ground.

Below: Without stabilisation, the radar would tend to command the aircraft to rise in a staircase-like flight path.

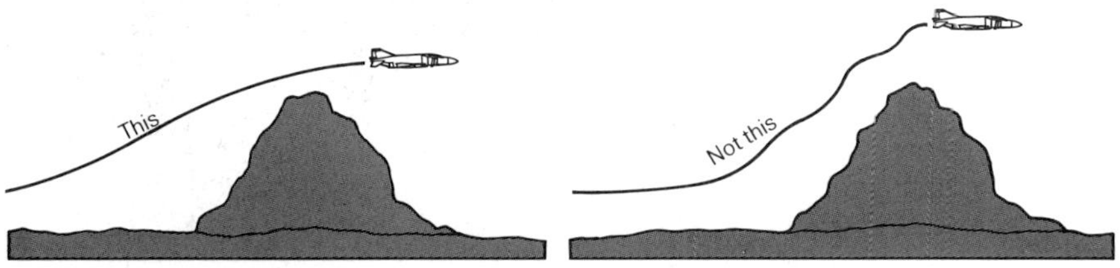

Below: After the peak is crossed and the aircraft begins to dive, maintaining the radar horizontal stabilisation would create the risk of a possible crash (see upper drawing)—the radar must be able to sense the approaching terrain during a dive. To overcome this problem, the APQ-99 directs its antenna downwards during a dive by an amount roughly half the aircraft's pitch angle. This results in a smooth flight path (as shown in the lower drawing).

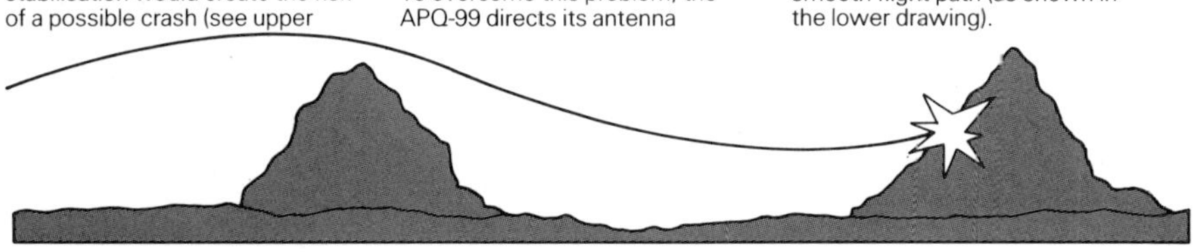

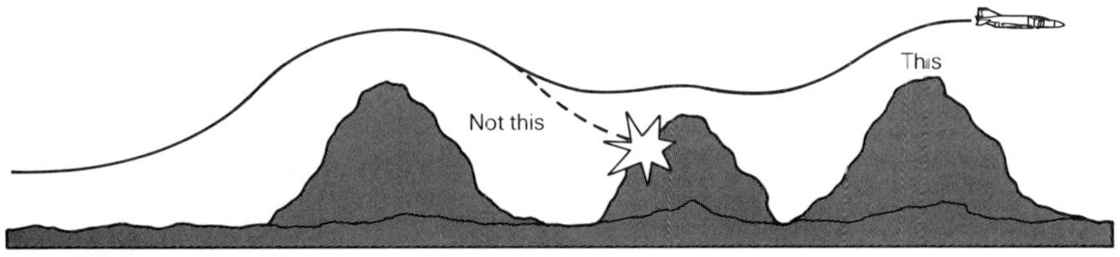

The APQ-99 system in action over rough terrain (upper drawing). As long as terrain does not impinge on the pre-set safety template, the aircraft will be safe. Note how the template remains horizontal for most of the time, but is depressed during a dive. The shape and size of the safety template is related to the selected cruise height. Following a command to climb, the faster an aircraft is flying, the closer it will approach the high ground (lower drawing).

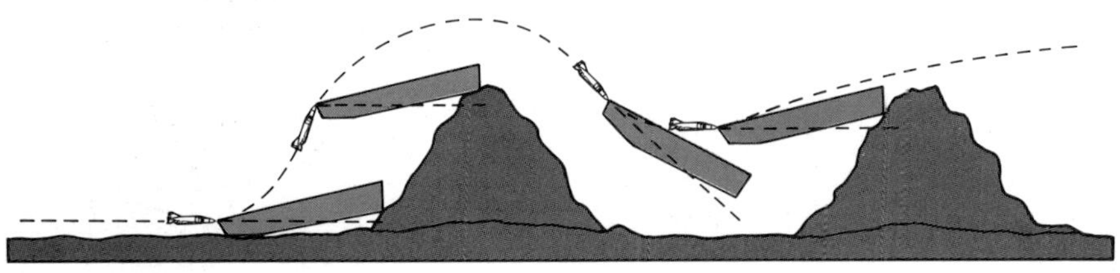

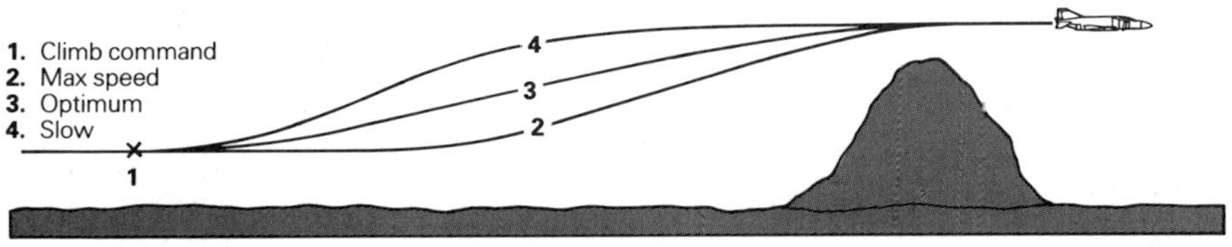

Many of the USAF sensors were highly classified, so could not be cleared for export. Customers ordering the RF-4E have in some cases had to accept an alternative equipment. Israel's F-4E(S) is equipped with the General Dynamics HIAC-camera of 66in (167cm) focal length, operating through side and bottom-mounted oblique windows in the aircraft nose. This version was supplied under a programme designated Peace Jack.

Recce Phantoms such as the RF-4B, -4C and -4E have been updated to match modern requirements. The original APQ-102A radar was replaced by the Goodyear UPD-4 synthetic-aperture sideways looking radar. The twin antennas are gimbal-mounted, and may be moved automatically in flight to maintain a constant look angle. The system can be set to a number of operating modes, recording fixed-target imagery only or mixed and moving target data.

Luftwaffe RF-4Es have been retrofitted with the newer Goodyear UPD-6 radar. This incorporates a data link which is used to transmit real-time radar data back to ground stations, a feature also incorporated in an extended-range version of the UPD-4.

Nav-attack systems

All versions of the F-4 carry complex navigation and attack systems. Standard systems on the F-4B were the ASN-39 dead-reckoning navigation computer, and AJB-3A bombing system. Twelve F-4Bs were assigned to the task of exploring automatic-landing techniques, and were given the designation F-4G (not to be confused with the later Wild Weasel configuration). Specialised avionics installed for this task included the ASW-21 two-way data link and an approach-power compensator.

Although the F-4C—first USAF version of the Phantom—was planned to be broadly similar to the existing USN F-4B, some avionics changes were necessary, including full flying controls and instrumentation in both cockpits and the installation of a Litton-built ASN-48 inertial navigation system. The AJB-7 bombing system selected for this aircraft was also to be used in the later F-4D, -4E, -4J, -4N and -4S.

The new avionics bay introduced by the F-4G was put to good use on the F-4D, housing new items of avionics such as the ASQ-91 weapon-release computer and sub-units of the ASG-22 lead-computing sighting system. A new ASN-63 inertial navigation set replaced the earlier ASN-48 and was to be used on the F-4E, -4G Wild Weasel and -4J.

To meet the appetite of these improved avionics suites, the aircraft's 20kVA engine-driven electrical generators were replaced by 30kVA units. Many of the earlier aircraft were eventually to be retrofitted with these uprated generators.

The new nav-attack avionics gave the F-4D an automatic air-to-ground weapon delivery capability, increasing bombing accuracy by a factor of three compared with that of the F-4C's manually-operated systems. The F-4Es introduced the Lear Siegler ARN-101 digital navigation and weapon-aiming system, which works in conjunction with the Pave Tack FLIR/laser designator.

Some versions have been updated with more modern equipment. Israeli F-4Es are now equipped with Litton LW-33 digital inertial navigation/attack system, while the USMC update programme for the RF-4B added the ASN-92 carrier alignment inertial navigation system (CAINS).

The most dramatic avionics upgrading is that proposed for the Super Phantom (see chapter on Development).

Armament

The end result of any combat mission is to get the ordnance on to the target. The Phantom can carry almost any air-to-air or air-to-surface weapon that the user air power might wish to deploy including missiles which had not even been conceived when the aircraft was designed. Delivery accuracy might not be up to the standards of today's high-technology fighters, but has been good enough for most of the wars to which the type has been committed, and in SE Asia Phantoms were able to carry out pinpoint attacks against small, high-value targets.

Above: Deployed in 1964, AGM-45 Shrike was the first weapon which allowed US aircrews to suppress defensive radars by destroying them or forcing them to switch off at a critical moment.

Although the single-seat F3H-G configuration originally studied would have carried a quartet of 20mm cannon, the Phantom was to enter service without a built-in gun. Back in the early 1950s, gun armament was considered obsolete by many operators. In the USA, Britain and the Soviet Union cannonless designs such as the F-86D, F-102, Lightning, MiG-19PM and Su-9 were to enter service. This mistaken trend continued into later designs such as the F-106 and Su-15, but represented a failure to appreciate that the era of fighter-versus-fighter combat was not yet dead. When Phantoms clashed with MiGs in the skies over North Vietnam, the need for an internal gun had to be learned the hard way.

For the F-4, the US Navy adopted an air-to-air armament of six AIM-7 Sparrow missiles or a mix of four AIM-7 plus four AIM-9 Sidewinders, weapons which first entered USN service back in 1956. The designers opted to carry the Sparrows mounted semi-flush beneath the lower fuselage, a move which reduced drag. Early flight trials with the F-4A confirmed the Phantom's ability to tote an ordnance load of up to 22,500lb (10,206kg) although a figure of 16,000lb (7,258kg) was adopted for initial service use of the F-4B. This ordnance load was carried on five wing and fuselage hard points.

Studies carried out the early 1950s had suggested that a salvo of two Sparrows fired against a target would have a kill probability of around 65 per cent, a significant improvement over the 45 per cent predicted for a volley of 72 unguided rockets (typical armament of many early-1950s American fighters). In practice, it was argued, the Sparrow-equipped aircraft would be able to fire at long range, inflicting heavy attrition on fighters armed with the simpler unguided rockets.

Such idealistic reasoning assumed that the Sparrow-equipped aircraft would be allowed to open fire against targets visible only as blips on the radar—identified as hostile only by the absence of an IFF response. But in Vietnam, the rules of air combat dictated that targets be visually identified before being engaged. This involved approaching the small and agile North Vietnamese MiG-17s and MiG-21s to a distance well below the minimum AIM-7 launch range, and often within the minimum for the AIM-9.

At such short ranges, gun armament was badly needed, so F-4 units had to improvise. US Navy F-4Bs were often fitted with Hughes Mk4 gun pods, while USAF F-4Cs were similarly upgraded with add-on gun armament. This normally took the form of SUU-16/A or SUU-23/A gun pods each carrying a 20mm calibre Vulcan rotary cannon plus 1,200 rounds of ammunition, but the smaller GAU-2B/A 7.62mm minipod machine-gun pods were often carried for air-to-ground strikes against personnel and soft-skinned vehicles.

Though acceptable as interim weapons, these pod-mounted guns imposed a performance penalty on the Phantoms, while their accuracy was less than that which would have been available with an internal gun: pylon mountings were designed to hold ordnance in place prior to release, but not to keep it axially aligned to the degree demanded by accurate gunnery. The US services took the lesson to heart, specifying a built-in gun for the later F-14, F-16, and F/A-18.

Introduction of built-in cannon armament for the Phantom had to await the F-4E. A reprofiled nose carries a single General Electric M61A1 rotary cannon with a fire rate of up to 100 rounds/sec. The entire gun system, complete with a 639-round magazine, is a single self-contained module which can be re-

Above: SUU-23/A gunpod ready for delivery at the General Electric works. The earlier SUU-16/A used a ram-air turbine to spin the barrels of the Vulcan cannon, but the -23 has an electric starting motor.

Below: Drag-inducing gunpods were not ideally suited to the demands of air-to-air combat, but gave the F-4 a powerful punch when strafing ground targets such as vehicle convoys or troop positions.

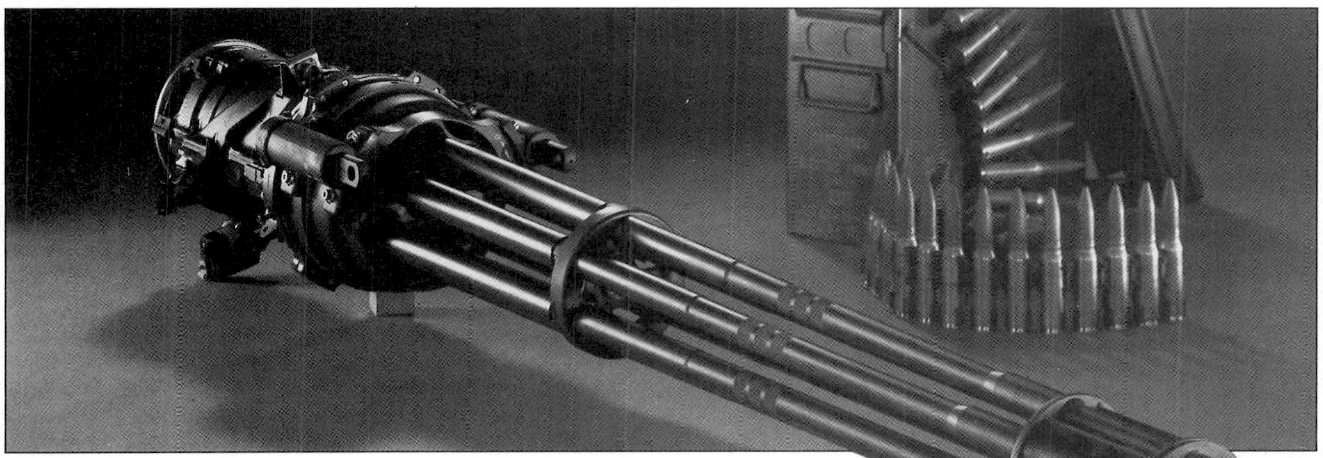

Left: M61 Vulcan cannon carried in SUU-23/A gunpods and in the nose of the F-4E. When the gun is firing, the six-barrelled assembly rotates. After a barrel has fired its round, a fresh barrel is brought into the firing position. As the assembly rotates, the breech of each newly-fired barrel is opened, the spent case ejected, a new round is loaded, and the breech is closed just before the barrel once again reaches the firing position. At the moment of firing, all six are at different but sequential points in this ejection/reloading/firing cycle.

moved for maintenance or replaced with another. Flying the aircraft without the gun installed is not recommended unless compensating ballast is carried in the nose. Without the weight of the gun, rotation at take-off could be somewhat abrupt.

The gun is hydraulically operated, and can reach its full fire rate in around half a second. The pilot may select a fire rate of 4,000 or 6,000 shots per minute using a "high/low" switch on the cockpit-mounted Multiple Weapons Control Panel, which also incorporates a "rounds left" counter. Approximately 630 of the 639 rounds are usable.

To prolong the life of the gun, it is recommended that bursts of fire should not be longer than three seconds. Minimum time between bursts is one second; the trigger is automatically inhibited for this period of time.

When the gun fires, a small door on the upper part of the nose automatically opens, admitting a flow of air to the gun. It remains open for 30 seconds after firing, clearing the gun compartment of fumes.

The Phantom's missiles

Experience of missile combat in the Vietnam War showed that the claims of the missile designers had been optimistic. Although more than 600 AIM-7 Sparrows and some 450 AIM-9 Sidewinders were fired in action, neither performed well. Part of the blame must lie with poor maintenance and the fact that many rounds were fired at targets which lay outside the specified performance envelope of the weapon concerned. The combat record of the Sparrow proved particularly disappointing. According to Congressional testimony released after the war, the "kill rate" of this missile was just under 10 per cent.

The original Sparrow I entered service in 1956 and used beam-riding guidance. The active-radar homing Sparrow II (AIM-7B) was abandoned by the USN while still in development, promoted as armament for the Canadian Avro CF-105 Arrow heavy interceptor, then finally cancelled. The definitive Sparrow III used semi-active radar homing (SARH).

AIM-7C was the first of the Sparrow III family to see service, arming the McDonnell F-3 Demon, but it was soon followed by the AIM-7D. Both carried a heavy 65lb (29kg) warhead of continuous-rod type with a lethal radius of around 125ft (38m), and triggered by contact and proximity fuzes, but the latter version was cleared for supersonic launch.

Right: Each SUU-23/A can hold 1,200 rounds of standard US M50 series 20mm ammunition. At the gun's maximum rate of fire of 6,000rpm, this 652lb (296kg) "warload" lasts for only 12 seconds of firing time.

Below: Now a museum exhibit at Wright Patterson AFB, Phantom BuAer No. 62-12200 spent most of its career as a trials aircraft. Originally built as an F-4B, it is seen here testing the F-4E gun installation.

Average range of the -7E when fired from the Phantom is around 13.8nm (25.5km)—a figure limited by the performance of the radar. Experience with the later F-14 Tomcat and its more powerful Hughes AWG-9 radar showed that reliable lock-on range of the -7E could be doubled.

Usable range depends on factors such as launch speed and engagement geometry. High-altitude range for a frontal engagement using the AIM-7E is reported to be between 7 and 8.6nm (13 and 16km), falling to around 3nm (5.5km) for a stern attack. Flight time for a 16nm (29.6km) engagement is around 40 seconds. Minimum ranges under the same conditions are probably 2nm (3.7km) and just under 1nm (1.85km) respectively.

AIM-7D and -7E were both deployed to Vietnam, with disappointing results. Combat firings gave a success rate well below the approximately 50 per cent scored on range "shoots", while the system proved almost useless against low-altitude or subsonically-manoeuvring targets. One squadron fired more than 20 rounds in combat at targets below 8,000ft (2,438m) without scoring a single "kill". The AIM-7E gave problems when mated to USAF F-4s, a problem overcome by a modification programme started in January 1969.

A policy of progressive improvement based on combat experience led to the more manoeuvrable AIM-7E2 variant with clipped wings plus improved guidance and fuzing, and the more reliable -7E3. (The later -7E4 was specifically designed for use with the F-14.)

Major improvement did not come until the introduction of the AIM-7F, whose developed started in 1972. The redesigned seeker of this weapon was greatly miniaturised, allowing the installation of a heavier 90lb (41kg) warhead and a longer and more powerful rocket motor. Maximum range of the -7F is roughly twice that of the -7E, flight times of up to 75 seconds being possible.

Above: US Navy F-4 of VX-4 fires a single Sparrow. Low smoke rocket motors were not available when the AIM-7 was designed; the dense plume therefore could give a "launch warning" to the intended victim.

Below: Test firing of a BAe Dynamics Sky Flash air-to-air missile. Although based on the AIM-7E airframe, warhead and propulsion system, this weapon has an all-new control and guidance system of advanced design.

Maximum range is more than 50nm (92.6km), but a typical long-range shot would probably be at around 30nm (55.5km) range. AIM-7F entered service in the late 1970s, and may have been the weapon used by Israel to down Syrian MiG-25 Foxbats.

British Phantom missiles

The UK selected the AIM-7E2 as interim armament for the F-4K and F-4M but opted to develop its own improved Sparrow for long term RAF use. Originally known as the Hawker Siddeley Dynamics XJ521, the new British Aerospace Dynamics Sky Flash combines the airframe, motor and warhead of the AIM-7E2 with an all new guidance and control section incorporating a solid-state monopulse seeker. The latter offers a higher resistance to electronic countermeasures than the conically-scanned unit carried by the AIM-7E and -7F.

Development trials of the British missile were conducted in the mid-1970s using the US test range at Point Mugu, and were observed by US personnel. The results were impressive, miss distances being much lower than those of existing radar-guided weapons. More than half the rounds fired scored direct hits on a target drone at a time when AIM-7 performance still left much to be desired.

The inevitable result was some degree of US interest in a possible Sky Flash purchase, and the start of a "Skyflash-knocking" campaign in the USA. Given the traditional US reluctance to procure foreign weapons—the much vaunted "two-way street" concept was probably the biggest non-event in the field of defence procurement in the 1970s—it was hardly surprising that Raytheon was contracted to develop a further-improved AIM-7M complete with monopulse seeker.

Sky Flash serves with the Royal Air Force as long-range armament for the Phantom and Tornado interceptors, but the decision not to proceed with the planned MK2 version cannot have helped its export prospects. Sole overseas user is the Royal Swedish Air Force.

Sidewinder's better record

The smaller and lighter Sidewinder heat-seeking missile emerged from the Vietnam War with a better reputation than did Sparrow. The original AIM-9B was a simple weapon with a maximum range of around 2.5nm (4.6km) at high altitude. Its uncooled seeker had a narrow look angle, so the missile had to be pointed very close to the target in order to obtain lock-on. The seeker tended to be distracted by sunlight, reflections from clouds and the general heat background from terrain.

AIM-9B was suitable for high altitude use only—altitudes of 3,000ft (914m) or more. A successful interception may not have depended on the full co-operation of the target (as some humorists have suggested), but the -9B appeared only to be effective in tail-chase engagements of non-manoeuvring targets. Combat experience in Vietnam showed that MiGs could break the lock of early-model Sidewinders by pulling tight turns. Lacking guidance signals, the US missile would then wander off course—what was termed "going ballistic".

Faced with these performance deficiencies, the US Navy developed the improved AIM-9D. This has an improved seeker cooled by liquid nitrogen (low temperature improves the infra-red detection capability of most types of detector element), a narrower field of view to improve signal-to-noise ratio, and a greater look angle. The USAF modified an AIM-9B to create the

Above: Two USAF F-4Es carry the classic "mix" of weaponry for air combat—four Sparrows, four Sidewinders and an internal cannon. These two aircraft carry enough firepower to maul badly or even wipe out an entire squadron of opponents.

-9E variant, which was shipped to Vietnam in early 1969. Improvements included a revised seeker with thermoelectric cooling, a greater look angle, and faster target tracking. AIM-9F was an -9B variant with an improved seeker, and was built in West Germany.

The AIM-9D gave the pilot much more freedom in planning his approach to the target, allowing shots at greater deflection angles. The later USN AIM-9G allowed the missile seeker to be slaved to the fighter's radar, while the -9H introduced solid-state electronics, plus double-delta canard control surfaces for increased manoeuvrability. The next generation USAF version was the AIM-9J, a rebuilt version of the -9B and -9E, broadly similar to the -9H.

Recent Sidewinder development has been a joint USAF/USN effort, resulting in the highly-successful AIM-9L "dogfight" missile. This can cope with highly-manoeuvrable targets and head-on engagements, and has displayed kill ratios in combat of 80 per cent or more. It entered service in 1978.

Pilots engaged in testing Sidewinder against low-level targets during trials in the late 1970s dubbed the missile "Groundwinder" because of the tendency of the seeker to respond to hot-spots on the desert terrain, but the new AIM-9M has a seeker better suited to detecting targets against such a difficult background. Many USAF rounds are currently being rebuilt to the -9P standard, while the -9N is an export version intended for Foreign Military Sales (FMS) programmes.

In 1964 the USAF updated Specific Operational Requirement 200 to substitute the Hughes AIM-4D Falcon infrared missile for the AIM-9B and -D Sidewinders carried by early F-4Cs. According to the Air Force, Falcon was cheaper and "more versatile" than the AIM-9D—the missile offered the ability to carry out lead-pursuit attacks rather than the simpler pure-pursuit attacks allowed by Sidewinder.

Falcon did not become operational on the F-4C until the summer of 1968, and its introduction does not seem to have been an unqualified success. By mid-1968, Falcon had replaced Sidewinder on the F-4C, but by April of the following year Sidewinder was back in use to supplement the Hughes missile. A similar "mix" of Falcons and Sidewinders also armed the F-4D. The unguided and nuclear-tipped Genie missile was originally specified as part of the armament of USAF F-4s, but saw little service.

UK Phantoms entered service with the USN AIM-9D. Following Britain's decision in the late 1970s not to proceed with the indigenous SRAAM (Short-Range Air-to-Air Missile), the UK MoD ordered the AIM-9L to replace the -9D.

Other foreign Phantoms

Two nations which operate the F-4 have developed their own heat-seeking missiles. Japan's F-4E(J) carry the Mitsubishi AAM-2, while Israel has developed the Rafael Shafrir and Python. Shafrir has demonstrated a kill rate of around 60 per cent during Middle East combat, while the newer Python 3 saw its first action during the 1982 air combats over the Bekaa Valley in Lebanon. Both weapons are probably available for use on the F-4. Israel has taken delivery of the AIM-9L, but use of this missile may be restricted to more modern aircraft such as the F-15 and F-16.

Below: The F-4M originally served with the RAF in Germany as a strike aircraft, complementing the shorter-ranged BAe Harrier GR.3. The survivors—now interceptors—still lack the internal cannon often needed in air combat.

Air-to-ground armament
The Phantom has been used to deliver many types of air-to-ground guided and unguided ordnance, and it is impossible to describe them all within the space available. The weapons listed here are all known to have been carried on the F-4, and represent a fair cross section of the total.

Normal high-explosive ordnance for US F-4s is one or more patterns of low-drag general purpose bomb. These include the Mk81 (250lb/113kg), Mk82 (500lb/227kg), M117 (750lb/340kg), and Mk83 (1,000lb/454kg). (All weight figures given are nominal. To take an example, the M117 weighs 823lb/373kg, including a 403lb/183kg explosive filling.) The Mk81 and Mk82 are often fitted with Snakeye fold-out retarders for use in low-level attacks, but despite its widespread use this system is reported to be somewhat unreliable.

During the Vietnam War, F-4 bomb attacks were often made from 45deg dives, with ordnance being released at around 7,000ft (2,133m). For high-accuracy attacks, or in areas were the flak was intense, bombs would be released at around 800ft (244m) from 15deg dives.

Much-favoured F-4 ordnance loading for close-support missions included the 500lb (227kg) Snakeye high-drag bomb, M117 750lb (340kg) bombs and napalm weapons such as the BLU-27 750lb (340kg/100 gallon) bomb. The M116A2 was a standard Fire Bomb (napalm weapon) of the 1950s and 1960s. It was 137 inches (348cm) long, 18.6 inches (47.2cm) in diameter, weighed 685lb (311kg) and was filled with 110 gallons of napalm. A smaller, 502lb (228kg) version only 110 inches (279cm) long was designated BLU-11/B 500lb Fire Bomb.

The SUU-30 bomblet dispenser is an 88 inch (223cm) long unit with a body made of sheet steel. Built in two halves and divided longitudinally, it can be used with several patterns of sub-munitions—the total weight varies from 718 to 818lb (326 to 371kg), depending on the type being carried. After weapon release, the fuze splits the body open so that the contents can be dispersed. Other dispensers include the 900lb (408kg) M36E2 incendiary cluster bomb, and the externally similar M30E2 chaff-filled bomb.

The Hughes Walleye laser-guided bomb entered combat service in South-east Asia in 1967. It consisted of a 1,000lb (454kg) warhead coupled with a miniaturised TV camera designed to lock onto and track ground targets. Prior to launch, the bomb transmitted TV imagery to a cockpit-mounted monitor screen. The aircrew would select a high-contrast aiming point by positioning a set of crosshairs, then release the weapon. The built-in guidance system gave the weapon high accuracy, and allowed attacks to be mounted from a modest stand-off range.

The parent aircraft uses a radio command link to monitor the flight by observing the TV imagery from the seeker. If the results of automatic homing are not satisfactory, the aircrew may take over the guidance task and fly the weapon into the target using manual controls.

First operational sorties (on March 11, 1967) were flown by US Navy A-4 Skyhawks, and saw the weapon tested against point targets such as small bridges and a barracks. The next day, the new weapon was used to attack the Thanh Hoa road/rail bridge on the Song Mah river. Although all three weapons impacted on the bridge and within five feet (1.5m) of one another, the target was not destroyed. This bridge had been regularly attacked since April 1965 as part of an attempt to interdict North Vietnamese rail traffic, but despite the expenditure of massive amounts of ordnance including 750lb (340kg) bombs and Bullpup missiles, the US Air Force and Navy had been unable to destroy it. At best, it was temporarily closed on several occasions while damage was repaired.

Walleye was later used to good effect on other bridges, but these early operational tests proved disappointing. USAF records show that 50 per cent of the Walleyes received in the later part of 1967 malfunctioned. An investigation into test and quality-control procedures seems to have solved the problem, since the weapon went on to establish a good reputation for accuracy and combat effectiveness. More than 3,600 Walleyes were delivered, and existing US stocks have been converted to the Walleye II Extended Range/Data Link standard. This has larger wings for longer range, and the built-in data link allows the launch aircraft to break away after weapon release, while another takes over the guidance task.

UK Phantoms were originally tasked with the strike role, and often carried the Hunting Engineering BL755 cluster bomb. This 613lb (278kg) store carries a total of 147 individual bomblets, and was recently upgraded to maintain its anti-armour effectiveness through the 1980s. The Rafael Armament Authority in Israel had developed a cluster munition designated TAL-1, and this may well be carried by Israeli Air Force F-4Es.

The 2.75 inch (6.9cm) folding-fin aircraft rocket (FFAR) is still widely used. Launchers carried on the F-4 include the LAU-3/A (19 rounds), plus the smaller LAU-59/A and -68A/A (seven rounds).

Not all F-4 conventional stores are lethal. The M129E1 leaflet bomb was a 750lb (340kg) unit carrying some 640lb (290kg) of propaganda leaflets. The body was made from glass-fibre, and a nose-mounted time-delay fuze was standard. Furthermore, during the Vietnam War the F-4 was often used to deliver special-purpose stores, including seismic and acoustic sensors which were dropped by night at low level.

Details of US tactical nuclear weapons are scarce, but several are known to have been allocated to US F-4 units. The Mk28 Mod 1FF "special bomb" is a 1960s-vintage nuclear weapon. Reported to be 92 inches (234cm) long and 18 inches (46cm) in diameter, it is probably a USN weapon and may be related to the Mk101 "Lulu" 1,200lb (544kg) nuclear depth bomb of similar dimensions. Also used on the F-4

Typical external stores, F-4F

The F-4F can carry a heavy warload as shown here (minus external fuel tanks); the Luftwaffe opted not to procure the AIM-7 Sparrow, relying instead on the AIM-9 Sidewinder.

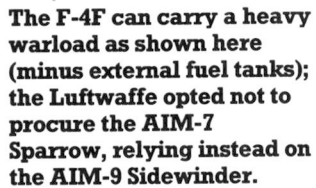

LAU-3A/A + 32A/A rocket launchers	x3	x3			x3			x3	x3
LAU-10A	x3	x3			x3			x3	x3
MLU-10/B land mine	x3	x3			x3			x3	x3
M-129E1 leaflet bomb	x3	x3			x6			x3	x3
M-117 general purpose bomb	x3	x3	MISSILE PROVISION	MISSILE PROVISION	x5	MISSILE PROVISION	MISSILE PROVISION	x3	x3
Mk 81 GP and/or retarded bomb	x6	x3			x6			x3	x6
Mk 82 GP and/or retarded bomb	x6	x3			x6			x3	x6
Mk 83 GP and/or retarded bomb	x2	x2			x3			x2	x2
Mk 84 GP and/or retarded bomb	x1				x1				x1
SUU-21 or MN-1A practice bomb					x1				x1
SUU-23 gun pod	x1				x1				x1
AB45-Y1 spray tank	x1								x1
AIM-9 Sidewinder		x2						x2	
Mk 12 smoke tank	x3	x3			x3			x3	x3

Above left: Although obsolete for air-to-air use, unguided rockets (such as these Matra 155s) are still effective against ground targets.

Left: The warload of iron bombs and unguided rocket launchers carried by this aircraft is typical of those first carried when the F-4C entered USAF service.

is the 13ft long (4m) B43, which offers a choice of five yields. A Phantom assigned to the nuclear strike role would normally carry three. More recent nuclear payloads are the B57 tactical weapon and the B61. The latter is available in at least six variants, five of which (Mods 0, 2, 3, 4, and 5) are intended for tactical use.

Weapons for the delivery of chemical agents include the 350lb(159kg) BLU-52 series (for CS), the 500lb (227kg) MC-1 store (containing 24 gallons of GB non-persistent agent), and the TMU-28/B spray tank for VX nerve gas. The latter store weighs 1,935lb (878kg) fully loaded, and would be carried on an outboard pylon. The spraying nozzle is mounted at the rear, and is tilted downwards 30 deg before the agent is released. VX is a highly persistent agent with high toxic effect, so the tank would be jettisoned when empty so as not to be a safety hazard to ground crew.

Right: F-4E releases iron bombs during a dive attack (note horizon angle). This initial attack will probably be followed by a precision strike using the Paveway laser-guided bomb still on an underwing pylon. The single LGB will be more militarily effective than the free-falling bombs.

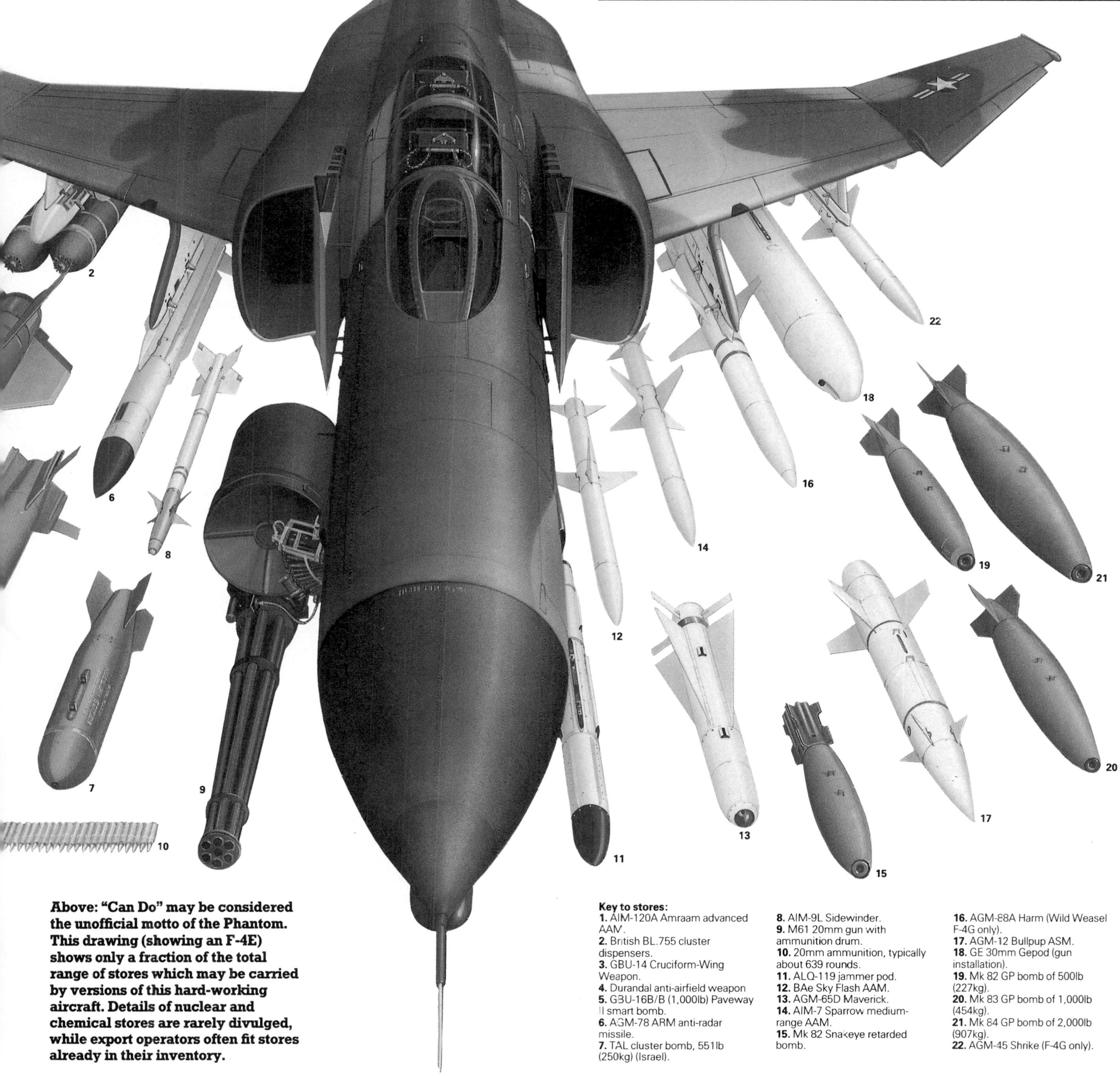

Above: "Can Do" may be considered the unofficial motto of the Phantom. This drawing (showing an F-4E) shows only a fraction of the total range of stores which may be carried by versions of this hard-working aircraft. Details of nuclear and chemical stores are rarely divulged, while export operators often fit stores already in their inventory.

Key to stores:
1. AIM-120A Amraam advanced AAM.
2. British BL.755 cluster dispensers.
3. GBU-14 Cruciform-Wing Weapon.
4. Durandal anti-airfield weapon
5. GBU-16B/B (1,000lb) Paveway II smart bomb.
6. AGM-78 ARM anti-radar missile.
7. TAL cluster bomb, 551lb (250kg) (Israel).
8. AIM-9L Sidewinder.
9. M61 20mm gun with ammunition drum.
10. 20mm ammunition, typically about 639 rounds.
11. ALQ-119 jammer pod.
12. BAe Sky Flash AAM.
13. AGM-65D Maverick.
14. AIM-7 Sparrow medium-range AAM.
15. Mk 82 Snakeye retarded bomb.
16. AGM-88A Harm (Wild Weasel F-4G only).
17. AGM-12 Bullpup ASM.
18. GE 30mm Gepod (gun installation).
19. Mk 82 GP bomb of 500lb (227kg).
20. Mk 83 GP bomb of 1,000lb (454kg).
21. Mk 84 GP bomb of 2,000lb (907kg).
22. AGM-45 Shrike (F-4G only).

By the time that the four-year long halt on bombing raids into North Vietnam was lifted in response to the invasion of the South on March 30, 1972, the US F-4s were equipped with newer models of "smart" bomb. The Rockwell HOBOS (HOming BOmb System) consisted of a 2,000lb or 3,000lb (907 or 1,360kg) bomb fitted with add-on tail fins and a nose-mounted TV guidance system. Like Walleye, this weapon locked on to high-contrast aiming points.

The Texas Instruments Paveway laser-guided bomb (LGB) was similar in concept to HOBOS, but in this case the nose-mounted sensor was a laser seeker. Targets for attack were illuminated with laser energy from a pod-mounted designator pod.

Combat debut for both types was in late spring and early summer of 1972 in the hands of the Phantom-equipped 8th Tactical Fighter Wing, based at Ubon in Thailand. High on the list of targets to be engaged with the new weapons was the troublesome Thanh Hoa rail bridge. It was finally downed as part of a campaign which saw a total of 106 bridges attacked between April 6 and June 30.

Even main battle tanks were found to be good targets for "smart" bomb attack. During one sortie, two Ubon-based F-4s knocked out a T-54 and a PT-76 light tank in three minutes. Working in conjunction with Rockwell OV-10 Bronco forward air control (FAC) aircraft equipped with the Pave Nail laser designator, USAF F-4s took a heavy toll of North Vietnamese armour during the critical months which followed the March 30 invasion of the South.

Development of HOBOS and Paveway continued during the 1970s. Latest Rockwell weapon is the GBU-15 long-range glide bomb, which is created by adding a TV or IR guidance seeker, tail-mounted control surfaces, and longitudinal strakes to standard Mk84 or M118E1 bombs.

The original Paveway I was supplanted from 1979 onwards by the Paveway II, which has folding wings and an improved seeker. Latest model is the Paveway III, designed for use at low level, and incorporating high-lift folding wings, a further-improved pattern of seeker, and microprocessor technology.

Simplest of the powered missiles which has armed the F-4 is the AGM-12 Bullpup, a command-guided weapon built in large numbers during the 1960s. Its modest performance permitted stand-off ranges of up to 10nm (18.5km), but simple weapons of this type were soon to be eclipsed by the more sophisticated homing missiles such as the Hughes AGM-65A Maverick.

More than 26,000 rounds of the TV-guided AGM-65A and B were delivered, mostly for use on the F-4. Like EO-guided bombs such as Walleye, Maverick relies on the operator identifying the target on a TV monitor, then positioning the aiming cross-hairs prior

Above: Enemy radar operators beware! This USAF F-4G Wild Weasel has the radar-sensing avionics plus Shrike, Standard ARM and Maverick firepower to put you out of business for life.

Below: Israel Aircraft Industries Gabriel Mk3 anti-ship missile on an F-4 testbed. The presence of a back-seater makes the F-4 ideal for tests.

Above: Development of the AGM-88A HARM (high-speed anti-radiation missile) has been protracted, but the Wild Weasel back-seaters are enthusiastic about the new weapon.

to launch. Maximum range is more than 10nm (18.5km) but seeker performance is limited by visibility, often a problem in Western Europe. The newer AGM-65D uses an imaging infra-red seeker, and may be used by day or night against point targets such as tanks, hangars, radar vans, buildings, fuel tanks and light naval craft.

Israeli F-4s probably carry the new IAI Gabriel Mk 3 anti-ship missile. Based on the original ship-launched weapon, the Mk 3 has a range of up to 32.3nm (60km). The dual-thrust rocket motor fitted to the naval weapon is replaced by a new pattern of sustainer with a longer burn time.

Two operating modes are possible. In Fire-and-Forget mode, the round cruises to the target area under inertial control, then turns on its X-band active-radar seeker for the final attack. This may lead to the wrong target being acquired and attacked, so Israeli tactical thinking favours Fire-and-Update mode. This allows the progress of the round to be observed using a track-while-scan radar, so that course corrections may be made in order to direct the round against the selected target before energising the seeker.

Specialised anti-radar missiles (ARMs) carried by Wild Weasel versions of the F-4 include the Texas Instruments AGM-45A Shrike. Many versions were built with passive seekers designed to home onto radar signals from a range of targets. Combat performance of these first-generation weapons was limited. Based on Sparrow, Shrike carried only a modest warhead, and could be confused if the crew of the radar being attacked detected the launch and switched off their transmitter. Some Shrike rounds were retrofitted with improved warheads and new rocket motors for use on USAF F-4s, while another Air Force programme corrected unspecified performance deficiencies.

The US Navy-developed General Dynamics AGM-78A and B Standard anti-radiation missiles were released for production in March 1968, and entered service the following year. Similar in concept to Shrike, these missiles were based on the RIM-66A naval SAM, and have a longer range, heavier warhead and Mach 2.5 cruise speed.

Most recent ARM is the Texas Instruments AGM-88 Harm (High Speed Anti-Radiation Missile), production deliveries of which started in December 1982. Development has been protracted, largely due to the need to improve the design to cope with the latest threats. When carried by the F-4G Wild Weasel, Harm operates in conjunction with the aircraft's McDonnell Douglas APR-3B radar warning and homing system.

Harm can be operated in three ways. In Self-Protect mode, the missile is fired against targets detected by the aircraft's radar-warning receiver. Seeker-Search mode allows the missile to carry out its own autonomous search for hostile emitters, while Pre-Brief mode allows the round to climb to height in order to search for targets whose radar parameters match values programmed into the missile just before launch.

As was the case with air-to-air armament, a number of missiles planned as F-4 armament were cancelled while still in development. The XAGM-79A and XASM-80A flak-suppression missiles were airburst weapons intended to kill the target by means of bomblets triggered by an altimeter fuze. Another experimental weapon whose development was spurred by the Vietnam War was the AGM-87, a modified Sidewinder designed to home in on ground IR sources such as vehicle headlights.

As is to be expected, the Phantom is used by many air arms as a test-bed on which to try out new weapons developments. One such case of special interest has been the Luftwaffe's research in 1983–84 into a new anti-armour weapon under development by Westinghouse and Germany's Messerschmitt-Bölkow-Blohm. Called Vebal Syndrom, it is a pod-mounted weapon system which launches inexpensive, unguided munitions rearward at an inclined angle from a low-flying aircraft so that the munitions follow a near-vertical trajectory and impact with the relatively vulnerable tops of armoured vehicles. Luftwaffe F-4Fs have made more than 500 flight passes with the weapon system, and during a demonstration scored three hits in three passes.

The system can detect and identify an armoured target, without the pilot having to operate it, by using laser-ranging radar which measures the target and makes comparisons with pre-stored data, an infrared sensor looking for hot spots which might indicate that the target has an engine, and a radiometer which indicates whether the target is made of metal. If the system is satisfied that the object is a valid target the munitions are discharged automatically. The system can be used in darkness and in poor weather provided visibility is sufficient to permit low flying; typical operating height would be between 100 and 300ft (about 30 and 90m) at speeds of 400 to 540 knots (roughly 740 to 1,000km/h).

Below: The plains of West Germany are ideal tank country, but the Luftwaffe's new Vebal Syndrom munitions dispenser is a new concept designed to destroy hostile AFVs.

Below: Launch of a Maverick air-to-surface missile from an F-4E from Eglin AFB. The TV-guided A and B versions are being supplemented by the new infra-red homing D round.

Performance

Some Mach 2 fighters clock up their "official" top speed only with difficulty and under the right conditions, but with the Phantom power and performance were available to spare. Vietnam War experience was to tarnish the aircraft's reputation, as stalling and spinning accidents increased attrition, but the fact remains that the F-4 has proven one of the safest combat aircraft of its generation, and one whose multirole performance was not to be eclipsed until the arrival of the F/A-18. Recent figures show it has a better safety record than F-16s replacing it in USAF service.

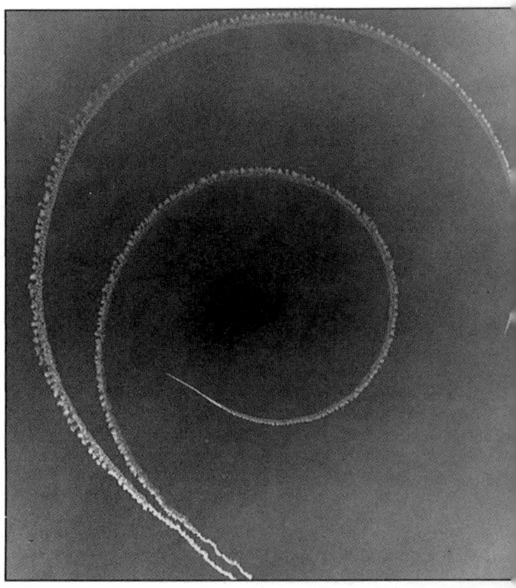

Above: As this Mach 1.2 "turning match" between an F-4E and an F-16 Fighting Falcon shows, the smaller, more modern aircraft has a clear edge, as could be expected, completing the 360deg with the Phantom lagging behind.

In January 1970 the Egyptian President Nasser visited the Soviet Union for high-level defence talks with the Soviet leadership. During the two and a half years of armed confrontation which had followed his country's shattering defeat at the hands of the Mirages of the Israeli Air Force, his own forces had been unable to maintain viable defences in the face of continuing Israeli air raids. Soviet officers seconded to Egypt were of the opinion that the problem lay not with the quality of the Soviet-supplied fighters, but with the poor morale and training of the Egyptian aircrew, but Nasser was determined to obtain better warplanes for his battered air arm. To his mind, the solution was simple—the Soviet Union must supply Egypt with aircraft in the performance class of the F-4 Phantoms flown by Israel.

This request caused some consternation in the Kremlin. To Nasser, the supply of aircraft able to match the Phantoms which were roaming almost unhindered deep into Egyptian air-space on regular bombing missions was a matter of necessity. To his Russian hosts, it was a matter of great embarrassment. Eventually they were forced to admit that the Soviet Union simply did not have an equivalent of the Phantom.

Whether the Egyptian delegation regarded this Soviet admission of technological inferiority as the truth, or just a polite means of refusing to release latest-generation warplanes for export has never been revealed, but the fact remains that they were in fact unable to match the F-4.

In terms of basic layout, the nearest Soviet equivalent to the Phantom was the Sukhoi Su-15 Flagon. This used a delta wing rather than the deep-chord design carried by the F-4 and was a pure interceptor rather than a multi-role combat aircraft able to "mix it" with opposing fighters or carry out strike missions. Although it was the best that the Soviet Union could offer. The first Su-15 units were only just entering Soviet Air Force service, so there could be no question of the type being cleared for export to an area where it might be compromised by being shot down over Israeli-controlled territory. Prototypes of the multi-role MiG-23 Flogger had flown in the mid-1960s, but the aircraft was still a year away from front-line service even in its interim AL-7F-engined form, while production of the definitive version had not yet begun.

The only way that the Soviet Union could help Egypt was to take upon themselves the task of defending the canal zone using Soviet aircraft (including a small detachment of Su-15s), missiles and personnel. The performance of Israel's Phantoms, and the lack of a comparable aircraft in the Soviet inventory a decade after the McDonnell aircraft entered service, led directly to Soviet intervention in the Middle East.

The description of the F-4 and its systems which appears in these pages makes no attempt to overlook some of the technical problems which the aircraft faced at different stages in its development and subsequent career. Nor, one suspects, would the team which created the F-4 wish to see their creation presented as "whiter-than-white". All aircraft have their share of minor problems, but the fighting record of the Phantom is the best testimonial to the fine qualities of a superb warplane. Anyone doubting that the F-4 was a triumph of aerospace engineering need only compare its career with that of the more pedestrian but ten years younger Su-15.

The F-4 has a "redline" (never-exceed) limit for normal flight of Mach 2.2, but this is imposed by the aluminium airframe rather than the aerodynamics and propulsion. Evidence of the ulti-

Above: Flying as a chase plane, a USAF F-4E tucks itself close in behind an air-launched cruise missile (ALCM) during a low-level test flight over the sea.

mate speed capability of the basic design was given in the Operation Skyburner attempt on the absolute speed record (November 22, 1961) described briefly in our opening chapter. The YF4H-1 prototype flown by Lt. Col. Robert B. Robinson of the USMC during this exercise had been fitted with engines incorporating water/menthol injection for pre-compressor cooling. After dropping his centreline fuel tank, Robinson accelerated to Mach 1.3, jettisoned his two wing tanks, then headed towards the measured course to fly two passes. The second run was started at more than Mach 2.5, and finished at Mach 2.62—an average speed was just over 1,606mph (2,584km/h).

Normal service ceiling is around 55,000 to 57,000ft (16,764 to 17,374m) in supersonic flight at full power, but the aircraft can do better in skilled hands. Maximum sustained height demonstrated by an F-4 was clocked up by Cdr. George W. Ellis, USN, during a record-breaking flight from Edwards AFB on December 6, 1961. Climbing to 60,000ft (18,288m) and reaching a speed of Mach 2.2, Ellis climbed at a constant airspeed to fly a measured course at an altitude of between 66,237 and 66,443ft (20,189 and 20,252m).

By trading speed for height in a zoom climb, even this figure may be comfortably exceeded. Under Operation Top Flight, Cdr. Lawrence E. Flint of the US Navy took a clean and partially-fuelled YFH4-1 prototype up to just under 50,000ft (15,240m) on December 6. Accelerating to a speed of more than Mach 2, he began a near-vertical "zoom" climb at full power, trading speed for height. Eventually the engines flamed out in the rarefied air, but Flint guided the aircraft up to a peak altitude of 98,557ft (30,040m) and a true airspeed of only 45kt (51.7mph, 83.3km/h). After relighting the engines at a lower altitude, he landed after a total sortie time of only 40 minutes.

The multi-role performance of the Phantom could not be matched by any serving Soviet aircraft in 1970, and still could not be matched by any other non-US type in the early 1980s. This is partly due to the fact that such multi-role "maid-of-all-work" aircraft are no longer fashionable. For example, the Panavia Tornado eclipses the performance of the F-4, but this internationally-developed warplane is fielded in individual dedicated interceptor and strike versions, neither of which could realistically be pressed into service in the opposite role.

The MiG-23 Flogger may have been drawn up to meet a Soviet Air Force requirement for a multi-role fighter—essentially a mini-Phantom, but it lacks the F-4's long range and massive load-carrying capability. It, too, rapidly evolved into variants customised for surface strike and air-to-air roles.

Only the new Su-27 Flanker offers the Soviet Union the ability comfortably to outperform the F-4 in air combat, but this new fighter is only just entering service a quarter of a century after the McDonnell design. According to intelligence sources, it is a dedicated air-superiority fighter, so it is unlikely to be able to match the Phantom's ground-attack capability.

F-4 exceeded expectations

Despite the large-scale use of high-technology design aids such as computers and wind tunnels, there is still a degree of luck involved in aircraft design. While many aircraft come out somewhere close to the specified performance, a few surpass the customer's expectations while others seem dogged by problems, ending up short of range, speed, ceiling or payload-carrying capability.

In the case of the F-4, all went better than designers dream of in their most

Left: Being a massive interceptor weighing around 20 tons, the Phantom may not seem every pilot's ideal mount for aerobatics, but the US Navy's Blue Angels team shows what the crowd-pleasing F-4 can do.

Below: The F-4 may have proven tricky to fly at low level, but this skilful pilot from the USAF Thunderbirds aerobatic team is not afraid of pulling a tight turn in the resilient Phantom.

High-low-high interdiction

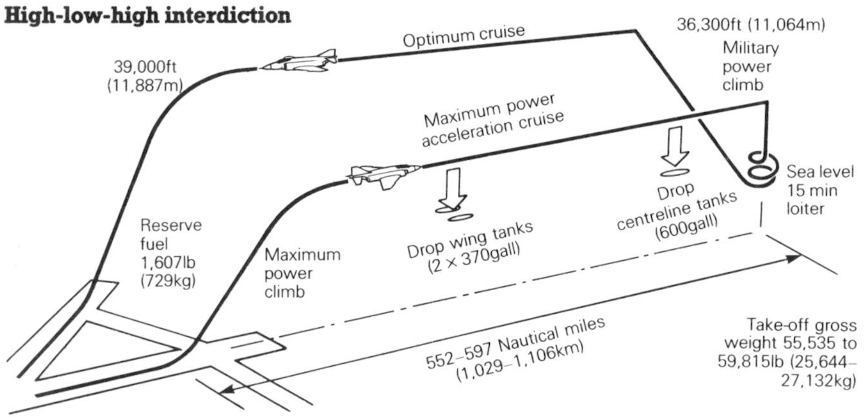

Close air support

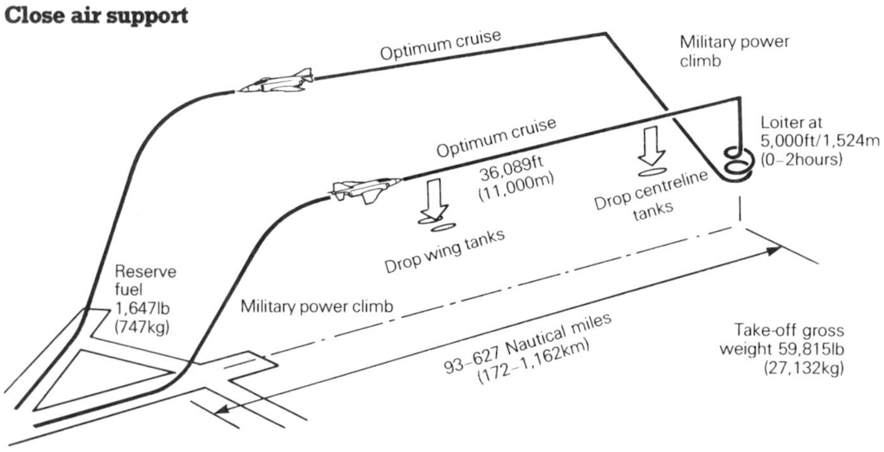

Combat air patrol

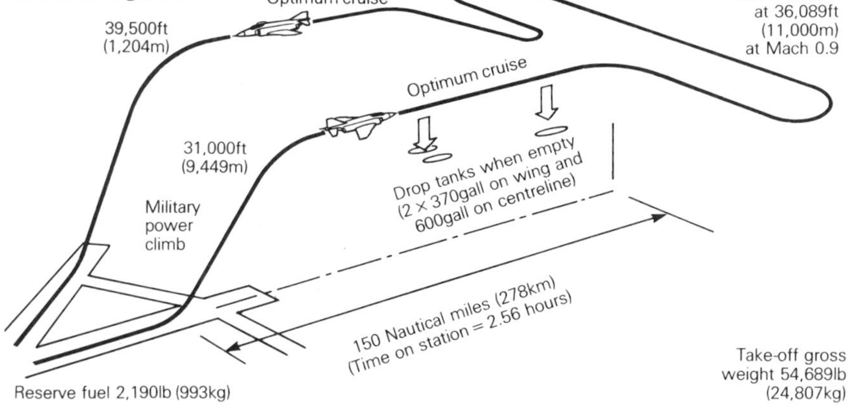

Point intercept mission

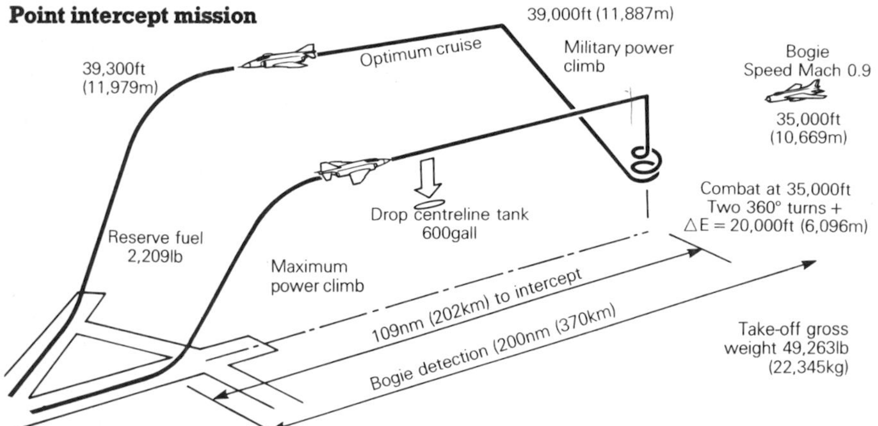

Counter air mission

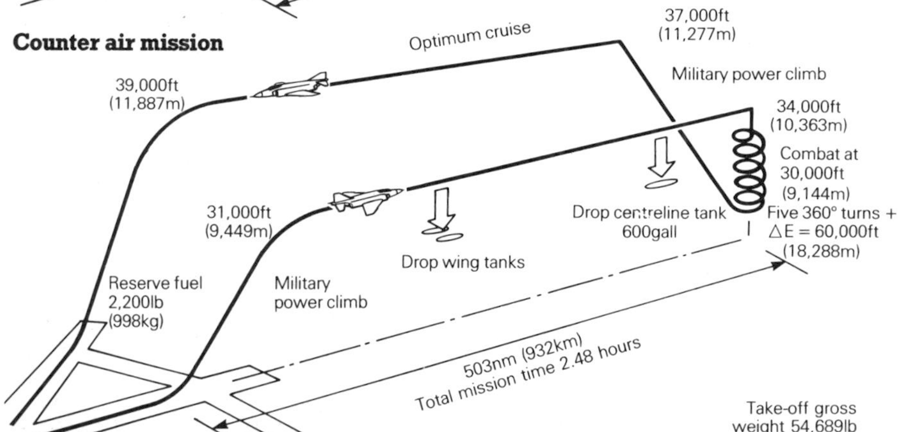

Above: Typical missions for the Phantom (with J79-GE-17 engines and M61A1 20mm nose gun) carrying the following payloads:

***Interdiction*—M117 bombs plus external fuel tanks (2 370gall; 1 600gall).**

***Close air support*—6 M117 bombs plus 1 external 600gall tank.**
***Combat air patrol*—2 AIM-9 plus 3 external tanks.**
***Intercept*—2 AIM-9 plus 1 600gall external tank.**
***Counter air*—2 AIM-9 plus 3 external tanks.**

Operational limits of the Phantom

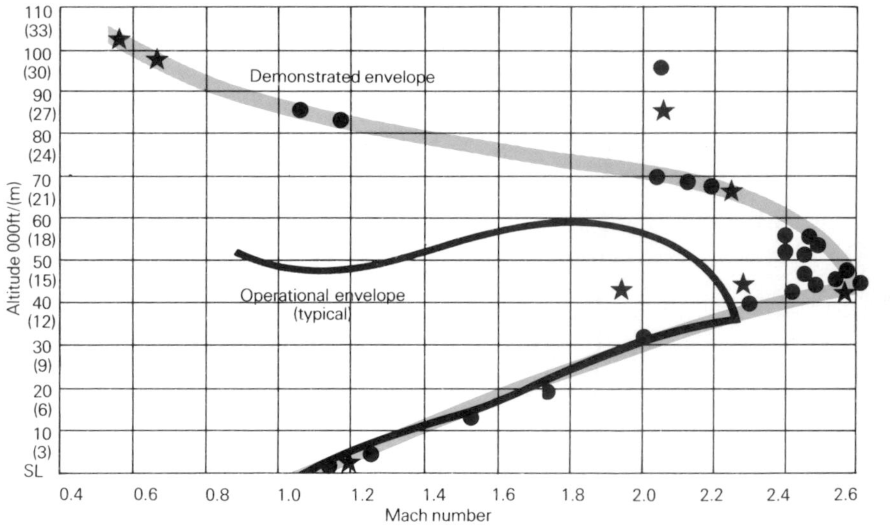

Above: The thick black line shows the operating limits of a clean Phantom, from Mach 1.8 at 60,000ft (18,288m) down to just over Mach 1.0 at low level, which is a good envelope even today. The blue line shows the limits determined by test flights. The black dots show measured performance points, while the stars show records set by the aircraft.

optimistic moments. Early flight tests of the F-4A showed that the performance was higher than anticipated. Combat weight was exactly the 36,817lb (16,700kg) specified, while many of the acceleration and climb-rate figures were well in excess of the specification.

Maximum speed of the prototypes in dry (military) thrust was marginally supersonic at Mach 1.01 instead of the specified Mach 0.99, while maximum speed in full afterburner was only just below the Mach 2.04 target. Tests even showed that the carriage of Sparrow missiles on the semi-buried hard points beneath the fuselage improved the handling under some flight conditions.

Top speed of most models is around Mach 2.2, but this soon drops once armament is added. Top speed of an F-4E is obtained at 36,000ft (10,973m), and is Mach 2.04 with a warload of four Sparrows or a single B28 nuclear weapon, Mach 1.78 with four Sparrows and two underwing tanks, and Mach 1.5 once a centreline tank is added. Aircraft fitted with elderly engines may not always manage Mach 2. Brochure performance claims should often be treated with some reserve, being notoriously prone to modification by "small print". However, the F-4 has the power to exceed its published figures with ease.

Even this impressive figure was later to be marginally exceeded during the final Operation High Jump climb-to-height flight on April 12, 1962. For the flights to 65,617 and 82,021ft (20,000 and 25,000m), the aircraft climbed to an intermediate level, accelerated, then pulled up into a further "zoom" climb. On the final sortie, the aircraft continued to climb beyond the 98,425ft (30,000m) mark, breaking the Operation Top Flight record a second or so later before coasting up to over 100,000ft (30,480m).

Zoom climbs can be flown as part of normal F-4 operations, thanks to these pioneering flights. Pilots are advised to keep the pitch angle below 60deg, and to retard the throttles once the engines flame out (usually between 67,000 and 70,000ft (20,422 and 21,336m). The engines require careful monitoring, and may have to be shut down completely above 70,000ft if they exceed temperature or overspeed limits. Even above this height, the engines will windmill sufficiently to provide electrical power and cockpit pressurisation.

Stabilator effectiveness drops away to a significant degree above 50,000ft (15,240m), but this should pose no problem. As the aircraft reaches the top of the climb, pilots are recommended to maintain an angle-of-attack (AOA) of between 3 and 8 units in order to keep the g loading on the aircraft at a safe positive value during recovery.

Flying the Phantom

It is difficult to describe in detail the flying qualities of an aircraft which exists in so many versions and which is flown from carriers and land bases, by many air arms with different operating procedures, so precise operating methods and figures may vary from those which follow (which assume operation from a land base).

The F-4 can weigh some 50,000lb (22,680kg) or more when ready to roll to the runway, so a fair degree of throttle is needed to get it moving. Once the aircraft starts moving, throttles may be retarded to idle. Taxi speeds have to be kept slow to minimise side stress on the tyres.

For take off from land, half flap is usually selected, since this setting gives less drag than full flaps and requires less air from the engines for boundary layer control. Trim change on flap retraction is minimised, and elevator effectiveness is increased, while the aircraft is easier to handle should an engine be lost at a critical moment. Engines are run up individually to around 85 per cent rpm for pre-flight test, since the brakes may find the urge of two J79s at full power difficult to restrain.

After running up both engines to around 80 per cent, brakes may be released and the take-off run begun. The throttles may then be taken to full military (dry thrust), then into afterburner. The crew are in no doubt that the burners have lit—at this point things start to happen fast. The rudder becomes effective at around 80kt (92mph, 148km/h), the elevators at around 110 to 115kt (126.5mph, 204km/h to 132mph, 213km/h). Pulling back on the stick to the aft stop will cause the nose to rise once the speed reaches 130 to 135kt (149.5mph, 241km/h to 155mph, 250km/h). Attitude should be held at between 10 and 12deg. of pitch by letting the stick forward, so that the aircraft can fly itself off once take-off speed is reached. Liftoff speed depends on air temperature and altitude. For an all-up weight of around 42,000lb (19,051kg) it will be around 140 to 150kts (161mph, 259km/h to 172.5mph, 278km/h).

This "stick hard back" approach causes some new pilots to hesitate, worried about the risk of scraping the tail or becoming airborne in a stalling aircraft. Experience has shown it to be

the best method of getting airborne. If the stick is held just an inch (2.54cm) forward of the fully-aft position, the speed at which the nose rotates to take-off attitude rises by some 10kt (11.5mph, 18.5km/h).

By the time the pilot has selected undercarriage up, his mount will have exceeded 160kt (184mph, 296km/h), the speed at which the flaps may be retracted. As the Phantom cleans up, a nose-up pitching tendency may be noted, but this is easily trimmed out and may even be put to some use. To prevent the aircraft reaching a speed beyond the limits for undercarriage and flap being extended, the pilot may hold the nose up to slow the build-up in speed.

At around 300kt (345mph, 556km/h), the afterburner may be shut down. Maximum speed in dry thrust is around 450kt (517mph, 834km/h), at low level.

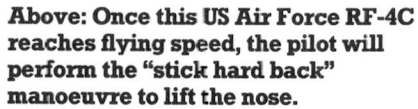

Above: Once this US Air Force RF-4C reaches flying speed, the pilot will perform the "stick hard back" manoeuvre to lift the nose.

Acceleration without the burner may seem slow after the take-off run, but is virtually identical with that of the F-5E.

Subsonic handling at medium altitudes (30,000 to 40,000ft/9,144 to 12,192m), is comfortable. The airbrakes may be extended at any speed, with minimal changes in pitch. Manoeuvring and handling qualities deteriorate below 300kt (345mph, 556km/h), so the F-4 is normally kept above this for all but approach and landing plus some tactical manoeuvres. High speed subsonic flight (above 475kt, 546mph, 880km/h) at altitudes below 15,000ft (4,572m) results in high aircraft response and low stick forces, so the tyro pilot must be careful of possible over-

Above: By the time this F-4's wheels are "in the well", flap retraction will be a priority task for the pilot as the speed builds up.

control leading to oscillations.

On the unslatted aircraft, buffeting starts soon after the nose is lifted above the normal cruise angle of attack (AOA), normally beginning at around 10 AOA units. (A rough conversion from AOA units into degrees can be done by subtracting 5.0.) Optimum turning performance is obtained at an angle of 19.2 units, and stability deteriorates rapidly once this is exceeded. The wing will generate lift out to just over 22 units but longitudinal stability about the lateral axis and lateral stability about the longitudinal axis are poor. The increase in lift does not normally warrant the decreased stability and the possibility of spin entry.

The slats have a marked effect on the handling characteristics of the F-4E, F-4F and F-4S. Onset of buffeting is just over 15 units, optimum turning performance comes at just over 20 units, and wing rocking is postponed to angles of attack of 25 to 28 units. During test flights of the F-4S, angles of attack of from 36 to 42 units were held for almost a minute.

F-4 stability increases at transonic speeds, but manoeuvrability remains good. As the speed picks up, the engines become more efficient, while the variable inlet moves to match the changing conditions. Acceleration beyond Mach 1.05 to 1.10 is better than that of the F-5E. Starting from maximum speed in military power of just below Mach 1.0 at 36,000ft (10,973m), the J79-GE-15 engined models (F-4C, -4D and RF-4E) can hit Mach 1.2 in around less than a minute after lighting the afterburner.

As Mach number continues to build up, the effectiveness of the horizontal stabiliser slowly decreases, roll rate decreases, and stick forces become high. Manoeuvrability is therefore limited, but remains acceptable at speeds of greater than Mach 2.0. There are no abnormal control problems at supersonic speeds out to the aircraft's Mach limits.

Despite having a ratio of top speed to landing speed of more than 12:1, the F-4 behaves well at low speeds and is not difficult to land. Once flying in the pattern at around 300kt (340mph, 556km/h), the pilot can reduce speed further, lowering the gear once below 250kt (287mph, 463km/h). Full-flap landings are normal, lowering being a two-stage operation conducted below 210kt (241mph, 389km/h). The flap switch is set momentarily to the ½ setting, then extended to full down.

The pilot may now turn on to the base leg, making his final approach at an angle-of-attack of 19.2 units. A speed-tone facility on the AOA indicator provides audible cues to enable the pilot to keep his attention on the outside world. At a height of between 20 and 30ft (6 and 9m), ground effect will tend to rotate the nose downwards. Maintaining the pitch angle will slightly reduce the landing speed, while ground effect will reduce the final sink rate during the last moments of flight. Sink rate for most of the final approach is typically around 700ft/min (213m/min).

Once on the ground, the pilot may chop the throttles to idle, then release the drag chute. Holding the nose up provides a degree of aerodynamic braking, but this cannot be maintained for long. After the speed has fallen by only around 20 to 25kt (23mph, 37km/h to 28mph, 46km/h), the nose will sink. At this point steering by rudder is no longer recommended, and the pilot will switch to a combination of nose wheel steering or slight pressure on the

Above: An RAF F-4M split seconds before touchdown. "Ground effect" tends to rotate the nose downwards during the last moments of descent.

Below: An Iranian F-4D taxies in with its braking parachute still attached. The 'chute is deployed soon after touchdown.

brakes, or even a combination of both.

Should an engine fail in flight, attempts may be made to relight it as soon as possible by setting the throttle to OFF, depressing and holding the ignition button, then advancing the throttle. A successful relight may be detected by rising exhaust temperature, followed by an increase in engine rpm.

If flight must be maintained on one engine, the basic rule is to apply a slight rudder deflection towards the failed engine. Flying on military power, the aircraft should be maintained at around 250kt (287mph, 463km/h), descending if necessary to a height where this speed may be maintained. Normal landing procedure is to select half flaps and to keep approach speeds on the high side to ensure good lateral control. Even with one engine out, the F-4 has sufficient thrust to cope with a wave-off, even without the use of afterburner.

Failures of both engines are more serious. If neither will relight, the pilot's manual summarises the best procedure in a single word—EJECT. It is possible to carry out a dead-stick landing, but this is only recommended if escape from the aircraft is for some reason impossible. Recommended landing procedure is to extend the gear at a speed of 210kt (241mph, 389km/h) at just over 10,000ft (3,048m), hold a 35 to 40deg. banked turn to get into the emergency pattern, maintain 210kt until on final approach, lower the flaps when necessary, then put the crippled aircraft on the runway at a touchdown speed of at least 145kt (167mph, 269km/h).

Fighting in the Phantom

The above details sketch out the rough shape of a typical sortie, but to gain an idea of how the F-4 may be handled in combat, one must throw away the brochure and talk to the user, and who better qualified as a user than an exmember of the F-5E-equipped "Aggressor" squadron at Alconbury, England, Captain Eric Coloney, who flew the F-4 before joining the elite Aggressors unit, and at the time he talked to Salamander Books was in the process of re-converting back to the F-4D with the 69th Tactical Fighter Squadron at Moody AFB, Georgia.

"It requires a lot of concentration to fly the Phantom well.... In my opinion, it would take a good 500hrs of intense flying to become very confident and familiar with the F-4—to be able to fly it well. By that I mean to be able to 'stick and rudder' it ... manoeuvre it the way it can and should be manoeuvred."

The F-4 was designed as a naval interceptor, not as a close-in dogfighter, so the pilot must be able to wring the optimum performance out of his aircraft in order to deal with faster-turning opponents. "It has to be manoeuvred aggressively ... primarily in the air-to-air role. The turn rate is not very high, due to the wing loading; the turn radius is quite large. Either offensively or defensively, the pilot must have rapid onset rates of g in order to get a turn started, and to help minimise his disadvantage against a better-turning aircraft."

Against an opponent who can pull 10deg. a second in his aircraft, while the F-4 pilot can only manage 8deg. a second, "if a guy gets started early enough in a Phantom and he gets to his eight degrees right away (that's purely a hypothetical number, although reasonably close), then he can minimise some of the turning inability (of the Phantom)."

Optimum tactics if flying against a small and highly agile opponent such as the MiG-21 or F-5E involve avoiding action on the other man's terms and relying on the F-4's strong points—particularly its missile firepower. "I'd try to keep well clear of him and shoot him all day long with Sparrows. I'd shoot him in the face with a Sparrow if I could; I'd shoot him in the beam; I'd shoot him on the tail.

"I would not point (my aircraft) at him very much, minimising my closing rate and the decrease in range. If I could make him do the jigging out there and run him out of knots, then maybe I'd go in for a gunshot.

"It's pretty well an accepted fact that if you have stern-only heat missiles, and the fellow sees you, he should be able to deny you a shot until you run out of gas—a heat shot is strictly a shot of opportunity."

The Phantom's safety record

One performance parameter rarely listed in reference books but seldom far from the minds of aircrew is safety. In this respect the Phantom was once again successful. Safety statistics for the initial service deployment were excellent. Operating the F-4B in 1965, USMC Fighter Attack Squadron VMFA-251 claimed to be the first to clock up 10,000 consecutive accident-free flying hours.

Right: A Royal Navy F-4K shown pulling a tight turn after releasing a volley of 2in rockets during a firepower demonstration for the Greek armed forces.

Below: A Bicentennially decorated F-4J (No. 153088) of the US Navy's "The Evaluators" squadron undergoing tests with fixed slats at Patuxent. It has an F-4B-style IR sensor housing.

Left: The crew of this turboprop-powered Tupolev Tu-95 Bear may have the throttles pushed to the firewall while overflying a US Navy cruiser, but their Phantom escort must have had no trouble keeping up with the lumbering Soviet intruder.

Below: The US Navy's Top Gun programme helped to hone the combat skills of aircrew destined for Vietnam. Here a USN Phantom is turning in towards an A-4 Skyhawk acting the "Aggressor" role, before pulling up into the sun, denying the Skyhawk lateral turning room and causing its pilot to lose visual contact.

When the F-4C entered USAF service, no major accidents were recorded in the first year of service. By the time that the USAF's F-4s had completed 20,000 hours of flying, only one major accident had been reported. The equivalent figures for other US Air Force fighters were:

F-100 Super Sabre	26
F-101 Voodoo	12
F-102 Delta Dagger	20
F-104 Starfighter	24
F-105 Thunderchief	8
F-106 Delta Dart	6
F-111	8

This good record was to be marred when the Phantom was sent to war in Southeast Asia. The demands of combat flying ruthlessly exposed the aircraft's greatest deficiency in flying qualities—unforgiving stall behaviour. Violent control movements below 10,000ft (3,048m) or at slow airspeeds could easily lead to a stall and subsequent spin, usually with fatal results—recovery from a fully-developed spin was difficult. This problem has received much publicity, but it must be seen in perspective if a balanced view of the F-4 handling characteristics is to be obtained.

The traditional piston-engined fighters and the early jets derived virtually all of their lift from the wings, but the massive fuselage needed to contain turbojets, fuel and avionics of the modern combat aircraft made it expedient for designers to use the fuselage to create part of the lift by making the lower surface as wide as possible. Wings and fuselage do not have the same stalling speed, while the modern engine location helps reduce the nose-heavy characteristic of piston-era spins. The modern fighter tends to have a flat spin attitude, and trickier handling near or close to the stall.

"Idiot-proof" aircraft

In the case of the F-4, the aircraft may require a high level of pilot skill to obtain the vital edge needed in air-to-air combat, but in most flight conditions it is generally forgiving and tolerant of the foibles of the newly-converted pilot. In the early 1960s, one experienced pilot described it as "the most idiot-proof piece of flying machinery I've seen".

The danger area with the F-4 lay at the point when aircrew were flying their mount close to the limits of its performance, and the margin between remaining in full control with some margin for error and being in an incipient spin was a small one. This condition was not associated with any particular altitude, airspeed, g loading or aircraft weight, but was more a characteristic of the pilot's flying habits and his understanding and feel for his F-4.

Captain Coloney describes high angle of attack handling of his F-4D as follows. "Use of aileron at high AOA results in adverse yaw and possible spin departure. If I go out there in the F-4D and pull anything beyond what is known as the 'on-speed' (which is 19.2 units of AOA) and deflect just a little bit of aileron, I can feel the airplane yaw back and forth. It results in a little bit of bank associated with the yaw, which is inherent in any swept-wing aircraft and called dihedral effect. The airplane starts gyrating back and forth and jerking all around with all this buffet at high AOA, telling the pilot—HEY, YOU'RE A ****!"

Left: USAF Phantoms "loaded for bear and looking for trouble" during Exercise Team Spirit. Asymmetric stores loadings such as those shown here create no handling problems.

Phantom in accidental spin-stall

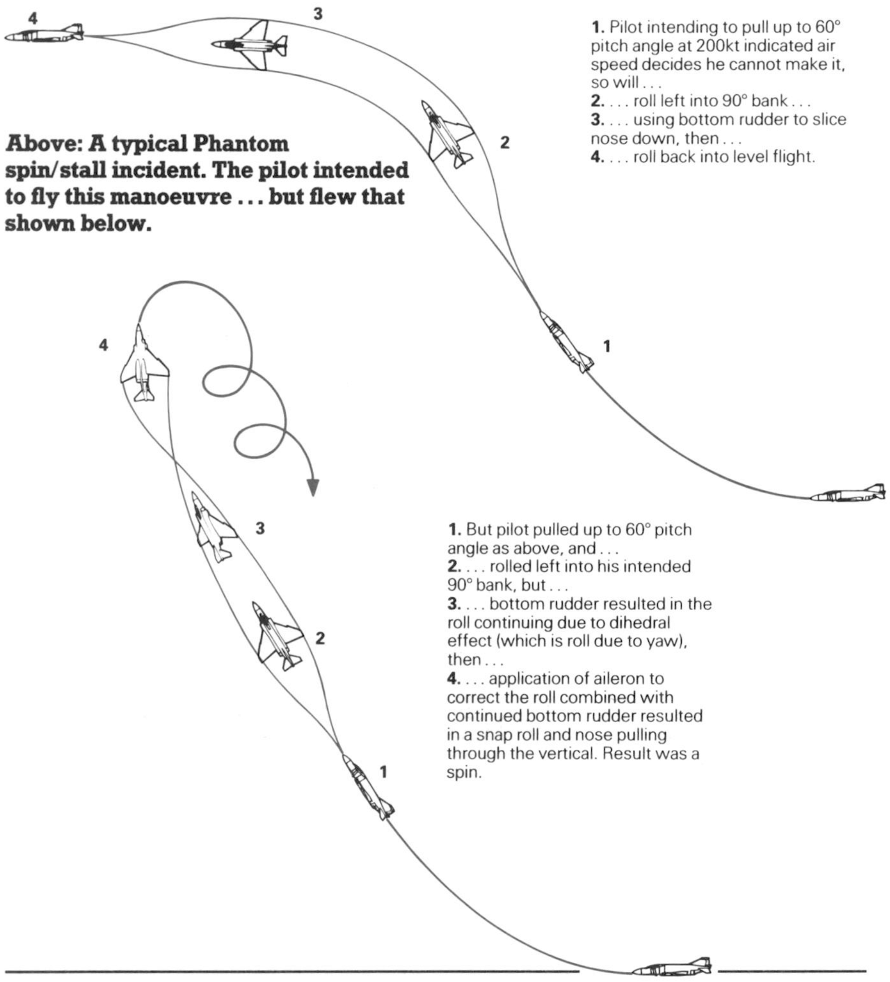
1. Pilot intending to pull up to 60° pitch angle at 200kt indicated air speed decides he cannot make it, so will . . .
2. . . . roll left into 90° bank . . .
3. . . . using bottom rudder to slice nose down, then . . .
4. . . . roll back into level flight.
1. But pilot pulled up to 60° pitch angle as above, and . . .
2. . . . rolled left into his intended 90° bank, but . . .
3. . . . bottom rudder resulted in the roll continuing due to dihedral effect (which is roll due to yaw), then . . .
4. . . . application of aileron to correct the roll combined with continued bottom rudder resulted in a snap roll and nose pulling through the vertical. Result was a spin.

Above: A typical Phantom spin/stall incident. The pilot intended to fly this manoeuvre . . . but flew that shown below.

Spinning from an Immelmann

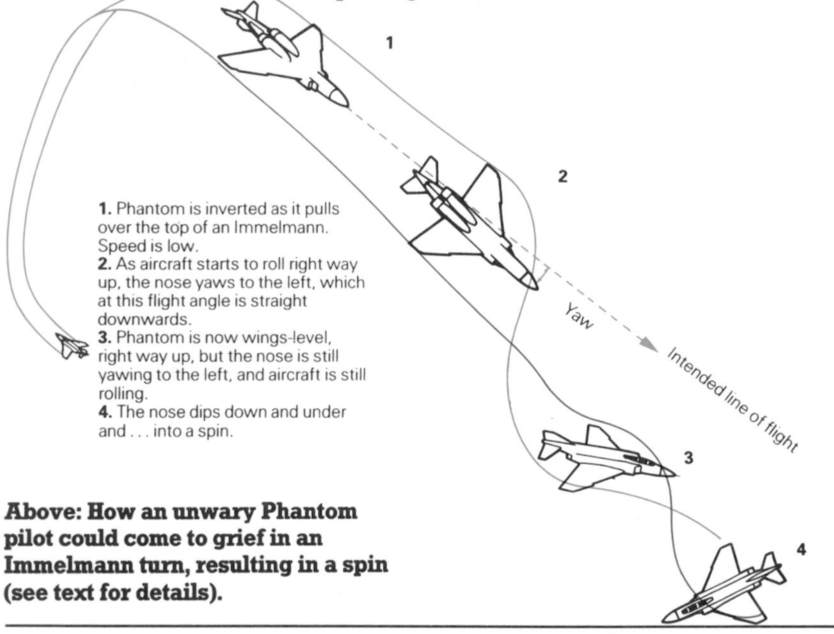
1. Phantom is inverted as it pulls over the top of an Immelmann. Speed is low.
2. As aircraft starts to roll right way up, the nose yaws to the left, which at this flight angle is straight downwards.
3. Phantom is now wings-level, right way up, but the nose is still yawing to the left, and aircraft is still rolling.
4. The nose dips down and under and . . . into a spin.
Yaw
Intended line of flight

Above: How an unwary Phantom pilot could come to grief in an Immelmann turn, resulting in a spin (see text for details).

Left: Ensign James Lainge ejects from the rear cockpit of a battle-damaged F-4B of VF-114 over the Tonkin Gulf on March 24, 1967. The pilot, Lt. Cmdr. Charles Southwick, also ejected safely.

Distracted by the fast-moving events in a dogfight, the less experienced Phantom "jockey" might not appreciate the warning signs in time to react. A typical combat incident might involve the pilot rolling out of an Immelman turn (a vertical climb or half-loop perhaps, with some aileron turning on the way up), with his speed a little low and the aircraft beginning to buffet. A little left aileron applied to quicken the roll might at first seem a good idea. As the nose yaws below the horizon, all seems well—that's the direction he wants to go—but when the wings come level and the nose still yaws left and the roll continues, it's too late to consult the rule book. The nose goes down and under and the aircraft is spinning.

Such a mistake is easy to make in combat, and can be fatal at low level. A single turn of a fully developed spin can result in the loss of 1,500 to 2,000ft (457 to 610m) of altitude. At low altitudes, prompt ejection may be the only recourse.

At higher altitudes, the recovery procedure from a normal oscillatory spin is to neutralise the ailerons and rudder at the first sign of trouble, while moving the stick smoothly forward. Throttles should be retarded to idle to reduce the possibility of flameout, unless the pilot considers his altitude to be marginal, requiring thrust for full recovery. If the aircraft does not respond rapidly, the drag chute may be released. Large oscillations in all axes may be experienced during the recovery, but may be minimised by forward stick.

More dangerous is the flat spin, which can develop within one or two turns after loss of control. The aircraft yaws by around 80deg. per second without noticeable changes in pitch or roll. No reliable method of recovery by using aerodynamic controls or the drag chute are known, so ejection is presumably the only solution.

Naval F-4 performance

Once documented and understood, the Phantom's stalling and spinning behaviour had been considered acceptable for a missile-armed naval interceptor. Tasked with protecting the fleet, naval versions would be vectored onto radar-detected targets—the need for tight manoeuvring was not anticipated. Attacks would be carried out with the aircraft in near-clean configuration (having dropped the external tanks), missiles being launched at long range in order to score its "kills".

At the time, the USN was convinced that manoeuvring performance could be built into the weapon rather than the platform. This philosophy was to lead in 1957 to the heavy and subsonic Douglas F6D-1 Missileer and its long-range 1,284lb (582kg) two-stage AAM-N-10 Eagle missile. Missileer was cancelled in 1960, and some of the Eagle technology was to be applied to the later AIM-54 Phoenix which arms the F-14 Tomcat.

In Vietnam, F-4 pilots found themselves dodging MiGs and SAMs while flying aircraft heavily loaded with ordnance. Low-level flight under such conditions was common, either during attacks on ground targets or as a result of losing height in a dogfight. These were the very conditions in which the aircraft's stall/spin behaviour were most troublesome and, by August 1971, more than 100 had been lost—perhaps as many as 150. (The USN and USMC admitted to losing 79; the USAF declined to release its figure but it is reported to have been higher.)

The USN did not accept that redesign was required, tackling the problem by improved training. The USAF response was to modify the aircraft. In 1970 the Air Force had started a programme to investigate methods of increasing F-4 manoeuvrability. This looked at wing leading and trailing edge flaps and slats, or leading-edge camber. The solution adopted for the F-4E involved the installation of manoeuvring slats. These replaced the original leading-edge blown flap, and extended at high angles of attack to increase lift (for full details of the modification see the chapter on Structure).

The slats were first tested on one of the original YF-4E in a project designated "Agile Eagle", and adopted for all F-4Es built from 1972 onwards (earlier F-4Es were retrofitted). "Slatted" F-4Es saw little service in Vietnam; only a few squadrons had reached that theatre by the end of the war.

Installation of the leading-edge slats had a dramatic effect on manoeuvre performance. According to McDonnell Douglas, the revised wing gives up to a third more lift. Turn radius being reduced by around 20 per cent—travelling at Mach 0.6 at 10,000ft (3,048m), a "slatted" F-4 can turn through 180deg. in 15 to 16 seconds, by which time the standard "un-slatted" aircraft can complete only three-quarters of the turn. Lateral directional stability was also increased at high angles of attack.

During the F-4S programme, USN F-4Js were eventually retrofitted with slats, perhaps an indirect admission that the USAF had been correct in adopting a hardware solution to the stall/spin problem.

The performance of the "Anglicised" F-4K and F-4M was disappointing, leading to suggestions that the resulting aircraft was the "slowest and most expensive" Phantom variant, with a tactical radius and combat ceiling well below that of the standard J79-powered aircraft. Problems with the engine reported in the "Propulsion" chapter kept the top speed of the Spey Phantom to Mach 2.1, while most of the other performance deficiencies have been blamed on the additional base drag created by the redesigned rear fuselage.

New "hot Phantom"

"Hottest" version of the F-4 would be the proposed PW 1120-powered Super Phantom. Maximum instantaneous turn rate of 13.5deg per second is limited by the airframe, and therefore would be identical to that of the existing aircraft, but sustained turn rate would increase from 9deg per second to 10.5. Thrust-to-weight ratio would rise from 0.76 to 0.92, boosting the climb rate at sea level from 41,300ft per minute to 51,000ft (12,588 to 15,545mpm). Acceleration time from Mach 0.9 to 1.6 at 36,000ft (10,973m) would be cut by 18 per cent. This class of performance may not match that of the latest dog fighters, but would do much to improve the Phantom's performance against opponents such as the agile MiG-21bis Fishbed and the fast-accelerating MiG-23 Flogger.

Despite its age, the F-4 should not be regarded as *passe*. Although outperformed by more modern aircraft, the Phantom can still "mix it" with the newer types and emerge victorious. Assuming that conventional wars will continue through the 1980s and 1990s, it seems only too likely that the F-4 will one day clash with latest-generation agile dogfighters such as the MiG-29 Fulcrum and Sukhoi Su-27 Flanker, or even

Steady state turn performance

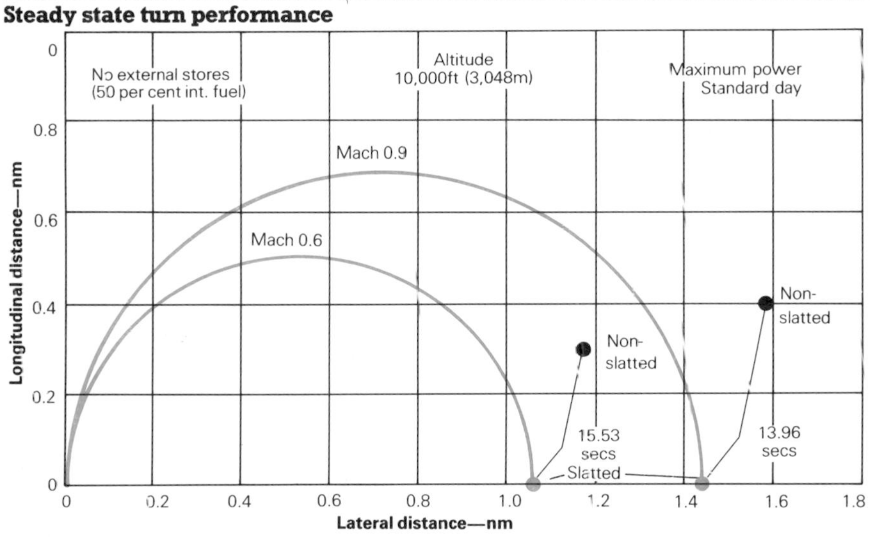

Above: The dramatic effect that the installation of wing slats had on the Phantom's turning performance is shown in this graph. The two curves show the turning ability at 10,000ft (3,048m) at Mach 0.6 (inner) and 0.9 (outer).

Below: The Phantom's specific power—the best means of measuring combat manoeuvring capability—was significantly improved by the wing slats. At Mach 0.9 at 10,000ft the slatted F-4E has a clear advantage above a load factor of 4.5

Specific power turn (slatted and non-slatted)

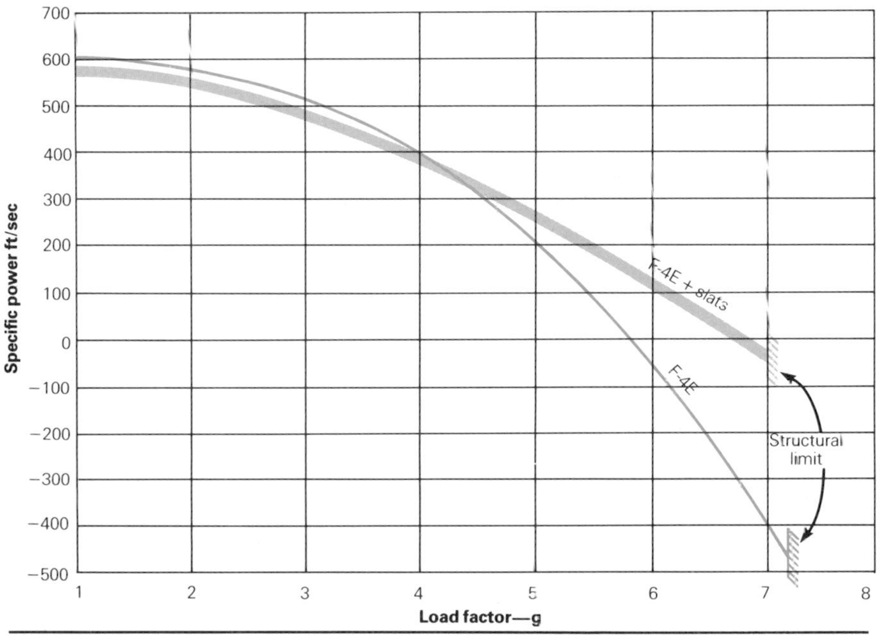

Above: An F-4B of Marine Fighter Squadron VMFA-115 prepares to touch down on *USS Enterprise* (CVAN-65).

Western types such as the Mirage 2000.

Some indication of how the Phantom would fare against such sophisticated opposition was given during 1981 and 1982 by the US Naval Reserve. The 1981 Fighter Airborne Early Warning Wing Pacific fighter derby saw VF-302 achieve the highest number of "kills", being placed second in a competition involving 12 squadrons, eight of which flew the F-14.

The 1982 Felix International Fighter Meet saw VF-201—equipped with aging and maintenance-hungry F-4Ns (rebuilt versions of the original F-4B)—take first place honours, achieving a 15:2 kill ratio over USAF and USN adversaries flying the more modern and manoeuvrable F-5E, F-14, F-15, and F-16. In some measure this performance is a tribute to the flying skills of the Reservist aircrew, but even they would acknowledge the part played by their veteran mounts. In the hands of an expert pilot, the Phantom is still a dangerous opponent and likely to remain so well into the 1990s.

Ultimate test of a warplane is air combat. Measured in this tough area, the performance of the F-4 has been excellent. The aircraft bore the brunt of the Vietnam War air combats, fighting in the post-1967 campaign of attrition between Egypt and Israel, the 1973 Yom Kippur War, the air battles over the Bekaa Valley in Lebanon, and taking part in the Iran/Iraq War. When an effective combat aircraft was needed, the Phantom was available and able to do the job. Its achievements created problems for the air arms it was used against and must have resulted in the expenditure of much midnight oil in the Mikoyan and Sukhoi design bureaux in the search for a suitable counter.

Units equipped with the Phantom have fought successfully against air arms equipped with high-performance fighters such as the MiG-21, MiG-23, Mirage 5 and Mirage F1. Some aircraft may be able to eclipse the McDonnell aircraft in one or more performance parameters, but such air battles have almost always seen the US aircraft on the winning side. (Politicians may on occasion have frittered away such military victory, but that is hardly the fault of the F-4 or its crews.)

Below: Afterburners blazing, a Phantom is reduced to a blur in the photographer's lens as it gathers take-off speed on a carrier catapult.

The Phantom in Combat

Above: Close air support: a Phantom hurtles in at low level to attack a North Vietnamese position while the grateful friendly ground forces wait to follow up. The F-4 is extremely capable of accurate ground attack.

The Phantom was adapted to fulfil many different combat missions, the most difficult of all being that of attaining air superiority. Over enemy territory, the advantage lies mainly with the defenders. Whether putting ordnance accurately on target, gathering intelligence, or battling with the lightweight, agile MiGs in the skies over North Vietnam or the Middle East, the Phantom proved itself a world beater. It has a good record against fighters of its own generation, and can be expected to perform well against more modern opponents.

The Phantom has seen action in two theatres of war, Southeast Asia and the Middle East. Of these, Southeast Asia was by far the most protracted, lasting officially from 1965 to 1973, and by far the best documented. During this period, Phantoms gradually superseded almost every other type of aircraft in almost every combat role, winning an unprecedented reputation for versatility in the process. They operated as air defence, air superiority, escort and strike fighters. As electronic countermeasures aircraft they carried chaff to confuse enemy radar systems. They carried out weather, pre-strike and post-strike reconnaissance. They were used for defence suppression, both as flak suppressors and in the Wild Weasel role. They flew both battlefield and deep interdiction missions by day and night. They even acted as forward air controllers in heavily defended areas, their speed rendering them less vulnerable than the traditional artillery spotters.

The war in Vietnam

The Phantom first saw action on August 6, 1964, when, following an incident in the Gulf of Tonkin involving US destroyers, a retaliatory strike was launched against North Vietnamese patrol boat bases. Five F-4Bs of VF-142 and VF-143 from the aircraft carrier USS *Constellation* took part in this operation.

The war in Vietnam truly commenced in 1965 when President Johnson authorised a limited campaign against North Vietnam. Carrier-based Navy Phantoms were in action from the outset, and were joined in April by Phantoms of the USMC and USAF. The Phantom was at first used for combat air patrol, and success in the air was not long in coming. On June 17, 1965, F-4Bs of VF-21 brought down two North Vietnamese Air Force MiG-17s with Sparrow missiles. The Air Force was not far behind, F-4Cs of 45 TFS downing two MiG-17s with Sidewinders on July 10.

The NVAF was equipped with MiG-17s, -19s and -21s, all single-seaters, all armed with cannon, and often carrying AA-2 Atoll heat-seeking missiles similar to the American Sidewinder. With the exception of later models of the MiG-21, these aircraft were slower than the Phantom; not that this mattered too much as V_{max} was never used in combat, since it took too long to attain, used too much fuel, and most of the fighting took place at altitudes where Mach 2 was not possible anyway.

All the Soviet-built fighters were highly manoeuvrable and could out-turn the Phantom, although at high subsonic speeds the MiG-17 had a control problem which gave a very slow rate of roll. From this it can be seen that the NVAF MiGs possessed a decided advantage in a close-range fight, but the Phantom, with its medium-ranged Sparrows, could attack from beyond visual distance. This was theoretically a tremendous advantage, as surprise is, and always has been, the dominant factor in air fighting.

Unfortunately identification posed a problem for US pilots, and after a couple of "own goals" were scored, visual identification had to be made in almost all circumstances. This, coupled with political constraints (for a long while the US rules of engagement stipulated that enemy aircraft could be shot down in the air but must not be destroyed on their airfields) made life difficult for the Phantom crews. As USAF Capt. Bill Jenkins commented years later, "The rules of engagement were such that I sometimes felt I needed a lawyer in the back seat instead of a WSO!".

The problem of foolproof beyond-visual-distance identification was never completely solved during the war, and this restricted the use of the Phantom's main asset. Furthermore, neither the Sparrow nor the Sidewinder proved very reliable; in Vietnam the Sparrow achieved a probability of kill (PK) of about 8 per cent; the Sidewinder about 15 per cent, although not too much significance should be attached to the different percentages as the Sidewinder was often used from easier tracking positions than was the Sparrow. The unreliability of both missiles led to a general practice of firing them in pairs, which was expensive, but gave a better chance of scoring.

Thus the fighting effectiveness of the Phantom was degraded by three factors; the difficulty of beyond-visual-range identification, the unreliability of the weapons and also, initially, the lack of a gun. Had the Phantom carried an internal gun from the outset, and a foolproof IFF been available, the North Vietnamese aircraft would have had a very hard time. As it was, the big American super-fighter gave considerably better than it got, as was shown by the events of May 10, 1972.

Phantoms Versus MiGs

Towards the end of 1971 it appeared that a large military buildup was under way in North Vietnam. In March 1972 the North launched a full-scale invasion of South Vietnam. Peace talks were still continuing in Paris, but on May 8 these were suspended by the Nixon administration, and Operation Linebacker was put into effect in an effort to force the Communists to negotiate seriously for a peaceful settlement. The United States imposed a naval blockade of the North and mined the waters around Haiphong and other ports. At the same time, the restrictions on bombing North Vietnam which had been imposed in 1968 were

Right: A USAF armourer makes a last minute check on AIM-7 Sparrow missiles prior to loading them onto Phantoms. The AIM-7 was the Phantom's primary air/air weapon in Southeast Asia.

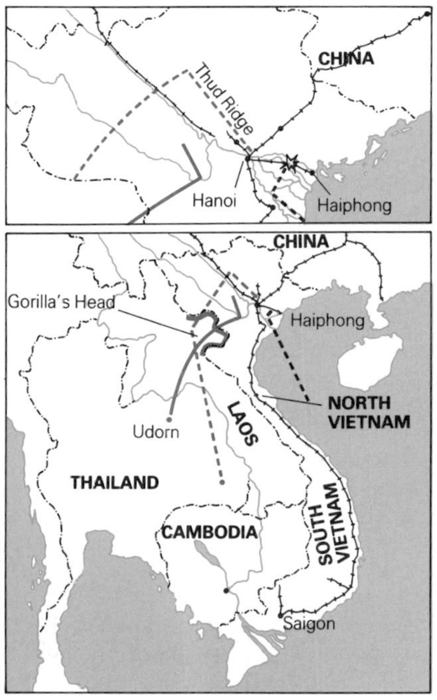

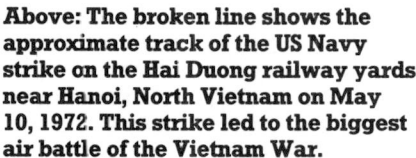

Above: The broken line shows the approximate track of the US Navy strike on the Hai Duong railway yards near Hanoi, North Vietnam on May 10, 1972. This strike led to the biggest air battle of the Vietnam War.

Above: Eight Phantoms drop their bombs in unison on instructions from the EB-66 lead ship. Weather and jungle often negated visual aiming.

lifted, and air strikes were launched against fuel, supply, and communications targets. The North Vietnamese Air Force rose in defence, and fierce air fighting took place, and it is against this background that the F-4 Phantom had what was probably its most successful day in air combat.

Before we recount the events of this day, it should be remembered that almost all the advantages lay with the defenders. The strike forces had to counter a highly sophisticated integrated ground/air defence system comprising AAA, SAMs, and fighters controlled by a comprehensive radar and communications network. The North Vietnamese fighters operated near their bases, whereas the Thailand-based American strike aircraft had to hit targets over 500 miles (800km) away.

This was the situation on May 10, 1972, when the USAF Tactical Fighter Wing (TFW) based at Ubon, in Thailand, were tasked to destroy the Paul Doumer bridge on the outskirts of Hanoi with Mk 84 guided bombs. It was a multiple strike; another wing loaded with 500lb (227kg) iron bombs was to hit the nearby railway marshalling yards at Yen Vien, and other communications targets.

It was a veritable air armada that set out that morning. At 08.00 hours eight chaff support Phantoms took off to rendezvous with their escort, a further four Phantoms. Their task was to lay a corridor of chaff down the line of the final run-in to the target to thwart the North Vietnamese radar and ground defences. At 08.20 hours, the strike force for the Paul Doumer bridge started to roll; four flights of four Phantoms, three flights carrying the new laser-guided bombs (LGBs), the fourth flight carrying electro-optical guided bombs (EOGBs). Yet more Phantoms joined them as escorts.

Meanwhile, 200 miles (320km) to the north-west, at Udorn in Thailand, the MIGCAPS (MiG Combat Air Patrols) were readying. They consisted of two flights of F-4D Phantoms of the "Triple Nickel", the 555th Tactical Fighter Squadron (TFS) belonging to the 432nd Tactical Reconnaissance Wing (TRW). Their task was to protect the strike force by engaging the defending fighters. To accomplish this, they had been assigned patrol areas which lay between the route of the main strike force and the MiG bases near Hanoi. First away was "Oyster" flight, whose assigned patrol area lay south of Yen Bai and west of Phuc Tho. They were followed, after a short delay because aircraft were not serviceable, by "Balter" flight.

Not only Phantoms were engaged on this mission. Supporting roles were being played by fifteen F-105G Thunderchiefs, Wild Weasel aircraft whose function was SAM suppression; and four EB-66 aircraft for electronic countermeasure support. The final factors in the airborne equation were the airborne refuelling tankers waiting high over Laos both on the outbound and homeward trips, without whom the mission could not have been flown, and the US Navy radar ship codenamed "Red Crown", waiting out in the Gulf of Tonkin to pass information on the MiG reaction, which was expected to be fierce.

The elements of the strike force flew north over Laos to meet the tankers at high altitude. having topped up their tanks, they sorted out their formation and, descending to 15,000ft (4,573m), headed north-eastward, towards the Red River and Thud Ridge. Meanwhile, Oyster flight had also refuelled and crossed the border between Laos and North Vietnam at the "Gorilla's Head". This was not a landmark; just a place where Laos bulges into North Vietnam, about 75 miles (120km) across, which on the map shows a distinct resemblance to the profile of a gorilla.

They were a very experienced flight. The leader, Oyster 01, was Major

Below: The Phantom carried a variety of stores in SE Asia. Here, a USAF F-4D of the 497 TFS, 8 TFW based at Ubon, Thailand, has both the underside and jettisonable fuel tanks painted black and carries three SUU-38 dispensers.

Above: It was often in order that Phantoms like this one from VF-21, USS *Midway*, could deliver their ordnance unmolested that F-4s had to engage manoeuvrable MiGs in aerial dogfights.

Oyster Flight: Detection Phase

Below: The initial phases of the combat between four F-4Ds of Oyster Flight and four NVAF MiG-21s are shown here.

Oyster Flight in Fluid Four

O1: Lodge and Locher.
O2: Markle and Eaves.
O3: Ritchie and DeBellevue.
O4: Feezel and Pettit.

Detection, closing and attack.

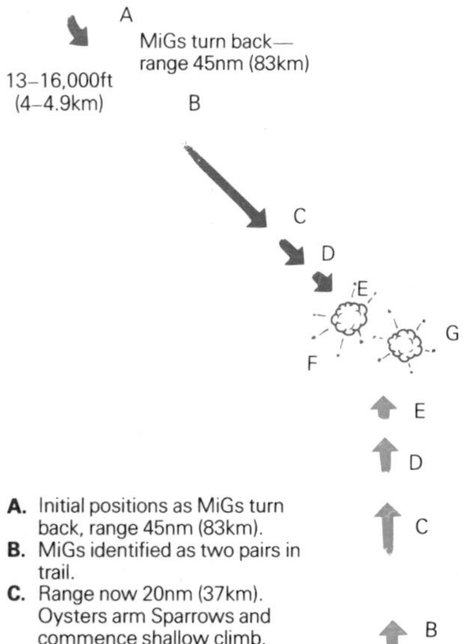

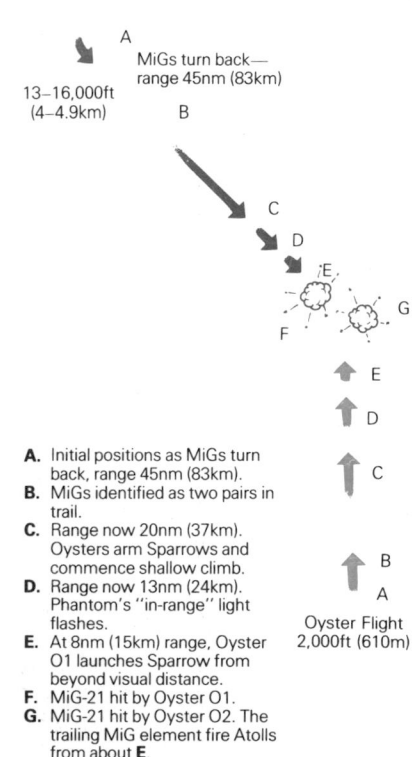

A. Initial positions as MiGs turn back, range 45nm (83km).
B. MiGs identified as two pairs in trail.
C. Range now 20nm (37km). Oysters arm Sparrows and commence shallow climb.
D. Range now 13nm (24km). Phantom's "in-range" light flashes.
E. At 8nm (15km) range, Oyster O1 launches Sparrow from beyond visual distance.
F. MiG-21 hit by Oyster O1.
G. MiG-21 hit by Oyster O2. The trailing MiG element fire Atolls from about **E**.

MiG-21 formation

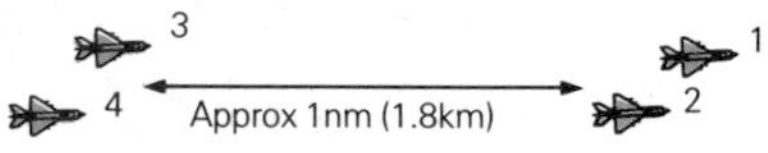

Robert Lodge, with Capt. Roger Locher as his Weapons Systems Operator (WSO). This team had already destroyed two MiG-21s. His wingman, Oyster O2, was Lt. John Markle, with Capt. Stephen Eaves in the back seat. Leading the second element, or pair, was Capt. Steve Ritchie, with Capt. Charles De-Bellevue as his WSO. His callsign was Oyster O3. His wingman in Oyster O4 was Lt. Thomas Feezel, with Capt. Lawrence Pettit as WSO.

Heading east-north-east, in the general direction of Hanoi, Oyster flight used the fuel in their centreline tanks, then jettisoned them. To minimise danger from SAMs and AAA, they reduced height to 3,000ft (915m), just above the effective limit of small arms fire, and increased speed to 500 knots (920km/h). This also reduced the chances of detection and interception considerably. As they left the foothills near the Black River, they made radio contact with Red Crown. Then when they were about 40nm (74km) short of Hanoi, they swung 90 degrees left and flew in the general direction of Yen Bai.

First signs of the enemy

So far the trip had been uneventful, but now Red Crown detected bandits airborne near Hanoi and radioed a warning. Oyster flight flew on with their radars searching the air ahead. Then Capt. Locher, the WSO in Oyster O1 picked up two radar contacts dead ahead at about 40nm (74km) range. Major Lodge moved Oyster flight into modified Fluid Four formation, with O2 (Markle) in fighting wing on his right, and O3 and O4 (Ritchie and Feezel) astern and wide on his left. At such low level, the vertical separation of the orthodox Fluid Four could not be carried out. It was a clear day, and the sun was almost exactly behind them.

At first the contacts moved away in a northerly direction, but at 45nm (83km) they turned around and came charging back. The projected track of the MiGs would take them across the path of the Phantoms from left to right. Radar soon identified the contacts as two pairs in approximately 1nm (1½km) trail, altitude between 13,000 and 16,000ft (4,600 to 4,900m). The trailing pair were at a lower altitude than the leaders. By now the Phantoms were hiding down at 2,000ft (600m) and their pilots rocked the twin throttle levers outboard through the detents to engage afterburner, and accelerated to supersonic speed.

At about 20nm (37km) range, they armed their AIM-7 Sparrows (with the exception of Feezel, whose radar had chosen this inconvenient moment to go down), and commenced a fast, shallow climb designed to bring the MiGs into the centre of the missile envelope. The radars were locked on and at 13nm (24km), a warning light flashed, indicating that the hostile aircraft were within range. The allowable steering error (ASE) on the radar display began to contract and at 8nm (13km) Lodge launched his first Sparrow at the leading MiG element. Trailing a plume of white smoke, it accelerated out in front and began tracking upwards at a shallow angle, but detonated when its motor burned out. With the range now down to 6nm (10km), Major Lodge fired a second Sparrow. It launched successfully and tracked upwards at a 20 degree angle. For several seconds it left a contrail, then came the flash of the detonation followed immediately by a reddish-orange fireball. A few seconds later, the crew of Oyster O1 were rewarded by the sight of a MiG-21 falling just off to their left, trailing fire and minus its left wing.

The trailing MiG element saw the explosion up ahead and correctly decided that they were under attack from head-on. They immediately launched their Atoll heat-homing missiles into the blue. While the Atoll has no head-on intercept capability, this was a perfectly valid ploy under the circumstances. No fighter pilot of any nationality would be prepared to watch missiles coming in his direction without taking avoiding action, which would almost certainly spoil his attack. In this instance, two things were wrong with the North Vietnamese pilot's reasoning. First the attack was not exactly head-on, and second, Oyster 2 (Markle and Eaves) had already locked onto the leader of the trailing element. Shortly after Lodge had fired his second Sparrow, Markle squeezed off two more in quick succession. By this time, the MiG was passing across the front of the Phantoms, and Markle's second Sparrow started tracking upwards and slightly to the right. Markle then spotted his MiG-21 target, ahead and crossing from left to right. As he watched, the big missile pulled lead and tracked right into it, causing a bright yellow explosion and shearing off the MiG's right wing.

At about this point, the Atolls fired by the trailing MiG element came sizzling over the top of Oysters O1 and O2. Instinctively, Major Lodge pulled hard up to the right in an oblique half loop which brought him out very close, about 200ft (60m) behind the surviving MiG-21 of the trailing element as it flashed past. To Capt. Locher in the back seat of Oyster O1, the MiG seemed to appear out of nowhere and almost collided with them.

Meanwhile Capt. Ritchie in Oyster O3 was getting into the fight. Lacking visual contact and acting on radar information, he pulled up to the right in a 4 to 5g turn. Rolling out at 18,000ft (5,500m) he sighted both MiGs; one off to the right with Major Lodge riding its tail, while the other was about 10,000ft (3,050m) away to the left and was turning back to rejoin. Capt. Ritchie selected the left MiG as his target and pulled to the inside of its turn, locking on his radar as he went. From a range of 6,000ft (1,800m) and 1,000ft (300m) below, he ripple-fired two Sparrows, both of them guided. The first passed close under the MiG without detonating, but the second scored a direct hit, causing a yellow fireball. From the back seat of Oyster O3, Capt. DeBellevue caught a glimpse of a dirty yellow parachute as they passed the falling MiG.

Attack from MiG-19s

While this was going on, Oyster O1 was still following his MiG, which, seemingly unaware of the huge Phantom peering up his tailpipe, was holding a gentle climbing turn to the right. With Lt. Markle holding fighting wing position, Major Lodge tried to drop back to effective missile range by using lag pursuit. He was far too close for his missiles to arm themselves and track, and none of the Phantoms carried guns. Intent on his quarry, Lodge failed to see the arrival of four MiG-19s that came storming in from his right rear and overshot. Lt. Markle broke away and radioed a warning to his leader as the bandits pulled back from 10 o'clock and came in behind the unsuspecting Phantom.

Lodge, intent on a second victory,

Oysters versus MiGs: The Manoeuvre Phase

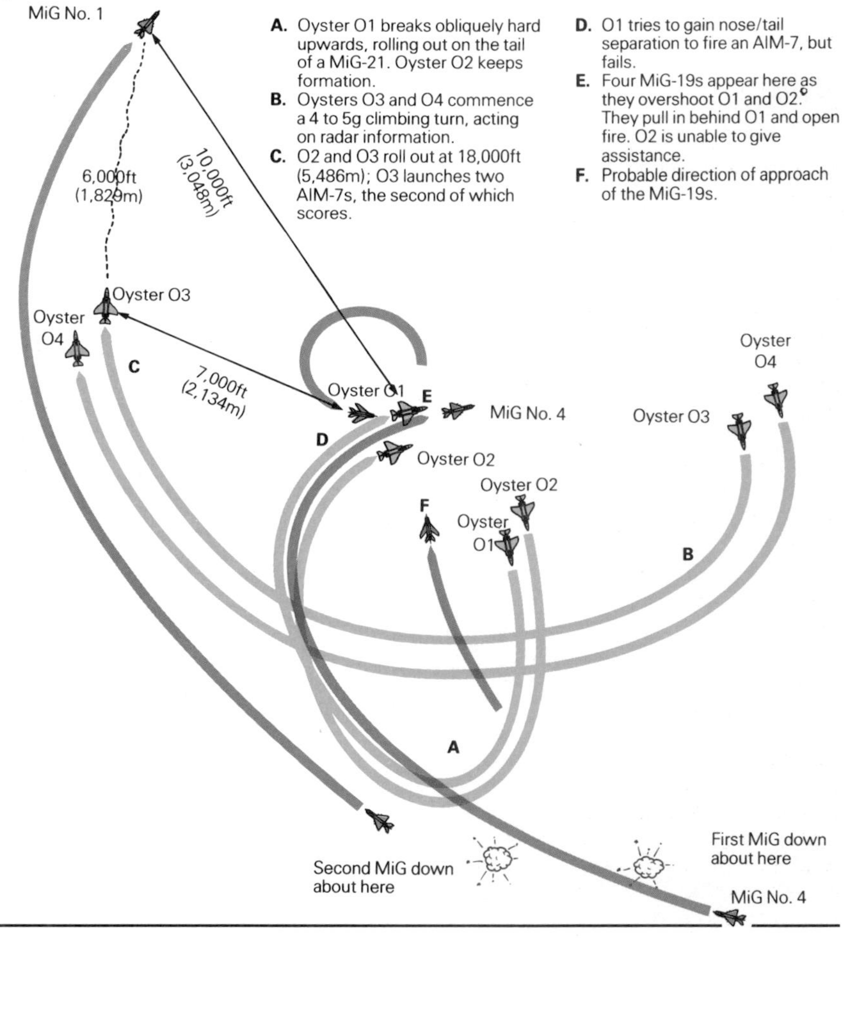

A. Oyster O1 breaks obliquely hard upwards, rolling out on the tail of a MiG-21. Oyster O2 keeps formation.
B. Oysters O3 and O4 commence a 4 to 5g climbing turn, acting on radar information.
C. O2 and O3 roll out at 18,000ft (5,486m); O3 launches two AIM-7s, the second of which scores.
D. O1 tries to gain nose/tail separation to fire an AIM-7, but fails.
E. Four MiG-19s appear here as they overshoot O1 and O2.
They pull in behind O1 and open fire. O2 is unable to give assistance.
F. Probable direction of approach of the MiG-19s.

Above: Oyster 03, the F-4D flown by Captains Ritchie and DeBellevue on May 10, 1972. Ritchie was to score his fifth victory with this aircraft only four months later.

hung in and fired a Sparrow from very close range which failed to guide, just before he in turn was hit by cannon fire from the MiG-19s. Neither Markle, who had broken into the new threat, nor Ritchie, off to the left and 1½ miles (2½km) in front, was in a position to give immediate assistance. Capt. Locher, in the back seat of Oyster 01, ejected and was rescued from the jungle nearly three weeks later. Major Lodge was killed. The remaining three Phantoms of Oyster flight, low on fuel and missiles, outnumbered by more manoeuvrable opponents, were in no position to enter a close turning flight. Afterburners blazing, they disengaged and headed back towards the border.

The 3 to 1 final score may not seem impressive, but had it not been for the intervention of the MiG-19s, it would probably have been 4 to nil. Oyster flight had tied up no less than one fifth of the North Vietnamese Air Force sorties launched against the strike force, which lost just one aircraft to a hit and run attack by a MiG-19. The Paul Doumer bridge was cut, and the Yien Vien railway yards sustained heavy damage. In short, the strike was a great success, thanks in no small measure to the action fought by Oyster flight, and the Phantom's superior weapons system which enabled kills to be scored from beyond visual distance, thus loading the dice in the initial encounter.

Eight-to-nil victory

During the early afternoon of the same day, US Navy Phantoms scored a momentous victory over the North Vietnamese MiGs, running up eight victories for no air to air losses, seven of them in one engagement. This encounter had several points of interest. First, the tactical situation was too confused for the beyond-visual-distance attack with radar-homing Sparrow missiles to be used. Second, the Phantom, often criticised for its lack of dogfighting capability, demonstrated that it could, if correctly handled, triumph in the close-combat arena, even though badly outnumbered. Third, a Phantom crew shot down three MiGs in one mission (the only time in the entire war that this feat was accomplished), becoming in the process the first American aces of the war. Fourth, one of the North Vietnamese casualties was their ranking ace, the top scorer of the war.

Carrier Wing 9, based on the USS *Constellation*, was tasked to strike the Hai Duong railway and storage depot, roughly midway between Hanoi and Haiphong. The strike force consisted of A-6s and A-7s, supported by a mixed force of Phantoms from fighting squadrons VF-92 and 96, flying Target Combat Air Patrol (TARCAP), MIGCAP, and Flak Suppression. Visibility was good above 10,000ft (3,050m), but hazy at lower levels.

At the left rear of the strike force were two Phantoms of VF-96; squadron callsign Showtime. Showtime 100 was flown by Lt. Randall Cunningham with Lt. (JG) William Driscoll as his Radar Intercept Officer (RIO). On his wing was Showtime 113, crewed by Lts. Brian Grant and Jerry Sullivan. They were Flak Suppressors. Their Phantoms were heavily laden, with a centreline tank, two AIM-7E-2 Sparrows under the belly, four AIM-9G Sidewinders and six 500lb (227kg) Rockeye cluster bombs on two triple ejector racks (TERs) under the wings.

The force crossed into North Vietnam at the Red River estuary and headed northwest. Due to the haze, they at first missed the target and were forced to turn south. This was unfortunate for two reasons. The defences had been well and truly alerted, and the strike aircraft were now committed to attacking down the same route from a north/south direction, and the defences were strong. The other pair of Flak Suppressors also went in from the same direction and were both hit by gunfire, which shot down Cdr. Blackburn, the Executive Officer of VF-92, and sent his wingman limping back to the carrier on one engine, somehow evading an attack by two MiG-21s en route.

Showtime 100 and 113 were unable to locate the AAA batteries but moved into fighting wing to attack a pre-briefed point to the right of a storage building. As they rolled in, two SAMs were fired at them but failed to guide. Within moments, the storage building collapsed, hit by one of the strike aircraft, so they rolled to the right and selected another target. This change of course left Showtime 113 slightly astern and 2,000ft (600m) out to the left of his leader. They released the Rockeyes and pulled up to the right, with Lt. Cunningham looking back over his right shoulder to observe the results of his attack.

As they climbed through 13,000ft (4,000m), with about 400kts (735km/h) on the clock, Showtime 113, who was falling astern in the right hand turn, sighted the enemy. Two MiG-17s were closing on Showtime 100 from 7 o'clock low at an estimated speed of 500kts (920km/h). Two more MiG-17s were following in 1nm (2km) trail. The leading MiG opened fire on Showtime 100 and tracer flashed past ahead of the Phantom. Showtime 100 broke hard left into him, and the MiG, controls stiffened by the speed, flashed past underneath, while his wingman, about 1,500ft (460m) further back, pulled up vertically and rolled across to the right. Showtime 100 reversed his turn back onto the leading MiG which was in a shallow left turn and, although it was still inside the minimum launch distance, squeezed off a Sidewinder. The MiG was travelling so fast that it opened the distance enough to allow the missile to home on the glowing afterburner. The Sidewinder scored a direct hit, and the MiG exploded.

The second MiG was still in position high on the right and Showtime 100 decided to try a "drag" manoeuvre. He unloaded and went into a gentle descending right turn, picking up speed as he went. Had the MiG attempted to follow, it would have set himself up for

Right: F-4Js of VF-92 and VF-96 on the aft flight deck of the carrier *USS Constellation*, September 5, 1972, shortly before a strike on targets in the Haiphong area.

Below: An AIM-7 Sparrow fired from an F-4D of the USAF 432nd TRW scores a direct hit on a MiG-19, May 1968. The thick white smoke plume is a typical Sparrow characteristic.

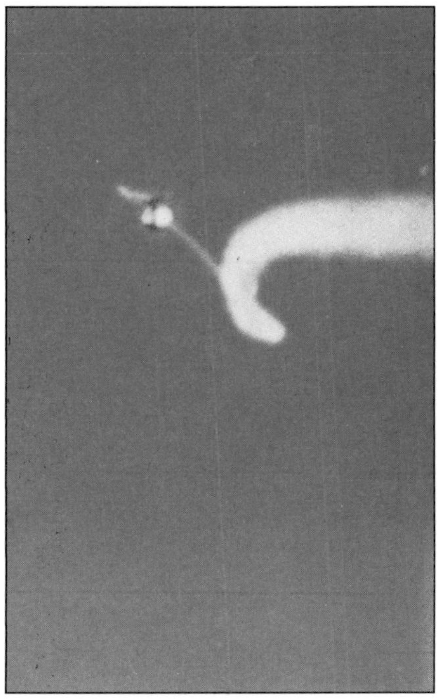

May 10, 1972, Showtime 100's First Victory

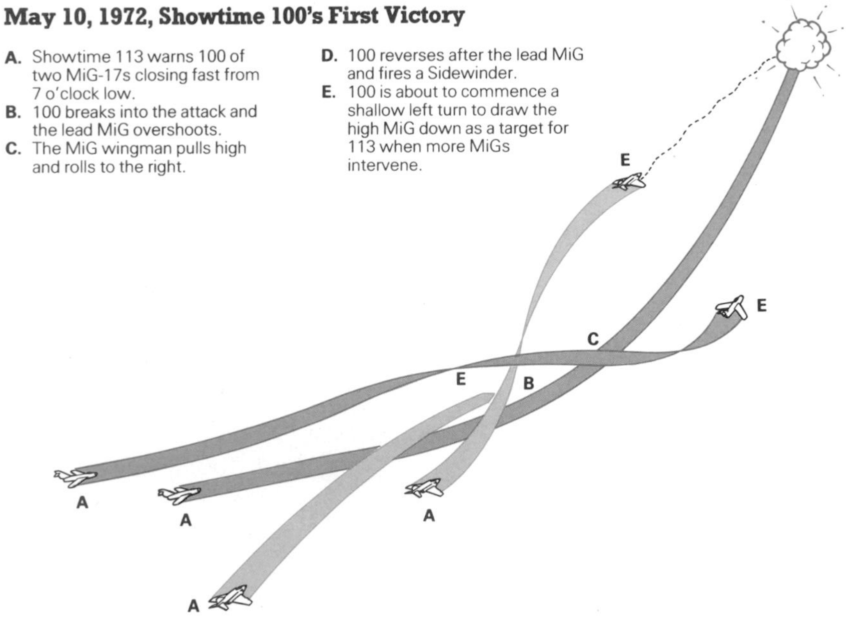
A. Showtime 113 warns 100 of two MiG-17s closing fast from 7 o'clock low.
B. 100 breaks into the attack and the lead MiG overshoots.
C. The MiG wingman pulls high and rolls to the right.
D. 100 reverses after the lead MiG and fires a Sidewinder.
E. 100 is about to commence a shallow left turn to draw the high MiG down as a target for 113 when more MiGs intervene.
A
A
A
A
B
C
E
E
E

Showtime 100's Second Victory

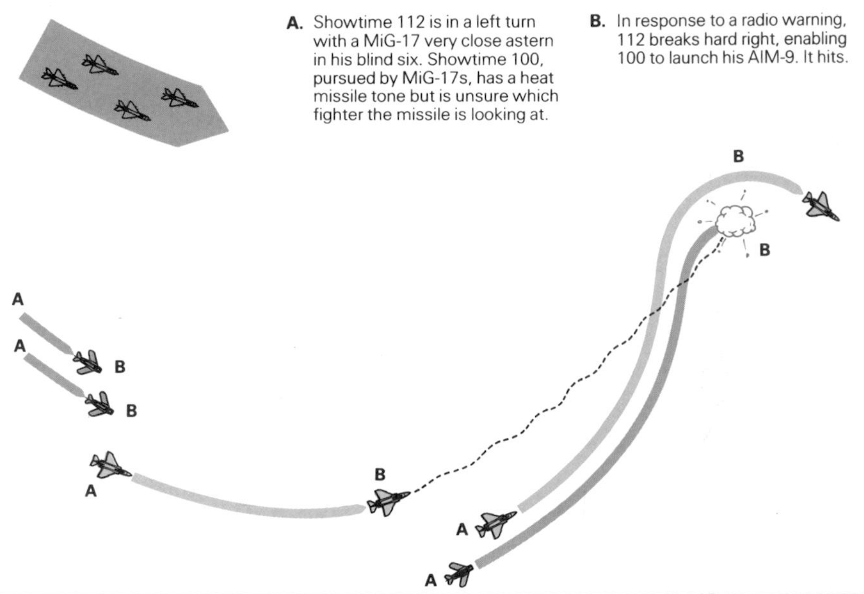
A. Showtime 112 is in a left turn with a MiG-17 very close astern in his blind six. Showtime 100, pursued by MiG-17s, has a heat missile tone but is unsure which fighter the missile is looking at.
B. In response to a radio warning, 112 breaks hard right, enabling 100 to launch his AIM-9. It hits.
A
A
A
A
A
B
B
B
B
B

an attack by Showtime 113. That was the plan, but in the event it was not to be. It was foiled by three more MiGs closing on Showtime 113's tail, and both Phantoms were forced to disengage and accelerate away out of range. With 500kts (920km/h) on the clock, they rejoined, moved into combat spread, and with plenty of fuel left, decided to re-enter the fight. They gained height and reversed course with an Immelmann. They still had centreline tanks on, and the TERs. The drag was a disadvantage in combat, but the centreline tanks could not safely be jettisoned at high speed, and dropping the TERs would have taken the Sidewinders with them.

Heading back into the fight at 12,000ft (3,660m), they looked down. Not far below was what Lt. Cunningham later described as "the awesome sight" of no less than eight MiG-17s in a Wagon Wheel. Worse still, three Phantoms were mixed up in it! Calling Showtime 113 to follow, Cunningham's Showtime 100 rolled down to the attack, hoping to get at the blind belly of a MiG. Moments later a Phantom broke upwards, hotly pursued by two MiG-17s. It passed close enough to Showtime 100 for Lt. Cunningham to identify it as Showtime 112, piloted by Cdr. Dwight Timm, with Lt. James Fox as his RIO. The Wagon Wheel broke up and a confused multi-bogey fight commenced.

In a combat of this nature, the electronic wizardry of the Phantom was of little use. The RIOs took their heads "out of their offices" and became a spare pair of eyes, keeping a lookout astern and passing a running commentary to their pilots, calling out sightings and differentiating them as either "threat" or "no threat". The pilots were thus given an all-round picture of the situation and could concentrate on attacking, leaving the RIOs to cover their rear.

Showtime 112, one of the MIGCAP flight, was in a left turn with a MiG-17 about 2,000ft (610m) astern and a MiG-21 a further 1,000ft (305m) behind that. But the worst threat to him was a MiG-17 which was at his 5 o'clock flying fighting wing on him. Because he was in a left turn, it was hidden beneath his belly, and was in position to pull in and start shooting. Showtime 100 was way back at 7 o'clock. Lt. Cunningham had a tone on a Sidewinder but the MiG-17 was so close to Showtime 112 that he could not be sure which aircraft it was looking at, and no Sidewinder can tell the difference between red and white star insignia! He called Showtime 112 to reverse his turn right and underneath to fling the MiG away from his tailpipe into a position where it could be safely fired at, but Cdr. Timm, aware of the two MiGs further back but not the close one, ignored the warning and kept on driving around the circle. Meanwhile four more MiG-17s had latched on behind Showtime 100 and were slowly closing. Two flashes, almost certainly the sun glinting on polished canopies, announced the arrival of a pair of MiG-19s rolling in from very high at 2 o'clock. The beleagured Showtime 100 reversed his turn to meet this new threat. The MiGs opened fire with cannon at long range, then pulled sharply up in a half loop and bored in again. Showtime 100 pulled up into them and held them at his 2 o'clock, giving them a difficult target. Again they fired and missed, then disengaged and vanished in the general direction of Hanoi.

Once more Showtime 100, still with the four MiGs in hot pursuit, set off to clear the MiG-17 from the tail of Showtime 112. By now, Showtime 112 was almost across the circle from Showtime 100, still in a left turn. Lt. Cunningham started to cut the corner, but the trailing MiGs turned inside him and closed the range. The lead aircraft opened fire with its cannon, the big 37mm looking like a blowlamp. The range was long, an estimated 2,500ft (760m), but tracer was passing the Phantom, which was doing over 550kts (1,000km/h). Cunningham slackened the turn and unloaded, opening the range again, with Lt. Driscoll in the back seat keeping a wary eye on their pursuers. They were now overtaking Showtime 112 fast, and again called Cdr. Timm to break right. A quick glance upwards showed yet more hostile fighters, MiG-21s this time, about 3,000ft (915m) above, and approaching from 9 o'clock.

At last Showtime 112 heeded their call and broke right. The MiG-17 that had been chasing him tried to follow, but its speed was about 400kts (740km/h) and its rate of roll was consequently slow. It was unable to follow the turn and, from about 20 degrees angle off, Showtime 100 got a good Sidewinder tone and launched. For the first time, Lt. Fox in the back seat of Showtime 112 saw the MiG that had been following them so closely. It was at 5 o'clock high, and at that precise moment the Sidewinder hit it. The North Vietnamese pilot ejected.

Below: The first Vietnam War Aces: US Navy aircrew Lt. Randy Cunningham and Lt. (jg) William Driscoll board their F-4J Phantom. Their success was largely due to excellent teamwork.

Showtime 100's Third Victory

Showtime 100's final kill on May 10, 1972 was in many ways a classic. The powerful but unmanoeuvrable Phantom was able to outfight an agile MiG-17 flown by an ace pilot.

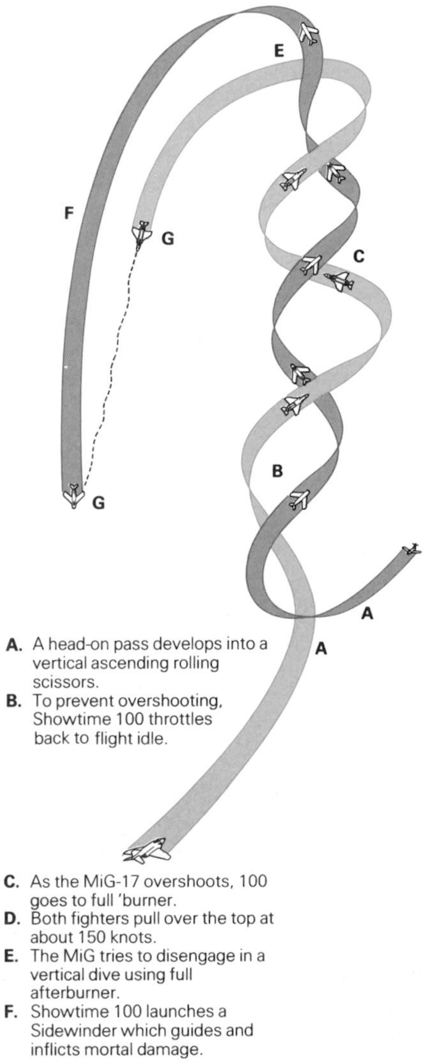

C. As the MiG-17 overshoots, 100 goes to full 'burner.

Showtime 100 looking for MiGs

Showtime 112's break to the right had set him up for the approaching MiG-21s and they rolled in to attack from astern. Showtime 100 turned left into them, passing them in the opposite direction while calling Showtime 112 to break left also. The MiGs, seeing their attack foiled, did not attempt to follow but climbed steeply away. Showtime 112 turned for the coast in a shallow dive while Showtime 100 made several hard clearing turns, looking for the four MiG-17s which had been chasing him, but they had vanished. The fight had lasted barely 105 seconds at this point and the big Phantom still had plenty of fuel and four missiles left. Many MiGs were still scattered around the sky while only two other Phantoms were to be seen, one of which was dead ahead with a MiG-17 closing him from 7 o'clock. A quick radio warning, allowed the threatened F-4 to accelerate away to safety. Outnumbered and with no support, Showtime 100 turned for the coast.

Until now, Showtime 100's crew had conducted a classic fight, exploiting the strong points of the Phantom's performance and avoiding the areas where the MiGs were superior. But when yet another MiG-17 hove into sight, approaching from head-on and slightly low, Lt. Cunningham made a serious error. As he had so often done in training, he nosed his gunless fighter down for a head-on pass, only to see the nose of the MiG erupt with cannon fire. He pulled vertically up to evade, expecting the MiG to bore straight on for home. It didn't. It pitched straight up, canopy to canopy with the Phantom, barely 30ft (9m) away. The heavy American fighter had much the better zoom climb, but this was of no advantage in the ascending rolling scissors which developed. Waiting until the MiG was nose high in the opposite direction, Showtime 100 disengaged and opened the distance, but made a further error by not running out in a straight line. The MiG started cutting across the curve, so Showtime 100 unloaded for extra energy, then once more pitched vertically upwards. The MiG-17, piloted by the North Vietnamese Air Force's leading ace, Colonel Tomb, cut the corner on the vertical manoeuvre and both aircraft ended in another ascending rolling scissors, with the lighter, more manoeuvrable Soviet-built fighter gradually gaining an advantage. Again the Phantom disengaged, unloaded, and ran out; this time far enough to give time to turn through 180 degrees and come back in from head-on. Once more both fighters pitched up into an ascending rolling scissors, but this time, rather than outzoom the MiG and be shot at, Lt. Cunningham chopped the throttles to idle. As soon as the MiG could be seen to be overshooting, he selected afterburner and pulled into the MiG's 7 o'clock, although at too close range to launch a missile. Both aircraft pulled over the top at about 150 knots (275km/h) and the MiG, afterburner blazing, attempted to disengage in a vertical dive. As the Phantom pursued, the range opened. Showtime 100 launched a Sidewinder which guided to the tail of the MiG-17, causing a little flash. This was followed by a small fire. The MiG, mortally hit, dived straight into the ground.

Again Showtime 100 turned for the coast. Yet another MiG-17 came in from 2 o'clock high. The Phantom turned into the attack but warnings came from Showtime 113, who was still in the area and about to join up, and another Showtime Phantom, crewed by Lts. Connelly and Blonski, who themselves had accounted for two MiG-17s during the action. Four more MiG-17s were at Showtime 100's 7 o'clock and cutting across the turn. They were foiled when, with a remarkable piece of quick thinking, Lt. Connelly fired an unguided Sparrow which passed over the top of Showtime 100. The MiGs saw the plume of white smoke as the missile hurtled towards them and broke away in all directions.

This had in many ways been a classic encounter. A handful of Phantoms from VF-96 had engaged an estimated 14 MiG-17s, four MiG-19s, and four MiG-21s, shooting down six MiG-17s for no loss. In addition, VF-92 had knocked down a MiG-21, and in a separate encounter an F-4B Phantom of VF-51 had accounted for a further MiG-17.

The final score for the day was Phantoms 11, MiGs 2, a highly satisfactory state of affairs for the United States air combat flyers. But far more than this a very damaging series of strikes had been carried out and the North Vietnamese Air Force had been unable to stop them.

Above: This was the Phantom actually flown by Cunningham and Driscoll on May 10, 1972, an F-4J BuAer No. 155800. It did not survive the mission.

Vietnam—a summary

The air fighting over North Vietnam lasted from the spring of 1965 to January 1973, but included a long period between April 1968 and March 1972 when strikes on the North were either halted or severely restricted by political leaders. Consequently, regular air fighting took place during only 43 months of the 7½-year conflict. During this time, USAF Phantoms were credited with 107½ air victories, USN Phantoms with 38, and USMC Phantoms with one.

Below: An early Sparrow-armed F-4E from USAF's 469 TFS, 388 TFW, based at Korat in 1972. The Sparrow had a poor record in the conflict in Southeast Asia, the missile achieving a kill ratio of under 10 per cent.

Above: Peace on earth? Not quite: but the decorated bombs indicate the festive season as F-4E No. 67-0379 of USAF 388 TFW sets out from Korat on a strike into North Vietnam.

Phantom losses in Southeast Asia (from June 6, 1965, to June 29, 1973)						
Version	**F-4C**	**RF-4C**	**F-4D**	**F-4E**	**Unknown**	**Totals**
Combat losses (air-air, Sam/AAA, others)	118	72	169	70	1	430
Operational losses (Collision, crash landings/t.o., others)	33	7	24	3	— n	67
Ground losses (Rocket/mortar attack, others)	9	4	1	—	—	14
Totals	**160**	**83**	**194**	**73**	**1**	**511**

When one considers the scale of operations, an average return of less than 3½ victories per month seems paltry. Yet three factors should be borne in mind. First, the main object of the North Vietnamese Air Force was to remain in being as an effective fighting force. Stubborn resistance, outnumbered as they were, could have led to their virtual destruction. Consequently there were not that many opportunities for the Phantoms to score. Second, the primary objective of the American strikes was to put munitions on target; in this they succeeded admirably, with minimal losses in air combat. Third, the manoeuvring dogfight had been considered a thing of the past and US pilots had not been trained for this type of fighting. Only the USN in the last years of the war remedied this situation, which in part explains the success of May 10, 1972. Six-to-nil in one fight while badly outnumbered is excellent by any standards. For once the Phantom pilots had sufficient targets and they made good use of their opportunities.

The Middle East War of Attrition, 1969–1970

The next nation to take the Phantom to battle was Israel. The War of Attrition was a static war fought across the Suez Canal, with neither Egypt nor Israel seeking to make territorial gains. The first Phantoms, F-4Es, arrived in Israel in September 1969 and were quickly in action against missile sites in Egypt. By the spring of 1970, Israeli Phantoms were ranging deep into Egypt, and targets in the Cairo area were hit.

Then in April, about 150 MiG-21s arrived to reinforce Egyption air defences, flown by Soviet volunteers. The Israelis ceased their deep penetration flights for a while, but a clash could not long be avoided. It came on July 30 when 16 Soviet-flown MiG-21s intercepted a mixed force of Phantoms and Mirages. Five MiGs were downed for no Israeli loss. A cease-fire was negotiated just eight days later, but not before Phantoms had raided Ras Banas on the Egyptian Red Sea coast, a distance of over 450 miles, and sunk a destroyer and a missile boat. Phantom losses in the war were described as "heavy".

Yom Kippur/Ramadan, 1973

This was a very short but concentrated war, whch started when Egypt and Syria simultaneously attacked Israel. The Egyptian ground forces crossed the Suez Canal under an umbrella of surface-to-air missiles, including large numbers of the very mobile SA-6 Gainful. Syria also deployed many Gainfuls in the Golan Heights. Air fighting was intense. Israel's *Heyl Ha'Avir*, with a first line strength of approximately 380 aircraft, including 121 F-4E Phantoms and six RF-4Es, suffered heavy losses, many of them in attacks on missile installations. Thirty-three F-4Es were lost. Despite a massive kill ratio claimed in air-to-air combat (including 14 by leading

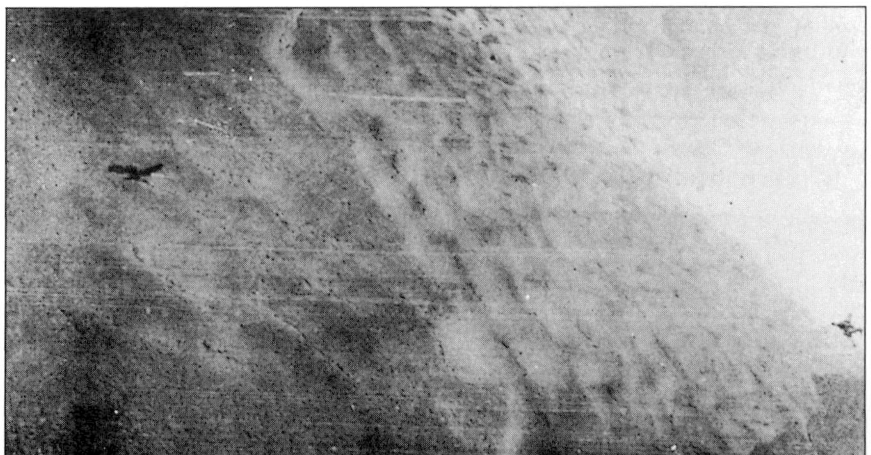

Below: A MiG-17 of the Egyptian air force uses full afterburner as it attempts to escape the pursuing Israeli Phantom over the Sinai Desert in 1973.

Right: The gun camera of an Israeli Phantom captures the last moments of an Egyptian air force MiG-21 (possibly piloted by a Soviet "volunteer"). Catastrophic damage and an uncontrollable fire have been caused by a direct hit from a heat missile.

ace, now Director of Operational Requirement, Colonel Israel Baharav), the Israelis have since been reported to be unwilling to use the Phantom in close combat against the MiG-21.

The Iran/Iraq war, 1980 onwards

No firm details of Iranian Phantom operations against Iraq are available, and those reports that do exist tend, understandably, to be conflicting. For example, it has been suggested that the Iranian Air Force (reportedly with undercover assistance from Israel) has kept a surprisingly large number of its 225 plus originally-delivered Phantoms airworthy, while the No. 44 edition of the Israeli-based *Defence Update International*, published in 1984, stated: "The Iranian Air Force survived the Iraqi opening attack, and the first phase of the war, although most of its aircraft were reportedly hardly operational. However, it was tested to its limits in 1982. Of the original quantity, only a few aircraft were in flying condition, with a small number of trained and experienced pilots. This reduced force had great difficulty in supporting the massive Iranian attacks in late 1982 and 1983. From a total number of 450 fighter aircraft before the revolution, there are now barely 50 fighters operational."

Presumably, Iran's Phantoms have faced a range of Iraqi aircraft including Mirage F.1EQ, MiG-19, MiG-21, MiG-23 and MiG-25, and apparently have launched a considerable number of strikes against Iraqi Army positions as well as Baghdad and, in 1981, the Rutba air base which houses squadrons of MiG-19/F6, MiG-21/F7, Su-7 and MiG-23. *Defence Update* further reports that dogfights have been few; the Iraqis have claimed to have engaged Phantoms operating with F-14 Tomcats which are presumed to be acting in the early warning role and as decoys to bring Iraqi fighters into close range so that they can be attacked by F-4s (despite the reports that Iran's Tomcats are no longer offensively operational).

Israel/Syria, 1982, and Lebanon

Although the Phantom has seen action in this conflict, the new F-15s and F-16s of the *Heyl Ha'Avir* have seen the major part of the fighting. Again, few details are available.

The Phantom is currently credited with 277½ victories in air combat. Records are incomplete, but known victims include 107 MiG-21s, 10 MiG-19s, and 53½ MiG-17s. The weapons used have varied. The Sparrow is known to have accounted for 64 victims, the Sidewinder and Shafrir heat-seekers share 96 victims and the Falcon is credited with five. Gunfire accounts for 22½ and the other 91 are undetermined, although at least five are ascribed to manoeuvring.

Above: An Israeli Air Force F-4E Phantom displays its wing slats in the extended position. Israeli military aircraft are rarely shown armed, and this one is no exception.

Below: An Israeli Phantom runs up its engines prior to takeoff. The smoky trail which is one characteristic that makes the Phantom vulnerable in combat is clearly to be seen here.

Right: Ultra-low flying is a good way of avoiding both detection and defensive fire. Here a fully armed Phantom storms low over the Sinai Desert inbound to the target, during the Yom Kippur War/War of Ramadan, October 1973.

Deployment

The distinctive shape of the Phantom makes it probably the most readily identifiable shape in the skies of the Western world. Described by a current pilot as "a kind of goofy looking airplane", it defies the age-old rule of thumb "If it looks right it probably is right." Appearance notwithstanding, it is rightly regarded as one of the all time greats, and has seen service quite literally around the world, from Japan to the Falklands. It has served with no fewer than 12 nations.

There were 5,195 F-4s built and flown, more than any other Western supersonic aircraft, and it is arguably the most successful aircraft of the post-war period. Its versatility is legend, and in its heyday it can literally be said to have formed the backbone of American air power, being widely used in the United States Navy, Marine Corps, and Air Force (including, latterly, the Air National Guard). Altogether 1,266 Phantoms were delivered to the USN and USMC, and 2,640 to the USAF.

Due to the world-wide commitments of the United States, Phantoms bearing the white star insignia have at one time or another been seen in almost every corner of the free world. American Phantoms have been based not only in the continental United States, but also in Alaska, Hawaii, the Philippines, Japan, Korea, South Vietnam, Thailand, Iceland, England, West Germany, Holland, and Spain. Furthermore, many other countries have operated the Phantom, which has taken the air (and often still does) sporting the insignia of Great Britain, Australia, West Germany, Israel, Spain, Greece, Turkey, Egypt, Japan, Korea and Iran. The ubiquitous Phantom has overflown the oceans of the world, borne by American and, to a lesser degree, British aircraft carriers. It has seen action in five "wars" to date; in Vietnam from 1965 to 1973; in the Middle East War of Attrition from 1969 to 1970; in the Yom Kippur War (or War of Ramadan) in 1973; in the continuing fracas between Iran and Iraq; and in the ongoing hostilities between Israel and Syria which started in 1982.

Over the past few years, the Phantom has been increasingly replaced by more modern weapons systems: for example, F-14 Tomcats and F/A-18 Hornets in USN and USMC service; F-15 Eagles and F-16 Fighting Falcons with the USAF. It has already been superseded in the strike role for Britain's Royal Air Force by the purpose-built Jaguar and will eventually be replaced in the interceptor role by the Tornado F.2 (air-defence variant – ADV).

Below: The United States Navy really had no requirement for a reconnaissance Phantom, and those RF-4Bs that were built entered the US Marine Corps. Over the years they have been continually upgraded and maintained by a process of cannibalisation. Consequently there are hardly any identical RF-4Bs. This example, from VMFP-3, is finished in low visibility two-tone grey. Others sport a three tone grey finish. The fox-head insignia on the tail is no longer used, and virtually all aircraft vary in detail.

Above: F-4S Phantoms prepare for catapult launch from USS *Constellation*, October 1983. The low visibility paint scheme has replaced previous gaudy squadron markings.

Left: Performing just one of its roles, an F-4E of 57 FIS, based at Keflavik, Iceland, makes a routine interception of a Soviet Tu-95 Bear.

Below: The most sophisticated Phantom to see operational service is the F-4G Wild Weasel. This particular example is from the US Air Force 81st TFS. Developed from the F-4E, the most noticeable external differences are the chin pod instead of the cannon fairing and a further pod on the fin.

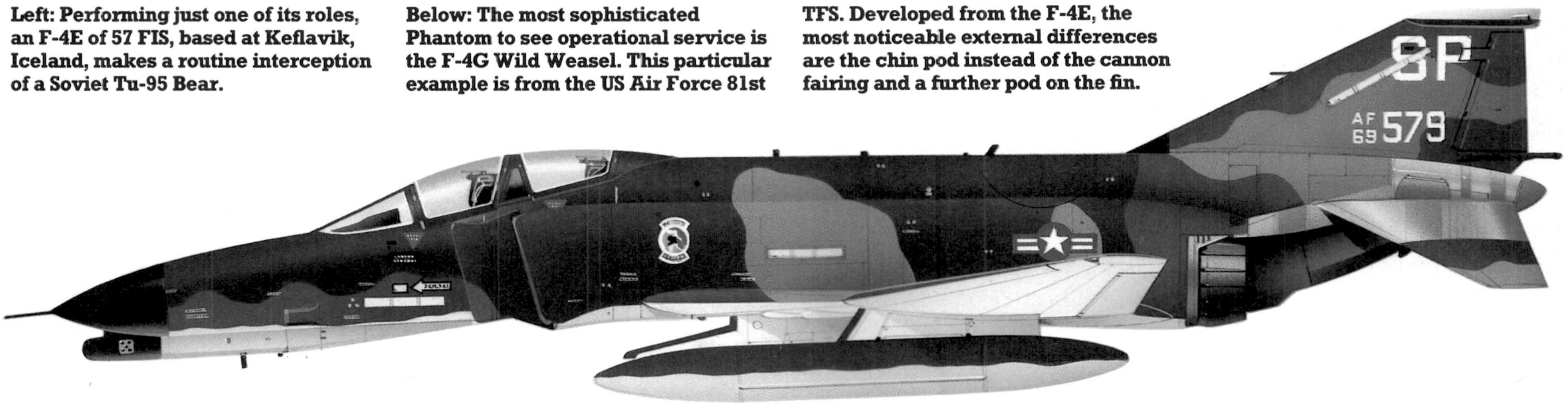

To be truthful, the Phantom is getting long in the tooth; after all, the aircraft first flew over a quarter of a century ago. There are even cases where sons are flying the same Phantoms that their fathers flew.

Considered an outstandingly long-ranged interceptor in its youth, the F-4 is now regarded as distinctively fuel-limited in this role. The pilot's work load is high; unless he is very experienced on the type he has to spend far too much time flying the aircraft, which reduces the time available to concentrate on other tasks in hand. It is an unforgiving aeroplane if pushed too hard at high AOA, and it is difficult to imagine it being able to hold its own in a knife-range dogfight against a modern fighter, no matter how skilfully handled.

Nevertheless, it will remain in service with many air arms for many years yet. Its continuing value is discussed in greater length in the chapter on combat, but one factor that will help prolong its active life is cost. It is far cheaper to refurbish the structure and upgrade the avionics of an elderly Phantom than it is to purchase a modern replacement such as the F-18 Hornet, which is currently being touted as its natural successor.

For first operational Phantom squadron, as distinct from training units, was VF-74 "Bedevilers". This squadron had had a relatively long history of operating jets from carriers, having previously operated Banshees, Cougars and Skyrays. After an initial familiarisation period on the type with training unit VF-121 Detachment Alpha at NAS Oceana, it received its full complement of 12 F-4Bs and became carrier-qualified aboard the USS *Saratoga*, making 198 day launches and 58 night arrested deck landings in the space of four days. In August 1962 the Phantom made its first extended deployment with the squadron, to the Mediterranean aboard USS *Forrestal*. VF-74 was to operate the Phantom for more than 20 years.

Because squadrons have been equipped for so long with Phantoms, it is inevitable that experience levels on the type are unprecedentedly high. It was once considered that 200 hours on type made for an experienced pilot, and that to have made 100 traps (as deck landings are commonly called in the USN) turned a pilot into a "greybeard". On the Phantom it is quite normal for a young pilot to have 100 hours on type before reaching an operational squadron. Over the time span that the Phantom has been in service, quite a few pilots have exceeded 4,000 hours on type, while traps in the high hundreds are quite commonplace.

Fairly typical was the deployment to the Indian Ocean of VF-102 "Diamondbacks" aboard USS *Independence* between December 1980 and June 1981. During this period, the "Diamondback" Phantoms flew more than 2,000 hours and made 1,185 traps. Their commanding officer, Cdr Dan Bunting, made his 1,000th trap during the cruise, a truly remarkable figure, which included his 300th night trap.

USAF Phantoms

The Phantom had been ordered for the USAF in 1962, originally with the designation F-110A. The first combat unit to be equipped was the 12th Tactical Fighter Wing at MacDill Air Force Base, Florida, with their first F-4C (as the F-110A had become) delivered in January 1966. By the following October the 12th TFW's Phantoms were ready for operations. No fewer than 16 of the 23 Wings in Tactical Air Command were eventually to be equipped with the type.

Its combat operational debut came on August 6, 1964 when Navy F-4Bs drawn from VF-142 and VF-143, flying from USS *Constellation*, were among aircraft from US 7th Fleet that struck at North Vietnamese patrol boat bases. In June of the following year the Phantom scored its first air combat victories, both Navy and Air Force Phantoms scoring in quick succession at the expense of North Vietnamese MiG-17s.

During the long-drawn out war in Southeast Asia, the Phantom served with great distinction in many roles, its versatility being such that it supplanted many other types, such as the Delta Dagger, Starfighter, Super Sabre, Voodoo and Thunderchief. One of the most spectacular feats achieved by Phantom units during the war was the long range deployment of the 49th TFW with no fewer than 72 F-4Ds from Holloman AFB in New Mexico to Takhli in Thailand. Codenamed Constant Guard III, the move was initiated during the early morning of May 4, 1972. The method was to team up sections of fighters with a KC-135 tanker to each section, providing in-flight refuelling en route. Overnight stops were made at Hickam Field, Oahu, and Guam. Some 71 of the 72 F-4Ds arrived at Takhli on schedule and combat operations commenced within 24 hours. The entire

Above: An F-4G Wild Weasel with two AGM-45 Shrike missiles banks steeply over Spangdahlem AB, Germany.

Below: Contrast in styles: F-4N of VF-111 Sundowners and (bottom) an F-4E in standard European camouflage.

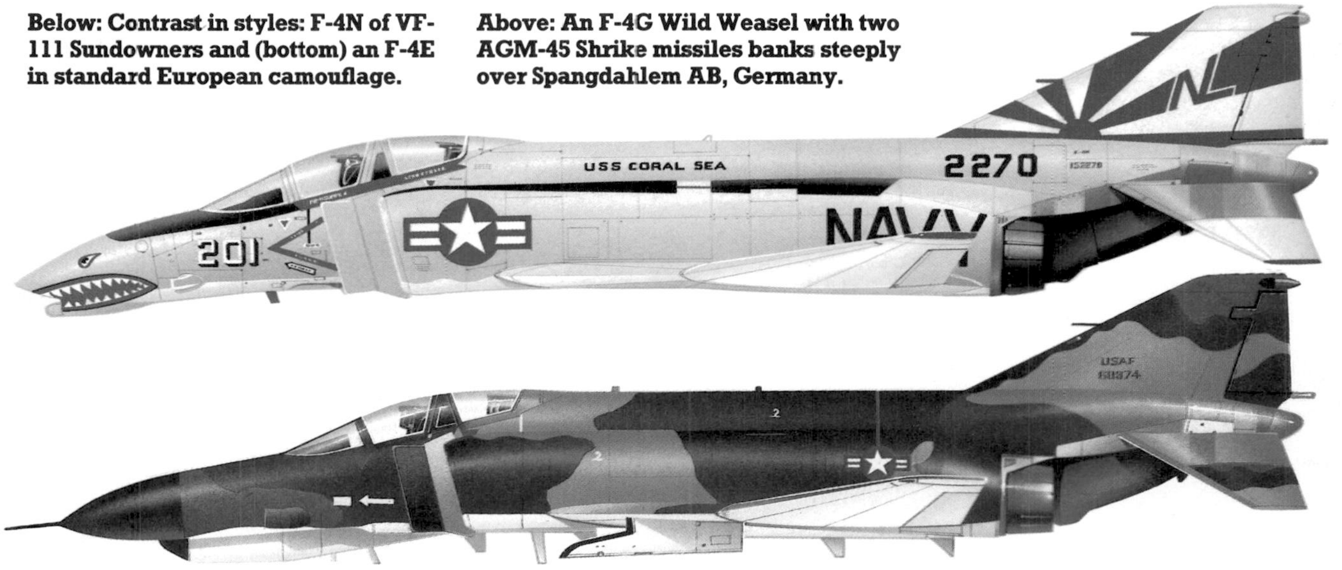

Wing, with its support crews and equipment was taken halfway across the world, and was in action in just a little more than a week!

Phantoms in foreign service

The sheer versatility of the Phantom attracted the attention of many air forces around the world. It was not cheap in terms of cost per aeroplane but, in terms of having one type that could perform several roles that normally required specialist machines, it was a bargain. Moreover, it was a proven all-round design. The multi-role aeroplane was at that time the fashion. A piece of doggerel seen on a notice board in a crew room at RAF Alconbury, England, in 1967 summed it up with advice to the passing reader that if one was a fighter-bomber pilot, all the others could kiss an unmentionable part of one's anatomy! It was therefore hardly surprising that the Phantom should enter the service of many nations other than the United States.

Royal Navy and Royal Air Force

The United Kingdom was the first foreign nation to buy the Phantom. Orders for the F-4K for the Royal Navy and the F-4M for the Royal Air Force were placed in September 1964 and May 1965, respectively. In British service, the F-4K was designated FG-1 and the F-4M became the FGR-2.

The first RN unit to equip with the Phantom was No. 700P Squadron, an intensive trials unit formed at Yeovilton on April 30, 1968. Its task complete, it disbanded during January 1969 and No. 767 Squadron was formed to act as the Phantom training unit. Due to cutbacks in defence spending, only one Royal Navy Phantom unit went to sea. This was No. 892 Squadron, which formed at Yeovilton on March 31, 1969. Its first taste of shipboard life came on board USS *Saratoga* in the Mediterranean in the autumn of 1969. The squadron joined HMS *Ark Royal* on June 12, 1970, although trials had also been held with HMS *Eagle*.

The life of the Phantom in RN service was to be relatively short; on November 27, 1978, ten Phantoms flew off the *Ark* for the last time as she approached Devonport at the end of her final voyage. The Phantoms landed at RAF St. Athan to be prepared for RAF service and No. 892 Squadron officially disbanded on December 15, temporarily ending fixed wing flying in the RN.

The Phantoms ordered for the RAF were originally the replace Hunters in the strike role, with reconnaissance and air defence as secondary tasks. The first squadron to equip was No. 6 at Coningsby, Lincolnshire, in May 1969. Over the next two and a half years, No. 54 Squadron at Coningsby, Nos. 14, 17 and 13 Squadrons at Bruggen in West

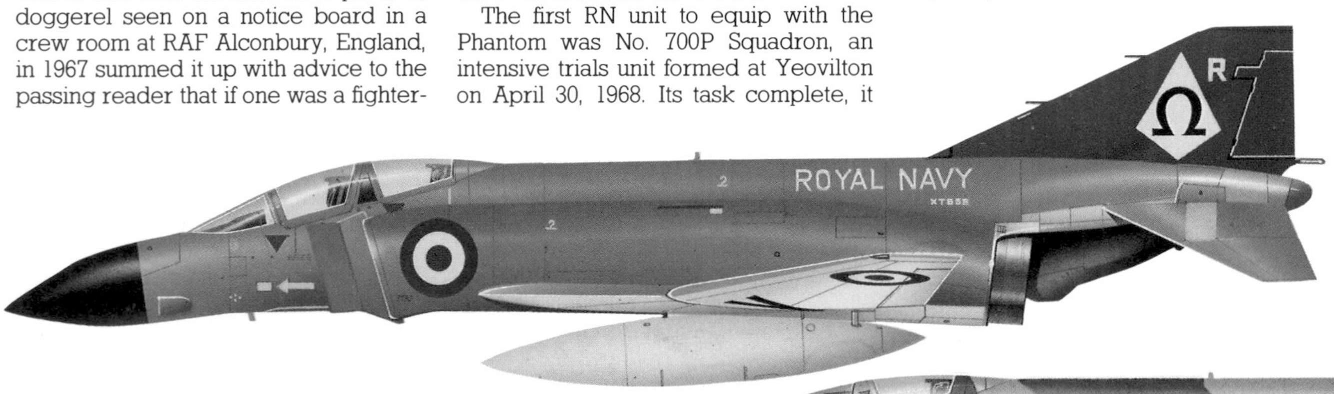

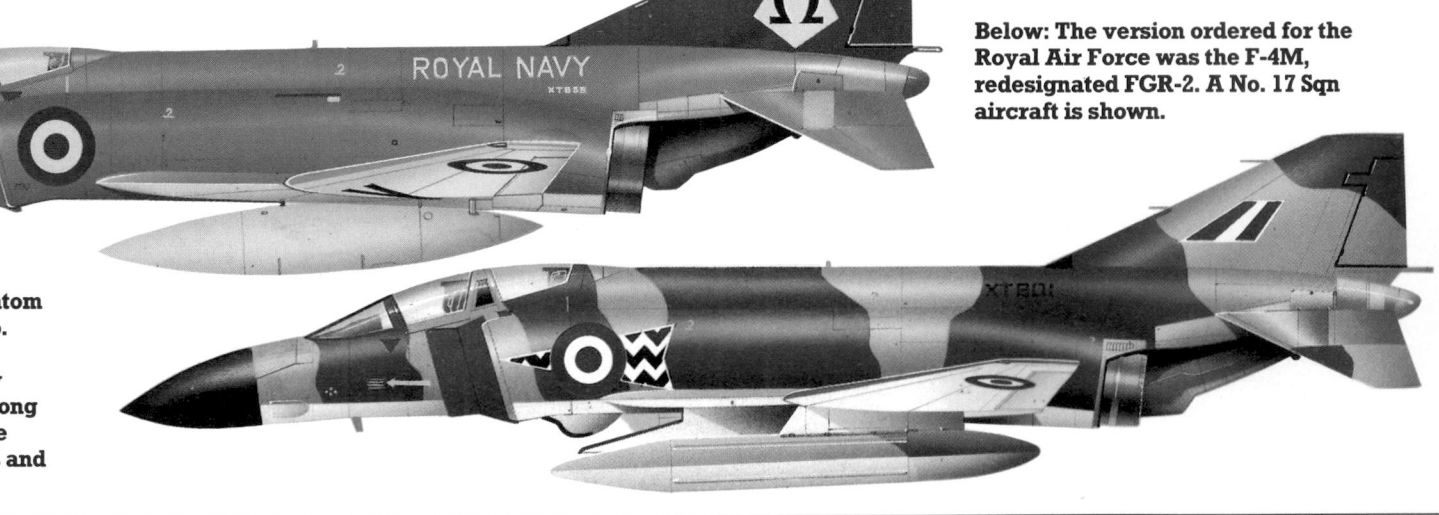

Left: The F-4K Phantom flew with No. 892 Sqn, Royal Navy, under the designation FG-1.

Below: The version ordered for the Royal Air Force was the F-4M, redesignated FGR-2. A No. 17 Sqn aircraft is shown.

Below: A pleasing study of a Phantom FGR-2 of the Royal Air Force's No. 111 Squadron over the Humber bridge. Sporting an air superiority grey finish, it is equipped for the long range interception role, with three external fuel tanks, four Sparrows and four Sidewinders.

Germany, and No. 2 Squadron at Laarbruch (also W. Germany) all followed. No. 2 Squadron specialised in tactical reconnaissance and its Phantoms were equipped with special pods for the purpose. All these squadrons were equipped with the FGR-2. Originally enough FG-1s had been ordered to equip two RN squadrons. The balance of FG-1s was given to No. 43 Squadron which formed at Leuchars, Scotland, in the air defence role.

From September 1974 the Jaguar started to replace Phantoms in the strike squadrons and their aircraft became available for air defence duties, replacing the Lightnings. Squadrons so equipped were No. 111 which joined No. 43 at Leuchars, on November 3, 1975, Nos. 23 and 56 at Wattisham, Suffolk, No. 29 at Coningsby and Nos. 19 and 92 at Wildenrath in West Germany. Overseas deployments by RAF Phantoms have also been made to Singapore, Cyprus, Malta, and to Decimomannu in Sardinia, while a detachment from No. 29 Squadron is currently based at Port Stanley in the Falkland Islands. The Phantom is likely to remain in British service until about 1990, but the Tornado F.2 will start to supersede it long before this.

Meanwhile the RAF will take delivery of 15 ex-USN F-4Js in August 1984. They will be based at Wattisham in Suffolk, where No. 74 "Tiger" Squadron will be reformed. Presumably, since the aircraft have J79 engines, USAF servicing facilities will be made available. They are currently being reworked in San Diego.

Iran

The next country to receive the Phantom, was Iran. In July 1967 McAIR received an order for F-4Ds, and deliveries to the *Niron Hayai Shahahanshahiye Iran* (Imperial Iranian Air Force) commenced in September 1968. Further orders increased the total numbers delivered to at least 227. By types

Above: Royal Navy Phantom FG-1 being stowed in the upper hangar below the flight deck of the now scrapped HMS *Ark Royal*. The size limitations of British aircraft carrier lifts meant the Phantom's radome had to be folded back (this feature not exclusive to UK Phantoms).

Phantom types delivered

Aircraft delivered to:	Type Total	Number	Remarks
Australia	F-4E	24	
	Total	24	(All from USAF inventory; 1 lost; 23 returned to USAF)
Egypt	F-4E	35	
	Total	35	All from USAF inventory
Germany	F-4E	10	
	RF-4E	88	
	F-4F	175	
	Total	273	(All from new production)
Greece	F-4E	56	
	RF-4E	6	
	Total	62	(All from new production)
Iran	F-4D	32	(All from new production)
	F-4E	177	(All from new production)
	RF-4E	16	Does not include: 6 RF-4E not delivered; cancellations
	Total	225	Does not include aircraft loaned by USAF
Israel	RF-4E	12	
	F-4E	204	162 from USAF inventory (including some supplied directly); 42 from new production; includes conversions to F-4P
	Total	216	
Japan	F-4E	15	2 complete airframes, 11 knockdown kits, 2 forward fuselage trial kits
	F-4EJ	125	Built by Mitsubishi
	RF-4E	14	
	Total	154	(All from new production)
Korea	F-4D	36	All from USAF inventory, at least 4 attritted
	F-4E	37	All from new production
	Total	73	
Spain	F-4C	40	includes at least 3 later attritted
	RF-4C	4	
	Total	44	All from USAF inventory
Turkey	F-4E	87	Includes 15 from USAF inventory, 72 from new production
	RF-4E	8	All from new production
	Total	95	Does not include: Possible additional transfers from USAF (number known) Rumoured transfers from Egypt (unlikely)
UK	F-4K	52	24 Royal Navy; 28 RAF
	F-4M	118	
	F-4J	15	Ex-US Navy, for RAF, 1984
	Total	185	
US Navy and	F-4A	47	(ex F4H-1, F4H-1F)
US Marine Corps	F-4B	651	(ex F4H-1) Includes: 27 F-4B loaned to USAF, 12 F-4G data-link aircraft, 44 QE-4B conversions, 243 F-4N conversions. Likely further QF-4B, QF-4N
	RF-4B	46	
	F-4J	522	Includes: at least 1 DF-4J conversion, 302 F-4S conversions, likely QF-4N conversions
	Total	1,266	F-4A USN only; RF-4B USMC only; F-4B, J, N, S aircraft routinely transferred between USN and USMC
US Air Force	F-4C	583	Includes 40 transferred to Spain (not 36 as reported elsewhere)
	YRF-4C	2	Includes conversion to YF-4E, F-4CCV, etc
	RF-4C	503	Includes 4 transferred to Spain
	F-4D	793	Includes some loaned to South Korea, 36 transferred to South Korea
	F-4E	993	Includes 24 loaned to Australia, 116 conversions to F-4G Wild Weasel, 162 transferred to Israel, some loaned to Israel, Iran, 58 "payback" aircraft purchased by Israel for USAF, 35 transferred to Egypt, 15 transfers to Turkey
	Total	2,874	(Lots of attrition) Does not include: 27 F-4B borrowed from USN, 32 F-4D new production for Iran, 42 F-4E from FMS as new production for Israel, F-4E new production for Germany (10); Greece (56); Iran (177); Japan (140); Turkey (72); South Korea (37)

Above: Armourers of No. 111 Sqn, RAF, service Martin-Baker seats. Traditionally, crew who eject provide a barrel of beer for the "plumbers!"

Above: An Iranian F-4E lifts off from Shiraz AB, August 1977. Iranian F-4s have flown many strikes against Iraq, some apparently operating with F-14s.

Below: Phantom FGR-2 of No. 111 Squadron, RAF. Note the camouflage finish in contrast to the photo at left, and also the lack of fin antenna.

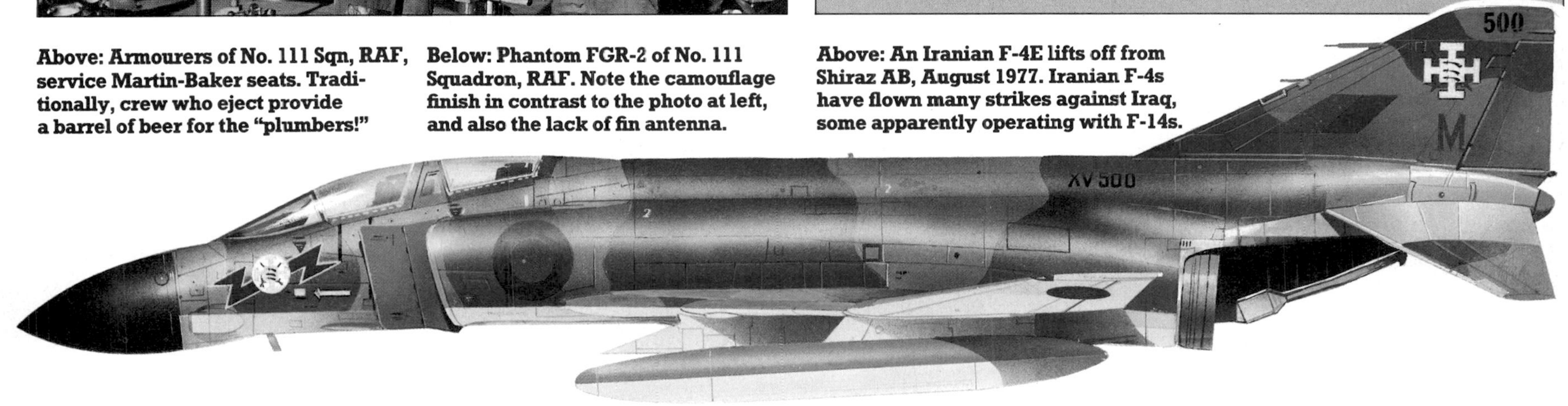

they were: 32 F-4Ds, 179 F-4Es, and 16 RF-4Es. They equipped a total of 11 squadrons, two of F-4Ds, eight of F-4Es and one of RF-4Es. Their known bases are at Tabriz, Shiraz, and Mehrabad. Had it not been for the revolution, even more would have entered the inventory, as six more RF-4Es had been completed but not delivered (including the last Phantom manufactured at St. Louis, No 5074) and a further 41 Phantoms were on order.

South Korea

The South Korean decision to acquire Phantoms was announced in February 1968, and the first six, F-4Ds from the USAF inventory, were handed over at Seoul on August 25, 1969. In all, 36 F-4Ds were supplied, supplemented later by 37 F-4Es. The Republic of Korea Air Force operates four Phantom squadrons, all from Taegu.

Australia

In the early 1960s the Royal Australian Air Force ordered the F-111, but serious delays in this project retarded delivery and to bridge the gap the US government offered to lease Australia 24 F-4Es with an option to buy. This offer was taken up, and the first Phantoms arrived in September 1970. These were operated by Nos. 1 and 6 Squadrons of No. 82 Bomber Wing, based in Amberley, Queensland, and No. 2 OCU. With the arrival of the F-111s nearly three years later the Phantoms were returned to the USA, minus an OCU machine that crashed into the sea off the coast of New South Wales on June 16, 1971. The last Phantom left Australia on June 22, 1973.

Israel

The *Heyl Ha'Avir* received its first Phantoms in September 1969. Israeli aircrews having been converting to the type at USAF's George AFB during the preceding six months. Typical Israeli security shrouds both quantity and deployment of the Israeli Phantoms but it is probable that about 204 F-4Es and 12 RF-4Es have been delivered and that a maximum of six squadrons were formed which have since been reduced. The *Heyl Ha'Avir* is also reported to operate a "mysterious" electronic warfare variant with the designation F-4P, of which three exist.

Another aircraft seen at Edwards AFB in 1976 where it was undergoing tests had the serial No. 69-7576 and featured a most unusual nose configuration and Israeli desert camouflage. At Edwards this bore the designation RF-4(X), although subsequent reports identify the designation RF-4E(S). Further details of this aircraft appear elsewhere in this book. The conversion was carried out by General Dynamics.

Above: A Republic of Korea F-4E, takes off from Taegu on an AGM-65A Maverick firing mission, February 19, 1979.

Below: Three F-4Es of the Royal Australian Air Force. These were on loan for three years pending arrival of F-111s swing-wing attack aircraft.

Below: An F-4E of the Israeli Air Force. The warload is two Gabriel anti-shipping missiles, for which an order has not yet been placed.

Below: An RF-4EJ of the Japanese Air Self-Defense Force. Japanese Phantoms were licence-built by Mitsubishi.

West Germany

The *Luftwaffe* became the next foreign Phantom user. The first of 88 RF-4Es on order arrived at Bremgarten on January 20, 1971 to commence the re-equipment of *Aufklarungsgeschwader* 51, replacing RF-104G Starfighters. The next unit to equip with Phantoms was *AKG* 52 at Leck. A further order followed, this time for 175 F-4Fs, the first of which arrived in May 1974. They went to re-equip two *Jagdgeschwadern*, *JG* 71 Richthofen at Wittmundhafen, and *JG* 74 Molders at Neufeld, and two *Jagdbombergeschwadern*, *JaboG* 35 at Pferdsfeld and *JaboG* 36 at Hopsten. At first, a dozen F-4Fs were held at USAF's George AFB for training purposes, but in 1977 they were transferred to Germany as attrition replacements and replaced at George by 10 F-4Es.

Spain

The *Erjecito del Aire* acquired a total of 36 ex-USAF F-4Cs, followed by four RF-4Cs. Delivery commenced in April 1971. The F-4Cs were given the Spanish designation C-12; the RF-4Cs became CR-12s. They were used to equip *Escadrones* 121 and 122 of *Ala* (Wing) No. 12 at Torrejon. The *Erjecito del Aire* has reportedly not been happy with the Phantoms, which operate in both the air defence and strike roles, and they are to be replaced with F-18 Hornets within the next few years.

Japan

The Japanese Air Self Defence Force (JASDF) received its first Phantoms on July 16, 1971. The first four aircraft were manufactured at St. Louis and a further nine were supplied in kit form for assembly in Japan, while the remainder were unique in that they were produced in Japan under licence, with Mitsubishi as the main contractor. Japanese Phantoms were basically F-4Es but were minus the IFR probe and some avionics units, notably the Rear Warning Radar. The in-flight refuelling probe is currently being retrofitted.

The first Japanese Phantom unit to be

Below: Israeli F-4E carrying the AGM-65 Maverick which was used effectively in the Yom Kippur war. This aircraft has also been seen carrying AIM-7s (aft left Sparrow well), ALQ-119 (V)-12 (forward left Sparrow well), 5 M117 bombs on centreline, AIM-9D on pylon at forward right Sparrow well, AIM-7E. (aft right Sparrow well), 3 M117 bombs (right inboard). 370gall fuel tank (both right and left outboard), M117s on centre and right stations of left inboard plus AIM-9D on left shoulder station.

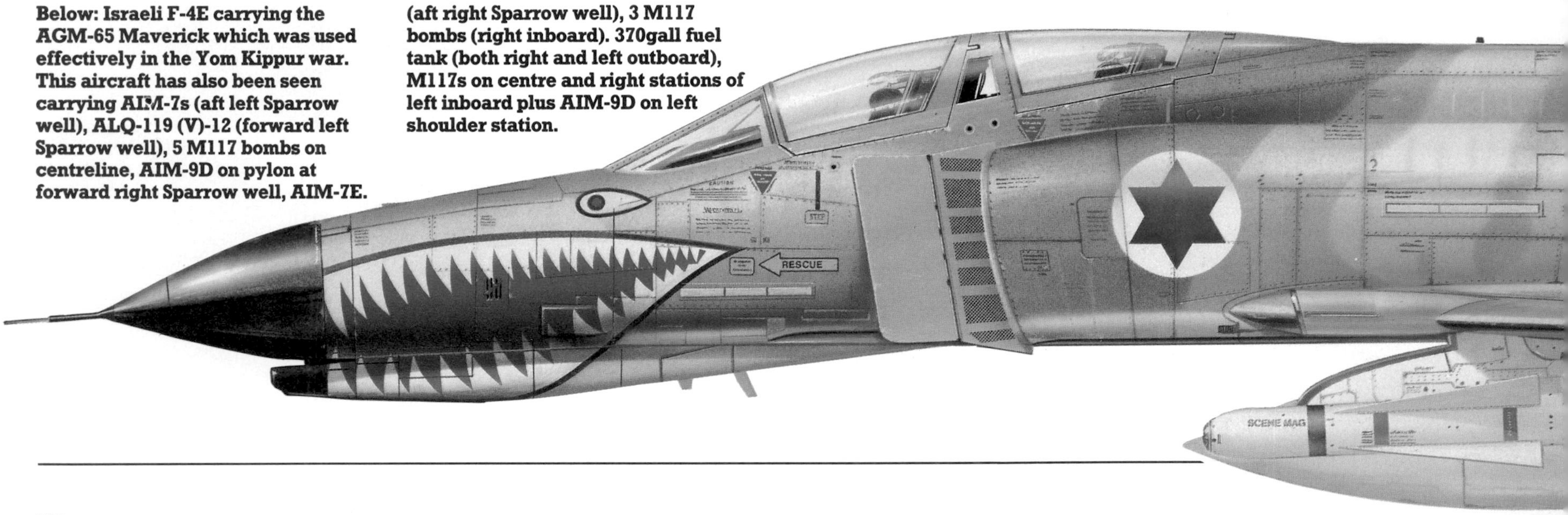

Above: A Luftwaffe F-4F of JaboG 36 taxies in at Rheine-Hopsten. The F-4F is a simpler, cheaper version of the F-4E. Luftwaffe also operates RF-4Es.

Above: An ex-US Air Force F-4E of the Air Force of the Arab Republic of Egypt, based at Cairo West, in June 1980.

Below: Spanish Air Force C12-23 (F-4C) interceptor of Escuadron 121 being readied for take-off from Torrejon.

Below: F-4E of the Turkish Air Force. By August 1984, Phantoms completed 10 years of service in Turkey, which also operates RF-4Es.

formed was the 301st *Hikotai*, at Hyakuri on July 1, 1973. Others followed over the next five years; 302nd *Hikotai* at Chitose, 303rd at Komatsu, 304th at Tsuiki and 305th at Naha, Okinawa. In addition, 14 St. Louis-built RF-4Es are operated out of Hyakuri by the 501st *Hikotai*, which belongs to the *Teisatsu Koku-tai* (Tactical Reconnaissance Group). Although strictly speaking F-4Es, Japanese Phantoms were often referred to as F-4EJs.

Greece
The *Helleniki Aeroporia* received its first Phantoms in March 1974. About 56 F-4Es and six RF-4Es have been delivered. the F-4Es are operated from Andravidha by the 117th *Pterige* (wing) which is made up of the 338th and 339th *Mira* (squadrons). The RF-4Es are believed to be operated out of Larissa by the 348th *Mira*.

Turkey
Turk Hava Kuvvetleri received its first Phantoms on August 30, 1974. It is believed that over 100 F-4Es and RF-4Es have been delivered at the time of writing, and it is known that No. 113 Squadron at Eskisehir and No. 162 Squadron at Bandirma both operate the type.

Egypt
The most recent Phantom user, the Air Force of the Arab Republic of Egypt, took delivery of 34 ex-USAF F-4Es during 1979. Air crews were given a crash course (no pun intended) in the USA, but ground crews received no training at all. Not surprisingly, a year later unserviceability reached a horrendous 75 per cent. Currently based at Cairo West, Egypt's remaining Phantoms may be procured by Turkey.

F-4 deployment shrinking
The once widespread United States Phantom presence has shrunk appreciably with the arrival of new aircraft types. At sea the F-14 Tomcat has taken over the lion's share of the fleet defence role, and the F/A-18 Hornet will make further inroads into the number of USN and USMC Phantoms deployed. USAF Phantom units are also much thinner on the ground.

In England, only the USAF 10th TRW remains at Alconbury, where they often unwittingly act as practice targets for marauding RAF Jaguars when they are on finals. The 48th TFW at Lakenheath now operates F-111s and the 81st TFW at Woodbridge flies A-10s. Phantom units based in West Germany were the 36th TFW at Bitberg, 50th TFW at Hahn, 52nd TFW at Spangdahlem, 86th TFW at Ramstein, and 26th TRW at Zweibrucken. Many of these units have re-equipped with F-15 Eagles and F-16 Fighting Falcons, and only the 52nd TFW, 86th TFW and 26th TRW retain the Phantom. The 32nd TFS at Soesterburg in Holland now flies F-15s, and the 401st TFW had F-16s. The only other USAF Phantom unit based in Europe is 57 FIS at Keflavik in Iceland.

Nor are things much different on the other side of the world. No more Phantoms are seen flying over Vietnam and Thailand. The 43rd TFS at Elmendorf, Alaska, has F-15s, as has the 18th TFW at Kadena AB, Okinawa, while the Wolfpack, the 8th TFW, based at Kunsan in Korea, now flies F-16s. For the moment Phantoms bearing the white star are still active with 154th FIG at Hickam Field, Oahu, and 3rd TFW at Clarke Field in the Philippines, while a few remain with the 51st Composite Wing in Korea.

Extending Phantom service
Plans to re-engine and otherwise improve many F-4s in foreign service (and perhaps some in USAF service, too) are discussed elsewhere in this book; there have also been suggestions that Phantoms which are gradually phased out of USAF service could be upgraded and sold to other air arms.

Left: The Hellenic Air Force has operated F-4Es for over 10 years. This picture of a 117 Wing Phantom in pristine condition was taken in May 1974. Greece also flies RF-4Es.

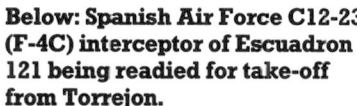

Glossary and abbreviations

AAA Anti-aircraft artillery
AIM- US designation for air-to-air missiles
AFB Air Force Base
Afterburner Device for boosting the thrust of a turbojet or turbofan by burning additional fuel in the efflux
AGM- US designation for air-to-surface missiles
AH-1 US Bureau of Aeronautics designation for mid-1950s twin J79 attack design
Algorithm Mathematical process for achieving a desired result
ALR- US designation for a radar-warning receiver
AMRAAM Advanced Medium-Range Air-to-Air Missile
Analogue Electronic system in which quantities are represented by electrical signals of variable characteristics, i.e. by electrical analogues
ANG Air National Guard
Anhedral Downward slope of a wing from root to tip
AOA Angle of attack
ASRAAM Advanced Short-Range Air-to-Air Missile
APG- US designation for nose-mounted fighter radar
APQ- US designation for jamming system
Aspect ratio Ratio of the span of a wing to its chord
AWG- US designation for a radar-based fire-control system
Boundary layer Layer of disturbed air which lies between the skin of a fast-moving airframe and the normal airflow
BLC Boundary-layer control—a system of blowing air over an aerodynamic surface to increase lift
Bypass ratio Ratio of the total airflow through a turbofan engine to that passing through the core section
Camber Curvature of the centreline of a wing aerofoil
CAP Combat air patrol (see also MIGCAP and TARCAP)
CCV Control-configured vehicle
c.g. Centre of gravity
Chord Imaginary line connecting the leading and trailing edge of a wing or other aerodynamic surface
Continuous-rod warhead Missile warhead which at point of explosion releases a large expanding metal ring designed to damage aircraft structure—more efficient at high altitude than a simple blast warhead
CRT Cathode-ray tube
DARPA Defense Advanced Research Projects Agency
dB Decibel (unit of gain or attenuation)
Digital Electronic system in which quantities are as on/off signals coded to represent numbers
Dihedral Upward slope of a wing from root to tip
DLGW Deck landing gross weight
ECM Electric countermeasures
E/F-band Radar frequencies from 2 to 4 GHz
Envelope Engineering term for the area defined by a series of limits
EOGB Electro-optical glide bomb
Esc see Escadrille and Escuadron
EW Electronic warfare
FBW Fly-by-wire (term for electrically signalled flight-control systems)
FLIR Forward-looking infra-red
F3H-G Original designation of Phantom design
F4H-1 Pre-1962 designation for Phantom
F-110 Early USAF designation for F-4C
g unit of acceleration
GAO General Accounting Office (an investigative branch of the US Congress)
GE General Electric
G/H band Radar frequencies from 4 to 8 GHz
GHz GigaHertz (Hertz × 1,000,000,000)
Heat shot Launch of a heat-seeking missile
HF High frequency
HUD Head-up display
Hz Hertz (unit of frequency)
IDFAF Israel Defence Force Air Force
IFF Identification Friend or Foe
IFR Instrument flight rules
IIR Imaging infra-red
I/J-band Radar frequencies from 8 to 12 GHz
INAS Inertial navigation and attack system
IOC Initial operating capability
IR infra-red
Iron bomb conventional free-falling high-explosive bomb
JTIDS Joint Tactical Information Distribution System
kHz kiloHertz (Hertz × 1,000)
kT Kiloton
Ku-band Radar frequencies from 12 to 18 GHz
LRU Line-replacable unit
Mach Unit equal to the speed of sound
MHz MegaHertz (Hz × 1,000,000)
MIGCAP MiG Combat Air Patrol
Monopulse Radar system able to measure range and bearing from a single returned pulse
MW Megawatt
Nav/attack navigation and attack (e.g. 'nav/attack system')
OCU Operational Conversion Unit
Pickle To release ordnance
Pipper Aiming mark in a gunsight or HUD
P&W Pratt & Whitney
PPI Plan position indicator
PRF Pulse repetition frequency
Proximity fuze Fuze which detonates if the target passes within a pre-set distance
Ps Engineering abbreviation for specific excess power
PSP Programmable signal processor
Pylon Load bearing structure often used to mate external stores such as drop tanks or ordnance to a hardpoint
Raster scan Method of building up a TV-style image on a CRT by scanning the image in a series of lines
R&D Research and development
Red Crown US Navy radar-equipped spotter ship based in Gulf of Tonkin during Vietnam War
RHAWS Radar homing and warning receiver
RWR Radar-warning receiver
SEAM Sidewinder Expanded Acquisition Mode
Semi-active homing Homing system which relies on detecting energy reflected from a target illuminated by an external source of radar or laser energy
s.f.c Specific fuel consumption (unit of fuel consumed per unit of thrust per hour)
Shaft Rotating assembly within a turbojet or turbofan engine which carries part or all of the compressor and turbine
Slat Small aerodynamic surface placed just ahead of a wing or tailplane, with a small gap between the two
Smart bomb free-falling bomb with built-in guidance system
Software One or more programmes for a computer
Solid-state Transistorised
Spar Load-bearing component running along the length of a wing
Special store/bomb Official terminology for a nuclear weapon
Spool Alternative designation for a shaft
Synthetic-aperture Radar technique by which a small antenna on a moving vehicle may simulate a larger unit in terms of resolution
TAC Tactical Air Command
TARCAP Target combat air patrol
TER Triple ejector rack
TFG Tactical Fighter Group
TFS Tactical Fighter Squadron
TFTS Tactical Fighter Training Squadron
TFW Tactical Fighter Wing
TISEO Target identification system—electro-optical
Trap Deck landing
Turbofan Engine in which part of the airflow from the compressor bypasses the core (hot section)
TWT Travelling-wave tube (power source used in many modern radar)
UHF Ultra-high frequency
USAF United States Air Force
USN United States Navy
USMC United States Marine Corps
VHF Very high frequency
VTAS Visual target acquisition system
Wild Weasel Aircraft equipped to home in onto and attack hostile radars
Wing loading Weight of an aircraft divided by the wing area
X-band Obsolescent designation for a range of frequencies from 8 to 12 GHz

Specifications

The Phantom changed remarkably little during its development life. Wingspan and wing area remained unchanged at 38.4ft (11.71m) and 530sq ft (49.26sq m) respectively, and height for all versions is 16ft 3in (4.96m). The empty weight rose from 28,000lb (12,700kg) to 30,000lb (13,608kg). All models could carry a maximum external load of 16,000lb (7,258kg). The variety of combinations of external loads render performance figures meaningless unless very heavily qualified. Suffice it to say that in clean condition, all models can exceed mach 2.10, have a combat ceiling of around 55,000ft (16,768m), a combat radius of more than 500 miles (805km), and an initial climb rate of between 28,000 and 32,000ft per minute (8,527 to 9,756m per min). But no combat Phantom ever has, nor ever will, go to war in a clean condition.

Version		A	B	RF-4B	C	RF-4C	D	E	RF-4E	F	G	J	K	M	N	S
Length	ft	58.2	58.2	62.9	58.2	62.9	58.2	63.0	63.0	63.0	63.0	58.2	57.6	58.9	58.2	58.2
	(Metres)	(17.74)	(17.74)	(19.18)	(17.74)	(19.18)	(17.74)	(19.21)	(19.21)	(19.21)	(19.21)	(17.74)	(17.56)	(17.96)	(17.74)	(17.74)
Weights	Empty lb	28,000[1]	28,000[1]	28,546	28,827	28,292	28,976	29,535	28,500[1]	31,000[1]		28,000[1]	30,000[1]	31,000[1]	28,000[1]	28,000[1]
	(kg)	(12,700)[1]	(12,700)[1]	(12,948)	(13,076)	(12,833)	(13,143)	(13,397)	(12,928)[1]	(14,061)[1]		(12,700)[1]	(13,608)[1]	(14,061)[1]	(12,700)[1]	(12,700)[1]
	Max. Take-off lb		54,600	54,600	59,689	58,000[2]	59,247	61,795	57,320	60,630		58,000[2]	58,000[2]	58,000[2]		
	(kg)		(24,766)	(24,766)	(27,075)	(26,309)[2]	(26,874)	(28,030)	(26,000)	(27,502)		(26,309)[2]	(26,309)[2]	(26,309)[2]		
Engines	Type	J79-2A	J79-8	J79-8	J79-15	J79-15	J79-15	J79-17	J79-17	J79-17	J79-17	J79-10	Spey 202	Spey 203	J79-18	J79-10
	Sea level static thrust-max. lb	16,150	17,000	17,000	17,000	17,000	17,000	17,900	17,900	17,900	17,900	17,900	20,515	20,515	17,000	17,900
	(kg)	(7,326)	(7,711)	(7,711)	(7,711)	(7,711)	(7,711)	(8,119)	(8,119)	(8,119)	(8,119)	(8,119)	(9,306)	(9,306)	(7,711)	(8,119)
	Sea level static thrust-mil lb	10,350	10,900	10,900	10,900	10,900	10,900	11,870	11,870	11,870	11,870	11,870	12,250	12,250	10,900	11,870
	(kg)	(4,695)	(4,944)	(4,944)	(4,944)	(4,944)	(4,944)	(5,384)	(5,384)	(5,384)	(5,384)	(5,384)	(5,557)	(5,557)	(4,944)	(5,384)
Air-to-air weapons (alternatives and combinations—8 missiles maximum)																
	Sparrow	4 to 6	4 to 6	—	4	—	4	4	—	—	2	4	4	4	4	4
	Sidewinder	—	4	—	4	—	4	4	—	4	4	4	4	4	4	4
	Shafrir (Israeli)	—	—	—	—	—	—	4	—	—	—	—	—	—	—	—
	Skyflash (RAF)	—	—	—	—	—	—	—	—	—	—	—	4	4	—	—
	Falcon	—	—	—	4	—	4	—	—	—	—	—	—	—	—	—
	Gun	—	Pod	—	Pod	—	Pod	M61-A1	—	M61-A1	—	Pod	Pod	Pod	Pod	Pod
Avionics	Fire control/radar	APQ-50	APQ-72	APQ-99	APQ-100	APQ-99	APQ-109	APQ-120	APQ-120	APQ-120[3]	APQ-120	AWG-10	AWG-11	AWG-12	AWG-10	AWG-10A
	Bombing system	AJB-3	AJB-3A	—	AJB-7	—	AJB-7	AJB-7	Varies		APR-38	AJB-7	AJB-7		AJB-7	AJB-7
	Optical sight	Fixed	Fixed	—	Fixed	—	ASG-22	ASG-26	with		APQ-30	Fixed	Fixed	LCOSS		
	INS	—	—	ASN-56	ASN-48	ASN-56	ASN-63	ASN-63	user		ASN-63	ASN-63		Ferranti		
	Nav. computer	ASN-39	ASN-39	ASN-46A	ASN46	ASN-46A	ASN-46A	ASN-46A	nation		ASN-46A	ASN-46A		INAS		
	Radar warning	—	APR-27	APR-27	APR-25/26	APR-25/26	APS-107	APR-36/37			APR-38	APR-32			APR-43	APR-43

Note: [1]Approximate. [2]Design load. [3]Simplified.

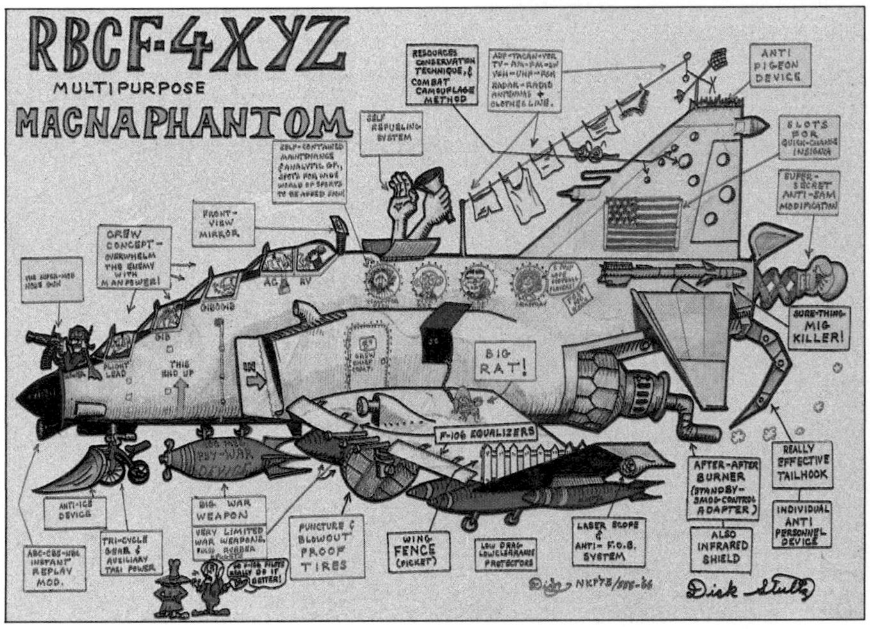

Chapter 10

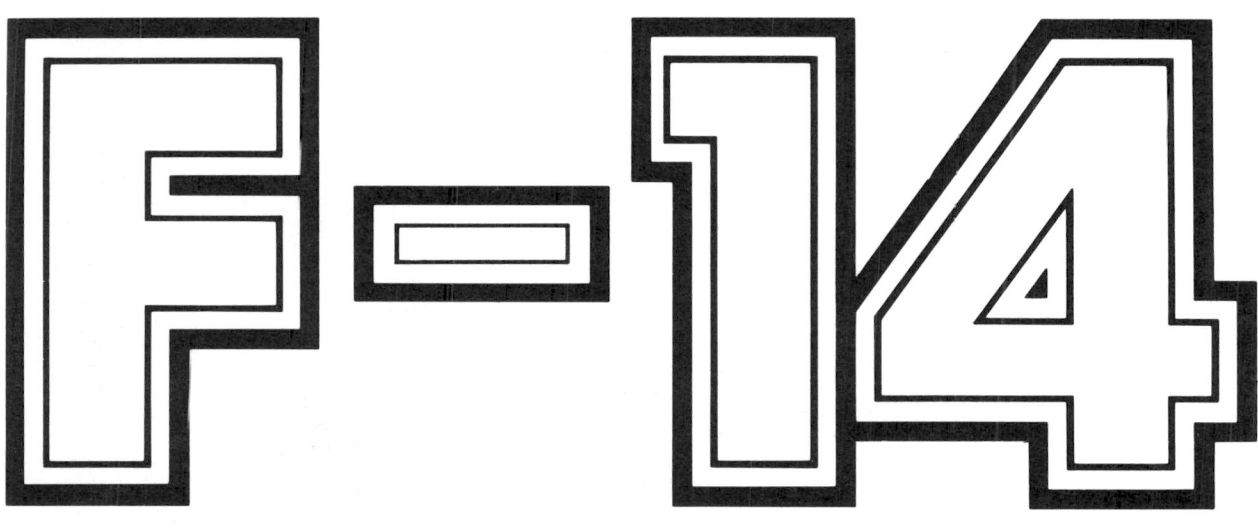

F-14

TOMCAT

Mike Spick

F-14 Tomcat

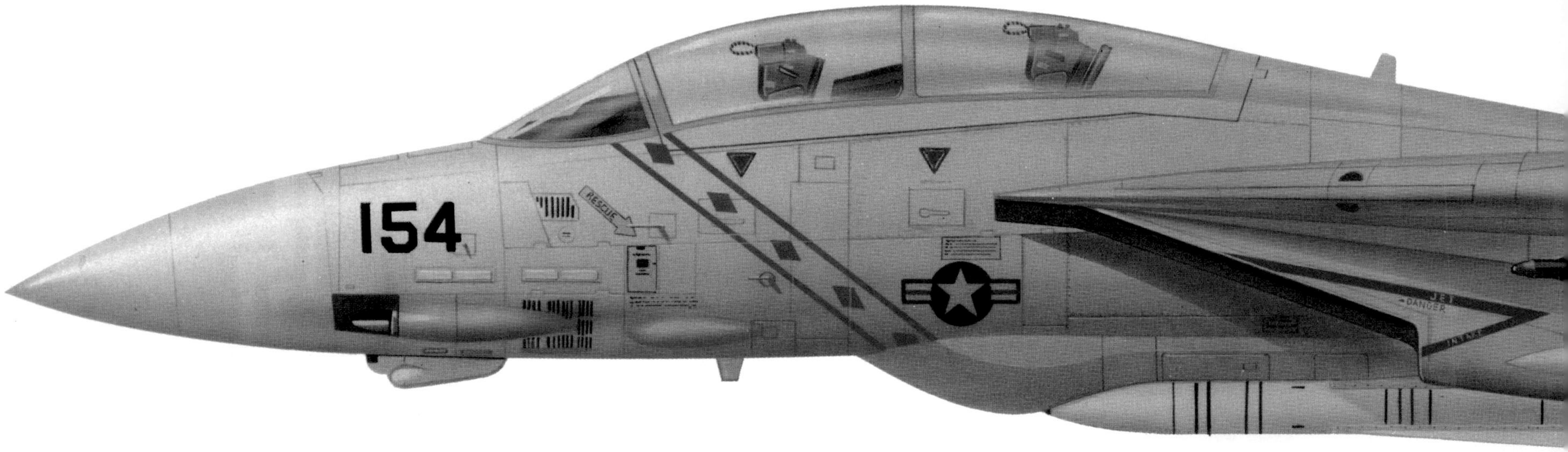

Contents

Acknowledgements

The author and editor would like to thank all those who have contributed information and pictures to this chapter. Photograph sources are credited at the beginning of the book, but particular thanks are due to Robert W. Kress, Lois Lovisolo, Brian Salisbury and H. J. Schonenberg of Grumman Aerospace Corporation; Dwight E. Weber of the General Electric Company Aircraft Engine Business Group; Kearney Bothwell of Hughes Aircraft Company Radar Systems Group; Marty J. Isham; Cdr Erwin Sharp, Lt Cdr Paul Williamson, Roy A. Grossnick and Anna C. Urband of the US Navy; and the 527th Aggressor Squadron, US Air Force.

Author

Mike Spick was born in London less than three weeks before the Spitfire made its maiden flight. Educated at Churchers College, Petersfield, he later entered the construction industry and carried out considerable work on RAF airfields. An interest in wargaming led him to a close study of air warfare and a highly successful first book, *Air Battles in Miniature* (Patrick Stephens, 1978). His subsequent work includes a historical study of the evolution of air combat tactics, *Fighter Pilot Tactics* (Patrick Stephens, 1983), and co-authorship of two previous Salamander books, *Modern Air Combat* (with Bill Gunston, 1983), and earlier chapters in this book, *F/A-18 Hornet*, *B-1B* and *F-4 Phantom II* (with Doug Richardson).

Introduction

The aircraft carrier has a vital part to play both in keeping the peace and in time of war. Seven-tenths of our planet is covered by salt water, the greater part of which is a neutral area in terms of air power. This is where the aircraft carrier comes into its own, as wherever it goes it converts roughly half a million square miles of surrounding air space into a friendly air defence zone, which a potential assailant must penetrate.

The huge United States Navy carriers are equipped with well balanced Air Wings which typically consist of two squadrons of fighters, two of attack aircraft and one of all-weather attack aircraft, supported by four tankers, four airborne early warning and four electronic warfare aircraft, plus a sizable complement of fixed and rotary wing anti-submarine machines. They are therefore capable of packing an enormous punch, both in offence and defence – and by the same token, they are prime targets for an enemy.

The vulnerability of land-based airfields is a matter of extreme concern to the military. Some degree of protection against conventional attack can be given to airfields by dispersal, coupled with hardened shelters, but no such alternative exists for an aircraft carrier, which perforce must cram over ninety aircraft, with their fuel, munitions and servicing requirements, into the smallest usable volume. In comparison with an airfield, a carrier can afford to absorb very little damage. Its survival depends on its own integral air defences and those of its accompanying ships, and the key is defence in depth: an attacking force must be detected, intercepted, and destroyed as far away as possible, so that if the first interception is only partially successful there is still time and space to effect another. But for this to work, a truly exceptional aircraft/detection system/weapon combination is needed. The F-14 Tomcat/Hughes AWG-9/AIM-54 Phoenix is that combination.

Like all major defence programmes, the Tomcat has had its share of detractors, mainly on the grounds of cost. It has had some problems, mainly with the engines, but a growth capability was built in from the outset, and the Tomcat looks set to remain in service into the next millenium.

Development

In March 1972 Admiral Elmo R. Zumwalt, Jr., Chief of Naval Operations, outlined the importance of the F-14 to the US Navy: "The F-14 weapon system is one of the highest-priority items in the Navy budget . . . It will be capable of tracking and evaluating multiple targets and of controlling up to six independent Phoenix missiles simultaneously. This multiple-shot capability is precisely what the Navy must possess if it is to survive and operate forces in the face of enemy air and missile concentrations. The increase in effectiveness over the single-shot F-4, or any single-shot fighter, is more than 4:1 when outnumbered by even moderately high-performance threats."

Above: Three of the 12 F-14 prototypes in flight. BuAer 157981 (nearest camera) demonstrates minimum sweep, 157983 (centre) has wings swept to 45deg, and 157991, the renumbered prototype 1X, has its wings fully swept.

Historical perspective shows that wars are won by offensive action, but one of the cardinal principles of war is that the base of such action must be secure enough to allow the striking forces freedom of action. Total security is of course impossible, and in the limited space of an aircraft carrier a balance between offensive and defensive forces must be struck.

Defence against air attack has traditionally been a process of attrition, breaking up attacks and degrading their effectiveness while striving to inflict unacceptable casualties on the attackers. Today, the defences form two layers: point defence, consisting of surface-to-air missiles (SAMs) and guns, plus fighters operating outside the SAM zone. Any attempt to operate defending fighters in the SAM zone is bound to lead to a degradation of the effectiveness of both, so the fighters must operate away from the carrier, but within the range of an effective detection and reporting system.

The 1950s saw fundamental advances in military aviation. Aircraft speeds increased greatly, reducing the time available for interception. More sinister still, stand-off weapons began to be developed that could be released at very long distances from the target. The requirement for a fleet air defence interceptor that emerged in 1955 stipulated an aircraft that could launch from the carrier, cruise out to a distance of 250nm (463km), stay on patrol at that radius, intercept and destroy intruders with AIM-7 Sparrow semi-active radar homing (SARH) missiles, then return to the carrier three hours after takeoff. This requirement resulted in the F-4 Phantom, which became operational in 1962.

Having initiated the programme that led to the Phantom, the US Navy immediately looked to the future. The projected threat appeared to be an aircraft that would approach at high speed to within about 200nm (368km) of the fleet, launch cruise missile type guided weapons, and retire to safety. Just one aircraft attacking in this manner would be difficult to counter, but a formation, each armed with two missiles . . . The missiles, once launched, would become the priority targets, but they were small and difficult to acquire on radar.

All in all, the larger, more readily detectable aircraft with its weapons still on board would be in many ways the easier target, but this entailed detection and interception at previously unheard-of distances. Excellent weapon system though the Phantom was, it would have to be in the right place at the right time to even attempt to cope with the problem. A permanent barrier of standing patrols appeared to be the only feasible solution, but with a total carrier complement of two Phantom squadrons (24 aircraft), this was hardly practicable. Something new was needed.

The answer proposed was to let the missiles rather than the interceptor do the work. There was nothing particularly outrageous about the idea; the Bomarc surface-to-air missile was already under development for just this purpose. Initially considered to be a pilotless interceptor (the propulsion test vehicle was given the experimental fighter designation XF-99), Bomarc A had a range of 200nm (370km) and a speed of between Mach 3 and Mach 4. Initial and mid-course guidance was from the ground, and active radar homing was used for the terminal guidance stage. Provided that a suitable missile could be developed, the main requirements for the aircraft were that it should carry a useful number of them, be capable of a long loiter (patrol) time and have excellent target detection and multiple target engagement capability, while at the same time being small enough to fit the lift on an aircraft carrier and light enough to land aboard without wrecking the arrestor gear.

Formal Requests for Proposals (RFPs) were issued in the summer of 1957. Fifteen companies competed for the missile contract, which was won by the Bendix Corporation Systems Division, of Ann Arbor, Michigan, with its AAM-N-10 Eagle proposal. Eagle was a large missile, 16.125ft (4.91m) long and with a launch weight of 1,284lb (852kg). Using tandem stages with solid-fuel motors, its maximum range was 110nm (204km), with a top speed of Mach 4. Westinghouse derived the pulse-Doppler seeker from its DPN-53 developed for the Bomarc B, which gave active homing over the final 10nm (16km), while Grumman was responsible for the airframe and propulsion system integration.

Above: An F-111B prototype equipped with four AIM-54 Phoenix missiles. The underwing missile pylons had to swivel to match the wing sweep, a problem not shared by the Tomcat with its fixed wing-glove pylons.

Below: (From left) Fleet Readiness Manager Emerson Fawkes, DCNO(AIR) Vice Admiral Tom Connolly, Programme Director Mike Pelehach, and Product Manufacturing Director Larry Mead.

The aircraft selected to carry Eagle was the Douglas Model D-766 Missileer, naval designation F6D. With an all-up weight not exceeding 50,000lb (22,680kg), it was to have been powered by two Pratt and Whitney TF-30-P2 unaugmented turbofans. Its high, unswept wing was optimized for economic cruise, and figures released at the time credited it with a maximum speed of Mach 0.8 and an endurance of between four and six hours. A Hughes high power pulse-Doppler and track-while-scan detection and missile control system was fitted. Three Eagles could be carried under each wing, and a further two could be fitted to the lower front fuselage.

The idea of an aircraft optimized to carry the heaviest possible air-to-air armament at the expense of performance and agility was far from new. Early in 1915, Lieutenant Colonel (later Marshal of the Royal Air Force Lord) Trenchard, then commanding 1st Wing, Royal Flying Corps, had recommended the development of a three-seat pusher-propelled fighter to carry two machine gunners. During the 1920s the Italian General Guilio Douhet postulated the use of 'battleplanes' – bombers fitted with extra guns and armour protection instead of a bombload. And in 1943 the US Army Air Forces put theory into practice by converting a handful of Boeing B-17 bombers into YB-40 gunships. For various reasons they were a failure. But the Missileer, with its battery of long-range Eagles, looked to be a feasible proposition for the simple reason that it would vastly outrange any possible opponent.

Interestingly enough, also under study at the same time was a USAF air defence concept codenamed 'Project Aerie'. This took the 'flying battleship' idea a stage further and was to have consisted of Boeing C-135As acting as airborne command centres and armed with no less than 24 Eagles. Project Aerie was stillborn, but the US Navy placed a study contract for the F6D in 1959.

The concept of a fighter that was no more than a slow, unwieldy missile carrier worried many people. Certainly it could fly the basic fleet air defence mission, which was to patrol at about 150nm (275km) out from the carrier at an altitude of 35,000ft (10,700m) while carrying at least six large missiles, detect and track bandits from ultra-long range, then kill them from a distance which rendered the Missileer safe from counter-attack. There were, however, certain disadvantages. Once the Missileer had expended its weapons, its only form of defence lay in flight, and it was comparatively slow – and lacking any self-defence capability, once overhauled, it would be hacked from the sky with relative ease.

Comparisons with the McDonnell Douglas F-4 Phantom, shortly to enter service in the fleet air defence role, were inevitable. The Phantom could not carry Eagle missiles, nor could it remain on station for more than a fraction of the time of the Missileer, but its tremendous rate of climb and Mach 2 capability enabled it to get out on station much faster, and to evade interception with ease once it had expended its missiles. It could also act as an escort fighter for the carrier's attack squadrons, which was totally beyond the capability of the Missileer.

The two horns of the dilemma can be summarized as follows: firstly, could an aircraft carrier, with its limited deck and hangar space, afford the luxury of a single-role aircraft, however capable it was in that role? Secondly, could the Navy afford to be without the undoubted interception capability of the Missileer/

Above: Grumman's response to the Navy's VFX Request for Proposals ran to a massive 37 volumes which occupied 54 binders, including a 42-page guide. Mike Pelehach (left) and President Llew Evans (in jacket) have something to smile about.

Below: The Tomcat as it nearly was – a mock-up of design 303E, submitted by Grumman in response to the Navy's VFX specification. In this rare picture, the single dorsal fin and one of the two ventral folding fins are clearly visible. The ventral folding fins would almost certainly have hampered quick engine changes.

Eagle combination? The uncertainty, generated in part by the lack of a historical precedent, lingered on until December 1960, when Thomas S. Gates, Jr., Secretary of Defense in the outgoing Eisenhower Administration, cancelled the Missileer. The flying battleship concept was once more put back on the shelf, although the Eagle and the weapon control system were allowed to continue for a while longer.

The administration of President John F. Kennedy took office on January 20, 1961, bringing with it a new Defense Secretary, Robert S. McNamara, and a new buzz-word, commonality. The idea of commonality had been around the DoD for a good few years, but its practical application was difficult. As applied to aircraft procurement, it implied an all-singing, all-dancing aeroplane that could perform many roles with equal facility, for both Air Force and Navy.

The advantage of such a multi-role machine was largely financial. The ability to carry out interception, air superiority, battlefield support, interdiction and reconnaissance missions, and to operate with equal ease from aircraft carriers or land bases, was bound to lead to large production runs, with attendant low unit costs. Spares, support, and training would also be greatly simplified. In other words, it meant either cheaper aeroplanes, or more aeroplanes for a fixed sum. The real irony was the fact that the only aircraft type ever to approach these goals, the Phantom, was entering service at precisely that moment.

Under the Kennedy administration, the new ideas and vigorous approach of comparatively young men was supposed to revitalize the nation, sweeping aside the caution of the older generation and the entrenched bureaucracy, compensating for experience with innovation and energy. McNamara was of this new breed. As a Vice-President of the Ford Motor Company, he had reorganized and streamlined the ailing industrial giant and generally knocked it into shape. Now he prepared to give the DoD the same treatment.

Defence costs generally defy comprehension; there are so many noughts as to make the figures meaningless. To McNamara, the scope for savings appeared almost limitless and commonality appeared to be the tool for the purpose, so one of his first acts was to examine the major new programmes.

It so happened that there were two major requirements for the near future. The first was the USAF specification SOR-183, issued in June 1960 and calling for a tactical strike fighter, later referred to as the TFX. The specification was demanding, including a low-level speed of Mach 1.2, a high-level speed of Mach 2.5, a radius of action with internal weapons of 800nm (1,475km), good short-field performance, and a ferry range sufficient to cross the Atlantic unrefuelled. The second requirement was, as we have seen, for a fleet air defence fighter (FADF) to fill the slot left vacant by the Missileer cancellation.

Meanwhile, the National Aeronautics and Space Administration (NASA) had been conducting studies in variable geometry. In mid-1959 they briefed

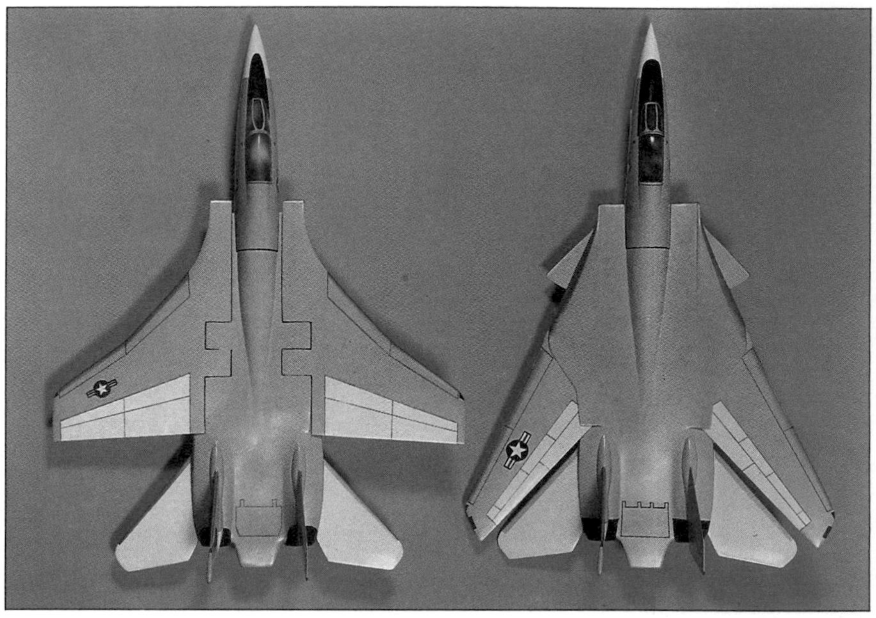

Above: Escalating costs caused by rocketing inflation forced radical alternatives to be considered, among them these two single-seat designs. The model on the right is still recognizable as a Tomcat and at this stage retains the glove vanes, while that on the left not only has a fixed wing, but also features narrower engine intakes, a revised canopy and more closely spaced fins.

Design 303-60

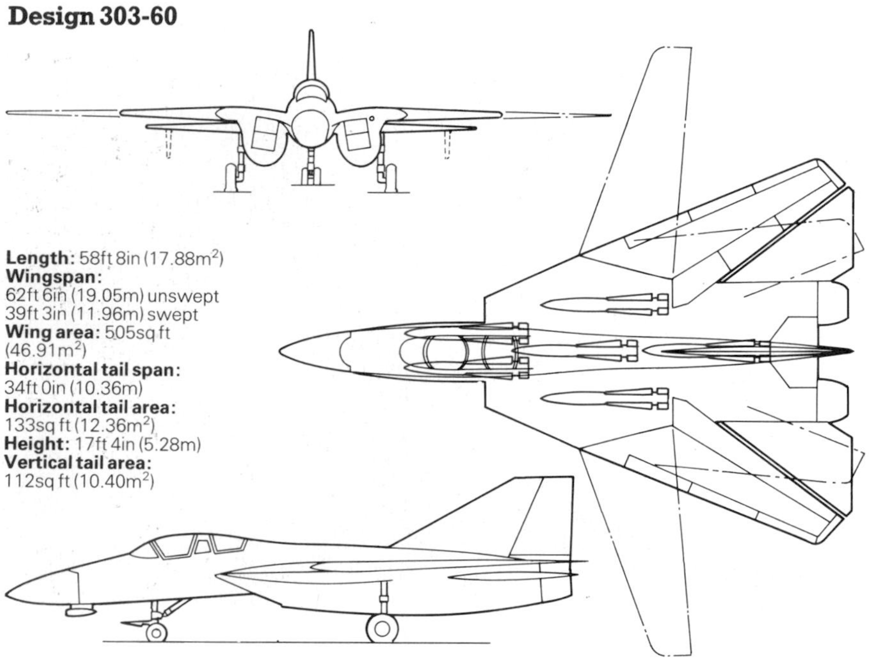

Length: 58ft 8in (17.88m^2)
Wingspan:
62ft 6in (19.05m) unswept
39ft 3in (11.96m) swept
Wing area: 505sq ft (46.91m^2)
Horizontal tail span: 34ft 0in (10.36m)
Horizontal tail area: 133sq ft (12.36m^2)
Height: 17ft 4in (5.28m)
Vertical tail area: 112sq ft (10.40m^2)

Design 303C

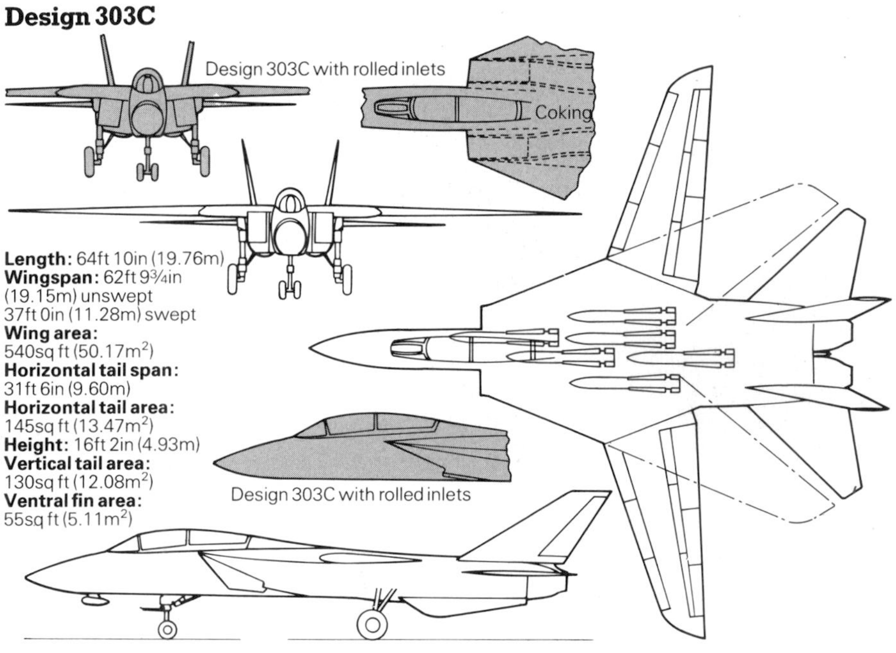

Length: 64ft 10in (19.76m)
Wingspan: 62ft 9¾in (19.15m) unswept
37ft 0in (11.28m) swept
Wing area: 540sq ft (50.17m^2)
Horizontal tail span: 31ft 6in (9.60m)
Horizontal tail area: 145sq ft (13.47m^2)
Height: 16ft 2in (4.93m)
Vertical tail area: 130sq ft (12.08m^2)
Ventral fin area: 55sq ft (5.11m^2)

Design 303E

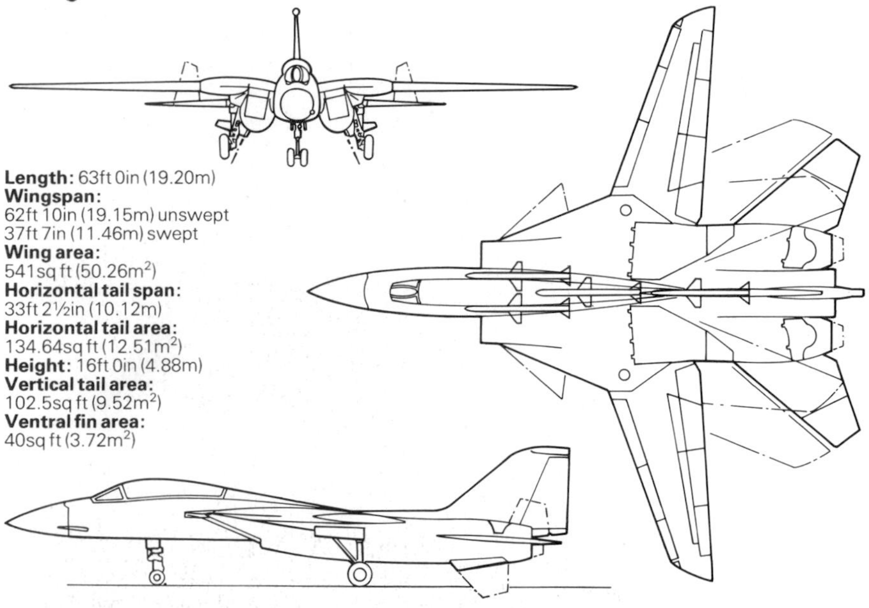

Length: 63ft 0in (19.20m)
Wingspan:
62ft 10in (19.15m) unswept
37ft 7in (11.46m) swept
Wing area: 541sq ft (50.26m^2)
Horizontal tail span: 33ft 2½in (10.12m)
Horizontal tail area: 134.64sq ft (12.51m^2)
Height: 16ft 0in (4.88m)
Vertical tail area: 102.5sq ft (9.52m^2)
Ventral fin area: 40sq ft (3.72m^2)

Design 303D

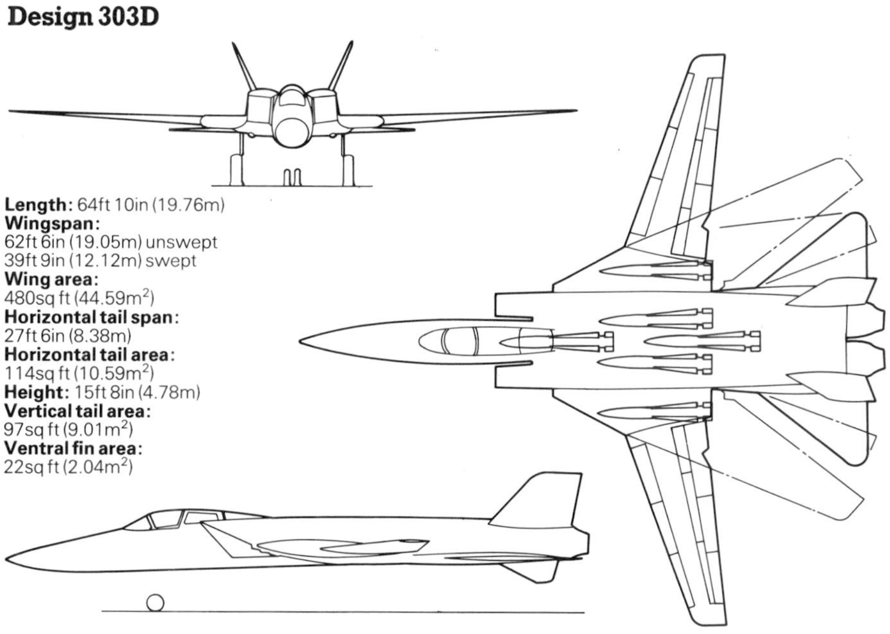

Length: 64ft 10in (19.76m)
Wingspan:
62ft 6in (19.05m) unswept
39ft 9in (12.12m) swept
Wing area: 480sq ft (44.59m^2)
Horizontal tail span: 27ft 6in (8.38m)
Horizontal tail area: 114sq ft (10.59m^2)
Height: 15ft 8in (4.78m)
Vertical tail area: 97sq ft (9.01m^2)
Ventral fin area: 22sq ft (2.04m^2)

Top: Design 303-60 was an assembly of reasonable goals rather than a mature design. A very high degree of oversweep was considered which entailed the outboard portions of the tailerons folding downwards.

Above: Design 303E emerged through 303A and B. Radical changes include the canopy, dorsal fin and taileron shape, and the addition of glove vanes and folding ventral fins. Main armament was to be four Sparrows.

Top: Design 303C featured twin fins and an orthodox submerged engine layout. A modification of this proposal envisaged the use of inlets rolled to the sides and intakes trunked inward in a 'coked', or area-ruled, fuselage.

Above: Design 303D combined a low-set variable-sweep wing with canted twin fins and submerged engines. Wind tunnel tests soon established that it would have been inferior to Design 303E in almost all areas.

senior US Navy officials on state-of-the-art variable-sweep configuration technology, and, applying it to a hypothetical naval fighter of the same weight as the proposed Missileer, demonstrated a performance potential sufficient to outclass any project then under consideration. NASA then repeated the exercise for the staff of USAF Tactical Air Command, but related to the then still only partially formulated SOR-183 requirement. Both Navy and Air Force issued study contracts to industry.

This was the situation when McNamara became Defense Secretary. It appeared to him that the two sets of requirements had much in common. The load-carrying ability of the TFX could be equated with the heavy load of large AAMs for the FADF, while the long ferry range of the TFX would match the extended patrol time of the Navy fighter. Both needed high speed at all altitudes, and the short-field performance of the TFX tallied with a slow carrier approach speed. The one really important point overlooked was that SOR-183 called for an attack aircraft: TFX should really have been TAX.

Convinced that a single type of tactical fighter could do both jobs, McNamara issued a formal recommendation on February 14, 1961, that both the Air Force and the Navy study a single basic design, to be developed in two versions to meet the needs of both services, but with maximum commonality. Naturally there were objections. Both requirements could be met by a twin-engined, two-seat swing-wing design, but there the resemblance ended, and on August 22, 1961, McNamara was told that a compromise aircraft capable of fulfilling both missions was not technically feasible. He reacted with a directive that it would be done, even going so far as to delineate certain design aspects, and instructed the Air Force to proceed with the development. With his Ford Motors background in mind, one cannot help but recall the saying attributed to the late Henry Ford: "You can have any colour you want so long as it's black!"

Naval TFX

After protracted hassles, General Dynamics was awarded the TFX contract in December 1962, with Grumman as principal subcontractor. Grumman, with a string of successful carrier fighters to its credit, and also previous swing-wing experience with the XF10F Jaguar, was to take primary responsibility for the development of the naval version. The Air Force variant was designated the F-111A, that for the Navy F-111B, and the two aircraft retained a high degree of commonality – the principal reason why the General Dynamics proposal had been accepted. The main difference between the F-111A and B was one of length, which in the naval version had to be held down to a size that could be accommodated by the carrier lifts.

The weapon system naturally varied according to the role, and the weapon control system developed for the Missileer, refined and designated AWG-9, was to be fitted to the F-111B. Meanwhile, the Eagle missile had been cancelled in what appears to have been part of the commonality purge. The Navy opposed this decision violently, and the technology was transferred from Bendix to Hughes, who began developing their own long-range missile, the AIM-54 Phoenix. The advantages of the same contractor developing both the missile and the detection/guidance/launch system were obvious, and Phoenix was the weapon selected for the new fleet air defence fighter.

The F-111B was in trouble from the outset. The concept of commonality dictated that the special needs of carrier operations, such as the ability to withstand repeated stresses of catapult launches and arrested landings, be incorporated into the basic design. This ensured a heavy aeroplane from the outset, and as development proceeded, so the weight increased. As if this were not enough, severe compressor stalls were experienced with the engines.

The first flight of the F-111B took place on May 18, 1965, and NPE 1 (Naval Preliminary Evaluation) was held during the following October. The findings were uniformly unfavourable, the F-111B proving inferior to the F-4 in almost every department. The windshield angle caused a serious reflection problem, and this, coupled with a high angle of attack (AOA) on the approach, caused pilots to lose sight of the carrier. Carrier landings are exciting enough without such problems. Further problems were experienced both with propulsion and in manoeuvrability, especially at supersonic speeds. It rapidly became obvious that despite the F prefix, the F-111B was not and never would be a fighter, nor was it suited for carrier operations.

Continued attempts to remedy the deficiencies were made, but despite Grumman's best efforts the problems, particularly that of excess weight, proved intractable. In May 1968 Congress refused further funding for the project. Work was halted in July and the contract officially terminated in December of that year. Ten years of effort had left the Navy no nearer acquiring the fighter it wanted. Or so it seemed.

Spurred on by the disastrous NPE 1 in October 1965, the Navy funded Grumman to prepare advanced fighter studies. Preliminary work began in January 1966, with more than 6,000 configurations being studied, and a process of elimination reduced these to a handful collec-

Design 303F

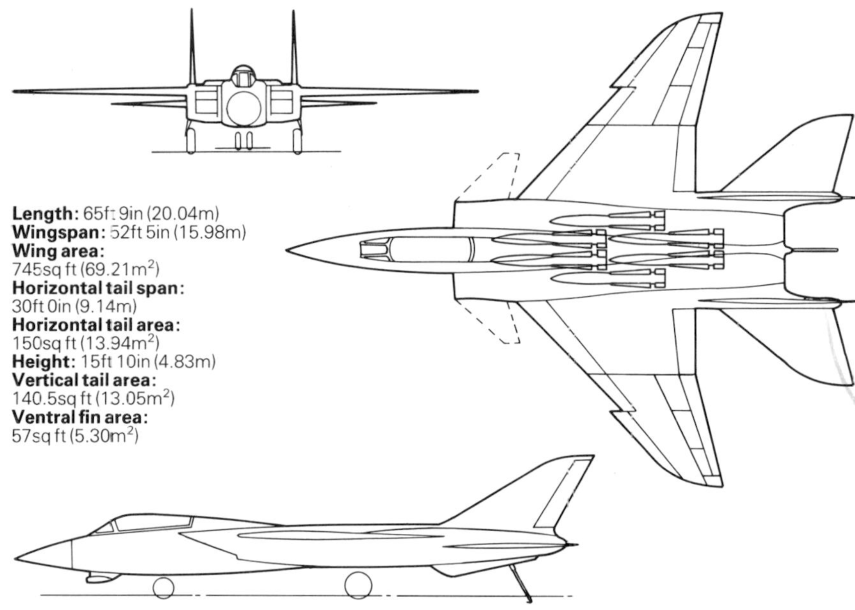

Length: 65ft 9in (20.04m)
Wingspan: 52ft 5in (15.98m)
Wing area: 745sq ft (69.21m²)
Horizontal tail span: 30ft 0in (9.14m)
Horizontal tail area: 150sq ft (13.94m²)
Height: 15ft 10in (4.83m)
Vertical tail area: 140.5sq ft (13.05m²)
Ventral fin area: 57sq ft (5.30m²)

Design 303G

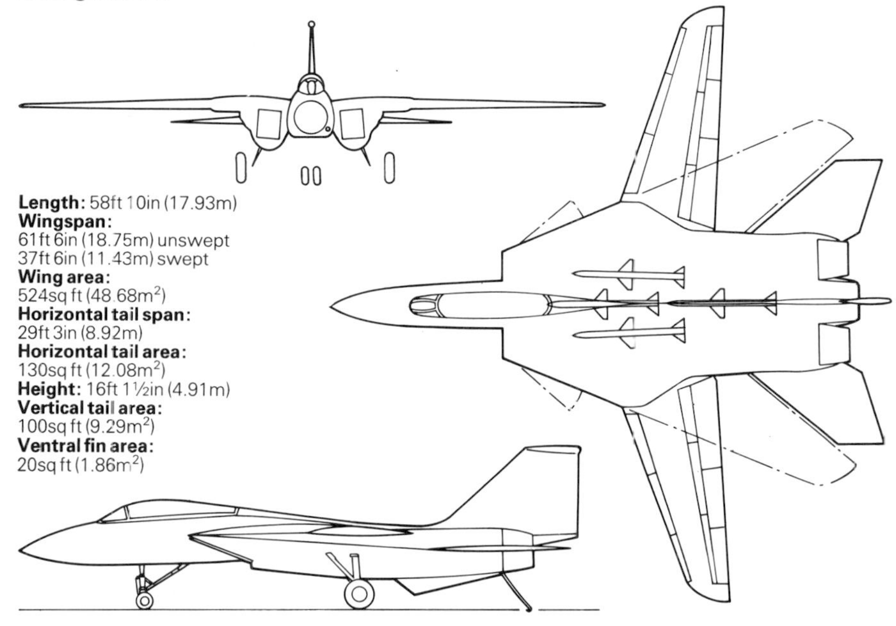

Length: 58ft 10in (17.93m)
Wingspan: 61ft 6in (18.75m) unswept
37ft 6in (11.43m) swept
Wing area: 524sq ft (48.68m²)
Horizontal tail span: 29ft 3in (8.92m)
Horizontal tail area: 130sq ft (12.08m²)
Height: 16ft 1½in (4.91m)
Vertical tail area: 100sq ft (9.29m²)
Ventral fin area: 20sq ft (1.86m²)

Top: Design 303F was a fixed-wing, submerged-engine proposal which, interestingly for 1968, considered the use of canard foreplanes. It was developed primarily to prove the advantages of variable sweep.

Above: Design 303G was studied to determine the extent to which the Phoenix requirement penalized the 303E as a fighter. The result was a smaller and lighter aircraft, but performance gains were marginal.

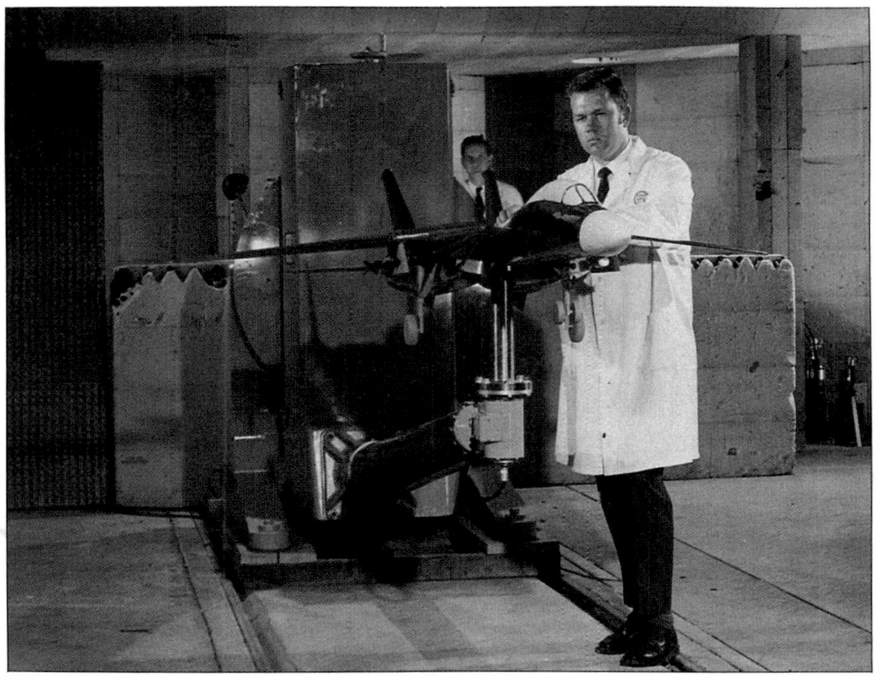

Above: A scale model of the Tomcat, now in its final form, is prepared for low-speed wind tunnel testing. Many thousands of hours of tests with models ranging from 1/7 to 1/48 scale were carried out.

Below: A 1/48 scale supersonic test model with a typical combat load of missiles. Surprisingly, the carriage of Phoenix in the tunnel between the engines is reported to cause no interference drag.

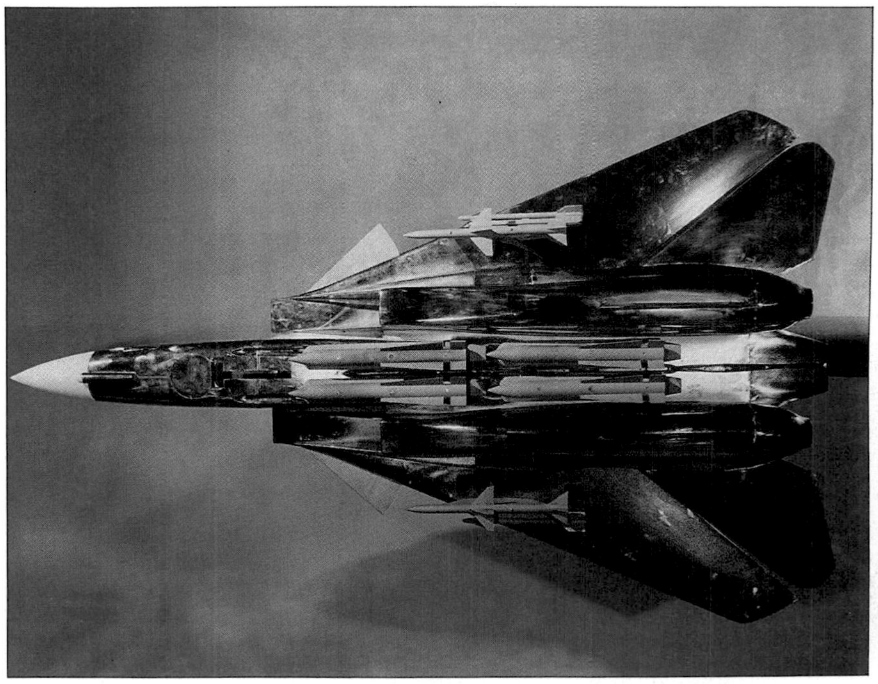

tively known as Project 303. The Admirals were encouraging, and in October 1967 Grumman made a formal proposal to the Navy. In essence, this consisted of a new airframe designed around the weapon control system and engines intended for the F-111B.

The Navy responded by forming Fighter Study Group II to examine the proposal, which became known as VFX-1. There also existed a second proposal called VFX-2 which was the same airframe and weapon control system wrapped around two Advanced Technology Engines (ATE) that were under development at that time. But more of VFX-2 later. Fighter Study Group II concluded that Project 303 was potentially vastly superior to the F-111B. For a start it was carrier-compatible, and it promised to have excellent close combat capability, a quality sadly lacking in the F-111B. It could therefore be used in the escort fighter role as well as fleet defence, and would obviously possess a 'fallout' capability for ground attack.

VFX-1 was Grumman Design No. 303-60. It has been described by the company as "more an assemblage of reasonable goals than a mature blend of aerodynamics, structures, electronics, and subsystems." This was soon to change.

As at January 1968, Design 303-60 featured a shoulder-mounted variable-sweep wing and widely spaced engines in pods. The undersides of the fuselage and engine pods were smoothly curved, and a single vertical tail surface of low aspect ratio was featured. Notwithstanding the other trouble encountered by the F-111B, the variable-sweep wing had fuctioned well and offered considerable advantages over a more orthodox layout. The concept was therefore adopted by Grumman for their new fighter.

The widely spaced engine pods were a direct result of experience with the F-111B. The Pratt & Whitney TF30 had proved to be very sensitive to high AOA and the quarter-cone inlet situated well downstream on the fuselage was less than ideal. Grumman's answer was to place the engines as far out from the fuselage nacelle as possible to minimize airflow interference, with the airstream running in a straight line from the front of the intake to the nozzle.

Original armament

The weapon control system was to be a modified Hughes AWG-9, but contrary to popular belief, the basic weaponry was to be Sparrow rather than Phoenix. The design philosophy was to produce an air superiority fighter first and a missile carrier second. Grumman's Robert W. Kress summed it up in June 1984: "We were totally preoccupied with producing a fighter, with a basic weapon fit of four AIM-7s and two AIM-9s. Then we sat back and figured how to screw six AIM-54s onto it without messing it up in its basic fighter role. That led to the palletized Phoenix carriage." (Phoenix missiles are carried on external flush-mounted low-drag racks, referred to as pallets). Design 303-60 was a large aeroplane and consequently heavy; the extensive use of exotic materials such as titanium and boron composites were to be incorporated into the structure to minimize the weight as far as possible.

Between January and September 1968 the design moved fast, and eight final configurations were in turn developed, examined, and discarded, with the exception of the one that was destined to emerge as the F-14. A minor nacelle modification turned 303-60 into 303A, then further modifications produced 303B the following month. By the end of June, enough further developments had occurred for a redesignation to 303E.

Other variants were running in parallel. Design 303C featured submerged engines and a shoulder-mounted variable sweep wing, while 303D also had submerged engines but with a low-set variable-sweep wing. Interestingly, both featured twin fins and ventral strakes. Wind tunnel tests and further studies revealed that 303D would have poor longitudinal stability, excessive drag due to lift at subsonic speeds, reduced maximum thrust in supersonic flight, and high fuel consumption at cruising speed. It was eliminated during April. A few weeks later, 303C was also eliminated as having a lower supersonic combat ceiling, and less growth potential than 303E.

As these two fell by the wayside, attention was turned to 303F, a submerged-engine design with a shoulder-mounted fixed wing, and 303G, a 'fighter only' variant whose AWG-10 weapon control system had no Phoenix capability. Designed to have the same mission capability as 303E, 303F had an empty weight calculated to be 2,520lb (1,143kg) heavier while takeoff gross weight (TOGW) panned out at 4,920lb (2,232kg) heavier than its variable-sweep rival. Most of the extra weight came from the need for a much larger wing – 745sq ft (69.24m^2) compared with 541sq ft (50.28m^2). In addition, the fixed wing had to be equipped with various trim and high lift devices to suit it for carrier operations. Even then it could not have met carrier suitability requirements when carrying six Phoenix and it was terminated in July of that year.

Design 303G was studied to establish the degree to which the Phoenix-armed fleet air defence mission requirement penalized the design as a pure fighter. Overall dimensions were smaller and both empty and TOGW weights were reduced, by 1,615lb (733kg) and 2,230lb (1,012kg) respectively. Calculations showed that only marginal gains in acceleration, combat ceiling, etc., were possible. As the Navy had been pushing for the long-range kill capability for many years, yet another Sparrow-armed fighter was hardly what it wanted. Furthermore, 303E had greater growth potential and greater attack capability.

Design evolution

Fighter design is a process of evolution, and it is instructive to examine the steps which led from 303-60 to 303E, and the reasons for them.

1) An increase in wing area from 505sq ft (46.93m^2) to 541sq ft (50.28^2) improved manoeuvrability, and also allowed a single-slotted hinged flap to be used rather than a complicated double-slotted extending flap.

2) A Grumman-designed convergent-divergent (con-di) iris nozzle increased maximum supersonic thrust.

3) The distance between the engine pods was reduced and forward fuselage depth increased. This improved area distribution, reduced wetted area and thus drag, and gave better single-engined control due to a reduction in the asymmetry of the thrust.

4) A revised trailing edge to the 'pancake' area between the nacelles reduced supersonic trim drag.

5) Wing aspect ratio was reduced from 8.15 to 7.28, yielding the minimum takeoff gross weight (TOGW).

6) The addition of a 'Mach Sweep Programmer' gave the pilot maximum combat agility and allowed the wing to be designed for a much lower static bending moment, thus making a considerable weight saving while reducing the flutter weight penalty.

Left: Round-the-clock working was needed to prepare the first Tomcat prototype for its maiden flight before Christmas 1970. Here it is being towed from the paint shop at dawn, masking still in place, for the next stage of preparation.

Above: The ill-fated first prototype, BuAer 147980, seen in the early part of its disastrous second flight on December 30, 1970. Minutes after this picture was taken, a series of hydraulic failures occurred.

Right: Flames and smoke erupt from the trees as Tomcat 1 crashes just short of the Calverton runway. Test pilots Miller and Smythe used their Martin Baker ejection seats – their parachutes can be seen above and in front of the fireball.

7) The addition of Direct Lift Control (DLC) for carrier approach gave a more stable glide path and a more consistent touch-down attitude.

8) A glove vane was incorporated to destabilize the aircraft in supersonic flight, thus reducing supersonic trim drag and improving supersonic manoeuvrability.

9) The addition of a 'speed bump' at the base of the vertical tail reduced supersonic drag.

10) Wing dihedral inboard and anhedral outboard produced better sealing at the sweep joint.

11) Wing thickness was revised from a constant 9 per cent to 10.65 tapering to 7 per cent, reducing structure weight and improving the buffet boundary.

12) The pallet concept for carrying Phoenix enabled the aircraft to operate at a lower weight when carrying Sparrows than would have been the case with a fixed mounting.

13) A revised horizontal tail planform as suggested by NASA to improve longitudinal stability also allowed the wing to be placed further to the rear to eliminate balance problems.

14) Improved external lines to upper and lower surfaces of the forward inlet reduced both drag and negative zero-lift moments at supersonic speeds.

15) Improved nose and canopy lines gave better supersonic cross-sectional area distribution, as well as better visibility from the cockpit. The F-14 was a trend-setter in the latter respect.

16) A lower positioning of the horizontal tail, another NASA suggestion to improve longitudinal stability, also insured against pitch-up at transonic speeds.

17) Revisions to the main landing gear fairing and horizontal tail actuator bump improved area ruling and lessened supersonic drag.

18) Deletion of the high-lift device on the glove leading edge reduced weight and complexity with no adverse effect on performance.

19) Cross-sectional area was redistributed to reduce wave drag.

20) A redesigned vertical tail similar in shape to that of the A-6 Intruder with an area reduction from 112sq ft ($10.41m^2$) on 303-60 to 102.5sq ft ($9.53m^2$) on 303E, plus sideways-retracting ventral fins totalling 40sq ft ($3.73m^2$) in area, were added.

At first sight the list seems formidable, but closer examination reveals it to be almost entirely a process of improvement, refining a basically sound design rather than seeking fixes because something was wrong.

The Navy issued a Request for Proposals for the VFX Specification to the aerospace industry in July 1968. The basic VFX requirements were a two-man crew seated in tandem, two engines

Below: Tomcat 12 (BuAer 157991) was redesignated 1X to replace the first prototype in the high-speed test and performance envelope exploration programme. Its first flight was made on August 30, 1971.

(the TF30-P-412 was expected to be used), an advanced weapon control system, and an air-to-air weapon load of either six Phoenix, or a combination from six AIM-7E or F Sparrows and four AIM-9 Sidewinders. An internal M61A 20mm multi-barrel cannon was mandatory. The 303E, by now a mature design, formed the basis of Grumman's submission.

Grumman's competitors for the VFX contract were General Dynamics, Ling-Temco-Vought, McDonnell Douglas, and North American Rockwell. By December, Grumman and McDonnell Douglas had emerged as the front runners, and on January 14, 1969, the DoD announced the award of the contract for the VFX fighter, now designated F-14, to Grumman. The contract was negotiated on a basis of six R&D aircraft and 463 production F-14As and Bs, although at that time, to update the fighter force of the USN and USMC would have required a total of 716 production aircraft. The Grumman proposal had at first been considerably more expensive than that of McDonnell, but had been negotiated downwards to within acceptable limits. Projected procurement was as follows: Lot I: 6 aircraft; Lot II: 6 aircraft; Lot III: 30 aircraft; Lots IV, V, VI, and VII: 96 aircraft each; and Lot VIII: 43 aircraft. On this basis, the unit cost per aircraft worked out at $12.4 million in FY 1970 terms.

Twin fins

One final major change occurred before the design was frozen in March 1969. Up to this point, Design 303E had featured a single fin, with two folding ventral fins to give the required directional stability and control. Early wind tunnel tests, performed on the 303B model, had confirmed the superiority of the single fin, particularly at high AOA, and it also possessed better wave drag qualities than twin fins, as well as weight and simplicity advantages.

However, at a very late date, the Navy objected to the complex ventral folding fins as being unsuitable for carrier operations. A further objection arose from the widely spaced engine thrust lines. In the event of a dynamic engine failure in high Mach number flight, at the critical external loading, a single fin might not have given sufficient directional stability without the extra area provided by the folding fins. As a direct result, the twin fins familiar to us today were adopted.

By this time, the need for the F-14 had become urgent. Three main factors were involved. Firstly, the abortive Missileer and F-111B projects had caused years of delay. Secondly, experience over North Vietnam had exposed the shortcomings of the F-4 Phantom in the close combat arena against the far from new Soviet-built MiG-17s and -21s. Thirdly, the nature of the threat was changing.

The Soviet Union was now producing a series of new fighters, among them the MiG-25 Foxbat. During the late 1960s the Foxbat had set a whole range of world records for speed, altitude, and rate of climb. Its very existence was interpreted to mean that the Soviets had made astounding technical advances, and as a result the Foxbat was credited with capabilities far in excess of those it actually possessed. For the next few years, the Foxbat was to become a sort of aerial bogeyman to the West. Something was needed to counter it.

That something was the Grumman F-14 Tomcat. The name had arisen fortuitously from a combination of the Grumman practice of naming its fighters after felines, and the enthusiasm for the project of Vice Admiral Tom Connolly, who at the time held the post of Deputy Chief of Naval Operations, Air (DCNO-AIR).

Above: The second prototype Tomcat, BuAer 147981, was assigned to low-speed, high AOA and spin testing. It is seen here in high AOA flight, in which the Tomcat excels. (Note the angle of the horizontal tails.)

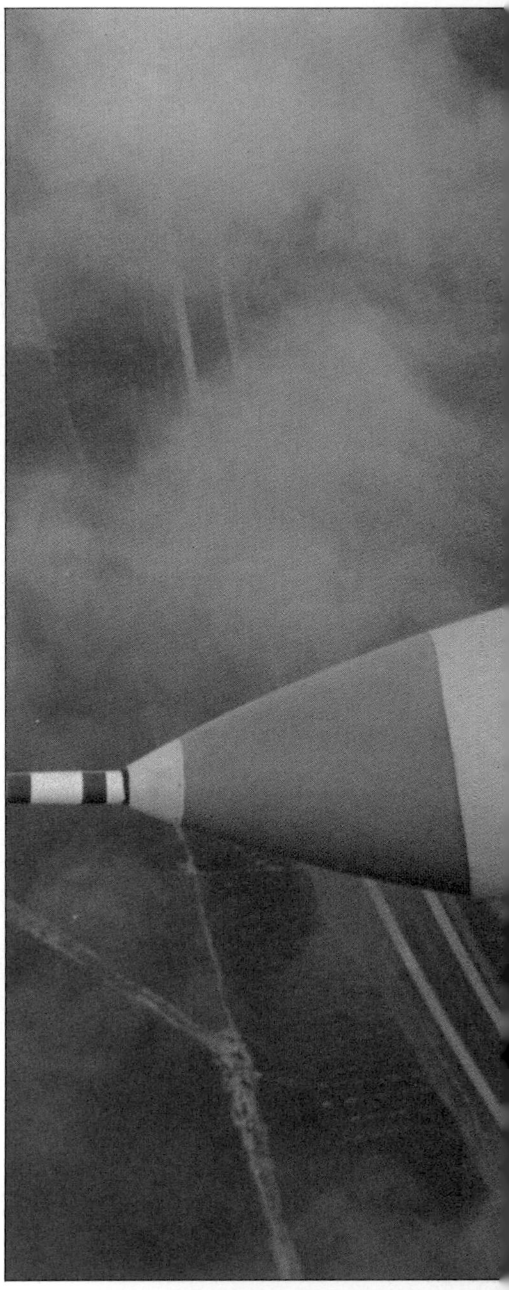

Right: A close-up view of Tomcat 2 showing the canard surfaces fitted before spin trials commenced in the spring of 1972. In the event, the Tomcat proved to be extremely resistant to spinning.

Left: With wings fully spread and everything – gear, flaps, slats and speedbrake – hanging out, Tomcat 2 flies slowly past the camera. The prominent ribs on the upper surface and the shape of the trailing edge of the pancake were later modified.

Right: In-flight refuelling played a large part in keeping the test programme on schedule by extending the duration of each flight. Here Tomcat 2 takes on fuel from a KA-6 equipped with a 'buddy pack'.

The project had been referred to from an early stage as 'Tom's Cat', and this was eventually formalized into Tomcat. Other names had been suggested, among them Alley Cat, rejected as being in questionable taste, and Seacat.

Meanwhile, an advanced technology engine known as the ATE was under development. Funded jointly by the USAF and US Navy, this was expected to produce a thrust of 28-30,000lb (12,700-13,600kg), for a weight saving of 800lb (363kg) per engine, and have a specific fuel consumption calculated to be 30 per cent better. The Tomcat was designed to accept the ATE with minimal modifications – the new engine promised considerable performance improvements, but to wait for it was to accept yet further postponement of the in-service date, which was scheduled for April 1973.

The decision was taken to proceed with all haste, using the flight-proven TF30-P-412 engines for the prototypes and early production models, a total of 67 aircraft. After this point, Tomcats were to be fitted with the ATE, with the designation F-14B, and the earlier model F-14As were to be retrofitted with the new engine. On the horizon was the F-14C, which was to feature advanced multimission avionics. The need for growth had been foreseen: what Grumman was tooling up to build was the world's most advanced fighter, designed to counter any present or projected threat, and capable of being progressively updated as required. It was a large aeroplane – "a big fighter to do a big job" was Grumman's comment – and it represented the pinnacle of technological achievement at that time.

Two years to first flight

Grumman, confident in its ability to win the VFX contract, had initiated fabrication of certain parts late in 1968. Now it was faced with the tremendous task of producing flyable hardware in just two years, successfully completing the flight test programme, and getting production aircraft into service by 1972.

The 'Ironworks', as Grumman was affectionately known to the Navy, tooled up to get the first prototype into the air in double-quick time, organized the production, including the extensive use of the expensive and intractable titanium, and set out to streamline the flight test programme. Under the terms of the contract, the maiden flight had to take place on or before January 31, 1971, while the US Navy Board of Inspection and Survey (BIS) trials were scheduled to take place just 17 months later – a very short time into which to compress a full flight test programme.

As the Tomcat project gathered momentum, the detractors were seizing upon it as a new duty scapegoat. Coming along, about two years behind in terms of an in-service date (and about level with the F-14B), was the USAF's new F-15 fighter. Civilian experts at the Pentagon started predicting that the F-14 could be out-manoeuvred by the MiG-21, while once again the familiar question arose as to why the two services could not agree on a common design, in this case inferring that the lighter and cheaper F-15 should be selected. Again the historical lesson that the process of converting a land-based fighter for carrier operations involved so much structural redesign as to make the exercise self-defeating, was being ignored. But both Secretary of Defense Melvin R. Laird and DCNO-AIR Vice Admiral Tom Connolly remained adamant that not only was the Tomcat the aircraft that the Navy wanted, but it was needed as soon as possible. The first Navy order, for 26 production aircraft, was placed in October 1970, and with this the possibility of cancellation faded.

The first prototype, BuAer (Bureau of Aeronautics number) 157980, was intended for high-speed testing and exploration of the flight performance envelope. Taxi trials started on December 14, 1970, and high-speed taxi runs were made six days later. The weather was not good on the following day (December 21) but the forecast for the next few days was worse. After consultation with high-ranking Navy observers, the test pilots took the decision to go.

With Grumman Chief Test Pilot Robert Smythe at the controls and Project Test Pilot William Miller in the rear seat, the big fighter lifted off the runway at Grumman's Calverton Field at 16:18. After circling the airfield twice at moderate speed and at low level, it touched down exactly at sunset after just ten minutes in the air. No attempt was made to vary the wing sweep on this flight, during which four dummy Sparrows were carried.

The next flight was scheduled as a test flight proper, with Miller at the controls and Smythe in the back seat, monitoring the instruments. The weather was bright and sunny on December 30, 1970, and the Tomcat lifted off the runway at 10:08. Accompanied by three chase aircraft, it headed southeast toward the test area over the Atlantic. Stability and control tests were carried out with the wheels down, then the gear was retracted and the speed gently increased from 133kt (245km/h) to 180kt (332km/h).

Twenty-five minutes into the flight, at an altitude of 14,000ft (4,270m), the pilot of a chase aircraft noticed what looked like smoke coming from the F-14. Simultaneously, Bill Miller reported a failure of the primary hydraulic system and announced that he was aborting the mission and returning, using the back-up flight system. The 'smoke' was actually leaking hydraulic fluid.

The early stages of the return flight were uneventful. At a distance of 4 miles (6km) out from Calverton, at an altitude of 2,500ft (750m), Miller blew down the landing gear with the nitrogen bottle and confirmed to the tower that both nose and main gears were down and locked. By this time he was within sight of the runway, but just when the emergency appeared to be over, the flight hydraulic system also failed, and in a last-ditch attempt to save the aircraft, Miller switched to the Combat Survival System. Designed to give enough control to allow a battle-damaged F-14 to egress from the combat zone and reach a safe area for the crew to eject, this system powered the rudders and tailerons only, but extremely skilful piloting might allow the valuable prototype to be landed safely.

On the final approach, however, the big fighter began a gentle longitudinal oscillation. Miller realized that he was no longer able to control it and decided to eject. The Martin Baker zero/zero seats worked as advertised, and the crew escaped unhurt from just above the treetops a split second before the F-14 impacted the ground about a mile short of the runway and caught fire.

Crash investigators were quickly on the scene, and on February 12 their findings were announced. Two ¼in (6.5mm) titanium hydraulic lines, one on each side of the fuselage, had both ruptured just behind the main landing gear, and loss of fluid had caused a catastrophic failure of both systems.

The Navy Accident Review Board concluded that the failures had been caused by "a highly improbable set of simultaneous conditions." At low engine settings used during the flight, the vibration frequency of the tubing matched that of the hydraulic pumps, setting up a resonance that caused the lines to fracture. This condition had been aggravated by a loose mounting connection. Shortly after, the pump in the combat survival system had become unserviceable, rendering this emergency system useless. The remedy for the fractured pipes was simple: the titanium tubes were replaced by heavier gauge stainless steel pipes.

Second prototype

After undergoing exhaustive ground testing of its hydraulic systems, the second prototype took to the air from Calverton on May 24, 1971. This flight, with Robert Smythe at the controls and Bill Miller in the back seat, lasted 58 minutes. It was uneventful, as was the second flight, lasting more than two hours, two days later. Only moderate speeds and altitudes were recorded on these flights, as this aircraft, BuAer 157981, was assigned to low speed, high AOA, and spin testing, and was specially instrumented and equipped for this task. To replace the crashed high speed test aircraft, No. 12, BuAer 157991, was accelerated through production and redesignated No. 1X, making its first flight on August 31 of that year, and going supersonic on September 16.

Although only the first dozen Tomcats were preproduction aircraft, a total of around 20 took part in the accelerated flight test programme, which had inevitably suffered some slippage as a result of the loss of the first prototype. Nine Tomcats had flown by the end of 1971, and all 20 by the following November.

The programme itself was very intensive. Calverton possessed an Automated Telemetry System (ATS), first used for the A-6 programme and consisting of a Control Data System CDC 6400 computer, with three CDC 1700 pre-processors. Each pre-processor could be linked to an individual aircraft, so that three Tomcats could undergo flight testing simultaneously. Also linked into the system was a laser ranging theodolite, used for tracking to an extreme degree of accuracy, and IFF. Flight test instruments on board each aircraft recorded literally hundreds of readings which were relayed to the ATS, processed by the computer and displayed to engineering test staff on the ground, either in real time or after a very short delay. Previously, the aircraft on test had to land back before the data could be retrieved and analysed.

Using ATS, most of the information was available in real time, while the remainder could be processed and made available before the end of the flight debrief. Real-time data gave quite startling advantages. Tests for thrust/drag, static and dynamic stability and structural flutter could be carried out simultaneously, and the real-time data enabled engineers on the ground to clear the aircraft for the next test sequence immediately, or alternatively rerun the test on the spot if necessary. No longer could adverse weather or a minor component failure negate a test flight; the flight could be immediately rescheduled to cover a new aspect. For weapon and avionic systems testing, the broadly comparable Systems Integration Test Station (SITS) was installed at the Pacific Missile Range at Point Mugu.

This dynamic flight testing at Calverton, involving Tomcats 1X, 2, 3, and 8, was backed up to a tremendous degree by in-flight refuelling (IFR). In particular, IFR made a large contribution to the high-speed flight tests, allowing up to three protracted afterburner runs per flight instead of the usual one. The endurance of a test flight thus became limited by weather or pilot fatigue rather than fuel, as in the past, while the proportion of takeoffs and landings to flight hours was dramatically reduced. Test flying on previous aircraft without IFR had produced an average of 1.3 hours

Above: Tomcat 3 (BuAer 157982) was the structural test aircraft. Comprehensively instrumented, it was responsible for proving both interceptor and fighter envelopes.

Below: Tomcat 4 (BuAer 157983) was the first Tomcat to be fitted with AWG-9 and AIM-54 missiles. The low-drag pallets and cranked wing pylon are clearly visible from this angle.

Right: Tomcat 5 (BuAer 157984) was the systems instrumentation aircraft, tasked with testing communication, navigation and weapon systems, as well as data link and countermeasures.

Typical test flight profile

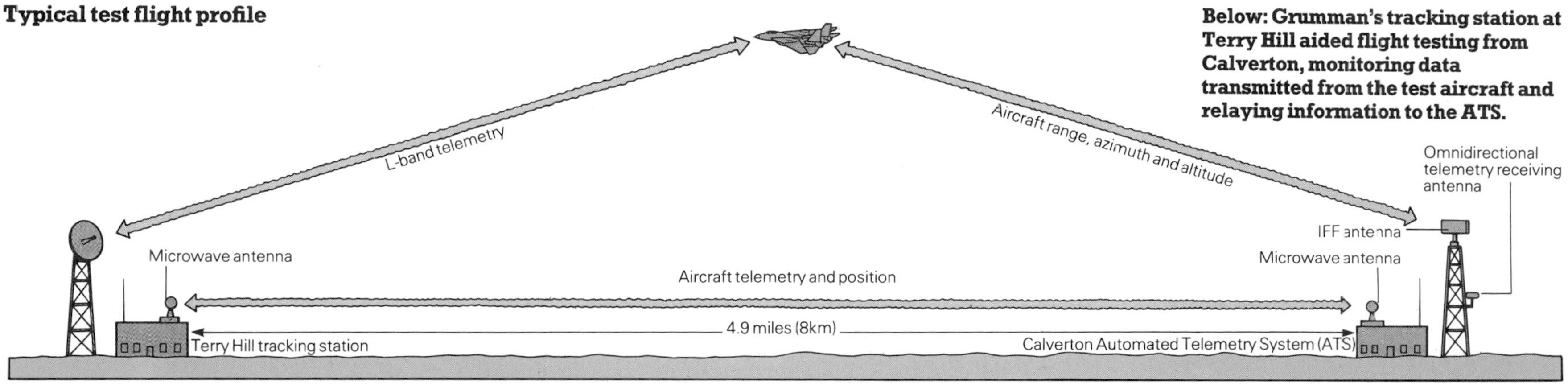

Below: Grumman's tracking station at Terry Hill aided flight testing from Calverton, monitoring data transmitted from the test aircraft and relaying information to the ATS.

per flight. The F-14 programme, with IFR, averaged 2.9 hours per flight, more than 200 per cent better.

The pace was hectic. The accelerated flight test programme was aimed at completing 3,600 flight test hours by the end of 1972, with the object of getting the F-14 into fleet service during the following year. In the course of 1971, the maximum number of flying hours in one day reached 12.5, while one single mission involved five in-flight refuellings. On one occasion, five test flights were made in one day.

The back-up effort required was prodigious. Three F-4 Phantoms were employed as high-speed chase aircraft, while low-speed chase duties were performed by three Grumman A-6s. A fourth A-6 augmented the low-speed chase aircraft and also dispensed smoke for high-speed, high-altitude airspeed calibration. The A-6s also acted as tankers, equipped with McDonnell Douglas 'buddy packs', holding 20,000lb (9,000kg) of transferable fuel; they were positioned where required by the IFF tracking station that augmented the ATS.

NPE 1 took place between December 2 and 16, 1971. The flight envelope that had been cleared by Grumman prior to the evaluation ranged from Mach 0.9 at sea level to Mach 1.8 at 35,000ft (10,700m).

The functions of the aircraft used in the flight test programme were as follows. No. 1, BuAer 157980, was assigned to high-speed testing and exploration of the flight performance envelope. As we have seen, it did not survive its second flight. No. 2, BuAer 157981, performed the low-speed and high AOA tests, followed later by stall/spin testing. For the latter, the variable geometry wings were at first fixed at a sweep angle of 20deg while the variable engine inlets were locked fully open, and an anti-spin parachute was fitted.

Intended to operate at low airspeeds and high AOA, No. 2 was the test aeroplane most likely to lose both engines in flight, so it was fitted with an emergency power unit. To provide power for the flight controls and an emergency electrical generator, a hydraulic pump driven by a Sundstrand hydrazine-powered turbine was fitted.

Grumman had set out to design and build a spinproof aeroplane, but early tests in NASA's Langley Research Center spin tunnel had shown a tendency for the scale models to enter a fast flat spin. Further tests with 1/10 scale radio-controlled models dropped from a helicopter failed to confirm this tendency, but Grumman was taking no chances. Before the spin test programme started in the Spring of 1972, Tomcat No. 2 was fitted with 6ft×2ft (1.83m×0.61m) canard surfaces on each side of the cockpit, as a precautionary measure. Later in 1972, this Tomcat was used for gun trials, firing the 20mm M61A multi-barrel cannon at speeds up to Mach 1.8. No. 2 was instrumented to record and transmit 325 different measurements via the ATS.

Replacement for Tomcat 1

Tomcat No. 12, BuAer 157991, was the next to take to the air. Redesignated No. 1X, it replaced 157980 in the flight test programme. Hydraulically powered shakers were attached to the wing and tail surfaces for flutter testing, and by December 1972 it had exceeded Mach 2.25. The most comprehensively instrumented of all the test aircraft, it could record and transmit no fewer than 647 different measurements via ATS.

Next off, on October 7, 1971, was No. 4, BuAer 157983. On October 30 it was flown to the Navy Missile Center (NMC) at Point Mugu, where it was fitted by Hughes with the AWG-9 fire control system and AIM-54 Phoenix missiles for evaluation. Also to Point Mugu on December 12 went No. 5, BuAer 157984, for systems instrumentation and compatibility testing. This covered navigation, communications, air-to-air and air-to-ground weapon systems, electronic countermeasures and data link.

No. 5 was followed to Point Mugu on January 15, 1972, by No. 6, BuAer 157985, which was scheduled take part in missile separation and weapon system compatibility tests. This aircraft was lost through an unfortunate accident on June 20, 1973, when an unarmed AIM-7E-2 Sparrow pitched up after launch and struck it, causing the Tomcat to catch fire. Both crew members ejected and were rescued from the sea. As a result of this accident, more powerful cartridges were used for missile ejection.

Tomcat No. 3, BuAer 157982, was the structural test vehicle, and first flew on December 28, 1971. Comprehensively fitted with strain gauges, it measured bending moments, torsion, and shear loads on the wings, fuselage and tail over the fighter interceptor envelope of 6.5g and weapons delivery envelope of 7.5g. A total of 477 different measurements could be recorded and transmitted.

No. 7, BuAer 157986, was the F-14B prototype, to test the new ATE engines. Holdups with the ATE delayed the first flight, which was made with the proven TF30-P-412 on one side and the new F401-PW-400 on the other, on September 12, 1973. No. 8, BuAer 157987, first flew on December 31, 1971, and was scheduled to provide contractual guarantee data for a production configuration aircraft. The first Tomcat to exceed an altitude of 56,000ft (17,000m), it was instrumented to record and transmit 164 different measurements. No. 9, BuAer 157988, went to Point Mugu to be used by Hughes to assist in the evaluation of the AWG-9 fire control system.

No. 10, BuAer 157989, was slated to undertake the carrier suitability proving programme. First flown on February 29, 1972, it was ferried to Naval Air Test Center (NATC) Patuxent River on April 6 for initial trials. These completed, it made the first Tomcat catapult launch from USS *Forrestal* on June 15, and its first arrested deck landing on the same carrier on June 28. It was lost on the following day in an unfortunate accident which claimed the life of test pilot Bill Miller. The annual air show at Patuxent River was to be held on June 30 and the Tomcat was scheduled to make two passes across the airfield at 1,000ft (300m), the first with the wings spread and the second with them swept back. On June 29, Miller was rehearsing for the show. It was a hazy day, and eyewitnesses saw the Tomcat flying low over Chesapeake Bay, then suddenly attempt to pull up. The big fighter mushed in, hitting the water tail first. Fortunately, the rear seat was unoccupied.

No. 11, BuAer 157990, joined the growing Tomcat contingent at Point Mugu for avionics systems compatibility testing on March 24, 1972. This included air-to-air evaluation, air-to-ground gunnery, automatic carrier landing system (ACLS), and antenna patterns. The ACLS, which had been successfully tested and used operationally by the F-4 Phantom, was designed to aid the recovery of aircraft at night or in marginal weather conditions. In such circumstances, the pilot couples his ACLS to the ACLS on the carrier, while the carrier ACLS acquires the aircraft on radar and tracks it, trans-

F-14 development milestones

Jan 1966	Preliminary studies started
Oct 1967	VFX concept formulated
May 1969	Funds for F-111B refused by Congress
Jun 21, 1968	RFP released to industry
Dec 13, 1968	Evaluation of proposals completed
Dec 15, 1968	Grumman and MCAIR proposals short-listed
Jan 5, 1968	Grumman and MCAIR final revisions submitted
Jan 14, 1968	Announcement of VFX award to Grumman
Feb 3, 1969	RTD&E contract signed
Mar 1969	Design frozen
Sep 16, 1969	Performance characteristics validated by NASA
Nov 1969	Engineering mockup and manufacturing assembly (EMMA) started
Feb 2, 1970	AWG-9 computer and development test equipment delivered to SITS, Point Mugu
Feb 27, 1970	ATE engine contract awarded to Pratt & Whitney; F-14B proposal submitted
May 18, 1970	XTF-30-P-412 ground test engine received from Pratt & Whitney and inlet compatibility testing started
Jul 9, 1970	Engine and inlet tests concluded
Jul 23, 1970	EMMA demonstration completed
Sep 30, 1970	F-14B contract signed
Dec 21, 1970	First flight
Sep 16, 1971	First supersonic flight
Dec 2-16, 1971	NPE I
Jun 15, 1972	First catapult launch from carrier
Jun 28, 1972	First arrested landing on carrier
Jul 6-Aug 15, 1972	NPE 2
Sep 28, 1972	First operational evaluation begun by test squadron VX-4
Dec 31, 1972	First delivery to RAG squadron VF-124
Oct 14, 1972	VF-1 and VF-2 commissioned at NAS Miramar
Oct 1973	BIS trials concluded
Sep 17, 1974	VF-1 and VF-2 deploy to sea aboard USS *Enterprise*
Jul 5, 1977	BuAer 157988 becomes the first Tomcat to reach 1,000 flight hours

mitting signals to the aircraft's auto-pilot which guide the aircraft straight onto the deck, making due allowance for the motion of the carrier. The frontal radar cross-section of the Tomcat causes 'glint' which leads to inaccuracies; consequently the ACLS is carried but not used operationally. Tomcat No. 12 was redesignated 1X as related earlier.

No. 13, BuAer 158612, made its maiden flight on May 2, 1972, then on August 2 entered Grumman's anechoic chamber at Calverton for intensive radiation and electro-magnetic compatibility tests. No. 14, BuAer 158613, was assigned to maintenance and reliability work at Calverton, while Nos 15 to 19, BuAer 158614 to 158618, were allotted to pilot training, although No. 17 was reassigned to Patuxent River to replace No. 10 on carrier suitability work. The final Tomcat to take part in the test programme, No. 20, BuAer 158620, was intended for climatic testing at Point Mugu, where it was to be 'cycled through the weather hangar' – an intriguing prospect! It later finished up at Patuxent River.

Meanwhile, cost problems were appearing. Grumman's original bid had been considerably higher than that of its main rival, McDonnell Douglas, and although it had been pared down subsequently it still remained higher. In evaluating the two fighters, cost had not been the only consideration for the Navy, and the contract had been awarded after an overall appraisal of the qualities of the two contenders on a value for money basis. Obviously, fleet air defence capability had weighed heavily with the assessors. The Tomcat was expensive, but it was clearly capable, and in time of war the loss of an aircraft carrier which might have been saved by better defensive equipment would be difficult to justify in terms of peacetime savings on aircraft procurement.

Cost escalation

Apart from the high initial cost of the Tomcat, however, other factors were emerging to boost the cost still higher. One was a reduction in company turnover, which meant that the Tomcat programme had to carry a higher proportion of the overheads than had originally been anticipated, but the main factor was inflation, which in the early 1970s started going through the roof. The contract for the F-14 contained set options to buy over a period of years, with an inflation content of 3 per cent on labour and 2 per cent on materials built in. This was the so-called total procurement package, and was one of the last such contracts to be issued.

The inflation percentages were insufficient to cover the true increases. This was not something that applied solely to Grumman, the aerospace industry, or even the United States: it was a world-wide trend, as readers in any country and any industry who were involved with fixed-price contracts during this period will remember with a shudder. To summarize the story, Grumman chairman E. Clinton Towl testified to the Senate Air Power Tactical Subcommittee that if the contract was enforced, the company would be compelled to close down. The importance to the security of the nation of Grumman products was such that a compromise was reached and production continued.

Above: Rotate! The tailerons reach a steep angle to pull the nosewheel off, while the blazing afterburners accentuate the wide spacing of the engines, and the pancake between.

Left: An extremely rare photo of Grumman's submission for the USAF improved manned interceptor, intended to replace the F-106. This never progressed beyond a mock-up.

Right: BuAer 157986 was the first and only F-14B, although it was intended as the definitive Tomcat. It flew just 33 hours with the F401-PW-400 Advanced Technology Engine.

Below: Only the paint job and the tail markings distinguish the F-14B from the F-14A. It was later used as the test airframe for the F101 Derivative Fighter Engine.

NPE 2 took place between July 6 and August 15, 1972, in two phases. Phase 2A was conducted at Calverton by a team from Patuxent River, headed by Commander George White. Aircraft Nos 2 and 8 were put through a demanding series of tests while configured with various combinations of Phoenix, Sparrow, Sidewinder, and drop tanks. The M61A cannon was also evaluated. Phase 2B was carried out at Point Mugu by a team led by Commander Frank Schluntz. Using aircraft Nos 5 and 9, they checked out the avionics and weapon system. A total of 178 flight hours in 72 flights was logged, and the final report contained this verdict: "Displayed outstanding performance characteristics and potential to accomplish the air superiority fighter and fleet air defence missions".

Flaws and modifications

Flight testing proceeded apace, with over 3,500 flight test hours recorded by June 1, 1973. Inevitably, problems were encountered. Initially it was found that buffetting was caused with the flaps down: a gap between the spoilers on the upper wing sections and the flaps was responsible, and closing the gap cured the problem. Fatigue cracks occurred in the beaver tail structure, and a minor redesign was necessary, while fibreglass skins in this area had to be replaced by metal. Vibration and fatigue caused the fin caps to be reinforced.

As had been feared, problems with spinning also began to be encountered. The Tomcat was a relatively vice-free aeroplane to fly; it was often described by its pilots as a pussycat in the air. It appeared to have no AOA limitations, and during tests had reached angles exceeding 90deg and negative angles of over 50deg. The negative angle was attained by a hard pull-up followed by a roll inverted. It remained controllable when well outside the normal flight envelope. But it could enter an irrecoverable flat spin, something which was to remain a vexed question for years.

The original Tomcat was designed with an Automatic Rudder Interconnect (ARI), which had been developed for use on aircraft which did not have leading edge wing flaps. The production machines featured manoeuvring wing slats which deployed automatically during hard manoeuvres. Like many other high-performance fighters, the Tomcat suffers from wing rock at high AOA. To roll the aircraft in this condition, the pilot must either use the rudder into the roll, or use rudder into but stick opposite to the direction of roll. The original ARI would command a large rudder input which could, and sometimes did, cause a flat spin. Once the spin was established, the crew had no option but to eject.

After an early loss of a production aircraft to this cause, the decision was taken to uncouple the signal inputs on AOA to the ARI, thus disabling the system. This still left the Tomcat with a wing rock and roll reversal problem, although to be fair, the Grumman fighter was more tractable than either the F-4

Above: Tomcats wearing a jagged rectilinear disruptive camouflage scheme reminiscent of the Luftwaffe in World War II. All identification has been painted over, but these are from VX-4 and are participants in AIMVAL/ACEVAL at Nellis in 1977.

Below: Another view of two of the six AIMVAL/ACEVAL Tomcats showing the disruptive paint scheme to advantage. These Block 90 F-14s were equipped with the Northrop TVSU for the evaluation, the equipment performing well in the clear skies above the Nevada desert.

Phantom or F-8 Crusader that it was designed to replace.

The method of using rudder into the roll but with opposite stick gave the fastest rate of roll, but in essence it was a pro-spin input, and if coupled with an engine stall, would easily turn into a flat spin. This had two consequences, both bad. The first was a small but steady attrition rate in fleet service attributable to this cause. The second was that inexperienced pilots tended to play safe, and did not handle the aircraft to the extremes of its capability. This was a problem that the Navy simply had to learn to live with, as they had lived with the unforgiving departure tendencies of the Phantom, but testing to overcome the problem continued.

New ARI

In 1980, a joint US Navy/NASA programme was instituted involving a new ARI. Tomcat 1X was extensively modified with spin prevention systems to carry out the flight testing. Modifications involved a spin chute, battery-driven hydraulic pumps to maintain pressure to the control surfaces in the event of a double engine stall, and extending canards. In a flat spin, a jettisoned canopy tends to remain in the vicinity of the aircraft, so an eject-through canopy and compatible seat were also fitted. Fitted with the new ARI, 1X carried out a three-year test programme at the Dryden Flight Research Facility at Edwards AFB, California.

Gradually, the system was evolved. The new ARI activates only when the AOA reaches about 33deg coupled with an excessive yaw rate. If the controls are set in a pro-spin direction, the ARI washes them out, allowing only 2deg of rudder input in a pro-spin direction; however, if they are against the spin, they are not modified. Roll reversal is reportedly eliminated, while wing rock has been suppressed. The handling qualities throughout the ACM envelope are significantly improved.

The flight test programme also produced engine stalling problems at high AOA. The TF30 had proved to be rather sensitive when used in the F-111, hence the widely spaced engine pods on the F-14. But provided that the power settings were left high, the engines appeared to be relatively stall-free at high AOA, although stalls did occur. It should however be noted that the TF30 had never previously flown in a real manoeuvring-type fighter, and that exploration of the high AOA regime came as a distinct culture shock to it. But as the ATE engine was scheduled to replace it as the definitive engine for the F-14, the TF30 was regarded as an interim measure and its shortcomings consequently seemed less significant.

Above: An F-14 attached to the Naval Air Test Center at Patuxent River goes off the ski jump. While it would appear to have little application for carrier operations other than with vertical-landing aircraft such as the Harrier, the ski jump, which can be erected in just two hours, seems to have possibilities when used to assist short takeoffs from a damaged airfield.

Below: VF-1 Wolfpack was the first fleet fighter squadron to equip with the Tomcat. Shore-based at NAS Miramar, VF-1 first deployed to sea aboard *Enterprise*.

In the long term, the question of powerplants for the Tomcat proved troublesome. The prototype F-14B, which first flew on September 12, 1973, was put through what was described as a reasonably successful test programme. The ATE, the powerful F401-PW-400, offered significant increases in thrust and improved fuel consumption, but it was pushing the technology of the times fairly hard, and two engines were reported to have exploded on the test rig prior to the first flight. With a large financial question mark hanging over the F-14 itself at this time, extra funds for further development were hard to come by, and tests with the F401 were finally suspended in April 1974. The F-14A, with its interim TF30 engine, was to be the definitive in-service model.

By 1974, as the number of F-14As in fleet service built up, the problems became really serious. During simulated combat missions flown by Navy pilots it was found that the compressor stalling was more serious than had been thought. This was coupled with a serious lack of reliability that on occasion caused catastrophic failure followed by fire. Much of the unreliability stemmed from the fact that the TF30-P-412 contained parts with short fatigue lives. To counter this, Pratt and Whitney developed the P-414, which among other design changes had a belt of armour around the fan section to contain the pieces of broken blade in the event of a failure.

The P-412 was gradually replaced by the P-414 in fleet service from February 1977 onwards. Further modifications

resulted in the P-414A, the first of which was delivered in December 1982. However, the stall problem could only partially be dealt with using the existing engine or its derivatives. At the time that the TF30 had been conceived, the constant high AOA work combined with the continual throttle movements used in modern fighter operations had not been foreseen, and the basic powerplant was just not designed to be worked that hard.

To return to the flight test programme, on the Pacific Missile Range, a dazzlingly successful series of AWG-9/AIM-54 Phoenix demonstrated both single and multi-shot capability against a wide variety of targets, details of which are given in the Avionics and Armament chapter. As an aeroplane, the Tomcat had demonstrated that it was a major advance on previous fleet fighters; now it showed an unparalleled capability as a weapon system in the fleet air defence role that remains unequalled.

Tomcats in service

BIS trials were successfully completed during October 1973, and the second batch of sea trials were flown from USS *Forrestal* off the Virginian Capes at the end of November. Three F-14s participated, notching up 54 catapult launches, 124 bolters and 56 traps during a seven day period, during which minimum wind over deck (WOD) requirements were evaluated, in addition to the approach power compensator (APC) and weapon systems. The first two Tomcat squadrons, VF-1 and VF-2, were commissioned at NAS Miramar on October 14, 1972, although the first production aircraft to be allocated to them, BuAer 158983, did not reach them until a year later. Also formed at Miramar was the first fleet training and Replacement Air Group (RAG) squadron, VF-124, previously equipped with F-8s. They received their first Tomcat, BuAer 158620, on the last day of 1972.

Although the Tomcat had been demonstrated to be a first class fighter and an unequalled weapon system, its escalating costs were still a source of worry. One of the arguments used against it was that four Phantoms could be purchased for the cost of one Tomcat. This argument, which overlooked the added crew, fuel and support costs of four Phantoms, was invalid for other reasons. It was doubtful whether four Phantoms could do the work of just one Tomcat in the fleet air defence role, while both aircraft occupied a comparable amount of deck space. Twenty-four Tomcats could therefore only be replaced by the same number of Phantoms, which would mean that the defensive capability of the carrier would be greatly reduced. The Navy's prime argument was that they really could not afford to be without the Tomcat.

As early as July 1971, the Secretary of Defense requested the Navy to examine the possibility of a navalized Eagle, the F-15N. McDonnell Douglas, makers of the F-15, the prototype of which had not at this time flown, produced a modification study which, not surprisingly, resulted in a considerable weight increase. The Navy's Fighter Study Group III, formed to carry out an independent examination of the project, concluded that even greater weight increases would result, and once Phoenix missiles were added, performance would fall while costs would increase, both to unacceptable levels.

New discussions were initiated in March 1973. This time the idea was to compare the F-15N, an austere variant of the F-14, an upgraded F-4, and proposals from other aerospace companies. Also under consideration was a return to the time-honoured method of selecting fighter aircraft – building rival prototypes then conducting a competitive flyoff. At this time the F-14B was still six months away from its first flight, and the projected F-14C lay still further in the future. The austere Tomcat proposal was therefore at first referred to as the F-14D.

The proposed changes gave it what can only be described as a negative improved capability. Among the modifications considered were four new weapon control systems, three of which had no Phoenix capability, and a modified Hughes AWG-9A, with the simultaneous tracking capability halved from 24 to 12, and the simultaneous engagement capability reduced from six Phoenix to four. The glove vane, DLC, and APC were to be deleted and the avionics made more austere.

By the following year, the F-14 Optimod, or F-14X, had emerged as a design study, with 38 airframe alterations, reduced avionics and modified engines. Also projected was the F-14T, so basic that it was regarded as a 'Model T' aeroplane. The whole idea was dropped in May 1974, one of the major influences being the high attrition rate of US-designed aircraft in the previous October's Arab-Israeli war. In a nutshell, the carrier air groups could not afford high attrition rates, so it made little sense to equip them with anything less than the very best, although one thing which did emerge from the discussions was the F/A-18 Hornet, a true dual-role fighter that could if necessary assist the Tomcat in the fleet air defence role, while largely supplanting it as an escort.

As with any other fighter, various updates took place over the years, although nothing of sufficient magnitude to warrant a redesignation. At sea, water intrusion caused electronic failures, and sealers, baffles and drain holes had to be incorporated. A Garrett AiResearch central air data computer was fitted in manufacturing batches from 1976 onward, along with a new ARC-159 UHF radio, both offering greatly improved reliability. And the manoeuvre flaps, previously controlled manually, were automated, operating as a function of Mach number, wing sweep angle, and

Above: A Wolfpack Tomcat carrying empty Phoenix pallets, and in the low-visibility finish currently favoured, during its later assignment to CVW-2 aboard USS *Ranger*.

Above right: A VF-2 Bounty Hunters Tomcat. VF-2 forms part of a Carrier Air Wing with VF-1 and the two squadrons deploy to sea together. This F-14 wears the tail code of CVW-14 and the colourful markings of that era.

Below: Tomcat 18 (BuAer 158617) was allotted to pilot training. It is seen here in the markings of VF-124 Gunfighters, the Pacific Coast Replacement Air Group, formed in 1972 and based at NAS Miramar, California.

AOA. This not only reduced the pilot's workload, but improved the sustained turning performance.

In the early 1970s, a dedicated reconnaissance variant, the RF-14, had been considered. Studies had been made, but the idea was dropped in 1974. Finally, the Tactical Airborne Reconnaissance Pod System (TARPS) was adopted. The TARPS was originally developed for the A-7, but no problems were encountered in fitting it on a modified F-14, although it neutralizes two Phoenix stations, and requires a control panel in the rear cockpit. F-14 TARPS can be modified back to carry six Phoenix, but the standard F-14A cannot be modified to carry TARPS. It is planned that one squadron on each carrier will have three TARPS F-14s. The pod has little effect on performance, just slightly increased buffet at high speeds and low altitudes. In all, 49 Tomcats have been modified.

New engines for the long overdue F-14B were still under development in 1980. In 1981, the F-14B prototype was fitted with the new General Electric F101 DFE engines for a 25-flight test programme, held between July and September of that year. The results were promising, and the F110-GE-400 augmented turbofan was developed from the DFE. The decision to use this engine in the F-14D (the B and C designations by now having been bypassed), and to retrofit the F-14A, was taken by the Navy in February 1984. The first engine was scheduled to be delivered to Grumman in November 1987, and its first flight in a Tomcat was expected to take place during the following year.

Running in parallel with the engine development was the advanced avionics fit planned for the F-14C. In the event, the F-14C was bypassed, and the F-14D programme announced in the summer of 1984 included a digital AWG-9 weapon system with new small-side lobe radar antenna, the Northrop AXX-1 Television Camera Set (TCS) and much other new avionic equipment, details of which are given in the relevant chapter. In all, some 300 new F-14Ds are planned, with production due to start in 1988, and the first D model scheduled to reach the Navy in March 1990. In the same time scale, an improvement programme for the F-14A avionic systems will be under way. The weapons fit is to standardize at four of the new digital AIM-54C Phoenix missiles, supplemented by four AIM-120 AMRAAMs. Sidewinder capability will be retained, with the AIM-9M the most likely weapon.

The Tomcat was planned from the outset to have plenty of room for growth, and production was expected to continue until 1995, with its service life extending well into the next millenium. The F-14 Tomcat was the first of a new breed of superfighters, and despite its comparatively old design will remain a force to be reckoned with for the foreseeable future. More recent fighters may hog the limelight, but it was the Tomcat that led the way.

Structure

In the period leading up to 1970, the technologically advanced nations demanded ever greater capability from their new jet fighters. They were expected to be able to operate with equal facility in fair weather or foul, as interceptors, air superiority fighters or tactical fighters with a strike capability, and these requirements resulted in ever-increasing size, complexity and cost. The F-14 Tomcat represented the apogee of this trend, being obviously large, undeniably complex and almost (but fortunately not quite) prohibitively expensive. Only its unique capabilities saved it from cancellation, but with a high proportion of exotic concepts in its design and advanced materials demanding new fabrication techniques in its structure, it represented the summit of the fighter designer's art.

Above: Grumman's design philosophy for the Tomcat was to space the engines well away from the fuselage, as seen here. The dielectric cone over the antenna hinges upwards.

It is many years since I first set eyes on a Tomcat, but my initial impressions have remained fresh. The general appearance was pleasing; from the side it looked sleek despite its size, the enormous, sharply raked intakes suggested immense power, and the large cockpit canopy gave the crew an excellent all-round view, something that had been missing from fighters for a long time. The twin fins were unusual in those days, but after all, this was supposed to be the shape of the future, and to support this view were the then very exotic variable sweep wings.

On walking round to view it from the rear, however, it suddenly looked a very strange bird indeed. For many years, twin-engined jet fighters had had the engines situated close together in the rear fuselage and the cockpit situated up in the front portion. Here was something very different. The huge engine nozzles were spaced many feet apart, connected by a flat area generally known as the pancake, with an oddly shaped beavertail trailing edge. Looking up toward the front, the cockpit just seemed to grow out of this flat area. A rapid walk round to the front confirmed this: there was no orthodox fuselage, just two rectangular intakes fronting engine pods that ran from front to back in straight lines, with a nacelle between them housing the radar and cockpit which tapered away smoothly into the pancake, while underneath, between the engine pods, was a very pronounced tunnel. This was all so different that it really did look like the shape of the future.

The fleet air defence role carrying Phoenix missiles demanded a large aircraft, and the F-14 is dimensionally large. It therefore could hardly help being fairly heavy, and there are weight constraints involved in carrier operations. Furthermore, the weight of any fighter has a habit of increasing during its service life as new bits are screwed on, and this can quickly exceed acceptable limits unless sufficient margin is allowed from the outset. Sheer weight had been one of the prime causes of the failure of the F-111B.

The structural design of the F-14 was therefore based on saving as much weight as possible by the use of advanced materials, in particular titanium alloy. By weight, this material accounts for approximately 25 per cent of the structure of the F-14, with 15 per cent steel, only 36 per cent of aluminium alloy, and 4 per cent of non-metallics, which last is made up of boron epoxy composites on the horizontal tail surfaces, fibreglass epoxy in the radome and ventral strakes, and acrylics in the windshield and canopy. This compares with the slightly later McDonnell Douglas F-15 Air Force fighter, which contains 26 per cent of titanium alloy, just over 37 per cent of aluminium, and 5.5 per cent of steel.

The desirable characteristics of titanium are its high strength to weight ratio, resistance to corrosion, which is essential in a maritime environment, and ability to withstand high temperatures. The alloy mostly used in the F-14 is Ti 6Al 4V, which contains 6 parts of aluminium and 4 parts of vanadium by weight. This alloy has very good welding characteristics, but is expensive and difficult to work. It had been used in fairly small quantities on many aircraft over the years, but a combination of cost and

Above: Instead of using pins, as on the F-111, the wing of the F-14 pivots on two spherical bearings, each held in a pair of lugs. One bearing can support the wing if the other fails.

difficulties in fabrication had restricted its use.

Titanium has a very high yield strength and a low modulus of elasticity. Consequently, it is difficult to shape cold, as it has a tendency to warp, wrinkle, or spring back, while tight bends or radii cause cracking. In the early 1960s, however, a major technological breakthrough increased fabrication potential and reduced costs. The method evolved was to preform individual parts with partially formed contours and flanges. They were then placed in a hot-forming press and creep-formed to their final size and shape at temperatures of 600-800deg C (1,050-1,470deg F), after which they were held in position for between 10 and 25 minutes to relieve the stress, thereby preventing wrinkling.

This was a tremendous advance, but it did not lend itself to efficient mass production. Grumman engineers decided that they could do better. They incorporated a die-cushion system in each of two conventional four-column presses, and added an electrically heated platen. This created a hot-forming process that allowed titanium sheet parts to be developed from flat pattern blanks in just the one operation, giving considerable savings in time, money, and equipment. Chem-milling is also used for shaping titanium sheets in some applications, and the old bogey of hydrogen embrittlement has been eliminated.

Hot isostatic pressing is also used to reduce wastage, which with titanium tends to be very high. In this process, titanium powder is poured into a mould, which is then sealed and pressurized with a chemically inert gas, before being heated to very high temperatures to produce a preformed part which is very close to the final shape required. This minimizes waste due to machining.

Titanium wing box

One of the most obvious applications of titanium in a variable sweep wing aeroplane is the wing carry-through box, which holds the pivots. This is inevitably a large and heavy structure which needs great strength to carry the in-flight loads. The corresponding item in the F-111 had been made of steel, part welded and part bolted together. Bolting is an excellent way of connecting things, but it does introduce discontinuities, as the stresses and strains are taken by the bolts and the areas surrounding the bolt holes. Suffice it to say that the F-111 experienced a few problems with its wing box assembly, and to avoid this, Grumman elected not only to manufacture the structure from titanium, but to produce an all-welded assembly. So large a component had never before been made from titanium, but the rewards, in the form of a 900lb (408kg) weight saving over the same product in steel, was great. The weight reduction also reduced the fuel load needed to meet mission requirements.

The wing box assembly was a large structure, 22ft (6.71m) long, made up of 35 sub-assemblies, which had to be carefully aligned before being placed in a vacuum chamber for electron-beam (EB) welding. For the production of the F-14, Grumman invested heavily in EB welding machines, five in all, including two of the biggest in the Western world. The largst was 32ft×10ft (9.76m×3.05m) and was capable of welding titanium wing planks 26ft (7.93m) long, while the machine used to weld the wing carry-

Left: The Tomcat begins to take shape. An abundance of precision measuring equipment is in evidence: theodolite and level in the foreground, and another level on the left wing box.

Right: Titanium alloy was widely used in the construction of the Tomcat – in the wing skins, for example, as well as in structural applications. The F-14's tailerons involved the first major structural use of composites.

Below: The widely separated engine pods and fuselage nacelle form a distinct tunnel. The extra keel area provided by this layout contributes to directional stability.

Below right: Seen from the rear, the Tomcat is unlike any other aircraft. The fuselage nacelle tapers away into the pancake, with its unique beaver tail between the nozzles.

Materials distribution

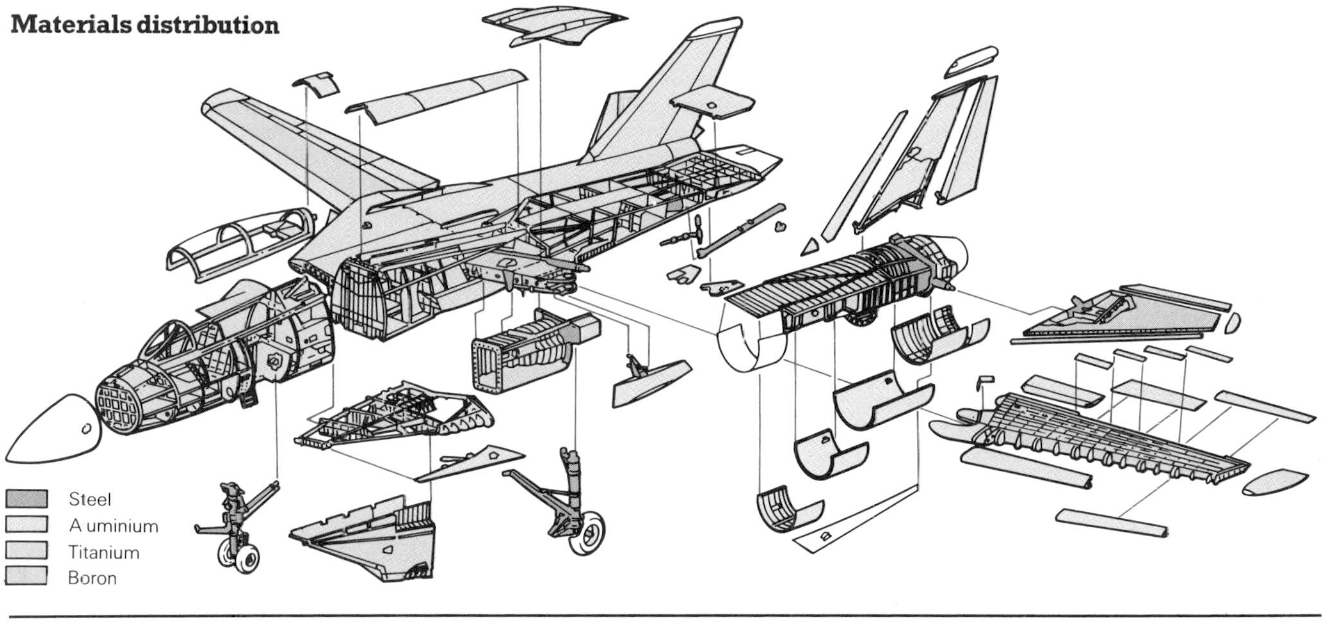

Above: Some idea of how much of the wing area is taken up with flaps and slats can be gained from this picture of a prototype Tomcat under construction. Also seen are the original beaver tail and speedbrake.

through boxes measured 25ft×11ft×9ft (7.62m×3.35m×2.74m). The vacuum chamber is necessary to maintain the high energy levels needed (60,000 volts), and to prevent atmospheric contamination of the weld. With the components in position, the chamber is closed and evacuated, and the machine operator uses a telescope to track the thin seam line of the joint.

Seventy welds are needed on each wing box assembly, and the machine is capable of operating at speeds of up to 60in (152.4cm) per minute. The energy of the electron beam is focussed on a spot roughly ⅛in (3mm) wide, and can penetrate up to 2½in (63.5mm) of titanium at a single pass. The resulting weld is very narrow, very strong, causes hardly any distortion, and needs little cleaning up on completion. The F-14 has had its share of problems, but the wing box was not one of them. So strong is it, that following the crash of the first prototype, the component was recovered intact from the wreck and put to use as a test fixture.

Wing design

No component of the airframe of a fighter affects its performance and flying characteristics as much as the wing. A wing of fixed shape and size is inevitably a compromise, optimized for a particular point in the flight performance envelope, and growing increasingly inefificient as the flight regimes diverge from that point. Wing design is therefore an attempt to meet the aerodynamic needs of widely varying flight conditions and operational requirements by building for the design point which gives the best results at contradictory extremes.

The Tomcat was designed to fulfil both the interceptor and the air superiority fighter functions. An interceptor needs endurance, economic cruise, then rapid acceleration to give its missiles maximum energy at launch, which extends their range and reduces their time of flight to the target, and consequently increases the probability of a kill. In passing, this little refinement seemed to have escaped the advocates of the subsonic Missileer.

An air superiority fighter also needs sparkling acceleration, both to catch an opponent and to disengage from the fight, and at the time when the Tomcat was designed it was also thought that a top speed exceeding Mach 2 was desirable. It also needs to be able to haul its nose around the horizon as fast as possible, both to bring its weaponry to bear on an evading target, and to crimp in the missile envelope of an assailant. If caught in a big multi-bogey dogfight – the furball, as American pilots call it – disengagement will be fraught with peril, and under certain circumstances it may well be preferable to stay and fight it out. This calls for two more desirable qualities, the ability to fly a slow-speed, high AOA engagement effectively, and combat persistence, which is the ability to outlast the enemy in the fight and force him to break off through fuel shortage.

While many of these qualities depend partially on the powerplant, all of them are influenced by the wing design to a greater or lesser degree. The precise requirements will also be conditioned by the altitude at which the engagement takes place. Many of these requirements aerodynamically oppose each other, while others occupy a middle ground. This is why the F-14 was designed with a variable sweep wing, so that each need is met by the best possible solution.

To see why this is so, we need to briefly examine the nature of lift and drag. Lift is created by the movement of air over the lifting surface, or wing, which creates a low pressure area. The pressure underneath the wing will either remain normal, or be higher than normal, which creates a tendency for the wing to move vertically, into the area of low pressure. The amount of lift created depends on three factors: the velocity of the airflow, the cross-sectional shape of the lifting surface, and the angle at which the lifting surface meets the airflow, which is known as the angle of attack (AOA). As AOA increases, so does lift, but only up to a certain point. If the AOA gets too steep, the smooth flow of air across the lifting surface will break down, destroying the lift completely.

The final factor affecting lift is wing loading. There is a limit to the amount of lift that any surface can provide. Hard turns cause accelerations, usually

Below: To meet the varying demands of different flight regimes, the wing reconfigures itself using leading edge slats and trailing edge flaps. The manoeuvre flap setting is only used at subsonic and transonic speeds.

Wing control surfaces

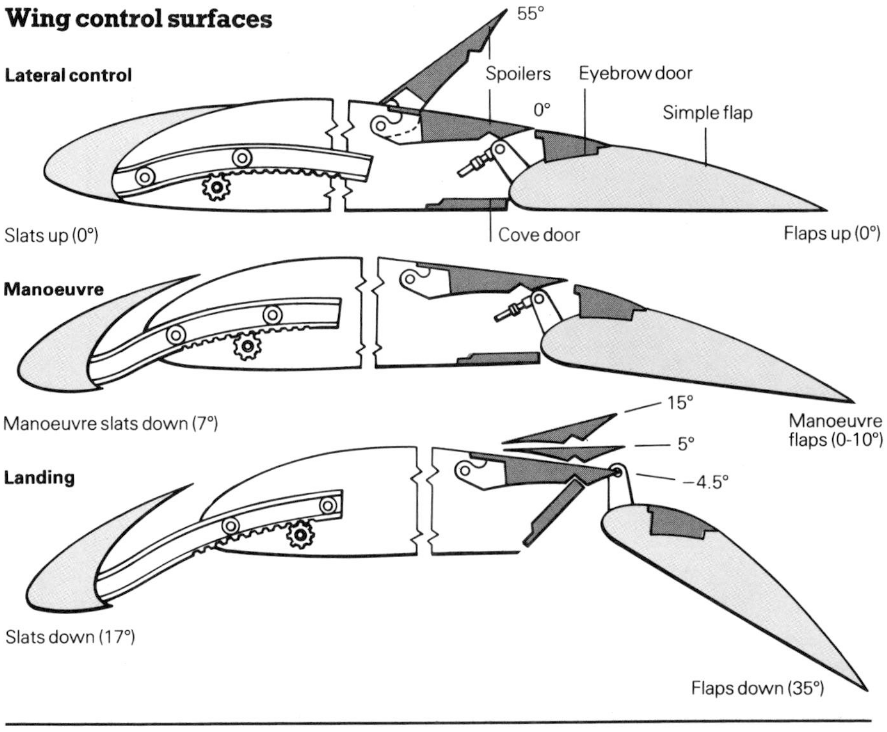

Above: The transparent mockup shown here taking shape is used to sort out the routings of hydraulic and fuel lines, also electric wiring. With large moving parts such as the wings, contact is to be avoided. The integral wing fuel tanks, shown here in forward and swept positions by time-lapse photography, are formed of aluminium frames with titanium alloy fuel-tight skin panels fixed with oversized rivets.

Above: The surrounding workstands convey something of the size of the big fighter as the first prototype takes shape. The speed bumps at the bases of the fins recommended by NASA are clearly apparent.

Above: A Tomcat of VF-124 showing the wings in the oversweep position. This is used to reduce the parking space required in the confines of a carrier. Despite early design studies, tail folding was not required.

Lift/drag control surfaces

Below: The wings of the Tomcat have no ailerons. Lateral control is by differentially moving tail surfaces assisted at subsonic speeds by the spoilers, which also give direct lift control for carrier landings.

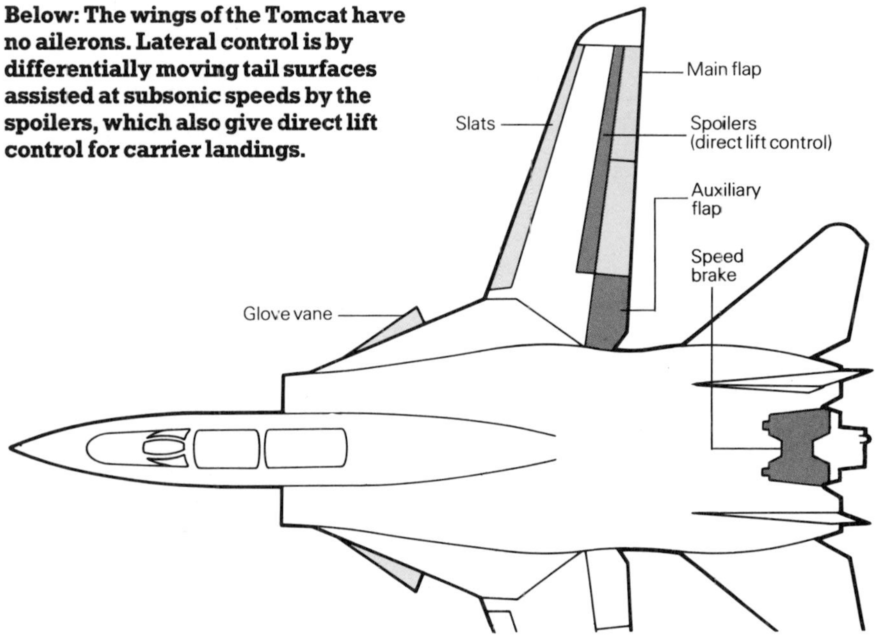

measured in terms of multiples of the force of gravity, or g forces. A wing area which is lifting an aeroplane weighing 40,000lb (18,144kg) suddenly finds itself having to cope with a weight of 160,000lb (72,576kg) if the aeroplane enters a 4g turn. It therefore has to find four times the lift, and high lift devices apart, it can only do that by increasing the AOA.

Drag comes basically in three forms: parasite, or profile drag, induced drag, and wave drag. In level flight, the profile drag of a wing is directly proportionate to its surface area. Profile drag also increases in direct proportion to the square of the speed (V^2). Thus the difference in profile drag at speeds of 200kt (370km/h) and 400kt (741km/h) is a factor of four – the velocity has doubled, but the drag has quadrupled. Induced drag is caused by creating lift with the wing, and is proportional to the span loading squared.

The best measurement of the aerodynamic efficiency of the wing is called the lift/drag (L/D) ratio. The obvious way of improving the L/D ratio is to decrease the span loading by increasing the ratio of the span squared to the wing area. This is known as the aspect ratio, and wings are often described as being either high or low aspect ratio. To illustrate the point, the long slender wing of the Lockheed U-2 is of high aspect ratio, while the short, broad wing of the Saab Viggen, for example, is of low aspect ratio. The final form of drag is called wave drag, which manifests itself only in the transonic speed region, dying away at about Mach 1.2.

The high aspect ratio wing is most advantageous at high lift, and the maximum L/D ratio is reached at increasingly high lift as the aspect ratio increases. High sustained and transient turn rates are best achieved by high aspect ratio wings. Sustained turn rate is in effect thrust-limited g, and is the product of thrust/weight (T/W) ratio and L/D ratio. All else being equal, the higher L/D ratio of the high aspect ratio wing gives a higher level of sustained manoeuvrability down to lower speeds than a fixed wing. It also permits transient turning out to the very edge of lift with a smaller loss of energy, than a low aspect ratio wing.

If we examined two wings of equal area, each creating equal lift, we would find that the higher aspect ratio wing has a lower AOA, and consequently less induced drag. The direct result of this is that the high aspect ratio wing needs less thrust to maintain both its lift, and the energy level of its aircraft. The reduction in drag also means that less thrust is needed to achieve the same performance than with a low aspect ratio wing, and by the same token, less fuel.

The beauty of a variable sweep wing is that it permits a fighter to have either a high or a low aspect ratio wing to suit the demands of the moment, and it converts from high to low aspect ratio by the simple process of sweeping the wings back. Now under some circumstances, a swept wing can be a desirable asset for a fighter. It reduces profile drag to assist rapid acceleration, and also delays the onset of compressibility and wave drag in the transonic region. An aircraft with a variable sweep wing can therefore redesign itself in flight, both in sweep angle and aspect ratio.

Wing control surfaces

The movable part of the Tomcat's wing is fitted with leading edge slats, trailing edge flaps, and spoilers on the top surface. Ailerons are not fitted, and lateral control is achieved primarily by means of differentially moving tailerons. The slats are in two sections, which run the full length of the leading edge from the wingtip cap to the trim line of the wing glove. They are simple slotted extending devices which operate at 7deg in the manoeuvre setting, and 17deg for the high-lift landing position.

The flaps are also in two sections and occupy the entire trailing edge. They are the single-slotted type, with a simple hinge, and have a maximum deflection angle of 35deg. Only the inboard flap section is used for take-off and landing. The flaps can be used to improve manoeuvrability by using a 'manoeuvre flap' setting of 10deg, combining with the slats to form wing camber and increase usable lift coefficient. This is used in subsonic and transonic flight only, as the air data computer monitors the flap deflection and prevents the Mach

Sweep Programmer (MSP) from sweeping the wings beyond 50deg when the manoeuvre flap setting is selected.

The spoilers, which are in four sections mounted on the upper surface of the wing, augment lateral control at subsonic speeds, operating only at sweep angles of less than 55deg. They are also used for direct lift control (DLC) on the final approach, and as lift dumpers after touchdown. DLC is pilot-activated by means of a switch on the throttle which deflects the spoilers to a neutral position of 7deg. Using a thumbwheel on the stick, the pilot can then command corrections to altitude while maintaining the same attitude. Deflections of the spoilers by this means give vertical accelerations of roughly 0.13g upwards and 0.07g downwards. In the event of a waveoff, retraction of the speed brakes automatically deactivates DLC and retracts the spoilers. As lift dumpers, the spoilers automatically deflect to a 55deg angle when the weight comes on the main gear. This kills lift and helps to shorten the landing run.

Combat agility

The airfoil selected for the wings was the NACA 64 A2, with a spanwise thickness ratio of 10.2 per cent at the pivot and 7 per cent at the tip. The wing area of 541sq ft (50.28m^2) was sized to achieve maximum combat agility through a combination of low wing loading and manoeuvre flaps and slats. The simple flap system was a design objective, and one which saved sufficient weight to offset the penalty of increasing the wing area. Originally, the aspect ratio at minimum sweep had been in excess of 8, which was absolutely out of sight for a fighter. Optimizing the aspect ratio at minimum sweep at 7.28 also reduced weight, and at this point shifted the determining factor for the six-Phoenix fleet air defence mission from available lift to single-engined rate of climb.

Another factor here is the pancake, which provides additional lifting area. The total lifting area of the F-14 is roughly 40 per cent greater than the defined wing area, which reduces bending moments in both the wings and the fuselage. It also produces an effective wing loading vastly lower than the reference wing loading, and for all practical purposes constitutes a third, low aspect ratio wing. This makes a significant contribution to the Tomcat's ability to fly at very high AOA, and remain under control at speeds outside the normal performance envelope. The lift on a high aspect ratio wing runs out quite suddenly at around 16deg AOA, whereas with a low aspect ratio surface such as the lifting body of the Tomcat, the lift curve gradually goes flat, with no abrupt break. Pilots have actually been in situations where the Tomcat has been flying on body lift alone, with the wings completely stalled!

In flight, the wing sweeps from the minimum of 20deg to the maximum of 68deg at a rate of 7.5deg/sec in level flight which reduces to just over 4deg/sec at a loading of 7.5g. To ease parking and general space problems in the limited confines of an aircraft carrier, there is an oversweep position of 75deg, which reduces the space occupied. In flight, there are four wing sweep modes. The most important of these is automatic, which is used in almost all flight conditions. It is controlled by the MSP, which uses outputs from the Central Air Data Computer (CADC) to give the optimum wing sweep angle for the flight conditions pertaining at the time.

In automatic mode, the sweep angle for takeoff and landing is 20deg, and at speeds of less than Mach 0.4 the wing sweeps through a mere 2deg. It then remains constant at 22deg up to Mach 0.75. Wing sweep really begins at this point, and the maximum sweep angle of 68deg is reached at Mach 1.2. The MSP was designed not only to improve agility, but also to reduce structural weight. It was obvious that a manual sweep mode would have to be provided, but in manual mode the MSP automatically limits the sweep angle as a function of Mach number and altitude. As this prevents the pilot from overstressing the airframe, the pivot bending moments design limit could be reduced by 30 per cent, or from 14.4×10^{6}in/lb, down to 11×10^{6}in/lb. This produced a substantial weight saving.

Manual sweep mode can therefore over-ride automatic mode. For example, if the pilot wants maximum acceleration, he can sweep the wings right back regardless of speed, but the electrons prevent him from over-extending them,

Below: Variable-sweep wings give a low AOA on finals and a good view over the nose for the pilot. The revised speedbrakes are evident as this Tomcat approaches the carrier.

Below: In-flight pictures of the Tomcat with the wings fully swept and the glove vanes extended are rare, but this Iranian formation is at high speed for the camera.

although there is a third mode, emergency, that allows the pilot to spread the wings as he wants them. Generally, the Tomcat is always flown in automatic mode. Manually optimizing the wing sweep during a manoeuvring combat would call for extremely fine judgement, adding considerably to the pilot's workload. In practice, MSP is always better.

The fourth and final mode is ground attack, which locks the wings at an angle of 55deg for bombing or strafing runs. A 55deg sweep angle provides a high-g load factor for heavy manoeuvring with a load of ordnance, and fixing the sweep removes one rapidly changing variable from the weapon release calculation.

Early experiments with variable sweep wings showed pronounced changes in what is called the static margin – the difference between the aircraft's centre of gravity and its aerodynamic centre. This was no problem when designing a fixed wing aeroplane, but with a variable sweep design both the lift and the weight were moving around. It was found that static margin changes could be minimized by locating the wing pivot well outboard of the aircraft centreline, which suited the widely spaced pod configuration chosen for the F-14 very nicely indeed, and the pivots are set 8.92ft (2.72m) out from the centreline.

Unlike the enormous wing pins used in the F-111 and Tornado, the Tomcat uses two spherical annular bearings for each wing. They are made of titanium alloy, and have Teflon-type and silver rhenium bearing surfaces. One bearing in each wing can fail without compromising the structural integrity of the wing. The loads on the pivot are focussed at a point which roughly corresponds to the centre of pressure of the wing, so that differential tension and compression in the lugs relieves to a certain extent the shear loads acting on the bearing.

The wing movement is powered by a pair of ball screw actuators which are coupled to keep the movement synchronized, while the closure between the fixed wing glove and moving wing section is done by a fairing assembly which 'breathes' as the wing moves back and forth. An air bag maintains the smooth contour of the aircraft when the wing is in the forward position, and is compressed as it sweeps aft, while the overwing fairing has external stiffeners.

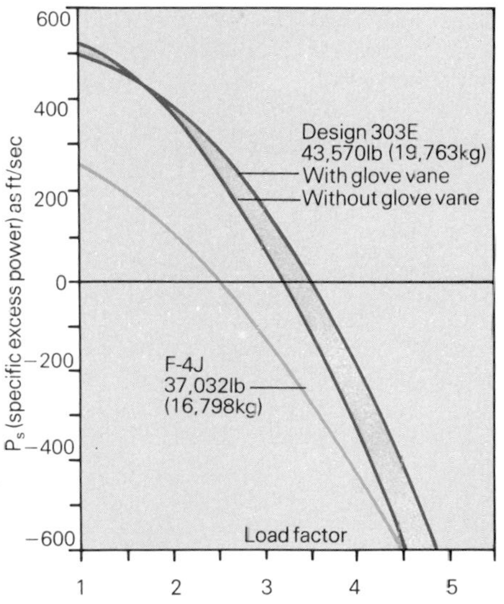

Above: The glove vane improves supersonic manoeuvrability by a considerable margin. These figures are for Mach 1.65 at 35,000ft (10,670m) with 50 per cent fuel.

As the wings sweep back, a high proportion of the lift also moves rearward, but very little of the weight, so that the centre of lift is well to the rear of the centre of gravity. This produces a nose-down moment which must be counterbalanced by a download on the horizontal tail surfaces to trim the aircraft as the wings sweep. At supersonic speeds, this produces excessive stability, which incidentally, is not confined to variable sweep fighters. It is most undesirable, because it reduces supersonic manoeuvrability. The F-111B had been described as 'absolutely awful' in this respect, unable to pull more than 2-3g at 35,000ft (10,670m) at high Mach numbers.

Glove vane

The solution was the brainchild of F-14 Project Manager Robert Kress, and consisted of a small, retractable triangular surface called a glove vane located in the leading edge of the wing glove. Controlled by the CADC, it automatically extends at speeds exceeding Mach 1.4. Its function is to destabilize the forward area of the aircraft, and relieve the downloads on the tail caused by trimming. As an example of its effect, at 68deg sweep angle and 4g acceleration, the net loading is reduced from 6,000lb to 4,000lb (2,721kg to 1,814kg). This reduces the airframe bending moments by some 12.5 per cent and permits a lighter structure. The glove vanes also enabled the F-14 to pull a 7½g turn at Mach 2, maintaining the loading as the speed wound down through Mach 1. At the time, this was practically unheard of, but a high premium had been placed on supersonic manoeuvre capability, partly because the F-111 had been so poor.

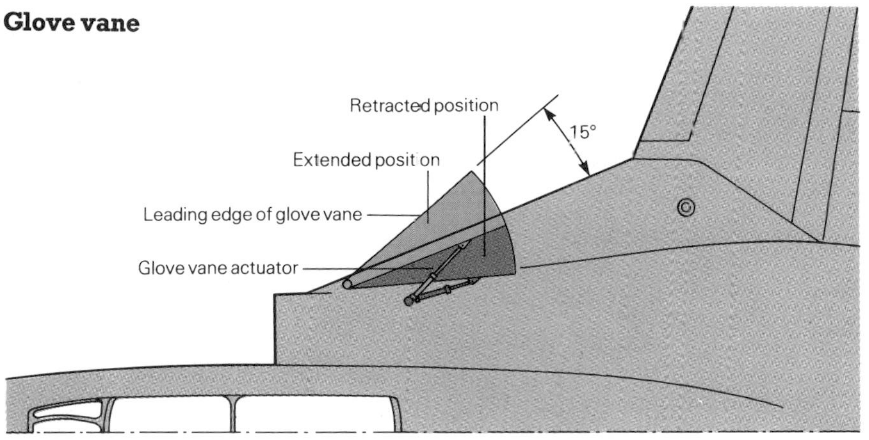

Above: A unique feature of the Tomcat is the glove vane, which improves supersonic manoeuvrability by destabilizing the forward area of the aircraft, reducing trim drag.

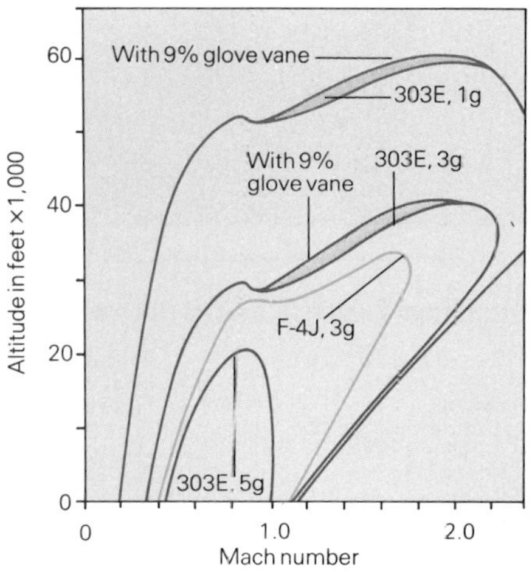

Above: The glove vane increases the flight performance envelope appreciably, as shown by the steady state boundaries for 1g and 3g (weights as in upper graph).

Below: The flattened pancake behind the cockpit acts virtually as a third, low aspect ratio wing, and greatly increases the lifting area. F-14A of VF-211 Checkmates.

The glove vane can be manually extended at speeds between Mach 1 and Mach 1.4, but is prevented from operating at sweep angles below 35deg at subsonic speeds as it would make the aircraft unstable in pitch. However, when the ground attack sweep mode is used, the vanes extend automatically to their full travel of 15deg at speeds exceeding Mach 0.35. The glove vane is hydraulically actuated, and pivots about its foremost angle at a maximum rate of about 10.5deg/sec.

Each wing is an integral fuel tank, although no special sealants are used. The wing skins are titanium alloy, Ti 6Al 4V on the upper surface and the slightly different Ti 6Al 4V 2Sn, with two parts of tin added, on the lower. The skins are creep-formed, and drilled by computerized methods. Oversized rivets are used and punched into the holes with such force and accuracy that they fuse into the metal, making a fuel-tight joint.

The fuselage is of semi-monocoque construction, with machined main frames and titanium longerons. The inlet duct support frame and engine support beams are also of titanium, while both the main gear support frame and the spectacle-shaped beam which carries the engine mounts and taileron connections are of steel. The stressed skin is generally of aluminium. The huge dielectric cone at the nose which houses the radar antenna is unusual in that it hinges upwards. The spacious cockpit, equipped with two Martin Baker GRU-7A ejection seats, rocket assisted to give a zero altitude, zero speed escape capability, is reached by means of an integral boarding ladder, which retracts into the left hand side of the nacelle, midway between the seats.

The speed brakes are situated well aft, extending above and below the pancake. They were deliberately oversized at the design stage for use in air combat manoeuvring. The dorsal speed brake has a total area of 8.6sq ft ($0.8m^2$) and operates in phase with the ventral brake, of 7.4sq ft ($0.69m^2$) area. The ventral speed brake is in two parts to operate around the arrester hook. Hydraulically operated, their maximum extension angle is 60deg, and the operating time to full extension is two seconds. Balancing the speed brakes in this under and over manner minimizes trim change when they are actuated. When the gear is lowered for landing, an interlock restricts the extension angle of the ventral speed brake to 18deg to provide sufficient ground clearance.

In the period when the F-14 was designed, there were no such luxuries as artificial stability and fly-by-wire, so the flight control system is largely mechanical. The F-111B had a considerable quantity of electronics in the flight control system, but early in the F-14 design stage, the decision was taken to use the proven spring and bobweight system. The wing sweep, slats, flaps, tailerons and rudders all have direct mechanical linkage, and only the spoilers are electrically driven. The result is a basically stable aeroplane which possesses flying qualities good enough to complete most missions even when stability augmentation and automatic systems operation are not functioning.

One of the obvious reactions to the unusual fuselage shape of the F-14 is, "Whatever happens to the airflow in the tunnel between the engine pods?" In fact, it was so obvious that it was the first question I put to Grumman when starting this work. Naturally Grumman had thought of it first, and NASA had been hard on their heels, but very extensive testing in all flight regimes, with and without external stores carried in the tunnel, failed to reveal any adverse flow

Grumman F-14A Tomcat cutaway

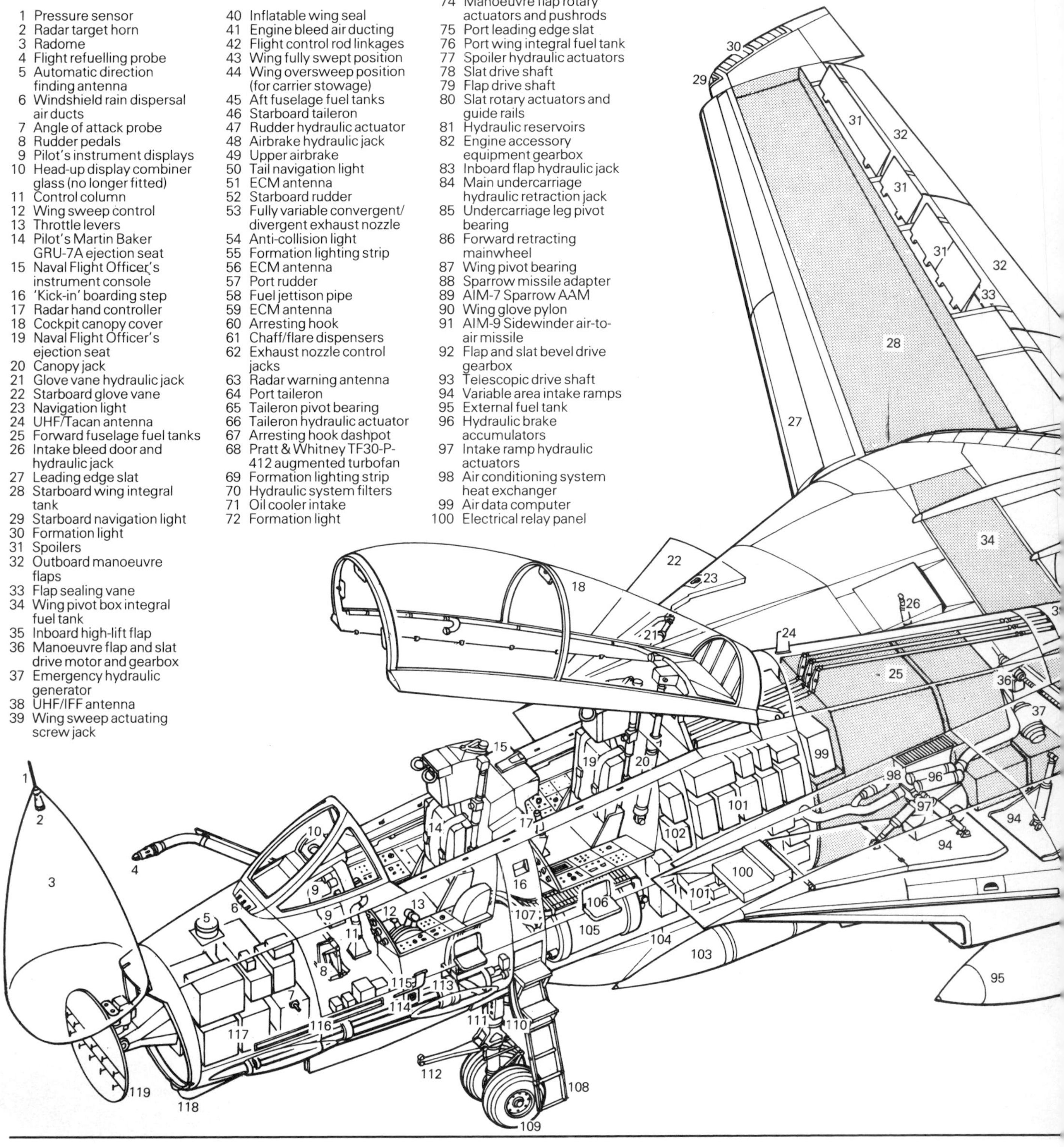

1 Pressure sensor
2 Radar target horn
3 Radome
4 Flight refuelling probe
5 Automatic direction finding antenna
6 Windshield rain dispersal air ducts
7 Angle of attack probe
8 Rudder pedals
9 Pilot's instrument displays
10 Head-up display combiner glass (no longer fitted)
11 Control column
12 Wing sweep control
13 Throttle levers
14 Pilot's Martin Baker GRU-7A ejection seat
15 Naval Flight Officer's instrument console
16 'Kick-in' boarding step
17 Radar hand controller
18 Cockpit canopy cover
19 Naval Flight Officer's ejection seat
20 Canopy jack
21 Glove vane hydraulic jack
22 Starboard glove vane
23 Navigation light
24 UHF/Tacan antenna
25 Forward fuselage fuel tanks
26 Intake bleed door and hydraulic jack
27 Leading edge slat
28 Starboard wing integral tank
29 Starboard navigation light
30 Formation light
31 Spoilers
32 Outboard manoeuvre flaps
33 Flap sealing vane
34 Wing pivot box integral fuel tank
35 Inboard high-lift flap
36 Manoeuvre flap and slat drive motor and gearbox
37 Emergency hydraulic generator
38 UHF/IFF antenna
39 Wing sweep actuating screw jack
40 Inflatable wing seal
41 Engine bleed air ducting
42 Flight control rod linkages
43 Wing fully swept position
44 Wing oversweep position (for carrier stowage)
45 Aft fuselage fuel tanks
46 Starboard taileron
47 Rudder hydraulic actuator
48 Airbrake hydraulic jack
49 Upper airbrake
50 Tail navigation light
51 ECM antenna
52 Starboard rudder
53 Fully variable convergent/divergent exhaust nozzle
54 Anti-collision lighting strip
55 Formation lighting strip
56 ECM antenna
57 Port rudder
58 Fuel jettison pipe
59 ECM antenna
60 Arresting hook
61 Chaff/flare dispensers
62 Exhaust nozzle control jacks
63 Radar warning antenna
64 Port taileron
65 Taileron pivot bearing
66 Taileron hydraulic actuator
67 Arresting hook dashpot
68 Pratt & Whitney TF30-P-412 augmented turbofan
69 Formation lighting strip
70 Hydraulic system filters
71 Oil cooler intake
72 Formation light
73 Port navigation light
74 Manoeuvre flap rotary actuators and pushrods
75 Port leading edge slat
76 Port wing integral fuel tank
77 Spoiler hydraulic actuators
78 Slat drive shaft
79 Flap drive shaft
80 Slat rotary actuators and guide rails
81 Hydraulic reservoirs
82 Engine accessory equipment gearbox
83 Inboard flap hydraulic jack
84 Main undercarriage hydraulic retraction jack
85 Undercarriage leg pivot bearing
86 Forward retracting mainwheel
87 Wing pivot bearing
88 Sparrow missile adapter
89 AIM-7 Sparrow AAM
90 Wing glove pylon
91 AIM-9 Sidewinder air-to-air missile
92 Flap and slat bevel drive gearbox
93 Telescopic drive shaft
94 Variable area intake ramps
95 External fuel tank
96 Hydraulic brake accumulators
97 Intake ramp hydraulic actuators
98 Air conditioning system heat exchanger
99 Air data computer
100 Electrical relay panel

Left: Once quantity production commenced, the main gear was fitted at an early stage to allow the Tomcats to move down the assembly line on their own wheels. Here the right main gear is being fitted.

Above: Block 90 aircraft, including some destined for Iran, move down the assembly line at Calverton in 1975. This assembly building is also used for A-6s, as is evidenced by the Intruder in the right foreground.

phenomena at all, not even interference drag when Phoenix missiles are carried. The increased wetted area caused by the podded configuration was responsible for a little extra drag, but this was considered to be offset by the improved stability of the layout, stability in pitch being enhanced by the aerofoil-like pancake, while extra stability in the directional plane was due to the keel area of the engine nacelles.

Tail configuration

As we saw in the previous chapter, twin fins replaced a single fin at a very late stage in the design. Twin fins do have one great advantage in that they reduce the adverse effects of body vortices at high AOA. A secondary advantage is, of course, systems redundancy in the event of battle damage.

The outward-canted ventral fins are in some flight conditions better than extra main fin area, as they are situated in a position where cross-flow induced by sideslip accelerates under the rear fuselage, which increases their effectiveness, while their low aspect ratio makes them very stiff and resistant to flexing. In sideslip conditions, the loading on them eases the torsion which the main fin loading exerts on the fuselage, while the rolling moment caused by sideslip opposes the rolling moment of the dorsal fins, thus reducing dihedral effect. Being situated in an undisturbed airflow, the ventral fins retain effectiveness at high AOA, and also help directional stability at high speeds. As recounted in the Development chapter, an automatic rudder interconnect was incorporated in the design from the outset, but handling problems caused it to be disconnected, although the hardware is still in position.

The horizontal tail surfaces are fully powered, all-moving surfaces with differential movement to provide control both in pitch and in roll. At wing sweep angles of more than 50deg these tailerons are the sole source of roll control, while at lower sweep angles the are augmented by the spoilers. The size of the tail surfaces was determined by the control requirements only. Stability was not a factor, since the wing and pivot were already located to provide this. The horizontal tail arm was determined by supersonic roll acceleration requirements, and the podded engine layout has an inherent lateral tail arm advantage, which resulted in a tail area 10 per cent smaller than that required for an equivalent submerged engine design. In this respect, it is interesting to compare the horizontal tail layout with that of the much more recent F-18 Hornet.

The F-14's tailerons are of multi-spar construction with 5 per cent thickness at the root, tapering to 3 per cent at the tip, with honeycomb leading edges and trailing edges, skinned with the very expensive boron epoxy composite. The F-14 was the first aircraft to employ advanced composites in a major structural application from the outset. Like other advanced composites, boron epoxy has outstanding strength and stiffness for a comparatively light weight, and is highly tolerant of damage, though in common with all advanced composite materials, damage repair is a problem area, research into which is still going on. Grumman developed a 'Band-Aid' answer, consisting of fibreglass and titanium discs as patches, hot-applied with a structural adhesive.

Providing air for the TF30 engines are two massive rectangular two-dimensional inlets, which rake back at a very acute angle. These inlets are placed 8in (20.3cm) out from the fuselage nacelle, which effectively isolates them from the forebody effect and obviates the need for a fuselage boundary layer air removal system, saving both weight and drag. The external compression type inlet is optimized for fighter operation and provides a stable airflow with low distortion levels. The upper intake surface is extended farther forward than the lower to improve high AOA performance.

The state of the art in jet engine design is that they cannot run using a supersonic airflow, and the air must be slowed down to subsonic speeds in the duct before it reaches the engine face. This is done by applying Bernouli's principle, which states that a moving fluid (in this case a gas) will slow down as it expands to occupy a greater volume. A movable hydraulic ramp system is used to adjust the volume of air entering the duct.

Two ramps are used, one hinged forward, the other hinged downstream to the airflow. The ramp movements are automatic, and are controlled by their own air data computer and hydraulic system which are independent of the CADC and main hydraulics. Air entering the inlet is compressed by the forward ramp. At transonic speeds this forms a shockwave, while at supersonic speeds four shocks are formed which decelerate and compress the air entering the inlet. Behind the forward ramp is a variable-size throat bleed slot, which cleans up the airflow by removing the

101 Avionics equipment bays
102 Electrical system equipment
103 AIM-54 Phoenix air-to-air missile
104 Phoenix missile pallet
105 Ammunition drum
106 Boarding step
107 Ammunition feed and link return chutes
108 Retractable boarding ladder
109 Forward retracting nosewheels
110 Nosewheel steering actuator
111 Carrier approach lights
112 Catapult launch strop
113 M61A-1 20mm six-barrel rotary cannon
114 Canopy emergency release
115 Pitot head
116 Formation lighting strips
117 Radar equipment bay
118 ECM antenna
119 AWG-9 pulse-Doppler flat plate radar scanner

Below: Cutaway drawing of what is arguably the world's most complex and certainly the world's most expensive fighter. The construction of the wing carry-through box, and the wing fuel tanks, which are skinned with titanium fixed with oversized rivets, and the main frame details, are all works of art in their way.

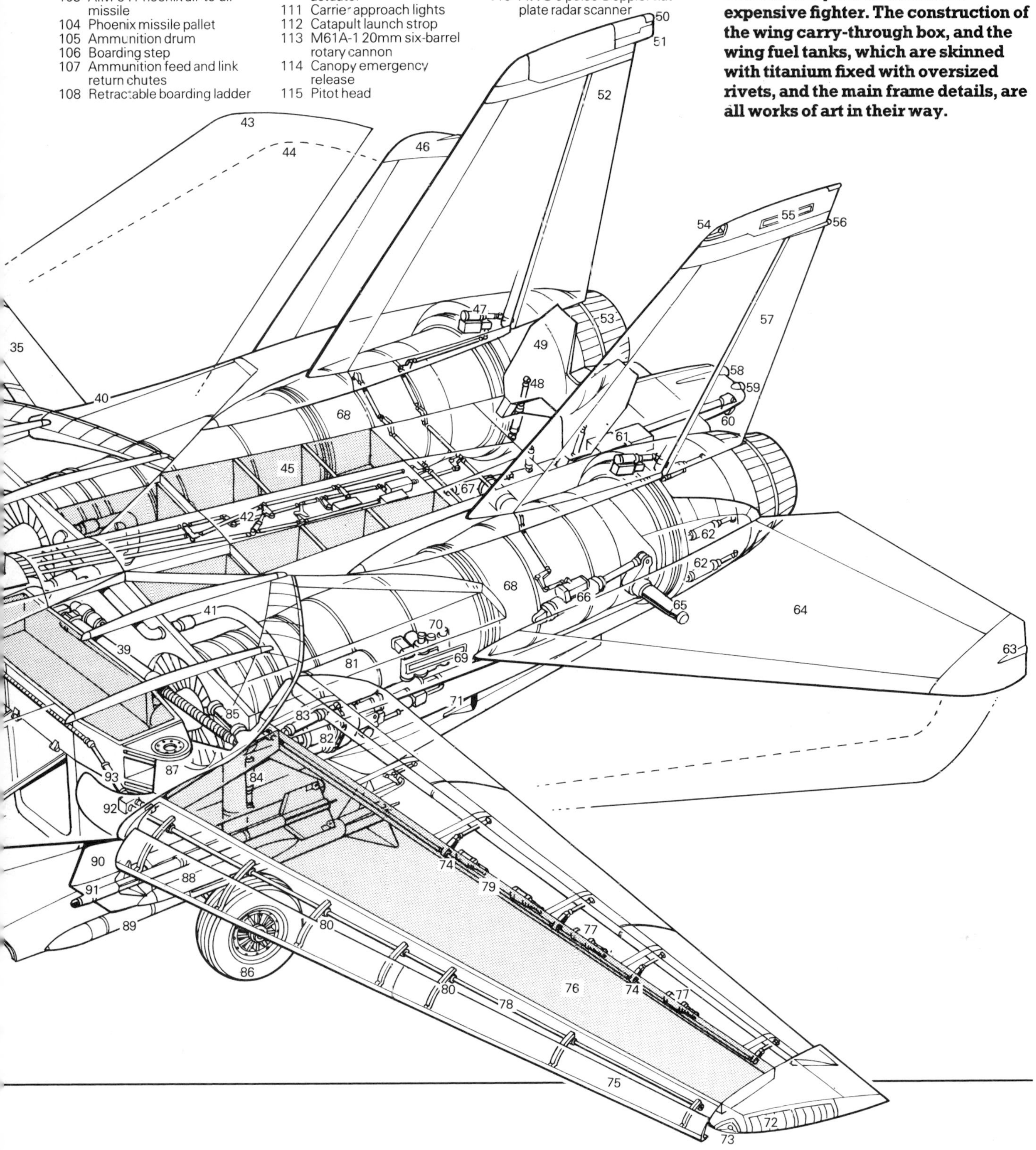

boundary layer, directs air down the face of the aft ramp and handles the bypass of excess air when necessary. Without the slot, flow separation would occur at ramp angles of 10-15deg.

Further compression takes place downstream of the ramp, in the subsonic diffuser duct. Because the air is clean (no boundary layer flow) and its local flow angle is optimized, rapid diffusion rates are possible, and the air which reaches the engine is of high quality. At speeds of up to Mach 0.5, the forward, external compression ramp is overcollapsed, while the aft, subsonic compression ramp collapses forward to contact the forward ramp and closes the bleed slot.

This configuration provides a 7.08sq ft (0.66m^2) capture area for takeoff and slow speed flight. Between Mach 0.5 and 1.2, the forward ramp deploys to form a continuous compression ramp at an angle of 3deg, while the aft ramp positions itself to match the forward ramp to provide a pre-scheduled throat bleed area. As the aft ramp is actuated, the bypass exit door on top of the duct opens, discharging any surplus air rearward with a low pressure drop, thus recovering most of the momentum as thrust. At velocities exceeding Mach 2, the operation of both ramps is scheduled according to a function of flight Mach number and AOA, but is biased by the duct exit Mach number to deliver the correct volume of air to the engine at the correct velocity. If the highly automated system fails at speeds of Mach 1.2 or higher, the ramps lock in position, while if a failure occurs at below this speed, they deploy into the fully open position.

At the other end of the engines are the nozzles. These are of the convergent/divergent type (con-di), and vary in area from 7.5sq ft (0.7m^2) in the fully open afterburning position, to 3.6sq ft (0.33m^2) when fully closed. Considered to be a significant breakthrough in fighter nozzle design when they were developed, the nozzles feature translating flaps, moving on curved rails which are attached to the rear of the afterburner shell. This layout, which produces some really graceful curves, passed a higher thrust than previous designs, and saved weight because it did not need a supply of cooling air.

The undercarriage, stressed for arrested landings on the heaving deck of a carrier at sea, accounts for a high proportion of the steel used in the structure. It consists of a twin-wheel steerable nose gear and single-wheel main gears, all of which retract forward. The nosewheel is housed under the cockpit and the main gears in the underside of the wing glove.

Launch procedure

Attached to the nosewheel strut is the catapult launch bar. Once it is in position over the shuttle, the Tomcat is made to 'kneel' by compressing the gear. Shortening it by 1.17ft (0.36m), gives the strut added strength for the launch, as well as eliminating any tendency the aircraft might have to lift off during the acceleration phase. As the fighter leaves the catapult, the compression is released, thrusting the nose up as the aircraft leaves the deck.

An early modification, introduced from BuAer 157981 on, is an automatic centering device for the nosewheel, which is actuated when the arrester hook is lowered. This prevents castoring as the aircraft rolls backwards from the arrester wires after landing. The brakes were originally of beryllium, but after an exhaustive test programme at Patuxent River in 1981, they have been replaced by carbon composite fitments. Carbon composites give high strength, low weight, and, most important, excellent thermal stability.

The airframe of the Tomcat has a design fatigue life of 6,000 flight hours, which at the current rate represents approximately 20 years. It has an induction cycle of 30 months, which means that after every 2½ years of operational usage it is returned to the Naval Air Rework Facility at Norfolk, Virginia. There it is refurbished, updated as required, and returned to service.

To achieve this long service life, a comprehensive structural test programme was carried out, the idea being to get the main design concepts structurally verified before the production line really got under way. In all, three aircraft and many individual components were assigned to the static and fatigue

Above: It was simpler to mount a stores pylon on the fixed portion of the wing, but the pylon had to be cranked to clear the main gear doors. The missile is an AIM-7F.

Below: Propelled by explosive bolts, the canopy goes up and back a split second before the ejection sequence is initiated in this static test. The crew are, of course, dummies.

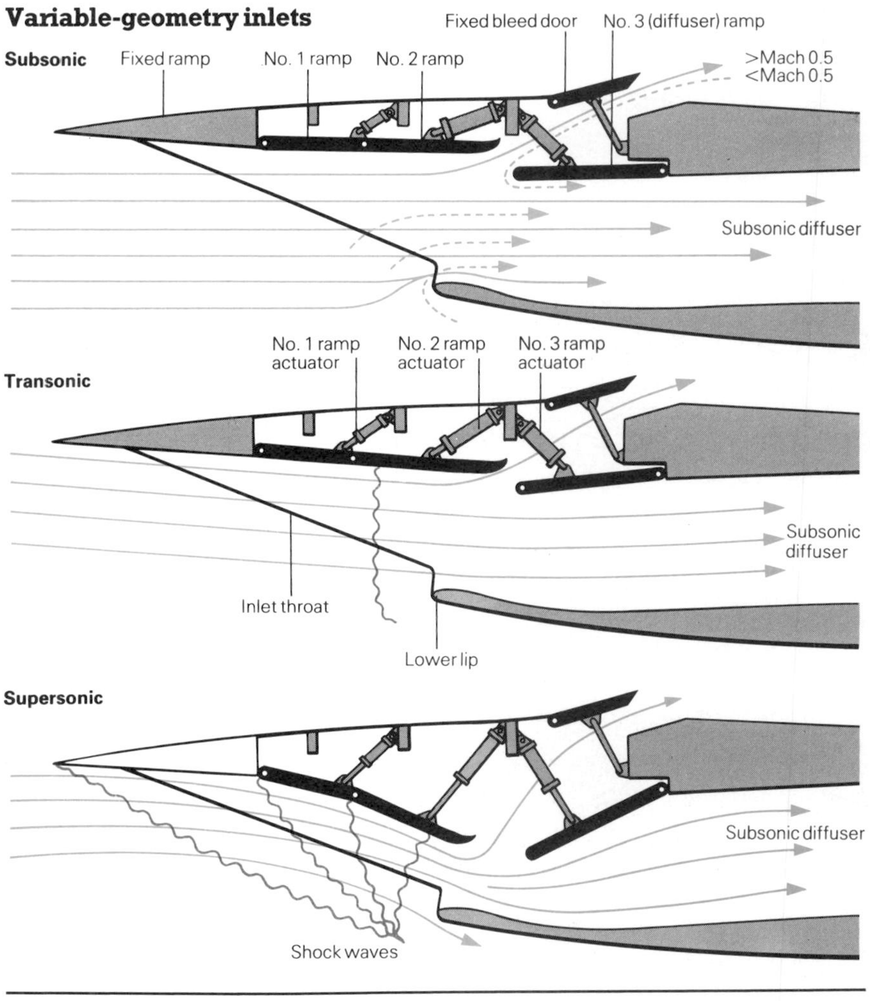

Below: As it was known from the start that the TF30 was a rather sensitive engine, design of the inlets was given careful thought. Three basic flight regimes had to be catered for: subsonic, transonic and supersonic, each of which demands high quality, non-turbulent air to be delivered to the compressor at subsonic speed. Three ramps and a bleed door are employed.

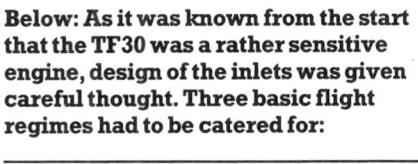

Above: Close view of the tunnel between the engine pods showing the large lifting area. Also clearly visible are three of the four Phoenix pallets, designed to carry the big missile without compromising the Tomcat in its Sparrow-armed fighter role. The front ends of the forward pallets are turned down to reduce drag when the missiles are carried.

Above: The widely spaced engine pods set well out from the forward fuselage, and their straight lines from intake to nozzle, are apparent in this shot of a Gunfighters F-14.

Below: A perfectly judged arrival, as this VF-2 Bountyhunters Tomcat returns to the *Enterprise* in 1974. The smoke seems to indicate that the pilot is using full dry thrust.

test programme. To relate them all would be tedious, but we can pick out some of the more important ones.

Qualification of the wing carry-through box and pivot structure started early in 1970. Both static and dynamic tests were carried out, with loadings reaching 128 per cent of the design limits, which were applied at wing sweep angles varying between 25deg and 68deg. To ensure that the friction levels of the pivot were acceptably low, the bearing was tested during wing sweeps at temperatures of −43deg C (−45deg F).

Next, a fatigue test was initiated on the structure, scheduled to last twice the anticipated life, or 12,000 equivalent flight hours (EFH). At 9,700 EFH, one of the lower lugs on the pivot structure failed. All the lugs on all the pivot structures were increased in thickness as a result of this mishap, and the assembly was then tested to destruction. This occurred at 23,760 EFH, nearly four times the design life. Also tested to more than twice the design life was the boron epoxy taileron. In this case, it was the test rig and not the component that failed, fully justifying Grumman's faith in this material.

Drop tests

The most structurally demanding part of the life of a carrier fighter is the continual series of arrested deck landings. A series of drop tests were run, up to the design limit sink rate of 24.7ft/sec (7.53m/sec). Over 500 drop tests were scheduled, culminating in a planned drop to failure in September 1972.

In the 1950s and 1960s, the complexity of modern aircraft tended to cause production tailbacks at the final assembly stage. To avoid this, the Ironworks used what they called the 'colony' concept. In essence, this was modular construction, with each major structural unit – wings, forward fuselage, and so on – completed as a module, then stuffed with all its plumbing and wiring and tested in its own area. Only at the final assembly stage did the completed modules come together on a final assembly line.

Powerplant

Technically, the most troubled aspect of the F-14 programme has been the engine. The TF30-P-412 augmented turbofan originally used was intended only as a stopgap until the new Advanced Technology Engine became available, but for various reasons the ATE was a non-starter and the Tomcat has soldiered on with two TF30 developments, the P-414 and the P-414A. Neither was ever entirely satisfactory, but a replacement was a long time in evolving: only in 1984 was the matter finally settled, with the selection of the F110-GE-400, but the new powerplant will not be in fleet service until 1990.

The design of the Pratt & Whitney JTF-10A turbofan, military designation TF30, was started on April 1, 1958. One of its first applications was to have been to power the Missileer; later, equipped for afterburning, or more correctly for a turbofan, augmentation, it was selected to propel the F-111, with a variant, the TF30-P-12, designed specifically for the Navy F-111B. The TF30 was the world's first augmented turbofan engine, and when the naval F-111B was cancelled, was the only suitable choice to power its successor.

It was recognized that the TF30 was not ideal; it was a bit short on thrust for the job that it was expected to do, and in the F-111 had suffered severely from compressor stalling. On the horizon was the new ATE, funded jointly by the Navy and the Air Force, which was expected to have less sensitivity, about 40 per cent greater thrust and a 30 per cent improvement in specific fuel consumption (sfc), as well as offering a considerable weight saving. The temptation surely existed for the Navy to wait for the new engine, but the existence of new Soviet fighter types, including the MiG-25 Foxbat, gave the F-14 programme added urgency. Consequently, the decision was taken to proceed with the TF30-powered F-14A, with the ATE-powered F-14B following about two years later. At the earliest reasonable moment (not the earliest possible: TF30s were too expensive to just throw away), the F-14A was to be retrofitted with the new engine.

The early definitive engine for the F-14A was the Pratt & Whitney TF30-P-412, a modified P-12. It produced 12,350lb (5,600kg) thrust in military power, increased to 20,900lb (9,480kg) at full augmentation, for a weight of 3,969lb (1,800kg); overall length was 19ft 7in (5.97m), and maximum diameter 4ft 2in (1.27m).

The P-412 was an axial flow turbofan, with the fan and low pressure compressor stages driven by the low pressure turbine stage. The three-stage fan had a pressure ratio of 2.14:1, and both the rotor and stator stages were of titanium. The six-stage low pressure compressor was also built of titanium, but with steel stator blades, while the high pressure compressor, made mainly of nickel alloy, had seven stages. The combustion chamber was can-annular with a steel casing, and contained eight Hastelloy X flame cans, with four dual-orifice burners in each. Behind this came the single-stage high pressure turbine, whose rotor blades and stators were of cobalt-based alloy to combat temperatures typically exceeding 1,000deg C (1,832deg F). The three-stage low pressure turbine was constructed of nickel-based alloy, while the augmentor consisted of a double wall outer duct, and an inner liner holding the five-zone burner system.

Turbofan advantages

The difference between a turbofan and a turbojet is that the turbofan's low pressure turbine takes energy from the hot jet to power large fan stages at the front of the engine. The fan stages take air from the inlet duct and pass it round the hot core of the engine proper, which reduces the average velocity of the core jet and the surrounding fan air combined, effectively reducing fuel consumption. In a turbojet, the afterburner operates in the engine exhaust gases, which have already had a high proportion of their oxygen burned, while the turbofan supplies a constant stream of oxygen-rich unburnt air through to the augmentation stage. The greater amount of oxygen allows more fuel to be used, which gives increased thrust. The ratio of air passing through the annular fan duct to that passing through the engine

Above: Seen here at full thrust on the test rig is an example of the Pratt & Whitney TF30 turbofan. At the front is a FOD screen intended to prevent birds being ingested.

Right: The TF30-P-412 engine was intended as an interim measure only but its replacement has been a long time coming. TF30 subtypes will power the Tomcat for many years yet.

core is known as the bypass ratio, and in the case of the TF30-P-412, is 0.9.

Experience with the F-111 programme had demonstrated that the TF30 family of engines were prone to compressor stalls. The blades of a compressor have sections like miniature air foils, and these will stall if the airflow meets them at more than a certain angle. It was known, however, that much of the compressor stalling problem encountered by General Dynamics arose from the design and position of the inlets. Aware of the difficulties, Grumman had done everything possible to get the engine inlets and ducts right, to the extent that, as described in the Development chapter, the engine airflow requirements influenced the layout of the airframe.

Early flight testing soon confirmed that Grumman had got it right, and compressor stalling, which could not reasonably have been expected to be eliminated entirely, seemed to have been confined to acceptable levels, even in high AOA flight, provided that the power levels were kept high. Specific fuel consumption was higher than had been anticipated when using augmentation, while more thrust would have been useful, even though the F-14 outperformed the Phantom in almost every department. The thrust to weight (t/w) ratio was only about 0.78, quite a low figure compared with the slightly later F-15's ratio of greater than unity. T/w ratio affects rate of climb, acceleration, and specific excess power (P_s) for manoeuvring flight. With more powerful engines all of these could be considerably improved, although the automatic wing sweep compensated to some extent by reducing drag, and the F-14 actually has much better performance than its modest t/w ratio implies. But apart from all these factors, it should be remembered that the TF30 was regarded merely as an interim solution pending the arrival of the ATE about two years later.

The ATE had arisen from an Air Force-funded technology demonstration programme in 1968, with Pratt & Whitney and General Electric as contenders, and

Below: With nozzles dilated an F-14 blasts off using all five stages of augmentation. Despite continual improvement the engine has proved to be unreliable in service.

a contract was awarded to Pratt & Whitney on February 27, 1970, for development of the ATE, in the shape of the F401-PW-400. Incidentally, the F100 powering the Air Force F-15 and F-16 was developed from the same base. The F401 and F100 were each optimized for their respective missions, and were therefore cousins rather than brothers, despite their common ancestry. The F401 was pushing the technology of the times pretty close to its limits, but the potential benefits were considerable. Rated at 28,000lb (12,700kg) augmented thrust, it would have raised the t/w ratio of the F-14 at combat weight to just over unity, with commensurate improvements in performance. Sfc was also claimed to be considerably better, especially with augmentation.

A mockup of the F401 was made, and a fit check accomplished in the nacelle of the EMMA mockup on September 15, 1970. This was followed by an installation and removal demonstration on April 28, 1971. Progress was slow, and the first ground test engine was not received by Grumman until November 22, 1972, by which time 19 Tomcats had flown. The first flight of the F401 took place on September 12, 1973, in BuAer 157986. It was mounted in one pod only, with a standard TF30-P-412 in the other. Meanwhile, the escalating costs of the F-14 were causing raised eyebrows, voices, and blood pressure. Even more money to improve it, when all the indications were that it was doing very nicely with its existing engines, was hard to obtain. The F401 had technical problems, as did its Air Force cousin, the F100, although these were not insoluble, but caught between the Scylla of technology and the Charybdis of cost, the F401 programme was suspended in April 1974.

This left the TF30-P-412 as the definitive Tomcat engine for the immediate future. As related, it had performed quite adequately during the flight test programme, but as the Tomcat entered fleet service and the numbers of aircraft in the squadrons mounted, problems with the powerplant slowly began to emerge. They did not manifest themselves quickly, for the simple reason that the numerical build-up was slow, and this made patterns hard to identify at first.

Problems emerge

The basic TF30 could, after years of service in the F-111, be considered a mature engine, but in the F-111 it had led a relatively easy life. Then, during the Tomcat test programme, the F-14 had been flown by both Grumman and Navy pilots of above average ability, on a careful and premeditated exploration of the flight performance envelope. But when the operational squadrons got their hands on it and started to amass flight hours at a high rate, it was a very different story, especially in air combat manoeuvring flights: excursions to 50deg AOA became a daily event, with the throttles being worked back and forward, in and out of afterburner.

Part of the trouble lay in the aerodynamic excellence of the Tomcat, which permitted manoeuvring that the Phantom or Crusader driver could only dream of. Both of these fighters, good though they undoubtedly were, were of the previous generation. The Phantom in particular tended to bleed off energy rapidly in a turning fight; the normal procedure was to keep the loud pedal firmly down to keep the energy levels up. The Tomcat, on the other hand, was so good in this respect that often pilots were forced to throttle back to maintain a good attacking position, then throttle up again. All this meant hard work for the engines, and they frankly didn't like it: they just had not been designed for such hard usage.

TF30-P-414 exhaust nozzle

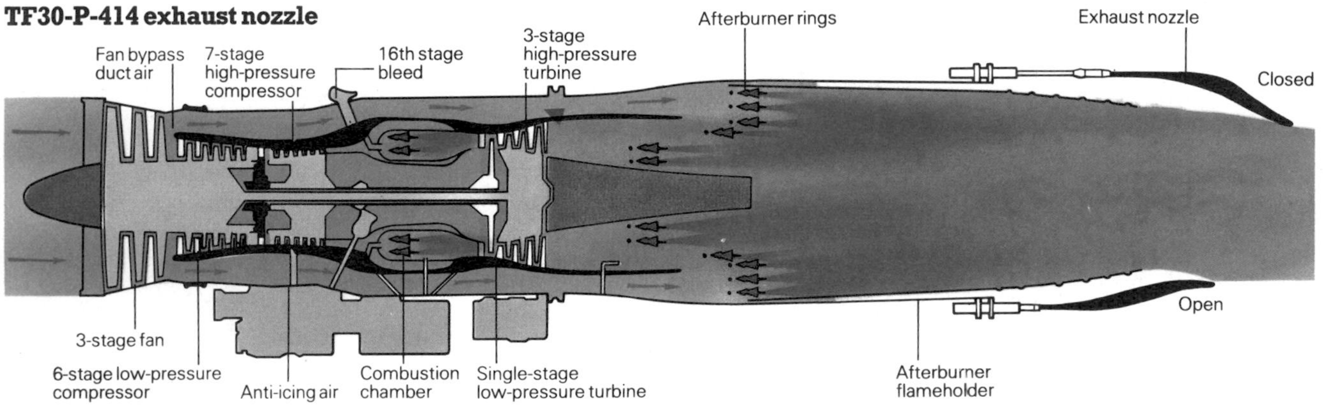

Left: Essentially a -412 modified to improve reliability and safety, the TF30-P-414 incorporated a certain amount of redesign plus steel containment casing around the first three fan stages. This increased the weight but provided no extra thrust.

Below: The -414 was unsatisfactory and further fixes produced the -414A seen here. A total of 31 further engine mods were made, and kits to modify the -414 were produced in addition to new engines. Less prone to compressor stalling than earlier models, the -414 suffered from the disadvantage of being smoky.

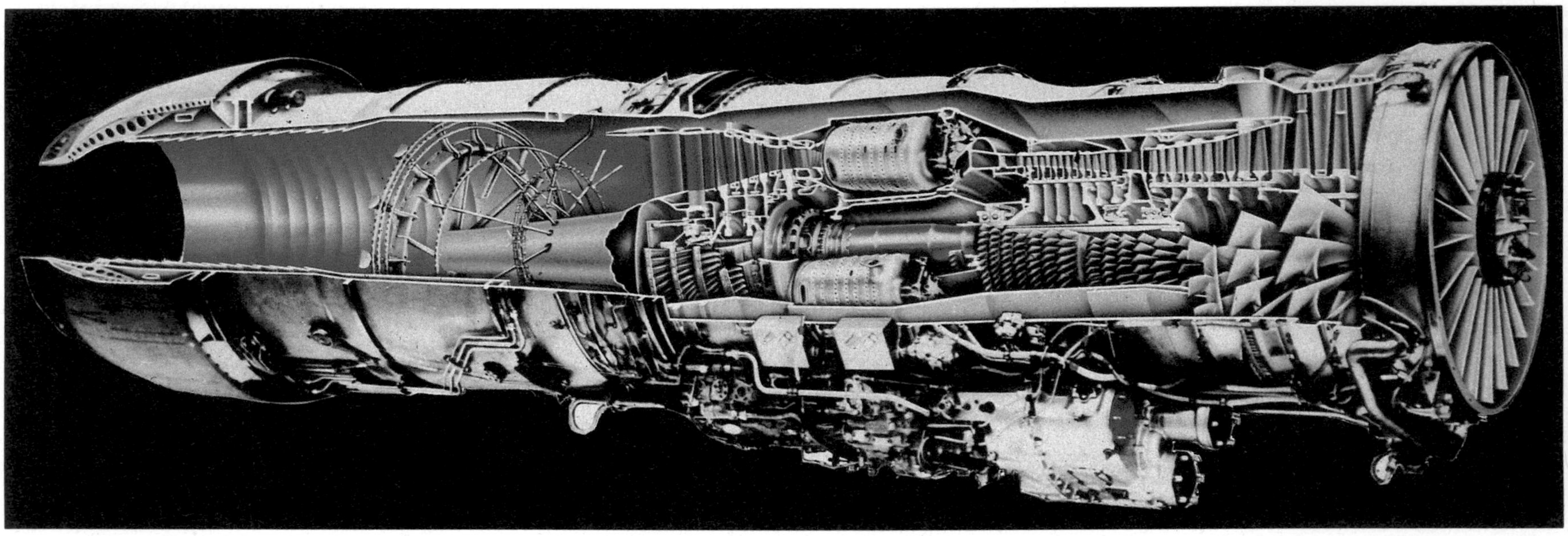

Below: The nozzles of jet engines are designed to expand the exhaust gases to reduce their pressure to roughly that of the outside air, which demands that their area should be variable. The nozzle designed for the TF30 as used in the Tomcat is a delicately engineered system of hydraulically actuated leaves mounted on rollers and sliding on a track.

Right: Tomcat variable nozzles. The upper illustration shows the normal military power setting, while the lower shows the nozzle fully dilated for afterburning.

TF30-P-414 internal layout

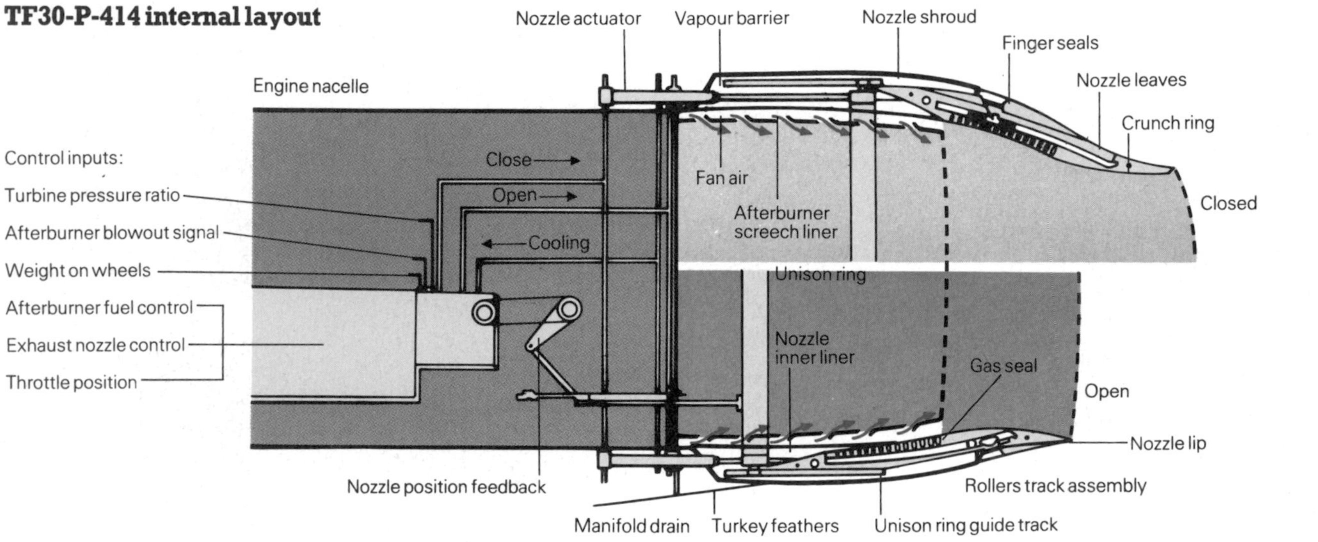

Exhaust nozzle positions

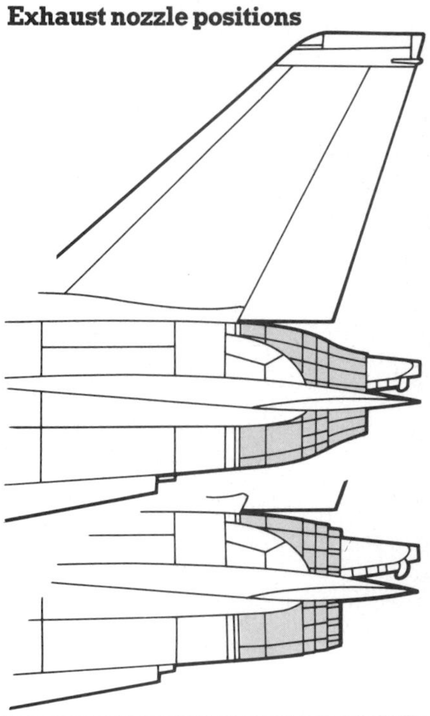

It had been thought that the hardest part of an engine's life was in prolonged full power running, but in fact these continued throttle transients took a far greater toll, and compressor stalls became frequent. Some were caused by high AOA at low power settings; others by afterburner 'pop', which is a result of delay in afterburner light-up: fuel momentarily accumulates in the tailpipe, where it is ignited by the hot core exhaust, causing a small explosion, which in turn causes pressure to back up through the engine, stalling the fan, the compressor, or both. The risk increased in proportion to the number of times that afterburner was either engaged or cancelled.

Back in 1972, the Navy anticipated that 1,000 flight hours would involve 597 afterburner lights, and 1,165 engine cycles, the definition of a cycle being a transition through all the power settings. These figures were subsequently shown to be way short of the mark: in 1979 the Naval Air Test Center installed low cycle fatigue monitors in the engines of 30 F-14As, and the results, gathered by late 1981, showed the true requirements to be no fewer than 2,250 afterburner lights and 10,549 engine cycles, increases of 277 and 805 per cent respectively!

With these unanticipated stress levels, it was little wonder that the TF30 had component failures, the most frequent of which, and potentially the most damaging, were failures of the fan blades. Unfortunately, at the design stage, no requirement had been laid down for blade containment. When a failure occurred, the broken blades sliced through almost everything in their path, causing considerable damage and rupturing fuel lines and tanks, which all too often resulted in fires. Several Tomcats were lost to this cause.

A programme of fixes was put in hand. Steel containment cases were installed around the first three fan stages, and the radius of the fan blade leading edges was increased, while the blades themselves were manufactured from a different titanium alloy which was less susceptible to stress corrosion cracking, the second to third stage fan air seal was modified, and the third stage fan rotor was redesigned. Fire containment measures also featured in the fixes. Titanium sheets were installed over the engine nacelles, while thin steel plates coated with an ablative substance helped to protect the flight control rods from the effect of engine fires. The flight control rods had been found to be particularly vulnerable to fires and a fire extinguisher bottle was added to the centreline trough area as well as to the engine nacelles.

Various fixes, plus a certain amount of redesign, led to a new engine variant, the TF30-P-414, essentially the P-412 with the fixes described in the previous paragraph. It was slightly heavier, turning the scales at just over 4,000lb (1,800kg), and it produced no extra thrust. A test programme, although resulting in the loss of the aircraft, cleared the new engine for installation in production machines. The accident happened during stall tests flown from NATC Patuxent River on February 22, 1977, when the test vehicle, fitted with one P-412 and one P-414 engine, stalled the P-414 at high AOA as intended while cutting the afterburner on the P-412 in and out. The stall occurred when the P-412 engine was at full power, causing a violent yaw, and the Tomcat immediately entered a fast, flat, irrecoverable spin, forcing the crew to eject. The pilot was picked up with minor injuries, but the NFO did not survive. We shall return to this point later.

The P-414 showed no performance advantages, providing the same thrust as its predecessor, but it did offer slightly

TF30 intake and exhaust hazards

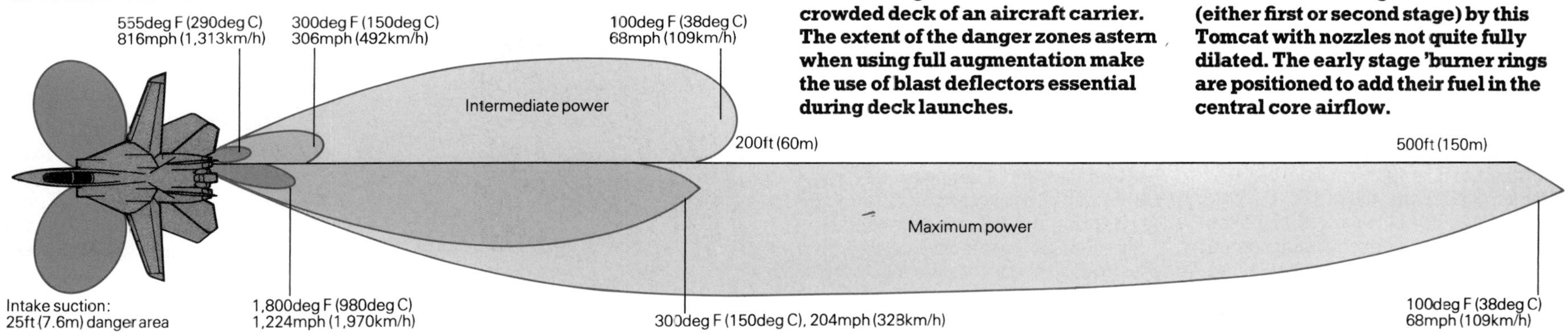

Left: The engines are a hazard on the crowded deck of an aircraft carrier. The extent of the danger zones astern when using full augmentation make the use of blast deflectors essential during deck launches.

Bottom: Limited augmentation is used (either first or second stage) by this Tomcat with nozzles not quite fully dilated. The early stage 'burner rings are positioned to add their fuel in the central core airflow.

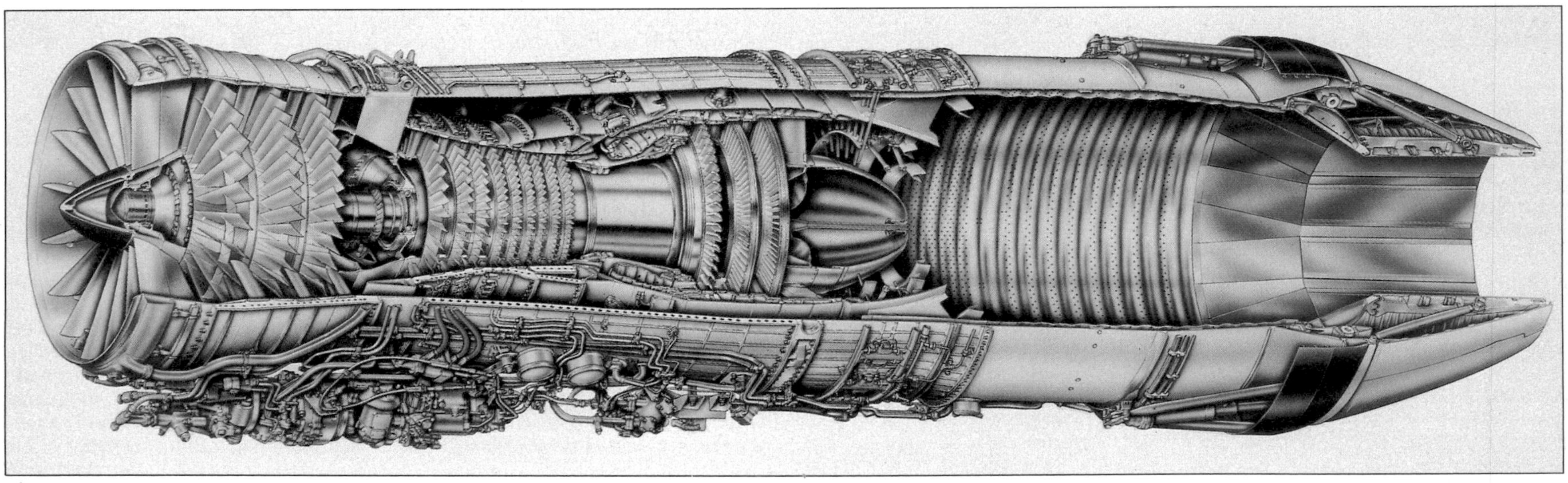

Above: The US Air Force General Electric F110-GE-100 was developed from the B-1's F101 via the F101DFE. Internally it is simpler than the TF30, and although more powerful, it is substantially smaller.

Below: The main difference between the -100 for the USAF and the -400 for the F-14 is the length. The basic F110 is shorter than the TF30 and has a 50in (127cm) steel tailpipe extension fitted to suit the F-14.

F110-GE-100/-400 profile section

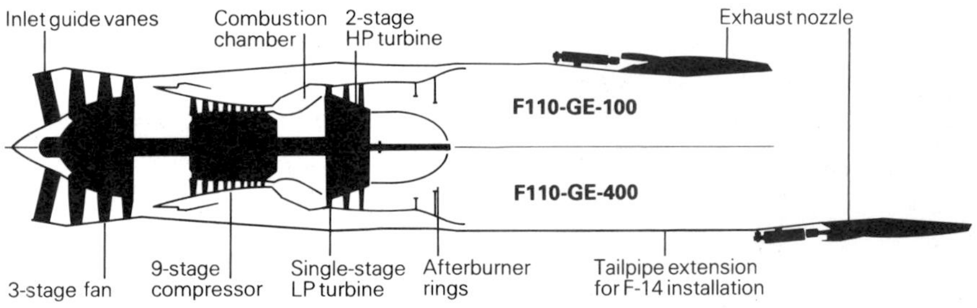

greater safety and reliability. The full extent of the problem would not become apparent until the figures were produced, although the loss statistics were bad enough. In the 35 months between January 1975 and November 1978, 31 Tomcats were lost to all causes. Of these, over 35 per cent were due to engine-related causes, and had it not been for the fan blade containment and fire prevention measures adopted, this figure might well have been higher. In two cases, *both* engines failed. The P-412 was replaced in fleet service between February 1977 and June 1979.

While the P-414 was a definite improvement over its predecessor, it was still far from satisfactory, a fact underlined by an engine up-grade programme consisting of 31 changes that was instituted by the Navy as early as October 1978, barely two-thirds of the way through the P-414 replacement programme. This had a fourfold purpose. It was intended to increase the low cycle fatigue life of all rotating components, to extend the inspection period for the hot section of the engine from 550 hours to 1,000 hours, to double the time between engine overhauls from 1,200 hours to 2,400 hours, and to reduce the stall rate. In the event, the inspection and overhaul targets were not achieved due to a vane in the third turbine disc burning through during testing in May 1981. Finding the cause of the failure and developing a cure would have caused unacceptable delays to the modification programme. The 31 changes were proved in two 2,400 hour accelerated simulated mission endurance tests, and were sufficient to warrant a change to the engine suffix: the P-414 now became the P-414A.

Sufficient kits to upgrade 1,007 engines from P-414 to P-414A configuration were issued to the Navy, the first being delivered to the Naval Air Rework Facility at Norfolk in October 1982. As the aircraft came in for their 30-month overhaul, so the modifications were made. At the same time, new production engines to P-414A standard replaced the P-414 on the production lines, the first of 158 new-build engines reaching the Navy during the following December.

The P-414A was more durable, and less prone to compressor stalling at low power settings than the P-414, but yet another problem was emerging: the exhaust was leaving a smoky trail. The F-14 is a big aeroplane and relatively easily spotted from a distance. Smoke made it even more visible and was one thing that it could really have done without. Pratt & Whitney instituted a programme to find a fix, but by mid-1984 no firm proposals had been made. Also in mid-1984, the manufacturers were still wrestling with the compressor stall problem, and were in the process of developing an automatic recovery system, although further improvements were not likely to become available for another two years.

In spite of numerous fixes, engine durability is still not all it might be, while the latest TF30 produces exactly the same thrust as it did 12 years ago. It is difficult not to be critical, and in a statement to the House Appropriations subcommittee of Congress in 1984, Navy Secretary John F. Lehman, Jr., pulled no punches. Referring to the TF30/F-14 combination, he called it "probably the worst engine/airframe mismatch we have had in many years. The TF30 is just a terrible engine and has accounted for 28.2 per cent of all F-14 crashes . . . the F-14 can perform its mission, but it has to be flown very carefully. You have to fly the engine, and cannot fly it in certain parts of the upper left-hand corner of the flight envelope (i.e., low speed, high altitude), without high risk."

Below: With a FOD screen and funnel fitted over the intake an F110 is tested at full thrust. The exhaust gases are drawn off through a noise and heat baffle at the rear.

Lehman, it should be pointed out, is not just a politician; he is also a pilot in the Navy Reserve, and therefore better qualified than most to make a statement of this kind. On the other hand, it does seem a trifle harsh. On the evidence, Pratt & Whitney were at least as much victims as villains of the piece. At the time of the Tomcat design inception the TF30 was the only engine in sight that appeared to be capable of doing the job, and the Navy expected that it would be used in the VFX competition by all tenderers. It was not foreseen that the flight performance of the airframe would be such as to make unprecedented demands on the engines, while if the problem was foreseeable, the user service was as well equipped as anyone to see it coming. In this context it should be remembered that both the F-15 and F-16 suffered engine problems arising from the same mission-related cause. And the final word on the subject must surely be that the TF30 was originally intended as a stopgap engine pending the availability of the ATE.

Replacement needed

Development of the advanced technology F401-PW-400 had been suspended in April 1974, but the need for more thrust, and incidentally, more dollars for development, lingered on. As the Tomcat entered fleet service, so the needs for greater durability, better sfc and stall-free performance were added to the shopping list. All of this pointed to a new engine, but as the Tomcat was committed to the TF30 for the time being, it was reasonable to hope that engine fixes could be devised to cover at least the durability and stalling problems. As we have seen, this was not to be, but there was no way of knowing that at the time.

By 1976 three new engines were emerging as possible TF30 replace-

ments. These were the Pratt & Whitney F401-PW-26C, which offered increased performance over the F-400, General Electric's F101-X, of which more later, and variants of the Allison TF41 as used in the A-7: the TF41-912-B31, an unaugmented engine offering approximately 18,000lb (8,165kg) of dry thrust, and the -B32, the same engine fitted with a variety of afterburners. No real action was taken, because although the Navy had $15m in the FY 1977 budget for a hardware competition for a follow-on engine no money was available in the FY 1978 budget to continue the programme. It therefore seemed pointless to engage the manufacturers in a competition with no future.

At the time, Pratt & Whitney were widely regarded as the most advanced of all the engine manufacturers. This caused some misgivings in government circles, partly due to the competition aspect, and partly because problems were being experienced with another Pratt & Whitney product, the F100 used to power the F-15 and F-16.

It was only sensible that both the USAF and the USN should pool their limited resources to develop a common powerplant which could be used as a replacement for both the TF30 and F100. Air Force Systems Command was directed to define a limited development programme by November 5, 1978, and a 30-month development contract was awarded to General Electric in March 1979. This would achieve two stated aims: to produce a fall-back engine for both services should such become essential; and to bring General Electric to a state of technical parity with Pratt & Whitney, thus solving the problem of future competition. The chosen engine was the F101-X, or, as it was to become known, the F101DFE (Derivative Fighter Engine). Its origins lay in the core of the F101, then under development for the Rockwell B-1 supersonic bomber, coupled with a scaled-up fan and augmentation from the F404 turbofan used to power the F-18 Hornet. In passing, it is interesting to note that the F404 was an exceptionally reliable and stall-free unit, in contrast to the TF30.

The development programme was unusual in that only three engines were to be built and tested, although two earlier 'boilerplate' F101-X demonstrators had logged 350 hours of test running in 1977-78. The first engine, No. 003, underwent systems and operability testing at General Electric's Evendale, Ohio, facility, while 004 was used for accelerated mission testing, also at Evendale. This involved 1,000 equivalent

Above: The original F-14B prototype is fitted with General Electric F101DFE engines prior to flight testing. Performance improvements justified the Super Tomcat label.

flight hours using the mission profile of the F-16, for which it was also under consideration, after which it was stripped down and inspected, then put back together for another 1,000 equivalent flight hours test using the mission profile of the Tomcat. This was completed in June 1981. The third engine, 005, was put through exhaustive altitude testing in the Naval Air Propulsion Test Center at Trenton, New Jersey, completing the schedule by February 1981. These three engines were then scheduled to be fitted into aircraft and flight tested, a procedure described by George E. Ward of General Electric as "pretty sporty."

Super Tomcat

The prototype F-14B, BuAer 157986, which had only flown for 33 hours in the development programme before being stored, was the obvious choice for this task. Dusted off, with F101 DFEs fitted and the legend 'Super Tomcat' blazoned across both fins, it lifted off from Calverton on July 14, 1981 for a flight test lasting an hour and a half. This was the start of a limited development programme of flight testing that lasted into late September. Actually, 24 flights were scheduled, 24 flights were recorded, but 30 takeoffs and landings were made. Odd? You bet, but if one returns and hot refuels, i.e., refuels with the engines running, then goes off again, it apparently only counts as one flight! Results were favourable, and a further 20 flights, involving some 70 flight hours, were carried out in the period ending March 1982.

The data obtained justified the Super Tomcat title. Time on station for CAP missions was increased by 34 per cent and combat radius for deck-launched intercepts was up by a staggering 62 per cent, while significantly better acceleration rates were achieved throughout the entire envelope. Thrust was up, sfc was down, and the engines had demonstrated remarkably stall-free performance. One tremendous advantage was that the available thrust was sufficient to allow the Tomcat to be catapult-launched at military power settings, as the use of full augmentation at takeoff from the carrier had led to a number of accidents directly attributable to compressor stalling. One of the few unfavourable test results was in airstarting the engines: a speed ex-

Above: The F110-GE-400, showing its steel tailpipe extension. The nozzle is based on that of the F404, while the gearbox and some components are rearranged to fit the Tomcat.

ceeding 450kt (830km/hr) was needed, which was too high to be practicable.

The Navy was very impressed, and by the summer of 1982 a re-engining programme was definitely on the cards, the only remaining question being the choice of engine. Pratt & Whitney had by this time taken their F100 and developed it into the PW1130, the thrust of which, at 27,410lb (12,430kg), was comparable to the DFE for a lighter installed weight. The PW1130 lagged the DFE in development by about 18 months, but the Navy was still interested in keeping competition between the two companies open. Meanwhile, full scale development of the F101DFE began in October 1982.

Finally, General Electric was selected by the Air Force to supply 120 DFEs, now designated F110-GE-100, for the F-16, with a proposed follow-on of more than 3,000 engines over the next few years. The announcement was made on February 3, 1984, and this strongly influenced the Navy. The Air Force order meant that economy would be achieved through large-scale production, also that most of the research and development costs had been met by the Air Force. The F110 was therefore chosen as the engine to power the F-14D, due to enter production in 1988. Apart from the economic factors, the F110 seemed a very suitable engine for the purpose. At the same time, a feasibility study was also put in hand to examine the possibility of retrofitting the F-14A with the new engine.

The designation of the new engine for Navy service became F110-GE-400. It varies slightly from the Air Force -100 in having a 50in (127cm) long steel tailpipe extension, and the gearbox and some components are rearranged to fit the Tomcat. The production qualification test is scheduled to commence towards the end of 1984.

The -400 has a bypass ratio of 0.85, with a three-stage fan, the blades of which are solid titanium, while the inlet guide vanes have variable trailing edge flaps. With a pressure ratio exceeding 3, the fan is the key to the engine's stall resistance, which is such that there are no restrictions on throttle movement throughout the entire operational range. For ease of repair, both the guide vanes and the fan blades are individually replaceable. The HP compressor has nine stages, the first three of which are variable. The blades are made of titanium in the front stages, changing to stainless steel towards the rear, where both temperature and pressure increase. The maximum pressure ratio developed is 11:1. The combustor is annular, with dual-cone nozzles which inject fuel into 20 scroll cups. These give a contra-rotating swirl effect to the airflow which ensures a satisfactory fuel/air mix in a very short distance.

The HP turbine is a single stage, with hollow airfoil section blades and vanes which are convection- and film-cooled by bleed air from the compressor, while the stationary shroud is segmented, being designed for cooling in such a way that the temperature expansion is compatible with that of the blades. In this way, constant clearance is provided for the blade tips. The LP turbine has two stages and is uncooled, driving the fan through the inner shaft which is concentric with the engine core. The blades in both are all individually replaceable.

F101 augmentation

The augmentation uses a convoluted flow mixer to mingle and burn flows from both the core and the fan. The flows mix in the plane of the flameholder, so that initial augmentation takes place in the hot, high-energy core stream, which gives much more reliable initial light-up than has been achieved on many turbofans, which in turn lessens the possibility of 'burner pop. Ignition is begun on the inner ring of the radial flameholder, and only when 90 per cent of the core flow is being burned is any fuel injected into the fan stream. This provides a relatively smooth increase in temperature over the augmentation range.

Below: The 'Super Tomcat' shows its paces for the camera during tests with the F101DFE engines in 1981. The extra power allows catapult launches without using 'burner.

Left: The carrier wings take their IFR tankers to sea with them. Here a Tomcat of VF-41 Black Aces takes on fuel from a Grumman KA-6D tanker of VF-355, also based on *Nimitz*.

Fuel tank locations

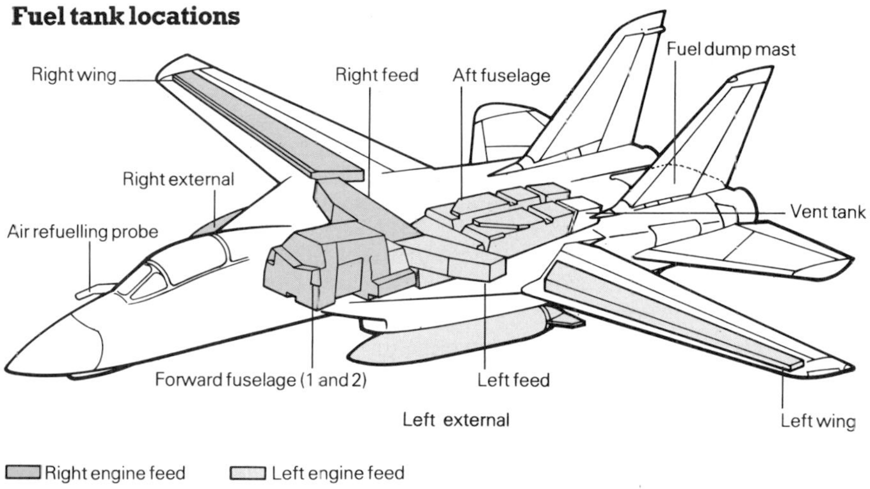

Above: A total of 16,200lb (7348kg) of fuel is carried internally in six tanks, including 2,000lb (907kg) in each wing; telescopic fuel lines adjust as the wing sweeps. The feed tanks are located in the wing box, and a further 3,800lb (1,724kg) can be carried in 'jugs', or external tanks.

Below: In-flight refuelling is standard to all Tomcats, allowing patrol time to be extended and combat radius to be increased. The retractable IFR probe is situated just below and in front of the cockpit, as this close-up of an Iranian machine shows; the ground refuelling point is below it.

A different exhaust nozzle is needed for the F110; this is a scaled-up version of the type used with the F404, with convergent-divergent flaps and seals, and outer flaps. If the F110-GE-400 lives up to its early promise, and there is no obvious reason why it should not, it will make the F-14D a very superior fighter in the air combat manoeuvring regime.

The fuel for the F-14 is generally JP-5, although JP-4 and -7 are both compatible. A total of 16,200lb (7,348kg) is carried internally in six areas: 4,700lb (2,132kg) is located in the forward fuselage, behind the cockpit; 4,400lb (1,996kg) is situated in the aft fuselage, where, incidentally, it was directly in line with stray blades from a disintegrating fan, a contributory factor to many in-flight fires; 2,000lb (907kg) is carried in each wing, utilizing telescopic fuel lines to accommodate changes in the angle of wing sweep; and the left and right feed tanks, mounted inside the wing carry-through box, contain 1,500lb (680kg) and 1,600lb (726kg) respectively.

The fuel dump outlet is situated on the trailing edge of the pancake, and connects to the aft fuselage tank. For in-flight refuelling, a retractable probe is located on the right-hand side of the fuselage nacelle, just ahead of the cockpit, while for ground refuelling a single point set low down beneath the IFR probe is used.

Information released at the time of the F-14 prototype's first flight stated that to achieve the Sparrow-armed air superiority mission radius of 500nm (921km), only 14,250lb (6,464kg) of fuel would be needed, but the additional capacity would be needed for the F-14B. The additional tankage was therefore included in all aircraft to save conversion at a later date; although the F-14B did not proceed, this proved to be a sound decision. The internal fuel load can also be supplemented by two external tanks, each holding 1,800lb (816kg) and carried on store stations 2 and 7.

Before we leave the subject of the Tomcat's propulsion, we should take a look at a question that has arisen quite frequently during the service life of the aircraft. The wide spacing of the engines resulted in a 4ft 6in (1.37m) moment arm between the centreline of the aircraft and the centreline of each engine. What was unarguable was that the dynamic failure of one engine while at full bore would cause a considerable asymmetric thrust loading, inducing a yawing moment. This appeared to have been a contributory factor in some F-14 accidents, although the precise degree to which it affected loss of control was unknown.

The loss of an F-14 during air combat manoeuvres at MCAS Yuma in 1983 was the final straw, and a test programme was instituted to investigate yaw characteristics under these conditions. A total of 22 sorties was made over the Edwards AFB test range, using the NASA Dryden facilities. The aircraft used was the early prototype Tomcat 1X, which was already equipped with many spin recovery aids. The tests were carried out at an altitude of 10,000ft (3,050m), but the engine functions were modified to simulate an altitude of 3,000ft (915m).

The final, and most demanding test in the series was flown by Grumman Chief Test Pilot Charles Sewell. It called for an AOA of 41deg, an airspeed of 150kt (276km/h) and both engines at maximum power. The right engine was then deliberately stalled by chopping the throttle to idle. The Tomcat pitched up to an angle of 72deg and developed a yaw rate of approximately 47deg/sec, while airspeed fell to a mere 25kt (46km/hr). Recovery was initiated and the effect was described as very positive, the Tomcat returning to normal controlled flight after about ten seconds. From this test, and the preceding flights in the series, it was concluded that the yawning moment was not a significant factor in causing loss of control.

Avionics and Armament

Writing in the spring of 1982, Commander John R. Wilson, Jr., Flight Test Officer of the F-14 Joint Evaluation Team, gave his verdict on the Tomcat's capabilities: "The F-14A is the most formidable and versatile fighter weapon system flying today. There are aircraft that fly faster or slower, but not both. Some fly higher, turn tighter, are better in the one-on-one visual ACM arena, but there is none, repeat none, that compares across the entire spectrum of fighter roles and missions, and *none* that can track 24 targets and selectively engage six targets simultaneously in the all-weather environment. It is the Phoenix/AWG-9 that really makes the F-14 unique among fighter aircraft."

The unique stand-off kill capability of the Tomcat against virtually any known or predicted type of target, from the ultra-high altitude, high speed Foxbat type, to tiny, wave-hugging cruise missiles, is conferred by the combination of the AIM-54 Phoenix missile and the Airborne Weapons Group Nine (AWG-9) avionic system for attack and detection, both produced by the Hughes Aircraft Company. AWG-9 is not just a radar. It is an integrated detection and weapon control system comprising a long-range, high-power multi-mode radar, an advanced fire control system, infra-red detection, computers and cockpit displays, and it also has a two-way data-link capability to enable it to transmit and receive information from surface ships and other aircraft.

The origins of AWG-9, like those of the Tomcat, date back to the Missileer, and were developed through the F-111B programme, though the design philosophy for AWG-9 as fitted to the Tomcat differs in principle from that developed for the F-111B. The F-14 was designed to be flown by the pilot rather than the black boxes, which was not the case in the earlier aircraft. Advanced technology (for the late 1960s) permitted a sizeable reduction in both weight and volume while increasing capability and giving more systems redundancy and back-up modes. In particular, a new generation of lightweight solid state computers provided major advantages, including the ability to simultaneously track up to 24 contacts while engaging six of them.

All weapons readiness is combined in a single control panel which, using the data from the sensors and/or the data link, advises the crew of the most effective weapon usage for the tactical situation. In addition, the computers permit extensive in-flight monitoring during non-critical phases of the mission, informing the crew of any malfunctions in the equipment, while all critical navigational functions are performed by the single Airborne Missile Control System (AMCS) computer. This eliminates the need for a separate navigational computer. Air-to-ground weapon release calculations are also made as required. AWG-9 was probably the most complicated airborne avionics system developed prior to the advent of databus technology.

As developed for the F-111B, AWG-9 had no Sparrow or Sidewinder capability and these had to be added, along with a tracking facility for the Vulcan cannon. New fighter attack modes were also incorporated. AWG-9 for the F-14 was more capable, cheaper, and 600lb (272kg) lighter than that for the F-111B. The first flight test of the reconfigured system took place in April 1970, in an adapted TA-3B.

While AWG-9 is an integrated system, it cannot be examined that way. To explain how it works, it must be considered unit by unit. The primary detection unit is the radar, which was based on the ASG-18 developed for the Mach 3 F-108 Rapier. Radar works rather like an echo sounder. It sends out a pulse, or stream of pulses, of electro-magnetic energy. The pulses weaken as the distance increases. If a pulse hits a solid object it bounces back, and can be 'heard' by the radar receiver.

Above: Tomcat 9 (BuAer 157988) launches a Phoenix missile in the first simulated Foxbat interception, in July 1972. This machine was bailed to the Hughes Aircraft Company during 1972-73; returned to the Navy in January 1974, it was assigned to PMTC and became the first Tomcat to reach 1,000 flight hours in June 1977.

The pulse attenuates in inverse proportion to the square of the distance covered, so that the echo is very faint by comparison with the pulse from which it emanated. For this reason, radar transmitters need to be very strong while the receivers should be extremely sensitive. AWG-9 has a very powerful radar, with a capacity of 10.2kW. This tremendous power is a great asset in long range detection, and also renders the radar less susceptible to electronic countermeasures (ECM), or jamming as it is generally known. Many jamming systems, particularly of the airborne type, are of relatively low power, and are unable to counter the AWG-9 emissions, which 'burn through' their signals.

Antenna performance

The radar antenna is a slotted planar array type, of 36in (914mm) diameter, the largest ever carried by a fighter. This type of antenna provides a higher gain than a parabolic dish antenna of comparable size, and is less vulnerable to certain types of jamming. Furthermore, the sidelobes, which are excess energy spilling over the side of the dish and causing erroneous returns, are much smaller. The planar array is also convenient for the location of interferometer identification/friend foe (IFF) antennas, which can also be used to obtain angular information.

The radiated energy is focussed into a narrow beam and pulses are transmitted, the number of pulses per second being referred to as the pulse repetition frequency (PRF). The antenna scans hydraulically and the echoes are received back while it is still aligned in pretty much the same direction as it was when the pulse was transmitted. From the received return a bearing angle can be obtained, and by measuring the time lapse between the emission and the return a distance can be established. In this connection, we are dealing with a time scale measured in microseconds.

Above: The radar components of AWG-9 are easily accessible for maintenance, as a Hughes technician demonstrates. They are all line replaceable units and the lifting handles can be seen. This enables faulty units to be quickly replaced. AWG-9 is self-testing and monitors itself in flight and on the ground.

The primary purpose of AWG-9 was to provide an ultra-long range detection and guidance facility for the Phoenix missile. For this it needed high power, and to achieve high power a high PRF is used. The greater the number of pulses transmitted per second, the higher the average power that is radiated, and the greater the detection range possible. High PRFs can be defined as exceeding 100,000 pulses a second.

So far we have described radar operating in the basic pulse mode. In the fleet air defence role, the Tomcat is likely to spend much of its time on station at medium and high altitudes, with the radar looking at or below the horizon. The pulses reflect back not only from aircraft, but also from the ground. In consequence, the radar picks up a multiplicity of echoes from the surface, generally referred to as 'clutter', amid which the return from a low flying aircraft would be lost. This poses a problem which is solved by the use of coherent pulse-Doppler radar.

Pulse-Doppler radar makes use of the Doppler shift, which is a frequency shift caused by relative speed, the time-honoured example of which is the change in pitch of the whistle of a locomotive as it rushes toward, past, then away from the listener. Exactly the same

Left: AWG-9 and Phoenix are the eyes and the claws of the Tomcat. The slotted planar array antenna, on which the IFF dipoles can be seen, is less vulnerable to jamming than a parabolic dish of comparable size. It is hydraulically actuated.

Right: Some idea of the complexity of AWG-9 can be gained from this simplified block diagram layout, in which can be seen the interplay of data and commands centred around the computer. Databus technology will streamline the system.

Below: AWG-9 components on display. The scale is given by the antenna, which is 36in (914mm) in diameter. Top right are controls and displays, top left are radar components. The upgraded AWG-9 system is digital and features four fewer units. The radar has a 10.2kW capacity.

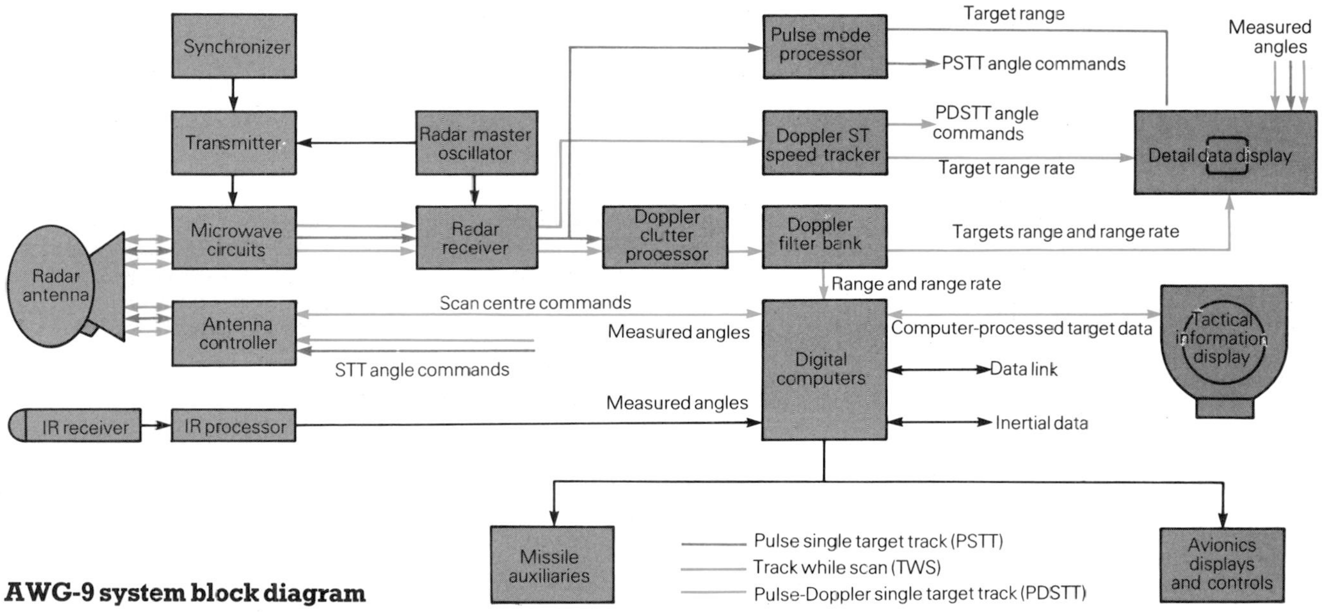

AWG-9 system block diagram

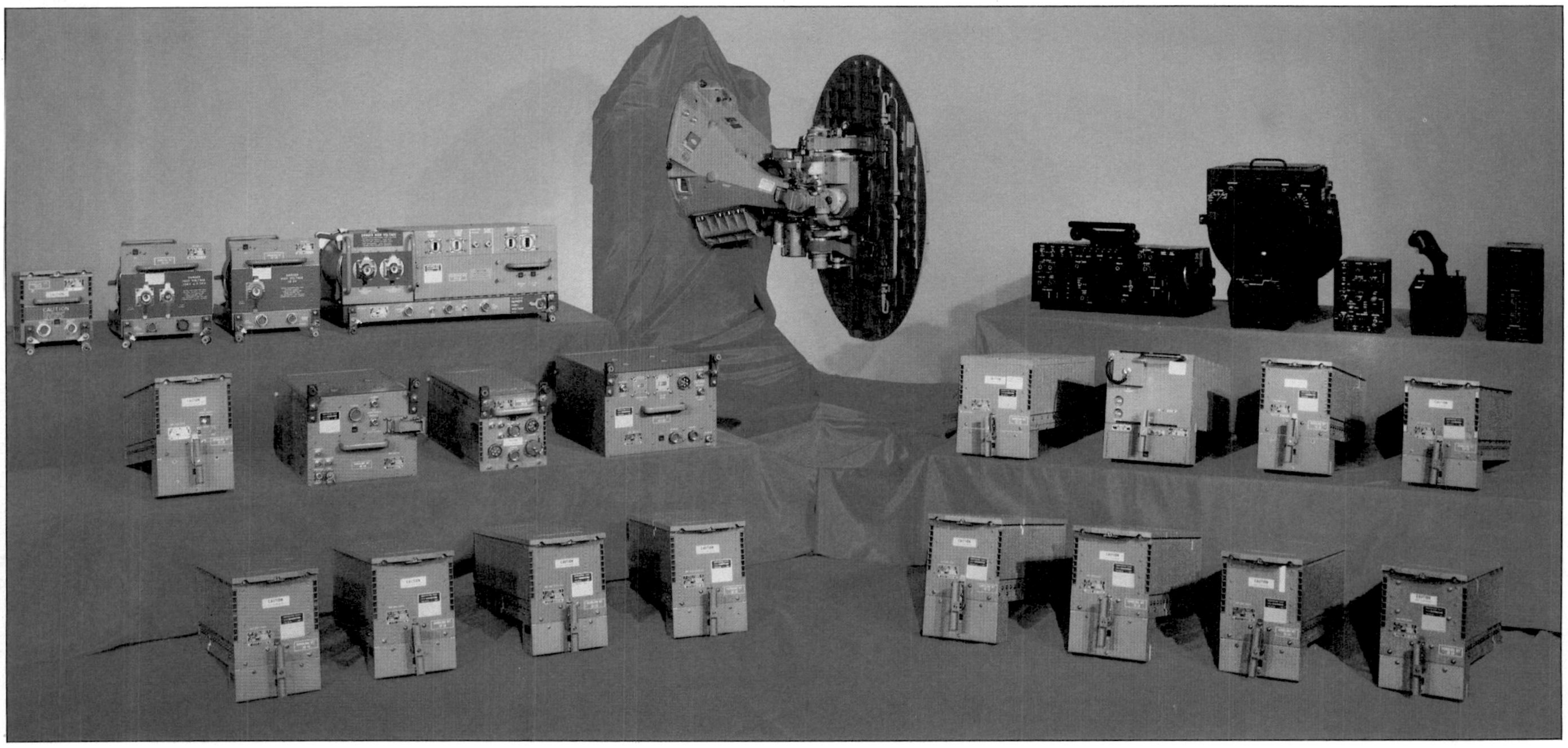

effect occurs with radar returns; the frequency of the returns from a moving object will vary from that of a stationary object, the variation in frequency being directly related to the relative speeds of the two objects.

Pulse-Doppler radar was made possible by the development of the gridded travelling wave tube (TWT) during the 1950s. The effect of the TWT is to increase the power level of a signal that is fed into it. It is very important to have each pulse exactly in phase with its neighbours, which is called coherence, and the TWT is pulsed with signals from a continuously running, ultra-stable coherent oscillator. In this manner, each pulse is transmitted precisely in phase with its fellows, so that any shift in frequency of the return can be detected and measured, giving the radar its look-down capability.

Returns from the ground naturally show a frequency shift as a result of the motion of the transmitting aircraft, but a moving contact will demonstrate a slightly different shift in almost all cases, and the ground returns can be filtered out by a bank of filters with graduated thresholds. These filters also grade the amount of shift, and by doing so determine the range rate, or speed differential, between the two aircraft. The ground returns having been eliminated, only moving objects are shown, which are almost certainly aircraft, and potential targets. Exceptions to this occur when a contact is moving at or close to right angles to the flight path of the transmitting fighter, or co-speed, heading away on the same flight path. In both cases, the contact's frequency shift will conform to that of the echoes received from the ground and will be filtered out with them, there being insufficient relative movement for detection.

High PRF is needed to give ultra-long distance detection, but it has one disadvantage. The time interval between pulses is so short that with distant contacts, several pulses will have been transmitted before the first echo is received, resulting in ambiguity as to which echo was engendered by which pulse. Frequently the radar return could be from a small contact at relatively close range, or a much larger and more distant contact. This difficulty is overcome by impressing a frequency modulation (FM) on a proportion of the pulses as a positive identifier.

Enhanced resolution

The change in the FM rate is detected by the computer by comparing the frequency difference between the modulated and unmodulated portions of the signal, while filters give improved range resolution to match the inherent resolution of the IFF system. At the same time, monopulse techniques and data processing are used to improve angular resolution which in normal search modes is rather coarse. The high PRF waveform is also limited in its ability to accurately measure range, while its ability to detect low closure rate contacts (i.e., tail-on, nearly co-speed) is poor.

On the other hand, AWG-9 radar is very versatile, and using the broad band gridded TWT it has 19 transmission channels available for pulse-Doppler search signals. Six of these channels are dedicated to Phoenix guidance, while a further five are used to provide semi-active guidance for Sparrows. The sheer number of channels permits adequate cover to minimize the effects of hostile ECM, while the TWT can accept different forms of modulation from the oscillator, allowing low as well as high PRFs to be used as circumstances dictate.

Vital parts of AWG-9 are the two cathode ray tube (CRT) displays in the NFO's cockpit. At the top of the panel is the 5in (12.4cm) Detail Data Display (DDD), which presents basic target data, while below it is situated the 10in (25.4cm) Tactical Information Display (TID). The TID presents processed information on a clutter-free screen showing the tactical situation with alphanumeric notation. Contacts are depicted together with their altitude and heading, identified as friendly or hostile, and, if hostile, assigned a firing priority as recommended by the computer, calculated on a pre-programmed 'greatest threat' basis. The NFO can override the computer-provided firing priority at his discretion.

The TID picture can be presented in two ways, either aligned with the F-14 with the fighter at the bottom of the scope pointing upwards, which depicts target motion in relation to the movement of both aircraft; or geostabilized with true north at the top of the screen and both the Tomcat and its targets shown. With a target on the TID, the NFO can instruct the computer to show its range, altitude, heading, and speed over the ground. The TID can also accept and display up to eight additional contacts from the ASW-27 two-way data link.

To ensure that the computer is tracking all targets, and to aid in the positive location of targets using ECM, the NFO monitors the information displayed on the DDD. The pilot also has a target display which is coupled into his Horizontal Situation Display (HSD) so that he has access to basically the same information as the NFO. Phoenix and Sparrow can be fired by either the pilot or the NFO, but only the pilot can launch Sidewinders.

The radar antenna of AWG-9 has a maximum scan pattern of 65deg to either side of the aircraft's centreline in azi-

AWG-9 pulse modes

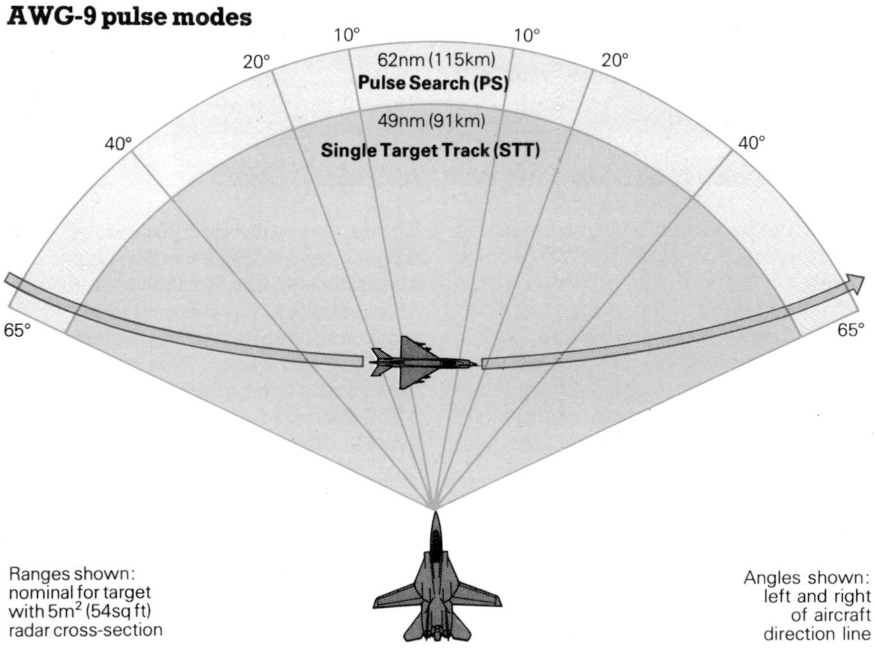

Above: Both pulse search and pulse single target track modes utilise the same scan patterns as pD (see below) but with reduced range. They are both effective against contacts at 90deg angle-off or with low closure rates.

Below: The pulse-Doppler modes give better range capability than pulse and also a look-down capability, but are ineffective against targets crossing at 90deg (see bottom right) due to lack of Doppler shift.

AWG-9 pulse-Doppler modes

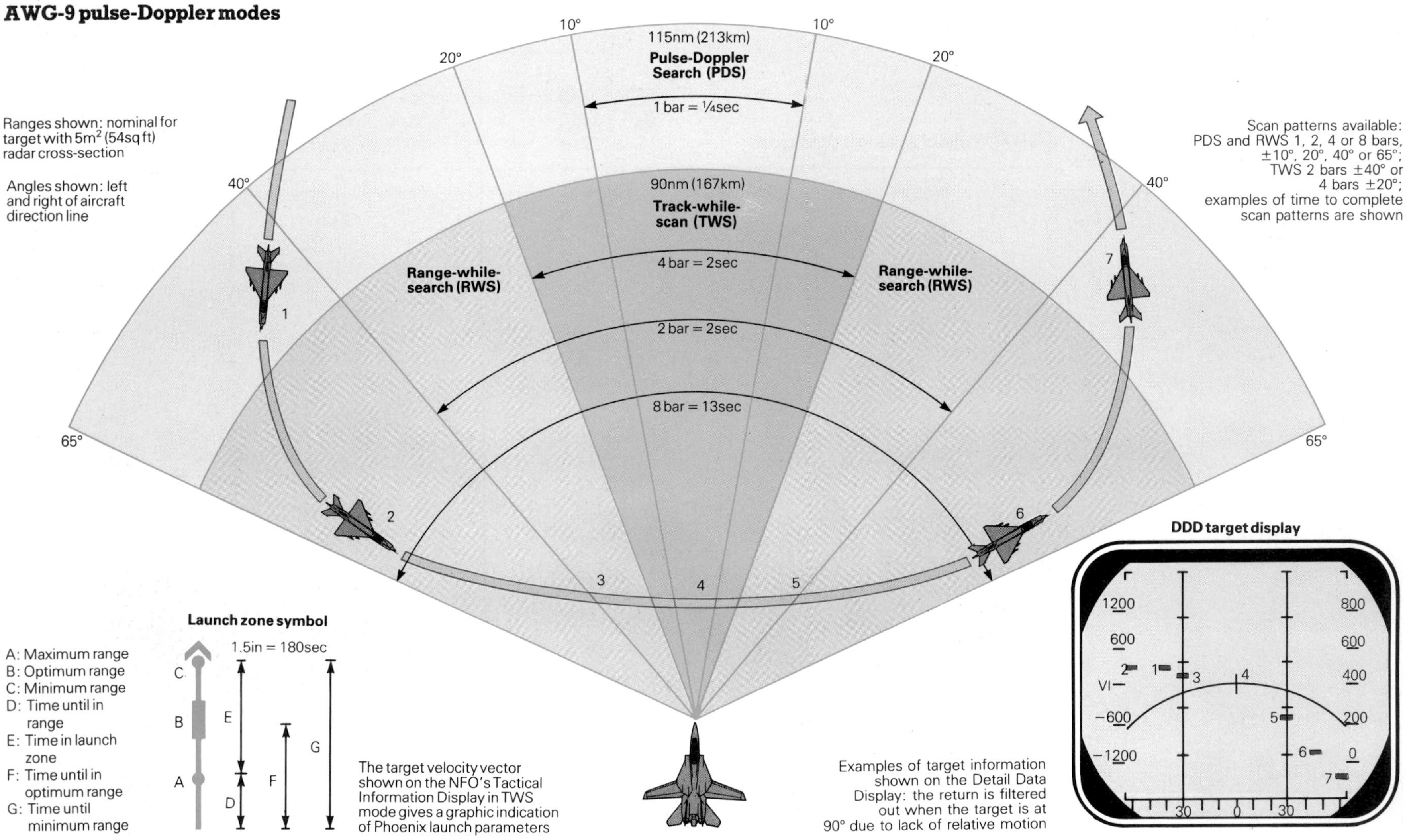

muth, and eight bars in elevation, the time cycle for the full scan being 13 seconds. The radar operates in six basic modes, four of which are pulse-Doppler, while the other two, used primarily for backup, are pulse only. The pulse-Doppler modes are: pulse-Doppler search (PDS), range while search (RWS), track while scan (TWS), and pulse-Doppler single target track (PDSTT).

PDS is used for long-range search and detection, using either the full antenna capability, or various reduced antenna programmes of 10deg, 20deg or 40deg to either side of the aircraft centreline coupled with one, two or four bars in elevation. The nominal detection range

Right: The NFO in the rear seat of a Tomcat is at the centre of a barrage of information, which can approach saturation point. Cockpit layout was designed by NFOs.

Below: Every inch of space is used. This view shows the left side console and the armament panel, on which can be seen various weapon switches and a clearly marked launch button.

Bottom: The NFO is the human end of AWG-9. His cockpit is dominated by the large circular TID and its hand control stick, with the smaller DDD just above. The NFO has a vital role to play in formulating tactics.

NFO's instrument panel and consoles

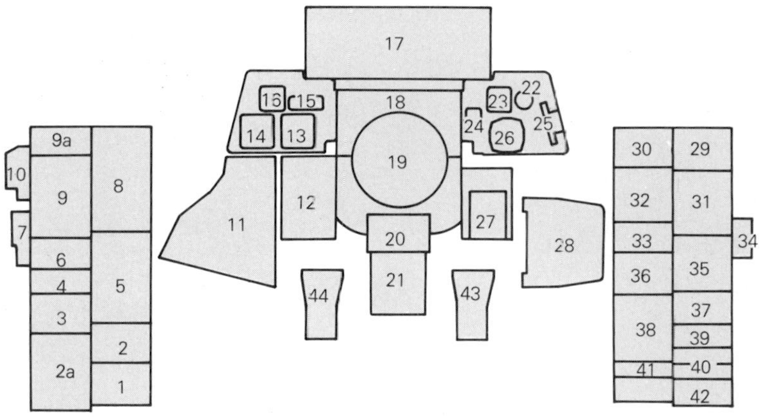

Left side console
1 G valve pushbutton
2 Oxygen vent airflow controls
2a Data stowage
3 Communications and navigation command control panel
4 Intercommunications system control panel
5 Integrated control panel
6 Tacan control panel
7 Liquid cooling controls
8 Computer address panel
9 Radar/infra-red/TV control panel
9a UHF communications selection panel
10 Eject command panel

Left vertical console
11 Armament panel

Left knee panel
12 System test/system power panel

Left instrument panel
13 Servopneumatic altimeter
14 Airspeed Mach indicator
15 UHF remote indicator
16 Standby attitude indicator

Centre panel
17 Detail data display panel

Centre console
18 Navigation control and data readout
19 Tactical information display
20 Tactical information control panel
21 Hand control unit

Right instrument panel
22 Fuel quantity totalizer
23 Clock
24 Threat advisory lights
25 Canopy jettison handle
26 Bearing distance heading indicator

Right knee panel
27 Caution advisory panel

Right vertical console
28 Multiple display indicator

Right side console
29 Digital data indicator
30 ECM display control panel
31 Data link reply and interior light control panel
32 ECM control panel
33 Defensive ECM controls
34 Defog control level
35 IFF transponder controls
36 ALE-39 programmer
37 AA1 control panel
38 Chaff/flare dispense panel
39 IFF antenna deployment and test panel
40 Radar beacon controls
41 KY-28 cryptographic system control panel
42 Electrical power test panel

Left and right foot wells
43 Microphone foot button
44 ICS foot button

is given as 115nm (212km) against fighter-sized targets with a 54sq ft (5m^2) radar cross-sectional area, though it is reported that jumbo-sized contacts can be detected as far away as 200nm (368km), and small cruise missiles at over 65nm (120km). Contact data is displayed on the DDD in terms of azimuth, elevation, and range rate, but not range. Boresight missile modes can be used in PDS.

RWS mode adds ranging to the long range search and detection by using FM techniques as described earlier, for a slight penalty in maximum detection range, which reduces to 90nm (166km) for a fighter-sized contact. The antenna programmes are the same as for PDS. The data is displayed on both the DDD and the TID.

TWS is the mode which sets AWG-9 apart from all other systems, with its ability to track 24 targets simultaneously. Ground testing has confirmed this capability, while a flight test has been carried out that successfully monitored seventeen, which was more of a headache for the ground controllers than for AWG-9.

In order to allow the computer to function correctly, contact data must be updated every two seconds; to achieve this, the field of scan has to be reduced to give coverage within this timescale. Two antenna patterns are compatible: plus and minus 40deg in azimuth combined with 2 bars elevation; and plus and minus 20deg in azimuth with 4 bars elevation. These enable the computer to store look angles, range, and range rate for each contact in a separate track file.

Intercept parameters

After a series of returns, the computer predicts where each contact should be and where the antenna should point on each subsequent scan. It then calculates missile intercept parameters based on stored launch envelopes, also launch priorities which are based primarily on the degree of threat indications. The designated targets are displayed on the TID, with a number indicating Phoenix launch order to their right. When the optimum launch position is achieved, the target symbol on the TID begins to flash, telling the crew they can launch.

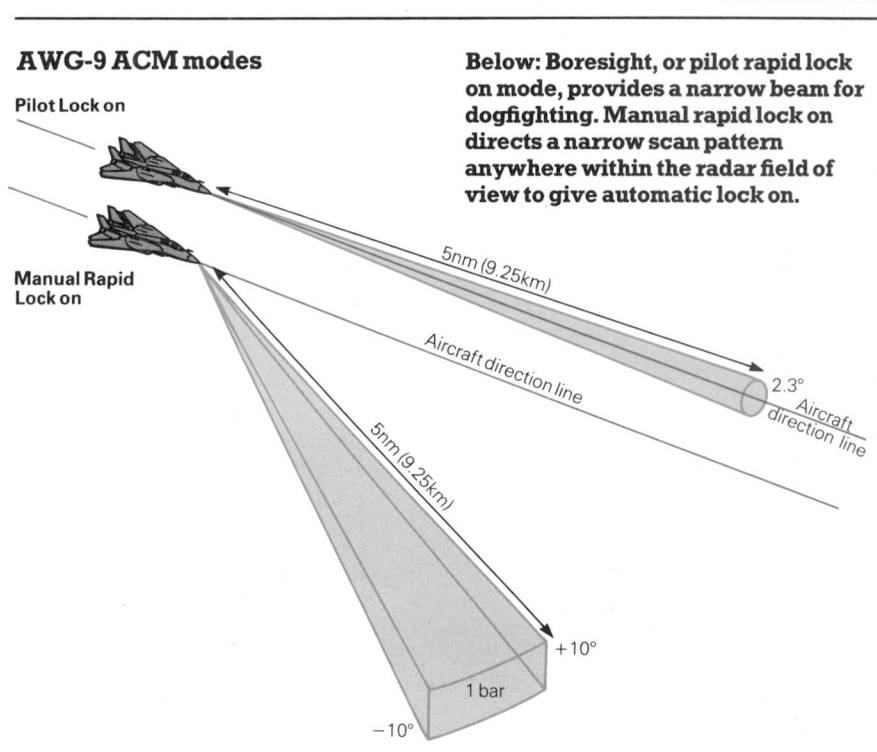

AWG-9 ACM modes

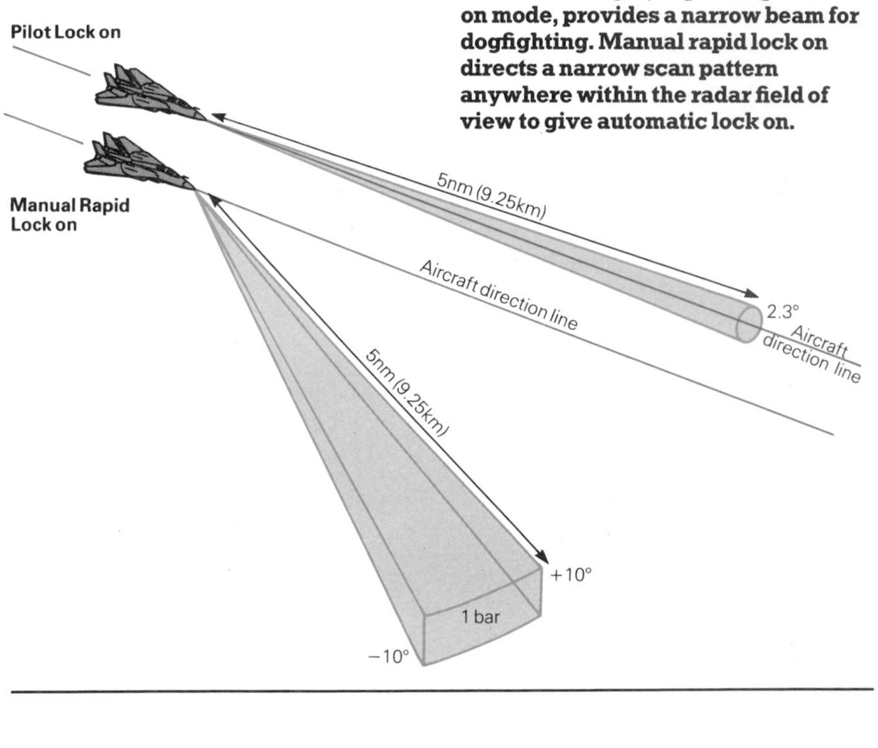

Below: Boresight, or pilot rapid lock on mode, provides a narrow beam for dogfighting. Manual rapid lock on directs a narrow scan pattern anywhere within the radar field of view to give automatic lock on.

Pilot's instrument panel and consoles

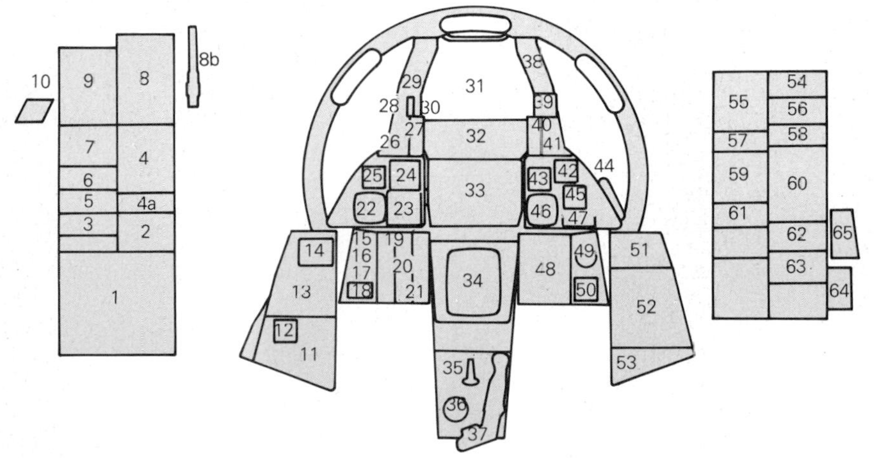

Left side console
1 G valve pushbutton
2 Oxygen vent airflow control panel
3 Communications and navigation command control panel
4 UHF (AN/ARC-159)
4a UHF communications selector panel
5 Tone/volume controls
6 Intercommunications system control panel
7 AFCS control panel
8 Throttle quadrant
8a Hydraulic hand pump
9 Inlet ramps/throttle controls
10 Target designate switch

Left vertical console
11 Fuel management panel
12 Control surface position indicator
12a Launch bar abort
13 Landing gear control panel
14 Wheels/flaps position indicator

Left knee panel
15 Engine pressure ratio indicator
16 Exhaust nozzle position indicator
17 Oil pressure indicator
18 Hydraulic pressure indicator
19 Electrical tachometer indicator
20 Thermocouple temperature indicator
21 Rate of flow indicator

Left instrument panel
22 Servopneumatic altimeter
23 Radar altimeter
24 Airspeed Mach indicator
25 Vertical velocity indicator
26 Left engine fuel shut-off
27 Angle of attack indicator

Left front windshield frame
28 Approach indexer
29 ACLS/AP/nosewheel steering engaged warning lights
30 Wheels/brakes warning lights

Centre panel
31 Head-up display
32 ACM panel
33 Vertical display indicator
34 Horizontal situation display
35 Pedal adjust handle
36 Brake pressure indicator
37 Control stick

Right front windshield frame
38 ECM warning light
39 Standby compass

Right instrument panel
40 Wing sweep indicator
41 Right engine fuel shutoff
42 Accelerometer
43 Standby attitude indicator
44 Canopy jettison handle
45 Clock
46 Bearing distance heading indicator
47 UHF remote indicator

Right knee panel
48 Fuel quantity indicator
49 Liquid oxygen quantity indicator
50 Cabin pressure altimeter

Right vertical console
51 Arresting hook panel
52 Displays control panel
53 Elevation lead panel

Right side console
54 Compass control panel
55 Caution advisory indicator
56 Tacan control panel
57 Master generator control panel
58 ARA-63 receiver-decoder control panel
59 Air conditioning controls
60 Master light control panel
61 External environmental control panel
62 Master test panel
63 Hydraulic transfer pump switch
64 Defog control panel
65 Windshield defog switch

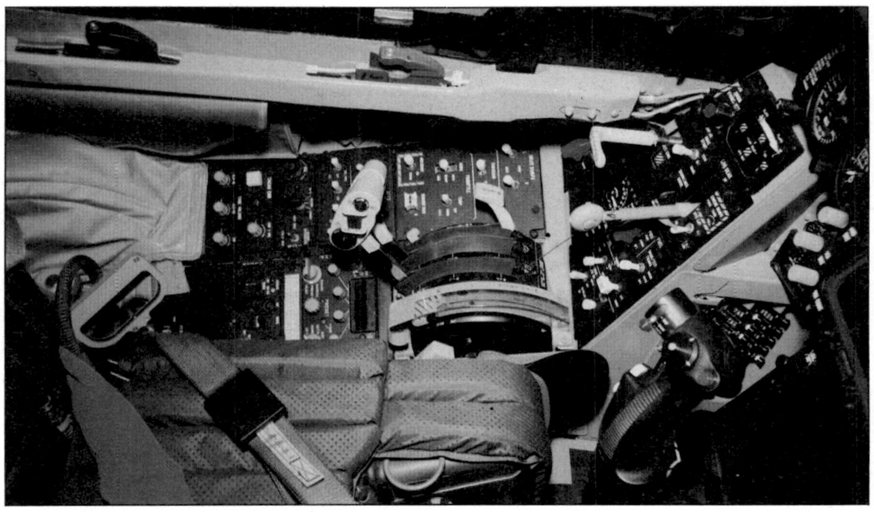

Left: The pilot's cockpit differs considerably from that of the NFO. The flight controls are in evidence, and the CRT displays are less dominant than in the rear position.

Above: The left console in the front cockpit is much simpler than that in the back, containing mainly engine controls plus Tacan and some other com/nav functions.

AWG-9 ACM modes

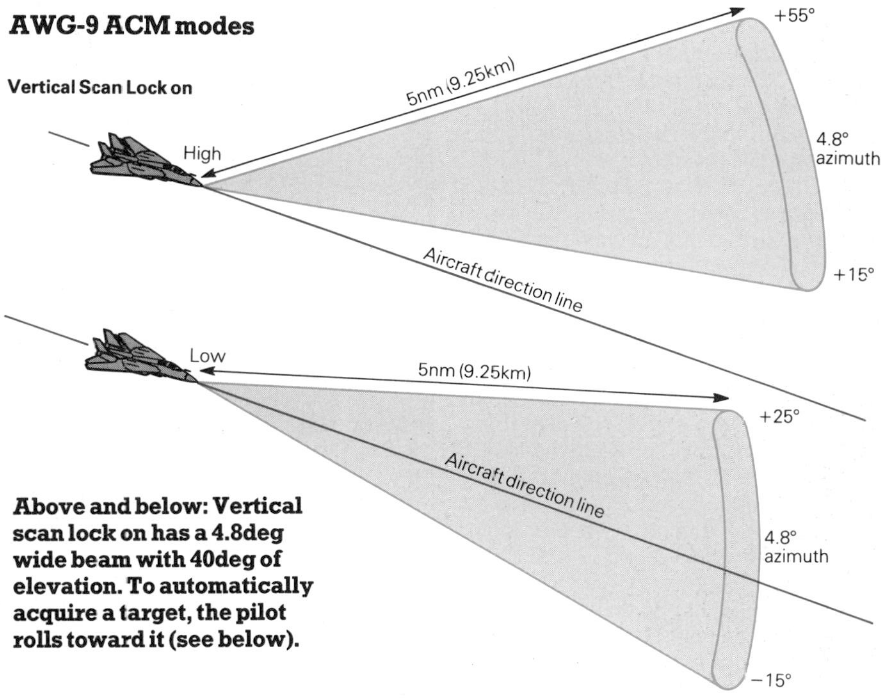

Above and below: Vertical scan lock on has a 4.8deg wide beam with 40deg of elevation. To automatically acquire a target, the pilot rolls toward it (see below).

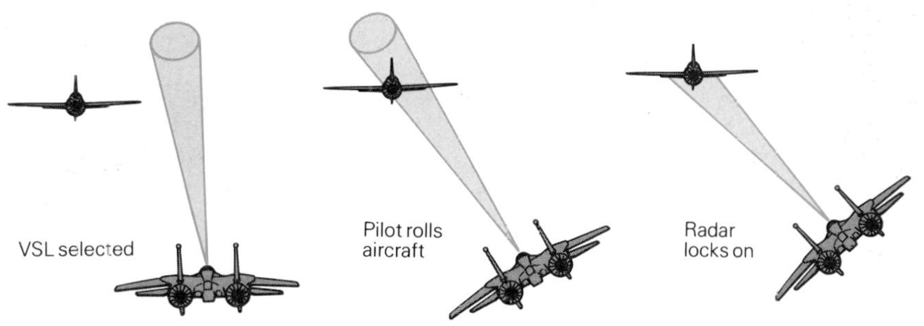

Left: The pilot's cockpit looks dated by modern standards, but in 1970 the air combat manoeuvre panel was an innovation, and some dials were replaced by tape instruments.

Above: Unlike more recent American fighters, the Tomcat is a two-seater. Each crewman has a well defined role and teamwork is the keynote, particularly for interception work.

Multiple Phoenix launches carried out in this manner are generally described as simultaneous attacks; this description is correct insofar as setting up the attack goes, but the missiles are necessarily fired one after the other in a predetermined order. TWS retains the nominal 90nm (166km) detection range for fighter-sized targets, but the maximum launch range for Phoenix in a multi-shot attack is stated as 52nm (96km). Mid-course guidance for Phoenix is provided by SARH until the terminal homing stage is reached, when the missile's active radar is used. In a multiple attack time-sharing is used to guide all the missiles.

TWS mode has one unusual advantage. With more conventional radars, the radar goes into attack mode, or locks on to the target prior to weapon release. Radar warning receivers in the target aircraft can detect the difference quite readily between a search scan, which simply indicates that someone is looking at them, and lock on, which indicates that a missile may very soon be on its way with hostile intent, but the TWS scan emissions are more difficult to identify as they appear to have the characteristics of a search mode rather than an attack mode. Warning of an inbound Phoenix is therefore minimal.

PDSTT is the mode used for the spectacular long-range Phoenix tests. It gives maximum range for tracking and also maximum range for a Phoenix launch. The antenna locks onto the target and the presented data includes range, range rate, and angle. PDSTT is also used for launching Sparrow and Sidewinder missiles. It employs a velocity track process, but it also incorporates a jamming angle track facility, for use against targets employing ECM, which provides range rate and angular data. Against standard fighter-sized targets, PDSTT provides a stated maximum launch range of 63nm (116km) for Phoenix, 38nm (70km) for AIM-7F Sparrow, and 10nm (16km) for Sidewinder. The earlier AIM-7E Sparrow needs continuous wave (CW) illumination on which to home; this is provided by a supplementary TWT in the transmitter.

Two pulse modes are used, mainly as backup for the pulse-Doppler modes. Pulse search is used for air-to-air search or for ground mapping. The antenna scan combinations are the same as for PDS, but naturally have no Doppler effect; range rate is therefore not available, just range and azimuth. Detection range reduces to 62nm (114km) for a fighter-sized target, but pulse search does have the advantage of being able to detect in the two blind areas of pD and can acquire bogeys at 90deg crossing angles or those with negligible closure rates.

Single target tracking

Pulse single target track is the other mode and is used in the conventional manner to lock on. It is compatible with all weapons, including the Vulcan cannon. Once acquired, the contact is displayed on the DDD together with its range. Phoenix can be used as a short range weapon using its active terminal homing, while CW illumination is provided for Sparrows, giving a maximum launch range of 18nm (33km) for the AIM-7E version and 29nm (53km) for the improved AIM-7F.

For close combat three modes are provided which give automatic lock on at ranges up to 5nm (9km). These are boresight, used in short-range attack or dogfight, which projects a 2.3deg wide beam along the axis of the Tomcat; vertical scan lock on, which is used to acquire a turning target; and a manual lock on mode. Vertical scan projects a narrow vertical beam in one of two positions, variable according to the needs of the moment. The first extends from 15deg to 55deg above the Tomcat datum line, while the second is from 15deg below datum to 25deg above, datum being a reference to the level axis of the Tomcat in the pitching plane. Above-datum acquisition permits missile launch without the nose being pointed directly at the target, while below-datum acquisition would be used for pulling lead on a hard-turning target.

Manual lock on uses a 20deg, 1-bar scan which gives lock on anywhere within the radar field of view to a range of 5nm (9km). Operated by the NFO, its use appears to require a high degree of communication and co-operation between the crew members, and for this reason it is unlikely to be used often. In all the close combat modes, the computer projects continuously updated weapon launch solutions through the Kaiser Aerospace Head Up Display (HUD) onto the windshield, which is used instead of a combiner glass.

An invaluable adjunct to the detection equipment of AWG-9 is its gimbal-mounted infra-red (IR) sensor, mounted in a pod beneath the nose of the aircraft. It possesses inherently better angular resolution than radar and can thus be used to confirm target azimuth and elevation. As it is a passive sensor, its use is undetectable, and it is sufficiently sensitive to gather data, including a rough assessment of range, to be used for either Phoenix or Sidewinder launch.

The IR detector can be used independently of the radar, for example to scan high while the radar searches downwards; or it can be slaved to the radar or vice versa so that the systems complement each other. It is especially effective in detecting high altitude after-burning targets, or rocket-propelled cruise missiles at long ranges, and in a heavy ECM environment it is an invaluable backup.

Weapon firing is actually performed by a separate computer, the AWG-15, while the problems inherent in using four different weapons, possibly in rapid succession and not in any particular order, are solved by using an integrated armament control system. A control and display indicator in the cockpit indicates, firstly, what selections a pilot should make for a particular weapon; secondly, when all necessary selections have been made; and thirdly, if an erroneous selection has been made. As an alternative, all weapon options can be pre-programmed and stored prior to takeoff, in which case a weapon is instantly prepared for launch at the touch of a switch.

A unique item for its time was the air combat manoeuvre panel, which consists of a single master panel mounted within the pilot's cone of vision. This contains the controls for rapid selection of all short-range weapons and was designed to be operated without the pilot risking losing visual contact with an opponent. This panel also gives the status of all remaining weapons, including the rounds remaining for the gun. Compared with the latest breed of fighter cockpit displays this sounds old hat, but in 1970 it was a major advance.

Another advance made possible in AWG-9 by computer technology was built-in test (BIT) capability. This provides both ground and in-flight monitoring of the equipment and, in the event of a malfunction in any of the 31 sub-assemblies that comprise AWG-9, can isolate the fault and at the same time advise the crew of the serviceable modes remaining, this enabling them to complete the mission using alternative means provided by systems redundancy. The bulk storage magnetic tape in the main AWG-9 computer has a capacity of about 70,000 words, of which nearly half are dedicated to BIT.

The computer network in the Tomcat would need a book of its own to describe its workings in full. Virtually all on-board computers, including AWG-9, are linked by the Computer Signal Data Converter (CSDC). It links AWG-9 data to the displays and their subsystems, and presents data from other systems, such as the Central Air Data Computer (CADC), which among other functions controls wing sweep, to AWG-9. It controls the two-way data link, the HUD, the cockpit displays, which are themselves computers, the INS, and data exchange between the cockpits.

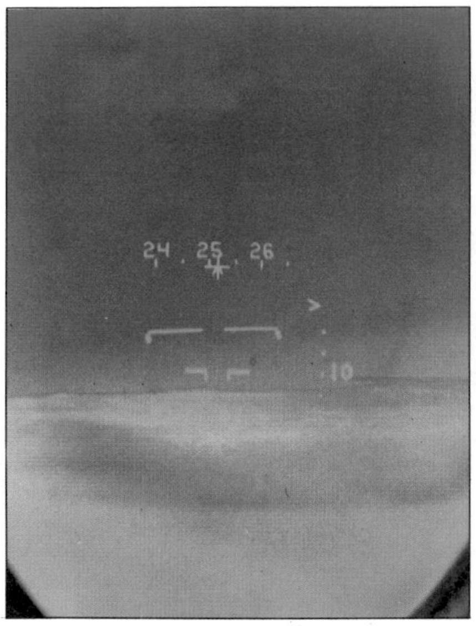

Above: The HUD projects data in symbolic and numeric format onto the windshield. It is focussed at infinity to aid the pilot in his visual search. Often, as seen here, contact is beyond visual distance.

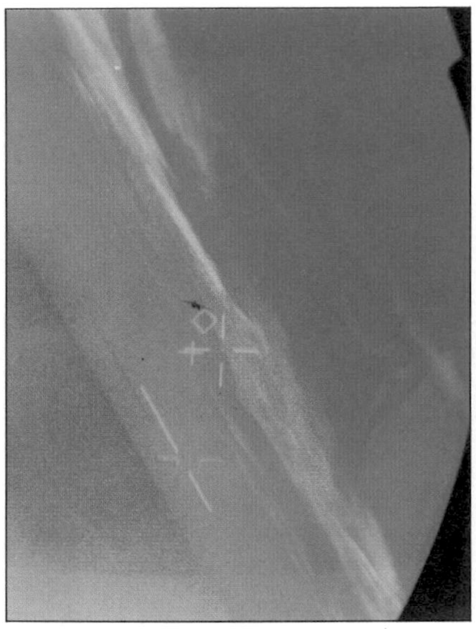

Above: Close combat! A Tomcat turns hard to keep out of the sights of a fellow squadron member. The long oblique line gives the horizon and the intersecting symbol the angle of bank of the attacking fighter.

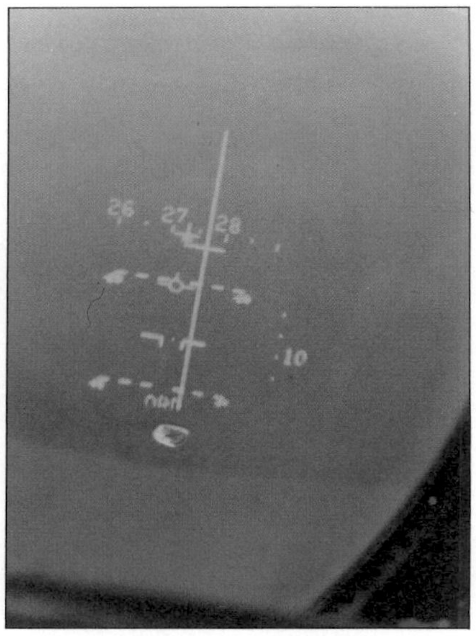

Above: An unseen opponent bores in but is detected and displayed on the pilot's windshield. The weapon is selected ready for use and the seconds tick away while the optimum firing solution is achieved.

Above: The Northrop TCS, mounted in place of the IR sensor, can provide positive identification at well beyond visual distance. Capable of working by nothing more than starlight, it gives cats' eyes to the Tomcat.

Below: Part of the update for AWG-9 is this digital display which is replacing the old analogue unit. The new DDD is much larger than the original and has a full range of brightness control, with greatly improved image quality. It incorporates a computer keyboard with software programmable switches – the key to future updates is seen as software changes using the flexibility provided by the new programmable signal processor.

Most of the computers are digital, but analogue types are used for the Automatic Flight Control System (AFCS). This is in two parts; autopilot, and stability augmentation in all three axes. The AFCS ties into the flight control system, and can automatically command altitude, attitude, heading, and approach. Another small analogue computer is used for fuel monitoring and management.

The two-way digital data link, ASW-27B, is what is known as a force multiplier. It provides automatic reception and display of targets outside the radar vision of the Tomcat from data transmitted from either a ship-board command centre, other Tomcats or the E-2C Hawkeye, while at the same time transmitting data on its own contacts. Thus the F-14 is enabled to operate in an integrated command data net, and the crew get a 360deg display of the area around them – a comforting thought if outnumbered in a confused situation. ASW-27B is also compatible with AWACS (Airborne Warning And Control System), NADGE (NATO Air Defence Ground Environment) and BADGE (Basic Air Defence Ground Environment), which enables the F-14 to operate equally effectively from land bases that have these facilities.

Given the age of the F-14 design, it would be rather surprising if no updating of equipment had taken place over the years. In fact, changes so far have been minimal, which speaks volumes for the essential rightness of the original equipment, although major changes are currently in the pipeline. Block 90 aircraft dating from FY 1975 and onward have been fitted with a new, more reliable CADC by Garrett AiResearch. This single-channel digital computer replaced the previous dual processor, while the Collins ARC-159 UHF radio, with a head-up presentation of frequency, was also fitted from this batch onward, again for increased reliability.

From the very outset, the F-14C variant had been envisaged as an aircraft containing future state-of-the-art avionics, which back in 1970 could not be envisaged fully. These updates have now taken shape, although apart from retrofits of the F-14A, the variant to carry them will be the F-14D. Most of these updates affect AWG-9. Reduced from 31 units to 27, the new system will feature greatly improved capability coupled with digital multi-function displays, the latter incorporating a new fully adjustable brightness control. One fault of the original was that it could be difficult to see in bright sunlight. New stores management and INS will also be fitted.

New dimension

Much of the improvement is accounted for by a new programmable signal processor capable of performing better than 7.2 million operations per second. This capacity to process data, added to the greater flexibility conferred by programmability, with rapid updates effected by software changes, will add a whole new dimension to AWG-9. Much information is gathered by the present equipment, in the form of radar returns, which cannot be retrieved by present means, whereas the improved AWG-9 will not only achieve greater range and accuracy but is reported to be able to identify contacts by Doppler returns both from their shapes, and from the characteristics of their powerplant.

Data bus technology will also play a part. A data bus can be pictured as a circular railway carrying data as passengers. Each passenger has a ticket to a particular station on the line, where he disembarks. The various sensors and computers in the system give each passenger (piece of data) a ticket (code) and put them on the train (data bus). Each piece of data then arrives at the correct destination for processing. No longer will data or commands be sent from one place to another through a maze of wires: instead, each system will recognize and extract its particular pieces of data by the code that prefixes them. In this manner, the entire data transfer system is simplified and the amount of complex wiring reduced.

At the heart of the system will be two Cubic Data Corporation AYK-14 computers which will integrate the flight and weapons control programmes. Also linked to the system will be the passive radar warning receivers (RWR) and the Joint Tactical Information Distribution System (JTIDS), a new two-way data link which incorporates secure voice communications and data transmissions.

Other equipment to be fitted includes the ALR-67 threat warning and recognition system and probably the ALQ-165 Advanced Self-Protection Jamming System (ASPJ). ALQ-165 is designed for maximum flexibility to meet new threat radars and counter them through programmability, by means of software changes. It consists of one high-band and one low-band transmitter, with two receivers to match, and a signal processor, all of which are line replaceable units (LRUs), plus antennas facing fore and aft. An augmented system has been proposed for the F-14D with a combined high-band transmitter/receiver in the fuselage to minimize the delay between receiving enemy signals and transmitting the deception signals. For the F-14A, a pod-mounted version is under consideration. A production decision is expected during the summer of 1985.

An interesting piece of kit that looks likely to become standard is the Northrop Television Camera System (TCS), the purpose of which is to provide positive visual identification of bogeys from well beyond normal visual distances. The idea is not new, having been suggested by Grumman for the F-14 as far back as 1970, but the first implementation came when F-14s were equipped with the broadly similar TISEO for the AIMVAL/ACEVAL exercise back in 1977, when it was judged to have been a success. On the other hand, TISEO-equipped F-4s were deployed to Europe, where it was not found to be particularly useful in the cloud-laden skies.

Nevertheless, further trials were held using Northrop's TVSU from which TCS was later developed, and an initial production contract was placed for TCS in 1981. TCS is a closed-circuit television system, with the camera mounted on a gimbal platform stabilized in both azimuth and elevation beneath the nose. Two modes are available: wide angle for

Tactical Airborne Reconnaissance Pod System (TARPS)

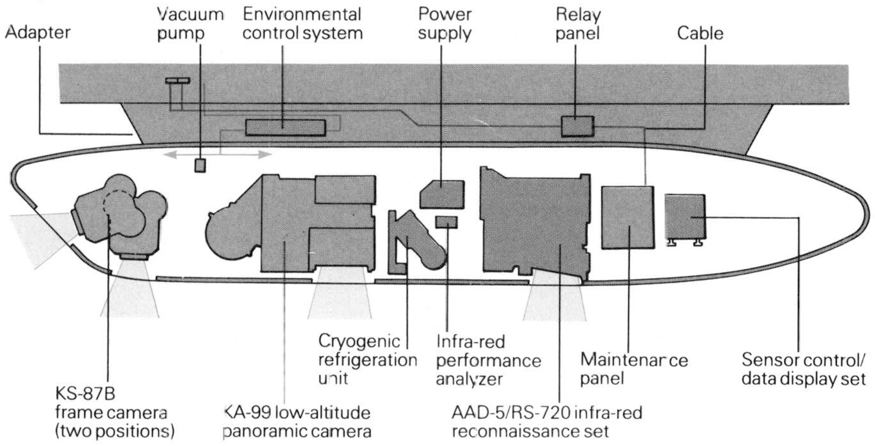

Above: TARPS is designed for the clear air medium to low altitude reconnaissance role. It is equipped with a frame camera for verticals and obliques, a panoramic camera, and an infra-red line-scanner.

Below: Some Tomcats have been specially modified to carry TARPS. Despite the bulk of the pod it has little effect on performance and this example is seen at supersonic speed with glove vanes extended.

target acquisition, and close-up for target identification. The mode is selected by the NFO.

A separate lens system is used for each mode, with two cameras and two vidicons, which are detectors which convert light impulses into electronic signals. The vidicons are very sensitive, and reportedly give satisfactory results on a clear starlit night. The cameras are normally slaved to the radar, and automatically lock on to the first contact acquired, although the NFO may direct the identification camera manually with the radar control stick. The picture is projected onto the radar display, and the displays in either cockpit may be operated independently for either video or radar. The target displays are stabilized automatically, despite aircraft movement, for as long as the target remains in the camera's field of view. One report goes so far as to credit TCS with the ability of permitting the Tomcat crew to examine their opponent's weapons fit to assist in formulating tactics.

As has been the case with many fighters, consideration was given to producing a dedicated reconnaissance version of the Tomcat. This reached the 'paper aeroplane' stage in 1974 before being dropped, mainly for lack of funds. Yet the need remained, and finally the Tactical Airborne Reconnaissance Pod System (TARPS) was adopted as an interim measure pending the introduction of a purpose-built machine, which in mid-1984 seemed most likely to materialize as an RF-18 Hornet.

The TARPS pod was originally developed for use by the A-7 Corsair and was adapted to fit the Tomcat, 49 of which have been modified to accept it. Electrical power and air conditioning had to be provided, along with modifications to the NFO's cockpit for TARPS operation controls. The pod is carried on the rear left Phoenix station, where it also neutralizes the rear right station, although there are no restrictions on the other missile stations. It can be fitted or dismounted in 30 minutes, and without it the Tomcat assumes its full fighter role, and even when the pod is carried performance degradation is reported to be negligible, while handling is hardly affected.

TARPS is designed for the low/medium altitude clear air reconnaissance role. It consists of a shell 17.29ft (5.27m) long and with a maximum width of 2.21ft (0.67m). Fully equipped it weighs 1,760lb (798kg). In the front bay is carried a KS-87B frame camera with two positions, forward oblique or vertical. Behind this is a KA-99 panoramic camera, which gives horizon to horizon coverage. Third in line is an AAD-5 IR line scanner, which provides a high-resolution record of the terrain along the aircraft's track. Behind this comes an ASQ-172 data display system, which is responsible for providing identifiable event marks on the film records for later interpretation. The intention is to attach three TARPS Tomcats to one squadron in each carrier air group. The first fleet squadron to deploy with TARPS was VF-84 aboard USS *Nimitz* in May 1981.

There are many other interesting avionics items aboard the F-14, but space precludes more than a brief listing. Among them are ALE-39 chaff and flare dispensers, the ALQ-100 ECM system, APX-72 IFF transponder, APR-25/45 radar warning receivers, ARC-51 and 159 UHF communications, ASN-92(V) INS, ARN-84 Tacan, and others of less import.

The Tomcat's weapons

The F-14 is a weapon system: its sole purpose is to carry weapons into the air to a position where they can be discharged at an enemy. The advanced airframe design, the engines and the clever electronic systems are all but a means to an end. Like all other modern fighters, Tomcat has an air-to-ground capability and can carry a maximum external load of about 14,500lb (6,577kg), but its extreme competence in the interception and air superiority roles have rendered it so vital to the defence of the carrier task force that it appears very unlikely that it will ever be called upon to operate as a fighter-bomber. In this connection, it should be remembered that security of base is one of the cardinal principles of war and the Tomcat is uniquely equipped to provide this. As a direct result, air to ground weaponry capability has not been developed beyond the 'iron bomb' stage. This leaves us to consider air-to-air weapons only.

The most important weapon carried by the Tomcat, and one that is carried by no other aircraft, is the AIM-54 Phoenix missile. Its origins lay in the Bendix Eagle, as outlined in the Development chapter, and in the Hughes GAR-9, later redesignated AIM-47A, a member of the Falcon family of missiles. AIM-47A was designed to be carried by the Mach 3.2-capable F-108 Rapier interceptor planned for the USAF. Midcourse guidance was by SARH to a range exceeding 100nm (161km), with IR terminal homing, and the signal for the SARH was to have been provided by the Hughes ASG-18 pulse-Doppler radar,

Phoenix high-altitude, high-speed trial

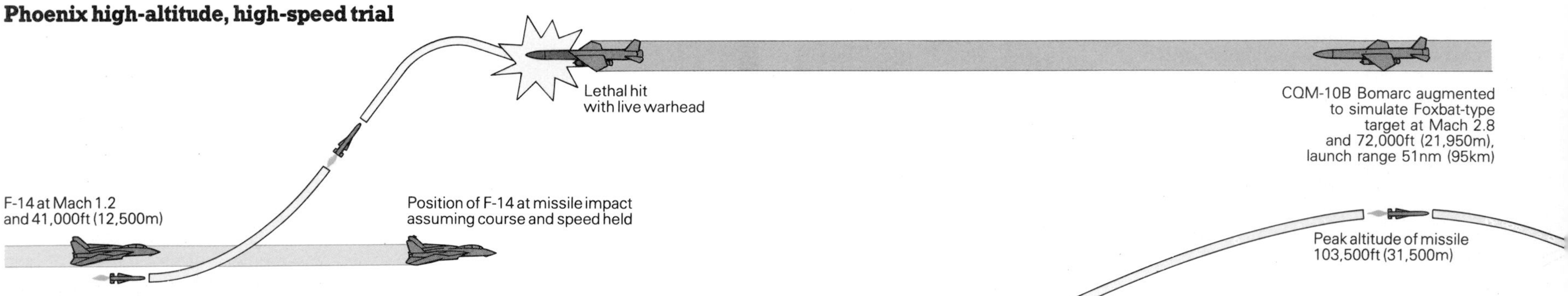

Above: One of the more spectacular Phoenix tests took place on May 5, 1975. The target was a Bomarc with augmentation to simulate a Foxbat flying at Mach 2.8 and an altitude of 72,000ft (21,950m). A Tomcat of VF-32 launched from the carrier *John F. Kennedy* and intercepted at a closing speed of Mach 4, destroying the drone from a launch range of 51nm (94km).

Phoenix long-range capability trial

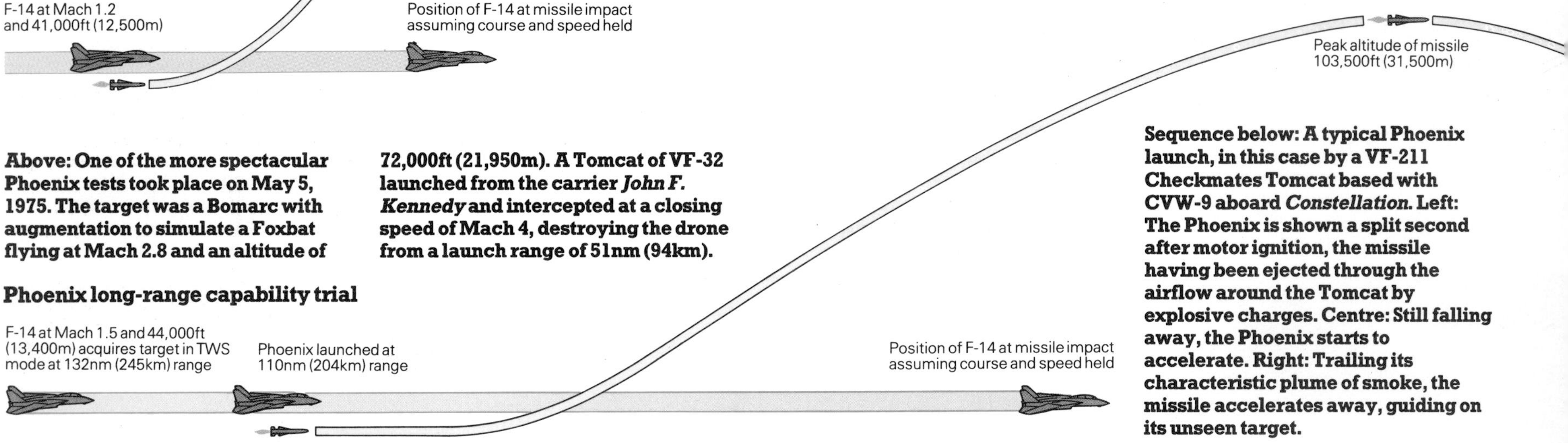

Sequence below: A typical Phoenix launch, in this case by a VF-211 Checkmates Tomcat based with CVW-9 aboard *Constellation*. Left: The Phoenix is shown a split second after motor ignition, the missile having been ejected through the airflow around the Tomcat by explosive charges. Centre: Still falling away, the Phoenix starts to accelerate. Right: Trailing its characteristic plume of smoke, the missile accelerates away, guiding on its unseen target.

AIM-54A Phoenix

Below: AIM-54A Phoenix differs from the later AIM-54C version only in the digital avionics and radar. Its manoeuvre capability is reported as being up to 25g.

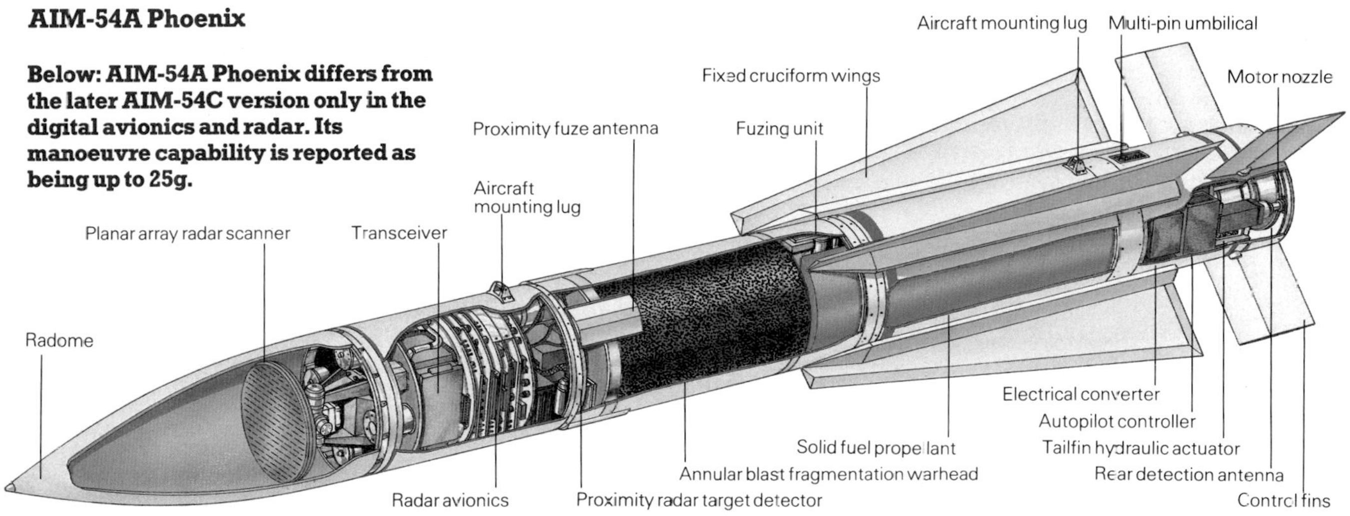

from which AWG-9 was developed. About 80 AIM-47As were built before cancellation.

AIM-54 Phoenix, reportedly so named because it arose from the ashes of its two predecessors, was selected to arm the F-111B, and Hughes received a contract in 1962. Originally designated AAM-N-11, Phoenix is a big, heavy air-to-air missile, 13ft (3.96m) long, 1.25ft (0.38m) in diameter and with a 3ft (0.914m) span, and the A variant weighs 975lb (443kg). Resembling its Falcon ancestor in shape and aerodynamic layout, it has cruciform wings and is controlled by hydraulically operated tail fins. This layout has low induced drag and gives excellent sustained manoeuvrability, even towards the end of its run.

For guidance, Phoenix has the battery-powered DSQ-26 system, consisting of a small planar array antenna and electronics for terminal homing using active radar; a transmitter/receiver electronics suite for semi-active mid-course guidance from AWG-9, which is used on a time-share basis in a multiple launch; and the autopilot. Phoenix can lose the Doppler return for up to 14 seconds, and still re-acquire its target.

The warhead is of the annular blast fragmentation type (continuous rod) and weighs 132lb (60kg). Detonation is either on impact with a DA fuze, or by the Downey Mk 334 proximity fuze, or, as a third option, a Bendix IR fuze. The propulsion unit is either a Rocketdyne Mk 47 or Aerojet Mk 60 long-burning motor, which gives an all-burnt speed of Mach 3.8, although some sources give a maximum speed of Mach 5 at very high altitude. In the design of the propulsion unit the trade-off was burn time against thrust; in the event, a single burn time and total impulse was selected.

To provide maximum range capability without incurring unacceptable size and weight penalties in the missile, it was decided to adopt a high midcourse trajectory, using altitudes where the rocket motor was at its most efficient and drag at a minimum. This had the added advantage that extra positional energy was gained in the form of altitude which could be converted back into kinetic energy for manoeuvre towards the end of the flight path. The active radar terminal homing has an approximate range of 10nm (18.5km), while maximum range is stated to be in excess of 100nm (185km).

Up to six Phoenix missiles are carried by the F-14: two on pylons situated on the wing gloves, and another four carried on semi-conformal pallets under the fuselage. The Tomcat was designed for the uncompromised fighter mission armed

Phoenix ECM capability trial

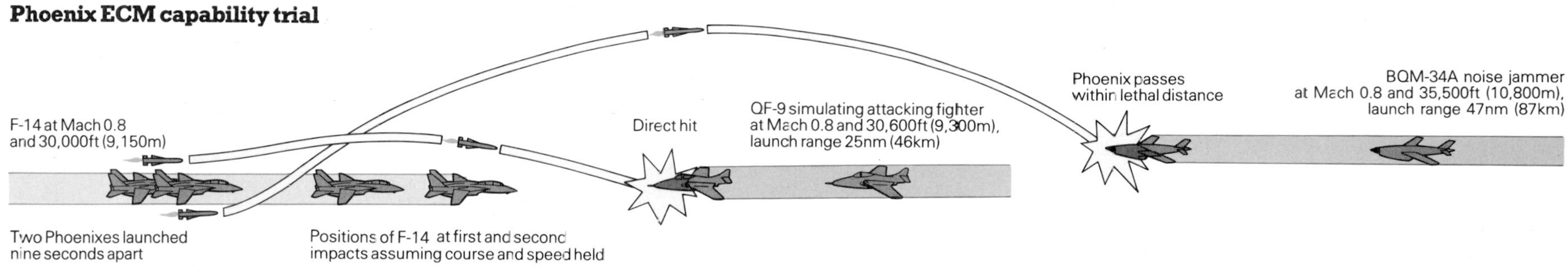

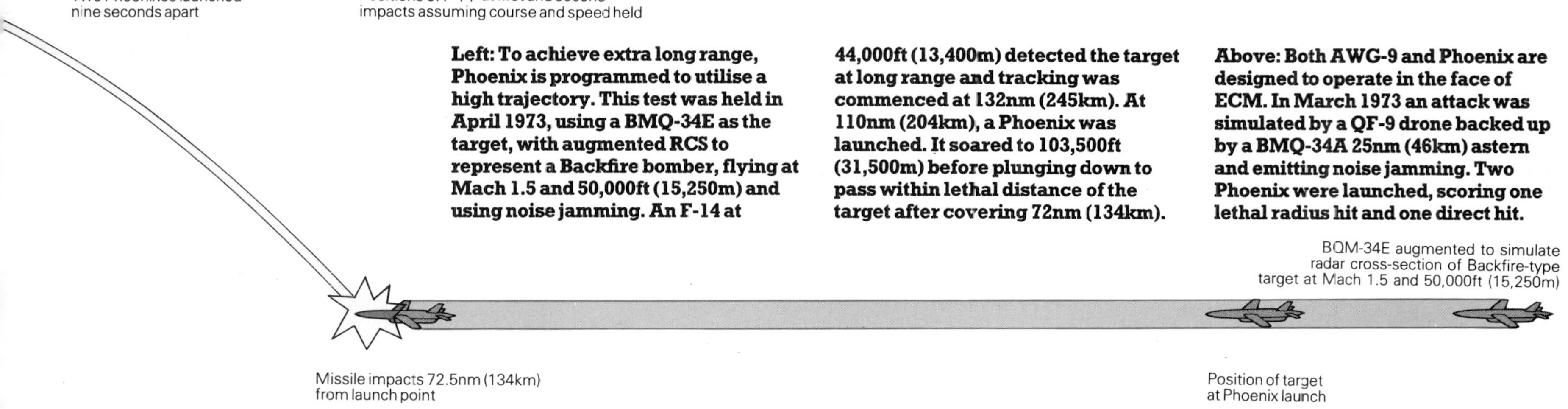

Left: To achieve extra long range, Phoenix is programmed to utilise a high trajectory. This test was held in April 1973, using a BMQ-34E as the target, with augmented RCS to represent a Backfire bomber, flying at Mach 1.5 and 50,000ft (15,250m) and using noise jamming. An F-14 at 44,000ft (13,400m) detected the target at long range and tracking was commenced at 132nm (245km). At 110nm (204km), a Phoenix was launched. It soared to 103,500ft (31,500m) before plunging down to pass within lethal distance of the target after covering 72nm (134km).

Above: Both AWG-9 and Phoenix are designed to operate in the face of ECM. In March 1973 an attack was simulated by a QF-9 drone backed up by a BMQ-34A 25nm (46km) astern and emitting noise jamming. Two Phoenix were launched, scoring one lethal radius hit and one direct hit.

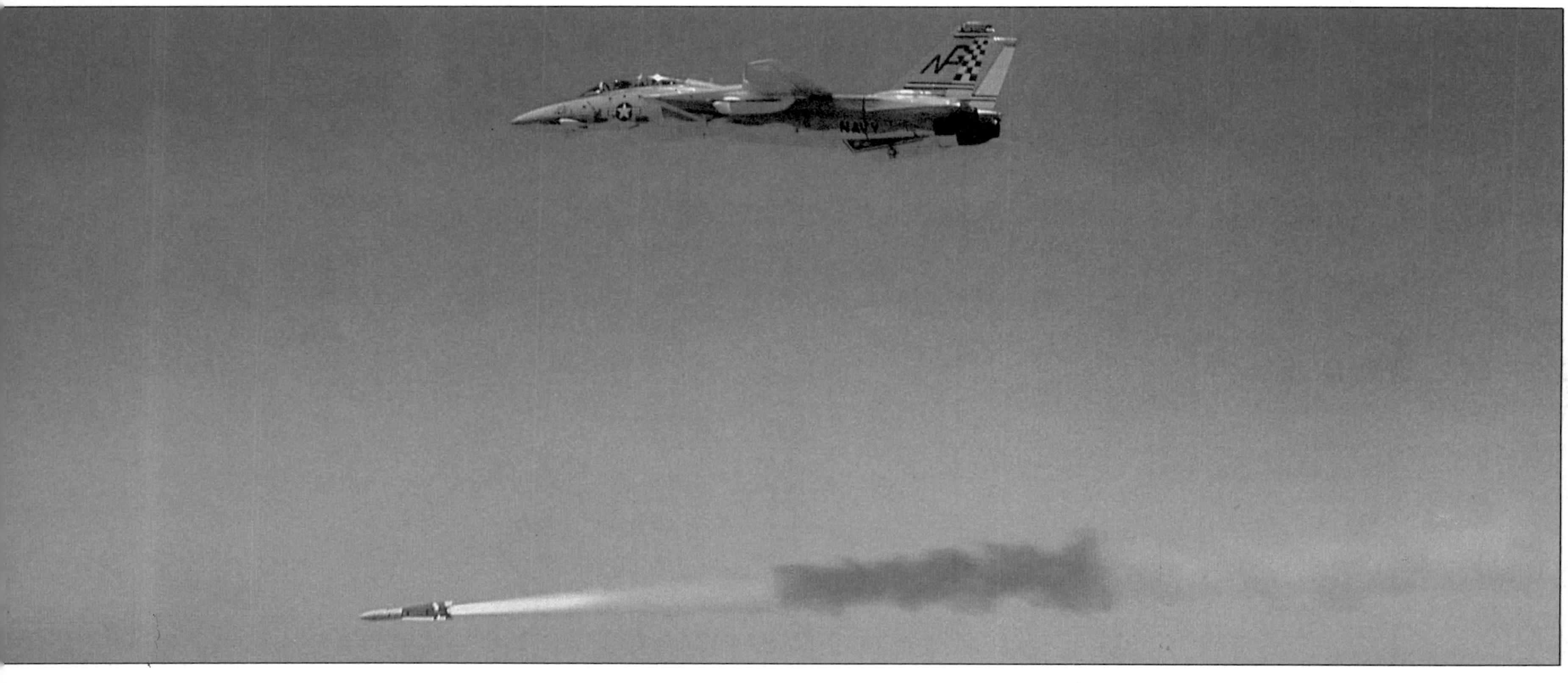

Phoenix cruise missile interception trial

Below: Sea-skimming cruise missiles are among the most dangerous threats surface ships have to counter. Hugging the waves at high subsonic speed, their small size makes them difficult to detect. In this test, an unaugmented BMQ-34A flying at Mach 0.75 and just 50ft (15m) was shot down by a Tomcat 22nm (41km) away from 10,000ft (3,050m).

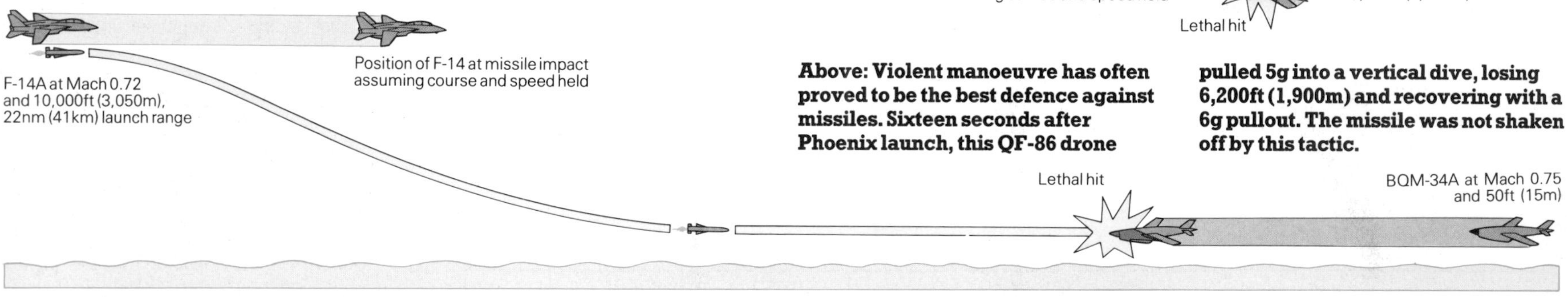

Phoenix manoeuvring target trial

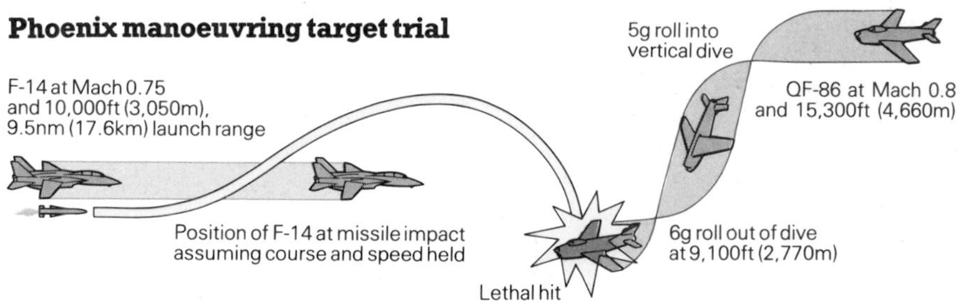

Above: Violent manoeuvre has often proved to be the best defence against missiles. Sixteen seconds after Phoenix launch, this QF-86 drone pulled 5g into a vertical dive, losing 6,200ft (1,900m) and recovering with a 6g pullout. The missile was not shaken off by this tactic.

with Sparrows semi-recessed into the underside of the fuselage for minimum drag. Phoenix needs a frequency decoder, wiring, and coolant lines as well as a launcher, and these were all incorporated into the pallets, which are only fitted when Phoenix are to be carried. The removal of these pallets saves both weight and drag when the Sparrow-armed fighter mission is flown, and does not compromise the recesses in which the Sparrows are carried.

Flight testing of Phoenix began at PMTC Point Mugu in 1965, using an A-3A Skywarrior as the trials aircraft, and the first interception was made on May 12, 1966, when a direct hit on a drone target was scored. The first multiple launch was made in March 1969 from an F-111B against two drones.

F-14 Phoenix trials

The Phoenix/Tomcat programme began in April 1972 with a jettison test. From this point, progress was rapid, and a dazzlingly successful series of tests, mainly with inert warheads but including some live, followed. Full details of Phoenix testing are impossible to give as between May 1972 and October 1980, in tests and in operational readiness exercises, no less than 155 production models of AIM-54A were launched, with a claimed success rate of 92 per cent. The success rate does not include failures in the equipment of the launching aircraft, nor failures in the augmentation of the drone targets. We can pick out some of the more spectacular tests – and not only those that were 100 per cent successful.

One of the reasons why the Navy had been so insistent on the Phoenix/Tomcat combination had been the need to counter the threat posed by the Soviet MiG-25, codenamed Foxbat by NATO. In July 1972, the first anti-Foxbat test took place at the PCMR. An AQM-37A Stiletto drone with radar augmentation to simulate the signature of the Foxbat was flown at an altitude of 82,000ft (25,000m) and a speed of Mach 2.2, and the intercepting Tomcat, flying at 47,000ft (14,300m) and Mach 1.2, launched a single Phoenix from a range of just under 35nm (64km). The big missile climbed unerringly and passed within lethal range of the target drone.

The first multiple launch from a Tomcat came during the following December, when BuAer 157983 launched two Phoenix at drones representing an aircraft and its previously-launched cruise missile. The cruise missile target was destroyed, but an anomaly in the second Phoenix caused one of its few failures.

A few days later, on December 20, the target was a simulated fighter wave consisting of three QT-33 drones, and two BQM-34s with their radar cross-sectional areas electronically augmented to the 32-54sq ft (3-5m^2) typical of the MiG-21 Fishbed. The five drones were staggered across a front 20nm (37km) wide at altitudes between 20,000ft and 25,000ft (6,100-7,600m), and their mean velocity was Mach 0.6, a reasonable fighter cruising speed. Higher up, at 31,500ft (9,600m), a single Tomcat armed with six AIM-54As moved to intercept at Mach 0.7. Using the pulse-Doppler radar to look down, detection was achieved at over 60nm (110km), and tracking, in the TWS mode, began at 50nm (92km). From a distance of 30nm (56km) the first missile was launched, followed during the next 45 seconds by three more. One QT-33 was destroyed by a direct hit, while the other three missiles all passed within the lethal distance of their targets. This was a most promising beginning.

Both AWG-9 and AIM-54 had been designed to operate in the face of electronic countermeasures. This ability was first put to the test in March 1973 when a raid was simulated by a QF-9 flying at Mach 0.8 and 30,600ft (9,300m), trailed by a BQM-34A 25nm (46km) astern, cospeed and at an altitude of 35,500ft (10,800m), which was emitting noise jamming to cover the lead drone. A Tomcat moved to intercept, and detected both targets at long range. Closing in at 30,000ft (9,150m) and Mach 0.8, it launched a Phoenix at the QF-9 from 25nm (46km) away, then just nine seconds later launched a second at the jamming drone from a distance of 47nm (87km). The QF-9 was destroyed by a direct hit, while the second Phoenix passed within lethal distance of its target.

Phoenix has what has been quaintly described as a 'home on jam' capability: its sensors tell it that it is being jammed; it then promptly homes on the source of the interference. Incidentally, it should be noted that most tests were carried out with inert warheads; drones are too expensive to merely throw away and are recovered for re-use when possible.

Air-to-air world record

The next test was to set a world record for air-to-air missiles. The new Soviet bomber codenamed Backfire was about to enter service, so in April 1973 a Backfire-type target was simulated by an augmented BQM-34E, flying at a speed of Mach 1.5 and an altitude of 50,000ft (15,250m), and using intermittent noise jamming. From 44,000ft (13,400m) the F-14 moved to intercept. It should be noted that the highest possible speed should be attained by all fighters engaging long-range targets in order to impart the maximum possible kinetic energy (in the form of their own velocity) to the missile on launch.

The Tomcat detected the oncoming target at very long range and started accelerating to Mach 1.5. Tracking

Below: The most spectacular test of all was the simultaneous six-on-six held on November 21, 1973. The targets were three unaugmented QT-33s and three augmented BMQ-34As flying in no discernable formation, staggered over a 15nm (27km) front at altitudes of 22-24,000ft (6,700-7,300m) and at speeds ranging from Mach 0.6 to 1.1. The opposing Tomcat ripple-fired six Phoenix in 38 seconds, scoring three direct hits, a lethal radius hit, one miss, and one no-test, giving an overall success rate of 80 per cent.

Phoenix simultaneous six-target capability trial

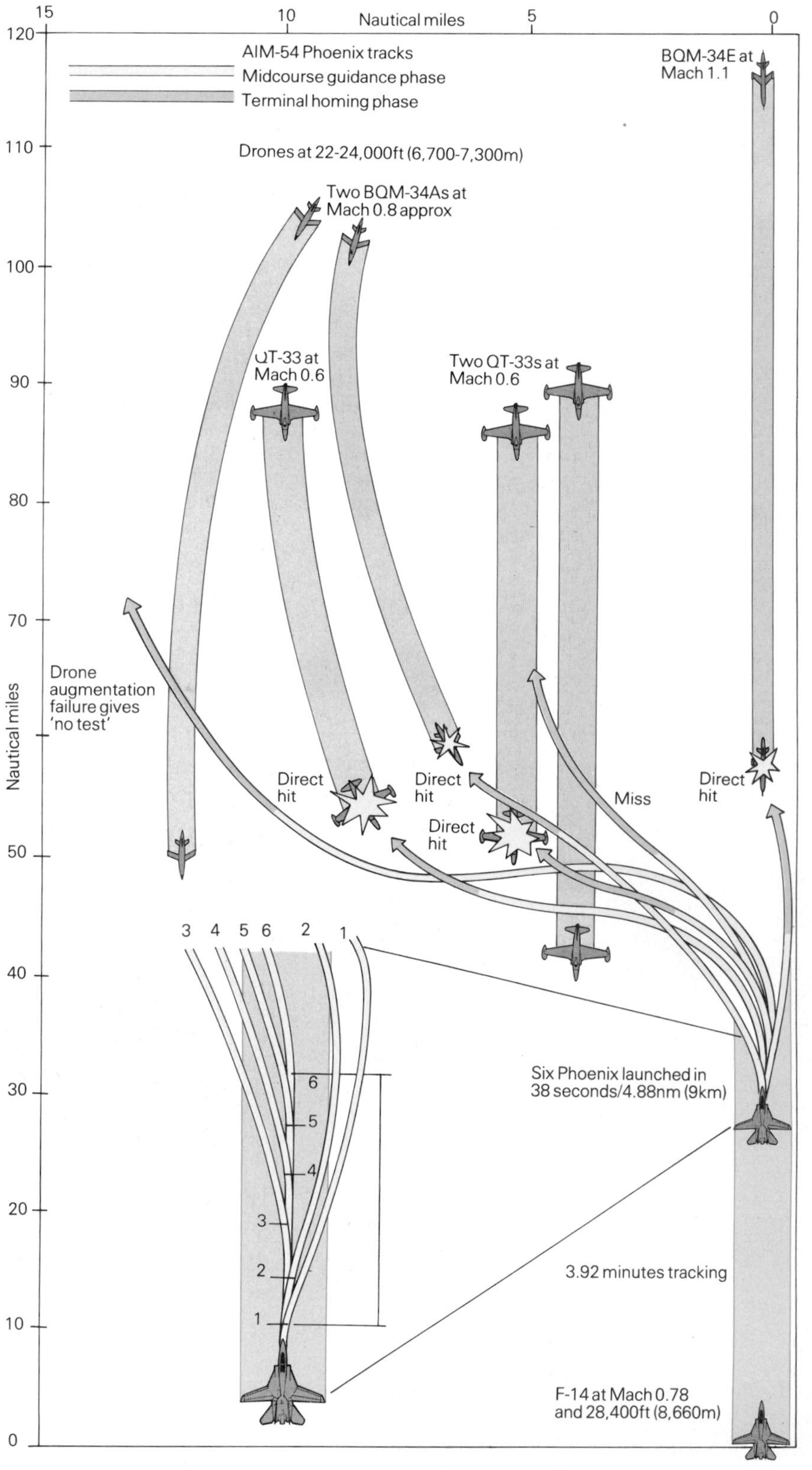

Above: A Phoenix, already attached to its pallet, is loaded onto the Tomcat mockup in a handling test. The pallet is an early type and does not feature the curved front of the model later adopted to reduce drag when carried in the front fuselage positions.

Right: The Tomcat wing missile pylons are located on the wing glove and are fixed. This 1967 photograph shows the swivelling pylon proposed for the F-111B – one of many unnecessary complications that compromised the earlier fighter.

began at 132nm (245km), and at a range of 110nm (204km) the Tomcat launched a single missile. Using its pre-programmed high trajectory to gain the required range, the big Phoenix soared up to a maximum altitude of 103,500ft (31,500m) before swooping down to pass within lethal distance of the target after a flight time of 2.62 minutes, during which time it covered a total horizontal distance of 72.5nm (134km). No other air-to-air missile has ever flown so high and so far to intercept.

The simultaneous six-target attack capability has been tested only once, on November 21, 1973. The simulated raid consisted of three QT-33s and three BQM-34s, augmented to fighter size and spread over a 15nm (27km) frontage, at altitudes ranging from 22,000 to 24,000ft (6,700-7,300m) and at speeds of between Mach 0.6 and Mach 1.1. Confronting them was an F-14 flown by Commander John R. Wilson Jr., Flight Test Officer of the F-14 Joint Evaluation Team, with Lieutenant Commander Jack Hawver in the back seat. At an altitude of 28,400ft (8,660m) and a speed of Mach 0.78, they detected the drones from ranges varying between 85 and 115nm (157-212km). The crew selected the first three targets, while the second three priorities were as recommended by the AWG-9 computer.

The first Phoenix was launched from a distance of 31nm (57km) and the other five followed within the space of 38 seconds, the shortest interval between launches being 3.5 seconds. In what must be one of the most expensive air-to-air missile tests ever conducted, four direct hits were scored, while a missile antenna malfunction caused one miss, and the failure of the augmentation in one of the drones caused both the Tomcat's AWG-9 and the AIM-54 aimed at it to break lock. This last was subsequently declared a 'no-test', which gave an 80 per cent success rate for the test.

Various other tests were carried out, some with live warheads. In one, a cruise missile type target skimming the waves at 50ft (15m) and Mach 0.75, was knocked down from a range of 22nm (41km). And in one of a number involving violently manoeuvring targets, a QF-86 drone pulled a 6g turn just four seconds after the Phoenix had been launched to try and break the radar lock. After

Below: Six Phoenix is the design load for the fleet air defence role. There is also provision for a Sidewinder to be carried on each wing pylon for close-range combat.

Above: Phoenix is the weapon most commonly associated with the Tomcat, but the F-14 was designed as a Sparrow-armed fighter. Here, Sparrows on their trolley have their fins fitted prior to loading.

Right: A Sparrow is launched from an F-14A of VF-41 Black Aces. The Sparrow has been much criticised for requiring its launching fighter to provide continuous illumination of the target during the homing phase.

174deg of turn, the missile caught up with it, having pulled 16g in the attempt. Also tested was a very short-range, tail-on aspect, active mode Phoenix launch.

Service evaluation

Most of the missile tests had been carried out either by test pilots or by the very experienced fliers of the Navy evaluation squadron VX-4, begging the question: how would the average squadron pilots and NFOs, often first-tour men, fare? The question was answered on May 5, 1975, during a three-day exercise by the squadrons of Carrier Air Wing One, based aboard USS *John F. Kennedy*, at sea off the coast of Jacksonville. A CQM-10B Bomarc missile augmented to represent a Foxbat was launched from Eglin AFB, Florida. Flying at a speed of Mach 2.8 and an altitude of 72,000ft (21,950m), it was intercepted by an F-14A of VF-32 Swordsmen. Piloted by Lieutenant Commander Andrews, with Lt(jg) Earl Kraay as his NFO, the Tomcat intercepted from 41,000ft (12,500m) at a speed of Mach 1.2, and launched an AIM-54A with a live warhead from a distance of 51nm (95km). In this test, an F-14A flown by a fleet squadron crew destroyed an ultra-fast, very high altitude target at a distance of 450nm (830km) from their carrier.

Impressive as the performance of Phoenix is, technology does not stand still, and it was a safe bet that any potential enemy would be busy trying to find the means to counter it. Since late 1977, many production models of Phoenix have been the AIM-54B version. This features sheet metal wings and fins instead of the previous honeycomb structure, digital guidance utilizing some micro-circuitry, non-liquid hydraulic and environmental conditioning systems, and generally simplified engineering. Production of the AIM-54A ceased in 1980 after more than 2,500 had been built, including a total of 484 which were supplied to the Imperial Iranian Air Force.

Development of the AIM-54C was begun by Hughes in 1977. Their philosophy was to upgrade selected components of the missile while retaining the basics, with only those modifications showing the greatest capability improvements to be adopted; 'nice to have' modifications were eliminated on cost grounds. The main focus was on improved reliability, better ECCM capability, and enhanced performance to cope with the projected threats through the 1990s.

The use of a programmable digital computer gives many advantages, including better high-altitude performance, increased ECCM logic, greater reliability, and the flexibility to accept further development through software rather than expensive hardware changes, while a digital autopilot and a strapdown inertial reference system improve accuracy and range, and enhanced target discrimination is provided by a new solid-state transmitter/receiver. The overall dimensions of Phoenix have not altered, but the weight has increased slightly to 1,008lb (457kg).

First AIM-54C launch

The first 15 engineering models of the AIM-54C were delivered from early 1980, and the first launch, against a supersonic QF-4 target, was made on June 2 of that year. The test, which used SARH throughout from a launch range believed to exceed 60nm (110km), was successful. The first pilot production model, from an initial batch of 30, was delivered on October 27, 1981, with full production starting in 1982.

Meanwhile, the search for better performance goes on, funded by Hughes rather than the Navy. At present under consideration are: a new low-sidelobe antenna to improve ECCM properties; a transmitter with higher power to give better burn-through capability against jamming; a lower noise level receiver to give greater sensitivity; and a rapid reprogramming capability.

We have spent a great deal of time describing the AIM-54 Phoenix. This is because it is a unique weapon. But while it inevitably overshadows the other weapons carried by the F-14, it should not do so to the point of exclusion.

Possible weapon combinations for the F-14 are: six AIM-54 and two AIM-9; four AIM-54 and four AIM-9; four AIM-54, two AIM-7 and two AIM-9; two AIM-54, three AIM-7 and two AIM-9; two AIM-54, one AIM-7 and four AIM-9; six AIM-7 and two

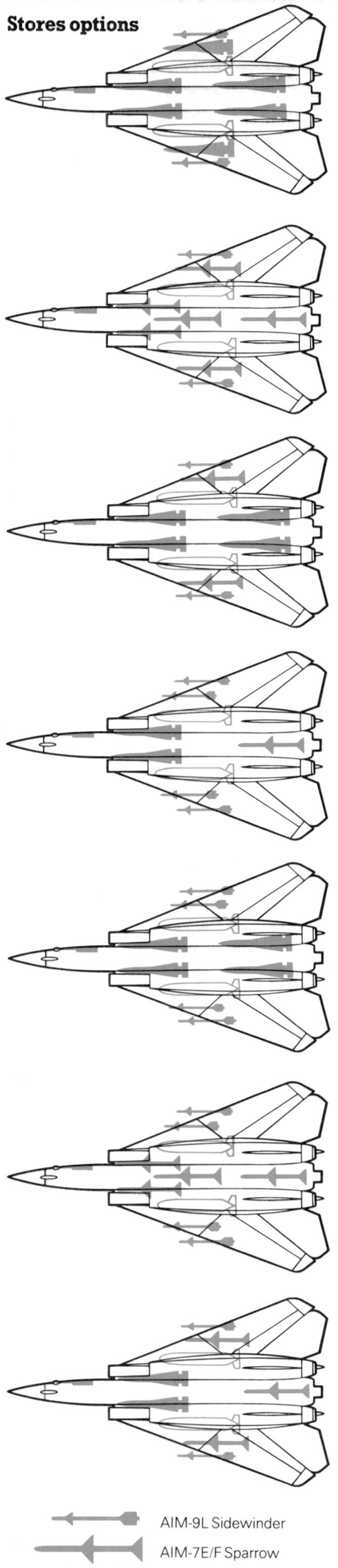

Above: Combat persistence depends on two factors – fuel status, and on-board kills – while the weapon load is also influenced by the mission. Here are shown some of the permutations of weapons available to the Tomcat, each providing either seven or eight on-board missile kills, while the gun provides backup for short-range work. Two external fuel tanks can be carried to increase range or patrol endurance without compromising weaponry or performance.

Above: Procurement of Phoenix has not been very high, and the full load of six is rarely carried. A typical external load for fleet air defence would be that shown here: four Phoenixes, two Sparrows (and later AMRAAM) and two Sidewinders. With the gun and two drop tanks, this will meet most foreseeable contingencies.

Right: Criticism of the Sparrow has led to the development of the launch and leave AIM-120 AMRAAM (Advanced Medium Range Air-to-Air Missile), seen here on the left pylon of this Pacific Missile Test Centre F-14 just prior to a test launch over the range during August 1982. It will largely replace Sparrow in the inventory.

AIM-9; or four AIM-7 and four AIM-9. From this it is clear that Tomcat can be configured for a wide variety of counter-air missions according to the needs of the moment. The M61A Vulcan cannon is carried with all the above combinations, while AIM-120 AMRAAM could replace AIM-7 Sparrow in five of them.

If Phoenix is the long-range weapon of the Tomcat, then the AIM-7 Sparrow covers the middle ground. At first sight it is difficult to justify the use of Sparrow as it does nothing that Phoenix does not do a great deal better, but on reflection it can be seen that Sparrow has virtues of its own. At 503lb (228kg) the AIM-7F is less than half the weight of Phoenix; it does not require the use of special pallets; and, carried semi-submerged, it has but a small fraction of the drag of the bigger missile. In consequence, the fighter performance of the Tomcat is not penalized by carrying a full bag of Sparrows, while the same cannot be said of the full six-Phoenix load.

Sparrow is also considerably cheaper, and therefore more cost-effective against heart-of-the-envelope targets. Finally, partly because it is cheaper, it is available in much larger numbers. One has only to consider the Phoenix procurement figures and match them with the number of F-14s in service to wonder how long Phoenix stocks would last if the necessity to use them arose.

Sparrow variants

Two main types of Sparrow are used by the Tomcat, the AIM-7E and the AIM-7F, while the AIM-7M may well be used in the future. AIM-7E is the more prolific of the two types, with a total production of 25,000. Lighter than the F variant, it weighs 452lb (205kg). It uses SARH with continuous wave illumination, has a 66lb (30kg) continuous-rod warhead, and is propelled by a Rocketdyne solid motor which gives it an all-burnt speed of Mach 3.7 and a range of 24nm (44km).

AIM-7E and earlier Sparrow variants were widely used in Vietnam, where its users were not very happy. Inadequate IFF techniques caused restrictions in use to visually identified targets in most cases, whereas Sparrow is essentially a beyond-visual-range (BVR) weapon, at its best against a non-manoeuvring target approaching from head-on. It also suffered from doubtful reliability so that pilots tended to launch it in pairs, which did nothing for its kill rate. When it worked, it worked very well, and in fact, all the kills of USAF Phantom aces Ritchie and Debellevue were scored with Sparrows. Notwithstanding, when at visual distance, pilots in Vietnam preferred to use the simpler and more reliable Sidewinder. Consequently Sparrow was in many cases used for the more difficult shots, which in part accounts for the fact that its probability of kill (PK) in Vietnam was much lower than that of Sidewinder.

AIM-7F, introduced in 1977, has improved solid-state electronics; a conical-scan slotted aerial which renders it less vulnerable to ECM; a larger, 88lb (40kg) continuous-rod warhead; and a Hercules Mk 58 high-impulse motor giving the missile a maximum velocity of about Mach 4 and a greatly increased range of 54nm (100km). A total of 19,000 F models are expected to have been produced by 1985. AIM-7F is compatible with pulse-Doppler as well as CW SARH.

A new model, AIM-7M, entered production in 1982. It features an inverse-process digital monopulse seeker which gives greater accuracy under adverse conditions. All Sparrows are 8in (20cm) in diameter and both E and F models are 12ft (3.66m) long, while AIM-7M is slightly longer. The control surfaces are triangular moving wings situated half-way along the body, with fixed fins at the tail.

Sparrow has come in for considerable criticism in recent years. Its SARH homing demands that the launching fighter illuminate the target all the way to impact, making it predictable for far too long. When Sparrow is used for a head-on attack, it is sometimes possible for the target to sight the illuminating fighter approaching in the distance and let fly with a launch-and-leave missile of its own, just seconds before it is destroyed by the oncoming Sparrow. This is a particularly valid point for the Tomcat, which by no stretch of the imagination could be described as a small fighter, and can be spotted at longer ranges than most. Swapping one for one is of course, no way to fight a war, but while the risk certainly exists, it appears to have been overstated.

A launch and leave missile is, of course, always preferable, and the long-term successor to Sparrow looks likely to be the Hughes AIM-120 AMRAAM (Advanced Medium Range Air-to-Air Missile). Its overall dimensions are similar to those of Sparrow to enable it to fit the same recessed missile wells, but at 326lb (148kg) it is much lighter. Its speed is stated to be Mach 4 and maximum range exceeds 26nm (48km). AMRAAM uses inertial midcourse guidance, and carries its own X-band radar for the terminal homing phase. It would therefore equate well with the multi-track, multi-shot capability of Tomcat's AWG-9.

AIM-9 Sidewinder

The short-range missile in the Tomcat's armoury is the heat-seeking AIM-9L Sidewinder. With an all-aspect tracking capability, the latest Sidewinders close the gap between the medium-range Sparrow and the ultra-short range Vulcan cannon. AIM-9L is a small missile, 9ft 4in (2.85m) long and just 5in (12.7cm) in diameter, with a weight of 188lb (85kg) and an annular blast fragmentation warhead weighing 25lb (11kg). With a stated range of 9.5nm (17km) and a maximum speed of Mach 2.5, it has a flight time of about 60 seconds. Both impact and proximity fuzes are fitted, and the seeker head uses argon-cooled indium antimonide, which is very sensitive to IR emissions.

The early Sidewinders could be used only from astern, homing on the hot jet efflux of the target aircraft, but AIM-9L is sufficiently sensitive to have an all-aspect capability, homing on those parts of the target aircraft that are heated by air friction, which show up well against the cold ambient background of the sky.

Sidewinder is a launch-and-leave weapon, and can easily be fitted to almost any aircraft, needing little more than launch rails, some wiring and switches, and earphones for the pilot. When armed, Sidewinder announces that it has acquired a target by emitting a noise often described as a growl, rising to a strident tone as it locks on. An IR homer is inherently more accurate than a radar-guided missile, as it can 'see' a heat source more clearly than a radar homer can sense the reflected emissions.

AIM-9L achieved a kill ratio of 73 per cent in the South Atlantic in 1982; in US Navy service, carried by the Tomcat, it has a 100 per cent record, although at the time of writing, only two missiles have been fired. Other Sidewinders are the AIM-9M, which is an upgraded L with improved motor and anti-countermeasures capability, while AIM-9N and P are essentially updates of the earlier E.

M61A1 Vulcan

The air-to-air weaponry of the Tomcat is rounded out by the M61A1 Vulcan cannon, which is located low on the port side of the forward fuselage. Guns were once considered obsolete as air-to-air weapons, but subsequent events proved this to be far from the case. The aircraft gun provides a very close range attack capability, with a secondary function for air-to-ground strafing. Guns may or may not score many kills in a future conflict, but they are sufficiently lethal to force an opponent to react honestly: he ignores them at his peril.

The Tomcat carries 675 rounds of 20mm M50 series ammunition, enough for a single seven-second burst, although as the Vulcan takes about one third of a second to wind up to its full firing rate of 6,000rds/min, a series of short bursts would give a longer total firing time. This colossal rate of fire gives an excellent chance of scoring hits on a rapidly crossing, high angle-off target, and will pump a simply enormous amount of lead into a low angle-off target in a very short space of time, provided that the aim is true.

M61A1 has six rifled barrels which rotate anti-clockwise. The high rate of fire dictates that a linkless feed is used, while the six barrels help to dissipate heat and reduce wear, extending the barrel life considerably. It is an exceptionally reliable gun, partly due to the fact that it is externally powered, and the feed does not rely on the gun's own action, which was the case with the previous generation of gas-operated revolver cannon. The stoppage rate of the M61A1 is about once in every 10,000 rounds.

At the design stage, Grumman designed a new captive boresight system for the gun, which dispensed with sighting ranges and eliminated the need for jacking or levelling the aircraft. A laser beam device is mounted on a forward bulkhead, using three close-tolerance pins. The beam is then directed into a collimating lens attached to the gun barrel, and a meter displays the amount of deviation from true boresighting. The gun mounts are then fine-tuned to eliminate the deviation.

As an air-to-air weapon, the gun is short on range and limited in capability. But while clever jamming devices may be produced to confound radar homing missiles, and flares may confuse heat-seekers, once within range there is no countermeasure against the gun other than manoeuvre. Regardless of whether the ether is solid with jamming, the sky full of decoy IRCM flares or all missiles have been expended, the Tomcat pilot still has a deadly weapon at his disposal, and what is more, it is a multi-shot weapon.

F-14A Tomcat weapons

Below: The number of different stores carried by the F-14 is unusually low for a modern fighter, but the Tomcat is too vital for fleet air defence against sophisticated modern threats to risk it being squandered as an attack aircraft. Although it was designed to have a secondary attack capability, this has been allowed to lapse. Even the TARPS pod was introduced only as an interim measure pending the entry into service of a purpose-built reconnaissance machine, and even then, the TARPS-modified Tomcats can be reconfigured quickly and easily into pure fighters.

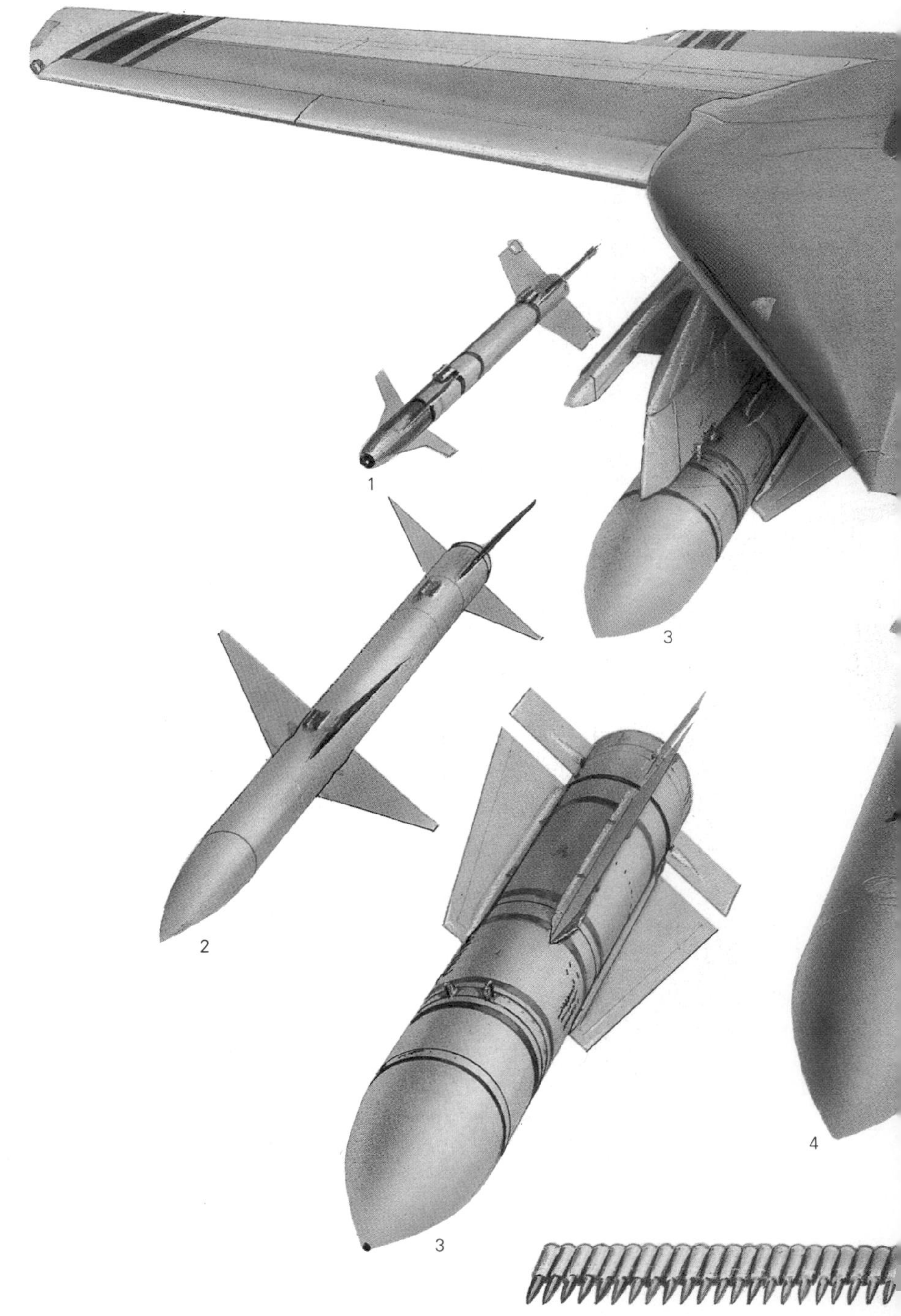

Below: The laser boresighting system is used to align an F-14's M61 cannon. In view of the long and medium range kill capability of the F-14's missile armament, a gun appears to be an anachronism, but experience in limited wars has shown that a gunless fighter is disadvantaged in close combat. The maximum rate of fire of the M61 is 6,000rds/min.

1 Ford AIM-9J Sidewinder infra-red homing air-to-air missile
2 Raytheon AIM-7E/F Sparrow semi-active radar homing air-to-air missile
3 Hughes AIM-54A Phoenix semi-active radar guided/ active radar terminal homing air-to-air missile
4 292 US gal (243Imp gal, 1,106l t) external fuel tank
5 20mm ammunition
6 General Electric M61A1 Vulcan 20mm cannon
7 675-round ammunition drum
8 Tactical Airborne Reconnaissance Pod System (TARPS), incorporating KS-87B serial frame camera, KA-99 panoramic camera and AAD-5 infra-red linescanner
9 Hughes Aircraft AIM-120 Advanced Medium Range Air-to-air Missile (AMRAAM) with inertial mid-course guidance and active radar terminal homing
10 Ford/Raytheon AIM-9L Sidewinder infra-red homing air-to-air missile
11 AIM-7 Sparrow training round

Below: An unusual shot of an F-14 carrying Snakeye retarded bombs, apparently on a specially designed rack. Air-to-ground is not part of the Tomcat training syllabus.

Performance and Handling

Set down in black and white, the performance figures for the F-14 Tomcat appear to offer little if any advantage over those for its predecessor, the F-4 Phantom. Maximum speed, service ceiling and rate of climb are all broadly similar, and only the AWG-9/Phoenix combination seems to offer any real gain. Yet air fighting consists of much more than long-range sniping, and the Tomcat is much more than a mere missile carrier. Once close combat is joined speed and height bleed off rapidly, and in this regime the Tomcat enjoys almost as great an advantage over the Phantom as it does at long ranges.

The Tomcat seems to have fallen into semi-obscurity during recent years. The reasons are not hard to find, but are as much to do with fashions and images as with logic. It has been followed into US service by the F-15 Eagle, F-16 Fighting Falcon and F/A-18 Hornet, all of which were designed as air superiority fighters with a one-man crew, a thrust/weight ratio of unity or slightly better, and fixed wings. The F-16 and F-18 also represented a trend toward a simple, austere and cheap fighter, a reaction against the relentless increases in size, cost and complexity which had reached their apogee with the F-14.

To deal with these points in reverse order, the small austere fighters were simply not capable of carrying out the fleet air defence role. Moreover, both, particularly the Hornet (described in a companion volume), have had new equipment added to increase their capability. No longer can either be described as either austere or cheap, particularly if measured against the yardstick of the Northrop F-20.

As for swing wings, they appear to have gone out of fashion in the West. The only Western fighter to utilize them since the Tomcat is the Tornado F.2, which fills a broadly comparable role. In the public mind, the inference is that variable geometry was an aberration which could well have been done without. As we saw in the Development chapter, this was simply not the case, and the Soviets, who over the last 15 years or so have produced a whole clutch of VG types, also appear to be convinced.

The low thrust/weight ratio is of course a valid criticism, and is widely acknowledged to be the main shortcoming of a fine aeroplane. As we have seen, however, more powerful engines have been in the pipeline since design inception, and lack of funds has been the main stumbling block. However, the F-14D should handle like a totally new aeroplane with the extra thrust of its new engines, and many F-14As will be retrofitted with them.

The main reason why the Tomcat has been overshadowed is that it was the first of a new generation, and those that followed were, originally at least, designed as air superiority fighters. Both the media and the public can more readily understand the concept of the air superiority fighter, and the spurious glamour of the dogfight has an instant appeal, unlike the cold-blooded sniper type killing ability of the Tomcat: the duellist always attracts more attention than the ambusher.

AWG-9 and Phoenix are an undoubtedly fearsome combination, but the publicity that they have attracted, while well earned, has tended to be counterproductive in that the Tomcat is all too often presented as a mere missile carrier, whereas it is also a remarkably fine close combat fighter in its own right. As an F-15 driver recently commented, "We think that we have the best dogfighter in the world, but we don't get slow against the gents in F-14s".

The 1970s trend towards single-seat fighters was not followed in the F-14, which is a two-holer. The reasons for this are partly technical and partly tactical. On the technical side, the complexity of the AWG-9 system requires a second crewman to obtain maximum results, particularly in a multi-target engagement or in an ECM environment. Detecting the launching of small air-to-surface missiles by a hostile radar contact demands full-time attention to the dis-

Above: A VF-84 Jolly Rogers Tomcat in a vertical climb. If the speed drops to zero at this angle, the aircraft slides backward before pitching nose-down. Recovery is simple.

Below: In the Korean war fighters had excellent rearward visibility, but the quest for greater speeds curtailed it badly. The Tomcat was the first modern fighter to reverse the trend and restore the rear view.

plays, as the launch indications may be of very brief duration and can easily be missed.

Again, as with all electronic gadgetry, part of the equipment will occasionally decide to sulk, invariably at the most inopportune moment. The NFO is then called upon to correct the problem, or to select alternative modes which will allow the mission to proceed. He also makes a valuable contribution to flight safety. A high proportion of accidents are caused by pilot error, often involving incorrect procedures. By monitoring procedures the second crewman provides a safeguard against error. It is very possible that Tomcat No. 10 might not have been lost had an NFO been aboard.

NFO's function

Tactically, the NFO performs many vital functions. It is his responsibility to structure the initial intercept and decide on the tactics to be used, basing his decisions on the information displayed as an all-round picture on his TID, although as the pilot is the aircraft commander, he can presumably exercise his own judgement, taking into account the different experience levels of himself and his NFO. Having said this, the NFO is hardly along for the ride; with information from two radios, data link and AWG-9 to deal with, he can get very close to saturation point.

In addition to all this, he must remain in constant communication with his pilot. If the fight closes to knife range, he then takes his head out of the office and becomes a spare pair of eyes checking 6 o'clock. Vietnam experience in 1972 showed that the NFOs made around 40 per cent of the visual MiG sightings, and this from the Phantom, with its notoriously poor rearward visibility. The all-round view from the F-14 makes sightings much easier, and with the rear arc under surveillance by his NFO, the pilot is relieved of a major chore and so able to concentrate much more on offensive action.

Combat formation

Back in World War II and Korea, fighters flew in basic sections of two aircraft, spaced roughly 900ft (275m) apart and, although circumstances varied, usually with the wingman, whose function it was to protect the leader, stepped back slightly. In this way, mutual cross-cover against gun attacks was maintained, but with the emergence of the relatively long-range homing missile such close spacing became redundant, as effective cover could no longer be given.

Fighters still operate in pairs, but the lateral spacing between them generally exceeds 5,000ft (1.5km) and is often combined with vertical separation. Visual cross-cover can still be given, but rapid intervention in a critical situation has become difficult (the previous close spacing made intervention totally impossible). What, in effect, the two-seat fighter does in close combat is provide the pilot with a wingman in very close formation, roughly 6ft (1.83m) behind him, as a lookout.

Pilot descriptions of flying the Tomcat are full of adjectives such as "amazingly controllable", "easy", and "vice-free". This praise comes from experienced pilots who have converted from the F-8 Crusader and the F-4 Phantom. The Phantom in particular had to be treated with care at low speeds, high weights, high AOA, or any combination of these three. By contrast, the Tomcat driver can generally "keep tugging on the pole 'til it hurts" as long as the engine settings are left high, without the risk of undue problems arising.

The Tomcat is very forgiving when flown into out-of-control manoeuvres and is highly spin-resistant except for a small region around 17 units AOA when not using slats. It will spin if pushed hard enough – a very fast, flat spin, with loadings nearing 6g, which is extremely difficult to get out of. The following observations of handling have been condensed from an article by Grumman Chief Test Pilot Charles Sewell written in 1973.

High AOA flight. The F-14 does not stall in the accepted sense as there is no g break or minimum control speed at any wing sweep. From the pilot's point of view, the airplane does not stall, and little change in flight characteristics in this condition is observable when carrying external stores, or with the speed brakes or manoeuvre flaps extended. At 22deg wing sweep and deceleration to a fully aft stick position, buffet commences at 14 units AOA, reaching moderate levels at 17 units and decreasing in intensity at about 24 units. Less buffet is experienced in proportion to the angle of wing sweep.

Above 24 units AOA, lateral stick deflection causes opposite yaw, which is countered by centering the stick and using opposite rudder. Above 24 units AOA, the stick should be kept centred, and the rudders used to control yaw and bank angle. With full aft stick, the actual AOA is about 38deg. The maximum rate of descent can reach 9,000ft (2,745m) per minute.

Yawing motion will, if unchecked, lead to roll owing to dihedral effect. Recovery to normal flight needs about 5,000ft (1,500m) of height, and is effected

F-14 dogfight performance

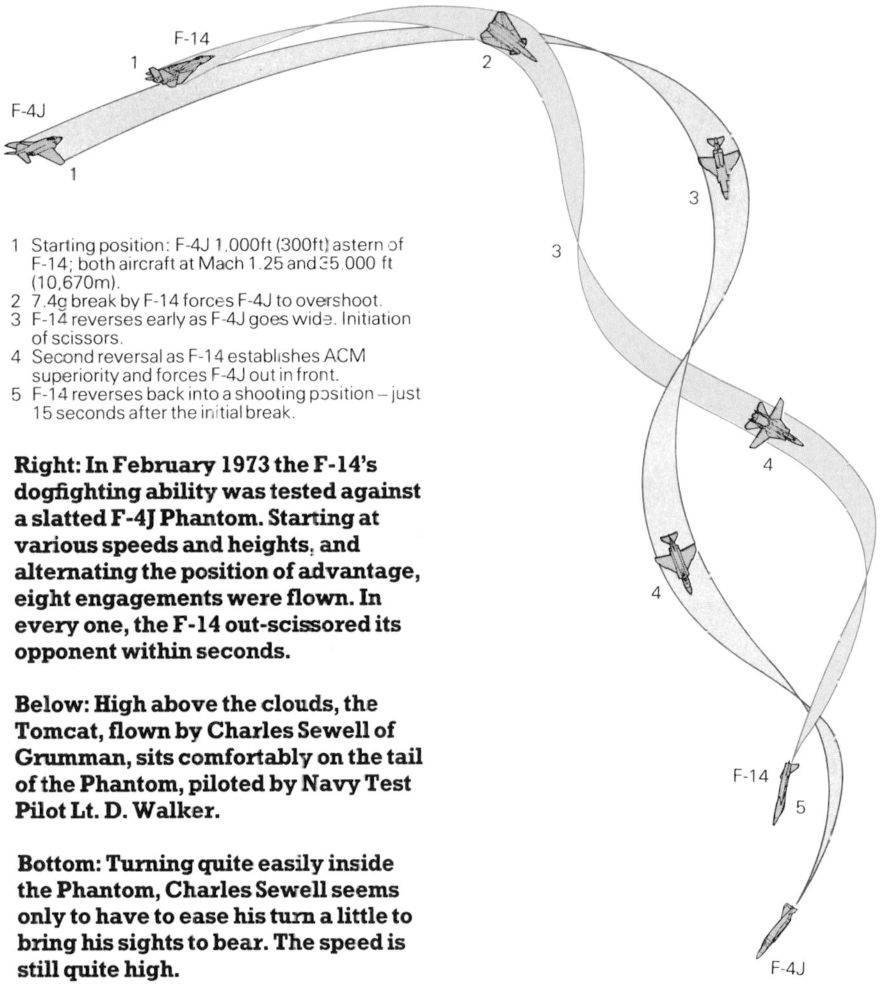

1 Starting position: F-4J 1,000ft (300ft) astern of F-14; both aircraft at Mach 1.25 and 35,000 ft (10,670m).
2 7.4g break by F-14 forces F-4J to overshoot.
3 F-14 reverses early as F-4J goes wide. Initiation of scissors.
4 Second reversal as F-14 establishes ACM superiority and forces F-4J out in front.
5 F-14 reverses back into a shooting position – just 15 seconds after the initial break.

Right: In February 1973 the F-14's dogfighting ability was tested against a slatted F-4J Phantom. Starting at various speeds and heights, and alternating the position of advantage, eight engagements were flown. In every one, the F-14 out-scissored its opponent within seconds.

Below: High above the clouds, the Tomcat, flown by Charles Sewell of Grumman, sits comfortably on the tail of the Phantom, piloted by Navy Test Pilot Lt. D. Walker.

Bottom: Turning quite easily inside the Phantom, Charles Sewell seems only to have to ease his turn a little to bring his sights to bear. The speed is still quite high.

by pushing the stick forward to decrease the AOA while maintaining lateral and directional control with the rudders, then pulling out into level flight when 17 units AOA is reached, holding 17 units with the engines in full military thrust, although if the afterburner is already engaged, it should be retained until the recovery is completed.

Vertical stall. If the Tomcat is allowed to decelerate to zero airspeed in a vertical or near-vertical position, it will slide backward before pitching down into a near-vertical dive. The nose-down pitch rate is about 20deg/sec with the wing sweep angle up to 50deg, increasing to about 30deg/sec at full sweep. At sweep angles exceeding 60deg the Tomcat will pitch down through the vertical before returning to it. Yaw and/or roll may sometimes be evident, but will damp out automatically as the airplane accelerates.

The Tomcat responds in pitch to control movements at all AOA and at airspeeds down to 100kt (184km/h) indicated. Recovery from the point of pitchover usually takes less than 10,000ft (3,050m) of altitude, and from zero airspeed is safely made 'hands-off', with the controls centralized. The pullout should be commenced at 200kt (368km/hr) indicated, maintaining 17 units AOA with full military thrust.

Inverted stall. Moderate application of full forward stick while flying inverted results in an AOA of about minus 30deg, which is off the AOA indicator. During inverted negative-g flight, the oil pressure indicators will drop to zero and the caution light will illuminate, but will return to normal on regaining positive-g flight. A caution here is that the load factor can exceed −2.5g. Recovery from the inverted stall is made by pulling the nose down, then rolling into a normal position with either rudder or lateral stick as the F-14 returns to positive-g flight.

In passing, the structural integrity of the Tomcat was convincingly demonstrated on September 11, 1980, when an aircraft of VF-24 flown by Lieutenants Blake Stichter and Chris Berg suffered a double malfunction, losing power to the flight controls. The fighter rolled nose-low inverted, and negative g pinned the crew against the canopy. In his effort to recover control, Stitcher broke the grip clean off the stick. The negative g and high speed precluded ejection, but Stichter pushed forward on the remainder of the stick and succeeded in arresting the dive after a bunt during which negative acclerations of 7-8 g were experienced. While climbing away, still inverted, the malfunction righted itself and control was regained. Despite the broken control column, the aircraft was successfully recovered aboard USS *Constellation*.

Takeoff or landing configuration stalls. With gear and flaps extended the F-14 exhibits divergent wing rock and yaw at about 28deg AOA. If the high AOA is maintained, yaw angles may reach 25deg and roll angles 90deg within six seconds. At the first sign of wing rock, the AOA should be reduced to less than 15 units. Recovery from a stall with gear and flaps down requires about 1,000ft (300m) of altitude, maintaining 15 to 16 units AOA at full military thrust.

Departing controlled flight. This can occur during manoeuvres in which roll is combined with increasing AOA, and is caused by the adverse yaw generated by the differentially moving tailerons. Warning of departure is given by adverse yaw combined with a decrease in the turn rate, and the Tomcat will sometimes 'hang up', the rate of turn practically ceasing while the angle of bank remains constant. The cure is to centralize the stick laterally and use rudder to continue the turn.

During air combat manoeuvres and all high AOA manoeuvring, the F-14 should be handled with generous use of the rudders, either leading or simultaneously with lateral stick movement. If the Tomcat 'hangs up' and the stick is not centralized laterally, roll reversal occurs at an AOA of about 25 units. The departure takes the form of a snap roll or series of snap rolls opposite to the direction of turn, acceleration occurring about all three axes, with roll rates of up to 120deg/sec and yaw rates of up to 60deg/sec, while the AOA increases to at least 45deg and the positive g loading almost doubles.

Recovery is effected by neutralizing rudders and lateral stick, then pushing the stick slowly forward to reduce the AOA to 17 units or less. If the yaw and roll motion does not cease, it should be controlled by using the stick in the direction of, and the rudders opposite to, the direction of the roll/yaw, neutralizing both controls when the motion stops. Level flight is then regained by holding 17 units AOA until the speed increases enough to permit a harder pullout.

Above: A Tomcat destined for Iran is put through its paces. Contrails stream from the wingtips in a tight turn, and water vapour can be seen near the wing sweep junction.

Compressor stalls

As Naval Secretary John F. Lehman stated in 1984, with the Tomcat you have to fly the engine and not just the airframe. Charles Sewell addressed this problem also, although at the time the article was written much exploration of the flight envelope remained to be done. His conclusions were that compressor stalls could occur at thrust settings of less than 85 per cent rpm, and sideslip at high AOA was found to increase the probability of an engine stall. About half the stalls encountered were self-clearing, reducing the throttle to the idle setting and reducing the AOA to 14 units or less. It was recommended that for high AOA operations, engine revolutions should be maintained at 88 per cent or above.

One problem encountered was that the engine stalls were often inaudible to the pilot, and could only be detected by monitoring the engine instruments – and at subsonic speeds the temperature in a stalled engine could quickly rise to destruction point if the throttle was not retarded in time. The handling procedures recommended to avoid engine stalls in a nose-high attitude with rapidly decreasing airspeed were: 1) if above 40,000ft (12,200m) in afterburner, slowly retard the throttles to full military thrust; 2) at less than 40,000ft (12,200m) in afterburner, leave the throttles well alone; 3) at any altitude and at any power setting less than full military, slowly advance the throttles to full military.

The pilots of the F-14D 'Super Tomcat' will not have these problems, the F110 being almost completely stall-free at high AOA and high yaw rates, while throttle 'slams' are possible throughout the entire flight regime.

In combat air patrol (CAP) configuration, with four AIM-54 Phoenix, two AIM-

Below: Afterburners blazing, a Tomcat of VF-84 blasts off the deck of *Nimitz* during the Teamwork 80 exercise, while a VF-41 aircraft is prepared for a catapult launch.

Above: A Tomcat of VF-142 Ghost Riders about to take the third wire aboard *Dwight D. Eisenhower* during Distant Drum in 1982. Along with VF-143, VF-142 forms part of CVW-7.

Below: Despite its size and weight, the Tomcat has a landing speed considerably slower than that of the Phantom: a Bounty Hunters F-14 about to land aboard *Enterprise*.

7 Sparrow and two AIM-9 Sidewinder, and carrying two 280US gal (1,060lit) drop tanks, the F-14A can remain approximately 50 minutes on station at a distance of 300nm (550km) from the carrier, the time on station increasing as the distance from the carrier decreases. This involves a fully augmented takeoff and climbout, with the cruise out to the CAP station and the return conducted at an economic speed and altitude.

With the same load, the F-14A has a combat radius of 134nm (247km) in the deck-launched intercept mission (DLI), using an augmented takeoff and an intercept run-out at Mach 1.5. It is anticipated that the greater power and lower sfc of the F110 engines will improve the performance of the Super Tomcat for these two missions to 1½ hours on station and 217nm (400km) respectively.

The original specification called for a maximum speed of Mach 2.4 and an acceleration time from Mach 0.8 to Mach 1.8 of 2.2 minutes. On an early test flight a Tomcat attained Mach 2.41 and was still accelerating when, the objective having been achieved, the test was curtailed. The acceleration time achieved on test was just two minutes. The maximum speed is generally quoted as Mach 2.34 at altitude and Mach 1.2 at sea level, though naturally these figures vary with the load. Maximum rate of climb at sea level exceeds 30,000ft/min (152m/sec) and the combat ceiling is better than 56,000ft (17,000m).

Takeoff and landing

From a land base, a fully augmented takeoff is achieved in 1,300ft (396m), the nosewheel liftoff speed varying between 95kt and 110kt (175-203km/h). The minimum landing roll is 2,700ft (823m). Landing can if necessary be accomplished with the wings fully swept, with the approach speed increased to about 160kt (295km/h), while single-engined bolters without augmentation and with the wings fully swept at an all-up weight of 57,000lb (25,855kg) have been demonstrated. Maximum takeoff weight is 74,349lb (33,724kg) and the design landing weight is 51,830lb (23,510kg).

Catapult launch from a carrier is regarded as easy: the Tomcat flies 'hands off' accelerating to 150kt (276km/h) in the space of 2.5sec. With a load of four Sparrows it can launch with a negative wind over deck of between 10 and 20kt (18-37km/h), while at maximum launch weight 10kt (18km/h) of wind over deck is needed.

For carrier landings the normal approach speed is 123kt (227km/h), although at light weights this can be reduced to 115kt (212km/h). In fact, the Tomcat can fly considerably more slowly than this, but the increased AOA necessary would ground the rear end before the wheels if a landing were attempted. The AOA on approach is a constant 10.8deg, held using DLC. This gives the pilot a visibility line over the nose of 15.5deg, which means that the waterline on the carrier is always in sight. On touchdown, the throttles are advanced to full military power, and if the hook fails to take a wire the big fighter flies straight past and off the deck again. The six-Phoenix CAP mission is rarely if ever flown from the deck of a carrier in training, as the weight of the missiles and their pallets makes recovery aboard rather marginal.

Below: At low speeds, with the gear, flaps and slats down and the spoilers, rudders and differentially moving tail surfaces all working, the F-14 has been likened to a turkey.

Combat and Deployment

The Tomcat is scheduled to equip 24 operational squadrons, or two for each large-deck carrier in the US Navy. It has seen little active service, but has demonstrated unparalleled effectiveness in the Fleet Air Defence role during exercises, making a conventional air attack on a carrier force a thankless task and even a long-range stand-off attack a venture fraught with peril. Many authorities regard huge super-carriers as too vulnerable to pose a viable threat: without the F-14 this would certainly be true, but the defence in depth offered by two Tomcat squadrons is a formidable gauntlet for any attacker to run.

The first United States Navy unit to fly the Tomcat was the test and evaluation squadron VX-4 Evaluators, based at NMC Point Mugu. Charged with evaluating systems and developing tactics, at one time the Evaluators had no less than nine Tomcats on charge. The first Tomcat squadron proper was the training unit, usually known as a Replacement Air Group (RAG), VF-124 Gunfighters, based at NAS Miramar. They were assigned as the west coast – and initially the only – F-14 training squadron in August 1972, receiving their first Tomcat, BuAer 158620, on the last day of that year.

The first fleet squadrons to be assigned were VF-1 Wolfpack and VF-2 Bounty Hunters, which were officially reactivated on October 14, 1972, at Miramar, under Commanders Rene W. Leeds and Richard L. Martin respectively. The crews functioned as part of VF-124 for the training period, which for Tomcat conversion typically lasts about ten months. The F-14 has no provision for flight controls in the rear cockpit and dual-control flying instruction in the accepted sense is not possible. Simulators are widely used in the initial instruction period, and few if any problems seem to have been met.

VF-1 and VF-2 were assigned to Carrier Air Wing (CVW) 14, aboard USS *Enterprise*. On completion of their training period with the Gunfighters, delivery of their aircraft began on October 31, 1973, with BuAer 158979, the 40th Tomcat to be built, while the 24th and last arrived at Miramar on April 26, 1974. The working up period and carrier qualifications completed, the two squadrons, now led by Commanders Edward J. Thaubald (VF-1) and Joseph A. Brantuas (VF-2), embarked aboard *Enterprise* at NAS Alameda, where the aircraft were unceremoniously hoisted aboard by crane. On the morning of September 17, 1974, the 75,700-ton nuclear powered carrier took the first operational Tomcat squadrons to sea.

The deployment, into the western Pacific and the Indian Ocean, was not uneventful. Besides covering the evacuation of Saigon for a brief period, Wolfpack and Bounty Hunters logged more

Above: First deployment, and the Tomcats of CVW-14 are hoisted on board *Enterprise* at Alameda in September 1974. A VF-1 aircraft is in midair and one from VF-2 waits.

Below: Aircraft of VF-143 Pukin' Dogs (at rear) and VF-142 Ghost Riders show off their bright paint schemes on their first deployment aboard *America* in 1976.

than 2,900 flight hours and 1,600 traps between them, 460 of the traps being at night. Lieutenant Commanders Grover Giles and his NFO, Roger McFillen, of VF-1, had gained the distinction of being the first squadron F-14 crew to become carrier qualified for day operations in March 1974. They now achieved the more dubious distinction of being the first active duty Naval aviators to take a Martin-Baker departure from the Tomcat when their fighter caught fire over the South China Sea on January 2, 1975. They survived their enforced bath, McFillen going on to command his own F-14 squadron at a later date. The fire was the first of far too many that led to F-14 losses. The deployment ended back at base in May 1975.

Meanwhile, other F-14 squadrons were forming. VF-14 Tophatters and VF-32 Swordsmen, sometimes called the

Above: The value of oversweep in minimizing parking space is shown. The carrier is *John F. Kennedy* and the Tomcat squadrons are VF-14 Tophatters and VF-32 Swordsmen.

Gypsies, were next, deploying aboard USS *John F. Kennedy* as CVW-1 on June 28, 1975, for a Mediterranean cruise. It was immediately prior to this deployment that the simulated Foxbat kill described in the Avionics and Armament chapter took place. Of particular interest during this trip was Exercise Lafayette. The French Air Force, using Mirage IIIs and Jaguars, launched 91 sorties against JFK, with the advantage of French ground control. The Tomcats of CVW-1, working with Grumman E-2C Hawkeyes for the first time, achieved a 100 per cent interception rate. The F-14 had started to prove itself as a fleet defence interceptor.

Tophatters and Swordsmen were followed into service by VF-142 Ghost Riders and VF-143 Pukin' Dogs. This unsalubrious name is an irreverent reference to the appearance of their unit emblem, a griffon. Forming CVW-6, VF-142 and 143 deployed to the Mediterranean aboard USS *America* in April 1976. In July of that year VF-1 and VF-2 returned to the Pacific aboard *Enterprise*, while VF-14 and VF-32, now reassigned to CVW-3 but still aboard *John F. Kennedy*, sailed out into the Atlantic for a NATO exercise between September and November.

Tomcat deployment

Squadron and name	First deployment and carrier	CVW	Remarks
VF-124 Gunfighters	— —	—	West Coast RAG
VF-101 Grim Reapers	— —	—	East Coast RAG
VF-1 Wolfpack	Sep 74 *Enterprise* (CVN-65)	14	To *Ranger* (CV-61) Sep 80
VF-2 Bounty Hunters	Sep 74 *Enterprise* (CVN-65)	14	as CVW-2
VF-14 Tophatters	Jun 75 *John F. Kennedy* (CV-67)	1	To *Nimitz* Sep 79 as CVW-8;
VF-32 Swordsmen	Jun 75 *John F. Kennedy* (CV-67)	1	to *JFK* Aug 80; to *Independence* (CV-62) 82 as CVW-6
VF-142 Ghost Riders	Apr 76 *America* (CV-66)	6	To *Dwight D. Eisenhower* (CVN-69)
VF-143 Pukin' Dogs	Apr 76 *America* (CV-66)	6	Jan 79 as CVW-7
VF-24 Checkertails	Apr 77 *Constellation* (CV-64)	9	Now called Renegades
VF-211 Checkmates	Apr 77 *Constellation* (CV-64)	9	
VF-114 Aardvaarks	Oct 77 *Kitty Hawk* (CV-63)	11	To *America* Mar 79 As CVW-11;
VF-213 Black Lions	Oct 77 *Kitty Hawk* (CV-63)	11	to *Enterprise* 82
VF-41 Black Aces	Dec 77 *Nimitz* (CVN-68)	8	
VF-84 Jolly Rogers	Dec 77 *Nimitz* (CVN-68)	8	
VF-51 Screaming Eagles	May 79 *Kitty Hawk* (CV-63)	15	To *Carl Vinson* (CVN-70) Mar 83
VF-111 Sundowners	May 79 *Kitty Hawk* (CV-63)	15	for round-the-world deployment
VF-11 Red Rippers	Jan 82 *John F. Kennedy* (CV-67)	3	
VF-31 Tomcatters	Jan 82 *John F. Kennedy* (CV-67)	3	
VF-102 Diamondbacks	May 82 *America* (CV-66)	1	
VF-33 Starfighters	May 82 *America* (CV-66)	1	Also known as Tarsiers
VF-74 Bedevilers	Jun 83 *Saratoga* (CV-60)	17	
VF-103 Sluggers	Jun 83 *Saratoga* (CV-60)	17	
VF-301 Devil's Disciples	— —	—	Reserve squadron formed Sep 84
VF-302 Stallions	— —	—	Reserve squadron formed 85

Headline news

This was the deployment that made headlines around the world when a Phoenix-carrying Tomcat went berserk on the flight deck and dived headlong overboard, the crew just managing to eject in time. As with all NATO exercises, units of the Soviet fleet had been hovering nearby; it was essential that the US Navy's latest air weapon was not compromised by being recovered by the wrong side. The efforts to recover both the aircraft and the much smaller

Left: In close combat the Tomcat is disadvantaged by its size, which makes it easy to see, and the original bright unit markings have been replaced by low visibility finish. The Pukin' Dogs transferred to *Eisenhower* in 1979.

missile were as costly as they were protracted, but were crowned with success after nearly eight weeks.

As Tomcats rolled off the production line, new squadrons continued to be formed, including the promised east coast RAG, based at Oceana, Virginia. VF-101 Grim Reapers were first tasked for this role in January 1976, their official designation as a Tomcat training squadron coming in July 1977. Details of Tomcat squadrons deployed to date are given in the accompanying table.

The Tomcat has seen virtually no action in USN service. TARPS Tomcats flew reconnaissance missions over Lebanon from USS *Independence* in December 1983, but the only combat involving the type took place in the Gulf of Sidra on August 19, 1981. This came during a two-day missile firing exercise in international waters of the southern Mediterranean. Despite the usual warning notices (NOTAMs) issued several days in advance, the first day of the exercise was marred by continual incursions of the Libyan Arab Air Force (LAAF). No fewer than 35 patrols of LAAF fighters approached the area, six of them actually entering it. In each case they were intercepted by the Tomcats from *Nimitz* and Phantoms from *Forrestal* operating in conjunction with E-2C Hawkeyes, and turned away without incident, apart from a certain amount of jockeying for position, which generally amounted to unscheduled dissimilar ACM training.

Fitter combat

The fatal encounter came early in the morning of the second day. Shortly after 0600, two Tomcats of VF-41 Black Aces launched from *Nimitz*. They were flown by the CO, Commander Henry Kleemann, with Lieutenant Dave Venlet as his NFO, and Lieutenant Larry Muczynski, with Lieutenant James Anderson in his back seat. Initially the two aircraft were assigned to different CAP stations, but as F-14s usually operate in pairs and Muczynski was on his own, Kleemann was sent to join him. They set up a north-south oriented racetrack pattern on the CAP station and waited, not really expecting anything to happen in this area, which had been quiet the previous day.

At about 0715 Venlet picked up a radar contact to the south, heading toward them. The contact climbed to the same altitude as the Black Aces pair, 20,000ft (6,100m), and accelerated to 540kt (995km/h), coming right at them. The Tomcats had been flying in combat spread, 5-10,000ft (1,500-3,000m) apart and in line abreast, with the section lead, Kleemann, on the left.

As they headed towards the contact, Muczynski gained some 6-8,000ft (1,800-2,400m) of altitude to obtain a better position from which to begin the interception, which was expected to be a repeat of the previous day's manoeuvring tussles. On the way, the Tomcats tried to 'sidestep' to gain lateral separation in order to be well placed to turn in behind the bogeys, but each time this was attempted the bogeys, obviously directed from the ground, turned into them and neutralized the angle. It became obvious that no advantage could be gained, so the Tomcats continued to close from nearly head-on. By this time, Muczynski had dropped back slightly, even though using stage five augmentation.

In Commander Kleemann's own words: "At approximately 8 miles (13km) I saw the section of two Su-22 Fitters on the nose (i.e., dead ahead). They were flying a formation we refer to as welded wing, within about 50ft (150m) of each other. The pass (was) nose to nose, with No. 102 (Kleemann's Tomcat) very nearly on the flight path with the two Fitters . . . I rolled my wings and began a (left) turn to keep the Fitters in sight and turn around and rendezvous on them. About 500ft (150m) above them and 1,000ft (300m) out in front, I observed a missile being fired from the right station of the Fitter." (Muczynski remembers it as the left side, launching with a bright orange flash and a smoke trail).

"As I saw the missile come off, I communicated to my wingman that we had been fired at. I then continued a very hard turn across their tails to come back and find them. I kept both of them in sight through this area. The lead Fitter did a climbing left-hand turn in the general direction of my wingman. I was initially turned around to go after the man who had fired, as I saw my wingman come in. He came into view in front of me, starting to come into a position behind the lead Fitter as he continued off in that direction. Since I saw that he had him under control, I switched my attention to the wing Fitter who had done a climbing right-hand turn.

"My Fitter was approaching the sun; as I intended to use a Sidewinder heat-seeking missile, I realised that that was not a good position to shoot. I waited about ten seconds until he cleared the sun, (then) fired my missile. The missile guided, struck him in his tailpipe area causing him to lose control of the airplane and he ejected within about five seconds."

Meanwhile, Lieutenant Muczynski had latched on to the leader and also launched a Sidewinder. It guided, and went straight up the Fitter's tailpipe. Muczynski, a bare half-mile astern, performed a 6g pull-up into the vertical to clear the debris. The encounter had lasted just 45 seconds.

In retrospect, it seems unlikely that the Libyan pilot had intended to open fire – missiles have been accidentally pooped off before now – but once done it could not be recalled, and the Black Aces gave him no further chance. This combat was a historic first, with all aircraft involved being variable geometry types.

Further intercepts were made that day. One, of considerable interest, turned out to be that old aerial bogeyman which years before had helped

Gulf of Sidra incident

Below: The Gulf of Sidra incident on August 19, 1981, is the only documented instance of the Tomcat in air combat. Both tactically and technically, the US Navy fighters proved superior to their opponents.

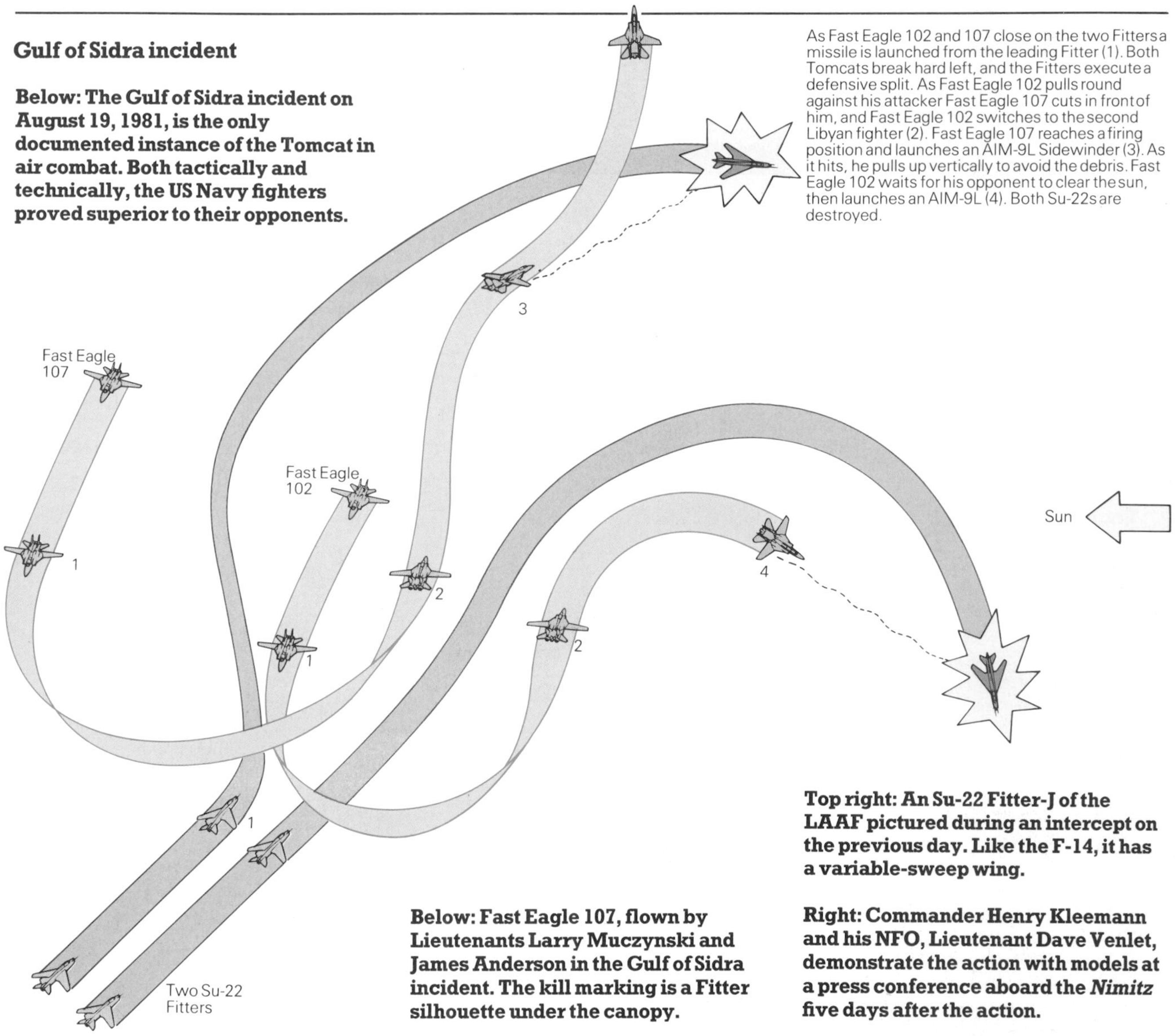

As Fast Eagle 102 and 107 close on the two Fitters a missile is launched from the leading Fitter (1). Both Tomcats break hard left, and the Fitters execute a defensive split. As Fast Eagle 102 pulls round against his attacker Fast Eagle 107 cuts in front of him, and Fast Eagle 102 switches to the second Libyan fighter (2). Fast Eagle 107 reaches a firing position and launches an AIM-9L Sidewinder (3). As it hits, he pulls up vertically to avoid the debris. Fast Eagle 102 waits for his opponent to clear the sun, then launches an AIM-9L (4). Both Su-22s are destroyed.

Top right: An Su-22 Fitter-J of the LAAF pictured during an intercept on the previous day. Like the F-14, it has a variable-sweep wing.

Right: Commander Henry Kleemann and his NFO, Lieutenant Dave Venlet, demonstrate the action with models at a press conference aboard the *Nimitz* five days after the action.

Below: Fast Eagle 107, flown by Lieutenants Larry Muczynski and James Anderson in the Gulf of Sidra incident. The kill marking is a Fitter silhouette under the canopy.

convince the USN of the need for the Tomcat, the MiG-25 Foxbat, also in Libyan service.

Lieutenant Commander Paul Williamson is an experienced NFO with just under 1,000 flight hours on the Tomcat and about 550 traps to his credit; at the time of the incident he was serving with VF-41. For this particular sortie he and his pilot, Lieutenant 'Junior' Thomas, were briefed about an hour and a half before launch, going over everything that they were expected to do on the mission, what they were expecting to see, what the Libyans might be expected to do, the anticipated tactics and counters. The briefing lasted roughly an hour, which left about 30 minutes to prepare to launch. Having completed the pre-flight checks on the aircraft, including checking the ordnance, they came to alert status, that is, in the aircraft and ready to start. Lieutenant Commander Williamson now takes up the story:

"We launched in good time and were vectored to a southeasterly station east of Misurata (the LAAF base) and joined with a fighter from our sister squadron VF-84. I believe the pilot was Commander Edward Andrews, the CO of VF-84. After a short time on station we were vectored almost due west to intercept two high-speed, relatively high-altitude aircraft which appeared to have launched from Misurata.

"We acquired the aircraft on radar and completed the intercept, identifying the aircraft as Foxbats. Naturally we were excited, but the intercept and escort of the Foxbats was relatively routine. Upon intercept, they made a few mild 360deg turns and then appeared to be returning to base. We broke off, but then had to intercept them again when they steadied up on an easterly heading (i.e., toward the fleet). Eventually they plugged in afterburner and departed, climbing to the west.

"I was impressed with the size and acceleration of the Foxbat, but because of (its) size, weight and wing configuration, I don't believe it would present much of a threat in a conventional turning fight. Its acceleration in afterburner is impressive, but understandable in view of its published high-altitude speed."

Early Phoenix tests had established the Tomcat's ability to destroy Foxbats at long range; Paul Williamson's account, similar to other intercepts carried out over the years, confirms the Tomcat's ascendancy in close combat over what was once thought to be its chief adversary. It would be very interesting to have a Foxbat pilot's opinion of the Tomcat.

Soviet Military Pilot 1st Class Colonel V. K. Babich uses several pages of his book *Fighters Change Tactics* (Moscow, 1983), to outline the Tomcat/AWG-9/Phoenix capabilities, but offers no thoughts other than to include a brief comment to the effect that at close quarters the Tomcat loses many of its advantages. This we can examine best by taking a ride with a pilot of the 527th Aggressor Squadron during a two versus two encounter against F-14s, in which the Tomcat's long-range detection and kill capability is degraded by introducing a requirement to visually identify (VID) them.

Aggressor combat

The exercise took place over the Mediterranean against Tomcats from USS *America*. The Aggressors flew Northrop F-5Es, used to simulate the MiG-21 for dissimilar air combat training. This was a standard exercise; there was nothing of an experimental or trial nature about it. This is the Aggressor's eye view of the ensuing engagement:

"The requirement to VID us, a much smaller aircraft (than the Tomcat), takes away one of the big advantages the Tomcat has: the Phoenix weapon system. It also takes away to a great extent the Sparrow capability, and brings them into a closer arena where we have the capability of seeing them visually at a greater range than they can see us, just because of the difference in size. It's quite a large aircraft; it's quite easy to see. You can probably figure on seeing a Tomcat in clear conditions at somewhere around 12nm (22km) if you have good vision, if you have some idea of where to look for it, and if you have the conditions in your favour, though you have to structure your intercept so that you are not looking into the sun. The first man to get a tallyho will obviously have an advantage.

"On this occasion we had GCI to make up for what we lacked with the radar,

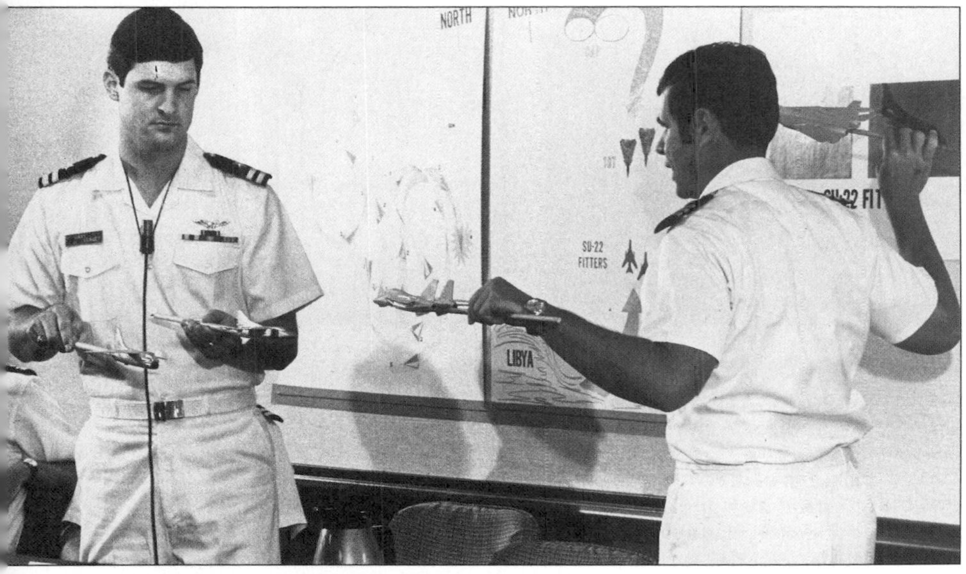

Below: Interception! A Tomcat of VF-111 Sundowners pulls alongside a Soviet Tu-95 Bear for a close look. The weapon fit appears to be a single Phoenix and one Sparrow.

and we planned to make the Tomcat's superior on-board radar work for us by using deception. Our tactics were to decoy the Tomcats by splitting up and allow them to find and lock on to our leader, while the second F-5E worked around behind them for a stern conversion.

"They entered the exercise area from the south, roughly line abreast and widely spaced, at medium altitude. We entered from the north at very high altitude, and when still a considerable distance away we executed a spacing manoeuvre which placed the lead F-5E at medium altitude and the other (myself) at low altitude. We were in line abreast and quite a few miles apart. Lead would be detected by the Tomcat's radar much more easily than myself. At the critical moment, the lead F-5E was to turn away as the decoy, luring the Tomcats after him, but staying just beyond the capability of their AIM-7 missiles, while ground control was to vector me in behind them.

"To start with, everything worked fine. We executed our space manoeuvre, our GCI was giving us information, the leading F-5E turned away for the decoy, and the Tomcats followed him. I should have been able to pull up into firing parameters on the second Tomcat, then quickly move into position to shoot the lead Tomcat, who was put in line abreast.

"It didn't work! As the Tomcats turned to follow the decoy they left their line abreast formation. Our GCI failed to detect this, and vectored me in on the lead Tomcat! I entered the fight at about 1.1 Mach, executing an Immelmann up towards the Tomcat. As I came up, the other Tomcat had radar contact; as I deployed into an attack position on his leader he called a Fox 2 (Sidewinder) shot on me.

"Our surprise attack had been foiled by two factors. The first was the Tomcat's tactics; the second was that their radar worked so well they had picked up the hidden threat, and they were enabled to get the first shot. Now they were free to concentrate on the remaining F-5E, which had turned back to assist. As it turned, both Tomcats called a good Fox 1 (Sparrow) shot on it. With the opposition eliminated, they linked up with a hard 90deg turn and exited the area to the southwest in line abreast formation."

The Aggressors are a highly trained and experienced squadron, well versed in adversary tactics, and it is no part of their function to give away easy kills. Yet despite having a course of action calculated to give them the best possible chance of success they lost out to a superior aeroplane and weapon system that was extremely well handled.

Above: Foxbat overflights of Iran ceased when Tomcats fired live Phoenix missiles on tests. Iran's F-14s appear to have taken little part in the current war against Iraq.

Below: Colourful squadron markings persist, as evidenced by this March 1983 shot of a VF-33 Starfighters aircraft aboard *America* during the squadron's first Atlantic deployment.

For the fleet air defence role, the Tomcat was designed to have a long loiter time. This equates well with a primary close combat requirement: to outlast the opponent in the dogfight. Modern fighters using afterburner gulp fuel at an alarming rate, and fuel shortage quickly forces them to disengage. The range and accuracy of modern missiles makes disengagement a perilous process, and therefore the longest possible combat endurance is vital. Endurance has yet another side, as experienced by Lieutenant Commander Williamson:

Benefit of endurance

"It was during the 1981 Mediterranean deployment with VF-41. We were on alert status aboard *Nimitz* one foul night with the rain lashing down. Just about midnight, the ship's radar picked up a contact coming straight for the fleet at 20,000ft (6,100m) and climbing. Just before we launched I looked back and could barely make out the island through the driving rain. We launched just after midnight and climbed out through the weather, intercepting the contact at 30,000ft (9,150m). It was an airliner, slightly off course. Conditions down below were impossible, so we just throttled right back for maximum endurance and just hung there. With the wings at minimum sweep, the Tomcat's ability to just hang in the air is pretty remarkable. The weather below slowly improved and we recovered aboard the *Nimitz* at around 4 am, having spent close to four hours aloft without in-flight refuelling."

Many nations have evaluated the Tomcat. Australia, Canada, Japan, Israel and Saudi Arabia have all looked but not bought. The basic criteria were cost, capability, and function, not necessarily in that order. Both Australia and Canada had limited budgets and they both really needed a dual-role machine. The Tomcat has a ground attack capability, but it has never really been developed to any extent. Today this does not feature in the Tomcat training programme, nor is it practised, although the gun is used for strafing. In the event, both countries settled for the F-18 Hornet. A statement to the Canadian Parliament on November 23, 1978, sums it up:

"Our numerical requirement of between 130 and 150 aircraft is critical to our capability to meet our domestic and European commitments. We are indeed disappointed that procurement of sufficient numbers of F-14s, F-15s, or Tornados could not be accommodated within our set budget . . . Our evaluation also revealed that acquisition of a mixed fleet would bring little or no benefit in terms of fleet size, and that operation of such a fleet would bring substantial liabilities . . ." The same reasoning held true for the RAAF also.

Of the other potential customers, Japan, Israel and Saudi Arabia bought the F-15, which is better for their particular circumstances. The Royal Air Force also evaluated the Tomcat and Eagle in the mid-1970s, in order to establish whether they could obtain a better aircraft for the same money as Tornado F.2, or an equal aircraft for less money and other advantages. In both cases the answer was negative.

No USAF Tomcats

Another potential customer to turn down the F-14 was the US Air Force. The F-106 Delta Dart used for continental air defence had entered service in 1959 and the final example was delivered in March 1961. A planned Mach 3 interceptor with long-range missiles, the F-108 Rapier, had been cancelled in September 1959, and repeated requests were made for an Improved Manned Interceptor (IMI).

The F-14 first emerged as a contender in June 1969, in competition with the F-106X and the YF-12. Later that year the USAF Sabre Defender Study informed the Air Staff that the most practicable Follow-On Interceptor (FOI) would be either the F-14B proposal or the F-15, but in December 1972 the USAF Sabre Select Study declared that the F-15 would be more cost effective than the F-14B.

In a re-evaluation completed in September 1976, an Interceptor Comparison Study compared the F-14, F-15, and F-16 and concluded that the F-15 was the best FOI based on cost-effectiveness, availability, logistics and operational capability. Bearing in mind the requirements

Above: Slightly less colourful are the markings of VF-102 Diamondbacks, VF-33's partners in CVW-1 The Diamondbacks 'stood up' as an F-14 squadron in May 1982.

Below: Contrast in styles. A Tomcat of the Atlantic fleet training squadron VF-101 Grim Reapers has low-vis markings. Even the warning triangles are a subdued grey.

of the continental air defence role, the last-mentioned item seems dubious, but the F-15 was selected.

The only other country to operate the Tomcat has been Iran. With the benefit of hindsight, it now seems incredible that the United States should sell such an advanced weapon system to a politically unstable country, but no doubt it seemed a good idea at the time.

Many reasons for the sale were evident. Firstly, Iran is an oil-rich country and could afford such weapons. Secondly, Iran borders the Soviet Union, whose Foxbats had been making reconnaissance overflights of the country, and it was desirable that these should be stopped. Thirdly, Iran supplied much of the oil used by the United States, which therefore had a vested interest in strengthening the country militarily. Fourthly, although this was after the purchase had been arranged, in August 1974, Congress voted to cut off the Navy loan that financed Grumman, which appeared to jeopardize the entire F-14 project. The Iranian government Bank Melli stepped into the breach with a loan which, to simplify the story, saved the day.

A total of 80 Tomcats were ordered by the Imperial Iranian Air Force, and the first three aircraft arrived at Mehrabad Air Base, Teheran, on January 27, 1976. The Iranian Tomcats are almost identical to those of the USN, but lack coding equipment, and have a diluter demand oxygen system and different harness locks. The transition period was not easy; at one point over 1,000 Grumman employees were sent to Iran to set up and maintain facilities for the IIAF. The 80th and last Iranian Tomcat was delivered in July 1978. Also delivered were 270 AIM-54A Phoenix missiles, out of a total order of 424. Meanwhile, the Foxbat overflights continued until August 1977, when the Shah of Iran personally ordered live Phoenix test firings against both high-speed, high-altitude, and very low level drone targets. Both tests were successful, and the Foxbat overflights ceased.

Revolution in Iran

In 1979 the Shah was overthrown, and the F-14s, in four squadrons based at Khatami and Shiraz, became the property of the Iranian Islamic Revolutionary Air Force. The war with Iraq broke out in 1980, but the Tomcats appear to have played little part. It is virtually certain that without American assistance the Phoenix missiles cannot be used, and very likely that the Sparrow capability has also since been lost.

The air war between the two sides was still in progress in late 1984, albeit at a low level of intensity. Reports described a 'handful' of F-14s being used as AWACS aircraft for defensive surveillance. On August 11, 1984, Baghdad radio claimed that Iraqi fighters had shot down three Tomcats into the sea off Bandar Khomeini, but the Iraqi authorities have declined to comment further. This is in any case no reflection on the Tomcat as a fighter; there is no means of knowing the circumstances surrounding the clash, such as system serviceability or state of crew training.

Notwithstanding its Iranian service, the Tomcat is a unique part of a unique weapons and detection complex. In US Navy service it will never fight alone, but will be backed up by E-2C Hawkeyes and another Grumman product, the EA-6B Prowler countermeasures aircraft. Any attacking force attempting to approach the fleet will be in for a thin time, and its ordeal will start when the electronic probing of AWG-9 reaches it at a distance from which it will be unable to retaliate. As their RWRs detect the threat, the attackers will immediately feel threatened. Even in a large formation, the attrition will be appalling, and will resemble an airborne game of Russian roulette.

Tactics for fleet air defence and air combat constantly change as new technology emerges, new threats are identified, and new ideas are defined. The Tomcat, and in particular the potent F-14D, are well equipped to rise to the occasion when needed.

Glossary and abbreviations

AAM Air-to-air missile
ACLS Automatic carrier landing system
ACM Air combat manoeuvring
AFB Air Force Base (USAF)
AFCS Automatic Flight control system
AIM Air interception missile
AIMVAL/ACEVAL Missile and air combat evaluation exercise held in Nevada in 1977
Alpha-numeric Information presented in the form of letters and/or numbers
AMCS Airborne missile control system
AMRAAM Advanced medium-range air-to-air missile (AIM-120)
Analogue Electronic system in which quantities are represented by electrical signals of variable characteristics, i.e., by electrical analogues
AOA Angle of attack (the angle at which an aircraft wing meets the airflow)
APC Approach power compensator
ARI Automatic rudder interconnect
Aspect ratio Ratio of wingspan^2 to wing area
ASPJ Advanced self-protection jammer
ATE Advanced technology engine (F401-PW-400, as installed in F-14B)
ATS Automatic telemetry system
AWG Airborne weapon control system
AWACS Airborne warning and control system
Azimuth Heading or direction in the horizontal plane
BADGE Basic air defence ground environment
BIS Board of Inspection and Survey
BIT Built-in test
Bogey Unidentified aircraft
Bolter Touch-and-go carrier landing
BuAer Bureau of Aeronautics (US Navy purchasing authority)
BVR Beyond visual range
Bypass ratio Ratio of total air passing through the engine to that passing through the core section
CADC Central air data computer
CAP Combat air patrol
Cdr Commander
CRT Cathode ray tube
CSDC Computer signal data converter
CW Continuous wave
DCNO-AIR Deputy Chief of Naval Operations, Air
DDD Detail data display
DFE Derivative fighter engine
Dielectric Radar non-reflecting material
Digital Electronic system in which quantities are represented as on/off signals coded to represent numbers
DLC Direct lift control
DoD Department of Defense (US)
Doppler Radar making use of shift in frequency of signals reflected from the earth's surface ahead of or behind an aircraft to give measurement of true groundspeed, or of signals reflected from earth and moving targets to indicate the latter
Drone Pilotless aircraft
EB Electron beam (welding)
ECCM Electronic counter-countermeasures
ECM Electronic countermeasures
EFH Equivalent flight hours (used in test programmes)
EMMA Engineering mockup and manufacturing assembly
Envelope Performance boundaries
FADF Fleet air defence fighter
FM Frequency modulation
FOI Follow-on interceptor
Fox one Pilot call on launching a Sparrow
Fox two Pilot call on launching a Sidewinder
FY Fiscal year (US)
g Unit of acceleration measured in terms of standard gravity
GCI Ground-controlled interception
Glint Apparent movement of the radar centre of a target
HP High pressure
HSD Horizontal situation display
HUD Head-up display
IFF Identification friend/foe
IFR In-flight refuelling
IMI Improved manned interceptor
Immelmann Pull-up manoeuvre
INS Inertial navigation system
IR Infra-red
JTIDS Joint tactical information distribution system
Knot/Kt Nautical mile per hour
kW kiloWatt
LAAF Libyan Arab Air Force
Lock on Radar attack mode
LP Low pressure
LRU Line replaceable unit
LtCdr Lieutenant Commander
Mach number Speed stated in terms of the local speed of sound
MCAS Marine Corps Air Station
MSP Mach sweep programmer
MTBF Mean time between failures
NACA National Advisory Committee on Aeronautics
NADGE NATO air defence ground environment
NAS Naval Air Station
NASA National Aeronautics and Space Agency
NATC Naval Air Test Center
Nm Nautical mile (= 1.15 statute miles, 1.85km)
NMC Naval Missile Center
NFO Naval Flight Officer
NPE Navy Preliminary Evaluation
Passive Non-emitting
pD Pulse-Doppler
PDS Pulse-Doppler Search
PDSTT Pulse-Doppler Single Target Track
Pitch Vertical movement or angle of aircraft longitudinal axis
PMTC Pacific Missile Test Center
PRF Pulse repitition frequency
P_s Specific excess power
PSP Programmable signal processor
R&D Research and development
RAG Replacement Air Group
RDT&E Research, development, test and evaluation
RFP Request for proposals
RWR Radar warning receiver
RWS Range-while-search
SAM Surface-to-air missile
SARH Semi-active radar homing
Sfc Specific fuel consumption (unit of fuel consumed per unit of thrust per hour)
SITS Systems Integration and Test Station
SOR Specific operational requirement
Tacan Tactical air navigation
Taileron Differentially-moving horizontal tail surfaces able to function as both elevator and aileron
TARPS Tactical airborne reconnaissance pod system
TCS Television camera set
TFX Experimental tactical fighter
TID Tactical information display
TISEO Target identification system, electro-optical
TOGW Takeoff gross weight
Trap Arrested deck landing
TVSU Television sight unit
T/w Thrust-to-weight (ratio)
TWS Track-while-scan
TWT Travelling wave tube
UHF Ultra high frequency
US gall US gallon (= 0.83 Imp gall; 3.785lit; 6.5lb [2.95kg] JP-4 fuel)
VF Fighter Squadron (US Navy)
VG Variable geometry
VID Visual identification
VX Test and Evaluation Squadron (US Navy)
WOD Wind over deck
Yaw Movement in azimuth

Specifications

Dimensions
Length: 62ft 8in (19.10m)
Wingspan: 64ft 1½in (19.55m) unswept
38ft 2½in (11.65m) swept
33ft 3½in (10.15m) overswept
Gross wing area: 565sq ft (52.49m^2)
Aspect ratio: 7.28 unswept
Height: 16ft 0in (4.88m)
Weights
Empty: 39,921lb (18,108kg)
Normal takeoff: 58,571lb (26,567kg)
Maximum: 74,349lb (33,724kg)
Power
Engines: 2 Pratt & Whitney TF30-P-412A or -414A
Maximum thrust: 20,900lb (93kN)
Internal fuel: 16,200lb (7,348kg)
External fuel: 3,800lb (1,724kg)
Performance
Vmax: Mach 2.34 at altitude
Mach 1.2 at sea level
Sea level rate of climb: 30,000ft/min (9,140m/min)
Service ceiling: 56,000ft (17,070m)
Maximum range: 1,740nm (3,220km)

F-14A

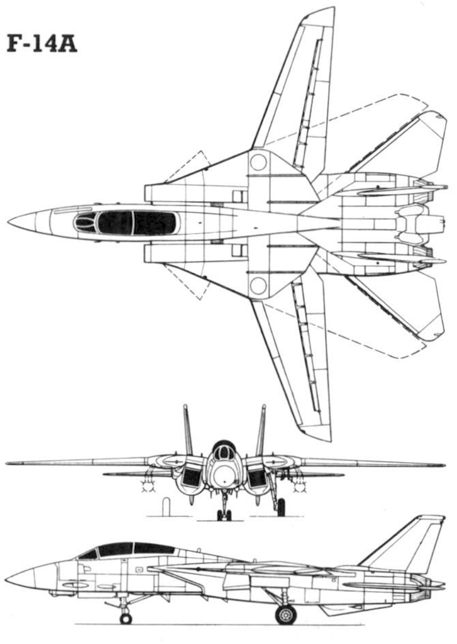

Data for F-14A; F-14D dimensions and weights are similar, but performance details have not been released.

Production

US Navy F-14A production

Contractor Nos. (and total)	Production Block	Fiscal year funded	BuAer Numbers
1-12* (12)	01-55	69-70	157980-7991
13-20 (8)	60	71	158612-8619
21-38 (18)	65	71	158620-8637
39-67 (29)	70	72	158978-9006
68-86 (19)	75	72	159007-9025
87-95 (9)	75	73	159421-9429
96-134 (39)	80	73	159430-9468
135-184 (50)	85	74	159588-9637
185-234 (50)	90	75	159825-9874
235-270 (36)	95	76	160379-0414
271-315 (45)	100	77	160652-0696
316-359 (44)	105	78	160887-0930
360-395 (36)	110	79	161133-1168
396-425 (30)	115	80	161270-1299
426-455 (30)	120	81	161416-1445
456-485 (30)	125	82	161597-1626
486-509 (24)	130	83	161850-1873
510-533 (24)	135	84	162588-2611
534-557 (24)	140	85	162688-2711

* No. 12 renumbered 1X after crash of first prototype.

PRINTED IN BELGIUM BY proost INTERNATIONAL BOOK PRODUCTION